THE NEW

LINGUISTIC

AND

EXEGETICAL

KEY TO THE

GREEK
NEW TESTAMENT

THE NEW

LINGUISTIC

AND

EXEGETICAL

KEY TO THE

GREEK

NEW TESTAMENT

CLEON L. ROGERS JR.
&
CLEON L. ROGERS III

ZondervanPublishingHouse

Grand Rapids, Michigan

A Division of HarperCollins*Publishers*

Requests for information should be addressed to:
Zondervan Publishing House
Academic and Professional Books
Grand Rapids, Michigan 49530

Library of Congress Cataloging-in-Publication Data

Rogers, Cleon L.
    The new linguistic and exegetical key to the Greek New Testament / Cleon L. Rogers, Jr. and Cleon
L. Rogers III.
        p. cm.
    Rev. ed. of: The linguistic key to the Greek New Testament / Fritz Rienecker. 1982.
    Includes bibliographical references.
    ISBN 0-310-20175-6 (hardcover)
    1. Bible. N.T. Greek–Language, style. 2. Bible. N.T. Greek–Translating. 3. Greek language, Bib-
lical–Glossaries, vocabularies, etc.   I. Rogers, Cleon L., 1955- . II. Rienecker, Fritz. Sprachlicher
Schlüssel zum griechischen Neuen Testament. English. III. Title.
BS1965.21998
225.4'8–dc21   97-45109
                                                                                    CIP

Typeset by Teknia Software

Printed in the United States of America

        03 04 05 06 07 08 09 / DC / 10 9 8 7

This work is dedicated to
V. Gail Martin Rogers,
a loving and faithful wife
as well as an exemplary mother and grandmother,
and to Kathy Louise Rogers,
also a loving, faithful, and exemplary wife.
Both of them embody the character
of the wise woman in Proverbs 31.

Table of Contents

Foreword

It has now been over twenty years since the *Linguistic Key to the Greek New Testament* first appeared in English, and we are thankful for the acceptance that it has received. There has, however, been a flood of significant literature in the area of New Testament studies since that time, so there is a real need for an "up-grade" of the book. Important contributions have been made in grammatical and lexical studies, and new tools, such as concordances, specialized lexica, and new texts, are now available. Illuminating background material in both Jewish and Greco-Roman cultures has appeared. New and helpful commentaries, as well as special studies both in journals and monographs dealing with various New Testament subjects, have been published. Many of these works have been consulted in the making of the present book. In fact, so much new material has been added and so many changes have been made that it has actually become a totally new book.

The original purpose–to provide a "key" to aid in the understanding of God's Word–has remained foremost; but this has also been expanded with the hope of making the work more useful for the exegesis of the New Testament by providing pertinent information to those who are studying a particular text. More grammatical explanations are given, especially in the use of the tenses, participles, and infinitives; more comments and references to historical works have been added, and a wider range of source material for further study has been included. The Greek words are each given a number (the Goodrick-Kohlenberger number), keying the total work to *The NIV Exhaustive Concordance*, thus expanding the availability of this book to include those who may not have a working knowledge of Greek. This will enable electronic publication of the book as well. All of this has lead to the new title, *The New Linguistic and Exegetical Key to the Greek New Testament*. It is our hope and prayer that the long hours of "delightful drudgery" spent in working on the New Testament will be used by the Lord to help those studying and preaching His eternal Word, which produces changes in their personal lives as well as the lives of those to whom they minister.

Many different grammars and commentaries have been consulted and cited in the work. The citation of a particular author or commentary does not necessarily mean that the given theological position or interpretation is accepted. The comment was simply deemed helpful in discussing the passage. Although we are aware of the many different approaches in New Testament studies, we decided to concentrate on the meaning and significance of the Greek text without a full discussion of the various approaches. In addition we have attempted to have various levels of comments, both for those with little knowledge of Greek as well as for the more advanced student.

It goes without saying that many people have helped in various ways in the preparation of this work, and they deserve a grateful word of thanks. It has been a personal joy for a "father-son" team to have been able to work together on this project. It has been a "team effort," with each making his own unique contribution. In a real sense it has also been a "family effort," for Gail (Cleon Jr.'s wife) and Kathy (Cleon III's wife) have been patient, long-suffering, and enduring as their husbands worked long hours. We all have experienced God's sustaining grace as Gail suffered a near-fatal heart attack as well as cancer. Each member of the family has had to bear the burden of stress during these times, but there was always a cheerful word of encouragement, and they deserve to be mentioned with a word of appreciation.

Charles's patient and caring medical help was often a source of strength. Sharon Breimhorst and her husband, Ditmar, and their daughters, Olivia and Geneviève, as well as Suzanne Assmann and her husband, Dieter, along with Esther, Stephan, and Philip Baxter, have provided "rays of sunshine," even when it appeared dark. Hannah, Cleon IV, Nathaniel, and Micah have also provided hours of joy and pleasure for Oma and Opa, as well as for Mom and Dad. The family heritage cannot be overlooked. Our lives have been positively influenced by the lives of our godly parents and grandparents, Cleon and Carrie Rogers and Albert and Inez Martin, and we thank God for them and for many other godly relatives as well.

There are others outside of the family who have provided invaluable assistance–colleagues, present and former students, friends, and those who have faithfully prayed for and supported us over the years. Without the encouragement and expert advice of those at Zondervan Publishing House, the work would not have been finished. We extend a special word of thanks and appreciation to Dr. Stan Gundry, Dr. Verlyn Verbrugge, Mr. Ed van der Maas, Mr. Philip Apol, Mrs. Becky Knapp, Dr. William D. Mounce, Ms. Courtney Boerstler, and other members of the Zondervan staff for their help and assistance, all of whom have worked hard to bring this book to completion.

There have also been various publishers who have graciously supplied many important works for this project and in this way have made a special contribution to the present work. We especially thank the following for providing some of their books to use in the revision: Moody; Baker; The Liturgical Press; Word; Broadman. Zondervan provided us with their *NIV Complete Bible Library* on CD, as well as many other books.

May the Lord see fit to use this combined effort to glorify His Name!

Cleon L. Rogers Jr. and Cleon L. Rogers III
Weidenhausen and Münchholzhausen, Germany
Easter in the year of our Lord 1998

Soli Deo gloria!

Abbreviations and Bibliography

NOTE: Standard abbreviations are used for the books of the Bible, the Apocrypha, the Pseudepigrapha, Jewish rabbinic literature, and the Dead Sea Scrolls.

A	Daniel R. Schwartz. *Agrippa I: The Last King of Judea*. Tübingen: J. C. B. Mohr [Paul Siebeck], 1990.
AA	Matthew Black. *An Aramaic Approach to the Gospels and Acts*[3]. Oxford: Clarendon, 1971.
AASS	Steven Thompson. *The Apocalypse and Semitic Syntax*. Society for New Testament Studies Monograph Series 52. Cambridge: Cambridge University Press, 1985.
AAT	Merrill F. Unger. *Archaeology and the New Testament*. Grand Rapids: Zondervan, 1962.
Abbott	T.K. Abbott. *A Critical and Exegetical Commentary on the Epistles to the Ephesians and the Colossians*. The International Critical Commentary. Edinburgh: T. & T. Clark, 1956.
ABD	David Noel Freedman (gen. ed.). *The Anchor Bible Dictionary.* 6 vols. New York: Doubleday, 1992.
Adamson	James Adamson. *The Epistle of James*. The New International Commentary on the New Testament. Grand Rapids: Eerdmans, 1977.
AHG	W. Ward Gasque & Ralph P. Martin (eds.). *Apostolic History and the Gospel*. Grand Rapids: Eerdmans, 1970.
AIA	Walter Müri. *Der Arzt im Altertum*. Darmstadt: Wissenschaftliche Buchgesellschaft, 1986.
AJA	*American Journal of Archaeology*
AJA	W. Harold Mare. *The Archaeology of the Jerusalem Area*. Grand Rapids: Baker, 1987.
ALAG	Scot McKnight. *A Light Among the Gentiles: Jewish Missionary in the Second Temple Period.* Minneapolis: Fortress, 1991.
Alex	Joseph Addison Alexander. *Commentary on the Acts of the Apostles*. Grand Rapids: Zondervan, 1956.
Alexander	Joseph Addison Alexander. *Commentary on the Gospel of Mark.* Grand Rapid: Zondervan, 1956.
Alford	Henry Alford. *The Greek Testament*. 5 vols. London: Rivingtons, 1855.
Allen	Willoughby C. Allen. *A Critical and Exegetical Commentary on the Gospel According to St. Matthew*. The International Critical Commentary. Edinburgh: T. & T. Clark, 1965.
AM	W.F. Albright and C.S. Mann. *Matthew*. The Anchor Bible. Garden City, N.Y.: Doubleday, 1971.
ANEP	James B. Pritchard (ed.). *Ancient Near Eastern Pictures*. Princeton: Princeton University Press, 1954.
ANET	James B. Pritchard (ed.). *Ancient Near Eastern Texts*. Princeton: Princeton University Press, 1955.

ANRW   H. Temporini & W. Hasse (gen. eds.). *Aufstieg und Niedergang der römischen Welt.* Berlin; Walter de Gruyter, 1972-.

ANT   Jack Finegan. *The Archeology of the New Testament.* Princeton: Princeton University Press, 1969.

ANTC   Edwin Yamauchi. *The Archaeology of New Testament Cities in Western Asia Minor.* Grand Rapids: Baker, 1980.

APC   Leon Morris. *The Apostolic Preaching of the Cross.* Grand Rapids: Eerdmans, 1956.

APM   Thorsten Moritz. *A Profound Mystery: The Use of the Old Testament in Ephesians.* Supplements to Novum Testamentum 85. Leiden: E.J. Brill, 1996.

Arndt   W.F. Arndt. *Bible Commentary: The Gospel According to St. Luke.* St. Louis: Concordia, 1956.

AS   G. Abbott-Smith. *A Manual Greek Lexicon of the New Testament.* Edinburgh: T. & T. Clark, 1936.

AT   Klaus Beyer. *Die aramäischen Texte vom Toten Meer.* Göttingen: Vandenhoeck & Ruprecht, 1984.

Attridge   Harold W. Attridge. *Hebrews.* Hermeneia. Philadelphia: Fortress, 1989.

Aune   David Aune. *Revelation:* Word Biblical Commentary. 3 vols. Dallas: Word, 1997.

AusBR   *Australian Biblical Review*

AUSS   *Andrews University Seminary Studies*

AUV   Otto Betz, Martin Hengel, and Peter Schmidt (eds.). *Abraham Unser Vater: Juden und Christen im Gespräch über die Bibel.* Festschrift für Otto Michel zum 60. Geburtstag. Leiden: E. J. Brill, 1963.

AVB   Etan Levine. *The Aramaic Version of the Bible: Contents and Context.* Beiheft zur *Zeitschrift für die alttestamentliche Wissenschaft.* Otto Kaiser (ed.). Berlin: Walter de Gruyter, 1988.

b.   Babylonian Talmud

BA   *Biblical Archaeologist*

BAFCS   Bruce W. Winter (ed.). *The Book of Acts in its First Century Setting.* 6 vols. Grand Rapids: Eerdmans, 1993-.

BAGD   Walter Bauer. *A Greek-English Lexicon of the New Testament.* William F. Arndt and F. Wilbur Gingrich (trans). Revised and augmented by F. Wilbur Gingrich and Frederick W. Danker from Walter Bauer's Fifth edition, 1958. Chicago: University of Chicago Press, 1979.

Bakker   W.F. Bakker. *The Greek Imperative.* Amsterdam: Adolf M. Hakkert, 1966.

Balch   David L. Balch. *Let Wives Be Submissive: The Domestic Code in 1 Peter.* Chico, Ca.: Scholars Press, 1981.

BAR   *Biblical Archaeology Review*

Barrett   C.K. Barrett. *The Gospel According to St. John: An Introduction with Commentary and Notes on the Greek Text.* London: SPCK, 1958.

Barrett   C.K. Barrett. *A Critical and Exegetical Commentary on the Acts of the Apostles. Vol. I Preliminary Introduction and Commentary on Acts I-XIV.* The International Critical Commentary. Edinburgh: T. & T. Clark, 1994.

Barrett   C.K Barrett. *The Epistle to the Romans.* New York, 1957.

Barrett   C.K. Barrett. *A Commentary on the First Epistle to the Corinthians.* London: Adam and Charles Black, 1968.

Barth   Marcus Barth. *Ephesians.* The Anchor Bible. 2 vols. Garden City, N.Y.: Doubleday, 1974.

BASHH   Colin J. Hemer. *The Book of Acts in the Setting of Hellenistic History.* Tübingen: J. C. B. Mohr [Paul Siebeck], 1989.

BASOR   *Bulletin of the American Schools of Oriental Research*

Bauckham   Richard J. Bauckham. *Jude, 2 Peter.* Word Biblical Commentary. Dallas: Word, 1983.

Bauernfeind   Otto Bauernfeind. *Kommentar und Studien zur Apostelgeschichte mit einer Einleitung von Martin Hengel.* WUNT 22. Tübingen: J. C. B. Mohr [Paul Siebeck], 1980.

BBC   Craig S. Keener. *The IVP Bible Background Commentary: New Testament.* Downers Grove: InterVarsity, 1994.

BBKA   Walter Bauer, Kurt Aland & Barbara Aland, *Griechisch-deutsches Wörterbuch zu den Schriften des Neuen Testaments und der frühchristlichen Literatur.* Berlin: Walter de Gruyter, 1988.

BBR   *Bulletin of Biblical Research*

BC   F.J. Foakes Jackson and Kirsopp Lake. *The Beginnings of Christianity,* 5 vols. London: Macmillan, 1920.

BDB   F. Brown, S.R. Driver and C.A. Briggs. *Hebrew and English Lexicon of the Old Testament.* Oxford: Oxford University Press, 1955.

BD, BDF   F. Blass and A. Debrunner. *A Greek Grammar of the New Testament.* Translated and revised by R.W. Funk. Chicago: University of Chicago Press, 1961.

BDG   Ingird Kitzberger. *Bau der Gemeinde: Das paulinische Wortfeld οἰκοδομή / ἐποικοδομεῖν.* Würzburg: Echter Verlag, 1986.

BE   Richard Longenecker. *Biblical Exegesis in the Apostolic Period.* Grand Rapids: Eerdmans, 1975.

Bean   George E. Bean. *Aegean Turkey.* London: John Murray, 1984.

Beare   Francis Wright Beare. *The Epistles of Peter.* Oxford: Basil Blackwell, 1958.

Beare   Francis Wright Beare. *The Epistles of the Philippians.* London: Adam and Charles Black, 1969.

Beare   Francis Wright Beare. *The Gospel According to Matthew: A Commentary.* Oxford: Basil Blackwell, 1981.

Beasley-Murray   George R. Beasley-Murray. *John.* Word Biblical Commentary. Waco, Tex.: Word, 1987.

Beasley-Murray   George R. Beasley-Murray. *Revelation.* The New Century Bible. Grand Rapids: Eerdmans, 1986.

Becker   Jürgen Becker. *Das Evangelium nach Johannes.* Ökumenischer Taschenbuch Kommentar zum Neuen Testament 4/1, 3rd. edition. GTB Siebenstern, Gütersloh: Gütersloher Verlag, 1991.

Bengel   John Albert Bengel. *Gnomon of the New Testament.* 5 vols. Edinburgh: T. & T. Clark, 1857.

Bernard   J.H. Bernard. *A Critical and Exegetical Commentary on the Gospel According to St. John.* The International Critical Commentary, 2 vols. Edinburgh: T. & T. Clark, 1969.

Best   Ernest Best. *A Critical and Exegetical Commentary on Ephesians.* The International Critical Commentary. Edinburgh: T. & T. Clark, 1998.

Best	Ernest Best. *A Commentary on the First and Second Epistles to the Thessalonians.* London: Adam and Charles Black, 1972.
Best	Ernest Best. *First Peter.* The New Century Bible. London: Oliphants, 1971.
Betz	Hans Bieter Betz. *Galatians.* Hermeneia: A Critical and Historical Commentary on the Bible. Philadelphia: Fortress, 1979.
Beyer	Klaus Beyer. *Semitische Syntax im Neuen Testament.* Göttingen: Vandenhoeck & Ruprecht, 1968.
BG	Maximillian Zerwick. *Biblical Greek.* Rome: Scripta Pontificii Instituti Biblici, 1963.
BHS	James D.G. Dunn. *Baptism in the Holy Spirit.* London: SCM, 1974.
Bib	*Biblica*
BibLeb	*Bibel und Leben*
Bib Sac	*Bibliotheca Sacra*
Bigg	Charles Bigg. *A Critical and Exegetical Commentary on the Epistles of St. Peter and St. Jude.* The International Critical Commentary. Edinburgh: T. & T. Clark, 1902.
BJRL	*Bulletin of the John Rylands University Library of Manchester*
BKC	John F. Walvoord and Roy B. Zuck. *The Bible Knowledge Commentary: An Exposition of the Scriptures by the Dallas Seminary Faculty, New Testament Edition Based on the New International Version.* Wheaton: Victor Books, 1983.
Blinzler	Josef Blinzler. *The Trial of Jesus.* Isabel and Florence McHugh (trans). Westminster: Newman, 1959.
Blomberg	Craig L. Blomberg. *Matthew: An Exegetical and Theological Exposition of Holy Scripture NIV Text.* The New American Commentary, vol. 22. Edited by David S. Dockery et al. Nashville: Broadman & Holman, 1992.
Blomberg	Craig Blomberg. *1 Corinthians.* The NIV Application Commentary. Grand Rapids: Zondervan, 1995.
Blomqvist	Jerker Blomqvist. *Greek Particles in Hellenistic Prose.* Lund, Sweden: C.W.K. Gleerup, 1969.
Blum	Edwin A. Blum, "John," in John F. Walvoord and Roy B. Zuck. *The Bible Knowledge Commentary: An Exposition of the Scriptures by the Dallas Seminary Faculty, New Testament Edition, Based on the New International Version.* Wheaton: Victor Books, 1983.
Blum	Edwin A. Blum. "1, 2 Peter, Jude" in *Expositor's Bible Commentary with The New International Version of the Holy Bible.* Vol. 12 (Hebrews, James, 1, 2 Peter, 1, 2, 3, John, Jude, Revelation). Frank E. Gaebelein and J.D. Douglas (eds.). Grand Rapids: Zondervan, 1984.
BN	*Biblische Notizen*
Bock	Darrel L. Bock. *Luke 1:1-9:50; 9:51-24:53.* Baker Exegetical Commentary on the New Testament. Moises Silva (ed.). Grand Rapids: Baker, 1994-96.
Bousset	Wilhelm Bousset. *Die Offenbarung Johannes.* Göttingen: Vandenhoeck & Ruprecht, 1906.
Bovon	Francois Bovon. *Das Evangelium nach Lukas.* 3 vols. Evangelisch-Katholischer Kommentar zum Neuen Testament. Neukirchen-Vluyn: Neukirchener Verlag, 1989-97.
Braun	Herbert Braun. *An die Hebräer.* Handbuch zum Neuen Testament. Tübingen: J. C. B. Mohr, 1984.

BRD   William Ramsay. *The Bearing of Recent Discovery on the Trustworthiness of the New Testament*. Grand Rapids: Baker, 1953.

Brooke   A.E. Brooke. *A Critical and Exegetical Commentary on the Johannine Epistles*. The International Critical Commentary. Edinburgh: T. & T. Clark, 1912.

Brooks   James A. Brooks. *Mark: An Exegetical and Theological Exposition of Holy Scripture NIV Text*. The New American Commentary, vol. 23. Edited by David S. Dockery et al. Nashville, Tenn.: Broadman & Holman, 1991.

Brown   Raymond E. Brown. *The Gospel According to John*. The Anchor Bible. 2 vols. Garden City, N.Y.: Doubleday, 1972.

Brown   Raymond E. Brown, *The Epistles of John*. The Anchor Bible. Garden City, N.Y.: Doubleday, 1982.

Brox   Norbert Brox. *Der erste Petrusbrief*. Evangelisch-katholischer Kommentar zum Neuen Testament. Neukirchen-Vluyn: Neukirchener Verlag, 1979.

Bruce   F.F. Bruce. *The Acts of the Apostles: The Greek Text with Introduction, Exposition and Notes*. Grand Rapids: Eerdmans, 1960.

Bruce   F.F. Bruce. *I and II Corinthians*. The New Century Bible. London: Oliphants, 1971.

Bruce   F.F. Bruce. *The Epistle to the Galatians: A Commentary on the Greek Text*. The New International Greek Testament Commentary. Grand Rapids: Eerdmans, 1982.

Bruce   F.F. Bruce. *The Epistles to the Colossians, to Philemon and to the Ephesians*. The New International Commentary on the New Testament. Grand Rapids: Eerdmans, 1981.

Bruce   F.F. Bruce. *1&2 Thessalonians*. Word Biblical Commentary. Dallas: Word, 1982.

Bruce   F.F. Bruce. *Commentary on the Epistle to the Hebrews*. Grand Rapids: Eerdmans, 1977.

Bruce-ET   F.F. Bruce. *Commentary on the Book of Acts: The English Text With Introduction, Exposition and Notes*. Grand Rapids: Eerdmans, 1960.

Bruner, Matt. Frederick Dale Bruner. *The Christbook: A Historical/Theological Commentary: Matthew 1-12*. Waco, Tex.: Word, 1987.

Bruner   Frederick Dale Bruner, *A Theology of the Holy Spirit: Pentecostal Experience and the New Testament Witness*. London: Hodder & Stoughton, 1971.

BS   Adolph Deismann. *Biblical Studies*. 2nd. edition. Alexander Grieve (trans). Edinburgh: T. & T. Clark, 1903

BTB   *Biblical Theology Bulletin*

BTNT   Roy B. Zuck and Darrell L. Bock, (eds.). *A Biblical Theology of the New Testament*. Chicago: Moody, 1994.

Buchanan   George Wesley Buchanan. *To the Hebrews*. The Anchor Bible. Garden City, N.Y.: Doubleday, 1972.

Buckland   W.W. Buckland. *A Textbook of Roman Law*. Cambridge: Cambridge University Press, 1932.

Bultmann   Rudolf Bultmann. *The Gospel of John*. Philadelphia: Fortress, 1971.

Bultmann   Rudolf Bultmann. *Der zweite Brief an die Korinther*. Kritisch-exegetischer Kommentar über das Neue Testament. Göttingen: Vandenhoeck & Ruprecht, 1976.

Bultmann   Rudolf Bultmann. *Die drei Johannesbriefe*. Kritisch-exegetischer Kommentar über das Neue Testament. Göttingen: Vandenhoeck & Ruprecht, 1967.

Burton   Ernest DeWitt Burton. *A Critical and Exegetical Commentary on the Galatians.* The International and Critical Commentary. Edinburgh: T. & T. Clark, 1956.

Byrne   Brendan Byrne. *Romans.* Sacra Pagina 6. A Michael Glazier Book. Collegeville, Minn.: Liturgical, 1996.

C   Martin Hengel. *Crucifixion.* Philadelphia: Fortress, 1977.

CAC   Fred O. Francis and Wayne A. Meeks (eds.). *Conflicts at Colossae: A Problem in the Interpretation of Early Christianity Illustrated by Selected Modern Studies.* Revised edition. Missoula, Mont: Scholars, 1975.

CAH   *The Cambridge Ancient History.* 12 vols. Cambridge: University Press, 1927-1975.

Caird   G.B. Caird. *The Gospel of Luke.* London: Penguin Books, 1963.

Caird   C.B. Caird. *The Revelation of St. John the Divine.* Black's New Testament Commentaries. London: Adam and Charles Black, 1966.

Carrington   Philip Carrington. *According to Mark: A Running Commentary on the Oldest Gospel.* Cambridge: University Press, 1960.

Carson   Donald A. Carson. "Matthew," in *Expositor's Bible Commentary with The New International Version of the Holy Bible.* Vol. 8 (Matthew, Mark, Luke). Frank E. Gaebelein and J.D. Douglas (eds.). Grand Rapids: Zondervan, 1984.

Carson   Donald A. Carson. *The Gospel According to John.* Grand Rapids: Eerdmans, 1991.

Catchpole   David R. Catchpole. *The Trial of Jesus.* Leiden: E.J. Brill, 1971.

CBB   L. Coenen, E. Beyereuther, H. Bietenhard. *Theologisches Begriffslexicon zum Neuen Testament.* 3 vols. Wuppertal: Brockhaus, 1971.

CBQ   *Catholic Biblical Quarterly*

CC   Stephen Benko and John J. O'Rourke. *The Catacombs and the Colosseum.* Valley Forge: Judson, 1971.

CCFJ   Karl Heinrich Rengstorf (ed.). *A Complete Concordance to Flavius Josephus.* 4 vols. Leiden: E.J. Brill, 1973-1983.

CD   Cairo Damascus Covenant

CDMG   Michael J. Wilkens. *The Concept of Disciple in Matthew's Gospel, as Reflected in the Use of the Term* μαθητής. Leiden: E.J. Brill, 1988.

CEC   Richard N. Longnecker. *The Christology of Early Jewish Christianity.* Studies in Biblical Theology. Second series 17. London: SCM, 1970.

CGP   Albert-Marie Denis. *Concordance Grecque des Pseudépigraphes d'Ancien Testament.* Louvain-la-Neuve: Université de Louvain, 1987.

CH   W.J. Conybeare and J.S. Howson. *The Life and Epistles of St. Paul.* Grand Rapids: Eerdmans, 1953.

CIC   Craig S. Wansink. *Chained in Christ: The Experience and Rhetoric of Paul's Imprisonments.* Sheffield: Sheffield Academic Press, 1996.

CIE   Werner Thiessen. *Christen in Ephesus: Die historische und theologische Situation in vorpaulinischer und paulinischer Zeit und zur Zeit der Apostelgeschichte und der Pastoralbriefe.* Tübingen: Francke Verlag, 1995.

Charles   R.H. Charles. *A Critical and Exegetical Commentary on the Revelation of St. John.* The International Critical Commentary, 2 vols. Edinburgh: T. & T. Clark, 1965.

CNT — Leon Morris. *The Cross in the New Testament*. Grand Rapids: Eerdmans, 1965.

Conzelmann — Hans Conzelmann. *Der erste Brief an die Korinther*. Kritschexegetischer Kommentar über das Neue Testament. Göttingen: Vandenhoeck & Ruprecht, 1969.

CPJ — Victor A. Tcherikover and Alexander Fuks (eds.). *Corpus Papyrorum Judaicarum*. Cambridge, Mass.: Harvard University Press, 1957-1964.

CPP — Dieter Zeller. *Charis bei Philon und Paulus*. Stuttgart: Verlag Katholisches Bibelwerk, 1990.

Cranfield — C. E. B. Cranfield. *The Gospel According to St. Mark*. The Cambridge Greek Testament Commentary. Cambridge: University Press, 1972.

Cranfield — C. E. B. Cranfield. *A Critical and Exegetical Commentary on the Epistle to the Romans*. The International Critical Commentary. 2 vols. Edinburgh: T. & T. Clark, 1975-79.

Cremer — Hermann Cremer. *Biblico-Theological Lexicon of the New Testament Greek*. William Urwick (trans). Edinburgh: T. & T. Clark, 1954.

Crouch — James E. Crouch. *The Origin and Intention of the Colossian Haustafel*. Göttingen: Vandenhoeck & Ruprecht, 1972.

CSP — William M. Ramsay. *The Cities of St. Paul*. London: Hodder and Stoughton, 1907.

DA — W.D. Davies and Dale C. Allison Jr. *A Critical and Exegetical Commentary on the Gospel According to Saint Matthew*. 3 vols. The International Critical Commentary. Edinburgh: T. & T. Clark, 1988–97.

Davids — Peter Davids. *The Epistle of James. A Commentary on the Greek Text*. The New International Greek Testament Commentary. Grand Rapids: Eerdmans, 1982.

Davids — Peter Davids. *The Epistle of 1 Peter*. The New International Commentary on the New Testament. Grand Rapids: Eerdmans, 1990.

DC — Dio Chrysostom

DCH — David J.A. Clines. *The Dictionary of Classical Hebrew*. Sheffield: Sheffield Academic Press, 1993-.

DCNT — G. Mussies. *Dio Chrysostom and the New Testament*. Leiden: E.J. Brill, 1972.

DDD — Karl van der Toorn, Bob Becking, Pieter W. van der Horst (eds.). *Dictionary of Deities and Demons in the Bible*. Leiden: E.J. Brill, 1995.

Delitzsch — Frank Delitzsch. *Commentary on the Epistle to the Hebrews*. Translated from the German by Thomas L. Kingsbury. 2 vols. Grand Rapids: Eerdmans, 1952.

DGRA — William Smith. *A Dictionary of Greek & Roman Antiquities*. London: John Murray, 1872.

Dibelius — Martin Dibelius. *An Die Kolosser, Epheser, An Philemon*. Handbuch zum Neuen Testament. Third edition. Newly revised by Heinrich Greeven. Tübingen: J. C. B. Mohr, 1953.

Dibelius — Martin Dibelius. *Die Pastoralbriefe*. Handbuch zum Neuen Testament. 4th edition, supplemented by Hans Conzelmann. Tübingen: J. C. B. Mohr, 1966.

Dibelius — Martin Dibelius and Heinrich Greeven. *A Commentary on the Epistle of James*. Hermeneia. Michael A. Williams (trans). Philadelphia: Fortress, 1976.

DJG — Joel B. Green, Scot McKnight, I. Howard Marshall (eds.). *Dictionary of Jesus and the Gospels*. Downers Grove: InterVarsity, 1992.

DJGE — Ismar Elbogen. *Der jüdische Gottesdienst in seiner geschichtlichen Entwicklung*. Hildesheim: Georg Olms Verlag, 1995.

DLNT	Ralph P.Martin and Peter Davids, *Dictionary of the Later New Testament and Its Development*. Downers Grove: InterVarsity, 1997.
DM	H.E. Dana and J. R. Mantey. *A Manual Grammar of the Greek New Testament*. New York: Macmillan, 1950.
DMTG	Richard J. Durling, *A Dictionary of Medical Terms in Galen*. Leiden: E.J. Brill, 1993.
DNP	Hubert Cancik & Helmuth Schneider (eds.). *Der Neue Pauly: Enzyklopädie der Antike*. Stuttgart: Verlag J.B Metzler, 1996-.
Dodd	C.H. Dodd. *The Interpretation of the Fourth Gospel*. Cambridge: University Press, 1958.
Dodd	C. H. Dodd. *The Epistle of Paul to the Romans*. London: Hodder & Stoughton, 1932.
DPL	Gerald F. Hawthorne and Ralph Martin (eds.). *Dictionary of Paul and His Letters*. Downers Grove: InterVarsity, 1993.
DRP	Günter Wagner. *Das Religionsgsechichtliche Problem von Römer 6, 1-11*. Zürich: Zwingli Verlag, 1962.
DRU	Hans Josepf Klauck. *Die religiöse Umwelt des Christentums*. 2 vols. I. *Stadt- und Hausreligion, Mysterienkulte, Volksglaube*. II. *Herrscher- und Kaiserkult, Philosophie, Gnosis*. Stuttgart: Verlag W. Kohlhammer, 1996.
DSS	Dead Sea Scrolls.
DSSE	Geza Vermes. *The Dead Sea Scrolls in English[3]*. Sheffield: Sheffield Academic Press, 1987.
DSST	Florentino García Martínez. *The Dead Sea Scrolls in Translation: The Qumran Texts in English*. Leiden: E.J. Brill, 1994.
DTM	Raymond E. Brown. *The Death of the Messiah: From Gethsemane to the Grave: A Commentary on the Passion Narratives in the Four Gospels*. 2 vols. The Anchor Bible Reference Library. David Noel Freedman (gen. ed). New York: Doubleday, 1994.
Dunn	James D.G. Dunn. *Romans*. Word Biblical Commentary, 2 vols. Dallas: Word, 1988.
Dunn	James D.G. Dunn. *The Epistle to the Colossians and to Philemon: A Commentary on the Greek Text*. The New International Greek Testament Commentary. Grand Rapids: Eerdmans, 1996.
DZ	Martin Hengel. *Die Zeloten: Untersuchungen zur jüdischen Freiheitsbewegung in der Zeit von Herodes I. bis 70 N. Chr*. Leiden: E. J. Brill, 1976.
Eadie	John Eadie. *Commentary on the Epistle of Paul to the Galatians*. Minneapolis: James and Klock, 1977.
Eadie	John Eadie. *Commentary on the Epistle to the Ephesians*. Grand Rapids: Zondervan, 1956.
Eadie	John Eadie. *Commentary on the Epistle of Paul to the Colossians*. Minneapolis: James and Klock, 1977.
EBC	Frank E. Gaebelein (gen. ed). *The Expositor's Bible Commentary*. Grand Rapids: Zondervan, 1976.
EBD	Gleason L. Archer. *Encyclopedia of Bible Difficulties*. Grand Rapids: Zondervan, 1982.
EC	Peter Marshall. *Enmity in Corinth: Social Conventions in Paul's Relations with the Corinthians*. Wissenschaftliche Untersuchungen zum Neuen Testament 2. Martin Hengel, Otfried Hofius, and Otto Michel (ed.). Reihe 23. Tübingen: J. C. B. Mohr [Paul Siebeck], 1987.
ECC	Vernon H. Neufeld. *The Earliest Christian Confessions*. Grand Rapids: Eerdmans, 1963.

Edersheim, *Temple*	Alfred Edersheim. *The Temple: Its Ministry and Services.* Grand Rapids: Eerdmans, 1954.
EDNT	Horst Balz and Gerhard Schneider. *Exegetical Dictionary of the New Testament.* Virgil P. Howard and James W. Thompson (trans). Grand Rapids: Eerdmans, 1990.
EGGNT	W.D. Chamberlain. *An Exegetical Grammar of the Greek New Testament.* New York: Macmillan. 1941.
EGT	W. Robertson Nicol (ed.). *The Expositor's Greek Testament.* 5 vols. Grand Rapids: Eerdmans, 1956.
EH	Karl Matthäus Woschitz. *Elpis Hoffnung: Geschichte, Philosophie, Exegese, Theologie eines Schlüsselbegriffs.* Wien: Herder, 1979.
EIW	Michael Lattke, *Einheit im Wort: Die spezifische Bedeutung von "agape," "agapan," und "filein" im Johannes-Evangelium.* Münich: Kösel-Verlag, 1975.
EJH	Herbert W. Bateman, IV. *Early Jewish Hermeneutics and Hebrews 1:5-13.* New York: Peter Lang, 1997.
Ellicott	Charles J. Ellicott. *A Critical and Grammatical Commentary on St. Paul's Epistle to the Galatians.* Boston: Draper and Halliday, 1867.
Ellicott	Charles J. Ellicott. *St. Paul's Epistle to the Ephesians: With a Critical and Grammatical Commentary, and a Revised Translation.* 4th Edition. London: Longman, Green, Reader and Dyer, 1868.
Ellicott	Charles J. Ellicott. *St. Paul's Epistle to the Philippians, the Colossians and Philemon.* London: Longman, Green, Reader and Dyer, 1865.
Ellicott	Charles J. Ellicott. *A Critical and Grammatical Commentary on St. Paul's Epistles to the Thessalonians.* Andover: Warten F. Draper, 1865.
Ellicott	Charles J. Ellicott. *The Pastoral Epistles of St. Paul.* Fifth corrected edition. London: Longmans, Green and Co., 1883.
Ellis	E. Earle Ellis. *The Gospel of Luke.* The New Century Bible. London: Nelson, 1966.
ELR	A. Trebel and K. M. King. *Everyday Life in Rome.* Oxford: Oxford University Press, 1958.
Epictetus	Epictetus, *Discourses*
ERE	Richard Duncan-Jones. *The Economy of the Roman Empire: Quantitative Studies.* 2nd. edition. Cambridge: Cambridge University Press, 1982.
ESB	Joseph A. Fitzmyer. *Essays on the Semitic Background of the New Testament.* Missoula, Mont.: Scholars, 1974.
ET	*Expository Times*
Evans	C.F. Evans. *Saint Luke.* TPI New Testament Commentaries. Philadelphia: Trinity, 1990.
EWNT	Horst Balz and Gerhard Schneider. *Exegetisches Wörterbuch zum Neuen Testament.* 2. Auflage. 3 vols. Stuttgart: Kohlhammer, 1992.
Fairbairn	Patrick Fairbairn. *Commentary on the Pastoral Epistles, First and Second Timothy, Titus.* Grand Rapids: Zondervan, 1956.
FAP	Rainer Riesner. *Die Frühzeit des Apostels Paulus.* Wissenschaftliche Untersuchungen im Neuen Testament 71. Martin Hengel and Otfried Hofius (eds.). Tübingen: J. C. B. Mohr [Paul Siebeck], 1994.

Fascher   Erich Fascher. *Der Erste Brief des Paulus an die Korinther.* Berlin: Evangelische Verlagsanstalt, 1975.

FCRR   H.H. Scullard. *Festivals and Ceremonies of the Roman Republic.* London: Thames and Hudson, 1981.

FCSS   Scott Bartchy. *First Century Slavery and First Corinthians 7:21.* Missoula, Mont.: Society of Biblical Literature, 1973.

Fee   Gordon D. Fee. *The First Epistle to the Corinthians.* The New International Commentary on the New Testament. Grand Rapids: Eerdmans, 1987.

FFB   *Fauna and Flora of the Bible: Helps for Translators.* Vol. XI. New York: United Bible Societies, 1972.

Filson   Floyd V. Filson. *The Gospel According to St. Matthew.* London: Adam and Charles Black, 1971.

Fitzmyer   Joseph A. Fitzmyer. *The Gospel According to Luke.* The Anchor Bible. 2 vols. Garden City, N.Y.: Doubleday, 1981, 1985.

Fitzmyer   Joseph A. Fitzmyer. *Romans.* The Anchor Bible. Garden City, N.Y.: Doubleday, 1993.

Ford   J. Massyngberde Ford. *Revelation.* The Anchor Bible. Garden City, N.Y.: Doubleday, 1975.

Frame   James Everett Frame. *A Critical and Exegetical Commentary on the Epistles of St. Paul to the Thessalonians.* The International Critical Commentary. Edinburgh: T. & T. Clark, 1953.

France   R.T. France. *The Gospel According to Matthew: An Introduction and Commentary.* Tyndale New Testament Commentaries. Leon Morris (ed.). Grand Rapids: Eerdmans, 1985.

FS   William Barclay. *Flesh and Spirit: An Examination of Galatians 5:19-23.* Grand Rapids: Baker, 1977.

FSLD   Donald A. Carson (ed.). *From Sabbath to Lord's Day.* Grand Rapids: Zondervan, 1982.

Fung   Ronald Y.K. Fung. *The Epistle to the Galatians.* The New International Commentary on the New Testament. Grand Rapids: Eerdmans, 1989.

Funk   Robert W. Funk. *A Beginning-Intermediate Grammar of Hellenistic Greek.* 3 vols. Missoula, Mont.: Society of Biblical Literature, 1973.

Furnish   Victor Paul Furnish. *II Corinthians.* The Anchor Bible. Garden City, N.Y.: Doubleday, 1984.

G   Seán Freyne. *Galilee from Alexander the Great to Hadrian 323 B.C.E. to 135 C.E.* Wilmington, Del.: Glazier, 1980.

GAM   William M. Ramsay. *The Historical Geography of Asia Minor.* Amsterdam: Adolf M. Hakkert, 1962.

Gaugler   Ernst Gaugler. *Der Epheserbrief.* Auslegung neutestamentlicher Schriften. Zurich: EVZ-Verlag, 1966.

Gaugler   Ernst Gaugler. *Die Johannesbriefe.* Auslegung neutestamentlicher Schriften. Zurich: EVZ-Verlag, 1964.

GB   Denis Baly. *The Geography of the Bible: A Study in Historical Geography.* New York: Harper, 1957.

GCDSS   James H. Charlesworth. *Graphic Concordance to the Dead Sea Scrolls.* Tübingen: J. C. B. Mohr [Paul Siebeck], 1991.

Geldenhuys   J. Norval Geldenhuys. *Commentary on the Gospel of Luke*. London: Marshall, Morgan & Scott, 1971.

GELRS   H.G. Liddell, Robert Scott, H. Stuart Jones (eds.). *A Greek English Lexicon: Revised Supplement*. F.G.W. Glare and A.A. Thompson (eds.). Oxford: Clarendon, 1996.

GELS   H.G. Liddell, Robert Scott, H. Stuart Jones (eds.). *A Greek English Lexicon: A Supplement*. E. A. Barber, P. Mass, M. Scheller, and M. L. West (eds.). Oxford: Clarendon, 1968.

GELTS   J. Lust, E. Eynikel, K. Hauspie (eds.). *A Greek-English Lexicon of the Septuagint. Parts I & II*. Stuttgart: Deutsche Bibelgesellschaft, 1992-1996.

GEW   Hjalmar Frisk. *Griechisches Etymologisches Wörterbuch*. Heidelberg: Carl Winter, 1973.

GG   Peter Stuhlmacher. *Gerechtigkeit Gottes bei Paulus*. Göttingen: Vandenhoeck & Ruprecht, 1966.

GGBB   Daniel B. Wallace. *Greek Grammar Beyond the Basics: An Exegetical Syntax of the New Testament*. Grand Rapids: Zondervan, 1996.

GGP   Francis Thomas Gignac. *A Grammar of the Greek Papyri of the Roman and Byzantine Periods*. Vol I Phonology; Vol II Morphology. Milan: Istituto Editoriale Cisalpino - La Goliardica, 1975-1981.

GGR   Martin P. Nilsson. *Geschichte der griechischen Religion*. 2 vols . Munich: C.H. Beck'sche Verlagsbuchhandlung, 1968.

GI   Nigel Turner. *Grammatical Insights Into the New Testament*. Edinburgh: T. & T. Clark, 1965.

Gifford   E. H. Gifford. *The Epistle of St. Paul to the Romans*. London: John Murray, 1886.

GIZ   Gerhard Pfohl (ed.). *Griechische Inschriften als Zeugnisse des privaten und öffentlichen Lebens*. München: Ernst Heimeran Verlag, 1965.

GLAJJ   Menahm Stern. *Greek and Latin Authors on Jews and Judaism*. 3 vols. Jerusalem: Israel Academy of Sciences and Humanities, 1974.

GLH   Louise Wells. *The Greek Language of Healing from Homer to New Testament Times*. Berlin: Walter de Gruyter, 1998.

GMP   Hans Dieter Betz (ed.). *The Greek Magical Papyri in Translation*. Chicago: University of Chicago Press, 1986.

Gnilka   Joachim Gnilka. *Das Matthaeusevangelium: 1. Teil Kommentar zu Kap. 1,1 - 13,58*. Herders theologischer Kommentar zum Neuen Testament. Freiburg: Herder, 1986.

Gnilka   Joachim Gnilka. *Das Evangelium nach Markus*. 2 vols. Evanglisch-katholischer Kommentar zum Neuen Testament. Neukirchen-Vluyn: Neukirchener Verlag, 1978.

Gnilka   Joachim Gnilka. *Der Epheserbrief*. Herders theologischer Kommentar zum Neuen Testament. Basel: Herder, 1971.

Gnilka   Joachim Gnilka. *Der Philipperbrief*. Herders theologischer Kommentar zum Neuen Testament. Freiburg: Herder, 1976.

Gnilka   Joachim Gnilka. *Der Kolosserbrief*. Herders theologischer Kommentar zum Neuen Testament. Freiburg: Herder, 1980.

GNT   James Moffatt. *Grace in the New Testament*. New York: Long and Smith, 1932.

Godet   Frederick L. Godet. *A Commentary on the Gospel of St. Luke*. 2 vols. Grand Rapids: Zondervan, 1969.

Godet	John Frederick L. Godet. *Commentary on the Gospel of John.* Grand Rapids: Zondervan, 1969.
Godet	Frederick L. Godet. *The Commentary on the Epistle to the Romans.* A. Cusin and Talbot W. Chambers (trans). Grand Rapids: Zondervan, 1956.
Godet	Frederick L. Godet. *Commentary on the First Epistle of St. Paul to the Corinthians.* A. Cusin (trans). 2 vols. Grand Rapids: Zondervan, 1957.
Goppelt	Leonhard Goppelt. *Der erste Petrusbrief.* Kritisch-exegetischer Kommentar über das Neue Testament. Ferdinand Han (ed.). Göttingen: Vandenhoeck & Ruprecht, 1977.
Gould	Ezra E. Gould. *A Critical and Exegetical Commentary on the Gospel According to Mark.* The International and Critical Commentary. Edinburgh: T. & T. Clark, 1896.
Govett	Robert Govett. *The Apocalypse Expounded by Scripture.* Abridged from 4 vol. edition 1864. London: Charles J. Thyme, 1920.
GPT	F.E. Peters. *Greek Philosophical Terms: A Historical Lexicon.* New York: New York University Press, 1967.
Grässer	Erich Grässer. *Der Brief an die Hebräer.* 2 vols. Evangelisch-katholischer Kommentar zum Neuen Testament. Neukirchen-Vluyn: Neukirchener Verlag, 1993-1997.
Green	Michael Green. *The Second Epistle of Peter and the General Epistle of Jude.* Tyndale New Testament Commentaries. London: Tyndale, 1970.
Grosheide	Frederick Grosheide. *Commentary on First Corinthians.* New International Commentaries on the New Testament. Grand Rapids: Eerdmans, 1970.
Grudem	Wayne Grudem. *1 Peter.* Tyndale New Testament Commentaries. Grand Rapids: Eerdmans, 1990.
Grundmann	Walter Grundmann. *Das Evangelium nach Lukas.* Theologischer Kommentar zum Neuen Testament. Edited by Otto Bauernfeind et al., 2nd. edition. Berlin: Evanglische Verlagsanstalt, 1966.
Grundmann	Walter Grundmann. *Der Brief des Judas und der zweite Brief des Petrus.* Theologischer Handkommentar zum Neuen Testament. Berlin: Evangelische Verlagsanstalt, 1986.
Guelich	Robert A. Guelich. *Mark.* Word Biblical Commentary. 2 vols. David A. Hubbard and Ralph P. Martin (gen. eds.). Dallas: Word, 1989.
Gundry	Robert H. Gundry. *Matthew: A Commentary on His Literary and Theological Art.* Grand Rapids: Eerdmans, 1982.
Gundry	Robert H. Gundry. *Mark: A Commentary on His Apology for the Cross.* Grand Rapids: Eerdmans, 1993.
Guthrie	Donald Guthrie. *Galatians.* The New Century Bible. London: Oliphants, 1969.
Guthrie	Donald Guthrie. *The Pastoral Epistles.* London: Tyndale, 1969.
GW	David Hill. *Greek Word and Hebrew Meanings: Studies in the Semantics of Soteriological Terms.* Cambridge: University Press, 1967.
HA	Harold Hoehner. *Herod Antipas.* Cambridge: University Press, 1967.
HAE	Johannes Renz & Wolfgang Röllig. *Handbuch der althebräischen Epigraphik.* 3 vols. Darmstadt: Wissenschaftliche Buchgesellschaft, 1995.
Haenchen	Ernst Haehnchen. *Johannes Evangelium: Ein Kommentar.* Ulrich Busse (ed.). Tübingen: J. C. B. Mohr [Paul Siebeck], 1980.
Haenchen	Ernst Haehnchen. *The Acts of the Apostles.* Philadelphia: Westminster, 1971.

Hagner	Donald A. Hagner. *Matthew.* Word Biblical Commentary. 2 vols. Dallas: Word, 1995.
Harrington	Wilfrid J. Harrington. *Revelation.* Sacra Pagina 16. Collegeville, Minn.: Liturgical Press, 1993.
Harris	Murray J. Harris. *Colossians & Philemon.* Exegetical Guide to the Greek New Testament. Grand Rapids: Eerdmans, 1991.
Hawthorne	Gerald F. Hawthorne. *Philippians.* Word Biblical Commentary. Dallas: Word, 1983.
HDB	James Hastings (ed.). *A Dictionary of the Bible.* 5 vols. Edinburgh: T. & T. Clark, 1901.
HDCG	James Hastings (ed.). *A Dictionary of Christ and the Gospels.* 2 vols. Edinburgh: T. & T. Clark, 1906.
Hendricksen	William Hendricksen. *New Testament Commentary: Matthew.* Grand Rapids: Baker, 1974.
Hendricksen	William Hendricksen. *New Testament Commentary: Colossians and Philemon.* Edinburgh: Banner of Truth Trust, 1974.
Hering	Jean Hering. *The Second Epistle of St. Paul to the Corinthians.* A.W. Heathcote & P.J. Allcock (trans). London: Epworth, 1967.
Herodotus	Herodotus, *History.*
Hewitt	Thomas Hewitt. *The Epistle to the Hebrews: An Introduction and Commentary.* Tyndale New Testament Commentary. Grand Rapids: Eerdmans, 1960.
HGAM	William. M. Ramsay. *The Historical Geography of Asia Minor.* Amsterdam: Adolf M. Hakkert, 1962.
HGS	Franz Passow. *Handwörterbuch der griechischen Sprache.* 4 vols. Darmstadt: Wissenschaftliche Buchgesellschaft, 1970.
Hill	David Hill. *The Gospel of Matthew.* The New Century Bible. London: Oliphants, 1972.
HJC	Frederic W. Madden. *History of Jewish Coinage and of Money in the Old and New Testament.* New York: KTAV, 1967.
HJP	Emil Schürer. *The History of the Jewish People in the Age of Jesus Christ (175 B.C-A.D.135).* New English edition revised and edited by Geza Verrnes and Fergus Millar. Vol. 1. Edinburgh: T. & T. Clark, 1973.
HK	Peter Richardson. *Herod: King of the Jews and Friend of the Romans.* Columbia, S.C.: University of South Carolina Press, 1996.
HVK	Uwe Wagner. *Der Hauptmann von Kafarnaum.* Wissenschaftliche Untersuchungen zum Neuen Testament 2. Martin Hengel, Otfried Hofius, and Otto Michel (eds.). Reihe 14. Tübingen: J. C. B. Mohr [Paul Siebeck], 1985.
HLIN	Stephen Farris. *The Hymns of Luke's Infancy Narratives: Their Origin, Meaning, and Significance.* Journal for the Study of the New Testament Supplement Series 9. Bruce D. Chilton and David J.A. Clines (eds.). Sheffield: JSOT, 1987.
Hodge	Charles Hodge. *Commentary on the Epistle to the Romans.* Grand Rapids: Eerdmans, 1953.
Hodge	Charles Hodge. *Commentary on the First Epistle to the Corinthians.* Grand Rapids: Eerdmans, 1953.
Hodge	Charles Hodge. *Commentary on the Second Epistle to the Corinthians.* Grand Rapids: Eerdmans, 1953.
Hodge	Charles Hodge. *A Commentary on the Epistle to the Ephesians.* Grand Rapids: Eerdmans, 1950.

Hofius	Otfried Hofius. *Der Christushymnus Philipper 2, 6-11*. Tübingen: J. C. B. Mohr, 1977.
HOG	David C. Verner. *The Household of God: The Social World of the Pastoral Epistles*. SBL Dissertaton Series 71. Chico, Ca.: Scholars, 1983.
Holz	Traugott Holz. *Der Erste Brief an die Thessalonicher*. Evangelisch-katholischer Kommentar zum Neuen Testament. Neukirchen-Vluyn: Neukirchener Verlag, 1986.
Hooker	Morna D. Hooker. *The Gospel According to St. Mark*. Black's New Testament Commentaries. Henry Chadwick (ed.). London: A. & C. Black, 1991.
Hort	F.J.A. Hort. *The First Epistle of St. Peter 1.1–2.17*. London: Macmillan, 1898; reprint Minneapolis: James and Klock, 1976.
Hort	F.J.A. Hort. *The Apocalypse of St. John I–III*. London: Macmillan, 1908; reprint Minneapolis: James and Klock, 1976.
Hoskyns	Edwyn Clement Hoskyns. *The Fourth Gospel*. Francis Noel Davey (ed.). London: Oxford University Press, 1972.
Houlden	J. L. Houlden. *A Commentary on the Johannine Epistles*. Black's New Testament Commentary. London: Adam and Charles Black, 1973.
HSB	Walter C. Kaiser, Jr., Peter H. Davids, F.F. Bruce, Manfred T. Brauch, (eds.). *Hard Sayings of the Bible*. Downers Grove: InterVarsity, 1996.
HTR	*Harvard Theological Review*
HTS	*Harvard Theological Studies*
Hughes	Philip E. Hughes. *Commentary on the Second Epistle to the Corinthians*. Grand Rapids, Eerdmans, 1971.
Hughes	Philip E. Hughes. *Commentary on the Epistle to the Hebrews*. Grand Rapids, Eerdmans, 1977.
IBD	J.D. Douglas (ed.). *The Illustrated Bible Dictionary*, 3 vols. Leicester: InterVarsity, 1986.
IDB	George Arthur Buttrick (ed.). *The Interpretator's Dictionary of the Bible*. 4 vols. Nashville: Abingdon, 1962.
IDB (Supp.)	Keith Crim (gen. ed). *The Interpreter's Dictionary of the Bible: Supplementary Vol.* Nashville: Abingdon, 1976.
IGNT	Stanley E. Porter. *Idioms of the Greek New Testament*. Sheffield: JSOT, 1992.
IMC	Wendell Lee Willis. *Idol Meat in Corinth: The Pauline Argument in 1 Corinthians 8 and 10*. SBL Dissertation Series 68. Chico, Ca.: Scholars, 1985.
Inter	*Interpretation*
IP	Craig L. Blomberg. *Interpreting the Parables*. Downers Grove: InterVarsity, 1990.
ISBE	Geoffery W. Bromiley. *The International Standard Bible Encyclopedia*. Fully revised. 4 vols. Grand Rapids: Eerdmans, 1979.
j.	Jerusalem Talmud
JAD	William A. Heth and Gordon J. Wenham. *Jesus and Divorce: The Problem with the Evangelical Consensus*. Nashville: Thomas Nelson, 1985.
JBL	*Journal of Biblical Literature*
JCHT	Georg Strecker (ed.). *Jesus Christus in Historie und Theologie*. Tübingen: J. C. B. Mohr [Paul Siebeck], 1975.

JCST — Ya'akov Meshorer. *Jewish Coins of the Second Temple Period*. Translated from the Hebrew by I.H. Levine. Tel-Aviv: Am Hasserer and Masada, 1967.

JDP — Josef Ernst. *Johannes der Täufer: Interpretation, Geschichte, Wirkungsgeschichte*. Berlin: Walter de Gruyter, 1989.

JETS — *Journal of the Evangelical Theological Society*

JG — Edwin A. Abbott. *Johannine Grammar*. London: Adam and Charles Black, 1906.

JHS — *Journal of Hellenic Studies*

JIU — Hans Walter Wolf. *Jesaja 53 im Urchristentum[4]*. Giessen: Brunnen Verlag, 1984.

JJ — Gustaf Dalman. *Jesus-Jeschua*. Darmstadt: Wissenschaftliche Buchgesellschaft, 1967.

JJS — *Journal of Jewish Studies*

JL — Rainer Riesner. *Jesus als Lehrer[3]*. Wissenschaftliche Untersuchungen zum Neuen Testament 2. Martin Hengel, Otfried Hofius, and Otto Michel (eds.). Reihe 7. Tübingen: J. C. B. Mohr [Paul Siebeck], 1988.

JLightfoot — John Lightfoot. *A Commentary on the New Testament from the Talmud and Hebraica: Matthew – I Corinthians*. 4 Vols. Grand Rapids: Baker, 1979.

JMJ — Helmuth L. Egelkraut. *Jesus' Mission to Jerusalem: A Redaction Critical Study of the Travel Narrative in the Gospel of Luke, Lk 9:51-19:48*. Frankfurt am Main: Peter Lang, 1976.

JMM — James B. Adamson. *James: The Man and His Message*. Grand Rapids: Eerdmans, 1989.

JNTU — Johannes Maier. *Jesus von Nazareth in der talmudischen Überlieferung*. Darmstadt: Wissenschaftliche Buchgesellschaft, 1978.

Johnson — Alan F. Johnson. "Revelation" in *Expositor's Bible Commentary with The New International Version of the Holy Bible*. Vol. 12 (Hebrews, James, 1, 2 Peter, 1, 2, 3, John, Jude, Revelation). Frank E. Gaebelein and J.D. Douglas (eds.). Grand Rapids: Zondervan, 1984.

Jos, *AA* — Josephus, *Against Appion*

Jos, *Life* — Josephus, *Life*

Jos, *JW* — Josephus, *Jewish Wars*

Jos, *Ant.* — Josephus, *Jewish Antiquities*

JosAsen — Joseph and Aseneth

JOT — R.T. France. *Jesus and the Old Testament: His Application of Old Testament Passages to Himself and His Mission*. Grand Rapids: Baker, 1982.

JPB — E.P. Sanders. *Judaism: Practice & Belief, 64 BCE - 66 CE*. London: SCM, 1992.

JPD — Ernst Bammel and C.F.D. Moule (eds.). *Jesus and the Politics of His Day*. Cambridge: Cambridge University Press, 1985.

JPF — S. Safrai and M. Stern (eds.). *The Jewish People in the First Century: Historical Geography, Political History, Social, Cultural and Religious Life and Institutions*. 2 vols. Compendia Rerum Iudaicarum ad Novum Testamentum. Philadelphia: Fortress , 1974-1976.

JQR — *Jewish Quarterly Review*

JS — Otto Betz, Klaus Haacker, Martin Hengel (eds.). *Josephus Studien. Untersuchungen zu Josephus, dem antiken Judentum und dem Neuen Testament*. Festschrift für Otto Michel. Göttingen: Vandenhoeck & Ruprecht, 1974.

JSNT   *Journal for the Study of the New Testament*

JSNTSS   Journal for the Study of the New Testament Supplement Series

JSP   *Journal for the Study of the Pseudepigrapha*

JTJ   Joachim Jeremias. *Jerusalem in the Times of Jesus*. London: SCM, 1969.

JTS   *Journal of Theological Studies* N.S. (New Series).

JURR   Mary E. Smallwood. *The Jews Under Roman Rule*. Leiden: E.J. Brill, 1981.

JZ   Fritz Herrenbrück. *Jesus und die Zöllner*. Wissenschaftliche Untersuchungen zum Neuen Testament 2. Martin Hengel, Otfried Hofius, and Otto Michel (eds.). Reihe 41. Tübingen: J. C. B. Mohr [Paul Siebeck], 1990.

KAI   Herbert Donner & Wolfgang Röllig. *Kanaanäische und aramäische Inschriften*. 3 vols. Wiesbaden: Otto Harrassowitz, 1971-1976.

Kaiser   Walter C. Kaiser Jr. *The Uses of the Old Testament in the New Testament*. Chicago: Moody, 1986.

Käsemann   Ernst Käsemann, *An die Römer*. Handbuch zum Neuen Testament. Tübingen: J. C. B. Mohr, 1974.

KB[3]   Ludwig Koehler and Walter Baumgartner. *Hebräisches und Aramäisches Lexikon zum Alten Testament*.[3] E. J. Brill: Leiden, 1967–1996.

Kelly   J.N.D. Kelly. *A Commentary on the Pastoral Epistles*. Black's New Testament Commentaries. London: Adam and Charles Black, 1972.

Kelly   J.N.D. Kelly. *A Commentary on the Epistles of Peter and Jude*. Black's New Testament Commentaries. London: Adam and Charles Black, 1969.

Kent   Homer A. Kent, Jr. *The Pastoral Epistles: Studies in I and II Timothy and Titus*. Chicago: Moody, 1975.

Kent   Homer A. Kent, Jr. *The Epistle to the Hebrews: A Commentary*. Winona Lake, Ind.: B. M. H. Books, 1974.

KGH   Carl Schneider. *Kulturgeschichte des Hellenismus*. 2 vols. München: Verlag C.H. Beck, 1967.

Kistemaker   Simon J. Kistemaker. *New Testament Commentary: First Epistle to the Corinthians*. Grand Rapids: Baker, 1993.

Klauck   Hans-Josef Klauck. *Der erste Johannesbrief*. Evangelisch-katholischer Kommentar zum Neuen Testament. Neukirchen-Vluyn: Neukirchener Verlag, 1991.

Klauck   Hans-Josef Klauck. *Der zweite und dritte Johannesbrief*. Evangelisch-katholischer Kommentar zum Neuen Testament. Neukirchen-Vluyn: Neukirchener Verlag, 1992.

Knowling   R. J. Knowling. *The Epistle of St. James*. Westminster Commentaries. London: Methuen, 1904.

KP   Konrad Ziegier & Walther Sontheimer (eds.). *Der kleine Pauly: Lexikon der Antike*. Munich: Alfred Druckenmüller, 1975.

Kuss   Otto Kuss. *Der Römer Brief*. Regensburg: Friedrick Pustet, 1963.

KVS   Robert Helbing. *Die Kasussyntax der Verba bei der Septuaginta*. Göttingen: Vandenhoeck & Ruprecht, 1928.

Lachs   Samuel Tobias Lachs. *A Rabbinic Commentary on the New Testament: The Gospels of Matthew, Mark and Luke*. Hobboken, N.J.: KTAV, 1987.

Ladd	George Eldon Ladd. *A Theology of the New Testament*. Grand Rapids: Eerdmans, 1974.
Ladd	George Eldon Ladd. *A Commentary on the Revelation of John*. Grand Rapids: Eerdmans, 1972.
LAE	Adolf Deissmann. *Light From the Ancient East*. Lionel R. M. Strachan (trans). London: Hodder & Stoughton, 1927.
Lane	William L. Lane. *The Gospel of Mark*. Grand Rapids: Eerdmans, 1974.
Lane	William L. Lane. *Hebrews*. Word Biblical Commentary. 2 vols. Dallas: Word, 1990.
LAW	*Lexikon der Antiken Welt*. Klaus Bartels and Ludwig Huber (eds.). Augsburg: Weltbild Verlag, 1995.
LC	Kirsopp Lake and Henry L. Cadbury. *The Beginnings of Christianity*. 4 vols. London: Macmillan, 1933.
LD	Charlton Lewis and Charles Short. *A Latin Dictionary*. Oxford: Clarendon, 1955.
LDC	Wilfrid Haubeck. *Loskauf durch Christus: Herkunft, Gestalt und Bedeutung des paulinischen Loskaufmotivs*. Giessen: Brunnen Verlag, 1985.
Lea and Griffin	Thomas D. Lea and Hayne P. Griffin Jr. *1, 2 Timothy, Titus*. The New American Commentary. David S. Dockery (gen. ed.). Nashville: Broadman & Holman, 1992.
Leaney	A. R. C. Leaney. *The Gospel According to St. John*. 2nd. edition. London: Adam and Charles Black, 1966.
Leidig	Edeltraut Leidig. *Jesu Gespräch mit der Samaritanärin und weitere Gespräche im Johannesevangelium*. Basel: Friedrich Reinhardt Kommisionsverlag, 1981.
Lenski	R. C. H. Lenski. *The Interpretation of St. Paul's I & II Epistles to the Corinthians*. Columbus, Ohio: Wartburg, 1956.
Lenski	R. C. H. Lenski. *The Interpretation of the Epistle to the Hebrews und the Epistle of James*. Minneapolis: Augsburg, 1966.
LGG	Henry Fanschawe Tozer. *Lectures on the Geography of Greece*. Chicago: Ares, 1974.
LHT	I. Howard Marshall. *Luke: Historian and Theologian*. Grand Rapids: Zondervan, 1970.
Liefeld	Walter L. Liefeld. "Luke," in *Expositor's Bible Commentary with The New International Version of the Holy Bible*. Vol. 8 (Matthew, Mark, Luke). Frank E. Gaebelein and J.D. Douglas (eds.). Grand Rapids: Zondervan, 1984.
Lietzmann	Hans Lietzmann. *An die Korinther I-II*. Handbuch zum Neuen Testament. Tübingen: J. C. B. Mohr, 1969.
LIF	Thomas R. Schreiner. *The Law and Its Fulfillment: A Pauline Theology of Law*. Grand Rapids: Baker, 1993.
Lightfoot	R. H. Lightfoot. *St. John's Gospel: A Commentary*. C.F. Evans (ed.). London: Oxford University Press, 1972.
Lightfoot	Joseph Barber Lightfoot. *The Epistle of St. Paul to the Galatians*. Grand Rapids: Zondervan, 1956.
Lightfoot	Joseph Barber Lightfoot. *St. Paul's Epistle to the Philippians*. Grand Rapids: Zondervan, 1953.
Lightfoot	Joseph Barber Lightfoot. *St. Paul's Epistle to the Colossians and to Philemon*. Grand Rapids: Zondervan, reprint of 1879 edition.

Lightfoot	Joseph Barber Lightfoot. *Notes on the Epistles of St. Paul (1 & II Thessalonians, 1 Corinthians 1-7, Romans 1-7, Ephesians 1:1-14)*. Grand Rapids: Zondervan, 1957.
Lincoln	Andrew T. Lincoln. *Ephesians*. Word Biblical Commentary. Dallas: Word, 1990.
Lindars	Barnabas Lindars. *The Gospel of John*. The New Century Bible. London: Oliphants, 1972.
LLAR	J.P.V.D. Baldson. *Life and Leisure in Ancient Rome*. New York: McGraw-Hill, 1970.
LN	Lohannes P. Louw and Eugene A. Nida (eds.). *Greek-English Lexicon of the New Testament Based on Semantic Domains*[2]. New York: United Bible Societies, 1989.
LNT	J. Duncan and M. Derrett. *Law in the New Testament*. London: Darton, Longman, & Todd, 1970.
Lock	Walter Lock. *A Critical and Exegetical Commentary on the Pastoral Epistles*. The International Critical Commentary. Edinburgh: T. & T. Clark, 1966.
Lohmeyer	Ernst Lohmeyer. *Die Briefe an die Philipper, und die Kolosser und an Philemon*. Kritisch-exegetischer Kommentar über das Neue Testament. Göttingen: Vandenhoeck & Ruprecht, 1964.
Lohse	Eduard Lohse. *Die Offenbarung des Johannes*. Das Neue Testament Deutsch. Göttingen: Vandenhoeck & Ruprecht, 1971.
Lohse	Eduard Lohse. *Colossians and Philemon*. Hermeneia. Philadelphia: Fortress, 1976.
Longenecker	Richard N. Longenecker. *Galatians*. Word Biblical Commentary. Dallas: Word, 1990.
Longenecker	Richard N. Longenecker. "Acts," in *Expositor's Bible Commentary*, vol. 9. Frank E. Gaebelein and J. D. Douglas (eds.). Grand Rapids: Zondervan, 1982.
LP	William M. Ramsay. *Luke the Physician and Other Studies in the History of Religion*. Grand Rapids: Baker, 1956.
LS	Henry George Liddell and Robert Scott. *A Greek-English Lexicon*. A new edition revised and augmented throughout by Henry Stewart Jones and Roderick McKenzie. Oxford: Oxford University Press, 1953.
LSC	William M. Ramsay. *The Letters to the Seven Churches of Asia*. London: Hodder & Stoughton, 1904.
LSCA	Colin J. Hemer. *The Letters to the Seven Churches of Asia and Their Local Setting*. Sheffield: JSOT, 1986.
LT	Alfred Edersheim. *The Life and Times of Jesus the Messiah*. 2 vols. Grand Rapids: Eerdmans, 1956.
LTH	J.E. Powell. *A Lexicon to Herodotus*. Hildesheim: Georg Olms Verlagsbuchhandlung, 1977.
Lührmann	Dieter Lührmann. *Das Markusevangelium*. Handbuch zum Neuen Testament. Hans Lietzmann, Günther Bornkamm, and Andreas Lindemann (eds.). Tübingen: J. C. B. Mohr [Paul Siebeck], 1987.
Lünemann	Gottlieb Lünemann. *Critical and Exegetical Commentary on the New Testament: The Epistles to the Thessalonians*. H. A. W. Meyer (ed.). Edinburgh: T. & T. Clark, 1880.
Lünemann	Gottlieb Lünemann. *Critical and Exegetical Commentary on the Epistle to the Hebrews*. The International Critical Commentary. H. A. W. Meyer (ed.). Edinburgh: T. & T. Clark, 1880.
Luz	Ulrich Luz. *Das Evangelium nach Matthäus (Mt 1-7)*. 3 vols. Evanglisch-katholischer Kommentar zum Neuen Testament. Edited by Josef Blank, Rudolf Schnackenburg, Eduard Schweizer, et al. Neukirchen-Vluyn: Neukirchener Verlag, 1985-1997.

LWGRA	Stanley K. Stowers. *Letter Writing in Greco-Roman Antiquity.* Library of Early Christianity 5. Philadelphia: Westminster, 1986.
M	James Hope Moulton. *A Grammar of New Testament Greek: Prolegomena.* Vol. 1. Edinburgh: T. & T. Clark, 1957.
M	(f. by the name of the tractate) *The Mishnah.* Herbert Danby (trans). London: Oxford University Press, 1967.
MacArthur	John MacArthur. *The MacArthur New Testament Commentary.* Chicago: Moody, 1986.
Marshall	I. Howard Marshall. *The Acts of the Apostles: An Introduction and Commentary.* The Tyndale New Testament Commentaries. Leicester: InterVarsity, 1980.
Marshall	I. Howard Marshall. *1 and 2 Thessalonians.* The New Century Bible Commentary. Grand Rapids: Eerdmans, 1983.
Marshall	I. Howard Marshall. *The Epistles of John.* The New International Commentary on the New Testament. Grand Rapids: Eerdmans, 1978.
Martin	Ralph P. Martin. *2 Corinthians.* Word Biblical Commentary. Dallas: Word, 1986.
Martin	Ralph P. Martin. *Carmen Christi: Philippians 2.5-11 in Recent Interpretation and in the Setting of Early Christian Worship.* Cambridge: University Press, 1967.
Martin	Ralph P. Martin. *Colossians: The Church's Lord and the Christian's Liberty.* Grand Rapids: Zondervan, 1973.
Martin	Ralph P. Martin. *James.* Word Biblical Commentary. Dallas: Word, 1988.
Martin, NCB	Ralph P. Martin. *Colossians and Philemon.* The New Century Bible. London: Oliphants, 1974.
Matera	Frank J. Matera. *Galatians.* Sacra Pagina. Collegeville, Minn.: Liturgical Press, 1992.
Mayor	Joseph B. Mayor. *The Epistles of St. James.* Grand Rapids: Zondervan, 1954.
Mayor	Joseph B. Mayor. *The Epistle of St. Jude and the Second Epistle of St. Peter.* Grand Rapids: Baker, 1965.
McKay	K.L. McKay, "The Use of the Perfect Down to the Second Century A.D.," *Bulletin of the Institute of Classical Studies of the University of London* 12 (1965): 1-21.
McNeile	A. H. McNeile. *The Gospel According to St. Matthew.* New York: Macmillan, 1955.
Meeks	Wayne A. Meeks. *The Prophet-King.* Leiden: E. J. Brill, 1967.
MET	R.T. France. *Matthew: Evangelist and Teacher.* Grand Rapids: Zondervan, 1989.
Meyer	Heinrich August Wilhelm Meyer. *Critical and Exegetical Commentary on the New Testament.* Translation revised and edited by William P. Dickson and Frederick Crombie, 20 vols. Edinburgh: T. & T. Clark, 1891.
MH	James Hope Moulton and William Francis Howard. *A Grammar of New Testament Greek: Accidence and Word Formation.* Vol. II. Edinburgh: T. & T. Clark, 1956.
MHW	Samuel S. Kottek. *Medicine and Hygiene in the Works of Flavius Josephus.* Leiden: E.J. Brill, 1994.
Michaeles	J. Ramsey Michaeles. *1 Peter.* Word Biblical Commentary. Dallas: Word, 1988.
Michel	Otto Michel. *Der Brief an die Römer.* Kritisch-exegetischer Kommentar über das Neue Testament. Göttingen: Vandenhoeck & Ruprecht, 1966.

Michel	Otto Michel. *Der Brief an die Hebräer.* Kritisch-exegetischer Kommentar über das Neue Testament. Göttingen: Vandenhoeck & Ruprecht, 1966.
Milligan	George Milligan. *St. Paul's Epistles to the Thessalonians.* Grand Rapids: Eerdmans, 1953.
MKG	G. Mussies. *The Morphology of Koine Greek, As Used in The Apocalypse of St. John: A Study in Bilingualism.* Leiden: E. J. Brill, 1971.
MLL	William K. Hobart. *The Medical Languages of St. Luke.* Grand Rapids: Baker, 1954.
MM	James Hope Moulton and George Milligan. *The Vocabulary of the Greek Testament.* London: Hodder & Stoughton, 1952.
MNTW	William Barclay. *More New Testament Words.* London: SCM, 1958.
Moffatt	James Moffatt. *A Critical and Exegetical Commentary on the Epistle to the Hebrews.* The International Critical Commentary. Edinburgh: T. & T. Clark, 1968.
Moffatt G	James Moffatt. *Grace in the New Testament.* New York: Long & Smith, 1932.
Moffatt L	James Moffatt. *Love in the New Testament.* London: Hodder and Stoughton, 1930.
Montefiore	Hugh Montefiore. *A Commentary on the Epistle to the Hebrews.* London: Adam and Charles Black, 1964.
Moo	Douglas Moo. *Romans.* The Wycliffe Exegetical Commentary. Chicago: Moody, 1991.
Moo, ER	Douglas Moo. *The Epistle to the Romans.* The New International Commentary on the New Testament. Grand Rapids: Eerdmans, 1996.
Moore	A. L. Moore. *The First and Second Thessalonians.* The Century Bible. London: Thomas Nelson, 1969.
Moore	George Foot Moore. *Judaism in the First Centuries of the Christian Era: The Age of Tannaim.* 3 vols. Cambridge: Harvard University Press, 1958.
Moorehouse	A.C. Moorehouse. *Studies in the Greek Negatives.* Cardiff: University of Wales Press, 1959.
Morris	Leon Morris. *The Gospel According to John.* London: Marshall, Morgan & Scott, 1972.
Morris	Leon Morris. *The Epistle to the Romans.* Grand Rapids: Eerdmans, 1988.
Morris	Leon Morris. *The First Epistle of Paul to the Corinthians.* Grand Rapids: Eerdmans, 1958.
Morris	Leon Morris. *The First and Second Epistles to the Thessalonians.* The New International Commentary on the New Testament. Grand Rapids: Eerdmans, 1959.
Morris, Studies	Leon Morris. *Studies in the Fourth Gospel.* Grand Rapids: Eerdmans, 1969.
Moule	C. F. D. Moule. *The Epistles to the Colossians and to Philemon.* The Cambridge Greek Testament Commentary. Cambridge: University Press, 1958.
Mounce	Robert H. Mounce. *The Book of Revelation.* The New International Commentary on the New Testament. Grand Rapids: Eerdmans, 1977.
Mounce	Robert H. Mounce. *Romans.* The New American Commentary. David S. Dockery (gen. ed.). Nashville: Broadman & Holman, 1995.
MP	Hubert Cancik. *Markus - Philologie.* Tübingen: J. C. B. Mohr [Paul Siebeck], 1983.
MPAT	Joseph A. Fitzmyer & Daniel J. Harrington. *A Manual of Palestinian Aramaic Texts.* Rome: Biblical Institute, 1978.
MRP	J.A. Ziesler. *The Meaning of Righteousness in Paul.* Cambridge: Cambridge University Press, 1972.

MS
C.H. Dodd. *More New Testament Studies.* Grand Rapids: Eerdmans, 1968.

MT
James Hope Moulton and Nigel Turner. *A Grammar of New Testament Greek: Syntax.* Vol. 3. Edinburgh: T. & T. Clark, 1963.

MT Style
James Hope Moulton and Nigel Turner. *A Grammar of New Testament Greek: Style.* Vol. 4. Edinburgh: T. & T. Clark, 1976.

Munck
Johannes Munck. *Christ and Israel: An Interpretation of Romans 9-11.* Philadelphia: Fortress, 1967.

Murray
John Murray. *The Epistle to the Romans.* 2 vols. New International Commentary on the New Testament. Grand Rapids: Eerdmans, 1971.

Mussner
Franz Mussner. *Der Galaterbrief.* Herders theologischer Kommentar zum Neuen Testament. Basel: Herder, 1974.

Mussner
Franz Mussner. *Der Jakobusbrief.* Herders theologischer Kommentar zum Neuen Testament. Freiburg: Herder, 1975.

N. Lightfoot
Neil R. Lightfoot. *Jesus Christ Today: A Commentary on the Book to the Hebrews.* Grand Rapids: Baker, 1976.

NBD
J. D. Douglas (ed.). *The New Bible Dictionary.* Grand Rapids: Eerdmans, 1962.

ND
Richard N. Longenecker and Merrill C. Tenney (eds.). *New Dimensions in New Testament Study.* Grand Rapids: Zondervan, 1974.

NDIEC
G.H.R. Horsley & S.R. Llewlyn (eds.) with collaboration of R.A. Kearsley. *New Documents Illustrating Early Christianity.* 8 vols. North Ryde, N.S.W.: Macquarie University and Grand Rapids: Eerdmans 1981-1998.

NIDNTT
Colin Brown (ed.). *The New International Dictionary of New Testament Theology.* 3 vols. Grand Rapids: Zondervan, 1975.

NIDOTTE
Willem A. VanGemerem (gen. ed). *New International Dictionary of Old Testament Theology & Exegesis.* 5 vols. Grand Rapids: Zondervan, 1997.

NIVAB
Carl G. Rassmussen. *NIV Atlas of the Bible.* Grand Rapids: Zondervan, 1989.

Nolland
John Nolland. *Luke.* Word Biblical Commentary. 2 vols. Dallas: Word, 1993.

Nov T
Novum Testamentum

NSV
Kenneth L. McKay. *A New Syntax of the Verb in New Testament Greek.* Frankfurt: Peter Lang, 1994.

NTCW
Allison A. Trites. *The New Testament Concept of Witness.* Cambridge: Cambridge University Press, 1977.

NTGS
Wesley J. Peshbacher. *New Testament Greek Syntax: An Illustrated Manual.* Chicago: Moody, 1995.

NTNT
Frederick Field. *Notes on the Translation of the New Testament.* Peabody, Ma.: Hendrickson, 1994.

NTRJ
David Daube. *The New Testament and Rabbinic Judaism.* New York: Arno, 1973.

NTS
New Testament Studies

NTW
William Barclay. *A New Testament Wordbook.* London: SCM, 1955.

NW
Georg Strecker and Udo Schnelle. *Neuer Wettstein: Texte zum Neuen Testament aus Griechentum und Hellenismus.* Band II: *Texte zur Briefliteratur und zur Johannesapokalypse.* Berlin: Walter de Gruyter, 1996.

Nygren	Anders Nygren. *Commentary on Romans*. Carl C. Rasmussen (trans). Philadelphia: Fortress, 1949.
O'Brien	Peter T. O'Brien. *Colossians, Philemon*. Word Biblical Commentary. Dallas: Word, 1982.
OCD	G. L. Hammond and H. H. Scullard (eds.). *Oxford Classical Dictionary*. 2nd. edition. Oxford: University Press, 1972).
OPG	Seyoon Kim. *The Origin of Paul's Gospel*. Wissenschaftliche Untersuchungen zum Neuen Testament 2. Martin Hengel, Otfried Hofius, and Otto Michel (eds.). Reihe 4. Tübingen: J. C. B. Mohr [Paul Siebeck], 1981.
OPSC	Dieter Georgi. *The Opponents of Paul in Second Corinthians*. Edinburgh: T. & T. Clark, 1987.
OTN	S. Lewis Johnson Jr. *The Old Testament in the New: An Argument for Biblical Inspiration*. Grand Rapids: Zondervan, 1980.
OTP	James H. Charlesworth (ed.). *The Old Testament Pseudepigrapha*. 2 vols. London: Darton, Longman & Todd, 1983-1985.
OTGPN	Douglas J. Moo. *The Old Testament in the Gospel Passion Narratives*. Sheffield: Almond, 1983.
P	Peter Pilhofer. *Philippi*. Band I. *Die erste christliche Gemeinde Europas*. Wissenschaftliche Untersuchungen zum Neuen Testament 87. Tübingen: J. C. B. Mohr [Paul Siebeck], 1995.
PAA	John Howard Schütz. *Paul and the Anatomy of Apostolic Authority*. Society for New Testament Studies Monograph Series 26. Cambridge: Cambridge University Press, 1975.
PAL	Richard N. Longenecker. *Paul, Apostle of Liberty: The Origin and Nature of Paul's Christianity*. Grand Rapids: Baker, 1977.
PAM	Victor C. Pfitzner. *Paul and the Agon Motif: Traditional Athletic Imagery in the Pauline Literature*. Leiden: E. J. Brill, 1967.
PAP	Kenneth E. Bailey. *Poet & Peasant: A Literary-Cultural Approach to the Parables in Luke*. Grand Rapids: Eerdmans, 1979.
PAPC	W. Bakker. *Pronomen Abundans and Pronomen Coniunctum*. Amsterdam: North-Holland Publishing Co., 1974.
PAT	Robert Jewett. *Paul's Anthropological Terms*. Leiden: E.J. Brill, 1971.
PB	Michael Zohary. *Pflanzen der Bibel*. Stuttgart: Calwer Verlag, 1983.
PCG	Edwin M. Yamauchi. *Pre-Christian Gnosticism*. London: Tyndale, 1973.
Pearson	Birger Albert Pearson. *The Pneumatikos-Psychikos Terminology*. Missoula, Mont.: Society of Biblical Literature, 1973.
Pesch	Rudolf Pesch. *Das Markusevangelium: Einleitung und Kommentar*. 2 vols. Herders Theologischer Kommentar zum Neuen Testament. Freiburg: Verlag Herder, 1976.
Pesch	Rudolf Pesch. *Die Apostelgeschichte*. Evangelisch katholischer Kommentar zum Neuen Testament. Josef Blank, Rudolf Schnackenburg, Eduard Schweizer, and Ulrich Wilckens (eds.). 2 vols. Neukirchen: Neukirchener Verlag, 1986.
PGL	W. H. Lampe. *A Patristic Greek Lexicon*. Oxford: Clarendon, 1968.
PIG	Winfried Elliger. *Paulus in Griechenland: Philippi, Thessaloniki, Athen, Korinth*. Stuttgart: Verlag Katholisches Bibelwerk, 1990.

PIGC	Werner Jaeger. *Paideia: The Ideals of Greek Culture*. 3 vols. Oxford: Basil Blackwell, 1939-1945.
PIP	Gordon P. Wiles. *Paul's Intercessory Prayers: The Significance of the Intercessory Prayer Passages in the Letters of Paul*. Society for New Testament Studies Monograph Series 24. Cambridge: Cambridge University Press, 1974.
PJP	Peder Borgen. *Philo, John, and Paul: New Perspectives on Judaism and Early Christianity*. Brown Judaic Studies 131. Edited by Jacob Neusner et al. Atlanta: Scholars, 1987.
PLG	Loveday Alexander. *The Preface to Luke's Gospel: Literary Convention and Social Context in Luke 1.1-4 and Acts 1.1*. Society for New Testament Studies Monograph Series 78. Cambridge: Cambridge University Press, 1993.
Pliny, NH	Pliny, *Natural History*.
PLL	William Dallmann, *Paul: Life and Letters*. St. Louis, Mo.: Concordia, 1929.
PLR	Joachim Marquardt. *Das Privatleben der Römer*. 2 vols. Darmstadt: Wissenschaftliche Buchgesellschaft, 1975.
Plummer	Alfred Plummer. *An Exegetical Commentary on the Gospel of Matthew*. Grand Rapids: Eerdmans, 1956.
Plummer	Alfred Plummer. *A Critical and Exegetical Commentary on the Gospel According to St. Luke*. The International Critical Commentary, 5th edition. Edinburgh: T. & T. Clark, 1952.
Plummer	Alfred Plummer. *A Critical and Exegetical Commentary on the Second Epistle of St. Paul to the Corinthians*. The International Critical Commentary. Edinburgh: T. & T. Clark, 1956.
Plummer	Alfred Plummer. *The Epistles of St. John*. The Cambridge Bible for Schools and Colleges. Cambridge: University Press, 1894.
POB	Harold N. Moldenke and Alma L. Moldenke. *Plants of the Bible*. New York: Roland, 1952.
Polhill	John B. Polhill. *Acts*. The New American Commentary. David S. Dockery (gen. ed). Nashville: Broadman & Holman, 1992.
Polybius	Polybius, *The Histories*.
PPP	Darrell L. Bock. *Proclamation from Prophecy and Pattern: Lucan Old Testament Christology*. Journal for the Study of the New Testament Supplement Series 12. David Hill and David E. Orton (eds.). Sheffield: JSOT, 1987.
Preisigke	Friedrich Preisigke. *Wörterbuch der griechischen Papyrussurkunden*. Heidelberg-Berlin: Selbsverlag des Herausgebers, 1924-31.
PRJ	W.D. Davies. *Paul and Rabbinic Judaism: Some Rabbinic Elements in Pauline Theology*. London: SPCK, 1965.
PSCZP	Lukas Bormann. *Philippi: Stadt & Christengemeinde zur Zeit des Paulus*. Leiden: E.J. Brill, 1995.
PSEB	Donald A. Hagner and Murray J. Harris (eds.). *Pauline Studies: Essays Presented to Professor F.F. Bruce on his 70th Birthday*. Grand Rapids: Eerdmans, 1980.
PS	J.N. Sevenster. *Paul and Seneca*. Leiden: E. J. Brill, 1961.
PTR	W.M. Ramsay. *St. Paul the Traveller and Roman Citizen*. London: Hodder & Stoughton, 1895.
PTW	Hans Dieter Betz. *Plutarch's Theological Writings and Early Christian Literature*. Leiden: E.J. Brill, 1975.

PVT	Joachim Gnilka. *Paulus von Tarsus: Zeuge und Apostel.* Herders theologischer Kommentar zum Neuen Testament Supplement Vol. Freiburg: Herder, 1996.
PWC	Charles Caldwell Ryrie. *The Place of Women in the Church.* New York: Macmillan, 1958.
PWR	G. Hamerton-Kelly. *Pre-existence Wisdom and the Son of Man.* Cambridge: Cambridge University Press, 1973.
Quinn	Jerome D. Quinn. *The Letter to Titus.* The Anchor Bible. Garden City, N.Y.: Doubleday, 1990.
Quintilian	Quintilian, *Institutio Oratoria.*
R	Johannes Friedrich, Wolfgang Pohlmann, Peter Stuhlmacher (eds.). *Rechtfertigung: Festschrift für Ernst Käsemann.* Tübingen: J. C. B. Mohr, 1976.
RA	C.G. Montefiore and H. Loewe (eds.). *A Rabbinic Anthology.* New York: Meridian,n.d.
RAC	Theodor Klauser (ed.). *Reallexikon für Antike und Christentum.* Stuttgart: Anton Hierseman, 1950-.
Rackham	Richard Belward Rackham. *The Acts of the Apostles.* Westminster Commentaries. London: Methuen, 1957.
Ramsay	William M. Ramsay. *A Historical Commentary of St. Paul's Epistle to the Galatians.* Grand Rapids: Baker, 1965.
Ramsay, LP	William M. Ramsay. *Luke the Physician and Other Studies in the History of Religion.* Grand Rapids: Baker, 1956.
RB	*Revue biblique*
RC	Stanislao Loffreda. *Recovering Capharnaum.* Jerusalem: Edizioni Custodia Terra Santa, 1985.
RCS	Naphtali Lewis & Meyer Reinhold (eds.). *Roman Civilization: Sourcebook II: The Empire.* New York: Harper & Row, 1966.
RE	A.H.M. Jones, *The Roman Economy: Studies in Ancient Economy and Administrative History.* P.A. Brunt (ed.). Oxford: Blackwell, 1974.
Reicke	Bo Ivar Reicke. *The Epistles St. James, Peter, and Jude.* The Anchor Bible. Garden City, N.Y.: Doubleday, 1964.
RevExp	*Review and Expositor*
RG	A. T. Robertson. *A Grammar of the Greek New Testament in the Light of Historical Research.* Nashville: Broadman & Holman, 1934.
RH	Robert Banks (ed.). *Reconciliation and Hope: New Testament Essays on Atonement and Eschatology.* Grand Rapids: Eerdmans, 1974.
RI	Leonhard Schumacher. *Römische Inschriften.* Stuttgart: Phillip Reclam Jun., 1988.
Richard	Earl J. Richard. *First and Second Thessalonians.* Sacra Pagina 11. Collegeville, Minn.: Liturgical Press, 1995.
Ridderbos	Herman N. Ridderbos. *The Epistle of Paul to the Churches of Galatia.* The New International Commentary on the New Testament. Grand Rapids: Eerdmans, 1970.
Riggenbach	Edward Riggenbach. *Der Brief an die Hebräer.* Leipzig: A. Deichert, 1913.
RK	Donald Verseput. *The Rejection of the Humble Messianic King.* European University Studies Vol. 291. Frankfurt: Peter Lang, 1986.

RM   Benno Przybylski. *Righteousness in Matthew and His World of Thought.* Society for New Testament Studies Monograph Series 41. Cambridge: Cambridge University Press, 1980.

RNE   Fergus Millar. *The Roman Near East 31 BC – AD 337.* Cambridge, Mass.: Harvard University Press, 1993.

Robinson   J. Armitage Robinson. *St. Paul's Epistle to the Ephesians.* London: Macmillan, 1914.

Ropes   James Hardy Ropes. *A Critical and Exegetical Commentary an the Epistle of St. James.* The International Critical Commentary. Edinburgh: T. & T. Clark, 1916.

RP   Archibald Robertson and Alfred Plummer. *A Critical and Exegetical Commentary on the First Epistle of St. Paul to the Corinthians.* The International Critical Commentary, 2nd. edition. Edinburgh: T. & T. Clark, 1955.

RPL   Max Kaser, *Roman Private Law.*[2] Rolf Dannenbring (trans). Durban: Butterworths, 1968.

RQ   *Römische Quartalschrift für christliche Alterlumskunde und Kirchengeschichte*

RWP   A. T. Robertson. *Word Pictures in the New Testament.* 6 vols. New York: Harper, 1930.

S   Otto Schwankl. *Die Sadduzäerfrage (Mk. 12, 18-27 par): Eine exegetisch-theologische Studie zur Auferstehungserwartung.* Bonner Biblische Beiträge 66. Frankfurt: Athenäum Verlag, 1987.

SA   Max Wilcox. *The Semitisms of Acts.* Oxford: Clarendon, 1965.

Sand   Alexander Sand. *Das Evangelium nach Matthäus: Übersetzt und Erklärt.* Regensburger Neues Testament. Jost Ekert and Otto Koch (eds.). Regensburg: Verlag Friederich Pustet, 1986.

Sanders   J. N. Sanders and B. A. Mastin. *The Gospel According to St. John.* London: Adam and Charles Black, 1968.

SAR   Solomon Schechter. *Some Aspects of Rabbinic Theology.* London: Adam and Charles Black, 1909.

SB   H. L. Strack and P. Billerbeck. *Kommentar zum Neuen Testament aus Talmud und Midrash.* 6 vols. Munich: C.H. Beck, 1965.

SBRP   William M. Ramsay. *The Social Basis of Roman Power in Asia Minor.* Amsterdam: Adolf M. Hakkert, 1967.

SBT   Robert H. Gundry. *Soma in Biblical Theology with an Emphasis on Pauline Anthropology.* Cambridge: Cambridge University Press, 1976.

SC   Peter Lampe. *Die stadtrömischen Christen in den ersten beiden Jahrhunderten.* Wissenschaftliche Untersuchungen zum Neuen Testament 2. Martin Hengel, Otfried Hofius, and Otto Michel (eds.). Reihe 18. Tübingen: J. C. B. Mohr [Paul Siebeck], 1987.

SCA   Richard C. Trench. *Commentary on the Epistles to the Seven Churches in Asia: Revelation II-III.* Sixth edition. Minneapolis: Klock and Klock, 1978, originally published in 1897.

Schelkle   Karl Hermann Schelkle. *Die Petrusbriefe, Der Judasbrief.* Herders theologischer Kommentar zum Neuen Testament. 3rd. edition. Freiburg: Herder, 1970.

Schille   Gottfried Schille. *Die Apostelgeschichte des Lukas.* Theologischer Handkommentar zum Neuen Testament. Erich Fascher, Joachim Rohde, and Christian Wolff (eds.). 2nd. edition. Berlin: Evangelische Verlagsanstalt, 1984.

Schl.   Adolf Schlatter. *Der Evangelist Matthäus.* Stuttgart: Calwer Verlag, 1963.

Schlatter	Adolf Schlatter. "Die Sprache und Heimat des Vierten Evangelisten," *Johannes und Sein Evangelium*, K. H. Gengstorf, (ed.). Darmstadt: Wissenschaftliche Buchgesellschaft, 1973.
Schlatter	Adolf Schlatter. *Die Kirche der Griechen im Urteil des Paulus: Eine Auslegung seiner Briefe an Timotheus und Titus.* Stuttgart: Calwer Verlag, 1958.
Schlier	Heinrich Schlier. *Der Brief an die Galater.* Kritisch-exegetischer Kommentar über das Neue Testament. Göttingen: Vandenhoeck & Ruprecht, 1965.
Schlier	Heinrich Schlier. *Der Brief an die Epheser.* Düsseldorf: Patmos Verlag, 1968.
Schnackenburg	Rudolf Schnackenburg. *Das Johannesevangelium.* Herders theologischer Kommentar zum Neuen Testament. 3 vols. Freiburg: Herder, 1971.
Schnackenburg	Rudolf Schanckenburg. *Der Brief an die Epheser.* Evangelisch-katholischer Kommentar zum Neuen Testament. Neukirchen-Vluyn: Neukirchener Verlag, 1982.
Schnackenburg	Rudolf Schnackenburg. *Die Johannesbriefe.* Herders theologischer Kommentar zum Neuen Testament. Basil: Herder, 1965.
Schneider	Gerhard Schneider. *Die Apostelgeschichte.* Herders theologischer Kommentar zum Neuen Testament. 2 vols. Freiburg: Herder, 1982.
Schrage	Wolfgang Schrage. *Der erste Brief an die Korinther.* Evangelisch-katholischer Kommentar zum Neuen Testament. 2 vols. Neukirchen-Vluyn: Neukirchener Verlag, 1991/1995.
Schürmann	Heinz Schürmann. *Das Lukasevangelium.* 2 vols. Herders theologischer Kommentar zum Neuen Testament. Freiburg: Verlag Herder, 1976-1993.
Schweizer	Eduard Schweizer. *Der Brief an die Kolosser.* Evangelisch-katholischer Kommentar zum Neuen Testament. Zürich: Benziger Verlag, 1976.
Schweizer	Eduard Schweizer. *Der Brief an die Kolosser.* Evangelisch-katholischer Kommentar zum Neuen Testament. Neukirchen-Vluyn: Neukirchener Verlag, 1976.
Scott	Walter Scott. *Exposition of the Revelation of Jesus Christ.* London: Pickering and Inglis, n.d.
SCS	Francis Lyall. *Slaves, Citizens, Sons: Legal Metaphors in the Epistles.* Grand Rapids: Zondervan, 1984.
SEH	M. Rosteovtzeff. *The Social & Economic History of the Roman Empire.* 2nd. edition, 2 vols. Oxford: Oxford University Press, 1960, 1963.
Seiss	Joseph Augustus Seiss. *The Apocalypse: Lectures on the Book of Revelation.* Grand Rapids: Zondervan, 1957.
Selwyn	Edward Gordon Selwyn. *The First Epistle of St. Peter.* London: Macmillan, 1958.
SF	Heinz-Werner Neudorfer. *Der Stephanuskreis in der Forschungsgeschichte seit F.C. Baur.* Giessen: Brunnen Verlag, 1983.
SG	Hans Licht. *Sittengeschichte Griechenlands.* Wiesbaden: R. Löwit, n.d.
SGP	George Milligan. *Selections from the Greek Papyri Edited with Translations and Notes.* Cambridge: University Press, 1912.
SH	William Sanday and Arthur C. Headlam. *A Critical and Exegetical Commentary on the Epistle to the Romans.* The International Critical Commentary. Edinburgh: T. & T. Clark, 1955.
Sherwin-White	A. N. Sherwin-White. *Roman Society and Roman Law in the New Testament.* Oxford: Oxford University Press, 1965.

SIG   Wilhelm Dittenberger. *Sylloge Inscriptionum Graecarum*. 4 vols. Hildesheim, Zürich, New York: Georg Olms Verlag, 1982.

Silva   Moisés Silva. *Philippians*. The Wycliffe Exegetical Commentary. Chicago: Moody, 1988.

Simpson   E.K. Simpson and F.F. Bruce. *Commentary on Ephesians and Colossians*. The New International Commentary on the New Testament. Grand Rapids: Eerdmans, 1975.

SIMS   Elliott C. Maloney. *Semitic Interference in Marcan Syntax*. SBL Dissertation Series 51. Chico, Ca.: Scholars, 1981.

SJT   *Scottish Journal of Theology*

SL   Robert A. Kraft. *Septuagintal Lexicography*. Missoula, Mont.: Scholars, 1975.

Smalley   Stephen S. Smalley. *1, 2, 3 John*. Word Biblical Commentary. Dallas: Word, 1984.

SMT   Ernest DeWitt Burton. *Syntax of the Moods and Tenses in New Testament Greek*. 3rd. edition. Edinburgh: T. & T. Clark, 1955.

SP   A.S. Hunt and C.C. Edgar (eds.). *Selected Papyri*. 2 vols. The Loeb Classical Library. Cambridge, Mass.: Harvard University Press, 1932.

SPC   Jerome Murphy-O'Connor. *St. Paul's Corinth: Texts and Archaeology*. Wilmington, Del.: Michael Glazier, 1983.

Spicq   Ceslas Spicq. *Saint Paul les Épîtres Pastorales*. 2 vols. Paris: J. Gabalda, 1969.

Spicq   Ceslas Spicq. *L'Épître aux Hebreux*. 2 vols. Paris: J. Gabalda, 1952-53.

SPJ   Ed L. Miller. *Salvation-History in the Prologue of John: The Significance of John 1:3/4*. Leiden: E.J. Brill, 1989.

SS   Marius Reiser. *Syntax und Stil des Markusevangeliums*. Wissenschaftliche Untersuchungen zum Neuen Testament 2. Martin Hengel, Otfried Hofius, and Otto Michel (eds.). Reihe 11. Tübingen: J. C. B. Mohr [Paul Siebeck], 1984.

SSAW   Lionel Casson. *Ships and Seamanship in the Ancient World*. Princeton: Princeton University Press, 1971.

SSM   W.D. Davies. *The Setting of the Sermon on the Mount*. Cambridge: University Press, 1966.

Stein   Robert Stein. *Luke*: The New American Commentary. David S. Dockery (gen. ed). Nashville: Broadman & Holman, 1992.

Stibbs   Alan M. Stibbs and Andrew F. Walls. *The First General Epistle of Peter*. Tyndale New Testament Commentaries. London: Tyndale, 1971.

Stonehouse   N. B. Stonehouse. *Origins of the Synoptic Gospels: Some Basic Questions*. London: Tyndale, 1964.

Stott   John R.W. Stott. *The Epistles of John*. Tyndale New Testament Commentaries. London: Tyndale, 1969.

Strabo   Strabo, *The Geography of Strabo*

Strecker   Georg Strecker. *Die Johannesbriefe*. Kritisch-exegetischer Kommentar über das Neue Testament. Göttingen: Vandenhoeck & Ruprecht, 1989.

Stuhlmacher   Peter Stuhlmacher. *Der Brief an die Römer*. Das Neue Testament Deutsch. Göttingen: Vandenhoeck & Ruprecht, 1989.

Stuhlmacher   Peter Stuhlmacher. *Der Brief an Philemon*. Evangelisch-katholischer Kommentar zum Neuen Testament. Zürich: Benziger Verlag, 1975.

Swete   Henry Barclay Swete. *The Apocalypse of St. John.* London: Macmillan, 1907.

Swete   Henry Barclay Swete. *The Gospel According to St. Mark.* Grand Rapids: Eerdmans, 1952.

T   Joseph Henry Thayer. *A Greek-English Lexicon of the New Testament.* New York: American Book Co., 1889.

TAA   John Camp. *The Athenian Agora.* London: Thames and Hudson, 1986.

Tasker   R.V.G. Tasker. *The Gospel According to St. Matthew.* Tyndale New Testament Commentaries. London: Tyndale, 1969.

Tasker   R.V.G. Tasker. *The Gospel According to St. John.* Tyndale New Testament Commentaries. London: Tyndale, 1970.

Tasker   R.V.G. Tasker. *The General Epistle of James.* Tyndale New Testament Commentaries. Grand Rapids: Eerdmans, 1956.

Taylor   Vincent Taylor. *The Gospel According to St. Mark.* London: Macmillan, 1957.

TB   *Tyndale Bulletin*

TBM   Raymond Brown. *The Birth of the Messiah.* Garden City, N.Y.: Doubleday, 1977.

TC   Bruce M. Metzger. *A Textual Commentary on the Greek New Testament.* London: United Bible Societies, 1971.

TDNT   Gerhard Kittel and Gerhard Friedrich (eds.). *Theological Dictionary of the New Testament.* 10 vols. Trans. G. F. Bromiley. Grand Rapids: Eerdmans, 1973.

TDOT   G.J. Botterweck and Helmer Ringgren (eds.). *Theological Dictionary of the Old Testament.* 7 vols. Grand Rapids: Eerdmans, 1973 - 95.

TFG   Hugo Odeberg. *The Fourth Gospel.* Amsterdam: B.R. Grüner B.V., 1974.

Tenny   Merrill C. Tenney. "John" in *Expositor's Bible Commentary,* vol. 9. Frank E. Gaebelein and J. D. Douglas (eds.). Grand Rapids: Zondervan, 1982.

THAT   Ernst Jenni and Claus Westermann. *Theologisches Handwörterbuch zum Alten Testament.* 2 vols. München: Chr. Kaiser Verlag, 1971.

Thomas   Robert L. Thomas. *Revelation 1-7; 8-22.* The Wycliffe Exegetical Commentary. 2 vols. Chicago: Moody, 1992-95.

Thrall   Margaret E. Thrall. *Greek Particles in the New Testament.* Leiden: E.J. Brill, 1962.

Thrall   Margaret E. Thrall. *A Critical and Exegetical Commentary on the Second Epistle to the Corinthians.* The International Critical Commentary. 2 vols. Edinburgh: T. & T. Clark. 1994.

ThZ   *Theologische Zeitschrift*

TJ   Cleon L. Rogers Jr. *The Topical Josephus: Historical Accounts That Shed Light on the Bible.* Grand Rapids: Zondervan, 1992.

TLNT   Ceslas Spicq. *Theological Lexicon of the New Testament.* Translated and edited by James D. Ernest. 3 vols. Peabody, Ma.: Hendrickson, 1994.

TLS   Shmuel Safrai (ed.). *The Literature of the Sages. First Part: Oral Tora, Halakha, Mishna, Tosefta, Talmud, External Tractates.* Compendia Rerum Iudaicarum ad Novum Testamentum. Philadelphia: Fortress, 1987.

Toussaint   Stanley D. Toussaint. *Behold The King: A Study of Matthew.* Portland: Multnomah, 1980.

Tr   Martin MacNamara. *Targum and Testament, Aramaic Paraphrases of the Hebrew Bible: A Light on the New Testament.* Grand Rapids: Eerdmans, 1972.

TRE   *Theologische Realenzyklopädie.*Berlin: Walter de Gruyter, 1976-.

Trench,   R. C. Trench. *Synonyms of the New Testament.* Grand Rapids: Eerdmans, 1953.
  Synonyms

TrinJ   *Trinity Journal*

TS   Ephraim E. Urbach. *The Sages: Their Concepts and Beliefs.* Cambridge, Mass.: Harvard University Press, 1987.

TSSI   John C.L. Gibson. *Textbook of Syrian Semitic Inscriptions.* 3 vols. Oxford: Clarendon, 1973-1982.

TWNT   G. Kittel and G. Friedrich (eds.). *Theologisches Wörterbuch zum Neuen Testament.* 10 vols. Stuttgart: Verlag M. Kohlhammer, 1933-1979.

TWOT   R. Laird Harris, Gleason L. Archer Jr., and Bruce K. Waltke (eds.). *Theological Wordbook of the Old Testament.* 2 vols. Chicago: Moody, 1980.

TZ   *Theologische Zeitschrift*

UBD   Merril F. Unger. *Unger's Bible Dictionary.* Chicago: Moody, 1957.

UFG   John Ashton. *Understanding the Fourth Gospel.* Oxford: Clarendon, 1991.

UJS   Günther Schwarz. *"Und Jesus Sprach": Untersuchungen zur aramäischen Urgestalt der Worte Jesu.* Stuttgart: Verlag W. Kohlhammer, 1985.

UTMC   George E. Cannon. *The Use of Traditional Materials in Colossians.* Macon, Ga: Mercer University Press, 1983.

V   Cilliers Breytenbach. *Versöhnung: Eine Studie zur paulinischen Soteriologie.* Wissenschaftliche Monographien zum Alten und Neuen Testament 60. Neukirchen-Vluyn: Neukirchener Verlag, 1989.

VA   Stanley E. Porter. *Verbal Aspect in the Greek of the New Testament with Reference to Tense and Mood.* Frankfurt: Peter Lang, 1989.

VANT   Buist M. Fanning. *Verbal Aspect in New Testament Greek.* Oxford: Clarendon, 1990.

VGG   Peter Stuhlmacher. *Versöhnung, Gesetz und Gerechtigkeit: Aufsätze zur biblischen Theologie.* Göttingen: Vandenhoeck & Ruprecht, 1981.

Vincent   Marvin R. Vincent. *A Critical and Exegetical Commentary on the Epistles to the Philippians and to Philemon.* The International Critical Commentary. Edinburgh: T. & T. Clark, 1955.

Vögtle   Anton Vögtle. *Der Judasbrief, Der zweite Petrusbrief.* Evangelisch-katholischer Kommentar zum Neuen Testament. Neukirchen-Vluyn: Neukirchener Verlag, 1994.

von Dobschütz   Ernst von Dobschütz. *Die Thessalonikerbriefe.* Göttingen: Vandenhoeck & Ruprecht, 1974.

VoxE   *Vox Evangelica*

VSSP   James Smith. *The Voyage and Shipwreck of St. Paul.* Minneapolis: James Family, 1979.

VT   *Vetus Testamentum*

WA   Joseph A. Fitzmyer. *A Wandering Aramean: Collected Aramaic Essays.* Society of Biblical Literature Monograph Series 25. Leander E. Keck and James L. Crenshaw (eds.). Chico, Ca.: Scholars, 1979.

Walvoord   John F. Walvoord. *The Revelation of Jesus Christ.* Chicago: Moody, 1966.

Wanamaker	Charles A. Wanamaker. *Commentary on 1 & 2 Thessalonians*. The New International Greek Testament Commentary. Grand Rapids: Eerdmans, 1990.
Weiss	Johannes Weiss. *Der erste Korinther Brief*. Göttingen: Vandenhoeck & Ruprecht, 1910.
Weiss	Hans-Friedrich Weiss. *Der Brief an die Hebräer*. Kritisch-exegetischer Kommentar über das Neue Testament. Göttingen: Vandenhoeck & Ruprecht, 1991.
Wessel	Walter W. Wessel. "Mark," in *Expositor's Bible Commentary with The New International Version of the Holy Bible*. Vol. 8 (Matthew, Mark, Luke). Frank E. Gaebelein and J.D. Douglas (eds.). Grand Rapids: Zondervan, 1984.
Westcott	Brooke Foss Westcott. *The Gospel According to St. John, The Greek Text with Introduction and Notes*. Grand Rapids: Eerdmans, 1954.
Westcott	Brooke Foss Westcott. *St. Paul's Epistle to the Ephesians*. Grand Rapids: Eerdmans, 1952.
Westcott	Brooke Foss Westcott. *The Epistle to the Hebrews*. Grand Rapids: Eerdmans, 1952.
Westcott	Brooke Foss Westcott. *The Epistles of John*. Cambridge: Macmillan, 1892.
Wiefel	Wolfgang Wiefel. *Das Evangelium nach Lukas*. Theologischer Kommentar zum Neuen Testament. Erich Fascher, Joachim Rohde, & Christian Wolf (eds.). Berlin: Evangelische Verlagsanstalt, 1988.
Wiesinger	August Wiesinger. *Biblical Commentary on St. Paul's Epistles to the Philippians, to Titus, and the First to Timothy (in Continuation of the Work of Olshausen)*. Edinburgh: T. & T. Clark, 1861.
Wilckens	Ulrich Wilckens. *Der Brief an die Römer*. 3 vols. Evangelisch-katholischer Kommentar zum Neuen Testament. Neukirchen-Vluyn: Neukirchener Verlag, 1982.
Williams	C. S. C. Williams. *The Acts of the Apostles*. Black's New Testament Commentaries. London: Adam and Charles Black, 1964.
Wilson	R. Macl. Wilson. *Galatians*. The New Century Bible Commentary. Grand Rapids: Eerdmans, 1987.
Windisch	Hans Windisch. *Der zweite Korintherbrief*. Kritisch-exegetischer Kommentar über das Neue Testament. Göttingen: Vandenhoeck & Ruprecht, 1970.
Witherington	Ben Witherington III. *John's Wisdom: A Commentary on the Fourth Gospel*. Louisville, Ky.: Westminster/John Knox, 1995.
WJ	Gustaf Dalman. *Die Worte Jesu*. Darmstadt: Wissenschaftliche Buchgesellschaft, 1965.
WSNT	Marvin R. Vincent. *Word Studies in the New Testament*. 2nd. edition. 2 vols. McLean, Va: MacDonald, 1888.
WTJ	*Westminster Theological Journal*
WTM	Jakob Levy. *Wörterbuch über die Talmudim und Midraschim*. 4 vols. Darmstadt: Wissenschaftliche Buchgesellschaft, 1963.
Wuest	Kenneth S. Wuest. *Galatians in the Greek New Testament*. Grand Rapids: Eerdmans, 1951.
WZZT	Shmuel Safari. *Die Wallfahrt im Zeitalter des Zweiten Tempels*. Forschungen zum jüdisch-christlichen Dialog 3. Yehuad Aschkenasy and Heinz Kremers (eds.). Dafna Mach (trans). Neukirchen-Vluyn:Neukirchener Verlag, 1981.
ZAH	*Zeitschrift für Althebraistik*
ZAW	*Zeitschrift für die alttestamentliche Wissenschaft*
ZNW	*Zeitschrift für die neutestamentliche Wissenschaft*

ZPEB   Merrill C. Tenney (gen. ed.). *The Zondervan Pictorial Encyclopedia of the Bible.* Grand Rapids: Zondervan, 1975.

ZThK   *Zeitschrift für Theologie und Kirche*

General Abbreviations

abs.	absolute		loc.	locative
acc.	accusative		LXX	Septuagint
adj.	adjective		masc.	masculine
adv.	adverb		mid.	middle
aor.	aorist		n.	neuter
Aram.	Aramaic		neg.	negative
art.	article		nom.	nominative
cf.	confer; compare		nr.	number
circum.	circumstantial		obj.	object
cl.	clause		obj. gen.	objective genitive
comp.	comparison		opt.	optative
cond.	condition, conditional		org.	original
conj.	conjunctive		p, pp	page (s)
const.	constative		part.	participle
cust.	customary		pass.	passive
dat.	dative		perf.	perfect
def.	definite; *also* defective		pers.	person, personal
dep.	deponent		pl.	plural
dimin.	diminutive		plperf.	pluperfect
dir.	direct		poss.	possessive
e.g.	exempli gratia; for example		pred.	predicate
epex.	epexegetical		pref.	prefix
esp.	especially		prep.	preposition
f, ff	following		pres.	present
fem.	feminine		pron.	pronoun
fig.	figuratively		purp.	purpose
fut.	future		refl.	reflexive
gen.	genitive		rel.	relative
Gr.	Greek		s.	see
Heb.	Hebrew		sing.	singular
hist.	historical		subj.	subjunctive
i.e.	id est; that is		subst.	substantive
imp.	imperative		suf.	suffix
impf.	imperfect		superl.	superlative
incep.	inceptive		synon.	synonymous
ind.	indicative		t.t.	technical term
indef.	indefinite		temp.	temporal
indir.	indirect		theol.	theological
inf.	infinitive		trans.	transitive
instr.	instrumental		v., vs., vv.	verse(s)
interj.	interjection		vb.	verb
intr.	intransitive		voc.	vocative
iterat.	iterative		Vulg.	Vulgate
Lat.	Latin		w.	with
lit.	literal, literally			

The Gospel of Matthew

Matthew 1

◆ **1** Βίβλος (# *1047*) book, different from βιβλίον (# *1161*), has a connotation of sacredness and veneration (AS). γενέσεως descriptive gen. origin, birth, genealogy, history, document (BAGD; DA; Luz; DJG, 253-59). The phrase may mean "geneological register" and refer to only Matt. 1:1-17 (Hagner). υἱοῦ Δαυὶδ son of David. Apposition. As a descendant of David, He has a legitimate claim to the throne of David (Cleon L. Rogers, Jr., "The Covenant of David in the New Testament: Part 2. The Davidic Covenant in the Gospels," *Bib Sac* 150 [1993]: 459; s. also Cleon L. Rogers, Jr., "The Promises to David in Early Judaism," *Bib Sac* 150 [1993]: 285-302). υἱοῦ Ἀβρααμ son of Abraham. Apposition. This traces Jesus' lineage back to the founding father of the nation of Israel and echoes the promises to Abraham that his offspring would bless all the peoples of the earth (Blomberg; Hagner). ◆ **2** ἐγέννησεν aor. ind. act. γεννάω (# *1164*) to beget; not necessarily immediate parentage, but merely direct descent (RWP). ◆ **6** βασιλέα acc. masc. sing. βασιλεύς (# *995*) king. Strikes the keynote of the book of Matthew. Jesus Christ as Son of David is king. ◆ **11** ἐπί w. gen. Means "at the time of" (MT, 3:271). τῆς μετοικεσίας (# *3578*) removal to another place of habitation, deportation (BAGD). The word should call to mind the hand of divine providence (DA). ◆ **16** Ἰωσήφ (# *2737*) Joseph. Joseph as the son of David is the legal father of Jesus and Jesus as his son is entitled to all his inheritance rights (Gnilka; SB, 1:35). Μαρίας (# *3451*) poss. gen. The syntax effects a displacement of Joseph in the progression of father begetting son and relates the generation of Jesus to his birth by Mary (Herman C. Waetjen, "The Genealogy as the Key to the Gospel according to Matthew," *JBL* 95 [1976]: 216). For the name "Mary" s. DA. ἐξ ἧς gen. fem. sing. John Nolland "Jechoniah and His Brothers" (*Matthew 1:11*) *BBR* 7 (1997): 169-78; Marshall D. Johnson, *The Purpose of Biblical Geneaologies* SNTS MS 8 2nd. ed. (Cambridge: Cambridge University Press, 1988). Means "from whom." The rel. pron. obviously refers to Mary, hinting at the virgin birth (Toussaint; France; GGBB, 336). ἐγεννήθη aor. ind. pass. γεννάω (# *1164*) to beget. The pass. means "to be conceived," or "to be born" (DA). λεγόμενος pres. pass. part. λέγω (# *3306*) to say, to name. For the textual variants in this v. s. DA; TBM,

62-64; TC, 2-7. ◆ **17** γενεαί fem. pl. γενεά (# *1155*) generation. The source of Matthew's information could have been the OT and certain "public registers" which were evidently available (Carson, 63; DA; SB, 1:1-6; JTJ, 275-302). δεκατέσσαρες (# *1280*) fourteen. The number is best explained as being the numerical value of the name "David" (DA; Carson, 70). ◆ **18** μνηστευθείσης aor. pass. part. (temp.) gen. fem. sing. gen. abs. "after his mother..." (s. BD, 218; RG, 514). μνηστεύω (# *3650*) to woo and win, betroth, pass. to be betrothed, to become engaged (BAGD). It was a formal pre-nuptial contract entered into before witnesses and could only be broken by a formal process of divorce (Hagner; M, Ketub. 1:2; 4:2; BBC). Aor. part. begins the sentence, the subject is first, and the pres. part. follows. It means that the action indicated by the part. accompanies the action of the main cl. (Schl., 11). For the custom of betrothal, marriage, and divorce s. M, Kiddushin; M, Gittin; Moore, *Judaism*, 1:119-26; JPF, 2:752-60; DA. πρὶν ἤ before (w. acc., w. inf.); s. VA, 388. συνελθεῖν aor. act. inf. συνέρχομαι (# *5302*) to come together (used of sexual intercourse), to live together as man and wife. In the papyrus marriage contracts it means "to marry" (BBKA; NDIEC, 3:85). εὑρέθη aor. ind. pass. εὑρίσκω (# *2351*) to find. The sense is "proved to be," or "to turn out to be" (DA). γαστρί dat. sing. γαστήρ (# *1143*) stomach, womb. ἔχουσα pres. act. part. nom. fem. sing. ἔχω (# *2400*) to have. ἐν γαστρὶ ἔχουσα to be pregnant. ἐκ indicates the source or cause from which something arises. πνεύματος gen. πνεῦμα (# *4460*) spirit; refers to the Holy Spirit. The art. is omitted owing to the prep. (McNeile). ◆ **19** ὤν pres. act. part. (causal) εἰμί (# *1639*) to be. θέλων pres. act. part. (causal) θέλω (# *2527*) to will, to desire. δειγατίσαι aor. act. inf. δειγματίζω (# *1258*) to expose publicly, to humiliate publicly (TDNT). ἐβουλήθη aor. ind. pass. (dep.) βούλομαι (# *1089*) to will, to make a decision after contemplation (TDNT; NIDNTT; EDNT; BBKA). "He came to a decision." λάθρα (# *3277*) secretly. It was a private arrangement whereby he drew up a bill of divorce himself, thus avoiding a complete public disgrace (McNeile; DA). ἀπολῦσαι aor. act. inf. ἀπολύω (# *668*) to release, to dismiss, to divorce, to send away one's wife or betrothed (BAGD; BBC). ◆ **20** ἐνθυμηθέντος aor. pass. (dep.) part. gen. masc. sing. ἐνθυμέομαι (# *1926*) to consider, to think about. Gen. abs.

"after he..." indicates the time of the vision and the vb. the state of mind: revolving the matter in thought without clear perception of outlet (EGT). ἰδού aor. imp. act. ὁράω (# 2629) to see, behold, used to draw attention. Points to the surprising, unexpected type of acion (Schl.). ἄγγελος (# 34) messenger, angel. κυρίου (# 3261) lord, ruler. Used in the OT sense for Yahweh especially when it is in the gen. (NIDNTT). κατ' = κατά (# 2848) in a dream (BD, 27). For the significance of dreams s. DJG, 199-200. ἐφάνη aor. ind. pass. φαίνομαι (# 5743) to appear, to show oneself. υἱός Δαυίδ "son of David." The form of the address summarizes the thought of the genealogy (McNeile; Cleon L. Rogers, Jr., "The Promises to David in Early Judaism," *Bib Sac* 150 [1993]: 285-302; "The Davidic Covenant in the Gospels: The Covenant of David in the New Testament," *Bib Sac* 150 [1993]: 485-78; DJG, 766-69). For the nom. instead of the voc. s. MT, 34. μὴ φοβηθῇς aor. subj. pass. (dep.) φοβέομαι (# 5828) to be afraid, to fear someone or something (w. μή = neg. imp. s. VA, 360). παραλαβεῖν aor. act. inf. παραλαμβάνω (# 4161) to take to oneself, to lead home, of one's wife, to take her into one's home (BAGD). γάρ for (cause). γεννηθέν aor. pass. part. γεννάω (# 1164) s.v. 2. ◆ **21** τέξεται fut. ind. mid. (dep.) τίκτω (# 5503) to give birth. καλέσεις fut. ind. act. καλέω (# 2813) to call, to name. For the fut. to express a command s. MT, 86; VA, 419. Ἰησοῦς (# 2652) Jesus, the Greek form of "Joshua," meaning "Yahweh saves." The name identifies Mary's Son as the one who brings Yahweh's promised eschatological salvation (Carson; s. DA; Hagner). σώσει fut. ind. act. σώζω (# 5392) to save, to rescue, to deliver. For a study of the word s. TDNT; NIDNTT; NTW, 114-21; TLNT; EDNT. λαόν (# 3295) people. In Matt. it refers to Israel, the OT people of God (Luz). ἁμαρτιῶν (# 281) sins. Many Jewish writings viewed the "Messianic Age" as one where sinners are removed and God's people cleansed and the Messiah leads the people in righteousness (SB, 1:70-74). ◆ **22** ὅλος (# 3910) all, whole (BAGD). The "all" refers to the universal providence of God, who knows all things before they come to pass and sees to it that all will be fulfilled (DA). γέγονεν perf. ind. act. γίνομαι (# 1181) to become, to happen (BD, 177). ἵνα (# 2671) w. subj. that, in order that. It indicates divine purpose (Gundry). πληρωθῇ aor. subj. pass. πληρόω (# 4444) to fulfill. The pass. implies God's activity (DA). ῥηθέν aor. pass. part. nom. masc. sing. λέγω (# 3306) to say, to speak. ὑπό by (w. pass). διά through. The prep. shows that the word was spoken by God and that the prophet was only a channel (DA; GGBB, 434). ◆ **23** παρθένος (# 4221) virgin. It translates the Heb. word עַלְמָה which means "a young lady w. high standing and noble qualities" s. Karen Engelken, *Frauen im Alten Israel* (Stuttgart, 1990); TLNT. ἕξει fut. ind. act. ἔχω (# 2400) (s.v. 18).

τέξεται fut. ind. mid. (s.v. 21). μεθερμηνευόμενον pres. pass. part. μεθερμηνεύω (# 3493) to interpret, to translate. μεθ' = μετά (# 3552) with (accompanying). The context of Isa. 7:14 indicates that the sign to Ahaz and the "House of David" was an assurance that the dynasty of David would not be destroyed. Immanuel, born of a virgin as the Son of David, is the fulfillment of the prophecy (s. Carson, 78-80). ◆ **24** ἐγερθείς aor. pass. part. nom. masc. sing. ἐγείρω (# 1586) trans. to awake, to arise, pass. to wake up, to awake (BAGD). When two actions are joined to one process, the aor. part. is placed before the aor. of the main vb. in order to prepare for the action of the main vb. (Schl. 23). προσέταξεν aor. ind. act. προστάσσω (# 4705) to prescribe, to order. παρέλαβεν aor. ind. act. s.v. 20. ◆ **25** ἐγίνωσκεν impf. ind. act. γινώσκω (# 1182) to know (used in sexual sense, similar to the Heb. word יָדַע "to know"). Impf. indicates the continual or unfulfilled action in the past. The delay in sexual union suits Joseph's original hesitation and preserves the virginity of the birth (Gundry). ἔτεκεν aor. ind. act. τίκτω (# 5503) Aor. views the promise as fulfilled (DA). ἐκάλεσεν aor. ind. act. καλέω (# 2813) Aor. points to the obedience of Joseph (DA; BBC).

Matthew 2

◆ **1** γεννηθέντος aor. pass. part. gen. masc. sing. γεννάω (# 1164) to beget, pass. to be born. Gen. abs. "after, when Jesus..." βασιλεύς (# 995) king. For the life of Herod the Great s. TJ, 17-35; HK; BBC; DJG, 317-26; Nikos Kokkinos, *The Herodian Dynasty: Origins, Role in Society and Eclipse* (Sheffield, 1997). ἰδού (# 2627) aor. imp. act. ὁράω behold (surprise). The word is used by Matthew 62 times (s. M, 1:11; E.J. Pryke, "ΙΔΕ and ID-OU," *NTS* 14 [1968]: 418-24). μάγος (# 3407) person or Babylonian priest or "wiseman" who is esp. acquainted w. the interpretation of stars and dreams as well as w. other things (TDNT; HDCG, 2:97-101; DA). ἀνατολή (# 424) rising of stars, then sunrise, pl. (BD, 78). The word for east means "from the rising" of the sun (RWP). The geographical meaning is orient. παρεγένοντο aor. ind. mid. (dep.) παραγίνομαι (# 4134) to come, to arrive, to be present (BAGD). ◆ **2** τεχθείς aor. part. pass. τίκτω (# 5503) to give birth, pass. to be born. εἴδομεν aor. ind. act. ὁράω (# 3972) to see. γάρ for (explanatory). ἀστέρα acc. sing. ἀστήρ (# 843) star. For the position of the poss. gen. αὐτοῦ s. BD, 148. The reference is evidently to Num. 24:17, which was taken by the Dead Sea community (CD 7:18-26; 1 QM 11:6) and other Jewish writings (Test. Levi 18:3) as referring to the "Messiah" (DA; Carson). ἤλθομεν aor. ind. act. ἔρχομαι (# 2262) to come. προσκυνῆσαι aor. act. inf. προσκυνέω (# 4686) to fall down and worship, to do obeisance to, to prostrate oneself before, used to designate the custom of prostrating oneself before a person and kissing his feet, the hem of his garment, the ground, and so forth (BAGD; NIDNTT; TDNT). Inf. expresses purp. ◆ **3 ἀκούσας** aor. act. part. (temp.) nom. masc. sing. ἀκούω (# 201) to hear. "when Herod heard...." **ἐταράχθη** aor. ind. pass. ταράσσω (# 5429) to shake together, to stir up; fig. to stir up, to disturb, to unsettle, to throw into confusion (BAGD). For Herod's fear s. R.T. France, "Herod and the Children," *Nov T* 21 (1979): 98-120; DJG, 317-22. ◆ **4 συναγαγών** aor. act. part. (temp.) nom. masc. sing. συνάγω (# 5251) to bring or call together, to gather. **ἀρχιερεύς** (# 797) chief or high priest (DJG, 634-36). **γραμματεύς** (# 1208) scribe (For chief priest and scribes s. HJP, 2:227-336; JPF, 2:600-612, 619-21; A.J. Saldarini, *Pharisees, Scribes, and Sadducees* [Wilmington, Del., 1988], 241-76; SB, 1:78-83; DA; DJG, 732-35). **ἐπυνθάνετο** impf. ind. mid. (dep.) πυνθάνομαι (# 4785) to inquire. Impf. suggests that Herod inquired repeatedly (RWP), or it may be incep.: "he began to inquire." **γεννᾶται** pres. ind. pass. γεννάω (# 1164) to be born. Prophetic pres. (McNeile). ◆ **5 εἶπαν** aor. ind. act. λέγω (# 3306). **γέγραπται** perf. ind. pass. γράφω (# 1211) to write. "It stands written" refers to the regulative and authoritative character of the document referred to (MM; BS, 112-14, 249-50). ◆ **6 γῆ** (# 1178) land, here in a territorial sense. The Davidic Messiah was expected to come from the tribe of Judah (DA). **οὐδαμῶς** (# 4027) certainly not, not at all. **ἐλαχίστη** (# 1788) superl. μικρός (# 3625) small, least in honor (McNeile). **ἡγεμόσιν** dat. pl. ἡγεμών (# 2450) ruler, leader. The word could translate the Hebrew מוֹשֵׁל and have the meaning "prince" (DA; TLNT). **ἐξελεύσεται** fut. ind. mid. (dep.) ἐξέρχομαι (# 2002) to go out. **ἡγούμενος** pres. pass. part. nom. masc. sing. ἡγέομαι (# 2451) to lead. Pres. part. used of men in any leading position (BAGD). **ὅστις** general rel. pron. "who." **ποιμανεῖ** fut. ind. act. ποιμαίνω (# 4477) to herd, to tend, to lead to pasture. Figurative of activity that protects, rules, governs (BAGD). ◆ **7 λάθρᾳ** (# 3277) adv. secretly. **καλέσας** aor. act. part. (temp.) nom. masc. sing. καλέω (# 2813) to call. **ἠκρίβωσεν** aor. ind. act. ἀκριβόω (# 208) to learn exactly or accurately (RWP). **φαινομένου** pres. mid. (dep.) part. φαίνομαι (# 5743) to appear. **ἀστέρος** star (s.v. 2). ◆ **8 πέμψας** aor. act. part. nom. masc. sing. πέμπω (# 4287) to send. **εἶπεν** aor. ind. act. λέγω (#3306). **πορευθέντες** aor. pass. (dep.) part. nom. masc. pl. πορεύομαι (# 4513) to go, to proceed on one's way. Part. here is attendant circumstance and can be translated as an imp. "go and inquire" (s. M, 230f). **ἐξετάσατε** aor. imp. act. ἐξετάζω (# 2004) to examine, to inquire. It is w. the implication of careful examination (LN, I: 409; NDIEC, 4:95-99). The aor. imp. forms in this verse point to specific commands which may indicate a sense of urgency (VANT, 381; VA, 351). **ἀκριβῶς** (# 209) adv. exactly, accurately (s. Lk. 1:3). **ἐπάν** (# 2054) w. subj. when, as soon as.

εὕρητε aor. subj. act. εὑρίσκω (# 2351) to find. **ἀπαγγείλατε** aor. imp. act. ἀπαγγέλλω (# 550) to report, w. possible focus on the source of the information (LN, 1:411). **ὅπως** (# 3968) w. subj., that, in order that. The word may suggest the manner or way in which the purp. is to be realized (LN, 1:785). **ἐλθών** aor. act. part. ἔρχομαι (# 2262) to come, to go. The part. is circumstantial and can be translated as a main vb. **προσκυνήσω** aor. subj. act. s.v. 2. ◆ **9 ἀκούσαντες** aor. act. part. (temp.) s.v. 3. "having heard." The king ought rather to have heard and assisted them (Bengel). **ἐπορεύθησαν** aor. ind. pass. (dep.) s.v. 8. **ἰδού** aor. imp. act. ὁράω to see, behold (s.v. 1). **εἶδον** aor. ind. act. ὁράω to see, s.v. 2. Here used as plperf. "They had seen" (Meyer). **προῆγεν** impf. ind. act. προάγω (# 4575) to lead ahead, to lead further, to go before. It kept on going before them until (**ἕως**) arriving at Bethlehem it took up its position (**ἐστάθη** aor. ind. pass. ἵστημι [# 2705] to stand still) right over the spot where the child was (EGT). **ἐπάνω** above, over (MT, 279). **οὗ** rel. where. ◆ **10 ἰδόντες** aor. act. part. ὁράω (# 3972) to see. Part. could be either temp. or causal. **ἐχάρησαν** aor. ind. pass. (dep.) χαίρω (# 5897) to rejoice, to be happy. **χαράν** (# 5915) joy. The cognate acc. or acc. of content repeating the content of the vb. itself (IBG, 32). ◆ **11 ἐλθόντες** (# 2262) aor. act. part. (temp.) nom. masc. pl. ἔρχομαι to come; "when they came...." **εἶδον** aor. ind. act. s.v. 2. **πεσόντες** aor. act. part. πίπτω (# 4406) to fall down. Part. of manner. **προσεκύνησαν** aor. ind. act. s.v. 2. The worship by falling down at one's feet, as indicated by this word, points the reader to the exalted position of the "Son of David" (Luz). It indicates homage given to a king (Hagner). **ἀνοίξαντες** aor. act. part. (temp.) nom. masc. pl. ἀνοίγω (# 487) to open. **θησαυρός** (# 2565) casket, receptacle for valuables (RWP). **προσήνεγκαν** aor. ind. act. προσφέρω (# 4712) to bring to, to present. **χρυσός** (# 5996) gold. **λίβανον** (# 3337) frankincense, a white resinous gum obtained from several kinds of certain trees in Arabia (BAGD; DA). **σμύρνα** (# 5043) myrrh. For the use of frankincense and myrrh s. Gus. W. Van Beek, "Frankincense and Myrrh," *BA* 23 (1960): 70-95; ABD, 2:854; 5:226-28; DA. The gifts are those fit for a king and it is well attested that the Jewish expectation was that both Jews and non-Jews would bring the Messiah gifts (Lachs, 10; SB, 1:83-84). ◆ **12 χρηματισθέντες** aor. pass. (dep). part. nom. masc. pl. χρηματίζομαι (# 5976) to be informed; in classical Gr. to do business, to manage public affairs, then to advise, to consult on public affairs. In later Gr. to give an authoritative answer, as by an oracle given to a worshiper who sleeps in the temple after making his petition, or to give a divine command or warning (McNeile; Beare; DA; TDNT). Causal part. **ἀνακάμψαι** aor. act. inf. ἀνακάμπτω (# 366) to bend or to turn back, to return (AS). Inf. gives the content of the warning. **ἀνεχώρησαν** aor. ind. act. ἀναχωρέω (# 432) to go away, to return; often used in the sense to take refuge from danger (MM). **χώρα** (# 6001) land, here homeland. For the location s. TBM, 168-70. ◆ **13** **ἀναχωρησάντων** aor. act. part. (gen. abs.) "when, after they ..." s.v. 12. **ἰδού** aor. imp. act. ὁράω to see, behold, s.v. 1. **φαίνεται** pres. ind. mid. (dep.) s.v. 7. The pres. may be hist. and add a vivid touch (Carson); or it may imply that the angel's appearance was concurrent w. the magi's departure (DA). **ἐγερθείς** aor. pass. part. nom. masc. sing. ἐγείρω (# 1586) to wake, pass. to wake up, to rise, to get up. Circum. part. used as part of the imp. **παράλαβε** aor. imp. act. παραλαμβάνω (# 4161) to take to oneself. Aor. imp. gives a specific command and adds a note of urgency. **φεῦγε** pres. imp. act. φεύγω (# 5771) to flee, to seek safety in flight (BAGD). **ἴσθι** pres. imp. act. εἰμί (# 1639) to be. **ἕως ἄν** (# 2401; 323) w. subj. until, until whenever; the ἕως is temp.; ἄν indicates that the time of fulfillment is indefinite (IBG, 133). **εἴπω** aor. subj. act. λέγω (# 3306) to say. **μέλλει** pres. ind. act. μέλλω (# 3516) to be about to, used w. the inf. to express imminence (BD, 181). **γάρ** (# 1142) for (explanatory). **ζητεῖν** pres. act. inf. ζητέω (# 2426) to seek. **ἀπολέσαι** aor. inf. act. ἀπόλλυμι (# 660) to ruin, to destroy, to kill (TDNT; NIDNTT). The gen. of the art. w. the inf. to express direct purp., "seek in order to kill" (DA). The back drop may be Exod. 1:16. ◆ **14 ἐγερθείς** aor. pass. part. (circum.) nom. masc. sing. ἐγείρω (# 1586) to arise. **παρέλαβεν** aor. ind. act. s.v. 13. **νυκτός** gen. sing. νύξ (# 3816) night. Gen. of time "during the night" (BD, 100). **ἀνεχώρησεν** aor. ind. act. s.v. 12. ◆ **15 ἦν** impf. ind. act. εἰμί (# 1639) to be. **ἵνα** (# 2671) w. the subj. that, in order that (to express purp.). **πληρωθῇ** aor. subj. pass. πληρόω (# 4444) to fulfill. For a study of this word related to OT quotations s. MET, 171-85. **ῥηθέν** aor. pass. part. λέγω (# 3306) to say. **ἐκάλεσα** aor. ind. act. s.v. 7. Matt. links Jesus to Israel typologically (R.T. France, "The Formula Quotations of Matthew 2 and the Problem of Communication," *NTS* 27 [1981]: 243-44). **υἱός** (# 5626) son (Gundry; Donald Verseput, "The Role and Meaning of the 'Son of God' Title in Matthew's Gospel," *NTS* 33 [1987]: 537, 542; DJG, 769-74). ◆ **16** **ἰδών** aor. act. part. temp. ὁράω (# 3972) to see. **ἐνεπαίχθη** aor. ind. pass. ἐμπαίζω (# 1850) to ridicule, to make fun of, to mock, to deceive, to trick (BAGD). Used in Exod. 10:2 (LXX) for God mocking the Egyptians. **ὑπό** by (w. pass.). **ἐθυμώθη** aor. ind. act. θυμόω (# 2597) to anger, pass. to be angry. Ingressive aor., "he became angry" (DA). **ἀποστείλας** aor. act. part. (circum.) ἀποστέλλω (# 690) to send. **ἀνεῖλεν** aor. ind. act. ἀναιρέω (# 359) to take away, to do away w., to kill. **παῖδας** acc. pl. παῖς (# 4090) youth, child. **διετοῦς** gen. pl. διετής (# 1453) two years old. **κατωτέρω** (# 3006) adv. under. There were probably about thirty children

under two years of age (France), but some have estimated under 20 (Hagner). **ἠκρίβωσεν** aor. ind. act. s.v. 7. ◆ **17 ἐπληρώθη** aor. ind. pass. s.v. 15. **ῥηθέν** aor. pass. part. s.v. 15. **διά** (# 1328) w. gen. expresses agency "through." **λέγοντος** (# 3306) pres. part. gen. sing. λέγω. The part. is used in a Semitic construction (BD, 216-17; s. 3:2). ◆ **18 ἠκούσθη** aor. ind. pass. s.v. 3. **κλαυθμός** (# 3088) crying, weeping. Nouns expressing actions are formed w. -μος (BD, 58, 59; also MH, 350-51, 355). **ὀδυρμός** (# 3851) lamentation, mourning. Ritualized wailing and crying as an expression of grief and sorrow at funerals (LN). **πολύς** (# 4498) much, great, loud. **κλαίουσα** pres. act. part. κλαίω (# 3081) to cry loudly, w. emphasis upon the noise accompanying the weeping (LN). **τέκνα** (# 5451) children. Acc. gives the cause of the weeping (LN). **ἤθελεν** impf. ind. act. θέλω (# 2527) to wish, to will. For the "potential" use of the impf. w. vbs. of "wishing," s. RG, 885. **παρακληθῆναι** aor. pass. inf. παρακαλέω (# 4151) pass. to be comforted. **ὅτι** (# 4022) because. ◆ **19 τελευτήσαντος** aor. act. part. τελευτάω (# 5462) to come to the end of one's life, to die; (temp.) gen. abs. "when," "after." Herod died 4 B.C. ◆ **20 λέγων** pres. act. part. λέγω s.v. 17. **πορεύου** pres. imp. mid. (dep.) s.v. 8. **τεθνήκασιν** perf. ind. act. θνήσκω (# 2598) to die, perf. to be dead. **γάρ** (# 1142) for (explanatory). **ζητοῦντες** (# 2426) pres. act. part. s.v. 13, to seek after something. To seek the soul of someone means to seek to kill him (DA). ◆ **21 ἐγερθείς** aor. pass. part. s.v. 14. **εἰσῆλθεν** aor. ind. act. εἰσέρχομαι (# 1656) to go in. ◆ **22 ἀκούσας** aor. act. part. s.v. 3. The part. could be temp. or causal. **βασιλεύει** pres. act. ind. βασιλεύω (# 996) to be king. Vbs. ending in -εύω indicate the exercise of a profession (MH, 398-400). For the life and deeds of Archelaus s. TJ. **ἀντί** (# 505) w. gen. instead of. Clear example of the prep. indicating substitution. **ἐφοβήθη** aor. ind. pass. (dep.) φοβέομαι (# 5828) to be afraid. Ingressive aor., "he became afraid." A state of severe distress, aroused by intense concern for impending pain, danger, or evil (LN). **ἐκεῖ** (# 1695) there, indicating motion (BD, 56; DA). **ἀπελθεῖν** aor. act. inf. ἀπέρχομαι (# 599) to go away, to depart, to go forth, to go to (BAGD). The inf. explains the "fear." **χρηματισθείς** aor. pass. part. s.v. 12. **ἀνεχώρησεν** aor. ind. act. ἀναχωρέω s.v. 12. ◆ **23 ἐλθών** aor. act. part. (temp.) **κατῴκησεν** aor. ind. act. κατοικέω (# 2997) to live, dwell, settle down. **λεγομένην** pres. pass. part. λέγω (# 3306) to say. **ὅπως** w. subj. in order that. **πληρωθῇ** (# 4444) aor. pass. subj. s.v. 15. **ῥηθέν** aor. pass. part. s.v. 15. **κληθήσεται** fut. ind. pass. καλέω (# 2813) s.v. 7. The variation in the "quotation formula" ("prophets," etc.) suggest that the general content of the OT is intended (SB, 1:92) and that the title "Nazarene" is a term of contempt and conveyed the humble, obscure origin of the king (France; R.T. France, "The Formula Quotations of

Matthew 2 and the Problem of Communication," *NTS* 27 [1981]: 247 f; DA; TMB, 207-213). It has also been suggested that the term "Nazarene" could refer to Jesus as a "Nazarite," or be a play on the Heb. word for "branch" and be a messianic designation (Hagner).

Matthew 3

◆ **1** ἐν δὲ ταῖς ἡμέραις ἐκείναις "In those days." Indefinite determination of time which points back to a date which has preceded it (Meyer). **παραγίνεται** pres. ind. mid. (dep.) παραγίνομαι (# *4134*) to come, to arrive, to be present. The hist. pres. introduces a new scene (DA). **βαπτιστής** (# *969*) baptizer. Most nouns ending in -της indicate one who performs an action (MH, 365ff). The Jewish method of "baptizing" was that the person immersed himself, but now John does the immersing (M, Mikwaoth; SB, 1:102-113). For the person of John the Baptist s. JDP; TJ, 63; Cleon L. Rogers, Jr., "The Davidic Covenant in the Gospels," *Bib Sac* 150 (1993): 469-70; John P. Meier, "John the Baptist in Josephus: Philology and Exegesis," *JBL* 111 (1992): 225-37; Blomberg; s. John 1:20. For a discussion of baptizing s. DJG, 55-58. **κηρύσσων** pres. act. part. κηρύσσω (# *3062*) to proclaim as a herald. Matthew uses this word for John, for Jesus, and for the disciples. He emphasizes the binding and official legalistic character of the proclamation (NIDNTT; TDNT). Part. describes the mode of John's coming. **ἔρημος** (# *2245*) desert, wilderness. Indicates the lower Jordan valley and possibly the eastern slopes of the valley (Robert W. Funk, "The Wilderness," *JBL* 78 [1959]: 205-214; Ernst, 278-84). ◆ **2** λέγων pres. act. part. λέγω (# *3306*) to say. Part. is used in a Semitic construction in connection w. a vb. of "speaking" and corresponds to לאמר. It can be translated as "thus" (VA, 138 f; BD, 216-17). **μετανοεῖτε** pres. imp. act. μετανοέω (# *3566*) to repent, to change one's thinking, to turn about. The primary sense in Judaism is always a change in man's attitude toward God and in the conduct of life. It involved the confession of sin, a prayer of remorse, and the forsaking of sin, all of which was a condition for the messianic redemption (Moore, *Judaism*, 1:507; s. SB, 1:162-72; TS, 462-471, 668-71; TDNT; NIDNTT; TLNT; DJG, 669-73). Pres. imp. gives a moral regulation (VANT, 355-64). **ἤγγικεν** perf. ind. act. ἐγγίζω (# *1581*) to draw near. Perf. indicates the state or cond. of "being near" (VA, 251-59), but not necessarily of "having arrived." **γάρ** (# *1142*) for (explanatory). **βασιλεία** (# *993*) kingdom, rule of a king. The rule of God on earth as promised in the OT. **οὐρανῶν** (# *4041*) gen. pl. heaven. The word is used as a substitute for the name of God (SB, 1:172). ◆ **3** ῥηθείς aor. pass. part. λέγω s.v. 2. **βοῶντος** pres. act. part. gen. sing. βοάω (# *1066*) to shout, to call out loudly. **ἑτοιμάσατε** aor. imp. act. ἑτοιμάζω (# *2286*) to prepare. Aor. looks at the total process (VA, 351). **εὐθείας**

adj. fem. pl. εὐθύς (# *2318*) straight. **ποιεῖτε** pres. act. imp. ποιέω (# *4472*) to make. The picture of road building refers to repentance (Carson). **τρίβους** acc. pl. τρίβος (# *5561*) a beaten path, a way that is familiar and well known (BAGD). The Qumran group interpreted this as the study of the Law. For the OT quotation in the DSS s. 1QS 8:14f; Fitzmyer, *Essays*, 3-58, esp. 34-36. John is to prepare the way for Jesus, so the people should be repentant and looking for the coming one (DA). ◆ **4** εἶχεν impf. ind. act. ἔχω (# *2400*) to have. Customary impf. denoting that which regularly or ordinarily occurs in the past time (DM, 188). **ἔνδυμα** (# *1903*), garment, clothing. **τριχῶν** gen. pl. θρίξ (# *2582*) hair. **καμήλου** (# *2823*) gen. (of material) camel. **ζώνη** (# *2483*) belt, girdle. **δερματίνος** (# *1294*) made out of leather. Adjectives ending in -ινος signify material, origin, or kind (MH, 359). **περί** w. acc. around. **ὀσφῦς** (# *4019*) waist. **τροφή** (# *5575*) food, nourishment. **ἦν** impf. ind. act. εἰμι. **ἀκρίδες** nom. pl. ἀκρίς (# *210*) grasshopper, locust. For locust as food s. DA; SB, 1:98-100. **μέλι** (# *3510*) honey. **ἄγριος** (# *67*) found in the open field, wild (BAGD). The rough dress and simple food of John highlight his preaching of repentance (Ernst, 289) and remind one of Elijah (DA; BBC). John's motive was ritual purity rather than asceticism (Harrington). ◆ **5** ἐξεπορεύετο impf. ind. mid. (dep.) ἐκπορεύομαι (# *1744*) to go out, to come out. Impf. shows the repetition of the act as the crowds kept going out to him (RWP). **πρός** w. acc. to. **περίχωρος** (# *4369*) neighboring subst. region, neighborhood. ◆ **6** ἐβαπτίζοντο impf. ind. pass. βαπτίζω (# *966*) to baptize, originally to dip under. Vbs. ending in -ίζω often are causative (MH, 409). Baptism symbolizes the putting off of the old life and identification w. the new life. For Jewish proselyte baptism s. SB, 1:102-112; ABD, 1:583-84; for the washings of the DSS in connection w. repentance s. 1QS 5:13-25; 2:25-31:13. **ἐξομολογούμενοι** pres. mid. (dep.) part. ἐξομολογέομαι (# *2018*) to confess, to acknowledge, to agree to, indicating a public acknowledgment (RWP; NDIEC, 8:173-74). Part. gives the attending circumstance of the baptism. ◆ **7** ἰδών aor. act. part. (temp.) ὁράω (# *3972*) to see. "When he saw...." **ἐρχομένους** pres. mid. (dep.) part. ἔρχομαι (# *2262*) to go, to come. **ἐπί** for, indicating purp. **εἶπεν** aor. ind. act. λέγω (# *2400*). **γέννημα** (# *1165*) that which is produced or born, child, offspring (BAGD). Nouns ending in -μα generally indicate the result of the action (MH, 355). **ἐχιδνῶν** gen. pl. ἔχιδνα (# *2399*) poison snake. Gen. of description. **ὑπέδειξεν** aor. ind. act. ὑποδείκνυμι (# *5683*) to show by tracing out, to make known (AS). **ὑπό** conveys the idea of thoughts making their way up into the mind (MH, 327). **φυγεῖν** aor. act. inf. φεύγω (# *5771*) to escape, to flee. Inf. explains the content of the main vb. It suggests the fleeing of snakes from a field when the harvest begins (McNeile).

μελλούσης pres. act. part. gen. fem. sing. μέλλω (# 3516) to be about to. Used w. inf. for the immediate fut. Part. is used as an adj. ◆ **8 ποιήσατε** aor. imp. act. ποιέω (# 4472). Aor. imp. speaks of a specific act. **οὖν** (# 4036) therefore. It draws conclusion from the preceding. **ἄξιον** (# 545) corresponding to, worthy. **μετανοίας** (# 3567) repentance, a change of mind s.v. 2. ◆ **9 δόξητε** aor. subj. act. δοκέω (# 1506) to suppose, to consider, to think. **μή** (# 3590) w. subj. = a neg. imp. "Do not suppose that you are to say" (BAGD). **ἑαυτοῖς** (# 1571) dat. pl. refl. pron. **πατήρ** (# 4252) father. John makes a reference to the merits of the fathers, particularly to the merits of Abraham. Abraham was represented sitting at the gate of Gehenna to deliver any Israelite who might have been consigned to its terrors (Edersheim, LT, 1:271; SB, 1:116-20; TS, 496-508). **λίθος** (# 3345) stone. Perhaps an illusion to the rabbinical use of rocks referring to the patriarchs and to their merits (SAR, 173). **ἐγεῖραι** aor. act. inf. ἐγείρω (# 1586) to raise up. The expression is Semitic for "cause to be born," "raise up a progeny" (DA). ◆ **10 ἤδη** (# 2453) already. The word is emphatic by its position (Beare). **ἀξίνη** (# 544) axe. **ῥίζα** (# 4844) root. **δένδρον** tree. The leaders and righteous were sometimes compared to trees (DA). **κεῖται** pres. ind. mid. (dep.) κεῖμαι (# 3023) to lie (BAGD). **ποιοῦν** pres. act. part. **ἐκκόπτεται** pres. ind. pass. ἐκκόπτω (# 1716) to cut down. A gnomic pres., a maxim or generalization, something that is always true (IBG, 8). ◆ **11 ἐν** (# 1877) instr. (BD, 104). **ὕδατι** dat. ὕδωρ (# 5623) water. **εἰς** (# 1651) w. acc. w. a view to. Perhaps also, "because of" (DM, 104). Baptism presupposes and expresses repentance (DA). **ὀπίσω** (# 3958) w. gen. after. **ἰσχυρότερος** comp. ἰσχυρός (# 2708) strong. He is stronger in spiritual power (John P. Meier, "John the Baptist in Matthew's Gospel," *JBL* 99 [1980]: 390). **μού** gen. of comp. "than I am." **οὗ** gen. sing. rel. pron. whose; "whose sandals." **ἱκανός** (# 2653) worthy, qualified (LN). **ὑπόδημα** (# 5687) sandal. **βαστάσαι** aor. act. inf. βαστάζω (# 1002) to pick up and to carry. A slave's office in Judea, Greece, and Rome (EGT). ◆ **12 πτύον** (# 4768) winnowing shovel, a forklike shovel, w. which the threshed grain was thrown into the wind (BAGD). Thus the components were separated by the wind according to weight (ABD, 1:97). **χειρί** (# 5931) hand. **διακαθαριεῖ** fut. ind. act. διακαθαρίζω (# 1351) to clean. δία is perfective and describes the carrying of action *through* to a definite result (MH, 301). **ἅλων** (# 272) threshing floor. Used of the threshed grain still lying on the threshing floor (BAGD). **συνάξει** fut. ind. act. συνάγω (# 5251) to gather together. **ἀποθήκη** (# 630) storehouse, barn. **ἄχυρον** (# 949) chaff. **κατακαύσει** fut. ind. act. κατακαίω (# 2876) to burn up, completely burned up. κατά is perfective (RWP). **ἀσβέστῳ** (# 812) unquenchable. Loc. dat. (in), or instr. dat. (by). ◆ **13 παραγίνεται** pres. ind.

mid. (dep.) παραγίνομαι s.v. 1. **βαπτισθῆναι** aor. inf. pass. Inf. used to express purp. s.v. 6. ◆ **14 διεκώλυεν** impf. ind. act. A conative impf. of διακωλύω (# 1361) to prevent; to try to prevent (RWP). **λέγων** pres. act. part. λέγω to say s.v. 2. **χρεία** (# 5970) need, necessity. **ἔρχῃ** pres. ind. mid. (dep.) ἔρχομαι (# 2262) s.v. 7. ◆ **15 ἀποκριθείς** aor. mid. (dep.) part. ἀποκρίνομαι (# 646) to answer. Semitic use of the part. s.v. 2. **εἶπεν** aor. ind. act. s.v. 7. **ἄφες** aor. imp. act. ἀφίημι (# 918) to allow. **γάρ** (# 1142) for (explanatory). **πρέπον ἐστίν** it is fitting, suitable, proper, right. **πληρῶσαι** aor. act. inf. πληρόω (# 4444) to fulfill. **δικαιοσύνη** (# 1466) righteousness. For various views on the meaning s. GW, 126-27; Carson; DA; TLNT; TDNT; Hagner. **ἀφίησιν** pres. ind. act. ἀφίημι hist. pres. ◆ **16 βαπτισθείς** aor. pass. part. (temp.) **ἀνέβη** aor. ind. act. ἀναβαίνω (# 326) to go up. **ἠνεῴχθησαν** aor. ind. pass. ἀνοίγω (# 487) to open. **εἶδεν** aor. ind. act. ὁράω (# 3972) to see. **καταβαῖνον** pres. act. part. καταβαίνω (# 2849) to go down, to come down. **ὡσεί** (# 6059) as, like. **περιστερά** (# 4361) dove. For numerous suggestions regarding the dove, s. DA; D.C. Allison, Jr., "The Baptism of Jesus and a New Dead Sea Scroll," *BAR* 18 (1992): 58-60. **ἐρχόμενον** pres. mid. (dep.) part. s.v. 7. ◆ **17 υἱός** (# 5626) son. **ἀγαπητός** (# 28) beloved. For verbal nouns ending in -ητος s. RG, 1095-97. **εὐδόκησα** aor. ind. act. εὐδοκέω (# 2305) to be pleased w. (Carson).

Matthew 4

◆ **1 τότε** (# 5538) then, at that time; in the NT esp. loved by Matt. He uses it 90 times. **ἀνήχθη** aor. ind. pass. ἀνάγω (# 343) to lead up. **ἔρημος** (# 2245) desert, wilderness. The wastelands on either side of the Jordan (Beare; DJG, 564-66). **πνεῦμα** (# 4460) Spirit. The gen w. the prep. **ὑπό** gives the agent. To be led by God's Spirit has as its result perfect subjection to and performance of God's will (DA). **πειρασθῆναι** aor. inf. pass. πειράζω (# 4279) to tempt, to try, to put one to the test, often w. the intent to do evil (Trench, *Synonyms*, 280-81; TLNT). Inf. expresses purp. The purp. of temptations, according to the rabbinical view, is the elevation of the one who has withstood the trial and the glorification of the divine righteousness; God does not place a person in the position of ruling unless He has tested him (SB, 1:135-36). **διάβολος** (# 1333) slanderer, devil (NIDNTT; SB, 1:136-49; DDD, 463-73; DJG, 163-72). ◆ **2 νηστεύσας** aor. act. part. (temp.) νηστεύω (# 3764) to fast. **ἡμέρας** (# 2465) days; **νύκτας** (# 3816) nights; accs. of time, "for forty days and forty nights." The period of forty days was often associated w. hardship, affliction, or punishment (DA). **ὕστερον** (# 5731) superl. adv. later, afterward. The superl. emphasizes the end of a series (BD, 34). **ἐπείνασεν** aor. ind. act. πεινάω (# 4277) to be hungry. ◆ **3 προσελθών** aor. act. part.

(temp.) προσέρχομαι (# 4665) to come to. "when he came...." **πειράζων** (# 4279) pres. act. part. Part. is used as a noun, "the one continually tempting." **εἰ** (# 1623) if. Introduces a cond. cl. which assumes the cond. to be a reality and the conclusion follows logically and naturally from that assumption. For this and other cond. clauses s. RG, 1004-1022. **υἱός** (# 5625) son. Emphatic by its position. **εἶ** pres. ind. act. 2nd. pers. sing. εἰμί (# 1639) to be. The devil assumes the deity of the Son. **εἰπέ** aor. imp. act. λέγω (# 3306). **ἵνα** that. Often used w. a vb. of "speaking" to denote a command (BD, 200). **γένωνται** aor. subj. mid. (dep.) γίνομαι (# 1181) to become. ◆ **4 ἀποκριθείς** aor. pass. (dep.) part. ἀποκρίνομαι (# 646) to answer (s. 3:15). **γέγραπται** perf. ind. pass. γράφω (# 1211) to write; perf. "it stands written." **ἐπ'** = ἐπί (# 2093) w. dat. That upon which a state of being, an action, or a result is based; hence, "to live on bread" (BAGD). **ζήσεται** fut. ind. mid. ζάω (# 2409) to live. **ῥήματι** dat. sing. ῥῆμα (# 4839) word, thing. The Heb. word means "thing" and the statement gives the positive reason for Jesus' action (Hagner). **ἐκπορευο- μένῳ** pres. mid. (dep.) part. ἐκπορεύομαι (# 1744) to go out, to come out. **διά** (# 1328) w. gen., through (instr.). **στόμα** (# 5125) mouth. The point Jesus makes is that man is to accept in trust everything that God ordains and not try to take things into his own hands and act apart from His will. ◆ **5 παραλαμβάνει** (# 4161) pres. ind. act. to take w., to lead. Hist. pres. w. vivid picturesqueness (RWP). **ἔστησεν** aor. ind. act. ἵστημι (# 2705) to place. **ἐπί** (# 2093) w. acc., on. **πτερύγιον** (# 4762) dimin. of πτέρυξ wing. Indicates the tip or extremity of anything, the pinnacle or summit of the temple (BAGD). This may have been the southeastern portico of the Temple. The height of the structure, plus the deep ravine below, could make one dizzy looking down (Jos., *Ant.*, 15:412; DA). ◆ **6 βάλε** aor. imp. act. βάλλω (# 965) to cast. **σεαυτόν** (# 4932) acc. refl. pron. 2nd. pers. **κάτω** (# 3004) adv. down. **γάρ** (# 1142) then, for (explanatory). **ὅτι** (# 4022) used as quotation marks to indicate that the words are quoted. For the recitative use s. RG, 1027-28. **ἐντελεῖται** fut. ind. mid. (dep.) ἐντέλλομαι (# 1948) to give an order, to command. **περί** (# 4309) w. gen., concerning. **ἐπί** (# 2093) w. gen., upon. **ἀροῦσιν** fut. ind. act. αἴρω (# 149) to lift up, to take up, to carry. **μήποτε** (# 3607) w. subj., lest. Used w. the subj. where the anxiety is directed towards warding off something still dependent on the will (BD, 188). **προσκόψῃς** aor. subj. act. προσκόπτω (# 4684) to strike against something, to stumble against something. If one is to live by faith, accepting everything coming from God, then God could be put to the test to see if He would really help. ◆ **7 ἔφη** impf. ind. act. φημί (# 5774) to say (VA, 444-46). **ἐκπειράσεις** fut. ind. act. ἐκπειράζω (# 1733). The ἐκ is intensive. "To put to a decisive test" (MH, 309). Fut. is used to render a categor-

ical injunction in the legal language of the OT (BD; BG, 94). ◆ **8 ὄρος** (# 4001) mountain. ὑψηλός (# 5734) high. **δείκνυσιν** pres. ind. act. δείκνυμι (# 1259) to show. The vb. has the significance of trying to explain or demonstrate or convince (DA). A vivid hist. pres. (RWP). **δόξαν** (# 1518) brightness, splendor, glory. ◆ **9 δώσω** fut. ind. act. δίδωμι (# 1443) to give. **ἐάν** (# 1569) w. subj. It introduces the cond. w. the prospects of fulfillment (RG, 1016ff). **πεσών** aor. act. part. πίπτω (# 4406) to fall down. Part. of manner. **προσκυνήσῃς** aor. subj. act. προσκυνέω (# 4686) to worship, to express by attitude and by position one's allegiance to regard to deity (LN; GGBB, 173; s. 2:2). ◆ **10 ὕπαγε** pres. imp. act. ὑπάγω (# 5632) to go away. **προσκυνήσεις** fut. ind. act. s.v. 9 **λατρεύσεις** fut. ind. act. λατρεύω (# 3302) to serve, to work for a reward, to work; in the NT used of religious service (NIDNTT). Pres. here expresses a categorical imp. (s.v. 7). ◆ **11 ἀφίησιν** pres. ind. act. ἀφίημι (# 918) to leave, to depart. **προσῆλθον** aor. ind. act. προσέρχομαι (# 4665) to come to. **διηκόνουν** impf. ind. act. διακονέω (# 1354) wait on someone, serve, minister incep. impf. "they began to minister." They brought him food (Bengel). ◆ **12 ἀκούσας** aor. act. part. (temp.) ἀκούω (# 201) to hear. "When he heard...." **παρεδόθη** aor. ind. pass. παραδίδωμι (# 4140) to hand over, to deliver over. **ἀνεχώρησεν** aor. ind. act. ἀναχωρέω (# 432) to go away, to depart, often to escape danger (MM). ◆ **13 καταλιπών** aor. act. part. καταλείπω (# 2901) to leave behind. **ἐλθών** aor. act. part. (temp.) ἔρχομαι (# 2262) to go, to come. **κατῴ- κησεν** aor. ind. act. κατοικέω (# 2997) to live. For the use of εἰς (# 1651) in this v. s. BD, 110f. **παραθαλασσία** (# 4144) situated on the sea. **ὅριον** (# 3990) border, pl. region. ◆ **14 ἵνα** (# 2671) w. subj. to express result, in order that. The divine determination (Meyer). **πλη- ρωθῇ** aor. subj. pass. πληρόω (# 4444) to fulfill. **ῥηθέν** aor. pass. part. λέγω (# 2400) to say. **λέγοντος** pres. act. part. gen. masc. sing. λέγω. For the use of the part. s. Matt. 3:2. ◆ **15 γῆ** (# 1178) earth, land. **ὁδόν** (# 3847) way, street. Adverbial acc. (MT, 247). **θαλάσσης** (# 2498) sea. Perhaps an obj. gen. "A way leading to the sea" (MT, 212). **πέραν** (# 4305) w. gen., on the other side, across. **ἐθνῶν** (# 1620) gen. pl. nation (pl. often heathen nations). Heb. designation was "circuit " or "district of the Gentiles" (HA, 53; for the composition of the area s. HA, 56-64). This was a district filled w. Gentiles (BBC). ◆ **16 καθήμενος** pres. pass./mid. (dep.) part. κάθημαι (# 2764) to sit, to reside (BAGD). **σκότει** dat. sing. σκότος (# 5030) darkness. Used of religious and moral darkness (BAGD). **εἶδεν** aor. ind. act. ὁράω (# 3972) to see. **ἀνέτειλεν** aor. ind. act. ἀνατέλλω (# 422) to rise, to dawn (intr.) ◆ **17 ἀπὸ τότε** (# 608; 5538) from then on. The words mark an important turning point and tie something new to what has just preceded it (Carson). **ἤρξατο** aor. ind. mid. (dep.) ἄρχομαι (# 806) to begin; w. inf. it either describes the beginning of a continuous action or marks a fresh start or phase in the narrative (McNeile). **κηρύσσειν** pres. act. inf. κηρύσσω (# 3062) to proclaim as a herald, to make an official proclamation (TDNT). Pres. pictures the carrying out of the ministry. **μετανοεῖτε** pres. act. imp. μετανοέω (# 3566) to change one's mind, to repent (s. Matt. 3:2). **ἤγγικεν** perf. ind. act. ἐγγίζω (# 1581) to draw near. The message of Jesus was the same as that of John the Baptist (s. 3:2).   ◆ **18 περιπατῶν** pres. act. part. περιπατέω (# 4344) to go about, to walk around. Part. expresses contemporaneous action. **παρά** w. acc., along. **λεγόμενος** pres. pass. part. λέγω (# 2400) to say, to name, pass. to be called, named. **βάλλοντας** (# 965) pres. act. part. acc. masc. pl. s.v. 6. **ἀμφίβληστρον** (# 312) casting net. A net which is thrown over the shoulders and spreads out into a circle as it falls upon the water. Stones were tied around the edges causing the net to sink rapidly, encompassing the fish. The net was lifted by a rope tied in the middle, thus gathering the stones together (Trench, *Synonyms*, 236; DA; BBC). **ἦσαν** impf. ind. act. εἰμί (# 1639) to be. **ἁλιεῖς** nom. pl. ἁλιεύς (# 243) fisher. For a discussion of fishing and fishermen s. Wilhelm H. Wuellner, *The Meaning of "Fishers of Men"* (Philadelphia: Westminster, 1967); William Radcliffe, *Fishing from the Earliest Times*, (Chicago: Ares Publ., 1974), 397-445; NDIEC, 5:95-114.   ◆ **19 δεῦτε** (# 1307) pl. of δεῦρο an adv. of place w. the force of a command. "Come here" (EGT). **ὀπίσω** (# 3958) w. gen., after. Used in the sense "be my pupils." The disciples were in constant attendance on their teacher (Meyer). **ποιήσω** fut. ind. act. ποιέω (# 4472) to make, to appoint to an office (McNeile).   ◆ **20 εὐθέως** (# 2311) at once. **ἀφέντες** aor. act. part. ἀφίημι (# 918) s.v. 11. **δίκτυον** (# 1473) net. For the different words for fishing nets s. Trench, *Synonyms*, 235-37. **ἠκολούθησαν** aor. ind. act. ἀκολουθέω (# 199) to follow. Often used of the willing and obedient disciple who follows his teacher as one who learns and serves. It involves personal commitment and cost (NIDNTT; Jack Dean Kingsbury, "The Verb Akolou-thein ["To Follow"] as an Index of Matthew's View of his Community," *JBL* 97 [1978]: 56-73; DJG, 176-78).   ◆ **21 προβάς** aor. act. part. (temp.) προβαίνω (# 4581) to go, to go ahead. **ἐκεῖθεν** (# 1696) from there. **εἶδεν** aor. ind. act. ὁράω (# 3972). **καταρτίζοντας** pres. act. part. καταρτίζω (# 2936) to make fitted, or equipped for a duty or function (McNeile). **ἐκάλεσεν** aor. ind. act. καλέω (# 2813) to call. ◆ **23 περιῆγεν** impf. ind. act. περιάγω (# 4310) to go about. **διδάσκων** pres. act. part. διδάσκω (# 1438) to teach. **συναγωγαῖς** dat. pl. συναγωγή (# 5252) synagogue. For information about the synagogue s. Moore, *Judaism*, 1:281-307; SB, 4:i, 115-88; JPF, 2:908-44; HJPE, 2:423-36; Rainer Riesner, "Synagogues in Jerusalem," BAFCS 4:179-211. **κηρύσσων** (# 3062) pres. act. part. s.v.

17. **θεραπεύων** pres. act. part. θεραπεύω (# 2543) to serve, to treat medically, to heal, to restore (BAGD; J.A. Comber, "The Verb therapeuo in Matthew's Gospel," *JBL* 97 [1978]: 431-34; GLH). The three participles–teaching, proclaiming, healing–summarize the Lord's work in Galilee (McNeile). **νόσος** (# 3798) sickness, disease, the chronic or serious disease. **μαλακία** (# 3433) sickness, the occasional sickness (RWP).   ◆ **24 ἀπῆλθεν** aor. ind. act. ἀπέρχομαι (# 599) to go away, to go out, to spread. **ἀκοή** (# 198) rumor, report. **προσήνεγκαν** aor. ind. act. προσφέρω (# 4712) to bring to. **ἔχοντας** pres. act. part. ἔχω (# 2400) to have. **ποικίλος** (# 4476) various kinds, diversified. **βασάνοις** (# 992) dat. pl. torture, torment, severe pain. The dat. = "those suffering w. severe pains." **συνεχομένους** pres. pass. part. συνέχω (# 5309) to hold together, pass. suffer from. The word underlines the severity of the ailment (DA). **δαιμονιζομένους** pres. pass. part. δαιμονίζομαι (# 1227) to be possessed by a demon. The casting out of demons was a sign of the eschatological age (DA; DJG, 166-69). **σεληνιαζομένους** pres. pass. part. σεληνιάζομαι (# 4944) to be brought under the influence of the moon, to be epileptic (MM). Adj. part. **παραλυτικός** (# 4166) lame, paralyzed. **ἐθεράπευσεν** aor. ind. act. θεραπεύω (# 2543) to heal. It is not "he treated them medically," but "he healed them" (DA).   ◆ **25 ἠκολούθησαν** aor. ind. act. s.v. 20. **ὄχλοι** (# 4063) (pl.) crowd, crowd of people. "many crowds" seems to be Matthew's way of saying "a great crowd" (DA). The crowds follow Jesus, showing him to be a charismatic figure, and as an audience, they respond w. reverence. They are contrasted w. the Jewish leaders, but are distinguished from the disciples. The crowd is also implicated in Jesus' death (DA; BBC).

Matthew 5

◆ **1 ἰδών** aor. act. part. (temp.) ὁράω (# 3972) to see. "When he saw...." **ὄχλος** (# 4063) crowd, crowd of people (s. Matt. 4:25). **ἀνέβη** aor. ind. act. ἀναβαίνω (# 326) to go up. **καθίσαντος** aor. act. part. gen. masc. sing. καθίζω (# 2767) to sit, to sit down. For rabbis' teaching sitting down s. DA; Carson. Temp. part. gen. abs. "after..." (BD, 218). **προσῆλθαν** aor. ind. act. προσέρχομαι (# 4665) to come to.   ◆ **2 ἀνοίξας** aor. act. part. ἀνοίγω (# 487) to open. **ἐδίδασκεν** impf. ind. act. διδάκω (# 1438) to teach. Incep. impf.: "he began to teach." For a study of the word "teaching" and its hist. context s. TDNT. For the purp. of the Sermon on the Mount s. J. Dwight Pentecost, "The Purpose of the Sermon on the Mount," *Bib Sac* 115 (1958): 128ff, 212ff, 313ff; SSM; Carson; D, 735-44; ABD, 5:1106-12.   ◆ **3 μακάριος** (# 3421) blessed, fortunate, happy, free from daily cares and worries. The word corresponds to the Heb. אֶשֶׁר (BAGD; DA, 431-42; TWAT, 1:481-85; THAT, 1:257-60; Walter Käser, "Beobachtungen zum alttestamentlichen Makarismus," *ZAW* 82 [1970]: 225-50; TLNT). Pred. adj. For a discussion of the beatitudes s. N. McEleney, "The Beatitudes of the Sermon on the Mount/Plain," 43 *CBQ* (1981): 1-13; DJG, 79-80. **πτω-χός** (# *4777*) poor, poor as a beggar. **πνεῦμα** (# *4460*) spirit. The dat. gives the sphere of the poverty (Mc-Neile). For the use of the phrase "poor in spirit" in DSS s. 1QM 14:7; 1QH 14:3; regarding the "poor," s. 1QM 11:9; 1QH 5:22. **αὐτῶν ἐστιν** "it belongs to them." **αὐτῶν** poss. gen. ◆ **4 πενθοῦντες** pres. act. part. πεν-θέω (# *4291*) to lament, to mourn for the dead. To grieve w. a grief which so takes possession of the whole being that it cannot be hid (Trench, *Synonyms*; TDNT). Adj. part. as subst. **παρακληθήσονται** fut. ind. pass. παρακαλέω (# *4151*) to comfort, pass. to find comfort, to receive comfort. ◆ **5 πραεῖς** nom. pl. πραΰς (# *4558*) meek, gentle. The humble and gentle attitude which expresses itself in a patient submissiveness to offense, free from malice and desire for revenge (R. Leivestad, "The Meekness and Gentleness of Christ, II Cor. X. 1," *NTS* 12 [1966]: 159; NTW 103-104; DA; TLNT). The word is used of the Messiah in Test. of Judah 24:1. **κληρονομήσουσιν** fut. ind. act. κληρονο-μέω (# *3099*) to inherit, to receive as a possession, to possess, to acquire (DA). **γῆ** (# *1178*) land, earth. For examples from the OT and Jewish lit. concerning inheriting the land s. SB, 1:197-200; Ps. 37:11; 1 Enoch 5:7; Jubilees 32:17-18; DA. ◆ **6 πεινῶντες** pres. act. part. πεινάω (# *4277*) to hunger, to hunger for something. Adj. part. as subst. Pres. indicates a continual attribute. **διψῶντες** pres. act. part. διψάω (# *1498*) to thirst. For vbs. in αω s. MH, 384. **δικαιοσύνη** (# *1466*) righteousness. It could mean the righteousness that God gives, or man's conduct in accordance w. the will of God, as in Matt. 5:20 (RM, 96-98). **χορτασθήσονται** fut. ind. pass. χορτάζω (# *5963*) to feed, to fill, to satisfy. Theol. pass. God is the agent (BG, 236). ◆ **7 ἐλεήμων** (# *1798*) merciful, sympathetic. **ἐλεηθήσονται** fut. ind. pass. ἐλεέω (# *1796*) to have mercy or pity, to be merciful or show mercy; pass. to find or be shown mercy (BAGD). It indicates being moved to pity and compassion by tragedy and includes the fear that this could happen to me (NIDNTT; TLNT). ◆ **8 καρδίᾳ** (# *2840*) heart. The heart is the center of the inner life of the person where all the spiritual forces and functions have their origin (TDNT). **ὄψονται** fut. ind. mid. (dep.) ὁράω (# *3972*) to see. To see God is to know God (DA). ◆ **9 εἰρηνοποιός** (# *1648*) one who makes peace. The word was used of kings who established peace (DA; SB, 1:215-18). S. also R. Schnackenburg, "Die Seligpreisung der Friedensstifter (Mt 5:9) im mattäischen Kontext," *BZ* 26 (1982): 161-78. **υἱοὶ θεοῦ** (# *5626; 2536*) "sons of God." The Heb. word for "son" often denotes the character of the parents as expressed by the child. **κληθήσονται** fut. ind. pass. καλέω (# *2813*) to call, to

name, pass. to be given a name. ◆ **10 δεδιωγμένοι** perf. pass. part. διώκω (# *1503*) to pursue, to persecute. **ἕνε-κεν** (# *1915*) w. gen. because of, on account of. The righteousness which is the cause of the persecution is "righteous conduct" (RM, 98; DA). ◆ **11 ὅταν** (# *4020*) w. subj., whenever. **ὀνειδίσωσιν** aor. subj. act. ὀνειδίζω (# *3943*) to reproach, to revile, to heap insults upon (BAGD). **διώξωσιν** aor. subj. act. διώκω (# *1503*). **εἴπωσιν** aor. subj. act. λέγω (# *3306*). **πᾶς** (# *4246*) every, each. It may be used to include everything belonging, in kind, to the class designated by the noun: "every kind of, all sorts of" (BAGD). **καθ'** = κατά (# *2848*) w. gen., against. Indicates the hostile relation (Schl.). **ψευδόμενοι** pres. mid. (dep.) part. ψεύδομαι (# *6017*) to lie. ◆ **12 χαίρετε** pres. imp. act. χαίρω (# *5897*) to rejoice, to be happy. **ἀγαλλιᾶσθε** pres. imp. mid. (dep.) ἀγαλλιάομαι (# *22*) to rejoice greatly. Pres. imps. call for an attitude. **μισθός** (# *3635*) reward (Carson, 138). **ἐδίωξαν** aor. ind. act. s.v. 11. ◆ **13 ἅλας** (# *229*) salt. For uses of salt s. DA; TDNT. **μωρανθῇ** aor. subj. pass. μωραίνω (# *3701*) to play the fool, to become foolish; of salt to become tasteless, insipid (RWP). **ἁλισθήσεται** fut. ind. pass. ἁλίζω (# *245*) to salt, to make salty; pass. to be salted. **ἰσχύει** pres. ind. act. ἰσχύω (# *2710*) strong, to be able, w. **οὐδέν** (# *4029*) to be good for nothing (BAGD). **εἰ μή** (# *1623; 3590*) except. **βληθέν** aor. pass. part. βάλλω (# *965*) to throw. **καταπατεῖσθαι** pres. inf. pass. καταπατέω (# *2922*) to tread down, to trample. Inf. explains the main vb. For an explanation of salt losing its savor and the idea of salt indicating productivity rather than preservation s. E.P. Deatrick, "Salt, Soil, Savor," *BA* 25 (1962): 41-48; BBC. ◆ **14 ὑμεῖς** "you!" (pl.), emphatic and contrastive. **φῶς** (# *5890*) light. Light was a metaphor for purity, knowledge of the truth, revelation at the presence of God (Carson, 139; for uses of the metaphor s. Luz). **κρυβῆναι** aor. inf. pass. κρύπτω (# *3221*) to hide; pass. to hide or conceal oneself. **ἐπάνω** w. gen., upon. **κειμένη** pres. mid. (dep.) part. κεῖμαι (# *3023*) to lie. Used of location of a place (BAGD). Some view this as a reference to the city of Jerusalem (DA), but it probably refers to cities often built of white limestone which would gleam in the sun (Carson, 139). ◆ **15 καίουσιν** pres. ind. act. 3rd. pers. pl. καίω (# *2794*) to light. **λύχνος** (# *3394*) oil lamp, a small clay lamp. **τιθέασιν** pres. ind. act. τίθημι (# *5502*) to set, to place. **μόδιος** (# *3654*) grain-measuring vessel containing about a peck (BAGD; DA). **λυχνία** (# *3393*) lampstand. **καί** (# *2779*) and, used to express purp. or result, "so that..." (BG,153). **λάμπει** pres. ind. act. λάμπω (# *3290*) to shine. Gnomic pres. here expressing general truths. For lamps and lampstands s. Robert H. Smith, "The Household Lamps of Palestine in New Testament Times," *BA* 29 (1966): 2-27; DA). ◆ **16 οὕτως** (# *4048*) so, makes the comp. **λαμψάτω** aor. imp. act. λάμπω s.v. 15. Aor. is used to express a specific command. The disciples of Jesus are to allow the light which they received from the heavenly Father through Jesus to shine in the world so that they may glorify God (TDNT). ἔμπροσθεν (# 1869) w. gen., before, in front of. ὅπως (# 3968) w. subj., in order that (purp.). ἴδωσιν aor. subj. act. ὁράω (# 3972) to see. καλός (# 2819) good, beautiful, pertaining to a positive moral quality, w. the implication of being favorably valued (LN). δοξάσωσιν aor. subj. act. δοξάζω (# 1519) to praise, to glorify. οὐρανός (# 4041) heaven. For the expression "Father in heaven" s. 6:9 (DJG, 273). ◆ **17** νομίσητε aor. subj. act. νομίζω (# 3787) to consider, to think. To regard something as presumably true, but without particular certainty (LN). The formula is a teaching device of Jesus, used to clarify his teaching and to avoid misunderstanding (Carson, 141; for the relation of this section to the previous context s. W.J. Dumbrell, "The Logic of the Role of the Law in Matthew v 1-20," *Nov T* 23 (1981): 1-21). Subj. is in a neg. command. μή (# 3590). ἦλθον aor. ind. act. ἔρχομαι (# 2262). καταλῦσαι aor. act. inf. καταλύω (# 2907) to tear down, to destroy, to annul. Inf. used to express purp. νόμος (# 3795) law. It refers to the Pentateuch. προφήτας (# 4737) "the prophets" refers to the rest of the OT (DA; Roger Beckwith, *The Old Testament Canon of the New Testament Church* [London: SPCK, 1985], 92, 107). πληρῶσαι aor. act. inf. πληρόω (# 4444) to fulfill. Inf. expresses purp. The meaning may be that Jesus fulfills the prophecies of the OT, or it could mean "to bring to its intended meaning," that is, "to present a definitive interpretation of the Law" (Hagner). For a discussion of this word and the meaning of the passage s. Carson, 141-45; C.F.D. Moule, "Fulfillment-Words in the New Testament: Use and Abuse," *NTS* 14 (1968): 316ff; DA; Robert Banks, "Matthew's Understanding of the Law: Authenticity and Interpretation in Matthew 5:17-20," *JBL* 93 (1974): 226-42; D.J. Moo,"Jesus and the Authority of the Mosaic Law," *JSNT* 20 (1984): 3-49; DJG, 456-58; LIF, 231-40; HSB, 355-58. ◆ **18** ἀμήν (# 297) (Heb. אָמֵן) certainly. For the Heb. word s. TWOT; DJG, 7-8; THAT; DCH; ABD, 1:184-86; NIDOTTE; Hagner. In Judaism the word was a strengthening or confirming answer or agreement w. another person's statement. For example, a prayer, praise, or oath (SB, 1:242f). Jesus did not use the word to apply to others but to introduce His own words. This gives strength and authority to what He says (s. 1QS 1:20; 2:10, 18; DA). παρέλθῃ aor. subj. act. παρέρχομαι (# 4216) to pass by, to come to an end. ἰῶτα (# 2740) the smallest Gr. letter used to represent the smallest Heb. letter (yod). κεραία (# 3037) horn, projection, hook as a part of a letter; perhaps it refers to the Heb. letter "waw" (BAGD). For various suggestions as to the meaning s. DA; Carson, 145; Lachs; Günther Schwarz, "ἰῶτα ἓν μία κεραία (Matthäus

5^18)," *ZNW* 66 (1975): 268-69; BBC. οὐ μή (# 4024; 3590) "not in any wise." For the double neg. s. M, 187-92; GGBB, 468. πάντα pl. acc. πᾶς (# 4246) everything. For the use of πᾶς s. IBG, 93-95; RG 771-74. γένηται aor. subj. mid. (dep.) γίνομαι (# 1181) to become, to come to pass, to happen. ◆ **19** ὃς ἐάν = ὃς ἄν (# 4005; 165) whoever. The rel. cl. has the character of a cond. cl. and refers to a general assertion or supposition (BD, 192). λύσῃ aor. subj. act. λύω (# 3395) to loose, to repeal, to annul, to abolish (BAGD). ἐλαχίστος (# 1788) superl., least, from μικρός small. Paronomasia–the reoccurrence of the same word in close proximity. The one who breaks the least commandment will be the least in the kingdom of heaven (BD, 258). διδάξῃ aor. subj. act. διδάσκω (# 1438) to teach. κληθήσεται fut. ind. pass. s.v. 9. ποιήσῃ aor. subj. act. ποιέω (# 4472) to do. μέγας (# 3489) large, great. The positive used for the superl., probably under Hebraic influence (MT, 31). ◆ **20** γάρ (# 1142) for. It gives an explanation of the previous statement. ὅτι (# 4022) used as quotation marks in a direct quotation. ἐάν (# 1569) if. It introduces a 3rd. class cond. cl., which views the cond. as probable or possible (RG, 1016-20). περισσεύσῃ aor. subj. act. περισσεύω (# 3455) to exceed, to overflow like a river out of its banks (RWP). δικαιοσύνη (# 1466) righteousness. It refers to the conduct demanded and characterized by the meticulous observance of the law (RM, 84). The demand is nothing less than perfection (Carson, 146). πλεῖον (# 4498) more, in a greater measure. Used as a heightened comp. (BD, 129). γραμματέων gen. pl. γραμματεύς (# 1208) scribe. gen. of comp. For a discussion of the Scribes and Pharisees s. TJ, 70-76; HJP, 2:322-25; EDNT; CCFJ, 1:393; BBC; s. also 2:4. οὐ μή (# 4024; 3590) emphatic neg. s.v. 18. εἰσέλθητε aor. subj. act. εἰσέρχομαι (# 1656) to go in, to come in, to enter. ◆ **21** ἠκούσατε aor. ind. act. ἀκούω (# 201) to hear. In the light of rabbinic parallels, the vb. could be translated, "you have understood" and refers to the interpretations given to the OT passage (NTRJ, 56). ἐρρέθη aor. ind. pass. λέγω (# 3306). ἀρχαίοις (# 792) old (dat. pl.), "to the old ones," men of earlier generations. Dat. is indir. obj., not agency (DA). For the "Oral Law" and "Halakha" of the Jewish rabbis s. TLS, 1:35-209; HJPE, 2:337-55; J.M. Baumgarten, "The Unwritten Law in the Pre-rabbinic Period," *Journal for the Study of Judaism in the Persian, Hellenistic and Roman Period* 3 (1972): 7-29. φονεύσεις fut. ind. act. φονεύω (# 5839) to murder, to kill. The fut. is used to express a moral command. φονεύσῃ aor. subj. act. φονεύω. ἔνοχος (# 1944) to be caught in, to be liable, to be guilty. ἔσται fut. ind. mid. (dep.) εἰμί (# 1639) to be. κρίσει dat. sing. κρίσις (# 3213) judging, judgment, trial, penalty, legal proceedings, judicial sentence, the court (DA). ◆ **22** ὀργιζόμενος pres. mid. (dep.) part. ὀργίζομαι (# 3974) to be angry, to be full of anger, to be furious (LN, 1:761). εἴπῃ aor. subj. act. λέγω. ῥακά (# 4819) fool, empty head. For examples s. SB, 1:278-79; TDNT; UJS, 30; R.A. Guelich, "Mt 5:22: Its Meaning and Integrity," ZNW 64 (1973): 39-40. The Aram. word ריק, meaning "empty, null & void, without effect," was used for a contract that was invalid and an offering without any effect (AT, 693-94). συνέδριον (# 5284) Sanhedrin, highest court of the Jews (s. Guelich, ZNW, 42-44). μωρέ voc. μωρός (# 3704) foolish, stupid. ῥακά expresses contempt for a man's head: "you stupid." μωρέ expresses contempt for his heart and character: "you scoundrel" (EGT). This type of language could lead to a murderous quarrel resulting in bloodshed (HSB, 359). γέεννα (# 1147) gehenna, the city dump of Jerusalem, as a picture of the final place of judgment for the wicked. For a description of the word s. TDNT; DJG, 310; BBC. ◆ 23 προσφέρῃς pres. subj. act. προσφέρω (# 4712) to bring, to present offerings and gifts. Subj. w. ἐάν (# 1569) used in a 3rd. class cond. cl. (s.v. 20). ἐπί (# 2093) w. acc., upon. θυσιαστήριον (# 2603) altar. For words ending in -τήριον meaning "place" s. RG, 154; MH, 343. κἀκεῖ = καὶ ἐκεῖ "and there." μνησθῇς aor. subj. pass. (dep.) μιμνήσκομαι (# 3630) to remember, to think about. ◆ 24 ἄφες aor. imp. act. ἀφίημι (# 918) to leave, to leave behind. ὕπαγε pres. imp. act. ὑπάγω (# 5632) to go, to leave behind. διαλλάγηθι aor. imp. pass. διαλλάσσομαι (# 1367) to reconcile; pass. to be reconciled. Denotes mutual concession after mutual hostility (Lightfoot, Notes, 288; V, 40-64). ἐλθών aor. act. part. (circum.) ἔρχομαι (# 2262) to come, to go. πρόσφερε pres. imp. act. s.v. 23. ◆ 25 ἴσθι pres. imp. act. εἰμί. εὐνοῶν pres. act. part. εὐνοέω (# 2333) to be well disposed, to make friends. Pres. part. is used in a periphrastic construction to express an imper. "be making friends w. your enemy quickly" (VA, 465; RG, 375; BD, 180). ἀντίδικος (# 508) opponent in a law case. ἕως ὅτου w. pres. ind. means "while," "as." εἶ pres. ind. act. εἰμί (# 1639) to be. ἐν τῇ ὁδῷ "in the way"; "on the way to court" (DA). μήποτε (# 3607) w. aor. subj. means "lest." Used in a neg. purp. clause expressing apprehension (BAGD). παραδῷ aor. subj. act. παραδίδωμι (# 4140) to give over, to turn over to. κριτής (# 3216) the one who makes a decision, judge. ὑπηρέτης (# 5677) helper, one who serves. φυλακή (# 5871) prison. βληθήσῃ fut. ind. pass. βάλλω (# 965) to throw, to cast. To be arrested and turned over to a judge is a projected possibility (subj.); then to be cast into prison becomes a very real expectation (VA, 415). ◆ 26 ἐξέλθῃς aor. subj. act. ἐξέρχομαι (# 2002) to come out, to go out. ἀποδῷς aor. subj. act. ἀποδίδωμι (# 625) to give back, to pay back. κοδράντης (# 3119) (Lat.) quadrans, a Roman coin or a coin used at the time of our Lord, worth about 1.5 cents (UBD, 724; HJC, 244-45; SB, 1:290-94). This indicates that the point at issue was money (DA). ◆ 27 ἠκούσατε aor. ind. act. s.v. 21. ἐρρέθη aor. ind. pass. s.v. 21. μοιχεύσεις fut. ind.

act. μοιχεύω (# 3658) to commit adultery. Fut. expresses a moral command. ◆ 28 βλέπων pres. act. part. βλέπω (# 1063) to see, to look upon. πρός (# 4639) w. inf. often expresses purp., but sometimes weakened to "with reference to." It may express tendency and ultimate goal rather than purp. (MT, 144; s. also M, 218). ἐπιθυμῆσαι aor. act. inf. ἐπιθυμέω (# 2121) to desire, to long for. Taken w. the acc. the meaning may be "that she may have sexual lust" (s. Klaus Haacker, "Der Rechtssatz Jesu zum Thema Ehebruch [Mt 5, 28]," Biblische Zeitschrift 21 [1977]: 113-16). ἐμοίχευσεν aor. ind. act. μοιχεύω s.v. 27. An aor. after a fut. cond. is, to a certain extent, futuristic (BD, 171; s. also RG, 846f). ◆ 29 σκανδαλίζει (# 4997) pres. ind. act. to cause to fall. The vb. means to stick in the trap that springs and closes the trap when the animal touches it (RWP). ἔξελε aor. imp. act. ἐξαιρέω (# 1975) to take out, to tear out. βάλε aor. imp. act. βάλλω (# 965) to throw, to cast. Aor. imps. call for specific actions. συμφέρει (# 5237) pres. ind. act. to be advantageous, profitable, good, useful. Followed by dat. of advantage. Here it is well translated "it is better for you ... than" (BAGD). ἵνα (# 2671) w. subj., that. This cl. is the subject of the vb. συμφέρει (RG, 992). ἀπόληται aor. subj. mid. (dep.) ἀπόλλυμι (# 660) to be destroyed, to be ruined, to be lost. βληθῇ aor. subj. pass. βάλλω. ◆ 30 χείρ (# 5931) hand. The "right hand" may be a reference to masturbation (DA; b. Nidda 13a-b; SB, 1:302-303). Here the cond. is assumed for the sake of argument (GGBB, 693; BBC). ἔκκοψον aor. imp. act. ἐκκόπτω (# 1716) to cut off. ἀπέλθῃ aor. subj. act. ἀπέρχομαι (# 599) to go away, to depart. ◆ 31 ἐρρέθη aor. ind. pass. λέγω s.v. 21. ἀπολύσῃ aor. subj. act. ἀπολύω (# 668) to release, to divorce. δότω aor. imp. act. 3rd. pers. sing. δίδωμι (# 1443) to give. ἀποστάσιον (# 687) bill of divorcement. The written notice was a protection to the wife (RWP). For the Jewish practice s. M, Gittin; SB, 1:303-312; AT, 307-308, 326; JAD; DJG, 192-97; s. Matt. 19:3. ◆ 32 παρεκτός (# 4211) w. gen., except. λόγος (# 3364) word, matter, reason. For rabbinical reasons for divorce s. BBC; SB, 1:312-20. πορνεία (# 4518) unchastity, fornication of every kind of unlawful sexual intercourse (BAGD); perhaps here incest (DA). For Jewish background to this v. see M.A.N. Bockmuehl, "Matthew 5.32; 19.9 in the Light of Pre-rabbinic Halakhah," NTS 35 (1989): 291-95. ποιεῖ pres. ind. act. ποιέω (# 4472) to make. W. inf. it means "to cause to make" (DB, 200). μοιχευθῆναι aor. inf. pass. μοιχεύω (# 3658) to commit adultery (BAGD). ἀπολελυμένην perf. pass. part. ἀπολύω (# 668) s.v. 31. γαμήσῃ aor. subj. act. γαμέω (# 1138) to marry, used of the man. μοιχᾶται pres. ind. pass. μοιχάω (# 3656) to cause one to commit adultery; pass. to be an adulterer, to commit adultery. ◆ 33 ἐπιορκήσεις fut. ind. act. ἐπιορκέω (# 2155) to swear falsely, to break an oath. ἀποδώσεις fut. ind. act. ἀποδίδωμι

◆ **43** ἠκούσατε aor. ind. act. ἀκούω s.v. 21. **ἐρρέθη** aor. ind. pass. **λέγω** pres. ind. act. s.v. 21. **ἀγαπήσεις** fut. ind. act. ἀγαπάω (# 26) to love. Fut. is used for injunctions in the legal language of the OT (BD, 183). **πλησίος** (# 4446) near, close by, neighbor, fellowman. **μισήσεις** fut. ind. act. μισέω (# 3631) to hate. For DSS instructions to hate the enemy s. 1QS 1:10; 2:4-9; 1QM 4:1. ◆ **44** ἀγαπᾶτε pres. imp. act. ἀγαπάω (# 26) Pres. imp. used to express a continual attitude. For a discussion of this command s. John Piper, *"Love Your Enemies:" Jesus' Love Command in the Synoptics and the Early Christian Paraenesis*, SNTSMS 38, Cambridge: Cambridge University Press, 1979; BBC. **προσεύχεσθε** pres. imp. mid. (dep.) προσεύχομαι (# 4667) to pray. **διωκόντων** pres. act. part. διώκω (# 1503) s.v. 10. ◆ **45** ὅπως (# 3968) w. subj. aor., in order that. **γένησθε** aor. subj. mid. (dep.) γίνομαι (# 1181) to become, to be. subj. in purp. cl. **ἀνατέλλει** pres. ind. act. ἀνατέλλω (# 422) to cause to rise, transitive and causative in meaning (BD, 163). **βρέχει** pres. ind. act. βρέχω (# 1101) to cause to rain. **ἐπὶ δικαίους** (# 1465) upon the righteous. The righteous are those who obey the law (RM, 103; DA). ◆ **46** ἀγαπήσητε aor. subj. act. ἀγαπάω (# 26) to love. Subj. w. ἐάν (# 1569) is used in a 3rd. class cond. cl. indicating that the cond. is a possibility. **ἀγαπῶντας** pres. act. part. **οὐχί** (# 4049) w. questions it expects a positive answer. **τελώνης** (# 5467) tax collector (TDNT; s. Matt. 9:9; JZ). ◆ **47** ἀσπάσησθε aor. subj. mid. (dep.) ἀσπάζομαι (# 832) to greet. More significant in the East; symbolic here of friendly relations implying a desire for God's blessing and peace (EGT, DA). For the subj. s.v. 46. **ἐθνικοί** (# 1618) gentile, heathen (DA). ◆ **48** ἔσεσθε pres. imp. mid. (dep.) εἰμί (# 1639). **ὑμεῖς** (# 5148) you (pl.) emphatic. **τέλειοι** (# 5455) perfect, mature. To obey Jesus' words is to love utterly: no more can be asked (DA). **οὐράνιος** (# 4039) heavenly, belonging to heaven, living in heaven.

Matthew 6

◆ **1** προσέχετε pres. imp. act. προσέχω (# 4668) to beware, to give heed to, to watch out for. Pres. calls for a constant vigil. **ποιεῖν** pres. act. inf. ποιέω (# 4472) to do. Inf. explains what is to be heeded. Used w. **δικαιοσύνη** (# 1466) meaning "to practice piety," and is the general title for acts of devotion and religious duty which conform to the will of God (GW, 129). **ἔμπροσθεν** (# 1869) w. gen., before, in the presence of. This should not be done in order to obtain reward (BBC). **πρός** (# 4639) to, indicates purp. **θεαθῆναι** aor. inf. pass. θεάομαι (# 2517) to see, to behold, to look at. **αὐτοῖς** dat. pl. αὐτός (# 899) "to be seen by them." Dat. of agency (MT, 240). **εἰ δὲ μή γε** but, if not, otherwise (Thrall, 9, 10). ◆ **2** ὅταν (# 4020) w. subj., when, whenever. **ποιῆς** pres. subj. act. The vb. is used w. the noun to form the

---

(# 625) to give away, to fulfill one's duty to someone, to keep oaths (BAGD). **ὅρκους** (# 3992) oaths, pl. even when one oath is intended (BAGD). For a Jewish view of oaths s. M, Shebuoth; SB, 1:321-36; also 1QS 5:8; DJG, 577-78; HSB, 361-62. ◆ **34** μὴ … ὅλως (# 3590; 3910) = an uncond. neg. (Schl., 182). **ὀμόσαι** aor. act. inf. ὄμνυμι / ὀμνύω (# 3923) to swear. Inf. is used w. dir. discourse (RG, 1060). **ὅτι** (# 4022) because. ◆ **35** ὑποπόδιον (# 5711) footstool. Some rabbinic authorities viewed oaths by heaven, by earth, and by one's own head as not binding (SB, 1:332-34; DA). ◆ **36** ὀμόσῃς aor. subj. act. s.v. 34. Subj. used in a neg. imp. **δύνασαι** pres. ind. act. 2nd. pers. sing. δύναμαι (# 1538) to be able. **τρίχα** acc. sing. θρίξ (# 2582) hair. **λευκός** (# 3328) bright, shining, white. Perhaps symbolic for wisdom. **ποιῆσαι** aor. act. inf. ποιέω (# 4472) to make. **μέλαιναν** acc. sing. μέλας (# 3506) black. Perhaps a symbol for youth (DA; BBC). One cannot swear by his head because he has no power over it (DA). ◆ **37** ἔστω pres. imp. act. 3rd. pers. sing. εἰμί (# 1639) to be. ◆ **38** ἠκούσατε aor. ind. act. s.v. 21. **ἐρρέθη** aor. ind. pass. s.v. 21. **ἀντί** (# 505) w. gen., instead of. **ὀδόντα** acc. sing. ὀδούς (# 3848) tooth. (SB, 1:337-41). ◆ **39** ἀντιστῆναι aor. act. inf. ἀνθίστημι (# 468) to set against, to set oneself against, to oppose, to resist, to withstand. Inf. in indir. discourse. **ῥαπίζει** pres. ind. act. ῥαπίζω (# 4824) to hit, to slap with the open hand (LN, 223). **σιαγόνα** acc. σιαγών (# 4965) cheek. To hit someone w. the right hand on the right cheek, one must hit backhanded, thus the reference may be to a "backhanded insult" (DA). **στρέψον** aor. imp. act. στρέφω (# 5138) to turn. ◆ **40** θέλοντι pres. act. part. (dat.) θέλω (# 2527) to will, to wish. Dat. as indir. obj. The anacoluthon construction w. the part. is Semitic and is used as a *casus pendens* (BD, 244; DA). **κριθῆναι** aor. inf. pass. κρίνω (# 3212) to judge; pass. to dispute, quarrel, debate, to go to law with someone (BAGD). Compl. inf. to the main vb. **χιτών** (# 5945) tunic. A sort of shirt or undergarment, and would be demanded by law (RWP; DA). **λαβεῖν** aor. act. inf. λαμβάνω (# 3284) to take. **ἄφες** aor. act. imp. ἀφίημι (# 918) to allow, to permit. **ἱμάτιον** (# 2668) garment, outer clothing, cloak. Exod. 22:26-27 and Deut. 24:12-13. ◆ **41** ἀγγαρεύσει fut. ind. act. ἀγγαρεύω (# 30) to compel, forcibly to impress someone to service, to compel him to serve whether he liked it or not (NTW, 16; NDIEC, 1:42; 2:77). **μίλιον** (# 3627) mile. A Roman mile, a thousand paces, then a fixed measure about 4,854 feet (BAGD). Acc. of space. ◆ **42** αἰτοῦντι pres. act. part. αἰτέω (# 160) to ask. **δός** aor. imp. act. δίδωμι (# 1443) to give. Imp. used in a specific command. **δανίσασθαι** aor. mid. inf. δανίζω (# 1247) to lend money; mid. to borrow money. (s. Deut. 15:7-11; for "lending" in Judaism s. SB, 1:346-53). **ἀποστραφῇς** aor. subj. pass. ἀποστρέφω (# 695) to turn away. Pass. to reject or repudiate someone (BAGD).

verbal idea; i.e., "to do alms," "to give alms." ἐλεημοσύνη (# 1797) kind deed, alms, charitable giving (BAGD). Nothing is more marked in rabbinic ethics than the stress laid upon charity in every sense of the word (RA, 412; for rabbinic views on charity s. RA, 412-39; Moore, *Judaism*, 2:162-79; SB, 4:536-38; RAC, 8:269-306; DA). **σαλπίσῃς** aor. subj. act. σαλπίζω (# 4895) to sound the trumpet, either in a figurative or literal sense (McNeile). It may refer to the blowing of the trumpet for the public fasts (Carson, 164), or to making the trumpet-shaped money-box resound by flinging the money hard (N.J. McEleney, "Does the Trumpet Sound or Resound? An Interpretation of Matthew 6²," *ZNW* 76 [1985]: 43-46; but BBC). Subj. is in a neg. command. **ὑποκριτής** (# 5695) actor, interpreter, one who impersonates another, hypocrite; one who assumes a role and identity that were not his own and performed for the audience's approval (RWP; R.A. Batey, "Jesus and the Theatre," *NTS* 30 [1984]: 563; Carson, 164). **ῥύμη** (# 4860) a narrow street. **ὅπως** (# 3968) w. subj., in order that. **δοξασθῶσιν** aor. subj. pass. δοξάζω (# 1519) to give honor, to praise, to glorify. **ἀπέχουσιν** pres. ind. act. ἀπέχω (# 600) to receive payment in full. Often used in the sense of receipting an account which has been paid in full (NTW, 17-20; LAE, 110-11). Perfective pres. denoting a produced state (VANT, 239). ◆ **3 ποιοῦντος** pres. act. part. (temp.) gen. masc. sing. ποιέω (# 4472) gen. abs. "when you...." **γνώτω** aor. imp. act. 3rd. pers. sing. γινώσκω (# 1182) to know. **ἀριστερός** (# 754) left. **δεξιός** (# 1288) right. ◆ **4 ᾖ** pres. subj. act. εἰμί (# 1639) to be. Subj. w. **ὅπως** (# 3968) used in a purp. cl. **ἀποδώσει** fut. ind. act. ἀποδίδωμι (# 625) to give back, to repay, to reward. Fut. is used to express the protasis of a Semitic cond.: "Do this and this will follow" (Beyer, 252-55). ◆ **5 προσεύχησθε** aor. subj. mid. (dep.) προσεύχομαι (# 4667) to pray (DJG, 623). The subj. w. the particle **ὅταν** (# 4020) generalizes the action: "whenever...." Perhaps there is a reference to the three hours of prayer: morning, afternoon (3 P.M.), and evening (DA; RA, 342-81). **ἔσεσθε** fut. ind. mid. (dep.) εἰμί (# 1639). Fut. w. the neg. **οὐκ** (# 4024) can express a prohibition in the legal language of the OT (BG, 149); but the fut. of εἰμί occurs for the imp. (BD, 49). **φιλοῦσιν** pres. ind. act. φιλέω (# 5797) to like, to love. Pres. indicates the habitual attitude. **γωνία** (# 1224) corner. **πλατεῖα** (# 4423) a wide street. **ἑστῶτες** perf. act. part. ἵστημι (# 2705) to stand. Standing was the usual attitude in prayer (McNeile). **φανῶσιν** aor. subj. pass. (dep.) φαίνομαι (# 5743) to appear, to show oneself. Subj. used in a purp. cl. ◆ **6 ταμεῖον** (# 5421) storeroom, innermost secret room (BAGD; BBC). **κλείσας** aor. act. part. κλείω (# 3091) to close. Temp. part., or it is part of the command. **πρόσευξαι** aor. imp. mid. (dep.) προσεύχομαι (# 4667) to pray. ◆ **7 βατταλογήσητε** aor. subj. act. βατταλογέω

(# 1006) to babble, either in the sense of repeating the words or chattering (RWP). Perhaps a reference to the heathen magical formulas, a repetition of meaningless sounds (F.W. Beare, "Speaking with Tongues," *JBL* 83 [1964]: 229; DJG, 623). For such texts s. GMP; for other views s. DA. **δοκοῦσιν** pres. ind. act. δοκέω (# 1506) to suppose, to think so. **πολυλογία** (# 4494) much speaking. **εἰσακουσθήσονται** fut. ind. pass. εἰσακούω (# 1653) to listen to, to hear and answer prayer. ◆ **8 ὁμοιωθῆτε** aor. subj. pass. ὁμοιόω (# 3929) to make like; pass. to be like. Subj. w. **μή** (# 3590) used in a prohibition. **οἶδεν** (# 3857) Def. perf. w. pres. meaning "to know." **χρείαν ἔχετε** w. gen., to have need of. **αἰτῆσαι** aor. act. inf. αἰτέω (# 160) to ask. Temp. inf. "before you ask." ◆ **9 οὕτως** (# 4048) so, in the following manner. It probably implies that this is an example of how to pray, rather than a formula to be mechanically repeated (DA; DJG, 619-23). **ἁγιασθήτω** aor. imp. pass. 3rd. pers. sing. ἁγιάζω (# 39) to treat as holy, to reverence (BAGD). The request is that the Holy One may secure before the whole world in a final and decisive way the holiness appropriate to His name, to which human beings will respond w. praise and exaltation (EDNT, 1:19; BBC). For the aor. imp. in prayers s. Bakker, 98-127; VA, 347-50; VANT, 380-82; GGBB, 487-88. ◆ **10 ἐλθέτω** aor. imp. act. 3rd. pers. sing. ἔρχομαι (# 2262) to come. The petition is for the future advent of God to establish His sovereignty on earth (McNeile). **γενηθήτω** aor. imp. pass. (dep.) 3rd. pers. sing. γίνομαι (# 1181) to become, to come to pass, to be done, to happen. ◆ **11 ἐπιούσιος** (# 2157) for the coming day (RWP). "The bread that we need, give us today, day after day" (s. Hagner; Harrington). For this translation and a study of the word s. TDNT; BAGD; DA; C.J. Hemer, "ἐπιούσιος," *JSNT* 22 (1984): 81-94; Luz. **δός** aor. imp. act. δίδωμι (# 1443) to give. Aor. looks at a specific request. ◆ **12 ἄφες** aor. imp. act. ἀφίημι (# 918) to let go, to cancel, to remit, to pardon; to remove the guilt resulting from wrongdoing (BAGD; LN, 1:503). **ὀφείλημα** (# 4052) debt, what is owed, one's due, a moral debt (BAGD; LN, 1:774). The word stresses a moral obligation. **ὡς** (# 6055) as, in the sense of because (BD, 236). **ἀφήκαμεν** aor. ind. act. ἀφίημι. Aor. may be timeless or refer to the recent past (VA, 129-30; VANT, 280-81). **ὀφειλέτης** (# 4050) debtor; one who is morally obligated. ◆ **13 εἰσενέγκῃς** aor. subj. act. εἰσφέρω (# 1662) to bring in, to lead into. There may be a reflective force here: "Do not let us fall victim" (DA). **πειρασμός** (# 4280) test, temptation. **ῥῦσαι** aor. imp. mid. (dep.) ῥύομαι (# 4861) to rescue, to deliver. ◆ **14 ἐάν** (# 1569) w. subj., if. Introduces a 3rd. class cond. cl., assuming that the cond. is possible. **ἀφῆτε** aor. subj. act. s.v. 12. **παράπτωμα** (# 4183) a false step, failure, transgression (LN, 1:774). ◆ **16 νηστεύητε** pres. subj. act. νηστεύω (# 3764) to fast, to sit and fast. Subj. w. the particle generalizes the action; s.v. 5. For Jewish fasting s. Moore, *Judaism*, 2:257-66; SB, 4:i, 77-144; DJG, 233-34; BBC. **γίνεσθε** pres. imp. mid. (dep.) γίνομαι (# *1181*). Neg. imp. forbids an habitual action. **σκυθρωπός** (# *5034*) sad, gloomy, sullen look which calls attention to the inward state of the person (s. LXX Gen. 40:7; Test. Simeon 4:1). **ἀφανίζουσιν** pres. ind. act. ἀφανίζω (# *906*) to render invisible or unrecognizable, of one's face; to disfigure, that is, w. ashes and by leaving the hair and beard unattended or by coloring the face to look pale as though fasting (McNeile). Perhaps there is a play on words w. **φανῶσιν**. They neglect their appearance in order that they may appear. **νηστεύοντες** pres. act. part. nom. masc. pl. νηστεύω to fast.   ◆ **17 νηστεύων** pres. act. part. (temp.). "When you (emphatic) fast...." **ἄλειψαι** aor. imp. mid. ἀλείφομαι (# *230*) to anoint oneself. This was not normally done during fasting (Lachs, 125). **νίψαι** aor. mid. imp. νίπτομαι (# *3782*) to wash oneself. Washing was usually for the purp. of eating (DA; DJG, 126-30).   ◆ **18 φανῇς** aor. subj. pass. (dep.) φαίνομαι (# *5743*) to appear, to show oneself (BAGD). Subj. w. **ὅπως** (# *3968*) used in a purp. cl. The neg. **μή** (# *3590*) is used w. the subj. to ward off something still dependent on the will (BD, 188).   ◆ **19 θησαυρίζετε** pres. act. imp. θησαυρίζω (# *2564*) to gather treasure. For the imp. w. the neg. s.v. 16. **ὅπου** (# *3963*) rel. where. The true value of any treasure is determined by its location (DA). **σής** (# *4962*) moth. The moth destroys that which is feeble; Job 4:19; 13:28 (DA). **βρῶσις** (# *1111*) eating, consuming, perhaps by an insect (BAGD; BBKA; EDNT). **ἀφανίζει** pres. ind. act. ἀφανίζω (# *906*) to ruin, destroy (BAGD; BBC). Gnomic pres. referring to a general truth. **διορύσσουσιν** pres. ind. act. διορύσσω (# *1482*) to dig through, to break in. Gnomic pres.   ◆ **20 ὅπου** (# *3963*) s.v. 19. For Jewish parallels s. DA; SB, 1:429-30.   ◆ **22 λύχνος** (# *3394*) light, lamp (s. Matt. 5:13; TDNT; for the eye as a lamp s. DA). **ἐάν** s.v. 14. **ἁπλοῦς** (# *604*) clear, sound, healthy, sincere, generous as the opposite of a grudging, selfish spirit (BAGD; DA). The moral sense of the word "sincere" occurs in Test. of Levi 13:1 ("walk in sincerity") and in an inscription to the god Men ("sincere soul") (MM; NDIEC, 3:20-21; Susan R. Garrett, "'Lest the Light in You Be Darkness': Luke 11:33-36 and the Question of Commitment," *JBL* 110 [1991]: 93-105, esp. 96-103). **φωτεινός** (# *5893*) shining brightly, light. A good eye is evidence of inner light (DA).   ◆ **23 ἐάν** (# *1569*) if. It introduces a 3rd. class cond. which assumes the cond. to be possible (s.v. 14). **εἰ** (# *1623*) if. It introduces a cond. assumed to be true. **πόσον** (# *4531*) adj. of number, magnitude, degree: how much, how great, how many (AS). "What a terrible kind of darkening that is" (McNeile). The conclusion of the argument from the lesser to the greater (s. Rom. 5:9).   ◆ **24 μισήσει** fut. ind. act. μισέω (# *3631*) to

hate; in this context to neglect, to disregard, to slight. Love and hate refer to faithful labor (DA). **ἀνθέξεται** fut. ind. mid. (dep.) ἀντέχομαι (# *504*) to hold fast to, to stick by. Used in the sense of sticking by one's rights (MM). For the local force of the prep. in composition s. MH, 297. **καταφρονήσει** fut. ind. act. καταφρονέω (# *2969*) to despise, to look down upon. The prep. indicates that the action is unfavorable to the obj. (MH, 316). Fut. forms in this v. are gnomic or omnitemporal expressing a general truth (VA, 423; RG, 876). **μαμωνᾷ** (# *3440*) possession, earthly goods, money, resources; that in which one has confidence (Carson, 178; DA; SB, 1:434; TDNT).   ◆ **25 μεριμνᾶτε** pres. imp. act. μεριμνάω (# *3534*) to be concerned for, to be anxious about, to think about something, to reflect (Sand). Imp. w. the neg. **μή** (# *3590*) is to stop an action in progress, or to forbid an attitude. **ψυχῇ** (# *6034*) soul, the life principle embodied in the body (McNeile). Dat. = dat. of advantage (MT, 238). **φάγητε** aor. subj. act. ἐσθίω (# *2266*) to eat. **πίητε** aor. subj. act. πίνω (# *4403*) to drink. **ἐνδύσησθε** aor. mid. subj. ἐνδύομαι (# *1907*) to clothe oneself with, to put on. The subjs. are deliberative in indir. discourse expressing hesitating questions (RG, 934-35; s.v. 31). **οὐχί** (# *4049*) in questions, expects a positive answer. **πλεῖον** comp. πολύς (# *4498*) much, much more. **τροφῆς** (# *5575*) food. Gen. of comp., "than." A rabbinic form of argumentation: "Will not God, having given the greater thing (ἡ ψυχή), supply the lesser things such as food and clothing?" (DA).   ◆ **26 ἐμβλέψατε** aor. imp. act. ἐμβλέπω (# *1838*) to look at, to consider. **σπείρουσιν** pres. ind. act. σπείρω (# *5062*) to sow seed. **θερίζουσιν** pres. ind. act. θερίζω (# *2545*) to harvest. **συνάγουσιν** pres. ind. act. συνάγω (# *5251*) to gather, to gather together. The pres. tenses are gnomic, stating general truths. **μᾶλλον** (# *3437*) more. Strengthens the comparative force of διαφέρετε (Meyer). **διαφέρετε** pres. ind. act. διαφέρω (# *1422*) to differ, to be different, to be worth more than, to be superior to (BAGD; for the type of argumentation s.v. 25; DA; BBC).   ◆ **27 μεριμνῶν** pres. act. part. μεριμνάω (# *3435*) s.v. 25 expresses means. **προσθεῖναι** aor. inf. act. προστίθημι (# *4707*) to add to. **ἡλικία** (# *2461*) size, age. The passage can refer to the length of life or to the size or stature of the person (TDNT; MM). **πῆχυς** (# *4388*) originally meant forearm, then cubit, as a length of measure–about 18 inches–or it can refer to a measure of time (BAGD).   ◆ **28 μεριμνᾶτε** pres. ind. act. s.v. 25. **καταμάθετε** aor. imp. act. καταμανθάνω (# *2908*) to learn thoroughly, to observe well, to consider carefully (AS), to understand, to take in this fact about (M, 117-18). **κρίνον** (# *3211*) lily, for the various flowers of the field (BAGD; DA; PB, 169-71). **αὐξάνουσιν** pres. ind. act. αὐξάνω (# *889*) to grow. **κοπιῶσιν** pres. ind. act. κοπιάω (# *3159*) to labor with wearisome effort, to toil (T). Not so much the actual exertion as the weariness which follows on this strain-ing of all his powers to the utmost (Trench, *Synonyms*, 378). **νήθουσιν** pres. ind. act. νήθω (# *3756*) to spin. Pres. tenses are gnomic. ◆ **29 περιεβάλετο** aor. ind. mid. περιβάλλω (# *4314*) to put around, to put on; mid. "to clothe oneself." ◆ **30 χόρτος** (# *5965*) grass. Mere weeds to be cut down and used as fuel (EGT). **ὄντα** pres. act. part. acc. masc. sing. εἰμί. "which is." **κλίβα-νος** (# *3106*) oven, furnace. A pottery oven often fired by burning grass inside (Carson, 181; BAGD; MM). **βαλλόμενον** pres. pass. part. βάλλω (# *965*) to cast. **ἀμ-φιέννυσιν** pres. ind. act. ἀμφιέννυμι (# *314*) to clothe. **ὀλιγόπιστοι** (# *3899*) little faith, a small amount of trust. The word is used of disciples in a trying situation (DA). ◆ **31 μεριμνήσητε** aor. subj. act. μεριμνάω s.v. 25. Aor. subj. w. **μή** (# *3590*) is used as a neg. imp., which either looks at a specific command (BD, 172; DA) or serves as a summary statement (VA, 354). **φάγωμεν** aor. subj. act. s.v. 25. **πίωμεν** aor. subj. ind. s.v. 25. **περιβα-λώμεθα** aor. subj. mid. s.v. 29. The subjs. are delibera-tive (s.v. 25; DM, 171; MT, 98-99). ◆ **32 ἔθνη** pl. ἔθνος (# *1620*) people, heathen. The non-Jewish pagans are the misguided, who because they do not know God, fail to trust in Him (DA). **ἐπιζητοῦσιν** pres. ind. act. ἐπιζητέω (# *2118*) to look for, to seek after. The prep. ἐπι is directive, indicating the concentration of the vb.'s action upon some object (MH, 312). Pres. indi-cates a continual seeking after. **οἶδεν** perf. ind. act. s.v. 8. **χρῄζετε** pres. ind. act. χρῄζω (# *5974*) to have need of, w. gen. ◆ **33 ζητεῖτε** (# *2426*) pres. imp. act. to seek. Pres. calls for a constant attitude. Imp. followed by the fut. forms the apodosis in a Semitic cond. cl. (Beyer, 252-55). **δικαιοσύνη** (# *1466*) righteousness, conduct in agreement w. God's will (GW, 129; RM, 89-91). **καί** (# *2779*) and, so. It introduces a result which comes from what precedes (BAGD). **προστεθήσεται** fut. ind. pass. προστίθημι (# *4707*) to add to, to put down to an account, to deliver allowances to someone (MM). Theol. pass.; God does the adding (DA). ◆ **34 μεριμνή-σητε** aor. subj. act. s.v. 31. **γάρ** (# *1142*) for; it gives the reason for the command (Richard A. Edwards, "Nar-rative Implications of *Gar* in Matthew," *CBQ* 52 [1990]: 636-55). **μεριμνήσει** fut. ind. act. μεριμνάω. s.v. 31. **ἑαυτῆς** (# *1571*) gen. refl. pron. 3rd. pers. For the gen. s. BD, 96. **κακία** (# *2798*) trouble, misfortune. Used in the sense of damage done to a crop by hail (MM). "Each day has enough trouble of its own" (BAGD).

Matthew 7

◆ **1 κρίνετε** pres. imp. act. κρίνω (# *3212*) to judge; habit of censoriousness, sharp, unjust criticism (RWP). The word is almost synonymous w. condemn (DA). Pres. imp. w. the neg. μή (# *3590*) forbids an attitude. **κριθῆτε** aor. subj. pass. κρίνω. It may refer to divine judgment or to human judgment (McNeile). For rab-

binic sayings such as "in the pot in which they cooked they were cooked" (Exod. Rabb.) s. Harrington; SB, 1:441-46; Hagner. ◆ **2 ἐν** (# *1877*) in instr. **κρίματι** dat. of κρίμα (# *3210*) judgment as a decision from a judge (Gnilka; MM, 360; s. Jos., *Ant.*, 14:321). **κριθήσεσθε** fut. ind. pass. s.v. 1. **μέτρῳ** dat. of μέτρος (# *3586*) measure, norm. **μετρεῖτε** pres. ind. act. μετρέω (# *3582*) to mea-sure. **μετρηθήσεται** fut. ind. pass. μετρέω. Theol. pass. referring to God's judgment (eschatological?). For OT and Jewish parallels s. SB, 1:444-46; H.P. Rüger, "'Mit welchem Maß ihr meßt, wird euch gemessen wer-den'," *ZNW* 60 (1969): 174-82; Gnilka. ◆ **3 τί** (# *5515*) why. **κάρφος** (# *2847*) a splinter, a piece of dry wood or chaff, a very small particle that may irritate (RWP). It denotes insignificance and stands for small moral de-fects (DA). **σῷ** dat. of σός (# *5050*) your. **δοκός** (# *1512*) beam, log. It stands for sizeable moral defects (DA; for Jewish parallels s. SB, 1:446-47). **κατανοεῖς** pres. ind. act. κατανοέω (# *2917*) to notice, to take note of, to per-ceive. ◆ **4 ἤ** (# *2445*) or. **ἐρεῖς** fut. ind. act. λέγω (# *3306*) to say. **ἄφες** aor. imp. act. ἀφίημι (# *918*) to al-low. Used w. the subj. to indicate permission (BD, 183-84). **ἐκβάλω** aor. subj. act. ἐκβάλλω (# *1675*) to cast out, to remove. The subj. is hortatory (or "projection" VA, 171-72) asking permission (BD, 183). **ἰδού** aor. imp. act. ὁράω (# *3972*) to see. Demonstrative particle, "Behold!" "Look!" It is used to emphasize the importance of the statement (BAGD). **ἡ δοκός** (# *1512*) beam, a log upon which planks in a house rest, a post sticking out gro-tesquely (RWP). The art. is used as the art. of previous reference or renewed mention (IBG, 117). ◆ **5 ἔκβαλε** aor. imp. act. ἐκβάλλω (# *1675*) to throw out. **τότε** (# *5538*) then, afterward. **διαβλέψεις** fut. ind. act. δια-βλέπω (# *1332*) to see clearly, sharply. The prep. is per-fective (MH, 301). **ἐκβαλεῖν** aor. act. inf. Const. aor. sums up the details without emphasis on the details (VANT, 395). ◆ **6 δῶτε** aor. subj. act. δίδωμι (# *1443*) to give; w. the neg. as an imp. The vb. is used in a general command w. an iterat. sense: "never give" (VANT, 355). **κυσίν** dat. pl. κύνων (# *3264*) dog. Dogs were vi-cious, wild, and considered to be unclean (s. Phil. 3:2). **βάλητε** aor. subj. act. βάλλω (# *965*) to cast. **μαργαρίτης** (# *3449*) pearl. Pearls were of great value and were used fig. of something of supreme value (DA; s. 1 Tim. 2:9). **ἔμπροσθεν** (# *1869*) w. gen., before. **χοῖρος** (# *5956*) a young pig, swine. The "dogs" and "pigs" are those who have abandoned themselves to vicious courses and are hard-hearted and blind (DA). Piglets and pup-pies are frequently associated w. heathen worship (ABD, 6:1143-44). **μήποτε** (# *3607*) w. ind. fut. and aor. subj., lest. **καταπατήσουσιν** fut. ind. act. καταπατέω (# *2922*) to trample. Fut. w. the following subj. may suggest that whereas it is likely the pigs will trample the pearls, they may not necessarily attack men (VA, 416). **ποσίν** dat. pl. πούς (# *4546*) foot. Instr. use of the prep. ἐν (# 1651) "with their feet." στραφέντες aor. pass. part. στρέφω (# 5138) to turn around. Circum. part. can be translated as a main vb. (DM, 228). ῥήξωσιν aor. subj. act. ῥήγνυμι (# 4838) to tear in pieces. Subj. to express neg. purp. (RG, 988). ◆ 7 αἰτεῖτε pres. imp. act. αἰτέω (# 160) to ask. Pres. is customary: "make it your habit to ask" (VANT, 333). δοθήσεται fut. ind. pass. δίδωμι (# 1443) to give. Fut. is used in a Semitic type of cond. cl. giving the results of carrying out the imp. (Beyer, 238-55). Theol. pass. shows that God acts (DA). ζητεῖτε pres. imp. act. ζητέω (# 2426) to seek. εὑρήσετε fut. ind. act. εὑρίσκω (# 2351) to find. κρούετε pres. imp. act. κρούω (# 3218) to knock. ἀνοιγήσεται fut. ind. pass. ἀνοίγω (# 487) to open. ◆ 8 αἰτῶν pres. act. part. nom. masc. sing. αἰτέω (# 160) to ask. ζητῶν pres. act. part. nom. masc. sing. κρούοντι pres. act. part. dat. masc. sing. ◆ 9 τίς (# 5516) (who) plus ἄνθρωπος (# 476) (person) means anyone. A Semitic use for the indef. pronominal adj. (DA, 81; BD, 246). μή (# 3590) used when a neg. answer to a question is expected. ἐπιδώσει fut. ind. act. ἐπιδίδωμι (# 2113) to give to. The prep. ἐπί is directive (MH, 312). ◆ 10 ἰχθύς (# 2716) fish. ὄφις (# 4058) snake. Stones on the shore and possible water snakes suggested themselves as substitute (McNeile). ◆ 11 εἰ (# 1623) if. Introduces a 1st. class cond. assuming the truth of the statement. ὄντες pres. act. part. nom. masc. pl. εἰμί (# 1639). Part. may be concessive, "even though...." οἴδατε perf. ind. act. οἶδα (# 3857) to know. Def. perf. w. pres. meaning. διδόναι pres. act. inf. δίδωμι (# 1443). Inf. used in indir. discourse. πόσῳ μᾶλλον "how much more?" The words introduce an argument from the "lesser to the greater" (s. Rom. 5:9; SB, 3:223-26). δώσει fut. ind. act. δίδωμι (# 1443) to give. αἰτοῦσιν pres. act. part. (dat. pl.) αἰτέω (# 160) to ask. ◆ 12 οὖν (# 4036) therefore. It sums up the sermon to this point (McNeile). ὅσα ἐάν whatever. Used as an indef. rel. (RG, 733). θέλητε pres. subj. act. θέλω (# 2527) to wish, to want. ποιῶσιν pres. subj. act. ποιέω (# 4472) to do, to make. ◆ 13 εἰσέλθατε aor. imp. act. εἰσέρχομαι (# 1656) to come in, to go in. στενός (# 5101) narrow. πύλη (# 4783) gate, of a city or temple (Luz). The figure may imply difficulty (DA), or hardships (s. 4 Ezra 7:6-12). ὅτι (# 4022) because. πλατεῖα fem. nom. sing. πλατύς (# 4426) wide. εὐρύχωρος (# 2353) wide, roomy, broad, spacious. The two words together connote a lack of striving, of work (DA). ἀπάγουσα pres. act. part. fem. sing. nom. ἀπάγω (# 552) to lead. Part. used as an adj. describing ὁδός (# 3847). ἀπώλεια (# 724) destruction. ◆ 14 τεθλιμμένη perf. pass. part. θλίβω (# 2567) to press, to be narrow, constricted. Part. used as a pred. adj. It may refer to troubles or a way of tribulations (Luz; DA). εὑρίσκοντες pres. act. part. εὑρίσκω (# 2351) to find. Adj. part. used as a noun. ◆ 15 προσέχετε pres. imp. act. προσέχω (# 4668) to turn one's mind to, to pay attention, to give

heed. πρός used w. vbs. meaning "to be on guard," "to give heed to" (BD, 83). οἵτινες (# 4015) nom. pl. ὅστις (# 4015) generic or generalized rel. pron. whoever, everyone who. ἐνδύμασιν dat. pl. ἔνδυμα (# 1903) clothing. Perhaps a reference to a dress worn by a prophet (EGT). λύκος (# 3380) wolf (TDNT). ἅρπαγες nom. pl. ἅρπαξ (# 774) raging, ravenous. ◆ 16 ἐπιγνώσεσθε fut. ind. mid. ἐπιγινώσκω (# 2105) to know, to recognize. Prep. in compound is directive. μήτι used in questions which expect a neg. answer (BD, 220; BAGD). συλλέγουσιν pres. ind. act. 3rd. pers. pl. συλλέγω (# 5198) to gather together. The 3rd. pers. pl. is impersonal and can be translated as pass. (RG, 820; GGBB, 402). ἄκανθα (# 180) thorn bushes. σταφυλή (# 5091) grape. τρίβολος (# 5560) thistle. σῦκον (# 5192) fig. ◆ 17 σαπρός (# 4911) decayed, rotten. Used of things unusable, unfit, bad (BAGD). ◆ 18 ποιεῖν pres. act. inf. ποιέω (# 4472) to make, to produce, to bear. Inf. supplements δύναται. Gnomic pres. For the variant ἐνεγκεῖν aor. act. inf. φέρω to bear s. TC, 20. ◆ 19 ἐκκόπτεται pres. pass. ind. ἐκκόπτω (# 1716) to cut down. ◆ 20 ἄρα (# 726) then, expresses an inference. Used to emphasize the preceding word. ◆ 21 κύριε (# 3261) voc. Lord. Often occurs as a form of polite address, but here it is more than that. It is addressed to Him in His supreme power in the last day (McNeile; s. WA, 115-42). εἰσελεύσεται fut. ind. mid. (dep.) εἰσέρχομαι (# 1656) to enter into. ποιῶν pres. act. part. ποιέω (# 4472) to do. Adj. part. used as a noun. ◆ 22 ἐροῦσιν fut. ind. act. λέγω (# 3306) to say. ὀνόματι (# 3950) name. Instr. dat. (McNeile; for other views s. DA). ἐπροφητεύσαμεν aor. ind. act. προφητεύω (# 4736) to prophesy, to speak for another (TDNT). ἐξεβάλομεν aor. ind. act. ἐκβάλλω (# 1675) to cast out. ἐποιήσαμεν aor. ind. act. ποιέω to do, to perform. ◆ 23 ὁμολογήσω fut. ind. act. ὁμολογέω (# 3933) to make a statement; in the legal sense to bear witness. An act of proclamation in which the relation of man to Jesus is expressed in a binding and valid form (TDNT). ὅτι (# 4022) recitative, used as quotation marks to introduce a direct quote. ἔγνων aor. ind. act. 1st. pers. sing. γινώσκω (# 1182) to know. The words "I never knew you" were used by the rabbis as a banish formula (SB, 1:469). ἀποχωρεῖτε pres. imp. act. ἀπο-χωρέω (# 713) to depart, to go away. ἐργαζόμενοι (# 2237) pres. mid. (dep.) part. to work. Adj. part. used as a subst. ἀνομία (# 490) lawlessness. The term here does not mean lack of law, but refers to a lax attitude of doing the will of God (S. James E. Davidson, "Anomia and the Question of an Antinomian Polemic in Matthew," JBL 104 [1985]: 617-35). ◆ 24 ὁμοιωθήσεται fut. ind. pass. ὁμοιόω (# 3929) to compare, to liken. Takes dat. Fut. refers to the last judgment (DA). φρονίμῳ (# 5861) understanding, practically wise, sensible (AS; NIDNTT). Dat. sing. ᾠκοδόμησεν aor. ind. act. οἰκοδομέω (# *3868*) to build. Perhaps a ref. to Prov. 9:1ff; 24:3.   ◆ **25 κατέβη** aor. ind. act. καταβαίνω (# *2849*) to go down, to fall down. **βροχή** (# *1104*) rain. Used in the papyri for artificial inundations (McNeile). **ἦλθον** aor. ind. act. ἔρχομαι (# *2262*). **ποταμοί** (# *4532*) rivers, flood. The torrents which fill the ravines after a heavy rain (DA). **ἔπνευσαν** aor. ind. act. πνεύω (# *4463*) to blow. **ἄνεμοι** (# *449*) winds. **προσέπεσαν** aor. ind. act. προσπίπτω (# *4700*) to fall upon. **ἔπεσεν** aor. ind. act. πίπτω (# *4406*) to fall. There is a play on words w. "fall" and "fall upon" (DA). **τεθεμελίωτο** plperf. ind. pass. θεμελιόω (# *2530*) to found, to lay the foundation. For the lack of the augment s. BD, 36.   ◆ **26 ἀνδρί** dat. sing. ἀνήρ (# *467*) man, male. Dat. w. vb. **μωρῷ** dat. sing. μωρός (# *3704*) foolish, unreflecting; foolish deeds, heart thoughts arising from a lack of knowledge or the inability to make correct decisions (s. NIDNTT; TDNT; TLNT). **ἄμμον** acc. sing. ἄμμος (# *302*) sand. w. prep. **ἐπί** (# *2093*) "upon the sand."   ◆ **27 προσέκοψαν** aor. ind. act. προσκόπτω (# *4684*) to strike against, to beat against. **πτῶσις** (# *4774*) fall.   ◆ **28 ἐγένετο** aor. ind. mid. (dep.) γίνομαι (# *1181*) to happen. For the construction s. Beyer, 41-60. **ἐτέλεσεν** aor. ind. act. τελέω (# *5464*) to complete, to end. **ἐξεπλήσσοντο** impf. ind. pass. ἐκπλήσσω (# *1742*) to amaze, to astound; pass. to be amazed, to be astounded, to be beside oneself. Impf. indicates continued amazement, as though the people returned to their homes still pondering what it all meant (DA). **ἐπί** (# *2093*) w. the dat. expressing the reason.   ◆ **29 γάρ** (# *1142*) for (explanatory). **διδάκων** pres. act. part. διδάσκω (# *1438*) to teach. Part. used in a periphastic construction which emphasizes the customary teaching function of Jesus (VA, 458; VANT, 315).

Matthew 8

◆ **1 καταβάντος** aor. act. part. καταβαίνω (# *2849*) to go down. Part. used as gen. abs. expressing contemporaneous time. **ἠκολούθησαν** aor. ind. act. ἀκολουθέω (# *199*) to follow, to be a traveling companion (EDNT).   ◆ **2 προσελθών** aor. act. part. (circum.) προσέρχομαι (# *4665*) to come to. "A leper came...." For the use of this vb. s. James R. Edwards, "The Use of Προσέρχεσθαι in the Gospel of Matthew," *JBL* 106 (1987): 65-74. **προσεκύνει** impf. ind. act. προσκυνέω (# *4686*) to worship by falling at the feet. Incep. impf. "he began to worship." **ἐάν** (# *1569*) w. subj., if. It indicates some doubt regarding the cond. The doubt is not about the power but about the will (EGT). **θέλῃς** pres. act. subj. θέλω (# *2527*) to wish, to will. **δύνασαι** pres. ind. pass. (dep.) δύναμαι (# *1538*) to be able. **καθαρίσαι** aor. act. inf. καθαρίζω (# *2751*) to cleanse. Compl. to the main vb.   ◆ **3 ἐκτείνας** aor. act. part. temp. masc. nom. sing. ἐκτείνω (# *1753*) to stretch out. **ἥψατο** aor. ind. mid. (dep.) ἅπτω (# *721*) to touch, to take hold of; used

w. the obj. in gen. **καθαρίσθητι** aor. imp. pass. καθαρίζω (# *2751*) to cleanse. **ἐκαθαρίσθη** aor. ind. pass.   ◆ **4 ὅρα** pres. imp. act. ὁράω (# *3972*) to see. **εἴπῃς** aor. subj. act. λέγω (# *3306*) to speak. Subj. expresses a neg. command (RG, 854, 932). **ὕπαγε** pres. imp. act. ὑπάγω (# *5632*) to go. **δεῖξον** aor. imp. act. δείκνυμι (# *1259*) to show. **προσένεγκον** aor. imp. act. προσφέρω (# *4712*) to bring to, to carry to, to offer. This was to take place at the Eastern Gate of the Temple (M, Sotah 1:5; Lev. 14:11). **προσέταξεν** aor. ind. act. προστάσσω (# *4705*) to instruct, to command. (s. Lev. 13-14). This included both inspection by a priest and sacrifices (JPB, 220; Hagner). For the Jewish view of leprosy s. SB, 4:745-63; BBC; ABD, 4:277-82; M, Negaim; 11QT 48:17. Judaism expected the removal of this affliction in the time of Messianic salvation (TDNT).   ◆ **5 εἰσελθόντος** aor. act. part. gen. masc. sing. εἰσέρχομαι (# *1656*) to go in, to come in. Temp. part. gen. abs. **προσῆλθεν** aor. ind. act. προσέρχομαι (# *4665*). **ἑκατόνταρχος** (# *1672*) leader of a hundred men, centurion (IDB, 1:547f; BC, 5:427-45; DJG, 548; Brian Dobson, "The Significance of the Centurion and 'Primipilaris' in the Roman Army and Administration," ANRW, 2:i, 392-433; BBC). **παρακαλῶν** pres. act. part. παρακαλέω (# *4151*) to call for help, to urge. Circum. part. or used to describe the manner, or even purp. of his coming.   ◆ **6 παῖς** (# *4090*) son; used here w. the meaning "servant." A friendly term of address which indicates that the one serving had a personal relation w. his master (Schl.). **βέβληται** perf. ind. pass. βάλλω (# *965*) to throw; pass. to lie on a sick bed. Perf. describes his cond. **παραλυτικός** (# *4166*) lame, paralyzed. **δεινῶς** (# *1267*) terribly. Used in the papyri of those who are seriously sick (MM, 138; NDIEC, 4:248). **βασανιζόμενος** pres. pass. part. βασανίζω (# *989*) to torment, to suffer physical pain and sickness (EDNT; NDIEC, 4:142). Part. used as an adj.   ◆ **7 ἐλθών** aor. act. part. ἔρχομαι (# *2262*) to come, to go. Part. could be temp. ("when I come ...") or circumstantial. **θεραπεύσω** fut. ind. act. θεραπεύω (# *2543*) to heal (s. Matt. 4:23). Fut. indicates a promise w. certainty (Schl.).   ◆ **8 ἀποκριθείς** aor. pass. (dep.) part. ἀποκρίνομαι (# *646*) to answer. For the Semitic construction s. 3:2. **ἔφη** impf. ind. act. φημί (# *5774*) to speak. **ἱκανός** (# *2653*) sufficient, worthy. According to rabbinical teaching, the entrance into a Gentile house made one defiled (M, Oholoth 18:7), but the centurion may have realized his moral guilt and Jesus' holiness (Gundry; BBC). **εἰσέλθῃς** aor. subj. act. εἰσέρχομαι (# *1656*) to enter. The unworthiness, explained by the subj., shows the humility of the centurion. **εἰπέ** aor. imp. act. λέγω (# *3306*) to speak. **λόγῳ** dat. sing. λόγος (# *3364*) word. Instr. dat., "with a word." The construction is Semitic and emphasizes the term "word" (Luz). **ἰαθήσεται** fut. ind. pass. ἰάομαι (# *2615*) to heal (GLH).   ◆ **9 ἐξουσίαν** (# *2026*) acc. sing. authority to rule, authority by virtue of office. W. prep. ὑπό (# 5679) and acc. it means "to be under the command, or rule" of someone (BAGD). πορεύθητι aor. imp. pass. (dep.) πορεύομαι (# 4513) to go, to march, perhaps w. the idea of continuity and distance (for a comparison in meaning to ἔρχομαι s. BD, 172; LN, 1:183). ἔρχου pres. imp. mid. (dep.) ἔρχομαι ποίησον aor. imp. act. ποιέω (# 4472) to do, to make. Aor. may point to a specific duty to be carried out. ◆ 10 ἀκούσας aor. act. part. temp. ἀκούω (# 201) to hear. "When he heard...." ἐθαύμασεν aor. ind. act. θαυμάζω (# 2513) to be amazed. ἀκολουθοῦσιν pres. act. part. ἀκολουθέω (# 199) s.v. 1. τοσαύτην fem. acc. τοσοῦτος (# 5537) so great. The word expresses quality: "faith as strong as this" (BAGD). εὗρον aor. ind. act. 1st. pers. sing. εὑρίσκω (# 2351) to find. ◆ 11 ἥξουσιν fut. ind. act. ἥκω (# 2457) to come. ἀνακλιθήσονται fut. ind. pass. (dep.) ἀνακλίνομαι (# 369) to recline at a table. Used of the Messianic banquet (BAGD; TDNT). For the Jewish custom of eating while reclining at table s. SB, 4:618f. ◆ 12 ἐκβληθήσονται fut. ind. pass. ἐκβάλλω (# 1675) to cast out. ἐξώτερον (# 2035) outer. Comp. in form only. κλαυθμός (# 3088) crying, weeping, w. emphasis upon the noise accompanying the weeping (LN, 1:304). βρυγμός (# 1106) biting, grinding of teeth. The wailing indicates suffering, the gnashing of teeth, despair (Meyer). ◆ 13 ἐπίστευσας aor. ind. act. 2nd. pers. sing. πιστεύω (# 4409) to believe. γενηθήτω aor. ind. pass. (dep.) 3rd. pers. sing. γίνομαι (# 1181) to be, to become, to happen. ἰάθη aor. ind. pass. ἰάομαι (# 2615) s.v. 8. ◆ 14 ἐλθών aor. act. part. (temp.) ἔρχομαι (# 2262) to come. "When he came...." εἶδεν aor. ind. act. ὁράω (# 3972) to see. πενθερά (# 4289) mother of the wife, mother-in-law. βεβλημένην perf. pass. part. βάλλω (# 965) s.v. 6. πυρέσσουσαν pres. act. part. πυρέσσω (# 4789) to have a fever. ◆ 15 ἥψατο aor. ind. mid. (dep.) ἅπτω (# 721) s.v. 3. ἀφῆκεν aor. ind. act. ἀφίημι (# 918) to depart. ἠγέρθη aor. ind. pass. ἐγείρω (# 1586) to wake; pass. to rise, to get up. διηκόνει impf. ind. act. διακονέω (# 1354) to wait on someone at the table, to serve. Obj. in acc. Incep. impf. "she began to serve." The previous aor. expresses a point, the impf. begins a linear action (Bakker, 26). ◆ 16 ὀψίας gen. sing. ὀψία (# 4070) evening. γενομένης aor. ind. mid. part. (dep.) gen. fem. sing. γίνομαι (# 1181) Gen. abs. "when it was evening." προσήνεγκαν aor. ind. act. προσφέρω (# 4712) to bring, to carry. δαιμονιζομένους pres. pass. part. δαιμονίζομαι (# 1227) to be possessed by a demon or an evil spirit. For the Jewish view of demons s. SB, 4:i, 501-35. ἐξέβαλεν (# 1675) aor. ind. act. s.v. 12. λόγῳ instr. dat. λόγος (# 3364) "With a word." ἔχοντας pres. act. part. ἔχω (# 2400) to have. W. the adv. κακῶς (# 2809) "to be ill, sick." ἐθεράπευσεν aor. ind. act. s.v. 7. For a discussion of these miracles to authenticate the message of Jesus s. DJG, 302-303. Aor. sums the in-

dividual acts of healing. ◆ 17 πληρωθῇ aor. subj. pass. πληρόω (# 4444) to fulfill. Subj. w. ὅπως (# 3968) used in a purp. cl. ῥηθέν aor. pass. part. λέγω (# 3306) to say. Part. used as a subst. αὐτός he, himself (emphatic; s. MT, 40-41). ἔλαβεν aor. ind. act. λαμβάνω (# 3284) to take, to take away. ἐβάστασεν aor. ind. act. βαστάζω (# 1002) to take away, to bear. For the quotation from Isa. 53 s. JIU, esp., 71-75. ◆ 18 ἰδών aor. act. part. (temp.) ὁράω (# 3972) to see. "When he saw...." ἐκέλευσεν aor. ind. act. κελεύω (# 3027) to command. For this vb. w. the aor. inf. s. BD, 174. ἀπελθεῖν aor. act. inf. ἀπέρχομαι (# 599) to go away, to leave. ◆ 19 προσελθών aor. act. part. temp. προσέρχομαι (# 4665) to come to. εἷς a (used as an indef. art. RWP). εἶπεν aor. ind. act. λέγω (# 3306) s.v. 8. διδάσκαλε (# 1437) teacher (voc.). For a study of this word and esp. the rabbi teacher position in Judaism s. TDNT; JL. ἀκολουθήσω fut. ind. act. ἀκολουθέω (# 199) s.v. 1. The word speaks of the rabbi teacher-student relation. ὅπου ἐάν (# 3963; 1569) w. subj., wherever. ἀπέρχῃ pres. mid. (dep.) subj. 2nd. pers. sing. ἀπέρχομαι (# 599). ◆ 20 ἀλώπεκες nom. pl. ἀλώπηξ (# 273) fox. φωλεός (# 5887) den, hole for animals. κατασκήνωσις (# 2943) dwelling place, nest. κλίνη pres. subj. act. κλίνω (# 3111) to incline, to lay. For the term "Son of Man" s. Carson, 209-13; DJG, 775-81. ◆ 21 ἕτερος (# 2283) another (RG, 748-50; BAGD). εἶπεν aor. ind. act. λέγω (s.v. 19). ἐπίτρεψον imp. act. ἐπιτρέπω (# 2205) to allow, to permit. Aor. views a specific act. ἀπελθεῖν aor. act. inf. ἀπέρχομαι (# 599) to go away (s.v. 18). θάψαι aor. act. inf. θάπτω (# 2507) to bury. Inf. completes the main vb. ◆ 22 ἀκολούθει pres. imp. act. s.v. 19. This is a call to discipleship. Pres. imp. points to a way of life. ἄφες aor. imp. act. ἀφίημι (# 918) to leave, to let, to allow. Aor. points to a definite act. νεκρούς acc. pl. νεκρός (# 3738) dead. Acc. w. inf. This may refer to the spiritual dead (Allen), or may have the meaning dying (AM). The urgency of following Jesus unreservedly is greater than burial duties (Hill). For the background of this passage s. Luke 9:59f; DJG, 187. ◆ 23 ἐμβάντι aor. act. part. dat. sing. ἐμβαίνω (# 1832) to step in, to embark. The part. is a dat. abs. (EGT) and is temp. ◆ 24 σεισμός (# 4939) shaking, used of a storm or an earthquake. ἐγένετο aor. ind. mid. (dep.) γίνομαι (# 1181) to become, to be. ὥστε (# 6063) so that; used w. the inf. to express results. καλύπτεσθαι pres. pass. inf. καλύπτω (# 2821) to cover over. The pres. graphically describes the action taking place. αὐτός he emphatic in contrast to the others. ἐκάθευδεν impf. ind. act. καθεύδω (# 2761) to sleep. Impf. "he kept on sleeping" stands in contrast to the aor. (MT, 66). ◆ 25 προσελθόντες aor. act. part. nom. masc. pl. s.v. 2. ἤγειραν aor. ind. act. s.v. 15. σῶσον aor. imp. act. σῴζω (# 5392) to save, to rescue. Aor. is used by people in straitened circumstances (Bakker, 130). ἀπολλύμεθα pres. ind. mid. ἀπόλλυμι

(# 660) to be destroyed (EDNT; GELTS, 53). Pres. tense vividly describes the dangerous situation. ◆ **26 δειλός** (# 1264) cowardly, timid, afraid. **ὀλιγόπιστοι** (# 3899) w. little trust, small in faith. It refers to its poor quality (Carson, 216). **ἐγερθείς** aor. pass. part. s.v. 15. Part. is temp. or circum. **ἐπετίμησεν** aor. ind. act. ἐπιτιμάω (# 2203) to rebuke. Suggests that the elements are treated as evil powers which must be subdued as a sign of the kingdom over which Christ is king (Hill; s. also Matt. 17:18). **γαλήνη** (# 1132) calm. The great calm is in contrast to the raging storm.   ◆ **27 ἄνθρωποι** (# 476) men, either the disciples in the boat (Filson) or the people who will subsequently hear (McNeile). **ποταπός** (# 4534) what sort of, what kind. **ὑπακούουσιν** pres. ind. act. ὑπακούω (# 5634) to listen to, to obey. Hist. pres.   ◆ **28 ἐλθόντος** (# 2262) aor. act. part. gen masc. sing. ἔρχομαι s.v. 14. Gen. abs. temp. part. **ὑπήντησαν** aor. ind. act. ὑπαντάω (# 5636) to meet, to meet up with (obj. in dat.). (LN, 1:192). **μνημείων** gen. pl. μνημεῖον (# 3646) monument, tomb. Possibly caves (Carson, 217). These were considered unclean (BBC). **ἐξερχόμενοι** pres. mid. (dep.) part. (circum.) ἐξέρχομαι (# 2002) to go out. **χαλεποί** (# 5901) hard, difficult, dangerous, violent (s. 2 Tim. 3:1). **ἰσχύειν** pres. act. inf. ἰσχύω (# 2710) to be strong, to be able. Used w. inf. Pres. indicates the continued inability. Inf. used to express actual results. **παρελθεῖν** aor. act. inf. προσέρχομαι (# 4216) to go by, to pass by. Aor. summarizes the various attempts to pass by.   ◆ **29 ἔκραξαν** aor. ind. act. κράζω (# 3189) to cry out, to scream. **τί ἡμῖν καὶ σοί** "What to us and you?" It represents a Heb. idiom suggesting the two parties have no common concern (Tasker; s. John 2:4). **ἦλθες** aor. ind. act. 2nd. pers. sing. ἔρχομαι s.v. 14. **βασανίσαι** aor. act. inf. βασανίζω s.v. 6. Inf. used to express purp.   ◆ **30 ἀγέλη** (# 36) herd. **χοίρων** gen. pl. χοῖρος (# 5956) pig, swine (gen. used as gen. of apposition or definition RG, 499). It was forbidden for Jews to raise pigs (M, Baba Kama, 7; SB, 1:492-93). **βοσκομένη** pres. pass. part. βόσκω (# 1081) to feed, to herd; pass. to graze (BAGD). Adj. part.   ◆ **31 παρεκάλουν** impf. ind. act. παρακαλέω (# 4151) to beseech, to beg. Impf. indicates they continually asked. **εἰ** (# 1623) if. The cond. is viewed as true. **ἀπόστειλον** aor. imp. act. ἀποστέλλω (# 90) to send. Aor. imp. looks at the specific request.   ◆ **32 εἶπεν** aor. ind. act. λέγω to say. s.v. 19. **ἐξελθόντες** aor. act. part. s.v. 28. Part. is temp. or circum. **ἀπῆλθον** aor. ind. act. s.v. 18. **ὥρμησεν** aor. ind. act. ὁρμάω (# 3994) to set out, to rush. **κρημνοῦ** (# 3204) (gen.) steep bank, precipice. The gen. w. the prep. is local, "over and down" (BD, 120). **ἀπέθανον** aor. ind. act. ἀποθνήσκω (# 633) to die (s. Mark 5:13). ◆ **33 βόσκοντες** pres. act. part. s.v. 30. **ἔφυγον** aor. ind. act. φεύγω (# 5771) to flee. **ἀπελθόντες** aor. act. part. (temp.) s.v. 18. **ἀπήγγειλαν** aor. ind. act. ἀπαγγέλω (# 550) to report.   ◆ **34 ἐξῆλθεν** aor. ind. act. s.v. 28.

ὑπάντησιν (# 5637) acc. sing. followed by the dat. meeting. The word is used sometimes for the meeting of an honored visitor outside a city (Gundry; for the grammatical use of this s. M, 14). **ἰδόντες** (# 3972) aor. act. part. temp. s.v. 18. **παρεκάλεσαν** aor. ind. act. s.v. 31. **μεταβῇ** aor. subj. act. μεταβαίνω (# 3553) to depart to another place. Subj. w. **ὅπως** (# 3968) gives the content of the request (BD, 200).

Matthew 9

◆ **1 ἐμβάς** aor. act. part. (temp.) ἐμβαίνω (# 1832) to step into, to embark. **διεπέρασεν** aor. ind. act. διαπεράω (# 1385) to cross over. **ἦλθεν** aor. ind. act. ἔρχομαι (# 2262) to come.   ◆ **2 προσέφερον** impf. ind. act. προσφέρω (# 4712) to bring to, to carry. Impf. suggests that they came bringing the man to Jesus as He arrived in Capernaum (Hill). **βεβλημένον** perf. pass. part. βάλλω (# 965) to throw, pass. to lie on a sick bed. s. 8:6. **ἰδών** aor. act. part. temp. ὁράω (# 3972) to see. "When he saw..." **αὐτῶν** (# 899) gen. pl. "their." Used of him who was borne, and of them who bore him (Bengel). **εἶπεν** aor. ind. act. λέγω (# 3306). **θάρσει** pres. imp. act. θαρσέω (# 2510) to be of good cheer, to have confidence and firmness of purp. in the face of danger or testing (LN, 1:306). Pres. imp. has an ingressive idea, "don't be fearful any longer, start to think positively about your situation" (VANT, 349). **ἀφίενται** pres. ind. pass. ἀφίημι (# 918) to depart; pass. to be forgiven (DJG, 241-43). Pres. means either "are in a state of remission" or "are at this moment remitted," an aoristic pres. (McNeile).   ◆ **3 βλασφημεῖ** pres. ind. act. βλασφημέω (# 1059) to speak evil of, to defame, to blaspheme. In Judaism it refers to words or deeds that impugn God's honor and injure His holiness, such as ascribing to oneself divine powers (EDNT). The penalty for this sin in the OT was death by stoning (BBC). ◆ **4 εἰδώς** perf. act. part. οἶδα (# 3857) to know. Def. perf. w. the pres. (For the variant **ἰδών** aor. act. part. s. TC, 24). **ἐνθυμήσις** (# 1927) reflection, thought. **ἱνατί** (# 2672) "In order that what might happen?" Why, for what reason? (BAGD). **ἐνθυμεῖσθε** pres. ind. mid. (dep.) ἐνθυμέομαι (# 1926) to consider, reflect, to think.   ◆ **5 εὐκοπώτερον** comp. εὔκοπος (# 2324) easy. **εἰπεῖν** aor. act. inf. λέγω (# 3306) to say. Inf. explains what is easier. **ἔγειρε** pres. imp. act. ἐγείρω (# 1586) intr. in imp. "Arise!" **περιπάτει** pres. imp. act. περιπατέω (# 4344) to walk, to go about. For the pres. imp. of this vb. s. VANT, 343-44. ◆ **6 εἰδῆτε** perf. subj. act. οἶδα s.v. 4. Subj. used in purp. cl. **ἀφιέναι** pres. act. inf. ἀφίημι (# 918) s.v. 2. Inf. explains authority. **ἐγερθείς** aor. pass. part. ἐγείρω (# 1586) pass. intr. to rise, to get up. Circum. part. used as imp. (VANT, 386; s. Matt. 28:19). **ἆρον** aor. imp. act. αἴρω (# 149) to lift up, to take up. Aor. imp. points to a specific act. **ὕπαγε** pres. imp. act. ὑπάγω (# 5632) to go, to go away. Pres. imp. used w. a vb. of motion.

◆ **7 ἐγερθείς** aor. pass. part. s.v. 6. **ἀπῆλθεν** aor. ind. act. ἀπέρχομαι (# 599) to depart. ◆ **8 ἰδόντες** aor. act. part. (temp.) pl. ὁράω (# 3972) to see, "when they saw this." **ἐφοβήθησαν** aor. ind. pass. (dep.) φοβέομαι (# 5828) to be afraid, to fear. **ἐδόξασαν** aor. ind. act. δοξάζω (# 1519) to praise, to glorify, to show honor (EDNT). **δόντα** aor. act. part. acc. sing. δίδωμι (# 1443) to give. **τοιαύτην** fem. acc. τοιοῦτος (# 5525) such as this, of such a kind. **ἀνθρώ-ποις** (# 476) dat. pl. "On behalf of men" (AM). ◆ **9 ἀράγω** pres. act. part. παράγω (# 4135) intr. to pass by. Temp. part expressing contemporaneous action. **εἶδεν** aor. ind. act. ὁράω (# 3972) to see. **καθήμενον** pres. mid. (dep.) part. κάθημαι (# 2764) to sit. Adj. part. **τε-λώνιον** (# 5468) tax office, probably near the beach in order to handle business connected w. ships coming to Galilee from the east side of the lake (Filson). For tax collectors and their position in Judaism s. TDNT; SB, 1:377-80; NDIEC, 5:103; JZ, 162-227; F. Herrenbrück, "Wer waren die 'Zöllner'?" *ZNW* 72 (1981): 178-94; J.R. Donahue, "Tax Collectors and Sinners," *CBQ* 33 (1971): 39-61; DJG, 804-807, particularly 805-806; BBC. **λεγόμενον** pres. pass. part.; here, "to be named." λέγω (# 3306) **ἀκολούθει** pres. imp. act. ἀκολουθέω (# 199) to follow; W. dat. "be My disciple," "attach yourself to My person in order to hear and follow Me" (Hill). **ἀναστάς** aor. act. part. (circum.) ἀνίστημι (# 482) to arise. **ἠκολούθησεν** aor. ind. act. ◆ **10 ἐγένετο** aor. ind. mid. (dep.) γίνομαι (# 1181) to become, to happen. **ἀνακειμένου** pres. mid. (dep.) part. ἀνάκειμαι (# 367) to recline at the table. Gen. abs. For a description of a Jewish banquet and reclining while eating s. SB, 4:ii, 611-39; BBC; DJG, 796-800. **ἁμαρτωλοί** (# 283) nom. pl. sinful, sinner. In this context, for those who either could not because of ignorance or would not observe the intricacies of the Jewish law as elaborated by the traditions of the scribes (Tasker). **ἐλθόντες** aor. act. part. nom. masc. pl. ἔρχομαι (# 2262). Circum. or temp. part. **συνανέκειντο** impf. ind. mid. (dep.). συνανάκει-μαι (# 5263) to recline together w. one at the table. ◆ **11 ἰδόντες** aor. act. part. s.v. 8. **ἔλεγον** impf. ind. act. λέγω (# 3306) incep. "they began to say...." ◆ **12 ἀκού-σας** aor. act. part. (temp.) ἀκούω (# 201) to hear. **ἰσχύον-τες** pres. act. part. nom. pl. ἰσχύω (# 2710) to be strong, to be healthy. **ἰατροῦ** (# 2620) gen. sing. (gen. w. the adj. χρείαν) doctor, physician. **κακῶς ἔχοντες** (# 2809; 2400) pres. act. part. w. adv. to have it bad, to be sick. ◆ **13 πορευθέντες** aor. pass. (dep.) part. πορεύομαι (# 4513) to go. Circum. part used as imp. **μάθετε** aor. imp. act. μανθάνω (# 3443) to learn; "go and learn." A common formula used by the rabbi (SB, 1:499). **ἔλεος** (# 1799) mercy. A rendering of the Hebrew word חֶסֶד, "covenant loyalty," "loyal love to God demonstrated by acts of mercy and loving-kindness." (D. Hill, "On the Use and Meaning of Hosea vi. 6 in Matthew's Gos-pel," *NTS* 24 [1977]: 107-119; TDOT; TLNT; DJG, 541-

43; s. Acts 13:34). **καλέσαι** aor. act. inf. καλέω (# 2813) to call. Inf. used to express purp. The same word used of inviting to a feast (AM). ◆ **14 προσέρχονται** pres. ind. mid. (dep.) προσέρχομαι (# 4665) to come to, to ap-proach. Hist. pres. **νηστεύομεν** pres. ind. act. νηστεύω (# 3764) to fast. ◆ **15 μή** (# 3590) used in questions which expect a neg. answer. **υἱοὶ τοῦ νυμφῶνος** "sons of the bridal chamber." A Hebrew idiom for wedding guests (RWP). **πενθεῖν** pres. act. inf. πενθέω (# 4291) to mourn, to be sad, to experience sadness or grief as the result of depressing circumstances or the cond. of per-sons (LN, 1:305). **ἐφ' ὅσον** so long as. A fast during the 7 day marriage feast was inappropriate. **ἐλεύσονται** fut. ind. mid. (dep.) ἔρχομαι (# 2262) to come. **ὅταν** (# 4020) w. subj., when, whenever. **ἀπαρθῇ** aor. subj. pass. ἀπαίρω (# 554) to take away, to remove. **νηστεύ-σουσιν** fut. ind. act. s.v. 14. ◆ **16 ἐπιβάλλει** pres. ind. act. ἐπιβάλλω (# 2095) to throw over, to lay on, to put on. Gnomic pres. **ἐπίβλημα** (# 2099) a patch. **ῥάκος** (# 4820) a piece of cloth. **ἄγναφος** (# 47) unshrunken, unbleached, new (BAGD). **παλαιῷ** dat. sing. παλαιός (# 4094) old. Old in the sense of worn out (Trench, *Syn-onyms* 249-53). **πλήρωμα** (# 4445) fullness, that which fills, a patch put on to fill a gap (McNeile). **χεῖρον** (# 5937) comp. κακός bad. "Worse." ◆ **17 νέον** (# 3742) new, fresh. "New wine" was a set phrase re-ferring to newly pressed grape juice, unfermented, or in the initial stages of fermentation (LN, 1:77). For the production of wine s. DJG, 870; R.J. Forbes, *Studies in Ancient Technology*, 3:72-80. **ἀσκός** (# 829) a leather bag, wineskin (BAGD). **εἰ δὲ μή γε** but, if not, otherwise (s. Matt. 6:1). **ῥήγνυνται** pres. ind. pass. ῥήγνυμι (# 4838) to tear, to burst. **ἐκχεῖται** pres. ind. pass. ἐκχέω (# 1772) to pour out. **ἀπόλλυνται** pres. ind. mid. ἀπόλλυμι (# 660) to be lost, to be destroyed. **συντηροῦνται** pres. ind. pass. συντηρέω (# 5337) protect, keep safe. The prep. is perfective (M, 113). Pres. tenses are gnomic. ◆ **18 λα-λοῦντος** pres. act. part. λαλέω (# 3281) to speak; gen. abs. to express contemporaneous time: "while he was speaking." **εἷς**, a (used as an indef. art., BAGD). **προσεκύνει** impf. ind. act. προσκυνέω (# 4686) to fall down and do reverence. The word here does not nec-essarily mean "worship," but shows deep courtesy (Carson, 230). Incep. impf. "he began...." **ὅτι** (# 4022) used as quotation marks to introduce a direct quota-tion. **ἐτελεύτησεν** aor. ind. act. τελευτάω (# 5462) to die. "Just now died" (RWP). Matthew has condensed the story (Carson, 230). **ἐπίθες** aor. imp. act. ἐπιτίθημι (# 2202) to place upon. Aor. imp. used of a specific act by one in difficult circumstances (s. Matt. 8:25). **ζήσεται** fut. ind. mid. (dep.) ζάω (# 2409) to live. For the form s. BD, 42; RG, 356. The fut. gives the results of fulfilling the plea and is a type of Semitic cond. cl. ◆ **19 ἐγερ-θείς** aor. pass. part. s.v. 6. **ἠκολούθησεν** aor. ind. act. ἀκολουθέω (# 199) to follow (followed by dat.).

◆ **20 αἱμορροοῦσα** pres. act. part. fem. sing. αἱμορροέω (# 137) to suffer w. a hemorrhage. In modern medical terminology, menorrhagia (Tasker). The person w. a flow of blood was unclean and anyone they touched was unclean (Lev. 15:25-33; M, Zabim, esp. 5:6-7; Harrington). For attempts to stop a flow s. b. Shab. 110a-b; SB, 1:520. **ἔτη** acc. pl. ἔτος (# 2291) year; acc. of time: "for twelve years." **προσελθοῦσα** aor. act. part. (circum.) προσέρχομαι (# 4665) to come to. **ἥψατο** aor. ind. mid. (dep.) ἅπτομαι (# 721) to touch, take hold (followed by gen.). **κράσπεδον** (# 3192) edge, border, hem or tassel which was worn on the four corners of the outer garment (Numb. 15:38-41; Deut. 22:12; BAGD; BBC; Hagner; Harrington; ABD 2:236; J. Milgrom, "Of Hems and Tassels: Rank, Authority and Holiness were Expres-sed in Antiquity by Fringes on Garments," *BAR* 9 [1983]: 61-65). Touching of the edge of a garment was often a humble and submissive sign of making a request, and may be the case here (Manfred Hutter, "Ein altorientalischer Bittgestus in Mt 9:20-22," *ZAW* 75 [1984]: 133-35). ◆ **21 ἐάν** (# 1569) w. subj., if. It views the cond. as possible. **ἅψωμαι** aor. subj. mid. (dep.) s.v. 20. **σωθήσομαι** fut. ind. pass. σῴζω (# 5392) to deliver, to save, to heal. Theol. pass. ◆ **22 στραφείς** aor. pass. part. (temp.) στρέφω (# 5138) to turn, to turn around. **θάρσει** pres. imp. act. s.v. 2. **σέσωκεν** perf. ind. act. s.v. 21. Perf. indicates "you have received healing and are now in perfect health" (GI, 33). **ἐσώθη** aor. ind. pass. σῴζω. ◆ **23 αὐλητής** (# 886) flute player. Even the poorest families were expected to provide two flute players and one wailing woman (M, Ket. 4:4; SB, 1:521-23; BBC). **θορυβούμενον** pres. pass. part. θορυβέω (# 2572) to throw into disorder; pass. be troubled, distressed, aroused, to be emotionally upset by a concern or anxiety (BAGD; LN, 1:314). Adj. use of the part. modifying ὄχλον. ◆ **24 ἀναχωρεῖτε** pres. imp. act. ἀναχωρέω (# 432) to go away. **ἀπέθανεν** aor. ind. act. ἀποθνῄσκω (# 633) to die. **καθεύδει** pres. ind. act. καθεύδω (# 2761) to sleep. Pres. stands in contrast to the aor.: "she has not died." **κατεγέλων** impf. ind. act. καταγελάω (# 2860) to laugh, to scorn. Obj. in gen. Prep. is perfective, the impf. indicates repeated laughter of scorn (RWP). ◆ **25 ἐξεβλήθη** aor. ind. pass. ἐκβάλλω (# 1675) to cast out. **εἰσελθών** aor. act. part. (circum.) εἰσέρχομαι (# 1656) to go in. **ἐκράτησεν** aor. ind. act. κρατέω (# 3195) take hold of, grasp, w. the gen. **ἠγέρθη** aor. ind. pass. s.v. 6. ◆ **26 ἐξῆλθεν** aor. ind. act. ἐξέρχομαι (# 2002) to go out. **φήμη** (# 5773) report, fame. ◆ **27 παράγοντι** pres. act. part. (temp.) dat. sing. s.v. 9. Dat. w. vb. **ἠκολούθησαν** aor. ind. act. s.v. 9. "As he was passing by...." **κράζοντες** pres. act. part. (circum.) κράζω (# 3189) to scream, to cry. Pres. indicates that they keep on crying out. **ἐλέησον** aor. imp. act. ἐλεέω (# 1796) to have compassion, to show mercy (EDNT; TDNT; NIDNTT; TLNT). Aor. imp. is a

call for a specific action from one in need. ◆ **28 ἐλθόντι** aor. act. part. dat. sing. ἔρχομαι (# 2262) (for the dat. s.v. 27). **πιστεύετε** pres. imp. act. πιστεύω (# 4409) to believe, to have faith, trust. **ποιῆσαι** aor. act. inf. ποιέω (# 4472) to do, to make. ◆ **29 ἥψατο** aor. ind. mid. (dep.) s.v. 20. **γενηθήτω** aor. imp. pass. (dep.) 3rd. pers. sing. γίνομαι (# 1181) to become, to happen. ◆ **30 ἠνεῴχθησαν** aor. ind. pass. ἀνοίγω (# 487) to open. **ἐνεβριμήθη** aor. ind. pass. (dep.) ἐμβριμάομαι (# 1839) to snort. (followed by dat.). As an expression of anger, to sternly warn (BAGD). **ὁρᾶτε** pres. imp. act. ὁράω (# 3972) to see, to see to it. **γινωσκέτω** pres. imp. act. 3rd. pers. sing. γινώσκω (# 1182) to know. ◆ **31 ἐξελθόντες** aor. act. part. ἐξέρχομαι (# 2002) to go out. Temp. part., "As they were going out ...," or circum. part. **διεφήμισαν** aor. ind. act. διαφημίζω (# 1424) to make known by word of mouth, to spread abroad (BAGD). ◆ **32 ἐξερχομένων** pres. mid. (dep.) part. gen. masc. pl. ἐξέρχομαι (# 2002) Gen. abs.: "As they departed...." **προσήνεγκαν** aor. ind. act. s.v. 2. **κωφόν** (# 3273) dull, deaf and dumb. **δαιμονιζόμενον** pres. pass. part. δαιμονίζομαι (# 1227) to be possessed by a demon (s. 8:16). ◆ **33 ἐκβληθέντος** aor. pass. part. ἐκβάλλω (# 1675) Gen. abs. "when the demon was cast out...." **ἐλάλησεν** aor. ind. act. λαλέω (# 3281) to speak. **ἐθαύμασαν** aor. ind. act. θαυμάζω (# 2513) to be amazed. **ἐφάνη** aor. ind. pass. (dep.) φαίνομαι (# 5743) to shine, to appear. ◆ **34 ἔλεγον** impf. ind. act. λέγω (# 3306) to say. Impf. indicates that the ferment was constantly in the background (Carson, 234). ◆ **35 περιῆγεν** impf. ind. act. περιάγω (# 4310) to go about. The three parts.–teaching, proclaiming, healing–summarize the ministry of Jesus as He went about from place to place (s. Mastt. 4:23; s. also S. Brown, "The Mission to Israel in Matt.'s Central Section," *ZNW* 69 (78): 73-90. ◆ **36 ἐσπλαγχνίσθη** aor. ind. pass. (dep.) σπλαγχνίζω (# 5072) to have pity, to be filled w. compassion, tenderness (MM). For a study of the word s. NIDNTT; TDNT. **ἐσκυλμένοι** perf. pass. part. σκύλλω (# 5035) to flay, to skin. Used in the papyri w. the meaning to distress, to harass, to worry, to trouble (MM). The people were harassed, importuned, bewildered by those who should have taught them (Allen). **ἐρριμμένοι** perf. pass. part. ῥίπτω (# 4849) to cast down, to prostrate, either from drunkenness or from a mortal wound (AM). Both parts. refer to the people as sheep, mishandled and lying helpless (McNeile; DJG, 751-52; ABD, 5:1190). The parts. are adj. and stress the cond. of the people due mainly to the lack of leadership. ◆ **37 θερισμός** (# 2546) harvesting. The ending indicates activity. It indicates either "spiritual susceptibility" (EGT) or judgment at the end of the age (Hill; DA). ◆ **38 δεήθητε** aor. imp. pass. (dep.) δέομαι (# 1289) to ask, to beg. W. gen. τοῦ κυρίου τοῦ θερισμοῦ "the Lord of the harvest" is the one who hires workers and sends them to the field (Gundry). He is portrayed as the owner who will enjoy the benefits of the harvest. οὖν (# 4036) drawing an inference based on the ripeness of the harvest. ἐκβάλῃ aor. subj. act. ἐκβάλλω (# 1675) to cast out; here, to send out.

Matthew 10

◆ **1** προσκαλεσάμενος aor. mid. part. προσκαλέω (# 4673) to call to oneself, to summon for a special task (BAGD). ἔδωκεν aor. ind. act. δίδωμι (# 1443) to give. ὥστε (# 6063) so that; w. the inf. to express purp. (BD, 197). ◆ **2** ἀπόστολος (# 693) apostle, one sent out. It indicates one sent out w. the personal authority and as a representative of the one sending (TDNT; NIDNTT; EDNT; TLNT; BBC). πρῶτος (# 4755) first. "First and foremost" (Tasker). ◆ **4** παραδούς aor. act. part. παρα-δίδωμι (# 4140) to give over, to betray. For views on the meaning of Iscariot s. Carson, 239-40; Lachs, 179; Mark 3:19; 14:10; Luke 6:16. ◆ **5** ἀπέστειλεν aor. ind. act. ἀποστέλλω (# 690) to send forth (s.v. 2). παραγγείλας aor. act. part. (circum.) παραγγέλλω (# 4133) to instruct, to give orders. ἐθνῶν gen. pl. ἔθνος (# 1620) people; pl. heathen, those who are not Jews. For the rationale of this command s. HSB, 375-76; BBC. ἀπέλ-θητε aor. subj. act. ἀπέρχομαι (# 599) to go away, to depart. Subj. w. the neg. μή (# 3590) to express a neg. imp. εἰσέλθητε aor. subj. act. εἰσέρχομαι (# 1656) to go in. ◆ **6** ἀπολωλότα perf. act. part. ἀπόλλυμι (# 660) to destroy, to lose, to perish (EDNT). Perf. stresses the state or cond. ◆ **7** πορευόμενοι (# 4513) pres. mid. (dep.) (circum.) part. is part of the command. ἤγγικεν perf. ind. act. ἐγγίζω (# 1581) to draw near (s. 3:2). ◆ **8** ἀσθενοῦντας pres. act. part. ἀσθενέω (# 820) to be without strength, to be sick. θεραπεύετε pres. imp. act. θερα-πεύω (# 2543) to heal. ἐγείρετε pres. imp. act. ἐγείρω (# 1586) to awaken, to raise. καθαρίζετε pres. imp. act. καθαρίζω (# 2751) to cleanse. ἐκβάλλετε pres. imp. act. ἐκβάλλω (# 1675) to cast out. The purp. is to authenticate the kingdom message. δωρεάν (# 1562) adv. as a gift, without payment, freely. ἐλάβετε aor. ind. act. λαμβάνω (# 3284) to take, to receive. δότε aor. imp. act. δίδωμι (# 1443) to give. For the aor. imp. s. VANT, 355. ◆ **9** κτήσησθε aor. subj. mid. (dep.) κτάομαι (# 3227) to procure for oneself, to get, gain, to acquire. χρυσός (# 5996) gold. ἄργυρος (# 738) silver. χαλκός (# 5910) acc. copper. ζώνη (# 2438) belt, girdle. Used for carrying money (RWP). For rabbinical parallels s. SB, 1:561-69. ◆ **10** πήρας (# 4385) traveling bag or bread bag, a beggar's collecting bag (LAE, 109). ῥάβδος (# 4811) staff. The staff or stick was used as a weapon against robbers (Luz). τροφῆς (# 5575) gen. food. Gen w. adj. The "Lord of the harvest" (Matt. 9:36) will supply through those who benefit from the teaching. ◆ **11** ἦν ἄν (# 4005; 165) acc. fem. sing. whatever; ὃς ἄν w. the subj. whoever. εἰσέλθητε aor. subj. act. εἰσέρχομαι

(# 1656) to enter. ἐξετάσατε aor. imp. act. ἐξετάζω (# 2004) to examine, to inquire, to question (s. Matt. 2:8). μείνατε aor. imp. act. μένω (# 3531) to remain. ἕως ἄν (# 2401; 165) w. the subj., as long as, until. ἐξέλθητε aor. subj. act. ἐξέρχομαι (# 2002) to go out. ◆ **12** εἰσ-ερχόμενοι pres. mid. (dep.) part. s.v. 11. Temp. or cond. part. ἀσπάσασθε aor. imp. mid. (dep.) ἀσπάζομαι (# 832) to greet. For Jewish greetings s. SB, 1:380-85. ◆ **13** ἐάν (# 1569) if, w. the subj. indicates the cond. is probable. ἦ pres. subj. act. εἰμί (# 1639). ἐλθάτω aor. imp. act. 3rd. pers. sing. ἔρχομαι (# 2262) to come. εἰ-ρήνη (# 1645) peace. Equivalent to the Hebrew *shalom* (שלום) indicating wholeness, prosperity, well being (AM; NIDNTT; TDNT; TLNT). Used as a greeting s.v. 12. ἐπιστραφήτω aor. imp. pass. 3rd. pers. sing. ἐπιστρέ-φομαι (# 2188) to turn about, to return. ◆ **14** δέξηται aor. subj. mid. (dep.) δέχομαι (# 1312) to receive as a guest. ἀκούσῃ aor. subj. act. ἀκούω (# 201) to hear. ἐξερ-χόμενοι pres. mid. (dep.) part. s.v. 11. ἐκτινάξατε aor. imp. act. ἐκτινάσσω (# 1759) to shake off. κονιορτός (# 3155) dust. "To shake off the dust" indicates total abandonment (Hill). For the Jewish custom s. SB, 1:571; Lachs, 180, 182. ◆ **15** ἀμήν (# 297) truly (s. 5:18). ἀνεκτότερον comp. ἀνεκτός (# 445) bearable, endurable. ἔσται fut. ind. mid. (dep.) εἰμί. κρίσεως gen. sing. κρίσις (# 3213) judgment, "day of" or "for judgment." For the lack of the art. s. BD, 134f. Comp. gen. ἤ (# 2445) "than." ◆ **16** ἰδού (# 2627) aor. imp. act. ὁράω (# 3972) to see, behold (s. Matt. 2:1). λύκος (# 3380) wolf. The figure denotes false prophets or some general menace, or here the Jewish adversaries (Hill). Israel often viewed itself as sheep among wolves (Gentiles) (BBC). γίνεσθε pres. imp. mid. (dep.) γίνομαι (# 1181) to become, to be. Pres. imp. calls for an attitude, or state of being. φρόνιμος (# 5861) (pred. adj.) understanding, wise, pertaining to understanding resulting from insight and wisdom (LN, 1:384). ὄφεις nom. pl. ὄφις (# 4058) snake. A symbol of cunningness or cleverness (TDNT; BAGD). ἀκέραιος (# 193) unmixed, pure, innocent. The word was used in an inscription of the innocence of a young girl who had died (NDIEC, 4:34). περιστερά (# 4361) dove. Used as a symbol of Israel–patient, submissive, faithful (Hill). ◆ **17** προσέχετε pres. imp. act. προσέχω (# 4668) to beware of. παραδώσουσιν fut. ind. act. παραδίδωμι (# 4140) s.v. 4. συνέδρια (# 5284) (acc. pl.) council. The pl. indicates the smaller local councils which were made up of 23 members (s. M. Sanh. 1, 6; SB, 1:575-76; TDNT). μαστιγώσουσιν fut. ind. act. μαστιγόω (# 3463) to whip, to flog (Deut. 25:2). ◆ **18** καί (# 2779)... δέ (# 1254) "and ... and." καί introduces that which is similar; δέ that which is different (EGT). ἀχθήσεσθε fut. ind. pass. ἄγω (# 72) to lead. ἔνεκεν (# 1915) w. gen. because of, for the sake of. ◆ **19** παραδῶσιν aor. subj. act. παραδίδωμι (# 4140) s.v. 4. μεριμνήσητε aor. subj. act.

μεριμνάω (# 3534) to be anxious, to have anxiety. Ingressive aor.: "do not become anxious" (RWP). **λαλήσητε** aor. subj. act. λαλέω (# 3281) to speak. **δοθήσεται** fut. ind. pass. δίδωμι (# 1443) to give. Theol. pass. suggests it is given from God. ◆ **20 λαλοῦντες** pres. act. part. s.v. 19. Part. used as a noun. **λαλοῦν** pres. act. part. n. sing. s.v. 19 **πνεῦμα** (# 4460) the Holy Spirit, not a promise of a universal outpouring, but an endowment of power for a specific kind of situation (GW, 250). ◆ **21 παραδώσει** fut. ind. act. s.v. 4. **ἐπαναστήσονται** fut. ind. mid. ἐπανίστημι (# 2060) to rise up against, to rebel. The prep. ἐπί is directive w. hostility implied (MH, 312). **γονεῖς** (# 1204) acc. pl. (only in pl.) parents (BAGD). **θανατώσουσιν** fut. ind. act. θανατόω to kill. ◆ **22 ἔσεσθε** fut. ind. mid. (dep.) εἰμί (# 1639). **μισούμενοι** pres. pass. part. μισέω (# 3631) to hate. The fut. of the vb. and the pres. part., used to form a periphrastic fut. pass., imply it will go on through the ages (RWP). **ὑπομείνας** aor. act. part. ὑπομονέω (# 5702) to remain under, to endure. **εἰς τέλος** (# 5465) "in the end," "finally," "until the end" (BAGD). **σωθήσεται** fut. ind. pass. σῴζω (# 5392) to save, to deliver. ◆ **23 διώκωσιν** pres. subj. act. διώκω (# 1503) to persecute. **φεύγετε** pres. imp. act. φεύγω (# 5771) to flee. **οὐ μή** (# 4024; 3590) certainly not, a strong and emphatic neg. (M, 188-92; GGBB, 468). **τελέσητε** aor. subj. act. τελέω (# 5464) to complete, to come to the end. **ἔλθῃ** aor. subj. act. ἔρχομαι (# 2262) to come. For various views on this v. s. Carson, 250-53. ◆ **25 ἀρκετόν** (# 757) enough, sufficient (followed by dat.). This is "sufficient in the eyes of God" (DA). **γένηται** aor. subj. mid. (dep.) γίνομαι (# 1181) to become. For the use of **ἵνα** (# 2671) not expressing purp. s. M, 206-209; here it introduces a cl. explaining "sufficient." **εἰ** (# 1623) if, views the cond. as true. **οἰκοδεσπότης** (# 3867) lord or head of the house. **ἐπεκάλεσαν** aor. ind. act. ἐπικαλέω (# 2126) to call, to name. The subject is the Jewish leaders (DA). **πόσῳ μᾶλλον** (# 4531; 3437) how much more. **οἰκιακός** (# 3865) member of a household, here in the sense of relative (BAGD). ◆ **26 φοβηθῆτε** aor. subj. pass. (dep.) φοβέομαι (# 5828) to be afraid, to fear. Subj. is used as an imp. Obj. of the vb. refers to those who oppose the disciples, probably the scribes and Pharisees (DA). **κεκαλυμμένον** perf. pass. part. καλύπτω (# 2821) to hide, to cover over. **ἀποκαλυφθήσεται** fut. ind. pass. ἀποκαλύπτω (# 636) to uncover; pass. to be revealed. Theol. pass. God will reveal. **γνωσθήσεται** fut. ind. pass. γινώσκω (# 1182) to know. ◆ **27 εἴπατε** aor. imp. act. λέγω (# 3306). **κηρύξατε** aor. imp. act. κηρύσσω (# 3062) to proclaim. ◆ **28 φοβεῖσθε** pres. imp. mid. (dep.) s.v. 26. For the use of this vb. w. μή as the translation of a Heb. idiom s. RG, 577. **ἀποκτεννόντων** pres. act. part. ἀποκτείνω (# 650) / ἀποκτέννω (for the form s. BD, 39) to kill, used of any way of depriving a person of life (BAGD). **δυναμένων** pres. pass. (dep.) part.

δύναμαι (# 1538) to be able to. Both parts. here are used as nouns and are objs. of the prep. ἀπό (# 608). **ἀποκτεῖναι** (# 650) aor. act. inf. **ἀπολέσαι** aor. act. inf. ἀπόλλυμι (# 660) to destroy. **γέεννη** (# 1147) Gehenna, hell (TDNT; Mark 9:43; Luke 12:5). ◆ **29 οὐχί** (# 4049) strong form of οὐ used in questions which expect a positive answer. **στρουθίον** (# 5141) sparrow. Sparrows were part of the diet of the poor and were of all birds the cheapest (DA; LAE, 272-75). **ἀσσαρίου** (# 835) gen. sing. The Roman "as," about one-sixteenth of a denarius (a day's wage), less than one-half cent (AM; HJC, 242-44; DJG, 805). Gen. of price. **πωλεῖται** pres. ind. pass. πωλέω (# 4797) to sell; pass. to offer for sale, to be sold. Cust. pres. **ἕν** (# 1651) n. one (for the construction ἕν ... οὐ, "no one, not one," s. BD, 159). **πεσεῖται** fut. ind. mid. (dep.) πίπτω (# 4406) to fall. **ἄνευ** (# 459) without; without the Father's presence or consent, or will. S. John G. Cook, "The Sparrow's Fall in Mt 10:29b," *ZAW* 79 (1988): 138-44. ◆ **30 ὑμῶν** your (pl.) emphatic position. **καί** (# 2779) even (ascensive) **τρίχες** nom. pl. θρίξ (# 2582) hair. **ἠριθμημέναι** perf. pass. part. ἀριθμέω (# 749) to count. Theol. pass. Part. used as pred. adj. ◆ **31 φοβεῖσθε** pres. imp. mid. (dep.) φοβέομαι (# 5828) to fear, to be afraid. **διαφέρετε** pres. ind. act. διαφέρω (# 1422) to be different, to be worth more than (w. gen. of comp.). ◆ **32 ὅστις** (# 4015) rel. pron. whoever. **ὁμολογήσει** fut. ind. act. ὁμολογέω (# 3933) to confess, to acknowledge, to affirm solidarity w. Him in action and even in death (Hill). Used w. the prep. **ἔμπροσθεν** (# 1869) before. It has the sense of a confession in a legal setting (DA). ◆ **33 ἀρνήσηται** aor. subj. mid. (dep.) ἀρνέομαι (# 766) to deny, to declare that one does not know or have dealings w. someone (Hill). **ἀρνήσομαι** fut. ind. mid. (dep.) ◆ **34 νομίσητε** aor. subj. act. νομίζω (# 3787) to think, to suppose. Subj. used as prohibition w. μή (# 3590) (GGBB, 469). **ἦλθον** aor. ind. act. ἔρχομαι (# 2262) to come. **βαλεῖν** aor. act. inf. βάλλω (# 965) to cast, to throw, to bring. Aor. inf. indicates a sudden hurling of the sword where peace is expected (RWP). Inf. of purp. ◆ **35 διχάσαι** aor. act. inf. διχάζω (# 1495) to divide in two, to set at variance. ◆ **37 φιλῶν** pres. act. part. φιλέω (# 5797) to love. The state of mind compelled naturally by sense and emotion (McNeile). **ὑπέρ** (# 5642) w. acc. beyond, more than. ◆ **38 σταυρός** (# 5089) cross. The emphasis is on self-renunciation to the point of being a lonely outcast (Hill; DA). ◆ **39 εὑρών** aor. act. part. εὑρίσκω (# 2351) to find. Part. used as a subst. **ἀπολέσει** fut. ind. act. ἀπόλλυμι (# 660) to lose. **ἀπολέσας** aor. act. part. Part. used as a subst. **εὑρήσει** fut. ind. act. εὑρίσκω (# 2351) ◆ **40 δεχόμενος** pres. mid. (dep.) part. δέχομαι (# 1312) to receive, to welcome. Part. used as noun. **ἀποστείλαντά** aor. act. part. ἀποστέλλω (# 690) to send. ◆ **41 εἰς ὄνομα** "in the name"; a Semitism meaning "because he is" (DA; BG, 35). **λήμψεται** fut. ind.

mid. (dep.) λαμβάνω (# 3284) to receive. **προφήτου** (# 4737) gen. sing. Gen. may be subjective meaning "reward offered by a righteous man" (GW, 137f). ◆ **42 ποτίσῃ** aor. subj. act. ποτίζω (# 4540) to give to drink. ἀπολέσῃ aor. subj. act. s.v. 39. The double neg. οὐ μή is very strong (GGBB, 468).

Matthew 11

◆ **1 ἐγένετο** aor. ind. mid (dep.) γίνομαι (# 1181) to become, to happen s. Matt. 7:28. **ἐτέλεσεν** aor. ind. act. τελέω (# 5464) to end, to complete. **διατάσσων** pres. act. part. διατάσσω (# 1411) to order, to direct, to command, to give detailed instruction as to what must be done (LN, 1:425). Here the word refers to the commissioning of the disciples, not the general teaching of Jesus (RK, 330). Part. complements the main vb. **μετέβη** aor. ind. act. μεταβαίνω (# 3553) to depart, followed by inf. of purpose. ◆ **2 ἀκούσας** aor. act. part. ἀκούω (# 201) to hear. Temp. or causal. **δεσμωτηρίῳ** (# 1303) dat. sing. prison, the ending expresses place (MH, 342f.). According to Josephus, John was brought to Machaerus, on the east side of the Jordan, and was put to death there (Jos., *Ant.* 18:119; TJ, 63-64; DJG, 388-89). **πέμψας** aor. act. part. πέμπω (# 4287) to send. ◆ **3 σύ** (# 5148) you (emphatic). **εἶ** (# 1639) pres. ind. act. 2nd. pers. sing. εἰμί to be. **ἐρχόμενος** pres. mid. (dep.) part. ἔρχομαι (# 2262) to come, to go, used w. the art. as a subst.: "the Coming One," virtually a title for the Messiah (Tasker; s. Matt. 21:9; 23:39); perhaps used by John in reference to the designation in Matt. 3:11, 12 (RK, 63-64). **προσδοκῶμεν** pres. subj. act. προσδοκάω (# 4659) to wait for, to expect. Deliberative subj. used in a reflective question: "Should we expect...." The form may be ind. RG, 934. ◆ **4 ἀποκριθείς** aor. pass. (dep.) part. ἀποκρίνομαι (# 646) to answer. s. 3:15. **πορευθέντες** aor. pass. (dep.) part. πορεύομαι (# 4513) to go. Circum. part. may be translated as an imp. **ἀπαγγείλατε** aor. imp. act. ἀπαγγέλλω (# 550) to report, to proclaim s. Matt. 2:8; 8:33. ◆ **5 ἀναβλέπουσιν** pres. ind. act. ἀναβλέπω (# 329) to see again; the prep. ἀνα has the force of "again" (MH, 295). **περιπατοῦσιν** pres. ind. act. περιπατέω (# 4344) to walk about. **καθαρίζονται** pres. ind. pass. καθαρίζω (# 2751) to cleanse; pass. to be cleansed. **ἐγείρονται** pres. ind. pass. ἐγείρω (# 1586) to rise, to be raised. For the Jewish expectation of the healing of diseases at the time of the Messiah s. SB, 1:593f; Lachs, 190; Luz. For the relation of this passage to Isa. s. DA, 1:438; RK, 66-69. These "Kingdom acts" were a revelation of the Messiah's identity (RK, 338). **πτωχός** (# 4777) poor, abject poverty (NTW, 110; s. Matt. 5:3). **εὐαγγελίζονται** pres. ind. pass. εὐαγγελίζω (# 2294) to evangelize, to bring the good news. ◆ **6 ὃς ἐάν** (# 4005; 1569) w. subj., whoever. The rel. sentence contains the cond. for the main cl. **σκανδαλισθῇ** aor. subj. pass. σκανδαλίζω (# 4997) to cause to

stumble, to fall into a trap or snare (TDNT; NTW; RK, 74). ◆ **7 πορευομένων** pres. mid. (dep.) part. πορεύομαι (# 4513) to go. Temp. part. gen. abs. "When they had departed...." **ἤρξατο** aor. ind. mid. (dep.) ἄρχομαι (# 806) to begin. **ἐξήλθατε** aor. ind. act. ἐξέρχομαι (# 2002) to go out, to come out. **θεάσασθαι** aor. mid. (dep.) inf. θεάομαι (# 2517) to see, to look at, to gaze at a show or demonstration (AM). Inf. of purp. **κάλαμον** (# 2812) acc. sing. reed. Obj. of the inf. "to see." **σαλευόμενον** pres. pass. part. σαλεύω (# 4888) to agitate, to shake. The expression may refer to that which is common: "weeds blown by the wind" (DA), or to a weak and unstable character (Gnilka; Carson, 263). ◆ **8 ἀλλά** (# 247) but, rather, or it has the force of "if not" (McNeile). **ἰδεῖν** aor. act. inf. ὁράω (# 3972) to see. Inf. of purp. **μαλακοῖς** (# 3434) dat. pl. soft; refers here to soft garments (for the use of adjs. as nouns s. IBG, 96). **ἠμφιεσμένον** perf. pass. part. ἀμφιέννυμι (# 314) to clothe; perf. pass., "to be dressed." Part. used as an adj. **φοροῦντες** pres. act. part. φορέω (# 5841) to wear constantly, denotes the repeated or habitual action (AS). Part. used as a noun, "those wearing...." ◆ **9 περισσότερον** (# 4358) comp. περισσός (# 4356) exceeding the usual number or size, extraordinary, remarkable, comp. greater (BAGD). **προφήτου** (# 4737) gen. of comp. The term "prophet" at that time could refer to an eschatalogical person (DA). ◆ **10 γέγραπται** perf. ind. pass. γράφω (# 1211) to write; perf. pass., "It stands written." **κατασκευάσει** fut. ind. act. κατασκευάζω (# 2941) to prepare, to make ready. ◆ **11 ἐγήγερται** perf. ind. pass. ἐγείρω (# 1586) to rise up, to appear on the stage of history (McNeile). **γεννητοῖς** (# 1168) dat. pl. born. For adj. w. this ending s. MH, 370. **μείζων** (# 3505) comp. μέγας (# 3489) large, great. Followed by gen. of comp. **μικρότερος** comp. μικρός (# 3625) small, little, the least. Comp. is used w. the force of superl. (RG, 667ff). No greater person has arisen than John the Baptist, because he stood on the threshold of the kingdom. Yet the least disciple who, through following Jesus, already participates in the reality of the kingdom is greater than John (Hill). ◆ **12 βιάζεται** pres. ind. mid. or pass. βιάζω (# 1041). The mid. form means to apply force, to enter forcibly. The pass. form means to be violently treated, to be oppressed, to suffer violence (BAGD; W.E. Moore, "ΒΙ-ΑΖΩ, ΑΡΠΑΖΩ and Cognates in Josephus," *NTS* 21 [1975]: 519-43; Gerd Häfner, "Gewalt gegen die Basileia? Zum Problem der Auslegung des 'Stürmerspruches' Mt 11:12," *ZNW* 83 [1992]: 21-51). For a discussion of the passage s. Carson, 265-68; RK, 90-99; NTRJ, 285-300; Hagner; Luz. One suggestion is that the word means "the use of property without the owner's consent." Thus the pass. is "to acquire possession of the Kingdom by force, i.e. without God's consent" (NDIEC, 7:130-62; esp. 159-62). **βιασταί** nom. pl. βιαστής (# 1043) one who uses violence. **ἁρπάζουσιν** pres. ind. act. ἁρπάζω (# 773) to snatch, to rob. Pres. may be conative, "They try to ..." (Carson, 267). ◆ **13** **ἐπροφήτευσαν** aor. ind. act. προφητεύω (# 4736) to prophesy. ◆ **14 δέξασθαι** aor. mid. (dep.) inf. δέχομαι (# 1312) to welcome, to receive. (s. 1QS 9:11). **μέλλων** pres. act. part. μέλλω (# 3516) to be about to do something, used w. the inf. to express fut. Part. used as a noun. ◆ **15 ὦτα** acc. pl. οὖς (# 4064) ear. **ἀκουέτω** pres. imp. act. 3rd. pers. sing. ἀκούω (# 201) Pres. imp. emphasizes the process or details of the action: "pay careful attention" (VANT, 365). ◆ **16 τίνι** dat. sing. τίς (# 5515) who. "To whom," dat. used w. the vb. **ὁμοιώσω** fut. ind. act. ὁμοιόω (# 3929) to compare, to liken to. Deliberative fut. used in a rhetorical question. This corresponds to the common Jewish way of introducing parables (s. SB, 2:7-9). **γενεάς** (# 1155) generation, "contemporaries" (DA; RK, 106-107). **καθημένοις** pres. mid. (dep.) part. dat. pl. κάθημαι (# 2764) to sit. Dat. w. the adj. **προσφωνοῦντα** pres. act. part. προσφωνέω (# 4715) to call to, to call out. Part. used as adj. ◆ **17 ηὐλήσαμεν** aor. ind. act. αὐλέω (# 884) to play the flute. **ὠρχήσασθε** aor. ind. mid. (dep.) ὀρχέομαι (# 4004) to dance. **ἐθρηνήσαμεν** aor. ind. act. θρηνέω (# 2577) to mourn, to lament. **ἐκόψασθε** aor. ind. mid. (dep.) κόπτομαι (# 3164) to strike one's self on the breast, a sign of sorrow. Just as stubborn children playing at the market places refuse to listen to their playmates, the generation of Jesus and John refused to listen to them (RK, 112-15; Dieter Zeller, "Die Bildlogik des Gleichnisses Mt 11:16 f. / Lk. 7:31 f.," *ZAW* 68 [1977]: 252-57). ◆ **18 ἦλθεν** aor. ind. act. ἔρχομαι (# 2262) to come. **ἐσθίων** pres. act. part. ἐσθίω (# 2266) to eat. **πίνων** pres. act. part. πίνω (# 4403) to drink. Parts. give the manner of "coming" and the pres. describe the customary action. ◆ **19 φάγος** (# 5741) glutton. **οἰνοπότης** (# 3884) wine drinker, drunkard. This charge has Deut. 21:20 in view and pictures a rebellious son who should be stoned (Gundry; RK, 111). **ἐδικαιώθη** aor. ind. pass. δικαιόω (# 1467) to declare righteous, to recognize as righteous, proved to be in the right and accepted by God (GW, 138). **ἀπό** (# 608) from, by. For the causal or instr. use s. IBG, 73. ◆ **20 ἤρξατο** aor. ind. mid. (dep.) s.v. 7. **ὀνειδίζειν** (# 3943) pres. act. inf. to reproach, revile, w. the implication of that individual being evidently to blame (LN, 1:437). **ἐγένοντο** aor. ind. mid. (dep.) 3rd. pers. pl. s.v. 1. **πλεῖσται** superl. πολύς (# 4498) much, "very many mighty works" (RWP). The elative use of the superl. (M, 79). **ὅτι** (# 4022) because, gives the reason for the accusation. **μετενόησαν** aor. ind. act. μετανοέω (# 3566) to repent s. Matt. 3:2. ◆ **21 εἰ** if, introduces a contrary to fact cond. cl. "If ... had been done ... would have repented" (MT, 91f.) **γενόμεναι** aor. mid. (dep.) part. γίνομαι (# 1181). Adj. part. translated as a rel. cl. "which were done...."

σάκκος (# 4884) sack, sackcloth. The fabric from which a sack is made is usually dark in color (BAGD). **σποδός** (# 5075) ashes. "Sackcloth and ashes" became a fixed phrase indicating sincerity (DA; SB, 1:605). ◆ **22** **ἀνεκτότερον** comp. ἀνεκτός (# 445) bearable, endurable. **ἔσται** fut. ind. mid. (dep.) εἰμί (# 1639). **ἤ** (# 2445) than, used w. comp. ◆ **23 ὑψωθήσῃ** fut. ind. pass. ὑψόω (# 5738) to lift up. The particle expects a neg. answer to the question. **καταβήσῃ** fut. ind. mid. (dep.) καταβαίνω (# 2849) to go down. **ἐγενήθησαν** aor. ind. pass. (dep.) γίνομαι (# 1181) to become, to be done, to happen. **ἔμεινεν** aor. ind. act. μένω (# 3531) to remain. Ind. used in a contrary to fact cond. cl. ◆ **25 ἀποκριθείς** aor. pass. (dep.) part. s.v. 4. **εἶπεν** aor. ind. act. λέγω (# 3306) to speak, to say. **ἐξομολογοῦμαι** (# 2018) pres. ind. mid. (dep.) to confess, often used in the LXX as the equivalent "to give praise" (AM; TDNT). **ἔκρυψας** aor. ind. act. 2nd. pers. sing. κρύπτω (# 3221) to hide. **ἀπεκάλυψας** aor. ind. act. 2nd. pers. sing. ἀποκαλύπτω (# 636) to unveil, to reveal. **νηπίοις** (# 3758) dat. pl. indir. obj. infant, minor. The babes are those who in the eyes of the world are weak and simple, but before God are the elect (DA). ◆ **26 πατήρ** (# 4252) father (nom. is used for voc. s. BD, 81). **ὅτι** (# 4022) because, introducing the reason for this contentment (EGT). **εὐδοκία** (# 2306) good pleasure, good will, satisfaction. **ἐγένετο** aor. ind. mid. (dep.) s.v. 1. ◆ **27 παρεδόθη** aor. ind. pass. παραδίδωμι (# 4140) to deliver over, to hand over, to pass on teaching (TDNT; TLNT). **ἐπιγινώσκει** pres. ind. act. ἐπιγινώσκω (# 2105) to know; sometimes it means "exact knowledge." It refers to personal, concentrated experiential knowledge (DA). The prep. is directive (MH, 312). **ἐάν** (# 1569) = ἄν (BD, 57), whomever. **βούληται** pres. subj. mid. (dep.) βούλομαι (# 1089) to will, to purp., to plan (LN, 1:357). **ἀποκαλύψαι** aor. act. inf. ἀποκλύπτω (# 636) to unveil, to reveal. For a discussion of the exegetical problems of this v. s. McNeile; RK, 143-44. ◆ **28 δεῦτε** (# 1307) adv. serving as a hortatory particle w. pl. "come!" "come on!" (BAGD). **κοπιῶντες** pres. act. part. nom. pl. κοπιάω (# 3159) to become weary, tired, to work hard. Pres. indicates the continual action. **πεφορτισμένοι** perf. pass. part. nom. pl. φορτίζω (# 5844) to burden. Perf. expresses a state of weariness (RWP). The demands of the Jewish teachers and the scribal traditions of the time have burdened the people (RK, 146; s. DA; Hagner; Luz). **κἀγώ** = καὶ ἐγώ (emphatic) "And I, in contrast to others." (cf. for example, Isa. 40:28-31). **ἀναπαύσω** fut. ind. act. ἀναπαύω (# 399) to cause to rest, to give rest, to refresh. The rest is the salvation for which they had striven, without the oppressive weight of legalism (RK, 148). ◆ **29 ἄρατε** aor. imp. act. αἴρω (# 149) to lift up, to take up. Aor. imp. points to a specific action. **ζυγός** (# 2433) yoke, symbol of obligation and subjection (Moore, *Judaism*, 1:465; SB, 1:608-610; ABD, 6:1026-27). **μάθετε** aor.

imp. act. μανθάνω (# 3443) to learn. πραΰς (# 4558) gentle, meek s. 5:5. ταπεινός (# 5424) lowly, humble. The word is used in Test. of Judah 24:1 of the Messiah. καί (# 2779) and, w. fut. introduces a result. εὑρήσετε fut. ind. act. εὑρίσκω (# 2351) to find. ἀνάπαυσις (# 398) refreshing, rest, refreshment. ◆ 30 χρηστός (# 5982) useful, comfortable. φορτίον (# 5845) burden. ἐλαφρόν (# 1787) light. To take the yoke of Jesus is not burdensome, but is characterized by humility and concern for the despised (Hill); s. Blaine Charette, "'To Proclaim Liberty to the Captives': Matthew 11:28-30 in the Light of OT Expectation," *NTS* 38 (1992): 290-97.

Matthew 12

◆ 1 ἐπορεύθη aor. ind. pass. (dep.) πορεύομαι (# 4513) to go. σπόριμος (# 5077) sown, grain fields, standing grain (BAGD). ἐπείνασαν aor. ind. act. πεινάω (# 4277) to hunger; incep. aor. "became hungry" (Tasker). ἤρξαντο aor. ind. mid. (dep.) ἄρχομαι (# 806) to begin. τίλλειν pres. act. inf. τίλλω (# 5504) to pluck, to pluck off. στάχυς (# 5092) head of grain. ἐσθίειν pres. act. inf. ἐσθίω (# 2266) to eat. Grains ripened after Passover, between April and June (DA). ◆ 2 ἰδόντες aor. act. part. (temp.) ὁράω (# 3972) to see. "When they saw...." εἶπαν aor. ind. act. λέγω (# 3306) to speak, to say. ποιοῦσιν pres. ind. act. ποιέω (# 4472) to do. Pres. points to an action taking place. ἔξεστιν (# 2003) pres. ind. act. it is lawful, it is allowed. Jewish tradition prohibited reaping or threshing on the Sabbath (M, Shabbath, 7, 2). For the Sabbath s. M, Shabbath; Moore, *Judaism*, 2:21-39; DA; JPB, 208-11; ABD, 851-56; Yong-Eui Yang, *Jesus and the Sabbath in Matthew's Gospel* JSNTSS 139 (Sheffield Academic Press, 1997). ◆ 3 ἀνέγνωτε aor. ind. act. ἀναγινώσκω (# 336) to read. The neg. in the question expects "yes" as the answer. ἐποίησεν aor. ind. act. ποιέω (# 4472) to do. ἐπείνασεν aor. ind. act. πεινάω (# 4277) to be hungry. ◆ 4 εἰσῆλθεν aor. ind. act. εἰσέρχομαι (# 1656) to go in, to come in. προθέσεως gen. sing. πρόθεσις (# 4606) setting forth, presentation, "loaves of presentation" (BAGD), the "shewbread." The bread before the Presence of the Lord consisted of twelve loaves in two rows on the table before the Holy of Holies (DA; SB, 3:719-33; ABD, 1:780-81). ἔφαγον aor. ind. act. ἐσθίω (# 2266) to eat. The pl. indicates that those w. David also ate of the bread (RK, 160). ἐξόν pres. act. part. ἔξεστι (# 2003) allowed, permitted; used w. inf. ἦν impf. ind. act. εἰμί (# 1639) to be. φαγεῖν aor. act. inf. ἐσθίω. Inf. explains what is not allowed. It was an act of God's mercy, which did not punish the deed of David and his friends (RK, 162). ◆ 5 βεβηλοῦσιν pres. ind. act. βεβηλόω (# 1014) to defile, to make common. Pres. points to a continual or habitual action. ἀναίτιος (# 360) guiltless, innocent. The requirements of the temple service profaned the temple, but the priest were con-

sidered innocent (SB, 1:620-22). ◆ 6 τοῦ ἱεροῦ (# 2639) gen. of comp.: "than the temple." μεῖζον (# 3505) n. comp. μέγας (# 3489) large, great. The n. can be used of persons when the emphasis is on some outstanding quality (MT, 21). Since the temple, as the symbol of God's presence, could set aside the Sabbath, Jesus had even greater right to do this (RK, 165; Carson, 281; ABD, 854-56; DJG, 816). ◆ 7 εἰ if. W. ἄν used for a contrary to fact cond. cl. ἐγνώκειτε plperf. ind. act. γινώσκω (# 1182) to know, to understand. The plperf. in the cond. cl. refers to past time. For the use of the plperf. in a cond. cl. s. DM, 290; VA, 304-306. ἔλεος (# 1799) mercy, loyalty (Matt. 9:13). This may be a reference to Jesus showing mercy (RK, 168-72; DJG, 542-43). κατεδικάσατε aor. ind. act. καταδικάζω (# 2868) to condemn in the legal sense (MM). ◆ 9 μεταβάς aor. act. part. (temp.) μεταβαίνω (# 3553) to depart. "After he departed...." ἦλθεν aor. ind. act. ἔρχομαι (# 2262) to come, to go. ◆ 10 ἔχων pres. act. part. ἔχω (# 2400) to have. Adj. part. ξηρός (# 3831) dried, withered, paralyzed (DA). ἐπηρώτησαν aor. ind. act. ἐπερωτάω (# 2089) to question. Pres. is directive (MH, 312). εἰ (# 1623) used to introduce a question. For this usage s. BD, 226. θεραπεῦσαι aor. act. inf. θεραπεύω (# 2543) to heal. The rabbis allowed help for the sick if the sick person's life was in danger (M, Zoma 8, 6; Hill). κατηγορήσωσιν aor. subj. act. κατηγορέω (# 2989) to accuse, to bring accusation against (w. gen.). A legal t.t. "to bring charges in a court" (BAGD). Subj. w. ἵνα (# 2671) used in a purp. cl. ◆ 11 ἔσται fut. ind. mid. (dep.) εἰμί (# 1639). ἕξει fut. ind. act. ἔχω (# 2400) to have. The words imply, "Can anyone of you imagine that ... ?" (VA, 422). ἐάν (# 1569) if. The cond. is probable. ἐμπέση aor. subj. act. ἐμπίπτω (# 1860) to fall into. βόθυνος (# 1073) ditch. οὐχί (# 4049) w. questions which expect a positive answer. κρατήσει fut. ind. act. κρατέω (# 3195) to take hold of. ἐγερεῖ fut. ind. act. ἐγείρω (# 1586) to raise up. ◆ 12 πόσῳ (# 4531) "how much?" διαφέρει pres. ind. act. διαφέρω (# 1422) to carry through; instr. to be worth more than, be superior to (BAGD; Matt. 10:31). προβάτου comp. gen. πρόβατον (# 4585) sheep. ὥστε (# 6063) wherefore, therefore (drawing a conclusion). ◆ 13 ἔκτεινον aor. imp. act. ἐκτείνω (# 1753) to stretch out. Aor. views a specific act. ἐξέτεινεν aor. ind. act. ἐκτείνω. When the Savior spoke, the man responded w. an obedient act of faith (RK). ἀπεκατεστάθη aor. ind. pass. ἀποκαθίστημι (# 635) to restore, to restore to the same cond. (s. 1 Kings 13:6; CCFJ, 1:186). ◆ 14 ἐξελθόντες aor. act. part. (temp.) ἐξέρχομαι (# 2002) to go out. συμβούλιον (# 5206) acc. plan, purpose (consultation and its result, BAGD). ἔλαβον aor. ind. act. λαμβάνω (# 3284) to take. ὅπως (# 3968) w. subj., in order that. ἀπολέσωσιν aor. subj. act. ἀπόλλυμι (# 660) to destroy. Their plan was to destroy Him, His following and ministry. ◆ 15 γνούς aor. act. part. masc. nom. sing. γινώσκω (# 1182) to know. Temp. or causal part. ἀνεχώρησεν aor. ind. act. ἀναχωρέω (# 432) to depart, to go away. ἠκολούθησαν aor. ind. act. ἀκολουθέω (# 199) to follow. ἐθεράπευσεν aor. ind. act. θεραπεύω (# 2543) to heal (s. Matt. 8:16). ◆ **16 ἐπετίμησεν** aor. ind. act. ἐπιτιμάω (# 2203) to rebuke (s. 8:26). **ποιήσωσιν** aor. subj. act. ποιέω (# 4472) to make. Vb. is used w. the double acc. "to make him known," "to reveal him" (BAGD). ◆ **17 πληρωθῇ** aor. subj. pass. πληρόω (# 4444) to fulfill (s. 1:22). Subj. w. **ἵνα** (# 2671) used in a purp. cl. indicating that the events of Jesus' ministry were divinely ordered (RK, 193). **ῥηθέν** aor. pass. part. λέγω (# 3306). Part. used as a subst.: "that which was spoken." Theol. pass. indicating that God spoke through Isaiah. For a discussion of the Servant of YHWH s. DJG, 744-47. ◆ **18 παῖς** (# 4090) child, servant, dependent (TDNT). **ἡρέτισα** aor. ind. act. αἱρετίζω (# 147) to choose. **εὐδόκησεν** aor. ind. act. εὐδοκέω (# 2305) to be pleased w., to be well pleased, to take pleasure in. **θήσω** fut. ind. act. τίθημι (# 5502) to place. **κρίσις** (# 3213) judgment, justice. It refers to the "divine verdict of God" (RK, 197). **ἔθνεσιν** (# 1620) dat. pl. indir. obj. people; pl. nations, Gentiles. **ἀπαγγελεῖ** fut. ind. act. ἀπαγγέλλω (# 550) to report, to proclaim. In the work of the servant, there is accomplished a work of righteousness, judgment, of justice for the Gentiles (Hill). ◆ **19 ἐρίσει** fut. ind. act. ἐρίζω (# 2248) to quarrel, to wrangle, to express differences of opinion w. at least some measure of antagonism or hostility (LN, 1:439; TLNT). It draws the picture of one who does not take action against those who wrong him (RK, 199). The Heb. word in Isa. 42:2 (פצ‎) could be used as a legal t.t. meaning "to cry out for legal help" (KB³, 976; WTM, 4:207-208; THAT, 2:567-75; TDOT). **κραυγάσει** fut. ind. act. κραυγάζω (# 3198) to cry (excitedly), to scream. **τις** anyone. **πλατείαις** dat. pl. πλατεῖα (# 4423) wide street. Note the contrast in Matt. 6:5 (DA). ◆ **20 κάλαμος** (# 2812) reed. **συντετριμμένον** perf. pass. part. συντρίβω (# 5341) to shatter, to crush. Perf. indicates the state or cond. **κατεάξει** fut. ind. act. κατάγνυμι (# 2682) to break (for the form s. BD, 50). **λίνον** (# 3351) flax, linen, lamp wick. **τυφόμενον** pres. pass. part. τύφω (# 5606) to produce smoke; pass. to smolder, glimmer. **σβέσει** fut. ind. act. σβέννυμι (# 4931) to extinguish (TLNT). The Servant will not add to the burden of the oppressed and the needy (RK, 260), but will accomplish his mission of bringing salvation to Gentiles in spite of opposition (TSS, 35-57). **ἐκβάλῃ** aor. subj. act. ἐκβάλλω (# 1675) to cast out, to bring forth. **εἰς νῖκος** unto victory. A translation of the Heb. term לָנֶצַח‎ meaning "successfully" (KB³, 676; DA). **κρίσιν** justice s.v. 18. ◆ **21 ἐλπιοῦσιν** fut. ind. act. ἐλπίζω (# 1827) to hope, to put one's hope in someone. W. obj. in dat. ◆ **22 προσηνέχθη** aor. ind. pass. προσφέρω (# 4712) to bring to, to bring. **δαιμονιζόμενος** pres.

mid./pass. part. δαιμονίζομαι (# 1227) to be possessed w. a demon, w. an evil spirit. **τυφλός** (# 5603) blind. **κωφός** (# 3273) dumb, mute. **ἐθεράπευσεν** (# 2543) aor. ind. act. s.v. 10. **ὥστε** (# 6063) w. inf. expresses results "so that." **λαλεῖν** pres. act. inf. λαλέω (# 3281) to speak. ◆ **23 ἐξίσταντο** impf. ind. mid. (dep.) ἐξίστημι (# 2014) to be beside oneself w. astonishment. Impf. vividly portrays the situation: "They were almost beside themselves w. excitement" (RWP). **ἔλεγον** impf. ind. act. λέγω (# 3306) to speak, to say. "They were continually saying" (iterat. impf. stressing the continous action) or "they began to say" (incep. impf. stressing the beginning action). **μήτι** (# 3614) generally expects a neg. answer, but can be used where there is doubt, "Can this possibly be the Son of David?" (BAGD; Cleon L. Rogers, Jr, "The Davidic Covenant in the Gospels," *Bib Sac* 150 [1993]: 461); for the "Son of David" as a designation for "the Messiah" s. Cleon Rogers, "The Promises to David in Early Judaism," *Bib Sac* 150 (1993): 285-302, Luz, 2:59-61. They can hardly believe what the facts seem to suggest (EGT). **οὗτος** this one (emphatic), this man (McNeile). ◆ **24 ἀκούσαντες** aor. act. part. (temp.) ἀκούω (# 201) to hear. **εἶπον** aor. ind. act. λέγω (# 3306). **ἄρχοντι** dat. sing. ἄρχων (# 807) ruler, prince. Dat. w. the prep. is "under the control of," or "in the power, authority of." For Beelzebub s. TDNT; SB, 1:631-35; DA, 2:195-96; ABD, 1:639; DDD, 294-96. ◆ **25 εἰδώς** perf. act. part. (causal) οἶδα (# 3857) to know. Def. perf. w. pres. meaning. **ἐνθύμησις** (# 1927) thought, reasoning. **μερισθεῖσα** aor. pass. part. μερίζω (# 3532) to divide. **ἐρημοῦται** pres. ind. pass. ἐρημόω (# 2246) to make into a wasteland, to depopulate (DA). Gnomic pres. **ἤ** (# 2445) or. **σταθήσεται** fut. ind. pass. ἵστημι (# 2705) to place, to set; pass. to stand, to stand firm. ◆ **26 εἰ** if. The cond. is assumed by the speaker to be true. **ἐμερίσθη** aor. ind. pass. 3rd. pers. sing. s.v. 25. Either a timeless aor. to be translated as a pres. (VA, 233), or a futuristic aor. viewing the fut. event as already fulfilled (VANT, 269). ◆ **27 Βεελζεβούλ** (# 1015) Baal, the prince, Satan (s.v. 24). ◆ **28 ἄρα** (# 726) then, introduces the conclusion based on the cond. and emphasizes the result (BAGD; EDNT). **ἔφθασεν** aor. ind. act. φθάνω (# 5777) to come before, to precede, to arrive (DA; RK, 228-29). ◆ **29 εἰσελθεῖν** aor. act. inf. εἰσέρχομαι (# 1656) to come in. **τοῦ ἰσχυροῦ** gen. ἰσχυρός (# 2708) strong, w. the art. it is used as a noun: "the strong one." The art. is generic, but hints at the particular strong man that is meant (McNeile). **σκεύη** acc. pl. σκεῦος (# 5007) vessel, pl. property. **ἁρπάσαι** aor. act. inf. ἁρπάζω (# 773) to snatch, to rob. **δήσῃ** aor. subj. act. δέω (# 1313) to bind. Subj. used in a type of cond. cl. "if not," **ἐὰν μή** (# 1623; 3590) "unless," "except." **διαρπάσει** fut. ind. act. διαρπάζω (# 1395) to plunder thoroughly. The prep. is perfective and describes the carrying of action through to a definite result (MH,

301). ◆ **30 συνάγων** pres. act. part. συνάγω (# *5251*) to gather together, to gather. Part. used as a subst. **σκορπίζει** pres. ind. act. σκορπίζω (# *5025*) to scatter. ◆ **31 βλασφημία** (# *1060*) abusive speech, blasphemy (TDNT; EDNT; Carson, 291-92). **ἀφεθήσεται** fut. ind. pass. ἀφίημι (# *918*) to release, to forgive. ◆ **32 εἴπη** aor. subj. act. λέγω (# *3306*) to say. **οὔτε ... οὔτε** "neither...nor." **μέλλοντι** pres. act. part. μέλλω (# *3516*) to be about to do. "In the coming age." ◆ **33 ἤ ... ἤ** (# *2445*) "either...or." **ποιήσατε** aor. imp. act. ποιέω (# *4472*) to make. Aor. imp. calls for a specific action. **σαπρόν** (# *4911*) acc. sing. bad, decayed, rotten. **γινώσκεται** pres. ind. pass. s.v. 15. ◆ **34 γεννήματα** that which is produced, child, offspring. **ἐχιδνῶν** gen. pl. ἔχιδνα (# *2399*) viper, snake. Descriptive gen.: "brood of vipers," a stinging rebuke to pharisaic hypocrisy (Hill). **περισσεύματος** gen. pl. περίσσευμα (# *4354*) abundance, overflow. ◆ **35 ἐκβάλλει** pres. ind. act. ἐκβάλλω (# *1675*) to bring forth. Gnomic pres. ◆ **36 ἀργός** (# *734*) useless, ineffective (Tasker). **λαλήσουσιν** fut. ind. act. λαλέω (# *3281*) to speak. **ἀποδώσουσιν** fut. ind. act. ἀποδίδωμι (# *625*) to render, to give back (w. **λόγον** "to give account"). ◆ **37 δικαιωθήση** fut. ind. pass. δικαιόω (# *1467*) to justify, to declare in the right. **καταδικασθήση** fut. ind. pass. καταδικάζω (# *2868*) to condemn. The pass. forms are theol. pass., indicating that God does the action. ◆ **38 ἀπεκρίθησαν** aor. ind. pass. (dep.) ἀποκρίνομαι (# *646*) to answer. **λέγοντες** pres. act. part. λέγω s.v. 32. **σημεῖον** (# *4956*) sign (TDNT). The sign was a request of legitimation of Jesus' ministry, thus continuing their unbelief (RK, 257). **ἰδεῖν** aor. act. inf. ὁράω (# *3972*) to see. ◆ **39 ἀποκριθείς** aor. pass. part. s.v. 38. **εἶπεν** aor. ind. act. λέγω (# *3306*) to say. **γενεά** (# *1155*) generation, contemporaries, the sum total of those born at the same time, expanded to include all those living at a given time (BAGD). **μοιχαλίς** (# *3655*) an adulteress, apostate, disobedient and unfaithful to God (Allen; s. 1 Enoch 93:9; Jubilees 23:16-21). **ἐπιζητεῖ** pres. ind. act. ἐπιζητέω (# *2118*) to seek after. Prep. is directive. It indicates not just looking for but demanding as a necessary preliminary to faith (Tasker). **δοθήσεται** fut. ind. pass. δίδωμι (# *1443*) to give. Theol. pass. ◆ **40 ὥσπερ** (# *6061*) just as. **κήτους** gen sing. κῆτος (# *3063*) sea monster, huge fish. For Jonah in Judaism s. SB, 1:642-49; DJG, 754-56. **ἡμέρας** acc. pl. ἡμέρα (# *2465*) acc. of time "for three days." According to Jewish reckoning a part of a day counted as a full day (SB, 1:649; RK, 261-62; 1 Sam. 30:12-13; HSB, 380-81). ◆ **41 ἀναστήσονται** fut. ind. mid. ἀνίστημι (# *482*) to rise up, to come forward, that is, as witnesses (Meyer). **κατακρινοῦσιν** fut. ind. act. κατακρίνω (# *2891*) to condemn. **μετενόησαν** aor. ind. act. μετανοέω (# *3566*) to repent. **εἰς** (# *1650*) because of (causal s. BD, 112; DM, 104). **πλεῖον** n. comp. πολύς (# *4498*) great, comp. "greater." It refers

to Jesus, not the kingdom or the proclamation (DA; RK, 269). The n. emphasizes quality as distinct from personal identity (Gundry). ◆ **42 βασίλισσα** (# *999*) queen. **νότου** gen. νότος (# *3803*) south wind, south, kingdom of the south. The ref. may be to 1 Kings 10:1-13. **ἐγερθήσεται** fut. ind. pass. ἐγείρω (# *1586*) to rise up. **ἦλθεν** aor. ind. act. ἔρχομαι s.v. 9. **περάτων** gen. pl. πέρας (# *4306*) border, end. **ἀκοῦσαι** aor. act. inf. ἀκούω (# *201*) to hear. Inf. used to express purp. **σοφία** (# *5053*) wisdom. Solomon was wise, but here is Wisdom itself (Bengel). ◆ **43 ἐξέλθη** aor. subj. act. ἐξέρχομαι (# *2002*) s.v. 14. Subj. w. **ὅταν** (# *4020*) is used in a generalized temp. cl. **διέρχεται** pres. ind. mid. (dep.) διέρχομαι (# *1451*) to go through, to pass through. **ἀνύδρων** gen pl. ἄνυδρος (# *536*) dry, waterless. For the habitation of demons as depicted in Judaism s. SB, 4:i, 515-19. **ζητοῦν** pres. act. part. ζητέω (# *2426*) to seek. Pres. indicates the continual action. Part. of manner. ◆ **44 ἐπιστρέψω** fut. ind. act. ἐπιστρέφω (# *2188*) to turn about, to return. Deliberative fut. showing intention (VA, 424). **ἐξῆλθον** aor. ind. act. 1st. pers. sing. s.v. 43. **ἐλθόν** aor. act. part. (circum.) n. nom. sing. ἔρχομαι (# *2262*) σχολάζοντα pres. act. part. σχολάζω (# *5390*) to have leisure time, to be unoccupied, stand empty. **σεσαρωμένον** perf. pass. part. σαρόω (# *4924*) to sweep, to sweep clean. **κεκοσμημένον** perf. pass. part. κοσμέω (# *3175*) to put into order, to decorate. Perf. parts. view the state or cond. The heart, though swept and decorated, remained empty (DA). ◆ **45 πονηρότερα** (# *4505*) comp. more evil. **ἑαυτοῦ** (# *1571*) gen. of comp., "than himself." **εἰσελθόντα** aor. act. part. s.v. 4. Circum. or temp. part. **κατοικεῖ** pres. ind. act. κατοικέω (# *2997*) to dwell, to settle down. The prep. of the vb. is perfectivizing (MH, 316). **ἔσχατος** (# *2274*) last, last thing, here "The last or latter cond." **χείρονα** (# *5937*) comp. of κακός bad. Comp. worse. **πρώτων** (# *4755*) gen. of comp. "the first or former cond." **ἔσται** fut. ind. mid. (dep.) εἰμί (# *1639*) Jesus applies the parable to those of that generation who have been blessed by His work, but have in unbelief rejected Him (RK, 274-76). ◆ **46 λαλοῦντος** pres. act. part. (temp.) gen. sing. s.v. 22. Gen. abs.: "while he was speaking." **εἱστήκεισαν** plperf. ind. act. ἵστημι (# *2705*) to stand, w. the sense of the impf. They had been standing while Jesus was speaking (EGT; VANT, 308). **ζητοῦντες** pres. act. part. (circum.) s.v. 43. **λαλῆσαι** aor. act. inf. λαλέω (# *3281*) to speak. Inf. used as obj. of the part. ◆ **47 εἶπεν** aor. ind. act. λέγω (# *3306*) to say. **ἑστήκασιν** perf. ind. act. ἵστημι s.v. 46. ◆ **48 ἀποκριθείς** aor. pass. part. s.v. 38. ◆ **49 ἐκτείνας** aor. act. part. (circum.) s.v. 13. **μαθητής** (# *3412*) disciple. Those who exemplify what Jesus requires of anyone desiring a relationship w. Him (CDMG, 139). ◆ **50 ὅστις** (# *4015*) general rel. pron., whoever. **ποιήση** aor. subj. act. s.v. 2. Here in the sense of obeying the commands of God.

Matthew 13

◆ **1 ἐξελθών** aor. act. part. ἐξέρχομαι (# 2002) to go out. Circum. or temp. part. **ἐκάθητο** impf. ind. mid. (dep.) κάθημαι (# 2764) to sit. A rabbi normally sat to teach s. Matt. 5:1. ◆ **2 συνήχθησαν** aor. ind. pass. συνάγω (# 5251) to gather together; pass. to assemble. **ἐμβάντα** aor. act. part. (circum.) acc. sing. ἐμβαίνω (# 1832) to embark, to get into. **καθῆσθαι** pres. mid. (dep.) inf. s.v. 1. Inf. expresses result. **αἰγιαλόν** (# 129) acc. w. prep. ἐπί (# 2093) shore, beach. **εἱστήκει** plperf. ind. act. ἵστημι (# 2705) to stand. Used in the impf. sense: had taken a stand and so stood (RWP). ◆ **3 ἐλάλησεν** aor. ind. act. λαλέω (# 3281) to speak. **παραβολαῖς** dat. pl. παραβολή (# 4130) parable. For the meaning of the word s. TDNT; NIDNTT; Carson, 301-304; DA; J.W. Sider, "Rediscovering the Parables: The Logic of the Jeremias Tradition," *JBL* 102 (1983): 61-83; ABD, 5:146-52; DJG, 591-601; BBC. **ἐξῆλθεν** aor. ind. act. s.v. 1. **σπείρων** pres. act. part. σπείρω (# 5062) to sow. Subst. part. ◆ **4 σπείρειν** pres. act. inf. Inf. w. prep. ἐν (# 1877) expressing contemporaneous time: "as he was sowing" (BD, 208). **ἔπεσεν** aor. ind. act. πίπτω (# 4406) to fall. **ἐλθόντα** aor. act. part. (temp.) nom. pl. n. ἔρχομαι (# 2262) to come. "When the birds came...." **κατέφαγεν** aor. ind. act. κατεσθίω (# 2983) to eat up. The prep. of the vb. is perfective: "to eat up completely." ◆ **5 πετρώδης** (# 4378) stony. **εἶχεν** impf. ind. act. ἔχω (# 2400) to have. **ἐξανέτειλεν** aor. ind. act. ἐξανατέλλω (# 1984) to spring up. **ἔχειν** (# 2400) pres. act. inf. ἔχω. Inf. used w. prep. διά (# 1328) to express cause. ◆ **6 ἀνατείλαντος** aor. act. part. (temp.) ἀνατέλλω (# 422) to rise (used of the sun). Gen. abs. **ἐκαυματίσθη** aor. ind. pass. καυματίζω (# 3009) to burn, to scorch. **ἐξηράνθη** aor. ind. pass. ξηραίνω (# 3830) to dry, to dry out, to become dry, to wither. ◆ **7 ἀκάνθας** (# 180) acc. pl. thorns. (PB, 153-67; FFB, 184-86) **ἀνέβησαν** aor. ind. act. ἀναβαίνω (# 326) to come up. **ἔπνιξαν** aor. ind. act. πνίγω (# 4464) to choke, to choke off; an effective aor. (RWP). ◆ **8 ἐδίδου** impf. ind. act. δίδωμι (# 1443) to give, yield. ◆ **9 ὦτα** acc. pl. οὖς, ὠτός (# 4044) ear. **ἀκουέτω** pres. imp. act. 3rd. pers. sing. ἀκούω (# 201) to hear. Pres. imp. in a specific command, emphasizing the process: "pay careful attention" (VANT, 365). ◆ **10 προσελθόντες** aor. act. part. (temp.) nom. masc. pl. προσέρχομαι (# 4665) to come to. **εἶπαν** aor. ind. act. λέγω (# 3306) to say. **λαλεῖς** pres. ind. act. λαλέω (# 3281) to speak. Hist. pres. ◆ **11 ἀποκριθείς** aor. pass. (dep.) part. ἀποκρίνομαι (# 646) to answer (s. 3:15). **δέδοται** perf. ind. pass. δίδωμι (# 1443) to give. Theol. pass. **γνῶναι** aor. act. inf. γινώσκω (# 1182) to know. Inf. describes the content of the vb. "to know." ◆ **12 δοθήσεται** fut. ind. pass. δίδωμι (# 1443) to give. **περισσευθήσεται** fut. ind. pass. περισσεύω (# 4355) to be more than enough, to be extremely rich or abundant. **ἀρθήσεται** fut. ind. pass. αἴρω (# 149) to take away. Theol. pass. ◆ **13 ὅτι** (# 4022) because. **βλέποντες** pres. act. part. βλέπω (# 1063) to see. **ἀκούοντες** pres. act. part. ἀκούω (# 201) to hear. The parts. refer to the Heb. inf. abs. (which strengthens the main vb.) as used in the quotation from Isa. 6:9, 10; s. Acts 28:26-27. **συνίουσιν** pres. ind act. συνίημι (# 5317) to gain insight, to comprehend, to understand (BAGD). ◆ **14 ἀναπληροῦται** pres. ind. pass. ἀναπληρόω to (# 405) fulfill; either "is being fulfilled" (Allen) or an aoristic pres. (RWP). Ind. points to an actual fact (Hagner). **λέγουσα** pres. act. part. fem. λέγω (# 3306) to say. **ἀκοῇ** (# 198) dat. sing. hearing, that which is heard, report, rumor. Cognate dat. used to translate the Heb. inf. abs. (BD, 106; BG, 128). **συνῆτε** aor. subj. act. s.v. 13. **βλέψετε** fut. ind. act. s.v. 13. **ἴδητε** aor. subj. act. ὁράω (# 3972) to see. ◆ **15 ἐπαχύνθη** aor. ind. pass. παχύνω (# 4266) to make fat, to make dull; pass. to become dull, to be insensitive (TDNT). **βαρέως** (# 977) adv., heavy. **ἤκουσαν** aor. ind. act. s.v. 13. **ἐκάμμυσαν** aor. ind. act. καμμύω (# 2826) to shut (fr. καταμύω "to shut down" RWP). **μήποτε** (# 3607) w. subj., lest, expressing neg. purp. **ἴδωσιν** aor. subj. act. s.v. 14. **ἀκούσωσιν** aor. subj. act. s.v. 13 **συνῶσιν** aor. subj. act. s.v. 13. **ἐπιστρέψωσιν** aor. subj. act. ἐπιστρέφω (# 2188) to turn about, to return. **ἰάσομαι** fut. ind. mid. (dep.) ἰάομαι (# 2615) to heal (GLH). ◆ **16 ὑμῶν** gen. pl., "your," emphatic, contrasted w. those (αὐτοῖς) described in v. 14 (McNeile). ◆ **17 ἐπεθύμησαν** aor. ind. act. ἐπιθυμέω (# 2121) to desire, to long for. **ἰδεῖν** aor. act. inf. s.v. 14. Inf. used as obj. **εἶδαν** aor. ind. act. s.v. 15. **ἀκοῦσαι** aor. act. inf. s.v. 13. **ἤκουσαν** aor. ind. act. ◆ **18 ὑμεῖς** nom. pl. "you"; emphatic standing in contrast to those who have rejected the teaching. **ἀκούσατε** aor. imp. act. s.v. 13. **σπείραντος** aor. act. part. s.v. 3. Part. as a subst. ◆ **19 ἀκούοντος** pres. act. part. (temp.) gen. abs. "While everyone is listening" (RWP). For the construction of the part. often considered as a Hebraic influence, casus pendens s. MH, 423-25. **συνιέντος** pres. act. part. συνίημι (# 5317) to comprehend, to understand. For the interpretation of this parable emphasizing the hearing and obeying of God's word in the light of Deut. 6:4-5 s. B. Gerhardsson, "The Parable of the Sower and its Interpretation," *NTS* 14 (1968): 165-93. **ἁρπάζει** pres. ind. act. ἁρπάζω (# 773) to snatch, to rob, to plunder. **ἐσπαρμένον** perf. pass. part. s.v. 3. **οὗτος** this, this one. Refers to the pers., not the seed (McNeile). **σπαρείς** aor. pass. part. s.v. 3. ◆ **20 ἀκούων** pres. act. part. s.v. 13; part. used as a subst. **λαμβάνων** pres. act. part. λαμβάνω (# 3284) to receive, to accept. Both parts. have one definite art. referring to the same person. ◆ **21 ἑαυτῷ** (# 1571) dat. refl. pron. in itself. **πρόσκαιρός** (# 4672) lasting for a time, temporary. **γενομένης** aor. mid. (dep.) part. (temp.) γίνομαι (# 1181) to become, to happen. Gen. abs. **θλίψεως** gen. sing. θλίψις (# 2568) pressure, tribulation (Trench, *Synonyms*, 292-304). **ἤ**

(# 2445) or. **σκανδαλίζεται** pres. ind. pass. σκανδαλίζω (# 4997) to cause to stumble, to cause to fall, to be tempted, to be caused to sin (BAGD).　◆ **22 σπαρείς** aor. pass. part. s.v. 3. **μέριμνα** (# 3533) care, concern, "worldly concerns and interest" (Hill). **ἀπάτη** (# 573) deceitfulness or pleasure (MM). **πλούτου** gen. sing. πλοῦτος (# 4458) riches; wealth (DJG, 705). Subj. gen. "riches which deceive." **συμπνίγει** pres. ind. act. συμπνίγω (# 5231) to choke, lit. "to choke together." For the perfectivizing prep. w. the vb. s. MH, 325f. **ἄκαρπος** (# 182) unfruitful.　◆ **23 συνιείς** pres. act. part. s.v. 13. **δή** a strengthening particle: "in reality" (EGT). **καρποφορεῖ** pres. ind. act. καρποφορέω (# 2844) to bring forth fruit, to produce. **ποιεῖ** pres. ind. act. ποιέω (# 4472) to do, to make, to produce.　◆ **24 παρέθηκεν** aor. ind. act. παρατίθημι (# 4192) to place along side, to put before. **ὁμοιώθη** aor. ind. pass. ὁμοιόω (# 3929) to compare. The pass. may be dep. and reflect the Aramaic formula to introduce a parable: "concerning the Kingdom of Heaven, it is as in the case of ..." (BG, 22; DA; DJG, 417-30). A timeless aor. (VA, 130, 234), or has a present stative meaning (VANT, 268, 280). **σπείραντι** aor. act. part. dat. sing. σπείρω (# 5062) to sow.　◆ **25 καθεύδειν** pres. act. inf. καθεύδω (# 2761) to sleep. Used w. dat. and the prep. **ἐν** (# 1877) to express contemporary time ("while"). **ἦλθεν** aor. ind. act. ἔρχομαι s.v. 4. **ἐπέσπειρεν** aor. ind. act. ἐπισπείρω (# 2178) to sow upon, to sow afterward, to resow (MM). **ζιζάνιον** (# 2429) a poisonous weed (possibly *Iloium* [*temulentum*]; or *Cephalaria syriaca*) which is related to wheat and in the early stages of growth is hard to distinguish from it (J. Jeremias, *The Parables of Jesus*, 224; FFB, 194-95; esp. PB, 161; BBC). **ἀνὰ μέσον** among, in the midst of, between (BAGD). **ἀπῆλθεν** aor. ind. act. ἀπέρχομαι (# 599) to go away.　◆ **26 ἐβλάστησεν** aor. ind. act. βλαστάνω (# 1506) to sprout, to put forth. **χόρτος** (# 5965) grass. **ἐποίησεν** aor. ind. act. s.v. 23. **ἐφάνη** aor. ind. pass. φαίνω (# 5743) pass. to appear, to become visible.　◆ **27 προσελθόντες** aor. act. part. (temp.) s.v. 10. **εἶπον** aor. ind. act. λέγω (# 3306) to say. **οὐχί** (# 4049) used in questions which expect a positive answer: "Isn't it so?" **ἔσπειρας** aor. ind. act. s.v. 3. **πόθεν** (# 4470) where? from where?　◆ **28 ἔφη** 3rd. pers. sing. of impf. ind. act. or 2nd. aor. ind. act. φημί (# 5774) to say (BAGD). **θέλεις** pres. ind. act. θέλω (# 2527) to wish, to want. For this word used to introduce a question w. the deliberative subj. s. BD, 185. **ἀπελθόντες** aor. act. part. (circum.) ἀπέρχομαι (# 599) to go out. **συλλέξωμεν** aor. subj. act. συλλέγω (# 5198) to bring together, to collect, to gather up. A deliberative subj. "shall we gather" (RG, 934).　◆ **29 φησιν** pres. ind. act. 3rd. pers. sing. s.v. 28. **μήποτε** (# 3607) lest, used to express apprehension (BD, 188). **συλλέγοντες** pres. act. part. (temp.) s.v. 28, contemporaneous action. **ἐκριζώσητε** aor. subj. act. ἐκριζόω (# 1748) to up-

root, to pull out by the roots.　◆ **30 ἄφετε** aor. imp. act. ἀφίημι (# 918) to leave, to leave alone. Aor. imp. used of a specific act. **συναυξάνεσθαι** pres. mid. inf. συναυξάνω (# 5277) to grow, to grow together. Inf. obj. of vb. **ἀμφότερα** (# 317) acc. pl. n., both. **ἐρῶ** fut. ind. act. λέγω (# 3306). **θερισταῖς** dat. pl. θεριστής (# 2547) harvester; the ending indicates the agent (MH, 365). **συλλέξατε** aor. imp. act. s.v. 28. **δήσατε** aor. imp. act. δέω (# 1313) to bind. **κατακαῦσαι** aor. act. inf. κατακαίω (# 2876) to burn up. The prep. in the vb. is perfective: not just "to burn," but "to burn up." Inf. w. **πρός** (# 4639) expresses purp. **συναγάγετε** aor. imp. act. συνάγω (# 5251) to gather together. **ἀποθήκη** (# 630) storage room, barn.　◆ **31 παρέθηκεν** aor. ind. act. s.v. 24. **κόκκῳ** dat. sing. κόκκος (# 3133) grain, a single grain. Dat. w. adj. like, similar. **σινάπεως** gen sing. σίναπι (# 4983) mustard, popularly viewed as the smallest of all seeds and planted in the field rather than in a garden (BAGD; SB, 1:668-69; PB, 93; FFB, 145-46). **λαβών** aor. act. part. s.v. 20. **ἔσπειρεν** aor. ind. act. s.v. 3.　◆ **32 ὅ** (# 4005) which, refers to grain, but n. by attraction (EGT). **μικρότερον** comp. μικρός (# 3625) small. **σπερμάτων** gen. pl. σπέρμα (# 5065) seed. Gen. of comp. The mustard seed is often used in rabbinic sources to describe something of minute size (Lachs, 225). **αὐξηθῇ** aor. subj. pass. αὐξάνομαι (# 889) to grow. Subj. w. **ὅταν** (# 4020) used in an indef. temp. cl. **μεῖζον** (# 3505) comp. μέγας large, great. **λαχάνων** gen. pl. λάχανον (# 3303) an edible plant, vegetable. gen. of comp. **ἐλθεῖν** aor. act. inf. ἔρχομαι (# 2262) to come. Inf. w. **ὥστε** (# 6063) expressing result. **κατασκηνοῦν** pres. act. inf. κατασκηνόω (# 2942) to live, to inhabit. Inf. expressing result.　◆ **33 ἐλάλησεν** aor. ind. act. s.v. 3. **ζύμη** (# 2434) dat. sing. leaven; dat. w. the adj. In this case it refers to old, fermented dough (DA). In Jewish imagery leaven refers to what is unclean or evil (Hill; DA; SB, 1:727-29; TDNT). **λαβοῦσα** aor. act. part. (circum.) fem. sing. λαμβάνω (# 3284) to take. **ἐνέκρυψεν** aor. ind. act. ἐνκρύπτω (# 1606) to hide, to conceal in. **ἀλεύρου** (# 236) gen. sing. wheat flour. **σάτα** (# 4929) n. acc. pl. σάτον seah. A Heb. measure of grain containing about a peck and a half (BAGD; SB, 1:670; ABD, 6:903; EBC, 1:610). This would be enough bread for 100 people (France). It is reported that the Greeks used 2/3 of an ounce of leaven for two half-pecks of flour, but for barley it was 2 pounds of leaven for every two and a half of barley (Pliny, NH, 18:103-4). **ἕως οὗ** until (BAGD). **ἐζυμώθη** aor. ind. pass. ζυμόω (# 2435) to ferment, to leaven.　◆ **34 ἐλάλει** impf. ind. act. λαλέω (# 3281) to speak. Impf. points to a regular practice, not merely to a single occasion (EGT).　◆ **35 πληρωθῇ** aor. subj. pass. πληρόω (# 4444) to fill, to fulfill. Subj. to express purp. s. Matt. 1:22. **ῥηθέν** aor. pass. part. λέγω (# 3306) to say. Part. used as subst., "that which was spoken." **ἀνοίξω** fut. ind. act. ἀνοίγω (# 487) to open. **ἐρεύξομαι** fut. ind.

mid. (dep.) ἐρεύγομαι (# 2243) to spew out, to bellow, to roar, to speak out loud, to utter (AS). **κεκρυμμένα** perf. pass. part. κρύπτω (# 3221) to hide. Perf. points to the state or cond., "that which was hidden." ◆ **36 ἀφείς** aor. act. part. (temp.) ἀφίημι (# 918) to dismiss, send away. **ἦλθεν** aor. ind. act. s.v. 25. **προσῆλθον** aor. ind. act. προσέρχομαι (# 4665) to come to. **διασάφησον** aor. imp. act. διασαφέω (# 1397) to explain, to make an obscurity clear by a thorough explanation (LN, 1:405); "make thoroughly clear right now" (RWP). ◆ **37 εἶπεν** aor. ind. act. λέγω (# 3306) to say. (For the construction s. Matt. 3:15.) ◆ **38 πονηροῦ** (# 4505) gen. sing. evil. "The sons of the evil one" = "those whose character is evil" (McNeile). ◆ **39 σπείρας** aor. act. part. s.v. 3. **συντέλεια** (# 5333) completion. (For "Completion of the Age" in Jewish apocalyptic lit. s. DA; SB, 1:671). ◆ **40 συλλέγεται** pres. ind. pass. s.v. 28. **πυρί** dat. sing. πῦρ, πυρός (# 4786) fire, instr. dat. **κατακαίεται** pres. ind. pass. s.v. 30. **ἔσται** fut. ind. mid. (dep.) εἰμί (# 1639). ◆ **41 ἀποστελεῖ** fut. ind. act. ἀποστέλλω (# 690) to send. **συλλέξουσιν** fut. ind. act. s.v. 28. **σκάνδαλα** (# 4998) acc. n. pl. the stick in a trap, the trap itself, the cause or occasion of stumbling. Here used of persons, "the devil's children," who work against God and try to cause as many as possible to fall (TDNT). **ποιοῦντας** pres. act. part. masc. acc. pl. s.v. 23. Vb. used w. subst. to express the verbal meaning; "to do lawlessness" = "to work lawlessness." ◆ **42 βαλοῦσιν** fut. ind. act. βάλλω (# 965) to throw, to cast. **κάμινος** (# 2825) furnace (BBC). **κλαυθμός** (# 3088) loud crying, weeping. **βρυγμός** (# 1106) gnashing, grinding. **ὀδόντων** gen. pl. ὀδούς, ὀδόντος (# 3848) tooth. "The gnashing of teeth" is used as an expression of anger and frustration of the damned (SB, 1:673). ◆ **43 ἐκλάμψουσιν** fut. ind. act. ἐκλάμπω (# 1719) to shine out, to shine forth, suggestive of the sun emerging from behind the cloud (EGT). ◆ **44 θησαυρῷ** dat. sing. θησαυρός (# 2565) treasure, treasure chest. Dat. w. adj. **κεκρυμμένῳ** perf. pass. part. κρύπτω (# 3221) to hide. It was common for people to bury valuables in the ground, esp. in dangerous times (DA; Jos., JW, 7:113). **εὑρών** aor. act. part. εὑρίσκω (# 2351) to find. For the Jewish Law regarding the finding and acquisition of a treasure s. LNT, 6-15. **ἔκρυψεν** aor. ind. act. κρύπτω (# 3221) to hide. **ἀπό** for, because of (for the causal use s. BD, 113). **ὑπάγει** pres. ind. act. ὑπάγω (# 5632) to go out. **πωλεῖ** pres. ind. act. πωλέω (# 4797) to sell. The point of the parable seems to be the determination to acquire the treasure (Luz). **ἀγοράζει** pres. ind. act. ἀγοράζω (# 60) to buy. The vbs. here are hist. pres. ◆ **45 ἐμπόρῳ** (# 1867) dat. sing. merchant. A wholesale dealer in contrast to a retailer (EDNT). Dat. w. adj. **ζητοῦντι** pres. act. part. dat. sing. ζητέω (# 2426) to seek, to look for. **μαργαρίτης** (# 3449) pearl. For a discussion of pearls in the ancient world s. 1 Tim. 2:9; DA. ◆ **46 εὑρών** aor. act. part. (temp.) s.v.

44. ἀπελθών aor. act. part. (temp.) ἀπέρχομαι (# 599) to go out. **πέπρακεν** perf. ind. act. πιπράσκω (# 4405) to sell. Perhaps an example of the aoristic perf., though the word has no aor. form (M, 142-45; MKG, 265; Luz). **εἶχεν** impf. ind. act. ἔχω (# 2400) to have, to possess. **ἠγόρασεν** aor. ind. act. ἀγοράζω (# 601) s.v. 44. ◆ **47 σαγήνη** (# 4880) dat. sing. dragnet, the long drawn-net or sweep-net. They are open to include a large extent of the sea, then drawn together and all which they contain is enclosed (Trench, *Synonyms*, 236). Dat. w. adj. **βληθείσῃ** aor. pass. part. fem. dat. sing. βάλλω (# 965) to cast. **γένους** gen. sing. γένος (# 1169) kind, sort, species (s. Jos., JW, 3:508). **συναγαγούσῃ** aor. act. part. fem. dat. sing. s.v. 2. ◆ **48 ἐπληρώθη** aor. ind. pass. s.v. 35. **ἀναβιβάσαντες** aor. act. part. (temp.) ἀναβιβάζω (# 328) to bring up, to pull up. The prep. in the vb. is a local (M, 295). **αἰγιαλός** (# 129) shore, beach. **καθίσαντες** aor. act. part. (temp.) καθίζω (# 2767) to sit, to take one's seat. **συνέλεξαν** aor. ind. act. s.v. 28. **ἄγγη** acc. pl. n. ἄγγος (# 35) vessel, container. **σαπρά** acc. pl. n. σαπρός (# 4911) worthless, unsuitable for eating (Hill). **ἔβαλον** aor. ind. act. βάλλω (# 965) to throw. ◆ **49 ἐξελεύσονται** fut. ind. mid. (dep.) ἐξέρχομαι (# 2002) to go out. **ἀφοριοῦσιν** fut. ind. act. ἀφορίζω (# 928) to separate, to set apart. ◆ **50 βαλοῦσιν** fut. ind. act. s.v. 42. ◆ **51 συνήκατε** aor. ind. act. συνίημι (# 5317) s.v. 13. **λέγουσιν** pres. ind. act. λέγω (# 3306) hist. pres. ◆ **52 μαθητευθείς** aor. pass. part. μαθητεύω (# 3411) to make a disciple, to be a disciple; pass. "to be discipled, to be instructed" (McNeile; Gundry; TDNT). Every scribe who is truly a disciple has been instructed (CDMG, 160-61). **βασιλείᾳ** (# 993) kingdom; dat. of reference "w. respect to the kingdom" (Hill; DM, 85). **καινά** n. pl. καινός (# 2785) new. It may refer to that which was not previously well known but significant (LN, 1:338). **παλαιά** n. pl. παλαιός (# 4094) old. It may refer to that which has existed continuously for a relatively long time (LN, 1:642; for various views as to the meaning s. DA). ◆ **53 ἐγένετο** aor. ind. mid. (dep.) γίνομαι s.v. 21. **ἐτέλεσεν** aor. ind. act. τελέω (# 5464) to end, to complete. **μετῆρεν** aor. ind. act. μεταίρω (# 3558) to change one's position, to depart (MM). ◆ **54 ἐλθών** aor. act. part. (temp.) ἔρχομαι (# 2262) to come. **πατρίδα** acc. sing. πατρίς (# 4258) fatherland, country, native place. **ἐδίδασκεν** impf. ind. act. διδάσκω (# 1438) to teach. Impf. may be incep.: "he began to teach," or it may suggest more than one occasion (Filson). **ἐκπλήσσεσθαι** pres. pass. inf. ἐκπλήσσω (# 1742) to amaze, to astound; pass. to be amazed, to be overwhelmed. Inf. used w. **ὥστε** (# 6063) to express results. ◆ **55 οὗτος** (# 4047) this one, this fellow; used contemptuously (Tasker). **τέκτονος** gen. sing. τέκτων (# 5454) carpenter, woodworker, builder (BAGD). The art. "the" w. carpenter indicates possibly that He was the only one in

the town, well-known to all (EGT). ◆ **57** ἐσκανδαλίζοντο impf. ind. pass. σκανδαλίζω (# 4997) pass. to be
offended, the opposite of "to believe in him." They refused to believe in Him (TDNT). ἄτιμος (# 872) without honor. ◆ **58** ἐποίησεν aor. ind. act. s.v. 23. ἀπιστία
(# 602) unbelief.

Matthew 14

◆ **1** ἤκουσεν aor. ind. act. ἀκούω (# 201) to hear.
τετραάρχης (# 5490) tetrarch, ruler over a quarter of a
region. The term was used to describe a petty ruler
(DA; HJPE, 1:334; KP, 5:632-33). For its use in Josephus
s. CCFJ, 4:181. For a study of Herod Antipas s. HA; TJ,
45-51; BBC; DJG, 322-25. ◆ **2** εἶπεν aor. ind. act. λέγω
(# 3306) to say. παισίν dat. pl. παῖς (# 4090) children,
servants, the courtiers (RWP). αὐτός he (emphatic), indicating the terror-stricken conscious (Meyer). Antipas feared not only the moral message of John, but he
also feared the political results of his preaching (Jos.,
Ant. 18:118; TJ, 63). ἠγέρθη aor. ind. pass. ἐγείρω
(# 1586) to awake; pass. to be raised. ἐνεργοῦσιν pres.
ind. act. ἐνεργέω (# 1919) to be at work in, to be operative in, to energize. Pres. emphasizes the continual activity. ◆ **3** κρατήσας aor. act. part. (circum.) κρατέω
(# 3195) to seize, to arrest. ἔδησεν aor. ind. act. δέω
(# 1313) to bind. ἀπέθετο aor. ind. mid. (dep.) ἀποτίθημι to put away. Prep. in the vb. has local force (M,
297f). John was imprisoned at the fortress Machaerus
on the east side of the Jordan (Jos., *Ant.* 18:119; TJ, 63).
◆ **4** ἔλεγεν impf. ind. act. s.v. 2. Impf. implies a repeated rebuke (McNeile). ἔξεστιν pres. ind. act. ἔξεστι
(# 2003) it is lawful, it is allowed. Followed by inf.
ἔχειν. Here "to have" is used in a marital or sexual
sense (DJG, 323). ◆ **5** θέλων pres. act. part. θέλω
(# 2527) to wish, to will, to want. Concess. part. "although he desired." ἀποκτεῖναι aor. act. inf. ἀποκτείνω
(# 650) to kill. ἐφοβήθη aor. ind. pass. (dep.) φοβέομαι
(# 5828) to fear. εἶχον impf. ind. act. ἔχω (# 2400) to
have, to consider, to look upon, to view (BAGD).
◆ **6** γενεσίοις dat. pl. γενέσια (# 1160) birthday celebration (RAC, 9:217-43; SB, 1:680-82). γενομένοις aor. mid.
(dep.) part. dat. pl. γίνομαι (# 1181) to become, to happen. Dat. is either a dat. abs. or a temp. dat. (IBG, 44-
45). ὠρχήσατο aor. ind. mid. (dep.) ὀρχέομαι (# 4004) to
dance, to represent by pantomime (LS, 1258; s. DGRA,
1004-1006; SB, 1:682). ἤρεσεν aor. ind. act. ἀρέσκω
(# 743) to please, to be pleasing to someone. ◆ **7** ὅθεν
(# 3854) from where (causal), because. ὡμολόγησεν aor.
ind. act. ὁμολογέω (# 3933) to confess on oath, to promise. This was an oath to do something, not a judicial
act. S also J.D.M. Derrett, "Herod's Oath and the Baptist's Head," *BZ* NF 9 (1965): 49-59, 233-46. δοῦναι aor.
act. inf. δίδωμι (# 1143) to give. Inf. gives the content of
the promise. αἰτήσηται aor. subj. mid. αἰτέω (# 160) to
ask, to request; mid. "to ask for oneself." ◆ **8** προ-

βιβασθεῖσα aor. pass. part. nom. fem. sing. προβιβάζω
(# 4586) to bring forward, to bring to the point, give
instructions (McNeile; BAGD). δός aor. imp. act. 2nd.
pers. sing. δίδωμι (# 1443). Aor. imp. used in a specific
request. φησίν pres. ind. act. φημί (# 5774) to say. Hist.
pres. πίνακι dat. sing. πίναξ (# 4402) a board, plank,
anything flat like a table or plate, dish (Hill; Harrington). ◆ **9** λυπηθείς aor. pass. part. λυπέω (# 3382)
to grieve, to pain; pass. become sad, sorrowful, distressed (BAGD). Concessive (although) or circum.
part. Ingressive aor. "becoming...." συνανακειμένους
pres. mid. (dep.) part. συνανάκειμαι (# 5263) to recline
together at the table. For the influence of the guest on
Antipas fulfilling his oath s. LNT, 352-55. ἐκέλευσεν
aor. ind. act. κελεύω (# 3027) to command, to order.
δοθῆναι aor. pass. inf. δίδωμι (# 1443). Inf. after a vb. of
commanding. ◆ **10** πέμψας aor. act. part. (circum.)
πέμπω (# 4287) to send. ἀπεκεφάλισεν aor. ind. act.
ἀποκεφαλίζω (# 642) to behead. For the death penalty
in Judaism s. SB, 1: 261-270; for beheading s. M, Sanh.
7. 1. For the death and circumstances surrounding
John's death s. DJG, 388-89. ◆ **11** ἠνέχθη aor. ind. pass.
φέρω (# 5770) to carry, to bring. ἐδόθη aor. ind. pass.
δίδωμι (# 1443) to give. κοράσιον (# 3166) girl. The dimin. "little girl" (Hill). She was probably about 12-14
years old (HA, 154-56). ἤνεγκεν aor. ind. act. φέρω
(# 5770) to carry (SB, 1:683). ◆ **12** προσελθόντες aor.
act. part. (circum.) προσέρχομαι (# 4665) to come to.
ἦραν aor. ind. act. αἴρω (# 149) to lift up, to carry away.
πτῶμα (# 4773) body, corpse. ἔθαψαν aor. ind. act.
θάπτω (# 2507) to bury. ἐλθόντες aor. act. part. (circum.) ἔρχομαι (# 2262) to come, to go. ἀπήγγειλαν aor.
ind. act. ἀπαγγέλλω (# 550) to report, to announce.
◆ **13** ἀκούσας aor. act. part. (temp.) ἀκούω (# 201) to
hear. "After he heard." ἀνεχώρησεν aor. ind. act.
ἀναχωρέω (# 432) to go away, to withdraw, to retire.
κατ' ἰδίαν (# 2848; 2625) for oneself, privately. ἠκολούθησαν aor. ind. act. ἀκολουθέω (# 199) to follow (w.
dat). πεζῇ (# 4270) by foot, by land (DA). ◆ **14** ἐξελθών aor. act. part. (temp.) ἐξέρχομαι (# 2002) to go
out; that is, disembark (Tasker). εἶδεν aor. ind. act.
ὁράω (# 3972) to see. ἐσπλαγχνίσθη aor. ind. pass. (dep.)
σπλαγχνίζομαι (# 5072) to pity, to have compassion on
(TLNT; s. Matt. 9:36). ἐθεράπευσεν aor. ind. act. θεραπεύω (# 2543) to heal. ἄρρωστος (# 779) without
strength, sick. ◆ **15** ὄψιος (# 4070) evening. γενομένης
aor. mid. (dep.) part. γίνομαι (# 1181) Gen. abs.
προσῆλθον aor. ind. act. s.v. 12. λέγοντες pres. act. part.
(circum.) λέγω (# 3306) to say. ὥρα hour, the hour for
the customary meal (Allen). παρῆλθεν (# 3306) aor. ind.
act. παρέρχομαι (# 4216) to go by, to pass. ἀπόλυσον aor.
imp. act. ἀπολύω (# 668) to dismiss, to send away. Aor.
imp. of a specific act. ἀπελθόντες aor. act. part. (circum.) ἀπέρχομαι (# 599) to go away. ἀγοράσωσιν aor.
subj. act. ἀγοράζω (# 60) to buy; subj. used to express

purp. ἑαυτοῖς (# 1571) dat. pl. refl. pron. 3rd. pers. Dat. of personal interest: "for themselves." ◆ 16 ἀπελθεῖν aor. act. inf. ἀπέρχομαι (# 599) to go away, epex. inf. explaining the need (IBG, 127). δότε aor. imp. act. δίδωμι (# 1443) to give. Aor. imp. used of a specific act. ὑμεῖς you (emphatic) stands in contrast w. their "send away" (RWP). φαγεῖν aor. act. inf. ἐσθίω (# 2266) to eat. ◆ 17 εἰ μή (# 1623; 3590) except. ἰχθύας acc. pl. ἰχθύς (# 2716) fish. Bread and fish form the basic diet of the poor of Galilee (Hill; DA; SB, 1:683-84). ◆ 18 εἶπεν aor. ind. act. λέγω (# 3306) to say. φέρετε pres. imp. act. φέρω (# 5770) to carry, to bring. ◆ 19 κελεύσας aor. act. part. κελεύω (# 3027) to command, generally designates verbal orders from a superior (Thayer). Temp. or circum. part. ἀνακλιθῆναι aor. pass. inf. ἀνακλίνω (# 369) to lay down; pass. to lie down, to sit down, to take one's place (at table) (Hill). λαβών aor. act. part. λαμβάνω (# 3284) to take. Temp. or circum. part. ἀναβλέψας aor. act. part. ἀναβλέπω (# 329) to look up. An outward sign of an inward dependence (DA). Temp. or circum. part. εὐλόγησεν aor. ind. act. εὐλογέω (# 2328) to bless, to express praise and thanks. It was customary to pray at the beginning of the meals and at the end as an expression of dependence on God for all man's needs and of gratitude for His constant goodness (Moore, *Judaism*, 2:216f; SB, 1:685f; M, Berakoth, 6-8). κλάσας aor. act. part. (temp.) κλάω (# 3089) to break. ἔδωκεν aor. ind. act. δίδωμι (# 1443) to give. ◆ 20 ἔφαγον aor. ind. act. ἐσθίω (# 2266) to eat. ἐχορτάσθησαν aor. ind. pass. χορτάζω (# 5963) to satisfy; pass. to be satisfied, to be filled; an effective aor., "to be completely satisfied" (RWP; Hagner). ἦραν aor. ind. act. αἴρω (# 149) to take up, to pick up. περισσεῦον pres. act. part. περισσεύω (# 4355) to exceed or remain over, to abound, to be in abundance. Part. used as subst. κοφίνος (# 3186) basket, probably a large, heavy basket for carrying things (BAGD; DA). ◆ 21 ἐσθίοντες pres. act. part. masc. nom. pl. s.v. 20. ἦσαν impf. ind. act. εἰμί (# 1639) to be. ὡσεί (# 6059) (w. numbers) about. χωρίς (# 6006) without, here, besides (DA). ◆ 22 ἠνάγκασεν aor. ind. act. ἀναγκάζω (# 337) to compel, to force, to urge strongly (BAGD; DA). ἐμβῆναι aor. act. inf. ἐμβαίνω (# 1832) to embark. Inf. gives the content of the compelling. προάγειν pres. act. inf. προάγω (# 4575) to go before. πέραν (# 4305) the other side. For the geographical problem s. Carson, 343. ἕως οὗ (# 2401; 4005) until, while (DA). ἀπολύσῃ aor. subj. act. ἀπολύω (# 668) to dismiss. ◆ 23 ἀπολύσας aor. act. part. (temp.) "after." ἀνέβη aor. ind. act. ἀναβαίνω (# 326) to go up. ὄρος (# 4001) mountain; here, hill country (AM). προσεύξασθαι aor. mid. (dep.) inf. προσεύχομαι (# 4667) to pray; inf. used to express purp. γενομένης aor. mid. (dep.) part. (temp.) γίνομαι (# 1181). ἦν impf. ind. act. εἰμί s.v. 21. ◆ 24 σταδίους acc. pl. στάδιον (# 5084) stade, about 600 feet (Filson; EBC, 1:611; ABD, 6:901). Acc.

of space. For the textual problem s. TC, 37; DA. ἀπεῖχεν impf. ind. act. ἀπέχω (# 600) to be distant, to be away. βασανιζόμενον pres. pass. part. βασανίζω (# 989) to torture, to torment, to harass (harassed by the waves, BAGD). κυμάτων gen. pl. κῦμα (# 3246) wave. ἄνεμος (# 449) wind. ◆ 25 τετάρτη...φυλακῇ dat. sing. the fourth watch, between 3 and 6 A.M. The Romans divided the night into four watches of three hours each, beginning at 6 P.M. (Tasker; Hendriksen). Dat. of time expressing a point of time (MT, 243). ἦλθεν aor. ind. act. ἔρχομαι (# 2262). περιπατῶν pres. act. part. περιπατέω (# 4344) to walk. Part. of manner: "he came walking." ◆ 26 ἰδόντες aor. act. part. (temp.) masc. nom. pl. ὁράω (# 3972) to see. "When they saw...." περιπατοῦντα pres. act. part. acc. sing. s.v. 25. ἐταράχθησαν aor. ind. pass. ταράσσω (# 5429) to be terrified. ὅτι (# 4022) used to indicate quotation marks in direct speech, recitative. φάντασμά (# 5753) appearance, apparition, ghost. ἔκραξαν aor. ind. act. κράζω (# 3189) to cry out, to scream. ◆ 27 ἐλάλησεν aor. ind. act. λαλέω (# 3281) to speak. θαρσεῖτε pres. imp. act. θαρσέω (# 2510) to be cheerful, to have courage, to have confidence and firmness of purp. in the face of danger (LN, 1:306). φοβεῖσθε pres. imp. mid. (dep.) φοβέομαι (# 5828) to be afraid. Pres. imp. w. the neg. μή (# 3590) indicates that an action in progress should discontinue (Bakker, 35ff; MKG, 247). ◆ 28 ἀποκριθείς aor. pass. (dep.) part. ἀποκρίνομαι (# 646) to answer. εἶπεν aor. ind. act. λέγω (# 3306). εἶ pres. ind. act. εἰμί (# 1639) to be. Ind. used in a first class cond. cl., assuming the reality of the cond. κέλευσον aor. imp. act. κελεύω (# 3027) to command. Generally followed by the aor. inf. w. the one receiving the order in the acc. (BAGD). ἐλθεῖν aor. act. inf. ἔρχομαι (# 2262). Inf. in indir. discourse. ◆ 29 ἐλθέ aor. imp. act. 2nd. pers. sing. ἔρχομαι. Aor. imp. used in a specific command (VANT, 345). καταβάς aor. act. part. (circum.) καταβαίνω (# 2849) to disembark, to go down. περιεπάτησεν aor. ind. act. περιπατέω (# 4344) to walk. That Peter walked on the water at Jesus' command indicates that Jesus had divine authority (DA). ◆ 30 βλέπων pres. act. part. (temp.) βλέπω (# 1063) to see. Expressing contemporaneous action. ἐφοβήθη aor. ind. pass. (dep.) φοβέομαι (# 5828) to be afraid. Ingressive aor.: "he became afraid." ἀρξάμενος aor. mid. (dep.) part. ἄρχομαι (# 806) to begin. w. inf. Temp. or causal part. καταποντίζεσθαι pres. pass. inf. καταποντίζω (# 2931) to throw into the sea, to drown; pass. to be sunk, to be drowned (BAGD). σῶσον aor. imp. act. σῴζω (# 5392) to rescue, to save. ◆ 31 ἐκτείνας aor. act. part. (circum.) ἐκτείνω to (# 1753) stretch out. ἐπελάβετο aor. ind. mid. (dep.) ἐπιλαμβάνομαι (# 2138) to take hold of, to grasp (w. gen.). ὀλιγόπιστε (# 3899) voc. masc. sing. ὀλιγόπιστος little faith. It is not "no faith," but a "deficiency in faith" (EDNT). εἰς τί (# 1650; 5516) "for what purpose?" "why?" (Carson, 346). ἐδίστασας aor. ind. act. διστάζω (# 1491) to doubt, not to trust (DA). ◆ **32 ἀναβάντων** aor. act. part. ἀναβαίνω (# 326) to go up, to embark. Gen. abs. **ἐκόπασεν** aor. ind. act. κοπάζω (# 3156) to stop, to cease, to rest. ◆ **33 προσεκύνησαν** aor. ind. act. προσκυνέω (# 4686) to fall down and worship. It includes awe and amazement (BBC). ◆ **34 διαπεράσαντες** aor. act. part. διαπεράω (# 1385) to pass over, to cross over. The prep. in the vb. describes the carrying of the action through to a definite result, describing a journey to a goal (M, 301). ◆ **35 ἐπιγνόντες** aor. act. part. (temp.) ἐπιγινώσκω (# 2105) to recognize. **ἀπέστειλαν** aor. ind. act. ἀποστέλλω (# 690) to send. **προσήνεγκαν** aor. ind. act. προσφέρω (# 4712) to bring to, to carry to. **τοὺς κακῶς ἔχοντας** pres. act. part. Subst. part. those having it bad, to be sick. ◆ **36 παρεκάλουν** impf. ind. act. παρακαλέω (# 4151) to ask, to beseech. Impf. indicates the continual asking. **ἅψωνται** aor. subj. mid. (dep.) ἅπτομαι (# 721) to touch (w. gen.) **κράσπεδον** (# 3192) edge, border, hem of a garment; possibly tassel, which the Israelite was obligated to wear on the four corners of his outer garment (BAGD; Lachs, 172; TDNT; SB, 4:276-92). **ἥψαντο** aor. ind. mid. (dep.) ἅπτομαι (# 721). **διεσώθησαν** aor. ind. pass. διασώζω (# 1407) to save, to heal completely. The prep. w. the vb. is perfective indicating a thorough healing (MH, 301f).

Matthew 15

◆ **1 Ἱεροσολύμων** (# 2647) gen. pl. Jerusalem. The rabbis of Jerusalem were held in high esteem and their wisdom was especially praised (SB, 1:691). **Φαρισαῖοι** (# 5757) Pharisees (TJ, 70-76; JPB, 380-451). ◆ **2 παραβαίνουσιν** pres. ind. act. παραβαίνω (# 4124) to transgress. Pres. points to a continual or habitual practice. **παράδοσις** (# 4142) tradition. The body of commentary added to the law and transmitted orally. The scribes and Pharisees regarded it as of equal importance w. the Law. It was later written and codified to form the Mishnah (Hill; Moore, *Judaism*, 1:251-62; SB, 1:691-95; TDNT, 6:661f; TLS, 1-262). **πρεσβύτερος** (# 4565) older, elder; pl. the learned ones (TDNT; DJG, 201-203). **νίπτονται** pres. ind. mid. (dir. mid.) νίπτω (# 3782) to wash. For the custom of hand washing s. M, Yadaim; SB, 1:695-704; LT, 2:10-15. Habitual pres. **ὅταν** (# 4020) w. subj., when, whenever. **ἐσθίωσιν** pres. subj. act. ἐσθίω (# 2266) to eat. ◆ **3 ἀποκριθείς** aor. pass. (dep.) part. ἀποκρίνομαι (# 646) to answer. **καί** also. **διά** (# 1328) w. acc., because of (RWP). **ἐντολή** (# 1953) commandment. Jesus counterattacks–the disciples transgress the unwritten tradition, they transgress God's commandment (Hill). This points to the pointlessness of observing the laws of ritual purity without moral righteousness (DJG, 130). ◆ **4 τίμα** pres. imp. act. τιμάω (# 5506) to honor. **κακολογῶν** pres. act. part.

κακολογέω (# 2800) to speak evil of, to insult. **ἤ** (# 2445) or. **τελευτάτω** pres. imp. act. 3rd. pers. sing. τελευτάω (# 5462) to die. W. the dat. as a translation of the Heb. inf. absolute: "let him surely die" (BG, 21). ◆ **5 ὅς ἄν** (# 4005; 165) w. subj., introduces a rel. cl. which forms the hypothetical cond. of a cond. sentence. **εἴπῃ** aor. subj. act. λέγω (# 3306). **δῶρον** (# 1565) gift, present, a reference to practice of korban in which a man dedicates his property to God and is not obligated to take care of his parents (Hill; M, Nedarim; SB, 1:711-17; J.D.M. Derrett, "KOPBAN, O ΕΣΤΙΝ ΔΩΡΟΝ," *NTS* 16 [1970]: 364-68; Hagner; Luz; s. Mk. 7:11). **ὠφεληθῇς** aor. subj. pass. ὠφελέω (# 6067) to profit, to benefit. ◆ **6 οὐ μή** (# 4024; 3590) not at all, a strong neg. (MT, 96). **τιμήσει** fut. ind. act. s.v. 4. "Need not honor" (BD, 184). **ἠκυρώσατε** aor. ind. act. ἀκυρόω (# 218) to make without authority, to make null and void, used in the papyri in the legal sense to cancel or make void a will or a debt (MM). Aor. looks at the accomplished fact. ◆ **7 ὑποκριταί** voc. pl. ὑποκριτής (# 5695) hypocrite, a legalist who manipulates the law w. casuistry and hair-splitting interpretations for his own benefit (AM, CXV-CXXIII). **ἐπροφήτευσεν** aor. ind. act. προφητεύω (# 4736) to prophesy. ◆ **8 χείλεσίν** dat. pl. χεῖλος (# 5927) lip. Instr. dat. **τιμᾷ** pres. ind. act. s.v. 4. **πόρρω** (# 4522) far, far away. **ἀπέχει** pres. ind. act. ἀπέχω (# 600) to be distant, to be far away. ◆ **9 μάτην** (# 3472) adv. in vain, to no end. **σέβονται** pres. ind. mid. (dep.) σέβομαι (# 4936) to worship; the honoring of God through acts of obedience to His will (NIDNTT; TDNT). **διδάσκοντες** pres. act. part. διδάσκω (# 1438) to teach. Part. of manner showing how the vain worship is being carried out. ◆ **10 προσκαλεσάμενος** aor. mid. (indir. mid.) part. (temp.) προσκαλέω (# 4673) to summon, to call to. **ἀκούετε** pres. imp. act. ἀκούω (# 201) to hear. **συνίετε** pres. imp. act. συνίημι (# 5317) to understand, to comprehend, to employ one's capacity for understanding and thus arrive at insight (LN, 1:380). ◆ **11 εἰσερχόμενον** pres. mid. (dep.) part. εἰσέρχομαι (# 1656) to come in, to go in. Part. used as subst. **κοινοῖ** pres. ind. act. κοινόω (# 3124) to make common, to defile (DJG, 130). **ἐκπορευόμενον** pres. mid. (dep.) part. ἐκπορεύομαι (# 1744) to go out, to go forth. ◆ **12 προσελθόντες** aor. act. part. (temp.) προσέρχομαι (# 4665) to come to. **οἶδας** (# 3857) perf. ind. act. 2nd. pers. sing. to know. Def. perf. w. pres. meaning. **ἀκούσαντες** aor. act. part. (temp.) ἀκούω (# 201) to hear. "When they heard." **ἐσκανδαλίσθησαν** aor. ind. pass. σκανδαλίζω (# 4997) to cause to stumble, indicating deep religious offense at the preaching of Jesus, which causes and includes denial and rejection of Jesus (TDNT). ◆ **13 φυτεία** (# 5884) plant, a cultivated plant (EGT), a figure common among Judaism (SB, 1:720-21) and the Dead Sea community (Hill; Gnilka; 1QS 8:5; 11:8). **ἦν** (# 4005) rel.

pron., which fem. sing. acc. ἐφύτευσεν aor. ind. act. φυτεύω (# 5885) to plant. ἐκριζωθήσεται fut. ind. pass. ἐκριζόω (# 1748) to tear out by the roots. Jesus is saying that the Pharisees were not truly part of God's planting and will be uprooted at the final judgment (Carson, 350; DA; BBC). ◆ 14 ἄφετε aor. imp. act. ἀφίημι (# 918) to leave, to leave alone. ὁδηγός (# 3843) guide. ὁδηγῇ pres. subj. act. ὁδηγέω (# 3842) to lead along the way. Subj. w. ἐάν (# 1569) used in 3rd. class cond. cl. which assumes the possibility of the cond. πεσοῦνται fut. ind. mid. (dep.) πίπτω (# 4406) to fall. ◆ 15 φράσον aor. imp. act. φράζω (# 5851) to explain, to interpret, sometimes w. the implication that the text in question is difficult or complex (LN, 1:405). ◆ 16 ἀκμήν (# 197) adverbial acc., still, places emphasis at the beginning of a sentence: "Even at this crucial juncture, are you without understanding?" (Hill). καί (# 2779) also. ἀσύνετος (# 852) without understanding, not comprehending s.v. 10. ◆ 17 νοεῖτε pres. ind. act. νοέω (# 3783) to comprehend, to understand, to comprehend something on the basis of careful thought and consideration (LN, 1:380). Ind. used in a question expecting the answer "yes." εἰσπορευόμενον pres. mid. (dep.) part. nom. n. sing. εἰσπορεύομαι (# 1660) to go in. Part. used as subst. χωρεῖ pres. ind. act. χωρέω (# 6003) to go out. Gnomic pres. ἀφεδρῶνα acc. sing. ἀφεδρών (# 909) drain, latrine. For sanitary conds. s. Edward Neufeld, "Hygiene Conditions in Ancient Israel," BA 34 (1971): 42-66; DJG, 125-32). ἐκβάλλεται pres. ind. pass. ἐκβάλλω (# 1675) to throw out. Gnomic pres. ◆ 18 κἀκεῖνα = καὶ ἐκεῖνα (# 2797) those things. κοινοῖ pres. ind. act. κοινόω (# 3124) to make common, to defile (BAGD). For a treatment of the laws of purity s. Roger P. Booth, Jesus and the Laws of Purity: Tradition History and Legal History in Mark 7, JSNTSS 13 (Sheffield: JSOT Press, 1986): 117-224. ◆ 19 διαλογισμός (# 1369) disputing, doubts, reason. Perhaps a reference to the evil impulse (DA). πορνεία (# 4518) illicit sexual activity (TDNT). κλοπαί nom. pl. κλοπή (# 3113) theft. βλασφημία (# 1060) slander, blaspheming (DJG, 75-77). For a comparison of the catalogues of sins in the NT and the ancient world s. DCNT, 67-70; DA; Luz. ◆ 20 κοινοῦντα pres. act. part. nom. n. pl. s.v. 18. χερσίν dat. pl. χείρ (# 5931) hand, dat. of means: "with unclean hands." φαγεῖν aor. act. inf. ἐσθίω (# 2266) to eat. Inf. used as noun. Subject of the vb. (BD, 205). ◆ 21 ἐξελθών aor. act. part. (temp.) ἐξέρχομαι (# 2002) to go out. ἀνεχώρησεν aor. ind. act. ἀναχωρέω (# 432) to depart. μέρη acc. pl. μέρος (# 3538) part, pl. region. For the social background of this region s. Gerd Theissen, "Lokal- und Sozialkolorit in der Geschichte von der syrophönikischen Frau (Mk 7:24-30)," ZAW 75 (1984): 202-25. ◆ 22 Χαναναία (# 5914) Canaanite. The term was perhaps used because these were the ancient enemies of Israel (DA; for more discussion s. BBC). ὁρίων

gen. pl. ὅριον (# 3990) boundary, pl. area. ἐξελθοῦσα aor. act. part. nom. fem. sing. ἐξέρχομαι (# 2002) s.v. 21. ἔκραζεν impf. ind. act. κράζω (# 3189) to cry out. Impf. indicates she kept on calling out (Filson). ἐλέησον aor. act. imp. ἐλεέω (# 1796) to have mercy, pity, to show mercy. Aor. imp. calls for a specific action. δαιμονίζεται pres. ind. pass. δαιμονίζομαι (# 1227) to be possessed w. a demon. ◆ 23 ἀπεκρίθη aor. ind. pass. (dep.) s.v. 3. προσελθόντες aor. act. part. προσέρχομαι (# 4665) to come to. Temp. or circum. part. ἠρώτουν impf. ind. act. ἐρωτάω (# 2263) to ask, to inquire, to request. Impf. pictures the continuous action in the past. ἀπόλυσον aor. imp. act. ἀπολύω (# 668) to send away. Possibly, "send her away w. her request granted" (Meyer; DA). Aor. imp. calls for a specific action. κράζει pres. ind. act. s.v. 22. Pres. is "she keeps continually calling out!" ὄπισθεν (# 3957) w. gen., after. (BD, 115). ◆ 24 ἀποκριθείς aor. pass. (dep.) part. s.v. 3. εἶπεν aor. ind. act. λέγω (# 3306). ἀπεστάλην aor. ind. pass. ἀποστέλλω (# 690) to send, to commission. S. 10:2, 5. Theol. pass., "sent by God." ἀπολωλότα perf. act. part. ἀπόλλυμι (# 660) to lose, to be lost (s. 10:6). ◆ 25 ἐλθοῦσα aor. act. part. (circum.) (fem.) ἔρχομαι (# 2262) to come, to go. προσεκύνει impf. ind. act. προσκυνέω (# 4686) to worship. The continual action of the impf. indicates her persistence (Filson). βοήθει pres. imp. act. βοηθέω (# 1070) to help, w. obj. in dat. Pres. imp. here pictures an excited request to begin an action which is not going on (Bakker, 83f; MKG, 272). ◆ 26 οὐκ (# 4024) not, used in a question expecting the answer "no." λαβεῖν aor. act. inf. λαμβάνω (# 3284) to take. βαλεῖν aor. act. inf. βάλλω (# 965) to cast, to throw. The infs. explain the adj. καλον. κυναρίοις dat. pl. κυνάριον (# 3249) dog, little dog. A house dog or lap dog in contrast to a dog of the street or farm (BAGD). Dat. as indir. obj. ◆ 27 ναί (# 3721) certainly. ψιχίον (# 6033) crumb, little morsel, dimin. form. πιπτόντων pres. act. part. gen. pl. s.v. 14. Part. as adj. Crumbs the size of a olive were to be gathered up (SB, 4:ii, 625-27; 4:i, 526). ◆ 28 γενηθήτω aor. imp. pass. (dep.) 3rd. sing. γίνομαι (# 1181) to become, to happen. Used w. dat. of personal interest. ἰάθη aor. ind. pass. ἰάομαι (# 2615) to heal. ◆ 29 μεταβάς aor. act. part. (temp.) μεταβαίνω (# 3553) to pass over, to withdraw, to depart. ἦλθεν aor. ind. act. s.v. 25. ἀναβάς aor. act. part. (temp.) ἀναβαίνω (# 326) to go up. ἐκάθητο impf. ind. mid. (dep.) κάθημαι (# 2764) to sit down, to sit. ◆ 30 προσῆλθον aor. ind. act. προσέρχομαι (# 4665) to come to. ἔχοντες pres. act. part. nom. masc. pl. ἔχω (# 2400) to have. μεθ' ἑαυτῶν (# 3552; 1571) refl. pron. 3rd. pers., "with themselves." χωλός (# 6000) lame. τυφλός (# 5603) blind (DJG, 81-82). κυλλός (# 3245) cripple, crippled, deformed; used of a limb of the body which is in any way abnormal or incapable of being used (BAGD). κωφός (# 3273) dumb, deaf. ἑτέρους, acc. pl. ἕτερος (# 2283) other. "Others different from those named" (BD, 161). ἔρριψαν aor. ind. act. ῥίπτω (# 4849) to cast, to fling, not carelessly but in haste (RWP). This implies acknowledgment of his lordship (Gundry; s. Test. Job 39:3). ἐθεράπευσεν aor. ind. act. θεραπεύω (# 2543) to heal. Aor. summarizes His acts. ◆ **31** θαυμάσαι aor. act. inf. θαυμάζω (# 2513) to marvel, to wonder at. Inf. w. ὥστε (# 6063) expresses results. βλέποντας pres. act. part. (temp.) acc. pl. βλέπω (# 1063) to see. Acc. w. inf. λαλοῦντας pres. act. part. λαλέω (# 3281) to speak, to talk. ὑγιεῖς acc. pl. ὑγιής (# 5618) well. περιπατοῦντας pres. act. part. acc. pl. περιπατέω (# 4344) to walk about. ἐδόξασαν aor. ind. act. δοξάζω (# 1519) to glorify, to praise. ◆ **32** προσκαλεσάμενος aor. mid. part. προσκαλέω (# 4673) to call, to summon. εἶπεν aor. ind. act. λέγω (# 3306). σπλαγχνίζομαι (# 5072) pres. ind. mid. (dep.) to have compassion, to be inwardly moved. ἡμέραι nom. pl. ἡμέρα (# 2465) day, a parenthetic nom. to express time (RG, 460; MT, 231; BD, 79-80). φάγωσιν aor. subj. act. ἐσθίω (# 2266) to eat. Indir. question w. the deliberative subj. (RWP). ἀπολῦσαι aor. act. inf. s.v. 23. νήστεις acc. pl. νῆστις (# 3765) not eating, hungry. μήποτε (# 3607) w. subj., lest. ἐκλυθῶσιν aor. subj. pass. ἐκλύομαι (# 1725) pass. to be without strength, to be weary (TLNT). ◆ **33** πόθεν (# 4470) where. ἡμῖν dat. ἐγώ (# 1609) dat. personal interest, "Where is there for us ...?" τοσοῦτος (# 5537) nom. pl. so much. χορτάσαι aor. act. inf. χορτάζω (# 5963) to satisfy, to fill w. food. Inf. expresses result. ◆ **34** πόσος (# 4531) how many. ἰχθύδια acc. pl. ἰχθύδιον (# 2715) dimin. small fish. For dimins. w. this ending s. MH, 344-46. They speak disparagingly of their provision (Bengel). ◆ **35** παραγγείλας aor. act. part. (temp.) παραγγέλλω (# 4133) to give instruction, to command. ἀναπεσεῖν aor. act. inf. ἀναπίπτω (# 404) to sit down, to recline for eating. It denotes the act rather than the stage (AS). Inf. w. vb. of commanding. ◆ **36** ἔλαβεν aor. ind. act. s.v. 26. ἰχθύας acc. pl. ἰχθύς (# 2716) fish. εὐχαριστήσας aor. act. part. (temp.) εὐχαριστέω (# 2373) to give thanks. ἔκλασεν aor. ind. act. κλάω (# 3089) to break. ἐδίδου impf. ind. act. δίδωμι (# 1443) to give. Impf. pictures the repeated giving. ◆ **37** ἔφαγον aor. ind. act. s.v. 32. ἐχορτάσθησαν aor. ind. pass. χορτάζω (# 5963) to fill to satisfy; pass. to eat one's fill, to be satisfied (BAGD). περισσεῦον pres. act. part. περισσεύω (# 4355) to be in abundance, to be in excess. Part. as subst. ἦραν aor. ind. act. αἴρω (# 149) to lift up. σπυρίδας acc. pl. σπυρίς (# 5083) basket, a flexible mat basket used for carrying fish or fruit (Tasker). ◆ **38** ἐσθίοντες pres. act. part. nom. masc. pl. ἐσθίω (# 2266) Part. as subst. ἦσαν impf. ind. act. εἰμί (# 1639). ◆ **39** ἀπολύσας aor. act. part. s.v. 23. ἐνέβη aor. ind. act. ἐμβαίνω (# 1832) to embark, to get into.

Matthew 16

◆ **1** προσελθόντες aor. act. part. (temp.) προσέρχομαι (# 4665) to come to. πειράζοντες pres. act. part. πειράζω (# 4279) to try, to test, to tempt, to obtain information to be used against a person by trying to cause someone to make a mistake (LN, 1:330; Trench, *Synonyms*; TLNT). Part. of manner describing how they asked. ἐπηρώτησαν aor. ind. act. ἐπερωτάω (# 2089) to ask, to ask for; prep. w. the vb. is directive and concentrates the vb.'s action upon some object (MH, 312). σημεῖον (# 4956) sign, here used in the sense of a proof of Jesus' power and eschatological office (DA). ἐπιδεῖξαι aor. act. inf. ἐπιδείκνυμι (# 2109) to show. For the prep. w. the vb. s. MH, 312. Inf. after a vb. of asking. ◆ **2** ἀποκριθείς aor. pass. (dep.) part. ἀποκρίνομαι (# 646) to answer (s. Matt. 4:4). ὄψιος (# 4070) evening. γενομένης aor. mid. (dep.) part. gen. fem. sing. γίνομαι (# 1181) to become, to happen; part. used as gen. abs. εὐδία (# 2304) fair or calm weather (RWP; DC 7,70). πυρράζει pres. ind. act. πυρράζω (# 4793) to be red like fire. ◆ **3** πρωΐ (# 4745) early morning. χειμών (# 5930) rainy, stormy weather. στυγνάζων pres. act. part. στυγνάζω (# 5145) to be or become dark, gloomy. γινώσκετε pres. ind. act. γινώσκω (# 1182) to know, w. inf. to know how to (BD, 199, 200). διακρίνειν pres. act. inf. διακρίνω (# 1359) to divide, to discern. For rabbinical weather rules s. SB, 1:727-28. δύνασθε pres. ind. mid. (dep.) δύναμαι (# 1538) to be able to. ◆ **4** μοιχαλίς (# 3655) adulterous. ἐπιζητεῖ pres. ind. act. ἐπιζητέω (# 2118) to seek, to seek after (for the prep. w. the vb. s. MH, 312). Pres. stresses the habitual action. δοθήσεται fut. ind. pass. δίδωμι (# 1443) to give. For a discussion of the sign of Jonah s. DJG, 754-56; Eugene H. Merrill, "The Sign of Jonah," *JETS* 23 (1980): 23-30. εἰ μή (# 1623; 3590) except. καταλιπών aor. act. part. (circum.) καταλείπω (# 2901) to leave behind. ἀπῆλθεν aor. ind. act. ἀπέρχομαι (# 599) to go away. ◆ **5** ἐλθόντες aor. act. part. (temp.) ἔρχομαι (# 2262) to come, to go. ἐπελάθοντο aor. ind. mid. (dep.) ἐπιλανθάνομαι (# 2140) to forget. λαβεῖν aor. act. inf. λαμβάνω (# 3284) to take. Inf. as obj. or epex. ◆ **6** ὁρᾶτε pres. imp. act. ὁράω (# 3972) to see, to beware. προσέχετε pres. imp. act. προσέχω (# 4668) to pay attention to, to give heed to. Pres. imp. calls for a constant watchfulness. ζύμη (# 2434) leaven. For the symbol of leaven s. 13:33. Jesus meant their teaching, the rigid legalism and casuistical sophistry of the Pharisees and the political opportunism and worldly materialism of the Sadducees (Tasker). ◆ **7** διελογίζοντο impf. ind. mid. (dep.) διαλογίζομαι (# 1368) to reason, to dispute. ἑαυτοῖς (# 1571) refl. pron. 3rd. pers. dat. pl. Either "each man in his own mind," or "among themselves" (EGT). ὅτι (# 4022) either causal (because) or recitative, indicating quotation marks. ἐλάβομεν aor. ind. act. λαμβάνω (# 3284). ◆ **8** γνούς aor. act. part.

masc. nom. sing. γινώσκω (# 1182) to know recognize. Temp. or causal part. ὀλιγόπιστος (# 3899) nom. pl. little faith, trust, confidence, assurance in the power of Christ to provide food as He had done before (Allen). ◆ 9 οὔπω (# 4037) not yet. νοεῖτε pres. ind. act. νοέω (# 3783) to grasp w. the mind, to understand. μνημονεύετε pres. ind. act. μνημονεύω (# 3648) to remember. κοφίνος (# 3186) basket (s. 14:20). ◆ 10 τετρακισχίλιοι (# 5483) four thousand. σπυρίς (# 5083) basket s. Matt. 15:37. ἐλάβετε aor. ind. act. λαμβάνω (# 3284) s.v. 7. ◆ 11 εἶπον aor. ind. act. λέγω (# 3306). ◆ 12 συνῆκαν aor. ind. act. συνίημι (# 5317) to comprehend, to understand and evaluate (LN, 1:380, 383). ◆ 13 ἐλθών aor. act. part. s.v. 5. μέρη acc. pl. μέρος (# 3538) part, pl. area, followed by gen. denoting the villages of the area (DA; BAGD). ἠρώτα impf. ind. act. ἐρωτάω (# 2263) to ask; incep. impf. "he began to question" (RWP). εἶναι pres. act. inf. εἰμί (# 1639) to be. Inf. in indir. discourse. ◆ 14 εἶπαν aor. ind. act. s.v. 5. οἱ μέν (# 3525) some. ἄλλοι (# 257) others. ἕτεροι (# 2283) others, distinguishing them not merely numerically but also generically (EGT). ἤ or. ◆ 15 λέγει pres. ind. act. λέγω (# 3306) to say. hist. pres. ὑμεῖς "you," emphatic & contrasting. ◆ 16 ἀποκριθείς aor. part. pass. (dep.) ἀποκρίνομαι to answer (s.v. 2). εἶ pres. ind. act. 2nd. pers. sing. εἰμί (# 1639). ὁ Χριστὸς (# 5986) the Messiah, the anointed one, used without the art. it has the character of a personal name, w. the art. it is a title of the one promised in the Old Testament (SB, 1:6ff; TDNT; DJG, 106-117; NIDNTT; EDNT, 3:1147-65, 1242; NIDOTTE; for a historical, but critical study s. Martin Karrer, Der Gesalbte [Göttingen: Vandenhoeck & Ruprecht, 1991]). ζῶντος pres. act. part. ζάω (# 2409) to live. God alone has life in Himself and gives life (DA; s. D. Verseput, "The Role and Meaning of the 'Son of God' Title in Matthew's Gospel," NTS 33 [1987]: 532-56). ◆ 17 μακάριος (# 3421) blessed, happy s. Matt. 5:3. σὰρξ καὶ αἷμα ("flesh and blood") is a Jewish way of referring to man in his entirety, but in his natural weakness. It had become a t.t. meaning "human agency" in contrast to divine agency (Hill; DA; TDNT). ἀπεκάλυψέν aor. ind. act. ἀποκαλύπτω (# 636) to unveil, to reveal. ◆ 18 κἀγώ = καὶ ἐγώ "I also." πέτρα (# 4376) fem. dat. sing. rock, cliff, ledge. Used by Josephus to describe the massive fitted stone blocks in the towers of Jerusalem (Jos., JW, 6:410), as contrasted w. the ordinary rocks that men carry around (πέτρος a small detachment of the massive ledge [RWP]) (Jos., JW, 5:174, note 175); also used of huge rocks suited for the foundation of buildings (s. 7:24; JosAsen 22:13). οἰκοδομήσω fut. ind. act. οἰκοδομέω (# 3868) to build. "Upon this rock of revealed truth I will build my church" (Allen). ἐκκλησία (# 1711) assembly, gathering, church (s. TDNT; NIDNTT; NTW). πύλαι nom. pl. πύλη (# 4783) gate. ᾅδου gen. sing. ᾅδης (# 87) hades, the underworld, death (TDNT; SB, 4:1016-29). κατισχύσουσιν fut. ind. act. κατισχύω (# 2996) to overpower, to have strength against, to gain mastery over (RWP). ◆ 19 δώσω fut. ind. act. δίδωμι (# 1443) to give. κλεῖδας acc. pl. κλείς (# 3090) key (BBC). δήσῃς aor. subj. act. δέω (# 1313) to bind. ἔσται δεδεμένον fut. ind. mid. (dep.) εἰμί w. perf. pass. part. δέω. λύσῃς aor. subj. act. λύω (# 3395) to loose. ἔσται λελυμένον fut. w. the perf. pass. part. This construction is the fut. perf. pass. periphrastic trans.: "will have been bound," "will have been loosed." It is the church on earth carrying out heaven's decisions, not heaven ratifying the church's decision (AM; for a discussion s. VA, 471-74; GI, 80-82; Gundry). ◆ 20 διεστείλατο aor. ind. mid. (dep.) διαστέλλομαι (# 1403) to instruct, to order. (Another reading has ἐπετίμησεν aor. ind. act. ἐπιτιμάω [# 2203] to reprove, to sternly warn, to seriously warn.) μηδενί dat. sing. indir. obj. μηδείς (# 3594) no one. εἴπωσιν aor. subj. act. λέγω (# 3306) to say, to tell. ◆ 21 ἤρξατο aor. ind. mid. (dep.) ἄρχομαι (# 806) to begin. The vb. is emphatic and indicates that a new stage in the self-revelation of Jesus has now been reached (Tasker). δεικνύειν pres. act. inf. δείκνυμι (# 1259) to show. δεῖ (# 1256) it is necessary, often w. the implication of inevitability (LN, 1:672) w. acc. and inf. ἀπελθεῖν aor. act. inf. s.v. 4. παθεῖν aor. act. inf. πάσχω (# 4248) to suffer. ἀποκτανθῆναι aor. pass. inf. ἀποκτείνω (# 650) to kill. ἡμέρα (# 2465) day. Dat. of time: "on the third day." ἐγερθῆναι aor. pass. inf. ἐγείρω (# 1586) pass. to be raised. ◆ 22 προσλαβόμενος aor. mid. part. προσλαμβάνω (# 4689) to take to oneself, to take aside. Temp. or circum. part. ἐπιτιμᾶν pres. act. inf. s.v. 20. ἵλεως (# 2664) gracious, merciful. "May God be gracious to you," that is, "may God in His mercy spare you this" (BAGD). It could be from חָלִילָה meaning, "far be it from you"(BD, 71; MT, 309). οὐ μή never, emphatic neg. ἔσται fut. ind. mid. (dep.) εἰμί. ◆ 23 στραφείς aor. pass. (w. refl. meaning BAGD) part. (circum.) στρέφω (# 5138) to turn, to turn oneself. ὕπαγε pres. imp. act. ὑπάγω (# 5632) to depart. Pres. imp. often is used to express an order involving motion (Bakker, 82; VANT, 343). ὀπίσω (# 3958) adv. as prep. w. gen., behind; here, phrase means "get out of my sight!" (BAGD). σκάνδαλον (# 4998) stumbling block, occasion to sin (TDNT; BBC). φρονεῖς pres. ind. act. φρονέω (# 5858) to set one's mind on, to be intent on. ◆ 24 θέλει pres. ind. act. θέλω (# 2527) to be willing, to purpose, generally based on a preference or desire (LN, 1:357). ἐλθεῖν aor. act. inf. s.v. 5. ἀπαρνησάσθω aor. imp. mid. (dep.) 3rd. pers. sing. ἀπαρνέομαι (# 565) to deny, to deny oneself, an act in wholly unselfish manner, give up his personality (BAGD). ἀράτω aor. imp. act. 3rd. pers. sing. αἴρω (# 149) to take up. Aor. imps. call for a specific and decisive action. ἀκολουθείτω pres. imp. act. 3rd. pers. sing. ἀκολουθέω (# 199) to follow after, used often in the sense of following like a disciple. The action called for by the aor. imps. stand at the beginning of the disciple's journey and is to be followed by a continued determination to stick to the chosen path indicated by the pres. imp. (DA). ◆ **25** ὃς ἐάν (# 4005; 1569) whoever. θέλῃ pres. subj. act. s.v. 24. σῶσαι aor. act. inf. σώζω (# 5392) to save. ἀπολέσει fut. ind. act. ἀπολέσῃ aor. subj. act. ἀπόλλυμι (# 660) to lose. ἕνεκεν (# 1915) w. gen. because of, for the sake of. εὑρήσει fut. ind. act. εὑρίσκω (# 2351) to find. ◆ **26** ὠφεληθήσεται fut. ind. pass. ὠφελέω (# 6067) to benefit, to help, to aid; pass. to have benefit, to profit. ἐάν (# 1569) introduces a supposed case (RWP). κερδήσῃ aor. subj. act. κερδαίνω (# 3045) to win, to gain, to make a profit. ζημιωθῇ aor. subj. pass. ζημιόω (# 2423) to suffer loss, to suffer confiscation (Allen). ἤ (# 2445) or. δώσει fut. ind. act. δίδωμι (# 1443) to give. ἀντάλλαγμα (# 498) something given in exchange. The prep. ἀντί (# 505) in the noun indicates reciprocity and implies the equivalence of the object to that against which it is set (MH, 297). A man must surrender his life and nothing less to God; no exchange is possible and nothing would compensate for such a loss (McNeile; BAGD). ◆ **27** μέλλει pres. ind. act. μέλλω (# 3516) to be about to, used w. the inf. to express the fut. ἀποδώσει fut. ind. act. ἀποδίδωμι (# 625) to give back, to repay. πρᾶξις (# 4552) deed, conduct; the sum of one's doings, including that self-denial, adherence to one's faith and confession (Meyer). ◆ **28** ἑστώτων perf. act. part. ἵστημι (# 2705) to stand. οἵτινες (# 4015) nom. pl. rel. pron., who. Used either in the sense of ὅς, or in the classical sense w. a generic meaning, that is, "which, as others of the same class" (IBG, 123-24; M, 91-92). γεύσωνται aor. subj. mid. (dep.) γεύομαι (# 1174) to taste, w. gen. ἕως ἄν (# 2401; 323) w. subj., until. ἴδωσιν aor. subj. act. ὁράω (# 3972) to see. Subj. in an indef. temp. clause. ἐρχόμενον pres. mid. (dep.) part. ἔρχομαι (# 2262) adj. part.

Matthew 17

◆ **1** μεθ' = μετά (# 3552) w. acc., after. ἕξ (# 1971) six. Means "on the sixth day" (McNeile), or "on the seventh day." Foster R. McCurley, Jr., "'And after Six Days' (Mark 9:2): A Semitic Literary Device," *JBL* 93 (1974): 67-81. παραλαμβάνει pres. ind. act. παραλαμβάνω (# 4161) to take w. Hist. pres. ἀναφέρει pres. ind. act. ἀναφέρω (# 429) to take up. Hist. pres. ὄρος ὑψηλόν acc. sing., high mountain. Mt. Tabor is the traditional site, but Mt. Hermon has been suggested (DA), as well as Mt. Meron (W. Liefeld, ND, 167). κατ' ἰδίαν (# 2848; 2625) by oneself, privately. ◆ **2** μετεμορφώθη aor. ind. pass. μεταμορφόω (# 3565) to transform, to change in form, a transformation that is outwardly visible. Jesus took the form of his heavenly glory (BBKA; DJG, 834-41). ἔμπροσθεν (# 1859) w. gen., before. ἔλαμψεν aor.

ind. act. λάμπω (# 3290) to shine, to gleam. Perhaps a reference to the Shekinah glory of God. S. 1 Enoch 14:18-22. ἐγένετο aor. ind. mid. (dep.) γίνομαι (# 1181) to become. λευκός (# 3328) bright, shining, gleaming. ◆ **3** ὤφθη aor. ind. pass. ὁράω (# 3972) to see. Pass. to be seen, to appear. For a sing. vb. w. a pl. subject s. BD, 74f. συλλαλοῦντες pres. act. part. συλλαλέω (# 5196) to talk w. Part. of manner, or temp.: "as they were conversing." ◆ **4** ἀποκριθείς aor. pass. (dep.) part. ἀποκρίνομαι (# 646) to answer. ἡμᾶς us, emphasized by its acc. position used w. the inf. εἶναι pres. act. inf. εἰμί. For the inf. explaining the adj. s. DM, 219. εἰ θέλεις (# 1623; 2527) "if you desire." In Hellenistic use equal to "please" (BD, 190). ποιήσω fut. ind. act. ποιέω (# 4472) to do, to make. For the cond. cl. s. VA, 294-96. σκηνάς acc. pl. σκηνή (# 5008) tent, booth, dwelling place. ◆ **5** λαλοῦντος pres. act. part. λαλέω (# 3281) to speak. Gen. abs. expressing contemporaneous time: "while he was speaking." νεφέλη (# 3749) cloud. The cloud indicates the presence of God (Leifeld, ND, 178). φωτεινός (# 5893) shining, bright, radiant. ἐπεσκίασεν aor. ind. act. ἐπισκιάζω (# 2173) to overshadow. Here the acc. pictures the motion of the cloud as it enveloped them (McNeile). λέγουσα pres. act. part. nom. fem. sing. λέγω (# 3306) to speak. It was the Shekinah from which the divine Voice proceeded (McNeile). ἀγαπητός (# 28) beloved. Often used of an only son (Leifeld, ND, 176). εὐδόκησα aor. ind. act. εὐδοκέω (# 2305) to be pleased w. ἀκούετε pres. imp. act. ἀκούω (# 201) to hear, to listen to; w. gen. to obey (DA). ◆ **6** ἀκούσαντες aor. act. part. (temp.), indicating antecedent action. "When they heard...." ἔπεσαν aor. ind. act. πίπτω (# 4406) to fall. ἐφοβήθησαν aor. ind. pass. (dep.) φοβέομαι (# 5828) to be afraid. Ingressive aor. "They became afraid." ◆ **7** προσῆλθεν aor. ind. act. προσέρχομαι (# 4665) to come to, to go to. ἁψάμενος aor. mid. (dep.) part. ἅπτομαι (# 721) to touch. Circum. part. w. gen. ἐγέρθητε aor. imp. pass. ἐγείρω (# 1586) to rise up; pass. to get up. Aor. imp. calls for a specific act. φοβεῖσθε pres. imp. mid. (dep.) s.v. 6. Pres. imp. w. the neg. indicates the action in progress should cease: "Stop being afraid!" (Bakker, 35ff). ◆ **8** ἐπάραντες aor. act. part. ἐπαίρω (# 2048) to lift up. εἶδον aor. ind. act. ὁράω (# 3972). εἰ μή (# 1623; 3590) except. The transfiguration is revelation and gives a divine confirmation of the sayings about the coming of the Son of Man (Leifeld, ND, 179). ◆ **9** καταβαινόντων pres. act. part. καταβαίνω (# 2849) to go down. Used as gen. abs. expressing contemporaneous time: "while they were going down." ἐνετείλατο aor. ind. mid. (dep.) ἐντέλλομαι (# 1948) to command. εἴπητε aor. subj. act. λέγω (# 3306) to speak, to tell. The prohibitive subj. implies that the action is not yet existent and should not arise (MKG, 273). ἕως οὗ (# 2401; 4005) until; used w. subj. to denote that the commencement of an event is dependent on circumstances (BAGD). **ἐγερθῇ** aor. subj. pass. ἐγείρω (# 1586) pass. to rise, to be raised. ◆ **10 ἐπηρώτησαν** aor. ind. act. ἐπερωτάω (# 2089) to ask, to inquire. **δεῖ** pres. ind. act. δέω (# 1256) it is necessary (w. acc. and inf.). **ἐλθεῖν** aor. act. inf. ἔρχομαι (# 2262) to come. (Mal. 4:5 [LXX 3:22-23]; Sirach 48:10-11. For the rabbinical teaching on Elijah s. SB, 4:764-98; TS, 658ff; Dale C. Allison, Jr., "'Elijah Must Come First," *JBL* 103 (1984): 256-58; DA; DJG, 206). ◆ **11 ἀποκαταστήσει** fut. ind. act. ἀποκαθίστημι (# 635) to restore to the former cond. (s. TDNT; EDNT). ◆ **12 ἦλθεν** aor. ind. act. ἔρχομαι (# 2262) to go. For the translation of the aor. into English s. M, 1:135ff. **ἐπέγνωσαν** aor. ind. act. ἐπιγινώσκω (# 2105) to know, to recognize, to acknowledge. **ἐποίησαν** aor. ind. act. ποιέω (# 4472) to do. **ἐν** (# 1877) here w. vb. "to do something to someone" (BD, 86). The reference is to John's execution (McNeile). **ἠθέλησαν** aor. ind. act. θέλω (# 2527) to will, to desire. For the aor. form s. BD, 36. **πάσχειν** pres. act. inf. πάσχω (# 4248) to suffer. Inf. used w. **μέλλει** to express fut. ◆ **13 συνῆκαν** aor. ind. act. συνίημι (# 5317) to understand, to comprehend. **εἶπεν** aor. ind. act. λέγω (# 3306) to say. ◆ **14 ἐλθόντων** aor. act. part. ἔρχομαι s.v. 10. Gen. abs. "when they came...." **γονυπετῶν** pres. act. part. nom. masc. sing. γονυπετέω (# 1206) to fall on the knees and beg (TDNT). ◆ **15 ἐλέησόν** aor. imp. act. ἐλεέω (# 1796) to have mercy, to show compassion s. 9:27; 15:22. **σεληνιάζεται** pres. ind. mid. (dep.) σεληνιάζομαι (# 4944) to be moonstruck, to have epilepsy. The sickness often was attributed to demons (SB, 1:758; RAC, 5:819-31; Luz; Lührmann, 274-79; AIA, 234-71; ABD, 6:12; DJG, 165). **πάσχει** pres. ind. act. s.v. 12. For the variant reading s. TC, 43; Gundry. **πίπτει** pres. ind. act. πίπτω (# 4406) to fall. Customary pres. (RG, 880). ◆ **16 προσήνεγκα** aor. ind. act. προσφέρω (# 4712) to bring to. **ἠδυνήθησαν** aor. ind. pass. (dep.) δύναμαι (# 1538) to be able w. inf. **θεραπεῦσαι** aor. act. inf. θεραπεύω (# 2543) to heal. ◆ **17 ἀποκριθείς** aor. pass. (dep.) part. s.v. 4. **ἄπιστος** (# 603) faithless, unbelieving. **διεστραμμένη** perf. pass. part. διαστρέφω (# 1406) distorted, twisted in two, corrupt (RWP). Perf. expresses a state or cond. consequent upon an action (K.L. McKay, "Syntax and Exegesis," *TB* 23 [1972]: 47f). **ἕως πότε** (# 2401; 4537) until when? how long? **ἔσομαι** fut. ind. mid. (dep.) εἰμί (# 1639) to be. **ἀνέξομαι** fut. ind. mid. (dep.) ἀνέχω (# 462) to bear up, to endure. Obj. in gen. after vb. of emotion (RG, 508). **φέρετε** (# 5770) pres. imp. act. φέρω to bring. In imp. the vb. is pres. (VANT, 347; BD, 173). ◆ **18 ἐπετίμησεν** aor. ind. act. ἐπιτιμάω (# 2203) to rebuke. The word of command that brought the hostile powers under control. H.C. Kee, "The Terminology of Mark's Exorcism Stories," *NTS* 14 (1968): 246; DJG, 166-68. **ἐξῆλθεν** aor. ind. act. ἐξέρχομαι (# 2002) to come out, to go out. **ἐθεραπεύθη** aor. ind. pass. s.v. 16. ◆ **19 προσελθόντες** aor. act.

part. προσέρχομαι (# 4665) to come to. Temp. or circum. part. **εἶπον** aor. ind. act. λέγω (# 3306) to say. **ἠδυνήθημεν** aor. ind. pass. δύναμαι (# 1538) w. inf. s.v. 16. **ἐκβαλεῖν** aor. act. inf. ἐκβάλλω (# 1675) to cast out. ◆ **20 ὀλιγόπιστος** (# 3898) little faith s. Matt. 6:30; 8:26; 14:31. **ἐάν** (# 1569) w. subj., if, used in a cond. cl. which assumes the possibility of the cond. **ἔχητε** pres. subj. act. ἔχω (# 2400). **σινάπεως** gen. sing. σίναπι (# 4983) mustard, mustard seed. Popularly considered the smallest of all seeds (BAGD). **ἐρεῖτε** fut. ind. act. λέγω (# 3306) to say. **μετάβα** aor. imp. act. μεταβαίνω (# 3553) to transfer, to move to another place. **μεταβήσεται** fut. ind. mid. (dep.) **ἀδυνατήσει** fut. ind. act. ἀδυνατέω (# 104) to be unable, to be impossible. ◆ **22 συστρεφομένων** pres. mid. (dep.) part. συστρέφομαι (# 5370) to gather together, to come together. Part. used as gen. abs. in a temp. sense. **παραδίδοσθαι** pres. pass. inf. παραδίδωμι (# 4140) to deliver over, hand over to the authority of (DA). Inf. w. **μέλλει** for fut. ◆ **23 ἀποκτενοῦσιν** fut. ind. act. ἀποκτείνω (# 650) to kill. **ἐγερθήσεται** fut. pass. ind. s.v. 7. **ἐλυπήθησαν** aor. ind. pass. λυπέω (# 3382) to cause pain, to grieve; pass. to become sad, sorrowful, distressed. Ingressive aor.: "they became distressed." ◆ **24 ἐλθόντων** aor. act. part. s.v. 14. gen. abs. **προσῆλθον** aor. ind. act. s.v. 7. **δίδραχμον** (# 1440) a double drachma. A coin worth two drachmas, approximately 36 cents. The amount required for the annual temple tax (BAGD; HJC, 235-40; DJG, 805). For the temple tax s. SB, 1:760-70; M, Shekalim; LNT, 247-65; W. Horsbury, "The Temple Tax," JPD, 265-86; HJPE, 2:270-72; DA; DJG, 805; BBC. **λαμβάνοντες** pres. act. part. λαμβάνω (# 3284) to take. Part. used as subst. "the ones collecting...." **εἶπαν** aor. ind. act. λέγω (# 3306). **τελεῖ** pres. ind. act. τελέω (# 5464) to complete, to pay. Customary pres. The neg. **οὐ** (# 4024) in the question expects the answer "yes." ◆ **25 ἐλθόντα** aor. act. part. (temp.) masc. sing. acc. s.v 14. part., acc. agreeing w. **αὐτόν. προέφθασεν** aor. ind. act. προφθάνω (# 4740) to anticipate, to get before one in doing a thing (RWP). "Jesus spoke to him first." For the use w. the part. s. RG, 1120. **τί σοι δοκεῖ** the impersonal use of δοκέω (# 1506) w. the dat. ("it appears" or "seems to be"). Here, "what do you think?" **τέλη** acc. pl. τέλος (# 5465) tax, tribute (JZ, 11, 31-34). **κῆνσος** (# 3056) tax. The former taxes on wares, the latter a tax on persons; that is, indir. and dir. taxation (EGT; SB, 1:770-71; DA; NDIEC, 3:70-71). **ἀλλότριος** (# 259) foreign, foreigners. ◆ **26 εἰπόντος** aor. part. act. masc. gen. sing. λέγω (# 3306) part. Used as gen. abs. "after he said." **ἔφη** impf. ind. act. φημί (# 5774) to say. **ἄρα** (# 726) then, draws an inference from the preceding. **γε** (# 1145) particle emphasizing the previous word. **ἐλεύθερος** (# 1801) free. Pred. adj. ◆ **27 σκανδαλίσωμεν** aor. subj. act. σκανδαλίζω (# 4997) to cause to stumble, to offend. Subj. w. **ἵνα** (# 2671) used to express purp. **πορευθείς** aor. pass. (dep.) part. πορεύομαι (# 4513) to go. Circum. part. used as imp. βάλε aor. imp. act. βάλλω (# 965) to cast. ἄγκιστρον (# 45) fishhook. ἀναβάντα aor. act. part. acc. sing. ἀναβαίνω (# 326) to come up. ἆρον aor. imp. act. αἴρω (# 149) to take, to lift up. ἀνοίξας aor. act. part. ἀνοίγω (# 487) to open. Circum. or temp. part. εὑρήσεις fut. ind. act. εὑρίσκω (# 2351) to find. στατῆρα acc. sing. στατήρ (# 5088) stater. A silver coin equal to 4 drachma, worth about 80 cents (BAGD; HJC, 239; DJG, 805). λαβών aor. act. part. λαμβάνω (# 3284) to take. Circum. part. used as imp. δός aor. imp. act. δίδωμι (# 1443) to give. ἀντί (# 505) w. gen., for, on behalf of, in the place of (GGBB, 365-67).

Matthew 18

◆ **1 προσῆλθον** aor. ind. act. προσέρχομαι (# 4665) to come to. **λέγοντες** pres. act. part. λέγω (# 3306) to say. **ἄρα** then; points back to the tax collection incident (RWP). **μείζων** (# 3505) comp. μέγας great. comp. used as superl (DA). **ἐστίν** pres. ind. act. εἰμί (# 1639) to be. Pres. points to the Kingdom in its present form of the church (Gundry). If the pres. is taken as fut. (BD, 168), the reference is to the fut. Kingdom (DA). ◆ **2 προσκαλεσάμενος** aor. mid. (dep.) part. προσκαλέω (# 4673) to call to oneself. **ἔστησεν** aor. ind. act. ἵστημι (# 2705) to place. ◆ **3 ἐάν** (# 1569) w. subj., if. Introduces a cond. cl. which assumes that the cond. is possible. **στραφῆτε** aor. subj. pass. στρέφω (# 5138) to turn about, to turn around; "unless you turn around so as to go in an opposite direction" (EGT). Pass. w. a refl. meaning (BAGD). **γένησθε** aor. subj. mid. (dep.) γίνομαι (# 1181) to become. **οὐ μή** (# 4024; 3590) double neg., not at all, emphatic negation. **εἰσέλθητε** aor. subj. act. εἰσέρχομαι (# 1656) to go in. ◆ **4 ὅστις** (# 4015) whoever. The pronoun is generic, indicating those who belong to this class (IGNT, 133). **ταπεινώσει** fut. ind. act. ταπεινόω (# 5427) to lower, to make low, to humble. **ἑαυτόν** (# 1571) acc. refl. pron., himself. The child is held up as the ideal of humility and unconcern for social status (Carson, 397; Gundry). "He will be the greatest who has the least idea that he is great" (McNeile). ◆ **5 ὅς ἐάν** (# 4005; 1569) whoever. **δέξηται** aor. subj. mid. (dep.) δέχομαι (# 1312) to receive, to receive as a guest, to welcome. Subj. in an indef. rel. cl. **τοιοῦτο** (# 5525) n. sing. such as this, of such a kind. **ἐπὶ τῷ ὀνόματί μου** "on the ground of my Name" (McNeile). ◆ **6 σκανδαλίσῃ** aor. subj. act. σκανδαλίζω (# 4997) to cause to fall, to offend, to cause to stumble. Subj. used w. the gen. rel. pronoun projecting a possibility (IGNT, 57). **πιστευόντων** pres. act. part. πιστεύω (# 4409) to put trust in (εἰς [# 1650]), to believe in. Adj. part. translated as a rel. cl. **συμφέρει** pres. ind. act. συμφέρω (# 5237) to be advantageous or profitable. The next cl. is the subject of the vb. "That a millstone be hung around his neck is advantageous for him" (RG, 992). **κρεμασθῇ**

aor. subj. pass. κρεμάννυμι (# 3203) to hang. **μύλος** (# 3685) millstone. This is a rotary mill. **ὀνικός** (# 3948) pertaining to a donkey; "a donkey-millstone" (BAGD; SB, 1:775-78). The large upper millstone driven by a donkey (EGT; Gnilka; ABD, 4:831-32; BBC). **τράχηλος** (# 5549) neck. **καταποντισθῇ** aor. subj. pass. καταποντίζω (# 2931) to flow into the sea; pass. to be drowned. **πελάγει** dat. sing. πέλαγος (# 4283) the open sea, depths of the sea (BAGD). ◆ **7 οὐαί** (# 4026) woe. Interj. of pain, displeasure, or threat, followed by dat. concerning whom the pain involves (BAGD; EDNT). **ἀπό** (# 608) w. gen. indicating the cause (BD, 113): "because of the stumblings, the reasons of offense" (TDNT). **ἀνάγκη** (# 340) necessary, necessity. **ἐλθεῖν** aor. act. inf. ἔρχομαι (# 2262) to come. Epex. inf. explaining what is necessary. **δι'** = διά (# 1328) w. gen., through. ◆ **8 εἰ** (# 1623) if. The cond. is viewed as true. **ἔκκοψον** aor. imp. act. ἐκκόπτω (# 1716) to cut off. **βάλε** aor. imp. act. βάλλω (# 965) to cast. **εἰσελθεῖν** aor. act. inf. εἰσέρχομαι (# 1656) to enter. Epex. inf. explaining what is better. **ἤ** (# 2445) than, used in a comp. **ἔχοντα** pres. act. part. ἔχω (# 2400) to have. **βληθῆναι** aor. inf. pass. βάλλω. **πῦρ** (# 4786) fire. **αἰώνιος** (# 173) everlasting. For the term "everlasting fire" s. 1QS 2:8; CD 2:5; 1 Enoch 90:24, 100:9, 108:3; Test. Zeb. 10:3. ◆ **9 ἔξελε** aor. imp. act. ἐξαιρέω (# 1975) to take out. **μονόφθαλμος** (# 3669) one eyed. **γέεννα** (# 1147) gehenna. Hell (TDNT; s. Mark, 9:43; Luke 12:5; DJG, 309-12). ◆ **10 ὁρᾶτε** pres. imp. act. ὁράω (# 3972) see, see to it. **καταφρονήσητε** aor. subj. act. καταφρονέω (# 2969) to despise. The subj. w. the neg. μή expresses a prohibition. It indicates that the action should not arise (MKG). **διὰ παντός** always. **βλέπουσι** pres. ind. act. βλέπω (# 1063) to see. The pres. emphasizes the continuous action. For references to guardian angels in Jewish and other literature s. DA; SB, 1:781-82; Lachs, 269; ABD, 1:254. ◆ **12 τί ὑμῖν δοκεῖ** "What do you think?" (s. Matt. 17:25). **γένηται** aor. subj. mid. (dep.) γίνομαι (# 1181) w. dat. indicates possession. "If a certain man had." Subj. **ἐάν** (# 1569) in a 3rd. class cond. cl. assuming the possibility of the cond. **ἀνθρώπῳ** dat. sing. ἄνθρωπος (# 476) dat. showing possession. **πλανηθῇ** aor. subj. pass. πλανάω (# 4414) to lead astray; pass. to go astray. **οὐχί** (# 4049) in questions expecting a positive answer. **ἀφήσει** fut. ind. act. ἀφίημι (# 918) to leave. **πορευθείς** aor. pass. (dep.) part. (circum.) πορεύομαι (# 4513) to go. **ζητεῖ** pres. ind. act. ζητέω (# 2426) to seek, to look for. Pres. indicates the continual search. **πλανώμενον** pres. pass. part. πλανάω (# 4414) Part. used as noun. ◆ **13 εὑρεῖν** aor. act. inf. εὑρίσκω (# 2351) to find. The inf. is used w. the vb.: "if he happened to find" (BD, 201). **χαίρει** pres. ind. act. χαίρω (# 5897) to rejoice, to be happy. The pres. emphasizes the continual joy, or gives a general (gnomic) statement (VANT, 224). **μᾶλλον ἤ** more than. **πεπλανημένοις** perf. pass. part. s.v. 12. ◆ **14 ἔμπροσθεν** (*# 1869*) w. gen., before. Targum expression used out of reverence to God, w. the meaning, "it is not the will of my Father" (TT, 95). **ἀπόληται** aor. subj. mid. ἀπόλλυμι (*# 660*) to perish. ◆ **15 ἁμαρτήσῃ** aor. subj. act. ἁμαρτάνω (*# 279*) to sin. Subj. w. **ἐάν** (*# 1569*) in cond. cl. w. the cond. viewed as possible. **ὕπαγε** pres. imp. act. ὑπάγω (*# 5632*) to go, to go forth. Pres. imp. often is used to express an order involving motion (Bakker, 2). **ἔλεγξον** aor. imp. act. ἐλέγχω (*# 1794*) to bring to light, to expose, w. the implication that there is adequate proof of wrongdoing (LN, 1:436). "Show him his fault while you are with him alone" (BAGD). **μεταξύ** (*# 3568*) w. gen., between. **ἀκούσῃ** aor. subj. act. ἀκούω (*# 201*) to hear, to listen to, to heed (DA) (w. obj. in gen.). **ἐκέρδησας** aor. ind. act. 2nd. pers. sing. κερδαίνω (*# 3045*) to win, to gain. ◆ **16 παράλαβε** aor. imp. act. παραλαμβάνω (*# 4161*) to take, to take with. **ἵνα** (*# 2671*) w. subj. to express purp. **μετά** (*# 3552*) w. gen., by. **σταθῇ** aor. subj. pass. ἵστημι (*# 2705*) to place; pass. to stand. For the necessity of two witnesses s. SB, 1:790-91; 11QT 61:6-7; 64:, 8-9; M, Sot. 1:1. ◆ **17 παρακούσῃ** aor. subj. act. παρακούω (*# 4159*) to ignore, to refuse to hear. The prep. indicates to hear "aside" (MH, 319). **εἰπέ** aor. imp. act. λέγω (*# 3306*) to speak. **ἐκκλησίᾳ** (*# 1711*) dat. sing. indir. obj. assembly, a small body of the Lord's followers (McNeile). **ἔστω** pres. imp. act. 3rd. pers. sing. εἰμί (*# 1639*). **σοι** dat. sing. ethical dat. "To you," "in your case" (BD, 103; RG, 539). **ἐθνικός** (*# 1618*) heathen. To treat someone as a heathen or toll collector involves breaking off fellowship (DA). ◆ **18 ὅσα ἐάν** (*# 4012; 1569*) whatever. **δήσητε** aor. subj. act. δέω (*# 1313*) to bind. Subj. in an indef. rel. clause. **ἔσται** fut. ind. act. εἰμί (*# 1639*) to be. **δεδεμένα** perf. pass. part. δέω For this construction s. Matt. 16:19. **λύσητε** aor. subj. act. λύω (*# 3395*) to loose. **λελυμένα** perf. pass. part. ◆ **19 ὅτι** (*# 4022*) = quotation marks (recitative use). **συμφωνήσωσιν** aor. subj. act. συμφωνέω (*# 5244*) to be in agreement; lit. "to produce a sound together." For the prep. s. MH, 324f. **οὗ** (*# 4005*) gen. sing. of the rel. pron., which. Gen. by attraction (MT, 324). **αἰτήσωνται** aor. subj. mid. αἰτέω (*# 160*) to ask, to request; mid. "to ask for oneself." For the view that this is not referring to prayer but the two parties pursuing their legal claims s. J. D. M. Darrett, "'Where Two or Three Are Convened in My Name ...': A Sad Misunderstanding," *Expository Times* 91 (1979): 83-86. **γενήσεται** fut. ind. mid. (dep.) γίνομαι (*# 1181*) to become, to happen, to be done. **αὐτοῖς** dat. pl. αὐτός (*# 899*). Dat. of personal interest / advantage: "for them." ◆ **20 οὗ** (*# 4024*) where. **συνηγμένοι** perf. pass. part. συνάγω (*# 5251*) to come together, to gather together. Perf. pictures the state of being gathered together. ◆ **21 προσελθών** aor. act. part. προσέρχομαι (*# 4665*) s.v. 1. Temp. or circum. part. **εἶπεν** aor. ind. act.

s.v. 17. **ποσάκις** (*# 4529*) "how many times?" "how often?" **ἁμαρτήσει** fut. ind. act. s.v. 15. **εἰς** (*# 1650*) w. acc., against. **ἀφήσω** fut. ind. act. ἀφίημι (*# 918*) to release, to forgive. **ἑπτάκις** (*# 2232*) seven times. Three times was considered the normal number of times to forgive (Allen; DA; SB, 1:795-96). ◆ **22 οὐ** (*# 4024*) not. Does not belong w. the vb. but w. **ἑπτάκις** (EGT). **ἑβδομηκοντάκις ἑπτά** seven times seventy, that is, unlimited (DA). ◆ **23 ὡμοιώθη** aor. ind. pass. ὁμοιόω (*# 3929*) to compare, to make like; pass. to be made like or to become like. **ἠθέλησεν** aor. ind. act. θέλω (*# 2527*) to will, to wish. **συνᾶραι** aor. inf. act. συναίρω (*# 5256*) to settle. W. **λόγον** (*# 3364*) "I compare accounts, make a reckoning" (LAE, 117). **δούλων** gen. pl. w. prep. δοῦλος (*# 1528*) servant, minister. It probably refers to the tax collectors who had contracted to raise a certain amount of taxes (LNT, 36; DJG, 805-806; JZ, 38-227; Jos., *Ant.*, 12:175-79). ◆ **24 ἀρξαμένου** aor. mid. (dep.) part. (temp.) ἄρχομαι (*# 806*) to begin. W. inf. Gen. abs. **συναίρειν** pres. act. inf. s.v. 23. Inf. used to complement the part. **προσηνέχθη** aor. ind. pass. προσφέρω (*# 4712*) to lead or bring to. Pass. may indicate that he was forced to appear. **ὀφειλέτης** (*# 4050*) debtor. **ταλάντων** (*# 5419*) gen. pl. τάλαντον talent. Gen. of description. A measure of weight, then a unit of coinage which was worth 6,000 denarii (BAGD; DJG, 805; s. Matt. 25:15). The debt here would be about $10 or $12 million dollars (RWP). It was an outrageous sum considering Galilee paid 200 talents yearly (Jos. *Ant.* 17.9.4; ABD, 2:115). ◆ **25 ἔχοντος** pres. act. part. ἔχω (*# 2400*) to have. Used as gen. abs., either temp. or causal (BD, 218). **ἀποδοῦναι** aor. act. inf. ἀποδίδωμι (*# 625*) to give back, to pay back; a t.t. for repaying a debt (Beat Weber, "Schulden erstatten - Schulden erlassen. Zum mattäischen Gebrauch einiger juristischer und monetärer Begriffe," *ZNW* 83 [1992]: 253-56). Inf. as obj. or compl. of the part. **ἐκέλευσεν** aor. ind. act. κελεύω (*# 3027*) (w. acc. and inf.) to command, to order, to state w. force and authority what others must do (LN, 1:425). **πραθῆναι** aor. pass. inf. πιπράσκω (*# 4405*) to sell. **ἀποδοθῆναι** aor. pass. inf. ἀποδίδωμι The two infs. are used w. the vb. κελεύω (BD, 201). For examples of punishment for unpaid debts s. DA; LAE, 270; NDIEC, 6:99; AT, 306-307; MPAT, 136-39. ◆ **26 πεσών** aor. act. part. πίπτω (*# 4406*) to fall. Part. of manner explaining the act of reverence. **προσεκύνει** impf. ind. act. προσκυνέω (*# 4686*) to fall down and worship, to do reverence to. Incep. impf., "he began to." **μακροθύμησον** aor. imp. act. μακροθυμέω (*# 3428*) to have patience. The word indicates one who has the power to avenge himself yet refrains from the exercise of this power (Trench, *Synonyms*, 195; TDNT; TLNT). The aor. imp. used by one in difficult circumstances is not intended to create an understanding but to display complete dependence on the one appealed to (Bakker, 100f). **ἀπο-**

δώσω fut. ind. act. s.v. 25. He was possibly asking for a loan, hoping that w. the revenues from the next year he could repay the debt (LNT, 39; BBC; ABD, 2:115; 3:424). ◆ **27 σπλαγχνισθείς** aor. pass. part. σπλαγχνίζω (# 5072) to be moved w. compassion, to experience great affection (LN, 1:295; TLNT). Part. could be causal. **ἀπέλυσεν** aor. ind. act. ἀπολύω (# 668) to release. Prep. in compound is perfective, indicating a complete release. **δάνειον** (# 1245) loan. This was a loan because the servant intended to try to pay it w. the next year's revenue (LNT, 1:39). **ἀφῆκεν** aor. ind. act. ἀφίημι (# 918) to pardon; "to cancel the loan" (BAGD). ◆ **28 ἐξελθών** aor. act. part. (circum.) ἐξέρχομαι (# 2002) to go out. **εὗρεν** aor. ind. act. εὑρίσκω (# 2351) to find. **ὤφειλεν** impf. ind. act. ὀφείλω (#4053) to owe a debt. **δηνάριον** (# 1324) denarius. A Roman silver coin worth about 18 cents. It was the workman's average daily wage (BAGD; s.v. 24). It was a six hundred-thousandth of his own remitted debt (McNeile). **κρατήσας** aor. act. part. (circum.) κρατέω (# 3195) to take hold of, to seize, to grab. **ἔπνιγεν** impf. ind. act. πνίγω (# 4464) to choke. Incep. impf. "he began choking." **ἀπόδος** aor. imp. act. ἀποδίδωμι (# 625) to pay back. **εἰ** if. Assumes the reality of the case. The expression of pitiless logic (Meyer). ◆ **29 πεσών** aor. act. part. (circum.) πίπτω (# 4406) to fall down. **παρεκάλει** impf. ind. act. παρακαλέω (# 4151) to beseech, to ask. Iterat. impf. indicates persistent requesting. ◆ **30 ἤθελεν** impf. ind. act. θέλω s.v. 23. Impf. of persistent refusal (RWP). **ἀπελθών** aor. act. part. ἀπέρχομαι (# 599) to go out. **ἔβαλεν** aor. ind. act. βάλλω (# 965) to cast, to throw. A person was imprisoned for interrogation purposes (RAC, 9:318-45). **ἀποδῷ** aor. subj. act. ἀποδίδωμι s.v. 28. **ὀφειλόμενον** pres. pass. part. s.v. 28 For imprisonment because of debt s.v. 25. ◆ **31 ἰδόντες** aor. act. part. (temp.) ὁράω (# 3972) to see. The fellow servants observe the actions complaining to the master. **γενόμενα** aor. mid. (dep.) part. s.v. 3. Part. used as subst. **ἐλυπήθησαν** aor. ind. pass. λυπέω (# 3382) s. Matt. 17:23. Ingressive aor. "they became sorrowful." **ἐλθόντες** aor. act. part. s.v. 7. **διεσάφησαν** aor. ind. act. διασαφέω (# 1397) to make clear, to explain, to inform in detail and w. clarity, to tell all, to report fully (BAGD; LN, 1:411). Prep. in compound is perfective (MH, 302). ◆ **32 προσκαλεσάμενος** aor. mid. part. s.v. 2. **ἀφῆκα** aor. ind. act. ἀφίημι s.v. 27. **παρεκάλεσας** aor. ind. act. 2nd. pers. sing. s.v. 29. ◆ **33 ἔδει** impf. ind. act. δεῖ (# 1250) "It is necessary," "one must," indicating logical necessity (w. acc. and inf.). Used in a question expecting a positive answer. **ἐλεῆσαι** aor. act. inf. ἐλεέω (# 1796) to show mercy and compassion, to be merciful. **ἠλέησα** aor. ind. act. ◆ **34 ὀργισθείς** aor. pass. (dep.) part. ὀργίζομαι (# 3974) to be angry w. someone. Ingressive aor. "to become angry." **παρέδωκεν** aor. ind. act. παραδίδωμι (# 4140) to deliver over. **βασανισταῖς** dat. pl. βασανιστής (# 991)

indir. obj. one who tortures, torturer. The defaulter is being punished in order to motivate him and those who care for him to raise the necessary funding (DA). **ἕως οὗ** (# 2401; 4005) until. **ἀποδῷ** aor. subj. act. ἀποδίδωμι s.v. 28. ◆ **35 ποιήσει** fut. ind. act. ποιέω (# 4472) to do. **ἀφῆτε** aor. subj. act. ἀφίημι (# 918) to forgive. Subj. w. ἐάν (# 1569) used in cond. cl. where the cond. is considered possible.

Matthew 19

◆ **1 ἐγένετο** aor. ind. mid. (dep.) γίνομαι (# 1181) to become, to happen. **ἐτέλεσεν** aor. ind. act. τελέω (# 5464) to end, to complete. **μετῆρεν** aor. ind. act. μεταίρω (# 3558) to depart, to move on (Carson, 334). **ἦλθεν** aor. ind. act. ἔρχομαι (# 2262) to come, to go. **ὅριον** (# 3390) border, pl. area, region. **πέραν** (# 4305) w. gen., the other side. ◆ **2 ἠκολούθησαν** aor. ind. act. ἀκολουθέω (# 199) to follow, w. dat. **ἐθεράπευσεν** aor. ind. act. θεραπεύω (# 2543) to heal. ◆ **3 προσῆλθον** aor. ind. act. προσέρχομαι (# 4665) to come to. **πειράζοντες** pres. act. part. πειράζω (# 4279) to try, to tempt. Part. expressing purp. (GGBB, 637-38). **εἰ** (# 1623) if, whether, used in indir. questions. **ἔξεστιν** (# 2003) pres. ind. act. "it is lawful, it is allowed." **ἀπολῦσαι** aor. act. inf. ἀπολύω (# 668) to release, to divorce. For Jewish divorce s. Matt. 5:31; AT, 307; Jos., *Ant.* 4:253; Carson, 411; Luz; BBC; ABD, 2:217-19. ◆ **4 ἀποκριθείς** aor. pass. (dep.) part. ἀποκρίνομαι (# 646) to answer. Semitic use of the part. w. vb. of speaking. **εἶπεν** aor. ind. act. λέγω (# 3306). **ἀνέγνωτε** aor. ind. act. ἀναγινώσκω (# 336) to read. Used w. the neg. οὐκ (#4024) in a question expecting a positive answer ("yes"). **κτίσας** aor. act. part. κτίζω (# 3231) to create. Part. used as subst. **ἄρσεν** acc. sing. ἄρσην (# 81) male. **θῆλυ** acc. sing. θηλύς (# 2559) female. **ἐποίησεν** aor. ind. act. ποιέω (# 4472) to do, to make. ◆ **5 εἶπεν** aor. ind. act. s.v. 4. **ἕνεκα** (# 1915) w. gen., because of. **καταλείψει** fut. ind. act. καταλείπω (# 2901) to leave. The prep. w. the vb. is perfective (MH, 316). **κολληθήσεται** fut. ind. pass. κολλάω (# 3140) to join closely together, to unite; pass. to cling. **ἔσονται** fut. ind. mid. (dep.) εἰμί (# 1639) to be. ◆ **6 ὥστε** (# 6063) therefore, draws a conclusion from the preceding. **συνέζευξεν** aor. ind. act. συνζεύγνυμι (# 5183) to yoke together, to join together, esp. of matrimony (BAGD). Aor. is timeless (RWP). **χωριζέτω** pres. imp. 3rd. pers. sing. χωρίζω (# 6004) to divide, to separate. Pres. imp. w. the neg. μή (# 3590) used to prohibit a general precept: "make it your practice not to..." (VANT, 337-38). ◆ **7 ἐνετείλατο** aor. ind. mid. (dep.) ἐντέλλομαι (# 1948) to command. **δοῦναι** aor. act. inf. δίδωμι (# 1443) to give. Inf. after vb. of commanding. **ἀπολῦσαι** aor. act. inf. ἀπολύω (# 668) s.v. 3. ◆ **8 ὅτι** (# 4022) "because," or the equivalent of quotation marks. **πρός** (# 4639) w. acc., in accordance w., in view of (BD, 124). With a view to (McNeile). **σκλη-**

ροκαρδία (# *5016*) hardness of heart. ἐπέτρεψεν aor. ind. act. ἐπιτρέπω (# *2205*) to allow, to permit. ἀπολῦσαι aor. act. inf. s.v. 3. γέγονεν perf. ind. act. γίνομαι (# *1181*) to become, to be. Perf. points to the continual state. ◆ **9 ὃς ἄν** (# *4005; 165*) whoever. The rel. cl. has the character of the cond. cl. in a cond. sentence. ἀπολύσῃ aor. subj. act. s.v. 3. Subj. in an indef. rel. cl. ἐπί (# *2093*) w. dat., on the basis of, because. πορνείᾳ (# *4518*) dat. sing. immorality, unchastity; every kind of unlawful sexual intercourse (BAGD; TDNT; EDNT; Carson, 413-14; Joseph Jensen, "Does *porneia* Mean Fornication? A Critique of Bruce Malina," *Nov T* 20 [1978]: 161-84; DJG, 643). γαμήσῃ aor. subj. act. γαμέω (# *1138*) to marry. Aor. views the event. μοιχᾶται pres. ind. mid. (dep.) μοιχάομαι (# *3656*) to commit adultery. Pres. views the continual action, and may be gnomic. ◆ **10 αἰτία** (# *162*) matter, case. συμφέρει pres. ind. act. συμφέρω (# *5237*) it is profitable, it is beneficial. γαμῆσαι aor. act. inf. s.v. 9. Epex. inf. explaining the vb. ◆ **11 χωροῦσιν** pres. ind. act. χωρέω (# *6003*) to make room, to have room for, to comprehend, to understand, to be able to accept a message and respond accordingly (BAGD; LN, 1:373). δέδοται perf. ind. pass. δίδωμι (# *1443*) to give. Theol. pass. ◆ **12 εὐνοῦχος** (# *2336*) eunuch, an emasculated man. The word may be taken literally or figuratively (TDNT; EDNT; EGT; SB, 1:805-807; s. NDIEC, 5:144; 3:40-41 where the word is used of a married woman). οἵτινες (# *4015*) nom. pl. ὅστις (# *4015*) "Which ones," indicates those belonging to a class (IGNT, 133). κοιλία (# *3120*) womb. ἐγεννήθησαν aor. ind. pass. γεννάω (# *1164*) to bear; pass. to be born. εὐνουχίσθησαν aor. ind. pass. εὐνουχίζω to make a eunuch, to castrate. εὐνούχισαν (# *2335*) aor. ind. act. ἑαυτούς reflex. pron. 3rd. pers. διά w. acc., because of. δυνάμενος pres. pass. (dep.) part. δύναμαι (# *1538*) to be able to. Part. used as subst.: "the one who...." χωρεῖν pres. act. inf. χωρείτω pres. imp. act. 3rd. pers. sing. s.v. 11. ◆ **13 προσηνέχθησαν** aor. ind. pass. προσφέρω (# *4712*) to bring to. Pass. may indicate that there were small children (Gnilka). ἐπιθῇ aor. subj. act. ἐπιτίθημι (# *2202*) to place upon. προσεύξηται aor. subj. mid. (dep.) προσεύχομαι (# *4667*) to pray. The placing of hands was a symbol of prayer and blessing (EGT; for the distinction between ordination and blessing, in laying on of hands s. NTRJ, 234). Subj. w. ἵνα used in purp. cl. ἐπετίμησαν aor. ind. act. ἐπιτιμάω (# *2203*) to rebuke (w. dat.). ◆ **14 ἄφετε** aor. imp. act. ἀφίημι (# *918*) to allow. κωλύετε pres. imp. act. κωλύω (# *3266*) to hinder. Pres. imp. w. the neg. μή (# *3590*) is used to stop an action in progress. ἐλθεῖν aor. act. inf. ἔρχομαι s.v. 1. Inf. used w. vb. of command. τοιούτων gen. pl. τοιοῦτος (# *5525*) such as this, of such a kind. Gen. of possession. Possessors of the kingdom are to be like children and all others who have the childlike spirit (McNeile). ◆ **15 ἐπιθείς** aor. act. part. (temp.) ἐπιτίθημι

s.v. 13. "After he had laid...." ἐπορεύθη aor. ind. pass. (dep.) πορεύομαι (# *4513*) to go, to leave. ◆ **16 προσελθών** aor. act. part. (circum.) s.v. 3. ποιήσω fut. ind. act. s.v. 4. σχῶ aor. subj. act. ἔχω (# *2400*) Ingressive aor. may get, may acquire (RWP). αἰώνιος (# *173*) eternal. Eternal life contains a temporal reference but stresses the qualitative reference. It refers to the Jewish concept of the life of the age to come (GW, 163-201; MNTW, 24-32). ◆ **17 ἐρωτᾷς** pres. ind. act. ἐρωτάω (# *2263*) to ask. εἰ (# *1623*) if, assumes the reality of the cond. εἰσελθεῖν aor. act. inf. εἰσέρχομαι (# *1656*) to come in, to go in. τήρησον aor. imp. act. (some mss. τήρει pres. imp. act.). τηρέω (# *5498*) to keep, to hold, to observe. ◆ **18 ποίας** (# *4481*) acc. pl. ποῖος which ones, or possibly what sort of (Filson). εἶπεν aor. ind. act. λέγω (# *3306*) to speak. Some mss. have ἔφη impf. ind. act. φημί to say. φονεύσεις fut. ind. act. φονεύω (# *5839*) to kill, to murder, to deprive a person of life by illegal, intentional killing (LN, 1:238; EDNT). μοιχεύσεις fut. ind. act. s.v. 9. κλέψεις fut. ind. act. κλέπτω (# *3096*) to steal. For the three categories of theft in Judaism s. SB, 1:810-13. ψευδομαρτυρήσεις fut. ind. act. ψευδομαρτυρέω (# *6018*) to give false witness, to perjure (AM). For the use of the fut. for the imp. under Semitic influence s. MH, 458; VA, 419; BG, 94. ◆ **19 τίμα** pres. imp. act. τιμάω (# *5506*) to honor. ἀγαπήσεις fut. ind. act. ἀγαπάω (# *26*) to love. πλησίον (# *4446*) acc. sing. the one near, neighbor. ◆ **20 νεανίσκος** (# *3734*) young man, used of a person until about the age of 40 (EDNT; Philo says until 28, Philo, *On Creation*, 105). ἐφύλαξα aor. ind. act. φυλάσσω (# *5875*) to guard, to observe. For the rabbinical teaching regarding the ability of a person keeping the whole Law s. SB, 1:814-16. ὑστερῶ pres. ind. act. ὑστερέω (# *5728*) to be in need of, to lack, to fail s. Rom. 3:23. ◆ **21 τέλειος** (# *5455*) perfect, complete, perhaps true, that is, true to God, true to the covenant (AM). Perhaps in the rabbinical sense of a completely righteous man, one who observes all of the commandments (Lachs, 331; SB, 1:816). εἶναι pres. act. inf. εἰμί (# *1639*). ὕπαγε pres. imp. act. ὑπάγω (# *5632*) to go. πώλησον aor. imp. act. πωλέω (# *4797*) to sell. Aor. imp. calls for a specific action. ὑπάρχοντα pres. act. part. acc. n. pl. ὑπάρχω (# *5639*) to be present, to be at one's disposal; part. possessions. δός aor. imp. act. δίδωμι (# *1443*) to give. πτωχός poor, abject poverty (s. 5:3; DJG, 704). ἕξεις fut. ind. act. ἔχω (# *2400*) to have. A Semitic type of cond. sentence w. the imp. followed by the fut. δεῦρο (# *1306*) adv. come, come here (used as imp.). ἀκολούθει pres. imp. act. ἀκολουθέω (# *199*) to follow (as a disciple). (MNTW, 32-37). ◆ **22 ἀκούσας** aor. act. part. (temp.) ἀκούω (# *201*) to hear. ἀπῆλθεν aor. ind. act. ἀπέρχομαι (# *599*) to go away. λυπούμενος pres. pass. part. (circum.) λυπέω (# *3382*) to make sorry; pass. to be sorry, to be sad. ἦν impf. ind. act. εἰμί (# *1639*). ἔχων pres. act.

part. ἔχω (# 2400) to have. Part. in a periphrastic construction (VA, 480). κτῆμα (# 3228) probably landed property, more definite than possessions (McNeile). ◆ 23 πλούσιος (# 4454) rich, very rich (DJG, 705). δυσκόλως (# 1552) (adv.) difficult, w. difficulty (RWP). εἰσελεύσεται fut. ind. mid. (dep.) εἰσέρχομαι (# 1656) to go, to come. ◆ 24 εὐκοπώτερον comp. εὔκοπος easy. κάμηλος (# 2823) camel. Acc. as subj. of the inf. τρυπήματος gen. sing. τρῆμα (# 5585) opening, eye. Gen. w. the prep. διά. ῥαφίδος gen. sing. ῥαφίς needle. A proverbial way of expressing something unusually difficult, well nigh impossible (Hill; Hendriksen). διελθεῖν aor. act. inf. διέρχομαι (# 1451) to go through. ἤ (# 2445) than. εἰσελθεῖν aor. act. inf. εἰσέρχομαι (# 1656) to enter. The two infs. used as the subj. of the verb (IBG, 127). ◆ 25 ἀκούσαντες aor. act. part. (temp.) ἀκούω (# 201). ἐξεπλήσσοντο impf. ind. pass. ἐκπλάσσω (# 1742) to be beside oneself, to be astonished, to be overwhelmed (BAGD). Impf. suggests a continuous mood culminating at that moment (EGT). λέγοντες pres. act. part. λέγω (# 3306) to say. Nom. masc. pl. ἄρα then; draws a logical conclusion. If this rich young ruler cannot be saved how can anyone else be saved (DJG, 704)? σωθῆναι aor. pass. inf. σῴζω (# 5392) to be rescued, to be saved (NTW; TDNT). ◆ 26 ἐμβλέψας aor. act. part. ἐμβλέπω (# 1838) to look at. τοῦτο this, refers to the being saved (Meyer). ◆ 27 ἀποκριθείς aor. pass. part. s.v. 4. ἡμεῖς we (emphatic). ἀφήκαμεν aor. ind. act. 1st. pl. ἀφίημι (# 918) to leave, to forsake. ἠκολουθήσαμεν aor. ind. act. s.v. 2. ἔσται fut. ind. mid. (dep.) εἰμί (# 1639) to be. ◆ 28 ἀκολουθήσαντες aor. act. part. s.v. 2. παλιγγενεσίᾳ (# 4098) dat. sing. regeneration, the new world. Jewish hopes awaited a renewal both of the land and of the entire world (Hill; HJPE, 2:537-38, 554; NIDNTT; SB, 3:840-47; 1QS 4:25; 1 Enoch 45:4-5, 72:1, 91:15-16; 2 Baruch 32:6; Gundry; Harrington). καθίσῃ aor. subj. act. καθίζω (# 2767) to seat, cause to sit. καθήσεσθε fut. ind. mid. (dep.) κάθημαι (# 2764) to sit. This is presented as a reward for the faithful. κρίνοντες pres. act. part. κρίνω (# 3212) to judge, to govern (McNeile). Part. of manner or circum. φυλάς acc. pl. φυλή (# 5876) tribe. Matthew meant Israel (Harrington). ◆ 29 ἑκατονταπλασίονα (# 1671) a hundredfold (some mss. have πολλαπλασίονα manifold s. TC, 50). λήμψεται fut. ind. mid. (dep.) λαμβάνω (# 3284) to take, to receive. κληρονομήσει fut. ind. act. κληρονομέω (# 3099) to inherit; here in the sense of obtain.

Matthew 20

◆ 1 οἰκοδεσπότῃ (# 3867) dat. sing. ruler of a house, householder. Dat. w. adj. ἐξῆλθεν aor. ind. act. ἐξέρχομαι (# 2002) to go out. πρωΐ (# 4745) early. "At the same time with early dawn" (RWP). μισθώσασθαι aor. mid. (dep.) inf. μισθόω (# 3636) to hire. Inf. expresses purp. ἀμπελών (# 308) vineyard. If God's generosity, in contrast to the merit system, is represented by such a man, then this must have been different from anyone they had encountered. For this parable in the light of the Jewish teaching s. SB, 4:484-500; Norman A. Huffman, "Atypical Features in the Parables of Jesus," *JBL* 97 (1978): 208-210; HSB, 389-91; BBC. ◆ 2 συμφωνήσας aor. act. part. συμφωνέω (# 5244) to agree s. 18:19. Circum. or temp. part. ἐκ (# 1666) for, represents the agreement (RWP). δηνάριον (# 1324) denarius, a Roman coin worth about 18 cents. A normal day's wage for laborers (BAGD; DJG, 805). ἡμέραν acc. ἡμέρα (# 2465) day. Acc. of time, "the whole day," or distributive, "per day" (BD, 88). ἀπέστειλεν aor. ind. act. ἀποστέλλω (# 690) to send. ◆ 3 ἐξελθών aor. act. part. s.v. 1. Circum. or temp. part. περί (# 4309) w. acc., about, used to express an undefined point of time: "around the third hour" (9:00 A.M.) (IGNT, 169). εἶδεν aor. ind. act. ὁράω (# 3972) to see. ἑστῶτας perf. act. part. ἵστημι (# 2705) to stand. Perf. denotes the state of standing idle (VANT, 136 ff). ἀργός (# 734) not working, idle. ◆ 4 ὑπάγετε pres. imp. act. ὑπάγω (# 5632) to go out. ᾖ pres. subj. act. εἰμί to be. δώσω fut. ind. act. δίδωμι (# 1443) to give. ◆ 5 ἀπῆλθον aor. ind. act. ἀπέρχομαι (# 599) to go out. ἐποίησεν aor. ind. act. ποιέω (# 4472) to do, to make. ὡσαύτως (# 6058) in the same way. ◆ 6 ἑνδεκάτην (# 1895) eleventh (hour), 5:00 P.M. The workday normally ended at 6:00 P.M. (SB, 2:442, 543). ἐξελθών aor. act. part. s.v. 3. εὗρεν aor. ind. act. εὑρίσκω (# 2351) to find. ἑστῶτας perf. act. part. s.v. 3. ◆ 7 ὅτι (# 4022) = quotation marks. ἐμισθώσατο aor. ind. mid. (dep.) s.v. 1. ◆ 8 ὀψίας gen. sing. ὄψιος (# 4070) evening. γενομένης aor. mid. (dep.) part. γίνομαι (# 1181) to become. Gen. abs. Payment according to Jewish law was at sunset, that is, 6 P.M. (s. Lev. 19:3; Tasker; Luz). ἐπιτρόπῳ dat. sing. ἐπίτροπος (# 2208) overseer, administrator. Indir. obj. κάλεσον aor. imp. act. καλέω (# 2813) to call. ἀπόδος aor. imp. act. ἀποδίδωμι (# 625) to give, to render, to pay. ἀρξάμενος aor. mid. (dep.) part. ἄρχομαι (# 806) to begin. Part. of manner describing how the payment was to be carried out. ◆ 9 ἐλθόντες aor. act. part. (temp.) ἔρχομαι (# 2262) to come. Aor. indicates antecedent action "when they had come...." ἔλαβον aor. ind. act. λαμβάνω (# 3284) to take, to receive. ἀνά (# 324) prep. used distributively "each, apiece" (BD, 110). ◆ 10 ἐνόμισαν aor. ind. act. νομίζω (# 3787) to think, to suppose. πλεῖον comp. πολύς (# 4498) more. λήμψονται fut. ind. mid. (dep.) λαμβάνω. ◆ 11 λαβόντες aor. act. part. (temp.) λαμβάνω. ἐγόγγυζον impf. ind. act. γογγύζω (# 1198) to murmur, to complain, to grumble. Incep. impf. "they began to...." κατά (# 2848) w. gen., against. ◆ 12 λέγοντες pres. act. part. λέγω (# 3306) μίαν acc. sing. fem. εἷς, μία, ἕν (# 1651) one. Acc. of time: "for one hour." ἐποίησαν aor. ind. act. ποιέω (# 4472) to do, here, to work. βαστάσασι aor. act.

part. βαστάζω (# *1002*) to bear, to carry. Part. used as subst. **καύσωνα** acc. sing. καύσων (# *3014*) heat. ◆ **13 ἀποκριθείς** aor. pass. (dep.) part. ἀποκρίνομαι (# *646*) to answer. **ἐνί** dat. sing. εἰς one. **ἑταῖρε** voc. sing. ἑταῖρος (# *2279*) friend. General address to someone whose name is not known (BAGD). It implies a rebuke (AM). **ἀδικῶ** pres. ind. act. ἀδικέω (# *92*) to treat unrighteously. **οὐχί** (# *4049*) in questions which expect a positive answer. **συνεφώνησάς** aor. ind. act. s.v. 2. ◆ **14 ἆρον** aor. imp. act. αἴρω (# *149*) take, take up. Aor. imp. used of a specific act. **σόν** (# *5050*) acc. sing. σός yours. **ὕπαγε** pres. act. imp. s.v. 4. Pres. imp. used w. a vb. of motion. **δοῦναι** aor. act. inf. δίδωμι (# *1443*) to give. ◆ **15 ἔξεστιν** (# *2003*) pres. ind. act., it is allowed, w. inf. Used in a question expecting a positive answer. **ποιῆσαι** aor. act. inf. s.v. 12. **ἐν** (# *1877*) either instr. (with) or local (on my property) (s. Jeremias, *Parables*). **ὀφθαλμός** (# *4057*) eye. "Evil eye" designates envy, and jealousy (Hill; SB, 1:833-35). ◆ **16 ἔσονται** fut. ind. mid. (dep.) εἰμί (# *1639*) to be. ◆ **17 ἀναβαίνων** pres. act. part. (temp.) ἀναβαίνω (# *326*) to go up. "As he was going up...." **παρέλαβεν** aor. ind. act. παραλαμβάνω (# *4161*) to take to the side. **κατ' ἰδίαν** (# *2848; 2625*) privately. ◆ **18 παραδοθήσεται** fut. ind. pass. παραδίδωμι (# *4140*) to give over, to hand over. A t.t. of police and courts: "hand over into the custody of" (BAGD). **κατακρινοῦσιν** fut. ind. act. κατακρίνω (# *2891*) to condemn. Prep. indicates action unfavorable to the object (MH, 316). The vb. indicates Jesus' death will follow a trial to establish legal responsibility (Hill). **θανάτῳ** dat. sing. θάνατος (# *2505*) death. Dat. w. vb., "condemn to death" (BD, 101). ◆ **19 παραδώσουσιν** fut. ind. act. s.v. 18. **ἐμπαῖξαι** aor. act. inf. ἐμπαίζω (# *1850*) to mock, to make fun of by pretending that he is not what he is or by imitating him in a distorted manner (EDNT; LN, 1:435). **μαστιγῶσαι** aor. act. inf. μαστιγόω (# *3463*) to scourge, to beat severely w. a whip, to flog (LN, 1:223; TDNT; RAC, 9:469-90; EDNT). **σταυρῶσαι** aor. act. inf. σταυρόω (# *5090*) to crucify. The Jews condemn, the Gentiles scourge and crucify (EGT). The infs. are used w. **εἰς τό** to express purp. **τρίτῃ** dat. sing. τρίτος (# *5569*) third. Dat. of time, "on the third day." **ἐγερθήσεται** fut. ind. pass. ἐγείρω (# *1586*) to raise up; pass. to rise, to be raised. ◆ **20 προσῆλθεν** aor. ind. act. προσέρχομαι (# *4665*) to come to; w. dat. **προσκυνοῦσα** pres. act. part. nom. fem. sing. προσκυνέω (# *4686*) to worship, to pay respect (TDNT; EDNT). **αἰτοῦσα** pres. act. part. (circum.) nom. fem. sing. αἰτέω (# *160*) to request, to ask. **τι** (# *5515*) something. ◆ **21 τί** "what?" **εἰπέ** aor. imp. act. λέγω (# *3306*) to speak. Aor. imp. used of a specific action. **καθίσωσιν** aor. subj. act. καθίζω (# *2767*) to cause to sit down, to seat. Subj. w. **ἵνα** (# *2671*) giving the content of the request. **δεξιός** (# *1288*) right. **εὐώνυμος** (# *2381*) left. Such locations indicate positions of honor and au-

thority, the middle was the most important person, then the right, then the left (Jos., *Ant*, 6:235; Lachs, 337; Carson, 431). ◆ **22 ἀποκριθείς** aor. pass. (dep.) part. s.v. 13. **οἴδατε** perf. ind. act. οἶδα (# *3857*) def. perf. w. a pres. meaning, to know. **αἰτεῖσθε** pres. ind. mid. αἰτέω (# *160*) to ask; mid. to ask for oneself. **δύνασθε** (# *1538*) pres. ind. pass. (dep.) to be able to. W. inf. **πιεῖν** aor. act. inf. πίνω (# *4403*) to drink. **ποτήριον** (# *4539*) acc. sing. n. cup. A metaphor of sorrow (Allen; *Martyr. of Isa.*, 5:13). ◆ **23 πίεσθε** fut. ind. mid. (dep.) 2nd. pers. pl. s.v. 22. **καθίσαι** aor. act. inf. s.v. 21. Inf. used as subst. **δοῦναι** aor. act. inf. s.v. 14. **ἡτοίμασται** perf. ind. pass. ἑτοιμάζω (# *2286*) to prepare. ◆ **24 ἀκούσαντες** aor. act. part. (temp.) ἀκούω (# *201*) to hear. **ἠγανάκτησαν** aor. ind. act. ἀγανακτέω to be moved w. indignation, to be indignant against what is judged to be wrong (LN, 1:762). They expressed their indignation (Tasker). ◆ **25 προσκαλεσάμενος** aor. mid. part. προσκαλέομαι (# *24*) to call to oneself. Temp. or circum. part. **ἄρχοντες** nom. pl. ἄρχω (# *807*) ruler, used here of earthly lordship in general (EDNT). **κατακυριεύουσιν** pres. ind. act. κατακυριεύω (# *2894*) to lord it over, to be master. Gnomic pres. indicating a general truth. **κατεξουσιάζουσιν** pres. ind. act. κατεξουσιάζω (# *2980*) to exercise authority over someone, to play the tyrant (RWP). W. gen. Gnomic. pres. ◆ **26 ἔσται** fut. ind. mid. (dep.) εἰμί (# *1639*). **θέλῃ** pres. subj. act. θέλω (# *2527*) to will, to desire. Subj. w. indef. rel. pron. **ὃς ἐάν**. **γενέσθαι** aor. mid. (dep.) inf. s.v. 8. **διάκονος** (# *1356*) servant, attendant (EDNT). ◆ **27 εἶναι** pres. act. inf. εἰμί. **δοῦλος** (# *1528*) slave. In the pagan world humility was regarded as a vice (Carson, 43). ◆ **28 ὥσπερ** (# *6061*) just as. **ἦλθεν** aor. ind. act. s.v. 9. **διακονηθῆναι** aor. pass. inf. διακονέω (# *1354*) to minister, to serve; pass., to be ministered to (EDNT). Inf. of purp. **διακονῆσαι** aor. act. inf. **δοῦναι** aor. act. inf. s.v. 14. **λύτρον** (# *3389*) ransom, the price paid for the release of a slave (AM; s. APC, 9-48; NTW, 76-83; GW, 49-81; TDNT; EDNT; LDC). **ἀντί** (# *505*) for, instead of. There is the notion of exchange and substitution (RWP). **πολλῶν** gen. pl. πολύς (# *4498*) many. A Semitic way of expressing "all" (Hill). ◆ **29 ἐκπορευομένων** pres. mid. (dep.) part. (temp.) ἐκπορεύομαι (# *1744*) to go out, to go forth; gen. abs. **ἠκολούθησεν** aor. ind. act. ἀκολουθέω (# *199*) to follow (w. dat.). ◆ **30 τυφλός** (# *5603*) blind (TDNT; SB, 1:524-25; EDNT; RAC, 2:433-46). **καθήμενοι** pres. mid. (dep.) part. κάθημι (# *2764*) to sit. **ἀκούσαντες** aor. act. part. (temp.) s.v. 24. **παράγει** pres. ind. act. παράγω (# *4138*) to go by. Hist. pres. describing the action in progress. **ἔκραξαν** aor. ind. act. κράζω (# *3189*) to cry out, to scream. **ἐλέησον** aor. imp. act. ἐλεέω (# *1796*) to have compassion, to show mercy. ◆ **31 ἐπετίμησεν** aor. ind. act. ἐπιτιμάω (# *2203*) to rebuke, to express strong disapproval (LN, 1:436). **σιωπήσωσιν** aor. subj. act. σιωπάω (# *4995*) to be quiet. Ingressive aor.

"they should be quiet." μεῖζον (# 3505) comp. μέγας great; "more." ◆ 32 στάς aor. act. part. (circum.) ἵστημι (# 2705) to stand. ἐφώνησεν aor. ind. act. φωνέω (# 5888) to call. ποιήσω aor. subj. act./fut. ind. act. s.v. 12. Deliberative subj. in a question. ◆ 33 ἀνοιγῶσιν aor. pass. subj. ἀνοίγω (# 487) to open. ◆ 34 σπλαγχνισθείς aor. pass. (dep.) part. σπλαγχνίζομαι (# 5072) to be moved w. compassion, to be inwardly moved (MNTW, 156ff; TDNT; EDNT). ἥψατο aor. ind. mid. (dep.) ἅπτομαι (# 712) to touch (w. gen.) ὀμμάτων gen. pl. ὄμμα (# 3921) eye; common in poetry (BAGD; MM). εὐθέως (# 2311) at once. ἀνέβλεψαν aor. ind. act. ἀναβλέπω (# 329) to see again. The prep. has the force of "again" (MH, 295). ἠκολούθησαν aor. ind. act. s.v. 29. Here it may have the force of "following as a disciple."

Matthew 21

◆ 1 ἤγγισαν aor. ind. act. ἐγγίζω (# 1581) to draw near. ἦλθον aor. ind. act. ἔρχομαι (# 2262) to come, to go. Ὄρος τῶν Ἐλαιῶν Mount of Olive Trees. ἀπέστειλεν aor. ind. act. ἀποστέλλω (# 690) to send. ◆ 2 πορεύεσθε pres. imp. mid. (dep.) πορεύομαι (# 4513) to go. κώμη (# 3267) village. κατέναντι (# 2978) w. gen., before, opposite (RG, 643). εὑρήσετε fut. ind. act. εὑρίσκω (# 2351) to find. ὄνος (# 3952) donkey (BBC). δεδεμένην perf. pass. part. δέω (# 1313) to bind. πῶλος (# 4798) a colt. λύσαντες aor. act. part. λύω (# 3395) to loose. Circum. part. w. force of an imp. ἀγάγετε aor. imp. act. ἄγω (# 72) to lead. ◆ 3 εἴπῃ aor. subj. act. λέγω (# 3306). Subj. w. ἐάν (# 1569) in a cond. cl. where the cond. is probable. ἐρεῖτε fut. ind. act. 2nd. pers. pl. λέγω. Fut. used as a command (VA, 419). ἀποστελεῖ fut. ind. act. s.v. 1. ◆ 4 γέγονεν perf. ind. act. γίνομαι (# 1181) to become, to happen. Perf. here functions as pluperf. (VA, 260). πληρωθῇ aor. subj. pass. πληρόω (# 4444) to fulfill. Subj. w. ἵνα (# 2671) used in purp. cl. ῥηθέν aor. pass. part. n. nom. sing. λέγω to say. Part. as noun: "that which was spoken." For Zech. 9:9 s. OTGPN, 173-82; SB, 1:842-45. ◆ 5 εἴπατε aor. imp. act. λέγω s.v. 3. πραΰς (# 4558) meek (s. Matt. 5:5). Adj. used as adverb describing the manner of His coming (RG, 549, 659). ἐπιβεβηκώς perf. act. part. ἐπιβαίνω (# 2094) to get up on, to mount; perf. mounted, sitting. Part. describing the manner of His coming. ὑποζύγιον (# 5689) beast of burden, donkey; lit. "under the yoke" (BAGD). The donkey pictures the peaceful character of the rider and those in Zech. were considered by the Rabbis to be the animal of the Messiah (RAC, 6:566; Lachs, 344; TDNT). For a discussion of the two animals s. OTGPN, 180-81; Carson, 438; Hagner. ◆ 6 πορευθέντες aor. pass. part. (circum.) s.v. 2. ποιήσαντες aor. act. part. (circum.) ποιέω (# 4472) to do, to make. συνέταξεν aor. ind. act. συντάσσω (# 5332) to command, to instruct. ◆ 7 ἤγαγον aor. ind. act. s.v. 2. ἐπέθηκαν aor. ind. act. ἐπιτίθημι (# 2202) to place upon.

ἐπεκάθισεν aor. ind. act. ἐπικαθίζω (# 2125) to seat oneself. ἐπάνω (# 2062) w. gen., upon, on. αὐτῶν (# 899) gen. pl., them, refers to the garments, not to the animals (RWP). ◆ 8 πλεῖστος superl. πολύς (# 4498) Rel. use of superl. "a huge growth" (IBG, 98). ἔστρωσαν aor. ind. act. στρώννυμι (# 5143) to spread out. For the spreading out of garments before kings in the OT and Judaism s. Lachs, 344; SB, 1:844-45. ἔκοπτον impf. ind. act. κόπτω (# 3164) to cut. Incep. impf. "they began...." ἐστρώννυον impf. ind. act. στρώννυμι. Impf. compared w. aor. shows the growing enthusiasm of the crowd (RWP). ◆ 9 προάγοντες pres. act. part. προάγω (# 4575) to proceed, to go before. ἀκολουθοῦντες pres. act. part. ἀκολουθέω (# 199) to follow. ἔκραζον impf. ind. act. κράζω (# 3189) to shout. Iterat. impf. pictures the repeated shouting (BBC). ὡσαννά (# 6057) Hosanna, a Heb. expression from Ps. 118:25. Originally "save, we pray." Here used as a cry of greeting, an homage: "glory, or hail, or welcome to David's son" (Hagner; Allen; SB, 1:845-50; EDNT; Cleon L. Rogers, Jr., "The Davidic Covenant in the Gospels," *Bib Sac* 150 [1993]: 462). εὐλογημένος perf. pass. part. εὐλογέω (# 2328) to praise, to bless. ἐρχόμενος pres. mid. (dep.) part. The one who is coming, perhaps a Messianic title (Hill; SB, 1:850). ὑψίστοις (# 5736) dat. pl. superl. ὕψηλος high. The highest heights = heaven, where the heavenly beings are called upon to praise God (BAGD; Lachs, 345). The angels are invoked to shout hosanna to God (McNeile). Ps. 118 was used liturgically at the Feasts of Tabernacles, Dedication, and Passover (Hill). This is a prayer that appears throughout the last week and anticipates the death and victory of the Messiah. ◆ 10 εἰσελθόντος aor. act. part. εἰσέρχομαι (# 1656) to come in, to go in; part. used as gen. abs. ἐσείσθη aor. ind. pass. σείω (# 4940) to shake, to stir. Shaken as by an earthquake (Filson). ◆ 11 ἔλεγον impf. ind. act. λέγω (# 3306) to say. Impf. indicates continual action: "They were continually saying." ◆ 12 εἰσῆλθεν aor. ind. act. ἔρχομαι s.v. 10. ἐξέβαλεν aor. ind. act. ἐκβάλλω (# 1675) to throw out (w. force). For a discussion s. DJG, 817-21. πωλοῦντας pres. act. part. masc. acc. pl. πωλέω (# 4797) to sell. ἀγοράζοντας pres. act. part. masc. acc. pl. ἀγοράζω (# 60) to buy. Part. used as subst., pres. indicates continual activity. κολλυβιστής (# 3142) moneychanger. For money changing and selling in the temple s. SB, 1:850-52; 763-65; LT, 1:367-74; WZZT, 185-88; J. Neusner, "Money-changers in the Temple: the Mishnah's Explanation," *NTS* 35 (1989): 287-90; M, Shek; BBC. The Temple business may have been under the control of the family of the High Priest (JTJ). κατέστρεψεν aor. ind. act. καταστρέφω (# 2951) to turn over. περιστερά (# 4361) dove. ◆ 13 γέγραπται perf. ind. pass. γράφω (# 1211) to write. Perf. means "it stands written" (MM). κληθήσεται fut. ind. pass. καλέω (# 2813) to call. ποιεῖτε pres. ind. act. s.v. 6. Pres. means "you are making...." **σπήλαιον** (# *5068*) cave, den. **ληστῶν** gen. pl. ληστής (# *3334*) robber. Jesus' action is in fulfillment of Mal. 3:1ff and is to be taken as a Messianic sign (Hill) s. also Neill Q. Hamilton, "Temple Cleansing and Temple Bank," *JBL* 83 (1964): 365-72; R.H. Hiers, "Purification of the Temple: Preparation for the Kingdom of God," *JBL* 90 (1971): 82-90; DJG, 816. ◆ **14 προσῆλθον** aor. ind. act. προσέρχομαι (# *4665*) to come to. **τυφλός** (# *5603*) blind **χωλός** (# *6000*) lame. **ἐθεράπευσεν** aor. ind. act. θεραπεύω (# *2543*) to heal. ◆ **15 ἰδόντες** aor. act. part. (temp.) ὁράω (# *3972*) to see. **θαυμάσιος** (# *2514*) wonderful; adj. used as noun "wonder," "wonderful things." **ἐποίησεν** aor. ind. act. s.v. 6. **κράζοντας** pres. act. part. s.v. 9. **λέγοντας** pres. act. part. λέγω (# *3306*) to say. Pres. part. points to the continual action. **ἠγανάκτησαν** aor. ind. act. ἀγανακτέω (# *24*) to be aroused, to be indignant against what is judged to be wrong, to be angry (BAGD; LN, 1:762). ◆ **16 εἶπαν** aor. ind. act. λέγω (# *3306*) to say. **ναί** (# *3721*) yes. **ἀνέγνωτε** aor. ind. act. ἀναγινώσκω (# *336*) to read. **θηλαζόντων** pres. act. part. θηλάζω (# *2558*) to suck, to nurse. Part. used as subst. **κατηρτίσω** aor. ind. mid. 2nd. pers. sing. καταρτίζω (# *2936*) to furnish, to prepare. Indir. mid., "you have prepared for yourself." For Ps. 8:3 in rabbinic lit. s. SB, 1:854-55. ◆ **17 καταλιπών** aor. act. part. (temp.) καταλείπω (# *2901*) to depart, to leave. **ἐξῆλθεν** aor. ind. act. ἐξέρχομαι (# *2002*) to go out. **ἔξω** outside. **ηὐλίσθη** aor. ind. pass. (dep.) αὐλίζομαι (# *887*) to spend the night, to find lodging. Not necessarily spending the night in the open (McNeile). Those coming to the feast first went to the Temple, then to their quarters, which were either in the city itself or in one of the surrounding villages (WZZT, 157-63). ◆ **18 πρωΐ** (# *4745*) early. **ἐπανάγων** pres. act. part. ἐπανάγω (# *2056*) to return. Temp. part. contemp. action. **ἐπείνασεν** aor. ind. act. πεινάω (# *4277*) to be hungry. ◆ **19 ἰδών** aor. act. part. s.v. 15. **συκῆν** acc. sing. συκῆ (# *5190*) fig tree. The fig tree symbolizes Jerusalem/Israel, which had become unfruitful (Gnilka; BBC). **μίαν** acc. sing. fem. εἷς one, used here as an indef. art. (BAGD; BD, 129). **ἦλθεν** aor. ind. act. s.v. 1. **εὗρεν** aor. ind. act. s.v. 2. **εἰ μή** (# *1623; 3590*) except. **φύλλα** acc. pl. n. φύλλον (# *5877*) leaf. **μόνον** only. Leaves would point to fruit, but sometimes the fruit fell off and there was nothing except leaves (Carson, 444; for the development of fruit on the trees s. SB, 1:856-58; M, Shebi, 4:7; 5:1). **γένηται** aor. subj. mid. (dep.) γίνομαι s.v. 4. Subj. w. **μηκέτι** (# *3600*) used in prohibition. **ἐξηράνθη** aor. ind. pass. ξηραίνω (# *3830*) to dry up; pass., to be dried up. **παραχρῆμα** (# *4202*) adv. at once, immediately, on the spot (Thayer). ◆ **20 ἐθαύμασαν** aor. ind. act. θαυμάζω (# *646*) to wonder at, to marvel. ◆ **21 ἀποκριθείς** aor. pass. (dep.) part. ἀποκρίνομαι (# *646*) to answer. **εἶπεν** aor. ind. act. λέγω (# *3306*) **ἔχητε** aor. subj. act. ἔχω (# *2400*)

to have. **διακριθῆτε** aor. subj. pass. διακρίω (# *1359*) to make a distinction; mid. & pass., to be at odds w. oneself, to be divided in mind, to waver, to doubt (RWP; BAGD). Subj. w. **ἐάν** (# *1569*) in a 3rd. class cond. cl. assuming the possibility of the cond. **ποιήσετε** fut. ind. act. s.v. 6. **κἄν** = καὶ ἐάν (# *2779; 1569*) even if. **εἴπητε** aor. subj. act. s.v. 3. **ἄρθητι** aor. imp. pass. αἴρω (# *149*) to take away, to remove. **βλήθητι** aor. imp. pass. βάλλω (# *965*) to cast, to throw. **γενήσεται** fut. ind. pass. (dep.) γίνομαι (# *1181*). ◆ **22 ὅσα** acc. pl. n. ὅσος (# *4012*) as great, how great, whatever; used w. making the expression more general ("whatever") (BAGD). **αἰτήσητε** aor. subj. act. αἰτέω (# *160*) to ask, to request. **πιστεύοντες** pres. act. part. πιστεύω (# *4409*) to believe, to trust. The part. expresses either cond. or manner. **λήμψεσθε** fut. mid. (dep.) λαμβάνω (# *3284*) to take, to receive. ◆ **23 ἐλθόντος** aor. act. part. masc. gen. sing. ἔρχομαι (# *2262*) s.v. 1. Part. used as gen. abs. **προσῆλθον** aor. ind. act. προσέρχομαι (# *4665*) s.v. 14. **διδάσκοντι** pres. act. part. (temp.) διδάσκω (# *1438*) to teach. "While he was teaching." Jesus was teaching in the porticoes around the Temple. **λέγοντες** pres. act. part. λέγω (# *3306*) to say. **ποίᾳ** dat. sing. ποῖος (# *4481*) what kind of? Qualitative interrogative pronoun (RG, 291, 740; IGNT, 137). **ἔδωκεν** aor. ind. act. δίδωμι (# *1443*) to give. ◆ **24 ἀποκριθείς** aor. pass. part. s.v. 21. **ἐρωτήσω** fut. ind. act. ἐρωτάω (# *2263*) to question, to ask. **ὃν ἐάν** which if. The rel. cl. has the character of a cond. (BD, 192). **εἴπητε** aor. subj. act. s.v. 3. Subj. used in a cond. cl. which is assumed to be possible. **ἐρῶ** fut. ind. act. 1st. sing. λέγω. ◆ **25 πόθεν** (# *4470*) where, from what source? **διελογίζοντο** impf. ind. mid. (dep.) διαλογίζομαι (# *1368*) to discuss, to reason w. thoroughness and completeness, to consider carefully (LN, 1:351). Impf. points to continual action describing their hopeless quandary (RWP). **εἴπωμεν** aor. subj. act. 1st. pers. pl. λέγω s.v. 3. Subj. w. **ἐάν** (# *1569*) in a cond. cl. where the cond. is assumed possible. **ἐρεῖ** fut. ind. act. 3rd. pers. sing. λέγω s.v. 24. **ἐπιστεύσατε** aor. ind. act. s.v. 22. ◆ **26 εἴπωμεν** aor. subj. act. s.v. 25. **φοβούμεθα** pres. ind. mid. (dep.) φοβέομαι (# *5828*) to be afraid, to fear. ◆ **27 ἀποκριθέντες** aor. pass. (dep.) part. s.v. 21. **εἶπαν** aor. ind. act. s.v. 25. For the use of 1st. aor. endings w. 2nd. aor. stems s. RG, 337-39. **οἴδαμεν** perf. ind. act. οἶδα (# *3897*) to know. Def. perf. w. pres. meaning. **ἔφη** impf. ind. act. φημί (# *5774*) to say. For the form of the vb. s. VA, 443-47. ◆ **28 τί ὑμῖν δοκεῖ** What does it seem to you? What do you think? (s. 17:25). **εἶχεν** impf. ind. act. ἔχω (# *2400*) to have. **προσελθών** aor. act. part. (circum.) s.v. 23. **ὕπαγε** pres. imp. act. ὑπάγω (# *5632*) to go forth. **ἐργάζου** pres. imp. mid. (dep.) ἐργάζομαι (# *2237*) to work. Pres. imp. is descriptive, emphasizing the process or the various details (VANT, 365). ◆ **29 For** the textual problems in v. 29-31 s. TC, 55-56; Carson, 449. **ἀποκριθείς** aor. pass. (dep.) part. s.v. 21. **εἶπεν** aor.

ind. act. s.v. 25. ὕστερον (# 5731) later. μεταμεληθείς aor. pass. part. μεταμέλομαι (# 3564) to be sorry, to be sorry afterward, to regret an action and change one's mind (RWP; TDNT; Trench, *Synonyms*, 255ff; NIDNTT; LN, 1:319, 373). ἀπῆλθεν aor. ind. act. ἀπέρχομαι (# 599) to go forth. ◆ 30 ὡσαύτως (# 6058) likewise. ἀποκριθείς aor. pass. (dep.) part. s.v. 21. ◆ 31 ἐκ (# 1666) of, used like the partitive gen. (BD, 90). ἐποίησεν aor. ind. act. s.v. 6. τελῶναι nom. pl. τελώνης (# 5467) tax collector. For the attitude towards this group s. JZ. πόρναι nom. pl. πόρνη (# 4520) prostitute (DJG, 643). προάγουσιν pres. ind. act. προάγω (# 4575) to go before, precede. For the prep. in the vb. s. MH, 322f. Pres. could express a general truth. ◆ 32 ἦλθεν aor. ind. act. s.v. 1. ἐν ὁδῷ δικαιοσύνης "with (in) the path of righteousness," that is, w. the message of righteousness. The obligation of obedience to the divine will as both preached and practiced by John (GW, 124-25; RM, 94-96; TLNT). ἐπιστεύσατε aor. ind. act. s.v. 22. ἰδόντες aor. act. part. (temp.) s.v. 15. μετεμελήθητε aor. ind. pass. s.v. 29. πιστεῦσαι aor. act. inf. s.v. 22. Inf. w. art. expresses either purp. or result (IBG, 128f.). ◆ 33 ἀκούσατε aor. imp. act. ἀκούω (# 201) to hear. οἰκοδεσπότης (# 3867) master of the house, a householder. ὅστις (# 4015) who, "like others of the same class who" (M, 91-92; IGNT, 133). ἐφύτευσεν aor. ind. act. φυτεύω (# 5885) to plant. φραγμός (# 5850) fence. Protection against wild beasts and a barrier to roving vine tendrils and prying eyes (McNeile; LNT, 292). περιέθηκεν aor. ind. act. περιτίθημι (# 4363) to place around, (w. dat.). ὤρυξεν aor. ind. act. ὀρύσσω (# 4002) to dig. ληνός (# 3332) winepress. The winepress consists of two parts, where the grapes were crushed and where the juice fell (McNeile; TDNT; ISBE, 4:1072; DJG, 871; DGRA, 958, 1137-38). ᾠκοδόμησεν aor. ind. act. οἰκοδομέω (# 3868) to build. πύργος (# 4788) tower. For the winedressers and watchmen (RWP; ZPEB, 5:883). ἐξέδετο aor. ind. mid. (mid.) ἐκδίδωμι (# 1686) to lease out. γεωργοῖς dat. pl. indir. obj. γεωργός (# 1177) farmer, tenant farmer. They had to pay a portion of the crops each year as their rent (Tasker; for the contracts of such agreements s. LNT, 292-95; for the work in vineyard s. the Roman writer Columella, *De Re Rustica*, 4-5). ἀπεδήμησεν aor. ind. act. ἀποδημέω (# 623) to go on a journey. It took four years before the fruit was ready (LNT, 295). ◆ 34 ἤγγισεν aor. ind. act. ἐγγίζω (# 1581) to draw near. ἀπέστειλεν aor. ind. act. ἀποστέλλω (# 690) to commission, to send as a representative (TDNT; EDNT). λαβεῖν aor. act. inf. s.v. 22. Inf. expressing purp. ◆ 35 λαβόντες aor. act. part. (circum.) λαμβάνω (# 3284) s.v. 22. ἔδειραν aor. ind. act. δέρω (# 1296) to flay, to skin, to beat. ἀπέκτειναν aor. ind. act. ἀποκτείνω (# 650) to kill. ἐλιθοβόλησαν aor. ind. act. λιθοβολέω (# 3344) to stone to death. ◆ 36 πλείονας comp. πολύς (# 4498) more. πρώτων gen. pl. πρῶτος (# 4755) first; Gen. of comp.,

"more than the first ones." ◆ 37 ὕστερον (# 5731) finally, at last, superl. emphasizing the end of a series (BD, 34) and is full of intense emotion and pathos (Hendriksen). ἐντραπήσονται fut. ind. pass. (pass. w. mid. sense) ἐντρέπω (# 1956) to make someone ashamed, to be put to shame, to have regard or respect for someone (BAGD). The fut. gives the father's projected expectation (VA, 424). ◆ 38 δεῦτε (# 1307) come, come on. ἀποκτείνωμεν aor. subj. act. s.v. 35. Hortatory subj., "let us kill." σχῶμεν aor. subj. act. ἔχω (# 2400) Hortatory subj., "let us get his inheritance" (RWP). The expectation was that the owner would give up hope of recovering his vineyard (LN, 303-306). ◆ 39 λαβόντες aor. act. part. s.v. 35. ἐξέβαλον aor. ind. act. ἐκβάλλω s.v. 12. ἀπέκτειναν aor. ind. act. s.v. 35. ◆ 40 οὖν (# 4036) therefore, draws the conclusion in form of a question directed to the listeners (s. Isa. 5:3). ἔλθῃ aor. subj. act. ἔρχομαι (# 2262) to come to, to go. Subj. w. ὅταν (# 4020) in an indef. temp. cl. ποιήσει fut. ind. act. ποιέω (# 4472) to do. ◆ 41 λέγουσιν pres. ind. act. λέγω (# 3306) to say. Hist. pres. The listeners give the answer and the application of the parable. κακός (# 2805) bad, pertaining to being bad, w. the implication of harmful and damaging (LN, 1:754). Adj. used as noun. κακῶς (# 2809) adv. badly, severely (BAGD). ἀπολέσει fut. ind. act. ἀπόλλυμι (# 660) to destroy. ἐκδώσεται fut. ind. mid. s.v. 33. ἀποδώσουσιν fut. ind. act. ἀποδίδωμι (# 625) to pay, to give back, to give over (s. Matt. 18:25). ◆ 42 ἀνέγνωτε aor. ind. act. s.v.16. This was an affront to their knowledge. λίθον acc. sing. λίθος (# 3345) stone. The acc. is inverse attraction of the antecedent to the case of the rel. (MT, 324). ἀπεδοκίμασαν aor. ind. act. ἀποδοκιμάζω (# 627) to reject after scrutiny, to declare useless (BAGD). οἰκοδομοῦντες pres. act. part. masc. nom. pl. οἰκοδομέω. Adj. part. w. the art. used as a noun: "the builders." Perhaps the religious leaders (OTGPN, 335). ἐγενήθη aor. ind. pass. (dep.) γίνομαι s.v.4. γωνία (# 1224) corner. The foundation stone at its farthest corner, w. which a building was begun–it firmly fixes its site and determines its direction (EDNT). ἐγένετο aor. ind. mid. (dep.) γίνομαι (# 1181) to become, to be. ◆ 43 ἀρθήσεται fut. ind. pass. αἴρω (# 149) to take away, to remove. δοθήσεται fut. ind. pass. δίδωμι (# 1443) to give. ἔθνει dat. sing. ἔθνος (# 1620) folk, nation. Indir. obj. ποιοῦντι pres. act. part. dat. sing. ποιέω (# 4472) to produce. ◆ 44 πεσών aor. act. part. πίπτω (# 4406) to fall. συνθλασθήσεται fut. ind. pass. συνθλάω (# 5314) to crush. πέσῃ aor. subj. act. πίπτω. λικμήσει fut. ind. act. λικμάω (# 3347) to break into small pieces or to scatter as dust (Allen; BBC). The stone of Dan. 2:44, 45 was viewed by the rabbis as the Messiah (SB, 1:877). ◆ 45 ἀκούσαντες aor. act. part. (temp.) masc. nom. pl. ἀκούω (# 201) to hear. ἔγνωσαν aor. ind. act. γινώσκω (# 1182) to know, to understand, to recognize. ◆ 46 ζητοῦντες pres. act. part. ζητέω

(# 2426) to seek, w. inf. Concessive part., "although...."
κρατῆσαι aor. act. inf. κρατέω (# 3195) to seize, to arrest.
ἐφοβήθησαν aor. ind. pass. (dep.) s.v. 26. **ἐπεί** (# 2075)
since, because. **εἰς** (# 1650), as, used w. the pred. acc. or
double acc. (RG, 481ff; IBG, 70). **εἶχον** impf. ind. act.
ἔχω (# 2400) to have, to hold to a view point.

Matthew 22

◆ **1 ἀποκριθείς** aor. pass. (dep.) part. ἀποκρίνομαι
(# 646). **εἶπεν** aor. ind. act. λέγω (# 3306) to say. ◆ **2**
ὡμοιώθη aor. ind. pass. ὁμοιόω (# 3929) to compare, to
make alike; pass. to be like. **ὅστις** (# 4015) rel. pron.
who, emphasizing the class or kind to which one belongs. **ἐποίησεν** aor. ind. act. ποιέω (# 4472) to make.
γάμους acc. pl. γάμος (# 1141) wedding feast; pl. because the festivities lasted for days (EGT; TDNT; for
Jewish wedding customs s. SB, 1: 501-17, 2:372-409;
JPF, 2:752-60; BBC; for a feast in general s. SB, 4:ii, 611-
39; LNT, 126-55; John 2:1). **υἱῷ** dat. sing. υἱός (# 5626)
son. Dat. of advantage, "for his son." ◆ **3 ἀπέστειλεν**
aor. ind. act. ἀποστέλλω (# 690) to send, to dispatch on
an official task. **καλέσαι** aor. act. inf. καλέω (# 2813) to
call, to summon. Inf. gives the purp. of the sending.
κεκλημένους perf. pass. part. καλέω. The words imply
the guest had been invited previously, the announcement now being that the feast was ready (McNeile).
ἤθελον impf. ind. act. θέλω (# 2527) to will, to want to.
Impf. pictures the repeated rejection. **ἐλθεῖν** aor. act.
inf. ἔρχομαι (# 2262) to come. ◆ **4 εἴπατε** aor. imp. act.
λέγω (# 3306) to say. **ἄριστον** (# 756) breakfast, toward
midday, when the series of meals connected w. the
marriage was to begin (Meyer). **ἡτοίμακα** perf. ind. act.
ἑτοιμάζω (# 2286) to prepare. Perf. denotes the responsibility of the subject or his authority to act (VANT,
148, 294). **ταῦρος** (# 5436) bull, steer. **σιτιστός** (# 4990)
fattened ones, verbal from the verb to feed w. wheat or
other grain, to fatten (RWP). **τεθυμένα** perf. pass. part.
θύω (# 2604) to slaughter. Perf. stresses the state. **δεῦτε**
(# 1307) "come!" ◆ **5 ἀμελήσαντες** aor. act. part.
ἀμελέω (# 288) to neglect, to be unconcerned, to pay
no attention, to not think about, and thus not respond
appropriately (LN, 1:356). **ἀπῆλθον** aor. ind. act. ἀπέρχομαι (# 599) to go out. **ὃς μὲν ... ὃς δέ** used indef.
"one...another" (BD, 131). ◆ **6 κρατήσαντες** aor. ind.
part. κρατέω (# 3195) to seize. **ὕβρισαν** aor. ind. act.
ὑβρίζω (# 5614) to treat in an arrogant or spiteful manner, to mistreat, to insult. Treatment which is calculated publicly to insult and openly to humiliate the
person who suffers from it (MNTW; TDNT). **ἀπέκτειναν** aor. ind. act. ἀποκτείνω (# 650) to kill. There is a
downward progress in the treatment. ◆ **7 ὠργίσθη**
aor. ind. pass. ὀργίζω (# 3974) to anger; pass. to be angry. Ingressive aor. "he became angry." **πέμψας** aor.
act. part. (circum.) πέμπω (# 4287) to send. **στράτευμα**
(# 5128) army, bands of soldiers (RWP). **ἀπώλεσεν** aor.

ind. act. ἀπόλλυμι (# 660) to destroy. **φονεῖς** acc. pl. φονεύς (# 5838) murderer. **ἐνέπρησεν** aor. ind. act. ἐμ-
πί(μ)πρημι (# 1856) to set on fire, to burn.   ◆ **8**
κεκλημένοι perf. pass. part. s.v. 3. **ἦσαν** impf. ind. act.
εἰμί (# 1639) to be.   ◆ **9 πορεύεσθε** pres. imp. mid.
(dep.) πορεύομαι (# 4513) to go. **οὖν** (# 4036) therefore,
draws a conclusion from the previous statement.
διέξοδος (# 1447) (w. the prep.) outlet, street crossing,
more probably the place where a street cuts through
the city boundary and goes out into the open country
(BAGD). **εὕρητε** aor. subj. act. εὑρίσκω (# 2351) to find.
Subj. used w. indef. rel. ὅσους ἐάν (# 4012; 1569). **καλέ-
σατε** aor. imp. act. καλέω s.v. 3. ◆ **10 ἐξελθόντες** aor.
act. part. ἐξέρχομαι (# 2002) to go out. Circum. or temp.
part. **συνήγαγον** aor. ind. act. συνάγω (# 5251) to gather
together. **εὗρον** aor. ind. act. s.v. 9. **τε...καί** "both
...and." **ἐπλήσθη** aor. ind. pass. πίμπλημι (# 4398) to
fill, to be full. **ἀνακειμένων** pres. mid. (dep.) part.
ἀνάκειμαι (# 367) to recline (at the table). Part. as subst. Gen. of content after vb. of filling.   ◆ **11 εἰσελθών**
aor. act. part. (temp.) εἰσέρχομαι (# 1656) to go in, to
come in. **θεάσασθαι** aor. mid. (dep.) inf. θεάομαι
(# 2517) to look at, to view; inf. of purp. **εἶδεν** aor. ind.
act. ὁράω (# 3972) to see. **ἐνδεδυμένον** perf. mid. part.
ἐνδύω (# 1907) to put on; mid. to clothe, to put on
clothes, to wear (BAGD). For the use of the neg. **οὐκ**
(# 4024) w. the part. s. M, 231f. **ἔνδυμα** (# 1903) acc. pl.
garment, clothes. Possibly a picture of a character thus
warning against false discipleship (HSB, 392). Only
clean and proper clothes were expected (AM; SB,
1:878, 882; LNT, 142).   ◆ **12 ἑταῖρε** voc. ἑταῖρος
(# 2279) friend (s. 20:13). **εἰσῆλθες** aor. ind. act. s.v. 11.
The king saw this as a personal insult (LNT, 142). **ἔχων**
pres. act. part. ἔχω (# 2400) to have. Part. of manner.
ἐφιμώθη aor. ind. pass. φιμόω (# 5821) to put to silence,
to muzzle. ◆ **13 διακόνοις** dat. pl. διάκονος (# 1356)
servant, minister. Indir. obj. **δήσαντες** aor. act. part. δέω
(# 1313) to bind. Circum. part. w. force of an imp. **ἐκβάλετε** aor. imp. act. ἐκβάλλω (# 1675) to cast out.
ἐξώτερος (# 2035) adjectival comp. of the adv. used as
superl.; fartherest, extreme, "the darkness fartherest
out" (BAGD; s. Matt. 8:12). One of the abiding hallmarks of life in prison was darkness (BAFCS, 3:199).
ἔσται fut. ind. mid. (dep.) εἰμί. **κλαυθμός** (# 3088) loud
crying, wailing. **βρυγμός** (# 1106) gnashing, grinding.
◆ **14 κλητός** (# 3105) called, invited. **ἐκλεκτός** (# 1723)
chosen, elect. ◆ **15 πορευθέντες** aor. pass. (dep.) part.
s.v. 9. **συμβούλιον** (# 5206) acc. sing. counsel, the engaging in joint planning so as to devise a course of common action, often w. a harmful or evil purp. (LN,
1:359). **ἔλαβον** aor. ind. act. λαμβάνω (# 3284) to take.
ὅπως (# 3968) in order that, introduces a purp. cl. (BD,
186). **παγιδεύσωσιν** aor. subj. act. παγιδεύω (# 4074) to
ensnare, to catch in a trap, to acquire information
about an error or fault, w. the purp. of causing harm,

to catch off guard, to catch in a mistake (LN, 1:330; BBC). ◆ **16** ἀποστέλλουσιν pres. ind. act. s.v. 3 Hist. pres. μετὰ τῶν Ἡρῳδιανῶν (# 2477) w. the Herodians. These supported Herod Antipas and were in favor of the taxes (Gundry; ISBE, 2:698; HA, 31-42; EDNT; DJG, 325). λέγοντες pres. act. part. (circum.) οἴδαμεν perf. ind. act. οἶδα (# 3857) to know. Def. perf. w. pres. meaning. μέλει (# 3508) pres. ind. act. It is a care or concern, you court no man's favor (BAGD). ◆ **17** εἰπέ aor. imp. act. λέγω (# 3306). τί σοι δοκεῖ "What do you think?" "What is it to you?" ἔξεστιν (# 2003) is it lawful. "Is it warranted by anything in the Law or the Scribal tradition?" (McNeile). δοῦναι aor. act. inf. δίδωμι (# 1443) to give. Inf. explains what is lawful. κῆνσος (# 3056) poll tax, to be paid by all males over 14 and females over 12, up to the age of 65 (McNeile; EDNT; DJG, 806; s. Jos., JW, 2:118). ◆ **18** γνούς aor. act. part. (causal) γινώσκω (# 1182) to know, to recognize. εἶπεν aor. ind. act. s.v. 17. πειράζετε pres. ind. act. πειράζω (# 4279) to tempt, to trap. ◆ **19** ἐπιδείξατε aor. imp. act. ἐπιδείκνυμι (# 2109) to show. νόμισμα (# 3790) coin. προσήνεγκαν aor. ind. act. προσφέρω (# 4712) to bring to. δηνάριον (# 1324) denarius. A Roman silver coin, a workman's average daily wage (BAGD; LNT, 329). ◆ **20** εἰκών (# 1635) image. ἐπιγραφή (# 2107) inscription. The imperial tax was paid in coins which bore the head of the emperor, and inscriptions which described the religious and cultic claims of the Caesar (JPD, 241-48; Luz; DJG, 805-806; Hill; LNT, 333; BBC). ◆ **21** ἀπόδοτε aor. imp. act. ἀποδίδωμι (# 625) to give back. It has the sense of rendering what is due (AM; LNT, 334). ◆ **22** ἀκούσαντες aor. act. part. (temp.) ἀκούω (# 201) to hear. ἐθαύμασαν aor. ind. act. θαυμάζω (# 2513) to be amazed. ἀφέντες aor. act. part. (circum.) ἀφίημι (# 918) to leave. ἀπῆλθαν aor. ind. act. ἀπέρχομαι (# 599) to depart s.v. 5. ◆ **23** προσῆλθον aor. ind. act. προσέρχομαι (# 4665) to come to. εἶναι pres. act. inf. εἰμί (# 1639) to be. Inf. used in indir. discourse. ἀνάστασιν acc. sing. ἀνάστασις (# 414) resurrection. Acc. as subj. of inf. For the Sadducees' view s. TJ, 76-81; DJG, 403; BBC. ἐπηρώτησαν aor. ind. act. ἐπερωτάω (# 2089) to ask about. Prep. in the vb. is directive. ◆ **24** ἀποθάνῃ aor. subj. act. ἀποθνήσκω (# 633) to die. Subj. w. ἐάν (# 1569) in cond. cl. ἔχων pres. act. part. (circum.) ἔχω (# 2400) ἐπιγαμβρεύσει fut. ind. act. ἐπιγαμβρεύω (# 2102) to become related by marriage, to marry as next of kin (BAGD; Deut. 25:5-10). For the Rabbinical teaching regarding the levirate marriage s. SB, 1:886-87; Lachs, 361; Sifre Deut. 288. ἀναστήσει fut. ind. act. ἀνίστημι (# 482) to raise up. ◆ **25** ἦσαν impf. ind. act. εἰμί to be. γήμας aor. act. part. (temp.) γαμέω (# 1138) to marry. "After he had married...." ἐτελεύτησεν aor. ind. act. τελευτάω (# 5462) to die. ἀφῆκεν aor. ind. act. ἀφίημι (# 918) to depart, to leave behind. ◆ **27** ὕστερος (# 5731) superl. latter, last, finally; here, "last of all"

(BAGD). ἀπέθανεν aor. ind. act. s.v. 24. ◆ **28** τίνος gen. sing. τίς (# 5515) interrogative pron., w. gen. showing possession. ἔσται fut. ind. mid. (dep.) εἰμί (# 1639). ἔσχον aor. ind. act. ἔχω (# 2400). ◆ **29** πλανᾶσθε pres. ind. pass. πλανάω (# 4414) to lead astray, pass. to go astray; to wander from the truth (BAGD; EDNT; LN, 1:374). εἰδότες perf. act. part. (causal) s.v. 16. ◆ **30** οὔτε...οὔτε (# 4046) "neither...nor." γαμοῦσιν pres. ind. act. γαμέω s.v. 25. γαμίζονται pres. ind. pass. γαμίζω (# 1139) to give a woman in marriage; pass., to be given in marriage. Gnomic pres. giving a general truth. Angels were created, not procreated. ◆ **31** ἀνέγνωτε aor. ind. act. ἀναγινώσκω (# 336) to read. Since the Sadduccees only accepted the Torah he quotes from Exod. 3:16. ῥηθέν aor. pass. part. λέγω (# 3306). Part. used as subst. ◆ **32** ζώντων pres. act. part. gen. pl. ζάω (# 2409) to live. The argument stands on the use of the gen. (McNeile). For the Rabbinical proofs for the resurrection s. SB, 1:892-97; S, 173-292. Part. used as subst. ◆ **33** ἀκούσαντες aor. act. part. s.v. 22. ἐξεπλήσσοντο impf. ind. pass. ἐκπλήσσω (# 1742) to be beside oneself, to be amazed, overwhelmed. ◆ **34** ἀκούσαντες aor. act. part. (temp.) s.v. 22. ἐφίμωσεν aor. ind. act. s.v. 12. συνήχθησαν aor. ind. pass. συνάγω (# 5251) to gather together. Pass. used in refl. sense: "to come together," "to assemble" (BAGD). ἐπὶ τὸ αὐτό together, at the same place, for the same thing (NIDNTT, 3:1194; Gundry). ◆ **35** ἐπηρώτησεν aor. ind. act. s.v. 23. νομικός (# 3788) lawyer, an expert in law, a man learned in the law of Moses, that is, a scribe belonging to the Pharisaic party (Hill; TDNT; NIDNTT; DJG, 732-34; SB, 1:898-900). For the textual problem s. TC, 59. πειράζων pres. act. part. s.v. 18. Part. of manner. ◆ **36** μεγάλη (# 3489) great. Positive of the adj. used as superl. "the greatest" (BD, 127). The Rabbis counted 613 laws; 248 positive and 365 negative (SB, 1:900-905). ◆ **37** ἔφη impf. ind. act. φημί (# 5774) to say. ἀγαπήσεις fut. ind. act. ἀγαπάω (# 26) to love. Fut. used as a categorical imp. (BG, 94). The terms heart, soul, understanding are overlapping categories, demanding love from the whole person (Carson, 464). ◆ **39** πλησίον (# 4446) adv. near; used as a noun, "neighbor." ◆ **40** κρέμαται pres. ind. mid. (dep.) κρεμάννυμι (# 3203) to hang. ◆ **41** συνηγμένων perf. pass. part. (temp.) s.v. 34. Gen. abs. ◆ **42** τοῦ Δαυίδ gen. of relationship (RG, 501f). For the Messiah as the Son of David s. SB, 1:525; Fitzmyer, *Essays*, 113-126; 4QFlor. 1:11-13; Cleon L. Rogers, Jr., "The Promises of David in Early Judaism," *Bib Sac* 150 (1993): 285-302; DJG, 766-69. ◆ **43** καλεῖ pres. ind. act. καλέω (# 2813) to call. ◆ **44** κάθου pres. imp. mid. (dep.) κάθημαι (# 2764) to sit. θῶ aor. subj. act. τίθημι (# 5502) to set, to place. ὑποκάτω (# 5691) under. For Ps. 110 s. SB, 4:452-65; David M. Hays, *Glory at the Right Hand: Psalm 110 in Early Christianity* (Nashville: Abingdon Press, 1973);

Cleon L. Rogers, Jr.,"The Davidic Covenant in Acts-Revelation," *Bib Sac* 151 (1994): 74; Luz. ◆ **46 ἐδύνατο** impf. ind. pass. (dep.) δύναμαι (# *1538*) to be able. **ἀποκριθῆναι** aor. pass. inf. s.v. 1. **ἐτόλμησεν** aor. ind. act. τολμάω (# *5528*) to dare. **ἐπερωτῆσαι** aor. act. inf. s.v. 23.

Matthew 23

◆ **1 ἐλάλησεν** aor. ind. act. λαλέω (# *3281*) to speak. For the literary problems of the chapter s. Carson, 469-71; Mark Alan Powell, "Do and Keep What Moses Says (Matthew 23:2-7)," *JBL* 114 (1995): 419-34; Hagner. For a discussion of scribes and Pharisees s. Luz; DJG, 732-35, 609-14. ◆ **2 καθέδρα** (# *2756*) chair. A soft seat w. a back (Jastrow, 2:1434). Not simply a metaphor, for there was an actual stone seat in front of the synagogue where the authoritative teacher sat (Hill; Gnilka). **ἐκάθισαν** aor. ind. act. καθίζω (# *2767*) to take a seat, to sit. Timeless aor. (RWP), but may be considered as ironic (Carson, 473). ◆ **3 εἴπωσιν** aor. subj. act. λέγω (# *3306*). **ποιήσατε** aor. imp. act. ποιέω (# *4472*) to do. Perhaps to be viewed as irony (Carson, 473). **τηρεῖτε** pres. imp. act. τηρέω (# *5498*) to observe. Aor. imp. indicates "start to do," the pres. "continue to observe" (Bakker, 434). **ποιεῖτε** pres. imp. act. **ποιοῦσιν** pres. ind. act. ποιέω to do. ◆ **4 δεσμεύουσιν** pres. ind. act. δεσμεύω (# *1297*) to bind, to tie on. **δυσβάστακτος** (# *1546*) hard to bear (for this reading s. TC, 59-60). **ἐπιτιθέασιν** pres. ind. act. ἐπιτίθημι (# *2202*) to place upon. **ὦμος** (# *6049*) shoulder. The "heavy burdens" are the meticulous instructions of the rabbinical interpretations imposed on the daily life of the people (SB, 1:911-13; Lachs, 366). They may refer to the attempts to gain notice by others (Gundry). **δακτύλῳ** dat. sing. δάκτυλος (# *1235*) finger. Instr. dat. "w. the finger." **κινῆσαι** aor. act. inf. κινέω (# *3075*) to move, to remove. ◆ **5 πρὸς τό** w. the inf. to express purp. (TDNT). **θεαθῆναι** aor. pass. inf. θεάομαι (# *2517*) to look upon, used in the sense of careful and deliberate vision which interprets its object (AS). **πλατύνουσιν** pres. ind. act. πλατύνω (# *4425*) to make wide. **φυλακτήριον** (# *5873*) means of protection, amulet, protective charms, phylacteries, small leather cases containing portions of Scripture. These were strapped to the left hand and to the forehead (SB, 4:250-276; HBD, 3:869-74; ZPEB, 4:786; JPF, 2:798-800; HJP, 2:480; BBC; ABD, 2:236; 5:368-70). **μεγαλύνουσιν** pres. ind. act. μεγαλύνω (# *3486*) to make large. **κράσπεδον** (# *3192*) fringes, tassels. These were worn on the corner of the outer garment in accord w. Num. 15:38f; Deut. 22:12 (SB, 4:277-92; JPF, 2:797-98; HJP, 2:480-81). The Pharisees lengthened theirs in order to call attention to their piety (Hill). ◆ **6 φιλοῦσιν** pres. ind. act. φιλέω (# *5797*) to love. **πρωτοκλισίαν** (# *4752*) place of honor at a dinner, beside the master of the house or host (BAGD). **δεῖπνον** (# *1270*) dinner, the main meal (s. Matt. 22:2). **πρω-**

τοκαθεδρία (# *4751*) chief seat. These were on the platform facing the congregation w. their backs to the chest in which the rolls of Scripture were kept. (McNeile; SB, 1:915-16; HJP, 2:446). ◆ **7 ἀσπασμός** (# *833*) greeting. Disciples were never to greet their masters since this implied a certain equality (AM). **καλεῖσθαι** pres. pass. inf. καλέω (# *2813*) to call. Epex. inf. describing what they love. **Ῥαββί** (# *4806*) master, teacher (TDNT; EDNT; SB, 1:916-18; DJG, 805). ◆ **8 κληθῆτε** aor. subj. pass. s.v. 7. Used w. the neg. **μή** (# *3590*) to express a prohibition of an action that should not arise. Pass. of permission. ◆ **9 καλέσητε** aor. subj. act. s.v. 7. Subj. used in a neg. command. ◆ **10 καθηγηταί** nom. pl. καθηγητής (# *2762*) guide, instructor, teacher, used as synon. of διδάσκαλος (LN, 1:416; Carson, 476). ◆ **11 μείζων** (# *3505*) comp. of μέγας greater. **ὑμῶν** gen. pl. ὑμεῖς comp. gen. "than you." **ἔσται** fut. ind. mid. (dep.) εἰμί. ◆ **12 ὑψώσει** fut. ind. act. ὑψόω (# *5738*) to lift up, to exalt. **ταπεινωθήσεται** fut. ind. pass. **ταπεινώσει** fut. ind. act. ταπεινόω (# *5427*) to make low, to humble. **ὑψωθήσεται** fut. ind. pass. ὑψόω. The pass. are theol. pass. indicating that God will perform the action (Beare). ◆ **13 οὐαί** (# *4026*) woe, horror. An interj. of pain, distress and warning. "How greatly one will suffer," "What terrible pain will come to one" (EDNT; LN, 1:243); followed by **ὅτι** (# *4022*), giving the reason for the pain. **κλείετε** pres. ind. act. κλείω (# *3091*) to shut, to lock. **εἰσέρχεσθε** pres. ind. mid. (dep.) εἰσέρχομαι (# *1656*) to go in, to come in. **εἰσερχομένους** pres. mid. part. Conative use of the pres. "Those who are in the process of entering–trying to enter" (McNeile). **ἀφίετε** pres. ind. act. ἀφίημι (# *918*) to allow. **εἰσελθεῖν** aor. act. inf. Inf. explains what they do not allow. ◆ **15 περιάγετε** pres. ind. act. περιάγω (# *4310*) to go about, to travel about. **ξηρός** (# *3831*) dry (land). **ποιῆσαι** aor. act. inf. ποιέω (# *4472*) to make. Inf. of purp. **προσήλυτος** proselyte (TDNT; Moore, *Judaism*, 1:323-53). **γένηται** aor. subj. mid. (dep.) γίνομαι (# *1181*) to become. **γεέννης** gen. sing. γέεννα (# *1147*) Gehenna; "son of Gehenna," one fitted and destined for Gehenna (McNeile; Hans Scharen, "Gehenna in the Synoptics," *Bib Sac* 149 [1992]: 324-37; 454-70; ABD, 2:926-28). **διπλότερον** comp. δίπλους (# *1486*) double. **ὑμῶν** gen. ὑμεῖς Gen. of comp., "than you." These converts "out-Phariseed" the Pharisees (Carson, 479). ◆ **16 ὅς ἄν** (# *4005; 323*) whoever. The rel. cl. has the character of a cond. **ὀμόσῃ** aor. subj. act. ὄμνυμι (# *3923*) to swear. Subj. w. indef. rel. cl. **ναῷ** dat. sing. ναός (# *3724*) temple. To swear by the Temple and the altar provides no surety for a creditor, but gold would (Gundry). **οὐδέν ἐστιν** (# *4029; 1639*) it is nothing, the formula for a nonbinding oath (EGT). **χρυσῷ** dat. sing. χρυσός (# *5996*) gold. **ὀφείλει** pres. ind. act. ὀφείλω (# *4053*) to be indebted, bound to performance, the formula for a binding oath (EGT). ◆ **17 μωροί** voc. / nom. pl. μωρός (# *3704*) foolish, fool. ἀγιάσας aor. part. act. ἁγιάζω (# 39) to sanctify, to make holy. Part. as adj. ◆ 18 θυσιαστηρίῳ dat. sing. θυσιαστήριον (# 2603) altar. It refers to the altar of incense and especially the horns of the altar (SB, 1:395; 932). ἐπάνω (# 2062) w. gen., upon. ◆ 19 μεῖζον (# 3505) comp. μέγας great. ἁγιάζον pres. act. part. s.v. 17. ◆ 20 ὁμόσας aor. act. part. s.v. 16. Part. used as subst.: "The one who...." ◆ 21 κατοικοῦντι pres. act. part. dat. sing. κατοικέω (# 2997) to dwell, to reside. ◆ 22 καθημένῳ pres. mid. (dep.) part. κάθημαι (# 2764) to sit. ◆ 23 ἀποδεκατοῦτε pres. ind. act. ἀποδεκατόω (# 620) to tithe, to give a tenth. Pres. indicates habitual tithing. For the tithe s. M, Maaseroth; M, Maaser Sheni (JPB, 148-69). Biblically, only grain, wine, and oil are to be tithed, but rabbinically, vegetables and greens were also included (Lachs, 370; SB, 1:932; 4:ii, 640-97). ἡδύοσμον (# 2455) sweet-smelling, mint. There were three kinds of mint which were used as a spice for meats, as a medication for headache and heart discomfort and its stems and leaves were scattered over the floors of the synagogues (PB, 88; FFB, 143; POB, 139-40; SB, 1:933). ἄνηθον (# 464) dill, used for seasoning, esp. the leaves for pickles, and as an antacid (PB, 88; FFB, 116; POB, 89; SB, 1:933). κύμινον (# 3248) cumin, used as spice, esp. for bread, and as medicine for cramps and its oil as a substance for perfume (Filson; PB, 88; POB, 46; FFB, 114; SB, 1:933). ἀφήκατε aor. ind. act. ἀφίημι (# 918) to leave, to neglect. βαρύτερα acc. pl. comp. βαρύς (# 987) heavy. Heavier, weightier, more important (Carson, 480). κρίσις (# 3213) justice. The respect for the rights of others which gives a just judgment (Hill). ἔλεος (# 1799) mercy s. Matt. 9:13. ἔδει impf. ind. act. δεῖ (# 1256) it is necessary. w. inf. Vbs. of obligation or necessity are in the impf. when the obligation has not been met (RG, 886). ποιῆσαι aor. act. inf. ποιέω (# 4472) to do, to accomplish. ἀφιέναι aor. act. inf. ἀφίημι (# 918) to leave undone, to neglect. Aor. w. a vb. of obligation points to a past action (RG, 886), or is omnitemporal (VA, 211). ◆ 24 διϋλίζοντες pres. act. part. διϋλίζω (# 1494) to strain out by filtering through (RWP). Note the prep. "through" in compound; s. MH, 300f. Part. used as a rel. cl. κώνωπα acc. sing. κώνωψ (# 3276) gnat. Straining out a gnat goes back to the practice of straining wine through a cloth or wicker basket (Lachs, 170). κάμηλος (# 2823) camel. καταπίνοντες pres. act. part. καταπίνω (# 2927) to swallow, to drink down. Note the prep. "down" in the compound. ◆ 25 ἔξωθεν (# 2033) outside. ποτήριον (# 4539) cup. παροψίδος gen. sing. παροψίς (# 4243) dish. For the cleaning of vessels s. M, Kleim; Jacob Neusner, "'First Cleanse the Inside'," NTS 22 (1976): 486-95; DJG, 125-30. ἔσωθεν (# 2277) inside. γέμουσιν pres. ind. act. γέμω (# 1154) to be full. ἁρπαγή (# 771) robbery, plunder; obtained by violent or dishonest practices (Filson). ἀκρασία (# 202) lack of self-control which

shows itself in an unrestrained desire for gain (McNeile; TDNT; Ps. of Sol. 4:3). ◆ 26 καθάρισον aor. imp. act. καθαρίζω (# 2751) to cleanse. Aor. imp. calls for a specific act. ἐντός (# 1955) inside. ἐκτός (# 1760) outside. For a discussion of this v. s. Carson, 481-82. ◆ 27 παρομοιάζετε pres. ind. act. παρομοιάζω (# 4234) to be like; w. dat. τάφος (# 5439) grave. κεκονιαμένοις perf. pass. part. κονιάω (# 3154) to make white, to whiten w. chalk or lime. Before the Passover it was customary to whitewash graves that people and the priest might not unintentionally touch them or contract ceremonial defilement (Allen; SB, 1:936-37). φαίνονται pres. ind. mid. (dep.) φαίνομαι (# 5743) to appear. ὡραῖος (# 6053) beautiful. The graves were beautiful because of their structure and art (Carson, 482; ABD, 1:791-94). ὀστέον (# 4014) bone. ◆ 28 μεστός (# 3550) full (w. gen.). ὑποκρίσεως gen. sing. ὑπόκρισις (# 5694) hypocrisy, pretense, outward show (BAGD). ἀνομία (# 490) lawlessness. For the alpha privative which negates the word s. Moorhouse, 41-68. ◆ 29 οἰκοδομεῖτε pres. ind. act. οἰκοδομέω (# 3868) to build. Pres. indicates a repeated action. κοσμεῖτε pres. ind. act. κοσμέω (# 3175) to put into order, to decorate. The erecting of monuments to mark the graves of Israel's heroes may have been initiated by Herod the Great's building of a monument at David's tomb. Such monuments may have had an expiatory character (Hill; SB, 1:936-37). ◆ 30 ἤμεθα impf. ind. mid. (dep.) 1st. pl. εἰμί (# 1639). ἄν (# 323) used to introduce the second part of a contrary to fact cond. cl. ◆ 31 ὥστε (# 6063) therefore, for this reason. μαρτυρεῖτε pres. ind. act. μαρτυρέω (# 3455) to testify. ἑαυτοῖς dat. pl. ἑαυτός (# 1571). Dat. of disadvantage: "against yourselves." φονευσάντων aor. act. part. φονεύω (# 5839) to kill, to murder, to deprive a person of life by illegal, intentional killing (LN, 1:238). ◆ 32 πληρώσατε aor. imp. act. πληρόω (# 4444) to fill, to fill up. "Perform then that w. the hand that which you cherish in the heart" (Bengel). μέτρον (# 3586) acc. sing. n. measure. The idea is that God can only tolerate so much sin; then he must respond in wrath (Carson, 484). ◆ 33 ὄφεις voc. pl. ὄφις (# 4098) snake. γέννημα (# 1165) that which is born, brood. For the background s. HSB, 395-97. ἐχιδνῶν gen. pl. ἔχιδνα (# 2399) a poisonous snake. (s. 3:7). φύγητε aor. subj. act. φεύγω (# 5771) to flee. Subj. is used in doubtful or deliberate question. "How shall (can) you escape?" (BD, 185; MKG, 244; Hendriksen). ◆ 34 διὰ τοῦτο because of this. The words point to an act that Jesus will do; because of the wicked reception more messengers will be sent, thus filling up the measure of iniquity and judgment will fall (Carson, 484). ἀποστέλλω (# 690) pres. ind. act. to send an official authoritative representative (TDNT; EDNT; TLNT). The pres. is "I am sending" (Gundry). ἀποκτενεῖτε fut. ind. act. ἀποκτείνω (# 650) to kill. σταυρώσετε fut. ind. act.

σταυρόω (# 5090) to crucify. μαστιγώσετε fut. ind. act. μαστιγόω (# 4363) to scourge. διώξετε fut. ind. act. διώκω (# 1503) to hunt, to pursue, to persecute. ◆ 35 ἔλθῃ aor. subj. act. ἔρχομαι (# 2262) to come, to go. Subj. used w. ὅπως (# 3968) to express results (IGNT, 235). αἷμα δίκαιον "innocent blood" (Hill). ἐκχυννόμενον pres. pass. part. ἐκχέω (# 1772) to shed, to pour out. Part. as adj. ἐφονεύσατε aor. ind. act. s.v. 31. μεταξύ (# 3568) between. For a discussion of the identity of Zachariah s. Carson, 485-86; SB, 1:940-43; Hagner. ◆ 36 ἥξει fut. ind. act. ἥκω (# 2457) to come. γενεά (# 1155) generation. ◆ 37 ἀποκτείνουσα pres. act. part. voc. fem. sing. ἀποκτείνω (# 650) to kill. λιθοβολοῦσα pres. act. part. voc. fem. sing. λιθοβολέω (# 3344) to stone. The part. w. the art. are almost substantives, "the killer of … the stoner of…" (McNeile; s. M, 127f). Pres. points to a repeated action. ἀπεσταλμένους perf. pass. part. ἀποστέλλω (# 690) to send, to commission someone for a special task giving them the authority of the one sending. ποσάκις (# 4529) how often. ἠθέλησα aor. ind. act. θέλω (# 2527) to want to, to wish. ἐπισυναγαγεῖν aor. act. inf. ἐπισυνάγω (# 2190) to gather together. For the double prep. w. the vb. s. MH, 312. ὃν τρόπον (# 5573) acc. sing. in the manner in which, like, in like manner (BAGD). ὄρνις (# 3998) bird, hen, the mother bird (McNeile). νοσσίον (# 3800) a young bird. πτέρυγας acc. pl. πτέρυξ (# 4763) wing (BBC). ἠθελήσατε aor. ind. act. θέλω to wish, to desire; showing purp. or resolve. ◆ 38 ἀφίεται pres. ind. pass. ἀφίημι (# 918) to leave, to abandon, pass. to be left (BAGD). ◆ 39 ἴδητε aor. subj. act. ὁράω (# 3972) to see. Subj. used in a prediction w. the emphatic neg. οὐ μή. (VA, 429). εἴπητε aor. subj. act. λέγω (# 3306) to say. εὐλογημένος perf. pass. part. εὐλογέω (# 2328) to bless, to praise, pass., blessed (Gundry). A quotation from Ps. 118:26.

Matthew 24

◆ 1 ἐξελθών aor. act. part. (temp.) ἐξέρχομαι (# 2002) to go out. ἐπορεύετο impf. ind. mid. / pass. (dep.) πορεύομαι (# 4513) to go, to precede. προσῆλθον (dep.) aor. ind. act. προσέρχομαι (# 4665) to come to. ἐπιδεῖξαι aor. act. inf. ἐπιδείκνυμι (# 2109) to show, to point out. Inf. of purp. οἰκοδομάς acc. pl. οἰκοδομή (# 3869) building. Pl. points to the various buildings of the Temple. For a description of the Temple s. TJ, 28-30, s. note #16; JPB, 51-72; DJG, 811-17; M, Middot. ◆ 2 ἀποκριθείς aor. part. pass. (dep.) ἀποκρίνομαι (# 646) to answer. ἀφεθῇ aor. subj. pass. ἀφίημι (# 918) to leave; pass, to be left. καταλυθήσεται fut. ind. pass. καταλύω (# 2907) to throw down, to destroy, to demolish. For the fulfillment s. TJ, 195ff. ◆ 3 καθημένου pres. part. mid. (dep.) κάθημαι (# 2764) to sit. κατ᾽ ἰδίαν (# 2848; 2625) privately. εἰπέ aor. imp. act. λέγω (# 3306) to say. πότε (# 4537) when. σημεῖον (# 4956) sign. παρουσίας (# 4242) presence, arrival, coming

(TDNT; NIDNTT; NTW). συντελείας (# 5333) end, consummation. For a prophetical study of Matt. 24-25 s. John F. Walvoord, "Christ's Olivet Discourse on the End of the Age," *Bib Sac* 128, 129 (1971-72); SB, 1:949; 4:ii, 799-976. Matthew supplies no answer regarding the destruction of the Temple (McNeile). ◆ 4 βλέπετε (# 1063) pres. imp. act. to beware. μή (# 3590) lest. πλανήσῃ aor. subj. act. πλανάω (# 4419) to lead astray, to cause to wander off the path, to cause someone to hold a wrong view and thus be mistaken (LN, 1:367). ◆ 5 ἐλεύσονται fut. ind. mid. (dep.) ἔρχομαι. (# 2262) to come, to go. πλανήσουσιν fut. ind. act. s.v. 4. ◆ 6 μελλήσετε fut. ind. act. μέλλω (# 3516) to be about to. For the use of this word to express the durative fut. s. MKG, 307 ("you will continually hear"). πολέμους (# 4483) acc. pl. war. ἀκοάς acc. pl. ἀκοή (# 198) rumor. ὁράτε pres. imp. act. ὁράω (# 3972) to see. For the use of the two imps. s. RG, 949. θροεῖσθε pres. imp. mid. / pass. (dep.) θροέομαι (# 2583) to cry aloud, to scream; pass. to be terrified by an outcry (RWP). The neg. μή (# 3590) w. imp. forbids a constant attitude. δεῖ (#1256) pres. ind. act. it is necessary. It gives a logical necessity. γενέσθαι aor. mid. (dep.) inf. γίνομαι (# 1181) to become, to happen. Inf. explaining what is necessary. τέλος (# 5465) end, goal, consummation. ◆ 7 ἐγερθήσεται fut. ind. pass. ἐρείρω (# 1586) pass. to rise up, to rise up against. ἔθνος (# 1620) folk, nation. λιμός (# 3350) famine. σεισμός (# 4939) earthquake. κατὰ τόπους (# 2848; 5536) in various places. For the distributive use of the prep. w. the acc. s. RG, 608. ◆ 8 ἀρχή (# 794) beginning. ὠδίν (# 6047) birth pangs, labor pains, travail. The Jews used the phrase to signify the time of unprecedented trouble which was to precede the Messianic salvation (Allen; HJP 2: ii, 154-56; Moore, *Judaism*, 2:361f; SB, 4:ii, 857-80). ◆ 9 παραδώσουσιν fut. ind. act. παραδίδωμι (# 4140) to deliver over. θλῖψις (# 2568) pressure, tribulation. ἀποκτενοῦσιν fut. ind. act. ἀποκτείνω (# 650) to kill. μισούμενοι pres. pass. part. μισέω (# 3631) to hate. διά w. acc. gives the reason for the hate. ◆ 10 σκανδαλισθήσονται fut. ind. pass. σκανδαλίζω (# 4997) to cause to stumble (TDNT). μισήσουσιν fut. ind. act. μισέω (# 3651) to hate. ◆ 11 ψευδοπροφήτης (# 6021) false prophet. ἐγερθήσονται fut. ind. pass. ἐγείρω (# 1586) pass. to rise, to appear (BAGD). ◆ 12 πληθυνθῆναι aor. pass. inf. πληθύνω (# 4437) to increase, to multiply; pass. to be multiplied, to grow. Prep. is used w. the inf. to express cause. (MT, 142f). ἀνομία (# 490) lawlessness (s. Matt. 23:28). ψυγήσεται fut. ind. pass. ψύχω (# 6038) to make cold; pass. to become cold. ◆ 13 ὑπομείνας aor. act. part. ὑπομένω (# 5702) to endure, to continue to bear up despite difficulty and suffering (LN, 1:308). σωθήσεται fut. ind. pass. σῴζω (# 5392) to save, to rescue; pass. to be delivered. ◆ 14 κηρυχθήσεται fut. ind. pass. κηρύσσω (# 3062) to preach, to proclaim. οἰκουμένη (# 3876) the inhabited earth. μαρτύριον (# 3451) witness. ἥξει fut. ind. act. ἥκω (# 2457) to come. Predictive fut. ◆ **15 ὅταν** whenever. **ἴδητε** aor. ind. subj. ὁράω (# 3972) to see. **βδέλυγμα** abomination, detestable thing, that which is repulsive. It was used in the LXX of idols and cultic objects and of a sacrilegious object or rite causing the desecration of a sacred place (GELTS, 79). **ἐρημώσεως** gen. ἐρήμωσις (# 2247) desolation. "An abominable thing that layeth waste" (McNeile; BBC). A reference to the Anti-Christ (the man of sin) s. 2 Thess. 2:3f (Hill). **ῥηθέν** aor. pass. part. λέγω (# 3306) to say. **ἑστός** perf. act. part. ἵστημι (# 2705) to place; perf. to stand. **ἀναγινώσκων** pres. act. part. ἀναγινώσκω (# 336) to read. **νοείτω** pres. imp. pass. νοέω (# 3783) to understand. ◆ **16 φευγέτωσαν** pres. imp. act. 3rd. pers. pl. φεύγω (# 5771) to flee. To Judeans, this means flight into the rugged Judean wilderness, whose cave-filled mountains were a traditional hideout (Gundry). ◆ **17 δῶμα** (# 1560) roof. **καταβάτω** aor. imp. act. 3rd. pers. sing. καταβαίνω to come down. **ἆραι** aor. inf. act. αἴρω (# 149) to pick up, to take. Inf. used to express purp. ◆ **18 ἐπιστρεψάτω** aor. imp. mid. 3rd. pers. sing. ἐπιστρέφω (# 2188) to turn about, to return. **ὀπίσω** (# 3958) back, behind. Aor. imps. call for a specific action. ◆ **19 οὐαί** (# 4026) woe. **γαστρί** dat. γαστήρ (# 1143) stomach. **ἐχούσαις** pres. act. part. fem. dat. pl. ἔχω (# 2400) to have something in the stomach, that is, to be pregnant. **θηλαζούσαις** pres. act. part. fem. θηλάζω (# 2558) to suck, to nurse. ◆ **20 προσεύχεσθε** pres. imp. mid. (dep.) προσεύχομαι (# 4667) to pray. **γένηται** aor. subj. mid. (dep.) γίνομαι (# 1181) to become. **φυγή** (# 5870) flight, escape. **χειμών** (# 5930) storm, winter. **σαββάτῳ** dat. σάββατον (# 4879). Dat. of time: "on the Sabbath." The winter dangers (heavy rains, high water) and the rules regarding profaning the Sabbath were to be avoided (Sand). ◆ **21 ἔσται** fut. ind. mid. (dep.) εἰμί (# 1639). **θλῖψις** (# 2568) pressure, tribulation. This unusual and unprecedented tribulation would be the birth pains of the Messiah in Jewish teaching s.v. 8. **γέγονεν** perf. ind. act. γίνομαι to become, to happen, to be. **γένηται** aor. subj. mid. (dep.) γίνομαι. The strong double neg. οὐ μή indicates that there will never be another tribulation like this one. ◆ **22 εἰ μή** (# 1623; 3590) if not, except, introduces a contrary to fact cond. cl. **ἐκολοβώθησαν** aor. ind. pass. κολοβόω (# 3143) to mutilate, to curtail, to shorten (BAGD). **ἐσώθη** aor. ind. pass. σῴζω (# 5392) to save, rescue. **ἐκλεκτός** (# 1723) elect, chosen. **κολοβωθήσονται** fut. ind. pass. κολοβόω. ◆ **23 εἴπῃ** aor. subj. act. λέγω (# 3306) to say. Subj. w. ἐάν (# 1569) in a 3rd. class cond. which views the cond. as possible. **πιστεύσητε** aor. subj. act. πιστεύω (# 4409) to trust, to believe; w. neg. μή (# 3590) it is a prohibition not to start an action. ◆ **24 ψευδόχριστος** (# 6023) false Christ. **δώσουσιν** fut. ind. act. δίδωμι (# 1443) to give. **τέρατα** pl.

τέρας (# 5469) wonder, that which is startling, imposing, amazement, waking (Trench, *Synonyms*; TDNT; NIDNTT). **πλανῆσαι** aor. inf. act. πλανάω (# 4414) s.v. 4. Inf. expresses result. ◆ **25 προείρηκα** perf. ind. act. προλέγω (# 4625) to say beforehand. Perf. indicates the abiding results of what was said. ◆ **26 εἴπωσιν** aor. subj. act. λέγω (# 3306). Subj. w. ἐάν (# 1569) in a 3rd. class cond. cl. s.v. 23. **ἐξέλθητε** aor. subj. act. ἐξέρχομαι (# 2002) to go out. **ταμείοις** dat. pl. ταμιεῖον (# 5421) hidden, secret room. **πιστεύσητε** aor. subj. act. s.v. 23. ◆ **27 ἀστραπή** (# 847) lightning. **ἀνατολῶν** gen. pl. ἀνατολή (# 424) east. **φαίνεται** pres. ind. mid. (dep.) φαίνομαι (# 5743) to shine. Gnomic pres. indicating that which is a general rule. **δυσμῶν** gen. pl. δυσμή (# 1553) west. Lightning is visible to all and so will be the coming of the Son of Man (Gnilka). **ἔσται** fut. ind. mid. (dep.) s.v. 21. ◆ **28 ὅπου ἐάν** (# 3963; 1569) w. subj. wherever. **πτῶμα** (# 4773) corpse, a fallen one. **συναχθήσονται** fut. ind. pass. συνάγω (# 5251) to gather together. **ἀετοί** (# 108) nom. pl. eagle, vulture (BAGD; Job 39:27-30). ◆ **29 εὐθέως** (# 2311) adv. immediately. **σκοτισθήσεται** fut. ind. pass. σκοτίζομαι (# 5029) to become dark, to be dark. **σελήνη** (# 4943) moon. **φέγγος** (# 5766) light, radiance. **ἀστέρες** pl. ἀστήρ (# 843) star. **πεσοῦνται** fut. ind. mid. (dep.) πίπτω (# 4406) to fall. **σαλευθήσονται** fut. ind. pass. σαλεύω (# 4888) to shake, to cause to move to and fro. These things indicate the coming of the end time (Lachs, 385; s. Isa. 24:23; 34:4; Joel 2:31; 3:15; 1 Enoch 80:1; Test. of Levi 4:1; Test. of Moses 10:5; b. Sanh. 91b; 1QM 18:5). ◆ **30 φανήσεται** fut. ind. pass. (dep. s. BD, 43) φαίνομαι (# 5743) to shine; pass. to appear, to make one's appearance (BAGD). **κόψονται** fut. ind. mid. κόπτω (# 3164) to strike, to strike the breast as a sign of mourning. **φυλαί** nom. pl. φυλή tribe. **ὄψονται** fut. ind. mid. (dep.) ὁράω (# 3972) to see. **ἐρχόμενον** pres. mid. (dep.) part. ἔρχομαι (# 2262) to go. Adj. part. **νεφέλη** (# 3749) cloud. **δόξης** (# 1518) glory. ◆ **31 ἀποστελεῖ** fut. ind. act. ἀποστέλλω (# 690) to send. **σάλπιγγος** gen. sing. σάλπιγξ (# 4894) trumpet. **ἐπισυνάξουσιν** fut. ind. act. ἐπισυνάγω (# 2190) to bring together, to gather together s. Matt. 23:37. **ἄνεμος** (# 449) wind. **ἄκρων** gen. pl. ἄκρον (# 216) end. ◆ **32 συκῆ** (# 5190) fig tree. **μάθετε** aor. imp. act. μαθάνω (# 3443) to learn. **κλάδος** (# 3080) branch. **γένηται** aor. subj. mid. (dep.) γίνομαι (# 1181) to become. Subj. used in an indef. temp. cl. w. ὅταν (# 4020). **ἁπαλός** (# 559) tender, that is, sprouts (BAGD). **φύλλα** nom. pl. φύλλον (# 5877) leaf. **ἐκφύῃ** pres. subj. act. ἐκφύω (# 1770) to put forth. Sing. vb. w. n. pl. subject. **θέρος** (# 2580) summer. ◆ **33 ἴδητε** aor. subj. act. ὁράω (# 3972) to see. Subj. w. ἕως ἄν (# 2401; 323) in an indef. temp. cl. **θύραις** dat. pl. θύρη (# 2598) door. The putting forth of the fig tree from its state of winter dryness symbolizes the future reviviscence of the Jewish people (Alford). ◆ **34 παρέλθῃ** aor. subj. act.

παρέρχομαι (# *4216*) to pass by, to pass away. **γενεά** (# *1155*) race, generation. ◆ **35 παρελεύσεται** fut. ind. mid. (dep.) παρέρχομαι. **παρέλθωσιν** aor. subj. act. παρέρχομαι. The dissolution of heaven and earth would constitute the end of the present age. "The world shall pass away and my prediction of it shall not fail" (McNeile). ◆ **36 οἶδεν** perf. ind. act. οἶδα (# *3857*) to know. Def. perf. w. pres. meaning. ◆ **37 ὥσπερ** (# *6061*) just as. Used in a comp. construction (BAGD). **ἔσται** fut. ind. mid. (dep.) εἰμί (# *1639*). **παρουσία** (# *4242*) presence, coming, arrival; used for the arrival or coming of the Caesar or a Ruler (EDNT; NDIEC, 1:46; 4:167-69; TDNT). ◆ **38 κατακλυσμός** (# *2886*) flood. **τρώγοντες** pres. act. part. τρώγω (# *5592*) to gnaw, to nibble, to munch, to chew raw fruit or vegetables (McNeile). **πίνοντες** pres. act. part. πίνω (# *4403*) to drink. **γαμοῦντες** pres. act. part. γαμέω (# *1138*) to marry. **γαμίζοντες** pres. act. part. γαμίζω (# *1139*) to give in marriage. Parts. are not periphrastic but are descriptive predicates (EGT; VA, 458-59). A description of a mode of life without concern and without any foreboding of an impending catastrophe (Meyer). **ἄχρι** (# *968*) w. gen. until. **εἰσῆλθεν** aor. ind. act. εἰσέρχομαι (# *1656*) to go in. **κιβωτός** (# *3066*) ark. ◆ **39 ἔγνωσαν** aor. ind. act. γινώσκω (# *1182*) to know. **ἦλθεν** aor. ind. act. ἔρχομαι (# *2262*) to go. **ἦρεν** aor. ind. act. αἴρω (# *149*) to lift up, to take away. For the days of Noah and the flood in Judaism s. SB, 1:961-66. ◆ **40 ἔσονται** fut. ind. mid. (dep.) εἰμί (# *1639*) to be. **παραλαμβάνεται** pres. ind. pass. παραλαμβάνω (# *4161*) to take along w., to take away. Pres. pictures what is fut. as though it were already taking place (Meyer). **ἀφίεται** pres. ind. pass. ἀφίημι (# *918*). The "taking" may indicate salvation and the "leaving" judgment (Gundry). ◆ **41 ἀλήθουσαι** pres. act. part. fem. pl. ἀλήθω (# *241*) to grind. The work usually performed by the lower order of female slaves (Meyer). **μύλος** (# *3685*) mill, mill stone. ◆ **42 γρηγορεῖτε** pres. imp. act. γρηγορέω (# *1213*) to watch. The word has ethical and religious overtones (Luz). Pres. imp. indicates a constant vigil. **ποίᾳ** dat. ποῖος (# *4481*) what kind; dat. of time. ◆ **43 ἐκεῖνο** refers to that which follows (BD, 151f). **γινώσκετε** pres. ind. or imp. act. s.v. 39 **εἰ** (# *1623*) w. ind. and **ἄν** (# *323*) to introduce a contrary to fact cond. cl. **ᾔδει** plperf. ind. act. οἶδα (# *3857*). Plperf. used w. past meaning. "If he were in a knowledgeable state" (VA, 306). **οἰκοδεσπότης** (# *3867*) ruler of the house. **φυλακῇ** (# *5871*) night watch. **ἐγρηγόρησεν** aor. ind. act. γρηγορέω (# *1213*). **εἴασεν** aor. ind. act. ἐάω (# *1572*) to allow. **διορυχθῆναι** aor. pass. inf. διορύσσω (# *1482*) to dig through, to break through. Dig through the tile roof or under the floor (RWP). Inf. supplements the vb. ἐάω. ◆ **44 γίνεσθε** pres. imp. mid. (dep.) γίνομαι (# *1181*) to become, to be. **ἕτοιμος** (# *2289*) ready. **ᾗ ... ὥρᾳ** (# *6052*) at which hour, dat. of time.

δοκεῖτε pres. ind. act. δοκέω (# *1506*) to think, to be of an opinion. ◆ **45 φρόνιμος** (# *5861*) sensible, thoughtful, wise. **κατέστησεν** aor. ind. act. καθίστημι (# *2770*) to appoint, to constitute. **οἰκετεία** (# *3859*) household slave. For the treatment of Heb. slaves s. SB, 4:698-744. **δοῦναι** aor. act. inf. δίδωμι (# *1443*) to give. Inf. expresses purp. ◆ **46 μακάριος** (# *3421*) happy (s. Matt. 5:3). **ἐλθών** aor. act. part. ἔρχομαι (# *2262*). The part. is used to express contemporaneous time: "When he comes." **εὑρήσει** fut. act. ind. εὑρίσκω (# *2351*) to find. **ποιοῦντα** pres. act. part. acc. masc. sing. ποιέω (# *4472*) to do, to make. Part. of manner, so performing as was assigned to him. ◆ **47 ὑπάρχουσιν** pres. act. part. ὑπάρχω (# *5639*) to exist, to be present, to be at one's disposal. Part. used as subst. ("possessions") (BAGD). **καταστήσει** fut. ind. act. καθίστημι s.v. 45. ◆ **48 εἴπῃ** aor. subj. act. λέγω (# *3306*) to say. Subj. w. ἐάν (# *1569*) used in 3rd. class cond. cl. viewing the cond. as a possibility. **χρονίζει** pres. ind. act. χρονίζω (# *5988*) to delay, to take time. ◆ **49 ἄρξηται** aor. subj. mid. (dep.) ἄρχομαι (# *806*) to begin. **τύπτειν** pres. act. inf. τύπτω (# *5597*) to strike, to beat. Inf. complements the vb. ἄρξηται. **σύνδουλος** (# *5281*) fellow servant. **ἐσθίῃ** pres. act. subj. ἐσθίω (# *2266*) to eat. **μεθυόντων** pres. act. part. μεθύω (# *3501*) to be drunk ("w. those who are drunken"). ◆ **50 προσδοκᾷ** pres. ind. act. προσδοκάω (# *4659*) to wait for, to expect. ◆ **51 διχοτομήσει** fut. ind. act. διχοτομέω (# *1497*) to cut in two. In Exod. 29:17 the vb. is used of dividing a sacrificial victim into pieces (McNiele; Hagner; s.v. 45). **μέρος** (# *3538*) lot, part. **θήσει** fut. ind. act. τίθημι (# *5502*) to place, to assign. **κλαυθμός** (# *3088*) loud crying.

Matthew 25

◆ **1 ὁμοιωθήσεται** fut. ind. pass. ὁμοιόω (# *3929*) to make alike, to compare, followed by dat. The kingdom is not like the virgins, but their story illustrates an aspect of it. (McNiele). Fut. alludes to the last judgment (Gundry). **παρθένος** (# *4221*) virgin. **λαβοῦσαι** aor. part. act. fem. pl. λαμβάνω (# *3284*) to take. **λαμπάς** (# *3286*) lamp, probably the so-called "Herodian" lamp (s. Matt. 5:15), or perhaps it refers to torches which were cloths soaked in olive oil (Jeremias, *Parables*), or maybe lanterns (Günther Schwartz, "Zum Vokabular von Matthäus XXV. 1-12," *NTS* 27 [1980/81]: 270). **ἐξῆλθον** aor. ind. act. ἐξέρχομαι (# *2002*) to go out. **ὑπάντησις** (# *5637*) meeting. This represents the betrothal, then the marriage. The bridegroom accompanied by his friends went to fetch the bride from her father's house and brought her back in procession to his own house where the marriage feast was held (Tasker; Carson, 513; SB, 1:500-518; JPFC, 2:757-60; HSB, 398-99; BBC). **νυμφίου** gen. sing. νυμφίος (# *3812*) bridegroom. Obj. gen. For variant readings s. TC, 62-63. ◆ **2 ἦσαν** impf. ind. act. εἰμί (# *1639*). **μωρός** (# *3704*) foolish. **φρόνιμος**

(# 5861) wise, sensible, thoughtful. They were wise because they were prepared (Carson, 513). ◆ 3 ἔλαβον aor. ind. act. λαμβάνω (# 3284) to take. ἔλαιον (# 1778) olive oil. Perhaps the meaning is rancid butter, which was used for lighting (Schwartz, NTS 27, 270). ◆ 4 ἀγγεῖον (# 31) vessel, flask, small jars w. a narrow neck (Jeremias, Parables). ◆ 5 χρονίζοντος pres. act. part. χρονίζω (# 5988) to delay, to take one's time. Part. used as gen. abs. Pres. suggests contemporary action. ἐνύσταξαν aor. ind. act. νυστάζω (# 3818) to nod, to become drowsy, to doze. Ingressive aor. "They all became drowsy" (BAGD). ἐκάθευδον impf. ind. act. καθεύδω (# 2761) to sleep. Incep. impf., "they began to nod off" (Hagner). They dropped off to sleep and then went on sleeping (RWP). ◆ 6 κραυγή (# 3199) cry, loud calling. γέγονεν perf. ind. act. γίνομαι (# 1181) to become, to happen. Perf. probably is used here as a hist. pres. (M, 146). S. also K.L. McKay, "The Use of the Ancient Greek Perfect Down to the End of the Second Century A.D.," Bulletin of the Institute of Classical Studies 12 (1965): 1-21. ◆ 7 ἠγέρθησαν aor. ind. pass. ἐγείρω (# 1586) to awaken, to arouse from sleep. ἐκόσμησαν aor. ind. act. κοσμέω (# 3175) to put in order, to trim the lamps, to make presentable. S. R.H. Smith, "The Household Lamps of Palestine in New Testament Times," BA 29 (1966): 5. If they were torches, it includes checking the rags, dipping them in oil, and setting them aflame (Gundry; s.v. 1). It may refer to lamps tied atop poles (Hagner). ◆ 8 εἶπαν aor. ind. act. λέγω (# 3306) to say. δότε aor. imp. act. δίδωμι (# 1443) to give. Aor. imp. looks at a specific urgent act. σβέννυνται pres. ind. pass. σβέννυμι (# 4931) to extinguish; pass. to go out. Pres. pictures the action in progress: "They are going out." ◆ 9 ἀπεκρίθησαν aor. ind. pass. (dep.) ἀποκρίνομαι (# 646) to answer. μήποτε (# 3607) probably, perhaps (BAGD). ἀρκέσῃ aor. subj. act. ἀρκέω (# 758) to be enough, sufficient. For the variant reading οὐ μή s. Carson, 514. πορεύεσθε pres. imp. mid. (dep.) πορεύομαι (# 4513) to go. πωλοῦντας pres. act. part. πωλέω (# 4797) to sell. Part. used as subst. ἀγοράσατε aor. imp. act. ἀγοράζω (# 60) to buy. Aor. imp. looks at the specific, urgent act. ◆ 10 ἀπερχομένων pres. mid. (dep.) part. ἀπέρχομαι (# 599) to go away. Part. used as gen. abs. "After they were gone away." ἀγοράσαι aor. act. inf. ἀγοράζω (# 60) to purchase. Inf. expresses purp. ἦλθεν aor. ind. act. ἔρχομαι (# 2262) to come. ἕτοιμος (# 2289) ready. εἰσῆλθον aor. ind. act. εἰσέρχομαι (# 1656) to enter into. γάμους (# 1161) pl. wedding festivities. ἐκλείσθη aor. ind. pass. κλείω (# 3091) to shut, to lock; effective aor. "to shut, to stay shut" (RWP; VANT, 159). ◆ 11 ὕστερον (# 5731) later. ἔρχονται pres. ind. mid. (dep.) ἔρχομαι to go. Hist. pres. κύριε voc. sing. κύριος (# 3261). The double voc. stresses the urgency of the plea (BD, 261). ἄνοιξον aor. act. imp. ἀνοίγω (# 487) to open. Aor. imp. looks at

the specific urgent act. ◆ 12 ἀποκριθείς aor. part. pass. (dep.) ἀποκρίνομαι (# 646) to answer. For the use of the part. s. 3:15. οἶδα (# 3857) perf. ind. act. def. perf. w. pres. meaning, to know. ◆ 13 γρηγορεῖτε pres. act. imp. γρηγορέω (# 1213) to watch, to be ready. A figurative extension of "to be awake," that is, "to be in continual readiness and alertness," "to be vigilant" (LN, 1:333). Pres. imp. calls for a continual, habitual alertness. ◆ 14 ἀποδημῶν pres. act. part. nom. masc. sing. ἀποδημέω (# 623) to go on a journey, about to go away from one's people, on the point of going abroad (RWP). Temp. or causal part. "When he was about to go away..." or "because he...." ἐκάλεσεν aor. ind. act. καλέω (# 2813) to call. παρέδωκεν aor. ind. act. παραδίδωμι (# 4140) to deliver over, to give to. ὑπάρχοντα pres. act. part. acc. n. pl. ὑπάρχω (# 5639) to exist. Part. used as a noun: goods, possession (BAGD). ◆ 15 ἔδωκεν aor. ind. act. δίδωμι (# 1443) to give. τάλαντον (# 5419) a measure of money worth 6,000 denarii, whose value varied from time to time and from place to place (Carson, 516; BAGD). One denarius was worth a day's wages (RWP; Gnilka; s. also Matt. 18:24). In a papyrus text around A.D. 100 the price for the ransom of a woman slave is given as 1000 drachmae of imperial silver (NDIEC, 6:64-66). When Antiochus VII besieged the city of Jerusalem and Hyrcanus robbed the tomb of David and took about 3000 talents, 300 of which he used to bribe Antiochus to remove the blockade and the rest to hire a mercenary force (Jos., JW, 1:61; for other references to talents in Josephus s. CCFJ, 4:155-56). κατὰ τὴν ἰδίαν δύναμιν "according to each individual's ability." ἀπεδήμησεν aor. ind. act. s.v. 14. ◆ 16 εὐθέως (# 2311) adv. immediately. πορευθείς aor. pass. (dep.) part. (temp.) πορεύομαι (# 4513) to travel. λαβών aor. part. act. λαμβάνω (# 3289). Part. used as subst. ἠργάσατο aor. ind. mid. (dep.) ἐργάζομαι (# 2237) to be active, to work. ἐκέρδησεν aor. ind. act. κερδαίνω (# 3045) to profit, to gain. ◆ 17 ὡσαύτως (# 6058) likewise. ◆ 18 ἀπελθών aor. act. part. (circum.) ἀπέρχομαι (# 599) to go away, to go out. ὤρυξεν aor. ind. act. ὀρύσσω (# 4002) to dig. ἔκρυψεν aor. ind. act. κρύπτω (# 3221) to hide. ἀργύριον (# 736) silver, money. For the burying of money to protect it from thieves s. SB, 1:971-72; LNT, 24; for the safekeeping of entrusted money s. M, Baba Metzia, 3:4-12. ◆ 19 ἔρχεται pres. ind. mid. (dep.) s.v. 10 Hist. pres. συναίρει λόγον μετά (# 5256; 3364; 3552) a commercial term, "to compare accounts," "to make a reckoning" (LAE, 117). ◆ 20 προσελθών aor. act. part. (temp.) προσέρχομαι (# 4665) to come to. προσήνεγκεν aor. ind. act. προσφέρω (# 4712) to bring to. παρέδωκας aor. ind. act. παραδίδωμι (# 4140) to deliver over, to entrust. ἴδε (# 2623) aor. imp. act. ὁράω to see. ἐκέρδησα aor. ind act. s.v. 16. ◆ 21 ἔφη impf. ind. act. φημί (# 5774) to say. εὖ (# 2292) adv. "well done!" "excellent!" (EGT). καταστήσω fut.

ind. act. καθίστημι (# 2770) to appoint. εἴσελθε aor. imp. act. εἰσέρχομαι (# 1656) to enter. χαρά (# 5915) joy. ◆ 22 εἶπεν aor. ind. act. λέγω (# 3306) to say. ◆ 24 εἰλη-φώς perf. act. part. λαμβάνω (# 3284) to take. Perf. points out that he still has what he had received: the possessor (VA, 379). ἔγνων aor. ind. act. γινώσκω (# 1182) to know. σκληρός (# 5017) hard, severe, harsh, demanding (LN, 1:757). θερίζων pres. act. part. θερίζω (# 2545) to harvest. ἔσπειρας aor. ind. act. 2nd. pers. sing. σπείρω (# 5062) to sow. συνάγων pres. part. act. συνάγω (# 5251) to gather. διεσκόρπισας aor. part. act. διασκορπίζω (# 1399) to scatter, to scatter seed or to winnow (BAGD). ◆ 25 φοβηθείς aor. pass. (dep.) part. (causal) φοβέομαι (# 5828) to be afraid. σόν (# 5050) yours. ◆ 26 ὀκνηρέ voc. sing. ὀκνηρός (# 3891) idle, lazy, pertaining to shrinking from or hesitating to en-gage in something worthwhile, possibly implying lack of ambition (LN, 1:769). ᾔδεις plperf. ind. act. οἶδα (# 3857) to know. Plperf. w. a past meaning. ◆ 27 ἔδει impf. act. ind. δεῖ (# 1256) it is necessary, w. acc. and inf. Impf. looks at the unfulfilled responsibility. βαλεῖν aor. inf. act. βάλλω (# 965) to throw; here, to bring. τρα-πεζίτης (# 5545) moneychanger, banker. Indir. obj. ἐλθών aor. part. act. ἔρχομαι (# 2262). ἐκομισάμην aor. ind. mid. κομίζω (# 3152) to bring; mid. to get back, re-cover. τόκος (# 5527) interest. The maximum rate for money loans in the empire was 12 percent (W.W. Buckland, *A Textbook of Roman Law*, 465). For invest-ments s. LNT, 22-24. ◆ 28 ἄρατε aor. imp. act. αἴρω (# 149) to lift up, to take away. δότε aor. imp. act. δίδω-μι (# 1443) to give. ἔχοντι pres. act. part. dat. masc. sing. ἔχω (# 2400) to have. Adj. part. used as subst.: "to the one who has...." ◆ 29 δοθήσεται fut. ind. pass. δίδωμι (# 1443) to give. περισσευθήσεται fut. ind. pass. περισσεύω (# 4355) to abound, to have an abundance, to make to abound. ἔχοντος pres. act. part. gen. sing. ἔχω (# 2400) to have. A Semitic construction of *casus pendens*. The part. is to be translated in the place of the resumptive pron.: "from the one who does not have" (s. McNiele; MH, 432f). ἀρθήσεται fut. ind. pass. αἴρω (# 149) to lift up, to take away. ◆ 30 ἀχρεῖος (# 945) useless, worthless. ἐκβάλετε aor. imp. act. ἐκβάλλω (# 1675) to cast out. ἐξώτερος (# 2035) outer, comp. form only (s. Matt. 8:12). The point of the parable is to be faithful w. that which God entrusts to you (LNT, 26-31). ◆ 31 ἔλθῃ aor. subj. act. ἔρχομαι (# 2262). Subj. in an undetermined temp. cl. w. ὅταν (# 4020). καθίσει fut. ind. act. καθίζω (# 2767) to sit, to take one's seat. ◆ 32 συναχθήσονται fut. ind. pass. συνάγω (# 5251) to gather together. ἔθνη nom. pl. ἔθνος (# 1620) nation, foreign nation, Gentile (BAGD; TDNT; EDNT). The ac-count describes the judgment of all humanity (Gun-dry). ἀφορίσει fut. ind act. ἀφορίζω (# 928) to separate. ποιμήν (# 4478) shepherd. ἔριφος (# 2253) kid, goat. ◆ 33 στήσει fut. ind. act. ἵστημι (# 2705) to place. ἐκ

(# 1666) from; here, on. The prep. here answers the question "where?" (BAGD). δέξιος (# 1288) right, on the right hand, indicating a status of high standing or honor (LN, 1:737). εὐώνυμος (# 2381) left, on the left hand, indicating a bad omen (Beare; Gnilka). For the use of the pl. w. words of directions s. BD, 77-78. ◆ 34 ἐρεῖ fut. ind. act. λέγω (# 3306). δεῦτε (# 1307) "come here!" εὐλογημένοι perf. pass. part. εὐλογέω to bless, to praise. κληρονομήσατε aor. imp. act. κληρονο-μέω (# 2328) to inherit, to receive an inheritance. ἡτοι-μασμένην perf. pass. part. ἑτοιμάζω (# 2286) to prepare. καταβολή (# 2856) foundation. ◆ 35 ἐπείνασα aor. ind. act. πεινάω (# 4277) to be hungry. To be hungry was a sign for being needy and poor (EDNT). ἐδώκατε aor. ind. act. δίδωμι (# 1443) to give. φαγεῖν aor. inf. act. ἐσ-θίω (# 2266) to eat. Inf. expresses purp. ἐδίψησα aor. ind. act. διψάω (# 1498) to be thirsty. ἐποτίσατε aor. ind. act. ποτίζω (# 4540) to drink (s. TJ, 60; Jos., *Ant.*, 18.193-94). ξένος (# 3828) stranger. There was often a general mistrust of strangers and they were in need of hospi-tality (EDNT). ἤμην impf. ind. mid. (dep.) 1st. pers. sing. εἰμί (# 1639) (s. BD, 49). συνηγάγετε aor. ind. act. συνάγω (# 5251) to bring together, to invite or receive as a guest (BAGD). ◆ 36 γυμνός (# 1218) naked. The word can be used of complete nakedness, or of inade-quate or meager clothing (EDNT). περιεβάλετε aor. ind. act. περιβάλλω (# 4314) to cast about, to clothe. ἠσθένησα aor. ind. act. ἀσθενέω (# 820) to be weak, to be sick. ἐπεσκέψασθε aor. ind. mid. (dep.) ἐπισκέπτομαι (# 2170) to go to see, esp. to visit the sick (BAGD). φυ-λακῇ (# 5871) place of guarding, prison. Prisons were generally a place of temporary confinement until the trial took place. To visit someone in prison was a dan-gerous undertaking (BAFCS 3; CIC, 78-95; Brian M. Rapske, "The Importance of Helpers to the Impris-oned Paul in the Book of Acts," *TB* 42 [1991]: 3-30). ἤλθατε aor. ind. act. ἔρχομαι (# 2262). All of these works were considered in Judaism as acts of kindness (Lachs, 394-94; SB, 4:i, 559-610). ◆ 37 ἀποκριθήσονται fut. ind. pass. (dep.) ἀποκρίνομαι (# 646) to answer. εἴδομεν aor. ind. act. ὁράω (# 3972) to see. πεινῶντα pres. part. act. s.v. 35. ἐθρέψαμεν aor. ind. act. τρέφω (# 5555) to nourish, to give to eat. διψῶντα pres. part. act. s.v. 35. ◆ 38 εἴδομεν aor. ind. act. ὁράω (# 3972) to see. περιεβάλομεν aor. ind. act. περιβάλλω (# 4314) to throw around, to cloth. ◆ 39 φυλακῇ s.v. 36. ἤλθομεν aor. ind. act., s.v. 36. For the dangers s. BAFCS, 3:388-92. ◆ 40 ἀποκριθείς aor. pass. part. (dep.) s.v. 37. ἐρεῖ fut. ind. act. s.v. 34. ἐφ' ὅσον in so far as (EGT). ἐποιή-σατε aor. ind. act. ποιέω (# 4472) to do. ἑνί dat. masc. sing. εἷς one. Indir. obj. ἐλαχίστων (# 1788) superl. μίκρος the least. ◆ 41 πορεύεσθε pres. imp. mid. (dep.) πορεύομαι (# 4513) to go. κατηραμένοι perf. pass. part. καταράομαι (# 2933) to curse (NIDNTT; TDNT). διαβό-λῳ dat. διάβολος (# 1333) slanderer, devil (SB, 1:983-

84). Dat. of disadvantage. ◆ **43 ἀσθενής** (*# 822*) weak, sick. ◆ **44 διηκονήσαμεν** aor. ind. act. διακονέω (*# 1354*) to serve, to minister, to take care of, by rendering humble service to; here, "we did not give you whatever you needed" (LN, 1:462). ◆ **46 ἀπελεύσονται** fut. ind. mid. (dep.) ἀπέρχομαι (*# 599*) to go out, to depart. **κόλασις** (*# 3136*) punishment, w. the implication of resulting severe suffering (TDNT; LN, 1:489; *Test. of Abraham*, 11:11).

Matthew 26

◆ **1 ἐγένετο** aor. ind. mid. (dep.) γίνομαι (*# 1181*) to become, to happen. **ἐτέλεσεν** aor. ind. act. τελέω (*# 5464*) to end, to bring to completion. **εἶπεν** aor. ind. act. λέγω (*# 3306*) to speak. ◆ **2 οἴδατε** perf. ind. act. οἶδα (*# 3857*) to know. Def. perf. w. pres. meaning. **πάσχα** (*# 4247*) passover (TDNT; Moore, *Judaism*, 2:40f; M, Pesahim; WZZT, 220-36; DJG, 237; JDB, 132-38). **παραδίδοται** pres. ind. pass. παραδίδωμι (*# 4140*) to deliver over, to betray. Used as a t.t. of police and courts: "hand over into the custody of" (BAGD; TLNT). Pres. is used to refer to the certainty of the fut. event (M, 120; VA, 230-31; VANT, 225). **εἰς τό** w. inf. indicates purp. **σταυρωθῆναι** aor. pass. inf. σταυρόω (*# 5090*) to crucify (TDNT; EDNT). ◆ **3 συνήχθησαν** aor. ind. pass. συνάγω (*# 5251*) pass. to gather together. This points to a meeting of the Sanhedrin (EGT; BBC). **ἀρχιερεύς** (*# 797*) high priest (DJG, 635). **πρεσβύτερος** (*# 4565*) elder. **αὐλή** (*# 885*) courtyard. **λεγομένου** pres. pass. part. λέγω (*# 3306*) to say; pass. to be called, to be named. **Καϊάφα** (*# 2780*) Caiaphas, Joseph Caiaphas, high priest from A.D. 18-36 (SB, 1:985; TDNT; JTJ; DJG, 635; ABD, 1:803-806; EDNT; HJPE, 2:230). ◆ **4 συνεβουλεύσαντο** aor. ind. mid. συμβουλεύω (*# 5205*) to give advice; mid. to counsel together. **ἵνα** (*# 2671*) w. subj. after a vb. of effort or plan (EGT). **δόλῳ** dat. sing. δόλος (*# 1515*) deceit, cunning, treachery, as they would trap a wild beast (RWP). Instr. dat. **κρατήσωσιν** aor. subj. act. κρατέω (*# 3195*) to seize, to take into custody, to arrest. **ἀποκτείνωσιν** aor. subj. act. ἀποκτείνω (*# 650*) to kill. ◆ **5 ἑορτῇ** (*# 2038*) dat. feast, festival. **θόρυβος** (*# 2573*) turmoil, uproar. **γένηται** aor. subj. mid. (dep.) γίνομαι (*# 1181*) to become, to happen. W. the increased number of people in the city and w. religious fervor and national messianism, the leaders were right in fearing the people (Carson, 524). ◆ **6 γενομένου** aor. part. mid. (dep.) γίνομαι s.v. 5. Gen. abs. temp. part. ◆ **7 προσῆλθεν** aor. ind. act. προσέρχομαι (*# 4665*) to come to. **ἔχουσα** pres. act. part. nom. fem. sing. ἔχω (*# 2400*) to have. **ἀλάβαστρον** (*# 223*) alabaster, then alabaster flask for ointment. A vessel w. a long neck which was broken off when the contents were used (BAGD). **μύρου** (*# 3693*) gen. sing. μύρον ointment, a highly perfumed or aromatic oil, perhaps from the nard plant (PB, 205; FFB, 151-52) or compound of such

substances. Gen. of content. **βαρύτιμος** (*# 988*) lit., heavy w. price, very expensive. The ointment was estimated at over 300 denarii, approximately a year's salary of a working man (McNiele; Carson, 526). **κατέχεεν** aor. ind. act. καταχέω (*# 2972*) to pour over, to pour down. **ἀνακειμένου** pres. mid. part. ἀνάκειμαι (*# 367*) to recline at the table. ◆ **8 ἰδόντες** aor. act. part. (temp.) ὁράω (*# 3972*) to see. **ἠγανάκτησαν** aor. ind. act. ἀγανακτέω (*# 24*) to be indignant, to be angry (s. 20:24). For the pl. s. GGBB, 405. **εἰς τί** "for what reason?" "why?" "but why to no purpose?" (LNT, 269). **ἀπώλεια** (*# 724*) destruction, waste. ◆ **9 ἐδύνατο** impf. ind. pass. (dep.) δύναμαι (*# 1538*) to be able to. Impf. points to the unfulfilled possibility. **πραθῆναι** aor. inf. pass. πιπράσκω (*# 4405*) to sell. Used w. gen. of price. **δοθῆναι** aor. inf. pass. δίδωμι (*# 1443*) to give. Almsgiving was probably expected from the passover pilgrims to accompany their worship (McNiele; WZZT, 214-15). ◆ **10 γνούς** aor. act. part. (temp.) γινώσκω (*# 1182*) to know. **κόπους παρέχετε** (*# 4218*) pres. ind. act. to cause someone trouble for someone (w. dat.). **ἠργάσατο** aor. ind. mid. (dep.) ἐργάζομαι to work, to do. ◆ **11 πτωχός** (*# 4777*) poor, poor as a beggar. **ἔχετε** pres. ind. act. ἔχω (*# 2400*) to have. The rabbis interpreted Deut. 15:11 to mean that even in the days of the Messiah, the poor would be present (Lachs, 401). ◆ **12 βαλοῦσα** aor. act. part. (temp.) βάλλω (*# 965*) to throw, of liquids, to pour. "When she poured...." **πρὸς τό** (*# 4639*) w. inf. to express purp. **ἐνταφιάσαι** aor. inf. act. ἐνταφιάζω (*# 1946*) to prepare for burial, to bury. **ἐποίησεν** aor. ind. act. ποιέω (*# 4472*) to do. ◆ **13 κηρυχθῇ** aor. subj. pass. κηρύσσω (*# 3062*) to proclaim as a herald, to preach. **λαληθήσεται** fut. ind. pass. λαλέω (*# 3281*) to speak. **μνημόσυνον** (*# 3649*) remembrance, memorial. ◆ **14 πορευθείς** aor. part. pass. (dep.) πορεύομαι (*# 4513*) to go. Circum. or temp. part. ◆ **15 δοῦναι** aor. inf. act. δίδωμι (*# 1443*) to give. **παραδώσω** fut. ind. act. παραδίδωμι s.v. 2. **ἔστησαν** aor. ind. act. ἵστημι (*# 2705*) to place, to place in the scales, to weigh (McNiele). **ἀργύριον** (*# 736*) silver money. The thirty shekels, a reference to Zech. 11:12. If a man's ox gored a servant he had to pay this amount (Exod. 21:32) (RWP). The total bribe was about a month's wages (Filson). ◆ **16 ἐζήτει** impf. ind. act. ζητέω (*# 2426*) to seek. **εὐκαιρία** (*# 2321*) the right time, opportunity. **παραδῷ** aor. subj. act. παραδίδωμι s.v. 2. ◆ **17 ἀζύμων** gen. ἄζυμα (*# 109*) unleavened bread, the Feast of Unleavened Bread. Celebrated in connection w. the Passover (s. Exod. 12:17ff; TDNT; SB, 1:987-88; JPB, 132-33; Hagner; Harrington). **προσῆλθον** aor. ind. act. προσέρχομαι (*# 4665*) s.v. 7. **ἑτοιμάσωμεν** aor. subj. act. ἑτοιμάζω (*# 2286*) to prepare. **φαγεῖν** aor. inf. act. ἐσθίω (*# 2266*) to eat. **πάσχα** Passover. For a discussion of the last supper s. DJG, 444-50. S.v. 2. ◆ **18 εἶπεν** aor. ind. act. λέγω (*# 3306*) to say. **ὑπάγετε** pres. imp. act. ὑπάγω (*# 5632*) to go. **δεῖνα**

(# *1265*) someone, a certain one. Used of a person or thing one cannot describe or does not wish to name (BAGD). **εἴπατε** aor. imp. act. **πρὸς σέ** (# *4639; 5148*) "w. you," "at your house." **ποιῶ** pres. ind. act. ποιέω (# *4472*) to do, to celebrate. ◆ **19 ἐποίησαν** aor. ind. act. ποιέω s.v. 18. **συνέταξεν** aor. ind. act. συντάσσω (# *5332*) to command, to give an order. **ἡτοίμασαν** aor. ind. act. ἑτοιμάζω (# *2286*) to prepare. ◆ **20 ὀψίας** (# *4070*) evening (BBC). **γενομένης** aor. mid. part. (dep.) γίνομαι s.v. 5. in gen. abs. **ἀνέκειτο** impf. ind. mid. (dep.) ἀνάκειμαι. s.v. 7. Impf. pictures the continual action. ◆ **21 ἐσθιόντων** pres. act. part. gen. abs. Temp. part., "while they were eating." **παραδώσει** fut. ind. act. s.v. 2. ◆ **22 λυπούμενοι** pres. pass. part. λυπέω (# *3382*) to make sad; pass. to be sad, to be distressed, to grieve (BAGD). **ἤρξαντο** aor. ind. mid. (dep.) ἄρχομαι (# *806*) to begin. **εἷς ἕκαστος** (# *1651; 1667*) each (intensified) (BD, 160). **μήτι** (# *3614*) used in a question which expects a neg. answer. ◆ **23 ἀποκριθείς** aor. pass. (dep.) part. ἀποκρίνομαι (# *646*) to answer. **ἐμβάψας** aor. act. part. ἐμβάπτω (# *1835*) to dip into. **τρυβλίῳ** dat. sing. τρύβλιον (# *5581*) a deep bowl. The food was dipped into a sauce composed of fruits, spices, and vinegar (McNiele). ◆ **24 ὑπάγει** pres. ind. act. ὑπάγω (# *5632*) to go away. A euphemism for dying (Gnilka). **γέγραπται** perf. ind. pass. γράφω (# *1211*) to write. **παραδίδοται** pres. ind. pass. παραδίδωμι (# *4140*) to betray. **ἐγεννήθη** aor. ind. pass. γεννάω (# *1164*) to bear, to be born. Used in a contrary to fact cond. cl. (VA, 295). ◆ **25 παραδιδούς** pres. act. part. παραδίδωμι to betray. **εἶπας** aor. ind. act. 2nd. pers. sing. λέγω (# *3306*) to say. "You (emphatic) said it." S.v. 64 for the significance of the statement. ◆ **26 λαβών** aor. act. part. λαμβάνω (# *3284*) to take. **εὐλογήσας** aor. act. part. εὐλογέω (# *2328*) to bless, to give thanks (s. TDNT). For the blessing used at such meals s. Hill; SB, 4:i, 61f; WZZT, 230ff; LT, 2:496; M, Berakoth 6-7; M, Pesahim 10. Parts. are temp. or circum. suggesting antecedent action. **ἔκλασεν** aor. ind. act. κλάω (# *3089*) to break. **δούς** aor. act. part. δίδωμι (# *1443*) s.v. 15. **λάβετε** aor. imp. act. λαμβάνω to take. **φάγετε** aor. imp. act. ἐσθίω (# *2266*) to eat. ◆ **27 ποτήριον** (# *4539*) cup. **εὐχαριστήσας** aor. act. part. εὐχαριστέω (# *2373*) to give thanks. **ἔδωκεν** aor. ind. act. δίδωμι (# *1443*) to give. **πίετε** aor. imp. act. πίνω (# *4403*) to drink. **πάντες** nom. pl. πᾶς (# *4246*) all. Nom. is the subj.: "all (of you) drink from it." ◆ **28 διαθήκη** (# *1347*) covenant (TDNT; NIDNTT; NTW; APC). **ἐκχυννόμενον** pres. pass. part. ἐκχύνω (# *1772*) to pour out. The shed blood indicates life given up in death (APC). ◆ **29 πίω** aor. subj. act. πίνω (# *4403*) to drink. **γένημα** (# *1163*) that which grows, fruit. **ἄμπελος** (# *306*) grapevine. ◆ **30 ὑμνήσαντες** aor. act. part. ὑμνέω (# *5630*) to sing hymns of praise. The second part of the Hallel (Pss. 113-118) was sung at the close of the Passover meal (BAGD; SB, 4:ii, 68-73; WZZT, 230, 288-90;

M, Pesahim 10:7). **ἐξῆλθον** aor. ind. act. ἐξέρχομαι (# *2002*) to go out. The meal was to be finished by midnight (M, Pes. 10:9). ◆ **31 σκανδαλισθήσεσθε** fut. ind. pass. σκανδαλίζω (# *4997*) to cause to stumble (TDNT). **πατάξω** fut. ind. act. πατάσσω (# *4250*) to strike, to hit. **ποιμένα** acc. sing. ποιμήν (# *4478*) shepherd. Here a picture of leadership (DJG, 752). **διασκορπισθήσονται** fut. ind. pass. διασκορπίζω (# *1399*) to scatter. For the prep. in the compound w. the meaning "to and fro" s. MH, 302. **ποίμνης** gen. sing. ποίμνη (# *4479*) flock. Gen. of content. For the quotation from Zech. 13:7 as the basis for Jesus' prediction s. OTGPN, 182-87. ◆ **32 ἐγερθῆναι** aor. inf. pass. ἐγείρω (# *1586*) to raise from the dead, to rise. Inf. w. the prep. **μετά** to express subsequent time ("after"). **προάξω** fut. ind. act. προάγω (# *4575*) to go before. ◆ **33 ἀποκριθείς** aor. pass. part. s.v. 23. **ἐγώ** (# *1609*) I (emphatic), in contrast to others. **σκανδαλισθήσονται** fut. ind. pass. σκανδαλίζω (# *4997*) to cause to stumble. The volative fut. expresses determination of the will (RG, 874). ◆ **34 ἔφη** impf. ind. act. φήμι (# *5774*) to say. **πρίν** (# *4570*) before, w. acc. and inf. **ἀλέκτωρ** (# *232*) rooster. **φωνῆσαι** aor. inf. act. φωνέω (# *5888*) to call; here, to crow. The cock crowing marked the third Roman watch 12-3 A.M. (McNiele). **ἀπαρνήσῃ** fut. ind. mid. (dep.) ἀπαρνέομαι (# *565*) to deny. The prep. of the compound perfectivizes the vb.: "to completely deny" (MH, 298). ◆ **35 δέῃ** pres. subj. act. δεῖ (# *1256*) it is necessary. **ἀποθανεῖν** aor. inf. act. ἀποθνήσκω (# *633*) to die. **οὐ μή** (# *4024; 3590*) emphatic neg. **εἶπαν** aor. ind. act. λέγω (# *3306*). ◆ **36 καθίσατε** aor. imp. act. καθίζω (# *2767*) to sit down. **αὐτοῦ** adv. of place, here. **ἕως οὗ** (# *2401; 4005*) w. subj., as long as, until, while. **ἀπελθών** aor. act. part. ἀπέρχομαι (# *599*) to go forth. **προσεύξωμαι** aor. subj. mid. (dep.) προσεύχομαι (# *4667*) to pray. ◆ **37 παραλαβών** aor. act. part. παραλαμβάνω (# *4161*) to take w. **ἤρξατο** impf. ind. mid. (dep.) ἄρχομαι s.v. 22. **λυπεῖσθαι** pres. inf. pass. s.v. 22. **ἀδημονεῖν** pres. inf. act. ἀδημονέω (# *86*) to be troubled, to be distressed. It implies a restless, distracted shrinking from some trouble or thought of trouble which nevertheless cannot be escaped (McNiele; s. *Test. Abraham*, 7:5). ◆ **38 περίλυπος** (# *4337*) lit., surrounded by sorrow, overwhelmed w. distress (EGT). For the prep. in this compound s. MH, 312f. **μείνατε** aor. imp. act. μένω (# *3531*) to remain. **γρηγορεῖτε** pres. imp. act. γρηγορέω (# *1213*) to watch, keep awake physically (McNiele). ◆ **39 προελθών** aor. act. part. προέρχομαι (# *4601*) to go before. **μικρόν** (# *3625*) a little, (adv.). Acc. a little way, a short distance. **ἔπεσεν** aor. ind. act. πίπτω (# *4406*) to fall. **προσευχόμενος** pres. mid. (dep.) part. προσεύχομαι (# *4667*) to pray. **παρελθάτω** aor. imp. act. 3rd. pers. sing. παρέρχομαι (# *4216*) to pass by. Aor. imp. indicates the feeling of dependence which leaves everything to the Father (Bakker, 101; for the cond. cl. s. VA, 294f). **ποτήριον** (# *4539*) cup. It refers to suffering, death, and the wrath of God (Carson, 543; EDNT). ◆ **40 εὑρίσκει** pres. ind. act. εὑρίσκω (*# 2351*) to find; hist. pres. **καθεύδοντας** pres. act. part. καθεύδω (*# 2761*) to sleep. **ἰσχύσατε** aor. ind. act. ἰσχύω (*# 2710*) to have strength, to be able. **ὥραν** acc. ὥρα (*# 6052*) hour. Acc. of time, "for one hour." **γρηγορῆσαι** aor. act. inf. γρηγορέω to watch s.v. 38. ◆ **41 προσεύχεσθε** pres. imp. mid. (dep.) προσεύχομαι (*# 4667*) to pray. **εἰσέλθητε** aor. subj. act. εἰσέρχομαι (*# 1565*) to go into. Subj. w. **ἵνα** (*# 2671*) gives the content, or expresses the purp. of the prayer. **πειρασμός** (*# 4280*) temptation. **πνεῦμα** (*# 4460*) spirit. **πρόθυμος** (*# 4609*) ready, willing. **σάρξ** (*# 4922*) flesh. The distinction is between man's physical weakness (flesh) and the noble desires of his will (willing spirit) (Hill). **ἀσθενής** (*# 822*) weak. ◆ **42 προσηύξατο** aor. ind. mid. (dep.) προσεύχομαι (*# 4667*) to pray. **εἰ** (*# 1623*) if, introduces a 1st. class cond., asserting something for the sake of argument (VA, 294-96). **παρελθεῖν** aor. inf. act. παρέρχομαι (*# 4216*) to pass by. **ἐὰν μή** (*# 1569; 3590*) if not, except, cond. of the 3rd. class undetermined. This delicate distinction between the cond. cls. accurately presents the real attitude of Jesus toward this subtle temptation (RWP). **γενηθήτω** aor. imp. pass. (dep.) 3rd. pers. sing. γίνομαι s.v. 5. ◆ **43 ἐλθών** aor. act. part. ἔρχομαι (*# 2262*) to go. Temp. or circum. part. **εὗρεν** aor. ind. act. εὑρίσκω (*# 2351*) to find. **βεβαρημένοι** perf. pass. part. βαρέω (*# 976*) to make heavy, to be heavy (w. sleep). Perf. emphasizes the present state. Adj. part. ◆ **44 ἀφείς** aor. act. part. (temp.) ἀφίημι (*# 918*) to leave. **εἰπών** aor. act. part. λέγω (*# 3306*) to say. ◆ **45 καθεύδετε** pres. imp. act. καθεύδω (*# 2761*) to sleep. **ἀναπαύεσθε** pres. imp. mid. (dep.) ἀναπαύομαι (*# 399*) to take one's rest. **ἤγγικεν** perf. ind. act. ἐγγίζω (*# 1581*) to draw near. **παραδίδοται** pres. ind. pass. s.v. 24. ◆ **46 ἐγείρεσθε** pres. imp. pass. s.v. 32. **ἄγωμεν** pres. subj. act. ἄγω (*# 72*) to go. Cohortative subj. means "let us go." **παραδιδούς** pres. act. part. s.v. 24. "The one who betrays." Judas sold information where Jesus could be found and taken inconspicuously (Blinzler). ◆ **47 λαλοῦντος** pres. act. part. λαλέω (*# 3281*) to speak, to say. Gen. abs., "while he was yet speaking." **ἦλθεν** aor. ind. act. ἔρχομαι s.v. 43. **μάχαιρα** (*# 3479*) sword. **ξύλον** (*# 3833*) wood, stick, club (McNiele). ◆ **48 ἔδωκεν** aor. ind. act. δίδωμι s.v. 27. **φιλήσω** aor. subj. act. φιλέω (*# 5797*) to love, to kiss. **κρατήσατε** aor. imp. act. s.v. 4. ◆ **49 προσελθών** aor. act. part. s.v. 7. **χαῖρε** pres. imp. act. χαίρω (*# 5897*) form of greeting, "hello." **κατεφίλησεν** aor. ind. act. καταφιλέω (*# 2968*) to kiss fervently, intensified by the prep. (RWP). A kiss expressing honor or reverence was common among the Rabbis (SB, 1:995). The disciple was not to greet the master first. This was a sign of insubordination (AM). ◆ **50 ἑταῖρε** voc. ἑταῖρος (*# 2279*) friend. **ἐφ᾽ ὅ** (*# 2093; 4005*) "for what?" "why?" (GI, 69-71; LAE, 125-31). **πάρει** pres. ind. act. 2nd. pers. sing. πάρειμι

(*# 4205*) to be present, to come. **ἐπέβαλον** aor. ind. act. ἐπιβάλλω (*# 2095*) to seize, to lay hands upon. **ἐκράτησαν** aor. ind. act. κρατέω (*# 3195*) to take into custody, apprehend. ◆ **51 ἐκτείνας** aor. act. part. (circum.) ἐκτείνω (*# 1753*) to stretch out. **ἀπέσπασεν** aor. ind. act. ἀποσπάω (*# 685*) to draw out. **πατάξας** aor. act. part. (circum.) s.v. 31. **ἀφεῖλεν** aor. ind. act. ἀφαιρέω (*# 904*) to take away, to cut off. **ὠτίον** (*# 6065*) ear. ◆ **52 ἀπόστρεψον** aor. imp. act. ἀποστρέφω (*# 695*) to turn away, to put away. **λαβόντες** aor. act. part. s.v. 26. **ἐν** by (instr. use of the prep.). **ἀπολοῦνται** fut. ind. mid. (dep.) ἀπόλλυμι (*# 660*) to perish. Gnomic fut. ◆ **53 δοκεῖς** pres. ind. act. δοκέω (*# 1506*) to suppose, to think. **οὐ** (*# 4024*) in the question expects a positive answer. **παρακαλέσαι** aor. inf. act. παρακαλέω (*# 4151*) to summon, to call to one's side for help. **παραστήσει** fut. ind. act. παρίστημι (*# 4225*) to stand by. Prep. in the compound is local (MH, 319). Both of these vbs. are used in connection w. military matters (EGT). **πλείω** comp. πολύς (*# 4498*) more than. **λεγιών** (*# 3305*) legion. The principle unit of the Roman army containing about 6,000 men (s. IDB, 3:110; BC, 5:427-31; DJG, 548-49; ABD, 5:789-91). The point is that his army is greater in number and greater in strength. ◆ **54 πληρωθῶσιν** aor. subj. pass. πληρόω (*# 4444*) to fulfill. Deliberative subj. used in a rhetorical question. **δεῖ** pres. ind. act. δέω to bind. s.v. 35. It expresses a logical necessity. **γενέσθαι** aor. inf. mid. (dep.) γίνομαι s.v. 5. Inf. used to complete the vb. ◆ **55 λῃστής** (*# 3334*) robber. One who uses violence to possess another's property, thus differing from a thief (EGT). **ἐξήλθατε** aor. ind. act. ἐξέρχομαι (*# 2002*) s.v. 30. **συλλαβεῖν** aor. inf. act. συλλαμβάνω (*# 5197*) to seize, to take. **καθ᾽ ἡμέραν** (*# 2848; 2465*) daily. **ἐκαθεζόμην** impf. ind. mid. (dep.) καθέζομαι (*# 2757*) to sit. Customary impf. **διδάσκων** (*# 1438*) pres. act. part. Part. of manner. ◆ **56 γέγονεν** perf. ind. act. γίνομαι (*# 1181*) to become, to happen. **ἀφέντες** aor. act. part. ἀφίημι s.v. 44. **ἔφυγον** aor. ind. act. φεύγω (*# 5771*) to flee. ◆ **57 κρατήσαντες** aor. act. part. s.v. 4. Temp. or circum. part. **ἀπήγαγον** aor. ind. act. ἀπάγω (*# 552*) to lead away. **ἀρχιερέα** acc. ἀρχιερεύς (*# 797*) high priest. For the trial of Jesus s. Catchpole; Blinzler; Sherwin-White, 24-47; Ernst Bammel, "The Trial before Pilate," JPD, 415-51; Carson, 549-52; DMM, 315-877; BBC. ◆ **58 ἠκολούθει** impf. ind. act. ἀκολουθέω (*# 199*) to follow, w. dat. The impf. pictures his continual following. **μακρόθεν** (*# 3427*) from afar, from a distance. **εἰσελθών** aor. act. part. (circum.) εἰσέρχομαι (*# 1656*) to go in, to come in. **ἐκάθητο** impf. ind. mid. (dep.) κάθημαι (*# 2764*) to sit. Impf. means "he was sitting." **ὑπηρέτης** (*# 5677*) servant, minister, helper. **ἰδεῖν** aor. inf. act. ὁράω (*# 3972*) to see. Inf. of purp. ◆ **59 συνέδριον** (*# 5284*) Sanhedrin. The Sanhedrin did not possess the general right of execution except in reference to the violation of the innermost

temple court (AM; Sherwin-White, 38ff.; s. Jonah Os-
trow, "Tannaitic and Roman Procedure in Homicide,"
Jewish Quarterly Review, 48 [1957-58]: 352-70; Luke
23:13). ἐζήτουν impf. ind. act. ζητέω (# 2426) to seek.
Impf. indicates the continual search. ψευδομαρτυρία
(# 6019) false witness. θανατώσωσιν aor. subj. act.
θανατόω (# 2506) to kill. Subj. w. ὅπως (# 3968) in a
purp. cl. ◆ 60 εὗρον aor. ind. act. εὑρίσκω (# 2351) to
find προσελθόντων aor. act. part. s.v. 7. Gen. abs. used
to express concession ("although"). ὕστερον (# 5731) at
last. ◆ 61 εἶπαν aor. ind. act. λέγω (# 3306) to say. οὗτος
(# 4047), "this one!" Derogatory in use. ἔφη impf. ind.
act. φημί (# 5774) to say s.v. 34. καταλῦσαι aor. inf. act.
καταλύω (# 2907) to destroy. διὰ τριῶν ἡμερῶν lit.,
through three days (EGT). οἰκοδομῆσαι aor. inf. act.
οἰκοδομέω (# 3868) to erect, to build. Desecration of a
sacred place was regarded as a capital offense in the
ancient world (Carson, 554). ◆ 62 ἀναστάς aor. act.
part. (circum.) ἀνίστημι (# 482) to stand up. ἀποκρίνῃ
pres. ind. mid. (dep.) 2nd. pers. sing. ἀποκρίνομαι
(# 646) to answer. καταμαρτυροῦσιν pres. ind. act.
καταματυρέω (# 2909) to give testimony against (w.
gen.). ◆ 63 ἐσιώπα impf. ind. act. σιωπάω (# 4995) to
be silent. Impf. pictures continual action in the past.
He continually remained silent during the various accusations. ἐξορκίζω pres. ind. act. ἐξορκίζω (# 2019) to
cause someone to take an oath, to charge someone
under oath, to put someone under oath using divine
names and titles renders the oath binding (McNeile).
ζῶντος pres. act. part. ζάω (# 2409) to live. εἴπῃς aor.
subj. act. λέγω (# 3306) to say. ◆ 64 εἶπας aor. ind. act.
λέγω to say. "You (emphatic) said it." The phrase is affirmative in content, and reluctant in formulation
(D.R. Catchpole, "The Answer of Jesus to Caiaphas
[Matthew 26:64]," *NTS* 17 [1971]: 213-26; Hagner).
πλήν (# 4440) moreover, indeed. "Yes, I am. Indeed I
tell you that you will see Me immediately vindicated"
(Thrall, 78). ὄψεσθε fut. ind. mid. (dep.) ὁράω (# 3972)
to see. καθήμενον pres. mid. (dep.) part. κάθημαι
(# 2764) s.v. 58. The right hand was a place of authority, prominence and privilege (Cleon L. Rogers, Jr. "The
Davidic Covenant in Acts-Revelation," *Bib Sac* 151
[1994]: 74). ◆ 65 διέρρηξεν aor. ind. act. διαρρήγνυμι
(# 1396) to rip, to tear. The tearing of the garment may
have been a spontaneous expression of real horror
(McNeile). Those judging the trial of a blasphemer
were required to stand and tear their garments upon
hearing the blasphemy (M, Sanhedrin 7:5; SB, 1:1006-
19). ἐβλασφήμησεν aor. ind. act. βλασφημέω (# 1059) to
blaspheme (TDNT; EDNT; RAC, 11:1190-93; DJG, 76-
77). ἠκούσατε aor. ind. act. ἀκούω (# 201) to hear.
◆ 66 τί ὑμῖν δοκεῖ used impersonally w. dat. "What is
it to you?" that is, "What do you think?" ἀποκριθέντες
aor. pass. (dep.) part. ἀποκρίνομαι (# 646) to answer.
ἔνοχος (# 1944) guilty, followed by gen. ◆ 67 ἐνέπτυ-

σαν aor. ind. act. ἐμπτύω (# 1870) to spit on. A sign of
the strongest rejection and contempt (NBD).
ἐκολάφισαν aor. ind. act. κολαφίζω (# 3139) to strike w.
the fist. ἐράπισαν aor. ind. act. ῥαπίζω (# 4824) to strike
w. a club; also to strike w. the open hand, esp. in the
face (BAGD; s. Isa 50:6). ◆ 68 προφήτευσον aor. imp.
act. προφητεύω (# 4736) to prophesy. παίσας aor. act.
part. παίω (# 4091) to hit, to strike. Part. used as subst.
"the one who hit...." ◆ 69 ἐκάθητο impf. ind. mid.
(dep.) κάθημαι (# 2764) to sit. προσῆλθεν aor. ind. act.
s.v. 7. ἦσθα impf. ind. mid. (dep.) εἰμί (# 1639) (BD, 49).
◆ 70 ἠρνήσατο aor. ind. mid. (dep.) ἀρνέομαι (# 766)
s.v. 34. οἶδα perf. ind. act. to know. Def. perf. w. pres.
meaning s.v. 2. For a discussion of the denials of Peter
s. Carson, 557-58. ◆ 71 ἐξελθόντα aor. act. part. ἐξέρχομαι s.v. 30. He retired into the dimmer light of the vestibule close to the gateway (McNeile). πυλών (# 4784)
gate, gateway, entrance. εἶδεν aor. ind. act. ὁράω
(# 3972) to see. ◆ 72 ὅρκος (# 3992) oath. ὅτι (# 4022) =
quotation marks, dir. speech. ◆ 73 ἑστῶτες perf. act.
part. ἵστημι (# 2705) to stand. λαλιά (# 3282) speech.
For the language and dialect of those of Galilee s. HA,
61-64; BBC; DJG, 434-44; SB, 1:156-59. δῆλος (# 1316)
clear, evident. ◆ 74 ἤρξατο aor. ind. mid. (dep.) s.v. 22.
καταθεματίζειν (# 3874) pres. act. inf. to curse, to wish
oneself accursed if he lies (TDNT). ὀμνύειν (# 3923)
pres. act. inf. to swear. Inf. used w. the vb. ἄρχω. ἐφώνησεν aor. ind. act. s.v. 34. ◆ 75 ἐμνήσθη aor. ind. pass.
(dep.) μιμνήσκομαι (# 3630) to remember. εἰρηκότος
perf. act. part. λέγω (# 3306) to say. ἔκλαυσεν aor. ind.
act. κλαίω (# 3081) to weep. πικρῶς (# 4396) bitterly.

Matthew 27

◆ 1 πρωΐα (# 4746) early morning. γενομένης aor.
mid. (dep.) part. γίνομαι (# 1181) to become, sometimes in the sense "to be"; gen. abs. συμβούλιον
(# 5206) consultation. ἔλαβον aor. ind. act. λαμβάνω
(# 3284) to take. Used w. the preceding word, to form a
plan, to consult, to plot (BAGD). The word refers to
the planning of strategy, the holding of a consultation,
but is not the interrogation of the accused or the examination of testimony (Catchpole, 191). ὥστε (# 6063)
that, used w. the inf. for purp., intended results (BD,
198). θανατῶσαι aor. inf. act. θανατόω (# 2506) to kill.
◆ 2 δήσαντες aor. act. part. (temp.) δέω (# 1313) to bind.
ἀπήγαγον aor. ind. act. ἀπάγω (# 552) to lead out. παρέδωκαν aor. ind. act. παραδίδωμι (# 4140) to deliver over.
ἡγεμόνι dat. sing. ἡγεμών (# 2450) governor, ruler. Indir.
obj. For material on Pontius Pilate s. TJ, 51-57; HA,
172-83. ◆ 3 ἰδών aor. act. part. (temp.) ὁράω (# 3972)
to see. παραδιδούς aor. act. part. παραδίδωμι (# 4140) to
deliver over, to betray. κατεκρίθη aor. ind. pass.
κατακρίνω (# 2891) to pronounce judgment against, to
condemn. μεταμεληθείς aor. pass. part. μεταμέλομαι
(# 3564) to regret, to repent, wishing it were undone

(EGT; s. Matt. 21:30). ἔστρεψεν aor. ind. act. στρέφω (# 5138) to bring back, to return. ◆ 4 ἥμαρτον aor. ind. act. ἁμαρτάνω (# 279) to sin. παραδούς aor. act. part. παραδίδωμι s.v. 2. Part. used to express manner. εἶπαν aor. ind. act. λέγω (# 3306) to say. ὄψῃ fut. ind. mid. 2nd. pers. sing. ὁράω (# 3972) see to it yourself, take care of that!, the volative fut. (BD, 183). ◆ 5 ῥίψας aor. act. part. ῥίπτω (# 4849) to throw, to put or lay down. Temp. or circum. part. He placed the money in the treasury (McNiele). If one wished to revoke a transaction but was refused, he could deposit the money in the Temple, thus revoking the matter (JTJ, 139; OTGPN, 200). ἀνεχώρησεν aor. ind. act. ἀναχωρέω (# 432) to depart, to go away. ἀπελθών aor. act. part. ἀπέρχομαι (# 599) to go out. ἀπήγξατο aor. ind. mid. ἀπάγω (# 551) dir. mid. to hang oneself (RWP). ◆ 6 λαβόντες aor. act. part. (circum.) λαμβάνω (# 3284) to take. ἔξεστιν (# 2003) pres. ind. act. ἔξειμι it is lawful. βαλεῖν aor. ind. act. βάλλω (# 965) to cast, to put. κορβανᾶς (# 3168) temple treasury (McNiele). τιμή (# 5507) price. The price of blood was pollution to the treasury (McNiele; Gnilka; Deut. 23:19). ◆ 7 ἠγόρασαν aor. ind. act. ἀγοράζω (# 60) to buy. κεραμεύς (# 3038) potter. ταφή (# 5438) grave. ξένοις dat. pl. ξένος (# 3828) stranger. Probably refers to the pilgrims who come to Jerusalem (Gnilka). Dat. of advantage. ◆ 8 ἐκλήθη aor. ind. pass. καλέω (# 2813) to call, to name. ◆ 9 ἐπληρώθη aor. ind. pass. πληρόω (# 4444) to fulfill. ῥηθέν aor. pass. part. λέγω (# 3306) to say. Probably a reference to Jer. 19:1-13 (HSB, 399-400). The betrayal for money led Matthew to Zech. 11:13 and the word "potter" led him to Jer. 19 (OTGPN, 207-10; Carson, 562-66; Gundry). τετιμημένου perf. pass. part. τιμάω (# 5506) to set a price on, to estimate, to value. ἐτιμήσαντο aor. ind. mid. τιμάω. ◆ 10 ἔδωκαν aor. ind. act. δίδωμι (# 1443) to give. εἰς (# 1650) here, for. συνέταξέν aor. ind. act. συντάσσω (# 5332) to arrange, to order. ◆ 11 ἐστάθη aor. ind. pass. ἵστημι (# 2705) to place. The sentence of the Sanhedrin had to be carried out by the procurator (Sherwin-White, 44ff). It is also suggested that the religious leaders sought to avoid responsibility by having a third party carry out the sentence (LNT, 422f). ἐπηρώτησεν aor. ind. act. ἐπερωτάω (# 2089) to question. σύ (# 5148) you (emphatic). The term "King of the Jews" indicated a leader of the resistance (Sherwin-White, 24). ἔφη impf. ind. act. φημί (# 5774) to say. (For the answer s. Matt. 26:64.) ◆ 12 ἐν τῷ (# 1877) w. inf. indicates contemporaneous time, while. κατηγορεῖσθαι pres. pass. inf. κατηγορέω (# 2989) to bring a change against. ἀπεκρίνατο aor. ind. mid. (dep.) ἀποκρίνομαι (# 646) to answer. ◆ 13 πόσα acc. pl. πόσος (# 4531) how much, how great, how many. καταμαρτυροῦσιν pres. ind. act. καταμαρτυρέω (# 2909) to witness against w. gen. ◆ 14 ἀπεκρίθη aor. ind. pass. (dep.) ἀποκρίνομαι (# 646) to answer. ῥῆμα (# 4839) word, thing. θαυ-

μάζειν pres. inf. act. θαυμάζω (# 2513) to be astonished, to wonder. Inf. w. ὥστε (# 6063) to express results. Those who did not defend themselves were given three opportunities of changing their mind before sentence was finally given against them (Sherwin-White, 25; s. Isa. 53:7). ◆ 15 εἰώθει plperf. ind. act. of the perf. form εἴωθα (# 1665) to be accustomed (BAGD). ἀπολύειν aor. inf. act. ἀπολύω (# 668) to release. The release was probably a royal prerogative by way of the Sanhedrin (JPD, 427). ἤθελον impf. ind. act. θέλω (# 2527) to wish, to desire. For the custom of releasing a prisoner at Passover and comments on M, Pesachim 7:6 s. Blinzler. One prisoner was released in remembrance of Israel's salvation from Egypt and Jews sought to buy back those taken captive (JPD, 427; BBC). ◆ 16 εἶχον impf. ind. act. ἔχω (# 2400) to have. ἐπίσημος (# 2168) outstanding, notorious. It may refer to the high reputation in which he was held by the more rebellious Jews (McNiele). λεγόμενον pres. pass. part. λέγω (# 3306) ◆ 17 συνηγμένων perf. pass. part. συνάγω (# 5251) to gather together, to assemble; gen. abs. ἀπολύσω fut. ind. act. ἀπολύω (# 668) to release. ◆ 18 ᾔδει plperf. ind. act. οἶδα (# 3857) to know. Def. perf. w. pres. meaning. φθόνος (# 5784) envy, jealousy, ill will against someone because of some real or presumed advantage by such a person (IDB, 2:806f; LN, 1:760). ◆ 19 καθημένου pres. mid. (dep.) part. κάθημαι (# 2764) to sit, to take one's seat; gen. abs. βῆμα (# 1037) tribunal, judicial bench. ἀπέστειλεν aor. ind. act. ἀποστέλλω (# 690) to send. δικαίῳ dat. sing. δίκαιος (# 1465) righteous, innocent (s. GW, 121f). Dat. of personal interest: "Let there be nothing between you and that innocent man!" (GI, 46). ἔπαθον aor. ind. act. πάσχω (# 4248) to suffer. ὄναρ (# 3941) dream; w. the prep. (κατά), "in a dream." ◆ 20 ἔπεισαν aor. ind. act. πείθω (# 4275) to persuade. αἰτήσωνται aor. subj. mid. αἰτέω (# 160) to ask, to request. ἀπολέσωσιν aor. subj. act. ἀπόλλυμι (# 660) to destroy. ◆ 21 ἀποκριθείς aor. pass. (dep.) part. ἀποκρίνομαι (# 646) to answer. ◆ 22 ποιήσω fut. ind. act. ποιέω (# 4472) to do. σταυρωθήτω aor. imp. pass. 3rd. pers. sing. σταυρόω (# 5090) to crucify. ◆ 23 ἐποίησεν aor. ind. act. ποιέω to do. ἔκραζον impf. ind. act. κράζω (# 3189) to scream; impf. pictures the continual action. The crowd clamored for crucifixion because it was cursed by God (s. Deut. 21:22-23; Gal. 3:13; TDNT under σταυρός; C, esp. 84-90; David J. Halperin, "Crucifixion, the Nahum Pesher, and the Rabbinic Penalty of Strangulation," JJS 32 [1981]: 32-46; Max Wilcox, "'Upon the Tree'-Deut 21:22-23 in the New Testament," JBL 96 [1977]: 85-99; Joseph A. Fitzmyer, "Crucifixion in Ancient Palestine, Qumran Literature, and the New Testament," CBQ 4 [1978]: 493-513). ◆ 24 ὠφελεῖ pres. ind. act. ὠφελέω (# 6067) to be of use, to profit. λαβών aor. act. part. (circum.) λαμβάνω (# 3284) to take. ἀπενίψατο aor. ind.

mid. ἀπονίπτω (# 672) to wash, to wash off. The mid. focuses on Pilate as if this symbolic act could remove real guilt (GGBB, 421). The practice of washing hands was a symbol for the removal of guilt (Tasker; Deut. 21:6; SB, 1:1032; Timothy B. Cargal, "'His Blood be Upon Us and Our Children': A Matthean Double Entendre?" NTS 37 [1991]: 104). ἀπέναντι (# 595) w. gen. over, against, before. (κατέναντι as variant reading, in the sight of, before [BAGD].) ◆ 25 εἶπεν aor. ind. act. λέγω (# 3306) to say. αἷμα (# 135) blood. Perhaps a reference both to taking responsibility and to the later offer of forgiveness through His blood (Timothy B. Cargal, "'His Blood be Upon Us and Our Children': A Matthean Double Entendre?" NTS 37 [1991]: 101-12). ◆ 26 ἀπέλυσεν aor. ind. act. ἀπολύω (# 668) to release. φραγελλώσας aor. act. part. φραγελλόω (# 5849) to scourge. This was either a part of the main punishment or was a separate punishment (Bammel, JPD, 440-41). For the horrible practice of scourging s. Blinzler; TDNT; RAC, 9:469-90; BAFCS, 3:14-15, 297-98; EDNT. παρέδωκεν aor. ind. act. παραδίδωμι (# 4140) to deliver over. It could be delivering over to the soldiers or to the Jews (Bammel, JPD, 436-51). σταυρωθῇ aor. subj. pass. σταυρόω (# 5090) to crucify. Subj. w. ἵνα (# 2671) used in a purp. cl. For more s.v. 23. ◆ 27 παραλαβόντες aor. act. part. παραλαμβάνω (# 4161) to take w. πραιτώριον (# 4550) the official residence of a governor (McNiele; BBC; Acts 23:35). This was either the Fortress of Antonia, at the northwest corner of the Temple Mount, or more likely the Palace of Herod, on the west side of the city. συνήγαγον aor. ind. act. συνάγω (# 5251) to gather together. ἐπ᾽ αὐτόν (# 2093; 899) upon him, around him, against him. σπεῖρα (# 5061) cohort s. 26:53. ◆ 28 ἐκδύσαντες aor. act. part. (temp.) ἐκδύω (# 1694) to undress. χλαμύδα acc. χλαμύς (# 5968) a man's outer garment, a cloak used by travelers and soldiers (BAGD). κόκκινος (# 3132) scarlet. This scarlet mantel on Jesus was a mock imitation of the royal purple (RWP). περιέθηκαν aor. ind. act. περιτίθημι (# 4363) to place around. ◆ 29 πλέξαντες aor. act. part. πλέκω (# 4428) to plait. στέφανος (# 5109) wreath, circlet. ἄκανθα (# 180) thorn. ἐπέθηκαν aor. ind. act. ἐπιτίθημι (# 2202) to place upon. The circlet of thorns was meant as a cheap (and painful) imitation of the radiant circlet depicted on the coins of Tiberius Caesar (AM). κάλαμος (# 2812) reed, corresponding to the scepter in the emperor's hand as depicted on the coins (AM). γονυπετήσαντες aor. act. part. γονυπετέω (# 1206) to fall on the knees. ἐνέπαιξαν aor. ind. act. ἐμπαίζω (# 1850) to ridicule, to make fun of, to mock (s. Matt. 20:19). χαῖρε (# 5897) "hail!" (s. Matt. 26:49). The soldiers used the familiar "Ave Caesar" in their mockery of Jesus (RWP). ◆ 30 ἐμπτύσαντες aor. act. part. ἐμπτύω (# 1870) to spit on. ἔλαβον aor. ind. act. λαμβάνω s.v. 24. ἔτυπτον impf. ind. act. τύπτω (# 5597) to

strike. Impf. indicates they repeatedly struck him on the head (Filson). ◆ 31 ἐξέδυσαν aor. ind. act. ἐκδύω (# 1694) to put on. ἀπήγαγον aor. ind. act. s.v. 2. εἰς τό (# 1650; 3836) w. inf. to express purp. σταυρῶσαι aor. inf. act. s.v. 22. ◆ 32 εὗρον aor. ind. act. εὑρίσκω (# 2351) to find. ἠγγάρευσαν aor. ind. act. ἀγγαρεύω (# 30) to compel, to forcibly press someone into compulsory service; a word evidently taken from the Persian postal service (NTW, 15-17; EDNT; NDIEC, 1:42; 2:77; McNiele). ἄρῃ aor. subj. act. αἴρω (# 149) to lift up, to carry. σταυρός (# 5089) cross (TDNT; Blinzler). ◆ 33 ἐλθόντες aor. act. part. (temp.) ἔρχομαι (# 2262) to come, to go. κρανίον (# 3191) skull. ◆ 34 ἔδωκαν aor. ind. act. s.v. 10. πιεῖν aor. act. inf. πίνω (# 4403) to drink. χολή (# 5958) that which is bitter, gall (EDNT). μεμιγμένον perf. pass. part. μείγνυμι (# 3502) to mix. A man about to be executed could beg a grain of incense (a narcotic) in wine in order to dull his senses and alleviate pain, and this was in accord w. Jewish custom (Hill; SB, 1:1037-38). γευσάμενος aor. mid. (dep.) part. γεύομαι (# 1174) to taste. ἠθέλησεν aor. ind. act. θέλω (# 2527) to desire. ◆ 35 σταυρώσαντες aor. act. part. σταυρόω (# 5090) to crucify s.v. 22. Temp. part. expressing contemporaneous action w. aor. in main vb. διεμερίσαντο aor. ind. mid. διαμερίζω (# 1374) to distribute, to distribute among themselves. The soldiers who carried out the sentence had a right to the clothes of the criminal (AM). This meant that Jesus was naked, which was in accord w. Jewish custom (SB, 1:1038). ◆ 36 καθήμενοι pres. mid. (dep.) part. s.v. 19. ἐτήρουν impf. ind. act. τηρέω (# 5498) to watch, to guard. The soldiers kept watch to prevent any rescue (Carson, 576). Impf. indicates the continual action. ◆ 37 ἐπέθηκαν aor. ind. act. ἐπιτίθημι (# 2202) to place upon, to place. ἐπάνω (# 2062) w. gen., over. αἰτία (# 162) cause, guilt. γεγραμμένην perf. pass. part. γράφω (# 1211) to write. The inscription was written w. black or red letters on a white background (Blinzler). ◆ 38 σταυροῦνται pres. ind. pass. σταυρόω (# 5090) to crucify. λησταί pl. λῃστής (# 3334) robber (s. Matt. 26:55). Though it was evidently normal to execute only one person a day, there is evidence that there were numerous executions on the same day (M, Sanh. 4:6; Jos., JW, 2:253; SB, 1:1039). ◆ 39 παραπορευόμενοι pres. mid. (dep.) part. παραπορεύομαι (# 4182) to pass alongside of, to pass by. ἐβλασφήμουν impf. ind. act. βλασφημέω (# 1059) to revile, to defame (TLNT). Impf. pictures the continual defaming. κινοῦντες pres. act. part. κινέω (# 3075) to move, to shake; to shake the head as a sign of scorn and derision (BAGD; SB, 1:1039; Ps. 22:7). ◆ 40 καταλύων pres. act. part. καταλύω (# 2907) to destroy. οἰκοδομῶν pres. act. part. οἰκοδομέω (# 3868) to build. Part. used as subst. Pres. is perhaps conative: "the one who tried to...." (VANT, 412). σῶσον aor. imp. act. σῴζω (# 5392) to save, to rescue. εἰ pres. ind. act.

εἰμί (# 1639) to be. Cond. w. εἰ (# 1623) assumes the reality for the sake of argument. κατάβηθι aor. imp. act. καταβαίνω (# 2849) to come down. Aor. points to a specific and immediate act. ◆ 41 ἐμπαίζοντες pres. act. part. (temp.) s.v. 29; contemporaneous action. ἔλεγον impf. ind. act. λέγω (# 3306) to say. Impf. indicates continual action: "they kept on saying." ◆ 42 ἔσωσεν aor. ind. act. σῴζω (# 5392) to save. σῶσαι aor. act. inf. σῴζω. Aor. points to the specific event and indicates a complete rescue from the cross. καταβάτω aor. imp. act. 3rd. pers. sing. καταβαίνω (# 2849) to come down. ◆ 43 πέποιθεν perf. ind. act. πείθω (# 4275) s.v. 20. Perf. has the pres. meaning of "to depend on," "to trust in" (BD, 176). ῥυσάσθω aor. imp. mid. (dep.) ῥύομαι (# 4861) to rescue. ◆ 44 τὸ αὐτό (# 899) the same thing. συσταυρωθέντες aor. pass. part. συσταυρόω (# 5365) to crucify together. ὠνείδιζον impf. ind. act. ὀνειδίζω (# 3943) to reproach, to heap insults upon. Incep. impf. means "they began to reproach him" (RWP). ◆ 45 ἐγένετο aor. ind. mid. (dep.) γίνομαι s.v. 1. ἕκτης gen. sing. ἕκτος (# 1761) sixth hour, that is, noon. The slaughtering of the Passover lamb, probably begun in the Temple at the 6th hour (WZZT, 223; SB, 4: i, 48-49); Josephus says from the ninth to the eleventh hour, or 3 to 5 P.M. (Jos., JW, 6:423). γῆ (# 1178) land, earth, indicating all of Palestine or the whole world (Hill). This could not have been an eclipse of the sun because the Passover was celebrated at the full moon. The darkness was a sign of God in mourning (SB, 1:1041-42). ◆ 46 ἀνεβόησεν aor. ind. act. ἀναβοάω (# 331) to cry out. ἠλί (# 2458) (Heb.) "my God!" λεμά (# 3316) (Heb.) why? σαβαχθάνι (# 4876) (Aram.) "Why did You forsake me?" (Allen). Not in the sense of depart, but abandon. In Ps. 22 the complaint is against God's silence in light of the unjust suffering by the Psalmist. θεέ voc. θεός (# 2536) God (BD, 25). ἐγκατέλιπες aor. ind. act. ἐγκαταλείπω (# 1593) to abandon, to leave in the lurch (for the prep. in compound s. MH, 305). ◆ 47 ἑστηκότων perf. act. part. ἵστημι (# 2705) to stand. ἀκούσαντες aor. act. part. (temp.) ἀκούω (# 201) to hear. φωνεῖ pres. ind. act. φωνέω (# 5888) to call. ◆ 48 δραμών aor. act. part. τρέχω (# 5556) to run. λαβών aor. act. part. λαμβάνω s.v. 24. Aor. presenting an action necessary for the main vb. σπόγγος (# 5074) sponge. πλήσας aor. act. part. πίμπλημι (# 4398) to fill (w. gen.) ὄξους gen. ὄξος (# 3954) sour wine, vinegar. Posca, a wine vinegar which was the favorite drink of soldiers and the lower ranks of society (BAGD; McNiele). περιθείς aor. act. part. περιτίθημι (# 4363) to place around; here, to put a sponge on a reed (BAGD). ἐπότιζεν impf. ind. act. ποτίζω (# 4540) to give to drink. The conative impf.: "they tried to give him to drink" (IBG, 9; RG, 885). ◆ 49 ἄφες aor. imp. act. ἀφίημι (# 918) to leave alone. ἴδωμεν aor. subj. act. ὁράω (# 3972) to see. Cohortative subj.: "Let us see." σώσων

fut. act. part. σῴζω (# 5392) to save, to rescue. The fut. part. used to express purp. (BD, 178, 215f). ◆ 50 κράξας aor. act. part. (temp.) κράζω (# 3189) s.v. 23. ἀφῆκεν aor. ind. act. ἀφίημι (# 918) to let go, to send away. Not the divine Spirit but the spirit of life (Hill). This suggests His sovereignty over the exact time of His own death (Carson, 580). ◆ 51 καταπέτασμα (# 2925) curtain, veil. For the veils of the temple s. LT, 2:611f; SB, 1:1043-46; Gundry; Jos., JW, 5:211-19; M, Shek. 8:4-5; M, Yoma 5:1. ἐσχίσθη aor. ind. pass. σχίζω (# 5387) to split, to divide, to tear apart. ἄνωθεν (# 540) from above. ἐσείσθη aor. ind. pass. σείω (# 4940) to shake (used of an earthquake). For extrabiblical references to this event s. LT, 2:610; Allen. ◆ 52 μνημεῖα pl. μνημεῖον (# 3646) tomb. ἀνεῴχθησαν aor. ind. pass. ἀνοίγω (# 487) to open. κεκοιμημένων perf. pass. part. κοιμάω (# 3121) to sleep, to fall asleep. ἠγέρθησαν aor. ind. pass. ἐγείρω (# 1586) to raise; pass. to rise s. HSB, 400-402. ◆ 53 ἐξελθόντες aor. act. part. ἐξέρχομαι (# 2002) to come out. Circum. or temp. part. ἔγερσις (# 1587) resurrection. εἰσῆλθον aor. ind. act. εἰσέρχομαι (# 1656) to come in, to go in. ἐνεφανίσθησαν aor. ind. pass. ἐμφανίζω (# 1872) to appear. ◆ 54 ἑκατόνταρχος (# 1672) leader of a hundred men, centurion. For Roman army divisions s. Matt. 25:53. τηροῦντες pres. act. part. τηρέω (# 5498) to watch, to guard. ἰδόντες aor. act. part. s.v. 3. γενόμενα pres. mid. (dep.) part. s.v. 1. ἐφοβήθησαν aor. ind. pass. (dep.) φοβέομαι (# 5828) to be afraid. ◆ 55 μακρόθεν (# 3427) from afar. θεωροῦσαι pres. act. part. nom. fem. pl. θεωρέω (# 2555) to look at (as a spectator) (AS). ἠκολούθησαν aor. ind. act. ἀκολουθέω (# 199) to follow. διακονοῦσαι pres. act. part. nom. fem. pl. διακονέω (# 1354) to minister. ◆ 57 ὀψίας gen. sing. ὄψιος (# 4070) late. Used w. the part. as a gen abs. w. the meaning "when evening came" (BAGD). γενομένης aor. mid. (dep.) part. s.v. 1. Gen abs. Jesus died shortly before 3 P.M. on Friday. The Sabbath would begin at sundown; before then, when all work ceased, the body should be buried (Filson). For material regarding the day of crucifixion–Friday–and the year–A.D. 33 s. Harold Hoehner, "Chronological Aspects of the Life of Christ Part IV: The Day of Christ's Crucifixion," Bib Sac 131 (1974): 241-64; "Part V: The Year of Christ's Crucifixion," Bib Sac 131 (1974): 332-48; DTM, 1350-78; DJG, 119-22. ἦλθεν aor. ind. act. ἔρχομαι s.v. 33. τοὔνομα = τὸ ὄνομα. ἐμαθητεύθη aor. ind. pass. μαθητεύομαι (# 3411) to be a disciple (TDNT). ◆ 58 προσελθών aor. act. part. (circum.) προσέρχομαι (# 4665) to come to. ᾐτήσατο aor. ind. mid. αἰτέω (# 160) to ask. Indir. mid. means "to ask for oneself." Bodies of criminals were sometimes given to their friends for burial (McNiele). ἐκέλευσεν aor. ind. act. κελεύω (# 3027) to command. ἀποδοθῆναι aor. inf. pass. ἀποδίδωμι (# 625) to give up, to give. ◆ 59 λαβών aor. act. part. λαμβάνω s.v. 24. ἐνετύλιξεν aor. ind. act. ἐντυλίσσω (# 1962) to wrap up.

For the wrapping of the body in linen in preparation for burial s. Blinzler; RAC, 2:198-200; DJG, 88-90; BBC. ◆ **60 ἔθηκεν** aor. ind. act. τίθημι (# *5502*) to place. **ἐλατόμησεν** aor. ind. act. λατομέω (# *3300*) to hew out of the rock. **προσκυλίσας** aor. act. part. (temp.) προσκυλίω (# *4685*) to roll, to roll up to. For the stone sealing the grave s. Carson, 584; SB, 1:1051; M, Ohol. 2:4. **ἀπῆλθεν** aor. ind. act. ἀπέρχομαι s.v. 5. ◆ **61 καθήμεναι** pres. mid. (dep.) part. s.v. 19. ◆ **62 ἐπαύριον** (# *2069*) on the next day, dat. of time. **παρασκευή** (# *4187*) preparation, the day of preparation. Friday, on which day everything had to be prepared for the Sabbath (BAGD). **συνήχθησαν** aor. ind. pass. συνάγω s.v. 17. ◆ **63 κύριε** voc. κύριος (# *3261*) lord, master. "Sir," used as a form of address to those in a high position (BAGD; MM). **ἐμνήσθημεν** aor. ind. pass. (dep.) μιμνήσκομαι (# *3630*) to remember. Ingressive aor. "we have just recalled" (RWP). **πλάνος** (# *4418*) deceiving as substantive, deceiver. **ζῶν** pres. act. part. nom. masc. sing. ζάω (# *2409*) to live. Temp. part. to express contemporaneous time: "while he was living...." **ἐγείρομαι** pres. ind. pass. ἐγείρω (# *1586*) pass. to be raised, to rise. Pres. of fut. reference, "I am going to rise." The action is viewed as in progress, carrying over into the future as he sees it; it affirms as well as predicts (VA, 231; VANT, 225; RG, 870). ◆ **64 κέλευσον** aor. imp. act. κελεύω (# *3027*) to command. **ἀσφαλισθῆναι** aor. inf. pass. ἀσφαλίζω (# *856*) to make safe, to guard. **μήποτε** (# *3607*) lest. **ἐλθόντες** aor. act. part. ἔρχομαι s.v. 33. **κλέψωσιν** aor. subj. act. κλέπτω (# *3096*) to steal. **εἴπωσιν** aor. subj. act. λέγω (# *3306*). **ἠγέρθη** aor. ind. pass. s.v. 52. **ἔσται** fut. ind. mid. (dep.) εἰμί (# *1639*) to be. Used after μήποτε (# *3607*) to express the feeling of apprehension (BD, 188). **πλάνη** (# *4415*) error, deception. **χείρων** (# *5937*) comp. κάκος bad; comp. worse. **πρώτης** gen. πρῶτος first. Gen. of comp. "as the first." ◆ **65 ἔφη** impf. ind. act. φημί (# *5774*) to say s.v. 11. **ἔχετε** pres. imp. act. ἔχω (# *2400*) to have. **κουστωδία** (# *3184*) (Lat.) watch, guard. S. William L. Craig, "The Guard at the Tomb," *NTS* 30 (1984): 273-81. **ὑπάγετε** pres. imp. act. ὑπάγω (# *5632*) to go forth. **ἀσφαλίσασθε** aor. imp. mid. ἀσφαλίζω (# *856*) to guard, to safeguard, to watch over someone. Here, "to watch over someone so he cannot escape." (BAGD). **οἴδατε** pres. ind. act. οἶδα. Def. perf. w. a pres. meaning s.v. 18. ◆ **66 πορευθέντες** aor. pass. (dep.) part. πορεύομαι (# *4513*) to go, to travel. **ἠσφαλίσαντο** aor. ind. mid. ἀσφαλίζω s.v. 65. **σφραγίσαντες** aor. act. part. (circum.) σφραγίζω (# *5381*) to seal, to use a seal to make something secure (LN, 1:60; MM; NDIEC, 2:191; TDNT; EDNT). Probably by a cord stretched across the stone and sealed at each end (RWP).

Matthew 28

◆ **1 ὀψέ** (# *4067*) w. gen., after; after the Sabbath (BAGD). **σαββάτων** gen. pl. σάββατον (# *4879*) Sabbath. Pl. was used for the names of festivals (BD, 78). **ἐπιφωσκούσῃ** pres. act. part. dat. sing. ἐπιφώσκω (# *2216*) to shine forth, to dawn. Dat. of time: "at the dawning." **ἦλθεν** aor. ind. act. ἔρχομαι (# *2262*) to come, to go. **θεωρῆσαι** aor. inf. act. θεωρέω (# *2555*) to see, to view. Inf. of purp. ◆ **2 σεισμός** (# *4939*) earthquake. **ἐγένετο** aor. ind. mid. (dep.) γίνομαι (# *1181*) to become, to happen. **γάρ** (# *1142*) for, explains the preceding. **καταβάς** aor. act. part. (circum.) καταβαίνω (# *2849*) to go down. **προσελθών** aor. act. part. (circum.) προσέρχομαι (# *4665*) to go to, to come to. **ἀπεκύλισεν** aor. ind. act. ἀποκυλίω (# *653*) to roll away. **ἐκάθητο** impf. ind. mid. (dep.) κάθημαι (# *2764*) to sit. **ἐπάνω** (# *2062*) w. gen., upon. ◆ **3 ἰδέα** (# *1624*) appearance. **ἀστραπή** (# *847*) lightning. **χιών** (# *5946*) snow. ◆ **4 φόβος** (# *5832*) fear. **αὐτοῦ** (# *899*) of him (obj. gen.). **ἐσείσθησαν** aor. ind. pass. σείω (# *4940*) to shake ("paralyzed w. fear"). The expression indicates faces waxen and immobile w. fear. (AM). **τηροῦντες** pres. act. part. τηρέω (# *5498*) to watch, to guard. Subst. part. **ἐγενήθησαν** aor. ind. pass. (dep.) γίνομαι (# *1181*) to become. ◆ **5 ἀποκριθείς** aor. pass. (dep.) part. ἀποκρίνομαι (# *646*) to answer. **φοβεῖσθε** pres. imp. act. φοβέομαι (# *5828*) to be afraid. Pres. imp. w. the neg. μή (# *3590*), "stop being afraid." **οἶδα** (# *3857*) perf. ind. act. to know. Def. perf. w. pres. meaning. **ἐσταυρωμένον** perf. pass. part. σταυρόω (# *5090*) to crucify. **ζητεῖτε** pres. ind. act. ζητέω (# *2426*) to seek. ◆ **6 ἠγέρθη** aor. ind. pass. ἐγείρω (# *1586*) to awaken, to raise; pass. to rise. **δεῦτε** (# *1307*) "come!" "come on!" Adv. used as hortatory particle (BAGD). **ἴδετε** aor. imp. act. ὁράω (# *3972*) to see. **ἔκειτο** impf. ind. mid. (dep.) κεῖμαι (# *3023*) to lie. ◆ **7 ταχύ** (# *5444*) quickly. **πορευθεῖσαι** aor. pass. part. nom. fem. pl. πορεύομαι (# *4513*) to go. Circum. part. to be translated as imp. It has both an ingressive force as well as an emphasis on the main vb. (GGBB, 643). **εἴπατε** aor. imp. act. λέγω (# *3306*) to say. **προάγει** pres. ind. act. προάγω (# *4575*) to go before. **ὄψεσθε** fut. ind. mid. (dep.) ὁράω (# *3972*) to see. ◆ **8 ἀπελθοῦσαι** aor. act. part. nom. fem. pl. ἀπέρχομαι (# *599*) to go away. **μνημεῖον** (# *3646*) tomb. **ἔδραμον** aor. ind. act. τρέχω (# *5556*) to run. **ἀπαγγεῖλαι** aor. act. inf. ἀπαγγέλλω (# *550*) to report, to bring news from (MH, 297). Inf. of purp. ◆ **9 ὑπήντησεν** aor. ind. act. ὑπαντάω (# *5636*) to meet. **χαίρετε** pres. imp. act. χαίρω (# *5897*) rejoice, to be glad. Used in greetings w. the meaning, "Greetings!" (EDNT). For the form of greeting s. Matt. 26:49. **ἐκράτησαν** aor. ind. act. κρατέω (# *3195*) to seize. **προσεκύνησαν** aor. ind. act. προσκυνέω (# *4686*) to kneel down, to worship. ◆ **10 ὑπάγετε** pres. imp. act. ὑπάγω (# *5632*) to go forth. **ἀπαγγείλατε** aor. imp. act. ἀπαγγέλλω (# *550*) to report, to announce, to proclaim, to tell, w. a possible focus on the source of information (LN, 1:411). **ἀπέλθωσιν** aor. subj. act. ἀπέρχομαι (# 599) to depart, go forth. Subj. w. ἵνα (# 2671) giving the content of the command. **ὄψονται** fut. ind. mid. (dep.) ὁράω (# 3972) to see. ◆ **11 πορευομένων** pres. mid. (dep.) part. πορεύομαι (# 4513) to go; gen. abs. **ἐλθόντες** aor. act. part. (circum.) ἔρχομαι (# 2262) to come. **γενόμενα** aor. mid. (dep.) part. γίνομαι (# 1181) to become, to happen. Part. used as subst., "the things that had happened." ◆ **12 συναχθέντες** aor. pass. part. (temp.) συνάγω (# 5251) to gather together, to assemble. **συμβούλιόν** (# 5206) consultation, plan, decision. **λαβόντες** aor. act. part. λαμβάνω (# 3284) to take. Used w. the preceding word to mean, "to form a plan," "to deceive," "to plot" (BAGD). Temp. or circum. part. **ἀργύριον** (# 736) silver. **ἱκανά** acc. pl. ἱκανός (# 2653) enough, large enough, much. **ἔδωκαν** aor. ind. act. δίδωμι (# 1443) to give. ◆ **13 νυκτός** gen. sing. νύξ (# 3816) night. Gen. of time "by night," "in the night-time." **ἔκλεψαν** aor. ind. act. κλέπτω (# 3096) to steal. **κοιμωμένων** pres. mid. (dep.) part. κοιμάομαι (# 3121) to sleep. Temp. part. to express contemporaneous time: "while we slept." ◆ **14 ἀκουσθῇ** aor. subj. pass. ἀκούω (# 201) to hear. Impersonal pass. "If this comes to a hearing, a trial" (EGT). Subj. w. ἐάν expressing cond. **πείσομεν** fut. ind. act. πείθω (# 4275) to persuade. **ἀμέριμνος** (# 291) without care. "We will put it right w. the Procurator, so that you need not trouble" (MM). **ποιήσομεν** aor. ind. act. ποιέω (# 4472) to do, to make (s. the discussion of the preceding word). ◆ **15 ἐποίησαν** aor. ind. act. ποιέω (# 4472) to do. **ἐδιδάχθησαν** aor. ind.

pass. διδάσκω (# 1438) to teach, to instruct. **διεφημίσθη** aor. ind. pass. διαφημίζω (# 1424) to make known by word or mouth, to spread the news about (BAGD). ◆ **16 ἐπορεύθησαν** aor. ind. pass. (dep.) πορεύομαι s.v. 7. **ἐτάξατο** aor. ind. mid. τάσσω (# 5435) to assign, to order; mid., to appoint by one's own authority (AS). ◆ **17 ἰδόντες** aor. act. part. s.v. 6. **ἐδίστασαν** aor. ind. act. διστάζω (# 1491) to doubt. The word refers to hesitation, indecision, and perhaps uncertainty (Hagner). ◆ **18 ἐδόθη** aor. ind. pass. δίδωμι s.v. 12. ◆ **19 πορευθέντες** aor. pass. (dep.) part. s.v. 7. For the translation of the part. as imp. as well as the setting of the term "to make disciples," s. Cleon Rogers, "The Great Commission," *Bib Sac* 130 (1973): 258-67; GGBB, 645; SSM, 455-57. **μαθητεύσατε** aor. imp. act. μαθητεύω (# 3411) to make a disciple. (Leon Morris, "Disciples of Jesus," *Jesus of Nazareth: Lord and Christ: Essays on the Historical Jesus and New Testament Christology* edited by Joel B. Green and Max Turner [Grand Rapids: Eerdmans, 1994], 112-27. **βαπτίζοντες** pres. act. part. βαπτίζω (# 966) to baptize. Part. of manner. ◆ **20 διδάσκοντες** pres. act. part. διδάσκω (# 1438) to teach. Part. of manner. **τηρεῖν** pres. inf. act. τηρέω (# 5498) to guard, to keep, to observe. Inf. gives the content of the teaching. **ἐνετειλάμην** aor. ind. mid. (dep.) ἐντέλλομαι (# 1948) to command. **ἡμέρας** acc. pl. ἡμέρα (# 2465) day. Acc. of time meaning "during all the days." **συντέλεια** (# 5333) completion, a point of time marking the end of a duration (LN, 1:638; Test. of Levi, 10:1-2; Test. of Benjamin 11:3; EDNT).

The Gospel of Mark

Mark 1

◆ **1** ἀρχή (# *794*) beginning, used without the article indicates it was intended as a title (M, 82). It is either the title for the whole gospel of Mark, for verses 1-13, or 1-8 (Cranfield; Gundry). εὐαγγέλιον (# *2295*) gospel, good news (Cranfield; TDNT; NTW; NIDNTT; EDNT; Guelich, 13-14; TLNT). The following gen. Ἰησοῦ Χριστοῦ is obj. gen. "the good news about Jesus Christ" (Taylor). For a discussion of this phrase and the prologue (1:1-15) s. Rudolf Pesch, "Anfang des Evangeliums Jesu Christi: Eine Studie zum Prolog des Markusevangeliums (Mk 1,1-15," *Die Zeit Jesu: Eine Festschrift für Heinrich Schaefer*, ed. Guenther Boernkamm and Karl Rahner, Freiburg i. Br.: Herder Verlag, 1970, pp. 108-44. ◆ **2** γέγραπται perf. ind. pass. γράφω (# *1211*) to write. Here perf., "it stands written." Refers to the regulative and authoritative character of the document (MM). For parallels in the DSS s. ESB, 8-10. κατασκευάσει fut. ind. act. κατασκεύω (# *2941*) to prepare, to make ready, to furnish. The word shifts the thought to the messenger's task (Guelich). ◆ **3** βοῶντος pres. act. part. βοάω (# *1066*) to shout, to cry out. ἑτοιμάσατε aor. imp. act. ἑτοιμάζω (# *2286*) to make ready. εὐθείας acc. εὐθύς (# *2318*) straight. ποιεῖτε pres. imp. act. ποιέω (# *4472*) to do, to make. τρίβους acc. pl. τρίβος (# *5561*) way, a beaten path (BAGD). ◆ **4** ἐγένετο aor. ind. mid. (dep.) γίνομαι (# *1181*) to become, to appear on the scene. It emphasizes His emergence in accordance w. the divine purpose (Taylor). βαπτίζων pres. act. part. βαπτίζω (# *966*) (TDNT; s. Matt. 3:6). Part. used as a subst.: "the one baptizing." Part. conveys a more dynamic tone than the subst. βαπτιστής (Guelich). A combination of 2 texts Isa. 40:1 and Mal. 3:1 (BBC). He is not continually baptizing, but this is a defining trait. κηρύσσων pres. act. part. κηρύσσω (# *3062*) to proclaim as a herald (NIDNTT; Cranfield). μετανοίας gen. sing. μετάνοια (# *3657*) a change of mind, repentance (Matt. 3:2; Cranfield). Gen. of source, "a baptism arising out of repentance," or gen. of description, "a baptism characterized by repentance" (Gundry, 43; SIMS, 166-69; GGBB, 80). ἄφεσις (# *912*) release, forgiveness (TDNT; NIDNTT). For the relation between baptism, repentance, and confession s. Gundry 43-44; Guelich; HSB, 404-6. ◆ **5** ἐξεπορεύετο impf. ind. mid. (dep.) ἐκπορεύομαι (# *1744*) to go out. Impf. "they were continually going out." ἐβαπτίζοντο impf. ind. pass. βαπτίζω (# *966*)

to baptize. Pass. of permission: "they were letting themselves be baptized" (Gundry, 44). Impf. indicates that they repeatedly came out and were being baptized. ἐξομολογούμενοι pres. mid. (dep.) part. ἐξομολογέομαι (# *2018*) to confess, to confess publicly, to avow openly (Taylor). It is possible that a spoken confession of sin preceded the actual baptism (Cranfield; BBC; DJG, 96-97). Part. expresing contemporary time. ◆ **6** ἦν impf. ind. act. εἰμί (# *1639*) used w. the two parts. ἐνδεδυμένος, ἐσθίων to form the periphrastic impf. and denotes habitual action "was clothed (as his custom was)" (Taylor). ἐνδεδυμένος perf. pass. part. ἐνδύω (# *1907*) to put on (clothing); perf., to be clothed. The acc. is normal after the pass. of this vb., (Cranfield). τρίχας acc. θρίξ (# *2582*) hair. δερμάτινος (# *1294*) made of leather. ὀσφύς (# *4019*) hip. ἐσθίων pres. act. part. ἐσθίω (# *2266*) to eat. For the form s. MH, 238. ἀκρίδας acc. pl. ἀκρίς (# *210*) grasshopper, locust. If a person vowed to abstain from flesh, he was permitted to eat fish or locusts (M, Hull. 8:1). Honey water was a substitute for wine. To eat only locust and honey indicated the refusal to eat meat or drink wine (Otto Böcher, "Ass Johannes der Täufer kein Brot Luk. vii. 33?" *NTS* 18 [1971/72]: 90-92, esp. 91). ◆ **7** ἐκήρυσσεν impf. ind. act. s.v. 4. λέγων pres. act. part. λέγω (# *3306*) to say, to speak. ἔρχεται pres. ind. mid. (dep.) ἔρχομαι (# *2262*) to come. Pres. sounds the note of immediacy (Taylor). This coming person is predicted in Isa. 5:26-27 and is messianic. S. Gordon D. Kirchhevel, "He That Cometh in Mark 1:7 and Matt. 24:30," *BBR* 4 (1994): 105-12. ἰσχυρότερος comp. ἰσχυρός (# *2708*) strong, mighty. μου gen. ἐγώ (# *1609*) gen. of comp. ("than I am.") ἱκανός (# *2653*) fit, sufficient, worthy. Denotes any kind of sufficiency or fitness (Gould). κύψας aor. act. part. κύπτω (# *3252*) to stoop. Epex. part. explaining the unworthiness. λῦσαι aor. act. inf. λύω (# *3395*) to loose. Compl. inf. to explain the main vb. ἱμάς (# *2666*) strap. The thong of the sandal which is held together (RWP). ὑπόδημα (# *5687*) sandal. For discussion of footwear s. ABD, 2:237. This was normally the service of a slave, but a disciple was not to render such a service to his teacher, lest he be mistaken for a Canaanite slave (b. Keth. 96a [Soncino edition]). αὐτοῦ (# *899*) his. For the pers. pronoun used after a rel. s. W.F. Bakker, *Pronomen Abundans and Pronomen Coniunctum*, (Amsterdam: North-Holland Publishing Co., 1974), 39; SIMS, 116-18. ◆ **8** ἐβάπτισα aor. ind. act. βαπτίζω (# *966*) to baptize. Aor. represents John's course as already fulfilled in the coming of Messiah (Swete; DJG, 57-58). **βαπτίσει** fut. ind. act. βαπτίζω. ◆ **9 ἐγένετο** aor. ind. mid. (dep.) γίνομαι (# 1181) to become, to happen, used to introduce a past event (SIMS, 81-86). **ἦλθεν** aor. ind. act. ἔρχομαι (# 2262) to come, to go. **ἐβαπτίσθη** aor. ind. pass. s.v. 4. ◆ **10 εὐθύς** (#2317) immediately, at once, so then; a favorite word of Mark occurring 41 times. Here it refers to the following vision and expresses continuity between John's and Jesus' ministry (Gundry, 47; Guelich; Taylor; David Daube, *The Sudden in the Scriptures* [Leiden: E.J. Brill, 1964], 46-51). **ἀναβαίνων** pres. act. part. ἀναβαίνω (# 326) to go up. Temp. part. expressing contemporaneous time. **εἶδεν** aor. ind. act. ὁράω (# 3972) to see. **σχιζομένους** pres. pass. part. σχίζω (# 5387) to divide, to split. Pres. part. indicates action already in progress (Cranfield). The idea is that of a fixed separation of heaven from earth, only to be broken in special circumstances (Taylor). **περιστερά** (# 4361) dove (s. Matt. 3:16; Gundry, 51). **καταβαῖνον** pres. act. part. καταβαίνω (# 2849) to come down. ◆ **11 εἶ** pres. ind. act. 2nd. pers. sing. εἰμί (# 1639) to be. **ἀγαπητός** (# 28) beloved. **εὐδόκησα** aor. ind. act. εὐδοκέω (# 2305) to be pleased. The statement is illative: *"therefore I am well pleased"* (Gundry, 49). ◆ **12 ἐκβάλλει** pres. ind. act. ἐκβάλλω (# 1675) to cast out, to drive out; hist. pres. where attention is drawn to an event or series of events (VA, 196; VANT, 231). ◆ **13 ἦν** impf. ind. act. s.v. 6. **πειραζόμενος** pres. pass. part. πειράζω (# 4279) to try, to test, to tempt, used here of an actual solicitation to evil (Gould). Pres. part. could be used to express purp. **διηκόνουν** impf. ind. act. διακονέω (# 1354) to serve, to minister to. Inceptive impf.: "they began to minister to." ◆ **14 παραδοθῆναι** aor. pass. inf. παραδίδωμι (# 4140) to deliver over, to deliver up as a prisoner (Cranfield; TLNT). Temp. use of the inf. w. the prep.: "after he was delivered over." **ἦλθεν** aor. ind. act. s.v. 9. **κηρύσσων** pres. act. part. s.v. 4. Part. of manner, purp., or circum. ◆ **15 λέγων** pres. act. part. s.v. 7. For a discussion of the Kingdom of God and Messsiah in early Jewish literature s. Michael Lahke "The Jewish Background of the Synoptic Concept, 'The Kingdom of God,'" in *The Kingdom of God*, edited by Bruce Chilton (Philadelphia: Fortress, 1984), 72-91. **ὅτι** (# 4022) recitative equivalent to quotation marks. **πεπλήρωται** perf. ind. pass. πληρόω (# 4444) to fulfill. (For this phrase s. Swete; Gundry, 69). **ἤγγικεν** perf. ind. act. ἐγγίζω (# 1581) to draw near. **μετανοεῖτε** pres. imp. act. μετανοέω (# 3566) to repent, to change one's mind (s.v. 4; Matt. 3:6). **πιστεύετε** pres. imp. act. πιστεύω (# 4409) (TDNT). Here w. the prep. **ἐν** (# 1877) probably a Semitism (Cranfield; for the Heb. construction אמן indicating a general continual acceptance as trustworthy s. Ernst Jenni, *Die hebräischen Präpositionen: Band 1: Die Präposition Beth* [Stuttgart, 1992], 254-55). ◆ **16 παράγων** pres.

act. part. παράγω (# 4135) to pass by, to go along. **εἶδεν** aor. ind. act. s.v. 10. **ἀμφιβάλλοντας** pres. act. part. ἀμφιβάλλω (# 311) to cast a net (Mendel Nun, "Cast Your Nets Upon the Waters," *BAR* 19 [1993]: 51ff). **ἦσαν** impf. ind. act. εἰμί (# 1639) to be. **ἁλιεύς** (# 243) fisherman (s. Matt. 4:18 BBC). ◆ **17 εἶπεν** aor. ind. act. λέγω (# 3306) to say. **δεῦτε** (# 1307) adv., come here. **ποιήσω** fut. ind. act. s.v. 3. W. the acc. and the inf. meaning "to cause someone to do something" (Cranfield). **γενέσθαι** aor. mid. (dep.) inf. γίνομαι s.v. 4. ◆ **18 ἀφέντες** aor. act. part. ἀφίημι (# 918) to leave **δίκτυον** (# 1473) net (s.v. 16). Temp. part. antecedent to "when he had left." **ἠκολούθησαν** aor. ind. act. ἀκολουθέω (# 199) to follow, to follow as a disciple. It implies personal adherence and association (Carrington). ◆ **19 προβάς** aor. act. part. προβαίνω (# 4581) to go forward. **ὀλίγον** (# 3900) adv. a little, a little further. **καταρτίζοντας** pres. act. part. καταρτίζω (# 2936) to put in order, mending, cleaning, folding, and making the nets ready for another night's fishing (Cranfield; s.v. 16; Nun, BAR). ◆ **20 ἐκάλεσεν** aor. ind. act. καλέω (# 2813) to call. **μισθωτός** a hired worker. The reference to "hired" indicates that the brothers were by no means poor (Hooker). **ἀπῆλθον** aor. ind. act. ἀπέρχομαι (# 599) to go forth. ◆ **21 εἰσπορεύονται** pres. ind. mid. (dep.) εἰσπορεύομαι (# 1660) to go in, hist. pres. **εἰσελθών** aor. act. part. εἰσέρχομαι (# 1656) to go in. **συναγωγή** (# 5252) synagogue (s. Matt. 4:23; TDNT; John C.H. Kaughlin, "Capernaum from Jesus' Time and After," *BAR* 19 [1993]: 54-61; RC, 32-49). **ἐδίδασκεν** impf. ind. act. διδάσκω (# 1438) to teach. Inceptive impf., "he began to teach" (Cranfield). ◆ **22 ἐξεπλήσσοντο** impf. ind. pass. ἐκπλήσσω (# 1742) to be astonished, to be amazed, to strike a person out of his senses by some strong feeling such as fear, wonder, or even joy (Gould). Impf. here corresponds to the impf. of teaching in v. 21, indicating that as long as he taught astonishment overwhelmed them (Gundry, 73). **διδάσκων** pres. act. part. διδάσκω (# 1438) to teach, used in the periphrastic construction. **ἐξουσία** (# 2026) authority. The authority of a rabbi or God-given authority (Cranfield; TDNT). **ἔχων** pres. act. part. ἔχω (# 2400) to have, to possess. Subst. use of part. "one who has." **γραμματεύς** (# 1208) scribe (s. Matt. 2:4; 5:20; EDNT; BBC; DJG, 732-35). ◆ **23 ἄνθρωπος** (# 476) man; the anarthrous use may be equivalent to the indef. pron. "someone" due to semitic influence (SIMS, 131-34; SS; 20-21). **ἀνέκραξεν** aor. ind. act. ἀνακράζω (# 371) to shout, indicating strong emotion, either the cries of the sufferer or of the unclean spirit (Taylor). ◆ **24 λέγων** pres. act. part. s.v. 7. **τί ἡμῖν καὶ σοί** An idiom meaning "what have we and you in common?" "Why do you interfere w. us?" "Mind your own business!" (Cranfield; Taylor; SIMS, 183-85; John 2:4). **ἦλθες** aor. ind. act. s.v. 9. **ἀπολέσαι** aor. act. inf. ἀπόλλυμι (# 660) to destroy. Inf. used to express purp. **οἶδα** (# 3857) perf. ind. act., to know. Def. perf. w. pres. meaning. For parallels to the spirit s. Taylor. ◆ **25 ἐπετίμησεν** aor. act. ind. ἐπιτιμάω (# 2203) to rebuke (s. Matt. 17:18). **φιμώθητι** aor. imp. pass. φιμόω (# 5821) to silence, to tie, to muzzle; to be muzzled, like an ox (RWP; Guelich). The command for silence refers to the demons' attempt to speak in self-defense (Pesch; Gundry, 77; for the meaning "banishing" or "binding" s. RAC, 174). **ἔξελθε** aor. imp. act. ἐξέρχομαι (# 2002) to go out. ◆ **26 σπαράξαν** aor. act. part. σπαράσσω (# 5057) to tear, to pull to and fro, to convulse. Medical writers used the word of the convulsive action of the stomach (Gould). **φωνῆσαν** aor. act. part. φωνέω (# 5888) to make a sound, to call out, to cry out. Temp. parts. Aor. expressing antecedent time ("after"). **ἐξῆλθεν** aor. ind. act. ἐξέρχομαι (# 2002) to go out. ◆ **27 ἐθαμβήθησαν** aor. ind. pass. θαμβέω (# 2501) to be astounded, to be amazed (Taylor). **ὥστε** (# 6063) used w. inf. and acc. to introduce a result cl. **συζητεῖν** pres. act. inf. συζητέω (# 5184) to question, to discuss. **καινή** (# 2785) new, in respect of quality as distinct from time (Cranfield). **ἐπιτάσσει** pres. act. ind. ἐπιτάσσω (# 2199) to command. **ὑπακούουσιν** pres. ind. act. ὑπακούω (# 5634) to obey. ◆ **28 ἐξῆλθεν** aor. ind. act. s.v. 26. **ἀκοή** (# 198) hearing, report, fame; followed by the obj. gen. **Γαλιλαίας** (# 1133) Galilee. Gen. of apposition, "the whole surrounding region, that is, Galilee" (Gundry, 85). ◆ **29 ἐξελθόντες** aor. act. part. (temp.) ἐξέρχομαι s.v. 26. Aor. expressing antecedent action. For the house of Peter and Andrew in Capernaum s. Kaughlin, "Capernaum from Jesus' Time and After," *BAR* 19 (Sept.-Oct., 1993): 54-61; RC, 50-64; 70-71. ◆ **30 πενθερά** (# 4289) mother-in-law. **κατέκειτο** impf. ind. mid. (dep.) κατάκειμαι (# 2879) to lie. **πυρέσσουσα** pres. act. part. πυρέσσω (# 4789) to suffer w. a fever, to be feverish (DMTG, 280). For a description of fever in the ancient world and its cure s. RAC, 7:877-909. ◆ **31 προσελθών** aor. act. part. (circum.) προσέρχομαι (# 4665) to come to. **ἤγειρεν** impf. ind. act. ἐγείρω (# 1586) to raise, to lift up. **κρατήσας** aor. act. part. κρατέω (# 3195) to take hold of; used w. partitive gen. Part. expresses contemporaneous action (Taylor), but logically necessary for the action of the main vb. **ἀφῆκεν** aor. ind. act. s.v. 18. **διηκόνει** impf. ind. act. διακονέω (# 1354) to wait on, to serve. Incep., "she began to serve." ◆ **32 ὄψιος** (# 4070) evening. The Sabbath has already passed (BBC). **γενομένης** aor. mid. part. (temp.) γίνομαι s.v. 4. Gen. abs. **ἔδυ** aor. ind. act. δύνω (# 1544) to go down, to set. For the form s. BD, 51. **ἔφερον** impf. act. ind. φέρω (# 5770) to carry, to bring. Impf. indicates they brought them in a steady stream (RWP). **ἔχοντας** pres. act. part. ἔχω (# 2400) to have. In this construction, "to have it bad," "to suffer from a sickness." **δαιμονιζομένους** pres. act. part. δαιμονίζω (# 1227) to be possessed by a demon. ◆ **33 ἐπισυνηγμένη** perf. pass. part. ἐπισυνάγω (# 2190) to gather together, to assemble. Part. used in a periphrastic

construction. The tense vividly describes the growing crowds (Taylor). **θύρα** (# 2598) door. The acc. dwells on the thought of the flocking up to the door which preceded, and the surging, moving, mass before it (Swete). Capernaum was on the highway between Beth-shan and Damascus, ideal for crowds coming by (RC, 63). ◆ **34 ἐθεράπευσεν** aor. ind. act. θεραπεύω (# 2543) to heal (GLH). **ποικίλαις** dat. pl. ποικίλος (# 4476) various kinds, diversified, manifold. Instr. dat. (SIMS, 181-82). **ἐξέβαλεν** aor. ind. act. ἐκβάλλω s.v. 12. **ἤφιεν** impf. ind. act. ἀφίημι (# 918) to allow. **λαλεῖν** pres. act. inf. λαλέω (# 3281) to speak. **ᾔδεισαν** plperf. ind. act. οἶδα (# 3857) to know. Def. perf. w. a pres. meaning. W. the plperf. the meaning is past or impf. ◆ **35 πρωΐ** (# 4745) early. **ἔννυχα** (# 1939) adv. at night. **ἀναστάς** aor. act. part. ἀνίστημι (# 482) to arise. Temp. or circum. part. Aor. indicates antecedent time. **ἐξῆλθεν** aor. ind. act. s.v. 26. **προσηύχετο** impf. ind. mid. (dep.) προσεύχομαι (# 4667) to pray. Impf. denotes what He was doing when He was sought by the others (Gould). ◆ **36 κατεδίωξεν** aor. ind. act. καταδιώκω (# 2870) to pursue closely, to follow down, to track down. Prep. in the vb. is perfective. ◆ **37 εὗρον** aor. ind. act. εὑρίσκω (# 2351) to find. **λέγουσιν** pres. ind. act. λέγω (# 3306) to say. Hist. pres. (Taylor). ◆ **38 ἄγωμεν** pres. subj. act. ἄγω (# 72) to lead, to go. Hortatory subj., "let us go." **ἀλλαχοῦ** (# 250) elsewhere. **ἐχομένας** pres. mid. part. ἔχω (# 2400). The mid. part. has the meaning "near," "neighboring." Adj. use of the part. **κωμόπολις** (# 3268) a small town having only the status of a village (Cranfield; SB, 2:3-4). Although Josephus' figure of 15,000 inhabitants in the smallest village in Galilee is an exaggeration, the area evidently had a great population (Jos., *J.W.*, 3:43; G., 103-104). **κηρύξω** aor. subj. act. s.v. 4. Subj. w. **ἵνα** (# 2671) expresses purp. **ἐξῆλθον** aor. ind. act. s.v. 26. Either leaving Capernaum or coming from the heavenly Father (Alexander; Guelich). ◆ **39 κηρύσσων** pres. act. part. s.v. 38. Expressing manner. ◆ **40 ἔρχεται** pres. ind. mid. (dep.) ἔρχομαι (# 2262) to go. Hist. pres. **λεπρός** (# 3320) leprous, used as a substitutive leper (DJG, 463-64; IDB, 3:111-13; Matt. 8:4). **παρακαλῶν** pres. act. part. παρακαλέω (# 4151) to ask for something earnestly and w. propriety, to request, to plead for (LN, 1:408). Part. of manner. **γονυπετῶν** pres. act. part. γονυπετέω (# 1206) to fall to the knees. It was a gesture of a sincere request (EDNT). **ἐάν** (# 1569) if. Indicates the cond. is uncertain. **θέλῃς** pres. subj. act. θέλω (# 2527) to will, to desire. **δύνασαι** pres. ind. pass. (dep.) 2nd. pers. sing. δύναμαι (# 1538) to be able, to be capable, to have the ability. **καθαρίσαι** aor. act. inf. καθαρίζω (# 2751) to cleanse, to make clean. Inf. complementing the main vb. ◆ **41 σπλαγχνισθείς** aor. pass. (dep.) part. (causal) σπλαγχνίζομαι (# 5072) to be inwardly disturbed, to be moved w. compassion (TDNT; EDNT). **ἐκτείνας** aor. act. part. (circum.) ἐκτείνω (# 1753) to stretch out. **ἥψατο** aor. ind. mid. (dep.) ἅπτομαι (# 721) to touch (w. obj. in gen.) Rather than Jesus becoming unclean, the leper became clean. **καθαρίσθητι** aor. imp. pass. s.v. 40. ◆ **42 ἀπῆλθεν** aor. ind. act. s.v. 20. **ἐκαθαρίσθη** aor. ind. pass. s.v. 40. Effective aor. pointing to the complete cleansing. The success is immediate: he is healed (Lührmann). ◆ **43 ἐμβριμησάμενος** aor. mid. (dep.) part. (circum.) ἐμβριμάομαι (# 1839) (w. dat.) to scold, censure, warn sternly (BAGD); "moved by deep feeling toward him" (Taylor; Cranfield), to growl (Gundry, 103). **ἐξέβαλεν** aor. ind. act. s.v. 12. ◆ **44 ὅρα** pres. imp. act. ὁράω (# 3972) to see. This vb. of caution is followed by an obj. cl. (SIMS, 75). **εἴπῃς** aor. subj. act. λέγω (# 3306) to talk, to speak. W. neg. **μηδέν** (#3594)used to forbid the starting of an action. **ὕπαγε** pres. imp. act. ὑπάγω (# 5632) to go, to go away. Pres. imp. used w. a vb. of motion. **δεῖξον** aor. imp. act. δείκνυμι (# 1259) to show. Aor. imp. used of a specific action. **προσένεγκε** aor. imp. act. προσφέρω (# 4712) to carry to, to bring an offering, to offer. **προσέταξεν** aor. ind. act. προστάσσω (# 4705) to command, to give an order. **μαρτύριον** (# 3457) witness, proof (Cranfield). ◆ **45 ἐξελθών** aor. act. part. (temp.) ἐξέρχομαι (# 2002) to go out. Possibly referring to Jesus, though more likely to the leper (J.Swetnam, "Some Remarks on the Meaning of ὁ δὲ ἐξελθών in Mark 1,45," *Bib* 68 [1987]: 245-49). **ἤρξατο** aor. ind. mid. (dep.) ἄρχομαι (# 806) to begin; to make known by word of mouth, to spread the news about (BAGD). **δύνασθαι** aor. mid. (dep.) inf. s.v. 40. Inf. w. **ὥστε** (# 6063) to express result. **εἰσελθεῖν** aor. act. inf. εἰσέρχομαι (# 1656) to go in. **ἤρχοντο** impf. ind. mid. (dep.) ἔρχομαι (# 2262). Impf. expresses the continual action in the past, "the people kept on coming." **πάντοθεν** (# 4119) from everywhere.

Mark 2

◆ **1 εἰσελθών** aor. act. part. (temp.) s. 1:45. **δι' ἡμερῶν** (# 1328; 2465)after some days. The prep. w. gen. has the idea of "through" and is used here temporarily "after" (BD, 119). For a discussion of 2:1-3:6, s. Joanna Dewey, *Markan Public Debate: Literary Technique, Concentric Structure, and Theology in Mark 2:1-3:6* (Chico, Ca.: Scholars Press, 1980). **ἠκούσθη** aor. ind. pass. ἀκούω (# 201) to hear. **ἐν οἴκῳ** (# 1877; 3875) at home, probably refers to the house of Peter and Andrew (Gundry, 110). For the omission of the article s. SIMS, 110. ◆ **2 συνήχθησαν** aor. ind. pass. συνάγω (# 5251) to gather together, to assemble. **ὥστε** (# 6063) w. inf. and the acc. to express result. **χωρεῖν** pres. act. inf. χωρέω (# 6003) to make room, to have space for, to contain. **τὰ πρὸς τὴν θύραν** either acc. of reference ("so that there was no longer room for them even about the door"), or to be taken w. inf. ("so that even the space about the door could no longer contain them") (Cranfield). Probably 50 people (BBC). **ἐλάλει** impf. ind. act. λαλέω

(# 3281) to speak. ◆ **3 ἔρχονται** pres. ind. mid. (dep.) ἔρχομαι (# 2262) hist. pres. **φέροντες** pres. act. part. φέρω (# 5770) to carry. Part. of manner. **παραλυτικός** (# 4166) paralyzed, one lame w. paralysis (DMTG, 259). **αἰρόμενον** pres. pass. part. αἴρω (# 149) to lift up, to carry. This causal part. underlines the severity of the case (Gundry, 111). ◆ **4 δυνάμενοι** pres. pass. (dep.) part. δύναμαι (# 1538) be able to. **προσενέγκαι** aor. act. inf. προσφέρω (# 4712) to carry, to bring to. Inf. to complement the main vb. **διά** (# 1328) w. acc., because of. **ἀπεστέγασαν** aor. ind. act. ἀποστεγάζω (# 689) to unroof, to remove the roof. **ἐξορύξαντες** aor. act. part. (temp.) ἐξορύσσω (# 2021) to dig out, to tear out. The roof probably was formed by beams and rafters across which matting, branches, and twigs, covered by hard-trodden earth, were laid (Taylor; BBC). **χαλῶσι** pres. ind. act. χαλάω (# 5899) to let down. This is not strange in the light of the rediscovered living quarters of Capernaum, where one-story rooms were covered by light roofs reached through a flight of steps from the courtyard (RC, 72). **κράβαττος** (# 3187) pallet. It was the poor man's bed (Swete; BAGD). **κατέκειτο** impf. ind. mid. (dep.) κατάκειμαι (# 2879) to lie, to lie down. Impf. may be customary. ◆ **5 ἰδών** aor. act. part. (temp.) ὁράω (# 3972) to see. **ἀφίενται** pres. ind. pass. ἀφίημι (# 918) to release, to forgive; an aoristic pres. indicating punctiliar action (RG, 864f). It could also be called a performative use of the pres., or an instantaneous pres., both describing the action which is accomplished in the very act of speaking (VANT, 187-90, 202). Here the agent is suppressed for rhetorical reasons (GGBB, 437). ◆ **6 ἦσαν** impf. ind. act. εἰμί (# 1639) used w. part. to build the periphrastic impf. **καθήμενοι** pres. mid. (dep.) part. κάθημαι (# 2764) to sit. **διαλογιζόμενοι** pres. mid. (dep.) part. διαλογίζομαι (# 1368) to reason, to debate, to balance accounts, to engage in some relatively detailed discussion of a matter (Taylor; LN, 1:407). Part. in periphrastic construction. ◆ **7 τί** (# 5515) why, interrogative pron. introducing a question expressing wonder or indig-nation (SIMS, 142f). **βλασφημεῖ** pres. ind. act. βλασφημέω (# 1059) to blaspheme, to slander God (TDNT; NIDNTT; EDNT). **ἀφιέναι** pres. act. inf. s.v. 5. **εἰ μή** (# 1623; 3590) except. ◆ **8 ἐπιγνούς** aor. act. part. (temp.) ἐπιγινώσκω (# 2105) to perceive, to recognize, to know. Aor. indicating antecedent time. **πνεύματι** dat. sing. πνεῦμα (# 4460) spirit; here "in himself" (Guelich). ◆ **9 εὐκοπώτερον** comp. of εὔκοπος (# 2324) w. easy labor, easy. **εἰπεῖν** aor. act. inf. λέγω (# 3306) to say. Epex. inf. explaining **εὐκοπώτερον**. **ἔγειρε** pres. imp. act. ἐγείρω (# 1586) to rise. **ἆρον** aor. imp. act. αἴρω (# 149) to take up. **περιπάτει** pres. imp. act. περιπατέω (# 4344) to walk about. The pres. imp. often is used to express an order involving motion (Bakker, 82; VANT, 343). ◆ **10 εἰδῆτε** perf. subj. act. οἶδα (# 3857) to know. Def. perf. w. pres. meaning. Subj. used w. **ἵνα** (# 2671) to express purp. **ἀφιέναι** pres. act.

inf. s.v. 5. Epex. inf. used to explain authority. For the title Son of Man s. Gundry, 118-20; Guelich, 89-94; HSB, 408-10; Hooker, 87-93. ◆ **11 ὑπαγε** pres. imp. act. ὑπάγω (# *5632*) to depart s. 1:44. ◆ **12 ἠγέρθη** aor. ind. pass. ἐγείρω (# *1586*) to raise; pass. to rise. **ἄρας** aor. act. part. (circum.) αἴρω (# *149*) to take. **ἐξῆλθεν** aor. ind. act. ἐξέρχομαι (# *2002*) to go out. **ἐξίστασθαι** pres. mid. (dep.) inf. ἐξίστημι (# *2014*) to amaze, to be amazed, to be beside oneself. Inf. used w. **ὥστε** (# *6063*) to express actual result. **δοξάζειν** pres. act. inf. δοξάζω (# *1519*) to praise, to give glory to (TDNT; NIDNTT; TLNT). Inf. expressing results. **λέγοντας** pres. act. part. acc. pl. λέγω (# *3306*) Part. gives the content of their praise. Acc. w. the subject of the inf. **εἴδομεν** aor. ind. act. ὁράω (# *3972*) to see. ◆ **13 ἤρχετο** impf. ind. mid. (dep.) ἔρχομαι (# *2262*) to come. **ἐδίδασκεν** impf. ind. act. διδάσκω (# *1438*) to teach. The two impfs. of this v. indicate the coming and going of successive groups of hearers (Taylor). ◆ **14 παράγων** pres. act. part. (temp.) παράγω (# *4135*) to go by, to pass along. **εἶδεν** aor. ind. act. s.v. 12. **καθήμενον** pres. mid. (dep.) part. s.v. 6. **τελώνιον** (# *5468*) customs office, toll house. (Matt. 9:9). It may have been a tax station on the trade route or a place for port duties and fishing tolls (BBC; DJG, 805-806; HA, 76). **ἀκολούθει** pres. imp. act. ἀκολουθέω (# *199*) to follow, to follow as a disciple (TDNT; EDNT; NIDNTT). **ἀναστάς** aor. act. part. (circum.) ἀνίστημι (# *482*) to get up, to rise up. **ἠκολούθησεν** aor. ind. act. ἀκολουθέω (# *199*) to follow, followed by dat. ◆ **15 κατακεῖσθαι** pres. mid. (dep.) inf. κατάκειμαι (# *2879*) to recline (at the table). Generally used of festive meals where entertainment was provided (Cranfield; SB, 4:ii, 611-39; DJG, 796-97). **τελῶναι** nom. pl. τελώνης (# *5467*) tax collector, not the Roman *publicani*, but native Jews who had been contracted to collect taxes in a town or small district (HA, 78; JZ, 22-37). **συνανέκειντο** impf. ind. mid. (dep.) συνανάκειμαι (# *5263*) to recline (at the table) together. **ἦσαν** impf. ind. act. εἰμί. (# *1639*) **ἠκολούθουν** impf. ind. act. s.v. 14. ◆ **16 ἰδόντες** aor. act. part. (temp.) s.v. 5. Aor. describes antecedent action, "when he saw." **ἔλεγον** impf. ind. act. s. v. 12. Inceptive impf., "they began to say." ◆ **17 ἀκούσας** aor. act. part. (temp.) ἀκούω (# *201*) to hear. Aor. describes antecedent action, "when he heard." **ἰσχύοντες** pres. act. part. ἰσχύω (# *2710*) to be strong, to be well, healthy. Part. used as subst. **ἰατροῦ** gen. sing. ἰατρός (# *2620*) doctor, physician. Gen. describes the need. **ἔχοντες** pres. act. part. ἔχω (# *2400*) to have. W. adv., "to have it bad," "to be sick." For parallels in D.C. s. DCNT, 52. **ἦλθον** aor. ind. act. ἔρχομαι (# *2262*) to come. **καλέσαι** aor. act. inf. καλέω (# *2813*) to call. Inf. of purp. ◆ **18 νηστεύοντες** pres. act. part. νηστεύω (# *3764*) to fast. Part. used w. impf. to form the periphrastic impf. (VA, 457), indicating that which was customary. ◆ **19 εἶπεν** aor. ind. act. s.v. 9. **μή** (# *3590*) used in a question expecting a neg. answer. **νυμφών**

(# *3812*) the bride chamber; **υἱοὶ τοῦ νυμφῶνος** refers to either the groomsmen or the wedding guests (Taylor; for the Semitic use of "son" indicating characteristic s. SIMS, 169). **ἐν ᾧ** (# *1877*; *4005*) in which time, while. ◆ **20 ἐλεύσονται** fut. ind. mid. (dep.) ἔρχομαι (# *2262*) to come. **ἀπαρθῇ** aor. subj. pass ἀπαίρω (# *554*) to take away. The aor. between the two fut. cls. indicates antecedent action and stresses the period of time after the bridegroom is removed (Guelich). ◆ **21 ἐπίβλημα** (# *2099*) a patch. Lit. "that which is placed upon." **ῥάκους** gen. sing. ῥάκος (# *4820*) cloth. Gen. of description or material. **ἀγναφος** (# *47*) new, that which was not treated by the fuller, a patch of undressed cloth (Taylor). **ἐπιράπτει** pres. ind. act. ἐπιράπτω (# *2165*) to sew on, gnomic pres. (GGBB, 524). **παλαιός** (# *4097*) old. **εἰ δὲ μή** otherwise, introduces the hypothetical results (Guelich). **αἴρει** pres. ind. act. s.v. 3. Here the meaning is "to tear." **πλήρωμα** (# *4445*) fullness, patch. **χεῖρον** (# *5937*) comp. of κακός (bad) worse. "A worse tear is the result" (SIMS, 111). **σχίσμα** (# *5388*) division, tear. A wedding requires good clothing and ample wine, so this section would follow naturally (Gundry, 133-34). ◆ **22 βάλλει** pres. ind. act. βάλλω (# *965*) to throw, to put. **νέος** (# *3742*) new, fresh. **ἀσκός** (# *829*) skin, leather bag or bottle, wineskin (Taylor). **ῥήξει** fut. ind. act. ῥήγνυμι (# *4838*) to rip (BBC). **ἀπόλλυνται** pres. ind. mid. ἀπόλλυμι (# *660*) to destroy, to ruin; mid. to be ruined (BAGD). ◆ **23 ἐγένετο** aor. ind. mid. (dep.) γίνομαι (# *1181*) to become, to happen, to come to pass. Used w. inf. to emphasize the actual occurrence of the action denoted by the vb. (BAGD; for the Semitic construction introducing a past event s. SIMS, 81, 85-86). **παραπορεύεσθαι** pres. mid. (dep.) inf. παραπορεύομαι (# *4182*) to pass by. For the use of the inf. w. the vb. **ἐγένετο** and the subject in the acc. s. SIMS, 85-86. **ἤρξαντο** aor. ind. mid. (dep.) ἄρχομαι (# *806*) to begin. **ποιεῖν** pres. act. inf. ποιέω (# *4472*) to make. Compl. inf. used w. the vb. ἄρχομαι. **τίλλοντες** pres. act. part. τίλλω (# *5504*) to pluck, to pick. Part. of manner. **στάχυς** (# *4719*) head or ear of grain. The word suggests the party was pushing its way through the corn where there was no path. As they went, they plucked the ears and ate (Swete). ◆ **24 ἔλεγον** impf. ind. act. λέγω (# *3306*) to say. Inceptive impf., "they began to say." **ἴδε** aor. imp. act. ὁράω (# *2632*) to see. **ἔξεστιν** (# *2003*) pres. ind. act. it is allowed, it is lawful. ◆ **25 ἀνέγνωτε** aor. ind. act. ἀναγινώσκω (# *336*) to read. **ἐποίησεν** aor. ind. act. ποιέω (# *4472*) to do. **ἔσχεν** aor. ind. act. ἔχω (# *2400*) to have. **ἐπείνασεν** aor. ind. act. πεινάω (# *4277*) to be hungry. ◆ **26 εἰσῆλθεν** aor. ind. act. s.v. 1. **ἐπί** w. gen., in time of or in the passage about (RWP). **τοὺς ἄρτους τῆς προθέσεως** (# *788*) the showbread. The twelve newly baked loaves of bread placed every Sabbath in two rows on a table before God in the Tabernacle and later eaten by priests (Lev. 24:5-9; HSB 412-14; Taylor).

ἔφαγεν aor. ind. act. ἐσθίω (# *2266*) to eat. φαγεῖν aor. act. inf. Inf. explains what was not lawful. ἔδωκεν aor. ind act. δίδωμι (# *1443*) to give. οὖσιν pres. act. part. dat. pl. εἰμί (# *1639*) to be. Part. as subst., "Those who were w. him." ◆ **27** διά (# *1328*) w. acc., because of, for. ἐγένετο aor. ind. mid. (dep.) γίνομαι (# *1181*) to become. ◆ **28** ὥστε (# *6063*) therefore. The word draws a logical conclusion.

Mark 3

◆ **1** ἐξηραμμένην perf. pass. part. ξηραίνω (# *3830*) to dry out, to become dry, to wither, to be withered (BBC). The perf. points to a withered state and may show that it was not from birth, but was the result of injury by accident or disease (RWP). ◆ **2** παρετήρουν impf. ind. act. παρατηρέω (# *4190*) to observe from the side, to observe minutely, going along as it were w. the object for the purp. of watching its movements (Swete). It was used for keeping a watchful eye on criminals, for watching out for a bowl lest it be stolen (MM). Galen used the subst. of empirical medical observation (DMTG, 260). It was also used of observing one's conduct to see if the person would act falsely toward another (*Letter of Aristeas*, 246:3). τοῖς σάββασιν dat. pl. Dat. of time: "on the Sabbath." For the use of pl. for names of festivals s. BD, 78. θεραπεύσει fut. ind. act. θεραπεύω (# *2543*) to heal. κατηγορήσωσιν aor. subj. act. κατηγορέω (# *2989*) w. gen. to accuse, to bring legal charges against. Subj. used in a purp. cl. ◆ **3** ἔχοντι pres. act. part. dat. sing. ἔχω (# *2400*) to have. Part. used as subst. ἔγειρε pres. imp. act. ἐγείρω (# *1586*) "stand up!" For the construction εἰς τὸ μέσον (# *1650*; *3545*) s. SS, 17; J.J. O'Rourke, "A Note Concerning the Use of EIS and EN in Mark," *JBL* 85 (1966): 349-51. ◆ **4** ἔξεστιν (# *2003*) pres. ind. act. it is allowed, it is lawful. ποιῆσαι aor. act. inf. ποιέω (# *4472*) to do. κακοποιῆσαι aor. act. inf. κακοποιέω (# *2803*) to do evil. Compl. infs. used to explain what is lawful. σῶσαι aor. act. inf. σῴζω (# *5392*) to save, to rescue, to heal (Pesch; for the Jewish idea of doing good on the Sabbath s. SB, 1:622-23; BBC). ἀποκτεῖναι aor. act. inf. ἀποκτείνω (# *650*) to kill. ἐσιώπων impf. ind. act. σιωπάω (# *4995*) to be silent. "They remained silent" (Guelich). ◆ **5** περιβλεψάμενος aor. mid. (dep.) part. περιβλέπω (# *4315*) to look around. The prep. compound is local (MH, 321f.). Temp. or circum. part. συλλυπούμενος pres. pass. part. συλλυπέομαι (# *5200*) to be grieved w., to feel sympathy, to feel sorry for (LN, 1:318). The prep. compound may be perfective ("utterly distressed") (MH, 325). πώρωσις (# *4801*) hardening. ἔκτεινον aor. imp. act. ἐκτείνω (# *1753*) to stretch out. ἐξέτεινεν aor. ind. act. ἀπεκατεστάθη aor. ind. pass. ἀποκαθίστημι (# *635*) to restore again. It indicates complete restoration (Guelich; MM). The subst. was used by Galen of recovery from sickness (DMTG, 63). ◆ **6** ἐξελθόντες aor. act. part. (temp.) ἐξέρχομαι

(# *2002*) to go out. συμβούλιον ἐδίδουν impf. ind. act. δίδωμι to give counsel, to plot (BAGD; Taylor; for the Herodians s. Gundry, 154; HA, 331-42; EDNT; DJG, 325). ὅπως (# *3968*) w. subj. to express purp. ἀπολέσωσιν aor. subj. act. ἀπόλλυμι (# *660*) to destroy. ◆ **7** ἀνεχώρησεν aor. ind. act. ἀναχωρέω (# *432*) depart. ἠκολούθησεν aor. ind. act. ἀκολουθέω (# *199*) to follow. ◆ **8** ἀκούοντες pres. act. part. ἀκούω (# *201*) to hear. Causal or temp. part. ἐποίει impf. ind. act. ποιέω (# *4472*) to do. "The things he was continually doing." ἦλθον aor. ind. act. ἔρχομαι (# *2262*) to come. ◆ **9** πλοιάριον (# *4449*) dimin., a small boat. προσκαρτερῇ pres. subj. act. προσκαρτερέω (# *4674*) w. dat. to attach oneself to, to wait on. The idea is that the boat is at the disposal of Jesus as a refuge from the crowd (Taylor). θλίβωσιν pres. subj. act. θλίβω (# *2567*) to pressure, to crowd. Subj. w. ἵνα (# *2671*) used in a neg. purp. cl. ◆ **10** ἐθεράπευσεν aor. ind. act. s.v. 2. ἐπιπίπτειν pres. act. inf. ἐπιπίπτω (# *2158*) to fall upon. Inf. w. ὥστε (# *6063*) to express results. ἅψωνται aor. subj. mid. (dep.) ἅπτομαι (# *721*) w. gen. to touch. Subj. used in a purp. cl. εἶχον impf. ind. act. ἔχω (# *2400*) to have. μάστιγας acc. pl. μάστιξ (# *3465*) whip, torment, suffering, disease, possibly thought of as divine chastisements (Alexander; BAGD; but s. Gundry, 162). ◆ **11** ἐθεώρουν impf. ind. act. θεωρέω (# *2555*) to see. Iterat. impf., "every time they saw." προσέπιπτον impf. ind. act. προσπίπτω (# *4700*) to fall before; it indicates servility (Gundry, 163). ἔκραζον impf. ind. act. κράζω (# *3189*) to cry out, to scream. Either iterat. "they cried repeatedly" or inceptive "they began to cry." ◆ **12** πολλά acc. pl. πολύς (# *4498*) much, very. ἐπετίμα impf. ind. act. ἐπιτιμάω (# *2203*) to rebuke, to sternly charge w. dat. ◆ **13** προσκαλεῖται pres. ind. mid. προσκαλέω (# *4673*) to summon, indir. mid., to call to oneself. It has the idea of "to call," "to select" (Guelich). ἤθελεν impf. ind. act. θέλω (# *2527*) to will, to want. The emphasis is on Jesus' initiative and choice (Gundry, 167). ἀπῆλθον aor. ind. act. ἀπέρχομαι (# *599*) to go forth, to go out. ◆ **14** ἐποίησεν aor. ind. act. ποιέω (# *4472*) to make, to appoint. ὠνόμασεν aor. ind. act. ὀνομάζω (# *3951*) to name. ὦσιν pres. subj. act. εἰμί (# *1639*) to be. W. the prep. μετ' (# *3552*) it indicates fellowship and discipleship. Subj. w. ἵνα (# *2671*) used in a purp. cl. ἀποστέλλῃ pres. subj. act. ἀποστέλλω (# *690*) to send as an official representive (TDNT; EDNT; BBC). Subj. used in purp. cl. κηρύσσειν pres. act. inf. κηρύσσω (# *3062*) to proclaim as a herald, to preach. Inf. expressing the purp. of the sending. ◆ **15** ἔχειν pres. act. inf. s.v. 10. Inf. expressing the purp. of the sending. ἐκβάλλειν pres. act. inf. ἐκβάλλω (# *1675*) to throw out, to cast out. Epex. inf. explaining the authority. ◆ **16** ἐπέθηκεν aor. ind. act. ἐπιτίθημι (# *2202*) to place upon, give a name. ◆ **17** υἱοὶ Βροντῆς sons of thunder. υἱός (# *5626*) followed by gen. expresses a characteristic (BAGD; SIMS, 169). It may indicate

rashness of disposition (Gundry, 169). For the suggestion that the transliteration Βοανηργές from Hebrew
means "Sons of (the) quaking (heavens)," s. John T.
Rook, "'Boanerges, Sons of Thunder' (Mark 3:17)," *JBL*
100 (1981): 94-95. ◆ **19 παρέδωκεν** aor. ind. act. παραδίδωμι (# *4140*) to deliver over, to betray. ◆ **20 συνέρ-
χεται** pres. ind. mid. (dep.) συνέρχομαι (# *5302*) to come
together (hist. pres.). **δύνασθαι** pres. mid. (dep.) inf. δύναμαι (# *1538*) to be able to, used w. **ὥστε** (# *6063*) to express actual result. **φαγεῖν** aor. act. inf. ἐσθίω (# *2266*) to
eat. Inf. w. vb. δύναμαι. ◆ **21 ἀκούσαντες** aor. act. part.
(temp.) ἀκούω (# *201*) to hear. Aor. indicating antecedent action: "when they had heard." **οἱ παρ' αὐτοῦ**
(#*4123; 899*) the ones w. him, his family (Cranfield;
Gundry, 171). **ἐξῆλθον** aor. ind. act. ἐξέρχομαι (# *2002*) to
go out (from Nazareth to Capernaum). **κρατῆσαι** aor.
act. inf. κρατέω to take hold of, to seize. The family
wanted to get hold of Jesus, to take control of His actions (Taylor). **ἐξέστη** aor. ind. act. ἐξίστημι (# *2014*) to be
out of one's mind. For the view that it was the crowd
that was out of control w. enthusiasm and Jesus' followers sought to calm them s. Henry Wansbrough,
"Mark 3:21 - Was Jesus Out of His Mind?" *NTS* 18
(1972): 231-35; David Wenham, "The Meaning of Mark
iii. 21," *NTS* 21 (1975): 295-300. ◆ **22 καταβάντες** aor.
act. part. καταβαίνω (# *2849*) to come down. Adj. use of
the part. **ἄρχοντι** pres. part. dat. masc. sing. ἄρχω
(# *807*) to be a ruler. Part. used as subst. meaning
"prince" (BAGD). For Beelzebub s. Matt. 12:24; Guelich; Lührmann. ◆ **23 προσκαλεσάμενος** aor. mid. (dep.)
part. s.v. 13. ◆ **24 ἐφ'** = ἐπί (# *2093*) w. acc., against.
μερισθῇ aor. subj. pass. μερίζω (# *3532*) to divide. Subj.
w. **ἐάν** (#*1569*) in a cond. cl. indicating a possibility.
σταθῆναι aor. pass. inf. ἵστημι (# *2705*) to stand, stand
firm, hold one's ground (BAGD). ◆ **25 δυνήσεται** fut.
ind. mid. (dep.) s.v. 20. **σταθῆναι** aor. pass. inf. s.v. 24.
◆ **26 εἰ** (# *1623*) if. Introduces a cond. cl. which the
speaker assumes to be true. "Suppose Satan to have actually risen up against himself .... then he is at this moment in unstable cond., his end has come" (Swete).
ἀνέστη aor. ind. act. ἀνίστημι (# *482*) to stand up, to rise
up. **ἐμερίσθη** aor. ind. pass. s.v. 24. ◆ **27 εἰσελθών** aor.
act. part. εἰσέρχομαι (# *1656*) to go in, to enter. Part. of
manner. **σκεύη** acc. pl. σκεῦος (# *5007*) vessel, pl. goods.
διαρπάσαι aor. act. inf. διαρπάζω (# *1395*) to plunder.
Prep. in compound is perfective: "to thoroughly ran-
sack" (RWP). **δήσῃ** aor. subj. act. δέω (# *1313*) to bind.
Subj. w. **ἐάν** (#*1569*) in a cond. cl. ◆ **28 ἀμήν** (# *297*)
(Heb.) truly. He solemnly guarantees the truth of what
He is about to say. It is the equivalent of "as I live, saith
the Lord" in the OT (Cranfield; Matt. 5:18; TDNT;
EDNT). **ἀφεθήσεται** fut. ind. pass. ἀφίημι (# *918*) to re-
lease, to forgive. **ἁμάρτημα** (# *280*) sin, the act of sin
(Swete). Apposition to **πάντα**, every. **βλασφημήσωσιν**
pres. subj. act. βλασφημέω (# *1059*) to slander, to blas-

pheme (BBC; DJG, 75-77). ◆ **29 βλασφημήσῃ** pres. subj.
act. s.v. 28. w. **ἄν** (# *165*) Subj. used in an indef. rel. cl.:
"whoever." **εἰς** (# *1650*) against. **ἄφεσις** (# *912*) release,
forgiveness. **ἔνοχος** (# *1944*) guilty of, liable, answerable; legal term followed by gen. denoting the crime
(BAGD; MM; Cranfield). ◆ **30 ὅτι** (# *4022*) because.
ἔλεγον impf. ind. act. λέγω (# *3306*) to say. Iterat. impf.,
"they were continually saying." They confused the
work of the *Holy* Spirit w. that of an *unclean* spirit
(Hooker). ◆ **31 ἔξω** (# *2032*) outside. It forms a contrast w. those seated around Him (Guelich). **στήκοντες**
pres. act. part. (adj.) στήκω (# *5112*) form from the perf.
of ἵστημι to stand (BAGD). **ἀπέστειλαν** aor. ind. act.
ἀποστέλλω (# *690*) to send. **καλοῦντες** pres. act. part. καλέω (# *2813*) to call. A request for an interview (Taylor).
Part. of manner telling how they send. ◆ **32 ἐκάθητο**
impf. ind. mid. (dep.) κάθημαι (# *2764*) to sit. **ζητοῦσιν**
pres. ind. act. ζητέω (# *2426*) to seek. ◆ **33 ἀποκριθείς**
aor. pass. part. (dep.) ἀποκρίνομαι (# *646*) to answer.
For the Semitic construction s. Matt. 3:12. ◆ **34 περιβλεψάμενος** aor. mid. part. s.v. 5. **κύκλῳ** (# *3241*) dat.
sing. κύκλος. Dat. of place (loc.) "in a circle." **ἴδε**
(# *2623*) aor. imp. act. ὁράω (# *3972*) to see.

Mark 4

◆ **1 ἤρξατο** aor. ind. mid. (dep.) ἄρχομαι (# *806*) to
begin (w. inf.). **συνάγεται** pres. ind. mid. / pass. συνάγω
(# *5251*) to gather; either mid. (in reflex.) to assemble,
come together, or pass. to be gathered together
(BAGD). **πλεῖστος** superl. of πολύς (# *4498*) much,
many. The elative use of the superl.: "a very large
crowd" (BD, 33; Guelich). **ἐμβάντα** aor. act. part. (circum.) ἐμβαίνω (# *1832*) to get in, to embark. **καθῆσθαι**
pres. mid. (dep.) inf. κάθημαι (# *2764*) to sit. Inf. w. **ὥστε**
(# *6063*) to express actual results. ◆ **2 ἐδίδασκεν** impf.
ind. act. διδάσκω (# *1438*) to teach. Inceptive impf., "he
began to teach." **παραβολή** (# *4130*) parable. A brief utterance connected w. a comparison or image (Lane;
Matt. 13:3; Cranfield; Lührmann). Dat. indicates the ve-
hicle used for teaching (Guelich). ◆ **3 ἀκούετε** pres.
imp. act. ἀκούω (# *201*) to hear, to listen, to pay attention and respond (LN, 1:373). This recalls the Shema of
Deut. 6:4 (Swete; also Matt. 13:19). **σπείρων** pres. act.
part. σπείρω (# *5062*) to sow (seed). Part. used as subst.
σπεῖραι aor. act. inf. Inf. of purp. ◆ **4 ἐγένετο** aor. ind.
mid. (dep.) γίνομαι (# *1181*) to become, to happen. For
the Semitic use s. SIMS, 85; 1:9. **ἔπεσεν** aor. ind. act.
πίπτω (# *4406*) to fall. **πετεινά** nom. pl. πετεινόν (# *4374*)
bird. **κατέφαγεν** aor. ind. act. κατεσθίω (# *2983*) to eat
up. Prep. in compound is perfective: "to eat up completely." ◆ **5 πετρώδης** (# *4378*) rocklike, stony, of shallow soil w. underlying rock (AS). **εἶχεν** impf. ind. act.
ἔχω (# *2400*) to have. **ἐξανέτειλεν** aor. ind. act. ἐξανατέλλω (# *1984*) to spring up. **ἔχειν** pres. act. inf. ἔχω to
have, **διά** (# *1328*) w. inf. expresses cause. ◆ **6 ἀνέτειλεν**

aor. ind. act. ἀνατέλλω (# 422) to rise (the sun) (BAGD).
ἐκαυματίσθη aor. ind. pass. καυματίζω (# 3009) to burn,
to scorch; it felt the burning heat (Swete). **ἐξηράνθη** aor.
ind. pass. ξηραίνω (# 3830) to dry up. ◆ **7 ἀκάνθας**
(# 1180) acc. pl. thorn. **ἀνέβησαν** aor. ind. act. ἀναβαίνω
(# 326) to go up, to grow up. Used in LXX of the springing up of vegetation (Taylor; GELTS, 26; Isa. 11:1).
συνέπνιξαν aor. ind. act. συμπνίγω (# 5231) to press
closely, to choke. Used of plants whose food and light
is cut off by weeds (BAGD). **ἔδωκεν** aor. ind. act. δίδωμι
(# 1443) to give, to yield. ◆ **8 ἐδίδου** impf. ind. act. δίδωμι (# 1443) to give (s.v. 7). Impf. w. the pres. parts. forms
a moving picture of ongoing emergence, growth, and
productivity (Gundry, 192). **ἀναβαίνοντα** pres. act. part.
ἀναβαίνω s.v. 7. **αὐξανόμενα** pres. pass. part. αὐξάνω
(# 889) to cause to grow; pass. to grow. Parts. describe
the manner of the yielding (BBC). **ἔφερεν** impf. ind. act.
φέρω (# 5770) to carry, to bear. ◆ **9 ἔλεγεν** impf. ind. act.
λέγω (# 2400) to speak. For the use in Mark s. Gundry,
187-89. **ὦτα** acc. pl. οὖς (# 4044) ear. **ἀκούειν** pres. act.
inf. Inf. of purp. **ἀκουέτω** pres. imp. act. 3rd. sing. s.v. 3.
◆ **10 ἐγένετο** aor. ind. mid. (dep.) γίνομαι s.v. 4. **κατὰ**
μόνας alone. **ἠρώτων** impf. ind. act. ἐρωτάω (# 2263) to
ask, to question. Inceptive impf., "they began to inquire." ◆ **11 μυστή-ριον** (# 3696) mystery, that which
man cannot know apart from God's revelation (TDNT;
NIDNTT; EDNT). **δέδοται** perf. ind. pass. δίδωμι
(# 1443) to give. Theol. pass. indicating that God is the
Giver. ◆ **12** For a discussion of the quotation s. HSB,
417-19. **βλέποντες** pres. act. part. βλέπω (# 1063) to see.
Part. as translation of the Heb. *inf. absolutus* (s. Matt.
13:14). **ἴδωσιν** aor. subj. act. ὁράω (# 3972) to see. Subj. w.
ἵνα (# 2671) to express purp. (for various possibilities s.
Guelich; Brooks). **συνιῶσιν** pres. subj. act. συνίημι
(# 5317) to comprehend, to understand. **ἐπιστρέψωσιν**
aor. subj. act. ἐπι-στρέφω (# 2188) to turn around, to repent (TDNT, EDNT; for the use in the LXX s. GELTS,
175). Subj. w. **μήποτε** (# 3607) to express a neg. purp.
(Guelich). For those who are not disciples the purpose
of the parables is to conceal the truth and to prevent repentance and forgiveness (Taylor). **ἀφεθῇ** aor. subj.
pass. ἀφίημι (# 918) to release, to forgive. ◆ **13 οἴδατε**
perf. ind. act. οἶδα (# 3857) to know. Def. perf. w. pres.
meaning. Used in a question expecting a positive answer. **γνώσεσθε** fut. ind. mid. (dep.) γινώσκω (# 1182) to
know. Οἶδα is used in reference to knowledge which
comes from intuition or insight, and γινώσκω of that
which is gained by experience or acquaintance (Swete;
but s. also Gundry, 207). ◆ **14 λόγος** (# 3364) word. The
seed represents the word, but since the seed fell into the
soil and became one w. it, the seed w. the soil also represents different kinds of hearers (Gundry, 205).
◆ **15 σπείρεται** pres. ind. pass. σπείρω s.v. 3. **ἀκούσωσιν**
aor. subj. act. ἀκούω (# 201) to hear. Subj. w. **ὅταν**
(# 4020) used in an indefinite temp. cl. **αἴρει** pres. ind.

act. αἴρω (# 149) to lift up, to take away. **ἐσπαρμένον**
perf. pass. part. σπείρω s.v. 3. Part. used as adj., perf.
stresses the state or cond. ◆ **17 πρόσκαιρος** (# 4672)
temporary, lasting for a time. **γενομένης** aor. mid. (dep.)
part. (temp.) γίνομαι (# 1181) to become, to happen.
Gen. abs., "when tribulation or persecution comes."
σκανδαλίζονται pres. ind. pass. σκανδαλίζω (# 4997) to
cause to stumble, to be offended. They are trapped at
once because their faith is so feeble (Taylor; TDNT;
EDNT). ◆ **19 μέριμνα** (# 3533) concern, care, a feeling of apprehension or distress in view of possible danger or misfortune (LN, 1:313). **ἀπάτη** (# 573) deceit,
deception, enticement (EDNT; BAGD). **ἐπιθυμία**
(# 2133) desire, longing. Prep. in the compound is directive: "having one's passion toward" (Taylor).
εἰσπορευόμεναι pres. mid. (dep.) part. εἰσπορεύομαι
(# 1660) to come in. Adj. use of the part. **συμπνίγουσιν**
pres. ind. act. συμπνίγω s.v. 7. ◆ **20 σπαρέντες** aor.
pass. part. σπείρω s.v. 3. **παραδέχονται** pres. ind. mid.
(dep.) παραδέχομαι (# 4138) to receive, to accept. This
denotes a favorable reception (Gould). **καρποφοροῦσιν**
pres. ind. act. καρποφορέω (# 2844) to bear fruit.
◆ **21 μήτι** (# 3614) used w. a question expecting a strong
neg. answer (Gould). A rabbinical way of expressing a
prohibition (LNT, 199f.). **ἔρχεται** pres. ind. mid. (dep.)
ἔρχομαι (# 2262). Perhaps an indication that Jesus was
thinking of Himself and His mission (Cranfield), or the
vb. may have the meaning "to be brought" (Gundry,
212; BAGD). **λύχνος** (# 3394) lamp (Matt. 5:15). The definite art. used here could refer to a special lamp, perhaps the Hanukkah lamp (LNT, 200). For the use of the
article in Mark s. SIMS, 104-11. **ἵνα** (# 2671) w. subj. to
express purp. or intent. **μόδιος** (# 3654) bushel. A dry
measure containing nearly two gallons (Taylor). **τεθῇ**
aor. subj. pass. τίθημι (# 5502) to place. The man who lit
the Hanukkah lamp. w. the intention of afterward covering or hiding it did not do his duty by lighting the
lamp (LNT, 207). **οὐχ** (# 4024) used in a question expecting a positive answer. **λυχνία** (# 3393) lampstand. It
was an iron holder w. a high foot (Pesch). The possible
interpretation of this difficult saying is "just as the little
light kindled at Hanukkah is intended to burn itself out
in praise of God and His miracles, so people did not
scruple to push it under the bed, so it is sinful to disregard Heavenly illumination or in any way to impair its
capacity to illuminate" (LNT, 207). ◆ **22 κρυπτός**
(# 3220) hidden. **φανερωθῇ** aor. subj. pass. φανερόω
(# 5746) to make clear, to manifest. Subj. to express
purp. **ἐγένετο** aor. ind. mid. (dep.) γίνομαι (# 1181) to become, to be. **ἀπόκρυφος** (# 649) secret, hidden. **ἔλθη** aor.
subj. act. ἔρχομαι. (# 2262) Subj. w. **ἵνα** (# 2671) used to
express purp. ◆ **23 ἀκουέτω** pres. imp. act. 3rd. pers.
sing. ἀκούω s.v. 3. ◆ **24 τί** acc. sing. τίς (# 5515) who,
what. Adv. acc. "how" (Gundry, 218). **μετρεῖτε** pres. ind.
act. μετρέω (# 3582) to measure. **μετρηθήσεται** fut. ind.

pass. **προστεθήσεται** fut. ind. pass. προστίθημι (# 4707) to add to. The pass. vbs. here may be the theol. pass. indicating that God does the action. "Your attention to the teaching will be the measure of the profit you will receive from it" (Swete). ◆ **25 δοθήσεται** fut. ind. pass. δίδωμι (# 1443) to give. **ἀρθήσεται** fut. ind. pass. αἴρω (# 149) to remove, to take away. Theol. pass. s.v. 24. ◆ **26 ἔλεγεν** impf. ind. act. λέγω s.v. 9. **βάλῃ** aor. subj. act. βάλλω (# 965) to cast. Subj. used w. **ὡς** (# 6055) in a cond. cl.: "as if a man would cast...." (RG, 974; Gundry, 223-24). ◆ **27 καθεύδῃ** pres. subj. act. καθεύδω (# 2761) to sleep. **ἐγείρηται** pres. subj. pass. ἐγείρω (# 1586) pass., to rise, to awaken. For the subj. s.v. 26. **νύκτα** acc. sing. νύξ (# 3816) night. Acc. of time. The sleeping and rising go on continually from day to day (RG, 470). **βλαστᾷ** pres. subj. act. βλαστάνω to grow. **μηκύνηται** pres. pass. subj. μηκύνω (# 3602) to make long; pass. to become long, to grow (BAGD). **ὡς** (# 6055) after vbs. of saying or thinking how (Taylor). ◆ **28 αὐτομάτη** (# 897) by itself, of something that happens without visible cause (BAGD; Rainer Stühlmann, "Beobachtungen und Überlegungen zu Markus iv. 26-29," *NTS* 19 [1972/73]: 153-62). **καρποφορεῖ** pres. ind. act. καρποφορέω (# 2844) to bear fruit, to produce. **χόρτος** (# 5965) grass, the green shoot. **εἶτα** (# 1663) then (BD, 19). **στάχυς** (# 5092) head or ear of grain. **σῖτος** (# 4992) wheat, grain. ◆ **29 παραδοῖ** aor. subj. act. παραδίδωμι (# 4140) to give over, to allow. Subj. w. **ὅταν** (# 4020) used in an indef. temp. cl. **δρέπανον** (# 1535) sickle. **παρέστηκεν** perf. ind. act. παρίστημι (# 4225) to place beside; perf. used of a point of time, "to be here," "to have come" (BAGD). ◆ **30 ὁμοιώσωμεν** aor. subj. act. ὁμοιόω (# 3929) to make alike, to compare. **θῶμεν** aor. subj. act. τίθημι (# 5502) to place. Used of setting forth an idea in symbolism (AS). The subjs. are deliberative or hortative subjs. used in a question of comtemplation (RG, 934; IGNT, 57f; IBG, 22). ◆ **31 κόκκῳ** dat. sing. κόκκος (# 3133) kernel, seed. Dat. of comparison. **σινάπεως** gen. sing. σίναπι (# 4983) mustard (Matt. 13:31). **σπαρῇ** aor. subj. pass. σπείρω s.v. 3. **μικρότερον** comp. μικρός (# 3625) small. Comp. used as superl. **ὄν** pres. act. part. nom. n. sing. εἰμί (# 1639) to be. Here, "being smallest" (Guelich; Gundry, 229). ◆ **32 μεῖζον** (# 3505) comp. μέγας (# 3489) large. Comp. used as superl. **λαχάνων** gen. pl. λάχανον (# 3303) plant, vegetable, gen. of comparison. **ποιεῖ** pres. ind. act. ποιέω (# 4472) to make, to produce. **κλάδος** (# 3080) branch. **δύνασθαι** pres. pass. (dep.) inf. δύναμαι (# 1538) to be able. Inf. w. **ὥστε** (# 6063) to express actual results. **κατασκηνοῦν** pres. act. inf. κατασκηνόω (# 2942) lit., to put up a tent, to dwell, to rest, to nest (Guelich). ◆ **33 τοιαύταις** dat. fem. pl. τοιοῦτος (# 5525) of such a kind, such as this. Instr. dat. **ἐλάλει** impf. ind. act. λαλέω (# 3281) to speak. **ἠδύναντο** impf. ind. pass. (dep.) δύναμαι s.v. 32. ◆ **34 χωρίς** (# 6006) w. gen. without. **ἐπέλυεν** impf. ind. act. ἐπιλύω

(# 2147) to untie, to release, to explain, to expound. ◆ **35 ὀψία** (# 4070) evening, late afternoon. **γενομένης** aor. mid. (dep.) part. γίνομαι (# 1181) to become; gen. abs. **διέλθωμεν** aor. subj. act. διέρχομαι (# 1451) to go through, to go across. For the prep. in compound s. MH, 300f. Hortatory subj. ◆ **36 ἀφέντες** aor. act. part. (temp.) ἀφίημι (# 918) to dismiss, to send away. **ἦν** impf. ind. act. εἰμί (# 1639) to be. ◆ **37 λαῖλαψ** (# 3278) furious storm, a hurricane, squall (Taylor; BBC). **ἐπέβαλλεν** impf. ind. act. ἐπιβάλλω (# 2095) throw upon; intr. to strike upon. "The waves were beating into the boat" (Gould). **ἤδη** (# 2453) already. **γεμίζεσθαι** pres. pass. inf. γεμίζω (# 1153) to fill; pass. to become full. Pres., "was filling up." Inf. w. **ὥστε** (# 6063) to express actual results. ◆ **38 πρύμνῃ** (# 4744) the stern of a ship. **προσκεφάλαιον** (# 4676) pillow, cushion. Presumably a rower's wooden or leathern seat used as a headrest (Taylor); or it may have been the pillow that was customarily kept for those not involved in sailing or fishing (Lane). **καθεύδων** pres. act. part. καθεύδω (# 2761) to sleep. Used in a periphrastic construction. **οὐ μέλει σοι** "Is it of no concern to you?" **ἀπολλύμεθα** pres. ind. mid. ἀπόλλυμι (# 660) to destroy, ruin. "We are in the process of perishing." Progressive pres. vividly describing the process. ◆ **39 διεγερθείς** aor. pass. part. (temp.) διεγείρω (# 1444) to wake up; to arouse completely (Taylor). **ἐπετίμησεν** aor. ind. act. ἐπιτιμάω (# 2203) to rebuke, to sternly warn (Matt. 17:18). **εἶπεν** aor. ind. act. λέγω (# 3306). The aor. vbs. stand in contrast to the pres. and impf. vbs. **σιώπα** pres. imp. act. σιωπάω (# 4995) to be silent. **πεφίμωσο** perf. imp. pass. φιμόω (# 5821) to muzzle, to silence. Perf., "to put the muzzle on and keep it on" (RG, 908; M, 110; MKG, 264f; VA, 362). **ἐκόπασεν** aor. ind. act. κοπάζω (# 3156) to grow weary, to cease. Used in the LXX of water in repose after a storm or flood (Swete; Gen. 8:1). **ἐγένετο** aor. ind. mid. (dep.) γίνομαι (# 1181) to become. **γαλήνη** (# 1132) calm. ◆ **40 δειλός** (# 1264) cowardly, timid, fearful, without courage (LN, 1:317-18). ◆ **41 ἐφοβήθησαν** aor. ind. pass. (dep.) φοβέομαι (# 5828) to be afraid. **φόβον** acc. sing. φόβος (# 5832) fear. For the cognate acc. s. RG, 477f; BD, 84f. **ὑπακούει** pres. ind. act. ὑπακούω (# 5634) to listen to, to obey, followed by dat.

Mark 5

◆ **1 ἦλθον** aor. ind. act. ἔρχομαι (# 2262) to come, to go. **πέραν** (# 4305) adv. of place used as a subst.; other side (BAGD). This ties the story to the previous one by indicating the arrival at the destination given in 4:35 (Guelich). For a discussion of the text problem and the location of the area s. Guelich; Gundry, 255-56. ◆ **2 ἐξελθόντος** aor. act. part. (temp.) ἐξέρχομαι (# 2202) to go out, to come out; gen. abs. "when he went out...." **ὑπήντησεν** aor. ind. act. ὑπαντάω (# 5636) to meet, followed by dat. ◆ **3 κατοίκησις** (# 2998) living quarters, dwelling. According to the Talmud there were four signs of madness: walking abroad at night, spending the night on a grave, tearing one's clothes, destroying what one was given (Lane; SB, 1:491). εἶχεν impf. ind. act. ἔχω (# 2400) to have. Customary impf. ἁλύσει dat. sing. ἅλυσις (# 268) chain. Instr. dat. ἐδύνατο impf. ind. pass. (dep.) δύναμαι (# 1538) to be able. Impf. indicates the unfulfilled action in the past. δῆσαι aor. act. inf. δέω (# 1313) to bind. ◆ **4** διά (# 1328) because, but here the construction indicates not the reason but the circumstances mentioned by way of explanation (Cranfield). πολλάκις (# 4490) often. πέδαις dat. pl. πέδη (# 4267) bonds for the feet, shackles. Instr. dat. δεδέσθαι perf. pass. inf. δέω (# 1313) to bind. Perf. indicates the cond. or state. διεσπάσθαι perf. pass. inf. διασπάω (# 1400) to tear apart. συντετρῖφθαι perf. pass. inf. συντρίβω (# 5341) to shatter, to smash, to crush. ἴσχυεν impf. ind. act. ἰσχύω (# 2710) to be strong. Impf. depicts the incomplete action in the past. δαμάσαι aor. act. inf. δαμάζω (# 1238) to tame. ◆ **5** διὰ παντὸς νυκτὸς καὶ ἡμέρας reflects the Jewish reckoning from sunset to sunset, "Through all the night and the day" (Gundry, 249). ὄρεσιν dat. pl. ὄρος (# 4001) mountain, hill (BAGD). κράζων pres. act. part. κράζω (# 3189) to cry out, to scream. This and the following part. used in a periphrastic construction emphasize the repeated action. κατακόπτων pres. act. part. κατακόπτω (# 2888) to cut to pieces. The prep. compound is perfective. His body in this way may have been gashed and scarred all over (Swete). ◆ **6** ἰδών aor. act. part. ὁράω (# 3972) to see. Temp. or causal part. μακρόθεν (# 3427) adv., from afar. ἔδραμεν aor. ind. act. τρέχω (# 5556) to run. προσεκύνησεν aor. ind. act. προσκυνέω (# 4686) to worship, to worship by falling on the knees; w. dat. ◆ **7** κράξας aor. act. part. (temp.) s.v. 5. "As he cried out...." τί ἐμοὶ καὶ σοί "What have I to do with you?" (Mark 1:24; SIMS, 183-85). ὕψιστος (# 5736) superl. most high. (s. Luke 1:32). ὁρκίζω (# 3991) pres. ind. act. to implore, to put under an oath, to cause someone to swear, to insist that one take an oath (LN, 1:441; TDNT; EDNT). Used w. double acc., where the second acc. shows by whom the oath is to be taken (DM, 95; BD, 83). βασανίσῃς aor. subj. act. 2nd. sing. βασανίζω (# 989) to torture. Subj. w. μή (# 3590) used in a neg. command. ◆ **8** ἔλεγεν impf. ind. act. λέγω (# 3306). Inceptive impf. "He began to say." ἔξελθε aor. imp. act. ἐξέρχομαι s.v. 2. Aor. imp. looks at a specific action expected. ◆ **9** ἐπηρώτα impf. ind. act. ἐπερωτάω (# 2089) to consult, to inquire of, to ask (Taylor). Inceptive impf. emphasizing the beginning, "he began to inquire." Λεγιών (# 3305) legion, a unit of the Roman army containing approximately six thousand men (Matt. 26:53; Gundry, 263). ◆ **10** παρεκάλει impf. ind. act. παρακαλέω (# 4151) to call to, to beseech, to plead w. Either inceptive impf. stressing the beginning; or iterat., stressing that they

repeatedly plead. ἀποστείλῃ aor. subj. act. ἀποστέλλω (# 690) to send away. Subj. used w. ἵνα (# 2671) giving the obj. of their request. ◆ **11** πρός (# 4639) w. dat. by, nearby. ἀγέλη (# 36) herd. χοίρων gen. pl. χοίρος (# 5956) pig, swine. Gen. of content. βοσκομένη pres. mid. part. βόσκομαι (# 1081) to graze, to feed. Part. used in a periphrastic construction. Jews were forbidden to raise pigs (M, Baba Kamma, 7:7). ◆ **12** παρεκάλεσαν aor. ind. act. s.v. 10. λέγοντες pres. act. part. λέγω (# 3306). πέμψον aor. imp. act. πέμπω (# 4287) to send. Aor. imp. calls for a specific act. w. a note of urgency. εἰσέλθωμεν aor. subj. act. εἰσέρχομαι (# 1656) to go into. Subj. w. ἵνα (# 2671) in a purp. cl. ◆ **13** ἐπέτρεψεν aor. ind. act. ἐπιτρέπω (# 2205) to allow, to give permission to. ἐξελθόντα aor. act. part. (temp.) nom. n. pl. ἐξέρχομαι (# 2202) to go out. Aor. indicating a logically antecedent action. εἰσῆλθον aor. ind. act. s.v. 12. ὥρμησεν aor. ind. act. ὁρμάω (# 3994) to set out, to rush. κατά (# 2848) w. gen., down. κρημνός (# 3204) cliff, precipice, steep bank. ὡς (# 6055) (w. numbers) about. ἐπνίγοντο impf. ind. pass. πνίγω (# 4464) to choke, to drown. Inceptive impf., "they began to drown." ◆ **14** βόσκοντες pres. act. part. βόσκω (# 1081) to feed, to graze a herd. Part. used as subst.: "the ones grazing the herd." ἔφυγον aor. ind. act. φεύγω (# 5771) to flee. ἀπήγγειλαν aor. ind. act. ἀπαγγέλλω (# 550) to bring news, to report. εἰς τὴν πόλιν καὶ εἰς τοὺς ἀγρούς for those in the city and for those in the fields. Not an incidence of εἰς (# 1650) used in the sense of ἐν (# 1877) (John J. O'Rourke, "A Note Concerning the Use of ΕΙΣ and ΕΝ in Mark," *JBL* 95 [1966]: 349-51). ἦλθον aor. ind. act. ἔρχομαι (# 2262) to go. ἰδεῖν aor. act. inf. ὁράω (# 3972) to see. Inf. of purp. γεγονός perf. act. part. γίνομαι (# 1181) to become, to happen. Perf. emphasizes the continuing state or cond. of that which had happened. Part. as subst. ◆ **15** θεωροῦσιν pres. ind. act. θεωρέω (# 2555) to see, to observe something w. continuity and attention, often w. the implication that what is observed is unusual (LN, 1:279). δαιμονιζόμενον pres. mid. (dep.) part. δαιμονίζομαι (# 1227) to be possessed by a demon. Imperfective part.: "the man who used to be (or, who had until now been) a demoniac." K.L. McKay, "Syntax in Exegesis," *TB* 23 (1972): 48. καθήμενον pres. mid. (dep.) part. κάθημαι (# 2764) to sit. ἱματισμένον perf. pass. part. ἱματίζω (# 2667) to clothe, to be clothed. Perf. emphasizing his pres. cond. or state. σωφρονοῦντα pres. act. part. σωφρονέω (# 5404) to be of sound mind, to be in one's right mind. The man was master of himself again (Swete; TDNT; NIDNTT; TLNT). ἐσχηκότα perf. act. part. ἔχω (# 2400) to have. Not an aoristic perf., but expressing a former state; i.e., "having had and now free of" (McKay, *TB* 23 [1972]: 48). ἐφοβήθησαν aor. ind. pass. (dep.) φοβέομαι (# 5828) to fear, to be afraid. ◆ **16** διηγήσαντο aor. ind. mid. (dep.) διηγέομαι (# 1455) to relate, to set out in detail

(Taylor). For the prep. compound s. MH, 301. ἰδόντες aor. act. part. ὁράω (# 3972) to see. Part. used as subst. ἐγένετο aor. ind. mid. (dep.) γίνομαι (# 1181) to become, to happen to, w. dat. ◆ **17** ἤρξαντο aor. ind. mid. (dep.) ἄρχομαι (# 806) to begin, w. inf. παρακαλεῖν pres. act. inf. s.v. 10. ἀπελθεῖν aor. act. inf. ἀπέρχομαι (# 599) to go away. Inf. in indir. discourse as obj. of the vb. παρακαλέω. ◆ **18** ἐμβαίνοντος pres. act. part. (temp.) ἐμβαίνω (# 1832) to get in, to embark. Gen. abs. παρεκάλει impf. ind. act. παρακαλέω s.v. 10. Inceptive impf. stresses the continual pleading. δαιμονισθείς aor. pass. part. δαιμονίζομαι (# 1227) to be possessed by a demon. ᾖ pres. subj. act. εἰμί to be. Subj. w. ἵνα (# 2671) used in a cl. as obj. of the vb. παρακαλέω. ◆ **19** ἀφῆκεν aor. ind. act. ἀφίημι (# 918) to release, to allow. ὕπαγε pres. imp. act. ὑπάγω (# 5632) to go, to go forth. Pres. imp. used w. a vb. of motion (VANT, 343). ἀπάγγειλον aor. imp. act. ἀπαγγέλλω s.v. 14. Aor. imp. used in a specific command. πεποίηκεν perf. ind. act. ποιέω (# 4472) to do. Perf. stresses the completed action w. a continuing result. ἠλέησεν aor. ind. act. ἐλεέω (# 1796) to show mercy, to be merciful (TDNT; EDNT). The change from perf. to aor. is deliberate. The man has received blessings which abide and which are a definite boon in his cure (Taylor). ◆ **20** ἀπῆλθεν aor. ind. act. s.v. 17. ἤρξατο aor. ind. mid. (dep.) s.v. 17. κηρύσσειν pres. act. inf. κηρύσσω (# 3062) to proclaim, to proclaim as a herald. ἐποίησεν aor. ind. act. ποιέω (# 4472) to do. Used w. dat. of advantage. ἐθαύμαζον impf. ind. act. θαυμάζω (# 2513) to marvel, to wonder, to be amazed. Inceptive impf. describing the continual action. ◆ **21** διαπεράσαντος aor. act. part. διαπεράω (# 1385) to cross over; gen. abs. συνήχθη aor. ind. pass. συνάγω (# 5251) to gather together, to assemble. For Mark's use of this vb. w. the prep. ἐπί (# 2093) s. Gundry, 278. ◆ **22** ἔρχεται pres. ind. (dep.) mid. ἔρχομαι (# 2262) to go. Hist. pres. ἀρχισυνάγωγος (# 801) leader or president of a synagogue. The official whose duty it was to take care of the physical arrangements for the worship services (BAGD; SB, 4:115-52; TDNT; BBC; for the pl. s. Gundry, 278). ἰδών aor. act. (temp.) part. s.v. 6. ◆ **23** παρακαλεῖ pres. ind. act. s.v. 10. Hist. pres. or inceptive pres. θυγάτριόν (# 2589) daughter. The dimin. appears to be used as a term of affection: "my little daughter" (Taylor). ἐσχάτως (# 2275) adv. last; ἐσχάτως ἔχει to be at the point of death (Gould; BAGD). ἐλθών aor. act. part. (circum.) s.v. 1. ἐπιθῇς aor. subj. act. ἐπιτίθημι (# 2202) to place upon. Used w. ἵνα (# 2671) in the sense of an imp.: "Do please come and lay ..." (IBG, 144). σωθῇ aor. subj. pass. σῴζω (# 5392) to save, to heal. ζήσῃ aor. subj. act. ζάω (# 2409) to live. Subj. w. ἵνα (# 2671) in a purp. cl. ◆ **24** ἀπῆλθεν aor. ind. act. s.v. 17. ἠκολούθει impf. ind. act. ἀκολουθέω (# 199) to follow. συνέθλιβον impf. ind. act. συνθλίβω (# 5315) to press together, to press upon. Impf. pictures the continual action in the past. ◆ **25** οὖσα pres. act.

part. nom. fem. sing. εἰμί (# 1639) to be. Adj. part. indicating the ongoing cond. (Gundry, 279). ῥύσει dat. sing. ῥύσις (# 4868) flow; she was suffering from vaginal bleeding (Hooker). The illness defiled her. She also defiled anything or anybody she touched (Guelich; BBC; Lev. 15:25; M, *Niddah* 2:2-7; M, *Zabim*). δώδεκα ἔτη (# 1557; 2291) acc. pl. twelve years; acc. of time. ◆ **26** παθοῦσα aor. act. part. nom. fem. sing. πάσχω (# 4248) to suffer. Concessive part., "although she suffered...." ἰατρός (# 2620) doctor. δαπανήσασα aor. act. part. nom. fem. sing. δαπανάω (# 1251) to spend, to spend freely. Used for expenses in a temple account of payment (MM; Preisigke, 1:319; Oxyrhynchus Papyri, 8:1143; GELTS, 95). ὠφεληθεῖσα aor. pass. part. (circum.) ὠφελέω (# 6067) to profit, to receive benefit; pass. to receive help. χεῖρον (# 5437) comp. κακός worse. ἐλθοῦσα aor. act. part. nom. fem. sing. ἔρχομαι (# 2262) ("she grew worse"). ◆ **27** ἀκούσασα aor. act. part. (temp.) nom. fem. sing. ἀκούω (# 201) to hear, "when he heard..." ἥψατο aor. ind. mid. (dep.) ἅπτομαι (# 721) to touch, w. obj. in gen. ◆ **28** ἔλεγεν impf. ind. act. s.v. 8. ἅψωμαι aor. subj. mid. (dep.) s.v. 27. Subj. in a cond. cl. which assumes the possibility of the cond. σωθήσομαι fut. ind. pass. s.v. 23. ◆ **29** ἐξηράνθη aor. ind. pass. ξηραίνω (# 3830) to dry, to dry up. πηγή (# 4380) spring, fountain, source. ἔγνω aor. ind. act. γίνωσκω (# 1182) to know, to recognize. σώματι dat. sing. σῶμα (# 5393). Dat. of place.: "She recognized in her body." ἴαται perf. ind. pass. ἰάομαι (# 2615) to heal (GLH). According to Jewish teaching, her touch should have made Jesus unclean (M, Zabim 5:1). But instead Jesus made her clean! μάστιγος gen. sing. μάστιξ (# 3465) scourge, plague. ◆ **30** ἐπιγνούς aor. act. part. (temp.) ἐπιγινώσκω (# 2105) to know, to recognize. ἐξελθοῦσαν aor. act. part. acc. fem. sing. s.v. 2. Part. used as obj. of the vb. ἐπιγινώσκω. ἐπιστραφείς aor. pass. (dep.) part. ἐπιστρέφω (# 2188) to turn; pass. to turn around. ἥψατο aor. ind. mid. (dep.), w. obj. in gen. (s.v. 27). ◆ **31** συνθλίβοντα pres. act. part. s.v. 24. Adj. part. ◆ **32** περιεβλέπετο impf. ind. mid. περιβλέπω (# 4315) to look, to look around, to look about oneself. Inceptive impf. (RG, 838), or the impf. views the action as continual and incomplete (VANT, 146, 165-66). ἰδεῖν aor. act. inf. ὁράω (# 3972) to see. Inf. of purp. ποιήσασαν aor. act. part. acc. fem. sing. ποιέω (# 4472) to do, to make. The fem. may indicate that Jesus knew the sex of the person healed (Gundry, 271). ◆ **33** φοβηθεῖσα aor. pass. (dep.) part. nom. fem. sing. s.v. 15. τρέμουσα pres. act. part. nom. fem. sing. τρέμω (# 5554) to shake, to tremble. εἰδυῖα perf. act. part. nom. fem. sing. of defective perf. οἶδα (# 3857) to know. Adj. parts. describing the woman. γέγονεν perf. act. part. s.v. 14. ἦλθεν aor. ind. act. ἔρχομαι s.v. 1. προσέπεσεν aor. ind. act. προσπίπτω (# 4700) to fall down before someone. εἶπεν aor. ind. act. λέγω (# 3306) to say. ◆ **34** σέσωκεν perf. ind. act. σῴζω s.v. 23. Perf. emphasizes the pres.

state as a result of an action. Perhaps Mark had a double meaning, the religious sense of the word being suggested as well as the sense to heal (Cranfield). ἴσθι pres. imp. act. εἰμί (# 1639) to be. The sense is "continue whole and well" (RWP; M, 174, 226). ◆ **35 λαλοῦντος** pres. act. part. (temp.) λαλέω (# 3281) to speak. Gen. abs. Pres. expressing contemporaneous action. **ἀπέθανεν** aor. ind. act. ἀποθηνήσκω (# 633) to die. Aor. stresses the occurrence of death (Gundry, 282). **σκύλλεις** pres. ind. act. 2nd. pers. sing. σκύλλω (# 5035) to flay, to skin; to trouble, to annoy. ◆ **36 παρακούσας** aor. act. part. παρακούω (# 4159) to hear beside, to overhear, to refuse to hear, to ignore (Taylor; Guelich). **λαλούμενον** pres. pass. part. s.v. 35. Adj. part. **φοβοῦ** pres. imp. mid. (dep.) φοβέομαι (# 5828) to fear, to be afraid. W. neg. μή (# 3590) to stop an action in progress: "stop fearing!" **πίστευε** pres. imp. act. πιστεύω (# 4409) to believe, to trust. ◆ **37 ἀφῆκεν** aor. ind. act. ἀφίημι (# 918) w. inf. to allow, to permit. **συνακολουθῆσαι** aor. act. inf. συνακολουθέω (# 5258) to follow along, to follow w. ◆ **38 θεωρεῖ** pres. ind. act. θεωρέω (# 2555) to see, to observe. Hist. pres. **θόρυβος** (# 2573) turmoil, uproar (Matt. 9:23f). **κλαίοντας** pres. act. part. κλαίω (# 3081) to cry, loud weeping (BBC). **ἀλαλάζοντας** pres. act. part. ἀλαλάζω (# 226) to shout, to wail. Two parts. explain the turmoil (Cranfield). For a description of the funeral tumult s. Lane. ◆ **39 εἰσελθών** aor. act. part. (temp.) s.v. 12. **θορυβεῖσθε** pres. ind. pass. θορυβέω (# 2572) to throw into disorder; pass. to be troubled, distressed, aroused. **καθεύδει** pres. ind. act. καθεύδω (# 2761) to sleep. The statement may mean that she has not yet been delivered over to the realm of death w. all its consequences (Lane). ◆ **40 κατεγέλων** impf. ind. act. καταγελάω (# 2860) w. gen. to laugh at, to deride, to jeer at. The prep. compound is perfective (Taylor). Inceptive impf., "They began ..." **ἐκβαλών** aor. act. part. ἐκβάλλω (# 1675) to throw out, to send out. **παραλαμβάνει** pres. ind. act. παραλαμβάνω (# 4161) to take; w. hist. pres. **εἰσπορεύεται** pres. ind. mid. (dep.) εἰσπορεύομαι (# 1660) to go in. **ἦν** impf. ind. act. εἰμί (# 1639) to be. ◆ **41 κρατήσας** aor. act. part. (circum.) κρατέω (# 3195) w. gen., to take hold of. The gen. suggests tenderness (GGBB, 132). **ταλιθα** (# 5420) (Aramaic: טַלְיְתָא) fem. form, youth (Gould; AT, 590). **κουμ** (# 3182) (Aramaic: קוּמִי) imp. arise! (UJS, 40-42). **μεθερμηνευόμενον** pres. pass. part. μεθερμηνεύω (# 3493) to translate. **κοράσιον** (# 3166) dimin., girl, little girl. **ἔγειρε** pres. imp. act. ἐγείρω (# 1586) to arise, get up. Pres. imp. suggests that the action should commence. ◆ **42 ἀνέστη** aor. ind. act. ἀνίστημι (# 482) to stand up, to arise, to get up. **περιεπάτει** impf. ind. act. περιπατέω (# 4344) to walk about. Inceptive impf., "she began to walk about." **ἐξέστησαν** aor. ind. act. ἐξίστημι (# 2014) to be astonished, to be bewildered. **ἐκστάσει** dat. sing. ἔκστασις (# 1749) confusion, bewilderment, amazement. "They were

quite beside themselves w. amazement" (BAGD). Instr. dat. ◆ **43 διεστείλατο** aor. ind. mid. (dep.) διαστέλλω (# 1403) to divide or distinguish; mid. to give an explicit order, to command (Swete). **γνοῖ** aor. subj. act. γινώσκω (# 1182) to know. Subj. w. ἵνα (# 2671) in a purp. cl. **εἶπεν** aor. ind. act. λέγω (# 3306) to say. **δοθῆναι** aor. pass. inf. δίδωμι (# 1443) to give. Inf. after a vb. of saying in indir. speech (Taylor). **φαγεῖν** aor. act. inf. ἐσθίω (# 2266) to eat. Inf. as subst. used as subject of the pass. inf. "Something to eat should be given to her."

Mark 6

◆ **1 ἐξῆλθεν** aor. ind. act. ἐξέρχομαι (# 2002) to go out. Jesus went from Capernaum to Nazareth. **ἀκολουθοῦσιν** pres. ind. act. ἀκολουθέω (# 199) to follow (w. dat.). Hist. pres. ◆ **2 γενομένου** aor. mid. (dep.) part. (temp.) γίνομαι (# 1181) to become, to happen. Gen. abs. "when it had become Sabbath." **ἤρξατο** aor. ind. mid. (dep.) ἄρχομαι (# 806) to begin, followed by inf. **ἀκούοντες** pres. act. part. ἀκούω (# 201) to hear. Adj. part. as subst. **ἐξεπλήσσοντο** impf. ind. pass. ἐκπλήσσω (# 1742) to amaze; pass. to be amazed, to be overwhelmed (Mark 7:37). **πόθεν** (# 4470) where, from where. **τούτῳ** dat. sing. Dat. of advantage. **δοθεῖσα** aor. pass. part. δίδωμι (# 1443) to give. Theol. pass. **τοιαῦται** nom. fem. pl. τοιοῦτος (# 5525) of such a kind, such as this (BAGD). **γινόμεναι** pres. mid. (dep.) part. γίνομαι. ◆ **3 τέκτων** (# 5454) builder, carpenter, woodworker, one who works w. hard material (Lane). It has been suggested Jesus worked in the nearby city of Sepphoris (R. A. Batey, "'Is Not This the Carpenter?'" *NTS* 30 [1984]: 249-58; BBC). **ἐσκανδαλίζοντο** impf. ind. pass. σκανδαλίζω (# 4997) to cause to stumble; pass. to be offended (TDNT). ◆ **4 ἄτιμος** (# 872) without honor, dishonored (Gundry, 292). For the alpha prefix forming the neg. s. Moorhouse, 41-68. **συγγενεῦσιν** dat. pl. συγγενής (# 5150) relative, kinsman. ◆ **5 ἐδύνατο** impf. ind. pass. (dep.) δύναμαι (# 1538) to be able, used w. inf. **ποιῆσαι** aor. act. inf. ποιέω (# 4472) to do. **ἀρρώστοις** dat. pl. ἄρρωστος (# 779) weak, sick. Galen often uses the noun ἀρρωστία to show illness (DMTG, 75). Dat. w. the prep. in the vb. **ἐπιθείς** aor. act. part. ἐπιτίθημι (# 2202) to place upon. Part of manner or means. **ἐθεράπευσεν** aor. ind. act. θεραπεύω (# 2543) to heal. ◆ **6 ἐθαύμαζεν** impf. ind. act. θαυμάζω (# 2513) to wonder, to be amazed. **περιῆγεν** impf. ind. act. περιάγω (# 4310) to go about, to go around. Impf. pictures the repeated action in the past. **διδάσκων** pres. act. part. διδάσκω (# 1438) to teach. Part. of manner: "He was going about teaching." This summary statement describes the teaching activity of Jesus around Nazareth (Guelich). ◆ **7 προσκαλεῖται** pres. ind. mid. (dep.) προσκαλέομαι (# 4673) to summons, to call. **ἤρξατο** aor. ind. mid. (dep.) ἄρχομαι (# 806) to begin s.v. 2. **ἐδίδου** impf. ind. act. δίδωμι (# 1443) to give. Impf. indicates the giving of authority to the groups of two, but is not to be confused w. a perf. implying the giving of authority today (Gundry, 301). ◆ **8 παρήγγειλεν** aor. ind. act. παραγγέλλω (# *4133*) to give instruction, to command. **αἴρωσιν** pres. subj. act. αἴρω (# *149*) to lift up, to take. Subj. w. **ἵνα** (# *2671*) used in a cl. which is the obj. of the vb. **ῥάβδος** staff. **πήρα** (# *4385*) leather pouch, wallet (Matt. 10:10). **ζώνη** (# *2438*) belt. Ancient custom was to keep small change in the girdle (Taylor; Matt. 10:9). ◆ **9 ὑποδεδεμένους** perf. mid. (dep.) part. ὑποδέομαι (# *5686*) to bind under, to put on shoes. **σανδάλιον** (# *4908*) sandals. The precipitous paths in Galilee make a staff and sandals necessary for protecting the feet and whole person (Gundry, 308). **ἐνδύσησθε** pres. mid. subj. ἐνδύω (# *1907*) mid., to clothe, to put on clothes. ◆ **10 εἰσέλθητε** aor. subj. act. εἰσέρχομαι (# *1656*) to go in, to come in. Subj. w. **ὅπου ἄν** in an indef. rel. cl. **μένετε** pres. imp. act. μένω (# *3531*) to remain. Pres. imp. expresses a distributive command (VANT, 367). **ἐξέλθητε** aor. subj. act. s.v. 1. ◆ **11 δέξηται** aor. subj. mid. (dep.) δέχομαι (# *1312*) to welcome, to receive. Subj. in an indef. rel. cl. **ἀκούσωσιν** aor. subj. act. s.v. 2. **ἐκπορευόμενοι** pres. mid. (dep.) part. ἐκπορεύομαι (# *1744*) to go out. Circum. part. to be translated as imp. (VANT, 386). **ἐκτινάξατε** aor. imp. act. ἐκτινάσσω (# *1759*) to shake, to shake off, to treat as unclean (BBC). **χοῦς** (# *5967*) earth, dust (Matt. 10:14). ◆ **12 ἐξελθόντες** aor. act. part. s.v. 1. **ἐκήρυξαν** aor. ind. act. κηρύσσω (# *3062*) to proclaim as a herald (TDNT; EDNT). **μετανοῶσιν** pres. subj. act. μετανοέω (# *3566*) to change one's mind, to repent (s. Matt. 3:2). Subj. w. **ἵνα** to express purp. ◆ **13 ἐξέβαλλον** impf. ind. act. ἐκβάλλω (# *1675*) to cast out, to drive out. **ἤλειφον** impf. ind. act. ἀλείφω (# *230*) to anoint w. oil. For the medicinal use of oil s. SB, 2:11-12; DMTG, 31; M, Shab. 14:4; TDNT; NIDNTT. **ἐθεράπευον** impf. ind. act. s.v. 5. The vbs. in impf. show the repeated action in the past. ◆ **14 ἤκουσεν** aor. ind. act. s.v. 2. Ἡρῴδης Herod, Herod Antipas (HA; TJ, 45-50). The term "king" represents a popular designation rather than an offical title (Guelich; Brooks). **ἐγένετο** aor. ind. mid. (dep.) s.v. 2. **ὄνομα** (# *3950*) name, reputation, fame (BAGD; Guelich). **βαπτίζων** pres. act. part. βαπτίζω (# *966*) to dip, to baptize (Matt. 3:6; TJ, 63-65). Part. used as subst. **ἐγήγερται** perf. ind. pass. ἐγείρω (# *1919*) to raise; pass., to rise, to be resurrected. Perf. indicates he has risen and is therefore alive and among us again (Swete). **ἐνεργοῦσιν** pres. ind. act. ἐνεργέω to be operative, to be at work; used of supernatural working (EDNT). ◆ **15 ἔλεγον** impf. ind. act. λέγω (# *3306*) Impf. stresses the repeated action in the past. ◆ **16 ἀκούσας** aor. act. part. (temp.) ἀκούω (# *201*) to hear. **ἀπεκεφάλισα** aor. ind. act. ἀποκεφαλίζω (# *642*) to take the head off, to behead. **ἠγέρθη** aor. ind. pass. s.v. 14. For a discussion of this passage s. HA, 184-97; TJ, 64-65. ◆ **17 αὐτός** he, himself, the aforementioned (BD, 145; SIMS, 113-16). **ἀποστείλας** aor. act.

part. (circum.) ἀποστέλλω (# *690*) to send, "he sent...." **ἐκράτησεν** aor. ind. act. κρατέω (# *3195*) to seize, to arrest. **ἔδησεν** aor. ind. act. δέω (# *1313*) to bind. According to Josephus, John was imprisoned at the fortress of Machaerus (Jos., *Ant.* 18:119; TJ, 63; also Roger Aus, *Water into Wine and the Beheading of John the Baptist,* Brown Judaic Studies 150 [Atlanta, Ga: Scholars Press, 1988], particularly 39-64). **ἐγάμησεν** aor. ind. act. γαμέω (# *1138*) to marry (HA, 131-36; TJ, 47-49). ◆ **18 ἔξεστιν** (# *2003*) it is lawful, it is allowed, followed by dat. and epex. inf. For the unlawfulness of this marriage s. HA, 137-46; BBC; DJG, 388-89; ABD, 3:175-76. ◆ **19 ἐνεῖχεν** impf. ind. act. ἐνέχω (# *1923*) to have it in for someone, to hold a grudge (Taylor). **ἤθελεν** impf. ind. act. θέλω (# *2527*) to will, to want. Impf. indicates unfulfilled action in the past. **ἀποκτεῖναι** aor. act. inf. ἀποκτείνω (# *650*) to kill. **ἠδύνατο** impf. ind. pass. (dep.) δύναμαι (# *1538*) (BD, 36). ◆ **20 ἐφοβεῖτο** impf. ind. mid. (dep.) φοβέομαι (# *5828*) to fear. Impf. pictures the continual fearing. **εἰδώς** perf. act. part. οἶδα (# *3857*) to know. Def. perf. w. a pres. meaning. Causal part. Josephus calls John a good man (Jos., *Ant.,* 18:117; TJ, 64). **συνετήρει** impf. ind. act. συντηρέω (# *5337*) to guard, to keep safe. The prep. compound is perfective (Taylor; M, 116). **ἠπόρει** impf. ind. act. ἀπορέω (# *679*) to be at a loss, in doubt, to be in perplexity, w. the implication of serious anxiety (LN, 1:381). **ἡδέως** (# *2452*) adv. gladly. **ἤκουεν** impf. ind. act. s.v. 16. Obj. gen. refers to Jesus. ◆ **21 γενομένης** aor. mid. (dep.) part. (temp.) γίνομαι (# *1181*) to become, to be. Gen. abs. **εὔκαιρος** (# *2322*) opportune, suitable, convenient. **γενεσίοις** dat. pl. γενέσια (# *1160*) birthday. For birthday celebrations in the ancient world s. RAC, 11:217-43. Dat. of time. Pl. used of festivals (BD, 107-108). **δεῖπνον** (# *1270*) dinner, banquet (SB, 4:ii, 611-39). **ἐποίησεν** aor. ind. act. s.v. 5. **μεγιστᾶσιν** dat. pl. μεγιστᾶνες (# *3491*) the great ones, courtiers (generally pl.) (BAGD). It refers to the inner circle of the king's government (Sherwin-White, 137). Dat. shows personal interest. **χιλίαρχος** (# *5941*) lit. the leader of a thousand soldiers; later, the commander of a cohort. Roughly equivalent to our present-day major or colonel (HA, 119; BAGD). The archaeological discoveries at Machaerus of a prison and two dining rooms fit the text (Gundry, 313). ◆ **22 εἰσελθούσης** aor. act. part. (temp.) gen. fem. sing. εἰσέρχομαι (# *1656*) to come in. Gen. abs. **ὀρχησαμένης** aor. mid. (dep.) part. ὀρχέομαι (# *4004*) to dance, not necessarily a sensual dance (HA, 157), but in Roman circles dancing was considered indecent and dances at banquets were generaly done by slaves or prostitutes (Lane; KP, 5:513-14; OCD, 312; DGRA, 1004-6). **ἤρεσεν** aor. ind. act. ἀρέσκω (# *743*) to please, w. dat. He not only took his brother's wife but wanted his wife's daughter. **συνανακειμένοις** pres. mid. (dep.) part. συνανάκειμαι (# *5263*) to recline at the table w. someone. **κοράσιον** (# *3166*) girl, dimin.

little girl, a young girl at or near marriageable age, probably around fourteen years old (HA, 151-56; Lane; BBC). **αἴτησον** aor. imp. act. αἰτέω (# 160) to ask, to request. Aor. imp. looks at a specific act. **θέλῃς** pres. subj. act. s.v. 19. Subj. in an indef. rel. cl. **δώσω** fut. ind. act. δίδωμι (# 1443) to give. Fut. used in a type of cond. cl. w. imp. stating the cond. ◆ **23 ὤμοσεν** aor. ind. act. ὀμνύω (# 3923) to swear. For the oath of Herod s. HA, 165-67; BBC. **αἰτήσῃς** aor. subj. act. s.v. 22. **ἥμισυς** (# 2468) half. ◆ **24 ἐξελθοῦσα** aor. part. nom. fem. sing. s.v. l. **αἰτήσωμαι** aor. subj. mid. αἰτέω (# 160) to ask. The change from act. to mid. is intentional and indicates the urgency of the request. Deliberative subj. (Taylor). ◆ **25 σπουδῇ** (# 5082) haste, speed. **ᾐτήσατο** aor. ind. mid. s.v. 24. **ἐξαυτῆς** (# 1994) immediately. **δῷς** aor. subj. act. δίδωμι (# 1443) to give. Subj. w. ἵνα (# 2671) in cl. giving the content of the request. **πίνακι** dat. sing. πίναξ a board, plate, dish, served as part of the dinner menu (BBC). ◆ **26 περίλυπος** (# 4337) surrounded by sorrow, sorrowful, very sad (14:34; Matt. 26:38). **γενόμενος** aor. mid. (dep.) part. (circum.) s.v. 21. **ὅρκους** acc. pl. ὅρκος (# 3992) oath. The pl. suggests repeated oaths (Taylor). Acc. w. prep. giving the cause of his sorrow, or of his unwillingness to set aside the promise (Gundry, 321). **ἠθέλησεν** aor. ind. act. s.v. 19. **ἀθετῆσαι** aor. act. inf. ἀθετέω (# 119) to set aside. He would not break faith w. her, disappoint her (Swete). Inf. w. the vb. of desire. ◆ **27 ἀποστείλας** aor. act. part. (circum.) ἀποστέλλω (# 690) to send, to commission, "The king sent...." **σπεκουλάτορα** acc. sing. σπεκουλάτωρ (# 5063) used to denote a member of the headquarters staff of a legionary commander in the Roman imperial army or of a provincial governor whose duties included the carrying out of executions; hence, "executioner" (Cranfield; EDNT). **ἐπέταξεν** aor. ind. act. ἐπιτάσσω (# 2199) to instruct, to command. **ἐνέγκαι** aor. act. inf. φέρω (# 5770) to carry, to bring. Inf. in indir. discourse. **ἀπελθών** aor. act. part. (circum.) ἀπέρχομαι (# 599) to go out. **ἀπεκεφάλισεν** aor. ind. act. s.v. 16. ◆ **28 ἤνεγκεν** aor. ind. act. φέρω s.v. 27. **ἔδωκεν** aor. ind. act. δίδωμι (# 1443) to give. ◆ **29 ἀκούσαντες** aor. act. part. (temp.) s.v. 2. **ἦλθον** aor. ind. act. ἔρχομαι (# 2262) to go, to come. **ἦραν** aor. ind. act. αἴρω (# 149) to take up, to take away. **πτῶμα** (# 4713) acc. sing. body, corpse. **ἔθηκαν** aor. ind. act. τίθημι (# 5502) to place. ◆ **30 συνάγονται** pres. ind. pass. συνάγω (# 5251) to gather together; pass. to be gathered together, to assemble (BAGD). Hist. pres. **ἀπήγγειλαν** aor. ind. act. ἀπαγγέλλω (# 550) to report, to inform. **ἐποίησαν** aor. ind. act. s.v. 5. **ἐδίδαξαν** aor. ind. act. διδάσκω (# 1438) to teach. ◆ **31 δεῦτε** (# 1307) Come! **ὑμεῖς αὐτοί** you yourselves. "I mean *you*" (Gundry, 322). **κατ' ἰδίαν** privately. **ἀναπαύσασθε** aor. imp. mid. (dep.) ἀναπαύω (# 399) to cease; mid. to rest, to regain strength, used of soldiers resting and of land being allowed to rest by lightly sowing crops (LS;

MM). Aor. imp. looks at a specific command (VANT, 334). **ὑπάγοντες** pres. act. part. ὑπάγω (# 5632) to depart, to go. Part. used in periphrastic construction. **φαγεῖν** aor. act. inf. ἐσθίω (# 2266) to eat. Epex. inf. explaining the vb. **εὐκαίρουν** impf. ind. act. εὐκαιρέω (# 2320) to have time, to have opportunity. ◆ **32 ἀπῆλθον** aor. ind. act. s.v. 27. ◆ **33 εἶδον** aor. ind. act. ὁράω (# 3972) to see. **ἐπέγνωσαν** aor. ind. act. ἐπιγινώσκω (# 2105) to know, to recognize. **πεζῇ** (# 4270) dat. sing. by foot. **συνέδραμον** aor. ind. act. συντρέχω (# 5340) to run together. **προῆλθον** aor. ind. act. προέρχομαι (# 4601) to go before. ◆ **34 ἐξελθών** aor. act. part. s.v. 1. **ἐσπλαγχνίσθη** aor. ind. pass. (dep.) σπλαγχνίζομαι (# 5072) to have pity, to feel sympathy, to be moved w. compassion (MNTW, 156-60; TDNT; NIDNTT; EDNT). **ἔχοντα** pres. act. part. ἔχω (# 2400) to have. Adj. part. **ποιμένα** acc. sing. ποιμήν (# 4478) shepherd. The figure denotes the lack of spiritual guidance and reflects an OT image (Gould; Guelich). **ἤρξατο** aor. ind. mid. (dep.) used w. inf. s.v. 2. ◆ **35 γενομένης** aor. mid. (dep.) part. s.v. 2. Gen. abs. Temp. part. indicates mid-to-late afternoon (Gundry, 329). **προσελθόντες** aor. act. part. (circum.) προσέρχομαι (# 4665) to come to. ◆ **36 ἀπόλυσον** aor. imp. act. ἀπολύω (# 668) to free, to release, to dismiss. **ἀπελθόντες** aor. act. part. s.v. 27. Circum. part. **κύκλῳ** (# 3241) adv. in a circle, surrounding. **ἀγοράσωσιν** aor. subj. act. ἀγοράζω (# 60) to purchase, to buy (at the market square). Subj. used in purp. cl. **φάγωσιν** aor. subj. act. ἐσθίω (# 2266) to eat. Subj. in an indef. cl. ◆ **37 ἀποκριθείς** aor. pass. (dep.) part. ἀποκρίνομαι (# 646) to answer. For the Semitic use of the part. s. Matt. 3:12. **δότε** aor. imp. act. s.v. 2. **φαγεῖν** aor. act. inf. s.v. 36. Inf. used as dir. obj. **ἀγοράσωμεν** aor. subj. act. s.v. 36. Deliberative subj. **δηναρίων** gen. pl. δηνάριον (# 1324) denar, a Roman coin worth about eighteen cents. It was the workman's average daily wage (BAGD; DJG, 805). **διακοσίων** gen. pl. διακόσιοι (# 1357) two hundred. This and the preceding gen. are gen. of price (SIMS, 166). **δώσομεν** fut. ind. act. δίδωμι (# 1443) to give. Fut. used in a type of purp. cl. "in order that we may give" (SS, 110). ◆ **38 ὑπάγετε** pres. imp. act. s.v. 31. **ἴδετε** aor. imp. act. ὁράω (# 3972) to see. **γνόντες** aor. act. part. (temp.) γινώσκω (# 1182) to know. Ingressive aor. (VANT, 414). ◆ **39 ἐπέταξεν** aor. ind. act. s.v. 27. **ἀνακλῖναι** aor. act. inf. or ἀνακλιθῆναι aor. pass. inf. ἀνακλίνω (# 369) act. (trans.) to cause to recline; pass. (intrans.) to recline (TC, 91). Inf. in indir. discourse. **συμπόσια** acc. pl. συμπόσιον (# 5235) originally a drinking party, then a party of guests of any kind, a company. Adv. acc. The repetition of the word indicates distribution (RWP). **χλωρός** (# 5952) green. **χόρτος** (# 5965) grass. ◆ **40 ἀνέπεσαν** aor. ind. act. ἀναπίπτω (# 404) to fall back, to recline. **πρασιά** (# 4555) a garden bed, refers to the arrangement in rows. It often was customary for the students of the rabbis to sit in rows which were compared to the rows of vines in the vineyard or to well-ordered gardens (SB, 2:13; Cranfield). ◆ **41 λαβών** aor. act. part. (temp.) λαμβάνω (# 3284) to take. **ἀναβλέψας** aor. act. part. (temp.) ἀναβλέπω (# 329) to look up. **εὐλόγησεν** aor. ind. act. εὐλογέω (# 2328) to praise, to give thanks, to bless. In Judaism it was a stringent rule that nothing should be eaten without thanking God before and after the meal (TDNT; Lane). **κατέκλασεν** aor. ind. act. κατακλάω (# 2880) to break up, to break into pieces. **ἐδίδου** impf. ind. act. δίδωμι (# 1443) to give. Impf. suggests the successive distributions of bread (Taylor). **παρατιθῶσιν** pres. subj. act. παρα-τίθημι (# 4192) to set before, to serve a meal. Subj. w. ἵνα (# 2671) used in a purp. cl. **ἐμέρισεν** aor. ind. act. μερίζω (# 3532) to divide. ◆ **42 ἔφαγον** aor. ind. act. ἐσθίω (# 2266) to eat. **ἐχορτάσθησαν** aor. ind. pass. χορτάζω (# 5963) to give to eat, to satisfy, to be filled, to be satisfied (w. food). ◆ **43 ἦραν** aor. ind. act. s.v. 8. **κλάσμα** (# 3083) piece, that which was broken. **κόφινος** (# 3186) a wicker-work basket in which the Jews carried food (Taylor; Matt. 14:20). ◆ **44 φαγόντες** aor. act. part. s.v. 36. Subst. part. ◆ **45 ἠνάγκασεν** aor. ind. act. ἀναγκάζω (# 337) to compel, to force. It implies that the disciples did not want to get into the boat and go ahead of Jesus (Gundry, 335). **ἐμβῆναι** aor. act. inf. ἐμβαίνω (# 1832) to embark. Inf. used as dir. obj. in indir. discourse. **προάγειν** pres. act. inf. προάγω (# 4575) to go before. The previous aor. inf. looks at the embarking as an event; pres. inf. views the motion of going. ◆ **46 ἀποταξάμενος** aor. mid. (dep.) part. (temp.) ἀπο-τάσσομαι (# 698) to depart, to say good-bye, w. dat. **ἀπῆλθεν** aor. ind. act. ἀπέρχομαι (# 599) to go away. **προσεύξασθαι** aor. mid. (dep.) inf. προσεύχομαι (# 4667) to pray. Inf. of purp. ◆ **47 γενομένης** aor. mid. (dep.) part. (temp.) γίνομαι (# 1181) to become, to be. Gen. abs. "When evening had come." Aor. indicates antecedent action. It generally refers to the late afternoon or early evening (Guelich). **μέσῳ** dat. sing. μέσος (# 3545) middle. ◆ **48 ἰδών** aor. act. part. (temp.) ὁράω (# 3972) to see, "when he saw..." **βασανιζομένους** pres. mid. / pass. part. βασανίζω (# 989) to test, to torture, to distress. Mid. would mean "tormenting themselves," that is, "straining" (Gundry, 335). Pres. pictures the continual action. **ἐλαύνειν** pres. act. inf. ἐλαύνω (# 1785) to drive, as of ships or chariots. They drove the boat w. oars (RWP). Pres. used for contemporaneous time. **ἐναντίος** (# 1885) against, w. dat. **τέταρτος** (# 5480) fourth. **φυλακή** (# 5871) watch. Implies the Roman reckoning of four night watches. It would be about three o'clock in the morning (Taylor). **περιπατῶν** pres. act. part. περι-πατέω (# 4344) to walk about; part. of manner. **ἤθελεν** impf. ind. act. s.v. 22. **παρελθεῖν** aor. act. inf. παρέρχομαι (# 4216) to go by, to pass by, to come by, to come along side of. For a discussion of various views s. Guelich; Gundry, 340-41; Lane. ◆ **49 ἰδόντες** aor. act. part. s.v.

48. **ἔδοξαν** aor. ind. act. δοκέω (# 1506) to suppose. **φάντασμα** (# 5753) an apparition, ghost. It was a popular belief that spirits of the night brought disaster (Lane). **ἀνέκραξαν** aor. ind. act. ἀνακράζω (# 371) to cry out, to scream. The appearance drew forth a shriek of terror (Swete). ◆ **50 εἶδον** aor. ind. act. ὁράω (# 3972) to see. **ἐταράχθησαν** aor. ind. pass. ταράσσω (# 5429) to shake together, to stir up, to unsettle, to throw into confusion. **ἐλάλησεν** aor. ind. act. λαλέω (# 3281) to speak. **θαρσεῖτε** pres. imp. act. θαρσέω (# 2510) to be brave, to be of good cheer, to have confidence and firmness of purpose in the face of danger or testing (LN, 1:306). **ἐγώ εἰμι** "It is I." It could be understood as the divine name "I am" (Hooker). **φοβεῖσθε** pres. imp. mid. (dep.) φοβέομαι (# 5828) to be afraid, to fear. Pres. imp. w. neg. μή (# 3590) used to prohibit an action in progress. ◆ **51 ἀνέβη** aor. ind. act. ἀναβαίνω (# 326) to go up. **ἐκόπασεν** aor. ind. act. κοπάζω (# 3156) to become tired, to cease. **ἐκ περισσοῦ** adv. beyond measure, exceedingly. **ἐξίσταντο** impf. ind. mid. (dep.) ἐξίστημι (# 2014) to be beside oneself, to be astonished, to be amazed. ◆ **52 συνῆκαν** aor. ind. act. συνίημι (# 5317) to comprehend, to understand. **πεπωρωμένη** perf. pass. part. πωρόω (# 4800) to harden, to form a callus (AS). Perf. pictures the state or cond. of hardness. ◆ **53 διαπεράσαντες** aor. act. part. (temp.) διαπεράω (# 1385) to pass over, to cross over. **ἦλθον** aor. ind. act. ἔρχομαι (# 2262) to come. **προσωρμίσθησαν** aor. ind. pass. (dep.) προσορμίζω (# 4694) mid. and pass. to land, to cast anchor. They brought the boat to the moorings, casting anchor, or lashing her to a post on the shore (Swete). ◆ **54 ἐξελθόντων** aor. act. part. (temp.) s.v. 1. Gen. abs **ἐπιγνόντες** aor. act. part. ἐπιγινώσκω (# 2105) to recognize. ◆ **55 περιέδραμον** aor. ind. act. περιτρέχω (# 4366) to run around, to run about. **ἤρξαντο** aor. ind. mid. (dep.) w. inf. s.v. 2. **κράβαττος** (# 3187) mattress, pallet, the poor man's bed (BAGD). **περιφέρειν** pres. act. inf. περιφέρω (# 4367) to carry about. Pres. stresses the repeated action. **ἤκουον** impf. ind. act. s.v. 2. ◆ **56 εἰσεπορεύετο** impf. ind. mid. (dep.) εἰσπορεύομαι (# 1660) to go in. Iterat. impf. indicates repeated action, "they came again and again." **ἀγρός** (# 69) field, farm, hamlet. **ἀγορά** (# 59) marketplace. **ἐτίθεσαν** impf. ind. act. τίθημι (# 5502) to place. For this form of the impf. s. BD, 47; MH, 202. **ἀσθενοῦντας** pres. act. part. ἀσθενέω (# 820) to be weak, to be sick. **παρεκάλουν** impf. ind. act. παρακαλέω (# 4151) to beseech, to plead w. Impf. indicates the continual beseeching. **κρασπέδου** gen. sing. κράσπεδον (# 3192) border, hem of a garment. It could refer to one of the four tassels worn by Jewish men. Each tassel had four blue and white threads to remind the wearer to do the commandments of the Lord (Guelich; SB, 4, i:277-92; ABD, 2:235-36). Gen. as dir. obj. of the vb. ἅπτομαι. **ἅψωνται** pres. subj. mid. (dep.) ἅπτομαι (# 721) w. gen. to touch. Subj. in a cl. as obj. of the

vb. ἥψαντο aor. ind. mid. ἅπτομαι. ἐσῴζοντο impf. ind. pass. σῴζω (# 5392) to save, to heal. Iterat. impf. used for repeated action.

Mark 7

◆ **1** συνάγονται pres. ind. pass. συνάγω (# 5251) to gather together, to assemble. ἐλθόντες aor. act. part. (circum.) ἔρχομαι (# 2262) to go, to come. ◆ **2** ἰδόντες aor. act. part. (temp.) ὁράω (# 3972) to see. κοινός (# 3123) common, profane, ritually unclean. χερσίν dat. pl. χείρ (# 5931) hand. Instr. dat. ἄνιπτος (# 481) unwashed. ◆ **3** πυγμῇ (# 4778) dat. sing. fist. The dat. could be modal ("w. the fist"), w. the fist held out while water is poured over it. It could be instr. dat., where the fist is rubbed in the hand to wash it; or it could be dat. of measure: "by elbow length" (Swete; Gundry, 360; Lane; BBC). νίψωνται aor. subj. mid. νίπτω (# 3782) to wash; mid. to wash oneself. Subj. used in a type of 3rd. class cond. cl. κρατοῦντες pres. act. part. κρατέω (# 3195) to seize, to hold to, to hold fast. Causal part. παράδοσις (# 4142) that which is handed down, tradition. The oral tradition which was passed along. ◆ **4** βαπτίσωνται aor. ind. mid. βαπτίζω (# 966) to immerse. A reference to the ritual bathing as prescribed by Jewish Law (Lane; TDNT; SB, 2:14). W.S. LaSor, "Discovering What Jewish Miqva'ot Can Tell Us About Christian Baptism," *BAR* 13 (1987): 52-59; Roger P. Booth *Jesus and the Laws of Purity,*, JSNTSSB (Sheffield: JSOT Press, 1986). Dir. mid. For the reading ῥαντίσωνται s. TC, 93; TDNT. Subj. w. ἐάν (# 1569) in a type of 3rd. class cond. cl. in which the cond. is viewed as possible. παρέλαβον aor. ind. act. παραλαμβάνω (# 4161) to receive, denoting the process of receiving a thing by transmission (Gould). κρατεῖν pres. act. inf. s.v. 3. Epex. inf. explaining the things delivered by tradition. Pres. indicates that they are habitually kept. ξεστῶν gen. pl. ξέστης (# 3829) pitcher, jug. Obj. gen. χαλκίων gen. pl. χάλκιον a bronze or copper vessel, kettle. κλίνη (# 3109) a place for those who are resting, couch, dining couch (BAGD). ◆ **5** ἐπερωτῶσιν pres. ind. act. ἐπερωτάω (# 2089) to ask, to inquire about something (s. 5:9). Hist. pres. περιπατοῦσιν pres. ind. act. περιπατέω (# 4344) to walk about, in the Hebraic sense of living or conducting one's life (Taylor). Pres. could point to a habitual action. ◆ **6** εἶπεν aor. ind. act. λέγω (# 3306). ἐπροφήτευσεν aor. ind. act. προφητεύω (# 4736) to prophesy. ὑποκριτής (# 5695) hypocrite; one who "speaks from under a mask." The word comes from the theater where the actors were only men and wore masks to portray the character (TDNT; EDNT; TLNT; R. A. Batey, "Jesus and the Theatre," *NTS* 30 [1984]: 563-74; Gundry, 361). γέγραπται perf. ind. pass. γράφω (# 1211) to write; perf., "it stands written." Often used to indicate the continuing authority of a binding document (MM). χείλεσιν dat. pl. χεῖλος (# 5927) lip. Instr. dat. τι-

μᾷ pres. ind. act. τιμάω (# 5506) to honor. πόρρω adv. far, far away. ἀπέχει pres. ind. act. ἀπέχω (# 600) to be away. ◆ **7** μάτην (# 3472) adv. in vain, to no purpose. σέβονται pres. ind. mid. (dep.) σέβω (# 4936) to worship; indicates a proper conduct in relation to those worthy of honor (NIDNTT; TDNT; EDNT). διδάσκοντες pres. act. part. διδάσκω (# 1438) to teach. Part. of means explaining how the worship is carried out. διδασκαλίας acc. pl. διδασκαλία (# 1436) teaching, doctrine, a definite course of instruction (Swete). Cognate acc. used as double acc.: "teaching the commandments of men as doctrine." ἔνταλμα (# 1945) commandment. ◆ **8** ἀφέντες aor. act. part. (circum.) ἀφίημι (# 918) to release, to leave, to forsake. κρατεῖτε pres. ind. act. κρατέω (# 3195) to hold on to, to keep. Pres. indicates an habitual action. παράδοσις (# 4142) that which is passed on, tradition; the oral law (commandments of men) w. its burdensome rules about ceremonial washings contravenes the divine intention and even sets it at naught (Taylor). ◆ **9** ἔλεγεν impf. ind. act. λέγω (# 3306). Incep. impf., "he began to speak." καλῶς (# 2822) well. Used here w. irony (BD, 262). ἀθετεῖτε (# 119) pres. ind. act. ἀθετέω to set aside, to reject, to cancel, to annul (MM; EDNT; GELTS). στήσητε aor. subj. act. ἵστημι (# 2705) to establish, to confirm, to make or consider valid (BAGD). Subj. w. ἵνα (# 2671) used in a purp. cl. ◆ **10** τίμα pres. imp. act. τιμάω (# 5506) to honor. κακολογῶν pres. act. part. κακολογέω (# 2800) to speak evil of, to insult. Part. used as subst. τελευτάτω pres. imp. act. 3rd. sing. τελευτάω (# 5462) to die. ◆ **11** εἴπῃ aor. subj. act. λέγω (# 3306). Subj. w. ἐάν (# 1569) in a 3rd. class cond. cl. where the cond. is possible. κορβᾶν (# 3167) offering, gift. A formula pronounced over some object to remove it from profane use (Joseph A. Fitzmyer, "The Aramaic Qorban Inscription from Jebel Hallet Et-Turi and Mark 7:11/Matt. 15:5," *JBL* 78 [1959]: 60-65. The inscription provides a contemporary parallel; TDNT; EDNT; Guelich; Brooks; BBC; Gundry, 363-64; s. Matt. 11:5). ὠφεληθῇς aor. subj. pass. ὠφελέω (# 6067) to help, to benefit; pass. to have benefit from, to profit. ◆ **12** οὐκέτι (# 4033) no longer. Once the formula was used (perhaps hastily), one evidently was not allowed to change one's mind (Cranfield). ἀφίετε pres. ind. act. ἀφίημι (# 918) w. inf. to allow. ποιῆσαι aor. act. inf. ποιέω (# 4472) to do. πατρί dat. sing. πατήρ (# 4252) father. Dat. of advantage. ◆ **13** ἀκυροῦντες pres. act. part. ἀκυρόω (# 218) to cancel, to render null and void, to revoke, to invalidate the authority of something (LN, 1:683). Often used of annulling wills and contracts (MM). παραδόσει dat. sing. παράδοσις s.v. 3. Instr. dat. ᾗ rel. pron. dat. fem. sing. Dat. by attraction for acc. as dir. obj. παρεδώκατε aor. ind. act. παραδίδωμι (# 4140) to give further, to pass on, to transmit by teaching. Used of passing on tradition. παρόμοιος (# 4235) similar, almost the same, like. Adj. used as subst.

ποιεῖτε pres. ind. act. s.v. 12. Pres. used of habitual action. ◆ **14 προσκαλεσάμενος** aor. mid. (indir. mid.) part. προσκαλέω (# 4673) to summons, to call someone to oneself. **ἀκούσατε** aor. imp. act. ἀκούω (# 201) to hear, to listen to, followed by obj. in gen. Often used to translate Heb. שָׁמַע s. Deut.6:4. **σύνετε** aor. imp. act. συνίημι (# 5317) to understand, to comprehend. Aor. imps. here call for specific action. ◆ **15 ἔξωθεν** (# 2033) adv. outside. **εἰσπορευόμενον** pres. mid. (dep.) part. εἰσπορεύομαι (# 1660) to go into. Part. used as subst. **κοινῶσαι** aor. act. inf. κοινόω (# 3124) to make common, to defile. **ἐκπορευόμενα** pres. mid. (dep.) part. ἐκπορεύομαι (# 1744) to go out. **κοινοῦντα** pres. act. part. κοινόω Adj. part. as subst. ◆ **17 εἰσῆλθεν** aor. ind. act. εἰσέρχομαι (# 1656) to go into. **ἐπηρώτων** impf. ind. act. ἐπερωτάω (# 2089) to ask, to inquire. Inceptive impf., "they began to question." ◆ **18 ἀσύνετος** (# 852) without understanding, not comprehending. It is the one who lacks discernment (Swete). **νοεῖτε** pres. ind. act. νοέω (# 3783) to understand, to apprehend. ◆ **19 κοιλία** (# 3120) stomach. **ἀφεδρῶν** (# 909) toilet. **καθαρίζων** pres. act. part. καθαρίζω (# 2751) to cleanse, to declare clean. **βρῶμα** (# 1109) food. ◆ **20 κοινοῖ** pres. ind. act. s.v. 15. ◆ **21 ἔσωθεν** (# 2277) inside. **διαλογισμός** consideration, thought. Not merely evil thoughts but evil devisings which issue in degraded acts and vices now mentioned (Taylor). **πορνεία** (# 4518) immorality, illicit sexual indulgence (TDNT). **κλοπαί** nom. pl. κλοπή (# 3113) theft. **φόνος** (# 5840) murder. ◆ **22 μοιχεία** (# 3657) adultery. **πλεονεξία** (# 4432) greed, the desire to have more, often at the expense of others (TDNT; NTW, 97-99; LN, 1:291-92). **πονηρία** (# 4504) bad, evil, wickedness (Trench, *Synonyms*). **δόλος** (# 1515) deceit. **ἀσέλγεια** (# 816) unrestrained, unbridled, shameless living; behavior completely lacking in moral restraint (NTW, 26-27; LN, 1:771). **ὀφθαλμὸς πονηρός** (# 4057; 4505) evil eye. Semitic expression for stinginess, envy, jealousy, a jealous grudge (Swete; Lane; SB, 2:14). **βλασφημία** (# 1060) blasphemy, slander. **ὑπερηφανία** (# 5661) pride, arrogance, haughtiness, contemptuousness, a state of ostentatious pride or arrogance bordering on insolence (LN, 1:765). **ἀφροσύνη** (# 932) foolish, senseless. Used esp. of religious insensibility (Cranfield). ◆ **24 ἀναστάς** aor. act. part. ἀνίστημι (# 482) to arise. It refers to Jesus standing up from a seated position after instructing the disciples (Gundry, 372). Circum. / temp. part. **ἀπῆλθεν** aor. ind. act. ἀπέρχομαι (# 599) to depart, to go out. **εἰσελθών** aor. act. part. (temp.) s.v. 17. **ἤθελεν** impf. ind. act. θέλω (# 2527) to will, to want, to want to, w. inf. **γνῶναι** aor. act. inf. γινώσκω (# 1182) to know. **ἠδυνήθη** aor. ind. pass. (dep.) δύναμαι (# 1538) to be able, an Ionic form for the aor. (Cranfield; MH, 234; GGP, 2:317-19). **λαθεῖν** aor. act. inf. λανθάνω (# 3291) to be hidden, concealed. Inf. w. the vb. δύναμαι. ◆ **25 ἀκούσασα** aor. act. part. (temp.) nom. fem. sing. ἀκούω (# 201) to hear.

ἧς rel. pron. gen. fem. sing. ὅς (# 4005). Semitic use followed by the redundant pers. pron. (SIMS, 116). **εἶχεν** impf. ind. act. ἔχω (# 2400) to have. **θυγάτριον** (# 2589) daughter, dimin. form used to express endearment. **ἐλθοῦσα** aor. act. part. (circum.) fem. s.v. 1. **προσέπεσεν** aor. ind. act. προσπίπτω (# 4700) to fall down. ◆ **26 γένει** dat. sing. γένος (# 1169) birth. Instr. dat. ("by birth"). **ἠρώτα** impf. ind. act. ἐρωτάω (# 2263) to ask, to request. Hist. pres. **ἐκβάλη** aor. subj. act. ἐκβάλλω (# 1675) to throw out, to cast out, to expel. Subj. used in noun cl. giving the content of the request. ◆ **27 ἔλεγεν** impf. ind. act. s.v. 9. **ἄφες** aor. imp. act. ἀφίημι (# 918) to allow. **πρῶτον** (# 4754) first. Implies the sequence of God's salvation; "to the Jew first" (Guelich). **χορτασθῆναι** aor. pass. inf. χορτάζω (# 5963) to feed; pass. to be full, to be satisfied. Inf. used to complete the vb. ἀφίημι. **λαβεῖν** aor. act. inf. λαμβάνω (# 3284) to take. Inf. explaining what is not good. **κυναρίοις** dat. pl. κυνάριον (# 3249) dog, dimin. little dog (Matt. 15:26). Indir. obj. The dimin. suggests the little dogs that were kept as pets (Cranfield). **βαλεῖν** aor. act. inf. βάλλω (# 965) to throw. ◆ **28 ἀπεκρίθη** aor. ind. pass. (dep.) ἀποκρίνομαι (# 646) to answer. **ὑποκάτω** (# 5691) under (w. gen.). **τραπέζης** (# 5544) gen. sing. table. **ψιχίον** (# 6033) crumb (dimin. form). ◆ **29 εἶπεν** aor. ind. act. λέγω (# 3306). **ὕπαγε** pres. imp. act. ὑπάγω (# 5632) to go away, to go. **ἐξελήλυθεν** perf. ind. act. ἐξέρχομαι (# 2002) to go out. Perf. indicates the pres. state or cond. (VA, 265). ◆ **30 ἀπελθοῦσα** aor. act. part. (temp.) nom. fem. sing. ἀπέρχομαι (# 599) to go out. **εὗρεν** aor. ind. act. εὑρίσκω (# 2351) to find. **βεβλημένον** perf. mid./pass. part. βάλλω (# 965) to cast, to lie. Perf. indicates the pres. state or cond. **ἐξεληλυθός** perf. act. part. s.v. 29. "When...." ◆ **31 ἐξελθών** aor. act. part. (temp.) s.v. 29. **ἦλθεν** aor. ind. act. s.v. 1. ◆ **32 φέρουσιν** pres. ind. act. φέρω (# 5770) to carry, to bring. Hist. pres. **κωφός** (# 3273) dumb, deaf. **μογιλάλος** (# 3652) speaking w. difficulty, having an impediment in speech (Cranfield). The recovery of hearing by the deaf was a note of the messianic age (Swete). **παρακαλοῦσιν** pres. ind. act. παρακαλέω (# 4151) to beseech, to plead. Hist. pres. This and the preceding hist. pres. stress the helpless plight of the man and the urgency of the people who bring him (Gundry, 383). **ἐπιθῇ** aor. subj. act. ἐπιτίθημι (# 2202) to place upon. Subj. used in a cl. as obj. of the vb. ◆ **33 ἀπολαβόμενος** aor. mid. part. (temp.) ἀπολαμβάνω (# 655) to take from, to draw a person aside privately to oneself. **ἔβαλεν** aor. ind. act. βάλλω (# 965) to throw; here in the sense of putting, placing. **δάκτυλος** (# 1235) finger. **ὦτα** acc. pl. οὖς (# 4044) ear. **πτύσας** aor. act. part. (temp.) πτύω (# 4772) to spit. For the custom of using spit s. SB, 2:15; Gundry, 389. **ἥψατο** aor. ind. mid. (dep.) ἅπτομαι (# 721) to touch, w. gen. as dir. obj. ◆ **34 ἀναβλέψας** aor. act. part. (temp.) ἀναβλέπω (# 329) to look up. **ἐστέναξεν** aor. ind. act. στενάζω (# 5100) to groan, to sigh. **ἐφφαθα** (*# 2395*) Aramaic ithpaal imp. sing. אֶתְפְּתַּח; (AT, 673; UJS, 13-15; MP, 79; Fred L. Horton, Jr., "Nochmals ἐφφαθά in Mk 7:34," *ZNW* 77 [1986]: 101-108). "Be opened," "be released." The idea is not of the particular part of the pers. being opened, but of the whole pers. being opened and released. It is the command that shatters the fetters by which Satan has held his victim bound (Cranfield). **διανοίχθητι** aor. imp. pass. διανοίγω (*# 1381*) to open, to open up. ◆ **35 ἠνοίγησαν** aor. ind. pass. ἀνοίγω (*# 487*) to open. **ἐλύθη** aor. ind. pass. λύω (*# 3395*) to loose. **ἐλάλει** impf. ind. act. λαλέω (*# 3281*) to speak. Inceptive impf., "he began to speak." **ὀρθῶς** (*# 3987*) adv. straight, correctly. ◆ **36 διεστείλατο** aor. ind. mid. (dep.) διαστέλλομαι (*# 1403*) to command, to charge. **λέγωσιν** pres. subj. act. λέγω (*# 3306*). Subj. in a cl. as obj. of the vb. **διεστέλλετο** impf. ind. mid. (dep.). **περισσότερον** (*# 4352*) comp. περισσός beyond measure, exceeding. Elative use of the comp. **ἐκήρυσσον** impf. ind. act. κηρύσσω (*# 3062*) to proclaim, to herald. Iterat. impf. expresses repeated action. ◆ **37 ὑπερπερισσῶς** (*# 5669*) adv., beyond all measure, exceedingly. **ἐξεπλήσσοντο** impf. ind. mid./pass. ἐκπλήσσω (*# 1742*) to be astounded (s. 1:22). **λέγοντες** pres. act. part. λέγω (*# 3306*). **πεποίηκεν** perf. ind. act. ποιέω (*# 4472*) to do, to make. Perf. denotes responsibility or credit of the subj. for having done the action (VANT, 295). **καί ... καί** both ... and. **λαλεῖν** pres. act. inf. λαλέω (*# 3281*) Inf. used as obj. of the vb.

Mark 8

◆ **1 ὄντος** pres. act. part. εἰμί (*# 1639*) to be. Gen. abs., temp. or causal (Gundry, 393). **ἐχόντων** pres. act. part. ἔχω (*# 2400*) to have. Gen. abs., temp. or causal part. **φάγωσιν** aor. subj. act. ἐσθίω (*# 2266*) to eat. Subj. in an indef. cl. **προσκαλεσάμενος** aor. mid. part. προσκαλέω (*# 4673*) to summons, to call someone to oneself. ◆ **2 σπλαγχνίζομαι** (*# 5072*) pres. ind. mid. (dep.) to be inwardly moved, to have compassion on (s. 6:34). **προσμένουσιν** pres. ind. act. προσμένω (*# 4693*) to remain w. someone, to stay. ◆ **3 ἀπολύσω** aor. subj. act. ἀπολύω (*# 668*) to release, to send away. Subj. in a 3rd. class cond. cl. w. the cond. as possible. **νήστεις** acc. pl. νῆστις (*# 3765*) not eating, hungry (for the form s. MH, 132). **ἐκλυθήσονται** fut. ind. pass. ἐκλύω (*# 1725*) to be weary, to become tired, to faint; "they will be exhausted" (Gould). **ἥκασιν** pres. ind. act. ἥκω (*# 2457*) to become, to have arrived. W. perf. meaning, "They have come and are here." For the form s. MH, 221. ◆ **4 ἀπεκρίθησαν** aor. ind. pass. (dep.) ἀποκρίνομαι (*# 646*) to answer. **δυνήσεται** fut. ind. mid. δύναμαι (*# 1538*) to be able. Deliberative fut. used in a question of deliberation. **χορτάσαι** aor. act. inf. χορτάζω (*# 5963*) to feed, to fill w. food, to satisfy. ◆ **5 ἠρώτα** impf. ind. act. ἐρωτάω (*# 2263*) to ask. **εἶπαν** aor. ind. act. λέγω (*# 3306*) to say. ◆ **6 ἀναπεσεῖν** aor. act. inf. ἀναπίπτω

(*# 404*) to recline. Inf. in indir. speech after a vb. of commanding. **λαβών** aor. act. part. (circum.) λαμβάνω (*# 3284*) to take. **εὐχαριστήσας** aor. act. part. (circum.) εὐχαριστέω (*# 2373*) to give thanks. **ἔκλασεν** aor. ind. act. κλάω (*# 3089*) to break. **ἐδίδου** impf. ind. act. δίδωμι (*# 1443*) to give; impf. suggests "to distribute" (s. Mark 6:41). **παρατιθῶσιν** pres. subj. act. παρατίθημι (*# 4192*) to serve (food). Subj. w. ἵνα (*# 2671*) in a purp. cl. **παρέθηκαν** aor. ind. act. ◆ **7 εἶχον** impf. ind. act. ἔχω (*# 2400*) to have. **ἰχθύδιον** (*# 2715*) dimin., small fish. **εὐλογήσας** aor. act. part. εὐλογέω (*# 2328*) to praise, to bless, to give thanks. Circum. or temp. part. **παρατιθέναι** pres. act. inf. s.v. 6. Inf. in indir. discourse. ◆ **8 ἔφαγον** aor. ind. act. s.v. 1. **ἐχορτάσθησαν** aor. ind. pass. s.v. 4. **ἦραν** aor. ind. act. αἴρω (*# 149*) to lift up, to pick up. **κλασμάτων** gen. pl. κλάσμα (*# 3083*) fragment. Gen. of content or description. It was common after a banquet to gather up the remaining pieces of bread at least the size of an olive (SB, 4:625). **σπυρίδας** acc. pl. σπυρίς (*# 4711*) a mat basket for provisions. In Acts 9:25 it is large enough to carry a man (Taylor). ◆ **9 ἀπέλυσεν** aor. ind. act. ἀπολύω (*# 668*) to release, to dismiss. ◆ **10 ἐμβάς** aor. act. part. ἐμβαίνω (*# 1832*) to get in, to embark. Circum. or temp. part. **ἦλθεν** aor. ind. act. ἔρχομαι (*# 2262*) to go, to come. ◆ **11 ἐξῆλθον** aor. ind. act. ἐξέρχομαι (*# 2002*) to go out, to come out. **ἤρξαντο** aor. ind. mid. (dep.) ἄρχομαι (*# 806*) to begin. **συζητεῖν** pres. act. inf. συζητέω (*# 5184*) to discuss, to debate, to argue, to express forceful differences of opinion (LN, 1:438). Inf. complements the vb. **ζητοῦντες** pres. act. part. ζητέω (*# 2426*) to seek. Part. expresses manner. **σημεῖον** (*# 4952*) acc. sing. sign. A sign from heaven may mean a sign from God, and may have been a request for an apocalyptic sign indicating God's help for His elect (Gundry, 402). **πειράζοντες** pres. act. part. πειράζω (*# 4279*) to try, to test, to tempt. Part. of purp. ◆ **12 ἀναστενάξας** aor. act. part. ἀναστενάζω (*# 417*) to sigh deeply. It expresses deep emotion (Guelich). **ζητεῖ** pres. ind. act. ζητέω (*# 2426*) to seek, to ask for. Pres. may indicate habitual action here. **εἰ** (*# 1623*) if, a strong negation. A Heb. oath formula w. the meaning "if I do such a thing, may I die!" (Taylor; MH, 468). **δοθήσεται** fut. ind. pass. δίδωμι (*# 1443*) to give. Theol. pass. indicating that God performs the action. ◆ **13 ἀφείς** aor. act. part. ἀφίημι (*# 918*) to leave, to depart. Circum. or temp. part. **ἐμβάς** aor. act. part. s.v. 10. **ἀπῆλθεν** aor. ind. act. ἀπέρχομαι (*# 599*) to go away, to depart. ◆ **14 ἐπελάθοντο** aor. ind. mid. (dep.) ἐπιλανθάνομαι (*# 2140*) to forget. **λαβεῖν** aor. act. inf. s.v. 6. Inf. complements the vb. **εἶχον** impf. ind. act. s.v. 7. ◆ **15 διεστέλλετο** impf. ind. mid. (dep.). διαστέλλομαι (*# 1403*) to charge, to command. **ὁρᾶτε** pres. imp. act. ὁράω (*# 3972*) to see, look out. Pres. imp. calls for continual action. **βλέπετε** pres. imp. act. βλέπω (*# 1063*) to see; w. the prep. ἀπό (*# 608*), to take heed, beware of.

Pres. imp. highlights the warning (Gundry, 408). ζύμη (# 2434) leaven. It indicates the permeating power of corruption, including the evil disposition of human beings (Gundry, 411; TDNT; Matt. 13:33). It is unbelief reflected in one's response to Jesus (Guelich). ◆ 16 διελογίζοντο impf. ind. mid. (dep.) διαλογίζομαι (# 1368) to reason, to discuss, to debate. ◆ 17 γνούς aor. act. part. γινώσκω (# 1182) to know. temp. / casual part. ούπω (# 4037) not yet. νοεῖτε pres. ind. act. νοέω (# 3783) to understand, to perceive. συνίετε pres. ind. act. συνίημι (# 5317) to bring together, to comprehend. πεπωρωμένην perf. pass. part. πωρόω (# 4800) to harden. Perf. indicates the state of hardness. Hardening flows on from the heart to the sight, the hearing, and the memory (Bengel; DJG, 81-82). ◆ 18 μνημονεύετε pres. ind. act. μνημονεύω (# 3648) to remember. The questions expect a positive answer. ◆ 19 ἔκλασα aor. ind. act. s.v. 6. κόφινος (# 3186) basket (s. Mark 6:43). ἤρατε aor. ind. act. s.v. 8. ◆ 22 παρακαλοῦσιν pres. ind. act. παρακαλέω (# 4151) to beseech, to plead w.; hist. pres. ἅψηται aor. subj. mid. (dep.) ἅπτομαι (# 721) w. gen., to grasp, to touch. Subj. in a noun cl. as obj. of the vb. ◆ 23 ἐπιλαβόμενος aor. mid. (dep.) part. ἐπιλαμβάνομαι (# 2138) w. gen., to take hold of, to place hands upon. Jesus must take hold of him because the man is blind (Gundry, 417). ἐξήνεγκεν aor. ind. act. ἐκφέρω (# 1766) to carry out. πτύσας aor. act. part. πτύω (# 4772) to spit (s. Mark 7:33; BBC). ὄμμα (# 3921) eye (DMTG). ἐπιθείς aor. act. part. ἐπιτίθημι (# 2202) to place upon. Circum. / temp. part. ἐπηρώτα impf. ind. act. ἐπερωτάω (# 2089) to ask a question. εἰ (# 1623) if. It introduces a direct quotation (BD, 226; NDIEC, 5:57-58; 6:183). ◆ 24 ἀναβλέψας aor. act. part. (temp.) ἀναβλέπω (# 329) to look up. The man involuntarily raised his eyes (Swete). ὁρῶ pres. ind. act. s.v. 15. περιπατοῦντας pres. act. part. περιπατέω (# 4344) to walk about. Adj. use of part. A suggested translation is "I can actually see people, for they look to me like trees–only they walk!" (Cranfield). ◆ 25 ἐπέθηκεν aor. ind. act. ἐπιτίθημι (# 2202) s.v. 23. διέβλεψεν aor. ind. act. διαβλέπω (# 1332) to see clearly. Aor. indicates the definite point at which the man achieved clear sight (Cranfield). ἀπεκατέστη aor. ind. act. ἀποκαθίστημι (# 635) to restore to the original state. Galen uses the subst. for the recovery from sickness (DMTG). ἐνέβλεπεν impf. ind. act. ἐμβλέπω (# 1838) to turn and fix the eyes upon, to see. Implies the power to concentrate the attention on a particular object (Swete). Impf. indicates the continuing action. τηλαυγῶς (# 5495) adv., clearly from afar. The meaning is that the man sees everything clearly at a distance (Taylor). ◆ 26 ἀπέστειλεν aor. ind. act. ἀποστέλλω (# 690) to send away. εἰσέλθης aor. subj. act. εἰσέρχομαι (# 1656) to go in, to come in. Used w. a neg. as a prohibition. ◆ 27 ἐξῆλθεν aor. ind. act. s.v. 11. ἐπηρώτα impf. ind. act. s.v. 23. εἶναι pres. act. inf. εἰμί (# 1639) to be. Inf. used

in indir. discourse. ◆ 28 εἶπαν aor. ind. act. λέγω (# 3306) to speak. ◆ 29 αὐτός pers. pron. Emphatic ("He Himself") suggests that he stands apart from the views mentioned (Gundry, 427). ὑμεῖς nom. pl. pers. pron. σύ (# 5148). Emphatic, "you, in contrast to the others." ἀποκριθείς aor. pass. (dep.) part. s.v. 4. εἶ pres. ind. act. εἰμί (# 1639) to be. ◆ 30 ἐπετίμησεν aor. ind. act. ἐπιτιμάω (# 2203) to rebuke, to sternly warn. λέγωσιν pres. subj. act. λέγω (# 3306) to say. Subj. used in cl. as obj. of the vb. ◆ 31 ἤρξατο aor. ind. mid. (dep.) s.v. 11. δεῖ (# 1256) pres. ind. act. "It is necessary," denotes a logical necessity (AS); followed by inf. παθεῖν aor. act. inf. πάσχω (# 4248) to suffer. ἀποδοκιμασθῆναι aor. pass. inf. ἀποδοκιμάζω (# 627) to reject after testing. ἀποκτανθῆναι aor. pass. inf. ἀποκτείνω (# 650) to kill. ἀναστῆναι aor. act. inf. ἀνίστημι (# 482) to rise. ◆ 32 παρρησία (# 4244) freely speaking, frankness, boldness of speech; used adverbially, "plainly" (Taylor). ἐλάλει impf. ind. act. λαλέω (# 3281) to speak. προσλαβόμενος aor. mid. (dep. / indir. mid.) part. (circum.) προσλαμβάνω (# 4689) to take to oneself. ἤρξατο aor. ind. mid. (dep.) s.v. 11. ἐπιτιμᾶν pres. act. inf. s.v. 30. ◆ 33 ἐπιστραφείς aor. pass. (dep.) part. (temp.) ἐπιστρέφω (# 2188) to turn around, to turn to. The Lord turned around sharply, as if to face the speaker (Swete). ἰδών aor. act. part. ὁράω (# 3972) to see. ἐπετίμησεν aor. ind. act. s.v. 30. ὕπαγε pres. imp. act. ὑπάγω (# 5632) to go away. φρονεῖς pres. ind. act. φρονέω (# 5858) to be minded, to think about. The vb. keeps in view the direction which thought takes (Taylor). Here it could mean "to take someone's side" (Cranfield). ◆ 34 προσκαλεσάμενος aor. mid. part. (temp.) s.v. 1. εἶπεν aor. ind. act. λέγω (# 3306) to say. ἀκολουθεῖν aor. act. inf. ἀκολουθέω (# 199) to follow after, to follow as a disciple, w. obj. in dat. (EDNT; HSB, 427-28). ἀπαρνησάσθω aor. imp. mid. (dep.) 3rd. sing. ἀπαρνέομαι (# 656) to deny. The basic idea is to say "no." It is to disown oneself, to turn away from the idolatry of self-centeredness (Cranfield). ἀράτω aor. imp. act. 3rd. pers. sing. αἴρω (# 149) to take up. The idea is taking up the cross beam and subjecting oneself to the shame and insult associated w. a cross (BBC; Gundry, 436; C). ἀκολουθείτω pres. imp. act. 3rd. sing. ἀκολουθέω to follow as a disciple. ◆ 35 θέλη pres. subj. act. θέλω (# 2527) to wish, to will. Subj. in an indef. rel. cl. ψυχή (# 6034) life, soul. σῶσαι aor. act. inf. σῴζω (# 5392) to rescue, to save. ἀπολέσει fut. ind. act. ἀπόλλυμι (# 660) to lose, to destroy, to ruin. σώσει fut. ind. act. σῴζω to rescue, to save. ◆ 36 τί (# 5515) in what way, adv. use (Gundry, 436). ὠφελεῖ pres. ind. act. ὠφελέω (# 6067) to have benefit, to profit. κερδῆσαι aor. act. inf. κερδαίνω (# 3045) to gain, to make a profit. Inf. used as subst. and subject of the vb. ὠφελέω. κόσμος (# 3180) world. Here used of the prizes of business and social life (Taylor). ζημιωθῆναι aor. pass. inf. ζημιόω (# 2423) to confiscate or find, to inflict a penalty of any kind; pass., to suffer loss, to loose (Swete; MM). ◆ **37** δοῖ aor. subj. act. δίδωμι (# 1443) to give. ἀντάλλαγμα (# 498) price. The price received in exchange for an article of commerce (Swete; BAGD; for the LXX usage s. GELTS). ◆ **38** ἐπαισχυνθῇ aor. subj. pass. ἐπαισχύνομαι (# 2049) w. acc. to be ashamed. Subj. used in indef. rel. cl. ἐπαισχυνθήσεται fut. ind. pass. ἔλθῃ aor. subj. act. s.v. 10. Subj. w. ὅταν (# 4020) in an indef. temp. cl.

Mark 9

◆ **1** ἔλεγεν impf. ind. act. λέγω (# 3306) to say. ἑστηκότων perf. act. part. ἵστημι (# 2705) in the perf., to stand. Subst. part. γεύσωνται aor. subj. mid. (dep.) γεύομαι (# 1174) to taste, w. gen. ἴδωσιν aor. subj. act. ὁράω (# 3972) to see. Subj. w. ἕως ἄν (# 2401; 165) in an indef. temp. cl. ἐληλυθυῖαν perf. act. part. acc. fem. sing. ἔρχομαι (# 2262) to come. Perf. indicates "already established" (GI, 42). The Transfiguration points forward to and is a foretaste of the Resurrection and of the Second Coming (Cranfield; DJG, 834-41). ◆ **2** παραλαμβάνει pres. ind. act. παραλαμβάνω (# 4161) to take w., hist. pres. μετεμορφώθη aor. ind. pass. μεταμορφόω (# 3565) to transform, an inward change that is outwardly visible (Matt. 17:2; TDNT; EDNT; Lane). ἔμπροσθεν (# 1869) before. ◆ **3** ἐγένετο aor. ind. mid. (dep.) γίνομαι (# 1181) to become, to happen. στίλβοντα pres. act. part. στίλβω (# 5118) to gleam, to glitter. Used of polished or bright surfaces (Taylor). λευκός (# 3328) white. λίαν (# 3336) very. γναφεύς (# 3326) bleacher, fuller, one who cleans woolen cloth by the use of nitrium (Lane). λευκᾶναι aor. act. inf. λευκαίνω (# 3326) to make white. The white shining clothes point to a heavenly being (Gnilka; Pesch). ◆ **4** ὤφθη aor. ind. pass. ὁράω (# 3972) to see; pass. to appear. ἦσαν impf. ind. act. εἰμί (# 1639) to be. Used w. part. to form the periphrastic construction. συλλαλοῦντες pres. act. part. συλλαλέω (# 5196) to talk together. ◆ **5** ἀποκριθείς aor. pass. (dep.) part. ἀποκρίνομαι (# 646) to answer. Pleonastic part. in a Semitic constr. εἶναι pres. act. inf. εἰμί (# 1639) to be. "It is a good thing that we are here" (Cranfield). ποιήσωμεν aor. subj. act. ποιέω (# 4472) to do, to make; a hortatory subj. σκηνή (# 5008) tent, booth. Peter was probably thinking of the booths used to celebrate the Feast of Tabernacles (Swete; s. Lev. 23:40-43). ◆ **6** ᾔδει plperf. ind. act. οἶδα (# 3857) to know. Def. perf. w. pres. meaning. ἀποκριθῇ aor. subj. pass. (dep.) s.v. 5. Subj. used to express uncertainty. ἔκφοβος (# 1769) terrified. The prep. in compound is intensive. ἐγένοντο aor. ind. mid. (dep.) s.v. 3. ◆ **7** ἐπισκιάζουσα pres. act. part. nom. fem. sing. ἐπισκιάζω (# 2173) to overshadow. The cloud indicates God's Shekinah or presence and may have the idea of complete envelopment (Hooker; Gundry, 460). Adj. part. ἀγαπητός (# 28) beloved. It indicates the special position of the Son. ἀκούετε pres. imp. act.

ἀκούω (# 201) to listen to, to hear. Used w. gen., indicating obj. ◆ **8** ἐξάπινα (# 1988) adv. suddenly. περιβλεψάμενοι aor. mid. part. περιβλέπω (# 4315) to look around. Indir. mid. representing the subj. as doing something for, to, or by himself. "The disciples themselves suddenly looking round..." (RG, 809). εἶδον aor. ind. act. ὁράω (# 3972) to see. ◆ **9** καταβαινόντων pres. act. part. (temp.) καταβαίνω (# 2849) to go down; gen. abs. διεστείλατο aor. ind. mid. (dep.) διαστέλλω (# 1403) to command. διηγήσωνται aor. subj. mid. (dep.) διηγέομαι (# 1455) to relate, to narrate, to tell. Subj. in a cl. as obj. of the vb. ἀναστῇ aor. subj. act. ἀνίστημι (# 482) to rise up, to arise. Subj. in an indef. temp. cl. ◆ **10** ἐκράτησαν aor. ind. act. κρατέω (# 3195) to grasp, to hold fast, to retain in their memory (Swete). συζητοῦντες pres. act. part. (circum.) συζητέω (# 5184) to seek together, to question, to dispute. ἀναστῆναι aor. act. inf. s.v. 9. Inf. used as subst. ◆ **11** ἐπηρώτων impf. ind. act. ἐπερωτάω (# 2089) to ask, to question, to inquire about. δεῖ (# 1256) pres. ind. act. δέω "It is necessary", w. inf. (s. Mark 8:31). ἐλθεῖν aor. act. inf. ἔρχομαι s.v. 1. For a discussion and lit. regarding Elijah's return s. Gundry, 483-85; W.C. Kaiser, "The Promise of the Arrival of Elijah in Malachi and the Gospels," *Grace Theological Journal* 3 (1982): 221-33; EDNT, 2:285-90, 1362. ◆ **12** ἔφη impf. ind. act. φημί (# 5774) to say, to speak. ἐλθών aor. act. part. (circum.) s.v. 1. ἀποκαθιστάνει pres. ind. act. ἀποκαθίστημι (# 635) to restore to the original cond. (TDNT). Futuristic pres. μέν ... καὶ πῶς "but how then?" For the adversative use of καί here s. SS, 112-13. γέγραπται perf. ind. pass. γράφω (# 1211) to write, perf., "it stands written," used of authoritative documents (MM). πάθη aor. subj. act. πάσχω (# 4248) to suffer. ἐξουδενηθῇ aor. pass. subj. ἐξουδενέω (# 2022) to consider as nothing, to despise. ◆ **13** καί (# 2779) also. ἐλήλυθεν perf. ind. act. ἔρχομαι (# 2262) to come. ἐποίησαν aor. ind. act. ποιέω (# 4472) to do. ἤθελον impf. ind. act. θέλω (# 2527) to wish, to want, to will. For a discussion of this passage and some of the exegetical problems s. Joel Marcus, "Mark 9,11-13: 'As It Has Been Written,'" *ZNW* 80 (1989): 42-63; Gundry, 483-86. ◆ **14** ἐλθόντες aor. act. part. (temp.) s.v. 1. εἶδον aor. ind. act. s.v. 8. συζητοῦντας pres. act. part. s.v. 10. ◆ **15** ἰδόντες aor. act. part. (temp.) ὁράω (# 3972) to see. ἐξεθαμβήθησαν aor. ind. pass. (dep.) ἐκθαυβέομαι (# 1701) to be amazed, to be extremely amazed. The prep. in the vb. is perfective (RWP). προστρέχοντες pres. act. part. (circum.) προστρέχω (# 4708) to run to someone. ἠσπάζοντο impf. ind. mid. (dep.) ἀσπάζομαι (# 832) to greet. ◆ **16** ἐπηρώτησεν aor. ind. act. s.v. 11. συζητεῖτε pres. ind. act. s.v. 10. Pres. pictures the continual action. ◆ **17** ἀπεκρίθη aor. ind. pass. (dep.) s.v. 5. ἤνεγκα aor. ind. act. φέρω (# 5770) to carry, to bring. ἔχοντα pres. act. part. ἔχω (# 2400) to have. Adj. part. ἄλαλος (# 228) dumb, not able to speak. ◆ **18** καταλάβῃ aor. subj. act. καταλαμβάνω (# 2898) to take hold of, to seize. Nouns related to this vb. were used as medical terms in reference to seizures and persons subjected to them (Swete; DMTG, 195). Subj. w. **ὅπου ἐάν** (# *3963; 1569*) used in an indef. temp. cl. Aor. is const., summing up the various acts of seizure. **ῥήσσει** pres. ind. act. ῥήσσω/ῥήγνυμι (# *4838*). The meaning of the vb. is either "to tear," "to rend," or "to strike or dash down" (Taylor). The related subst., ῥῆγμα ("breakage," "fracture"), was often used by Galen in connection w. σπάσμα ("convulsion," "spasm") (DMTG, 283). Iterat. pres. depicting the repeated action. "He is continually foaming." **ἀφρίζει** pres. ind. act. ἀφρίζω (# *930*) to foam. Iterat. pres. **τρίζει** pres. ind. act. τρίζω (# *5563*) to grind. Used of any sharp or grinding sound (Swete). Galen used the word of involuntary gnashing (DMTG, 313). **ξηραίνεται** pres. ind. pass. ξηραίνω (# *3830*) to dry out, to wither. It pictures complete exhaustion (Taylor). **εἶπα** aor. ind. act. 1st pers. sing. λέγω (# *3306*) to say. **ἐκβάλωσιν** aor. subj. act. ἐκβάλλω (# *1675*) to throw out, to cast out, to drive out. Subj. used in a cl. as obj. of the vb. **ἴσχυσαν** aor. ind. act. ἰσχύω (# *2710*) to be strong, to be able. ◆ **19 ἀποκριθείς** aor. pass. (dep.) part. s.v. 5. Pleonastic use of the part. **ἔσομαι** fut. ind. mid. (dep.) εἰμί (# *1639*). **ἀνέξομαι** fut. ind. mid. (dep.) ἀνέχομαι (# *462*) to endure, to put up w. Obj. in gen. (RG, 508). ◆ **20 ἤνεγκαν** aor. ind. act. φέρω (# *5770*) to carry, to bring. **ἰδών** aor. act. part. (temp.) ὁράω (# *3972*) to see. **συνεσπάραξεν** aor. ind. act. συσπαράσσω (# *5360*) to tear to pieces, to pull about, to convulse. **πεσών** aor. act. part. (circum.) πίπτω (# *4406*) to fall. **ἐκυλίετο** impf. ind. pass. κυλίω (# *3244*) to roll, to roll oneself (BAGD). Iterat. impf. pictures the repeated action in the past. **ἀφρίζων** pres. act. part. (circum.) s.v. 18. ◆ **21 ἐπηρώτησεν** aor. ind. act. s.v. 11. **γέγονεν** perf. ind. act. s.v. 3. Perf. emphasizes the state or cond. **παιδιόθεν** (# *4085*) from childhood. For the use of the adv. w. the strengthening prep. s. MH, 164. ◆ **22 ἔβαλεν** aor. ind. act. βάλλω (# *965*) to throw. Const. aor. summarizing the action that had taken place often (**πολλάκις**). **ἀπολέσῃ** aor. subj. act. ἀπόλλυμι (# *660*) to destroy. Subj. in a purp. cl. **δύνῃ** pres. subj. pass. (dep.) 2nd. pers. sing. δύναμαι (# *1538*) to be able. Used in a first class cond. cl. where the cond. is judged to be true (RWP; for the form s. MH, 206; GGP, 2:384). **βοήθησον** aor. imp. act. βοηθέω (# *1070*) to assist in supplying what may be needed, to help (LN, 1:485). Aor. calls for specific help, w. a note of urgency (Bakker, 83). **σπλαγχνισθείς** aor. pass. (dep.) part. (circum.) σπλαγχνίζομαι (# *5072*) to be inwardly moved, to have compassion. ◆ **23 εἶπεν** aor. ind. act. λέγω (# *3306*). **τὸ εἰ δύνῃ** The article has the effect of making this cl. into a noun: "as to your 'if you can'!" (Cranfield; Taylor; RG, 766). **πιστεύοντι** pres. act. part. dat. sing. πιστεύω (# *4409*) to believe, to trust. Part. used as subst. Dat. of advantage. ◆ **24 κράξας** aor. act. part. κράζω (# *3189*) to scream, to cry out. **ἔλεγεν** impf. ind. act. λέγω (# *3306*)

s.v. 1. **βοήθει** pres. imp. act. s.v. 22. Pres. imp. may call for continual help in relation to his unbelief (VA., 350). ◆ **25 ἐπισυντρέχει** pres. ind. act. ἐπισυντρέχω (# *2192*) to run together. The prep. compound is directive. The word describes a crowd converging on a single point, perhaps from several directions (Taylor). **ἐπετίμησεν** aor. ind. act. ἐπιτιμάω (# *2203*) to command, to rebuke, to charge (Matt 17:18). **ἔξελθε** aor. imp. act. ἐξέρχομαι (# *2002*) to come out. Aor. imp. calls for an immediate and specific action. **εἰσέλθῃς** aor. subj. act. εἰσέρχομαι (# *1656*) to go into. Subj. used w. the neg. **μηκέτι** (# *3600*) to form a prohibition: "don't ever go in again!" ◆ **26 κράξας** aor. act. part. s.v. 24. **σπαράξας** aor. act. part. (circum.) σπαράσσω (# *5057*) to tear, to pull to and fro, to convulse (BAGD; s. 1:26). **ἐξῆλθεν** aor. ind. act. s.v. 25. **ἐγένετο** aor. ind. mid. (dep.) s.v. 3. **ὥστε** (# *6063*) used w. inf. to express actual results. **ἀπέθανεν** aor. ind. act. ἀποθνήσκω (# *633*) to die. ◆ **27 κρατήσας** aor. act. part. (circum.) s.v. 10; w. gen. to seize, to take hold of. **ἤγειρεν** aor. ind. act. ἐγείρω (# *1586*) to raise. **ἀνέστη** aor. ind. act. ἀνίστημι (# *482*) to stand up. ◆ **28 εἰσελθόντος** aor. act. part. (temp.) s. v. 25. Gen. abs. **ἐπηρώτων** impf. ind. act. s.v. 11. Inceptive impf. **ἠδυνήθημεν** aor. ind. pass. (dep.) δύναμαι (# *1538*) to be able, w. inf. **ἐκβαλεῖν** aor. act. inf. s.v. 18. ◆ **29 εἶπεν** aor. ind. act. λέγω (# *3306*) s.v. 1. **ἐξελθεῖν** aor. act. inf. s.v. 25. ◆ **30 ἐξελθόντες** aor. act. part. (temp.) s.v. 25. **παρεπορεύοντο** impf. ind. mid. (dep.) παραπορεύομαι (# *4182*) to travel, to travel along. **διά** w. gen., through. **ἤθελεν** impf. ind. act. s.v. 13. **γνοῖ** aor. subj. act. γινώσκω (# *1182*) to know. Subj. used in a noun cl. which is the obj. of the vb. ◆ **31 ἐδίδασκεν** impf. ind. act. διδάσκω (# *1438*) to teach. **γάρ** (# *1142*) for. It gives the explanation of the preceding. **παραδίδοται** pres. ind. pass. παραδίδωμι (# *4140*) to deliver over (Cranfield; TLNT). Futuristic pres. It startles and arrests attention. It affirms and gives a sense of certainty (RG, 870). Pass. is perhaps the theol. pass. (but s. Gundry, 506-7). **ἀποκτενοῦσιν** fut. ind. act. ἀποκτείνω (# *650*) to kill. Futuristic pres. **ἀποκτανθείς** aor. pass. part. (circum.) **μετά** (# *3552*) w. acc., after. **ἀναστήσεται** fut. ind. mid. s.v. 9. ◆ **32 ἠγνόουν** impf. ind. act. ἀγνοέω (# *51*) not to understand, not to know, to be ignorant. They did not expect the Messiah to suffer, but to conquer. **ἐφοβοῦντο** impf. ind. mid. (dep.) φοβέομαι (# *5828*) to fear, to be afraid. **ἐπερωτῆσαι** aor. act. inf. s.v. 11. Epex. inf. explaining the fear. ◆ **33 ἦλθον** aor. ind. act. s.v. 1. **γενόμενος** aor. mid. (dep.) part. s.v. 3. Temp. part. **ἐπηρώτα** impf. ind. act. s.v. 11. **διελογίζεσθε** impf. ind. mid. (dep.) διαλογίζομαι (# *1368*) to discuss, to dispute, to engage in some relatively detailed discussion (LN, 1:407, 351). ◆ **34 ἐσιώπων** impf. ind. act. σιωπάω (# *4995*) to be silent. **διελέχθησαν** aor. ind. pass. (dep.) διαλέγομαι (# *1363*) to contend, to dispute, to discuss, to conduct a discussion. The prep. in the compound recalls the two parties in a conversation (MH, 302). **μείζων**

(*# 3505*) comp. μέγας great. Comp. used here to express the superl. (BD, 32). ◆ **35 καθίσας** aor. act. part. (temp.) καθίζω (*# 2767*) to take a seat, to sit down. **ἐφώνησεν** aor. ind. act. φωνέω (*# 5888*) to call. The certain degree of loudness w. this vb. shows the vigor w. which Jesus exercises authority over the disciples (Gundry, 509). **εἶναι** pres. act. inf. s.v. 5. **ἔσται** fut. ind. mid. (dep.) s.v. 5. ◆ **36 λαβών** aor. act. part. (temp.) λαμβάνω (*# 3284*) to take. **ἔστησεν** aor. ind. act. ἵστημι (*# 2705*) to place. **ἐναγκαλισάμενος** aor. mid. (dep.) part. ἐναγκαλίζομαι (*# 1878*) to take in one's arms, to embrace. **εἶπεν** aor. ind. act. λέγω s.v. 18. ◆ **37 τοιοῦτος** (*# 5525*) of such a character, character, such a one. **δέξηται** aor. subj. mid. (dep.) δέχομαι (*# 1312*) to receive, to welcome. Subj. w. **ἄν** (*# 323*) used in an indef. rel. cl. **δέχηται** pres. subj. mid. (dep.) δέχομαι. Pres. subj. stresses the greater importance of receiving Jesus (VA, 326). **ἐπί** (*# 2093*) w. dat., because of, on the ground of (Taylor). **ἀποστείλαντα** aor. act. part. ἀποστέλλω (*# 690*) to send, to commission w. a special assignment and w. the authority of the one sending (TDNT; EDNT). Adj. part. ◆ **38 ἔφη** impf. ind. act. s.v. 12. **εἴδομεν** aor. ind. act. s.v. 8. **ἐκβάλλοντα** pres. act. part. s.v. 18. Part. as subst. **ἐκωλύομεν** impf. ind. act. κωλύω (*# 3266*) to prevent, to hinder. Impf. is conative: "we sought to stop him" (Taylor; M, 129). **ὅτι** (*# 4022*) because. **ἠκολούθει** impf. ind. act. ἀκολουθέω (*# 199*) to follow, to follow as a disciple. ◆ **39 κωλύετε** pres. imp. act. κωλύω (*# 3266*) Pres. imp. used w. neg. **μή** (*# 3590*) to stop an action in progress (MKG, 272). **ποιήσει** fut. ind. act. ποιέω (*# 4472*) to do, to perform. **δυνήσεται** fut. ind. mid. (dep.) δύναμαι (*# 1538*) to be able. **κακολογῆσαι** aor. act. inf. κακολογέω (*# 2800*) to speak evil of. ◆ **40 καθ'** = κατά (*# 2848*) w. gen., against. **ὑπέρ** (*# 5642*) w. gen., for. ◆ **41 ποτίσῃ** aor. subj. act. ποτίζω (*# 4540*) to give to drink. Subj. w. **ἄν** (*# 323*) used in an indef. rel. cl. **ἀπολέσῃ** aor. subj. act. s.v. 22. ◆ **42 σκανδαλίσῃ** aor. subj. act. σκανδαλίζω (*# 4997*) to cause to stumble, to cause someone to stumble in his faith (Cranfield). Subj. w. **ἄν** (*# 323*) used in an indef. rel. cl. **πιστευόντων** pres. act. part. πιστεύω (*# 4409*) to believe, to trust. Part. as subst. **περίκειται** pres. ind. mid. (dep.) περίκειμαι (*# 4329*) to place about, to place around. The picture is evidently that of placing the person's head through the hole, so that he is wearing the millstone as a collar (Gundry, 512). **μύλος ὀνικός** (*# 3685; 3948*) the upper millstone. The millstone turned by a donkey, in contrast w. the handmill served by a woman (Taylor; ABD, 4:831-32). **τράχηλος** (*# 5549*) throat, neck. **βέβληται** perf. ind. pass. βάλλω s.v. 22. Perf. emphasizes the state or cond. Perhaps the intent was to prevent the person from being buried, which would have been a disgrace J. Duncan M. Derrett, "ΜΥΛΟΣ ΟΝΙΚΟΣ (Mk 9:42)," *ZNW* 76 (1985): 284. ◆ **43 σκανδαλίζῃ** pres. subj. act. s.v. 42. Subj. used in a 3rd. class cond. cl. which assumes the possibility of the

cond. **ἀπόκοψον** aor. imp. act. ἀποκόπτω (*# 644*) to cut off. Aor. imp. calls for a specific act. **κυλλός** (*# 3245*) crooked, cripple, deformed, also club-footed (LS; s. DMTG, 214). **εἰσελθεῖν** aor. act. inf. s.v. 25. Epex. inf. explaining καλόν (positive of the adj. used w. ἤ (*# 2445*) to form the comparative). **ἔχοντα** pres. act. part. ἔχω (*# 2400*) to have. **ἀπελθεῖν** aor. act. inf. ἀπέρχομαι (*# 599*) to go away. **γέεννα** (*# 1147*) Gehenna, hell (TDNT; Hans Scharen, "Gehenna in the Gospels," *Bib. Sac.* 149 [1992]: 324-37; 454-70; Chaim Milikowsky, "Which Gehenna? Retribution and Eschatology in the Synoptic Gospels and in Early Jewish Texts," *NTS* 34 [1988]: 238-49; ABD, 2:926-28; DJG, 310-12). **ἄσβεστος** (*# 812*) unquenchable. ◆ **45 βληθῆναι** aor. pass. inf. βάλλω s.v. 22. ◆ **47 ἔκβαλε** aor. imp. act. ἐκβάλλω (*# 1675*). **μονόφθαλμος** (*# 3669*) one-eyed. ◆ **48 σκώληξ** (*# 5038*) worm. Used to emphasize the unending destruction and decay of the pers. (TDNT). The maggots that constantly feed on the garbage in the Valley of Hinnom and the fires that constantly burn there stand for the eternal torment of sinners (Gundry, 514). **τελευτᾷ** pres. ind. act. τελευτάω (*# 5462*) to come to an end, to die. **σβέννυται** pres. ind. pass. σβέννυμι (*# 4931*) to extinguish, to put out. ◆ **49 ἁλισθήσεται** fut. ind. pass. ἁλίζω (*# 245*) to salt. For a discussion of the meaning s. Gundry, 526-28. ◆ **50 ἅλας** (*# 229*) salt, salt grain. **ἄναλος** (*# 383*) not salty. **γένηται** aor. subj. mid. (dep.) s.v. 3. Subj. w. **ἐάν** (*# 1569*) in a 3rd. class cond. cl. which assumes the possibility of the cond. **ἀρτύσετε** fut. ind. act. ἀρτύω (*# 789*) to prepare, specifically to season. **ἔχετε** pres. imp./ind. act. ἔχω (*# 2400*) to have. **εἰρηνεύετε** pres. imp./ind. act. εἰρηνεύω (*# 1644*) to be peaceable, to keep peace. For a discussion of the passage and of salt, s. Michael Lattke, "Salz der Freundschaft in Mk 9:50c," *ZNW* 75 (1984): 44-59; HSB, 430-31.

Mark 10

◆ **1 ἀναστάς** aor. act. part. ἀνίστημι (*# 482*) to arise, to indicate the beginning of an action (usually motion) expressed by another vb., to set out, to get ready (BAGD). For a discussion of the chapter and its ethics s. Dan O. Via, *The Ethics of Mark's Gospel in the Middle of Time* (Philadelphia: Fortress Press, 1985). **συμπορεύονται** pres. ind. mid. (dep.) συμπορεύομαι (*# 5233*) to accompany, to travel w. someone. **εἰώθει** plperf. ind. act. of the perf. form εἴωθα (*# 1665*) to be accustomed to. The form is used here as an impf. (RWP). **ἐδίδασκεν** impf. ind. act. διδάσκω (*# 1438*) to teach. There is absolutely no reason for rejecting that Jesus spoke here in Greek (J.N. Sevenster, *Do You Know Greek?*, 190; JL, 382-92, 510-12; VA, 111-56). ◆ **2 προσελθόντες** aor. act. part. (temp.) προσέρχομαι (*# 4665*) to come to. Aor. indicating the logically necessary action before that of the main vb. **ἐπηρώτων** impf. ind. act. ἐπερωτάω (*# 2089*) to ask, to question. **ἔξεστιν** (*# 2003*) pres. ind. it is allowed, it is lawful. **ἀπολῦσαι** aor. act. inf. ἀπολύω (# 668) to release, to divorce, to divorce by means of a bill of divorcement (EDNT; RAC, 6:707-19; TRE, 9:318-25). Inf. explains what is lawful. For a discussion s. HSB, 431-35. **πειράζοντες** pres. act. part. πειράζω (# 4279) to tempt, to try, here in a neg. sense. Part. indicating purp. ◆ **3 ἀποκριθείς** aor. pass. (dep.) part. ἀποκρίνομαι (# 646) to answer. Semitic use of the pleonastic part. (MH, 453). **εἶπεν** aor. ind. act. λέγω (# 3306). **ἐνετείλατο** aor. ind. mid. (dep.) ἐντέλλομαι (# 1948) to command. ◆ **4 ἐπέτρεψεν** aor. ind. act. ἐπιτρέπω (# 2205) to allow. It was permission, not a command. **βιβλίον ἀποστασίου** (# 1046; 687) bill of divorcement (Matt. 5:31; AT, 307-8; M, Gittin). **γράψαι** aor. act. inf. γράφω (# 1211) to write. Inf. is epex. to the vb. ἐπιτρέπω. **ἀπολῦσαι** aor. act. inf. s.v. 2. Epex. inf. ◆ **5 πρός** w. acc., in accordance w., in view of (BD, 124). **σκληροκαρδία** (# 5016) hardness of heart, stubborn insensitivity (LN, 1:766; Klaus Berger, "Hartherzigkeit und Gottes Gesetz, die Vorgeschichte des antijüdischen Vorwurfs in Mc 10:5," ZNW 61 [1970]: 1-47). **ἔγραψεν** aor. ind. act. s.v. 4. ◆ **6 ἄρσεν** acc. sing. ἄρσην (# 781) male. **θῆλυς** (# 2559) female. **ἐποίησεν** aor. ind. act. ποιέω (# 4472) to make. ◆ **7 ἕνεκεν** (# 1915) w. gen., because of. **καταλείψει** fut. ind. act. καταλείπω (# 2901) to leave. **προσκολληθήσεται** fut. ind. pass. προσκολλάω (# 4681) to glue on; pass. to be stuck to, to stick or cleave to; fig. to adhere closely to, to be faithfully devoted to, to be joined to (LS; BAGD; MM). For the textual problem s. TC, 104-5. ◆ **8 ἔσονται** fut. ind. mid. (dep.) 3rd. pl. εἰμί (# 1639) to be. ◆ **9 συν-έζευξεν** aor. ind. act. συζεύγνυμι (# 5183) to yoke together, to join together, used of marriage (BAGD; Preisigke, 2:539; MM; NTRJ, 368-69). **χωριζέτω** pres. imp. act. χωρίζω (# 6004) to separate, to divide. ◆ **10 ἐπηρώτων** impf. ind. act. s.v. 2. ◆ **11 ἀπολύση** aor. subj. act. s.v. 2. Subj. w. ἄν (# 323) in an indef. rel. cl. **γαμήση** aor. subj. act. γαμέω (# 1138) to marry. **μοιχᾶται** pres. ind. pass. μοιχάω (# 3656) to commit adultery; pass. to cause to commit adultery (BAGD). ◆ **12 ἀπολύσασα** aor. act. part. nom. fem. sing. s.v. 2. For Jesus' teaching on marriage and divorce and the woman divorcing the man s. NTRJ, 362-72; LNT, 363-88; Ernst Bammel, "Markus 10:11f. und das jüdische Eherecht," ZNW 61 (1970): 93-101; Gundry, 543; SB 2:23; JAD. ◆ **13 προσέφερον** impf. ind. act. προσφέρω (# 4712) to bring to, to carry to. **ἅψηται** aor. subj. mid. (dep.) ἅπτομαι (# 721) w. gen. to touch. Subj. used w. ἵνα (# 2671) to express purp. The purpose of the touching is to obtain a blessing (Taylor; SB, 1:807). **ἐπετίμησαν** aor. ind. act. ἐπιτιμάω (# 2203) to rebuke. ◆ **14 ἰδών** aor. act. part. (temp.) ὁράω (# 3972) to see. **ἠγανάκτησεν** aor. ind. act. ἀγανακτέω (# 24) to be vexed, to be indignant. Ingressive aor., "to become indignant" (Gould). **ἄφετε** aor. imp. act. ἀφίημι (# 918) to allow, w. inf. **κωλύετε** pres. imp. act. κωλύω (# 3266) to hinder. Neg. pres. imp. call-

ing for the stopping of an action in progress. **τοιούτων** gen. pl. τοιοῦτος (# 5525) of such a kind, of such a character. Poss. gen. (Gundry, 544). ◆ **15 δέξηται** aor. subj. mid. (dep.) δέχομαι (# 1312) to receive, to welcome. The idea is to submit to God's rule. Subj. w. ἄν (# 323) in an indef. rel. cl. **εἰσέλθη** aor. subj. act. εἰσέρχομαι (# 1656) to come in, to enter into. ◆ **16 ἐναγκαλισάμενος** aor. mid. (dep.) part. (circum.) ἐναγκαλίζομαι (# 1878) to embrace, to take in one's arms. **κατευλόγει** impf. ind. act. κατευλογέω (# 2986) to wish one well, to bless. The force of the prep. in the compound is intensive. He blessed them fervently, in no perfunctory way, but w. emphasis (Swete). Iterat. impf. pictures the repeated action. **τιθείς** aor. act. part. τίθημι (# 5502) to place. Part. of manner. ◆ **17 ἐκπορευομένου** pres. mid. (dep.) part. (temp.) ἐκπορεύομαι (# 1744) (# 4708) to go out, to go out on a journey. **προσδραμών** aor. act. part. (temp.) προστρέχω to run to. **γονυπετήσας** aor. act. part. (circum.) γονυπετέω (# 1206) to fall to one's knees. Falling on the knees is an expression of homage and petition toward human beings and God (EDNT). **ἐπηρώτα** impf. ind. act. s.v. 2. **ποιήσω** fut. ind. act. or aor. subj. act. s.v. 6. **κληρονομήσω** fut. ind. act. or aor. subj. act. κληρονομέω (# 3099) to inherit. Inheriting eternal life was a fixed expression in Judaism (Lane; Pesch; Ps. of Sol. 14:10). ◆ **18 εἶπεν** aor. ind. act. λέγω (# 3306) to say, to speak. **ἀγαθός** (# 19) intrinsically good, good. In reference to God, "perfect" (NIDNTT; TDNT; EDNT). ◆ **19 οἶδας** perf. ind. act. 2nd. pers. sing. οἶδα (# 3857) to know. Def. perf. w. a pres. meaning. **φονεύσης** aor. subj. act. φονεύω (# 5839) to kill, to murder. Aor. subj. forms in prohibitions forbid the whole act ever being done: "never do..." (VANT, 337). **μοιχεύσης** aor. subj. act. μοιχεύω (# 3658) to commit adultery. **κλέψης** aor. subj. act. κλέπτω (# 3096) to steal. **ψευδομαρτυρήσης** aor. subj. act. ψευδομαρτυρέω (# 6018) to bear false witness, to give false testimony (BAGD). **ἀποστερήσης** aor. subj. act. ἀποστερέω (# 691) to rob, to deprive, to defraud of. Used of keeping back wages from one hired, and in classical Gr. of refusing to return goods or money deposited w. another for safe keeping (Taylor). **τίμα** pres. imp. act. τιμάω (# 5506) to honor. Pres. imp. stands in contrast to the previous aor. subj. forms and calls for a continual action. Perhaps this emphasis in due to the youth of the person (s. Gundry, 553). ◆ **20 ἔφη** impf./aor. ind. act. φημί (# 5774) to say. For a discussion of the vb. form, either aor. or impf. s. VA, 443-46. **ἐφυλαξάμην** aor. ind. mid. φυλάσσω (# 5875) to guard, to keep (on mid. as possible influence from the LXX s. BAGD). Aor. is intended to sum up his accomplishments. **νεότητος** gen. sing. νεότης (# 3744) youth. It has reference to a boy's twelfth year when he assumed the yoke of the commandments and was held responsible for their performance (Lane). ◆ **21 ἐμβλέψας** aor. act. part. (circum.) ἐμβλέπω (# 1838) to look at. **ἠγάπησεν** aor. ind. act.

ἀγαπάω (# 26) to love, to have love for someone, based on sincere appreciation and high regard (LN, 1:293-94; EDNT; TDNT). **σε** acc. sing. σύ (# 5148) you. Acc. of general reference: "so far as you are concerned" (Gundry, 554). **ὑστερεῖ** pres. ind. act. ὑστερέω (# 5728) to come short of, to fail, to be lacking (Taylor; Rom. 3:23). **ὕπαγε** pres. imp. act. ὑπάγω (# 5632) to go. **πώλησον** aor. imp. act. πωλέω (# 4797) to sell, to offer for sale (LS). **δός** aor. imp. act. δίδωμι (# 1443) to give. Aor. imp. calls for a specific act. **ἕξεις** fut. ind. act. ἔχω (# 2400) to have. Imp. w. the fut. form a Semitic cond. cl. (Beyer, 238-55; SS, 120-21). **δεῦρο** (# 1306) Come! **ἀκολούθει** pres. imp. act. ἀκολουθέω to follow, (# 199) to follow as a disciple. Pres. imp. indicates the continual following as a disciple. ◆ **22 στυγνάσας** aor. act. part. (circum.) στυγνάζω (# 5145) to be sad, to become sad. Used of the saddening of the face of nature or the human face. Used of a dark stormy night or the somber, gloomy man who broods over unwelcome thoughts (Swete). **ἀπῆλθεν** aor. ind. act. ἀπέρχομαι (# 599) to go away. **λυπούμενος** pres. mid. (dep.) part. λυπέομαι (# 3382) to be sad, to be sorry. Circum. / causal part. **ἦν** impf. ind. act. εἰμί (# 1639) to be. **ἔχων** pres. act. part. ἔχω (# 2400) to have. Part. in a periphrastic construction. ◆ **23 περιβλεψάμενος** aor. mid. part. (circum.) περιβλέπω (# 4315) to look around. **δυσκόλως** (# 1552) w. difficulty. **χρήματα** acc. pl. χρῆμα (# 5975) a thing one uses; pl. wealth, riches, money gotten by selling (Taylor; Gundry, 564). **εἰσελεύσονται** fut. ind. mid. (dep.) εἰσέρχομαι (# 1656) to go in. ◆ **24 ἐθαμβοῦντο** impf. ind. pass. θαμβέω (# 2501) to scare, to terrify; pass. to be amazed. **ἀποκριθείς** aor. pass. (dep.) part. s.v. 3. **εἰσελθεῖν** aor. act. inf. s.v. 23. Epex. inf. explaining what is difficult. ◆ **25 εὐκοπώτερος** comp. εὔκοπος (# 2324) easy, without trouble. **τρυμαλιά** (# 5584) hole, perforation, opening. **ῥαφίδος** gen. sing. ῥαφίς (# 4827) needle. **διελθεῖν** aor. act. inf. διέρχομαι (# 1451) to go through. Epex. inf. explaining what is easy. ◆ **26 ἐξεπλήσσοντο** impf. ind. mid. / pass. ἐκπλήσσω (# 1742) pass. to be amazed, to be overwhelmed. **σωθῆναι** aor. pass. inf. σώζω (# 5392) to rescue, to save. ◆ **27 ἐμβλέψας** aor. act. part. s.v. 21. **ἀδύνατος** (# 105) impossible. ◆ **28 ἤρξατο** aor. ind. mid. (dep.) ἄρχομαι (# 806) to begin, w. inf. **ἀφήκαμεν** aor. ind. act. ἀφίημι (# 918) to leave. **ἠκολουθήκαμεν** perf. ind. act. ἀκολουθέω (# 199) to follow, to follow as a disciple, w. dat. Perf. indicates "we have left all and are following you." ◆ **29 ἔφη** impf. ind. act. s.v. 20. **ἀφῆκεν** aor. ind. act. s.v. 28. **ἕνεκεν** (# 1915) because of, on account of. ◆ **30 ἐὰν μή** (# 1569; 3590) if he does not, more freely, without (Taylor). **λάβῃ** aor. subj. act. λαμβάνω (# 3284) to take, to receive. Subj. in a cond. cl. (VA, 308; Beyer, 119-20). **ἑκατονταπλασίονα** (# 1671) a hundred times as much, or as many; one hundredfold. **διωγμός** (# 1501) persecution. **ἐρχομένῳ** pres. mid. part. ἔρχομαι (# 2262) to come. ◆ **31 ἔσονται** fut. ind. mid. (dep.) εἰμί (# 1639) to be. ◆ **32 ἦσαν** impf. ind. act. εἰμί to be. Used w. part. in a periphrastic constr. **ἀναβαίνοντες** pres. act. part. ἀναβαίνω (# 326) to go up. **ἦν** impf. ind. act. s.v. 22. **προάγων** pres. act. part. προάγω (# 4575) to go before, to precede, to lead forward. Part. in a periphrastic construction. **ἐθαμβοῦντο** impf. ind. pass. s.v. 24. **ἀκολουθοῦντες** pres. act. part. s.v. 21. Part. used as subst. (Gundry, 570). **ἐφοβοῦντο** impf. ind. mid. (dep.) φοβέομαι (# 5828) to fear, to be afraid. **παραλαβών** aor. act. part. (circum.) παραλαμβάνω (# 4161) to take w., to take along. **ἤρξατο** aor. ind. mid. (dep.) s.v. 28. **μέλλοντα** pres. act. part. μέλλω (# 3516) to be about to. Part. used w. the pres. inf. to express a fut. w. a durative value: "the things which will be happening" (MKG, 307). **συμβαίνειν** pres. act. inf. συμβαίνω, (# 5201) to happen, to come about. Used w. dat., "to happen to." ◆ **33 παραδοθήσεται** fut. ind. pass. παραδίδωμι (# 4140) to deliver over (s. Mark 9:31). **κατακρινοῦσιν** fut. ind. act. κατακρίνω (# 2891) to condemn, to make a decision against someone. ◆ **34 ἐμπαίξουσιν** fut. ind. act. ἐμπαίζω (# 1850) to mock, to play his game w. someone (TDNT; EDNT; Luke 22:63). **ἐμπτύσουσιν** fut. ind. act. ἐμπτύω (# 1870) to spit on. **μαστιγώσουσιν** fut. ind. act. μαστιγόω (# 3463) to beat w. a whip, to scourge. **ἀποκτενοῦσιν** fut. ind. act. ἀποκτείνω (# 650) to kill. **ἀναστήσεται** fut. ind. mid. ἀνίστημι (# 482) to rise, to rise up. ◆ **35 προσπορεύονται** pres. ind. mid. (dep.) προσπορεύομαι (# 4702) to come to. Hist. pres. **αἰτήσωμεν** aor. subj. act. αἰτέω (# 160) to ask, to request. For a discussion to the parallel passage in Matt. 20:22 s. HSB, 440-41. Subj. w. **ἐάν** (# 1569) in an indef. rel. cl. **ποιήσῃς** aor. subj. act. s.v. 6. Subj. w. **ἵνα** (# 2671) in a cl. as obj. of vb. ◆ **36 ποιήσω** aor. subj. act. s.v. 6. Deliberative subj. "What shall I do...?" ◆ **37 δός** aor. imp. act. s.v. 21. Aor. imp. calls for a specific action w. a note of urgency. **καθίσωμεν** aor. subj. act. καθίζω (# 2767) to sit, to take one's seat. Subj. in cl. as obj. of vb. ◆ **38 οἴδατε** perf. ind. act. s.v. 19. **αἰτεῖσθε** pres. ind. mid. αἰτέω (# 160) to ask, to request. Mid. somewhat stronger than the act. "to ask for oneself" (M, 160; TDNT). **πιεῖν** aor. act. inf. πίνω (# 4403) to drink. **ποτήριον** (# 4539) acc. sing. cup. The cup belongs to the royal banquet at which the king sits beside his most honored guests. It also is associated w. the allotted share of joy or suffering which is the portion of men and of nations in the course of their life (Swete). **βαπτισθῆναι** aor. pass. inf. βαπτίζω (# 966) to dip, to baptize, to immerse. Here it means to be overwhelmed by some difficult experience or ordeal (LN, 1:286). His death and sufferings are compared to a raging flood of sorrow (EDNT). ◆ **39 πίεσθε** fut. ind. mid. (dep.) s.v. 38. **βαπτισθήσεσθε** fut. ind. pass. s.v. 38. ◆ **40 καθίσαι** aor. act. inf. s.v. 37. Inf. used as subst. **δοῦναι** aor. act. inf. δίδωμι (# 1443) s.v. 21. Inf. as subst. **ἡτοίμασται** perf. ind. pass. ἑτοιμάζω (# 2286) to make ready, to prepare. Perf. indicates it has been prepared and stands ready. ◆ **41 ἀκούσαντες** aor. act. part. (temp.) ἀκούω (# *201*) to hear. **ἤρξαντο** aor. ind. mid. (dep.) s.v. 28. **ἀγανακτεῖν** pres. act. inf. s.v. 14. ◆ **42 προσκαλεσάμενος** aor. mid. part. (circum.) προσκαλέομαι (# *4673*) to call to oneself, to summon. **δοκοῦντες** pres. act. part. δοκέω (# *1506*) to appear, to suppose. Possibly "those who aspire to rule" (but s. Cranfield). **ἄρχειν** pres. act. inf. ἄρχω (# *806*) w. gen. to rule over. Compl. inf. w. vb. "to begin." **κατακυριεύουσιν** pres. ind. act. κατακυριεύω (# *2894*) w. gen. to be lord over, to rule over. The compound prep. in the vb. gives the sense of using lordship over people to their disadvantage and to one's own advantage (Cranfield). Gnomic pres. indicating a general truth. **κατεξουσιάζουσιν** pres. ind. act. w. gen. κατεξουσιάζω (# *2980*) to exercise authority over. The prep. κατά in compound vbs. indicates unfavorableness to an obj. (MH, 316). ◆ **43 θέλῃ** pres. subj. act. θέλω (# *2527*) to want, to will, w. inf. Subj. w. ἄν (# *323*) in an indef. rel. cl. **γενέσθαι** aor. mid. (dep.) inf. γίνομαι (# *1181*) to become, to be. **ἔσται** fut. ind. mid. (dep.) εἰμί (# *1639*) to be. ◆ **44 εἶναι** pres. act. inf. εἰμί. ◆ **45 καὶ γάρ** either emphatic ("for the Son of Man Himself") (Taylor) or "for also." The Son of Man is not exempt from this rule; His kingship is also that of service and not of lordship (Gould). **ἦλθεν** aor. ind. act. ἔρχομαι (# *2262*) to come. **διακονηθῆναι** aor. pass. inf. διακονέω (# *1354*) to serve, to minister; pass., to be ministered to. **διακονῆσαι** aor. act. inf. **δοῦναι** aor. act. inf. δίδωμι (# *1443*) to give. Infs. express purp. **λύτρον** (# *3389*) acc. sing. ransom; the price paid for release (Matt. 20:28; Cranfield; LDC, 239-49). **ἀντί** (# *505*) w. gen., instead of, in place of. It is the prep. of substitution. He took our place (CNT, 54; GGBB, 365-67; NIDNTT, 3:1179-80; EDNT). ◆ **46 ἐκπορευομένου** pres. mid. (dep.) part. (temp.) s.v. 17. Gen. abs. **προσαίτης** (# *4645*) beggar. The prep. compound is directive and indicates to ask to or for oneself (MH, 324). **προσαιτῶν** a variant reading (TC, 108), pres. act. part. προσαιτέω (# *4644*) to beg. Part. of manner. **ἐκάθητο** impf. ind. mid. (dep.) κάθημαι (# *2764*) to sit. Iterat. or customary impf.: "he used to sit," "it was his custom to sit" (RG, 884). ◆ **47 ἀκούσας** aor. act. part. (temp.) s.v. 41. **ἤρξατο** aor. ind. mid. (dep.) s.v. 28. **κράζειν** pres. act. inf. κράζω (# *3189*) to cry out, to scream. **υἱὲ Δαυίδ** voc. sing. For the title "Son of David" s. Cleon Rogers, Jr., "The Promises to David in Early Judaism," *Bib Sac* 150 (1993): 285-302; "The Davidic Covenant in the Gospels," *Bib Sac* 150 (1993): 458-78. **ἐλέησον** aor. imp. act. ἐλεέω (# *1796*) to have mercy, to show mercy (TDNT). ◆ **48 ἐπετίμων** impf. ind. act. s.v. 13. Impf. indicates they continually rebuked him. **σιωπήσῃ** aor. subj. act. σιωπάω (# *4995*) to keep silent, to be silent. Subj. w. ἵνα (# *2671*) in a obj. cl. **ἔκραζεν** impf. ind. act. s.v. 47. "He continually cried out." ◆ **49 στάς** aor. act. part. (circum.) ἵστημι (# *2705*) to stand, to remain. By standing still Jesus allows the

blind man to come to him. (BBC). **φωνήσατε** aor. imp. act. φωνέω (# *5888*) to call. **φωνοῦσιν** pres. ind. act., hist. pres. **θάρσει** pres. imp. act. θαρσέω (# *2510*) to be cheerful, to have courage. **ἔγειρε** pres. imp. act. ἐγείρω (# *1586*) to rise, arise. ◆ **50 ἀποβαλών** aor. act. part. (temp.) ἀποβάλλω (# *610*) to throw off. **ἀναπηδήσας** aor. act. part. ἀναπηδάω (# *403*) to jump up, to spring up. **ἦλθεν** aor. ind. act. ἔρχομαι (# *2262*). ◆ **51 ἀποκριθείς** aor. pass. part. s.v. 3. **Ῥαββουνι** (# *4808*) voc. sing. my great One, master, teacher (TDNT; EDNT; SB, 2:25; UJS, 29; AUV, 432-33). **ἀναβλέψω** aor. subj. act. ἀναβλέπω (# *329*) to look up, to see again, to regain sight (MH, 295). ◆ **52 ὕπαγε** pres. imp. act. s.v. 21. **σέσωκεν** perf. ind. act. s.v. 26. Perf. emphasizes the state or cond. of being healed. **ἀνέβλεψεν** aor. ind. act. s.v. 51. **ἠκολούθει** impf. ind. act. s.v. 21. Inceptive impf. "he began to follow."

Mark 11

◆ **1 ἐγγίζουσιν** pres. ind. act. ἐγγίζω (# *1581*) to be near, to draw near. Hist. pres. **ἀποστέλλει** pres. ind. act. ἀποστέλλω (# *690*) to send w. authority, to commission. Hist. pres. ◆ **2 ὑπάγετε** pres. imp. act. ὑπάγω (# *5632*) to go forth, to go. **κατέναντι** (# *2978*) adv. opposite. **εἰσπορευόμενοι** pres. mid. (dep.) part. (temp.) εἰσπορεύομαι (# *1660*) to go in, to come in (DJG, 854-59). **εὑρήσετε** fut. ind. act. εὑρίσκω (# *2351*) to find. **πῶλος** (# *4798*) the young of any animal, generally a horse, but in the LXX and the papyri also the colt or foal of a donkey (Taylor). **δεδεμένον** perf. pass. part. δέω (# *1313*) to bind. Perf. part. describes the cond. (VA, 395). **ἐκάθισεν** aor. ind. act. καθίζω (# *2767*) to sit, to take one's seat. The fact that no one had ridden on the animal is obviously a reference to the Messiah's Donkey of Gen. 49:11 and Zech. 9:9 (Pesch). **λύσατε** aor. imp. act. λύω (# *3395*) to loosen, to untie. Aor. looks at the specific act. **φέρετε** pres. imp. act. φέρω (# *5770*) to bring. Pres. imp. used of a specific act w. a vb. of motion (VANT, 347-48). ◆ **3 εἴπῃ** aor. subj. act. λέγω (# *3306*) to say. Subj. in a 3rd. class cond. cl., which assumes the possibility of the cond. **ποιεῖτε** pres. ind. act. ποιέω (# *4472*) to do, to make. **εἴπατε** aor. imp. act. λέγω **αὐτοῦ** gen. sing. αὐτός It refers to the animal and could be the obj. gen. w. **χρείαν** (# *5970*), or the poss. gen. w. **κύριος** (# *3261*) (Gundry, 624; Pesch). In the light of the Roman system of official transport, it has been suggested that the words **κύριος αὐτοῦ** refer to an unspecified legitimate claimant who promises to return the animal when finished w. it (NDIEC, 1:43; J.D.M. Derrett, "Law in the NT: The Palm Sunday Colt," *Nov T* 13 [1971]: 241-58. Jesus as King had the privilege of using the animal for transportation. ◆ **4 ἀπῆλθον** aor. ind. act. ἀπέρχομαι (# *599*) to go out. **εὗρον** aor. ind. act. s.v. 2. **ἄμφοδον** (# *316*) a city quarter surrounded and crossed by streets; thus street; here, "outside, in the street"

(BAGD). ◆ **5 ἑστηκότων** perf. act. part. ἵστημι (# 2705) perf., to stand. Part. used as subst. **ἔλεγον** impf. ind. act. λέγω (# 3306). **λύοντες** pres. act. part. s.v. 2. Part. used to complete the vb. ◆ **6 εἶπαν** aor. ind. act. λέγω to say, s.v. 3. **ἀφῆκαν** aor. ind. act. ἀφίημι (# 918) to allow. ◆ **7 ἐπιβάλλουσιν** pres. ind. act. ἐπιβάλλω (# 2095) to place upon, to cast upon; hist. pres. ◆ **8 ἔστρωσαν** aor. ind. act. στρώννυμι (# 5143) to spread out. **στιβάς** (# 5115) kind of bed or mattress made of straw, rushes, reeds, leaves, etc. Here leaves, leafy branches (BAGD). **κόψαντες** aor. act. part. (circum.) κόπτω (# 3164) to cut. The paving of the road for about two miles makes for a red-carpet effect, magnifying the VIP Jesus (Gundry, 626; BBC). ◆ **9 προάγοντες** pres. act. part. προάγω (# 4575) to go before. Part. as subst. **ἀκολουθοῦντες** pres. act. part. ἀκολουθέω (# 199) to follow. Part. as subst. **ἔκραζον** impf. ind. act. κράζω (# 3189) to cry out, to scream. Impf. pictures the continual action. "They screamed out repeatedly." **ὡσαννά** (# 6059) (Heb.) hosanna; save, we pray; save now (Matt. 21:9; Pesch). **εὐλογημένος** perf. pass. part. εὐλογέω (# 2328) to bless, to give thanks (TDNT; EDNT; NIDNTT). ◆ **10 ὑψίστοις** dat. pl. ὕψιστος (# 5736) the highest, pl. heaven. ◆ **11 εἰσῆλθεν** aor. ind. act. εἰσέρχομαι (# 1656) to go in, to come in. **περιβλεψάμενος** aor. mid. part. (temp.) περιβλέπω (# 4315) to look about, to look around. **ὄψιος** (# 4070) adj. late. **οὔσης** pres. act. part. (causal) εἰμί (# 1639) to be. Gen. abs., "since the hour was already late" (BAGD). **ἐξῆλθεν** aor. ind. act. ἐξέρχομαι (# 2002) to go out. ◆ **12 ἐπαύριον** (# 2069) adv., tomorrow, used w. the noun ἡμέρα understood; "on the next day" (BAGD). **ἐξελθόντων** aor. act. part. s.v. 11. Gen. abs., temp. or circum. part. Aor. indicates the logically necessary action. **ἐπείνασεν** aor. ind. act. πεινάω (# 4277) to be hungry. Ingressive aor., "he became hungry." For a discussion of the cursing s. HSB, 441-42. ◆ **13 ἰδών** aor. act. part. (temp.) ὁράω (# 3972) to see. Aor. describing an antecedent action. **συκῆ** (# 5190) fig tree. **μακρόθεν** (# 3427) adv., from afar off. **ἔχουσαν** pres. act. part. ἔχω (# 2400) to have. Adj. part. **φύλλα** acc. pl. φύλλον (# 5877) leaf; pl. leaves, foliage. **ἦλθεν** aor. ind. act. ἔρχομαι (# 2262) to come, to go. **ἄρα** (# 726) so then, consequently; "in these circumstances" (Lane). **εὑρήσει** fut. ind. act. s.v. 2. **ἐλθών** aor. act. part. (temp.) ἔρχομαι (# 2262) to come. **εὗρεν** aor. ind. act. s.v. 2. **ἦν** impf. ind. act. εἰμί to be. **σῦκον** (# 5192) fig. In the Messianic age figs and all other products of nature will always be in season. (Richard H. Hiers, "Not the Season for Figs," *JBL* 87 [1968]: 394-400; BBC). This indicates the promised OT kingdom would not be established at this time. ◆ **14 ἀποκριθείς** aor. pass. (dep.) part. ἀποκρίνομαι (# 646) to answer, to reply. **εἶπεν** aor. ind. act. λέγω (# 3306) to say. **φάγοι** aor. opt. act. ἐσθίω (# 2266) to eat. Opt. here expresses prohibition (M, 165). **ἤκουον** impf. ind. act. ἀκούω (# 201) to hear. ◆ **15 εἰσελθών** aor. act.

part. (temp.) s.v. 11. **ἤρξατο** aor. ind. mid. (dep.) ἄρχομαι (# 806) to begin, w. inf. **ἐκβάλλειν** pres. act. inf. ἐκβάλλω (# 1675) to cast out, to drive out. **πωλοῦντας** pres. act. part. πωλέω (# 4797) to sell. Part. as subst. **ἀγοράζοντας** pres. act. part. ἀγοράζω (# 60) to buy. Part. as subst. **τράπεζας** (# 5544) table, the table on which moneychangers display their coins (BAGD). **κολλυβιστής** (# 3142) moneychanger (Matt. 21:12). They were necessary to change money for the pilgrims (DJG, 806; BBC). **καθέδρα** (# 2756) seat, chair. **περιστερά** (# 4361) pigeon. **κατέστρεψεν** aor. ind. act. καταστρέφω (# 2951) to turn down, to overthrow, to turn over. For a discussion of this in the light of its background s. Craig A. Evans, "Jesus' Action in the Temple: Cleansing or Portent of Destruction," *CBQ* 51 (1989): 237-70. ◆ **16 ἤφιεν** impf. ind. act. ἀφίημι (# 918) to allow. **διενέγκῃ** aor. subj. act. διαφέρω (# 1422) to carry through. No one was allowed to enter the Temple Mount w. his staff, sandal, wallet, or w. dust on his feet (M, Berakoth, 9:5; Swete). ◆ **17 ἐδίδασκεν** impf. ind. act. διδάσκω (# 1438) to teach. Incep. impf., "he began to teach." **ἔλεγεν** impf. ind. act. λέγω (# 3306). **γέγραπται** perf. ind. pass. γράφω (# 1211) to write. Quoting Isa. 56:7; Jer. 7:11. Used w. οὐ (# 4024) in a question expecting a positive answer. **κληθήσεται** fut. ind. pass. καλέω (# 2813) to call. **πεποιήκατε** perf. ind. act. ποιέω s.v. 3. Perf. emphasizes the past action w. a continuing state or result. **σπήλαιον** (# 5068) acc. sing. hole, den, cave. **λῃστής** (# 3334) robber, bandit, one who robs by force and violence (LN, 1:585; TDNT). ◆ **18 ἤκουσαν** aor. ind. act. ἀκούω (# 201) to hear. **ἐζήτουν** impf. ind. act. ζητέω (# 2426) to seek. Impf. pictures the repeated action. **ἀπολέσωσιν** aor. subj. act. ἀπόλλυμι (# 660) to destroy, to ruin. Subj. used in obj. cl. **ἐφοβοῦντο** impf. ind. act. mid. (dep.) φοβέομαι (# 5828) to be afraid, to fear. **ἐξεπλήσσετο** impf. ind. act. mid. (dep.) ἐκπλήσσομαι (# 1742) to be astounded, to be amazed. ◆ **19 ἐγένετο** aor. ind. mid. (dep.) γίνομαι (# 1181) to become. "When it got late" (Cranfield). **ἐξεπορεύοντο** impf. ind. act. mid. (dep.) ἐκπορεύομαι (# 1744) to go out. Impf. points to habitual action: "Whenever it became late, they would go out of the city" (Gundry, 647). ◆ **20 παραπορευόμενοι** pres. mid. (dep.) part. (temp.) παραπορεύομαι (# 4182) to pass by. **εἶδον** aor. ind. act. ὁράω (# 3972) to see. **ἐξηραμμένην** perf. pass. part. ξηραίνω (# 3830) to dry up, to wither. Perf. pictures the abiding results (Taylor). **ῥίζα** (# 4844) root. This implies the process took place in a day and strikes at the very source of the tree's life, emphasizing the power of Jesus' curse (Gundry, 648). ◆ **21 ἀναμνησθείς** aor. pass. (dep.) part. ἀναμιμνήσκομαι (# 389) to remember, to be reminded. Circum. / temp. part. **ἴδε** (# 2623) aor. imp. act. ὁράω to see. **κατηράσω** aor. ind. mid. (dep.) 2nd. sing. καταράομαι (# 2933) to curse. **ἐξήρανται** perf. ind. pass. s.v 20. Perf. stresses the completion and permanance of the effect produced by Jesus' word (Gun-

dry, 648). ◆ **22** ἀποκριθείς aor. pass. (dep.) part. s.v. 14.
ἔχετε pres. imp. act. ἔχω (# 2400) to have. Pres. imp. calls
for a continual attitude. ◆ **23** εἴπῃ aor. subj. act. s.v. 3.
Subj. w. ἄν (# 323) in an indef. rel. cl. **ἄρθητι** aor. imp.
pass. αἴρω (# 149) to lift up; pass., to be lifted up. **βλήθη-**
τι aor. imp. pass. βάλλω (# 965) to throw. Both aor. imps.
call for specific things, while the pass. describes the action to be done. **διακριθῇ** aor. subj. pass. (dep.) διακρίνομαι (# 1359) to hesitate, to doubt, to waver back and
forth in judgment (s. MH, 302). Subj. in indef. rel. cl.
πιστεύῃ pres. subj. act. πιστεύω (# 4409) to believe, to
trust, w. obj. of belief in subst. cl. **λαλεῖ** pres. ind. act. λαλέω (# 3281) to speak, to say. **γίνεται** pres. ind. mid.
(dep.) γίνομαι (# 1181) to become. Futuristic pres. depicting a process going on in the pres., but w. termination in the fut. (VANT, 221); or incohative pres.
describing an act just beginning (RG, 880). **ἔσται** fut.
ind. mid. (dep.) εἰμί (# 1639) to be. **αὐτῷ** dat. sing. αὐτός
Dat. of personal interest, or advantage. ◆ **24** προσεύ-
χεσθε pres. ind. mid. (dep.) προσεύχομαι (# 4667) to
pray. **αἰτεῖσθε** pres. ind. mid. αἰτέω (# 160) to ask, to ask
for oneself (s. Mark 10:38). **πιστεύετε** pres. imp. act. s.v.
23. **ἐλάβετε** aor. ind. act. λαμβάνω (# 3284) to receive.
Used w. ὅτι (# 4022) as obj. of vb. ◆ **25** στήκετε pres.
ind. act. στήκω (# 5112) to stand (BAGD). **προσευχόμενοι**
pres. mid. (dep.) part. s.v. 24. **ἀφίετε** pres. imp. act.
ἀφίημι (# 918) to forgive (TDNT; EDNT; NIDNTT). **ἀφῇ**
aor. subj. act. Subj. used in purp. cl. **παράπτωμα** (# 4183)
a false step, a fall from the right course, an error, a mistake in judgment, a blunder, transgression (Swete;
Trench, *Synonyms*; TDNT; NIDNTT; EDNT). ◆ **27** περι-
πατοῦντος pres. act. part. (temp.) περιπατέω (# 4344) to
walk about. Gen. abs., "While he was walking
around." He was evidently walking around in the por-
ticos of the Temple.   ◆ **28** ἔλεγον impf. ind. act. s.v.
5. **ποιεῖς** pres. ind. act. ποιέω (# 4472) to do. Pres. points
to the continual action. **ἔδωκεν** aor. ind. act. δίδωμι
(# 1443) to give. **ποιῇς** pres. subj. act. ποιέω. Subj. w. ἵνα
(# 2671) used in purp. cl. ◆ **29** εἶπεν aor. ind. act. s.v. 3.
ἐπερωτήσω fut. ind. act. ἐπερωτάω (# 2089) to ask a
question. **ἀποκρίθητε** aor. imp. pass. (dep.), w. dat. s.v.
14. **ἐρῶ** fut. ind. act. λέγω (# 3306). Fut. used in a Semitic
type of cond. cl. w. imp. w. **καί** and fut. (Beyer, 238). The
answering of a question w. a question was a common
Rabbinical method (Hooker).   ◆ **30** ἐξ οὐρανοῦ "from
heaven" means from God (Lührmann). **ἦν** impf. ind.
act. εἰμί (# 1639) to be. **ἀποκρίθητε** aor. imp. pass. (dep.)
s.v. 29. ◆ **31** διελογίζοντο impf. ind. mid. (dep.) διαλογίζομαι (# 1368) to discuss, to dispute. **εἴπωμεν** aor. subj.
act. s.v. 3. Subj. w. ἐάν (# 1569) in a 3rd. class cond. cl.
w. the cond. assumed as possible. **ἐρεῖ** fut. ind. act. λέγω
s.v. 29. **ἐπιστεύσατε** aor. ind. act., w. dat. as obj. s.v. 23.
◆ **32** εἴπωμεν aor. subj. act. s.v. 3. Subj. continues the
cond. cl. w. another possibility (s.v. 31). **ἐφοβοῦντο** impf.
ind. mid. (dep.) s.v. 18. The apodosis of the cond. sen-

tence is suppressed out of the strong emotion of fear
and is a form of anacoluthon or aposiopesis (RG, 1203).
εἶχον impf. ind. act. ἔχω (# 2400) to have, to hold, to
think (BD, 204). ◆ **33** ἀποκριθέντες aor. pass. (dep.)
part. s.v. 14. **οἴδαμεν** perf. ind. act. perf. οἶδα (# 3857) to
know. Def. perf. w. pres. meaning.

Mark 12

◆ **1** ἤρξατο aor. ind. mid. (dep.) ἄρχομαι (# 806) to
begin, w. inf. **λαλεῖν** pres. act. inf. λαλέω (# 3281) to
speak, compl. inf. to main vb. **ἀμπελών** (# 308) vineyard. For a study of this parable in the light of Jewish
law s. LNT, 286-308; Martin Hengel, "Das Gleichnis
von den Weingärtnern Mc 12, 1-12 im Lichte der Zeno-
papyri und der rabbinischen Gleichnisse," ZNW 59
[1968]: 1-39; BBC. **ἐφύτευσεν** aor. ind. act. φυτεύω
(# 5885) to plant. **περιέθηκεν** aor. ind. act. περιτίθημι
(# 4363) to place around. **φραγμόν** acc. sing. φραγμός
(# 5850) a fence, wall, hedge. This was necessary to
keep the vines from running over another's property
(LNT, 292). It also was for protection against wild animals (Taylor). **ὤρυξεν** aor. ind. act. ὀρύσσω (# 4002) to
dig. **ὑπολήνιον** (# 5700) acc. sing. the trough for the
juice under the press in which the grapes were crushed
(Cranfield). **ᾠκοδόμησεν** aor. ind. act. οἰκοδομέω (# 3868)
to build. **πύργος** (# 4788) tower. **ἐξέδετο** aor. ind. mid.
ἐκδίδωμι (# 1686) to give out, to farm out, to lease. For
the mid. form s. GGP, 2:394; MH, 212. **γεωργός** (# 1177)
farmer, tenant farmer. Those who had made a contract
w. the landlord to tend the vineyard in return for part
of its produce (LNT, 293f). **ἀπεδήμησεν** aor. ind. act.
ἀποδημέω (# 623) to travel, to make a trip; here, to travel to a foreign country (Hengel, "Das Gleichnis," 21).
◆ **2** ἀπέστειλεν aor. ind. act. ἀποστέλλω (# 690) to send,
to commission, w. the authority of the one sending.
καιρῷ dat. sing. καιρός (# 2789) time. Dat. of time. **λάβῃ**
aor. subj. act. λαμβάνω (# 3284) to take, to receive. Subj.
w. ἵνα (# 2671) in a purp. cl. Normally the first time
wine could be made from the vineyard grapes was the
fourth year; it was for personal use the fifth year (Lev.
19:23-25). The fruit of the vineyard was possibly the
vegetables grown between the vines. It was necessary
for the owner to receive a token payment of the harvest
in order to retain ownership (LNT, 295; Pesch). Often
one would have to pay one quarter of the produce
(BBC). ◆ **3** λαβόντες aor. act. part. (circum.) s.v. 2. **ἔδει-**
ραν aor. ind. act. δέρω (# 1296) to beat. **ἀπέστειλαν** aor.
ind. act. s.v. 2. **κενός** (# 3031) adv. empty. For parallels
s. Hengel, "Das Gleichnis," 26-31.   ◆ **4** ἐκεφαλίωσαν
aor. ind. act. κεφαλαιόω (# 3052) to strike on the head.
ἠτίμασαν aor. ind. act. ἀτιμάζω (# 870) to dishonor, to
insult. ◆ **5** ἀπέκτειναν aor. ind. act. ἀποκτείνω (# 650) to
kill. **δέροντες** pres. act. part. s.v. 3. **ἀποκτέννοντες** pres.
act. part. For the form ἀποκτέννω / ἀποκτέννυμι s. MH,
245; RG, 1213. ◆ **6** ἕνα acc. sing. εἷς (# 1651) one. Em-

phatic position separated from its noun υἱόν (Gundry, 686). εἶχεν impf. ind. act. ἔχω (# 2400) to have. ἀγαπητός (# 28) beloved. ἐντραπήσονται fut. ind. pass. ἐντρέπω (# 1956) pass., to reverence, to respect. ◆ 7 εἶπαν aor. ind. act. λέγω (# 3306) to say, followed by dir. discourse w. ὅτι (# 4022) used as quotation marks (DM, 252). κληρονόμος (# 3101) heir. The one who would take over the property. δεῦτε (# 1307) Come! (BD, 184). ἀποκτείνωμεν pres. or aor. subj. act. s.v. 5. Hortatory subj., "Let us kill...." Since the owner of the vineyard had not received payment for three years, the tenants hoped to destroy the evidence by killing the son and thus to have a claim to the vineyard (LNT, 300-306). ἔσται fut. ind. mid. (dep.) εἰμί (# 1639) to be. ◆ 8 λαβόντες aor. act. part. s.v. 3. Temp. or circum. part. ἀπέκτειναν aor. ind. act. s.v. 5. ἐξέβαλον aor. ind. act. ἐκβάλλω (# 1675) to cast out, to throw out. ◆ 9 ποιήσει fut. ind. act. ποιέω (# 4472) to do, to make. ἐλεύσεται fut. ind. mid. (dep.) ἔρχομαι (# 2262) to come, to go. ἀπολέσει fut. ind. act. ἀπόλυμι (# 660) to destroy, to ruin. δώσει fut. ind. act. δίδωμι (# 1443) to give. ◆ 10 ἀνέγνωτε aor. ind. act. ἀναγινώσκω (# 336) to read. ἀπεδοκίμασαν aor. ind. act. ἀποδοκιμάζω (# 627) to reject, to reject after examining. οἰκοδομοῦντες pres. act. part. οἰκοδομέω (# 3868) to build. Part. as subst., "the builders." ἐγενήθη aor. ind. pass. (dep.) γίνομαι (# 1181) to become. γωνία (# 1224) corner. For the grammatical structure of this v. s. MH, 423f; Taylor. ◆ 11 ἐγένετο aor. ind. mid. (dep.) s.v. 10. θαυμαστή (# 2515) wonderful, incomprehensible. ◆ 12 ἐζήτουν impf. ind. act. ζητέω (# 2426) to seek, w. inf. Impf. emphasizes they repeatedly sought. κρατῆσαι aor. act. inf. κρατέω (# 3195) to seize. ἐφοβήθησαν aor. ind. pass. (dep.) φοβέομαι (# 5828) to fear, to be afraid of. ἔγνωσαν aor. ind. act. γινώσκω (# 1181) to know, to recognize. πρὸς αὐτούς w. reference to them (Lane). ἀφέντες aor. act. part. ἀφίημι (# 918) to leave. For the Semitic use of the redundant part. s. MH, 452-54. ἀπῆλθον aor. ind. act. ἀπέρχομαι (# 599) to go away. ◆ 13 ἀποστέλλουσιν pres. ind. act. s.v. 2. Hist. pres. ἀγρεύσωσιν aor. subj. act. ἀγρεύω (# 65) to catch or take by hunting or fishing (AS; s. *Joseph and Asenath*, 21:21; GELTS, 1:5). Subj. w. εἰ (# 1623) in purp. cl. λόγῳ dat. λόγος (# 3364). Instr. dat. ◆ 14 ἐλθόντες aor. act. part. s.v. 9. Circum./temp. part. οἴδαμεν perf. ind. act. οἶδα (# 3857) to know. Def. perf. w. pres. meaning. ἀληθής (# 239) true, upright (Taylor). εἶ pres. ind. act. 2nd. sing. εἰμί (# 1639). μέλει σοι you are not concerned about. ἔξεστιν (# 2003) pres. ind. act; it is lawful, w. inf. δοῦναι aor. inf. act. δίδωμι (# 1443) to give. Here in the sense of pay taxes, compl. inf. to main vb. "Is it lawful to give?" κῆνσος (# 3056) tribute, poll tax (Matt. 22:17). δῶμεν aor. subj. act. δίδωμι; deliberative subj. used in a question. ◆ 15 εἰδώς perf. act. part. (causal) οἶδα s.v. 14. ὑπόκρισις (# 5694) hypocrisy, pretense, outward show (BAGD); an attempt to evade the law (s. Mark 7:6).

φέρετε pres. imp. act. φέρω (# 5770) to carry, to bring. ἴδω aor. subj. act. ὁράω (# 3972) to see. Subj. in purp. cl. ◆ 16 ἤνεγκαν aor. ind. act. φέρω s.v. 15. εἰκών (# 1635) image (Paul Corby Finey, "The Rabbis and the Coin Portrait [Mark 12:15b, 16]: Rigorism Manqué," *JBL* 112 [1993]: 629-44). ἐπιγραφή (# 2107) inscription (Matt. 22:20). εἶπαν aor. ind. act. s.v. 7. ◆ 17 ἀπόδοτε aor. imp. act. ἀποδίδωμι (# 625) to give back, to pay. The compound vb. implies that the tribute is a debt (Swete; s. W. Stenger, *Gebt dem Kaiser, was des Kaisers ist!" Eine sozialgeschichtliche Untersuchung zur Besteuerung Palästinas in neutestamentlichen Zeit* [Marburg: Wenzel, 1987]; HSB, 443-45). ἐξεθαύμαζον impf. ind. act. ἐκθαυμάζω (# 1703) to be astounded, to be amazed. Prep. in compound may be perfective: "completely astonished" (MH, 309). ◆ 18 εἶναι pres. act. inf. εἰμί (# 1639) to be. Inf. in indir. discourse. For a discussion of the resurrection in Jewish teaching s. S, 142-292; for the Sadducees' view s. TJ, 77-78; BBC; DJG, 403. ἐπηρώτων impf. ind. act. ἐπερωτάω (# 2089) to question. λέγοντες pres. act. part. λέγω (# 3306). For the Semitic construction of the part. s. MH, 454. ◆ 19 ἔγραψεν aor. ind. act. γράφω (# 1211) to write, w. dat. as indir. obj. ἀποθάνῃ aor. subj. act. ἀποθνήσκω (# 633) to die. Subjs. w. ἐάν (# 1569) here are in a cond. cl. assuming the possibility of the cond. καταλίπῃ aor. subj. act. καταλείπω (# 2901) to leave behind. ἀφῇ aor. subj. act. ἀφίημι (# 918) to leave. λάβῃ aor. subj. act. s.v. 2. For the change from dir. to indir. discourse and the imp. force of the subj. s. Gundry, 701; BD, 247; VANT, 382, 385. ἐξαναστήσῃ aor. subj. act. ἐξανίστημι (# 1985) to raise up. For the quote from Deut. 25:5; Gen. 38:8 s. S, 338-45; SB, 1:886-87. ◆ 20 ἔλαβεν aor. ind. act. s.v. 2. ἀποθνήσκων pres. act. part. (temp.) s.v. 19. ἀφῆκεν aor. ind. act. s.v. 19. ◆ 21 ἀπέθανεν aor. ind. act. s.v. 19. καταλιπών aor. act. part. (circum.) s.v. 19. ◆ 22 ἀφῆκαν aor. ind. act. s.v. 19. For the story in its Jewish setting s. S., 345-52. ◆ 23 ἀναστῶσιν aor. subj. act. ἀνίστημι (# 482) to rise up, to rise. Subj. w. ὅταν (# 4020) in an indef. temp. cl.: "whenever they might rise." ἔσται fut. ind. mid. (dep.) εἰμί s.v. 14. ἔσχον aor. ind. act. ἔχω (# 2400) to have. ◆ 24 ἔφη impf. ind. act. φημί (# 5774) to say, to speak (s. Mark 10:20). πλανᾶσθε pres. ind. pass. πλανάω (# 4414) to lead astray, to cause to wander, to deceive; pass. to go astray, to be deceived, to be misled (BAGD; TDNT; EDNT; S, 357). εἰδότες perf. act. part. (causal) οἶδα (# 3857) s.v. 14. ◆ 25 ἀναστῶσιν aor. subj. act. s.v. 23. γαμοῦσιν pres. ind. act. γαμέω (# 1138) to marry. Fut. pres. or gnomic pres. indicating a general truth that will exist at the Resurrection. γαμίζονται pres. ind. pass. γαμίζω (# 1139) to give in marriage. For a discussion of no marriage in eternity for the angels s. S, 368-81. ◆ 26 ἐγείρονται pres. ind. pass. ἐγείρω (# 1586) to rise, to be raised. Theol. pass. (Gundry, 703). ἀνέγνωτε aor. ind. act. s.v. 10. Used w. οὐκ (# 4024) in a question expecting a positive answer.

For the quotation from Exod. 3:6 s. Gundry, 703-704: S., 381-403. ◆ **27 ζώντων** pres. act. part. ζάω (# 2409) to live (as applied to God s. S, 406-14). **πλανᾶσθε** pres. ind. pass. s.v. 24. This answers the question of v. 24: "You are decieved, aren't you...?"; "You are much deceived!" (Gundry, 704). ◆ **28 προσελθών** aor. act. part. (circum.) προσέρχομαι (# 4665) to come to. **ἀκούσας** aor. act. part. (temp.) ἀκούω (# 201) w. gen. to hear, to listen to. **συζη-τούντων** pres. act. part. συζητέω (# 5184) to examine to-gether, to dispute. Supplemental part. w. the vb. ἀκούω. **ἰδών** aor. act. part. (temp.) ὁράω (# 3972) to see. **ἀπεκρίθη** aor. ind. pass. (dep.) ἀποκρίνομαι (# 646) to answer. **ἐπηρώτησεν** aor. ind. act. s.v. 18. ◆ **29 ἄκουε** pres. imp. act. s.v. 28. ◆ **30 ἀγαπήσεις** fut. ind. act. ἀγαπάω (# 26) to love. Fut. w. the force of the imp. is a translation of the Heb. impf. used as a jussive (MH, 458; BG, 94). ◆ **31 πλησίος** (# 4446) the next one, neighbor. **μείζων** (# 3505) comp. μέγας great. **τούτων** gen. τοῦτο this. Gen. of comparison. ◆ **33 ἀγαπᾶν** pres. act. inf. s.v. 30. Inf. used as subst. **σύνεσις** (# 5304) understanding. **περισ-σότερον** (# 4358) comp. περισσός beyond measure, over and above, more exceeding. **πάντων** gen. pl. πᾶς (# 4246) all, every. Gen. of comparison. **ὁλοκαύτωμα** (# 3906) burnt offering. **θυσία** (# 2602) sacrifice. ◆ **34 ἰδών** aor. act. part. (temp.) ὁράω (# 3972) to see. **νουνεχῶς** (# 3807) wisely, thoughtfully, w. understand-ing (LN, 1:384). **ἀπεκρίθη** aor. ind. pass. (dep.) s.v. 28. **μακράν** (# 3426) acc. sing. far. Acc. fem. used as an adv. (Taylor). **ἐτόλμα** impf. ind. act. τολμάω (# 5528) to dare, w. inf. **ἐπερωτῆσαι** aor. act. inf. s.v. 18. ◆ **35 ἀποκριθείς** aor. pass. part. s.v. 28. For the Semitic use of the part. s. MH, 453. **διδάσκων** pres. act. part. διδάσκω (# 1438) to teach; part. of manner. ◆ **36 κάθου** pres. imp. mid. (dep.) κάθημαι (# 2764) to sit, to sit down. **θῶ** aor. subj. act. τίθημι (# 5502) to place, to set, to establish, to make. **ὑποκάτω** (# 5691) w. gen., under. For this section s. Matt. 22:41-46; Cleon L. Rogers, Jr., "The Davidic Covenant in the Gospels," *Bib. Sac.* 150 (1993): 463-64; BBC. ◆ **37 ἤκουεν** impf. ind. act. s.v. 28. **ἡδέως** (# 2452) adv. gladly. ◆ **38 βλέπετε** pres. imp. act. βλέπω (# 1063) to see, to beware of. **θελόντων** pres. act. part. (adj.) θέλω (# 2527) to desire, to wish, w. inf. **στολαῖς** dat. pl. στολή (# 5124) cloak; not only the cloak worn by the common people, but esp. the cloak of honor, of the scholars or of-ficers (Jastrow, 1:537; SB, 2:31-33; BBC). **περιπατεῖν** pres. act. inf. περιπατέω (# 4344) to walk about. **ἀσπασμός** (# 833) greetings. Walking around in such robes and being greeted in the market places make a pair (Gun-dry, 719). ◆ **39 πρωτοκαθεδρία** (# 4751) the chief seat, the bench in the synagogues in front of the ark where the Scriptures were contained while facing the congre-gation. It was reserved for the officials and persons of high distinction (LT, 1:436). **πρωτοκλισία** (# 4752) first or chief place at the table. The place of the most honored guest on the couch around the table (Swete). **δεῖπον**

(# 1270) dinner, the main meal, generally in the evening (SB, 4:611-39; LT, 2:205-210). ◆ **40 κατεσθίοντες** pres. act. part. κατεσθίω (# 2983) to devour, to eat up. **χηρῶν** gen. pl. χήρα (# 5939) widow. Widows were helpess in the society of the day, and the scribes are accused of sponging on the hospitality of people of limited means (Lane; EDNT; TDNT; NIDNTT; BBC). Part. as subst. **προφάσει** dat. sing. πρόφασις (# 4733) alleged motive or cause, esp. a motive or cause that is falsely alleged; pre-text, pretense (Cranfield; Harry Fleddermann, "A Warning about the Scribes [Mark 12:37b-40]," *CBQ* 44 [1982]: 62-63). Dat. of manner. **προσευχόμενοι** pres. mid. (dep.) part. προσεύχομαι (# 4667) to pray. **λήμψονται** fut. ind. mid. (dep.) λαμβάνω (# 3284) to take, to receive. ◆ **41 καθίσας** aor. act. part. (temp.) καθίζω (# 2767) to sit, to take one's seat. Aor. showing antecedent action. **κατέναντι** (# 2978) w. gen., opposite. **γαζοφυλακεῖον** (# 1126) treasury. Probably a reference to the thirteen trumpet-like chests placed at intervals around the walls of the court of the women in the Herodian temple (Swete; SB, 2:37-45; BBC; DJG, 812). **ἐθεώρει** impf. ind. act. θεωρέω (# 2555) to watch, to observe. Impf. pictures his repeated watching of the different persons who passed by. **χαλκός** (# 5910) copper, brass, bronze mon-ey. **πλούσιος** (# 4454) rich, very rich. **ἔβαλλον** impf. ind. act. βάλλω (# 965) to throw, to place "they were repeat-edly casting." This was above and beyond the tithe and Temple tax. For the tithe and Temple tax s. JPB, 146-69. ◆ **42 ἐλθοῦσα** aor. act. part. nom. fem. sing. s.v. 9. Cir-cum. or temp. part. **πτωχή** (# 4777) adj. fem. poor, abject poverty, referring to one who has literally nothing and is in imminent danger of real starvation (NTW, 110). **ἔβαλεν** aor. ind. act. βάλλω (# 965) to throw. **λεπτόν** (# 3321) the smallest Jewish coin. A small copper coin worth normally about one-eighth of a cent (BAGD; Lane; HJC, 296-302; DJG, 805). **κοδράντης** (# 3119) a Roman coin equal to about a fourth of a cent (BAGD). Mark gives the Roman coinage for the benefit of his readers (Taylor). ◆ **43 προσκαλεσάμενος** aor. mid. part. (temp.) προσκαλέομαι (# 4673) to summons, to call to oneself. **πλεῖον** comp. πολύς (# 4498) much; "more." **πάντων** s.v. 33. **βαλλόντων** pres. act. part. βάλλω s.v. 41. ◆ **44 περισσεύοντος** pres. act. part. περισσεύω (# 4355) to be in abundance. Part. used as subst. **ὑστερήσεως** gen. sing. ὑστέρησις (# 5730) deficiency, want, need. **εἶχεν** impf. ind. act. ἔχω (# 2400) to have, to possess. **βίον** acc. sing. βίος (# 1050) living, livelihood, the means by which life is sustained (AS).

Mark 13

◆ **1** For a discussion of this chapter as well as its history of interpretation s. George R. Beasley-Murray, *Jesus and the Last Days: The Interpretation of the Olivet Discourse* (Peabody, Mass.: Hendrickson Publishers, 1993). **ἐκπορευομένου** pres. mid. (dep.) part. (temp.) ἐκπορεύομαι (# 1744) to go out. Gen. abs. ἴδε (# 2623) aor. imp. act. ὁράω to see. ποταπός (# 4534) what sort of, how fashioned. οἰκοδομαί nom. pl. οἰκοδομή (# 3869) building. Pl. refers to the whole Temple complex (Gundry, 735; for a description of the temple s. Jos., JW, 5:184-247; Ant., 15: 380-425; JPB, 51-72; TJ, 28-30; DJG, 811-14). ◆ 2 ἀφεθῇ aor. subj. pass. ἀφίημι (# 918) to leave. Subj. w. the two negatives is emphatic (RG, 1174). καταλυθῇ aor. subj. pass. καταλύω (# 2907) to destroy, to completely demolish (RWP). For the destruction of the Temple s. TJ, 190-98. ◆ 3 καθημένου pres. mid. (dep.) part. (temp.) κάθημι (# 2764) to sit down. Gen. abs. ἐπηρώτα impf. ind. act. ἐπερωτάω (# 2089) to question, to ask. Inceptive impf., "they began to ask." For grammatical remarks on this section s. VA, 433-35. ◆ 4 εἰπόν aor. imp. act. λέγω (# 3306). For the form s. MH, 58; GGP, 2:337. μέλλῃ pres. subj. act. μέλλω (# 3516) to be about to. Used w. inf. to express the fut. Subj. w. ὅταν (# 4020) in an indef. temp. cl. συντελεῖσθαι pres. pass. inf. συντελέω (# 5334) to complete, to bring to an end. Prep. in the compound is perfective (Taylor). ◆ 5 ἤρξατο aor. ind. mid. (dep.) ἄρχομαι (# 806) to begin, w. inf. βλέπετε pres. imp. act. βλέπω (# 1063) to see, to watch out, to beware, s. vv. 9, 23, 33. πλανήσῃ aor. subj. act. πλανάω (# 4414) to lead astray, to cause to wander, to deceive. For revolutionary movements s. DJG, 688-98. Subj. in a neg. purp. cl. ◆ 6 ἐλεύσονται fut. ind. mid. (dep.) ἔρχομαι (# 2262) to go, to come. ἐπὶ τῷ ὀνόματί μου on the basis of my name. That is, coming and saying that they are the Christ just as he had done (Gundry, 737). πλανήσουσιν fut. ind. act. s.v. 5. ◆ 7 ἀκούσητε aor. subj. act. ἀκούω (# 201) to hear. πόλεμος (# 4483) war. θροεῖσθε pres. imp. pass. θροέω (# 2583) to raise an outcry; pass., of the alarm occasioned by a sudden cry or of mental uneasiness in general, to be inwardly aroused, to be disturbed or frightened (Swete; BAGD). Pres. imp. w. the neg. has the idea "do not immediately be alarmed" (MKG, 272). δεῖ (# 1256) pres. ind. act. it is necessary, w. inf. Shows divine necessity. γενέσθαι aor. mid. (dep.) inf. γίνομαι (# 1181) to become, to happen. ◆ 8 ἐγερθήσεται fut. ind. pass. ἐγείρω (# 1586) to rise up. ἔσονται fut. ind. mid. (dep.) εἰμί (# 1639). σεισμός (# 4939) earthquake. κατά (# 2848) distributive use of the prep.; "from place to place," "everywhere," "here and there." λιμός (# 3350) famine. ἀρχή (# 794) beginning. ὠδίνων gen. pl. ὠδίν (# 6047) birth pains (Matt. 24:8). For the form s. MH, 135. ◆ 9 παραδώσουσιν fut. ind. act. παραδίδωμι (# 4140) to deliver over. συνέδριον (# 5284) (BBC; DJG; 728-32; ABD, 5:975-80) a local Jewish council, court (Moore, Judaism, 261). δαρήσεσθε fut. ind. pass. δέρω (# 1296) to beat. ἡγεμόνων gen. pl. ἡγεμών (# 2450) ruler, governor. σταθήσεσθε fut. ind. pass. ἵστημι (# 2705) to place, to set, to stand. μαρτύριον (# 3457) witness. For the threefold aspect of this witness s. Cranfield. αὐτοῖς

dat. pl. αὐτός (# 899). Dat. of disadvantage: "against them." ◆ 10 κηρυχθῆναι aor. pass. inf. κηρύσσω (# 3062) to preach, to proclaim as a herald. Inf. w. δεῖ (s.v. 7). ◆ 11 ἄγωσιν pres. subj. act. ἄγω (# 72) to lead. Subj. w. ὅταν (# 4020) in an indef. rel. cl. Pres. subj. used when the issue personally affects those present (VA, 326). παραδιδόντες pres. act. part. s.v. 9. Part. of manner. προμεριμνᾶτε pres. imp. act. προμεριμνάω (# 4628) to concern oneself, to be anxious beforehand. Pres. imp. denotes simultaneous action w. another action (VANT, 391). λαλήσητε aor. subj. act. λαλέω (# 3281) to speak. Subj. w. ἐάν (# 1569) in an indef. cl. δοθῇ aor. subj. pass. δίδωμι (# 1443) to give. Theol. pass. indicating that God is the giver. λαλεῖτε pres. imp. act. λαλέω. λαλοῦντες pres. act. part. Part. as subst. ◆ 12 παραδώσει fut. ind. act. s.v. 9. παραδίδωμι to betray. ἐπαναστήσονται fut. ind. act. ἐπανίστημι (# 2060) to rise up against. γονεῖς acc. pl. γονεύς (# 1204) pl. parents. θανατώσουσιν fut. ind. act. θανατόω (# 2506) to kill. ◆ 13 ἔσεσθε fut. ind. mid. (dep.) εἰμί (# 1639) to be. μισούμενοι pres. pass. part. μισέω (# 3631) to hate. Part. as predicate adj., or as part of a fut. periphrastic construction (RG, 889; VA, 464). ὑπομείνας aor. act. part. ὑπομένω (# 5702) to remain under, to endure patiently, to continue to bear up despite difficulty and suffering (LN, 1:308; TDNT; EDNT). σωθήσεται fut. ind. pass. σῴζω (# 5392) to rescue, deliver, to save. ◆ 14 ἴδητε aor. subj. act. s.v. 1. Subj. w. ὅταν (# 4020) in an indef. temp. cl. βδέλυγμα (# 1007) that which is detestable, abomination. ἐρημώσεως gen. sing. ἐρήμωσις (# 2247) making into a desert, desolating, desolation (Matt. 24:15; BBC). ἑστηκότα perf. act. part. ἵστημι (# 2705) to stand (perf.). ἀναγινώσκων pres. act. part. ἀναγινώσκω (# 336) to read. Part. as subst. νοείτω pres. imp. act. νοέω (# 3783) to understand, to comprehend. φευγέτωσαν pres. imp. act. 3rd. pl. φεύγω (# 5771) to flee. ◆ 15 καταβάτω aor. imp. act. καταβαίνω (# 2849) to come down. εἰσελθάτω aor. imp. act. εἰσέρχομαι (# 1656) to go in. Aor. imp. prohibits the whole act. ἆραι aor. act. inf. αἴρω (# 149) to take away, to remove. Inf. used to express purp. ◆ 16 ἐπιστρεψάτω aor. imp. act. 3rd. pers. sing. ἐπιστρέφω (# 2188) to turn about. ἆραι aor. act. inf. s.v. 15. ◆ 17 ἐχούσαις pres. act. part. dat. fem. pl. ἔχω (# 2400) to have. Used in the idiom "to have something in the stomach," "to be pregnant." θηλαζούσαις pres. act. part. fem. dat. pl. θηλάζω (# 2558) to nurse, to suck. Part. as subst. ◆ 18 προσεύχεσθε pres. imp. mid. (dep.) προσεύχομαι (# 4667) to pray. γένηται aor. subj. mid. (dep.) γίνομαι (# 1181) to become, to be. Subj. in an obj. cl. χειμῶνος (# 5930) wintertime. ◆ 19 ἔσονται fut. ind. mid. (dep.) εἰμί (# 1639) to be. γέγονεν perf. ind. act. s.v. 18. τοιαύτη (# 5525) of such a kind, of such a character. It emphazies the severity of the tribulation (Gundry, 777). ἔκτισεν aor. ind. act. κτίζω (# 3231) to make, to create. This increases the emphasis on unprecedented severity (Gundry, 777). ◆ **20 ἐκολόβωσεν** aor. ind. act. κολοβόω (# 3143) to shorten. **ἐσώθη** aor. ind. pass. s.v. 13. Ind. used in a 2nd. class cond. cl. (contrary to fact). **ἐξελέξατο** aor. ind. mid. ἐκλέγω (# 1721) to choose; mid. to choose out, to pick out for oneself. ◆ **21 εἴπῃ** aor. subj. act. λέγω (# 3306). Subj. w. **ἐάν** (# 1569) in a 3rd. class cond. assuming the possibility of the cond. **πιστεύετε** pres. imp. act. πιστεύω (# 4409) to believe, to trust. Pres. imp. calls for a continual rejection of the false claims. ◆ **22 ἐγερθήσονται** fut. ind. pass. ἐγείρω (# 1586) to raise; pass. to rise, to appear on the scene (BAGD). **δώσουσιν** fut. ind. act. δίδωμι (# 1443) to give. For the variant reading ποιήσουσιν (fut. ind. act.) s. TC, 112. **ἀποπλανᾶν** pres. act. inf. ἀποπλανάω (# 675) to lead astray, to cause to wander. The prep. compound is either local or perfective, to lead away (MH, 297). Inf. w. **πρός** (# 4639) to indicate subjective purp. (Taylor). ◆ **23 προείρηκα** perf. ind. act. προλέγω (# 4625) to say beforehand. Perf. indicates the abiding results of what was predicted. ◆ **24 σκοτισθήσεται** fut. ind. pass. σκοτίζω (# 5029) to darken, to make dark. **σελήνη** (# 4943) moon. **δώσει** fut. ind. act. s.v. 22. **φέγγος** (# 5766) acc. sing. light, ray, beam. ◆ **25 ἔσονται** fut. ind. mid. (dep.) εἰμί (# 1639) to be, used w. pres. part. to form a fut. periphrastic construction (VA, 483). **πίπτοντες** pres. act. part. πίπτω (# 4406) to fall. **σαλευθήσονται** fut. ind. pass. σαλεύω (# 4888) to shake. For OT and Jewish references concerning the celestial disaster s. Gundry, 783; EDNT. ◆ **26 ὄψονται** fut. ind. mid. (dep.) ὁράω (# 3972) to see. **ἐρχόμενον** pres. mid. (dep.) part. ἔρχομαι (# 2262) to go. Part. as adj. ◆ **27 ἀποστελεῖ** fut. ind. act. ἀποστέλλω (# 690) to send, to commission; to send w. a special task, as a representative w. the authority of the one sending. **ἐπισυνάξει** fut. ind. act. ἐπισυνάγω (# 2190) to assemble, to gather together. **ἄκρου** gen. sing. ἄκρον (# 216) end, extreme limit (BAGD). ◆ **28 συκῆ** (# 5190) fig tree. **μάθετε** aor. imp. act. μανθάνω (# 3443) to learn. **κλάδος** (# 3080) branch. **ἀπαλός** (# 559) tender; pred. adj. The fig tree is mentioned because in Palestine, where most trees are evergreens, oaks, or olives, the rising of the sap in its branches and the appearance of leaves is a sure sign that winter is past (Taylor; Lane). **γένηται** aor. subj. mid. (dep.) s.v. 18. Subj. w. **ὅταν** (# 4020) in an indef. temp. cl. **ἐκφύῃ** pres. subj. act. ἐκφύω (# 1770) to put forth, to sprout. **φύλλα** acc. pl. φύλλον (# 5877) leaf; pl. foliage. **γινώσκετε** pres. imp. / ind. act. γινώσκω (# 1182) to know, to recognize. **θέρος** (# 2550) summer. ◆ **29 ἴδητε** aor. subj. act. ὁράω (# 3972) to see. Subj. w. **ὅταν** (# 4020) in an indef. temp. cl. **γινόμενα** pres. mid. (dep.) part. γίνομαι (# 1181) "When you see these things happening." ◆ **30 παρέλθῃ** aor. subj. act. παρέρχομαι (# 4216) to pass by, to pass away. For the subj. w. the double neg. οὐ μή s. RG, 929; IBG, 22. **γενεά** (# 1155) generation, race (Swete). **μέχρις οὗ** (# 3588; 4005) until. **γένηται** aor. subj. mid. (dep.) γίνομαι (# 1181) to be-

come, to happen. Subj. in an indef. temp. cl. ◆ **31 παρελεύσονται** fut. ind. mid. (dep.) s.v. 30. ◆ **32 οἶδεν** perf. ind. act. οἶδα (# 3857) to know. Def. perf. w. pres. meaning. ◆ **33 ἀγρυπνεῖτε** pres. imp. act. ἀγρυπνέω (# 70) to chase sleep away, to be watchful, to be alert, to be on the lookout for, to be vigilant (MH, 290; LN, 1:333). Pres. imp. calls for a constant vigil. ◆ **34 ἀπόδημος** (# 624) to be away from home, to be away on a journey. **ἀφείς** aor. act. part. (circum.) ἀφίημι (# 918) to leave, "he left." **δούς** aor. act. part. (circum.) δίδωμι (# 1443) to give, "he gave." Aor. giving antecedent action. **θυρωρός** (# 2601) doorkeeper, the one who stood guard at the entrance of a courtyard which served several houses (SB, 2:47; BBC). **ἐνετείλατο** aor. ind. mid. (dep.) ἐντέλλομαι (# 1948) to command. **γρηγορῇ** pres. subj. act. γρηγορέω (# 1213) to watch, to keep awake, to be on the alert (BAGD). Subj. in a obj. cl. ◆ **35 γρηγορεῖτε** pres. imp. act. s.v. 34. **ὀψέ** (# 4067) evening. **μεσονύκτιον** (# 3543) midnight, acc. of time. **ἀλεκτοροφωνίας** gen. sing. ἀλεκτοροφωνία (# 231) the crowing of a rooster. "At cockcrow," the name of the third watch of the night (12-3 a.m.) (BAGD; BBC). Gen. of time. **πρωΐ** (# 4745) early morning. These four words denote the four watches of the night, from six at night to six in the morning (Gould). ◆ **36 ἐλθών** aor. act. part. ἔρχομαι (# 2262) temp. or cond. part. Aor. giving antecedent action. **ἐξαίφνης** (# 1978) suddenly. **εὕρῃ** aor. subj. act. εὑρίσκω (# 2351) to find. Subj. in a neg. purp. cl. **καθεύδοντας** pres. act. part. καθεύδω (# 2761) to sleep. Adj. part. complementary to main vb.

Mark 14

◆ **1 ἦν** impf. ind. act. εἰμί (# 1639) to be. Here equivalent to, "was about to be." Mark looks back on the event as past (Swete). **πάσχα** (# 4247) Passover, the Passover Lamb, the Passover Feast, or the Passover Meal (Matt. 26:2; DJG, 236-41; SB, 4:41-76). **ἄζυμος** (# 109) unleavened, the Feast of Unleavened Bread celebrated in connection w. Passover. For the days of the week involved s. Gundry, 801. **ἐζήτουν** impf. ind. act. ζητέω (# 2426) to seek. Impf. pictures the repeated attempts without success. **δόλος** (# 1515) deceit, guile, trickery. **κρατήσαντες** aor. act. part. (circum.) κρατέω (# 3195) to seize. **ἀποκτείνωσιν** aor. subj. act. ἀποκτείνω (# 650) to kill. Pres. emphasizes their murderous intent (Gundry, 801). ◆ **2 ἑορτῇ** (# 2038) dat. sing. feast. **μήποτε** (# 3607) lest, used to express neg. purp. **ἔσται** fut. ind. mid. (dep.) εἰμί to be. Fut. ind. represents the danger as real and imminent, and adds force to the depreciation (Swete). **θόρυβος** (# 2573) tumult, uproar, riot. ◆ **3 ὄντος** pres. act. part. (temp.) εἰμί (# 1639). Gen. abs. **κατακειμένου** pres. mid. (dep.) part. (temp.) κατάκειμαι (# 2879) to recline at the table, Gen. abs. **ἦλθεν** aor. ind. act. ἔρχομαι (# 2262) to come, to go. **ἔχουσα** pres. act. part. ἔχω (# 2400) to have. **ἀλάβαστρον** (# 223) an alabaster vase (s. Matt. 26:7). Unguents kept best in alabaster boxes [*alabastris*] (Pliny, NH, 13:19). μύρου gen. sing. μύρον (# 3693) sweet-smelling oil, perfume. Gen. of content. νάρδος (# 3726) spikenard, nard. A plant native to India (BAGD; s. PB, 205; POB, 148-49) that had a "foremost place among perfumes" (Pliny, NH, 12:42). The raw product cost 100 denarii a pound, and its leaves cost anywhere from 40 to 75 denarii, depending on the size (Pliny, NH, 12:44). In 13:20 Pliny says the cost for the finished product is more than 400 denarii. πιστικός (# 4410) genuine, pure (Taylor; LN, 1:703). πολυτελοῦς gen. sing. πολυτελής (# 4500) very expensive, having great cost (MH, 285; BBC). συντρίψασα aor. act. part. nom. fem. sing. συντρίβω (# 5341) to crush. The breaking of the flask was perhaps the expression of the wholeheartedness of her devotion (Cranfield). It dramatizes the outpouring of all the contents by making the flask henceforth unusable (Gundry, 813). κατέχεεν aor. ind. act. καταχέω (# 2972) to pour down, to pour over, w. gen. ◆ 4 ἀγανακτοῦντες pres. act. part. ἀγανακτέω (# 24) to be unwilling, to be angry, to be indignant against what is judged to be wrong (LN, 1:762). Part. used as pred. adj. or as periphrastic w. ἦσαν. ἀπώλεια (# 724) destruction, ruin, waste. γέγονεν perf. ind. act. γίνομαι (# 1181) to become, to happen, to be. For a similar complaint that perfumes serve the most superfluous of all forms of luxury, because unguents lose their scent and die at once when used s. Pliny, NH, 13:20. ◆ 5 ἠδύνατο aor. ind. mid. (dep.) δύναμαι (# 1538) to be able, w. inf. πραθῆναι aor. pass. inf. πιπράσκω (# 4405) to sell. ἐπάνω (# 2062) over, above, more than. For the price of the perfume s.v. 3. δοθῆναι aor. pass. inf. δίδωμι (# 1443) to give. ἐνεβριμῶντο impf. ind. mid. (dep.) ἐμβριμάομαι (# 1839) to snort, an expression of anger and displeasure, to warn sternly. w. dat. (BAGD; s. Mark 1:43). ◆ 6 ἄφετε aor. imp. act. ἀφίημι (# 918) to leave, to leave alone. Aor. imp. here calls for immediate cessation of the action. παρέχετε pres. ind. act. παρέχω (# 4218) to cause. In this context "to cause trouble." ἠργάσατο aor. ind. mid. (dep.) ἐργάζομαι (# 2237) to work, to do. ◆ 7 θέλητε pres. subj. act. θέλω (# 2527) to wish, to will, to want to. Subj. w. ὅταν (# 4020) in an indef. temp. cl. ποιῆσαι aor. act. inf. ποιέω (# 4472) to do. ◆ 8 ἔσχεν aor. ind. act. ἔχω (# 2400) to have. ἐποίησεν aor. ind. act. s.v. 7. προέλαβεν aor. ind. act. προλαμβάνω (# 4624) to take beforehand, to anticipate. For the Jewish aspect of performimg a deed in advance s. NTRJ, 313. μυρίσαι aor. act. inf. μυρίζω (# 3690) to anoint. Epex. inf. explaining the main vb. ἐνταφιασμός (# 1947) preparation for burial, or the burial (Taylor; BAGD). The anointing w. expensive perfume gives Him dignity in burial so as to erase the shame of the coming crucifixion (Gundry, 804; NTRJ, 312). ◆ 9 κηρυχθῇ aor. subj. pass. κηρύσσω (# 3062) to preach, to herald. Subj. w. ὅπου ἐάν (# 3963;

1569) in an indef. cl. λαληθήσεται fut. ind. pass. λαλέω (# 3281) to speak, to tell. μνημόσυνον (# 3649) memorial. ◆ 10 ἀπῆλθεν aor. ind. act. ἀπέρχομαι (# 599) to go out. παραδοῖ aor. subj. act. παραδίδωμι (# 4140) to deliver over. Subj. in a purp. cl. ◆ 11 ἀκούσαντες aor. act. part. (temp.) ἀκούω (# 201) to hear. ἐχάρησαν aor. ind. pass. χαίρω (# 5897) to rejoice, to be glad. ἐπηγγείλαντο aor. ind. mid. (dep.) ἐπαγγέλλομαι (# 2040) to promise, w. epex. inf. δοῦναι aor. act. inf. δίδωμι (# 1443) to give. ἐζήτει impf. ind. act. s.v. 1. Inceptive impf., "he began to seek ..." or iterat. impf., "he sought continually...." εὐκαίρως (# 2323) conveniently, well-timed, opportunely. ◆ 12 ἔθυον impf. ind. act. θύω (# 2604) to slay, to sacrifice (an animal). Customary impf. ἀπελθόντες aor. act. part. (circum.) s.v. 10. ἑτοιμάσωμεν aor. subj. act. ἑτοιμάζω (# 2286) to prepare. Deliberative subj. in an obj. cl. (SIMS, 75-76). φάγῃς aor. subj. act. ἐσθίω (# 2266) to eat. Subj. w. ἵνα (# 2671) in purp. cl. ◆ 13 ὑπάγετε pres. imp. act. ὑπάγω (# 5632) to go forth. Pres. imp. w. a vb. of motion. ἀπαντήσει fut. ind. act. ἀπαντάω (# 560) to meet, w. dat. κεράμιον (# 3040) acc. sing. a jar or vessel of pottery. ὕδατος gen. sing. ὕδωρ (# 5623) water. Gen. of content. βαστάζων pres. act. part. βαστάζω (# 1002) to carry. Adj. part. ἀκολουθήσατε aor. imp. act. ἀκολουθέω (# 199) to follow, w. dat. ◆ 14 εἰσέλθῃ aor. subj. act. εἰσέρχομαι (# 1656) to go in. Subj. w. ὅπου ἄν (# 3963; 323) in an indef. rel. cl. εἴπατε aor. imp. act. λέγω (# 3306). οἰκοδεσπότης (# 3867) master of the house, landlord. κατάλυμα (# 2906) inn, guest room (Taylor). The citizens of Jerusalem provided rooms for the pilgrims free of charge (WZZT, 160; JPF, 2:903). φάγω aor. subj. act. s.v. 12. ◆ 15 δείξει fut. ind. act. δείκνυμι (# 1259) to show. ἀνάγαιον (# 333) a room upstairs. ἐστρωμένον perf. pass. part. στρώννυμι (# 5143) to spread out; or perhaps to be provided w. carpeted couches on which the guests reclined. (Swete; Taylor; NTNT, 39). Adj. part. ἕτοιμος (# 2289) ready, prepared. ἑτοιμάσατε aor. imp. act. ἑτοιμάζω (# 2286) to prepare, get ready. ◆ 16 ἐξῆλθον aor. ind. act. ἐξέρχομαι (# 2002) to go out. ἦλθον aor. ind. act. s.v. 3. εὗρον aor. ind. act. εὑρίσκω (# 2251) to find. ἡτοίμασαν aor. ind. act. s.v. 15. ◆ 17 γενομένης aor. mid. (dep.) part. gen. abs. s.v. 4. This could include late afternoon before sunset as well as twilight after sunset (Gundry, 835; BBC). ◆ 18 ἀνακειμένων pres. mid. (dep.) part. (temp.) ἀνάκειμαι (# 367) to recline at the table. One would recline on the cushions around the table and eat. Gen. abs. ἐσθιόντων pres. act. part. ἐσθίω (# 2266) to eat. Gen. abs. παραδώσει fut. ind. act. παραδίδωμι s.v. 10. ◆ 19 ἤρξαντο aor. ind. mid. (dep.) ἄρχομαι (# 806) to begin, w. inf. λυπεῖσθαι pres. mid. (dep.) inf. λυπέομαι (# 3382) to be sad, to be sorrowful. εἰς κατὰ εἷς (# 1651; 2848) one by one. (Taylor; SIMS, 154, 226, 372). μήτι (# 3614) "Not I, is it?" It suggests a possibility, only to negate it (Gundry, 836). ◆ 20 ἐμβαπτόμενος pres. mid.

(indir. mid. "for oneself") part. ἐμβάπτω (# 1835) to dip in. Part. used as subst. τρύβλιον (# 5581) bowl. The pieces of bread were dipped into the sauce or relish. This intimate relationship is broken by betrayal (BBC). ◆ 21 γέγραπται perf. ind. pass. γράφω (# 1211) to write. Perf. "it stands written" (MM). παραδίδοται pres. ind. pass. s.v. 10. Futuristic pres. ἐγεννήθη aor. ind. pass. γεννάω (# 1164) to bear; pass. to be born. Ind. in a 2nd. class cond. cl. which assumes the cond. to be contrary to fact. ◆ 22 λαβών aor. act. part. (temp.) λαμβάνω (# 3284) to take. εὐλογήσας aor. act. part. (temp.) εὐλογέω (# 2328) to give thanks, to praise, to bless. ἔκλασεν aor. ind. act. κλάω (# 3089) to break. ἔδωκεν aor. ind. act. δίδωμι (# 1443) to give. λάβετε aor. imp. act. λαμβάνω (# 3284) to take. For the celebration of the meal s. SB, 4:41-76; HSB, 448-50; BBC. ◆ 23 εὐχαριστήσας aor. act. part. (temp.) εὐχαριστέω (# 2373) to thank, to say thanks. ἔπιον aor. ind. act. πίνω (# 4403) to drink. ◆ 24 διαθήκη (# 1347) covenant, testament, will (s. Matt. 26:28). ἐκχυννόμενον pres. pass. part. ἐκχέω (# 1772) to pour out, to shed. Blood was used in the treaty ceremony to indicate that disobedience to the covenant stipulations would result in death. ὑπέρ (# 5642) w. gen., for; either in the sense of "for the benefit of," or "instead of" (EDNT; NIDNTT, 3:1196-97). ◆ 25 πίω aor. subj. act. s.v. 23. For the construction the double neg. οὐ μή (# 4024; 3590) s. RG, 929-30. γενήματος gen. sing. γένημα (# 1163) that which is produced, fruit. For references to the messanic banquet s. Gundry, 844. ◆ 26 ὑμνήσαντες aor. act. part. ὑμνέω (# 5630) to sing a hymn. The Passover meal was concluded w. the singing of the last part of the Hallel, ending w. Psalm 118; the meal was to be over by midnight (WZZT, 232, 288-90; M, Pesahim, 7-9). This last song, Ps. 118, appears throughout the last week of Christ's earthly life starting w. the triumphal entry. The psalm emphasizes the treachery of friends; the assurance of deliverance and the coming coronation of the Messianic King. ἐξῆλθον aor. ind. act. s.v. 16. ◆ 27 σκανδαλισθήσεσθε fut. ind. pass. σκανδαλίζω (# 4997) to cause to stumble, to offend; pass. to be offended; to be tripped up and fall into sin because of some baneful influence (Gundry, 844; TDNT; EDNT; NIDNTT; TLNT). γέγραπται perf. ind. pass. s.v. 21. πατάξω fut. ind. act. πατάσσω (# 4250) to strike, to hit. ποιμένα acc. sing. ποιμήν (# 4478) shepherd. διασκορπισθήσονται fut. ind. pass. διασκορπίζω (# 1399) to scatter. ◆ 28 ἐγερθῆναι aor. pass. inf. ἐγείρω (# 1586) to rise up; pass. to be raised. Inf. w. prep. μετά (# 3552) "after I am raised." προάξω fut. ind. act. προάγω (# 4575) to go forward, to go before. The word may continue the shepherd image and mean "to lead" (Pesch). ◆ 29 ἔφη impf. ind. act. φήμι (# 5774) to say (VA, 443-46). σκανδαλισθήσονται fut ind. pass. s.v. 27. Fut. in a cond. cl. expressing "expectaion" (VA, 315). ◆ 30 ἀλέκτορα acc. ἀλέκτωρ (# 232) rooster.

φωνῆσαι aor. act. inf. φωνέω (# 5888) to call, to make a sound, to crow, indicating the coming dawn (BBC). Inf. w. prep. πρίν (# 4570) "before." ἀπαρνήσῃ aor. subj. mid. (dep.) ἀπαρνέομαι (# 565) to deny. For a discussion of the textual problems s. Markus Öhler, "Der zweimalige Hahnschrei der Markuspassion: Zur Textüberlieferung von Mk 14, 30.68.72," ZNW 85 (1994): 145-50. ◆ 31 ἐκπερισσῶς (# 1735) beyond measure, exceedingly. ἐλάλει impf. ind. act. s.v. 9. Inceptive impf. δέῃ pres. subj. act. δεῖ (# 1256) it is necessary, w. inf. Subj. w. ἐάν (# 1569) in cond. cl. assuming the possibility of the cond. συναποθανεῖν aor. act. inf. συναποθνήσκω (# 5271) to die together. ἀπαρνήσομαι fut. ind. mid. (dep.) s.v. 30. For the construction s. BD, 184; RG 929. ◆ 32 Γεθσημανί (# 1149) Gethsemane (Heb. / Aram. "press of oils" Lane; ISBE, 2:457-58; ABD, 2:997-98). καθίσατε aor. imp. act. καθίζω (# 2767) to sit, take one's seat. προσεύξωμαι aor. subj. mid. (dep.) προσεύχομαι (# 4667) to pray. Subj. in a temp. cl. ◆ 33 ἤρξατο aor. ind. mid. (dep.), w. inf. s.v. 19. ἐκθαμβεῖσθαι pres. mid. (dep.) inf. ἐκθαμβέομαι (# 1701) to be amazed, to be distressed. Here denotes a being in the grip of a shuddering horror given the dreadful prospect before him (Cranfield). ἀδημονεῖν pres. act. inf. ἀδημονέω (# 86) to be sorely troubled, to be in anguish, to be upset (Taylor; LN, 1:315). ◆ 34 περίλυπος (# 4337) very sorrowful, surrounded w. sorrow, very sad. Prep. in compound is perfective (Gundry, 854) or intensive: "having excessive sorrow" (MH, 322). μείνατε aor. imp. act. μένω (# 3531) to remain. Aor. calls for a specific action (VANT, 334). γρηγορεῖτε pres. imp. act. γρηγορέω (# 1213) to be awake, to be watchful, to watch. Pres. imp. lays stress on the watching (VA, 355). ◆ 35 προελθών aor. act. part. προέρχομαι (# 4601) to go forward, to go farther. μικρόν (# 3625) adv. a little. ἔπιπτεν impf. ind. act. πίπτω (# 4406) to fall. Iterat. impf. pointing to the repeated prayers (Gundry, 854), or descriptive impf. describing the action as a moving-picture show (RG, 883). προσηύχετο impf. ind. mid. (dep.) s.v. 32. Impf. may be inceptive: "he began to pray." παρέλθῃ aor. subj. act. παρέρχομαι (# 4216) to go by, to pass by. The substance of the prayer is given in indir. speech (Taylor). ◆ 36 παρένεγκε aor. imp. act. παραφέρω (# 4195) to take away, to remove. ◆ 37 καθεύδοντας pres. act. part. καθεύδω (# 2761) to sleep. Adj. part. ἴσχυσας aor. ind. act. ἰσχύω (# 2710) to be strong, to be able, w. inf. γρηγορῆσαι aor. act. inf. s.v. 34. ◆ 38 προσεύχεσθε pres. imp. mid. (dep.) s.v. 32. Pres. imp. calls for a continual attitude in prayer. ἔλθητε aor. subj. act. ἔρχομαι (# 2262) to go, to enter. Subj. w. ἵνα (# 2671) in a neg. purp. cl. πρόθυμος (# 4609) willing, eager, ready. ἀσθενής (# 822) weak, without strength. ◆ 39 ἀπελθών aor. act. part. (circum.) s.v. 10. προσηύξατο aor. ind. mid. (dep.) s.v. 32. εἰπών aor. act. part. λέγω (# 3306) to say. Part. of manner. ◆ 40 ἐλθών aor. act. part. (temp.) s.v. 38. εὗρεν aor. ind.

act. s.v. 16. **καταβαρυνόμενοι** pres. pass. part. καταβαρύνω (# 2852) to be weighed down, to be heavy. Part. as pred. adj. **ἤδεισαν** plperf. ind. act. οἶδα (# 3857) to know. Def. plperf. w. impf. meaning. **ἀποκριθῶσιν** aor. subj. pass. (dep.) ἀποκρίνομαι (# 646) to answer. ◆ **41 καθεύδετε** pres. imp. act. s.v. 37. Pres. imp. calls for the continuation of an action in progress. It stresses the exasperation of Jesus (Gundry, 857). **ἀναπαύεσθε** pres. imp. mid. (dep.) ἀναπαύομαι (# 399) to cease, to rest. **ἀπέχει** pres. ind. act. ἀπέχω (# 600) it is sufficient, enough of this! For possible meanings s. Cranfield; Gundry, 856-57; NTNT, 39. **ἦλθεν** aor. ind. act. s.v. 3. **παραδίδοται** pres. ind. pass. s.v. 10. Pres. describes the action as it is taking place. ◆ **42 ἐγείρεσθε** pres. imp. pass. s.v. 28. **ἄγωμεν** pres. subj. act. ἄγω (# 72). Cohortative subj., "let us go." **παραδιδούς** pres. act. part. s.v. 10. Part. as subst. **ἤγγικεν** perf. ind. act. ἐγγίζω (# 1581) to draw near. ◆ **43 λαλοῦντος** pres. act. part. (temp.) λαλέω (# 3281) to speak. Gen. abs. w. contemporaneous time. **παραγίνεται** pres. ind. mid. (dep.) παραγίνομαι (# 4134) to come to. Hist. pres. **μαχαιρῶν** gen. pl. μάχαιρα (# 3479) sword, knife (BAGD; NTNT, 76-77; TJ, 107-108; EDNT). **ξύλον** (# 3833) wood, a stout stick or perhaps a club (Swete). ◆ **44 δεδώκει** plperf. ind. act. δίδωμι (# 1443) to give. For the plperf. without the augment s. BD, 36. **παραδιδούς** pres. act. part. s.v. 10. **σύσσημον** (# 5361) a sign, signal, a sign which has been previously agreed upon as having a particular meaning or significance (LN, 1:443). **φιλήσω** fut. ind. act. φιλέω (# 5797) to kiss (BBC). For the *casus pendens* construction followed by a resumptive pronoun s. SIMS, 86-88. **κρατήσατε** aor. imp. act. s.v. 1. **ἀπάγετε** pres. imp. act. ἀπάγω (# 552) to lead forth, to lead away. **ἀσφαλῶς** (# 857) adv., safely. ◆ **45 ἐλθών** aor. act. part. (circum.) s.v. 38. **προσελθών** aor. act. part. (temp.) προσέρχομαι (# 4665) to come to. **κατεφίλησεν** aor. ind. act. καταφιλέω (# 2968) to kiss fervently (Matt. 26:49). The compound indicates a prolonged kissing designed to give the crowd a chance to see the one to be seized (Cranfield). ◆ **46 ἐπέβαλον** aor. ind. act. ἐπιβάλλω (# 2095) to place, to lay hands upon in a hostile sense (Swete). **ἐκράτησαν** aor. ind. act. s.v. 1. ◆ **47 παρεστηκότων** perf. act. part. παρίστημι (# 4225) to stand by, to be present w. someone (BAGD). Adj. part. **σπασάμενος** aor. mid. (dep.) part. (circum.) σπάομαι (# 5060) to draw out, to draw. **ἔπαισεν** aor. ind. act. παίω (# 4091) to strike, to hit. **ἀφεῖλεν** aor. ind. act. ἀφαιρέω (# 904) to cut off. **ὠτάριον** (# 6064) acc. sing. dimin., ear. ◆ **48 ἀποκριθείς** aor. pass. (dep.) part. ἀποκρίνομαι (# 646) to answer. For the redundant use of the part. s. MH, 453. **λῃστής** (# 3334) robber. **ἐξήλθατε** aor. ind. act. s.v. 16. **συλλαβεῖν** aor. act. inf. συλλαμβάνω (# 5197) to arrest, to take as prisoner. Inf. of purp. ◆ **49 ἤμην** impf. ind. act. εἰμί (# 1639) to be. **διδάσκων** pres. act. part. διδάσκω (# 1438) to teach. Part. of manner. **ἐκρατήσατε** aor. ind.

act. s.v. 1. **πληρωθῶσιν** aor. subj. pass. πληρόω (# 4444) to fill, to fulfill. Subj. in a purp. cl. w. ἵνα (# 2671). ◆ **50 ἀφέντες** aor. act. part. (circum.) ἀφίημι (# 918) to leave, to forsake. **ἔφυγον** aor. ind. act. φεύγω (# 5771) to flee. ◆ **51 νεανίσκος** (# 3734) youth, young man. It has been suggested that this was John Mark (Gundry, 861; Lane). **συνηκολούθει** impf. ind. act. συνακολουθέω (# 5258) to follow along w. someone, w. dat. Impf. describes the continual action in the past. **περιβεβλημένος** perf. pass. part. περιβάλλω (# 4314) to put around, to put on, to be clothed ("having a sheet 'wrapped about' his naked body," NTNT, 40). **σινδών** (# 4984) fine linen cloth or a garment made out of it (Cranfield). Either a light summer square hastily caught up or a night dress (Swete). For the clothing of that time s. JPB, 123. **γυμνός** (# 1218) naked, possibly in the sense of light clad (Taylor). The shedding of a garment under high emotional feeling may picture the idea that Jesus was deserted by all (Howard M. Jackson, "Why the Youth Shed His Cloak and Fled Naked: The Meaning and Purpose of Mark 14:51-52," *JBL* 116 [1997]: 273-89). **κρατοῦσιν** pres. ind. act. s.v. 1. Hist. pres. or conative pres.: "they tried to seize...." ◆ **52 καταλιπών** aor. act. part. (circum.) καταλείπω (# 2901) to leave behind. **ἔφυγεν** aor. ind. act. s.v. 50. ◆ **53 ἀπήγαγον** aor. ind. act. s.v. 44. **συνέρχονται** pres. ind. mid. (dep.) συνέρχομαι (# 5302) to accompany, to go w. Hist. pres. ◆ **54 μακρόθεν** (# 3427) from a distance, from afar. **ἠκολούθησεν** aor. ind. act. ἀκολουθέω (# 199) to follow, w. dat. **αὐλή** (# 885) courtyard. An enclosed space, open to the sky, near a house or surrounded by buildings (BAGD). **συγκαθήμενος** pres. mid. (dep.) part. συγκάθημαι (# 5153) to sit together. **θερμαινόμενος** pres. mid. (dir. mid.) part. θερμαίνομαι (# 2548) to warm oneself. The two parts. are used in a periphrastic construction. **φῶς** (# 5890) acc. sing. light, fire. ◆ **55 συνέδριον** (# 5284) the Sanhedrin (TDNT; EDNT; HJPE, 2:199-226; JPFC, 1:379-400; Sidney B. Honig, *The Great Sanhedrin* [New York: Bloch Publishing Co., 1953]; M, Sanhedrin; b. Sanhedrin; John 11:47). For the legal violations of the trial s. Gundry, 893; BBC; DJG, 845-48. For the Roman interest s. DTM 1:666-68, 676-710. **ἐζήτουν** impf. ind. act. s.v. 1. **θανατῶσαι** aor. act. inf. θανατόω (# 2506) to kill. Inf. w. εἰς (# 1650) for purp. **ηὔρισκον** impf. ind. act. s.v. 16. Conative impf. indicating the unfulfilled action. ◆ **56 ἐψευδομαρτύρουν** impf. ind. act. ψευδομαρτυρέω (# 6018) to give a false witness. **ἴσαι** nom. pl. fem. ἴσος (# 2698) equal in number, size, quality, of testimony given by witnesses; consistent (BAGD). ◆ **57 ἀναστάντες** aor. act. part. (circum.) ἀνίστημι (# 482) to stand up, to rise up. ◆ **58 ἠκούσαμεν** aor. ind. act. ἀκούω (# 201) to hear. **καταλύσω** fut. ind. act. καταλύω (# 2907) to destroy. A new temple was expected after driving out the Romans (BBC). **χειροποίητος** (# 5935) made w. human hands. **ἀχειροποίητος** (# 942) not made w. human hands. For

the significance of the endings s. M, 221. **οἰκοδομήσω**
fut. ind. act. οἰκοδομέω (# *3868*) to build. ◆ **59 ἴση** equal
s.v. 56. ◆ **60 ἐπηρώτησεν** aor. ind. act. ἐπερωτάω (# *2089*)
to question. **ἀποκρίνῃ** pres. ind. mid. (dep.) 2nd. pers.
sing. ἀποκρίνομαι (# *646*) to answer. Iterat. pres. **καταμαρτυροῦσιν** pres. ind. act. καταμαρτυρέω (# *2909*) to
witness against, w. gen. ◆ **61 ἐσιώπα** impf. ind. act.
σιωπάω (# *4995*) to be silent. Perhaps this was in accord
to the current view of the Messiah (J. C. O'Niel, "The Silence of Jesus," *NTS* 15 [1969]: 153-67, esp. 165-67). **ἀπεκρίνατο** aor. ind. mid. (dep.) s.v. 60. **ἐπηρώτα** impf. ind.
act. s.v. 60. Inceptive impf. ◆ **62 ἐγώ εἰμι** "I am" (Matt.
26:64). **ὄψεσθε** fut. ind. mid. (dep.) ὁράω (# *3972*) to see.
καθήμενον pres. mid. (dep.) part. κάθημαι (# *2764*) to sit.
For a discussion of this messianic claim as the Son of
God s. Martin Hengel *The Son of God: The Origin of
Christology and the History of Jewish-Hellenistic Religion,*
trans. J. Bowden (London: SCM, 1976, 41-56). Adj. part.
ἐρχόμενον pres. mid. (dep.) part. s.v. 3. ◆ **63 διαρρήξας**
aor. act. part. (temp.) διαρρήγνυμι (# *1396*) to tear into,
to rip (Matt. 26:65; BBC). ◆ **64 ἠκούσατε** aor. ind. act.
ἀκούω (# *201*) to hear, w. gen. **βλασφημία** (# *1060*) slander, blasphemy. For blasphemy in connection w. v. 62 s.
Catchpole, 135-41; Gundry, 915; and for the Jewish
view of Jesus s. JNTU, esp. 217-38; M, Sanhedrin 6:4.
φαίνεται pres. ind. mid. φαίνω (# *5743*) to appear. **κατ-
έκριναν** aor. ind. act. κατακρίνω (# *2891*) to decide
against, to condemn. **ἔνοχος** (# *1944*) guilty, w. gen. explaining the charge, which here is at the end of the sentence for emphasis (BD, 98). **εἶναι** pres. act. inf. εἰμί
(# *1639*). Epex. inf. explaining the condemnation.
◆ **65 ἤρξαντο** aor. ind. mid. (dep.) s.v. 19 w. compl. inf.
ἐμπτύειν pres. act. inf. ἐμπτύω (# *1870*) to spit on, w. dat.
περικαλύπτειν pres. act. inf. περικαλύπτω (# *4328*) to
cover all around, to blindfold. **κολαφίζειν** pres. act. inf.
κολαφίζω (# *3139*) to strike w. the fist, derived from the
word meaning "knuckles" (MH, 407). Pres. infs. picture the repeated action. **προφήτευσον** aor. imp. act.
προφητεύω (# *4736*) to prophesy. This seems to be in accord w. the Jewish view of Isa. 11:2-4, which indicates
that the Messiah could judge by smell without seeing
(Lane; b, Sanhedrin 93b). **ὑπηρέτης** (# *5677*) helper, assistant, officer. These were evidently the armed guards
of the Temple (JPB, 28). **ῥάπισμα** (# *4825*) a slap on the
cheek w. the open hand (Taylor). **ἔλαβον** aor. ind. act.
s.v. 22. "They caught him w. blows" (Swete). ◆ **66
ὄντος** pres. act. part. (temp.) εἰμί. Gen. abs. **παιδισκῶν**
gen. pl. παιδίσκη (# *4087*) a female slave, maid.
◆ **67 ἰδοῦσα** aor. act. part. (temp.) ὁράω (# *3972*) to see.
θερμαινόμενον pres. mid. (dir. mid.) part. s.v. 54. **ἐμβλέ-
ψασα** aor. act. part. ἐμβλέπω (# *1838*) to look at. This
may indicate that she looked straight at him (Cranfield). **ἦσθα** impf. ind. mid. (dep.) 2nd. pers. sing. εἰμί
(# *1639*) to be. For the form s. MH, 203; GGP, 2:403.
◆ **68 ἠρνήσατο** aor. ind. mid. (dep.) ἀρνέομαι (# *766*) to

say no, to deny. **οἶδα** (# *3856*) perf. ind. act. to know.
Def. perf. w. pres. meaning (VA, 281-87). **ἐπίσταμαι**
(# *2179*) pres. ind. mid. (dep.) to understand. **ἐξῆλθεν**
aor. ind. act. s.v. 16. **προαύλιον** (# *4580*) acc. sing., the
vestibule leading to the courtyard. ◆ **69 παρεστῶσιν**
perf. act. part. (dat. masc. pl.) παρίστημι (# *4225*) perf. to
stand by, to be a bystander. Part. as subst. Dat. as indir.
obj. ◆ **70 ἠρνεῖτο** impf. ind. mid. (dep.) s.v. 68. Impf.
suggests repeated denials (Cranfield). ◆ **71 ἀναθε-
ματίζειν** pres. act. inf. ἀναθεματίζω (# *354*) to curse.
Peter invokes an anathema on himself if his denials are
false (Swete). **ὀμνύναι** pres. act. inf. ὄμνυμι/ὀμνύω
(# *3923*) to swear. For the form s. MH, 251; GGP, 2:375-
77. ◆ **72 ἐφώνησεν** aor. ind. act. s.v. 30. **ἀνεμνήσθη** aor.
ind. pass. ἀναμιμνήσκω (# *389*) to remind, pass., to remember. **εἶπεν** aor. ind. act. λέγω (# *3306*) to say.
φωνῆσαι aor. act. inf. s.v. 30. Inf. w. **πρίν** (# *4570*) to express antecedent time ("before"). **ἀπαρνήσῃ** aor. subj.
mid. (dep.) s.v. 30. **ἐπιβαλών** aor. act. part. (temp.) ἐπιβάλλω (# *2095*) to throw upon; to put his mind on
(RWP), to set about to, to begin (BD, 162; M, 131; NTNT,
41-43). **ἔκλαιεν** impf. ind. act. κλαίω (# *3081*) to weep, to
cry; inceptive impf. "began to cry."

Mark 15

◆ **1 πρωΐ** (# *4745*) early, at daybreak, from five to
six a.m. (Swete; BBC). It was common for the Roman
officials to be at work very early (Sherwin-White, 45).
συμβούλιον (# *5206*) council, counsel. W. the part. **ποιήσαντες** aor. act. part. ποιέω (# *4472*) to make, the meaning could be either "to reach a decision," or "to hold
consultation" (BAGD; Taylor). The variant reading,
ἑτοιμάσαντες, seems to support the latter (TC, 117; Gundry, 929). **δήσαντες** aor. act. part. (temp.) δέω (# *1313*) to
bind. **ἀπήνεγκαν** aor. ind. act. ἀποφέρω (# *708*) to carry
away, to take away. Used in the papyri of one who is
transferred from a village prison to the prison of the
metropolis (M, 39). **παρέδωκαν** aor. ind. act. παραδίδωμι
(# *4140*) to turn over, to deliver over to. ◆ **2 ἐπηρώτησεν**
aor. ind. act. ἐπερωτάω (# *2089*) to question. The prep.
in compound is directive. **Πιλᾶτος** (# *4397*) Pilate (TJ,
51-57). **ἀποκριθείς** aor. pass. (dep.) part. ἀποκρίνομαι
(# *646*) to answer. For the Semitic construction s. MH,
453. ◆ **3 κατηγόρουν** impf. ind. act. κατηγορέω (# *2989*)
to accuse. Iterat. impf. pictures the repeated accusations. ◆ **4 ἐπηρώτα** impf. ind. act. s.v. 2. **ἀποκρίνῃ** pres.
ind. mid. (dep.) 2nd. pers. sing. s.v. 2. Used in a question expecting a positive answer. **ἴδε** (# *2623*) aor. imp.
act. ὁράω to see; "look here!" **πόσα** nom. pl. πόσος
(# *4531*) how large, pl. how many. **κατηγοροῦσιν** pres.
ind. act. s.v. 3. Hist. pres., or indicating the action in
progress. ◆ **5 ἀπεκρίθη** aor. ind. pass. (dep.) s.v. 2. **θαυ-
μάζειν** pres. act. inf. θαυμάζω (# *2513*) to be astounded,
to wonder, to be amazed. Inf. w. **ὥστε** (# *6063*) to express actual result. Subject of the inf. in acc. ◆ **6 ἀπέλυ-**

εν impf. ind. act. ἀπολύω (# 668) to release. Customary impf., "it was customary to release," "he was in the habit of releasing" (Gould). παρῃτοῦντο impf. ind. mid. (dep.) or indir. mid. παραιτέομαι (# 4148) to ask from another, to beg. ◆ 7 ἦν impf. ind. act. εἰμί (# 1639) to be. λεγόμενος pres. pass. part. λέγω (# 3306) to say; pass. to be called. Βαραββᾶς Barabbas (MP, 74; EDNT). στασιαστής (# 5086) insurrectionist, rebel, revolutionary (BAGD). δεδεμένος perf. pass. part. δέω (# 1313) to bind. Part. as pred. adj. στάσις (# 5087) rebellion, insurrection. φόνος (# 5840) murder. πεποιήκεισαν plperf. ind. act. ποιέω (# 4472) to do, to make, to commit. For the lack of the augment s. BD, 36. ◆ 8 ἀναβάς aor. act. part. (circum.) ἀναβαίνω (# 326) to go up. ἤρξατο aor. ind. mid. (dep.) ἄρχομαι (# 806) to begin, w. inf. αἰτεῖσθαι pres. mid. inf. αἰτέω (# 160) to ask, to request; indir. mid., to ask for oneself. ἐποίει impf. ind. act. ποιέω, (# 4472) to do, to make. Customary impf. ◆ 9 ἀπεκρίθη aor. ind. pass. (dep.) s.v. 2. ἀπολύσω fut. ind. act. s.v. 6. ◆ 10 ἐγίνωσκεν impf. ind. act. γινώσκω (# 1182) to know. φθόνος (# 5784) jealousy, a state of ill will toward someone because of some real or presumed advantage experienced by such a person (LN, 1:760). παραδεδώκεισαν plperf. ind. act. παραδίδωμι (# 4140) to deliver over. ◆ 11 ἀνέσεισαν aor. ind. act. ἀνασείω (# 411) to stir up, to encite. ἀπολύσῃ aor. subj. act. s.v. 6. Subj. in purp. cl. ◆ 12 ἀποκριθείς aor. pass. (dep.) part. s.v. 2. ποιήσω fut. ind. act. s.v. 8. Deliberative fut. ◆ 13 ἔκραξαν aor. ind. act. κράζω (# 3189) to cry out, to scream. σταύρωσον (# 5090) aor. imp. act. σταυρόω to crucify. For a summary of recent research s. DTM, 2:884-99. ◆ 14 ἐποίησεν aor. ind. act. s.v. 8. ◆ 15 βουλόμενος pres. mid. (dep.) part. (causal) βούλομαι (# 1089) to will, to wish, to want. ἱκανός (# 2653) sufficient. Used in the idiom "to satisfy" (Taylor; RG, 1385). ποιῆσαι aor. act. inf. s.v. 8. παρέδωκεν aor. ind. act. s.v 10. φραγελλώσας aor. act. part. (temp.) φραγελλόω (# 5849) to flog (Matt. 27:26; Gundry, 938-39). σταυρωθῇ aor. subj. pass. s.v. 13. Subj. w. ἵνα (# 2671) in purp. cl. ◆ 16 ἀπήγαγον aor. ind. act. ἀπάγω (# 552) to lead out, to lead away. αὐλή (# 855) courtyard (s. 14:54). πραιτώριον (# 4550) the official residence of a governor. Here it is either Herod's palace (BBC) or the Tower of Antonia (Taylor). συγκαλοῦσιν pres. ind. act. συγκαλέω (# 5157) to call together. Hist. pres. ◆ 17 ἐνδιδύσκουσιν pres. ind. act. ἐνδιδύσκω (# 1898) to put on, to dress. Hist. pres. πορφύρα (# 4525) purple. The cloak of one of the soldiers, possibly a castoff and faded rag, but w. color enough left in it to suggest the royal purple (Swete; BBC). περιτιθέασιν pres. ind. act. περιτίθημι (# 4363) to place about. πλέξαντες aor. act. part. (circum.) πλέκω (# 4428) to braid, plait (out of thorns). For the ending signifying material s. MH, 359. ◆ 18 ἤρξαντο aor. ind. mid. (dep.) ἄρχομαι (# 806) to begin, w. inf. ἀσπάζεσθαι pres. mid. (dep.) inf. ἀσπάζομαι (# 832) to greet. χαῖρε pres. imp. act. χαίρω (# 5897) to

rejoice, to be glad. As a greeting, "Good day," "Hail to you," "Glad to see you," "How do you do?" (BAGD). ◆ 19 ἔτυπτον impf. ind. act. τύπτω (# 5597) to strike, to hit. Impf. looks at the repeated action. καλάμῳ dat. sing. κάλαμος (# 2812) reed. Instr. dat. ἐνέπτυον impf. ind. act. ἐμπτύω (# 1870) to spit on. τιθέντες pres. act. part. τίθημι (# 5502) to place. Used w. γόνατα (# 1205) to kneel. A Latinism for genua ponere (IBG, 192). Part. of manner. προσεκύνουν impf. ind. act. προσκυνέω (# 4686) to worship, to pay homage, a mockery in terms of Caesar worship or oriental ideas of kingship (Taylor). Impf. describes the continual action in the past. ◆ 20 ἐνέπαιξαν aor. ind. act. ἐμπαίζω (# 1850) to mock (TDNT; EDNT). Effective aor. pointing to the completion of the action. ἐξέδυσαν aor. ind. act. ἐκδύω (# 1694) to take off, to remove (clothing). ἐνέδυσαν aor. ind. act. ἐνδύω (# 1907) to put on. σταυρώσωσιν aor. subj. act. s.v. 13. Subj. in purp. cl. w. ἵνα (# 2671). ◆ 21 ἀγγαρεύουσιν pres. ind. act. ἀγγαρεύω (# 30) to compel, forcibly to impress someone into service, to compel him to serve whether he likes it or not (NTW, 16; NDIEC, 1:42; 2:77; BS, 86-87; MM). Hist. pres. παράγοντα pres. act. part. παράγω (# 4135) to pass by. Adj. part. ἐρχόμενον pres. mid. (dep.) part. (temp.) ἔρχομαι (# 2262) to go, to come. "As he was coming...." ἄρῃ aor. subj. act. αἴρω (# 149) to lift up, to take up. Subj. w. ἵνα (# 2671) in a cl. giving the content of the compelling. ◆ 22 μεθερμηνευόμενον pres. pass. part. μεθερμηνεύω (# 3493) to translate. Part. as pred. adj. κρανίον (# 3191) skull. ◆ 23 ἐδίδουν impf. ind. act. δίδωμι (# 1443) to give. The conative impf., "they tried to give" (Swete). ἐσμυρνισμένον perf. pass. part. σμυρνίζω (# 5046) to drug w. myrrh. In accordance w. Jewish customs, based on Proverbs 31:6, wine drugged w. myrrh was given in order to dull the senses (Cranfield). ἔλαβεν aor. ind. act. λαμβάνω (# 3284) to take, to receive. ◆ 24 σταυροῦσιν pres. ind. act. s.v. 13. Hist. pres. διαμερίζονται pres. ind. mid. διαμερίζω (# 1374) to distribute; mid. to divide among themselves. The soldier's clothing, provided from home or by his own means, reduced the amount of deductions from his stipend. This may explain why the soldiers cast lots for Jesus' garment (BBC; NDIEC, 6:158-59). βάλλοντες pres. act. part. βάλλω (# 965) to throw. Part. of means or manner. κλῆρος (# 3102) lot; that is, pebble or small stick (BAGD) possibly out of sheep bone. A certain combination of the highest number would win (LAW, 2861). ἄρῃ aor. subj. act. s.v. 21. Subj. in an indef. cl. ◆ 25 ἦν impf. ind. act. εἰμί (# 1639) to be. τρίτη third (about 9 o'clock). ἐσταύρωσαν aor. ind. act. s.v. 13. Aor. may be culminative, viewing the total crucifixion, or it may be ingressive, stressing the beginning of the crucifixion. ◆ 26 ἐπιγραφή (# 2107) inscription. αἰτία (# 162) cause, reason; here as legal t.t.: guilt, crime, charge, accusation (EDNT; BBC). ἐπιγεγραμμένη perf. pass. part. ἐπιγράφω (# 2108) to inscribe, to write upon (Matt.

27:37). ◆ **27 σταυροῦσιν** pres. ind. act. σταυρόω (# *5090*) to crucify. **λῃστάς** acc. pl. λῃστής (# *3334*) robber, insurrectionist (BAGD). **δεξιῶν** (# *1288*) right side, right hand. **εὐωνύμων** (# *2381*) left side, .left hand. ◆ **29 παραπορευόμενοι** pres. mid. (dep.) part. παραπορεύομαι (# *4182*) to go by, to pass by. Part. as subst. **ἐβλασφήμουν** impf. ind. act. βλασφημέω (# *1059*) to slander, to blaspheme (s. Mark 14:64; TLNT). Iterat. impf. stresses the repeated action. **κινοῦντες** pres. act. part. κινέω (# *3075*) to move, to shake. Part. of manner. Pres. indicates contemporaneous action. **οὐά** (# *4025*) ah! or ha!, indicating wonder, real or assumed (Taylor; SB, 2:52). **καταλύων** pres. act. part. καταλύω (# *2907*) to destroy, to demolish. Part. as subst. **οἰκοδομῶν** pres. act. part. οἰκοδομέω (# *3868*) to build. ◆ **30 σῶσον** aor. imp. act. σώζω (# *5392*) to save, to rescue. The jest was the harder to endure since it appealed to the consciousness of power held back only by the self-restraint of a sacrificed will (Swete). **καταβάς** aor. act. part. καταβαίνω (# *2849*) to come down, to go down. Part. of means. ◆ **31 ἐμπαίζοντες** pres. act. part. (circum.) ἐμπαίζω s.v. 20. **ἔσωσεν** aor. ind. act. s.v. 30. **σῶσαι** aor. act. inf. s.v. 30. ◆ **32 καταβάτω** aor. imp. act. s.v. 30. **ἴδωμεν** aor. subj. act. s.v. 4. Subj. w. ἵνα (# *2671*) in purp. cl. **πιστεύσωμεν** aor. subj. act. πιστεύω (# *4409*) to believe, to trust. Subj. in purp. cl. **συνεσταυρωμένοι** perf. pass. part. συσταυρόω (# *5365*) to co-crucify, to crucify together, τὸ crucify w. someone. Perf. emphasizes the state or cond. perhaps a generic pl. in light of Luke 23:39 (GGBB, 405). **ὠνείδιζον** impf. ind. act. ὀνειδίζω (# *3943*) to reproach, to insult. Impf. indicates the repeated action of the past. ◆ **33 γενομένης** aor. mid. (dep.) part. γίνομαι (# *1181*) to become, to happen. Gen. abs. **ἕκτος** sixth. The sixth hour was 12 noon. **ἐγένετο** aor. ind. mid. (dep.) γίνομαι. ◆ **34 ἐνάτῃ** dat. sing. ninth (3:00 p.m.). **ἐβόησεν** aor. ind. act. βοάω (# *1066*) to cry out, to shout, to cry aloud. **ἐλωι** (# *1836*) My God. **λεμα** (# *3316*) why? **σαβαχθανι** (# *4876*) you have forsaken me. (Matt. 27:46). **μεθερμηνευόμενον** pres. pass. part. s.v. 22. **ἐγκατέλιπες** aor. ind. act. 2nd. pers. sing. ἐγκαταλείπω (# *1593*) to forsake, to leave in the lurch, to provide no help. ◆ **35 παρεστηκότων** perf. act. part. παρίστημι (# *4225*) perf. to be a bystander, to stand aside. Part. as subst. **ἀκούσαντες** aor. act. part. (temp.) ἀκούω (# *201*) to hear. Aor. indicating antecedent action. **ἴδε** aor. imp. act. s.v. 4. **φωνεῖ** pres. ind. act. φωνέω (# *5888*) to call. ◆ **36 δραμών** aor. act. part. (circum.) τρέχω (# *5556*) to run. **γεμίσας** aor. act. part. γεμίζω (# *1153*) to fill. **σπόγγος** (# *5074*) sponge. **ὄξος** (# *3954*) sour wine (Matt. 27:48; RAC, 6:635-46). **περιθείς** aor. act. part. (circum.) περιτίθημι (# *4363*) to place around, to wrap around. **ἐπότιζεν** impf. ind. act. ποτίζω (# *4540*) to give to drink. Conative impf., "they tried to give." **ἄφετε** aor. imp. act. ἀφίημι (# *918*) to leave, to leave alone. **ἴδωμεν** aor. subj. act. s.v. 4. Cohortative subj., "let us see." **καθελεῖν** aor.

act. inf. καθαιρέω (# *2747*) to take down. Inf. of purp. ◆ **37 ἀφείς** aor. act. part. s.v. 36. In this context, "having uttered" (Cranfield). **ἐξέπνευσεν** aor. ind. act. ἐκπνέω (# *1743*) to breathe out, to expire, to die. ◆ **38 καταπέτασμα** (# *2925*) curtain, veil (Matt. 27:51). **ἐσχίσθη** aor. ind. pass. σχίζω (# *5387*) to split; pass. to be torn. ◆ **39 ἰδών** aor. act. part. s.v. 4. **κεντυρίων** (# *3035*) centurion (Acts. 10:1; EDNT; TJ, 101). **ἐναντίας** (# *1885*) opposite. **υἱὸς θεοῦ** Son of God. Anarthrous predicate and its position emphasize nature and character (John 1:1). For a discussion of this incidence s. Gundry, 973-75. ◆ **40 ἦσαν** impf. ind. act. εἰμί (# *1639*). **ἀπὸ μακρόθεν** from afar. **θεωροῦσαι** pres. act. part. nom. fem. pl. θεωρέω (# *2555*) to see, to view, to watch. Adj. part. ◆ **41 ἠκολούθουν** impf. ind. act. ἀκολουθέω to follow, to follow as a disciple. **διηκόνουν** impf. ind. act. διακονέω (# *199*) to serve, to minister to. The word implies material support w. dat. Customary impf. **συναναβᾶσαι** aor. act. part. συναναβαίνω (# *5262*) to go up together, to go up w., used w. dat. Adj. part. ◆ **42 γενομένης** aor. mid. (dep.) part. temp. s.v. 33. Gen. abs. Aor. indicates antecedent action. **παρασκευή** (# *4187*) preparation. Here used technically of the day of preparation for a Sabbath or the Passover (Taylor). **προσάββατον** (# *4640*) the day before the Sabbath, that is, Friday (BAGD). ◆ **43 ἐλθών** aor. act. part. (circum.) s.v. 21. **εὐσχήμων** (# *2363*) prominent, noble, influential, wealthy (Taylor). **βουλευτής** (# *1085*) counselor, a member of the Sanhedrin (Swete). **προσδεχόμενος** pres. mid. (dep.) part. προσδέχομαι (# *4657*) to await, to expect. Part. in a periphrastic construction. **τολμήσας** aor. act. part. (temp.) τολμάω (# *5528*) to dare, to have courage, to be brave enough. "He summoned up courage" (BAGD). **εἰσῆλθεν** aor. ind. act. εἰσέρχομαι (# *1656*) to go in. **ἠτήσατο** aor. ind. mid. αἰτέω s.v. 8. ◆ **44 ἐθαύμασεν** aor. ind. act. s.v. 5. **τέθνηκεν** perf. ind. act. θνῄσκω (# *2569*) to die; perf. to be dead. The prep. ἀπό is left off, because there is no need for perfectivizing (M, 114; VA, 255). **προσκαλεσάμενος** aor. mid. part. προσκαλέω (# *4673*) to summons, to call to oneself (BAGD). **ἐπηρώτησεν** aor. ind. act. s.v. 2. **ἀπέθανεν** aor. ind. act. ἀποθνῄσκω (# *633*). The distinction in tenses is noticeable. Perf. implies an existing cond.; aor. describes an observed event (Taylor). ◆ **45 γνούς** aor. act. part. (temp.) γινώσκω (# *1182*) to know. **ἐδωρήσατο** aor. ind. mid. (dep.) δωρέομαι (# *1563*) to give, to present, to bestow. The vb. suggests a gracious act (Taylor). **πτῶμα** (# *4773*) one that is fallen, corpse. This word was chosen to strengthen the fact of death (Pesch). For the general Roman view of not burying traitors s. Raymond E. Brown, "The Burial of Jesus (Mark 15:42-47)," *CBQ* 50 (1988): 234-36; and for the Jewish view of burying even those crucified before sunset s. Deut. 21:23; M, Sanhedrin 6:4-5; Jos., *J.W.*, 4:317; Brown, "The Burial," 236-38; BBC. ◆ **46 ἀγοράσας** aor. act. part. (temp.) ἀγοράζω (# *60*) to buy. **σινδών** (# *4984*) fine linen. **καθελών** aor. act. part. (temp.) s.v. 36. **ἐνείλη-σεν** aor. ind. act. ἐνειλέω (# 1912) to wrap, to roll, to wrap in (Matt. 27:59; Gnilka, 334-36). **ἔθηκεν** aor. ind. act. τίθημι (# 5502) to place, to put, to lay. A variant reading is κατέθηκεν aor. ind. act. κατατίθημι (# 2960) to lay down, to place a body in a tomb (BAGD). **λελατο-μημένον** perf. pass. part. λατομέω (# 3300) to hew, to cut out of stone. Adj. part. **προσεκύλισεν** aor. ind. act. προσ-κυλίω (# 4685) to roll to, to roll up. Rock tombs were common in the neighborhood of Jerusalem, sometimes containing chambers and sometimes a single room, provided w. a bench or shelf on which the body was placed. The entrance was closed by a large flat stone rolled or pushed into position (Taylor). ◆ **47 ἐθεώρουν** impf. ind. act. s.v. 40. **τέθειται** perf. ind. pass. τίθημι (# 5502) to place, to lay.

Mark 16

◆ **1 διαγενομένου** aor. mid. (dep.) part. διαγίνομαι (# 1335) to pass, to elapse. Gen. abs., "when the Sab-bath was over," after sunset on the day following the crucifixion (Swete). **ἠγόρασαν** aor. ind. act. ἀγοράζω (# 60) to buy. **ἄρωμα** (# 808) spice, probably perfumed oils rather than aromatic herbs (Taylor). **ἐλθοῦσαι** aor. act. part. (circum.) ἔρχομαι (# 2262) to come, to go. **ἀλείψωσιν** aor. subj. act. ἀλείπω (# 230) to anoint (BBC). Subj. w. ἵνα (# 2671) in purp. cl. ◆ **2 ἀνατείλαντος** aor. act. part. (temp.) ἀνατέλλω (# 422) to rise, used of the sun rising. Gen. abs. ◆ **3 ἀποκυλίσει** fut. ind. act. ἀποκυλίω (# 653) to roll away. **ἡμῖν** dat. pl. ἐγώ (# 1609); dat. of personal interest, "for us." ◆ **4 ἀναβλέψασαι** aor. act. part. (temp.) ἀναβλέπω (# 329) to look up. **θεωροῦσιν** pres. ind. act. θεωρέω (# 2555) to see, hist. pres. **ἀποκεκύλισται** perf. ind. pass. s.v. 3. Perf. indi-cates the state or cond. after a completed action. **σφόδρα** (# 5379) very, extremely (BAGD). ◆ **5 εἰσελθοῦσαι** aor. act. part. (temp.) εἰσέρχομαι (# 1656) to go in. **εἶδον** aor. ind. act. ὁράω (# 3972) to see. **καθήμενον** pres. mid. (dep.) part. κάθημαι (# 2764) to sit. Adj. part. **περιβεβλη-μένον** perf. pass. part. περιβάλλω (# 4314) to place around; perf. pass. to be clothed w. **στολήν** (# 5124) acc. sing. robe, esp. a long-flowing robe (BAGD). For the acc. w. vb. of dressing s. BD, 86. **ἐξεθαμβήθησαν** aor. ind. pass. (dep.) ἐκθαμβέομαι (# 1701) to be amazed. The women were startled and awestricken (Swete). ◆ **6 ἐκθαμβεῖσθε** pres. imp. mid. (dep.) s.v. 5. Pres. imp. w. the neg. μή (# 3590) indicates the stopping of an ac-tion in progress. **ζητεῖτε** pres. ind. act. ζητέω (# 2426) to seek, to look for. **ἐσταυρωμένον** perf. pass. part. σταυρόω (# 5090) to crucify. Perf. indicates the state or cond. Adj. part. **ἠγέρθη** aor. ind. pass. ἐγείρω (# 1586) to raise; pass. to rise. **ἴδε** (# 2632) aor. imp. act. ὁράω to see; "look!" **ἔθηκαν** aor. ind. act. τίθημι (# 5502) to place, to lay. ◆ **7 ὑπάγετε** pres. imp. act. ὑπάγω (# 5632) to go forth, to go. Pres. imp. w. a vb. of motion (VANT, 341-44).

εἴπατε aor. imp. act. λέγω (# 3306) to say, to tell. **ὄψεσθε** fut. ind. mid. (dep.) ὁράω (# 3972) to see. ◆ **8 ἐξελθοῦσαι** aor. act. part. (circum.) ἐξέρχομαι (# 2002) to go out. **ἔφυγον** aor. ind. act. φεύγω (# 5771) to flee. **εἶχεν** impf. ind. act. ἔχω (# 2400) to have. Used w. emotions (BAGD). **τρόμος** (# 5571) trembling, fear. **ἔκστασις** (# 1749) bewilderment. **ἐφοβοῦντο** impf. ind. mid. (dep.) φοβέομαι (# 5828) to fear, to be afraid. ◆ **9** For the textual problem concerning Mark 16:9-20 s. TC, 122-26; John W. Burgon, *The Last Twelve Verses of the Gospel According to Mark*; William R. Farmer, *The Last Twelves Verses of Mark*; DJG, 523-24; Pesch, 2:544-59. **ἀναστάς** aor. act. part. (temp.) ἀνίστημι (# 482) to rise. **ἐφάνη** aor. ind. pass. (dep.) φαίνομαι (# 5743) to appear. **ἐκβεβλήκει** plperf. ind. act. ἐκβάλλω (# 1675) to cast out, to drive out. ◆ **10 πορευθεῖσα** aor. pass. (dep.) part. (temp.) πορεύομαι (# 4513) to go. **ἀπήγγειλεν** aor. ind. act. ἀπαγγέλλω (# 550) to report, to announce. **γενο-μένοις** aor. mid. (dep.) part. dat. masc. pl. γίνομαι (# 1181) to become, to happen, to be. Part. as subst. **πεν-θοῦσι** pres. act. part. πενθέω (# 4291) to mourn. **κλαίουσιν** pres. ind. act. κλαίω (# 3081) to cry, to weep. ◆ **11 κἀκεῖνοι** = καὶ ἐκεῖνοι (# 2797). **ἀκούσαντες** aor. act. part. (temp.) ἀκούω (# 201) to hear. **ζῇ** pres. ind. act. ζάω (# 2409) to live, to be alive. **ἐθεάθη** aor. ind. pass. θεάομαι (# 2517) to see, to behold, to look at; pass. to be seen. **ἠπίστησαν** aor. ind. act. ἀπιστέω (# 601) to disbe-lieve, to refuse to believe. ◆ **12 περιπατοῦσιν** pres. act. part. dat. masc. pl. περιπατέω (# 4344) to walk about, to go about. Indir. obj. **ἐφανερώθη** aor. ind. pass. φανερόω (# 5746) to make clear, to make visible; pass. to become visible, to be revealed, to appear. **μορφῇ** (# 3671) form (Phil. 2:6). **πορευομένοις** pres. mid. (dep.) part. dat. masc. pl. πορεύομαι (# 4513) to go. ◆ **13 ἀπελθόντες** aor. act. part. ἀπέρχομαι (# 599) to go away, to depart. For the Semitic use of the part. s. MH, 452. **ἀπήγγειλαν** aor. ind. act. s.v. 10. **ἐπίστευσαν** aor. ind. act. πιστεύω (# 4409) to believe. ◆ **14 ἀνακειμένοις** pres. mid. (dep.) part. ἀνάκειμαι (# 367) to recline at the table. Adj. part. **ἐφανερώθη** aor. ind. pass. s.v. 12. **ὠνείδισεν** aor. ind. act. ὀνειδίζω (# 3943) to rebuke, to insult. **σκληροκαρδία** (# 5016) hard-heartedness. **θεασαμένοις** aor. mid. (dep.) part. s.v. 11. Part. as subst. **ἐγηγερμένον** perf. pass. part. s.v. 6. Perf. indicates the state or cond. after the com-pleted act. ◆ **15 εἶπεν** aor. ind. act. λέγω (# 3306) to say. **πορευθέντες** aor. pass. (dep.) part. s.v. 12. Circum. part. w. force of imp. (Matt. 28:19). **κηρύξατε** aor. imp. act. κηρύσσω (# 3062) to preach, to proclaim. ◆ **16 πιστεύσας** aor. act. part. s.v. 13. Part. as subst. **βαπ-τισθείς** aor. pass. part. βαπτίζω (# 966) to baptize. Part. as subst. **σωθήσεται** fut. ind. pass. σώζω (# 5392) to res-cue, to save. **ἀπιστήσας** aor. act. part. s.v. 11. **κατακριθή-σεται** fut. ind. pass. κατακρίνω (# 2891) to decide against, to condemn. ◆ **17 πιστεύσασιν** aor. act. part. s.v. 13. Part. as subst. Dat. as obj. of παρακολουθέω.

παρακολουθήσει fut. ind. act. παρακολουθέω (# 4158) to follow, to accompany, to follow along the side, w. dat. **ἐκβαλοῦσιν** fut. ind. act. ἐκβάλλω (# 1675) to cast out. **λαλήσουσιν** fut. ind. act. λαλέω (# 3281) to speak. ◆ **18 ὄφεις** acc. pl. ὄφις (# 4058) snake. **ἀροῦσιν** fut. ind. act. αἴρω (# 149) to lift up, to pick up. **θανάσιμος** (# 2503) deadly. **πίωσιν** aor. subj. act. πίνω (# 4403) to drink. Subj. in a 3rd. class cond. cl. assuming the possibility. **βλάψῃ** aor. subj. act. βλάπτω (# 1055) to harm, to injure. **ἄρρωστος** (# 779) weak, sick. **ἐπιθήσουσιν** fut. ind. act. ἐπιτίθημι (# 2202) to place upon. **ἕξουσιν** fut. ind. act.

ἔχω (# 2400) to have. Used w. **καλῶς** (# 2822) it means "to be well," "to be healthy." ◆ **19 λαλῆσαι** aor. act. inf. s.v. 17. Temp. use of inf. w. **μετά** (# 3552) ("after"). **ἀνελήμφθη** aor. ind. pass. ἀναλαμβάνω (# 377) to take up. **ἐκάθισεν** aor. ind. act. καθίζω (# 2767) to sit down, to take one's seat. ◆ **20 ἐξελθόντες** aor. act. part. (circum.) s.v. 8. **ἐκήρυξαν** aor. ind. act. s.v. 15. **συνεργοῦντος** pres. act. part. συνεργέω (# 5300) to work along w., to cooperate w. Gen. abs. **βεβαιοῦντος** pres. act. part. βεβαιόω (# 1011) to confirm. **ἐπακολουθούντων** pres. act. part. ἐπακολουθέω (# 2051) to follow, to accompany.

The Gospel of Luke

For a discussion of the research on Luke, s. E. Bovon, *Luke the Theologian: Thirty Years of Research (1950-83)*, PTMS 12 (Allison Park, Pa.: Pickwick, 1987). See also I. Howard Marshall, *Luke: Historian and Theologian*, 13-20; DJG, 495-510.

Luke 1

◆ **1 ἐπειδήπερ** (# 2077) inasmuch as, since. A triple compound particle ("since," "truly," "indeed") expressing cause w. reference to a fact already well known (Arndt; Godet; BD, 238). For a study of this section s. PLG. **ἐπεχείρησαν** aor. ind. act. ἐπιχειρέω (# 2217) to put the hand to, to undertake, to attempt. Without thought of censure, the other writers are mentioned as precedents rather than failures (BC, 2:493). **ἀνατάξασθαι** aor. mid. (dep.) inf. ἀνατάσσομαι (# 421) to arrange in a row, to draw up again, in order; that is, to arrange afresh so as to show the sequence of events; perhaps referring to an orderly written account (Plummer; Marshall). Epex. inf. explaining ἐπεχείρησαν. **διήγησις** (# 1456) narrative. It indicates a narration of a verified and well-witnessed report (I.I. Du Plessis, "Once More: The Purpose of Luke's Prologue," *Nov T* 16 [1974]: 263; Fitzmyer, 292). **πεπληροφορημένων** perf. pass. part. πληροφορέω (# 4442) to fill completely, to fulfill, either in the sense of to be fully persuaded or to be accomplished (Arndt; BAGD; LAE, 86; Fitzmyer, 293). ◆ **2 παρέδοσαν** aor. ind. act. παραδίδωμι (# 4140) to deliver, to transmit in both oral and written form (Ellis; BBC). **αὐτόπται** nom. pl. αὐτόπτης (# 898) eyewitness, seeing something for oneself, one who has personal experience, those who know the facts at first hand (Evans; PLG, 120). This reflects the conviction that the Christian faith is rooted not in speculative creation but in hist. reality (Ellis). The eyewitnesses are Luke's guarantee of a true report (Du Plessis, 265). Used in medical language of a personal examination of disease or of the parts of the body (WSNT; MLL, 89-90; PLG,121; for other uses s. Evans; PLG, 34-41; 121-23; BASHH, 322). **ὑπηρέται** nom. pl. ὑπηρέτης (# 5677) minister. They not only had personal knowledge of the facts but also practical experience of the facts (Plummer). The word was used of medical assistants or attendants (MLL, 88-89; PLG, 123). **γενόμενοι** aor. mid. (dep.) part. (adj.) γίνομαι (# 1181) to become, to be. Part. w. one art. and the two substs. point to one

group, the Twelve (Fitzmyer, 294). ◆ **3 ἔδοξε** aor. ind. act. δοκέω (# 1506) to appear, to seem. **κἀμοί** = καὶ ἐμοί. ἐμοί used impersonally w. dat. of advantage; "it appeared good to me also." **παρηκολουθηκότι** perf. act. part. (temp.) dat. masc. sing. παρακολυθέω (# 4158) to follow along, to investigate, to be thoroughly familiar w. the whole affair (Nolland; Fitzmyer; Evans; PLG, 128-30). Indicates the mental tracing, investigating, whereby one arrives at a knowledge of the matter (Meyer). Perf. emphasizes the state reached after investigation ("after having"). **ἄνωθεν** (# 540) from the beginning, from the first, thoroughly (PLG, 130). **ἀκριβῶς** (# 209) accurately, carefully, precisely, exactly (PLG, 131). Used by Galen to describe his accurate investigation before writing one of his works (MLL, 251) and was used to indicate the accurate information gained by a doctor questioning the patient (Rufus, *Interrogationes*, 1; AIA, 64-65). Points to the painstaking character of research (Arndt). **καθεξῆς** (# 2759) in order, one after the other, successively; in an orderly fashion (Gerhard Schneider, "Zur Bedeutung von καθεξῆς im lukanischen Doppelwerk," *ZNW* 68 [1977]: 128-31; BC, 2:504; Fitzmyer, 298-99; PLG, 131-32, 95). It could refer to topical order or chronological order. **γράψαι** aor. act. inf. γράφω (# 1211) to write. Epex. inf. w. the vb. δοκέω. **κράτιστε** voc. sing. κράτιστος (# 3196) most noble, most excellent, honorary form of address used to persons who hold a higher official or social position than the speaker (BAGD). ◆ **4 ἐπιγνῶς** aor. subj. act. ἐπιγινώσκω (# 2105) to know. The prep. compound emphasizes a directive knowledge (M, 312). Subj. w. ἵνα (# 2671) expressing purp. **κατηχήθης** aor. ind. pass. κατηχέω (# 2994) to instruct, to sound down into the ears, teach orally (Plummer; PLG, 139). **ἀσφάλεια** (# 854) certainty, safety, security, the truth about some matters reported or discussed, a reliable account (BC, 2:509; Evans). The position of the word gives its solemn emphasis. Theophilus shall know that the faith he has embraced has an impregnable hist. foundation (Plummer). Luke wants to give him certainty by supplying him w. a historically verified and complete account (Du Plessis, "The Purpose...," 270; s. also Terrance Callan, "The Preface of Luke–Acts and Historiography," *NTS* 31 [1985]: 580; BASHH, 326). There may be a contrast w. the oral instruction (PLG, 140-41). ◆ **5 ἐγένετο** aor. ind. mid. (dep.) s.v. 2 (s. 2:1). **ἐφημερία**

(# *2389*) daily service; then, a course (מִשְׁמֶרֶת) of priests who were on duty for a week. The whole body of priests was divided into twenty-four families or courses of service (JPB, 78; HJPE, 2:245-50; SB, 2:55-68; JPF, 2:587-96). Ἐλισάβετ (# *1810*) Elizabeth, meaning My God is the one by whom to swear, or My God is fortune (Fitzmyer, 322). ◆ **6** ἦσαν impf. ind. act. εἰμί (# *1639*) to be. ἀμφότεροι (# *317*) both. ἐναντίον (# *1883*) before. πορευόμενοι pres. mid. (dep.) part. πορεύομαι (# *4513*) to go. Hebraic expression indicating conduct or way of life. Part. may be periphrastic. ἐντολαῖς dat. pl. ἐντολή (# *1953*) commandment. δικαιώμασιν dat. pl. δικαίωμα (# *1468*) ordinance, righteous demands, things declared right (TDNT). ἄμεμπτος (# *289*) blameless, unblamed (Trench, *Synonyms*, 380). ◆ **7** στεῖρα (# *5069*) barren, sterile. Green argues that Luke consciously builds parallels to the Abrahamic story. (Joel B. Green, "The Problem of a Beginning: Israel's Scripture in Luke 1-2," *BBR* 4 [1994]: 61-86; BBC). προβεβηκότες perf. act. part. προβαίνω (# *4581*) to go forward, to advance. Part. as pred. adj. This heightens the miracle that follows (Nolland). ◆ **8** ἐγένετο aor. ind. mid. (dep.) s.v. 2. For the Semitic construction w. prep. ἐν (# *1877*) and inf. expressing contemporaneous time s. Arndt; Beyer, 34-42. ἱερατεύειν pres. act. inf. ἱερατεύω (# *2634*) to be a priest, to function as a priest. For vbs. w. this ending indicating the exercise of a profession s. MH, 398; DJG, 634-35. τάξει dat. sing. τάξις (# *5423*) row, order. The temple service of an order was for one week (from Sabbath to Sabbath) twice a year and at certain Feasts (s.v. 5; SB, 2:58-63; M, Sukk. 5:7). ◆ **9** ἔθος (# *1621*) acc. sing. custom. ἔλαχε aor. ind. act. λαγχάνω (# *3275*) to receive, to obtain something by lot, to be appointed or chosen by lot. The casting of lots took place twice a day at the morning and at the evening offering of incense (Plummer; J. Lightfoot, 2:15-16; M, Tamid, 3:1; 5:2; b, Yoma 25a). θυμιᾶσαι aor. act. inf. θυμιάω (# *2594*) to burn incense, to offer incense as a sacrifice (SB, 2:71-75; M, Yoma 5:1; M, Tamid 5:4; 6:2, 3; LT, 1:137). This was a high privilege and came only once in a lifetime (TBM, 259). Epex. inf. explaining what was obtained by lot. εἰσελθών aor. act. part. (circum.) εἰσέρχομαι (# *1656*) to go in. ◆ **10** προσευχόμενον pres. mid. (dep.) part. προσεύχομαι (# *4667*) to pray. Periphrastic part. θυμίαμα (# *2592*) incense, offering of incense. Incense was offered in the morning and in the evening (Exod. 30:7-8), and with the mention of the crowd it was probably the evening offering, at around 3:00 P.M. (Fitzmyer, 324; Nolland). ◆ **11** ὤφθη aor. ind. pass. ὁράω (# *3972*) to see; pass. to appear. ἑστώς (# *2705*) perf. act. part. ἵστημι perf. to stand. θυσιαστήριον (# *2603*) altar of incense. The right side was the south side, and the angel would be between the altar and the golden candlestick (Plummer; SB, 2:79; BBC). ◆ **12** ἐταράχθη aor. ind. pass. ταράσσω

(# *5429*) to shake together, to stir up, to trouble, to disturb, to throw into confusion (BAGD). ἰδών aor. act. part. (temp.) ὁράω (# *3972*) to see. Aor. gives the logically necessary action antecedent to the main vb. ἐπέπεσεν aor. ind. act. ἐπιπίπτω (# *2158*) to fall upon. ◆ **13** φοβοῦ pres. imp. mid. (dep.) φοβέομαι (# *5828*) to fear, to be afraid. Pres. imp. w. neg. μή (# *3590*) is used to prohibit an action in progress (GGBB, 724). εἰσηκούσθη aor. ind. pass. εἰσακούω (# *1653*) to hear, to listen to, to attend to. For the effect of the prep. compound s. MH, 304. δέησις (# *1255*) request, prayer. Implies personal need (Plummer). γεννήσει fut. ind. act. γεννάω (# *1164*) to bear, to give birth. καλέσεις fut. ind. act. καλέω (# *2813*) to call, to name. Fut. used w. the force of an imp. Ἰωάννης John. The name means "Yahweh has given grace or favor" (Evans). ◆ **14** ἔσται fut. ind. mid. (dep.) εἰμί (# *1639*). ἀγαλλίασις (# *21*) rejoicing, refers to a demonstrative rejoicing (Arndt). It indicates the joy and happiness that arises from the experience of God's saving action (Marshall). χαρήσονται fut. ind. pass. (dep.) χαίρω (# *5897*) to be glad, to rejoice. ◆ **15** σίκερα (# *4975*) acc. sing. strong drink, beer (Fitzmyer, 326). Denotes any intoxicating beverage prepared from either grain or fruit (IDB, 4:448). For regulations regarding a Nazarite s. M, Nazir; SB, 2:80-88. πίῃ fut. ind. mid. (dep.) πίνω (# *4403*) to drink. Fut. w. double neg. οὐ μή (# *4024; 3590*) for strong denial of a fut. action. πλησθήσεται fut. ind. pass. πίμπλημι (# *4398*) to fill. κοιλία (# *3120*) body cavity, womb, uterus. The expression means either "from birth" (BAGD) or "before birth," "prenatal" (Godet; Nolland). ◆ **16** ἐπιστρέψει fut. ind. act. ἐπιστρέφω (# *2188*) to turn about, to cause to return, to convert. It conveys the idea of turning from idolatry and sin to love and serve God (Marshall; s. Mal. 2:6). ◆ **17** προελεύσεται fut. ind. mid. (dep.) προσέρχομαι (# *4601*) to go before. ἐπιστρέψαι aor. act. inf. s.v. 16. Inf. of purp. ἀπειθεῖς acc. pl. ἀπειθής (# *579*) disobedient. Obj. of the inf. ἐπιστρέψαι. For the construction s. Marshall. ἑτοιμάσαι aor. act. inf. ἑτοιμάζω (# *2286*) to prepare, to make ready. Inf. of purp. κατεσκευασμένον perf. pass. part. (adj.) κατασκευάζω (# *2941*) to furnish, to equip, to prepare. Perf. emphasizes the state of preparedness. It was used of the outfitting of a ship, a city, or an army (Bovon; EDNT). This was the spiritual preparation of Israel for the coming of the King. For the Rabbinic discussion of repentance and redemption s. TS, 668-74. ◆ **18** εἶπεν aor. ind. act. λέγω (# *3306*). γνώσομαι fut. ind. mid. (dep.) γινώσκω (# *1182*) to know, to recognize. προβεβηκυῖα perf. act. part. nom. fem. sing. s.v. 7. ◆ **19** ἀποκριθείς aor. pass. (dep.) part. ἀποκρίνομαι (# *646*) to answer. For the Hebraic construction of the part. s. MH, 453. παρεστηκώς perf. act. part. παρίστημι (# *4225*) to stand, to stand beside; implies ministering (Plummer). For Gabriel and the ministry before the Lord s. SB, 2:89-98. ἀπεστάλην aor. ind. pass. ἀποστέλλω (# 690) to send, to send w. authority, to accomplish a mission (TDNT; NIDNTT). Theol. pass. indicating that God had commissioned him. λαλῆσαι aor. act. inf. λαλέω (# 3281) to speak. Inf. of purp. εὐαγγελίσασθαι aor. mid. (dep.) inf. εὐαγγελίζομαι (# 2294) to bring good news. Inf. of purp. ◆ 20 ἔσῃ fut. ind. mid. (dep.) 2nd. pers. sing. εἰμί (# 1639) to be. σιωπῶν pres. act. part. σιωπάω (# 4995) to be silent. Part. of the stative vb. used in a periphrastic construction (VANT, 317-18; VA, 483). δυνάμενος pres. pass. (dep.) part. δύναμαι (# 1538) to be able. Part. in periphrastic construction. λαλῆσαι aor. act. inf. s.v. 19. γένηται aor. subj. mid. (dep.) s.v. 2. Subj. in an indef. temp. cl. ἐπίστευσας aor. ind. act. πιστεύω (# 4409) to believe. πληρωθήσονται fut. ind. pass. πληρόω (# 4444) to fulfill, to fill. It is used of the completion of a specified or divinely predestined time (Evans). καιρόν acc. sing. time, καιρός (# 2789) a specific time. It is the point of time in God's determination (Fitzmyer, 328). ◆ 21 ἦν impf. ind. act. εἰμί (# 1639). προσδοκῶν pres. act. part. προσδοκάω (# 4659) to expect, to wait for. While it took a little time to throw incense on the heated altar this delay troubled the people (BBC). Part. in a periphrastic construction. ἐθαύμαζον impf. ind. act. θαυμάζω (# 2513) to marvel, to be astounded, to wonder at. Impf. pictures the continual action. χρονίζειν pres. act. inf. χρονίζω (# 5988) to delay. Inf. used w. the prep. expressing contemporaneous time: "while he delayed" (MH, 450; IGNT, 201). They were waiting for him to come out and lead in the blessing of the people (Nolland; M, Tamid, 6:2). ◆ 22 ἐξελθών aor. act. part. (temp.) ἐξέρχομαι (# 2002) to go out. Aor. indicating antecedent action. ἐδύνατο impf. ind. pass. (dep.) s.v. 20, w. inf. ἐπέγνωσαν aor. ind. act. ἐπιγινώσκω (# 2105) to know, to recognize. ὀπτασία (# 3965) vision. ἑώρακεν perf. ind. act. ὁράω (# 3972) to see. Perf. indicates the abiding results on the subject. διανεύων pres. act. part. διανεύω (# 1377) to nod. Part. used in a periphrastic construction indicating continuous action (IBG, 16). διέμενεν impf. ind. act. διαμένω (# 1373) to remain. The prep. in the compound is perfective. Both the compound and the tense emphasize the fact that it was not a mere temporary seizure (Plummer). ◆ 23 ἐγένετο aor. ind. mid. (dep.) s.v. 2. ἐπλήσθησαν aor. ind. pass. s.v. 15. λειτουργία (# 3311) ministry; literally, service rendered to the people. Used in the religious sense denoting the service a priest renders to God (Arndt). ἀπῆλθεν aor. ind. act. ἀπέρχομαι (# 599) to go away. ◆ 24 συνέλαβεν aor. ind. act. συλλαμβάνω (# 5197) to conceive, to become pregnant. For the medical use of the term s. MLL, 91-92; DMTG, 304. περιέκρυβεν impf. ind. act. περικρύβω (# 4332) to conceal, to hide, w. the ref. pron. "she hid herself." The compound vb. implies all-round, complete conceal-

ment (Plummer; BD, 39). ◆ 25 πεποίηκεν perf. ind. act. ποιέω (# 4472) to do. Perf. implies the state or cond. as a result of the completed action. ἐπεῖδεν aor. ind. act. ἐφοράω (# 2393) to look upon, to concern oneself w., to look w. favor on someone (BAGD). ἀφελεῖν aor. act. inf. ἀφαιρέω (# 904) to take away. Inf. used as object of the vb. or to express results (Schürmann; TBM, 264). ὄνειδος (# 3945) reproach, disgrace, insult (BAGD). Barrennesss was regarded as a severe reproach by Jewish women (Marshall; SB, 2:98). ◆ 26 ἀπεστάλη aor. ind. pass. s.v. 19. ᾗ dat. sing. fem. ὅς (# 4005) rel. pron. Dat. of respect (IGNT, 98). ◆ 27 παρθένος (# 4221) virgin. ἐμνηστευμένην perf. pass. part. μνηστεύω (# 3650) pass. to be engaged (s. Matt. 1:18; SB, 2:374, 376, 393-98). ᾧ dat. sing. ὅς (# 4005) rel. pron. Dat. of respect s.v. 26. ◆ 28 εἰσελθών aor. act. part. (temp.) s.v. 9. κεχαριτωμένη perf. pass. part. χαριτόω (# 5923) to bestow grace, to show favor to someone. Here it is the divine favor for a special vocation (Moffat, Grace, 100; Robinson, Ephesians, 226; TDNT; Test. of Joseph 1:6). ◆ 29 διεταράχθη aor. ind. pass. διαταράσσω (# 1410) to confuse, to perplex. The prep. compound intensifies the vb. ταράσσω. διελογίζετο impf. ind. mid. (dep.) διαλογίζομαι (# 1368) to reason, to debate, to consider, to reckon up different reasons (RWP). ποταπός (# 4534) what sort of, what kind. of. εἴη pres. opt. act. εἰμί (# 1639) to be. The opt. may be in indir. discourse (BD, 195; GGBB, 483), dir. discourse (VA, 176), or the potential opt. (BG, 119). ◆ 30 φοβοῦ pres. imp. mid. (dep.) s.v. 13. εὗρες aor. ind. act. εὑρίσκω (# 2351) to find. ◆ 31 συλλήμψῃ fut. ind. mid. (dep.) 2nd. pers. sing. s.v. 24. τέξῃ fut. ind. mid. (dep.) τίκτω (# 5503) to bear, to give birth. καλέσεις fut. ind. act. καλέω (# 2813) to call. Fut. as command (s. 1:13). ◆ 32 ἔσται fut. ind. mid. (dep.) εἰμί (# 1639). ὕψιστος (# 5736) superl. the highest, the most high. The term "the Most High" was used in early Judaism for Yahweh (Cleon L. Rogers, Jr., "The Davidic Covenant in the Gospels," Bib Sac 150 [1993]: 465; SB, 2:99-100; Fitzmyer, 248; WA, 90-93). κληθήσεται fut. ind. pass. s.v. 31. δώσει fut. ind. act. δίδωμι (# 1443) to give. For the significance of the Throne of David s. Cleon L. Rogers, Jr., "The Promises to David in Early Judaism," Bib Sac 150 [1993]: 285-302; "The Davidic Covenant...," Bib Sac 150 [1993]: 466; Godet). ◆ 33 βασιλεύσει fut. ind. act. βασιλεύω (# 996) to be king, to reign. ἐπὶ τὸν οἶκον Ἰακώβ (# 2093; 3875; 2609) over the house of Jacob. This refers to the Twelve Tribes of Israel (Nolland; Rogers, "Davidic Covenant in the Gospels," Bib Sac, 465). ◆ 34 εἶπεν aor. ind. act. λέγω (# 3306) to say. γινώσκω (# 1182) pres. ind. act. to know. Perfective pres. emphasizing that the results of a past action are still continuing (GGBB, 532). Used here in the sexual sense: "I have had no relations w. a man" (TBM, 289). ◆ 35 ἐπελεύσεται fut. ind. mid. (dep.) ἐπέρχομαι

(# 2088) to come upon. ἐπισκιάσει fut. ind. act. ἐπισκιάζω (# 2173) to overshadow. Though the words in themselves do not have sexual meanings, they do here explain how the male part in reproduction is provided (Bovon). γεννώμενον pres. pass. part. s.v. 13. Part. used as subst. κληθήσεται fut. ind. pass. s.v. 13. "The child shall be called holy, the Son of God," or "The holy child shall be called the Son of God" (Schürmann; Marshall; Fitzmyer, 351-52; IBG, 107). ◆ 36 συγγενίς (# 5151) relative, kinswoman. The degree of kinship is not certain, but it implies the kinship of John and Jesus (Fitzmyer, 352). συνείληφεν perf. ind. act. s.v. 24. Perf. stresses the state or cond. γήρει dat. sing. γῆρας (# 1174) old age. μήν (# 3604) nom. sing. month. καλουμένη pres. pass. part. s.v. 13. Dat. of pers. interest, "for the one called barren." ◆ 37 ἀδυνατήσει fut. ind. act. ἀδυνατέω (# 104) to be impossible. ῥῆμα (# 4839) word; here, thing, matter (NTNT, 46). ◆ 38 γένοιτο aor. opt. mid. (dep.) γίνομαι (# 1181) to become, to happen. The opt. generally is used to express a wish (BD, 194). Here it is an expression of submission (Plummer). ἀπῆλθεν aor. ind. act. s.v. 23. ◆ 39 ἀναστᾶσα aor. act. part. nom. fem. sing. ἀνίστημι (# 482) to arise. For the Semitic use of the redundant part. s. MH, 453. ἐπορεύθη aor. ind. pass. (dep.) πορεύομαι (# 4513) to go, to travel. ◆ 40 εἰσῆλθεν aor. ind. act. s.v. 9. ἠσπάσατο aor. ind. mid. (dep.) ἀσπάζομαι (# 832) to greet. ◆ 41 ἐγένετο aor. ind. mid. (dep.) s.v. 38. ἤκουσεν aor. ind. act. ἀκούω (# 201) to hear. ἐσκίρτησεν aor. ind. act. σκιρτάω (# 5015) to leap, to jump. This is a sign of his prenatal sensitivity to the prophetic Spirit (BBC). βρέφος (# 1100) unborn child, embryo, baby, infant (BAGD). ἐπλήσθη aor. ind. pass. s.v. 15, w. gen. of content. ◆ 42 ἀνεφώνησεν aor. ind. act. ἀναφωνέω (# 430) to call out. εὐλογημένη perf. pass. part. εὐλογέω (# 2328) to bless. The term could imply, "to praise" or "to provide benefits" (LN, 1:750). W. the latter meaning the pass. would be the theol. pass., indicating that God acted graciously in choosing Mary as the mother of the Messiah. Perf. indicates the state or cond. after an action. ἐν γυναιξίν "among women." Hebraic way of expressing a superl. (BD, 128; BG, 48). εὐλογημένος perf. pass. part. εὐλογέω The meaning "praise" is in view here. ◆ 43 ἔλθῃ aor. subj. act. ἔρχομαι (# 2262) to come, to go. Subj. w. ἵνα (# 2671) in an explanatory noun cl. (Marshall). ◆ 45 μακάριος (# 3421) happy (s. Matt. 5:3). πιστεύσασα aor. act. part. πιστεύω (# 4409) to believe, to trust. ὅτι (# 4022) because, giving the reason for the happiness, or that, giving the content of the belief (Nolland; Marshall). λελαλημένοις perf. pass. part. λαλέω (# 3281) to speak. Dat. of respect, a fullfillment with respect to that which was told her. For a discussion of the song s. DJG, 525-26. ◆ 47 μεγαλύνει pres. ind. act. μεγαλύνω (# 3486) to make large, to magnify, to exalt, to praise (BAGD). ἠγαλλίασεν aor. ind.

act. ἀγαλλιάω (# 22) to rejoice, to be glad, to be overjoyed, w. ἐπί which gives the reason for the joy (BAGD; KVS, 256). The aor. may be understood as a stative, as the Hebrew stative perf. which implies a past action, but emphasizes the pres. cond. resulting from the completed action (VANT, 276-80; for various views s. VA, 131-32; Fitzmyer, 366; Nolland; HLIN, 117). ◆ 48 ἐπέβλεψεν aor. ind. act. ἐπιβλέπω (# 2098) to look upon. It was often used of loving care (Marshall). ταπείνωσις (# 5428) lowliness, humiliation, humble station, afflicted state (Nolland; EDNT; TMB, 336, 350-55; HLIN, 118-19). μακαριοῦσιν fut. ind. act. μακαρίζω (# 3420) to call or consider blessed, happy, fortunate. ◆ 49 ἐποίησεν aor. ind. act. s.v. 25. μοι dat. sing. ἐγώ (# 1609) I. Dat. of advantage, or personal interest. ◆ 50 ἔλεος (# 1799) mercy. LXX translation of חֶסֶד, God's gracious loyalty to His covenant promises (Matt. 9:13; Marshall). φοβουμένοις pres. mid. (dep.) part. s.v. 13. Fearing God is the OT description of piety (Plummer). Part. as subst. ◆ 51 ἐποίησεν aor. ind. act. ποιέω (# 4472) to do, to make; here, to display. Constative aor. summarizing God's activity. For various views of the aor. here s. VA, 132-33; VANT, 268-69, 273-74; HLIN, 114-16. βραχίονι dat. sing. βραχίων (# 1098) arm. OT image of God's power, esp. as manifested in the Exodus (Nolland). Perhaps an allusion to Ps. 103:17 (BBC). διεσκόρπισεν aor. ind. act. διασκορπίζω (# 1399) to scatter. Often used in the LXX for God scattering disobedient Israel or the enemies of His people (Bovon). ὑπερήφανος (# 5662) haughty, arrogant. διανοίᾳ (# 1379) dat. sing. thought, thinking, a particular manner or way of thinking, disposition, attitude (LN, 1:350). Frequently in the Psalms and Wisdom literature the enemies of God are described as arrogant, self-sufficient, and unwilling to acknowledge His sovereignty (Evans; Isa. 2:12; Pss. Sol. 17:8; SB, 2:101-106). Dat. of respect (Marshall) or loc. dat. ◆ 52 καθεῖλεν aor. ind. act. καθαιρέω (# 2747) to bring down. ὕψωσεν aor. ind. act. ὑψόω (# 5738) to lift up (s. Prov. 3:34; Isa. 2:11-12). ◆ 53 πεινῶντας pres. act. part. πεινάω (# 4277) to hunger, to be hungry. Ps. 107:9. Part. as subst. ἐνέπλησεν aor. ind. act. ἐμπίμπλημι (# 1855) to fill, to fill quite full, to satisfy, w. gen. of content (KVS, 144). For the use in the LXX s. GELTS, 146. πλουτοῦντας pres. act. part. πλουτέω (# 4456) to be rich, to be very rich. Part. as subst. ἐξαπέστειλεν aor. ind. act. ἐξαποστέλλω (# 1990) to send out. Used w. adv. acc. ◆ 54 ἀντελάβετο aor. ind. mid. (dep.) ἀντιλαμβάνω (# 514) mid. to lay hold of in order to support or to succour; to help, to come to the aid of someone, w. gen. as obj. (Plummer; BAGD; for the LXX s. GELTS, 40-41; KVS, 126-27; for the papyri s. MM; Preisigke, 1:135-36). The prep. in compound may connote grasping while squarely facing the obj. (MH, 297). μνησθῆναι aor. pass. (dep.) inf. μιμνῄσκομαι (# 3630) to remember, to recall,

w. gen. as obj. (BAGD). The inf. to express result (BD, 198) or to explain the help (HLIN, 125). ἐλέους gen. sing. s.v. 50. The covenant w. Abraham is in view here (TBM, 338). ◆ **55 ἐλάλησεν** aor. ind. act. λαλέω (# 3281) to speak; here, to promise (Bovon). For the syntax of **τῷ Ἀβραάμ** s. Marshall. **εἰς τὸν αἰῶνα** forever. The covenant w. Abraham is viewed as eternal. ◆ **56 ἔμεινεν** aor. ind. act. μένω (# 3531) to remain. **μῆνας** acc. pl. s.v. 36. Acc. of time. **ὑπέστρεψεν** aor. ind. act. ὑποστρέφω (# 5715) to return. ◆ **57 ἐπλήσθη** aor. ind. pass. s.v. 15. **τεκεῖν** aor. act. inf. s.v. 31. Epex. inf. explaining time. **ἐγέννησεν** aor. ind. act. s.v. 13. ◆ **58 ἤκουσαν** aor. ind. act. ἀκούω (# 201) to hear. **ἐμεγάλυνεν** impf. ind. act. s.v. 47. **συνέχαιρον** impf. ind. act. συγχαίρω (# 5176) to rejoice together. ◆ **59 περιτεμεῖν** aor. act. inf. περιτέμνω (# 4362) to cut around, to circumcise (TDNT; EDNT; NIDNTT; SB, 4:23-40, esp. 23-27; TRE, 5:714-24; RAC, 2:159-69; BBC). **ἐκάλουν** impf. ind. act. s.v. 13. Conative impf., "they were attempting to name him" (Arndt). ◆ **60 ἀποκριθεῖσα** aor. pass. part. nom. fem. sing. s.v. 19. **κληθήσεται** fut. ind. pass. s.v. 13. ◆ **61 εἶπαν** aor. ind. act. 3rd. pers. pl. λέγω (# 3306) to say. **καλεῖται** pres. ind. pass. s.v. 13. ◆ **62 ἐνένευον** impf. ind. act. ἐννεύω (# 1935) to nod, to signal by nodding. Incep. impf., "they began to signal by nodding." The art. used here introduces an indir. question (RG, 766). **θέλοι** pres. opt. act. θέλω (# 2527) to will, to want. Opt. used in indir. discourse (BD, 195) or as a less probable future (GGBB, 484, 700). **καλεῖσθαι** pres. pass. inf. s.v. 13. ◆ **63 αἰτήσας** aor. act. part. (circum.) αἰτέω (# 160) to ask for, to request. Aor. indicating an antecedent action. **πινακίδιον** (# 4400) a small tablet, small wooden boards, covered w. a film of wax, were used (Ellis; SB, 2:108). In medical language it was used for a physician's notebook or tablet (MLL, 95-96; MM; Preisigke, 2:305). **ἔγραψεν** aor. ind. act. γράφω (# 1211) to write. **ἐθαύμασαν** aor. ind. act. θαυμάζω (# 2513) to be amazed. ◆ **64 ἀνεῴχθη** aor. ind. pass. ἀνοίγω (# 487) to open. Theol. pass. **παραχρῆμα** (# 4202) immediately. **ἐλάλει** impf. ind. act. λαλέω (# 3281) to speak. Incep. impf., "he began to speak." **εὐλογῶν** pres. act. part. εὐλογέω (# 2328) to bless, to praise. Part. of manner. ◆ **65 ἐγένετο** aor. ind. mid. (dep.) γίνομαι (# 1181) to become, to be, to come to be. **περιοικοῦντας** pres. act. part. περιοικέω (# 4340) to live around, to live by, neighboring. Part. as subst. **ὀρεινῇ** (# 3978) dat. sing. hill country. **διελαλεῖτο** impf. ind. pass. διαλαλέω (# 1362) to discuss, to talk w. The prep. compound and the iterat. impf. indicate it was continuous talk back and forth between the people (RWP). ◆ **66 ἔθεντο** aor. ind. mid. τίθημι (# 5502) to place, to lay. **ἔσται** fut. ind. mid. (dep.) εἰμί (# 1639) to be. Deliberative fut. used in a question. ◆ **67 ἐπλήσθη** aor. ind. pass. πίμπλημι (# 4398) to fill, w. gen. of content. **ἐπροφήτευσεν** aor. ind. act. προφητεύω (# 4736) to prophesy, to speak for

God (BBC). For a summary discussion of the song s. DJG, 895-96. ◆ **68 ἐπεσκέψατο** aor. ind. mid. (dep.) ἐπισκέπτομαι (# 2170) to look upon, to visit. **λύτρωσις** (# 3391) redemption, release. The reference here is no doubt to political redemption, but it is accompanied by and based upon moral and spiritual reformation (Plummer; s. 2:38). ◆ **69 ἤγειρεν** aor. ind. act. ἐγείρω (# 1586) to wake, to raise up. The idea of God raising someone up points to His role as governor of history and sender of salvation (PPP, 72). **κέρας** (# 3043) acc. sing. horn. Used as a symbol of power, strength and authority (TDNT; SB, 2:110-11; Fitzmyer, 383; Rogers, "The Davidic Covenant in the Gospels," *Bib Sac* 150 [1993]: 467). ◆ **70 ἐλάλησεν** aor. ind. act. λαλέω (# 3281) to speak; here in the sense of promise. ◆ **71 σωτηρίαν** (# 5401) acc. sing. deliverance, salvation. Salvation is seen in terms of physical deliverance so that the pious can give spiritual service to God (PPP, 72). **μισούντων** pres. act. part. gen. masc. pl. μισέω (# 3631) to hate (s. Gen. 12:3). Part. as subst. ◆ **72 ποιῆσαι** aor. act. inf. ποιέω (# 4472) to do, to perform (s.v. 51). Inf. expresses the purp. of **ἤγειρεν** aor. ind. act. s.v. 69. **ἔλεος** (# 1799) mercy, covenant loyalty (s.v. 50). **μνησθῆναι** aor. pass. inf. s.v. 54, w. gen. as obj. Used in parallelism w. "to render covenant loyalty." The covenant w. Abraham promised a seed through whom redemption for Israel and blessings for all people would come (Gen. 12:1-3). ◆ **73 ὤμοσεν** aor. ind. act. ὀμνύω (# 3923) to swear. **δοῦναι** aor. act. inf. δίδωμι (# 1443) to give. Inf. gives the content and purp. of the oath (Plummer). ◆ **74 ἀφόβως** (# 925) without fear, fearless. **ῥυσθέντας** aor. pass. part. ῥύομαι (# 4861) to rescue, to deliver. Part. as subst. **λατρεύειν** pres. act. inf. λατρεύω (# 3302) to serve (s. Heb. 12:28). ◆ **75 ὁσιότητι** dat. sing. ὁσιότης (# 4009) piety, devoutness, personal piety or devoutness which arises out of respect for the eternal laws (TDNT; Eph. 4:24). ◆ **76 κλη-θήσῃ** fut. ind. pass. 2nd. pers. sing. s.v. 13. Here, "acknowledged as," for the calling brings to expression what the child is (TBM, 372). **προπορεύσῃ** fut. ind. mid. (dep.) 2nd. pers. sing. προπορεύομαι (# 4638) to go before, to go forth. **ἑτοιμάσαι** aor. act. inf. s.v. 17. Inf. of purp. ◆ **77 δοῦναι** aor. act. inf. δίδωμι (# 1443) to give. Inf. of purp. ◆ **78 σπλάγχνον** (# 5073) compassion, the heart of mercy (Arndt; TDNT). **ἔλεος** (# 1799) mercy; here, "tender mercy"; s. Test. of Zeb. 7:3; 8:2, 6; 1QS 1:22; 2:1; 1QH 1:30-31 (Nolland; TDNT). **ἐπισκέψεται** fut. ind. mid. (dep.) s.v. 68. **ἀνατολή** (# 424) rising of a heavenly body or a growing shoot, branch. It refers to the Davidic Messiah as a Light that arises or as a Branch (s. PPP, 73; HLIN, 140-41; TBM, 373-74; Marshall; Fitzmyer, 387; BBC). ◆ **79 ἐπιφᾶναι** aor. act. inf. ἐπιφαίνω (# 2210) to appear, to show oneself. Inf. of purp. **καθημένοις** pres. mid. (dep.) part. κάθημαι (# 2764) to sit. Part. as subst. **κατευθῦναι** aor. act. inf. κατευθύνω (# 2985) to make straight, to guide. Inf. may be purp. or epex. to the first inf. (Marshall; Schürmann). ◆ **80** ηὔξανεν impf. ind. act. αὐξάνω (# *889*) to grow. ἐκραταιοῦτο impf. ind. pass. κραταιόω (# *3194*) to grow strong. Impf. indicates He continued to grow strong. ἀναδείξεως gen. sing. ἀνάδειξις (# *345*) manifestation, commissioning, installation (BAGD; Fitzmyer, 389).

Luke 2

◆ **1** ἐγένετο aor. ind. mid. (dep.) γίνομαι (# *1181*) to become, to happen. Used as an introductory formula w. the prep. ἐν (# *1877*) giving the time. For the use of this vb. in Luke s. Plummer, 45; Beyer, 31-33; VA, 120-26. ἐξῆλθεν aor. ind. act. ἐξέρχομαι (# *2002*) to go out. ἀπογράφεσθαι pres. mid. inf. ἀπογράφω (# *616*) to register, to record; mid. to register oneself, or permissive mid., to allow oneself to be enrolled (GGBB, 426). Inf. expresses either the content or the purp. of the edict. οἰκουμένην acc. sing. οἰκουμένη (# *3876*) world, the inhabited earth. Acc. as subj. of the inf. ◆ **2** ἀπογραφή (# *615*) enrollment, tax registration. πρώτη (# *4755*) first, before. For the latter translation s. Nolland; Wayne Brindle, "The Census of Quirinius: Luke 2:2," *JETS* 27 (1984): 43-52; GGBB, 305-6; BBC. ἡγεμονεύοντος pres. act. part. ἡγεμονεύω (# *2448*) to govern, to be governor. For the system of taxation and the problem of the governorship of Quirinius s. Arndt; William Ramsey, *The Bearing of Recent Discovery on the Trustworthiness of the New Testament* (London: Hodder & Stoughton, 1915), 238-300; Harold Hoehner, "Chronological Aspects of the Life of Christ: The Date of Christ's Birth," *Bib Sac* 130 (1974): 340-48; DJG, 66-69; and other bibliographical references by HA, 299; Nolland, 94-96; Marshall; Fitzmyer, 399-405; Sherwin-White, 162-71; NDIEC, 6:112-32. It has been suggested that Quirinius had authority over Syria at two different times, or the census here was before Quirinius. ◆ **3** ἐπορεύοντο impf. ind. mid. (dep.) πορεύομαι (# *4513*) to go, to travel. Impf. pictures the continual action in the past. For a discussion of each going to his own town s. NDIEC, 6:112-32. ἀπογράφεσθαι pres. mid. inf. s.v. 1. Inf. of purp.   ◆ **4** ἀνέβη aor. ind. act. ἀναβαίνω (# *326*) to go up. καλεῖται pres. ind. pass. καλέω (# *2813*) to call, to name. εἶναι pres. act. inf. εἰμί (# *1639*) to be. Inf. w. prep. giving the reason.   ◆ **5** ἀπογράψασθαι aor. mid. inf. s.v. 1. Inf. of purp. ἐμνηστευμένη perf. pass. part. μνηστεύω (# *3650*) pass. to be engaged (s. Matt. 1:18). οὔσῃ pres. act. part. εἰμί. ἐγκύῳ dat. sing. ἔγκυος (# *1607*) pregnant (MLL, 92). ◆ **6** εἶναι pres. act. inf. s.v. 4. Inf. w. prep. ἐν (# *1877*) in, to express time s.v. 1. ἐπλήσθησαν aor. ind. pass. πίμπλημι (# *4398*) to fill, to fulfill. τεκεῖν aor. act. inf. τίκτω (# *5503*) to give birth. Epex. inf. explaining αἱ ἡμέραι (# *2465*). ◆ **7** ἔτεκεν aor. ind. act. s.v. 6. πρωτότοκον (# *4758*) firstborn. ἐσπαργάνωσεν aor. ind. act.

σπαργανόω (# *5058*) to wrap in strips of cloth intended to strengthen the back and bones and to provide proper growth. It indicated the maternal care (Wisd. Sol. 7:4; Ezek. 16:4; s. 11 QtgJob 38:9), and the rank of the child was indicated by the splendor and costliness of the bands (HDCG, 2:685; TBM, 399; DGRA, 634; MLL, 99). ἀνέκλινεν aor. ind. act. ἀνακλίνω (# *369*) to lay down, to place in a reclining position. φάτνη (# *5764*) dat. sing. trough or box for feeding cattle, stable (IDB, 3:257; TDNT; BBC). καταλύματι dat. sing. κατάλυμα (# *2906*) lodging, inn, guest room. For a description of a possibly similar building s. RWP; Fitzmyer, 408; DJG, 69. ◆ **8** ποιμένες nom. pl. ποιμήν (# *4478*) shepherd. Shepherds had a low reputation and were looked upon w. great suspicion (TDNT; SB, 2:113). ἦσαν impf. ind. act. εἰμί (# *1639*) used w. part. to form a periphrastic construction. ἀγραυλοῦντες pres. act. part. ἀγραυλέω (# *64*) lit., to make the field the courtyard, to spend their life in the open air (Plummer). The Jews made a distinction between a flock in a stall and a flock which was kept outside in the fields (SB, 2:114-16). φυλάσσοντες pres. act. part. φυλάσσω (# *5875*) to guard. ◆ **9** ἐπέστη aor. ind. act. ἐφίστημι (# *2392*) to come upon suddenly and unexpectedly (NTNT). περιέλαμψεν aor. ind. act. περιλάμπω (# *4334*) to shine around. ἐφοβήθησαν aor. ind. pass. (dep.) φοβέομαι (# *5828*) to be afraid, followed by the cognate acc. used adverbially: "fear a great fear," "to fear greatly" (BD, 84-85). ◆ **10** φοβεῖσθε pres. mid. (dep.) imp. Pres. imp. w. neg. μή (# *3590*) indicating the prohibition of an action in progress. ◆ **11** ἐτέχθη aor. ind. pass. τίκτω (# *5503*) to give birth. ἔσται fut. ind. mid. (dep.) εἰμί (# *1639*) followed by dat. of personal interest. ◆ **12** εὑρήσετε fut. ind. act. εὑρίσκω (# *2351*) to find. ἐσπαργανωμένον perf. pass. part. s.v. 7. κείμενον pres. mid. (dep.) part. κεῖμαι (# *3023*) to lie down, to be lying down. ◆ **13** ἐξαίφνης (# *1978*) suddenly. ἐγένετο aor. ind. mid. (dep.) s.v. 1. στρατιά (# *5131*) army, a band of soldiers; this army, however, announces peace (Bengel). Perhaps heavenly attendents in God's royal entourage (DJG, 9). αἰνούντων pres. act. part. masc. gen. pl. αἰνέω (# *140*) to praise. The pl. construction is according to sense (RWP). ◆ **14** εὐδοκίας (# *2306*) good pleasure. It refers to God's good pleasure, those upon whom God's favor rests (Arndt; Marshall; ESB, 101-104; Schürmann; David Flusser, "Sanktus und Gloria," AUV, 129-52; for the phrase in DSS s. 1QH 4:32, 33; 11:9; 1QS 8:6). ◆ **15** ἐγένετο aor. ind. mid. (dep.) s.v. 1. ἀπῆλθον aor. ind. act. ἀπέρχομαι (# *599*) to go away. ἐλάλουν impf. ind. act. λαλέω (# *3281*) to speak. Impf. is incep. and pictures the repeated action. διέλθωμεν aor. subj. act. διέρχομαι (# *1451*) to pass through, to go through. Prep. in compound refers to passing through from one place to another (MH, 300-03). Hortatory subj., "let us go." δή (# *1314*) indeed. It has the force of urgency (Arndt). ἴδωμεν aor. subj. act. ὁράω (# 3972) to see. Hortatory subj. γεγονός perf. act. part. (adj.) γίνομαι (# 1181) to become, to happen. ἐγνώρισεν aor. ind. act. γνωρίζω (# 1192) to make known. ◆ 16 ἦλθαν aor. ind. act. 3rd. pl. ἔρχομαι (# 2262) to go. σπεύσαντες aor. act. part. σπεύδω (# 5067) to hurry, part. of manner. "They came in a hurry." ἀνεῦραν aor. ind. act. ἀνευρίσκω (# 461) to find. Prep. in compound implies a successful search in finding the object (Plummer; MH, 295-96). ◆ 17 ἰδόντες aor. act. part. (temp.) ὁράω (# 3972) to see. Aor. indicating antecedent action. This is logically necessary for the main vb. ("when they had seen this"). λαληθέντος aor. pass. part. (adj.) λαλέω (# 3281) to speak. ◆ 18 ἀκούσαντες aor. act. part. ἀκούω (# 201) to hear. Adj. part. used as subst. ἐθαύμασαν aor. ind. act. θαυμάζω (# 2513) to wonder, to be amazed. ◆ 19 συνετήρει impf. ind. act. συντηρέω (# 5337) to keep in mind, to hold or treasure up (in one's memory) (BAGD). The difficult events that happened are to be retained in order to be interpreted correctly (TBM, 406). Impf. pictures the continual action in the past. συμβάλλουσα pres. act. part. συμβάλλω (# 5202) to reflect upon ("placing together for comparison" [RWP]), to interpret, often w. divine help (TBM, 407). ◆ 20 ὑπέστρεψαν aor. ind. act. ὑποστρέφω (# 5715) to return. αἰνοῦντες pres. act. part. αἰνέω (# 140) to praise. Part. of manner. ἤκουσαν aor. ind. act. ἀκούω (# 201) to hear. εἶδον aor. ind. act. ὁράω to see s.v. 17. ◆ 21 ἐπλήσθησαν aor. ind. pass. s.v. 6. περιτεμεῖν aor. act. inf. περιτέμνω (# 4362) to circumcise. For the rite of circumcision among the Jews s. 1:59. Epex. inf. ἐκλήθη aor. ind. pass. s.v. 4. κληθέν aor. pass. part. s.v. 4. συλλημφθῆναι aor. pass. inf. συλλαμβάνω (# 5197) to conceive, to become pregnant; s. 1:24. Inf. w. prep. πρό (# 4574) w. a temp. meaning, "before," (RG, 1091). ◆ 22 καθαρισμός (# 2752) cleansing. The birth of a boy made the mother unclean for 7 days; she had to remain at home for 40 days without touching anything holy. She then was to offer the sacrifice at the Nicanor Gate on the east of the Court of the Women (JPB, 219; SB, 2:119-20; BBC; DJG, 130; Lev. 12:1-8). αὐτῶν gen. pl. αὐτός (# 899) their. It may refer to Mary and Joseph, indicating family solidarity, or it may refer to the purification of Mary and to the redemption of the firstborn (Stein; Marshall). ἀνήγαγον aor. ind. act. ἀνάγω (# 343) to lead up. παραστῆσαι aor. act. inf. παρίστημι (# 4225) to present. Inf. of purp. For the redemption of the firstborn s. Exod. 13:2-12; SB, 2:120. ◆ 23 γέγραπται perf. ind. pass. γράφω (# 1211) to write. Perf. is used of documents whose legal authority remains (MM; Stein). διανοῖγον pres. act. part. διανοίγω (# 1380) to open. Adj. use of the part. κληθήσεται fut. ind. pass. καλέω s.v. 4. ◆ 24 δοῦναι aor. act. inf. δίδωμι (# 1443) to give. Inf. of purp. εἰρημένον perf. pass. part. λέγω (# 3306) to say, to speak; here, commanded. Perf. indicates the abiding

results. ζεῦγος (# 2414) yoke, pair. τρυγών (# 5583) turtledove, dove. νοσσός (# 3801) young, offspring, particularly used of birds. περιστερά (# 4361) pigeon, tamed pigeon. This was the offering of the poor who could not afford a lamb. The doves had to reach a certain stage of growth, but the pigeons had to be young (Plummer; J Lightfoot, 3:39; SB, 2:123-24; M, Hullin 1:5). ◆ 25 εὐλαβής (# 2327) cautious, esp. conscientious; here, conscientious in matters of religion (Plummer; BAGD), pious in religious observance (Evans). προσδεχόμενος pres. mid. (dep.) part. προσδέχομαι (# 4657) to wait for, to expect. Part. in a periphrastic construction. παράκλησις (# 4155) consolation. A comprehensive term for the fulfillment of the messianic hope; the hope for God's eschatological restoration of the theocracy to Israel (SB, 2:124; Fitzmyer, 427; TDNT). ◆ 26 κεχρηματισμένον perf. pass. part. χρηματίζω (# 5976) to impart a revelation, to instruct, to warn. In the papyri the word meant to transact business, as well as a revelation from a deity (MM). Part. in a periphrastic construction. ἰδεῖν aor. act. inf. s.v. 15. Inf. explains the instruction. ἴδῃ aor. act. subj. s.v. 15. Subj. w. ἄν (# 323) in an indef. temp. cl. w. πρὶν ἢ ἄν (# 4570; 2445; 323), before. ◆ 27 ἦλθεν aor. ind. act. s.v. 16. εἰσαγαγεῖν aor. act. inf. εἰσάγω (# 1652) to bring in. Inf. w. prep. ἐν (# 1877) in a temp. sense, while (RG, 1072). ποιῆσαι aor. act. inf. ποιέω (# 4472) to do, to perform, to effect. εἰθισμένον perf. pass. part. ἐθίζω (# 1616) to be accustomed or used to. Perf. part. as subst.: "the custom"; here, "according to the custom of the Law." ◆ 28 ἐδέξατο aor. act. mid. (dep.) δέχομαι (# 1312) to receive, to welcome. ἀγκάλας acc. pl. ἀγκάλη (# 44) arm, bent as to receive something (BAGD). εὐλόγησεν aor. ind. act. εὐλογέω (# 2328) to bless, to thank God as the source of blessing. It was the custom in Jerusalem to bring a small child to a rabbi that he might bless the child and pray for it (SB, 2:138). ◆ 29 ἀπολύεις pres. ind. act. ἀπολύω (# 668) to dismiss, send away; here, to allow to die. Pres. ind., "You are dismissing your servant" (Stein; Marshall; HLIN, 146-47; ABD, 4:1155-56). An alternate meaning is a permissive sense: "Now you can dismiss your servant." ◆ 30 εἶδον aor. ind. act. s.v. 20. ◆ 31 ἡτοίμασας aor. ind. act. ἑτοιμάζω (# 2286) to prepare. ◆ 32 φῶς (# 5890) light. In apposition to salvation, defining its nature (HLIN, 148). ◆ 33 θαυμάζοντες pres. act. part. s.v. 18. Part. in a periphrastic construction. ◆ 34 κεῖται pres. ind. mid. of an old def. vb. κεῖμαι (# 3023), here used as the pass. of τίθημι to place, to appoint, to be destined (RWP; Bovon). πτῶσις (# 4774) fall, falling, used of the collapse of a house and in the LXX for the effect of judgment on the wicked (BAGD; Evans; 1QH 2:8). ἀνάστασις (# 414) rising, refers to rising up out of humiliation or oppression (Evans). ἀντιλεγόμενον pres. pass. part. ἀντιλέγω

(# 515) to speak against, to contradict, to oppose. The Son experiences contradiction from the world, reaching its culmination in the crucifixion (Meyer). ◆ 35 δι-ελεύσεται fut. ind. mid. (dep.) διέρχομαι (# 1451) to pass through. ῥομφαία (# 4855) a large, wide, double-edged sword. Such a weapon signifies extreme anguish (Plummer; Bovon). ἀποκαλυφθῶσιν aor. subj. pass. ἀποκαλύπτω (# 636) to unveil, to reveal. Used w. ὅπως to express purp. of κεῖται in v. 34 (Arndt). διαλο-γισμός (# 1369) consideration, thought, scheme, an undertone of hostility is suggested (Leaney). ◆ 36 προβεβηκυῖα perf. act. part. προβαίνω (# 4581) to advance. ζήσασα aor. act. part. (adj.) ζάω (# 2409) to live. παρθενία (# 4220) virginity. ◆ 37 ἀφί-στατο impf. ind. mid. (dep.) ἀφίστημι (# 923) to depart. Impf. indicates the continual but unfulfilled action in the past. λα-τρεύουσα pres. act. part. (adj.) λατρεύω (# 3302) to minister. The datives indicate how she served and the acc. of time indicates how long she served (GGBB, 202). ◆ 38 ἐπιστᾶσα aor. act. part. ἐφίστημι (# 2392) to approach, to come up, to stand by. ἀνθωμολογεῖτο impf. ind. mid. (dep.) ἀνθωμολογέομαι (# 469) to give thanks. The compound prep. in the vb. indicates thanksgiving in return for benefits (M, 297). Incep. impf. ἐλάλει impf. ind. act. λαλέω (# 3281) to speak, to say. προσ-δεχομένοις pres. mid. (dep.) part. dat. masc. pl. προσ-δέχομαι (# 4657) to expect, to wait for. Part. used as subst. Dat. as indir. obj. λύτρωσις (# 3391) redemption, deliverance. Many of the coins struck by the Jews as they declared their independence from Rome read, "to the redemption of Israel" (Rogers, "The Davidic Covenant in the Gospels," *Bib Sac* 150 [1993]: 466-67). ◆ 39 ἐτέλεσαν aor. ind. act. τελέω (# 5464) to complete. ἐπέ-στρεψαν aor. ind. act. ἐπιστρέφω (# 2188) to return. ◆ 40 ηὔξανεν impf. ind. act. αὐξάνω (# 889) to grow. ἐκραταιοῦτο impf. ind. pass. κραταιόω (# 3194) to make strong; pass. to be strengthened, to grow strong. The emphasis is upon total physical vigor, not mere muscular strength (LN, 1:269). Impf. pictures the continual action in the past. πληρούμενον pres. pass. part. πληρόω (# 4444) to fill. Part. could be manner describing how he developed. σοφία (# 5053) dat. sing. wisdom. The word was frequently used in the LXX to translate חָכְמָה, the ability to apply knowledge (esp. of God's instruction) to matters of life (s. M.V. Fox, "Words for Wisdom: חכומה and בינה; ערמה and מזמה; עצה and חושיה," *Zeitschrift für Althebräistik* 6 [1993]: 149-69). Instr. dat. giving also the content (KVS, 145). ◆ 41 ἐπορεύοντο impf. ind. mid. (dep.) πορεύομαι (# 4513) to go, to travel, to make a journey. Customary impf. According to the Law the men were to go to three celebrations a year (Exod. 34:23; Deut. 16:16; JPB, 130; WZZT, 20; SB, 2:141-44). Impf. could be incep., emphasizing the beginning of this particular trip: "they began to travel." ◆ 42 ἐγένετο aor. ind. mid. (dep.) s.v.

1. ἐτῶν gen. pl. ἔτος (# 2291) year; here, twelve years old. The Jewish father was required to acquaint the children with the Law, and when the child turned 13 he was required to fulfill the Law. Jesus' parents were perhaps getting him accustomed to the Law by taking him to the Feast of the Passover when he was twelve (SB, 2:144-47; Fitzmyer, 440; BBC; DJG, 236-37). ἀνα-βαινόντων pres. act. part. s.v. 4. Gen. abs. ◆ 43 τελει-ωσάντων aor. act. part. (temp.) τελειόω (# 5457) to end, to complete. Gen. abs. Aor. describes the antecedent, logically necessary action to the main vb. ὑποστρέφειν pres. act. inf. ὑπο-στρέφω (# 5715) to return. Inf. w. prep. ἐν (# 1877) to express contemporaneous time. ὑπέμειν-εν aor. ind. act. ὑπομένω (# 5702) to remain behind. ἔγν-ωσαν aor. ind. act. γινώσκω (# 1182) to know. ◆ 44 νομίσαντες aor. act. part. (causal) νομίζω (# 3787) to suppose, to believe. εἶναι pres. act. inf. εἰμί (# 1639) to be. Inf. used to complete the vb., giving the content of their supposition. It was common for pilgrims to travel together to the Feast in organized groups (WZZT, 121-27). ἦλθον aor. ind. act. ἔρχομαι (# 2262) to go. ὁδόν acc. sing. ὁδός (# 3847) way; acc. of space (GGBB, 202). A day's journey was 20-25 miles (Stein). ἀνεζήτουν impf. ind. act. ἀναζητέω (# 349) to look for, to seek. The prep. denotes thoroughness, and the iterat. impf. gives the repeated action: "They searched up and down, back and forth, a thorough search and prolonged" (RWP). ◆ 45 εὑρόντες aor. act. part. s.v. 12. Temp. or causal part. ὑπέστρεψαν aor. ind. act. s.v. 43. ἀναζητοῦντες pres. act. part. (circum.) s.v. 44. ◆ 46 ἐγένετο aor. ind. mid. (dep.) γίνομαι (# 1181) to happen, to occur. εὗρον aor. ind. act. s.v. 12. καθεζόμενον pres. mid. (dep.) part. καθέζομαι (# 2757) to sit. ἐπερωτῶντα pres. act. part. ἐπερωτάω (# 2089) to ask a question, to inquire. The prep. compound is directive (MH, 312). For questions and answers in the rabbinical method of teaching s. SB, 2:150; JL, 115, 196-97. ◆ 47 ἐξίσταντο impf. ind. mid. (dep.) ἐξίστημι (# 2014) to be amazed, to be astonished. Impf. pictures the continual action of the past. Jesus appears as a pupil who astonishes His teachers by the understanding apparent in His questions and answers (Marshall). ◆ ἰδόντες aor. act. part. (temp.) s.v. 15. ἐξεπλάγησαν aor. ind. pass. ἐκπλήσσω (# 1742) to strike out, to drive out by blow; pass. to be overwhelmed, to be astonished. ἐποίησας aor. ind. act. 2nd. pers. sing. s.v. 27. ὀδυνώμενοι pres. pass. part. ὀδυνάω (# 3849) to suffer pain, used of mental and spiritual pain. Here, "We have been anxiously looking for you" (BAGD; for the medical use s. DMTG, 249; MLL, 32-33). ἐζητοῦμεν impf. ind. act. ζητέω (# 2426) to look for, to seek. Impf. indicates the continual searching ("to look all over"). ◆ 49 ἐζητεῖτε impf. ind. act. s.v. 48. ᾔδειτε plperf. ind. act. of the def. perf. οἶδα (# 3857) to know. Ind. used w. οὐκ (# 4024) in a question expecting a positive answer. δεῖ (# 1256) pres. ind. act. it is neces-

sary, followed by inf. ◆ **50 συνῆκαν** aor. ind. act. συνίημι (# 5317) to bring together, to understand, to comprehend. **ἐλάλη-σεν** aor. ind. act. s.v. 15. ◆ **51 κατέβη** aor. ind. act. καταβαίνω (# 2849) to go down. **ἦν** impf. ind. act. εἰμί (# 1639) used w. the following pres. part. as a periphrastic emphasizing the continual obedience (Fitzmyer, 445; VA, 459). **ὑποτασσόμενος** pres. pass. part. ὑποτάσσω (# 5718) pass. submit oneself, to subordinate oneself, to obey. **διετήρει** impf. ind. act. διατηρέω (# 1413) to keep, to guard safely. The prep. in compound is perfective and describes the carrying of action through to a definite result (M, 301). ◆ **52 προέκοπτεν** impf. ind. act. προκόπτω (# 4621) to advance. **ἡλικία** (# 2461) dat. sing. height, stature, or perhaps age (Fitzmyer, 446; MM). Dat. of sphere, indicating the area of advancement.

Luke 3

◆ **1 ἡγεμονία** (# 2449) leadership, government, reign. The fifteenth year of Tiberius was probably about A.D. 27-29 since he was made emperor on Sept. 17, A.D. 14 (HA, 307-12; s. also FAP, 31-52, esp. 35-36; BBC; Dietmar Kienast, *Römishe Kaisertabelle: Grundzüge einer Kaiserchronologie* [Darmstadt: Wissenschaftliche Buchgesellschaft, 1996], 77). **ἡγεμονεύοντος** pres. act. part. (temp.) gen. masc. sing. ἡγεμονεύω (# 2448) to be governor. Gen. abs. Pres. indicating a contemporaneous action. For Pilate s. TJ, 51-57. **τετραρχοῦντος** pres. act. part. (temp.) τετραρχέω (# 5489) to be tetrarch; that is, a governor of one of four provinces, later a governor of any division (Plummer; TJ, 43). Gen. abs. For the life and times of Herod Antipas s. HA; Harold Hoehner, "Chronological Aspects of the Life of Christ: The Commencement of Christ's Ministry," *Bib Sac* 131 (1974): 147-62; TJ, 45-51. ◆ **2 ἐγένετο** aor. ind. mid. (dep.) γίνομαι (# 1181) to become, to happen (s. 2:1). ◆ **3 ἦλθεν** aor. ind. act. ἔρχομαι (# 2262) to come, to go. **κηρύσσων** pres. act. part. κηρύσσω (# 3062) to proclaim, to preach, to herald. Part. of manner explaining how he came. For John's preaching of baptism and repentance s. Matt. 3:1, 2. ◆ **4 γέγραπται** perf. ind. pass. γράφω (# 1211) to write. Perf. means "it stands written," used of a quote from an authoritative script (MM). **βοῶντος** pres. act. part. βοάω (# 1066) to shout, to call aloud. **ἑτοιμάσατε** aor. imp. act. ἑτοιμάζω (# 2286) to prepare. **ποιεῖτε** pres. imp. act. ποιέω (# 4472) to do, to make. **τρίβος** (# 5561) way, path. ◆ **5 φάραγξ** (# 5754) a valley shut in by precipices, a ravine (Plummer). **πληρωθήσεται** fut. ind. pass. πληρόω (# 4444) to fill. **βουνός** (# 1090) hill. **ταπεινωθήσεται** fut. ind. pass. ταπεινόω (# 5427) to make low. **σκολιός** (# 5021) crooked, curved. **εὐθείαν** acc. sing. εὐθύς (# 2318) straight. For the use of εἰς w. acc. for the pred., w. εἰμί s. KVS, 64. **τραχεῖαι** nom. pl. τραχύς (# 5550) uneven, rough. **λείας** acc. pl. λεῖος (# 3308) smooth, even.

These are metaphors of repentance (Stein). ◆ **6 ὄψεται** fut. ind. mid. (dep.) ὁράω (# 3972) to see. ◆ **7 βαπτισθῆναι** aor. pass. inf. βαπτίζω (# 966) to baptize (s. Matt. 3:6). Inf. of purp. **ἐχιδνῶν** gen. pl. ἔχιδνα (# 2399) snake, poisonous snake. The expression is intended to convey the repulsive and destructive character of those described (Fitzmyer, 467). Descriptive gen. For a similar expression ("adder or snake eggs") in DSS s. CD 5:14. **ὑπέδειξεν** aor. ind. act. ὑποδείκνυμι (# 5683) to show, to show under, to point out, to give a tip or private hint (RWP). **φυγεῖν** aor. act. inf. φεύγω (# 5771) to flee. Inf. w. vb. ὑποδείκνυμι. **μελλούσης** pres. act. part. gen. fem. sing. μέλλω (# 3516) to be about to. Adj. part. ("coming wrath") (Isa. 24; Fitzmyer, 468; SB, 4, ii:857-72; Moore, *Judaism*, 2:360-63). ◆ **8 ποιήσατε** aor. imp. act., ποιέω (# 4472) to do, to make, to produce. Aor. imp. calls for a specific action. Fruit implies a life of deeds (Stein). **ἄρξησθε** aor. subj. mid. (dep.) ἄρχομαι (# 806) to begin, w. inf. Used in a Semitic construction: "do not say" (Arndt; M, 455). **ἐγεῖραι** aor. act. inf. ἐγείρω (# 1586) to awake, to raise up. For this v. s. Matt. 3:9. ◆ **9 ἀξίνη** (# 544) axe. **κεῖται** pres. ind. pass. κεῖμαι (# 3023) used as perf. pass. of τίθημι to lie (s. 2:34; BAGD). **ποιοῦν** pres. ind. act. 3rd. pers. sing. s.v. 8. Habitual pres. indicating the consistent character. **ἐκκόπτεται** pres. ind. pass. ἐκκόπτω (# 1716) to cut off. Gnomic pres. indicating that which generally occurs. ◆ **10 ἐπηρώτων** impf. ind. act. ἐπερω-τάω (# 2089) to question, to inquire about. Prep. in compound is directive pointing to a specific subject. Incep. impf., "they began to ask." **ποιήσωμεν** aor. subj. act. s.v. 8. Deliberative subj., "what shall we do?" ◆ **11 ἀποκριθείς** aor. pass. (dep.) part. ἀποκρίνομαι (# 646) to answer. For the Semitic construction s. MH, 453. **χιτών** (# 5945) the tunic, garment worn next to the skin, made by sewing two sheets of fabric together w. a space in the middle for the head and neck (JPB, 123; EDNT; ABD, 2:235-37). Two tunics may have been worn to protect against the cold (Marshall). **μεταδότω** aor. imp. act. 3rd. pers. sing. μεταδίδωμι (# 3556) to give, to share. Aor. imp. calls for a specific action. It also stresses a general principle in a distributive sense; each is to do the action once (VANT, 354-55). **βρῶμα** (# 1109) food. Pl. is used w. the idea of food supplies (EDNT). **ποιείτω** pres. imp. act. 3rd. sing. s.v. 4. Pres. imp. gives a general principle in an iterat. sense. ◆ **12 ἦλθον** aor. ind. act. s.v. 3. **τελῶναι** nom. pl. τελώνης (# 5467) tax collector (BAGD). **βαπτισθῆναι** aor. pass. inf. s.v 7. Inf. of purp. **ποιήσωμεν** aor. subj. act. s.v. 8. ◆ **13 διατεταγμένον** perf. pass. part. διατάσσω (# 1411) to command, to prescribe. Part. used as subst. in a comp. **πράσσετε** pres. imp. act. πράσσω (# 4556) to do, to extort, to exact tribute (Plummer). Pres. imp. gives a general principle (s. VA, 355). ◆ **14 ἐπηρώτων** impf. ind. act. s.v. 10. **καί** also. **στρατευόμενοι** pres. mid. (dep.) part. στρατεύομαι

(# *5129*) to be a soldier, to serve as a soldier (TJ, 101-115; BBC). **διασείσητε** aor. subj. act. διασείω (# *1398*) to extort money by violence; literally, to shake violently; that is, to shake down (BAGD). Used in the papyri in the sense "to intimidate" (MM). **συκοφαντήσητε** aor. subj. act. συκοφαντέω (# *5193*) to accuse falsely, to extort by blackmail (Arndt; for soldiers' discontentment, corruption, and bribes s. NDIEC, 6:158; Tacitus, *Annals* 1, 16-17 ["Truly the army is a harsh, unrewarding profession! Body and soul are reckoned at two and a half sesterces a day–and with this you have to find clothes, weapons, and bribes for brutal company commanders if you want to avoid chores"]). The subj. here forbids the whole act from occurring and adds a note of urgency (VANT, 337, 339). **ἀρκεῖσθε** pres. imp. pass. ἀρκέω (# *758*) pass. to be enough, to be sufficient. **ὀψώνιον** food, ration, pay. The average soldier received 225 denarii a year (a denarius, worth about 18 cents, was the normal day's wages) from which deductions were made for food, clothing, and arms (OCD, 1014; NDIEC, 6:157-59). For the meaning of "provisions," "shoppings," s. C.C. Caragounis, "ΟΨΩΝΙΟΝ: A Reconsideration of Its Meaning," *Nov T* 16 (1974): 49-51. ◆ **15 προσδοκῶντος** pres. act. part. προσδοκάω (# *4659*) to await w. expectation. Gen. abs. Temp. part. expressing contemporaneous time. **διαλογιζομένων** pres. mid. (dep.) part. διαλογίζομαι (# *1368*) to discuss, to reason, to debate. Gen. abs. **μήποτε** (# *3607*) whether, perhaps; interrogative particle in an indir. question (BAGD). **εἴη** pres. opt. act. εἰμί (# *1639*) to be. Opt. in indir. speech. ◆ **16 ἀπεκρίνατο** aor. ind. mid. (dep.) ἀποκρίνομαι (# *646*) to answer. For the use of the aor. mid. instead of the aor. pass. s. MM; BG, 74. **ἰσχυρότερος** comp. ἰσχυρός (# *2708*) strong, mighty; comp. stronger, followed by gen. of comp. **ἱκανός** (# *2653*) sufficient, worthy. **λῦσαι** aor. act. inf. λύω (# *3395*) to loose. Epex. inf. explaining ἱκανός. **ἱμάντα** acc. pl. ἱμάς (# *2666*) leather strap (s. Mark 1:7); dat. of sphere indicating place and means of baptism (GGBB, 155). **βαπτίσει** fut. ind. act. βαπτίζω (# *966*) to baptize. ◆ **17 πτύον** (# *4768*) winnowing shovel (Matt. 3:12). **διακαθᾶραι** aor. act. inf. διακαθαίρω (# *1350*) to thoroughly clean, to clean out. Inf. of purp. **ἅλων** (# *272*) threshing floor. **συναγαγεῖν** aor. act. inf. συνάγω (# *5251*) to gather together. Inf. of purp. **ἀποθήκη** (# *630*) storehouse, barn. **ἄχυρον** (# *949*) chaff. Chaff was used not only for making bricks, but as fuel for fires (MM; BAGD). **κατακαύσει** fut. ind. act. κατακαίω (# *2876*) to burn, to burn up. **ἀσβέστῳ** dat. sing. ἄσβεστος (# *812*) unquenchable. Used w. instr. dat. ◆ **18 παρακαλῶν** pres. act. part. παρακαλέω (# *4151*) to urge, to exhort, to encourage. Part. of manner. **εὐηγγελίζετο** impf. ind. mid. (dep.) εὐαγγελίζομαι (# *2294*) to proclaim the good news (TDNT; EDNT; NIDNTT). This was the good news of the coming of the Messiah

and His Kingdom. ◆ **19 ἐλεγχόμενος** pres. pass. part. ἐλέγχω (# *1794*) to bring to light, to expose, to convict or convince someone of something, to reprove (BAGD). For John and Herod Antipas s. TJ, 63-64; HA, 110-71. Part. of cause. **ἐποίησεν** aor. ind. act. s.v. 4. ◆ **20 προσέθηκεν** aor. ind. act. προστίθημι (# *4707*) to add to. "He added this also on top of all–he shut up John in prison" (Plummer). **κατέκλεισεν** aor. ind. act. κατακλείω (# *2881*) to shut up; literally, to shut down. According to Josephus he was brought in chains to the fortress of Machaerus on the east side of the Jordan (TJ, 63-64; Jos., *Ant.*, 18.119; *J.W.*, 7.163-95). ◆ **21 ἐγένετο** aor. ind. mid. (dep.) γίνομαι (# *1181*) to become, to happen (s. 1:8). **βαπτισθῆναι** aor. pass. inf. s.v. 16. Inf. used w. prep. to express time. **βαπτισθέντος** aor. pass. part. (temp.) s.v. 16. Gen. abs. **προσευχομένου** pres. mid. (dep.) part. (temp.) προσεύχομαι (# *4667*) to pray. Gen. abs. **ἀνεῳχθῆναι** aor. pass. inf. ἀνοίγω (# *487*) to open. Temp. inf. w. prep. ἐν (# *1877*). ◆ **22 καταβῆναι** aor. act. inf. καταβαίνω (# *2849*) to come down. Temp. inf. s.v. 21. **σωματικῷ** dat. sing. σωματικός (# *5394*) bodily. Loc. dat. **εἴδει** dat. sing. εἶδος (# *1626*) form, outward appearance (BAGD). This expresses the reality of what was seen (Marshall). **γενέσθαι** aor. mid. (dep.) inf. s.v. 21 (s. 1:8; 2:1). **εὐδόκησα** aor. ind. act. εὐδοκέω (# *2305*) to have pleasure, to be pleased. ◆ **23 ἀρχόμενος** pres. mid. (dep.) part. (temp.) s.v. 8. It refers to Jesus beginning His ministry (Plummer). **ὡσεί** (# *6059*) about, around. A person's age frequently was given in multiples of five. Luke's chronology is only very general (Ellis; s. also v. 1). **ἐνομίζετο** impf. ind. pass. νομίζω (# *3787*) to suppose.

Luke 4

◆ **1 ὑπέστρεψεν** aor. ind. act. ὑποστρέφω (# *5715*) to return, to depart (Marshall). **ἤγετο** impf. ind. pass. ἄγω (# *72*) to lead. Impf. pictures the continual action in the past. ◆ **2 πειραζόμενος** pres. pass. part. πειράζω (# *4279*) to try, to tempt, here in the bad sense (Bovon). Pres. part. here may express purp. (Matt. 4:1; RG, 891). For a discussion of the temptation s. DJG, 821-27. **ἔφαγεν** aor. ind. act. ἐσθίω (# *2266*) to eat. **συντελεσθεισῶν** aor. pass. part. (temp.) συντελέω (# *5334*) to finish, to complete. The prep. compound is perfective. Gen. abs. **ἐπείνασεν** aor. ind. act. πεινάω (# *4277*) to be hungry. ◆ **3 εἰπέ** aor. imp. act. λέγω (# *3306*) to say, to speak. **γένηται** aor. subj. mid. (dep.) γίνομαι (# *1181*) to become. Subj. w. ἵνα (# *2671*) in purp. cl. ◆ **4 ἀπεκρίθη** aor. ind. pass. (dep.) ἀποκρίνομαι (# *646*) to answer. **γέγραπται** perf. ind. pass. γράφω (# *1211*) to write. Perf. used to indicate the lasting authority of what was written (MM). **ζήσεται** fut. ind. mid. ζάω (# *2409*) to live. For the fut. mid. s. BD, 42; RG, 356. ◆ **5 ἀναγαγών** aor. act. part. (temp.) ἀνάγω (# *343*) to lead up. **ἔδειξεν** aor. ind. act. δείκνυμι (# *1259*) to show. **ἐν στιγμῇ χρόνου** in a point of time. It intimates the kingdoms were represented, not in a series of pageants, but simultaneously (Plummer). ◆ **6 δώσω** fut. ind. act. δίδωμι (# 1443) to give. **παραδέδοται** perf. ind. pass. παραδίδωμι (# 4140) to deliver over. Perf. indicates the present possession. ◆ **7 προσκυνήσῃς** aor. subj. act. προσκυνέω (# 4686) to worship, to worship by falling on the knees. Subj. in a 3rd. class cond. cl., w. the cond. considered as a possibility. **ἔσται** fut. ind. mid. (dep.) εἰμί (# 1639) to be. ◆ **8 ἀποκριθείς** aor. pass. part. s.v. 4. For the construction s. 3:11. **προσκυνήσεις** fut. ind. act. s.v. 7. **λατρεύσεις** fut. ind. act. λατρεύω (# 3302) to perform religious rites as part of worship, to minister, to serve (LN, 1:533). ◆ **9 ἤγαγεν** aor. ind. act. s.v. 1. **ἔστησεν** aor. ind. act. ἵστημι (# 2705) to place, to stand. **εἶ** pres. ind. act. εἰμί (# 1639). Ind. in a 1st. class cond., in which the speaker assumes the reality of the cond. **βάλε** aor. imp. act. βάλλω (# 965) to throw. For a discussion of this location in the temple s. BBC. ◆ **10 γέγραπται** perf. ind. pass. s.v. 4. **ἐντελεῖται** fut. ind. mid. (dep.) ἐντέλλομαι (# 1948) to command, to give instructions. **διαφυλάξαι** aor. act. inf. διαφυλάσσω (# 1428) to guard carefully, to watch over closely, to preserve, used esp. for divine guardianship (MM; GELTS, 112). Prep. in compound is intensive or perfective. Inf. in indir. speech, or as obj. of the vb. of speaking. ◆ **11 ἀροῦσιν** fut. ind. act. αἴρω (# 149) to lift up. **μήποτε** (# 3607) w. subj., lest, to express neg. purp. **προσκόψῃς** aor. subj. act. προσκόπτω (# 4684) to strike against, to stumble on. ◆ **12 ἀποκριθείς** aor. pass. part. (dep.) s.v. 4. **εἴρηται** perf. ind. pass. λέγω (# 3306) to say. **ἐκπειράσεις** fut. ind. act. ἐκπειράζω (# 1733) to tempt, to test, to try, to test out. Prep. in compound might suggest the daring of the act or the effort to put to a decisive test (MM, 309). ◆ **13 συντελέσας** aor. act. part. συντελέω (# 5334) to complete, to finish. **ἀπέστη** aor. ind. act. ἀφίστημι (# 923) to depart. ◆ **14 ὑπέστρεψεν** aor. ind. act. s.v. 1. **ἐξῆλθεν** aor. ind. act. ἐξέρχομαι (# 2002) to go out. ◆ **15 ἐδίδασκεν** impf. ind. act. διδάσκω (# 1438) to teach. Impf. emphasizes the continuing action. Possibly iterat.: "He taught time and again in their synagogues." **δοξαζόμενος** pres. pass. part. (circum.) δοξάζω (# 1519) to glorify, to praise, to hold in high esteem. Possibly result (GGBB, 638). ◆ **16 ἦλθεν** aor. ind. act. ἔρχομαι (# 2262) to come, to go. **τεθραμμένος** perf. pass. part. (adj.) τρέφω (# 5555) to nourish, to bring up, to rear. **εἰσῆλθεν** aor. ind. act. εἰσέρχομαι (# 1656) to go in. **εἰωθός** (# 1665) perf. act. part. of an old form ἔθω, to be accustomed. Synagogue attendance was expected of every devout Jew (Ellis). For a discussion of synagogue s. DJG, 781-84. **ἀνέστη** aor. ind. act. ἀνίστημι (# 482) to stand up. **ἀναγνῶναι** aor. act. inf. ἀναγινώσκω (# 336) to read. Inf. of purp. The ruler of the synagogue could appoint one or more persons to read the Scriptures (a section of Law and of the Prophets). For the

reading of the Scripture in the synagogue service and the service itself s. M, Meg. 4; TT, 36-53; SB, 4:i, 153-88; Moore, *Judaism*, 1:291-307; HJP, 2:447-63; JPFC, 2:914-33. ◆ **17 ἐπεδόθη** aor. ind. pass. ἐπιδίδωμι (# 2113) to give to, to hand over. **ἀναπτύξας** aor. act. part. (temp.) ἀναπτύσσω (# 408) to unroll, to unroll a book in scroll form (BAGD). For the variant form, ἀνοίξας (aor. act. part. ἀνοίγω to open), s. TC, 137. **εὗρεν** aor. ind. act. εὑρίσκω (# 2351) to find. This may indicate that the passages from the Prophets to be read were not yet fixed and Jesus deliberately sought out this passage (Fitzmyer, 532). **γεγραμμένον** perf. pass. part. s.v. 4. Part. used w. ἦν to form the plperf. pass.: "It stood in writing" (Marshall; VA, 469). ◆ **18 εἴνεκεν** (# 1641) because of. Prep. preceded by gen. of the rel. pron. (RG, 425). **ἔχρισεν** aor. ind. act. χρίω (# 5987) to anoint. **εὐαγγελίσασθαι** aor. mid. (dep.) inf. εὐαγγελίζομαι (# 2294) to proclaim good news. Inf. of purp. **πτωχός** (# 4777) poor. For a discussion and summary of the research on the poor in Lukan theology s. Joel B. Green, "Good News to Whom?" in *Jesus of Nazareth: Lord and Christ: Essays on the Historical Jesus and New Testament Christology*, eds. Joel B. Green and Max Turner (Grand Rapids: Eerdmans, 1994), 59-74, esp. 60-61. **ἀπέσταλκεν** perf. ind. act. ἀποστέλλω (# 690) to send, to send as an authoritative representative (TDNT). **κηρύξαι** aor. act. inf. κηρύσσω (# 3062) to preach, to proclaim as a herald. Inf. of purp. **αἰχμαλώτοις** dat. pl. αἰχμάλωτος (# 171) prisoner captured in war, captive. Dat. as indir. obj. **ἄφεσις** (# 912) release from captivity, pardon, forgiveness (BAGD). **ἀνάβλεψις** (# 330) restoration of sight. **ἀποστεῖλαι** aor. act. inf. ἀποστέλλω. Inf. of purp. **τεθραυσμένους** perf. pass. part. θραύω (# 2575) to break in pieces, to shatter. Perf. emphasizes the state or cond. Part. as subst. **ἐν ἀφέσει** in release; used w. the vb. in the sense of "to set free" (Marshall). ◆ **19 ἐνιαυτός** (# 1929) year. **δεκτός** (# 1283) acceptable. That in which He is pleased to show humanity extraordinary favors (Godet). In a DSS text concerning Melchizedek, this passage is believed to refer to the tenth and final Year of Jubilee, in which there is freedom from the debt of sin, atonement, and judgment (11Q13 [11QMelch]; ESB, 245-67; DJG, 396-97). ◆ **20 πτύξας** aor. act. part. (temp.) πτύσσω (# 4771) to fold, to roll together. **ἀποδούς** aor. act. part. (temp.) ἀποδίδωμι (# 625) to give back. **ὑπηρέτης** (# 5677) minister, attendant. The use of the art. identifies him as a typical attendant (GGBB, 217). He was responsible to return the scroll to its place (SB, 4:i, 147). **ἐκάθισεν** aor. ind. act. καθίζω (# 2767) to sit down, to take one's seat. The one teaching generally sat to teach. For a study of the sermon s. Asher Finkel, "Jesus' Sermon at Nazareth," AUV, 106-15. **ἦσαν** impf. ind. act. εἰμί (# 1639) to be. **ἀτενίζοντες** pres. act. part. ἀτενίζω (# 867) to look or gaze intently, w. dat. The prefix of the word is not alpha privative but copulative or intensive (RWP). Part. in a periphrastic construction. ◆ **21 ἤρξατο** aor. ind. mid. (dep.) ἄρχομαι (# 806) to begin, w. inf. **πεπλήρωται** perf. ind. pass. πληρόω (# 4444) to fill, to fulfill. Perf. stresses the state or cond. (VANT, 295-96) and has the sense of a pres. (BD, 176). The passage was fulfilled in the Messianic age. The listeners took offense since they did not see the Messiah before them (BBC). ◆ **22 ἐμαρτύρουν** impf. ind. act. μαρτυρέω (# 3455) to be a witness, to testify, w. dat. of advantage ("to testify for him"). Incep. impf. **ἐθαύμαζον** impf. ind. act. θαυμάζω (# 2513) to wonder, to be amazed, to admire. Incep. impf. **ἐκπορευομένοις** pres. mid. (dep.) part. (adj.) ἐκπορεύομαι (# 1744) to go out. **οὐχί** (# 4049) used in a question expecting a positive answer: "this is..., isn't it?" ◆ **23 εἶπεν** aor. ind. act. λέγω (# 3306) to say. **πάντως** (# 4122) adv. (in answers to questions) certainly! **ἐρεῖτε** fut. ind. act. λέγω to say. "You will go on to say to me" (Marshall). **ἰατρέ** voc. masc. sing. ἰατρός (# 2620) doctor, physician. **θεράπευσον** aor. imp. act. θεραπεύω (# 2543) to heal (GLH). **ἠκούσαμεν** aor. ind. act. ἀκύω (# 201) to hear. **γενόμενα** aor. mid. (dep.) part. (adj.) s.v. 3. **ποίησον** aor. imp. act. ποιέω (# 4472) to do, to perform. Aor. imp. calls for a specific action. ◆ **24 εἶπεν** aor. ind. act. s.v. 23. ◆ **25 ἐκλείσθη** aor. ind. pass. κλείω (# 3091) to shut, to close. Theol. pass. **ἐπί** for, about. **ἐγένετο** aor. ind. mid. (dep.) s.v. 3. ◆ **26 ἐπέμφθη** aor. ind. pass. πέμπω (# 4287) to send. Theol. pass. ◆ **27 ἐπί** w. gen., at the time of. **ἐκαθαρίσθη** aor. ind. pass. καθαρίζω (# 2751) to cleanse. ◆ **28 ἐπλήσθησαν** aor. ind. pass. πίμπλημι (# 4398) to fill. **θυμοῦ** gen. θυμός (# 2596) anger; partitive gen. used w. **ἐπλήθησαν**. The construction indicates the control and domination of the total person. The mob could not legally execute capital punishment in dicating their great anger (BBC). **ἀκούοντες** pres. act. part. s.v. 23. ◆ **29 ἀναστάντες** aor. act. part. ἀνίστημι (# 482) to arise, to get up. **ἐξέβαλον** aor. ind. act. ἐκβάλλω (# 1675) to throw out, to drive out. **ἤγαγον** aor. ind. act. s.v. 1. **ὀφρύς** (# 4059) brow, ridge. **ᾠκοδόμητο** plperf. ind. pass. οἰκοδομέω (# 3868) to build; intensive plperf. emphasizing the results that existed in the past time. It makes no comment about the present (GGBB, 584). **κατακρημνίσαι** aor. act. inf. κατακρημνίζω (# 2889) to throw someone over a cliff. Inf. used w. **ὥστε** to express intended result (RWP; GGBB, 591; Takamitsu Muraoka, "Purpose or Result?: Ὥστε in Biblical Greek," *NovT* 15[1972]: 205-19; J. L. Boyer, "The Classification of Infinitives: A Statistical Study," *Grace Theological Journal* 6 [1985]: 11-12). ◆ **30 διελθών** aor. act. part. (circum.) διέρχομαι (# 1451) to pass through, to go through. **ἐπορεύετο** impf. ind. mid. (dep.) πορεύομαι (# 4513) to go, to go away. ◆ **31 κατῆλθεν** aor. ind. act. κατέρχομαι (# 2982) to go down. **διδάσκων** pres. act. part. διδάσκω (# 1438) to teach. Part. w. impf. **ἦν** in periphrastic construction expressing continual or re-

peated action. ◆ **32 ἐξεπλήσσοντο** impf. ind. pass. ἐκπλήσσω (# 1742) pass. to be astounded, to be so amazed as to be practically overwhelmed, to be greatly astounded (LN, 1:312-13). Impf. pictures the repeated action in the past. ◆ **33 ἀνέκραξεν** aor. ind. act. ἀνακράζω (# 371) to cry out, to scream out. ◆ **34 ἔα** (# 1568) ah! Interjection of anger or dismay, displeasure or surprise (Fitzmyer, 545). It may be taken as the imp. of ἐάω w. the meaning "let (me) alone" (Schürmann; Nolland). **τί ἡμῖν καὶ σοί** "What is it to us and to you?" "What do we have in common?" "Do not meddle w. me!" (Marshall; s. John 2:4). **ἦλθες** aor. ind. act. 2nd. pers. sing. s.v. 16. **ἀπολέσαι** aor. act. inf. ἀπόλλυμι (# 660) to destroy, to ruin. Inf. of purp. **οἶδα** (# 3857) to know. Def. perf. w. pres. meaning. ◆ **35 ἐπετίμησεν** aor. ind. act. ἐπιτιμάω (# 2203) to charge, to sternly command (Matt. 17:18; cf. 1QM 14:10). **φιμώθητι** aor. imp. pass. φιμόω (# 5821) to muzzle; pass. to be silent. Aor. imp. calls for a specific action. **ἔξελθε** aor. imp. act. s.v. 14. **ῥίψαν** aor. act. part. nom. n. sing. ῥίπτω (# 4849) to throw, to fling. In medicine the word was used of convulsive fits and similar affections (MLL, 2). Part. of manner telling how the demon came out. **βλάψαν** aor. act. part. (circum.) βλάπτω (# 1055) to damage, to injure. In medicine the word indicated the damage done to the system by a disease. Here it means that no permanent bodily damage was done to the man (MLL, 2). ◆ **36 ἐγένετο** aor. ind. mid. (dep.) s.v. 3. **συνελάλουν** impf. ind. act. συλλαλέω (# 5196) to talk together, to discuss. Impf. pictures the repeated action in the past. ◆ **37 ἐξεπορεύετο** impf. ind. mid. (dep.) ἐκπορεύομαι (# 1744) to go out. Impf. pictures the repeated action. **ἦχος** (# 2491) echo, report. ◆ **38 ἀναστάς** aor. act. part. (temp.) s.v. 16. **εἰσῆλθεν** aor. ind. act. εἰσέρχομαι (# 1656) to go into. **συνεχομένη** pres. pass. part. συνέχω (# 5309) pass. to be held by something, to suffer. Part. is used in a periphrastic construction. **πυρετῷ** dat. πυρετός (# 4790) fever. The ancient physicians distinguished fevers by the terms great and small. For this and the previous word s. MLL 3, 4. Instr. dat. **ἠρώτησαν** aor. ind. act. ἐρωτάω (# 2263) to ask, to request. They (those in the house) made a request on her behalf (Nolland). ◆ **39 ἐπιστάς** aor. act. part. (temp.) ἐφίστημι (# 2392) to stand by or near, to approach. **ἐπάνω** (# 2062) over. Jesus stepped up to the bed or rug on which the patient lay and bent over her (Arndt). **ἐπετίμησεν** aor. ind. act. s.v. 35. **ἀφῆκεν** aor. ind. act. ἀφίημι (# 918) to leave. **ἀναστᾶσα** aor. act. part. s.v. 16. **διηκόνει** impf. ind. act. διακονέω (# 1354) to serve, to minister. Incep. impf., "she began to minister." ◆ **40 δύνοντος** pres. act. part. (temp.) δύνω (# 1544) to go down (of the sun), to set. Gen. abs. **εἶχον** impf. ind. act. ἔχω (# 2400) to have. **ἀσθενοῦντας** pres. act. part. ἀσθενέω (# 820) to be weak, to be sick. Part. as subst. **ἤγαγον** aor. ind. act. s.v. 1. **ἐπιτιθείς** aor. act. part. ἐπιτίθημι (# 2202) to place

upon. Part. of means. "He healed by placing...." ἐθε-
ράπευεν impf. ind. act. s.v. 23.   ◆ 41 ἐξήρχετο impf.
ind. mid. (dep.) s.v. 14. κραυγάζοντα pres. act. part.
κραυγάζω (# 3198) to scream, to cry out. Part. of manner, telling how the demons came out. ἐπιτιμῶν pres.
act. part. s.v. 35. εἴα impf. ind. act. ἐάω (# 1572) to allow. λαλεῖν pres. act. inf. λαλέω (# 3281) to speak. Inf.
completing the vb. ᾔδεισαν plperf. ind. act. οἶδα
(# 3857) s.v. 34. εἶναι pres. act. inf. εἰμί. (# 1639) Inf. in
indir. discourse. The subject of the inf. is αὐτόν (# 899)
◆ 42 γενομένης aor. mid. (dep.) part. (temp.) s.v. 3., gen.
abs. ἐξελθών aor. act. part. (temp.) s.v. 14. ἐπορεύθη aor.
ind. pass. (dep.) πορεύομαι (# 4513) to go. ἐπεζήτουν
impf. ind. act. ἐπιζητέω (# 2118) to seek after, to look
for. Prep. marks the direction of the search (Plummer).
Impf. describes the continual action. κατεῖχον impf.
ind. act. κατέχω (# 2988) to hold back, to restrain. Conative impf. "they tried to restrain him." πορεύεσθαι
pres. mid. (dep.) inf. s.v. 30. Inf. explaining what they
tried to do.   ◆ 43 εἶπεν aor. ind. act. λέγω (# 3306) to
say. εὐαγγελίσασθαι aor. mid. (dep.) inf. s.v. 18. Inf. explaining what is necessary. δεῖ (# 1265) pres. ind. act.
"it is necessary." It gives a logical necessity. ἀπεστάλην
aor. ind. pass. ἀποστέλλω (# 690) to send, to send as an
official representative (TDNT; NIDNTT; EDNT).

Luke 5
◆ 1 ἐγένετο aor. ind. mid. (dep.) γίνομαι (# 1181) to
become, to happen (s. 2:1). ἐπικεῖσθαι pres. mid. inf.
ἐπίκειμαι (# 2130) to lie upon, to press around, to press
upon. It describes the physical pressure of the crowd
as they seek to hear Jesus (Marshall). Inf. w. prep. ἐν
(# 1877) for contemporaneous time. ἀκούειν pres. act.
inf. ἀκούω (# 201) hear. ἑστώς perf. act. part. ἵστημι
(# 2705) perf. to stand. Part. in a periphrastic construction w. impf. ἦν.   ◆ 2 εἶδεν aor. ind. act. ὁράω (# 3972)
to see. πλοῖα acc. pl. πλοῖον (# 4450) boat; here, small
boat, an open craft some twenty to thirty feet in length
(Ellis; Shelley Wachsmann, "The Galilee Boat–2,000-
Year-Old Hull Recovered Intact," *BAR* 16 [1988]: 18-
33). ἑστῶτα perf. act. part. s.v. 1. ἁλιεῖς nom. pl. ἁλιεύς
(# 243) fisherman (Mendel Nun, "Cast Your Nets
Upon the Waters: Fish and Fishermen in Jesus' Time,"
BAR 19 [1993]: 46-56, 70; Matt. 4:18-19). ἀποβάντες aor.
act. part. ἀποβαίνω (# 609) to go away, to disembark.
Circum. or temp. part. ἔπλυνον impf. ind. act. πλύνω
(# 4459) to wash, to clean. Impf. pictures the continual
action.   ◆ 3 ἐμβάς aor. act. part. ἐμβαίνω (# 1832) to
get in, to embark. ἠρώτησεν aor. ind. act. ἐρωτάω
(# 2263) to ask, to request. ἐπαναγαγεῖν aor. act. inf.
ἐπανάγω (# 2056) to put out to sea. Inf. as obj. of the vb.
ὀλίγον (# 3900) adv. a little. καθίσας aor. act. part. καθίζω (# 2767) to sit down. ἐδίδασκεν impf. ind. act.
διδάσκω (# 1438) to teach. Incep. impf., "he began

teaching."   ◆ 4 ἐπαύσατο aor. ind. mid. (dep.) παύω
(# 4264) to cease, to stop. λαλῶν pres. act. part. λαλέω
(# 3281) to speak. Part. completes the vb. ἐπανάγαγε
pres. imp. act. s.v. 3. χαλάσατε aor. imp. act. χαλάω
(# 5899) to let down. A nautical term for lowering
cargo or boats (RWP). ἄγρα (# 62) catch.   ◆ 5 ἀποκριθείς aor. pass. (dep.) part. ἀποκρίνομαι (# 646) to
answer (MH, 453; VA, 138). ἐπιστάτα voc. sing.
ἐπιστάτης (# 2181) overseer, director, master, implying
authority and used here of one who has the right to
give orders (Plummer). κοπιάσαντες aor. act. part. κοπιάω (# 3159) to work, to work w. effort, to work hard,
implying difficulties and trouble (LN, 1:515). Concessive part., "although we have worked." ἐλάβομεν aor.
ind. act. λαμβάνω (# 3284) to take, to receive. ἐπί
(# 2093) w. dat., "in reliance on Your Word" (Arndt).
χαλάσω fut. ind. act. s.v. 4.   ◆ 6 ποιήσαντες aor. act.
part. (temp.) ποιέω (# 4472) to do. συνέκλεισαν aor.
ind. act. συγκλείω (# 5168) to close together. ἰχθύων
gen. pl. ἰχθύς (# 2716) fish. The kind of fish caught in
the nets was very probably the Tilapia Galilee ("musht
abiad," or "amnun"), known as St. Peter's fish (M.
Nun, "Fish and Fishermen," *BAR* 19 [1993]: 48-52).
Descriptive gen. διερρήσσετο impf. ind. pass. διαρρήγνυμι (# 1396) to rip apart; pass. to burst. Incep. impf., "they began to break apart."   ◆ 7 κατένευσαν aor.
ind. act. κατανεύω (# 2916) to motion to. μέτοχος
(# 3581) partner. ἐλθόντας aor. act. part. (adj.) ἔρχομαι
(# 2262) to come. συλλαβέσθαι aor. mid. inf. συλλαμβάνω (# 5197) to take hold together, to help; w. dat. as
obj. Inf. explaining motioning of the disciples. ἦλθον
aor. ind. act. ἔρχομαι. ἔπλησαν aor. ind. act. πίμπλημι
(# 4398) to fill. βυθίζεσθαι pres. pass. inf. βυθίζω
(# 1112) to cause to sink; pass. to sink. Inf. used w.
ὥστε to express actual result. Pres. is incep., "it began
to sink" (Arndt).   ◆ 8 ἰδών aor. act. part. (temp.) ὁράω
(# 3972) to see. προσέπεσεν aor. ind. act. προσπίπτω
(# 4700) to fall down before (w. dat.). γόνασιν dat. pl.
γόνυ (# 1205) knee. ἔξελθε aor. imp. act. ἐξέρχομαι
(# 2002) to depart, to go away. ἁμαρτωλός (# 283) sinful. Pred. adj.   ◆ 9 θάμβος (# 2502) amazement.
περιέσχεν aor. ind. act. περιέχω (# 4321) to surround, to
encompass, to seize. ὧν gen. pl. ὅς rel. pron. Gen. by
attraction. συνέλαβον aor. ind. act. συλλαμβάνω
(# 5197) to catch.   ◆ 10 κοινωνός (# 3128) partner, associate, one who shares, stronger than the term used in
v. 7. It denotes an association and a common undertaking (Godet; TDNT; NIDNTT; MNTW). φοβοῦ pres.
imp. mid. (dep.) φοβέομαι (# 5828) to fear, w. the neg.
μή (# 3590) indicating a prohibition of existing action.
ἔσῃ fut. ind. mid. (dep.) 2nd. pers. sing. εἰμί (# 1639).
ζωγρῶν pres. act. part. ζωγρέω (# 2436) to capture alive,
to catch alive (Matt. 4:18-19; BBC). Part. in a periphrastic fut. construction emphasizing linear or durative action (VA, 464; MT, 89; MKG, 307).   ◆ 11 καταγαγόντες

aor. act. part. (temp.) κατάγω (# 2864) to lead down; nautical term to bring boats to land. ἀφέντες aor. act. part. (temp.) ἀφίημι (# 918) to leave. ἠκολούθησαν aor. ind. act. ἀκολουθέω (# 199) to follow, to follow as a disciple (TDNT; NIDNTT; Fitzmyer, 569). ◆ **12** ἐγένετο aor. ind. mid. (dep.) s.v. 1. εἶναι pres. act. inf. εἰμί. Inf. w. prep. ἐν (# 1877) to express contemporaneous time. λέπρα (# 3319) leprosy (s. Matt. 8:4; for the medical use of this term s. DJG, 463-64; MLL, 5-6; DMTG, 219-20; MHW, 42-46; SB, 4:ii, 745-63; 11Q19 [Temple] 48:14-49:1). ἰδών aor. act. part. (temp.) s.v. 8. Aor. indicating antecedent action. πεσών aor. act. part. (circum.) πίπτω (# 4406) to fall. ἐδεήθη aor. ind. pass. δέομαι (# 1289) to want for oneself, to beg, to request. θέλῃς pres. subj. act. θέλω (# 2527) to want, to will. Subj. w. ἐάν (# 1569) in a 3rd. class cond. cl., assuming the possibility of the reality of the cond. δύνασαι pres. ind. pass. (dep.) δύναμαι (# 1538) to be able. καθαρίσαι pres. act. inf. καθαρίζω (# 2751) to cleanse. Inf. supplementing the vb. δύνασαι. ◆ **13** ἐκτείνας aor. act. part. (circum.) ἐκτείνω (# 1753) to stretch out. ἥψατο aor. ind. mid. (dep.) ἅπτομαι (# 721) to touch, w. obj. in gen. καθαρίσθητι aor. imp. pass. s.v. 12. Aor. imp. calls for a specific action. ἀπῆλθεν aor. ind. act. ἀπέρχομαι (# 599) to go away, to depart. ◆ **14** παρήγγειλεν aor. ind. act. παραγγέλλω (# 4133) to command, to charge. εἰπεῖν aor. act. inf. λέγω (# 3306). Inf. after a vb. of commanding. ἀπελθών aor. act. part. s.v. 13. Circum. part. taking the grammatical sense of the main vb. δεῖξον; imp. thrust. (VANT, 386). δεῖξον aor. imp. act. δείκνυμι (# 1259) to show. προσένεγκε aor. imp. act. προσφέρω (# 4712) to carry to, to offer a sacrifice. προσέταξεν aor. ind. act. προστάσσω (# 4705) to instruct, to command, to give detailed instructions as to what must be done (LN, 1:425; s. Lev. 14:4-20; M, Neg. 14; M, Zeb. 5:5; 10:5; M, Par. 11:8). μαρτύριον witness, proof. ◆ **15** διήρχετο impf. ind. mid. (dep.) διέρχομαι (# 1451) to go through, to spread abroad. Impf. indicates the fame of Jesus kept going (RWP). συνήρχοντο impf. ind. mid. (dep.) συνέρχομαι (# 5302) to accompany, to travel w. someone. ἀκούειν pres. act. inf. s.v. 1. Inf. of purp. θεραπεύεσθαι pres. pass. inf. θεραπεύω (# 2543) to heal. Inf. of purp. ◆ **16** ὑποχωρῶν pres. act. part. ὑποχωρέω (# 5723) to withdraw, to slip away secretly (RWP). Part. in a periphrastic construction. προσευχόμενος pres. mid. (dep.) part. προσεύχομαι (# 4667) to pray. Part. in periphrastic construction. Both periphrastics show his habit of withdrawing and praying (VA, 481). ◆ **17** ἐγένετο aor. ind. mid. (dep.) s.v. 1. διδάσκων pres. act. part. διδάσκω (# 1438) to teach. Part. in periphrastic construction stressing the continuing progress of his teaching, thus giving the context of the controversy (Fitzmyer, 581). καθήμενοι pres. mid. (dep.) part. κάθημαι (# 2764) to sit. νομοδιδάσκαλος (# 3791) teacher of the law. Used in the rabbinical writings of those who

give *halacha,* i.e., authoritative interpretations of Scripture (Ellis). ἐληλυθότες perf. act. part. ἔρχομαι (# 2262) to come, to go. Part. in a periphrastic construction (VA, 469). ἰᾶσθαι pres. mid. (dep.) inf. ἰάομαι (# 2615) to heal. Inf. w. εἰς (# 1650) to express purp. (MT, 143). ◆ **18** φέροντες pres. act. part. (adj.) φέρω (# 5770) to carry. παραλελυμένος perf. pass. part. παραλύω (# 4168) to weaken, to disable. Perf. emphasizes the state or cond. of paralysis. Luke is in strict agreement w. the medical writers in using the vb. instead of the more popular adj. (MLL, 6; s. DMTG, 259). ἐζήτουν impf. ind. act. ζητέω (# 2426) to seek. Conative impf. pictures the unfulfilled attempt. εἰσενεγκεῖν aor. act. inf. εἰσφέρω (# 1662) to carry in. Inf. as obj. of vb., completing it. θεῖναι aor. act. inf. τίθημι (# 5502) to lay, to place. Inf. as obj. of the vb. ◆ **19** εὑρόντες aor. act. part. (temp.) εὑρίσκω (# 2351) to find. ποίας (# 4481) gen. fem. sing., what sort of. Gen. of place: "by what sort of (way)" (BD, 99). εἰσενέγκωσιν aor. subj. act. s.v. 18. Deliberative subj. of dir. question retained in the indir. (RWP). ἀναβάντες aor. act. part. (circum.) ἀναβαίνω (# 326) to go up. They went up the stairs on the outside (BBC). κέραμος (# 3041) tile. Because of the Gentile influence in Palestine at the time it would not be unusual for Jewish homes to have had tile roofs (Geldenhuys). διά (# 1328) followed by gen., through. καθῆκαν aor. ind. act. καθίημι (# 2768) to let down. κλινίδιον (# 3110) (dimin. of κλίνη) pallet, stretcher. For examples where the word is used of a light couch for carrying the sick s. MLL, 116. ◆ **20** ἰδών aor. act. part. (temp.) s.v. 8. ἀφέωνται perf. ind. pass. ἀφίημι (# 918) to release, to forgive (TDNT; NIDNTT; EDNT). Perf. indicates a completed state and expresses the abiding force of the forgiveness (Marshall). Pass. is the theol. pass. indicating that God has forgiven the sins (Stein). ◆ **21** ἤρξαντο aor. ind. mid. (dep.) ἄρχομαι (# 806) to begin, w. inf. διαλογίζεσθαι pres. mid. (dep.) inf. διαλογίζομαι (# 1368) to reason w., to debate w., to consider, to engage in some relatively detailed discussion of a matter (LN, 1:407). Inf. w. vb. of beginning. ἀφεῖναι aor. act. inf. s.v. 20. Inf. completing vb. εἰ μή (# 1623; 3590) except. ◆ **22** ἐπιγνούς aor. act. part. ἐπιγινώσκω (# 2105) to know, to recognize. The prep. in compound is directive and the vb. implies a thorough and accurate knowledge (Plummer). Temp. or causal part. ἀποκριθείς aor. pass. (dep.) part. s.v. 5. ◆ **23** εὐκοπώτερον comp. εὔκοπος (# 2324) easy; comp., easier. εἰπεῖν aor. act. inf. λέγω (# 3306) to say. Epex. inf. ἔγειρε pres. imp. act. ἐγείρω (# 1586) arise. περιπάτει pres. imp. act. περιπατέω (# 4344) to walk about. For vbs. of motion used in the pres. imp. s. VANT, 343-44. ◆ **24** εἰδῆτε perf. subj. act. οἶδα (# 3857) to know. Def. perf. w. pres. meaning. υἱὸς τοῦ ἀνθρώπου Son of Man s. Darrell L. Bock, "The Son of Man in Luke 5:24," *BBR* 1 (1991): 109-21. ἀφιέναι pres. act. inf. s.v. 20. Epex. inf.

explaining ἐξουσίαν. ἄρας aor. act. part. αἴρω (# 149) to lift up, to take up. πορεύου pres. imp. mid. (dep.) πορεύομαι (# 4513) to go. ◆ **25** ἀναστάς aor. act. part. (circum.) ἀνίστημι (# 482) to stand up. κατέκειτο impf. ind. mid. (dep.) κατάκειμαι (# 2879) to lie; customary impf., "upon which he used to lie." ἀπῆλθεν aor. ind. act. s.v. 13. δοξάζων pres. act. part. δοξάζω (# 1519) to glorify, to praise. Part. of manner explaining how he departed. ◆ **26** ἔλαβεν aor. ind. act. s.v. 5. ἐδόξαζον impf. ind. act. s.v. 25. Impf. stresses the continual action. ἐπλήσθησαν aor. ind. pass. s.v. 7. εἴδομεν aor. ind. act. s.v. 2. παράδοξος (# 4141) incredible; lit. "things which are contrary to opinion or belief" (Arndt). In medicine the word was used of an unusual or unexpected recovery from illness (MLL, 71). It was used of an athlete to mean "wonderful," "admirable" (MM; Preisigke, 2:241). ◆ **27** ἐξῆλθεν aor. ind. act. s.v. 8. ἐθεάσατο aor. ind. mid. (dep.) θεάομαι (# 2517) to see, to observe, to look at. τελώνιον (# 5468) tax station, custom house (s. Mark 2:14; BBC; DJG, 805-6). ἀκολούθει pres. imp. act. s.v. 11 (Bovon). ◆ **28** καταλιπών aor. act. part. (circum.) καταλείπω (# 2901) to leave, to forsake. ἀναστάς aor. act. part. s.v. 25. ἠκολούθει impf. ind. act. s.v. 11. Incep. impf., "he began to follow him as a disciple." ◆ **29** ἐποίησεν aor. ind. act. s.v. 6. δοχή (# 1531) banquet. For a description of a Jewish banquet s. SB, 4:611-639; DJG, 798-99. ἦσαν impf. ind. act. εἰμί. κατακείμενοι pres. mid. (dep.) part. s.v. 25. Here, to recline at the table. Part. in a periphrastic construction. ◆ **30** ἐγόγγυζον impf. ind. act. γογγύζω (# 1197) to murmur, to complain, to grumble, to express one's discontent (LN, 1:432; EDNT; BAGD). Impf. pictures the continual action. ◆ **31** ἀποκριθείς aor. pass. (dep.) part. s.v. 5. ὑγιαίνοντες pres. act. part. ὑγιαίνω (# 5617) to be well. Part. as subst. ἰατροῦ gen. sing. ἰατρός (# 2620) physician, surgeon (DMTG, 182). Gen. w. adj. χρείαν (# 5970) need. ◆ **32** ἐλήλυθα perf. ind. act. s.v. 7. καλέσαι aor. act. inf. καλέω (# 2813) to call. Inf. expresses purp. ◆ **33** νηστεύουσιν pres. ind. act. νηστεύω (# 3764) to fast (Geldenhuys). Pharisees frequently fasted twice a week (BBC). Iterat. pres. πυκνός (# 4781) frequent, numerous. As adv. (acc. pl.) often, frequently (BAGD). δέησις (# 1255) request, prayer. ποιοῦνται pres. ind. mid. s.v. 6. Indir. mid., "to do something for oneself" (BAGD). ◆ **34** μή (# 3590) used in a question expecting a neg. answer. νυμφών (# 3813) marriage hall, wedding room. The Hebraic expression (υἱοὺς τοῦ νυμφῶνος) designates the attendants of the bridegroom (Arndt; Marshall; DJG, 88). ἐν ᾧ (# 1877; 4005) while, so long as. ποιῆσαι aor. act. inf. s.v. 6. Inf. w. vb. δύνασθε. νηστεῦσαι aor. act. inf. s.v. 33. Inf. w. previous inf.: "to make to fast," "to cause to fast," "to fast." ◆ **35** ἐλεύσονται fut. ind. mid. (dep.) ἔρχομαι (# 2262) to come. ἀπαρθῇ aor. subj. pass. ἀπαίρω (# 554) to take away, implying rejection and violent death (Ellis).

Subj. in an indef. temp. cl. νηστεύσουσιν fut. ind. act. s.v. 33. ◆ **36** ἐπίβλημα (# 2099) patch. σχίσας aor. act. part. (temp.) σχίζω (# 5387) to tear, to rip. εἰ δὲ μή γε but if otherwise (Plummer). σχίσει fut. ind. act. συμφωνήσει fut. ind. act. συμφωνέω (# 5244) to fit, to harmonize, to agree. ◆ **37** ῥήξει fut. ind. act. ῥήγνυμι to tear, to burst (BBC). ἐκχυθήσεται fut. ind. pass ἐκχέω (# 1772) to pour out. ἀπολοῦνται fut. ind. mid. ἀπόλλυμι (# 660) to ruin, to lose. ◆ **38** βλητέον (# 1064) verbal adj. from βάλλω (# 965) one must put (s. M, 221). ◆ **39** πιών aor. act. part. (temp.) πίνω (# 4403) to drink. "After drinking." χρηστός (# 5982) good, useful, pleasant.

Luke 6

◆ **1** ἐγένετο aor. ind. mid. (dep.) γίνομαι (# 1181) to become, to happen (s. 2:1). Followed by prep. ἐν (# 1877) w. infin. expressing contemporaneous time. σαββάτῳ dat. sing. σάββατον (# 4879) Sabbath. For the Jewish regulations regarding the Sabbath s. M, Shab., where 7:2 forbids reaping, threshing, and winnowing. (b. Shab.; Matt. 12:2). Dat. of time: "on a sabbath." For discussion of the Sabbath controversies s. DJG, 716-19. διαπορεύεσθαι pres. mid. (dep.) inf. διαπορεύομαι (# 1388) to go through. Inf. w. prep. ἔτιλλον impf. ind. act. τίλλω (# 5504) to pluck, to pick. ἤσθιον impf. ind. act. ἐσθίω (# 2266) to eat. Impf. pictures the continual action in the past. στάχυς (# 5092) ear of grain. ψώχοντες pres. act. part. (circum.) ψώχω (# 6041) to rub. χερσίν dat. pl. χείρ (# 5931) hand. Instr. dat. ◆ **2** εἶπαν aor. ind. act. λέγω (# 3306). ◆ **3** ἀποκριθείς aor. pass. (dep.) part. ἀποκρίνομαι (# 646) to answer. For the use of the part. s. MH, 453-54; VA, 137-38. ἀνέγνωτε aor. ind. act. ἀναγινώσκω (# 336) to read. ἐποίησεν aor. ind. act. ποιέω (# 4472) to do. ἐπείνασεν aor. ind. act. πεινάω (# 4277) to be hungry. Ingressive aor., "when he became hungry." ◆ **4** εἰσῆλθεν aor. ind. act. εἰσέρχομαι (# 1656) to go in. λαβών aor. act. part. (circum.) λαμβάνω (# 3284) to take. ἔφαγεν aor. ind. act. ἐσθίω to eat. ἔδωκεν aor. ind. act. δίδωμι (# 1443) to give. φαγεῖν aor. act. inf. ἐσθίω Epex. inf. explaining what is not lawful. ◆ **5** ἔλεγεν impf. ind. act. s.v. 2. Incep. impf., "he proceeded to say." ◆ **6** ἐγένετο aor. ind. mid. (dep.) s.v. 1. εἰσελθεῖν aor. act. inf. s.v. 4. διδάσκειν pres. act. inf. διδάσκω (# 1438) to teach. For prep. w. inf. s.v. 1. δεξιά (# 1288) right. There is a mark of particularity here such as a physician would observe (MLL, 7). ξηρός (# 3831) dried, withered. ◆ **7** παρετηροῦντο impf. ind. mid. παρατηρέω (# 4190) to observe, to watch closely, esp. w. sinister intent perhaps from looking sideways out of the corner of one's eyes (Plummer). θεραπεύει pres. ind. act. θεραπεύω (# 2543) to treat medically, to heal. εὕρωσιν aor. subj. act. εὑρίσκω (# 2351) to find. Subj. in a purp. cl. κατηγορεῖν pres. act. inf. κατηγορέω (# 2989) w. gen., to accuse. Epex. inf. explaining the obj. of the vb. ◆ **8 ᾔδει** plperf. ind. act. of the def. perf. οἶδα (# 3857) to know. **ἔχοντι** pres. act. part. (adj.) masc. dat. sing. ἔχω (# 2400) to have. **ἔγειρε** pres. imp. act. ἐγείρω (# 1586) arise. **στῆθι** aor. imp. act. ἵστημι (# 2705) to stand. For the aor. imp. expressing a specific command and the use of the pres. imp. s. VANT, 328, 348-49. **ἀναστάς** aor. act. part. ἀνίστημι (# 482) to stand up. Temp. or circum. part. **ἔστη** aor. ind. act. ἵστημι to stand. ◆ **9 ἐπερωτῶ** pres. ind./subj. act. ἐπερωτάω (# 2089) to ask, to direct a question to someone. Hortatory subj. if taken as subj.: "Let me ask." **ἀγαθοποιῆσαι** aor. act. inf. ἀγαθοποιέω (# 16) to do good. Epex. inf. explaining **ἔξεστιν** (# 5392). **κακοποιῆσαι** aor. act. inf. κακοποιέω (# 2803) to do evil. **σῶσαι** aor. act. inf. σῴζω (# 5392) to save, to rescue, to heal. **ἀπολέσαι** aor. act. inf. ἀπόλλυμι (# 660) to destroy, to ruin. ◆ **10 περιβλεψάμενος** aor. mid. part. περιβλέπω (# 4315) to look about. The mid. voice gives a personal touch (RWP). **ἔκτεινον** aor. imp. act. ἐκτείνω (# 1753) to stretch out. Aor. imp. calls for a specific act. **ἀπεκατεστάθη** aor. ind. pass. ἀποκαθίστημι (# 635) to completely restore. Used as a medical t.t. to cure (BAGD; for the subst. s. Acts 3:21; MLL, 194; DMTG, 63). ◆ **11 ἐπλήσθησαν** aor. ind. pass. πίμπλημι (# 4398) to fill, w. gen. **ἄνοια** (# 486) madness, mad fury, a loss of reason which is caused by extreme excitement (Plummer); it expresses the hardness of heart in Jesus' critics (Fitzmyer, 611). **διελάλουν** impf. ind. act. διαλαλέω (# 1362) to discuss, to speak back and forth. For the force of the prep. in compound s. MH, 302. **ποιήσαιεν** aor. opt. act. ποιέω (# 4472) to do. Potential opt. expressing hesitancy, a weighing of possibilities (Arndt). ◆ **12 ἐγένετο** aor. ind. mid. (dep.) s.v. 1. **ἐξελθεῖν** aor. act. inf. ἐξέρχομαι (# 2002) to go out. Inf. w. prep. expressing contemporaneous time. **προσεύξασθαι** aor. mid. (dep.) inf. προσεύχομαι (# 4667) to pray. Inf. used to express purp. **διανυκτερεύων** pres. act. part. διανυκτερεύω (# 1381) to watch through the night. Medical writers used it of whole night vigils (RWP; MLL, 117). Part. used in a periphrastic construction. ◆ **13 προσεφώνησεν** aor. ind. act. προσφωνέω (# 4715) to summons, to call to. **ἐκλεξάμενος** aor. mid. (dep.) part. ἐκλέγομαι (# 1721) to choose, to select. The word implies the telling over (λέγειν) in preference to others (ἐκ) for one's own advantage (mid.) (Plummer). **ὠνόμασεν** aor. ind. act. ὀνομάζω (# 3951) to name, to give a name to. ◆ **15 καλούμενον** pres. pass. part. καλέω (# 2813) to call; pass. to be named. **ζηλωτής** (# 2421) zealous, referring to the personal character (BC, 1:425), or zealot, referring to a political party which radically opposed the Roman rule (s. IDB, 4:936; H. P. Kingdon, "The Origins of the Zealots," *NTS* 19 [1972]: 74-81; DZ; EDNT; Fitzmyer, 619; ABD, 6:1043-54). ◆ **16 ἐγένετο** aor. ind. mid. (dep.) γίνομαι (# 1181) to become. **προδότης** (# 4595) one who delivers over, betrayer. ◆ **17 κατα-**

βάς aor. act. part. (temp.) καταβαίνω (# 2849) to go down. **ἔστη** aor. ind. act. s.v. 8. **πεδινός** (# 4268) flat, level. **παράλιος** (# 4163) along the sea, seacoast. ◆ **18 ἦλθον** aor. ind. act. ἔρχομαι (# 2262) to come. **ἀκοῦσαι** aor. act. inf. ἀκούω (# 201) to hear, w. obj. in gen. Inf. of purp. **ἰαθῆναι** aor. pass. inf. ἰάομαι (# 2615) to heal (GLH). Inf. of purp. **ἐνοχλούμενοι** pres. pass. part. ἐνοχλέω (# 1943) to trouble. For medical examples of the word s. MLL, 8; for demons and disease s. MHW, 139, 162-63. **ἐθεραπεύοντο** impf. ind. pass. s.v. 7. ◆ **19 ἐζήτουν** impf. ind. act. ζητέω (# 2426) to seek. Impf. pictures the continual or repeated action. **ἅπτεσθαι** pres. mid. (dep.) inf. ἅπτομαι (# 721) to touch (w. gen.). Epex. inf. explaining **ἐζήτουν**. **ἐξήρχετο** impf. ind. mid. (dep.) ἐξέρχομαι (# 2002) to go out. Impf. pictures the continual action in the past. **ἰᾶτο** impf. ind. mid. s.v. 18. ◆ **20 ἐπάρας** aor. act. part. (temp.) ἐπαίρω (# 2048) to lift up. ◆ **21 πεινῶντες** pres. act. part. s.v. 3. Part. as subst. **χορτασθήσεσθε** fut. ind. pass. χορτάζω (# 5963) to feed animals, to fill, to satisfy; pass. to be satisfied. In the OT this could indicate a gift from God (Bovon). Theol. pass. indicating that God does the filling. **κλαίοντες** pres. act. part. κλαίω (# 3081) to cry, to weep. It expresses mourning and sorrow of all kinds (Marshall; TDNT; EDNT). Part. as subst. **γελάσετε** fut. ind. act. γελάω (# 1151) to laugh. It functions as a divine pass.: "God will cause you to laugh" (Stein). ◆ **22 μισήσωσιν** aor. subj. act. μισέω (# 3631) to hate. Subj. in an indef. temp. cl. **ἀφορίσωσιν** aor. subj. act. ἀφορίζω (# 928) to mark off from by a boundary, to separate; excommunication from the congregation as well as from social intercourse; to outlaw (Plummer; Fitzmyer, 635). **ὀνειδίσωσιν** aor. subj. act. ὀνειδίζω (# 3943) to reproach, to heap insults on. **ἐκβάλωσιν** aor. subj. act. ἐκβάλλω (# 1675) to cast out, to throw out. Subj. in an indef. temp. cl. ◆ **23 χάρητε** aor. imp. pass. χαίρω (# 5897) to rejoice. **σκιρτήσατε** aor. imp. act. σκιρτάω (# 5015) to skip, to jump, to leap. Aor. imp. calls for a specific act. **κατὰ τὰ αὐτά** (# 2848; 899) in just the same way (Fitzmyer, 635). **ἐποίουν** impf. ind. act. ποιέω (# 4472) to do. Customary impf. indicating a habitual or characteristic action (VANT, 246). ◆ **24 ἀπέχετε** pres. ind. act. ἀπέχω (# 600) to receive. The word was used in a commercial sense to acknowledge the receipt of full payment (MM; LAE, 110f). Beyond the present possession of riches these people have nothing to hope for (Arndt). ◆ **25 ἐμπεπλησμένοι** perf. pass. part. ἐμπίμπλημι (# 1855) to fill up, to satisfy. Perf. indicates a continual state. Part. as subst. **πεινάσετε** fut. ind. act. s.v. 3. **γελῶντες** pres. act. part. s.v. 21. **πενθήσετε** fut. ind. act. πενθέω (# 4291) to mourn. **κλαύσετε** fut. ind. act. κλαίω (# 3081) s.v. 21. For the form s. MH, 244; GGP, 273. ◆ **26 εἴπωσιν** aor. subj. act. λέγω (# 3306) to say. Subj. in an indef. temp. cl. **ἐποίουν** aor. ind. act. s.v. 23. ◆ **27 ἀκούουσιν** pres. act. part. dat. masc. pl. ἀκούω

(# *201*) to hear, to hear and obey. Part. as subst. ἀγα-πᾶτε pres. imp. act. ἀγαπάω (# *26*) to love. ποιεῖτε pres. imp. act. s.v. 23. Pres. imp. calls for a constant attitude. As a contrast in the DSS community s. 1QS 1:9-10; for parallels s. Nolland; Luise Schottroff, "Gewaltverzicht und Feindesliebe in der urchristlichen Jesustradition," JCHT, 197-221; esp. 204-13. ◆ **28** εὐλογεῖτε pres. imp. act. εὐλογέω (# *2328*) to bless. The granting or acknowledgment of power leading to success. Here general kindness shown to enemies (NIDNTT; TDNT; EDNT). καταρωμένους pres. mid. (dep.) part. καταράομαι (# *2933*) to curse, the attempt to bring evil, harm, or injury upon someone by means of a statement (NIDNTT; TDNT; LN, 1:442). προσεύχεσθε pres. imp. mid. (dep.) s.v. 12. ἐπηρεαζόντων pres. act. part. ἐπηρεάζω (# *2092*) to abuse, to mistreat, to display a despiteful spirit (Arndt). ◆ **29** τύπτοντι pres. act. part. dat. sing. τύπτω (# *5597*) to hit, a violent blow w. the fist rather than a contemptuous slap (Plummer). Part. as subst. σιαγόνα acc. sing. σιαγών (# *4965*) cheek, jawbone. A blow to the right cheek was a grievous insult (BBC). πάρεχε pres. imp. act. παρέχω (# *4218*) to offer. αἴροντος pres. act. part. gen. masc. sing. αἴρω (# *149*) to take, to take away. ἱμάτιον (# *2668*) coat, outward garment. χιτῶνα acc. sing. χιτών (# *5945*) undergarment (s. Matt. 5:40). κωλύσῃς aor. subj. act. κωλύω (# *3266*) to hinder, to prevent. Subj. used w. neg. μή (# *3590*) to express a prohibition. ◆ **30** αἰτοῦντι pres. act. part. αἰτέω (# *160*) to ask, to request. δίδου pres. imp. act. δίδωμι (# *1443*) to give. Pres. imp. may be iterat. ἀπαίτει pres. imp. act. ἀπαιτέω (# *555*) to ask for something back. Neg. pres. imp. forbids the habitual action. ◆ **31** θέλετε pres. ind. act. θέλω (# *2527*) to will, to desire. ποιῶσιν pres. subj. act. s.v. 23. Subj. w. ἵνα (# *2671*) in a obj. cl. For parallels to the Golden Rule s. Nolland; Fitzmyer, 639-40. ◆ **32** ἀγαπᾶτε pres. ind. act. s.v. 27. Ind. used in a 1st. class cond. cl., which assumes the reality of the cond. Pres. generalizes the thought (Marshall). ἀγαπῶντας pres. act. part. Part. as subst. χάρις (# *5921*) thanks, favor. ◆ **33** ἀγαθοποιῆτε pres. subj. act. ἀγαθοποιέω (# *16*) to do good. Subj. w. ἐάν (# *1569*) used in a 3rd. class cond. cl. w. the cond. assumed as probable. ◆ **34** δανίσητε aor. subj. act. δανίζω (# *1247*) to lend money (BBC). Subj. w. ἐάν (# *1569*) in 3rd. class cond. cl. assuming the possibility of the cond. λαβεῖν aor. act. inf. λαμβάνω (# *3284*) to take, to receive. Inf. as obj. of vb. ἀπολάβωσιν aor. subj. act. ἀπολαμβάνω (# *655*) to receive again. Subj. used in purp. cl. τὰ ἴσα (# *2698*) similar services in return (Marshall). ◆ **35** ἀπελπίζοντες pres. act. part. ἀπελπίζω (# *594*) to hope to have something in return (Arndt) or to give up in despair (Plummer). Used in medical language to denote a disease one despairs of curing (MLL, 118f). Part. of manner. ◆ **36** γίνεσθε pres. imp. mid. (dep.) s.v. 1. οἰκτίρμονες nom. pl. οἰκτίρμων (# *3881*) merciful,

compassionate (TDNT; NIDNTT). ◆ **37** κρίνετε pres. imp. act. κρίνω (# *3212*) to judge. The disciples are forbidden to ursurp the place of God in judging and condemning other people (Marshall). Pres. imp. calls for a continual attitude. κριθῆτε aor. subj. pass. Futuristic subj. used w. οὐ μή (# *4024; 3590*) for emphatic denial (RG, 930). καταδικάζετε pres. imp. act. καταδικάζω (# *2868*) to condemn, to pass sentence against. Pres. imp. calls for a continual attitude. ἀπολύετε pres. imp. act. ἀπολύω (# *668*) to release, to forgive. Pres. imp. is iterat. ἀπολυθήσεσθε fut. ind. pass. The reference is to personal insults and injuries (Marshall). ◆ **38** δίδοτε pres. imp. act. s.v. 30. δοθήσεται fut. ind. pass. s.v. 30. Imp. followed by a fut. ind. indicates a Semitic type of cond. sentence (Beyer, 238). πεπιεσμένον perf. pass. part. (adj.) πιέζω (# *4390*) to press down. Perf. views the state or cond. σεσαλευμένον perf. pass. part. σαλεύω (# *4888*) to shake. ὑπερεκχυννόμενον pres. mid. part. ὑπερεκχύννω (# *5658*) to overflow. The picture is of grain poured into a container, pressed down and then shaken so that every little corner is filled and the grain is poured in until it runs over (Arndt). δώσουσιν fut. ind. act. 3rd. pers. pl. δίδωμι s.v. 30. 3rd. pers. pl. is used impersonally, sometimes when the subject is God (BD, 72). κόλπος (# *3146*) the fold formed by a loose garment overhanging a belt (Plummer), or it may be the lap, in which case the skirt becomes the receptacle (Nolland). μετρεῖτε pres. ind. act. μετρέω (# *3582*) to measure. ἀντιμετρηθήσεται fut. ind. pass. ἀντιμετρέω (# *520*) to measure back again. Prep. in compound expresses reciprocal action (MH, 297). For Jewish parallels s. Hans Peter Rüger, "'Mit welchem Maß ihr meßt, wird euch gemessen werden,'" ZNW 60 (1969): 174-82. ◆ **39** ὁδηγεῖν pres. act. inf. ὁδηγέω (# *3842*) to lead, to show the way. ἐμπεσοῦνται fut. ind. mid. (dep.) ἐμπίπτω (# *1860*) to fall in. ◆ **40** κατηρτισμένος perf. pass. part. (temp.) καταρτίζω (# *2936*) to complete, to finish, to equip. When the disciple has received complete preparation from his teacher, he will equal but not surpass his teacher. (Meyer). ◆ **41** κάρφος (# *2847*) splinter, anything small and dry. δοκός (# *1512*) beam. The main beam receiving the other beams in a roof or floor (Plummer). κατανοεῖς pres. ind. act. κατανοέω (# *2917*) to notice, to observe carefully, to consider, to look at w. reflection. ◆ **42** δύνασαι pres. ind. pass. (dep.) 2nd. pers. sing. δύναμαι (# *1538*) to be able. ἄφες aor. imp. act. ἀφίημι (# *918*) to leave, to leave alone, to allow. ἐκβάλω aor. subj. act. ἐκβάλλω (# *1675*) to cast out, to remove. βλέπων pres. act. part. βλέπω (# *1063*) to see. Circum. or temp. part. For the use of οὐ (# *4024*) w. the part. s. BD, 222. ἔκβαλε aor. imp. act. διαβλέψεις fut. ind. act. διαβλέπω (# *1332*) to see clearly, to see accurately. ἐκβαλεῖν aor. act. inf. Inf. of purp. or result. ◆ **43** ποιοῦν pres. ind. part. ποιέω (# *4472*) to do, to produce. Gnomic pres. ◆ **44 γινώσκεται** pres. ind. pass. γινώσκω (# 1182) to know, to recognize. Gnomic pres. **ἀκανθῶν** gen. pl. ἄκανθα (# 180) thorn bush. **συλλέγουσιν** pres. ind. act. συλλέγω (# 5198) to gather. Gnomic pres. **σῦκα** acc. pl. σῦκον (# 5192) figs. **βάτος** (# 1003) a bramble bush. **σταφυλή** (# 5091) a cluster of grapes, a bunch of grapes. **τρυγῶσιν** pres. ind. act. τρυγάω (# 5582) to pick grapes, to gather fruit. Gnomic pres. ◆ **45 προφέρει** pres. ind. act. προφέρω (# 4734) to bring forth. Gnomic pres. **λαλεῖ** pres. ind. act. λαλέω (# 3281) to speak. Gnomic pres. ◆ **46 καλεῖτε** pres. ind. act. s.v. 15. Iterat. pres. indicating a repeated action. ◆ **47 ἀκούων** pres. act. part. ἀκούω (# 201) to hear, to listen to, to hear and obey. Part. as subst. **ποιῶν** pres. act. part. s.v. 43. The parts. imply the continued action necessary to receive Jesus' blessing (Arndt). **ὑποδείξω** fut. ind. act. ὑποδείκνυμι (# 5683) to show, to point out. ◆ **48 οἰκοδομοῦντι** pres. act. part. (adj.) dat. sing. οἰκοδομέω (# 3868) to build. Dat. w. the adj. **ἔσκαψεν** aor. ind. act. σκάπτω (# 4999) to dig. **ἐβάθυνεν** aor. ind. act. βαθύνω (# 959) to make deep, to deepen. **ἔθηκεν** aor. ind. act. τίθημι (# 5502) to lay. **θεμέλιον** (# 2529) acc. sing. foundation. **πλημμύρης** (# 4439) a flood. **γενομένης** aor. mid. (dep.) part. (temp.) s.v. 1. Gen. abs. **προσέρηξεν** aor. ind. act. προσρήγνυμι (# 4703) to break against. **ἴσχυσεν** aor. ind. act. ἰσχύω (# 2710) to be strong, to be able, w. inf. **σαλεῦσαι** aor. act. inf. σαλεύω (# 4888) to shake, to cause to move to and fro, to cause to totter (BAGD). **οἰκοδομῆσθαι** perf. pass. inf. οἰκοδομέω Perf. indicates that the house has been build and stands firm. Inf. w. prep. to express cause. ◆ **49 ἀκούσας** aor. act. part. s.v. 47. Part. as subst. **ποιήσας** aor. act. part. s.v. 47. Aor. sums up the lack of obedience. **οἰκοδομήσαντι** aor. act. part. s.v. 48. **συνέπεσεν** aor. ind. act. συμπίπτω (# 5229) to fall together. **ῥῆγμα** (# 4837) breaking, ruin, collapse. Used of a breach in a dam (MM). As a medical term, laceration or rupture (MLL, 56).

Luke 7

◆ **1 ἐπειδή** (# 2076) after. Normally causal, but the word is temp. here (RWP). **ἐπλήρωσεν** aor. ind. act. πληρόω (# 4444) to fulfill, to end, to conclude, to finish a task (Marshall). **εἰσῆλθεν** aor. ind. act. εἰσέρχομαι (# 1656) to go in. ◆ **2 ἑκατόνταρχος** (# 1672) leader of a hundred men, centurion (s. Matt. 8:5; Acts 10:1; IDB, 1:547f; TJ, 101). **ἤμελλεν** impf. ind. act. μέλλω (# 3516) to be about to. Used w. inf. to express fut. Impf. w. inf. expresses futurity or intention reckoned from a moment in the past: "he was going to die," "he was at the point of death" (MKG, 307). **τελευτᾶν** pres. act. inf. τελευτάω (# 5462) to die. **ἔντιμος** (# 1952) costly, valuable, honored. Used w. the dat. of reference **αὐτῷ** (# 899). ◆ **3 ἀκούσας** aor. act. part. (temp.) ἀκούω (# 201) to hear. **ἀπέστειλεν** aor. ind. act. ἀποστέλλω (# 690) to send, to send someone to carry out a task w.

the authority of the one sending (TDNT). **ἐρωτῶν** pres. act. part. (circum.) ἐρωτάω (# 2263) to ask, to request. **ἐλθών** aor. act. part. (circum.) ἔρχομαι (# 2262) to come. **διασώσῃ** aor. subj. act. διασῴζω (# 1407) to save, to rescue, to heal. Medical writers used the term w. the meaning to escape from a severe illness or an epidemic, to get through the attack (MLL, 10). ◆ **4 παραγενόμενοι** aor. mid. (dep.) part. παραγίνομαι (# 4134) to come to. Part. as subst. **παρεκάλουν** impf. ind. act. παρακαλέω (# 4151) to call for help, to appeal to, to urge. Impf. emphasizes the continual urging. **σπουδαίως** (# 5081) eagerly, earnestly. **ᾧ** dat. sing. ὅς (# 4005) rel. pron. For a possible Latinism s. BD, 8. **παρέξῃ** fut. ind. mid. (dep.) 2nd. pers. sing. παρέχομαι (# 4218) to grant something to someone. ◆ **5 ἀγαπᾷ** pres. ind. act. ἀγαπάω (# 26) to love. Pres. pictures the continual action. **ᾠκοδόμησεν** aor. ind. act. οἰκοδομέω (# 3868) to build. Aor. pictures the act demonstrating the love. ◆ **6 ἐπορεύετο** impf. ind. mid. (dep.) πορεύομαι (# 4513) to go. **μακράν** (# 3426) adv. far. **ἀπέχοντος** pres. act. part. (temp.) ἀπέχω (# 600) to be away. Gen. abs. **ἔπεμψεν** aor. ind. act. πέμπω (# 4287) to send. **σκύλλου** pres. imp. pass. σκύλλω (# 5035) to skin, to flay, to trouble, to bother, to annoy; pass. to trouble oneself (BAGD; MM). Pres. imp. w. the neg. calls for the ending of an action in progress. **ἱκανός** (# 2653) sufficient, worthy, pertaining to being adequate, qualified for something (LN, 1:679). **στέγη** (# 5094) roof. **εἰσέλθῃς** aor. subj. act. s.v. 1. Subj. in a cl. explaining **ἱκανός**, or in a result cl. ◆ **7 ἠξίωσα** aor. ind. act. ἀξιόω (# 546) to judge or consider worthy. **ἐλθεῖν** aor. act. inf. s.v. 3. Epex. inf. explaining the main vb. **εἰπέ** aor. imp. act. λέγω (# 3306) to speak. Aor. imp. calls for a specific act. **ἰαθήτω** aor. imp. pass. 3rd. pers. sing. ἰάομαι (# 2615) to heal. ◆ **8 τασσόμενος** pres. pass. part. τάσσω (# 5435) to place or station, to appoint, to put someone over, to put in charge. Pres. part. is adjectival: "For I am a man who is habitually placed under authority" (Plummer). **πορεύθητι** aor. imp. pass. (dep.) s.v. 6. **ἔρχου** pres. imp. mid. (dep.) s.v. 3. **ποίησον** aor. imp. act. ποιέω (# 4472) to do. For harsh and strict discipline in the army s. TJ, 112. ◆ **9 ἐθαύμασεν** aor. ind. act. θαυμάζω (# 2513) to wonder, to be amazed at someone, to marvel at some object (LN, 1:312). **στραφείς** aor. pass. part. (temp.) στρέφω (# 5138) to turn; pass. to turn around. **ἀκολουθοῦντι** pres. act. part. dat. masc. sing. ἀκολουθέω (# 199) to follow, w. obj. in dat. **τοσαύτην** acc. sing. fem. τοσοῦτος (# 5537) so great, so large. **εὗρον** aor. ind. act. εὑρίσκω (# 2351) to find. For a comparison of the accounts in Matt. and Luke s. Zane C. Hodges, "The Centurion's Faith in Matthew and Luke," *Bib Sac* 121 (1964): 321-32. ◆ **10 ὑποστρέψαντες** aor. act. part. (temp.) ὑποστρέφω (# 5715) to return. **πεμφθέντες** aor. pass. part. s.v. 6. Part. as subst. **ὑγιαίνοντα** pres. act. part. (adj.) masc. acc. sing. ὑγιαίνω (# 5617) to be healthy. The servant was not only cured but was also in good health (MLL, 11; s. DMTG, 316). ◆ **11 ἐγένετο** aor. ind. mid. (dep.) γίνομαι (# 1181) to become, to happen (s. 2:1). **ἐξῆς** (# 2009) adv. of time, next, in a series, of time on the next day, afterward (BAGD). **ἐπορεύθη** aor. ind. pass. (dep.) s.v. 6. **καλουμένην** pres. pass. part. καλέω (# 2813) to call. The town of Nain was located between Nazareth and Capernaum (ZPEB, 4:358-60; Fitzmyer, 658). **συνεπορεύοντο** impf. ind. mid. (dep.) συμπορεύομαι (# 5233) to travel together. ◆ **12 ἤγγισεν** aor. ind. act. ἐγγίζω (# 1581) to draw near, to approach, w. dat. **ἐξεκομίζετο** impf. ind. pass. ἐκκομίζω (# 1714) to carry out, esp. to bury. Impf. pictures the burial procession in progress. **τεθνηκώς** perf. act. part. θνήσκω (# 2569) to die; perf. to be dead. Part. as subst. **μονογενής** (# 3666) only, only child. **χήρα** (# 5939) widow. Jesus' compassion on the weeping widow, who for the second time (first her husband) had been robbed of her provider and protector, is probably to be understood as a Messianic act. (TDNT). **ἱκανός** (# 2653) here, much, many, numerous. According to Jewish custom, everyone of the village was to take part in the funeral procession. In Galilee the men went before the open coffin (SB, 4: i:579-80; s. Matt. 9:23). ◆ **13 ἰδών** aor. act. part. (temp.) ὁράω (# 3972) to see. **ἐσπλαγχνίσθη** aor. ind. pass. σπλαγχνίζομαι (# 5072) to be inwardly moved w. compassion, to have compassion upon (TDNT; EDNT; NIDNTT; TLNT). **κλαῖε** pres. imp. act. κλαίω (# 3081) to cry, to weep loudly. The pres. imp. w. neg. **μή** (# 3590) indicates the discontinuing of an action in progress. ◆ **14 προσελθών** aor. act. part. (temp.) προσέρχομαι (# 4665) to come to. **ἥψατο** aor. ind. mid. (dep.) ἅπτομαι (# 721) to touch, w. gen. This exposed him to uncleanness (BBC). **σορός** (# 5049) an open coffin, a portable frame on which the body was laid (Arndt). **βαστάζοντες** pres. act. part. βαστάζω (# 1002) to carry. Part. as subst. **ἔστησαν** aor. ind. act. ἵστημι (# 2705) to stand. **ἐγέρθητι** aor. imp. pass. ἐγείρω (# 1586) to raise; pass. to rise up. Aor. imp. calls for a specific act. ◆ **15 ἀνεκάθισεν** aor. ind. act. ἀνακαθίζω (# 361) to sit up. Used by medical writers to describe patients sitting up in bed (MLL, 11). **ἤρξατο** aor. ind. mid. (dep.) ἄρχομαι (# 806) to begin, w. inf. **λαλεῖν** pres. act. inf. λαλέω (# 3281) to speak, to utter a sound (Arndt). **ἔδωκεν** aor. ind. act. δίδωμι (# 1443) to give. ◆ **16 ἔλαβεν** aor. ind. act. λαμβάνω (# 3284) to take, to seize. **ἐδόξαζον** impf. ind. act. δοξάζω (# 1519) to glorify, to hold in high esteem. Incep. impf., "they began to glorify...." **ἠγέρθη** aor. ind. pass. s.v. 14. **ἐπεσκέψατο** aor. ind. mid. (dep.) ἐπισκέπτομαι (# 2170) to look at, to go to see, to visit. Used of God's gracious visitation in bringing salvation (BAGD). ◆ **17 ἐξῆλθεν** aor. ind. act. ἐξέρχομαι (# 2002) to go out. ◆ **18 ἀπήγγειλαν** aor. ind. act. ἀπαγγέλλω (# 550) to report. **προσκαλεσάμενος** aor. mid. part. προσκαλέω

(# 4673) to call to, to summons (mid., to oneself). ◆ **19 ἔπεμψεν** aor. ind. act. s.v. 6. **εἶ** pres. ind. act. εἰμί (# 1639) to be. **προσδοκῶμεν** pres. ind. act. or subj. (deliberative subj.) προσδοκάω (# 4659) to wait for, to expect. ◆ **20 παραγενόμενοι** aor. mid. (dep.) part. s.v. 4. **ἀπέστειλεν** aor. ind. act. s.v. 3. ◆ **21 ἐθεράπευσεν** aor. ind. act. θεραπεύω (# 2543) to treat medically, to heal. **μαστίγων** gen. pl. μάστιξ (# 3465) whip, scourge, plague, suffering. **ἐχαρίσατο** aor. ind. mid. (dep.) χαρίζομαι (# 5919) to be gracious to, to graciously grant. **βλέπειν** pres. act. inf. βλέπω (# 1063) to see. Inf. as obj. ◆ **22 ἀποκριθείς** aor. pass. (dep.) part. ἀποκρίνομαι (# 646) to answer. For the Semitic use s. MH, 453. **πορευθέντες** aor. pass. (dep.) part. s.v. 6. Circum. part. w. imp. force (VANT, 386). **ἀπαγγείλατε** aor. imp. act. ἀπαγγέλλω s.v. 18. Aor. imp. calls for a specific act. **εἴδετε** aor. ind. act. s.v. 13. **ἠκούσατε** aor. ind. act. s.v. 3. **ἀναβλέπουσιν** pres. ind. act. ἀναβλέπω (# 329) to see again. Iterat. pres. For the prep. ἀνά in compound s. MH, 295. **περιπατοῦσιν** pres. ind. act. περιπατέω (# 4344) to walk about. **καθαρίζονται** pres. ind. pass. καθαρίζω (# 2751) to cleanse. Iterat. pres. ◆ **23 σκανδαλισθῇ** aor. subj. pass. σκανδαλίζω (# 4997) to cause to stumble, to take offense (TDNT). Subj. in an indef. rel. cl. ◆ **24 ἀπελθόντων** aor. act. part. (temp.) ἀπέρχομαι (# 599) to go away. Gen. abs. **ἄγγελος** (# 34) messenger. **ἤρξατο** aor. ind. mid. (dep.) s.v. 15. **ἐξήλθατε** aor. ind. act. s.v. 17. **τί** why? or what? (s. Beyer, 100-102; Marshall) **θεάσασθαι** aor. mid. (dep.) inf. θεάομαι (# 2517) to see, to watch. Inf. of purp. **σαλευόμενον** pres. pass. part. σαλεύω (# 4888) to shake. It refers to an insignificant thing or person. They did not go out to see an insignificant person (Stein). ◆ **25 ἰδεῖν** aor. act. inf. s.v. 13. Inf. of purp. **μαλακός** (# 3434) soft. It is used to describe clothes of fine material (Marshall). **ἠμφιεσμένον** perf. pass. part. ἀμφιέννυμι (# 314) to clothe, to dress. For the acc. used w. the pass. s. BD, 87. **ἔνδοξος** (# 1902) distinguished, splendid. **τρυφῇ** (# 5588) dat. sing. indulgent, luxurious. **ὑπάρχοντες** (# 5639) pres. act. part. ὑπάρχω to be, to exist. Part. as subst. translated as a rel. cl. **βασίλειον** (# 994) palace. ◆ **26 ναί** (# 3721) yes, certainly! A strong emphatic particle, confirming a preceding statement (DM, 262). **περισσότερον** (# 4358) comp. περισσός remarkable (in the comp. περισσός, together w. its adv. and comp. is a colloquial substitute for μᾶλλον, μάλιστα [BAGD 651]). **προφήτου** gen. sing. προφητής (# 4737) prophet. Gen. of comp. ◆ **27 γέγραπται** perf. ind. pass. γράφω (# 1211) to write. Perf. used for authoritative documents or writings (MM). **κατασκευάσει** fut. ind. act. κατασκευάζω (# 2941) to prepare, to build, to construct. ◆ **28 μείζων** (# 3505) comp. μέγας great; comp., greater. **Ἰωάννου** gen. Ἰωάννης (# 2722) John. Gen. of comp. **μικρότερος** comp. μικρός (# 3625) small. Comp. used as superl.: "least," "smallest" (RG, 667-69). **αὐτοῦ** gen. αὐτός (# 899) gen.

of comp. ◆ **29 ἀκούσας** aor. act. part. (temp.) s.v. 3. **ἐδικαίωσαν** aor. ind. act. δικαιόω (# 1467) to declare righteous, to consider as righteous, to justify. Here, "to recognize and acknowledge the righteousness of God" (GW, 138). **βαπτισθέντες** aor. pass. part. βαπτίζω (# 966) to baptize. Temp. or circum. part. ◆ **30 ἠθέτησαν** aor. ind. act. ἀθετέω (# 119) to set aside, to annul. Used of grain rejected by the inspector as unfit for food (MM). **βαπτισθέντες** aor. pass. part. (causal) s.v. 29. ◆ **31 ὁμοιώσω** fut. ind. act. ὁμοιόω (# 3929) to compare. Deliberative fut. used as a question of deliberation. ◆ **32 παιδίον** (# 4086) child. **καθημένοις** pres. mid. (dep.) part. (adj.) κάθημαι (# 2764) to sit. **προσφωνοῦσιν** pres. act. part. (adj.) dat. masc. pl. προσφωνέω (# 4715) to call to. **ηὐλήσαμεν** aor. ind. act. αὐλέω (# 884) to play the flute. **ὠρχήσασθε** aor. ind. mid. (dep.) ὀρχέομαι (# 4004) to dance. **ἐθρηνήσαμεν** aor. ind. act. θρηνέω (# 2577) to mourn, to lament. **ἐκλαύσατε** aor. ind. act. κλαίω (# 3081) to weep. Both John and Jesus were rejected (Marshall). ◆ **33 ἐλήλυθεν** perf. ind. act. ἔρχομαι (# 2262) to come. **ἐσθίων** pres. act. part. ἐσθίω (# 2266) to eat. Part. of manner telling how he came. Habitual pres. **πίνων** pres. act. part. πίνω to drink (# 4403) Part. of manner. Habitual pres. ◆ **34 φάγος** (# 5741) glutton. **οἰνοπότης** (# 3884) wine drinker, drunkard. The pred. without the art. stresses the character or quality (s. John 1:1). ◆ **35 ἐδικαιώθη** aor. ind. pass. s.v. 29; Matt. 11:19. ◆ **36 ἠρώτα** impf. ind. act. ἐρωτάω (# 2263) to ask, to ask someone to do something. Incep. impf.: "He began to ask." **φάγῃ** aor. subj. act. ἐσθίω (# 2266) to eat. Subj. used in a cl. which is the obj. of the vb. (RG, 991-94). **εἰσελθών** aor. act. part. (temp.) s.v. 1. **κατεκλίθη** aor. ind. pass. κατακλίνω (# 2884) to cause to lie down; pass. to recline at the table. ◆ **37 ἦν** impf. ind. act. εἰμί (# 1639) to be. **ἁμαρτωλός** (# 283) sinful, devoted to sin (RWP). Pred. adj. without the art. stresses the character or quality (s.v. 34). **ἐπιγνοῦσα** aor. act. part. (temp.) ἐπιγινώσκω (# 2105) to know, "having learned definitely" (Arndt). **κατάκειται** pres. ind. mid. (dep.) κατάκειμαι (# 2879) to lie down, to recline on a dining couch (BAGD). **κομίσασα** aor. act. part. (temp.) κομίζω (# 3152) to bring. **ἀλάβαστρον** (# 223) alabaster, a very soft stone from which flasks or vases were made for the keeping of perfume (Arndt; Mark 14:3). **μύρου** gen. sing. μύρον (# 3693) ointment, perfume; gen. of content. ◆ **38 στᾶσα** aor. act. part. ἵστημι (# 2705) to stand. Circum. part. or part. of manner. **κλαίουσα** pres. act. part. (circum.) s.v. 13. The outward act of weeping is the result and expression of the inward state of grief, repentance, or joy over the forgiveness of sin (Geldenhuys; Stein). **δάκρυσιν** dat. pl. δάκρουν (# 1232) tear. Instr. dat. **ἤρξατο** aor. ind. mid. (dep.) s.v. 15. **βρέχειν** pres. act. inf. βρέχω (# 1101) to wet. Jesus was reclining and she was standing behind him, thus wetting his feet w. her tears (Marshall). **θριξίν** dat. pl. θρίξ (# 2582) hair.

Instr. dat. **ἐξέμασσεν** impf. ind. act. ἐκμάσσω (# 1726) to wipe off, to dry. **κατεφίλει** impf. ind. act. καταφιλέω (# 2968) to kiss, to kiss affectionately. Kissing the feet was a common mark of deep reverence, esp. to leading rabbis (Plummer; SB, 1:995; TDNT; Fitzmyer, 689). **ἤλειφεν** impf. ind. act. ἀλείφω (# 230) to anoint. Not the religious, but the general word for anoint (Trench, *Synonyms*, 136; 2 Sam. 12:20); but s. the use of the word in the LXX for anointing priests in Exod. 40:15; Num. 3:3 (GELTS, 18; s. also Jos., *Ant.*, 6:165). **μύρῳ** s.v. 37. Instr. dat. ◆ **39 ἰδών** aor. act. part. (temp.) s.v. 13. **καλέσας** aor. act. part. (adj.) καλέω (# 2813) to call, to invite. **ἦν** impf. ind. act. s.v. 37. **ἐγίνωσκεν** impf. ind. act. γινώσκω (# 1182) to know. Used w. **ἄν** (# 323) in a contrary to fact cond. sentence (GGBB, 663). **ποταπή** (# 4534) what sort of? Literally, from what country? (AS). **ἅπτεται** pres. ind. mid. (dep.) s.v. 14. Pres. pictures the action in progress. ◆ **40 ἀποκριθείς** aor. pass. (dep.) part. s.v. 22. **σοί** dat. sing. σύ (# 5148) 2nd. pers. personal pron. Indir. obj. **εἰπεῖν** aor. act. inf. s.v. 7. Epex. inf. **εἰπέ** aor. imp. act. s.v. 7. ◆ **41 χρεοφειλέτης** (# 5971) debtor, one who owes an obligation or debt (RWP). **δανιστής** (# 1250) moneylender, a professional moneylender (Arndt). Herod Agrippa I was deeply in debt to many moneylenders (Jos., *Ant.*, 18:147; TJ, 57-62). **ὤφειλεν** impf. ind. act. ὀφείλω (# 4053) to owe. **δηνάριον** (# 1324) denarius. A Roman silver coin worth normally about 18 cents. It was a workman's average daily wage (BAGD). **πεντακόσια** (# 4296) acc. pl. five hundred. For high debts incurred in the Roman Empire s. Nolland. **πεντήκοντα** (# 4299) acc. pl. fifty. ◆ **42 ἐχόντων** pres. act. part. (causal) ἔχω (# 2400) to have. Gen. abs. **ἀποδοῦναι** aor. act. inf. ἀποδίδωμι (# 625) to pay back, to give back. Inf. as dir. obj. **ἐχαρίσατο** aor. ind. mid. (dep.) s.v. 21. He made them a present of what they owed (Plummer). **πλεῖον** comp. πολύς (# 4498) much; comp. more. **ἀγαπήσει** fut. ind. act. ἀγαπάω (# 26) to love; perhaps here to feel the deepest thankfulness (Fitzmyer, 690). ◆ **43 ὑπολαμβάνω** (# 5696) pres. ind. act. to take up, to assume, to suppose w. an air of supercilious indifference (Plummer). **ὀρθῶς** (# 3987) adv. rightly, correctly. **ἔκρινας** aor. ind. act. 2nd. pers. sing. κρίνω (# 3212) to judge. ◆ **44 στραφείς** aor. pass. part. (temp.) s.v. 9. **ἔφη** impf./aor. ind. act. φημί (# 5774) to say. For the form s. VA, 443-46. **εἰσῆλθον** aor. ind. act. s.v. 1. **ἔδωκας** aor. ind. act. 2nd. pers. sing. s.v. 15. It could be translated, "you did not pour any water on my feet," indicating not that Simon had failed to perform normal rules of etiquette, but that he had failed to show any expression of love whatever (Otfried Hofius, "Fußwaschung als Erweis der Liebe: Sprachliche und sachliche Anmerkungen zu Lk 7,44b," *ZNW* 81 [1990]: 171-77; BBC). **ἔβρεξεν** aor. ind. act. s.v. 38. **ἐξέμαξεν** aor. ind. act. s.v. 38. ◆ **45 φίλημα** (# 5799) kiss. The kiss in public was not a general practice among Jews of the Second Temple era, but was a special sign of respect (William Klassen, "The Sacred Kiss in the New Testament. An Example of Social Boundary Lines," *NTS* 39 [1993]: 122-35; esp. 123-26; Hofius, "Fußwaschung...," 176; SB, 1:995). **διέλιπεν** impf. ind. act. διαλείπω (# 1364) to stop, to cease. **καταφιλοῦσα** pres. act. part. s.v. 38. Part. supplements the vb. ◆ **46 ἐλαίῳ** dat. sing. ἔλαιον (# 1778) olive oil. Instr. dat. **ἤλειψας** aor. ind. act. s.v. 38. For the anointing and washing of the body s. SB, 1:426-429. ◆ **47 οὗ χάριν** because of which, on account of. **ἀφέωνται** perf. ind. pass. ἀφίημι (# 918) to release, to forgive. Perf. indicates the continuing results or state of a completed act. **ἠγάπησεν** aor. ind. act. s.v. 42. **ἀφίεται** pres. ind. pass. Gnomic pres. ◆ **49 ἤρξαντο** aor. ind. mid. (dep.) s.v. 15. **συνανακείμενοι** pres. mid. (dep.) part. συνανάκειμαι (# 5263) to sit at the table together, to recline at the table together. Part. as subst. **ἀφίησιν** pres. ind. act. s.v. 47. ◆ **50 σέσωκεν** perf. ind. act. σῴζω (# 5392) to rescue, to save, to deliver. It was her faith, not her love, that saved her (Caird). Perf. indicates the continuing results of a completed action. **πορεύου** pres. imp. mid. (dep.) s.v. 6.

Luke 8

◆ **1 ἐγένετο** aor. ind. mid. (dep.) γίνομαι (# 1181) to become, to happen (s. 2:1). The formula often is used to introduce a temp. element (Beyer, 29-62). **καθεξῆς** (# 2759) gen. sing. one after the other, successively, afterward (s. 1:3). **διώδευεν** impf. ind. act. διοδεύω (# 1476) to pass through, to travel through. **κατὰ πόλιν** from city to city. Distributive use of the prep. (RG, 608). **κηρύσσων** pres. act. part. (circum.) κηρύσσω (# 3062) to proclaim as a herald. ◆ **2 τεθεραπευμέναι** perf. pass. part. θεραπεύω (# 2543) to treat medically, to heal. Perf. emphasizes the pres. state or cond. Part. in a plperf. periphrastic constr. (VA, 466; VANT, 321). **καλουμένη** pres. pass. part. (adj.) καλέω (# 2813) to call, to name. **ἐξεληλύθει** plperf. ind. act. ἐξέρχομαι (# 2002) to come out. Plperf. of completed action highlights the antecedent past while still implying the past state consequent upon it (VANT, 307). ◆ **3 ἐπίτροπος** (# 2208) overseer, finance minister, one who is concerned w. the finances and personal property of an owner (HA, 303f). **διηκόνουν** impf. ind. act. διακονέω (# 1354) to minister, to provide; rel. pron. for those w. a person to minister to them. They were persons of substance (Plummer). Impf. pictures the continual ministering or providing. ◆ **4 συνιόντος** pres. act. part. (temp.) σύνειμι (# 5290) to come together. Gen. abs. **ἐπιπορευομένων** pres. mid. (dep.) part. ἐπιπορεύομαι (# 2164) to go on a journey to, to go to. Gen. abs., epex. explaining the preceding gen. abs. (Marshall). ◆ **5 ἐξῆλθεν** aor. ind. act. ἐξέρχομαι (# 2002) to go out. **σπείρων** pres. act. part. σπείρω (# 5062) to sow. Part. as

subst. **σπεῖραι** aor. act. inf. Inf. of purp. **σπείρειν** pres. act. inf. Inf. w. prep. **ἐν** (# 1877) to express contemporaneous time: "as he was sowing." **ἔπεσεν** aor. ind. act. πίπτω (# 4406) to fall. **κατεπατήθη** aor. ind. pass. καταπατέω (# 2922) to trample on, to trample down. **κατέφαγεν** aor. ind. act. κατεσθίω (# 2983) to eat up. Prep. in compound is perfective. ◆ **6 κατέπεσεν** aor. ind. act. καταπίπτω (# 2928) to fall down. **φυέν** aor. pass. part. (temp.) φύω (# 5886) to spring up, to sprout, to grow. In medical terms it was used for the growth of parts of the body, of diseases and of vegetation (MLL, 58). **ἐξηράνθη** aor. ind. pass. ξηραίνω (# 3830) to dry up. **ἔχειν** pres. act. inf. ἔχω (# 2400) to have. Inf. w. prep. to express cause. **ἰκμάς** (# 2657) moisture. It could be used as the medical expression for the juices of the body, of plants, and of the earth (MLL, 57). ◆ **7 ἄκανθα** (# 180) thorns, thorn bush. **συμφυεῖσαι** aor. pass. part. nom. fem. pl. συμφύω (# 5243) to grow together. This was a t.t. in medical language for the closing of wounds, ulcers, the uniting of nerves, bones, etc. (MLL, 59; DMTG, 304). **ἀπέπνιξαν** aor. ind. act. ἀποπνίγω (# 678) to choke, to choke off so as to exterminate (Plummer). ◆ **8 ἐποίησεν** aor. ind. act. ποιέω (# 4472) to make, to produce. **ἐφώνει** impf. ind. act. φωνέω (# 5888) to call. Impf. is best interpreted as denoting repeated action (Arndt). **ἀκούειν** pres. act. inf. ἀκούω (# 201) to hear. Inf. of purp. **ἀκουέτω** pres. imp. act. 3rd. pers. sing. ◆ **9 ἐπηρώτων** impf. ind. act. ἐπερωτάω (# 2089) to ask, to direct questions to. Incep. impf., "they began...." **εἴη** pres. opt. act. εἰμί. Opt. of indir. discourse, a mark of elegant speech (Arndt). ◆ **10 δέδοται** perf. ind. pass. δίδωμι (# 1443) to give. Theol. pass. indicating that God is the subject. **γνῶναι** aor. act. inf. γινώσκω (# 1182) to know. Inf. as dir. obj. **λοιποῖς** dat. pl. λοιπός (# 3370) the rest. Those outside the circle of Christ's disciples (Plummer). Dat. as indir. obj. **ἵνα** (# 2671) w. subj. introduces a purp. or result cl. (Stein). **βλέποντες** pres. act. part. βλέπω (# 1063) to see. Part. used to translate the Heb. inf. abs. (Isa. 6:9) in a concessive sense (Beyer, 266). Conveys the idea, "you may look and look again, but you will never see" (Marshall). **συνιῶσιν** pres. subj. act. συνίημι (# 5317) to understand, to comprehend. ◆ **11 τοῦ θεοῦ** (#2536) subjective gen. "A word which comes from God" (RWP). ◆ **12 ἀκούσαντες** aor. act. part. s.v. 8. Part. as subst. **πιστεύσαντες** aor. act. part. (temp.) πιστεύω (# 4409) to believe, to trust. **σωθῶσιν** aor. subj. pass. σῴζω (# 5392) to save, to rescue. Theol. pass. Subj. used in a purp. or result cl. (s.v. 10). ◆ **13 ἀκούσωσιν** aor. subj. act. s.v. 8. Subj. in an indef. temp. cl. **δέχονται** pres. ind. mid. (dep.) δέχομαι (# 1312) to welcome, to receive. **πρὸς καιρόν** for a time, temporarily. **ἀφίστανται** pres. ind. mid. (dep.) ἀφίστημι (# 923) to go away, to withdraw, to fall away. ◆ **14 πεσόν** aor. act. part. πίπτω (# 4406) to fall. Part. as subst. **πορευόμενοι** pres. mid.

(dep.) part. (temp.) πορεύομαι (# *4513*) to go. "As they go on their way" (Arndt). **συμπνίγονται** pres. ind. pass. συμπνίγω (# *5231*) to choke, to choke until dead. Prep. in compound is perfective (MH, 325). **τελεσφοροῦσιν** pres. ind. act. τελεσφορέω (# *5461*) to bear fruit to maturity, to bring to maturity. ◆ **15 κατέχουσιν** pres. ind. act. κατέχω (# *2988*) to hold down, to hold fast. **καρποφοροῦσιν** pres. ind. act. καρποφορέω (# *2844*) to bear fruit. ◆ **16 λύχνος** (# *3394*) lamp (s. Matt. 5:15). **ἅψας** aor. act. part. ἅπτω (# *721*) to light. **καλύπτει** pres. ind. act. καλύπτω (# *2821*) to hide, to cover. Gnomic pres. **σκεύει** dat. sing. σκεῦος (# *5007*) vessel, jar, dish (BAGD). Instr. dat. ("cover it w. a vessel"). **κλίνης** (# *3109*) gen. sing. bed, couch. **τίθησιν** pres. ind. act. τίθημι (# *5502*) to set in place. Gnomic pres. **λυχνία** (# *3393*) lampstand. **εἰσπορευόμενοι** pres. mid. (dep.) part. εἰσπορεύομαι (# *1660*) to go in. Part. as subst. **βλέπωσιν** pres. subj. act. βλέπω s.v. 10. Subj. w. ἵνα (# *2671*) in a purp. cl. For this s. Mark 4:21f. ◆ **17 κρυπτόν** (# *3220*) hidden. **γενήσεται** fut. ind. mid. (dep.) s.v. 1. **ἀπόκρυφον** (# *649*) hidden, hidden away from the public eye (Plummer). **γνωσθῇ** aor. subj. pass. γινώσκω (# *1182*) to know. **ἔλθῃ** aor. subj. act. ἔρχομαι (# *2262*) to come. Subj. used w. double neg. οὐ μή (# *4024; 3590*) (BD, 184; VA, 416). ◆ **18 ἔχῃ** pres. subj. act. ἔχω (# *2400*) to have, to possess. Subj. w. ἄν (# *165*) in an indef. rel. cl. **δοθήσεται** fut. ind. pass. δίδωμι (# *1443*) to give. Theol. pass. **ἀρθήσεται** fut. ind. pass. αἴρω (# *149*) to take away. Theol. pass. ◆ **19 παρεγένετο** aor. ind. mid. (dep.) παραγίνομαι (# *4134*) to come. **ἠδύναντο** impf. ind. mid. (dep.) δύναμαι (# *1538*) to be able, w. inf. **συντυχεῖν** aor. act. inf. συντυγχάνω (# *5344*) (w. dat.) to come together w., to join, to contact. ◆ **20 ἀπηγγέλη** aor. ind. pass. ἀπαγγέλλω (# *550*) to report. **ἑστήκασιν** perf. ind. act. ἵστημι (# *2705*) to stand. Perf. indicates the state or cond.: "they are standing." **ἰδεῖν** aor. act. inf. ὁράω (# *3972*) to see. **θέλοντες** pres. act. part. (circum.) θέλω (# *2527*) to want to, to desire, w. inf. ◆ **21 ἀποκριθείς** aor. pass. (dep.) part. ἀποκρίνομαι (# *646*) to answer (s. MH, 453). ◆ **22 ἐγένετο** aor. ind. mid. (dep.) s.v. 1. **ἐνέβη** aor. ind. act. ἐμβαίνω (# *1832*) to go in, to get in, to embark. **διέλθωμεν** aor. subj. act. διέρχομαι (# *1451*) to go through. Prep. in compound emphasizes the passing through a point and the arrival at the destination (MH, 300ff). Hortatory subj. **ἀνήχθησαν** aor. ind. pass. ἀνάγω (# *343*) to lead up, to put out to sea. For a discussion of the Sea of Galilee s. ABD, 2:899-901. ◆ **23 πλεόντων** pres. act. part. (temp.) πλέω (# *4434*) to sail. Gen. abs. **ἀφύπνωσεν** aor. ind. act. ἀφυπνόω (# *934*) to fall asleep. Probably on the elevated stern using a wooden or leather-covered helmsman's seat (BBC). Ingressive aor. **κατέβη** aor. ind. act. καταβαίνω (# *2849*) to come down, to go down. **λαῖλαψ** (# *3278*) a violent storm, a whirlwind or tornado (Arndt). **συνεπληροῦντο** impf. ind. pass. συμπληρόω

(# *5230*) to fill completely. The prep. in compound is perfective (MH, 325). Impf. pictures the process of completely filling. **ἐκινδύνευον** impf. ind. act. κινδυνεύω (# *3073*) to be in danger. ◆ **24 προσελθόντες** aor. act. part. (temp.) προσέρχομαι (# *4665*) to come to. **διήγειραν** aor. ind. act. διεγείρω (# *1444*) to wake up. **ἐπιστάτα** voc. sing. ἐπιστάτης (# *2181*) master, overseer (s. 5:5). **ἀπολλύμεθα** pres. ind. mid. ἀπόλλυμι (# *660*) to destroy; mid. to perish. Pres. pictures the action in progress. **διεγερθείς** (# *1444*) aor. pass. part. (circum.). **ἐπετίμησεν** aor. ind. act. ἐπιτιμάω (# *2203*) to rebuke (s. Matt. 17:18). **κλύδων** (# *3114*) wave, a boisterous surge, a violent agitation (RWP). **ἐπαύσαντο** aor. ind. mid. παύω (# *4264*) to cease, to stop. **γαλήνη** (# *1132*) calm, stillness. ◆ **25 φοβηθέντες** aor. pass. part. (circum.) φοβέομαι (# *5828*) to be afraid. **ἐθαύμασαν** aor. ind. act. θαυμάζω (# *2513*) to wonder, to be amazed. ◆ **26 κατέπλευσαν** aor. ind. act. καταπλέω (# *2929*) to sail down; i.e., from the high seas toward the coast. **ἀντιπέρα** (# *527*) opposite. "Opposite Galilee," that is, "on the east shore of the Lake of Gennesaret" (BAGD). ◆ **27 ἐξελθόντι** aor. act. part. (temp.) s.v. 5. Dat. used w. the vb. **ὑπήντησεν** aor. ind. act. ὑπαντάω (# *5636*) to meet someone, w. dat. **ἐνεδύσατο** aor. ind. mid. ἐνδύω (# *1709*) to put on, to clothe oneself. **ἱμάτιον** (# *2668*) the outer garment, clothes; here, any kind of garment (Arndt). **ἔμενεν** impf. ind. act. μένω (# *3531*) to remain; customary impf. ◆ **28 ἰδών** aor. act. part. (temp.) s.v. 20. **ἀνακράξας** aor. act. part. ἀνακράζω (# *371*) to cry out. Part. of manner. **προσέπεσεν** aor. ind. act. προσπίπτω (# *4700*) to fall forward, to fall down before, w. dat. **βασανίσῃς** aor. subj. act. βασανίζω (# *989*) to rub on a touchstone, to test the genuineness, to examine, to torture. The NT has merely the general sense of inflicting bodily or mental pain (Arndt; TDNT; MLL, 63; NIDNTT; EDNT). Subj. used in a neg. command. ◆ **29 παρήγγειλεν** aor. ind. act. παραγγέλλω (# *4133*) to command, to charge. A number of manuscripts have the impf. παράγγελλεν, which would emphasize repeated action or be incep. (Fitzmyer, 738). **ἐξελθεῖν** aor. act. inf. s.v. 5. Inf. in indir. discourse. **συνηρπάκει** plperf. ind. act. συναρπάζω (# *5275*) to seize by violence, to drag away. The prep. in compound is perfective and denotes the establishment of a permanent hold (M, 113): "seize and keep a firm hold of" (MM). **ἐδεσμεύετο** impf. ind. pass. δεσμεύω (# *1297*) to bind. Impf. could be iterat. **ἁλύσεσιν** dat. pl. ἅλυσις (# *268*) chain. Instr. dat. **πέδαις** dat. pl. πέδη (# *4267*) fetter, bond for the feet. It could be made of hair or of material that was used in the manufacture of ropes (Arndt). **φυλασσόμενος** pres. pass. part. (circum.) φυλάσσω (# *5875*) to guard, to watch. **διαρρήσσων** pres. act. part. (circum.) διαρρήγνυμι (# *1396*) to tear into. The prep. intensifies the meaning of the vb. (RWP). **ἠλαύνετο** impf. ind. pass. ἐλαύνω (# *1785*) to drive as the wind drives clouds (BAGD).

Impf. pictures the repeated action. ◆ **30** ἐπηρώτησεν aor. ind. act. s.v. 9. **Λεγιών** (# 3305) legion (s. Matt. 26:53; Evans). **εἰσῆλθεν** aor. ind. act. εἰσέρχομαι (# 1656) to go into. ◆ **31** **παρεκάλουν** impf. ind. act. 3rd. pl. παρακαλέω (# 4151) to ask, to beseech. Impf. is incep. or stresses the continual begging. **ἐπιτάξῃ** aor. subj. act. ἐπιτάσσω (# 2199) to enjoin or change. Subj. used in an obj. cl. **ἄβυσσος** (# 12) abyss, depth, underworld. The prison of disobedient spirits (TDNT; Ellis; Cremer; EDNT; 1 Enoch 10:4-6; 18:11-16; Jubilees 5:6-10). **ἀπελθεῖν** aor. act. inf. ἀπέρχομαι (# 599) to go away. Inf. in indir. discourse. ◆ **32** **βοσκομένη** pres. pass. part. (adj.) βόσκω (# 1081) to feed; pass. to graze. **ἐπιτρέψῃ** aor. subj. act. ἐπιτρέπω (# 2205) to allow. Subj. in a obj. cl. **εἰσελθεῖν** aor. act. inf. s.v. 30. Inf. as dir. obj. ◆ **33** **ἐξ-ελθόντα** aor. act. part. (temp.) s.v. 5. **ὥρμησεν** aor. ind. act. ὁρμάω (# 3994) to rush. **κρημνός** (# 3204) a steep and rocky slope (Plummer). **ἀπεπνίγη** aor. ind. pass. s.v. 7. ◆ **34** **ἰδόντες** aor. act. part. (temp.) s.v. 20. **βόσκοντες** pres. act. part. s.v. 32. Part. as subst. **γεγονός** perf. act. part. γίνομαι (# 1181) to become, to happen. Part. as subst. **ἔφυγον** aor. ind. act. φεύγω (# 5771) to flee. **ἀπήγγειλαν** aor. ind. act. s.v. 20. ◆ **35** **ἐξῆλθον** aor. ind. act. s.v. 5. **ἰδεῖν** aor. act. inf. s.v. 20. Inf. of purp. **εὗρον** aor. ind. act. εὑρίσκω (# 2351) to find. **καθήμενον** pres. mid. (dep.) part. (adj.) κάθημαι (# 2764) to sit. **ἱματισμένον** perf. pass. part. ἱματίζω (# 2667) to clothe. Perf. part. emphasizes the state or cond. **σωφρονοῦντα** pres. act. part. σωφρονέω (# 5404) to be of sound mind, to be in one's right mind. Used of mental health in contrast to madness (BAGD). **ἐφοβήθησαν** aor. ind. pass. (dep.) φοβέομαι (# 5828) to be afraid, to fear. ◆ **36** **ἀπήγγειλαν** aor. ind. act. s.v. 20. **ἐσώθη** aor. ind. pass. σῴζω (# 5392) to rescue, to save, to heal. **δαι-μονισθείς** aor. pass. part. δαιμονίζομαι (# 1227) to be possessed by an evil spirit. ◆ **37** **ἠρώτησεν** aor. ind. act. ἐρωτάω (# 2263) to ask, to request. **ἀπελθεῖν** aor. act. inf. s.v. 31. **συνείχοντο** impf. ind. pass. συνέχω (# 5309) to hold together; pass. to be seized. **ἐμβάς** aor. act. part. (temp.) s.v. 22. **ὑπέστρεψεν** aor. ind. act. ὑποστρέφω (# 5715) to return. ◆ **38** **ἐδεῖτο** impf. ind. mid. (indir. mid., "ask for oneself") δέομαι (# 1289) to ask, to request, to beg. Iterat. impf. pictures the continual asking. **ἐξεληλύθει** plperf. ind. act. s.v. 5. **εἶναι** pres. act. inf. εἰμί (# 1639) to be. Inf. in indir. discourse. **ἀπέλυσεν** aor. ind. act. ἀπολύω (# 668) to release, to send away, to dismiss. ◆ **39** **ὑπόστρεφε** pres. imp. act. s.v. 37. **διη-γοῦ** pres. imp. mid. (dep.) διηγέομαι (# 1455) to tell, to describe. **ἀπῆλθεν** aor. ind. act. s.v. 31. **κηρύσσων** pres. act. part. s.v. 1. Part. of manner. **ἐποίησεν** aor. ind. act. ποιέω (# 4472) to do. ◆ **40** **ὑποστρέφειν** pres. act. inf. s.v. 37. Inf. w. prep. ἐν (# 1877) to express contempora-neous time. **ἀπεδέξατο** aor. ind. mid. (dep.) ἀποδέχομαι (# 622) to receive, to welcome, implying a cordial re-ception (EGT). **προσδοκῶντες** pres. act. part. προσδοκάω

(# 4659) to await, to expect. Part. in a periphrastic con-struction. A vivid picture of the attitude of the people toward Jesus (RWP). ◆ **41** **ἦλθεν** aor. ind. act. s.v. 17. **ὑπῆρχεν** impf. ind. act. ὑπάρχω (# 5639) to be. **πεσών** aor. act. part. (circum.) s.v. 5. **παρεκάλει** impf. ind. act. s.v. 31. Incep. impf. or stressing the continual pleading. **εἰσελθεῖν** aor. act. inf. s.v. 30. Inf. in indir. discourse, or dir. obj. ◆ **42** **μονογενής** (# 3666) only child. **ἀπέ-θνησκεν** impf. ind. act. ἀποθνήσκω to die. Impf. mean-ing ("she is dying") is from the viewpoint of the father (Plummer). **ὑπάγειν** pres. act. inf. ὑπάγω (# 5632) to go away, to depart. Inf. w. prep. ἐν (# 1877) to express con-temporaneous time. **συνέπνιγον** impf. ind. act. s.v. 14. The prep. expresses the pressing together all around him (Plummer). ◆ **43** **οὖσα** pres. act. part. (adj.) nom. fem. sing. εἰμί (# 1639). **ῥύσις** (# 4868) flow (s. Mark 5:25; for the medical use of the word s. MLL, 15-16). **προσαναλώσασα** aor. act. part. προσαναλίσκω or προσ-αναλόω (# 4649) to spend lavishly (BAGD). For the tex-tual problem s. TC, 145. **ἴσχυσεν** aor. ind. act. ἰσχύω (# 2710) to be able, w. inf. **θεραπευθῆναι** aor. pass. inf. s.v. 2. ◆ **44** **προσελθοῦσα** aor. act. part. (circum.) s.v. 24. **ἥψατο** aor. ind. mid. (dep.) ἅπτομαι (# 721) to touch, w. gen. **κράσπεδον** border, perhaps the tassel, one on each corner of the overgarment (Arndt). **ἔστη** aor. ind. act. ἵστημι (# 2705) to stand. Used among medical writ-ers to denote the stoppage of bodily discharges (MLL, 15). ◆ **45** **ἁψάμενος** aor. mid. (dep.) part. s.v. 44. **ἀρνουμένων** pres. mid. (dep.) part. ἀρνέομαι (# 766) to say no, to deny. Gen. abs. **συνέχουσιν** pres. ind. act. συνέχω (# 5309) to press hard (BAGD). Pres. indicates the action in progress. **ἀποθλίβουσιν** pres. ind. act. ἀπο-θλίβω (# 632) to crush, to press upon, to crowd. Used of pressing out grapes (RWP). ◆ **46** **ἔγνων** aor. ind. act. s.v. 10. **ἐξεληλυθυῖαν** perf. act. part. (adj.) acc. fem. sing. s.v. 1. ◆ **47** **ἰδοῦσα** aor. act. part. (temp.) s.v. 20. **ἔλαθεν** aor. ind. act. λανθάνω (# 3291) to escape notice, to be hidden (BAGD). **τρέμουσα** pres. act. part. τρέμω (# 5554) to tremble. Part. of manner. **προσπεσοῦσα** aor. act. part. (circum.) s.v. 28. **ἥψατο** aor. ind. mid. (dep.) s.v. 44. **ἀπήγγειλεν** aor. ind. act. s.v. 20. **ὡς** how, that. **ἰάθη** aor. ind. pass. ἰάομαι (# 2615) to heal. ◆ **48** **σέσωκεν** perf. ind. act. s.v. 36. Perf. indicates the state as the result of a completed action. **πορεύου** pres. imp. mid. (dep.) πορεύομαι (# 4513) to go. ◆ **49** **λαλοῦντος** pres. act. part. (temp.) λαλέω (# 3281) to speak. Gen. abs. expressing contemporaneous time: "while he was speaking." **τέθνηκεν** perf. ind. act. θνήσκω (# 2569) to die; perf. to be dead. **σκύλλε** pres. imp. act. σκύλλω (# 5035) to trouble, to cause inconvenience to, to an-noy. Pres. imp. w. neg. μή (# 3590) used to discontinue an action in progress. ◆ **50** **ἀκούσας** aor. act. part. (temp.) s.v. 8. **ἀπεκρίθη** aor. ind. pass. (dep.) s.v. 21. **φοβοῦ** pres. imp. mid. (dep.) s.v. 25. **πίστευσον** aor. imp. act. s.v. 12. Note the change of tense ("cease to fear;

only make an act of faith" [Plummer]). **σωθήσεται** fut.
ind. pass. s.v. 36. Fut. ind. in a Semitic type of cond. cl.
preceded by the imp. and **καί** (# 2779) (Beyer, 238-54).
◆ **51 ἐλθών** aor. act. part. (temp.) s.v. 17. **ἀφῆκεν** aor.
ind. act. ἀφίημι (# 918) to allow, w. inf. **εἰσελθεῖν** aor.
act. inf. s.v. 30. ◆ **52 ἔκλαιον** impf. ind. act. κλαίω
(# 3081) to weep loudly. **ἐκόπτοντο** (# 3164) impf. ind.
mid. (dir. mid.) κόπτω to beat the breast or head in
mourning (s. Matt. 9:23; BBC). **κλαίετε** pres. imp. act.
used w. a neg. as a command to stop the action which
is in progress. **ἀπέθανεν** aor. ind. act. ἀποθνήσκω (# 633)
to die. **καθεύδει** pres. ind. act. καθεύδω (# 2761) to
sleep. Pres. stresses the action in progress. ◆ **53 κατε-**
γέλων impf. ind. act. καταγελάω (# 2860) to deride, to
laugh scornfully at (used w. gen.). Incep. impf., "they
began to ridicule." **εἰδότες** perf. act. part. (causal) of the
def. perf. οἶδα (# 3857) to know. ◆ **54 κρατήσας** aor. act.
part. (temp.) κρατέω (# 3195) to grasp, to take hold of,
w. gen. **ἐφώνησεν** aor. ind. act. φωνέω (# 5888) to call
aloud. **ἔγειρε** pres. imp. act. ἐγείρω (# 1586) to rise up,
to get up. For a discussion of the idiomatic use of the
pres. imp. of this vb. s. VANT, 348-49. ◆ **55 ἐπέστρεψεν**
aor. ind. act. ἐπιστρέφω (# 2188) to return. Prep. in compound is directive (MH, 312). **ἀνέστη** aor. ind. act. ἀ-
νίστημι (# 482) to arise, to stand up. **διέταξεν** aor. ind.
act. διατάσσω (# 1411) to instruct, to command. **δοθῆναι**
aor. pass. inf. δίδωμι (# 1443) to give. Inf. in indir. discourse, or as dir. obj. of the vb. **φαγεῖν** aor. act. inf. ἐσθίω (# 2266) to eat. Inf. as obj. of the previous inf. ◆ **56**
ἐξέστησαν aor. ind. act. ἐξίστημι (# 2014) to be beside
oneself, to be greatly astounded. **παρήγγειλεν** aor. ind.
act. s.v. 29. **εἰπεῖν** aor. act. inf. λέγω (# 3306) to speak, to
tell. Inf. in indir. discourse, or dir. obj. of the vb. **γε-**
γονός perf. act. part. s.v. 34. Part. as subst.

Luke 9

◆ **1 συγκαλεσάμενος** aor. mid. part. (temp.) συγκαλέω (# 5157) to call together, to summons. **ἔδωκεν** aor.
ind. act. δίδωμι (# 1443) to give. **ἐξουσία** (# 2026) authority (TDNT; NIDNTT). **θεραπεύειν** pres. act. inf.
θεραπεύω (# 2543) to treat medically, to heal. Epex. inf.
explaining the authority and power. ◆ **2 ἀπέστειλεν**
aor. ind. act. ἀποστέλλω (# 690) to send out, to send out
as an official or authoritative representative (TDNT;
EDNT). **κηρύσσειν** pres. act. inf. κηρύσσω (# 3062) to
preach, to proclaim as a herald. Inf. of purp. **ἰᾶσθαι**
pres. mid. (dep.) inf. ἰάομαι (# 2615) to heal.
◆ **3 αἴρετε** pres. imp. act. αἴρω (# 149) to take. **ἔχειν**
pres. act. inf. ἔχω (# 2400) to have. Inf. used to express
a command (RG, 1092; BD, 196). ◆ **4 εἰσέλθητε** aor.
subj. act. εἰσέρχομαι (# 1656) to come into, to go into.
Subj. in an indef. cl. **μένετε** pres. imp. act. μένω (# 3531)
to remain. **ἐξέρχεσθε** pres. imp. mid. (dep.) ἐξέρχομαι
(# 2002) to go out. The pres. imps. are iterat., applying
to repeated incidents. ◆ **5 δέχωνται** pres. subj. mid.

(dep.) δέχομαι (# 1312) to receive, to welcome. Subj. in
an indef. cl. **κονιορτός** (# 3155) dust. **ἀποτινάσσετε** pres.
imp. act. ἀποτινάσσω (# 701) to shake off. An act symbolizing the severance of all association. Jews returning to Palestine from pagan territory were expected to
do the same (Fitzmyer, 754; BC, 5:269-77; BBC; Matt.
10:14). ◆ **6 διήρχοντο** impf. ind. mid. (dep.) διέρχομαι
(# 1451) to go through. Iterat. impf. **εὐαγγελιζόμενοι**
pres. mid. (dep.) part. εὐαγγελίζομαι (# 2294) to proclaim good news. Part. of manner. ◆ **7 ἤκουσεν** aor.
ind. act. ἀκούω (# 201) to hear. **τετραάρχης** (# 5490) tetrarch. Luke calls Herod Antipas by his correct title
(HA, 149; TJ, 46; DJG, 324). **γινόμενα** pres. mid. (dep.)
part. γίνομαι (# 1181) to become, to happen. Part. as
subst. **διηπόρει** impf. ind. act. διαπορέω (# 1389) to be
perplexed, to be thoroughly at a loss, unable to find a
way out (RWP). Impf. pictures his continual state of
mind. **λέγεσθαι** pres. pass. inf. λέγω (# 3306) to say. Inf.
w. prep. to express cause. **ἠγέρθη** aor. ind. pass. ἐγείρω
(# 1586) to raise; pass. to rise. For discussion of the
popular opinion regarding the supposed resurrection
of John s. HA, 187-89. ◆ **8 ἐφάνη** aor. ind. pass. φαίνω
(# 5743) to appear. **ἀνέστη** aor. ind. act. ἀνίστημι
(# 482) to raise up, to rise. ◆ **9 ἀπεκεφάλισα** aor. ind.
act. ἀποκεφαλίζω (# 642) to behead (TJ, 63-64). **ἐζήτει**
impf. ind. act. ζητέω (# 2426) to seek. Impf. pictures the
continual seeking. **ἰδεῖν** aor. act. inf. ὁράω (# 3972) to
see. The statement could be taken as a form of sarcasm
or irony (HA, 190f). Inf. as dir. obj. ◆ **10 ὑποστρέ-**
ψαντες aor. act. part. (temp.) ὑποστρέφω (# 5715) to return. **διηγήσαντο** aor. ind. mid. (dep.) διηγέομαι
(# 1455) to report, to narrate, to tell. **ἐποίησαν** aor. ind.
act. ποιέω (# 4472) to do, to accomplish. **παραλαβών**
aor. act. part. (circum.) παραλαμβάνω (# 4161) to take
someone along as a traveling companion. **ὑπεχώρησεν**
aor. ind. act. ὑποχωρέω (# 5723) to withdraw. **κατ᾿ ἰδίαν**
(# 2848; 2625) privately, alone. **καλουμένην** pres. pass.
part. καλέω (# 2813) to call, to name. ◆ **11 γνόντες**
aor. act. part. γινώσκω (# 1182) to know, to recognize.
Temp. or causal part. **ἠκολούθησαν** aor. ind. act.
ἀκολουθέω (# 199) to follow. **ἀποδεξάμενος** aor. mid.
(dep.) part. ἀποδέχομαι (# 622) to receive, to welcome
(s. 8:40). **ἐλάλει** impf. ind. act. λαλέω (# 3281) to speak.
Incep. impf. **ἰᾶτο** impf. ind. mid. (dep.) s.v. 2. Impf. pictures the repeated action. ◆ **12 ἤρξατο** aor. ind. mid.
(dep.) ἄρχομαι (# 806) to begin, w. inf. **κλίνειν** pres. act.
inf. κλίνω (# 3111) to bend, to bow down. Intr. to decline; used of the day coming to an end, probably between 3:00 and 6:00 P.M. (Arndt). **προσελθόντες** aor. act.
part. (temp.) προσέρχομαι (# 4665) to come to. **ἀπόλυσον**
aor. imp. act. ἀπολύω (# 668) to release, to dismiss. Aor.
imp. calls for a specific act. **πορευθέντες** aor. pass.
(dep.) part. (circum.) πορεύομαι (# 4513) to go, to journey. **καταλύσωσιν** aor. subj. act. καταλύω (# 2907) lit., to
unharness the pack animals, to rest, to find lodging

(BAGD; MM). Subj. w. ἵνα (# *2671*) in purp. cl. εὕρωσιν aor. subj. act. εὑρίσκω (# *2351*) to find. ἐπισιτισμός (# *2169*) provision, food, esp. provisions for a journey (RWP); (s. Gen. 42:25; 45:21; Exod. 12:39). Subj. w. ἵνα (# *2671*) in purp. cl. ◆ **13 δότε** aor. imp. act. s.v. 1. Aor. imp. calls for a specific act. **φαγεῖν** aor. act. inf. ἐσθίω (# *2266*) to eat. Inf. as dir. obj. **ἀγοράσωμεν** aor. subj. act. ἀγοράζω (# *60*) to buy, to buy in the marketplace. Subj. is used in 3rd. class cond. cl. w. εἰ (# *1623*) instead of ἐάν (RWP). ◆ **14 κατακλίνατε** aor. imp. act. κατακλίνω (# *2884*) to recline, to have someone to sit down to eat (LN, 1:219). **κλισία** (# *3112*) a group of people eating together, a company reclining. **ἀνὰ πεντήκοντα** (# *324; 4299*) groups of about fifty. ◆ **15 ἐποίησαν** aor. ind. act. s.v. 10. **κατέκλιναν** aor. ind. act. s.v. 14. ◆ **16 λαβών** aor. act. part. (temp.) λαμβάνω (# *3284*) to take, to receive. **ἀναβλέψας** aor. act. part. (temp.) ἀναβλέπω (# *329*) to look up. Both parts. express antecedent action. **εὐλόγησεν** aor. ind. act. εὐλογέω (# *2328*) to bless, to give thanks. **κατέκλασεν** aor. ind. act. κατακλάω (# *2880*) to break. **ἐδίδου** impf. ind. act. s.v. 1. Impf. pictures the repeated act of giving. **παραθεῖναι** aor. act. inf. παρατίθημι (# *4192*) to place before, to serve food. Jesus' act would remind a Jew of the miracle of the manna (Ellis). Inf. of purp. ◆ **17 ἔφαγον** aor. ind. act. s.v. 13. **ἐχορτάσθησαν** aor. ind. pass. χορτάζω (# *5963*) to feed, to satisfy. **ἤρθη** aor. ind. pass. αἴρω (# *149*) to take up. **περισσεῦσαν** aor. act. part. περισσεύω (# *4355*) to be in abundance, to be left over. Part. as subst. **κόφινοι** nom. pl. κόφινος (# *3186*) basket (s. Mark 6:43). Nom. in apposition to the subject. ◆ **18 ἐγένετο** aor. ind. mid. (dep.) γίνομαι (# *1181*) to become, to happen, w. prep. and inf. expressing contemporaneous time (s. 8:1). **εἶναι** pres. act. inf. εἰμί (# *1639*). **προσευχόμενον** pres. mid. (dep.) part. προσεύχομαι (# *4667*) to pray. Part. in a periphrastic construction. **κατὰ μόνας** alone. **συνῆσαν** impf. ind. act. σύνειμι (# *5289*) w. dat., to be together. **ἐπηρώτησεν** aor. ind. act. ἐπερωτάω (# *2089*) to question, to direct a question to. **εἶναι** pres. act. inf. Inf. in indir. speech. ◆ **19 ἀποκριθέντες** aor. pass. (dep.) part. ἀποκρίνομαι (# *646*) to answer. For the Semitic use s. MH, 453. **ἀνέστη** aor. ind. act. s.v. 8. ◆ **20 Χριστόν** acc. sing. χριστός (# *5986*) the anointed, the Christ (TDNT; NIDNTT; DJG, 106-17; EDNT). Acc. is used w. the unexpressed inf. (RWP). ◆ **21 ἐπιτιμήσας** aor. act. part. ἐπιτιμάω (# *2203*) to rebuke, to sternly charge. Part. of manner. **παρήγγειλεν** aor. ind. act. παραγγέλλω (# *4133*) to command, to order. Used esp. of transmitted orders of a military commander (AS). **λέγειν** pres. act. inf. λέγω (# *3306*) to say. Inf. as obj. or in indir. speech. ◆ **22 εἰπών** aor. act. part. λέγω (# *3306*) to say. **δεῖ** (# *1256*) pres. ind. act., it is necessary, w. inf. It gives a logical necessity. It refers not to fate but to the will of God (Evans). **παθεῖν** aor. act. inf. πάσχω (# *4248*) to suffer. **ἀποδοκιμασθῆναι** aor. pass. inf.

ἀποδοκιμάζω (# *627*) to reject after investigation; to judge someone or something as not being worthy or genuine and thus something to be rejected (Plummer; LN, 1:365; TDNT). **ἀποκτανθῆναι** aor. pass. inf. ἀποκτείνω (# *650*) to kill. **ἐγερθῆναι** aor. pass. inf. s.v. 7. The infs. here are dependent on the vb. δεῖ. ◆ **23 ἀρνησάσθω** aor. imp. mid. (dep.) 3rd. sing. ἀρνέομαι (# *766*) to say no, to deny. **ἀράτω** aor. imp. act. s.v. 3. Taking up one's cross refers to the attitude of self-denial (Marshall). This refers to carrying the horizontal beam (*patibulum*) to the place of crucifixion past a mocking, jeering mob (BBC). It is the readiness to renounce self and be ready to die a shameful death. **καθ᾽ ἡμέραν** (# *2848; 2465*) day by day, daily. **ἀκολουθείτω** pres. imp. act. s.v. 11. Here the word indicates to follow as a disciple (TDNT; EDNT). ◆ **24 θέλῃ** pres. subj. act. θέλω (# *2527*) to will, to want to, w. inf. Subj. in an indef. rel. cl. **σῶσαι** aor. act. inf. σῴζω (# *5392*) to save, to rescue. **ἀπολέσει** fut. ind. act. ἀπόλλυμι (# *660*) to lose, to destroy (EDNT). **ἀπολέσῃ** aor. subj. act. Subj. in an indef. rel. cl. **σώσει** fut. ind. act. ◆ **25 ὠφελεῖται** pres. ind. pass. ὠφελέω (# *6067*) to help, to benefit, to be of use. **κερδήσας** aor. act. part. (cond.) κερδαίνω (# *3045*) to gain, to win. The word is often used of the pursuit of wealth, earthly riches, business success (Fitzmyer, 788). **ἀπολέσας** aor. act. part. s.v. 24. **ζημιωθείς** aor. pass. part. ζημιόω (# *2423*) to suffer loss, to receive damage (NTNT, 61; Preisigke; s. Mark 8:36). ◆ **26 ἐπαισχυνθῇ** aor. subj. pass. ἐπαισχύνομαι (# *2049*) to be ashamed, in the eyes of men. Subj. w. ἄν (# *323*) in an indef. rel. cl. **ἐπαισχυνθήσεται** fut. ind. pass. **ἔλθῃ** aor. subj. act. ἔρχομαι (# *2262*) to go, to come. Subj. in an indef. temp. cl. ◆ **27 ἑστηκότων** perf. act. part. ἵστημι (# *2705*) to stand. Part. in a periphrastic construction. **γεύσωνται** aor. subj. mid. (dep.) γεύομαι (# *1174*) to taste, w. obj. in gen. Subj. w. double neg. strongly negating an action. **ἴδωσιν** aor. subj. act. ὁράω (# *3972*) to see. Futuristic subj. (RWP). ◆ **28 ἐγένετο** aor. ind. mid. (dep.) γίνομαι (# *1181*) (s. 2:1). **παραλαβών** aor. act. part. (circum.) s.v. 10. **ἀνέβη** aor. ind. act. ἀναβαίνω (# *326*) to go up. **προσεύξασθαι** aor. mid. (dep.) inf. s.v. 18. Inf. of purp. ◆ **29 προσεύχεσθαι** pres. mid. (dep.) inf., s.v 18. Inf. w. prep. ἐν (# *1877*) to express contemporaneous time ("while"); s. BD, 208. **εἶδος** (# *1626*) appearance. **λευκός** (# *3328*) white. **ἐξαστράπτων** pres. act. part. (adj.) ἐξαστράπτω (# *1993*) to flash forth as lightning, to gleam. For a discussion of the Transfiguration s. DJG, 834-41. ◆ **30 συνελάλουν** impf. ind. act. συλλαλέω (# *5196*) to speak together, to converse. Impf. pictures the continued conversation. ◆ **31 ὀφθέντες** aor. pass. part. (adj.) ὁράω (# *3972*) to see; pass. to appear. **ἔξοδος** (# *2016*) departure, going out. The word contains the ideas both of death and ascension (Godet). **ἤμελλεν** impf. ind. act. μέλλω (# *3516*) to be about to; w. inf. to express the fut. In the impf. it expresses fut. or intention reckoned from a moment in the past (MKG, 307). The concept of divine appointment or determination is evident (Arndt). ♦ **32 βεβαρημένοι** perf. pass. part. (adj.) βαρέω (# *976*) to make heavy, to burden; pass. to be heavy. Perf. pictures the state or cond. **διαγρηγορή-σαντες** aor. act. part. (circum.) διαγρηγορέω (# *1340*) to remain awake. The force of the prep. is either to remain awake in spite of desire to sleep or to become thoroughly awake (RWP; MH, 301). **εἶδον** aor. ind. act. ὁράω (# *3972*) to see. **συνεστῶτας** perf. act. part. (adj.) συνίστημι (# *5319*) to stand together. ♦ **33 διαχωρίζεσθαι** pres. mid. inf. διαχωρίζω (# *1431*) to divide; mid. to depart. Inf. w. prep. to express time. **εἶναι** pres. act. inf. εἰμί. (# *1639*) Epex. inf. **ποιήσωμεν** aor. subj. act. s.v. 10. Hortatory subj. **εἰδώς** perf. act. part. οἶδα (# *3857*) to know. Def. perf. w. pres. meaning. Circum. or causal part. ♦ **34 ἐπεσκίαζεν** impf. ind. act. ἐπισκιάζω (# *2173*) to overshadow. Incep. impf. **ἐφοβή-θησαν** aor. ind. pass. (dep.) φοβέομαι (# *5828*) to be afraid. **εἰσελθεῖν** aor. act. inf. s.v. 4. Inf. w. prep. to express contemporaneous time. ♦ **35 ἐκλελεγμένος** perf. pass. part. (adj.) ἐκλέγω (# *1721*) to choose. Perf. pictures the state or cond. **ἀκούετε** pres. imp. act. ἀκούω (# *201*) to hear, listen to, w. the gen. ♦ **36 γενέσθαι** aor. mid. (dep.) inf. s.v. 18. Inf. w. prep. **ἐν** (# *1877*) to express time (after). **εὑρέθη** aor. ind. pass. εὑρίσκω (# *2351*) to find. **ἐσίγησαν** aor. ind. act. σιγάω (# *4967*) to be silent. Ingressive aor., "they became silent." **ἀπήγ-γειλαν** aor. ind. act. ἀπαγγέλλω (# *550*) to report. **ἑώρα-καν** plperf. ind. act. ὁράω (# *3972*) to see. ♦ **37 ἐγένετο** aor. ind. mid. (dep.) s. 2:1. **ἑξῆς** (# *2009*) afterward. **κατελθόντων** aor. act. part. (temp.) κατέρχομαι (# *2982*) to come down, to go down. Gen. abs. **συνήντησεν** aor. ind. act. συναντάω (# *5267*) to meet, w. dat. ♦ **38 ἐβόησεν** aor. ind. act. βοάω (# *1066*) to call out, to cry out for help. **ἐπιβλέψαι** aor. act. inf. ἐπιβλέπω (# *2098*) to look upon, to regard w. compassion (Arndt; KVS, 282). **μονογενής** (# *3666*) only child. This son was extremely important since he would provide in old age and would carry on the name (BBC). ♦ **39 ἐξαίφνης** (# *1978*) suddenly. The word was used in medical language for sudden attacks of speechlessness, spasms, etc. (MLL, 19). **σπαράσσει** pres. ind. act. σπαράσσω (# *5057*) to tear. Hist. pres. **ἀφρός** (# *931*) foam. Used by medical writers to describe the symptoms of epilepsy. Probably the disease through which the demons exerted their power over this child (MLL, 17). **μόγις** (# *3653*) hardly, w. difficulty. **ἀποχωρεῖ** pres. ind. act. ἀποχωρέω (# *713*) to leave, to depart. **συντρῖβον** pres. act. part. (circum.) συντρίβω (# *5341*) to crush together, to mishandle, to bruise (Fitzmyer, 808; cf. σύν-τριμμα fracture, abrasion, DMTG, 306). ♦ **40 ἐδεήθην** aor. ind. pass. (dep.) δέομαι (# *1289*) to ask, to plea, to beg, to ask for w. urgency (LN, 1:408), w. gen. of pers. (BAGD). **ἐκβάλωσιν** aor. subj. act. ἐκβάλλω (# *1675*) to

cast out. Subj. in an obj. cl. **ἠδυνήθησαν** aor. ind. pass. (dep.) δύναμαι (# *1538*) to be able. ♦ **41 ἀποκριθείς** aor. pass. (dep.) part. s.v. 19. **διεστραμμένη** perf. pass. part. (adj.) διαστρέφω (# *1406*) to make twisted, turned, distorted. Perf. stresses the state or cond. **ἔσομαι** fut. ind. mid. (dep.) εἰμί (# *1639*). **ἀνέξομαι** fut. ind. mid. (dep.) ἀνέχομαι (# *462*) to bear w., to endure, w. gen. **προσ-άγαγε** aor. imp. act. προσάγω (# *4642*) to bring to, to lead to. Aor. imp. w. a vb. of motion (VANT, 341-48). ♦ **42 προσερχομένου** pres. mid. (dep.) part. (temp.) προσέρχομαι (# *4665*) to come to. Gen. abs. expressing contemporaneous time, "as he was coming." **ἔρρηξεν** aor. ind. act. ῥήγνυμι (# *4838*) to throw down. The word is used of boxers knocking down, and of wrestlers throwing an opponent (Plummer). **συνεσπάραξεν** aor. ind. act. συσπαράσσω (# *5360*) to tear, to pull about, to convulse. **ἐπετίμησεν** aor. ind. act. s.v. 21; Matt. 17:18. **ἰάσατο** aor. ind. mid. (dep.) s.v. 2. **ἀπέδωκεν** aor. ind. act. ἀποδίδωμι (# *625*) to give back. ♦ **43 ἐξεπλήσ-σοντο** aor. ind. mid. (dep.) ἐκπλήσσομαι (# *1742*) to be beside oneself, to be astonished, to be so amazed as to be practically overwhelmed (LN, 1:312). **μεγαλειότητι** dat. sing. μεγαλειότης (# *3484*) majesty, grandeur, sublimity (Marshall). **θαυμαζόντων** pres. act. part. (temp.) θαυμάζω (# *2513*) to wonder, to be amazed. Gen. abs. **ἐποίει** impf. ind. act. s.v. 10. ♦ **44 θέσθε** aor. imp. mid. (dep.) τίθημι (# *5502*) to place, to lay. The meaning of the expression is "store them in your memory" (Arndt). **μέλλει** pres. ind. act. s.v. 31. **παραδίδοσθαι** pres. pass. inf. παραδίδωμι (# *4140*) to deliver over, to betray. ♦ **45 ἠγνόουν** impf. ind. act. ἀγνοέω (# *51*) to be ignorant, not to know. **παρακεκαλυμμένον** perf. pass. part. (adj.) παρακαλύπτω (# *4152*) to conceal. Perf. stresses the state or cond. **αἴσθωνται** aor. subj. mid. (dep.) αἰσθάνομαι (# *150*) to possess the power of perception, to perceive (BAGD). Subj. in purp. cl. **ἐφο-βοῦντο** impf. ind. mid. (dep.) s.v. 34. **ἐρωτῆσαι** aor. act. inf. ἐρωτάω (# *2263*) to ask, to question. Epex. inf. explaining the fear. ♦ **46 εἰσῆλθεν** aor. ind. act. s.v. 4. **τό** the definite art. used before indir. speech (BD, 140). **εἴη** pres. opt. act. εἰμί (# *1639*) to be. Opt. used in indir. question in a context of doubt and perplexity (RG, 940; MKG, 240ff). **μείζων** (# *3505*) comp. μέγας great. Comp. used as superl., "greatest." **αὐτῶν** gen. αὐτός; gen. of comp. ♦ **47 εἰδώς** perf. act. part. οἶδα (# *3857*). Def. perf. w. pres. meaning, s.v. 33. Temp. or causal part. **ἐπιλαβόμενος** aor. mid. (dep.) part. (circum.) ἐπιλαμ-βάνομαι (# *2138*) to take, to take hold of. **ἔστησεν** aor. ind. act. ἵστημι (# *2705*) to place, to stand. ♦ **48 δέξηται** aor. subj. mid. (dep.) s.v. 5. Subj. in an indef. rel. cl. **ἀποστείλαντα** aor. act. part. s.v. 2. Part. as subst. **μικρό-τερος** comp. μικρός (# *3625*) little, small. Comp. used as the superl., "least" (BD, 32; GGBB, 298). **ὑπάρχων** pres. act. part. ὑπάρχω (# *5639*) to be. Part. as subst. **μέγας** (# *3489*) great. The thought is "great in God's eyes"

(Stein). Positive used as superl. (BD, 127; MT, 31). ◆ **49** ἀποκριθείς aor. pass. part. s.v. 19. εἴδομεν aor. ind. act. ὁράω s.v. 36. ἐκβάλλοντα pres. act. part. (adj.) s.v. 40. Iterat. pres. indicating a repeated action. ἐκωλύομεν impf. ind. act. κωλύω (# 3266) to hinder, to prevent. Conative impf., "We tried to prevent...." ἀκολουθεῖ pres. ind. act. s.v. 11. Pres. indicates continual action. ◆ **50** κωλύετε pres. imp. act. s.v. 49. Pres. imp. used w. a neg. here means "do not continue" or "do not always" (MKG, 272). ◆ **51** ἐγένετο aor. ind. mid. (dep.) s.v. 18. συμπληροῦσθαι pres. pass. inf. συμπληρόω (# 5230) to fill, to fulfill. Used in the fulfillment of a divine plan (TDNT). Inf. w. prep. ἐν (# 1877) to express time, "while the days leading up to His taking up were being fulfilled" (Marshall). ἀναλήμψεως gen. sing. ἀνάλημψις (# 378) taking up, lifting up. It could refer to His death or to His ascension (Arndt; Marshall). Gen. of description. ἐστήρισεν aor. ind. act. στηρίζω (# 5114) to fix firmly. "To set the face" is a Hebraism implying fixedness of purp., esp. in the prospect of difficulty or danger (Plummer; JMJ, 79-81; Fitzmyer, 828; C.A. Evans, "'He Set His Face': A Note on Luke 9, 51," *Biblica* 63 [1982]: 545-48; Gen. 31:21; Jer. 42:15, 17; Dan. 11:17; 1QS 2:12; 1QH 8:16). πορεύεσθαι pres. mid. (dep.) inf. s.v. 12. Inf. of purp. ◆ **52** ἀπέστειλεν aor. ind. act. s.v. 2. πορευθέντες aor. pass. (dep.) part. (circum.) s.v. 12. εἰσῆλθον aor. ind. act. s.v. 4. ἑτοιμάσαι aor. act. inf. ἑτοιμάζω (# 2286) to prepare. Inf. w. ὡς (# 6055) to express purp. (BD, 197-98). ◆ **53** ἐδέξαντο aor. ind. mid. (dep.) s.v. 5. πρόσωπον (# 4725) face. Semitic use means "person" or "he" (SB, 2:165; Marshall). πορευόμενον pres. mid. (dep.) part. s.v. 12. Periphrastic vb. part. w. impf. ἦν. ◆ **54** ἰδόντες aor. act. part. (temp.) s.v. 9. εἴπωμεν aor. subj. act. λέγω (# 3306) to speak. Deliberative subj. preceded by a vb. of desire (BD, 185). καταβῆναι aor. act. inf. καταβαίνω (# 2849) to go down, to come down. Inf. expressing purp. or result. ἀναλῶσαι aor. act. inf. ἀναλόω (# 384) to consume, to destroy. For the use of the word in the LXX s. GELTS, 30. Prep. in compound is perfective (MH, 296). Inf. of purp. or result. ◆ **55** στραφείς aor. pass. part. (temp.) στρέφω (# 5138) to turn. ἐπετίμησεν aor. ind. act. s.v. 21. ◆ **56** ἐπορεύθησαν aor. ind. pass. (dep.) s.v. 12. ◆ **57** ἀκολουθήσω fut. ind. act. s.v. 11. For a discussion s. Matt. 28:19; DJG, 186-88. Deliberative fut. indicating intention (VA, 424). ἀπέρχῃ pres. subj. mid. (dep.) ἀπέρχομαι (# 599) to go away. Subj. in an indef. rel. cl. ◆ **58** ἀλώπεκες nom. pl. ἀλώπηξ (# 273) fox. φωλεός (# 5887) den, hole for animals. κατασκήνωσις (# 2943) encampments, roost (Plummer). κλίνη pres. subj. act. κλίνω (# 3111) to lay. Subj. in indef. rel. cl. (RWP). ◆ **59** ἀκολούθει pres. imp. act. s.v. 11. The word indicates to follow as a disciple (TDNT). Pres. imp. would indicate a lifestyle. ἐπίτρεψόν aor. imp. act. ἐπιτρέπω (# 2205) to allow. Aor. calls for a spe-

cific act. ἀπελθόντι aor. act. part. (circum.) s.v. 57. θάψαι aor. act. inf. θάπτω (# 2507) to bury. According to Jewish tradition, the obligation to bury a relative took precedence over religious duties and was considered an obligatory act of love (Ellis; SB, 4:578ff; M, Berakoth, 3:l; Roy A. Harrisville, "Jesus and the Family," *Interp.* 23 [1969]: 432). Inf. of purp. ◆ **60** ἄφες aor. imp. act. ἀφίημι (# 918) to allow, w. inf. νεκρός (# 3738) dead. "Let the (spiritually) dead bury the (physically) dead" (Marshall). ἀπελθών aor. act. part. s.v. 57. Circum. part. w. the force of an imp. (VANT, 386). διάγγελλε pres. imp. act. διαγγέλλω (# 1334) to publish everywhere, to proclaim far and wide (Arndt). ◆ **61** ἀποτάξασθαι aor. mid. (dep.) inf. ἀποτάσσομαι (# 698) to detach, to separate; to set myself apart from, bid farewell to those who that are at my house (Plummer). ◆ **62** ἐπιβαλών aor. act. part. ἐπιβάλλω (# 2095) to place upon, to place the hand upon. Part. as subst. ἄροτρον (# 770) acc. sing. plow (ABD, 6:1115-16). βλέπων pres. act. part. βλέπω (# 1063) to see, to look. Part. as subst. Pres. indicates a continual looking. εὔθετος (# 2310) well-placed, fit, suitable, useable. It was used of those suitable for a place or office (MM; Preisigke). In medical writers it meant "well adapted to," "well arranged" (MLL, 75).

Luke 10

◆ **1** ἀνέδειξεν aor. ind. act. ἀναδείκνυμι (# 344) to show forth, to display, to make public, esp. a person's appointment to an office (Plummer). ἀπέστειλεν aor. ind. act. ἀποστέλλω (# 690) to send out, to send out as an official authoritative representative (TDNT). ἀνὰ δύο (# 324; 1545) distributive, by twos. For the textual problem s. TC, 150-51; Bock. ἤμελλεν impf. ind. act. μέλλω (# 3516) to be about to, w. inf. for the fut. (s. 7:2). ◆ **2** δεήθητε aor. imp. pass. (dep.) δέομαι (# 1289) to pray, to ask someone for something, w. gen. ἐκβάλῃ aor. subj. act. ἐκβάλλω (# 1675) to drive out, to cast out. Subj. w. ὅπως (# 3968) in an obj. cl. giving the content of the prayer. ◆ **3** ὑπάγετε pres. imp. act. ὑπάγω (# 5632) to go, to go forth. Pres. imp. w. a vb. of motion. ἄρνας acc. pl. ἀρήν (# 748) lamb. For the figure of lambs and wolves s. Marshall; Fitzmyer, 847; TDNT; 1 Enoch 89:13-27. ◆ **4** βαστάζετε pres. imp. act. βαστάζω (# 1002) to carry. Here the pres. imp. w. neg. indicates "do not always" (MKG, 272). βαλλάντιον (# 964) acc. sing. purse, an old word for moneybag (RWP; Bovon). ἀσπάσησθε aor. subj. mid. (dep.) ἀσπάζομαι (# 832) to greet. ◆ **5** εἰσέλθητε aor. subj. act. εἰσέρχομαι (# 1656) to go in. Subj. w. ἄν (# 323) in an indef. rel. cl. λέγετε pres. imp. act. λέγω (# 3306) to say. εἰρήνη (# 1645) peace, used in Semitic sense of שׁלום (*shalom*), wholeness, prosperity, salvation (TDNT; NIDNTT; TDOT; EDNT; GELTS, 130). ◆ **6** ᾖ pres. subj. act. εἰμί (# 1639) to be. Subj. w. ἐάν (# 1569) in 3rd. class cond. cl., where the possibility of the cond. is assumed. **υἱὸς εἰρήνης** son of peace. In the Semitic sense of "one characterized by wholeness," that is, "one who has been born of peace and is also destined for the peace of others" (William Klassen, "'A Child of Peace' [Luke 10.6] in First Century Context," *NTS* [1981]: 488-506, esp. 501; also Marshall; SB, 2:166). **ἐπαναπαήσεται** fut. ind. pass. (dep.) ἐπαναπαύομαι (# *2058*) to rest upon. **εἰ δὲ μή γε** but if not, otherwise (Thrall, 10). **ἀνακάμψει** fut. ind. act. ἀνακάμπτω (# *366*) to return. ◆ **7 μένετε** pres. imp. act. μένω (# *3531*) to remain. **ἐσθίοντες** pres. act. part. (circum.) ἐσθίω (# *2266*) to eat. **πίνοντες** pres. act. part. (circum.) πίνω (# *4403*) to drink. **μισθοῦ** (# *3635*) gen. sing. wage, pay. The saying does not appear to be found in Jewish lit. (JJ, 210). Gen. w. the adj. **ἄξιος** (# *545*) ("worthy"). **μεταβαίνετε** pres. imp. act. μεταβαίνω (# *3553*) to change a place, to leave, to depart. The force of the prep. involves the idea of change (MH, 318). ◆ **8 εἰσέρχησθε** pres. subj. mid. (dep.) s.v. 5. Subj. in an indef. rel. cl. **δέχωνται** pres. subj. mid. (dep.) δέχομαι (# *1312*) to receive, to welcome. **παρατιθέμενα** pres. pass. part. παρατίθημι (# *4192*) to set (food) before someone. Part. as subst. ◆ **9 θεραπεύετε** pres. imp. act. θεραπεύω (# *2543*) to treat medically, to heal. **ἤγγικεν** perf. ind. act. ἐγγίζω (# *1581*) to draw near; perf. to be at hand (s. Matt. 3:2). ◆ **10 ἐξελθόντες** aor. act. part. (temp.) ἐξέρχομαι (# *2002*) to go out. **εἴπατε** aor. imp. act. λέγω (# *3306*) to say, to speak. ◆ **11 καί** (# *2779*) even. Ascensive use; the thing that is added is out of the ordinary and rises to a climax like the crescendo in music (RG, 1181). **κονιορτός** (# *3155*) dust. **κολληθέντα** aor. pass. part. (adj.) κολλάω (# *3140*) to cling to. For the medical examples of the word s. MLL, 128. **ἀπομασσόμεθα** pres. ind. mid. ἀπομάσσω (# *669*) to wipe off, to rub off w. the hands (RWP; for medical usages s. MLL, 111). Pres. indicates that the saying accompanies the action (Marshall). ◆ **12 ἀνεκτότερον** comp. ἀνεκτός (# *445*) bearable, endurable. The word is used in a Christian letter of the 4th century to describe a sick lady who has gotten better: "Her cond. seems ... to be more tolerable (ἀνεκτότερον), as she can sit up" (Oxyrhynchus Papyri 939, 25; also NDIEC, 4:247; MM). ◆ **13 ἐγενήθησαν** aor. ind. pass. (dep.) γίνομαι (# *1181*) to become, to happen. **γενόμεναι** aor. mid. (dep.) part. Part. as adj. **σάκκος** (# *4884*) sackcloth. From the Heb. or Aramaic word meaning a cloth made of rough goat's hair to cover the naked body as a sign of mourning or penitence (Fitzmyer, 854). **καθήμενοι** pres. mid. (dep.) part. κάθημαι (# *2764*) to sit. Circum. part. or part. of manner. **μετενόησαν** aor. ind. act. μετανοέω (# *3566*) to change the mind, to repent. Ind. w. **ἄν** (# *323*) in a contrary to fact. cond. cl. ◆ **15 μή** (# *3590*) used in questions which expect the answer "no." **ὑψωθήσῃ** fut. ind. pass. ὑψόω (# *5738*) to lift up, to exalt. "You don't expect to be exalted..., do you?" (Fitzmyer,

850). **ᾅδου** gen. sing. ᾅδης (# *87*) Hades, like the OT Sheol (שְׁאוֹל). It means death, grave, or the realm of death (Ellis; TDNT; TDOT; NIDOTTE; NIDNTT; EDNT; SB, 4:ii, 1016-29; 1 Enoch 102:5, 11; 1QH 3:9, 16, 19; Fitzmyer, 855). **καταβήσῃ** fut. ind. mid. καταβαίνω (# *2849*) to go down. Perhaps an allusion to Isa. 14:13, 15 (Marshall). ◆ **16 ἀκούων** pres. act. part. ἀκούω (# *201*) to hear, to listen to, w. gen. Part. as subst. **ἀθετῶν** pres. act. part. ἀθετέω (# *119*) to set aside, to reject. Part. as subst. **ἀποστείλαντα** aor. act. part. s.v. 1. Part. as subst. ◆ **17 ὑπέστρεψαν** aor. ind. act. ὑποστρέφω (# *5715*) to turn about, to return. **ὑποτάσσεται** pres. ind. pass. ὑποτάσσω (# *5718*) to subject; pass. to be in subjection. The word was used in a magical text in the papyri for the subjection of evil spirits and demons (LAE, 258, 263). Pres. could be iterat. ◆ **18 ἐθεώρουν** impf. ind. act. θεωρέω (# *2555*) to see, to be a spectator. Impf. points to what was constantly repeated. Every expulsion of demons meant a fall of Satan (Arndt). **ἀστραπή** (# *847*) lightning. **πεσόντα** aor. act. part. (adj.) πίπτω (# *4406*) to fall. ◆ **19 δέδωκα** perf. ind. act. δίδωμι (# *1443*) to give. Perf. means, "I have given to you, so that you now possess it" (Geldenhuys). **πατεῖν** pres. act. inf. πατέω (# *4251*) to walk. Epex. inf. explaining the **ἐξουσία**. **ὄφεων** gen. pl. ὄφις (# *4058*) snake. **ἀδικήσῃ** aor. subj. act. ἀδικέω (# *92*) to commit an injustice, to harm, to do wrong. Subj. w. double neg. **οὐ μή** (# *4024; 3590*) for a strong denial. ◆ **20 χαίρετε** pres. imp. act. χαίρω (# *5897*) to rejoice. Pres. imp. w. neg. **μή** (# *3590*) indicates that this should not be one's attitude. **ἐγγέγραπται** perf. ind. pass. ἐγγράφω (# *1582*) to write in, to record. For the Jewish concept of various heavenly books s. SB, 2:169-176, and for references to passages s. Stein. Perf. indicates the completed state. Theol. pass. indicating that God has done the action. ◆ **21 ἠγαλλιάσατο** aor. ind. mid. (dep.) ἀγαλλιάω (# *22*) to rejoice, to be overjoyed, to experience a state of great joy and gladness, often involving verbal expression and bodily movement (LN, 1:303; TDNT; NIDNTT; EDNT). **ἐξομολογοῦμαι** pres. ind. mid. (dep.) ἐξομολογέομαι (# *2018*) to confess publicly, to praise, to thank. **ἀπέκρυψας** aor. ind. act. 2nd. pers. sing. ἀποκρύπτω (# *648*) to conceal, to hide. **ἀπεκάλυψας** aor. ind. act. ἀποκαλύπτω (# *636*) to unveil, to reveal. **ἐγένετο** aor. ind. mid. (dep.) γίνομαι (# *1181*) to become, to be. "In this way good pleasure has come into being before you," referring, in a reverential way, to God's gracious action of revealing to the elect (Fitzmyer, 873). ◆ **22 παρεδόθη** aor. ind. pass. παραδίδωμι (# *4140*) to give over, to pass on, to transfer. **βούληται** pres. subj. mid. (dep.) βούλομαι (# *1089*) to will, to consider carefully, to make a decision after careful consideration, w. inf. (EDNT; TDNT; NIDNTT). **ἀποκαλύψαι** aor. act. inf. s.v. 21. ◆ **23 στραφείς** aor. pass. part. (temp.) στρέφω (# *5138*) to turn; pass. (w. refl. meaning) to turn toward, to turn to (BAGD). **βλέποντες** pres. act. part. (adj.) βλέπω (# 1063) to see. ◆ **24 ἠθέλησαν** aor. ind. act. θέλω (# 2527) to wish, to desire, to want, w. inf. **ἰδεῖν** aor. act. inf. ὁράω (# 3972) to see. **εἶδαν** aor. ind. act. ὁράω. **ἀκοῦσαι** aor. act. inf. s.v. 16. **ἤκουσαν** aor. ind. act. s.v. 16. ◆ **25 νομικός** (# 3788) jurist, lawyer. One conversant w. the law, its interpretation and application (TDNT; EDNT; Matt. 22:35). **ἀνέστη** aor. ind. act. ἀνίστημι (# 482) to stand up, to rise for a question or participation in an argument (Arndt). Perhaps this was a gruff, unexpected gesture (Bovon). **ἐκπειράζων** pres. act. part. ἐκπειράζω (# 1733) to try, to test, to tempt. A recognized religious authority is testing the unofficial teacher to see whether He gives the right answers (Marshall). Circum. part. or expressing purp. **ποιήσας** aor. act. part. ποιέω (# 4472) to do. Part. of means ("by doing"). **κληρονομήσω** fut. ind. act. κληρονομέω (# 3099) to receive as inheritance, to receive a share allotted to you (Arndt). ◆ **26 γέγραπται** perf. ind. pass. γράφω (# 1211) to write. Perf. was used for authoritative documents ("it stands written") (MM). **ἀναγινώσκεις** pres. ind. act. ἀναγινώσκω (# 336) to read. "How do you read?" i.e., "May I hear your authorities w. exposition?" (LNT, 224). ◆ **27 ἀποκριθείς** aor. pass. (dep.) part. ἀποκρίνομαι (# 646) to answer. Semitic use of the part. (MH, 453). **ἀγαπήσεις** fut. ind. act. ἀγαπάω (# 26) to love. For the fut. used in a Semitic way to express a command s. BG, 94. **πλησίον** (# 4446) acc. sing. neighbor. Samaritans and foreigners were excluded from this category (Marshall). ◆ **28 ὀρθῶς** (# 3987) straight, correctly. **ἀπεκρίθης** aor. ind. pass. (dep.) s.v. 27. **ποίει** pres. imp. act. s.v. 25. Pres. imp. calls for a habitual and continual way of life. **ζήσῃ** fut. ind. mid. ζάω (# 2409) to live. Imp. w. **καί** (# 2779) and fut. forms a cond. type sentence. For this Semitic construction s. Beyer, 238-55; MH, 421. ◆ **29 θέλων** pres. act. part. s.v. 24. Part. may be causal. **δικαιῶσαι** aor. act. inf. δικαιόω (# 1467) to declare righteous, to justify, to clear oneself of a charge. The lawyer wishes to vindicate himself w. a question implying he did not know precisely what his duty was (GW, 133). **μου** gen. sing. ἐγώ (# 1609). Personal pron. emphasized by its position, "Who is *my* neighbor?" ◆ **30 ὑπολαβών** aor. act. part. (circum.) ὑπολαμβάνω (# 5696) to take up, to take up the discussion. **κατέβαινεν** impf. ind. act. καταβαίνω (# 2849) to go down. Impf. vividly describes the action. **ἀπὸ Ἱερουσαλὴμ εἰς Ἱεριχώ** from Jerusalem to Jericho. For a description of the area s. Jos., *JW*, 4:451-474; SB, 2:177-81. The distance of about 150 furlongs (approximately 11 1/2 miles) is desert and rocky (Jos., *JW*, 4:474). **λῃσταῖς** dat. pl. λῃστής (# 3334) robber, one who uses force in robbing. Dat. w. prep. in the vb. **περιέπεσεν** aor. ind. act. περιπίπτω (# 4346) to fall among, to be encompassed by, to be surrounded by robbers. A common experience on the road to Jericho

(RWP; SB, 2:181-82). **ἐκδύσαντες** aor. act. part. (temp.) ἐκδύω (# 1694) to remove the clothing, to strip. **ἐπιθέντες** aor. act. part. (temp.) ἐπιτίθημι (# 2202) to place upon; here, to inflict blows upon someone. **ἀπῆλθον** aor. ind. act. ἀπέρχομαι (# 599) to go away. **ἀφέντες** aor. act. part. (circum.) ἀφίημι (# 918) to leave. **ἡμιθανής** (# 2467) half dead. ◆ **31 συγκυρία** (# 5175) coincidence. This had not been prearranged or planned (Arndt). **ἰδών** aor. act. part. (temp.) ὁράω (# 3972) to see. **ἀντιπαρῆλθεν** aor. ind. act. ἀντιπαρέρχομαι (# 524) to pass by along on the other side, to pass alongside (παρά) of, facing, or being opposite (ἀντί). He came alongside, then stepped over to the opposite side of the road to avoid ceremonial contamination w. a stranger, or one who might be dead (RWP; Fitzmyer, 887). The priest and the Levite were obligated according to the law to help a neighbor in need. They also were obligated not to defile themselves by touching a dead body. Since defilement prevented their service in the temple and eating of the tithe, they chose to pass by on the opposite side rather than to take a chance on defilement (LNT, 211-17). ◆ **32 ἐλθών** aor. act. part. (temp.) ἔρχομαι (# 2262) to go, to come. The Levites served in the temple helping the priest and were responsible for the music. For the priests and Levites s. JPB, 77-102; Luke 1:5. ◆ **33 Σαμαρίτης** (# 4901) Samaritan (s. 9:52; John 4:3-15; SB, 1:538-60; Bock). The word stands first in the sentence for emphasis (Evans). **ὁδεύων** pres. act. part. (temp.) ὁδεύω (# 3841) to travel, to be on a journey ("As he was traveling"). **ἦλθεν** aor. ind. act. s.v. 32. **ἐσπλαγχνίσθη** aor. ind. pass. (dep.) σπλαγχνίζομαι (# 5072) to be deeply moved w. compassion, to have compassion (TDNT; EDNT; MNTW, 156-60). The irony is that a foreigner, not included in the Jewish definition of a neighbor, is the one who showed himself neighbor to the unfortunate Jew (Ellis). ◆ **34 προσελθών** aor. act. part. (circum.) προσέρχομαι (# 4665) to come to. (Contrast ἀντιπαρέχομαι v. 31.) The Samaritan was moved by compassion, and this obviated fears about his own contamination (LNT, 217). **κατέδησεν** aor. ind. act. καταδέω (# 2866) to bind up. Used in medical language of binding up wounds, ulcers, etc. (MLL, 27; BBC). **τραύματα** acc. pl. τραῦμα (# 5546) wound, hurt (DMTG, 312). The pl. points to the severe cond. of the man. **ἐπιχέων** pres. act. part. (circum.) ἐπιχέω (# 2219) to pour upon. For the medical use of this term as well as the medicinal use of oil and wine s. MLL, 28-29. **ἐπιβιβάσας** aor. act. part. (circum.) ἐπιβιβάζω (# 2097) to set upon. **κτῆνος** (# 3229) acc. sing. animal, animal used for riding (BAGD). **ἤγαγεν** aor. ind. act. ἄγω (# 72) to lead. **πανδοχεῖον** (# 4106) inn. A large structure w. shelter for man and beast (Arndt). **ἐπεμελήθη** aor. ind. pass. (dep.) ἐπιμελέομαι (# 2150) to care for, w. obj. in gen. Used in medical language of care taken of the sick or some injured part of the body

(MLL, 29). ◆ **35 ἐκβαλών** aor. act. part. (circum.) ἐκβάλλω (# 1675) to throw out, to take out. **ἔδωκεν** aor. ind. act. δίδωμι (# 1443) to give. **δηνάριον** (# 1324) denarius. A Roman coin worth about 18 cents. It was the workman's average daily wage (BAGD; DJG, 805; ABD, 1:1086-87). **πανδοχεῖ** dat. sing. πανδοχεύς (# 4107) innkeeper. Indir. obj. **ἐπιμελήθητι** aor. imp. pass. (dep.) s.v. 34. **προσδαπανήσῃς** aor. subj. act. προσδαπανάω (# 4655) to spend besides, to spend in addition. Subj. in an indef. rel. cl. **ἐπανέρχεσθαι** pres. mid. (dep.) inf. ἐπανέρχομαι (# 2059) to come back again. Inf. w. prep. **ἐν** (# 1877) to express time: "When I return." **ἀποδώσω** fut. ind. act. ἀποδίδωμι (# 625) to give back, to pay back. For the Samaritan's utter trust in making the innkeeper his agent, esp. in light of his lack of legal recourse s. LNT, 218. ◆ **36 δοκεῖ** pres. ind. act. δοκέω (# 1506) to appear, to seem, w. dat. **γεγονέναι** perf. act. inf. s.v. 13. Inf. as obj. of the vb. **ἐμπεσόντος** aor. act. part. (adj.) ἐμπίπτω (# 1860) to fall in, to fall among. ◆ **37 ποιήσας** aor. act. part. ποιέω (# 4472) to do, w. the adj., to show. He could not bring himself to say, "the Samaritan!" **ἔλεος** (# 1799) mercy. For the Heb. content of this word s. TDNT; NIDNTT; EDNT. **πορεύου** pres. imp. mid. (dep.) πορεύομαι (# 4513) to go. **ποίει** pres. imp. act. ποιέω to do. "Do constantly," in the sense of lifelong action (Geldenhuys). ◆ **38 πορεύεσθαι** pres. mid. (dep.) inf. s.v. 37. Inf. w. prep. to express contemporaneous time. **εἰσῆλθεν** aor. ind. act. s.v. 5. **ὑπεδέξατο** aor. ind. mid. (dep.) ὑποδέχομαι (# 5685) to receive, to welcome as a guest. ◆ **39 τῇδε** dat. fem. sing. ὅδε, this one here (RG, 696). **καλουμένη** pres. pass. part. καλέω (# 2813) to call; pass. to be named. **παρακαθεσθεῖσα** aor. pass. (dep.) part. (temp.) nom. fem. sing. παρακαθέζομαι (# 4149) to sit beside. She is eager to hear the teaching (BBC). **ἤκουεν** impf. ind. act. s.v. 16. Impf. pictures the continual listening. ◆ **40 περιεσπᾶτο** impf. ind. mid. (dep.) περισπάομαι (# 4352) to be pulled or dragged away, to become or be distracted. She was drawn about in different directions (Plummer). **ἐπιστᾶσα** aor. act. part. (circum.) ἐφίστημι (# 2392) to place upon, to come to. **μέλει** (# 3508) pres. ind. act. used impersonally w. dat., **μέλει σοι** "to be of concern to you" (BAGD). **κατέλιπεν** impf. ind. act. καταλείπω (# 2901) to leave, to forsake. Impf. expresses the continuance of the neglect (Plummer). **διακονεῖν** pres. act. inf. διακονέω (# 1354) to minister, esp. to serve at the table. Inf. of purp. or result. **εἰπέ** aor. imp. act. λέγω (# 3306) to speak. Aor. imp. calls for a specific act. **συναντιλάβηται** aor. subj. mid. (dep.) συναντιλαμβάνομαι (# 5269) to help. The mid. voice w. the prep. in compound means to take hold of oneself at the end of a task together w. another (RWP). ◆ **41 ἀποκριθείς** aor. pass. (dep.) part. s.v. 27. **μεριμνᾷς** pres. ind. act. μεριμνάω (# 3534) to be concerned, to be overly concerned, to be anxious, to have care (BAGD). It refers to

an agitated state of mind (Geldenhuys). **θορυβάζῃ** pres. ind. pass. θορυβάζω (# 2571) to cause trouble; pass. to be troubled or distracted. ◆ **42 ἐξελέξατο** aor. ind. mid. (indir. mid.) ἐκλέγομαι (# 1721) to choose, to choose for oneself, for one's benefit (GGBB, 421). **ἀφαιρεθήσεται** fut. ind. pass. ἀφαιρέω (# 904) to take away.

Luke 11

◆ **1 ἐγένετο** aor. ind. mid. (dep.) γίνομαι (# 1181) to become, to happen, followed by prep. w. inf. indicating time (Luke 8:1). **εἶναι** pres. act. inf. εἰμί (# 1639) to be. Inf. w. prep. for contemporaneous time. **προσευχόμενον** pres. mid. (dep.) part. προσεύχομαι (# 4667) to pray. Part. in a periphrastic construction. **ἐπαύσατο** aor. ind. mid. (dep.) παύομαι (# 4264) to stop, to cease. **δίδαξον** aor. imp. act. διδάσκω (# 1438) to teach. **προσεύχεσθαι** pres. mid. (dep.) inf. Inf. as dir. obj. ◆ **2 προσεύχησθε** pres. subj. mid. (dep.) s.v. 1. Subj. in an indef. temp. cl. **λέγετε** pres. imp. act. λέγω (# 3306) to say. Pres. imp. here is iterat. **πάτερ** voc. sing. πατήρ (# 4252) father; suggesting that the Father will grant what's best. The prayer has as contextual background the family relationship between a father and son (TDNT; NIDNTT; EDNT). **ἁγιασθήτω** aor. imp. pass. ἁγιάζω (# 39) to declare holy, to treat as holy (Arndt). It indicates a respect and reverence due to a heavenly Father. **ἐλθέτω** aor. imp. act. 3rd. pers. sing. ἔρχομαι (# 2262) to come. ◆ **3 ἐπιούσιος** (# 2157) daily, for the coming day (s. Matt. 6:11; Fitzmyer, 908-909; EDNT; TDNT). **δίδου** pres. imp. act. δίδωμι (# 1443) to give. Pres. is iterat., "give time after time." The father was to provide for the family. ◆ **4 ἄφες** aor. imp. act. ἀφίημι (# 918) to release, to forgive. **ὀφείλοντι** pres. act. part. ὀφείλω (# 4053) to owe, to owe a debt. For sins viewed as a debt to God s. TDNT. The family members were to be at harmony w. one another. **εἰσενέγκῃς** aor. subj. act. εἰσφέρω (# 1662) to lead into, to bring into. "Do not permit the foes of our soul to catch us in their net" (Arndt). The father was to protect the family. ◆ **5 ἕξει** fut. ind. act. ἔχω (# 2400) to have. Deliberative fut. in a rhetorical question (RG, 875), w. nuance: "Can you imagine going to a neighbor, asking for help to entertain a friend and getting this response?" (PAP, 121). **μεσονυκτίου** gen. sing. μεσονύκτιον (# 3543) midnight. Gen. of time ("about midnight") (BAGD). Often one traveled at night because of the heat during the day (PAP, 121; Bovon). **εἴπῃ** aor. subj. act. λέγω s.v. 2. Deliberative subj. **φίλε** voc. φίλος (# 5813) friend. The point of the story seems to turn on the concept of friendship, esp. the responsibilities of loyalty, faithfulness, helpfulness, unselfishness, etc., connected w. it (RAC, 8:418-34; TDNT; EDNT; Jos., *J.W.*, 1:390; TJ, 20). **χρῆσον** aor. imp. act. κίχρημι (# 3079) to lend. Distinct from "to lend on interest" as a matter of business. It means "to allow the use of" as a friendly act (Plummer; LXX Ps.

111 [112]:5). ἄρτος (# 788) bread, loaf of bread. To feed a guest w. a partial loaf left from another meal would be an insult (PAP, 122). ◆ 6 ἐπειδή (# 2076) because. παρεγένετο aor. ind. mid. (dep.) παραγίνομαι (# 4134) to arrive, to come to. παραθήσω fut. ind. act. παρατίθημι (# 4192) to set before. The reputation of a whole community is at stake and the host is asking the sleeper to fulfill his duty to the guest of the village (PAP, 122-23). ◆ 7 κἀκεῖνος ἔσωθεν and *that one from within*. The demonstrative pron. is used in a derogatory sense. ἀποκριθείς aor. pass. (dep.) part. ἀποκρίνομαι (# 646) to answer (s. 10:27). κόπος (# 3160) tiring work, trouble. πάρεχε pres. imp. act. παρέχω (# 4218) to cause, to make; κόπους πάρεχε "to cause trouble for someone," "to bother someone" (BAGD). Pres. imp. w. the neg. μή (# 3590) indicates the stopping of an action in progress. κέκλεισται perf. ind. pass. κλείω (# 3091) to lock. The noise would wake the children sleeping on the floor (BBC). Perf. indicates the state after the completed action. εἰς (# 1650) w. force of ἐν (BG, 33). ἀναστάς aor. act. part. ἀνίστημι (# 482) to arise, to get up. The part. could be cond.: "even if I get up," or else circum. δοῦναι aor. act.inf. δίδωμι (# 1443) to give. Inf. completes the vb. Vv. 5-7 could be an extended question, "Can you imagine having a friend and going to him with a sacred request to help you entertain a guest, and then he offers silly excuses about sleeping children and a barred door?" (PAP, 124). ◆ 8 ἀναίδεια (# 357) lack of feeling of shame, shamelessness, ruthlessness, a bold act out of ignorance (PAP, 125-33; Alan F. Johnson, "Assurance for Man: The Fallacy of Translating *Anaideia* by 'Persistence' in Luke 11:5-8," *JETS* 22 [1979]: 123-31; CCFJ, 1:92; Nolland). The man got up because he wanted to avoid the shame of being a faithless friend and a horrible host (PAP, 132-33). The word may refer to the one requestion and the meaning would be, "If among humans a request is granted because the request is rude and out of ignorance, how much more will your heavenly Father grant your request" (Klyne Snodgrass, "*Anaideia* and the Friend at Midnight [Luke 11:8]," *JBL* 116 [1997]: 505-20). ἐγερθείς aor. pass. part. (circum.) ἐγείρω (# 1586) to arise, to get up. δώσει fut. ind. act. s.v. 7. χρῄζει pres. ind. act. χρῄζω (# 5974) to need, to have need of, w. gen. ◆ 9 αἰτεῖτε pres. imp. act. αἰτέω (# 160) to ask, to request. Pres. imp. here is customary; i.e., "make it your habit," "respond in this way whenever it is called for"; here, "if you ask at any time, it will be given you" (VANT, 433). δοθήσεται fut. ind. pass. s.v. 7. Theol. pass., God is the Giver. ζητεῖτε pres. imp. act. ζητέω (# 2426) to seek. εὑρήσετε fut. ind. act. εὑρίσκω (# 2351) to find. κρούετε pres. imp. act. κρούω (# 3218) to knock. ἀνοιγήσεται fut. ind. pass. ἀνοίγνυμι, ἀνοίγω (# 487) to open. Theol. pass., the heavenly Father will do more than the friend; His reputation as a father is reliable. For the

construction of the imp. followed by the fut. as a type of cond. cl. s. 10:28. ◆ 10 λαμβάνει pres. ind. act. λαμβάνω (# 3284) to receive. Iterat. or customary pres. ◆ 11 τίνα acc. sing. masc. interrogative pron. τίς who? what sort of? (BAGD). αἰτήσει fut. ind. act. s.v. 9. Deliberative fut. used in a question which expects the answer "no" (s.v. 5): "of what sort of father from your midst would a son ask a fish, and he would give him...?" The point has to do with the kind of earthly father that would do such a thing. ὄφιν acc. sing. ὄφις (# 4058) snake. ἐπιδώσει fut. ind. act. ἐπιδίδωμι (# 2113) to give over, to hand to. ◆ 12 ᾠόν (# 6051) acc. sing. egg. ◆ 13 οὖν (# 4036) therefore, draws a conclusion. ὑπάρχοντες pres. act. part. (adj.) ὑπάρχω (# 5639) to be, to exist. οἴδατε perf. ind. act. οἶδα (# 3857) to know. Def. perf. w. pres. meaning. διδόναι pres. act. inf. s.v. 7. πόσῳ μᾶλλον how much more? Introduces a rabbinical type of argument (*Qal wahomer*) which argues from the lesser to the greater (Stein; SB, 3:223-26). The heavenly Father's reputation as a father is reliable. ◆ 14 ἐκβάλλων pres. act. part. ἐκβάλλω (# 1675) to throw out, to cast out. Part. in a periphrastic construction, "he was in the process of casting out ... (VA, 481). κωφός (# 3273) dumb, not able to speak. ἐγένετο aor. ind. mid. (dep.) s.v. 1, w. gen. abs. for time. ἐξελθόντος aor. act. part. (temp.) ἐξέρχομαι (# 2002) to go out. Gen. abs. ἐλάλησεν aor. ind. act. λαλέω (# 3281) to speak. ἐθαύμασαν aor. ind. act. θαυμάζω (# 2513) to wonder, to marvel. ◆ 15 εἶπον aor. ind. act. λέγω (# 3306) to say. ἄρχοντι dat. sing. ἄρχων (# 807) leader, prince (s. Matt. 12:24, 27). ◆ 16 πειράζοντες pres. act. part. (circum.) πειράζω (# 4279) to test, to try, to tempt. ἐζήτουν impf. ind. act. s.v. 9. ◆ 17 εἰδώς perf. act. part. (temp.) οἶδα. Def. perf. w. pres. meaning s.v. 13. διανόημα (# 1378) thought, the content of thinking and reasoning (LN, 1:351). The word indicates to think through or distinguish intent or purp. (RWP). εἶπεν aor. ind. act. s.v. 15. διαμερισθεῖσα aor. pass. part. (adj.) nom. fem. sing. διαμερίζω (# 1374) to divide into. ἐρημοῦται pres. ind. pass. ἐρημόω (# 2246) to make empty, to destroy, to make desolate. Gnomic. pres. indicating a general statement that is always true. οἶκος ἐπὶ οἶκον one house falls on another (in civil strife or civil war) (Marshall; Fitzmyer, 921). ◆ 18 διεμερίσθη aor. ind. pass. s.v. 17. Ind. used in a 1st. class cond. cl. where the cond. is assumed as true for the sake of argument. σταθήσεται fut. ind. pass. ἵστημι (# 2705) to stand. ἐκβάλλειν pres. act. inf. s.v. 14. Inf. in indir. speech. ◆ 19 υἱοί nom. pl. υἱός (# 5626) son. Here equivalent to "your own people" (Arndt). ἔσονται fut. ind. mid. (dep.) εἰμί (# 1639) to be. ◆ 20 δάκτυλος (# 1235) finger. Jesus works through God's power without the use of rings, charms, and incantations (Fitzmyer, 922; s. Robert W. Wall, "'The Finger of God': Deuteronomy 9:10 and Luke 11:20," *NTS* 33 [1987]: 144-50). ἐκβάλλω pres. ind. act. s.v. 14. Ind. in a 1st. class cond. cl. Pres. is habitual or iterat. **ἔφθασεν** aor. ind. act. φθάνω (# 5777) to come, to arrive at. The rule of God is present in the person of Jesus. ◆ **21 ἰσχυρός** (# 2708) strong. Adj. used as subst. **καθωπλισμένος** perf. pass. part. (adj.) καθοπλίζω (# 2774) to arm fully, to equip. Prep. in compound is perfective. **φυλάσσῃ** pres. subj. act. φυλάσσω (# 5875) to guard. Subj. in an indef. temp. cl. **αὐλή** (# 885) courtyard, palace. ◆ **22 ἐπάν** when, w. subj. **ἰσχυρότερος** comp. ἰσχυρός; comp., "stronger than he is." **αὐτοῦ** gen. αὐτός; gen. of comp. **ἐπελθών** aor. act. part. (circum.) ἐπέρχομαι (# 2088) to come upon. **νικήσῃ** aor. subj. act. νικάω (# 3771) to conquer. **πανοπλία** (# 4110) complete armor, a word indicating the soldier's outfit such as shield, sword, lance, helmet, etc. (RWP; Eph. 6:11; TJ, 106-10). **αἴρει** pres. ind. act. αἴρω (# 149) to take away. **ἐπεποίθει** plperf. ind. act. πείθω (# 4275) to trust. **σκῦλα** acc. pl. σκῦλον (# 5036) booty, spoils. The armor and weapons taken from the body of a slain enemy (BAGD). **διαδίδωσιν** pres. ind. act. διαδίδωμι (# 1344) to distribute. ◆ **23 ὤν** pres. act. part. εἰμί (# 1639). Part. as subst. **συνάγων** pres. act. part. συνάγω (# 5251) to lead together, to gather together. Part. as subst. **σκορπίζει** pres. ind. act. σκορπίζω (# 5025) to scatter, to scatter out. The picture is one of gathering the flock of sheep, or scattering them (Marshall, Evans). ◆ **24 ἐξέλθῃ** aor. subj. act. ἐξέρχομαι (# 2002) to go out. Subj. w. **ὅταν** (# 4020) in an indef. temp. cl. **διέρχεται** pres. ind. mid. (dep.) διέρχομαι (# 1451) to pass through, to go through. **ἄνυδρος** (# 536) waterless (s. Matt. 12:43). **ζητοῦν** pres. act. part. ζητέω (# 2426) to seek. Part. of manner. **εὑρίσκον** pres. act. part. (temp.) s.v. 9. **ὑποστρέψω** fut. ind. act. ὑποστρέφω (# 5715) to turn back, to return. **ἐξῆλθον** aor. ind. act. ◆ **25 ἐλθόν** aor. act. part. (temp.) s.v. 2. **σεσαρωμένον** perf. pass. part. (adj.) σαρόω (# 4924) to sweep out, to clean. **κεκοσμημένον** perf. pass. part. (adj.) κοσμέω (# 3175) to arrange in order. Perf. parts. emphasize the state or cond. ◆ **26 πονηρότερα** comp. of πονηρός (# 4505) evil, wicked (TDNT; EDNT; NIDNTT). **ἑαυτοῦ** gen. of comp., than himself. **εἰσελθόντα** aor. act. part. (temp.) εἰσέρχομαι (# 1656) to go in. **κατοικεῖ** pres. ind. act. κατοικέω (# 2997) to dwell, to take up residence. Prep. in compound indicates taking up a permanent abode (Plummer). **χείρονα** (# 5937) comp. κακός bad; comp., worse. **πρώτων** gen. pl. πρῶτος (# 4755) first; gen. of comp. Pl., "the first things." ◆ **27 ἐγένετο** aor. ind. mid. (dep.) s.v. 1, w. prep. **ἐν** (# 1877) and inf. expressing time. **λέγειν** pres. act. inf. λέγω (# 3306) to speak. Inf. w. prep. for contemporaneous action. **ἐπάρασα** aor. act. part. (circum.) nom. fem. sing. ἐπαίρω (# 2048) to lift up. **κοιλία** (# 3120) womb, belly, abdomen (DMTG, 206). **βαστάσασα** aor. act. part. (adj.) βαστάζω (# 1002) to carry. **μαστοί** nom. pl. μαστός (# 3466) breast (DMTG, 231). **ἐθήλασας** aor. ind. act.

2nd. pers. sing. θηλάζω (# 2558) to suck, to nurse. ◆ **28 μενοῦν** (# 3528) rather. The word is used in a corrective sense: "What you have said is true as far as it goes, but the blessedness of Mary consists in the fact that she shares in the blessedness of those who hear the Word of God and keep it" (Thrall). **ἀκούοντες** pres. act. part. ἀκούω (# 201) to hear, to hear and obey. Pres. stresses the continual action. **φυλάσσοντες** pres. act. part. φυλάσσω (# 5875) to guard, to keep. Both parts. used as subst. ◆ **29 ἐπαθροιζομένων** pres. mid. part. (temp.) ἐπαθροίζω (# 2044) to throng together, to crowd upon. Prep. in compound is directive, indicating the concentration of the vb.'s action upon some object (MH, 312). Gen. abs. **ἤρξατο** aor. ind. mid. (dep.) ἄρχομαι (# 806) to begin, w. inf. **δοθήσεται** fut. ind. pass. s.v. 7. Theol. pass. indicating God as the Giver. ◆ **30 ἐγένετο** aor. ind. mid. (dep.) s.v. 1. ◆ **31 νότος** (# 3803) south. **ἐγερθήσεται** fut. ind. pass. s.v. 8. **κατακρινεῖ** fut. ind. act. κατακρίνω (# 2891) to condemn. **ἦλθεν** aor. ind. act. s.v. 2. **ἀκοῦσαι** aor. act. inf. s.v. 28. Inf. to express purp. **πλεῖον** comp. πολύς (# 4498) many, great; comp., greater (w. gen. of comp.). ◆ **32 ἀναστήσονται** fut. ind. mid. (dep.) s.v. 7. **μετενόησαν** aor. ind. act. μετανοέω (# 3566) to change one's mind, to repent. **εἰς** (# 1650) at, because of w. acc. For this meaning of the prep. s. BD, 112; DM, 104. ◆ **33 λύχνος** (# 3394) lamp, oil lamp (s. Matt. 5:15). **ἅψας** aor. act. part. (circum.) ἅπτω (# 721) to light. **κρύπτη** a dark and hidden place, a cellar. **τίθησιν** pres. act. ind. τίθημι (# 5502) to place, to put. Gnomic pres. **μόδιος** (# 3654) a bushel, a peck measure, a grain measure (s. Mark 4:21ff). **λυχνία** (# 3393) lampstand. **εἰσπορευόμενοι** pres. mid. (dep.) part. (temp.) εἰσπορεύομαι (# 1660) to go in. **βλέπωσιν** pres. subj. act. βλέπω (# 1063) to see. Subj. in purp. cl. ◆ **34 ἁπλοῦς** (# 604) single, as opposed to double or faulty and distorted vision (Arndt; Matt. 6:22). It would indicate that one should focus his or her eye on God alone, so that nothing can cause one to compromise integrity toward the Lord (Susan R. Garrett, "'Lest the Light in You Be Darkness': Luke 11:33-36 and the Question of Commitment," *JBL* 110 [1991]: 93-105, esp. 99). **ᾖ** pres. subj. act. εἰμί (# 1639) to be. Subj. w. **ὅταν** (# 4020) in an indef. temp. cl. **φωτεινός** (# 5893) shining, brilliant. **ἐπάν** (# 2054) whenever, after, w. subj. **σκοτεινός** (# 5027) dark. ◆ **35 σκόπει** pres. imp. act. σκοπέω (# 5023) to see, to look upon, to watch. **μή** (# 3590) whether. Here used like an indir. question (RG, 1045). ◆ **36 ἔχον** pres. act. part. ἔχω (# 2400) to have. **ἀστραπῇ** (# 847) dat. sing. flash, lightning. Instr. dat. **ἔσται** fut. ind. mid. (dep.) εἰμί (# 1639). Perhaps the fut. is to be taken as an imp. (Gottfried Nebe, "Das ἔσται in Lk 11,36–ein neuer Deutungsvorschlag," *ZNW* 83 [1992]: 108-14). **φωτίζῃ** pres. subj. act. φωτίζω (# 5894) to illuminate, to enlighten. Jesus warns those who will test him, by pointing out that on the Day of Judgement all will stand in heavenly light and the light will reveal those who are fully committed to Christ (Garrett, "Luke 11:33-36 and Commitment," *JBL* 110 [1991]: 105). ◆ 37 λαλῆσαι aor. act. inf. s.v. 14. Inf. w. prep. ἐν (# 1877) to express contemporaneous time, "while he is speaking...." ἐρωτᾷ pres. ind. act. ἐρωτάω (# 2263) to ask, to question. Hist. pres. ἀριστήσῃ aor. subj. act. ἀριστάω (# 753) to eat, to eat breakfast. It may be the morning meal after the return from morning prayers (RWP; SB, 2:204). The upper class Jews had two meals on weekdays, a light meal in mid-morning and a main meal in the late afternoon (Marshall). Subj. in indir. speech in a obj. cl. εἰσελθών aor. act. part. (circum.) s.v. 26. ἀνέπεσεν aor. ind. act. ἀναπίπτω (# 404) to recline, to fall back on a sofa or lounge (RWP). ◆ 38 ἰδών aor. act. part. (temp.) ὁράω (# 3972) to see. ἐθαύμασεν aor. ind. act. s.v. 14. ἐβαπτίσθη aor. ind. pass. βαπτίζω (# 966) to dip, to wash; pass. to wash oneself. The dir. mid. is probably causative since Jesus was a guest in a Pharisee's house, "did not first have himself washed" (GGBB, 424). For the washing of hands s. Matt. 15:2. ◆ 39 νῦν (# 3814) now (logical). ἔξωθεν (# 2033) outside. πίνακος gen. sing. πίναξ (# 4402) platter, dish. For household utensils s. JPFC, 2:740-43. καθαρίζετε pres. ind. act. καθαρίζω (# 2751) to clean. Habitual pres. ἔσωθεν (# 2277) inside. γέμει pres. ind. act. γέμω (# 1154) to be full of, w. gen. ἁρπαγή (# 771) robbery, robbing. It points to covetousness and greed (Arndt). ◆ 40 ἄφρονες voc. pl. ἄφρων (# 933) foolish, ignorant, pertaining to not employing one's understanding, particularly in practical matters (LN, 1:387). οὐχ (# 4024) neg. part. used in a question expecting a positive answer. ποιήσας aor. act. part. ποιέω (# 4472) to make. Part. as subst. ◆ 41 πλήν (# 4440) however, nevertheless. In this case, possibly introducing an inference (Thrall, 23; s. 22:21). ἐνόντα pres. act. part. ἔνειμι (# 1913) to be in; those things which are within; i.e., the heart. "Give your heart as alms, let your heart go out to the poor." For this and other suggestive meanings s. Arndt; Fitzmyer, 947. Part. as subst. δότε aor. imp. act. s.v. 3. ἐλεημοσύνη (# 1797) mercy, compassion, alms. ◆ 42 οὐαί (# 4026) woe, alas. Denotes a grieving giving up to judgment (Ellis). ἀποδεκατοῦτε pres. ind. act. ἀποδεκατόω (# 620) to pay a tenth, to tithe (JPB, 146-69; Matt. 23:23). ἡδύοσμον (# 2455) mint (POB, 139-40; PB, 88; Matt. 23:23). πήγανον (# 4379) rue. A strong-smelling herb w. gray-green leaves and lemon-yellow clusters of flowers (IDB, 4:129; POB, 208). λάχανον (# 3303) vegetable, plant. Whatever is used for food and is kept watch over and grows from the soil is subject to tithes (M, Maaseroth; also SB, 4:640-97). παρέρχεσθε pres. ind. mid. (dep.) παρέρχομαι (# 4216) to go by, to pass by, to neglect, to disobey. Habitual pres. ἔδει impf. ind. act. δεῖ (# 1256) it is necessary, w. inf. ποιῆσαι aor. act. inf. s.v. 40. παρεῖναι aor. act. inf. παρίημι (# 4223) to leave

undone, to neglect, to let pass (BAGD). ◆ 43 ἀγαπᾶτε pres. ind. act. ἀγαπάω (# 26) to love. Habitual pres. πρωτοκαθεδρία (# 4751) chief seat, place of honor, the best seat. This was a semicircular bench around the ark facing the congregation (Plummer). ◆ 44 μνημεῖα nom. pl. μνημεῖον (# 3646) tomb. Pred. nom. ἄδηλα nom. pl. ἄδηλος (# 83) unseen, inconspicuous. περιπατοῦντες pres. act. part. (adj.) περιπατέω (# 4344) to walk about. οἴδασιν perf. ind. act. s.v. 13. ◆ 45 ἀποκριθείς aor. pass. (dep.) part. s.v. 7. ὑβρίζεις pres. ind. act. ὑβρίζω (# 5614) to insult, to mistreat, to treat shamefully (MNTW; TDNT). ◆ 46 φορτίζετε pres. ind. act. φορτίζω (# 5844) to burden, to burden down; double acc. Habitual pres. φορτία acc. pl. φορτίον (# 5845) burden. δυσβάστακτα acc. pl. δυσβάστακτος (# 1546) difficult, heavy to bear. δακτύλων gen. pl. δάκτυλος (# 1235) finger. προσψαύετε pres. ind. act. προσψαύω (# 4718) to touch, w. dat. A term used by medical writers to describe the feeling, very gently, of a sore or tender part of the body or the pulse (MLL, 62). The scribes escape the obligations they place on others (Marshall). ◆ 47 οἰκοδομεῖτε pres. ind. act. οἰκοδομέω (# 3868) to build. Habitual pres. ἀπέκτειναν aor. ind. act. ἀποκτείνω (# 650) to kill. ◆ 48 συνευδοκεῖτε pres. ind. act. συνευδοκέω (# 5306) to approve of, to entirely approve of. ◆ 49 ἀποστελῶ fut. ind. act. ἀποστέλλω (# 690) to send, to send as an authoritative official representative. Fut. is like the Heb. prophetic perf., which views the fut. spoken of w. the certainty of a past event (Stein). ἀποκτενοῦσιν fut. ind. act. s.v. 47. διώξουσιν fut. ind. act. διώκω (# 1503) to persecute. ◆ 50 ἐκζητηθῇ aor. subj. pass. ἐκζητέω (# 1699) to require, to demand back, to require as a debt (Plummer). Subj. in a purp. cl. dependent on the vb. ἀποστέλλω in v. 49 (Marshall). Theol. pass., indicating that God holds them responsible. ἐκκεχυμένον perf. pass. part. ἐκχέω (# 1772) to pour out, to shed. Perf. stresses the state or cond. of lasting results. καταβολή (# 2856) foundation. ◆ 51 ἀπολομένου aor. mid. (dep.) part. (adj.) ἀπόλλυμι (# 660) to destroy, to loose; mid. to perish. μεταξύ (# 3568) between, w. gen. ἐκζητηθήσεται fut. ind. pass. s.v. 50. ◆ 52 ἤρατε aor. ind. act. αἴρω (# 149) to take away. κλεῖδα acc. sing. κλείς (# 3090) key. The key of knowledge is the key that opens the treasures of knowledge; it is the right interpretation of Scripture (Arndt). εἰσήλθατε aor. ind. act. s.v. 26. εἰσερχομένους pres. mid. (dep.) part. s.v. 26. Part. as subst. ἐκωλύσατε aor. ind. act. κωλύω (# 3266) to hinder. ◆ 53 ἐξελθόντος aor. act. part. (temp.) s.v. 14. Gen. abs., "after he had gone out...." ἤρξαντο aor. ind. mid. (dep.) s.v. 29, w. inf. δεινῶς (# 1267) adv., terribly. ἐνέχειν pres. act. inf. ἐνέχω (# 1923) to have it in for someone, to have a grudge against someone. ἀποστοματίζειν pres. act. inf. ἀποστοματίζω (# 694) to pry w. questions, to entice to answers. Originally to dictate what is to be learned by heart and recited (Plummer). **πλειόνων** comp. πολύς (# 4498) much, many. Comp. as the positive (BG, 50). ◆ **54 ἐνεδρεύοντες** pres. act. part. (circum.) ἐνεδρεύω (# 1910) to prepare an ambush, to lie in wait. **θηρεῦσαι** aor. act. inf. θηρεύω (# 2561) to ensnare, to catch in hunting, to hunt (RWP). Inf. of purp. Their purp. was ultimately to kill him.

Luke 12

◆ **1 ἐν οἷς** in which things or circumstances, in the meantime (RWP). **ἐπισυναχθεισῶν** aor. pass. part. (temp.) ἐπισυνάγω (# 2190) to gather together. Gen. abs. **καταπατεῖν** pres. act. inf. καταπατέω (# 2922) to trample on, to walk on. Inf. w. **ὥστε** (# 6063) to express result. **ἤρξατο** aor. ind. mid. (dep.) ἄρχομαι (# 806) to begin, w. inf. **προσέχετε** pres. imp. act. προσέχω (# 4668) to beware, to take heed. Pres. imp. calls for a continual attitude. ◆ **2 συγκεκαλυμμένον** perf. pass. part. συγκαλύπτω (# 5158) to hide, to conceal completely, to cover up. Perf. looks at the completed cond. w. abiding results. Part. as subst. **ἀποκαλυφθήσεται** fut. ind. pass. ἀποκαλύπτω (# 636) to uncover, to reveal. **γνωσθήσεται** fut. ind. pass. γινώσκω (# 1182) to know. ◆ **3 ἀνθ' ὧν** = ἀντὶ ὧν (# 505; 4005) on account of which things, because. Or it may mean "therefore" (Marshall). **εἴπατε** aor. ind. act. λέγω (# 3306) to say, to speak. **ἀκουσθήσεται** fut. ind. pass. ἀκούω (# 201) to hear. **ἐλαλήσατε** aor. ind. act. λαλέω (# 3281) to speak. **ταμιεῖον** (# 5421) store chamber, secret room. **κηρυχθήσεται** fut. ind. pass. κηρύσσω (# 3062) to proclaim, to herald. For a discussion of these vv. s. JMJ, 159-60. ◆ **4 φίλοις** dat. pl. φίλος (# 5813) friend. It is as companions of Jesus that the disciples are esp. precious to God (Evans, 11:5). Apposition, indir. obj. **φοβηθῆτε** aor. subj. pass. (dep.) φοβέομαι (# 5828) to be afraid, to fear; w. prep. **ἀπό** (# 608) "to be afraid of" (KVS, 29-30). Subj. w. the neg. is used to prohibit the starting of an action. **ἀποκτεινόντων** pres. act. part. ἀποκτείνω (# 650) to kill. Part. as subst. **μετὰ ταῦτα** (# 3552; 4047) after these things. **ἐχόντων** pres. act. part. ἔχω (# 2400) to have. Part. as subst. **περισσότερον** (# 4358) comp. περισσός remarkable (s. 7:26). **ποιῆσαι** aor. act. inf. ποιέω (# 4472) to do. Inf. as dir. obj. ◆ **5 ὑποδείξω** fut. ind. act. ὑποδείκνυμι (# 5683) to show. **φοβήθητε** aor. imp. pass. (dep.), here w. acc. s.v. 4. Aor. imp. gives a note of urgency (VANT, 339-40). **ἀποκτεῖναι** aor. act. inf. s.v. 4. Inf. w. prep. **μέτα** (# 3552) expressing subsequent time: "after he has killed" (VA, 388). **ἔχοντα** pres. act. part. s.v. 4. Part. as subst. referring to God (Fitzmyer, 959). **ἐμβαλεῖν** aor. act. inf. ἐμβάλλω (# 1833) to throw into. Epex. inf. explaining **ἐξουσίαν. γέεννα** (# 1147) the valley Gehenna, hell (Fitzmyer, 959; TDNT; DJG, 310-11; Mark 9:43). **ναί** (# 3721) yes, certainly. ◆ **6 οὐχί** (# 4049) strengthened form of οὐ, not. Used in a question expecting the answer "yes." **στρου-**

θίον (# 5141) dimin. sparrow. Sparrows were regarded as good to eat and sought after by the poor since they were very inexpensive (Fitzmyer, 960; SB, 1:583; LAE, 272-74; BBC). **πωλοῦνται** pres. ind. pass. πωλέω (# 4797) to sell; pass. to offer for sale. Iterat. pres. **ἀσσαρίων** gen. pl. ἀσσάριον (# 837) the sixteenth part of a denarius worth approximately one cent (Arndt). Gen. of price. **ἐπιλελησμένον** perf. pass. part. ἐπιλανθάνομαι (# 2140) to forget, to be forgotten, to neglect, overlook, care nothing about, to escape one's notice (BAGD). Perf. indicates the state or cond. ◆ **7 τρίχες** nom. pl. θρίξ (# 2582) hair. **ἠρίθμηνται** perf. ind. pass. ἀριθμέω (# 749) to count; pass. to be counted. Perf. indicates the lasting results. **φοβεῖσθε** pres. imp. mid. (dep.) s.v. 4. W. the neg. **μή** (# 3590), "stop being afraid" or "do not always be afraid." **διαφέρετε** pres. ind. act. w. gen. διαφέρω (# 1422) to differ, to be superior to (Plummer; s. Matt. 10:29). The difference is not quantitative, but qualitative (Fitzmyer, 960). Pres. indicates the continual state. ◆ **8 ὃς ἄν** (# 4005; 165) whoever. **ὁμολογήσῃ** aor. subj. act. ὁμολογέω (# 3933) to agree, to confess. The expression w. prep. is Semitic and means "to state about a person what one knows to be true" (Arndt). Subj. in an indef. rel. cl. **ὁμολογήσει** fut. ind. act. ὁμολογέω (# 3933) to confess. ◆ **9 ἀρνησάμενος** aor. mid. (dep.) part. ἀρνέομαι (# 766) to say no, to deny. Part. as subst. **ἀπαρνηθήσεται** fut. ind. pass. ἀπαρνέομαι (# 565) to deny. Prep. in compound is perfective (MH, 298). Theol. pass. indicating that God is the subject of the action. ◆ **10 ἐρεῖ** fut. ind. act. λέγω (# 3306) to speak. Fut. used indef. in a cond.-like statement (VA, 432; BD, 192). **εἰς** (# 1650) against. **ἀφεθήσεται** fut. ind. pass. ἀφίημι (# 918) to release, to forgive, w. dat. (TDNT; EDNT; Fitzmyer, 965). Theol. pass. indicating that God is the one who forgives. **βλασφημήσαντι** aor. act. part. dat. sing. βλασφημέω (# 1059) to slander, to blaspheme (TDNT; NIDNTT; EDNT). Part. as subst. Dat. w. vb. ◆ **11 εἰσφέρωσιν** pres. subj. act. εἰσφέρω (# 1662) to bring into, to lead in. Subj. w. **ὅταν** (# 4020) in an indef. temp. cl. **μεριμνήσητε** aor. subj. act. μεριμνάω (# 3534) to be concerned, to be anxious. Subj. used to express a prohibition. **ἀπολογήσησθε** aor. subj. pass. ἀπολογέομαι (# 664) to defend oneself. Subj. in a prohibition. **εἴπητε** aor. subj. act. s.v. 10. Subj. in a prohibition. ◆ **12 διδάξει** fut. ind. act. διδάσκω (# 1438) to teach. **δεῖ** (# 1256) pres. ind. act. it is necessary, giving a logical necessity; w. inf. **εἰπεῖν** aor. act. inf. s.v. 10. ◆ **13 εἰπέ** aor. imp. act. s.v. 10. Aor. imp. for a specific request. **μερίσασθαι** aor. mid. inf. μερίζω (# 3532) to divide; mid. to divide something w. another. Inf. in indir. speech. For a copy of a will and a discussion of inheritance s. NDIEC, 6:27-47; for Jewish regulations s. M, Baba Bathra, 8-9; SB, 3:545-53. ◆ **14 κατέστησεν** aor. ind. act. καθίστημι (# 2770) to appoint, to constitute, w. double acc. **μεριστής** (# 3537) divider, one who divides.

◆ **15 ὁρᾶτε** pres. imp. act. ὁράω (# 3972) to see, to beware. Pres. imp. calls for a continual attitude. **φυλάσσεσθε** pres. imp. mid. (dir. mid.) φυλάσσω (# 5875) to guard; mid. to guard oneself against something, to look out for, to avoid (BAGD). **πλεονεξία** (# 4432) covetousness, greediness. The greedy desire to have more, a strong desire to acquire more and more material possessions or to possess more things than other people have, all irrespective of need (Plummer; LN, 1:291-92; MNTW; TDNT). **περισσεύειν** pres. act. inf. περισσεύω (# 4355) to be in abundance. Inf. w. prep. as a subst., or epex. (MT, 146; RWP). ◆ **16 πλούσιος** (# 4454) rich, very rich. **εὐφόρησεν** aor. ind. act. εὐφορέω (# 2369) to produce well, to be fruitful. It was a covenant blessing to have a good harvest (Deut. 28:8). The word was used by Josephus of a plentiful olive crop in Galilee (Jos., J.W., 2:592). In medical writers it was used of a woman who was fruitful, or of countries or climates producing disease (MLL, 144). ◆ **17 διελογίζετο** impf. ind. mid. (dep.) διαλογίζομαι (# 1368) to consider, to think over, to reason. Impf. pictures the continual action in the past, or is incep.: "he began to reason." **ποιήσω** aor. subj. act. ποιέω (# 4472) to do, to make. Deliberative subj. in a question of contemplation. **συνάξω** fut. ind. act. συνάγω (# 5251) to gather together, to harvest. ◆ **18 καθελῶ** fut. ind. act. καθαιρέω (# 2747) to tear down. Volitive fut. indicating purp. and determination of the will (RG, 874). **ἀποθήκας** acc. pl. ἀποθήκη (# 630) storehouse, granary, barn. There were large grain silos in Sepphoris (BBC). **μείζονας** (# 3505) comp. μέγας great; comp., greater. **οἰκοδομήσω** fut. ind. act. οἰκοδομέω (# 3868) to build. Volitive fut. ◆ **19 ἐρῶ** fut. ind. act. λέγω (# 3306) to say. Volitive fut. **κείμενα** pres. mid. part. (adj.) κεῖμαι (# 3023) to lie. Here used of goods stored up. **ἀναπαύου** pres. imp. mid. (dep.) ἀναπαύομαι to rest, to take one's rest. Pres. imp. views the continual action expected by the rich farmer. **φάγε** aor. imp. act. ἐσθίω (# 2266) to eat. **πίε** aor. imp. act. πίνω (# 4403) to drink. Aor. imps. look at the specific actions within the expected period. **εὐφραίνου** pres. imp. mid. (dep.) εὐφραίνομαι (# 2370) to be happy. Pres. imp. stresses the continual action as habitual. Note the frequency of the egotistic assertions marking the superficial self-confidence of the speaker (Fitzmyer, 973). ◆ **20 ἄφρων** (# 933) voc. sing. without reason, senseless, foolish, expressing a reckless and inconsiderate habit of mind (AS). **ἀπαιτοῦσιν** pres. ind. act. ἀπαιτέω (# 555) to ask from someone, to require. Impersonal pl. (GGBB, 403). The rabbis used the 3rd. pl. to avoid saying "God" (RWP). Futuristic pres. **ἡτοίμασας** aor. ind. act. 2nd. pers. sing. ἑτοιμάζω (# 2286) to prepare. **τίνι** dat. sing. τίς (# 5515) interrogative pron. what? Dat. of advantage or possession. **ἔσται** fut. ind. mid. (dep.) εἰμί (# 1639) to be. ◆ **21 θησαυρίζων** pres. act. part. θησαυρίζω (# 2564) to treasure

up. Habitual pres. Part. as subst. **ἑαυτῷ** (# 1571) dat. sing. refl. pron. Dat. of interest ("for himself"). **πλουτῶν** pres. act. part. πλουτέω (# 4456) to be rich. W. prep. **εἰς** (# 1650), "to be rich in," or "toward God" (BAGD). ◆ **22 μεριμνᾶτε** pres. imp. act. μεριμνάω (# 3534) to be concerned about, to worry about, to have anxious concern (LN, 1:313; Bovon). Pres. imp. w. neg. prohibits an attitude. **ψυχῇ** (# 6034) dat. sing. soul, life; it refers to the whole human being (Stein). Dat. of interest (BD, 101). **φάγητε** aor. subj. act. s.v. 19. Deliberative subj. in indir. discourse, s.v. 17. **ἐνδύσησθε** aor. subj. mid. (dep.) ἐνδύομαι (# 1907) to put on, to clothe oneself. ◆ **23 πλεῖον** comp. πολύς (# 4498) much; comp., more. **τροφῆς** gen. sing. τροφή (# 5575) nourishment, food, sustenance. Gen. of comp. **ἐνδύματος** gen. sing. ἔνδυμα (# 1903) clothing. Gen. of comp. ◆ **24 κατανοήσατε** aor. imp. act. κατανοέω (# 2917) to understand, to take knowledge of, to perceive, to give careful consideration to some matter, to think very carefully, to consider closely (LN, 1:350). **κόρακας** acc. pl. κόραξ (# 3165) crow, raven. The name covers the whole of the crow tribe (Plummer). They are cared for by God even though they are unclean birds (Fitzmyer, 978). **σπείρουσιν** pres. ind. act. σπείρω (# 5062) to sow seed. Gnomic pres. **θερίζουσιν** pres. ind. act. θερίζω (# 2545) to harvest. **τρέφει** pres. ind. act. τρέφω (# 5555) to nourish, to sustain. Gnomic pres. indicating that which is always true. **πόσῳ μᾶλλον** by how much more? For this construction s. 11:13. ◆ **25 μεριμνῶν** pres. act. part. s.v. 22. Part. of means ("by being concerned"). **ἡλικία** (# 2461) stature, a measure of space used here for a small unit of time ("age") (Arndt). **προσθεῖναι** aor. act. inf. προστίθημι (# 4707) to add to. Inf. after the vb. **δύναται**. **πῆχυς** (# 4388) cubit, a measure of length about 18 inches (BAGD). Here it may refer to a temp. measurement: "a small amount of time on one's life" (Stein; Fitzmyer, 978-79). ◆ **26 οὖν** (# 4036) therefore, draws a conclusion from the preceding. **ἐλάχιστον** (# 1788) superl. ὀλίγος small, slight; superl., least, smallest. **δύνασθε** pres. ind. pass. (dep.) δύναμαι (# 1538) to be able. Ind. in a 1st. class cond. cl., assuming the reality of the cond. **μεριμνᾶτε** pres. ind. act. s.v. 22. ◆ **27 κατανοήσατε** aor. imp. act. s.v. 24. **κρίνα** acc. pl. κρίνον (# 3211) lily. The word is used generically for many lily-like flowers; beautiful wild flowers (Fitzmyer, 979; PB, 169). **κοπιᾷ** pres. ind. act. κοπιάω (# 3159) to work. Gnomic pres. **νήθει** pres. ind. act. νήθω (# 3756) to spin. **περιεβάλετο** aor. ind. mid. περιβάλλω (# 4314) to put around oneself, to clothe. ◆ **28 χόρτος** (# 5965) grass. **ὄντα** pres. act. part. (adj.) εἰμί (# 1639) to be. **αὔριον** (# 892) tomorrow. **κλίβανος** (# 3106) oven, furnace. **βαλλόμενον** pres. pass. part. (adj.) βάλλω (# 965) to throw, to cast. Gnomic pres. **ἀμφιέζει** pres. ind. act. ἀμφιάζω, ἀμφιέζω (# 313) to clothe. For the form s. BD, 39. **πόσῳ μᾶλλον** by how much more (s. 11:13). **ὀλιγόπιστοι** (*# 3899*) voc. pl. small faith, little faith. ◆ **29 ζητεῖτε** pres. imp. act. ζητέω (*# 2426*) to seek. Pres. imp. w. neg. **μή** (*# 3590*) forbids an attitude. **φάγητε** aor. subj. act. s.v. 22. **πίητε** aor. subj. act. πίνω (*# 4403*) to drink. **μετεωρίζεσθε** pres. imp. pass. μετεωρίζω (*# 3577*) to be raised from the ground, suspended in midair, to be anxious, to be worried, to be put in a state of anxiety (Arndt; BAGD; EDNT; MM; TDNT; TLNT; CCFJ, 3:99; Jos., *Ant.*, 16.135). Permissive pass., "do not let yourself be worried." ◆ **30 ἐπιζητοῦσιν** pres. ind. act. ἐπιζητέω (*# 2118*) to seek, to look for. Pres. indicates the constant attitude. **οἶδεν** perf. ind. act. οἶδα (*# 3857*) to know. Def. perf. w. pres. meaning. **χρῄζετε** pres. ind. act. χρῄζω (*# 5974*) to need, w. obj. in gen. ◆ **31 πλήν** (*# 4440*) however, adversative use (Thrall, 21; s. 22:21). **ζητεῖτε** pres. imp. act. s.v. 29. Pres. imp. calls for continual action or lifestyle. **προστεθήσεται** fut. ind. pass. s.v. 25. For the imp. followed by the fut. as a type of cond. sentence s. 10:28. ◆ **32 φοβοῦ** pres. imp. mid. (dep.) s.v. 4. Pres. imp. w. neg. forbids a continual attitude of fear. **εὐδόκησεν** aor. ind. act. εὐδοκέω (*# 2305*) to have pleasure, to be pleased. **δοῦναι** aor. act. inf. δίδωμι (*# 1443*) to give. Epex. inf. explaining εὐδόκησεν. ◆ **33 πωλήσατε** aor. imp. act. πωλέω (*# 4797*) to sell. Aor. imp. calls for a specific act. **ὑπάρχοντα** pres. act. part. ὑπάρχω (*# 5639*) to exist, to be at one's disposal. Part. as subst.: what belongs to someone, property, possessions (BAGD). **δότε** aor. imp. act. s.v. 32. **ἐλεημοσύνη** (*# 1797*) compassion, alms, contribution (TDNT; EDNT; NIDNTT; TLNT; SB, 4:536-58; Stein, 52-54). **ποιήσατε** aor. imp. act. ποιέω (*# 4472*) to make. **βαλλάντιον** (*# 964*) moneybag, purse. The following phrase indicates that this refers to receptacles for heavenly treasure (Marshall). **παλαιούμενα** pres. pass. part. (adj.) παλαιόω (*# 4096*) to make old; pass. to become old. **ἀνέκλειπτος** (*# 444*) unfailing, inexhaustible. **σής** (*# 4962*) moth. **διαφθείρει** pres. ind. act. διαφθείρω (*# 1425*) to corrupt, to spoil, to destroy. Prep. in compound is perfective. ◆ **34 καί** (*# 2779*) also. **ἔσται** fut. ind. mid. (dep.) εἰμί (*# 1639*) to be. ◆ **35 ἔστωσαν** pres. imp. act. 3rd. pers. pl. εἰμί (*# 1639*). **ὀσφῦς** (*# 4019*) hips, waist. **περιεζωσμέναι** perf. pass. part. περιζώννυμι (*# 4322*) to fasten up the garments w. a belt, to adjust the long ankle-length robe to ensure readiness for action or departure; a commom OT instruction for readiness or service (Fitzmyer, 987). Part. used in a perf. pass. periphrastic imp. construction. Perf. has the meaning, "be the kind of person who never needs to be told to gird them up, because he will always live in this cond." (GI, 41). **καιόμενοι** pres. pass. part. καίω (*# 2794*) to light, to keep burning, to burn (BAGD). Periphrastic pres. imp., "already burning and continuously burning" (RWP). ◆ **36 προσδεχομένοις** pres. mid. (dep.) part. (adj.) προσδέχομαι (*# 4657*) to await, to expect. Dat. w. the adj. **ὅμοιοι** ("like"). **ἀναλύσῃ** aor. subj.

act. ἀναλύω (*# 386*) to break up, to loose, to untie, to depart, to return. The picture is the breaking up of a feast or a camp (Plummer). Subj. in an indir. question w. the interrogative adv. **ποτέ** when (RWP; BAGD). **γάμων** gen. pl. γάμος (*# 1141*) marriage, wedding; pl. wedding celebration or simply banquet (Marshall). **ἐλθόντος** aor. act. part. (temp.) ἔρχομαι (*# 2262*) to go, to come. Gen. abs. **κρούσαντος** aor. act. part. (temp.) κρούω (*# 3218*) to knock. Gen. abs. **ἀνοίξωσιν** aor. subj. act. ἀνοίγνυμι, ἀνοίγω (*# 487*) to open. Subj. w. **ἵνα** (*# 2671*) in a purp. cl. ◆ **37 ἐλθών** aor. act. part. (temp.) s.v. 36. **εὑρήσει** fut. ind. act. εὑρίσκω (*# 2351*) to find. **γρηγοροῦντας** pres. act. part. (adj.) γρηγορέω (*# 1213*) to remain awake, to watch. **περιζώσεται** fut. ind. mid. s.v. 35. **ἀνακλινεῖ** fut. ind. act. ἀνακλίνω (*# 369*) to cause to recline, esp. at a table. **παρελθών** aor. act. part. (temp.) παρέρχομαι (*# 4216*) to go along, to come to, to come. **διακονήσει** fut. ind. act. διακονέω (*# 1354*) to serve, esp. at the table. ◆ **38 φυλακῇ** (*# 5871*) dat. sing. guard, watch. The Jewish system was to divide the night into 3 equal watches, each having 4 hours (6-10, 10-2, 2-6), but the Roman system had 4 watches of 3 hours (6-9, 9-12, 12-3, 3-6) (SB, 1:688-91; Fitzmyer, 988). Dat. of time: "sometime in the second or third watch." **ἔλθη** aor. subj. act. s.v. 36. Subj. in a 3rd. class cond. cl., which assumes the possibility of the cond. **εὕρη** aor. subj. act. s.v. 37. ◆ **39 γινώσκετε** pres. imp. act. γινώσκω (*# 1182*) to know. **ᾔδει** plperf. ind. act. οἶδα s.v. 30. Ind. in a 2nd. class cond. cl., w. a contrary to fact. cond. **ἀφῆκεν** aor. ind. act. ἀφίημι (*# 918*) to allow, to permit. **διορυχθῆναι** aor. pass. inf. διορύσσω (*# 1482*) to dig through, to break in. Epex. inf. explaining what would not be allowed. ◆ **40 γίνεσθε** pres. imp. mid. (dep.) γίνομαι (*# 1181*) to become, to be. Pres. imp. calls for continual state of readiness. **ἕτοιμος** (*# 2289*) ready, prepared. Pred. nom. **δοκεῖτε** pres. ind. act. δοκέω (*# 1506*) to suppose, to think. ◆ **42 ἄρα** (*# 726*) then, therefore. Used in questions to draw an inference from what precedes, or simply to enliven the question (BAGD). **οἰκονόμος** (*# 3874*) steward, a trusted slave commissioned w. the responsibility of the oversight of various duties in the household (TDNT; NIDNTT; EDNT). **φρόνιμος** (*# 5861*) wise, understanding, resulting from insight and wisdom (LN, 1:384). **καταστήσει** fut. ind. act. καθίστημι (*# 2770*) to appoint, to commission. **θεραπεία** (*# 2542*) ministry, household, a body of domestic servants (RWP). **διδόναι** pres. act. inf. δίδωμι (*# 1443*) to give. Inf. of purp. **σιτομέτριον** (*# 4991*) acc. sing. a measured portion of food, ration (Plummer). ◆ **43 ποιοῦντα** pres. act. part. (adj.) s.v. 33. ◆ **45 εἴπη** aor. subj. act. λέγω (*# 3306*) to say. Subj. w. **ἐάν** (*# 1569*) in a 3rd. class cond. cl. assuming the possibility of the cond. **χρονίζει** pres. ind. act. χρονίζω (*# 5988*) to take time, to delay. With his absence the slave could abuse his authoritiy (BBC). **ἔρχεσθαι** pres. mid. (dep.) inf. s.v.

36. Epex. inf. explaining the vb. **χρονίζει**. **ἄρξηται** aor. subj. mid. (dep.) ἄρχομαι (# 806) to begin, w. inf. **τύπτειν** pres. act. inf. τύπτω (# 5597) to beat. **ἐσθίειν** pres. act. inf. ἐσθίω (# 2266) to eat. **πίνειν** pres. act. inf. πίνω (# 4403) to drink. **μεθύσκεσθαι** pres. mid. (dep.) inf. μεθύσκομαι (# 3499) to be drunk, to become drunk, to get drunk. ◆ **46 ἥξει** fut. ind. act. ἥκω (# 2457) to come. **προσδοκᾷ** pres. ind. act. προσδοκάω (# 4659) to expect. **διχοτομήσει** fut. ind. act. διχοτομέω (# 1497) to cut in two pieces. This could be literal or metaphorical (Marshall). **θήσει** fut. ind. act. τίθημι (# 5502) to place, to give. ◆ **47 γνούς** aor. act. part. (adj.) s.v. 39. **ἑτοιμάσας** aor. act. part. (adj.) ἑτοιμάζω (# 2286) to be ready, to be prepared. **ποιήσας** aor. act. part. s.v. 33. **δαρήσεται** fut. ind. pass. δέρω (# 1296) to skin, to flay, to flog. For customs regarding old Jewish slavery s. SB, 4:698-744; for the beating of a slave s. NDIEC, 4:63-67. ◆ **48 ὀλίγος** (# 3900) few. Adj. w. subst. ("blows") to be supplied (BD, 85). The punishment of the one who sinned in ignorance is less severe (Stein). **ἐδόθη** aor. ind. pass. s.v. 32. Theol. pass. **ζητηθήσεται** fut. ind. pass. ζητέω (# 2426) to seek, to require. Theol. pass.: God gives and God requires. **παρέθεντο** aor. ind. mid. (dep.) παρατίθημι (# 4192) to give over, to commit, to entrust. **περισσότερον** (# 4358) comp. περισσός remarkable (s. 7:26). **αἰτήσουσιν** fut. ind. act. αἰτέω (# 160) to ask from someone, to require great endowments or a great responsibility, w. acc. (Arndt). ◆ **49 ἦλθον** aor. ind. act. s.v. 36. **βαλεῖν** aor. act. inf. βάλλω (# 965) to cast, to throw. Inf. of purp. **τί θέλω εἰ** "How I wish that..." (RWP). **ἀνήφθη** aor. ind. pass. ἀνάπτω (# 409) to kindle, to set on fire. Fire may indicate how the coming of God's Kingdom divides people into two camps (Stein; Marshall). ◆ **50 βαπτισθῆναι** aor. pass. inf. βαπτίζω (# 966) to baptize; in a metaphorical sense of being overwhelmed by a catastrophe (Marshall; Stein). Epex. inf. explaining the word **βάπτισμα** (# 967). **συνέχομαι** pres. ind. pass. συνέχω (# 5309) pass. to be afflicted, to suffer. **τελεσθῇ** aor. subj. pass. τελέω (# 5464) to complete, to finish, to end. Subj. in an indef. temp. cl. ◆ **51 παρεγενόμην** aor. ind. mid. (dep.) παραγίνομαι (# 4134) to arrive, to come. **δοῦναι** aor. act. inf. s.v. 32. Inf. of purp. **διαμερισμός** (# 1375) division. ◆ **52 ἔσονται** fut. ind. mid. (dep.) εἰμί (# 1639) to be. **διαμεμερισμένοι** perf. pass. part. (adj.) διαμερίζω (# 1374) to divide, to divide into. ◆ **53 διαμερισθήσονται** fut. ind. pass. s.v. 52. ◆ **54 ἴδητε** aor. subj. act. ὁράω (# 3972) to see. Subj. in an indef. temp. cl. **ἀνατέλλουσαν** pres. act. part. (adj.) ἀνατέλλω (# 422) to rise. **δυσμῶν** gen. pl. δυσμή (# 1553) going down, setting of the sun; pl. west. **ὄμβρος** (# 3915) rain. Generally the rain came from the Mediterranean in the west. For the rain and climate in Palestine s. GB, 41-66; NIVAB, 24-26; ABD, 5:119-26. ◆ **55 νότος** (# 3803) south wind. Dir. obj. of **ἴδητε**. **πνέοντα** pres. act. part. (adj.) πνέω (# 4463)

to blow. **καύσων** (# 3014) hot, burning. "It will be a scorcher!" (Fitzmyer, 1000). For a vivid description of the hot winds s. GB, 67-70. ◆ **56 δοκιμάζειν** pres. act. inf. δοκιμάζω (# 1507) to examine, to prove, to come to a conclusion after an examination. Inf. as obj. of the vb. **οἴδατε** ("You know how to") perf. ind. act. οἶδα (# 3857). Def. perf. w. pres. meaning. ◆ **57 κρίνετε τὸ δίκαιον** judge the right, pronounce just judgment (LAE, 117). ◆ **58 ἀντίδικος** (# 508) opponent, adversary in a law case. **δός** aor. imp. act. δίδωμι (# 1443) to give. Used w. **ἐργασίαν** (# 2238) as a Latinism meaning "to take pains," "to make an effort" (BAGD; LAE, 116). **ἀπηλλάχθαι** perf. pass. inf. ἀπαλλάσσω (# 557) to free; pass. to be released from, to be rid of. Used here in a legal sense where the perf. emphasizes a state of completion: "to be rid of him for good" (RWP). It was used in the papyri of one getting rid of the plots of evil men (NDIEC, 4:155; MM). **κατασύρῃ** pres. subj. act. κατασύρω (# 2955) to drag away. Subj. in a neg. result cl. **παραδώσει** fut. ind. act. παραδίδωμι (# 4140) to deliver over, to turn over. **πράκτωρ** (# 4551) officer, the subordinate officer carrying out the judgment of the court, the officer of a debtor's court (Arndt; Fitzmyer, 1003; Marshall). **βαλεῖ** fut. ind. act. βάλλω (# 965) to throw, to cast. For a discussion of debt obligations s. NDIEC, 6:99-105. ◆ **59 ἐξέλθῃς** aor. subj. act. ἐξέρχομαι (# 2002) to come out. Subj. w. double neg. for a strong prohibition. **λεπτόν** (# 3321) acc. sing. a small copper coin worth about one-eighth of a cent (BAGD; s. Mark 12:42). **ἀποδῷς** aor. subj. act. ἀποδίδωμι (# 625) to give back, to pay back. Subj. in an indef. temp. cl.

Luke 13

◆ **1 παρῆσαν** impf. ind. act. πάρειμι (# 4205) to be present, to come. Impf., "they had come," "they had just arrived" (BAGD; Fitzmyer, 1006). **ἀπαγγέλλοντες** pres. act. part. (circum.) ἀπαγγέλλω (# 550) to report. **ἔμιξεν** aor. ind. act. μείγνυμι (# 3502) to mix. It has been suggested that this incident occurred at a Passover, perhaps the year before Jesus' death (Ellis; HA, 175ff; for Pilate s. TJ, 51-57; DJG, 615-17). ◆ **2 ἀποκριθείς** aor. pass. (dep.) part. ἀποκρίνομαι (# 646) to answer. For the Semitic construction s. MH, 453. **δοκεῖτε** pres. ind. act. δοκέω (# 1506) to suppose. **παρά** (# 4123) more than. **ἐγένοντο** aor. ind. mid. (dep.) γίνομαι (# 1181) to become, to be. **πεπόνθασιν** perf. ind. act. πάσχω (# 4248) to suffer. ◆ **3 μετανοῆτε** pres. subj. act. μετανοέω (# 3566) to change the mind, to repent. Subj. w. **ἐάν** (# 1569) in a 3rd. class cond. cl. in which the speaker assumes the possibility of the cond. **ἀπολεῖσθε** fut. ind. mid. ἀπόλλυμι (# 660) to perish. ◆ **4 ἔπεσεν** aor. ind. act. πίπτω (# 4406) to fall. **πύργος** (# 4788) tower. **ἀπέκτεινεν** aor. ind. act. ἀποκτείνω (# 650) to kill. **ὀφειλέτης** (# 4050) debtor, sinner. The idea of sin as a debt to God was well-known (TDNT; EDNT; WJ, 334-44). **κατοι-**

κοῦντας pres. act. part. κατοικέω (# 2997) to dwell, to live. Part. as subst. ◆ 5 οὐχί (# 4049) introduces a question which expects a positive answer. ὡσαύτως (# 6058) likewise, in the same manner. ◆ 6 εἶχεν impf. ind. act. ἔχω (# 2400) to have. πεφυτευμένην perf. pass. part. (adj.) φυτεύω (# 5885) to plant. ἀμπελών (# 308) vineyard. For the planting and cultivating of a vineyard s. Pliny, NH, 17:156-214; Columella, *De Arboribus*, 21; BBC. ἦλθεν aor. ind. act. ἔρχομαι (# 2262) to come. ζητῶν pres. act. part. ζητέω (# 2426) to seek, to look for. Part. expressing purp. "I have come in order to seek fruit." εὗρεν aor. ind. act. εὑρίσκω (# 2351) to find. ◆ 7 ἀμπελουργός (# 307) vineyard keeper (SB, 1:869-75). ἔτη nom. pl. ἔτος (# 2291) year; parenthetical nom. used to express time (BD, 79). It was four years from the time of planting that mature fruit was expected (LNT, 295; M, Orlah; Lev. 19:23-25). Here the three years are counted from the time when the fig tree would normally be expected to bear, not from the time of planting (RWP). ἔκκοψον aor. imp. act. ἐκκόπτω (# 1716) to cut off. ἱνατί (# 2672) why? καί (# 2779) also, in addition (Plummer). καταργεῖ pres. ind. act. καταργέω (# 2934) to make idle, to make ineffective, to use up. ◆ 8 ἄφες aor. imp. act. ἀφίημι (# 918) to allow. ἔτος acc. sing. s.v. 7. Acc. of time expressing duration. σκάψω aor. subj. act. σκάπτω (# 4999) to dig. Subj. w. ἕως ὅπου (# 2401; 3963) in a temp. cl. βάλω aor. subj. act. βάλλω (# 965) to throw. κόπρια acc. pl. κόπριον (# 3162) manure, fertilizer. For the work of digging and fertilizing s. SB, 2:198. ◆ 9 ποιήσῃ aor. subj. act. ποιέω (# 4472) to make, to produce. Subj. in 3rd. class cond. cl., assuming the possibility of the cond. τὸ μέλλον (# 3516) next year, for the future. For the construction of this sentence in the suppression or breaking off under the influence of strong emotion s. Arndt; RG, 1203; NTNT, 67. εἰ δὲ μή γε (# 1623; 1254; 3590; 1145) but if not, otherwise, w. γε used for greater emphasis (Thrall, 10). ἐκκόψεις fut. ind. act. s.v. 7. Fut. used to express a command. The parable applies to the need of Israel and its religious leaders to repent before God's coming judgment (Arndt; IP, 269). ◆ 10 διδάσκων pres. act. part. διδάσκω (# 1438) to teach. Part. in a periphrastic construction highlighting the continual action in the past. ◆ 11 ἔχουσα pres. act. part. ἔχω (# 2400) to have. ἀσθένεια (# 819) weakness, sickness. "A spirit of infirmity" may be an Aramaism, indicating that the sickness was caused by this spirit (Fitzmyer, 1012; SB, 2:198; 4:i, 521, 524-26). ἔτη acc. pl. s.v. 7. Acc. of time expressing duration. συγκύπτουσα pres. act. part. συγκύπτω (# 5174) to bend together. Medical word for curvature of the spine (RWP). The illness has been diagnosed as *spondylitis ankylopoitica* or *skoliasis hysterica* (Marshall). δυναμένη pres. pass. (dep.) part. δύναμαι (# 1538) to be able, w. inf. ἀνακύψαι aor. act. inf. ἀνακύπτω (# 376) to bend up, to raise oneself up, to stand erect. Galen used it of

straightening the vertebrae of the spine (MLL, 21). εἰς τὸ παντελές (# 1650; 4117) complete, at all. Either to be taken w. inf. ("to raise herself at all") or w. part. ("completely unable") (Marshall). ◆ 12 ἰδών aor. act. part. (temp.) ὁράω (# 3972) to see. προσεφώνησεν aor. ind. act. προσφωνέω (# 4715) to call to. ἀπολέλυσαι perf. ind. pass. 2nd. pers. sing. ἀπολύω (# 668) to release, to free someone (acc.) from something (gen). Perf. indicates, "you have been freed and are in the state of freedom" (Arndt). The word is used in medical writers for the releasing from disease; i.e., relaxing tendons, membranes, etc. (MLL, 21). The power of the evil spirits was to be broken when the days of the Messiah came (SB, 4:i, 521, 527). ◆ 13 ἐπέθηκεν aor. ind. act. ἐπιτίθημι (# 2202) to lay upon, to place upon. παραχρῆμα (# 4202) at once, immediately. ἀνωρθώθη aor. ind. pass. ἀνορθόω (# 494) to straighten up again. A medical term meaning, "to straighten, to put into natural position, abnormal or dislocated parts of the body" (MLL, 22). ἐδόξαζεν impf. ind. act. δοξάζω (# 1519) to glorify. Incep. impf. "she began to glorify." ◆ 14 ἀποκριθείς aor. pass. (dep.) part. s.v. 2. ἀγανακτῶν pres. act. part. (circum.) ἀγανακτέω (# 24) to be aroused, to be indignant against what is judged to be wrong, to be angry (LN, 1:762). ἐθεράπευσεν aor. ind. act. θεραπεύω (# 2543) to treat medically, to heal. δεῖ (# 1256) pres. ind. act., it is necessary, w. inf. explaining the necessity. ἐργάζεσθαι pres. mid. (dep.) inf. ἐργάζομαι (# 2237) to work. ἐρχόμενοι pres. mid. (dep.) part. ἔρχομαι (# 2262) to come. Circum. part. as imp. θεραπεύεσθε pres. imp. pass. ◆ 15 ἀπεκρίθη aor. ind. pass. (dep.) s.v. 2. ὑποκριταί voc. pl. ὑποκριτής (# 5695) hypocrite, casuist (TDNT; EDNT; TLNT). τῷ σαββάτῳ dat. sing. σάββατον (# 4879) Sabbath. Dat. of time ("on the Sabbath"). βοῦν acc. sing. βοῦς (# 1091) ox. ὄνος (# 3952) donkey. φάτνη (# 5764) stable, stall, feeding trough. ἀπαγαγών aor. act. part. (circum.) ἀπάγω (# 552) to lead out. ποτίζει pres. ind. act. ποτίζω (# 4540) to give to drink. Pres. tenses here are customary. For examples from the Mishnah and DSS s. Marshall; SB, 2:199-200; M, Shab. 5:1-4; M, Erub. 2:1-4; CD 11:5, 13-14; Luke 14:5. ◆ 16 θυγάτηρ (# 2588) daughter. θυγατέρα Ἀβραάμ (acc. sing.) "daughter of Abraham." It indicates that she has the faith of Abraham and is a member of God's people (s. 4 Macc. 11:28-29; the mother of the seven martyrs is called a "daughter of Abraham" because of her bravery and faith). The nation of Israel was also referred to as the daughter of Abraham (SB, 2:200). οὖσαν pres. act. part. (adj.) εἰμί (# 1639) to be. ἔδησεν aor. ind. act. δέω (# 1313) to bind. ἔδει impf. ind. act., w. inf. δεῖ (# 1256) it is necessary. It gives the logical necessity. λυθῆναι aor. pass. inf. λύω (# 3395) to loose, to free, to release. Epex. inf. explaining what is necessary. ◆ 17 λέγοντος pres. act. part. (temp.) λέγω (# 3306) to say, to speak. Gen. abs. κατησχύνοντο impf. ind. pass. καταισχύνω (# 2875) to be ashamed, to humiliate, to disgrace (LN, 1:310). Impf., "they were being put to shame." **ἀντικείμενοι** pres. mid. (dep.) part. ἀντίκειμαι (# 512) to be opposed, to resist. Part. as subst. **ἔχαιρεν** impf. ind. act. χαίρω (# 5897) to rejoice. Impf. describes the continous action. **ἐνδόξοις** (# 1902) glorious, splendid, wonderful (LN, 1:696). **γινομένοις** pres. mid. (dep.) part. (adj.) s.v. 2. "They were rejoicing over the glorious things being done by Him." ◆ **18 ὁμοιώσω** fut. ind. act. ὁμοιόω (# 3929) to compare, to make alike. Deliberative fut. in a rhetorical question. ◆ **19 κόκκος** (# 3133) grain. **σινάπεως** gen. sing. σίναπι (# 4983) mustard (s. Matt. 13:31). **λαβών** aor. act. part. (circum.) λαμβάνω (# 3284) to take. **ἔβαλεν** aor. ind. act s.v. 8. **κῆπος** (# 3057) garden. **ηὔξησεν** aor. ind. act. αὐξάνω (# 889) to grow. **ἐγένετο** aor. ind. mid. (dep.) γίνομαι (# 1181) to become. **κατεσκήνωσεν** aor. ind. act. κατασκηνόω (# 2942) to dwell, to make a nest. ◆ **20 εἶπεν** aor. ind. act. s.v. 17. **ὁμοιώσω** fut. ind. act. s.v. 18. ◆ **21 ζύμη** (# 2434) dat. sing. leaven. **λαβοῦσα** aor. act. part. (circum.) s.v. 19. **ἐνέκρυψεν** aor. ind. act. ἐγκρύπτω (# 1606) to hide. **ἀλεύρου** gen. sing. ἄλευρον (# 236) flour. Descriptive gen. **σάτα** acc. pl. σάτον (# 4929) seah. A Jewish measure for grain about a peck and a half (BAGD). **ἐζυμώθη** aor. ind. pass. ζυμόω (# 2435) to leaven, to ferment. For this parable s. Matt. 13:33. ◆ **22 διεπορεύετο** impf. ind. mid. (dep.) διαπορεύομαι (# 1388) to journey through, to pass through. Impf. pictures the continual action, "he continued on his journey" (Fitzmyer, 1024). **κατά** (# 2848) w. acc., distributive use ("from village to village"). **διδάσκων** pres. act. part. (circum.) s.v. 10. **πορεία** (# 4512) journey. **ποιούμενος** pres. mid. part. s.v. 9 ("making his way to Jersualem") (RWP). ◆ **23 εἰ** (# 1623) if. Used to introduce a dir. question and is either a Hebraism or an ellipsis (RG, 1176, 1024). **σῳζόμενοι** pres. pass. part. σῴζω (# 5392) to rescue, to save. Part. as subst. ◆ **24 ἀγωνίζεσθε** pres. imp. mid. (dep.) ἀγωνίζομαι (# 76) to engage in an athletic contest, to strive, to strive to do something w. great intensity and effort, to make every effort to, w. inf. (LN, 1:663). **εἰσελθεῖν** aor. act. inf. εἰσέρχομαι (# 1656) to go in. Epex. inf. **στενῆς** gen. sing. στενός (# 5101) narrow. Descriptive gen. **ζητήσουσιν** fut. ind. act. s.v. 6. **ἰσχύσουσιν** fut. ind. act. ἰσχύω (# 2710) to be strong, to be able. ◆ **25 ἐγερθῇ** aor. subj. pass. ἐγείρω (# 1586) to rise; pass. to raise, to get up. **ἀποκλείσῃ** aor. subj. act. ἀποκλείω (# 643) to lock up. **ἄρξησθε** aor. subj. mid. (dep.) ἄρχομαι (# 806) to begin, w. inf. Subj. here used in an indef. temp. cl. **ἑστάναι** perf. act. inf. ἵστημι (# 2705) to stand. **κρούειν** pres. act. inf. κρούω (# 3218) to knock. **ἄνοιξον** aor. imp. act. ἀνοίγω (# 487) to open. Aor. imp. calling for a specific act may also have a note of urgency. **ἀποκριθείς** aor. pass. part. s.v. 2. **ἐρεῖ** fut. ind. act. λέγω (# 3306) s.v. 17. **οἶδα** (# 3857) perf. ind. act. to know. Def. perf. w. pres. meaning. **πόθεν** (# 4470) where, from

where. "I do not know where you come from." ◆ **26 ἄρξεσθε** fut. ind. mid. (dep.) s.v. 25. **ἐφάγομεν** aor. ind. act. ἐσθίω (# 2266) to eat. **ἐπίομεν** aor. ind. act. πίνω (# 4403) to drink. **πλατεῖα** (# 4423) wide, wide street. **ἐδίδαξας** aor. ind. act. s.v. 10. ◆ **27 ἀπόστητε** aor. imp. act. ἀφίστημι (# 923) to depart, to go away. Aor. imp. has a note of finality. **ἐργάται** nom. pl. ἐργάτης (# 2239) worker; obj. gen. follows, "workers of unrighteousness." ◆ **28 ἔσται** fut. ind. mid. (dep.) εἰμί (# 1639) to be. **κλαυθμός** (# 3088) loud crying, wailing. **βρυγμός** (# 1106) grinding, gnashing of teeth. The chattering or gnashing of the teeth indicates suffering or the anger directed against the master (Marshall). **ὄψεσθε** aor. subj. mid. (dep.) ὁράω (# 3972) to see. Subj. in an indef. temp. cl. **ἐκβαλλομένους** pres. pass. part. ἐκβάλλω (# 1675) to cast out, to drive out. ◆ **29 ἥξουσιν** fut. ind. act. ἥκω (# 2457) to come. **ἀνατολῶν** gen. pl. ἀνατολή (# 424) east. **δυσμῶν** gen. pl. δυσμή (# 1553) west. For the pl. used for the four directions s. BD, 77-78. **βορρᾶ** (# 1080) north. For the form in Koine s. GGP, 20-21. **νότου** gen. sing. νότος (# 3803) south. **ἀνακλιθήσονται** fut. ind. pass. ἀνακλίνω (# 369) to recline (at the table). ◆ **30 ἔσονται** fut. ind. mid. (dep.) s.v. 28. ◆ **31 προσῆλθαν** aor. ind. act. προσέρχομαι (# 4665) to come to. **ἔξελθε** aor. imp. act. ἐξέρχομαι (# 2002) to go out. **πορεύου** pres. imp. mid. (dep.) πορεύομαι (# 4513) to go. **ἐντεῦθεν** (# 1949) from here. This incident probably took place just before Jesus left Galilee (HA, 218). **ἀποκτεῖναι** aor. act. inf. s.v. 4. Evidently a threat by Herod to get out of Antipas' domain (HA, 219f). Inf. w. the vb. **θέλει**. ◆ **32 πορευθέντες** aor. pass. (dep.) part. (circum.) πορεύομαι (# 4513) to go; w. imp. force (VANT, 386). **εἴπατε** aor. imp. act. s.v. 17. **ἀλώπεκι** dat. sing. ἀλώπηξ (# 273) fox. The person described as a fox is looked down upon as weak and wily, lacking real power and dignity (HA, 220, 343-47; Bovon; BBC). Epictetus says that foxes are "rascals of the animal kingdom" and men like them are "slanderous and malicious" (Epictetus, *Discourses*, 1.3.7-8; DNP, 4:687. The form used in the descriptions was normally fem. (DNP, 4:687). **ἴασις** (# 2617) healing, cure. **ἀποτελῶ** pres. ind. act. ἀποτελέω (# 699) to complete, to perform. For the medical use of these two terms s. MLL, 23-24. **σήμερον καὶ αὔριον** acc. sing. The expression "today and tomorrow" means "day by day." Along w. the reference to the third day it is a Semitic idiom for a short and definite period (HA, 221). **τελειοῦμαι** pres. ind. pass. τελειόω (# 5457) to complete, to finish. Here it is pass. and means "I am brought to completion" (HA, 222). ◆ **33 δεῖ** (# 1256) pres. ind. act. it is necessary, w. inf. giving a logical necessity. **ἐχομένῃ** pres. mid. part. dat. ἔχω (# 2400) to have; mid. used of time, immediately, following (BAGD). Here, "the next day" (Plummer). Dat. of time. **πορεύεσθαι** pres. mid. (dep.) inf. s.v. 32. **ἐνδέχεται** pres. ind. mid. ἐνδέχομαι (# 1896) impersonal, it is possible, it is fitting. Here, "it will not do," "it is impossible," the idea of necessity entering in (BAGD; Arndt; MM). **ἀπολέσθαι** aor. mid. inf. s.v. 3. Epex. inf. explaining what is impossible. It is not destined that Herod would kill Jesus, but Jerusalem would (Fitzmyer, 1032). ◆ **34 ἀποκτείνουσα** pres. act. part. (adj.) ἀποκτείνω (# 650) to kill. Pres. may indicate the repeated action, indicating the ever-present attitude toward heaven-sent messengers (Fitzmyer, 1036). **λιθοβολοῦσα** pres. act. part. (adj.) λιθοβολέω (# 3344) to stone. **ἀπεσταλμένους** perf. pass. part. ἀποστέλλω (# 690) to send, to send out as an authoritative representative (TDNT; EDNT). Part. as subst. **ἠθέλησα** aor. ind. act. θέλω (# 2527) to wish, to desire, w. inf. **ἐπισυνάξαι** aor. act. inf. ἐπισυνάγω (# 2190) to gather together. **ὃν τρόπον** (# 4005; 5573) in like manner, just as. **ὄρνις** (# 3998) hen. **νοσσιά** (# 3799) nest, brood. **πτέρυγας** acc. pl. πτέρυξ (# 4763) wing. **ἠθελήσατε** aor. ind. act. Aor. points to the finality of the decision. ◆ **35 ἀφίεται** pres. ind. pass. ἀφίημι (# 918) to leave, to forsake. It means "you have it entirely to yourselves to possess and protect, for God no longer dwells in it and protects it" (Plummer). **ἴδητε** aor. subj. act. ὁράω (# 3972) to see. Subj. w. strong negation οὐ μή (# 4024; 3590) (NSV, 74). **ἥξει** fut. ind. act. s.v. 29. **εἴπητε** aor. subj. act. λέγω (# 3306) to say. Subj. in an indef. temp. cl. **εὐλογημένος** perf. pass. part. εὐλογέω (# 2328) to bless, to praise. Part. as subst.

Luke 14

◆ **1 ἐγένετο** aor. ind. mid. (dep.) γίνομαι (# 1181) to become, to happen (s. 8:1). **ἐλθεῖν** aor. act. inf. ἔρχομαι (# 2262) to come, to go. Inf. w. prep. ἐν (# 1877) to express time (MT, 145). **φαγεῖν** aor. act. inf. ἐσθίω (# 2266) to eat; inf. of purp. Normally there were two main meals in the day, but on the Sabbath there were three. The Sabbath meal, which was prepared the day before and kept warm (M, Shab. 3:1-6; 4:1-2), was around noon (Jos., *Life*, 279), after the synagogue service, and it was common to invite guests to the Sabbath meal (SB, 2:202-203; Fitzmyer, 1040-41). **ἦσαν** impf. ind. act. εἰμί (# 1639) to be. **παρατηρούμενοι** pres. mid. part. παρατηρέω (# 4190) to stand by the side and watch (s. 6:7). Part. in a periphrastic construction. The mid. and act. have the same meaning (BAGD; RG, 811, "redundant mid."). ◆ **2 ἰδού** (# 2627) aor. imp. ὁράω (# 3972) to see, to behold. Used as particle meaning "behold," "look." **ὑδρωπικός** (# 5622) dropsy. A medical term denoting a person suffering from dropsy, a disease in which the body swells up due to fluid forming in the cavities and tissues (Marshall; MLL, 24; DMTG, 318; SB, 2:203-04). ◆ **3 ἀποκριθείς** aor. pass. (dep.) part. ἀποκρίνομαι (# 646) to answer (s. 13:2). **ἔξεστιν** pres. ind. act. ἔξεστι(ν) (# 2003) it is lawful, it is allowed, w. inf. **θεραπεῦσαι** aor. act. inf. θεραπεύω (# 2543) to han-

dle medically, to heal. Epex. inf. ◆ **4 ἡσύχασαν** aor. ind. act. ἡσυχάζω (# 2483) to be silent. Ingressive aor., "they became silent" (RWP). **ἐπιλαβόμενος** aor. mid. (dep.) part. (circum.) ἐπιλαμβάνομαι (# 2138) to take hold of. **ἰάσατο** aor. ind. mid. (dep.) ἰάομαι (# 2615) to heal. **ἀπέλυσεν** aor. ind. act. ἀπολύω (# 668) to release (s. 13:12). ◆ **5 βοῦς** (# 1091) ox. **φρέαρ** (# 5853) acc. sing. well. **πεσεῖται** fut. ind. mid. (dep.) πίπτω (# 4406) to fall. **ἀνασπάσει** fut. act. ind. ἀνασπάω (# 413) to pull up, to pull out. In the DSS it was forbidden to give help to an animal on the Sabbath, either to pull it out of a ditch or help deliver the young (CD, 11:13-15). ◆ **6 ἴσχυσαν** aor. ind. act. ἰσχύω (# 2710) to be strong, to be able, w. inf. **ἀνταποκριθῆναι** aor. pass. (dep.) inf. ἀνταποκρίνομαι (# 503) to answer back, to reply. For the force of the prep. compound s. MH, 297. ◆ **7 ἔλεγεν** impf. ind. act. λέγω (# 3306) to speak. Incep. impf., "he began to tell...." **κεκλημένους** perf. pass. part. καλέω (# 2813) to call, to invite. Part. as subst. **ἐπέχων** pres. act. part. (causal) ἐπέχω (# 2091) to hold the mind on something, to notice. He directed His attention to this (Plummer). **πρωτοκλισία** (# 4752) chief seat, the first place. In a group of three cushions or couches used for reclining, the one in the center was the place of honor (SB, 4:611-35). **ἐξελέγοντο** impf. ind. mid. ἐκλέγω (# 1721) to choose; mid., to choose for oneself. Customary impf. ◆ **8 κληθῇς** aor. subj. pass. s.v. 7. Subj. w. ὅταν (# 4020) in an indef. temp. cl. **κατακλιθῇς** aor. subj. pass. (dep.) κατακλίνομαι (# 2884) to sit down, to recline (esp. when eating). Subj. w. neg. to express prohibition, implying the action does not yet exist and should not arise (MKG, 273). **ἐντιμότερος** comp. ἔντιμος (# 1952) honored. **σου** gen. σύ you. Than you; gen. of comp. ᾖ pres. subj. act. εἰμί (# 1639) to be. Subj. used is a cl. where fear is implied: "for fear that there might be..." (NSV, 142). **κεκλημένος** perf. pass. part. s.v. 7. ◆ **9 ἐλθών** aor. act. part. (cond.) ἔρχομαι (# 2262) to come. "If he comes...." **καλέσας** aor. act. part. s.v. 7. Part. as subst. **ἐρεῖ** fut. ind. act. λέγω s.v. 7. **δός** aor. imp. act. δίδωμι (# 1443) to give. Aor. imp. calls for a specific act. **ἄρξῃ** fut. ind. mid. (dep.) ἄρχομαι (# 806) to begin, w. inf. The vb. marks the contrast between the brief, self-assumed promotion and the permanent merited humiliation (Plummer). **αἰσχύνη** (# 158) shame. **κατέχειν** pres. act. inf. κατέχω (# 2988) to take, to hold down. ◆ **10 κληθῇς** aor. subj. pass. s.v. 7. Subj. w. ὅταν (# 4020) in an indef. temp. cl. **πορευθείς** aor. pass. (dep.) part. πορεύομαι (# 4513) to go. Circum. part. w. imp. force (VANT, 386; NSV, 82). **ἀνάπεσε** aor. imp. act. ἀναπίπτω (# 404) to fall back, to lie back, to recline at the table. **ἔλθῃ** aor. subj. act. s.v. 1. Subj. in an indef. temp. cl. **κεκληκώς** perf. act. part. s.v. 9. **ἐρεῖ** fut. ind. act. λέγω (# 3306) to say. Used w. ἵνα (# 2671), here perhaps to express results rather than purp. (Plummer; RG, 984f). **προσανάβηθι** aor. imp. act. προσαναβαίνω

(# *4646*) to come up to. It pictures the host as beckoning the guest to come up to him (Arndt). **δόξα** (# *1518*) praise, fame, honor; here, honored (Marshall). **συνανακειμένων** pres. mid. part. συνανάκειμαι (# *5263*) to recline at the table together (w. dat.). Part. as subst. ◆ **11** **ὑψῶν** pres. act. part. ὑψόω (# *5738*) to lift up, to exalt. **ταπεινωθήσεται** fut. ind. pass. ταπεινόω (# *5427*) to make low, to humble. Subst. part. pres. points to a habit of life. **ὑψωθήσεται** fut. ind. pass. ◆ **12 κεκληκότι** perf. act. part. dat. sing. s.v. 7. **ποιῇς** pres. subj. act. ποιέω (# *4472*) to make. Subj. w. **ὅταν** (# *4020*) in an indef. temp. cl. Iterat. pres. **ἄριστον** (# *756*) acc. sing. breakfast, the early morning meal (11:37; SB, 2:204-206). **δεῖπνον** (# *1270*) acc. sing. dinner, the main meal (SB, 4:611-39). **φώνει** pres. imp. act. φωνέω (# *5888*) to call, to invite. Pres. imp. means "do not habitually invite." It is the exclusive invitation of rich neighbors that is forbidden (Plummer). **συγγενεῖς** acc. pl. συγγενής (# *5150*) relative. **γείτονας** acc. pl. γείτων (# *1150*) neighbor. **ἀντικαλέσωσιν** aor. subj. act. ἀντικαλέω (# *511*) to invite in return. For the reciprocal action expressed in the prep. s. MH, 297. Subj. w. **μήποτε** (# *3607*) to express purp. or a conjectured probability (BAGD). **καὶ αὐτοί** emphatic, even they (Fitzmyer, 1047). **γένηται** aor. subj. mid. (dep.) s.v. 1. **ἀνταπόδομα** (# *501*) repayment. ◆ **13 δοχή** (# *1531*) reception, banquet. It could be a reference to the messianic victory banquet after the destruction of His enemies (LNT, 126-55). **ποιῇς** pres. subj. act. s.v. 12. Subj. w. **ὅταν** (# *4020*) in an indef. temp. cl. **κάλει** pres. imp. act. s.v. 7. **ἀνάπειρος** (# *401*) crippled, maimed. Prep. is intensive ("very maimed") (Plummer). For the term πηρός in medical language s. MLL, 148-49. **χωλός** (# *6000*) lame. ◆ **14 ἔσῃ** fut. ind. mid. (dep.) 2nd. pers. sing. εἰμί (# *1639*) to be. **ἀνταποδοῦναι** aor. act. inf. ἀνταποδίδωμι (# *500*) to pay back again, to pay back in return. Inf. as obj. **ἀνταποδοθήσεται** fut. ind. pass. Theol. pass. indicating that God is the subject. ◆ **15 ἀκούσας** aor. act. part. (temp.) ἀκούω (# *201*) to hear. **συνανακειμένων** pres. mid. (dep.) part. s.v. 10. **φάγεται** fut. ind. mid. (dep.) ἐσθίω (# *2266*) to eat. ◆ **16 ἐποίει** impf. ind. act. s.v. 12. Impf., "he was in the process of making...." **ἐκάλεσεν** aor. ind. act. s.v. 7. ◆ **17 ἀπέστειλεν** aor. ind. act. ἀποστέλλω (# *690*) to send, to send out as an official and authoritative representative (TDNT; EDNT). **εἰπεῖν** aor. act. inf. s.v. 7. Inf. of purp. **κεκλημένοις** perf. pass. part. s.v. 7. **ἔρχεσθε** pres. imp. mid. (dep.) s.v. 9. ◆ **18 ἤρξαντο** aor. ind. mid. (dep.) ἄρχομαι (# *806*) to begin, w. inf. **ἀπὸ μιᾶς** (# *608; 1877*) unanimously, w. one accord (BD, 126). **παραιτεῖσθαι** pres. mid. (dep.) inf. παραιτέομαι (# *4148*) to ask someone for something. When used w. invitations, "to make an excuse," "to beg off" (RWP; BAGD; NDIEC, 3:78). For a discussion of the excuses s. LNT, 137-38; Humphrey Palmer, "Just Married, Cannot Come," *Nov T* 18 (1976):

241-57. **ἠγόρασα** aor. ind. act. ἀγοράζω (# *60*) to buy. **ἀνάγκη** (# *340*) necessity, constraint; "I am obliged." He would have to see if the field had depreciated in value (LNT, 137). **ἐξελθών** aor. act. part. (circum.) ἐξέρχομαι (# *2002*) to go out. **ἰδεῖν** aor. act. inf. ὁράω (# *3972*) to see. Epex. inf. explaining the **ἀνάγκην**. **ἐρωτῶ** pres. ind. act. ἐρωτάω (# *2263*) to ask, to request. **ἔχε** pres. imp. act. ἔχω (# *2400*) to have, to consider. "Consider me excused" (BAGD; NSV, 106). **παρῃτημένον** perf. pass. part. παραιτέομαι. (# *4148*) For the construction s. RWP; Fitzmyer, 1056. ◆ **19 ζεύγη** acc. pl. ζεῦγος (# *2414*) yoke. **ἠγόρασα** aor. ind. act. s.v. 18. **δοκιμάσαι** aor. act. inf. δοκιμάζω (# *1507*) to try out, to prove by testing. Inf. of purp. ◆ **20 ἔγημα** aor. ind. act. γαμέω (# *1138*) to marry. (Deut. 20:5-7; 24:5; Palmer, "Just Married" *NovT* 18 [1976]: 242). **ἐλθεῖν** aor. act. inf. s.v. 9. ◆ **21 παραγενόμενος** aor. mid. part. (temp.) παραγίνομαι (# *4134*) to come. **ἀπήγγειλεν** aor. ind. act. ἀπαγγέλλω (# *550*) to report. **ὀργισθείς** aor. pass. part. ὀργίζομαι (# *3974*) to be angry, to be very angry, to be furious (LN, 1:761). Ingressive aor., "to become angry." **οἰκοδεσπότης** (# *3867*) ruler of a house. **ἔξελθε** aor. imp. act. s.v. 18. Aor. imp. calls for immediate action. **πλατεῖα** (# *4423*) wide, wide street. **ῥύμας** acc. pl. ῥύμη (# *4860*) street, lane. **ἀναπείρους** acc. pl. s.v. 13. lame, cripple. The physically blemished were barred from full participation in Jewish worship. This was also stressed in the Qumran community (Ellis; 1QSa 2:4-10). **εἰσάγαγε** aor. imp. act. εἰσάγω (# *1652*) to lead in, to bring in. ◆ **22 γέγονεν** perf. ind. act. s.v. 1. Perf. stresses the completed state or abiding results. **ἐπέταξας** aor. ind. act. ἐπιτάσσω (# *2199*) to command, to give an order. ◆ **23 φραγμός** (# *5850*) hedge, fence. The vineyards, gardens, or fields surrounded by hedges or fences (Fitzmyer, 1057). Poor travelers were accustomed to camping in the shelter of the hedges and fences (Arndt). **ἀνάγκασον** aor. imp. act. ἀναγκάζω (# *337*) to compel. The compelling was by persuasion (Plummer). Aor. imp. stresses the urgency. **εἰσελθεῖν** aor. act. inf. s. 13:24. Inf. as dir. obj. **γεμισθῇ** aor. subj. pass. γεμίζω (# *1153*) to fill; pass. to become full. Subj. w. **ἵνα** (# *2671*) in a purp. cl. ◆ **24 κεκλημένων** perf. pass. part. s.v. 7. **γεύσεται** fut. ind. mid. (dep.) γεύομαι (# *1174*) to taste, to eat, w. obj. in gen. There shall be no food sent to them as a token of recognition (LNT, 141). ◆ **25 συνεπορεύοντο** impf. ind. mid. (dep.) συνπορεύομαι (# *5233*) to go together, to accompany, w. dat. **στραφείς** aor. pass. part. (circum.) στρέφω (# *5138*) to turn oneself, to turn. ◆ **26 μισεῖ** pres. ind. act. μισέω (# *3631*) to hate. It signifies loving less (Arndt; Fitzmyer, 1063). For the rabbinical teaching regarding preferential treatment of the teacher over the father s. M, Baba Netzia 2, 11. Ind. in a cond. cl. which the speaker assumes to be true. **εἶναι** pres. act. inf. s.v. 14. ◆ **27 βαστάζει** pres. ind. act. βαστάζω (# *1002*) to carry, to bear. Pres. views a continual or habitual action. σταυ-ρός (# 5089) cross. For the concept of discipleship s. Matt. 28:19. ◆ **28 θέλων** pres. act. part. (adj.) θέλω (# 2527) to wish, to desire, w. inf. **πύργος** (# 4788) tower, some sort of fortification to protect a house, land, or vineyard (Fitzmyer, 1065). **οἰκοδομῆσαι** aor. act. inf. οἰκοδομέω (# 3868) to build. **καθίσας** aor. act. part. (circum.) καθίζω (# 2767) to sit down. This represents long and serious consideration (Plummer). **ψηφίζει** pres. ind. act. ψηφίζω (# 6028) to count, to calculate. Gnomic pres. indicating that which generally takes place. **δα-πάνη** (# 1252) cost. **ἀπαρτισμός** (# 568) completion, to finish off, to finish up. For the force of the prep. s. MH, 299. ◆ **29 θέντος** aor. act. part. (temp.) τίθημι (# 5502) to place, to lay. Gen. abs. **θεμέλιος** (# 2529) foundation. **ἰσχύοντος** pres. act. part. (causal) s.v. 6. Gen. abs. **ἐκ-τελέσαι** aor. act. inf. ἐκτελέω (# 1754) to bring to completion, to finish successfully. **θεωροῦντες** pres. act. part. θεωρέω (# 2555) to see, to watch. Part. as subst. **ἄρξωνται** aor. subj. mid. (dep.), w. inf. s.v. 9. Subj. in a neg. purp. cl. of apprehension (NSV, 141-42; BD, 188). **ἐμπαίζειν** pres. act. inf. ἐμπαίζω (# 1850) to mock, to make fun of someone, to ridicule, to taunt, w. dat. ◆ **30 λέγοντες** pres. act. part. s.v. 7. Part. explaining the ridiculing. **οὗτος** this man, derogatory sense, used sarcastically in derision. **ἤρξατο** aor. ind. mid. (dep.), w. inf. s.v. 9. **οἰκοδομεῖν** pres. act. inf. s.v. 28. **ἴσχυσεν** aor. ind. act. s.v. 6. ◆ **31 πορευόμενος** pres. mid. (dep.) part. s.v. 10. Temp. or cond. part. **συμβαλεῖν** aor. act. inf. συμ-βάλλω (# 5202) to throw together, to fight, w. dat. **πό-λεμος** (# 4483) war. **καθίσας** aor. act. part. (circum.) s.v. 28. **βουλεύσεται** fut. ind. mid. (dep.) βουλεύομαι (# 1086) to confer, to take counsel, to deliberate w. one-self. **ἐν** by, with. Instr. use of the prep. (RWP). **ὑπαντῆσαι** aor. act. inf. ὑπαντάω (# 5636) to meet, w. dat. Epex. inf. explaining what might be possible. **ἐρ-χομένῳ** pres. mid. (dep.) part. s.v. 1. Part. as subst. ◆ **32 εἰ δὲ μή γε** but if not, otherwise (Thrall, 10). **πόρρω** (# 4522) far. **ὄντος** pres. act. part. (temp.) εἰμί to be. Gen. abs. **πρεσβεία** (# 4561) embassy, delegation. **ἀποστείλας** aor. act. part. (circum.) s.v. 17. **ἐρωτᾷ** pres. ind. act. s.v. 18. ◆ **33 ἀποτάσσεται** pres. ind. mid. (dep.) ἀποτάσσομαι (# 698) to say good-bye to, to re-nounce, to forsake, to willingly give up or set aside what one possesses, w. dat. (LN, 1:566; s. NDIEC, 1:58-9). **ὑπάρχουσιν** pres. act. part. dat. n. pl. ὑπάρχω (# 5639) to exist, to be at one's disposal. Part. as subst., "what belongs to someone, property, possessions" (BAGD). **δύναται** pres. ind. pass. (dep.) δύναμαι (# 1538) to be able, w. inf. It is not a matter of "one *may* not," but "one *can* not!" **εἶναι** pres. act. inf. s.v. 1. ◆ **34 οὖν** (# 4036) to be sure (DM, 255). **ἅλας** (# 229) salt; s. Evans for the symbol of salt. **μωρανθῇ** aor. subj. pass. μωραίνω (# 3701) to make foolish, to make useless (Matt. 5:13; Marshall). Subj. w. ἐάν (# 1569) in a 3rd.

class cond. cl. in which the speaker assumes the cond. to be possible. **ἀρτυθήσεται** fut. ind. pass. ἀρτύω (# 789) to equip, to make ready, to season (Fitzmyer, 1069). ◆ **35 κοπρία** (# 3161) manure heap, rubbish heap. **εὔθε-τος** (# 2310) fit, suitable. **βάλλουσιν** pres. ind. act. βάλλω (# 965) to throw out. Impersonal pl. used to express pass. Gnomic pres. **ἀκούειν** pres. act. inf. ἀκούω (# 201) to hear. Inf. of purp. **ἀκουέτω** pres. imp. act. 3rd. pers. sing.

Luke 15

◆ **1 ἦσαν** impf. ind. act. εἰμί (# 1639) to be. Used w. the part. in a periphrastic construction. **ἐγγίζοντες** pres. act. part. ἐγγίζω (# 1581) to come near, w. dat. **ἀκούειν** pres. act. inf. ἀκούω (# 201) to hear. Inf. of purp., "they were coming in order to hear." ◆ **2 διεγόγγυζον** impf. ind. act. διαγογγύζω (# 1339) to murmur, to murmur among themselves, throughout their whole company (Plummer; Bock). For the abuses of tax collectors s. NDIEC, 8:68-74; DJG, 805-6). Impf. pictures the continual action. **προσδέχεται** pres. ind. mid. (dep.) προσδέχο-μαι (# 4657) to receive, to welcome. The vb. often implies hospitality and it is assumed that the guest brings honor to the house where he is invited (PAP, 143). **συνεσθίει** pres. ind. act. συνεσθίω (# 5303) to eat together, to eat w. someone, w. dat. The pres. tenses here stress a habitual conduct. ◆ **3 εἶπεν** aor. ind. act. λέγω (# 3306) to say, to speak. ◆ **4 ἔχων** pres. act. part. (adj.) ἔχω (# 2400) to have, to possess. **ἀπολέσας** aor. act. part. (cond.) ἀπόλλυμι (# 660) to lose. The act. may indicate that the shepherd takes responsibility for the losing of the sheep (PAP, 149). **καταλείπει** pres. ind. act. καταλείπω (# 2901) to leave. W. the neg. οὐ (# 4024) in a question expecting the answer "yes." Pres. indicates habitual action. **ἀπολωλός** perf. act. part. ἀπόλυμμι Perf. indicates the state or cond. Part. as subst. **εὕρη** aor. subj. act. εὑρίσκω (# 2351) to find. Subj. in an indef. temp. cl. ◆ **5 εὑρών** aor. act. part. (temp.) s.v. 4. **ἐπιτίθη-σιν** pres. ind. act. ἐπιτίθημι (# 2202) to place upon. **ὦμος** (# 6049) shoulder. **χαίρων** pres. act. part. χαίρω (# 5897) to rejoice. Part. of manner. The shepherd rejoices, al-though the process of restoration calls for the arduous task of carrying the sheep for some distance (PAP, 148). ◆ **6 ἐλθών** aor. act. part. (temp.) ἔρχομαι (# 2262) to come. **συγκαλεῖ** pres. ind. act. συγκαλέω (# 5157) to call together. Pres. tenses are hist. pres., making the story lively and vivid. **γείτων** (# 1150) neighbor. **συγχάρητε** aor. imp. act. συγκαίρω (# 5176) to rejoice together. Aor. imp. calls for a specific act, w. a note of urgency. Friends and neighbors were to try to help find a lost animal and would rejoice when it was found (Exod. 23:4; Deut. 22:1-3; J. Duncan and M. Derrett, "Fresh Light on the Lost Sheep and the Lost Coin," *NTS* 26 [1979]: 36-60; esp. 38-40). **εὗρον** aor. ind. act. 1st. pers. sing. s.v. 4. **ἀπολωλός** perf. act. part. s.v. 4. Just as the

shepherd's friends rejoice so God's friends should rejoice when He recovers that which was lost (BBC). ◆ 7
ἔσται fut. ind. mid. (dep.) εἰμί (# 1639) to be. μετανοοῦντι pres. act. part. μετανοέω (# 3566) to change the
mind, to repent (s. Matt. 3:2). ἤ (# 2445) than. Used w.
the positive of the adj. to form a comp. construction.
χρεία (# 5970) need, necessity. ◆ 8 δραχμάς acc. pl.
δραχμή (# 1534) drachma. A Greek silver coin worth
normally about 18 or 19 cents. It was the price of a
sheep or one-fifth the price of an ox (BAGD; EDNT;
DJG, 805; Fitzmyer, 1081; Marshall). ἔχουσα pres. act.
part. (adj.) s.v. 4. ἀπολέσῃ aor. subj. act. s.v. 4. Subj. in a
3rd. class cond. cl. in which the speaker assumes the
cond. might be possible. ἅπτει pres. ind. act. ἅπτω
(# 721) to light. Used w. the neg. in a question
("doesn't she light?") expecting the answer "yes." σα-
ροῖ pres. ind. act. σαρόω (# 4924) to sweep, to clean.
ζητεῖ pres. ind. act. ζητέω (# 2426) to search. ἐπιμελῶς
(# 2151) carefully, diligently. The prep. compound is
directive. It is directed concern (MH, 312). εὕρῃ aor.
subj. act. s.v. 4. Subj. in an indef. temp. cl. ◆ 9 εὑροῦσα
aor. act. part. (temp.) nom. fem. sing. s.v. 4. φίλας acc.
pl. φίλη (# 5813) female friend, girl friend. εὗρον aor.
ind. act. s.v. 4. ἀπώλεσα aor. ind. act. s.v. 4. ◆ 10 ἐνώπιον (# 1967) in the presence of, w. gen. μετανοοῦντι pres.
act. part. s.v. 7. ◆ 11 εἶπεν aor. ind. act. s.v. 3. εἶχεν
impf. ind. act. s.v. 4. Impf. used for a vivid description.
◆ 12 νεώτερος comp. νέος (# 3742) new, young; comp.,
younger. δός aor. imp. act. δίδωμι (# 1443) to give. Aor.
imp. calls for a specific act. w. a note of urgency. The
request of the son that the father give him his inheritance while the father was in good health was an insult
w. the implication, "Father, I cannot wait for you to
die!" (PAP, 164). ἐπιβάλλον pres. act. part. (adj.).
ἐπιβάλλω (# 2095) to fall to, to be appropriate. It is the
share which hypothetically is bound to come to him
(LNT, 106). μέρος (# 3538) portion, part. οὐσία (# 4045)
possession, property. The younger son's part was
probably about two-ninths (LNT, 109) or one third
(Fitzmyer, 1087). διεῖλεν aor. ind. act. διαιρέω (# 1349)
to divide. The father made a formal and legal division
of his goods. The son's responsibility to his family did
not cease with his legal claims (LNT, 108ff). ◆ 13 συναγαγών aor. act. part. (temp.) συνάγω (# 5251) to gather
together. Perhaps in the sense, "to turn everything into
cash" (BAGD; MM). The buyer of the property was
not to possess it before the death of the father (s. M,
Baba Bathra 8, 7). ἀπεδήμησεν aor. ind. act. ἀποδημέω
(# 623) to be out of the land, to be away from home, to
go on a journey to a distant country. διεσκόρπισεν aor.
ind. act. διασκορπίζω (# 1399) to scatter, to scatter in
various directions, to squander (Arndt). ζῶν pres. act.
part. ζάω (# 2409) to live. Part. of means or manner.
ἀσώτως (# 862) adv. without saving, dissolutely. Used
of debauched and profligate living (TDNT). ◆ 14

δαπανήσαντος aor. act. part. (temp.) δαπανάω (# 1251)
to spend, to spend completely, w. the implication of
uselessly and therefore wastefully (LN, 1:575). Gen.
abs. ἐγένετο aor. ind. mid. (dep.) γίνομαι (# 1181) to become, to arise, to happen. ἤρξατο aor. ind. mid. (dep.)
ἄρχομαι (# 806) to begin, w. inf. ὑστερεῖσθαι pres. mid.
(dep.) inf. ὑστερέομαι (# 5728) to come late, to be behind, to fall short, to be in want, to suffer need. ◆ 15
πορευθείς aor. pass. (dep.) part. (circum.) πορεύομαι
(# 4513) to go. ἐκολλήθη aor. ind. pass. κολλάω (# 3140)
to glue together, to join. It denotes that he forced himself on a citizen of the country (Arndt). ἔπεμψεν aor.
ind. act. πέμπω (# 4287) to send. βόσκειν pres. act. inf.
βόσκω (# 1081) to feed, to graze. Inf. of purp. χοῖρος
(# 5956) pig. He was occupied in the most degraded
occupation known to the Jews (LNT, 112). The polite
way a Middle Easterner gets rid of unwanted hangers-
on is to assign them a task he knows they will refuse
(PAP, 170). ◆ 16 ἐπεθύμει impf. ind. act. ἐπιθυμέω
(# 2121) to desire, to long for. Impf. expresses an unfulfilled desire. χορτασθῆναι aor. pass. inf. χορτάζω
(# 5963) to feed, to fill; pass. to eat one's fill, to be satisfied (BAGD). Epex. inf. explaining the desire. κεράτιον
(# 3044) little horn, carob pods. The pods of the carob
tree whose sweet-tasting pods were shaped like little
horns (RWP; POB, 72-73; PB, 63). The rabbis considered this the equivalent of being in the direst need
(Leaney). Perhaps it is better to see this as a wild carob
plant, whose berries are black and bitter w. no nourishment and hardly filling (PAP, 173). ἤσθιον impf. ind.
act. ἐσθίω (# 2266) to eat. ἐδίδου impf. ind. act. δίδωμι
(# 1443) to give. Nobody would give him anything
else, anything suitable (Fitzmyer, 1088). ◆ 17 ἐλθών
aor. act. part. ἔρχομαι (# 2262) to come; here, to come to
oneself, to repent. He is motivated by hunger and re-
pents for having lost the money (PAP, 176, cf. 173-76).
ἔφη impf. ind. act. φημί (# 5774) to say. μίσθιος (# 3634)
hired worker. These were workers who were paid at
the end of the day and did not form part of the household (Fitzmyer, 1089). περισσεύονται pres. ind. mid.
(indir. mid., "for themselves") περισσεύω (# 4355) to be
in abundance, to cause to abound, to make extremely
rich, used of persons who receive something in great
abundance (BAGD). ◆ 18 ἀναστάς aor. act. part.
(temp.) ἀνίστημι (# 482) to stand up, to get up. πορεύσομαι fut. ind. mid. (dep.) s.v. 15. Volitive fut. indicating a decision or intention of the will (RG, 889; NSV,
52). ἐρῶ fut. ind. act. λέγω (# 3306) to say. πάτερ voc.
sing. πατήρ (# 4252) father. ἥμαρτον aor. ind. act.
ἁμαρτάνω (# 279) to sin. He sinned against God and
his father in disobeying the fifth commandment. Having squandered his goods, he was not able to fulfill his
moral obligation to his father (LNT, 111f). ◆ 19 κληθῆναι aor. pass. inf. καλέω (# 2813) to call, to name.
Epex. inf. explaining the adj. ἄξιος. ποίησον aor. imp.

act. ποιέω (# 545) to do, to make. He wants to be made a hired worker, which means he would not live at home eating his brother's bread and would be able to earn money to gain back what he had lost (PAP, 178). Aor. imp. calls for a specific act. w. a sense of urgency. ◆ **20 ἦλθεν** aor. ind. act. ἔρχομαι (# 2262) to come. **ἀπέχοντος** pres. act. part. (temp.) ἀπέχω (# 600) to be far off. Gen. abs. ("while"). **εἶδεν** aor. ind. act. ὁράω (# 3972) to see. **ἐσπλαγχνίσθη** aor. ind. pass. σπλαγχνίζομαι (# 5072) to be deeply moved w. compassion (MNTW; TDNT; EDNT; TLNT). Part of the compassion was that the father knew the humiliation that the son faced in the village (PAP, 180-82). **δραμών** aor. act. part. (circum.) τρέχω (# 5556) to run. An Oriental nobleman w. flowing robes never runs anywhere, but in his deep compassion the father did (PAP, 181). **ἐπέπεσεν** aor. ind. act. ἐπιπίπτω (# 2158) to fall upon. **τράχηλος** (# 5549) neck. **κατεφίλησεν** aor. ind. act. καταφιλέω (# 2968) to kiss, to kiss fervently, the sign of forgiveness (Jeremias, *Parables*). ◆ **22 ἐξενέγκατε** aor. imp. act. ἐκφέρω (# 1766) to bring out. Aor. imp. calls for a specific act. w. a note of urgency. **στολή** (# 5124) robe, a stately robe. Instead of medals of honor, robes were given. He is treated as the guest of honor (Jeremias). The best robe would be the father's robe which he wore on special occasions (PAP, 185). **ἐνδύσατε** aor. imp. act. ἐνδύω (# 1907) to clothe, to dress. **δότε** aor. imp. act. δίδωμι (# 1443) to give. **δακτύλιος** (# 1234) ring, signet ring. He is to consider himself as his father's deputy (LNT, 113; BBC). **ὑπόδημα** (# 5687) sandal, shoe. A sign that the servants accepted him as master and that he is a free man in the house (LNT, 114; PAP, 185). ◆ **23 φέρετε** pres. imp. act. φέρω (# 5770) to bring, to carry. Pres. imp. here is idomatic and may be due to the idea of motion involved in the vb. (VANT, 347). **μόσχος** (# 3675) a young animal, calf. **σιτευτόν** (# 4988) fattened. **θύσατε** aor. imp. act. θύω (# 2604) to kill, to slaughter. The killing of the fatted calf is the height of hospitality (LNT, 14). **φαγόντες** aor. act. part. ἐσθίω (# 2266) to eat. Circum. or temp. part. ("when we eat"). **εὐφρανθῶμεν** aor. subj. pass. (dep.) εὐφραίνομαι (# 2370) to make merry, to rejoice, to be happy. Hortatory subj., "Let us be happy." A calf indicates that the whole village was invited and that this was a sort of covenant banquet to reconcile the son to the whole community (PAP, 186-87). ◆ **24 ὅτι** (# 4022) because. **ἦν** impf. ind. act. εἰμί (# 1639) to be. **ἀνέζησεν** aor. ind. act. ἀναζάω (# 348) to live again, to begin to live (GI, 150). **ἀπολωλώς** perf. act. part. ἀπόλλυμι (# 660) used in sense of the mid. to be ruined, to be lost (BAGD). Part. in a periphrastic construction, "he was in a state of destruction" (VA, 470). **εὑρέθη** aor. ind. pass. εὑρίσκω (# 2351) to find. **ἤρξαντο** aor. ind. mid. (dep.) s.v. 14., w. inf. ◆ **25 πρεσβύτερος** (# 4565) comp. πρέσβυς old; comp., older. **ἤγγισεν** aor. ind. act. ἐγγίζω

(# 1581) to come near. **ἤκουσεν** aor. ind. act. ἀκούω (# 201) to hear, w. obj. in gen. **συμφωνία** (# 5246) music. It means a band of players or singers (Plummer). **χορός** (# 5962) choral dance, dancing. The older son heard a loud, boisterous, joyous celebration in progress as he approached the house (PAP, 192). ◆ **26 προσκαλεσάμενος** aor. mid. part. (temp.) προσκαλέω (# 4673) to summons, to call to oneself. **ἐπυνθάνετο** impf. ind. mid. (dep.) πυνθάνομαι (# 4785) to inquire, to question. Impf. indicates that he kept asking various questions, perhaps to find out if his brother was rich or poor (PAP, 194). **εἴη** pres. opt. act. εἰμί (# 1639) to be. Opt. used in indir. discourse corresponding to the potential opt. of the dir. question (BD, 195). ◆ **27 ἤκει** pres. ind. act. ἤκω (# 2457) w. the perf. meaning, to have come, to be present (BAGD). **ἔθυσεν** aor. ind. act. s.v. 23. **ὑγιαίνοντα** pres. act. part. (adj.) ὑγιαίνω (# 5617) to be healthy (MLL, 10). **ἀπέλαβεν** aor. ind. act. ἀπολαμβάνω (# 655) to receive back. ◆ **28 ὠργίσθη** aor. ind. pass. ὀργίζω (# 3974) to be angry, to become angry. Ingressive aor. **ἤθελεν** impf. ind. act. θέλω (# 2527) to wish, to desire, to want to, w. inf. **εἰσελθεῖν** aor. act. inf. εἰσέρχομαι (# 1656) to go in. **ἐξελθών** aor. act. part. (circum.) ἐξέρχομαι (# 2002) to go out. **παρεκάλει** impf. ind. act. παρακαλέω (# 4151) to entreat, to beseech, to beg, to plead. Iterat. impf. indicates "he kept on beseeching him" (RWP). ◆ **29 ἀποκριθείς** aor. pass. (dep.) part. ἀποκρίνομαι (# 646) to answer. For the Semitic use of the part. s. MH, 453. **παρῆλθον** aor. ind. act. παρέρχομαι (# 4216) to pass by, to neglect, to transgress. Aor. indicates not even once in contrast w. so many years of service (RWP). **ἔδωκας** aor. ind. act. 2nd. pers. sing. s.v. 16. **ἔριφος** (# 2253) kid, young goat. This was far less value than a fatted calf (Fitzmyer, 1091). Worth at the most about 20 cents (Arndt). **εὐφρανθῶ** aor. subj. pass. (dep.) s.v. 23. Subj. w. **ἵνα** (# 2671) in a purp. cl. ◆ **30 οὗτος** this one. Used contemptuously. **καταφαγών** aor. act. part. (adj.) κατεσθίω (# 2983) to eat up, to devour. The prep. is perfective. ◆ **31 εἶπεν** aor. ind. act. λέγω (# 3306) to say. **εἶ** pres. ind. act. 2nd. pers. sing. εἰμί (# 1639). **σά** acc. pl. poss. adj. σός (# 5050) yours. ◆ **32 εὐφρανθῆναι** aor. pass. inf. s.v. 23. **χαρῆναι** aor. pass. inf. χαίρω (# 5897) to rejoice, to be glad. Infs. are emphasized by the position. **ἔδει** impf. ind. act. δεῖ (# 1256) it is necessary, one must; w. inf. It gives a logical necessity. The parable was told to entreat the respectable Jews to rejoice w. God over the restoration of sinners (Caird).

Luke 16

◆ **1 καί** (# 2779) also, connects this parable w. what has just been related (Arndt). **εἶχεν** impf. ind. act. ἔχω (# 2400) to have. **οἰκονόμος** (# 3874) steward, manager of an estate. One who has been given the authority and responsibility to handle the affairs of the estate for the owner. He was chosen because he was hard-working, zealous, competent, and faithful–not too young, but not too old (between 35-65) (LNT, 52; TDNT; TLNT; Columella, *De Re Rustica*, 11:16-265). In this case, the estate manager may have been responsible for land rentals (PAP, 91-94). **διεβλήθη** aor. ind. pass. διαβάλλω (# 1330) to bring charges w. hostile intent, either falsely and slanderously or justly (BAGD). It means being accused behind one's back (NTNT, 69). **ὡς** (# 6055) because. Used w. part. for giving the alleged ground of a charge against one (RWP). **διασκορπίζων** pres. act. part. διασκορπίζω (# 1399) to scatter, to squander. It refers to the steward's wastefulness, carelessness, and neglect of duty (Geldenhuys). Pres. indicates that this was a continual process. ◆ **2** **φωνήσας** aor. act. part. (temp.) φωνέω (# 5888) to call. **ἀπόδος** aor. imp. act. ἀποδίδωμι (# 625) to give back, to render. Aor. imp. calls for a specific action w. a note of urgency. **λόγος** (# 3364) account. **οἰκονομία** (# 3873) stewardship, trusted responsibility. This involved a presentation and examination of records, receipts, disbursements, cash on hand and the settlement of accounts (TLNT, 2:572). This was not only a demand for a statement of accounts but also a dismissal or firing of the steward, but he is not jailed (Marshall; PAP, 96-98). **δύνῃ** pres. ind. pass. (dep.) 2nd. pers. sing. δύναμαι (# 1538) to be able, w. inf. For the form s. BD, 46. **οἰκονομεῖν** pres. act. inf. οἰκονομέω (# 3872) to be a steward, to exercise the responsibility of managing an estate (s.v. 1). ◆ **3** **ποιήσω** aor. subj. act. ποιέω (# 4472) to do. Deliberative subj., "what shall I do?" **ἀφαιρεῖται** pres. ind. mid. ἀφαιρέω (# 904) to take away from. Pres. indicates that the process was taking place but had not yet been made public (PAP, 98). **σκάπτειν** pres. act. inf. σκάπτω (# 4999) to dig. Digging is the hardest kind of work (BAGD). **ἐπαιτεῖν** pres. act. inf. ἐπαιτέω (# 2050) to ask for something, to beg. Epex. inf. explaining what he would be ashamed of. **αἰσχύνομαι** (# 159) pres. ind. mid. (dep.) to be ashamed. ◆ **4** **ἔγνων** aor. ind. act. γινώσκω (# 1182) to know. "I've got it"; it is a burst of daylight to the puzzled, darkened man (RWP). **ποιήσω** fut. ind. act. s.v. 3. **μετασταθῶ** aor. subj. pass. μεθίστημι (# 3496) to remove, to transfer. **δέξωνται** aor. subj. mid. (dep.) δέχομαι (# 1312) to receive, to welcome. His purpose was to win a place of acceptance. Subj. w. **ἵνα** (# 2671) in purp. cl. ◆ **5** **προσκαλεσάμενος** aor. mid. part. (temp.) προσκαλέω (# 4673) to summons, to call someone to oneself. **χρεοφειλέτης** (# 5972) debtor. **ὀφείλεις** pres. ind. act. ὀφείλω (# 4053) to owe, to owe a debt. ◆ **6** **βάτος** (# 1004) bath. A Heb. liquid measure between eight and nine gallons (BAGD) a yield of 150 trees worth 1,000 denarii (BBC). **ἐλαίου** gen. sing. ἔλαιον (# 1778) olive oil. Gen. of content or description. **εἶπεν** aor. ind. act. λέγω (# 3306) to say. **δέξαι** aor. imp. mid. (dep.) δέχομαι (# 1312) to re-

ceive. Aor. imp. has a note of urgency. **γράμμα** (# 1207) writing, reference to a written contract. **καθίσας** aor. act. part. καθίζω (# 2767) to sit down. Circum. part. w. sense of the imp. **γράψον** aor. imp. act. γράφω (# 1211) to write. Aor. imp. is specific and urgent. It has been suggested that the steward was releasing the debtors from unlawful interest (usury), which was condemned by biblical law (LNT, 56-74), but this may have been a case where it was not money, but produce from the coming harvest. At any rate, he is acting in the name of his lord and the debtors are happy w. the reduction (PAP, 100-101). He forgives in the name of the master about 500 denarii (BBC). **πεντήκοντα** (# 4299) acc. pl., but not declinable, fifty. Each reduction amounted to about 500 denarii (PAP, 101). ◆ **7** **κόρος** (# 3174) corn. A measure for grain, flour, etc., between ten and twelve bushels (BAGD); a yield of about 100 acres worth about 2,500 denarii (BBC). ◆ **8** **ἐπῄνεσεν** aor. ind. act. ἐπαινέω (# 2046) to praise. If the lord had reversed the steward's action, the debtors would have been upset, but by accepting the decision the community views him as a generous person; thus the steward has actually brought honor to his lord (PAP, 101-2, 106-7). **ἀδικία** (# 94) unrighteous, refers to his previous cond. **φρονίμως** (# 5862) adv., wisely. In this context it means "cleverness and skill deployed in self-preservation" (PAP, 106). **ἐποίησεν** aor. ind. act. ποιέω (# 4472) to do, to make, to act. **φρονιμώτεροι** comp. φρόνιμος (# 5861) wise; comp., wiser. This clever rascal was wise enough to place his total trust in the quality of mercy experienced at the beginning of the story. That trust was vindicated. Disciples need the same kind of wisdom (PAP, 107). ◆ **9** **ποιήσατε** aor. imp. act. s.v. 8. The point is how one should use his money generally (Bock). **ἐκ** (# 1666) of, by, apart from. The translation "and not" has been suggested (Pasquale Colella, "Zu Lk 16:7," *ZNW* 64 [1973]: 125). **μαμωνᾶς** (# 3440) mammon, livelihood, possession. For a comprehensive listing of the examples of this word s. H.P. Rüger, "Μαμωνᾶς," *ZNW* 64 [1973]: 127-31; TDNT; EDNT; Fitzmyer, 1109; Matt. 6:24. **ἐκλίπῃ** aor. subj. act. ἐκλείπω (# 1722) to fail, where the unrighteous mammon ceases to be of service (Arndt). Subj. w. **ὅταν** (# 4020) in an indef. temp. cl. **δέξωνται** aor. subj. mid. (dep.) s.v. 6. to welcome, to receive. 3rd. pl. is indef. and is like a pass., or refers to God (SB, 2:221). **αἰώνιος** (# 173) eternal. **σκηνάς** acc. pl. σκηνή (# 5008) tent (TDNT; SB, 2:221). ◆ **10** **ἐλαχίστῳ** (# 1788) dat. sing. superl. ὀλίγος few; elative superl., very little (RWP). ◆ **11** **ἐγένεσθε** aor. ind. mid. (dep.) γίνομαι (# 1181) to become, to be, to prove to be (Plummer). Ind. in a 1st. class cond. cl. which assumes the reality of the cond. **ἀληθινός** (# 240) true, real, genuine, authentic (BAGD; TLNT). Adj. used as subst. **πιστεύσει** fut. ind. act. πιστεύω (# 4409) to have faith in, to entrust; w. dir. obj. in acc. and indir. obj. in dat. ◆ **12** ἀλλοτρίῳ dat. sing. ἀλλότριος (# 259) another's, that which belongs to another. ὑμέτερος (# 5629) yours, your own. The treasure of heaven will be their own inalienable possession (Marshall). δώσει fut. ind. act. δίδωμι (# 1443) to give. ◆ **13** οἰκέτης (# 3860) slave, a household servant. It means people in service, including all the servants in the household (TLNT, 1:384). δουλεύειν pres. act. inf. δουλεύω (# 1526) to be enslaved, to serve as a slave. Inf. completes the vb. Pres. inf. denoted the continual action of service. μισήσει fut. ind. act. μισέω (# 3631) to hate. Futs. in this context are gnomic, indicating a general truth. ἀγαπήσει fut. ind. act. ἀγαπάω (# 26) to love. ἀνθέξεται fut. ind. mid. (dep.) ἀντέχομαι (# 504) to cling to, to hold fast to someone, to be devoted to (MM). καταφρονήσει fut. ind. act. καταφρονέω (# 2969) to despise, to scorn, to disdain, denoting a lack of respect, w. gen. (TDNT; TLNT). ◆ **14** ἤκουον impf. ind. act. ἀκούω (# 201) to hear, to listen. Impf. pictures the continual action, "they were listening." φιλάργυρος (# 5795) lover of money (TLNT). For the greed of the Pharisees s. SB, 1:222; 4:i, 336-39. ὑπάρχοντες pres. act. part. (adj.) ὑπάρχω (# 5639) to exist, to be. ἐξεμυκτήριζον impf. ind. act. ἐκμυκτηρίζω (# 1727) to turn up the nose, to show disrespect or contempt; to sneer at (Arndt; LN, 1:435; TLNT, 2:534-35; TDNT; s. Ps. 2:4). ◆ **15** δικαιοῦντες pres. act. part. δικαιόω (# 1467) to justify, to declare righteous. Part. as subst. Pres. part. is conative, "the ones who are trying to justify themselves." ὑψηλός (# 5734) high, exalted, lifted up. βδέλυγμα (# 1007) abomination, that which is detestable. It orginally meant something that offends on account of its stench (Arndt). ◆ **16** εὐαγγελίζεται pres. ind. mid. (dep.) εὐαγγελίζομαι (# 2294) to proclaim or announce as good news (TLNT). βιάζεται pres. ind. mid. βιάζομαι (# 1041) to use force, to force one's way. Conative pres., "everybody tries to press into it" (Arndt). For the mid. force s. BS, 258; for the possible pass. meaning ("each one is urged," or "expressly invited to enter") s. TLNT, 1:290-91; Fitzmyer, 1117. ◆ **17** εὐκοπώτερον comp. εὔκοπος (# 2324) easy; comp., easier. παρελθεῖν aor. act. inf. παρέρχομαι (# 4216) to go by, to pass away. Epex. inf. explaining what is easier. κεραία (# 3037) horn, one of the little horns or minute projections which distinguish Heb. letters (Plummer). Acc. as subject of the inf. πεσεῖν aor. act. inf. πίπτω (# 4406) to fall. Epex. inf. ◆ **18** ἀπολύων pres. act. part. ἀπολύω (# 668) to release, to divorce. Part. as subst. γαμῶν pres. act. part. γαμέω (# 1138) to marry. μοιχεύει pres. ind. act. μοιχεύω (# 1358) to commit adultery. Gnomic pres. indicating a general truth. ἀπολελυμένην perf. pass. part. acc. fem. sing. ἀπολύω. (# 668) Christ has spoken of the continual obligation of the law; He now gives an isolated example (Meyer). ◆ **19** δέ (# 1254) and, now. For the

connection of thoughts in this chapter s. LNT, 78-99. ἐνεδιδύσκετο impf. ind. mid. (dep.) ἐνδιδύσκομαι (# 1898) to dress oneself in something, to clothe oneself, w. acc. Customary impf., "he customarily clothed himself." πορφύρα (# 4525) purple. βύσσος (# 1116) fine linen. The outer garment was dyed purple, the inner garment was of fine linen made of flax (Arndt). εὐφραινόμενος pres. mid. (dep.) part. εὐφραίνομαι (# 2370) to be glad, to enjoy oneself. Part. in a periphrastic construction emphasizing the continual action in the past. λαμπρῶς (# 3289) splendidly, sumptuously, extravagantly, lavishly (TLNT, 2:366). ◆ **20** πτωχός (# 4777) poor, poor as a beggar (TDNT; MNW; EDNT). ἐβέβλητο plperf. ind. pass. βάλλω (# 965) to throw, to place. He had been placed there and was still there. πυλών (# 4784) gate. It refers to the large ornamental gateway to a mansion (Marshall). εἰλκωμένος perf. pass. part. (adj.) ἑλκόω (# 1815) to be full of sores. A medical term meaning to be ulcerated (MLL, 31; DMTG, 148). ◆ **21** ἐπιθυμῶν pres. act. part. ἐπιθυμέω (# 2121) to desire, to long for. Luke uses this word w. the inf. to express the unfulfilled desire or longing (Jeremias, *Parables*). χορτασθῆναι aor. pass. inf. χορτάζω (# 5963) to satisfy, to feed until one is full. Inf. as obj. πιπτόντων pres. act. part. (adj.) πίπτω (# 4406) to fall. He wanted to be allowed to crawl under the table after the guest had departed and to share the scraps w. the dogs (LNT, 89). ἀλλὰ καί (# 247; 2779) further, what is more. The two particles are combined in a progressive sense, "and worse than all" (Thrall, 14; Marshall). κύνες nom. pl. κύων (# 3264) dog. ἐπέλειχον impf. ind. act. ἐπιλείχω (# 2143) to lick. The prep. ἐπί could be local ("to lick over") (RWP). ἕλκη acc. pl. ἕλκος (# 1814) wound, ulcer (MLL, 32; s.v. 20). ◆ **22** ἐγένετο aor. ind. mid. (dep.) γίνομαι (# 1181) to become, to happen, w. inf. (s. 2:1). ἀποθανεῖν aor. act. inf. ἀποθνήσκω (# 633) to die. ἀπενεχθῆναι aor. pass. inf. ἀποφέρω (# 708) to carry away. κόλπος (# 3146) bosom. It indicates the place of honor at a banquet (s. John 13:23; Jeremias, *Parables*; SB, 2:225-27). ἀπέθανεν aor. ind. act. ἐτάφη aor. ind. pass. θάπτω (# 2507) to bury. ◆ **23** ᾅδῃ dat. sing. ᾅδης (# 87) hades, the underworld, the place of the dead (TDNT; SB, 4:ii:1016-29). ἐπάρας aor. act. part. (temp.) ἐπαίρω (# 2048) to lift up. ὑπάρχων pres. act. part. (circum.) ὑπάρχω (# 5639) to exist, to be. βάσανος (# 992) torment, torture. Originally the touchstone by which metals were tested, then the rack for torturing people (RWP; TWNT; EDNT; NIDNTT; SB, 4:1016-165). ὁρᾷ pres. ind. act. ὁράω (# 3972) to see. Hist. pres. ◆ **24** φωνήσας aor. act. part. (circum.) φωνέω (# 5888) to call, to cry out. ἐλέησον aor. imp. act. ἐλεέω (# 1796) to have mercy on, to show mercy, to see someone in dire need, to have compassion on them, and to give help to remove the need (TLNT; NIDNTT). πέμψον aor. imp. act. πέμπω (# 4287) to send. Both aor. imps. are used in the state of emergency, a cry for help (Bakker, 100). **βάψῃ** aor. subj. act. βάπτω (# *970*) to dip. **ἄκρον** (# *216*) acc. sing. tip. **δάκτυλος** (# *1235*) finger. **ὕδατος** gen. sing. ὕδωρ (# *5623*) water. Gen. w. the vb. indicating the thing into which something was dipped (Marshall; BD, 95). **καταψύξῃ** aor. subj. act. καταψύχω (# *2976*) to cool off, to make cool. For medical examples s. MLL, 32. Subj. w. **ἵνα** (# *2671*) in a purp. cl. **ὀδυνῶμαι** pres. ind. pass. ὀδυνάω (# *3849*) to cause pain; pass. to feel pain, to be in anguish, to be in severe pain (BAGD; MM). For medical examples of the word s. MLL, 32-33; DMTG, 249. Pres. indicates the continual suffering. For the end of kings, rulers, and the landlords at the coming of the Son of Man s. 1 Enoch 63. ◆ **25 μνήσθητι** aor. imp. pass. (dep.) μιμνῄσκομαι (# *3630*) to remember. **ἀπέλαβες** aor. ind. act. ἀπολαμβάνω (# *655*) to take from, to receive. **παρακαλεῖται** pres. ind. pass. παρακαλέω (# *4151*) to encourage, to comfort. **ὀδυνᾶσαι** pres. ind. pass. s.v. 24. For the form s. BD, 45. ◆ **26 μεταξύ** (# *3568*) w. gen., between. **χάσμα** (# *5926*) division, chasm. **ἐστήρικται** perf. ind. pass. στηρίζω (# *5114*) to set up, to firmly establish. Perf. indicates that which stands fixed. Theol. pass. indicating that God made the great chasm. **θέλοντες** pres. act. part. θέλω (# *2527*) to wish, to want, w. inf. Part. as subst. **διαβῆναι** aor. act. inf. διαβαίνω (# *1329*) to pass through. **δύνωνται** pres. subj. pass. (dep.) δύναμαι (# *1538*) to be able, w. inf. Subj. w. **ὅπως** (# *3968*) in a result cl. **διαπερῶσιν** pres. subj. act. διαπεράω (# *1385*) to cross over. Subj. in a result cl. ◆ **27 ἐρωτῶ** pres. ind. act. ἐρωτάω (# *2263*) to ask. **πέμψῃς** aor. subj. act. s.v. 24. The rich man showed love for his brothers but had no love for Lazarus (LNT, 90). Subj. in an obj. cl. ◆ **28 διαμαρτύρηται** pres. subj. mid. (dep.) διαμαρτύρομαι (# *1371*) to witness to, to warn. The prep. compound may mean "bear witness successfully" or "bear witness thoroughly, earnestly" (Plummer). Subj. in a purp. cl. **καί** (# *2779*) too, also. **ἔλθωσιν** aor. subj. act. ἔρχομαι (# *2262*) to come, to go. Subj. used in a neg. purp. cl. ◆ **29 ἀκουσάτωσαν** aor. imp. act. 3rd. pl. ἀκούω (# *201*) to hear, to hear and obey, w. obj. in gen. ◆ **30 πορευθῇ** aor. subj. pass. (dep.) πορεύομαι (# *4513*) to go, to make a journey. Subj. w. **ἐάν** (# *1569*) in a 3rd. class cond. cl. in which the speaker assumes the possibility of the cond. **μετανοήσουσιν** fut. ind. act. μετανοέω (# *3566*) to repent, to change one's mind. ◆ **31 ἀκούουσιν** pres. ind. act. s.v. 29. Ind. in a 2nd. class cond. cl. in which the speaker views the cond. as contrary to fact. **ἀναστῇ** aor. subj. act. ἀνίστημι (# *482*) to rise, to rise up. Subj. w. **ἐάν** (# *1569*) in a 3rd. class cond. assuming the possibility of the cond. **πεισθήσονται** fut. ind. pass. πείθω (# *4275*) to persuade. The story teaches the necessity of giving earnest heed to the warnings of God's Word. For a discussion of extra-biblical parallels s. Richard

Bauckham, "The Rich Man and Lazarus: The Parable and the Parallels," *NTS* 37 (1991): 225-46.

Luke 17

◆ **1 εἶπεν** aor. ind. act. λέγω (# *3306*) to say. For the construction **εἶπεν πρός** s. Fitzmyer, 116. **ἀνένδεκτος** (# *4510*) impossible, from the vb. meaning "to admit to oneself"; hence, "inadmissible," "unallowable" (RWP). **ἐλθεῖν** aor. act. inf. ἔρχομαι (# *2262*) to come. Inf. used either as the subject (IBG, 129) or to express design (Plummer). ◆ **2 λυσιτελεῖ** pres. ind. act. λυσιτελέω (# *3387*) lit., it pays the taxes, repays the outlay, it is well, it is advantageous, it is worth its while (Plummer). **μυλικός** (# *3683*) that which belongs to the mill (millstone). **περίκειται** pres. ind. mid. (dep.) περίκειμαι (# *4329*) to place around, to be placed around. **τράχηλος** (# *5549*) neck. **ἔρριπται** perf. ind. pass. ῥίπτω (# *4849*) to throw, to hurl (s. Matt. 18:6; Mark 9:42). **σκανδαλίσῃ** aor. subj. act. σκανδαλίζω (# *4997*) to cause to stumble (TDNT; EDNT). Subj. w. **ἵνα** (# *2671*) like the inf. in a comparative cl. (BD, 201; NSV, 135). ◆ **3 προσέχετε** pres. imp. act. προσέχω (# *4668*) to give attention, to take heed. Pres. imp. calls for a continual attitude. **ἁμάρτῃ** aor. subj. act. ἁμαρτάνω (# *279*) to sin. Subj. w. **ἐάν** (# *1569*) in a 3rd. class cond. cl., in which the speaker assumes the possibility of the cond. **ἐπιτίμησον** aor. imp. act. ἐπιτιμάω (# *2203*) to rebuke, to warn sternly, w. dat. The vb. has the nuance of a frank, but gentle admonition: politely tell him that he is wrong. This is to be done instead of harboring a grudge (Fitzmyer, 1140). Aor. imp. calls for a specific act. **μετανοήσῃ** aor. subj. act. μετανοέω (# *3566*) to change one's mind, to repent. Subj. w. **ἐάν** (# *1569*) in a cond. cl. assuming the possibility of the cond. **ἄφες** aor. imp. act. ἀφίημι (# *918*) to release, to forgive, to pardon. Aor. imp. calls for a specific act which is complete, but the completed act may be repeated (VANT, 367). ◆ **4 ἑπτάκις** (# *2232*) seven times. Symbolizes any large number (Arndt). **ἡμέρας** gen. sing. ἡμέρα (# *2465*) day. Gen. of time. **ἁμαρτήσῃ** aor. subj. act. s.v. 3. Subj. w. **ἐάν** (# *1569*) in a cond. cl., assuming the possibility of the cond. For the first aor. form used in Hellenistic Gr. instead of the 2nd. aor. form s. BD, 41; MH, 214; GGP, 2:290-97. **εἰς** (# *1650*) against. **ἐπιστρέψῃ** aor. subj. act. ἐπιστρέφω (# *2188*) to turn to. Subj. w. **ἐάν** (# *1569*) in a cond. cl. assuming the possibility of the cond. **ἀφήσεις** fut. ind. act. 2nd. pers. s.v. 3. ◆ **5 πρόσθες** aor. imp. act. προστίθημι (# *4707*) to add to, to give in addition, to increase. It involves increasing the substance rather than adding a new substance (GI, 51). ◆ **6 κόκκος** (# *3133*) grain. **σινάπεως** gen. sing. σίναπι (# *4983*) mustard. Gen. of description. **ἐλέγετε** impf. ind. act. λέγω (# *3306*) to speak, to say. Impf. in a contrary to fact cond. cl. The vb. in the cond. is pres. ind. in a 1st. class cond. cl. (giving a mixed cond. sentence [RWP; BD, 189] rather than the normal impf. This implies the disciples had some faith (GI, 51). **συκάμινος** (# *5189*) mulberry tree, or maybe the fig-mulberry (BAGD; Marshall; RWP). It designates a large tree whose roots were very strong and was not to be planted within 37 feet of a cistern (SB, 2:234; Fitzmyer, 1144). The use of the art. is deictic, pointing to a particular tree (GGBB, 221). **ἐκριζώθητι** aor. imp. pass. ἐκριζόω (# *1748*) to rip out by the roots, to uproot. The pass. may be a theol. pass. indicating that God is to perform the act. **φυτεύθητι** aor. imp. pass. φυτεύω (# *5885*) to plant. **ὑπήκουσεν** aor. ind. act. ὑπακούω (# *5634*) to listen to, to obey. Used in a contrary to fact cond. cl. ◆ **7 ἔχων** pres. act. part. ἔχω (# *2400*) to have. Adj. part. modifying τίς (# *5515*). **ἀροτριῶντα** pres. act. part. (adj.) ἀροτριάω (# *769*) to plow. **ποιμαίνοντα** pres. act. part. (adj.) ποιμαίνω (# *4477*) to be a shepherd. Pres. indicates the continual work that the servant does. **εἰσελθόντι** aor. act. part. (temp.) (dat.) εἰσέρχομαι (# *1656*) to come in. Dat. in agreement w. αὐτῷ (# *899*). **ἐρεῖ** fut. ind. act. λέγω (# *3306*) to say. Used in a question expecting the answer "no" (Stein). **εὐθέως** (# *2311*) immediately. **παρελθών** aor. act. part. παρέρχομαι (# *4216*) to come to. Circum. part. w. the nuance of the imp. **ἀνάπεσε** aor. imp. act. ἀναπίπτω (# *404*) to fall back, to recline at the table. ◆ **8 οὐχί** (# *4049*) strengthened form of οὐ used in a question expecting the answer "yes." **ἑτοίμασον** aor. imp. act. ἑτοιμάζω (# *2286*) to prepare. Aor. imp. calls for a specific act. **δειπνήσω** fut. ind. act. δειπνέω (# *1268*) to eat, to dine, to eat the main meal (LS). **περιζωσάμενος** aor. mid. (dir. mid.) part. περιζώννυμι (# *4322*) to gird yourself about, to tie up your tunic so that it will not interfere w. your movements (Arndt). Circum. part. as imp. **διακόνει** pres. imp. act. διακονέω (# *1354*) to minister, to serve (at the table). Pres. imp. emphasizes the details of the service: "Serve me throughout the meal in the various duties of such table service" (VANT, 353). **φάγω** aor. subj. act. ἐσθίω (# *2266*) to eat. **πίω** aor. subj. act. πίνω (# *4403*) to drink. Effective aor.; both subjs. in an indef. temp. cl.: "until I finish eating and drinking." **μετά** (# *3552*) w. acc., after. **φάγεσαι** fut. ind. mid. (dep.) ἐσθίω. Fut. as command or permission. **πίεσαι** fut. ind. mid. (dep.) πίνω. This reflects the current custom (Geldenhuys). ◆ **9 μή** (# *3590*) used in questions expecting the answer "no." **χάρις** (# *5921*) grace, thanks. Here, "to have gratitude toward one" (RWP). **ἐποίησεν** aor. ind. act. ποιέω (# *4472*) to do, to accomplish. **διαταχθέντα** aor. pass. part. διατάσσω (# *1411*) to order, to command. Part. as subst. The point is that slaves have to carry out their duties without expecting to thereby place their masters under obligation (Marshall). ◆ **10 ποιήσητε** aor. subj. act s.v. 9. Subj. w. ὅταν (# *4020*) in an indef. temp. cl. **λέγετε** pres. imp. act. s.v. 7. **ὅτι** (# *4022*) equivalent to quotation marks. **ἀχρεῖος** (# *945*)

unprofitable, useless, unworthy, as an expression of modesty (Marshall). For the alpha privative s. Moorhouse, 41-68. **ὠφείλομεν** impf. ind. act. ὀφείλω (# *4053*) to be obligated, to owe a debt, to be morally obligated, w. inf. **ποιῆσαι** aor. act. inf. s.v. 9. **πεποιήκαμεν** perf. ind. act. s.v. 9. Perf. indicates the abiding results of the completed action. ◆ **11 ἐγένετο** aor. ind. mid. (dep.) γίνομαι (# *1181*) to become, to happen, w. prep. and inf. in a Semitic construction (s. 2:1). **πορεύεσθαι** pres. mid. (dep.) inf. πορεύομαι (# *4513*) to go, to travel. Inf. w. prep. ἐν (# *1877*) to express contemporaneous time. **διήρχετο** impf. ind. mid. (dep.) διέρχομαι (# *1451*) to go through. Impf. pictures the progressive action in the past. ◆ **12 εἰσερχομένου** pres. mid. (dep.) part. (temp.) s.v. 7. Gen. abs. **ἀπήντησαν** aor. ind. act. ἀπαντάω (# *560*) to meet, to encounter. **ἔστησαν** aor. ind. act. ἵστημι (# *2705*) to stand. **πόρρωθεν** (# *4523*) far away, at a distance (concerning leprosy s. Matt. 8:4). ◆ **13 ἦραν** aor. ind. act. αἴρω (# *149*) to lift up. **ἐλέησον** aor. imp. act. ἐλεέω (# *1796*) to have mercy on, to have compassion on, to see one in need who may not deserve the misfortune, to feel sorrow and compassion and to seek to help the one in need (TDNT; EDNT; NIDNTT; TLNT). Aor. imp. has a note of urgency. ◆ **14 ἰδών** aor. act. part. (temp.) ὁράω (# *3972*) to see. **πορευθέντες** aor. pass. (dep.) part. s.v. 11. Circum. part. w. nuance of an imp. **ἐπιδείξατε** aor. imp. act. ἐπιδείκνυμι (# *2109*) to show. Aor. imp. calls for a specific act. **ἐγένετο** aor. ind. mid. (dep.) s.v. 11. **ὑπάγειν** pres. act. inf. ὑπάγω (# *5632*) to go. Inf. w. prep. ἐν (# *1877*) to express contemporaneous time. **ἐκαθαρίσθησαν** aor. ind. pass. καθαρίζω (# *2751*) to cleanse. ◆ **15 ἰάθη** aor. ind. pass. ἰάομαι (# *2615*) to heal. **ὑπέστρεψεν** aor. ind. act. ὑποστρέφω (# *5715*) to turn around, to return. **δοξάζων** pres. act. part. δοξάζω (# *1519*) to esteem, to glorify, to praise, to cause someone to have a good opinion of another (TDNT; TLNT). Part. of manner. ◆ **16 ἔπεσεν** aor. ind. act. πίπτω (# *4406*) to fall. **εὐχαριστῶν** pres. act. part. εὐχαριστέω (# *2373*) to be thankful, to give thanks. Part. of manner. **καὶ αὐτός** (# *2779; 899*) and *he*, emphatic (Plummer; Stein). ◆ **17 ἀποκριθείς** aor. pass. (dep.) part. ἀποκρίνομαι (# *646*) to answer. For the Semitic use of the part. s. MT, 155ff. **ἐκαθαρίσθησαν** aor. ind. pass. s.v. 14. ◆ **18 εὑρέθησαν** aor. ind. pass. εὑρίσκω (# *2351*) to find. W. the part. it can denote the state of one's being or action in which one is involved (BAGD; GELTS, 189). **ὑποστρέψαντες** aor. act. part. (adj.) s.v. 15. **δοῦναι** aor. act. inf. δίδωμι (# *1443*) to give. Inf. of purp. εἰ μή (# *1623; 3590*) except. **ἀλλογενής** (# *254*) one of another race, foreigner. ◆ **19 ἀναστάς** aor. act. part. ἀνίστημι (# *482*) to rise up. Circum. part. w. nuance of imp. Yet this action is necessary for the completion of the action of the main vb. **πορεύου** pres. imp. mid. (dep.) s.v. 11. **σέσωκεν** perf. ind. act. σῴζω (# *5392*) to rescue, to save, to heal. Perf. indicates the state or cond. ◆ **20 ἐπερωτηθείς** aor. pass. part. (temp.) ἐπερωτάω (# *2089*) to ask a question, to direct a question to. **ἀπεκρίθη** aor. ind. pass. (dep.) s.v. 17. **παρατήρησις** (# *4191*) observation, a watching closely. Used by medical writers to denote empirical medical observation of disease (MLL, 153; DMTG, 260). Here the idea is the watching for premonitory signs, i.e., a sort of eschatological timetable (Fitzmyer, 1160). ◆ **21 ἐροῦσιν** fut. ind. act. s.v. 7. **ἐντός** (# *1955*) w. gen. within, in the midst of, among (Arndt; BAGD; Stein; Marshall; Fitzmyer, 1161; Cleon L. Rogers, Jr., "The Davidic Covenant in the Gospels," *Bib Sac* 150 [1993]: 470-71). ◆ **22 ἐλεύσονται** fut. ind. mid. (dep.) ἔρχομαι s.v. 1. **ἐπιθυμήσετε** fut. ind. act. ἐπιθυμέω (# *2121*) to desire, to long for. Prep. in compound is directive. **ἰδεῖν** aor. act. inf. ὁράω (# *3972*) to see. Inf. as dir. obj. **ὄψεσθε** fut. ind. mid. (dep.) ὁράω. ◆ **23 ἀπέλθητε** aor. subj. act. ἀπέρχομαι (# *599*) to go away, to depart. Subj. w. neg. is used as a prohibition; the aor. indicates do not start the action. **διώξητε** aor. subj. act. διώκω (# *1503*) to pursue. ◆ **24 ἀστραπή** (# *847*) lightning. **ἀστράπτουσα** pres. act. part. (adj.) ἀστράπτω (# *848*) to flash, to lightning. **ἐκ τῆς** (# *1666*) the word χώρας (# *6001*) (region) is to be supplied. "From one place on earth to another place on earth" (Marshall). **λάμπει** pres. ind. act. λάμπω (# *3290*) to shine. Gnomic pres. **ἔσται** fut. ind. mid. (dep.) εἰμί (# *1639*) to be. ◆ **25 δεῖ** pres. ind. act. δεῖ (# *1256*) it is necessary; giving a logical necessity, w. inf. **παθεῖν** aor. act. inf. πάσχω (# *4248*) to suffer. Epex. inf. explaining the necessity. **ἀποδοκιμασθῆναι** aor. pass. inf. ἀποδοκιμάζω (# *627*) to reject as unworthy or unfit after examination (TDNT; LN, 1:31; GELTS, 50). ◆ **26 ἐγένετο** aor. ind. mid. (dep.) s.v. 11. ◆ **27 ἤσθιον** impf. ind. act. ἐσθίω (# *2266*) to eat. **ἔπινον** impf. ind. act. s.v. 8. **ἐγάμουν** impf. ind. act. γαμέω (# *1138*) to marry. **ἐγαμίζοντο** impf. ind. pass. γαμίζω (# *1139*) to give in marriage. The impfs. vividly portray the continual action of the past time. They were not merely living their ordinary lives, but they were wholly given up to external things (Plummer). **εἰσῆλθεν** aor. ind. act. s.v. 7. **κιβωτός** (# *3066*) ark. **ἦλθεν** aor. ind. act. s.v. 1. **κατακλυσμός** (# *2886*) flood; from the vb. meaning "to dash against," signifying an overwhelming inundation (Arndt). **ἀπώλεσεν** aor. ind. act. ἀπόλλυμι (# *660*) to ruin, to destroy. The last three vbs. in the aor. stand in contrast to the previous impfs. (RWP). ◆ **28 ἠγόραζον** impf. ind. act. ἀγοράζω (# *60*) to buy, to purchase at the marketplace. **ἐπώλουν** impf. ind. act. πωλέω (# *4797*) to sell. **ἐφύτευον** impf. ind. act. φυτεύω (# *5885*) to plant. **ᾠκοδόμουν** impf. ind. act. οἰκοδομέω (# *3868*) to build. ◆ **29 ᾗ** fem. sing. dat. rel. pron. ὅς (# *4005*) which. Dat. of time, "on which day." **ἐξῆλθεν** aor. ind. act. ἐξέρχομαι (# *2002*) to go out. **ἔβρεξεν** aor. ind. act. βρέχω (# *1101*) to rain. Rather than used impersonally, the subject of the vb. is probably the Lord (BD, 72). **θεῖον**

(# *2520*) acc. sing. sulphur, brimstone. ◆ **30 ἀποκαλύπτεται** pres. ind. pass. ἀποκαλύπτω (# *636*) to unveil, to reveal. The futuristic use of the pres. gives a confident assertion intended to arrest attention w. a vivid and realistic tone (MT, 63). Theol. pass. ◆ **31 καταβάτω** aor. imp. act. 3rd. pers. sing. καταβαίνω (# *2849*) to come down. Aor. imp. forbids the beginning of an action. **ἆραι** aor. act. inf. αἴρω (# *149*) to lift up, to take. Inf. of purp. **ἐπιστρεψάτω** aor. imp. act. 3rd. pers. sing. s.v. 4. ◆ **32 μνημονεύετε** pres. imp. act. μνημονεύω (# *3648*) to remember. It means to pay attention to something and so to be warned (Marshall). Pres. imp. calls for a constant attitude. ◆ **33 ζητήσῃ** aor. subj. act. ζητέω (# *2426*) to seek, to attempt, to try, w. inf. Subj. w. **ὃς ἄν** (# *4005; 165*) in an indef. rel. cl. **περιποιήσασθαι** aor. mid. inf. περιποιέω (# *4347*) to preserve (mid.) for oneself, to preserve one's life. Inf. as dir. obj. **ἀπολέσει** fut. ind. act. s.v. 27. **ἀπολέσῃ** aor. subj. act. s.v. 27. Subj. **ὃς ἄν** in an indef. rel. cl. **ζῳογονήσει** fut. ind. act. ζῳογονέω (# *2441*) to give life to, to make alive, to preserve a life. ◆ **34 ἔσονται** fut. ind. mid (dep.) s.v. 24. **παραλημφθήσεται** fut. ind. pass. παραλαμβάνω (# *4161*) to accept, to receive, to take. It could mean take for judgment or for salvation (Marshall). **ἀφεθήσεται** fut. ind. pass. ἀφίημι (# *918*) to leave. ◆ **35 ἀλήθουσαι** pres. act. part. nom. fem. pl. ἀλήθω (# *241*) to grind. ◆ **37 ἀποκριθέντες** aor. pass. (dep.) part. s.v. 17. **ἀετός** (# *108*) eagle, vulture (Fitzmyer, 1173). **ἐπισυναχθήσονται** fut. ind. pass. ἐπισυνάγω (# *2190*) to gather together.

Luke 18

◆ **1 πρός** (# *4639*) used w. inf. indicating purp., but is sometimes weakened to "w. reference to" (MT, 144). **δεῖν** pres. act. inf. δεῖ (# *1256*) it is necessary, giving a logical necessity. **προσεύχεσθαι** pres. mid. (dep.) inf. προσεύχομαι (# *4667*) to pray. Pres. inf. w. **πάντοτε** (# *4121*) stresses a continual action. Epex. inf. explaining the necessity. **αὐτούς** acc. pl. αὐτός (#*899*). Acc. as subject of the inf. **ἐγκακεῖν** pres. act. inf. ἐγκακέω (# *1591*) to give in to evil, to become weary, to lose heart, to turn coward (RWP). Real courage requires that we leave the problem w. God (J. M. Derrett, "Law in the New Testament: The Unjust Judge," *NTS* 18 [1972]: 191). In the most desperate circumstances they must continue to ask doggedly and intensely and never desist. It is not so much a matter of omission as of relaxing one's efforts, giving up rather than continuing the fight (TLNT, 1:398-99). ◆ **2 φοβούμενος** pres. mid. (dep.) part. (adj.) φοβέομαι (# *5828*) to fear, to be afraid. **ἐντρεπόμενος** pres. mid. (dep.) part. (adj.) ἐντρέπομαι (# *1956*) to turn to confusion, to put to shame; mid. to reverence. In these respects he showed disregard for God's Law, which demanded love for God and his neighbor. ◆ **3 χήρα** (# *5939*) widow. A widow would go to court without an advocate only in a desperate situation (Derrett, *NTS*, 188; TDNT; EDNT; NIDNTT; NDIEC, 3:20). **ἤρχετο** impf. ind. mid. (dep.) ἔρχομαι (# 2262) to come. Iterat. impf., "she came over and again!" **ἐκδίκησον** aor. imp. act. ἐκδικέω (# 1688) to avenge someone, to procure justice for someone. Here, "to render justice by upholding the innocent and punishing the guilty" (Stein), "take up my case" (Derrett, *NTS*, 187). Aor. imp. calls for a specific act w. a tone of urgency. **ἀντιδίκου** gen. sing. ἀντίδικος (# 508) adversary, opponent (in court). ◆ **4 ἤθελεν** impf. ind. act. θέλω (# 2527) to wish, to want to. Impf. pictures his continual rejection. **εἰ καί** (# 2779; 1623) if, also, even if. W. this construction the cond. is treated as a matter of indifference. The matter is belittled (RG, 1026f). ◆ **5 γε** (# 1145) a particle of emphasis. "Yet because she troubles me" (Plummer). **παρέχειν** pres. act. inf. παρέχω (# 4218) to cause, to bring about (BAGD). **παρέχειν κόπον** (# 3160) to cause trouble, torment, suffering. "Since this woman is exasperating me" (TLNT, 2:326). Inf. w. prep. διά (# 1328) to express cause. **ἐρχομένη** pres. mid. (dep.) part. s.v. 3. Pres. indicates the continual coming; the part. could be cond. or manner. **ὑπωπιάζῃ** pres. subj. act. ὑπωπιάζω (# 5724) to strike in the eye, to give a black eye to. Here in the sense of "to annoy" (Plummer) or "to disgrace" in the sense of losing prestige (Derrett, *NTS*, 190ff; Marshall). Subj. w. ἵνα (# 2671) in a neg. purp. cl. ◆ **6 ἀκούσατε** aor. imp. act. ἀκούω (# 201) to hear. ◆ **7 ποιήσῃ** aor. subj. act. ποιέω (# 4472) to do, to make. Subj. in a question w. the double neg. οὐκ μή (# 4024; 3590) to express an affirmation (BD, 184). **ἐκδίκησις** (# 1689) vengeance, w. the vb. ποιέω, "to vindicate," "to punish the offenders" (Marshall). A t.t. for administrative justice (Derrett, *NTS*, 186). **βοώντων** pres. act. part. (adj.) βοάω (# 1066) to cry aloud, to call for help. **ἡμέρας καὶ νυκτός** (# 2465; 2779; 3816) gen. sing.; gen. of time: during the day and the night. **μακροθυμεῖ** pres. ind. act. μακροθυμέω (# 3428) to be patient, to delay, to extend a period of time on the basis of a particular mental attitude, to be slow to (LN, 1:646). God will not delay (Derrett, *NTS*, 189; Arndt). ◆ **8 ποιήσει** fut. ind. act. s.v. 7. **ἐλθών** aor. act. part. (temp.) ἔρχομαι s.v. 3. ◆ **9 πεποιθότας** perf. act. part. πείθω (# 4275) to persuade; perf. to be persuaded, to be convinced, to have confidence in, to trust in. Perf. expresses persistence in a state of confidence (TLNT, 3:67). Adj. part. as subst. **ἐξουθενοῦντας** pres. act. part. ἐξουθενέω (# 2024) to regard as nothing, to despise, to treat w. contempt, to despise someone or something on the basis that it is worthless or of no value (LN, 1:763). ◆ **10 ἀνέβησαν** aor. ind. act. ἀναβαίνω (# 326) to go up. **προσεύξασθαι** aor. mid. (dep.) inf. προσεύχομαι (# 4667) to pray. There were two periods reserved in the Temple for public prayer at the third hour (9:00 A.M.) and at the ninth hour (3:00 P.M.) (Fitzmyer, 1186; SB, 2:696-702). Inf. of purp. **τελώνης**

(# 5467) tax collector (JZ). ◆ **11 σταθείς** aor. pass. part. (circum.) ἵστημι (# 2705) to stand. **προσηύχετο** impf. ind. mid. (dep.) s.v. 10. Incep. impf., "he began to pray." **εὐχαριστῶ** pres. ind. act. εὐχαριστέω (# 2373) to be thankful, to give thanks. It was customary to began a prayer w. a note of thanksgiving. In this case it turned out to be an expression of self-admiration (Arndt). **ἅρπαγες** nom. pl. ἅρπαξ (# 774) swindler, extortioner, robber (LAE, 316f). Pred. nom. **μοιχός** (# 3659) adulterer. **οὗτος** this one! Used in a contemptuous sense. ◆ **12 νηστεύω** (# 3764) pres. ind. act. to fast (TDNT; SB, 2:241ff, 4:77-144; M, Taanith; DJG, 233). Pres. pictures a continual lifestyle. **δὶς τοῦ σαββάτου** (# 1489; 4879) twice a week, on Mondays and Thursdays (Plummer; Fitzmyer, 1187). **ἀποδεκατῶ** pres. ind. act. ἀποδεκατόω (# 620) to tithe, to pay a tenth. For the tithe at the time of the NT s. JPB, 146-69. **κτῶμαι** pres. ind. mid. (dep.) κτάομαι (# 3227) to own, to possess. ◆ **13 μακρόθεν** (# 3427) from afar, far off. Probably just within the confines of the court of Israel (Fitzmyer, 1188). **ἑστώς** perf. act. part. (circum.) s.v. 11. **ἤθελεν** impf. ind. act. s.v. 4. **ἐπᾶραι** aor. act. inf. ἐπαίρω (# 2048) to lift up. **ἔτυπτεν** impf. ind. act. τύπτω (# 5597) to strike, to hit. **στῆθος** (# 5111) acc. sing. breast. The breast or heart was regarded as the seat of sin; hence the act is one of grief or contrition (Marshall). **ἱλάσθητι** aor. imp. pass. ἱλάσκομαι (# 2661) to propitiate; pass. to be propitiated, to be merciful or gracious; to forgive (Ps. 79:9 [78 LXX]; APC, 125-185; TDNT; GW, 23-48; V, 84-100, esp. 87, 98; K. Grayston, "ἱλάσκεσθαι and Related Words in LXX," *NTS* 27 [1981]: 640-56; NIDNTT; NDIEC, 3:25). ◆ **14 κατέβη** aor. ind. act. καταβαίνω (# 2849) to go down. **δεδικαιωμένος** perf. pass. part. δικαιόω (# 1467) to justify, to declare righteous. Perf. looks at the completed state; i.e., the state of having been declared to be in the right (TDNT; APC, 224-74). Theol. pass. indicating that God is the One justifying. **ὑψῶν** pres. act. part. ὑψόω (# 5738) to lift up, to exalt. **ταπεινωθήσεται** fut. ind. pass. ταπεινόω (# 5427) to make low, to humble. **ταπεινῶν** pres. act. part. Part. as subst. **ὑψωθήσεται** fut. ind. pass. ◆ **15 προσέφερον** impf. ind. act. προσφέρω (# 4712) to bring to. Impf. pictures the continual action in the past. **βρέφη** acc. pl. βρέφος (# 1100) baby, infant. **ἅπτηται** pres. subj. mid. (dep.) ἅπτομαι (# 721) to touch, w. gen. Iterat. pres., "He touched one after the other" (RWP). Subj. in a purp. cl. **ἰδόντες** aor. act. part. (temp.) ὁράω (# 3972) to see. **ἐπετίμων** impf. ind. act. ἐπιτιμάω (# 2203) to rebuke. Incep. impf., "they began to rebuke." ◆ **16 προσεκαλέσατο** aor. ind. mid. προσκαλέω (# 4673) to summons, to call to oneself. **ἄφετε** aor. imp. act. ἀφίημι (# 918) to allow. **ἔρχεσθαι** pres. mid. (dep.) inf. s.v. 3. Epex. inf. explaining what is to be allowed. **κωλύετε** pres. imp. act. κωλύω (# 3266) to hinder, to forbid. Pres. imp. w. the neg. calls for an action in progress to cease (VANT, 365). ◆ **17 δέξηται** aor. subj. mid. (dep.) δέχομαι (# 1312) to receive, to welcome. Subj. in an indef. rel. cl. **εἰσέλθη** aor. subj. act. εἰσέρχομαι (# 1656) to go into. Subj. w. double neg. **οὐ μή** (# 4024; 3590) for strong negation. It has been suggested that the following accounts of the rich young ruler, the blind man, and Zacchaeus reflect how one is to receive the Kingdom as children; that is, a sudden, single-minded attraction to an object or person (Stephen Fowl, "Receiving the Kingdom of God as a Child: Children and Riches in Luke 18:15ff," *NTS* 39 [1993]: 153-58). ◆ **18 ἐπηρώτησεν** aor. ind. act. ἐπερωτάω (# 2089) to question, to ask a question, to direct a question to someone, to ask about. Prep. in compound is directive. **ποιήσας** aor. act. part. (circum.), s.v. 7. **κληρονομήσω** fut. ind. act. κληρονομέω (# 3099) to receive as an inheritance, to inherit. ◆ **19 ἀγαθός** (# 19) good (EDNT; for various views s. Fitzmyer, 1199). **εἰ μὴ εἷς** "except one," that is God. ◆ **20 οἶδας** perf. ind. act. οἶδα (# 3857) to know. Def. perf. w. a pres. meaning. **μοιχεύσῃς** aor. subj. act. μοιχεύω (# 3658) to commit adultery. Used w. neg. **μή** (# 3590) as a prohibition forbidding that the action should arise (MKG, 273). **φονεύσῃς** aor. subj. act. φονεύω (# 5839) to murder, to commit murder. **κλέψῃς** aor. subj. act. κλέπτω (# 3096) to steal. **ψευδομαρτυρήσῃς** aor. subj. act. ψευδομαρτυρέω (# 6018) to be a false witness, to give false witness. **τίμα** pres. imp. act. τιμάω (# 5506) to honor. ◆ **21 ἐφύλαξα** aor. ind. act. φυλάσσω (# 5875) to guard, to keep, to observe. Complexive aor. looking at his total life as a whole. ◆ **22 ἀκούσας** aor. act. part. (temp.) s.v. 6. **λείπει** pres. ind. act. λείπω (# 3309) to be lacking. **πώλησον** aor. imp. act. πωλέω (# 4797) to sell. Aor. imp calls for a decisive and specific action. **διάδος** aor. imp. act. διαδίδωμι (# 1344) to distribute. Prep. compound implies the giving to various ones (MH, 302). **ἕξεις** fut. ind. act. ἔχω (# 2400) to have. For the construction of an imp. followed by the fut. indicating a type of a cond. sentence s. Beyer, 238-55. **δεῦρο** (# 1306) come! **ἀκολούθει** pres. imp. act. ἀκολουθέω (# 199) to follow, to follow as a disciple, w. dat. (TDNT; EDNT). ◆ **23 περίλυπος** (# 4337) surrounded by sorrow, extremely sorrowful. Pred. adj. **ἐγενήθη** aor. ind. pass. (dep.) γίνομαι (# 1181) to become. ◆ **24 ἰδών** aor. act. part. (temp.) s.v. 15. **γενόμενον** aor. mid. (dep.) part. s.v. 23. **δυσκόλως** (# 1552) adv. difficult. ◆ **25 εὐκοπώτερον** comp. εὔκοπος (# 2324) easy, without difficulty; comp., easier. **τρῆμα** (# 5557) hole, eye of a needle. **βελόνη** (# 1017) needle. Used in medical writers of a surgical needle used in operations (MLL, 60f). **εἰσελθεῖν** aor. act. inf. s.v. 17. Epex. inf. explaining what is easier. ◆ **26 ἀκούσαντες** aor. act. part. ἀκούω (# 201) to hear, to listen. Part. as subst. **σωθῆναι** aor. pass. inf. σῴζω (# 5392) to save, to rescue. ◆ **27 εἶπεν** aor. ind. act. λέγω (# 3306) to say. **ἀδύνατα** nom. pl. ἀδύνατος (# 105) powerless, im-

potent, impossible (BAGD). Nom. as subject. ◆ **28 ἀφέντες** aor. act. part. (circum.) s.v. 16. Here "to forsake," "to leave." **ἠκολουθήσαμεν** aor. ind. act. s.v. 22. ◆ **29 ἀφῆκεν** aor. ind. act. ἀφίημι to allow (s.v. 28). **γονεῖς** acc. pl. γονεύς (# 1204) only. In pl. γονεῖς parents. **ἕνεκεν** (# 1915) because of, on account of. ◆ **30 [ἀπο]λάβη** aor. subj. act. ἀπολαμβάνω (# 655) to receive, to receive in return, to recover, to get back (BAGD). Subj. **οὐχὶ μή** (# 4049; 3590) in a strong double neg. statement. **πολλαπλασίων** (# 4491) having many folds, manifold, much more, many times as much (MM). ◆ **31 παραλαβών** aor. act. part. (circum.) παραλαμβάνω (# 4161) to take along; the notion of taking aside is involved but not prominent (Plummer). **τελεσθήσεται** fut. ind. pass. τελέω (# 5464) to bring to completion, to complete. Theol. pass. indicating that God is the One who acts. **γεγραμμένα** perf. pass. part. γράφω (# 1211) to write. Perf. indicates the completed state of an authoritative document (MM). ◆ **32 παραδοθήσεται** fut. ind. pass. παραδίδωμι (# 4140) to deliver over to. **ἔθνεσιν** dat. pl. ἔθνος (# 1620) Gentile. **ἐμπαιχθήσεται** fut. ind. pass. ἐμπαίζω (# 1850) to mock (s. 22:63). **ὑβρισθήσεται** fut. ind. pass. ὑβρίζω (# 5614) to treat outrageously, to treat someone contemptuously in an insolent and arrogant way, to treat abusively (MNTW; TDNT; LN, 1:433, 757; CCFJ, 4:225). **ἐμπτυσ-θήσεται** fut. ind. pass. ἐμπτύω (# 1870) to spit on. ◆ **33 μαστιγώσαντες** aor. act. part. (temp.) μαστιγόω (# 3463) to scourge (s. Matt. 27:26; TDNT). **ἀποκτενοῦσιν** fut. ind. act. ἀποκτείνω (# 650) to kill. **ἀναστήσεται** fut. ind. mid. ἀνίστημι (# 482) to rise. ◆ **34 συνῆκαν** aor. ind. act. συνίημι (# 5317) to comprehend, to understand. They did not understand how the messianic King could die! **κεκρυμ-μένον** perf. pass. part. (adj.) κρύπτω (# 3221) to conceal, to hide. Theol. pass. **ἐγίνωσκον** impf. ind. act. γινώσκω (# 1182) to know. ◆ **35 ἐγένετο** aor. ind. mid. (dep.) (s. 2:1). **ἐγγίζειν** pres. act. inf. ἐγγίζω (# 1581) to come near. Inf. w. prep. **ἐν** (# 1877) to express contemporaneous time. **ἐκάθητο** impf. ind. mid. (dep.) κάθημαι (# 2764) to sit. **ἐπαιτῶν** pres. act. part. (circum.) ἐπαιτέω (# 2050) to ask for, to beg. ◆ **36 ἀκούσας** aor. act. part. (temp.) s.v. 6., w. gen. as obj. **διαπορευομένου** pres. mid. (dep.) part. διαπορεύομαι (# 1388) to travel through, to pass through. **ἐπυνθάνετο** impf. ind. mid. (dep.) πυνθάνομαι (# 4785) to inquire. Incep. impf., "he began to inquire." **εἴη** pres. opt. act. εἰμί (# 1639) to be. Opt. in indir. speech. ◆ **37 ἀπήγγειλαν** aor. ind. act. ἀπαγγέλλω (# 550) to report. ◆ **38 ἐβόησεν** aor. ind. act. s.v. 7. **υἱὲ Δαυίδ** voc. sing. For the significance of the expression s. Cleon L. Rogers, Jr., "The Davidic Covenant in Early Judaism," and "The Davidic Covenant in the New Testament," *Bib Sac* 150 (1993): 285-302; 458-78. **ἐλέησον** aor. imp. act. ἐλεέω (# 1796) to have mercy on (s. 17:13). Aor. imp. calls for a specific act w. a note of urgency. ◆ **39 προάγοντες** pres. act. part. προάγω

(# *4575*) to go before. Part. as subst. ἐπετίμων impf. ind. act. s.v. 15. Incep. impf. σιγήσῃ aor. subj. act. σιγάω (# *4967*) to be silent, to be quiet. Subj. in obj. cl. ἔκραζεν impf. ind. act. κράζω (# *3189*) to shout, to scream. Impf. pictures the repeated action, "he continued screaming." ◆ **40** σταθείς aor. pass. part. (temp.) s.v. 11. ἐκέλευσεν aor. ind. act. κελεύω (# *3027*) to order, to command. ἀχθῆναι aor. pass. inf. ἄγω (# *72*) to lead. Inf. in indir. speech. ἐγγίσαντος aor. act. part. (temp.) s.v. 35. Gen. abs. ἐπηρώτησεν aor. ind. act. s.v. 18. ◆ **41** ποιήσω fut. ind. act. s.v. 7. Fut. in an obj. cl. ἀναβλέψω aor. subj. act. ἀναβλέπω (# *329*) to look up, to see again, to regain sight (s. MH, 295). ◆ **42** ἀνάβλεψον aor. imp. act. σέσωκεν perf. ind. act. s.v. 26. Perf. points to the completed cond. ◆ **43** ἀνέβλεψεν aor. ind. act. s.v. 41. ἠκολούθει impf. ind. act. s.v. 22. Incep. impf., "he began to follow." δοξάζων pres. act. part. δοξάζω (# *1519*) to glorify (s. 17:15). ἰδών aor. act. part. (temp.) s.v. 15. ἔδωκεν aor. ind. act. δίδωμι (# *1443*) to give. αἶνος (# *142*) praise, the speaking of the excellence of a person (LN, 1:429).

Luke 19

◆ **1** εἰσελθών aor. act. part. (circum.) εἰσέρχομαι (# *1656*) to go in. διήρχετο impf. ind. mid. (dep.) διέρχομαι (# *1451*) to go through, to pass through. ◆ **2** καλούμενος pres. pass. part. (adj.) καλέω (# *2813*) to call; pass. to be named. ἀρχιτελώνης (# *803*) chief tax collector, superintendent of tax collectors. Although the term itself is not found in Gr., it is a literal translation of the Heb. *rav mokhes* (JZ, 277). He was in the service of the government or foreign bankers who had bought the privilege of collecting taxes (Arndt). For tax collectors and the Jewish view of them as using force and fraud to gain riches s. LNT, 280ff; TDNT; JZ; BBC; DJG, 804-6; NDIEC, 8:47-76. πλούσιος (# *4454*) rich, very rich. ◆ **3** ἐζήτει impf. ind. act. ζητέω (# *2426*) to seek. Impf. pictures his continual effort. ἰδεῖν aor. act. inf. ὁράω (# *3972*) to see. Epex. inf. explaining ἐζήτει. ἠδύνατο impf. ind. pass. (dep.) δύναμαι (# *1538*) to be able, w. inf. ἀπό (# *608*) (w. gen.) from, here in a causal sense. The multitude was the source of the hindrance (Plummer). ἡλικία (# *2461*) stature, size. ◆ **4** προδραμών aor. act. part. (circum.) προτρέχω (# *4731*) to run before. ἀνέβη aor. ind. act. ἀναβαίνω (# *326*) to go up, to climb up. συκομορέα (# *5191*) fig-mulberry tree. It has leaves like those of the mulberry tree, and fruit like that of a fig tree. It grows to a height of 30-40 feet w. a crown of 120 feet in diameter. The trunk is short w. twisted main branches near the ground making it easy to climb (Arndt; POB, 106-08; PB, 68-69). ἴδῃ (# *1697*) aor. subj. act. s.v. 3. Subj. in a purp. cl. ἐκείνης gen. sing. ἐκεῖνος (# *1697*) w. the word "way" to be understood. Gen. used in connection w. the prep. in the compound vb., or else adverbial in use (RWP; MT, 16).

ἤμελλεν impf. ind. act. μέλλω (# *3516*) to be about to, w. the inf. to express fut. Impf. w. inf. expresses futurity reckoned from a moment in the past: "He was going to pass through" (MKG, 307). διέρχεσθαι pres. mid. (dep.) inf. s.v. 1. ◆ **5** ἦλθεν aor. ind. act. ἔρχομαι (# *2262*) to come. ἀναβλέψας aor. act. part. ἀναβλέπω (# *329*) to look up. Circum. or temp. part. σπεύσας aor. act. part. σπεύδω (# *5067*) to hurry. Circum. part. used as imp. (Matt. 28:19). κατάβηθι aor. imp. act. καταβαίνω (# *2849*) to come down. Aor. imp. calls for a specific action w. a note of urgency. δεῖ (# *1256*) pres. ind. act. it is necessary, giving a logical necessity, w. inf. μεῖναι aor. act. inf. μένω (# *3531*) to remain, to stay. Jesus was putting pressure on him to clean up his life so that He could visit w. him (LNT, 283). ◆ **6** κατέβη aor. ind. act. s.v. 5. ὑπεδέξατο aor. ind. mid. (dep.) ὑποδέχομαι (# *5685*) to welcome, to receive as a guest. χαίρων pres. act. part. χαίρω (# *5897*) to rejoice, to be glad. Part. of manner. ◆ **7** ἰδόντες aor. act. part. (temp.) s.v. 3. διεγόγγυζον impf. ind. act. διαγογγύζω (# *1339*) to express discontent in an emphatic way, to murmur, to complain, to grumble w. one another (LN, 1:433). Incep. impf., "they began to grumble." εἰσῆλθεν aor. ind. act. s.v. 1. καταλῦσαι aor. act. inf. καταλύω (# *2907*) to take up one's quarters, to lodge, to rest. Inf. of purp. It was thought to be wicked to eat the fruit of a person whose earnings were tainted (LNT, 281). ◆ **8** σταθείς aor. pass. part. ἵστημι (# *2705*) to stand up, to step up to say something (BAGD). ἥμισυς (# *2468*) half. ὑπαρχόντων pres. act. part. ὑπάρχω (# *5639*) that which one has, possessions. εἰ (# *1623*) if. Introduces a 1st. class cond. cl. in which the subject views the cond. as real. ἐσυκοφάντησα aor. ind. act. συκοφαντέω (# *5193*) originally, one who shows the fig, that is, one who makes w. his hand the sign known as the "fig," a gesture meant to "misrepresent in an outrageous way" (MM); to bring false charges, to inform, to obtain through extortion or blackmail, used frequently of blackmail by officials (LS; s. also A. C. Mitchell, "The Use of συκοφαντεῖν in Luke 19:8: Further Evidence in Zacchaeus's Defense," *Bib.* 72 [1991]: 546-47). ἀποδίδωμι (# *625*) pres. ind. act. to pay back, to give back. Futuristic pres. indicating the intention (Dennis Hamm, "Luke 19:8 Once Again: Does Zacchaeus Defend or Resolve?" *JBL* 107 [1988]: 431-37). τετραπλοῦν (# *5486*) four times, fourfold. If a person was convicted for wrongdoing in matters of tax collecting, he could be fined from three to tenfold (JZ, 278-80). In later Roman law there was a fourfold penalty required (Buckland, 582; s. esp. 576-83; RPL, 212-13). His intention to make restoration indicates his repentence, making it possible for Jesus to eat w. him without contamination and indicating that he is now a new man (LNT, 283ff; SB, 2:250-51). ◆ **9** ἐγένετο aor. ind. mid. (dep.) γίνομαι (# *1181*) to become, to happen, to come. υἱὸς Ἀβραάμ a son of Abraham. Although he is a physical descendant of Abraham by birth, the anarthrous construction stresses his characteristic as having faith as Abraham did. ◆ **10 ζητῆσαι** aor. act. inf. ζητέω (# 2426) to seek, to look for. Inf. of purp. **σῶσαι** aor. act. inf. σῴζω (# 5392) to save, to rescue. Inf. of purp. **ἀπολωλός** perf. act. part. ἀπόλλυμι (# 660) to ruin, to destroy, to be lost. Perf. pictures the state or condition. Part. used as subst. ◆ **11 ἀκουόντων** pres. act. part. (temp.) ἀκούω (# 201) to hear, to listen to. Gen. abs. **προσθείς** aor. act. part. προστίθημι (# 4707) to add. Here used in the Hebraic sense of an adv.: again, further. For the Hebraic adverbial use of an auxiliary vb. s. MH, 445f. **εἶναι** pres. act. inf. εἰμί (# 1639) to be. Inf. prep. to express cause, "because He was near Jerusalem" (MT, 142). **δοκεῖν** pres. act. inf. δοκέω (# 1506) to seem, to appear, to suppose. **αὐτούς** acc. pl. αὐτός (# 899) they; to the ones listening to Him. Acc. as subject of the inf. **παραχρῆμα** (# 4202) immediately. **ἀναφαίνεσθαι** pres. pass. inf. ἀναφαίνω (# 428) pass., to dawn, to appear, to manifest itself. Inf. w. **μέλλει** to express fut.　◆ **12 εὐγενής** (# 2302) of noble birth. A significant term, since to be a member of the aristocracy was highly prized (Arndt; s. NDIEC, 2:58-60). **ἐπορεύθη** aor. ind. pass. (dep.) πορεύομαι (# 4513) to go, to travel. **λαβεῖν** aor. act. inf. λαμβάνω (# 3284) to receive. Inf. of purp. **ὑποστρέψαι** aor. act. inf. ὑποστρέφω (# 5715) to return. Inf. of purp.　◆ **13 καλέσας** aor. act. part. (temp.) καλέω (# 2813) to call, to summons. **ἔδωκεν** aor. ind. act. δίδωμι (# 1443) to give. **μνᾶ** (# 3641) mina. A Gr. monetary unit, w. the Attic mina being worth in normal times about eighteen to twenty dollars, or about 100 drachmas (BAGD; SEH, 1:471ff). A drachma was the pay for a day's work and this would be about 3 months' wages (Stein). The small sum indicates this is a test of faithfulness (Marshall). **πραγματεύσασθε** aor. imp. mid. (dep.) πραγματεύομαι (# 4549) to carry on business, esp. as a banker or trader (Plummer; NDIEC, 2:58-59; 4:12-13; MM; Preisigke, 2:350). For business ventures in the ancient world, esp. involving private companies and investments, s. LNT, 17-31; Jones, 114-39; E. Badian, *Publicans and Sinners. Private Enterprise in the Service of the Roman Republic* (Oxford: Basil Blackwell, 1972), esp. 67-81; SEH, 1:130-91; 255-352. **ἐν ᾧ** (# 1877; 4005) while, until (BD, 193). ◆ **14 πολῖται** nom. pl. πολίτης (# 4489) citizen. **ἐμίσουν** impf. ind. act. μισέω (# 3631) to hate. This would refer to the Jewish rejection of Jesus (Stein). Impf. indicates the habitual hate. **ἀπέστειλαν** aor. ind. act. ἀποστέλλω (# 690) to send, to send as an official authoritative representative. **πρεσβεία** (# 4561) embassy, delegation (TLNT). **βασιλεῦσαι** aor. act. inf. βασιλεύω (# 996) to be king, to rule as king. ◆ **15 ἐγένετο** aor. ind. mid. (dep.) s.v. 9. **ἐπανελθεῖν** aor. act. inf. ἐπανέρχομαι (# 2059) to return again. Aor. inf. used w. prep. **ἐν** (# 1877) to express time: "after he returned" (MT, 145). **λαβόντα** aor.

act. part. (temp.) s.v. 12; "after he had received." **φωνηθῆναι** aor. pass. inf. φωνέω (# 5888) to call. Inf. in indir. discourse (RG, 1036). **δεδώκει** plperf. ind. act. s.v. 13. **γνοῖ** aor. subj. act. γινώσκω (# 1182) to know. Subj. in a purp. cl. **διεπραγματεύσαντο** aor. ind. mid. (dep.) διαπραγματεύομαι (# 1390) to gain by trading, to earn in business. The compound points to the result of the activity enjoined (Arndt). ◆ **16 παρεγένετο** aor. ind. mid. (dep.) παραγίνομαι (# 4134) to come on the scene, to come, to present oneself. Consummative aor. emphasizing the cessation of an act or state, "when he arrived..." (GGBB, 560). **προσηργάσατο** aor. ind. mid. (dep.) προσεργάζομαι (# 4664) to produce in addition, to gain. The prep. compound indicates "in addition," "besides," "more" (RWP). ◆ **17 εὖγε** (# 2301) well, indeed, excellent, well done. **ἐλαχίστῳ** (# 1788) superl. μικρός little, small; superl., very little. **πιστός** (# 4412) faithful, trustworthy, dependable, reliable (LN, 1:377). **ἐγένου** aor. ind. mid. 2nd. pers. sing. s.v. 9. **ἴσθι** pres. imp. act. εἰμί (# 1639) to be. Used in a periphrastic construction w. the part. **ἔχων** (# 2400) (VA, 465). ◆ **18 ἦλθεν** aor. ind. act. s.v. 5. **ἐποίησεν** aor. ind. act. ποιέω (# 4472) to make. ◆ **19 γίνου** pres. imp. mid. (dep.) s.v. 9. ◆ **20 εἶχον** impf. ind. act. ἔχω (# 2400) to have. **ἀποκειμένην** perf. pass. part. ἀπόκειμαι (# 641) to lay aside, to put away. **σουδαρίῳ** dat. sing. σουδάριον (# 5051) (from Latin) a face cloth for wiping perspiration, corresponding to our handkerchief (BAGD). To hide the money in a cloth was a safe hiding place and a breach of faithfulness required of a servant (LNT, 24). ◆ **21 ἐφοβούμην** impf. ind. mid. (dep.) φοβέομαι (# 5828) to be afraid, to fear. **αὐστηρός** (# 893) harsh, severe; originally that which is harsh and stringent in taste. It signifies a person who would not permit any trifling, one who was strict and exacting, who expects to get blood out of a stone (Arndt; Trench, 47f; MM; 2 Macc. 14:30). Anarthrous pred. adj. stresses the character or quality. **εἶ** pres. ind. act. εἰμί (# 1639) to be. **αἴρεις** pres. ind. act. αἴρω (# 149) to lift up, to take away. **ἔθηκας** aor. ind. act. τίθημι (# 5502) to place, to lay, to set, to put down. **θερίζεις** pres. ind. act. θερίζω (# 2545) to reap. **ἔσπειρας** aor. ind. act. 2nd. pers. sing. σπείρω (# 5062) to sow. ◆ **22 ᾔδεις** plperf. ind. act. of the def. perf. οἶδα (# 3857) to know. Def. perf. w. pres. meaning. ◆ **23 ἔδωκας** aor. ind. act. s.v. 13. **τράπεζα** (# 5544) table, banker's table. Banks would take in a deposit, pay interest on money invested, and change money into various currencies (s. KP, 1:819-21; OCD, 160-61; Jones, 187-88; SEH, 1:180ff, plate XXIV, picture 4; MM). **ἐλθών** aor. act. part. ἔρχομαι (# 2262) to come, to go. Part. forms a cond. cl. of a contrary to fact cond. sentence (BD, 182). **τόκῳ** dat. sing. τόκος (# 5527) interest on money loaned. A papyrus text states, "I have paid the interest ... at the rate of a stater (= 4 drachmas [BAGD]) per mina" (MM; Preisigke, 2:606). In Rome the interest rate of a bank was set at 12% per annum (KP, 1:820; NDIEC, 6:107). ἔπραξα aor. ind. act. πράσσω (# 4556) to make, to collect. Used of collecting taxes, duties, and interest (BAGD). ◆ **24** παρεστῶσιν perf. act. part. dat. pl. παρίστημι (# 4225) to stand by. Part. as subst. Dat. as indir. obj. ἄρατε aor. imp. act. αἴρω (# 149) to take, to take away. Aor. calls for a specific act w. a note of urgency. δότε aor. imp. act. s.v. 13. ἔχοντι pres. act. part. dat. sing. ἔχω (# 2400) to have. Part. as subst. Dat. as indir. obj. ◆ **26** δοθήσεται fut. ind. pass. s.v. 13. ἀρθήσεται fut. ind. pass. s.v. 24. ◆ **27** πλήν (# 4440) moreover. Here the meaning is progressive, "and, what is more" (Thrall, 23; s. 22:21). θελήσαντας aor. act. part. θέλω (# 2527) to will, to want, w. inf. Part. as subst. βασιλεῦσαι aor. act. inf. s.v. 14. ἀγάγετε aor. imp. act. ἄγω (# 72) to lead. κατασφάξατε aor. imp. act. κατασφάζω (# 2956) to slaughter, to cut down. ἔμπροσθεν (# 1869) w. gen., before. ◆ **28** εἰπών aor. act. part. (temp.) λέγω (# 3306) to say, to speak. ἐπορεύετο impf. ind. mid. (dep.) s.v. 12. Incep. impf., "he began to go," "he continued traveling." ἀναβαίνων pres. act. part. s.v. 4. Epex. part. explaining how he continued his journey. ◆ **29** ἐγένετο aor. ind. mid. (dep.) s.v. 9. ἤγγισεν aor. ind. act. ἐγγίζω (# 1581) to be near, to come near. For a discussion of the triumphal entry s. DJG, 854-59. καλούμενον pres. pass. part. καλέω (# 2813) to call; pass., to be called, to be named. ἀπέστειλεν aor. ind. act. s.v. 14. ◆ **30** ὑπάγετε pres. imp. act. ὑπάγω (# 5632) to go, to go forth. εἰσπορευόμενοι pres. mid. (dep.) part. (temp.) εἰσπορεύομαι (# 1660) to go in, to come in. εὑρήσετε fut. ind. act. εὑρίσκω (# 2351) to find. πῶλος (# 4798) a young animal, a young donkey, colt (TDNT; EDNT). δεδεμένον perf. pass. part. (adj.) δέω (# 1313) to bind, to tie. ἐκάθισεν aor. ind. act. καθίζω (# 2767) to sit. This would indicate that it was fit for a king (Fitzmyer, 1249). One is to think of a young, un-ridden animal tethered alongside its mother, which would naturally accompany the young animal (Marshall). λύσαντες aor. act. part. λύω (# 3395) to loose. Circum. part. w. the meaning of an imp. (VANT, 385-86). ◆ **31** ἐρωτᾷ pres. subj. act. ἐρωτάω (# 2263) to question, to ask, to inquire. ἐρεῖτε fut. ind. act. λέγω (# 3306) to say. Fut. used as a command (VA, 419-20; NSV, 52). ◆ **32** ἀπελθόντες aor. act. part. (temp.) ἀπέρχομαι (# 599) to go away, to go out. ἀπεσταλμένοι perf. pass. part. s.v. 14. Part. as subst. εὗρον aor. ind. act. s.v. 30. ◆ **33** λυόντων pres. act. part. s.v. 30. Gen. abs. ◆ **35** ἤγαγον aor. ind. act. ἄγω (# 72) to lead. ἐπιρίψαντες aor. act. part. (circum.) ἐπιρίπτω (# 2166) to throw upon. ἐπεβίβασαν aor. ind. act. ἐπιβιβάζω (# 2097) to place upon. The act is regarded as one of honor; such homage was a sign of kingship (Marshall). ◆ **36** πορευομένου pres. mid. (dep.) part. (temp.) s.v. 12. Gen. abs. ὑπεστρώννυον impf. ind. act. ὑποστρώννυμι (# 5716) to spread out under. Impf. pic-

tures the continual and repeated action. ◆ **37** ἐγγίζοντος pres. act. part. (temp.) s.v. 29. Gen. abs. καταβάσει dat. sing. κατάβασις (# 2853) going down, descent. This was the western slope, going down to the Kidron Valley (Fitzmyer, 1250). ἤρξαντο aor. ind. act. mid. (dep.) ἄρχομαι (# 806) to begin, w. inf. χαίροντες pres. act. part. χαίρω (# 5897) to rejoice. Part. of manner. αἰνεῖν pres. act. inf. αἰνέω (# 140) to praise. ὧν gen. pl. ὅς (# 4005) rel. pron. Gen. by attraction. εἶδον aor. ind. act. ὁράω (# 3972) to see. ◆ **38** εὐλογημένος perf. pass. part. εὐλογέω (# 2328) to bless, to praise. Adj. part. as pred. adj. A quotation similar to Ps. 118:26. ◆ **39** ἐπιτίμησον aor. imp. act. ἐπιτιμάω (# 2203) to rebuke, to warn, to threaten. Aor. imp. calls for a specific act w. a note of urgency. The Pharisees recognize that the crowd's claims have messianic character. ◆ **40** ἀποκριθείς aor. pass. (dep.) part. ἀποκρίνομαι (# 646) to answer. For the Semitic use s. MH, 453. ἐάν (# 1569) used here in a 1st. class cond. cl. where the cond. is assumed as real (RWP; BD, 189). σιωπήσουσιν fut. ind. act. σιωπάω (# 4995) to be quiet, to be silent. κράξουσιν fut. ind. act. κράζω (# 3189) to cry out, to scream. ◆ **41** ἰδών aor. act. part. (temp.) s.v. 37. ἔκλαυσεν aor. ind. act. κλαίω (# 3081) to cry, to weep, w. emphasis upon the noise accompanying the weeping (LN, 1:104). The word means to lament w. sobs (Arndt). ◆ **42** εἰ (# 1623) if, introduces a contrary to fact cond. cl. w. the conclusion broken off and not expressed (RWP; BD, 255). ἔγνως aor. ind. act. 2nd. pers. sing s.v. 15. καὶ σύ (# 2779; 5148) emphatic, even you! ἐκρύβη aor. ind. pass. κρύπτω (# 3221) to conceal, to hide. ◆ **43** ὅτι (# 4022) that, introducing the obj. of ἔγνως (Marshall); or "for," giving an explanation of why Jesus weeps over the city. ἥξουσιν fut. ind. act. ἥκω (# 2457) to come. For a firsthand report of the Roman siege and destruction of Jerusalem s. TJ, 156-209. παρεμβαλοῦσιν fut. ind. act. παρεμβάλλω (# 4212) to throw or raise up beside. χάρακα acc. pl. χάραξ (# 5918) stake. Here the sing. is collective designating the palisades, a wall made of stakes erected by Roman soldiers during the siege of the city (Arndt; s. Jos., *J.W.*, 5:260). σοι dat. sing. σύ (# 5148) you. "Against you." Dat. w. the prep. in the vb. περι-κυκλώσουσιν fut. ind. act. περικυκλόω (# 4333) to encircle. συνέξουσιν fut. ind. act. συνέχω (# 5309) to hold together, to press hard, to crowd someone, to hem someone in. πάντοθεν (# 4119) from all sides. ◆ **44** ἐδαφιοῦσιν fut. ind. act. ἐδαφίζω (# 1610) to level to the ground, to dash against the ground (Geldenhuys; NTNT, 74). ἀφήσουσιν fut. ind. act. ἀφίημι (# 918) to leave. As Titus entered Jerusalem the Beautiful on the morning of Sept. 26, after the destruction, he is reported to have said, "God indeed has been with us in the war. God it was who brought down the Jews from these strongholds; for what power have human hands or engines against these towers?" (Jos., *JW*, 6:411; TJ,

201). ἐπισκοπή (# *2175*) visitation, visitation of divine power, mostly in the good sense (BAGD). ◆ **45 εἰσελθών** aor. act. part. (temp.) s.v. 1 (DJG, 816). **ἤρξατο** aor. ind. mid. (dep.) s.v. 37. **πωλοῦντας** pres. act. part. πωλέω (# *4797*) to sell. Part. as noun "those who sell," "sellers." ◆ **46 γέγραπται** perf. ind. pass. γράφω (# *1211*) to write. Perf. indicates "it stands written," and was used for authoritative documents (MM). **ἔσται** fut. ind. mid. (dep.) εἰμί (# *1639*) to be. **ἐποιήσατε** aor. ind. act. s.v. 18. **σπήλαιον** (# *5068*) acc. sing. cave, den. **λῃστῶν** gen. pl. λῃστής (# *3334*) robber. For this incident, s. Matt. 21:12. ◆ **47 διδάσκων** pres. act. part. διδάσκω (# *1438*) to teach. Part. used in a periphrastic construction stressing the continual action. **ἐζήτουν** impf. ind. act. s.v. 3. Impf. pictures the repeated action which was not completed. **ἀπολέσαι** aor. act. inf. ἀπόλλυμι (# *660*) to destroy. Epex. inf. explaining what was attempted. ◆ **48 εὕρισκον** impf. ind. act. εὑρίσκω (# *2351*) to find. Impf. indicates they were not to succeed, in spite of their searching and meditating (Arndt). **ποιήσωσιν** aor. subj. act. s.v. 18, deliberative subj. **ἐξεκρέματο** impf. ind. mid. (dep.) ἐκκρεμάννυμι (# *1717*) to hang upon. **αὐτοῦ** gen. sing. αὐτός. It is not clear if it is the obj. of the vb. ("they hung on Him") or of the part. ("they were listening to Him") (Fitzmyer, 1270). **ἀκούων** pres. act. part. ἀκούω (# *201*) to hear, to listen to. Part. of manner or circum. part.

Luke 20

◆ **1 ἐγένετο** aor. ind. mid. (dep.) γίνομαι (# *1181*) to become, to happen (s. 2:1). **διδάσκοντος** pres. act. part. (temp.) διδάσκω (# *1438*) to teach. Gen. abs. "While he was teaching." The Court of the Gentiles surrounded by pillared halls was a popular place for teachers (DJG, 812). **εὐαγγελιζομένου** pres. mid. (dep.) part. (temp.) εὐαγγελίζομαι (# *2294*) to proclaim good news (TLNT; TDNT; TLNT). Gen. abs. **ἐπέστησαν** aor. ind. act. ἐφίστημι (# *2392*) to stand by, to approach. ◆ **2 εἶπαν** aor. ind. act. λέγω (# *3306*) to say, to speak. **λέγοντες** pres. act. part. λέγω. Pleonastic part. in Semitic construction (MH, 454). **εἰπόν** aor. imp. act. λέγω Aor. imp. calls for a specific action w. a note of urgency. **ποίᾳ** dat. sing. ποῖος (# *4481*) what kind. **ποιεῖς** pres. ind. act. ποιέω (# *4472*) to do, to perform. Pres. points to what He is in the process of doing. **δούς** aor. act. part. δίδωμι (# *1443*) to give. Part. as subst. The former question is more general, the latter more precise (Noland). ◆ **3 ἀποκριθείς** aor. pass. (dep.) part. ἀποκρίνομαι (# *646*) to answer. Semitic use of the redundant part. (MH, 453). **ἐρωτήσω** fut. ind. act. ἐρωτάω (# *2263*) to question, to ask. **εἴπατε** aor. imp. act. s.v. 2. ◆ **4 ἐξ οὐρανοῦ** from heaven; a circumlocution for "from God" (Stein). **ἦν** impf. ind. act. εἰμί (# *1639*) to be. ◆ **5 συνελογίσαντο** aor. ind. mid. (dep.) συλλογίζομαι (# *5199*) to bring together accounts, to reason, to

reason together, to calculate, to reflect together (TLNT). **εἴπωμεν** aor. subj. act. s.v. 2. Subj. w. **ἐάν** (# *1569*) in a 3rd. class cond. cl. in which the cond. is considered as a possibility. **ἐρεῖ** fut. ind. act. λέγω to say. **ἐπιστεύσατε** aor. ind. act. πιστεύω (# *4409*) to believe, w. obj. in dat. ◆ **6 καταλιθάσει** fut. ind. act. καταλιθάζω (# *2902*) to stone, to throw stones down upon. Prep. in compound may be perfective: "to stone to death" (Fitzmyer, 1275). **πεπεισμένος** perf. pass. part. πείθω (# *4275*) to persuade. Perf. indicates a settled state of persuasion (RWP). Part. is either in a periphrastic construction or is a pred. adj. **εἶναι** pres. act. inf. εἰμί (# *1639*). Inf. in indir. speech. ◆ **7 ἀπεκρίθησαν** aor. ind. pass. (dep.) s.v. 3. **εἰδέναι** perf. act. inf. οἶδα (# *3857*) to know. Def. perf. w. pres. meaning. Inf. in indir. speech. This is an unexpected answer from the chief priests and teachers of the Law. ◆ **8 εἶπεν** aor. ind. act. s.v. 2. **ποιῶ** pres. ind. act. s.v. 2. ◆ **9 ἤρξατο** aor. ind. mid. (dep.) ἄρχομαι (# *806*) to begin, w. inf. **ἐφύτευσεν** aor. ind. act. φυτεύω (# *5885*) to plant. **ἐξέδετο** aor. ind. mid. (dep.) ἐκδίδωμι (# *1686*) to lease, to give out (MM). **ἀπεδήμησεν** aor. ind. act. ἀποδημέω (# *623*) to leave the country, to go on a journey. **χρόνους ἱκανούς** (# *5989*; *2653*) acc. pl., for a long time. Acc. of time expressing duration. For this parable s. Mark 12:1-12; also Charles A. Kimball, "Jesus' Exposition of Scripture in Luke 20:9-19: An Inquiry in Light of Jewish Hermeneutics," *BBR* 3 (1993): 77-93. ◆ **10 ἀπέστειλεν** aor. ind. act. ἀποστέλλω (# *690*) to send; to send as an authoritative representative (TDNT). **δώσουσιν** fut. ind. act. δίδωμι (# *1443*) to give. Fut. w. **ἵνα** (# *2671*) to express purp. w. a sense of expectation (VA, 415; RWP). **ἐξαπέστειλαν** aor. ind. act. ἐξαποστέλλω (# *1990*) to send out, to send away. **δείραντες** aor. act. part. (temp.) δέρω (# *1296*) to flay, to beat. ◆ **11 προσέθετο** aor. ind. mid. (dep.) προστίθημι (# *4707*) to add. Used in the Hebraic sense of "again" (BAGD; s. 19:11). **πέμψαι** aor. act. inf. πέμπω (# *4287*) to send. Inf. as complement of the vb. **προσέθετο** (BD, 200). **ἀτιμάσαντες** aor. act. part. (temp.) ἀτιμάζω (# *869*) to dishonor. ◆ **12 τραυματίσαντες** aor. act. part. (temp.) τραυματίζω (# *5547*) to wound. For the medical use of the term s. DMTG, 312. **ἐξέβαλον** aor. ind. act. ἐκβάλλω (# *1675*) to throw out. ◆ **13 ποιήσω** fut. ind. act. or aor. subj. act. ποιέω (# *4472*) to do. Deliberative fut. or subj. in a question of contemplation (RWP). **πέμψω** fut. ind. act. s.v. 11. **ἴσως** (# *2711*) perhaps, probably, presumably (MM). **ἐντραπήσονται** fut. ind. pass. (dep.) ἐντρέπομαι (# *1956*) to show respect to, to have regard for, to respect (BAGD). ◆ **14 ἰδόντες** aor. act. part. (temp.) ὁράω (# *3972*) to see. **διελογίζοντο** impf. ind. mid. (dep.) διαλογίζομαι (# *1368*) to reason, to discuss. Incep. impf., "they began to discuss." **ἀποκτείνωμεν** pres./aor. subj. act. ἀποκτείνω (# *650*) to kill. Hortatory subj., "let us kill." **γένηται** aor. subj. mid. (dep.) s.v. 1. Subj. in a

purp. or result cl.   ◆ **15** ἐκβαλόντες aor. act. part.
(temp.) s.v. 12. ἀπέκτειναν aor. ind. act. s.v. 14. οὖν
(# 4036) therefore, drawing a conclusion from the story
so far (s. Isa. 5:3-5). ποιήσει fut. ind. act. s.v. 13.   ◆ **16**
ἐλεύσεται fut. ind. mid. (dep.) ἔρχομαι (# 2262) to come.
ἀπολέσει fut. ind. act. ἀπόλλυμι (# 660) to destroy. δώσει
fut. ind. act. s.v. 2. ἀκούσαντες aor. act. part. (temp.) ἀκούω (# 201) to hear. The subject would be the audience
of v. 9. γένοιτο aor. opt. mid. (dep.) s.v. 1. The only use
of this phrase outside Paul's epistles. The meaning is
"may the whole story never happen!" (Arndt; Rom.
3:4). The audience recognizes the justice and yet the
extremeness of the lord's punishment of people performing such horrible acts (VA, 175).   ◆ **17** ἐμβλέψας
aor. act. part. (circum.) ἐμβλέπω (# 1838) to look at, to
fix one's gaze upon. γεγραμμένον perf. pass. part. (adj.)
γράφω (# 1211) to write; perf., it stands written. For the
legal and authoritative implications of this word s. BS,
112ff; MM. a quotation from Ps. 118:22. ἀπεδοκίμασαν
aor. ind. act. ἀποδοκιμάζω (# 627) to reject after examination, to reject as unworthy or unfit (GELTS, 50).
οἰκοδομοῦντες pres. act. part. οἰκοδομέω (# 1868) to
build. Part. as subst., "the builders." ἐγενήθη aor. ind.
pass. (dep.) s.v. 1. γωνία (# 1224) corner. It may be a
foundation stone binding two walls at the corner, or it
may be a keystone locking into place the stones of an
arch (Nolland).   ◆ **18** πεσών aor. act. part. (adj.) πίπτω
(# 4406) to fall. συνθλασθήσεται fut. ind. pass. συνθλάω
(# 5314) to shatter. πέσῃ aor. subj. act. πίπτω Subj. in an
indef. rel. cl. λικμήσει fut. ind. act. λικμάω (# 3347) to
winnow chaff from grain, to blow away like chaff, to
sweep out of sight or out of existence (Plummer). For
the meaning "to grind to powder" s. BS, 225f; MM;
Fitzmyer, 1286.   ◆ **19** ἐζήτησαν aor. ind. act. ζητέω
(# 2426) to seek, to try, w. inf. ἐπιβαλεῖν aor. act. inf.
ἐπιβάλλω (# 2095) to place upon, to lay hands upon
someone. ἐφοβήθησαν aor. ind. pass. (dep.) φοβέομαι
(# 5828) to be afraid, to fear. ἔγνωσαν aor. ind. act. γινώσκω (# 1182) to know, to recognize. πρός (# 4639) in
reference to, w. respect to.   ◆ **20** παρατηρήσαντες aor.
act. part. (circum.) παρατηρέω (# 4190) to watch intently (s. 6:7). ἀπέστειλαν aor. ind. act. s.v. 10. ἐγκάθετος
(# 1588) spy, agent, someone hired to trap one by crafty
words, one who is hired to lie in wait (RWP; Fitzmyer,
1294). Used in Job 19:12 for one "set in ambush"
(GELTS, 126; s. also Jos., JW, 2.27; 6.286). ὑποκρινο-
μένους pres. mid. (dep.) part. (adj.) ὑποκρίνομαι
(# 5693) to pretend; they play the role of righteous people to spy on Jesus (TLNT, 3:409; s. TDNT). εἶναι pres.
act. inf. εἰμί (# 1639) to be. Epex. inf. ἐπιλάβωνται aor.
subj. mid. ἐπιλαμβάνω (# 2138) to lay hold upon, to
seize, w. double gen. (αὐτοῦ λόγου), the first being the
dir. obj., the second being epex.; "to catch him [in his]
word" (Fitzmyer, 1295). Subj. w. ἵνα (# 2671) in a purp.
cl. ὥστε (# 6063) w. inf. Used to express intended result

(BD, 198). The sense would be, "such words as it
would enable them to hand him over" (IBG, 143).
παραδοῦναι aor. act. inf. παραδίδωμι (# 4140) to deliver
over. ἀρχῇ dat. sing. ἀρχή (# 794) rule, office, domain,
sphere of influence (BAGD). Indir. obj. ἡγεμόνος gen.
sing. ἡγεμών (# 2450) governor. Gen. goes w. both of
the preceding nouns (Marshall).   ◆ **21** ἐπηρώτησαν aor.
ind. act. ἐπερωτάω (# 2089) to direct a question to
someone, to ask. οἴδαμεν perf. ind. act. οἶδα (# 3857) to
know. Def. perf. w. pres. meaning. λαμβάνεις pres. ind.
act. λαμβάνω (# 3284) to receive. Used in the expression
"to accept the face," which is a Hebraism meaning "to
regard w. favor," "to show partiality" (Geldenhuys).
Pres. indicates the habitual practice.   ◆ **22** ἔξεστιν pres.
ind. act. ἔξεστι (# 2003) it is allowed, it is lawful, w. inf.
The question is framed as a question in the law. The
authority and ability of Jesus as a teacher was being
tested (LNT, 315-23). φόρος (# 5843) tribute. δοῦναι aor.
act. inf. s.v. 10. Epex. inf. explaining ἔξεστιν.   ◆ **23**
κατανοήσας aor. act. part. (temp.) κατανοέω (# 2917) to
take note of, to perceive, to consider carefully. πανουργία (# 4111) lit., readiness to do anything, skill, in the
neg. sense craftiness, trickery, treachery (BAGD; LN,
1:771).   ◆ **24** δείξατε aor. imp. act. δείκνυμι (# 1259) to
show. δηνάριον (# 1324) acc. sing. denarius. A Roman
silver coin with a picture of Caesar (s. Matt. 22:20; H.
StJ. Hart, "The Coin of 'Render unto Caesar...' [A Note
on Some Aspects of Mark 12:13-17; Matt. 22:15-22;
Luke 20:20-26]," JPD, 241-48; BBC). εἰκόνα acc. sing.
εἰκών (# 1635) image. ἐπιγραφή (# 2107) inscription.
Some feel Jesus was alluding to Ecclesiastes 7:2 (LNT,
324-28).   ◆ **25** τοίνυν (# 5523) therefore, draws an inference and a consequence from the preceding (BD, 235).
ἀπόδοτε aor. imp. act. ἀποδίδωμι (# 625) to render, to
give what is proper and due, to pay (Marshall). Jesus'
answer is that human governments are to be obeyed as
long as they do not conflict w. God's law and obedience to God (LNT, 333-37). τὰ τοῦ θεοῦ (# 2536). The
gen. indicates to whom the things are to be paid, probably indicating the dedication of one's whole life (Fitzmyer, 1297; F.F Bruce, "Render to Caesar," JPD, 261; s.
Nolland for a discussion of the gen. here).   ◆ **26** ἴσχυσαν aor. ind. act. ἰσχύω (# 2710) to be able, w. inf. ἐπιλα-
βέσθαι aor. mid. (dep.) inf. s.v. 20. θαυμάσαντες aor. act.
part. (circum.) θαυμάζω (# 2513) to marvel, to wonder.
ἐσίγησαν aor. ind. act. σιγάω (# 4967) to be silent, to become silent. Ingressive aor.   ◆ **27** προσελθόντες aor.
act. part. (temp.) προσέρχομαι (# 4665) to come to, to
approach. ἀντιλέγοντες pres. act. part. ἀντιλέγω (# 515)
to speak in opposition to, to oppose, to contradict, to
deny. εἶναι pres. act. inf. εἰμί (# 1639) to be. Inf. in indir.
speech. For the Sadducees s. TJ, 76-81; Acts 23:8-9.
ἐπηρώτησαν aor. ind. act. s.v. 21.   ◆ **28** ἔγραψεν aor.
ind. act. s.v. 17. ἀποθάνῃ aor. subj. act. ἀποθνήσκω
(# 633) to die. Subj. in a 3rd. class cond. cl. where the

cond. is viewed as possible. **ἄτεκνος** (# *866*) childless. **ᾖ** pres. subj. act. εἰμί (# *1639*) to be. Subj. in 3rd. class cond. cl. **λάβῃ** aor. subj. act. s.v. 21. Subj. in a noun cl. as obj. of the vb. ἔγραψεν. **ἐξαναστήσῃ** aor. subj. act. ἐξανίστημι (# *1985*) to raise up out of, to raise up. Subj. in noun cl. For the levirate marriage s. Deut. 25:5-10; M, Yebamoth; Fitzmyer, 1304; Donald A. Leggett, *The Levirate and Goel Institutions in the Old Testament* (Cherry Hill, N.J.: Mack Publishing Company, 1974); ABD, 1:765; 4:296-97. ◆ **29 λαβών** aor. act. part. (temp.) s.v. 21. **ἀπέθανεν** aor. ind. act. s.v. 28. ◆ **31 ἔλαβεν** aor. ind. act. s.v. 21. **κατέλιπον** aor. ind. act. καταλείπω (# *2901*) to leave behind. **ἀπέθανον** aor. ind. act. s.v. 28. ◆ **33 γίνεται** pres. ind. mid. (dep.) s.v. 1. Futuristic pres. **ἔσχον** aor. ind. act. ἔχω (# *2400*) to have, w. double acc. ("to have her as wife"). ◆ **34 οἱ υἱοὶ τοῦ αἰῶνος τούτου** the sons of this age (world). **γαμοῦσιν** pres. ind. act. γαμέω (# *1138*) to marry. Gnomic or habitual pres. indicating a constant practice. **γαμίσκονται** pres. ind. pass. γαμίσκω (# *1140*) to give in marriage; pass., to be given in marriage, used of the woman (BAGD). Gnomic or habitual pres. ◆ **35 καταξιωθέντες** aor. pass. part. καταξιόω (# *2921*) to consider worthy. Part. as subst. translated as a rel. cl. ("the ones who..."). **τυχεῖν** aor. act. inf. τυγχάνω (# *5593*) to attain, to meet, to experience, w. gen. Epex. inf. explaining the part. καταξιωθέντες ◆ **36 ἀποθανεῖν** aor. act. inf. s.v. 28. **ἰσάγγελοι** nom. pl. ἰσάγγελος (# *2694*) angel-like, equal to angels. Pred. adj. **ὄντες** pres. act. part. (causal) εἰμί (# *1639*). ("Since they sons of the resurrection.") They participate in the age to come (Fitzmyer, 1306). ◆ **37 ἐγείρονται** pres. ind. pass. ἐγείρω (# *1586*) to raise, to be raised. Futuristic pres. **καί** (# *2779*) even, also. **ἐμήνυσεν** aor. ind. act. μηνύω (# *3606*) to disclose, to inform, to reveal. Used esp. of making known what was secret or known only to a select few (Plummer; LN, 1:412). ◆ **38 ζώντων** pres. act. part. ζάω (# *2409*) to live. Part. as subst. **αὐτῷ** dat. sing. αὐτός (# *899*) ("to Him"). Dat. of respect, indicating a relationship (IGNT, 97-98); they are alive as far as God is concerned (Marshall). **ζῶσιν** pres. ind. act. ◆ **39 ἀποκριθέντες** aor. pass. (dep.) part. s.v. 3. **εἶπας** aor. ind. act. λέγω (# *3306*) to say. ◆ **40 ἐτόλμων** impf. ind. act. τολμάω (# *5528*) to dare, w. inf. **ἐπερωτᾶν** pres. act. inf. s.v. 21. Epex. inf. ◆ **41 εἶναι** pres. act. inf. s.v. 27. Inf. in indir. speech. For a discussion of this passage s. Cleon L. Rogers, Jr., "The Davidic Covenant in the Gospels," *Bib Sac* 150 (1993): 463-64. ◆ **42 κάθου** pres. imp. mid. (dep.) κάθημαι (# *2764*) to sit. **ἐκ δεξιῶν μου** at my right hand. The king is accorded a place of honor by Yahweh Himself, a sign of blessing on his rule (Fitzmyer, 1315). ◆ **43 θῶ** aor. subj. act. τίθημι (# *5502*) to place, to make. Subj. w. **ἕως ἄν** (# *2401; 165*) in an indef. temp. cl. **ὑποπόδιον** (# *5711*) acc. sing. footstool. Double acc. used predicatively. It predicates something of a noun already in the acc. ("as...") (IBG,

35). ◆ **44 καλεῖ** pres. ind. act. καλέω (# *2813*) to call. ◆ **45 ἀκούοντος** pres. act. (temp.) part. s.v. 16. Gen. abs. ◆ **46 προσέχετε** pres. imp. act. προσέχω (# *4668*) to give heed to, to be aware of. Pres. imp. calls for a continual action. **θελόντων** pres. act. part. (adj.) θέλω (# *2527*) to wish, to want to, w. inf. **περιπατεῖν** pres. act. inf. περιπατέω (# *4344*) to walk about. **στολαῖς** dat. pl. στολή (# *5124*) robe, a stately robe generally reaching to the feet or, train-like, sweeping the ground (Trench, *Synonyms*, 186). Lawyers and officers used these in more ornamented or voluminous fashion as a mark of distinction (Fitzmyer, 1318; SB, 2:31-33). **φιλούντων** pres. act. part. (adj.) φιλέω (# *5797*) to love, to be fond of. **πρωτοκαθεδρία** (# *4751*) seat of honor. For the seat of honor at the synagogue and at banquets s. 11:43; Mark 12:39. ◆ **47 κατεσθίουσιν** pres. ind. act. κατεσθίω (# *2983*) to eat up. Habitual pres. **προφάσει** dat. sing. πρόφασις (# *4733*) actual motive, valid excuse, falsely alleged motive, pretext (BAGD). **μακρά** acc. μακρός (# *3431*) long. It is not the length of prayers, but the motive that is criticized. **λήμψονται** fut. ind. mid. (dep.) s.v. 21. **περισσότερον** (# *4358*) comp. περισσός remarkable (s. 7:26).

Luke 21

◆ **1 ἀναβλέψας** aor. act. part. (temp.) ἀναβλέπω (# *329*) to look up. **εἶδεν** aor. ind. act. ὁράω (# *3972*) to see. **βάλλοντας** pres. act. part. (adj.) βάλλω (# *965*) to throw. Pres. indicates the continual action. **γαζοφυλάκιον** (# *1126*) contribution box (s. Mark 12:41). **πλούσιος** (# *4454*) rich, very rich. Gifts were brought for various reasons, and the one making the offering declared the amount and purp. to the priest; in this way it was possible to know how much various people brought (SB, 2:38-39; Marshall; M, Shek. 2:4-5; 6:5-6). ◆ **2 χήρα** (# *5939*) widow. The plight of a widow without a husband to provide was grievous (EDNT; TDNT; TDOT). **πενιχρός** (# *4293*) needy, poor. It describes the person for whom life and living is a struggle (NTW; Fitzmyer, 1322). **λεπτά** acc. pl. λεπτόν (# *3321*) the smallest bronze coin (s. Mark 12:42). ◆ **3 πτωχή** (# *4777*) poor, poor to the point of having nothing at all and being forced to beg in order to survive. (Arndt; TDNT; Fitzmyer, 1322; NTW). **πλεῖον** comp. of πολύς (# *4498*) much; comp., more. **πάντων** gen. pl. πᾶς (# *4246*) all. Gen. of comparison. **ἔβαλεν** aor. ind. act. s.v. 1. ◆ **4 περισσεύοντος** pres. act. part. gen. n. sing. περισσεύω (# *4355*) to be in abundance, to be in excess. Part. as subst. **αὐτοῖς** dat. pl. αὐτός. Poss. dat. ("their abundance"). **ἔβαλον** aor. ind. act. s.v. 1. **ὑστέρημα** (# *5729*) lack, poverty. It is more than poverty; it signifies destitution (Arndt). **βίος** (# *1050*) living, livelihood (s. Mark 12:44). **εἶχεν** impf. ind. act. ἔχω (# *2400*) to have. Her generous giving came from her great faith! ◆ **5 λεγόντων** pres. act. part. (temp.) λέγω (# *2400*) to

say, to speak. Gen. abs. ἀναθήμασιν dat. pl. ἀνάθημα
(# 356) a gift dedicated to God. Used of costly offerings
presented to the gods and suspended or exposed to
view in the temple. It expresses that which is dedicated to God for its own honor as well as for God's glory
(Trench, *Synonyms*, 16ff). Instr. dat. κεκόσμηται perf.
ind. pass. κοσμέω (# 3175) to adorn. Perf. indicates a
state or cond. For the beauty of the Temple s. TJ, 28-30;
Jos., *J.W.*, 5.222-24; ABD, 6:364-65. For example, the
amount of gold on the exterior of the Temple was so
great that it was said when the sun shone it virtually
blinded the onlookers. In Rabbinic sources it is said,
"No one has seen a truly beautiful building unless he
has seen the Temple" (b. Baba Bathra, 3b). ◆ **6** ταῦτα
(# 4047) these things. Acc. of general reference (RWP).
Also explained as an independent nom. (M, 69; DM,
70). **θεωρεῖτε** pres. ind. act. θεωρέω (# 2555) to see, to
look at, to observe something w. continuity, often w.
the implication that what is observed is something unusual (LN, 1:279). **ἐλεύσονται** fut. ind. mid. (dep.) ἔρχομαι (# 2262) to come. **ἀφεθήσεται** fut. ind. pass. ἀφίημι
(# 918) to leave. **καταλυθήσεται** fut. ind. pass. καταλύω
(# 2907) to destroy, to destroy completely. For the destruction of the temple by the Romans s. TJ, 193-96.
◆ **7** **ἐπηρώτησαν** aor. ind. act. ἐπερωτάω (# 2089) to direct a question to, to ask. **ἔσται** fut. ind. mid. (dep.) εἰμί
(# 1639) to be. **μέλλη** pres. subj. act. μέλλω (# 3516) to be
about to; w. inf. to express fut. (MKG, 307). Subj. w.
ὅταν (# 4020) in an indef. temp. cl. **γίνεσθαι** pres. mid.
(dep.) inf. γίνομαι (# 1181) to become, to happen. The
question becomes the springboard for the eschatological discourse proper (Fitzmyer, 1331). ◆ **8** **βλέπετε**
pres. imp. act. βλέπω (# 1063) to see, to beware. Pres.
imp. calls for a constant vigil. **πλανηθῆτε** aor. subj.
pass. πλανάω (# 4414) to deceive, to lead astray; pass.
to be led astray. Subj. w. neg. **μή** (# 3590) to express a
command not to start an action. Pass. of permission:
"Do not allow yourselves to be deceived." **ἐλεύσονται**
fut. ind. mid. (dep.) s.v. 6. **ἐπὶ τῷ ὀνόματί μου** in my
name. Perhaps the idea is "claiming the name 'Messiah' which rightfully belongs to me" (Marshall; Nolland). **ἐγώ εἰμι** (# 1609; 1639) I am. That is, "I am the
Messiah" (Stein; Marshall; Evans). **ἤγγικεν** perf. ind.
act. ἐγγίζω (# 1581) to draw near, to be near. **πορευθῆτε**
aor. subj. pass. (dep.) πορεύομαι (# 4513) to go. Subj. w.
neg. **μή** (# 3590) as a command not to start an action.
◆ **9** **ἀκούσητε** aor. subj. act. ἀκούω (# 201) to hear. Subj.
w. **ὅταν** (# 4020) in an indef. temp. cl. **πόλεμος** (# 4483)
armed conflict, war, battle, conflict (BAGD). **ἀκαταστασία** (# 189) disturbance, upheaval, revolution. **πτοηθῆτε**
aor. subj. pass. πτοέω (# 4765) to be terrified as the result of something which startles or alarms, to be very
frightened (LN, 1:317). Subj. w. neg. **μή** (# 3590) to prevent an action from beginning. **δεῖ** pres. ind. act.
(# 1256) it is necessary, giving a logical necessity, w. inf.

γενέσθαι aor. mid. (dep.) inf. s.v. 7. ◆ **10** **ἔλεγεν** impf.
ind. act. s.v. 5. Impf., "He continued talking." **ἐγερθήσεται** fut. ind. pass. ἐγείρω (# 1586) to raise; pass. to
rise. ◆ **11** **σεισμός** (# 4939) earthquake. **κατὰ τόπους**
(# 2848; 5536) everywhere, various places, distributive
use of prep. **λιμός** (# 3350) hunger, famine. **λοιμός**
(# 3369) pestilence, plague, disease. For the medical
use of the word s. DMTG, 225. **φόβητρα** nom. pl.
φόβητρον (# 5831) terrible sight or event, horror. For the
signs that were reported to have happened just before
the destruction of Jerusalem in A.D. 70 s. TJ, 197-98.
◆ **12** **πρό** (# 4574) prep. w. gen., before. The prep. is
used of time (Plummer). **ἐπιβαλοῦσιν** fut. ind. act.
ἐπιβάλλω (# 2095) to throw upon, to lay (hands) upon;
w. the idea of violence; to arrest (MM). **διώξουσιν** fut.
ind. act. διώκω (# 1503) to pursue, to persecute. **παραδιδόντες** pres. act. part. παραδίδωμι (# 4140) to deliver
over. Part. of manner describing the persecution.
ἀπαγομένους pres. pass. part. ἀπάγω (# 552) to lead
away as a prisoner or condemned man (BAGD). A t.t.
in Athenian legal language (EGT). Circum. part. or
part. of manner. ◆ **13** **ἀποβήσεται** fut. ind. mid. (dep.)
ἀποβαίνω (# 609) to turn out, w. dat. of advantage.
"This will lead to [an opportunity] for you for witness" (RWP; Nolland). ◆ **14** **θέτε** aor. imp. act. τίθημι
(# 5502) to place, to determine. Aor. imp. calls for a
specific act. **προμελετᾶν** pres. act. inf. προμελετάω
(# 4627) to practice beforehand, to prepare. The proper
term for preparing a speech (Geldenhuys). Epex. inf.
explaining the command. **ἀπολογηθῆναι** aor. pass. inf.
ἀπολογέομαι (# 664) to defend oneself (EDNT). Inf. as
obj. of the previous inf. ◆ **15** **δώσω** fut. ind. act. δίδωμι
(# 1443) to give. **στόμα** (# 5125) acc. sing. mouth; here,
the power of speech (Exod. 4:10-17). **σοφία** (# 5053)
wisdom, the choice of matter and form (Plummer).
δυνήσονται fut. ind. pass. (dep.) δύναμαι (# 1538) to be
able, w. inf. **ἀντιστῆναι** aor. act. inf. ἀνθίστημι (# 468)
to stand against, to withstand, to resist. **ἀντειπεῖν** aor. act.
inf. ἀντιλέγω (# 515) to speak against, to refute. **ἀντικείμενοι** pres. mid. (dep.) part. ἀντίκειμαι (# 512) to lie
over against, to be opposed. Part. as subst.: opponent,
enemy, adversary (BAGD). For the prep. in compound
s. MH, 297. ◆ **16** **παραδοθήσεσθε** fut. ind. pass. παραδίδωμι (# 4140) to deliver over. **γονέων** gen. pl. γονεύς
(# 1204) parent. **θανατώσουσιν** fut. ind. act. θανατόω
(# 2506) to kill. **ἐξ** (# 1666) out of. Partitive gen. w. the
prep. used as the obj. ("some of you") (BD, 91). ◆ **17**
ἔσεσθε fut. ind. mid. (dep.) εἰμί (# 1639). Used w. part.
to form a periphrastic construction stressing the continual action or state. **μισούμενοι** pres. pass. part. μισέω
(# 3631) to hate. ◆ **18** **ἀπόληται** aor. subj. mid. ἀπόλλυμι (# 660) to destroy, to perish. Subj. w. double neg. **οὐ
μή** (# 4024; 3590) for a strong denial.   ◆ **19** **ὑπομονῇ**
dat. sing. ὑπομονή (# 5705) lit., remaining under; patience, endurance, courageous and constant tenacity

w. hopeful expectancy, indicating an active endurance which opposes the evil while patiently waiting on the Lord (TDNT; NIDNTT; TLNT). W. the prep. ἐν (# 1877) may indicate the sphere rather than means. κτήσασθε aor. imp. mid. (dep.) κτάομαι (# 3227) to possess, to acquire. For the variant reading κτήσεσθε (fut. ind. mid.) s. TC, 173. ◆ **20** ἴδητε aor. subj. act. s.v. 1. Subj. w. ὅταν (# 4020) in an indef. temp. cl. κυκλουμένην pres. pass. part. (adj.) κυκλόω (# 3240) to encircle. στρατόπεδον (# 5136) army camp. For the Roman siege of Jerusalem s. TJ, 174-204. γνῶτε aor. imp. act. γινώσκω (# 1182) to know, to recognize. Aor. calls for a specific act. ἤγγικεν perf. ind. act. s.v. 8. ◆ **21** φευγέτωσαν pres. imp. act. 3rd. pers. pl. φεύγω (# 5771) to flee. Pres. imp. vbs. in this v. give general precepts or prohibit them (VANT, 338). ἐκχωρείτωσαν pres. imp. act. 3rd. pl. ἐκχωρέω (# 1774) to go out. εἰσερχέσθωσαν pres. imp. mid. (dep.) 3rd. pl. εἰσέρχομαι (# 1656) to go into to enter. ◆ **22** ἐκδικήσεως gen. sing. ἐκδίκησις (# 1689) punishment, vengeance. Gen. of description. πλησθῆναι aor. pass. inf. πίμπλημι (# 4398) to fill, to fulfill. Inf. of purp. γεγραμμένα perf. pass. part. (adj.) γράφω (# 1211) to write. Perf. was used of authoritative documents (MM). For the OT character of this prophecy s. C.H. Dodd, *More New Testament Studies*, 74-80. ◆ **23** ἐχούσαις pres. act. part. dat. fem. pl. ἔχω (# 2400) to have; ἐν γαστρὶ ἔχειν to be pregnant. Part. as subst. Dat. of disadvantage. θηλαζούσαις pres. act. part. dat. fem. pl. θηλάζω (# 2558) to nurse, to breast-feed. Adj. part. as subst. Dat. of disadvantage. ἀνάγκη (# 340) distress, calamity. ὀργή (# 3973) wrath, deep-seated anger. ◆ **24** πεσοῦνται fut. ind. mid. (dep.) πίπτω (# 4406) to fall. αἰχμαλωτισθήσονται fut. ind. pass. αἰχμαλωτίζω (# 170) to take captive. ἔσται fut. ind. mid. (dep.) s.v. 7. πατουμένη pres. pass. part. πατέω (# 4251) to walk on, to tread on. Part. in a periphrastic construction. ἄχρι οὗ (# 948; 4005) until, whenever, w. subj. πληρωθῶσιν aor. subj. pass. πληρόω (# 4444) to fill, to fulfill. It is possible that Luke understands the final signs (vv. 25-33) to follow the Gentile times and, if so, a fut. repossession by the Jews is anticipated (Ellis; Marshall). Subj. in an indef. temp. cl. ◆ **25** ἔσονται fut. ind. mid. (dep.) s.v. 17. σημεῖα nom. pl. σημεῖον (# 4956) sign. Jesus now answers the question of v. 7 about "the sign." συνοχή (# 5330) distress, dismay. ἀπορία (# 680) dat. sing. perplexity. ἤχους gen. sing. ἦχος (# 2492) roaring. Gen. of possession, shading over into an expression of cause: "perplexity caused by the roaring of the sea" (Arndt). σάλου gen. sing. σάλος (# 4893) rolling or tossing motion, esp. of the waves in a rough sea (BAGD). The fabric of the universe shows signs of breaking up and there is panic on the earth (Marshall). ◆ **26** ἀποψυχόντων pres. act. part. (temp.) ἀποψύχω (# 715) to breathe out, to faint, to expire. For the medical use s. MLL, 166. Gen. abs. προσδοκία (# 4660) expectation.

Used w. the prep. ἀπό giving the cause of the fainting or expiring. ἐπερχομένων pres. mid. (dep.) part. ἐπέρχομαι (# 2088) to come upon. Adj. part. modifying the word "things," which is to be supplied (Fitzmyer, 1349). οἰκουμένη (# 3876) dat. sing. inhabited earth, the land that is built upon. σαλευθήσονται fut. ind. pass. σαλεύω (# 4888) to shake. ◆ **27** ὄψονται fut. ind. mid. (dep.) ὁράω (# 3972) to see. ἐρχόμενον pres. mid. (dep.) part. (adj.) s.v. 6. ◆ **28** ἀρχομένων pres. mid. (dep.) part. (temp.) ἄρχομαι (# 806) to begin, w. inf. Gen. abs. γίνεσθαι pres. mid. (dep.) inf. s.v. 7. ἀνακύψατε aor. imp. act. ἀνακύπτω (# 376) to stand erect, to be elated. Used of being elated after sorrow (Plummer; MLL, 21). Aor. imp. calls for a specific act. w. a note of urgency. ἐπάρατε aor. imp. act. ἐπαίρω (# 2048) to lift up. ἀπολύτρωσις (# 667) redemption, release for the payment of a price, complete deliverance (APC, 37-48; TDNT; NIDNTT; EDNT; GW, 71ff). The word suggests not just redemption from sin but redemption from political oppression and establishment of an independent Jewish state. It is found on a coin struck ca. 133-34, "First year of the Redemption of Israel" (ABD, 1:1081 fig. m). ◆ **29** ἴδετε aor. imp. act. s.v. 27. ◆ **30** προβάλωσιν aor. subj. act. προβάλλω (# 4582) to put forth, to sprout. Subj. in an indef. temp. cl. βλέποντες pres. act. part. βλέπω (# 1063) to see. Circum. part., "you see for yourselves." The construction stresses that no other instruction will be necessary (Fitzmyer, 1353). θέρος (# 2550) summer. ◆ **31** ἴδητε aor. subj. act. s.v. 29. Subj. w. ὅταν (# 4020) in an indef. temp. cl. γινόμενα pres. mid. (dep.) part. (adj.) s.v. 7. Pres. indicates that the occurrence would be taking place as they watched. γινώσκετε pres. imp. act. s.v. 20. ◆ **32** παρέλθῃ aor. subj. act. παρέρχομαι (# 4216) to go by, to pass away. For the term "last generation" in DSS s. 1QpHab 2:7; 7:2; CD 1:12; Bock. Subj. w. a double neg. οὐ μή (# 4024; 3590) for a strong denial. γένηται aor. subj. mid. (dep.) s.v. 7. Subj. in an indef. temp. cl. ◆ **33** παρελεύσονται fut. ind. mid. (dep.) s.v. 32. The second form is fut. w. a double neg. expressing a strong denial. Jesus identifies the permanence of His prophetic utterance w. the constancy of Yahweh's word found in the OT (Fitzmyer, 1353). ◆ **34** προσέχετε pres. imp. act. προσέχω (# 4668) to give attention, to give heed. Pres. imp. calls for a constant vigil. βαρηθῶσιν aor. subj. pass. βαρέω (# 976) to weigh down, to depress. Subj. w. μήποτε in a neg. purp. cl.; warding off something still dependent on the will (BD, 188). κραιπάλη (# 3190) dat. sing. drunken nausea. Signifies the distressing aftereffects of intoxication (Arndt; for medical examples of the word s. MLL, 167). μέθη (# 3494) dat. sing. drunkenness. Dat. w. prep. expressing the instrument causing the depression. μέριμνα (# 3533) care, worry, anxiety, a feeling of apprehension or distress in view of possible danger or misfortune (LN, 1:313). βιωτικός (# 1053) belonging to daily life, worldly, secular, everyday (MH, 379). **ἐπιστῇ** aor. subj. act. ἐφίστημι (# 2392) to come upon (suddenly and unexpectedly). Subj. w. **μήποτε** (# 3607) in a neg. purp. or result cl. **αἰφνίδιος** (# 167) suddenly, unexpectedly. ◆ **35 παγίς** (# 4075) snare, trap. **ἐπεισελεύσεται** fut. ind. mid. (dep.) ἐπεισέρχομαι (# 2082) to come in over. **καθημένους** pres. mid. (dep.) part. κάθημαι (# 2764) to sit, to dwell. Part. as subst. ◆ **36 ἀγρυπνεῖτε** pres. imp. act. ἀγρυπνέω (# 70) to be awake, to stay awake, be alert, to be watchful; to make an effort to learn of what might be a potential future threat (LN, 1:333; GELTS, 5). **δεόμενοι** pres. mid. (dep.) part. δέομαι (# 1289) to request, to pray. Part. of manner telling how one should be alert. **κατισχύσητε** aor. subj. act. κατισχύω (# 2996) to have the strength to, to be able to, w. inf. Subj. in a purp. cl. **ἐκφυγεῖν** aor. act. inf. ἐκφεύγω (# 1767) to flee, to escape. **μέλλοντα** pres. act. part. (adj.) s.v. 7. as subst. **γίνεσθαι** pres. mid. (dep.) inf. s.v. 7. Inf. used w. the part. **μέλλοντα** to express fut.: "the things about to happen." **σταθῆναι** aor. pass. inf. ἵστημι (# 2705) to stand. Inf. w. the vb. **κατισχύσητε**. ◆ **37 ἦν** impf. ind. act. εἰμί (# 1639). **διδάσκων** pres. act. part. διδώσκω (# 1438) to teach. Part. in a periphrastic construction stressing the continual action in the past. **νύκτας** acc. pl. νύξ (# 3816) night. Acc. of time. **ἐξερχόμενος** pres. mid. (dep.) part. (temp.) ἐξέρχομαι (# 2002) to go out. **ηὐλίζετο** impf. ind. mid. (dep.) αὐλίζομαι (# 887) to spend the night, to find lodging. ◆ **38 ὤρθριζεν** impf. ind. act. ὀρθρίζω (# 3983) to rise, to come, early in the morning. Impf. indicates the customary action for this time. **ἀκούειν** pres. act. inf. ἀκούω (# 201) to hear. Inf. of purp.

Luke 22

◆ **1 ἤγγιζεν** impf. ind. act. ἐγγίζω (# 1581) to be near, to draw near. **λεγομένη** pres. pass. part. λέγω (# 3306) to say; pass., to be called, to be named. ◆ **2 ἐζήτουν** impf. ind. act. ζητέω (# 2426) to seek. Impf. indicates continual action, but not a special meeting of the Sanhedrin (Arndt). **τό** n. sing. ὁ (# 3836) The def. art. functions as quotation and makes clear the substantival idea of the indir. question (RG, 766). **ἀνέλωσιν** aor. subj. act. ἀναιρέω (# 359) to take away, to do away w., to kill. Deliberative subj. in indir. question (RWP). **ἐφοβοῦντο** impf. ind. mid. (dep.) φοβέομαι (# 5828) to be afraid, to fear. ◆ **3 εἰσῆλθεν** aor. ind. act. εἰσέρχομαι (# 1656) to go in, to come in. **καλούμενον** pres. pass. part. καλέω to call. **Ἰσκαριώτης** (# 269) Iscariot. For a discussion of the possible meanings of the term s. ABD, 3:1091-92; EDNT, 2:491-93, 1366-67; DTM, 2:1410-18. **ὄντα** pres. act. part. (adj.) εἰμί (# 1639) to be. ◆ **4 ἀπελθών** aor. act. part. ἀπέρχομαι (# 599) to depart, to go away. Circum. or temp. part. **συνελάλησεν** aor. ind. act. συλλαλέω (# 5196) to talk together, to confer w. **τό** n. sing. s.v. 2. **παραδῷ** aor. subj. act. παραδίδωμι

(# 4140) to hand over, to deliver over. Deliberative subj. (RWP). ◆ **5 ἐχάρησαν** aor. ind. pass. χαίρω (# 5897) to rejoice, to be glad. **συνέθεντο** aor. ind. mid. συντίθημι (# 5338) to make an agreement together. **δοῦναι** aor. act. inf. δίδωμι (# 1443) to give. Epex. inf. explaining the agreement. ◆ **6 ἐξωμολόγησεν** aor. ind. act. ἐξομολογέω (# 2018) to consent, to promise. Prep. in compound is intensive: "he fully consented," "agreed out and out" (NTNT, 75). **ἐζήτει** impf. ind. act. s.v. 2. **εὐκαιρία** (# 2321) opportunity, convenient time, the right time (s. Heb. 4:16). **παραδοῦναι** aor. act. inf. s.v. 4. Epex. inf. explaining εὐκαιρίαν. **ἄτερ** (# 868) w. gen., without, apart from. ◆ **7 ἦλθεν** aor. ind. act. ἔρχομαι (# 2262) to come. Perfective aor., "to arrive." **ἔδει** impf. ind. act. δεῖ (# 1256) it is necessary, w. inf. **θύεσθαι** pres. pass. inf. θύω (# 2604) to offer, to slay. For suggestions regarding the time s. Fitzmyer, 1382. ◆ **8 ἀπέστειλεν** aor. ind. act. ἀποστέλλω (# 690) to send w. delegated authority. **εἰπών** aor. act. part. λέγω (# 3306) to say. Semitic use of the redundant part. **πορευθέντες** aor. pass. (dep.) part. πορεύομαι (# 4513) to go. Circum. part. used as imp. (VANT, 386). **ἑτοιμάσατε** aor. imp. act. ἑτοιμάζω (# 2286) to prepare, to make ready. Aor. imp. calls for a specific act. **φάγωμεν** aor. subj. act. ἐσθίω (# 2266) to eat. Subj. w. **ἵνα** (# 2671) in a purp. cl. ◆ **9 ἑτοιμάσωμεν** aor. subj. act. s.v. 8. Deliberative subj. ◆ **10 εἰσελθόντων** aor. act. part. (temp.) s.v. 3. Gen. abs. **συναντήσει** fut. ind. act. συναντάω (# 5267) to meet, w. dat. **βαστάζων** pres. act. part. (adj.) βαστάζω (# 1002) to carry. **ἀκολουθήσατε** aor. imp. act. ἀκολουθέω (# 199) to follow, w. dat. ◆ **11 ἐρεῖτε** fut. ind. act. λέγω s.v. 8. Fut. used as imp. **κατάλυμα** (# 2906) guest room (BAGD; s. 2:7). **φάγω** aor. subj. act. s.v. 8. Futuristic or deliberative subj. (RWP). It could be tantamount to a purp. cl. (Marshall). ◆ **12 δείξει** fut. ind. act. δείκνυμι (# 1259) to show. **ἀνάγαιον** (# 333) acc. sing. an upstairs room, an extra room built onto the flat roof of a typical Palestinian house (Marshall). **ἐστρωμένον** perf. pass. part. (adj.) στρώννυμι (# 5143) to spread out. Here the term could indicate the floor consisting of tiles, but more likely it describes the room as furnished, supplied w. rugs and couches (Arndt). ◆ **13 ἀπελθόντες** aor. act. part. (temp.) ἀπέρχομαι (# 599) to go out. **εὗρον** aor. ind. act. εὑρίσκω (# 2351) to find. **εἰρήκει** plperf. ind. act. λέγω (# 3306) to say. **ἡτοίμασαν** aor. ind. act. s.v. 8. ◆ **14 ἐγένετο** aor. ind. mid. (dep.) γίνομαι (# 1181) to become, to be. ("When it was sundown.") **ἀνέπεσεν** aor. ind. act. ἀναπίπτω (# 404) to recline (at the table); lit. to fall back. ◆ **15 ἐπιθυμία** (# 2123) dat. sing. desire. **ἐπεθύμησα** aor. ind. act. ἐπιθυμέω (# 2121) to desire, to long for. For the Hebraic construction w. the dat. of the verbal substitutive w. the cognate vb. as a translation of the Heb. inf. abs. s. BD, 106; Fitzmyer, 1395. **φαγεῖν** aor. act. inf. s.v. 8. Epex. inf. explaining the desire. **παθεῖν** aor. act. inf. πάσχω (# 4248) to suffer. Inf. w. prep. **πρό**

(# *4574*) to express time, "before I suffer" (MT, 144). ◆ **16 φάγω** aor. subj. act. s.v. 8. Subj. w. a double neg. **οὐ μή** (# *4024; 3590*) for a strong denial. **πληρωθῇ** aor. subj. pass. **πληρόω** (# *4444*) to fill, to fulfill. The subject is probably the Passover (maybe as the Messianic Banquet [Stein]) and pass. is the theol. pass. indicating that God is the One who does the action (Marshall). ◆ **17 δεξάμενος** aor. mid. (dep.) part. (temp.) **δέχομαι** (# *1312*) to receive. The cup was handed to Him (Plummer). **εὐχαριστήσας** aor. act. part. **εὐχαριστέω** (# *2373*) to bless, to give thanks. The blessing or thanksgiving for the wine was, "Blessed art Thou, O Eternal, King of the Universe, the Creator of the fruit of the vine" (M, Berakhoth 6:2; Marshall; SB, 4: ii, 627-34). **εἶπεν** aor. ind. act. s.v. 8. **λάβετε** aor. imp. act. **λαμβάνω** (# *3284*) to take. **διαμερίσατε** aor. imp. act. **διαμερίζω** (# *1374*) to distribute. ◆ **18 πίω** aor. subj. act. **πίνω** (# *4403*) to drink. Subj. w. a double neg. **οὐ μή** (# *4024; 3590*) for a strong denial. **ἔλθῃ** aor. subj. act. s.v. 7. Subj. in an indef. temp. cl. ◆ **19 λαβών** aor. act. part. (temp.) s.v. 17. **εὐχαριστήσας** aor. act. part. s.v. 17. **ἔκλασεν** aor. ind. act. **κλάω** (# *3089*) to break. The word is used in the NT of dividing up bread at a meal (Marshall). **ἔδωκεν** aor. ind. act. **δίδωμι** (# *1443*) to give. **διδόμενον** pres. pass. part. (adj.) **ποιεῖτε** pres. imp. act. **ποιέω** (# *4472*) to do. Pres. imp. calls for a repeated action. **ἀνάμνησις** (# *390*) remembrance, memorial. The Passover Meal was a memorial for the Jews to remind them of their past and give them hope for a future and final deliverance (SB, 2:256). ◆ **20 δειπνῆσαι** aor. act. inf. **δειπνέω** (# *1268*) to dine, to eat a meal. Inf. w. prep. **μέτα** (# *3552*) to express time ("after") (MT, 143). **διαθήκη** (# *1347*) covenant, will (s. Matt. 26:28). **ἐκχυννόμενον** pres. pass. part. **ἐκχύννω** (ἐκχέω) (# *1772*) to pour out, to shed. "To shed blood" meant to murder (BAGD; Gen. 9:6). ◆ **21 πλήν** (# *4440*) however. Here it seems to indicate a breakoff in the thought and a transition to a different point (Thrall, 22; also the detailed study of this word in Blomqvist, 75-100). **παραδιδόντος** pres. act. part. (adj.) s.v. 4. ◆ **22 ὡρισμένον** perf. pass. part. **ὁρίζω** (# *3988*) to mark off the boundary, to determine. The perf. indicates a state arising from a completed action in the past. Theol. pass. indicates that what was about to happen would occur because God had ordained it (Stein). Part. as subst. ◆ **23 ἤρξαντο** aor. ind. mid. (dep.) **ἄρχομαι** (# *806*) to begin, w. inf. **συζητεῖν** pres. act. inf. **συζητέω** (# *5184*) to discuss w., to dispute, to express forceful differences of opinion without necessarily having a presumed goal of seeking a solution (LN, 1:438-39). **εἴη** pres. opt. act. **εἰμί** (# *1639*) to be. Opt. in indir. speech, a mark of culture (Arndt). **μέλλων** pres. act. part. **μέλλω** (# *3516*) to be about to. Used w. inf. to express fut. (MKG, 307). Part. as subst. **πράσσειν** pres. act. inf. **πράσσω** (# *4556*) to do, to accomplish. ◆ **24 ἐγένετο** aor. ind. mid. (dep.) s.v. 14. **καί** even, also.

φιλονεικία (# *5808*) contentiousness; lit. love of strife, contention, readiness or desire to argue or quarrel (Arndt; LN, 1:439). **δοκεῖ** pres. ind. act. **δοκέω** (# *1506*) to seem to be, w. inf. **εἶναι** pres. act. inf. s.v. 23. **μείζων** (# *3505*) comp. **μέγας** great; comp., greatest. ◆ **25 κυριεύουσιν** pres. ind. act. **κυριεύω** (# *3259*) to be lord or master, to rule over, w. gen. Gnomic pres. indicating a general truth. **ἐξουσιάζοντες** pres. act. part. **ἐξουσιάζω** (# *2027*) to have authority over, w. gen. Part. as subst. **εὐεργέται** nom. pl. **εὐεργέτης** (# *2309*) one who does good deeds, benefactor. This was a title given to gods, princes, and other outstanding persons; it became a t.t. for the benefactor-protector of a city, people, or of the whole human race (BAGD; MM; EDNT; RAC, 6:848-60; TDNT; TLNT). **καλοῦνται** pres. ind. pass. **καλέω** (# *2813*) to call; pass. to be called. ◆ **26 γινέσθω** pres. imp. mid. (dep.) 3rd. sing. s.v. 14. Pres. imp. calls for a continual attitude. **νεώτερος** comp. **νέος** (# *3742*) young, the lowest in rank (Plummer). Comp. used as superl.: "the youngest." **ἡγούμενος** pres. mid. (dep.) part. **ἡγέομαι** (# *2451*) to lead, to be the leader. Part. as subst. **διακονῶν** pres. act. part. **διακονέω** (# *1354*) to serve, to minister, to render assistance or help by performing certain duties, often of a humble or menial nature (LN, 1:460). ◆ **27 ἀνακείμενος** pres. mid. (dep.) part. **ἀνάκειμαι** (# *367*) to recline at the table. Part. as subst. **οὐχί** (# *4049*) used in a question expecting a positive answer, "It is the one who reclines at the table, isn't it?" **ἐγώ** I (emphatic). "I am the one who is serving." ◆ **28 διαμεμενηκότες** perf. act. part. **διαμένω** (# *1373*) to remain throughout. The idea of persistent loyalty is enforced by the compound vb., the perf. tense, and the prep. ("who have perseveringly remained w. me and continue to do so" [Plummer]). ◆ **29 διατίθεμαι** pres. ind. mid. (dep.) **διατίθημι** (# *1416*) to decree, to ordain, to assign. **διέθετο** aor. ind. mid. (dep.) **διατίθημι**. ◆ **30 ἔσθητε** pres. subj. act. **ἐσθίω** s.v. 8. Subj. w. noun cl. as obj. of the vb. **διατίθεμαι**. **πίνητε** pres. subj. act. s.v. 18. **καθήσεσθε** fut. ind. mid. (dep.) **κάθημαι** (# *2764*) to sit. **κρίνοντες** pres. act. part. (circum.) **κρίνω** (# *3212*) to judge. The Passover celebrated two events, the deliverance from Egypt and the anticipated coming Messianic deliverance (Ellis). There may be a reference here to Ps. 122:4-5 (Fitzmyer, 1416). This would refer to final restoration of Israel and the fut. Kingdom to be set up at the return of Christ (s. Stein). ◆ **31 ἐξῃτήσατο** aor. ind. mid. **ἐξαιτέω** (# *1977*) to ask for, to demand, to demand the surrender of (Marshall; TDNT). The mid. voice indicates the personal interest of Satan (Arndt). **σινιάσαι** aor. act. inf. **σινιάζω** (# *4985*) to sift, to separate the chaff from the wheat (Fitzmyer, 1424; Marshall). Inf. of purp. ◆ **32 ἐδεήθην** aor. ind. pass. **δέομαι** (# *1289*) to ask for, to pray, to voice a petition based on a real need (Arndt). **ἐκλίπῃ** aor. subj. act. **ἐκλείπω** (# *1722*) to leave off, to fail utterly. Prep. in compound is perfective (MH, 309). Subj. w. **ἵνα** (# 2671) used in an obj. cl. **ἐπιστρέψας** aor. act. part. (temp.) ἐπιστρέφω (# 2188) to turn, to return. **στήρισον** aor. imp. act. στηρίζω (# 5114) to establish, to support, to strengthen. Aor. imp. calls for a specific act. ◆ **33** **πορεύεσθαι** pres. mid. (dep.) inf. πορεύομαι (# 4513) to go. Epex. inf. explaining **ἕτοιμος**. ◆ **34 φωνήσει** fut. ind. act. φωνέω (# 5888) to make a sound, to call. Here, to crow. **ἀπ-αρνήσῃ** aor. subj. mid. (dep.) 2nd. sing. ἀπαρνέομαι (# 656) to deny. Subj. in an indef. temp. cl. **εἰδέναι** perf. act. inf. οἶδα (# 3857) to know. Def. perf. w. pres. meaning. Inf. in indir. speech. ◆ **35 ἀπέστειλα** aor. ind. act. ἀποστέλλω (# 690) to send as an official representative. **ἄτερ** (# 868) prep. w. gen., without. **βαλ-λάντιον** (# 964) moneybag, purse. **πήρα** (# 4385) knapsack, wallet. **ὑπόδημα** (# 5687) sandal, a leather sole that is fastened to the foot by straps (BAGD). **μή** (# 3590) neg. in a question expecting the answer "no." **ὑστερήσατε** aor. ind. act. ὑστερέω (# 5728) to lack (s. Ps. 23:1 [LXX 22:1]). **οὐθενός** (# 4029) not a thing! (Fitzmyer, 1431). ◆ **36 ἀράτω** aor. imp. act. 3rd. pers. sing. αἴρω (# 149) to take up. **πωλησάτω** aor. imp. act. 3rd. pers. sing. πωλέω (# 4797) to sell. **ἀγορασάτω** aor. imp. act. 3rd. pers. sing. ἀγοράζω (# 60) to buy. The aor. imps. call for a specific action. For various interpretations s. Fitzmyer, 1431-32. The idea may be, "Prepare for difficult times" (Marshall). ◆ **37 γεγραμμένον** perf. pass. part. γράφω (# 1211) to write. Perf. was used for authoritative documents (MM). Part. used as subst. **δεῖ** pres. ind. act., w. inf. s.v. 7. It indicates the divine necessity. **τελεσθῆναι** aor. pass. inf. τελέω (# 5464) to complete. The bringing to completion of what one wills or what another wills (TDNT). **ἐλογίσθη** aor. ind. pass. λογίζομαι (# 3357) to count, to reckon, to consider, to class. ◆ **39 ἐξελθών** aor. act. part. (temp.) ἐξέρχομαι (# 2002) to go out. For a discussion of the Mount of Olives in Luke s. DJG, 266-67. **ἠκολούθησαν** aor. ind. pass. s.v. 10. ◆ **40 γενόμενος** aor. mid. (dep.) part. (temp.) s.v. 14. **προσεύχεσθε** pres. imp. mid. (dep.) προσεύχομαι (# 4667) to pray. Pres. imp. calls for a continual action on the part of the disciples (VANT, 353). **εἰσελθεῖν** aor. act. inf. s.v. 3. The idea is either "to fall into temptation" or "to succumb to temptation" (DTM, 1:159). Inf. of purp. ◆ **41 ἀπεσπάσθη** aor. ind. pass. ἀποσπάω (# 685) to tear away; pass., to withdraw (Fitzmyer, 1441). **θείς** aor. act. part. τίθημι (# 5502) to place; here, to kneel down. One normally stood, but this stresses the urgency and humility of Jesus (Marshall). Circum. part. or part. of manner. **προσηύχετο** impf. ind. mid. (dep.) s.v. 40. Incep. impf. stressing the beginning; it also pictures repeated action. ◆ **42 εἰ** (# 1623) if. Introduces a cond. cl. which is considered to be true. **βούλει** pres. ind. act. βούλομαι (# 1089) to will, to desire. It carries the tone of a preordained, divine decision, somewhat more deliberate than θέλω (DTM, 1:171).

παρένεγκε aor. imp. act. παραφέρω (# 4195) to carry by, to remove. **ποτήριον** (# 4539) acc. sing. cup. For a discussion of the meaning of "the cup," s. DTM, 1:168-71; C. A. Blaising, "Gethsemane: A Prayer of Faith," *JETS* 22 (1979): 333-43. **πλήν** (# 4440) either a balancing adversative particle ("nevertheless") or introducing a cond. ("on the cond. that") (Thrall, 69ff; s.v. 21). **γινέσθω** pres. imp. mid. (dep.) 3rd. pers. sing. s.v. 14. Pres. imp. calls for a continued and continual action (VANT, 380-82; VA, 350). ◆ **43 ὤφθη** aor. ind. pass. ὁράω (# 3972) to see; pass. to appear. **ἐνισχύων** pres. act. part. ἐνισχύω (# 1932) to strengthen. The strengthening role of the angel is like that of a trainer who readies the athlete (DTM, 1:189; for the medical use s. MLL, 80-81). Adj. or circum. part. ◆ **44 γενόμενος** aor. mid. (dep.) part. (temp.) s.v. 14. **ἀγωνία** (# 75) dat. sing. conflict (an athletic conflict), struggle; sweat is often mentioned in the struggle (DTM, 1:189; for the medical use s. MLL, 81-82). **ἐκτενέστερον** comp. ἐκτενῶς (# 1757) eagerly, earnestly; comp., more earnestly, fervently. **προσηύχετο** impf. ind. mid. (dep.) s.v. 40. **ἐγένετο** aor. ind. mid. (dep.) s.v. 14. **ἱδρώς** (# 2629) sweat. **ὡσεί** (# 6059) as, introduces a comparison; the sweat became so profuse that it flowed to the ground as freely as if it were drops of blood (DTM, 1:185; Marshall). **θρόμβος** (# 2584) thick clots. Used in medical language for a clot of coagulated blood (MLL, 82-83; DMTG, 180; DTM, 1:184-86). **αἵματος** gen. sing. αἷμα (# 135) blood. Descriptive gen. **καταβαίνοντος** pres. act. part. (adj.) καταβαίνω (# 2849) to go down, to fall down. ◆ **45 ἀναστάς** aor. act. part. (temp.) ἀνίστημι (# 482) to stand up. The standing up indicates that Jesus has stopped praying and is also a sign of vigor (DTM, 1:192-93). **ἐλθών** aor. act. part. (temp.) s.v. 7. **εὗρεν** aor. ind. act. s.v. 13. **κοιμωμένους** pres. mid. (dep.) part. (adj.) κοιμάομαι (# 3121) to sleep. **λύπη** (# 3383) sorrow, grief, anxiety. Gen. w. prep. **ἀπό** (# 608) ("because of sorrow"). It has been suggested that when sorrow had exhausted one, sleep came (DTM, 1:193; s. also MLL, 84-85). ◆ **46 καθεύδετε** pres. ind. act. καθεύδω (# 2761) to sleep. **ἀναστάντες** aor. act. part. s.v. 45. Circum. part. w. the nuance of the main vb. **προσεύχεσθε**; imp. thrust (s. Luke 15:14). **εἰσέλθητε** aor. subj. act. s.v. 3. ◆ **47 λαλοῦντος** pres. act. part. (temp.) λαλέω (# 3281) to speak. Gen. abs. "While he was speaking...." **λεγόμενος** pres. pass. part. (adj.) λέγω (# 3306) to say; pass. to be called or named. **προήρχετο** impf. ind. mid. (dep.) προέρχομαι (# 4601) to go before. **ἤγγισεν** aor. ind. act. s.v. 1. **φιλῆσαι** aor. act. inf. φιλέω (# 5797) to kiss. Inf. of purp. ◆ **48 φιλήματι** dat. sing. φίλημα (# 5799) kiss (s. DTM, 1:255). Instr. dat. **παρα-δίδως** pres. ind. act. 2nd. pers. sing. s.v. 4. ◆ **49 ἰδόντες** aor. act. part. (temp.) s.v. 43. **ἐσόμενον** fut. mid. (dep.) part. εἰμί (# 1639) to be. Part. as subst., "what was about to happen." **εἰ** (# 1623), particle normally used when indir. question is due to an ellipsis, "tell us whether we shall strike" (Arndt). **πατάξομεν** fut. ind. act. πατάσσω (# *4250*) to strike (w. a sword). ◆ **50** **ἐπάταξεν** aor. ind. act. s.v. 49. **ἀφεῖλεν** aor. ind. act. ἀφαιρέω (# *904*) to take away, to cut off. **οὖς** acc. n. sing. (# *4044*) ear. ◆ **51 ἀποκριθείς** aor. pass. (dep.) part. ἀποκρίνομαι (# *646*) to answer. Semitic use of the pleonastic part. **ἐᾶτε** pres. imp. act. ἐάω (# *1572*) to allow. Perhaps the idea is, "allow them to continue w. the arrest" (VANT, 353; for various views s. Marshall). **ἁψάμενος** aor. mid. (dep.) part. ἅπτομαι (# *721*) to touch, w. obj. in gen. Part. of manner. **ὠτίου** gen. sing. ὠτίον (# *6005*) ear. **ἰάσατο** aor. ind. mid. (dep.) ἰάομαι (# *2615*) to heal. ◆ **52 παραγενομένους** aor. mid. (dep.) part. (adj.) παραγίνομαι (# *4134*) to come, to arrive, to be present. **ἀρχιερεύς** (# *797*) high priest (DTM, 1:404-11; 2:1425-26). **στρατηγός** (# *5130*) guard, captain (of the Temple) (BAGD; DTM, 2:1430-31; HJP, 2:277-79; JPB, 81-82). **πρεσβύτερος** (# *4565*) an older one, elder (DTM, 2:1428-29). **λῃστής** (# *3334*) robber. **ἐξήλθατε** aor. ind. act. s.v. 39. **ξύλον** (# *3833*) wood, club. ◆ **53 ὄντος** pres. act. part. εἰμί (# *1639*) to be. Gen. abs. **ἐξετείνατε** aor. ind. act. ἐκτείνω (# *1753*) to stretch out. ◆ **54 συλλαβόντες** aor. act. part. συλλαμβάνω (# *5197*) to seize, to arrest. Circum. or temp. part. **ἤγαγον** aor. ind. act. ἄγω (# *72*) to lead, to lead away. **εἰσήγαγον** aor. ind. act. εἰσάγω (# *1652*) to lead into. **ἠκολούθει** impf. ind. act. s.v. 10. ◆ **55 περιαψάντων** aor. act. part. (probably gen. abs.) περιάπτω (# *4312*) to kindle around, to make a good fire that blazes all over (RWP). **αὐλή** (# *885*) courtyard (DTM, 1:593-95). **συγκαθισάντων** aor. act. part. συγκαθίζω (# *5154*) to sit together. Nights in March and early April can be very chilly, and it was the custom of soldiers to keep fires burning through the night (DTN, 1:594-95). Gen. abs. **ἐκάθητο** impf. ind. mid. (dep.) s.v. 30. ◆ **56 ἰδοῦσα** aor. act. part. (temp.) nom. fem. sing. s.v. 49. **ἀτενίσασα** aor. act. part. (circum.) nom. fem. sing. ἀτενίζω (# *867*) to gaze at, to look steadily at, to stare, w. dat. ◆ **57 ἠρνήσατο** aor. ind. mid. (dep.) ἀρνέομαι (# *766*) to say no, to deny. Two meanings are implicit: "to refuse to recognize" and "to abandon and deny solidarity w. someone" (Ellis). **οἶδα** (# *3857*) perf. ind. act. to know. Def. perf. w. pres. meaning. ◆ **58 μετὰ βραχύ** (# *3552; 1099*) after a little while. **ἔφη** impf. ind. act. φημί (# *5774*) to say. **καὶ σύ** (# *2779; 5148*) even you *too*! Emphatic by position (Fitzmyer, 1464). **εἶ** pres. ind. act. 2nd. pers. sing. εἰμί (# *1639*). ◆ **59 διαστάσης** aor. act. part. (temp.) διΐστημι (# *1460*) to go away, to pass. Gen. abs. **διϊσχυρίζετο** impf. ind. mid. (dep.) διϊσχυρίζομαι (# *1462*) to make oneself strong, to make an emphatic declaration, to insist (RWP).   ◆ **60 παραχρῆμα** (# *4202*) immediately. **λαλοῦντος** pres. act. part. (temp.) s.v. 47. Gen. abs. **ἐφώνησεν** aor. ind. act. s.v. 34. **ἀλέκτωρ** (# *232*) rooster. The second cockcrow was associated w. dawn (DTM, 1:605-07).   ◆ **61 στραφείς** aor. pass. part. στρέφω

(# *5138*) to turn, to turn oneself. **ἐνέβλεψεν** aor. ind. act. ἐμβλέπω (# *1838*) to look at, w. dat. **ὑπεμνήσθη** aor. ind. pass. (dep.) ὑπομιμνήσκομαι (# *5703*) to remember. **πρίν** (# *4570*) w. inf., before. **φωνῆσαι** aor. act. inf. s.v. 34. **ἀπαρνήσῃ** fut. ind. mid. (dep.) 2nd. pers. sing. s.v. 34. ◆ **62 ἐξελθών** aor. act. part. (temp.) s.v. 39. **ἔκλαυσεν** aor. ind. act. κλαίω (# *3081*) to weep. **πικρῶς** (# *4396*) adv. bitterly. For a comparison of this section w. Mark's account s. Catchpole, 160-74; DTM, 2:587-626; esp. 590-91. ◆ **63 συνέχοντες** pres. act. part. (adj.) συνέχω (# *5309*) to hold together, to hold in custody (BAGD). **ἐνέπαιζον** impf. ind. act. ἐμπαίζω (# *1850*) to play a game w., to mock, to make fun of someone by imitating him in a distorted manner (LN, 1:435; EDNT; TDNT; D.L. Miller, "*Empaizen*: Playing the Mock Game [Luke 22:63-64]," *JBL* 90 [1971]: 309-13; DTM, 1:581-84; for the use in the LXX s. GELTS, 146). Incep. impf., "They began mocking...." **δέροντες** pres. act. part. δέρω (# *1296*) to flay, to beat. For this word in reference to the beating of a slave s. NDIEC, 4:63-67. Part. of manner or temp. ◆ **64 περικαλύψαντες** aor. act. part. (temp.) περικαλύπτω (# *4328*) to put a veil around, to blindfold. **ἐπηρώτων** impf. ind. act. ἐπερωτάω (# *2089*) to question. Impf. is incep. or pictures the questioning over and again in this game of blindman's bluff. **προφήτευσον** aor. imp. act. προφητεύω (# *4736*) to prophesy. Aor. imp. calls for a specific act. **παίσας** aor. act. part. παίω (# *4091*) to strike, to hit. Part. as subst. ◆ **65 βλασφημοῦντες** pres. act. part. (adj.) βλασφημέω (# *1059*) to slander, to blaspheme, to speak against someone in such a way as to harm or injure his or her reputation (LN, 1:434). **ἔλεγον** impf. ind. act. s.v. 13. Impf. pictures the continual action. ◆ **66 ἐγένετο** aor. ind. mid. (dep.) s.v. 14. **συνήχθη** aor. ind. pass. συνάγω (# *5251*) to come together, to assemble. For a discussion of the political background w. special focus on the Jewish legal power and the Sanhedrin s. DTM, 1:328-72. **ἀπήγαγον** aor. ind. act. ἀπάγω (# *552*) to lead away. ◆ **67 εἰπόν** aor. imp. act. s.v. 13. Aor. imp. calls for a specific act w. a note of urgency. **εἴπω** aor. subj. act. Subj. w. ἐάν (# *1569*) in a 3rd. class cond. cl. in which the speaker assumes the possibility of the cond. **πιστεύσητε** aor. subj. act. πιστεύω (# *4409*) to believe. Subj. w. double neg. for a strong denial. ◆ **68 ἐρωτήσω** aor. subj. act. ἐρωτάω (# *2263*) to question, to ask. Subj. in a 3rd. class cond. cl. **ἀποκριθῆτε** aor. subj. pass. (dep.) s.v. 51. Subj. w. double neg. for a strong denial. It might be that Jesus has in mind the earlier refusal of the Jewish leaders to enter into dialogue w. him and take up an honest position (Marshall). ◆ **69 ἔσται** fut. ind. mid. (dep.) εἰμί (# *1639*) to be. **καθήμενος** pres. mid. (dep.) part. s.v. 30. Part. in a periphrastic construction. ◆ **70 ἔφη** impf. ind. act. s.v. 58. For the answer of Jesus s. Mark 14:62. ◆ **71 ἠκούσαμεν** aor. ind. act. ἀκούω (# *201*) to hear. For the charge of blasphemy s. Matt. 26:65; Mark 14:63-64;

DTM, 1:520-27, 530-47; Darrell L. Bock, "The Son of Man and the Debate over Jesus' Blasphemy," *Jesus of Nazareth: Lord and Christ: Essays on the Historical Jesus and New Testament Christology,* ed. by Joel B. Green and Max Turner (Grand Rapids: Eerdmans, 1994), 181-84; DJG, 76-77.

Luke 23

◆ **1 ἀναστάν** aor. act. part. (temp.) ἀνίστημι (# 482) to arise. **ἤγαγον** aor. ind. act. ἄγω (# 72) to lead. ◆ **2 ἤρξαντο** aor. ind. mid. (dep.) ἄρχομαι (# 806) to begin, w. inf. **κατηγορεῖν** pres. act. inf. κατηγορέω (# 2989) to speak against someone, to accuse, w. gen. A legal t.t.: "to bring a charge against someone" (EDNT; BAGD; NDIEC, 1:28-29). **τοῦτον** acc. sing. οὗτος (# 4047) this one, used contemptuously. **εὕραμεν** aor. ind. act. εὑρίσκω (# 2351) to find. Indicates either "to catch in the act" or "to discover by investigation" (Plummer). **διαστρέφοντα** pres. act. part. (adj.) διαστρέφω (# 1406) to turn this way and that, to distort, to pervert, implying sedition (RWP). This political charge is one that tyrants often made of their opponents and may be related to Deut. 13:1-6; 18:20-22, which speaks of a false prophet who turns people away fom the Lord God (DTM, 1:739). Pres. may be conative, "He is trying...." **καί** that is, introducing two examples of the political perversion. **κωλύοντα** pres. act. part. (adj.) κωλύω (# 3266) to forbid. **διδόναι** pres. act. inf. δίδωμι (# 1443) to give, to pay. The accusation brought against Jesus is presented by Luke as being purely political in content (Blinzler). Epex. inf giving the content of κωλύοντα. **λέγοντα** pres. act. part. λέγω (# 3306) to say. Adj. part. indicating the second aspect of the attempted perversion. **Χριστὸν βασιλέα** (# 5986; 995) acc. sing. "Messiah King" (DTM, 1:740). Pred. acc. w. the inf. **εἶναι** pres. inf. act. εἰμί (# 1639) to be. Inf. in indir. speech. This is also a revolutionary charge, but in more personal terms (Evans). They are playing on the fears of a Roman governor that this Jew may be trying to restore a kingdom that Rome had supplanted 25 years before (DTM, 1:740; DJG, 687-98). ◆ **3 ἠρώτησεν** aor. ind. act. ἐρωτάω (# 1163) to question, to ask. **ἀποκριθείς** aor. pass. (dep.) part. ἀποκρίνομαι (# 646) to answer. Pleonastic use of the part. (MH, 453). **ἔφη** impf./aor. ind. act. φημί (# 5774) to say. ◆ **4 αἴτιος** (# 165) cause, case, guilty. Either "I find no case" or "I find nothing guilty" (DTM, 1:742). ◆ **5 ἐπίσχυον** impf. ind. act. ἐπισχύω (# 2196) to grow strong, to insist. The prep. in compound indicates "to add up in strength" and the impf. indicates they kept insisting (RWP). **ἀνασείει** pres. ind. act. ἀνασείω (# 411) to stir up, to incite. Pres. indicates the continual action. **διδάσκων** pres. act. part. διδάσκω (# 1438) to teach. Part. of manner explaining how Jesus was inciting the people. **ἀρξάμενος** aor. mid. (dep.) part. ἄρχομαι (# 806) to begin.

◆ **6 ἀκούσας** aor. act. part. (temp.) ἀκούω (# 201) to hear. **ἐπηρώτησεν** aor. ind. act. ἐπερωτάω (# 2089) to question, to ask. ◆ **7 ἐπιγνούς** aor. act. part. ἐπιγινώσκω (# 2105) to know, to recognize. The prep. compound is directive. It directs the vb.'s action upon some object (MH, 312). **ἀνέπεμψεν** aor. ind. act. ἀναπέμπω (# 402) to send, to send up. In this case for judicial examination (Arndt; DTM, 1:765). Pilate evidently sent Jesus to Herod Antipas as a diplomatic move to try to please Herod. He also felt that Herod would reach the same conclusion of innocence in this awkward case (HA, 233-39). Perhaps Pilate sent Jesus to Herod Antipas as a sort of preliminary investigation (DTM, 1:766; BBC; DJG, 848). **ὄντα** pres. act. part. (adj.) εἰμί (# 1639) to be. ◆ **8 ἰδών** aor. act. part. (temp.) ὁράω (# 3972) to see. **ἐχάρη** aor. ind. pass. (dep.) χαίρω (# 5897) to rejoice, to be glad. **λίαν** (# 3336) very. **ἐξ ἱκανῶν χρόνων** from many times; that is, for a long time. **θέλων** pres. act. part. θέλω (# 2527) to will, to want to, w. inf. Part. in a periphrastic construction, which catches the intensity of Herod's wish (DTM, 1:768). **ἰδεῖν** aor. act. inf. ὁράω (# 3972). **ἀκούειν** pres. act. inf. s.v. 6. Inf. w. prep. **διά** (# 1328) expressing cause. **ἤλπιζέν** impf. ind. act. ἐλπίζω (# 2527) (# 1827) to hope. The periphrastic construction and the impf. indicate the continuation of the wishing and hoping (Plummer). **ἰδεῖν** aor. act. inf. Inf. as obj. of the vb. **γινόμενον** pres. mid. (dep.) part. γίνομαι (# 1181) to become, to do, to perform. ◆ **9 ἐπηρώτα** impf. ind. act. s.v. 6. Impf. pictures the repeated questioning. Impf. may be conative, "he tried to question" (DTM, 1:771). **οὐδέν** (# 4029) acc. sing. nothing. It may be used adverbially ("not at all") or as the dir. obj. ("nothing") (DTM, 1:772). **ἀπεκρίνατο** aor. ind. mid. (dep.) s.v. 3. ◆ **10 εἱστήκεισαν** plperf. ind. act. ἵστημι (# 2705) to place; perf. to stand. **εὐτόνως** (# 2364) adv. at full pitch, vigorously (HA, 240). **κατηγοροῦντες** pres. act. part. s.v. 2. Circum. part. or part. of manner. ◆ **11 ἐξουθενήσας** aor. act. part. (circum.) ἐξουθενέω (# 2024) to count as nothing, to treat w. contempt, to despise. **στρατεύμασιν** dat. pl. στράτευμα (# 5128) army. Here the pl. may indicate only a modest detachment of soldiers, his bodyguard (HA, 241). **ἐμπαίξας** aor. act. part. (temp.) ἐμπαίζω (# 1850) to play a game w., to mock (s. 22:63). **περιβαλών** aor. act. part. περιβάλλω (# 4314) to throw about, to put on. Part. of manner telling how they mocked Jesus. **ἐσθῆτα** acc. sing. ἐσθής (# 2264) robe. **λαμπράν** acc. sing. λαμπρός (# 3287) bright. Such a robe was used of the candidate for an office. Jesus was ridiculed and mocked as the candidate for the kingship of the Jews (HA, 243). **ἀνέπεμψεν** aor. ind. act. s.v. 7. Here, "to send back." ◆ **12 ἐγένοντο** aor. ind. mid. (dep.) s.v. 8. **προϋπῆρχον** impf. ind. act. προϋπάρχω (# 4732) to be before, to exist previously, w. part. (BD, 213). **ἔχθρα** (# 2397) dat. sing. enmity, open hostility. **ὄντες** pres. act. part. εἰμί (# 1639) to be. ◆ **13 συγκαλε-**

σάμενος aor. mid. part. (circum.) συγκαλέω (# 5157) to call together, to summons. "He called them together about himself" (HA, 243). ◆ **14 προσηνέγκατε** aor. ind. act. προσφέρω (# 4712) to bring to. **ἀποστρέφοντα** pres. act. part. ἀποστρέφω (# 695) to turn someone away from, to pervert. "To seduce the people from their allegiance" (Plummer). Part. as subst. Conative pres.: "as one trying to seduce the people." **ἀνακρίνας** aor. act. part. (temp.) ἀνακρίνω (# 373) to examine, to examine judicially (s. DTM 1:766-68, 791). Effective aor., examined and reached a conclusion. **εὗρον** aor. ind. act. εὑρίσκω (# 2351) to find. Const. aor. **ὧν** gen. pl. rel. pron. ὅς (# 4005) who, which. "Of which things." **κατηγορεῖτε** pres. ind. act. s.v. 2. ◆ **15 πεπραγμένον** perf. pass. part. πράσσω (# 4556) to do, to practice. The perf. looks at the abiding results of an act which was done. Adj. part. as subst. Agency expressed by the dat. **αὐτῷ** (# 899) "by him." ◆ **16 παιδεύσας** aor. act. part. παιδεύω (# 4084) to teach, to admonish. "To give him a lesson," either by beating or warning (Sherwin-White, 27). It would be a minor beating that would be the whole penalty (DTM, 1:793). Temp. part. means, "After I have...." **ἀπολύσω** fut. ind. act. ἀπολύω (# 668) to release. ◆ **18 ἀνέκραγον** aor. ind. act. ἀνακράζω (# 371) to cry out. **παμπληθεί** (# 4101) all together. **αἶρε** pres. imp. act. αἴρω (# 149) to take away. Pres. imp. is the emotional and impatient command to become involved in the action of taking away (Bakker, 82-83; also VANT, 350-51; VA, 356). **ἀπόλυσον** aor. imp. act. ἀπολύω (# 668) to release, set free. Effective aor. draws attention to the terminating point: "release him quickly and decisively." For a discussion of the identity of Barabbas s. DTM, 1:796-800; Fitzmyer, 1490-91. ◆ **19 στάσις** (# 5087) uprising, insurrection, riot, revolt. **γενομένην** aor. mid. (dep.) part. (adj.) s.v. 8. **φόνον** acc. sing. φόνος (# 5840) murder. Acc. w. prep. **διά** (# 1328) giving the cause. **βληθείς** aor. pass. part. βάλλω (# 965) to throw, to cast. One was placed in prison until information about the accused could be gathered. ◆ **20 προσεφώνησεν** aor. ind. act. προσφωνέω (# 4715) to call to, to call out, to address someone. **θέλων** pres. act. part. (causal). s.v. 8. **ἀπολῦσαι** aor. act. inf. s.v. 18. ◆ **21 ἐπεφώνουν** impf. ind. act. ἐπιφωνέω (# 2215) to call forth, to shout, to yell. The prep. in compound means "against" (Marshall). Impf. pictures the continuous action. **σταύρου** pres. imp. act. σταυρόω (# 5090) to crucify. The pres. imp. is full of emotion for the people are irritated even more by the evasive answers of Pontius Pilate (Bakker, 83).   ◆ **22 ἐποίησεν** aor. ind. act. ποιέω (# 4472) to do. **εὗρον** aor. ind. act. s.v. 14.   ◆ **23 ἐπέκειντο** impf. ind. mid. (dep.) ἐπίκειμαι (# 2130) lit., to lie upon, to press upon, to be urgent. The vb. was used for the rush and swirl of a tempest (RWP). **αἰτούμενοι** pres. mid. (indir. mid., "for oneself") part. αἰτέω (# 160) to ask. Part. used to complement the vb. ἐπέ-

κειντο. **σταυρωθῆναι** aor. pass. inf. s.v. 21. Epex. inf. explaining their request. **κατίσχυον** impf. ind. act. κατισχύω (# 2996) to gain power over, to prevail. Prep. in compound indicates an unfavorable action (MH, 316). Incep. impf., "... began to prevail." ◆ **24 ἐπέκρινεν** aor. ind. act. ἐπικρίνω (# 2137) to give a sentence, to pronounce a legal decision, the final decision (Arndt). **γενέσθαι** aor. mid. (dep.) inf. s.v. 8. Epex. inf. explaining the judgment that was pronounced. ◆ **25 ἀπέλυσεν** aor. ind. act. s.v. 18. **βεβλημένον** perf. pass. part. s.v. 19. **ᾐτοῦντο** impf. ind. mid. s.v. 23. **παρέδωκεν** aor. ind. act. παραδίδωμι (# 4140) to deliver over. ◆ **26 ἀπήγαγον** aor. ind. act. ἀπάγω (# 552) to lead away. **ἐπιλαβόμενοι** aor. mid. (dep.) part. ἐπιλαμβάνομαι (# 2138) to seize, to lay hold upon (s. Mark 15:21). **ἐρχόμενον** pres. mid. (dep.) part. ἔρχομαι (# 2262) to come. **ἐπέθηκαν** aor. ind. act. ἐπιτίθημι (# 2202) to place upon. The condemned person generally had to carry the crossbeam behind the nap of the neck like a yoke (DTM, 2:913). **φέρειν** pres. act. inf. φέρω (# 5770) to carry. Inf. of purp. ◆ **27 ἠκολούθει** impf. ind. act. ἀκολουθέω (# 199) to follow. **ἐκόπτοντο** impf. ind. mid. κόπτω (# 3164) to cut off; mid., to hit oneself on the chest as a sign of mourning (BAGD). **ἐθρήνουν** impf. ind. act. θρηνέω (# 2577) to lament, to wail. For the Jewish mourning for the dead s. SB, 4:i, 582-609. ◆ **28 στραφείς** aor. pass. part. (circum.) στρέφω (# 5138) to turn; pass., w. reflexive meaning, to turn oneself, to turn around, to turn toward (BAGD). **κλαίετε** pres. imp. act. κλαίω (# 3081) to weep, to cry. Pres. imp. w. the neg. **μή** (# 3590) indicates the stopping of an action in progress. **πλήν** (# 4440) but. Used in in adversative function (Thrall, 21, 68; s. 22:21). ◆ **29 ἐροῦσιν** fut. ind. act. λέγω (# 3306) to say. **μακάριαι** nom. pl. fem. μακάριος (# 3421) blessed, happy (s. Matt. 5:3). **στεῖρα** (# 5096) sterile, childless. **κοιλία** (# 3120) stomach, womb (DMTG, 206). **ἐγέννησαν** aor. ind. act. γεννάω (# 1164) to bear, to give birth. **μαστός** (# 3466) breast. **ἔθρεψαν** aor. ind. act. τρέφω (# 5555) to nourish, to give nourishment. The blessing falls on the childless women who will not have to give children as booty to death (Fitzmyer, 1498; DTM, 2:923). ◆ **30 ἄρξονται** fut. ind. mid. (dep.) s.v. 2. **πέσετε** aor. imp. act. πίπτω (# 4406) to fall. **βουνοῖς** dat. pl. βουνός (# 1090) hill. Indir. obj. **καλύψατε** aor. imp. act. καλύπτω (# 2821) to hide, to conceal. ◆ **31 ὑγρός** (# 5619) moist. **ξύλον** (# 3833) wood. **ξηρός** (# 3831) dry. The proverb perhaps from the carpentry profession. The meaning is if an innocent person has to suffer so severely, what will happen to those who are guilty? (Arndt; DTM, 2:925-27; SB, 2:263-64). **γένηται** aor. subj. mid. (dep.) s.v. 8. Deliberative subj. in a question of contemplation (RWP).   ◆ **32 ἤγοντο** impf. ind. pass. s.v. 1. **ἕτεροι** (# 2283) other, of a different kind. **κακοῦργος** (# 2806) wrongdoer, criminal. **ἀναιρεθῆναι** aor. pass. inf. ἀναιρέω (# 359) to take up, to take away, to put to death. Inf. of purp. ◆ **33** ἦλθον aor. ind. act. s.v. 26. **καλούμενον** pres. pass. part. (adj.) καλέω (# 2813) to call, to name. **κρανίον** (# 3191) skull, upper part of the head (DMTG, 211). **ἐσταύρωσαν** aor. ind. act. s.v. 21. For crucifixion s. Blinzler; C; TDNT; DJG, 147-49; ABD, 1:1207-10; DTM, 2:885-87 (w. bibliography), 945-52. ◆ **34** ἄφες aor. imp. act. ἀφίημι (# 918) to release, to forgive. Aor. imp. calls for a specific act. **οἴδασιν** perf. ind. act. οἶδα (# 3857) to know. Def. perf. w. pres. meaning. "They" includes both Romans and Jews (DTM, 2:973). **διαμεριζόμενοι** pres. mid. part. (circum.) διαμερίζω (# 1374) to divide up into parts for oneself, to distribute. **ἔβαλον** aor. ind. act. s.v. 19. **κλῆρος** (# 3102) lot; that is, a pebble, small stick, etc. (BAGD; Blinzler). ◆ **35** εἱστήκει plperf. ind. act. s.v. 10. Plperf. here has the import of the impf. (DTM, 2:991). **θεωρῶν** pres. act. part. (circum.) θεωρέω (# 2555) to watch, to observe. **ἐξεμυκτήριζον** impf. ind. act. ἐκμυκτηρίζω (# 1727) to turn up the nose at, to mock (s. Luke 16:14; s. also Gal. 6:7). Impf. expresses continual action, "they kept sneering" (Fitzmyer, 1504; BBC). **ἔσωσεν** aor. ind. act. σώζω (# 5392) to rescue, to save. It refers to the healing work of Jesus, and the cl. is equivalent to a cond. (Marshall). **σωσάτω** aor. imp. act. 3rd. pers. sing. ◆ **36** ἐνέπαιξαν aor. ind. act. s.v. 11. **προσερχόμενοι** pres. mid. (dep.) part. (circum.) προσέρχομαι (# 4665) to come to. Prep. in compound may give the meaning, "to come forward" (DTM, 2:997). **ὄξος** (# 3954) acc. sing. vinegar, a sour wine drink (s. Matt. 27:48; DTM, 2:997). **προσφέροντες** pres. act. part. προσφέρω (# 4712) to bring to. Their offering of cheap wine is a burlesque gift to the King (DTM, 2:997). ◆ **37** εἰ pres. ind. act. 2nd. pers. sing. εἰμί (# 1639) to be. Used in a 1st. class cond. cl. in which the speaker assumes the reality of the cond. Here it is sarcasm. **σῶσον** aor. imp. act. s.v. 35. ◆ **38** ἐπιγραφή (# 2107) inscription (s. Matt. 27:37; DTM, 2:962-68). ◆ **39** κρεμασθέντων aor. pass. part. κρεμάννυμι (# 3203) to hang; mid. to be hanging (BAGD). **ἐβλασφήμει** impf. ind. act. βλασφημέω (# 1059) to blaspheme, to slander. **οὐχί** (# 4049) Used in questions expecting a positive answer ("You are, aren't you?"). A more bitter taunt than "if thou art" (Plummer). ◆ **40** ἐπιτιμῶν pres. act. part. (circum.) ἐπιτιμάω (# 2203) to rebuke. **ἔφη** impf./aor. ind. act. s.v. 3. **φοβῇ** pres. ind. mid. (dep.) φοβέομαι (# 5828) to be afraid, to fear. ◆ **41** μὲν ... δέ (# 3525; 1254) on the one hand ... on the other hand. **δικαίως** (# 1469) adv. justly. **ἐπράξαμεν** aor. ind. act. s.v. 15. **ἀπολαμβάνομεν** pres. ind. act. ἀπολαμβάνω (# 655) to receive, to receive in return, to receive back (BAGD; MH, 298). **ἄτοπος** (# 876) out of place, out of line, wrong. ◆ **42** μνήσθητι aor. imp. pass. (dep.) μιμνήσκομαι (# 3630) to recall to mind, to remember (BAGD). A prayer petition found on gravestones that one be remembered at the resurrection (E. E. Ellis, "Present and Future Eschatology in Luke,"

NTS 12 [1965]: 36). **ἔλθῃς** aor. subj. act. s.v. 26. Subj. w. **ὅταν** (# 4020) in an indef. temp. cl. ◆ **43** παράδεισος (# 4137) paradise; a Persian word meaning a park or enclosed garden, then used in Judaism as the abode of the redeemed between death and the resurrection (TDNT; SB, 2:264-69; DTM, 2:1010-13). ◆ **44** ἕκτη (# 1761) six. According to Jewish reckoning 12 noon. **ἐγένετο** aor. ind. mid. (dep.) γίνομαι (# 1181) to become, to be. **ἐνάτη** (# 1888) ninth, that is, 3:00 P.M. ◆ **45** ἐκλιπόντος aor. act. part. (causal) ἐκλείπω (# 1722) to fail, to leave out, to fail utterly. Gen. abs. **ἐσχίσθη** aor. ind. pass. σχίζω (# 5387) to rip, to tear. Theol. pass. **καταπέτασμα** (# 2925) curtain, veil (Ellis; DTM, 2:1098-113; Matt. 27:51). ◆ **46** φωνήσας aor. act. part. (temp.) φωνέω (# 5888) to call, to cry out. **παρατίθεμαι** pres. ind. mid. παρατίθημι (# 4192) mid. to deposit w. another, to give someone charge, to commit, to entrust (BAGD). Ps. 31:6 (LXX 30) was used in later rabbinical tradition as an evening prayer (Fitzmyer; SB, 2:269; BBC). **εἰπών** aor. act. part. (temp.) λέγω (# 3306) to say. **ἐξέπνευσεν** aor. ind. act. ἐκπνέω (# 1743) to breathe out, to expire, to die. ◆ **47** ἰδών aor. act. part. (temp.) s.v. 8. **γενόμενον** aor. mid. (dep.) part. s.v. 44. Part. used as subst.: "that which happened." **ἐδόξαζεν** impf. ind. act. δοξάζω (# 1519) to glorify. Incep. impf., "he began to glorify." **ὄντως** (# 3953) adv. truly, certainly. **δίκαιος** (# 1465) righteous, innocent (DTM, 2:1163-67; TLNT, 1:320-26; TDNT). ◆ **48** συμπαραγενόμενοι aor. mid. (dep.) part. (adj.) συμπαραγίνομαι (# 5219) to come together, to arrive along w. **θεωρία** (# 2556) show, spectacle. **θεωρήσαντες** aor. act. part. (temp.) s.v. 35. **γενόμενα** aor. mid. (dep.) part. s.v. 44. **τύπτοντες** pres. act. part. τύπτω (# 5597) to strike. **στῆθος** (# 5111) breast, chest. **ὑπέστρεφον** impf. ind. act. ὑποστρέφω (# 5715) to return. Incep. impf. ◆ **49** εἱστήκεισαν plperf. ind. act. s.v. 10. **γνωστός** (# 1196) known. The reference is to Jesus' friends rather than His relatives (Marshall). **συνακολουθοῦσαι** pres. act. part. (adj.) nom. fem. pl. συνακολουθέω (# 5258) to follow along w., to accompany. **ὁρῶσαι** pres. act. part. (circum.) nom. fem. pl. ὁράω (# 3972) to see. ◆ **50** βουλευτής (# 1085) council member. This marks Joseph as a member of the Sanhedrin (Arndt). **ὑπάρχων** pres. act. part. (adj.) ὑπάρχω (# 5639) to exist, to be. ◆ **51** συγκατατεθειμένος perf. pass. part. συγκατατίθημι (# 5163) to put down the same vote as, to agree w., to consent to (Marshall). Periphrastic construction. Luke wants to clarify parenthetically and yet emphatically that though Joseph was a member of the Sanhedrin, he had not stood in agrement w. their decision to kill Jesus (VA, 485). **προσεδέχετο** impf. ind. mid. (dep.) προσδέχομαι (# 4657) to wait for, to expect. Impf. pictures his continual attitude of waiting. ◆ **52** προσελθών aor. act. part. (temp.) s.v. 36. **ᾐτήσατο** aor. ind. mid. (indir. mid., to ask for oneself) αἰτέω (# 160) to ask, to request. ◆ **53** καθελών aor. act. part. (temp.)

καθαιρέω (# 2747) to take down. **ἐνετύλιξεν** aor. ind. act. ἐντυλίσσω (# 1962) to wrap, to wrap in, to wrap up. For burial customs in the Mishnah s. DTM, 2:1243-44. **ἔθηκεν** aor. ind. act. τίθημι (# 5502) to place. **λαξευτός** (# 3292) cut in a rock, hewn. For the type of tomb s. DTM, 2:1247-51. **κείμενος** pres. pass. part. κεῖμαι (# 3023) lie down, used in periphrastic construction. ◆ 54 **παρασκευή** (# 4187) preparation. Here Friday must be meant, as the next cl. makes clear (Marshall). **ἐπέφωσκεν** impf. ind. act. ἐπιφώσκω (# 2216) to dawn, to give light. In a figurative way, to approach (Arndt). Incep. impf., "began to approach." ◆ 55 **κατακολουθήσαι** aor. act. part. (circum.) nom. fem. pl. κατακολουθέω (# 2887) to follow after. The prep. compound describes following right over an intervening space until the goal is reached (MH, 316). **συνεληλυθυῖαι** perf. pass. (dep.) part. nom. fem. pl. συνέρχομαι (# 5302) to come w., to accompany. Part. in a periphrastic construction. **ἐθεάσαντο** aor. ind. mid. (dep.) θεάομαι (# 2517) to see, to observe, to watch. **ἐτέθη** aor. ind. pass. τίθημι (# 5502) to place. ◆ 56 **ὑποστρέψασαι** aor. act. part. (temp.) nom. fem. pl. s.v. 48. **ἡτοίμασαν** aor. ind. act. ἑτοιμάζω (# 2286) to prepare. For a discussion of burial practice s. DJG, 88-90. **ἄρωμα** (# 808) spice, sweet-smelling herbs (Arndt). **μύρον** (# 3693) ointment. It probably means scented oil and/or ointment which was applied to the corpse (DTM, 2:1258). **σάββατον** (# 4879) acc. sing. Sabbath. From sundown at the end of the day of Passover until sundown ending the Sabbath (Fitzmyer, 1543). Acc. of time. **ἡσύχασαν** aor. ind. act. ἡσυχάζω (# 2483) to rest.

Luke 24

◆ 1 **ὄρθρου βαθέως** (# 3986; 960) gen. sing. early; lit., "at deep dawn." Gen. of time (RWP). **ἦλθον** aor. ind. act. ἔρχομαι (# 2262) to come. **φέρουσαι** pres. act. part. (circum.) nom. fem. pl. φέρω (# 5770) to bring, to carry. **ἡτοίμασαν** aor. ind. act. ἑτοιμάζω (# 2286) to prepare. ◆ 2 **εὗρον** aor. ind. act. εὑρίσκω (# 2351) to find. **ἀποκεκυλισμένον** perf. pass. part. ἀποκυλίω (# 653) to roll away. For a description of tombs found near Jerusalem, fitted w. huge circular stone discs set in a transverse channel hollowed out of stone s. Fitzmyer, 1544. Perf. indicates the completed state or condition. ◆ 3 **εἰσελθοῦσαι** aor. act. part. (temp.) nom. fem. pl. εἰσέρχομαι (# 1656) to go into. For the empty tomb s. Zane C. Hodges, "The Women and the Empty Tomb," *Bib Sac* 123 (1966): 301-9; W. L. Craig, "The Historicity of the Empty Tomb of Jesus," *NTS* 31 (1985): 39-67. ◆ 4 **ἐγένετο** aor. ind. mid. (dep.) γίνομαι (# 1181) to become, to happen, w. prep. and inf. (s. 8:1). **ἀπορεῖσθαι** pres. mid. (dep.) inf. ἀπορέω (# 679) to be at a loss, to be perplexed. Temp. use of the inf. w. the prep. ἐν (# 1877) ("while"). **ἐπέστησαν** aor. ind. act. ἐφίστημι (# 2392) to come upon suddenly or unexpectedly and

stand by, to step up as suddenly, to burst upon one (RWP). **ἀστραπτούσῃ** pres. act. part. (adj.) dat. fem. sing. ἀστράπτω (# 848) to flash, lightning. ◆ 5 **ἔμφοβος** (# 1873) afraid, frightened. **γενομένων** aor. mid. (dep.) part. s.v. 4. Gen. abs. **κλινουσῶν** pres. act. part. gen. fem. pl. κλίνω (# 3111) to bend, to bow. Gen. abs. **ζητεῖτε** pres. ind. act. ζητέω (# 2426) to seek. **ζῶντα** pres. act. part. ζάω (# 2409) to live. Part. as subst., "the living one." ◆ 6 **ἠγέρθη** aor. ind. pass. ἐγείρω (# 1586) to raise; pass. to be raised, to rise. **μνήσθητε** aor. imp. pass. μιμνῄσκομαι (# 3630) to remember. **ἐλάλησεν** aor. ind. act. λαλέω (# 3281) to say, to speak. ◆ 7 **δεῖ** (# 1256) pres. ind. act. it is necessary, w. inf. It gives a logical necessity. **παραδοθῆναι** aor. pass. inf. παραδίδωμι (# 4140) to deliver over. **σταυρωθῆναι** aor. pass. inf. σταυρόω (# 5090) to crucify. **ἡμέρᾳ** (# 2465) dat. sing. day. Dat. of time. **ἀναστῆναι** aor. act. inf. ἀνίστημι (# 482) to stand up, to rise. ◆ 8 **ἐμνήσθησαν** aor. ind. pass. (dep.) w. obj. in gen. s.v. 6. ◆ 9 **ὑποστρέψασαι** aor. act. part. (temp.) nom. fem. pl. ὑποστρέφω (# 5715) to return. **ἀπήγγειλαν** aor. ind. act. ἀπαγγέλλω (# 550) to report. ◆ 10 **ἦσαν** impf. ind. act. εἰμί (# 1639) to be. **ἔλεγον** impf. ind. act. λέγω (# 3306) to say. to tell. Impf. indicates the repeated action. ◆ 11 **ἐφάνησαν** aor. ind. pass. (dep.) φαίνομαι (# 5743) to appear, to show oneself, to appear to be, to seem to be (BAGD). **λῆρος** (# 3333) idle talk, nonsense, babbling, delirium. Used in medical language of the wild talk of the sick during delirium (MLL, 178; TLNT). **ἠπίστουν** impf. ind. act. ἀπιστέω (# 601) to disbelieve. The impf. pictures the continual disbelief. ◆ 12 **ἀναστάς** aor. act. part. (circum.) s.v. 7. **ἔδραμεν** aor. ind. act. τρέχω (# 5556) to run. **παρακύψας** aor. act. part. (circum.) παρακύπτω (# 4160) to peer in, stretching forward to get a good look (MM; NTNT, 80-81; Fitzmyer, 1547). **ὀθόνιον** (# 3856) linen cloth, bandage used in preparing a corpse for burial (BAGD; Fitzmyer, 1547-48; MM). **ἀπῆλθεν** aor. ind. act. ἀπέρχομαι (# 599) to come or go away, to depart. **θαυμάζων** pres. act. part. θαυμάζω (# 2513) to be amazed, to marvel. Part. of manner. **γεγονός** perf. act. part. s.v. 4. Part. as subst., "that which had happened." Perf. indicates the abiding results. ◆ 13 **ἦσαν** impf. ind. act. s.v. 10. **πορευόμενοι** pres. mid. part. πορεύομαι (# 4513) to go. Part. in a periphrastic constr. **ἀπέχουσαν** pres. act. part. (adj.) acc. fem. sing. ἀπέχω (# 600) to be at a distance. **στάδιον** (# 5084) stade. A measure of distance about 607 feet; 60 stade, about seven miles. (RWP). For a discussion of the village and its location s. Fitzmyer, 1561-62; Nolland, 1196, 1201; Marshall; ABD, 2:497-98; ZPEB, 2:299-301. ◆ 14 **ὡμίλουν** impf. ind. act. ὁμιλέω (# 3917) to talk w., to converse. **συμβεβηκότων** perf. act. part. (adj.) συμβαίνω (# 5201) to happen, to occur. It perhaps indicates the lingering results. ◆ 15 **ἐγένετο** aor. ind. mid. (dep.) s.v. 4. **συζητεῖν** pres. act. inf. συζητέω (# 5184) to investigate together, to discuss. Inf.

w. prep. ἐν (# 1877) expressing contemporaneous action. αὐτός (# 899) himself, emphatic use (IBG, 121). ἐγγίσας aor. act. part. ἐγγίζω (# 1581) to come near. Circum. or temp. part. συνεπορεύετο impf. ind. mid. (dep.) συμπορεύομαι (# 5233) to go w., to travel w. Impf. pictures the continual action. ◆ 16 ἐκρατοῦντο impf. ind. pass. κρατέω (# 3195) to lay hold of, to take possession, to hold, to restrain. They were blocked or restrained by supernatural power (Ellis). ἐπιγνῶναι aor. act. inf. ἐπιγινώσκω (# 2105) to know, to recognize. Inf. expressing result. ◆ 17 ἀντιβάλλετε pres. ind. act. ἀντιβάλλω (# 506) to place or put against, to exchange words, to argue about. For the reciprocal action indicated by the prep. compound s. MH, 297. περιπατοῦντες pres. act. part. (temp.) περιπατέω (# 4344) to walk ("while you were walking"). ἐστάθησαν aor. ind. pass. ἵστημι (# 2705) to stand. They stopped in their tracks (Marshall). σκυθρωπός (# 5034) w. a sad, gloomy, or sullen look. ◆ 18 ἀποκριθείς aor. pass. (dep.) part. ἀποκρίνομαι (# 646) to answer. Pleonastic use of the part. παροικεῖς pres. ind. act. παροικέω (# 4228) to live as a stranger, to inhabit or live in. "Have you been living alone (all by yourself)?" (RWP). ἔγνως aor. ind. act. γινώσκω (# 1182) to know. ◆ 19 ποῖα (# 4481) what kind of? what sort of? ἐγένετο aor. ind. mid. (dep.) s.v. 4. ◆ 20 ὅπως (# 3968) that, how, in what way? introducing an indir. question (BAGD; Marshall). παρέδωκαν aor. ind. act. s.v. 7. ἐσταύρωσαν aor. ind. act. s.v. 7. ◆ 21 ἠλπίζομεν impf. ind. act. ἐλπίζω (# 1827) to hope. Impf. used w. a vb. of wishing. It indicates failure to realize the desire or the perception that it cannot be realized (SMT, 15). μέλλων pres. act. part. μέλλω (# 3516) to be about to. Part. as subst. Used w. pres. inf. to express durative fut. (MKG, 307). λυτροῦσθαι pres. mid. inf. λυτρόω (# 3390) to redeem, to release by payment of a price, to fulfill the obligation of the OT family protector, kinsman redeemer, Heb. גֹּאֵל go'el (DCH, 2:293-95; THAT; NIDOTTE; TDNT; NIDNTT; APC, 9-59; TLNT). ἀλλά γε καί moreover. The second and third of these particles form a combination expressing a progressive idea reinforced by the one in the mid. for the sake of emphasis (Thrall, 12-15). ἄγει pres. ind. act. ἄγω (# 12) to lead, to spend time. Used impersonally, "one is keeping the third day," or personally, "he (that is, Jesus) is already spending the third day since" (BAGD; Arndt; BD, 72). ἐγένετο aor. ind. mid. (dep.) s.v. 4. ◆ 22 ἐξέστησαν aor. ind. act. ἐξίστημι (# 2014) to amaze, to startle. γενόμεναι aor. mid. (dep.) part. s.v. 4. Circum. or temp. part. ὀρθρινός (# 3984) early. ◆ 23 εὑροῦσαι aor. act. part. (temp.) nom. fem. pl. s.v. 2. ἦλθον aor. ind. act. s.v. 1. λέγουσαι pres. act. part. (circum.) nom. fem. pl. λέγω (# 3306) to say. ὀπτασία (# 3965) appearance, vision. ἑωρακέναι perf. act. inf. ὁράω (# 3972) to see. Inf. in indir. discourse. ζῆν pres. act. inf. s.v. 5. Inf. in indir. dis-

course. ◆ 24 ἀπῆλθόν aor. ind. act. ἀπέρχομαι (# 599) to go away, to go out. εὗρον aor. ind. act. s.v. 2. εἶδον aor. ind. act. ὁράω s.v. 23. ◆ 25 ἀνόητοι nom. pl. voc. ἀνόητος (# 485) not understanding, unintelligent, foolish, pertaining to unwillingness to use one's mental faculties in order to understand (LN, 1:386). βραδεῖς nom. pl. voc. βραδύς (# 1096) slow, dull. πιστεύειν pres. act. inf. πιστεύω (# 4409) used w. the prep. ἐπί (w. dat.) to believe on, to repose one's trust upon, suggesting more of a state (M, 68). Epex. inf. explaining the dullness (BD, 206-07). ἐλάλησαν aor. ind. act. s.v. 6. ◆ 26 οὐχί (# 4049) Used in questions expecting a positive answer (is it not true?). ἔδει impf. ind. act. s.v. 7. παθεῖν aor. act. inf. πάσχω (# 4248) to suffer (TDNT; for the suffering Messiah s. Isa. 52:13-15; 53; SB, 2:273-99; JIU; TDNT under παῖς θεοῦ; the somewhat neg. approach HJP, 2:547-54). Epex. inf. explaining the logical necessity. εἰσελθεῖν aor. act. inf. s.v. 3. Isa. 52:13-15 and 53 picture the Messiah's suffering and then His glory. ◆ 27 ἀρξάμενος aor. mid. (dep.) part. (circum.) ἄρχομαι (# 806) to begin. διερμήνευσεν aor. ind. act. διερμηνεύω (# 1450) to interpret, to explain. The vb. is used of interpreting a foreign language (Plummer). ◆ 28 ἤγγισαν aor. ind. act. s.v. 15. ἐπορεύοντο impf. ind. mid. (dep.) s.v. 13. προσεποιήσατο aor. ind. mid. (dep.) προσποιέω (# 4701) to act as though, to pretend. He would have departed if they had not begged Him to remain (Plummer). πορρώτερον comp. πόρρω (# 4522) far ahead, forward; comp., farther. πορεύεσθαι pres. mid. (dep.) inf. s.v. 13. Epex. inf. explaining the main vb. ◆ 29 παρεβιάσαντο aor. ind. mid. (dep.) παραβιάζομαι (# 4128) to use force to accomplish something, to urge strongly, to prevail upon; effective aor., "they successfully constrained Him" (Arndt). μεῖνον aor. imp. act. μένω (# 3531) to remain. Aor. imp. calls for a specific action w. a note of urgency. κέκλικεν perf. ind. act. κλίνω (# 3111) to decline (used of the day), to approach its end. εἰσῆλθεν aor. ind. act. s.v. 3. μεῖναι aor. act. inf. μένω. Inf. of purp. ◆ 30 ἐγένετο aor. ind. mid. (dep.) s.v. 4. κατακλιθῆναι aor. pass. (dep.) inf. κατακλίνομαι (# 2884) to sit down, to lie down, to recline (when eating). Inf. w. prep. to express time ("while") (MT, 145). λαβών aor. act. part. (temp.) λαμβάνω (# 3284) to take, to receive. εὐλόγησεν aor. ind. act. εὐλογέω (# 2328) to bless, to give thanks. κλάσας aor. act. part. (temp.) κλάω (# 3089) to break. ἐπεδίδου impf. ind. act. ἐπιδίδωμι (# 2113) to give to, to distribute. Incep. impf., "He began...." ◆ 31 διηνοίχθησαν aor. ind. pass. διανοίγω (# 1380) to open. Theol. pass., indicating that God had opened their eyes (Fitzmyer, 1568). ἐπέγνωσαν aor. ind. act. ἐπιγινώσκω (# 2105) to recognize. ἄφαντος (# 908) invisible. ◆ 32 καιομένη pres. mid. (dep.) part. καίομαι (# 2394) to burn. Periphrastic construction emphasizing continuance of the emotion (Plummer). ἐλάλει impf. ind. act. s.v. 6. διήνοιγεν impf. ind. act. s.v. 31.

◆ 33 ἀναστάντες aor. act. part. (circum.) s.v. 7. αὐτῇ τῇ ὥρᾳ (# *899; 6052*) in the same hour. Dat. of time. ὑπέστρεψαν aor. ind. act. s.v. 9. εὗρον aor. ind. act. s.v. 2. ἠθροισμένους perf. pass. part. (adj.) ἀθροίζω (# *125*) to gather together, to assemble. ◆ 34 ὄντως (# *3953*) adv., truly, certainly. ἠγέρθη aor. ind. pass. s.v. 6. ὤφθη aor. ind. pass. ὁράω (# *3972*) to see; pass., to appear. ◆ 35 ἐξηγοῦντο impf. ind. mid. (dep.) ἐξηγέομαι (# *2007*) to lead out, to rehearse, to explain. Incep. impf. ἐγνώσθη aor. ind. pass. γινώσκω (# *1182*) to know, to make known. κλάσει dat. sing. κλάσις (# *3082*) breaking. ◆ 36 λαλούντων pres. act. part. (temp.) s.v. 6. Gen. abs. ἔστη aor. ind. act. ἵστημι (# *2705*) to stand. ◆ 37 πτοηθέντες aor. pass. part. (circum.) πτοέω (# *4765*) to terrify; pass. to be terrified, to be alarmed, to be frightened. γενόμενοι aor. mid. (dep.) part. (circum.) s.v. 4. ἐδόκουν impf. ind. act. δοκέω (# *1506*) to suppose, to believe, to seem, w. inf. θεωρεῖν pres. act. inf. θεωρέω (# *2555*) to see, to watch. ◆ 38 τεταραγμένοι perf. pass. part. ταράσσω (# *5429*) to agitate, to stir up, to shake up, to trouble. Periphrastic construction. διαλογισμός (# *1369*) consideration, esp. doubt. ἀναβαίνουσιν pres. ind. act. ἀναβαίνω (# *326*) to come up, to arise. ◆ 39 ἴδετε aor. imp. act. ὁράω s.v. 34. ψηλαφήσατε aor. imp. act. ψηλαφάω (# *6027*) to touch, to feel. πνεῦμα (# *4460*) spirit, bodiless independent being of a person after death (Fitzmyer, 1576). ὀστέα acc. pl. ὀστεον (# *4014*) bone. ἔχοντα pres. act. part. (adj.) ἔχω (# *2400*) to have. ◆ 40 ἔδειξεν aor. ind. act. δείκνυμι (# *1259*) to show. For the textual problem of this v. s. TC, 187; Marshall. ◆ 41 ἀπιστούντων pres. act. part. (temp.) ἀπιστεύω (# *601*) to disbelieve. Gen. abs. θαυμαζόντων pres. act. part. θαυμάζω (# *2513*) to wonder, to be amazed. Gen. abs. βρώσιμος (# *1110*) eatable. ἐνθάδε (# *1924*) here. ◆ 42 ἐπέδωκαν aor. ind. act. ἐπιδίδωμι (# *2113*) to give to. ἰχθύος gen. sing. ἰχθύς (# *2716*) fish. Partitive gen. (BD, 90-91). ὀπτός (# *3966*) roasted, baked, broiled. μέρος (# *3538*) acc. sing. part of something. ◆ 43 λαβών aor. act. part. s.v. 30. ἔφαγεν aor. ind. act. ἐσθίω (# *2266*) to eat. ◆ 44 ὤν pres. act. part. (temp.) εἰμί (# *1639*) to be. ("While I was yet w. you.") πληρωθῆναι aor. pass. inf. πληρόω (# *4444*) to fill, to fulfill. Inf. w. δεῖ s.v. 7. γεγραμμένα perf. pass. part. γράφω (# *1211*) to write. Perf. was used for legal binding documents whose authority lasted (MM). ◆ 45 διήνοιξεν aor. ind. act. s.v. 31. συνιέναι pres. act. inf. συνίημι (# *5317*) to understand, to comprehend. Inf. of result. ◆ 46 γέγραπται perf. ind. pass. s.v. 44. παθεῖν aor. act. inf. s.v. 26. Inf. in indir. discourse. ἀναστῆναι aor. act. inf. s.v. 7. ◆ 47 κηρυχθῆναι aor. pass. inf. κηρύσσω (# *3062*) to proclaim, to preach, to herald (TDNT; EDNT). Inf. in indir. discourse. ◆ 49 ἀποστέλλω (# *690*) pres. ind. act. to send out, to send out as a personal authoritative representative (TDNT; NIDNTT; EDNT). καθίσατε aor. imp. act. καθίζω (# *2767*) to sit, to spend some time in a place (Plummer). ἐνδύσησθε aor. subj. pass. ἐνδύω (# *1907*) to clothe; pass. to be clothed. Subj. w. ἕως οὗ (# *2401; 4005*) in an indef. temp. cl. ◆ 50 ἐξήγαγεν aor. ind. act. ἐξάγω (# *1974*) to lead out. ἐπάρας aor. act. part. (temp.) ἐπαίρω (# *2048*) to lift up. ◆ 51 ἐγένετο aor. ind. mid. (dep.) s.v. 4. εὐλογεῖν pres. act. inf. s.v. 30. Inf. w. prep. to express contemporaneous time (MT, 145). διέστη aor. ind. act. διΐστημι (# *1460*) to set apart, to separate, to part, to depart. ἀνεφέρετο impf. ind. pass. ἀναφέρω (# *429*) to carry through. ◆ 52 προσκυνήσαντες aor. act. part. (temp.) προσκυνέω (# *4686*) to worship. ὑπέστρεψαν aor. ind. act. s.v. 33. ◆ 53 εὐλογοῦντες pres. act. part. s.v. 30. Periphrastic part. or part. of manner. For the reason of the disciples' joy s. Plummer.

The Gospel of John

For a discussion of the authorship of this Gospel s. Westcott, IX-LXVII; Morris, *Studies* 139-292; Adolf Schlatter, "Die Sprache und Heimat des Vierten Evangelisten," *Johannes und Sein Evangelium*, K.H. Rengstorf (ed.), 28-201; Eugen Ruckstuhl, *Die literarische Einheit des Johannesevangeliums* (Göttingen: Vandenhoeck & Ruprecht, 1987); Eugen Ruckstuhl and Peter Dschulnigg, *Stilkritik und Verfasserfrage im Johannesevangelium* (Göttingen: Vandenhoeck & Ruprecht, 1991). For an overview of the prologue see M. Rissi, "John 1,1-18," *Interpretation* 31 (1977): 395-401; J.A.T. Robinson, "The Relationship of the Prologue to the Gospel of St. John," *NTS* 9 (1962/63): 120-29; R.G. Hamerton-Kelly, *Pre-existence, Wisdom and the Son of Man* (Cambridge, 1973); DJG, 368-83; s. Haenchen for further bibliography.

John 1

◆ **1** ἀρχῇ (# *794*) dat. sing. beginning. Refers to a period before creation and is more qualitative than temp. (Brown). Without the art. it can refer to any possible beginning. While there is a deliberate allusion to Gen 1:1 here, there are also numerous contrasts (Haenchen; TDNT; NIDNTT; GELTS, 64). ἦν impf. ind. act. εἰμί (# *1639*) to be. Impf. expresses continuous timeless existence (Bernard) and is contrasted w. ἐγένετο of v. 3 (Barrett). It relates here not to the act of creation, but to what existed when creation came into being, namely, the Word (Beasley-Murray). The Word existed in the past at any beginning. πρός (# *4639*) toward, to. Here, "with," showing accompaniment ("w. God"), or "toward God"; i.e., relationship (Brown). θεός (# *2536*) God. The word occurs without the art. It is the predicate emphasizing quality: "the Word has the same nature as God" (Phillip B. Harner, "Qualitative Anarthrous Predicate Nouns," *JBL* 92 [1973]: 75-78; DM, 139-40; GGBB, 266-69). ὁ λόγος nom. λόγος (# *3364*) word. Possibly a description of Jesus from the OT designating Him as the divine and ultimate Revealer of God's wisdom and power (Brown; Morris; Hoskyns; s. further Bernard; Dodd; Beasley-Murray, 6-10; Carson; TDNT; NIDNTT; Ladd, 237-42; Burton L. Mack, *Logos und Sophia* [Göttingen: Vandenhoeck and Ruprecht, 1973]; ABD, 4:348-56, esp. 352-53; DJG, 481-84, 376-77). Perhaps the best view is to view the art. as indicating *par excellence* (GGBB, 222-23), and "word" from the context of rhetoric, w. the meaning "The Communicator *par excellence*." The word was used w. the art. as a nickname for Protagoras, because of his eloquence and ability to communicate (LS, 1059; HGS, 2:78; s. also Jos., *JW*, 1:234, 515). As THE WORD, Jesus reveals the Father to the creation (s.v. 18). Borgen discusses that it is an exposition of Gen. 1:1, assuming Philo's exegesis; s. Haenchen, 145-47, for further bibliography. ◆ **2** οὗτος (# *4047*) demonstrative pron. nom. masc. this. It implies and emphasizes the whole previous definition (Westcott). ◆ **3** πάντα δι' αὐτοῦ "all things (were) through Him." This phrase seems to be particularly appropriate to describe the role of the Logos vis-à-vis God and the world (Schlatter). ἐγένετο aor. ind. mid. (dep.) γίνομαι to become. The creative activity is viewed as one event in contrast to the continuous existence in vv. 1-2 (RWP; Tenny). χωρίς (# *6006*) prep. w. gen., without, apart. It implies here both causality and presence (Brown). γέγονεν perf. ind. act. γίνομαι (# *1181*) For the possible grammatical constructions s. Brown; 1QH 1:20; 1QS 3:15. Perf. here emphasizes the existing results along with the accomplished action. The emphasis here is not on the process of creation, as previously, but on the product of creation. For the textual problem s. TC, 195-96; Kurt Aland, "Über die Bedeutung eines Punktes: Eine Untersuchung zu Joh 1, 3/4," *ZNW* 69 (1968): 174-209; Schnackenburg; SPJ, 17-44. For various interpretations of vv. 3-4 s. SPJ, 45-89. ◆ **4** ζωή (# *4237*) life. The right and power to bestow activity, to make alive. Here it points to one particular part of creation: mankind (Lightfoot). All that is created continually owes its existence to him (Becker; DJG, 469-71). φῶς (# *5890*) light. That which enables men to recognize the operation of God in the world (Hoskyns). The emphasis is on the source and purpose of the light (Carson; Peder Borgen, *LOGOS Was the True Light and Other Essays on the Gospel of John* [Trondheim: Tapir Publishers, 1983]; cf. also R.E. Brown, "The Qumran Scrolls and the Johannine Gospel and Epistles," *CBQ* 17 [1955]: 403-419; 559-74; BTNT, 203-204; DJG, 472-73). τῶν ἀνθρώπων gen. pl. ἄνθρωπος man. Obj. gen., light for men to see how they are and how God is. ◆ **5** σκοτία (# *5028*) dat. sing. darkness. Darkness is viewed as opposite and opposed to the light. Fig. of speech that describes the cond. of the world darkened by sin. **φαίνει** pres. ind. act. φαίνω (# 5743) to shine. Pres. indicates, "the light keeps on giving light" (RWP). **κατέλαβεν** aor. ind. act. καταλαμβάνω (# 2898) to seize, to grasp, to overcome, to grasp w. the mind, to understand. Const. aor. viewing the total action in contrast to the light that continues to shine. Perhaps John combined the two verbal meanings–the darkness neither understood nor quenched the light (Barrett). Here the vb. could also refer to acknowledging and receiving the truth of the revelation (Beasley-Murray); for discussion of the options s. *PJP*, 89-92. He concludes it means "seize," "overcome in an undesirable or hostile manner." For the importance of life and darkness in DDS s. 1QS 1:9-10; 2:16; 3:13; 3:20; 1 QM 1:7, 9; Morris, *Studies*, 324f; Ladd, 234-36; J.H. Charlesworth, "A Critical Comparison of the Dualism in 1QS iii, 12-iv, 26 and the 'Dualism' contained in the Fourth Gospel," *NTS* 15 (1969): 389-418. This v. is almost a summary of the Gospel: 1. Light invades the realm of darkness; 2. Satan and his subjects resist the light, but are unable to thwart its power; 3. the light is victorious in spite of the opposition. (Blum; Tenny). ◆ **6 ἀπεσταλμένος** perf. pass. part. ἀποστέλλω (# 690) to send, to commission, to send as an authoritative personal representative (TDNT; EDNT). Perf. stressing the existing result. Adj. part. giving a description of the man who appeared. The prep. indicates the permanent character of his mission (Morris). John was divinely commissioned and equipped to prepare for the coming light; thus his witness was valid. This is the reason for his testimony concerning the true nature of the light (Beasley-Murray; Carson; Blum; Morna D. Hooker, "John the Baptist and the Johannine Prologue," *NTS* 16 [1969/70]: 354-58; DJG, 383-91). **παρά** (# 4123) w. gen., from, from the side of. It does not indicate the same close relation as v. 1 (Morris). John is to prepare for the coming Light (PJP, 86). ◆ **7 ἦλθεν** aor. ind. act. ἔρχομαι (# 2262) to come. **μαρτυρήσῃ** aor. subj. act. μαρτυρέω (# 3455) to witness, to be a witness. Const. aor. viewing all the various actions of his testimony as a whole. The effectiveness of his witness is visible in vv. 19-51. **εἰς** (# 1650) prep., to. Used as an idiom with the vb. to give the purp. of the coming, to testify. Subj. w. **ἵνα** (# 2671) to explain the previous (Barrett), or to express purp. **πιστεύσωσιν** aor. subj. act. πιστεύω (# 4409) to believe. Subj. w. ἵνα to express the purp. of the witness, that or so that people believe in the light. ◆ **8 ἦν** impf. ind. act. s.v. 1. **ἐκεῖνος** (# 1697) that one, referring to John in contrast to Christ. **μαρτυρήσῃ** aor. subj. act. s.v. 7. **περὶ τοῦ φωτός** concerning the light. John was the lamp, not the light itself (*PJP*, 89). ◆ **9 ἀληθινός** (# 240) real, genuine, authentic. The opposite is not necessarily false, but impf., shadowy. Christ is the perf. light in whose radiance all other lights seem dim (Bernard;

Morris). He is the true light, the genuine and ultimate self-disclosure of God to man (Carson; TDNT; NIDNT; MM; TLNT). **φωτίζει** pres. ind. act. φωτίζω (# 5894) to shed light upon, to bring light, to enlighten, to instruct. Customary pres., indicating that this is the general habit. Only He can make clear for every individual the meaning and purpose of his or her life; it is not that he literally enlightens everyone (Lightfoot; Carson). This helps man to see God and himself. Pres. indicates the revelation is only in Him (Bultmann), or that it continually shines in the present darkness, not referring to universal salvation or revelation. It may mean that the conception of the Torah's light coming with Moses is the model for the coming of Logos light (*PJP*, 88). **ἐρχόμενον** pres. mid. (dep.) part., s.v. 7. Adj. part. expressing contemporaneous action to the main vb. **φωτίζει**. It could refer to each person born, or more like to Christ as the light who came into the world (Brown). It seems best to take it as the antecedent to the light. In light of 3:19; 12:46 it should refer grammatically to Christ coming into the world. Cf. various options for the meaning here (*PJP*, 87; Carson). ◆ **10 ἔγνω** aor. ind. act. 3rd. pers. sing. γινώσκω (# 1182) to know, to recognize; more than intellectual knowledge, but rather "to be in right relation" (Morris). The lack of recognition was not due to the light, but due to the willful rejection of man, caused by sin (s. John 12:37-43). ◆ **11 ἴδια** acc. n. pl. ἴδιος. (# 2625) one's own, belonging to one, personal. It describes the land and people of Israel as being the home and family of God (Westcott; NIDNTT, 2:838-39; W. Pryor, "Jesus and Israel in the Fourth Gospel – John 1:11," *Nov T* 32 [1990]: 201-18; LS; Thucydides, *History*, 1.141; TLNT). It emphasizes that they should have been familiar with His person, His coming and His claims, as well as the great tragedy of their ultimate rejection. **παρέλαβον** aor. ind. act. παραλαμβάνω (# 4161) to receive, to take to one's side; a common vb. meaning "to welcome" (RWP). Aor. pictures the action independent of time. ◆ **12 ὅσοι** nom. ὅσος (# 4012) as many as. This introduces a *casus pendus*, a dangling construction which is resumed by the subsequent pron. **αὐτοῖς** dat. pl. αὐτός (# 899) (GGBB, 51-52; Bernard; MH, 423ff). The unbelief of John 1:11 is not universal. **ἔλαβον** aor. ind. act. λαμβάνω (# 3284) to receive. **ἔδωκεν** aor. ind. act. δίδωμι (# 1443) to give, used here in the sense of give permission. While there is human responsibility to act upon the offer of faith, it requires a divine action to bestow this privilege. **γενέσθαι** aor. mid. (dep.) inf. γίνομαι (# 1181) to become. Epex. inf. completing the verbal thought of **ἐξουσίαν** (# 2026). By nature men are not the children of God; only by receiving Christ do they gain the right to become the children of God or enjoy the benefits of the salvation that comes from the Jews (John 4:22; Barrett; Beasley-

Murray). **πιστεύουσιν** pres. act. part. πιστεύω (# *4409*) to believe, to trust, to put one's faith in (BAGD; TDNT; NIDNTT; Dennis R. Lindsey, *Josephus and Faith: πίστις & πιστεύειν as Faith Terminology in the Writings of Flavius Josephus & in the New Testament* (Arbeiten zur Geschichte des Antiken Judentums und des Urchristentums 19; Leiden: Brill 1993). It is the appropriate response to revelation (DJG, 224-25). Part. w. the prep. **εἰς** (# *1650*) indicating an active commitment to a person. It is the acceptance of Jesus and what He claims to be as well as a committing of one's life to Him (Brown; M, 67-68). ◆ **13 αἱμάτων** gen. pl. αἱμά (# *135*) blood. Perhaps the blood of father and mother, but it is better to view the pl. in the Semitic sense of bloodshed, blood, or violence (DCH, 2:443-44; GELTS, 11) or bloodshed at the altar (*Epistle of Aristeas,* 88, 90). This and the following phrases emphasize that no human agency is or can be responsible for such a birth (Barrett). **σαρκός** gen. sing. σάρξ (# *4922*) flesh. Gen. indicates the source of the will. Here the word "flesh" is not a wicked principle opposite to God, but rather the sphere of the natural, the powerless, and the superficial (Brown). It stands in contrast to the divine will, emphasizing "earthly humanity's transitoriness and subjection to death" (EDNT). **ἐγεννήθησαν** aor. ind. pass. γεννάω (# *1164*) to give birth, to bear; pass. to be born. Vb. is used of the new birth and the new source of life. Const. aor. viewing the total action. ◆ **14 σάρξ** flesh (s.v. 13). Here it stands for the whole man, a synecdoche (Brown). It shows that Christ shared in man's creaturely weakness (Beasley-Murray). **ἐγένετο** aor. ind. mid. (dep.) s.v. 3. The word came on the human scene as flesh, man (Barrett). This change in state stands in contrast to its permanent cond. in 1:1 (Tenny, 31; s. J. Painter, "Christology and the Fourth Gospel," *AusBR* 31 [1983]: 45-62). **ἐσκήνωσεν** aor. ind. act. σκηνόω (# *5012*) to live in a tent, to settle. Ingressive aor., to take up one's temporary dwelling place (Bernard). The flesh of Jesus Christ is the new localization of God's presence on earth; Jesus is the replacement of the ancient tabernacle (Brown). His body is now the physical location of the divine presence; an incarnation, becoming flesh, not coming into existence. The Word is the ultimate manifestation of the presence of God amongst human beings (Carson). This may also allude to the attendant temp. limitations of human life and environment s. John 3:17; 6:38-42, 51; 7:29; 8:23; 10:36; 16:28 (Tenny, 33). **ἐθεασάμεθα** aor. ind. mid. (dep.) θεάομαι (# *2517*) to watch as in a theater, to view, to contemplate (Brown, 502). Const. aor. viewing his whole life as one event to behold. To attribute to the word θεάομαι in such a context purely a spiritual sense is to set at nought the evidence (Godet, *John*). This could also refer to the revelation of glory in terms of the signs performed (2:11), the being lifted up on

the cross (19:35), and the Easter resurrection (20:24-29; Beasley-Murray). This clearly manifested glory was not perceived by all, as the Gospel goes on to show (Carson). **δόξαν** (# *1518*) glory, that which brings honor and praise to someone. Here the manifestation of God's presence and power which is visible to Israel during the wilderness wandering. Now it is visible in the person of Christ (Dodd, 207; TDNT; TLNT). Possibly this refers to the glory seen in the miracles mentioned in John (Haenchen). **μονογενοῦς** acc. sing. μονογενής (# *3666*) only, unique. The word emphasizes the unique relationship that the Father has to the Son (Morris; EDNT; s. also John 3:16). It does not suggest the idea of begotten by one alone, by one Father without the assistance of a mother. Instead, it suggests the unique position to the father and thus his unique ability to reveal the Father (Gen. 22:2; Beasley-Murray). For the textual problem s. *PJP,* 97. **πλήρης** (# *4441*) full. In apposition to **δόξαν** (Carson). **χάριτος** gen. sing. χάρις (# *5921*) grace (TDNT; TLNT). **ἀλήθεια** (# *237*) truth. These terms used together are based on the OT concepts of grace (loving loyalty) and truth related to God's loyalty and faithfulness to His covenant and covenant people (Barrett). For the OT background s. Lester J. Kuyper, "Grace and Truth: An Old Testament Description of God and Its Use in the Johannine Gospel," *Interpretation* 18 (1964): 3-19; TDNT; Matt. 9:13; 12:7; Zane Hodges, "Problem Passages in the Gospel of John 1. Grace after Grace," *Bib Sac* 135 (1978): 34-45. In John's Gospel it often represents "eternal reality as revealed to men–either the reality itself or the revelation of it" (Dodd, 177; DJG, 860-62). Here it suggests the personal nature of the reality of God and the revelation (Beasley-Murray). ◆ **15 μαρτυρεῖ** pres. ind. act. s.v. 7. Hist. pres. adding vividness to the account or iterat., suggesting the repeated testimony of John concerning Jesus. It may also suggest that John's testimony continues (Beasley-Murray). **κέκραγεν** perf. ind. act. κράζω (# *3189*) to cry, to cry out. A rabbinic t.t. for the loud voice of prophet who intends to be heard (Hoskyns). Perf. possibly pictures the ringing of the message in the ears of the hearers (Bernard; but s. M, 147). It may also be presenting John's witness comprehensively, as a summary of all the action (Carson). **πρῶτός μου ἦν** "He was before me." Jesus is superior to John in terms of might, priority in status and in time (Beasley-Murray). ◆ **16 πληρώματος** gen. sing. πλήρωμα (# *4445*) fullness, that which is filled (in the pass. sense) or that which fills (act. sense) (Morris; TDNT). **καί** (# *2779*) even, resumptive. **ἀντί** (# *505*) instead of, either the idea of replacement (the old covenant replaced by the new covenant [Brown]), or the idea of accumulation–the total life is of grace as it perceives one grace is exchanged only for another (Barrett). Fresh grace replaces grace received and perpetually so; thus the grace is inexhaustible (Beasley-Murray; Tenny, 33). A more likely alternative view is that the Old Testament Law (a token of grace) is replaced by the revelation through Christ (a new grace) (Carson). ◆ **17** ὅτι (# 4022) that, explanatory of the preceding cl. (Haenchen). ἐδόθη aor. ind. pass. δίδωμι (# 1443) to give. Const. aor. with the action being viewed as a whole. This underscores the contrast to the grace given through the Mosaic Law and the grace that appears with the advent of Christ. This is a dominant theme throughout the prologue. (Eldon Jay Epp, "Wisdom, Torah, Word: The Johannine Prologue and the Purpose of the Fourth Gospel," in *Current Issues in Biblical and Patristic Interpretation: Studies in Honor of Merrill C. Tenney Presented by His Former Students* [Grand Rapids: Eerdmans, 1975], 136-38). Divine passive not mentioning explicitly God as the subject. ◆ **18** θεός (# 2536) God. The anarthrous use of the noun emphasizes his nature, not just his person. Thus no one has seen the essence of true deity (Tenny, 34). The background is Exod. 33:20. In Christ there is the full revelation of God (HSB, 492-93). ἑώρακεν perf. ind. act. ὁράω (# 3972) to see, to behold, to view. Perf. indicating the action has not taken place at any time. πώποτε (# 4799) ever, yet at any time. ὤν pres. act. part. εἰμί (# 1639) to be. κόλπον (# 3146) bosom. A Heb. idiom expressing the intimate relationship of child and parent, or of friends (Tasker), or a position of honor (John 13:23; TDNT). Here it suggests intimate fellowship. εἰς w. a stative vb. does not express motion, but affirms the intimate relationship (GGBB, 360). ἐξηγήσατο aor. ind. mid. (dep.) ἐξηγέομαι to lead out, to explain, to rehearse facts, to recount a narrative. Often used for a publishing or explaining of divine secrets (Barrett; TLNT). Only the Son, who has the very nature of God, is able to give an authentic exposition of God to man. This is a t.t. of the exposition of the Laws by the rabbis. This exposition is particularly authoritative due to his unity with God (Beasley-Murray). As a result he displays the nature of the invisible Father (Blum). Const. aor. viewing Christ's life as a continuing revelation of the Father. Consequently, the rest of the Gospel is Christ's unfolding revelation of God the Father (Carson). ◆ **19** μαρτυρία (# 3456) witness. The miracle of the incarnation calls for witnesses to substantiate its reality (Tenney; M.C. Tenney, "The Meaning of Witness in John," *Bib Sac* 132 [1975]: 229-41). ἀπέστειλαν aor. ind. act. s.v. 6. Λευίτης (# 3324) Levite. Perhaps the Levites accompanied the priests here as members of the Temple police (Haenchen; JTJ, 207-13). ἐρωτήσωσιν aor. subj. act. ἐρωτάω (# 2263) to ask, to question. Subj. w. ἵνα (# 2671) indicates the purp. of the sending. There does not seem to be any hostile intent, but there seems to be a legitimate function of inquiring concerning John's self-understanding. C.J.A. Hick-

ling, "Attitudes to Judaism in the Fourth Gospel," *L'Evangile de Jean, Sources, Rédaction, Theologie*, ed. M. de Jonge (Louvain: University Press, 1977), 347-54. ◆ **20** ὡμολόγησεν aor. ind. act. ὁμολογέω (# 3933) to agree, to confess. Const. aor. viewing the total action. ἠρνήσατο aor. ind. mid. (dep.) ἀρνέομαι (# 766) to deny. The first term marks the ready self-devotion of the testimony, the second its completeness (Westcott). The terms taken together suggest "he declared without any qualification, avowing" (Brown). Even his denials constituted part of his witness to the true Christ (Carson). For a discussion of John s. TJ, 63-65; E. Bammel, "The Baptist in Early Christian Tradition," *NTS* 18 (1971): 95-128; W. Wink, *John the Baptist in the Gospel Tradition*, Society for New Testament Studies Monograph Series 7 (Cambridge, 1968), 87-115; Martin Stowasser, *Johannes der Täufer im Vierten Evangelium: Eine Untersuchung zu seiner Bedeutung für die johannische Gemeinde*, OeBS 12 (Klosterneuburg: Öesterreichisches Katholisches Bibelwerk, 1992); R.L. Webb, *John the Baptizer and Prophet: A Socio-Historical Study*, JSNTSS 62 (Sheffield: JSOT, 1991). Carl H. Kraeling, *John the Baptist* (New York: C. Scribner's Sons, 1951); ABD, 3:887-99. Χριστός (# 5986) Christ, Messiah. S. M. de Jonge, "Jewish Expectations about the 'Messiah' according to the Fourth Gospel," *Jesus Stranger from Heaven and Son of God*, (Missoula, Mont.: Scholars, 1977), 77-116; DJG, 114-17. ◆ **21** ἠρώτησαν aor. ind. act. s.v. 19. ἀπεκρίθη aor. ind. pass. (dep.) ἀποκρίνομαι (# 646) to answer. Ἠλίας (# 2460) Elijah. This expectation is based on Mal. 4:5-6; cf. Mark 9:11-12; ABD, 2:465-66; BBC; DJG, 203-206. ὁ προφήτης (# 4737) the prophet. The art. refers to the known or promised prophet intended by Deut. 18:15 (Meyer; s. also the study of background material in Meeks; 1QS 9:11; Beasley-Murray). ◆ **22** δῶμεν aor. subj. act. δίδωμι (# 1443) to give. Subj. w. ἵνα (# 2671) to express purp. πέμψασιν aor. act. part. (temp.) masc. dat. pl. πέμπω (# 4287) to send. Aor. indicating antecedent time. ◆ **23** ἔφη impf. ind. act. φημί (# 5773) to say, to speak (VA, 444-47). βοῶντος pres. act. part. βοάω (# 1066) to shout, to cry out. It describes the cry which answers to strong feeling (Westcott). εὐθύνατε aor. imp. act. εὐθύνω (# 2316) straighten, to make straight. ◆ **24** ἀπεσταλμένοι perf. pass. part. s.v. 6. ◆ **25** ἠρώτησαν aor. ind. act. s.v. 19. Here the question turns from his identity to his authority (Haenchen). βαπτίζεις pres. ind. act. βαπτίζω (# 966) to baptize. Pres. pictures the repeated action. ◆ **26** ἀπεκρίθη aor. ind. pass. (dep.) s.v. 21. Here John renounces all three Messianic titles, viewing himself only as one who prepares the way. ἕστηκεν perf. ind. act. ἵστημι (# 5112) to stand. Perf. suggests "there is one who has taken his stand in your midst: the hidden Messiah is present in Israel" (Beasley-Murray). The other variant readings have insufficient support, while the perf. fits into the context and John's usage nicely (TC, 199). **οἴδατε** perf. ind. act. οἶδα (# 3857) to know. Def. perf. w. a pres. meaning. For a discussion of the meaning and its contrast to its synonym s. Brown, Appendix 1; VA, 281-87. ◆ **27 ἐρχόμενος** aor. pass. (dep.) part. ἔρχομαι (# 2262) to go, to come. **ἵνα** (# 2671) used here w. the adj. **ἄξιος** (# 545) worthy; w. the subj. where normally the inf. is used (RWP; Mark 1:7). **αὐτοῦ** repeated after the rel. pron. and best regarded as a Semitism (Barrett). **ἱμάντα** acc. ἱμάς (# 2666) leather strap. **ὑπόδημα** (# 5687) sandal, shoe. Loosing and carrying sandals was a duty of a slaves and a disciple was exempt from this because of its menial character (Bernard; Talmud, Keth 96a; SB, 1:121). This then reflects the exalted nature of Jesus (Tenney). John's baptism is to prepare for the appearance of the yet hidden Messiah (Beasley-Murray). ◆ **28 ἐγένετο** aor. ind. mid. (dep.) s.v. 3. **Βηθανίᾳ** Bethany beyond the Jordan. The present location is unknown; perhaps a small wadi close to Jericho (ABD, 1:703-705) or it may refer to Batanea (OT Bashan) in the north-east of Palestine (Carson; Rainer Riesner, "Bethany Beyond the Jordan [John 1:28]: Topography, Theology and History in the Fourth Gospel," TB 38 [1987]: 29-63. ◆ **29 ἐπαύριον** (# 2069) adv. tomorrow; that is, on the following day. The word "day" in the dat. (dat. of time) is understood (RWP). In vv. 29, 35, 43 this phrase occurs; in John 2:1 it is **ἡμέρα τῇ τρίτῃ** ("the third day"). Thus there seems to be a beginning of a series of days here (Haenchen). This series culminates in the first sign. For a discussion of proposed parallels between these days and the last week of Christ's life s. Tenney, 38-39. **ἴδε** (# 2623) aor. act. imp. ὁράω to see ("behold"). This favorite word of John is no longer a real imp. expressing a command but an exclamation to draw attention (Morris; SB, 2:371; NIDNTT; P. Fiedler, *Die Formel "und siehe" im Neuen Testament*, 1969). **ἀμνός** (# 303) lamb. Evidently a reference to the various uses of the lamb as a sacrifice in the OT (ABD, 4:132.). All that this sacrifice foreshadowed was perfectly fulfilled in the sacrifice of Christ (Morris). Here referring to the innocence and mildness of a lamb. It emphasizes not only the vicarious suffering, but his unprotesting suffering. This makes a lamb a perfect substitute for sins in contrast to the daily sacrifice of the lamb (J Lightfoot). For the possible specific references of what was intended s. Morris; Brown. S. C.K. Barrett, "The Lamb of God," NTS 1 (1954/55): 210-18; G. Ashbey, "The Lamb of God," JTS (1977): 63ff; (1978): 62ff; D. Brent Sandy, "John the Baptist's 'Lamb of God' Affirmation in Its Canonical and Apocalyptic Milieu," JETS 34 (1991): 447-59. The figs. of the lion and the lamb are combined in the T. Jos. 19:8f; s. also the T. Benj. 3; J.C. O'Neill, "The Lamb of God in the Testaments of the Twelve Patriarchs," JSNT 1 (1979): 2-30; DJG, 432-34. **αἴρων** pres. act. part. αἴρω

(# 149) to lift up, to take away, to carry off, to bear (TDNT). Pres. is the futuristic (Brown) or timeless (Bultmann) or hist. (Godet). **ἁμαρτία** (# 281) sin. The sing. here refers to the mass of sin and the subsequent guilt incurred (Godet; Hoskyns). ◆ **30 γέγονεν** perf. ind. act. s.v. 3. **πρῶτος** (# 4755) first, as a comp. It has a temp. significance, "before" (Brown). Here the priority stems from his preexistence (Blum). ◆ **31 ᾔδειν** plperf. ind. act. οἶδα (# 3857) to know. Def. perf. w. pres. meaning. Plperf. refers to a past event, or is a remote stative aspect (VA, 287-90). **φανερωθῇ** aor. subj. pass. φανερόω (# 5746) to manifest, to make clear, to reveal. **ἦλθον** aor. ind. act. ἔρχομαι (# 2262) to come. ◆ **32 ἐμαρτύρησεν** aor. ind. act. μαρτυρέω (# 3455) to witness. Const. aor. viewing John's witness to Jesus as the Messiah as a whole. **τεθέαμαι** perf. ind. mid. (dep.) s.v. 14. Resultative perf. emphasizes the continuing effects of the past action. **καταβαῖνον** pres. act. part. καταβαίνω (# 2849) to come down. **ὡς** (# 6055) as. **περιστερά** (# 4361) dove. **ἔμεινεν** aor. ind. act. μένω (# 3531) to remain. Const. aor. suggests the dove's remaining as a whole. For the phrase "Son of God" s. Beasley-Murray, 25-26. ◆ **33 ᾔδειν** plperf. ind. act. οἶδα to know. Def. perf. w. pres. meaning (s.v. 31). **πέμψας** aor. act. part. s.v. 22. Subst. part. **βαπτίζειν** pres. act. inf. s.v. 25. Inf. of purp. **εἶπεν** aor. ind. act. λέγω (# 3306) to say. **ἴδῃς** aor. subj. act. 2nd. pers. sing. ὁράω. Subj. w. indef. rel. **ἄν** (# 165) suggests "any one who." **καταβαῖνον** pres. act. part. (adj.) s.v. 32. **μένον** pres. act. part. (adj.) nom. n. sing. s.v. 32. For the idea of ritual cleansing with water and the cleansing of the spirit s. 1QS 3:7, 8; 4:21. ◆ **34 ἑώρακα** perf. ind. act. s.v. 18. **μεμαρτύρηκα** perf. ind. act. s.v. 32. Perf. emphasizes that his testimony was continuous up to the time of speaking (Bernard). ◆ **35 εἱστήκει** plperf. ind. act. ἵστημι (# 2705) to stand. Plperf. indicates that they were standing before the conversation commenced. **ἐκ** (# 1666) out of, from; used here to circumscribe a partitive gen. (Haenchen). ◆ **36 ἐμβλέψας** aor. act. part. ἐμβλέπω (# 1838) to look at; signifies an intent, earnest gazing (Bernard). **ἀμνός** (# 303) lamb (s. John 1:29). **περιπατοῦντι** pres. act. part. περιπατέω (# 4344) to walk. **ἴδε** aor. imp. act. ὁράω to see (s.v. 29). ◆ **37 ἤκουσαν** aor. ind. act. ἀκούω (# 201) to hear. Const. aor. viewing the conversation and the talking as a whole. **λαλοῦντος** pres. act. part. λαλέω (# 3281) to speak. For John's use of this vb. s. Morris. **ἠκολούθησαν** aor. ind. act. ἀκολουθέω (# 199) to follow as a disciple. They followed in the sense of literally walking with him and as his disciples. They turned their loyalty to him as a result of hearing the conversation (TNDT). ◆ **38 στραφείς** aor. pass. part. στρέφω (# 5138) to turn, to turn around. **θεασάμενος** aor. mid. (dep.) part. (temp.) θεάομαι (# 2517) to see; s.v. 14. Aor. is necessarily antecedent to his question. **Τί ζητεῖτε** "What do you seek?" Here the question is understood as "where do you live?" However, the significance here seems to be, "What do you seek in life?" (Blum). ῥαββί (Heb.) rabbi; lit., my great one; teacher (TDNT; ABD, 5:600-602). μεθερμηνευόμενον pres. pass. part. μεθερμηνεύω (# *3493*) to translate, to interpret. ◆ **39 ἔρχεσθε** pres. imp. mid. (dep.) ἔρχομαι (# *2262*) to come s.v. 7. **ὄψεσθε** fut. imp. mid. ὁράω (# *3972*) to see. For the imp. followed by καί and the fut. as a Semitic type of cond. cl. s. Beyer, 238-58. ἦλθαν aor. ind. act. ἔρχομαι s.v. 7. **εἶδαν** aor. ind. act. ὁράω to see. The time was either 10 A.M. (Roman time) or 4 P.M. K. Hanhnart, "About the Tenth Hour" ... on Nisan 15 (John 1, 40), in *L'Evangile de Jean* BETL 44 Gembloux/Leuven 1977, 335-46; IBC, 1:594-95. ◆ **40 ἀκουσάντων** aor. act. part. (adj.) ἀκούω (# *201*) to hear. **ἀκολουθησάντων** aor. act. part. s.v. 37. ◆ **41 εὑρίσκει** pres. ind. act. εὑρίσκω (# *2351*) to find. Hist. pres. **πρῶτον** (# *4754*) first, taken either as an adv. (i.e., he found his own brother first and later found someone else) or as an adj.: the first thing he did was to find his brother (Tasker). **εὑρήκαμεν** perf. ind. act. εὑρίσκω to find. **Μεσσίας** (# *3549*) the anointed, Messiah, Christ. Perhaps looking forward to John 20:31. For the term s. NIDNTT; TDNT; EDNT; UFG, 238-79; Matt. 16:16. **μεθερμηνευόμενον** pres. pass. part. (adj.) μεθερμηνεύω (# *3493*) to translate, to interpret. ◆ **42 ἤγαγεν** aor. ind. act. ἄγω (# *72*) to lead. **ἐμβλέψας** aor. act. part. ἐμβλέπω (# *1838*) to look upon. Aor. part. indicates that he looked before he spoke. **κληθήσῃ** fut. ind. pass. καλέω (# *2813*) to call. **ἑρμηνεύεται** pres. ind. pass. ἑρμηνεύω (# *2257*) to translate, to interpret. ◆ **43 ἠθέλησεν** aor. ind. act. θέλω (# *2527*) to will, to want. Aor. indicates "he resolved" w. the subject probably Jesus (Morris). **ἐξελθεῖν** aor. act. inf. ἐξέρχομαι (# *2002*) to go out. Compl. inf. to the main vb. **εὑρίσκει** pres. ind. act. s.v. 41. **ἀκολούθει** pres. imp. act. ἀκολουθέω s.v. 37. ◆ **45 ἔγραψεν** aor. ind. act. γράφω (# *1211*) to write. The prominent position of the vb. may indicate that Philip and Nathanael had previously discussed the fulfillment of these Scriptures (Morris). A major theme in John is that Jesus fulfills the OT (Carson). Moses (Deut. 18:18-19) and the prophets (Isa. 52:13-53:12; Dan. 7:13; Mic. 5:2-4; Mal. 3:1-4) predicted Messiah's coming. ◆ **46 τι ἀγαθόν** anything good. A scornful question (Barrett) due to the low regard for Nazareth. **ἔρχου** pres. imp. mid. (dep.), s.v. 7. Imp. is inviting rather than commanding. Pres. imp. is common w. a vb. of motion (VANT, 341-48; esp., 344-45). ◆ **47 ἐρχόμενον** pres. mid. (dep.) part. s.v. 7. **ἀληθῶς** (# *242*) truly. H. Kuhli, "Nathanael – "Wahrer Israelit"? Zum angeblischen attributiven Gebrauch von ἀληθῶς in Joh 1,47," *BN* 9 (1979): 11-19. **δόλος** (# *1515*) deceit, cunning, treachery. It indicates his religious and moral integrity (Lindars). ◆ **48 πόθεν** (# *4470*) where. **γινώσκεις** pres. ind. act. γινώσκω (# *1182*) to know. **ἀπεκρίθη** aor. ind. pass. (dep.) ἀποκρίνομαι s.v.

21. **φωνῆσαι** aor. act. inf. φωνέω (# *5888*) to call. Inf. w. prep. **πρό** (# *4574*) to express time ("before") (MT, 144). **ὄντα** pres. act. part. εἰμί (# *1639*) to be. **συκῆ** (# *5190*) fig tree. The rabbis often sat under a fig tree for study or for teaching (Bultmann). The fig tree portrays a place of peace and prosperity, safety and leisure (1 Kings 4:25; Mic. 4:4; Zech. 3:10). Perhaps it was a place of meditation on the Law (Tenney; Blum; s. also J.R. Michaels "Nathanael under the Fig-Tree [Jn 1, 48; 4, 19]" *ET* 78 [1966/67]: 182f; C.F.D. Moule, "A Note on "Under the Fig tree in John 1,48.50," *JTS* 5 [1954]: 210f. For a discussion of the fig tree see FFB, 118-19; Oded Boronski, *Agriculture in Iron Age Israel*, 114-16; POB, 103-07; PB, 58-59). The supernatural knowledge of Christ, not the fig tree, is emphasized (Carson). **εἶδον** aor. ind. act. ὁράω (# *3972*) to see. ◆ **49 ἀπεκρίθη** aor. ind. pass. (dep.) s.v. 21. **σὺ βασιλεὺς εἶ τοῦ Ἰσραήλ** "You are King over Israel." Without the art. the character or quality is stressed (s.v. 1 θεός). A confession as to the person and office of Christ (Bengel). ◆ **50 ὑποκάτω** (# *5691*) w. gen., under. **μείζω** (# *3505*) comp. μέγας great; comp., greater. Perhaps this refers to the miracles in the following chapters. **τούτων** pl. gen. τοῦτο; gen. of comp. referring to his supernatural knowledge. **ὄψῃ** fut. ind. mid. (dep.) ὁράω (# *3972*) to see. ◆ **51 ὄψεσθε** fut. ind. mid. (dep.) ὁράω to see. **ἀνεῳγότα** perf. act. part. ἀνοίγω (# *487*) to open. Perf. indicates the completed state ("to be opened"). A reference to Jacob's vision in Gen. 28:10ff (Bernard). For more discussion s. HSB, 493-95. **ἀναβαίνοντας** pres. act. part. ἀναβαίνω (# *326*) to go up. The thought is that the Son of man is the means of bridging the gap between earth and heaven (Morris).

John 2

◆ **1 γάμος** (# *1141*) wedding. For the Jewish custom regarding weddings s. SB 2:372-79; IDB, 3:285f; LNT, 228-46; H. Granquist, *Marriage Conditions in a Palestinian Village* 2 vols. (New York: AMS Press, 1975), 1931-35; JPFC, 2:752-60. **ἐγένετο** aor. ind. mid. (dep.) γίνομαι (# *1181*) to become. For a discussion of this passage s. B. Olsson, *Structure and Meaning in the Fourth Gospel: A Text-Linguistic Analysis of John 2:1-11 and 4:1-42* (Gleerup, 1974); R. Schnackenburg, *Das erste Wunder Jesu* (Freiburg: Herder, 1951); W. Luetgehetmann, *Die Hochzeit von Kana (Joh 2,1-11)*, 1989. For a discussion of the structure of 2:1-4:54 s. Carson, 166. **Κανὰ τῆς Γαλιλαίας** Cana of Galilee. The exact location is unknown. It was in the area around Nazareth. Thus it would have taken 2-3 days to travel from Jerusalem to Cana of Galilee. ◆ **2 ἐκλήθη** aor. ind. pass. καλέω (# *2813*) to call, to invite. Const. aor. viewing the complete action. For the moral obligation of the guests to bring gifts and the duty of reciprocation

s. *LNT*, 229-34. ♦ **3 ὑστερήσαντος** aor. act. part. (temp.) ὑστερέω (# 5728) to fall short, to run short, to fail. Gen. abs. Aor. describes action that is antecedent and logically necessary for the action of the main vb. Usually the wedding was seven days of feasting. No reason is mentioned for the shortage of wine. Failure by the groom to provide adequately for the guests was a social disgrace (Tenney; *BBC*). ♦ **4 τί ἐμοὶ καὶ σοί** "What is it to Me and to you?" ("You have no right to blame Me. The problem is taken care of.") It is an answer of remonstrance, of putting off and impatient urging (*LNT*, 238-43). There are two ways of understanding this (1) What business is that of ours? (2) What authority do you have over me? (Tenney). For the various views see C.P. Ceroke, "The Problem of Ambiguity in John 2,4," *CBQ* 21 (1959): 316-40; O. Baechli, "Was habe ich mit Dir zu schaffen?" *ThZ* 33 (1977): 69-80; *GGBB*, 150-51. **γύναι** voc. γυνή (# 1222) woman. Voc. is not disrespectful, but a certain disassociation is present (Schnackenburg) Jos., *Ant.*, 17:74 uses the term as a sign of affection. **ἥκει** pres. ind. act. ἥκω (# 2457) to have come, to be present (*BAGD*). **ὥρα** (# 6052) hour. "I shall choose the appropriate moment," referring to His intention to provide the needed wine, and to reveal his glory. The reference is not immediately to his death. It is the beginning of the journey which through the cross climaxes in his exaltation (*LNT*, 142; for similar expressions s. 7:6, 8, 30; 8:20; 12:23; 13:1; 17:1). ♦ **5 ὅ τι ἄν** (# 4005; 5515; 323) whatever. **λέγῃ** pres. subj. act. λέγω (# 3306) to speak, to say. Subj. w. **ἄν** expresses a generalization. Mary anticipates some immediate action or utterance from her Son. Thus the meaning is, "Whatever he may be shortly saying to you" (*JG*, 376-77). **ποιήσατε** aor. imp. act. ποιέω (# 4472) to do. Aor. imp. has a note of urgency here (*EGGNT*, 86), "do immediately." ♦ **6 λίθιναι** (# 3343) stone. Adjs. w. this ending generally signify material, origin, or kind (MH, 359). Stone was used because it did not itself contract uncleanness (Barrett; *SB*, 2:406-07; R. Deines, *Jüdische Steingefäße und pharisäische Frömmigkeit. Ein archäolog.-historischer Beitrag zum Verständnis von Joh 2,6 und der jüdischen Reinheitshalacha z. Zeit Jesu* [Tübingen: J.C.B. Mohr], 1993). **ὑδρία** (# 5620) waterpot. **κείμεναι** pres. mid. (dep.) part. κεῖμαι (# 3023) to lie, to stand (of vessels). Adj. part. describing the location. **χωροῦσαι** pres. act. part. χωρέω (# 6003) to have room for, to contain. Adj. part. describing the content. **ἀνά** (# 324) each, prep. used in a distributive sense (*JG*, 222-23). **μετρητής** (# 3583) measure; a liquid measure about nine gallons or 36 liters each (*BAGD*; *ABD*, 6:905). ♦ **7 γεμίσατε** aor. imp. act. γεμίζω (# 1153) to fill, to fill w. (w. gen.). Authoritative imp. (*JG*, 319). **ἐγέμισαν** aor. ind. act. **ἕως ἄνω** (# 2401; 539) up to the brim. There was no room left for adding anything to the water in the jars (Bernard). ♦ **8 ἀντλήσατε** aor. imp. act. ἀντλέω (# 533) to

draw, to draw out. Often used of drawing water from a well, but here from a water jar (Brown; *TLNT*, 1:131-33; Gen. 24:13; Isa. 12:3; cf. Jos., *JW*, 4:472). Aor. imp. has a note of urgency (*EGGNT*, 86). There is intentionally no description of the method of the miracle, only of the person performing it. **φέρετε** pres. imp. act. φέρω (# 5770) to carry. Pres. progressive suggesting that the action should continue. Frequently, the pres. imp. occurs with vbs. of motion. **ἀρχιτρίκλινος** (# 804) superintendent of a banquet whose duty it was to arrange the table and food (AS; *BBC*). **ἤνεγκαν** aor. ind. act. φέρω to carry. Const. aor. viewing the total action. ♦ **9 ἐγεύσατο** aor. ind. mid. (dep.) γεύομαι (# 1174) to taste. Const. aor. viewing the total action. **γεγενημένον** perf. mid. (dep.) part. γίνομαι (# 1181) to become. Perf. emphasizes the state or cond. arising from a past completed action. Here it also emphasizes the antecedent action of the quite recent events (*JG*). **ᾔδει** plperf. ind. act. οἶδα (# 3857) to know. Def. perf. w. pres. meaning **πόθεν** (# 4470) where, from where, indicating source. **ἠντληκότες** perf. act. part. ἀντλέω s.v. 8. Perf. part. emphasizes the antecedent action of the quite recent events (*JG*). **φωνεῖ** pres. ind. act. φωνέω (# 5888) to call, to call out. Hist. pres., adding vividness to the account. **νυμφίος** (# 3812) groom. Called since he was ultimately responsible for the food and drink. ♦ **10 τίθησιν** pres. ind. act. τίθημι (# 5502) to place; here, to serve. **μεθυσθῶσιν** aor. subj. pass. μεθύσκω (# 3499) pass. to become drunk, to be drunk. Subj. w. **ὅταν** (# 4020) describes the general time ("whenever"). The words do not imply that the guests were already drunk (Sanders). **ἐλάσσω** (# 1781) comp. μικρός small; comp., lesser, inferior; used as the opposite of **καλόν** (# 2819) to describe less good wine served at the end of a meal (*TLNT*). **τετήρηκας** perf. ind. act. τηρέω (# 5498) to guard, to keep back, to preserve. Perf. describing the continuing result of his withholding the wine. The point of the miracle is that Christianity is an advance over Judaism. God has kept his best gift until last (Blum; *DJG*, 873). ♦ **11 ἐποίησεν** aor. ind. act. ποιέω (# 4472) to do. Const. aor. emphasizing the total action. **ἀρχή** (# 794) beginning (implying that there was more to come). **σημεῖον** (# 4956) sign, an act or miracle w. a meaning designed to lead to belief in Jesus as the Messiah, the Son of God. This is a personal mark, identifying sign, or distinctive in respect to the true character and nature of Christ (Schnackenburg; Brown; *TDNT*; *TLNT*; H. van der Loos, "The Miracles of Jesus," *NTS* 9 [1965]: 590-618; *DJG*, 555-56). It was also designed to show the type of ministry he was to have, one of transformation. (Jos., *Ant.*, 2:274, 280 states God uses miracles to convince people). **ἐφανέρωσεν** aor. ind. act. φανερόω (# 5746) to manifest, to make visible, to make clear. Const. aor. viewing all the actions in the miracle as part of the manifestation of His glory. His Messianic glory was manifested in the abundance of wine which was the OT figure for joy in the final days (Brown). ἐπίστευσαν aor. ind. act. πισ-τεύω (# 4409) to believe in, to trust in. Const. aor. picturing their belief as a whole, or ingressive aor. picturing their entrance into the state of belief. ◆ **12 μετὰ τοῦτο** after this. This common connective within John is without any reference to a particular length of time (Carson). **κατέβη** aor. ind. act. καταβαίνω (# 2849) to go down. Const. aor. viewing the journey as a whole. If Cana is on the northwest shore of Galilee, then they went down in a literal sense (Carson). **ἔμειναν** aor. ind. act. μένω (# 3531) to remain. Const. aor. viewing the staying as a whole. ◆ **13 πά-σχα** (# 4247) Passover. This feast was celebrated on the 14-15 of Nisan (Exod. 12:6). Two other Passovers are mentioned in John (6:4; 11:55; 12:1; 13:1). For a discussion of the pilgrimages to the Passover s. WZZT. For a discussion of the way of celebrating Passover cf. the Mishnah tractate Pesahim. **ἀνέβη** aor. ind. act. ἀναβαίνω (# 326) to go up. This describes the pilgrimage to Jerusalem. It could simply refer to the geographic height or to the importance of the capital and Temple. For a discussion of this pericope s. R.H. Hiers, "The Purification of the Temple: Preparation for the Kingdom of God," *JBL* 90 (1971): 82-90; DJG, 819-20. ◆ **14 εὗρεν** aor. ind. act. εὑρίσκω (# 2351) to find. **ἱερῷ** dat. ἱερόν (# 2639) temple. Here it is a reference to the Court of the Gentiles, not the sanctuary per se (2:19-20). For a summary of the history and description of this temple s. ABD, 6:364-68; JPB, 54-72. **πωλοῦντας** pres. act. part. πωλέω (# 4797) to sell. Subst. part. used as a noun indicating not only their profession, but the activity. Pres. parts. indicate action contemporaneous to the main vb. For a discussion of the trade and commerce, particularly to enrich the family of Annas s. JTJ, 48-49. **βόας** pl. βοῦς (# 1091) ox. **πρόβατον** (# 4585) sheep. **περιστερά** (# 4361) pigeon. These were the animals used for the Temple sacrifices. Pigeons were for the poor, oxen for the very wealthy (M, Sheq. 5:3; SB 1:851). **κερματιστής** (# 3048) money changer, properly one who exchanges large money into small (Morris). Money changers were required because the Jews were not allowed to mint their own coins. The Roman coins, w. images of the emperor as deity, were blasphemous to the Jewish leaders. For this reason the Temple tax and sacrifices had to be paid in silver didrachmas of Tyre. For a picture s. ABD, 1:1081 fig. o. According to the Mishnah (M, Sheq. 1:1, 3) they were to collect the tax before the Feast (beginning the 25th of Adar) inside the Temple precincts. At times they cheated in assisting in transactions, particularly in converting or selling animals for the temple service (M, Ker. 1:7; M, Shek. 7:4; JCST; Beasley-Murray; ABD, 1:1086-87; JTJ, 48-49). **καθημένους** pres. mid. (dep.) part. κάθημαι (# 2764) to sit. Subst. part. At times a money changer

also functioned as a banker charging interest and a 4-6 percent transaction fee for exchanging coins of different origins. The temple tax, based on Neh. 10:32-33, was for the upkeep of the temple (ABD, 6:340). ◆ **15 ποιήσας** aor. act. part. ποιέω (# 4472) to make. Aor. indicates antecedent time to the main vb. ἐξέβαλεν. **φρα-γέλλιον** (# 5848) whip, scourge. No sticks or weapons were allowed in the temple precinct (Brown). This is a Latin loanword, *flagellum*, the dem. form of *flagrum* (BAGD; MM; for a discussion of the incident in general s. DJG, 817-21; particularly in John s. DJG, 819-20). A lash made of cords or thongs made from the ox's hide was attached. The purpose was for whipping horses, slaves, or criminals (*DGRA,* 539-40). **σχοινίον** (# 5389) cord, probably of twisted rushes (Westcott). **ἐξέβαλεν** aor. ind. act. ἐκβάλλω (# 1675) to cast out, to drive out. Const. aor. viewing the action as a whole. He drove out the animals. **κολλυβιστῶν** gen. κολλυβιστής (# 3142) money changer. Poss. gen., indicating to whom the coins belonged. The action is not directed against the worshippers, but against those who detract from true worship (Beasley-Murray). **ἐξέχεεν** aor. ind. act. ἐξέχω (# 1772) to pour out. For the unusual form s. MH 215, 265. **κέρμα** (# 3047) small coin, usually copper; change (BAGD; MM). **τράπεζα** (# 5544) table. **ἀνέτρεψεν** aor. ind. act. ἀνατρέφω (# 418) to turn over. ◆ **16 πωλοῦσιν** pres. act. part. πωλέω (# 4797) to sell. Used here as an noun with an obj. ("the sellers of pigeons"). **ἄρατε** aor. imp. act. αἴρω (# 149) to lift up, to take away. **ποιεῖτε** pres. imp. act. ποιέω (# 4472) to make; used w. neg. **μή** (# 3590) to prohibit an action in progress. **ἐμπορίου** gen. ἐμπόριον (# 1866) a place of trade, a house of merchandise. Gen. of apposition (Barrett) or epex. gen. (BAGD). Here the selling location takes the place of the action of selling. The attack here is that they think one can purchase God's favor through sacrifice (Schlatter; Richard Bauckham, "Jesus' Demonstration in the Temple," in *Law and Religion: Essays on the Place of the Law in Israel and Early Christianity* ed. Barnabas Lindars [London: SPCK, 1988], 72-89). ◆ **17 ἐμνήσθη-σαν** aor. ind. pass. (dep.) μιμνήσκομαι (# 3630) to remember. **γεγραμμένον** perf. pass. part. γράφω (# 1211) to write. Periphrastic part. **ζῆλος** (# 2419) zeal, followed by the obj. gen. **τοῦ οἴκου σου** zeal for thine house (Tasker). A quotation from Ps. 69:9. The zeal for God would ultimately lead Jesus to his death. His vehemence demonstrates his inward passion for the Father and the Father's interest (Tenney). **καταφάγεται** fut. ind. mid. (dep.) κατεσθίω (# 2983) to eat up, to consume. Pred. fut. describing a fut. event. ◆ **18 ἀπε-κρίθησαν** aor. ind. pass. (dep.) ἀποκρίνομαι (# 646) to answer. **οὖν** (# 4036) in response. For the responsive use of the particle s. DM, 254. **σημεῖον** sign. s.v. 11 (s. Morris, 684-91; Peter Riga, "Signs of Glory: The Use of 'Semeion'in St. John's Gospel," *Interpretation* 17 [1963]:

402-424). The question is one of credentials (Carson). δεικνύεις pres. ind. act. δείκνυμι (# 1259) to show. Pres. indicating an immediate fut. action: "What sign are you going to show us?" ὅτι (# 4022) because (JG, 157). ποιεῖς pres. ind. act. ποιέω (# 4472) to do. Pres. points to the things that Jesus was in the process of doing. ◆ 19 ἀπεκρίθη aor. ind. pass. (dep.) ἀποκρίνομαι s.v. 18. λύσατε aor. imp. act. λύω (# 3395) to loose, to destroy. The construction by over 1,000 workers was ongoing (ABD, 6:365). It is a permissive or concessive imp., not a command (RWP; JG, 321-22; contra GGBB, 490-97). Or it is a type of cond. cl.: "If you destroy..." (VA, 352-53). ἐν within; temp. use of the prep. "after an interval of three days" (JG, 255). ἐγερῶ fut. ind. act. ἐγείρω (# 1586) to raise up. For the imp. followed by the fut. s. 1:39. This may refer to the restoration of the Temple by Messiah (Tg Isa. 53:5). ◆ 20 οἰκοδομήθη aor. ind. pass. οἰκοδομέω (# 3868) to build, to erect. Complexive aor. summing up the completed building, though it is not yet completed (it was completed in A.D. 63) (Brown; Harold W. Hoehner, "Chronological Aspects of the Life of Christ," *Bib Sac* 131 [1974]: 49-52; VANT, 172; 257-58; cf. GGBB, 560-61; for DSS instructions concerning temple building s. Yigael Yadin, "The Temple Scroll," *BA* 30 [1967]: 137-39). Since the building was started about 20 or 19 B.C. this year must be between 27 or 28 A.D. (SB, 2:411ff; Jos., *Ant.* 15:380-425; *JW*, 1:401; 5:184-247; for a discussion on the chronological problem as well as the building of the temple in Josephus cf. *TJ*, 28-30. Hoehner understands the aor. to refer to a completed edifice finished 18/17 B.C. Thus this year would be 29/30 A.D. Harold W. Hoehner, *Chronological Aspects of the Life of Christ*, 40-43. ◆ 21 For the misunderstanding by the Jewish leaders s. O. Cullmann, "Der johannische Gebrauch doppeldeutiger Ausdrücke als Schlüssel zum Verständnis des vierten Evangeliums," *TZ* 4 (1948): 360-72; D.A. Carson, "Understanding Misunderstandings in the Fourth Gospel," *TB* 13 (1982): 59-91. ◆ 22 ἠγέρθη aor. ind. pass. ἐγείρω s.v. 19. Const. aor. including both his death and resurrection. ἐμνήσθησαν aor. ind. pass. (dep.) μιμνήσκομαι (# 3630) to remember, w. gen. αὐτοῦ gen. sing. αὐτός (# 899). Gen. as an obj. The content of what they remembered is given in the ὅτι cl. Only after the resurrection did the disciples understand the meaning of this statement (Schlatter). ◆ 23 θεωροῦντες pres. act. part. θεωρέω (# 2555) to see. Part. is causal or temp. Pres. indicates contemporaneous action. S. Donald Guthrie, "Importance of Signs in the Fourth Gospel," *VoxE* 5 (1967): 72-83; Zane C. Hodges, "Untrustworthy Believers Joh 2,23-25," *Bib Sac* 135 (1978): 139ff. ἐποίει impf. ind. act. ποιέω s.v. 18. Progressive impf. to vividly describe the past action in progress. ◆ 24 αὐτός pron. emphasizes the contrast between the others and Jesus (GGBB, 349). δέ (# 1254) in contrast,

on the other hand. ἐπίστευεν impf. ind. act. πιστεύω (# 4409) to trust, to entrust oneself. Prog. impf. to vividly describe the past action. It could be customary, describing Jesus' custom of not entrusting the full meaning of his mission to everyone. The use of the vb. is parallel to 1 Thess. 2:4; Gal. 2:7; 1 Cor. 9:17; 1 Tim. 1:11; cf. also Jos., *Ant.*, 20:183; *JW*, 5:567; MM; BAGD; Schlatter). γινώσκειν pres. act. inf. γινώσκω (# 1182) to know. διά (# 1328) with the art. inf. describes the cause. For them he was a great healer, not necessarily a great Savior (Blum). ◆ 25 μαρτυρήσῃ aor. subj. act. μαρτυρέω (# 3455) to witness, to give witness. "God, who knows everything and is everywhere present, from whom nothing is hidden, is the witness *par excellence*" (TLNT). Const. aor. describing his knowledge as a whole. ἐγίνωσκεν impf. ind. act. γινώσκω s.v. 24. Cust. impf. indicating that he regularly knew what was in man. What is in a man is hidden from another; only God knows (SB, 2:412; GGBB, 228-29).

John 3

◆ 1 δέ (# 1254) and, but. This can be in contrast to the preceding and suggest that Nicodemus was open. Or it can be a continuation of the narrative, not necessarily as a point in thought (Carson, 185-86; JG, 104-106). ἄνθρωπος (# 476) man, a man of the Pharisees. An unusual expression probably linked to the closing of the previous chapter, so as to bring out Jesus' knowledge of man (Morris). For two opposite portrayals s. Michael Goulder, "Nicodemus," *SJT* 44 (1991): 153-68 and M. de Jonge, "Nicodemus and Jesus: Some Observations on Misunderstandings and Understanding in the Fourth Gospel," *BJRL* 53 (1970-71): 337-59; ABD, 4:1105-106. For a discussion of the Pharisees s. TJ, 70-76; Alan Watson, *Jesus and the Jews: The Pharisaic Tradition in John* (Athens, Ga.: University of Georgia Press, 1995); ABD, 5:289-303; DJG, 609-14. ἄρχων (# 807) leader. At least an influential Pharisee, perhaps a member of the Sanhedrin (BAGD; Haenchen; Schlatter; SB, 2:412-19). ◆ 2 ἦλθεν aor. ind. act. ἔρχομαι (# 2262) to come. οἴδαμεν perf. ind. act. οἶδα (# 3857) to know. Def. perf. w. a pres. meaning. The 1st. pl. may be a reference to others among the Sanhedrin who believe or at least are interested. ἐλήλυθας perf. ind. act. ἔρχομαι to come; a consummative perf. emphasizing not only the completion of the process of coming, but the state of Christ's presence in Israel. This is not a reference to Christ's preexistence but a recognition that God was peculiarly with him (Carson). σημεῖον (# 4956) sign (s. John 2:11, 18) Here it is plural even though only one sign has been mentioned by John (Carson). The miracles authenticated the message (SB, 2:420; Baba Meci'a 59b; s. also Acts 2:22; Schlatter). ᾖ pres. subj. act. εἰμί (# 1639) to be. Subj. w. ἐάν (# 1569), except. The im-

plied question is, "who are you really?" (Carson).
◆ **3** ἀπεκρίθη aor. ind. pass. (dep.) ἀποκρίνομαι (# 646)
to answer. γεννηθῇ aor. subj. pass. γεννάω (# 1164).
Pass. can either mean to be born or begotten (Brown).
Subj. w. ἐάν in a cond. cl. where the cond. is possible.
The emphasis here is on receiving a new origin. This
birth is attributed to the Spirit (NIDNTT, 3:179).
ἄνωθεν (# 540) from above; the heavenly word from
whose power a man must be renewed (s. 3:31; 19:11,
23; Schnackenburg; Tenney). Perhaps a circumlocution
for God (BBC). This is an adaptation of the Jewish
hope of a new creation (Beasley-Murray; SB, 1:420-23).
Advs. with the suffix -θεν answer the question
"whence?" "from where?" (BD, 56). The word can also
mean "again," "anew" (Acts 26:5). The translation "re-
born from above" includes both meaning of the word
(Morris). This also stands in contrast to the belief that
being of the seed of Abraham was sufficient (J Lightfoot). ἰδεῖν aor. inf. act. ὁράω (# 3972) to see. Here to
experience, encounter, participate in at the end of the
age (Brown). Compl. inf. to the main vb. δύναται. Aor.
points to the total experience. The need is for transformation (Carson). βασιλείαν τοῦ θεοῦ kingdom of God.
It points to God's rule. Used almost as a synonym for
eternal life (DJG, 429). ◆ **4** γεννηθῆναι aor. pass. inf.
γεννάω s.v. 3. Compl. inf. to the main vb. δύναται.
γέρων (# 1173) old. ὤν pres. act. part. εἰμί (# 1639) to be.
Circum. part. describing a contemporaneous cond.
κοιλία (# 3120) stomach, womb. δεύτερον (# 1309) second, a second time. εἰσελθεῖν aor. act. inf. εἰσέρχομαι
(# 1656) to go into. Compl. inf. to the main vb. δύναται. γεννηθῆναι aor. pass. inf. γεννάω s.v. 3. ◆ **5** γεννηθῇ
ἐξ ὕδατος καὶ πνεύματος "born of water and spirit."
For a discussion of the various views s. Carson; Zane
C. Hodges, "Water and Spirit – John 3,5," *Bib Sac* 135
(1978): 206ff; Linda Belleville, "'Born of Water and
Spirit': John 3:5," *TrinJ* N.S. 2 (1981): 125-41; HSB, 495-
96; BBC; DJG, 347-48, 575-76. Witherington wants to
see water as physical birth (Ben Witherington III, "The
Waters of Birth: John 3:5 and 1 John 5:6-8," *NTS* 35
[1989]: 155-60). The phrase explains the previous
ἄνωθεν (# 540) and καί (# 2779) is explanatory in the
sense of "that is." Thus there is an equation between
water and the spirit. ◆ **6** γεγεννημένον perf. pass. part.
s.v. 3. Perf. conveys that which has been born and
presently comes before us in this light (Westcott). This
shows the necessity of a new birth in order to become
children of God (Carson). ἐκ (# 1666) prep., from; indicates the source or sphere. ◆ **7** θαυμάσῃς aor. subj. act.
θαυμάζω (# 2513) to wonder, to marvel. Aor. subj. is a
categorical prohibition: "Do not marvel at all!" (which
he had done in v. 4) (BD, 337,2). Perhaps the idea of
the vb. here is to stumble or reject; s. 5:28 for the same
meaning (Schlatter). δεῖ (# 1256) pres., ind. act. it is
necessary (w. inf.). ὑμᾶς pl. σύ (# 5148) you; the pl.

here stands in contrast to the sing. of addressing Nicodemus. This application is broader than simply Nicodemus. This explains the generalizing τίς (# 5516) in
vv. 3, 5 (Carson). ◆ **8** πνεῦμα (# 4460) wind. Perhaps
there is a play on words here or it is figurative; the
wind itself has no will. θέλει pres. ind. act. θέλω
(# 2527) to desire. πνεῖ pres. ind. act. πνέω (# 4463) to
blow. Gnomic pres. suggesting what normally occurs
(IBG, 8). πόθεν (# 4470) where, from what place. ποῦ
(# 4544) where, to what place. γεγεννημένος perf. pass.
part. s.v. 3. The point of the comp. seems to be that the
Spirit as the wind is not understandable or controlla-
ble. Yet the effects are undeniable and unmistakable
(Carson). ◆ **9** γενέσθαι aor. mid. (dep.) inf. γίνομαι
(# 1181) to become; to be; to happen. ταῦτα (# 4047)
fem. pl. αὕτη; this is a summary of the discussion so
far. ◆ **10** ὁ διδάσκαλος (# 1437) the teacher. The art.
emphasizes this status of Nicodemus as a great teacher (Barrett). This is ironic, the "well-known teacher"
who does not know this simple truth (JG). As a Pharisee, he was considered among "the most accurate interpreters of the Laws" (Jos., *JW*, 2:162; *Life*, 191; *TJ*, 72-
73). The sharp rebuke stands in contrast to his leadership position. Based on the study of the Hebrew Bible
he should have but did not understand this (Carson).
◆ **11** οἴδαμεν perf. ind. act. s.v. 2. λαλοῦμεν pres. ind.
act. λαλέω (# 3281) to speak. Pres. indicates the action
in progress. ἑωράκαμεν perf. ind. act. ὁράω (# 3972) to
see. Perf. indicates the resulting cond. of having seen.
μαρτυροῦμεν pres. ind. act. μαρτυρέω (# 3455) to witness to, to bear witness. λαμβάνετε pres. ind. act. λαμβάνω (# 3284) to receive. The problem here is not
intellectual, but one of believing the witness (Carson).
◆ **12** εἰ (# 1623) if; the fact of fulfillment is assumed to
be fulfilled (SMT, 244). ἐπίγεια n. pl. ἐπίγειος (# 2103)
earthly. εἴπω aor. subj. act. λέγω (# 3306) to say. Subj.
suggests doubt. ἐπουράνιος heavenly. For the terms
"earthly" and "heavenly" s. Schnackenburg. The
earthly things may refer to the conds. necessary to
enter the kingdom of God, while the heavenly things
refer to the conds. of the established kingdom on earth
(Carson).   ◆ **13** ἀναβέβηκεν perf. ind. act. ἀναβαίνω
(# 326) to go up, to ascend. Perf. indicates "no man
has gained the height of heaven" (Morris). εἰ μή
(# 1623; 3590) except. Since he is the only one who has
come from heaven, he alone can speak authoritatively
of it (Carson). He alone by virtue of his descent from
heaven is authorized and empowered by the Father to
achieve the salvation of the divine sovereignty (Beasley-Murray). καταβάς aor. act. part. καταβαίνω
(# 2849) to descend, to come down. Subst. part. to describe here the qualifications of the Son of Man. Aor.
indicates action logically antecedent, though the action could be temporally simultaneous. ◆ **14** ὕψωσεν
aor. ind. act. ὑψόω (# 5738) to lift up, to make high.

Const. aor. referring to the action as a whole. In John it refers both to the lifting up on the cross as well as the exaltation to heaven (TDNT). ὄφις (# *4058*) snake; cf. Num. 21:4-9; 2 Kings 18:4; ABD, 5:1117. ὑψωθῆναι aor. pass. inf. ὑψόω. Compl. inf. to the impersonal vb. δεῖ (# *1256*) pres. ind. act. w. inf., it is necessary to, giving a logical necessity. τὸν υἱὸν τοῦ ἀνθρώπου Son of Man. S. the discussion in Schackenburg. ◆ **15 πιστεύων** pres. act. part. πιστεύω (# *4409*) to believe. Subst. part. πᾶς ὁ (# *4246*) anyone who. Pres. expresses simultaneous action. ἔχῃ pres. subj. act. ἔχω (# *2400*) to have. Subj. w. ἵνα (# *2671*) to express purp.; the purp. of the exaltation is that those who believe obtain eternal life. αἰώνιος (# *173*) eternal. Eternal life is the life of the age to come which is gained by faith, cannot be destroyed, and is a pres. possession of the one who believes (GW, 191-201; Brown, 505-508; Dodd, 144-50). ◆ **16 οὕτως γάρ** just as the acquisition of eternal life is grounded in the lifting up of the Son, so the lifting up of the Son is grounded in the love of God (Carson). ἠγάπησεν aor. ind. act. ἀγαπάω (# *26*) to love (TDNT; TLNT; EDNT; James Moffatt, *Love in the New Testament* [London: Hodder and Stoughton, 1929]; Brown, 497ff; EIM, 64-85). Const. aor. viewing all God's individual actions of loving the world as a whole. κόσμος (# *3180*) world (N.H. Cassem, "A Grammatical and Contextual Inventory of the Use of κόσμος in the Johannine Corpus with some Implications for a Johannine Cosmic Theology," *NTS* 19 [1972]: 81-91; TDNT). ὥστε (# *6063*) w. ind. to express actual result (RG, 1000; BAGD; Carson). μονογενῆ (# *3666*) unique, only one of this kind (EDNT; TDNT; GELTS, 309; Wisdom 7:22; D. Moody, "God's Only Son," *JBL* 72 [1953]: 213-19). ἔδωκεν aor. ind. act. δίδωμι (# *1443*) to give. The giving points to His grace (s. Isa. 9:6). Const. aor. viewing all God's individual actions in sending His Son. πᾶς ὁ πιστεύων this construction has a generalizing tendency; perhaps a gnomic pres. (GGBB, 620-27); "anyone who believes." ἀπόληται aor. subj. mid. ἀπόλλυμι (# *660*) to destroy, to perish (TDNT). Subj. w. ἵνα (# *2671*) and neg. μή (# *3590*) to express neg. purp. of the giving. ◆ **17 ἀπέστειλεν** aor. ind. act. ἀποστέλλω (# *690*) to send, to send as an authoritative representative (TDNT; EDNT). This may be a preparation for v. 19, because the word is used for emitting light (TLNT, 1:186). κρίνῃ aor. subj. act. κρίνω (# *3212*) to decide, to judge, to condemn, as a contrast w. σωθῇ (Morris). The vb. suggests not just the process of sentencing, but the ensuing condemnation (NIDNNT, 2:362-67). Const. aor. viewing the total action. σωθῇ aor. subj. pass. σῴζω (# *5392*) to rescue, to save. Subjs. w. ἵνα (# *2671*) to express purp. In light of John 9:39 one should understand the statement that Jesus came into a world already condemned in order to save some (Carson). ◆ **18 πιστεύων** pres. act. part. πιστεύω to believe s.v. 16.

κρίνεται pres. ind. pass. s.v. 17. The change to the pres. is durative or progressive, suggesting a sentence presently being executed. κέκριται perf. ind. pass. κρίνω to judge. Perf. indicates he has already been judged and presently is under the sentence (JG, 352). πεπίστευκεν perf. ind. act. πιστεύω to believe. Perf. indicates he has entered into a continuing state of belief (Morris). ◆ **19 κρίσις** (# *3213*) judgment. Here as the process of judging, not the sentence of condemnation (Morris). Men are judged by the work and person of Jesus (Barrett). God's great saving act has become a means of judgment through the perverted reaction of people. (Beasley-Murray). φῶς (# *5890*) light. The revelation brings to light what man truly is (TDNT; s. John 1:4). The difference in men is their response to the light (Tenny; Zane C. Hodges, "Coming to the Light–John 3:20-21," *Bib Sac* 135 [1978]: 314-22; E.R. Achtemeier, "Jesus Christ, the Light of the World: The Biblical Understanding of Light and Darkness," *Interpretation* 17 [1963]: 439-49). ἐλήλυθεν perf. ind. act. ἔρχομαι (# *2262*) to come. Perf. indicates the abiding results of His coming. ἠγάπησαν aor. ind. act. s.v. 16. ◆ **20 φαῦλα** (# *5765*) bad, foul, worthless. πράσσων pres. act. part. πράσσω (# *4556*) to do. Pres. indicates simultaneous actions. His evil deeds demonstrate his rejection of Christ, the light of God. ἐλεγχθῇ aor. subj. pass. ἐλέγχω (# *1794*) to bring to light, expose; properly sifted, tried, tested and then, if need be, convicted; to show how faulty they are and to reprove; to state that someone has done wrong, w. the implication that there is adequate proof of such wrongdoing; to prove (Westcott; LN, 1:436; NIDNTT; TDNT; CCFJ, 2:73). Subj. w. ἵνα (# *2671*) to express purp. ◆ **21 ποιῶν** pres. act. part. ποιέω (# *4472*) to do, practice. For the construction ποιῶν τὴν ἀλήθειαν in DDS s. 1QS 1:5; 5:3; 8:2. φανερωθῇ aor. subj. pass. φανερόω (# *5746*) to manifest, to bring to light. ὅτι (# *4022*) gives the content of what is manifested. εἰργασμένα perf. pass. part. ἐργάζομαι (# *2237*) to work, to produce by work. Perf. points to the permanence of such works (Morris; JG, 344). ἐν θεῷ (# *1877*; *2536*) Instr. use of the prep., giving the reason for the permanence of the deeds (BD, 117-18; BAGD). ◆ **22 μετὰ ταῦτα** (# *3552*; *4047*) after these things. There is no indication of length of time. The previous conversation took place in Jerusalem, while the following was in the Judean hillside (Carson). ἦλθεν aor. ind. act. ἔρχομαι s.v. 2. διέτριβεν impf. ind. act. διατρίβω (# *1417*) to remain, to spend some time. Durative impf. presenting the staying as in progress, but prior to the time of writing. ἐβάπτιζεν impf. ind. act. βαπτίζω (# *966*) to baptize. Iterat. impf. points to the repeated action. ◆ **23 βαπτίζων** pres. act. part. βαπτίζω s.v. 22. In light of John 4:2 the disciples baptized, not Jesus himself. παρεγίνοντο impf. ind. mid. (dep.) παραγίνομαι (# *4134*) to come on the scene, to appear, to come. Iterat. impf. indicates "they kept on coming again and again." ἐβαπτίζοντο impf. ind. pass. βαπτίζω to baptize. ◆ **24 γάρ** (# *1142*) explains why John is still baptizing. **βεβλημένος** perf. pass. part. βάλλω (# *965*) to throw, to cast. Part. in a periphastic construction indicating that John was not yet in prison (VA, 485). This gives an indication of the earliest ministry of Christ. Based on Mark 1:14 the Galilean ministry began after the incarceration (Carson). ◆ **25 ἐγένετο** aor. ind. mid. (dep.) γίνομαι (# *1181*) to become, to arise. Const. aor. describing the total controversy. **οὖν** (# *4036*) now, to indicate the continuation of a subject from one thought to another (DM, 254). **ζήτησις** (# *2428*) questioning, controversy, debate concerning a controversial subject (BAGD), even of a legal dispute (MM). **ἐκ** (# *1666*) from. The dispute arose from and originated w. the disciples of John (Barrett). **καθαρισμός** (# *2752*) cleansing, purification. This is not concerning baptism, but concerning ritual cleansings (John 2:6; Carson). It refers to agricultural purification in a physical or cultic sense (BAGD; NIDNTT, 3:102, citing the Michigan papyri 185,16; cf. also A.R.C. Leaney, *The Rule of Qumran and its Meaning* [London: SCM Press, 1966], 141f, 191f; Roger P. Booth, *Jesus and the Laws of Purity: Tradition, History, and Legal History* [Sheffield: The University of Sheffield, 1986]; MM; DJG, 125-31). ◆ **26 μεμαρτύρηκας** perf. ind. act. s.v. 11. Perf. describes antecedent action: "who you witnessed to in the past, yet people are still following because of your testimony." **ἴδε** (# *2623*) aor. imp. act. ὁράω to see. Used to point out something that the speaker wishes to draw attention to (BAGD). ◆ **27 ἀπ-εκρίθη** aor. ind. pass. (dep.) ἀποκρίνομαι to answer. s.v. 3. **ἦ** pres. subj. act. εἰμί (# *1639*) to be. **δεδομένον** perf. pass. part. δίδωμι (# *1443*) to give. Part. used in a periphrastic w. ἐάν (# *1569*) construction to express the perf. subj. Subj. expresses the cond.; it is possible for the cond. to be fulfilled. ◆ **28 μαρτυρεῖτε** pres. ind. act. μαρτυρέω (# *3455*) to witness. Their witness to John's role is contrasted to John's previous witness concerning Christ (v. 26). **ἀπεσταλμένος** perf. pass. part. s.v. 17. **ἔμπροσθεν** (# *1869*) before. ◆ **29 ἔχων** pres. act. part. ἔχω (# *2400*) to have. **νύμφη** (# *3811*) bride. **νυμφίος** (# *3812*) bridegroom. **φίλος τοῦ νυμφίου** the friend of the groom. The groom's closest friend who takes care of arranging the wedding. He was to ensure that the ceremony encountered no difficulties (Brown; Jastrow, 2:1543; Carson; SB, 1:45-46, 500-501; DJG, 86-88). **ἑστηκώς** perf. act. part. ἵστημι (# *2705*) to stand. Subst. part. **τὴν φωνὴν τοῦ νυμφίου** the voice of the groom is thought to be the triumph shout by which the bridegroom announced to his friends outside that he had been united to a virginal bride (Beasley-Murray; Schnackenburg). **ἀκούων** pres. act. part. (adj.) s.v. 8, w. obj. in gen. **πεπλήρωται** perf. ind. pass. πληρόω (# *4444*) to fill, to fulfill. Perf. indicates the continuing effects of this joy. ◆ **30 αὐξάνειν**

pres. act. inf. αὐξάνω (# *889*) to grow, to increase. Inf. complements the impersonal vb. δεῖ, which gives a logical necessity. Durative or iterat. pres. (BD, 172). **ἐλαττοῦσθαι** pres. pass. inf. ἐλαττόω (# *1738*) to make less, inferior, to decrease. Inf. complements the impersonal vb. δεῖ. ◆ **31 ἄνωθεν** from above s.v. 3. **ἐπάνω** (# *2062*) above, w. gen. **ὤν** pres. act. part. s.v. 4. ◆ **32 ἑώρακεν** perf. ind. act. ὁράω s.v. 11. Perf. indicates the past action. **ἤκουσεν** aor. ind. act. ἀκούω (# *201*) to hear. Const. aor. viewing the hearing of the total speech. ◆ **33 λαβών** aor. act. part. λαμβάνω (# *3284*) to take, to receive. **ἐσφράγισεν** aor. ind. act. σφραγίζω (# *5381*) to seal, to certify, to acknowledge as a seal does on a document. It indicates authenticity or ownership (TDNT; BAGD; MM; BBC). Const. aor. viewing the total action of sealing. **ὅτι** (# *4022*) is either causal cl. or it could give the content of the seal. ◆ **34 ὅν** (# *4005*) the antecedent is omitted; often a demonstrative pron., here it would be in the nom. case ("the one, whom..."). **ἀπέστειλεν** aor. ind. act. s.v. 17. **ῥῆμα** (# *4839*) word, that which is spoken. **μέτρον** (# *3586*) measure. The Father gives to the Son without measure (Morris). ◆ **35 ἀγαπᾷ** pres. ind. act. ἀγαπάω (# *26*) to love. Pres. describes the ongoing relationship between the Father and Son. **δέδωκεν** perf. ind. act. δίδωμι (# *1443*) to give, to entrust, to place into one's authority (Gen. 39:8; 29:12; BAGD). Perf. indicates the lasting results of the Son receiving the authority over all things. ◆ **36 πιστεύων** pres. act. part. πιστεύω (# *4409*) to believe. Subst. part. to describe the characteristics necessary. Pres. describes the simultaneous action of the part. and the main vb. **ζωὴν αἰώνιον** (# *2437; 173*) eternal life. Since life is in the Son the believer has this life when he is united to him by faith (Beasley-Murray). **ἀπειθῶν** pres. act. part. ἀπειθέω (# *578*) to be disobedient. Disbelief is regarded in its activity (Westcott). **ὄψεται** fut. ind. mid. (dep.) ὁράω (# *3972*) to see. It means to participate in God's kingdom and is interchangeable with faith (Lindars; NIDNTT, 3:516). **ὀργή** (# *3973*) wrath. This played a role in the preaching of John the Baptist (John 1:6ff, 19-28; Matt. 3:7; Mk. 1:3-8; Lk. 3:2-17). Only by faith in Messiah can one escape the wrath. While the future holds the full manifestation of the wrath, present unbelief places one presently under wrath (NIDNTT; TDNT; DJG, 411). God's wrath is not a sudden gust or passion, but the settled displeasure of God against sin (Tenny).

John 4

◆ **1** For a discussion of this pericope s. Edeltraud Leidig, *Jesus Gespräch mit der Samaritanerin und weitere Gespräche im Johannesevangelium* (Basel: Friederich Reinhardt Kommissionsverlag, 1981); I.H. Marshall, "The Problem of NT Exegesis (John 4,1-45)," *JETS* 17

(1974): 67-73. Hendrikus Boers, *Neither on this Mountain Nor in Jerusalem: A Study of John 4*, SBLMS 35 (Atlanta: Scholars Press, 1988); Teresa Okure, *The Johannine Approach to Mission*, WUNT 31 (Tübingen: J.C.B Mohr, 1988). For several contrasts between Nicodemus and the Samaritan woman, and Christ and the Samaritan woman s. Blum, 284. This interview again demonstrates the truth of John 2:25; for the similarities; also Mary M. Pazdan, "Nicodemus and the Samaritan Woman: Contrasting Models of Discipleship," *BTB* 17 (1987): 145-48; Carson, 214-15. οὖν (# 4036) when, now; indicates a succession of either time or events (DM, 253). ἔγνω aor. ind. act. γινώσκω (# 1182) to know. ὅτι (# 4022) gives the content of his knowledge. He did this in order to avoid conflict with the Pharisees. ἤκουσαν aor. ind. act. ἀκούω (# 201) to hear. ὅτι gives the content of what the Pharisees heard. It introduces indir. discourse here (GGBB, 458). While the Pharisees were throughout the land, in John they seem to be concentrated in Jerusalem (John 1:24; 7:32, 45-48; 8:13; 9:13, 15; 11:46ff, 57; 12:19, 42) (Schlatter). πλείονας comp. πολύς (# 4498) much; comp., more. ἤ (# 2445) than, used to complete the comp. ◆ 2 καίτοι γε (# 2793) although (BD, 234; Thrall; Blomquist, 35-45). ἐβάπτιζεν impf. ind. act. βαπτίζω (# 966) to baptize. The durative or customary impf. emphasizing the repeated act. This is to show that Jesus was not just another baptizer or even an imitator of John the Baptist (Beasley-Murray, 58). He used his disciples as the agents (Carson). ◆ 3 ἀφῆκεν aor. ind. act. ἀφίημι (# 918) to leave. ἀπῆλθεν aor. ind. act. ἀπέρχομαι (# 599) to go out. Aor. in both vbs. describe the journey from Judea to Galilee. Since Jesus was working on God's timetable and since he also now saw the end of his ministry he withdrew to avoid the present conflict (Blum). ◆ 4 ἔδει impf. ind. act. δεῖ (# 1256) it is necessary, to have to, w. inf. Not geographical necessity in light of Jos., *Ant.*, 20:118; *JW*, 2:232; *Life*, 269, referring to Jewish travellers passing through Samaria (Carson). Rather, the vb. gives a divine necessity, meaning that God's will or plan is involved (Brown). It may anticipate the statement in John 4:42 that Jesus is the Savior of the world, and not just the Jews. διὰ τῆς Σαμαρείας (# 1328; 4899).This was the shortest way from Judea to Galilee. Normally, a Jew would not pass through Samaria, since the Samaritans even made the land impure. S. ABD, 5:940-47; James D. Purvis, "The Samaritans and Judaism," in *Early Judaism and Its Modern Interpreters*, ed. by Robert A. Kraft and George W.E. Nickelsburg, 81-98, particularly 87-90; idem., *The Samaritan Pentateuch and the Origin of the Samaritan Sect* (Cambridge: Harvard University Press, 1968); idem., "The Fourth Gospel and the Samaritans," *Nov T* 17 (1976): 161-98; Jürgen Zangenberg, *ΣΑΜΑΡΕΙΑ. Antike Quellen zur Geschichte und Kultur der Samaritaner in*

deutscher Übersetzung (Tübingen: A. Francke Verlag, 1994); DJG, 40. Impf. ἔδει is used w. a necessity in the past. Josephus comments, "It was absolutely necessary for those who would go quickly to pass through that country (Samaria), for by that road you may, in three days, go from Galilee to Jerusalem" (Jos., *Life*, 269). διέρχεσθαι pres. mid. (dep.) inf. διέρχομαι (# 1451) to pass through. Compl. inf. to the impersonal vb. ἔδει. ◆ 5 Συχάρ (# 5373) this may be modern day 'Askar, on the shoulder of Mount Ebal, opposite of Mount Gerizim (Carson). λεγομένην pres. pass. part. λέγω (# 3306) to say; pass. to have the name. πλησίον (# 4446) w. gen., near to, near. χωρίον (# 6005) piece of land, parcel. ἔδωκεν aor. ind. act. δίδωμι (# 1443) to give. Const. aor. viewing the action of purchasing and giving as a whole (cf. Gen. 33:19; 48:22; Josh. 24:32). A.F. Wedel, "John 4:5-36," *Interp.* 31 (1977): 406-12.   ◆ 6 πηγή (# 4380) well, spring. This well was over 90 ft. deep. There was a rounded stone at the top. A hole was cut in the top so that a leather bucket could be lowered to the underground spring (Schlatter). The following discussion revolves around the contrast of well water and living water suggesting the life and salvation of the kingdom (Beasley-Murray). While the well here is dug out, it is fed by an underground spring, providing then fresh water (Carson). κεκοπιακώς perf. act. part. κοπιάω (# 3159) to labor, to grow weary from work (TLNT). Perf. emphasizes the state of weariness, frequently beginning before the action of the main vb. Part. is either causal or temp. It describes a trait of Jesus. ὁδοιπορία (# 3845) walking, journey. This is a metonymy (cause for the effect). The journey is mentioned; the weariness is meant. ἐκαθέζετο impf. ind. mid. (dep.) καθέζομαι (# 2757) to sit, to be sitting. Impf. is progressive describing a vivid past action. οὕτως (# 4048) thus, so, either modifying the vb. ἐκαθέζετο or the part. κεκοπιακώς (Brown). ἐπί (# 2093) w. dat., upon; "upon the curbstone of the well" (RWP). ὡς (# 6055) w. numbers, about; (i.e., about noon, the natural time to rest while the sun was at its height [Bernard; BBC]). ◆ 7 ἔρχεται pres. ind. mid. (dep.) ἔρχομαι (# 2262) to come. Hist. pres. ἀντλῆσαι aor. act. inf. ἀντλέω (# 533) to draw. Inf. expresses the purp. of her coming. Possibly the woman's public shame (s.v. 16ff; BBC) caused her to come alone (Carson). δός aor. imp. act. δίδωμι (# 1443) to give. This is a polite request, yet with a note of urgency. πεῖν aor. act. inf. πίνω (# 4403) to drink. Compl. inf. to the main vb. giving the content of the request with the dir. object (water) understood. ◆ 8 ἀπεληλύθεισαν plperf. ind. act. ἀπέρχομαι (# 599) to go away. Plperf. describes the antecedent action of the disciples. They had left, leaving Jesus alone. ἀγοράσωσιν aor. subj. act. ἀγοράζω (# 60) to buy at the marketplace. Subj. w. ἵνα (# 2671) describes the purp. of their leaving. ◆ 9 ὤν pres. act. part. εἰμί

(# *1639*) to be. Part. in apposition to **σύ** Concessive use of the part., "even though you are a Jew." The inherited suspicions and animosities were intensified when the Samaritan was a woman (Carson). According to the Mishnah a Cuthean (Samaritan) woman was considered completely unclean (M, Niddah 4:1). **οὔσης** pres. act. part. εἰμί to be. Part. used appositionally; pres. indicates a contemporaneous status, thus heightening the distinction between the two. **συγχρῶνται** pres. ind. act. συγχράομαι (# *5178*) to have dealings w., to use together w.; s. D.R. Hall, "The Meaning of *synchraomai* in John 4,9," *ET* 83 (1972): 56-57. Jews do not use vessels w. Samaritans for fear of becoming unclean (Barrett; Morris; M, Niddah 4:1; SB, 1:538-60; D. Daube, "Jesus and the Samaritan Woman: The Meaning of συνχράομαι," *JBL* 69 [1950]: 137-47; Matt. 10:5). Customary or gnomic pres., indicating the Jewish custom. ◆ **10 ἀπεκρίθη** aor. ind. pass. (dep.) ἀποκρίνομαι (# *646*) to answer. **ᾔδεις** plperf. ind. act. of the def. perf. οἶδα (# *3857*) to know. Ind. in a 2nd. class cond. cl. in which the speaker assumes the cond. is contrary to fact. **δωρεά** (# *1561*) gift, donation. This could refer either to the Torah as God's gift, or better to eternal life which Christ will offer her (Carson). This deals with the legal aspect of the gift (TDNT). In a letter it refers to the Emperor's beneficium to the soldiers (MM). It could possibly be referring to Jesus himself, the gift of God, that is the one who is speaking to you (NIDNTT). **ᾔτησας** aor. ind. act. αἰτέω (# *160*) to ask. Const. aor. describing the upcoming conversation. **ἔδωκεν** aor. ind. act. δίδωμι (# *1443*) to give. **ζῶν** pres. act. part. ζάω (# *2409*) to live; attributive use of the part. Part. describes an attribute of the water; that is, fresh, flowing water in contrast to brackish water from a cistern or a well, but also water creating and maintaining life (Barrett; Beasley-Murray; SB, 2:433-36). For the expression in DSS s. CD 19:34. There it means the law which is a well of living water. This expression often refers to YHWH and his salvation in the OT (Prov. 13:14; 18:4; Isa. 12:3; Jer. 2:13; 17:13). Jesus' request is only an opening to the rest of the conversation. Jesus focuses the conversation on three things: 1. Who is he? 2. What is the gift of God? 3. What is the living water? (Blum). Here the thirsty traveler becomes the true giver of thirst-quenching water (Becker). In light of SB, 2:433-36 it is tempting to view this water as the revelation brought by the Revealer (Becker) or the gift bestowed by the revelation (Beasley-Murray), i.e., the eternal life mediated by the Spirit (Carson). ◆ **11 κύριε** (# *3261*) sir; not christological, but a polite address. **ἔχεις** pres. ind. act. ἔχω (# *2400*) to have. Progressive pres. indicating pres. possession here. **ἄντλημα** (# *534*) bucket for drawing water. The response of the woman is controlled by her misunderstanding of the conversation (Beasley-Murray). **φρέαρ** (# *5853*) well. **βαθύ** (# *960*)

deep. The well is still over 100 feet (30 m) deep. (Carson). **οὖν** (# *4036*) therefore, then; the lack of the bucket and the depth of the well make it impossible to draw the desired water. Even the great patriarch Jacob had to use a bucket. ◆ **12 μή** (# *3590*) expecting a neg. reply. **μείζων** (# *3505*) comp. μέγας great; comp., greater. **πατρός** gen. πατήρ (# *4252*) father; gen. of comp. **ἔδωκεν** aor. ind. act. δίδωμι (# *1443*) to give. Const. aor. viewing the action of giving as a whole. **θρέμματα** (# *2576*) cattle. **ἔπιεν** aor. ind. act. πίνω (# *4403*) to drink. Const. aor. viewing the action of drinking as a whole. ◆ **13 πίνων** pres. act. part. πίνω s.v. 12. Attributive part. to describe a generalizing tendency. It is in apposition to **πᾶς** (# *4246*) ("all who ...") (RG, 772). **διψήσει** fut. ind. act. διψάω (# *1498*) to thirst, to be thirsty. Predictive fut. here describes what will certainly happen. Jesus means here nothing in the world offers one true satisfaction (Schlatter). ◆ **14 πίῃ** aor. subj. act. πίνω s.v. 12. Subj. w. **ἄν** (# *323*) generalizes: anyone who, anyone in general, without any particular individual in mind (EGGNT). **οὗ** (# *4005*) rel. pron. has been attracted to the gen. of its antecedent. **δώσω** fut. ind. act. δίδωμι s.v. 12. Fut. gives the fut. cond. in which the following will be fulfilled. The water given by Jesus liberates because it is what one deeply longs for and fulfills human needs (Schlatter). This water satisfies the thirst for God (cf. Isa. 12:3; 55:1). **γενήσεται** fut. ind. mid. (dep.) γίνομαι (# *1181*) to be, to become. The water that Jesus will give will change the person by becoming a spring itself. **ἁλλομένου** pres. mid. (dep.) part. ἅλλομαι (# *256*) to spring up, leap. In simple apposition. Used of quick movement by living beings like jumping (Brown). **εἰς** (# *1650*) could be understood to give the purp. or result. It could also give the goal of the water, leading the recipient to eternal life (Schlatter). ◆ **15 δός** aor. imp. act. δίδωμι s.v. 12. Imp. is used as a request or entreaty. **ἵνα** (# *2671*) gives the content or result of the preceding request. **διψῶ** pres. subj. act. διψάω s.v. 13. **διέρχωμαι** pres. subj. mid. (dep.) διέρχομαι (# *1451*) to go, to come (BAGD). **ἐνθάδε** (# *1924*) here. **ἀντλεῖν** pres. act. inf. ἀντλέω s.v. 7. Inf. gives the purp. of her coming to the well. ◆ **16 ὕπαγε** pres. imp. act. ὑπάγω (# *5632*) to go. Pres. imp. often is used to express an order involving motion (Bakker, 82). Here the imps. are dir. commands for the woman to follow. They are given in the necessary and chronological sequence. **φώνησον** aor. imp. act. φωνέω (# *5888*) to call. Aor. imp. may have a note of urgency to it (*EGGNT*, 86). **ἐλθέ** aor. imp. act. ἔρχομαι (# *2262*) to go. ◆ **17 ἀπεκρίθη** aor. ind. pass. (dep.) ἀποκρίνομαι (# *646*) to answer. **καλῶς** (# *2822*) adv., well; used here in the sense of truthfully (EDNT). Jesus commends her formal truthfulness, while gently exposing the truth (Carson). **ὅτι** (# *4022*) gives the content of her speech. ◆ **18 ἔσχες** aor. ind. act. ἔχω (# *2400*) to have. Const. aor. viewing all five marriages as a whole. According to rabbinic teaching, a woman was to be married only twice or at most three times (SB, 2:437; C.M. Carmichel, "Marriage and the Samaritan Woman," NTS 26 [1980]: 332-46). ἀληθές acc. ἀληθής (# 239) truly. "This is a true thing" (RWP). εἴρηκας perf. ind. act. λέγω (# 3306) to say. Perf. emphasizes the completion of her speech and confession. ◆ 19 θεωρῶ pres. ind. act. θεωρέω (# 2555) to see, to perceive. προφήτης (# 4737) prophet. The word is used with a wide range of meaning. At this point it may not denote a full-orbed OT prophet or messianic figure (Carson), but prophetic quality (GGBB, 265-66). ◆ 20 προσεκύνησαν aor. ind. act. προσκυνέω (# 4686) to worship. Aor. views the entire process of worship ever since the establishment of the Samaritan temple or religion as one whole act. προσκυνεῖν pres. act. inf. Compl. inf. to the main vb. δεῖ (# 1256) pres. ind. act. it is necessary. R.J. Bull, "An Archaeological Context of Understanding John 4, 20," BA 38 (1975): 54-59. The different location in worship was a major difference between the Jews and Samaritans. For a discussion of the OT background s. Otto Betz, "'To Worship God in Spirit and Truth:' Reflections on John 4, 20-26," Standing before God: Studies on Prayer in Scripture and Tradition with Essays: Festschrift John M. Oesterreicher, KTAV, 1981, 53-72. ◆ 21 ὅτι (# 4022) indir. discourse or possibly causal. πίστευε pres. imp. act. πιστεύω (# 4409) to believe. Pres. imp. may have the notion of linear or continuing action (EGGNT). ὥρα (# 6052) hour. "The eschatological hour, initiating the new age of the kingdom of God–when worship of the Father will be tied to no place" (Beasley-Murray). προσκυνήσετε fut. ind. act. προσκυνέω s.v. 20. The conversation concerning the controversy of the location of worship should not be understood against the rival temple built in the Persian period and destroyed by John Hyrcanus in 128 B.C. ◆ 22 ὅτι (# 4022) because; causal. The question is what is it giving the reason to: just to the immediate cl. or to the two that precede. This then goes beyond the location of worship to the object of worship (Becker). σωτηρία (# 5401) deliverance, salvation. What is meant is that salvation is available through Jesus, who was born as fulfillment of the covenant with Abraham. Samaritans must participate in the salvation that comes from the Jews (TDNT; TLNT; NIDNTT; Carson). ◆ 23 ἔρχεται pres. ind. mid. (dep.) ἔρχομαι (# 2262) to go, to come. Futuristic pres. to emphasize the certainty of coming. ἀληθινός (# 240) true, genuine. προσκυνητής (# 4687) worshiper. προσκυνήσουσιν fut. ind. act. προσκυνέω s.v. 20. τοιούτους (# 5525) such, of such a kind. ζητεῖ pres. ind. act. ζητέω (# 2426) to seek. Continuous pres. emphasizing John's point that this type of worship is what God seeks at all times. Possibly progressive emphasizing that God is presently look-

ing for such worshipers. προσκυνοῦντας pres. act. part. προσκυνέω to worship (TDNT; EDNT). ◆ 24 πνεῦμα (# 4460) spirit. The predicate without the art. emphasizes the character and nature (s. John 1:1; GGBB, 270). As a spirit he is not bound to a location as the Jews and Samaritans would have him bound. "God is invisible, life-giving and unknowable unless he chooses to reveal himself" (Carson). ἐν (# 1877) "in." Prep. gives the sphere or manner in which one must worship. προσκυνεῖν pres. act. inf. προσκυνέω s.v. 20. Compl. inf. to the impersonal δεῖ (# 1256). ◆ 25 ἔλθῃ aor. subj. act. ἔρχομαι s.v. 23. Subj. adds a degree of uncertainty ("whenever"). ἀναγγελεῖ fut. ind. act. ἀναγγέλλω (# 334) to announce. The word is used of the fresh and authoritative message of the advocate in John 16:13ff (Westcott). The Messiah is the supernatural person who will declare the divine truth to men (Barrett). This will be His recognizing trait. ◆ 26 λαλῶν pres. act. part. λαλέω (# 3281) to speak. Pres. emphasizes the ongoing action. Part. in simple apposition to ἐγώ ◆ 27 ἐπὶ τούτῳ (# 2093; 4047) this indicates a shift in the story with the return of the disciples (Becker). ἐθαύμαζον impf. ind. act. θαυμάζω (# 2513) to be astonished, to marvel. It denotes incredulous surprise (MM). Ingressive impf., "they began to wonder." The surprise arises because He was talking to a woman, which was held to be improper, esp. for a rabbi. One does not talk to a woman publicly on the street, not one's own wife, and particularly not to another woman, due to the gossip of the people (Schlatter; s. M, Aboth 1:5; b. Qidd. 70a; Moore, Judaism, 2:269f; SB, 2:438). ἐλάλει impf. ind. act. λαλέω s.v. 26. Durative impf. describing the whole conversation in the past tense. μέντοι (# 3530) really, actually. ◆ 28 ἀφῆκεν aor. ind. act. ἀφίημι (# 918) to leave. Const. aor. viewing the action as a whole. οὖν (# 4036) now. This should not be understood logically, but chronologically. ὑδρία (# 5620) water jar (BAGD). It must be fairly large, since in Gen. 24:14 it could provide enough water for camels to drink. She leaves her water bucket behind in haste. This indicates her desire to return; or perhaps it allows Jesus to drink from it (Schlatter). ◆ 29 δεῦτε (# 1307) adv. serving as hortatory particle: come! come on! (BAGD). ἴδετε aor. imp. act. ὁράω (# 3972) to see. Aor. imp. often has a sense of urgency, entreaty, command, a polite command. ἐποίησα aor. ind. act. ποιέω (# 4472) to do. Const. aor. viewing all her actions as a whole. This is consonant with the Samaritans' understanding of the "Taheb" as restorer and revealer of the truth (Beasley-Murray; BBC). μήτι (# 3614) not necessarily expecting a neg. answer, but rather a cautious, tentative opinion (Schnackenburg; M, 193). Χριστός (# 5986) for her Jesus is not just a prophet or the prophet, but the Messiah (Becker; DJG, 114-17). ◆ 30 ἐξῆλθον aor. ind. act. ἐξέρχομαι (# 2002) to go out.

Const. aor. viewing the action as a whole. **ἤρχοντο** impf. ind. mid. (dep.) ἔρχομαι (# 2262) to go. Impf. pictures the long procession as they approached Jesus (RWP), "they began coming." ◆ **31 ἐν τῷ μεταξύ** (# 1877; 3590) in the meanwhile; that is, before the Samaritan villagers arrived (Bernard). Another indication of a shift in the story line. **ἠρώτων** impf. ind. act. ἐρωτάω (# 2263) to question, to ask. Impf. may suggest the very recent past or the action as still ongoing; or it may be incep. **φάγε** aor. imp. act. ἐσθίω (# 2266) to eat. Aor. imp. calls for a specific act w. a note of urgency. This section moves from the water for the woman to the bread for the disciples (Beasley-Murray). ◆ **32 βρῶσιν** (# 1111) food, properly the process of eating but here synon. w. food (Barrett). **φαγεῖν** aor. act. inf. ἐσθίω s.v. 31. Here the inf. describes the purp. of having the bread. ◆ **33 ἀλλήλους** acc. pl. ἀλλήλων (# 253) each other, a reciprocal pron. **μή** (# 3590) used in questions expecting the answer no. **ἤνεγκεν** aor. ind. act. φέρω (# 5770) to carry, to bring. ◆ **34 βρῶμα** (# 1109) food. **ἵνα** (# 2671) does not express purp., but rather introduces a noun cl. used as subject or pred. nom. explaining what the food is (M, 208). A person lives from that for which he lives (Schlatter). **πέμψαντος** aor. act. part. πέμπω (# 4287) to send. **τελειώσω** aor. subj. act. τελειόω (# 5457) to accomplish, to finish, to bring to consummation; to complete, to bring to completion that work which was begun by the Father (BAGD; Schnackenburg). Subj. w. **ἵνα** (# 2671) cl. explaining what His food is. ◆ **35 τετράμηνος** (# 5485) the fourth month. **θερισμός** (# 2546) harvest. Four months intervened between the end of sowing and the beginning of harvest (Barrett; s. also "The Gezer Calendar," ANET, 320; IBD, "Calendar"; ABD, 1:816-20). There is a question, whether this is a simple proverbial saying, or whether the saying describes the time of year (Becker; W.G.E. Watson, "Antecedents of a New Testament Proverb," VT 20 [1970]: 368-70). Usually the period between sowing and harvest was six months, but the interval from the latest date of sowing to the beginning of the harvest was four months (Beasley-Murray; SB, 2:439-40). Here the word is used in a fig. sense, indicating the spiritual readiness of the Samaritans. He had just sown the seed through his conversation with the woman; now the harvest is already at hand with the population streaming out of the city (Carson). **ἐπάρατε** aor. imp. act. ἐπαίρω (# 2048) to lift up. Imp. here is used as entreaty, inviting them to see that the fields are ready for the harvest. Aor. here indicates a note of urgency and a specific action (EGGNT, 86). **θεάσασθε** aor. imp. mid. (dep.) θεάομαι (# 2517) to look at, to contemplate (John 1:14). The disciples should not only see the people streaming out of the city, but contemplate the meaning and significance of this. **χώρα** (# 6001) field, open country (BAGD). Used

here of people coming to Christ. **λευκαί** pl. λευκός (# 3328) white. Perhaps referring to the people in their white clothes (Morris). Jesus' work–to do the will of the one who sent him–cannot be postponed, since the harvest is now (Becker). ◆ **36 θερίζων** pres. act. part. θερίζω (# 2545) to harvest. Subst. part. describing a man in his role as sower. The pres. suggests durative action. The harvest is already ongoing (Becker). **μισθός** (# 3635) reward, recompense. **σπείρων** pres. act. part. σπείρω (# 5062) to sow. **ὁμοῦ** (# 3938) together. Both should rejoice though each had a different responsibility, one at the end of the harvest, the other is necessary for its initiation. **χαίρῃ** pres. subj. act. χαίρω (# 5897) to rejoice. Subj. w. **ἵνα** (# 2671) expresses result. This proverb is used differently than in Lev. 26:10; Deut. 28:30; Mic. 6:15; Matt. 25:26, where it largely has a neg. connotation. Here it indicates the difference of roles in the service of the kingdom of God. Each worker may rejoice in the total harvest (Beasly-Murray). ◆ **37 ἐν τούτῳ** (# 1877; 4047) in this. It may refer to the previous (v. 36) but more probably to the following (v. 38) (Barrett). **ἀληθινός** (# 240) true, dependable; here an accurate proverb in contrast to the previous one. ◆ **38 ἀπέστειλα** aor. ind. act. ἀποστέλλω (# 690) to send, to send as an official and authoritative representative. Const. aor. viewing the action of sending as whole. This would include not only the actual sending out, but also the preparation and work. It refers to the general purp. of their calling (Carson). **θερίζειν** pres. act. inf. s.v. 36. Compl. inf. is giving the purp. of the sending. **κεκοπιάκατε** perf. ind. act. κοπιάω s.v. 6. Consummative perf. emphasizing the completion of the work antecedent to the time of sending. **κόπος** (# 3160) work, labor. **εἰσεληλύθατε** perf. ind. act. εἰσέρχομαι (# 1656) to go into, to enter into; used here in a fig. sense to come to enjoy; to enjoy the fruit of one's labor (BAGD). Consummative perf. emphasizing that the disciples have already been sent and are enjoying the fruit of the previous work. ◆ **39 ἐπίστευσαν** aor. ind. act. πιστεύω (# 4409) to believe. Const. aor. emphasizes the action in its entirety; possibly an ingressive aor. emphasizing the entrance into the state or cond. This acceptance of Jesus as Christ by the Samaritans stands in sharp contrast to the rejection by the Pharisees (vv. 1-3). **μαρτυρούσης** pres. act. part. μαρτυρέω (# 3455) to give witness, to testify. She has joined John the Baptist in testifying to Jesus as the Messiah (Beasley-Murray). **ἐποίησα** aor. ind. act. ποιέω (# 4472) to do. Const. aor. viewing her life as a whole. ◆ **40 ἠρώτων** impf. ind. act. ἐρωτάω (# 2263) to ask, to request. Iterat. impf., "they kept on asking him." **μεῖναι** aor. act. inf. μένω (# 3531) to remain. Compl. inf. giving the content of the request. **ἔμεινεν** aor. ind. act. μένω to remain. The following indicates that he stayed and taught about his person and his mission (Schlatter). A shocking action to the Jews then (BBC). ◆ **41 τὸν λόγον αὐτοῦ** "his word." This is a further development from the reference to word of the woman in v. 39. Their belief is not based on a secondhand report, but a firsthand encounter. ◆ **42 λαλιά** (# *3282*) speech. Not in the sense of gossip but as human and outward speech about something (Schnackenburg). **ἀκηκόαμεν** perf. ind. act. ἀκούω (# *201*) to hear. Consummative perf. emphasizes the previous report that was heard (past act) and accepted (present result). **ἀληθῶς** (# *242*) truly, in the sense of certainly. This is great insight into the true nature of Christ, while the Pharisees rejected these claims (vv. 1-2). **σωτὴρ τοῦ κόσμου** (# *5400; 3180*) "savior of the world." The term "savior of the world" often was used of the Roman emperor (LAE, 364f; TDNT; Craig R. Koester, "'The Savior of the World' (John 4:42)," *JBL* 109 [1990]: 665-80). The emphasis in this story is not on the woman or the Samaritans, but on the person of Christ. The Samaritans believed based on Deut. 18:15-18 promising another Moses to come and initiate divine favor. This is a title applied to Jesus in that he fulfills the hopes of the Samaritans, Jews, and the world of nations (Beasley-Murray; cf. John MacDonald, *The Theology of the Samaritans* [Philadelphia: Westminster, 1964], 365ff). ◆ **43 ἐξῆλθεν** aor. ind. act. ἐξέρχομαι to go out (s.v. 30). Jesus and his disciples leave the Samaritan city of Sychar and continue on northward into Galilee, continuing the journey from 4:3. ◆ **44 ἐμαρτύρησεν** aor. ind. act. μαρτυρέω to witness s.v. 39. **πατρίδι** dat. sing. πατρίς (# *4258*) homeland, one's own part of the country (BAGD). For a discussion of the word s. Carson. ◆ **45 οὖν** (# *4036*) then, therefore (DM, 253f). **ἦλθεν** aor. ind. act. ἔρχομαι (# *2262*) to go, to come. Const. aor. describing the total journey. **ἐδέξαντο** aor. ind. mid. (dep.) δέχομαι (# *1312*) to receive, to welcome. Const. aor. describing the reception as a whole. **ἑωρακότες** perf. act. part. ὁράω (# *3972*) to see. Perf. part. often refers to recent events in John (JG, 366; # *2506*). **ἐποίησεν** aor. ind. act. ποιέω (# *4472*) to do, to make. Const. aor. describing the ministry as a whole. **ἑορτή** (# *2038*) feast; here referring to the Passover (BAGD). ◆ **46 βασιλικός** (# *997*) belonging to the king, royal officer. Either a person of royal blood or a servant of the king (Brown); perhaps here an official in the army of Herod Agrippa (Beasley-Murray), since the term describes the soldiers of King Mithridates (BAGD); s. also A.H. Mead, "The βασιλικός in John 4:46-53," *JSNT* 23 (1985): 69-72. **ἠσθένει** impf. ind. act. ἀσθενέω (# *820*) to be sick. Prog. impf. indicates the vivid past or perhaps that the illness is still going on. ◆ **47 ἀκούσας** aor. act. part. ἀκούω (# *201*) to hear. Temp. use of the circum. part., "when he heard." Aor. describes action as the basis for the main vb. **ἀπῆλθεν** aor. ind. act. ἀπέρχομαι (# *599*) to go out. The journey from Capernaum to Cana was about 18 miles (Becker).

ἠρώτα impf. ind. act. s.v. 31. Incep. impf. ("began to ask") or iterat. impf. ("asked repeatedly"). The vb. occurs here in the sense of petition, not in the sense to ask a question (Schlatter; MM). **ἵνα** (# *2671*) w. subj. gives the content of the request. **καταβῇ** aor. subj. act. καταβαίνω (# *2849*) to go down, to descend; used to indicate a direction away from Jerusalem. **ἰάσηται** aor. subj. mid. (dep.) ἰάομαι (# *2615*) to heal. This is the actual purp. of his coming and the request. **ἤμελλεν** impf. ind. act. μέλλω (# *3516*) to be about to, w. inf. ("was going to die," "was at point of death"). For the use of the inf. to express futurity reckoned from a moment in the past s. MKG, 307. ◆ **48 σημεῖον** (# *4956*) sign (John 2:11). **τέρατα** pl. τέρας (# *5469*) wonder. Directs attention to the miraculous, but in the NT the word is not used alone (Morris). **ἴδητε** aor. subj. act. ὁράω (# *3972*) to see. Subj. occurs to express uncertainty in the cond. His faith required the support of sight (Westcott). **πιστεύσητε** aor. subj. act. πιστεύω (# *4409*) to believe. The pl. indicates the individual was representative of a whole class (Bernard). ◆ **49 κατάβηθι** aor. imp. act. καταβαίνω (# *2849*) to go down. Aor. imp. indicates a note of urgency. **πρίν** (# *4570*) w. inf. **ἀποθανεῖν** aor. act. inf. ἀποθνῄσκω (# *633*) to die. This suggests the urgency of the request. He is not so much interested in the signs and wonders, but in the healing powers of Jesus (Carson). **παιδίον** (# *4086*) child. The word does not necessarily mean a small child. ◆ **50 πορεύου** pres. imp. mid. (dep.) sing. πορεύομαι (# *4513*) to go, to travel. Pres. imp. emphasizes the durative nature of the journey. **ζῇ** pres. ind. act. ζάω (# *2409*) to live; Semitic, covering both recovery from illness and return to life from death (Brown). Pres. is futuristic indicating the certainty of the healing. **ἐπίστευσεν** aor. ind. act. πιστεύω (# *4409*) to believe. His belief consisted of thinking that Jesus can heal even from a distance. **λόγῳ** dat. λόγος (# *3364*) word. Here the object of the faith is the revelation of Christ. Here is an example of a positive response in faith to the revelation of Christ through a sign. **ἐπορεύετο** impf. ind. mid. (dep.) πορεύομαι to travel. This is the outward expression of his faith in Christ's revelation. ◆ **51 καταβαίνοντος** pres. act. part. καταβαίνω s.v. 49. Gen. abs. implying "as" or "because" (JG, 84); "while on his way." **ὑπήντησαν** aor. ind. act. ὑπαντάω (# *5636*) to meet. The viewpoint of the action has changed. The servants now are the subjects of the action. The dat. **αὐτῷ** (# *899*) describes who is being met. **ὅτι** (# *4022*) introduces the dir. discourse. ◆ **52 ἐπύθετο** aor. ind. mid. (dep.) πυνθάνομαι (# *4785*) to inquire. Ingressive aor. views the initiation of the conversation. **οὖν** (# *4036*) now; not a temp. but a logical connection. **κομψότερον** (# *3153*) adv. comp. κομψός nicely; comp., better. **ἔσχεν** aor. ind. act. ἔχω (# *2400*) to have. Used w. the preceding adv. meaning "to be well"; w. the ingressive aor. "to get better" (Barrett).

ἐχθές (# 2396) yesterday. For the reckoning of time s. Norris; IBD, "Time." ἀφῆκεν aor. ind. act. ἀφίημι (# 918). ◆ **53** ἔγνω aor. ind. act. γινώσκω (# 1182) to know s.v. 1. The Father knows that the words of Jesus had an immediate effect (Schlatter). καί (# 2779) and; introduces the result of the encounter with Christ. ◆ **54** δεύτερον (# 1311) again, the second (sign). The term "again" is pleonastic (Brown). Both signs are means of Christ revealing Himself (Becker). Though demonstrating that Jesus is the promised One they are also hidden. The miracle at the wedding and this healing were not openly public. ἐλθών aor. act. part. ἔρχομαι (# 2262) to go. Aor. describes the logically antecedent action to the main vb.

John 5

◆ **1** ἀνέβη aor. ind. act. ἀναβαίνω (# 326) to go up. ◆ **2** ἔστιν pres. ind. act. εἰμί (# 1639) to be. Hist. pres. (Schnackenburg; contra GGBB, 531; D.B. Wallace "John 5, 2 and the Date of the Fourth Gospel, *Bib* 71 (1990): 177-205. προβατικῇ (# 4583) having to do w. sheep. Either sheep gate or sheep pool (Morris; Barrett). An adj. modifying an understood noun, such as gate or market. This allows for κολυμβήθρα (# 3148) (diving pool, sheep pool) to be nom. (Carson). For a discussion of the variant see Barrett; TC, 207-208. For the identification as the pool of St. Anne s. Morris; Schnackenburg; Carson. ἐπιλεγομένη pres. pass. part. ἐπιλέγω (# 2141) to name, to be named. ἔχουσα pres. act. part. ἔχω (# 2400) to have. The attributive part. is used in place of a rel. cl. For a discussion of the pool see John Wilkinson, *The Jerusalem Jesus Knew: An Archaeological Guide to the Gospels* (Thames & Hudon, 1978); Joachim Jeremias, *The Rediscovery of Bethsesda* (Louisville: Southern Baptist Theological Seminary, 1966); David J. Witkamp, "John 5,2 and the Pool of Bethesda," *NTS* 12 (1965/66): 392-404; AJA, 166-68, 238-40; BBC; DJG, 41.   ◆ **3** κατέκειτο impf. ind. mid. (dep.) κατακείομαι (# 2879) to lie; customary impf., "a multitude used to lie." ἀσθενούντων pres. act. part. ἀσθενέω (# 820) to be weak, to be sick. Subst. part. as a noun to describe a weakened cond., a sick person (BAGD). τυφλός (# 5603) blind. χωλός (# 6000) lame. ξηρός (# 3831) dry, withered, disabled w. atrophied limbs, a wasting disease (Brown; BAGD). ◆ **4** For the textual problem and the omission of this v. s. TC, 209. ◆ **5** ἀσθενεία (# 819) weakness, sickness. Based on v. 7 his illness prevented him from going to the water himself. Nothing more can be inferred from the text. ◆ **6** ἰδών aor. act. part. ὁράω (# 3972) to see. Circum. part. temp.: "when Jesus saw." Jesus is the one who initiates the miracle (Becker) κατακείμενον pres. mid. (dep.) part. κατακείμαι s.v. 3. γνούς aor. act. part. γινώσκω (# 1182) to know. Circum. part. causal, "because

he knew," or temp., "when he became aware" (Carson). ὑγιής (# 5618) whole, well, restored to health (BAGD). γενέσθαι aor. mid. (dep.) inf. γίνομαι (# 1181) to become. Compl. inf. to the vb. θέλεις "do you desire to become well?" ◆ **7** ἀπεκρίθη aor. ind. pass. (dep.) ἀποκρίνομαι (# 646) to answer. ἀσθενῶν pres. act. part. nom. masc. sing. ἀσθενέω s.v. 3. Subst. part. to emphasize this trait of the man. ταραχθῇ aor. subj. pass. ταράσσω (# 5429) to trip up, to trouble. Subj. w. ὅταν (# 4020) to express an indef. time ("whenever"). βάλῃ aor. subj. act. βάλλω (# 965) to throw, to bring. It may express the necessary haste of movement (Westcott). Here in the sense of "quickly put" (BAGD). Subj. w. ἵνα (# 2671) to express purp. ◆ **8** ἔγειρε pres. imp. act. ἐγείρω (# 1586) to rise. For the idiomatic use of the pres. imp. of this vb. s. VANT, 348-49. ἆρον aor. imp. act. αἴρω (# 149) to pick up, to lift up. Aor. imp. calls for a specific act and has a note of urgency. κράβαττος (# 3187) mat, pallet, mattress used by the poor as bedding (Brown; MM). The command to carry the light mat shows the completeness of the healing (Carson). περιπάτει pres. imp. act. περιπατέω (# 4344) to walk about. Pres. imp. w. vb. of motion (VANT, 343-44). ◆ **9** ἐγένετο aor. ind. mid. (dep.) γίνομαι (# 1181) to become. ἦρεν aor. ind. act. αἴρω s.v. 8. This action will introduce the reaction of the Jewish leaders. περιεπάτει impf. ind. act. περιπατέω to walk around. Incep. impf., "he began to walk about." σάββατον (# 4879) Sabbath (ABD, 5:853-56). The exegetical significance is not just a chronological statement, but that healing on the Sabbath caused controversy. The carrying does not contradict the OT law, but does break the tradition of the elders (Carson; BBC; DJG, 716-19, 218-19; SB, 2:454-61; Matt. 12:2). ◆ **10** τεθεραπευμένῳ perf. pass. part. θεραπεύω (# 2543) to treat medically, to heal. Perf. pictures his state or cond. and puts some stress on the permanence of the cure (Morris). Perf. describes an event in the recent past. Instead of rejoicing over the healing, the Jewish leaders, ironically, only find fault (Carson). ἔξεστιν pres. ind. act. ἔξεστι (# 2003) it is lawful, it is allowed, w. inf. ἆραι aor. act. inf. αἴρω s.v. 8. Compl. inf. to the main vb. ◆ **11** ἀπεκρίθη aor. ind. pass. (dep.) s.v. 7. ποιήσας aor. act. part. ποιέω (# 4472) to do, to make. Subst. part. Aor. describes antecedent action, "the one who made me well." ◆ **12** ἠρώτησαν aor. ind. act. ἐρωτάω (# 2263) to ask. εἰπών aor. act. part. λέγω (# 3306) to say, to speak. Attributive part. to ὁ ἄνθρωπος. ◆ **13** ἰαθείς aor. pass. part. ἰάομαι (# 2615) to heal. Subst. part. Aor. portrays antecedent time. In this story the persons are referred to by their activities, "the one who said," "the one who was healed," etc. ᾔδει plperf. ind. act. οἶδα (# 3857) to know. Def. perf. w. pres. meaning. ἐξένευσεν aor. ind. act. ἐκνεύω (# 1728) to turn the head aside, to dodge, to turn aside (Barrett; NTNT, 88; GELTS, 138; Jos., *Ant.*, 7:83; 9:120). Jesus was no longer visible to the man healed (BAGD). ὄντος pres. act. part. (causal) εἰμί (# 1639) to be. Gen. abs., "because there was a crowd in the place." (JG, 84). ◆ **14** μετὰ ταῦτα after these things; after the Jewish leaders had interrogated the man; no specific time is in mind. ἴδε (# 2623) aor. imp. act. ὁράω to see. γέγονας perf. ind. act. γίνομαι (# 1181) to become. Perf. emphasizes the action in the recent past, w. results of the healing continuing. ἁμάρτανε pres. act. imp. ἁμαρτάνω (# 279) to sin. Pres. imp. w. the neg., "do not continue to sin any longer." Sin in the man's life may have occasioned the illness. This may have been the reason for Jesus healing this particular man (Carson). χεῖρον (# 5937) comp. κακός bad, evil; comp., worse. It is something worse than the physical ailment. γένηται aor. subj. mid. (dep.) γίνομαι to become. Subj. w. ἵνα (# 2671) to express purp. ◆ **15** ἀνήγγειλεν aor. ind. act. ἀναγγέλλω (# 334) to report. He reported to the officials the name of the one who healed him (BAGD). ποιήσας aor. act. part. s.v. 11. ◆ **16** διὰ τοῦτο (# 1328; 4047) because of this; because the man identified the healer as Jesus. ἐδίωκον impf. ind. act. διώκω (# 1503) to persecute. Incep. impf., "they began to persecute." There is a marked shift here from a simple hesitation about Christ to a controversy and ultimately an official rejection of Christ (Carson, 240). ἐποίει impf. ind. act. ποιέω to do. Impf. could be incep. (Morris) or better, customary: "he was in the habit of doing" (Westcott). ◆ **17** ἀπεκρίνατο aor. ind. mid. (dep.) s.v. 7. The mid. indicates a legal force, to make answer to the charge, to make a defense (Morris; MM). Even though the opponents' statements are not mentioned, the answer should be viewed as a response to these charges (Carson). The response indicates that the charges against the man of carrying his bed were only a pretense to the real charge of Jesus healing on the Sabbath (Becker). The basis of the answer is that while God's creative activity ceased after 6 days, his activity of rewarding and punishing did not (Haenchen). ◆ **18** ἐζήτουν impf. ind. act. ζητέω (# 2426) to seek. Impf. is either progressive, indicating the action in progress, or iterat.: "they kept on seeking to kill him." ἀποκτεῖναι aor. act. inf. ἀποκτείνω (# 650) to kill. Inf. indicates the purp. of the searching and complements the main vb. ἔλυεν impf. ind. act. λύω (# 3395) to loose, to break, in the sense of disregarding their traditions. ἴσος (# 2698) equal. He claims to be God. ποιῶν pres. act. part. ποιέω (# 4472) to do. In rabbinic teaching a rebellious son is said to make himself equal w. his father (Lightfoot). Breaking the Law concerning the Sabbath was serious, but claiming God as his own Father was blasphemy (Carson). ◆ **19** ποιεῖν pres. act. inf. ποιέω s.v. 18. βλέπῃ pres. subj. act. βλέπω (# 1063) to see. ποιοῦντα pres. act. part. ποιέω to do. ποιῇ pres. subj. act. ποιέω to do. Subj. w. ἄν (# 323) for a generalizing tendency. Perfect Son-

ship involves perfect identity of will and action with the Father (Westcott; s. Isa. 42:1). ◆ **20** γάρ (# 1142) for. Explains how the Son can do the Father's will (Carson). φιλεῖ pres. ind. act. φιλέω (# 5797) to love; from the original meaning, "treat someone as one of their own" developed the meaning, "the natural inclination to a relative, love for a relative"; then the meaning, "to love" (TDNT; TLNT; Brown; 3:16). Pres. indicates the ongoing love of the Father for the Son. δείκνυσιν pres. ind. act. δείκνυμι (# 1259) to show, to demonstrate. μείζονα (# 3505) comp. μέγας large, great; comp., greater. τούτων gen. of comp., w. ἔργα referring to the healings. θαυμάζητε pres. subj. act. θαυμάζω (# 2513) to be astonished, to wonder. Subj. w. ἵνα (# 2671) to express purp. ◆ **21** γάρ (# 1142) for. Introduces an illustration of the principal of vv. 19-20 (Carson). ἐγείρει pres. ind. act. ἐγείρω (# 1586) to raise. ζωοποιεῖ pres. ind. act. ζωοποιέω (# 2443) to make alive. There seems to be a play on words here. Just as the Father physically gives life to the dead so the Son gives spiritual life to the spiritually dead. This was an activity belonging exclusively to God and may be anticipatory of John 11 (Carson). ◆ **22** δέδωκεν perf. ind. act. δίδωμι (# 1443) to give; in the sense of granting authority. Resultative perf. stressing the pres. results of the Son's authority due to the Father's past action. ◆ **23** τιμῶσι pres. subj. act. τιμάω (# 5506) to honor. Subj. w. ἵνα (# 2671) to express result, possibly purp. τιμῶν pres. act. part. τιμάω to honor. Subst. part. Pres. used to describe a trait or attitude. πέμψαντα aor. act. part. πέμπω (# 4287) to send. Adj. part. to describe the past actions of the Father sending the Son. Jesus is equal in activity and honor (Carson). ◆ **24** ἀκούων pres. act. part. ἀκούω (# 201) to hear. Subst. part. ("the one who"), used here in the sense of meeting a cond. πιστεύων pres. act. part. πιστεύω (# 4409) to believe. πέμψαντι aor. act. part. πέμπω s.v. 23. αἰώνιος (# 173) eternal (s. 3:15). κρίσις (# 3213) judgment. Includes fut. judgment and also the judgment that was in process throughout the ministry of Jesus (Barrett). μεταβέβηκεν perf. ind. act. μεταβαίνω (# 3553) to go or pass from one place to another, to transform, to move one's living quarters (Schnackenburg). Perf. indicates the completed state; the believer has passed into eternal life which begins here (Bernard). The place from which and to which is given with ἐκ (# 1666) and εἰς (# 1650) (BAGD; s. 1 John 3:14). Part of the Son's mission is to bring both life and judgment. ◆ **25** ἀκούσουσιν fut. ind. act. ἀκούω s.v. 24, to hear and do, to be obedient as commonly used in the OT (Barrett); to hear and to appropriately act upon what has been heard. There is a double reference here to the physically dead and the spiritually dead. Just as Jesus healed by his word, so he makes those alive by his word (Carson). ἀκούσαντες aor. act. part. ἀκούω to hear. ζήσουσιν fut. ind. act. ζάω (# 2437) to live. Refers to the spiritually dead being made alive (Tasker). ◆ **26** ὥσπερ … οὕτως "just as . . . so also"; explicates the comp. between the Father and the Son. **ἔδωκεν** aor. ind. act. δίδωμι (# 1443) to give. **ἔχειν** pres. act. inf. ἔχω (# 2400) to have. Compl. inf. to the main vb. ◆ **27** κρίσιν ποιεῖν to execute judgment. Compl. inf. to the main vb. **ἔδωκεν**. **ὅτι** because. **υἱὸς ἀνθρώπου** Son of Man (DJG, 775-81). Without the art. emphasizing humanity or equal to the expression w. the art. (Morris). Here the concept of the Son of God in the previous discussion (vv. 19-26) is expanded. ◆ **28** θαυμάζετε pres. imp. act. θαυμάζω (# 2513) to wonder, to be astonished. w. the neg. μή (# 3590) prohibits an action in progress. **μνημεῖον** (# 3646) grave; this strengthens the contrast between the physically and spiritually dead. Those who are physically dead obey the Son while those who are spiritually dead do not. **ἀκούσουσιν** pres. act. part. ἀκούω s.v. 24. Subst. part. Here used in the sense of "obey." ◆ **29** ἐκπορεύσονται fut. ind. mid. (dep.) ἐκπορεύομαι (# 1744) to go out. **ποιήσαντες** aor. act. part. ποιέω (# 4472) to do; to practice virtue (BAGD). Aor. describes the antecedent action, here the fulfilling of a cond. **ἀνάστασις** (# 414) resurrection. The following gen. is result or purp. **φαῦλος** (# 5765) bad, worthless. **πράξαντες** aor. act. part. πράσσω (# 4556) to do. Subst. part. The two parts. describe the two types of individuals and their ensuing destinies. ◆ **30** δίκαιος (# 1465) righteous, corresponding to God's standard. **πέμψαντος** aor. act. part. πέμπω to send s.v. 23. The authority of passing judgment is derived from the sending agent, the Father Himself. ◆ **31** ἀληθής (# 239) true, genuine in the sense of legally acceptable. The legal principle here is from Deut. 19:15 where man can not be convicted of a crime on the testimony of one witness (Brown; s. also M, Kethoboth, 2:9; SB, 2:227-29.). For a structure of the discourse s. U.C. von Wahlde, "Literary Structure and Theological Argument in Three Discourses with the Jews in the Fourth Gospel," *JBL* 103 (1984): 575-84. ◆ **32** ἄλλος (# 257) another. Not the Baptist, but the Father (Barrett). **μαρτυρῶν** pres. act. part. μαρτυρέω (# 3455) to witness. Used substantivally to emphasize the person witnessing. Pres. describes the contemporaneous action. The testimony is going on presently. **περί** (# 4309) concerning; this prep. gives the object of the testimony, while the dat. would suggest advantage for the person (BAGD). **οἶδα** (# 3857) perf. ind. act. to know. Def. perf. w. pres. meaning. ◆ **33** ἀπεστάλκατε perf. ind. act. ἀποστέλλω (# 690) to send, to send as an authoritative representative. The reference is to the religious leaders who examined John the Baptist (s. John 1:19-27). Now Jesus offers corroborative evidence for his claim, namely the following witnesses: John the Baptist (33-35); God the Father (36-38); and the Scriptures (39-47) (Carson). **μεμαρτύρηκεν** perf. ind. act. μαρ-

τυρέω (# 3455) to witness. Perf. indicates the testimony of John still has value (Brown). Those of Qumran considered themselves as witnesses of the truth and sons of the truth (1QS 8:6; 4:5; 1QM 17:8; 1QH 6:29). **τῇ ἀληθείᾳ** (# 237) dat. of interest; if the truth refers to the person of Christ. It can refer to his testimony of the Coming One or to his testimony that Jesus is the truth (Haenchen). ◆ **34** σωθῆτε aor. subj. pass. σῴζω (# 5392) to save, to rescue. The pass. may express divine agency. Subj. w. ἵνα (# 2671) to express purp. ◆ **35** λύχνος (# 3394) lamp (Matt. 5:15). A hypocatastasis referring to John the Baptist. Thus he combines the themes of witness and light. He is not the light but a lightbearer, suggesting that his light was from a higher source (Carson). **καιόμενος** pres. pass. part. καίω (# 2794) to light; pass. to burn. The emphasis is on the process and result of the light burning (BAGD). Adj. part. to describe the activity of the lamp. Pres. indicates the ongoing testimony of John the Baptist. **φαίνων** pres. act. part. φαίνω (# 5743) to shine, to give light, to be bright (BAGD) **ἠθελήσατε** aor. ind. act. θέλω (# 2527) to wish, to want to. Const. aor. describes the whole process of encounter with and reaction to John. **ἀγαλλιαθῆναι** aor. pass. (dep.) inf. ἀγαλλιάομαι (# 22) to be glad, to be overjoyed, to exult (BAGD). Compl. inf. is used as a complement to the main vb. Aor. suggests the simple event of their rejoicing without reference to duration or results. ◆ **36** μείζω comp. s.v. 20. Predicate acc. **γάρ** (# 1142) for. The miracles Christ has done are greater than the testimony of John. They are part of the Father's testimony (Carson). Thus they constitute two witnesses, the Father and the works themselves (Becker). **δέδωκεν** perf. ind. act. δίδωμι (# 1443) to give. The consummative perf. emphasizes the completion of the Father giving the Son specific tasks to accomplish. **τελειώσω** aor. subj. act. τελειόω (# 5457) to complete. Consummative aor. emphasizes the completion of the works that Christ was to do. Subj. w. ἵνα (# 2671) indicates purp. or result. **ἀπέσταλκεν** perf. ind. act. ἀποστέλλω (# 690) to send. Resultative perf. emphasizing that the present miracles are due to the Father's previous commissioning. ◆ **37** πέμψας aor. act. part. s.v. 23. **μεμαρτύρηκεν** perf. ind. act. μαρτυρέω (# 3455) to witness. Resultative perf. emphasizing the continuing effect of the Father's witness. The Father is the third witness to the validity of Christ's claims. **ἀκηκόατε** perf. ind. act. ἀκούω (# 201) to hear. Resultative perf. They have not in the past, nor do they now, accept the Father's revelation and testimony. **εἶδος** (# 1626) appearance, form. **ἑωράκατε** perf. ind. act. ὁράω (# 3972) to see. ◆ **38** μένοντα pres. act. part. (adj.) μένω (# 3531) to remain. "The word, which would remain in you." **ἀπέστειλεν** aor. ind. act. ἀποστέλλω (# 690) to send. Consumative aor. emphasizing the completion of the fact that he is already here.

◆ **39 ἐραυνᾶτε** pres. ind. act. ἐραυνάω (# 2236) to search, to investigate. Customary pres. suggesting their long–standing habit of searching the Scriptures. The form could be imp., but the context demands the ind. (Carson). Corresponding to the Heb. t.t. used by the rabbis and in the Qumran literature for the study of the Scripture (Schnackenburg; Sir. 17:11; 45:5; Bar. 4:1; Pss. Sol. 14:1f; Becker). **ὅτι** (# 4022) because. **μαρτυροῦσαι** pres. act. part. nom. fem. pl. μαρτυρέω s.v. 37. Pres. emphasizes the contemporaneous aspect of the witness; that is, the Scriptures continue to witness to the claims of Christ. While there is no explicit passage mentioned, it is a comprehensive hermeneutical key (Carson). ◆ **40 ἐλθεῖν** aor. act. inf. ἔρχομαι (# 2262) to come. Compl. inf. to the main vb. **ἔχητε** pres. subj. act. ἔχω (# 2400) to have. Subj. w. **ἵνα** (# 2671) to express purp. ◆ **41 δόξαν** (# 1518) glory, in the sense of approval. If he was the kind of Messiah they wanted, all would follow. There were a number of messianic pretenders before A.D. 70 (Jos., *Ant.* 20:97–99, 171–72; *JW,* 2:258–65. S. P.W. Barnett, "The Jewish Sign Prophets–A.D. 40–70–Their Intentions and Origins," *NTS* 27 [1981]: 679–97; DJG, 688–98). ◆ **42 ἔγνωκα** perf. ind. act. γινώσκω (# 1182) to know. The resultative perf. suggests the present knowledge Christ has of them based on his past experience. **ὅτι** (# 4022) gives the content of the knowledge. ◆ **43 ἐλήλυθα** perf. ind. act. ἔρχομαι (# 2262) to go. Resultative perf. emphasizes the completion of the coming, and the present aspect, his presence. **ἔλθη** aor. subj. act. ἔρχομαι to go. Const. aor. viewing the total action. Subj. w. **ἐάν** (# 1569) in a 3rd. class cond. cl. which views the cond. as possible. **λήμψεσθε** fut. ind. mid. (dep.) λαμβάνω (# 3284) to receive. ◆ **44 πιστεῦσαι** aor. act. inf. πιστεύω (# 4409) to believe. Compl. inf. to the main vb. **δύνασθε** (# 1538). **λαμβάνοντες** pres. act. part. λαμβάνω (# 3284) to receive. Part. is either causal ("because") or cond. ("if you"). Pres. emphasizes the contemporaneous action. It is not possible to believe while seeking man's approval. **καί** (# 2779) and; connects the two main vbs. ◆ **45 δοκεῖτε** pres. imp. act. δοκέω (# 1506) to think, suppose. Pres. imp. w. **μή** (# 3590) suggests the cessation of an ongoing action. **κατηγορήσω** fut. ind. act. κατηγορέω (# 2989) to accuse, w. gen. A legal t.t. to bring charges in court (BAGD). **κατηγορῶν** pres. act. part. κατηγορέω. Pres. part. perhaps having the force of the fut. (BD, 175). Tragically, Moses will not support, but condemn them for their disbelief (DJG, 562). **ἠλπίκατε** perf. ind. act. ἐλπίζω (# 1827) to hope. Perf. indicates that the hope continues in the pres. and is not merely and emotion of the past (Bernard). ◆ **46 ἐπιστεύετε** impf. ind. act. πιστεύω s.v. 44. Impf. in a contrary-to-fact cond. cl. **ἔγραψεν** aor. ind. act. γράφω (# 1211) to write. Const. aor. viewing the writing more as a whole, with the finished product, not the process,

in mind. ◆ **47 πιστεύετε** pres. ind. act. s.v. 44. Ind. in a 1st. class cond. cl. which assumes the reality of the cond. **πιστεύσετε** fut. ind. act. Their rejection of Christ is a continuation of the rejection of the OT prophets and Scriptures.

John 6

◆ **1 ἀπῆλθεν** aor. ind. act. ἀπέρχομαι (# 599) to go away, to depart. **πέραν** (# 4305) the other side (of the shore). For a collection of essays on this chapter s. R. Alan Culpepper, *Critical Readings of John 6* (Leiden: E.J. Brill, 1996). ◆ **2 ἠκολούθει** impf. ind. act. ἀκολουθέω (# 199) to follow, w. dat. Impf. denotes the continuous action: "they kept following" (Morris). **ἐθεώρουν** impf. ind. act. θεωρέω (# 2555) to be a spectator, to watch, to notice (BAGD). The miracles and signs attracted great attention. **ἀσθενούντων** pres. act. part. ἀσθενέω (# 820) to be weak, to be sick. Subst. part. ◆ **3 ἀνῆλθεν** aor. ind. act. ἀνέρχομαι (# 456) to go up, to come up. **ἐκάθητο** impf. ind. mid. (dep.) κάθημαι (# 2764) to sit down, to sit, to be, to live (BAGD). ◆ **4 ἦν** impf. ind. act. εἰμί (# 1639) to be. For the Passover s. Matt. 26:2; Luke 22:1; J Lightfoot, 3:301-302. ◆ **5 ἐπάρας** aor. act. part. ἐπαίρω (# 2048) to lift up. Temp. or circum. part. Aor. indicates antecedent action to the main vb. **θεασάμενος** aor. mid. (dep.) part. θεάομαι (# 2517) to see, to view. **ἀγοράσωμεν** aor. subj. act. ἀγοράζω (# 60) to buy at the marketplace. Deliberative subj. in a question. **φάγωσιν** aor. subj. act. ἐσθίω (# 2266) to eat. Subj. w. **ἵνα** to express purp. ◆ **6 πειράζων** pres. act. part. πειράζω (# 4279) to test. Used here in the neutral sense of testing (Morris; TLNT). Pres. indicates contemporaneous action. Circum. part. expressing his motive. **ᾔδει** plperf. ind. act. of the def. perf. οἶδα (# 3857) to know. **ἔμελλεν** impf. ind. act. μέλλω (# 3516) to be about to. Used w. the inf. to express the immediate fut. (MKG, 307). **ποιεῖν** pres. act. inf. ποιέω (# 4472) to do. ◆ **7 δηνάριον** (# 1324) denarius. A Roman silver coin normally worth about 18 cents; it was a day's wages (BAGD; IBD; ABD, 1:1086; DJG, 805). Gen. of price, "for two hundred denarii." **βραχύ** (# 1099) short, small; used of quantity in a small amount: a little (BAGD). **λάβη** aor. subj. act. λαμβάνω (# 3284) to receive. Subj. w. **ἵνα** (# 2671) to express purp. ◆ **9 παιδάριον** (# 4081) lad, small boy, a double dimin. (Brown). **κρίθινος** (# 3209) made of barley. For adj. w. this suffix signifying material, origin or kind s. MH, 359. **ὀψάριον** (# 4066) cooked food eaten w. bread, tidbit, w. a special meaning of pickled or preserved fish (BAGD; MM; NDIEC, 2:92; Barrett). ◆ **10 ποιήσατε** aor. imp. act. ποιέω (# 4472) to do. In the sense of "make" or "command." Jesus himself makes the preparation for the miracle (Becker). Aor. imp. calls for a specific act. **ἀναπεσεῖν** aor. act. inf. ἀναπίπτω (# 404) to recline, to sit down.

Inf. in indir. discourse giving the content of the command. **χόρτος** (# *5965*) grass, hay; almost always of grass standing in a field (BAGD). **τόπῳ** dat. τόπος (# *5536*) place, area, location, region. **ἀνέπεσαν** aor. ind. act. ἀναπίπτω. **ὡς** (# *6055*) w. numbers, about. ◆ **11 οὖν** (# *4036*) used in a temp. sense, then, or used to introduce an act of special solemnity (JG, 168-69). **ἔλαβεν** aor. ind. act. λαμβάνω (# *3284*) to receive, to take. **εὐχαριστήσας** aor. act. part. εὐχαριστέω (# *2373*) to give thanks. Not a sacramental reference (Bernard). For examples of the prayers s. SB, 4:627-34. **διέδωκεν** aor. ind. act. διαδίδωμι (# *1344*) to distribute. **ἀνακειμένοις** pres. mid. (dep.) part. ἀνάκειμαι (# *367*) to recline (at the table). Subst. part. Pres. indicates contemporaneous activity. **ἤθελον** impf. ind. act. θέλω (# *2527*) to wish, to desire. ◆ **12 ἐνεπλήσθησαν** aor. ind. pass. ἐμπίπλημι (# *1855*) to fill up, to fill; pass. to be satisfied (w. enough to eat). Const. aor. viewing the total action of both the eating and being satisfied. **συναγάγετε** aor. imp. act. συνάγω (# *5251*) to gather together. Ingressive aor. suggests the beginning of the action, "start picking up." This is not only a Jewish custom so that nothing is wasted (SB, 4:626ff; 2:479; BBC), but it shows the greatness of the miracle (Becker). The leftovers were for the ones who served (J Lightfoot, 3:302). **περισσεύσαντα** aor. act. part. περισσεύω (# *4355*) to be in abundance, to be left over. Adj. part. describing the food. **ἀπόληται** aor. mid. (dep.) subj. ἀπόλλυμι (# *660*) to perish, to be lost. Subj. w. **ἵνα** (# *2671*) to express purp. ◆ **13 συνήγαγον** aor. ind. act. συνάγω s.v. 12. Const. aor. viewing all the actions of the gathering. **ἐγέμισαν** aor. ind. act. γεμίζω (# *1153*) to fill. **κόφινος** (# *3186*) basket, probably of wicker (Morris); of various sizes but usually a large, heavy basket for carrying things; typical of the Jews (BAGD). **βεβρωκόσιν** perf. act. part. βιβρώσκω (# *1048*) to eat. Significant in that there is more left over after the meal than before. ◆ **14 ἰδόντες** aor. act. part. (temp.) ὁράω (# *3972*) to see. Aor. describing antecedent action. **ἐποίησεν** aor. ind. act. ποιέω (# *4472*) to do. Const. aor. summarizing all the actions necessary in performing the miracle. **ἔλεγον** impf. ind. act. λέγω (# *3306*) to say. Incep. impf., "they began to say." **ὁ προφήτης** (# *4737*) the prophet (s. John 1:21; Meeks, 87-91; 1QS 9:11). **ἐρχόμενος** pres. mid. (dep.) part. (adj.) ἔρχομαι (# *2262*) to come. ◆ **15 γνούς** aor. act. part. γινώσκω (# *1182*) to know. Causal part. w. aor. indicating antecedent action. Jesus knew about their future actions beforehand; thus he acted to avoid being made king for the wrong reasons. **μέλλουσιν** pres. ind. act. μέλλω (# *3516*) to be about to. W. inf. to indicate an imminent future. **ἁρπάζειν** pres. act. inf. ἁρπάζω (# *773*) to rob, to seize. A violent word w. connotations of force (Brown). They wanted to make him king for the wrong motives, which he rejected by withdrawing. **ποιήσωσιν** aor. subj. act. s.v. 14. Subj. w. **ἵνα** (# *2671*) to indicate purp.

ἀνεχώρησεν aor. ind. act. ἀναχωρέω (# *432*) to depart, to go away. The departure here is a preparation for the next miracle (Becker). ◆ **16 ἐγένετο** aor. ind. mid. (dep.) γίνομαι (# *1181*) to become. "When evening came." **κατέβησαν** aor. ind. act. καταβαίνω (# *2849*) to go down. ◆ **17 ἐμβάντες** aor. act. part. ἐμβαίνω (# *1832*) to embark, to get into (a boat). Temp. part w. aor. showing antecedent action. **ἤρχοντο** impf. ind. mid. (dep.) ἔρχομαι (# *2262*) to go, travel. Impf. may be conative, "they were trying to cross," or emphasize continuing action, "they were in process of crossing" (Morris). **ἐγεγόνει** plperf. ind. act. s.v. 16. Now it is no longer evening, but darkness has set in. **ἐληλύθει** plperf. ind. act. ἔρχομαι to go. Plperf. indicating antecedent action. ◆ **18 πνέοντος** pres. act. part. πνέω (# *4463*) to blow. Gen. abs. **διεγείρετο** impf. ind. pass. διεγείρω (# *1444*) to wake up, to arouse, pass., "was becoming aroused" (BAGD). ◆ **19 ἐληλακότες** perf. act. part. (temp.) ἐλαύνω (# *1785*) to row. **στάδιον** (# *5084*) stade, about 607 feet (BAGD). The lake is about 13 miles long and at its greatest width 8 miles wide (IDB, 2:348; ZPEB, 2:643-48; ABD, 2:899-901). **περιπατοῦντα** pres. act. part. (adj.) περιπατέω (# *4344*) to walk about. Pres. indicates contemporaneous action. **ἐφοβήθησαν** aor. ind. pass. (dep.) φοβέομαι to be afraid. Used in the pass. to describe fear, alarm, fright (BAGD). Ingressive aor., "they became afraid." ◆ **20 φοβεῖσθε** pres. imp. mid. (dep.) φοβέομαι (# *5828*) to be afraid. Pres. imp. w. a neg. μή to prohibit an action in progress. ◆ **21 οὖν** (# *4036*) used in a temp. sense, then (s.v. 11). **ἤθελον** impf. ind. act. s.v. 11. **λαβεῖν** aor. act. inf. λαμβάνω (# *3284*) to take, in the sense of take someone up into the boat (BAGD). **ὑπῆγον** impf. ind. act. ὑπάγω (# *5632*) to go to. The direction is given by the prep. εἰς (# *1650*); progressive impf., "to which land they had been going" (RWP). ◆ **22 ἑστηκώς** perf. act. part. ἵστημι (# *2705*) to stand. **εἶδον** aor. ind. act. ὁράω (# *3972*) to see. **πλοιάριον** (# *4449*) small ship, boat. **εἰ μή** (# *1623*; *3590*) except. **συνεισῆλθεν** aor. ind. act. συνεισέρχομαι (# *5291*) to go into together. Prep. in compound indicates the accompaniment and the goal. **ἀπῆλθον** aor. ind. act. ἀπέρχομαι (# *599*) to go. ◆ **23 ἦλθεν** aor. ind. act. ἔρχομαι (# *2262*) to go; here in the sense, to arrive. **ἔφαγον** aor. ind. act. ἐσθίω (# *2266*) to eat. **εὐχαριστήσαντος** aor. act. part. (temp.) s.v. 11. Gen. abs. Aor. indicates antecedent action. ◆ **24 ἐνέβησαν** aor. ind. act. s.v. 17. **ζητοῦντες** pres. act. part. (circum.) ζητέω (# *2426*) to seek. ◆ **25 εὑρόντες** aor. act. part. (temp.) εὑρίσκω (# *2351*) to find. Aor. indicating antecedent action. **εἶπον** aor. ind. act. λέγω (# *3306*) to say. **γέγονας** perf. ind. act. 2nd. pers. sing. γίνομαι (# *1181*) to become, to be. Perf. brings two ideas together: "When did you come?" and "How long have you been here?" (Morris). ◆ **26 ἀπεκρίθη** aor. ind. pass. (dep.) ἀποκρίνομαι (# *646*) to answer. **σημεῖον** (# *5946*) sign s.

John 2:18. **ἐφάγετε** aor. ind. act. s.v. 5. **ἐχορτάσθητε** aor. ind. pass. χορτάζω (# 5963) to feed, to feed until full, to be satisfied (w. food). ◆ **27 ἐργάζεσθε** pres. mid. (dep.) imp. ἐργάζομαι (# 2237) to work, to earn by working (Barrett). Pres. imp. w. the neg. μή (# 3590) in this case may be conative: "stop trying to earn" (Barrett). **βρῶσις** (# 1111) food. **ἀπολλυμένην** pres. mid. part. (adj.) s.v. 12. **μένουσαν** pres. act. part. (adj.) μένω (# 3531) to remain. This food remains forever and also has the effect of producing a life that lasts forever (Morris). **δώσει** fut. ind. act. δίδωμι (# 1443) to give. **ἐσφράγισεν** aor. ind. act. σφραγίζω (# 5381) to seal, to certify (s. John 3:33). The sacrificial animals were examined and sealed if perfect. Perhaps the thought of Christ as an accepted sacrifice is indicated (Westcott). Perhaps in the sense of attestation that the Son of Man gives true, nonperishable food (NIDNTT). ◆ **28 ποιῶμεν** pres. subj. act. s.v. 10. Deliberative subj., "What shall we do?" **ἐργαζώμεθα** pres. subj. mid. (dep.) s.v. 27. Subj. w. ἵνα (# 2671) to express purp. The meaning here is "to perform a work" (Barrett). **ἔργα τοῦ θεοῦ** the works of God; the works that God desires of men (Brown; BBC). Descriptive gen., indicating the kind of works. One work is mentioned in the following verse, which is belief in the mission of Jesus given by the Father. ◆ **29 πιστεύητε** pres. subj. act. πιστεύω (# 4409) to believe. Subj. w. ἵνα (# 2671) as explanatory of the work (Barrett). **ἀπέστειλεν** aor. ind. act. ἀποστέλλω (# 690) to send, to send as an authoritative representative (TDNT; TLNT; EDNT). ◆ **30 ἴδωμεν** aor. subj. act. ὁράω (# 3972) to see. The miracle he had just performed was not enough for them (Becker). Subj. w. ἵνα (# 2671) to express purp. ◆ **31 μάννα** (# 3445) manna. The miraculous provision of the manna in the desert provided the rabbi w. suitable language to describe the rich gifts of God in the messianic age (Hoskyns; SB, 2:481; TFG, 238-50; P. Borgen, *Bread from Heaven: An Exegetical Study of the Concept of Manna in the Gospel of John and the Writings of Philo* [Leiden: E.J. Brill, 1965]; and his updated discussion, PJP, 121-44). They expected in the endtime limitless, supernatural provision of manna (Becker; s. Apoc. Bar. 29:8). **γεγραμμένον** perf. pass. part. γράφω (# 1211) to write. Perf. was used for important authoritative documents (MM). **ἔδωκεν** aor. ind. act. δίδωμι (# 1443) to give. **φαγεῖν** aor. act. inf., s.v. 5. Inf. of purp. ◆ **32 οὖν** (# 4036) then, either temp. as a response or logical inference ("therefore, because of their misunderstanding"). **δέδωκεν** perf. ind. act. δίδωμι s.v. 31. Perf. implies, "Moses has never given you true bread" (JG, 333). **δίδωσιν** pres. ind. act. Pres. indicates the standing offer. ◆ **33 καταβαίνων** pres. act. part. καταβαίνω (# 2849) to come down, to descend. Subst. part. Jesus is no longer simply the provider of bread, but also the gift of God, just as the bread was in the OT (Becker). **διδούς** pres. act. part. s.v. 31. Pres. de-

picts the offer in progress. In Rabbinical circles the "Bread from Heaven" was spiritual food from the spiritual world (TFG, 240). ◆ **34 δός** aor. imp. act. δίδωμι s.v. 31. Aor. imp. calls for a specific act w. a note of urgency. ◆ **35 ὁ ἄρτος τῆς ζωῆς** the bread that gives life; that is, everlasting life (Morris). The gen. could be called a verbal gen. (Carson). For a discussion of the "I am" sayings s. DJG, 354-56. **ἐρχόμενος** pres. mid. (dep.) part. (subst.) s.v. 14. Here in the sense, come in belief. Part. emphasizes the performance of the act of belief (Becker). **πεινάσῃ** aor. subj. act. πεινάω (# 4277) to be hungry. Subj. w. οὐ μή (# 4024; 3590) to express strong denial (M, 187-92; GGBB, 468-69). **πιστεύων** pres. act. part. s.v. 29. **διψήσει** fut. ind. act. διψάω (# 1498) to thirst, to be thirsty, to suffer from thirst. **πώποτε** (# 4799) ever. ◆ **36 εἶπον** aor. ind. act. s.v. 25. It may refer to v. 26; or to words like them spoken at an earlier time (Westcott). **ἑωράκατε** perf. ind. act. ὁράω s.v. 30. Perf. here emphasizes the completion of the action w. the resultant cond., yet without the appropriate response emphasized by the following perf. ◆ **37 δίδωσιν** pres. ind. act. s.v. 31. Pres. is used here where the Son awaits; in v. 39 the perf. expresses the gift as completed in the will of Father (Morris). **ἥξει** fut. ind. act. ἥκω (# 2457) to come. Specific fut., "will certainly come." ◆ **38 καταβέβηκα** perf. ind. act. καταβαίνω (# 2849) to go down, to come down. Perf. emphasizing the completion of the act w. its results: He has come down and is here. **ποιῶ** pres. subj. act. s.v. 6. Subj. w. ἵνα (# 2671) to express purp. **πέμψαντος** aor. act. part. (subst.) πέμπω (# 4287) to send. ◆ **39 ἀπολέσω** aor. subj. act. ἀπόλλυμι (# 660) to destroy, to lose. "That I should not lose one of the whole company" (Barrett; TDNT). **ἀναστήσω** aor. subj. act. ἀνίστημι (# 482) to raise up. Subj. w. ἵνα (# 2671) explaining the content of the will. Here it indicates the final resurrection as the beginning of the anticipated kingdom. ◆ **40 θεωρῶν** pres. act. part. θεωρέω (# 2555) to see. Subst. part. **ἔχῃ** pres. subj. act. ἔχω (# 2400) to have. Subj. w. ἵνα (# 2671) explains the content of the will. Not as fut. but as pres. already a divine power before the resurrection (Westcott). **ἀναστήσω** aor. subj. act. or fut. ind. act. ἀνίστημι (# 482) to raise up. The volitive fut., a promise (RWP). If subj. then parallel to ἔχῃ expressing the content of the Father's will. ◆ **41 ἐγόγγυζον** impf. ind. act. γογγύζω (# 1197) to murmur, to grumble, to complain, as a sign of displeasure or perhaps unbelief (GELTS, 92; TDNT; EDNT). Incep. impf., "they began to complain." This reaction is in sharp contrast to the later reaction of belief in 6:68-69 (Becker). **οὖν** (# 4036) then; logical connection. **καταβάς** aor. act. part. (adj.) s.v. 16. ◆ **42 οὗτος** this one. An element of discouragement, w. a note of disgust or despisement (Brown). **οἴδαμεν** perf. ind. act. οἶδα (# 3857) to know. Def. perf. w. a pres. meaning. **καταβέβηκα** perf. ind. act. s.v. 38. ◆ **43 γογγύ-**

ζετε pres. act. imp. s.v. 41. Pres. imp. w. a neg. μή (# 3590) to stop an action in progress. ◆ **44** ἐλθεῖν aor. act. inf. ἔρχομαι (# 2262) to come. Inf. w. vb. δύναται. πέμψας aor. act. part. (adj.) s.v. 38. ἑλκύσῃ aor. subj. act. ἑλκύω (# 1816) to draw. For the possible implications of this word, such as the idea of resistance–"to take possession of," "to bring near"–referring to the conversion of proselytes s. Morris; Barrett. The word was used in rabbinic lit. as the expression of a religious experience (TFG, 266). ἀναστήσω fut. ind. act. s.v. 40. ◆ **45** γεγραμμένον perf. pass. part. s.v. 31. ἔσονται fut. ind. mid. (dep.) εἰμί (# 1639) to be. διδακτός (# 1435) taught; the substantivized verbal adj. as a pass., w. gen. (θεοῦ) to designate the agent (MT, 134). ἀκούσας aor. act. part. (adj.) ἀκούω (# 201) to hear. μαθών aor. act. part. (adj.) μανθάνω (# 3443) to learn. ◆ **46** ἑώρακέν perf. ind. act. ὁράω s.v. 30. Perf. emphasizing the abiding results. No one has seen the Father; thus they cannot know him. ὤν pres. act. part. εἰμί (# 1639) to be. ◆ **47** πιστεύων pres. act. part. s.v. 29. Subst. part. ἔχει pres. ind. act. ἔχω (# 2400) to have. Pres. indicates continual possession. ◆ **48** ἐγώ (# 1609) I. Emphatic, "I, alone," "I, in contrast to any other." ◆ **49** ἔφαγον aor. ind. act. ἐσθίω (# 2266) to eat. Const. aor. viewing the forty years of eating as a whole. ἀπέθανον aor. ind. act. ἀποθνήσκω (# 633) to die. ◆ **50** καταβαίνων pres. act. part. καταβαίνω (# 2849) to come down. φάγῃ aor. subj. act. ἐσθίω (# 2266) to eat. ἀποθάνῃ aor. subj. act. ἀποθνήσκω (# 633) s.v. 49. Subj. w. ἵνα (# 2671) to express purp. ◆ **51** ζῶν pres. act. part. (adj.) ζάω (# 2409) to live. καταβάς aor. act. part. s.v. 38. φάγῃ aor. subj. act. s.v. 50. 3rd. class cond. w. ἐάν (# 1569) viewing the cond. as possible. It refers to the act of appropriating Christ (Morris). ζήσει fut. ind. act. ζάω. δέ (# 1254) an unusual position for the particle, but introducing a fresh thought (Barrett). ὑπέρ (# 5642) w. gen., for, in behalf of, for the sake of. ◆ **52** ἐμάχοντο impf. ind. mid. (dep.) μάχομαι (# 3481) to fight, to wage a war of words (RWP); incep. impf. δοῦναι aor. act. inf. δίδωμι (# 1443) to give. Compl. inf. w. vb. δύναται. ◆ **53** φάγητε aor. subj. act. s.v. 50. Subj. w. ἐάν (# 1569) in a 3rd. class cond. cl. viewing the cond. as a possibility. πίητε aor. subj. act. πίνω (# 4403) to drink. The Law of Moses forbade the drinking of blood and eating of meat w. the blood still in it; here it refers to the violent death of Jesus on the cross (Carson; s. also HSB, 498-500). ◆ **54** τρώγων pres. act. part. τρώγω (# 5592) to nibble, to munch, to eat audibly, to crunch. Pres. points to a continuing appropriation (Morris). Subst. part. describing the trait w. a possibly cond. idea. πίνων pres. act. part. s.v. 53. ἀναστήσω fut. ind. act. s.v. 39. ◆ **55** βρῶσις (# 1111) food. Pred. nom. ἀληθής (# 239) true, genuine. πόσις (# 4530) drink. ◆ **56** μένει pres. ind. act. μένω (# 3531) to remain, to abide. Pres. indicates a continual abiding. ◆ **57** ἀπέ-

στειλεν aor. ind. act. s.v. 29. ζῶ pres. ind. act. s.v. 51. διά (# 1328) w. acc., because of. καί (# 2779) also. ζήσει fut. ind. act. s.v. 51. ◆ **58** καταβάς aor. act. part., s.v. 38. ἔφαγον aor. ind. act. s.v. 31. ἀπέθανον aor. ind. act. ἀποθνήσκω (# 633) to die. ζήσει fut. ind. act. ζάω s.v. 51. ◆ **59** συναγωγῇ (# 5252) dat. sing. gathering, synagogue. διδάσκων pres. act. part. (temp.) διδάσκω (# 1438) to teach. Pres. expressing contemporaneous action. ◆ **60** σκληρός (# 5017) dried, rough, harsh. ἀκούειν pres. act. inf. ἀκούω (# 201). "To hear w. appreciation" (Morris). Compl. inf. w. vb. δύναται. ◆ **61** εἰδώς perf. act. part. οἶδα s.v. 42. Temp. or causal part. σκανδαλίζει pres. ind. act. σκανδαλίζω (# 4997) to cause to stumble, to offend (TLNT; TDNT; EDNT). ◆ **62** θεωρῆτε pres. subj. act. θεωρέω (# 2555) to see. For the possible constructions of this elliptical sentence s. Brown; Barrett. ἀναβαίνοντα pres. act. part. (temp.) ἀναβαίνω (# 326) to go up, to ascend. Pres. expressing contemporaneous action, "while he is ascending." πρότερον (# 4728) formerly. ◆ **63** ζωοποιοῦν pres. act. part. (adj.) ζωοποιέω (# 2443) to make alive. ὠφελεῖ pres. ind. act. ὠφελέω (# 6067) to profit, to be useful. λελάληκα perf. ind. act. λαλέω (# 3281) to speak. Perf. emphasizing the completed action of the past conversation and its continuing results. ◆ **64** ᾔδει plperf. ind. act. οἶδα (# 3857) to know. Def. perf. w. pres. meaning. παραδώσων fut. act. part. παραδίδωμι (# 4140) to deliver over, to betray. Subst. part. indicating the trait by which the person is known. ◆ **65** εἴρηκα perf. ind. act. λέγω (# 3306) to say, to tell, to speak. ἐλθεῖν aor. act. inf. ἔρχομαι (# 2261) to go. Compl. inf. w. vb. δύναται. ᾖ pres. subj. act. εἰμί (# 1639) to be. δεδομένον perf. pass. part. δίδωμι (# 1443) to give. Used here to form the periphrastic perf. pass. subj. ◆ **66** ἐκ τούτου (# 4047) either "for this reason" or "from this time" (Barrett). ἀπῆλθον aor. ind. act. s.v. 1. περιεπάτουν impf. ind. act. s.v. 19. ◆ **67** μή (# 3590) used in a question expecting the answer no. καί (# 2779) also. ◆ **68** ἀπεκρίθη aor. ind. pass. (dep.) s.v. 26. ἀπελευσόμεθα fut. ind. mid. (dep.) ἀπέρχομαι (# 599) to go away; in the sense, "to whom should we turn." Here is the clear sense of hearing resulting in belief, which results in eternal life. ◆ **69** πεπιστεύκαμεν perf. ind. act. πιστεύω (# 4409) to believe. Perf. implies, "we have come to a place of faith and continue there" (Morris). ἐγνώκαμεν perf. ind. act. γινώσκω (# 1182) to know. Perf. implies "we have recognized the truth and hold it" (Barrett). ὁ ἅγιος (# 41) the Holy One, dedicated by God to convey the words of eternal life to mankind (Tasker). ◆ **70** ἐξελεξάμην aor. ind. mid. ἐκλέγω (# 1721) to select, to choose out for oneself. διάβολος (# 1333) slanderer, devil (DJG, 171-72). Satan has made Judas his ally, a subordinate devil (Barrett). Monadic noun not requiring art. (GGBB, 249). ◆ **71** ἔμελλεν impf. ind. act. s.v. 6.

παραδιδόναι pres. act. inf. s.v. 64. Inf. w. μέλλω expressing near fut.

John 7

◆ **1 περιεπάτει** impf. ind. act. περιπατέω (# 4344) to walk, to conduct one's life, to pass one's time. Impf. of customary action (Barrett). **ἤθελεν** impf. ind. act. θέλω (# 2527) to will to desire, to want to, w. inf. **περιπατεῖν** pres. act. inf. **ἐζήτουν** impf. ind. act. ζητέω (# 2426) to seek, w. inf. Impf. pictures the progressive attitude (RWP). **ἀποκτεῖναι** aor. act. inf. ἀποκτείνω (# 650) to kill. Epex. inf. explaining what they were seeking to do. Perhaps this refers back to 5:18. ◆ **2 ἑορτή** (# 2038) feast, festival. **σκηνοπηγία** (# 5009) the setting up of tents or dwellings. For the popular, great, and holy Feast of Tabernacles s. SB, 2:774-812; Edersheim, *Temple*, 268-287; WZZT, 238-54; Jos., *Ant.*, 8:100; M, Sukkah; BBC; DJG, 235-41. This was one of the three great feasts. It lasted a week from 15 to 21 of Tishri (September / October). It concluded on the eighth day with a great celebration of music, dancing, and prayer for rain. It was a harvest festival for the grape, fruit, and olive crops. ◆ **3 μετάβηθι** aor. imp. act. μεταβαίνω (# 3553) to leave, to depart. Aor. imp. calls for a specific act w. a note of urgency. **ἐντεῦθεν** (# 1949) from here. **ὕπαγε** pres. imp. act. ὑπάγω (# 5632) to go. Pres. imp. of a vb. of motion. **ἵνα** (# 2671) w. the fut. ind. which may put a slight emphasis on the actuality of beholding (Morris). **θεωρήσουσιν** fut. ind. act. θεωρέω (# 2555) to see. The brothers want Jesus to show off His miraculous power in Jerusalem (Brown). ◆ **4 κρυπτῷ** dat. (# 3220) hidden, secret. **παρρησίᾳ** dat. (# 4244) open, public. "Public" was considered anything in the presence of ten Israelites (SB, 2:486). **φανέρωσον** aor. imp. act. φανερόω (# 5746) to manifest, to make clear. ◆ **5 ἐπίστευον** impf. ind. act. πιστεύω (# 4409) to believe. Impf. pictures the continual attitude. Though they believed that Jesus might be able to dazzle Jerusalem w. miracles, they themselves had not begun to perceive the meaning of what they had already beheld (Barrett). ◆ **6 καιρός** (# 2789) time, the suitable time, the favorite opportunity (Morris). **ἕτοιμος** (# 2289) ready, in the sense of present (BAGD). ◆ **7 μισεῖν** pres. act. inf. μισέω (# 3631) to hate. Compl. inf. w. the vb. **δύναται**. ◆ **8 ἀνάβητε** aor. imp. act. ἀναβαίνω (# 326) to go up, to ascend. Aor. imp. indicates the action should start. Perhaps Jesus uses a play on words w. the term "ascend" (Brown), or He simply is refusing to go w. the disciples at that time (Morris). **ταύτην** (# 4047) this, there, "this kind of feast"; not necessarily the particular feast, but this kind of feast to be received with applause (J Lightfoot). **πεπλήρωται** perf. ind. pass. πληρόω (# 4444) to fill, to fulfill. Resultative perf. showing that the state or results have not

yet arrived. ◆ **9 εἰπών** aor. act. part. (temp.) λέγω (# 3306) to say. Aor. suggests logically antecedent action. **ἔμεινεν** aor. ind. act. μένω (# 3531) to remain. ◆ **10 ἀνέβησαν** aor. ind. act. ἀναβαίνω s.v. 8. **φανερῶς** (# 5747) adv., openly. This is the exact opposite of what the brothers had desired (v. 4). ◆ **11 οὖν** (# 4036) temp. use, then. **ἐζήτουν** impf. ind. act. ζητέω s.v. 1. Iterat. impf., "continually sought him." ◆ **12 γογγυσμός** (# 1198) murmuring, complaint, grumbling. Perhaps here muttering, as of men who did not dare to speak plainly and loudly what they felt (Westcott). It may also convey the idea of dispute, since there was no agreement concerning Jesus. Based on Deut. 13 the charge was very serious (BBC). ◆ **13 μέντοι** (# 3530) particle, mostly adversative; though, to be sure, indeed, however (BAGD). **παρρησίᾳ** (# 4244) openly, boldly, w. confidence. The basic idea in the word is freedom of speech, when the word flowed freely (Morris; TLNT). **ἐλάλει** impf. ind. act. λαλέω (# 3281) to speak. ◆ **14 μεσούσης** pres. act. part. (temp.) μεσόω (# 3548) to be in the middle. Gen. abs. **ἀνέβη** aor. ind. act. s.v. 8. **ἐδίδασκεν** impf. ind. act. διδάσκω (# 1438) to teach. Incep. impf., "he began to teach." Instead of revealing himself through miracles and signs, Jesus reveals himself through his revelatory teaching. The temple courts were a common place for popular teachers (BBC). ◆ **15 ἐθαύμαζον** impf. ind. act. θαυμάζω (# 2513) to wonder, to marvel at. Impf. vividly describes the ongoing action. **γράμματα** (# 1207) letters, education. Refers particularly to rabbinical learning under another rabbi (Brown). **οἶδεν** perf. ind. act. οἶδα (# 3857) to know. Def. perf. w. pres. meaning. **μεμαθηκώς** perf. act. part. μανθάνω (# 3443) to learn, to study. Perf. emphasizes the status of his education, not having passed through the school of the master (Godet; BBC). ◆ **16 ἀπεκρίθη** aor. ind. pass. (dep.) ἀποκρίνομαι (# 646) to answer. **πέμψαντος** aor. act. part. (subst.) πέμπω (# 4287) to send. ◆ **17 θέλῃ** pres. subj. act. θέλω (# 2527) to want to, w. inf.; that is, "if it be any man's will to do His will" (Westcott). **γνώσεται** fut. mid. (dep.) ind. γινώσκω (# 1182) to know. **πότερον** (# 4538) interrogative used in a disjunctive question ("whether") (BAGD). ◆ **18 λαλῶν** pres. act. part. (subst.) λαλέω (# 3281) to speak. Pres. indicates contemporaneous action, "the one who presently speaks." **ζητῶν** pres. act. part. ζητέω s.v. 1. Adj. part. describes the character trait of the one who speaks the truth. Here in the sense of try to obtain, possess, desire. (BAGD). **πέμψαντος** aor. act. part. πέμπω (# 4287) to send. Aor. part. indicates logically or temporally antecedent action. ◆ **19 δέδωκεν** perf. ind. act. δίδωμι (# 1443) to give. Perf. emphasizes the result of the past giving and thus their present possession. **ζητεῖτε** pres. ind. act., w. inf. s.v. 1. **ἀποκτεῖναι** aor. act. inf. s.v. 1. ◆ **20 ἀπεκρίθη** aor. ind. pass. (dep.) s.v 16. ◆ **21 ἐν** ἔργον one work, a reference to the healing in John 5:1-15 (Brown). ἐποίησα aor. ind. act. ποιέω (# 4472) to do. ◆ **22** δέδωκεν perf. ind. act. δίδωμι s.v. 19. περιτομή (# 4364) circumcision. Here it is more than the simple rite, but all the work that is involved in preparing for and carrying out the rite (SB, 4:23-30; TDNT; RAC, 2:159-69; TRE, 5:714-24; NIDNTT; EDNT; BBC). ◆ **23** λυθῇ aor. pass. subj. λύω (# 3395) to loose, to break laws, to annul, to cancel (AS). Subj. w. ἵνα (# 2671) for purp. or perhaps result. This argumentation is from the lesser to the greater (SB, 2:488; b. Sabb 132a; Haenchen). χολᾶτε pres. ind. act. χολάω (# 5957) to be angry, to be enraged; preferring anger over defilement (MM; NDIEC, 4:175-76). ὑγιής (# 5618) well, healthy. ◆ **24** κρίνετε pres. imp. act. κρίνω (# 3212) to judge. Pres. imp. w. the neg. indicates the stopping of a action which is in progress. ὄψις (# 4071) appearance. They should recognize the true nature of the matter. ◆ **25** ἔλεγον impf. ind. act. λέγω (# 3306) to say. Incep. impf. he "began to say...." οὐχ (# 4024) neg. in a question expecting a positive answer. ζητοῦσιν pres. ind. act. s.v. 1. ἀποκτεῖναι aor. act. inf. s.v. 1. ◆ **26** ἴδε (# 2623) aor. imp. act. ὁράω to see. μήποτε (# 3607) whether, perhaps. "Can it be possible that...?" (Barrett). ἔγνωσαν aor. ind. act. γινώσκω (# 1182) to know; here in the sense of accept or approve. ◆ **27** πόθεν (# 4470) where, from where. ἔρχεται pres. mid. (dep.) subj. ἔρχομαι (# 2262) to come. Subj. w. ὅταν (# 4020) in an indef. temp. cl. The Jewish idea was that the Messiah would remain in some unknown place until He appeared to Israel (SB, 2:48-89; Carson; TFG, 283). ◆ **28** ἔκραξεν aor. ind. act. κράζω (# 3189) to cry out. Used by John to introduce solemn pronouncements (Barrett). διδάσκων pres. act. part. (temp.) διδάσκω (# 1438) to teach. ἐλήλυθα perf. ind. act. ἔρχομαι s.v. 27. Perf. emphasizing the present results of the past action. ἀληθινός (# 240) true; denotes genuineness. God is the ultimate reality (Barrett). πέμψας aor. act. part. πέμπω s.v. 18. Subst. part. to describe a characterizing trait. ◆ **29** ἀπέστειλεν aor. ind. act. ἀποστέλλω (# 690) to send, to send as an authoritative representative. ◆ **30** οὖν (# 4036) therefore. Because of His claim to be sent from God (Westcott). πιάσαι aor. act. inf. πιάζω (# 4389) to seize, to arrest. Compl. inf. w. vb. ἐζήτουν. ἐπέβαλεν aor. ind. act. ἐπιβάλλω (# 2095) to cast upon, to lay hands upon. ἐληλύθει plperf. ind. act. ἔρχομαι (# 2262) to come, here in the sense of arrive (John 4:5). ◆ **31** ἐπίστευσαν aor. ind. act. πιστεύω (# 4409) to believe. ἔλθῃ aor. subj. act. ἔρχομαι s.v. 27. Subj. w. ὅταν (# 4020) whenever. πλείονα comp. πολύς (# 4498) much, many; comp., more. ποιήσει fut. ind. act. ποιέω (# 4472) to do. ὧν gen. ὅς (# 4005); gen. of comp. ἐποίησεν aor. ind. act. ποιέω to do. The variant of the pres. appears to be a scribal correction (TC, 217). Const. aor. viewing the total action (s. M. de Jonge,

"Jewish Expectations about the 'Messiah' according to the Fourth Gospel," NTS 19 [1972]: 246-70). ◆ **32** ἄκουσαν aor. ind. act. ἀκούω (# 201) to hear. γογγύζοντος pres. act. part. γογγύζω (# 1197) to murmur. ὑπηρέτης (# 5677) attendant. Here temple police (Brown; BBC). πιάσωσιν aor. subj. act. πιάζω (# 4389) to arrest. Subj. w. ἵνα (# 2671) to express purp. ◆ **33** πέμψαντα aor. act. part. (subst.) s.v. 18. ◆ **34** ζητήσετε fut. ind. act. ζητέω (# 2426) to seek. εὑρήσετε fut. ind. act. εὑρίσκω (# 2351) to find. ἐλθεῖν aor. act. inf. ἔρχομαι (# 2262) to go. Compl. inf. ◆ **35** μέλλει pres. ind. act. μέλλω (# 3516) to be about to, w. inf. for the fut. (s. 6:6). διασποράν (# 1402) dispersion, diaspora. Jews living outside Palestine (TDNT; JPFC, 1:117-83, 183-215, 464-503). The following gen. describes the area of the dispersion (Schnackenburg). ◆ **36** εἶπεν aor. ind. act. λέγω (# 3306). ζητήσετε fut. ind. act. s.v. 1. ◆ **37** ἐσχάτῃ (# 2274) last. At dawn during the Feast of Tabernacles the priests took water from the Pool of Siloam in a golden vessel and brought it to the temple. As they approached the Water Gate the trumpets sounded–a short blast, a long one, then another short one. At the morning offering the water along w. wine was poured on the altar from two silver bowls. Perhaps at this time Jesus stood and cried out w. a loud voice (Edersheim, *The Temple*, 281f; Morris; SB, 2:799-805; WZZT, 243-45; Beasley-Murray; M, Sukkah 4:9-10; BBC). εἰστήκει plperf. ind. act. ἵστημι (# 2705) to stand. ἔκραξεν aor. ind. act. κράζω (# 3189) to cry out s.v. 28. διψᾷ pres. subj. act. διψάω (# 1498) to thirst. Subj. w. ἐάν (# 1569) in a 3rd. class cond. in which the cond. is viewed as possible. For more discussion s. B.H. Grisby, "'If Any Man Thirsts ...' Observations on the Rabbinic Background of John 7,37-39," Bib 67 (1986): 101-8. ἐρχέσθω pres. mid. (dep.) imp. 3rd. pers. sing. ἔρχομαι (# 2262) to come. For a convenient summary of the options and solutions s. Juan B. Cortes, "Yet Another Look at Jn 7, 37-38," CBQ 29 (1967): 79-84. πινέτω pres. imp. act. 3rd. sing. πίνω (# 4403) to drink. ◆ **38** πιστεύων pres. act. part. πιστεύω (# 4409) to believe. Subst. part. describing a necessary character trait. καθώς (# 2777) just as. For the use and construction s. Morris; Brown. ποταμοί nom. pl. ποταμός (# 4532) river. For the importance of water s. DJG, 869-70. κοιλίας (# 3120) stomach. Denotes the hidden, innermost recesses of the human body (BAGD). Here perhaps referring to the heart or the center of the person; s., for example, Prov. 4:23. ῥεύσουσιν fut. ind. act. ῥέω to flow. ζῶντος pres. act. part. (adj.) ζάω (# 2409) to live. ◆ **39** περὶ τοῦ πνεύματος concerning the Spirit. In a later rabbinical discussion regarding the playing of flutes by the ceremony of pouring out the water–if it takes precedent over the Sabbath–Rabbi Jehosua ben Levi connects the expression "House of Drawing Water" to Isa. 12:3 to indicate the "drawing of the Holy

Spirit" who produces joy (j. Sukkah, 5; WZZT, 245; BBC). ἔμελλον impf. ind. act. μέλλω to be about to; s.v. 35. λαμβάνειν pres. act. inf. λαμβάνω (# 3284) to take; compl. inf. πιστεύσαντες aor. act. part. πιστεύω (# 4409) to believe. οὐδέπω (# 4031) not yet. ἐδοξάσθη aor. ind. pass. δοξάζω (# 1519) to glorify. ◆ **40 ἀκούσαντες** aor. act. part. ἀκούω (# 201) to hear. ὁ προφήτης (# 4737) the prophet; s. John 6:14. ◆ **41 ἔλεγον** impf. ind. act. s.v. 25. Iterat. impf., indicating what various people were saying. μή (# 3590) neg. used to introduce a question expecting a neg. answer, "He is not … is he?" ◆ **42 οὐχ** (# 4024) neg. used to introduce a question expecting a positive answer. σπέρμα (# 5065) seed, ancestry. For the Messiah as a descendant of David and His birth in Bethlehem s. Cleon L. Rogers Jr., "The Promises to David in Early Judaism," *Bib Sac* 150 (1993): 285-302; Matt. 2:5-6; DJG, 766-69. ◆ **43 σχίσμα** (# 5388) division, split. ἐγένετο aor. ind. mid. (dep.) γίνομαι (# 1181) to become; here, arose. ◆ **44 ἤθελον** impf. ind. act. s.v. 1. πιάσαι aor. act. inf. πιάζω s.v. 32; compl. inf. ◆ **45 ἠγάγετε** aor. ind. act. ἄγω (# 72) to lead; here, to bring. ◆ **46 ἀπεκρίθησαν** aor. ind. pass. (dep.) s.v. 16. οὐδέποτε (# 4030) never, not at any time. ἐλάλησεν aor. ind. act. λαλέω (# 3281) to speak; const. aor. viewing the action as a whole. ◆ **47 πεπλάνησθε** perf. ind. pass. πλανάω (# 4414) to lead astray, to deceive. Perf. emphasizing the past deception which does not allow the recognition of the truth and its continuing results. ◆ **48 ἐπίστευσεν** aor. ind. act. πιστεύω (# 4409) to believe. ◆ **49 γινώσκων** pres. act. part. γινώσκω (# 1182) to know; here, in the sense of intimately acquainted, trained in. ἐπάρατος (# 2063) accursed. For examples of how the learned rabbis despised those who were not concerned w. the law s. SB, 2:494-519; Barrett; BBC. ◆ **50 ἐλθών** aor. act. part. nom. masc. sing. ἔρχομαι (# 2262) to go. Part. as subst., "the one who." ὤν pres. act. part. εἰμι (# 1639) to be. ◆ **51 ἀκούσῃ** aor. subj. act. ἀκούω (# 201) to hear. Subj. w. ἐάν (# 1569) to express a cond. γνῷ aor. subj. act. γινώσκω (# 1182) to know; here in the sense, to be informed. ◆ **52 ἐραύνησον** aor. imp. act. ἐραυνάω (# 2236) to search, to examine, to investigate completely (BAGD). ἴδε aor. imp. act. s.v. 26. ◆ **53 ἐπορεύθησαν** aor. ind. pass. (dep.) πορεύομαι (# 4513) to go. For a discussion of the text problem of this pericope s. TC, 219; Daniel B. Wallace, "Reconsidering 'The Story of Jesus and the Adultress Reconsidered'" *NTS* 39 (1993): 290-96, w. bibliography.

John 8

◆ **1 ἐπορεύθη** aor. ind. pass. (dep.) πορεύομαι (# 4513) to go. Const. aor. viewing the travel as a whole. ◆ **2 ὄρθρος** (# 3986) daybreak, early in the morning; gen. of time. παρεγένετο aor. ind. mid. (dep.) παραγίνομαι (# 4134) to come to. ἤρχετο impf. ind. mid.

(dep.) ἔρχομαι (# 2262) to come. **καθίσας** aor. act. part. (temp.) καθίζω (# 2767) to sit down. Aor. indicates antecedent action. ἐδίδασκεν impf. ind. act. διδάσκω (# 1438) to teach; incep. impf., "he began to teach." ◆ **3 μοιχεία** (# 3657) adultery. According to Lev. 20:10 and Deut. 22:22 adultery was punishable by death (SB, 2:519; for a discussion s. D. Lührmann, "Die Geschichte von einer Sünderin…," *NTS* 32 [1990]: 289-316). κατειλημμένην perf. pass. part. καταλαμβάνω (# 2898) to seize, to take often with hostile intent, catch, detect; esp. detection of adultery (BAGD). Perf. indicates "taken w. shame upon her." It points to her continuing character as an adulteress (Morris). It has been suggested that the husband set a deliberate trap in order to divorce her or have her stoned (LNT, 160-64; Morris). στήσαντες aor. act. part. ἵστημι (# 2705) to place, to stand. Aor. part. suggests the logically and temporally antecedent action to the following vb. ◆ **4 κατείληπται** perf. ind. pass. καταλαμβάνω to seize s.v. 3. αὐτοφώρῳ (# 900) (caught) in the act. Used of catching a thief or one in adultery (BAGD). μοιχευομένη pres. mid. part. μοιχεύομαι (# 3658) to commit adultery. Pres. suggests contemporaneous action to the main vb. They seized her just as adultery was in process. ◆ **5 ἐνετείλατο** aor. ind. mid. (dep.) ἐντέλλομαι (# 1948) to command. τοιαύτας (# 5525) such a one. λιθάζειν pres. act. inf. λιθάζω (# 3342) to stone. Inf. in indir. discourse. Only under the cond. of the persistence, after previous warning and after the actual witness of act by two competent witnesses, was one to be stoned for adultery (LNT, 160ff). ◆ **6 πειράζοντες** pres. act. part. πειράζω (# 4279) to tempt, to test, here in a neg. sense. He would violate either Roman law forbidding capital punishment or Jewish law contradicting Moses. ἔχωσιν pres. subj. act. ἔχω (# 2400) to have. Subj. to express purp. κατηγορεῖν pres. act. inf., w. the gen. κατηγορέω (# 2989) to accuse. Inf. as obj. They wanted to know if she could lawfully be stoned, under the circumstances (LNT, 174). κύψας aor. act. part. (circum.) κύπτω (# 3252) to stoop. δακτύλῳ dat. δάκτυλος (# 1235) finger. Writing w. the finger was symbolic of divine legislation (LNT, 177). Instr. dat. κατέγραφεν impf. ind. act. καταγράφω (# 2863) to write down, to register (MM). Incep. impf., "he began to write down." Perhaps he was beginning to register the complaints or accusations. It has been suggested that Jesus wrote down Exod. 23:1b about it being wrong to join w. the wicked; here, meaning the conspiracy against the woman (LNT, 175-82; BBC). ◆ **7 ἐπέμενον** impf. ind. act. ἐπιμένω (# 2152) to remain. Impf., "as they continued to stay." ἐρωτῶντες pres. act. part. (circum.) ἐρωτάω (# 2263) to ask. ἀνέκυψεν aor. ind. act. ἀνακύπτω (# 376) to raise oneself up, to stand erect, to look up. ἀναμάρτητος (# 387) without sin. Used generally of innocence (Hoskyns). βαλέτω aor. imp. 3rd. sing.

βάλλω (# 965) to throw. Jesus insists upon the innocence and therefore the competence of the accuser and witness (LNT, 182). In this sense he is asking that the law be followed. ◆ **8 κατακύψας** aor. act. part. (circum.) κατακύπτω (# 2893) to stoop down. **ἔγραφεν** impf. ind. act. γράφω (# 1211) write. Impf., "He continued writing." It is suggested that He wrote Exod. 23:7a, a command to keep away from a false matter and leave judgment and retribution to God (LNT, 138f). ◆ **9 ἀκούσαντες** aor. act. part. (subst.) ἀκούω (# 201) to hear. Aor. is logically antecedent to the main vb. **ἐξήρχοντο** impf. ind. act. mid. (dep.) ἐξέρχομαι (# 2002) to go out. Incep. or iterat. impf., "they began to go out and continued one by one." **ἀρξάμενοι** aor. mid. (dep.) part. ἄρχομαι (# 806) to begin. **κατελείφθη** aor. ind. pass. καταλείπω (# 2901) to leave alone. **οὖσα** pres. act. part. εἰμί (# 1639) to be. ◆ **10 ἀνακύψας** aor. act. part. (circum.) s.v. 7. **κατέκρινεν** aor. ind. act. κατακρίνω (# 2891) to condemn. ◆ **11 πορεύου** pres. mid. (dep.) imp. πορεύομαι (# 4513) to go. Pres. imp. w. a vb. of motion. **μηκέτι** (# 3600) no longer. **ἁμάρτανε** pres. imp. act. ἁμαρτάνω (# 279) to sin. She is a typical example of a forgiven sinner. Grace gives the chance to start over again (Becker). ◆ **12 αὐτοῖς** them. It can refer to the Pharisees and the crowds in the temple (RWP). **ἐλάλησεν** aor. ind. act. λαλέω (# 3281) to speak. **φῶς** (# 5890) light. For the meaning of this and the description of the Jewish ceremony of lighting the huge golden candlesticks at the Feast of the Tabernacles s. M, Sukkah 5:2-4; Barrett; BBC; Morris; 1QS 3:20; 4:8; 1QM 17:6; CD 5:18. **ἀκολουθῶν** pres. act. part. ἀκολουθέω (# 199) to follow, to follow as a disciple (TDNT). Subst. part. to express a necessary trait as well as a cond. **περιπατήσῃ** aor. subj. act. περιπατέω (# 4344) to walk, to walk about. Subj. w. double neg. for a strong denial. **ἕξει** fut. ind. act. ἔχω (# 2400) to have, obtain. ◆ **13 εἶπον** aor. ind. act. λέγω (# 3306) to say. ◆ **14 ἀπεκρίθη** aor. ind. pass. (dep.) ἀποκρίνομαι (# 646) to answer. In his answer Jesus now suggests that His is not the only testimony. **οἶδα** (# 3857) perf. ind. act. to know. Def. perf. w. pres. meaning. **πόθεν** (# 4470) where, from where. **ἦλθον** aor. ind. act. ἔρχομαι (# 2262). **ποῦ** (# 4544) where, where to. ◆ **15 κατά** (# 2848) w. the acc., according to. It gives the norm of judgment ("after the flesh") and draws attention to the imperfection of their judgment (Morris). ◆ **16 ἀληθινός** (# 240) true, verified, here in the sense of accurate (Brown; TLNT). **πέμψας** aor. act. part. (subst.) πέμπω (# 4287) to send. ◆ **17 γέγραπται** perf. ind. pass. γράφω (# 1211) to write. Perf. means "it stands written," suggesting legal authority (MM). ◆ **18 μαρτυρῶν** pres. act. part. μαρτυρέω (# 3455) to witness. Subst. part. as a pred. nom. Pres. indicates contemporaneous action. ◆ **19 ᾔδειτε** plperf. ind. act. οἶδα to know (s.v. 14). Plperf. in a contrary to fact cond. cl. ◆ **20 ῥῆμα**

(# 4839) speech. **ἐν** by, denoting nearness (Brown). **γαζοφυλάκιον** (# 1126) treasury. Probably situated in the Court of the Women (Barrett; BBC; Mark 12:41f; Luke 21:1f). **διδάσκων** pres. act. part. διδάσκω (# 1438) to teach. Temp. part. w. pres. indicates contemporaneous action. **ἐπίασεν** aor. ind. act. πιάζω (# 4389) to seize, to arrest. This comment shows that the time of the capture of Christ was divinely ordained and planned. **ἐληλύθει** plperf. ind. act. ἔρχομαι (# 2262) to come, to go. ◆ **21 ὑπάγω** (# 5632) pres. ind. act. to go away. Fut. pres. referring to His death (Carson). **ζητήσετε** fut. ind. act. ζητέω (# 2426) to seek; here, seek in the sense of follow. **ἀποθανεῖσθε** fut. ind. mid. (dep.) ἀποθνήσκω (# 633) to die. **ἐλθεῖν** aor. act. inf. ἔρχομαι s.v. 20. Compl. inf. w. vb. **δύνασθε**. The goal of the journey is the Father; the time will be after the ascension. ◆ **22 μήτι** (# 3614) Introduces a hesitant question, "You don't suppose … do you? (M, 170; Matt. 12:23). **ἀποκτενεῖ** fut. ind. act. ἀποκτείνω (# 650) to kill; here, due to the reflexive pron., in the sense of "to commit suicide" **ἑαυτόν** himself. Those who commit suicide are excluded from eternal life according to Jewish tradition (SB, 1:1027ff). ◆ **23 κάτω** (# 3004) below, beneath. **ἄνω** (# 539) above. Jewish t.t. for heavenly and earthly (Schnackenburg). Both terms are further explained in the v. ◆ **24 ὅτι** (# 4022) introducing the dir. discourse. **ἀποθανεῖσθε** fut. ind. mid. (dep.) s.v. 21. Dying in one's sin left no opportunity for repentance (BBC). **πιστεύσητε** aor. subj. act. πιστεύω (# 4409) to believe. Aor. means, "make an act of faith," "come to believe" (Morris). Subj. w. **ἐάν** (# 1569) in a 3rd. class cond. in which the possibility of the cond. is assumed. **ὅτι** (# 4022) gives the content of the belief or faith. ◆ **25 τὴν ἀρχήν** adverbial acc., from the beginning, at all. For this difficult construction s. Brown; Schnackenburg. ◆ **26 πέμψας** aor. act. part. (subst.) πέμπω (# 4287) to send. Aor. indicates antecedent action, "the one who has sent." ◆ **27 ἔγνωσαν** aor. ind. act. γινώσκω (# 1182) to know; here in the sense of fully recognize. **ἔλεγεν** impf. ind. act. λέγω (# 3306) to speak, to talk about. ◆ **28 ὑψώσητε** aor. subj. act. ὑψόω (# 5738) to lift up. A reference both to the cross and to the exaltation as well as the event of salvation (Barrett; TDNT). Subj. w. **ὅταν** (# 4020) in an indef. temp. cl. **γνώσεσθε** fut. ind. mid. (dep.) s.v. 27. **ἐδίδαξεν** aor. ind. act. διδάσκω (# 1438) to teach, instruct. ◆ **29 πέμψας** aor. act. part. s.v. 16. **ἀφῆκεν** aor. ind. act. ἀφίημι (# 918) to leave. Const. aor. **ἀρεστά** pl. ἀρεστός (# 744) verbal adj. of ἀρέσκω to please, "the things pleasing." ◆ **30 λαλοῦντος** pres. act. part. (temp.) λαλέω (# 3281) to speak. Gen. abs., giving necessary information to the cl., without being part of the cl. Pres. indicating contemporaneous action, "while he was speaking." **ἐπίστευσαν** aor. ind. act. s.v. 24. ◆ **31 πεπιστευκότας** perf. act. part. (adj.) s.v. 24. Perf. suggests the lasting effects of the past action. Perhaps referring to those who have made an outward profession (Morris; but s. also Schnackenburg). **μείνητε** aor. subj. act. μένω (# 3531) to remain. Those who are not fickle but genuine disciples remain in His teaching (Carson). Subj. w. **ἐάν** (# 1569) in a 3rd. class cond. w. some probability of fulfillment. **ἀληθῶς** (# 242) adv. truly. ◆ **32 γνώσεσθε** fut. ind. mid. (dep.) s.v. 27. **ἐλευθερώσει** fut. ind. act. ἐλευθερόω (# 1802) to free; liberation from sin, a synonym for salvation (Barrett). ◆ **33 ἀπεκρίθησαν** aor. ind. pass. (dep.) ἀποκρίνομαι s.v. 14. **δεδουλεύκαμεν** perf. ind. act. δουλεύω (# 1526) to be enslaved, to serve as a slave. Perf. w. the emphasis on the present results of the past action. There is a misunderstanding on their part or a play on words by Jesus. Jesus is speaking not of their social but of their spiritual cond. They have no need of a Savior since they consider themselves children of Abraham (BBC; Becker). While they are physically descents of Abraham, their actions are in stark contrast (DJG, 3-4, 6). **γενήσεσθε** fut. ind. mid. (dep.) γίνομαι (# 1181) to become. ◆ **34 ποιῶν** pres. act. part. ποιέω (# 4472) to do, to practice. Subst. part. describing the trait or class of those doing the action (SMT 56). ◆ **36 ἐλευθερώσῃ** aor. subj. act. s.v. 32. **ὄντως** (# 3953) really, actually. **ἔσεσθε** fut. ind. mid. εἰμί (# 1639) to be. ◆ **37 οἶδα** (# 3857) perf. ind. act. to know. Def. perf. w. a pres. meaning. **ἀποκτεῖναι** aor. act. inf. s.v. 22. Epex. inf. explaining ζητεῖτε. **ὅτι** (# 4022) because, giving the reason. **χωρεῖ** pres. ind. act. χωρέω (# 6003) to make room for, to contain. They have never really made room for His word at all (Tasker). Here fig. in the sense of open-hearted or comprehending (BAGD). ◆ **38 ἑώρακα** perf. ind. act. ὁράω (# 3972) to see. Perf. would seem to imply that Jesus had a preexistent vision which continues into the pres. (Brown). **ἠκούσατε** aor. ind. act. ἀκούω to hear s.v. 9. **ποιεῖτε** pres. ind./imp. act. ποιέω s.v. 34 (Westcott). ◆ **39 ἀπεκρίθησαν** aor. ind. pass. (dep.) ἀποκρίνομαι (# 646) to answer. **ἐστε** pres. ind. act. εἰμί (# 1639) to be. Ind. in a 1st. class cond. cl. in which the speaker assumes the reality of the cond. ◆ **40 ἀποκτεῖναι** aor. act. inf. s.v. 22. Compl. inf. **ἄνθρωπον** in apposition to με. **λελάληκα** perf. ind. act. λαλέω (# 3281) to speak. The resultative perf. indicates the past speech, but the effects of the speech linger on. ◆ **41 πορνείας** (# 4518) fornication, unlawful sexual relation. **γεγεννήμεθα** perf. ind. pass. γεννάω (# 1164) to bear; pass. to be born. Perf. stressing their continued existence based on the past act of birth. ◆ **42 ἠγαπᾶτε** impf. ind. act. ἀγαπάω (# 26) to love. Used in a contrary to fact cond. cl., "If God were your Father..." (but he is not). **ἐξῆλθον** aor. ind. act. ἐξέρχομαι (# 2002) to go out. **ἥκω** (# 2457) pres. ind. act. to come, to be pres. **ἐλήλυθα** perf. ind. act. ἔρχομαι to go, to come. **ἀπέστειλεν** aor. ind. act. ἀποστέλλω (# 690) to send, to send as an authoritative

representative (TDNT). If they loved the Father they would recognize His messenger. Their rejection of His revelation through his messenger demonstrates their rejection of the Father. ◆ **43 λαλιά** (# 3282) speech. Denotes the form of expression, the outward shape of the discourse (Morris). **γινώσκετε** pres. ind. act. γινώσκω (# 1182) to know; here in the sense of to recognize or accept. **λόγος** (# 3364) word. Signifies the content (Morris). **ἀκούειν** pres. act. inf. ἀκούω (# 201) to hear; here in the sense of obey or understand. Compl. inf. ◆ **44 διάβολος** (# 1333) slanderer, devil (DDD, 463-73; 1369-80). Their father stands in sharp contrast to the Father of Jesus (Becker; TFG, 303). For the construction here s. BD, 140. **ἐπιθυμία** (# 2123) desire; the deeds according to his desires; to act in accordance with the desires (BAGD). **πατρός** gen. πατήρ (# 4252) father gen. of source ("coming from the devil") or possibly gen. of quality ("devilish desires"). **ἀνθρωποκτόνος** (# 475) murderer. Because he robbed Adam of immortality (Barrett). **ἕστηκεν** impf. ind. act. στήκω (# 5112) to stand, to stand fast. For a discussion of the textual problem s. TC, 226. **λαλῇ** pres. subj. act. λαλέω (# 3281) to speak. Subj. w. indef. temp. cl. ("whenever"). **ψεῦδος** (# 6022) lie. **ψεύστης** (# 6026) liar. ◆ **45 ἐγὼ δέ** I on the other hand. Placed first for emphasis (Bernard). **πιστεύετε** pres. ind. act. πιστεύω (# 4409) to believe. Pres. describes their present state of belief. They give credence to a lie rather than the truth. ◆ **46 ἐλέγχει** pres. ind. act. ἐλέγχω (# 1794) to convict, to prove, to convince w. proof. ◆ **47 ὤν** pres. act. part. εἰμί (# 1639) to be. Pres. describes a contemporaneous action. Subst. part. to describe a trait. **ἐκ τοῦ θεοῦ** out of God. gen. of source. ◆ **48 ἀπεκρίθησαν** aor. ind. pass. (dep.) ἀποκρίνομαι (# 646) to answer. **καλῶς** (# 2822) adv., well. The meaning here is, "Are we not right in saying?" (Barrett). **Σαμαρίτης** (# 4901) Samaritan, as a derogatory term of disrespect (s. John 4:4; BBC). ◆ **49 ἀτιμάζετε** pres. ind. act. ἀτιμάζω (# 869) to dishonor; here in the sense of treat shameful, insult (BAGD). ◆ **50 ζητῶν** pres. act. part. ζητέω (# 2426) to seek. Part. as subst. **καί** (# 2779) and, also. **κρίνων** pres. act. part. (subst.) κρίνω (# 3212) to judge. ◆ **51 τηρήσῃ** aor. subj. act. τηρέω (# 5498) to guard, to keep, to observe. Subj. w. **ἐάν** in 3rd. class cond. assuming that it is possible to fulfill the cond. **θεωρήσῃ** aor. subj. act. θεωρέω (# 2555) to see. Here in the sense of experience death. Subj. w. double neg. **οὐ μή** (# 4024; 3590) for a strong denial. ◆ **52 ἐγνώκαμεν** perf. ind. act. s.v. 27. Perf. emphasizes the present state of knowledge, "now we know for sure." **ἀπέθανεν** aor. ind. act. ἀποθνῄσκω (# 633) to die. Const. aor. describing their death. **γεύσηται** aor. subj. mid. (dep.) γεύομαι (# 1174) to taste, w. obj. in gen. Here fig. in the sense of come to know (SB, 1:751ff; BAGD; NIDNTT, 2:271). ◆ **53 μείζων** (# 3505) comp. μέγας great; comp., greater. **πατρός** gen. πατήρ (# 4252) father. gen. of comp., "greater than the father." **ποιεῖς** pres. ind. act. ποιέω (# 4472) to do, here in the sense of make oneself out to be, to claim to be. ◆ **54 ἀπεκρίθη** aor. ind. pass. (dep.) s.v. 14. **δοξάσω** aor. subj. act. δοξάζω (# 1519) to glorify (TLNT; TDNT; EDNT). Subj. w. **ἐάν** (# 1569) in a 3rd. class cond. cl. which assumes the possibility of the cond. **δοξάζων** pres. act. part. Subst. part. ◆ **55 ἐγνώκατε** perf. ind. act. s.v. 27. Perf. indicates the continuing results. **εἴπω** aor. subj. act. λέγω (# 3306) to say. Subj. w. **κἄν** (# 2779; 323) in a 3rd. class cond. cl. assuming the possibility of the cond. **ἔσομαι** fut. ind. mid. εἰμί (# 1639). ◆ **56 ἠγαλλιάσατο** aor. ind. mid. (dep.) ἀγαλλιάω (# 22) to rejoice, to be overjoyed (Morris). This refers to the joy that results from salvation. Here Abraham anticipated it (EDNT). The basis for this may be a rabbinic interpretation of Gen. 17:17 (Philo, *De mut. nom.*, 154ff; TFG, 306-8; Haenchen; SB, 2:525-26). **ἴδη** aor. subj. act. ὁράω (# 3972) to see. Subj. w. **ἵνα** (# 2671) to express content of the seeing (IBG, 145f). **εἶδεν** aor. ind. act. ὁράω (# 3972) to see. **ἐχάρη** aor. ind. pass. (dep.) χαίρω (# 5897) to be glad, to rejoice. ◆ **57 ἑώρακας** perf. ind. act. ὁράω s.v. 56. ◆ **58 γενέσθαι** aor. inf. mid. (dep.) γίνομαι (# 1181) to become; to come into existence (Morris). Note the contrast w. ἐγὼ εἰμί, "I am" (D. M. Ball, *'I Am' in John's Gospel: Literary Function, Background, and Theological Implications* [Sheffield: Sheffield Academic Press, 1996]); (s. John 1:1; also TFG, 308-10). Inf. w. the prep. **πρίν** (# 4570) to express time ("before") (MT, 144). ◆ **59 ἦραν** aor. ind. act. αἴρω (# 149) to lift up, to pick up. Perhaps they picked up stones from the ongoing construction of the Temple (BBC). **βάλωσιν** aor. subj. act. βάλλω (# 965) to throw. Subj. w. **ἵνα** (# 2671) to express purp. **ἐκρύβη** aor. ind. pass. κρύπτω (# 3221) to hide, to conceal.

John 9

◆ **1 παράγων** pres. act. part. (temp.) παράγω (# 4135) to go by, to pass by. Pres. expresses contemporaneous action: "while he was passing by." **εἶδεν** aor. ind. act. ὁράω (# 3972) to see. **τυφλός** (# 5603) blind. He starts physically and spiritually blind, but ends his blindness (DJG, 81-82). **γενετή** (# 1162) birth. Thus there was no sin he actively participated in. This also indicates the severity of the illness (Becker). ◆ **2 ἠρώτησαν** aor. ind. act. ἐρωτάω (# 2263) to question, to ask. **λέγοντες** pres. act. part. λέγω (# 3306) to say. Part. used here as quotation marks to introduce the following dir. discourse. **ἥμαρτεν** aor. ind. act. ἁμαρτάνω (# 279) to sin. For the rabbis it was possible to sin while in the womb (SB, 2:528-30; J Lightfoot). **γονεῖς** (# 1204) parents. Thus he would be suffering for his parents' sin (BBC). **ἵνα** (# 2671) so that, expressing result (RG, 997f). **γεννηθῇ** aor. subj. pass. γεννάω (# 1164) to bear; pass. to be born. ◆ **3 ἀπεκρίθη** aor. ind. pass. (dep.)

ἀποκρίνομαι (# 646) to answer. **φανερωθῇ** aor. subj. pass. φανερόω (# 5746) to make clear, to manifest; here in the sense of to bring to the spotlight. Subj. w. **ἵνα** (# 2671) to express purp. ◆ **4 δεῖ** (# 1256) pres. ind. act. it is necessary, w. inf. giving a logical necessity. **ἐργάζεσθαι** pres. mid. (dep.) inf. ἐργάζομαι (# 2237) to work. Compl. inf. The acc. **ἡμᾶς** functions as the subject of the inf. **πέμψαντος** aor. act. part. (subst.) πέμπω (# 4287) to send. Aor. indicates antecedent action. **ἡμέρα** (# 2465) day; here meaning daylight in contrast to the darkness of the night. **ἔρχεται** pres. ind. mid. (dep.) ἔρχομαι (# 2262) to come. Pres. futuristic or predictive, "night will certainly come." **δύναται** pres. ind. pass. (dep.) δύναμαι (# 1538) to be able, w. inf. Gnomic pres. **ἐργάζεσθαι** pres. mid. (dep.) inf. ἐργάζομαι to work. Compl. inf. ◆ **5 ὦ** pres. subj. act. εἰμί (# 1639) to be, to be present. Subj. w. **ὅταν** (# 4020) in indef. temp. cl., "whenever I am present." The Light is to give guidance through revelation (s. John 1:4). ◆ **6 ἔπτυσεν** aor. ind. act. πτύω (# 4772) to spit. The curative value of saliva was highly esteemed in antiquity (Morris; Barrett). **χαμαί** (# 5912) on the ground. An old adv., either dat. or loc. (RWP). **ἐποίησεν** aor. ind. act. ποιέω (# 4472) to do, to make. **πηλός** (# 4384) mud, clay. For the forbidding of kneading on the Sabbath, s. M, Shabbath 7:2. **πτύσμα** (# 4770) saliva, spittle. **ἐπέχρισεν** aor. ind. act. ἐπιχρίω (# 2222) to anoint, to smear, spread an eye salve on the eyes. Used in a report of healing and also to describe the wax that receives the impression of the seal (BAGD; MM). For a discussion of the textual problem s. TC, 227-28. ◆ **7 ὕπαγε** pres. imp. act. ὑπάγω (# 5632) to go. Pres. imp. w. a vb. of motion. **νίψαι** aor. imp. act. νίπτω (# 3782) to wash, to wash one for myself, bathe in a pool (BAGD). Aor. usually indicates that the action should commence. This could be an authoritative imp. (JG, 319.) **κολυμβήθρα** (# 3148) pool. This pool was located in the Lower City close to the end of Hezekiah's underground conduit (BBC). **ἑρμηνεύεται** pres. ind. pass. ἑρμηνεύω (# 2257) to translate. **ἀπεσταλμένος** perf. pass. part. ἀποστέλλω (# 690) to send. It was from Siloam that the water used in the libations at the Feast of the Tabernacles was drawn (Barrett). **ἀπῆλθεν** aor. ind. act. ἀπέρχομαι (# 599) to go away. **οὖν** (# 4036) now, therefore, based on the command of Jesus. **ἐνίψατο** aor. ind. mid. νίπτω. **ἦλθεν** aor. ind. act. ἔρχομαι (# 2262) to come. **βλέπων** pres. act. part. βλέπω (# 1063) to see. Part. of manner, he returned as one who sees. ◆ **8 γείτονες** pl. γείτων (# 1150) neighbor. Often used to describe an adjacent locality. **θεωροῦντες** pres. act. part. (subst.) θεωρέω (# 2555) to see. Pres. indicates contemporaneous and continual action, "those who were seeing." **προσαίτης** (# 4645) beggar. **καθήμενος** pres. mid. (dep.) part. κάθημαι (# 2764) to sit. **προσαιτῶν** pres. act. part. προσαιτέω (# 4644) to ask from someone, to beg (MH, 324).

Pres. indicates he had his regular place and was a familiar figure (RWP). ◆ **9 ἔλεγον** impf. ind. act. λέγω (# 3306) to say. Iterat. impf. indicating the various things the different ones said. ◆ **10 ἠνεῴχθησαν** aor. ind. pass. ἀνοίγω (# 487) to open. Used here fig. ("to be able to see"). Const. aor. viewing the total process. ◆ **11 ἀπεκρίθη** aor. ind. pass. (dep.) ἀποκρίνομαι (# 646) to answer. **λεγόμενος** pres. pass. part. λέγω (# 3306) to call; pass. to be named. **ἐπέχρισεν** aor. ind. act. s.v. 6. **ὕπαγε** pres. imp. act. s.v. 7. **νίψαι** aor. imp. mid. (dir. mid. "wash oneself") s.v. 7. This is a dir. quotation of the commands of Jesus. **ἀπελθών** aor. act. part. ἀπέρχομαι (# 599) to go away. Aor. for both parts. describes antecedent action necessary for the action of the main vb. **νιψάμενος** aor. mid. (dir. mid.) part. s.v. 7. **ἀνέβλεψα** aor. ind. act. ἀναβλέπω (# 329) to see again. Ingressive aor. describes the beginning of his sight ("I began to see"). The addition of the prep. **ἀνα** (again) has the idea of restoration to a proper state; not that he had seen before, since he had been blind from birth. ◆ **12 οἶδα** (# 3857) perf. ind. act. to know. Def. perf. w. a pres. meaning. ◆ **13 ἄγουσιν** pres. ind. act. ἄγω (# 72) to lead. Hist. pres. giving a vivid description of the action. ◆ **14 ἦν** impf. ind. act. εἰμί (# 1639) to be. **ἐν ᾗ ἡμέρᾳ** the day on which. **ἐποίησεν** aor. ind. act. ποιέω (# 4472) to do, to make. **ἀνέῳξεν** aor. ind. act. ἀνοίγω (# 487) to open. ◆ **15 ἠρώτων** impf. ind. act. ἐρωτάω s.v. 2. Iterat. impf. emphasizes the repeated questioning, "they repeatedly asked." **ἀνέβλεψεν** aor. ind. act. ἀναβλέπω s.v. 11. **ἐπέθηκεν** aor. ind. act. ἐπιτίθημι (# 2202) to place. **ἐνιψάμην** aor. ind. mid. νίπτω s.v. 7. ◆ **16 ἁμαρτωλός** (# 283) sinful. This should be understood here to mean "mortal." **τοιαῦτα** pl. τοιοῦτος (# 5525) such a thing, such as this. **σχίσμα** (# 5388) division. ◆ **17 λέγουσιν** pres. ind. act. λέγω (# 3306) to say; hist. pres. **ἠνεῴξέν** aor. ind. act. ἀνοίγω s.v. 10. ◆ **18 ἐπίστευσαν** aor. ind. act. πιστεύω (# 4409) to believe. **ἐφώνησαν** aor. ind. act. φωνέω (# 5888) to call. **ἀναβλέψαντος** aor. act. part. ἀναβλέπω s.v. 11. Subst. part. to emphasize the newly acquired sight which precipitated the discussion. Gen. of relationship. ◆ **19 ἠρώτησαν** aor. ind. act. ἐρωτάω s.v. 2. This is to discredit the testimony of the blind man who was healed. **ἐγεννήθη** aor. ind. pass. γεννάω (# 1164) pass. to be born. **ἄρτι** (# 785) now (in contrast to your claims that he was born blind). ◆ **20 ἀπεκρίθησαν** aor. ind. pass. (dep.) s.v. 3. **ἐγεννήθη** aor. ind. pass. s.v. 2. ◆ **21 ἤνοιξεν** aor. ind. act. ἀνοίγω s.v. 10. **ἐρωτήσατε** aor. act. imp. ἐρωτάω s.v. 2. Aor. imp. calls for a specific act and suggests by implication they should stop asking them. It is amazing that in the whole discussion no one considers the great miracle or the benefits to the man who was previously blind. **ἡλικία** (# 2461) age, full age, to come to maturity, one who is 13 years and one day old (SB, 2:534). **λαλήσει** fut. ind. act. λαλέω (# 3281) to

speak. ◆ **22 ἐφοβοῦντο** impf. ind. mid. (dep.) φοβέομαι (# 5828) to fear. Mid. suggests that they were afraid of what would happen to them. **γάρ** (# 1142) because. This gives the reason for their fear. **συνετέθειντο** plperf. ind. mid. (dep.) συντίθημι (# 5338) to agree. Consummative plperf. emphasizes that the decision had been made at least before the conversation with the parents, more probably at the initiation of their investigation. **ὁμολογήσῃ** aor. subj. act. ὁμολογέω (# 3933) to confess. Subj. w. **ἐάν** (# 1569) in a 3rd. class cond. cl. where the cond. is viewed as possible. **ἀποσυνάγωγος** (# 697) to be excommunicated, to be separated from the synagogue (Brown; SB, 4:293-333). **γένηται** aor. subj. mid. (dep.) γίνομαι (# 1181) to become, to be. ◆ **23 ἡλικίαν ἔχει** to have age; to have (be) the age of legal maturity (BAGD). ◆ **24 δός** aor. imp. act. δίδωμι (# 1443) to give. Aor. imp. calls for a specific act w. a note of urgency. He should confess his guilt of associating with Jesus and accept the Sabbath Law (Becker). ◆ **25 ἀπεκρίθη** aor. ind. pass. (dep.) s.v. 3. **ὢν** pres. act. part. εἰμί (# 1639) to be. Concessive part. Pres. describing a previous, yet long-lasting state. ◆ **26 ἐποίησεν** aor. ind. act. s.v. 6. **σοι** dat. σύ (to you). Dat. of personal interest. ◆ **27 ἠκούσατε** aor. ind. act. ἀκούω (# 201) to hear. Used here not just of acoustically hearing, but accepting as true. **μή** (# 3590) Used in questions expecting a neg. answer. He recognizes their hostile attitude to Jesus. **γενέσθαι** aor. mid. (dep.) inf. γίνομαι s.v. 22. Compl. inf. ◆ **28 ἐλοιδόρησαν** aor. ind. act. λοιδορέω (# 3366) to abuse, to revile or harshly criticize, including curses and defamation (TDNT; TLNT). **μαθητής** (# 3412) disciple (TDNT; EDNT). ◆ **29 λελάληκεν** perf. ind. act. λαλέω s.v. 21; here in the sense of "reveal." **πόθεν** (# 4470) from where. ◆ **30 θαυμαστός** (# 2515) wonderful, remarkable. **ἤνοιξέν** aor. ind. act. ἀνοίγω s.v. 10. ◆ **31 θεοσεβής** (# 2538) devout, God-fearing. **ᾖ** pres. subj. act. εἰμί (# 1639) to be. Subj. w. **ἐάν** (# 1569) expresses cond. **ποιῇ** pres. subj. act. ποιέω (# 4472) to do. ◆ **32 ἠκούσθη** aor. ind. pass. ἀκούω (# 201) to hear. **ἠνεῴξέν** aor. ind. act. ἀνοίγω s.v. 10. The fact that there was a miracle indicates that God answered the prayers of Jesus; thus he is devout and God-fearing (Becker). **γεγεννημένου** perf. pass. part. s.v. 2. Perf. here describes antecedent action with the emphasis on the resulting state. ◆ **33 ἠδύνατο** imp. ind. pass. (dep.) δύναμαι (# 1538) to be able. Used in a contrary to fact cond. cl. (RG, 922f, 1014ff). **ποιεῖν** pres. act. inf. ποιέω s.v. 31. Compl. inf. to the main vb. ◆ **34 ἀπεκρίθησαν** aor. ind. pass. (dep.) s.v. 3. **ἐγεννήθης** aor. ind. pass. γεννάω s.v. 2. **ὅλος** (# 3910) totally, pred. nom. (RWP). **ἐξέβαλον** aor. ind. act. ἐκβάλλω (# 1675) to throw out; here in the sense of excommunicated from the synagogue. ◆ **35 ἐξέβαλον** aor. ind. act. ἐκβάλλω s.v. 34. **εὑρών** aor. act. part. (temp.) εὑρίσκω (# 2351) to find. ◆ **36 καί** (# 2779) Used to introduce the apodosis, which here is a question and has the force "who then" (under the circumstances set forth in the protasis) (BD, 227). **πιστεύσω** aor. subj. act. πιστεύω s.v. 18. Subj. w. **ἵνα** (# 2671) describing the result. ◆ **37 ἑώρακας** perf. ind. act. ὁράω (# 3972) to see. Perf. emphasizes the continuing results. "You have seen and still are seeing." **λαλῶν** pres. act. part. λαλέω s.v. 21. Part. describes the ongoing action of speaking. ◆ **38 ἔφη** impf. ind. act. φημί (# 5774) to say, to speak. **προσεκύνησεν** impf. ind. act. προσκυνέω (# 4686) to worship. Incep. impf., "he began to worship." The act of bowing down to worship is used in John 4:20-24 to describe the worship due to God (Brown). ◆ **39 βλέποντες** pres. act. part. βλέπω (# 1063) to see. Pres. describes contemporaneous action. Concessive part., "even though they cannot see, can see." **βλέπωσιν** pres. subj. act. βλέπω. **γένωνται** aor. subj. mid. (dep.) γίνομαι (# 1181) to become, to be. ◆ **40 ἄκουσαν** aor. ind. act. ἀκούω (# 201) to hear. **ὄντες** pres. act. part. εἰμί (# 1639) to be. **μή** (# 3590) expecting a neg. answer: "We are not blind, are we?" ◆ **41 ἦτε** pres. subj. act. εἰμί (# 1639) to be. **εἴχετε** impf. ind. act. ἔχω (# 2400) to have. Used in a contrary to fact cond. cl. The addition of **ἄν** (# 323) produces the effect of italicizing εἰ (# 1623) (M, 200). Here there is a play on words. They are blind to their sin in the belief they can see. Those who are blind and recognize their need see how one truly is before God.

John 10

◆ **1 εἰσερχόμενος** pres. mid. (dep.) part. εἰσέρχομαι (# 1656) to go in. Subst. part. Pres. to describe an action that is a characteristic trait. **αὐλή** (# 885) courtyard, sheepfold; here seemingly a yard in front of the house, surrounded by a stone wall probably topped w. briers (Brown; BBC). **ἀναβαίνων** pres. act. part. (subst.) ἀναβαίνω (# 325) to go up, to climb over. **ἀλλαχόθεν** (# 249) from another place. He does not use the acceptable entrance (Becker). **κλέπτης** (# 3095) thief, one who steals. **λῃστής** (# 3334) robber, bandit. The combination may denote a readiness to engage in violence as well as dishonesty (Morris). In both cases their intentions are less than ideal.   ◆ **2 ποιμήν** (# 4478) shepherd (TDNT; NIDNTT; Ezek. 34). The main responsibility of the shepherd was to keep the flock intact, to protect and to provide for the sheep. Jesus' mission is marked by a caring concern, even willingness, to die for the sheep (ABD, 5:1187-90; DJG, 751-53). Though John portrays the shepherd's devotion to duty, they were generally despised (NIDNTT; JTJ, 305-12; PAP, 147-48).   ◆ **3 θυρωρός** (# 2601) doorkeeper. Perhaps an undershepherd or one fold served more than one flock and had an independent porter (Barrett). **ἴδια** pl. ἴδιος (# 2625) one's own. **φωνεῖ** pres. ind. act. φωνέω (# 5888) to call. **κατ' ὄνομα** (# 2848; 3950) by

name. Eastern shepherds commonly give names to their sheep, descriptive of some trait or characteristic of the animal (Bernard). ◆ **4 ἐκβάλῃ** aor. subj. act. ἐκβάλλω (# 1675) to drive out. The word has an air of force (Morris). Subj. w. **ὅταν** (# 4020) in an indef. temp. cl. ("whenever"). **ἔμπροσθεν** (# 1869) w. the gen., before, in front of. **οἴδασιν** perf. ind. act. οἶδα (# 3857) to know. Def. perf. w. pres. meaning. Here in the sense of recognize and follow him. They will find rest and security with him. ◆ **5 ἀλλότριος** (# 259) stranger. **οὐ μή** (# 4024; 3590) strong neg., certainly not! (GGBB, 468-69). **ἀκολουθήσουσιν** fut. ind. act. ἀκολουθέω (# 199) to follow, w. obj. in dat. **φεύξονται** fut. ind. mid. (dep.) φεύγω (# 5771) to flee. The sheep do not recognize his voice, nor does he demonstrate concern for the sheep. ◆ **6 παροιμία** (# 4231) proverb, parable (Barrett). **ἔγνωσαν** aor. ind. act. γινώσκω (# 1182) to know, to recognize. Const. aor., describing their lack of understanding during the whole conversation. **ἐλάλει** impf. ind. act. λαλέω (# 3281) to speak. Impf. describes the antecedent action. ◆ **7 θύρα** (# 2598) door, gate. Jesus is the door through which the sheep pass and the door through which alone men can rightly approach the sheep (Hoskyns). **τῶν προβάτων** gen. pl. πρόβατον (# 4585) sheep. Obj. gen., "for the sheep." ◆ **8 ἦλθον** aor. ind. act. ἔρχομαι (# 2262) to come. **ἤκουσαν** aor. ind. act. ἀκούω (# 201) to hear. Here in the sense of obey. For a discussion of the case of the obj. s. BD, 95. ◆ **9 εἰσέλθῃ** aor. subj. act. εἰσέρχομαι (# 1656) to enter into. Subj. w. **ἐάν** (# 1569) in a 3rd. class cond. cl. viewing the cond. as possible ("some may enter"). **σωθήσεται** fut. ind. pass. σῴζω (# 5392) to save, to rescue. Here in the sense of being safely within the confines of the shepherd's protection, not just in the confines of the shelter. **ἐξελεύσεται** fut. ind. mid. (dep.) ἐξέρχομαι (# 2002) to go out. **νομή** (# 3786) pasture. **εὑρήσει** fut. ind. act. εὑρίσκω (# 2351) to find. For the requirement of sheep's food and water s. ABD, 6:1127. ◆ **10 εἰ μή** (# 1623; 3590) except. **κλέψῃ** aor. subj. act. κλέπτω (# 3096) to steal. Subj. w. **ἵνα** (# 2671) here gives the purp. of the coming. It is selfish and self-serving, instead of out of concern for the sheep. **θύσῃ** aor. subj. act. θύω (# 2604) to slaughter, to kill for food (Morris). **ἀπολέσῃ** aor. subj. act. ἀπόλλυμι (# 660) to destroy. The word includes injury of a violent nature, destruction, and ruin (NIDNTT). They do not allow the sheep to fully develop. This is the commentary of Christ on the present leaders of Israel. **ἔχωσιν** pres. subj. act. ἔχω (# 2400) to have. **περισσόν** (# 4356) abundance, superfluous, more than is really necessary (Sanders); "have it to the full," "to have a surplus" (Bernard). ◆ **11 καλός** (# 2819) good, beautiful, in the sense of ideal or model of perfection (Brown; Barrett); this in contrast to the previous shepherds. **τίθησιν** pres. ind. act. τίθημι (# 5502) to place. **ὑπέρ** (# 5642)

w. gen., on behalf of, for the benefit of. This means to place one's life at risk on behalf of the sheep (Becker). ◆ **12 μισθωτός** (# *3638*) a hired man, one paid to do his work (Morris). **ὤν** pres. act. part. nom. masc. sing. εἰμί (# *1639*) to be. Pres. part. here used as a subst. to describe a characterizing trait. **λύκος** (# *3380*) wolf; used here to connote danger. **ἐρχόμενον** pres. mid. (dep.) part. acc. masc. sing. ἔρχομαι (# *2262*) to come. Part. used here to vividly portray the approaching danger. **ἀφίησιν** pres. ind. act. ἀφίημι (# *918*) to forsake, to leave. Hist. pres.: to vividly portray the action. **ἁρπάζει** pres. ind. act. ἁρπάζω (# *773*) to snatch, to seize, to take suddenly and vehemently, to drag away. Often used to describe violence and speed (TDNT). **σκορπίζει** pres. ind. act. σκορπίζω (# *5025*) to scatter. ◆ **13 μέλει** pres. ind. act. μέλλω (# *3508*) w. dat. **αὐτῷ** (# *899*) to be of concern to someone. ◆ **14 γινώσκουσι** pres. ind. act. γινώσκω (# *1182*) to know; here, not just an intellectual awareness, but a mutual relationship (Haenchen). This is a frequent picture of a proper relationship w. God (Hos. 6:6; Jer. 31:34). ◆ **16 δεῖ** (# *1256*) pres. ind. act. it is necessary, one must (w. the inf.) **ἀγαγεῖν** aor. act. inf. ἄγω (# *72*) to lead. Compl. inf. **ἀκούσουσιν** fut. ind. act. ἀκούω (# *201*) to listen to. **γενήσονται** fut. ind. mid. (dep.) γίνομαι (# *1181*) to become, to be. **ποίμνη** (# *4479*) flock. ◆ **17 λάβω** aor. subj. act. λαμβάνω (# *3284*) to take, to receive. Subj. w. **ἵνα** (# *2671*) to express purp. (Barrett). ◆ **18 αἴρει** pres. ind. act. αἴρω (# *149*) to take away. Despite its early support, the alternate reading ἦρεν (aor. from the same vb.) does not have the widespread distribution as the other reading (TC, 231). **ἐξουσία** (# *2026*) authority (Schnackenburg). **θεῖναι** aor. act. inf. τίθημι (# *5502*) to lay down. **λαβεῖν** aor. act. inf. λαμβάνω s.v. 17. Compl. inf. to complete the main vb. **ἔλαβον** aor. ind. act. λαμβάνω. ◆ **19 σχίσμα** (# *5388*) division, split. **ἐγένετο** aor. ind. mid. (dep.) γίνομαι s.v. 16; here, to arise. ◆ **20 μαίνεται** pres. ind. mid. (dep.) μαίνομαι (# *3419*) to rage, to rave, to be mad. It was Jewish belief that demons could cause violent, insane behavior (ABD, 2:140-41; DDD, 452-53). ◆ **21 δαιμονιζομένου** pres. mid. part. gen. masc. sing. δαιμονίζω (# *1227*) to be possessed w. an evil spirit. For the Jewish view of demons s. SB, 4:501-35. One who has a demon was not to be listened to (TDNT). **μή** (# *3590*) used in hesitant questions expecting the answer "no." **ἀνοῖξαι** aor. act. inf. ἀνοίγω (# *487*) to open. Compl. inf. ◆ **22 ἐγένετο** aor. ind. mid. (dep.) γίνομαι s.v. 16. **ἐγκαίνια** (# *1589*) renewal, rededication. Used here for the Feast of Dedication or Hanukkah commemorating the cleansing and dedication by the Maccabees (1 Macc. 4:36-59; 2 Macc. 10:1-8; Edersheim, *Temple*, 333-36; Jerry R. Lancaster and R. Larry Overstreet, "Jesus' Celebration of Hanukkah in John 10," *Bib Sac* 152 [1995]: 318-33; BBC). **χειμών** winter. The eight-day feast began on the 25th of the month

of Kislev (December). This is called by Josephus the Feasts of Lights (Jos., *Ant.*, 12:319-326). The great candelabrum was brought into the Temple. Its lamps were lit so that they gave light in the Temple (2 Macc. 1:8; 10:3; J. VanderKam, "Hannukah: Its Timing and Significance According to 1 and 2 Maccabees," *JSP* 1 [1987]: 23-40; ABD, 2:123-25). ◆ **23 περιεπάτει** impf. ind. act. περιπατέω (# *4344*) to walk about. Progressive impf. picturing the walking in progress, or iterat. impf. picturing the repeated walking with occasional stops and starts. **στοᾷ** (# *5119*) porch w. columns (Edersheim, *Temple*, 43f; Acts 3:11; 5:12; JPB, 64-68; DJG, 812-13; BBC). ◆ **24 ἐκύκλωσαν** aor. ind. act. κυκλόω (# *3240*) to encircle. **οὖν** (# *4036*) then; temp. use of the particle. **ἕως πότε** how long? **αἴρεις** pres. ind. act. αἴρω (# *149*) to lift up. s.v. 18. Here "to hold in suspense"; lit., "to take away our life" (Brown). **εἶ** pres. ind. act. εἰμί to be. The cond. is phrased in such a way that the statement is assumed to be true. **εἰπέ** aor. imp. act. λέγω (# *3306*) to say. Aor. imp. calls for a specific act w. a note of urgency. **παρρησίᾳ** (# *4244*) adv., openly, plainly. The answer should be a simple "yes" or "no" so that they can understand. ◆ **25 ἀπεκρίθη** aor. ind. pass. (dep.) ἀποκρίνομαι (# *646*) to answer. **εἶπον** aor. ind. act. λέγω s.v. 24. Const. aor. describing his past relationship (in word and deed) with them as a revelation of his true identity. ◆ **27 ἀκολουθοῦσιν** pres. ind. act. ἀκολουθέω (# *199*) to follow, here in the sense of obey. Pres. tenses here are customary or habitual. This is the expected action of the sheep. ◆ **28 ἀπόλωνται** aor. subj. mid. ἀπόλλυμι (# *660*) to be lost. **ἁρπάσει** fut. ind. act. ἁρπάζω (# *773*) to drag away s.v. 12. **ἐκ τῆς χειρός** gen. fem. sing. Gen. of separation, "out of the hand." **πατρός** gen. masc. sing. πατήρ (# *4252*) father. Gen. of possession, "of the Father." ◆ **29 δέδωκεν** perf. ind. act. δίδωμι (# *1443*) to give. Perf. indicates the resulting state from the past action. **πάντων** gen. πᾶς all; gen. of comparison. **μεῖζον** (# *3505*) comp. μέγας large, big; comp., greater. Here perhaps "powerful." **ἁρπάζειν** pres. act. inf. ἁρπάζω s.v. 28. Compl. inf. ◆ **30 ἕν** (# *1651*) n., one thing. Identity is not asserted, but essential unity is (Morris). ◆ **31 ἐβάστασαν** aor. ind. act. βαστάζω (# *1002*) to take up. **πάλιν** (# *4099*) again (s. 8:59). **λιθάσωσιν** aor. subj. act. λιθάζω (# *3342*) to stone. Subj. w. **ἵνα** (# *2671*) expresses purp. They wanted to stone him for blasphemy. This is the reaction to his open answer as they had requested in John 10:24. ◆ **32 ἔδειξα** aor. ind. act. δείκνυμι (# *1259*) to show. **ποῖος** (# *4481*) which kind of. **λιθάζετε** pres. ind. act. λιθάζω s.v. 31. Pres. is either tendential ("you want to stone me?") or conative ("you are attempting to stone me"). ◆ **33 ἀπεκρίθησαν** aor. ind. pass. (dep.) ἀποκρίνομαι s.v. 25. **περί** (# *4309*) w. gen. used with vbs. of charging, censuring, judging to express cause, on account of, because of (BAGD). **ὧν** pres. act. part. s.v. 12. Concessive part., "even though you are a man." ◆ **34 γεγραμμένον** perf. pass. part. nom. n. sing. γράφω (# *1211*) to write. For a discussion of the quotation from Ps. 82:6 s. A.T. Hanson, "John's Citation of Psalm 82 in John 10:33-36," *NTS* 11 (1964/65): 158-62; "John's Citation of Ps 82 Reconsidered," *NTS* 13 (1966/67): 363-67; SB, 2:539-41; OTN, 21-37, esp. 33; HSB, 279-80. If rulers are called gods in the Hebrew Scriptures, how much more does one who authenticates himself by miracles have this right (Becker). **εἶπα** aor. ind. act. λέγω (# *3306*) to say. ◆ **35 λυθῆναι** aor. pass. inf. λύω (# *3395*) to break, to set aside, to nullify (Brown). Comp. inf. to the main vb. **γραφή** (# *1210*) Scripture. It means any particular passage of Scripture (Lindars). ◆ **36 ἡγίασεν** aor. ind. act. ἁγιάζω (# *39*) to set apart, to sanctify, to consecrate. The -άζω ending suggests to make holy. Here to set apart for a specific task (TDNT; EDNT) **ὅν** rel. pron., whom. Used in the rel. cl. which is an acc. of reference (Barrett). **ἀπέστειλεν** aor. ind. act. ἀποστέλλω (# *690*) to send. ◆ **37 ποιῶ** pres. ind. act. ποιέω (# *4472*) to do. Ind. in a 2nd. class cond. where the cond. is assumed to be true. ◆ **38 πιστεύητε** pres. subj. act. πιστεύω (# *4409*) to believe, w. obj. in dat. Subj. in a 3rd. class cond. cl. w. **κἄν** (# *2779; 323*) where the cond. is viewed as possible. **πιστεύετε** pres. imp. act. Imp. here is an invitation; pres. is gnomic. **γνῶτε** aor. subj. act. γινώσκω (# *1182*) to know. Aor. indicates "that ye may come to know" (Morris). Subj. w. **ἵνα** (# *2671*) indicates purp. **γινώσκητε** pres. subj. act. γινώσκω; and keep on knowing (Morris). ◆ **39 ἐζήτουν** impf. ind. act. ζητέω (# *2426*) to seek. Iterat. impf. to describe their repeated attempts to stone him. "They repeatedly sought to stone him." **πιάσαι** aor. inf. act. πιάζω (# *4389*) to seize. **ἐξῆλθεν** aor. ind. act. ἐξέρχομαι (# *2002*) to go out, here in the sense of escape. **χειρός** gen. fem. sing. χείρ (# *5931*) hand, used here fig. as power. ◆ **40 ἀπῆλθεν** aor. ind. act. ἀπέρχομαι (# *599*) to go away. **πέραν** (# *4305*) w. the gen., the other side. **βαπτίζων** pres. act. part. βαπτίζω (# *966*) to baptize. Pres. part. indicates contemporaneous action to the main vb. Here the action is in the past. **ἔμεινεν** aor. ind. act. μένω (# *3531*) to remain, to stay. ◆ **41 ἦλθον** aor. ind. act. ἔρχομαι (# *2262*) to come, to go. **ἐποίησεν** aor. ind. act. ποιέω s.v. 37. **ἀληθής** (# *239*) true. Here in the sense of accurate. ◆ **42 ἐπίστευσαν** aor. ind. act. πιστεύω s.v. 38.

John 11

◆ **1 ἀσθενῶν** pres. act. part. ἀσθενέω (# *820*) to be weak, to be sick. Part. used in a periphrastic construction. ◆ **2 ἀλείψασα** aor. act. part. ἀλείπω (# *230*) to anoint (s. 12:1-8.) **μύρῳ** dat. μύρον (# *3693*) ointment, perfume. **ἐκμάξασα** aor. act. part. ἐκμάσσω (# *1726*) to wipe. Perhaps a proleptic aor. from this event, but past

from the event of writing (Haenchen). **θριξίν** dat. pl. θρίξ (# *2582*) hair. Instr. dat., "with her hair." **ἠσθένει** impf. ind. act. ἀσθενέω s.v. 1. The type of illness is not mentioned, but it is clearly fatal (Becker). ◆ **3 ἀπέστειλαν** aor. ind. act. ἀποστέλλω (# *690*) to send. **ἴδε** (# *2623*) aor. imp. act. ὁράω to see. ◆ **4 ἀκούσας** aor. act. part. (temp.) ἀκούω (# *201*) to hear. Aor. indicates antecedent action, "after Jesus had heard." **πρὸς θάνατον** w. a view to death. This construction is more reassuring, indicating the sickness is not dangerous (Bernard). **δοξασθῇ** aor. subj. pass. δοξάζω (# *1519*) to glorify. Subj. w. **ἵνα** (# *2671*) expresses purp. Const. aor. shows that through all the following action God is glorified. This could also be a proleptic aor.: "God will certainly be glorified." Then the reference is not just to the illness, but to the future resurrection of Lazarus. ◆ **5 ἠγάπα** impf. ind. act. ἀγαπάω (# *26*) to love. This statement is necessary to heighten the contrast between his attitude of love and concern and his lack of action. ◆ **6 ἤκουσεν** aor. ind. act. ἀκούω (# *201*) to hear. **ἔμεινεν** aor. ind. act. μένω (# *3531*) to remain. ◆ **7 ἔπειτα** (# *2083*) then. **ἄγωμεν** pres. subj. act. ἄγω (# *72*) to go. Hortatory subj., "let us go." **πάλιν** (# *4099*) again. ◆ **8 ἐζήτουν** impf. ind. act. ζητέω (# *2426*) to seek. **λιθάσαι** aor. act. inf. λιθάζω (# *3342*) to stone. Compl. inf. to the main vb. ◆ **9 ἀπεκρίθη** aor. ind. pass. (dep.) ἀποκρίνομαι (# *646*) to answer. **περιπατῇ** pres. subj. act. περιπατέω (# *4344*) to walk, to walk about. Subj. w. **ἐάν** (# *1569*) in 3rd. class cond. cl. where the cond. is considered possible. **προσκόπτει** pres. ind. act. προσκόπτω (# *4684*) to stumble and consequently suffer harm. Used of the blind and of the darkness of night (Tob. 11:10; Prov. 3:23; Jer. 13:16; BAGD). It is tacitly assumed that if a man can see he can avoid the obstacles and thus avoid falling. This is particularly true given the narrow and stony roads in Palestine (Haenchen). The point here is that Jesus is aware of the short time before his approaching fall. He is clearly aware of the plans to terminate him (TDNT). Gnomic pres. ◆ **11 κεκοίμηται** perf. ind. pass. κοιμάω (# *3121*) to sleep, to fall asleep. Perf. emphasized the pres. state. The word is used here as a euphemism for death (Brown). **ἐξυπνίσω** aor. subj. act. ἐξυπνίζω (# *2030*) to awake someone out of sleep. Subj. with **ἵνα** (# *2671*) expresses purp. The disciples do not realize that the cost of giving life is Jesus' death (BBC). ◆ **12 εἶπαν** aor. ind. act. λέγω (# *3306*) to say. **κεκοίμηται** perf. ind. pass. κοιμάω (# *3121*) to sleep, to fall asleep. Cond. cl. assumes that he has died. **σωθήσεται** fut. ind. pass. σῴζω (# *5392*) to rescue, to recover from illness (Barrett). ◆ **13 εἰρήκει** plperf. ind. act. λέγω s.v. 12. Plperf. expresses antecedent action. **ἔδοξαν** aor. ind. act. δοκέω (# *1506*) to suppose. **κοιμήσις** (# *3122*) sleep. **ὕπνου** gen. ὕπνος (# *5678*) sleep; gen. of description or possibly obj. gen. (RWP). ◆ **14 τότε** (# *5538*) then. **παρρησία**

(# 4244) openly, without a fig. expression, which could be misunderstood (Haenchen). ἀπέθανεν aor. ind. act. ἀποθνήσκω (# 633) to die. Const. aor. simply stating the fact of his death. ◆ **15** πιστεύσητε aor. subj. act. πιστεύω (# 4409) to believe. Aor. points to a single act ("to come to have faith") (Brown). Subj. w. ἵνα (# 2671) giving the result. This cl. gives the result of Christ not being present. ἤμην impf. ind. act. εἰμί (# 1639) to be present. ἄγωμεν pres. subj. act. ἄγω (# 72) to lead. Here intr., to go (BAGD). Hortatory subj., "let us go." ◆ **16** λεγόμενος pres. pass. part. λέγω s.v. 12. Here "who is called" or "with the name." συμμαθητής (# 5209) fellow-disciple. Ind. obj. ἄγωμεν s.v. 15. ◆ **17** ἐλθών aor. act. part. (temp.) ἔρχομαι (# 2262) to come, to go. Aor. indicates antecedent action, "when he had come." εὖρεν aor. ind. act. εὑρίσκω (# 2351) to find. τέσσαρας ἡμέρας acc. of measure, answering the question how long? "For 4 days." The soul stayed near the body for three days (SB, 2:544). Thus there was no hope for Lazarus (Haenchen). ἔχοντα pres. act. part. (circum.) ἔχω (# 2400) to have; here act. intr., to be, to be situated (BAGD). Pres. expressing contemporaneous action. ◆ **19** ἐληλύθεισαν plperf. ind. act. ἔρχομαι s.v. 17. Plperf. expresses antecedent action with an emphasis on the result. "They had come and were there." παραμυθήσωνται aor. subj. mid. (dep.) παραμυθέομαι (# 4170) to comfort, to console. Subj. w. ἵνα (# 2671) expresses purp. For the Jewish custom s. SB, 4:592-607; LT, 2:316-20. ◆ **20** ὑπήντησεν aor. ind. act. ὑπαντάω (# 5636) to meet. ἐκαθέζετο impf. ind. mid. (dep.) καθέζομαι (# 2757) to sit, to be sitting down. ◆ **21** εἶπεν aor. ind. act. λέγω (# 3306) to say, to speak. οὖν (# 4036) then. ἦς impf. ind. act. εἰμί (# 1639) to be. Used in a contrary to fact cond. cl.: "If you had been here, but you were not, then my brother would not have died, but he did." They believed in the power of Jesus to perform a miracle, but they did not contemplate his power to raise the dead. For them his power stopped where a doctor's ability ceases (Becker). ἀπέθανεν aor. ind. act. ἀποθνήσκω (# 633) to die. ◆ **22** οἶδα perf. ind. act. (# 3857) to know. Def. perf. w. a pres. meaning. αἰτήσῃ aor. subj. act. αἰτέω (# 160) to ask. Subj. with ἄν (# 323) generalizes ("whatever"). δώσει fut. ind. act. δίδωμι (# 1443) to give. ◆ **23** ἀναστήσεται fut. ind. mid. (dep.) ἀνίστημι (# 482) to rise. For Jewish references to the resurrection s. Barrett; DJG, 677-78. ◆ **24** ἀναστήσεται fut. ind. mid. (dep.) s.v. 23. ◆ **25** πιστεύων pres. act. part. πιστεύω (# 4409) to believe. Part. used as subst. ("anyone who"). ἀποθάνῃ aor. subj. act. s.v. 21. Subj. w. κἄν in 3rd. class cond. cl. expressing concession ("although he dies") (RWP). ζήσεται fut. ind. mid. (dep.) ζάω (# 2409) to live. ◆ **26** ζῶν pres. act. part. ζάω s.v. 25. πιστεύων pres. act. part. πιστεύω s.v. 25. ἀποθάνῃ aor. subj. act. s.v. 21. ◆ **27** πεπίστευκα perf. ind. act. s.v. 25. Perf. indicates a faith once given and perma-

nently remaining (Morris). ὅτι (# 4022) gives the content of the faith. ἐρχόμενος pres. mid. (dep.) part. ἔρχομαι (# 2262) to come. Subst. use of the part. to give a characteristic or trait. ◆ **28** εἰποῦσα aor. act. part. (temp.) λέγω s.v. 21. Aor. indicates antecedent action. ἀπῆλθεν aor. ind. act. ἀπέρχομαι (# 599) to go away. ἐφώνησεν aor. ind. act. φωνέω (# 5888) to call. λάθρα (# 3277) secretly. πάρεστιν pres. ind. act. πάρειμι (# 4205) to be present. ◆ **29** ἠγέρθη aor. ind. pass. ἐγείρω (# 1586) to raise; pass. to rise. ταχύ (# 5444) quickly. ἤρχετο impf. ind. mid. (dep.) ἔρχομαι (# 2262) to come, to go. ◆ **30** ἐληλύθει plperf. ind. act. s.v. 17. ὑπήντησεν aor. ind. act. ὑπαντάω (# 5636) to meet. ◆ **31** ὄντες pres. act. part. εἰμί (# 1639) to be. παραμυθούμενοι pres. mid. (dep.) part. (temp.) παραμυθέω s.v. 19. Pres. shows contemporaneous action. ἰδόντες aor. act. part. (temp.) ὁράω (# 3972) to see. Aor. shows antecedent action. ἀνέστη aor. ind. act. ἀνίστημι (# 482) to stand up, to get up. ἐξῆλθεν aor. ind. act. ἐξέρχομαι (# 2002) to go out. ἠκολούθησαν aor. ind. act. ἀκολουθέω (# 199) to follow. δόξαντες aor. act. part. δοκέω (# 1506) to think, to suppose. Aor. indicates antecedent action. Causal part., "because they supposed that." κλαύσῃ aor. subj. act. κλαίω (# 3081) weep, to cry. Subj. w. ἵνα (# 2671) expresses purp. ◆ **32** ἦλθεν aor. ind. act. ἔρχομαι s.v. 17. ἰδοῦσα aor. act. part. (temp.) ὁράω s.v. 31. Aor. indicates antecedent action. ἔπεσεν aor. ind. act. πίπτω (# 4406) to fall. λέγουσα aor. act. part. λέγω s.v. 21. ἦς impf. ind. act. εἰμί s.v. 21. ἀπέθανεν aor. ind. act. s.v. 21. ◆ **33** εἶδεν aor. ind. act. ὁράω s.v. 31. κλαίουσαν pres. act. part. κλαίω s.v. 31. Pres. part. indicates contemporaneous action; she was crying then. συνελθόντας aor. act. part. συνέρχομαι (# 5302) to go together, to go w. someone. Subst. part. w. art. Aor. indicates the antecedent action ("who had come together"). ἐνεβριμήσατο aor. ind. mid. (dep.) ἐμβριμάομαι (# 1839) to snort as an expression of anger, to be moved w. the deepest emotions, to express violent displeasure (MM). Perhaps the anger was at what was looked on as a manifestation of Satan's kingdom of evil (Brown). ἐτάραξεν aor. ind. act. ταράσσω (# 5429) to shake, to trouble, to be disturbed, to shudder. His own emotion and the experience from which it is His purp. to deliver men (J Lightfoot). ◆ **34** τεθείκατε perf. ind. act. τίθημι (# 5502) to place, to lay. Consummative perf. indicates the completion of the action in the past. ἔρχου pres. imp. mid. (dep.) ἔρχομαι (# 2262) to come. Imp. is a polite request. Pres. suggests that the action of Jesus coming should continue. ἴδε (# 2623) aor. imp. act. ὁράω to see. Aor. imp. suggests the beginning of the action; he should start looking. ◆ **35** ἐδάκρυσεν aor. ind. act. δακρύω (# 1233) to shed tears. Aor. suggests "he burst into tears" (Morris). ◆ **36** ἴδε aor. imp. act. ὁράω s.v. 34. Aor. suggests that they should start to see. This is used to call attention to the tears of Christ.

ἐφίλει impf. ind. act. φιλέω (# 5797) to love. ◆ **37** ἐδύνατο impf. ind. pass. (dep.) δύναμαι (# 1538) to be able. Here this describes Jesus' ability to heal and restore. ἀνοίξας aor. act. part. ἀνοίγω (# 487) to open. Aor. used to describe antecedent action. Subst. part. to describe Jesus' characteristic of healing. ποιῆσαι aor. act. inf. ποιέω (# 4472) to do. The following cl. expresses their hoped-for action. οὗτος (# 4047) this one, referring to Lazarus. ἀποθάνῃ aor. subj. act. ἀποθνῄσκω (# 633) to die. Subj. w. ἵνα (# 2671) to express purp. or to give the content of the action. ◆ **38** πάλιν (# 4099) again, a second time. ἐμβριμώμενος pres. mid. part. ἐμβριμάομαι (# 1839) to snort as an expression of anger s.v. 33. μνημεῖον (# 3646) grave. This is the response to the invitation in v. 34. σπήλαιον (# 5068) cave, probably w. a horizontal shaft which was used as a grave (Barrett). ἐπέκειτο impf. ind. mid. (dep.) (# 2130) ἐπίκειμαι pass. to lie upon, to cover (BAGD; MM). ◆ **39** ἄρατε aor. imp. act. αἴρω (# 149) to take away. Aor. indicates that they should start removing the stone. Imp. here expresses a positive command. The stone would be extremely heavy in order to keep beasts of prey out of the tomb (J Lightfoot; BBC). τετελευτηκότος perf. act. part. τελευτάω (# 5462) to come to an end, to lose one's life, thus to die (NIDNTT). Subst. part. emphasizing the specific, that he has died. Perf. emphasizes the continuing results of the past. Gen. describes the family relationship. ὄζει pres. ind. act. ὄζω to smell, to give off an odor pleasant or unpleasant. "By this time the smell must be offensive" (BAGD). This indicates the hopelessness of the situation. There is no life, the body already decaying. ◆ **40** οὐκ (# 4024) neg. in a question expecting the answer "yes." πιστεύσῃς aor. subj. act. πιστεύω (# 4409) to believe. Subj. w. ἐάν (# 1569) in a 3rd. class cond. cl. in which the cond. is viewed as possible. ὄψῃ aor. ind. act. ὁράω (# 3972) to see; perhaps here to observe in action. ◆ **41** ἦραν aor. ind. act. αἴρω s.v. 39, lit., lifting up the stone. ἦρεν aor. ind. act. Here lifting up the eyes toward heaven in prayer; cf. Ps. 123:1; Isa. 51:6. ἤκουσας aor. ind. act. ἀκούω (# 201) to hear. Proleptic aor. The answer to the prayer is still future–the resurrection of Lazarus–but the certainty of the outcome is underscored w. the aor. ◆ **42** ᾔδειν plperf. ind. act. οἶδα (# 3857) to know. περιεστῶτα perf. act. part. περιΐστημι (# 4325) perf. to stand about, to stand around. Perf. part. here is used with a present meaning to describe the presence of the crowd. ◆ **43** φωνῇ (# 5889) sound, voice. Instr. dat., "with a loud voice." ἐκραύγασεν aor. ind. act. κραυγάζω (# 3198) to shout. δεῦρο (# 1306) adv. of place used as an imp.: here! Jesus' command is wonderfully succinct: "Here! Outside!" (Morris). ◆ **44** τεθνηκώς perf. act. part. θνῄσκω (# 2569) to die; perf. to be dead. Subst. part. to emphasize the fact that he is dead. Perf. indicates the results of the death; i.e., that he is dead.

This then forms the stark contrast to the vb. Even though he is dead he still walks. δεδεμένος perf. pass. part. δέω (# 1313) to bind. Perf. suggests the result of the past binding; the circum. use of the part. indicates his cond. while he walked. For a discussion of this binding s. BBC. τοὺς πόδας καὶ τὰς χεῖρας acc. of reference with respect to "hand and foot." κειρία (# 3024) bandage, grave clothes. Instr. dat. "with grave clothes." ὄψις (# 4071) face. σουδάριον (# 5051) (Latin) napkin, a cloth used for wiping off perspiration. There is some reason to think that only the faces of the poor were covered in this way (Barrett). περιεδέδετο plperf. ind. pass. περιδέω (# 4317) to bind about, to bind around. λύσατε aor. imp. act. λύω (# 3395) to loose. Both imps. suggest a command for the action to begin. ἄφετε aor. imp. act. ἀφίημι (# 918) to release, to let go; i.e., from the bandages that held him. ◆ **45** ἐλθόντες aor. act. part. (adj.) ἔρχομαι s.v. 17. Aor. describes the antecedent aor. Both parts. may express either a temp. or causal relationship. θεασάμενοι aor. mid. (dep.) part. θεάομαι (# 2517) to see, to behold, to view. They had come and were there to be eyewitnesses to the miracle. ἐποίησεν aor. ind. act. ποιέω (# 4472) to do. ἐπίστευσαν aor. ind. act. πιστεύω (# 4409) to believe. ◆ **46** ἀπῆλθον aor. ind. act. ἀπέρχομαι (# 599). ◆ **47** συνήγαγον aor. ind. act. συνάγω (# 5251) to summon together, to call together. συνέδριον (# 5284) Sanhedrin, the supreme council made up of the most powerful and influential leaders at a particular time (TDNT; ABD, 5:975-80; BBC; DJG, 728-32. For a more technical discussion s. A. Buechler, *The Political and Social Leaders of the Jewish Community of Sepphoris in the Second and Third Centuries* [London, 1909]; S.B. Hoenig, *The Great Sanhedrin* [Philadelphia, 1953]; H. Mantel, *Studies in the History of the Sanhedrin* [Cambridge: Harvard U. Press, 1961]). ποιοῦμεν pres. ind. act. ποιέω s.v. 45. "What are we now doing?" It implies the answer "nothing" (Barrett). ὅτι (# 4022) because. It is impossible to deny the miracle (Haenchen). ◆ **48** ἀφῶμεν aor. subj. act. ἀφίημι s.v. 44. Subj. with ἐάν (# 1569) expresses a cond. πιστεύσουσιν fut. ind. act. πιστεύω s.v. 45. ἐλεύσονται fut. ind. mid. (dep.) ἔρχομαι (# 2262) to come; here in a fig. sense of coming in a hostile manner. ἀροῦσιν fut. ind. act. αἴρω s.v. 39. Here, take away in a hostile manner to destroy. ◆ **49** ὤν pres. act. part. εἰμί (# 1639) to be. ἐνιαυτός (# 1929) year, "that fateful year" (Morris) i.e., the year of Christ's death; gen. of time (MT, 235). It may be ironic showing the power of the Romans to depose him (BBC). ◆ **50** συμφέρει pres. ind. act. συμφέρω (# 5237) it is profitable, it is to one's advantage. ἀποθάνῃ aor. subj. act. ἀποθνῄσκω (# 633) to die. Subj. w. ἵνα (# 2671) expresses the content of his hope or prophesy. ὑπέρ (# 5642) w. gen., on behalf of, or for the benefit of is probably what Caiaphas meant. Yet the use of this prep. suggests not just benefit, but substitution. **ἀπόληται** aor. subj. mid. (dep.) ἀπόλλυμι (# 660) to perish. Subj. can express the result. More probably it is parallel to the preceding cl., expressing the content of the hope. The high priest is attempting to maintain his political standing (Haenchen; DJG, 635-36; ABD, 1:803-806). ◆ **51 ἀφ' ἑαυτοῦ** not on his own account; i.e., intentionally. **ἐπροφήτευσεν** aor. ind. act. προφητεύω (# 4736) to prophecy. For unintentional prophecy among the rabbis s. Hoskyns; SB, 2:546. **ὅτι** (# 4022) gives the content of the prophecy. **ἔμελλεν** impf. ind. act. μέλλω (# 3516) to be about to; s. 6:6. **ἀποθνῄσκειν** pres. act. inf. ἀποθνῄσκω s.v. 50. Compl. inf. to main vb. ◆ **52 ἔθνους** gen. n. sing. ἔθνος (# 1620) nation. **διεσκορπισμένα** perf. pass. part. (adj.) διασκορπίζω (# 1399) to scatter. Perf. suggests not just the past action, but the lingering results of this action; they were scattered in the past and remain that way even up to the time of writing. Sin scatters men, but salvation in Christ brings them together (Morris). **συναγάγῃ** aor. subj. act. συνάγω (# 5251) to gather. Used here of gathering something that is scattered afar. Used literally of the harvest; here, perhaps of the harvest at the end of the age (NIDNTT). ◆ **53 οὖν** (# 4036) then, now (DM, 253). **ἐβουλεύσαντο** aor. mid. (dep.) ind. βουλεύομαι (# 1086) to will, to take counsel. Const. aor. portrays their plans over a period of time as a whole. That which had been a desire before now becomes a settled plan (Westcott). **ἵνα** (# 2671) introduces the content of their plan. **ἀποκτείνωσιν** aor. subj. act. ἀποκτείνω (# 650) to kill. Subj. w. ἵνα to express purp. ◆ **54 οὖν** (# 4036) therefore. Denotes a much stricter sequence of thought than is common in this Gospel (Morris). **παρρησίᾳ** (# 4244) openly. Dat. of manner. **περιεπάτει** impf. ind. act. περιπατέω (# 4344) to walk about. Incep. impf., "from that day on he could no longer walk about openly." **ἀπῆλθεν** aor. ind. act. ἀπέρχομαι (# 599) to walk away, to depart. **λεγομένην** pres. pass. part. λέγω (# 3306) to say, to call; pass. to have the name; Adj. part. connotes, "which is called," "with the name." ◆ **55 πάσχα** (# 4247) Passover s. John 2:13; Matt. 26:2. **ἀνέβησαν** aor. ind. act. ἀναβαίνω (# 326) to go up. This is in accordance with the Jewish practice of pilgrimage (WZZT). **ἁγνίσωσιν** aor. subj. act. ἁγνίζω (# 49) to sanctify, to purify (Brown). Subj. w. ἵνα (# 2671) to express purp. ◆ **56 ἐζήτουν** impf. ind. act. ζητέω (# 2426) to seek. Incep. impf., "they began to seek Jesus." Here the people seek Jesus, while the fears of v. 8 become reality in v. 57. **ἑστηκότες** perf. act. part. ἵστημι (# 2705) to stand. Temp. part., "while they were standing." **δοκεῖ ὑμῖν** lit., "what does it seem to you?" or "what do you think?" **ἔλθῃ** aor. subj. act. ἔρχομαι (# 2262) to come. Subj. w. double neg. **οὐ μή** (# 4024; 3590) suggests strong doubt (RWP; GGBB, 468-69). **ἑορτή** (# 2038) feast, referring to the Passover. ◆ **57 δεδώκεισαν** plperf. ind. act. δίδωμι (# 1443) to give (or is-

sue). Plperf. may indicate the permanent nature of the order (Morris). **γνῷ** aor. subj. act. γινώσκω to know. Subj. w. **ἐάν** (# 1569) in a 3rd. class cond. where the μηνύω (# 3606) to make known, to report; to give information to the authorities (MM). Subj. w. **ἵνα** (# 2671) to express the content of the order. **ὅπως** (# 3968) to express purp. (BD, 186f). **πιάσωσιν** aor. subj. act. πιάζω (# 4389) to seize, to arrest. Subj. w. **ἵνα** (# 2671) to express purp.

John 12

◆ **1 πρό** (# 4574) before. For the use of the prep. here s. M, 100f. **ἐξ ἡμερῶν τοῦ πάσχα** "six days before the Passover." This may be given to show that there was over a week of examination of the true Passover lamb, namely, Jesus. For a discussion of the chronology s. DJG, 119-22. **ἦλθεν** aor. ind. act. ἔρχομαι (# 2262) to come. **ἤγειρεν** aor. ind. act. ἐγείρω (# 1586) to raise. ◆ **2 ἐποίησαν** aor. ind. act. ποιέω (# 4472) to do, to make; here to prepare. **δεῖπνον** (# 1270) banquet (SB, 4:611-39). **διηκόνει** impf. ind. act. διακονέω (# 1354) to minister, to serve tables. **ἀνακειμένων** pres. mid. (dep.) part. ἀνάκειμαι (# 367) to recline at the table. ◆ **3 λαβοῦσα** aor. act. part. nom. fem. sing. λαμβάνω (# 3284) to take. Part. of attendant circumstance. Aor. indicates antecedent action, "she had taken." **λίτρα** (# 3354) a (Roman) pound (12 ounces) (BAGD). An extravagant amount (BBC). **μύρου** gen. μύρον (# 3693) nard, ointment of nard (Pliny, NH, 12:42-44). It could cost 100 denarii a pound. **νάρδος** (# 3726) spikenard, a fragrant oil derived from the root and spike (hair stem) of the nard plant which grows in the mountains of northern India (Brown). **πιστικός** (# 4410) fit to be trusted, genuine (MH, 379f). **πολύτιμος** (# 4501) of great worth, expensive. This was an expression of her great love for Jesus. **ἤλειψεν** aor. ind. act. ἀλείφω (# 230) to anoint. **ἐξέμαξεν** aor. ind. act. ἐκμάσσω (# 1726) to wipe off, to dry off. **ἐπληρώθη** aor. ind. pass. πληρόω (# 4444) to fill. **ὀσμή** (# 4011) odor. **μύρου** gen. of source. ◆ **4 μέλλων** pres. act. part. μέλλω (# 3516) to be about to (s. John 6:6). Adj. part. to show Judas' actions in a certain light. **παραδιδόναι** pres. act. inf. παραδίδωμι (# 4140) to betray. Compl. inf. "who was about to betray." ◆ **5 ἐπράθη** aor. ind. pass. πιπράσκω (# 4405) to sell. **δηνάριον** (# 1324) denarius. A Roman silver coin worth normally about 18 cents. A workman's average daily wage (BAGD). Thus an average worker would need approximately ten months to earn this much. **ἐδόθη** aor. ind. pass. δίδωμι (# 1443) to give, to donate. ◆ **6 πτωχῶν** pl. πτωχός (# 4777) poor. Pl. to describe a class of people. **ἔμελεν** impf. ind. act. μέλει (# 3508) to have concern for, w. dat. Customary impf. to describe his longstanding practice–that is, he never was concerned for the poor. **γλωσσόκομον** (# 1186) a small box or case; originally one for the mouthpiece of a flute (Morris; MM). ἔχων pres. act. part. (temp.) ἔχω (# 2400) to have, to hold. Pres. part. used to describe contemporaneous action; that is, while he was holding the bag he said this. βαλλόμενα pres. pass. part. acc. neut. pl. βάλλω (# 965) to throw, to put. Subst. use of the part. to describe the money contributed to the common purse. ἐβάσταζεν impf. ind. act. βαστάζω (# 1002) to carry, to take away, to steal (BS, 257). ◆ **7** ἄφες aor. imp. act. ἀφίημι (# 918) to leave alone. Aor. imp. here describes the beginning of a categorical command for action, which in itself is durative: "Start leaving her alone." ἐνταφιασμός (# 1947) preparation for burial. τηρήσῃ aor. subj. act. τηρέω (# 5498) to keep. Subj. to express purp., "that she might keep" (Brown). ◆ **9** ἔγνω aor. ind. act. γινώσκω (# 1182) to know. ἦλθον aor. ind. act. ἔρχομαι (# 2262) to come, to go. ἴδωσιν aor. subj. act. ὁράω (# 3972) to see. Subj. w. ἵνα (# 2671) expresses the purp. for their coming. ◆ **10** ἐβουλεύσαντο aor. ind. mid. (dep.) βουλεύομαι (# 1086) to take counsel. ἀποκτείνωσιν aor. subj. ind. ἀποκτείνω (# 650) to kill. The subj. w. ἵνα (# 2671) expresses the content of their decision. ◆ **11** ὑπῆγον impf. ind. act. ὑπάγω (# 5634) to go. Here it means that many of the Jews left their former Jewish allegiance and way of life to become disciples (Barrett). ἐπίστευον impf. ind. act. πιστεύω to believe. Iterat. impf. pictures the repeated action, while the incep. impf. would emphasize the beginning of the action. ◆ **12** ἐλθών aor. act. part. (temp.) ἔρχομαι s.v. 9. Aor. describing the antecedent action, "when the crowd had come." The sing. views them as a collective subject. ἀκούσαντες aor. act. part. ἀκούω (# 201) to hear. The pl. emphasizes the actions of individuals. Aor. part. also shows antecedent action. Temp. or causal part.: "when they heard" or "because they heard." ◆ **13** ἔλαβον aor. ind. act. λαμβάνω (# 3284) to take; here in the sense of cut and take into their hand. βαία pl. βάϊον (# 961) palm branch. φοινίκων pl. φοῖνιξ (# 5836) palm tree; the palm branches of the palm tree (RWP). To carry palms was a mark of triumphant homage to a victor or a king (Bernard; s. also W.R. Farmer, "The Palm Branches in John 12:13," *JTSt* 3 (1952): 62-66; DJG, 857-58. ἐξῆλθον aor. ind. act. ἐξέρχομαι (# 2002) to go out. ὑπάντησις (# 5637) meeting. The special idea of the word was official welcome of a newly arrived dignitary (M, 14). ἐκραύγαζον impf. ind. act. κραυγάζω (# 3198) to shout. Incep. impf., "they began to cry out," or iterat. impf., "they continually cried out." ὡσαννά (# 6057) hosanna (Matt. 21:9). This is the beginning of the references to Ps. 118 which appear throughout the last week of Christ's earthly life. εὐλογημένος perf. pass. part. nom. masc. sing. εὐλογέω (# 2328) to bless, to attribute power to (NIDNTT; TDNT). Part. here is used as an imp., though it is not related to any vb. in the context. ἐρχόμενος pres. mid. (dep.) part. ἔρχομαι s.v. 9. Subst. use of the part. Pres.

describes the ongoing action. The following phrase "king of Israel" is a further explanation of the one who is coming. ἐν ὀνόματι (# 1877; 3950) "in the name of" suggests the power and authority as an authorized representative. ◆ **14** εὑρών aor. act. part. εὑρίσκω (# 2351) to find. It could mean "to find after a search" or "to find by agency of others" (Barrett). ὀνάριον (# 3942) dimin. donkey. ἐκάθισεν aor. ind. act. καθίζω (# 2767) to sit down. ◆ **15** φοβοῦ pres. imp. mid. (dep.) φοβέομαι (# 5828) to fear. Pres. imp. is to stop an action in progress or to forbid an attitude. πῶλος (# 4798) colt, young animal, young donkey. ὄνος (# 3952) donkey. καθήμενος pres. mid. (dep.) part. κάθημαι (# 2764) to sit down. Attendant part. ("He was sitting") or temp. part. ("while he was sitting"). ◆ **16** ἔγνωσαν aor. ind. act. γινώσκω (# 1182) to know. ἐδοξάσθη aor. ind. pass. δοξάζω (# 1519) to glorify (TLNT). ἐμνήσθησαν aor. ind. pass. (dep.) μιμνήσκομαι (# 3630) to remember. γεγραμμένα perf. pass. part. nom. neut. pl. γράφω (# 1211) to write. ἐποίησαν aor. ind. act. ποιέω (# 4472) to do, to happen. ◆ **17** ἐμαρτύρει impf. ind. act. μαρτυρέω (# 3455) to give testimony to, to bear witness. Iterat. impf. pictures the continual action and they proclaimed what had been done as testimony to the power of Jesus (Barrett). οὖν (# 4036) then, now, indicating a succession of events (DM, 253). ὤν pres. act. part. εἰμί (# 1639) to be. Pres. part. denotes a continued action antecedent to that of the principal vb. (SMT, 58). ἐφώνησεν aor. ind. act. φωνέω (# 5888) to call. ἤγειρεν aor. ind. act. ἐγείρω (# 1586) to raise. Const. aor., viewing all the surrounding actions as a whole. ◆ **18** ὑπήντησεν aor. ind. act. ὑπαντάω (# 5636) to meet. ἤκουσαν aor. ind. act. ἀκούω (# 201) to hear. πεποιηκέναι perf act. inf. ποιέω s.v. 16. Compl. inf. to the main vb. ἤκουσαν explaining what they had heard. Perf. emphasizes the continuing results of the past action. ◆ **19** εἶπαν aor. ind. act. λέγω (# 3306) to say. θεωρεῖτε pres. imp. act. θεωρέω (# 2555) to see. ἀπῆλθεν aor. ind. act. ἀπέρχομαι (# 599) to go out. ◆ **20** Ἕλλην (# 1818) a Greek; Greeks by birth (Schnackenburg), or those of non-Jewish birth (Barrett). ἀναβαινόντων pres. act. part. (adj.) ἀναβαίνω (# 326) to go up. προσκυνήσωσιν aor. subj. act. προσκυνέω (# 4686) to worship. Subj. w. ἵνα (# 2671) expresses the purp. of their travel to Jerusalem. For the worship of half proselytes s. SB, 2:548-51. ◆ **21** προσῆλθον aor. ind. act. προσέρχομαι (# 4665) to come to, to go to. ἠρώτων impf. ind. act. ἐρωτάω (# 2263) to ask, to make a request. λέγοντες pres. act. part. λέγω s.v. 19. ἰδεῖν aor. act. inf. ὁράω (# 3972) to see. Compl. inf. to the main vb. θέλομεν. ◆ **23** ἐλήλυθεν perf. ind. act. ἔρχομαι s.v. 9. Perf. emphasizes the past action and the continuing present results. δοξασθῇ aor. subj. pass. s.v. 16. ◆ **24** κόκκος (# 3133) seed, grain. πεσών aor. act. part. (circum.) πίπτω (# 4406) to fall.

ἀποθάνῃ aor. subj. act. ἀποθνήσκω (# 633) to die. Subj. w. ἐάν (# 1569) in a 3rd. class cond. cl. where the cond. is viewed as possible. ◆ **25** φιλῶν pres. act. part. φιλέω (# 5797) to love. μισῶν pres. act. part. μισέω (# 3631) to hate. φυλάξει fut. ind. act. φυλάσσω (# 5875) to guard, to preserve. The use of this vb. indicates that the life is a pres. possession which will extend into eternity (Schnackenburg). ◆ **26** διακονῇ pres. subj. act. διακονέω (# 1354) to serve. ἀκολουθείτω pres. act. imp. 3rd. pers. sing. ἀκολουθέω (# 199) to follow, to follow as a disciple (TDNT). The sense is that a man must follow Jesus if he would serve Him (Tasker). εἰμί (# 1639) pres. ind. act. to be; pres. of anticipation. He refers to the state of the celestial glory of Jesus as the promise (Godet). ἔσται fut. ind. mid. (dep.) εἰμί to be. διακονῇ pres. subj. act. διακονέω. τιμήσει fut. ind. act. τιμάω (# 5506) to honor. ◆ **27** τετάρακται perf. pass. ind. ταράσσω (# 5429) to trouble (s. John 11:33). Perf. emphasizes the state or cond. εἴπω aor. subj. act. λέγω (# 3306) to speak; deliberative subj. This is a rhetorical question that reveals the human shrinking from death (Morris). ἦλθον aor. ind. act. ἔρχομαι s.v. 9. ◆ **28** δόξασον aor. imp. act. δοξάζω s.v. 16. ἐδόξασα aor. ind. act. δοξάσω fut. ind. act. ◆ **29** ἑστώς perf. act. part. (adj.) ἵστημι (# 2705) to stand. ἀκούσας aor. act. part. (temp.) ἀκούω s.v. 18. Aor. to describe antecedent action, "after they had heard." βροντή (# 1103) thunder. γεγονέναι perf. mid. (dep.) inf. γίνομαι (# 1181) to be, to become. Inf. used in indir. discourse. λελάληκεν perf. ind. act. λαλέω (# 3281) to speak. ◆ **30** ἀπεκρίθη aor. ind. pass. (dep.) ἀποκρίνομαι (# 646) to answer. γέγονεν perf. ind. act. γίνομαι s.v. 29. ◆ **31** τοῦ κόσμου (#3180) obj. gen. (judgment for the world). ἄρχων pres. act. part. (subst.) ἄρχω (# 806) to rule. ἐκβληθήσεται fut. ind. pass. ἐκβάλλω (# 1675) to cast out, to throw out. This is a neg. picture of acquiring the title to the world (PJP, 175). ◆ **32** ὑψωθῶ aor. pass. subj. ὑψόω (# 5738) to lift up. Subj. w. ἐάν (# 1569) in a 3rd. class cond. where the cond. is viewed as possible. Here this is a clear reference to the coming crucifixion and the following exaltation (Becker). ἑλκύσω fut. ind. act. ἑλκύω (# 1816) to drag, to draw. ◆ **33** σημαίνων pres. act. part. σημαίνω (# 4955) to signify, to indicate. Now to be considered a t.t. for the prophecy of an oracle (TDNT). Circum. part. explaining what he was saying. ἤμελλεν impf. ind. act. μέλλω (# 3516) to be about to, w. inf. for the immediate fut. ἀποθνήσκειν pres. act. inf. ἀποθνήσκω (# 633) to die. ◆ **34** ἀπεκρίθη aor. ind. pass. (dep.) ἀποκρίνομαι (# 646) to answer. ἠκούσαμεν aor. ind. act. ἀκούω (# 201) to hear. Aor. is const. to describe their hearing over a long period. δεῖ (# 1256) pres. ind. act. it is necessary, w. inf. giving a logical necessity. ὑψωθῆναι aor. pass. inf. ὑψόω s.v. 32. ◆ **35** περιπατεῖτε pres. imp. act. περιπατέω (# 4344) to walk, to walk about; fig. here in the sense of live, or conduct one's

life. S. also M. Bampfylde, "More Light on John 12:34," JSNT 17 (1983): 87-89. καταλάβῃ aor. subj. act. καταλαμβάνω (# 2898) to overcome, to overtake (s. 1:5). Subj. w. ἵνα (# 2671) describes purp. or result. περιπατῶν pres. act. part. περιπατέω. Subst. part. describes a trait. Pres. refers to either a contemporary trait or a continuing characteristic. οἶδεν perf. ind. act. οἶδα (# 3857) to know. Def. perf. w. pres. meaning. Here in the sense of recognize the way and direction in which he is walking. ◆ **36** πιστεύετε pres. imp. act. πιστεύω (# 4409) to believe. υἱοὶ φωτός "sons of light." This is a common designation in the DSS to express those who faithfully follow God and live in a right relationship with Him (1QS 1:9; 2:16; 1QM 1:1-2, etc.). γένησθε aor. subj. mid. (dep.) γίνομαι (# 1181) to become. Subj. w. ἵνα (# 2671) expresses purp. or result. ἐλάλησεν aor. ind. act. λαλέω (# 3281) to speak. ἀπελθών aor. act. part. ἀπέρχομαι (# 599) to go away. ἐκρύβη aor. ind. pass. κρύπτω (# 3221) to conceal, to hide; pass. to hide oneself. ◆ **37** τοσαῦτα pl. τοσοῦτος (# 5537) so many. πεποιηκότος perf. act. part. ποιέω (# 4472) to do; gen. abs. Perf. points to the permanent character (Morris). ἔμπροσθεν (# 1869) w. the gen., before, in the presence of. ἐπίστευον impf. ind. act. πιστεύω s.v. 36. Iterat. impf. emphasizes the repeated unbelief or the continual stubbornness of the unbelief (Schnackenburg). ◆ **38** πληρωθῇ aor. subj. pass. πληρόω (# 4444) to fulfill. Subj. w. ἵνα (# 2671) expresses purp. ἐπίστευσεν aor. ind. act. πιστεύω s.v. 36. ἀκοῇ (# 198) report. βραχίων (# 1098) arm. ἀπεκαλύφθη aor. ind. pass. ἀποκαλύπτω (# 636) to reveal. ◆ **39** ἠδύναντο impf. ind. pass. (dep.) δύναμαι (# 1538) to be able to. πιστεύειν pres. act. inf. πιστεύω s.v. 36. Compl. inf. to the main vb. ◆ **40** τετύφλωκεν perf. ind. act. τυφλόω (# 5604) to be blind. Perf. emphasizes the continuing state. ἐπώρωσεν aor. ind. act. πωρόω (# 4800) to harden. It describes the formation of a callus in a part of the body (Westcott). ἴδωσιν aor. subj. act. ὁράω s.v. 9. For a discussion of the quotation from Isa. 6:10, s. C.A. Evans, "The Function of Isaiah in 6,9-10 in Mark and John," Nov T 24 (1992): 124-38. τοῖς ὀφθαλμοῖς dat. pl. ὀφθαλμός (# 4057) eye. Instr. dat. νοήσωσιν aor. subj. act. νοέω (# 3783) to understand, to comprehend. Perhaps ingressive aor., "to come to realize" (M, 117). στραφῶσιν aor. subj. pass. στρέφω (# 5138) pass. to be converted. It has the sense of a middle voice, "to turn themselves" (Brown). Subj. w. ἵνα (# 2671) expresses result. ◆ **41** εἶδεν aor. ind. act. ὁράω s.v. 9. ◆ **42** ὅμως μέντοι (# 3940; 3530) nevertheless even, but yet even (RWP). ὡμολόγουν impf. ind. act. ὁμολογέω (# 3933) to confess. Impf. marks the continued shrinking from the act of faith (Westcott). ἀποσυνάγωγος (# 697) excommunicated, expelled from the synagogue. γένωνται aor. subj. act. γίνομαι (# 1181) to become. Subj. w. ἵνα (# 2671) expresses purp. ◆ **43** ἠγάπησαν aor. ind. act. ἀγαπάω (# 26) to love. τὴν δόξαν τῶν ἀνθρώπων glory of men. For the term "glory of men" in DSS s. 1Q 4:23. Gen. describes the source of the glory. ◆ **44 ἔκραξεν** aor. ind. act. κράζω (# 3189) to shout, to cry out. This section is a summary of the public appeal of Jesus in John (Becker). **πιστεύων** pres. act. part. nom. masc. sing. πιστεύω s.v. 36. Subst. part. to describe a character trait. **πέμψαντα** aor. act. part. acc. masc. sing. πέμπω (# 4287) to send. Aor. part. describes antecedent action. ◆ **45 θεωρῶν** pres. act. part. nom. masc. sing. θεωρέω (# 2555) to see. **πέμψαντα** s.v. 44. Part. as subst. ◆ **46 ἐλήλυθα** perf. ind. act. ἔρχομαι (# 2262) to come. Perf. emphasizes the past action and the continuing present results. **μείνῃ** aor. subj. act. μένω (# 3531) to remain. Subj. w. ἵνα (# 2671) to express purp. ◆ **47 ἀκούσῃ** aor. subj. act. ἀκούω (# 201) to hear. Subj. w. ἐάν (# 1569) in a 3rd. class cond. where the cond. is considered to be possible. **φυλάξῃ** aor. subj. act. φυλάσσω (# 5875) to guard, to preserve. Subj. w. ἵνα (# 2671) gives the purp. of the coming, not to judge but to save. ◆ **48 ἀθετῶν** pres. act. part. ἀθετέω (# 119) to set aside, to reject. **λαμβάνων** pres. act. part. λαμβάνω (# 3284) to accept, to receive. **κρίνοντα** pres. act. part. κρίνω (# 3212) to judge. **κρινεῖ** fut. ind. act. κρίνω. ◆ **49 πέμψας** aor. act. part. (temp.) πέμπω s.v. 44. Aor. describes antecedent action. **δέδωκεν** perf. ind. act. δίδωμι (# 1443) to give. **εἴπω** aor. subj. act. λέγω (# 3306) to say. **λαλήσω** aor. subj. act. λαλέω (# 3281) to speak. Subj. used in an indir. question. ◆ **50 καθώς ... οὕτως** (# 2777; 4048) "just... as." **εἴρηκεν** perf. ind. act. λέγω s.v. 49. Perf. indicates the past action as well as the lasting effects.

John 13

◆ **1** This begins the second major section of the Gospel of John: the Return to the Father (John 13:1–20:29). **εἰδώς** perf. act. part. of the def. perf. οἶδα (# 3857) w. a pres. meaning, to know. Either concessive or causal part., "even though" or "because he knew." **ὅτι** (# 4022) that gives the content of the knowledge. **ἦλθεν** aor. ind. act. ἔρχομαι (# 2262) to come, to go. Aor. expresses what has just happened (M, 135). **μεταβῇ** aor. subj. act. μεταβαίνω (# 3553) to depart, to transfer (Barrett). Subj. w. ἵνα (# 2671) expresses the content of the hour. **ἀγαπήσας** aor. act. part. ἀγαπάω (# 26) to love (TLNT; TDNT; s. John 3:16; EIW, 138-49). Aor. indicates antecedent action. Causal part. describing the motivation: "because he had loved them." Love becomes an important concept in this section of Christ's dealing w. His disciples (Dodd, 398ff). **ἴδιος** (# 2625) own; "those belonging to him." **εἰς τέλος** (# 1650; 5465) to the end or to the utmost. Perhaps both meanings are intended (Morris). **ἠγάπησεν** aor. ind. act. ἀγαπάω. Const. aor. describes the following actions as part of his love. ◆ **2 γινομένου** aor. mid. (dep.) part. γίνομαι

(# 1181) to become. Gen. abs. offers important information, unrelated grammatically to the cl. Pres. indicates contemporaneous action, "while it was supper." The textual variant could originate from Matt. 26:6. **βεβληκότος** perf. act. part. βάλλω (# 965) to throw, to place or put something into the heart (BAGD). Perf. part. indicates a preceding action w. the continuing results. **παραδοῖ** aor. subj. act. παραδίδωμι (# 4140) to betray, to deliver over. Subj. w. ἵνα (# 2671) gives the purp. of the Satanic influence. ◆ **3 εἰδώς** perf. act. part. (causal) οἶδα s.v. 1. Perf. describes antecedent time. This then is the basis or motivation for his confidence: "because he already knew." **ἐξῆλθεν** aor. ind. act. ἐξέρχομαι (# 2002) to go out. ◆ **4 ἐγείρεται** pres. ind. pass. ἐγείρω (# 1586) to arise; hist. pres. **λαβών** aor. act. part. (temp.) λαμβάνω (# 3284) to take. Aor. describes an antecedent action. **λέντιον** (# 3317) linen, towel; a Lat. loan word (linteum) (BAGD; MM; SB, 2:556f). **διέζωσεν** aor. ind. act. διαζώννυμι (# 1346) to tie around oneself, a normal preparation for menial service. The Emperor Caligula humiliated high-ranking members of the Roman Senate by making them serve him at a meal–"standing napkin (linteo) in hand either at the head of his couch, or at his feet" (Suetonius, "Gaius Caligula," *The Lives of the Caesars*, 4:26). ◆ **5 νιπτήρ** (# 3871) basin or jug. Washing was done by pouring water over the feet from one vessel into another (Morris). **ἤρξατο** aor. ind. mid. (dep.) ἄρχομαι (# 806) to begin. **νίπτειν** pres. act. inf. νίπτω (# 3782) to wash. Compl. inf. to the main vb. **ἐκμάσσειν** pres. act. inf. ἐκμάσσω (# 1726) to wipe off. **λεντίῳ** dat., s.v. 4. Instr. dat. **διεζωσμένος** perf. pass. part. διαζώννυμι s.v. 4. Perf. describes the enduring effect of the past action ("with which he had girded himself"). It was the duty of the non-Jewish servant to wash the feet of his master. A Jewish slave was not required to do this (SB, 2:557; BBC; DJG, 749-50; ABD, 2:828-29). ◆ **6 σύ** and **μου**, both prons. are emphatic, w. special stress on the second (Bernard). ◆ **7 ἀπεκρίθη** aor. ind. pass. (dep.) ἀποκρίνομαι (# 646) to answer. **γνώσῃ** fut. ind. act. γινώσκω (# 1182) to know. ◆ **8 οὐ μή** (# 4024; 3590) not in any wise; used as an emphatic neg. **νίψῃς** aor. subj. act. νίπτω s.v. 5. Aor. subj. is used to express a prohibition forbidding the occurrence of an action (BD, 184). **μέρος** (# 3538) part. Jesus' answer points us to a washing free from sin, which only Christ can give (Morris). ◆ **9 λέγει** pres. ind. act. λέγω (# 3306) to say. Hist. pres. making the narrative very vivid. **μὴ...μόνον ἀλλὰ καὶ...καί** "not...only, but both...and...." ◆ **10 λελουμένος** perf. pass. part. λούω (# 3374) to wash, to bathe. The former vb. tends to be used for washing a part of the body; here for the whole body (Brown). Perf. part. indicates a past action w. continuing results; thus emphasizing the state and character of one who has been bathed. **νίψασθαι** aor. mid. inf. νίπτω s.v. 5.

καθαρός (# 2754) clean. Jesus symbolically declares the complete purification through the humiliation by the death of the Messiah (Hoskyns). ◆ **11 ἤδει** plperf. ind. act. οἶδα s.v. 1. Plperf. has an impf. meaning for this def. vb. **παραδιδόντα** pres. act. part. παραδίδωμι s.v. 2. Subst. part. indicates the trait or characteristic of Judas. ◆ **12 ἔνιψεν** aor. ind. act. νίπτω s.v. 5. **ἔλαβεν** aor. ind. act. λαμβάνω (# 3284) to take, to receive. **ἀνέπεσεν** aor. ind. act. ἀναπίπτω (# 404) to recline, to recline at the table. **πεποίηκα** perf. ind. act. ποιέω (# 4472) to do. Perf. here describes the completed action in the recent past w. continuing results in a most vivid manner. ◆ **13 φωνεῖτε** pres. ind. act. φωνέω (# 5888) to call, to address. Used for addressing one w. his title (RWP). **ὁ διδάσκαλος** (# 1437) nom. teacher; the articular nom. used in an address (M, 70; BD, 81; JG, 94-95). ◆ **14 ἔνιψα** aor. ind. act. νίπτω s.v. 5. **ὀφείλετε** pres. ind. act. ὀφείλω (# 4053) to owe a debt, to be obligated. Used to express human and ethical obligations (NIDNTT; TDNT). **νίπτειν** pres. act. inf. Compl. inf. to the main vb. ◆ **15 ὑπόδειγμα** (# 5682) example, pattern, illustration (Barrett; MM). **ἔδωκα** aor. ind. act. δίδωμι (# 1443) to give. **ἐποίησα** aor. ind. act. **ποιῆτε** pres. subj. act. ποιέω (# 4472) to do. The subj. w. ἵνα (# 2671) expresses purp., "I have given you the illustration, so that you do it." ◆ **16 μείζων** (# 3505) comp. μέγας great; comp., greater. Here in terms of authority and position. Used w. the gen. of comparison. **ἀπόστολος** (# 693) in a non-technical sense, "messenger." **πέμψαντος** aor. act. part. (subst.) πέμπω (# 4287) to send. Aor. indicating the logically necessary or antecedent action. ◆ **17 εἰ** (# 1623) if; used w. the ind. introducing a 1st. class cond. It carries the implication that in fact they did know them (Morris). **ἐάν** (# 1569) introduces a cond. cl. which has less certainty (Morris). ◆ **18 ἐξελεξάμην** aor. ind. mid. ἐκλέγομαι (# 1721) to choose, to select for oneself. **πληρωθῇ** aor. pass. subj. πληρόω (# 4444) to fill, to fulfill (Matt. 5:17). **τρώγων** pres. act. part. τρώγω (# 5592) to chew, to eat. Subst. part. to emphasize a certain trait that is contemporaneous. **ἐπῆρεν** aor. ind. act. ἐπαίρω (# 2048) to lift up. **πτέρνα** (# 4761) heel. The same word occurs in the Greek translation of Gen. 3:16. ◆ **19 γενέσθαι** aor. mid. (dep.) inf. γίνομαι (# 1181) to be. Inf. w. prep. **πρό** (# 4574) before, to indicate antecedent time ("before it happens"). **πιστεύσητε** aor. subj. mid. πιστεύω (# 4409) to believe. Subj. w. ἵνα (# 2671) expresses result. **γένηται** aor. subj. mid. (dep.) γίνομαι here, to happen. Subj. w. ὅταν (# 4020) expresses an indef. time period ("whenever"). The prediction of the betrayal is proof of his deity. ◆ **20 λαμβάνων** pres. act. part. λαμβάνω (# 3284) to receive. Subst. part. to describe a character trait in the sense of a cond. **πέμψω** fut. ind. act. πέμπω (# 4287) to send. **πέμψαντα** aor. ind. act. πέμπω. Subst. part. to describe a defining action. ◆ **21 εἰπών** aor. act. part. (temp.) λέγω (# 3306) to say.

Aor. describes an antecedent action which becomes the basis for the main action. **ἐταράχθη** aor. ind. pass. ταράσσω (# 5429) to trouble, to be disturbed; used of mental and spiritual agitation (BAGD; John 11:33). The accompanying dat. gives the sphere in which he was troubled. **ἐμαρτύρησεν** aor. ind. act. μαρτυρέω (# 3455) to bear witness. Used here in the sense of making an important and solemn declaration (Barrett). **παραδώσει** fut. ind. act. παραδίδωμι s.v. 2. Predictive fut., "one will betray me shortly." ◆ **22 ἔβλεπον** impf. ind. act. βλέπω (# 1063) to look at, to see. Incep. impf., "they began to look at one another." **ἀπορούμενοι** pres. mid. part. ἀπορέω (# 679) to be at loss, to be disturbed; to dispute, to contest (NIDNTT, 1:454; TDNT; GELTS, 54; MM). ◆ **23 ἀνακείμενος** pres. mid./pass. (dep.) part. ἀνάκειμαι (# 367) to lie at the table, to recline. The custom was to use pillows while on the floor in order to eat. This was to show the rest and freedom enjoyed by Israel through God's redemption (b. Pesachim 99b; M, Pesachim 10:1; J Lightfoot, 3:392; BBC). **ἐν τῷ κόλπῳ** (# 3146) "at his breast," indicating that he was next to Jesus; thus he naturally would be the one to ask. **ἠγάπα** impf. ind. act. ἀγαπάω (# 26) to love. ◆ **24 νεύει** pres. ind. act. νεύω (# 3748) to nod, to signal by nodding the head, to gesture. Hist. pres. to vividly portray the action. **πυθέσθαι** aor. mid. (dep.) inf. πυνθάνομαι (# 4785) to inquire. Inf. to show purp., "he nodded in order to ask." This suggests that Peter was across from Jesus in a u-form shaped seating arrangement. **εἴη** aor. subj. act. εἰμί (# 1639), to be. Subj. in an indir. question. ◆ **25 ἀναπεσών** aor. act. part. ἀναπίπτω (# 404) to lean back, to lie down, to recline (BAGD). **στῆθος** (# 5111) chest. For the seating arrangement and other customs of a meal s. SB, 4:611-39; LT, 2:493-95. ◆ **26 βάψω** fut. ind. act. βάπτω (# 970) to dip. This may refer to eating the appetizers and sauces in remembrance of Israel's bitter slavery in Egypt (M, Pesachim 10:2-3). **ψωμίον** (# 6040) this small piece of bread. **δώσω** fut. ind. act. δίδωμι (# 1443) to give. **βάψας** aor. act. part. βάπτω. This suggests that Judas was on the other side of Jesus, opposite John. ◆ **27 μετὰ τὸ ψωμίον** "after the bread" is elliptical. One should supply the vb. "to dip," that is, "after dipping the morsel of bread." **εἰσῆλθεν** aor. ind. act. εἰσέρχομαι (# 1656) to go in. **ποίησον** aor. imp. act. ποιέω (# 4472) to do. **τάχιον** comp. ταχέως quickly; comp., more quickly (Morris). ◆ **28 ἔγνω** aor. ind. act. γινώσκω (# 1182) to know. **ἀνακειμένων** pres. mid. (dep.) part. ἀνάκειμαι (# 367) to recline. Subst. part. Pres. indicates contemporaneous action. ◆ **29 ἐδόκουν** impf. ind. act. δοκέω (# 1506) to suppose. **ἐπεί** (# 2075) since, because. **γλωσσόκομον** (# 1186) bag, purse (s. John 12:6). **ἀγόρασον** aor. imp. act. ἀγοράζω (# 60) to buy. This may suggest that this Passover meal was the day before the actual Passover. **δῷ** aor. subj. act. δίδωμι s.v. 26. This was perhaps to provide a Passover for the poor (M, Pesachim 10:1). Subj. w. **ἵνα** (# *2671*) gives the purp., "that he should give something to the poor." ◆ **30 λαβών** aor. act. part. λαμβάνω (# *3284*) to take. Aor. indicates antecedent action. Temp. part., "after he had taken, then...." **ἐξῆλθεν** aor. ind. act. ἐξέρχομαι (# *2002*) to go out. **νύξ** (# *3816*) night. The meal was to be eaten between 6 P.M. and 12 A.M. (M, Pesachim 10:1, 9). Perhaps the departure was earlier, indicating that the meal had just started and it was just becoming dark. It was the time when the darkness would attempt to overcome the light (1:5). ◆ **31 ἐξῆλθεν** aor. ind. act. ἐξέρχομαι s.v. 30. **ἐδοξάσθη** aor. ind. pass. δοξάζω (# *1519*) to glorify. Used intransitively, "to display one's importance, greatness, or glory." It indicates that God has made a full display of His glory in the person of the Son of man (G.B. Caird, "The Glory of God in the Fourth Gospel: An Exercise in Biblical Semantics," *NTS* 15 [1969]: 265-77). ◆ **32 δοξάσει** fut. ind. act. δοξάζω s.v. 31. ◆ **33 τεκνίον** (# *5448*) little child. Dimin. expressing affection (Morris). **ζητήσετε** fut. ind. act. ζητέω (# *2426*) to seek. **ἐλθεῖν** aor. act. inf. ἔρχομαι (# *2262*) to go. Compl. inf. to the main vb. ◆ **34 ἀγαπᾶτε** pres. subj. act. ἀγαπάω (# *26*) to love. Subj. w. **ἵνα** (# *2671*) expresses result. It gives the content of the new commandment. **καθώς** (# *2777*) just as, giving the standard or manner of love. **ἠγάπησα** aor. ind. act. ἀγαπάω. This is the commandment of the New Covenant (Brown). ◆ **35 γνώσονται** fut. ind. mid. (dep.) γινώσκω to know s.v. 7. **ἔχητε** pres. subj. act. ἔχω (# *2400*) to have. Subj. w. **ἐάν** (# *1569*) expresses a 3rd. class cond. ◆ **36 ἀπεκρίθη** aor. ind. pass. (dep.), s.v. 28. **δύνασαι** pres. ind. pass. (dep.) 2nd. pers. sing. δύναμαι (# *1538*) to be able to, w. inf. **ἀκολουθῆσαι** aor. act. inf. ἀκολουθέω (# *199*) to follow, to follow as a disciple. Inf. is compl. to the main vb. **ἀκολουθήσεις** fut. ind. act. This refers perhaps to his manner of death. **ὕστερον** (# *5731*) later. ◆ **37 ἀκο-λουθῆσαι** aor. act. inf. s.v. 36. **ὑπὲρ σοῦ** for you. This is the motive and goal for Jesus. **θήσω** fut. ind. act. τίθημι (# *5502*) to lay down. ◆ **38 θήσεις** fut. ind. act. τίθημι s.v. 37. **φωνήσῃ** aor. subj. act. φωνέω (# *5888*) to call, to crow (s. Matt. 26:34, 74-75; Mark 14:30, 72-73; Luke 22:34, 60-61). Consummative aor. to emphasize the culmination or climax of crowing. **ἀρνήσῃ** aor. subj. mid. (dep.) ἀρνέομαι (# *766*) to deny.

John 14

◆ **1 ταρασσέσθω** pres. imp. pass. 3rd. pers. sing. ταράσσω (# *5429*) to trouble (s. John 11:33). Pres. subj. w. neg. **μή** (# *3590*) indicates the stopping of the action in progress (MKG, 272). Pass. imp. indicates permission, "Do not allow" or "permit your hearts to be troubled." This command is necessary based on the downcast mood of the disciples. They had just heard about the coming absence of Jesus and that Peter would deny him. **πιστεύετε** pres. imp. act. πιστεύω (# *4409*) to believe. Jesus is urging His followers to continue to believe and in this way not to let their hearts be troubled (Morris). ◆ **2 μοναί** pl. μονή (# *3665*) dwelling place. John may be referring to places where the disciples can dwell in peace by remaining w. the Father (Brown). **ἑτοιμάσαι** aor. act. inf. ἑτοιμάζω (# *2286*) to prepare. Inf. to express the purp. of his going. ◆ **3 ἐάν** (# *1569*) here, when (Brown; BBC). **πορευθῶ** aor. subj. pass. (dep.) πορεύομαι (# *4513*) to go. **ἑτοιμάσω** aor. subj. act. ἑτοιμάζω s.v. 2. Subj. expresses a cond. that will surely be fulfilled. **παραλήμψομαι** fut. ind. mid. παραλαμβάνω (# *4161*) to take w. someone. **ἦτε** pres. subj. act. εἰμί (# *1639*) to be. Subj. expresses result. The argument is if he goes to prepare a place (and he is), then it is only reasonable to assume that he will return in order to take the disciples w. him so that they can be where he is as well. ◆ **4 οἴδατε** perf. ind. act. οἶδα (# *3857*) to know. Def. perf. w. pres. meaning. ◆ **5 εἰδέναι** perf. act. inf. οἶδα s.v. 4. Compl. inf. to the main vb. ◆ **6 καί** (# *2779*) Epex. use of the particle, giving an additional explanation to ὁδός (# *3847*): "I am the Way; that is to say, the Truth and the Life" (s. BD, 228). The repetition of the definite art. may refer to Christ as the real truth, life, etc., and all other truths and lives are transitory (BG, 57; MT, 178). **ἔρχεται** pres. ind. mid./pass. (dep.) ἔρχομαι (# *2262*) to go. Gnomic pres., "No one ever comes to the Father except through me." ◆ **7 ἐγνώκατε** perf. ind. act. γινώσκω (# *1182*) to know. The cond. cl. could be a 1st. class cond., where the cond. is assumed to be true (VA, 294-95), or a 2nd. class cond. where the cond. is viewed as contrary to fact (for a discussion s. Brown). **ἀπ' ἄρτι** (# *608; 785*) from now on. **ἑωράκατε** perf. ind. act. ὁράω to see (# *3972*). Consummative perf. emphasizes the completed action in the past, as well as the lasting results. In the past three years they had seen Jesus. ◆ **8 δεῖξον** aor. imp. act. δείκνυμι (# *1259*) to show. Aor. imp. suggests that the action should begin: "start showing us the Father." **ἀρκεῖ** pres. ind. act. ἀρκέω (# *758*) to be strong, to be enough, to be sufficient. This would be enough to stop their anxiety. ◆ **9 τοσούτῳ χρόνῳ** (# *5537; 5989*) so great, so long a time. **ἔγνωκάς** perf. ind. act. γινώσκω s.v. 7. **ἑωρακώς** perf. act. part. ὁράω s.v. 7. Subst. part. emphasizes the person doing the action. Perf. stresses the result of the action. **ἑώρακεν** perf. ind. act. ὁράω. ◆ **10 μένων** pres. act. part. μένω (# *3531*) to remain. Subst. part. emphasizing the person who carries out the trait or fulfills this cond. Pres. emphasizes a durative aspect. ◆ **12 πιστεύων** pres. act. part. πιστεύω s.v. 1. Subst. part. emphasizes the person who carries out the trait or fulfills this cond. Pres. emphasizes a durative aspect. **ποιήσει** fut. ind. act. ποιέω (# *4472*) to do. **μείζο-**

να (# 3505) comp. μέγας great; comp., greater. Gen. of comp. ◆ **13 αἰτήσητε** aor. subj. act. αἰτέω (# 160) to ask. Subj. w. **ἄν** (# 165) adds a more generalized promise. **δοξασθῇ** aor. subj. pass. δοξάζω (# 1519) to glorify. Subj. w. **ἵνα** (# 2671) describes the purp. (why Jesus will answer prayer). ◆ **14 αἰτήσητε** aor. subj. act. αἰτέω s.v. 13. Subj. w. **ἐάν** (# 1569) in a 3rd. class cond. cl. where the cond. is viewed as possible. ◆ **15 ἀγαπᾶτε** pres. subj. act. ἀγαπάω (# 26) to love. Subj. in a 3rd. class cond. cl. in which the speaker views the cond. as possible. **τηρή- σετε** fut. ind. act. τηρέω (# 5498) to guard, to keep, in the sense of obey. The variant (aor. imp.) accords less well w. the following ἐρωτήσω. ◆ **16 ἐρωτήσω** fut. ind. act. ἐρωτάω (# 2263) to ask. Generally used of the prayers of Jesus Himself (Bernard). **παράκλητος** (# 4156) advocate, comforter. For the meaning of this term s. Brown, 2:1135-44; MNTW; NIDNTT; TDNT; D.A. Carson, "The Function of the Paraklese and John 16:7-11," *JBL* 98 (1979): 547-66; ABD, 5:152-54. **δώσει** fut. ind. act. δίδωμι (# 1443) to give. This is the content of the request. **ᾖ** pres. subj. act. εἰμί (# 1639) to be. Subj. w. **ἵνα** (# 2671) could be purp. or show result, "so that he will be with you forever." ◆ **17 ἀληθείας** gen. ἀλή- θεια (# 237) truth. Attributive gen., "the spirit charac- terized by truth." **λαβεῖν** aor. act. inf. λαμβάνω (# 3284) to receive. Compl. inf. to the main vb. ◆ **18 ἀφήσω** fut. ind. act. ἀφίημι (# 918) to leave, to forsake. **ὀρφανός** (# 4003) orphan; used of the children left without a fa- ther and used of disciples left without the master (Bar- rett). Used as an acc. apposition, "to leave you as orphans" or "in the position of orphans." Orphans were an especially pitiful and needy group in the soci- ety (TDNT; EDNT; SB, 2:562). ◆ **19 ζήσετε** fut. ind. act. ζάω (# 2409) to live. ◆ **20 γνώσεσθε** fut. ind. mid. (dep.) γινώσκω (# 1182) to know. ◆ **21 ἔχων** pres. act. part. ἔχω (# 2400) to have. **τηρῶν** pres. act. part. τηρέω s.v. 15. Subst. part. as subject of cl. in a *casus pendens* construction, followed by a resumptive pron. (MH, 423). **ἀγαπῶν** pres. act. part. ἀγαπάω s.v. 15. The art. is used here w. the pred. signifying that the pred. is iden- tical w. the subject and the only one of its kind (Harn- er, 75; John 1:1). In all three pres. parts. there is the emphasis on the durative aspect. **ἀγαπηθήσεται** fut. ind. pass. ἀγαπάω. **ἀγαπήσω** fut. ind. act. **ἐμφανίσω** fut. ind. act. ἐμφανίζω (# 1872) to reveal, to manifest, to make visible. The presentation in a clear, conspicuous form (Westcott). ◆ **22 γέγονεν** perf. ind. act. γίνομαι (# 1181) to be, to become. **μέλλεις** pres. ind. act. μέλλω (# 3516) to be about to (s. 6:6). **ἐμφανίζειν** pres. act. inf. ἐμφανίζω s.v. 21. Compl. inf. to the main vb. ◆ **23 ἀπε- κρίθη** aor. ind. pass. (dep.) ἀποκρίνομαι (# 646) to an- swer. **ἐλευσόμεθα** fut. ind. mid. (dep.) ἔρχομαι (# 2262) to go, to come. **ποιησόμεθα** fut. ind. mid. (dep.) ποιέω s.v. 12. The 1st. pl. includes the Father and the Son. ◆ **24 ἀγαπῶν** pres. act. part. ἀγαπάω s.v. 15. Subst. part.

to emphasize the person who does this. It is similar to fulfilling a cond. **πέμψαντός** aor. act. part. πέμπω (# 4287) to send. Aor. part. emphasizes the antecedent action as the basis for the main vb. ◆ **25 λελάληκα** perf. ind. act. λαλέω (# 3281) to speak. Perf. emphasiz- es the completed action. **μένων** pres. act. part. μένω s.v. 10. Temp. part. emphasizing the durative aspect of Jesus' ministry, "while I was with you." ◆ **26 πέμψει** fut. ind. act. πέμπω s.v. 24. **διδάξει** fut. ind. act. διδάσκω (# 1438) to teach. **ὑπομνήσει** fut. ind. act. ὑπομιμνήσκω (# 5703) to cause to remember, to bring to remem- brance. ◆ **27 ταρασσέσθω** pres. pass. imp. 3rd. pers. sing. ταράσσω s.v. 1. **δειλιάτω** pres. act. imp. 3rd. pers. sing. δειλιάω (# 1262) to be afraid, to be cowardly, to be timid. ◆ **28 ἠκούσατε** aor. ind. act. ἀκούω (# 201) to hear. Aor. describes the immediate past. **εἶπον** aor. ind. act. λέγω (# 3306) to speak. **ἠγαπᾶτε** impf. ind. act. ἀγα- πάω s.v. 15. Impf. in a 2nd. class cond. cl. (Carson). **ἐχάρητε** aor. ind. pass. (dep.) χαίρω (# 5897) to rejoice. **μείζων** comp. s.v. 12. Comp. is constructed w. the gen.: "greater than I," in the sense position not essence (HSB, 503-505). ◆ **29 εἴρηκα** perf. ind. act. λέγω s.v. 28. Consummative perf. emphasizing the completion of the action. Here Christ predicts before it happens. **πρίν** (# 4570) before, used w. the inf. to express time. **γενέσθαι** aor. mid. (dep.) inf. γίνομαι s.v. 22. Inf. w. prep. **πρίν** (# 4570) "before" to express antecedent ac- tion. **γένηται** aor. subj. mid. (dep.) γίνομαι. Subj. w. **ὅταν** (# 4020) in an indef. temp. cl. ("whenever"). **πιστεύσητε** aor. subj. act. πιστεύω s.v. 1. Aor. may mean "come to trust" (Morris). Subj. w. **ἵνα** (# 2671) express- es purp. Purp. of this prediction of the coming of the Spirit is to produce faith and confidence in His word. ◆ **30 λαλήσω** fut. ind. act. λαλέω s.v. 25. **ἄρχων** (# 807) pres. act. part. (subst.) ἄρχω to rule. ◆ **31 γνῶ** aor. subj. act. γινώσκω (# 1182) to know. Subj. w. **ἵνα** (# 2671) in a purp. cl. **ἐνετείλατο** aor. ind. mid. (dep.) ἐντέλλομαι (# 1948) to command, to give orders. **ἐγείρεσθε** pres. imp. pass. ἐγείρω (# 1586) to arise; pass. to rise, to get up; here, of those who had been sitting (BAGD). **ἄγω- μεν** pres. subj. act. ἄγω (# 72) to go. Hortatory subj., "Let us go." The Passover meal had to be completed by midnight.

John 15

◆ **1 ἄμπελος** (# 306) vine. For the Jewish symbol of the vine s. Barrett; Hoskyns; DJG, 867-68. **ἀληθινός** (# 240) true, genuine; cf. Isa. 5:1-2, 7; Hos. 10:1; Jer. 2:21; Ezek. 15; Ps. 80:9-12, 15f; Lev Rabba 36: 2; SB, 2:563. This is one of the most prized of plants and thus represents the most privileged among nations and men. It is also emphasized by being placed after the emphatic **ἐγώ εἰμι** and by the use of the adj. following the noun (Schnackenburg). This refers to the idea of a fruitful Israel obedient to God. For a description of the vine as the temple representing Israel s. Josephus, *Ant.*,15:11:3; *JW*, 5:5:4; 5:20; Tacitus, *Historiae*, 5:5. γεωργός (# 1177) farmer, one who tills soil. Refers here in a specialized way to a vinedresser (Brown). G.S. Haaf, "The Physiology of the Vine and the Branches: John 15:1-9," *The Lutheran Church Quarterly* 11 (1938): 404; George Johnston, "The Allegory of the Vine: An Exposition of John 15:1-17," *Canadian Journal of Theology* 3 (1957): 150-58; R. Borig, *Der Wahre Weinstock: Untersuchungen zu Jo 15,1-10* Munich, 1967; P. Albenda, "Grapevines in Ashurbanipal's Garden," *BASOR* 92 (1974): 215 / 5-17; *Columella*, a treatise about agriculture in the Roman world, particularly books 2-4 about the treatment and care of grape vines. ◆ **2** κλῆμα (# 3097) cane, shoot of a vine (Morris). φέρον pres. act. part. φέρω (# 5770) to carry, to bear. αἴρει pres. ind. act. αἴρω (# 149) to lift up, to take away. The light pruning was done by snapping off the tips by hand so that the wood would grow longer (*Columella*, Book 4, 6:4; 7:1; Oded Borowski, *Agriculture in Iron Age Israel: The Evidence from Archaeology and the Bible*, 108-110). καθαίρει pres. ind. act. καθαίρω (# 2748) to cleanse; here in the sense of "cleanse by pruning" (Bernard). A method of viticulture consisted of training the vines on trellises, poles, or trees (4-6 feet high), which provided a canopy-like form (*Columella*, Book 4, 18-19). Whether poles or trees were used, grapes grown this way were easier to harvest since the bunches hung down from the vine and hence were more accessible (*ANEP*, fig. 19). To train the vine for maximum yield the vinedresser had to prune (זמר) excessive branches (Num. 13:23). The time of pruning was after the winter was over, usually during the fall before the vines became dormant. It involved cutting into the wood. This needed to be done in the fall lest there be new vegetative growth at the cut (*Columella*, Book 4, 6:5). For the first five years, the plant needed the fall pruning every year; thereafter only every third year (*Columella*, Book 4, 6:5). πλείονα comp. πολύς (# 4498) much; comp., greater, more. φέρῃ pres. subj. act. φέρω to carry, used fig., to bear. Subj. w. ἵνα (# 2671) to express purp. ◆ **3** διά (# 1328) w. acc., the cause of. λελάληκα perf. ind. act. λαλέω (# 3281) to speak. Perf. may suggest that the word may remain w. them (Morris). ◆ **4** μείνατε aor. imp. act. μένω (# 3531) to remain. Ingressive aor. They should begin to stay in Christ. S. Jürgen Heise, *Bleiben: Menein in den Johanneischen Schriften.* φέρειν pres. act. inf. φέρω s.v. 2. Compl. inf. to the main vb. μένῃ pres. subj. act. μένω. μένητε pres. subj. act. μένω. Subj. w. ἐάν (# 1569) expresses a cond. ◆ **5** μένων pres. act. part. μένω s.v. 4. Subst. part. emphasizes the person who must fulfill a particular trait. χωρίς (# 6006) w. the gen., without, apart from. ποιεῖν pres. ind. act. ποιέω (# 4472) to do; here, to accomplish. ◆ **6** μένῃ aor. subj. act. μένω s.v. 4. Subj. w.

ἐάν (# 1569) expresses cond. ἐβλήθη aor. ind. pass. βάλλω (# 965) to throw. ἔξω (# 2032) out; here, out of the vineyard (Morris). ἐξηράνθη aor. ind. pass. ξηραίνω (# 3830) to dry out; pass. to become dry, to wither. συνάγουσιν pres. ind. act. συνάγω (# 5251) to gather together. The subject ("they") may refer to the unnamed servants (Bernard), or it may be the Semitic custom of using the 3rd. pers. pl. as the pass. (Brown). καίεται pres. ind. pass. καίω (# 2794) to burn. Gnomic pres., for what generally occurs. ◆ **7** μείνητε aor. subj. act. μένω s.v. 4. θέλητε pres. subj. act. θέλω (# 2527) to desire. Subj. expresses a more generalized thought. αἰτήσασθε aor. imp. mid. αἰτέω (# 160) to ask; mid., to ask for oneself. γενήσεται fut. ind. mid. (dep.) γίνομαι (# 1181) to do, to happen. ◆ **8** ἐν τούτῳ (# 1877; 4047) in this; the pron. looks back, and at the same time the thought already indicated is developed in the words that follow (Westcott). ἐδοξάσθη aor. ind. pass. δοξάζω (# 1519) to glorify (TDNT; TLNT). Aor. views the glorification as complete (Morris). φέρητε aor. subj. act. φέρω (# 5770) to carry; here, to bear. γένησθε aor. subj. mid. (dep.) γίνομαι s.v. 7. Subj. w. ἵνα (# 2671) expresses result or purp. (γενήσεσθε fut. ind. mid. [dep.], a variant reading. If the fut. is adopted it has a kind of independence: "and then you will become" [BD, 186; TC, 246].) ◆ **9** ἠγάπησεν aor. ind. act. ἀγαπάω (# 26) to love. μείνατε aor. imp. act. μένω s.v. 4. Aor. imp. suggests an action that should commence. ◆ **10** τηρήσητε aor. subj. act. τηρέω (# 5498) to guard, to observe. Subj. ἐάν (# 1569) in 3rd. class cond. cl. where the cond. is believed possible. μενεῖτε fut. ind. act. μένω s.v. 4. τετήρηκα perf. ind. act. τηρέω. ◆ **11** λελάληκα perf. ind. act. λαλέω (# 3281) to speak. ᾖ pres. subj. act. εἰμί (# 1639) to be. Subj. w. ἵνα (# 2671) expresses purp. πληρωθῇ aor. subj. pass. πληρόω (# 4444) to fulfill. ◆ **12** ἀγαπᾶτε pres. subj. act. s.v. 9. Subj. w. ἵνα (# 2671) expresses the content of the command. ἠγάπησα aor. ind. act. ἀγαπάω. ◆ **13** μείζονα (# 3505) comp. μέγας great; comp., greater. Used w. a gen. of comp. The ἵνα (# 2671) cl. w. the subj. is explanatory (Barrett). θῇ aor. subj. act. τίθημι (# 5502) to lay, to lay down. For examples of this type of heroics s. BBC. ◆ **14** ποιῆτε pres. subj. act. ποιέω (# 4472) to do. Subj. expresses cond. ◆ **15** εἴρηκα perf. ind. act. λέγω (# 3306) to speak, to say. ἤκουσα aor. ind. act. ἀκούω (# 201) to hear. ἐγνώρισα aor. ind. act. γνωρίζω (# 1192) to make known. Aor. contemplates the completed work of Christ (Barrett). ◆ **16** ἐξελέξασθε aor. ind. mid. ἐκλέγομαι (# 1721) to choose, to choose for oneself. ἐξελεξάμην aor. ind. mid. ἔθηκα aor. ind. act. τίθημι (# 5502) to lay, to place. ὑπάγητε aor. ind. act. ὑπάγω (# 5632) to go, to go forth. αἰτήσητε aor. subj. act. αἰτέω s.v. 7. Subj. w. ἄν (# 165) here is generalizing. δῷ aor. subj. act. δίδωμι (# 1443) to give. Subj. w. ἵνα (# 2671) expresses result. ◆ **17** ταῦτα (# 4047) these. It indicates all that Jesus has commanded them is designed to teach them the lesson of mutual love (SM; DJG, 135-36). ◆ **18 γινώσκετε** pres. imp. act. γινώσκω (# *1182*) to know; here in the sense of "recognize." **μεμίσηκεν** perf. ind. act. μισέω (# *3631*) to hate. Perf. points to a permanent attitude (Morris). ◆ **19 ἦτε** impf. ind. act. εἰμί (# *1639*) to be. **ἄν** used in a contrary to fact cond. cl. **ἐφίλει** impf. ind. act. φιλέω (# *5797*) to love. **ἐξελεξάμην** aor. ind. mid. ἐκλέγω s.v. 16. ◆ **20 μνημονεύετε** pres. imp. act. μνημονεύω (# *3648*) to remember, followed by gen. Pres. suggests that they should continue to remember these words. **ἐδίωξαν** aor. ind. act. διώκω (# *1503*) to persecute. **διώξουσιν** fut. ind. act. **ἐτήρησαν** aor. ind. act. τηρέω (# *5498*) to keep, to guard, to obey. **τηρήσουσιν** fut. ind. act. ◆ **21 ποιήσουσιν** fut. ind. act. ποιέω (# *4472*) to do. **πέμψαντα** aor. act. part. πέμπω (# *4287*) to send. Subst. part. emphasizing the person performing the act. Durative pres. ◆ **22 ἦλθον** aor. ind. act. ἔρχομαι (# *2262*) to go. **ἐλάλησα** aor. ind. act. λαλέω (# *3281*) to speak. **εἴχοσαν** impf. ind. act. ἔχω (# *2400*) to have. Impf. w. this ending is common in the LXX and occurs in the papyri and inscriptions (RWP; MH, 194f; GGP, 2:332). **πρόφασις** (# *4733*) excuse. It is what is put forth to justify it, whether the real reason or a mere excuse (Morris). ◆ **23 μισῶν** pres. act. part. μισέω s.v. 18. Subst. part. emphasizing the person performing the act. Durative pres. ◆ **24 ἐποίησα** aor. ind. act. ποιέω s.v. 21. **εἴχοσαν** impf. ind. act. ἔχω s.v. 22. Iterat. impf. emphasizing their repeated sin. **ἑωράκασιν** perf. ind. act. ὁράω (# *3972*) to see. **μεμισήκασιν** perf. ind. act. μισέω s.v. 18. ◆ **25 πληρωθῇ** aor. subj. pass. πληρόω (# *4444*) to fulfill. **γεγραμμένος** perf. pass. part. γράφω (# *1211*) to write. **ἐμίσησάν** aor. ind. act. μισέω s.v. 18. **δωρεάν** (# *1562*) without cause. ◆ **26 ἔλθῃ** aor. subj. act. ἔρχομαι s.v. 22. **παράκλητος** comforter (s. 14:16). **μαρτυρήσει** fut. ind. act. μαρτυρέω (# *3455*) to bear witness. ◆ **27 μαρτυρεῖτε** pres. imp. act. μαρτυρέω s.v. 26. It could be understood also as ind. (Brown).

John 16

◆ **1 λελάληκα** perf. ind. act. λαλέω (# *3281*) to speak. **σκανδαλισθῆτε** aor. subj. pass. σκανδαλίζω (# *4997*) to cause to stumble (TDNT). Subj. w. **ἵνα** (# *2671*) expresses purp. or result. ◆ **2 ἀποσυναγώγους** (# *697*) expelled from the synagogue. **ποιήσουσιν** fut. ind. act. ποιέω (# *4472*) to do, to make, to make you into. **ἔρχεται** pres. ind. mid. (dep.) ἔρχομαι (# *2262*) to come, to go. Pres. is futuristic depicting the certain fut. event as already taking place. **ἀποκτείνας** aor. act. part. (temp.) ἀποκτείνω (# *650*) to kill. Subst. part. emphasizing the person acting. Aor. emphasizes antecedent action or action that is necessary for the main vb. The murder of the disciples will be the necessary action of the enemies' service to God. **δόξῃ** aor. subj. act. δοκέω (# *1506*) to suppose. **λατρεία** (# *3301*) service. Denotes

worship as well as the more general idea of serving God (Morris). **προσφέρειν** pres. inf. act. προσφέρω (# *4712*) to carry. Compl. inf. to complete the main vb. ◆ **3 ποιήσουσιν** fut. ind. act. ποιέω s.v. 2. Futuristic pres. portraying the certain fut. event as already in process. **ἔγνωσαν** aor. ind. act. γινώσκω (# *1182*) to know. ◆ **4 λελάληκα** perf. ind. act. λαλέω s.v. 1. **ἔλθῃ** aor. subj. act. ἔρχομαι s.v. 2. Subj. w. **ὅταν** (# *4020*) generalizes. **μνημονεύητε** pres. subj. act. μνημονεύω (# *3648*) to remember. Subj. w. **ἵνα** (# *2671*) expresses purp. **ἤμην** impf. ind. mid. εἰμί (# *1639*) to be. ◆ **5 πέμψαντα** aor. act. part. πέμπω (# *4287*) to send. Subst. part. to emphasize the person sending. Aor. shows antecedent action. **ἐρωτᾷ** pres. ind. act. ἐρωτάω (# *2263*) to ask. ◆ **6 λελάληκα** perf. ind. act. λαλέω s.v. 1. **πεπλήρωκεν** perf. ind. pass. πληρόω (# *4444*) to fulfill. Intensive perf. focusing on the continuing results: "they remain sad." ◆ **7 συμφέρει** pres. ind. act. συμφέρω (# *5237*) it is expedient, it is of an advantage, it is profitable. **ἀπέλθω** aor. subj. act. ἀπέρχομαι (# *599*) to go away. In this case the subj. w. **ἵνα** (# *2671*) expresses purp. In the following the subj. w. **ἐάν** (# *1569*) is in a 3rd. class cond. where the cond. is viewed as possible. **παράκλητος** comforter (s. 14:16). **ἐλεύσεται** fut. ind. mid. (dep.) ἔρχομαι s.v. 2. **πορευθῶ** aor. subj. pass. (dep.) πορεύομαι (# *4513*) to go, to go away. **πέμψω** fut. ind. act. πέμπω s.v. 5. Just as the Father has sent the Son, so the Son will send the Spirit. ◆ **8 ἐλθών** aor. act. part. ἔρχομαι s.v. 2. Aor. describes an antecedent action necessary for the completion of the main vb. Thus it is antecedent to the main vb., even though the coming is still future from the speaker's standpoint. **ἐλέγξει** fut. ind. act. ἐλέγχω (# *1794*) to expose, to convict, to cross-examine for the purp. of convincing or refuting an opponent; esp. used of legal proceedings (Morris). **δικαιοσύνη** (# *1466*) righteousness. Christ's own righteousness as the standard and source (MRP, 143; TDNT; TLNT; EDNT, 1:1146). **κρίσεως** gen. κρίσις (# *3213*) judgment. ◆ **9 ὅτι** (# *4022*) because or that. For the possible construction s. Barrett. **πιστεύουσιν** pres. ind. act. πιστεύω (# *4409*) to believe. Durative pres., their long-standing refusal to believe. ◆ **10 οὐκέτι** (# *4033*) no longer. **θεωρεῖτε** pres. ind. act. θεωρέω (# *2555*) to see. Futuristic pres. describes a future event w. great certainty, "they certainly will not see me." ◆ **11 κέκριται** perf. ind. pass. κρίνω (# *3212*) to judge. Perf. emphasizes the completed act of judging the present ruler of the world. ◆ **12 βαστάζειν** pres. act. inf. βαστάζω (# *1002*) to bear. The basic idea is that they cannot understand now (Brown). Inf. is compl. to the main vb. ◆ **13 ἔλθῃ** aor. ind. act. ἔρχομαι s.v. 2. Subj. w. **ὅταν** (# *4020*) is generalizing, "whenever he comes." **ἀληθείας** gen. ἀλήθεια, truth (# *237*); attributive or descriptive, giving the trait of the Spirit. **ὁδηγήσει** fut. ind. act. ὁδηγέω (# *3842*) to show the way; a guide who introduces the traveler into an unknown country (Godet). **λαλήσει** fut. ind. act. λαλέω s.v. 1. **ἐρχόμενα** pres. mid. (dep.) part. (subst.) ἔρχομαι s.v. 2. **ἀναγγελεῖ** fut. ind. act. ἀναγγέλλω (# 334) to proclaim. ◆ **14 δοξάσει** fut. ind. act. δοξάζω (# 1519) to glorify. **λήμψεται** fut. ind. mid. (dep.) λαμβάνω (# 3284) to take. **ἀναγγελεῖ** fut. ind. act. ἀναγγέλλω s.v. 13. Repetition of this word puts emphasis on this aspect of the Spirit's work (Morris). ◆ **16 ὄψεσθε** fut. ind. mid. (dep.) ὁράω (# 3972) to see. ◆ **18 οἴδαμεν** perf. ind. act. οἶδα (# 3857) to know. Def. perf. w. pres. meaning. ◆ **19 ἔγνω** aor. ind. act. γινώσκω (# 1182) to know. **ἤθελον** impf. ind. act. θέλω (# 2527) to desire, to want to. **ἐρωτᾶν** pres. act. inf. ἐρωτάω (# 2263) to ask. Compl. inf. to the main vb. **ὄψεσθε** fut. ind. mid. ὁράω s.v. 16. ◆ **20 κλαύσετε** fut. ind. act. κλαίω (# 3081) to cry, to weep. **θρηνήσετε** fut. ind. act. θρηνέω (# 2577) to mourn. The reference is to the loud wailing and lamentation that is the customary reaction to death in the Near East (Brown). **χαρήσεται** fut. ind. mid. (dep.) χαίρω (# 5897) to rejoice. **λυπηθήσεσθε** fut. ind. pass. λυπέω (# 3382) pass. to be sad. **γενήσεται** fut. ind. mid. (dep.) γίνομαι (# 1181) to become, to be. ◆ **21 τίκτῃ** pres. subj. act. τίκτω (# 5503) to give birth. Subj. w. **ὅταν** (# 4020) in an indef. temp. cl. **ἦλθεν** aor. ind. act. ἔρχομαι s.v. 2; here, to arrive. **γεννήσῃ** aor. subj. act. γεννάω (# 1164) to give birth. The previous pres. depicts the woman in the act of childbirth; aor. here sees the process as complete (Morris). **μνημονεύει** pres. ind. act. μνημονεύω s.v. 4, w. obj. in gen. Gnomic pres. **ἐγεννήθη** aor. ind. pass. γεννάω. ◆ **22 ὄψομαι** fut. ind. act. ὁράω s.v. 16. **χαρήσεται** fut. ind. pass. χαίρω s.v. 20. ◆ **23 ἐρωτήσετε** fut. ind. act. ἐρωτάω s.v. 19. **αἰτήσητε** aor. subj. act. αἰτέω (# 160) to ask. Subj. in an indef. rel cl. w. **ἄν τι. δώσει** fut. ind. act. δίδωμι (# 1443) to give. ◆ **24 ᾐτήσατε** aor. ind. act. αἰτέω s.v. 23. **αἰτεῖτε** imp. act. αἰτέω. Pres. imp. suggests that the petition should continue. **λήμψεσθε** fut. ind. mid. (dep.) λαμβάνω (# 3284) to receive. **ἦ** pres. subj. act. εἰμί. **πεπληρωμένη** perf. pass. part. πληρόω s.v. 6; used to form the periphrastic perf. subj. pass. Subj. w. **ἵνα** (# 2671) expresses purp. ◆ **25 παροιμία** (# 4231) proverb. In John, "dark sayings," "figures of speech" (BAGD; MM). Abbott understands it as a brief, not a dark saying (Abbott, *Johannine Vocabulary*, 219ff). **λελάληκα** perf. ind. act. λαλέω s.v. 1. Perf. emphasizes the durative action in the past. **ἔρχεται** pres. mid. (dep.) act. ἔρχομαι s.v. 2. Pres. is fut., but it emphasizes the certainty of the coming fact. **λαλήσω** fut. ind. act. λαλέω. **ἀπαγγελῶ** fut. ind. act. ἀπαγγέλλω (# 550) to speak, to proclaim. ◆ **26 αἰτήσεσθε** fut. ind. mid. αἰτέω s.v. 23. **ἐρωτήσω** fut. ind. act. ἐρωτάω s.v. 19. ◆ **27 πεφιλήκατε** perf. ind. act. φιλέω (# 5797). **πεπιστεύκατε** perf. ind. act. πιστεύω (# 4409) to believe. Perf. implies a continuous attitude of life (Brown). **ἐξῆλθον** aor. ind. act. ἐξέρχομαι (# 2002) to go out. ◆ **28 ἐλήλυθα** perf. ind. act. ἔρχομαι s.v. 2.

◆ **29 ἴδε** (# 2623) aor. imp. act. ὁράω to see. Used almost as a deictic particle to draw attention. ◆ **30 οἴδαμεν** perf. ind. act. οἶδα to know. s.v. 18. **ἐξῆλθες** aor. ind. act. ἐξέρχομαι s.v. 27. ◆ **31 ἀπεκρίθη** aor. ind. pass. (dep.) ἀποκρίνομαι (# 646) to answer. ◆ **32 ἐλήλυθεν** perf. ind. act. ἔρχομαι s.v. 2. **σκορπισθῆτε** aor. subj. pass. σκορπίζω (# 5025) to scatter. Subj. used w. **ἵνα** (# 2671) to explain **ὥρα** (# 6052). **ἀφῆτε** aor. subj. act. ἀφίημι (# 918) to forsake. ◆ **33 λελάληκα** perf. ind. act. λαλέω s.v. 1. **ἔχητε** pres. subj. act. ἔχω (# 2400) to have. Subj. w. **ἵνα** (# 2671) expresses result. **ἔχετε** pres. ind. act. ἔχω. **θαρσεῖτε** pres. imp. act. θαρσέω (# 2510) to have courage, to be courageous. **νενίκηκα** perf. ind. act. νίκω (# 3771) to conquer. Perf. denotes an abiding victory (Morris).

John 17

◆ **1 ἐλάλησεν** aor. ind. act. λαλέω (# 3281) to speak. **ἐπάρας** aor. act. part. ἐπαίρω (# 2048) to lift up. Part. is attendant circumstance or temp. Aor. indicates an antecedent action to the main vb. (ἐλάλησεν): "After he had lifted up his eyes, he spoke." **ἐλήλυθεν** perf. ind. act. ἔρχομαι (# 2262) to come. Perf. indicates a completed past action and emphasizes the results: "The hour has come and is here." **δόξασον** aor. imp. act. δοξάζω (# 1519) to glorify. Aor. imp. calls for a specific act and portrays the action as beginning: "Start to glorify." **δοξάσῃ** aor. subj. act. δοξάζω. Subj. w. **ἵνα** (# 2671) expresses purp. or result. ◆ **2 ἔδωκας** aor. ind. act. δίδωμι (# 1443) to give. **δέδωκας** perf. ind. act. Perf. denotes the permanence of the gift (Morris). **δώσῃ** aor. subj. act. ◆ **3 ἵνα** (# 2671) that, explanatory use. **γινώσκωσιν** pres. subj. act. γινώσκω (# 1182) to know. Subj. w. **ἵνα** expresses the content of eternal life. It could also express the result. **ἀπέστειλας** aor. ind. act. ἀποστέλλω (# 690) to send, to send as a personal authoritative representative (TDNT). ◆ **4 ἐδόξασα** aor. ind. act. δοξάζω s.v. 1. Const. aor. looking at his whole past life in which he glorified God. **τελειώσας** aor. act. part. τελειόω (# 5457) to complete, accomplish, make perfect. This completion is the necessary basis for his coming glorification. It looks back upon the completed life of Jesus, and probably upon His death too (Barrett). **ἵνα** (# 2671) expresses either purp. or it is explanatory (Brown). **ποιήσω** aor. subj. act. ποιέω (# 4472) to do. ◆ **5 δόξασόν** aor. imp. act. δοξάζω s.v. 1. **εἶχον** impf. ind. act. ἔχω (# 2400) to have. **εἶναι** pres. act. inf. εἰμί (# 1639) to be. Inf. used w. **πρό** (# 4574) to express antecedent action. ◆ **6 ἐφανέρωσα** aor. ind. act. φανερόω (# 5746) to make clear, to reveal. Aor. sums up the work of the ministry and is parallel to v. 4 (Barrett). **ἔδωκας** aor. ind. act. δίδωμι (# 1443) to give. **τετήρηκαν** perf. ind. act. τηρέω (# 5498) to keep. For the form s. BD, 44. ◆ **7 ἔγνωκαν** perf. ind. act. γινώσκω

(# 1182) to know. **δέδωκας** perf. ind. act. δίδωμι s.v. 6. ♦ **8 ἔδωκας** aor. ind. act. δίδωμι s.v. 6. **ἔλαβον** aor. ind. act. λαμβάνω (# 3284) to take, to receive. **ἔγνωσαν** aor. ind. act. γινώσκω s.v. 3. **ἐξῆλθον** aor. ind. act. ἐξέρχομαι (# 2002) to go out. **ἀπέστειλας** aor. ind. act. ἀποστέλλω s.v. 3. ♦ **9 δέδωκας** perf. ind. act. δίδωμι s.v. 6. ♦ **10 δεδόξασμαι** perf. ind. pass. δοξάζω s.v. 1. Perf. indicates the state of glorification and may be proleptic, pointing forward to the certain glory yet to come (Morris). ♦ **11 τήρησον** aor. imp. act. τηρέω s.v. 6. **ἐν** (# 1877) in, both local and instr. They are to be both marked w. and protected by the divine name (Brown). **δέδωκας** perf. ind. act. δίδωμι s.v. 6. **ὦσιν** pres. subj. act. εἰμί (# 1639) to be. Subj. expresses purp. or result w. **ἵνα** (# 2671). ♦ **12 ἤμην** impf. ind. mid. (dep.) εἰμί s.v. 11. **ἐτήρουν** impf. ind. act. τηρέω s.v. 6. Customary impf. indicates that he kept them over a longer period of time. **δέδωκας** perf. ind. act. δίδωμι s.v. 6. **ἐφύλαξα** aor. ind. act. φυλάσσω (# 5875) to guard. Aor. sums up the process represented by the impf. ἐτήρουν (Barrett). **ἀπώλετο** aor. ind. mid. ἀπόλλυμι (# 660) to destroy, to be lost, to perish. **ἀπώλεια** (# 724) destruction, perdition, damnation (Brown). Attributive gen., i.e., "the son deserving perdition" or "the son characterized by perdition." **πληρωθῇ** aor. subj. pass. πληρόω (# 4444) to fulfill. Subj. w. **ἵνα** (# 2671) expresses result. ♦ **13 ἔχωσιν** pres. subj. act. ἔχω (# 2400) to have. **πεπληρωμένην** perf. pass. part. (adj.) πληρόω s.v. 12. Perf. indicates that the action is completed. ♦ **14 ἐμίσησεν** aor. ind. act. μισέω (# 3631) to hate. ♦ **15 ἄρῃς** aor. subj. act. αἴρω (# 149) to lift up, to take away. Subj. w. **ἵνα** (# 2671) indicates the content of the request. **τηρήσῃς** aor. subj. act. τηρέω s.v. 6. Subj. w. **ἵνα** (# 2671) indicates the content of the request. ♦ **17 ἁγίασον** aor. imp. act. ἁγιάζω (# 39) to sanctify, to set apart and dedicate a person or thing to the service of God and to dedicate as a sacrifice (Hoskyns). Aor. imp. may suggest that the action begin. Certainly there is at least a timeless or gnomic idea here. **ἀλήθεια** (# 237) truth. For the construction without the article s. John 1:1. ♦ **18 ἀπέστειλας** aor. ind. act. ἀποστέλλω s.v. 3. Aor. describes a past action that has been completed. **ἀπέστειλα** aor. ind. act. ἀποστέλλω. Proleptic aor. referring to the commission after the resurrection (Morris). ♦ **19 ὦσιν** pres. subj. act. εἰμί s.v. 11. Subj. w. **ἵνα** (# 2671) is used to express purp. or result. The vb. is used here to form a periphrastic construction. **ἡγιασμένοι** perf. pass. part. ἁγιάζω s.v. 17. ♦ **20 πιστευόντων** pres. act. part. πιστεύω (# 4409) to believe. Pres. part. emphasizes a continuing trait. ♦ **21 ἵνα** (# 2671) so that, that. The first two cls. express the content of prayer and the third expresses purp. (Brown). **ὦσιν** pres. subj. act. εἰμί s.v. 11. **πιστεύῃ** pres. subj. act. πιστεύω s.v. 20. Subj. w. **ἵνα** (# 2671). **ὅτι** (# 4022) that, introducing the content of the belief. **ἀπέστειλας** aor. ind. act. ἀποστέλλω s.v. 3. Consummative aor. empha-

sizing the end of the action, "He has been sent and is here." ♦ **22 δέδωκα** perf. ind. act. δίδωμι s.v. 6. Perf. emphasizes the result of a past action. **ὦσιν** pres. subj. act. εἰμί s.v. 11. ♦ **23 ὦσιν** pres. subj. act. εἰμί s.v. 11. **τετελειωμένοι** perf. pass. part. τελειόω s.v. 4, complete, to accomplish, to make perfect (BAGD). Used in a periphrastic construction to form the perf. pass. Subj. w. **ἵνα** (# 2671) used to express purp. Perf. indicates a permanent state as the goal and final result (RWP). **γινώσκῃ** pres. subj. act. γινώσκω (# 1182) to know. **ἠγάπησας** aor. ind. act. ἀγαπάω (# 26) to love. ♦ **24 δέδωκας** perf. ind. act. δίδωμι s.v. 6. **ἵνα** (# 2671) that, used to express the content of the desire. **θεωρῶσιν** pres. subj. act. θεωρέω (# 2555) to see. Subj. w. **ἵνα** (# 2671) to express result. **ἠγάπησάς** aor. ind. act. ἀγαπάω s.v. 23. ♦ **25 καί** (# 2779) both; i.e., both the world ... and these (Morris). **ἔγνω** aor. ind. act. γινώσκω s.v. 7. ♦ **26 ἐγνώρισα** aor. ind. act. γνωρίζω (# 1192) to make known. **ᾖ** pres. subj. εἰμί (# 1639) to be. Subj. w. **ἵνα** (# 2671) to express purp. or better result.

John 18

♦ **1 εἰπών** aor. act. part. λέγω (# 3306) to say. Aor. part. expresses antecedent time ("after"). **ἐξῆλθεν** aor. ind. act. ἐξέρχομαι (# 2002) to go out. **χείμαρρος** (# 5929) brook. One containing water perhaps only in the winter (Barrett). Thus there was no water at this time. **κῆπος** (# 3057) garden. Refers to a plot of land where vegetables or flowers are planted and sometimes trees as well (Brown). These gardens often contained palms, fruit trees, flowers, even vegetables (MM). Such gardens were forbidden in Jerusalem (SB, 1:992f). **εἰσῆλθεν** aor. ind. act. εἰσέρχομαι (# 1656) to go in. ♦ **2 ᾔδει** plperf. ind. act. of the def. perf. οἶδα (# 3857) to know. **παραδιδούς** pres. act. part. παραδίδωμι (# 4140) to betray, to deliver over. Subst. part. here emphasizing the character trait. For a discussion of the traitor Judas s. DJG, 406-8. **συνήχθη** aor. ind. pass. συνάγω (# 5251) to gather together; here, to meet. Const. aor. without making a statement concerning the manner or duration of the action. ♦ **3 λαβών** aor. act. part. λαμβάνω (# 3284) to take. Aor. part. indicates antecedent action necessary for the completion of the action of the main vb. For a discussion of extrabiblical sources s. DJG, 841-43. For a discussion of and bibliography to the passion narratives s. DJG, 842-54; DTM. **σπεῖρα** (# 5061) cohort (Morris). **ὑπηρέτης** (# 5677) minister, the temple police (Brown; BBC). **φανῶν** gen. pl. φανός torch (# 5749). **λαμπάδων** gen. λαμπάς (# 3286) lantern, lamp. Some were certainly necessary in spite of the new moon at Passover. **ὅπλον** (# 3960) weapon. ♦ **4 εἰδώς** pres. act. part. οἶδα s.v. 2. Aor. indicates antecedent action. Jesus knew the answer even before asking. Concessive part., "even though he knew." ♦ **5** ἀπεκρίθησαν aor. ind. pass. (dep.) ἀποκρίνομαι (# 646) to answer. εἱστήκει plperf. ind. act. ἵστημι (# 2705) perf., to stand. παραδιδούς pres. act. part. παραδίδωμι (# 4140) to betray; used as subst. part., "the traitor." ◆ 6 ἀπῆλθον aor. ind. act. ἀπέρχομαι (# 599) to go away. ἔπεσαν aor. ind. act. πίπτω (# 4406) to fall. χαμαί (# 5912) to the ground. ◆ 7 ἐπηρώτησεν aor. ind. act. ἐπερωτάω (# 2089) to question, to ask. ◆ 8 ἀπεκρίθη aor. ind. pass. (dep.) ἀποκρίνομαι s.v. 5. ἄφετε aor. imp. act. ἀφίημι (# 918) to allow. ὑπάγειν pres. act. inf. ὑπάγω (# 5632) to go away. Here in the sense of unimpeded, or without being arrested (BAGD). Inf. is compl. to the main vb. ◆ 9 πληρωθῇ aor. subj. pass. πληρόω (# 4444) to fulfill. Subj. w. ἵνα (# 2671) to express result or purp. δέδωκας perf. ind. act. δίδωμι (# 1443) to give. ἀπώλεσα aor. ind. act. ἀπόλλυμι (# 660) to perish, to be lost; here, lose (BAGD). ◆ 10 ἔχων pres. act. part. ἔχω (# 2400) to have; here, to have in one's possession. Part. of attendant circumstance. Pres. describes that the sword is presently in Peter's possession. εἵλκυσεν aor. ind. act. ἑλκύω (# 1816) to draw, to drag. Here literally to draw out a sword (BAGD). ἔπαισεν aor. ind. act. παίω (# 4091) to strike. ἀπέκοψεν aor. ind. act. ἀποκόπτω (# 644) to cut off. ὠτάριον (# 6064) dimin. ear, the external part of the ear (Brown). δεξιός (# 1288) right. ◆ 11 βάλε aor. act. imp. βάλλω (# 965) to throw, to place. Aor. imp. is either ingressive, "begin to put the sword away"; or const., giving a categorical command without describing the progress: "put it away." θήκη (# 2557) scabbard; here, the receptacle into which a thing is put (Barrett). δέδωκεν perf. ind. act. δίδωμι s.v. 9. Perf. emphasizes the results of a completed act. πίω aor. subj. act. πίνω (# 4403) to drink. ◆ 12 συνέλαβον aor. ind. act. συλλαμβάνω (# 5197) to seize, to take into custody. ἔδησαν aor. ind. act. δέω (# 1313) to bind. ◆ 13 πενθερός (# 4290) father-in-law (Jos., *Ant.*, 18:34-35; 26; b. Pesachim 573; BBC). ◆ 14 συμφέρει pres. ind. act. συμφέρω (# 5237) impersonal use; it is useful, it is advantageous. ἀποθανεῖν aor. act. inf. ἀποθνήσκω (# 633) to die. Inf. is compl. to the main vb. ◆ 15 ἠκολούθει impf. ind. act. ἀκολουθέω (# 199) to follow. γνωστός (# 1196) known. This provided him access to the house. συνεισῆλθεν aor. ind. act. συνεισέρχομαι (# 5291) to go in together. αὐλή (# 885) courtyard. ◆ 16 εἱστήκει plperf. ind. act. s.v. 5. ἐξῆλθεν aor. ind. act. ἐξέρχομαι s.v. 1. θυρωρός (# 2601) doorkeeper. εἰσήγαγεν aor. ind. act. εἰσάγω (# 1652) to lead into. The subject is uncertain; the meaning might be, "he brought Peter in," or "she admitted Peter" (Morris). ◆ 17 παιδίσκη (# 4087) maidservant. ◆ 18 εἱστήκεισαν s.v. 16. ἀνθρακιά (# 471) charcoal fire. πεποιηκότες perf. act. part. ποιέω (# 4472) to make. Perf. part. describes antecedent action emphasizing the result. They had made the fire and it was burning. ψῦχος (# 6036) cold. Snow and ice were possible during Nisan (JLightfoot, 3:420). ἐθερ-

μαίνοντο impf. ind. mid. (dep.) θερμαίνομαι (# 2548) to warm oneself. ἑστώς perf. act. part. (temp.) ἵστημι s.v. 5; "while he was standing." θερμαινόμενος pres. mid. part. θερμαίνομαι. ◆ 19 οὖν (# 4036) then, now. Here it indicates a succession of events (DM, 253f). ἠρώτησεν aor. ind. act. ἐρωτάω (# 2263) to question. Incep. impf., "he began to question him," or iterat. impf., "he questioned him continually." ◆ 20 ἀπεκρίθη aor. ind. pass. (dep.) ἀποκρίνομαι s.v. 5. λελάληκα perf. ind. act. λαλέω (# 3281) to speak. Perf. emphasizes the results of his past teaching. His teaching is public record. ἐδίδαξα aor. ind. act. διδάσκω (# 1438) to teach. ἐλάλησα aor. ind. act. λαλέω. ◆ 21 ἐρώτησον aor. imp. act. ἐρωτάω (# 2263) to ask, to question. Ingressive aor., "begin to ask them" (not me). ἀκηκοότας perf. act. part. ἀκούω (# 201) to hear. Perf. stresses the result of their hearing. They have heard and thus know. Subst. part. to emphasize a particular trait, "those who have heard." ἴδε aor. imp. act. ὁράω to see. οἴδασιν perf. ind. act. οἶδα (# 3857) to know; a perf. w. pres. meaning. ◆ 22 εἰπόντος aor. act. part. (temp.) λέγω (# 3306) to speak. Aor. stresses the antecedent action as the basis for the action of the main vb. Gen. abs., "when he had spoken..." παρεστηκώς perf. act. part. παρίστημι (# 4225) to stand along side of. Subst. perf. part. Perf. emphasizes the result, that he is present and positioned there. ἔδωκεν aor. ind. act. δίδωμι (# 1443) to give. ῥάπισμα (# 4825) slap, a blow on the face w. the flat on the hand (Barrett). Certainly illegal (BBC). ◆ 23 ἀπεκρίθη aor. ind. pass. (dep.) ἀποκρίνομαι s.v. 5. μαρτύρησον aor. imp. act. μαρτυρέω (# 3455) to testify ("produce some evidence of it") (Brown). Aor. imp. may suggest that they should start w. the evidence, if they have any. δέρεις pres. ind. act. δέρω (# 1296) to strike, to flay; here, to strike someone in the face (BAGD). ◆ 24 ἀπέστειλεν aor. ind. act. ἀποστέλλω (# 690) to send. δεδεμένον perf. pass. part. δέω (# 1313) to bind. Perf. emphasizes the results of the binding; i.e., he was bound. ◆ 25 ἑστώς perf. act. part. (temp.) ἵστημι s.v. 5. θερμαινόμενος pres. mid. (dep.) part. θερμαίνομαι s.v. 18. The repetition of these words brings the scene back to Peter (John 18:18). εἶπον aor. ind. act. λέγω s.v. 22. The subject is not named, but presumably is the servants and police mentioned in v. 18 (Brown). εἶ pres. act. ind. 2nd. sing. εἰμί (# 1639) to be. ἠρνήσατο aor. ind. mid. (dep.) ἀρνέομαι (# 766) to deny. Incep. aor., "he began to deny it." ◆ 26 συγγενής (# 5150) relative. ὤν pres. act. part. εἰμί s.v. 25. Part. of attendant circumstance giving the reason for the more intimate knowledge than that of a mere onlooker. ἀπέκοψεν aor. ind. act. ἀποκόπτω (# 644) to cut off. ὠτίον (# 6065) ear. εἶδον aor. ind. act. ὁράω (# 3972) to see. κῆπος garden s.v. 1. ◆ 27 ἀλέκτωρ (# 232) rooster. ἐφώνησεν aor. ind. act. φωνέω (# 5888) to call, here, to crow. ◆ 28 πρωΐ (# 4745) early. It was common for Romans to start their day early (BBC). **μιανθῶσιν** aor. subj. pass. μιαίνω (# 3620) to defile. Subj. w. **ἵνα** (# 2671) to express purp. Ironically, they were more concerned about ritual cleanness than social justice. **φάγωσιν** aor. subj. act. ἐσθίω (# 2266) to eat. Subj. w. **ἵνα** (# 2671) in both cls. expresses the purp. or motive for their actions. **πάσχα** (# 4247) Passover, not necessarily referring to the Passover season (Tasker). If they become unclean their Passover will not be counted as valid. Thus their sacrifice should be burned (M, Pesachim, 7:8-10; 8:6-8). ◆ **29 ἐξῆλθεν** aor. ind. act. ἐξέρχομαι s.v. 1 **φησίν** aor. ind. act. φημί (# 5774) to say. **κατηγορία** (# 2990) legal accusation for a lawsuit (MM). ◆ **30 ἀπεκρίθησαν** aor. ind. pass. (dep.) ἀποκρίνομαι s.v. 5. **ποιῶν** pres. act. part. ποιέω (# 4472) to do, here, to commit evil deeds. Subst. part. shows one who does evil; i.e., an evildoer. The emphasis is on the personal trait of committing evil. **παρεδώκαμεν** aor. ind. act. παραδίδωμι (# 4140) to deliver over, to hand over; here in a legal sense of to deliver up to prison or for judgment (MM). ◆ **31 λάβετε** aor. imp. act. λαμβάνω (# 3284) to take. Aor. imp. is a momentary command given for a specific situation. **κρίνατε** aor. imp. act. κρίνω (# 3212) to judge. Aor. imp. here could be ingressive, "start judging him yourselves." **ἔξεστιν** pres. ind. act. ἔξεστι(ν) (# 2003) it is lawful, it is allowed. **ἀποκτεῖναι** aor. act. inf. ἀποκτείνω (# 650) to kill. Inf. is compl. to the main vb. Aor. portrays here an undefined action without reference to its beginning, duration, or completion (Morris, 786ff; Sherwin-White, 35-43). ◆ **32 πληρωθῇ** aor. subj. pass. πληρόω (# 4444) to fulfill. Subj. w. **ἵνα** (# 2671) describes result. **σημαίνων** pres. act. part. σημαίνω (# 4955) to signify, to indicate. Part. of attendant circumstance. **ἤμελλεν** impf. ind. act. μέλλω (# 3516) to be about to. For the construction w. the inf. to express the fut. s. 6:6. **ἀποθνῄσκειν** pres. act. inf. ἀποθνῄσκω (# 633) to die. Inf. is compl. to the main vb. ◆ **33 εἰσῆλθεν** aor. ind. act. εἰσέρχομαι (# 1656) to enter. Pilate conducts an inquiry (*cognitio*) upon which he makes his decision. **ἐφώνησεν** aor. ind. act. φωνέω s.v. 27. **βασιλεὺς τῶν Ἰουδαίων** (# 995; 2681) "the king of the Jews." ◆ **34 ἀπεκρίθη** aor. ind. pass. (dep.) ἀποκρίνομαι s.v. 5. ◆ **35 παρέδωκαν** aor. ind. act. παραδίδωμι s.v. 30. ◆ **36 ἠγωνίζοντο** impf. ind. mid. (dep.) ἀγωνίζομαι (# 76) to fight. Impf. implies they would be fighting now (Morris). If Christ's kingdom were earthly his servants would not permit the capture or betrayal of the commander. **παραδοθῶ** aor. subj. pass. παραδίδωμι s.v. 30. Subj. w. **ἵνα** (# 2671) expresses purp. or result. **νῦν** (# 3814) nontemp. use following a cl. expressing an unfulfilled cond.–"but as it is," "but as the case now stands" (Thrall, 21). **ἐντεῦθεν** (# 1949) from here, giving the source or sphere of the kingdom. ◆ **37 οὐκοῦν** (# 4034) an argumentative particle seeking a definite answer: "very well; so you are a king?" (Barrett) **γεγέννημαι**

perf. ind. pass. γεννάω (# 1164) to bear; pass. to be born. While John does not develop the concept of Christ's birth, he clearly develops the purp. of Christ's coming to witness to and reveal the truth. **ἐλήλυθα** perf. ind. act. ἔρχομαι (# 2262) to come. **μαρτυρήσω** aor. subj. act. μαρτυρέω (# 3455) to witness. Subj. w. **ἵνα** (# 2671) expresses the purp. of his coming. **ἀληθείᾳ** (# 237) truth, here perhaps the truth about himself, but also about God and man. ◆ **38 εἰπών** aor. act. part. (temp.) λέγω (# 3306) to say. Aor. describing antecedent action to the main vb., "After he said this." ◆ **39 συνήθεια** (# 5311) custom (Blinzler). **ἀπολύσω** fut. ind. act. ἀπολύω (# 668) to release. Referring to a pardoning of a condemned man (*indulgentia*) or an acquittal before judgment (*abolitio*) (BBC). ◆ **40 ἐκραύγασαν** aor. ind. act. κραυγάζω (# 3198) to scream. **λῃστής** (# 3334) robber, highway bandit; here probably revolutionary, insurrectionist (DJG, 688-98). They chose to release a revolutionary rather than a righteous man.

John 19

◆ **1 ἔλαβεν** aor. ind. act. λαμβάνω (# 3284) to take. **ἐμαστίγωσεν** aor. ind. act. μαστιγόω (# 3463) to scourge (Matt. 27:26) (BBC). ◆ **2 πλέξαντες** aor. act. part. πλέκω (# 4428) to plait. **ἄκανθα** (# 180) thorn (Brown). Portraying him in mockery as a vassal king. **ἐπέθηκαν** aor. ind. act. ἐπιτίθημι (# 2202) to place upon. **πορφύρα** (# 4526) purple (Morris). **περιέβαλον** aor. ind. act. περιβάλλω (# 6314) to cast about, to put around, to wrap about, to clothe (MM). ◆ **3 ἤρχοντο** impf. ind. mid. (dep.) ἔρχομαι (# 2262) to come. **χαῖρε** pres. imp. act. χαίρω (# 5897) to greet; here hail! followed by the nom. of address w. the article: "Hail, you king!"(Barrett). **ἐδίδοσαν** impf. ind. act. δίδωμι (# 1443) to give. Iterat. impf. speaks of repeated action. **ῥάπισμα** slap (18:22). ◆ **4 ἐξῆλθεν** aor. ind. act. ἐξέρχομαι (# 2002) to go out. **ἴδε** (# 2623) aor. imp. act. ὁράω to see. **γνῶτε** aor. subj. act. γινώσκω (# 1182) to know. Subj. w. **ἵνα** (# 2671) expresses result. ◆ **5 ἐξῆλθεν** aor. ind. act. s.v. 4. **φορῶν** pres. act. part. φορέω (# 5841) to wear, to carry. Part. of manner, describing how he was when he was brought out. Pres. indicates that the action is contemporaneous. **ἀκάνθινος** (# 181) thorny, made of thorns. For the suffix indicating material s. MH, 459. ◆ **6 εἶδον** aor. ind. act. ὁράω (# 3972) to see. **ἐκραύγασαν** aor. ind. act. κραυγάζω (# 3198) to scream. **σταύρωσον** aor. imp. act. σταυρόω (# 5090) to crucify. Aor. imp. suggests a specific, immediate command or petition. **λάβετε** aor. imp. act. λαμβάνω s.v. 1. This is returning Jesus to the Jewish custody. Because they did not have the right of capital punishment, they would not be able to crucify him. Thus Pilate was rejecting the Jewish request. There was no reason for a Roman court to condemn him. ◆ **7 ἀπεκρίθησαν** aor. ind. pass. (dep.)

ἀποκρίνομαι (# 646) to answer. ὀφείλει pres. ind. act. ὀφείλω (# 4053) to be necessary. ἀποθανεῖν aor. act. inf. ἀποθνήσκω (# 633) to die. Compl. inf. to the main vb. "It is necessary for him to die." ἐποίησεν aor. ind. act. ποιέω (# 4472) to make, to do. Here to make oneself to be, to claim to be. John uses this word significantly in light of John 18:30. This is the evil that they claimed against him. ◆ 8 ἤκουσεν aor. ind. act. ἀκούω (# 201) to hear. μᾶλλον (# 3437) more. ἐφοβήθη aor. ind. pass. (dep.) φοβέομαι (# 5828) to fear, to be afraid. ◆ 9 εἰσῆλθεν aor. ind. act. εἰσέρχομαι (# 1656) to go into. ἔδωκεν aor. ind. act. δίδωμι (# 1443) to give. ◆ 10 ἀπολῦσαι aor. act. inf. ἀπολύω (# 668) to release. Inf. is compl. to the main vb. σταυρῶσαι aor. act. inf. σταυρόω s.v. 6. Compl. inf. to main vb. ◆ 11 ἀπεκρίθη aor. ind. pass. (dep.) ἀποκρίνομαι s.v. 7. δεδομένον perf. pass. part. δίδωμι s.v. 9. ἄνωθεν (# 540) from above (s. 3:3). παραδούς aor. act. part. παραδίδωμι (# 4140) to deliver over, to betray. Subst. part. to emphasize this trait of Judas as a traitor. Aor. describes antecedent action. μείζονα (# 3505) comp. μέγας great; comp., greater. ◆ 12 ἐζήτει impf. ind. act. ζητέω (# 2426) to seek. Conative impf. implies a series of attempts which were shouted down (Brown). ἀπολῦσαι aor. act. inf. ἀπολύω s.v. 10. Inf. is compl. to the main vb. ἐκραύγασαν aor. ind. act. κραυγάζω s.v. 6. Iterat. impf., "they shouted repeatedly," or incep. impf., "they began to shout." ἀπολύσῃς aor. subj. act. ἀπολύω. Subj. w. ἐάν (# 1569) expresses cond. φίλος τοῦ Καίσαρος a friend of Caesar. The phrase amici Caesaris (friend of Caesar) is a technical term designating the elite in the Roman government loyal to the emperor. To lose or forego this designation meant political death. Hoehner, Chronological Aspects of the Life of Christ (Grand Rapids: Zondervan, 1977), 111-12; s. Ernst Bammel, "φίλος τοῦ Καίσαρος," Theologische Literaturzeitung 77 (1952): 205-10; E. Stauffer, Jesus and His Story, 108-10; Witherington, 303-6; BBC; DJG, 615-17. ποιῶν pres. act. part. ποιέω s.v. 7; here, to claim to be. Subst. part. to emphasize this trait. Pres. indicates contemporaneous action. Used w. πᾶς it means "anyone who." ◆ 13 ἀκούσας aor. act. part. ἀκούω s.v. 8; w. the gen., to listen to, to obey. This accusation would have been certain death under the suspicious Tiberias. Thus Pilate, to save himself, gave way under this threat. ἤγαγεν aor. ind. act. ἄγω (# 72) to lead. ἐκάθισεν aor. ind. act. καθίζω (# 2767) to sit down, to take one's seat. βῆμα (# 1037) judgment seat (Blinzler). λιθόστρωτος (# 3346) paved w. stone, used of a mosaic or tesselated pavement (LS). λεγόμενον pres. pass. part. λέγω (# 3306) to say; pass. to have the name. ◆ 15 ἆρον aor. imp. act. αἴρω (# 149) to take away. σταυρώσω fut. ind. act. σταυρόω s.v. 6. J.A. Fitzmeyer, "Crucifixion in Ancient Palestine, Qumran Literature, and the New Testament," CBQ 40 (1978): 493-513; ABD, 1:1206-210. ἀπεκρίθησαν

aor. ind. pass. (dep.) ἀποκρίνομαι s.v. 7. ◆ 16 παρέδωκεν aor. ind. act. παραδίδωμι (# 4140) to take away, to turn over, here, in judgment. σταυρωθῇ aor. subj. pass. σταυρόω s.v. 6. Subj. w. ἵνα (# 2671) to express purp. παρέλαβον aor. ind. act. παραλαμβάνω (# 4161) to take, to take custody of. The vb.'s subject is probably the soldiers (Morris). ◆ 17 βαστάζων pres. act. part. βαστάζω (# 1002) to carry. Part. of manner explaining in what manner he went out. Pres. indicates contemporaneous activity. He carried the horizontal cross beam (patibulum), usually stripped naked, out to the stake. These were about 10 feet high and were reused (BBC). ἐξῆλθεν aor. ind. act. ἐξέρχομαι s.v. 4. ◆ 18 ἐσταύρωσαν aor. ind. act. σταυρόω s.v. 6. ◆ 19 ἔγραψεν aor. ind. act. γράφω (# 1211) to write. It was common to post the crime (HSB, 505-6). ἔθηκεν aor. ind. act. τίθημι (# 5502) to place. γεγραμμένον perf. pass. part. γράφω. Periphrastic part. ◆ 20 ἀνέγνωσαν aor. ind. act. ἀναγινώσκω (# 336) to read. ἐσταυρώθη aor. ind. pass. σταυρόω s.v. 6. ◆ 21 γράφε pres. imp. act. γράφω s.v. 19. Pres. imp. indicates that Pilate should stop writing; that is, he should change the inscription. ◆ 22 γέγραφα perf. ind. act. γράφω s.v. 19. Perf. marks the permanence and abiding character of his act. It was the expression of a legal decision (Bernard). Without the threat of disloyalty to Caesar, Pontius Pilate shows once again his unyielding character and spiteful contempt for the Jews. The sign (tilulus) was designed as an insult and a warning to those who opposed the Roman emperor. ◆ 23 ἔλαβον aor. ind. act. s.v. 1. ἐποίησαν aor. ind. act. ποιέω s.v. 7. χιτῶνα (# 5945) tunic, shirt, a garment worn next to the skin underneath the rest of the garments (BAGD; MM). ἄραφος (# 731) without a seam. ὑφαντός (# 5733) woven. ◆ 24 σχίσωμεν aor. subj. act. σχίζω (# 5387) to divide, to split; hortatory subj, "let us not divide." λάχωμεν aor. subj. act. λαγχάνω (# 3275) to obtain by casting lots, to cast lots. πληρωθῇ aor. subj. pass. πληρόω (# 4444) to fulfill. This is interpreted as a fulfillment of Ps. 22:18. For the ancient Jewish understanding of Ps. 22 s. SB, 2:574-80. διεμερίσαντο aor. ind. mid. διαμερίζω (# 1374) to divide, to distribute; mid. to divide among themselves. ἔβαλον aor. ind. act. βάλλω (# 965) to throw, to cast. οὖν (# 4036) so then; resumptive (MT, 337). ◆ 25 εἱστήκεισαν plperf. ind. act. ἵστημι (# 2705) perf. to stand. ◆ 26 ἰδών aor. act. part. ὁράω (# 3972) to see. Temp. part., "when he saw." Aor. indicates antecedent action. Here Jesus honors his mother by providing for her (BBC). παρεστῶτα perf. act. part. παρίστημι (# 4225) to stand alongside. ἠγάπα impf. ind. act. ἀγαπάω (# 26) to love. ◆ 27 ἔλαβεν aor. ind. act. λαμβάνω s.v. 1. ◆ 28 εἰδώς perf. act. part. οἶδα (# 3857) to know. Def. perf. w. pres. meaning. τετέλεσται perf. ind. pass. τελέω (# 5464) to bring to an end. It has the connotation of completion (Brown). τελειωθῇ aor. subj. pass.

τελειόω (# *5457*) to accomplish. Used here in the sense of the fulfillment of Scripture (Morris). Subj. used here w. ἵνα (# *2671*) to express result. ◆ **29 σκεῦος** (# *5007*) vessel. ἔκειτο impf. ind. mid. (dep.) κεῖμαι (# *3023*) to set. ὄξος (# *3954*) vinegar, a diluted vinegary wine drunk by soldiers and laborers (Brown). σπόγγος (# *5074*) sponge. ὕσσωπος (# *5727*) hyssop (BBC; ABD, 2:812). περιθέντες aor. act. part. περιτίθημι (# *4363*) to put around. προσήνεγκαν aor. ind. act. προσφέρω (# *4712*) to bring to someone. ◆ **30 ἔλαβεν** aor. ind. act. λαμβάνω s.v. 1. τετέλεσται perf. ind. pass. τελέω s.v. 28. κλίνας aor. act. part. κλίνω (# *3111*) to bow. Aor. describes an antecedent action. Temp. part., "after bowing his head." παρέδωκεν aor. ind. act. s.v. 16. It is to give up voluntarily (Bernard). ◆ **31 μείνῃ** aor. subj. act. μένω (# *3531*) to remain. Subj. w. ἵνα (# *2671*) expresses purp. ἠρώτησαν aor. ind. act. ἐρωτάω (# *2263*) to ask. The second ἵνα w. subj. expresses the content of the request. κατεαγῶσιν aor. subj. pass. κατάγνυμι (# *2862*) to break. The word is used of breaking a reed, wood, or causing a wound (BAGD; MM). Often this was done w. iron clubs (BBC). σκέλος (# *5003*) leg. ἀρθῶσιν aor. subj. pass. αἴρω (# *149*) to take away; here, in the sense of take down from the cross, to remove. ◆ **32 ἦλθον** aor. ind. act. ἔρχομαι (# *2262*) to come, to go. κατέαξαν aor. ind. act. κατάγνυμι s.v. 31. συσταυρωθέντος aor. pass. part. (subst.) συσταυρόω (# *5365*) to co-crucify, to crucify together. Aor. indicates an antecedent action to the main vb. ◆ **33 ἐλθόντες** aor. act. part. (temp.) ἔρχομαι s.v. 32. Aor. describes antecedent action, "when they had come." εἶδον aor. ind. act. ὁράω (# *3972*) to see. τεθνηκότα perf. act. part. θνήσκω (# *2569*) to die. Perf. emphasizes the completed results of the action. He had already died and thus was dead. κατέαξαν s.v. 32. ◆ **34 λόγχῃ** (# *3365*) spearhead, lance, a shaft tipped w. an iron point (Morris), perhaps a *pilum* (BBC). πλευρά (# *4433*) side. ἔνυξεν aor. ind. act. νύσσω (# *3817*) to stab, to pierce. J.R. Michaels, "The Centurion's Confession and the Spear Thrust (Jn. 19,34ff.)," *CBQ* 29 (1967): 102-109. ἐξῆλθεν aor. ind. act. ἐξέρχομαι (# *2002*) to come out. A possible translation is, "and there came out immediately blood, even fluid (water)," which may be an allusion to the Passover (J.M. Ford. "Mingled Blood From the Side of Christ [John 19:34]," *NTS* 15 [1969]: 337-38). ◆ **35 ἑωρακώς** perf. act. part. (subst.) ὁράω s.v. 33. Perf. emphasizes the results of the past action. The author circumscribes himself this way. μεμαρτύρηκεν perf. ind. act. μαρτυρέω (# *3455*) to bear witness. Perf. signifies "he has said it on a permanent record" (Morris). πιστεύσητε pres. subj. act. πιστεύω (# *4409*) to believe. Subj. w. ἵνα (# *2671*) expresses purp. This purp. cl. probably modifies the whole idea in the v. (Brown). ◆ **36 ἐγένετο** aor. ind. mid. (dep.) γίνομαι (# *1181*) to become, to happen. πληρωθῇ aor. subj. pass. πληρόω s.v. 24. Subj.

w. ἵνα (# *2671*) expresses purp. ὀστοῦν (# *4014*) bone. συντριβήσεται fut. ind. pass. συντρίβω (# *5341*) to shatter, to crush. ◆ **37 ὄψονται** fut. ind. mid. (dep.) ὁράω s.v. 33; here, to recognize who he is; a quotation from Zech. 12:10. ἐξεκέντησαν aor. ind. act. ἐκκεντέω (# *1708*) to pierce, in the sense of kill. ◆ **38 μετὰ δὲ ταῦτα** (# *3552; 1254; 4047*) after these things, events. ἠρώτησεν aor. ind. act. ἐρωτάω (# *2263*) to ask, to petition. ὤν pres. act. part. εἰμί (# *1639*) to be. κεκρυμμένος perf. pass. part. κρύπτω (# *3221*) to hide, to conceal. Adverbial part. (Barrett). Perf. emphasizes the results of the action. He had hidden himself and was anonymous. ἄρῃ aor. subj. act. αἴρω (# *149*) to take. Subj. w. ἵνα (# *2671*) indicates the content of the request. ἐπέτρεψεν aor. ind. act. ἐπιτρέπω (# *2205*) to allow, to permit. ἦλθεν aor. ind. act. ἔρχομαι (# *2262*) to come. ἦρεν aor. ind. act. αἴρω. ◆ **39 ἐλθών** aor. act. part. (subst.) ἔρχομαι s.v. 38. Aor. indicates an antecedent action. φέρων pres. act. part. φέρω (# *5770*) to carry. Pres. indicates contemporaneous action. Part. describes the manner in which he came carrying a mixture. μίγμα (# *3623*) mixture. σμύρνης gen. σμύρνα (# *5043*) myrrh. Gen. of material describing what the mixture was made of. ἀλόη (# *264*) aloe. A powdered aromatic sandalwood used for perfuming bedding or clothes. Its purp. probably was to counteract unpleasant odor and slow down corruption (Brown). λίτρα (# *3354*) a Roman pound (12 ounces) (BAGD). A lavish expression of devotion (BBC). ◆ **40 ἔλαβον** aor. ind. act. λαμβάνω s.v. 1. ἔδησαν aor. ind. act. δέω (# *1313*) to bind. ὀθόνιον (# *3856*) linen bandage. The body is wrapped in the bandages, the spices sprinkled between the folds (Barrett; Blinzler). ἄρωμα (# *808*) spices, aromatic oil (Brown). ἐνταφιάζειν pres. inf. act. ἐνταφιάζω (# *1946*) to bury. Epex. inf. to the noun ἔθος (# *1621*) custom. ◆ **41 ἐσταυρώθη** aor. ind. pass. σταυρόω s.v. 6. τεθειμένος perf. pass. part. τίθημι (# *5502*) to place; here, to bury. ◆ **42 ἔθηκαν** aor. ind. act. τίθημι s.v. 41. For the form s. BD, 47f. Aor. is consummative emphasizing the completion of the action. Possibly a preliminary burial.

John 20

◆ **1 οὔσης** pres. act. part. (temp.) gen. fem. sing. εἰμί (# *1639*) to be. Gen. abs. Pres. is contemporaneous: "while it was still dark." For a discussion of the accounts s. HSB, 506-8; DJG, 673-88. ἠρμένον perf. pass. part. αἴρω (# *149*) to take away. This seems to imply that the stone was lifted out of the groove in which it ran. Perf. may give an air of finality (Morris). ◆ **2 ἐφίλει** impf. ind. act. φιλέω (# *5797*) to love. Durative impf. showing an action continuing over a period of time. ἦραν aor. ind. act. αἴρω s.v. 1. οἴδαμεν perf. ind. act. οἶδα (# *3857*) to know. Def. perf. w. pres. meaning.

ἔθηκαν aor. ind. act. τίθημι (# 5502) to place (s. 19:42). ◆ 3 ἐξῆλθεν aor. ind. act. ἐξέρχομαι (# 2002) to go out. ἤρχοντο impf. ind. mid. (dep.) ἔρχομαι (# 2262) to go, to come, here in the sense of arrive. ◆ 4 ἔτρεχον impf. ind. act. τρέχω (# 5556) to run. ὁμοῦ (# 3938) together. προέδραμεν aor. ind. act. προτρέχω (# 4708) to run before, to outrun (Brown). τάχιον (# 5441) comp. adv. ταχέως quickly; comp., more quickly. ἦλθεν aor. ind. act. ἔρχομαι s.v. 3, here to arrive. ◆ 5 παρακύψας aor. act. part. παρακύπτω (# 4160) to bend over. The vb. conveys the idea of bending over; i.e., to see something better–"to peer into," "to peep into" (Morris). In this case the object must be supplied. Aor. indicates an action necessary and antecedent to the main action. Temp. part., "after peering into the grave he saw." κείμενα pres. mid. (dep.) part. κεῖμαι (# 3023) to lie. εἰσῆλθεν aor. ind. act. εἰσέρχομαι (# 1656) to go into. This disciple hesitated to go into the grave. ◆ 6 ἀκολουθῶν pres. act. part. ἀκολουθέω (# 199) to follow. Part. of attendant circumstance. Pres. indicates contemporaneous action. ὀθόνιον (# 3856) grave cloth. These were linen and cloth bandages. This linen cloth appears to come from Egypt (BAGD; MM). ◆ 7 σουδάριον (# 5051) handkerchief, a cloth used to wipe off perspiration, probably the size of a small towel or large napkin (Brown). ἐντετυλιγμένον perf. pass. part. ἐντυλίσσω (# 1962) to wrap in a neat pile. ◆ 8 εἰσῆλθεν aor. ind. act. εἰσέρχομαι s.v. 5. ἐλθών aor. act. part. (temp.) ἔρχομαι s.v. 3, here arrived. Aor. indicating antecedent action ("who had arrived first"). εἶδεν aor. ind. act. ὁράω (# 3972) to see. ◆ 9 ᾔδεισαν plperf. ind. act. οἶδα s.v. 2. ὅτι (# 4022) that, introducing the content. ἀναστῆναι aor. act. inf. ἀνίστημι (# 482) to rise. Compl inf. to the main vb. ◆ 10 ἀπῆλθον aor. ind. act. ἀπέρχομαι (# 599) to go out. ◆ 11 εἱστήκει plperf. ind. act. ἵστημι (# 2705) perf. to stand. κλαίουσα pres. act. part. κλαίω (# 3081) to cry, to weep. ἔκλαιεν aor. ind. act. κλαίω. παρέκυψεν aor. ind. act. παρακύπτω to bend over (s.v. 5). ◆ 12 καθεζομένους pres. mid. (dep.) part. καθέζομαι (# 2757) to sit down. Part. of manner describing how the angels were when seen. ἔκειτο impf. ind. mid. (dep.) κεῖμαι s.v. 5. ◆ 13 ἦραν aor. ind. act. αἴρω s.v. 1. ἔθηκαν aor. ind. act. τίθημι (# 5502) to place. ◆ 14 εἰποῦσα aor. act. part. (temp.) λέγω (# 3306) to say. Aor. indicates antecedent action. "After saying this." ἐστράφη aor. ind. pass. στρέφομαι (# 5138) to turn around. ἑστῶτα perf. act. part. ἵστημι s.v. 11. UFG, 227-28. ᾔδει plperf. ind. act. οἶδα to know. Def. perf. w. pres. meaning s.v. 2. Plperf. used as an impf. ◆ 15 δοκοῦσα pres. act. part. δοκέω (# 1506) to suppose. ὅτι (# 4022) that, giving the content of the belief. κηπουρός (# 3058) gardener. ἐβάστασας aor. ind. act. βαστάζω (# 1002) to carry, to carry away. εἰπέ aor. imp. act. λέγω (# 3306) to say. Imp. is a polite request. Ingressive aor.: "please start to tell me," or const. aor. "please tell me

right now." ἔθηκας aor. ind. act. τίθημι s.v. 13. ἀρῶ fut. ind. act. αἴρω s.v. 1. ◆ 16 στραφεῖσα aor. act. part. (temp.) nom. fem. sing. στρέφομαι s.v. 14. Aor. indicates antecedent action. "After she turned, she said." W. her back previously turned she now faces him and recognizes who he is. ◆ 17 ἅπτου pres. imp. mid. (dep.) ἅπτομαι (# 721) w. the gen., to touch, to grasp, to cling. Jesus is asking her not to hold onto Him (Brown). Pres. imp. used as a prohibition suggests that she should stop touching him. ἀναβέβηκα perf. ind. act. ἀναβαίνω (# 326) to ascend, to go up. πορεύου pres. mid. (dep.) imp. πορεύομαι to go. Perhaps pres. indicates that the action should done and continued. ◆ 18 ἀγγέλλουσα pres. act. part. ἀγγέλλω (# 33) to report. Pres. indicates contemporaneous action w. the main vb. ἑώρακα perf. ind. act. ὁράω s.v. 8. Perf. emphasizes the result of the action. ◆ 19 οὔσης pres. act. part. (temp.) εἰμί (# 1639) to be. Gen. abs.; "when it was evening." κεκλεισμένων perf. pass. part. κλαίω (# 3091) to shut. Gen. abs., "with shut or locked doors." Perf. emphasizes the result of the action–they were shut. Usually a heavy bolt slid through rings attached to the door and the frame. ἦλθεν aor. ind. act. ἔρχομαι (# 2262) to come, to go. ἔστη aor. ind. act. ἵστημι s.v. 11. εἰρήνη (# 1645) peace; a normal greeting but significant in light of their fear. ◆ 20 εἰπών aor. act. part. λέγω s.v. 15. Aor. indicates antecedent action. Temp. part., "after saying...." ἔδειξεν aor. ind. act. δείκνυμι (# 1259) to show. πλευρά (# 4433) side. ἐχάρησαν aor. ind. pass. χαίρω (# 5897) to be glad, to rejoice. ἰδόντες aor. act. part. s.v. 8. Aor. indicates antecedent action. Temp. or causal part., "when or because they saw him." ◆ 21 ἀπέσταλκεν perf. ind. act. ἀποστέλλω (# 690) to send. Perf. emphasizes the completion of the act of sending and the conclusion of the mission. ◆ 22 ἐνεφύσησεν aor. ind. act. ἐμφυσάω (# 1874) to breathe upon. This is a preparatory event different from Pentecost (Hoskyns; Morris). λάβετε aor. imp. act. λαμβάνω (# 3284) to receive. ◆ 23 ἀφῆτε aor. subj. act. ἀφίημι (# 918) to release, to forgive. ἀφέωνται pres. ind. pass. ἀφίημι. κρατῆτε pres. subj. act. κρατέω (# 3195) to hold, to retain. The church, not the apostles, is now given authority to declare that certain sins are forgiven and certain sins are retained (Morris). κεκράτηνται pres. ind. pass. κρατέω. ◆ 24 ἦλθεν aor. ind. act. ἔρχομαι s.v. 3. ◆ 25 ἑωράκαμεν perf. ind. act. ὁράω s.v. 8. ἴδω aor. subj. act. ὁράω. Subj. w. ἐάν (# 1569) expresses cond. ἧλος (# 2464) nail. δάκτυλος (# 1235) finger. πιστεύσω aor. subj. act. πιστεύω (# 4409) to believe. ◆ 26 κεκλεισμένων perf. pass. part. s.v. 19. The doors are locked due to their fear of the Jews. The story is now built around the repetition of the key words. ἔστη aor. ind. act. ἵστημι (# 2705) to stand. ◆ 27 φέρε pres. act. imp. φέρω (# 5770) to bring, to take. Pres. imp. here shows that the action should continue. ἴδε (# 2623) aor.

imp. act. ὁράω (# 3972) to see. **βάλε** aor. imp. act. βά-λλω (# 965) to throw; here, to put, place, lay (BAGD). Aor. imp. suggests that the action should start. **γίνου** pres. mid. (dep.) imp. γίνομαι (# 1181) to become. Pres. imp. here is progressive. ◆ **28 ἀπεκρίθη** aor. ind. pass. (dep.) ἀποκρίνομαι (# 646) to answer. ◆ **29 ἑώρακας** perf. ind. act. ὁράω s.v. 8. **πεπίστευκας** perf. ind. act. πιστεύω s.v. 25. **ἰδόντες** aor. act. part. ὁράω. **πιστεύσαντες** aor. act. part. πιστεύω. ◆ **30 ἐνώπιον** (# 1967) w. gen., in the presence of, before. **γεγραμμένα** perf. pass. part. γράφω (# 1211) to write. ◆ **31 γέγραπται** perf. ind. pass. γράφω s.v. 30. Perf. indicates that what he has written stands (Morris). **πιστεύσητε** pres. subj. act. πιστεύω s.v. 25. Subj. w. ἵνα (# 2671) to express purp. **πιστεύοντες** pres. act. part. Part. of manner, "by believing." **ἔχητε** pres. subj. act. ἔχω (# 2400) to have, to obtain. Subj. w. ἵνα (# 2671) to express purp. or result.

John 21

◆ **1 ἐφανέρωσεν** aor. ind. act. φανερόω (# 5746) to manifest, to make visible, to show oneself, to appear. ◆ **3 ἁλιεύειν** pres. act. inf. ἁλιεύω (# 244) to fish. Inf. of purp., "in order to fish," taking up their previous profession. **ἐξῆλθον** aor. ind. act. ἐξέρχομαι (# 2262) to go out. **ἐνέβησαν** aor. ind. act. ἐμβαίνω (# 1832) to get in, to embark. **ἐπίασαν** aor. ind. act. πιάζω (# 4389) to catch. Usually fishing took place at night in order to catch more and sell in the morning (BBC). ◆ **4 πρωΐας** (# 4746) early morning. **γενομένης** pres. mid. (dep.) part. (temp.) γίνομαι (# 1181) to become, gen. abs. Pres. indicates contemporaneous action, "while day was already breaking," or "when it was early morning" (BAGD). **ἔστη** aor. ind. act. ἵστημι (# 2705) to stand. **αἰγιαλός** (# 129) shore, beach. **ᾔδεισαν** plperf. ind. act. οἶδα (# 3857) to know. Plup. used as an impf. ◆ **5 προσφάγιον** (# 4709) relish. Here best understood as some staple article of food of the genus fish. A part of an ordinary meal (MM). **ἀπεκρίθησαν** aor. ind. pass. (dep.) ἀποκρίνομαι (# 646) to answer. ◆ **6 βάλετε** aor. imp. act. βάλλω (# 965) to throw. Ingressive aor. ("start throwing") or const. aor. describing a categorical command without a reference to its duration ("throw"). **δίκτυον** (# 1473) net, casting net. **εὑρήσετε** fut. ind. act. εὑρίσκω (# 2351) to find. **ἔβαλον** aor. ind. act. βάλλω. **ἑλκύσαι** aor. act. inf. ἑλκύω (# 1816) to draw, haul, drag (BAGD). Inf. to express purp. **ἴσχυον** impf. ind. act. ἰσχύω (# 2710) to be strong, to be able. Obedience to Christ, not luck, is the important thing (Morris). ◆ **7 ἠγάπα** impf. ind. act. ἀγαπάω (# 26) to love. **ἀκούσας** aor. act. part. ἀκούω (# 201) to hear. **ἐπενδύτης** (# 2087) outer garment. Peter was working in a loincloth, but for the sake of modesty and reverence he put on his outer garment (Brown). **διεζώσατο** aor. ind. mid. διαζώννυμι (# 1346) to gird oneself by pulling up

the tunic and allowing a fold to fall over the belt. ◆ **8 ἦλθον** aor. ind. act. ἔρχομαι (# 2262) to come. **ὡς** w. numbers, about, approximately. **πηχῶν** gen. πῆχυς (# 4388) cubit, about 18 inches. Here, about a hundred yards away (BAGD). **σύροντες** pres. act. part. (temp.) σύρω (# 5359) to draw, to drag. Pres. suggests contemporaneous action. While Peter was wading or swimming ashore, the others follow in the boat dragging a net filled w. fish behind them. ◆ **9 ἀπέβησαν** aor. ind. act. ἀποβαίνω (# 609) to get out, to disembark. **ἀνθρακιά** (# 471) charcoal fire. **κειμένην** pres. mid. (dep.) part. κεῖμαι (# 3023) to lie there (BAGD). **ὀψάριον** (# 4066) fish. Normally refers to dried or preserved fish but here used to describe freshly caught fish (Brown). **ἐπικείμενον** pres. mid. (dep.) part. ἐπίκειμαι (# 2130) to lie upon; here used of fish lying on it (BAGD). ◆ **10 ἐνέγκατε** aor. imp. act. φέρω (# 5770) to bring, to carry. Ingressive aor., "start bringing." ◆ **11 ἀνέβη** aor. ind. act. ἀναβαίνω (# 326) to go up. Here used of embarking on a ship (Morris). **εἵλκυσεν** aor. ind. act. ἑλκύω s.v. 6. **ὄντων** pres. act. part. εἰμί (# 1639) to be. Gen. abs., concessive part. ("although"). Pres. suggests contemporaneous action. **ἐσχίσθη** aor. ind. pass. σχίζω (# 5387) to tear, to trip, to break; here, to rip under the weight of the fish. ◆ **12 ἀριστήσατε** aor. imp. act. ἀριστάω (# 753) to take breakfast, which was the first meal of the day (Barrett). **ἐτόλμα** impf. ind. act. τολμάω (# 5528) to dare. **ἐξετάσαι** aor. act. inf. ἐξετάζω (# 2004) to inquire, to ask. **εἰδότες** perf. act. part. οἶδα (# 3857) to know. Def. perf. w. pres. meaning. ◆ **14 ἐφανερώθη** aor. ind. pass. φανερόω (# 5746) to appear. **ἐγερθείς** aor. ind. pass. ἐγείρω (# 1586) to rise. ◆ **15 ἠρίστησαν** aor. ind. act. ἀριστάω s.v. 12. **πλέον** comp. πολύς (# 4498) much, comp., more than. Gen. of comparison (Brown). **φιλῶ** pres. ind. act. φιλέω (# 5797) to love. For a discussion of the this word and its synonym in the context s. Morris. **βόσκε** pres. imp. act. βόσκω (# 1081) to feed as a herdsman, to tend. Pres. imp. calls for a habitual feeding. **ἀρνίον** (# 768) lamb. ◆ **16 ποίμαινε** pres. imp. act. ποιμάνω (# 4477) to shepherd, to tend to sheep. **προβάτιον** (# 4585) sheep. ◆ **17 ἐλυπήθη** aor. ind. pass. λυπέω (# 3382) pass. to be sad. ◆ **18 νεώτερος** comp. νέος (# 3742) young; comp., younger. **ἐζώννυες** impf. ind. act. ζώννυμι (# 2439) to gird oneself. **περιεπάτεις** impf. ind. act. περιπατέω (# 4344) to go about. **ἤθελες** impf. ind. act. θέλω (# 2527) to desire, to want to. **γηράσῃς** aor. subj. act. γηράσκω (# 1180) to become old. **ἐκτενεῖς** fut. ind. act. ἐκτείνω (# 1753) to stretch out. **ζώσει** fut. ind. act. ζώννυμι. **οἴσει** fut. ind. act. φέρω (# 5770) to carry. ◆ **19 σημαίνων** pres. act. part. σημαίνω (# 4955) to signify. **δοξάσει** fut. ind. act. δοξάζω (# 1519) to glorify. **εἰπών** aor. act. part. λέγω (# 3306) to say. **ἀκολούθει** pres. imp. act. ἀκολουθέω (# 199) to follow. ◆ **20 ἐπιστραφείς** aor. pass. part. (temp.) ἐπιστρέφω (# 2188) to turn about.

Aor. indicates antecedent action, "when he turned around, he saw." ἠγάπα impf. ind. act. ἀγαπάω (# 26) to love. ἀκολουθοῦντα pres. act. part. ἀκολουθέω s.v. 19. ἀνέπεσεν aor. ind. act. ἀναπίπτω (# 404) to lean, to recline at the table. παραδιδούς pres. act. part. (subst.) παραδίδωμι (# 4140) to betray, to deliver over. ◆ **21** ἰδών aor. act. part. ὁράω (# 3972) to see. ◆ **22 θέλω** pres. subj. act. s.v. 18. μένειν pres. inf. act. μένω (# 3531) to remain. Compl. inf. to the main vb. ◆ **23 ἐξῆλθεν** aor. ind. act. s.v. 3. ἀποθνήσκει pres. ind. act. ἀποθνήσκω

(# 633) ◆ **24 μαρτυρῶν** pres. act. part. μαρτυρέω (# 3455) to testify, to give witness. **γράψας** aor. act. part. γράφω (# 1211) to write. ◆ **25 ἐποίησεν** aor. ind. act. ποιέω (# 4472) to do. **γράφηται** pres. subj. pass. γράφω s.v. 24. **χωρῆσαι** aor. act. inf. χωρέω (# 6003) to have room for, to hold, to contain. This indicates selectivity. (For a defense of the integrity and importance of this chapter to the entire Gospel s. S. S. Smalley, "The Sign in John 2," *NTS* 20 [1974]: 275-88.)

Acts

Acts 1

For a bibliographical discussion of Acts s. John C. Hurd, *A Bibliography of NT Bibliographies*, (New York: Seabury Press, 1966) 32-34; A. J. Matill, Jr. *A Classified Bibliography of Literature on the Acts of the Apostles* (Leiden: E. J. Brill, 1966).

◆ **1** μέν (# 3525) on the one hand. Normally followed by δέ ("on the other hand"), but not in this case (Marshall; PLG, 143-44). **πρῶτον** (# 4755) first, used for πρότερον ("former"). The first of two, not implying a third (RG, 662; Schneider; Barrett; PLG, 144). **λόγος** (# 3364) book, treaty. This was a customary name for a division of the work which covered more than one roll of papyrus (LC; PLG, 144-45). For a discussion of the relation between the Gospel of Luke and Acts s. I. Howard Marshall, "Acts and the 'Former Treatise,'" BAFCS, 1:163-82; BASHH, 30-43; Hubert Cancik, "The History of Culture, Religion, and Institutions in Ancient Historiography: Philological Observations Concerning Luke's History," *JBL* 116 (1997): 673-95. **ἐποιησάμην** aor. ind. mid. ποιέω (# 4472) to make. Mid. is the usual construction for mental acts (RWP; BG, 228). **ὧ** voc. O (Barrett). **ὧν** gen. pl. ὅς (# 4005) rel. pron. Gen. by attraction. **ἤρξατο** aor. ind. mid. (dep.) ἄρχομαι (# 806) to begin, w. inf. The vb. is emphatic and is not a Semitic auxiliary (as suggested by SA, 125-26). As the Gospel tells us what Jesus began to do and teach, so Acts tells what He continued to do and teach by His Holy Spirit (Bruce). **ποιεῖν** pres. act. inf. ποιέω (# 4472) to do, to make. **διδάσκειν** pres. act. inf. διδάσκω (# 1438) to teach. A very adequate summary of both the contents and the interests of the Third Gospel (Barrett). For comparisons of this preface to other ancient historical writings s. BAFCS, 1:1-82; PLG, 11-41, 147-67, 213-29; BASHH, 63-100. ◆ **2** ἐντειλάμενος aor. mid. (dep.) part. (temp.) ἐντέλλομαι (# 1948) to instruct, to command. **διὰ πνεύματος ἁγίου** through (by) the Holy Spirit; to be taken w. the part. ἐντειλάμενος (Barrett). **ἐξελέξατο** aor. ind. mid. (indir. mid., "for oneself") ἐκλέγω (# 1721) to select, to choose. **ἀνελήμφθη** aor. ind. pass. ἀναλαμβάνω (# 377) to take up. Used of the ascension of Christ (Haenchen). For the textual problems of this v. s. Barrett; TC, 273-77; BC, 3:256-61. ◆ **3** παρέστησεν aor. ind. act. παρίστημι (# 4205) to present. **ζῶντα** pres. act. part. ζάω (# 2409) to live, to be alive. Adj. part. as part of a double acc. construction: "he presented Himself as living." **παθεῖν** aor. act. inf. πάσχω (# 4248) to suffer. Inf. w. the prep. **μετά** (# 3552) to express time ("after") (MT, 143). **τεκμήριον** (# 5447) sign, proof; convincing and decisive proof (BAGD; MM). In logic demonstrative proof (LC); in medical language demonstrative evidence, a sure symptom (MLL, 184; LS); in legal language proof from which there was no getting away, an indication which is irrefutable and indisputable (Quintilian, 5, ix, 3-4; 3 Macc. 3:24). **δι' ἡμερῶν τεσσεράκοντα** (# 1328; 2465; 5477) at intervals during forty days (RWP). **ὀπτανόμενος** pres. mid. (dep. "appearing to them" [Barrett]) part. ὀπτάνομαι (# 3964) to let oneself be seen, to appear to someone. It is not used in the sense of a vision (Haenchen; MM). Part. of manner showing how he presented Himself alive. **λέγων** pres. act. part. λέγω (# 3306) to say, to speak. Iterat. pres. **τὰ περὶ τῆς βασιλείας τοῦ θεοῦ** the things concerning the Kingdom of God. The pl. art. w. the prep. expresses generalities (Cleon L. Rogers, Jr., "The Davidic Covenant in Acts-Revelation," *Bib Sac* 151 [1994]: 71-72). The phrase looks forward to the question in v. 6 (Barrett). ◆ **4** συναλιζόμενος pres. mid. (dep.) part. (temp.) συναλίζω (# 5259) lit., to eat w., or possibly to dwell w. (Bruce - ET). For a discussion of the textual problem s. Barrett; TC, 278-79. **παρήγγειλεν** aor. ind. act. παραγγέλλω (# 4133) to command. **χωρίζεσθαι** pres. pass. (dep.) inf. χωρίζομαι (# 6004) to depart. Inf. gives the content of the command. **περιμένειν** pres. act. inf. περιμένω (# 4338) to wait for. **ἠκούσατε** aor. ind. act. ἀκούω (# 201) to hear, w. obj. in gen. ◆ **5** ὅτι (# 4022) because. **ἐβάπτισεν** aor. ind. act. βαπτίζω (# 966) to baptize. **βαπτισθήσεσθε** fut. ind. pass. ◆ **6** μὲν οὖν (# 3525; 4036) so then. A favorite formula of Acts in opening a new story, which is nevertheless connected w. what goes before (LC). **συνελθόντες** aor. act. part. (temp.) "When (after) they had gathered together." συνέρχομαι (# 5302) to come together. **ἠρώτων** impf. ind. act. ἐρωτάω (# 2263) to question, to ask. Incep. impf., "they began to ask." **εἰ** (# 1623) if. It introduces a dir. question. **ἀποκαθιστάνεις** pres. ind. act. ἀποκαθιστάνω (# 634/635) to restore, to restore to a former state. An eschatological term for the restoration of the right order through God in the end time (Haenchen; TDNT; EDNT; RAC, 1:510-16; Schneider; CD, 19:6,9; for the

Jewish expectations s. Moore, *Judaism*, 2:323-76; SB, 4:799-976; TS, 649-90; HJP, 2:488-554). Futuristic pres., "Are you restoring?" (Barrett). ◆ **7 εἶπεν** aor. ind. act. λέγω (# *3306*) to say. **ὑμῶν** gen. pl. σύ (# *5148*); possessive gen. in pred.: "it is not your concern" (BD, 89; RG, 497). **γνῶναι** aor. act. inf. γινώσκω (# *1182*) to know. Epex. inf. explaining what does not belong to them. Jesus refuses to answer the question, not in respect of the matter itself but in of the time inquired after (Meyer; John A. McLean, "Did Jesus Correct the Disciples' View of the Kingdom?" *Bib Sac* 151 [1994]: 215-27). **χρόνος** (# *5989*) time, a period of time. **καιρός** (# *2789*) time, the right moment (s. 1 Thess. 5:1; Rogers, "Davidic Covenant in Acts-Rev.," *Bib Sac* 151 [1994]: 73). **ἔθετο** aor. ind. mid. (dep.) τίθημι (# *5502*) to place, to set. ◆ **8 λήμψεσθε** fut. ind. mid. (dep.) λαμβάνω (# *3284*) to receive. **ἐπελθόντος** aor. act. part. (temp.) ἐπέρχομαι (# *2088*) to come upon. Gen. abs. **ἔσεσθε** fut. ind. mid. (dep.) εἰμί (# *1639*) to be. **μου** gen. sing. 1st. pers. pron. ἐγώ (# *1609*); emphatic by position. Either poss. gen. ("my witnesses") or obj. gen. ("of/for me"). **μάρτυρες** nom. pl. μάρτυς witness (TDNT; TLNT; DPL; 974-75). **ἐσχάτου** gen. sing. ἔσχατος (# *2274*) last, end (s. James M. Scott, "Luke's Geographical Horizon," BAFCS 2:483-544; also E. Earle Ellis, "'The End of the Earth' [Acts 1:8]," *Bulletin for Biblical Research* 1 (1991): 123-32). ◆ **9 εἰπών** aor. act. part. (temp.) s.v. 7. **βλεπόντων** pres. act. part. (temp.) βλέπω (# *1063*) to see, to watch. Gen. abs. ("while"). **ἐπήρθη** aor. ind. pass. ἐπαίρω (# *2048*) to lift up. Theol. pass. **νεφέλη** (# *3749*) cloud. Symbolic of the Shekinah, the visible manifestation of the divine presence and glory (Longenecker, 258). **ὑπέλαβεν** aor. ind. act. ὑπολαμβάνω (# *5696*) to take up, to receive (BAGD). ◆ **10 ἀτενίζοντες** pres. act. part. ἀτενίζω (# *867*) to gaze. Used in medical texts to denote a peculiar fixed look (MLL, 76). Periphrastic part. indicating continual action and forming a backdrop for a punctual event (VA, 457). **ἦσαν** impf. ind. act. s.v. 8. **πορευομένου** pres. mid. (dep.) part. (temp.) πορεύομαι (# *4513*) to go. Gen. abs. **παρειστήκεισαν** plperf. ind. act. παρίστημι (# *4225*) perf. to stand. **ἐσθήσεσι** dat. pl. ἐσθής (# *2264*) clothing. For the dat. form s. BAGD; GGP, 47-48. ◆ **11 ἑστήκατε** perf. ind. act. ἵστημι (# *2705*) perf. to stand. **ἀναλημφθείς** aor. pass. part. (adj.) s.v. 2. **ἐλεύσεται** fut. ind. mid. (dep.) ἔρχομαι (# *2262*) to go, to come. He will come as he has gone (Barrett). **ἐθεάσασθε** aor. ind. mid. (dep.) θεάομαι (# *2517*) to see, to watch. **πορευόμενον** pres. mid. (dep.) part. (adj.) s.v. 10. ◆ **12 ὑπέστρεψαν** aor. ind. act. ὑποστρέφω (# *5715*) to return. **καλουμένου** pres. pass. part. (adj.) καλέω (# *2813*) to call; pass., to be called, to be named. **Ἐλαιῶνος** gen. sing. ἐλαιών (# *1779*) olive yard, olivet (DJG, 43-44). Nouns w. this suffix denote a place where persons or things are found (Bruce). **ἔχον** pres. act. part. (adj.) ἔχω (# *2400*) to have, to be. A Sab-

bath day's journey was 2000 cubits (2000 medium size steps) or almost 1 mile (SB, 2:509-94; Marshall; Barrett; BBC). ◆ **13 εἰσῆλθον** aor. ind. act. εἰσέρχομαι (# *1656*) to go into. **ὑπερῷον** (# *5673*) an upstairs room, an upper story or a room on a flat roof (Barrett; SB, 594). Traditionally the study and the room for prayer of a rabbi (LC; SB, 2:594). **ἀνέβησαν** aor. ind. act. ἀναβαίνω (# *326*) to go up. **καταμένοντες** pres. act. part. καταμένω (# *2910*) to remain. For part. in a periphrastic construction s.v. 10. The prep. in compound conveys the perfective idea (Kistemaker). ◆ **14 προσκαρτεροῦντες** pres. act. part. προσκαρτερέω (# *4674*) to be strong, to be steadfast (like the English "carry on") (RWP; TLNT; TDNT). For part. in a periphrastic construction s.v. 10. **ὁμοθυμαδόν** (# *3924*) together w. one mind or purpose. ◆ **15 ἀναστάς** aor. act. part. (temp.) ἀνίστημι (# *482*) to arise. **ἐπὶ τὸ αὐτό** all together. The phrase seems to be a semitechnical term like "in church fellowship" (Bruce; TC, 305; Bradley Blue, "Acts and the House Church," BAFCS, 2:131-35). **ἑκατὸν εἴκοσι** (# *1667*; *1663*) one hundred twenty. In Jewish law a minimum of 120 Jewish men was required to establish a community w. its own council (Marshall; SB, 2:594-95; M, Sanh. 1:6). ◆ **16 ἔδει** impf. ind. act. δεῖ (# *1256*) it is necessary, giving a logical necessity, w. inf. **πληρωθῆναι** aor. pass. inf. πληρόω (# *4444*) to fulfill. **προεῖπεν** aor. ind. act. προλέγω (# *4625*) to say beforehand. **γενομένου** aor. mid. (dep.) part. γίνομαι (# *1181*) to become, to be. Gen. abs. **ὁδηγοῦ** gen. sing. ὁδηγός (# *3843*) guide. **συλλαβοῦσιν** aor. act. part. dat. pl. συλλαμβάνω (# *5197*) to seize, to arrest. Dat. of interest. Part. as subst. ◆ **17 κατηριθμημένος** perf. pass. part. καταριθμέω (# *2935*) to number, used of the inclusion of someone in a list (Barrett). Periphrastic part., "he had been numbered among us" (VA, 485). **ἔλαχεν** aor. ind. act. λαγχάνω (# *3275*) to obtain by lot; here, to obtain the rank (LC; for the council of 12 men and 3 priests in DSS s. 1QM 8:1f). ◆ **18 ἐκτήσατο** aor. ind. mid. (dep.) κτάομαι (# *3227*) to acquire, to get for oneself (GGBB, 424). **ἀδικίας** gen. sing. ἀδικία (# *94*) unrighteousness. Obj. gen., "the reward he received for his unrighteousness"; or a Semitic adjectival gen., "his unrighteous reward" (Bruce). **πρηνής** (# *4568*) head first, flat on the face (EGT; s. DTM, 2:1405-06). **γενόμενος** aor. mid. (dep.) part. (circum.) s.v. 16. **μέσος** (# *3545*) middle, in the middle (DTM, 2:1405). **ἐλάκησεν** aor. ind. act. λακέω (# *3279*) to crack, to burst. An accompanying noise is implied (Bruce). **ἐξεχύθη** aor. ind. pass. ἐκχέω (# *1772*) to pour out. **σπλάγχνα** pl. σπλάγχνον the inward organs, the intestines. ◆ **19 γνωστόν** (# *1196*) known. **ἐγένετο** aor. ind. mid. (dep.) s.v. 16. **κατοικοῦσιν** pres. act. part. κατοικέω (# *2997*) to dwell, to live, to be at home. Part. as subst. **κληθῆναι** aor. pass. inf. s.v. 12. Inf. w. ὥστε (# *6063*) to express actual results. **Ἀκελδαμάχ** (# *192*) Akeldama, Aramaic term (Barrett; TRE, 3:603; SA 87-89). ◆ **20 γέγραπται** perf. ind. pass. γράφω (# *1211*) to write. Perf. used for authoritative documents whose authority abides (MM). **γενηθήτω** aor. imp. pass. (dep.) 3rd. pers. sing. s.v. 16. **ἔπαυλις** (# *2068*) homestead, a country house, cottage, cabin, office (RWP; MM; NDIEC 3:71; GELTS, 166; Barrett). **ἔστω** pres. imp. act. εἰμί s.v. 8. **κατοικῶν** pres. act. part. s.v. 19. Part. as subst. **ἐπισκοπή** (# *2175*) office (GELTS, 174; TDNT). **λαβέτω** aor. imp. act. s.v. 8. ◆ **21 δεῖ** pres. ind. act. s.v. 16, w. the inf. **γενέσθαι** in v. 22. **συνελθόντων** aor. act. part. συνέρχομαι (# *5302*) to come together, to go together, to accompany. Adj. part. taken up by **τουτῶν** in v. 22 (Barrett). Const. aor. viewing the action in its entirety (VANT, 415). **ἐν παντὶ χρόνῳ** during the whole time (Schneider). **εἰσῆλθεν** aor. ind. act. s.v. 13. **ἐξῆλθεν** aor. ind. act. ἐξέρχομαι (# *2002*) to go out. The expression "to go in and out among us" is a Semitic idiom for familiar and unhindered association (Longenecker, 265; Deut. 31; 2 Sam. 3:25; Ps. 121:8; Schneider). The aor. tenses are const. (RWP). ◆ **22 ἀρξάμενος** aor. mid. (dep.) part. (adj.) s.v. 1; the nom. refers to Jesus (RWP; Barrett). **ἀνελήμφθη** aor. ind. pass. s.v. 2. **γενέσθαι** aor. mid. (dep.) inf. s.v. 16. Inf. w. **δεῖ** from v. 21. ◆ **23 ἔστησαν** aor. ind. act. ἵστημι (# *2705*) to set up; here, to nominate (Alex). The subject is not mentioned, but it is probably all who were present (Schneider; LC). **καλούμενον** pres. pass. part. (adj.) s.v. 12. **ἐπεκλήθη** aor. ind. pass. ἐπικαλέω (# *2126*) to give a name; pass. to be named. ◆ **24 προσευξάμενοι** aor. mid. part. (temp.) προσεύχομαι (# *4667*) to pray. **κύριε** voc. sing. κύριος (# *3261*) lord. **καρδιογνῶστα** voc. sing. καρδιογνώστης (# *2841*) knower of the heart. A favorite expression of post-apostolic Christianity (Haenchen). **ἀνάδειξον** aor. imp. act. ἀναδείκνυμι (# *344*) to show. Aor. imp. calls for a specific act w. a note of urgency. **ἐξελέξω** aor. ind. mid. 2nd. pers. s.v. 2. ◆ **25 λαβεῖν** aor. act. inf. s.v. 8. Epex. inf. or inf. of purpose. **παρέβη** aor. ind. act. παραβαίνω (# *4124*) to go aside, to turn aside. **πορευθῆναι** aor. pass. (dep.) inf. s.v. 10. Inf. of purpose. ◆ **26 ἔδωκαν** aor. ind. act. δίδωμι (# *1443*) to give. **ἔπεσεν** aor. ind. act. πίπτω (# *4406*) to fall. **συγκατεψηφίσθη** aor. ind. pass. συγκαταψηφίζω (# *5164*) mid., to join in a vote of condemnation; pass., to be chosen (by a vote), together w.; thus, to be added (BAGD). The method employed by the Jews was to put the names written on stones into a vessel and shake it until one fell out (LC).

Acts 2

◆ **1 συμπληροῦσθαι** pres. pass. inf. συμπληρόω (# *5230*) to fill completely; of time, to approach, to come. Inf. w. prep. to express time ("when," "in the approaching of") (Longenecker, 247; MT, 145; Luke 9:51). **πεντηκοστῆς** (# *4300*) gen. sing. Pentecost. For the Jewish celebration of Pentecost s. TDNT; SB, 2:597-

602; Edersheim, *Temple,* 206-7; WZZT, 236-38. ◆ **2 ἐγένετο** aor. ind. mid. (dep.) γίνομαι (# *1181*) to become, to be, to happen. **ἄφνω** (# *924*) suddenly. **ἦχος** (# *2491*) sound, noise. Used in Luke 21:25 for the roar of the sea. It was "an echoing sound as of a mighty wind borne vibrantly" (RWP). **φερομένης** pres. pass. part. (adj.) φέρω (# *5770*) to carry; pass. to be driven. **πνοῆς** gen. sing. πνοή (# *4466*) wind. Gen. of description. **ἐπλήρωσεν** aor. ind. act. πληρόω (# *4444*) to fill. **οἶκος** (# *3910*) house. This was probably either a rented house or a house that a believer had let them use (Blue, "Acts and the House Church," BAFCS, 2:133-34). **καθήμενοι** pres. mid. (dep.) part. κάθημαι (# *2764*) to sit. Periphrastic construction. ◆ **3 ὤφθησαν** aor. ind. pass. ὁράω (# *3972*) to see; pass. to appear. **διαμεριζόμεναι** pres. mid./pass. part. (adj.) διαμερίζω (# *1374*) to distribute; mid. parting themselves asunder or distributing themselves (RWP). **γλῶσσα** (# *1185*) tongue, tongue-shaped. **ὡσεί** (# *6059*) as. **πυρός** gen. sing. πῦρ (# *4786*) fire. Gen. of description. **ἐκάθισεν** aor. ind. act. καθίζω (# *2767*) to take one's seat, to sit. Fire was said to have rested on Rabbis as they studied or disputed (SB, 2:603-4). A flame or tongue of fire is depicted on some Roman coins as resting over the head of the person and probably indicates the dawn of a new age (Richard Oster, "Numismatic Windows into the Social World of Early Christianity: A Methodological Inquiry," *JBL* 101 [1982]: 212-14). **ἕκαστον** (# *1667*) acc. sing. each. Each one present received the Spirit without conditions (Bruner, 163). The coming of the Spirit was an historical event, which, along w. the atoning death of the Messiah (forgiveness of sins), formed the basis for the New Covenant (s. Jer. 31:31-37; Ezek. 11:19; 36:26-27). ◆ **4 ἐπλήσθησαν** aor. ind. pass. πίμπλημι (# *4398*) to fill. **ἤρξαντο** aor. ind. mid. (dep.) ἄρχομαι (# *806*) to begin, w. inf. **λαλεῖν** pres. act. inf. λαλέω (# *3281*) to speak. **ἑτέραις γλώσσαις** (# *2283; 1185*) in other kinds of tongues; that is, languages (Schneider; EDNT). **ἐδίδου** impf. ind. act. δίδωμι (# *1443*) to give. Iterat. impf., indicating the giving one after another. **ἀποφθέγγεσθαι** pres. mid. (dep.) inf. ἀποφθέγγομαι (# *710*) to utter, to speak. Used of weighty or oracular utterance (Bruce), but not for ecstatic speech (Haenchen; Schneider). Inf. as dir. obj. The filling w. the Spirit was an experience to be repeated on several occasions, but the Spirit-baptism took place once for all (Bruce-ET). ◆ **5 κατοικοῦντες** pres. act. part. κατοικέω (# *2997*) to dwell, to reside in a place (RWP). Periphrastic part. **εὐλαβεῖς** nom. pl. εὐλαβής (# *2327*) pious, devout. This could refer to Jewish pilgrims who had come to the Feast (SB, 2:604), or to Jews from the Diaspora who had moved to Jerusalem and were now permanent residents (Schneider), or to both (RWP). ◆ **6 γενομένης** aor. mid. (dep.) part. (temp.) s.v. 2. Gen. abs. **συνῆλθεν** aor. ind. act. συνέρχομαι (# *5302*) to come together. **συνεχύθη** aor. ind. pass. συγχέω (# *5177*) to pour together, to confound, to be perplexed, to cause such astonishment as to bewilder and dismay, to cause consternation (LN, 1:313). It describes the surprising effect of the miracle (Haenchen). **ἤκουον** impf. ind. act. ἀκούω (# *201*) to hear. Impf. may be iterat. **διαλέκτῳ** dat. sing. διάλεκτος (# *1365*) dialect, manner of speech (Bruce). Luke's choice of this word indicates that the speaking in tongues was the use of other languages (Bruner, 164). Loc. dat. **λαλούντων** pres. act. part. s.v. 4. Part. in gen. is either the obj. of the vb., ἤκουν, or is gen. abs. ("as they were speaking"). ◆ **7** **ἐξίσταντο** impf. ind. mid. ἐξίστημι (# *2014*) to be beside oneself, to be astonished. **ἐθαύμαζον** impf. ind. act. θαυμάζω (# *2513*) to wonder, to marvel. ◆ **8 ἐγεννήθημεν** aor. ind. pass. γεννάω (# *1164*) to bear; pass. to be born. ◆ **10 ἐπιδημοῦντες** pres. act. part. (adj.) ἐπιδημέω (# *2111*) to be away from home, to be on a journey. ◆ **11 προσήλυτος** (# *4670*) proselyte. In the LXX used of a sojourner in the land of Israel, later to denote those Gentiles who undertook the complete observance of the Jewish law and had to be circumcised, baptized, and offer sacrifices (Bruce; TDNT; SB, 2:715-23; EDNT; ALAG, 30-89; BAFCS, 5:19-49; BC, 5:74-96; for the names of the areas mentioned s. BASHH, 222-23; Barrett; SB, 2:606-14). **λαλούντων** pres. act. part. s.v. 4. **μεγαλεῖα** acc. pl. μεγαλεῖος (# *3483*) mighty deeds. ◆ **12 ἐξίσταντο** impf. ind. mid. s.v. 7. **διηπόρουν** impf. ind. act. διαπορέω (# *1389*) to be at a loss, to be perplexed, to be very confused (LN, 1:381). For the text variant, διηποροῦντο (impf. ind. mid.) s. Barrett; TC, 294. **εἶναι** pres. act. inf. εἰμί (# *1639*) to be. Inf. w. the vb. θέλω (lit., "what does this wish to be?") "What does this mean?" (RWP). ◆ **13 διαχλευάζοντες** pres. act. part. διαχλευάζω (# *1430*) to mock, to ridicule. The prep. compound indicates the flinging of ridicule at another party (MH, 302). **γλεύκους** gen. sing. γλεῦκος (# *1183*) sweet wine, probably the fresh wine which has not yet been kept long enough and is still fermenting (LC). It is suggested that it was wine mixed w. honey—sometimes honey and spices (SB, 2:614). For the making and preserving of sweet wine by sealing it, immersing it in cold water, or burying it for 6 to 8 weeks, after which it was good for a year (ἀεὶ γλεῦκος, *semper mustum*) s. Columella, *De Re Rustica*, 12:27-29; Pliny, NH, 14:83-85; DGRA, 1202. Gen. w. the vb. μεστόω (# *3551*) indicating the thing by which they were intoxicated. **μεμεστωμένοι** perf. pass. part. μεστόω to fill; pass. to be full. The perf. emphasizes the state or condition. ◆ **14 σταθείς** aor. pass. part. (circum.) ἵστημι (# *2705*) to stand up, to rise. **ἐπῆρεν** aor. ind. act. ἐπαίρω (# *2048*) to lift up. **ἀπεφθέγξατο** aor. ind. mid. (dep.) s.v. 4. **κατοικοῦντες** pres. act. part. s.v. 5. **ἔστω** pres. imp. act. εἰμί (# *1639*) to be. For the construction, "Let it be known," as introducing facts that the speak-

er intends to list s. SA, 90-91. **ἐνωτίσασθε** aor. imp. mid. (dep.) ἐνωτίζομαι (# *1969*) to give ear to. For the use of the word in the LXX s. KVS, 157-58; GELTS, 156. ◆ **15 ὑπολαμβάνετε** pres. ind. act. ὑπολαμβάνω (# *5696*) to assume, to be of the opinion that (BAGD). **μεθύουσιν** pres. ind. act. μεθύω (# *3501*) to be drunk. **ὥρα τρίτη τῆς ἡμέρας** the third hour of the day, or 9:00 A.M. Although it seems that the early meal was after the morning prayers which ended around the fourth hour (10:00 A.M.) (SB, 2:615; LC), it may be that Peter simply means it is too early to find men drunk (Barrett). ◆ **16 εἰρημένον** perf. pass. part. λέγω (# *3306*) to say. Part. as subst. ◆ **17 ἔσται** fut. ind. mid. (dep.) s.v. 14. **ἐκχεῶ** fut. ind. act. ἐκχέω (# *1772*) to pour out. **προφητεύσουσιν** fut. ind. act. προφητεύω (# *4736*) to speak forth for someone, to prophecy. **ὄψονται** fut. ind. mid. (dep.) ὁράω (# *3972*) to see. **ἐνυπνιασθήσονται** fut. ind. pass. (dep.) ἐνυπνιάζομαι (# *1965*) to dream. ◆ **19 δώσω** fut. ind. act. δίδωμι (# *1443*) to give. **ἀτμίδα** acc. pl. ἀτμίς (# *874*) vapor. **καπνοῦ** gen. sing. καπνός (# *2837*) smoke. Gen. of description. ◆ **20 μεταστραφήσεται** fut. ind. pass. μεταστρέφω (# *3570*) to change, to turn into. The prep. compound has the idea of change (MH, 318). **ἐλθεῖν** aor. act. inf. ἔρχομαι (# *2262*) to come. Inf. w. **πρίν** (# *4570*) to express time ("before"). **ἐπιφανῆ** acc. sing. ἐπιφανής (# *2212*) splendid, glorious. The word has the idea of effective help and indicates that the Day of the Lord is awesome (TLNT; NDIEC, 4:148; MM). ◆ **21 ἐπικαλέσηται** aor. subj. mid. ἐπικαλέω (# *2126*) to call upon. Subj. w. **ἄν** (# *323*) in an indef. rel. cl. **σωθήσεται** fut. ind. pass. σῴζω (# *5392*) to save, to rescue. ◆ **22 ἀκούσατε** aor. imp. act. ἀκούω (# *201*) to hear. Aor. imp. calls for a specific act w. a note of urgency. **ἀποδεδειγμένον** perf. pass. part. (adj.) ἀποδείκνυμι (# *617*) to appoint, to designate (LC), to authenticate (Haenchen). Perf. indicates the lasting results. **οἷς** dat. pl. ὅς (# *4005*) Dat. by attraction. **ἐποίησεν** aor. ind. act. ποιέω (# *4472*) to do. ◆ **23 ὡρισμένῃ** perf. pass. part. ὁρίζω (# *3988*) to mark off by boundaries, to determine. The perf. emphasizes a state of completion. God had willed the death of Jesus (RWP). **βουλῇ** (# *1087*) dat. sing. purpose, decision, counsel. Instr. dat. foreknowledge (GGBB, 288). **ἔκδοτον** (# *1692*) given up, delivered up. For verbal adj. w. this ending s. M, 221f. **προσπήξαντες** aor. act. part. προσπήγνυμι (# *4699*) to nail to. Part. of manner showing how they killed Him. **ἀνείλατε** aor. ind. act. ἀναιρέω (# *359*) to kill. Here human freedom and divine necessity join hands (Haenchen). ◆ **24 ἀνέστησεν** aor. ind. act. ἀνίστημι (# *482*) to raise up. **λύσας** aor. act. part. λύω (# *3395*) to release, to loose. Part. of manner. **ὠδῖνας** acc. pl. ὠδίν (# *6047*) pain; pl. birth pains. For possible views of the meaning s. Barrett. **δυνατόν** (# *1543*) verbal adj. "To be able," w. inf. **κρατεῖσθαι** pres. pass. inf. κρατέω (# *3195*) to hold fast. ◆ **25 προορώμην** impf.

ind. mid. (dep., LC) προοράω (# 4632) to see beforehand; "to have before one's eyes" (Haenchen). Impf. indicates that the Lord is continually before him. **σαλευθῶ** aor. subj. pass. σαλεύω (# 4888) to shake. pass. to be moved. Subj. w. ἵνα (# 2671) in a purp. cl. The quotations follow the midrashic exegetical rules of linking passages together which have the same words–here, "at my right hand" (Longenecker, 279; BE, 32-38). ◆ **26 ηὐφράνθη** aor. ind. pass. (dep.) εὐφραίνομαι (# 2370) to rejoice, to gladden; pass. to be glad (GELTS, 190; KVS, 257-58). **ἠγαλλιάσατο** aor. ind. mid. (dep.) ἀγαλλιάομαι (# 22) to be glad, to rejoice exceedingly (GELTS, 2; KVS, 255-58). **ἔτι δὲ καί** (# 2285; 1254; 2779) and yet also, besides, moreover. **κατασκηνώσει** fut. ind. act. κατασκηνόω (# 2942) to dwell, to live in a tent (John 1:14). ◆ **27 ἐγκαταλείψεις** fut. ind. act. ἐγκαταλείπω (# 1593) to abandon, to leave behind, to desert, to forsake (GELTS, 126-27; TLNT). **δώσεις** fut. ind. act. s.v. 19. **ἰδεῖν** aor. act. inf. ὁράω (# 3972) to see. Inf. as dir. obj. **διαφθορά** (# 1426) corruption. ◆ **28 ἐγνώρισας** aor. ind. act. γνωρίζω (# 1192) to make known. **πληρώσεις** fut. ind. act. πληρόω (# 4444) to fulfill, to fill, w. gen. = "to fill w." ◆ **29 ἐξόν** pres. act. part. ἔξεστιν (# 2003) it is lawful, it is allowed, w. inf. The vb. εἰμί is to be supplied forming a periphrastic construction (RWP). **εἰπεῖν** aor. act. inf. s.v. 16. **καί** (# 2779) also. **ἐτελεύτησεν** aor. ind. act. τελευτάω (# 5462) to die. **ἐτάφη** aor. ind. pass. θάπτω (# 2507) to bury. ◆ **30 ὑπάρχων** pres. act. part. (causal) ὑπάρχω (# 5639) to exist, to be. **εἰδώς** perf. act. part. οἶδα perf. w. pres. meaning, to know. **ὤμοσεν** aor. ind. act. ὀμνύω (# 3923) to swear; w. dat., to swear w. an oath. **ὀσφύς** (# 4019) loins, as the place of the reproductive organs–"fruit of his loins"; i.e., one of his descendants (Bruce; BAGD). **καθίσαι** aor. act. inf. καθίζω (# 2767) to cause to sit, to appoint, to install (BAGD). Epex. inf. giving the content of that which was sworn (s. 2 Sam. 7:8-18; Ps. 89:3-4; Cleon L. Rogers, Jr., "The Promises to David in Early Judaism," *Bib Sac* 150 [1993]: 285-302). ◆ **31 προϊδών** aor. act. part. προοράω (# 4632) to see beforehand s.v. 25. Circum. or causal part. **ἐλάλησεν** aor. ind. act. λαλέω (# 3281) to speak. **ἐγκατελείφθη** aor. ind. pass. s.v. 27. ◆ **32 ἀνέστησεν** aor. ind. act. s.v. 24. The resurrection of Jesus is based on the covenant promise that God unconditionally swore to David. An eternal kingdom demands an eternal King, not a dead one. **μάρτυρες** witness s. 1:8. ◆ **33 ὑψωθείς** aor. pass. part. (temp.) ὑψόω (# 5738) to lift up, to exalt. **λαβών** aor. act. part. (temp.) λαμβάνω (# 3284) to receive. **ἐξέχεεν** aor. ind. act. ἐκχέω (# 1772) to pour out. ◆ **34 ἀνέβη** aor. ind. act. ἀναβαίνω (# 326) to ascend. **κάθου** pres. imp. mid. s.v. 2. ◆ **35 θῶ** aor. subj. ind. τίθημι (# 5502) to place, to set, to make. Subj. w. an indef. temp. cl. (s. RWP). ◆ **36 ἀσφαλῶς** (# 857) assuredly. Used to emphasize the conclusion which he is about to draw from

his three texts (EGT). **γινωσκέτω** pres. imp. act. γινώσκω (# 1182) to know, to recognize. **ἐποίησεν** aor. ind. act. ποιέω (# 4472) to make, to appoint, to cause actually to become, used of the holder of an official position (Barrett). Here w. double acc., "God appointed Him both Lord and Messiah." **ἐσταυρώσατε** aor. ind. act. σταυρόω (# 5090) to crucify. ◆ **37 ἀκούσαντες** aor. act. part. (temp.) ἀκούω (# 201) to hear. **κατενύγησαν** aor. ind. pass. κατανύσσομαι (# 2920) to pierce, to sting sharply, pass. to be pierced, stabbed (BAGD). Used of painful emotion, which penetrates the heart as if stinging (Meyer). **ποιήσωμεν** aor. subj. act. s.v. 36. Deliberative subj., "What shall we do?" ◆ **38 μετανοήσατε** aor. imp. act. μετανοέω (# 3566) to change one's mind, to repent (s. Matt. 3:2). Aor. imp. calls for specific act w. a note of urgency. **βαπτισθήτω** aor. imp. pass. 3rd. pers. sing. βαπτίζω (# 966) to baptize. Baptism was the outward sign of repentance (Bruce). Pass. of permission: "let each one of you allow himself to be baptized." **εἰς** (# 1650) for, or because of (DM, 104; contra GGBB, 369-71). The phrase could be connected with the command, "repent." **λήμψεσθε** fut. ind. mid. (dep.) s.v. 33. ◆ **39 ὅσους** acc. pl. ὅσος (# 4012) as many as; w. ἄν which makes the expression more general: all those who, whoever (BAGD). **προσκαλέσηται** aor. subj. mid. (dep.) προσκαλέομαι (# 4673) to call to, to call upon. Subj. w. an indef. rel. pron. ◆ **40 πλείοσιν** dat. pl. comp. πολύς (# 4498) much, many; comp., many more (Barrett). Instr. dat. **διεμαρτύρατο** aor. ind. mid. (dep.) διαμαρτύρομαι (# 1371) to make a solemn attestation or call to witness. The perfective use of the prep. compound (RWP). **παρεκάλει** impf. ind. act. παρακαλέω (# 4151) to exhort, to encourage (TDNT). Impf. pictures the repeated action. **σώθητε** aor. imp. pass. s.v. 21. Pass. suggests, "let yourselves be saved," "accept salvation" (Barrett). **σκολιός** (# 5021) crooked, twisted. It refers to a generation that is wayward, perverse, rebellious (TLNT, 1:389). ◆ **41 ἀποδεξάμενοι** aor. mid. (dep.) part. ἀποδέχομαι (# 622) to receive, to welcome. Adj. part. as subst. **ἐβαπτίσθησαν** aor. ind. pass. s.v. 38. **προσετέθησαν** aor. ind. pass. προστίθημι (# 4707) to add to. Luke does not say anything about the newly baptized ones speaking in tongues, although according to v. 38 they did receive the Holy Spirit (Haenchen). **τρισχίλιαι** three thousand. For a defense of the historical reliability of the number against a background of some 100-120,000 inhabitants in Jerusalem at that time s. Wolfgang Reinhardt, "The Population Size of Jerusalem and the Numerical Growth of the Jerusalem Church," BAFCS, 4:237-65. ◆ **42 ἦσαν** impf. ind. act. εἰμί (# 1639) to be. **προσκαρτεροῦντες** pres. act. part. προσκαρτερέω (# 4674) to be firm, persevere, remain faithful to a person or task. In regard to prayer, the idea is constant diligence, effort that never lets up, confident waiting for results (TLNT, 3:193; s. 1:14).

Part. in a periphrastic construction stressing the continual action. **τῇ διδαχῇ τῶν ἀποστόλων** in the teaching of the apostles. Dat. of sphere, indicating the area of the steadfast devotion. It refers to a body of material considered authoritative because it was the message about Jesus of Nazareth proclaimed by accredited apostles (Longenecker, 289). **κλάσει** dat. sing. κλάσις (# 3082) breaking. The breaking of bread refers either to an ordinary meal or to the celebration of the Lord's Supper (LC). Dat. of sphere. ◆ **43 ἐγίνετο** impf. ind. mid. (dep.) s.v. 2. ◆ **44 πιστεύοντες** pres. act. part. πιστεύω (# 4409) to believe. Adj. part. as subst. **εἶχον** impf. ind. act. ἔχω (# 2400) to have. **κοινά** acc. pl. κοινός (# 3123) common. For the DSS group and their common goods s. TJ, 88; Barrett; and among the Christians s. Schneider, 290-95; BC, 5:140-51; BAFCS, 4:323-56. ◆ **45 κτῆμα** (# 3228) possession, personal property. **ἐπίπρασκον** impf. ind. act. πιπράσκω (# 4405) to sell. Customary impf., "they sold from time to time" (RWP). **διεμέριζον** impf. ind. act. s.v. 3. ◆ **46 κλῶντες** pres. act. part. κλάω (# 3089) to break. **μετελάμβανον** impf. ind. act. μεταλαμβάνω (# 3561) to partake of, to share in. **ἀφελότητι** dat. sing. ἀφελότης (# 911) singleness, generosity (Bruce). ◆ **47 αἰνοῦντες** pres. act. part. αἰνέω (# 140) to praise. **ἔχοντες** pres. act. part. ἔχω s.v. 44. The parts. are circum. or are to be taken in a periphrastic construction. **προσετίθει** impf. ind. act. s.v. 41. Impf. indicates the repeated action. **σωζομένους** pres. pass. part. s.v. 21. Theol. pass., indicating that God performed the action.

Acts 3

◆ **1 ἀνέβαινον** impf. ind. act. ἀναβαίνω (# 326) to go up; descriptive impf. They were ascending the terraces to the temple court (RWP). **ἐνάτη** (# 1888) ninth. The afternoon prayer in connection w. the evening offering, was from 12:30 P.M. to 6:00 P.M., w. 3:00 P.M. (the ninth hour) being the average time (SB, 2:696-703, esp. 698; Jos., *Ant.*, 14:65; BBC). ◆ **2 ὑπάρχων** pres. act. part. (adj.) ὑπάρχω (# 5639) to exist, to be. **χωλός** (# 6000) lame, cripple. **ἐβαστάζετο** impf. ind. pass. βαστάζω to carry. Impf. denotes the action was simultaneous to the going up (Meyer). **ἐτίθουν** impf. ind. act. τίθημι (# 5502) to place. Customary impf. **λεγομένην** pres. pass. part. λέγω (# 2400) to say; pass., to be called, to be named. **Ὡραίαν** acc. sing. ὡραῖος (# 6053) beautiful. This is possibly the famous Nicanor Gate, which was covered w. Corinthian bronze and located outside the sanctuary on the east (Barrett; Haenchen; Edersheim, *Temple*, 47; SB, 2:620-25; Jos., *JW*, 5:201, 204-5; BBC; JTJ, 117-18; ABD, 1:631-32; TJ, 30). **αἰτεῖν** pres. act. inf. αἰτέω to ask, to beg. Inf. of purp. **ἐλεημοσύνη** (# 1797) alms (s. Matt. 6:2). **εἰσπορευομένων** pres. mid. (dep.) part. εἰσπορεύομαι (# 1660) to go into. Adj. part.

as subst. ◆ **3 ἰδών** aor. act. part. (temp.) ὁράω (# 3972) to see. **μέλλοντας** pres. act. part. μέλλω (# 3516) to be about to, w. the inf. **εἰσιέναι** pres. act. inf. εἴσειμι (# 1655) to go in. **ἠρώτα** impf. ind. act. ἐρωτάω (# 2263) to ask, to request. **λαβεῖν** aor. act. inf. λαμβάνω (# 3284) to receive. Inf. in indir. speech as obj. of the vb. ◆ **4 ἀτενίσας** aor. act. part. (circum.) ἀτενίζω (# 867) to gaze, to look upon intently. **βλέψον** aor. imp. act. βλέπω (# 1063) to see, to look. ◆ **5 ἐπεῖχεν** impf. ind. act. ἐπέχω (# 2091) to hold fast, to aim at, to fix one's attention upon, w. dat. **προσδοκῶν** pres. act. part. (circum.) προσδοκάω (# 4659) to expect, to wait for. **λαβεῖν** aor. act. inf. s.v. 3. Epex. inf. explaining the expectation. ◆ **6 ὑπάρχει** pres. ind. act. s.v. 2. **ἐν τῷ ὀνόματι** (# 1899; 3950) in the name of; not a magic formula, but gives the authority and power (Barrett). **περιπάτει** pres. imp. act. περιπατέω (# 4344) to walk about. For the use of the pres. imp. w. this vb. s. VANT, 343-44. ◆ **7 πιάσας** aor. act. part. πιάζω (# 4389) to seize. Circum. part. or part. of manner. **ἤγειρεν** aor. ind. act. ἐγείρω (# 1586) to raise up. **παραχρῆμα** (# 4202) immediately. **ἐστερεώθησαν** aor. ind. pass. στερεόω (# 5105) to make firm, solid; ingressive aor., "to become strong." In medical language applied to the bones in particular (MLL, 35). **βάσις** (# 1000) foot. **σφυδρόν** (# 5383) ankle, ankle bone (LC). ◆ **8 ἐξαλλόμενος** pres. mid. (dep.) part. (circum.) ἐξάλλομαι (# 1982) to leap out, to leap up. **ἔστη** aor. ind. act. ἵστημι (# 2705) to stand. **περιεπάτει** impf. ind. act. s.v. 6. Incep. impf., "he began walking around." **εἰσῆλθεν** aor. ind. act. εἰσέρχομαι (# 1656) to go in. **περιπατῶν** pres. act. part. s.v. 6. **ἁλλόμενος** pres. mid. (dep.) part. (circum.) ἅλλομαι (# 256) to leap, to spring up. **αἰνῶν** pres. act. part. αἰνέω (# 140) to praise. ◆ **9 εἶδεν** aor. ind. act. ὁράω (# 3972) to see. **αἰνοῦντα** pres. act. part. s.v. 8. Luke adds this to prepare for and underline the theological meaning of the miracle (Barrett). ◆ **10 ἐπεγίνωσκον** impf. ind. act. ἐπιγινώσκω (# 2105) to recognize, to know. Incep. impf. "they began to perceive" (RWP). **καθήμενος** pres. mid. (dep.) part. (adj.) κάθημαι (# 2764) to sit. **ἐπλήσθησαν** aor. ind. pass. πίμπλημι (# 4398) to fill, w. gen. indicating that w. which one is filled. **θάμβος** (# 2502) amazement, a state of astonishment due to both the suddenness and the unusualness of the phenomenon (LN, 1:311). **ἐκστάσεως** gen. sing. ἔκστασις (# 1749) being besides oneself, confusion, a state of intense amazement, to the point of being beside oneself w. astonishment (BAGD; LN, 1:312). **συμβεβηκότι** perf. act. part. dat. sing. συμβαίνω (# 5201) to happen to, w. dat. For an example of the neg. sense ("the calamity which happened") s. NDIEC, 1:63. Perf. pictures the continuing results. ◆ **11 κρατοῦντος** pres. act. part. (temp.) κρατέω (# 3195) to hold. Gen. abs. ("while he was holding") **συνέδραμεν** aor. ind. act. συντρέχω (# 5340) to run together. **στοά** (# 5119) roofed colonnade, portico

(BAGD). The Portico of Solomon was on the east side of the Temple Mount, in double rows supported by high columns of pure white marble, w. the ceiling panels of cedar (Jos., *JW*, 5:184, 190; Jos., *Ant.*, 15:396-401; 20:221-22; SB, 2:625-26). ◆ **12 ἰδών** aor. act. par. s.v. 3. **ἀπεκρίνατο** aor. ind. mid. (dep.) ἀποκρίνομαι (# 646) to answer. **ἐπὶ τούτῳ** over this, either the healed man (masc.) or the act of healing (n.) (Haenchen). **εὐσεβείᾳ** (# 2354) dat. sing. piety, godliness (TDNT; EDNT; RAC, 6:985-1052) Instr. dat. **πεποιηκόσιν** perf. act. part. dat. pl. ποιέω (# 4472) to do, to perform, to cause, to bring about; w. inf. which expresses the result of an action—"as though we had caused him to walk" (BAGD). Perf. looks at the abiding results and expresses responsibility in a context of praise (K. L. McKay, "On the Perfect and Other Aspects in New Testament Greek," *Nov T* 23 [1981]: 317). **περιπατεῖν** pres. act. inf. s.v. 6. ◆ **13 ἐδόξασεν** aor. ind. act. δοξάω (# 1519) to glorify, to honor, to exalt, to magnify, to display one's greatness (TLNT, 1:376; GELTS, 119). **παῖδα** acc. sing. παῖς (# 4090) child, servant (TDNT). Peter must have Isa. 52:13-15; 53:1-12 in mind when he was speaking of the exaltation of the Servant after the suffering (JIU, 86-90; Barrett). **παρεδώκατε** aor. ind. act. παραδίδωμι (# 4140) to deliver over, a legal and judicial term which became a t.t. for Jesus' passion (TLNT, 3: 21-23). **ἠρνήσασθε** aor. ind. mid. (dep.) ἀρνέομαι (# 766) to deny. **κρίναντος** aor. act. part. κρίνω (# 3212) to judge. Gen. abs., "when he judged" (temp.), or "although he decided to release" (concessive). "You wanted your Messiah condemned; Pilate had judged that he should be released" (Barrett). **ἀπολύειν** pres. act. inf. ἀπολύω (# 668) to release. Inf. as dir. obj. ◆ **14 ᾐτήσασθε** aor. ind. mid. (indir. mid., "ask for oneself") αἰτέω (# 160) to ask. **χαρισθῆναι** aor. pass. inf. χαρίζομαι (# 5919) to do a favor, to give over to. In the legal context, to release (TDNT; Bruce). ◆ **15 ἀρχηγός** (# 795) originator, author, leader (Haenchen; TDNT; EDNT; Heb. 2:10; Barrett). It may mean Prince, equivalent to נָשִׂיא, and portray Jesus as the fulfillment of the Davidic hope (George Johnston, "Christ as Archegos," *NTS* 27 [1980/81]: 381-85). **ἀπεκτείνατε** aor. ind. act. ἀποκτείνω (# 650) to kill. **ἤγειρεν** aor. ind. act. s.v. 7. ◆ **16 θεωρεῖτε** pres. ind. act. θεωρέω (# 2555) to see, to watch. **οἴδατε** perf. ind. act. οἶδα (# 3859) to know. Def. perf. w. pres. meaning. **ἐστερέωσεν** aor. ind. act. s.v. 7. **ἔδωκεν** aor. ind. act. δίδωμι (# 1443) to give. **ὁλοκληρία** (# 3907) wholeness, completeness, soundness in all parts, to be in good health (MM; NDIEC, 1:132-33; 4:161-62; TLNT). In medical use the adj. indicates entire, complete soundness of body (MLL, 193). ◆ **17 κατὰ ἄγνοιαν** (# 2848; 53) according to/in ignorance. This allows those wanting to repent the opportunity for forgiveness (EDNT; for the word in the LXX, s. GELTS, 4). **ἐπράξατε** aor. ind. act. πράσσω (# 4556) to do.

◆ **18 προκατήγγειλεν** aor. ind. act. προκαταγγέλλω (# 4615) to report beforehand, to announce fully beforehand (RWP). **παθεῖν** aor. act. inf. πάσχω (# 4248) to suffer. Epex. inf. explaining the message of the prophets. **ἐπλήρωσεν** aor. ind. act. πληρόω (# 4444) to fulfill. ◆ **19 μετανοήσατε** aor. imp. act. μετανοέω (# 3566) to change one's mind, to repent (s. Matt. 3:2). Aor. imp. calls for a specific act w. a note of urgency. **ἐπιστρέψατε** aor. imp. act. ἐπιστρέφω (# 2188) to turn to. The prep. compound is directive (MH, 312). **ἐξαλειφθῆναι** aor. pass. inf. ἐξαλείφω (# 1981) to wash over, to wipe out, to obliterate, to cancel a debt (NTW; Col. 2:14). Inf. w. **εἰς** (# 1650) to express purp. ◆ **20 ἔλθωσιν** aor. subj. act. ἔρχομαι (# 2262) to come. Subj. w. **ὅπως ἄν** to express purpose. **ἀναψύξεως** gen. sing. ἀνάψυξις (# 433) breathing space, cooling, relaxation, relief. Gen. of description. The phrase indicates the refreshing relief of the eschatological salvation promised to Israel, "the restoration of all things" (Cleon L. Rogers, Jr., "The Davidic Covenant in Acts-Revelation," *Bib Sac* 151 [1994]: 73; TLNT; TDNT; EDNT; Pesch). For the medical use s. MLL, 166-67; TLNT, 1:120. **ἀποστείλῃ** aor. subj. act. ἀποστέλλω (# 690) to send. Subj. used to express purp. **προκεχειρισμένον** perf. pass. part. (adj.) προχειρίζομαι (# 4741) to choose for oneself, to select, to appoint, to officially designate (TLNT; NDIEC, 3:82; MM; MLL, 202-03). It could have the sense of, "to make one ready to act," "to put one in the state of readiness," indicating that Jesus has been put in a state of readiness to act as Messiah (Barrett). It has been inferred that if the Jewish nation had accepted the gospel then, the kingdom of God would have been established speedily on earth. The nation as a whole declined this offer, and Acts records the progressive acceptance of the gospel by the Gentiles (Bruce). ◆ **21 δεῖ** (# 1256) pres. ind. act. it is necessary; giving the logical necessity, w. inf. **δέξασθαι** aor. mid. (dep.) inf. δέχομαι (# 1312) to receive. **ἀποκατάστασις** (# 640) restoration. The establishment of all that had been promised in the OT (Williams; s. 1:6). **ἐλάλησεν** aor. ind. act. λαλέω (# 3281) to speak. ◆ **22 ἀναστήσει** fut. ind. act. ἀνίστημι (# 482) to raise up. S. 4Q Testim 5-9; 1QS 9:11. **ἀκούσεσθε** fut. ind. mid. ἀκούω (# 201) to hear, to listen to, to obey. **λαλήσῃ** aor. subj. act. s.v. 21. Subj. w. **ἄν** in an indef. rel. cl. ◆ **23 ἐξολεθρευθήσεται** fut. ind. pass. ἐξολεθρεύω (# 2017) to destroy, to utterly destroy; perfective use of the prep. in compound. ◆ **24 καθεξῆς** (# 2759) in order, in succession. **ἐλάλησαν** aor. ind. act. s.v. 21. **κατήγγειλαν** aor. ind. act. καταγγέλλω (# 2859) to proclaim. ◆ **25 διέθετο** aor. ind. mid. διατίθημι (# 1416) to take a covenant. **[ἐν]ευλογηθήσονται** fut. ind. pass. ἐνευλογέω (# 1922) to bless. The universal blessing to all families of the earth through the Messiah as Abraham's seed is emphasized without annulling the other promises of the

Covenant (s. Gal.3:8). ◆ **26 ὑμῖν** dat. pl. σύ (# *5148*) ("to you"). Dat. of personal interest ("for you"). Although the universal blessing in the Messiah is for all people, it is first (πρῶτον) for those of Israel who will accept it by faith. **ἀναστήσας** aor. act. part. (circum.) s.v. 22; here, "to raise from the dead," or perhaps the idea is God brought him on the stage of history (Barrett). **ἀπέστειλεν** aor. ind. act. ἀποστέλλω (# *690*) to send, to send as an official representative. **εὐλογοῦντα** pres. act. part. εὐλογέω (# *2328*) to bless. Part. expressing purp. (RG, 991). **ἀποστρέφειν** pres. act. inf. ἀποστρέφω (# *695*) to turn from, to turn someone from something (Barrett). Subst. inf. w. prep. giving the content of the blessing (BBC).

Acts 4

◆ **1 λαλούντων** pres. act. part. (temp.) λαλέω (# *3281*) to speak. Gen. abs., "while they were speaking." **ἐπέστησαν** aor. ind. act. ἐφίστημι (# *2392*) to come upon, w. dat. **ὁ στρατηγὸς τοῦ ἱεροῦ** captain of the temple. He had the supreme charge of order in and around the temple (HJP, 2:278; SB, 2:628-31; JTJ, 163; Edersheim, *Temple*, 147-48; DTM, 2:1430-31). ◆ **2 διαπονούμενοι** pres. mid. (dep.) part. (causal) διαπονέομαι (# *1387*) to be annoyed, to be worked up, to be indignant, to be strongly irked or provoked at somebody (LN, 1:763). Perfective use of the prep. in compound (RWP). **διδάσκειν** pres. act. inf. διδάσκω (# *1438*) to teach. Inf. w. prep. **διά** (# *1328*) expressing cause. **καταγγέλλειν** pres. act. inf. καταγγέλλω (# *2859*) to proclaim, to report. Inf. w. prep. expressing cause. **ἐν τῷ Ἰησοῦ** (# *1877; 2652*) by (instr.) Jesus, or in the case of Jesus (Barrett). ◆ **3 ἐπέβαλον** aor. ind. act. ἐπιβάλλω (# *2095*) to lay hands upon. **ἔθεντο** aor. ind. mid. (dep.) τίθημι (# *5502*) to place. **τήρησις** (# *5499*) keeping, prison; place of custody, probably in one of the chambers of the temple (RWP). ◆ **4 ἀκουσάντων** aor. act. part. ἀκούω (# *201*) to hear. Part. as subst. **ἐπίστευσαν** aor. ind. act. πιστεύω (# *4409*) to believe. **ἐγενήθη** aor. ind. pass. (dep.) γίνομαι (# *1181*) to become, to be. Used to end an addition sum (MH, 173). **χιλιάδες πέντε** five thousand (s. Acts 2:41). ◆ **5 ἐγένετο** aor. ind. mid. (dep.) s.v. 4; here used in a Semitic construction w. prep. and inf. (MH, 425-28; Beyer, 31-33). **συναχθῆναι** aor. pass. inf. συνάγω (# *5251*) to come together, to convene. Inf. as subject of the vb. ("they were gathered together"). ◆ **6 ἦσαν** impf. ind. act. εἰμί (# *1639*) to be. **ἐκ γένους ἀρχιερατικοῦ** from the high priestly family (s. JTJ, 193-97). For the historical knowledge displayed by Luke s. DJG; BASHH, 108, 161. ◆ **7 στήσαντες** aor. act. part. (temp.) ἵστημι (# *2705*) to place, to set, to stand. **ἐπυνθάνοντο** impf. ind. mid. (dep.) πυνθάνομαι (# *4785*) to inquire. Incep. impf. stressing the beginning of a continuing or re-

peated action. **ἐποιήσατε** aor. ind. act. ποιέω (# *4472*) to do, to perform. ◆ **8 πλησθείς** aor. pass. part. (circum.) πίμπλημι (# *4398*) to fill. ◆ **9 ἀνακρινόμεθα** pres. ind. pass. ἀνακρίνω (# *373*) to examine, to interrogate (GELTS, 29). In Attic Gr. it refers to a preliminary hearing, but later to any legal inquiry (LC). **εὐεργεσίᾳ** (# *2307*) dat. sing. good deed, w. obj. gen. **σέσωται** perf. ind. pass. σώζω (# *5392*) to save, to heal. Perf. indicates the continuing results of the completed action. ◆ **10 ἔστω** pres. imp. act. 3rd. pers. sing. εἰμί s. 2:14. **ἐσταυρώσατε** aor. ind. act. σταυρόω (# *5090*) to crucify. **ἤγειρεν** aor. ind. act. ἐγείρω (# *1586*) to raise. **παρέστηκεν** perf. ind. act. παρίστημι (# *4225*) to stand, to stand before someone. ◆ **11 ἐξουθενηθείς** aor. pass. part. (adj.) ἐξουθενέω (# *2024*) to despise, to disdain, to despise someone or something on the basis that it is worthless or of no value (LN, 1:763; GELTS, 162). **γενόμενος** aor. mid. (dep.) part. s.v. 4. **γωνία** (# *1224*) corner, either the highest cornerstone right under the roof, or the cornerstone under the building, or the keystone (RWP; TDNT). ◆ **12 δεδομένον** perf. pass. part. (adj.) δίδωμι (# *1443*) to give. Perf. indicates the abiding results. Theol. pass., indicating that God performed the act. **δεῖ** (# *1256*) pres. ind. act. it is necessary, giving the logical necessity, w. inf. **σωθῆναι** aor. pass. inf. σώζω s.v. 9. Jesus Christ is the only source and ground of salvation available for mankind (Barrett). ◆ **13 θεωροῦντες** pres. act. part. (temp.) θεωρέω (# *2555*) to see. **παρρησία** (# *4244*) boldness, freedom of speech, liberty of language, the courageous and unhindered freedom of speech in proclaiming the word about Jesus (TLNT; EDNT; Stanley B. Morrow, "*Parrhesia* and the New Testament," CBQ 44 [1982]: 431-46; Barrett). Here of the confidence and forthrightness w. which the apostles spoke under the prompting of the Holy Spirit (Bruce). **καταλαβόμενοι** aor. mid. (dep.) part. (temp.) καταλαμβάνω (# *2898*) to grasp, to perceive; mid. indicates the grasping w. the mind (Bruce). **ἀγράμματοι** (# *63*) nom. pl. uneducated, unable to write (NDIEC, 5:12-13; MM). Here it denotes the lack of rabbinic training (Meyer) or lack of rhetorical training (BBC). **ἰδιῶται** nom. pl. ἰδιώτης (# *2626*) layman, one who is not an expert; unskilled, commoner, one who has no training or specialty in contrast to experts and professionals (Bruce; TLNT). **ἐθαύμαζον** impf. ind. act. θαυμάζω (# *2513*) to be amazed. Incep. impf. **ἐπεγίνωσκον** impf. ind. act. ἐπιγινώσκω (# *2105*) to recognize, to realize. ◆ **14 βλέποντες** pres. act. part. (temp.) βλέπω (# *1063*) to see. **ἑστῶτα** perf. act. part. (adj.) ἵστημι (# *2705*) to stand. **τεθεραπευμένον** perf. pass. part. (adj.) θεραπεύω (# *2543*) to treat medically, to heal (GLH). Perf. indicates the continuing results of a completed act. **εἶχον** impf. ind. act. ἔχω (# *2400*) to have, to be able (Barrett). **ἀντειπεῖν** aor. act. inf. ἀντιλέγω (# *515*) to say something against, to speak against, to contradict.

Epex. inf. explaining οὐδέν ("nothing"). ◆ **15 κελεύ-σαντες** aor. act. part. (temp.) κελεύω (# 3027) to command. **ἀπελθεῖν** aor. act. inf. ἀπέρχομαι (# 599) to go out, to depart. Inf. as dir. obj. **συνέβαλλον** impf. ind. act. συμβάλλω (# 5202) to confer, to hold a discussion (Barrett). ◆ **16 ποιήσωμεν** aor. subj. act. s.v. 7. Deliberative subj.: "What shall we do w. these men?" **γνωστόν** (# 1196) known; publicly known (Barrett). **γέγονεν** perf. ind. act. s.v. 4. Perf. indicates the abiding results. ◆ **17 πλεῖον** comp. πολύς (# 4498) much; comp., more. ἐπὶ πλεῖον any farther (spacial), or any longer (temporal) (BAGD). **διανεμηθῇ** aor. subj. pass. διανέμω (# 1376) to distribute, to divide into portions, to spread abroad (EGT; NDIEC, 2:193-94). Subj. w. ἵνα (# 2671) in a neg. purp. cl. **ἀπειλησώμεθα** aor. subj. mid. (dep.) ἀπειλέω (# 580) to threaten. Hortatory subj.: "let us threaten." **λαλεῖν** pres. act. inf. λαλέω s.v. 1. Epex. inf. giving the content of the threat. ◆ **18 καλέσαντες** aor. act. part. (temp.) καλέω (# 2813) to call, to summon. **παρήγγειλαν** aor. ind. act. παραγγέλλω (# 4133) to command, to order, to announce what must be done (LN, 1:426). **καθόλου** (# 2773) at all. **φθέγγεσθαι** pres. mid. (dep.) inf. φθέγγομαι (# 5779) lit., to produce a sound; then, to speak, to utter, to proclaim (BAGD). Epex. inf. explaining the command. **διδάσκειν** pres. act. inf. διδάσκω (# 1438) to teach. Epex. inf. ◆ **19 ἀπο-κριθέντες** aor. pass. (dep.) part. ἀποκρίνομαι (# 646) to answer. For the Semitic use of the redundant part. s. MH, 453. **εἶπον** aor. ind. act. λέγω (# 3306) to say. **ἀκού-ειν** pres. act. inf. ἀκούω (# 201) to hear, to hear and obey. Obedience to God is of overriding importance (Barrett). Epex. inf. explaining what is right (**δίκαιον**). **κρίνατε** aor. imp. act. κρίνω (# 3212) to judge, to decide. Perfective aor., "you reach a decision," "you make the decision." ◆ **20 δυνάμεθα** pres. ind. pass. (dep.) δύναμαι (# 1538) to be able, w. inf. **εἴδαμεν** aor. ind. act. ὁράω (# 3972) to see. **ἠκούσαμεν** aor. ind. act. s.v. 19. **λαλεῖν** pres. act. inf. s.v. 1. The double neg. represents a strong affirmative: "We must speak at all cost" (Barrett). ◆ **21 προσαπειλησάμενοι** aor. mid. (dep.) part. (temp.) προσαπειλέω (# 4653) to threaten further. The prep. compound indicates "in addition" (Bruce; Jos., *Ant.* 14:170). **ἀπέλυσαν** aor. ind. act. ἀπο-λύω (# 668) to release. **εὑρίσκοντες** pres. act. part. (causal) εὑρίσκω (# 2351) to find. (M, 230). **κολάσωνται** aor. subj. mid. (dep.) κολάζομαι (# 3134) to prune, to curb, to correct, to punish (RWP). Subj. in indir. question (RWP). **ἐδόξαζον** impf. ind. act. δοξάζω (# 1519) to glorify (s. 3:13). Impf. indicates the continual action. **γε-γονότι** perf. act. part. s.v. 4. Part. as subst. Perf. indicates the abiding results. ◆ **22 γέγονει** plperf. ind. act. s.v. 4. ◆ **23 ἀπολυθέντες** aor. pass. part. (temp.) s.v. 21. **ἦλθον** aor. ind. act. ἔρχομαι (# 1181) to come, to go. **ἀπήγγειλαν** aor. ind. act. ἀπαγγέλλω (# 550) to report. ◆ **24 ἀκούσαντες** aor. act. part. s.v. 19. **ἦραν** aor. ind.

act. αἴρω to lift up. **Δέσποτα** voc. sing. δεσπότης (# 1305) lord, sovereign lord, one who holds complete power or authority over another (LN, 1:479; TDNT; NDIEC, 4:144). A word used in connection w. servants (Bruce). It was used in the LXX to translate אֲדֹנָי אָדוֹן (Master, Lord) (TDOT; TWOT; DCH; NIDOTTE). **ποιή-σας** aor. act. part. ποιέω (# 4472) to do, to make. Part. as subst. ◆ **25 ἱνατί** (# 4672) why? for what reason? Used for ἵνα τί γένηται "in order that what might happen" (BAGD; RG, 739; IBG, 139). **ἐφρύαξαν** aor. ind. act. φρυάσσω (# 5865) to snort, to neigh like a horse, to prance or stamp the ground, to put on lofty airs, to be arrogant, haughty, insolent (BAGD; RWP). **ἐμελέτησαν** aor. ind. act. μελετάω (# 3509) to devise, to plan. ◆ **26 παρέστησαν** aor. ind. act. παρίστημι (# 4225) to stand, to stand by someone. **συνήχθησαν** aor. ind. pass. συνάγω (# 5251) to gather together. ◆ **27 ἔχρισας** aor. ind. act. 2nd. pers. sing. χρίω (# 5987) to anoint, to anoint to an office (TDNT; EDNT). ◆ **28 ποιῆσαι** aor. act. inf. ποιέω (# 4472) to do. Inf. of purp. **προώρισεν** aor. ind. act. προορίζω (# 4633) to determine beforehand, to mark out with a boundary before, to predestine, to decide beforehand (TDNT; EDNT; NDNTT, 1:695-95). **γενέσθαι** aor. mid. (dep.) inf. s.v. 4. Epex. inf. explaining the determined decision. ◆ **29 ἔπιδε** aor. imp. act. ἐφοράω (# 2078) to look upon. Aor. imp. calls for a specific action w. a note of urgency. **ἀπειλάς** acc. pl. ἀπειλή (# 581) threat. **δός** aor. imp. act. δίδωμι (# 1443) to give. **παρρησία** s.v. 13. **λαλεῖν** pres. act. inf. s.v. 1. Inf. as dir. obj. ◆ **30 ἐκτείνειν** pres. act. inf. ἐκ-τείνω (# 1753) to stretch out. Inf. w. prep. ἐν (# 1877) expressing contemporaneous action. The phrase seems to be explanatory of **δός** (Barrett). **γίνεσθαι** aor. mid. (dep.) inf. s.v. 4. Inf. of purp. ◆ **31 δεηθέντων** aor. pass. (dep.) part. (temp.) δέομαι (# 1289) to pray, to make a request. Gen. abs. **ἐσαλεύθη** aor. ind. pass. σαλεύω (# 4888) to shake; shook as w. an earthquake, a sign of divine assent (Bruce). **συνηγμένοι** perf. pass. part. s.v. 26. Periphrastic part. **ἐπλήσθησαν** aor. ind. pass. πίμπλημι (# 4398) to fill. **ἐλάλουν** impf. ind. act. s.v. 1. Impf. could be incep. or indicate that they continued speaking boldly. ◆ **32 πιστευσάντων** aor. act. part. πιστεύω (# 4409) to believe. Adj. part. as subst. **ὑπαρ-χόντων** pres. act. part. ὑπάρχω (# 5639) to exist, to be. Pl. part. as subst. ("possessions"). **αὐτῷ** dat. sing. αὐ-τός (# 899) Dat. of possession. **ἴδιος** (# 2625) particular, private, one's own, often in contrast to κοινός ("common") (TLNT). **εἶναι** pres. act. inf. εἰμί (# 1639) to be. Inf. in indir. speech. ◆ **33 δυνάμει** dat. sing. δύναμις (# 1539) power, strength, ability, capability (BAGD). Instr. dat. **ἀπεδίδουν** impf. ind. act. ἀποδίδωμι to give, (# 625) to give back, to render. ◆ **34 ἐνδεής** (# 1890) in need, needy. **κτήτορες** nom. pl. κτήτωρ (# 3230) owner. Frequent in papyri for owners of real estate (Bruce; MM; NDIEC, 2:89). **πωλοῦντες** pres. act. part. (circum.)

πωλέω (# *4797*) to sell. Iterat. pres. indicating repeated action. ἔφερον impf. ind. act. φέρω (# *5770*) to bring. Iterat. impf. πιπρασκομένων pres. pass. part. πιπράσκω (# *4405*) to sell. Part. as subst. ◆ **35** ἐτίθουν impf. ind. act. s.v. 3. Iterat. impf. διεδίδετο impf. ind. pass. διαδίδωμι (# *1344*) to distribute. Iterat. impf. καθότι in proportion as, according as. εἶχεν impf. ind. act. ἔχω (# *2400*) to have. ◆ **36** ἐπικληθείς aor. pass. part. (adj.) ἐπικαλέω (# *2126*) to name, to call by the surname. μεθερμηνευόμενον pres. pass. part. μεθερμηνεύω (# *3493*) to translate. υἱός (# *5626*) son; used here in the Semitic sense of the leading characteristic of the person. παράκλησις (# *4155*) encouragement, exhortation, comfort; here, "son of exhortation"; that is, "preacher" (Barrett). ◆ **37** πωλήσας aor. act. part. (temp.) s.v. 34. ἤνεγκεν aor. ind. act. φέρω s.v. 34. ἔθηκεν aor. ind. act. s.v. 3. For the common ownership of goods s. 2:44; 1QS 1:12f.

Acts 5

◆ **1** Ἀνανίας (# *393*) Ananias. Transcription of חֲנַנְיָה ("Yahweh shows mercy," "God is gracious") w. Greek ending (Schneider; SB, 2:634). Σαπφίρῃ dat. sing. Σάπφιρα (# *4912*) Sapphira. Greek form of the Aramaic name שַׁפִּירָא ("The Beautiful") (Schneider; SB, 2:634; for both names w. examples s. BASHH, 224; HAE, 2:68; AT, 718). ἐπώλησεν aor. ind. act. πωλέω (# *4797*) to sell. κτῆμα (# *3228*) acc. sing. n. possession, landed property (Bruce). ◆ **2** ἐνοσφίσατο aor. ind. mid. (dep.) νοσφίζομαι (# *3802*) to embezzle, to secretly take a part of a larger quantity which had been given to one as a trust. It was used in the LXX (Josh 7:1) of Achan (LC; TLNT; MM). Indir. mid. "he kept back ... for himself" (GGBB, 421). συνειδυίης perf. act. part. fem. sing. σύνοιδα (# *5323*) to share knowledge w., to be implicated. ἐνέγκας aor. act. part. (temp.) φέρω (# *5770*) to carry, to bring. ἔθηκεν aor. ind. act. τίθημι (# *5502*) to place. ◆ **3** ἐπλήρωσεν aor. ind. act. πληρόω (# *4444*) to fill, to control. ψεύσασθαι aor. mid. (dep.) inf. ψεύδομαι (# *6017*) to lie, to lie to someone, to try to deceive by lying (BAGD; KVS, 105-6; Barrett). Inf. of purp. or result. καί (# *2779*) epex., "that is, in that you embezzled" (Pesch). νοσφίσασθαι aor. mid. inf. s.v. 2. ◆ **4** οὐχί (# *4049*) introduces a question expecting a positive answer. μένον pres. act. part. (temp.) μένω (# *3531*) to remain; referring to κτῆμα in v. 1 (Schneider); "While (so long as) it remained unsold, it remained yours, didn't it?" ἔμενεν impf. ind. act. μένω. πραθέν aor. pass. part. (temp.) πιπράσκω (# *4405*) to sell. "When it was sold, it was still under your authority, wasn't it?" ὑπῆρχεν impf. ind. act. ὑπάρχω (# *5639*) to exist, to be. τί ὅτι Why (it is) that...? Elliptical construction (Bruce). ἔθου aor. ind. mid. τίθημι s.v. 2. ἐψεύσω aor. ind. mid. (dep.) s.v. 3. ◆ **5** ἀκούων pres. act.

part. ἀκούω (# *201*) to hear. Temp. part. indicating contemporaneous action. πεσών aor. act. part. (circum.) πίπτω (# *4406*) to fall. ἐξέψυξεν aor. ind. act. ἐκψύχω (# *1775*) to breathe out, to expire. A term used by medical writers (MLL, 37; Barrett). ἐγένετο aor. ind. mid. (dep.) γίνομαι (# *1181*) to become, to be. ἀκούοντας aor. act. part. Part. as subst. ◆ **6** ἀναστάντες aor. act. part. ἀνίστημι (# *482*) to arise. For the Semitic construction s. BG, 126f. συνέστειλαν aor. ind. act. συστέλλω (# *5366*) to gather together, to draw together, to wrap up. It could indicate the laying out of a corpse, or covering it w. a shroud, or simply preparing for burial (Barrett; LC; MLL, 38). ἐξενέγκαντες aor. act. part. ἐκφέρω (# *1766*) to carry out. Used in the technical sense to carry out for burial (Bruce). Circum. or temp. part. ἔθαψαν aor. ind. act. θάπτω (# *2507*) to bury. ◆ **7** διάστημα (# *1404*) interval (of time, or space) (NDIEC, 4:86; GELTS, 109). It is to be taken as subject of the vb. ἐγένετο (Barrett). εἰδυῖα perf. act. part. (circum.) nom. fem. sing. οἶδα (# *3857*) to know. γεγονός perf. act. part. s.v. 5. Subst. part., "the thing that had happened." Perf. indicates the lasting results. εἰσῆλθεν aor. ind. act. εἰσέρχομαι (# *1656*) to come in. ◆ **8** ἀπεκρίθη aor. ind. pass. ἀποκρίνομαι (# *646*) to answer. εἰπέ aor. imp. act. λέγω (# *3306*) to say. τοσούτου gen. sing. τοσοῦτος (# *5537*) so large, so much. Gen. of price. ἀπέδοσθε aor. ind. mid. ἀποδίδωμι (# *625*) to give back; mid., to sell. ναί (# *3721*) yes. ◆ **9** συνεφωνήθη aor. ind. pass. συμφωνέω (# *5244*) to agree together; impersonal use w. the dat., "It was agreed together by you, or for you" (RWP). πειράσαι aor. act. inf. πειράζω (# *4279*) to tempt, to put to the test (TLNT, 3:82-83). θαψάντων aor. act. part. s.v. 6. ἐξοίσουσιν fut. ind. act. ἐκφέρω s.v. 6. ◆ **10** ἔπεσεν aor. ind. act. s.v. 5. ἐξέψυξεν aor. ind. act. s.v. 5. εἰσελθόντες aor. act. part. (temp.) s.v. 7. εὗρον aor. ind. act. εὑρίσκω (# *2351*) to find. ἐξενέγκαντες aor. act. part. s.v. 6. ἔθαψαν aor. ind. act. s.v. 6. ◆ **11** ἐγένετο aor. ind. mid. (dep.) s.v. 5. ἀκούοντας aor. act. part. s.v. 5. Part. as subst. Both the believers and those who heard had great fear. ◆ **12** ἐγίνετο impf. ind. mid. (dep.) s.v. 5. The impf. pictures the repeated occurrence. ὁμοθυμαδόν w. one accord. In Hellenistic Gr., "together" (LC). ἐν τῇ στοᾷ Σολομῶντος in the Portico of Solomon (s. 3:11). This seems to be the regular meeting place for the Christians (Barrett). ◆ **13** ἐτόλμα impf. ind. act. τολμάω (# *5528*) to dare, w. inf. κολλᾶσθαι pres. pass. inf. κολλάω (# *3140*) to join, to approach. Perhaps w. the idea of attaching oneself without a regular introduction (Bruce; Christoph Burchard, "Fussnoten zum neutestamentlichen Griechisch," ZNW 61 [1970]: 159-60). ἐμεγάλυνεν impf. ind. act. μεγαλύνω (# *3486*) to make large, to magnify, to praise, to glorify (TLNT, 2:459-60). ◆ **14** μᾶλλον (# *3437*) even more (Barrett). προσετίθεντο impf. ind. pass. προστίθημι (# *4707*) to add to. The impf. pictures the repeated action. κυρίῳ dat. sing. κύριος (# *3261*) lord. Dat. could be taken either w. the main vb., "added to the Lord," or w. the part., "believers on the Lord" (Pesch). πιστεύοντες pres. act. part. πιστεύω (# *4409*) to believe. Part. as subst. ◆ **15** καί (# *2779*) even. πλατεῖα (# *4423*) street. ἐκφέρειν pres. act. inf. s.v. 6. Inf. w. ὥστε (# *6063*) to express result looking back to the general context, but esp. v. 12a. (Bauernfeind). τιθέναι pres. act. inf. τίθημι s.v. 2. Inf. of result. κλινάριον (# *3108*) bed, little bed. κράβαττος (# *3187*) pallet, camp bed (RWP; EGT). ἐρχομένου pres. mid. (dep.) part. (temp.) ἔρχομαι (# *2262*) to come, to go. Gen. abs. κᾶν at least (Barrett). ἐπισκιάσῃ aor. subj. act. ἐπισκιάζω (# *2173*) to overshadow, w. dat. It is not the effect of Peter's shadow but of the presence and power of God which Peter represented (Barrett). ◆ **16** συνήρχετο impf. ind. mid. (dep.) συνέρχομαι (# *5302*) to come together. Impf. pictures the repeated action in the past. πέριξ (# *4339*) adv. surrounding. φέροντες pres. act. part. φέρω (# *5770*) to carry. Circum. part. ὀχλουμένους pres. pass. part. ὀχλέω (# *4061*) to trouble, to torment. For the medical use s. MLL, 7-8. ἐθεραπεύοντο impf. ind. pass. θεραπεύω (# *2543*) to heal. Impf. pictures the repeated action. ◆ **17** ἀναστάς aor. act. part. (circum.) s.v. 6. οὖσα pres. act. part. εἰμί (# *1639*). Used here in the sense of introducing some technical phrase w. the meaning "local," "current," "existing" (Bruce; MT, 151-52). ἐπλήσθησαν aor. ind. pass. πίμπλημι (# *4398*) to fill. ζήλου gen. sing. ζῆλος (# *2419*) jealousy, envy, a particularly strong feeling of resentment and jealousy against someone (LN, 1:760; TDNT; NIDNTT). Gen. of content indicating that with which they were filled. ◆ **18** ἐπέβαλον aor. ind. act. ἐπιβάλλω (# *2095*) to place upon, to lay hands upon someone (s. 4:3). ἔθεντο aor. ind. mid. s.v. 15. δημόσιος (# *1323*) dat. sing. publicly (adv.), or public (adj.). The latter refers to the *Custodia publica* or public prison indicating a more severe form of imprisonment (Schille; BAGD; SB, 2:635, 1:679). ◆ **19** διὰ νυκτός (# *1328; 3816*) at night (BD, 199). ἀνοίξας aor. act. part. (circum.) ἀνοίγω (# *487*) to open. ἐξαγαγών aor. act. part. (circum.) ἐξάγω (# *1974*) to lead out. εἶπεν aor. ind. act. λέγω (# *3306*) to say, to speak. ◆ **20** πορεύεσθε pres. imp. mid. (dep.) πορεύομαι (# *4513*) to go. σταθέντες aor. pass. part. ἵστημι (# *2705*) to stand; pass. to take a stand (RWP). Circum. part. w. the idea of an imp. (s. VANT, 386). λαλεῖτε pres. imp. act. λαλέω (# *3281*) to speak. The idea of the pres. imp. may be "Continue the act of speaking," "Resume speaking and continue to do so." ◆ **21** ἀκούσαντες aor. act. part. (circum.) ἀκούω (# *201*) to hear, to obey. εἰσῆλθον aor. ind. act. s.v. 7. ὄρθρον acc. sing. ὄρθρος (# *3986*) dawn, early morning, daybreak. Acc. w. prep. ὑπό (# *5679*) as acc. of time: "under the dawn," "about dawn" (RWP; TLNT, 1:51). ἐδίδασκον impf. ind. act. διδάσκω (# *1438*) to teach. Incep. impf., "they began to teach." παραγενό-

μενος aor. mid. (dep.) part. (temp.) παραγίνομαι (# *4134*) to come on the scene, to appear. συνεκάλεσαν aor. ind. act. συγκαλέω (# *5157*) to call together, to summons. καί (# *2779*) that is (epex.) (BG, 154). ἀπέστειλαν aor. ind. act. ἀποστέλλω (# *690*) to send. δεσμωτήριον (# *1303*) place of confinement, prison. ἀχθῆναι aor. pass. inf. ἄγω (# *72*) to lead. Inf. of purp. Some see it as a pass. inf. after a vb. of commanding, as in Latin (MT, 138; BD, 200). ◆ **22** ὑπηρέτης (# *5677*) helper, assistant, temple guard (Barrett; s. 4:1). εὗρον aor. ind. act. s.v. 10. ἀναστρέψαντες aor. act. part. (temp.) ἀναστρέφω (# *418*) to turn again, to return again. ἀπήγγειλαν aor. ind. act. ἀπαγγέλλω (# *550*) to report. ◆ **23** εὕρομεν aor. ind. act. s.v. 10. κεκλεισμένον perf. pass. part. (adj.) κλείω (# *3091*) to close, to shut, to lock. The perf. emphasizes that it was shut tight (RWP). ἀσφαλείᾳ (# *854*) dat. sing. safety, security. W. the prep. ἐν (# *1877*) to express manner ("most securely") (BD, 118; NDIEC, 3:149; 154; TLNT, 1:217). φύλακας acc. pl. φύλαξ (# *5874*) guard. ἑστῶτας perf. act. part. (adj.) s.v. 20. ἀνοίξαντες aor. act. part. (temp.) s.v. 19. ◆ **24** ἤκουσαν aor. ind. act. s.v. 21. στρατηγός (# *5130*) captain of the temple guard (s. 4:1). διηπόρουν impf. ind. act. διαπορέω (# *1389*) to be perplexed (s. 2:12). Incep. impf. γένοιτο aor. opt. mid. (dep.) γίνομαι (# *1181*) to become, to be; here "as to what this would become." The conclusion of a cond. cl. w. the cond. ("if the thing should be allowed to go on") not expressed (RWP). "What will be the end, or result, of this?" (Barrett). It may refer to the past, "What could have happened to them?" (NSV, 110). ◆ **25** παραγενόμενος aor. mid. (dep.) part. (temp.) s.v. 21. ἀπήγγειλεν aor. ind. act. s.v. 22. ἔθεσθε aor. ind. mid. s.v. 2. ἑστῶτες perf. act. part. s.v. 20. Periphrastic part. ("The men are standing in the Temple"). διδάσκοντες pres. act. part. s.v. 21. Periphrastic part. The first part. gives the author's view of the apostles' condition or state, and the second the progress they are making (VA, 456). Parts. may have a loose attachment to the vb. εἰμί and be circum. (NSV, 9). ◆ **26** ἀπελθών aor. act. part. (temp.) ἀπέρχομαι (# *599*) to go away. ἦγεν aor. ind. act. s.v. 21. They were leading them slowly and no doubt and solemnly (RWP). μετὰ βίας (# *3552; 1040*) w. force, w. violence. ἐφοβοῦντο impf. ind. mid. (dep.) φοβέομαι (# *5828*) to be afraid, to fear. λιθασθῶσιν aor. subj. pass. λιθάζω (# *3342*) to stone. Subj. in a neg. purp. cl. w. a vb. of fearing (RWP; NSV, 141). ◆ **27** ἀγαγόντες aor. act. part. s.v. 21. ἔστησαν aor. ind. act. ἵστημι (# *2705*) to place, to stand. ἐπηρώτησεν aor. ind. act. ἐπερωτάω (# *2089*) to question, to put a question to, to interrogate. ◆ **28** παραγγελίᾳ (# *4132*) dat. sing. Instr. dat. used like the Heb. inf. abs. (SA, 151; Barret; MH, 443). παρηγγείλαμεν aor. ind. act. παραγγέλλω (# *4133*) to command, to charge. Often used as a legal term indicating a summons to court or the complaint against the defendant (LC). Ind. w. **οὐ** (# 4024) in a question expecting a positive answer. **διδάσκειν** pres. act. inf. s.v. 21. Inf. as dir. obj. of the vb. παρηγγείλαμεν. **πεπληρώκατε** perf. ind. act. πληρόω (# 4444) to fill. Perf. emphasizes the continuing result. **βούλεσθε** pres. ind. mid. (dep.) βούλομαι (# 1089) to want to, w. inf. **ἐπαγαγεῖν** aor. act. inf. ἐπάγω (# 2042) to bring upon. ◆ **29 ἀποκριθείς** aor. pass. part. s.v. 8. Pleonastic use of the part. (MH, 453). **πειθαρχεῖν** pres. act. inf. πειθαρχέω (# 4272) to obey one in authority, to obey willingly, to let oneself be persuaded, to willingly comply w. a rule; w. dat. (EGT; TLNT; MM; NDIEC, 2:105). Epex. inf. w. **δεῖ** (# 1256) (logical necessity). ◆ **30 ἤγειρεν** aor. ind. act. ἐγείρω (# 1586) to raise. **διεχειρίσασθε** aor. ind. mid. (dep.) διαχειρίζομαι (# 1429) to take in hand, to do away w. A euphemism for "kill" (MH, 302). **κρεμάσαντες** aor. act. part. κρεμάννυμι (# 3203) to hang. Part. of manner, or means (s. 10:39). ◆ **31 ἀρχηγός** s. 3:15. Double acc., "God has exalted this One as Prince and Savior." **ὕψωσεν** aor. ind. act. ὑψόω (# 5738) to lift up, to exalt. **δοῦναι** aor. act. inf. δίδωμι (# 1443) to give, to grant. Inf. of purpose. ◆ **32 καί...καί** (# 2779) both ... and. **ἔδωκεν** aor. ind. act. δίδωμι s.v. 31. **πειθαρχοῦσιν** pres. act. part. dat. pl. s.v. 29. Part. as subst., dat. as indir. obj. ◆ **33 ἀκούσαντες** aor. act. part. s.v. 5. Part. as subst. **διεπρίοντο** impf. ind. pass. διαπρίω (# 1391) to saw through; pass. to be cut to the quick, to be infuriated (BAGD). Incep. impf. **ἐβούλοντο** impf. ind. mid. (dep.) s.v. 28, w. inf. Impf. indicates the incompleted action. **ἀνελεῖν** aor. act. inf. ἀναιρέω (# 359) to kill. ◆ **34 ἀναστάς** aor. act. part. (temp.) s.v. 6. **Γαμαλιήλ** (# 1137) Gamaliel. Gamaliel I, the Elder, worked from A.D. 25-50 and was a highly respected teacher. When he died it was said that the glory of the Law ceased and purity and abstinence died (M, Sotah 6:15; SB 2:636-36; ABD, 2:904-906; BBC; HJP, 2:367-68; Barrett; for the Chief Priests, Sadducees, Pharisees, and Sanhedrin in Acts s. BAFCS, 4:115-77). He was also Paul's teacher (s. 22:3). **ἐκέλευσεν** aor. ind. act. κελεύω (# 3027) to command. **ποιῆσαι** aor. act. inf. ποιέω (# 4472) to do, to make; here, "to put the men outside for a little while." Inf. gives the content of the command. ◆ **35 προσέχετε** pres. imp. act. προσέχω (# 4668) to give heed, to pay attention; "hold your mind (νοῦς, not expressed) for or on yourselves" (RWP). **πράσσειν** pres. act. inf. πράσσω (# 4556) to do. Inf. w. **μέλλετε** (# 3516) to express fut., "What you are about to do." ◆ **36 ἀνέστη** aor. ind. act. s.v. 6. **Θευδᾶς** Theudas. For name and the historical difficulties here, s. NDIEC, 4:183-85; BASHH, 162-63; Barrett; Longenecker, 322-23; SB, 2:639-40. **εἶναι** pres. act. inf. εἰμί (# 1639) to be. Inf. in indir. speech. **προσεκλίθη** aor. ind. pass. προσκλίνομαι (# 4679) to attach oneself to, to follow, w. dat. **ἀνῃρέθη** aor. ind. pass. s.v. 33. **ἐπείθοντο** impf. ind. mid. πείθω (# 4275) to convince, to persuade, to be convinced, persuaded, to

obey, w. dat. (BAGD). **διελύθησαν** aor. ind. pass. διαλύω (# 1370) to scatter, to destroy. **ἐγένοντο** aor. ind. mid. (dep.) s.v. 5. ◆ **37 ἀνέστη** aor. ind. act. s.v. 6. **ἀπέστησεν** aor. ind. act. ἀφίστημι (# 923) to cause to revolt, to mislead (DJG, 688-98; DPL, 812-19; BBC). **ἀπώλετο** aor. ind. mid. (dep.) ἀπόλλυμι (# 660) to destroy, to perish. **διεσκορπίσθησαν** aor. ind. pass. διασκορπίζω (# 1399) to scatter. ◆ **38 ἀπόστητε** aor. imp. act. ἀφίστημι (# 923) keep away from. **ἄφετε** aor. imp. act. ἀφίημι (# 918) to leave, to leave alone. **ᾖ** pres. subj. act. εἰμί (# 1639) to be. Subj. w. **ἐάν** (# 1569) in a 3rd. class cond. cl. which assumes the possibility of the cond. **καταλυθήσεται** fut. ind. pass. καταλύω (# 2907) to destroy; to loosen down like a falling house (RWP). ◆ **39 εἰ** (# 1623) if. Used in a 1st. class cond. cl. where the cond. is assumed to be true. For the cond. here s. BG, 104-5; NSV, 169-70; VA, 310; Barrett. **δυνήσεσθε** fut. ind. pass. (dep.) δύναμαι (# 1538) to be able, w. inf. **καταλῦσαι** aor. act. inf. s.v. 38. **θεομάχος** (# 2534) fighting against God, one who strives against God (NIDNTT, 3:962; 3 [Greek] Bar., 2:7). **εὑρεθῆτε** aor. subj. pass. εὑρίσκω (# 2351) to find. Subj. w. **μή** (# 3590) in a cl. of apprehension, where the warding off of anxiety is still dependent on the will (BD, 188). **ἐπείσθησαν** aor. ind. pass. s.v. 36. Effective aor. indicating that the persuading was successful. ◆ **40 προσκαλεσάμενοι** aor. mid. (dep.) part. (temp.) προσκαλέομαι (# 4673) to summons someone. A legal t.t., "to call in" (BAGD). **δείραντες** aor. act. part. δέρω (# 1296) to flog, to beat. The punishment was for minor offenses (EGT). Perhaps this was the "forty stripes minus one," as in 2 Cor. 11:24 (Schneider), or the *Makkat mardut* ("stripes of correction") given for rebellion and resistance (s. Sven Gallas, "'Fünfmal vierzig weniger eins....' Die an Paulus vollzogenen Synagogalstrafen nach 2 Kor 11, 24," *ZNW* 81 [1990]: 178-91, esp. 190). **παρήγγειλαν** aor. ind. act. s.v. 28. **λαλεῖν** pres. act. inf. λαλέω (# 3281) to sound, make sounds. Inf. gives the content of the command. Pres. w. the neg. indicates that they are not to continue speaking, or that they are to stop the action in progress. **ἀπέλυσαν** aor. ind. act. ἀπολύω (# 668) to release. ◆ **41 ἐπορεύοντο** impf. ind. mid. (dep.). πορεύομαι (# 4513) to go. **χαίροντες** pres. act. part. χαίρω (# 5897) to rejoice. Part. of manner. **κατηξιώθησαν** aor. ind. pass. καταξιόω (# 2921) to consider worthy. Theol. pass. indicating that God considered them worthy. **ἀτιμασθῆναι** aor. pass. inf. ἀτιμάζω (# 869) to dishonor. Epex. inf. ◆ **42 ἐπαύοντο** impf. ind. mid. (dep.) παύομαι (# 4264) to cease, w. part.

Acts 6

◆ **1 πληθυνόντων** pres. act. part. πληθύνω (# 4437) to fill; here intr., to increase. Gen. abs. expresses contemporaneous time, but also gives the cause for the problem to be described (SF, 325). **ἐγένετο** aor. ind. mid. (dep.) γίνομαι (# 1181) to become, to arise. **γογγυσμός** (# 1198) murmuring, complaining, discontent. Used in the LXX of Israel murmuring (Exod. 16:7, 8; GELTS, 92). In the papyri it occurs in a letter from a doctor to his mother in which he says he has not been able to send his brother to her because he could not leave the patients, "lest there be some murmuring against us" (NDIEC, 4:143-44; s. TDNT). **Ἑλληνιστής** (# 1821) Hellenist. The word seems to refer to the Greek-speaking Jewish believers of the Diaspora in contrast to the Hebrew, or Aramaic-speaking Jewish Christians (SF, 19-85, 219-34, 309, 329-31; Longenecker, 327-30; Barrett; LC; BC, 5:59-74; Martin Hengel, "Zwischen Jesus und Paulus. Die 'Hellenisten', die 'Sieben' und 'Stephanas' [Apg 6, 1-15; 7, 54-8, 3]," ZThK 72 [1975]: 151-206; Edvin Larsson, "Die Hellenisten und die Urgemeinde," NTS 33 [1987]: 205-25; Schneider, 406-16; for the composition of the Jerusalem church s. BAFCS, 4:213-36). **παρεθεωροῦντο** impf. ind. pass. παραθεωρέω (# 4145) to look beyond, to overlook, to neglect. **διακονία** (# 1355) dat. sing. ministry. It suggests a daily dispensation of alms or of food to the widows (LC; TDNT; SF, 86-102, 234-40, 310). Perhaps it was an adaptation of the Jewish system of *tamhuy* ("poor bowl"), a daily distribution among the poor travellers who were in Jerusalem that consisted of bread, beans, and fruit; or the *quppah* ("poor basket"), a weekly dole for the poor of Jerusalem consisting of food, clothing, and enough money to buy food for 14 days (JTJ, 131; SB, 2:643-47; Haenchen). **καθημερινός** (# 2766) daily. **χήρα** (# 5939) widow. Perhaps a reference to the widows of those from the Diaspora who had come to Jerusalem late in life. Their widows were now left destitute (Haenchen). ◆ **2 προσκαλεσάμενοι** aor. mid. part. (temp.) προσκαλέω (# 4673) to call to oneself, to summon. **ἀρεστός** (# 744) fitting, pleasing, satisfactory; w. dat. of reference (here, "to us all," "to us Twelve," "to God" [Barrett]). **καταλείψαντας** aor. act. part. (cond.) καταλείπω (# 2901) to leave behind, to abandon. **διακονεῖν** pres. act. inf. διακονέω (# 1354) to minister to, to serve. Epex. inf. explaining **ἀρεστόν**. ◆ **3 ἐπισκέψασθε** aor. imp. mid. (dep.) ἐπισκέπτομαι (# 2170) to oversee, to supervise, here, "seeking w. a view to appointment (Barrett). **μαρτυρουμένους** pres. pass. part. (adj.) μαρτυρέω (# 3455) to give testimony, to bear witness, to be well reported of (BS, 256; LAE, 88). **ἑπτά** (# 2231) seven. Perhaps this is analogous to the "seven of a city" which made up the local board of a Jewish community (SB, 2:641; SF, 126-32; 249-51). **καταστήσομεν** fut. ind. act. καθίστημι (# 2770) to appoint. The twelve were to give their approval to the congregation's selection of the seven (Bruce). ◆ **4 προσκαρτερήσομεν** fut. ind. act. προσκαρτερέω (# 4674) to hold fast to, to continue in (s. 1:14). ◆ **5 ἤρεσεν** aor. ind. act. ἀρέσκω (# 743) to please.

ἐξελέξαντο aor. ind. mid. ἐκλέγω (# 1721) to select, to choose. **Νικόλαον προσήλυτον Ἀντιοχέα** (# 3775; 4670; 522) Nicolas, a proselyte (one who has come over from paganism to Judaism, a convert [BAGD]) from Antioch. For a discussion of this person s. SF, 132-44; ABD, 4:1107-8.. ◆ **6 ἔστησαν** aor. ind. act. ἵστημι (# 2705) to place, to stand. **προσευξάμενοι** aor. mid. (dep.) part. (temp.) προσεύχομαι (# 4667) to pray. **ἐπέθηκαν** aor. ind. act. ἐπιτίθημι (# 2202) to place upon. The whole company of believers, not only the apostles, laid their hands on the seven men, signifying the blessing which accompanies the committing and undertaking of a new kind of ministry (Barrett). It indicates the identification with and unity of those involved in the act. For Jewish material s. SB, 2:647-61; NTRJ, 224-46. ◆ **7 ηὔξανεν** impf. ind. act. αὐξάνω (# 889) to grow. The impf. pictures the continual growth. The Word of God, as the apostles continued to preach it, had continually increasing influence and effect (Barrett). **ἐπληθύνετο** impf. ind. pass. s.v. 1. **σφόδρα** (# 5379) very, greatly, extremely. **ὑπήκουον** impf. ind. act. ὑπακούω (# 5634) to listen to, to obey, w. dat. ◆ **8 χάριτος** gen. sing. χάρις (# 5921) grace. It could indicate God's favor to Stephen, or the spiritual charm or winsomeness of Stephen; that is, the power which flows from God (Longenecker, 334; NIDNTT, 2:119). Gen. of content. **ἐποίει** impf. ind. act. ποιέω (# 4472) to do, to perform. Impf. pictures the repeated action. ◆ **9 ἀνέστησαν** aor. ind. act. ἀνίστημι (# 482) to arise. For a discussion of the adversaries of Stephen and the places referred to s. SF, 158-63, 266-69; Barrett; SB, 2:65. **λεγομένης** pres. pass. part. (adj.) λέγω (# 3306) to say; here, "so called." **συζητοῦντες** pres. act. part. συζητέω (# 5184) to dispute, to question together, to express forceful differences of opinion without necessarily having a presumed goal of seeking a solution (LN, 1:438-39), w. dat. ◆ **10 ἴσχυον** impf. ind. act. ἰσχύω (# 2710) to be strong, to be able to, w. inf. **ἀντιστῆναι** aor. act. inf. ἀνθίστημι (# 468) to stand against, to successfully withstand, w. dat. **ᾧ** dat. sing. **ὅς** (# 4005) rel. pron. Instr. dat. ("w. which"). **ἐλάλει** impf. ind. act. λαλέω (# 3281) to speak. ◆ **11 ὑπέβαλον** aor. ind. act. ὑποβάλλω (# 5680) to put up, to prompt. It applies to the secret instigation of persons supplied w. suggestions of what they are to say, much as in the modern frame-up (LC; BAGD; MM). **ἀκηκόαμεν** perf. ind. act. ἀκούω (# 201) to hear, w. gen. **λαλοῦντος** pres. act. part. s.v. 10. Part. used to complete the vb. **ἀκηκόαμεν**. ◆ **12 συνεκίνησαν** aor. ind. act. συγκινέω (# 5167) to throw into a commotion, to stir violently, to incite. **ἐπιστάντες** aor. act. part. (circum.) ἐφίστημι (# 2392) to come upon. Ingressive aor., "they rushed at him" (RWP). **συνήρπασαν** aor. ind. act. συναρπάζω (# 5275) to seize. **ἤγαγον** aor. ind. act. ἄγω (# 72) to lead. ◆ **13 ἔστησάν** aor. ind. act. s.v. 6. **ψευδής** (# 6014) false, lying. For a discussion of the charges and whether the witnesses lied or misrepresented the words of Stephen s. SF, 172-82, 270-77, 312-13. **παύεται** pres. ind. mid. (dep.) παύομαι (# 4264) to cease; w. part. ♦ **14 ἀκηκόαμεν** perf. ind. act. s.v. 11. **καταλύσει** fut. ind. act. καταλύω (# 2907) to destroy (s. Matt. 24:2; Mark 13:2; Luke 21:6). **ἀλλάξει** fut. ind. act. ἀλλάσσω (# 248) to change. **ἔθη** acc. pl. ἔθος (# 1621) custom, law. It covers both written and oral tradition (Barrett). **παρέδωκεν** aor. ind. act. παραδίδωμι (# 4140) to give over, to transmit. Stephen saw clearly the inevitability of a break w. Judaism. He may have spoken of the transitory character of the Mosaic ceremonies (Bruce). ♦ **15 ἀτε-νίσαντες** aor. act. part. (temp.) ἀτενίζω (# 867) to gaze, to look at intently. **καθεζόμενοι** pres. mid. (dep.) part. καθέζομαι (# 2757) to sit. Part. as subst. **εἶδον** aor. ind. act. ὁράω (# 3972) to see.

Acts 7

♦ **1 εἰ** (# 1623) introduces a direct question. The accused is asked to defend himself against the charge (Haenchen). **ἔχει** pres. ind. act. ἔχω (# 2400) to have; to hold; lit., "Do these things hold thus?" (RWP). The question means, "Are the facts stated in the accusation true?" "Do you admit the charge?" (Barrett). ♦ **2 ἔφη** impf./aor. ind. act. φημί (# 5774) to say (s. VA, 443-46). **ἀκούσατε** aor. imp. act. ἀκούω (# 201) to hear, to listen to. Aor. imp. calls for a specific act. **ὤφθη** aor. ind. pass. ὁράω (# 3972) to see; pass. to appear. **ὄντι** pres. act. part. (temp.) dat. masc. sing. εἰμί (# 1639) to be. For extra-biblical Jewish accounts at the time of the Second Temple s. *The Apocalypse of Abraham* 1-8; *Jub.* 11-12. **κατοικῆσαι** aor. act. inf. κατοικέω (# 2997) to live, to be at home. Inf. used w. **πρὶν ἤ** to express antecedent time ("before") (MT, 140). ♦ **3 ἔξελθε** aor. imp. act. ἐξέρχομαι (# 2002) to go out. **συγγένεια** (# 5149) kinship, relatives. **δεῦρο** (# 1306) adv., here. In this case used as imp., "come!" "come here!" **δείξω** aor. subj. act. δείκνυμι (# 1259) to show. Subj. w. **ἄν** (# 323) in an indef. rel. cl. ♦ **4 ἐξελθών** aor. act. part. (temp.) s.v. 3. **κατῴκησεν** aor. ind. act. s.v. 2. **ἀποθανεῖν** aor. act. inf. ἀποθνήσκω (# 633) to die. Inf. w. prep. **μετά** (# 3552) to express subsequent time: "after he died." **μετῴκισεν** aor. ind. act. μετοικίζω (# 3579) to cause to dwell, to settle. The idea of transfer or change is indicated by the prep. compound (MH, 318). **κατοικεῖτε** pres. ind. act. s.v. 2. The fact that Jews were living in the land given to Abraham indicated God's faithfulness to His Word. ♦ **5 ἔδωκεν** aor. ind. act. δίδωμι (# 1443) to give. **ἐν αὐτῇ** in it, perhaps referring to Mesopotamia or Haran rather than Canaan. **βῆμα** acc. sing. step; "stepping of a foot" (RWP). **ἐπηγγείλατο** aor. ind. mid. (dep.) ἐπαγγέλλομαι (# 2040) to promise. **δοῦναι** aor. act. inf. δίδωμι (# 1443) Epex. inf. explaining the promise. **κατάσχεσις** (# 2959) possession. **ὄντος** pres. act. part. εἰμί. Gen.

abs., concessive ("although"). ♦ **6 ἐλάλησεν** aor. ind. act. λαλέω to speak. **ἔσται** fut. ind. mid. (dep.) εἰμί s.v. 2. **πάροικος** (# 259) foreign, alien, sojourner. Translation of the Heb. גֵּר *ger*, one who lives in a foreign land but has certain rights (TDOT; TWOT; DCH). **ἀλλότριος** foreign. **δουλώσουσιν** fut. ind. act. δουλόω (# 1530) to make someone a slave, to be enslaved. **κακώσουσιν** fut. ind. act. κακόω (# 2808) to treat badly, to harm, to mistreat. **ἔτη τετρακόσια** 400 years. This is probably a round figure (Longenecker, 340; for a discussion of Jewish views of the 400 years s. SB, 2:668-71). ♦ **7 δουλεύσουσιν** fut. ind. act. δουλεύω (# 1526) to be a slave, to serve as a slave. For the fut. ind. w. **ἐάν** (# 1569) s. BD, 192. **ἐξελεύσονται** fut. ind. mid. (dep.) s.v. 3. **λατρεύσουσιν** fut. ind. act. λατρεύω (# 3302) to worship in service, to perform religious rites as part of worship, to venerate, to worship (LN, 1:533). ♦ **8 ἔδωκεν** aor. ind. act. s.v. 5. **διαθήκη** (# 1347) treaty, covenant (TDNT; IDB, 1:714-23; DCH; TDOT; TWOT). The sign of the covenant w. Abraham was circumcision (Cleon L.Rogers, Jr., "The Covenant with Abraham and Its Historical Setting," *Bib Sac* 127 [1970]: 241-56; Lawrence H. Schiffman, "The Rabbinic Understanding of Covenant," *RevExp* 84 [1987]: 289-98). **οὕτως** (# 4048) so, thus. It implies, the covenant having been made, he begot Isaac (Barrett). **ἐγέννησεν** aor. ind. act. γεννάω (# 1164) to beget. **περιέτεμεν** aor. ind. act. περιτέμνω (# 4362) to circumcise. ♦ **9 ζηλώσαντες** aor. act. part. (causal) ζηλόω (# 2420) to boil w. zeal, then w. envy, to be jealous (RWP; GELTS, 194). **ἀπέδοντο** aor. ind. mid. ἀποδίδωμι (# 625) to give away; mid., to sell. ♦ **10 ἐξείλατο** aor. ind. mid. ἐξαιρέω (# 1975) to take out; mid. to set free, to rescue, to deliver. The prep. in compound is perfective. **ἔδωκεν** aor. ind. act. s.v. 5. **κατέστησεν** aor. ind. act. καθίστημι (# 2770) to appoint. **ἡγούμενον** pres. mid. (dep.) part. ἡγέομαι (# 2451) to rule, to govern. Part. as subst. ♦ **11 ηὕρισκον** impf. ind. act. εὑρίσκω (# 2351) to find. **χόρτασμα** (# 5964) food. Originally of animals, later in the sense of human food as well (Bruce). ♦ **12 ἀκούσας** aor. act. part. ἀκούω (# 201) to hear. Temp. or causal part. **ὄντα** pres. act. part. s.v. 2. Part. in indir. discourse ("heard of corn being in Egypt") (RWP). **ἐξαπέστειλεν** aor. ind. act. ἐξαποστέλλω (# 1990) to send out. ♦ **13 ἐν τῷ δευτέρῳ** (# 1877; 1309) on the second occasion, on the second visit (Barrett). **ἀνεγνωρίσθη** aor. ind. pass. ἀναγνωρίζω (# 341) to make known; pass. (w. dat.), "let himself be recognized" (BD, 103). For the textual variant ἐγνωρίσθη s. TC, 344; Barrett. **φανερόν** nom. sing. φανερός (# 5745) manifest, known, plain, evident. Pred. nom. **ἐγένετο** aor. ind. mid. (dep.) γίνομαι (# 1181) to become, to be. ♦ **14 ἀποστείλας** aor. act. part. (circum.) ἀποστέλλω (# 690) to send. **μετεκαλέσατο** aor. ind. mid. μετακαλέομαι (# 3559) to summon, to call to oneself. ♦ **15 κατέβη** aor. ind. act. καταβαίνω (# 2849) to go down. **ἐτελεύτη-**

σεν aor. ind. act. τελευτάω (# *5462*) to die. ◆ **16 με-τετέθησαν** aor. ind. pass. μετατίθημι (# *3572*) to transfer, to move from one place to another. The prep. in compound has the idea of change (MH, 318). **ἐτέθησαν** aor. ind. pass. τίθημι (# *5502*) to place. **ὠνήσατο** aor. ind. mid. (dep.) ὠνέομαι (# *6050*) to buy, w. gen. of price. It could have been that Abraham had purchased this first, then Jacob repurchased it later (EBD, 379-81). ◆ **17 καθώς** when (Barrett). **ἤγγιζεν** impf. ind. act. ἐγγίζω (# *1581*) to draw near, to be near. **ἧς** gen. sing. ὅς (# *4005*) rel. pron. Gen. by attraction. **ὡμολόγησεν** aor. ind. act. ὁμολογέω (# *3933*) to agree, to promise. **ηὔξησεν** aor. ind. act. αὐξάνω (# *889*) to grow. **ἐπληθύνθη** aor. ind. pass. πληθύνω (# *4437*) pass. to multiply, to increase. ◆ **18 ἀνέστη** aor. ind. act. ἀνίστημι (# *482*) to arise. **ᾔδει** plperf. ind. act. οἶδα (# *3857*) def. perf. w. pres. meaning, to know. Plperf. = impf. ◆ **19 κατασοφισάμενος** aor. mid. (dep.) part. κατασοφίζομαι (# *2947*) to exploit, to deal wisely. It implies crafty or deceitful ill treatment, to exploit by means of craftiness and cunning, to take advantage of (LC; LN, 1:758). Part. of manner. **ἐκάκωσεν** aor. ind. act. s.v. 6. **ποιεῖν** pres. act. inf. ποιέω (# *4472*) to do, to make. Epex. inf. used to explain content of the ill-treatment, involving some idea of purpose: "so that," "in that he made" (Bruce; BD, 206). **βρέφος** (# *1100*) infant. **ἔκθετος** (# *1704*) exposed, cast out. **ζωογονεῖσθαι** pres. pass. inf. ζωογονέω (# *2441*) to produce life. Here to preserve life (Haenchen; MM; TLNT). Inf. w. εἰς (# *1650*) expressing purp. ◆ **20 ἐγεννήθη** aor. ind. pass. γεννάω (# *1164*) to produce a child, to beget; pass., to be born. **ἀστεῖος** (# *842*) belonging to the city, w. city manners and polish, elegant, fine (RWP). Luke probably means that Moses was an entirely satisfactory child, without physical or mental handicap (Barrett). **θεῷ** dat. sing. θεός (# *2536*) God. Ethical dat., "fair to God" (RWP; GGBB, 147). **ἀνετράφη** aor. ind. pass. ἀνατρέφω (# *427*) to bring up, to nourish. ◆ **21 ἐκτεθέντος** aor. pass. part. (temp.) ἐκτίθημι (# *1758*) to set out, to expose. Gen. abs., "after he had been set out." **ἀνείλατο** aor. ind. mid. (dep.) ἀναιρέω (# *359*) to lift up. Used of acknowledging or adopting as one's child (Bruce; MM; NDIEC, 2:7-10). For the custom of adopting an exposed child s. NDIEC, 2:9-10. **ἀνεθρέψατο** aor. ind. mid. (indir. mid., "for herself") s.v. 20. **εἰς υἱόν** (# *1650; 5626*) acc. w. εἰς used for the predicate acc. is probably due to Semitic influence (BD, 86; GELTS, 131; but s. M, 71-72; KVS, 61). ◆ **22 ἐπαιδεύθη** aor. ind. pass. παιδεύω (# *4084*) to train a child, to instruct, to educate. Josephus said that he was educated ("brought up" ἐτρέφετο) with the utmost care (Jos., *Ant.*, 2:236). Philo states that teachers from various parts of the world instructed Moses in math, geometry, music, hieroglyphics, Egyptian, Greek, and Assyrian Wisdom (Philo, *De Vita Mosis*, I, 21-24; SB, 2:678-79; s. also James Henry Breasted, *A*

History of Egypt [London: Hodder & Stoughton, 1950], 98-102; Adolf Erman & Hermann Ranke, *Ägypten und ägyptisches Leben im Altertum* [Hildesheim: Gerstenberg Verlag, 1981], 374-428). ◆ **23 ἐπληροῦτο** impf. ind. pass. πληρόω (# *4444*) to fulfill, to complete. **ἀνέβη** aor. ind. act. ἀναβαίνω (# *326*) to go up, to come up. Used of things coming up into one's mind (AS; SA, 63-64). **ἐπισκέψασθαι** aor. mid. (dep.) inf. ἐπισκέπτομαι (# *2170*) to visit, to go to see w. one's own eyes, to help if possible (RWP). Epex. inf. explaining what came into his mind. ◆ **24 ἰδών** aor. act. part. (temp.) ὁράω (# *3972*) to see. **ἀδικούμενον** pres. pass. part. (adj.) ἀδικέω (# *92*) to wrong, to act unjustly toward; pass. to suffer injustice. **ἠμύνατο** aor. ind. mid. ἀμύνομαι (# *310*) to avenge oneself, to retaliate, to help, to come to the aid of someone (BAGD). **ἐποίησεν** aor. ind. act. s.v. 19. The vb. is used w. the noun expressing the verbal aspect of the noun; "to avenge," "to take vengeance." **καταπονουμένῳ** pres. pass. part. καταπονέω (# *2930*) to subdue, to torment, to oppress. Dat. of advantage, "for the one being oppressed." **πατάξας** aor. act. part. πατάσσω (# *4250*) to strike, to hit. Part. of manner explaining how he took vengeance. ◆ **25 ἐνόμιζεν** impf. ind. act. νομίζω (# *3787*) to suppose. **συνιέναι** pres. act. inf. συνίημι (# *5317*) to comprehend, to understand. Inf. in indir. discourse. **δίδωσιν** pres. ind. act. s.v. 5. **συνῆκαν** aor. ind. act. συνίημι. ◆ **26 ἐπιούσῃ** dat. fem. sing. ἔπειμι (# *2079*) on the following day (BAGD). Dat. of time. **ὤφθη** aor. ind. pass. s.v. 2. Not the idea of a vision, but he appeared suddenly and unexpected (RWP). **μαχομένοις** pres. mid. part. (dep.) μάχομαι (# *3481*) to fight. "As they were fighting" (Barrett). **συνήλλασσεν** impf. ind. act. συναλλάσσω (# *5261*) to reconcile. Conative impf., "tried to reconcile." **εἰπών** aor. act. part. λέγω (# *3306*) to say. Part. of manner. **ἀδικεῖτε** pres. ind. act. s.v. 24. ◆ **27 ἀδικῶν** pres. act. part. s.v. 24. Part. as subst. **ἀπώσατο** aor. ind. mid. (dep.) ἀπωθέομαι (# *723*) to push away from oneself. **κατέστησεν** aor. ind. act. s.v. 10; w. double acc. **δικαστής** (# *1471*) judge. ◆ **28 μή** (# *3590*) used in a question expecting a neg. answer. **ἀνελεῖν** aor. act. inf. ἀναιρέω (# *359*) to kill. **θέλεις** pres. ind. act. θέλω (# *2527*) to desire, to wish, to plan to, w. inf. **ἀνεῖλες** aor. ind. act. 2nd. pers. sing. **ἐχθές** (# *2396*) yesterday. ◆ **29 ἔφυγεν** aor. ind. act. φεύγω (# *5771*) to flee. **ἐγένετο** aor. ind. mid. (dep.) s.v. 13. **πάροικος** s.v. 6. **ἐγέννησεν** aor. ind. act. s.v. 20. ◆ **30 πληρωθέντων** aor. pass. part. (temp.) s.v. 23. Gen. abs. **ὤφθη** aor. ind. pass. s.v. 2. **φλογί** dat. sing. φλόξ (# *5825*) flame. According to Philo, the burning fire described the plight of the nation at that time (Philo, *De Vita Mosis*, I, 68-70). ◆ **31 ἰδών** aor. act. part. (temp.) s.v. 24. **ἐθαύμαζεν** impf. ind. act. θαυμάζω (# *2513*) to wonder, to be amazed at. **ὅραμα** (# *3969*) appearance, sight. **προσερχομένου** pres. mid. (dep.) part. (temp.) προσέρχομαι (# *4665*) to come to. Gen. abs. **κατανοῆσαι** aor. act. inf. κατανοέω (# *2917*) to take knowledge of, to take notice of; "to master the mystery." The prep. in compound indicates the completion of a mental process (M, 117). Inf. of purp. ◆ **32 ἔντρομος** (# *1958*) pertaining to extreme terror or fear, often accompanied by trembling; trembling w. fear (LN, 1:317). **γενόμενος** aor. mid. (dep.) part. s.v. 13. Causal or circum. part. **ἐτόλμα** impf. ind. act. τολμάω (# *5528*) to dare, w. inf. **κατανοῆσαι** aor. act. inf. s.v. 31. ◆ **33 λῦσον** aor. imp. act. λύω (# *3395*) to loose. **ἔστηκας** perf. ind. act. ἵστημι (# *2705*) to stand. Perf. is intr., "to stand" (NSV, 23). Whenever the Shekinah appeared the wearing of sandals is prohibited (SB, 2:681). ◆ **34 εἶδον** aor. ind. act. ὁράω (# *3972*) to see. **κάκωσις** (# *2810*) ill treatment. **στεναγμοῦ** gen. sing. στεναγμός (# *5099*) sighing, groaning as the result of deep concern or stress (LN, 1:305). Gen. as dir. obj. **ἤκουσα** aor. ind. act. ἀκούω (# *201*) to hear, w. obj. in gen. **κατέβην** aor. ind. act. s.v. 15. **ἐξελέσθαι** aor. mid. (indir. mid., "for myself") inf. ἐξαιρέω (# *1975*) to take out, to deliver. Inf. of purp. **δεῦρο** (# *1306*) "come!" **ἀποστείλω** aor. subj. act. s.v. 14. Hortatory subj., "let me send!" ◆ **35 ἠρνήσαντο** aor. ind. mid. (dep.) ἀρνέομαι (# *766*) to say no to, to deny; here, not to recognize or acknowledge (Schneider; EDNT). **εἰπόντες** aor. act. part. s.v. 26. **κατέστησεν** aor. ind. act. s.v. 10, w. double acc. **λυτρωτής** (# *3392*) one who ransoms, one who sets free, redeemer. In Judaism Moses was the human agent of God's redemption, and here Moses could be considered as a type of Christ (Barrett; LDC, 134, 221, 271; Longenecker, 339). **ἀπέσταλκεν** perf. ind. act. s.v. 14. **ὀφθέντος** aor. pass. part. (adj.) s.v. 2. ◆ **36 ἐξήγαγεν** aor. ind. act. ἐξάγω (# *1974*) to lead out. **ποιήσας** aor. act. part. s.v. 19. Part. of manner explaining how he led them out. Ἐρυθρᾷ dat. sing. ἐρυθρός (# *2261*) red. ◆ **37 εἴπας** aor. act. part. (adj.) s.v. 26. **ἀναστήσει** fut. ind. act. ἀνίστημι to raise up, to awaken (s.v. 18; 3:22). ◆ **38 γενόμενος** aor. mid. (dep.) part. s.v. 13. Part. as subst. **ἐκκλησία** (# *1711*) dat. sing. assembly, a group which is gathered together, congregation of Israelites (BAGD). **λαλοῦντος** pres. act. part. (adj.) λαλέω (# *3281*) to speak. **ἐδέξατο** aor. ind. mid. (dep.) δέχομαι to receive, to welcome. **ζῶντα** pres. act. part. (adj.) ζάω (# *2409*) to live. **δοῦναι** aor. act. inf. s.v. 5. Inf. of purp. ◆ **39 ἠθέλησαν** aor. ind. act. s.v. 28, w. inf. **ὑπήκοος** (# *5675*) obedient, w. dat. **γενέσθαι** aor. mid. (dep.) inf. s.v. 13. **ἀπώσαντο** aor. ind. mid. (indir. mid. [RWP]) s.v. 27. **ἐστράφησαν** aor. ind. pass. στρέφω (# *5138*) to turn. ◆ **40 ποίησον** aor. imp. act. s.v. 19. **προπορεύσονται** fut. ind. mid. (dep.) προπορεύομαι (# *4638*) to go before, to precede, as Jehovah had gone before them in the pillar of cloud and as images were carried by the heathen in their marches (Alex). Fut w. rel. pron. οἵ to express purpose (RWP). **ὁ γὰρ Μωϋσῆς οὗτος** For this Moses (nom. sing.). Nom. abs. (*nominativus pendens*) giving the logical subj. followed by a pron., in the case re-

quired by the syntax (BG, 9; BD, 243; PAPC). **ἐξήγαγεν** aor. ind. act. s.v. 36. **οἴδαμεν** perf. ind. act. s.v. 18. **ἐγένετο** aor. ind. mid. (dep.) s.v. 13. Josephus says that the Hebrews were deeply distressed and thought that Moses had been killed by wild animals or that God had taken him, but he does not mention the making of the golden calf (Jos., *Ant.*, 3:95-98). ◆ **41 ἐμοσχοποίησαν** aor. ind. act. μοσχοποιέω (# *3674*) to make a calf. **ἀνήγαγον** aor. ind. act. ἀνάγω (# *343*) to lead up, to bring a sacrifice (MM). **εὐφραίνοντο** impf. ind. mid. (dep.) εὐφραίνομαι (# *2370*) to rejoice, to cheer, to be glad (GELTS, 190; KVS, 257-58). Impf. pictures the continuing action. ◆ **42 ἔστρεψεν** aor. ind. act. s.v. 39. **παρέδωκεν** aor. ind. act. παραδίδωμι (# *4140*) to deliver over. **λατρεύειν** pres. act. inf. s.v. 7, w. dat. Inf. of result or purpose. **τῇ στρατιᾷ τοῦ οὐρανοῦ** the army (host) of heaven, the heavenly bodies worshipped as deities (Barrett). **γέγραπται** perf. ind. pass. γράφω (# *1211*) to write. Perf. indicates the permanence of the authoritative record (MM). **βίβλῳ** dat. sing. βίβλος (# *1047*) book (Matt. 1:1). **μή** (# *3590*) neg. in a question which expects a neg. answer, "You did not bring your offerings to the true God, did you?" (Barrett). **σφάγιον** (# *5376*) animal sacrifice. **προσηνέγκατε** aor. ind. act. προσφέρω (# *4712*) to bring to, to sacrifice. ◆ **43 ἀνελάβετε** aor. ind. act. ἀναλαμβάνω (# *377*) to take up, to take. **ἄστρον** (# *849*) acc. sing. star, constellation. Perhaps a reference to the Assyrian and Egyptian worship of the planet Saturn as god (Bruce - ET). **ἐποιήσατε** aor. ind. act. s.v. 19. **προσκυνεῖν** pres. act. inf. προσκυνέω (# *4686*) to worship, to prostrate oneself, to do reverence to (NIDNTT, 2:875). **μετοικιῶ** fut. ind. act. μετοικίζω (# *3579*) to remove to a new abode, to cause to migrate (s.v. 4). **ἐπέκεινα** (# *2084*) w. gen., beyond. For the OT quote of Amos 5:26 in DSS s. CD 7:14-21; Barrett. ◆ **44 διετάξατο** aor. ind. mid. (dep.) διατάσσομαι (# *1411*) to command. **λαλῶν** pres. act. part. s.v. 38. Part. as subst. **ποιῆσαι** aor. act. inf. s.v. 19. Inf. in indir. discourse. **ἑωράκει** plperf. ind. act. ὁράω (# *3972*) to see. ◆ **45 εἰσήγαγον** aor. ind. act. εἰσάγω (# *1652*) to bring in. **διαδεξάμενοι** aor. mid. (dep.) part. διαδέχομαι (# *1342*) to receive through another, to receive in succession (RWP; BAGD). **κατάσχεσις** (# *2959*) possession. **ἐξῶσεν** aor. ind. act. ἐξωθέω (# *2034*) to drive out. ◆ **46 εὗρεν** aor. ind. act. εὑρίσκω (# *2351*) to find. **ᾐτήσατο** aor. ind. mid. αἰτέω to ask; mid. to ask a favor for oneself. **εὑρεῖν** aor. act. inf. Inf. in indir. discourse. **σκήνωμα** (# *5013*) acc. sing. tent, dwelling place. Used by David in the humility of his request (Meyer). ◆ **47 οἰκοδόμησεν** aor. ind. act. οἰκοδομέω (# *3868*) to build. **αὐτῷ** dat. sing. αὐτός. Dat. of advantage, or personal interest, "for Him." ◆ **48 ὕψιστος** (# *5736*) The most High. In Hellenistic texts used for Zeus, but in the LXX used to translate עליון (*Elyon*) (EDNT; SB, 2:99; TDNT; Barrett). **χειροποίητος** (# *5935*) made w. human hands. **κατοικεῖ** pres. ind. act. s.v. 2. Gnomic pres., indicating that which is always true. ◆ **49** ὑποπόδιον (# *5711*) footstool. ποῖον (# *4481*) acc. sing. what kind of? what sort of? οἰκοδομήσετε fut. ind. act. s.v. 47. καταπαύσεως gen. sing. κατάπαυσις (# *2923*) rest. Gen. of description. ◆ **50** οὐχί (# *4049*) strengthened form of the neg. οὐ used in a question expecting a positive answer. ἐποίησεν aor. ind. act. s.v. 19. ◆ **51** σκληροτράχηλοι voc. pl. σκληροτράχηλος (# *5019*) stiff-necked. When a donkey or horse refuses to go on, it tightens and stiffens its neck; so the expression means stubborn disobedience, hardening or obstinace in rebellion (TLNT, 3:260). Used in the LXX to describe the rebellious tendency of Israel (LC; BBC). ἀπερίτμητος (# *598*) uncircumcised. They are uncircumcised heathen not in their flesh, but in readiness to hear and accept God's word (Barrett; SB 2:683-84; *Gen. Rab.*, 26; *Jub.* 1:23; 1QpHab 11:13; 1QS 5:5). ἀντιπίπτετε pres. ind. act. ἀντιπίπτω (# *528*) to fall against, to resist. Pres. indicates habitual action. ◆ **52** οὐκ (# *4024*) neg. in a question expecting a positive answer. ἐδίωξαν aor. ind. act. διώκω (# *1503*) to persecute, pursue. ἀπέκτειναν aor. ind. act. ἀποκτείνω (# *650*) to kill. προκαταγγείλαντας aor. act. part. προκαταγγέλλω (# *4615*) to announce beforehand. Part. as subst. ἐλεύσεως gen. sing. ἔλευσις (# *1803*) coming. A messianic term denoting Messiah's advent (Bruce). προδόται nom. pl. προδότης (# *6595*) traitor, betrayer. Pred. nom. φονεῖς nom. pl. φονεύς (# *5838*) murderer. ἐγένεσθε aor. ind. mid. (dep.) s.v. 13. Effective aor. ◆ **53** οἵτινες nom. pl. ὅστις (# *4015*) indef. rel. pron. used here to indicate persons belonging to a certain class (BAGD; BD, 153; RG, 728; NSV, 143-44). ἐλάβετε aor. ind. act. λαμβάνω (# *3284*) to receive. ἐφυλάξατε aor. ind. act. φυλάσσω (# *5875*) to observe, to keep. They accused Stephen of teaching against the Law; he accuses them of not keeping the Law! ◆ **54** ἀκούοντες pres. act. part. (temp.) s.v. 34. διεπρίοντο impf. ind. pass. διαπρίω (# *1391*) to cut to the quick (s. 5:33). Incep. impf. ἔβρυχον impf. ind. act. βρύχω (# *1107*) to bite w. loud noise, to grind or gnash the teeth. Incep. impf., "they began" (RWP). ◆ **55** ὑπάρχων aor. act. part. (circum.) ὑπάρχω (# *5639*) to exist, to be. ἀτενίσας aor. act. part. (circum.) ἀτενίζω (# *867*) to gaze. εἶδεν aor. ind. act. ὁράω (# *3972*) to see. ἑστῶτα perf. act. part. (adj.) s.v. 33. He is standing as advocate to plead Stephen's cause before God and to welcome him into God's presence (Marshall; SF, 199-207, 313-14; Barrett). ◆ **56** εἶπεν aor. ind. act. λέγω (# *3306*) to say. θεωρῶ pres. ind. act. θεωρέω (# *2555*) to see. διηνοιγμένους perf. pass. part. διανοίγω (# *1380*) to open. Perf. indicates the state or condition, "standing open." ◆ **57** κράξαντες aor. act. part. (circum.) κράζω (# *3189*) to scream. συνέσχον aor. ind. act. συνέχω (# *5309*) to hold, to hold together. ὥρμησαν aor. ind. act. ὁρμάω (# *3994*) to rush. ◆ **58** ἐκβαλόντες aor. act. part. (temp.) ἐκβάλλω (# *1675*) to

throw out. ἐλιθοβόλουν impf. ind. act. λιθοβολέω (# *3344*) to stone. Incep. impf., "they began." For stoning as punishment for blasphemy s. SB, 2:685-86; 1:1013; and for the killing of Stephen in the light of Roman law s. DTM, 1:369-71; SF, 186-96. ἀπέθεντο aor. ind. mid. ἀποτίθημι (# *700*) to put away, to put down. καλουμένου pres. pass. part. (adj.) καλέω (# *2813*) to call; pass. to be named. Σαῦλος (# *4930*) Saul. The Greek meaning of the word σαῦλος as an adj. described the swinging movement of certain animals; then the loose, wanton walk of a prostitute; then the idea of sensual pride (LS, 1586; HGS, 2, ii:1385; T.J. Leary, "Paul's Improper Name," *NTS* 38 [1992]: 467-69). ◆ **59** ἐπικαλούμενον pres. mid. (dep.) part. (temp.) ἐπικαλέω (# *2126*) to call upon, to call to. "As he was calling...." δέξαι aor. imp. mid. (dep.) s.v. 38. ◆ **60** θείς aor. act. part. τίθημι (# *5502*) to place; here, to kneel down. γόνατα acc. pl. γόνυ (# *1205*) knee. ἔκραξεν aor. ind. act. s.v. 57. στήσῃς aor. subj. act. ἵστημι (# *2705*) to lay, to establish. The neg. is equivalent to "forgive" (LC). εἰπών aor. act. part. s.v. 56. ἐκοιμήθη aor. ind. pass. (dep.) κοιμάομαι (# *3121*) to go to sleep; an unexpectedly beautiful word for so brutal a death (Bruce).

Acts 8

◆ **1** συνευδοκῶν pres. act. part. συνευδοκέω (# *5306*) to agree w., to approve of, to have pleasure w.; used w. dat. Part. in a periphrastic construction describing a condition, not a momentary excitement (Haenchen). ἀναιρέσει dat. sing. ἀναίρεσις (# *358*) killing, murder. ἐγένετο aor. ind. mid. (dep.) γίνομαι (# *1181*) to become, to be, to happen, to arise. διωγμός (# *1501*) persecution. διεσπάρησαν aor. ind. pass. διασπείρω (# *1401*) to scatter, to disperse. ◆ **2** συνεκόμισαν aor. ind. act. συγκομίζω (# *5172*) to gather up for burial (LC; NTNT, 117). The prep. in compound is perfective: the burial in completed (Barrett). ἐποίησαν aor. ind. act. ποιέω (# *4472*) to make. Used to verbalize the meaning of the subst. κοπετός (# *3157*) beating the breast, mourning, lamentation (LN, 1:530). For the burial of one who has been executed s. SB, 2:685-87; M, Sanh. 6:5-6; Barrett. ◆ **3** ἐλυμαίνετο impf. ind. mid. (dep.) λυμαίνομαι (# *3381*) to devastate, to ruin. Used of physical injury, particularly of the mangling by wild beast (LC). Impf. pictures the continual action. κατά w. acc. used in the distributive sense: "from house to house." εἰσπορευόμενος pres. mid. (dep.) part. εἰσπορεύομαι (# *1660*) to go into. Part. of manner or means, explaining how he was inflicting injury. σύρων pres. act. part. σύρω (# *5359*) to drag. παρεδίδου impf. ind. act. παραδίδωμι (# *4140*) to deliver over, to deliver over to prison (TLNT, 3:23). Prisons were places of custody until the person was tried (ABD, 5:468-69; OCD, 879). ◆ **4** διασπαρέντες aor. pass. part. s.v. 1. Part. as subst. διῆλθον aor. ind. act. διέρχομαι (# 1451) to go through. εὐαγγελιζόμενοι pres. mid. (dep.) part. (circum.) εὐαγγελίζομαι (# 2294) to proclaim good news. ◆ 5 κατελθών aor. act. part. (temp.) κατέρχομαι (# 2982) to go down. ἐκήρυσσεν impf. ind. act. κηρύσσω (# 3062) to proclaim, to preach. Impf. could be incep. and emphasize the repeated action. ◆ 6 προσεῖχον impf. ind. act. προσέχω (# 4668) to give heed to, w. dat. Used in the sense of paying attention and giving a favorable response (Bruce). Impf. pictures the repeated action. λεγομένοις pres. pass. part. λέγω (# 3306) to say, to speak. Part. as subst. ἀκούειν pres. act. part. ἀκούω (201) to hear. Articular inf. w. subject in acc. and w. ἐν (# 1877) expressing contemporaneous time. βλέπειν pres. act. inf. βλέπω (# 1063) to see. ἐποίει impf. ind. act. s.v. 2. Impf. pictures repeated action. ◆ 7 ἐχόντων pres. act. part. ἔχω (# 2400) to have. Part. as subst. βοῶντα pres. act. part. βοάω (# 1066) to call aloud. Part. of manner explaining how the unclean spirits came out. ἐξήρχοντο impf. ind. mid. (dep.) ἐξέρχομαι (# 2002) to come out. Impf. pictures repeated action. παραλελυμένοι perf. pass. part. (adj.) παραλύω (# 4168) to be weakened, to be disabled. Luke's use of the vb. instead of the adj. is in strict agreement w. that of the medical writers (MLL, 6). Perf. indicates the state or condition. ἐθεραπεύθησαν aor. ind. pass. θεραπεύω (# 2543) to heal. ◆ 8 ἐγένετο aor. ind. mid. (dep.) s.v. 1. ◆ 9 προϋπῆρχεν impf. ind. act. προϋπάρχω (# 4732) to be before, to exist previously. μαγεύων pres. act. part. μαγεύω (# 3405) to practice magic. He was a peripatetic practitioner in the occult who had illicit dealings w. the supernatural and made money from it (J.D.M. Derrett, "Simon Magus [Acts 8:9-24]," ZNW 73 [1982]: 53; Barrett; for the word s. TDNT; Arthur Darby Nock, "Paul and the Magus," BC, 5:164-82; NIDNT, 2:552-62). Part. w. the previous vb. to form a periphrastic construction: "he was existing previously practicing magic" (RWP). ἐξιστάνων pres. act. part. ἐξίστημι (# 2014) to astonish, to amaze, to cause one to be beside himself. λέγων pres. act. part. s.v. 6. εἶναι pres. act. inf. εἰμί (# 1639) to be. Inf. in indir. discourse, "saying that he was someone great" (NSV, 100). ◆ 10 προσεῖχον impf. ind. act. s.v. 6. καλουμένη pres. pass. part. καλέω (# 2813) to call; pass., to be named. The part. shows that the adj. Μεγάλη is a title, w. ἡ δύναμις τοῦ θεοῦ as a synonym for God (NDIEC, 1:107; 3:32; s. Barrett). ◆ 11 προσεῖχον impf. ind. act. s.v. 6. ἱκανῷ χρόνῳ dat. sing., for a long time. Temp. dat. used for a duration of time (MT, 243). μαγείαις dat. pl. μαγεία (# 3404) magic, magical acts. Instr. dat. ἐξεστακέναι perf. act. inf. s.v. 9. Perf. indicates the abiding result, or state (VA, 392). Articular inf. w. διά (# 1328) to express cause, "because for a long time he had amazed them with his magic" (NSV, 125). ◆ 12 ἐπίστευσαν aor. ind. act. πιστεύω (# 4409) to believe, w. dat. εὐαγγελιζομένῳ pres. mid. (dep.) part. s.v.

4. Temp. part., "when he proclaimed the good news." ἐβαπτίζοντο impf. ind. pass. βαπτίζω (# 966) to baptize. They received baptism, but had nevertheless not yet received the Holy Spirit (Bruner, 173f). Impf. pictures the repeated action. ◆ 13 ἐπίστευσεν aor. ind. act. s.v. 12. βαπτισθείς aor. pass. part. (temp.) s.v. 12. προσκαρτερῶν pres. act. part. προσκαρτερέω (# 4674) to attend constantly, to adhere to. Part. w. ἦν in a periphrastic construction. θεωρῶν pres. act. part. (temp.) θεωρέω (# 2555) to see, to watch. γινομένας pres. mid. (dep.) part. (adj.) s.v. 1. ἐξίστατο impf. ind. mid. s.v. 9. ◆ 14 ἀκούσαντες aor. act. part. (temp.) s.v. 6. δέδεκται perf. ind. mid. (dep.) δέχομαι (# 1312) to receive, to welcome. Perf. indicates the abiding result. ἀπέστειλαν aor. ind. act. ἀποστέλλω (# 690) to send, to send as an official authoritative representative (TDNT; EDNT). ◆ 15 καταβάντες aor. act. part. (temp.) καταβαίνω (# 2849) to descend, to go down. προσηύξαντο aor. ind. mid. (dep.) προσεύχομαι (# 4667) to pray. λάβωσιν aor. subj. ind. λαμβάνω (# 3284) to receive. Subj. w. ὅπως (# 3968) to express purp. The reception of the Holy Spirit through the apostles from Jerusalem evidently was related to the conflict between the Jews and Samaritans (Longenecker, 359; for the Samaritans s. HJP, 2:16-20; A.D. Crown [ed.], The Samaritans [Tübingen, 1989]; ABD, 5:940-47; Luke 10:33; John 4:9; Jürgen Zangenberg, ΣΑΜΑΡΕΙΑ Antike Quellen zur Geschichte und Kultur der Samaritaner in deutscher Übersetzung [Tübingen:A. Franke Verlag, 1994]). ◆ 16 οὐδέπω (# 4031) not yet. ἦν impf. ind. act. εἰμί (# 1639) to be. ἐπιπεπτωκός perf. act. part. ἐπιπίπτω (# 2158) to fall upon. Part. in a periphrastic construction: "The Holy Spirit never was in a state of having fallen upon any of them" (VA). βεβαπτισμένοι perf. pass. part. s.v. 12. Part. w. ὑπῆρχον in a periphrastic construction. ὑπῆρχον impf. ind. act. ὑπάρχω (# 5639) to exist, to be present, to be. ◆ 17 ἐπετίθεσαν impf. ind. act. ἐπιτίθημι (# 2202) to lay upon. The iterat. impf. emphasizing the repetition (MT, 67). ἐλάμβανον impf. ind. act. s.v. 15. ◆ 18 ἰδών aor. act. part. (temp.) ὁράω (# 3972) to see. δίδοται pres. ind. pass. δίδωμι (# 1443) to give. προσήνεγκεν aor. ind. act. προσφέρω (# 4712) to bring to. χρῆμα (# 5975) pl. money. ◆ 19 δότε aor. imp. act. s.v. 18. Aor. imp. calls for a specific act w. a note of urgency. ἐπιθῶ aor. subj. act. s.v. 17. Subj. w. ἐάν (# 1569) in an indef. rel. cl. λαμβάνῃ pres. subj. act. s.v. 15. Subj. in a purp. cl. ◆ 20 εἴη pres. opt. act. εἰμί s.v. 16. Opt. used to express a wish that can be fulfilled (RG, 939; MKG, 241). ἀπώλεια (# 724) destruction, ruin, injury, the end of earthly existence (NIDNTT; TDNT). W. prep. εἰς (# 1650) indicating direction and thus destiny (Barrett). δωρεά (# 1561) gift, free gift. ἐνόμισας aor. ind. act. νομίζω (# 3787) to suppose. κτᾶσθαι pres. mid. (dep.) inf. κτάομαι (# 3227) to obtain. Inf. as obj. of the vb. ◆ 21 σοι dat. sing. σύ (# 5148) Dat. of advantage or

poss. dat. **μερίς** (# *3535*) part of a whole, share, portion (BAGD). **κλῆρος** (# *3102*) lot, allotment, inheritance. Either he does not have part in the authority to give the Holy Spirit, or he does not share in the message (the Word) of the Lord (Pesch; Barrett). **εὐθεῖα** fem. sing. εὐθύς (# *2318*) straight, right. **ἔναντι** (# *1882*) prep. w. gen., before, in the presence of. ◆ **22 μετανόησον** aor. imp. act. μετανοέω (# *3566*) to change one's mind, to repent. Aor. imp. calls for a specific act w. a note of urgency. **δεήθητι** aor. imp. pass. (dep.) δέομαι (# *1289*) to ask for, to pray. **ἀφεθήσεται** fut. ind. pass. ἀφίημι (# *918*) to forgive. For the construction w. the part. s. IBG, 158. Theol. pass. indicating that God forgives. **ἐπίνοια** (# *2154*) thought, intent, plot. Used in the bad sense of evil or hostile schemes or stratagems (LC). ◆ **23 χολή** (# *5958*) gall, bitter anger, bitter poison. **πικρία** bitterness. **σύνδεσμος** (# *5278*) bond. Perhaps the meaning is, "You are full of bitter poison, bound by unrighteousness" (Barrett). **ὁρῶ** pres. ind. act. ὁράω (# *3972*) to see, to perceive. **ὄντα** pres. act. part. εἰμί s.v. 16. Part. used to complete the vb. or in indir. discourse (RWP). ◆ **24 ἀποκριθείς** aor. pass. (dep.) part. ἀποκρίνομαι (# *646*) to answer. Pleonastic part. **δεήθητε** aor. imp. pass. s.v. 22. **ἐπέλθη** aor. subj. act. ἐπέρχομαι (# *2088*) to come upon. Subj. w. ὅπως (# *3968*) expressing the content of the prayer. **ὧν** gen. pl. ὅς (# *4005*) rel. pron. Gen. by attraction to the case of the unexpressed antecedent τουτῶν (RWP). **εἰρήκατε** perf. ind. act. λέγω (# *3306*) to say. ◆ **25 δια-μαρτυράμενοι** aor. mid. (dep.) part. διαμαρτύομαι (# *1371*) to testify, to bear witness, to solemnly declare (MH, 302). Part. as subst. **λαλήσαντες** aor. act. part. λαλέω (# *3281*) to speak. **ὑπέστρεφον** impf. ind. act. ὑποστρέφω (# *5715*) to return. **εὐηγγελίζοντο** impf. ind. mid. (dep.) s.v. 4. For the importance of the conversion of the Samaritans s. C.H.H. Scobie, "The Origins and Development of Samaritan Christianity," *NTS* 19 (1973): 390-414; R.J. Coggins, "The Samaritans and Acts," *NTS* 28 (1982): 423-34; BHS, 55-72. ◆ **26 ἐλάλησεν** aor. ind. act. s.v. 25. **ἀνάστηθι** aor. imp. act. ἀνίστημι (# *482*) to arise. **πορεύου** pres. imp. mid. (dep.) πορεύομαι (# *4513*) to go. **μεσημβρία** (# *3540*) midday, noon. Noon was no time to travel over hot desert country and this unusual action ensured that Philip would meet the Ethiopian (Barrett). **αὕτη ἐστὶν ἔρημος** this was a desert. "This" may refer to the road (Schneider), or to the uninhabited wilderness on the way from Jerusalem to Gaza along the Roman route leading southwest through Eleutheropolis w. Ein Yael as a stopover (Yehudah Rapuano, "Did Philip Baptize the Eunuch at Ein Yael?" *BAR* 16 [1990]: 44-49). ◆ **27 ἀναστάς** aor. act. part. s.v. 26. **ἐπορεύθη** aor. ind. pass. (dep.) s.v. 26. **Αἰθίοψ** (# *134*) Ethiopian. Ethiopia refers to modern-day Sudan (Barrett). **εὐνοῦχος** (# *2336*) a castrated person, eunuch, chaste, faithful in marriage, high-ranking official (TDNT; EDNT; NDIEC,

3:40-41; LN, 1:482; BAGD). **δυνάστης** (# *1541*) a man of power, a leading man of authority (Barrett). **Κανδάκης** (# *2833*) gen. sing. Candace; title for the queen of Ethiopia, a name that has been passed on through a succession of queens (Pliny, *NH*, 26:186; BAGD; BBC; ABD, 1:837). **ἐληλύθει** plperf. ind. act. ἔρχομαι (# *2262*) to come, to go. **προσκυνήσων** fut. act. part. προσκυνέω (# *4686*) to worship. Part. expressing purp. ◆ **28 ὑπο-στρέφων** pres. act. part. s.v. 25. Part. in a periphrastic construction (VA, 461), or simply a descriptive adj. (Barrett). **καθήμενος** pres. mid. (dep.) part. κάθημαι (# *2764*) to sit. **ἅρμα** (# *761*) wagon, probably an ox wagon or little more than a flat board on wheels (Bruce; Barrett). **ἀνεγίνωσκεν** impf. ind. act. ἀναγινώσκω (# *336*) to read. One was to study by reading aloud so one would not forget, and it was considered good to contemplate religious things while travelling (SB, 2:687, 273). Impf. pictures continual action. ◆ **29 εἶπεν** aor. ind. act. λέγω s.v. 6. **πρόσελθε** aor. imp. act. προσέρχομαι (# *4665*) to go to. **κολλήθητι** aor. imp. pass. κολλάω (# *3140*) to bind close together; pass. to join oneself to, w. dat. (BAGD). ◆ **30 προσδραμών** aor. act. part. (circum.) προστρέχω (# *4708*) to run to. **ἤκουσεν** aor. ind. act., w. gen. s.v. 6. **ἆρα** (# *727*) interrogative particle w. the intensive particle γε (# *1145*) indicate doubt on Philip's part: "Do you really understand what you are reading?" (RWP; IBG, 158). ◆ **31 δυ-ναίμην** pres. opt. mid. (dep.) δύναμαι (# *1538*) to be able to. Opt. w. ἄν (# *323*) in a dir. question expressing what is merely thought: "Of course I do not (fully) understand, *for* how should I be able to do so, unless...?" (BD, 194; Barrett). **ὁδηγήσει** fut. ind. act. ὁδηγέω (# *3842*) to show the way, to lead, to instruct. **παρεκάλεσεν** aor. ind. act. παρακαλέω (# *4151*) to invite, to call upon for help, to request, w. inf. (BAGD). **ἀναβάντα** aor. act. part. (circum.) ἀναβαίνω (# *326*) to get up, to come up. **καθίσαι** aor. act. inf. s.v. 28. ◆ **32 περιοχή** (# *4343*) passage. Equivalent to the Heb. עִנְיָן indicating both content and place (SB, 2:687-88). For Isa. 53 s. SB, 1:481; Luke 24:25-27; JIU, 90-93. **ἀνεγίνωσκεν** impf. ind. act. s.v. 28. **σφαγή** (# *5375*) slaughter. **ἤχθη** aor. ind. pass. ἄγω (# *72*) to lead. **κείραντος** pres. act. part. κείρω (# *3025*) to shear. Part. as subst. **ἄφωνος** (# *936*) without sound, dumb. **ἀνοίγει** pres. ind. act. ἀνοίγω (# *487*) to open. ◆ **33 ἤρθη** aor. ind. pass. αἴρω (# *149*) to lift up, to take away. **διηγήσεται** fut. ind. mid. (dep.) διηγέομαι (# *1455*) to relate, to narrate. ◆ **34 ἀποκριθείς** aor. pass. (dep.) part. s.v. 24. ◆ **35 ἀνοίξας** aor. act. part. (circum.) s.v. 32. **ἀρξάμενος** aor. mid. (dep.) part. (circum.) ἄρχομαι (# *806*) to begin. **εὐηγγελίσατο** aor. ind. mid. (dep.) s.v. 4. ◆ **36 ἐπορεύοντο** impf. ind. mid. (dep.) s.v. 26. **ἦλθον** aor. ind. act. s.v. 27. **κωλύει** pres. ind. act. κωλύω (# *3266*) to prevent, to forbid. **βαπτισθῆναι** aor. pass. inf. βαπτίζω (# *966*) to baptize. Epex. inf. giving what was to be forbidden. ◆ **37** For the textual problem of this v. s. TC, 359-60; Barrett. ◆ **38 ἐκέλευσεν** aor. ind. act. κελεύω (# 3027) to command. **στῆναι** aor. act. inf. ἵστημι (# 2705) to stand. Inf. gives the content of the command. **κατέβησαν** aor. ind. act. s.v. 15. **ἐβάπτισεν** aor. ind. act. s.v. 36. ◆ **39 ἀνέβησαν** aor. ind. act. s.v. 31. **ἥρπασεν** aor. ind. act. ἁρπάζω (# 773) to snatch, to carry off to a different place (Barrett). **εἶδεν** aor. ind. act. ὁράω (# 3972) to see. **ἐπορεύετο** impf. ind. act. s.v. 26. **χαίρων** pres. act. part. χαίρω (# 5897) to rejoice, to be happy. Part. of manner. ◆ **40 εὑρέθη** aor. ind. pass. (dep.) εὑρίσκω (# 2351) to find; idiomatic for "he came" (GI, 158). **διερχόμενος** pres. mid. (dep.) part. (circum.) s.v. 4. **εὐηγγελίζετο** impf. ind. mid. (dep.) s.v. 4. Impf. pictures the repeated action. **ἐλθεῖν** aor. act. inf. s.v. 27. Articular inf. w. ἕως (# 2401) in a temp. cl. ("until").

Acts 9

◆ **1 ἐμπνέων** pres. act. part. (circum.) ἐμπνέω (# 1863) to breathe in, to inhale, w. gen. indicating what was breathed. Threats and murder were the atmosphere in which he breathed and by which he lived (EGT; BD, 95-94). It could have the meaning of "to breathe out," "to fume," indicating that Saul threatened the disciples w. death (NDIEC, 4:147). Pres. w. ἔτι (# 2285) expresses the continual action, indicating that Saul's fierce opposition did not abate w. time (Barrett). **ἀπειλή** (# 581) threat. This was the legal warning (Longenecker, 368). **φόνος** (# 5840) murder, killing. **προσελθών** aor. act. part. (circum.) προσέρχομαι (# 4665) to come to. ◆ **2 ᾐτήσατο** aor. ind. mid. αἰτέω (# 160) to request, to ask for oneself. **ἐπιστολή** (# 2186) letter. These were letters of recommendation to commend Saul to the Jewish synagogue (SB, 2:689; BBC). Saul was going as an official representative (שליח) of the Sanhedrin (Barrett). **Δαμασκός** (# 1242) Damascus. For Damascus, about 135 miles northwest of Jerusalem, and its large Jewish population at this time, of which some 10,500 to 18,000 were massacred just before the revolt against Rome s. ABD, 2:5-8; Jos., JW, 2:559-61; 7:368; HJP, 2:127-30; RNE, 310-19; SB, 2:689-90; Barrett. **εὕρῃ** aor. subj. act. εὑρίσκω (# 2351) to find. Subj. w. **ἐάν** (# 1569) in a 3rd. class cond. cl. assuming the possibility of the cond. **ὁδός** (# 3847) way; "The Way," referring to the mode of life (TDNT; EDNT; NIDNTT, 3:935-43; Barrett; for a discussion of the DSS parallels s. ESB, 281-84). **ὄντας** pres. act. part. (adj.) εἰμί (# 1639) to be. The separation of the part. from the obj. may indicate a measure of uncertainty ("any who might be...") (Barrett). **δεδεμένους** perf. pass. part. (adj.) δέω (# 1313) to bind. Perf. emphasizes the state or condition. **ἀγάγῃ** aor. subj. act. ἄγω (# 72) to lead. Subj. w. **ὅπως** (# 3968) to express purp. ◆ **3 πορεύεσθαι** pres. mid. (dep.) inf. πορεύομαι (# 4513) to go, to travel. Ar-

ticular inf. w. prep. ἐν (# 1877) expressing contemporaneous time. **ἐγένετο** aor. ind. mid. (dep.) γίνομαι (# 1181) to become, to happen. For the construction w. a prep. and inf. s. Beyer, 36; MH, 427; MT, 144-45. **ἐγγίζειν** pres. act. inf. ἐγγίζω (# 1581) to draw near, to approach, w. dat. Inf. expressing contemporaneous time: "as he was approaching...." **ἐξαίφνης** (# 1978) suddenly. **περιήστραψεν** aor. ind. act. περιαστράπτω (# 4313) to flash around. **φῶς** (# 5890) light. Perhaps a reference to the Shekinah, the manifestation of the Presence of the Lord (s. TS, 37-65). The light was the physical representation or accompaniment of the divine glory of Christ (Barrett). ◆ **4 πεσών** aor. act. part. (temp.) πίπτω (# 4406) to fall. **ἤκουσεν** aor. ind. act. ἀκούω (# 201) to hear, w. acc. Paul both perceived a sound and distinguished the words that were spoken (Barrett). **λέγουσαν** pres. act. part. (adj.) acc. fem. sing. λέγω (# 3306) to say, to speak. ◆ **5 εἶπεν** aor. ind. act. λέγω. **εἶ** pres. act. ind. εἰμί (# 1639) to be. **κύριε** voc. sing. κύριος (# 3261) Lord. This is more than just the polite "sir," for Saul is aware that he is confronted by a superhuman being (Barrett). For the view that Saul came to consider the exalted Christ as the image of God through this experience s. OPG, 193-268. **διώκεις** pres. ind. act. διώκω (# 1503) to persecute. Pres. indicates the continual action. For a discussion of the conversion and call s. DPL, 156-63. ◆ **6 ἀλλά** (# 247) but. Introduces the imp., which adds something new to the context (Haenchen). **ἀνάστηθι** aor. imp. act. ἀνίστημι (# 482) to arise. **εἴσελθε** aor. imp. act. εἰσέρχομαι (# 1656) to go into. **λαληθήσεται** fut. ind. pass. λαλέω (# 3281) to tell, to speak. For the construction of an imp. followed by καί (# 2779) and the fut., forming a Semitic type of cond. cl. s. Beyer, 238-55. **ποιεῖν** pres. act. inf. ποιέω (# 4472) to do. Epex. inf. w. δεῖ: "what is necessary to do." ◆ **7 συνοδεύοντες** pres. act. part. (adj.) συνοδεύω (# 5321) to accompany, to travel w. someone, w. dat. **εἱστήκεισαν** plperf. ind. act. ἵστημι (# 2705) to stand. **ἐνεός** (# 1917) speechless. **ἀκούοντες** pres. act. part. s.v. 4. The obj. in gen. may indicate that they heard a sound, but did not understand the words (RWP; M, 66; Gert Steuernagel, "ΑΚΟΥΟΝΤΕΣ ΜΕΝ ΤΗΣ ΦΩΝΗΣ [Apg 9.7]: Ein Genitiv in der Apostelgeschichte," NTS 35 [1989]: 619-24). Circum. or concessive part. **θεωροῦντες** pres. act. part. (circum.) θεωρέω (# 2555) to see. ◆ **8 ἠγέρθη** aor. ind. pass. ἐγείρω (# 1586) to raise; pass. to rise. **ἀνεῳγμένων** perf. pass. part. ἀνοίγω (# 487) to open. For the form s. BD, 53. Part. as gen. abs., either temp. or concessive. **ἔβλεπεν** impf. ind. act. βλέπω (# 1063) to see. **χειραγωγοῦντες** pres. act. part. χειραγωγέω (# 5932) to lead by the hand. Circum. part. or part. of manner explaining how they led him. **εἰσήγαγον** aor. ind. act. εἰσάγω (# 1652) to lead into. ◆ **9 βλέπων** pres. act. part. s.v. 8. Part. as pred. adj. or in a periphrastic construction. **ἔφαγεν** aor.

ind. act. ἐσθίω (# 2266) to eat. ἔπιεν aor. ind. act. πίνω (# 4403) to drink. ◆ **10** εἶπεν aor. ind. act. s.v. 5. ὅραμα (# 3969) vision. Not necessary a night vision, but a condition in which the person's consciousness is opened for a heavenly message (Haenchen). ◆ **11** ἀναστάς aor. act. part. s.v. 6. Circum. part. w. the idea of imp. πορεύθητι aor. imp. pass. (dep.) s.v. 3. ῥύμη (# 4860) street. καλουμένην pres. pass. part. (adj.) καλέω (# 2813) to call; pass. to be called, to be named. Εὐθεῖαν acc. sing., εὐθύς (# 2318) straight. The name of the street which was the main east-west axis of the city (Barrett). For directions (σημασία) given to find houses, esp. for the delivery of letters s. BASHH, 226; NDIEC, 7:29-45. ζήτησον aor. imp. act. ζητέω (# 2426) to seek. Ταρσέα acc. sing. Ταρσεύς (# 5432) Tarsus. For this Hellenistic city, w. its university, its famous philosophers, its harbor, its control of the famous Cilician Gates in the Tarsus mountains, and the city where Cicero visited, and where Cleopatra met Anthony, s. CSP, 85-244; ISBE, 4:734-36; ABD, 6:333-34; DC, "The Thirty-third Discourse, or First Tarsic Discourse"; "The Thirty-fourth Discourse or Second Tarsic Discourse"; Strabo, XIV, 5:11-15. ◆ **12** εἶδεν aor. ind. act. ὁράω (# 3972) to see. εἰσελθόντα aor. act. part. (adj.) s.v. 6. ἐπιθέντα aor. act. part. (adj.) ἐπιτίθημι (# 2202) to place upon. ἀναβλέψῃ aor. subj. act. ἀναβλέπω (# 329) to see again, to regain sight (LC). Subj. w. ὅπως (# 3968) expressing purpose. ◆ **13** ἀπεκρίθη aor. ind. pass. (dep.) ἀποκρίνομαι (# 646) to answer. ἤκουσα aor. ind. act. s.v. 4. ἐποίησεν aor. ind. act. s.v. 6. ◆ **14** δῆσαι aor. act. inf. s.v. 2. Epex. inf. explaining ἐξουσίαν. ἐπικαλουμένους pres. mid. (dep.) part. ἐπικαλέομαι (# 2126) to call upon. ◆ **15** πορεύου pres. imp. mid. (dep.) s.v. 3. σκεῦος (# 5007) vessel, instrument. The word means implements in general (LC). Nom. used as pred. nom. ἐκλογῆς gen. sing. ἐκλογή (# 1724) choice, selection. Gen. of quality used in the Hebraic sense: "instrument of choice"; i.e., "chosen vessel" (Bruce; Kistemaker). βαστάσαι aor. act. inf. βαστάζω (# 1002) to bear, to carry. Epex. inf. giving the use and purpose of the σκεῦος. ◆ **16** ὑποδείξω fut. ind. act. ὑποδείκνυμι (# 5683) to show, to make plain. παθεῖν aor. act. inf. πάσχω (# 4248) to suffer. Inf. w. δεῖ giving the necessity. ◆ **17** ἀπῆλθεν aor. ind. act. ἀπέρχομαι (# 599) to go away, to go forth. εἰσῆλθεν aor. ind. act. s.v. 6. ἐπιθείς aor. act. part. (circum.) s.v. 12. ἀπέσταλκεν perf. ind. act. ἀποστέλλω (# 690) to send, to send as an authoritative representative (TDNT; EDNT). Perf. indicates the abiding effect of the authoritative sending. ὀφθείς aor. pass. part. ὁράω (# 3972) to see; pass. to been seen, to appear. ἤρχου impf. ind. mid. (dep.) ἔρχομαι (# 2262) to go, to come. Impf. gives a picture of him moving along. ἀναβλέψῃς aor. subj. act. s.v. 12. Subj. w. ὅπως (# 3968) gives the purp. of the sending. πλησθῇς aor. subj. pass. πίμπλημι (# 4398) to fill.

◆ **18** ἀπέπεσαν aor. ind. act. ἀποπίπτω (# 674) to fall off. λεπίς (# 3318) scaly substance, flakes (LC; for the medical use of the term s. MLL, 39). ἀνέβλεψεν aor. ind. act. s.v. 12. ἀναστάς aor. act. part. (circum.) s.v. 6. ἐβαπτίσθη aor. ind. pass. βαπτίζω (# 966) to baptize. ◆ **19** λαβών aor. act. part. (temp.) λαμβάνω (# 3284) to receive. ἐνίσχυσεν aor. ind. act. ἐνισχύω (# 1932) to receive strength. ἐγένετο aor. ind. mid. (dep.) s.v. 3. ◆ **20** ἐκήρυσσεν impf. ind. act. κηρύσσω (# 3062) to preach, to proclaim as a herald. Incep. impf., "he began to preach." ὅτι (# 4022) that. It introduces what he preached about Jesus. ◆ **21** ἐξίσταντο aor. ind. mid. ἐξίστημι (# 2014) to be beside oneself, to be amazed. οὐχ not. Used in a question expecting a positive answer. πορθήσας aor. act. part. πορθέω (# 4514) to destroy, to ravage, to destroy or sack a city, to destroy any human fellowship (Haenchen; LC). Adj. part. as subst.; used as pred. nom. w. the art. indicating that the subject and pred. are the same. ἐπικαλουμένους pres. mid. (dep.) part. ἐπικαλέω (# 2126) mid. to call upon someone for help, to call upon a deity, to invoke (BAGD; Barrett). ἐληλύθει plperf. ind. act. s.v. 17. Plperf. indicates that the purp. was now a thing of the past and the state resulting from it was no longer in effect (BD, 178; VANT, 308). δεδεμένους perf. pass. part. (adj.) s.v. 2. ἀγάγῃ aor. subj. act. s.v. 2. Subj. w. ἵνα (# 2671) in a purp. cl. ◆ **22** μᾶλλον (# 3437) rather; giving a contrast w. his previous conduct. ἐνεδυναμοῦτο impf. ind. pass. ἐνδυναμόω (# 1904) to receive power, to fill w. power. It is used of religious and spiritual strength (EGT). Impf. pictures the continual increase of strength. συνέχυννεν impf. ind. act. συγχύννω (for the form συγχέω (# 5177) s. MH, 195, 214) to pour together, to confuse, to confuse by reason, to confound, to throw into consternation (BAGD; LS). He tied them in knots! (Barrett). κατοικοῦντας pres. act. part. (adj.) κατοικέω (# 2997) to live, to be at home, to dwell. συμβιβάζων pres. act. part. συμβιβάζω (# 5204) to prove, putting together, to cause something to be known as certain and therefore dependable, to instruct (LN, 1:340; MM). Used here of putting the prophetic Scriptures alongside their fulfillment (Bruce). Part. of manner explaining how Saul confounded them. ◆ **23** ἐπληροῦντο impf. ind. pass. πληρόω (# 4444) to fulfill. Impf. w. time ("as time went on"), indicating that the Jews felt the situation was daily becoming more intolerable (LC). συνεβουλεύσαντο aor. ind. mid. (dep.) συμβουλεύομαι (# 5205) to counsel together, to plot. ἀνελεῖν aor. act. inf. ἀναιρέω (# 359) to kill. Luke seems to use the word in reference to the Jews killing Jesus and Christians (Mark Harding, "On the Historicity of Acts: Comparing Acts 9.23-5 with 2 Corinthians 11.32-2," *NTS* 39 [1993]: 524-29). Epex. inf. explaining the content of their planning. ◆ **24** ἐγνώσθη aor. ind. pass. γινώσκω (# 1182) to know. ἐπιβουλή (# 2101) plot.

παρετηροῦντο impf. ind. mid. παρατερέω (# *4190*) to watch, to observe (s. Luke 6:7). ἡμέρας ... νυκτός (# *2465; 3816*) by day and by night; gen. of time. ἀνέλωσιν aor. subj. act. ἀναιρέω s.v. 23. Subj. w. ὅπως (# *3968*) to express purp. For this incident s. 2 Cor. 11:32-33; BASHH, 163-64; 215. ◆ **25** λαβόντες aor. act. part. λαμβάνω (# *3284*) to take. Circum. part. or Semitic pleonastic (auxiliary) use (SA, 125; AA, 125; but s. Barrett). μαθητής (# *3412*) disciple, convert; ("his converts" s. Barrett). νυκτός gen. sing. νύξ (# *3816*) night. Gen. of time. ("by night"). τεῖχος (# *5446*) wall, city wall (BAGD). Gen. w. prep. διά (# *1328*) ("through"). καθῆκαν aor. ind. act. καθίημι (# *2768*) to let down. χαλάσαντες aor. act. part. χαλάω (# *5899*) to slacken, to loosen, to lower (Barrett). Part. of means, explaining how they let him down through the city wall. σπυρίδι dat. sing. σπυρίς (# *5083*) basket, a large woven basket suitable for hay and straw or for bales of wool (LC). ◆ **26** παραγενόμενος aor. mid. (dep.) part. (temp.) παραγίνομαι (# *4134*) to arrive. ἐπείραζεν impf. ind. act. πειράζω (# *4279*) to try, to attempt. Impf. pictures the repeated attempts. κολλᾶσθαι pres. mid. (dir. mid.) inf. κολλάω (# *3140*) to join up w., w. dat. (s. 5:13). Epex. inf. explaining what he attempted. ἐφοβοῦντο impf. ind. mid. (dep.) φοβέομαι (# *5828*) to be afraid, to fear. πιστεύοντες pres. act. part. πιστεύω (# *4409*) to believe. Causal part. giving the reason why they were afraid. ◆ **27** ἐπιλαβόμενος aor. mid. (dep.) part. (circum.) ἐπιλαμβάνομαι (# *2138*) to take hold of, to be concerned w., to take an interest in. It occurs in the papyri in the sense of "taking a care or concern upon oneself" (Preisigke, 1:561). ἤγαγεν aor. ind. act. s.v. 2. διηγήσατο aor. ind. mid. (dep.) διηγέομαι (# *1455*) to narrate, to relate, to describe. The subject could be either Paul or Barnabas, but more likely it is Barnabas (Barrett). εἶδεν aor. ind. act. s.v. 12. ἐλάλησεν aor. ind. act. s.v. 6. ἐπαρρησιάσατο aor. ind. mid. (dep.) παρρησιάζομαι (# *4245*) to speak freely, openly, boldly (s. 4:13). ◆ **28** εἰσπορευόμενος pres. mid. (dep.) part. εἰσπορεύομαι (# *1660*) to go in. "Going in and going out" implies the regular conduct of life (Barrett). Part. in a periphrastic construction. ◆ **29** ἐλάλει impf. ind. act. s.v. 6. συνεζήτει impf. ind. act. συζητέω (# *5184*) to dispute, to argue. Impf. indicates Paul argued often (Haenchen). ἐπεχείρουν impf. ind. act. ἐπιχειρέω (# *2217*) to put the hand to, to try. Impf. indicates the incomplete or unsuccessful action. ἀνελεῖν aor. act. inf. s.v. 24. Epex. inf. explaining συνεζήτει. ◆ **30** ἐπιγνόντες aor. act. part. (temp.) ἐπιγινώσκω (# *2105*) to realize, to know, to recognize. The vb. without any object is perhaps idiomatic (LC). κατήγαγον aor. ind. act. κατάγω (# *2864*) to lead down. ἐξαπέστειλαν aor. ind. act. ἐξαποστέλλω (# *1990*) to send away. ◆ **31** ἐκκλησία (# *1711*) church, congregation of Christians. The sing. possibly refers to the church at Jerusalem, whose members were dispersed

throughout Judea, Galilee, and Samaria (K.N. Giles, "Luke's Use of the term ΕΚΚΛΗΣΙΑ' with Special Reference to Acts 20.28 and 9.31," *NTS* 31 [1985]: 135-42). καθ᾽ ὅλης (# *2848; 3910*) throughout (BD, 120). εἶχεν impf. ind. act. ἔχω (# *2400*) to have. οἰκοδομουμένη pres. pass. part. (adj.) οἰκοδομέω (# *3868*) to build, to edify, to build up (TDNT; EDNT; BDG). πορευομένη pres. mid. (dep.) part. s.v. 3. παράκλησις (# *4155*) comfort, encouragement, followed by subjective gen. ἐπληθύνετο impf. ind. pass. πληθύνω (# *4437*) to increase, to multiply. ◆ **32** ἐγένετο aor. ind. mid. (dep.) s.v. 3. For the Semitic construction s. M, 16f; Beyer 29-62. διερχόμενον pres. mid. (dep.) part. (temp.) διέρχομαι (# *1451*) to pass through. διὰ πάντων through all; that is, through all the areas mentioned in v. 31 (Haenchen). κατελθεῖν aor. act. inf. κατέρχομαι (# *2982*) to go down; that is, to come down from Jerusalem (LC). Inf. w. ἐγένετο. κατοικοῦντας pres. act. part. (adj.) s.v. 22. ◆ **33** εὗρεν aor. ind. act. εὑρίσκω (# *2351*) to find. κατακείμενον pres. mid. (dep.) part. (adj.) κατάκειμαι (# *2879*) to be lying down. κράβαττος (# *3187*) mattress, mat. In the papyri it refers to a "poor man's bed" (NDIEC, 2:15; Mark 2:4). For the spelling s. BD, 24; MH, 102; GGP, 1:65-66, 77. παραλελυμένος perf. pass. part. παραλύω (# *4168*) pass., to be paralyzed. Perf. indicates the state or condition. Adj. part. as pred. adj. ◆ **34** ἰᾶται pres. ind. mid. (dep.) ἰάομαι (# *2615*) to heal (GLH). Aoristic pres. (RWP; RG, 864; BD, 166; VANT, 202-03; but s. VA, 55). If the accent were ἴαται the form would be perf. (MH, 60; Barrett). ἀνάστηθι aor. imp. act. s.v. 6. Aor. imp. calls for a specific act w. a note of urgency. στρῶσον aor. imp. act. στρώννυμι (# *5143*) to make one's bed; that is "to pack it up," since he will no longer need it (Barrett), or to get ready to eat (Bruce; LC). ἀνέστη aor. ind. act. s.v. 6. ◆ **35** εἶδαν aor. ind. act. ὁράω (# *3972*) to see. κατοικοῦντες pres. act. part. s.v. 22. Adj. part. as subst. Σαρών (# *4926*) (Heb. שָׁרוֹן) Sharon, the Plain of Sharon; the coastal plain which at that time was thickly populated and famous for its fruitfulness, its wine and the poor quality of earth for making bricks (Barrett; ABD, 5:1161-63; SB, 2:693-94). For the form s. MH, 149. οἵτινες nom. pl. ὅστις (# *4015*) who (s. 7:53; but s. also MKG, 174; BG, 68). ἐπέστρεψαν aor. ind. act. ἐπιστρέφω (# *2188*) to turn to. ◆ **36** μαθήτρια (# *3413*) fem. sing. a (woman) disciple. Ταβιθά (# *5412*) Tabitha (Aramaic טְבִיתָא female gazelle, deer [AT, 588, 381; SA, 109; SB, 2:694]). διερμηνευομένη pres. pass. part. (adj.) διερμηνεύω (# *1450*) to translate. Δορκάς (# *1520*) Dorcas. The name was used both by Greeks and Jews (NDIEC, 4:177-78; MM; BASHH, 226). Josephus refers to an assassin named John, son of Dorcas (Jos., *JW*, 4:145). ὧν gen. pl. ὅς (# *4005*) rel. pron., which. Gen. by attraction. ἐποίει impf. ind. act. ποιέω (# *4472*) to do. Customary impf., "which she continually did." For good works and alms by the

Jews s. SB, 4, i:559-610. ◆ **37** ἐγένετο aor. ind. mid. (dep.) s.v. 3, 32. **ἀσθενήσασαν** aor. act. part. (circum.) acc. fem. sing. ἀσθενέω (# 820) to be weak, to be sick. **ἀποθανεῖν** aor. act. inf. ἀποθνήσκω (# 633) to die. Inf w. vb. in a Semitic construction. **λού-σαντες** aor. act. part. λούω (# 3374) to wash. It was a widespread custom to wash the body in preparation for burial (Barrett). **ἔθη-καν** aor. ind. act. τίθημι (# 5502) to place, to put. **ὑπερῴῳ** dat. sing. ὑπερῷον (# 5673) upper room (s. Acts 1:13). ◆ **38** οὔσης pres. act. part. (causal) gen. fem. sing. εἰμί (# 1639) to be. Gen. abs. Lydda was about 10 miles from Joppa, or a three-and-one-half-hour journey by foot (Longenecker, 382; Schneider). **ἀκούσαντες** aor. act. part. ἀκούω (# 201) to hear. Temp. or causal part. **ἀπέστειλαν** aor. ind. act. s.v. 17. **παρακαλοῦντες** pres. act. part. (circum.) παρακαλέω (# 4151) to ask, to beseech, to urge. **ὀκνήσῃς** aor. subj. act. ὀκνέω (# 3890) to delay. Ingressive aor.; subj. in a prohibition (RWP). **διελθεῖν** aor. act. inf. s.v. 32. Epex. inf. explaining the vb. ◆ **39** ἀναστάς aor. act. part. (circum.) s.v. 6. **συνῆλθεν** aor. ind. act. συνέρχομαι (# 5302) to go with, to accompany. **παραγενόμενον** aor. mid. (dep.) part. (temp.) s.v. 26. **ἀνήγαγον** aor. ind. act. ἀνάγω (# 343) to lead up. **παρέστησαν** aor. ind. act. παρίστημι (# 4225) to come to and stand by. A vivid picture of this group of widows as they stood around Peter (RWP). **χήρα** (# 5939) widow. **κλαίουσαι** pres. act. part. (adj.) nom. fem. pl. κλαίω (# 3081) to weep, to cry loudly. **ἐπι-δεικνύμεναι** pres. mid. part. ἐπιδείκνυμι (# 2109) to show, to display. Perhaps the mid. indicates the exhibitors owned and were wearing Tabitha's gift (LC). **ἐποίει** impf. ind. act. s.v. 36. **οὖσα** pres. act. part. (temp.) nom. fem. sing. εἰμί, "while she was with them." ◆ **40** ἐκβαλών aor. act. part. (temp.) ἐκβάλλω (# 1675) to put out. **θείς** aor. act. part. τίθημι (# 5502) to place, to put, to bow one's knees. **γόνατα** acc. pl. γόνυ (# 1205) knee. **προσηύξατο** aor. ind. mid. (dep.) προσεύχομαι (# 4667) to pray. **ἐπιστρέψας** aor. act. part. (temp.) s.v. 35. **Ταβιθά** voc. sing. **ἀνάστηθι** aor. imp. act. s.v. 6. **ἤνοιξεν** aor. ind. act. s.v. 8. **ἰδοῦσα** aor. act. part. (temp.) nom. fem. sing. ὁράω (# 3972) to see. **ἀνεκάθισεν** aor. ind. act. ἀνακαθίζω (# 361) to sit up. ◆ **41** δούς aor. act. part. (temp.) δίδωμι (# 1443) to give. **ἀνέστησεν** aor. ind. act. s.v. 6. **φωνήσας** aor. act. part. (temp.) φωνέω (# 5888) to call. **παρέστησεν** aor. ind. act. παρίστημι (# 4225) to present. **ζῶσαν** pres. act. part. acc. fem. sing. ζάω (# 2409) to live. Adj. part. used in a double acc. construction. ◆ **42** γνωστός (# 1196) known. **ἐγένετο** aor. ind. mid. (dep.) s.v. 3. **ἐπίστευσαν** aor. ind. act. s.v. 26. Ingressive aor., "many came to believe." ◆ **43** ἐγένετο aor. ind. mid. (dep.) s.v. 3; for the Semitic construction s.v. 32. **μεῖναι** aor. act. inf. μένω (# 3531) to remain. Inf. w. vb. **βυρσεῖ** dat. sing. βυρσεύς (# 1114) tanner. The work of a tanner was defiling according to Jewish law (LC; M, Ketuboth. 7:10; SB, 2:695; JTJ, 301-12; Barrett).

Acts 10

◆ **1** ἑκατοντάρχης (# 1672) centurion (s. T.R.S. Broughton, "The Roman Army," BC, 5:427-45; TJ, 101; HK, 60-69; Brian Dobson, "The Significance of the Centurion and 'Primipilaris' in the Roman Army and Administration," ANRW, 2, i, 392-433; CC, 201-4). **σπεῖρα** (# 5061) cohort, about 600 men, the tenth part of a legion (BAGD; NDIEC, 5:159-61). For the *cohors II Italic(a) c(iuium) R(omanorum)* s. Broughton, BC, 5:441-43; Bruce, BASHH, 164; Barrett). It is suggested that Cornelius may have been retired and settled in Caesarea (BC, 5:443). ◆ **2** εὐσεβής (# 2356) pious. **φοβούμενος** pres. mid. (dep.) part. φοβέομαι (# 5828) to fear. These two terms denote Gentiles who, though not full proselytes, attached themselves to the Jewish religion, practicing its monotheistic and imageless worship (Bruce; BAFCS, 5:51-126; ALAG, 98; BBC; TDNT; BC, 5:74-96; SB, 2:715-23; Barrett; Conrad H. Gempf, "The God-Fearers," BASHH, 444-47; Thomas M. Finn, "The God-fearers Reconsidered," CBQ 47 [1985]: 75-84; EDNT]. **ποιῶν** pres. act. part. (adj.) ποιέω (# 4472) to do; used w. the subst. expressing the verbal idea of the subst., "to give alms." **ἐλεημοσύνη** (# 1797) alms (s. Matt. 6:2). **δεόμενος** pres. mid. (dep.) part. (adj.) δέομαι (# 1289) to ask, to pray. **διὰ παντός** (# 1328; 4246) always. ◆ **3** εἶδεν aor. ind. act. ὁράω (# 3972) to see. **φανερῶς** (# 5747) adv. clearly. **περὶ ὥραν ἐνάτην** around the ninth hour (s. 3:1). **εἰσελθόντα** aor. act. part. (adj.) εἰσέρχομαι (# 1656) to come in. **εἰπόντα** aor. act. part. λέγω (# 3306) to say, to speak. ◆ **4** ἀτενίσας aor. act. part. (temp.) ἀτενίζω (# 867) to gaze. **γενόμενος** aor. mid. (dep.) part. γίνομαι (# 1181) to become, to be. Adj. or circum. part. **ἀνέβησαν** aor. ind. act. ἀναβαίνω (# 326) to ascend, to go up. **μνημόσυνον** (# 3649) remembrance. ◆ **5** πέμψον aor. imp. act. πέμπω (# 4287) to send. Aor. imp. calls for a specific act w. a note of urgency. **μετάπεμψαι** aor. imp. mid. μεταπέμπω (# 3569) to send for. The mid. indicates the sending of another for one's own sake (RWP). **ἐπικαλεῖται** pres. ind. pass. ἐπικαλέω (# 2126) to call; pass. to be named. ◆ **6** ξενίζεται pres. ind. pass. ξενίζω (# 3826) to receive as a guest, to entertain as a stranger. **ᾧ** dat. sing. ὅς (# 4005) rel. pron. Dat. of poss., "whose house is along the sea." For addresses or instructions as to how to find places where a message is to be delivered s. NDIEC, 7:29-45. ◆ **7** ἀπῆλθεν aor. ind. act. ἀπέρχομαι (# 599) to go away from, to depart. **φωνήσας** aor. act. part. (temp.) φωνέω (# 5888) to call. **οἰκετῶν** gen. pl. οἰκέτης (# 3860) household servant. **στρατιώτης** (# 5132) soldier. The soldier may have been retired but remained w. Cornelius (Barrett). **εὐσεβῆ** pious s.v. 2. **προσκαρτερούντων** pres. act. part. προσκαρτερέω (# 4674) to attach oneself to, to wait on, to be faithful to someone, to be true to someone, to remain faithfully attached to someone, w. dat. (BAGD; TLNT, 3:191). Adj. part. referring to both the soldier and the servants. Habitual pres. indicating their constant character. ◆ **8 ἐξηγησάμενος** aor. mid. (dep.) part. (temp.) ἐξηγέομαι (# *2007*) to relate, to explain. **ἀπέστειλεν** aor. ind. act. ἀποστέλλω (# *690*) to send, to send as personal representative w. authority to carry out a task. ◆ **9 τῇ ἐπαύριον** (# *2069*) on the following day. **ὁδοιπορούντων** pres. act. part. (temp.) ὁδοιπορέω (# *3844*) to journey. Gen. abs., "While they were travelling." It was about 30 miles between Joppa and Caesarea; they may have gone by foot, or on horseback (Barrett; Bruce; LC). **ἐγγιζόντων** pres. act. part. (temp.) ἐγγίζω (# *1581*) to draw near, to approach, w. dat. **ἀνέβη** aor. ind. act. ἀναβαίνω (# *326*) to go up. **προσεύξασθαι** aor. mid. (dep.) inf. προσεύχομαι (# *4667*) to pray. Inf. of purp. **περὶ ὥραν ἕκτην** around the sixth hour; i.e., 12 noon. Peter had probably not eaten anything and chose this time as an early afternoon or offering prayertime, since one was not to eat immediately before the prayertime (SB, 2:698-99). For a discussion of the number of daily prayers, their time and content s. SB, 2:696-702; JPB, 196-97; 202-08; 4Q 503. ◆ **10 ἐγένετο** aor. ind. mid. (dep.) γίνομαι (# *1181*) to become, to be. **πρόσπεινος** (# *4698*) pred. adj. very hungry. **ἤθελεν** impf. ind. act. θέλω (# *2527*) to will, to want to, w. inf. Impf. indicates the incomplete action or desire. **γεύσασθαι** aor. mid. (dep.) inf. γεύομαι (# *1174*) to taste, to eat, to eat a meal (Barrett). **παρασκευαζόντων** pres. act. part. (temp.) παρασκευάζω (# *4186*) to prepare. Gen. abs. **ἔκστασις** (# *1749*) ecstasy, trance, a state in which a man stands outside himself (Bruce). ◆ **11 θεωρεῖ** pres. ind. act. θεωρέω (# *2555*) to see, to watch. Hist. pres. **ἀνεῳγμένον** perf. pass. part. ἀνοίγω (# *487*) to open. Perf. part. indicates the state or condition. **καταβαῖνον** pres. act. part. (adj.) καταβαίνω (# *2849*) to go down, to come down, to descend. **σκεῦος** vessel, thing, container (BAGD). **ὀθόνη** (# *3855*) linen cloth, a sheet of cloth used for various things: a woman's dress, sails of a ship, or bandages (Barrett). **ἀρχαῖς** dat. pl. ἀρχή (# *794*) corner. These two words (ἀρχαῖς ὀθόνη) were a technical medical phrase ("the ends of a bandage") to describe the sheet (MLL, 218). Instr. dat. **καθιέμενον** pres. pass. part. (adj.) καθίημι (# *2768*) to let down. ◆ **12 ὑπῆρχεν** impf. ind. act. ὑπάρχω (# *5639*) to exist, to be. **τετράπους** (# *5488*) four-footed (animals). **ἑρπετόν** (# *2260*) creeping animal, reptile (GELTS, 181). **πετεινόν** (# *4374*) bird. ◆ **13 ἐγένετο** aor. ind. mid. (dep.) s.v. 10. **ἀναστάς** aor. act. part. ἀνίστημι (# *482*) to arise. Circum. part. w. the idea of an imp. as in the vb. **θῦσον** aor. imp. act. θύω (# *2604*) to slay, to sacrifice, to kill. Perhaps used in the sense of to sacrifice as a religious act (Barrett; SB, 2:703; but s. Bruce). **φάγε** aor. imp. act. ἐσθίω (# *2266*) to eat. Aor. imp. calls for a specific act w. a note of urgency. ◆ **14 μηδαμῶς** (# *3592*) not at all, by no means. **ἔφαγον** aor. ind. act. s.v. 13. For the possible Semitic construction w. the neg. s. BG,

150-51. **κοινός** (# *3123*) common, that which comes into contact w. anything and everything and is therefore ordinary, profane, or ceremonially unclean (DJG, 125-28; BAGD; TDNT). **ἀκάθαρτον** (# *176*) unclean, impure, in ritual or cultic sense (GELTS, 14). ◆ **15 ἐκαθάρισεν** aor. ind. act. καθαρίζω (# *2751*) to cleanse, to purify. There was a later rabbinic teaching that in the days of the Messiah the rules regarding unclean foods would be lifted (SB, 4, ii:1147; 1163). **κοίνου** pres. imp. act. κοινόω (# *3124*) to consider common, to count as profane (LC). Pres. imp. w. the neg. **μή** (# *3590*) implies that he is not to go on doing what he is already doing (Bruce). ◆ **16 ἐγένετο** aor. ind. mid. (dep.) s.v. 10. **ἀνελήμφθη** aor. ind. pass. ἀναλαμβάνω (# *377*) to take up. Theol. pass. indicating that God did the action. ◆ **17 διηπόρει** impf. ind. act. διαπορέω (# *1389*) to be perplexed. The original meaning, intensified by the prep. in compound, is "to be completely at a loss what road to take" (RWP). **εἴη** pres. opt. act. εἰμί (# *1639*) to be. Opt. in a deliberative question (RG, 940; 1044). **εἶδεν** aor. ind. act. ὁράω (# *3972*) to see. **ἀπεσταλμένοι** perf. pass. part. (adj.) s.v. 8. **διερωτήσαντες** aor. act. part. (circum.) διερωτάω (# *1452*) to ask. The prep. in compound intensifies and gives the meaning, "to ask constantly or continually" (EGT). **ἐπέστησαν** aor. ind. act. ἐφίστημι (# *2392*) to approach, to stand before. **πυλών** (# *4784*) gate, esp. of the larger gate at the entrance of large buildings; gateway, entrance, house door (BAGD). ◆ **18 φωνήσαντες** aor. act. part. (temp.) s.v. 7. **ἐπυνθάνοντο** impf. ind. mid. (dep.) πυνθάνομαι (# *4785*) to inquire. Incep. impf. **εἰ** (# *1623*) if, whether. Introduces either a dir. or indir. quotation (LC). **ἐνθάδε** (# *1924*) here. ◆ **19 διενθυμουμένου** pres. mid. (dep.) part. (temp.) διενθυμέομαι (# *1445*) to think about, to think through and through, in and out (RWP). Gen. abs., "as he was contemplating...." **ζητοῦντές** pres. act. part. ζητέω (# *2426*) to seek. Circum. or adj. part. ◆ **20 ἀναστας** aor. act. part. s.v. 13. **κατάβηθι** aor. imp. act. s.v. 11. **πορεύου** pres. imp. mid. (dep.) πορεύομαι (# *4513*) to go. Pres. imp. occurs w. a vb. of motion (VANT, 341-42). **διακρινόμενος** pres. mid. (dep.) part. διακρίνομαι (# *1359*) to question, to doubt. Part. of manner, telling how he is to go, that is, w. which attitude he is to go. **ἀπέσταλκα** perf. ind. act. s.v. 8. ◆ **21 καταβάς** aor. act. part. (circum.) s.v. 11. **ζητεῖτε** pres. ind. act. s.v. 19. **πάρεστε** pres. ind. act. πάρειμι (# *4205*) to be present. "What is the reason for which you are here?" ◆ **22 μαρτυρούμενος** pres. pass. part. (adj.) μαρτυρέω (# *3455*) to give witness. For the pass., s. 6:3. **ἐχρηματίσθη** aor. ind. pass. (dep.) χρηματίζομαι (# *5976*) to do business, to consult an oracle, to instruct, to give a divine warning, to make known a divine revelation, to make known God's message (Bruce; RWP; MM; NDIEC, 4:176; LN, 1:339; TDNT; GELTS, 519). **μεταπέμψασθαι** aor. mid. (dep.) inf. μεταπέμπω

(# 3569) to send after, to send for someone. Inf. gives the content of the divine message. ἀκοῦσαι aor. act. inf. ἀκούω (# 201) to hear, to hear and obey. ◆ 23 εἰσκαλεσάμενος aor. mid. (dep.) part. (temp.) εἰσκαλέομαι (# 1657) to call in, to invite in. ἐξένισεν aor. ind. act. s.v. 6. ἀναστας aor. act. part. (circum.) s.v. 13. ἐξῆλθεν aor. ind. act. ἐξέρχομαι (# 2002) to go out, to depart. συνῆλθον aor. ind. act. συνέρχομαι (# 5302) to accompany, to go w. ◆ 24 προσδοκῶν pres. act. part. προσδοκάω (# 4659) to expect, to await, to direct the mind toward anything (RWP). Part. in a periphrastic construction emphasizing the constant expectancy and waiting, as well as building a backdrop for a punctual event (VA, 457-60). συγκαλεσάμενος aor. mid. (dep.) part. (temp.) συγκαλέομαι (# 5157) to call together, to summon. συγγενής (# 5150) relative. This may be a hint that Cornelius was retired. ἀναγκαῖος (# 338) intimate, familiar. The most intimate friend, close enough to be like blood relations; one who is explicitly trusted (TLNT, 1:98-99; Barrett; NDIEC, 1:132-33). ◆ 25 ἐγένετο aor. ind. mid. (dep.) s.v. 10. For the construction s. 9:3. εἰσελθεῖν aor. act. inf. s.v. 3. The construction of the inf. w. the gen. of the art. is probably a Semitic influence and supposes some futurity: "it happened, when Peter was about to go in" (BG, 133; RG, 1067). συναντήσας aor. act. part. (temp.) συναντάω (# 5267) to meet, w. dat. πεσών aor. act. part. πίπτω (# 4406) to fall. Part. of manner. προσεκύνησεν aor. ind. act. προσκυνέω to worship. ◆ 26 ἤγειρεν aor. ind. act. ἐγείρω (# 1586) to raise up. ἀνάστηθι aor. imp. act. s.v. 13.   ◆ 27 συνομιλῶν pres. act. part. (temp.) συνομιλέω (# 5326) to talk w. συνεληλυθότας perf. act. part. συνέρχομαι (# 5302) to come together, to gather.   ◆ 28 ἔφη impf./aor. ind. act. φημί (# 5774) to say, to speak (VA, 441-47). ἐπίστασθε pres. ind. pass. (dep.) ἐπίσταμαι (# 2179) to understand, to be acquainted w. (BAGD). ὡς (# 6055) as, that, used to introduce an obj. cl. ἀθέμιτος (# 116) unlawful, contrary to the divinely constituted order of things, breaking a taboo. It denotes profanity (LC). κολλᾶσθαι pres. mid. inf. καλλάω (# 3140) to join, to keep company w. someone. Habitual pres. Epex. inf. explaining what is not lawful. προσέρχεσθαι pres. mid. (dep.) inf. προσέρχομαι (# 4665) to go to. Epex. inf. ἀλλόφυλος (# 260) of another tribe; one that is not a Jew. Not every intercourse w. Gentiles was absolutely prohibited, but what rendered a Jew ceremonially unclean was, such as entering a Gentile house or handling articles belonging to Gentiles (Bruce; SB, 4, ii:353-414; Barrett). κἀμοί = καὶ ἐμοί but to me (emphatic)." For the adverbial use of the particle s. BG, 153. ἔδειξεν aor. ind. act. δείκνυμι (# 1259) to show. λέγειν pres. act. inf. λέγω (# 3306) to say, to call. Inf. as obj. of the vb. ἔδειξεν. ◆ 29 ἀναντιρρήτως (# 395) adv. not speaking back, without raising any objection. ἦλθον aor. ind. act. ἔρχομαι (# 2262) to come, to go. μεταπεμ-

φθείς aor. pass. part. (temp.) s.v. 22. πυνθάνομαι pres. ind. mid. (dep.) s.v. 18. τίνι λόγῳ (# 5516; 3364) for what reason (RWP). μετεπέμψασθε aor. ind. mid. (dep.) s.v. 22. ◆ 30 ἔφη impf./aor. ind. act. s.v. 28. ἤμην impf. ind. mid. (dep.) εἰμί (# 1639) Used w. the part. in a periphrastic construction. τὴν ἐνάτην (# 1888) the ninth (hour); acc. of time, indicating either "all the ninth hour" (RWP) or "at what time?" Or it may be a cognate acc., meaning "the ninth-hour prayer" (IBG, 34). προσευχόμενος pres. mid. (dep.) part. s.v. 9. ἔστη aor. ind. act. ἵστημι (# 2705) to stand. ἐσθῆτι dat. sing. ἐσθής (# 2264) clothing. λαμπρός (# 3287) shining, bright. ◆ 31 εἰσηκούσθη aor. ind. pass. εἰσακούω (# 1653) to hear, to attend to (MH, 304). Theol. pass. indicating that God did the action. ἐμνήσθησαν aor. ind. pass. μιμνήσκω (# 3630) to remember. ◆ 32 πέμψον aor. imp. act. s.v. 5. μετακάλεσαι aor. imp. mid. (dep.) μετακαλέομαι (# 3559) to call to oneself, to summon. ◆ 33 ἐξαυτῆς (# 1994) at once. ἔπεμψα aor. ind. act. s.v. 5. καλῶς (# 2822) well. Used w. the aor. mid. part. παραγενόμενος as a means of expressing a polite request: "please do so and so," "You did well to come," "You were so kind to come" (Bruce; Barrett; MM). ἐποίησας aor. ind. act. ποιέω (# 4472) to do. πάρεσμεν pres. ind. act. s.v. 21. ἀκοῦσαι aor. act. inf. s.v. 22. Inf. of purp. προστεταγμένα perf. pass. part. (adj.) προστάσσω (# 4705) to command. Perf. indicates the abiding state. Cornelius is a military man and he employs a military term (RWP). ◆ 34 ἀνοίξας aor. act. part. s.v. 11. Pleonastic or temp. part. καταλαμβάνομαι pres. ind. mid. (dep.) καταλαμβάνω (# 2898) to grasp w. the mind, to perceive. προσωπολήμπτης (# 4720) lit., acceptor of faces, or persons; to have favorites, one who shows partiality (LC; BAGD). ◆ 35 ἐργαζόμενος pres. mid. (dep.) part. ἐργάζομαι (# 2237) to work, to do. To work righteousness is used in its widest sense but may denote almsgiving (Bruce). It is not that righteousness is itself acceptable, but in the Jewish tradition it is that which leads to acceptability (MRP, 132; Barrett; Schille). Part. as subst. δεκτός (# 1283) acceptable, w. dat. ◆ 36 ἀπέστειλεν aor. ind. act. s.v. 8. Though the v. is difficult to translate the sense is clear; God sent to the children of Israel the good news of peace through Jesus Christ (Barrett). εὐαγγελιζόμενος pres. mid. (dep.) part. εὐαγγελίζω (# 2294) to proclaim good news (TDNT; TLNT; NIDNNT). Circum. part. or part. of manner explaining how God sent His word. οὗτος (# 4047) nom. masc. sing. this one; emphatic, "He, yes He, is Lord of all" (Barrett). ◆ 37 οἴδατε perf. ind. act. οἶδα (# 3857) to know. Def. perf. w. pres. meaning. γενόμενον aor. mid. (dep.) part. (adj.) γίνομαι (# 1181) to become, to happen, to take place. ἀρξάμενος aor. mid. (dep.) part. (adj.) ἄρχομαι (# 806) to begin. ἐκήρυξεν aor. ind. act. κηρύσσω (# 3062) to proclaim, to preach. ◆ 38 ὡς (# 6055) how; perhaps a translation of the Aramaic rel.

pron. ד, or of Heb. שׁ or אֲשֶׁר in a resumptive pron. construction (SA, 116-18; Barrett). ἔχρισεν aor. ind. act. χρίω (# 5987) to anoint (TDNT; NIDNTT; EDNT). διῆλθεν aor. ind. act. διέρχομαι (# 1451) to pass through, to go about from place to place. Const. aor. summing up the series of acts He did time after time (MT, 72; BD, 171). εὐεργετῶν pres. act. part. εὐεργετέω (# 2308) to do well, to do good or beneficial deeds. Possibly w. reference to the royal title of Hellenistic kings (LC; DC, I, 34; NDIEC, 1:63-64; 7:233-41). Part. of manner, telling how he went about, that is, what he did. ἰώμενος pres. mid. (dep.) part. ἰάομαι (# 2615) to heal. Both pres. parts. indicate His habitual action. καταδυναστευομένους pres. pass. part. καταδυναστεύω (# 2872) to oppress, to exploit, to dominate someone (BAGD). Adj. part. as subst. ◆ **39** ἐποίησεν aor. ind. act. ποιέω (# 4472) to do. ἀνεῖλαν aor. ind. act. ἀναιρέω (# 359) to kill. κρεμάσαντες aor. act. part. κρεμάννυμι (# 3203) to hang. ξύλον (# 3833) wood (J.M. Baumgarten, "Does TLH in the Temple Scroll Refer to Crucifixion?" *JBL* 91 [1972]: 472-481). Seneca speaks of "the accursed tree" (Seneca; *Epistle* 101.14; DTM, 1:947; s. 5:30). Part. of means explaining by what means they killed Him. ◆ **40** τοῦτον acc. sing. τοῦτο (# 4047) this one! emphatic, "this very One!" ἤγειρεν aor. ind. act. ἐγείρω (# 1586) to raise. ἔδωκεν aor. ind. act. δίδωμι (# 1443) to give; here, to make, w. inf. In this sense it seems to be a Semitism or a type of septuagintalism (LC; SA, 64-65). ἐμφανῆς (# 1871) visible. γενέσθαι aor. mid. (dep.) inf. s.v. 4. Inf. as obj. of the vb. ◆ **41** προκεχειροτονημένοις perf. pass. part. (adj.) προχειροτονέω (# 4742) to choose or designate by hand, to choose beforehand (RWP). They were previously hand-picked. συνεφάγομεν aor. ind. act. συνεσθίω (# 5303) to eat w. someone. συνεπίομεν aor. ind. act. συμπίνω (# 5228) to drink w. someone. ἀναστῆναι aor. act. inf. s.v. 13. Inf. w. prep. μετά (# 3552) to express time ("after He arose"). ◆ **42** παρήγγειλεν aor. ind. act. παραγγέλλω (# 4133) to command, to charge. κηρύξαι aor. act. inf. s.v. 37. Inf. in indir. speech, giving the content of the command. διαμαρτύρασθαι aor. mid. (dep.) inf. διαμαρτύρομαι (# 1371) to witness, to testify to. (s. 2:40). ὡρισμένος perf. pass. part. (adj.) ὁρίζω (# 3988) to mark out the boundary, to ordain, to designate, to appoint. ζώντων pres. act. part. ζάω (# 2409) to live. Part. as subst. ◆ **43** λαβεῖν aor. act. inf. λαμβάνω (# 3284) to receive. Inf. in indir. speech. πιστεύοντα pres. act. part. πιστεύω (# 4409) to believe. Adj. part. in acc. as subject of the inf. ◆ **44** λαλοῦντος pres. act. part. (temp.) λαλέω (# 3281) to speak. Gen. abs., "as he was speaking." This happened before he had finished what he meant to say (Alex). ἐπέπεσεν aor. ind. act. ἐπιπίπτω (# 2158) to fall upon. ἀκούοντας aor. act. part. s.v. 22. Adj. part. as subst. ◆ **45** ἐξέστησαν aor. ind. act. ἐξίστημι (# 2014) to be beside oneself, to be out of one's senses, to be amazed (BAGD). The great amazement

among the believing Jews was evidently because the Jews felt that God's presence was only in the Land of Israel or, when outside the Land, only among the Israelites (SB, 2:705). συνῆλθαν aor. ind. act. s.v. 23. ἐκκέχυται perf. ind. pass. ἐκχέω (# 1772) to pour out. Perf. indicates the continuing results. ◆ **46** ἤκουον impf. ind. act. s.v. 22., w. obj. in gen. λαλούντων pres. act. part. s.v. 8. Adj. or temp. part: "as they were speaking...." μεγαλυνόντων pres. act. part. μεγαλύνω (# 3486) to magnify, to praise. Adj. temp. or part., "As they were magnifying...." ἀπεκρίθη aor. ind. pass. (dep.) ἀποκρίνομαι (# 646) to answer. ◆ **47** μήτι (# 3614) used in a question expecting a neg. answer, "no one is able to hinder..., are they?" κωλῦσαι aor. act. inf. κωλύω (# 3266) to hinder, to forbid. βαπτισθῆναι aor. pass. inf. βαπτίζω (# 966) to baptize. Inf. after a vb. of hindering or forbidding (BD, 206-7). ἔλαβον aor. ind. act. s.v. 43. The Gentiles had received the baptism of the Spirit just as the Jews had at Pentecost. ◆ **48** προσέταξεν aor. ind. act. προστάσσω (# 4705) to give an order, to order. βαπτισθῆναι aor. pass. inf. s.v. 47. Inf. in indir. speech giving the content of the order. ἠρώτησαν aor. ind. act. ἐρωτάω (# 2263) to ask, to request. ἐπιμεῖναι aor. act. inf. ἐπιμένω (# 2152) to remain. Inf. in indir. speech giving the content of the request. ἡμέρας acc. pl. ἡμέρα (# 2465) day. Acc. of time ("for some days").

Acts 11

◆ **1** ἤκουσαν aor. ind. act. ἀκούω (# 201) to hear. ὄντες pres. act. part. (adj.) εἰμί (# 1639) to be. ἐδέξαντο aor. ind. mid. (dep.) δέχομαι (# 1312) to receive, to welcome. ◆ **2** ἀνέβη aor. ind. act. ἀναβαίνω (# 326) to go up. διεκρίνοντο impf. ind. mid. (dep.) διακρίνομαι (# 1359) to take issue, to take sides against, to dispute w. someone (RWP; Barrett). For the force of the prep. compound indicating to and fro, s. MH, 302. Incep. impf., "They began to debate." οἱ ἐκ περιτομῆς (# 1666; 4364) The ones of circumcision, evidently referring to Jewish believers (Longenecker, 397). ◆ **3** λέγοντες pres. act. part. λέγω (# 3306) to say. Pleonastic part. ὅτι (# 4022) = quotation marks, introduces a dir. quotation, or has the meaning "Why?" (Barrett). εἰσῆλθες aor. ind. act. εἰσέρχομαι (# 1656) to go into. ἔχοντας pres. act. part. (adj.) ἔχω (# 2400) to have, to be. συνέφαγες aor. ind. act. συνεσθίω (# 5303) to eat w. someone, w. dat. ◆ **4** ἀρξάμενος aor. mid. (dep.) part. (circum.) ἄρχομαι (# 806) to begin. Not pleonastic, but graphically showing how Peter began at the beginning and gave the full story (RWP). ἐξετίθετο impf. ind. mid. ἐκτίθημι (# 1758) to set forth, to explain, to provide additional information, a deliberate and detailed narrative (RWP; LN, 1:406). καθεξῆς (# 2759) in order, in succession. ◆ **5** ἤμην impf. ind. mid., s.v. 1. προσευχόμενος pres. mid. (dep.) part. προσεύχομαι (# 4667) to pray. Periphrastic part. **εἶδον** aor. ind. act. ὁράω (# *3972*) to see. **ἐκστάσει** dat. sing. ἔκστασις (# *1749*) trance (s. 10:10). **καταβαῖνον** pres. act. part. (adj.) καταβαίνω (# *2849*) to go down, to come down. **ὀθόνη** (# *3855*) a sheet made of fine linen. **ἀρχαῖς** corner s. 10:11. **καθιεμένην** pres. pass. part. (adj.) καθίημι (# *2768*) to let down. **ἦλθεν** aor. ind. act. ἔρχομαι (# *2262*) to come. ◆ **6 ἀτενίσας** aor. act. part. (temp.) ἀτενίζω (# *867*) to gaze. "As I was gazing at it...." **κατενόουν** impf. ind. act. κατανοέω (# *2917*) to put the mind down, to understand, to take notice of. **εἶδον** aor. ind. act. s.v. 5. **τετράπους** (# *5488*) four-footed. **θηρίον** (# *2563*) wild animal **ἑρπετόν** (# *2260*) reptile. ◆ **7 ἤκουσα** aor. ind. act. s.v. 1. **ἀναστάς** aor. act. part. ἀνίστημι (# *482*) to rise up, to get up. Circum. part. w. idea of an imp. **θῦσον** aor. imp. act. θύω (# *2604*) to slay (s. 10:13). **φάγε** aor. imp. act. ἐσθίω (# *2266*) to eat. ◆ **8 μηδαμῶς** (# *3592*) not at all. **εἰσῆλθεν** aor. ind. act. s.v. 3. ◆ **9 ἀπεκρίθη** aor. ind. pass. (dep.) ἀποκρίνομαι (# *646*) to answer. **ἐκαθάρισεν** aor. ind. act. καθαρίζω (# *2751*) to cleanse. **κοίνου** pres. imp. mid. κοινόω (# *3124*) to make common; mid. to consider common (s. 10:15). Pres. imp. w. neg. **μή** (# *3590*) is a call to stop an action in progress, or it forbids a habitual attitude. ◆ **10 ἐγένετο** aor. ind. mid. (dep.) γίνομαι (# *1181*) to become, to be, to happen. **ἀνεσπάθη** aor. ind. pass. ἀνασπάω (# *413*) to pull up. ◆ **11 ἐπέστησαν** aor. ind. act. ἐφίστημι (# *2392*) to come upon and stand by. **ἦμεν** impf. ind. act. εἰμί (# *1639*) to be. **ἀπεσταλμένοι** perf. pass. part. (adj.) ἀποστέλλω (# *690*) to send. ◆ **12 εἶπεν** aor. ind. act. λέγω (# *3306*) to say. **συνελθεῖν** aor. act. inf. συνέρχομαι (# *5302*) to go w., to accompany. Inf. in indir. speech. **διακρίναντα** aor. act. part. διακρίνω (# *1359*) to make a distinction; here, possibly w. the meaning "without hesitation" (LC). **ἦλθον** aor. ind. act. s.v. 5. **εἰσήλθομεν** aor. ind. act. s.v 3. ◆ **13 ἀπήγγειλεν** aor. ind. act. ἀπαγγέλλω (# *550*) to announce, to report. **εἶδεν** aor. ind. act. s.v. 6. **σταθέντα** aor. pass. part. (adj.) ἵστημι (# *2705*) pass. to stand. **εἰπόντα** aor. act. part. s.v. 12. **ἀπόστειλον** aor. imp. act. s.v. 11. **μετάπεμψαι** aor. imp. mid. μεταπέμπω (# *3569*) to send for. **ἐπικαλούμενον** pres. pass. part. ἐπικαλέω (# *2126*) to call; pass. to be called, to be named. ◆ **14 λαλήσει** fut. ind. act. λαλέω (# *3281*) to speak. **σωθήσῃ** fut. ind. pass. σώζω (# *5392*) to rescue, to save (TDNT; EDNT; NIDNTT; TLNT). ◆ **15 ἄρξασθαι** aor. mid. (dep.) inf. ἄρχομαι (# *806*) to begin, w. inf. Inf. w. prep. **ἐν** (# *1877*) to express contemporaneous time: "When I began to speak." **με** sing. acc. 1st. pers. pron. ἐγώ (# *1609*) I. Acc. as subject of the inf. **λαλεῖν** pres. act. inf. s.v. 14. **ἐπέπεσεν** aor. ind. act. ἐπιπίπτω (# *2158*) to fall upon. **ὥσπερ** (# *6061*) just as. This indicates that the baptism of the Spirit on the Jewish believers in Jerusalem had its counterpart for believing Gentiles here. ◆ **16 ἐμνήσθην** aor. ind. pass. (dep.) μιμνήσκομαι (# *3630*) to remember, w. gen. **ἐβάπ-**

τισεν aor. ind. act. βαπτίζω (# *966*) to baptize. **βαπτισθήσεσθε** fut. ind. pass. ◆ **17 ἴσην** acc. sing. ἴσος (# *2698*) same, identical. **δωρεά** (# *1561*) free gift. **ἔδωκεν** aor. ind. act. δίδωμι (# *1443*) to give. **πιστεύσασιν** aor. act. part. (adj.) πιστεύω (# *4409*) to believe. The vb. w. the prep. **ἐπί** (# *2093*) may indicate the turning away from former objects to a new personal object of faith in whom one has confidence (NIDNTT, 3:1212). **ἤμην** impf. ind. mid., s.v. 11. Used in a question which is the apodosis of the cond. sentence: "If..., who was I, that I was able to hinder God?" (RWP; Barrett). **κωλῦσαι** aor. act. inf. κωλύω (# *3266*) to forbid. Epex. inf. explaining the adj. **δυνατός** (# *1543*). ◆ **18 ἀκούσαντες** aor. act. part. (temp.) s.v. 1. **ἡσύχασαν** aor. ind. act. ἡσυχάζω (# *2483*) to be silent. Ingressive aor., "they became silent." **ἐδόξασαν** aor. ind. act. δοξάζω (# *1519*) to glorify, to cause to have a good opinion of someone, to praise (TLNT, 1:376-78). Their opposition ceased and their praise began (Bruce). **ἔδωκεν** aor. ind. act. s.v. 17. ◆ **19 διασπαρέντες** aor. pass. part. διασπείρω (# *1401*) to scatter. Adj. part. as subst. **ἀπό** is causal: "on account of," "because of" (Gen. 9:11 LXX; GELTS, 48; NIDNTT, 3:1180). **γενομένης** aor. mid. (dep.) part. s.v. 10. **διῆλθον** aor. ind. act. διέρχομαι (# *1451*) to pass through, to go about. **Φοινίκης** (# *5834*) Phoenicia; not the provincial name, but denoting the narrow coastal plain between Lebanon and the Mediterranean (Barrett). **Ἀντιοχείας** (# *522*) Antioch on the Orontes. This very rich and great city, located 15 miles inland on the left bank of the Orontes River, ranking third in the Roman Empire (behind Rome & Alexandria) (Jos., *JW*, 3:29), was the capital of Syria. It had a large Jewish population (Jos., *JW*, 7:43-45) and was also famous for the suburban resort area, Daphne, which was a symbol in the Roman Empire for Antioch's depravity. Herod the Great paved the main street w. polished marble because of the muddy street and as a protection from the rain, adorned it with a colonnade (Jos., *JW* 1:425; s. also Barrett; OCD, 71, 313; BBC; RAC, 1:461-69; TRE, 3:99-103; ABD, 1:265-69; KP, 1:386; AAT, 170-80). **λαλοῦντες** pers. act. part. (circum.) s.v. 14. ◆ **20 ἐλθόντες** aor. act. part. (temp.) s.v. 5. **ἐλάλουν** impf. ind. act. s.v. 14. Incep. impf., "they began speaking and continued." **Ἑλληνιστής** (# *1821*) a Greek-speaking person. It may refer to Greek-speaking persons who had some contact w. the Jews (Longenecker, 398-400). For the text problem s. TC, 386-89. **εὐαγγελιζόμενοι** pres. mid. (dep.) part. (circum.) εὐαγγελίζομαι (# *2294*) to tell the good news (TDNT; EDNT; IDNTT; TLNT). ◆ **21 ἦν** impf. ind. act. εἰμί (# *1639*). **πιστεύσας** aor. act. part. (adj.) s.v. 17. **ἐπέστρεψεν** aor. ind. act. ἐπιστρέφω (# *2188*) to turn to (TDNT; EDNT). ◆ **22 ἠκούσθη** aor. ind. pass. s.v. 1. **οὔσης** pres. act. part. (adj.) gen. fem. sing. εἰμί s.v. 21. **ἐξαπέστειλαν** aor. ind. act. ἐξαποστέλλω (# *1990*) to send out, to dispatch, to send out as an authoritative representative (TDNT). **διελθεῖν** aor. act. inf. s.v. 19. Epex. inf., explaining the sending. ◆ **23 παραγενόμενος** aor. mid. (dep.) part. (temp.) παραγίνομαι (# 4134) to arrive. **ἰδών** aor. act. part. (temp.) ὁράω (# 3972) to see. **ἐχάρη** aor. ind. pass. χαίρω (# 5897) to be glad, to rejoice. **παρεκάλει** impf. ind. act. παρακαλέω (# 4151) to exhort, to encourage. Impf. pictures the continual encouraging. **πρόθεσις** (# 4606) purpose; w. purpose of heart, that is, w. determination (Bruce; LC). **προσμένειν** pres. act. inf. προσμένω (# 4693) to remain, to stay w., to continue (BAGD). ◆ **24 προσετέθη** aor. ind. pass. προστίθημι (# 4707) to add to. Theological pass., indicating that God did the action. ◆ **25 ἐξῆλθεν** aor. ind. act. ἐξέρχομαι (# 2002) to go out. **ἀναζητῆσαι** aor. act. inf. ἀναζητέω (# 349) to search for. The prep. compound means to seek up and down, back and forth, to make a thorough search till success comes (RWP). Inf. of purp. ◆ **26 εὑρών** aor. act. part. (temp.) εὑρίσκω (# 2351) to find. **ἤγαγεν** aor. ind. act. ἄγω (# 72) to lead, to bring. **ἐγένετο** aor. ind. mid. (dep.) s.v. 10. **ἐνιαυτὸν ὅλον** for a whole year; acc. of time. **συναχθῆναι** aor. pass. inf. συνάγω (# 5251) to gather together, to be taken in as a guest (LC). Inf. as subject the vb. ἐγένετο (RWP). **διδάξαι** aor. act. inf. διδάσκω (# 1438) to teach, to give instruction. Const., or complexive aor. giving a summary of the deeds (BD, 171). Inf. as subject. **χρηματίσαι** aor. act. inf. χρηματίζω (# 5976) to bear a name, to be called, to be named, to bear a title (Jos., *JW*, 2:488; BAGD; TWNT). Inf. as subject. **Χριστιανός** (# 5985) Christian, adherents of the Anointed One (Barrett; EDNT; TDNT; Haenchen; BC, 5:383-86). ◆ **27 κατῆλθον** aor. ind. act. κατέρχομαι (# 2982) to come down. ◆ **28 ἀναστάς** aor. act. part. (circum.) s.v. 7. **ἐσήμανεν** impf. ind. act. σημαίνω (# 4955) to signify, to make known. **λιμόν** acc. sing. λιμός (# 3350) famine. Famine in the ancient world had to do not only with a shortage of food, but also w. the inability to transport it, as well as appealing to those w. money, like some of Antioch's citizens (s. Jos., *JW*, 7:42-45), to provide help (FAP, 112-19; Bruce W. Winter, "Acts and Food Shortages," BAFCS, 2:72-76). Acc. as subject of the inf. **μέλλειν** pres. act. inf. μέλλω (# 3516) to be about to. Inf. as obj. of vb. ἐσήμανεν. **ἔσεσθαι** fut. mid. (dep.) inf. εἰμί (# 1639) to be. Used w. μέλλω to express the fut. (MKG, 308). **οἰκουμένη** (# 3876) world, inhabited earth. For local and widespread famines in that time s. K.S. Gapp, "The Universal Famine under Claudius," *HTR* 28 (1935): 258-65; FAP, 112-21; BASHH, 164-65; Colin J. Hemer, "Observations on Pauline Chronology," PSEB, 5-6; B.W. Winter, BAFCS, 2:59-78. **ἐγένετο** aor. ind. mid. (dep.) s.v. 10. **ἐπὶ Κλαυδίου** at the time of Claudius. Possibly around A.D. 41/42 (FAP, 121; BC, 5:452-55). For Claudius s. Suetonius, "The Deified Claudius," *The Lives of the Caesars*, V.; Barrett. ◆ **29 εὐπορεῖτο** impf. ind. mid. εὐπορέω (# 2344) to be well off, to have

plenty; here "according to his financial ability" (BAGD). **ὥρισαν** aor. ind. act. ὁρίζω (# 3988) to fix a boundary, to determine, to appoint; "they arranged." Perhaps each one set aside a fixed sum out of his property or income as a contribution to the fund (Bruce). **πέμψαι** aor. act. inf. πέμπω (# 4287) to send. Inf. as dir. obj. ◆ **30 ἐποίησαν** aor. ind. act. ποιέω (# 4472) to do. **ἀποστείλαντες** aor. act. part. s.v. 11. Part. explaining πέμψαι.

Acts 12

◆ **1 κατ᾽ ἐκεῖνον δὲ τὸν καιρόν** "And at that time." This was probably at the beginning of Herod Agrippa's rule, ca. A.D. 41 or early 42 (FAP, 104-8; BBC; ABD 1:98-100). **ἐπέβαλεν** aor. ind. act. ἐπιβάλλω (# 2095) to cast upon, to lay hands on, to seize. **Ἡρῴδης** Herod, that is, Herod Agrippa I, (grandson of Herod the Great) who had grown up in Rome, was a friend of Gaius & Claudius, was noted for spending huge sums of money, and ruled over Palestine for three years (s. TJ, 57-63; A; BAFCS, 4:19; s.v. 23). **κακῶσαι** aor. act. inf. κακόω (# 2808) to afflict, to do harm to. For vbs. w. this ending having a factitive or instr. meaning s. MH, 394f. In addition to political motives for Agrippa's persecution of the church, there may have also been his own personal aspirations to be recognized as a messianic ruler (FAP, 109-10; A, 119-24). Inf. of purp. ◆ **2 ἀνεῖλεν** aor. ind. act. ἀναιρέω (# 359) to kill. **μαχαίρη** dat. sing. μάχαιρα (# 3479) sword. Instr. dat. For execution w. the sword at that time, which may indicate that the charge was political, s. Barrett; Haenchen; SB, 2:706; Acts 7:58. ◆ **3 ἰδών** aor. act. part. (temp.) ὁράω (# 3972) to see. **ἀρεστός** (# 744) pleasing, verbal adj., w. dat. (RWP). **προσέθετο** aor. ind. mid. (dep.) προστίθημι (# 4707) to add to, to proceed, w. inf. A Semitic construction common in OT (Barrett; Bruce; MH, 445). **συλλαβεῖν** aor. act. inf. συλλαμβάνω (# 5197) to arrest. **αἱ ἡμέραι τῶν ἀζύμων** days of unleavened bread. For the Feast of Unleavened Bread s. IDB, 3:663f; TDNT; M, Pesahim; WZZT, 207-36. ◆ **4 πιάσας** aor. act. part. (temp.) πιάζω (# 4389) to seize, to catch. **ἔθετο** aor. ind. mid. τίθημι (# 5502) to place. Mid. expresses the fact that Herod Agrippa I was acting in accordance w. his own intended purp. (Barrett). The imprisonment was very probably in the Fortress Antonia, rebuilt by Herod the Great and located at the northwest corner of the Temple (TJ, 24; ANT, 156-61; AJA, 160-66; Jos., *JW*, 1:401, 5:238-46). **παραδούς** aor. act. part. παραδίδωμι (# 4140) to deliver over. **τέσσαρσιν** dat. pl. τέσσαρες (# 5475) four (BAGD). **τετράδιον** (# 5482) quaterion, a company of four soldiers for each of the four night watches of three hours (LC; Barrett; BBC). **φυλάσσειν** pres. act. inf. φυλάσσω (# 5875) to guard, to watch. Inf. of purpose. Pres. indicates that they were to continually guard Peter. **βουλόμενος** pres. mid. (dep.) part. (circum.) βούλομαι (# 1089) to plan, to will, w. inf. **ἀναγαγεῖν** aor. act. inf. ἀνάγω (# 343) to lead up. Peter was in the inner prison or lower ward and so would be led up (RWP). The idea was to bring him up for public execution (Barrett). ◆ **5 μὲν … δέ** affirmative particle used correlatively: on the one hand … on the other hand (BAGD). **ἐτηρεῖτο** impf. ind. pass. τηρέω (# 5498) to guard, to watch. Impf. pictures the continual action. **ἦν** impf. ind. act. εἰμί (# 1639) used w. the pres. part. to form a periphrastic construction. **ἐκτενῶς** (# 1757) adv. earnestly (LC). The word combines the ideas of perseverance ("without letting up") and intensity ("w. fervor, urgently") and is used of the great cries of prayer (s. Luke 22:44) (TLNT, 1:457-61, w. examples!). **γινομένη** pres. mid. (dep.) (for pass. s. VA, 482) part. γίνομαι (# 1181) to become, to be, to happen. Periphrastic part. ◆ **6 ἤμελλεν** impf. ind. act. μέλλω (# 3516) to be about to. Impf. used w. the inf. to express intention reckoned from a moment in the past (MKG, 307). **προαγαγεῖν** aor. act. inf. προάγω (# 4575) to lead out. In the language of the law court, to bring before (BAGD). **ἦν** impf. ind. act. s.v. 5. Impf. w. the pres. part. to form a periphrastic construction. **κοιμώμενος** pres. pass. part. κοιμάω (# 3121) to sleep. **μεταξύ** (# 3568) between. **δεδεμένος** perf. pass. part. δέω (# 1313) to bind. Perf. indicates the state or condition. **ἁλύσεσιν** dat. pl. ἅλυσις (# 268) chain. Instr. dat. **ἐτή-ρουν** impf. ind. act. τηρέω to watch, to guard. ◆ **7 ἐπέ-στη** aor. ind. act. ἐφίστημι (# 2392) to stand by, to suddenly come on the scene (BAGD). **ἔλαμψεν** aor. ind. act. λάμπω (# 3290) to shine. **οἴκημα** (# 3862) room; euphemism for prison (LC). **πατάξας** aor. act. part. (temp.) πατάσσω (# 4250) to strike, to hit. **πλευρά** (# 4433) side. **ἤγειρεν** aor. ind. act. ἐγείρω (# 1586) to wake up someone. **ἀνάστα** aor. imp. act. ἀνίστημι (# 482) to rise up, to get up. Aor. imp. calls for a specific action w. a note of urgency. **τά-χει** dat. sing. τάχος (# 5443) hurry, quickness. Used w. prep. adverbially: "in a hurry," "quickly" (IBG, 78). **ἐξ-έπεσαν** aor. ind. act. ἐκπίπτω (# 1738) to fall off. There were magic spells to cause chains to fall off or to open doors (CIC, 92; GMP, 159-60, 277). ◆ **8 εἶπεν** aor. ind. act. λέγω (# 3306) to say. **ζῶσαι** aor. imp. mid. ζώννυμι (# 2439) to gird oneself, to bind the tunic w. a wide belt. During the night the long-flowing undergarment was loosened, then fastened up by day, so as not to impede movements (EGT). **ὑπόδησαι** aor. imp. mid. ὑποδέω (# 5686) to bind under, to tie on sandals. **ἐποίησεν** aor. ind. act. ποιέω (# 4472) to do. **περιβαλοῦ** aor. imp. mid. περιβάλλω (# 4314) to throw about (oneself), to put on. **ἀκολούθει** pres. imp. act. ἀκολουθέω (# 199) to follow, w. dat. The aor. imps. call for specific acts; the pres. here is used w. a vb. of motion describing the maze-like journey that followed; "keep behind me" (Barrett; VANT, 345-46). ◆ **9 ἐξελθών** aor. act. part.

ἐξέρχομαι (# 2002) to go out. Circum. or temp. part. **ἠκολούθει** impf. ind. act. s.v. 8. Incep. impf.: "he began to follow." **ᾔδει** plperf. ind. act. of def. perf. οἶδα (# 3857) to know. Plperf. used here as impf. **γινόμενον** pres. mid. (dep.) part. s.v. 5. Adj. part. as subst. **ἐδόκει** impf. ind. act. δοκέω (# 1506) to suppose, to think. **ὅρα-μα** acc. sing. vision. **βλέπειν** pres. act. inf. βλέπω (# 1063) to see. Inf. as obj. giving an indir. assertion (RWP). ◆ **10 διελθόντες** aor. act. part. (temp.) διέρχομαι (# 1451) to go through. **ἦλθαν** aor. ind. act. ἔρχομαι (# 2262) to go, to come. **πύλη** (# 4783) gate. **σιδηρᾶν** acc. sing. σιδηροῦς (# 4969) iron. **φέρουσαν** pres. act. part. (adj.) acc. fem. sing. φέρω (# 5770) to carry, to lead. **αὐ-τόματος** (# 897) automatically, of its own accord, often indicating something supernatural (LC; TLNT, 1:231-34; Josh. 6:5; GELTS, 71). **ἠνοίγη** aor. ind. pass. ἀνοίγω (# 487) to open. A type of theological pass. (TLNT, 1:231). **ἐξελθόντες** aor. act. part. (temp.) s.v. 9. **προῆλθον** aor. ind. act. προέρχομαι (# 4601) to go forward, to proceed; here, to go one block farther (BAGD). **ῥύμην** acc. sing. ῥύμη (# 4860) street or alley. They went along the main street until its intersection (LC). Acc. of extent, of space (BD, 88). **ἀπέστη** aor. ind. act. ἀφίστημι (# 923) to go away, to depart (note v. 7 ἐφίστημι). ◆ **11 γενόμενος** aor. mid. (dep.) part. (temp.) s.v. 5. W. **ἐν ἑαυτῷ** (# 1877; 1571) ("coming to himself"). **εἶπεν** aor. ind. act. λέγω (# 3306) to say. **οἶδα** (# 3857) perf. ind. act. def. perf. w. pres. meaning, to know. **ἐξαπέστειλεν** aor. ind. act. ἐξ-αποστέλλω (# 1990) to send out. **ἐξείλατο** aor. ind. mid. ἐξαιρέω (# 1975) to take out of; mid. to rescue, to take away, to liberate and place the one delivered in the hands of the agent of deliverance (TLNT, 2:14-17). **προσδοκία** (# 4660) expectation. ◆ **12 συνιδών** aor. act. part. (temp.) συνοράω (# 5328) to see together, to see clearly, to be aware of, to perceive, "having realized the position" (Bruce; NTNT, 120). For the perfective force of the prep. compound s. MH, 325. **ἦλθεν** aor. ind. act. s.v. 10. **ἐπικαλουμένου** pres. pass. part. ἐπικαλέω (# 2126) to call, to be called, to be named. **οὗ** (# 4005) where. **ἦσαν** impf. ind. act. s.v. 5. **ἱκανός** (# 2653) considerable, many. **συνηθροισμένοι** perf. pass. part. συναθροίζω (# 5255) to bring together; pass. to be gathered, to meet. **προσευχόμενοι** pres. mid. (dep.) part. προσεύχομαι (# 4667) to pray. Part. w. **ἦσαν** to form the periphrastic impf. The praying apparently had been going on all night (RWP). ◆ **13 κρούσαντος** aor. act. part. (temp.) κρούω (# 3218) to knock. Gen. abs. **πυλών** (# 4784) gateway, entrance. The gate entrance was separated from the living quarters by a courtyard (Haenchen). **προσῆλθεν** aor. ind. act. προσέρχομαι (# 4665) to come to. **ὑπακοῦσαι** aor. act. inf. ὑπακούω to answer the door. Used technically of the doorkeeper, whose duty it is to listen for the signals of those who wish to enter, and to admit them if they are entitled to do so (BAGD). Inf. of purp. ◆ **14 ἐπιγνοῦσα** aor. act.

part. (temp.) nom. fem. sing. ἐπιγινώσκω (# 2105) to recognize. ἤνοιξεν aor. ind. act. s.v. 10. εἰσδραμοῦσα aor. act. part. (circum.) εἰστρέχω (# 1661) to run in. ἀπήγγειλεν aor. ind. act. ἀπαγγέλλω (# 550) to report. ἑστάναι perf. act. inf. ἵστημι (# 2705) to stand. Inf. in indirect discourse (IBG, 153). ◆ 15 μαίνη pres. ind. mid. (dep.) 2nd. pers. sing. μαίνομαι (# 3419) to be mad, to be crazy. For the medical use of the vb. and noun, s. DMTG, 230; MLL, 267; MHW, 145-48. διϊσχυρίζετο impf. ind. mid. (dep.) διϊσχυρίζομαι (# 1462) to insist. An old word of vigorous and confident assertion, originally "to lean upon" (RWP). Used in a papyrus text of a dispute between two parties, one of which affirms a matter confidently (NDIEC, 2:81). ἔχειν pres. act. inf. ἔχω (# 2400) to have, to hold; here, it is, the situation is so (BAGD). Inf. in indirect discourse. ◆ 16 ἐπέμενεν impf. ind. act. ἐπιμένω (# 2152) to remain, to continue. κρούων pres. act. part. s.v. 13. Supplementary part. used to indicate the action that was continued (BD, 213). ἀνοίξαντες aor. act. part. (temp.) s.v. 10. εἶδαν aor ind. act. s.v. 3. ἐξέστησαν aor. ind. act. ἐξίστημι (# 2014) to be amazed, to be beside oneself. ◆ 17 κατασείσας aor. act. part. (temp.) κατασείω (# 2939) to signal or motion to w. the hand. σιγᾶν pres. act. inf. σιγάω (# 4967) to be silent. Epex. inf. explaining what his motioning w. the hand meant. διηγήσατο aor. ind. mid. (dep.) διηγέομαι (# 1455) to relate, to narrate. ἐξήγαγεν aor. ind. act. ἐξάγω (# 1974) to lead out. ἀπαγγείλατε aor. imp. act. s.v. 14. ἐξελθών aor. act. part. (circum.) s.v. 9. ἐπορεύθη aor. ind. pass. (dep.) πορεύομαι (# 4513) to go. ◆ 18 γενομένης aor. mid. (dep.) part. (temp.) s.v. 5. Gen. abs. τάραχος (# 5431) commotion. ἄρα (# 726) therefore, then; inferential particle. ἐγένετο aor. ind. mid. (dep.) s.v. 5. ◆ 19 ἐπιζητήσας aor. act. part. ἐπιζητέω (# 2118) to look for. Concessive part. εὑρών aor. act. part. εὑρίσκω (# 2351) to find. Part. w. καί giving a contrast, "and yet did not find" (BD, 227). ἀνακρίνας aor. act. part. ἀνακρίνω (# 373) to examine, to question thoroughly. ἐκέλευσεν aor. ind. act. κελεύω (# 3027) to command. ἀπαχθῆναι aor. act. pass. inf. ἀπάγω (# 552) to lead away. Perhaps used in the sense of "to arrest," "to lead off to prison"; but the stronger sense, "to lead off to execution," is called for here (Barrett). According to Justinian's Code (Codex Justinianus 9.4.4) a guard who allowed a prisoner to escape became liable to the same penalty as had awaited the prisoner (Bruce; Barrett). Inf. in indir. discourse. κατελθών aor. act. part. (circum.) κατέρχομαι (# 2982) to go down. διέτριβεν impf. ind. act. διατρίβω (# 1417) to remain. ◆ 20 θυμομαχῶν pres. act. part. θυμομαχέω (# 2595) to fight desperately; here "to be furious," "to be exasperated" (Bruce). Part. w. ἦν as periphrastic. ὁμοθυμαδόν (# 3924) together, w. one accord. παρῆσαν impf. ind. act. πάρειμι (# 4205) to be present. πείσαντες aor. act. part. (circum.) πείθω (# 4275) to persuade.

κοιτῶν (# 3131) bedroom; lit., "the one over the bedroom of the king." Used as a title for a highly respected person w. considerable responsibility, who was in charge of the king's bedroom and personal affairs (LC; LN, 1:86); A, 113; Epictetus 4, vii, 1, 19-20). ᾐτοῦντο impf. ind. mid. αἰτέω (# 160) to ask. Incep. impf., "they began to ask for peace." Mid. "to ask for one's self." τρέφεσθαι pres. pass. inf. τρέφω (# 5555) to feed, to support, to provide w. food. The Phoenician cities depended largely on the grain fields of Galilee for their food, and Herod had cut off their supply (Rackham). Inf. w. διά (# 1328) is causal. βασιλικός (# 997) royal, belonging to a king. For adj. ending w. this suffix s. MH, 378. ◆ 21 τακτῇ dat. sing. τακτός (# 5414) set, appointed. Dat. of time. According to Josephus, it was a festival in honor of the emperor (Jos., Ant., 19:343), possibly on the first of August, his birthday (Bruce), or in October 43 at the Caesarean games to honor the emperor (A, 145-46; 109-11). ἐνδυσάμενος aor. mid. part. (temp.) ἐνδύω (# 1907) to put on, to dress. ἐσθής (# 2264) clothing, raiment. According to Josephus, it was an impressive robe made of silver which glittered in the sun as he entered the theater at daybreak (Bruce, ET; BBC; TJ, 61-62; Jos., Ant., 19:344). καθίσας aor. act. part. (temp.) καθίζω (# 2767) to sit down; ingressive aor. to take one's seat. ἐδημηγόρει impf. ind. act. δημηγορέω (# 1319) to make a speech. Incep. impf., "he began to make a speech." ◆ 22 ἐπεφώνει impf. ind. act. ἐπιφωνέω (# 2215) to cry out loudly, to cheer (LC). θεός God; here, "a god." Emphatic by its position. Josephus says the people went on to flatter him by saying, "May you be propitious to us, and if we have hitherto feared you as a man, yet henceforth we agree that you are more than mortal in your being," and, Josephus adds, "the king did not rebuke them nor did he reject their flattery as impious" (Jos., Ant., 19:345-46). ◆ 23 ἐπάταξεν aor. ind. act. πατάσσω (# 4250) to strike, to hit. ἀνθ' ὧν (# 505; 4005) because. ἔδωκεν aor. ind. act. δίδωμι (# 1443) to give. γενόμενος aor. mid. (dep.) part. (circum.) s.v. 5. σκωληκόβρωτος (# 5037) eaten by worms. The word is used of diseased grain (MM). ἐξέψυξεν aor. ind. act. ἐκψύχω (# 1775) to die, to breathe out. A term used by medical writers (MLL, 37). For the life and death of Herod Agrippa I s. Jos., Ant., 18:126-309; 19:1-227, 292-366; HJP 1:442-54; TJ, 57-62; ABD, 1:98-100. ◆ 24 ηὔξανεν impf. ind. act. αὐξάνω (# 889) to grow. Impf., "continued to grow." ἐπληθύνετο impf. ind. pass. πληθύνω (# 4437) to increase. Luke means that the Word of God increased in effectiveness (Barrett). ◆ 25 ὑπέστρεψαν aor. ind. act. ὑποστρέφω (# 5715) to return. πληρώσαντες aor. act. part. (temp.) πληρόω (# 4444) to fill, to fulfill. Perhaps this refers to them taking financial help from the church in Antioch to Jerusalem. συμπαραλαβόντες aor. act. part. (circum.)

συμπαραλαμβάνω (# 5221) to take someone along w. ἐπικληθέντα aor. pass. part. (adj.) s.v. 12.

Acts 13

◆ **1 κατά** (# 2848) w. acc., distributed throughout (RWP). **οὖσαν** pres. act. part. (adj.) acc. fem. sing. εἰμί (# 1639) to be. "The existing church," "the local church" (Barrett, M, 228). **καλούμενος** pres. pass. part. καλέω (# 2813) to call; pass. to be named. **Νίγερ** (# 3769) Lat. black, dark-complexioned (BAGD). **Λούκιος ὁ Κυρηναῖος** Lucius the Cyrenian. Cyrene was the capital city of the North African district of Cyrenaica, which was combined w. Crete in 27 BC as a senatorial province and ruled by a proconsul (BAGD; HJP, 3:61-62, 94; BC, 5:498-95). **σύντροφος** (# 5343) nourished together, brought up together, foster brother, a companion in education, playmate, intimate friend (BS, 310-12; BBC; MM; NDICE, 3:37-39; BAGD; *Josephus and Aseneth* 10:4; 18:8; Jos. *JW*, 1:215). Manean was a close friend of Herod Antipas and was probably brought up w. him in the court of Jerusalem (JTJ, 88; HA, 14; 305-06). ◆ **2 λειτουργούντων** pres. act. part. (temp.) λειτουργέω (# 3310) to serve. Used in classical Gr. to describe the service voluntarily rendered to the state; then it indicated the performing of services which the state required from citizens who were specially qualified by their wisdom or wealth. Later it was used to describe any kind of service. In NT times it was the word for the service that a priest or servant rendered in a temple. Perhaps the service rendered here was that of prayer (NTW, 74-76; TLNT; TDNT). Gen. abs., "while they were continuing to serve." **νηστευόντων** pres. act. part. (temp.) νηστεύω (# 3764) to fast. Gen. abs. **εἶπεν** aor. ind. act. λέγω (# 3306) to say. **ἀφορίσατε** aor. imp. act. ἀφορίζω (# 928) to mark off w. boundary, to separate. **δή** (# 1314) particle, used here to emphasize the imp. (Bruce). **μοι** dat. sing. ἐγώ (# 1609); "for me." Dat. of personal interest, or advantage. **προσκέκλημαι** perf. ind. mid. προσκαλέω (# 4673) to call, to call to one's service (Bruce). Perf. emphasizes that the divine decision was already made before it was revealed (Haenchen). For the omission of the prep. w. the rel. pron. s. NSV, 149. ◆ **3 νηστεύσαντες** aor. act. part. (temp.) s.v. 2. **προσευξάμενοι** aor. mid. (dep.) part. (temp.) προσεύχομαι (# 4667) to pray. **ἐπιθέντες** aor. act. part. ἐπιτίθημι (# 2202) to place upon. The laying on of hands here expressed the fellowship w. the two and the recognition of the divine call (Bruce; SB, 2:647-61; s. 6:6). **ἀπέλυσαν** aor. ind. act. ἀπολύω (# 668) to release, to let go, to send off. ◆ **4 αὐτοί** (# 899) they. The pron. is used here unemphatic (Haenchen; IBG, 121). **ἐκπεμφθέντες** aor. pass. part. (circum.) ἐκπέμπω (# 1734) to send out. **κατῆλθον** aor. ind. act. κατέρχομαι (# 2982) to go down. For the seaport of Antioch, Seleucia, locat-

ed about five miles up the Orontes from the Mediterranean, and perhaps even at that time a Roman naval station s. AAT, 179-80; ZPEB, 5:331-34; ABD, 5:1075-6; RNE, 87-88; 103-4; 257-58; KP, 5.85. **ἀπέπλευσαν** aor. ind. act. ἀποπλέω (# 676) to sail away. For travel in the ancient world, both overland and by ship s. Brian M. Rapske, "Acts, Travel and Shipwreck," BAFCS, 2:1-47. For the island of Cyprus s. AAT, 181-86; ABD, 1:1228-30; Alaana Nobbs, Cyprus," BAFCS, 2:279-89; Thomas W. Davis, "A History of American Archaeology in Cyprus," BA 52 (1989): 163-69; Stuart Swiny, "Prehistoric Cyprus: A Current Perspective," BA 52 (1989): 178-91; Demetrios Michaelides, "The Early Christian Mosaics of Cyprus," BA 52 (1989): 192-202. ◆ **5 γενόμενοι** aor. mid. (dep.) part. (temp.) γίνομαι (# 1181) to become; here in the sense, "to arrive." **κατήγγελλον** impf. ind. act. καταγγέλλω (# 2859) to report, to proclaim. Incep. impf., "they began to proclaim." **εἶχον** impf. ind. act. ἔχω (# 2400) to have. **ὑπηρέτης** (# 5677) assistant, attendant, a helper who willingly submits himself to carrying out the will of the one over him (TDNT; TLNT). Double acc., "they had John as an assistant." ◆ **6 διελθόντες** aor. act. part. (temp.) διέρχομαι (# 1451) to pass through. **εὗρον** aor. ind. act. εὑρίσκω (# 2351) to find. **μάγος** (# 3407) magician (BC, 5:164-88; for the widespread use of magic and magic incantations s. 8:9; Pliny, *NH*, 30:1-28; GMP). **ψευδοπροφήτης** (# 6021) false prophet. ◆ **7 ἀνθύπατος** (# 478) proconsul, one who is head of the government in a senatorial province, that is, the provinces of the Roman people (BAGD; RNE, 31-32). For a discussion of Sergius Paulus and the inscriptions s. BRD, 150-72; AAT, 185-86; Barrett; BASHH, 166-67; esp. FAP, 121-26 and Nobbs, BAFCS, 2:282-89; Bastian Van Elderen, "Some Observations on Paul's First Missionary Journey," AHG, 151-56; BBC; ABD, 5:205-206; for a more neg. view, s. BC, 5:455-59. **συνετός** (# 5305) intelligent, being able to understand and evaluate, insightful (LN, 1:384). **προσκαλεσάμενος** aor. mid. (dep.) part. (circum.) προσκαλέομαι (# 4673) to call to oneself, to summon. **ἐπεζήτησεν** aor. ind. act. ἐπιζητέω (# 2118) to seek, to look for. **ἀκοῦσαι** aor. act. inf. ἀκούω (# 201) to hear. Epex. inf. explaining what he sought. ◆ **8 ἀνθίστατο** impf. ind. mid. ἀνθίστημι (# 468) to stand against, to withstand. Impf. pictures the continual action and may be conative: "he tried to oppose." **Ἐλύμας** (# 1829) Elymas. For the rare and obscure Semitic name s. BASHH, 227-28; Barrett. **μεθερμηνεύεται** pres. ind. pass. μεθερμηνεύω (# 3493) to translate. **ζητῶν** pres. act. part. ζητέω (# 2426) to seek. Part. of manner explaining how he tried to oppose them. **διαστρέψαι** aor. act. inf. διαστρέφω (# 1406) to pervert, to distort, to divert. For the force of the prep. compound, s. MH, 302. Epex. inf. explaining what he sought to do. ◆ **9 ὁ καί** (# 2779) who is also. For this phrase and the use of double names s. BS, 313-17;

Haenchen; SB, 2:711-13; NDIEC, 1:89-96; TLNT, 2:41-43. For the names Saul and Paul s. 7:58; FAP, 126-29; Colin J. Hemer, "The Name of Paul," *TB* 36 (1985): 179-83; NDIEC, 1:94; SB, 2:711-13; DPL, 679-91. It may be that Paul (an upperclass name in the Roman onomasticon) had both names from birth (NDIEC, 1:94). **πλησθείς** aor. pass. part. (adj.) πίμπλημι (# 4398) to fill, w. gen. of content. **ἀτενίσας** aor. act. part. (adj.) ἀτενίζω (# 867) to gaze at someone or something. This is not the evil eye used by the rabbis to inflict punishment (Haenchen; SB, 2:713-15). ◆ **10 δόλου** gen. sing. δόλος (# 1515) deceit, treachery, craft. Properly bait for fish, then any cunning contrivance for deceiving or catching (LS). Gen. of content. **ῥαδιουργία** (# 4816) ease in doing, recklessness, wickedness, unscrupulousness (LN, 1:775). Used in the papyri in the general sense of false pretenses (MM), and in a list of criminal charges w. the meaning "fraud" (NDIEC, 1:59-61). **υἱέ** voc. sing. υἱός (# 5626) son. **ἐχθρέ** voc. sing. ἐαθρός (# 2398) hostile, hated, enemy, one engaged in open and active hostility arising out of hate. **παύσῃ** fut. ind. mid. (dep.), παύομαι (# 4264) to cease, w. part. Volitive fut. slightly imp. w. an implied reproach (Bruce; RG, 847). **διαστρέφων** pres. act. part. s.v. 8. Pres. may be conative, "Will you not cease trying to pervert?" He was making straight roads crooked (Barrett). ◆ **11 ἔσῃ** fut. ind. mid. 2nd. pers. sing. εἰμί (# 1639) to be. **βλέπων** pres. act. part. (adj.) βλέπω (# 1063) to see. **ἔπεσεν** aor. ind. act. πίπτω (# 4406) to fall. **ἀχλύς** (# 944) cloud. Used by medical writers of an inflammation which brings a cloudy appearance into the eye (LC; MLL, 44). **περιάγων** pres. act. part. (circum.) περιάγω (# 4310) to go about. **ἐζήτει** impf. ind. act. ζητέω (# 2426) to seek, to look for. **χειραγωγός** (# 5933) one who leads another by the hand (s. 9:8; 22:11). ◆ **12 ἰδών** aor. act. part. (temp.) ὁράω (# 3972) to see. **γεγονός** perf. act. part. γίνομαι (# 1181) to become, to happen. Part. as subst., "that which happened." **ἐπίστευσεν** aor. ind. act. πιστεύω (# 4409) to believe. **ἐκπλησσόμενος** pres. mid. (dep.) part. (circum.) ἐκπλήσσομαι (# 1742) to be astonished. ◆ **13 ἀναχθέντες** aor. pass. part. (temp.) ἀνάγω (# 343) to lead up; in mid./pass. a nautical t.t., to set sail (BAGD). **ἦλθον** aor. ind. act. ἔρχομαι (# 2262) to come. εἰς Πέργην τῆς Παμφυλίας unto Perga of Pamphylia; that is, "They proceeded to Pamphylia, to the special point Perga" (PTR, 89. For a description of this area and the small province of Pamphylia s. LC; Barrett; CH, 124-29; Anthony D. Macro, "The Cities of Asia Minor Under the Roman Imperium," ANRW, 2, 7, 2:663-67; G. Walter Hansen, "Galatia," BAFCS, 2:377-95). **ἀποχωρήσας** aor. act. part. (circum.) ἀποχωρέω (# 713) to depart, to leave, to desert. **ὑπέστρεψεν** aor. ind. act. ὑποστρέφω (# 5715) to return. For suggestions as to the reason John Mark left, s. Barrett. ◆ **14 διελθόντες** aor. act. part. (temp.) s.v. 6. They probably

took the paved Roman road, *Via Sebaste* (David French, "Acts and the Roman Roads of Asia Minor," BAFCS, 2:51-53; David French, "The Roman Road-System of Asia Minor" ANRW 2, 7, 2:698-729; GAM, 47). **παρεγένοντο** aor. ind. mid. (dep.) παραγίνομαι (# 4134) to arrive. Ἀντιόχειαν τὴν Πισιδίαν Pisidian Antioch, that is Antioch in Phrygia near Pisidia (Longenecker, 422; Barrett; CSP, 247-314). This was the home of one of the wealthiest business families in Pisidian Antioch, the family of Sergius Paullus and he may have suggested that Paul visit his city (G. Walter Hansen, "Galatia," BAFCS, 2:386-87; Nobbs, "Cyprus," BAFCS, 2:287). **ἐκάθισαν** aor. ind. act. καθίζω (# 2767) to take one's seat. ◆ **15 ἀνάγνωσις** (# 342) reading. The service consisted of the Shema, prayer by the leader, reading of the law and prophets, and a sermon by a member of the congregation (Bruce; Moore, *Judaism* 1:281-307; TDNT; SB, 4:153-88; HJP, 2:447-54; JPF, 2:914-37; DJGE, 107-331). **ἀπέστειλαν** aor. ind. act. ἀποστέλλω (# 690) to send. **ἀρχισυνάγωγος** (# 801) head of the synagogue. One of his duties was to select the readers and the speakers for the service (RWP; s. NDIEC, 4:213-20; HJP, 2:433-36). **λόγος παρακλήσεως** word of encouragement, exhortation, that is, a sermon (Barrett; s. also David A. deSilva, "Paul's Sermon in Antioch of Pisidia," *Bib Sac* 151 [1994]: 32-49). **λέγετε** pres. imp. act. λέγω (# 3306) to speak. ◆ **16 ἀναστάς** aor. act. part. ἀνίστημι (# 482) to stand up. Temp. or circum. part. **κατασείσας** aor. act. part. κατασείω (# 2939) to shake down, to shake or wave as a signal (AS). **φοβούμενοι** pres. mid. (dep.) part. φοβέομαι (# 5828) to fear. Paul may be addressing Jews and proselytes or just Jews who fear God (Barrett; SB, 2:715-23; s. 10:2). **ἀκούσατε** aor. imp. act. ἀκούω (# 201) to hear, to listen. For an analysis of Paul's sermon according to the method of rabbinical preaching s. J. W. Bowker, "Speeches in Acts: A Study in Proem and Yellammedenu Form," *NTS*, 14 (1967): 96-111; DJGE, 194-98. Aor. imp. calls for a specific act w. a note of urgency. ◆ **17 ἐξελέξατο** aor. ind. mid. ἐκλέγω (# 1721) to choose, to elect. Mid. indicates a selection for oneself. **ὕψωσεν** aor. ind. act. ὑψόω (# 5738) to exalt. **παροικία** dat. sing. sojourn, living in a place as a stranger or foreigner (s. 7:6; TDNT; TDOT). **βραχίονος** gen. sing. βραχίων (# 1098) arm. The uplifted arm was a symbol of God's power at work for Israel (BAGD; SB, 2:723-24). **ἐξήγαγεν** aor. ind. act. ἐξάγω to lead out. ◆ **18 ὡς** (# 6055) approximately (w. numbers). **τεσσερακονταετής** (# 5478) forty years. **ἐτροποφόρησεν** aor. ind. act. τροποφορέω (# 5574) to bear or put up w. someone, to endure, implying extensive patience (LC; LN, 1:308). For the variant reading **ἐτροφοφόρησεν** aor. ind. act. τροφοφορέω (# 5578) "he cared for them" s. TC, 405-6; Barrett; LC. ◆ **19 καθελών** aor. act. part. (temp.) καθαιρέω (# 2747) to destroy. **κατεκληρονόμησεν** aor. act. ind.

κατακληρονομέω (# *2883*) to divide according to lot, to distribute an inheritance, to take for a possession, to give for a possession (Bruce). ◆ **20 ὡς ἔτεσιν τετρακοσίοις καὶ πεντήκοντα** about 450 years. S. Eugene H. Merrill, "Paul's Use of 'About 450 Years' in Acts 13:20," *Bib Sac* 138 (1981): 246-57. **ἔδωκεν** aor. ind. act. δίδωμι (# *1443*) to give. ◆ **21 κἀκεῖθεν** (# *2796*) from that time, after that (Barrett). **ἠτήσαντο** aor. ind. mid. αἰτέω (# *160*) to ask; mid. to ask for oneself, to avail oneself of one's right to ask (BG, 76). **ἔδωκεν** aor. ind. act. s.v. 20. ◆ **22 μεταστήσας** aor. act. part. (temp.) μεθίστημι (# *3496*) to remove, to depose. **ἤγειρεν** aor. ind. act. ἐγείρω (# *1586*) to raise up. **αὐτοῖς** dat. pl. αὐτός (# *899*). Dat. of personal interest. **εἰς βασιλέα** (# *1650; 993*) as king. The prep. w. the acc. replaces the predicate (M, 71; s. also BD, 86; KVS, 51-65). **εἶπεν** aor. ind. act. λέγω (# *3306*) to say. **μαρτυρήσας** aor. act. part. μαρτυρέω (# *3455*) to bear witness, to testify. Part. used to explain the vb. **εὗρον** aor. ind. act. s.v. 6. **ποιήσει** fut. ind. act. ποιέω (# *4472*) to do. **θέλημα** (# *2525*) will. David will do all the several things willed by God (Barrett). ◆ **23 τούτου** gen. sing. οὗτος (# *4047*); "from the seed of *this one*." Placed first for emphasis. **ἤγαγεν** aor. ind. act. ἄγω (# *72*) to lead. Here "God fulfilled His promise to Israel" (Barrett). ◆ **24 προκηρύξαντος** aor. act. part. προκηρύσσω (# *4619*) to proclaim beforehand. Gen. abs. **εἴσοδος** (# *1658*) entrance, coming. It refers to the entry of Jesus upon his public ministry (Barrett). ◆ **25 ἐπλήρου** impf. ind. act. πληρόω (# *4444*) to fulfill, to complete. Impf. indicates that John had not finished his course at the time referred to (LC). **ὑπονοεῖτε** pres. ind. act. ὑπονοέω (# *5706*) to suppose, to suspect. The prep. compound conveys the idea of thoughts making their way up into the mind (MH, 327). **εἶναι** pres. act. inf. εἰμί (# *1639*) to be. Inf. in indir. discourse. **οὗ** gen. sing. ὅς (# *4005*) rel. pron. used w. the adj. ἄξιος. **ὑπόδημα** (# *5687*) sandal. **λῦσαι** aor. act. inf. λύω to (# *3395*) loose. Epex. inf. explaining the adj. ◆ **26 γένους** gen. sing. γένος (# *1169*) race, stock, descendants. "Descendants of Abraham" was a title of honor for those who were Jews by birth (Schneider). Gen. of description. **φοβούμενοι** pres. mid. (dep.) part. s.v. 16. Part. as subst. w. the art. indicates another group of listeners besides the Jews. **ἐξαπεστάλη** aor. ind. pass. ἐξαποστέλλω (# *1990*) to send out. Theol. pass. ◆ **27 κατοικοῦντες** pres. act. part. κατοικέω (# *2997*) to live, to dwell. Part. as subst. **ἀγνοήσαντες** aor. act. part. (causal) ἀγνοέω (# *51*) to be ignorant, to not recognize. **ἀναγινωσκομένας** pres. pass. part. ἀναγινώσκω (# *336*) to read. Customary or iterat. pres. **κρίναντες** aor. act. part. (temp.) κρίνω (# *3212*) to judge, to condemn. **ἐπλήρωσαν** aor. ind. act. s.v. 25. ◆ **28 αἰτία** (# *162*) reason, charge; w. gen. giving the reason for a capital punishment (BAGD). **εὑρόντες** aor. act. part. s.v. 6. Concessive part. ("although"). **ἠτήσαντο** aor. ind. mid.

s.v. 21. **ἀναιρεθῆναι** aor. pass. inf. ἀναιρέω (# *359*) to put to death. Inf. in indir. discourse. ◆ **29 ἐτέλεσαν** aor. ind. act. τελέω (# *5464*) to complete. **γεγραμμένα** perf. pass. part. γράφω (# *1211*) to write. Part. as subst. **καθελόντες** aor. act. part. (temp.) καθαιρέω (# *2747*) to take down. A t.t. for removal after crucifixion (AS). **ἔθηκαν** aor. ind. act. τίθημι (# *5502*) to place. ◆ **30 ἤγειρεν** aor. ind. act. s.v. 22. ◆ **31 ὤφθη** aor. ind. pass. ὁράω (# *3972*) to see. **πλείους** acc. pl. comp. πολύς (# *4498*) much, many. Used here w. no sense of comparison (LC), or w. the idea, "more than a few days" (RWP). **συναναβᾶσιν** aor. act. part. συναναβαίνω (# *5262*) to accompany, to go up w. someone. Adj. part. as subst. ◆ **32 γενομένην** aor. mid. (dep.) part. (adj.) s.v. 5. ◆ **33 ἐκπεπλήρωκεν** perf. ind. act. ἐκπληρόω (# *1740*) to fulfill. Perf. emphasizes the completed action w. continuing results. **τέκνοις** dat. pl. τέκνον (# *5451*) child. Dat. of advantage or interest. **ἀναστήσας** aor. act. part. ἀνίστημι (# *482*) to raise up. Part. of means explaining how God fulfilled the promise. **γέγραπται** perf. ind. pass. s.v. 29. Perf. was used for important documents which had continual binding authority (MM). **γεγέννηκα** perf. ind. act. γεννάω (# *1164*) to beget, to bring forth (GELTS, 88). The day of the king's anointing was ideally the day in which he was born into a new relation of sonship toward Jehovah (Bruce). For the connecting of two passages, 2 Sam. 7 and Psalm 2, s. Longenecker, 426; 4Q174 (4QFlor). ◆ **34 ἀνέστησεν** aor. ind. act. s.v. 33. **μέλλοντα** pres. act. part. μέλλω (# *3516*) to be about to. Used w. inf. to express the fut. (MKG, 307). Part. could express purp. or result. **ὑποστρέφειν** pres. act. inf. ὑποστρέφω (# *5715*) to return. **εἴρηκεν** perf. ind. act. λέγω (# *3306*) to say. **ὅτι** (# *4022*) recitative, equivalent to quotation marks. **δώσω** fut. ind. act. s.v. 20. **ὅσιος** (# *4008*) pious, divine decrees, in contrast to human statutes (BAGD; EDNT). The word is used to translate the Heb. *hesed* (חֶסֶד), which means conduct in accordance w. the covenant and refers here to the inviolable covenant w. David (Nelson Glueck, *Hesed in the Bible*, [Cincinnati: The Hebrew Union College Press, 1967], 78; Katharine Doob Sackenfeld, *The Meaning of Hesed in the Hebrew Bible* [Missoula, Mont.: Scholars Press, 1978]; Gordon R. Clark, *The Word Hesed in the Hebrew Bible*, [Sheffeld: Sheffeld Academic Press, 1993]; TDOT). ◆ **35 δώσεις** aor. ind. act. 2nd. pers. sing, s.v. 20. **ἰδεῖν** aor. act. inf. ὁράω (# *3972*) to see. Jesus was raised from the dead so that He as the Son of David can in the future rule over Israel (Marshall; Cleon Rogers, Jr., "The Davidic Covenant in Acts-Revelation," *Bib Sac* 151 [1994]: 75). ◆ **36 ὑπηρετήσας** aor. act. part. (temp.) ὑπηρετέω (# *5676*) to serve (TDNT). **βουλῇ** dat. sing. Instr. dat. Probably both datives should be taken w. the part., "After David had served in his generation by the will of God..." (Barrett). **ἐκοιμήθη** aor. ind. pass. κοιμάω (# *3121*) pass. to sleep, to fall asleep, to die (s.

7:60). **προσετέθη** aor. ind. pass. προστίθημι (# *4707*) to add. An expression arising from the practice of burying families together (Alford; also "Gather," NIDOTTE). **εἶδεν** aor. ind. act. ὁράω s.v. 35. ◆ **37 ἤγειρεν** aor. ind. act. s.v. 22. ◆ **38 ἔστω** pres. act. imp. εἰμί (# *1639*) to be. **καταγγέλλεται** pres. ind. pass. καταγγέλλω (# *2859*) to proclaim, to announce. Pres. indicates here the action in progress. **ἠδυνήθητε** aor. ind. pass. (dep.) δύναμαι (# *1538*) to be able, w. inf. **δικαιωθῆναι** aor. pass. inf. δικαιόω (# *1467*) to justify, to declare righteous; a legal term indicating the pronouncement of a judge that a person is in the right (TDNT; APC; TLNT; EDNT). The law could never justify anyone from anything. Complete justification is afforded by Christ to every believer (Bruce). ◆ **39 πιστεύων** pres. act. part. πιστεύω (# *4409*) to believe. Part. as subst. **δικαιοῦται** pres. ind. pass. s.v. 38. Iterat. or customary pres.; every time someone believes he is justified. Theol. pass. indicating that God is the one who justifies. ◆ **40 οὖν** (# *4036*) therefore. Draws a conclusion from the previous. **μή** (# *3590*) lest. Neg. particle used to express neg. purp. (RG, 987). **ἐπέλθῃ** aor. subj. act. ἐπέρχομαι (# *2088*) to come upon, to happen to. Used of what time brings and generally unpleasant (BAGD; KVS, 84-85; 279). **εἰρημένον** perf. pass. part. s.v. 34. Part. as subst. ◆ **41 ἴδετε** aor. imp. act. ὁράω s.v. 35. **καταφρονητής** (# *2970*) one who despises, despiser, one who "thinks down" on another, scoffer, indicating a lack of respect or consideration; as translation of *bagad* (בָּגַד to betray, to be disloyal [DCH]); in the OT it means "arrogant traitor" (TLNT). **θαυμάσατε** aor. imp. act. θαυμάζω (# *2513*) to wonder, to be amazed. **ἀφανίσθητε** aor. imp. pass. ἀφανίζω (# *906*) to vanish away; pass. to be made to vanish, to destroy utterly so as to be invisible (LC). The aor. imps. call for a specific act w. a note of urgency. **πιστεύσητε** aor. subj. act. s.v. 39. Subj. w. double neg. **οὐ μή** (# *4024; 3590*) for a strong negation used as the apodosis in a 3rd. class cond. cl. **ἐκδιηγῆται** pres. subj. mid. (dep.) ἐκδιηγέομαι (# *1687*) to declare, to relate or tell in detail. The double prep. in compound indicates "to declare right through to the end" (MH, 311). Subj. w. **ἐάν** (# *1569*) in a 3rd. class cond. cl. in which the cond. is considered to be possible. ◆ **42 ἐξιόντων** pres. act. part. ἔξειμι (# *1996*) to go out. Gen. abs., temp. expressing contemporaneous time. **παρεκάλουν** impf. ind. act. παρακαλέω (# *4151*) to ask, to urge, to beseech. Incep. impf., "they began to beseech." **μεταξύ** (# *3568*) between; commonly used to mean "next" (Bruce). **λαληθῆναι** aor. pass. inf. λαλέω (# *3281*) to speak. Inf. in indir. discourse. Although there was midweek meetings in the synagogue on Monday and Thursday, the majority would be occupied during the week and would not be able to attend until the next Sabbath (Barrett). ◆ **43 λυθείσης** aor. pass. part. (temp.) fem. gen. sing. λύω (# *3395*) to

loose; here to break up the synagogue meeting (Barrett). Gen. abs. **ἠκολούθησαν** aor. ind. act. ἀκολουθέω (# *199*) to follow, w. dat. **σεβομένων** pres. mid. (dep.) part. (adj.) σέβομαι (# *4936*) to be devout, to worship (TDNT; EDNT; NIDNTT, 2:90-95). **προσήλυτος** (# *4670*) proselyte; Gentiles who had adopted Judaism and been circumcised, baptized and offered a sacrifice (TDNT; SB, 2:715-23; BC, 5:74-96; EDNT; JTJ, 320-34; Barrett; Acts 2:11). **προσλαλοῦντες** pres. act. part. (circum.) προσλαλέω (# *4688*) to talk w., to talk to. **ἔπειθον** impf. ind. act. πείθω (# *4275*) to persuade; conative impf. "they were trying to persuade" (RWP); "urged" (Bruce). ◆ **44 ἐρχομένῳ** pres. mid. (dep.) part. ἔρχομαι (# *2262*) to come; "on the following Sabbath" (Schneider; Haenchen). **σχεδόν** (# *5385*) almost. **συνήχθη** aor. ind. pass. συνάγω (# *5251*) to gather together. **ἀκοῦσαι** aor. act. inf. ἀκούω (# *201*) to hear. Inf. of purp. ◆ **45 ἰδόντες** aor. act. part. (temp.) s.v. 12. **ἐπλήσθησαν** aor. ind. pass. s.v. 9. **ζῆλος** (# *2419*) jealousy, envy, a particularly strong feeling of resentment and jealously against someone (LN, 1:760; NIDNTT, 3:1166-68). **ἀντέλεγον** impf. ind. act. ἀντιλέγω (# *515*) to speak against, to contradict. Conative impf., "they tried to contradict." **λαλουμένοις** pres. pass. part. (adj.) s.v. 42. **βλασφημοῦντες** pres. act. part. βλασφημέω (# *1059*) to blaspheme, to slander, to defame. Circum. part., or part. of means explaining how they tried to contradict. ◆ **46 παρρησιασάμενοι** aor. mid. (dep.) part. (circum.) παρρησιάζομαι (# *4245*) to be bold; also suggests abnormal eloquence and emotion (LC; Acts 9:27). **ἦν** impf. act. ind. εἰμί (# *1639*) **ἀναγκαῖος** (# *338*) urgently necessary, compelling, pressing need (TLNT). **λαληθῆναι** aor. pass. inf. s.v. 42. Epex. inf. explaining the necessity. **ἐπειδή** (# *2076*) since, because. **ἀπωθεῖσθε** pres. ind. mid. (dep.) ἀπωθέω (# *723*) to push away from oneself, to reject, to repudiate. **στρεφόμεθα** pres. ind. pass. (dep.) στρέφομαι (# *5138*) to turn oneself. Pres. indicates an action in progress. ◆ **47 ἐντέταλται** perf. ind. mid. (dep.) ἐντέλλομαι (# *1948*) to command. **τέθεικα** perf. ind. act. τίθημι (# *5502*) to place. **εἶναί** pres. act. inf. εἰμί to be (# *1639*). Inf. of purp. **ἕως ἐσχάτου τῆς γῆς** unto the end of the earth (s. 1:8). ◆ **48 ἀκούοντα** pres. act. part. (temp.) s.v. 44. **ἔχαιρον** impf. ind. act. χαίρω (# *5897*) to be glad, to rejoice. Incep. impf., "they began to rejoice." **ἐδόξαζον** impf. ind. act. δοξάζω (# *1519*) to glorify, to praise (TLNT). **ἐπίστευσαν** aor. ind. act. s.v. 12. **ἦσαν** impf. act. ind. εἰμί s.v. 47. **τεταγμένοι** perf. pass. part. τάσσω (# *5435*) to put in place, to appoint; perhaps here in the sense "enrolled," "inscribed" (Bruce; MM). For passages w. the idea of enrollment in God's book of the saved (Exod. 32:33; Ps. 69:28; Dan. 12:1; 1 Enoch 47:3; Jubilees, 30:20) s. Barrett; SB, 2:726). Part. in a periphrastic construction, "those who were in a state of appointment to eternal life believed" (VA, 466), or part. forming the plperf. pass. (NSV, 9). ◆ **49 διεφέρετο** impf. ind. pass. διαφέρω (*# 1422*) to carry through. The Word was carried through the whole region (Barrett). ◆ **50 παρώτρυναν** aor. ind. act. παροτρύνω (*# 4241*) to incite, to stir up. **εὐσχήμων** (*# 2363*) prominent, of high standing; here, perhaps "rich" (LC; TDNT; for wealthy women in the ancient world s. David W.J. Gill, "Acts and the Urban Élites," BAFCS, 2:114-17). **ἐπήγειραν** aor. ind. act. ἐπεγείρω (*# 2074*) to rouse up, to excite, to stir up. **ἐξέβαλον** aor. ind. act. ἐκβάλλω (*# 1675*) to cast out. ◆ **51 ἐκτιναξάμενοι** aor. mid. (dep.) part. ἐκτινάσσομαι (*# 1759*) to shake off. **κονιορτός** (*# 3155*) dust. The shaking off of dust might mean the missionaries clear themselves of all further responsibilities (BC, 5:271). **ἦλθον** aor. ind. act. s.v. 44. **εἰς Ἰκόνιον** to Iconium. They evidently took the paved Roman highway, *Via Sebaste* (French, BAFCS, 2:53; s.v. 14. For the city of Iconium s. CSP, 317-82; CH, 145-49; ABD, 3:357-58; AAT, 194-97. ◆ **52 ἐπληροῦντο** impf. ind. pass. πληρόω (*# 4444*) to fill, w. gen. of content.

Acts 14

◆ **1 ἐγένετο** aor. ind. mid. (dep.) γίνομαι (*# 1181*) to become, to happen, to take place. For the construction of this vb. w. the inf. s. Luke 2:1. **κατὰ τὸ αὐτό** together; or perhaps "in the same way" or "at one time" (LC). **εἰσελθεῖν** aor. act. inf. εἰσέρχομαι (*# 1656*) to go into. **λαλῆσαι** aor. act. inf. λαλέω (*# 3281*) to speak. **πιστεῦσαι** aor. act. inf. πιστεύω (*# 4409*) to believe. Inf. w. ὥστε (*# 6063*) to express actual result (RG, 1000). ◆ **2 ἀπειθήσαντες** aor. act. part. ἀπειθέω (*# 578*) to disobey, used here as the opposite of believe. Unbelief and disobedience are both involved in the rejection of the gospel (Bruce). Part. as subst. **ἐπήγειραν** aor. ind. act. ἐπεγείρω (*# 2074*) to excite, to stir up. **ἐκάκωσαν** aor. ind. act. κακόω (*# 2808*) to make evil, to injure, to irritate (LC). ◆ **3 διέτριψαν** aor. ind. act. διατρίβω (*# 1417*) to stay, to remain. **παρρησιαζόμενοι** pres. mid. (dep.) part. (circum.) παρρησιάζομαι (*# 4245*) to speak freely, to be bold (s. 9:27). **ἐπί** (*# 2093*) w. dat., upon the basis of, in reliance upon (IBG, 50). **μαρτυροῦντι** pres. act. part. (adj.) μαρτυρέω (*# 3455*) to testify, to bear witness. Iterat. pres. indicating the repeated action. **διδόντι** pres. act. part. δίδωμι (*# 1443*) to give. The part. indicates how the witness was carried out (Haenchen). **γίνεσθαι** pres. mid. (dep.) inf. s.v. 1. Inf. as obj. of what was given. ◆ **4 ἐσχίσθη** aor. ind. pass. σχίζω (*# 5387*) to split, to divide. **ἦσαν** impf. ind. act. εἰμί (*# 1639*) to be. ◆ **5 ἐγένετο** aor. ind. mid. (dep.) s.v. 1. **ὁρμή** (*# 3995*) impulse, inclination, attempt. W. the vb. γίνομαι (lit., "an impulse happens") to make a decision, to carry out some action, but w. emphasis upon the impulse involved (TDNT; LN, 1:360). **ὑβρίσαι** aor. act. inf. ὑβρίζω (*# 5614*) to mistreat, to treat shamefully. It expresses

insult and outrageous treatment which is calculated publicly to insult and humiliate the person who suffers from it (MNTW, 83; TDNT). Epex. inf. explaining the impulsive decision. **λιθοβολῆσαι** aor. act. inf. λιθοβολέω (*# 3344*) to stone. ◆ **6 συνιδόντες** aor. act. part. (temp.) συνοράω (*# 5328*) to see together, to become conscious of, to perceive; "to get wind of it" (Bruce). **κατέφυγον** aor. ind. act. καταφεύγω (*# 2966*) to flee, to take refuge. Used in the Koine as a kind of technical expression for suppliants fleeing or resorting to anyone for help (MM). **Λύστρα** (*# 3388*) Lystra. For the city s. AAT, 197-99; CH, 147-59; SBRP, 180-83; CSP, 407-19; ABD, 4:426-27. **Δέρβη** (*# 1292*) Derbe. For the city, s. AAT, 199-200; Bastiaan Van Elderen, "Some Archaeological Observations on Paul's First Missionary Journey," AHG, 156-61; CSP, 383-404; ABD, 2:144-45. ◆ **7 εὐαγγελιζόμενοι** pres. mid. (dep.) part. εὐαγγελίζομαι (*# 2294*) to proclaim good news. Part. used w. **ἦσαν** in a periphrastic construction emphasizing the continual action. ◆ **8 ἀδύνατος** (*# 105*) without strength, weak, impotent. For the medical use of this term s. MLL, 46. **ἐκάθητο** impf. ind. mid. (dep.) κάθημαι (*# 2764*) to sit. Customary use of the impf., "he used to sit" (DM, 188). **κοιλία** (*# 3120*) womb. **περιεπάτησεν** aor. ind. act. περιπατέω (*# 4344*) to walk, to walk about. ◆ **9 ἤκουσεν** aor. ind. act. ἀκούω (*# 201*) to hear, w. gen. A variant reading has the impf. ἤκουεν, which would picture the continual action of listening. **λαλοῦντος** pres. act. part. s.v. 1. Part. as subst. **ἀτενίσας** aor. act. part. (circum.) ἀτενίζω (*# 867*) to gaze. **ἰδών** aor. act. part. ὁράω (*# 3972*) to see. Temp. or circum. part. **σωθῆναι** aor. pass. inf. σώζω (*# 5392*) to save, to rescue, to heal. Inf. combines here both purpose and result (RWP). ◆ **10 εἶπεν** aor. ind. act. λέγω (*# 3306*) to say. **ἀνάστηθι** aor. imp. act. ἀνίστημι (*# 482*) to stand up. **ἥλατο** aor. ind. mid. (dep.) ἅλλομαι (*# 256*) to leap, to jump up. **περιεπάτει** impf. ind. act., s.v. 8. Incep. impf., "he began to walk." Note the use of the previous aor. w. the impf. here. ◆ **11 ἰδόντες** aor. act. part. (temp.) s.v. 9. **ἐποίησεν** aor. ind. act. ποιέω (*# 4472*) to do. **ἐπῆραν** aor. ind. act. ἐπαίρω (*# 2048*) to lift up. **Λυκαονιστί** (*# 3378*) adv., in the Lycaonian language (BAGD; for the language s. BASHH, 110-11). **ὁμοιωθέντες** aor. pass. part. (circum.) ὁμοιόω (*# 3929*) to make like, to become like. **κατέβησαν** aor. ind. act. καταβαίνω (*# 2849*) to come down. Ovid (*Metamorphoses* 8:626-742) relates a legend of Zeus and Hermes visiting the Phrygian hill country disguised as ordinary men. They were rejected by all except an elderly couple who welcomed them. The couple was rewarded and the others punished (Hansen, "Galatia," BAFCS, 2:394). ◆ **12 ἐκάλουν** impf. ind. act. καλέω (*# 2813*) to call, to name. **Δία** (*# 2416*) Zeus. He was the most widely worshiped god in Galatia and is often linked w. Hermes (Hansen, "Galatia," BAFCS, 2:393; BASHH,

111; David W.J. Gill & Bruce Winter, "Acts and Roman Religion," BAFCS, 2:81-85; for information concerning Zeus and Hermes s. GGR, 1:385-427, 501-10; F. Graf, "Zeus," DDD, 1758-71; L.H. Martin, "Hermes," DDD, 771-83; Cilliers Breytenbach, "Zeus und der lebendige Gott: Anmerkungen zu Apostelgeschichte 14.11-17," NTS 39 [1993]: 396-413; BBC; ABD, 5:811-12). ἐπειδή (# 2076) since, because. ἡγούμενος pres. mid. (dep.) part. ἡγέομαι (# 2451) to lead. Part. as a noun, "the leader of the talk." ◆ **13** ὄντος pres. act. part. εἰμί s.v. 4. ταῦρος (# 5436) bull, ox. Bulls were used in several cults and were an expensive animal to kill (Gill & Winter, "Acts and Roman Religion," BAFCS, 2:83). στέμμα (# 5098) garland, wreath, either made of flowers or wool used to adorn the victim (BAGD; Williams). πυλών (# 4784) gate. The great gateway which led into the temple area (Rackham). ἐνέγκας aor. act. part. (circum.) φέρω (# 5770) to bring. ἤθελεν impf. ind. act. θέλω (# 2527) to wish, to want to, w. inf. Desiderative impf. used in expressing a wish (IBG, 9). θύειν pres. act. inf. θύω (# 2604) to sacrifice. ◆ **14** ἀκούσαντες aor. act. part. (temp.) s.v. 9. διαρρήξαντες aor. act. part. διαρρήγνυμι (# 1396) to rip in two. This was to indicate that they had heard blasphemy (Barrett; M, Sanh. 7:5). Temp. or circum. part. ἐξεπήδησαν aor. ind. act. ἐκπηδάω (# 1737) to leap out, to rush out. The prep. compound retains its local force (Haenchen). κράζοντες pres. act. part. (circum.) κράζω (# 3189) to scream. ◆ **15** ποιεῖτε pres. ind. act. s.v. 11. Pres. describes action in progress. ὁμοιοπαθής (# 3926) w. the same nature. Used of similar feelings, circumstances, and experiences (BAGD). μάταιος (# 3469) vain, empty, futile, lacking in content, emphasizing the aimlessness, the leading to no object or end (LN, 1:625; Trench, Synonyms, 180f; TDNT). The word was used of false gods in contrast to the true God (EDNT). ἐπιστρέφειν pres. act. inf. ἐπιστρέφω (# 2188) to turn fr. something to something or someone. Epex. inf. explaining the good news they were proclaiming. ζῶντα pres. act. part. (adj.) ζάω (# 2409) to live. ἐποίησεν aor. ind. act. s.v. 11. ◆ **16** παρῳχημέναις perf. mid. (dep.) part. παροίχομαι (# 4233) to go by. Adj. part., "bygone generations." εἴασεν aor. ind. act. ἐάω (# 1572) to permit, to allow, w. inf. πορεύεσθαι pres. mid. (dep.) inf. πορεύομαι (# 4513) to go. ◆ **17** καίτοι (# 2792) and yet. ἀμάρτυρος (# 282) without a witness. For the prefix used to negate the meaning of the word s. Moorhouse, 61ff. αὐτόν (# 899) himself (Barrett). ἀφῆκεν aor. ind. act. ἀφίημι (# 918) to leave. ἀγαθουργῶν pres. act. part. ἀγαθουργέω (# 14) to do good. The parts. here are either causal (RWP) or explanatory: "in that He did good" (EGT; Barrett). οὐρανόθεν (# 4040) from heaven. For the ending of the adv. w. the ablative quality of indicating source, s. MH, 164. ὑετός rain, heavy shower (LS). Zeus was considered to be a weather god and had the names Ὑέτιος

("Rainy," "Rainbringer," LS, 1846) and Ὄμβριος ("Thunder-storm," LS, 1221) (DDD, 1768-70; GGR, 1:391-401). διδούς pres. act. part. δίδωμι (# 1443) to give. καρποφόρος (# 2845) fruitbearing, fruitful. Zeus was also considered to be a fertility god (GGR, 1:401-2). ἐμπιπλῶν pres. act. part. ἐμπίμπλημι (# 1855) to fill, w. gen. of content. The pres. parts. indicate habitual action. Paul contrasts the true God with the false gods. τροφή (# 5575) enjoyment, joy, delight (BAGD). εὐφροσύνη (# 2372) gladness, cheerfulness. ◆ **18** μόλις (# 3660) scarcely, barely, w. effort. κατέπαυσαν aor. ind. act. καταπαύω (# 2924) to restrain, to cause to cease. The prep. compound is perfective. The articular inf. in the gen. case, used w. a neg. μή (# 3590) following this vb., is a common Gr. idiom (RG, 1171). θύειν pres. act. inf. s.v. 13. Epex. inf. ◆ **19** ἐπῆλθαν aor. ind. act. ἐπέρχομαι (# 2088) to come upon, to come to. πείσαντες aor. act. part. (temp.) πείθω (# 4275) to persuade, to get someone on one's side (Barrett). λιθάσαντες aor. act. part. (temp.) λιθάζω (# 3342) to stone. ἔσυρον impf. ind. act. σύρω (# 5359) to drag. νομίζοντες pres. act. part. (causal) νομίζω (# 3787) to suppose. τεθνηκέναι perf. act. inf. θνήσκω (# 2569) to die; perf. to be dead. The perf. emphasizes the state or condition. Inf. as obj. in indir. discourse. ◆ **20** κυκλωσάντων aor. act. part. (temp.) κυκλόω (# 3240) to encircle. Gen. abs. ἀναστάς aor. act. part. (temp.) ἀνίστημι (# 482) to arise, to get up. εἰσῆλθεν aor. ind. act. εἰσέρχομαι s.v. 1. ἐπαύριον (# 2069) tomorrow, the next day. ἐξῆλθεν aor. ind. act. ἐξέρχομαι (# 2002) to go out of. ◆ **21** εὐαγγελισάμενοι aor. mid. (dep.) part. (temp.) εὐαγγελίζομαι s.v. 7. μαθητεύσαντες aor. act. part. (temp.) μαθητεύω (# 3411) to make a disciple (s. Matt. 28:19). ὑπέστρεψαν aor. ind. act. ὑποστρέφω (# 5715) to return. ◆ **22** ἐπιστηρίζοντες pres. act. part. (circum.) ἐπιστηρίζω (# 2185) to strengthen. Pres. indicates the repeated action. παρακαλοῦντες pres. act. part. (circum.) παρακαλέω (# 4151) to exhort, to encourage. The word is used of exhorting troops who are about to go into battle (MNTW, 134; TDNT). ἐμμένειν pres. act. inf. ἐμμένω (# 1844) to remain in, to continue in. Inf. as obj. πίστει dat. sing. πίστις (# 4411) faith. W. the art. it may indicate the body of Christian doctrine. διὰ πολλῶν θλίψεων through many tribulations, stresses, pressures. This is not the means of getting into the kingdom of God, but indicates the circumstances along the way. δεῖ (# 1256) pres. ind. act. it is necessary; expressing a logical necessity determined by the circumstances, w. acc. and inf. εἰσελθεῖν aor. act. inf. s.v. 20. ◆ **23** χειροτονήσαντες aor. act. part. χειροτονέω (# 5936) to elect by show of hands, to appoint. Here the selection was made by Paul and Barnabas (Haenchen). κατ᾽ ἐκκλησίαν (# 2848; 1711) from church to church. The prep. is used here distributively. πρεσβύτερος (# 4565) an older person, elder. These were the spiritual leaders of the

churches (TDNT; EDNT, NIDNTT, 1:192-200). **προσευξάμενοι** aor. mid. (dep.) part. (temp.) προσεύχομαι
(# 4667) to pray. **νηστειῶν** gen. pl. νηστεία (# 3763) fasting. **παρέθεντο** aor. ind. mid. (dep.) παρατίθημι (# 4192)
to place before, mid. to deposit w. another, to commend a person to the care of another (MM). **πεπιστεύ-
κεισαν** plperf. ind. act., s.v. 1. ◆ **24 διελθόντες** aor. act.
part. (temp.) διέρχομαι (# 1451) to pass through. **ἦλθον**
aor. ind. act. ἔρχομαι (# 2262) to come. ◆ **25 λαλήσαντες** aor. act. part. (temp.) s.v. 1. **κατέβησαν** aor. ind.
act. s.v. 11. ◆ **26 ἀπέπλευσαν** aor. ind. act. ἀποπλέω
(# 676) to sail, to sail from. **ἦσαν** impf. ind. act. εἰμί
(# 1639). **παραδεδομένοι** perf. pass. part. παραδίδωμι
(# 4140) to deliver over to, to commit. The part. is used
in a perf. pass. periphrastic construction. **χάριτι** dat.
sing. χάρις (# 5921) grace. Here w. special reference to
the protective care of God who watches over His people and esp. over His missionaries (Barrett). **ἐπλήρωσαν** aor. ind. act. πληρόω (# 4444) to fulfill, to
complete. ◆ **27 παραγενόμενοι** aor. mid. (dep.) part.
(temp.) παραγίνομαι (# 4134) to arrive. **συναγαγόντες**
aor. act. part. (temp.) συνάγω (# 5251) to gather together. **ἀνήγγελλον** impf. ind. act. ἀναγγέλλω (# 334) to report, to carry back good tidings, to inform, to provide
information, w. the implication of considerable detail
(EGT; LN, 1:411; s. NDIEC, 4:10-17; GELTS, 26-27).
Impf. pictures the repeated action. **ἐποίησεν** aor. ind.
act. s.v. 11. **ἤνοιξεν** aor. ind. act. ἀνοίγω (# 487) to open.
◆ **28 διέτριβον** impf. ind. act. διατρίβω (# 1417) to stay,
to remain.

Acts 15

◆ **1 κατελθόντες** aor. act. part. (temp.) κατέρχομαι
(# 2982) to come down. **ἐδίδασκον** impf. ind. act. διδάσκω (# 1438) to teach. Incep. impf., "They began to teach
and kept it up" (RWP). **περιτμηθῆτε** aor. subj. pass.
περιτέμνω (# 4362) to circumcise. Subj. w. **ἐάν** (# 1569)
in a 3rd. class cond. cl. which assumes that the cond. is
possible. **ἔθει** dat. sing. ἔθος (# 1621) habit, custom, law
(TLNT). Instr. or causal dat. (MT, 242). **δύνασθε** pres.
ind. mid./pass. (dep.) δύναμαι (# 1538) to be able, w.
inf. **σωθῆναι** aor. pass. inf. σῴζω (# 5392) to rescue, to
save. Theol. pass. indicating that God saves. ◆ **2 γενομένης** aor. mid. (dep.) part. (temp.) γίνομαι (# 1181) to
become, to be, to come about, to arise. Gen. abs. **στάσις**
(# 5087) uprising, standing up in opposition to or disagreement w. someone, faction, discord, heated quarrel (LN, 1:439; TLNT, 1:287). **ζήτησις** (# 2428)
questioning, dispute, discussion. **ἔταξαν** aor. ind. act.
τάσσω (# 5435) to arrange. The subject of the vb. implies that the brethren at Antioch appointed Paul and
Barnabas as their delegates (LC). **ἀναβαίνειν** aor. act.
inf. ἀναβαίνω (# 326) to go up. Inf. as obj., or epex. inf.
explaining what was arranged. **ζήτημα** (# 2427) ques-

tion, controversial question, issue (BAGD). ◆ **3
προπεμφθέντες** aor. pass. part. προπέμπω (# 4636) to accompany, to help on one's journey w. food, money by
arranging for companions, means of travel, etc., to
send on one's way (BAGD). **διήρχοντο** impf. ind. mid.
(dep.) διέρχομαι (# 1451) to pass through. Impf. pictures the action of the past as it was in progress. **ἐκδιη-
γούμενοι** pres. mid. (dep.) part. (circum.) ἐκδιηγέομαι
(# 1687) to narrate, to tell in detail (s. 13:41). **ἐπιστροφή**
(# 2189) turning to, conversion. **ἐποίουν** impf. ind. act.
ποιέω (# 4472) to do, to make; here used in the sense
"to cause", "to bring about," w. the dat. of advantage
(BAGD). ◆ **4 παραγενόμενοι** aor. mid. (dep.) part.
(temp.) παραγίνομαι (# 4134) to arrive. **παρεδέχθησαν**
aor. ind. pass. παραδέχομαι (# 4138) to receive, to welcome. **ἀνήγγειλαν** aor. ind. act. ἀναγγέλλω (# 334) to report. **ἐποίησεν** aor. ind. act. s.v. 3. ◆ **5 ἐξανέστησαν** aor.
ind. act. ἐξανίστημι (# 1985) to arise. The prep. in compound is perfective (MH, 308f). **αἵρεσις** (# 146) group,
party. It does not refer to a heresy or sect in the modern
sense (LC). **πεπιστευκότες** perf. act. part. πιστεύω
(# 4409) to believe. Adj. part. as subst. Perf. indicates
the lasting state or condition. **δεῖ** (# 1256) pres. ind. act.
it is necessary, w. inf. **περιτέμνειν** pres. act. inf. s.v. 1.
αὐτούς acc. pl. αὐτός (# 899) they; acc. used w. inf. It refers to Gentile believers or perhaps those like Titus,
among Paul's companions, who were not circumcised
(Williams). **παραγγέλλειν** pres. act. inf. παραγγέλλω
(# 4133) to command, to charge. Used esp. of the transmitted orders of a military commander (AS). **τηρεῖν**
pres. act. inf. τηρέω (# 5498) to guard, to keep, to observe. Inf. in indir. discourse. ◆ **6 συνήχθησαν** aor. ind.
pass. συνάγω (# 5251) to gather together, to assemble.
ἰδεῖν aor. act. inf. ὁράω (# 3972) to see, to examine and
evaluate (Schille). Inf. of purpose. ◆ **7 γενομένης** aor.
mid. (dep.) part. (temp.) s.v. 2. "After much discussion...." **ἀναστάς** aor. act. part. (circum.) ἀνίστημι
(# 482) to arise. **εἶπεν** aor. ind. act. λέγω (# 3306) to say,
to speak. **ὑμεῖς** nom. pl. pers. pron. σύ (# 5148) you;
emphatic. **ἐπίστασθε** pres. ind. mid. (dep.) ἐπίσταμαι
(# 2179) to understand, to possess information about,
w. the implication of an understanding of the significance of such information (LN, 1:335). **ἐξελέξατο** aor.
ind. mid. ("to chose for oneself") ἐκλέγομαι (# 1721) to
select, to make a choice. **ἀκοῦσαι** aor. act. inf. ἀκούω
(# 201) to hear. Inf. either to define the choice or to express result. **πιστεῦσαι** aor. act. inf. s.v. 5. ◆ **8 καρδιογνώστης** (# 2841) one who knows the heart (s. 1:24).
ἐμαρτύρησεν aor. ind. act. μαρτυρέω (# 3455) to bear
witness. Used in the sense of confirmation or approval
(TDNT). **δούς** aor. act. part. δίδωμι (# 1443) to give, to
grant. Part. indicates how the approval was expressed
(Haenchen). ◆ **9 διέκρινεν** aor. ind. act. διακρίνω
(# 1359) to make a difference, distinction. **μεταξύ**
(# 3568) between. **πίστει** dat. sing. πίστις (# 4411) faith.

Instr. dat. ("through"); emphatic by position. **καθαρίσας** aor. act. part. καθαρίζω (# 2751) to clean, to cleanse. Part. is either causal or explanatory. ◆ **10** **πειράζετε** pres. ind. act. πειράζω (# 4279) to try, to tempt. It recalls Israel tempting God in the wilderness (TLNT, 3:84-85). Pres. may be conative (s. James 1:13). **ἐπιθεῖναι** aor. act. inf. ἐπιτίθημι (# 2202) to place upon. Epex. inf. explaining their tempting God (Bruce). **ζυγός** (# 2433) yoke. Used in Jewish writers in the sense of obligation, but here the figure suggests a burden rather than a religious duty (LC; SB, 1:608-10; 2:728). **ἰσχύσαμεν** aor. ind. act. ἰσχύω (# 2710) to be strong, to be able, to have the ability to, w. inf. (BAGD). **βαστάσαι** aor. act. inf. βαστάζω (# 1002) to carry a load, to bear a burden. ◆ **11 σωθῆναι** aor. pass. inf. σῴζω s.v. 1. Inf. in indir. discourse: "We believe that we are saved through grace ..." (RWP). **καθ' ὃν τρόπον** (# 2848; 4005; 5573) in like manner. ◆ **12 ἐσίγησεν** aor. ind. act. σιγάω (# 4967) to be quiet. Ingressive aor., "to become silent." **ἤκουον** impf. ind. act. ἀκούω (# 201) to hear, to listen to, w. gen. Impf. pictures the past action in progress. **ἐξηγουμένων** pres. mid. (dep.) part. ἐξηγέομαι (# 2007) to explain, to go through or lead out a narrative of events, to recount; to provide detailed information in a systematic way, to relate in full (RWP; TLNT; LN, 1:411; GELTS, 160). Temp. part, "as they told at length." **ἐποίησεν** aor. ind. act. ποιέω (# 4472) to do. ◆ **13 σιγῆσαι** aor. act. inf. s.v. 12. Inf. w. prep. μετά expressing time ("after"). **ἀπεκρίθη** aor. ind. pass. (dep.) ἀποκρίνομαι (# 646) to answer. **ἀκούσατε** aor. imp. act. s.v. 12. Aor. imp. calls for a specific act. ◆ **14 ἐξηγήσατο** aor. ind. mid. (dep.) s.v. 12. **ἐπεσκέψατο** aor. ind. mid. (dep.) ἐπισκέπτομαι (# 2170) to look upon, to visit, to make provision for (BAGD; NDIEC, 2:69). Here it means that God made provision for the call of the Gentiles (LC). **λαβεῖν** aor. act. inf. λαμβάνω (# 3284) to receive. Epex. inf. or inf. of purpose. **τῷ ὀνόματι αὐτοῦ** (# 3950; 899) for His Name. Dat. of personal interest. ◆ **15 συμφωνοῦσιν** pres. ind. act. συμφωνέω (# 5244) to agree, to be in agreement w., to be in harmony w. (Cleon Rogers, Jr., "The Davidic Covenant in Acts-Revelation," *Bib Sac* 151 [1994]: 76; TLNT). **γέγραπται** perf. ind. pass. γράφω (# 1211) to write. Perf. ("it stands written") used of important documents whose authority abides (MM). ◆ **16 ἀναστρέψω** fut. ind. act. ἀναστρέφω (# 418) to turn again. **ἀνοικοδομήσω** fut. ind. act. ἀνοικοδομέω (# 488) to build again, to rebuild. **σκηνή** (# 5008) tent, booth. Translation of the Heb. סֻכָּה (*succoth*), which was a flimsy booth made of branches intertwined together and laid over a frame, also seems to refer to the Davidic dynasty (Rogers, Jr., "Davidic Cov. in Acts and Rev.," *Bib Sac* 151 [1994]: 77-78). **πεπτωκυῖαν** perf. act. part. (adj.) acc. fem. sing. πίπτω (# 4406) to fall, to collapse. **κατεσκαμμένα** perf. pass. part. (adj.) κατασκάπτω (# 2940) to turn down, to ruin.

The perf. part. emphasizes the condition "the ruined portions of it" (RWP). **ἀνορθώσω** fut. ind. act. ἀνορθόω (# 494) to erect again, to rebuild, to restore. ◆ **17** **ἐκζητήσωσιν** aor. act. subj. ἐκζητέω (# 1699) to seek out. Subj. w. ὅπως (# 3968) to express purp. (MT, 105). **κατάλοιπος** (# 2905) rest, remaining. **ἐπικέκληται** perf. ind. pass. ἐπικαλέω (# 2126) to call upon, to call a name over someone, to designate the latter as the property of the former (BAGD). **ἐπ' αὐτούς** over them. The use of a pron. repeating the relative is due to Semitic influence (BD, 65; PAPC, 33-42; for the use of the OT quote in DSS s. CD 7:15; 4QFlor. 1:12). ◆ **18 γνωσός** (# 1196) known. This may be a comment James added to mean, "we cannot be in opposition to the expressed will of God ... but only God knows for certain how everything fits together and is to be fully understood" (Longenecker, 447). ◆ **19 κρίνω** (# 3212) pres. ind. act. to judge, to decree. It is the definite sentence of a judge, and implies that he is acting by personal authority (LC). **παρενοχλεῖν** pres. act. inf. παρενοχλέω (# 4214) to trouble, to annoy, to cause extra difficulty and hardship by continual annoyance, w. dat. (LN, 1:245; MM; NDIEC, 4:166-67). Pres. means "stop annoying" (LC). Inf. in indir. discourse. **ἐπιστρέφουσιν** pres. act. part. (adj.) ἐπιστρέφω (# 2188) to turn to. Pres. part. is an acknowledgment of a work actually in progress (EGT). ◆ **20 ἐπιστεῖλαι** aor. act. inf. ἐπιστέλλω (# 2182) to send, to send to, to instruct. In the papyri the general use related to sending a letter or other written communications, but in official documents it had the meaning "instruct," "enjoin" (MM). Inf. in indir. discourse dependent on the vb. κρίνω in v. 19. **ἀπέχεσθαι** pres. mid. (dep.) inf. ἀπέχω (# 600) mid. to keep away from, to abstain from, w. gen. (BAGD). Inf. in indir. discourse giving the content of the instruction. **ἀλίσγημα** (# 246) pollution, contamination. Jeremiah is said to have taught the people to keep away from the pollutions of the Gentiles of Babylon (*Paraleipomena Jeremiou* 7:32 [4 Baruch 7:37]; OTP, 2:423). It implies ritual rather that moral pollution (LC). **πορνεία** (# 4518) illicit sexual relation. Perhaps used here to refer to the breaking of the Jewish marriage law prohibiting those of close kin to marry (Bruce; TDNT; SB, 2:729-30). **πνικτός** (# 4465) strangled, choked to death. Used in Jewish writings of animals which died a natural death or were killed without having the blood drained from them, so that the "life in the blood" was considered strangled (BAGD; SB, 2:730-34; Exod. 22:31; Lev. 17:15; Deut. 14:21). **αἷμα** (# 135) blood. For the Jewish regulation against eating blood, s. SB, 2:734-39; CD, 4:6; 11QT, 53:6; DCH, 2:443. ◆ **21 κατὰ πόλιν** from city to city; distributive use of the prep. **κηρύσσοντας** pres. act. part. κηρύσσω (# 3062) to preach, to proclaim. Iterat. pres. Part. as subst. **ἀναγινωσκόμενος** pres. pass. part. ἀναγινώσκω (# 336) to read. For the reading of the OT and the preaching in the synagogue service s. 13:15; SB, 4:154-88. ◆ **22** ἔδοξε aor. ind. act. δοκέω (# *1506*) to seem to be; it seems good, w. dat. and inf. It is the t.t. in Gr. of all periods for voting or passing a measure in the assembly (LC). **ἐκλεξαμένους** aor. mid. (indir. mid., "to chose for oneself") part. (temp.) ἐκλέγω (# *1721*) to choose. **πέμψαι** aor. act. inf. πέμπω (# *4287*) to send. Epex. inf. explaining what they thought was good. **καλούμενον** pres. pass. part. (adj.) καλέω (# *2813*) to call; pass. to be named. **ἡγουμένους** pres. mid. (dep.) part. ἡγέομαι (# *2451*) to lead. Part. as subst., leaders. ◆ **23** **γράψαντες** aor. act. part. γράφω (# *1211*) to write. Nom. abs. (RG, 459). **χαίρειν** pres. act. inf. χαίρω (# *5897*) to greet. Abs. (independent) inf. as epistolary inf. common in letters (RG, 1093; RWP; VA, 377; BAGD; NDIEC, 7:35-36, 8:127-28; NSV, 82). ◆ **24** **ἐπειδή** (# *2076*) since, seeing that. **ἠκούσαμεν** aor. ind. act. s.v. 7. **ἐξελθόντες** aor. act. part. (adj.) ἐξέρχομαι (# *2002*) to go out. **ἐτάραξαν** aor. ind. act. ταράσσω (# *5429*) to disturb, to throw into confusion, to agitate, used for mental uncertainty and confusion; to cause acute emotional distress or turbulence (Haenchen; TLNT; LN, 1:315). **ἀνασκευάζοντες** pres. act. part. ἀνασκευάζω (# *412*) to destroy, to pervert. It means reversing what has been done, tearing down what has been built, or cancelling what has been agreed upon (LC). Also, a military metaphor, for plundering a town (Bruce). Conative pres., "they tried to...." Part. of manner, explaining how they disturbed. **διεστειλάμεθα** aor. ind. mid. (dep.) διαστέλλομαι (# *1403*) to order, to give strict commands. ◆ **25** **γενομένοις** aor. mid. (dep.) part. (adj.) γίνομαι (# *1181*) to become, to be. **ὁμοθυμαδόν** (# *3924*) to be of one soul, together, unanimously, in unity, brotherly harmony. Used of the unanimity of a synod, of creditors, of husband and wife, of brothers (TLNT; MM). ◆ **26** **ἄνθρωπος** (# *476*) man. Used in apposition to describe the character of those chosen. **παραδεδωκόσι** perf. act. part. (adj.) παραδίδωμι (# *4140*) to deliver over, to turn over, to entrust (BAGD; TLNT). Perf. indicates the state or condition of their character. ◆ **27** **ἀπεστάλκαμεν** perf. ind. act. ἀποστέλλω (# *690*) to send, to send as an official representative. **ἀπαγγέλλοντας** pres. act. part. ἀπαγγέλλω (# *550*) to report. Part. may be used to express purp. (LC). ◆ **28** **ἔδοξεν** aor. ind. act. s.v. 22. **πλέον** comp. πολύς (# *4498*) much; comp., more, greater. **ἐπιτίθεσθαι** pres. mid. (dep.) inf. ἐπιτίθημι (# *2202*) to place upon, to add to. Inf. in indir. discourse. **ἐπάναγκες** (# *2055*) adv. by compulsion, bound by necessity, necessarily; here, "the necessary things" (BAGD; Jos., *Ant.*, 16:365; for a discussion of the difficulties w. the word, s. LC). ◆ **29** **ἀπέχεσθαι** pres. mid. (dep.) inf. w. gen., s.v. 20. Inf. in indir. discourse. **εἰδωλόθυτον** (# *1628*) that which is offered to an idol. **διατηροῦντες** pres. act. part. (cond.) διατηρέω (# *1413*) to keep carefully, to observe carefully. **πράξετε**

fut. ind. act. πράσσω (# *4556*) to do, indicating the action of a moral and responsible being (MM); w. εὖ (adv.), to do right, or to prosper (LC; MM). **ἔρρωσθε** perf. pass. imp. ῥώννυμι (# *4874*) to make strong, to be made strong, to keep well, farewell. Common at the close of letters (RWP; MM; NDIEC, 7:26-27; VA, 362). ◆ **30** **ἀπολυθέντες** aor. pass. part. (temp.) ἀπολύω (# *668*) to release, to dismiss. **κατῆλθον** aor. ind. act. κατέρχομαι (# *2982*) to go down. **συναγαγόντες** aor. act. part. (temp.) s.v. 6. **ἐπέδωκαν** aor. ind. act. ἐπιδίδωμι (# *2113*) to give over, to deliver. In later Gr. a t.t. for sending in a report or handing over a letter (Bruce; NDIEC, 7:35). ◆ **31** **ἀναγνόντες** aor. act. part. (temp.) s.v. 21. **ἐχάρησαν** aor. ind. pass. s.v. 23. Ingressive aor., "they burst into exultant joy" (RWP). **παράκλησις** (# *4155*) encouragement (TDNT; EDNT). ◆ **32** **ὄντες** pres. act. part. (adj.) εἰμί (# *1639*) to be. **παρεκάλεσαν** aor. ind. act. παρακαλέω (# *4151*) to exhort, to encourage, to comfort (MNTW, 134; TDNT; EDNT). **ἐπεστήριξαν** aor. ind. act. ἐπιστηρίζω (# *2185*) to strengthen, to cause someone to become stronger in the sense of more firm and unchanging in attitude or belief (LN, 1:678; GELTS, 175). ◆ **33** **ποιήσαντες** aor. act. part. (temp.) ποιέω (# *4472*) to do; here, to spend time. **ἀπελύθησαν** aor. ind. pass. s.v. 30. **ἀποστείλαντας** aor. act. part. s.v. 27. Adj. part. as subst. ◆ **35** **διέτριβον** impf. ind. act. διατρίβω (# *1417*) to remain, to spend time. **διδάσκοντες** pres. act. part. (circum.) διδάσκω (# *1438*) to teach. **εὐαγγελιζόμενοι** pres. mid. (dep.) part. (circum.) εὐαγγελίζομαι (# *2294*) to proclaim the good news, to evangelize. ◆ **36** **εἶπεν** aor. ind. act. λέγω (# *3306*) to say. **ἐπιστρέψαντες** aor. act. part. s.v. 19. Circum. part. w. idea of the imp. in the main vb. (VANT, 386). **ἐπισκεψώμεθα** aor. mid. (dep.) subj. s.v. 14. Hortatory subj., "let us visit." **κατηγγείλαμεν** aor. ind. act. καταγγέλλω (# *2859*) to proclaim. This vb. w. prep. in compound often emphasizes the solemn style of the proclamation (CBB). **ἔχουσιν** pres. ind. act. ἔχω (# *2400*) to have; here, "how they have it," "how their state is," their internal and external Christian condition (Meyer). ◆ **37** **ἐβούλετο** impf. ind. mid. (dep.) βούλομαι (# *1089*) to will, to want, to wish, w. inf. Impf. indicates Barnabas stuck to his decision (RWP). **συμπαραλαβεῖν** aor. act. inf. συμπαραλαμβάνω (# *5221*) to take along together w., to take someone along as a helper (MM). The pres. inf. in v. 38 compared to the aor. inf. here indicates to have someone w. them day by day (M, 130). **καλούμενον** pres. pass. part. s.v. 22. ◆ **38** **ἠξίου** impf. ind. act. ἀξιόω (# *546*) to consider worthy, to consider suitable, w. inf. He did not think Mark fit or worthy to be taken w. them (Alex.). For a milder view of the situation w. the idea that the impf. indicates that Paul merely requested, and not even pressingly s. GI, 95. **ἀποστάντα** aor. act. part. (adj.) ἀφίστημι (# *923*) to depart, to desert, to give up. **συνελθόντα** aor. act. part.

συνέρχομαι (# *5302*) to go w. someone, to accompany. **συμπαραλαμβάνειν** pres. act. inf. s.v. 37. ◆ **39 ἐγένετο** aor. ind. mid. (dep.) s.v. 2. **παροξυσμός** (# *4237*) irritation, provocation, quarrel, severe argument based on intense difference of opinion, sharp argument (TDNT; LN, 1:440; LS, 1343). **ἀποχωρισθῆναι** aor. pass. inf. ἀποχωρίζω (# *714*) to separate, to depart. Inf. to express result (RG, 999). **παραλαβόντα** aor. act. part. (adj.) παραλαμβάνω (# *4161*) to take w. **ἐκπλεῦσαι** aor. act. inf. ἐκπλέω (# *1739*) to sail away. Inf. expressing result. The quarrel had at least one good result, that two missionary expeditions set out instead of one (Bruce). ◆ **40 ἐπιλεξάμενος** aor. mid. (indir. mid., to chose for oneself) part. (circum.) ἐπιλέγω (# *2141*) to choose, to select. **ἐξῆλθεν** aor. ind. act. ἐξέρχομαι (# *2002*) to go out. **παραδοθείς** aor. pass. part. s.v. 26. ◆ **41 διήρχετο** impf. ind. mid. (dep.) s.v. 3. This time Paul went by foot. Though the exact route is not mentioned, he may have passed through the Cilian Gates or a more westerly road, between Seleuia to Laranda to Derbe. (David French, "Acts and the Roman Roads of Asia Minor," BAFCS, 2:53-54; 54; Schneider). Paul left probably in the spring of A.D. 49 on the second mission trip (BASHH, 269; BAFCS, 2:398-99; FAP, 286). **ἐπιστηρίζων** pres. act. part. (circum.) s.v. 32.

Acts 16

◆ **1 κατήντησεν** aor. ind. act. καταντάω (# *2918*) to come down to, to arrive at. **ἦν** impf. act. ind. εἰμί (# *1639*) to be. **πιστός** (# *4412*) faithful, believing (in Christ) (BAGD). That Timothy's mother was Jewish and married to a Greek was illegal according to Jewish law, but children from such a marriage were considered Jewish because of the mother (SB, 2:741). ◆ **2 ἐμαρτυρεῖτο** impf. ind. pass. μαρτυρέω (# *3455*) to bear witness; pass. to be well spoken of, to be approved (EDNT; BAGD; MM; BS, 265). ◆ **3 ἠθέλησεν** aor. ind. act. θέλω (# *2527*) to wish, to want to, w. inf. **ἐξελθεῖν** aor. act. inf. ἐξέρχομαι (# *2002*) to go out. A person generally did not travel alone, but w. several companions. **λαβών** aor. act. part. (circum.) λαμβάνω (# *3284*) to take. **περιέτεμεν** aor. ind. act. περιτέμνω (# *4362*) to circumcise. **ὄντας** pres. act. part. (adj.) εἰμί s.v. 1. **ᾔδεισαν** plperf. ind. act. οἶδα (# *3857*) def. perf. w. pres. meaning, to know. W. def. perf. the plperf. is equivalent to the impf. (MH, 221). **ὑπῆρχεν** impf. ind. act. ὑπάρχω (# *5639*) to be, to exist. The impf. probably indicates that his father was dead (Bruce). ◆ **4 διεπορεύοντο** impf. ind. mid. (dep.) διαπορεύομαι (# *1388*) to travel through. **παρεδίδοσαν** impf. ind. act. παραδίδωμι (# *4140*) to deliver over, to pass on authoritative teaching (TLNT; TDNT). Impf. indicates they kept on delivering them in city after city (RWP). **φυλάσσειν** pres. act. inf. φυλάσσω (# *5875*) to guard, to observe. Inf. ex-

pressing purp. (IBG, 139). **δόγμα** (# *1504*) decree, decision. The noun is derived from the vb. δοκέω which is used in 15:22, 28. **κεκριμένα** perf. pass. part. κρίνω (# *3212*) to decide. Perf. emphasizes the permanence of the conclusion (RWP). ◆ **5 ἐστερεοῦντο** impf. ind. pass. στερεόω (# *5105*) to make firm, to strengthen (s. 3:7). **ἐπερίσσευον** impf. ind. act. περισσεύω (# *4355*) to increase. Impf. indicates the continual increase. ◆ **6 διῆλθον** aor. ind. act. διέρχομαι (# *1451*) to go through. This part of the journey was certainly carried out on unpaved tracks or paths (French, BAFCS, 2:56). For the areas of Phyrygia and Galatia and the problems involved s. G. Walter Hansen, "Galatia," BAFCS, 2:377-95; FAP, 251-54; BASHH, 112. **κωλυθέντες** aor. pass. part. κωλύω (# *3266*) to hinder, to prevent, to cause something not to happen (LN, 1:165. Part. could be causal and the action is simultaneous or antecedent w. the main vb., not a subsequent action (RWP). For a discussion of the aor. part. possibly expressing subsequent action s. BG, 87f; G.M. Lee, "The Past Participle of Subsequent Action," *Nov T* 17 (1975): 199. **λαλῆσαι** aor. act. inf. λαλέω (# *3281*) to speak. Epex. inf. explaining what the Holy Spirit prevented. ◆ **7 ἐλθόντες** aor. act. part. ἔρχομαι (# *2262*) to come, to go. **ἐπείραζον** impf. ind. act. πειράζω (# *4279*) to try, to attempt. Impf. indicating incomplete action. **πορευθῆναι** aor. pass. (dep.) inf. πορεύομαι (# *4513*) to travel, to go. Epex. inf. explaining what they attempted. **εἴασεν** aor. ind. act. ἐάω (# *1572*) to allow. ◆ **8 παρελθόντες** aor. act. part. (temp.) παρέρχομαι (# *4216*) to pass by. **κατέβησαν** aor. ind. act. καταβαίνω (# *2849*) to go down. The way from Mysia to Troas is uncertain (W. P. Bowers, "Paul's Route through Mysia: A Note on Acts XVI.8," *JTS* n.s. 30 [1979]: 507-11; BASHH, 112-13; FAP, 260-61). **Τρῳάς** (# *5590*) Troas. For the city s. Colin J. Hemer, "Alexandria Troas," *TB* 26 (1975): 79-112; KP, 5:977-83; Paul Trebilco, "Asia," BAFCS, 2:357-59; Thomas Pekáry, "Kleinasien unter römischer Herrschaft," ANRW 2, 7, 2:613-17. A grave marker just outside the city, reads, "*Resta, viator, et lege*" ("Stand still, oh traveller, and read") (H. Geist & G. Pfohl, *Römische Grabinschriften* [München: Ernst Heimeran Verlag, 1969], 25) ◆ **9 ὅραμα** (# *3969*) vision. **ὤφθη** aor. ind. pass. ὁράω (# *3972*) to see; pass., to appear. **ἦν** impf. act. ind. εἰμί s.v. 1. **ἑστώς** perf. act. part. ἵστημι (# *2705*) perf. to stand. Part. in a periphrastic construction. Perf. part. indicating the man in a state of standing contrasts w. the pres. part. ("beseeching") which indicates the activity which he is in progress of performing (VA, 482). **παρακαλῶν** pres. act. part. παρακαλέω (# *4151*) to encourage, to beseech, to entreat (s. 15:32). Part. in a periphrastic construction. **διαβάς** aor. act. part. διαβαίνω (# *1329*) to pass through, to come over. Circum. part. expressing a command (Matt. 28:19; BG, 129; VANT, 386). **βοήθησον** aor. imp. act. βοηθέω (# *1070*) to help, to assist in supplying what may be needed (LN, 1:458). Aor. imp. calls for a specific action w. a note of urgency. For the view that the man of Macedonia was Luke s. PTR, 202; P, 153-59. For the area of Macedonia s. David W.J. Gill, "Macedonia," BAFCS, 2:397-417; LGG, 199-21; KP, 3:910-19. ◆ **10** ὡς (# *6055*) when, after (BD, 237.38). εἶδεν aor. ind. act. ὁράω s.v. 9. ἐζητήσαμεν aor. ind. act. ζητέω (# *2426*) to seek. 1st. pers. pl. subject is the beginning of the first long "we passage," continuing to the arrest of Paul and Silas in Philippi (LC; BASHH, 312-34; Colin J. Hemer, "First Person Narrative in Acts 27-28," *TB* 36 [1985]: 79-110; Stanley E. Porter, "The 'We' Passages," BAFCS, 2:545-74). ἐξελθεῖν aor. act. inf. s.v. 3. Epex. inf. explaining what they sought to do. συμβιβάζοντες pres. act. part. συμβιβάζω (# *5204*) to put together, to conclude, to infer. Causal or circum. part. προσκέκληται perf. ind. mid. προσκαλέω (# *4673*) to call, to call to a special task (BAGD). Perf. refers to the continuation of the narrative (VA, 262). εὐ-αγγελίσασθαι aor. mid. (dep.) inf. εὐαγγελίζομαι (# *2294*) to proclaim the good news (TDNT; TLNT). Inf. of purp. ◆ **11** ἀναχθέντες aor. pass. part. (temp.) ἀνάγω (# *343*) to lead up; pass.; to set sail. εὐθυδρομήσαμεν aor. ind. act. εὐθυδρομέω (# *2312*) to run a straight course; that is, they found a favorable wind, probably from the northeast, enabling them to make Samothrace (LC). Samothrace, an island in the northeast part of the Aegean Sea, was a conspicuous landmark, dominated by a 5000-foot-high mountain; it was also called Poseidon's Island, the Greek god of the waters, earthquakes, and horses (BASHH, 113; Longenecker, 459). ἐπιούσῃ (# *2079*) on the following (day); dat. of time, w. the word "day" to be supplied. Νέαν Πόλιν acc. sing. Nea Polis, a seaport about 10-12 miles from Philippi (BASHH, 113; BAFCS, 2:410). ◆ **12** πρώτη (# *4755*) first. Perhaps here a leading city of the district of Macedonia; or the conjectured gen. (πρώτης) may indicate a city of the first district of Macedonia (Macedonia was divided into four districts; Gill, "Macedonia," BAFCS, 2:401; TC, 444-46; BASHH, 113-14; Sherwin-White, 93-95; P, 159-65). κολωνία colony. A Roman colony was like a piece of Rome or Italy transplanted abroad and settled by army veterans. It enjoyed special privileges such as *libertas* (self-government w. two magistrates [*duoviri*]); *immunitas* (freedom from tribute and taxes); *jus Italicum* (under the laws of Rome) (Bruce; LC, 1:657; CC, 175; DGRA, 315-20; CH, 223-26). For the city of Philippi, s. BAFCS, 2:411-13; AAT, 216-19; CH, 222-23; NW, 2:ii:653-54; P, 1-113; PSCZP, 11-84). It was just outside Philippi that Octavius and Mark Anthony defeated Cassius and Brutus, the assassins of Julius Caesar (CAH, 10:22-25). ἦμεν impf. act. ind. εἰμί s.v. 1. δια-τρίβοντες pres. act. part. διατρίβω (# *1417*) to remain. Part. in a periphrastic construction. ἡμέρας acc. pl. ἡμέρα (# *2465*) day. Acc. of time, "for certain days."

◆ **13** ἐξήλθομεν aor. ind. act. s.v. 3. ποταμός (# *4532*) river. The river would be the Gangites (Angites) which flows into the Strymon (Williams). The omission of the art. is one of the touches of familiarity which shows the hand of one who knew Philippi well (PTR, 213; s. RG, 792). οὗ where. For a discussion of the geographical location s. P, 165-174; Valerie A. Abrahamsen, *Women and Worship at Philippi: Diana/ Artemis and Other Cults in the Early Christian Era* (Portland, Me.: Astarte Shell, 1995). ἐνομίζομεν impf. ind. act. νομίζω (# *3787*) to suppose, to be the custom. For the textual problem here s. TC, 447. προσευχή (# *4666*) prayer, a place of prayer (BS, 222). εἶναι pres. act. inf. εἰμί s.v. 1. Inf. in indir. discourse. καθίσαντες aor. act. part. (temp.) καθίζω (# *2767*) to take one's seat, to sit down. ἐλαλοῦμεν impf. ind. act. λαλέω (# *3281*) to speak. Incep. impf., "we began to speak." συνελθούσαις aor. act. part. dat. fem. pl. συνέρχομαι (# *5302*) to come together, to gather. Part. as subst. To form a synagogue there had to be ten male heads of households; since this was evidently not the case, they met by the river to pray (Longenecker, 460). ◆ **14** Λυδία (# *3376*) Lydia. For the name s. BASHH, 231. πορφυρόπωλις (# *4527*) one who sells purple. The purple dye could come from three sources: the shellfish murex (the most expensive), the kermes oak, and the madder root (NDIEC, 2:25-26; 3:54; s. esp. P, 174-82) Thyatira was famous for its dyeing (PTR, 214). There was a great demand for this fabric as it was used for the official Roman toga (RWP; Pliny, NH, 9:124-41). For the cloth industry under the Roman Empire s. RE, 350-64. Since Lydia was a business woman w. a household, it has been suggested that she was a freedwoman, a widow, or divorcee w. at least three children so that she came under the *Ius liberorum*, which allowed a woman of her status to conduct business without her husband (NDIEC, 25-32; 3:53-55; 4:93; David W.J. Gill, "Acts and the Urban Elite," BAFCS, 2:114-18). σεβομένη pres. mid. (dep.) part. σέβομαι (# *4936*) to worship, to fear, to be devout (s. 13:43). ἤκουεν impf. ind. act. ἀκούω (# *201*) to hear, to listen to. Impf. pictures the attentive listening. διή-νοιξεν aor. ind. act. διανοίγω (# *1380*) to open. Prep. in compound suggests, "to open up wide or completely," like a folding door (RWP). "To open the heart" indicates that the Lord caused her to understand (BAGD; EDNT) or that He caused her to have an open mind w. a willingness to learn and evaluate fairly (LN, 1:332). προσέχειν pres. act. inf. προσέχω (# *4668*) to hold to, to give heed to, to pay attention to (BAGD). Inf. expressing result. λαλουμένοις pres. pass. part. s.v. 6. Part. used as subst. ◆ **15** ἐβαπτίσθη aor. ind. pass. βαπτίζω (# *966*) to baptize. ὁ οἶκος αὐτῆς (# *3875; 899*) her house. Her household probably included servants and other dependents, perhaps some of the women of v. 13 (Bruce). Perhaps the church began to meet in her house. For the house church s. Bradley Blue, "Acts and the House Church," BAFCS, 2:119-222. **κεκρίκατε** perf. ind. act. κρίνω (# 3212) to judge, to decide. Perf. indicates the lasting result. Ind. in a 1st. class cond. cl. in which the speaker assumes the reality of the cond. **εἶναι** pres. act. inf. εἰμί s.v. 1. Inf. used as obj. **εἰσελθόντες** aor. act. part. εἰσέρχομαι (# 1656) to go in. Circum. part. w. force of the imp. (s.v. 9). **μένετε** pres. imp. act. μένω (# 3531) to remain. **παρεβιάσατο** aor. ind. mid. (dep.) παραβιάζομαι (# 4128) to urge strongly, to insist. ◆ **16 ἐγένετο** aor. ind. mid. γίνομαι (# 1181) to become, to happen. For the construction s. Beyer, 45f. **πορευομένων** pres. mid. (dep.) part. (temp.) s.v. 7. Gen. abs. **παιδίσκη** (# 4087) slave girl. **ἔχουσαν** pres. act. part. acc. sing. fem. ἔχω (# 2400) to have. **πύθων** (# 4780) python, divination, prophecy. The word was used for the serpent that guarded the Delphic oracle and later was slain by Apollo. The word came to designate a spirit of divination, then also a ventriloquist believed to have such a spirit dwelling in his belly (BAGD; LC; TDNT; EDNT; DPL, 210-11; KP, 4:1280; GGR, 1:550). The word is in apposition to "spirit." **ὑπαντῆσαι** aor. act. inf. ὑπαντάω (# 5636) to meet. Inf. w. ἐγένετο ("It happened ... she met us"). **παρεῖχεν** impf. ind. act. παρέχω (# 4218) to bring in, to provide, to supply. Impf. pictures a steady source of income (RWP). **μαντευομένη** pres. mid. (dep.) part. μαντεύομαι (# 3446) to soothsay, to give an oracle. It refers to the tumult of the mind, the fury, the temporary madness of these who were supposed to be possessed by the god during the time they delivered their oracles (Trench, *Synonyms*, 22). In the LXX it always is employed of lying prophets (EGT). Instr. part., explaining how they made their gain. ◆ **17 κατακολουθοῦσα** pres. act. part. κατακολουθέω (# 2887) to follow after, w. dat. Prep. in compound indicates the following after someone over an intervening space (MH, 316). Causal or temp. part. **ἔκραζεν** impf. ind. act. κράζω (# 3189) to scream. Impf., because she did it many days (Bruce). **δοῦλοι τοῦ θεοῦ τοῦ ὑψίστου** servants of the highest God. Though this may have been a Jewish designation for the true God, it might have also been understood as a pagan designation for Zeus or another deity (BAFCS, 3:117; BBC; P.R. Trebilco, "Paul and Silas – 'Servants of the Most High God,'" JSNT 36 [1989]: 51-73; NDIEC, 1:25-29; P, 182-88; for worship at Philippi s. Valerie A. Abrahamsen, *Women and Worship at Philippi: Diana/ Artemis and Other Cults in the Early Christian Era*, [Portland, Me.: Astarte Shell, 1995]). **καταγγέλλουσιν** pres. ind. act. καταγγέλλω (# 2859) to proclaim. **ὁδὸν σωτηρίας** a way of salvation. The implication is that the girl was denying an exclusive way of salvation (BAFCS, 3:117). ◆ **18 ἐποίει** impf. ind. act. ποιέω (# 4472) to do. Impf. indicates continual action, "she kept on doing it." **διαπονηθείς** aor. pass. part. (temp.)

διαπονέω (# 1387) to be worked up, to be indignant (s. 4:2). Ingressive aor., "he became irritated." **ἐπιστρέψας** aor. act. part. (temp.) ἐπιστρέφω (# 2188) to turn to. **εἶπεν** aor. ind. act. λέγω (# 3306) to say. **παραγγέλλω** (# 4133) pres. act. ind. to command, w. dat. and inf. The word is esp. used of the transmitted orders of a military commander (AS). **ἐξελθεῖν** aor. act. inf. s.v. 3. Inf. as obj. in indir discourse. **ἐξῆλθεν** aor. ind. act. ◆ **19 ἰδόντες** aor. act. part. (temp.) ὁράω (# 3972) to see. **κύριοι** nom. pl. κύριος (# 3261) lord, owner. The owners of the girl were probably Roman veterans, themselves Roman citizens, retired from military service and well known in Philippi, who were property owners with material wealth and a good family heritage (BAFCS, 3:119-20). **ἐξῆλθεν** aor. ind. act. s.v. 3. **ἐπιλαβόμενοι** aor. mid. (dep.) part. (circum.) ἐπιλαμβάνομαι (# 2138) to take hold of, to seize, to catch. **εἵλκυσαν** aor. ind. act. ἑλκύω (# 1816) to drag. **ἀγορά** (# 59) marketplace. Here it indicates the courthouse (LC). Every eighth day for the Romans was a market day called *Nundinae* ("ninth-day affairs"), during which court was held (LLAR, 58-65; 79-81; FCRR, 42-50). Business was conducted from early morning till midday, with courts beginning around 9:00 A.M. (LLAR, 24). **ἄρχοντας** acc. pl. ἄρχων (# 807) ruler, magistrate. A general Greek name for the magistrates of a city (Gill, "Macedonia," BAFCS, 2:412). For their function in a Roman colony s. LC; Sherwin-White, 74f. ◆ **20 προσαγαγόντες** aor. act. part. (temp.) προσάγω (# 4642) to lead to. **στρατηγός** (# 5130) leader of an army, general, city official. The author uses the most common Hellenistic title to render the untranslatable term *duoviri* (Sherwin-White, 93; Gill, "Macedonia," BAFCS, 2:412). After the pattern of the consuls at Rome, the chief magistrates of a Roman colony were two in number and their official title was *duoviri* ("the two men"). They were attended by two *lictores* (s.v. 35) who carried bundles of rods called *virgae* which were symbols of their right to use physical coercion or corporal punishment (Rackham; BAFCS, 3:123-24; P, 193-99). **εἶπαν** aor. ind. act. λέγω (# 3306) to say. **ἐκταράσσουσιν** pres. ind. act. ἐκταράσσω (# 1752) to trouble, to agitate, to throw into confusion. The prep. compound is perfective, "to cause utter confusion" (MH, 309). Pres. indicates a continual action. **ὑπάρχοντες** pres. act. part. (adj.) s.v. 3. ◆ **21 καταγγέλλουσιν** pres. ind. act. s.v. 17. **ἔθη** acc. pl. ἔθος (# 1621) custom. **ἔξεστιν** (# 2003) pres. ind. act. it is lawful; impersonal use, it is allowed, w. inf. **παραδέχεσθαι** pres. mid. (dep.) inf. παραδέχομαι (# 4138) to receive, to adopt. **ποιεῖν** pres. act. inf. s.v. 18. The two charges were causing riots and the introduction of an alien religion. (Sherwin-White, 78-83; P, 189-93). Since Paul was a Jew, the charges may reflect an awareness of Claudius' recent edict and the Roman soldiers refusal to observe Jewish rituals (BAFCS,

3:117-18). οὖσιν pres. act. part. (adj.) εἰμί s.v. 1. ◆ **22** συνεπέστη aor. ind. act. συνεφίστημι (# 5308) to rise up together, to join in an attack (BAGD). The crowd seems to be orderly, and it was not uncommon for watching and participating assemblies to gather for informal or legal proceedings (BAFCS, 3:122-23). περιρήξαντες aor. act. part. (temp.) περιρήγνυμι (# 4351) to strip off all around. The magistrates had the clothes of the apostles torn off (Bruce). ἐκέλευον impf. ind. act. κελεύω (# 3027) to command. The official order generally given was, "Go, lictors; strip off their garments; let them be scourged" (CH, 234). ῥαβδίζειν pres. act. inf. ῥαβδίζω (# 4810) to beat w. rods or sticks. The beating w. rods (Latin *verberatio*), a means of police coercion, was done by the lictors (s.v. 35) and could be a cruel, bloody process w. lethal results (TDNT; KP, 5:1186; s. H. Last, "Coercitio," RAC, 3:235-43; BAFCS, 3:124-25). The punishment was considered appropriate for those causing civic disturbance (BAFCS, 3:125). The *Lex Porciae de Tergo Civium* prohibited the scourging of Roman citizens without appeal (OCD, 604; BAFCS, 3:47-56). Perhaps Paul did not claim his rights as a Roman citizen at this time because he feared delay in checking his claim and, most of all, because it would have compromised his Jewishness, his Gospel message, and the young church at Philippi (BAFCS, 3:129-34). ◆ **23** ἐπιθέντες aor. act. part. (temp.) ἐπιτίθημι (# 2202) to lay on. ἔβαλον aor. ind. act. βάλλω (# 965) to throw. φυλακή (# 5871) place of guarding, prison. A person was placed in a prison until he could be tried before the proconsul, either at the capital of the province, or the nearest assize city (Sherwin-White, 82-83). παραγγείλαντες aor. act. part. παραγγέλλω (# 4133) to give orders, to command, to instruct (BAGD). δεσμοφύλακι dat. sing. δεσμοφύλαξ (# 1302) jailer, keeper of a prison who had the sole responsibility for running the prison and its security. He may have been a military officer, a retired soldier, or a public slave (BAFCS, 3:261-63; for prison personnel s. BAFCS, 3:244-61; CIC, 86-89; Pliny, the Younger, Letter 10). Indir. obj. ἀσφαλῶς (# 857) safely. τηρεῖν pres. act. inf. τηρέω (# 5498) to watch, to guard, to keep. Inf. in indir. discourse. ◆ **24** παραγγελία (# 4132) command, instruction. λαβών aor. act. part. (temp.) λαμβάνω (# 3284) to receive. ἐσώτερος (# 2278) inner. The comp. has perhaps superl. force ("innermost") (Bruce). The first part of a Roman prison (*communiora*) had light and fresh air; the second part (*interiora*) was shut off by iron gates; the third part (*tullianum*) was a dungeon where those who had committed the most serious crimes and those of the lowest level of society were kept awaiting execution (CH, 234; DGRA, 240-41; BAFCS, 3:20-22, 126). ἠσφαλίσατο aor. ind. mid. (dep.) ἀσφαλίζω (# 856) to make safe, to secure, to guard someone so that he cannot escape (BAGD). ξύλον (# 3833) acc. sing. wood, stock. A

Roman instrument of torture w. more than two holes for the legs so that they could be forced widely apart into a position which soon became intolerably painful. It was probably used as a security precaution in this case (LC; RAC 8:112-41, esp. 118; BAFCS, 3:126-27). ◆ **25** κατὰ τὸ μεσονύκτιον (# 2848; 3543) about midnight. One of the abiding hallmarks of life in prison was darkness. Nightfall robbed the prisoner of what little light there was and at midnight there was total darkness (BAFCS, 3:199-200). Since business was concluded generally by noon, Paul and Silas had been beaten in the morning and held in the inner prison in stocks, unable to move their legs, for about 12 hours. προσευχόμενοι pres. mid. (dep.) part. (circum.) προσεύχομαι (# 4667) to pray. ὕμνουν impf. ind. act. ὑμνέω (# 5630) to sing a hymn of praise addressed directly to God (Trench, *Synonyms,* 297; TDNT; EDNT; NIDNTT, 3:668-70). The joyful hymns were for praise, not release, and their stark contrast to the distress, complaint and/or anxious petition which might be expected was a witness to those in the prison (BAFCS, 3:339). Impf. pictures continual singing. ἐπηκροῶντο impf. ind. mid. (dep.) ἐπακροάομαι (# 2053) to listen to, w. the probable implication of one's own interest (LN, 1:283), w. gen. Employed in medical language for the placing of the ear to the human body in order to detect the nature of internal disease by the sound (MLL, 234). The prep. compound is directive indicating the closest attention (BAFCS, 3:202). Impf. indicates that the missionaries held their attention throughout (Williams). ◆ **26** ἄφνω (# 924) suddenly. σεισμός (# 4939) shaking, earthquake. ἐγένετο aor. ind. mid. (dep.) s.v. 16. σαλευθῆναι aor. pass. inf. σαλεύω (# 4888) to shake. Inf. w. ὥστε (# 6063) to express result. θεμέλιον (# 2528) foundation, base. δεσμωτήριον (# 1303) prison. ἠνεῴχθησαν aor. ind. pass. ἀνοίγω (# 487) to open. παραχρῆμα (# 4202) immediately. δεσμά nom. pl. δεσμός (# 1301) bond, shackle. N. pl. is collective (GGP, 2:96-97). ἀνέθη aor. ind. pass. ἀνίημι (# 479) to loosen, to release. ◆ **27** ἔξυπνος (# 2031) out of sleep, awake, aroused. γενόμενος aor. mid. (dep.) part. s.v. 16. Temp. or circum. part. ἰδών aor. act. part. (temp.) ὁράω (# 3972) to see. ἀνεῳγμένας perf. pass. part. s.v. 26. Perf. indicates the state ("standing open"). σπασάμενος aor. mid. (dep.) part. (temp.) σπάω (# 5060) to draw. μάχαιρα (# 3479) sword. ἤμελλεν impf. ind. act. μέλλω (# 3516) to be about to. W. inf. expressing futurity or intention reckoned from a moment in the past (MKG, 307). ἀναιρεῖν pres. act. inf. ἀναιρέω (# 359) to kill. νομίζων pres. act. part. (causal) νομίζω (# 3787) to suppose, to presume, w. inf. ἐκπεφευγέναι perf. act. inf. ἐκφεύγω (# 1767) to flee, to escape. The prep. is perfective, indicating a successful escape (MH, 310). Perf. indicates the continuing result. It was evidently dark and he could not see. He was accountable for how he kept the prisoners and laxness in the method of constraint, especially if the prisoners escaped, was punishable (BAFCS, 3:390-91). ◆ **28 ἐφώνησεν** aor. ind. act. φωνέω (# 5888) to call. **πράξῃς** aor. subj. act. πράσσω (# 4556) to do. The aor. subj. w. the neg. is used in a specific command to prohibit the beginning of an action (MKG, 273; VANT, 337-38). **ἐσμεν** pres. act. ind. εἰμί s.v. 1. ◆ **29 αἰτήσας** aor. act. part. (circum.) αἰτέω (# 160) to ask. **φῶς** (# 5890) light. **εἰσεπήδησεν** aor. ind. act. εἰσπηδάω (# 1659) to leap in, to rush in, to burst in (MM). **γενόμενος** aor. mid. (dep.) part. (circum.) s.v. 16. **προσέπεσεν** aor. ind. act. προσπίπτω (# 4700) to fall down before someone, w. dat. ◆ **30 προαγαγών** aor. act. part. (temp.) προάγω (# 4575) to lead forth, to bring out. **ἔφη** aor. ind. act. φημί (# 5774) to say. **κύριοι** voc. pl. κύριος (# 3261) sir. Polite form of address. **δεῖ** (# 1256) pres. inf. act. it is necessary, indicating a logical necessity, w. inf. **ποιεῖν** pres. act. inf. s.v. 18. **σωθῶ** aor. subj. pass. σώζω (# 5392) to rescue, to save. Subj. w. **ἵνα** (# 2671) to express purpose. The cry indicates that he had not simply kept the apostles but had in fact abused them (BAFCS, 3:264). ◆ **31 εἶπαν** aor. ind. act. λέγω (# 3306) to say. **πίστευσον** aor. imp. act. πιστεύω (# 4409) to believe, to put one's faith and confidence in. Aor. imp. calls for a specific act w. a note of urgency. **σωθήσῃ** fut. ind. pass. s.v. 30. For the use of the imp. followed by **καί** (# 2779) and the fut. to form a type of Hebraic cond. cl. s. Beyer, 238-55; also GGBB, 402. ◆ **32 ἐλάλησαν** aor. ind. act. λαλέω (# 3281) to speak. ◆ **33 παραλαβών** aor. act. part. παραλαμβάνω (# 4161) to take w. **ἔλουσεν** aor. ind. act. λούω (# 3374) to wash. For the use of this word w. the prep. s. BS, 227; NDIEC, 3:20. ◆ **34 ἀναγαγών** aor. act. part. (temp.) ἀνάγω (# 343) to bring up. **παρέθηκεν** aor. ind. act. παρατίθημι (# 4192) to set before. An individual table was placed beside each guest (Bruce). The jailor was taking a great risk in helping the prisoners, especially in providing a meal; it could have cost him his life (BAFCS, 3:392). **ἠγαλλιάσατο** aor. ind. mid. (dep.) ἀγαλλιάομαι (# 22) to rejoice, to be full of joy. **πανοικεί** (# 4109) w. one's whole household. An expression common in the closing greetings of private letters (MM). **πεπιστευκώς** perf. act. part. s.v. 31. Causal (VA, 399) or supplementary part. w. a vb. of emotion: "He was filled w. joy at having a firm faith in God" (NSV, 66). Perf. indicates the state of having believed. ◆ **35 γενομένης** aor. mid. (dep.) part (temp.) s.v. 16. Gen. abs. **ἀπέστειλαν** aor. ind. act. ἀποστέλλω (# 690) to send. **ῥαβδοῦχος** (# 4812) lictor, rod-bearer. They were attendants serving the magistrate who prepared his way and carried out punishments and summons (OCD, 609; s.v. 20). **λέγοντες** pres. act. part. s.v. 18. **ἀπόλυσον** aor. act. imp. ἀπολύω (# 668) to release. ◆ **36 ἀπήγγειλεν** aor. ind. act. ἀπαγγέλλω (# 550) to report. **ἀπέσταλκαν** perf. ind. act. s.v. 35. **ἀπολυθῆτε** aor.

subj. pass. s.v. 35. Subj. w. **ἵνα** (# 2671) to express purp. **ἐξελθόντες** aor. act. part. s.v. 3. Circum. part. w. force of the imp. (s.v. 9). **πορεύεσθε** pres. mid. (dep.) imp. s.v. 7. ◆ **37 ἔφη** impf./aor. ind. act. s.v. 30. **δείραντες** aor. act. part. (temp.) δέρω (# 1296) to flay, to skin, to strike. **δημοσίᾳ** (# 1323) publicly. **ἀκατάκριτος** (# 185) uncondemned, or possibly untried, without a trial (LC). Paul seems to be accusing the Philippian magistrates of being guilty of serious procedural irregularities owing to their faulty assumptions, the result being that Roman citizens had been unjustly punished (BBC; BAFCS, 3:302). **ὑπάρχοντας** pres. act. part. s.v. 20. Concessive part., "although we are Romans." **ἔβαλαν** aor. ind. act. s.v. 23. **λάθρα** (# 3277) secretly. **ἐκβάλλουσιν** pres. ind. act. ἐκβάλλω (# 1675) to throw out. **οὐ** (# 4024) no! **ἐλθόντες** aor. act. part. s.v. 7. Circum. part. w. force of the imp., "let them come themselves (αὐτοί). **ἐξαγαγέτωσαν** aor. imp. act. ἐξάγω (# 1974) to lead out, to conduct. A Roman citizen could travel anywhere within Roman territory under the protection of Rome (Longenecker, 466). ◆ **38 ἐφοβήθησαν** aor. ind. pass. (dep.) φοβέομαι (# 5828) to be afraid. Ingressive aor., "they became afraid." **ἀκούσαντες** aor. act. part. (temp.) ἀκούω (# 201) to hear. ◆ **39 ἐλθόντες** aor. act. part. (temp.) s.v. 7. **παρεκάλεσαν** aor. ind. act. παρακαλέω (# 4151) to call, to summon. **ἐξαγαγόντες** aor. act. part. (temp.) s.v. 37. **ἠρώτων** impf. ind. act. ἐρωτάω (# 2263) to ask. Incep. impf., or it stresses the repeated request. **ἀπελθεῖν** aor. act. inf. ἀπέρχομαι (# 599) to go forth, to go out. Inf. in indir. discourse. ◆ **40 ἐξελθόντες** aor. act. part. s.v. 3. **εἰσῆλθον** aor. ind. act. εἰσέρχομαι (# 1656) to go into. **ἰδόντες** aor. act. part. s.v. 19. **παρεκάλεσαν** aor. ind. act. παρακαλέω (# 4151) to encourage, to comfort.

Acts 17

◆ **1 διοδεύσαντες** aor. act. part. διοδεύω (# 1476) to take the road through. The road was the *Via Egnatia* (Gill, "Macedonia," BAFCS, 2:409-10; FAP, 297–99; P, 199-205). This vb. probably was chosen to emphasize the way (Bruce). Temp. part., or perhaps part. of means, "By taking the road." **ἦλθον** aor. ind. act. ἔρχομαι (# 2262) to go, to come. The city of Thessalonica, located on the *Via Egnatia*, was 267 miles from the Adriatic coast, about halfway along the road (Gill, BAFCS, 2:409-10; for a Roman milestone found close to the city s. NDIEC, 1:81; ABD, 4:831-32). It had become a "free city" in 42 B.C. and with its warm springs (*Thermae*) and public buildings around a market place (*Agora*), linked to a stoa, it was one of the most heavily populated cites of the area, having some 100,000 inhabitants including the settlements outside the city wall (Gill, BAFCS, 2:414-15; FAP, 296-301; ABD, 6:523-27; NW, 2:ii:767-68). For the religion of the city s. Charles Edson, "State Cults of Thessalonica (Macedonia II)," *Harvard Studies in Classical Philogy* 51 (1940): 127-36; C. Edson, "Cults of Thessalonica (Macedonia III)," *HTR* 41 (1948): 153-204; Karl P. Donfried, "The Cults of Thessalonia and the Thessalonian Correspondence," *NTS* 31 (1985): 336-56. ◆ **2 εἰωθός** (*# 1665*) pref. act. part. acc. n. sing. ἔθω to be accustomed. Part. as subst.: custom, habit, "as Paul's custom was" (BAGD). **εἰσῆλθεν** aor. ind. act. εἰσέρχομαι (*# 1656*) to go into. **ἐπὶ σάββατα τρία** three Sabbath days, but not necessarily three weeks (LC, 202-03). **διελέξατο** aor. ind. mid. (dep.) διαλέγομαι (*# 1363*) to reason, to argue, to dispute, to revolve in the mind, to teach w. the method of question and answer, to give a discourse, but always w. the idea of intellectual stimulus (RWP; LN, 1:439). **γραφῶν** gen. pl. γραφή (*# 1210*) writing, Scriptures. The OT was the source of authority for Paul and the Jews. ◆ **3 διανοίγων** pres. act. part. διανοίγω (*# 1380*) to open. Part. of means explaining how Paul argued. **παρατιθέμενος** pres. mid. part. παρατίθημι (*# 4192*) to place alongside, to allege, to present evidence, to establish evidence to show that something is true (LN, 1:673; MM; Preisigke, 2:258). Here it is the bringing forward of proof passages of Scripture (EGT). Pres. part. emphasizes the continuing action and describes the means or methods of Paul's reasoning and argumentation. **ἔδει** impf. ind. act. δεῖ (*# 1256*) it is necessary, w. inf. giving a logical necessity. **παθεῖν** aor. act. inf. πάσχω (*# 4248*) to suffer. **ἀναστῆναι** aor. act. inf. ἀνίστημι (*# 482*) to rise. **καταγγέλλω** (*# 2859*) pres. ind. act. to proclaim. The word often emphasizes the elevated and solemn style of the proclamation (NIDNTT, 3:45; TDNT). ◆ **4 ἐπείσθησαν** aor. ind. pass. πείθω (*# 4275*) to persuade; pass. to be persuaded. **προσεκληρώθησαν** aor. ind. pass. προσκληρόω (*# 4677*) to allot, to assign; pass. to be attached, to join w., w. dat. (BAGD). **σεβομένων** pres. mid. (dep.) part. (adj.) σέβομαι (*# 4936*) to be devout, pious, to be God-fearing (s. 10:2). **πολὺ γυναικῶν τε τῶν πρώτων** "and many of the leading women." The Gr. worshipers and the women were perhaps of the social elite (BAFSC, 2:113). ◆ **5 ζηλώσαντες** aor. act. part. (causal) ζηλόω (*# 2420*) to be jealous, to feel strong envy and resentment against someone (LN, 1:760). **προσλαβόμενοι** aor. mid. (dep.) part. προσλαμβάνω (*# 4689*) to take to oneself, to accept in the circle of acquaintances, to take along w. oneself as companion or helper (BAGD). **ἀγοραῖος** (*# 61*) market people, one who hangs out at the marketplace, loafer, gangster, or country people who brought their goods to the *agora* to have them sold (Bruce; BAGD; LS; DGRA, 35-36). The *agora* was originally an open place where the king met the people; it later became the open place where the citizens gathered; then it indicated the open place around which important government buildings were located, as well as stores,

where one could buy the necessities of life, it corresponded to the Latin *Forum*. Business was usually carried from 9:00 A.M. to 12 noon on the market days (*Nundinae*) (DGRA, 32-36; TAA; LLAR, 59-61). **ὀχλοποιήσαντες** aor. act. part. (temp.) ὀχλοποιέω (*# 4062*) to gather a crowd, to collect a mob. **ἐθορύβουν** impf. ind. act. θορυβέω (*# 2572*) to cause an uproar, to trouble, to throw into confusion. Incep. impf., "they began to trouble...." **ἐπιστάντες** aor. act. part. (temp.) ἐφίστημι (*# 2392*) to stand before, to approach, to appear. **ἐζήτουν** impf. ind. act. ζητέω (*# 2426*) to seek, to try. **προαγαγεῖν** aor. act. inf. προάγω (*# 4575*) to lead before, to bring out before. Epex. inf. explaining what they attempted. **δῆμος** (*# 1322*) people, crowd gathered for any purp. (BAGD). ◆ **6 εὑρόντες** aor. act. part. (temp.) εὑρίσκω (*# 2351*) to find. **ἔσυρον** impf. ind. act. σύρω (*# 5359*) to drag. **πολιτάρχης** (*# 4485*) ruler of the city. Used mainly of the Macedonian title for the non-Roman magistrates of a city (generally five in number), whose duties were, among other things, to confirm decisions made by the Demos, and to maintain peace and order in their city. The title is found in numerous inscriptions, the majority of which come from northern Greece and some 40% from the city of Thessalonica (LC; G.H.R. Horsley, "The Politarchs," BAFCS, 2:419-31; ADB, 6:386-89; NDIEC, 2:34-35; FAP, 314-15; Bruce). **βοῶντες** pres. act. part. (circum.) βοάω (*# 1066*) to shout. **ἀναστατώσαντες** aor. act. part. ἀναστατόω (*# 415*) to stir up sedition, to upset. Used in a letter of a bad little boy whose mother said, "He drives me mad" (LAE, 202). **πάρεισιν** pres. ind. act. πάρειμι (*# 4205*) to be present. Perfective pres. indicating an action as well as a condition or state (VANT, 230-40). ◆ **7 ὑποδέδεκται** perf. ind. mid. (dep.) ὑποδέχομαι (*# 5685*) to receive, to entertain. **ἀπέναντι** (*# 595*) against, opposed to. **πράσσουσι** pres. ind. act. πράσσω (*# 4556*) to do, to practice. **λέγοντες** pres. act. part. λέγω (*# 3306*) to say. Part. explaining how they are doing things against the Caesar. **εἶναι** pres. act. inf. εἰμί (*# 1639*) to be. Inf. in indir. discourse. The accusation was not only political in nature, but also religious because of the imperial cult (Gill & Winter, BAFCS, 2:93-103; S.R.F. Price, "Gods and Emperors: The Greek Language of The Roman Imperial Cult," *JHS* 104 [1984]: 79-95). ◆ **8 ἐτάραξαν** aor. ind. act. ταράσσω (*# 5429*) to stir up, to confuse, to trouble. **ἀκούοντας** pres. act. part. (temp.) ἀκούω (*# 201*) to hear, to listen to. ◆ **9 λαβόντες** aor. act. part. (temp.) λαμβάνω (*# 3284*) to take. **ἱκανόν** (*# 2653*) acc. sing. security, bail. It is equivalent to the Latin *satis accipere* which is used in connection w. the offering and giving of security in civil and criminal procedures (Sherwin-White, 95; MM; Preisigke, 1:693-94). **ἀπέλυσαν** aor. ind. act. ἀπολύω (*# 668*) to release. For the relation of these events to things mentioned in 1 and 2 Thess. s. Bruce; FAP, 325-26. ◆ **10 διὰ νυκτός**

(# *1328; 3816*) in the night, during or in the course of the night (IBG, 56). **ἐξέπεμψαν** aor. ind. act. ἐκπέμπω (# *1734*) to sent out, to send away. For the city of Berea s. Gill, "Macedonia," BAFCS, 2:415-16; CH, 261-62. **οἵτινες** nom. pl. ὅστις (# *4015*) who. **παραγενόμενοι** aor. mid. (dep.) part. (temp.) παραγίνομαι (# *4134*) to arrive. **ἀπῄεσαν** impf. ind. act. ἄπειμι (# *583*) to go away, to go; "they went their way to the synagogue" (LC). **♦ 11 ἦσαν** impf. ind. act. εἰμί s.v. 7. **εὐγενέστεροι** comp. εὐγενής (# *2302*) noble birth, well-born, noble-minded (BAGD); comp., more noble. The word is used not only for noble birth but also for noble sentiments, character, morals; thus the Jews of Berea were more noble in character than those of Thessalonica in their welcome and cordial treatment of the apostles (TLNT). **οἵτινες** nom. pl. ὅστις s.v. 10. Those belonging to the same class; used to emphasize a characteristic quality, by which a preceding statement is to be confirmed (BAGD; IBG, 124). **ἐδέξαντο** aor. ind. mid. (dep.) δέχομαι (# *1312*) to receive, to welcome. **προθυμία** (# *4608*) willingness, eagerness. It indicates a positive disposition, goodwill in the heightened sense of eagerness and ardor and is a compliment that honors its subject (TLNT; TDNT; EDNT). **καθ' ἡμέραν** (# *2848; 2465*) day by day, daily. **ἀνακρίνοντες** pres. act. part. ἀνακρίνω (# *373*) to examine, to sift up and down, to make careful and exact research as in legal processes; to try to learn the nature or truth of something by the process of careful study, evaluation, and judgment (RWP; GELTS, 29; LN, 1:331). **ἔχοι** pres. opt. act. ἔχω (# *2400*) to have. Opt. in indir. question, "if these things have it so" (MT, 130; RG, 1043). **♦ 12 ἐπίστευσαν** aor. ind. act. πιστεύω (# *4409*) to believe, to trust in. **εὐσχήμων** (# *2363*) respectable, noble, used of appearance, outward bearing, of correct moral conduct, or of high social class; that is, a special class of citizens who were the most well-thought-of and well-to-do in a town or city (TLNT; NDIEC, 2:86; MM; Gill, "Acts and the Urban Elite," BAFCS, 2:117). **♦ 13 ἔγνωσαν** aor. ind. act. γινώσκω (# *1182*) to know. Ingressive aor., "to come to know." **κατηγγέλη** aor. ind. pass. s.v. 3. **ἦλθον** aor. ind. act. s.v. 1. **σαλεύοντες** pres. act. part. σαλεύω (# *4888*) to shake, to cause to waver, to agitate, to incite. Shaking the crowd like an earthquake (RWP). Part. expressing purp. **ταράσσοντες** pres. act. part. s.v. 8. Part. expressing purpose. **♦ 14 ἐξαπέστειλαν** aor. ind. act. ἐξαποστέλλω (# *1990*) to send out. **πορεύεσθαι** pres. mid. (dep.) inf. πορεύομαι (# *4513*) to go, to travel. Epex. inf. explaining ἐξαπέστειλαν. **ὑπέμειναν** aor. ind. act. ὑπομένω (# *5702*) to remain, to remain behind. The prep. in compound means, "to tarry *behind*" (MH, 327). **♦ 15 καθιστάνοντες** pres. act. part. (temp.) καθίστημι (# *2770*) to bring down to a place. **ἤγαγον** aor. ind. act. ἄγω (# *72*) to lead, to conduct. **λαβόντες** aor. act. part. (circum.) λαμ-

βάνω (# *3284*) to take, to receive. **ἐντολή** (# *1953*) instruction. **ὡς τάχιστα** (# *6055; 5441*) as quickly as possible. **ἔλθωσιν** aor. subj. act. s.v. 1. Subj. w. **ἵνα** (# *2671*) used as obj. in an indir. command (RG, 1046). **ἐξῄεσαν** impf. ind. act. ἔξειμι (# *1996*) to go out. **♦ 16 ἐκδεχομένου** pres. mid. (dep.) part. (temp.) ἐκδέχομαι (# *1683*) to expect, to wait for. Gen. abs. For the city of Athens s. David W.J. Gill, "Achaia," BAFCS, 2:441-48; TAA; Daniel J. Geagan, "Roman Athens: Some Aspects of Life and Culture," ANRW 2.7.1, 371-437; CH, 266-96; AAT, 232-42; BBC; ABD, 1:513-18; Pausanias, "Attica," *Description of Greece*, 1. i-xliv. **παρωξύνετο** impf. ind. pass. παροξύνω (# *4236*) to stimulate, to provoke to wrath, to irritate; pass. to be angry (s. 15:39). **θεωροῦντος** pres. act. part. θεωρέω (# *2555*) to see, to observe. Paul probably could distinguish the statues of the gods from those of ordinary men because the former had no inscriptions (DCNT, 125). Temp. or causal part. **κατείδωλος** (# *2977*) full of images. For the prep. compound and the coining of this word s. MH, 317. The prep. may mean "thick with," "luxuriant with" as used of vegetation (R.E. Wycherly, "St. Paul at Athens," *JTS*, n.s. 19 [1968]: 619, 620). Perhaps Paul was standing in the *Stoa Poikile* and saw the various temples housing the imperial cult as well as other temples and altars (Gill, "Achaia," BAFCS, 2:443-45). **οὖσαν** pres. act. (adj.) part. εἰμί s.v. 7. **♦ 17 διελέγετο** impf. ind. mid. (dep.) s.v. 2. Impf. pictures the repeated action. **σεβομένοις** pres. mid. (dep.) part. s.v. 4. Part. as subst. **ἀγορᾷ** (# *59*) dat. sing. agora, forum, marketplace as the economic, political, and cultural center of the city (s.v. 5; Gill, "Achaia," BAFCS, 2:445-56). **παρατυγχάνοντας** pres. act. part. παρατυγχάνω (# *4193*) to happen to be near or present. The idea of chance is not necessarily implied (MM). Part. as subst. **♦ 18 συνέβαλλον** impf. ind. act. συμβάλλω (# *5202*) to throw together, to discuss, to meet, to quarrel. For the Epicureans and Stoics s. Bruce. **ἔλεγον** impf. ind. act. λέγω (# *3306*) to say. **θέλοι** pres. opt. act. θέλω (# *2527*) to wish, to want to, w. inf. Potential opt. used in an incomplete cond. cl. w. the protasis implied. "What would he wish to say, if he could say anything?" "What might he be trying to say?" (M, 174; IBG, 151). **σπερμολόγος** (# *5066*) seed picker. A slang term first used of birds that pick up grain, then of men who pick up odds and ends in the market, and then applied to men who were zealous seekers of the second rate at second hand, and finally to generally worthless persons–"this character" (LC; MM; PTR, 242-43; TLNT, 3:268-69). **ξένος** (# *3828*) strange, foreign. **δαιμονίων** gen. pl. δαιμόνιον (# *1228*) deity, divinity (BAGD). Obj. gen. **καταγγελεύς** (# *2858*) announcer, proclaimer, preacher (BAGD). **εἶναι** pres. act. inf. εἰμί s.v. 7. Inf. in indir. discourse. **εὐηγγελίζετο** impf. ind. mid. (dep.) εὐαγγελίζομαι (# *2294*) to proclaim good news (TDNT; TLNT). ◆ **19** ἐπιλαβόμενοι aor. mid. part. (circum.) ἐπιλαμβάνω (# *2138*) to take hold of. Ἄρειος πάγος (# *740*) the Areopagus or Hill of Ares (Mars Hill). The word is to be understood either as the geographic place or a governmental council in the city of Athens. Among the many functions of this council was supervising education, particularly controlling the many visiting lecturers, and checking on the introduction of new or unauthorized religions (BAGD; PTR, 245; LC; BBC; DPL, 51-54; DGRA, 126-29). For the suggestion that the whole incident took place near the northwest angle of the Agora in or near the Stoa Basileios s. C.J. Hemer, "Paul at Athens: A Topographical Note," *NTS* 20 (1974): 341-50; BASHH, 117. It could have been that the council met on the geographical location of the Hill of Ares (Gill, "Achaia," BAFCS, 2:448). ἤγαγον aor. ind. act. s.v. 15. δυνάμεθα pres. ind. pass. (dep.) δύναμαι (# *1538*) to be able to, w. inf. γνῶναι aor. act. inf. s.v. 13. λαλουμένη pres. pass. part. (adj.) λαλέω (# *3281*) to speak. ◆ **20** ξενίζοντα pres. act. part. ξενίζω (# *3826*) to receive as a guest, to entertain, to surprise or astonish w. something new or strange. Part. as subst., "surprising things" (BAGD). εἰσφέρεις pres. ind. act. εἰσφέρω (# *1662*) to bring into. γνῶναι aor. act. inf. s.v. 13. εἶναι pres. act. inf. s.v. 7. ◆ **21** ἐπιδημοῦντες pres. act. part. ἐπιδημέω (# *2111*) to reside as a foreigner. Part. as subst. ηὐκαίρουν impf. ind. act. εὐκαιρέω (# *2320*) to have time, to have leisure or opportunity. Accompanied by the prep. it means "to devote one's leisure to" (AS). Customary impf. οὐδὲν ἕτερον ... ἤ (# *4029; 2283; 2445*) "nothing else than" (BAGD). λέγειν pres. act. inf., s.v. 18. Epex. inf. explaining the vb. ηὐκαίρουν. ἀκούειν pres. act. inf. s.v. 8. καινότερον comp. καινός (# *2785*) new; comp., newer. The comparison can often have the force of a superl. (D, 127). The true comparison would mean, "something newer than what they had heard" (RG, 665). ◆ **22** σταθείς aor. pass. part. ἵστημι (# *2705*) to stand. Circum. or temp. part. ἐν μέσῳ (# *1877; 3545*) in the midst of. Perhaps indicating "in the midst of the council" rather than "in the middle of the hill." ἔφη aor. ind. act. φημί (# *5774*) to say, to speak. δεισιδαιμονεστέρους comp. δεισιδαίμων (# *1273*) God-fearing, religious, superstitious; comp., very religious. It expresses respect for or fear of the supernatural which according to its nature can be either piety or superstition (Williams; LC; TLNT). Here the comp. means "more religious than usual" (RWP). The Athenians were often praised for their piety (TLNT, 1:308; s. also the references given here). θεωρῶ pres. ind. act. s.v. 16. ◆ **23** διερχόμενος pres. mid. (dep.) part. (temp.) διέρχομαι (# *1451*) to pass through. γάρ for, giving an explanation of the previous statement. ἀναθεωρῶν pres. part. (temp.) ἀναθεωρέω (# *355*) to look at, to observe. The prep. compound is perfective (MH, 296). σέβασμα

(# *4934*) object of worship or religious reverence (NIDNTT, 2:91-92). εὗρον aor. ind. act. s.v. 6. βωμός (# *1117*) altar. ἐπεγέγραπτο plperf. ind. pass. ἐπιγράφω (# *2108*) to inscribe. Ἀγνώστῳ θεῷ (# *58; 2536*) to (the) an unknown God. For examples and evidences of altars to unknown gods in and around Athens s. BC, 5:240-46; Haenchen; Gill, "Achaia," BAFCS, 2:446-47; BASHH, 117; BBC. ἀγνοοῦντες pres. act. part. ἀγνοέω (# *51*) not to know, to be ignorant. Concessive part, "although you do not know him...." εὐσεβεῖτε pres. ind. act. εὐσεβέω (# *2355*) to reverence, to respect, to worship. Customary pres. καταγγέλλω (# *2859*) pres. ind. act. s.v. 3. Pres. points to an action in progress. ◆ **24** ποιήσας aor. act. part. (adj.) ποιέω (# *4472*) to make. ὑπάρχων pres. act. part. (causal) ὑπάρχω (# *5639*) to exist, to be. χειροποίητος (# *5935*) made w. human hands. Perhaps Paul alludes to the many temples there which were made w. human hands. κατοικεῖ pres. ind. act. κατοικέω (# *2997*) to dwell, to be at home. Pres. refers to a truth that is always true. ◆ **25** ἀνθρώπινος (# *474*) human. Adj. w. this ending signifies material, origin, or kind (MH, 359). θεραπεύεται pres. ind. pass. θεραπεύω (# *2543*) to care for, to attend, to serve. προσδεόμενος pres. mid. (dep.) part. προσδέομαι (# *4656*) to want, to need in addition. Cond. part, "as if He needed anything" (RWP). αὐτός (# *899*) he. Emphatic, "He Himself." διδούς pres. act. part. (causal) δίδωμι (# *1443*) to give. (Schneider). ◆ **26** ἐποίησεν aor. ind. act. s.v. 24. κατοικεῖν pres. act. inf. s.v. 24. Inf. as obj. ὁρίσας aor. act. part. ὁρίζω (# *3988*) to mark out boundaries, to determine. The aor. part. is not later in time than the main vb. The determination of man's home preceded his creation in the divine plan (M, 133). προστεταγμένους perf. pass. part. προστάσσω (# *4705*) to appoint, to assign, to prescribe, to fix. Perf. indicates the abiding results. καιρός (# *2787*) time, season. It could refer to the seasons or to the historical epoch (Polhill). ὁροθεσία (# *3999*) boundary. It could refer to the inhabitable areas of the planet, or to the boundaries between nations (Polhill). ◆ **27** ζητεῖν pres. act. inf. ζητέω (# *2426*) to seek. Inf. of purp. (RWP). ψηλαφήσειαν aor. opt. act. ψηλαφέω (# *6027*) to touch, to feel. The vb. gives the idea of groping after God in the darkness when the light of His full revelation is not available (Bruce). Opt. in a type of incomplete cond. sentence expressing aim or purp. (MT, 127; RG, 1021; VA, 311-12). εὕροιεν aor. opt. act. εὑρίσκω (# *2351*) to find. καί γε (# *2779; 1145*) and yet, although, a concessive expression (Bruce; Thrall, 37f). ◆ **28** ζῶμεν pres. ind. act. ζάω (# *2409*) to live. κινούμεθα pres. ind. mid./pass. κινέω (# *3075*) to move. Simultaneously the vb. might mean "we are moved by Him" and "we move in Him" (DCNT, 127). ποιητής (# *4475*) poet. εἰρήκασιν perf. ind. act. λέγω (# *3306*) to say. For the quotations from the Gr. poet Aratus and also possibly from Epimenides s. BC, 5:246-51; Polhill, Longenecker, 476. τοῦ gen. sing. ὁ (# 3836) the. Gen. of source or origin: "from the one," "from him." γένος (# 1169) descendant of common ancestor (BAGD). ◆ **29** ὑπάρχοντες pres. act. part. s.v. 24; Causal part., "since we are...." ὀφείλομεν pres. ind. act. ὀφείλω (# 4053) to be obligated, ought to, w. inf. νομίζειν pres. act. inf. νομίζω (# 3787) to suppose, to think. χρυσίον (# 5992) gold. ἄργυρος (# 738) silver. χάραγμα (# 5916) an engraved work, an inscription engraved. Dat. w. adj. ὅμοιον. τέχνης (# 5492) gen. sing. art, skill, trade (BAGD). Gen. of description. ἐνθύμησις (# 1927) thought, reflection, design, the content of thinking and reasoning (LN, 1:351). θεῖος divine; as subst., divine being, divinity (BAGD). Subject of inf. εἶναι pres. act. inf. εἰμί s.v. 7. Inf. in indir. discourse as obj. of the inf. νομίζειν. Dio Chrysostom considered sculpture to be one source of man's conception of the divine (DCNT, 128; DC XII, 44, 80). If they had genuinely accepted Paul's major premise that God is Creator, they would have had to acknowledge their own self-idolatry and need for repentance (Polhill). ◆ **30** ἀγνοίας gen. sing. ἄγνοια (# 53) ignorance. Gen. of description. ὑπεριδών aor. act. part. ὑπεροράω (# 5666) to overlook. A frequent vb. in the LXX applied to a thing which is not attended to, but left without favorable help or without severe punishment (Bengel). Concessive part. ("although"). παραγγέλλει pres. ind. act. παραγγέλλω (# 4133) to command, to order, to instruct. πανταχοῦ (# 4116) everywhere. μετανοεῖν pres. act. inf. μετανοέω (# 3566) to change one's thinking, to repent; a complete turnabout from their false worship and a turning to God (Polhill). Inf. in indir. discourse. ◆ **31** καθότι (# 2776) in view of the fact that. ἔστησεν aor. ind. act. ἵστημι (# 2705) to set, to appoint. κρίνειν pres. act. inf. κρίνω (# 3212) to judge. Used w. μέλλει to express the fut. ἐν ἀνδρί by a man. For the use of the prep. expressing agency, s. the examples quoted by Haenchen. ᾧ dat. sing. ὅς (# 4005) rel. pron. Dat. by attraction. ὥρισεν aor. ind. act. s.v. 26. παρασχών aor. act. part. (circum.) παρέχω (# 4218) to furnish, to show, to provide; w. πίστιν, to bring forward evidence, proof, guarantee (RWP; BAGD; TLNT, 3:112). ἀναστήσας aor. act. part. ἀνίστημι (# 482) to raise. Temp. part. or part. of means. ◆ **32** ἀκούσαντες aor. act. part. (temp.) s.v. 8. ἐχλεύαζον impf. ind. act. χλευάζω (# 5949) to mock, to sneer, to scoff. Incep. impf., "they began to scoff." ἀκουσόμεθα fut. ind. mid. s.v. 8, w. gen. as obj. ◆ **33** ἐξῆλθεν aor. ind. act. ἐξέρχομαι (# 2002) to go out. ◆ **34** κολληθέντες aor. pass. part. κολλάομαι (# 3140) to join (s. 5:13; 9:26; 10:28). ἐπίστευσαν aor. ind. act. πιστεύω (# 4409) to believe. Ἀρεοπαγίτης (# 741) member of the Areopagus. It is the correct title for a member of the court (BASHH, 119). Δάμαρις (# 1240) Damaris. For the name s. BASHH, 232.

Acts 18

◆ **1** χωρισθείς aor. pass. (dep.) part. (temp.) χωρίζομαι (# 6004) to depart. ἦλθεν aor. ind. act. ἔρχομαι (# 2262) to go, to come. For the city of Corinth s. James Wiseman, "Corinth and Rome I: 228 B.C.-A.D. 267," ANRW, 2.7.1:438-548, esp. 509-21; SPC; David W.J. Gill, "Achaia," BAFCS, 2:448-53; Victor Paul Furnish, "Corinth in Paul's Time–What Can Archaeology Tell Us?" *BAR* 15 (1988): 14-27; NW, 2:ii:235-37. ◆ **2** εὑρών aor. act. part. (temp.) εὑρίσκω (# 2351) to find. ὀνόματι dat. sing. ὄνομα (# 3950) name. Instr. dat. (RG, 487), or dat. of respect (BD, 105): "named," "by name." For the names s. BASHH, 132-33; for a discussion of Priscilla and Aquila s. CIE, 87-89. γένει dat. sing. γένος (# 1169) race, stock. Dat. of respect, "by birth" (BD, 105). προσφάτως (# 4711) recently. ἐληλυθότα perf. act. part. (adj.) masc. acc. sing. ἔρχομαι s.v. 1. διατεταχέναι perf. act. inf. διατάσσω (# 1411) to decree, to order. Inf. w. διά (# 1328) to express cause. χωρίζεσθαι pres. mid./pass. inf. χωρίζω (# 6004) to separate; pass. to be separated, to take one's departure, to go away (BAGD). Epex. inf. giving the content of the order. The edict was given in A.D. 49, probably due to the unrest in the Jewish quarters of Rome, which may have arisen because Christians preached that Jesus was the Messiah (for this and the decree of Claudius to expel the Jews from Rome s. SPC, 130-40 [texts and discussion]; FAP, 139-80; SC; 4-8; BASHH, 167-68; Andrew D. Clarke, "Rome and Italy," BAFCS, 2:469-71; BC, 5:295f, 495f; JPF, 1:180-83). προσῆλθεν aor. ind. act. προσέρχομαι (# 4665) to come to. ◆ **3** ὁμότεχνος (# 3937) the same trade. Aquila and Priscilla probably had a small private business making tents or awnings (SC, 158-64; BBC). εἶναι pres. act. inf. εἰμί (# 1639) to be. Inf. w. διά (# 1328) to express cause. ἔμενεν impf. ind. act. μένω (# 3531) to remain. ἠργάζετο impf. ind. mid. (dep.) ἐργάζομαι (# 2237) to work. ἦσαν impf. ind. act. εἰμί. σκηνοποιός (# 5010) tentmaker, leather worker, tent-cloth worker (BAGD; LC; DPL, 925-27). Tents were used for soldiers, for those attending the Isthmian Games, for passengers of ships w. a stopover; awnings were used to cover the Forum in Rome, to cover walkways, as protection from the sun in private houses or at the beach and in the theater; leather was used for coats, curtains, and tents; linen was used for sails and for awnings (Peter Lampe, "Paulus–Zeltmacher," *Biblische Zeitschrift* 31 [1987]: 256-61; SC, 156-58; SB, 2:746-47; Pliny, *NH*, 19:23-25). Perhaps Paul and Aquila used one of the small shops which have been excavated in Corinth and thereby were able to contact people w. the gospel (SPC, 167-70; Lampe, "Paulus–Zeltmacher," *Biblische Zeitschrift* 31 [1987]: 260-61; also Ronald F. Hock, "Paul's Tentmaking and the Problem of His Social Class," *JBL* 97 [1979]: 555-64; R.F. Hock, "The Workshop as a Social Setting for Paul's Missionary

Preaching," *CBQ* 41 [1979]: 438-50). The rabbis emphasize the necessity of learning a trade: "Excellent is the study of the law together w. worldly occupation, for toil in them both puts sin out of mind" (M, Aboth 2,2; SB, 2:745-46). At Tarsus there was a large group of linen workers (DC, 34:21). The church at Corinth met in Aquila and Priscilla's house, and when they went to Ephesus, the church there also used their house as a meeting place (Brad Blue, "Acts and the House Church," BAFCS, 2:173; Rom. 16:3-5; 1 Cor. 16:19). The church probably also met in the houses of Titus Justus, Gaius (Rom. 16:23), Stephanus, and Crispus. Before Paul left it numbered around 100 people (Blue, "Acts and the House Church," BAFCS, 2:174-77). ◆ **4** **διελέγετο** impf. ind. mid. (dep.) διαλέγομαι (# *1363*) to discuss, to dispute, to argue (s. 17:2). Iterat. impf. indicating the repeated action. **ἔπειθεν** impf. ind. act. πείθω (# *4275*) to persuade. Iterat. impf. or conative, "he tried to persuade." ◆ **5** **κατῆλθον** aor. ind. act. κατέρχομαι (# *2982*) to go down. **συνείχετο** impf. ind. mid. συνέχω (# *5309*) to hold together, to grip, to compel; mid. to devote oneself to, to be occupied w. or absorbed in something, to be wrapped up. "Paul was wholly absorbed in preaching" (BAGD); "He was completely wrapped up in this ministry" (TLNT, 3:338). Incep. impf., "He began to devote himself...." When Silas and Timothy came down to Corinth, Paul was able to give all his time to preaching (LC). **διαμαρτυρόμενος** pres. mid. (dep.) part. διαμαρτύρομαι (# *1371*) to testify, to solemnly declare. The prep. in compound is intensive (IBG, 88). Part. of manner, explaining how Paul devoted himself. ◆ **6** **ἀντιτασσομένων** pres. mid. (dep.) part. (temp.) ἀντιτάσσομαι (# *530*) to oppose, to resist. Gen. abs. **βλασφημούντων** pres. act. part. (temp.) βλασφημέω (# *1059*) to slander, to blaspheme. **ἐκτιναξάμενος** aor. mid. part. ἐκτινάσσω (# *1759*) to shake off, to shake out (BC, 5:269-75; Mark 6:11). **εἶπεν** aor. ind. act. λέγω (# *3306*) to say. **πορεύσομαι** fut. ind. mid. (dep.) πορεύομαι (# *4513*) to go. ◆ **7** **μεταβάς** aor. act. part. (temp.) μεταβαίνω (# *3553*) to go away, to leave. **εἰσῆλθεν** aor. ind. act. εἰσέρχομαι (# *1656*) to go into. Paul moved his place of teaching from the synagogue, but he did not move from Aquila's house (BASHH, 197, 208). **σεβομένου** pres. mid. (dep.) part. (adj.) σέβομαι (# *4936*) to fear, to reverence, to worship (s. 10:2). **ἦν** impf. ind. act. εἰμί (# *1639*) to be. **συνομοροῦσα** pres. act. part. (adj.) συνομορέω (# *5327*) to be right next to, to adjoin, w. dat. ◆ **8** **ἀρχισυνάγωγος** (# *801*) leader of the synagogue (s. 13:15). **ἐπίστευσεν** aor. ind. act. πιστεύω (# *4409*) to believe, to believe in, w. dat. (M, 67). **ἀκούοντες** pres. act. part. (temp.) ἀκούω (# *201*) to hear. Pres. indicates a repeated act. **ἐπίστευον** impf. ind. act. Impf. pictures the repeated action. **ἐβαπτίζοντο** impf. ind. pass. βαπτίζω (# *966*) to baptize. ◆ **9** **εἶπεν** aor. ind. act. λέγω s.v. 6. **φοβοῦ** pres. imp. mid. (dep.) φοβέομαι (# *5828*) to be

afraid. Pres. imp. w. the neg. **μή** (# *3590*) may indicate the discontinuing of an action in progress (MKG, 272), or it may be used in prohibitory general precepts (VANT, 335-40). **λάλει** pres. imp. act. λαλέω (# *3281*) to speak. Pres. imp. may be, "continue to speak," "keep on speaking." **σιωπήσῃς** aor. subj. act. σιωπάω (# *4995*) to be silent. Aor. subj. w. a neg. **μή** (# *3590*) to prevent the beginning of an action which is not in progress (MKG, 273; VANT, 335). ◆ **10** **ἐπιθήσεται** fut. ind. mid. (dep.) ἐπιτίθημι (# *2202*) to place upon; mid. to set upon, to attack, w. dat. (BAGD). **κακῶσαι** aor. act. inf. κακόω (# *2808*) to do harm, to injure. Inf. expresses either purp. or result. ◆ **11** **ἐκάθισεν** aor. ind. act. καθίζω (# *2767*) to sit, to remain. **ἐνιαυτὸν καὶ μῆνας ἕξ** acc. of time, for a year and six months. This indicates the total time of Paul's ministry here (FAP, 186). **διδάσκων** pres. act. part. (circum.) διδάσκω (# *1438*) to teach. ◆ **12** **ἀνθύπατος** (# *478*) proconsul. Roman head of the government in a senatorial province, but the emperor still had influence on the office (RNE,31-32). Claudius in A.D. 44 returned Achaia to a senatorial province (Gill, "Acahia," BAFCS, 2:436; BBC; Seutonius, *Claudius*, 25:3). **ὄντος** pres. act. part. (temp.) εἰμί s.v. 7. Gen. abs., "while Gallio was proconsul." Annaeus Novatus, known as Gallio, was the brother of Seneca, the philosopher and tutor of Nero. He was, according to an inscription at Delphi, proconsul in Corinth between A.D. 51 and 52; however he may have broken off his term because of alleged health problems. Paul probably appeared before him sometime between July and October in A.D. 51 (SPC, 141-52, 173-76; FAP, 180-89; BASHH, 119, 168-69, 214; Colin J. Hemer, "Observations on Pauline Chronology," PSEB, 6-9, 16-18; KP, 2:686; BC, 5:460-64; IDB, 2:351; ABD, 2:901-03; Gill, "Acahia," BAFCS 2:436-37, 449-40). **κατεπέστησαν** aor. ind. act. κατεφίστημι (# *2987*) to rise up against someone. **ὁμοθυμαδόν** (# *3924*) w. one mind, together. **ἤγαγον** aor. ind. act. ἄγω (# *72*) to lead. **βῆμα** (# *1037*) acc. sing. speaker's platform, from which official proclamations might be read, or an important magistrate might give an address. This was equivalent to the Roman *Rostra* (DGRA, 995-96). In Corinth it was a marble structure located in the middle of the South Stoa, on the upper level of the Agora, flanked by stairways leading up from the lower level of the Agora. On the lower level before the Bema was a square stone platform where those appearing before the Bema stood (Wiseman, "Corinth," ANRW, 2, 7:515-16; SPC, 28-29; FAP, 185; E. Dinkler, "Das Bema zu Korinth: Archäologische, lexikographische, rechtsgeschichtliche und ikonographische Bemerkungen zu Apg 18,12-17," *Signum Crucis* [Tübingen: J.C.B. Mohr [Paul Siebeck], 1967]). ◆ **13** **λέγοντες** pres. act. part. s.v. 6. **παρὰ τὸν νόμον** (# *4123*; *3795*) against (contrary to) the law. It could refer to either the Roman or Jewish law and may mean contrary to the allowed religions, or contrary to the decrees of Claudius, which allowed the Jews to worship according to their customs, or contrary to the Mosaic Law (Sherwin-White, 101-4; FAP, 187; Polhill). **ἀναπείθει** pres. ind. act. ἀναπείθω (# 400) to persuade; in a neg. sense to seduce, to mislead (MM). The prep. compound is perfective and suggests success (MH, 296). Pres. indicates a continual action. **σέβεσθαι** pres. mid. (dep.) inf. s.v. 7. Inf. as obj. of the vb. ◆ **14 μέλλοντος** pres. act. part. (temp.) μέλλω (# 3516) to be about to. Used w. inf. to express fut. Gen. abs. **ἀνοίγειν** pres. act. inf. ἀνοίγω (# 487) to open. **ἦν** impf. ind. act. εἰμι s.v. 7. Ind. in a 2nd. class cond. cl. where the speaker considers the cond. as contrary to fact. **ἀδίκημα** (# 93) nom. sing. unrighteous deed, wrong, crime (BAGD). **ῥᾳδιούργημα** (# 4815) a prank, crime; particularly implies fraud and deception, swindle (LC; MM; TLNT, 219-20; s. 13:10). **κατὰ λόγον** (# 2848; 3364) according to reason. It may be used w. the vb. in the legal sense: "to accept in accordance w. a charge," "to accept a complaint on court," "to admit a complaint to judgment" (LN, 553). **ἀνεσχόμην** aor. ind. mid. (dep.) ἀνέχομαι (# 462) to bear w., to tolerate. Used of listening patiently while others are allowed to speak (Bruce). ◆ **15 ὄψεσθε** fut. ind. mid. (dep.) ὁράω (# 3972) to see. Volitive fut. w. the force of the imp. (RG, 874; VA, 420). **κριτὴς ἐγὼ τούτων οὐ βούλομαι εἶναι** "A judge of these things I do not desire to be." These are the exact words of a Roman magistrate refusing to exercise his *arbitrium iudicatis* within a matter *extra ordinem* (Sherwin-White, 102). It is within the competence of the judge to decide whether to accept a novel charge or not (Sherwin-White, 100). It may be that Gallio shared the anti-Semitic feelings of his brother Seneca, who dedicated to him such writings as *De Ira* ("Concerning Anger") or *De Vita Beata* ("Concerning the Happy Life") (FAP, 186-87; GLAJJ, 1:429-34). ◆ **16 ἀπήλασεν** aor. ind. act. ἀπελαύνω (# 590) to drive away. A stronger term than just "to send away" (Haenchen). ◆ **17 ἐπιλαβόμενοι** aor. mid. (dep.) part. (temp.) Perhaps by the force of his lictors' rods (BBC). ἐπιλαμβάνομαι (# 2138) to take, to lay hold of. Sosthenes, the ruler of the synagogue (s. 1 Cor. 1:1), may have been beaten because he was a believer or because the indifference of Gallio led to an anti-Semitic attack (Polhill). **ἔτυπτον** impf. ind. act. τύπτω (# 5597) to beat; incep. impf., "they began to beat." **ἔμελεν** impf. ind. act. μέλω used impersonally (μέλει # 3508) or personally w. dat., to be concerned about something, to pay attention to (BAGD). For Paul's experience before Gallio in the light of Roman law and for a defense of its integrity s. Sherwin-White, 99-107. ◆ **18 προσμείνας** aor. act. part. (temp.) προσμένω (# 4693) to remain. **ἡμέρας ἱκανάς** acc. pl. Acc. of time, "for a considerable number of days." Exactly how long this was is not certain (FAP, 185-86). **ἀποτα-**

ξάμενος aor. mid. (dep.) part. (temp.) ἀποτάσσομαι (# 698) to say farewell. **ἐξέπλει** impf. ind. act. ἐκπλέω (# 1739) to sail out. Sailing was less expensive, easier, and faster than land travel (BBC). Incep. impf., "they began to sail." **κειράμενος** aor. mid. part. κείρομαι (# 3025) to shear; mid., to have one's hair cut. **εἶχεν** impf. ind. act. ἔχω (# 2400) to have. **εὐχή** (# 2376) vow. A temporary Nazarite vow of thirty days could be taken to seek divine blessing in an undertaking, to express thanksgiving, or to seek deliverance from illness. During this time abstinence from wine was practiced and the hair was not cut. The cutting of the hair marked the termination of the vow (Bruce; LC; SB, 2:747-51; Polhill; M, Nazir). ◆ **19 κατήντησαν** aor. ind. act. καταντάω (# 2918) to arrive. **εἰς Ἔφεσον** (# 1650; 2387) in Ephesus. For the great city of Ephesus s. Paul Trebilco, "Asia," BAFCS, 2:302-59; AAT, 248-63; Merrill M. Parvis, "Ephesus in the Early Christian Era," *BA* 3 (1945): 61-73; Floyd V. Filson, "Ephesus and the New Testament," *BA* 3 (1945): 73-80; CH, 419-33; Bean, 128-150; LSC, 210-36; LSCA, 35-56; Dieter Knibbe & Wilhelm Alzinger, "Ephesos vom Beginn der römischen Herrschaft in Kleinasien bis zum Ende der Principatzeit," ANRW, 2, 7:748-830; ANTC, 79-114. **κατέλιπεν** aor. ind. act. καταλείπω (# 2901) to leave behind. **αὐτοῦ** (# 899) there. **εἰσελθών** aor. act. part. s.v. 7. **διελέξατο** aor. ind. mid. (dep.) διαλέγομαι (# 1363) to reason, to dispute, to argue, w. dat. (s. 17:2). ◆ **20 ἐρωτώντων** pres. act. part. ἐρωτάω (# 2263) to ask, to request. Gen. abs. (concessive), "although they asked him...." **πλείονα** acc. sing. πλείων comp. πολύς (# 4498) many, comp., more. **μεῖναι** aor. act. inf. μένω (# 3531) to remain. Inf. in indir. discourse giving the content of the request. **ἐπένευσεν** aor. ind. act. ἐπινεύω (# 2153) to approve by a nod, to consent. ◆ **21 ἀποταξάμενος** aor. mid. (dep.) part. (temp.) s.v. 18. **εἰπών** aor. act. part. (temp.) λέγω s.v. 6. **ἀνακάμψω** fut. ind. act. ἀνακάμπτω (# 366) to turn back, to return again. Volitive fut. expressing a decision of the will (RG, 874). **θέλοντος** pres. act. part. θέλω (# 2527) to will, to purpose, w. inf. Gen. abs., cond. **ἀνήχθη** aor. ind. pass. ἀνάγω (# 343) to lead or bring up; as nautical t.t., to put a ship to sea; mid. or pass., to put to sea, to set sail (BAGD). ◆ **22 κατελθών** aor. act. part. (temp.) κατέρχομαι (# 2982) to go down, to come down. **Καισάρεια** (# 2791) Caesarea on the Sea. This was the larger harbor city built by Herod the Great and as headquarters of the governor of Judea. **ἀναβάς** aor. act. part. (temp.) ἀναβαίνω (# 326) to go up, to disembark. **ἀσπασάμενος** aor. mid. (dep.) part. (temp.) ἀσπάζομαι (# 832) to greet. "After he had greeted the church...." **κατέβη** aor. ind. act. καταβαίνω (# 2849) to go down. ◆ **23 ποιήσας** aor. act. part. (temp.) ποιέω (# 4472) to do; here, to spend time. **ἐξῆλθεν** aor. ind. act. ἐξέρχομαι (# 2002) to go out. **διερχόμενος** pres. mid. (dep.) part. (circum.) διέρχομαι

(# *1451*) to pass through. **καθεξῆς** (# *2759*) in order, successively. **ἐπιστηρίζων** pres. act. part. (circum.) ἐπιστηρίζω (# *2185*) to strengthen (TLNT, 3:291-95). ◆ **24 γένει** race s.v. 2. **λόγιος** (# *3360*) learned, eloquent, master of the art of oratory, learned, scholarly, well-read, as a title of honor; eminent or quite distinguished man, a man of culture (MM; TLNT). **κατήντησεν** aor. ind. act. s.v. 19. **δυνατός** (# *1543*) powerful, strong. **ὤν** pres. act. part. adj. εἰμί s.v. 7. For a discussion of Apollos s. CIE, 43-60; DPL, 37-39; ABD, 1:301; L. D. Hurst, "Apollos, Hebrews and Corinth," *SJT* 38 (1985): 503-13. ◆ **25 ἦν** impf. act. ind. εἰμί s.v. 7. **κατηχημένος** perf. pass. part. κατηχέω (# *2994*) to inform, to instruct, to teach by repeating, dinning into the ears, to teach orally by word of mouth (RWP; TLNT; TDNT; NIDNTT, 3:771-72; EDNT). Part. in a periphrastic construction, "he had been taught." **ζέων** pres. act. part. ζέω (# *2417*) to boil. Lit., "boiling over in his spirit," that is, full of enthusiasm (Bruce). Part. in a periphrastic construction. **ἐλάλει** impf. ind. act. λαλέω (# *3281*) to speak. Impf. indicates customary action. **ἐδίδασκεν** impf. ind. act. διδάσκω (# *1438*) to teach. **ἀκριβῶς** (# *209*) accurately. **ἐπιστάμενος** pres. pass. (dep.) part. ἐπίσταμαι (# *2179*) to know, to understand, to be acquainted w. (BAGD). Concessive part., "although he knew only...." ◆ **26 ἤρξατο** aor. ind. mid. (dep.) ἄρχομαι (# *806*) to begin, w. inf. **παρρησιάζεσθαι** pres. mid. (dep.) inf. παρρησιάζομαι (# *4245*) to speak freely, to speak openly, to be bold (BAGD; TLNT, 3:60; s. 2:29; 13:46; 14:3). **ἀκούσαντες** aor. act. part. (temp.) ἀκούω (# *201*) to hear, w. gen. **προσελάβοντο** aor. ind. mid. (dep.) προσλαμβάνομαι (# *4689*) to take to oneself. **ἀκριβέστερον** comp. (s.v. 25); more accurately. **ἐξέθεντο** aor. ind. mid. (dep.) ἐκτίθημι (# *1758*) to set forth, to explain. ◆ **27 βουλομένου** pres. mid. (dep.) part. (temp.) βούλομαι (# *1089*) to want to, to desire, to decide, w. inf. Gen. abs. **διελθεῖν** aor. act. inf. s.v. 23. **προτρεψάμενοι** aor. mid. (dep.) part. προτρέπομαι (# *4730*) to urge forward, to push on, to encourage, to exhort. The Corinthians were probably urged to write Apollos a letter of recommendation (TLNT, 3:202). **ἔγραψαν** aor. ind. act. γράφω (# *1211*) to write. **ἀποδέξασθαι** aor. mid. (dep.) inf. ἀποδέχομαι (# *622*) to welcome, to receive, to accept gladly. Inf. in indir. discourse. **παραγενόμενος** aor. mid. (dep.) part. (temp.) παραγίνομαι (# *4134*) to arrive. **συνεβάλετο** aor. ind. mid. (dep.) συμβάλλω (# *5202*) to throw together, to help, to be helpful. **πεπιστευκόσιν** perf. act. part. πιστεύω (# *4409*) to believe. Part. as subst. Perf. emphasizes the state of belief. ◆ **28 εὐτόνως** (# *2364*) vigorously. **διακατηλέγχετο** impf. ind. mid. (dep.) διακατελέγχομαι (# *1352*) to refute, to confute w. rivalry in a contest (RWP). The two preps. in compound may be a double perfective indicating success in confuting and convicting (MH, 301-2). **δημοσίᾳ** (# *1323*) publicly. **ἐπιδεικνύς** pres. act. part.

ἐπιδείκνυμι (# *2109*) to set forth, to point out, to prove. Part. of manner, explaining how Apollos successfully refuted the Jews. **εἶναι** pres. act. inf. εἰμί s.v. 7. Epex. inf. indicating what he proved.

Acts 19

◆ **1 ἐγένετο** aor. ind. mid. (dep.) γίνομαι (# *1181*) to become, to happen, w. prep. and inf. for time. For this Semitic construction s. Luke 2:1. **εἶναι** pres. act. inf. εἰμί (# *1639*) to be. Inf. w. ἐν (# *1877*) to express contemporaneous time. **διελθόντα** aor. act. part. (temp.) διέρχομαι (# *1451*) to pass through. **τὰ ἀνωτερικὰ μέρη** higher, upper regions. It may refer to the upper country, the region above and behind Ephesus (Williams). It may, however, refer to the higher-lying and more direct route from Antioch to Ephesus (PTR, 265; HGAM, 164f.). **[κατ]ελθεῖν** aor. act. inf. κατέρχομαι (# *2982*) to go or come down. Inf. w. ἐν (# *1877*) for time. **εὑρεῖν** aor. act. inf. εὑρίσκω (# *2351*) to find. Inf. w. prep. expresses time. ◆ **2 εἶπεν** aor. ind. act. λέγω (# *3306*) to say. **εἰ** (# *1623*) if, whether. Particle used to introduce a direct question may be due to the translation of the Heb. interrogative particle (RG, 916; BD, 226). **ἐλάβετε** aor. ind. act. λαμβάνω (# *3284*) to receive. **πιστεύσαντες** aor. act. part. πιστεύω (# *4409*) to believe. Temp. part. expressing contemporaneous action: "on believing," that is, "when you became Christians" (LC). The coincident aor. part. is doctrinally important (M, 131). **ἠκούσαμεν** aor. ind. act. ἀκούω (# *201*) to hear. ◆ **3 εἰς** (# *1650*) into. Used w. the baptismal formula ("into the name of"). For a discussion of the meaning and the suggestion that it characterized the rite in a fundamental way—that is, a "Jesus baptism" or a "John baptism"—s. Lars Hartman, "Into the Name of Jesus," NTS 20 (1974): 432-440. **ἐβαπτίσθητε** aor. ind. pass. βαπτίζω (# *966*) to baptize. ◆ **4 ἐβάπτισεν** aor. ind. act. s.v. 3. **μετανοίας** gen. sing. μετάνοια (# *3567*) change of mind, repentance (s. Matt. 3:2). Descriptive gen. **λέγων** pres. act. part. (temp.) s.v. 2. "When he spoke to the people." **ἐρχόμενον** pres. mid. (dep.) part. ἔρχομαι (# *2262*) to come. Adj. part. as subst. Part. w. the prep. is placed first in the clause to give prominence, thus stressing the preparatory nature of John's ministry (Bruce). **μετ' αὐτόν** (# *3552; 899*) after him; that is, after John. **πιστεύσωσιν** aor. subj. act. s.v. 2. Subj. w. ἵνα (# *2671*) gives both a content and the purp. (Alford). These disciples' real deficiency was not their baptism; they failed to recognize Jesus as the one whom John had proclaimed, as the promised Messiah (Polhill). ◆ **5 ἀκούσαντες** aor. act. part. (temp.) s.v. 2. **ἐβαπτίσθησαν** aor. ind. pass. s.v. 3. ◆ **6 ἐπιθέντος** aor. act. part. ἐπιτίθημι (# *2202*) to place upon. **ἦλθε** aor. ind. act. ἔρχομαι s.v. 4. **ἐλάλουν** impf. ind. act. λαλέω (# *3281*) to speak. Incep. impf., "they began to speak." **ἐπροφήτευον** impf. ind.

act. προφητεύω (# 4736) to speak for someone, to prophesy. Incep. impf. For an explanation of this event in the light of the transitional period s. Roy L. Aldrich, "The Transition Problem in Acts," *Bib Sac* 114 (1957): 235-242; also BHS, 83-89. ◆ **7** ἦσαν impf. ind. act. εἰμί s.v. 1. ◆ **8** εἰσελθών aor. act. part. (temp.) εἰσέρχομαι (# 1656) to go in. ἐπαρρησιάζετο impf. ind. mid. (dep.) παρρησιάζομαι (# 4245) to speak freely, to speak boldly (s. 18:26). Impf. pictures the repeated action. μήν (# 3604) month. διαλεγόμενος pres. mid. (dep.) part. διαλέγομαι (# 1363) to discuss, to dispute, to argue (s. 17:2). Part. of manner explaining how he was speaking boldly. πείθων pres. act. part. πείθω (# 4275) to persuade. ◆ **9** ἐσκληρύνοντο impf. ind. pass. σκληρύνω (# 5020) to harden; pass. to be or become hardened, to be obstinate (Bruce; TLNT). ἠπείθουν impf. ind. act. ἀπειθέω (# 578) to be disobedient, to refuse to believe. κακολογοῦντες pres. act. part. κακολογέω (# 2800) to speak evil about. Part. of manner explaining how they were obstinate and disobedient. ἀποστάς aor. act. part. (temp.) ἀφίστημι (# 923) to depart, to withdraw. ἀφώρισεν aor. ind. act. ἀφορίζω (# 928) to separate. καθ' ἡμέραν (# 2465) daily. διαλεγόμενος pres. mid. (dep.) part. (circum.) s.v. 8. σχολῇ (# 5391) dat. sing. lecture hall. It has been suggested that it refers to a guild hall, or not to a hall at all but to a group of people, perhaps students of Tyrannos (Paul Trebilco, "Asia," BAFCS, 2:311-12; NDIEC, 1:129-30; CIE, 91-92). For the name of Tyrannos as found in Ephesus s. NDIEC, 5:113; 6:196-98; BASHH, 120-21, 134; Trebilco, "Asia," BAFCS, 2:312). The day's work activity ended at 11:00 A.M. Paul worked manually from daybreak until 11:00 A.M., then devoted the next five hours to the still more exhausting business of Christian dialectic (Bruce; LC; LLAR, 21-29). ◆ **10** ἐγένετο aor. ind. mid. (dep.) s.v. 1. κατοικοῦντας pres. act. part. κατοικέω (# 2997) to live, to dwell. Part. as subst. ἀκοῦσαι aor. act. inf. s.v. 2. Inf. w. ὥστε (# 6063) to express actual result (RG, 999). ◆ **11** τυχούσας aor. act. part. (adj.) τυγχάνω (# 5593) to hit upon, to happen. Here it means "not common," "extraordinary" (AS). It indicates that which is unusual or extraordinary (Bruce). ἐποίει impf. ind. act. ποιέω (# 4472) to do, to perform. Impf. pictures the continual action. ◆ **12** ἀσθενοῦντας pres. act. part. ἀσθενέω (# 820) to be weak, to be sick. ἀποφέρεσθαι pres. pass. inf. ἀποφέρω (# 708) to carry away. Inf. w. ὥστε (# 6063) to express result, s.v. 10. χρώς (# 5999) skin. σουδάριον (# 5051) sweat rag, cloths worn around the head and used to wipe the sweat off (LC; BS, 223). σιμικίνθιον (# 4980) apron. These were worn by the working men (Rackham). Perhaps the word means "belt" (Trebilco, "Asia," BAFCS, 2:313-14). ἀπαλλάσσεσθαι pres. pass. inf. ἀπαλλάσσω to free, to release; pass. to be released, to be cured, to leave, to depart, to be rid of (NDIEC, 4:155; for the frequent occurrence of this word in the

medical writers s. MLL, 47). Inf. expressing result. ἐκπορεύεσθαι pres. mid. (dep.) inf. ἐκπορεύομαι (# 1744) to go out. Inf. expressing result. ◆ **13** ἐπεχείρησαν aor. ind. act. ἐπιχειρέω (# 2217) to lay hands on, to attempt, to undertake. περιερχομένων pres. mid. (dep.) part. (adj.) περιέρχομαι (# 4320) to go about. ἐξορκιστής (# 2020) exorcist. For Jewish views on demonism and exorcism s. SB, 4:501-35; DPL, 209-11; DJG, 165; Jos., *Ant.* 8:45-49; MHW, 136; TJ, 97. ὀνομάζειν pres. act. inf. ὀνομάζω (# 3951) to name, to pronounce a name over someone (BAGD). λέγοντες pres. act. part. λέγω (# 3306) to say. Part. of manner indicating how they pronounced the name of Jesus over the possessed person. ὁρκίζω (# 3991) pres. ind. act. to cause to swear, to adjure, to charge. For such forms of exorcism s. F.V. Filson, "Ephesus and the New Testament," *BA* 8 (1945): 73-80; LC; GMP; MM; BS, 274-300. κηρύσσει pres. ind. act. κηρύσσω (# 3062) to preach, to proclaim. Pres. indicates the continual or repeated action. ◆ **14** ἦσαν impf. ind. act. εἰμί s.v. 1. Impf. w. part. in a periphrastic construction. Σκευᾶ (# 5005) Sceva. His name may mean "left-handed" (BASHH, 234; MM; ABD, 5:1004). ἀρχιερεύς (# 797) high priest. He may have been from one of the priestly families from which a high priest came (the Western reading of "priest" may thus be correct [Polhill]); or he may have tried to impress others by this title (BASHH, 121). ποιοῦντες pres. act. part. s.v. 11. ◆ **15** ἀποκριθέν aor. pass. (dep.) part. ἀποκρίνομαι (# 646) to answer. Semitic use of the pleonastic part. εἶπεν aor. ind. act. λέγω s.v. 13. ἐπίσταμαι (# 2179) pres. ind. pass. (dep.) to know, to possess information about, w. the implication of an understanding of the significance of such information (LN, 1:335). ◆ **16** ἐφαλόμενος aor. mid. (dep.) part. (circum.) ἐφάλλομαι (# 2383) to leap, to jump, to spring upon like a panther (RWP). κατακυριεύσας aor. act. part. (circum.) κατακυριεύω (# 2894) to become master of, to subdue. The prep. compound is perfective and indicates an action unfavorable to its object (MH, 316). ἀμφότεροι (# 317) both, all (Haenchen; MM). ἴσχυσεν aor. ind. act. ἰσχύω (# 2710) to be strong, to overcome. γυμνός (# 1218) naked. τετραυματισμένους perf. pass. part. (adj.) τραυματίζω (# 5547) to wound. Perf. emphasizes the state or condition. ἐκφυγεῖν aor. act. inf. ἐκφεύγω (# 1767) to flee, to escape. Inf. w. ὥστε (# 6063) to express actual result (s.v. 10). ◆ **17** ἐγένετο aor. ind. mid. (dep.) s.v. 1. γνωστός (# 1196) known, w. dat. Pred. adj. κατοικοῦσιν pres. act. part. s.v. 10. Part. as subst. The population of the city at that time is generally estimated at between 200,000-250,000, making Ephesus the third largest city in the empire after Rome and Alexandria (Trebilco, "Asia," BAFCS 2:307). ἐπέπεσεν aor. ind. act. ἐπιπίπτω (# 2158) to fall upon. ἐμεγαλύνετο impf. ind. pass. μεγαλύνω (# 3486) to make large, to magnify. Theol.

pass., indicating that God did the action. ◆ **18** πε-πιστευκότων perf. act. part. (adj.) s.v. 2. Part. as subst. Perf. indicates the state of belief. **ἤρχοντο** impf. ind. mid. (dep.) s.v. 6. Impf. pictures the repeated action, "they kept coming, one after another" (RWP). **ἐξομολο-γούμενοι** pres. mid. (dep.) part. (circum.) ἐξομολογέω (# *2018*) to confess, to make public confession, to acknowledge a fact publicly, often in reference to previous bad behavior (LN, 1:420). **ἀναγγέλλοντες** pres. act. part. ἀναγγέλλω (# *334*) to make known. **πρᾶξις** (# *4552*) deed. A t.t. for a specific magical spell (BS, 323). ◆ **19** περίεργος (# *4319*) things belonging to magic. Also a t.t. for a magical spell (BS, 323; BAGD; DPL, 580-83; BBC; MM; NDIEC, 1:47-49; 6:109-96; GMP; for the well-known "Ephesian Letters" [Ἐφέσια Γράμματα], which were six magical terms thought to be words of power s. Trebilco, "Asia," BAFCS, 2:314; CIE, 95f). **πραξάντων** aor. act. part. (adj.) πράσσω (# *4556*) to do, to practice; here, to practice magic. Part. as subst. **συνενέγκαντες** aor. act. part. (temp.) συμφέρω (# *5237*) to bring together. **κατέκαιον** impf. ind. act. κατακαίω to burn up. Prep. in compound is perfective, "to completely burn up." Books were burned in public in order to repudiate the contents of the books, so the new believers were openly repudiating their own previous involvement in magic (Trebilco, "Asia," BAFCS, 2:315). Impf. indicates the repeated action. **συνεψή-φισαν** aor. ind. act. συμψηφίζω (# *5248*) to reckon together, to calculate. **εὗρον** aor. ind. act. εὑρίσκω (# *2351*) to find. **ἀργυρίου** gen. sing. ἀργύριον (# *736*) silver, silver pieces. Gen. of price, "worth fifty thousand pieces of silver," which, if it was the drachma (one drachma was the average daily wage), was about $35,000 (Polhill). ◆ **20** ηὔξανεν impf. ind. act. αὐξάνω (# *889*) to grow. Impf. pictures the continual growth. **ἴσχυεν** impf. ind. act. ἰσχύω s.v. 16. ◆ **21 ἐπληρώθη** aor. ind. pass. πληρόω (# *4444*) to fulfill, to complete. **ἔθετο** aor. ind. mid. τίθημι (# *5502*) to place, to purpose. **δι-ελθών** aor. act. part. (temp.) s.v. 1. "After passing through." **πορεύεσθαι** pres. mid. (dep.) inf. πορεύομαι (# *4513*) to go, to travel. Inf. as obj. of the vb. **ἔθετο**. **εἰπών** aor. act. part. (circum.) λέγω (# *3306*) to say. **γενέσθαι** aor. mid. (dep.) inf. s.v. 1. Inf. is used w. **μετά** (# *3552*) to express time ("after") (MT, 143). **δεῖ** (# *1256*) pres. ind. act. it is necessary, w. inf. **καί** (# *2779*) also. **ἰδεῖν** aor. act. inf. ὁράω (# *3972*) to see. ◆ **22 ἀποστείλας** aor. act. part. (temp.) ἀποστέλλω (# *690*) to send, to send as an official representative. **διακονούντων** pres. act. part. διακονέω (# *1354*) to minister, to serve as an assistant (EDNT; TDNT; NIDNTT, 3:544-49). Part. as subst. **Ἔραστος** (# *2235*) Erastus. This may have been the city official whose name was found on an inscription in Corinth (Blue, "Act and the House Church," BAFCS, 2:177; SPC, 37; Gerd Thiessen, "Soziale Schichtung in der korinthischen Ge-

meinde," *ZNW* 65 [1974]: 237-46; D.W.J. Gill, "Erastus the Aedile," *TB* 40 [1989]: 293-301; Gill, "Acts and the Urban Elite," BAFCS, 2:112; A.D. Clark, "Another Corinthian Erastus Inscription," *TB* 42 [1991]: 146-51; Rom. 16:23). **ἐπέσχεν** aor. ind. act. ἐπέχω (# *2091*) to stay, to wait. ◆ **23 ἐγένετο** aor. ind. act. mid. (dep.) s.v. 1, Luke 8:1. **τάραχος** (# *5431*) trouble, uproar, disturbance. For a description of such disturbances in the ancient world s. Trebilco, "Asia," BAFCS, 2:338-42. ◆ **24 ἀργυροκόπος** (# *737*) silversmith. For an inscription of a silversmith at Ephesus, a sacred official whose duties were also civic s. NDIEC, 4:5-10; 127-29; BASHH, 235-36; Trebilco, "Asia," BAFCS, 2:336; CIE, 100-108). **ποιῶν** pres. act. part. s.v. 11. **ναός** (# *3724*) temple, shrine. Although shrines of terra cotta and marble have been found during excavations, no silver shrines have come to light thus far. However, theft, war, and plunder would decrease the number of shrines that survived, and any object of precious metal might be destroyed or melted down for other uses (F. Filson, "Ephesus and the New Testament," *BA* 8 [1945]: 73-80). A small terra cotta shrine representing the goddess Artemis sitting in a niche w. her lions beside her has been found, as well as depictions of her wearing a miniature of the temple on her head. In the seventh century silver pins carrying a bee, the sacred animal of Artemis Ephesia, were found; these may have been in vogue in the Roman period. They were used in the homes and in public processions (PTR, 278; Trebilco, "Asia," BAFCS, 2:336-38; DDD, 174). **παρείχετο** impf. ind. mid. παρέχω (# *4218*) to furnish, to supply. Mid. accents the part that Demetrius played as the leader of the guild of silversmiths (RWP). **τεχνίταις** dat. pl. τεχνίτης (# *5493*) craftsman, artisan. Dat. of personal interest. **ἐργασία** (# *2238*) work, gain, profit. ◆ **25 συναθροίσας** aor. act. part. (temp.) συναθροίζω (# *5255*) to assemble, to gather together. He was organizing the whole trade in a protest (Bruce). **εἶπεν** aor. ind. act. λέγω s.v. 21. **ἐπίστασθε** pres. ind. mid. pass. s.v. 15. **εὐπορία** (# *2345*) wealth, affluence. For the wealth of the Temple of Artemis, which was a bank as well as a place of asylum s. Trebilco, "Asia," BAFCS, 2:324-26; DC, 31:54. ◆ **26 θεωρεῖτε** pres. ind. act. θεωρέω (# *2555*) to see. **Ἐφέσου** gen. Ἔφεσος (# *2387*). Gen. of place, at Ephesus (RWP; RG, 494; M, 73). **σχεδόν** (# *5385*) almost. **οὗτος** (# *4047*) this. Used here to express contempt (RG, 697; MT, 44). **πείσας** aor. act. part. (temp.) πείθω s.v. 8. **μετέστησεν** aor. ind. act. μεθίστημι (# *3496*) to change, to pervert. The prep. compound has the idea of change (MH, 318). **γινόμενοι** pres. mid. (dep.) part. (adj.) s.v. 1. ◆ **27 κινδυνεύει** pres. ind. act. κινδυνεύω (# *3073*) to be in danger. **ἡμῖν** dat. pl. ἐγώ (# *1609*). Dat. of disadvantage: "danger for us." **μέρος** (# *3538*) acc. sing. part, trade. Acc. as subject of the inf. **ἀπελεγ-μός** (# *591*) exposure, rejection after examination, disrepute (RWP). Possibly a Latinism (*in redargutionem venire*: "to fall into contempt," "to be mocked at" LD, 1538; EDNT). **ἐλθεῖν** aor. act. inf. s.v. 4. Epex. inf. explaining the danger. **θεά** (# 2516) goddess. Those who worshipped Artemis of Ephesus called her the Lady (Κυρία), Saviour (Σώτειρα), heavenly goddess (οὐράνιος θεὸς Ἄρτεμις Ἐφεσία), Queen of the Cosmos (Βασιληῒς κόσμου) and looked to her for safety, health, protection, deliverance, answers to their prayers, and general benevolence. In mythology she was the twin sister of Apollo and as Mistress of the Animals, Artemis the Huntress, she ruled over fertility, esp. of women, protected hunted animals, sent wild animals against her enemies, or killed women in childbirth. Her worship consisted of sacrifice, prayer, religious processions to feasts, games, and festivals. In Ephesus the month of Artemisison (March-April) was sacred to her and all its days were holy days in which celebrations were held and all judicial activity ceased (KP, 1:618-25; BC, 5:251-56; Trebilco, "Asia," BAFCS, 2:316-57; RAC, 1:714-18; GGR, 1:481-500; 2:342-43, 368-69; DDD, 167-80; DNP, 2:53-60; NDIEC, 4:74-82; 6:196-206). **λογισθῆναι** aor. pass. inf. λογίζομαι (# 3357) to reckon, to judge, to consider. Epex. inf. explaining the danger. **μέλλειν** pres. act. inf. μέλλω (# 3516) to be about to, used w. inf. to express fut. Epex. inf. explaining the danger. **καθαιρεῖσθαι** pres. pass. inf. καθαιρέω (# 2747) to tear down, to destroy, to dispose of. w. gen. Inf. w. μέλλω to express fut. **μεγαλειότης** (# 3484) greatness, majesty. The famous temple, which was considered one of the seven wonders of the world, was about four times as large as the Parthenon in Athens and was richly adorned w. the works of the greatest painters and sculptors of the age. It was used as a bank as well as a place of asylum (BC, 5:252-53; Trebilco, "Asia," BAFCS, 2:322-24; Strabo XIV. 1. 22-23; Anton Bammer, *Das Heiligtum der Artemis von Ephesos* [Graz, Austria: Akademische Druck-u. Verlagsanstalt, 1984]; ABD, 2:545; ANTC, 102-8). **σέβεται** pres. ind. mid. (dep.) σέβομαι (# 4936) to worship. She had sanctuaries all over the world, even in Spain (DDD, 175-76; Trebilco, "Asia," BAFCS, 2:332-36). ◆ **28 ἀκούσαντες** aor. act. part. (temp.) ἀκούω (# 201) to hear. **γενόμενοι** aor. mid. (dep.) part. (causal) s.v. 1. **θυμοῦ** gen. sing. θυμός (# 2596) anger, violent anger. Gen. of content. **ἔκραζον** impf. ind. act. κράζω (# 3189) to scream. Incep. impf., "they began screaming." ◆ **29 ἐπλήσθη** aor. ind. pass. πίμπλημι (# 4398) to fill. **συγχύσεως** gen. sing. σύγχυσις (# 5180) confusion. Gen. of content. **ὥρμησαν** aor. ind. act. ὁρμάω (# 3994) to rush. **ὁμοθυμαδόν** (# 3924) together, w. one mind, w. one accord. **θέατρον** (# 2519) acc. sing. theater. The great theater of Ephesus was the regular meeting place of the assembly (Sherwin-White, 87). The large theater was approximately 495 ft. in diameter and would accommodate approxi-

mately 24,500 persons (Merrill M. Parvis, "Ephesus in the Early Christian Era," *BA* 8 [1945]: 61-73; Trebilco, "Asia," BAFCS, 2:348-50). **συναρπάσαντες** aor. act. part. (circum.) συναρπάζω (# 5275) to seize, to take w. force. The prep. compound is perfective (MH, 325). **συνέκδημος** (# 5292) traveling companion. ◆ **30 βουλομένου** pres. mid. (dep.) part. βούλομαι (# 1089) to will, to plan to, w. inf. **εἰσελθεῖν** aor. act. inf. s.v. 8. **δῆμος** (# 1322) crowd, popular assembly. **εἴων** impf. ind. act. ἐάω (# 1572) to allow. ◆ **31 Ἀσιάρχης** (# 825) Asiarch, title of a civic administrative official who served for a fixed term. They proposed motions in the city councils and gave undertakings to council and assembly (R.A. Kearsley, "The Asiarchs," BAFCS, 2:363-76; NDIEC, 4:46-55; ABD, 1:495-97; DPL, 547; ANTC, 109-10; for an older discussion s. BC, 5:256-262). **ὄντες** pres. act. part. εἰμί (# 1639) to be. Adj. or maybe causal part. **φίλος** (# 5813) friend. For the concept of friendship in the ancient world, s. TLNT; TDNT; RAC, 8:418-34; EC, 1-34; 130-64; John T. Fitzgerald (ed.), *Greco-Roman Perspectives on Friendship* (Atlanta: Scholars Press, 1997). **πέμψαντες** aor. act. part. (circum.) πέμπω (# 4287) to send. **παρεκάλουν** impf. ind. act. παρακαλέω (# 4151) to ask, to beseech, to plead. **δοῦναι** aor. act. inf. δίδωμι (# 1443) to give. Inf. in indir. discourse. ◆ **32 ἦν** impf. ind. act. εἰμί s.v. 31, used w. perf. part. in a periphrastic construction. **ἐκκλησία** (# 1711) assembly, gathering of a group of people; here, a mob (RWP). **συγκεχυμένη** perf. pass. part. συγχέω (# 5177) to pour together, to confuse. Perf. emphasizes the state or condition in a periphrastic construction. **πλείους** comp. πολύς (# 4498) many; comp. as superl., most of, the majority. **ᾔδεισαν** plperf. ind. act. of def. perf. οἶδα (# 3857) to know. **συνεληλύθεισαν** plperf. ind. act. συνέρχομαι (# 5302) to come together. ◆ **33 συνεβίβασαν** aor. ind. act. συμβιβάζω (# 5204) to bring together, to prove, to instruct (Haenchen). **προβαλόντων** aor. act. part. προβάλλω (# 4582) to put forward. Gen. abs. **κατασείσας** aor. act. part. κατασείω (# 2939) to motion w. the hand, to shake down; here it indicates the rapid waving of the hand up and down to get a hearing (RWP). **ἤθελεν** impf. ind. act. θέλω (# 2527) to will, to want to, w. inf. **ἀπολογεῖσθαι** pres. mid. inf. ἀπολογέομαι (# 664) to defend oneself. Perhaps Alexander was defending the Jewish rights granted them by the Romans (Robert F. Stoops, Jr., "Riot and Assembly: The Social Context of Acts 19:23-41," *JBL* 108 [1989]: 73-91). ◆ **34 ἐπιγνόντες** aor. act. part. (temp.) ἐπιγινώσκω (# 2105) to know, to recognize. **ἐγένετο** aor. ind. mid. (dep.) s.v. 1. **κραζόντων** pres. act. part. s.v. 28. **μεγάλη** (# 3489) great. The word was used in connection w. Artemis as well as other pagan deities (Trebilco, "Asia," BAFCS, 2:318). ◆ **35 καταστείλας** aor. act. part. (temp.) καταστέλλω (# 2948) to calm down, to quiet down. **γραμματεύς** (# 1208) town clerk. This was one of the highest local Ephesian officials in the city government of that day (Sherwin-White, 86-87; Trebilco, "Asia," BAFCS, 2:351). **νεωκόρος** (# 3753) temple guardian, temple warden, protector of the temple, used of those responsible for the administration of the temple and its sacrifices and festivals (Sherwin-White, 88-89; NDIEC, 6:203-6; Trebilco, "Asia," BAFCS, 2:329-31; Richard Oster, "Numismatic Windows into the Social World of Early Christianity: A Methodological Inquiry," *JBL* 101 [1982]: 214-18). **οὖσαν** pres. act. part. (adj.) fem. sing. acc. εἰμί s.v. 31. **διοπετής** (# 1479) fallen from Zeus, fallen from heaven, an image fallen from heaven. Used also of objects like meteorites which fell from the sky. This was probably the answer to Paul's claim that gods made w. hands are not gods (Trebilco, "Asia," BAFCS, 2:351-53; DDD, 178-79). ◆ **36 ἀναντίρρητος** (# 394) incontestable, not to be contradicted, undeniable (BAGD). The prefix has the force of a negative (Moorhouse, 47-68). **ὄντων** pres. act. part. (causal) εἰμί s.v. 31. Gen abs. **δέον** pres. act. part. δεῖ (# 1256) it is necessary. Part. in a periphrastic construction, "it is binding for you to be prepared" (VA, 479). **κατεσταλμένους** perf. pass. part. s.v. 35. **ὑπάρχειν** pres. act. inf. ὑπάρχω (# 5639) to exist, to be. Epex. inf. explaining what is necessary. **προπετής** (# 4637) rash, reckless, thoughtless. **πράσσειν** pres. act. inf. πράσσω (# 4556) to do. Epex. inf. ◆ **37 ἠγάγετε** aor. ind. act. ἄγω (# 72) to lead. **ἱερόσυλος** (# 2645) temple robber, one who commits sacrilege (Trebilco, "Asia," BAFCS, 2:354). **βλασφημοῦντας** pres. act. part. βλασφημέω (# 1059) to slander, to blaspheme. **τὴν θεόν** (# 2536) goddess. The fem. art. w. the masc. noun was the regular term for the great goddess of the city. The town clerk uses the t.t. (Bruce). ◆ **38 ἔχουσι** pres. ind. act. ἔχω (# 2400) to have. Ind. in a 1st. class cond. cl. where the speaker assumes the reality of the cond. **λόγος** (# 3364) matter, case. **ἀγοραῖος** (# 61) market day. In Rome every eighth day was a market day and when the people came to town, the courts were open for business (FCRR, 43). The Jewish market days or court days were on Monday (2nd. day of the week) and Thursday (5th day of the week) (SB, 2:751-53). The word was then a rendering of the Latin term *conventus*, which in the provinces was a time the proconsul set in which the people could convene for court (DGRA, 357-58). **ἄγονται** pres. ind. pass. ἄγω (# 72) to hold court; "the courts are in session" (BAGD, 13). **ἀνθύπατος** (# 478) proconsul. Generalizing pl.: "There are such people as proconsuls" (Trebilco, "Asia," BAFCS, 2:356). **ἐγκαλείτωσαν** pres. imp. act. 3rd. pers. pl. ἐγκαλέω (# 1592) to accuse, to call one in, to bring a charge against (RWP). ◆ **39 περαιτέρω** (# 4304) comp. πέρα further, beyond (BAGD). **ἐπιζητεῖτε** pres. ind. act. ἐπιζητέω (# 2118) to look for, to seek after. **ἔννομος** (# 1937) lawful. The t.t. for the regularly appointed meeting of the people. For

the accuracy of this terminology and of Luke's description of the entire event s. Sherwin-White, 84-92. **ἐπιλυθήσεται** fut. ind. pass. ἐπιλύω (# 2147) to explain, to decide, to settle. ◆ **40 κινδυνεύομεν** pres. ind. act. s.v. 27. **ἐγκαλεῖσθαι** pres. pass. inf. s.v. 38, w. gen. giving the charge. Epex. inf. explaining the danger. **ὑπάρχοντος** pres. act. part. s.v. 36. Gen. abs. **δυνησόμεθα** fut. ind. pass. (dep.) δύναμαι (# 1538) to be able to, w. inf. **ἀποδοῦναι** aor. act. inf. ἀποδίδωμι (# 625) to give account. **συστροφή** (# 5371) disorderly gathering, commotion. **εἰπών** aor. act. part. (temp.) λέγω s.v. 21. **ἀπέλυσεν** aor. ind. act. ἀπολύω (# 668) to dismiss.

Acts 20

◆ **1 παύσασθαι** aor. mid. (dep.) inf. παύομαι (# 4264) to cease. Inf. w. prep. μετά (# 3552) to express time (s. 19:21), "after the tumult had ceased." **μεταπεμψάμενος** aor. mid. (dep.) part. (temp.) μεταπέμπω (# 3569) to send after, to send for, to summon. **παρακαλέσας** aor. act. part. παρακαλέω (# 4151) to encourage, to exhort (TDNT; EDNT). **ἀσπασάμενος** aor. mid. (dep.) part. ἀσπάζομαι (# 832) to greet, to draw to oneself in embrace, either in greeting or farewell. Here it is farewell (RWP). **ἐξῆλθεν** aor. ind. act. ἐξέρχομαι (# 2002) to go out. **πορεύεσθαι** pres. mid. (dep.) inf. πορεύομαι (# 4513) to go, to travel. Inf. expressing purp. Paul had sent Titus to Corinth to find out their reaction to his "painful letter of tears," but when Titus did not meet him in Troas, he left for Macedonia (2 Cor. 2:3-4, 12-13), where he met Titus (probably at Philippi), wrote 2 Cor., and then finally went to Corinth, where he wrote Romans, and w. the collection for the saints in Jerusalem set out for Jerusalem (Polhill; CH, 434-73). For the collection s. DPL, 143-47. ◆ **2 διελθών** aor. act. part. (temp.) διέρχομαι (# 1451) to go through. **παρακαλέσας** aor. act. part. (temp.) s.v. 1. This evidently was Paul's ministry in Troas (2 Cor. 2:12). **λόγῳ** dat. sing. λόγος (# 3364) word. Instr. dat. **ἦλθεν** aor. ind. act. ἔρχομαι (# 2262) to go, to come. ◆ **3 ποιήσας** aor. act. part. ποιέω (# 4472) to make; w. time, to spend time. **μῆνας** acc. pl. μήν (# 3604) month. Acc. to express the extent of time answering the question, "How long?" (BD, 88; RG, 469f). **γενομένης** aor. mid. (dep.) part. (temp.) γίνομαι (# 1181) to become, to be, to develop. Gen. abs. **ἐπιβουλή** (# 2101) plot. Perhaps the plot was to kill Paul as he took a pilgrim ship carrying Jews to the Passover (PTR, 287; Haenchen). **αὐτῷ** dat. sing. αὐτός (# 899). Dat. of disadvantage, "against him." **μέλλοντι** pres. act. part. (temp.) μέλλω (# 3516) to be about to. Used w. inf. to express fut. **ἀνάγεσθαι** pres. mid. (dep.) part. ἀνάγω (# 343) to set sail, to put out to sea (BAGD). **ἐγένετο** aor. ind. mid. (dep.) γίνομαι. **γνώμη** (# 1191) opinion, decision; "to be of the opinion," "he decided." **ὑποστρέφειν** pres. act. inf. ὑποστρέφω (# 5715) to return. Epex. inf. used to explain the decision (IBG, 127). ◆ **4 συνείπετο** impf. ind. mid. (dep.) συνέπομαι (# 5299) to accompany, w. dat. For the names of the ones mentioned s. BASHH, 236-37; NDIEC, 3:91-93. ◆ **5 προελθόντες** aor. act. part. (circum.) προέρχομαι (# 4601) to go before, to go ahead. **ἔμενον** impf. ind. act. μένω (# 3531) to remain, to wait for. The 1st. pers. pl. ("we") begins again. ◆ **6 ἐξεπλεύσαμεν** aor. ind. act. 1st. pers. pl. ἐκπλέω (# 1739) to set sail, to sail away. **μετὰ τὰς ἡμέρας τῶν ἀζύμων** after the days of the Feast of Unleavened Bread. This perhaps indicates that Paul celebrated Easter w. the church at Philippi (Marshall). **ἤλθομεν** aor. ind. act. s.v. 2. **διετρίψαμεν** aor. ind. act. διατρίβω (# 1417) to spend, to stay. ◆ **7 συνηγμένων** perf. pass. part. (temp.) συνάγω (# 5251) to gather together; pass. to assemble. Gen. abs. **κλάσαι** aor. act. inf. κλάω (# 3089) to break. Inf. expressing purp. The Lord's Supper was accompanied by a larger fellowship meal (1 Cor. 11:20). This incident probably took place on Sunday night (according to Roman reckoning), w. Paul's departure on Monday morning (Polhill). **διελέγετο** impf. ind. mid. (dep.) διαλέγομαι (# 1363) to instruct, to teach (s. 17:2). Impf. pictures the continual action in the past. **μέλλων** pres. act. part. (causal) s.v. 3. Used w. inf to express fut. **ἐξιέναι** pres. act. inf. ἔξειμι (# 1996) to go out. **τῇ ἐπαύριον** (# 2069) on the next day, tomorrow. **παρέτεινεν** impf. ind. act. παρατείνω (# 4189) to stretch beside, to prolong. **μεσονύκτιον** (# 3543) midnight. ◆ **8 ἦσαν** impf. act. ind. εἰμί (# 1639) to be. **λαμπάς** (# 3286) torch, lamp, w. a wick and space for oil (BAGD; EDNT). **ὑπερῴῳ** dat. sing. ὑπερῷον (# 5673) upstairs. **οὗ** (# 4023) where. **συνηγμένοι** perf. pass. part. s.v. 7. Adj. part. as pred. adj. or part. in a periphrastic construction. ◆ **9 καθεζόμενος** pres. mid. (dep.) part. (adj.) καθέζομαι (# 2757) to sit. **θυρίδος** gen. sing. θυρίς (# 2600) window. **καταφερόμενος** pres. pass. part. (temp.) καταφέρω (# 2965) to bear down; to drop off to sleep. Pres. tense describes the progressive action. The hot, oily atmosphere caused by the crowd and the torches made it difficult for one who had probably put in a hard day's work to keep awake. As a medical doctor, Luke would be interested in the cause of the deep sleep (Bruce; MLL, 47-50). **ὕπνῳ** dat. sing. ὕπνος (# 5678) sleep. Instr. dat. **βαθύς** (# 960) deep. **διαλεγομένου** pres. mid. (dep.) part. (temp.) s.v. 7. Gen. abs., "while Paul was instructing." **πλεῖον** comp. πολύς (# 4498) much; comp., more; w. prep. for time, at length, too long (BAGD). **κατενεχθείς** aor. pass. part. (temp.) καταφέρω (# 2965). The perfective aor. in contrast to the pres. part. indicates that sleep finally overtook him and he fell fast asleep (Alford; RWP). **ἔπεσεν** aor. ind. act. πίπτω (# 4406) to fall. **τρίστεγος** (# 5566) third story. **κάτω** (# 3004) down. **ἤρθη** aor. ind. pass. αἴρω (# 149) to lift up, to pick up. ◆ **10 καταβάς** aor. act. part. (circum.) καταβαίνω

(# 2849) to go down. **ἐπέπεσεν** aor. ind. act. ἐπιπίπτω (# 2158) to fall upon, w. dat. **συμπεριλαβών** aor. act. part. (circum.) συμπεριλαμβάνω (# 5227) to embrace, to take hold, to gather around. **εἶπεν** aor. ind. act. λέγω (# 3306) to say. **θορυβεῖσθε** pres. imp. mid. (dep.) θορυβέομαι (# 2572) to throw into disorder, to be troubled, to be distressed. Pres. imp. w. the neg. **μή** (# 3590) indicates the stopping of an action in progress (MKG, 272). ◆ **11 ἀναβάς** aor. act. part. (temp.) ἀναβαίνω (# 326) to go up. **κλάσας** aor. act. part. (temp.) s.v. 7. **γευσάμενος** aor. mid. (dep.) part. (temp.) γεύομαι (# 1174) to taste, to eat. **ὁμιλήσας** aor. act. part. ὁμιλέω (# 3917) to be in company w., to converse w. This second discourse, which lasted from midnight till dawn, was probably more informal and conversational (RWP). **αὐγή** (# 879) daylight, dawn. **ἐξῆλθεν** aor. ind. act. s.v. 1. ◆ **12 ἤγαγον** aor. ind. act. ἄγω (# 72) to lead. **ζῶντα** pres. act. part. ζάω (# 2409) to live. Adj. part. without the art. emphasizes the character or quality. **παρεκλήθησαν** aor. ind. pass. s.v. 1. **μετρίως** (# 3585) adv. moderately. Used w. neg., **οὐ** (# 4024) "no small measure," "exceedingly," "greatly" (MM). ◆ **13 προελθόντες** aor. pass. part. (circum.) s.v. 5. **ἀνήχθημεν** aor. ind. pass. s.v. 3. The first pers. pl. includes Luke and the others, but not Paul. **Ἄσσος** (# 840) Assos. Located on the southern coast of the Troad, about 20 miles from Troas, opposite the northern end of the island of Lesbos was on the coast road from Adramyttiun to Troas (Trebilco, "Asia," BAFCS, 2:359; ABD 4:878-79; Polhill; ANTC, 21-29). **μέλλοντες** pres. act. part. (circum.) s.v. 3., w. inf. to express fut. **ἀναλαμβάνειν** pres. act. inf. ἀναλαμβάνω (# 377) to take up, to take along as a traveling companion, to take on board (BAGD). **διατεταγμένος** perf. mid. (dep.) part. διατάσσομαι (# 1411) to give orders, to give instruction. Periphrastic part. **μέλλων** pres. act. part. s.v. 3. Causal part, "because he was about to go by foot"; or possibly a second periphrastic (VA, 461). **πεζεύειν** pres. act. inf. πεζεύω (# 4269) to go by foot, to travel by land (LC). ◆ **14 ὡς** (# 6055) when, as. **συνέβαλλεν** impf. ind. act. συμβάλλω (# 5202) to bring together, to meet. Impf. may imply that Paul was seen and taken in by boat as he was nearing Assos (Bruce). Some manuscripts have the aor. instead of the impf. (BC, 3:194). **ἀναλαβόντες** aor. act. part. (temp.) s.v. 13. "After we took him on board." **ἤλθομεν** aor. ind. act. s.v. 2. ◆ **15 ἀποπλεύσαντες** aor. act. part. (temp.) ἀποπλέω (# 676) to sail away. **ἐπιούσῃ** (# 2079) on the following day (the word "day" is to be supplied). Dat. of time. **κατηντήσαμεν** aor. ind. act. καταντάω (# 2918) to arrive, to reach a destination. **ἄντικρυς** (# 513) opposite, face to face w. (RWP). **παρεβάλομεν** aor. ind. act. παραβάλλω (# 4125) to throw alongside, to approach, to come near. As a t.t. in seamen's speech, "to come near by ship," "to cross over" (BAGD). It might mean they stopped here

(Schneider) or that they just passed by (Polhill). ἐχομένη pres. mid. part. ἔχω (# 2400) to have; used in the idiom, "on the following (day)." The trip from Mitylene to Miletus was three days; because of the dangerous coastal waters they only sailed during the day (Pesch). ἤλθομεν aor. ind. act. s.v. 2. The city was located on the southwest coast of Asia Minor near the mouth of the Maeander River thirty miles south of Ephesus (Trebilco, "Asia," BAFCS, 2:360-62; KP, 3:1295-98; D. Boyd, "Miletus," IBD Suppl., 597-98; ANTC, 115-27). ◆ **16 κεκρίκει** plperf. ind. act. κρίνω (# 3212) to decide. Plperf. indicates that Paul had reached a decision and remained w. it (s. VA, 278, 287-90). **παραπλεῦσαι** aor. act. inf. παραπλέω (# 4179) to sail by, to bypass. Inf. in indir. discourse explaining Paul's decision. **γένηται** aor. mid. (dep.) subj. s.v. 3. W. dat., "that it might not happen to him" (RWP). Subj w. **ὅπως** (# 3968) to express purp. **χρονοτριβῆσαι** aor. act. inf. χρονοτριβέω (# 5990) to spend time, to lose or waste time (BAGD). Epex. inf. explaining what Paul did not want to happen. **ἔσπευδεν** impf. ind. act. σπεύδω (# 5067) to hurry. **εἴη** pres. opt. act. εἰμί s.v. 8. Opt. in a 4th. class cond. cl. where the possibility is remote and it expresses an uncertain expectation associated w. an effort to attain something (RWP; BG, 138; VA, 311). **γενέσθαι** aor. mid. (dep.) inf. s.v. 3. Epex. inf. explaining the possibility. ◆ **17 πέμψας** aor. act. part. (circum.) πέμπω (# 4287) to send. **μετεκαλέσατο** aor. ind. mid. (dep.) μετακαλέω (# 3559) to call to oneself, to summon. The prep. compound has the idea of change; that is, to call from one place to another (MH, 318; RWP). **πρεσβύτερος** (# 4565) older person, elder as a church office, leader in the church (TDNT; NIDNTT, 1:192-201). ◆ **18 παρεγένοντο** aor. ind. mid. (dep.) παραγίνομαι (# 4134) to arrive. **εἶπεν** aor. ind. act. λέγω (# 3306) to say. **ἐπίστασθε** pres. ind. pass. (dep.) ἐπίσταμαι (# 2179) to know, to understand, primarily expressing the knowledge obtained by proximity to the thing known; then knowledge viewed as a result of a prolonged practice (T). **ἐπέβην** aor. ind. act. ἐπιβαίνω (# 2094) to step on, to set foot on. **τὸν πάντα χρόνον** (# 4246; 5989) for the whole time; acc. of time. It refers to calendar time, not opportune time (Kistemaker). **ἐγενόμην** aor. ind. mid. (dep.) s.v. 3. ◆ **19 δουλεύων** pres. act. part. δουλεύω (# 1526) to carry out the duties of a slave, to serve as a slave (TDNT; NIDNTT, 3:592-98; EDNT; TLNT, 1:380-86). Part. of manner describing Paul's manner among them. **ταπεινοφροσύνη** (# 5425) humility, the quality of unpretentious behavior, the recognition of one's own weakness as well as the recognition of God's power (LN, 1:748; Trench, *Synonyms*, 148-153; TDNT; TLNT, 3:369-71; EDNT; NIDNTT, 2:259-64; R. Leivestad, "Ταπεινός-ταπεινόφρων," *Nov T* 8 [1966]: 36-47). **δάκρυον** (# 1232) tear. Jeremiah was known as the weeping prophet of the OT (Jer. 9:1 [LXX 8.23]). πει-

ρασμός (# 4280) test, trial (TLNT). **συμβάντων** aor. act. part. (adj.) συμβαίνω (# 5201) to come together, to happen to, w. dat. **ἐπιβουλή** (# 2101) plot, a plan for treacherous activity against someone (LN, 1:359; GELTS, 168). ◆ **20 ὑπεστειλάμην** aor. ind. mid. (dep.) ὑποστέλλω (# 5713) to draw back in fear, to shrink from, w. gen. of separation. The opposite of speaking boldly. **συμφερόντων** pres. act. part. συμφέρω (# 5237) to be profitable, to be of an advantage. Part. as subst. **ἀναγγεῖλαι** aor. act. inf. ἀναγγέλλω (# 334) to announce, to proclaim. Epex. inf. explaining the vb. ὑπεστειλάμην. **διδάξαι** aor. act. inf. διδάσκω (# 1438) to teach. Epex. inf. **δημοσίᾳ** (# 1323) publicly. **κατ' οἴκους** (# 2848; 3875) from house to house. Perhaps a reference to the various houses where the believers met (Bradley Blue, "Acts and the House Church," BAFCS, 2:119-222). ◆ **21 διαμαρτυρόμενος** pres. mid. (dep.) part. διαμαρτύρομαι (# 1371) to testify (s. 2:40). Part. of manner, explaining how he served the Lord or how he did nor shrink back. Ἰουδαίοις τε καὶ Ἕλλησιν to both Jews and Greeks. Dat. as indir. obj. ◆ **22 δεδεμένος** perf. pass. part. δέω (# 1313) to bind. Perf. emphasizes the state or condition. Part. of manner explaining in what condition he is going, or the part. may be causal. **πνεύματι** dat. sing. πνεῦμα (# 4460) spirit; Holy Spirit. Dat. of agency., "bound by the Spirit." **πορεύομαι** (# 4513) pres. ind. mid. (dep.) to go. Futuristic pres., describing a process going on in the present w. its termination to be reached only in the fut. (VANT, 221-22). **ἐν αὐτῇ** in it; that is, in Jerusalem. **συναντήσοντα** fut. act. part. (adj.) συναντάω (# 5267) to meet w., to happen to, w. dat. **εἰδώς** perf. act. part. (circum.) οἶδα (# 3857) to know. ◆ **23 πλήν** (# 4440) except that, only; conjunction w. a limitive force (Thrall, 20). **κατὰ πόλιν** (# 2848; 4484) from city to city. **λέγον** pres. act. part. n. nom. sing. λέγω (# 3306) to say. Semitic use of the pleonastic part. **μένουσιν** pres. ind. act. s.v. 5. Pres. indicates a continual condition. ◆ **24 οὐδενὸς λόγου ποιοῦμαι τὴν ψυχὴν τιμίαν ἐμαυτῷ** I reckon my life of no account (Bruce; RWP). **ὡς** (# 6055) used w. inf. to express purp.: "in order that" (RG, 987). **τελειῶσαι** aor. act. inf. τελειόω (# 5457) to complete, to finish, to reach a goal. **δρόμος** (# 1536) run, course. The description of his ministry as a footrace is also common in his letters (Polhill; PAM; 2 Tim. 4:7). **ἔλαβον** aor. ind. act. λαμβάνω (# 3284) to receive. **διαμαρτύρασθαι** aor. mid. (dep.) inf. s.v. 21. Epex. inf. explaining his ministry. **χάριτος** gen. sing. χάρις (# 5921) grace. Gen. of content giving the content of the good news. ◆ **25 οἶδα** perf. ind. act. to know. Def. perf. w. pres. meaning s.v. 22. **ὄψεσθε** fut. ind. mid. (dep.) 2nd. pers. pl. ὁράω (# 3972) to see. **διῆλθον** aor. ind. act. s.v. 2. **κηρύσσων** pres. act. part. κηρύσσω (# 3062) to proclaim as a herald, to preach (TDNT; EDNT). Part. of manner explaining his action as he was among them. ◆ **26 μαρτύρομαι** (# 3458) pres. ind.

mid. (dep.) to testify to, to assert. **αἷμα** (# 135) blood. In this connection Paul means, "I am free of blame in reference of each one, if he (on account of unbelief) falls a prey to death" (Meyer). ◆ **27 ὑπεστει-λάμην** aor. ind. mid. (dep.) s.v. 20. **ἀναγγεῖλαι** aor. act. inf. s.v. 20. ◆ **28 προσέχετε** pres. imp. act. προσέχω (# 4668) to take heed, to pay attention to. Pres. imp. calls for an habitual action. **ἔθετο** aor. ind. mid. τίθημι (# 5502) to place, to appoint. **ἐπίσκοπος** (# 2176) overseer, guardian, bishop, one who has the responsibility of caring for the spiritual concerns (LN, 1:463; TDNT; EDNT). It is significant that the pl. is used for the one church at Ephesus (s. Phil. 1:1). **ποιμαίνειν** pres. act. inf. ποιμαίνω (# 4477) to shepherd, to tend or feed the flock. Inf. of purp. **περιεποιήσατο** aor. ind. mid. (indir., "for oneself") περιποιέω (# 4347) to secure, to acquire (TLNT; TDNT; EDNT). **ἴδιος** (# 2625) own, personal (s. Bruce; Polhill). ◆ **29 εἰσελεύσονται** fut. ind. mid. (dep.) εἰσέρχομαι (# 1656) to go into, to come into. **ἄφιξις** (# 922) departure. **λύκος** (# 3380) wolf. The ferocious wolf terrorized the shepherds, attacking above all the ewes. Metaphorically, the wolf symbolized the wicked exploiter of the weak, who ruin, extort, and reduce their subjects to servitude and was often used to describe false teachers or active enemies of the faith (TLNT; Polhill; 4 Ezra; 1 Enoch 89:13-27; T. Gad 1:3). **βαρύς** (# 987) heavy, difficult to bear, savage, fierce, cruel (TLNT, 2:416). **φειδόμενοι** pres. mid. (dep.) part. (adj.) φείδομαι (# 5767) to spare, w. gen. ◆ **30 ἀναστήσονται** fut. ind. mid. (dep.) ἀνίστημι (# 482) to arise, to rise up. **αὐτῶν** your own selves. **λαλοῦντες** pres. act. part. λαλέω (# 3281) to speak. Adj. or circum. part. **διεστραμμένα** perf. pass. part. διαστρέφω (# 1406) to turn aside, to twist, to pervert, to distort. Part. as subst., "things having been distorted." Perf. stresses the continuing state or condition. **ἀποσπᾶν** pres. act. inf. ἀποσπάω (# 685) to draw out, to tear away, to attract (BAGD). Inf. of purp. ◆ **31 γρηγορεῖτε** pres. imp. act. γρηγορέω (# 1213) to stay awake, to watch, be alert. Pres. imp. indicates a continual watchfulness. **μνημονεύοντες** pres. act. part. (circum.) μνημονεύω (# 3648) to remember. **τριετία** (# 5562) three years. **νύκτα** acc. sing. νύξ (# 3816) night. Acc. of time. **ἐπαυσάμην** aor. ind. mid. (dep.) παύομαι (# 4264) to cease, to stop. **νουθετῶν** pres. act. part. νουθετέω (# 3805) to put something in someone's mind, to instruct, to provide instruction as to correct behavior and belief, to warn, to admonish, to instruct one who has gone astray by warning him of the danger, admonishing him to return (TDNT; TLNT; LN, 1:415; NIDNTT, 1:567-69). Supplementary part. describing what Paul did not stop doing. ◆ **32 παρατίθεμαι** pres. ind. mid. (dep.) παρατίθημι (# 4192) to commit to, to entrust someone to the care or protection of someone, to deposit for safekeeping, w. acc. and dat. (TLNT, 3:24-27; BAGD). The Temple of Artemis in Ephesus

was an asylum and bank for depositing valuables. **δυναμένῳ** pres. pass. (dep.) part. (adj.) δύναμαι (# 1538) to be able to, w. inf. **οἰκοδομῆσαι** aor. act. inf. οἰκοδομέω (# 3868) to build, to build up. **δοῦναι** aor. act. inf. δίδωμι (# 1443) to give, to grant. **ἡγιασμένοις** perf. pass. part. ἁγιάζω (# 39) to set apart, to sanctify. Perf. indicates the condition. Part. as subst. ◆ **33 ἀργύριον** (# 736) silver. **χρυσός** (# 5996) gold. **ἱματισμός** (# 2669) clothing. **ἐπεθύμησα** aor. ind. act. ἐπιθυμέω (# 2121) to desire, to covet, w. gen. ◆ **34 αὐτοί** (# 899) you yourselves. Intensive pers. pron. **γινώσκετε** pres. ind. act. γινώσκω (# 1182) to know. **οὖσιν** pres. act. part. εἰμί (# 1639) to be. Part. as subst., "the ones with me." **ὑπηρέτησαν** aor. ind. act. ὑπηρετέω (# 5676) to serve, to minister (TDNT; EDNT). ◆ **35 ὑπέδειξα** aor. ind. act. ὑποδείκνυμι (# 5683) to show under one's eyes, to give an object lesson, to show (RWP). **κοπιῶντας** pres. act. part. κοπιάω (# 3159) to work, to toil. The vb. emphasizes the hardness of the work and the weariness it brings (LC). Part. of means, indicating how the help was provided. **δεῖ** (# 1256) pres. ind. act., it is necessary, giving a logical necessity, w. inf. **ἀντιλαμβάνεσθαι** pres. mid. (dep.) inf. ἀντιλαμβάνω (# 514) to help, to take another's part, to succour, w. gen. (EGT; MM). **ἀσθενούντων** pres. act. part. ἀσθενέω (# 820) to be sick, to be weak. Part. as subst. **μνημονεύειν** pres. act. inf. s.v. 31. Inf. explaining the necessity. **αὐτός** (# 899) He, himself. Emphatic. pron. **εἶπεν** aor. ind. act. λέγω (# 3306) to say. **διδόναι** pres. act. inf. s.v. 32. Epex. inf. explaining what is more blessed. **λαμβάνειν** pres. act. inf. λαμβάνω (# 3284) to receive. Epex. inf. ◆ **36 εἰπών** aor. act. part. (temp.) s.v. 35. "After he said...." **θείς** aor. act. part. (temp.) τίθημι (# 5502) to place, to put. **γόνατα** acc. pl. γόνυ (# 1205) knee; "to place the knee," "to kneel." **προσηύξατο** aor. ind. mid. (dep.) προσεύχομαι (# 4667) to pray. ◆ **37 κλαυθμός** (# 3088) crying, weeping. **ἐγένετο** aor. ind. mid. (dep.) γίνομαι (# 1181) to become, to be, to happen. **ἐπιπεσόντες** aor. act. part. (circum.) ἐπιπίπτω (# 2158) to fall upon. **τράχηλος** (# 5549) neck. **κατεφίλουν** impf. ind. act. καταφιλέω (# 2968) to kiss (s. Mark 14:45). Incep. impf., "they began to kiss." ◆ **38 ὀδυνώμενοι** pres. mid. (dep.) part. (circum.) ὀδυνάομαι (# 3849) to be distressed, to be moved by pain, to sorrow. **μάλιστα** (# 3436) especially. **ᾧ** dat. sing. rel. pron. ὅς (# 4005) Dat. by attraction. **εἰρήκει** plperf. ind. act. λέγω s.v. 35. **μέλλουσιν** pres. ind. act. μέλλω (# 3516) to be about to. W. inf. to express fut. **θεωρεῖν** pres. act. inf. θεωρέω (# 2555) to see. **προέπεμπον** impf. ind. act. προπέμπω (# 4636) to send forward, to accompany, to escort (BAGD).

Acts 21

◆ **1 ἐγένετο** aor. ind. mid. (dep.) γίνομαι (# 1181) to become, to be, to happen. For the Semitic construction

s. Luke 2:1. ἀναχθῆναι aor. pass. inf. ἀνάγω (# 343) mid. or pass. to put out to sea, to set sail. Temp. use of the inf. w. ὡς (# 6055). ἀποσπασθέντας aor. pass. part. (temp.) ἀποσπάω (# 685) to tear away, to part. It speaks of the painful parting of friends. εὐθυδρομήσαντες aor. act. part. (temp.) εὐθυδρομέω (# 2312) to run a straight course. The prevailing wind was northeast (Bruce). ἤλθομεν aor. ind. act. ἔρχομαι (# 2262) to come. The island of Cos, famous for its temple to Asclepius, the god of healing, was a major shipping port exporting excellent wine, costly ointments, purple dye, and fabrics of a transparent texture. It was also the birthplace of Hippocrates, the father of medicine (Scott T. Carroll, "Cos," ABD, 1:1161-62; CH, 556). τῇ ἑξῆς (# 1971) on the next day (w. the word "day" supplied). Ῥόδος (# 4852) Rhodes (CH, 557-59; AAT, 291). It was probable that they left Miletus on Sunday, May, 1, reached Cos on the same day; then reached Rhodes on Monday, May 2; Patara on Tuesday, May 3; Myra on Wednesday, May 4; and Tyre on May 7 (PRT, 294). ◆ 2 εὑρόντες aor. act. part. (temp.) εὑρίσκω (# 2351) to find. διαπερῶν pres. act. part. (adj.) διαπεράω (# 1385) to cross over. ἐπιβάντες aor. act. part. (temp.) ἐπιβαίνω (# 2094) to embark, to go aboard. ἀνήχθημεν aor. ind. pass. s.v. 1. ◆ 3 ἀναφάναντες aor. act. part. ἀναφαίω (# 428) to cause to appear, probably a nautical t.t., "to sight" (BAGD). The word lit. means "to make visible to oneself," that is, by drawing near (BD, 163). καταλιπόντες aor. act. part. (circum.) καταλείπω (# 2901) to leave behind. εὐώνυμος (# 2381) left, on the left side. ἐπλέομεν impf. ind. act. πλέω (# 4434) to sail. Impf., "we continued to sail." κατήλθομεν aor. ind. act. κατέρχομαι (# 2982) to come down. ἐκεῖσε (# 1698) there. ἀποφορτιζόμενον pres. mid. (dep.) part. ἀποφορτίζομαι (# 711) to make light, to unload. Impf. periphrastic construction used as the customary or progressive impf., "the ship had the characteristic of" (BD, 175; RG, 884). γόμος (# 1203) freight, cargo. ◆ 4 ἀνευρόντες aor. act. part. (temp.) ἀνευρίσκω (# 461) to seek out, to find by searching. The prep. compound is perfective (MH, 296). ἐπεμείναμεν aor. ind. act. ἐπιμένω (# 2152) to remain. ἔλεγον impf. ind. act. λέγω (# 3306) to say, to tell. Perhaps in the sense of conative, "they tried to tell." ἐπιβαίνειν pres. act. inf. ἐπιβαίνω s.v. 2. Inf. in indir. discourse. ◆ 5 ἐγένετο aor. ind. mid. (dep.) s.v. 1. ἐξαρτίσαι aor. act. inf. ἐξαρτίζω (# 199) to fulfill, to complete. Here in the sense of accomplishing the days; that is, finishing the time, the seven days, during which we had to remain for the cargo to be unloaded and for other business (EGT). Temp. use of the inf. ἐξελθόντες aor. act. part. (temp.) ἐξέρχομαι (# 2002) to go out. ἐπορευόμεθα impf. ind. mid. (dep.) πορεύομαι (# 4513) to go, to travel. Impf. indicates the continuing of the journey. προπεμπόντων pres. act. part. (temp.) προπέμπω (# 4636) to accompany, to escort (s. 20:38).

Gen. abs. θέντες aor. act. part. τίθημι (# 5502) to place, to kneel down. γόνυ (# 1205) knee. αἰγιαλός (# 129) beach. προσευξάμενοι aor. mid. (dep.) part. (temp.) προσεύχομαι (# 4667) to pray. ◆ 6 ἀπησπασάμεθα aor. ind. mid. (dep.) ἀπασπάζομαι (# 571) to give parting greetings, to say farewell. ἀνέβημεν aor. ind. act. ἀναβαίνω (# 326) to embark, to get on board. ὑπέστρεψαν aor. ind. act. ὑποστρέφω (# 5715) to return. ◆ 7 διανύσαντες aor. act. part. διανύω (# 1382) to accomplish, to complete, to arrive (GELTS, 107; 2 Macc. 12:17); here perhaps w. the meaning, "to continue the voyage" (NTNT, 134-35; BAGD; NDIEC, 1:77; LC). The prep. has the idea of carrying an action through to a definite result (MH, 301). κατηντήσαμεν aor. ind. act. καταντάω (# 2918) to arrive. Ptolemais was also called Acco (Moshe Dothan, "Acco," ABD, 1:51-53). ἀσπασάμενοι aor. mid. (dep.) part. (temp.) ἀσπάζομαι s.v. 6. ἐμείναμεν aor. ind. act. μένω (# 3531) to remain. ἡμέραν acc. sing. ἡμέρα (# 2465) day. Acc. of time, "for one day." ◆ 8 τῇ ἐπαύριον (# 2069) on the next day. The distance of 40 miles suggests the travel was by boat (BBC). ἐξελθόντες aor. act. part. (temp.) s.v. 5. ἤλθομεν aor. ind. act. s.v. 1. This was Caesarea on the Sea (s. 18:22). εἰσελθόντες aor. act. part. εἰσέρχομαι (# 1656) to go into. εὐαγγελιστής (# 2296) evangelist, one who brings the good news. A possible secular use of the word describes one as the proclaimer of the oracle announcements (MM). Words ending w. this suffix indicate the agent who performs the action (MH, 360). ὄντος pres. act. part. (adj.) εἰμί (# 1639) to be. ἐμείναμεν aor. ind. act. s.v. 7. ◆ 9 ἦσαν impf. ind. act. εἰμί s.v. 8. τούτῳ...ἦσαν there was to this one; that is, "this one had...." θυγάτηρ (# 2588) daughter. παρθένος (# 4221) virgin (TLNT, TDNT; EDNT). προφητεύουσαι pres. act. part. (adj.) fem. nom. pl. προφητεύω (# 4736) to prophesy. ◆ 10 ἐπιμενόντων pres. act. part. (temp.) s.v. 4. Gen. abs. πλείους comp. πολύς (# 4498) much, many; comp., more. "More days than we expected" (RWP). κατῆλθεν aor. ind. act. s.v. 3. ◆ 11 ἐλθών aor. act. part. (temp.) s.v. 1. ἄρας aor. act. part. αἴρω (# 149) to lift up, to take. ζώνη (# 2438) belt. δήσας aor. act. part. (temp.) δέω (# 1313) to bind, to tie. εἶπεν aor. ind. act. λέγω (# 3306) to say. οὗ gen. sing. rel. pron. ὅς (# 4005). Gen. of possession. δήσουσιν fut. ind. act. δέω. παραδώσουσιν fut. ind. act. παραδίδωμι (# 4140) to deliver over to. The actions of the Jews caused Paul's Roman imprisonment (GGBB, 412). ◆ 12 ἠκούσαμεν aor. ind. act. ἀκούω (# 201) to hear. παρεκαλοῦμεν impf. ind. act. παρακαλέω (# 4151) to urge, to exhort. Conative impf., "we tried to persuade him from going up" (RWP). ἐντόπιος (# 1954) one belonging to the place, resident. ἀναβαίνειν pres. act. inf. ἀναβαίνω (# 326) to go up (s.v. 6). Inf. expressing purp. or inf. in indir. discourse. The pres. inf. indicates "to stop going up" (Bruce). ◆ 13 ἀπεκρίθη aor. ind. pass. (dep.) ἀποκρίνομαι (# 646) to answer. **ποιεῖτε** pres. ind. act. ποιέω (# 4472) to do. Used w. the part. to express the action of the part. **κλαίοντες** pres. act. part. κλαίω (# 3081) to weep, to cry. **συνθρύπτοντες** pres. act. part. συνθρύπτω (# 5316) to crush together, to break up, to pound to bits, to pound, to break one's heart (LC; BAGD; Polhill). The word was used by Josephus to describe the stone in Nebuchadnezzar's dream which broke the image into pieces (Jos., *Ant.*, 10:207). The idea may be "to exert pressure on someone because of a decision" (EDNT). For the medical use of θρύπτω as a t.t for the crushing of a calculus s. MLL, 249; LS, 807. **δεθῆναι** aor. pass. inf. s.v. 11. Epex. inf. explaining the readiness of Paul. **καί** (# 2779) also, even. **ἀποθανεῖν** aor. act. inf. ἀποθνήσκω (# 633) to die. Epex. inf. **ἑτοίμως ἔχω** (# 2290; 2400) to have readiness; here, to be ready (BAGD). ◆ **14 πειθομένου** pres. pass. part. πείθω (# 4275) to persuade. Gen. abs., temp. or causal. **ἡσυχάσαμεν** aor. ind. act. ἡσυχάζω (# 2483) to be still, to be quiet. Ingressive aor., "we became silent." **εἰπόντες** aor. act. part. (circum.) λέγω s.v. 11. **κυρίου** gen. sing. κύριος (# 3261) Lord. Possessive gen. placed first for emphasis. **γινέσθω** pres. imp. mid. (dep.) s.v. 1. ◆ **15 ἐπισκευασάμενοι** aor. mid. (dep.) part. (temp.) ἐπισκευάζομαι (# 2171) to prepare, to pack up (LC). **ἀνεβαίνομεν** impf. ind. act. s.v. 6. Incep. impf., "we started to go up." ◆ **16 συνῆλθον** aor. ind. act. συνέρχομαι (# 5302) to go w. someone, to accompany. **ἄγοντες** pres. act. part. ἄγω (# 72) to lead, to bring. adj. part., nom. pl agreeing w. τινες understood (RWP), "who brought us to Mnason." **ξενισθῶμεν** aor. subj. pass. ξενίζω (# 3826) to entertain guests, to show hospitality. The subj. used here in the rel. cl. to express purp. (BD, 191; RG, 955, 989). **ἀρχαίῳ** dat. sing. ἀρχαῖος (# 792) old, early. It may mean that he was a disciple from Pentecost, the beginning of the church (EGT; BASHH, 170). ◆ **17 γενομένων** aor. mid. (dep.) part. (temp.) s.v. 1. Gen. abs. **ἀσμένως** (# 830) w. joy, gladly. **ἀπεδέξαντο** aor. ind. mid. (dep.) ἀποδέχομαι (# 622) to welcome, to receive. ◆ **18 τῇ ἐπιούσῃ** (# 2157) on the next (day). **εἰσῄει** impf. ind. act. εἴσειμι (# 1655) to go into. **παρεγένοντο** aor. ind. mid. (dep.) παραγίνομαι (# 4134) to arrive. ◆ **19 ἀσπασάμενος** aor. mid. (dep.) part. (temp.) s.v. 6, 7. **ἐξηγεῖτο** impf. ind. mid. (dep.) ἐξηγέομαι (# 2007) to narrate, to explain in detail (TLNT). For the prep. compound s. MH, 310. Incep. impf., "he began to explain." **καθ᾽ ἓν ἕκαστον** (# 1667) one by one. He explained the events of his second and third missionary journeys (Schneider). **ὧν** gen. pl. rel. pron. ὅς (# 4005) Gen. by attraction to the unexpressed antecedent τουτων instead of the normal acc. (RWP). **ἐποίησεν** aor. ind. act. s.v. 13. Complexive aor. summarizing all of the things God had done among the Gentiles through Paul's ministry. ◆ **20 ἀκούσαντες** aor. act. part. s.v. 12. **ἐδόξαζον** impf. ind. act. δοξάζω (# 1519) to glorify. Incep. impf. **εἶπον** aor.

ind. act. λέγω s.v. 11. **θεωρεῖς** pres. ind. act. θεωρέω (# 2555) to see, to come to understand as a result of perception (LN, 1:381). **μυριάς** (# 3689) myriad, tens of thousands. Gr. idiom for a great number (LC). **πεπιστευκότων** perf. act. part. (adj.) πιστεύω (# 4409) to believe. Perf. emphasizes the lasting state or condition. **ζηλωτής** (# 2421) zealous. The word here does not indicate the political party of the Zealots (Bruce). For a description of the political party s. H.P. Kingdon, "Who Were the Zealots and Their Leaders in A.D. 66?" *NTS* 17 (1970): 68-72; ABD, 6:1043-54; DJG, 696-97; TJ, 159. **ὑπάρχουσιν** pres. ind. act. ὑπάρχω (# 5639) to exist, to be. Pres. indicates the existing situation. ◆ **21 κατηχήθησαν** aor. ind. pass. κατηχέω (# 2994) to instruct, to inform. For Jewish attacks against Paul found in extrabiblical Jewish writings s. SB, 2:753-55. **ἀποστασία** (# 686) apostasy, falling away. **διδάσκεις** pres. ind. act. διδάσκω (# 1438) to teach. Customary pres. indicating a continual, habitual action. **περιτέμνειν** pres. act. inf. περιτέμνω (# 4362) to circumcise. Inf. in indir. discourse. **περιπατεῖν** pres. act. inf. περιπατέω (# 4344) to walk, to conduct one's life. ◆ **22 πάντως** (# 4122) certainly, of course; originally a word of assurance ("by all means"), it has been weakened and could be uncertain in force ("probably") (LC; G.M. Lee, Πάντως Perhaps? *ZNW* 64 [1973]: 152). **ἀκούσονται** fut. ind. mid. (dep.) s.v. 12. **ἐλήλυθας** perf. ind. act. ἔρχομαι (# 2262) to come. ◆ **23 ποίησον** aor. act. imp. ποιέω (# 4472) to do; here, to take a vow. Aor. imp. calls for a specific act. **εὐχή** (# 2376) vow (SB, 2:755-61; s. 18:18). **ἔχοντες** pres. act. part. (adj.) ἔχω (# 2400) to have. ◆ **24 παραλαβών** aor. act. part. παραλαμβάνω (# 4161) to take, to take w. someone. Circum. part. w. force of an imp. (VANT, 386). **ἁγνίσθητι** aor. imp. pass. ἁγνίζω (# 49) to purify. The pass. is used here as a refl. pass.: "purify yourself" (RG, 819). Perhaps the four had become impure during their vow and needed to undergo a purification lasting seven days. Paul was perhaps considered impure because he had been travelling in Gentile countries (SB, 2:757-59; Polhill). **δαπάνησον** aor. imp. act. δαπανάω (# 1251) to spend money on someone, to pay the expenses. It was necessary for one with a Nazirite vow to bring three offerings (a sin-offering, a whole-offering, and a peace-offering) at the end of his vow (M, Nazir, 5:7). When Agrippa I came to power in Palestine, he paid for the offerings of a considerable number of poor Nazirites (Jos., *Ant.*, 19:294). A certain Simeon ben Shetah was to have divided equally the cost for three hundred Nazirites w. King Alexander Jannai, but freed 150 of them (TS, 572; SB, 2:755-56). **ξυρήσονται** fut. ind. mid. ξυράω (# 3834) to shave; mid. to shave oneself, to let oneself be shaved. Fut. ind. used w. **ἵνα** (# 2671) to express purp. (MT, 100; RG, 984). At the end of the vow the person had his head shaved (M, Nazir, 3; SB, 2:755-56). **γνώ-**

σονται fut. ind. mid. (dep.) γινώσκω (# 1182) to know, to recognize, to realize. Fut. may be dependent on ἵνα to express purp. ὦν gen. pl. rel. pron. ὅς (# 4005). Gen. by attraction to an unexpressed antecedent τουτῶν (RWP). κατήχηνται perf. ind. pass. s.v. 21. στοιχεῖς pres. ind. act. στοιχέω (# 5123) to be in line w., to follow in someone's footsteps, to walk, to conduct one's life, to live in conformity w. some presumed standard or set of customs (BAGD; LN, 1:505). Pres. refers to a constant, habitual action. αὐτός (# 899) emphasis, you yourself. φυλάσσων pres. act. part. φυλάσσω (# 5875) to guard, to observe. Part. of manner. Pres. points to a customary or habitual action. ◆ 25 πεπιστευκότων perf. act. part. s.v. 20. ἐπεστείλαμεν aor. ind. act. ἐπιστέλλω (# 2182) to send to, to send a message by letter, to write. From the usage of the word in official documents, the meaning readily passed over into "instruct," "enjoin" (MM). κρίναντες aor. act. part. κρίνω (# 3212) to decide, to determine, to judge. Part. gives the content of the writing. φυλάσσεσθαι pres. mid. (dir. mid., "to guard oneself") inf. s.v. 24. Inf. in indir. discourse. εἰδωλόθυτον (# 1628) acc. sing. meat offered to an idol. It refers to sacrificial meat, part of which was burned on the altar, part of which was eaten at a solemn meal in the temple, and part of which was sold in the market for home use (BAGD). πνικτός (# 4465) strangled. For the instructions s. 15:29. ◆ 26 ἐχομένῃ ἡμέρᾳ (# 2400; 2465) on the following day; dat. of time. ἁγνισθείς aor. pass. part. (temp.) s.v. 24. εἰσήει impf. ind. act. s.v. 18. διαγγέλλων pres. act. part. διαγγέλλω (# 1334) to announce, to declare. Circum. part. or part. expressing purp. ἐκπλήρωσις (# 1741) fulfillment. ἕως οὗ until; w. aor. pass. ind. it contemplates the final result (RWP). προσηνέχθη aor. ind. pass. προσφέρω (# 4712) to bring an offering, to offer. ὑπέρ (# 5642) on behalf of, instead of (IBG, 64). προσφορά (# 4714) offering. ◆ 27 ἔμελλον impf. ind. act. μέλλω (# 3516) to be about to. W. inf. to express futurity or intention reckoned from a moment in the past: "the days were going to be completed" (MKG, 307). συντελεῖσθαι pres. pass. inf. συντελέω (# 5334) to complete. The completion of the seven days evidently refers to the completion of the time required for the purification (s.v. 24; SB, 2:757-61). θεασάμενοι aor. mid. (dep.) part. (adj.) θεάομαι (# 2517) to see, to observe. συνέχεον impf. ind. act. συγχέω (# 5177) to pour together, to cause confusion, to stir up. Incep. impf. pictures the beginning of a continual action. ἐπέβαλον aor. ind. act. ἐπιβάλλω (# 2095) to place upon, to place hands upon, to seize. ◆ 28 κράζοντες pres. act. part. (circum.) κράζω (# 3189) to scream. βοηθεῖτε pres. imp. act. βοηθέω (# 1070) to help. Pres. imp. here emphasizes the process or the various details of the help (VANT, 365). πανταχῇ (# 4114) everywhere. διδάσκων pres. act. part. (adj.) s.v. 21. Pres. stresses the continual and habitual action. εἰσήγαγεν

aor. ind. act. εἰσάγω (# 1652) to lead into, to bring into. κεκοίνωκεν perf. ind. act. κοινόω (# 3124) to make common, to defile. Perf. pictures the abiding condition. The temple was holy and was to be kept holy and pure. It was a capital offense for a Gentile to be found within the barrier (for the inscription w. text and translation s. LAE, 80-81; Jos., JW, 5:193-96) which divided the court of the Gentiles from the court of Israel (JPB, 70-76; LC; Longenecker, 521-22; M, Kelim 1:8; M, Middoth, 2:3). ◆ 29 ἦσαν impf. ind. act. εἰμί (# 1639) w. part. to form a periphrastic construction. γάρ (# 1142) for, gives the explanation for their action. προεωρακότες perf. act. part. προοράω (# 4632) to see previously, to see before. ἐνόμιζον impf. ind. act. νομίζω (# 3787) to suppose. εἰσήγαγεν aor. ind. act. s.v. 28. ◆ 30 ἐκινήθη aor. ind. pass. κινέω (# 3075) to move. ἐγένετο aor. ind. mid. (dep.) s.v. 1. συνδρομή (# 5282) running together, forming of a mob (BAGD). ἐπιλαβόμενοι aor. mid. (dep.) part. ἐπιλαμβάνομαι (# 2138) to seize. εἷλκον impf. ind. act. ἕλκω (# 1816) to drag. ἐκλείσθησαν aor. ind. pass. κλείω (# 3091) to shut. The Levitical temple police closed the doors separating the temple from the court of the Gentiles (Haenchen; JPB, 81-82). ◆ 31 ζητούντων pres. act. part. (circum.) ζητέω (# 2426) to seek, to try to, w. inf. ἀποκτεῖναι aor. act. inf. ἀποκτείνω (# 650) to kill. ἀνέβη aor. ind. act. ἀναβαίνω (# 326) to go up. The Roman soldiers were stationed in the Fortress of Antonia, at the northwest corner of the Temple area, and were responsible to quiet any trouble that might arise in and around the temple area (TJ, 25; BAFCS, 3:137-38). φάσις (# 5762) information, report, news (MM). χιλίαρχος (# 5941) the leader of a thousand soldiers, the military tribune, the commander of a cohort, about six hundred men (BAGD). These usually were young men doing military service at the beginning of their official career (BC, 5:428; KP, 5:947-48; OCD, 1091-92; DGRA, 502-4; Schneider; s. 22:24). συγχύννεται pres. ind. pass. s.v. 27. ◆ 32 ἐξαυτῆς (# 1994) immediately. παραλαβὼν aor. act. part. (circum.) s.v. 24. ἑκατοντάρχης (# 1672) leader of a hundred men, centurion (s. 10:1). κατέδραμεν aor. ind. act. κατατρέχω (# 2963) to run down. ἰδόντες aor. act. part. (temp.) ὁράω (# 3972) to see. ἐπαύσαντο aor. ind. mid. (dep.) παύομαι (# 4264) to stop, to cease, w. supplementary part. τύπτοντες pres. act. part. τύπτω (# 5597) to beat. ◆ 33 ἐγγίσας aor. act. part. (temp.) ἐγγίζω (# 1581) to draw near, to be near. ἐπελάβετο aor. ind. mid. (dep.) s.v. 30. ἐκέλευσεν aor. ind. act. κελεύω (# 3027) to command. δεθῆναι aor. pass. inf. s.v. 11. Inf. in indir. discourse. ἁλύσεσι dat. pl. ἅλυσις (# 268) chain. Instr. dat. δυσί dat. pl. δύο (# 1545) two. ἐπυνθάνετο impf. ind. mid. (dep.) πυνθάνομαι (# 4785) to investigate, to inquire. Incep. impf., "he began to inquire." εἴη pres. opt. act. εἰμί (# 1639) to be. Opt. in indir. discourse (RG, 1044). πεποιηκώς perf. act. part.

s.v. 13. Part. in periphrastic construction.   ◆ 34
ἐπεφώνουν impf. ind. act. ἐπιφωνέω (# 2215) to call to.
Impf. pictures the continual action, "they kept on
shouting." δυναμένου pres. pass. (dep.) part. (causal)
δύναμαι (# 1538) to be able to, w. inf. Gen. abs. γνῶναι
aor. act. inf. s.v. 24. ἀσφαλής (# 855) not slipping, not
falling, certainty; here, certain, precise, or exact knowledge (TLNT, 1:217). ἐκέλευσεν aor. ind. act. s.v. 33.
ἄγεσθαι pres. pass. inf. ἄγω s.v. 16. Inf. in indir. discourse. παρεμβολή (# 4213) camp, barracks, headquarters (BAGD). These were the barracks of the Roman
garrison called Antonia, located northwest of the temple and connected to the temple by two flights of
stairs (BC, 5: 478f; Jos., JW, 238-47; s.v. 31). ◆ 35 ἐγένετο aor. ind. mid. (dep.) s.v. 1. ἀναβαθμός (# 325) step.
These were the steps leading from the temple area up
to the fortress (s.v. 34). συνέβη aor. ind. act. συμβαίνω
(# 5201) to happen. βαστάζεσθαι pres. pass. inf.
βαστάζω (# 1002) to carry. Epex. inf. explaining what
happened. βία (# 1040) force, violence. Acc. w. prep.
διά (# 1328) to mean, "because of the violence of the
crowd."   ◆ 36 ἠκολούθει impf. ind. act. ἀκολουθέω
(# 199) to follow. Impf. pictures the action in progress.
κράζοντες pres. act. part. (circum.) s.v. 28. αἶρε pres.
imp. act. s.v. 11. For a discussion of the pres. imp. here
s. VANT, 350-51. ◆ 37 μέλλων pres. act. part. s.v. 27 w.
inf. to express the immediate fut., "As he was about to
be taken into the headquarters." εἰσάγεσθαι pres. pass.
inf. s.v. 28. ἔξεστιν pres. ind. act. ἔξεστι(ν) (# 2003) it is
allowed, w. inf. Here in a question, "Am I allowed."
εἰπεῖν aor. act. inf. λέγω (# 3306). ἔφη aor. ind. act. φημί
(# 5774) to say, to speak. Ἑλληνιστί (# 1822) adv. in the
Greek language (BAGD). γινώσκεις pres. ind. act. s.v.
24; "Do you understand in the Greek language?"
◆ 38 οὐκ (# 4024) neg. in a question expecting a positive answer: "You are..., aren't you?" ἀναστατώσας
aor. act. part. (adj.) ἀναστατόω (# 415) to cause a revolt,
to instigate an uprising. ἐξαγαγών aor. act. part. (adj.)
ἐξάγω (# 1974) to lead out. σικάριος (# 4974) sicarius,
assassin. Radical assassins opposing the Romans were
armed w. short daggers (sica) under their cloaks, mingled w. the crowd, struck down their opponents, then
pretended to call for help. One could not even trust a
friend (Jos., JW, 2:254-57; TJ, 157-58; DJG, 695-96; BBC;
Schneider). The Egyptian mentioned was a Jew who
proclaimed himself a prophet. He gathered a large following w. the intent to lead them to the Mount of Olives, where, at his command, the walls of Jerusalem
would collapse. His force was attacked by Felix; the
Egyptian himself escaped (Jos., JW, 2:261-63; Ant.,
20:167-72; BBC; HJP, 1:464). For revolutionary movements s. DPL, 812-19. ◆ 39 εἶπεν aor. ind. act. λέγω s.v.
37. ἄσημος (# 817) insignificant, unimportant, obscure
(BAGD; MM). As a medical term it indicated a disease
without well-marked symptoms (MLL, 249). πολίτης

(# 4489) citizen. At this point Paul appeals to being a
citizen of Tarsus, rather than of Rome so as not to
alienate the Jews (BAFCS, 3:140-43). For the city of
Tarsus and Paul's citizenship there s. Strabo, 6:311,
341-353; DC 33-34; BAFCS, 3:72-83; PVT, 21-27; s. 9:30;
11:25. ἐπίτρεψόν aor. imp. act. ἐπιτρέπω (# 2205) to permit, to allow, w. inf. λαλῆσαι aor. act. inf. λαλέω
(# 3281) to speak.   ◆ 40 ἐπιτρέψαντος aor. act. part.
(temp.) s.v. 39. Gen. abs. ἑστώς perf. act. part. (adj.)
ἵστημι (# 2705) to stand. κατέσεισεν aor. ind. act.
κατασείω (# 2939) to wave w. the hand (s. 19:33). χειρί
dat. sing. χείρ (# 5931) hand. Instr. dat. γενομένης aor.
mid. (dep.) part. (temp.) s.v. 1. Gen. abs. προσεφώνησεν
aor. ind. act. προσφωνέω (# 4715) to speak to, to deliver
a speech. For the speeches in Acts s. BASHH, 415-27;
Conrad Gempf, "Public Speaking and Published Accounts," BAFCS, 1:259-303; W. Ward Gasque, "The
Speeches of Acts: Dibelius Reconsidered," ND, 232-50.
Ἑβραΐδι διαλέκτῳ (# 1579; 1365) in the Hebrew dialect.
Although it is generally accepted that Aramaic was
used by the Jews at this time, Hebrew may have also
been spoken (J.M. Grintz, "Hebrew as the Spoken and
Written Language in the Last Days of the Second Temple," JBL 79 [1960]: 32-47; Robert H. Gundry, "The
Language Milieu of First-Century Palestine: Its Bearing on the Authenticity of the Gospel Tradition," JBL
83 [1964]: 409-18).

Acts 22

◆ 1 πατέρες voc. pl. πατήρ (# 4252) father. The
term may indicate that members of the Sanhedrin
were present (Schneider). ἀκούσατε aor. imp. act.
ἀκούω (# 201) to hear, to listen to, w. gen. ἀπολογία
(# 665) defense. The personal pron. is to be taken w.
the noun, "hear my defense" (Bruce). ◆ 2 ἀκούσαντες
aor. act. part. (temp.) s.v. 1. προσεφώνει impf. ind. act.
προσφωνέω (# 4715) to speak to, to address. Impf. indicates the action in progress. μᾶλλον (# 3437) more,
rather. παρέσχον aor. ind. act. παρέχω (# 4218) to offer,
to provide, to give. ἡσυχία (# 2484) quietness. A vivid
picture of the sudden hush that swept over the vast
mob (RWP).   ◆ 3 ἐγώ (# 1609) I, emphatic. Ἰουδαῖος
(# 2681) Jewish. The anarthrous pred. stresses the character. γεγεννημένος perf. pass. part. (adj.) γεννάω
(# 1164) to bear; pass. to be born. For Paul's birth in
Tarsus s. Simon Légasse, "Paul's Pre-Christian Career
according to Acts," BAFCS, 4:366-72; s. 21:39. ἀνατε-
θραμμένος perf. pass. part. (adj.) ἀνατρέφω (# 427) to
nourish, to nurse up, to bring up. ἐν τῇ πόλει ταύτῃ
(# 1877; 4047; 4484) in this city. This could refer to Tarsus (GI, 83-85), or more likely, to Jerusalem (E.F. Harrison, "Acts 22:3–A Test Case for Luke's Reliability,"
ND, 251-53; Légasse, "Paul's Pre-christian Career according to Acts," BAFCS, 4:373-79; PVT, 27-33). Γαμα-

λιήλ Gamaliel (s. 5:34; for a defense of the historical accuracy of the statement s. Harrison, ND, 251-60). πεπαιδευμένος perf. pass. part. (adj.) παιδεύω (# 4084) to instruct, to train. For Jewish education s. CC, 154f; JL, 98-245. ἀκρίβεια (# 205) strictness, exactness (Luke 1:3). ζηλωτής (# 2421) zealot, zealous (s. 21:20). ὑπάρχων pres. act. part. (adj.) ὑπάρχω (# 5639) to exist, to be. τοῦ θεοῦ (# 2536) of God. Obj. gen. would be "zealous for God." Paul's former life had been marked by a zeal for the Law that matched or exceeded that of his accusers (Polhill). ◆ 4 ἐδίωξα aor. ind. act. διώκω (# 1503) to pursue, to hunt an animal, to persecute. δεσμεύων pres. act. part. δεσμεύω (# 1297) to bind, to put in chains. Part. of manner explaining how he persecuted. Pres. indicates a repeated action. παραδιδούς pres. act. part. παραδίδωμι (# 4140) to deliver over (TLNT). Part. of manner. ◆ 5 μαρτυρεῖ pres. ind. act. μαρτυρέω (# 3455) to testify to, to bear witness to. πρεσβυτέριον (# 4564) the elderhood, the Sanhedrin (Schneider; JPF, 1:379-400). δεξάμενος aor. mid. (dep.) part. (temp.) δέχομαι (# 1312) to receive. ἐπορευόμην impf. mid. (dep.) πορεύομαι (# 4513) to travel, to go. Impf. pictures the action in progress. ἄξων fut. act. part. ἄγω (# 72) to lead. Fut. part. expressing purp. (BD, 178). ἐκεῖσε (# 1698) there, to that place. If the original force ("to that place") be pressed, it refers to those Christians who had gone to Damascus to escape the persecution in Jerusalem (Bruce). ὄντας pres. act. part. εἰμί (# 1639) to be. Part. as subst. δεδεμένους perf. pass. part. (adj.) δέω (# 1313) to bind. τιμωρηθῶσιν aor. subj. pass. τιμωρέω (# 5512) to punish. Subj. w. ἵνα (# 2761) expressing purp. ◆ 6 ἐγένετο aor. ind. mid. (dep.) γίνομαι (# 1181) to become, to be, to happen. For the Semitic construction s. Luke 8:1; NSV, 57. πορευομένῳ pres. mid. (dep.) part. (temp.) s.v. 5; "while going." (Dat. agrees w. μοι: "it happened to me..." [RWP]). ἐγγίζοντι pres. act. part. (temp.) ἐγγίζω (# 1581) to draw near, to come near. περὶ μεσημβρίαν around midday, noon. ἐξαίφνης (# 1978) suddenly. περιαστράψαι aor. act. inf. περιαστράπτω (# 4313) to shine all around (s. 9:3). Inf. w. ἐγένετο (RG, 1042-43). ◆ 7 ἔπεσα aor. ind. act. πίπτω (# 4406) to fall. ἔδαφος (# 1611) acc. sing. ground. ἤκουσα aor. ind. act. ἀκούω (# 201) to hear, w. gen. W. the gen. it may mean, "to hear, but not necessarily understand," w. the emphasis on the physical perception (M, 64; RG, 506; BG, 24-25; NSV, 105-06; but s. GI, 87-90; IBG, 36-37). διώκεις pres. ind. act. s.v. 4. Pres. indicates either a customary action or an action in progress (VANT, 207). ◆ 8 ἀπεκρίθην aor. ind. pass. (dep.) ἀποκρίνομαι (# 646) to answer. εἶπέν aor. ind. act. λέγω (# 3306) to say. ἐγώ I! (emphatic). σύ (# 5148) you! (emphatic). ◆ 9 ὄντες pres. act. part. s.v. 5. Part. as subst. ἐθεάσαντο aor. ind. mid. (dep.) θεάομαι (# 2517) to see, to view. ἤκουσαν aor. ind. act. s.v. 7. Here w. acc., "to hear and understand" (cf. v. 7). λαλοῦντος pres. act. part. λαλέω

(# 3281) to speak. Adj. part. as subst. μοι (# 1609) to me. Indir. obj. ◆ 10 εἶπον aor. ind. act. 1st. pers. sing, s.v. 8. ποιήσω aor. subj. act. ποιέω (# 4472) to do. Deliberative subj. in a question. ἀναστάς aor. act. part. ἀνίστημι (# 482) to stand up, to arise. Circum. part. w. force of an imp. πορεύου pres. imp. mid. (dep.) s.v. 5. Pres. imp. of a vb. of motion. λαληθήσεται fut. ind. pass. s.v. 9. τέτακται perf. ind. pass. τάσσω (# 5435) to command. Perf. stresses the completed state w. lasting results. ποιῆσαι aor. act. inf. Inf. in indir. discourse. ◆ 11 ἐνέβλεπον impf. ind. act. ἐμβλέπω (# 1838) to look at, to see, to have sight. Impf. pictures the continuing condition in the past. δόξης (# 1518) gen. sing. glory, splendor, brilliance, dazzling, luminous, brightness (TLNT; TDNT; GELTS, 119). χειραγωγούμενος pres. pass. part. (circum.) χειραγωγέω (# 5932) to lead by the hand. συνόντων pres. part. act. σύνειμι (# 5289) to be present, to accompany, to be with someone. Part. as subst. ἦλθον aor. ind. act. ἔρχομαι (# 2262) to come. ◆ 12 εὐλαβής (# 2327) pious, godly, pertaining to being reverent toward God (LN, 1:533; GELTS, 187; NIDNTT, 2:90-91; TDNT). μαρτυρούμενος pres. pass. part. s.v. 5. κατοικούντων pres. act. part. κατοικέω (# 2997) to live, to dwell, to inhabit. Part. as subst. ◆ 13 ἐλθών aor. act. part. (temp.) s.v. 11. ἐπιστάς aor. act. part. (temp.) ἐφίστημι (# 2392) to come to, to stand before. εἶπεν aor. ind. act. s.v. 8. ἀδελφέ voc. sing. ἀδελφός (# 81) brother. A term used to designate members of the Christian community (BS, 87-88; LAE, 107; for the Jewish usage s. SB, 2:765-66). ἀνάβλεψον aor. imp. act. ἀναβλέπω (# 329) to see again, to look up. The vb. has both meanings (MH, 295). ἀνέβλεψα aor. ind. act. ◆ 14 εἶπεν aor. ind. act. s.v. 8. προεχειρίσατο aor. ind. mid. (dep.) προχειρίζομαι (# 4741) to take into one's hands beforehand, to plan, to purpose, to determine (RWP). γνῶναι aor. act. inf. γινώσκω (# 1182) to know, to know by experience. Epex. inf. explaining what was purposed. ἰδεῖν aor. act. inf. ὁράω (# 3972) to see. Epex. inf. τὸν δίκαιον (# 1465) acc. sing. the righteous one. A messianic title (s. 3:14; 7:52; Polhill; TLNT, 1:323-24). ἀκοῦσαι aor. act. inf. s.v. 1. Epex. inf. ◆ 15 ἔσῃ fut. ind. mid. εἰμί s.v. 5. αὐτῷ dat. sing. αὐτός (# 899). Dat. of personal advantage, a witness ("for Him"). ὧν gen pl. rel. pron. ὅς (# 4005). Gen. by attraction to the unexpressed obj. gen. τουτῶν (of the things, which...") (RWP). ἑώρακας perf. ind. act. ὁράω (# 3972). Perf. denotes the continuing effect on Paul of having seen the Lord, what establishes him permanently as an apostle (BD, 176). ἤκουσας aor. ind. act. s.v. 1. ◆ 16 μέλλεις pres. ind. act. μέλλω (# 3516) to be about to, denoting an intended action: "to intend," "to propose," "to have in mind" (BAGD). ἀναστάς aor. act. part. s.v. 10. Circum. part. w. force of imp. βάπτισαι aor. imp. mid. βαπτίζω (# 966) to baptize. Causative mid., "get yourself baptized" (RG, 808; GGBB, 426). ἀπόλουσαι aor. act. inf. ἀπολούω

(# 666) to wash away. **ἐπικαλεσάμενος** aor. mid. (dep.) part. ἐπικαλέω (# 2126) to call upon. Part. of means or manner; the calling upon the Lord effects the washing away of sin. ◆ **17 ἐγένετο** aor. ind. mid. (dep.) s.v. 6. **ὑποστρέψαντι** aor. act. part. (temp.) ὑποστρέφω (# 5715) to return. Dat. of time (NSV, 57; IBG, 43). **προσευχομένου** pres. mid. (dep.) part. (temp.) προσεύχομαι (# 4667) to pray. Gen. abs., "while I was praying." **γενέσθαι** aor. mid. (dep.) inf. γίνομαι; w. subject in acc. Inf. in a Semitic construction w. ἐγένετο (s.v. 6). **ἔκστασις** (# 1749) trance, a vision accompanied by an ecstatic psychological state (LN, 1:489; NIDNTT, 1:527-28; TDNT). ◆ **18 ἰδεῖν** aor. act. inf. ὁράω (# 3972) to see. Inf. w. vb. **λέγοντα** pres. act. part. (adj.) λέγω (# 3306) to say. **σπεῦσον** aor. imp. act. σπεύδω (# 5067) to hurry, hurry up. Aor. imp. calls for a specific act w. a note of urgency. **ἔξελθε** aor. imp. act. ἐξέρχομαι (# 2002) to go out. **ἐν τάχει** (# 1877; 5444) quickly. **παραδέξονται** fut. ind. mid. (dep.) παραδέχομαι (# 4138) to receive, to welcome. ◆ **19 εἶπον** aor. ind. act. λέγω s.v. 18. **κύριε** voc. sing. κύριος (# 3261) Lord. **ἐπίστανται** pres. ind. pass. ἐπίσταμαι (# 2179) to understand. **ἤμην** impf. ind. mid. εἰμί used w. part. to form a periphrastic construction emphasizing continual action in the past. **φυλακίζων** pres. act. part. φυλακίζω (# 5872) to put into prison. Periphrastic part. **δέρων** pres. act. part. δέρω (#1296) to flay, to skin, to beat, to flog. Periphrastic part. **πιστεύοντας** pres. act. part. πιστεύω (# 4409) to believe. Part. as subst. ◆ **20 ἐξεχύννετο** impf. ind. pass. ἐκχύννω (# 1772) to pour out, to shed. Impf. pictures the action in progress. **αὐτός** (# 899) emphatic, I, myself! **ἐφεστώς** perf. act. part. ἐφίστημι (# 2392) to stand by. Part. w. impf. ἤμην to form a periphrastic construction. **συνευδοκῶν** pres. act. part. συνευδοκέω (# 5306) to consent, to be pleased w. Periphrastic part. **φυλάσσων** pres. act. part. φυλάσσω (# 5875) to guard, to watch. Periphrastic part. **ἀναιρούντων** pres. act. part. ἀναιρέω (# 359) to do away w. someone, to destroy, to kill (BAGD). Part. as subst. Pres. pictures the act in progress, "of the ones who were doing away w. him." ◆ **21 εἶπεν** aor. ind. act. λέγω s.v. 18. **πορεύου** pres. imp. mid. (dep.) s.v. 5. **ἐξαποστελῶ** fut. ind. act. ἐξαποστέλλω (# 1990) to send out, to send as an official representative w. the authority of the one sending (TDNT; EDNT). ◆ **22 ἤκουον** impf. ind. act. s.v. 1, w. obj. in gen. (s.v. 7). Impf., "they continued listening...." **ἐπῆραν** aor. ind. act. ἐπαίρω (# 2048) to lift up. **λέγοντες** pres. act. part. λέγω s.v. 18. Pleonastic use of the part. **αἶρε** pres. imp. act. αἴρω (# 149) to take away. For the use of the pres. imp. of this vb. s. VANT, 350-51. **τοιοῦτος** (# 5525) of such a kind, such as this, such a person. Used either in such a way that a definite individual w. his special characteristics is thought of, or that any bearer of certain definite qualities is meant (BAGD). **καθῆκεν** impf. ind. act. καθήκω (# 2763) to be

proper or fitting; usually impersonal, "it comes to someone," "it is proper," "it is fitting" w. the implication of moral judgement involved, w. inf. explaining what is fitting (BAGD; LN, 1:627). Vbs. expressing obligation or necessity are used in the impf. when the obligation is not lived up to, or has not been met (RG, 886). **ζῆν** pres. act. inf. ζάω (# 2409) to live. Pres. means to go on living, to continue to live. ◆ **23 κραυγαζόντων** pres. act. part. (temp.) κραυγάζω (# 3198) to scream, to cry out. Gen. abs., "as they were screaming." **ῥιπτούντων** pres. act. part. ῥιπτέω (# 4849) to throw off. Perhaps here it means to shake, to wave (LC). Gen. abs. **κονιορτός** (# 3155) dust. **βαλλόντων** pres. act. part. βάλλω (# 965) to throw. Gen. abs. **ἀέρα** acc. sing. ἀήρ (# 113) air. ◆ **24 ἐκέλευσεν** aor. ind. act. κελεύω (# 3027) to command. **χιλίαρχος** (# 5941) leader of a thousand men, tribune (s. 21:31). He appears as the commander-in-chief in Jerusalem. Probably commander of a *Cohors Italica*, which had tribunes as officers (HJP, 1:366; Sherwin-White, 155; BAFCS, 3:144). **εἰσάγεσθαι** pres. pass. inf. εἰσάγω (# 1652) to lead in, to bring in. Inf. in indir. discourse. **εἴπας** aor. act. part. (temp.) λέγω s.v. 18. For the form of the aor. s. BD, 43. **μάστιξιν** dat. pl. μάστιξ (# 3465) whip, lash, mostly pl. lashing or lashes w. a whip of knotted cords or knucklebones and lead pellets (BAGD; BAFCS, 3:139, 447). Instr. dat. **ἀνετάζεσθαι** aor. pass. inf. ἀνετάζω (# 458) to examine. The word was used of government clerks whose business it was to examine documents and glue them into books (MM). Scourging was not only a punishment, but also the simplest method of getting the truth or a confession. It was the legal method of examining a slave or alien (LC; BBC). **ἐπιγνῶ** aor. subj. act. ἐπιγινώσκω (# 2105) to recognize, to know. The prep. compound is directive (MH, 312). Subj. w. ἵνα (# 2671) for purp. **ἐπεφώνουν** impf. ind. act. ἐπιφωνέω (# 2215) to call to, to shout at. ◆ **25 προέτειναν** aor. ind. act. προτείνω (# 4727) to stretch forward; probably the t.t. for tying up a person for a whipping (Bruce). **ἱμᾶσιν** dat. pl. ἱμάς (# 2666) strap, thong. Instr. dat. ("tied w. straps"), or dat. of purp. ("for the whip") (BAGD; LC). **εἶπεν** aor. ind. act. s.v. 18. **ἑστῶτα** (# 2705) perf. act. part. (adj.) ἵστημι perf. to stand. **εἰ** (# 1623) if. It introduces a hypothetical question designed for clarification on a point of Roman trial procedure (BAFCS, 3:143). **ἀκατάκριτος** (# 185) uncondemned. **ἔξεστιν** (# 2003) pres. ind. act. (impersonal) it is lawful, w. inf. **μαστίζειν** pres. act. inf. μαστίζω (# 3464) to whip, to scourge. The oblique way Paul insinuates his Roman citizenship highlights his desire not to undercut his religious commitment to Judaism as well as his readiness to suffer without complaint if his question is disregarded (BAFCS, 3:143). ◆ **26 ἀκούσας** aor. act. part. s.v. 1. **προσελθών** aor. act. part. προσέρχομαι (# 4665) to come to, to go to. Circum. or temp. part. **ἀπήγγειλεν** aor. ind. act. ἀπαγγέλλω

(# *550*) to report. **μέλλεις** pres. ind. act. s.v. 16. W. inf. for the immediate fut. **ποιεῖν** pres. act. inf. ποιέω (# *4472*) to do. **γάρ** (# *1142*) for, giving the reason for his excited question. ◆ **27 προσελθών** aor. act. part. (circum.) s.v. 26. **λέγε** pres. imp. act. λέγω s.v. 18. For the pres. imp. s. VANT, 351. **σύ** (# *5148*) you, emphatic position, a question of surprise (Meyer). **εἶ** pres. ind. act. εἰμί (# *1639*). **ἔφη** aor. ind. act. φημί (# *5774*) to say. ◆ **28 ἀπεκρίθη** aor. ind. pass. (dep.) s.v. 8. **κεφαλαίου** gen. sing. κεφάλαιον (# *3049*) capital, sum. Gen. of price (BD, 97). Claudius' wife and members of her court would sell (for a bribe!) citizenship rights for their own personal gain (Polhill; Dio Cassius, *Roman History*, 60:17, 5; Sherwin-White, 164-65). **πολιτεία** (# *4486*) citizenship. The tribune is seeking more personal information for the purpose of comparing his status w. that of Paul's (BAFCS, 3:144). For a discussion of Roman citizenship and Acts s. Sherwin-White, 144-85; A.N. Sherwin-White, *The Roman Citizenship* (Oxford: Clarendon Press); Sherwin-White, "The Roman Citizenship: A Survey of its Development into a World franchise," ANRW, 1, 2:23; Endre Ferenczy, "Rechtshistorische Bemerkungen zur Ausdehnung des römischen Bürgerrechts und zum *ius Italicum* unter dem Prinzipat," ANRW, 2, 14:1018-58; FAP, 129-39; BAFCS, 3:83-90; CC, 176; DPL, 140-41; ABD, 5:804-5. **ἐκτησάμην** aor. ind. mid. (dep.) κτάομαι (# *3227*) to obtain. **γεγέννημαι** perf. ind. pass. γεννάω (# *1164*) to bear; pass. to be born. Not to be taken in the sense of "to become"; rather, it indicates Paul's father was a Roman citizen and Paul was born w. this right (Sherwin-White, 151). Within 30 days after birth a Roman citizen was registered in the public record office (BAFCS, 3:130-31). Citizenship may have been proven by certificates on small wooden blocks (*testatio*) or metal certificates (*diploma militaris*) as carried by the soldiers (Sherwin-White, 148-51; BAFCS, 3:131-33). This gave Paul a higher status than the tribune, thus making the tribune's position very precarious (BAFCS, 3:144-45) ◆ **29 ἀπέστησαν** aor. ind. act. ἀφίστημι (# *923*) to stand away, to depart. **μέλλοντες** pres. act. part. s.v. 16, w. inf. for fut. **ἀνετάζειν** pres. act. inf. s.v. 24. **ἐφοβήθη** aor. ind. pass. (dep.) φοβέομαι (# *5828*) to be afraid. **ἐπιγνούς** aor. act. part. (temp.) s.v. 24. **δεδεκώς** perf. act. part. δέω s.v. 5. Part. used w. **ἦν** (# *2069*) in a periphrastic construction. ◆ **30 τῇ ἐπαύριον** "on the next (day). **βουλόμενος** pres. mid. (dep.) part. (temp.) βούλομαι (# *1089*) to will, to wish, w. inf. **γνῶναι** aor. act. inf. s.v. 14. **ἀσφαλές** (# *855*) certainty (s. 21:34). **τὸ τί κατηγορεῖται** of what he was being accused. This is an explanation of the preceding word **ἀσφαλές** (RWP). The art. used w. the indir. interrogative makes the cl. substantival, but it does not change the meaning (MT, 182). **ἔλυσεν** aor. ind. act. λύω (# *3395*) to loose, to release. The term indicates at least a further slackening of cus-

todial arrangements for Paul (BAFCS, 3:146). **ἐκέλευσεν** aor. ind. act. s.v. 24. **συνελθεῖν** aor. act. inf. συνέρχομαι (# *5302*) to come together, to convene. Inf. in indir. discourse. **καταγαγών** aor. act. part. (temp.) κατάγω (# *22864*) to lead down. **ἔστησεν** aor. ind. act. ἵστημι (# *2705*) (trans.) to place, to stand.

Acts 23

◆ **1 ἀτενίσας** aor. act. part. (temp.) ἀτενίζω (# *867*) to gaze, to look at intently. "As Paul intently looked at the Sanhedrin...." **εἶπεν** aor. ind. act. λέγω (# *3306*) to say, to speak. **συνείδησις** conscience (TLNT; TDNT; EDNT; Rom. 2:15). **πεπολίτευμαι** perf. ind. mid. (dep.) πολιτεύομαι (# *4488*) to live as a citizen, w. all of the rights and obligations; to live, in the religious sense (Haenchen). Perf. indicates the continuing results. **θεῷ** dat. sing. θεός (# *2536*) God. Dat. of personal interest, "for God" (RWP). ◆ **2 ὁ ἀρχιερεὺς Ἀνανίας** (# *797; 393*) the high priest Ananias. He was the son of Nebedeus and as a Sadducee held the office from c. A.D. 47-58, but then was removed from office. He was known for his greed, wealth, and brutality and was murdered in A.D. 66 by the Zealots because of his friendliness w. the Romans (SB, 2:766; ABD, 1:225; BASHH, 170-71; BBC; HJP, 2:231; Longenecker, 530; Jos., *JW*, 2:243, 409, 426, 429, 441-42; *Ant.*, 20:103, 131, 205-6, 208-10, 213). **ἐπέταξεν** aor. ind. act. ἐπιτάσσω (# *2199*) to command, to charge. **παρεστῶσιν** perf. act. part. masc. dat. pl. παρίστημι (# *4225*) to stand near or by someone, w. dat. Part. as subst. **τύπτειν** pres. act. inf. τύπτω (# *5597*) to strike, to hit. Inf. in indir. discourse. ◆ **3 εἶπεν** aor. ind. act. s.v. 1. **μέλλει** pres. ind. act. μέλλω (# *3516*) to be about to, w. inf. for the immediate fut.; here in a type of predictive curse (LC). **τοῖχε** voc. sing. τοῖχος (# *5526*) wall. **κεκονιαμένε** perf. pass. part. voc. κονιάω (# *3154*) to whitewash. The whitewashed wall contrasted the decent exterior w. the unclean contents (Bruce). Paul may be referring to Ezek. 13:10-12, where the whitewashed wall is about to collapse because of God's coming judgment (Polhill); or it may be a reference to Lev. 14:33-53. For the figure in the DSS s. CD 8:12; 19:25. **καὶ σύ** "and you!" Emphatic expressing indignation (RWP). **κάθη** pres. ind. mid. (dep.) 2nd. pers. sing. κάθημαι (# *2764*) to sit. For the form s. BD, 50. **κρίνων** pres. act. part. (circum.) κρίνω (# *3212*) to judge. **παρανομῶν** pres. act. part. (circum.) παρανομέω (# *4174*) to act contrary to the law. **κελεύεις** pres. ind. act. κελεύω to command. **τύπτεσθαι** pres. pass. inf. s.v. 2. Inf. in indir. discourse. ◆ **4 παρεστῶτες** perf. act. part. s.v. 2. Part. as subst. **λοιδορεῖς** pres. ind. act. 2nd. pers. sing. λοιδορέω (# *3366*) to abuse, to reproach, to heap abuse upon, to insult, to speak in a highly insulting manner (LN, 1:433; TLNT; TDNT). ◆ **5 ἔφη** impf./aor. ind. act. φημί (# *5774*) to speak, to say. **ᾔδειν** plperf. ind. act. οἶδα

(# *3857*) to know. Def. perf. w. pres. meaning; w. pl-perf. forming the past (VA, 281-87). Perhaps Paul did not recognize the high priest because of weak eyesight; or he spoke w. irony (Bruce). γέγραπται perf. ind. pass. γράφω (# *1211*) to write. Perf. used of binding documents whose authority remains (MM). ἐρεῖς fut. ind. act. λέγω s.v. 1. Fut. in a Semitic command (BG, 94-95). κακῶς (# *2809*) (adv.) evil, in an evil manner. ◆ 6 γνούς aor. act. part. (temp.) γινώσκω (# *1182*) to know, to recognize. ἔκραζεν impf. ind. act. κράζω (# *3189*) to scream. Incep. impf., "he began to cry out." υἱὸς Φαρισαίων (# *5626*; *5757*) the son of a Pharisee. That Paul's father was a Pharisee implies that he had lived in Palestine until adulthood (Légasse, "Paul's Pre-Christian Career According to Acts," BAFCS, 4:376-77; for the teaching of the Pharisees s. TJ, 70-76; Steve Mason, *Flavius Josephus on the Pharisees* [Leiden: E.J. Brill, 1991]). καί (# *2779*) that is; used to explain the hope: "that is, the resurrection from the dead." κρίνομαι pres. ind. pass. s.v. 3. Pres. indicates an action that is in progress. For the various legal terms used in Paul's triads s. A.A. Trites, "The Importance of Legal Scenes and Language in the Book of Acts." *Nov T* (1974), 278-84. ◆ 7 εἰπόντος aor. act. part. (temp.) s.v. 1. Gen. abs. ἐγένετο aor. ind. mid. (dep.) γίνομαι (# *1181*) to become, to happen, to arise. στάσις (# *5087*) sedition, revolution, riot. ἐσχίσθη aor. ind. pass. σχίζω (# *5387*) to split, to divide. ◆ 8 γάρ (# *1142*) for, giving the explanation for the division. λέγουσιν pres. ind. act. s.v. 1. Pres. indicates the habitual action or standard teaching. εἶναι pres. act. inf. εἰμί (# *1639*) to be. Inf. in indir. assertion (RWP). For the teaching of the Sadducees s. TJ, 76-81, esp. 78-79; Benedict T. Viviano & Justin Taylor, "Sadducees, Angels, and the Resurrection," *JBL* 111 (1992): 496-98; ABD, 5:892-93; David Daube, "On Acts 23: Sadducees and Angels," *JBL* 109 (1990): 492-97; SB, 4, i:339-52; J. Le Mayne, *Les Sadducées* (Paris: Gabalda, 1972); Mark 12:18-27. ὁμολογοῦσιν pres. ind. act. ὁμολογέω (# *3933*) to confess, to agree, to acknowledge. ◆ 9 ἐγένετο aor. ind. mid. (dep.) s.v. 7. κραυγή (# *3199*) scream, cry, clamor. ἀναστάντες aor. act. part. ἀνίστημι (# *482*) to rise up. Circum. or temp. part. διεμάχοντο impf. ind. mid. (dep.) διαμάχομαι (# *1372*) to fight, to fight it out. The prep. compound indicates a fierce fighting between, back and forth (RWP; s. GELTS, 106). εὑρίσκομεν pres. ind. act. εὑρίσκω (# *2351*) to find. ἐλάλησεν aor. ind. act. λαλέω (# *3281*) to speak. Part of the sentence is suppressed under the influence of a strong emotion: "What if a spirit or an angel has spoken to him?" (RG, 1203). ◆ 10 γινομένης pres. mid. (dep.) part. (temp.) s.v. 7. Gen. abs. φοβηθείς aor. pass. (dep.) part. (causal) φοβέομαι (# *5828*) to be afraid, to fear. διασπασθῇ aor. subj. pass. διασπάω (# *1400*) to tear into. For the force of the prep., s. MH, 302. Subj. w. μή (# *3590*) in an expression of apprehension to ward off

an impending danger (BD, 188). ἐκέλευσεν aor. ind. act. s.v. 3. καταβάν aor. act. part. (circum.) καταβαίνω (# *22849*) to go down. ἁρπάσαι aor. act. inf. ἁρπάζω (# *773*) to seize, to snatch, to take by force. Inf. in indir. discourse giving the content of the command. ◆ 11 τῇ δὲ ἐπιούσῃ νυκτί (# *1254*; *2157*; *3816*) in the following night. Dat. of time. ἐπιστάς aor. act. part. (circum.) ἐφίστημι (# *2392*) to come upon, to stand by, w. dat. A t.t. for a revelatory experience ("The Prisoner Paul's Divine Helper in Acts," BAFCS, 3:419). εἶπεν aor. ind. act. s.v. 1. θάρσει pres. imp. act. θαρσέω (# *2510*) to be brave, to be courageous, to have confidence, be unafraid. It can refer to courage displayed in the midst of danger (TLNT; GELTS, 202). (For the idiomatic pres. imp., almost like an exclamation s. VANT, 349-50). διεμαρτύρω aor. ind. mid. (dep.) 2nd. sing. διαμαρτύρομαι (# *1371*) to testify, to give witness, to solemnly declare (MH 302). δεῖ pres. ind. act. it is necessary, giving a logical necessity, w. inf. Here it could indicate a divine necessity (BAFCS, 3:420). μαρτυρῆσαι aor. act. inf. μαρτυρέω (# *3455*) to be a witness. ◆ 12 γενομένης aor. mid. (dep.) part. (temp.) s.v. 7. ποιήσαντες aor. act. part. (circum.) ποιέω (# *4472*) to make. συστροφή (# *5371*) conspiracy, plot, a plan devised by a number of persons who agree to act against someone (LC; LN, 1:359). ἀνεθεμάτισαν aor. ind. act. ἀναθεματίζω (# *354*) to place oneself under a curse, to invoke divine harm if what is said is not true or if one does not carry out what has been promised, to take a vow, w. refl. pron. (LN, 1:442-43; NIDNTT, 1:413-15; TDNT). For the Jewish teaching on vows s. M, Nedarim. φαγεῖν aor. act. inf. ἐσθίω (# *2266*) to eat. Epex. inf. explaining the vow. πίειν aor. act. inf. πίνω (# *4403*) to drink. Epex. inf. ἀποκτείνωσιν aor. subj. act. ἀποκτείνω (# *650*) to kill. Subj. in an indef. temp. cl. ◆ 13 ἦσαν impf. ind. act. εἰμί s.v. 8. πλείους comp. πολύς (# *4498*) much; comp., more than. συνωμοσία (# *5350*) conspiracy, plot, a swearing together (RWP). ποιησάμενοι aor. mid. part. s.v. 12. Adj. part. as subst. ◆ 14 προσελθόντες aor. act. part. (circum.) προσέρχομαι (# *4665*) to come to. εἶπαν aor. ind. act. s.v. 1. ἀνάθεμα (# *353*) curse, that which is set aside for destruction (TDNT; GELTS, 28; Lev. 27:28; Deut. 13:16 LXX) γεύσασθαι aor. mid. inf. γεύομαι (# *1174*) to taste, to eat, w. gen. ἀποκτείνωμεν aor. subj. act. s.v. 12. ◆ 15 ἐμφανίσατε aor. imp. act. ἐμφανίζω (# *1872*) to give information, to lay information before. Here used in a semi-technical sense (LC). καταγάγῃ aor. subj. act. κατάγω (# *2864*) to lead down. Subj. w. ὅπως (# *3968*) to express purp. μέλλοντας pres. act. part. s.v. 3. Part. w. ὡς (# *6055*) giving the alleged reason: "as if," "as though" (RWP). διαγινώσκειν pres. act. inf. διαγινώσκω (# *1336*) to decide, to determine. A legal t.t.; here, to determine his case by thorough investigation (BAGD; NDIEC, 1:49). ἀκριβέστερον adv. comp. ἀκριβῶς (# *209*) exactly, accurately; comp., more accurate. **ἐγγίσαι** aor. act. inf. ἐγγίζω (# *1581*) to be near, to draw near. Inf. w. **πρό** (# *4574*) to express time ("before he comes near"). **ἐσμεν** pres. ind. act. εἰμί s.v. 8. **ἀνελεῖν** aor. act. inf. ἀναιρέω (# *359*) to kill. Epex. inf. explaining their readiness. On the way between Antonia and the council chambers, they would ambush and kill Paul (Polhill). This was common especially in these years (BBC). ◆ **16 ἀκούσας** aor. act. part. (temp.) ἀκούω (# *201*) to hear. **ὁ υἱὸς τῆς ἀδελφῆς Παύλου** (# *5626; 80*) the son of Paul's sister. The visit of Paul's nephew is unusual and because he was young the soldiers deemed him harmless (BAFCS, 3:149). **ἐνέδρα** (# *1909*) ambush, treacherous ambush (MM). **παραγενόμενος** aor. mid. (dep.) part. (temp.) παραγίνομαι (# *4134*) to come, to arrive. Here either in the sense of having been present or having arrived (at the barracks) (Bruce). **εἰσελθών** aor. act. part. (temp.) εἰσέρχομαι (# *1656*) to go in. **ἀπήγγειλεν** aor. ind. act. ἀπαγγέλλω (# *550*) to report. ◆ **17 προσκαλεσάμενος** aor. mid. (dep.) part. (temp.) προσκαλέω (# *4673*) to call to oneself, to summon. **ἑκατονταρχῶν** gen. pl. ἑκατονάρχης (# *1672*) centurion. Partitive gen.: "one of the centurions" (BD, 90-91). **ἔφη** aor. ind. act. s.v. 5. **ἀπάγαγε** aor. imp. act. ἀπάγω (# *522*) to lead out, to lead away. (Some mss. [ℵ, B, etc.] have ἄπαγε pres. imp. act.) **ἔχει** pres. ind. act. ἔχω (# *2400*) to have, to possess. **ἀπαγγεῖλαι** aor. act. inf. s.v. 16. Epex. inf. explaining the content of what the young man has. ◆ **18 παραλαβών** aor. act. part. (circum.) παραλαμβάνω (# *4161*) to take along. **ἤγαγεν** aor. ind. act. ἄγω (# *72*) to lead, to bring. **φησίν** pres. ind. act. s.v. 5. Hist. pres. **προσκαλεσάμενος** aor. mid. part. (circum.) s.v. 17. **ἠρώτησεν** aor. ind. act. ἐρωτάω (# *2263*) to ask, to request. **ἀγαγεῖν** aor. act. inf. ἄγω. Inf. in indir. discourse giving the content of the request. **ἔχοντα** pers. act. part. s.v. 17. Adj. or causal part. **λαλῆσαι** aor. act. inf. λαλέω (# *3281*) to say. Epex. inf. ◆ **19 ἐπιλαβόμενος** aor. mid. (dep.) part. (circum.) ἐπιλαμβάνω (# *2138*) to take, to take hold of, w. gen. He took hold of his hand so as to give confidence to the youth (Bengel). **ἀναχωρήσας** aor. act. part. (temp.) ἀναχωρέω (# *432*) to withdraw. For the prep. compound, s. MH, 295. **ἐπυνθάνετο** impf. ind. mid. (dep.) πυνθάνομαι (# *4785*) to inquire. Incep. impf., "he began to inquire." **ἔχεις** pres. ind. act. s.v. 17. **ἀπαγγεῖλαι** aor. act. inf. s.v. 16. ◆ **20 εἶπεν** aor. ind. act. s.v. 1. **συνέθεντο** aor. ind. mid. (dep.) συντίθημι (# *5338*) to place together, to arrange, to agree. **ἐρωτῆσαι** aor. act. inf. s.v. 18. Epex. inf. explaining what they had arranged. **ὅπως** (# *3968*) that (w. subj. giving the content of their request). **αὔριον** (# *892*) tomorrow. **καταγάγῃς** aor. subj. act., s.v. 15. **μέλλον** pres. act. part. s.v. 3. **ἀκριβέστερον** s.v. 15. **πυνθάνεσθαι** pres. mid. (dep.) inf. πυνθάνομαι (# *4785*) to ask, to examine. Inf. w. **μέλλον** for the immediate fut. ◆ **21 πεισθῇς** aor. subj. pass. πείθω (# *4275*) to persuade; pass. to be persuad-

ed, to consent, to obey. Aor. subj. w. neg. **μή** (# *3590*) indicates forbidding the starting of an action not in progress. Permissive pass., "do not let yourself be persuaded." **ἐνεδρεύουσιν** pres. ind. act. ἐνεδρεύω (# *1910*) to lie in ambush, to lie in wait for. Fut. pres., "they are going to ambush him." **ἀνεθεμάτισαν** aor. ind. act. s.v. 12. **φαγεῖν** aor. act. inf. s.v. 12. Epex. inf. **πιεῖν** aor. act. inf. s.v. 12. Epex. inf. **ἀνέλωσιν** aor. subj. act. s.v. 15. Subj. in an indef. temp. cl. **προσδεχόμενοι** pres. mid. (dep.) part. (adj.) προσδέχομαι (# *4657*) to wait for, expect. **ἐπαγγελία** (# *2039*) command, announcement, consent (LS). The word often means promise, but its original sense is a favorable message (LC). ◆ **22 ἀπέλυσε** aor. ind. act. ἀπολύω (# *668*) to release. **παραγγείλας** aor. act. part. (circum.) παραγγέλλω (# *4133*) to command, to charge. **ἐκλαλῆσαι** aor. act. inf. ἐκλαλέω (# *1718*) to speak out, to divulge. Inf. in an indirect command. For this construction and also the change to direct quotation s. RG, 1046-47. **ἐνεφάνισας** aor. ind. act. 2nd. pers. sing. s.v. 15. ◆ **23 προσκαλεσάμενος** aor. mid. part. s.v. 17. **εἶπεν** aor. ind. act. s.v. 1. **ἑτοιμάσατε** aor. imp. act. ἑτοιμάζω (# *2286*) to make ready, to prepare. Aor. imp. calls for a specific act w. a note of urgency. **πορευθῶσιν** aor. subj. pass. πορεύομαι (# *4513*) to go, to travel. W. **ὅπως** (# *3968*) to express purp. **δεξιολάβους** acc. pl. δεξιολάβος (# *1287*). The spearman, bowman, slinger, or perhaps bodyguard (BAGD); "taking (a spear) in the right hand." In military phraseology the spear was always connected w. the right, as the shield w. the left (MH, 273). **ἀπὸ τρίτης ὥρας τῆς νυκτός** at the third hour of the night; that is, about 9:00 P.M. (RWP). In the light of the general unrest in Judea (David W.J. Gill, "Acts and Roman Policy in Judaea," BAFCS, 4:15-25; JURR, 256-92; HJP, 1:455-83; JPF, 1:359-72; Jos., *JW*, 2:223-341; *Ant.*, 20:104-255), the sending of some 470 troops was an adequate preparation which wisely avoided the very real perils of travel (BAFCS, 3:154). Since this force consisted of one-third of the garrison in Jerusalem, they needed to return immediately. ◆ **24 κτήνη** acc. pl. κτῆνος (# *3229*) animal, domesticated animal, animal used for riding; mostly in pl. as collective, horses or mules (BAGD; LC). **παραστῆσαι** aor. act. inf. παρίστημι (# *4225*) to stand by, to provide. Inf. in indir. discourse (RG, 1046-47). **ἐπιβιβάσαντες** aor. act. part. (circum.) ἐπιβιβάζω (# *2097*) to cause to sit upon, to mount. **διασώσωσι** aor. subj. act. διασώζω (# *1407*) to rescue, to bring through safely. The prep. compound describes carrying action through to a definite result (MH, 301). Subj. w. **ἵνα** (# *2671*) to express purp. **ἡγεμόνα** acc. sing. ἡγεμών (# *2450*) governor. Felix, a freedman and the brother of Pallas, most influential w. the Emperor Claudius, was appointed governor of Judaea by him. Tacitus said of him, "Antonius Felix indulged in every kind of cruelty and immorality, wielding a king's authority with all the instincts of a slave" (Tacitus, *The Histories*, 5:9). He also said of Felix, "He believed himself free to commit any crime" (Tacitus, *Annals*, 12:54). For his person and rule s. HJP, 1:460-66; JURR, 269-70; JPF, 1:365-68; BAFCS, 4:21-25; BBC; Jos. *JW*, 2:247-70; *Ant.*, 20:137-47; 20:173-81. ◆ **25 γράψας** aor. act. part. (circum.) γράφω (# *1211*) to write. **ἔχουσαν** pres. act. part. (adj.) ἔχω (# *2400*) to have. **τύπος** (# *5596*) type, copy, replication. The value of copies of letters would lie precisely in their being made verbatim (NDIEC, 1:77-78). The contents of the speech may have been read in court before Felix (BASHH, 347-48; s.v. 34). For the use of these words to introduce the contents of a letter s. 1 Macc. 11:29; 3 Macc. 3:30; Jos., *Ant.*, 11:215; NDIEC, 1:72-76; 4:41. ◆ **26 κράτιστος** (# *3196*) most excellent, excellency, a polite term of address. Indir. obj. **χαίρειν** (# *5897*) pres. act. inf. χαίρω to greet. Inf. was common in the intro. of a letter expressing greetings (VA, 377). ◆ **27 συλλημφθέντα** aor. pass. part. (adj.) συλλαμβάνω (# *5197*) to arrest, to seize. **μέλλοντα** pres. act. part. s.v. 3. Adj. part. w. inf. to express the immediate fut. **ἀναιρεῖσθαι** pres. pass. inf. s.v. 15. **ἐπιστάς** aor. act. part. (temp.) ἐφίστημι s.v. 11. "When I came on the scene...." **ἐξειλάμην** aor. ind. mid. (dep.) ἐξαιρέω (# *1975*) to rescue, to take out. **μαθών** aor. act. part. (temp.) μανθάνω (# *3443*) to learn. ◆ **28 βουλόμενος** pres. mid. (dep.) part. (causal) βούλομαι (# *1089*) to will, to wish, w. inf. **ἐπιγνῶναι** aor. act. inf. ἐπιγινώσκω (# *2105*) to know. The prep. in compound is directive; that is, knowledge directed toward a particular obj. **ἐνεκάλουν** impf. ind. act. ἐγκαλέω (# *1592*) to accuse; "to call in" perjoratively; that is, calling a man in to accuse him, to bring charges against, w. dat. (MH, 305). **κατήγαγον** aor. ind. act. s.v. 15. ◆ **29 εὗρον** aor. ind. act. εὑρίσκω (# *2351*) to find. **ἐγκαλούμενον** pres. pass. part. s.v. 28. Supplementary part. denoting the state of being or the action in which someone is involved (BAGD, 325; BD, 215-15). **ζήτημα** (# *2427*) question, dispute. **ἄξιον** (# *545*) acc. sing. worthy, w. gen. **ἔχοντα** pres. act. part. s.v. 25. Supplementary part. **ἔγκλημα** (# *1598*) accusation, legal charge. ◆ **30 μηνυθείσης** aor. pass. part. μηνύω (# *3606*) to disclose, to inform, to report. Gen. abs. **ἔσεσθαι** fut. mid. (dep.) inf. εἰμί s.v. 8. Inf. in indir. discourse (RG, 877). **ἐξαυτῆς** (# *1994*) at once. **ἔπεμψα** aor. ind. act. πέμπω (# *4287*) to send. Epistolary aor. (Bruce). **παραγγείλας** aor. act. part. (circum.) s.v. 22. **κατηγόροις** dat. pl. κατήγορος (# *2991*) accuser. Dat. as indir. obj. **λέγειν** pres. act. inf. s.v. 1. Inf. in indir. discourse. The tribune's letter is designed to put himself in a good light as protector of a Roman citizen, explaining that there is actually no charge against Paul worthy of death and ordering the accusers to appear in person before Felix to press their charges. Paul's situation is also helped by the letter (BAFCS, 3:152-53). ◆ **31 διατεταγμένον** perf. pass. part. (adj.) διατάσσω

(# *1411*) to command. **ἀναλαβόντες** aor. act. part. (circum.) ἀναλαμβάνω (# *377*) to take up, to conduct. **ἤγαγον** aor. ind. act. s.v. 18. **Ἀντιπατρίς** (# *526*) Antipatris. The ancient city of Aphek about 26 miles south of Caesarea was renamed by Herod the Great and was an important crossroad town in the Roman period (Moshe Kochavi, "Antipatris," ABD, 1:272-74; Martin Hengel, "The Geography of Palestine in Acts," BAFCS, 4:64-67). ◆ **32 τῇ δὲ ἐπαύριον** (# *1254; 2069*) And on the following (day). **ἐάσαντες** aor. act. part. (circum.) ἐάω (# *1572*) to allow, w. inf. **ἀπέρχεσθαι** pres. mid. (dep.) inf. ἀπέρχομαι (# *599*) to go out, to depart. **ὑπέστρεψαν** aor. ind. act. ὑποστρέφω (# *5715*) to return. ◆ **33 εἰσελθόντες** aor. act. part. (circum.) εἰσέρχομαι (# *1656*) to go into. **ἀναδόντες** aor. act. part. (circum.) ἀναδίδωμι (# *347*) to give up, to hand over. **παρέστησαν** aor. ind. act. παρίστημι (# *4225*) to present, as a legal t.t., to bring before a judge (BAGD). ◆ **34 ἀναγνούς** aor. act. part. (temp.) ἀναγινώσκω (# *336*) to read. **ἐπερωτήσας** aor. act. part. (circum.) ἐπερωτάω (# *2089*) to question, to ask. **ποῖος** (# *4481*) what kind of, what sort of. **ἐπαρχεία** (# *2065*) province. **πυθόμενος** aor. mid. (dep.) part. s.v. 19. Felix probably was trying to avoid trying the case, but Cilcia was at that time under the authority of the Legate of Syria, to whom Felix was responsible; so Felix was forced into handling the case (BAFCS, 3:355). ◆ **35 διακούσομαι** fut. ind. mid. (dep.) διακούω (# *1358*) to listen through; a legal term for holding a hearing (LC). **ἔφη** aor. ind. act. s.v. 5. **παραγένωνται** aor. subj. mid. (dep.) παραγίνομαι (# *4134*) to arrive, to be present. Subj. w. **ὅταν** (# *4020*) in an indef. temp. cl. **κελεύσας** aor. act. part. (circum.) s.v. 3. **πραιτώριον** (# *4550*) praetorium, originally the headquarters of the praetor or military commander; then the official residence of the Roman provincial governor. The word is used here of the palace in Caesarea, built by Herod the Great, which served as a residence for the procurator and had numerous rooms (Bruce; BAFCS, 3:155-58; B. Burrell, K. Gleason, and E. Netzer, "Uncovering Herod's Seaside Palace," *BAR* 19 [1993]: 50-57, 76; Robert L. Hohlfelder, "Caesarea," ADB, 1:789-803). **φυλάσσεσθαι** pres. pass. inf. φυλάσσω (# *5875*) to guard. Inf. in indir. discourse. Paul was placed under strict restraint, perhaps even in bonds in a cell (BAFCS, 3:157).

Acts 24

◆ **1 κατέβη** aor. ind. act. καταβαίνω (# *2849*) to go down. Paul's accusers had imposing political, social, and economic Jewish status which was superior to Paul's status; however, Paul was a Roman citizen (BAFCS, 3:158-59). **ῥήτωρ** (# *4842*) public speaker, orator, a speaker in court, attorney, a lawyer acquainted w. Roman and Jewish law (Haenchen; MM; SGP, 48-51; Preisigke, 2:442; BAFCS, 3:159). **ἐνεφάνισαν** aor.

ind. act. ἐμφανίζω (# 1872) to reveal, to inform, to bring an accusation, to indict, to bring formal charges against someone (BAGD; NDIEC, 2:104; MM). ἡγεμών (# 2450) governor. For the legal aspects and accuracy of this section s. Sherwin-White, 48-70; BC, 5:306-38; BAFCS, 3:158-72. ◆ **2 κληθέντος** aor. pass. part. (temp.) καλέω (# 2813) to call, to summons. Gen. abs. ἤρξατο aor. ind. mid. (dep.) ἄρχομαι (# 806) to begin, w. inf. **κατηγορεῖν** pres. act. inf. κατηγορέω (# 2989) to accuse, to bring a legal accusation against someone (BAGD; TDNT). The speeches could be analyzed according to the rhetorical arrangement of that time as follows: for Tertullus: vv. 2b-3 *exordium* (the introduction); v. 5 *narratio* (the statement of facts); vv. 6-8 *confirmatio (probatio)* (the proof), w. *peroratio* (the conclusion) at v. 8; for Paul: v. 10b *exordium*; v. 11 *narratio*; vv. 12-13 *probatio* or *confirmatio*; vv. 14-18 *refutatio* (the refutation); vv. 19-21 *peroratio* (Bruce Winter, "The Importance of the *Captatio Benevolentia* in the Speeches of Tertullus and Paul in Acts 24:1-21," *JTS* 42 [1991]: 505-31; BAFCS, 3:159; Quintilian, *Institutio Oratoria*, 3:9; Aristotle, "The Art of Rhetoric," 3:13-19; Cicero, *De Oratore*, 2). **τυγχάνοντες** pres. act. part. (circum.) τυγχάνω (# 5593) to happen to, to happen, to come about, w. gen. The Romans prided themselves in preserving the peace and such a comment was sure to win favor (Polhill). **διόρθωμα** (# 1480) reform, improvements in internal administration (BAGD). **γινομένων** pres. mid. (dep.) part. (causal) γίνομαι (# 1181) to become, to come about, to happen. Gen. abs. **ἔθνει** dat. sing. ἔθνος (# 1620) nation. Dat. of advantage or personal interest. **πρόνοια** (# 4630) forethought, foresight. ◆ **3 πάντη** (# 4118) in every way (adv. of manner). **πανταχοῦ** (# 4116) in every place, everywhere (adv. of place). The two words used together are rhetorical alliteration (Bruce). **ἀποδεχόμεθα** pres. ind. mid. (dep.) ἀποδέχομαι (# 622) to welcome, to acknowledge, to praise. **κράτιστε** voc. sing. κράτιστος (# 3196) most excellent. Honorary form of address used to persons who hold a higher official or social position (BAGD). ◆ **4 πλεῖον** comp. πολύς (# 4498) much; comp., any more, any longer. **ἐγκόπτω** (# 1601) pres. subj. act. to cut in, to hinder or perhaps here to make weary, to delay (LC; TDNT). Subj. w. ἵνα (# 2671) to express purp. **παρακαλῶ** pres. ind. act. παρακαλέω (# 4151) to urge, to beg, beseech. **ἀκοῦσαι** aor. act. inf. ἀκούω (# 201) to hear, to listen to. Inf. giving the content of the request. **σε** acc. sing. σύ (# 5148) Subj. of the inf. **ἡμῶν** gen. pl. ἐγώ (# 1609). Obj. of the vb. **συντόμως** (# 5339) briefly. **ἐπιεικείᾳ** (# 2116) dat. sing. mildness, moderation, clemency, the quality of justice which treats people w. mercy; the quality of gracious forbearing (LN, 1:749; TDNT; TLNT; NTW, 38; EDNT; Phil. 4:5). Instr. dat. or dat. of cause. ◆ **5 εὑρόντες** aor. act. part. εὑρίσκω (# 2351) to find. Circum. or causal part. **λοιμός** (# 3369) pest, plague, pestilence, adj., pestilen-

tial, diseased; used of birds of prey or people who are dangerous to the public; a public menace (BAGD; DMTG, 225). The point is to create the right atmosphere–Paul was a political, not a theological, offender (LC; Sherwin-White, 50; BAFCS, 3:160-61). Double acc. giving the quality found in the person. **κινοῦντα** pres. act. part. (adj.) κινέω (# 3075) to stir up, to incite. Pres. indicates an habitual action. **στάσις** (# 5087) uprising, revolt, sedition. This charge was very serious (BAFCS, 3:160). **οἰκουμένη** (# 3876) world, the inhabited earth. For a similar charge found in a letter of Claudius to the Alexandrines s. Sherwin-White, 51. **πρωτοστάτης** (# 4756) ringleader, used of a man in the front rank (Bruce; s. NDIEC, 4:244). By calling Paul a ringleader, Tertullus ascribes to him full responsibility for the troubles (BAFCS, 3:161). **αἵρεσις** (# 146) party, sect. ◆ **6 ἐπείρασεν** aor. ind. act. πειράζω (# 4279) to attempt, to try, w. inf. In 21:28 Paul was accused of actually profaning the temple, here the charge is weakened to the attempt (BAFCS, 3:162). **βεβηλῶσαι** aor. act. inf. βεβηλόω (# 1014) to make accessible to everybody, to profane, to desecrate, to pollute, to defile (TLNT; TDNT; GELTS, 79). The Roman general Titus accuses the Jerusalem rebels under John of themselves defiling the temple even after the Romans permitted them to kill any Gentile, even Roman citizens, who crossed the barrier to the temple (Jos, *JW*, 6:124-26). **ἐκρατήσαμεν** aor. ind. act. κρατέω (# 3195) to seize, to arrest. A slight euphemism for mob lynching! (Williams). ◆ **8 δυνήσῃ** fut. ind. pass. (dep.) 2nd. pers. sing. δύναμαι (# 1538) to be able, w. inf. **ἀνακρίνας** aor. act. part. ἀνακρίνω (# 373) to examine. The word often is used of the interrogation of a prisoner (LC). Part. of means indicating how he was to get the information. **ἐπιγνῶναι** aor. act. inf. ἐπιγινώσκω (# 2105) to recognize, to know, to get at the facts (Bruce). The prep. in compound is directive; that is, the knowing is concentrated on one thing. **ὧν** gen. pl. rel. pron. ὅς (# 4005). Gen. by attraction, or a double gen. after the vb. ἀνακρίνας (BAGD, 423). **κατηγοροῦμεν** pres. ind. act. s.v. 2. Pres. pictures the action in progress. **αὐτοῦ** gen. sing. αὐτός (# 899). Gen. after the vb. of accusing. ◆ **9 συνεπέθεντο** aor. ind. mid. συνεπιτίθημι (# 5298) to join in the attack, to attack together. **φάσκοντες** pres. act. part. φάσκω (# 5763) to say, to speak, to insist. The vb. often seems to mean an assertion against a challenge (LC). Part. of means explaining how they joined the attack. **ἔχειν** pres. act. inf. ἔχω (# 2400) to have, here; "to be," "the things are so." Inf. in indir. discourse. ◆ **10 ἀπεκρίθη** aor. ind. pass. (dep.) ἀποκρίνομαι (# 646) to answer. For a summary of the elements of a defense speech s. BBC. **νεύσαντος** aor. act. part. (temp.) νεύω (# 3748) to wave, to motion w. the hand to someone, w. dat. Gen. abs. **λέγειν** pres. act. inf. λέγω (# 3306) to speak. Inf. of purp. **ὄντα** pres. act. part. (causal) εἰμί (# 1639) to be.

"Because you have been a judge for many years." The period that Paul had in mind could have been as long as nine years, since Felix had occupied a subordinate office in Samaria from A.D. 48, before he became procurator (BAFCS, 3:162; BASHH, 129). ἐπιστάμενος pres. mid. (dep.) part. ἐπίσταμαι (# 2179) to know, to understand. εὐθύμως (# 2315) w. good courage, cheerfully. ἀπολογοῦμαι pres. ind. mid. (dir. mid.) ἀπολογέομαι (# 664) to defend oneself, to speak in one's own defense (BAGD).   ◆ 11 δυναμένου pres. pass. (dep.) part. (causal) w. inf. s.v. 8. Gen. abs. ἐπιγνῶναι aor. act. inf. s.v. 8. πλείους nom. pl. comp. πολύς (# 4498) many (BD, 16); comp., more; here, more than. (RG, 666). The twelve days probably refer to the time between his arrival in Jerusalem and his arrest; twelve days was hardly enough time to start a rebellion (Polhill). ἀνέβην aor. ind. act. ἀναβαίνω (# 326) to go up. προσκυνήσων fut. act. part. προσκυνέω (# 4686) to worship. Fut. part. to express purp.   ◆ 12 εὗρον aor. ind. act. s.v. 5. διαλεγόμενον pres. mid. (dep.) part. (adj.) διαλέγομαι (# 1363) to discuss, to teach, to dispute (s. 17:2). ἐπίστασις (# 2180) attack, onset (BAGD). ποιοῦντα pres. act. part. ποιέω (# 4472) to do, to cause; used to express the verbal idea of the noun. οὔτε … οὔτε (# 4046) neither … nor.   ◆ 13 παραστῆσαι aor. act. inf. παρίστημι (# 4225) to place alongside to prove, to provide proof, to substantiate; to put evidence alongside of argument (LC). δύνανται pres. ind. pass. (dep.) s.v. 8. κατηγοροῦσιν pres. ind. act. s.v. 2.   ◆ 14 ὁμολογῶ pres. ind. act. ὁμολογέω (# 3933) to agree with, to confess, to admit. λατρεύω (# 3302) pres. ind. act. to serve, to worship, to worship through service, w. dat. (NIDNTT, 3:549-51; TDNT; EDNT). Pres. indicates habitual action: "continually worship by service." πατρῷος (# 4262) ancestral. Paul insisted that he had not forsaken the faith of his fathers (Bruce). πιστεύων pres. act. part. (circum.) πιστεύω (# 4409) to believe; here w. dat. γεγραμμένοις perf. pass. part. γράφω (# 1211) to write. Perf. emphasizes the permanent state of authority of that which was written (MM). ◆ 15 ἐλπίς (# 1828) hope (s. Klaus Haacker, "Das Bekenntnis des Paulus zur Hoffnung Israels nach der Apostelgeschichte des Lukas," NTS 31 [1985]: 437-51). ἔχων pres. act. part. (circum.) s.v. 9. προσδέχονται pres. ind. mid. (dep.) προσδέχομαι (# 4657) to welcome, to wait for. ἀνάστασις (# 414) resurrection. Acc. as subject of the inf. μέλλειν pres. act. inf. μέλλω (# 3516) to be about to. Epex. inf. explaining the hope, or inf. in an indir. assertion (RWP). ἔσεσθαι fut. mid. (dep.) inf. εἰμί s.v. 10. For the construction w. the fut. inf. as being closer to classical Gr. s. MT, 79; MKG, 308.   ◆ 16 ἐν τούτῳ (# 1877; 4047) therefore; the causal or instr. use of the prep. (BG, 40). ἀσκῶ pres. ind. act. ἀσκέω (# 828) to practice, to exercise, to take pains, to drill; here w. inf., "I do my best" (BAGD; NDIEC, 2:58-60; 3:153).

The word has a note of moral strictness about it, without the later sense of asceticism (Bruce). The pres. could be conative, "I try to do my best," or customary pres. (VANT, 205-08). ἀπρόσκοπος (# 718) without offense, unharmed, uninjured, blameless. In the papyri it is used to refer to the maintenance of an unspoiled record in one's self-judgment, or of one who has been protected from harm (LC; NDIEC, 1:54-56). συνείδησις (# 5287) conscience (TLNT; TDNT; EDNT; NIDNTT, 348-51). ἔχειν pres. act. inf. s.v. 9. διὰ παντός (# 1328; 4246) always.   ◆ 17 πλειόνων (# 4498) gen. pl. comp.; here, ἐλεημοσύνας acc. pl. ἐλεημοσύνη (# 1797) kind. deed, alms, charitable giving (BAGD; GELTS, 144). ποιήσων fut. act. part. s.v. 12. Fut. part. to express purp. παρεγενόμην aor. ind. mid. (dep.) παραγίνομαι (# 4134) to come, to arrive. προσφορά (# 4714) offering.   ◆ 18 ἐν αἷς (# 1877; 4005) with which, referring to the offering of v. 17. εὗρον aor. ind. act. s.v. 5. ἡγνισμένον perf. pass. part. (adj.) ἁγνίζω (# 49) to sanctify, to dedicate, to purify. Perf. indicates the state or condition.   ◆ 19 τινὲς δὲ ἀπὸ τῆς Ἀσίας Ἰουδαῖοι but some of the Jews from Asia. No vb. appears for these words. Paul stops to note their absence, a Pauline anacoluthon (RWP). ἔδει impf. ind. act. δεῖ (# 1256) it is necessary, w. inf. giving a logical necessity. Impf. indicates the unfulfilled obligation (RWP). παρεῖναι pres. act. inf. πάρειμι (# 4205) to be present. κατηγορεῖν pres. act. inf. s.v. 2. The Roman law was very strong against accusers who abandoned their charges. The Jews from Asia are the ones to bring the charges; the present accusers are disqualified (Sherwin-White, 52; BAFCS, 3:163). ἔχοιεν pres. opt. act. s.v. 9. Opt. is used to express the cond. of a 4th. class cond. cl. indicating the remoteness of the hypothesis (RG, 1020f). The cond. cl. is mixed w. the apodosis of the 2nd. class; that is contrary to fact (RG, 1022).   ◆ 20 αὐτοὶ οὗτοι these themselves. εἰπάτωσαν aor. imp. act. λέγω (# 3306). Aor. imp. calls for a specific act. εὗρον aor. ind. act. s.v. 5. ἀδίκημα (# 93) acc. sing. wrong, crime. στάντος aor. act. part. (temp.) ἵστημι (# 2705) to stand. Gen. abs.   ◆ 21 ἤ (# 2445) than, what else than, except (RWP). ἧς gen. sing. rel. pron. ὅς (# 4005) Gen. by attraction instead of acc. as dir. obj. ἐκέκραξα aor. ind. act. κράζω (# 3189) to scream out. ἑστώς perf. act. part. (temp.) s.v. 20. κρίνομαι pres. ind. pass. κρίνω (# 3212) to judge.   ◆ 22 ἀνεβάλετο aor. ind. mid. (dep.) ἀναβάλλομαι (# 327) to postpone. A legal t.t. to adjourn a trial (BAGD). Felix was within his rights to postpone the trial without a verdict (BAFCS, 3:164). ἀκριβέστερον adv. comp. ἀκριβῶς (# 209) accurately, carefully (BAGD); s. 23:15. The comp. is used in the sense of elative superl., "knowing for certain" (BG, 49). εἰδώς perf. act. part. οἶδα (# 3857) to know. Def. perf. w. pres. meaning. Circum. part. or perhaps causal. He could have gotten his information from his wife Drusilla (EGT; s.v. 24). εἴπας aor. act. part. (circum.) s.v.

20. **καταβῇ** aor. subj. act. s.v. 1. Subj. in an indef. temp. cl. **διαγνώσομαι** fut. ind. mid. (dep.) διαγινώσκω (# 1336) to examine, to determine, to decide. Lysias was the only independent witness as to the fact of any civil disturbance (Sherwin-White, 53). ◆ **23 διαταξά-μενος** aor. mid. (dep.) part. διατάσσω (# 1411) to command. **τηρεῖσθαι** pres. pass. inf. τηρέω (# 5498) to guard. Inf. in indir. discourse. **ἔχειν** pres. act. inf. s.v. 9. **ἄνεσις** (# 457) relaxing, indulgence, privilege, free custody. He was still bound w. a light chain, but the indulgence involved food, visits from friends, and the remission from the severe form of custody; he was probably kept in the palace that Herod had built (EGT; BAFCS, 3:167-72). **κωλύειν** pres. act. inf. κωλύω (# 3266) to forbid, to hinder, to prevent. Inf. in indir. discourse. **ὑπηρετεῖν** pres. act. inf. ὑπηρετέω (# 5676) to minister to, w. dat. Epex. inf. explaining what was not to be forbidden. ◆ **24 παραγενόμενος** aor. mid. (dep.) part. (temp.) s.v. 17. **γυναικί** dat. sing. γυνή (# 1222) wife. **οὔσῃ** pres. act. part. (adj.) εἰμί (# 1639). Felix was married three times, once to the granddaughter of Cleopatra and Anthony; then to Drusilla, the daughter of Agrippa I, who was six years old when her father died (s. 12:23; Jos. *Ant.*, 19:354) and fourteen when Felix assumed office. Shortly thereafter, she was married to Azizus king of Emensa, but Felix, enchanted by her beauty, got a magician from Cyprus to persuade her to leave her husband and marry him, even though it was against her ancestral (Jewish) laws. She was probably about sixteen years old. Their son, Agrippa, and his wife died in the eruption of Mount Vesuvius (Jos., *Ant.*, 20:141-44; ABD, 2:783; HJP, 1:461-62; JURR, 270; BBC; Richard D. Sullivan, "The Dynasty of Judaea in the First Century," ANRW, 2, 8:329-31). **μετεπέμψατο** aor. ind. mid. (dep.) μεταπέμπομαι (# 3569) to send for, to summons. **ἤκουσεν** aor. ind. act. s.v. 4. Here w. gen. as obj. ◆ **25 διαλεγομένου** pres. mid. (dep.) part. s.v. 12. Gen. abs. **δικαιοσύνη** (# 1466) righteousness, justice in the widest sense, the rendering to everyone his due. (Alex.; TLNT, 1:331; TDNT; EDNT, 1:784-96, 1146; NDIEC, 4:144-45). **ἐγκράτεια** (# 1602) self-control; the control of the passions and desires, often used regarding the control of sexual desires; here it may include Felix's bribe-taking tendencies (Polhill; TDNT; TLNT; EDNT; H. Chadwick, "Enkratia," RAC, 5:343-65; Gal. 5:23). **κρίμα** (# 3210) judgment. **μέλλοντος** pres. act. part. (adj.) s.v. 15. **ἔμφοβος** (# 1873) afraid, terrified, frightened (BAGD; GELTS, 148). Truth makes Felix fear even a prisoner in bonds (Bengel). **γενόμενος** aor. mid. (dep.) part. (circum.) s.v. 2. Ingressive aor., "he became afraid" (RWP), or simply, "he was afraid" (NTNT, 139). **ἀπεκρίθη** aor. ind. pass. (dep.) s.v. 10. **ἔχον** pres. act. part. s.v. 9. Part. in the idiom, "as for the present" or "holding the now"; acc. of time (RWP). **πορεύου** pres. imp. mid. (dep.) πορεύομαι (# 4513) to go.

μεταλαβών aor. act. part. (temp.) μεταλαμβάνω (# 3561) to receive, to have. An idiom meaning "to have spare time." The prep. in compound implies a different or subsequent occasion (LC). **μετακαλέσομαι** fut. ind. mid. (dep.) μετακαλέω (# 3559) to send for. ◆ **26 ἅμα** (# 275) at the same time. **καί** (# 2779) also. **ἐλπίζων** pres. act. part. (causal) ἐλπίζω (# 1827) to hope. Pres. indicates his continual hope. **χρῆμα** (# 5975) pl. money. Although bribes were legally forbidden, the practice was widespread, extending even to Caesar himself (BAFCS, 3:62-67, 166-67; Polhill). **δοθήσεται** fut. ind. pass. δίδωμι (# 1443) to give. **πυκνότερον** adv. comp. πυκνός (# 4781) frequent, numerous; either in the comp. sense, "the more often" (because of his financial expectations), or used as an elative superl., "very often" (Bruce). **μεταπεμπόμενος** pres. mid. (dep.) part. (circum.) s.v. 24. **ὡμίλει** impf. ind. act. ὁμιλέω (# 3917) to converse w., to talk to, w. dat. Impf. pictures the repeated action. For a discussion of the reasons why Felix did not render a verdict s. BAFCS, 3:164-67. ◆ **27 διετία** (# 1454) two years. **πληρωθείσης** aor. pass. part. (temp.) πληρόω (# 4444) to fulfill, to complete. Gen. abs. **ἔλαβεν** aor. ind. act. λαμβάνω (# 3284) to take. **διάδοχος** (# 1345) successor. Used in the idiom "to take a successor," "to be succeeded by someone." There was evidently widespread dissatisfaction from political and religious unrest, esp. when Felix attacked the Jews in Caesarea in their fight w. the Syrians over equal citizenship (Jos., *Ant.*, 20:173-78; JW, 2:266-70; for a summary of the events during the rule of Felix and the events leading to the appointment of Festus s. JPF, 1:462-70; JURR, 269–70, 286–88; BC, 5:464-67). **θέλων** pres. act. part. θέλω (# 2527) to wish, to want, w. inf. **χάριτα** acc. sing. χάρις (# 5921) gift, favor. For the form of the acc. s. BD, 27; MH, 132; GGP, 2:52-53. **καταθέσθαι** aor. mid. (dep.) inf. κατατίθημι (# 2960) to lay down, to grant or do someone a favor. **κατέλιπε** aor. ind. act. καταλείπω (# 2901) to leave behind, to leave. **δεδεμένον** perf. pass. part. (adj.) δέω (# 1313) to bind. Perf. stresses the condition. Paul was evidently kept in the palace that Herod had built, where the procurator lived. He was probably in lightened custody, which, however, did not keep him from being chained (BAFCS, 3:167-72).

Acts 25

◆ **1 Φῆστος** (# 5776) Porcius Festus. He was appointed by Nero to succeed Felix. After trying to put down some of the unrest in the land caused by the bandits, or *sicarii*, he died in office in A.D. 62. Before Albinus, his successor, took office in Oct. 62, Ananus, the Jewish priest, had James, the half-brother of Jesus and leader in the church at Jerusalem, killed (Jos., *JW*, 2:271; *Ant.*, 20:182-203; HJP, 1:467-68; ABD, 2:794-95;

JURR, 271; KP, 4:1059; JPFC, 1:368-70; BC, 5:464-67). ἐπιβάς aor. act. part. (temp.) ἐπιβαίνω (# 2094) to enter, to come into, to set foot upon, w. dat. ἐπαρχεία (# 2065) dat. sing. province, the district governed by a prefect (LC). ἀνέβη aor. ind. act. ἀναβαίνω (# 326) to go up. ◆ 2 ἐνεφάνισαν aor. ind. act. ἐμφανίζω (# 1872) to make known, to bring charges against (s. 24:1). παρεκάλουν impf. ind. act. παρακαλέω (# 4151) to encourage, to beseech, to urge. ◆ 3 αἰτούμενοι pres. mid. (indir. mid., "to ask for oneself") part. αἰτέω (# 160) to ask, to request. Supplementary part. explaining the urging of the Jewish leaders. μεταπέμψηται aor. subj. mid. (dep.) μεταπέμπομαι (# 3569) to summon; subj. used w. ὅπως (# 3968) to express purp. or to give the content of the request. ἐνέδρα (# 1909) ambush, plot (s. 23:16). ποιοῦντες pres. act. part. (causal) ποιέω (# 4472) to do, to make. ἀνελεῖν aor. act. inf. ἀναιρέω (# 359) to kill. Epex. inf. explaining the plot. κατὰ τὴν ὁδόν along the way. ◆ 4 ἀπεκρίθη aor. ind. pass. (dep.) ἀποκρίνομαι (# 646) to answer. τηρεῖσθαι pres. pass. inf. τηρέω (# 5498) to guard, to watch over. Inf. in indirect discourse. Pres. indicates the action in progress, εἰς (# 1650) in, at. The prep. is used in a local sense without expressing motion (BD, 110-12; BG, 33-34). μέλλειν pres. act. inf. μέλλω (# 3516) to be about to. Inf. in indir. discourse. ἐν τάχει (# 1877; 5443) quickly, soon. ἐκπορεύεσθαι pres. mid. (dep.) inf. ἐκπορεύομαι (# 1744) to go out, to depart. Inf. w. μέλλω to express the immediate fut. ◆ 5 Οἱ ἐν ὑμῖν δυνατοί the men of power or influence among you. A phrase used frequently for the Jewish notables. The word δυνατοί may include the ability to speak as well as the prestige of position (LC). φησίν pres. ind. act. φημί (# 5774) to say. Hist. pres. συγκαταβάντες aor. act. part. (temp.) συγκαταβαίνω (# 5160) to come down together, to go down together. ἄτοπος (# 876) not in place, improper. κατηγορείτωσαν pres. imp. act. κατηγορέω (# 2989) to accuse, to bring a charge against. ◆ 6 διατρίψας aor. act. part. (temp.) διατρίβω (# 1417) to spend, to stay. πλείους comp. πολύς (# 4498) many; here, not more than eight or ten days. καταβάς aor. act. part. (circum.) καταβαίνω (# 2849) to go down. τῇ ἐπαύριον (# 2069) on the next day. Dat. of time. καθίσας aor. act. part. (temp.) καθίζω (# 2767) to sit down, to take one's seat. This was a necessary formality in order that his decision might have legal effect (Bruce). βῆμα (# 1037) judicial bench. ἐκέλευσεν aor. ind. act. κελεύω (# 3027) to command. ἀχθῆναι aor. pass. inf. ἄγω (# 72) to lead, to bring. Inf. in indir. discourse giving the content of the command. ◆ 7 παραγενομένου aor. mid. (dep.) part. (temp.) παραγίνομαι (# 4134) to arrive, to come, to be present. Gen. abs. περιέστησαν aor. ind. act. περιίστημι (# 4325) to stand around. καταβεβηκότες perf. act. part. (adj.) s.v. 6. βαρέα acc. pl. βαρύς (# 987) heavy, weighty, serious. αἰτίωμα (# 166) charges. Used in the papyri in the

sense of blame (MM; SGP, 65-68; Preisigke, 1:39). καταφέροντες pres. act. part. (circum.) καταφέρω (# 2965) to bring against, to bring down upon. Pres. could be incep. and picture the repeated bringing of the charges. ἴσχυον impf. ind. act. ἰσχύω (# 2710) to be strong, to be able, w. inf. Impf. pictures the repetition and reiteration that took the place of proof (RWP). ἀποδεῖξαι aor. act. inf. ἀποδείκνυμι (# 617) to prove, to demonstrate. ◆ 8 ἀπολογουμένου pres. mid. part. ἀπολογέομαι (# 664) to defend oneself. Gen. abs. ἥμαρτον aor. ind. act. ἁμαρτάνω (# 279) to sin, to offend, to do wrong. ◆ 9 θέλων pres. act. part. θέλω (# 2527) to want to, to desire to, w. inf. τοῖς Ἰουδαίοις (# 2681) dat. pl. for the Jews. Dat. of advantage or personal interest. χάρις (# 5921) favor. καταθέσθαι aor. mid. (dep.) inf. κατατίθημι (# 2960) to grant (s. 24:27). ἀποκριθείς aor. pass. (dep.) part. s.v. 4. For the Semitic use of the pleonastic part. s. MH, 453-54. εἶπεν aor. ind. act. λέγω (# 3306) to say. ἀναβάς aor. act. part. (circum.) s.v. 1. κριθῆναι aor. pass. inf. κρίνω (# 3212) to judge. ◆ 10 εἶπεν aor. ind. act. s.v. 9. ἑστώς perf. act. part. ἵστημι (# 2705) to stand. Part. w. εἰμί in a periphrastic construction (VA, 483-84). οὗ (# 4023) where. δεῖ (# 1256) pres. ind. act. w. inf., "it is necessary to," giving a logical necessity. με acc. sing. ἐγώ; (# 1609) subject of inf. κρίνεσθαι pres. pass. inf. s.v. 9. ἠδίκησα perf. ind. act. ἀδικέω (# 92) to do that which is not right, to commit a crime. Perf. emphasizes the completes action w. the resulting condition. καί (# 2779) also. κάλλιον adv. comp. καλῶς (# 2822) good. Comp. used as an elative superl., very well. ◆ 11 ἀδικῶ pres. ind. act. s.v. 10. Here, "I am guilty" is an Attic use (Bruce). The perf. (πέπραχα) is used for individual trespasses, the pres. only for the general result (BD, 186). Another view is that the pres. refers to his being involved in wrongdoing and the perf. captures the state of affairs of one who has done such things (VA, 303; VANT, 296). πέπραχα perf. ind. act. πράσσω (# 4556) to do, to commit. παραιτοῦμαι pres. ind. mid. (dep.) παραιτέομαι (# 4148) to ask, to excuse oneself (BAGD). "I beg myself off," an idiomatic use of Hellenistic Gr. (LC). Found on an inscription where it indicates that a wrestler declined, or threw in the towel (NDIEC, 3:78). Conative pres., "I am not trying to beg myself off" (SMT, 8). ἀποθανεῖν aor. act. inf. ἀποθνήσκω (# 633) to die. Inf. w. the art. as the object of the vb. (MT, 140; IBG, 127). ἐστιν pres. ind. act. εἰμί (# 1639) to be. Here it means "exists" and is used in a 1st. class cond. assuming the reality of the cond. (RWP). ὧν gen. pl. rel. pron. ὅς (# 4005) Gen. by attraction to the case of the unexpressed antecedent τουτῶν (RWP). κατηγοροῦσιν pres. ind. act. s.v. 5. Pres. indicates a continual action, "they keep accusing me." χαρίσασθαι aor. mid. (dep.) inf. χαρίζομαι (# 5919) to give freely or graciously as a favor, to pardon. Here (and v. 16) it is the giving of a man to those who wish to harm him (BAGD). **ἐπικαλοῦμαι** pres. ind. mid. (dep.) ἐπικαλέω (# 2126) to call upon, to appeal. According to the Roman right of *provocatio* a Roman citizen had the right to be tried before Caesar. For a discussion of this right and its relation to Acts and Luke's historical accuracy s. Sherwin-White, 57-70; NDIEC, 4:8-385; BBC; TLNT, 2:43, and the excellent discussion, along w. a description of a Roman coin depicting the process, BAFCS, 3:48-56. ◆ **12 συλλαλήσας** aor. act. part. συλλαλέω (# 5196) to talk w., to discuss w. **ἀπεκρίθη** aor. ind. pass. s.v. 4. **ἐπικέκλησαι** perf. ind. mid. (dep.) 2nd. pers. sing. s.v. 11. Perf. indicates the settled state. **πορεύσῃ** fut. ind. mid. (dep.) πορεύομαι (# 4513) to go. ◆ **13 διαγενομένων** aor. mid. (dep.) part. (temp.) διαγίνομαι (# 1335) to pass by, to intervene. Gen. abs. "After certain days had passed." **Ἀγρίππας** (# 68) King Agrippa II, the son of Agrippa I (s. Acts 12:1), was brought up in Rome. When his father died, he was only a youth of seventeen, and for this reason Claudius did not give him the territory of Agrippa I. A few years later, however, he was given the kingdom of his recently deceased uncle Herod of Chalis in northern Palestine. He also received the right to appoint the high priest. Later he exchanges Chalis for the territory of Bathanaea, Trachonitis, and Gaulanitis. In addition, Nero gave him northern Galilee. He remained a friend of Rome until his death under Domitian in A.D. 92/93, and during his life, he enjoyed the friendship of Josephus, Vespasian, and Titus. His sister, Bernice, was his mistress, which caused a scandal even in Rome. He antagonized the Jews when he enlarged his palace in Jerusalem so he could watch what was going on in the temple (HJP, 1:471-83; JURR; R.D. Sullivan, "The Dynasty of Judaea in the First Century," ANRW, 2, 8:329-45; JPF, 1:300-304, 367-72; Jos., *JW*, 2:220-632; 3:29-68, 443-540; *Ant.*, 19:360-62; 20:9-12, 104-214; *Life*, 362-67; *AA*, 1:51; HJC, 113-33; BBC; JCST, 81-87, 141-53; Polhill). **Βερνίκη** (# 1022) Bernice. As daughter of Agrippa I, she was Agrippa's and Drusilla's sister. Upon the death of her husband (and uncle!), Herod of Chalis, she lived w. her brother, Agrippa II. When this incestuous love affair caused much unrest in Rome, Agrippa sent her away. She became the mistress of the Roman general (and later emperor), Titus, who also finally ditched her (HJP, 1:471-83; BBC; ABD, 1:677-78; BASHH, 173; Polhill). **κατήντησαν** aor. ind. act. καταντάω (# 2918) to come down, to arrive. **ἀσπασάμενοι** aor. mid. (dep.) part. (circum.) ἀσπάζομαι (# 832) to greet. The greeting and arrival coincided (Haenchen). ◆ **14 πλείους** comp. πολύς (# 4498) many; comp., many more. **διέτριβον** impf. ind. act. s.v. 6. **ἀνέθετο** aor. ind. mid. (dep.) ἀνατίθημι (# 423) to lay before, to communicate w. a view to consultation (MM). **καταλελειμμένος** perf. pass. part. καταλείπω (# 2901) to

leave behind. Part. in a periphrastic construction (VA, 484). ◆ **15 γενομένου** aor. mid. (dep.) part. (temp.) γίνομαι (# 1181) to become, to be. Gen. abs. **ἐνεφάνισαν** aor. ind. act. s.v. 2. **αἰτούμενοι** pres. mid. (indir. mid., "for oneself") part. s.v. 3. **καταδίκη** (# 2869) sentence, condemnation (MM; Preisigke, 1:749). ◆ **16 ἀπεκρίθην** aor. ind. pass. (dep.) s.v. 4. **χαρίζεσθαι** pres. pass. inf. s.v. 11. Epex. inf. explaining the custom of the Romans. **πρὶν ἤ** before. **κατηγορούμενος** pres. pass. part. s.v. 5. **ἔχοι** pres. opt. act. ἔχω (# 2400) to have. Opt. is used in a temp. cl., but is due to indir. discourse (RG, 970). **τόπος** (# 5536) place, opportunity. **ἀπολογίας** gen. sing. ἀπολογία (# 665) defense, legal defense. Obj. gen., "opportunity for a defense" (RWP). **λάβοι** aor. opt. act. λαμβάνω (# 3284) to receive. **ἔγκλημα** (# 1598) charge, accusation (s. 23:29). ◆ **17 συνελθόντων** aor. act. part. (temp.) συνέρχομαι (# 5302) to come together. Gen. abs. **ἐνθάδε** (# 1924) here. **ἀναβολήν** (# 332) delay, postponement. **ποιησάμενος** aor. mid. part. (circum.) ποιέω (# 4472) to do, to make, gives a verbal idea to the noun: "I did not delay." **τῇ ἑξῆς** on the next (day). Dat. of time. **καθίσας** aor. act. part. (temp.) s.v. 6. **ἐκέλευσα** aor. ind. act. s.v. 6. **ἀχθῆναι** aor. pass. inf. s.v. 6. Inf. in indir. discourse. ◆ **18 σταθέντες** aor. act. part. (temp.) ἵστημι (# 2705) to stand. **ἔφερον** impf. ind. act. φέρω (# 5770) to bring. Impf. indicates the repeated charges (RWP). **ὧν** gen. pl. rel. pron. ὅς (# 4005). The antecedent (πονηρῶν) is incorporated into the rel. cl. and the acc. of the rel. is attracted to the case (gen. pl.) of the antecedent (RG, 718). **ὑπενόουν** impf. ind. act. ὑπονοέω (# 5706) to suppose, to suspect, to have an opinion based on scant evidence, often w. the implication of regarding a false opinion as true (LN, 1:370; MM). ◆ **19 δεισιδαιμονία** (# 1272) fear of or reverence for the divinity, superstition, religion (BAGD; TLNT; EDNT). **εἶχον** impf. ind. act. s.v. 16. **τεθνηκότος** perf. act. part. (adj.) θνήσκω (# 2569) to die; perf. to be dead. **ἔφασκεν** impf. ind. act. φάσκω (# 5763) to say, to affirm, to insist (s. 24:9). Impf. pictures the repeated avowal. **ζῆν** pres. act. inf. ζάω (# 2409) to live. Pres. indicates the continual living; to be alive. Inf. in indir. discourse. ◆ **20 ἀπορούμενος** pres. mid. (dep.) part. (causal) ἀπορέομαι (# 679) to be perplexed, to be in doubt which way to turn, w. the implication of serious anxiety (RWP; LN, 1:381). **ἔλεγον** impf. ind. act. λέγω (# 3306) to say. **βούλοιτο** pres. opt. mid. (dep.) βούλομαι (# 1089) to wish, to will, w. inf. Opt. in indir. discourse. **κρίνεσθαι** pres. pass. inf. s.v. 9. ◆ **21 ἐπικαλεσαμένου** aor. mid. (dep.) part. s.v. 11. Gen. abs., temp. or causal. **τηρηθῆναι** aor. pass. inf. s.v. 4. Inf. in indir. discourse as obj. of the vb. ἐπικαλεσαμένου. **Σεβαστός** (# 4935) revered, worthy of reverence, august. A translation of Lat. "August" and designation of the Roman emperor (BAGD). **διάγνωσις** (# 1338) decision. A legal term; here, to be kept in custody for the emperor's decision (*cognitio*) (BAGD; MM; NDIEC, 1:47-49; 4:86; Jos., *JW*, 2:17). ἐκέλευσα aor. ind. act. s.v. 6. τηρεῖσθαι pres. pass. inf. s.v. 4. Inf. in indir. discourse. ἀναπέμψω fut. ind. or aor. subj. act. ἀναπέμπω (# 402) to send up, to send to a superior. It indicates the sending of a prisoner to a superior tribunal (LC). Subj. or fut. in an indef. temp. cl. ◆ **22** ἐβουλόμην impf. ind. mid. (dep.) s.v. 20. "I should like," w. inf. (Bruce). αὐτός (# 899) myself. ἀκοῦσαι aor. act. inf. ἀκούω (# 201) to hear, w. obj. in gen. φησίν pres. ind. act. s.v. 5. ἀκούσῃ fut. ind. act. 2nd. pers. sing., w. obj. in gen. ◆ **23** τῇ ἐπαύριον (# 2069) on the next day. ἐλθόντος aor. act. part. (temp.) ἔρχομαι (# 2262) to come. Gen. abs. φαντασία (# 5752) pomp, pageantry. εἰσελθόντων aor. act. part. (temp.) εἰσέρχομαι (# 1656) to go into. Gen. abs., temp. ἀκροατήριον audience chamber, doubtless in Herod's praetorium (Bruce). κατ' ἐξοχην (# 2848; 2029) prominence par excellence. κελεύσαντος aor. act. part. s.v. 6. Gen. abs. ἤχθη aor. ind. pass. ἄγω s.v. 6. ◆ **24** φησιν pres. ind. act. s.v. 5. Hist. pres. βασιλεῦ voc. sing. βασιλεύς (# 995) king, one who exercises the office of a king. συμπαρόντες pres. act. part. nom. (as voc.) pl. συμπάρειμι (# 5223) to be present together. Adj. part. as subst. θεωρεῖτε pres. ind. act. θεωρέω (# 2555) to see, to view. Pres. indicates the action in progress, "you are looking at this one." ἐνέτυχον aor. ind. act. ἐντυγχάνω (# 1961) to meet, to approach, to appeal, to petition, w. dat. βοῶντες pres. act. part. βοάω (# 1066) to scream, to yell. Part. of manner explaining how they petitioned him. δεῖν pres. act. inf. δεῖ (# 1256) it is necessary, giving a logical necessity based on the circumstances at hand, w. inf. Inf. in indir. discourse. ζῆν pres. act. inf. ζάω (# 2409) to live. ◆ **25** ἐγώ (# 1609) I. Emphatic and contrastive: "I, in contrast to them." κατελαβόμην aor. ind. mid. (dep.) καταλαμβάνω (# 2989) to seize; mid. to grasp, to understand. πεπραχέναι perf. act. inf. s.v. 11. Inf. in indir. discourse as obj. of the vb. Perf. indicates the abiding results or condition. The perf. inf. is used by Luke to emphasize one of his major themes–Paul was never found guilty of violating the law in his preaching (VA, 393). αὐτοῦ (# 899) himself. ἐπικαλεσαμένου aor. mid. (dep.) part. (causal) s.v. 11. Gen. abs. ἔκρινα aor. ind. act. s.v. 9. Effective aor., "I judged," "I decided," "I have reached a decision." πέμπειν pres. act. inf. πέμπω (# 4287) to send. Inf. in indir. discourse. ◆ **26** ἀσφαλής (# 855) certain, sure, definite. γράψαι aor. act. inf. γράφω (# 1211) to write. Inf. as obj., or epex. inf. explaining ἀσφαλές. προήγαγον aor. act. ind. 1st. pers. sing. προάγω (# 4575) to lead before. μάλιστα (# 3436) especially. ἀνάκρισις (# 374) investigation, hearing, esp. preliminary hearing (BAGD). γενομένης aor. mid. (dep.) part. (temp.) s.v. 15. Gen. abs., "after the hearing has taken place." σχῶ aor. subj. act. s.v. 16. Subj. w. ὅπως (# 3968) to express purp. γράψω aor. subj. act., or fut. ind. act. Subj. or fut. in indir. speech

(RG, 1044). ◆ **27** ἄλογος (# 263) unreasonable, without reason, senseless (MM). δοκεῖ pres. ind. act. δοκέω (# 1506) to seem, to appear; impersonal w. dat., "it seems to me." πέμποντα pres. act part. s.v. 25. αἰτία (# 162) charge. σημάναι aor. act. inf. σημαίνω (# 4955) to signify, to indicate. Epex. inf. explaining what seems to be unreasonable.

Acts 26

◆ **1** ἔφη impf./aor. ind. act. φημί (# 5774) to speak. For material regarding Agrippa II s. 25:13. ἐπιτρέπεται pres. ind. pass. ἐπιτρέπω (# 2205) to allow; impersonal pass. w. inf. (sometimes w. part. VA, 390), "it is allowed for you to speak" (BD, 164). Aoristic or instantaneous pres. used of an action coincident in time w. the act of speaking, and conceived of as a simple event done in a moment (SMT, 9; VANT, 202-3). ἐκτείνας aor. act. part. ἐκτείνω (# 1753) to stretch out. Temp. or circum. part. This was not a gesture for silence, but rather the out-stretched hand of an orator (Polhill; for the use of hand gestures as prescribed for ancient Rhetoric s. Quintilian, 11, 3:85-124). ἀπελογεῖτο impf. ind. mid. ἀπολογέομαι (# 664) to defend oneself. Incep. impf., "he began to make his defense." ◆ **2** ὧν gen. pl. rel. pron. ὅς (# 4005). ἐγκαλοῦμαι pres. ind. pass. ἐγκαλέω (# 1592) to accuse, to bring legal charges against someone (BAGD). Pres. indicates the action in progress or the repeated continual action. ἥγημαι perf. ind. mid./pass. (dep.) ἡγέομαι (# 2451) to consider, to regard. The perf. here carries the sense of the pres., "I consider" (BD, 176). μακάριος (# 3421) happy, fortunate (TDNT; TLNT; EDNT). μέλλων pres. act. part. μέλλω (# 3516) to be about to. Used w. the inf. to express the impending fut. Causal part. giving the reason for Paul's feeling. ἀπολογεῖσθαι pres. mid. inf. s.v. 1. This v. gives Paul's brief *capitatio benevolentiae* (Polhill; s. 24:2). ◆ **3** μάλιστα (# 3436) especially. This may go w. the whole following phrase, giving a special reason for Paul's pleasure, or only w. the following word "because you are specially expert" (Bruce). γνώστης (# 1195) one who knows, expert (LAE, 367; MM). ὄντα pres. act. part. (causal) εἰμί (# 1639) to be. δέομαι (# 1289) pres. ind. mid. (dep.) to ask, to beg. μακροθύμως (# 3430) adv. patiently. ἀκοῦσαι aor. act. inf. ἀκούω (# 201) to hear, to listen to, w. gen. Inf. in indir. discourse. ◆ **4** μὲν οὖν (# 3525; 4036) well, then (Bruce). βίωσις (# 1052) manner of life, way of life, daily life (LN, 1:506). νεότης (# 3744) youth. ἀρχή (# 794) beginning; explains what precedes–the commencement of his training, which was not only among his own nation, but also esp. in Jerusalem (EGT; Simon Légasse "Paul's Pre-Christian Career According to Acts," BAFCS, 4:373-89). γενομένην aor. mid. (dep.) part. (adj.) γίνομαι (# 1181) to become, to be. ἴσασι perf. ind.

act. 3rd. per. pl. οἶδα (# 3857) to know. Def. perf. w. pres. meaning. For the use of the old form instead of the vernacular Hellenistic s. MH, 221. ◆ 5 προγινώσκοντες pres. act. part. προγινώσκω (# 4589) to know before, to know previously. ἄνωθεν (# 540) from the beginning, for a long time. The word deals w. a condition now existent and long standing (LC); from the beginning of his public education in Jerusalem (EGT). θέλωσι pres. subj. act. θέλω (# 2527) to want to, w. inf. Subj. w. ἐάν (# 1569) in a 3rd. class cond. where the speaker assumes the possibility of the cond. μαρτυρεῖν pres. act. inf. μαρτυρέω (# 3455) to testify, to bear witness to. ἀκριβεστάτην superl. ἀκριβής (# 207) accurate, strict. The true superl. force, "strictest" (Bruce). αἵρεσις (# 146) party, school of thought, religious party (TDNT; EDNT). θρησκεία (# 2579) religion, rite, worship. It indicates the practical side of religion, its customs (LC; MM; TLNT). ἔζησα aor. ind. act. ζάω (# 2409) to live, to conduct one's life. Constantive aor. summing up his previous life (VANT, 257-59, 262). Φαρισαῖος (# 5757) nom. sing. Nom. modifying the vb. ἔζησα "I lived as a Pharisee" (BAGD). For the life of the Pharisees s. TJ, 70-76. ◆ 6 ἐλπίς (# 1828) hope. ἐπαγγελίας gen. sing. ἐπαγγελία (# 2039) promise. Descriptive gen. explaining the hope. γενομένης aor. mid. (dep.) part. (adj.) s.v. 4. For the connection between the eschatological hope of Israel and the resurrection of the dead s. Klaus Haacker, "Das Bekenntnis Paulus zur Hoffnung Israels nach der Apostelgeschichte des Lukas," NTS 31 (1985): 437-51. ἕστηκα perf. ind. act. ἵστημι (# 2705) perf. to stand. κρινόμενος pres. pass. part. (circum.) κρίνω (# 3212) to judge. ◆ 7 δωδεκάφυλον (# 1559) twelve tribes. It indicates that Israel saw itself as composed of twelve tribes (Polhill). ἐκτενείᾳ (# 1755) dat. sing. fervor, unfailing intensity (TLNT; TDNT). Used in the papyri w. the meaning "effort" (MM). Used w. prep. ἐν (# 1877) adverbially, "earnestly," "intently." νύκτα καὶ ἡμέραν (# 3816; 2779; 2465) night and day; acc. sing. Acc. of time. λατρεῦον pres. act. part. (circum.) λατρεύω (# 3302) to worship, to serve, to perform religious rites as a part of worship (LN, 1:533). Pres. indicates a continual and habitual action. ἐλπίζει pres. ind. act. ἐλπίζω (# 1827) to hope. Pres. indicates the continual attitude. καταντῆσαι aor. act. inf. καταντάω (# 2918) to go down, to arrive, to attain. Used in the papyri as a t.t for the inheritance that comes to an heir (BAGD; MM; TLNT; TDNT; NIDNTT, 1:324-25). Inf. as obj. of the vb. ἐγκαλοῦμαι pres. ind. pass. s.v. 2. ◆ 8 ἄπιστος (# 603) unbelievable, incredible. Double acc. after a vb. of considering (BD, 85-87; RG, 479-84). κρίνεται pres. ind. pass. κρίνω s.v. 6. εἰ (# 1623) if, that. Introduces a 1st. class cond. assuming the reality of the cond. (RWP); or it is the same as ὅτι ("that") (BG, 138). ἐγείρει pres. ind. act. ἐγείρω (# 1586) to raise. ◆ 9 ἐγὼ μὲν οὖν (# 2670; 3525; 4036) I then. In-

troduces a reference to his past way of life (Schneider; s.v. 4). ἔδοξα aor. ind. act. δοκέω (# 1506) to seem, to think, w. inf. ἐμαυτῷ (# 1831) myself. The use of the refl. pron. strengthens the subject of the sentence (Haenchen; MT, 42). δεῖν pres. act. inf. δεῖ (# 1256) impersonal w. inf, it is necessary. Inf. in indir. discourse. That Paul considered his persecuting zeal within God's will is perhaps implied by his use of the divine "must" (Polhill). ἐναντίος (# 1885) in opposition to. πρᾶξαι aor. act. inf. πράσσω (# 4556) to do. ◆ 10 ἐποίησα aor. ind. act. ποιέω (# 4472) to do. Aor. sums up his activity. κατέκλεισα aor. ind. act. κατακλείω (# 2881) to shut up, to shut down like a trap door (RWP). λαβών aor. act. part. (circum.) λαμβάνω (# 3284) to receive. ἀναιρουμένων pres. pass. part. (temp.) ἀναιρέω (# 359) to kill. Gen. abs. κατήνεγκα aor. ind. act. καταφέρω (# 2965) to bring down, to cast down. Used w. the following word "to cast down my pebble (ψῆφος)" (a black one). The ancient Greeks used white pebbles for acquittal, black ones for condemnation (RWP; BAGD; EDNT; LS; DGRA, 971). For Paul as persecutor s. Légasse, BAFCS, 4:379-89; PVT, 34-40. ◆ 11 κατὰ πάσας τὰς συναγωγάς from synagogue to synagogue. Distributive used of the prep. For synagogues in Jerusalem and Palestine s. Rainer Riesner, "Synagogues in Jerusalem," BAFCS, 4:179-211. τιμωρῶν pres. act. part. (temp.) τιμωρέω (# 5512) to punish, w. the implication of causing people to suffer what they deserve (LN, 1:490). The synagogue punishment of scourging is probably intended (Haenchen). The noun is used in the papyri w. the possible idea of capital punishment (NDIEC, 1:47-49). "As I punished them." Pres. indicates the repeated action. ἠνάγκαζον impf. ind. act. ἀναγκάζω (# 337) to force, to compel, w. inf. Conative impf., "I tried to compel them." He does not say that he succeeded in making them blaspheme (Bruce). περισσῶς (# 4360) exceedingly, beyond measure, extremely. ἐμμαινόμενος pres. mid. (dep.) part. ἐμμαίνομαι (# 1841) to be enraged, to be so furiously angry w. someone as to be almost out of one's mind, to be insanely angry, to be furiously enraged (LN, 1:762; BAGD). Circum. or causal part. ἐδίωκον impf. ind. act. διώκω (# 1503) to hunt, to pursue, to persecute. Impf. indicates the repeated action. ◆ 12 ἐν οἷς in which things, under these circumstances (Bruce). πορευόμενος pres. mid. (dep.) part. (temp.) πορεύομαι (# 4513) to go, to travel. ἐπιτροπῆς (# 2207) gen. sing. permission; "w. the order, commission." Paul was a commissary (Bengel). τῆς art. used as a rel. pron. ἀρχιερέων gen. pl. ἀρχιερύς (# 797) high priest. Gen. of source, "from the chief priests." ◆ 13 ἡμέρας μέσης (# 2465; 3545) midday. Gen. of time. κατὰ τὴν ὁδόν along the way. εἶδον aor. ind. act. ὁράω (# 3972) to see. βασιλεῦ voc. sing. βασιλεύς (# 995), O king! οὐρανόθεν (# 4040) from heaven. ὑπὲρ τὴν λαμπρότητα brighter. Prep. used in a comp. **τοῦ ἡλίου** (# *2463*) than the sun. Gen. of comp. Perhaps the light was the Shekinah presence of the risen Christ (TS, 37-65). **περιλάμψαν** aor. act. part. (adj.) περιλάμπω (# *4334*) to shine around. **πορευομένους** pres. mid. (dep.) part. s.v. 12. Adj. part. as subst. ◆ **14 καταπεσόντων** aor. act. part. καταπίπτω (# *2928*) to fall down. A common reaction to revelation. Gen. abs. **ἤκουσα** aor. ind. act. ἀκούω (# *201*) to hear, w. acc. **λέγουσαν** pres. act. part. (adj.) λέγω (# *3306*) to speak. The voice was directed to Paul. **τῇ Ἑβραΐδι διαλέκτῳ** (# *1579; 1365*) in the Hebrew language. Dat. of means. **διώκεις** pres. ind. act. s.v. 11. **σκληρός** (# *5017*) difficult. **σοι** for you. **κέντρα** acc. pl. κέντρον (# *3034*) goad. A sharp-pointed stick used to prod an ox at the plow (LC). **λακτίζειν** pres. act. inf. λακτίζω (# *3280*) to kick. Epex. inf., explaining what was difficult. Pres. indicates a repeated action. Perhaps this was a common proverb of the time (Polhill). ◆ **15 εἶπα** aor. ind. act. s.v. 14. **ἐγώ ... σύ** I ... you! The personal prons. are emphatic. The emphasis of this account is on Paul's commissioning (Charles W. Hedrick, "Paul's Conversion/Call: A Comparative Analysis of the Three Reports in Acts," *JBL* 100 [1981]: 415-32). ◆ **16 ἀνάστηθι** aor. imp. act. ἀνίστημι (# *482*) to rise up, to arise. Aor. imp. calls for a specific act. **στῆθι** aor. imp. act. ἵστημι (# *2705*) to stand. **ὤφθην** aor. ind. pass. ὁράω (# *3972*) to see; pass. to appear to, w. dat. **προχειρίσασθαι** aor. mid. (dep.) inf. προχειρίζομαι (# *4741*) to determine, to appoint (s. 22:14). Epex. inf. explaining **τοῦτο**. **ὑπηρέτης** (# *5677*) servant, helper, assistant (BAGD; TLNT). It was used of a doctor's assistant (MLL, 88). **εἶδες** aor. ind. act. s.v. 13. **ὀφθήσομαι** fut. ind. pass. ὁράω. ◆ **17 ἐξαιρούμενος** pres. mid. (indir. mid., "for oneself") part. (circum.) ἐξαιρέω (# *1975*) to rescue, to take out, to choose. **ἀποστέλλω** (# *690*) pres. ind. act. to send or commission as an authoritative representative (TDNT; EDNT; TLNT). Instantaneous pres. indicating an action done at the moment of speaking (VANT, 202-3). ◆ **18 ἀνοῖξαι** aor. act. inf. ἀνοίγω (# *487*) to open. Inf. of purp., or epex. inf. explaining the commission. **ἐπιστρέψαι** aor. act. inf. ἐπιστρέφω (# *2188*) to turn. Inf. of purp., but subordinate to and explanatory of the previous inf. (EGT). **λαβεῖν** aor. act. inf. λαμβάνω (# *3284*) to take, to receive. Again, subordinate to the previous inf., expressing the final result aimed at (EGT). **ἄφεσις** (# *912*) settlement, forgiveness, release (TDNT; TLNT). **κλῆρος** (# *3102*) share, part, portion, inheritance. **ἡγιασμένοις** perf. pass. part. ἁγιάζω (# *39*) to sanctify. Adj. part. as subst. Perf. emphasizes the state or condition. **πίστει** dat. sing. πίστις (# *4411*) faith. Instr. dat., "through/by faith." **τῇ** which. Art. as rel. pron. ◆ **19 ὅθεν** (# *3854*) therefore. This rel. adv. gathers up all that Paul had said (RWP). **βασιλεῦ** voc. sing. s.v. 13. **ἐγενόμην** aor. ind. mid. (dep.) s.v. 4. Aor. summarizes Paul's life after this to the present. **ἀπειθής**

(# *579*) disobedient, w. dat. **ὀπτασίᾳ** (# *3965*) dat. sing. vision. ◆ **20 χώραν** acc. sing. χώρα (# *6001*) district, place, region. Acc. of extent of space (RG, 469; for the text problem s. TC, 495-96). **ἀπήγγελλον** impf. ind. act. ἀπαγγέλλω (# *550*) to proclaim. Impf. pictures the repeated action of proclamation in the various locations mentioned. **μετανοεῖν** pres. act. inf. μετανοέω (# *3566*) to change one's thinking, to repent. Inf. in indir. discourse giving the content of the proclamation. **ἐπιστρέφειν** pres. act. inf. ἐπιστρέφω (# *2188*) to turn to. Inf. in indir. discourse. **πράσσοντας** pres. act. part. (circum.) πράσσω (# *4556*) to do, to practice. ◆ **21 ἕνεκα** (# *1915*) because of, on account of, w. gen. **συλλαβόμενοι** aor. mid. (dep.) part. (temp.) συλλαμβάνω (# *5197*) to seize. **ὄντα** pres. act. part. (temp.) εἰμί (# *1639*) to be. Action contemporary w. the part. **συλλαβόμενοι**: "while I was in the temple." **ἐπειρῶντο** impf. ind. mid. (dep.) πειράομαι (# *4281*) to try, to attempt, w. inf. Conative impf. emphasizing the unsuccessful attempt. **διαχειρίσασθαι** aor. mid. (dep.) inf. διαχειρίζομαι (# *1429*) to take in hand, to lay hands on, to kill. ◆ **22 ἐπικουρία** (# *2135*) aid, help, w. the possible implication of assistance provided by an ally (LN, 1:459; MM; BBKA; NDIEC, 3:67-68). **τυχών** aor. act. part. (causal) τυγχάνω (# *5593*) to obtain, w. gen. **τῆς** (# *3836*) def. art. as rel. pron. ("which"). **ἕστηκα** perf. ind. act. ἵστημι (# *2705*) to stand. It emphasizes Paul's stability and fidelity (RWP). **μαρτυρόμενος** pres. mid. (dep.) part. (circum.) μαρτύρομαι (# *3458*) to witness, to testify. **ἐκτός** (# *1760*) except. Prep. w. gen. **λέγων** pres. act. part. (circum.) λέγω (# *3306*) to say, to speak. **ἐλάλησαν** aor. ind. act. λαλέω (# *3281*) to speak. **μελλόντων** pres. act. part. (adj.) μέλλω (# *3516*) to be about to, w. inf. to express the immediate fut. **γίνεσθαι** pres. mid. (dep.) inf. s.v. 4. The demonstration from Scripture that the Messiah must suffer and arise from the dead is a familiar pattern in Acts (Polhill). ◆ **23 εἰ** (# *1623*) if, that, whether (s.v. 8; RWP; Haenchen). It gives the content of the OT message. **παθητός** (# *4078*) suffer, subject to suffering, capable of suffering (BD, 36; RG, 157). **μέλλει** pres. ind. act. s.v. 22. **καταγγέλλειν** pres. act. inf. καταγγέλλω (# *2859*) to proclaim. Inf. w. **μέλλει** to express fut. ◆ **24 ἀπολογουμένου** pres. mid. (dep.) part. (temp.) s.v. 1. Gen. abs. **φωνῇ** dat. sing. φωνή (# *5889*) voice. Instr. dat. **φησιν** pres. ind. act. φημί s.v. 1. Hist. pres. **μαίνῃ** pres. ind. mid. (dep.) 2nd. pers. sing. μαίνομαι (# *3419*) to be mad, to be out of one's mind, to be insane. Those people are called crazy whose words or actions fly in the face of common sense, whose reasoning or conduct is not understood, who do not observe propriety and decorum (TLNT, 2:430; TDNT; MM; LN, 1:353; NIDNTT, 1:528-29; for the medical metaphor in Josephus s. MHW, 145-48; for references in Dio Chrysostom s. DCNT, 132-34). **Παῦλε** voc. sing. Παῦλος (# *4263*) Paul. **γράμμα** (# *1207*) the body of information acquired in school or from the study of writing, learning, education, elementary knowledge and higher learning (LN, 1:328; BAGD; MM). **μανίαν** (# *3444*) acc. sing. insane, crazy, mad. **περιτρέπει** pres. ind. act. περιτρέπω (# *4365*) to turn, to turn around, to turn from one state to (εἰς) its opposite (BAGD). Pres. indicates the process as taking place. ◆ **25 κράτιστε** voc. sing. κράτιστος (# *3196*) most excellent. (s. 24:3). **ἀληθείας** gen. sing. ἀλήθεια (# *2317*) truth. Gen. of description, without the art. indicating the character. **σωφροσύνη** (# *5408*) sobriety, soundness of mind, rational, good sense, sensible, the opposite of madness. It indicates the condition of an entire command over the passion and desires (Trench, *Synonyms*, 69f; TLNT; TDNT; GPT, 179-80; BAGD; LN, 1:384; EDNT; NIDNTT, 501-2). Paul says he is speaking words which are understandable and capable of being proven, which do not have to do w. ecstasy (TDNT). **ἀποφθέγγομαι** (# *710*) pres. ind. mid. (dep.) to speak. Pres. indicates the action in progress. ◆ **26 ἐπίσταται** pres. ind. pass. (dep.) ἐπίσταμαι (# *2179*) to know, to understand, to be acquainted w., to possess information about, w. the implication of understanding the significance of such information (BAGD; LN, 1:335). **παρρησιαζόμενος** pres. mid. (dep.) part. (circum.) παρρησιάζομαι (# *4245*) to speak openly, to speak boldly, to speak freely. **λαλῶ** pres. ind. act. s.v. 22. **λανθάνειν** pres. act. inf. λανθάνω (# *3291*) to be hidden, to escape notice. Pres. indicates that Paul regards the whole course of events as still unfinished, w. Agrippa watching it (LC). Inf. in indir. discourse after the vb. πείθομαι. **γωνία** (# *1224*) corner. **πεπραγμένον** perf. pass. part. πράσσω, s.v. 9. Part. in a periphrastic construction. Perf. indicates the abiding result. The expression "not in a corner" occurs often in Greek philosophical writings where the philosophers are accused of withdrawing into their ivory towers and avoiding the people in the markets and streets (Polhill). ◆ **27 πιστεύεις** pres. ind. act. πιστεύω (# *4409*) to believe, w. dat., to give assent to. Ind. used in a question. **οἶδα** (# *3857*) perf. ind. act. to know. Def. perf. w. pres. meaning. ◆ **28 ἐν ὀλίγῳ** in a short time, rapidly (LC). **πείθεις** pres. ind. act. 2nd. pers. sing. πείθω (# *4275*) to persuade. Conative pres., "you are trying to...." **Χριστιανός** (# *5985*) Christian (s. 11:26). Double acc., "to make me a Christian." **ποιῆσαι** aor. act. inf. ποιέω (# *4472*) to make, to do, "in short, you are trying to persuade me to act the Christian" (Bruce). ◆ **29 εὐξαίμην** aor. opt. mid. (dep.) εὔχομαι (# *2377*) to wish, to pray. Potential opt. used in the conclusion of an unexpressed 4th. class cond. cl. expressing what would happen on the fulfillment of some supposed condition (MT, 121f; RG, 1021; VA, 172-74). **καὶ ... καί** (# *2779*) both ... and. The phrase here may mean "w. few or many words" (Williams) or "concerning both small and great" (BD, 41). **ἀκούοντας** pres. act. part. s.v. 3.

Obj. in gen. Adj. part. as subst. **γενέσθαι** aor. mid. (dep.) inf. s.v. 4. Inf. as obj. of the vb. εὐξαίμην. **παρεκτός** (# *4211*) except. For the chains of a prisoner s. BAFCS, 3:206-9. ◆ **30 ἀνέστη** aor. ind. act. ἀνίστημι (# *482*) to stand up. **συγκαθήμενοι** pres. mid. (dep.) part. συγκάθημαι (# *5153*) to sit together, to sit w. Adj. part. as subst. ◆ **31 ἀναχωρήσαντες** aor. act. part. (temp.) ἀναχωρέω (# *432*) to retire, to depart. **ἐλάλουν** impf. ind. act. s.v. 22. Impf. continues the action and describes the eager conversation of the dignitaries about Paul's wonderful speech (RWP). **ἄξιος** (# *545*) worthy, w. gen. **πράσσει** pres. ind. act. s.v. 9. Customary pres., referring to his customary conduct, not just his behavior at the hearing (VANT, 208). ◆ **32 ἔφη** impf./aor. ind. act. s.v. 1. **ἀπολελύσθαι** perf. pass. inf. ἀπολύω (# *668*) to release, to free. **ἐδύνατο** impf. ind. pass. (dep.) δύναμαι (# *1538*) to be able, w. inf. Impf. in the conclusion of a 2nd. class cond. cl., where the condition is contrary to fact (RG, 1014) or gives an assertion for the sake of argument (VA, 294-96). **ἐπεκέκλητο** plperf. ind. mid. (dep.) ἐπικαλέω (# *2126*) to appeal, to call upon. Plperf. expresses more than the aor. would have; Paul's appeal to Caesar was not a mere act in the past, but had put him in a definite position in the eyes of the law (Bruce).

Acts 27

◆ **1 ἐκρίθη** aor. ind. pass. κρίνω (# *3212*) to judge, to decide, to determine. **ἀποπλεῖν** pres. act. inf. ἀποπλέω (# *676*) to sail out, to sail. Articular inf. w. κρίνω probably translates the Heb. inf. abs. (RWP; RG, 1067). **ἡμᾶς** we; acc. pl. ἐγώ (# *1609*). Acc. as subject of the inf. S. Colin J. Hemer, "First Person Narration in Acts 27-28," *TB* 36 (1985): 75-109. **παρεδίδουν** impf. ind. act. παραδίδωμι (# *4140*) to deliver over. **δεσμώτης** (# *1304*) prisoner. Prisoners were kept below deck, or were allowed to camp on deck in the open or under tiny temporary shelters (BAFCS, 3:295), but they were expected to pay for their own food (BAFCS, 3:224). **ἑκατοντάρχης** (# *1672*) centurion. **σπείρης** gen. sing. σπεῖρα (# *5061*) cohort. Descriptive gen., "belonging to the cohort." **Σεβαστός** (# *4935*) worthy of reverence, Augusta, emperor. An honorary title frequently given to auxiliary troops (BAGD; BC, 5:443f; HJP 1:364). For references to this cohort s. BASHH, 132-33; NDIEC, 6:159-60. For sea travel s. Brian M. Rapske, "Acts, Travel and Shipwreck," BAFCS, 2:22-46; FAP, 280-82; VSSP. ◆ **2 ἐπιβάντες** aor. act. part. (temp.) ἐπιβαίνω (# *2094*) to embark, to go aboard, w. dat. **Ἀδραμυττηνός** Adramyttium, a city located along the NW coast of the Roman province of Asia. The ship was probably a small privately-owned trading vessel (*oraria navis*), not a government ship, and was homeward bound from Caesarea; it would be natural for Julius to find a ship bound for Rome in one of the Lycian ports (ABD, 1:80; BASHH, 133; BAFCS, 3:375). μέλλοντι pres. act. part. (adj.) μέλλω (# 3516) to be about to, w. inf. to express the immediate fut. πλεῖν pres. act. inf. πλέω (# 4434) to sail. ἀνήχθημεν aor. ind. pass. ἀνάγω (# 343) to put out to sea. ὄντος pres. act. part. εἰμί (# 1639) to be. Gen. abs. Aristarchus, a Macedonian of Thessalonica, is called a fellow prisoner by Paul in his letter to the Colossians (VSSP, 64; s. 19:29; 20:4; Col. 4:10). ◆ 3 τῇ τε ἑτέρᾳ (# 5445; 2283) and on another (the next) (day). Dat. of time. κατήχθημεν aor. ind. pass. κατάγω (# 2864) to lead down; pass., used of ships and seafarers, to put in at a harbor (BAGD). From Caesarea to Sidon was approximately 67 miles, so they must have had a fair or at least a leading wind, probably westerly (VSSP, 64). The stop was probably to load or unload cargo (Polhill; VSSP, 64). φιλανθρώπως (# 5793) adv. humanely, kindly. χρησάμενος aor. mid. (dep.) part. χράομαι (# 5968) to use, to deal w., to show to, to conduct oneself in a particular manner w. regards to some person, w. dat.(LN, 1:505). Causal or circum. part. ἐπέτρεψεν aor. ind. act. ἐπιτρέπω (# 2225) to allow, w. inf. πορευθέντι aor. pass. (dep.) part. dat. sing. πορεύομαι (# 4513) to go. Adj. part. as instr. dat. ("by coming to his friends"), or circum. part. Paul was permitted to see his friends, but probably under the watchful eye of a soldier (BAFCS, 3:270). ἐπιμέλεια (# 2149) attention, care. Although the word appears in medical writers for the care and attention for the sick (MLL, 269-70), it had a wider range of usages, including providing the material assistance for sustaining life (TLNT; BAFCS, 3:223-24). Here it may indicate that Paul obtained from them the things necessary for the voyage (Alford). τυχεῖν aor. act. inf. τυγχάνω (# 5593) to obtain, to receive, w. gen. Inf. w. vb. ◆ 4 κἀκεῖθεν (# 2796) and from there. ἀναχθέντες aor. pass. part. s.v. 2. ὑπεπλεύσαμεν aor. ind. act. ὑποπλέω (# 5709) to sail by the side of an island in such a way that the island protects the ship from the wind (BAGD). ἀνέμους acc. pl. ἄνεμος (# 449) wind. The prevailing wind through the summer months was west or northwest so the ship sailed east and north of the island (Bruce; for the various winds s. BC, 5:338-44; Colin J. Hemer, "Euraquilo and Melita," JTS 26 [1975]: 100-111; SSAW, 270-73; Pliny, NH, 2:117-31). εἶναι pres. act. inf. εἰμί s.v. 2. Inf. w. prep. διά (# 1328) to express cause. ἐναντίος (# 1885) contrary, against. ◆ 5 πέλαγος (# 4283) open sea. διαπλεύσαντες aor. act. part. (temp.) διαπλέω (# 1386) to sail across. κατήλθομεν aor. ind. act. κατέρχομαι (# 2982) to come down. Μύρα Myra. This was a principal port for the Alexandrian grain-ships, and was precisely the place where Julius would expect to find a ship sailing to Italy in the imperial service (BASHH, 134; SSAW, 297). The Western text says that it took 15 days (δι' ἡμερῶν δεκαπέντε) (TC, 497; BC, 3:241), which

is a fair estimate (Marshall). ◆ 6 κἀκεῖ (# 2795) and there. εὑρών aor. act. part. εὑρίσκω (# 2351) to find. πλοῖον (# 4450) acc. sing. ship. For ancient ships like this one s. VSSP, 181-244; B.M. Rapske, "Acts, Travel and Shipwreck," BAFCS, 2:29-35; N. Hirschfeld, "Part I: The Ship of Saint Paul – Historical Background;" M. A. Fitzgerald, "Part II: The Ship of Saint Paul–Comparative Archaeology," BA 53 [1990]; Elisha Linder, "Excavating an Ancient Merchantman," BAR 18 [1992]: 24-35; SSAW, 157-200). πλέον pres. act. part. (adj.) acc. n. sing. s.v. 2. ἐνεβίβασεν aor. ind. act. ἐμβιβάζω (# 1837) to cause to enter, to put on board. The ship they got on seems to have been a grain ship. Egypt was the chief granary of Rome and the grain trade between Rome and Egypt was of the greatest importance (Bruce; for the important grain traffic s. Rapske, "Acts, Travel and Shipwreck," BAFCS, 2:25-29; NDIEC, 7:112-29; BBC). ◆ 7 ἱκανός (# 2653) many. βραδυπλοοῦντες pres. act. part. (temp.) βραδυπλοέω (# 1095) to sail slowly. μόλις (# 3660) w. difficulty. γενόμενοι aor. mid. (dep.) part. γίνομαι (# 1181) to be, to become. Temp. or circum. part. The words express the delays which a ship experiences in working windward (VSSP, 75). κατὰ τὴν Κνίδον (# 2848; 3118) down along Cnidius. Cndius was a seaport on the western tip of a peninsula jutting into the Mediterranean between the islands of Cos and Rhodes (ABD, 1:1066-67). προσεῶντος pres. act. part. (causal) προσεάω (# 4661) to permit to go farther. Gen. abs. With northwest winds and a westerly current, the ship was able to slowly make its way from Myra to Cndius; when unfavorable wind did not allow them to continue sailing westward, they had to turn south and sail under Crete in the direction of Salmone (Strabo, Geography, 3:17; BASHH, 135-36; VSSP, 76-77). ὑπεπλεύσαμεν aor. ind. act. s.v. 4. ◆ 8 παραλεγόμενοι pres. mid. (dep.) part. (circum.) παραλέγομαι (# 4162) a nautical t.t., to sail past, to coast along (BAGD). This was doubtless by hugging the shore and using every breach of land breeze that they managed to creep slowly along (LC). ἤλθομεν aor. ind. act. ἔρχομαι (# 2262) to come. καλούμενον pres. pass. part. (adj.) καλέω (# 2813) to call; pass; to be named. Λιμένας acc. pl. λιμήν (# 3348) harbor, port; here, "Fair Havens." The farthest point which an ancient ship, navigating under the lee of Crete, could reach w. northwest winds. It was a small bay protected by islands, but was not a very good winter harbor (VSSP, 81-84; Bruce; BASHH, 136; ABD, 2:744). ◆ 9 διαγενομένου aor. mid. (dep.) part. (temp.) διαγίνομαι (# 1335) to come in between, to intervene, to pass. Gen. abs. ὄντος pres. act. part. (causal) εἰμί s.v. 2. Gen. abs. ἐπισφαλής (# 2195) dangerous. πλοῦς (# 4453) voyage, navigation. The period from May 27 to September 14 was safe for sea travel; from March 10 to May 26 and from September 14 to November 11, when weather and sea conditions were quite changeable, it was considered risky. The period from November 11 to March 10 was extremely dangerous. The danger was not only storms, but also the reduced visibility of the sun and stars (which was essential for navigation) caused by persistent cloud cover in these months (Rapske, "Acts, Travel and Shipwreck," BAFCS, 2:24; Williams; NDIEC, 4:115-16). **καί** (# 2779) even. **νηστεία** (# 3763) fast. The Fast was the Day of Atonement. In A.D. 59 the Fast was on October 5th and Luke indicates travel was more dangerous than ever (Bruce; LC). This was probably just before the Feast of Tabernacles (5 days after the Fast), which the Jews considered to be the beginning of the dangerous time for sea travel (SB, 2:771-72; BASHH, 137-38). **παρεληλυθέναι** perf. act. inf. παρέρχομαι (# 4216) to pass by. Inf. w. **διά** (# 1328) to express cause. **παρῄνει** impf. ind. act. παραινέω to warn, to offer advice, to indicate strongly to someone what he should plan to do, to advise strongly, to urge (LN, 1:422). Impf. pictures the repeated action. ◆ **10** **λέγων** pres. act. part. λέγω (# 3306) to say. Part. introduces the content of the advice. **ἄνδρες** voc. pl. ἀνήρ (# 467) man. **θεωρῶ** pres. ind. act. θεωρέω (# 2555) to see, to perceive, to come to understand as a result of perception (LN, 1:381). **ὕβρις** (# 5615) injury, disaster, damage caused by the elements (BAGD; TDNT). The word could be used of a loss at sea (Williams). For shipping contracts limiting liability in the case of loss by an act of God s. NDIEC, 6:83-86. **ζημία** (# 2422) loss. **φορτίου** (# 5845) gen. sing. freight, cargo. Obj. gen. "loss of cargo." **καί** (# 2779) also. **μέλλειν** pres. act. inf. μέλλω (# 3516) to be about to; w. inf to express immediate fut. Inf. in indir. discourse after the vb. θεωρῶ. **ἔσεσθαι** fut. mid. (dep.) inf. εἰμί s.v. 2. "The voyage is going to be..." (VA, 489; MKG, 308). ◆ **11** **κυβερνήτῃ** dat. sing. κυβερνήτης (# 3237) pilot, a professional navigator, the officer responsible for its safe navigation and for the discipline of the crew (LC; TLNT, 2:543; SSAW, 300-302, 316). Dat. as obj. of the vb. **ναύκληρος** (# 3729) captain, owner, one leasing a ship, transport official; here, he could have been a merchant ship owner, who usually acted as captain of his own ship, or one who is chartering to transport grain for Rome (Bruce; PTR, 324f; TLNT; BASHH, 138-39; NDIEC, 4:116-17; SSAW, 314-21). **ἐπείθετο** impf. ind. mid. (dep.) πείθω (# 4275) to yield, to persuade; mid. to be persuaded, to obey, w. dat. **μᾶλλον ... ἤ** (# 3437; 2445) rather than. **λεγομένοις** pres. pass. part. s.v. 10. Adj. part. as subst.: "that which was spoken by Paul." ◆ **12** **ἀνεύθετος** (# 460) unsuitable. **ὑπάρχοντος** pres. act. part. (causal) ὑπάρχω (# 5639) to exist, to be. Gen. abs. **παραχειμασία** (# 4200) wintering. **πλείονες** comp. πολύς (# 4498) much; comp., the majority, most (BAGD, 689). **ἔθεντο** aor. ind. mid. (dep.) τίθημι (# 5502) to place, to put; here "to take counsel," "to give counsel." **ἀναχ-**

θῆναι aor. pass. inf. s.v. 2. Epex. inf. explaining the counsel. **δύναιντο** pres. opt. pass. (dep.) δύναμαι (# 1538) to be able to, w. inf. Opt. in a 4th class cond. cl. w. the idea of purp. implied (RWP; VA, 311-12). **καταντήσαντες** aor. act. part. καταντάω (# 2918) to come to, arrive. Part. of means ("by arriving"), or temp. ("after arriving"). **Φοῖνιξ** (# 5837) Phoenix. For the location of the harbor as being Phineka, on the coast of Crete a few miles farther west s. R. M. Ogilvie, "Phoenix," *JTS* n.s. 9 (1958): 308-14; BASHH, 139-40; Polhill; NDIEC, 4:115; Raspke, "Acts, Travel and Shipwreck," BAFCS, 2:37. **παραχειμάσαι** aor. act. inf. παραχειμάζω (# 4199) to spend the winter. **βλέποντα** pres. act. part. (adj.) βλέπω (# 1063) to see, to look. **κατὰ λίβα** (# 2848; 3355) southwest. **κατὰ χῶρον** (# 2848; 6008) northwest (BASHH, 139-40; Polhill). ◆ **13** **ὑποπνεύσαντος** aor. act. part. (temp.) ὑποπνέω (# 5710) to blow under, to blow softly, gently. Gen. abs. **νότος** (# 3803) south wind. **δόξαντες** aor. act. part. (circum.) δοκέω (# 1506) to suppose, to seem, to appear to, w. inf. **πρόθεσις** (# 4606) plan, purpose. **κεκρατηκέναι** perf. act. inf. κρατέω (# 3195) to seize, to obtain. The south wind was ideal for reaching Phoenix, enabling them to cling to the coast around Cape Matala, about 4 miles west, and then bear westnorthwest across the bay of Mesará, some 34 miles to Phoenix (BASHH, 141; VSSP, 97-98). **ἄραντες** aor. act. part. (circum.) αἴρω (# 149) to lift up, to take up, to weigh anchor. **ἆσσον** (# 839) comp. ἄγχι until; comp., nearer, closer (BAGD). **παρελέγοντο** impf. ind. mid. (dep.) s.v. 8. ◆ **14** **μετ᾽ οὐ πολύ** after not much time. **ἔβαλεν** aor. ind. act. βάλλω (# 965) to throw, to dash, to rush. Here in this context, "there rushed down from it (Crete)" (Bruce; for the use of the prep. w. gen. meaning "down from," s. RG, 606). **τυφωνικός** (# 5607) tempestuous. The word refers to the whirling motion of the clouds and sea caused by the meeting of opposite currents of air like a typhoon (Bruce; VSSP, 102-3). For adjs. w. this suffix meaning "pertaining to," "w. the characteristic of," s. MH, 378. Perhaps as the ship rounded Cape Matala a violent wind rushed down, striking the ship broadside (Polhill). **Εὐρακύλων** (# 2350) northeast wind, Euraquilo, "Northeaster," the deadly winter storm known by the sailors as the *gregale* (BASHH, 141-42; Colin J. Hemer, "Euraquilo and Melita," *JTS* 26 [1975]: 100-11; BC, 5:344; Polhill; Raspke, "Acts, Travel and Shipwreck," BAFCS, 2:38-39). ◆ **15** **συναρπασθέντος** aor. pass. part. (circum.) συναρπάζω (# 5275) to seize violently. It was as if the ship was seized by a great monster (RWP). Gen. abs. **δυναμένου** pres. mid./pass. (dep.) part. w. inf. s.v. 12. **ἀντοφθαλμεῖν** pres. act. inf. ἀντοφθαλμέω (# 535) to face into; lit. "facing the eye." Perhaps the origin of the phrase lay in the custom of putting an eye on each side of the bow of the ship (VSSP, 98; Williams). **ἐπιδόντες** aor. act. part. (circum.) ἐπιδίδωμι (# 2113) to give way to, w. dat. **ἐφερόμεθα** impf. ind. pass. φέρω (# 5770) to carry; here, "we were being carried," "we were being driven." Impf. pictures the continual action. ◆ **16 νησίον** (# 3761) little island. For the possibility that some nouns w. this ending do not have a dimin. meaning s. MH, 340ff. **ὑποδραμόντες** aor. act. part. ὑποτρέχω (# 5720) to run under (for protection against the wind). The sailors knew that their only hope was in the smooth waters behind Cauda; thus they kept the ship w. its head in the wind and let it drift w. the right side towards the wind (PTR, 328). **καλούμενον** pres. pass. part. s.v. 8. **Καῦδα** (# 3007) Cauda. A small island 23 miles south of Crete. As the ship passed by the island, it gave the crew time to make some preparations for the storm (ABD, 1:878; VSSP, 95-96). **ἰσχύσαμεν** aor. ind. act. ἰσχύω (# 2710) to have the strength to, to be able to, w. inf. μόλις s.v. 7. **περικρατής** (# 4331) having power, bringing in command. Used here w. the inf., "to get the boat under control" (BAGD). **γενέσθαι** aor. mid. inf. s.v. 7. **σκάφης** gen. sing. σκάφη (# 5002) dinghy, a small boat which was sometimes towed or sometimes kept on deck, used for landing or for pulling the ship's head around or for unloading cargo (LC; SSAW, 330; 335-36). The Latin t.t. was *scapha*. The difficulty of bringing in the boat was no doubt due to its being waterlogged (BASHH, 143). Gen. w. the adj., "control over." ◆ **17 ἄραντες** aor. act. part. (temp.) s.v. 13. **βοηθείαις** dat. pl. βοήθεια (# 1069) help; pl. helps, tackle. It means either ropes, sails, or perhaps the maneuvers dictated by the professional skill of the sailors (LC). Here it probably refers to the cables used to secure the ship (BASHH, 143). **ἐχρῶντο** impf. ind. mid. (dep.) χράομαι (# 5968) to use, w. dat. **ὑποζωννύντες** pres. act. part. ὑποζώννυμι (# 5690) to undergird, to brace. A nautical t.t. used of securing the ship. This could be done in a number of ways: (1) by placing exterior cables transversely around the bottom of the hull, called "frapping," probably the best solution; (2) by exterior cables longitudinally around the hull from bow to stern on either side; (3) transverse interior braces across the hold; (4) interior braces lengthwise across the hold (Henry J. Cadbury, "Ὑποζώματα," BC, 5:345-54; VSSP, 108-9; BASHH, 143; Polhill; SSAW, 91-92). Part. of purp. or explaining the use of the helps. One possible reason for securing the ship in this manner is that the wet grain could expand and split the ship (Raspke, "Acts, Travel and Shipwreck," BAFCS, 2:35). **φοβούμενοι** pres. mid. (dep.) part. (circum.) φοβέομαι (# 5828) to be afraid, to fear. μή (# 3590) lest, used after a vb. of fear expressing apprehension (BD, 188). **τὴν Σύρτιν** (# 5358) the Syrtis. This extensive zone of sandbars and quicksands of the coast of North Africa, some 400 miles south of Cauda, was notorious as a navigational hazard and often mentioned in first-century literature in this regards ("Syrtey, whose very name

strikes terror," Jos., *JW*, 2:381; BASHH, 144; Polhill; Pliny, *NH*, 5:26-28). **ἐκπέσωσιν** aor. subj. act. ἐκπίπτω (# 1738) nautical t.t., to drift off course, to run aground (BAGD; Schneider). Subj. after a vb. of fearing. **χαλάσαντες** aor. act. part. (circum.) χαλάω (# 5899) to lower, to let down. **σκεῦος** (# 5007) acc. sing. gear. The phrase "lowering the gear" could mean either lowering the sail, dropping the sea anchor, or lowering such gear as sail, rigging, anchors, cables, etc.; that is, removing all superfluous sail and rigging (Bruce; VSSP, 111-12; BASHH, 143). **ἐφέροντο** impf. ind. pass. s.v. 15. Impf. pictures the continual action. ◆ **18 σφοδρῶς** (# 5380) adv. very, exceedingly. **χειμαζομένων** pres. pass. part. χειμάζομαι (# 5928) to expose to bad weather, to toss in a storm. Gen. abs. **τῇ ἑξῆς** (# 2009) on the following (day). **ἐκβολή** (# 1678) throwing out, jettisoning. **ἐποιοῦντο** impf. ind. mid. (dep.) ποιέω (# 4472) to do, to make. w. the subst.; as a t.t. for throwing the cargo overboard in order to save the ship (LC; Schneider). Incep. impf., "they began to throw things overboard." ◆ **19 τῇ τρίτῃ** (# 5569) on the third (day) (dat. of time). **αὐτόχειρες** (# 901) with their own hands. This emphatic word marks a climax of precautionary operations (Bruce). **σκεύη** (# 5006) gear, presumably spare sails and tackle (LC; Bruce; Schneider). **ἔρριψαν** aor. ind. act. ῥίπτω (# 4849) to throw, to hurl. ◆ **20 ἥλιος** (# 2463) sun. **ἄστρων** (# 843) star. The sun and stars were used in navigation. **ἐπιφαινόντων** pres. act. part. ἐπιφαίνω (# 2210) to appear. Gen. abs., temp. or causal. **χειμών** (# 5930) storm. **ὀλίγου** (# 3900) little, small. Used in the sense of degree: οὐκ ὀλίγος "not a small," that is, "great," "severe" (BAGD). **ἐπικειμένου** pres. mid. (dep.) part. ἐπίκειμαι (# 2130) to lie upon. Used to describe the pressure of a violent tempest (T); gen. abs. **λοιπόν** (# 3370) finally. **περιῃρεῖτο** impf. ind. pass. περιαιρέω (# 4311) to take away, to remove. The force of the prep. compound could be local, but is perhaps better as intensive (MH, 321). Impf. implies that the situation was continually getting worse (Bruce). **σῴζεσθαι** pres. pass. inf. σῴζω (# 5392) to save, to rescue, to deliver. Epex. inf. explaining the hope. ◆ **21 ἀσιτία** (# 826) without food. They had no appetite. For the medical use of this word, s. MLL, 276; DMTG, 82. **ὑπαρχούσης** pres. act. part. (temp.) s.v. 12. Gen. abs. **σταθείς** aor. pass. part. (circum.) ἵστημι (# 2705) to put; aor. pass., to stand, to step up or to stand to say something or make a speech (BAGD). **εἶπεν** aor. ind. act. λέγω (# 3306) to say. **ἔδει** impf. ind. act. δεῖ (# 1256) it is necessary, w. inf. giving a logical necessity. Impf. gives a condition which should have been, but is not (Schneider). **πειθαρχήσαντας** aor. act. part. (circum.) πειθαρχέω (# 4272) to listen to, to obey, w. dat. **ἀνάγεσθαι** pres. pass. inf. s.v. 2. **κερδῆσαι** aor. act. inf. κερδαίνω (# 3045) to gain. The word may have the sense of "gain by avoiding what would be detrimental," or "to incur," "to obtain" (LC). ◆ **22 παραινῶ** pres. ind. act. s.v. 9. **εὐθυμεῖν** pres. act. inf. εὐθυμέω (# 2313) to be of good cheer, to reassure, to comfort, to regain composure. In medicine, it refers to the sick keeping up their spirits. The noun εὐθυμία means a good interior disposition, courageous good humor, an optimistic outlook that causes the heart to swell and preserves or favors the appearance of that internal equilibrium that constitutes good health (MLL, 270-80; TLNT; NDIEC, 1:132-33; MM). Inf. in indir. discourse (NSV, 81). **ἀποβολή** (# 613) loss. **γάρ** (# 1142) for, giving a causal explanation. **ἔσται** fut. mid. ind. εἰμί s.v. 2. **πλήν** (# 1142) except (s. Luke 22:21). ◆ **23 παρέστη** aor. ind. act. παρίστημι (# 4225) to stand beside, to appear before. **νυκτί** dat. sing. νύξ night. Dat. of time. **θεοῦ** gen. sing. θεός (# 2536) God. Emphatic by its position. Gen. of possession or gen. of source: "a messenger (angel) from the God of...." **οὗ** gen. sing. rel. pron. ὅς (# 4005) Gen. of possession, "whose I am," "to whom I belong." **ᾧ** dat. sing. rel. pron. ὅς. Dat. as obj. of the vb. **λατρεύω** (# 3302) pres. ind. act. to worship, to serve, w. dat. Pres. indicates the continual, habitual service. ◆ **24 φοβοῦ** pres. imp. mid. (dep.) s.v. 17. Pres. imp. used w. neg. μή (# 3590) to stop an action in progress. **Παῦλε** voc. sing. Παῦλος (# 4263). **Καῖσαρ** (# 2790) Caesar. **σε** acc. sing. personal pron. σύ (# 5248) Acc. as subject of the inf. **δεῖ** pres. ind. act., w. inf. s.v. 21. It speaks of the divine necessity (s. C.H. Cogsgrove, "The Divine ΔΕΙ in Luke-Acts," *Nov T* 26 [1984]: 178). **παραστῆναι** aor. act. inf. s.v. 23. **κεχάρισται** perf. ind. mid. (dep.) χαρίζομαι (# 5919) to give, to grant, to graciously give. "God has given as a present...." (Bruce). Perf. emphasizes the lasting effects of God's giving. ◆ **25 εὐθυμεῖτε** pres. imp. act. s.v. 22. Pres. imp. calls for a continual attitude. **καθ' ὃν τρόπον** according to the manner, in the same way as (BAGD). **λελάληται** perf. ind. pass. λαλέω (# 3281) to speak. Perf. emphasizes the abiding result of what was spoken. ◆ **26 ἐκπεσεῖν** aor. act. inf. s.v. 17. Inf. w. δεῖ expressing necessity. ◆ **27 τεσσαρεσκαιδεκάτη** (# 5476) fourteen. The time is probably reckoned from Cauda to Malta, some 475 miles (VSSP, 126-27; BASHH, 145). **ἐγένετο** aor. ind. mid. (dep.) s.v. 7. **διαφερομένων** pres. pass. part. διαφέρω (# 1422) to carry through, to drive about. The idea here is "drifting across" (LC). Gen. abs. **Ἀδρίας** (# 102) Adria. Not the modern Adriatic Sea, but according to the ancient writers it referred to the sea between Crete and Malta, that is, the Ionaian Sea and the north-central Mediterranean between Greece and Italy (BASHH, 145-46; Polhill). **κατὰ μέσον τῆς νυκτός** "along about the middle of the night." **ὑπενόουν** impf. ind. act. ὑπονοέω (# 5706) to think, to suspect. The prep. compound conveys the idea of thoughts making their way up into the mind (MH, 327). Incep. impf., "they began to suppose." **προσάγειν** pres. act. inf. προάγω (# 4642) to come

near, to approach. They began to suspect that land was near (approaching) them (BAGD). Inf. in indir. discourse. ◆ **28 βολίσαντες** aor. act. part. βολίζω (# 1075) to throw down the lead into the sea, to take soundings (RWP). A sounding lead was hollow on the underside, which was filled w. tallow or grease to bring up samples of the sea bottom (BASHH, 147; SSAW, 246). **εὗρον** aor. ind. act. εὑρίσκω (# 2351) to find. **ὀργυιά** (# 3976) fathom, about six feet; as a nautical t.t. used to measure the depth of water (BAGD). **εἴκοσι** (# 1633) twenty. The depth would have been about 120 feet. **βραχύ** (# 1099) little, short. **διαστήσαντες** aor. act. part. (temp.) διΐστημι (# 1460) to go away, to pass; here, either after a short interval, perhaps about half an hour (Bruce; VSSP, 131), or after they had sailed a short distance farther (BAGD). **δεκαπέντε** (# 1278) fifteen. This would have been a depth of about 90 feet. ◆ **29 φοβούμενοι** pres. mid. (dep.) part. (causal) s.v. 17. **μή** lest (s.v. 17). **τραχύς** (# 5550) rough, rocky. **ἐκπέσωμεν** aor. subj. act., s.v. 17. **πρύμνα** (# 4744) stern. **ῥίψαντες** aor. act. part. (circum.) s.v. 19. **ἄγκυρα** (# 46) anchor. Cast from the stern, the anchors were to act as a brake keeping the prow of the ship pointing to the shore (Bruce; for ancient anchors s. N. Hirschfeld, "The Ship of St. Paul–Pt 1," *BA* 53 [1990]: 25-30; SSAW, 250-58). **ηὔχοντο** impf. ind. mid. (dep.) εὔχομαι (# 2377) to pray, to wish for. Impf. pictures the continual action. **γενέσθαι** aor. mid. (dep.) inf. s.v. 7. Inf. in indir. discourse giving the content of their prayers. ◆ **30 ζητούντων** pres. act. part. (temp.) ζητέω (# 2426) to seek, to attempt to, w. inf. Gen. abs. **φυγεῖν** aor. act. inf. φεύγω (# 5771) to flee. **χαλασάντων** aor. act. part. (temp.) s.v. 17. Gen. abs. s.v. 16. **προφάσει** dat. sing. πρόφασις (# 4733) pretext, pretense. Instr. dat. **πρῷρα** (# 4749) bow, prow. **μελλόντων** pres. act. part. s.v. 2, w. inf. to express immediate fut. **ἐκτείνειν** pres. act. inf. ἐκτείνω (# 1753) to stretch out, to let out. ◆ **31 εἶπεν** aor. ind. act. s.v. 21. **μείνωσιν** aor. subj. act. μένω (# 3531) to remain. Subj. in a 3rd. class cond. cl. which assumes the possibility of the cond. **σωθῆναι** aor. pass. inf. s.v. 20. **δύνασθε** pres. ind. pass. s.v. 12. ◆ **32 ἀπέκοψαν** aor. ind. act. ἀποκόπτω (# 644) to cut off. **σχοινίον** (# 5389) rope. **εἴασαν** aor. ind. act. ἐάω (# 1572) to let, to allow, to permit, w. inf. **ἐκπεσεῖν** pres. act. inf. s.v. 17; here, to fall off. ◆ **33 ἄχρι οὗ** until; here, w. the impf., "until it was about to become day"; that is, "before daybreak" (Haenchen; BD, 193). **ἤμελλεν** impf. ind. act. s.v. 2. **γίνεσθαι** pres. mid. (dep.) inf. s.v. 7. **παρεκάλει** impf. ind. act. παρακαλέω (# 4151) to encourage, to exhort. Impf. pictures the repeated action. Vbs. of asking and commanding have the idea of an incomplete action in the past, since they await a fulfillment in a further action by another agent (MT, 164). **μεταλαβεῖν** aor. act. inf. μεταλαμβάνω (# 3561) to take, to partake of food, w. gen. **τεσσαρεσκαιδεκάτην** (# 5476) fourteenth. Acc. of duration of time (RWP). **προσ-**

δοκῶντες pres. act. part. προσδοκάω (# *4659*) to wait. Circum. or supplementary part. διατελεῖτε pres. ind. act. διατελέω (# *1412*) to accomplish, to continue. προσλαβόμενοι aor. mid. part. προσλαμβάνω (# *4689*) to take; mid. to take to oneself. Probably Paul means that they had taken no regular meals, only bits of food now and then (RWP). ◆ **34** πρός (# *4639*) w. gen., in the interest of (BD, 125). σωτηρία (# *5401*) deliverance. Paul's advice was meant to restore calm as well as to strengthen the crew for the tasks ahead (BASHH, 149). ὑπάρχει pres. ind. act. s.v. 12. θρίξ (# *2582*) hair. ἀπολεῖται fut. ind. mid. (dep.) ἀπόλλυμι (# *660*) to perish, to be lost. The expression is proverbial in the OT, meaning the saving of life (LC). ◆ **35** εἴπας aor. act. part. (temp.) s.v. 21. λαβών aor. act. part. λαμβάνω (# *3284*) to take. Circum. or temp. part. εὐχαρίστησεν aor. ind. act. εὐχαριστέω (# *2373*) to thank, to give thanks, w. dat. Giving thanks for one's food was a normal Jewish custom (Bruce). ἐνώπιον πάντων in the presence of all, before all. Paul was not ashamed to express his thanksgiving openly. κλάσας aor. act. part. (temp.) κλάω (# *3089*) to break. In a Jewish household the father broke the bread as a signal to begin the meal (BAGD). ἤρξατο aor. ind. mid. (dep.) ἄρχω (# *806*) to begin, w. inf. ἐσθίειν pres. act. inf. ἐσθίω (# *2266*) to eat. ◆ **36** εὔθυμοι (# *2314*) nom. pl. cheerful, assured, confident (s.v. 22). Pred. adj. γενόμενοι aor. mid. (dep.) part. (circum.) s.v. 7. πάντες καὶ αὐτοί all of them also. προσελάβοντο aor. ind. mid. s.v. 33. τροφῆς (# *5575*) gen. sing. food, nourishment. Partitive gen., "to take from," "to eat of" (RWP; RG, 519; BD, 93). ◆ **37** ἤμεθα impf. ind. mid. εἰμί s.v. 2. For this Hellenistic form s. BD, 49; GGP, 404. ψυχαί nom. pl. ψυχή (# *6034*) soul, life, person (BAGD). διακόσιαι ἑβδομήκοντα ἕξ 276. The ship was probably large enough to accommodate more (BASHH; Josephus claims that 600 were aboard the ship he was enroute to Rome that suffered shipwreck, Jos., *Life*, 15). ◆ **38** κορεσθέντες aor. pass. part. (temp.) κορέννυμι (# *3170*) to satisfy. ἐκούφιζον impf. ind. act. κουφίζω (# *3185*) to lighten. Incep. impf., "they began to make the ship lighter." ἐκβαλλόμενοι pres. mid. (dep.) part. ἐκβάλλω (# *1675*) to throw out. The grain may have been loaded in sacks, thus making it easier to throw overboard (Raspke, "Acts, Travel and Shipwreck," BAFCS, 2:31-32; SSAW, 199-200). ◆ **39** ἐγένετο aor. ind. mid. (dep.) s.v. 7. ἐπεγίνωσκον impf. ind. act. ἐπιγινώσκω (# *2105*) to know, to recognize. κόλπος (# *3146*) bay. κατενόουν impf. ind. act. κατανοέω (# *2917*) to perceive. Impf. may indicate that one after another of them noticed (Bruce). ἔχοντα pres. act. part. (adj.) ἔχω (# *2400*) to have. αἰγιαλός (# *129*) beach, a sandy beach, in contradistinction to a rocky coast (VSSP, 140). ἐβουλεύοντο impf. ind. mid. (dep.) βουλεύομαι (# *1086*) to take counsel, to decide, to plan, w. inf. Impf. shows the process of deliberation and doubt

(RWP). δύναιντο pres. opt. pass. s.v. 12. Opt. in a 4th. class cond. cl. viewing the cond. as less probable. ἐξῶσαι aor. act. inf. ἐξωθέω (# *2034*) to drive out; as a seaman's t.t., to beach, to run ashore (BAGD). ◆ **40** περιελόντες aor. act. part. (circum.) περιαιρέω (# *4311*) to take away, to cast off. The prep. compound is intensive (MH, 321). They cut off the anchors and let them fall into the sea (VSSP, 141; BASHH, 151). εἴων impf. ind. act. ἐάω (# *1572*) to allow. ἀνέντες aor. act. part. (circum.) ἀνίημι (# *479*) to loosen, to release. ζευκτηρία (# *2415*) band, lashing, strap. The word is used in the papyri in connection w. the mechanism of a water wheel (MM). On the ship these served to lift the steering oars when the ship was at anchor to prevent them from banging around (BASHH, 151; SSAW, 228). During the storm the rudders, large paddles on each side of the ship, had been lifted and tied down; now they were untied and let down into the water for guidance (Polhill; VSSP, 141). πηδάλιον (# *4382*) rudder (SSAW, 224-28). ἐπάραντες aor. act. part. (circum.) ἐπαίρω (# *2048*) to set, to hoist. ἀρτέμων foresail, the forward mast or the sail on it (LC). It refers to the small bowsprit sail, slanting low over the bows in order to be hoisted rapidly (BASHH, 151; VSSP, 141; SSAW, 242-43). πνεούσῃ pres. act. part. πνέω (# *4463*) to blow. Dat. of direction, "to the blowing (wind)." The cutting away of the anchors, the loosing of the bands of the rudder and the hoisting of the sail, performed simultaneously, put the ship immediately under control (BASHH, 151). κατεῖχον impf. ind. act. κατέχω (# *2988*) to hold down. Incep. impf., "they began to hold the ship steadily for the beach" (RWP). ◆ **41** περιπεσόντες aor. act. part. περιπίπτω (# *4346*) to fall around, to encounter, to fall into; here, to strike a reef (BAGD). Circum. or temp. part. διθάλασσος (# *1458*) w. the sea on both sides. Perhaps they ran onto a sand bank, a reef (BAGD), or a mud bank (BASHH, 151). ἐπέκειλαν aor. ind. act. ἐπικέλλω (# *2131*) to run ashore (BASHH, 151). ναῦς (# *3570*) ship. πρῷρα (# *4749*) the forepart, bow or prow of a ship s.v. 30. ἐρείσασα aor. act. part. (circum.) nom. fem. sing. ἐρείδω (# *2242*) to jam fast, to become firmly fixed. ἔμεινεν aor. ind. act. μένω (# *3531*) to remain. ἀσάλευτος (# *810*) unmovable, unshakable. πρύμνα (# *4744*) back part of the ship, stern. ἐλύετο impf. ind. pass. λύω (# *3395*) to loosen, to break up. Incep. impf., "the stern began to break up." βία (# *1040*) force, violence. ◆ **42** βουλή (# *1087*) plan, intent, decision. ἐγένετο aor. ind. mid. (dep.) s.v. 7. ἀποκτείνωσιν aor. act. subj. ἀποκτείνω (# *650*) to kill. Subj. w. ἵνα (# *2671*) giving the content of the plan. μή (# *3590*) lest. ἐκκολυμβήσας aor. act. part. ἐκκολυμβάω (# *1713*) to swim away. Part. of means, "by swimming away." διαφύγῃ aor. subj. act. διαφεύγω (# *1423*) to escape. The pres. in compound is perfective, "to escape successfully." Subj. in a neg. result cl. ◆ **43** βουλόμενος pres. mid.

(dep.) part. βούλομαι (# *1089*) to wish, to want to, w. inf. **διασῶσαι** aor. act. inf. διασῴζω (# *1407*) to save, to rescue. The prep. compound describes the carrying of action through to a definite result, "to bring safely through" (MH, 301). The centurion was apparently impressed w. Paul's continued pronouncements and warnings, the conviction and authority w. which he delivered them, and their prescient character as revealed in the unfolding events (B. Raspke, BAFCS, 3:271). **ἐκώλυσεν** aor. ind. act. κωλύω (# *3266*) to hinder. **βούλημα** (# *1088*) plan, intention. Gen. w. a vb. of hindering. **ἐκέλευσεν** aor. ind. act. κελεύω (# *3027*) to command. **δυναμένους** pres. pass. part. w. inf. s.v. 12. Part. as subst. **κολυμβᾶν** pres. act. inf. κολυμβάω (# *3147*) to swim. **ἀπορίψαντας** aor. act. part. (circum.) ἀπορίπτω (# *681*) to leap off. **ἐξιέναι** pres. act. inf. ἔξειμι (# *1996*) to go out; here, to go on land. Inf. in indir. discourse giving the content of the command. ◆ **44 οὓς μὲν ... οὓς δέ** some ... others. **σανίσιν** dat. pl. σανίς (# *4909*) board, plank. Instr. dat. **ἐγένετο** aor. ind. mid. (dep.) s.v. 7. **διασωθῆναι** aor. pass. inf. s.v. 43. Inf. w. **ἐγένετο** (s. Luke 2:1). "It happened that all were rescued."

Acts 28

◆ **1 διασωθέντες** aor. pass. part. (temp.) διασῴζω (# *1407*) to rescue completely (s. 27:43). **ἐπέγνωμεν** aor. ind. act. ἐπιγινώσκω (# *2105*) to know, to recognize. **Μελίτη** (# *3514*) Melita. The island is to be identified as Malta. (ABD, 4:489-90). For this and other suggestions s. BASHH, 152; Polhill; B. Rapske, "Acts, Travel and Shipwreck," BAFCS, 2:41-43; O.F.A. Meinardus, "St. Paul Shipwrecked in Dalmatia," *BA* 39 (1976): 145-47; Alfred Suhl, "Gestrandet! Bermerkungen zur Streit über die Romfahrt des Paulus," ZThK 88 (1991): 1-28; Jürgen Wehnert, "'... und da erfuhren wir, daß die Insel Kephallenia heißt.' Zur Auslegung von Apg 27-28 und ihrer Methode," ZThK 88 (1991): 169-80. **καλεῖται** pres. ind. pass. καλέω (# *2813*) to call; pass., to be named. ◆ **2 βάρβαρος** (# *975*) one who does not speak Greek, foreigner. The Maltese were Phoenicians speaking some dialect of Punic or Phoenician (LC; for text from Malta s. BASHH, 152; KAI, 1:14; 2:76-79; TSSI. 3:72-77). **παρεῖχον** impf. ind. act. παρέχω (# *4218*) to offer, to provide, to show. Impf. may indicate their habit (RWP). **τυχοῦσαν** aor. act. part. (adj.) τυγχάνω (# *5593*) to hit, to meet w. Part. used w. the neg. **οὐ** (# *4024*) means not common, not ordinary, extraordinary (BAGD). **φιλανθρωπία** (# *5792*) love for humankind, kindness toward people, hospitality. This noble virtue, a key word in the Hellenistic period, is expressed especially as solicitude, a willingness to serve, and in effective liberalities; it is a form of generosity (TLNT; TDNT; EDNT). The word was also applied to the medical profession (MLL, 296-97). **ἅψαντες** aor. act.

part. (temp.) ἄπτω (# *721*) to light (a fire). **γάρ** (# *1142*) for: particle explaining their generosity. **πυρά** (# *4787*) fire, bonfire, a fire of brush wood in the open (LC). **προσελάβοντο** aor. ind. mid. (indir. RWP) προσλαμβάνω (# *4689*) to receive, to take to; "they brought us all to it" (Bruce). **ὑετός** (# *5624*) rain. **ἐφεστῶτα** perf. act. part. ἐφίστημι (# *2392*) to set upon, to be present, "the rain that stood upon them"; that is, "the pouring rain" (RWP). **ψῦχος** (# *6036*) acc. sing. cold. ◆ **3 συστρέψαντος** aor. act. part. (temp.) συστρέφω (# *5370*) to twist together, to roll together in a bundle. Gen. abs., "as he was...." **φρύγανον** (# *5866*) brush, dry wood, brush wood. **ἐπιθέντος** aor. act. part. (temp.) ἐπιτίθημι (# *2202*) to place upon. Gen. abs. **ἔχιδνα** (# *2399*) snake, viper; usually a poisonous snake (BAGD; Pliny, NH, 8:85-86). The snake as an agent of vengeance was a common idea (BASHH, 153). **θέρμη** (# *2546*) heat. **ἐξελθοῦσα** aor. act. part. (circum.) ἐξέρχομαι (# *2002*) to come out. **καθῆψεν** aor. ind. act. καθάπτω (# *2750*) to fasten on to, to bite, w. gen. (LC). For the medical use of the term indicating the introduction of poison matter into the body s. MLL, 288. ◆ **4 εἶδον** aor. ind. act. ὁράω (# *3972*) to see. **κρεμάμενον** pres. mid. (dep.) part. (adj.) κρεμάννυμι (# *3203*) to hang. **θηρίον** (# *2563*) animal, beast, wild beast. Term used by medical writers of venomous serpents (MLL, 51). **ἔλεγον** impf. ind. act. λέγω (# *3306*) to say. Incep. impf., "they began to say." **πάντως** (# *4122*) adv., perhaps (s. 21:22). **φονεύς** (# *5838*) murderer. Pred. nom. without the art. stresses the character. **διασωθέντα** aor. pass. part. s.v. 1. Adj. part. or concessive part., "although he was rescued." **δίκη** (# *1472*) justice; perhaps a reference to justice as the goddess Dike, who was to report all the unrighteous deeds of mankind to Zeus immediately so that people would have to pay for their crimes (DDD, 467-80; Rackham; TDNT; TLNT). **ζῆν** pres. act. inf. ζάω (# *2409*) to live. **εἴασεν** aor. ind. act. ἐάω (# *1572*) to allow, to let, w. inf. ◆ **5 ἀποτινάξας** aor. act. part. ἀποτινάσσω (# *701*) to shake off. **ἔπαθεν** aor. ind. act. πάσχω (# *4248*) to suffer. **κακός** (# *2805*) harm, evil, bad effect. ◆ **6 προσεδόκων** impf. ind. act. προσδοκάω (# *4659*) to await, to expect. Impf. pictures the continuing action: they stood watching him for some time (Bruce). **μέλλειν** pres. act. inf. μέλλω (# *3516*) to be about to, w. inf. to express the immediate fut. Inf. as obj. of the vb. **προσεδόκων**. **πίμπρασθαι** pres. pass. inf. πίμπρημι (# *4399*) to swell. It was the usual medical word for inflammation (MLL, 50). **καταπίπτειν** pres. act. inf. καταπίπτω (# *2928*) to fall down. For the medical use of the term, s. MLL, 50f. **ἄφνω** (# *924*) suddenly. **νεκρόν** (# *3738*) acc. sing. dead. Acc. of manner. **ἐπὶ πολύ** for a long (time). **προσδοκώντων** pres. act. part. προσδοκάω (# *4659*) Gen. abs. Pres. indicates the continual waiting. **θεωρούντων** pres. act. part. θεωρέω (# *2555*) to see, to watch. Gen. abs. **ἄτοπος** (# *876*) out of place, harm. The word was used in medical language to denote anything unusual in the symptoms of a disease or something that was deadly or fatal (MLL, 289). γινόμενον pres. mid. (dep.) part. (adj.) γίνομαι (# 1181) to become, to be, to happen. μεταβαλόμενοι pres. mid. (dep.) part. (circum.) μεταβάλλω (# 3554) to change one's mind. ἔλεγον impf. ind. act. s.v. 4. Incep. impf., "they began to say." εἶναι pres. act. inf. εἰμί (# 1639). Inf. in indir. discourse. θεός (# 2536) god. Pred. acc. w. inf.; without the art. the character is stressed. ◆ 7 ὑπῆρχεν impf. ind. act. ὑπάρχω (# 5639) to exist, to be. χωρία (# 6005) land, property. πρώτῳ dat. sing. πρῶτος (# 4755) first. The term may be a title or it may be a designation of honor (SPT, 343; BASHH, 153; Polhill). Dat. of ownership or possession. ὄνομα (# 3950) name. ἀναδεξάμενος aor. mid. (dep.) part. (adj.) ἀναδέχομαι (# 346) to receive, to welcome. τρεῖς ἡμέρας for three days; acc. pl., acc. of time. φιλοφρόνως (# 5819) friendly, courteously, hospitably. ἐξένισεν aor. ind. act. ξενίζω (# 3826) to entertain as guest, to receive and give lodging to a guest. Hospitality is a virtue practiced marvelously by the pagans from the time of Homer (TLNT, 2:559; EDNT). ◆ 8 ἐγένετο aor. ind. mid. (dep.) s.v. 6. For the Semitic construction s. Luke 2:1. πυρετοῖς dat. pl. πυρετός (# 4790) fever. Instr. dat. δυσεντερίῳ dat. sing. δυσεντέριον (# 1548) dysentery. For the medical use of these terms s. MLL, 52-53; DMTG, 135, 280; MHW, 32, 39, 41, 116, 154-55. Instr. dat. συνεχόμενον pres. pass. part. (adj.) συνέχω (# 5309) to be sick; to be afflicted w. attacks (LC). κατακεῖσθαι pres. mid. (dep.) inf. κατάκειμαι (# 2879) to lie down, to be lying down; used of sick people (BAGD). Inf. used w. the vb. ἐγένετο, "It happened that he was lying down sick." The sickness may have been the Malta fever, caused by infected milk of the Maltese goats (BASHH, 153-54). εἰσελθών aor. act. part. (temp.) εἰσέρχομαι (# 1656) to come into. προσευξάμενος aor. mid. (dep.) part. (temp.) προσεύχομαι (# 4667) to pray. ἐπιθείς aor. act. part. (temp.) ἐπιτίθημι (# 2202) to place upon. ἰάσατο aor. ind. mid. (dep.) ἰάομαι (# 2615) to heal. ◆ 9 γενομένου aor. mid. (dep.) part. (temp.) s.v. 6. Gen. abs. ἔχοντες pres. act. part. ἔχω (# 2400) to have; w. ἀσθενείας to have sicknesses, to be sick. Adj. part. as subst. προσήρχοντο impf. ind. mid. (dep.) προσέρχομαι (# 4665) to come to. Iterat. impf. pictures the repeated action. ἐθεραπεύοντο impf. ind. pass. θεραπεύω (# 2543) to treat medically, to heal. Iterat. impf. ◆ 10 τιμαῖς dat. pl. τιμή (# 5507) price, value, honor, respect. Instr. dat. ἐτίμησαν aor. ind. act. τιμάω (# 5506) to honor, to show respect. The context opposes the possible rendering, "paid us large fees" (LC; Polhill). ἀναγομένοις pres. mid. (dep.) part. ἀνάγω (# 343) to sail. Temp. part. as dat. of time: "When we were sailing," "at the time we were going to sail." ἐπέθεντο aor. ind. mid. (dep.) ἐπιτίθημι (# 2202) to place upon, (s.v. 8), to put on board.

◆ 11 μετὰ δὲ τρεῖς μῆνας and after three months. This was very probably in early February and the crew wanted to leave at the earliest moment they could expect favorable spring winds so they could get to Ostia and reload the cargo for the return journey to Alexandria (BASHH, 154). ἀνήχθημεν aor. ind. pass. (dep.) s.v. 10. παρακεχειμακότι perf. act. part. (adj.) παραχειμάζω (# 4199) to spend the winter. They found another giant grain carrier of Alexandrian registry (Polhill). παράσημος (# 4185) figurehead, sign. These were both fore and aft and ships were sometimes named after the guardian deity (SSAW, 344-60). Διόσκουροι (# 1483) the Dioscuri, Castor and Pollux, twin sons of Zeus and Leda, who were protectors of those in need and popular in Egypt (BAGD; DDD, 490-93; GGR, 1:406-11; RAC, 3:1122-38; KP, 2:92-94; Haenchen; SSAW, 357, 367). In an inscription from around 500 B.C. the following occurs: "For Castor and Pollux, the sons of Jupiter." They were considered to be gods who were to help in time of need (RI, 109 Text #25). ◆ 12 καταχθέντες aor. pass. (dep.) part. κατάγω (# 2864) to go down, to land. Συράκουσαι (# 5352) Syracuse. A Greek city on the southeast coast of Sicily (ABD, 6:270-71). ἐπεμείναμεν aor. ind. act. ἐπιμένω (# 2152) to remain there. The prep. compound is directive (MH, 312). ἡμέρας acc. pl. ἡμέρα (# 2465) day. Acc. of duration of time. The delay of three days may have been due to weather or to loading or unloading cargo (Haenchen; BASHH, 154). ◆ 13 περιελόντες aor. act. part. (temp.) περιαιρέω (# 4311) to take away, to weigh anchor (TC, 501). An alternate reading is περιελθόντες aor. act. part. περιέρχομαι (# 4320) to go around (TC, 500-501). κατηντήσαμεν aor. ind. act. καταντάω (# 2918) to arrive. Ῥήγιον (# 4836) Rhegium. It was an important harbor at the toe of Italy (Longenecker, 566) They were waiting for a southerly wind to carry them through the straits for a rapid passage to Puteoli (BASHH, 154). ἐπιγενομένου aor. mid. (dep.) part. (temp.) ἐπιγίνομαι (# 2104) to arise, to come on. Gen. abs. νότος (# 3803) south wind. δευτεραῖος (# 1308) on the 2nd. day. Ποτίολοι (# 4541) Puteoli. This was the port where the passengers were set ashore, but the cargo of grain was taken to Portus, the new harbor built by Claudia at Ostia (BASHH, 154-55; SSAW, 283-85). ◆ 14 οὗ (# 4023) where. εὑρόντες aor. act. part. (circum.) εὑρίσκω (# 2351) to find. παρεκλήθημεν aor. ind. pass. παρακαλέω (# 4151) to ask, to urge; "we were invited" (LC). It may be that Luke found the Christians and the centurion may have been glad to have such accommodations, rather than having to billet the party, as was the government practice (BAFCS, 3:272-75; NDIEC 1:36-45; 7:58-92; for Christians at Puteoli s. BASHH, 155). ἐπιμεῖναι aor. act. inf. s.v. 12. Inf. in indir. discourse as obj. of the vb. τὴν Ῥώμην (# 4873) Rome. The art. would denote Rome as the goal of the entire journey (BD, 137). ◆ **15 κἀκεῖθεν** (# 2796) and from there. **ἀκούσαντες** aor. act. part. (temp.) ἀκούω (# 201) to hear. **ἦλθαν** aor. ind. act. ἔρχομαι (# 2262) to come. **ἀπάντησις** (# 561) meeting. Ἀππίου Φόρον (# 716; 5842) Appi Forum. A stopping place on the Appian Way about 43 miles from Rome (BASHH, 156). **Τριῶν Ταβερνῶν** *Tres Tabernae*, a roadside house 33 miles from Rome on the Appian Way (LC; BBC). **ἰδών** aor. act. part. (temp.) ὁράω (# 3972) to see. **εὐχαριστήσας** aor. act. part. (circum.) εὐχαριστέω (# 2373) to give thanks. **ἔλαβε** aor. ind. act. λαμβάνω (# 3284) to take. **θάρσος** (# 2511) acc. sing. courage, confidence in the midst of trial (TLNT). ◆ **16 εἰσήλθομεν** aor. ind. act. s.v. 8. **ἐπετράπη** aor. ind. pass. ἐπιτρέπω (# 2205) to allow, to permit, w. inf. **μένειν** pres. act. inf. μένω (# 3531) to remain. **καθ' ἑαυτόν** (# 2848; 1571) by himself, privately, in his own quarters. (s.v. 30). **φυλάσσοντι** pres. act. part. φυλάσσω (# 5875) to guard. Paul was not in prison but in the custody of a soldier detailed to guard him (LC). He was still bound to a soldier by a light chain so that he could not go in and out as he pleased (EGT; s. esp. BAFCS, 3:206-9). For conditions of a prisoner s. BAFCS, 3:195-225. Paul was probably allowed to live in rented quarters, which could have been a small room in an upper story of a house not far from the *Castra Praetoria*. He would have been required to provide his own food; else he received a grain ration (BAFCS, 3:227-42). The guards were taken from the Praetorian Guard, commanded at this time by Afranius Burrus. He died later in A.D. 62 during the purges by Nero (BBC). ◆ **17 ἐγένετο** aor. ind. mid. (dep.) s.v. 6, 8. **συγκαλέσασθαι** aor. mid. inf. συγκαλέω (# 5157) to call together; mid., to call to one's side, to summon (BAGD). Under certain circumstances, Roman practice allowed free access to the prisoner during the day, but enforced solitude through the night (BAFCS, 3:384, 180-81). **ὄντας** pres. act. part. (adj.) εἰμί (# 1639) to be. **πρῶτος** (# 4755) first, leading, leaders. Josephus says that 8,000 Jews appeared against Archelaus in Rome (Jos., *JW*, 2:80). Modern estimates of the number of Jews at Rome in the first century range between 10,000 to 50,000 (BAFCS, 3:330-31; Schneider). **συνελθόντων** aor. act. part. (temp.) συνέρχομαι (# 5302) to come together, to assemble. Gen. abs. **ἔλεγεν** impf. ind. act. s.v. 4. Incep. impf. **ἐναντίος** (# 1885) contrary, hostile. **ποιήσας** aor. act. part. ποιέω (# 4472) to do. Concessive part. ("although..."). **λαῷ** dat. sing. λαός (# 3295) people. Dat. of disadvantage. W. the art. it refers to his people, that is, the Jews. **ἔθεσι** dat. pl. ἔθος (# 1621) custom, common usage, legal rule (TLNT). Dat. of disadvantage. **δέσμιος** (# 1300) nom. sing. prisoner. Nom. w. pass. vb. but no art. stresses the character: "I was delivered over as a prisoner." **παρεδόθην** aor. ind. pass. παραδίδωμι (# 4140) to deliver over. ◆ **18 οἵτινες** (# 4015) nom. pl. who, used for the normal rel., esp.

after part. where the rel. pron. could be confused w. the art. (BD, 153). **ἀνακρίναντες** aor. act. part. (temp.) ἀνακρίνω (# 373) to legally examine, to try (s. 24:8). **ἐβούλοντο** impf. ind. mid. βούλομαι (# 1089) to will, to want to, w. inf. Impf. indicates the desire was not realized. **ἀπολῦσαι** aor. act. inf. ἀπολύω (# 668) to release. **ὑπάρχειν** pres. act. inf. s.v. 7. Inf. w. **διά** (# 1328) expressing cause. ◆ **19 ἀντιλεγόντων** pres. act. part. ἀντιλέγω (# 515) to speak against, to object. Gen. abs., temp. or causal. Pres. indicates the repeated action. **ἠναγκάσθην** aor. ind. pass. ἀναγκάζω (# 337) to compel, to force, w. inf. It refers to a logical compelling brought about by the circumstances (EDNT). **ἐπικαλέσασθαι** aor. mid. inf. ἐπικαλέω (# 2126) to appeal to (s. 25:11, 12). **ἔχων** pres. act. part. ἔχω (# 2400) to have. **ὡς** (# 6055) w. the part. giving the alleged reason is common in Gr. (RWP). **κατηγορεῖν** pres. act. inf. κατηγορέω (# 2989) to accuse, to bring an accusation against someone, w. gen. Epex. inf. explaining τι. ◆ **20 παρεκάλεσα** aor. ind. act. s.v. 14. **ἰδεῖν** aor. act. inf. ὁράω (# 3972) to see. Inf. in indir. discourse. **προσλαλῆσαι** aor. act. inf. προσλαλέω (# 4688) to talk to. **ἕνεκεν** (# 1915) because of. **ἅλυσις** (# 268) chain. **περίκειμαι** (# 4329) pres. ind. mid. (dep.) to lie around, to wear. Security against escape in light custody conditions usually called for a chain which would bind the prisoner by the wrist to his soldier guard, and this would probably have been a light chain rather than a heavy one (BAFCS, 3:181). ◆ **21 εἶπαν** aor. ind. act. λέγω s.v. 4. **γράμμα** (# 1207) letter. **ἐδεξάμεθα** aor. ind. mid. (dep.) δέχομαι (# 1312) to receive. Perhaps the ship Paul was on was one of the first to arrive in Italy after the winter, thus explaining why there had been no communication from the Jews in Jerusalem (Munck). **παραγενόμενός** aor. mid. (dep.) part. (circum.) παραγίνομαι (# 4134) to come. **ἀπήγγειλεν** aor. ind. act. ἀπαγγέλλω (# 550) to report. **ἐλάλησεν** aor. ind. act. λαλέω (# 3281) to speak. ◆ **22 ἀξιοῦμεν** pres. ind. act. ἀξιόω (# 546) to consider worthy, to think right or proper, w. inf. **ἀκοῦσαι** aor. act. inf. s.v. 15. **φρονεῖς** pres. ind. act. φρονέω (# 5858) to think. **γνωστός** (# 1196) known. **πανταχοῦ** (# 4116) everywhere. **ἀντιλέγεται** pres. ind. pass. ἀντιλέγω (# 515) to speak against, to oppose. ◆ **23 ταξάμενοι** aor. mid. (indir. mid.) part. τάσσω (# 5435) to arrange, to appoint. **ἦλθον** aor. ind. act. s.v. 15. **ξενία** (# 3825) lodging. The living quarters that Paul had rented (Haenchen; s.v. 16). **πλείονες** comp. πολύς (# 4498) much; comp., even more, in greater numbers (BAGD). **ἐξετίθετο** impf. ind. mid. ἐκτίθημι (# 1758) to lay out, to set forth. Perhaps the mid. indicates that the apostle vindicates his own conduct (EGT). **διαμαρτυρόμενος** pres. mid. (dep.) part. διαμαρτύρομαι (# 1371) to testify, to bear witness. Circum. part. explaining how he set forth his message. **πείθων** pres. act. part. (circum.) πείθω (# 4275) to persuade. Pres. may be conative, "he was trying to persuade." **πρωΐ** (# 4745) early. **ἑσπέρα** (# 2270) evening. ◆ **24 ἐπείθοντο** impf. ind. pass. s.v. 23. Impf. either pictures the repeated action or is incep., "some began to be persuaded" (RWP). **λεγομένοις** pres. pass. part. s.v. 4. Adj. part. as subst. Instr. dat. **ἠπίστουν** impf. ind. act. **ἀπιστέω** (# 601) to disbelieve. For the alpha as a neg. prefix s. Moorhouse 41-68. ◆ **25 ἀσύμφωνος** (# 851) out of harmony, without agreement. **ὄντες** pres. act. part. (causal) **εἰμί** (# 1639). **ἀπελύοντο** impf. ind. mid. **ἀπολύω** (# 668) to dismiss; mid. to loose oneself, to depart. **εἰπόντος** aor. act. part. s.v. 4. Gen. abs. **ἐλάλησεν** aor. ind. act. s.v. 21. ◆ **26 πορεύθητι** aor. imp. pass. (dep.) **πορεύομαι** (# 4513) to go. **εἰπόν** aor. imp. act. s.v. 4. **ἀκοῇ** (# 198) dat. sing. hearing. Dat. of manner as translation of the Heb. inf. abs. to emphatically reinforce the idea of the vb. (BG, 21). **ἀκούσετε** fut. ind. act. s.v. 15. **συνῆτε** aor. subj. act. **συνίημι** (# 5317) to comprehend, to understand. Subj. w. double neg. **οὐ μή** (# 4024; 3590) as emphatic denial. **βλέποντες** pres. act. part. **βλέπω** (# 1063) to see. Part. as translation of Heb. inf. abs. (BG, 21). **βλέψετε** fut. ind. act. **ἴδητε** aor. subj. act. **ὁράω** (# 3972) to see. ◆ **27 ἐπαχύνθη** aor. ind. pass. **παχύνω** (# 4266) to make fat, to become fat, to make dull, pass. to become dull (TDNT). **ὠσίν** dat. pl. **οὖς** (# 4044) ear. Instr. dat. **βαρέως** (# 977) adv. heavy, heavily, w. difficulty; w. vb. **ἤκουσαν**, "to be hard of hearing" (BAGD). **ἤκουσαν** aor. ind. act. s.v. 15. **ἐκάμμυσαν** aor. ind. act. **καμμύω** (# 2826) to shut, to close the eyes. **ἴδωσιν** aor. subj. act. s.v. 26. Subj. in a neg. purp.

cl. **ἀκούσωσιν** aor. subj. act. s.v. 15. Subj. in neg. purp. cl. **συνῶσιν** aor. subj. act., s.v. 26. **ἐπιστρέψωσιν** aor. subj. act. **ἐπιστρέφω** (# 2188) to turn, to turn back. Subj. in a neg. purp. cl. **ἰάσομαι** fut. ind. mid. (dep.) s.v. 8. ◆ **28 ἔστω** pres. act. imp. act. **εἰμί** s.v. 25. **ἀπεστάλη** aor. ind. pass. 3rd. pers. sing. **ἀποστέλλω** (# 690) to send (TDNT; EDNT; TLNT, 1:186-94). **αὐτοί** (# 899) they, in contrast to the unbelieving Jews (RWP). **ἀκούσονται** fut. ind. mid. (dep.) s.v. 15. ◆ **30 ἐνέμεινεν** aor. ind. act. **ἐμμένω** (# 1844) to remain. **διετίαν ὅλην** two whole years. Acc. of time. Maybe the two years indicate that the time period for Paul's accusers to appear had elapsed (BC, 5:330; BBC). It is better, however, to assume that Paul stood before Nero, but was acquitted and released (BASHH, 157-58, 390-404; BAFCS, 3:191). **μισθώματι** dat. pl. **μίσθωμα** (# 3637) contract price, rent, rented lodging (BAGD; BAFCS, 3:327). **ἀπεδέχετο** impf. ind. mid. (dep.) **ἀποδέχομαι** (# 622) to receive, to welcome. Impf. pictures the repeated action. **εἰσπορευομένους** pres. mid. (dep.) part. **εἰσπορεύομαι** (# 1660) to go into, to come to. Adj. part. as subst. ◆ **31 κηρύσσων** pres. act. part. (circum.) **κηρύσσω** (# 3062) to proclaim, to preach. **διδάσκων** pres. act. part. (circum.) **διδάσκω** (# 1438) to teach. Pres. indicates the repeated action. **ἀκωλύτως** (# 219) adv. without hindrance. The adv. is of constant occurrence in legal documents in the papyri (MM). For the ending of the book of Acts s. BASHH, 383-87.

Romans

Romans 1

◆ **1 Παῦλος** (# *4263*) Paul. Nom. used in the address of a letter. For the form and sending of letters in the ancient world s. NDIEC, 7:1-57; DPL, 550-53; LAE, 146-215; RAC, 2:564-84; KP, 2:324-27; John Lee White, *The Form and Function of the Body of the Greek Letter* (Missoula, Mont.: Scholar's Press, 1972); White, *The Form and Structure of the Official Petitions: A Study in Greek Epistolography* (Missoula, Mont.: Scholar's Press, 1972); Chan-Hie Kim, *Form and Structure of the Familiar Greek Letter of Recommendation* (Missoula, Mont.: Scholar's Press, 1972); Stanley K. Stowers, *Letter Writing in Greco-Roman Antiquity*; vol. 5, Library of Early Christianity, Wayne A. Meeks (ed.) (Philadelphia: Westminster Press, 1986); Franz Schneider und Werner Stenger, *Studien zum neutestamentlichen Briefformular* (Leiden: E.J. Brill, 1978); Joseph A. Fitzmyer, "Some Notes on Aramaic Epistolography," *JBL* 93 (1974): 201-25; ABD, 4:290-93. **δοῦλος** (# *1528*) slave, bondservant. The term emphasizes the bondage and the belonging to another (TDNT; Dunn; SCS, 27-46; Philemon 21). The following gens. show possession: as a slave he belonged to Christ Jesus. **κλητός** (# *3105*) called. Verbal adj. w. this ending usually has pass. sense (BG, 47; N, 221). **ἀπόστολος** (# *693*) apostle, one commissioned by another, who bears the authority of the one who commissions him (TLNT; TDNT; EDNT; Fitzmyer, 231-32). Pred. nom., "called to be an apostle." **ἀφωρισμένος** perf. part. pass. ἀφορίζω (# *928*) to mark off, to separate by a boundary. Perf. suggests the continuing result of the past action. Adj. part. in apposition to ἀπόστολος (Cranfield). The absence of the article w. the words in v. 1 indicates the nature or quality (BG, 55). **εὐαγγέλιον** (# *2295*) acc. sing. good news, gospel (TLNT; TDNT; Stuhlmacher; Wilckens, 74-75). ◆ **2 προεπηγγείλατο** aor. ind. mid. (dep.) προεπαγγέλλω (# *4600*) to promise before, to promise previously or in advance. **γραφαῖς** dat. pl. γραφή (# *1210*) writing, Scripture. The absence of the article throws the stress on ἁγίαις (SH). ◆ **3 περὶ τοῦ υἱοῦ αὐτοῦ.** The phrase "concerning his Son" is to be connected closely w. the word εὐαγγέλιον (Lightfoot, *Notes*). **γενομένου** aor. mid. (dep.) part. (adj.) γίνομαι (# *1181*) to become. The vb. indicates a change in existence and focuses on the Son of God coming into human existence (Moo). **σπέρματος** gen. sing. σπέρμα (# *5065*) seed, descendant. According to his humanity the Messiah

was a descendant of David and will ultimately fulfill the covenant promises which were made to David (Cleon L. Rogers, Jr., "The Davidic Covenant in Acts-Revelation," *Bib Sac* 151 [1994]: 78-79; Byrne). ◆ **4 ὁρισθέντος** aor. pass. part. adj. ὁρίζω (# *3988*) to mark out the boundary, to decree, to appoint, to designate (Dunn; S. Lewis Johnson, Jr., "The Jesus that Paul Preached," *Bib Sac* 128 [1971]: 129f; L. C. Allen, "The Old Testament Background of [προ] ὁρίζω in the New Testament," *NTS* 17 [1970]: 104-108; TDNT). **ἁγιωσύνης** (# *43*) holiness. Here it indicates a spirit or disposition of holiness which characterized Christ spiritually (Johnson, 132; EDNT). ◆ **5 ἐλάβομεν** aor. ind. act. λαμβάνω (# *3284*) to take, to receive. The pl. refers only to Paul. It is his stylistic method of avoiding the emphasize on "I" (Kuss). **ἀποστολή** (# *2779*) apostleship, the office of the apostle. **ὑπακοή** (# *5633*) obedience. ◆ **7 οὖσιν** pres. act. part. εἰμί (# *1639*) to be. Pres. describes their present location in Rome. For a study of the early Christians in Rome s. Peter Lampe, *Die stadtrömischen Christen in den ersten beiden Jahrhunderten* [Tübingen, 1987]; DPL, 850-55). **ἀγαπητοῖς** (# *28*) beloved. For verbal adjs. w. this ending s.v. 1. ◆ **8 καταγγέλλεται** pres. ind. pass. καταγγέλλω (# *2859*) to proclaim, to report, to publicly report (Barrett). Pres. suggests continuing activity. ◆ **9 λατρεύω** (# *3302*) to serve, to serve for pay; then to do service for a deity (TDNT). Plutarch: "The god whom the priestess serves understands and hears" [*Moralia*, 512e], and others use the term in this way (NW, 2, i:1-2). **ἐν τῷ πνεύματι** (#*1877*; *4460*) with (in) my spirit. It is by using spirit that Paul renders God service (Barrett). **ἐν τῷ εὐαγγελίῳ** (# *1877*; *2295*) "in the gospel." Prep. here denotes the external sphere (Lightfoot, *Notes*). **ἀδιαλείπτως** (# *90*) adv., without ceasing, constantly (TLNT). The word was used for a continuous cough (MM) and Josephus used it for the incessant attacks of the Romans against Jotapatha (TJ, 127; Jos., *JW*, 3:155-57) or for the continual hammering of a battering ram against the walls of Jerusalem (TJ, 181; Jos., *JW*, 5:298-302; CCFJ, 1:24). **μνεία** (# *3644*) remembrance, mention. ◆ **10 δεόμενος** pres. mid. part. (dep.) δέομαι (*1289*) to pray, to make a request. Epex. part. or part. of manner explaining how or what Paul prayed. Often Jews prayed several hours a day (BBC). **εἴ πως** (# *1623*; *4803*) if perhaps. By omitting the apodosis of the cond. cl. the first cl. may be taken as a wish (MT, 91). **εὐοδωθήσομαι** fut. ind. pass. εὐδόω (# *2338*) to be led along a good road, to cause one to journey prosperously, to make one succeed (Dunn; Godet). **ἐν τῷ θελήματι τοῦ θεοῦ** (# *2525; 2536*) in the will of God. The expression occurs often in private letters (BS, 252). A Jewish prayer for travel says, "May it be your will, Oh Lord our God, that you lead us in peace, and that you sustain us in peace that you save me from the hand of every enemy..." (b. Berakoth, 29b). **ἐλθεῖν** aor. inf. act. ἔρχομαι (# *2262*) to come. Inf. expressing purp. or result. ◆ **11 ἐπιποθῶ** pres. ind. act. ἐπιποθέω (# *2160*) to long for. Prep. in compound marks the direction of the desire (SH). **ἰδεῖν** aor. inf. act. ὁράω (# *3972*) to see. Epex. inf. explaining the desire. **μεταδῶ** aor. subj. act. μεταδίδωμι (# *3566*) to share w. someone. Subj. w. **ἵνα** (# *2671*) expresses the purp. of his coming. **χάρισμα** (# *5922*) a gift freely and graciously given, a favor bestowed (BAGD; TLNT). **πνευματικόν** (# *4461*) spiritually, pertaining to the spirit. The suffix indicates a dynamic relation to the idea involved in the root (MH, 378). **στηριχθῆναι** aor. inf. pass. στηρίζω (# *5114*) to strengthen. Pass. indicates it is God who will strengthen (Godet). Articular inf. w. prep. **εἰς** (# *1650*) to express purp. (MT, 143). It should be understood as modifying the impartation of the gift. Const. aor. viewing the action as a whole, not in its individual aspects. ◆ **12 συμπαρακληθῆναι** aor. inf. pass. συμπαρακαλέω (# *5220*) to encourage together, to encourage mutually. Here it signifies "I w. you, Christians at Rome" (Godet). Inf. to express purp. ◆ **13 ἀγνοεῖν** pres. inf. act. ἀγνοέω (# *51*) to be ignorant. Compl. inf. to the main vb. **ἀδελφοί** voc. pl. ἀδελφός (# *81*) "brothers." The word was used of those who belonged to the same religious group and here makes the appeal more personal and affective (Dunn; Fitzmyer, 246; BS, 87-88; MM; NDIEC, 2:29, 50, 63; 4:56; 5:73). **προεθέμην** aor. ind. mid. (dep.) προτίθημι (# *4729*) to place before, to purpose, to intend. **ἐλθεῖν** aor. inf. act. ἔρχομαι (# *2262*) to come. Compl. inf. to the main vb. **ἐκωλύθην** aor. ind. pass. κωλύω (# *3266*) to hinder. **δεῦρο** (# *1306*) adv., here, until now. **καρπός** (# *2843*) fruit. **σχῶ** aor. subj. act. ἔχω (# *2400*) to have, to get. Subj. w. **ἵνα** (# *2671*) to express purp. The idea expressed is that of gathering fruit (Murray). ◆ **14 βάρβαρος** (# *975*) one who does not speak Gr. properly, one who speaks an unintelligible language; then applied to people who did not familiarly use Gr. and so were regarded as uncultured (Dodd; Fitzmyer, 250-51; NW, 2, i:3-6; BBC; 1 Cor. 14:11). **σοφός** (# *5055*) wise. **ἀνόητος** (# *485*) ignorant, not understanding. **ὀφειλέτης** (# *4050*) one who owes a debt. For the binding obligation placed upon debtors in the ancient world s. SEH, 1:382f. ◆ **15 τὸ κατ᾽ ἐμέ** either to be taken as the subject w. the next word as the predicate, "for my part, I am all readiness" (EGT), or else the prep. is to be taken as a circumlocution for the poss. gen, "my

readiness" (BD, 120). **πρόθυμος** (# *4609*) ready, willing, eager. **εὐαγγελίσασθαι** aor. mid. (dep.) inf. εὐαγγελίζομαι (# *2294*) to evangelize, to proclaim the good news. Epex. inf. to explain what he is willing to do. ◆ **16 ἐπαισχύνομαι** (# *2049*) pres. ind. mid. (dep.) to be ashamed. **πιστεύοντι** pres. act. part. πιστεύω (# *4409*) to believe. Pres. expresses continuous action. **Ἕλληνι** dat. sing. Ἕλλην (# *1818*) Greek. Here it refers to anyone who is not a Jew (Gifford). ◆ **17 δικαιοσύνη θεοῦ** (# *1466; 2536*) righteousness of God. The phrase could mean "the righteous standing which God gives" or "the righteous character which God is" or "the righteous activity which comes from God." For a review of these meaning s. MRP, 9-14; Cranfield; Dunn; Moo; Fitzmyer, 257-63; VGG, 87-116; Wilckens, 202-33; GG, 78-84; DPL, 827-37. **ἐν αὐτῷ** (# *1877; 899*) in it; that is, in the gospel. **ἀποκαλύπτεται** pres. ind. pass. ἀποκαλύπτω (# *636*) to reveal. **ἐκ πίστεως** (# *1666; 4411*) out of faith. The prep. here may indicate the source of the righteousness. For the various interpretations of his source of the righteousness s. S. Lewis Johnson, Jr., "The Gospel that Paul Preached," *Bib Sac* 128 (1971): 336f; Moo; Dunn. **γέγραπται** perf. ind. pass. γράφω (# *1211*) to write. Perf. emphasizes the permanent and authoritative character of that which was written (MM). **ζήσεται** fut. ind. mid. ζάω (# *2409*) to live. ◆ **18 ἀποκαλύπτεται** pres. ind. pass. ἀποκαλύπτω (# *636*) to reveal. The word need not be totally eschatological, but has the sense of God's displeasure at sin, the sense that God will not overlook sin (Lightfoot, *Notes*). Theol. pass. indicating God as the agent revealing his wrath. **ὀργή** (# *3973*) wrath. The word indicates the deep-seated anger of God against sin. This anger arises from His holiness and righteousness (TDNT; NIDNTT, 1:106-08; EDNT; Trench, *Synonyms*, 130-34; Cranfield). **ἀσέβεια** (# *813*) ungodliness. **ἀδικία** (# *94*) unrighteousness. The first represents impiety toward God and the second injustice toward men (Hodge). **ἀλήθεια** (# *237*) truth. The knowledge of God as communicated to the human conscience (Godet). **ἀδικία** (# *94*) dat. sing. unrighteousness. Dat. of sphere or possibly instr. **κατεχόντων** pres. act. part. gen. masc. pl. κατέχω (# *2988*) to hold down, to suppress, to hold fast or firmly. Adj. part. to emphasize a trait. Conative pres., "trying to hold down." ◆ **19 διότι** (# *1484*) because. It gives the reason of that which precedes (Godet). **γνωστός** (# *1196*) known or knowable. **ἐφανέρωσεν** aor. ind. act. φανερόω (# *5745*) to make clear, to manifest. Gnomic aor. It is always manifest or observable. ◆ **20 ἀόρατος** (# *548*) unseen, invisible. For the use of the prefix as a neg. s. Moorhouse, 41-66. **κτίσεως** gen. sing. κτίσις (# *3232*) creation. **κόσμου** gen. sing. κόσμος (# *3180*) world. Obj. gen., "at the creation of the world." **ποιήμασιν** dat. pl. ποίημα (# *4473*) that which is made. It refers to the source from which our perception of the invisible things is derived, to gain an insight into (TDNT). Instr. dat. (Moo). **νοούμενα** pres. pass. part. nom. n. pl. νοέω (# 3783) to perceive, to gain an insight into (TDNT). **καθορᾶται** pres. ind. pass. καθοράω (# 2775) to see, to see clearly or plainly, distinctly (LS). The force of the prep. compound is intensive, or it may relate to the direction of sight: "contemplated" (SH). **τε** (# 5445) and, both. It joins words closely which have between themselves a close or logical affinity (MT, 339). **ἀΐδιος** (# 132) eternal. **θειότης** (# 2522) divinity, divine nature, a summary term for the attributes which constitute deity (SH; for this term and its contrast w. the word "deity" as used in Col. 2:9 s. TDNT; Cranfield; Trench, *Synonyms*, 7-10). **εἶναι** pres. inf. act. εἰμί (# 1639) to be. That gods existed was denied by no one (BBC). Articular inf. used w. prep. **εἰς** (# 1650) to express purp. or result (MT, 143). The purpose of natural revelation is to leave man without a justifiable excuse before God (Moo, 121-24; for examples from the ancient world s. NW, 2. i:13-22). **ἀναπολόγητος** (# 406) without excuse, without legal defense (Lightfoot, *Notes*; EDNT; BAGD). Josephus uses the word in the sense of "unanswered," "without defense" (CCFJ, 1:107). Dio Chrysostom sets his oration in the form of a discussion between Philip of Macedonia and his son Alexander and in their discussion concerning Homer the young Alexander says he will not let Homer go undefended (ἀναπολόγητον) (DC, "The Second Discourse on Kingship," 2:39). ◆ **21 γνόντες** aor. act. part. nom. masc. pl. γινώσκω (# 1182) to know. For the Jewish teaching regarding the Gentiles knowing God's demands s. SB, 3:36-46. Concessive part., "although they recognized" (Moo). Aor. suggests an antecedent action forming the basis of the main vb. **ἐδόξασαν** aor. ind. act. δοξάζω (# 1519) to form an opinion about, to glorify. Const. aor. viewing the total action. **ηὐχαρίστησαν** aor. ind. act. εὐχαρίζω (# 2273) to give thanks, to be thankful. **ἐματαιώθησαν** aor. ind. pass. ματαιόω (# 3471) to render futile, worthless; pass. to be given over to worthlessness, think about worthless things, to be foolish (BAGD). **διαλογισμός** (# 1369) reason; here, inward questions (Lightfoot, *Notes*). **ἐσκοτίσθη** aor. ind. pass. σκοτίζω (# 5029) to darken. Ingressive aor. "to become darkened." **ἀσύνετος** (# 852) unintelligent, without insight. ◆ **22 φάσκοντες** pres. act. part. circum. φάσκω (# 5763) to affirm, to assert. **εἶναι** pres. inf. act. εἰμί (# 1639) to be. Inf. in indir. discourse. **ἐμωράνθησαν** aor. ind. pass. μωραίνω (# 3701) to make foolish; pass. to become foolish. ◆ **23 ἤλλαξαν** aor. ind. act. ἀλλάσσω (# 248) to exchange. They exchanged one thing for another (Hodge). **δόξα** (# 1518) glory, splendor, majesty (TDNT; TLNT; EDNT). It refers to the manifest majesty of God (Cranfield). **ἀφθάρτου** gen. sing. ἄφθαρτος (# 915) incorruptible, not subject to corruption, immortal, imperishable (Fitzmyer, 283). Gen. of quality. **ὁμοίωμα** (# 3930)

likeness, implies a resemblance which may be accidental. **εἰκόνος** gen. εἰκών (# 1635) image; this presupposes an archetype of which it is a copy (Lightfoot, *Notes*; Dunn). Gen. of apposition or explanation. **φθαρτός** (# 5778) corruptible. **πετεινά** (# 4374) (pl.) birds. **τετράποδος** (# 5488) four-footed. **ἑρπετά** (# 2260) (pl.) creeping things, snakes. For examples from the ancient world s. NW, 2, i:26-30; Fitzmyer, 284-85. ◆ **24 διό** (# 1475) therefore. **παρέδωκεν** aor. ind. act. παραδίδωμι (# 4140) to deliver over, to hand over, often w. a judicial aspect (Gifford; SB, 3:62f; TLNT). **ἐπιθυμία** (# 2123) lust, desire. **καρδιῶν** gen. καρδία (# 2840) heart. Gen. of source, "the desires coming from their heart." **ἀκαθαρσία** (# 174) uncleanness. It refers to sexual aberration (Murray). **ἀτιμάζεσθαι** pres. inf. pass. ἀτιμάζω (# 869) to dishonor. Inf. is epex. (Barrett) or result (Cranfield). ◆ **25 μετήλλαξαν** aor. ind. act. μεταλάσσω (# 3563) to change w., to exchange. The word suggests a volitional choice. **ἐσεβάσθησαν** aor. ind. pass. σεβάζομαι (# 4933) to worship, to show reference to. **ἐλάτρευσαν** aor. ind. act. λατρεύω (# 3302) to serve (s.v. 9). **παρά** (# 4123) w. acc., more than. Used to express the comp. and here means virtually "instead of" (BD, 123f). **κτίσαντα** aor. act. part. acc. masc. sing. κτίζω (# 3231) to create. Part. as a subst. to emphasize this action as characteristic. **εὐλογητός** (# 2329) blessed. ◆ **26 διὰ τοῦτο** (# 1328; 4047) for this reason, giving the justification for the ensuing judgment. **παρέδωκεν** aor. ind. act. παραδίωμι (# 4140) to turn over to (s.v. 24). **πάθος** (# 4079) passion or a passionate desire. It represents the passive, ungoverned aspect of evil desire as opposed to ἐπιθυμία, which is the active and also the more comprehensive term (AS). **ἀτιμία** (# 871) dishonor, disgrace. For the prefix as a neg. s.v. 20. Here, gen. of description or quality, "desires characterized by disgrace," or "disgraceful desires," "passions which bring dishonor (Byrne). **θήλειαι** pl. θῆλυς (# 2559) female. **μετήλλαξαν** aor. ind. act. μεταλλάσσω (# 3563) to exchange. **φυσικός** (# 5879) natural, that which pertains to nature (for the meaning of the suffix s. MH, 378). **χρῆσις** (# 5979) use, function, esp. of sexual intercourse (BAGD). Lesbian love (Tribadism) was common in the ancient world (NW, 2, i:39-40; SG, 224-34; KP, 4:1546-48; Fitzmyer, 285-86; DPL, 413-15; BBC). ◆ **27 ὁμοίως** (# 3931) likewise. **ἄρσενες** pl. ἄρσην (# 781) male. **ἀφέντες** aor. act. part. nom. masc. pl. ἀφίημι (# 918) to leave, to forsake. Part. expressing manner. Aor. expresses antecedent action as the basis for the main vb. **ἐξεκαύθησαν** aor. ind. pass. ἐκκαίω (# 1706) to set on fire; pass. to be consumed, to be inflamed. **ὄρεξις** (# 3979) desire, passionate desire (TLNT). It is always the reaching out after and toward an object, w. the purpose of drawing that after which it reaches to itself, and making it its own (Trench, *Synonyms*, 326). **ἀσχημοσύνη** (# 859) shameless or disgraceful act, obscenity (Barrett). **κατεργαζόμενοι** pres. mid.

(dep.) part. κατεργάζομαι (# 2981) to work, to accomplish. For the perfectivizing force of the prep. compound s. M, 112f. ἀντιμισθία (# 521) reward, penalty. Prep. in compound emphasizes the reciprocal nature of the transaction (BAGD). ἔδει impf. ind. act. δεῖ (# 1256) it is necessary. πλάνη (# 4415) error. For the Jewish view of sexual perversion of the heathen s. SB, 3:64-74. For homosexuality in the ancient world s. David E. Malick, "The Condemnation of Homosexuality in Romans 1:26-27," *Bib Sac* 150 [1993]: 327-40; NW, 2, i:32-50; KP, 4:1583-84; SG, 286-344. ἀπολαμβάνοντες pres. act. part. nom. masc. pl. ἀπολαμβάνω (# 655) to receive, to receive back, to receive one's due (SH). ◆ **28 καθώς** (# 2777) just as; drawing a comparison between man and God's actions. ἐδοκίμασαν aor. ind. act. δοκιμάζω (# 1507) to test, to put to the test, to make a decision after a trial. They tested God at first and turned aside from Him (RWP). ἐπίγνωσις (# 2106) cognizance, knowledge. ἔχειν pres. inf. act. ἔχω (# 2400) to have. Inf. is exepeg. to the main vb. παρέδωκεν aor. ind. act. παραδίδωμι (# 4140) to turn over, to give up to. ἀδόκιμος (# 99) rejected, rejected after a trial, failing the test, disqualified, useless (Cranfield). νοῦς (3808) mind, the reasoning faculty, esp. as concerns moral action (SH). ποιεῖν pres. inf. act. ποιέω (# 4472) to do. Inf. expresses result. καθήκοντα pres. act. part. acc. masc. pl καθήκω (# 2763) that which is proper, or fitting, moral, according to one's duty (BAGD). The word was a t.t. of Stoic philosophy (TDNT; Barrett; Dunn; NW, 2, i:52-54). ◆ **29 πεπληρωμένους** pres. pass. part. πληρόω (# 4444) to fill. πλεονεξία (# 4432) greediness, consuming ambition, greed, the insatiable desire to have more even at the expense of harming others (Lightfoot, *Notes*; NTW, 97ff; TDNT; TLNT). μεστός (# 3550) full. φθόνος (# 5784) envy. φόνος (# 5840) murder. ἔριδος gen. ἔρις (# 2251) strife, wrangling. δόλος (# 1515) deceit, cunning, treachery. κακόηθεια (# 2799) malice, the tendency to put the worst construction upon everything (SH; Trench, *Synonyms*, 38-40). ψιθυριστης (# 6031) whisperer, the man who pours his poison against his neighbor by whispering in the ear (Godet). ◆ **30 κατάλαλος** (# 2897) speaking evil against others, slanderous, slanderer. The prep. compound indicates the action of the word is unfavorable to its object (MH, 316). θεοστυγής (# 2539) "hated of God" (pass.) or "haters of God" (active) (Gifford; Kuss). ὑβριστής (# 5616) a man arrogant and insolent. The word contains a mixture of cruelty and pride. The proud insolence and contempt for others who suffer (Trench, *Synonyms*, 202-5; Cranfield; MNTW, 77-85; TDNT). ὑπερήφανος (# 5662) proud, arrogant, one who shows himself above others. It is the proud, insolent, self-sufficient person who in his heart sets himself upon a pedestal above all others, even above God (Trench, *Synonyms*, 101f; MNTW, 85-89; TDNT). ἀλάζων (# 225) boastful, bragger, one who

makes empty boasts and false promises, often for the purpose of gain (Trench, *Synonyms*, 98-101; MNTW, 38-42; TDNT). ἐφευρετής (# 2388) inventor. γονεῦσιν dat. γονεῖς (# 1204) parents. ἀπειθής (# 579) disobedient. ◆ **31 ἀσύνετος** (# 852) senseless. ἀσύνθετος (# 853) covenant-breaker, faithless to an agreement. ἀστόργος (# 845) unloving, without tenderness. It refers to the lack of the feelings of natural tenderness, as seen in a mother who exposes or kills her child, a father who abandons his family, or children who neglect their aged parents (Godet). ἀνελεήμων (# 446) unmerciful, without pity. ◆ **32 δικαίωμα** (# 1468) that which is declared right, judgment, ordinance (TDNT; MRP, 209). ἐπιγνόντες aor. act. part. ἐπιγινώσκω (# 2105) to know. Aor. suggests antecedent time. It is the basis for the action of the main vb. Concessive part., "even though they fully knew, they approved of evil." πράσσοντες pres. act. part. πράσσω (# 4556) to do, to carry out, to practice. συνευδοκοῦσιν Pres. ind. act. συνευδοκέω (# 5306) to heartily approve (SH). Iterat. pres., "They approved time and again." For a list of vices s. DPL, 962-63; ABD, 6:857-59.

Romans 2

◆ **1 διό** (# 1475) therefore. It refers either to the preceding section (1:18-32)–this assumes that the person addressed in 2:1 admits to the sin of all men (Cranfield)–or only to v. 32, or to that which follows in Chapter 2 (Murray). εἶ pres. ind. act. 2nd. sing. εἰμί (# 1639) to be. The 2nd. pers. is a vivid address (Rom. 2:17; 8:2; 9:19; 11:17; 13:3; 14:4, 10, 15, 20-22; Cranfield). ἄνθρωπε voc. sing. ἄνθρωπος man (# 476). "O man," "sir." This may be a diatribe in which the speaker puts the words in the mouth of his opponent. Then he proceeds to answer the objection. (S.K. Stowers, *The Diatribe in Paul's Letter to the Romans*, SBLDS 57 [Chico, Ca.: Scholars Press, 1981]; Mounce.) ἀναπολόγητος (# 406) without excuse, without defense. The pref. ἀν- means "without." The related word ἀπολογέομαι is used in a judicial sense to describe a legal petition or defense (MM). κρίνων pres. act. part. κρίνω (# 3212) to judge. Subst. part. used to emphasize an ongoing trait. Iterat. pres., "judging repeatedly" or habitual "judging all the time." The use of πᾶς (# 4246) w. the part. means "every one who ...." This could be referring to the Jew or the morally superior Gentile (Cranfield). ἐν (# 1877) dat. of rule or standard, "in accordance to the standard." κατακρίνεις pres. ind. act. κατακρίνω (# 3212) to judge against, to condemn. πράσσεις pres. ind. act. πράσσω (# 4556) to do, to practice. Gnomic pres. describing the habit of the one who judges. ◆ **2 ὅτι** (# 4022) that, giving the content of knowledge. κρίμα (# 3210) judgment, decision, either good or bad (RWP). θεοῦ gen. sing. θεός (# 2536) God. Subjective gen., "judgment by God." τοιαῦτα (# 5525) such as this, of such a kind. **πράσσοντας** pres. act. part. πράσσω (# *4556*) to do, to practice. Subst. part. used to emphasis a trait or characteristic. ◆ **3 λογίζῃ** pres. ind. mid. (dep.) 2nd. pers. sing. λογίζω (# *3357*) to reckon, to consider, to suppose. **ὅτι** (# *4022*) that, giving the content of the hope. **σύ** (# *5148*) you, emphatic used to strengthen the contrast between the one who judges and the judged. **ἐκφεύξῃ** fut. ind. mid. (dep.) ἐκφεύγω (# *1767*) to flee, to escape, to seek safety in flight (BAGD). ◆ **4 πλούτου** gen. sing. πλοῦτος (# *4458*) richness. Gen. due to the vb. **χρηστότητος** gen. χρηστότης (# *5983*) kindness in general, as expressed in giving favors (Hodge; TDNT; EDNT; TLNT). Gen. of description, "rich kindness." **ἀνοχή** (# *496*) patience. It is that forbearance or suspense of wrath, that truce w. the sinner, which by no means implies that the wrath will not be executed at last (Trench, *Synonyms*, 200). **μακροθυμία** (# *3429*) longsuffering; a long holding out of the mind before it gives room to action or passion, a state of emotional calm in the face of provocation or misfortune and without complaint or irritation (Trench, *Synonyms*, 196; LN, 1:307; TDNT; Moo; EDNT). **καταφρονεῖς** pres. ind. act. καταφρονέω (# *2969*) to look down on, to despise, to think lightly, to have the wrong idea about someone, "to entertain wrong ideas about God's goodness" (BAGD). **ἀγνοῶν** pres. act. part. ἀγνοέω (# *51*) to be ignorant, to ignore (Barrett). Part. of manner, describing how they have the wrong idea about God's goodness. **ἄγει** pres. ind. act. ἄγω (# *72*) to lead; conative pres. "to try to lead" (Käsemann). ◆ **5 σκληρότης** (# *5018*) hardness, stubbornness (Morris). **ἀμετανόητος** (# *295*) unrepentant. **θησαυρίζεις** pres. ind. act. θησαυρίζω (# *2564*) to store up, to treasure up. The idea is gradual accumulation (Lightfoot, *Notes*). Ironically they do not store something valuable or beneficial, but something that will justly destroy them. **σεαυτῷ** (# *4932*) dat. sing., yourself. Dat. of disadvantage. **ὀργῆς** gen. sing. ὀργή (# *3973*) wrath (s. 1:18). Gen. of description telling what kind of day is intended. **ἀποκαλύψεως** gen. sing. ἀποκάλυψις (# *637*) unveiling, revelation. Gen. of description. **δικαιοκρισία** (# *1464*) just judgment, judgment according to that which is right. It denotes God's justice in the narrow, even distributive sense (MRP, 189). **θεοῦ** (# *2536*) s.v. 2. God. Subjective gen., justice meted out by God. The words refer to the final judgment of God (Dunn; Morris). ◆ **6 ἀποδώσει** fut. ind. act. ἀποδίδωμι (# *625*) to give back, to recompense. Used in the papyri for the paying of debt or restoring of a due of any kind (MM). **ἔργα** pl. ἔργον (# *2240*) work, deed. Perhaps Paul is quoting from the OT (Dunn; Byrne; s. LXX Ps. 61:13). ◆ **7 ὑπομονή** (# *5705*) patience, endurance, bearing up under (TLNT; TDNT; EDNT). **ἀφθαρσία** (# *914*) incorruptible, immortality. **ζητοῦσιν** pres. act. part. dat. pl. ζητέω (# *2426*) to seek. Subst. part. to emphasize a defining trait. Dat. of advantage.

◆ **8 ἐριθεία** (# *2249*) selfish ambition (BAGD; Barrett; Dunn; Fitzmyer, 302; Phil. 2:3). This perhaps gives their motivation. **ἀπειθοῦσι** pres. act. part. (adj.) ἀπειθώ (# *578*) to be disobedient. **πειθομένοις** pres. mid. part. πείθω (# *4275*) to obey, to be obedient, w. dat. Part. as subst. **ἀδικίᾳ** (# *94*) unrighteousness. **ὀργὴ καὶ θυμός** (# *3973; 2779; 2596*) anger, rage. Perhaps a hendiadys, "burning anger." (For this and the following word s. Trench, *Synonyms*, 130-34; TDNT.) ◆ **9 θλῖψις** (# *2568*) pressure, tribulation. **στενοχωρία** (# *5103*) anguish, torturing confinement, hemmed in w. no way out (SH; Dunn). **κατεργαζομένου** pres. mid. (dep.) part. κατεργάζομαι (# *2981*) to do, to accomplish (s. Rom. 1:27). ◆ **10 ἐργαζομένῳ** pres. mid. (dep.) part. ἐργάζομαι (# *2237*) to work, to do. Pres. indicates a complete continual action, but no one is able to do this perfectly (Moo). ◆ **11 προσωπολημψία** (# *4721*) respective persons, the accepting of the appearance of a pers. A Hebraic term for partiality. The oriental custom of greeting was to bow one's face to the ground. If the one greeted accepted the person, he was allowed to lift his head again (TDNT; SB, 3: 79-83). ◆ **12 ὅσοι** (# *4012*) as many as; those belonging to the same class or group. **ἀνόμως** (# *492*) adv. without the law, lawless. **ἥμαρτον** (# *279*) aor. ind. act. ἁρματάνω to sin. Timeless aor. (RWP). **ἀπολοῦνται** fut. ind. mid. (dep.) ἀπόλλυμι (# *660*) to perish. **κριθήσονται** fut. ind. pass. κρίνω (# *3212*) to judge (s.v. 1). ◆ **13 ἀκροατής** (# *212*) one who hears. **ποιητής** (# *4475*) one who does. For the ending of these two nouns indicating the agent who performs the action s. MH, 364f. **δικαιωθήσονται** fut. ind. pass. δικαιόω (# *1467*) to justify, to declare righteous, to declare in the right. Some vbs. w. -οω endings are causative ("to make ..."), but others are "delocutive" indicating a pronouncement, or declaration (TDNT; EDNT; APC, 224-80; GW, 82-162; MRP; DPL, 517-23; Delbert Hillers, "Delocutive Verbs in Biblical Hebrew," *JBL* 86 [1967]: 320-24; Cleon L. Rogers, Jr., "A Study of the Greek Words for Righteousness" [unpublished dissertation; Dallas Theological Seminary: Dallas, Texas, 1962]). ◆ **14 ὅταν** (# *4020*) w. subj., whenever. **ἔχοντα** pres. act. part. (adj.) ἔχω (# *2400*) to have. **φύσει** dat. sing. φύσις (# *5882*) nature. Instr. dat. **ποιῶσιν** pres. subj. act. ποιέω (# *4472*) to do, to conduct oneself. Subj. in an indef. temp. cl. **ἔχοντες** pres. act. part. ἔχω (# *2400*) to have. **νόμος** (# *3795*) law. All men show by their acts that they have a knowledge of right and wrong (Hodge; Morris; Moo; BBC; for examples from the ancient world s. NW, 2, i:71-86). ◆ **15 ἐνδείκνυνται** pres. ind. mid. (dep.) ἐνδείκνυμι (# *1892*) to demonstrate, to show. The word implies an appeal to facts (SH). **γραπτός** (# *1209*) written. **συμμαρτυρούσης** pres. act. part. gen. fem. sing. συμμαρτυρέομαι (# *5210*) to testify w., to confirm, to testify in support of someone or something (BAGD). **συνείδησις** (# *5287*) conscience. Paul regarded conscience as performing in the gentile world roughly the same function as was the Law performed among the Jews. (Margaret E. Thrall, "The Pauline Use of Συνείδησις," *NTS* 14 [1967]: 124; TDNT; TLNT; EDNT; Fitzmyer, 311; Dunn; Byrne). **μεταξύ** (# 3568) between. **κατηγορούντων** pres. act. part. κατηγορέω (# 2989) to speak against, to accuse, to bring a legal accusation against someone. Gen. abs. **ἀπολογουμένων** pres. mid. (dep.) part. ἀπολογέομαι (# 664) to excuse, to defend, to offer a legal defence. Adj. part. or perhaps gen abs., temp. part., "while their conscience either accuses or excuses them." ◆ **16 κρίνει** pres. ind. act. κρίνω (# 3212) to judge. Pres. indicates the certainty of the fut. event. **κρυπτός** (# 3220) hidden. ◆ **17 ἐπονομάζῃ** pres. ind. pass. 2nd. sing. ἐπονομάζω (# 2226) to put a name upon; pass., to have a name imposed, to bear the name (SH). **ἐπαναπαύῃ** pres. ind. mid. 2nd. sing. ἐπαναπαύω (# 2058) to rest upon, to rely upon (Michel). **καυχᾶσαι** pres. ind. mid. (dep.) 2nd. sing. καύομαι (# 3016) to boast, to pride oneself in. ◆ **18 δοκιμάζεις** pres. ind. act. δοκιμάζω (# 1507) to test, to examine, to approve after testing. **διαφέροντα** pres. act. part. διαφέρω (# 1422) to carry through, to differ, to excel, to be worth more than (BAGD). The part. could mean either "the things which excel" or "the things which differ." Here it refers to the most delicate shades of the moral life alluding to the legal casuistry in which the Jewish schools excelled (Godet). **κατηχούμενος** pres. pass. part. κατηχέω (# 2994) to instruct. ◆ **19 πέποιθας** perf. ind. act. πείθω (# 4275) to persuade, to be persuaded, to put one's trust in. **ὁδηγός** (# 3843) guide, one who leads the way (RWP). ◆ **20 παιδευτής** (# 4083) educator, teacher, schoolmaster. The word has the idea of discipline, correction, as well as teaching (SH). **ἀφρόνων** gen. pl. ἄφρων (# 933) unthinking, foolish, ignorant, obj. gen. **νήπιος** (# 3758) infant. **μόρφωσις** (# 3673) form, rough sketch, penciling of the form, the outline of the framework without the substance (Lightfoot, *Notes*). ◆ **21 διδάσκων** pres. act. part. διδάσκω (# 1438) to teach. **κηρύσσων** pres. act. part. κηρύσσω (# 3062) to preach. **κλέπτειν** pres. inf. act. κλέπτω (# 3096) to steal. Inf. in indir. discourse, or perhaps the translation of a Heb. inf. absolute following a part. ◆ **22 λέγων** pres. act. part. λέγω (# 3306) to say. **μοιχεύειν** pres. inf. act. μοιχεύω (# 3658) to commit adultery. Inf. in indir. discourse. **βδελυσσόμενος** pres. mid. (dep.) part. βδελύσσομαι (# 1009) to abhor, to detest. **εἴδωλον** (# 1631) idol. **ἱεροσυλεῖς** pres. ind. act. ἱεροσυλέω (# 2644) to rob a temple. Perhaps a reference to the robbing of heathen temples (Kuss; SB, 3:113). For the Jewish opposition to heathen idolatry s. Moore, *Judaism*, 1:362f; SB, 3:111f. ◆ **23 καυχᾶσαι** pres. ind. mid. (dep.) καυχάομαι (# 3016) to boast. Pres. emphasizing the simple statement of fact that they boast. **παραβάσεως** (# 4126) overstepping, transgression, breaking. w. a following obj. gen.

(BAGD). **ἀτιμάζεις** pres. ind. act. ἀτιμάζω (# 869) to dishonor. Pres. is either customary or iterat. In this case the emphasis is on the repeated action of dishonoring God. Pres. could also be progressive with the emphasis being on the action of dishonoring God in progress. ◆ **24 βλασφημεῖται** pres. ind. pass. βλασφημέω (# 1059) to blaspheme. **γέγραπται** perf. ind. pass. γράφω (# 1211) to write; here used to introduce an authoritative quotation (MM). ◆ **25 περιτομή** (# 4364) circumcision **ὠφελεῖ** pres. ind. act. ὠφελέω (# 6067) to help, to be of benefit, to be of use (BAGD). Gnomic pres. Used to express customary action and general truths (SMT, 8). **πράσσῃς** pres. subj. act. πράσσω (# 4556) to do, to practice. Pres. emphasizes the continual doing of the law. **παραβάτης** (# 4127) transgressor, one who steps across a line (RWP). **νόμου** gen. sing. νόμος (# 3795) law. Obj. gen., "against the law." **ῇς** pres. subj. act. εἰμί (# 1639) to be. **ἀκροβυστία** (# 213) uncircumcision. For the importance of circumcision in Judaism s. Moore, *Judaism*, 2:16-21; TDNT; SB, 4:23-40; JPB, 213-14; Gal. 2:3. **γέγονεν** perf. ind. act. γίνομαι (# 1181) to become. Perf. emphasizes the continuing state of results. ◆ **26 δικαίωμα** (# 1468) ordinance, righteous to man (s. 1:32). **φυλάσσῃ** pres. subj. act. φυλάσσω (# 5875) to guard, to observe. **λογισθήσεται** fut. ind. pass. λογίζομαι (# 3357) to regard (s.v. 3). ◆ **27 κρινεῖ** fut. ind. act. κρίνω (# 3212) to judge (s.v. 1). **τελοῦσα** pres. act. part. τελέω (# 5464) to bring to an end, to complete, to fulfill. **διά** (# 1328) w. gen., with. Used to describe the attendant circumstances; that is, w. all your advantages of circumcision and the possession of written law (SH). ◆ **28 φανερός** (# 5745) visible, open to sight, manifest. ◆ **29 οὗ** gen. sing. ὅς (# 4005) rel. pron.; the antecedent is Ἰουδαῖος. **ἔπαινος** (# 2047) praise. **ἐξ** (# 1666) from. Prep. w. gen. describes the source.

Romans 3

◆ **1 περισσός** (# 4356) advantage, that which encircles a thing, that which is in excess, over and above (SH). **ὠφέλεια** (# 6066) benefit, usefulness. For the use of the rhetorical question to express clarity s. BD, 262. **περιτομή** (# 4364) circumcision. Gen. of source, "benefit derived from circumcision." The article and the pl. vb. in v. 2 show that it refers to the nation. Fig. use of circumcision (metonymy); here circumcision the sign is used to describe the covenant and its ensuing benefits. Paul is thinking of the promises of the Abrahamic Covenant as the superiority that Israel had (S. Lewis Johnson, Jr., "Studies in Romans: The Jews and the Oracles of God," *Bib Sac* 130 [1973]: 239). ◆ **2 πρῶτον** (# 4754) first, in the first place. **ἐπιστεύθησαν** aor. ind. pass. πιστεύω (# 4409) to entrust; pass. to be entrusted w. **λόγιον** (# 3359) saying, oracle. Here the reference is to the OT promises. (Johnson, "The Jews and the Oracles of God," 240-46; Byrne). Acc. is used after a pass.

vb. ◆ **3 ἠπίστησαν** aor. ind. act. ἀπιστεύω (# *601*) to disbelieve, to refuse to believe; or w. meaning to be unfaithful (SH). For the prefix as a neg. s. Rom. 1:20. **ἀπιστία** (# *602*) unbelief, unfaithfulness. **καταργήσει** fut. ind. act. καταργέω (# *2934*) to render inactive, to render invalid (SH). ◆ **4 γένοιτο** aor. opt. mid. (dep.) γίνομαι (# *1181*) to be, to become. In this phrase, "let it not be." It expresses the abhorrence of an inference which may be falsely drawn from the argument (SMT, 79; Dunn). Opt. expresses a wish, here a negative one or abhorrence (GGBB, 482). **γινέσθω** pres. imp. mid. (dep.) γίνομαι (# *1181*). Here, be found; that is, become, relatively to our apprehension (Lightfoot, *Notes*). **δέ** (# *1254*) but. The contrast suggests "though every man be found a liar" (RWP). **ἀληθής** (# *239*) true. **καθώς** (# *2777*) just as. **γέγραπται** perf. ind. pass. γράφω (# *1211*) to write. Perf. emphasizing the completed state and the continual authority of that which is written. **δικαιωθῇς** aor. subj. pass. δικαιόω (# *1467*) to declare right, to justify; pass. to be declared to be in the right (s. 2:13). **νικήσεις** fut. ind. act. νικέω (# *3771*) to be victorious, to conquer. **κρίνεσθαι** pres. inf. mid./pass. κρίνω (# *3212*) to judge. For the use of the inf. w. the prep. to express contemporary action s. MT, 144f. ◆ **5 ἀδικία** (# *94*) unrighteousness. **συνίστησιν** pres. ind. act. συνίστημι (# *5319*) to bring together, to commend, to demonstrate, to bring out something (BAGD). The word developed from meaning to appoint as a technical legal term to meaning establish, prove (MM). Used in a 1st. class cond. cl. where the cond. is assumed for the sake of argument to be true (BG, 103). **ἐροῦμεν** fut. ind. act. λέγω (# *3306*) to say. **ἐπιφέρων** pres. act. part. ἐπιφέρω (# *2214*) to inflict. The cl. expects the answer "no" (Barrett) ◆ **6 γένοιτο** aor. opt. mid. (dep.) γίνομαι (# *1181*) (s.v. 4). **ἐπεί** (# *2075*) since, if that were so; that is, "if the inflicting of punishment necessarily implied injustice" (SH). **κρινεῖ** fut. ind. act. κρίνω (# *3212*) to judge (s.v. 4). ◆ **7 ἐν** (# *1877*) by, through. For the instr. use of the prep. s. MT, 252f. **ψεῦσμα** (# *6025*) lie. **ἐπερίσσευσεν** aor. ind. act. περισσεύω (# *4355*) to be in abundance, to increase. **κἀγώ** (# *2743*) = καὶ ἐγώ. The word **καί** (# *2779*) then, is used to introduce the main cl. of a cond. cl. and connotes a previously expressed circumstance (BG, 155). **ἁμαρτωλός** (# *283*) sinful, sinner. **κρίνομαι** pres. ind. pass. κρίνω (# *3212*) to judge s.v. 4. ◆ **8 μή** (# *3590*) used in a rhetorical question expecting the answer "no" (RWP; Cranfield; Kuss; Byrne). **βλασφημούμεθα** pres. ind. pass. βλασφημέω (# *1059*) to slander, to blaspheme (TLNT; TDNT). **ὅτι** (# *4022*) recitative, equivalent to quotation marks (RG, 951f). **φασίν** pres. ind. act. φημί (# *5774*) to say. **λέγειν** pres. inf. act. λέγω (# *3306*) to say, to speak. Inf. in indir. discourse. **ποιήσωμεν** aor. subj. act. ποιέω (# *4472*) to do, to commit. Hortatory subj. "let us do," or deliberative subj., "shall we commit." **ἔλθη** aor. subj. act. ἔρχομαι

(# *2262*) to come. Subj. w. **ἵνα** (# *2671*) to express purp. **ὧν** gen. pl. ὅς (# *4005*) rel. pron., whose. It refers to all who draw these antinomian inferences (Lightfoot, *Notes*; Dunn). **κρίμα** (# *3210*) judgment. **ἔνδικος** (# *1899*) just. For this passage s. S. Lewis Johnson, Jr., "Studies in Romans: Divine Faithfulness, Divine Judgment, and the Problem of Antinomianism," *Bib Sac* 130 (1973): 329-37; Cranfield; Moo; C.H. Cosgrove, "What if Some Have Not Believed? The Occasion and Thrust of Romans 3:1-8," *ZNW* 78 (1987): 90-105. ◆ **9 προεχόμεθα** pres. ind. mid./pass. προέχω (# *4604*) to excel, to be first; mid., to have an advantage or to hold something before oneself for protection; pass., to be excelled, to be in a worse position (BAGD; SH; Käsemann; Moo; Fitzmyer, 330-31; Byrne). **πάντως** (# *4122*) not all together, only in a limited sense, not at all (Barrett; S. Lewis Johnson, Jr., "Studies in Romans: The Universality of Sin," *Bib Sac* 131 [1974]: 166; Fitzmyer, 331). **προῃτιασάμεθα** aor. ind. mid. (dep.) προαιτιάομαι (# *4577*) to make a previous accusation, to accuse previously, to incriminate previously. It belongs to the language of the bar (Godet). **εἶναι** pres. inf. act. εἰμί (# *1639*) to be. Inf. in indir. discourse. ◆ **10 γέγραπ-ται** perf. ind. pass. γράφω (# *1211*) to write. Perf. indicates the permanent and authoritative character of that which is written (MM). **δίκαιος** (# *1465*) righteous, meeting God's standard. Pred. nom. without the article stresses the character. **εἷς** (# *1651*) one. For the composite character of the following quotation s. Fitzmyer, *Essays*, 66f; Dunn; Cranfield. ◆ **11 συνίων** pres. act. part. συνίω (# *5317*) to understand. Part. as subst. **ἐκζητῶν** pres. act. part. ἐκζητέω (# *1699*) to seek out. Part. as subst. Pres. indicates an habitual action. ◆ **12 ἐξέκλιναν** aor. ind. act. ἐκκλίνω (# *1712*) to turn away from, to turn aside from. **ἅμα** (# *275*) together. **ἠχρεώθησαν** aor. ind. pass. ἀχρεόομαι (# *946*) to be worthless, to be useless. The idea of the Heb. word (אלח, DCH, 1:289) is to go bad or sour like milk (Lightfoot, *Notes*; Dunn). Ingressive aor., "to become worthless." **ποιῶν** pres. act. part. ποιέω (# *4472*) (s.v. 8). **χρηστότητα** acc. pl. χρηστότης (# *5983*) goodness in the widest sense, w. the idea of utility (SH). ◆ **13 τάφος** (# *5439*) grave. **ἀνεῳγμένος** perf. pass. part. ἀνοίγω (# *487*) to open. **λάρυγξ** (# *3296*) throat. **ἐδολιοῦσαν** impf. ind. act. δολιόω (# *1514*) to deceive, to practice or use deceit. For impf. of contract vbs. w. the aor. ending s. MH, 195. **ἰός** (# *2675*) poison. **ἀσπίς** (# *835*) asp, the Egyptian cobra (RWP). The emphasis here is not just on evil, but the quick, fatal poison (ZPEB, 5:366; DDD, 1407-10). **χεῖλος** (# *5667*) lip. ◆ **14 ἀρᾶς** (# *725*) curse (TDNT). **πικρία** (# *4394*) bitterness. **γέμει** pres. ind. act. γεμέω (# *1154*) to be full. ◆ **15 ὀξεῖς** pl. ὀξύς (# *3955*) swift, fast. **ἐκχέαι** aor. inf. act. ἐκχέω (# *1772*) to pour, to shed. **αἷμα** (# *135*) blood. Used here as an expression of violence or murder. Perhaps Prov. 1:16 is alluded to. ◆ **16 σύντριμμα** (# *5342*) destruction, ruin, fracture (MM). ταλαιπωρία (# 5416) misery. ◆ **17 ὁδός** (# 3847) way, path. εἰρήνη (# 1645) peace. Gen. to characterize the path. ἔγνωσαν aor. ind. act. γινώσκω (# 1182) to know. Const. aor. emphasizing the action without ref. to time. ◆ **18 ἀπέναντι** (# 595) before, in the presence of. ◆ **19 οἴδαμεν** perf. ind. act. οἶδα (# 3857) to know. Def. perf. w. a pres. meaning (VA, 281-87). ὅσα acc. pl. ὅσος (# 4012) as much; here, whatever things. λέγει pres. ind. act. λέγω (# 3306) to speak. λαλεῖ pres. ind. act. λαλέω (# 3281) to speak. The first vb. calls attention to the substance of what is spoken, the second to the outward utterance (SH). ἵνα (# 2671) w. subj. to express purp. or result (BD, 198; Fitzmyer, 337). φραγῇ aor. subj. pass. φράσσω (# 5852) to shut, to stop, to close or stop the mouth, so that the man must remain silent (BAGD). It gives the imagery of a courtroom connoting the situation of the defendant who has no more to say in response to the charges brought against him (Moo). ὑπόδικος (# 5688) liable to judgment or to punishment; a legal term meaning "to answer to," "to bring under the cognizance of." It indicates someone who is guilty in the sense of having offended against the law and so made himself liable to prosecution and punishment (Cranfield). It was used in the papyri of officials who were held answerable (MM). γένηται aor. subj. mid. (dep.) γίνομαι (# 1181) to become. Subj. w. the previous ἵνα (# 2671) to express purp. or result. τῷ θεῷ (# 2536) before God. Dat. shows that God is the judicial authority concerned and that He is the injured party (Cranfield). ◆ **20 διότι** (# 1484) because. ἐξ ἔργων νόμου (# 1666; 2240; 3795) from the works of the law. (s. the discussion of this by Dunn; Byrne, w. bibliography). δικαιωθήσεται fut. ind. pass. δικαιόω (# 1467) to declare righteous, to justify. Fut. may indicate that this will never be the case. The whole context has reference to a judicial trial and verdict (SH; Moo, 212-18; s. 2:13). Theol. pass. indicating God is the agent of the action. ἐπίγνωσις (# 2106) recognition, knowledge. The prep. w. the gen. indicates "through," "by means of" (IBG). ◆ **21 πεφανέρωται** perf. ind. pass. φανερόω (# 5746) to make manifest, to make clear. Perf. emphasizes the state or condition (K.L. McKay, "The Use of the Ancient Greek Perfect Down to the Second Century A.D.," *Bulletin of the Institute of Classical Studies of the University of London* 12 (1965): 1-21). μαρτυρουμένη pres. pass. part. (adj.) μαρτυρέω (# 3455) to testify, to bear witness. ◆ **22 διὰ πίστεως Ἰησοῦ Χριστοῦ** "through faith in Jesus Christ." Gen. is best understood as obj. gen., rather than subjective gen., "the faithfulness of Jesus Christ" (Moo; Dunn; GGBB, 114-15). εἰς πάντας (# 1650; 4246) unto all, for all. πιστεύοντας pres. act. part. πιστεύω (# 4409) to believe. Adj. part. to describe a necessary characteristic. διαστολή (# 1405) difference, distinction. ◆ **23 ἥμαρτον** aor. ind. act. ἁμαρτάνω (# 279) to sin, to miss the mark (TDNT;

EDNT; BBC; NIDNTT, 3:577-83). Aor. may be constantive, summarizing the sins of people throughout the past in a single moment, or it may refer to the sinning of all people in Adam (s. 5:12; Moo; Dunn; VA, 222; VANT, 258-59; GGBB, 503). ὑστεροῦνται pres. ind. mid. ὑστερέω (# 5728) to come too late, to miss, to fail to reach, to be lacking, to come short of, w. gen. (BAGD; TDNT; TLNT). Pres. indicates a continual action. There is a continuous failing. δόξα (# 1518) glory, the manifestation of God's perfection (s. Rom. 1:23). The following gen., θεοῦ (# 2536), could be objective, failing to give God glory; or subjective, failing to receive the glory God gives; or poss., either failing to receive the glory God gives, or failing to conform to His image (Murray). ◆ **24 δικαιούμενοι** pres. pass. part. δικαιόω (# 1467) to justify. Pres. is iterat. and emphasizes the repeated action in each case (RWP). For the grammatical connection and use of the part. s. SH; Murray; Cranfield. δωρεάν (# 1562) freely, as a gift without payment, gratis, for nothing (Fitzmyer, 347). Adv. acc. χάριτι dat. sing. χάρις (# 1562) grace, free help to one who is undeserving (TDNT; EDNT; TLNT). Instr. dat. ἀπολύτρωσις (# 667) redemption, release, or deliverance of the payment of a price (APC, 37-48; GW, 71f; TDNT; LDC; TLNT; I. Howard Marshall, "The Development of the Concept of Redemption in the New Testament," RH, 153-69). ◆ **25 προέθετο** aor. ind. mid. (dep.) προτίθημι (# 4729) to place before; mid. to purpose, to design or to set forth publicly (SH). ἱλαστήριον (# 2663) that which expiates or propitiates, the means of expiation or the place of propitiation (for example, the OT mercy seat) (BBC; DPL, 784-86; APC, 167-74; GW, 38-47; TDNT; Dunn; VGG, 120-31; Wilckens, 233-43). αἵματι dat. sing. αἷμα (# 135) blood. It indicates a life given up in death and refers to the sacrificial death of Christ (Moo; APC, 108-24). The phrase could be taken w. πίστεως (Hodge), or better w. ἱλαστήριον (Morris). ἔνδειξις (# 1893) demonstration, sign, proof. διά (# 1328) w. acc., because of. πάρεσις (# 4217) passing over; Christ died and thereby manifested God's righteousness because in the past God had merely overlooked man's sins (Barrett; MRP, 210). προγεγονότων perf. act. part. προγίνομαι (# 4588) to happen before, to happen previously. Perf. views the continuing condition. The prep. compound is temp. ◆ **26 ἀνοχῇ** (# 496) patience, forbearing (s. 2:4). εἶναι pres. inf. act. εἰμί (# 1639) to be. Articular inf. w. εἰς (# 1650) to express purp. or result. δικαιοῦντα pres. act. part. acc. masc. sing. δικαιόω (# 1467) to justify (s.v. 24). Part. as subst. ◆ **27 καύχησις** (# 3018) boasting. ἐξεκλείσθη aor. ind. pass. ἐκκλείω (# 1710) to shut out, to exclude. Theol. pass. indicating that God is the agent (Dunn). ποῖος (# 4481) what sort of? what kind of? νόμος (# 3795) law. Justification through keeping of the law would lead to boasting. ◆ **28 λογιζόμεθα** pres. ind. mid. (dep.) λογίζομαι (# 3357) to reckon. **δικαιοῦσθαι** pres. inf. pass. δικαιόω (# 1467) to justify (s.v. 24). Inf. in indir. discourse. ◆ **29 οὐχί** (# 4049) introduces a rhetorical question expecting a positive answer. ◆ **30 εἴπερ** (# 1642) if, if on the whole. Used of a thing which is assumed to be (T). **δικαιώσει** fut. ind. act. δικαιόω (# 1467) to justify (s.v. 24). **ἀκροβυστία** uncircumcision. ◆ **31 καταργοῦμεν** pres. ind. act. καταργέω (# 2934) to render inactive (s.v. 3). **γένοιτο** aor. opt. mid. (dep.) γίνομαι (# 1181) to be (s.v. 4). **ἱστάνομεν** pres. ind. act. ἵστημι or ἱστάνω (# 2705) to establish.

Romans 4

◆ **1 ἐροῦμεν** fut. ind. act. λέγω (# 3306) to say. **εὑρηκέναι** perf. inf. act. εὑρίσκω (# 2351) to find. The dominant thought in this usage is that of being granted a favored standing before someone who has the power to withhold or bestow the favor he chooses (Dunn). Inf. in indir. discourse (BD, 203-204). **προπάτωρ** (# 2848) forefather, ancestor. ◆ **2 ἐδικαιώθη** aor. ind. pass. δικαιόω (# 1467) to justify, to declare righteous (s. 2:13). Theol. pass. indicating that God is the agent. Ind. w. **εἰ** (# 1623) in a 1st. class cond. cl. which assumes the reality of the cond. for the sake of argument. **καύχημα** (# 3017) boasting, ground of boasting (SH). For the righteousness of Abraham in Jewish thinking s. SB, 3:186-201; *Jub.*, 23:10; Roy A. Harrisville, III, *The Figure of Abraham in the Epistles of St. Paul: In the Footsteps of Abraham* (San Francisco: Mellen Research University Press, 1992), 47-135; 185-204; BBC; CPP, 164-68; DPL, 1-9. ◆ **3 γάρ** (# 1142) for. To be taken as an argumentative particle showing why Abraham has no ground of boasting (Barrett). **ἐλογίσθη** aor. ind. pass. λογίζομαι (# 3357) to reckon to one's account. In the language of an accountant the word means "to enter in the account book" (Ramsay, LP, 286f; Fitzmyer, 373). The use of the Heb. construction in Gen. 15:6 (חֹשֵׁב לֹ) shows that the meaning is *not* that faith is considered the equivalent of righteousness, but rather that God reckoned to him a status of righteousness that Abraham did not have (Moo; חשׁב in TDOT). ◆ **4 ἐργαζομένῳ** pres. mid. (dep.) part. ἐργάζομαι (# 2237) to work. Part. as subst. Dat. of advantage or personal interest. **μισθός** (# 3635) pay, wage, salary (MM). **λογίζεται** pres. ind. pass. λογίζομαι (# 3357) (s.v. 3). **ὀφείλημα** (# 4052) debt, that which is owed, moral obligation (s. 1:14). ◆ **5 ἐργαζομένῳ** pres. mid. (dep.) part. ἐργάζομαι (# 2237) (s.v. 4). Part. as subst. **πιστεύοντι** pres. act. part. dat. masc. sing. πιστεύω (# 4409) to believe. Part. as subst. used to emphasize a trait. **δικαιοῦντα** pres. act. part. acc. masc. sing. δικαιόω (# 1467) to justify (s.v. 2). Part. as subst. **ἀσεβῆς** (# 815) ungodly. A very strong word used to place the gratuity of the gift in the strongest light (Lightfoot, *Notes*). ◆ **6 καθάπερ** (# 2749) even as. For Paul's use of the rabbinical exegetical principle of comparing the same

word used in two passages s. Barrett; Cranfield. **μακαρισμός** (# 3422) declaration of blessedness (T). The ending of the word indicates a state or cond. (MH, 355). ◆ **7 μακάριος** (# 3421) blessed, happy (TLNT; Matt. 5:3). **ἀφέθησαν** aor. ind. pass. ἀφίημι (# 918) to forgive. **ἀνομία** (# 490) lawlessness. **ἐπεκαλύφθησαν** aor. ind. pass. ἐπικαλύπτω (# 2128) to cover over. ◆ **8 οὐ μή** (# 4024; 3590) not ever. For this emphatic neg. use s. M, 188f; BG, 149f. **λογίσηται** aor. subj. mid. (dep.) λογίζομαι (# 3357) to reckon. Subj. w. emphatic neg. ◆ **9 περιτομή** (# 4364) circumcision. **ἀκροβυστία** (# 213) uncircumcision. The prep. here w. acc. primarily designates movement toward, in this sense "for" (IBG, 49). ◆ **10 ὄντι** pres. act. part. (temp.) εἰμί (# 1639) to be. Pres. expressing contemporaneous time, "when he was...." ◆ **11 σημεῖον** (# 4956) sign; distinguishing mark by which something is known (BAGD). **ἔλαβεν** aor. ind. act. λαμβάνω (# 3284) to take. **σφραγῖδα** acc. sing. σφραγίς (# 5382) seal. That which clearly attests or validates the authority of a claim or status to the outside world (Dunn). **δικαιοσύνης** gen. sing. δικαιοσύνη (# 1466) righteousness. That sign of circumcision simply confirms righteousness through faith that was already pres. (BAGD; BBC; TDNT). **λογισθῆναι** aor. inf. pass. λογίζομαι (# 3357) to reckon (s.v. 3). Inf. to express purp. (contemplated result) or actual result (RWP). ◆ **12 στοιχοῦσιν** pres. act. part. στοιχέω (# 5123) to walk, to follow in the footsteps. A well-known military term meaning "to march in file" (SH; Moo). **ἴχνεσιν** dat. ἴχνος (# 2717) footstep, track. ◆ **13 νόμου** (# 3795) the context of law. The prep. w. gen. indicates attendant circumstances (Barrett) or is instr. (Moo). The word law without the article refers to law which falls into this category (Murray). **ἐπαγγελία** (# 2039) promise. **κληρονόμος** (# 3101) heir. For the Jewish view of Abraham as heir of the world and that this was achieved through his law righteousness s. SB, 3:204-209. **εἶναι** pres. inf. act. εἰμί (# 1639) to be. Epex. inf. in apposition to ἐπαγγελία (Moo). ◆ **14 κεκένωται** perf. ind. pass. κενόω (# 3033) to empty. Perf. emphasizes a state or condition brought about by a previous condition. **κατήργηται** perf. ind. pass. καταργέω (# 2934) to annul, to render inoperative. Perf. indicates the abiding condition. The cond. cl. of this v. could be classified as a 2nd. class cond. cl. where the cond. is not true (IBG, 148). ◆ **15 ὀργή** (# 3973) wrath (s. 1:18). **κατεργάζεται** pres. ind. mid. (dep.) κατεργάζομαι (# 2981) to work, to produce. **οὐ** (# 4024) where. **παράβασις** (# 4126) transgression, stepping over the mark. ◆ **16 βέβαιος** (# 1010) solid, durable, valid, a legally guaranteed security, reliable, dependable, certain, sure (Lightfoot, *Notes*; MM; Dunn; TLNT). **σπέρμα** (# 5065) seed. ◆ **17 γέγραπται** perf. ind. pass. γράφω (# 1211) to write. **ὅτι** (# 4022) recitative, equal to quotation marks. **τέθεικα** perf. ind. act. τίθημι (# 5502) to place, to appoint. This was part of the covenant promise given to Abraham. Perf. indicates the abiding result. **κατέναντι** (# *2978*) opposite to, in the presence of. For this prep. s. MH, 129. **ἐπίστευσεν** aor. ind. act. πιστεύω (# *4409*) to believe. **ζῳοποιοῦντος** pres. act. part. (adj.) gen. masc. sing. ζῳοποιόω (# *2443*) to make alive. Refers to God's ability to give a child to Abraham and Sarah in their old age (Godet). The designation of God as "lifegiver" corresponds to the second of the Jewish Eighteen Benedictions (Byrne). **καλοῦντος** pres. act. part. καλέω (# *2813*) to call. **ὄντα** pres. act. part. εἰμί (# *1639*) to be. Part. as subst. ◆ **18** **ἐλπίδα** acc. ἐλπίς (# *1828*) hope. Here lit. "against (or beyond) hope," "in hope"; that is, "hoping against hope" (Barrett; EH, 501-6). **γενέσθαι** aor. mid. (dep.) inf. γίνομαι (# *1181*) to become. Articular inf. w. prep. εἰς (# *1650*) to express purp. **εἰρημένον** perf. pass. part. λέγω (# *3306*) to say. Subst. use of part. Perf. emphasizes the past result w. lingering effects: "that which has been spoken." **ἔσται** fut. ind. mid. (dep.) εἰμί (# *1639*) to be. ◆ **19** **ἀσθενήσας** aor. act. part. ἀσθενέω (# *820*) to be weak; ingressive aor. w. neg. **μή** (# *3590*), "without becoming weak" (SH). Causal or circum. part. **κατενόησεν** aor. ind. act. κατανοέω (# *2917*) to see clearly, to discern. For the prep. compound s. M, 117. **νενεκρωμένον** perf. pass. part. (adj.) νεκρόω (# *3739*) to kill; pass., to die. Perf. emphasizes the completed state or cond. (s. Rom. 3:21). **ἑκατονταετής** (# *1670*) a hundred years. **που** (# *4543*) about. **ὑπάρχων** pres. act. part. ὑπάρχω (# *5639*) to exist, to be. **νέκρωσις** (# *3740*) death, deadness. For nouns w. this suffix s. MH, 373. ◆ **20** **διεκρίθη** aor. ind. pass. διακρίνω (# *1359*) to separate, to divide into, to be divided in one's own mind, to waiver (RWP). **ἐνεδυναμώθη** aor. ind. pass. ἐνδυναμόω (# *1904*) to strengthen; pass., to be strengthened, to be empowered. **δούς** aor. act. part. δίδωμι to give (# *1443*) to give. Circum. part., "and gave glory to God." ◆ **21** **πληροφορηθείς** aor. pass. part. πληροφορέω (# *4442*) to fill completely, to convince fully; pass., to be fully convinced, assured (BAGD; TDNT). Causal. part. or circum. **ἐπήγγελται** perf. ind. pass. ἐπαγγέλλω (# *2040*) to promise. **ποιῆσαι** aor. inf. act. ποιέω (# *4472*) to do. Compl. inf. w. δυνατός (# *1543*), "he was able to do." ◆ **22** **ἐλογίσθη** aor. ind. pass. λογίζομαι (# *3357*) to reckon to one's account. (s.v. 3). ◆ **23** **ἐγράφη** aor. ind. pass. γράφω (# *1211*) to write. ◆ **24** **μέλλει** pres. ind. act. μέλλω (# *3516*) to be about to. Used w. inf. to express fut. (MKG, 307). **λογίζεσθαι** pres. inf. act. (s.v. 22). Compl. inf. to the main vb. **πιστεύουσιν** pres. act. part. πιστεύω (# *4409*) to believe. **ἐγείραντα** aor. act. part. ἐγείρω (# *1586*) to raise. Part. as subst. ◆ **25** **παρεδόθη** aor. ind. pass. παραδίδωμι (# *4140*) to deliver up. Perhaps a reference to Isa. 53:12 (Lightfoot, *Notes*). Theol. pass. (Dunn). **διά** (# *1328*) w. acc., because of. The first prep. here could be causal, the second final (MRP, 196; Dunn). Both preps. could have a prospective reference

(Murray), or the first could be retrospective ("because of") and the second prospective ("for the sake of") (Moo). **παράπτωμα** (# *4183*) transgression, a falling along-side, a false step, transgression (TDNT; Cremer, 498f). **ἠγέρθη** aor. ind. pass. ἐγείρω (# *1586*) to raise. **δικαίωσις** (# *1470*) justification, the judicial vindication and justification (TDNT; MRP, 196).

Romans 5

◆ **1** **δικαιωθέντες** aor. pass. part. δικαιόω (# *1467*) to justify, to declare to be in the right (s. 2:13). Aor. part. expressing antecedent time before the main vb. It could be either temp. or casual. Aor. points to a completed action. Theol. pass. indicating that God has done the action upon the subject. **εἰρήνη** (# *1645*) peace. It denotes the outward situation of being in a relationship of peace with God as shown by the prep. **πρός** (Moo; Dunn; Fitzmyer, 395; Cranfield). **ἔχομεν** pres. ind. act. ἔχω (# *2400*) to have, to possess. For the variant reading ἔχωμεν (pres. subj. act.; hortatory subj. "let us enjoy the possession of peace" s. TC, 511; M, 35, 110, 247, 249; Stanley E. Porter, "The Argument of Romans 5: Can a Rhetorical Question Make a Difference?" *JBL* 110 [1991]: 662-65; GGBB, 464). **πρός** (# *4639*) with. It denotes a friendly relationship (BD, 124; NIDNTT, 3:1204). ◆ **2** **καί** (# *2779*) also (Godet). **προσαγωγή** (# *4643*) access, introduction (SH; Moo; MM; EDNT). **ἐσχήκαμεν** perf. ind. act. ἔχω (# *2400*) to have. Perf. emphasizes the completed state: "to have received and still possess" (M, 238). **ἑστήκαμεν** perf. ind. act. ἵστημι (# *2705*) perf. to stand. **καυχώμεθα** pres. ind./subj. mid. (dep.) καυχάομαι (# *3016*) to boast. It here means a triumphant, rejoicing confidence in God (Barrett). Ind., "we are boasting;" or hortatory subj, "let us continue to boast." ◆ **3** **καί** (# *2779*) also. **ἐν ταῖς θλίψεσιν** (# *1877*; *3836*; *2568*) in the tribulations. The word refers to pressures, hardships, and sufferings, the distress brought about by outward circumstances (SH; TDNT; Trench, *Synonyms*, 202f; Dunn). **εἰδότες** perf. act. part. (causal) of the def. vb. οἶδα (# *3857*) to know; "because we know." **ὅτι** (# *4022*) that, introducing the content of the knowledge. **ὑπομονή** (# *5705*) patient endurance, patiently waiting in hope (TDNT; NIDNTT; TLNT). **κατεργάζεται** pres. ind. mid. (dep.) κατεργάζομαι (# *2981*) to produce. The prep. compound is perfective, carrying the action of the main vb. to its conclusion (M, 112f). ◆ **4** **δοκιμή** (# *1509*) approved character, the quality of being approved as a result of tests and trials (BAGD; SH). ◆ **5** **ἐλπίς** (# *1828*) hope. This is the faithful trust in God's promises for the future in the midst of trials (EH, 510). **καταισχύνει** pres. ind. act. καταισχύνω (# *2875*) to put to shame. Pres. indicates a continuing action, "will never put us to shame." **ὅτι** (# *4022*) because, giving the reason hope will not cause shame or disappointment. **ἡ ἀγάπη τοῦ θεοῦ** (# *27*; *2536*) the love of God. Subjective gen., "the love which God has for us" (Moo; Dunn; EH, 511; GGBB, 121). ἐκκέχυται perf. ind. pass. ἐκχέω (# 1772) to pour out. The word denotes both abundance and diffusion (Lightfoot, *Notes*). The idea of spiritual refreshment and encouragement is conveyed through the metaphor of watering. Perf. indicates a completed state or continuing results (s. 3:21 for the perf.). δοθέντος aor. pass. part. δίδωμι (# 1443) to give. Adj. part. to emphasize this as a trait. Aor. indicates a logically antecedent action. Theol. pass., indicating that God is the giver. ◆ 6 ἔτι γάρ (# 2285; 1142) if indeed. Thrall discusses the textual problem and concludes that the combination is used to introduce a fact of which one was absolutely certain (Thrall, 89f). Some opt for the reading εἰς τί γάρ and translate, "For to what purpose did Christ, while we were helpless, die at the right time for the ungodly" (Porter, "The Argument of Romans 5: Can a Rhetorical Question Make a Difference?" *JBL* 110 [1991]: 666). ὄντων pres. act. part. (temp.) εἰμί (# 1639) to be. Gen. abs. Pres. expressing contemporaneous action ("while"). ἀσθενής (# 820) weak, helpless (Moo). He did not wait for us to start helping ourselves, but died for us when we were altogether helpless (Cranfield). κατὰ καιρόν (# 2848; 2789) at the appropriate time, at the very time (Moo; Dunn). ὑπὲρ ἀσεβῶν (# 5642; 815) for ungodly ones. The prep. has the idea of substitution as well as benefit (Moo; Porter, "The Argument of Romans 5: Can a Rhetorical Question Make a Difference?" *JBL* 110 [1991]: 668; NIDNTT, 3:1196-97). ἀπέθανεν aor. ind. act. ἀποθνήσκω (# 633) to die. Aor. views the act of dying as a finished deed. ◆ 7 μόλις (# 3660) w. difficulty, scarcely, hardly. ὑπὲρ δικαίου (# 5642; 1465) for a righteous (man). For a discussion of the structure of this v. s. Frederik Wisse, "The Righteous Man and the Good Man in Romans 5:7," *NTS* 19 (1972): 91-93. ἀποθανεῖται fut. ind. mid. (dep.) ἀποθνήσκω (# 633) to die. Gnomic fut. (GGBB, 571). τάχα (# 5440) perhaps, possibly, probably. τολμᾷ pres. ind. act. τολμάω (# 5528) to dare. ἀποθανεῖν aor. inf. act. ἀποθνήσκω (# 633) to die. Compl. inf. w. the vb. τολμᾷ. ◆ 8 συνίστησιν pres. ind. act. συνίστημι (# 5319) to bring together, to demonstrate. ὄντων pres. act. part. (temp.) gen. n. pl. εἰμί (# 1639) to be. Gen. abs. Pres. expressing contemporaneous time. ἀπέθανεν aor. ind. act. ἀποθνήσκω (# 633) to die. ◆ 9 μᾶλλον (# 3437) more; here, "much more," an argument from the greater to the less (RWP). The point is, since God has already done the really difficult thing, justified the impious sinner, we may be absolutely confident that He will do what is by comparison very easy, namely, save from His wrath at the last those who are already righteous in His sight (Cranfield). For examples of this method of argument among the rabbis s. SB, 3:223-26; EJH, 11-12; for this in the Greek diatribe s. Porter, "The Argument of Romans 5: Can a Rhetorical

Question Make a Difference?" *JBL* 110 (1991): 668. δικαιωθέντες aor. pass. part. (causal) δικαιόω (# 1467) to justify. Aor. points to the completed action. Theol. pass. ἐν τῷ αἵματι (# 1877; 3836; 135) in the blood (s. 3:25). Instr. use of the prep., giving the means of the justification. σωθησόμεθα fut. ind. pass. σῴζω (# 5392) to save, to rescue, to deliver. Here it means the consummation of that work of which justification is the commencement. It is a preservation from all causes of destruction and points to the final salvation (Hodge; Cranfield; TDNT). Theol. pass. indicating that God is the one who saves. ◆ 10 ἐχθρός (# 2398) enemy. ὄντες pres. act. part. εἰμί (# 1639) to be. Concessive or temp. part. Pres. indicates contemporaneous action, "while we were enemies" or "even though we were still enemies at that time." κατηλλάγημεν aor. ind. pass. καταλλάσσω (# 2904) to exchange, to exchange enmity for friendship, to reconcile (ACP, 187; TDNT; MNTW, 102-06; V; Cilliers Breytenbach, "Versöhnung, Stellvertretung und Sühne: Semantische und traditionsgeschichtliche Bemerkungen am Beispiel der paulinischen Briefe," *NTS* 39 [1993]: 59-79; I. Howard Marshall, "The Meaning of 'Reconciliation'," *Unity and Diversity in New Testament Theology: Essays in Honor of George E. Ladd*, Robert A. Guelich, ed, [Grand Rapids: Eerdmans, 1978], 153-69). The prep. compound is perfective and means "to effect a thorough change back, reconciled" (MH, 298). Aor. points to the completed action (V, 154). Theol. pass. ind. in a 1st. class cond. cl. which assumes the reality of the cond. πολλῷ μᾶλλον (# 4498; 3437) by how much more (s.v. 9). καταλλαγέντες aor. pass. part. (causal) Aor. indicates antecedent action and points to a completed action. Theol. pass. σωθησόμεθα fut. ind. pass. σῴζω (# 5392) to save (s.v. 9). ◆ 11 οὐ μόνον δέ, ἀλλὰ καί (# 4024; 3667; 1254; 247; 2779) not only, but also. It indicates that for all that he has already said, he has something more to say (Dunn; Moo). καυχώμενοι pres. mid. part. (circum.) καυχάομαι to boast (# 3016) (s.v. 2). καταλλαγή (# 2903) reconciliation (s.v. 10). ἐλάβομεν aor. ind. act. λαμβάνω (# 3284) to take. ◆ 12 For a study of this section s. Marty L. Reid, *Augustinian and Pauline Rhetoric in Romans Five: A Study in Early Christian Rhetoric* (Lewiston, N.Y.: Mellen Biblical Press, 1996). διὰ τοῦτο (# 1328; 4047) because of this. (For a discussion of the phrase as being retrospective, prospective, or illative, introducing an inference from the preceding s. Moo, 363-64; S. Lewis Johnson, Jr., "Romans 5:12: An Exercise in Exegesis and Theology," ND, 301). εἰσῆλθεν aor. ind. act. εἰσέρχομαι (# 1656) to come into. διῆλθεν aor. ind. act. διέρχομαι (# 1451) to pass through. It contains the force of distribution: "made its way to each individual member of the race" (SH). ἐφ' ᾧ (# 2093; 4005) perhaps best understood as causal ("because") (F.W. Danker, "Romans 5:12: Sin Under Law," *NTS* 14 [1968]: 424-39; but s. also GI, 116f; for various ways of understanding the phrase s. Fitzmyer, 413-17; Cranfield; Johnson, ND, 303-5; GGBB, 342-43). The reason why death has come to all men is that death is universal in that sin is universal (Johnson, ND, 305). ἥμαρτον aor. ind. act. ἁμαρτάνω (# 279) to sin. For the relation between Adam sinning and the sin of mankind s. Johnson, ND, 298-316, esp. 305-316; Moo. ◆ **13** ἄχρι (# 948) until w. gen. ἐλλογεῖται pres. ind. pass. ἐλλογέω (# 1824) to charge to one's account (MM). ὄντος pres. act. part. gen. n. sing. εἰμί (# 1639) to be. ◆ **14** ἐβασίλευσεν aor. ind. act. βασιλεύω (# 996) to rule as king, to be a king, here in the sense of control or determine the destiny of. ἁμαρτήσαντας aor. act. part. ἁμαρτάνω (# 279) to sin. ὁμοίωμα (# 3930) likeness. It denotes a resemblance which may be purely accidental (AS). παράβασις (# 4126) transgression. τύπος (# 5596) type. The word means a visible mark left by some object. (TDNT). μέλλοντος pres. act. part. μέλλω (# 3516) to be about to. Subst. part., "the one who is coming." ◆ **15** οὐχ (# 4024) the neg. here and in v. 16 can be understood as introducing a rhetorical question expecting the answer "yes" (C.C. Caragounis, "Romans 5.15-16 in the Context of 5.12-21: Contrast or Comparison?" *NTS* 31 [1985]: 142-48). παράπτωμα (# 4183) transgression (s. 4:25; Trench, *Synonyms*, 239f). χάρισμα (# 5922) grace gift, an act of grace (Godet; TDNT; NIDNTT, 2:115-24; EDNT). ἀπέθανον aor. ind. act. ἀποθνῄσκω to die (# 633) (s.v. 6). πολλῷ μᾶλλον (# 4498; 3437) how much more (s.v. 9; s. also John T. Kirby, "The Syntax of Romans 5.12: a Rhetorical Approach," *NTS* 33 [1987]: 283-86). δωρεά (# 1561) gift, the act of giving (Godet). ἐπερίσσευσεν aor. ind. act. περισσεύω (# 4355) to be more than enough, to abound. ◆ **16** ἁμαρτήσαντος aor. act. part. (adj.) gen. masc. sing. ἁμαρτάνω (# 279) to sin (s.v. 12). δώρημα (# 1564) gift. It denotes the concrete gift, the blessing bestowed (Godet). κρίμα (# 3210) judgment, decision. κατάκριμα (# 2890) condemnation, judgment against someone. For the force of the prep. compounds s. MH, 316. δικαίωμα (# 1468) justification, acquittal, the righteous status that results from God's justifying action (MRP, 198f; Moo). ◆ **17** ἐβασίλευσεν aor. ind. act. βασιλεύω (# 996) to rule. Constative viewing the action over a period of time. περισσεία (# 4353) more than enough, abundance. λαμβάνοντες pres. act. part. λαμβάνω (# 3284) to receive. It is the gift which man receives, imputed not infused (SH). Subst. part. βασιλεύσουσιν fut. ind. act. βασιλεύω (# 996) to be king, to rule as a king. ◆ **18** ἄρα (# 726) therefore. It gives a summation of the doctrine set forth in the whole passage, from v. 12 onward (Murray). δικαίωσις (# 1468) justification. ζωῆς gen. sing. ζωή (# 2437) life. Gen. may be epex. (MT, 214; BG, 16-17); or, perhaps better, gen. of result ("justification which leads to life") (BD, 92; Cranfield; Moo; Byrne). ◆ **19** παρακοή (# 4157) disobedience (Dunn). κατασταθήσονται fut. ind. pass. καθίστημι

(# 2770) to set down, to constitute, to establish. ◆ **20** παρεισῆλθεν aor. ind. act. παρέρχομαι (# 4216) to come in alongside, to enter a state of things already existing (SH). πλεονάσῃ aor. subj. act. πλεονάζω (# 4429) to be, or to become more, to be pres. in abundance. Here it is probably intr. (Lightfoot, *Notes*). Subj. w. ἵνα (# 2671) to express purp. ἐπλεόνασεν aor. ind. act. πλεονάζω (# 4429). ὑπερεπερίσσευσεν aor. ind. act. ὑπερπερισσεύω (# 5668) to abound more exceedingly. The prep. compound magnifies (MH, 326). ◆ **21** βασιλεύσῃ aor. subj. act. βασιλεύω (# 996) (s.v. 17). Subj. w. ἵνα (# 2671) used to express purp. αἰώνιος (# 173) eternal. Eternal life is not only related to the fut., but is organically related to the actual life lived and is a pres. possession of the believer (GW, 189f).

Romans 6

◆ **1** ἐροῦμεν fut. ind. act. λέγω (# 3306) to say. Used here in a rhetorical question. ἐπιμένωμεν pres. subj. act. ἐπιμένω (# 2152) to stay, to remain, to reside in. Pres. indicates practice of sin as a habit. Deliberate subj. in a rhetorical question (RWP). πλεονάσῃ aor. subj. act. πλεονάζω (# 4429) to be in abundance, to abound, to cause to increase. Subj. w. ἵνα (# 2671) to express purp. ◆ **2** γένοιτο aor. opt. mid. (dep.) γίνομαι (# 1181) to be, to happen (s. 3:4). Opt. in an expression rejecting a false conclusion. ἀπεθάνομεν aor. ind. act. ἀποθνῄσκω (# 633) to die. Death was "in God's sight, w. God's seal and pledge of the fact in baptism, providing freedom from sin and with the assurance of final victory" (Cranfield). τῇ ἁμαρτίᾳ (# 281) w. respect to sin; dat. of reference or respect (BD, 105f), or dat. of disadvantage w. the vb. ἀποθνῄσκω, indicating that one has changed one's state to the detriment of sin (Moo). ἔτι (# 2285) still. ζήσομεν fut. ind. act. ζάω (# 2409) to live; that is, at any fut. time after our death (Meyer). A deliberative future expressing "oughtness" (GGBB, 570). ◆ **3** ἀγνοεῖτε pres. ind. act. ἀγνοέω (# 51) not to know, to be ignorant. Paul does not use the mystery religions of the day as the base of his teaching in this section (DRP; Dunn). ὅσοι nom. pl. ὅσος (# 4012) as many as, those belonging to a class or group, "all of us who" (BAGD; Moo). ἐβαπτίσθημεν aor. ind. pass. βαπτίζω (# 966) to baptize (s. 1 Cor. 10:2; 12:13). W. the prep. it indicates "movement into in order to become involved with or part of," no longer referring directly to the ritual act; the pass. is a theol. pass. (Dunn). ◆ **4** συνετάφημεν aor. ind. pass. συνθάπτω (# 5313) to bury together. The words w. σύν indicate the communality of believers rooted in a dependence upon their communality with Christ (Dunn). διὰ τοῦ βαπτίσματος (# 967) through baptism. εἰς τὸν θάνατον (# 2505) into the death. The prep. conveys the notation of incorporation into (Lightfoot, *Notes*). ὥσπερ (# 6061) just as, even so. ἠγέρθη aor. subj. pass. ἐγείρω (# 1586) pass. to be raised, to rise. Subj. w. ἵνα (# 2671) to express purp. or result. **καινότητι** dat. sing. καινότης (# 2786) freshness, newness. The idea of the word is "strangeness," and therefore a change (Lightfoot, *Notes*). **ζωῆς** (# 2437) life. Gen. of apposition, "newness, that is, life" (DPL, 553-55). **περιπατήσωμεν** aor. subj. act. περιπατέω (# 4344) to walk, to walk about, to conduct one's life (TDNT). Subj. w. **ἵνα** (# 2671) to express purp. ◆ **5 σύμφυτος** (# 5242) grown together w. The process of grafting may be in mind (Barrett). **γεγόναμεν** perf. ind. act. γίνομαι (# 1181) to become. Perf. indicates the abiding state or condition. Ind. w. **εἰ** (# 1623) in a 1st. class cond. cl. assuming the reality of the cond. **ὁμοίωμα** (# 3930) likeness, copy, form (Moo; s. Rom. 5:14). The following fut. shows that the word does not refer to baptism (DRP, 293-94). Associative dat. w. **σύμφυτοι** (Moo). **ἀναστάσεως** gen. sing. ἀνάστησις (# 386) resurrection. Descriptive gen. w. **ὁμοιώματι. ἐσόμεθα** fut. ind. mid. (dep.) εἰμί (# 1639) to be. ◆ **6 γινώσκοντες** pres. act. part. γινώσκω (# 1182) to know. Pres. indicates contemporaneous action. Causal part., "because we know." **παλαιός** (# 4094) old. The "old man" could refer to the evil inclination of Jewish teaching (s. Gal. 5:17; SB, 4, i:466-83; TS, 471-82; PRJ, 25-27), or to what we were in Adam (Moo; Cranfield; DPL, 9-14). **συνεσταυρώθη** aor. ind. pass. συσταυρόω (# 5365) to crucify together. **καταργηθῇ** aor. subj. pass. καταργέω (# 2934) to render inoperative, to make inactive. **μηκέτι** (# 3600) no longer. **δουλεύειν** pres. inf. act. δουλεύω (# 1526) to be a slave, to serve as a slave. Articular inf. to express purp. ◆ **7 ἀποθανών** aor. act. part. ἀποθνήσκω (# 633) to die. Aor. describes antecedent action. Part. is substantive, expressing a characteristic. **δεδικαίωται** perf. ind. pass. δικαιόω (# 1467) to justify, to declare to be in the right. Here the word means either to be declared to be free from sin or to be acquitted from sin (MRP, 200f). ◆ **8 ἀπεθάνομεν** aor. ind. act. ἀποθνήσκω (# 633) to die (s.v. 7). **συζήσομεν** fut. ind. act. συζάω (# 2409) to live together. ◆ **9 εἰδότες** perf. act. part. οἶδα (# 3857) to know. Def. perf. w. pres. meaning. **ἐγερθείς** aor. pass. part. (causal) ἐγείρω (# 1586) to raise. **κυριεύει** pres. ind. act. κυριεύω (# 3259) to be lord over, to rule over, w. gen. The idea of master and slave is pres., (SH). Durative pres. "continue to rule." ◆ **10 ὃ γάρ** stands for τὸν γὰρ θάνατον, ὅν (Cranfield; RWP). **ἀπέθανεν** aor. ind. act. ἀποθνήσκω (# 633) to die (s.v. 7). **ἐφάπαξ** (# 2384) once for all. **ὃ δέ** stands for τὴν δὲ ζωήν, ἥν (Cranfield). **ζῇ** pres. ind. act. ζάω (# 2409) to live. ◆ **11 λογίζεσθε** pres. imp. mid. (dep.) λογίζομαι (# 3357) to consider, to reckon. Pres. imp. could mean "do this continuously" or "continue doing this" (MKG, 272). **εἶναι** pres. inf. act. εἰμί (# 2462) to be. Compl. to the main vb. "Continually consider yourselves to be dead to sin." **ζῶντας** pres. act. part. ζάω (# 2409) to live. Part. used as a substantive. The dat. w. part. could be dat. of respect or dat. of personal interest or advantage (DM, 84). ◆ **12 βασιλευέτω**

pres. imp. act. βασιλεύω (# 996) to be king, to rule as king. Pres. imp. w. neg. **μή** (# 3590) means either "do not always," or "do not continue," or else gives a prohibition of a general command, "do not make it your habit" (MKG, 272; VANT, 335-40). **θνητός** (# 2570) mortal, subject to death. **ὑπακούειν** pres. inf. act. ὑπακούω (# 5634) to listen to, to obey. Articular inf. w. prep. **εἰς** (# 1650) expresses either purp. or result (MT, 143). **ἐπιθυμία** (# 2123) desire. The prep. compound is directive. The basic meaning, "drive," "passion," is directed to an object (TDNT; Godet). ◆ **13 πα-ριστάνετε** pres. imp. act. παρίστημι (# 4225) to place beside, to put at one's disposal, to present, to make something available to someone (Kasemann; LN, 1:567; BBC). For the meaning of the pres. imp. w. neg. s.v. 12. **μέλη** acc. pl. μέλος (# 3517) member. A synecdoche (part for the whole) meaning "your body." **ὅπλον** (# 3960) tool, weapon. Sin is regarded as a sovereign (v. 12) who demands the military service of its subjects, levies their quota of arms (v.13), and gives them their soldier's pay of death (v. 23) (Lightfoot, *Notes*). **ἀδικία** (# 94) unrighteousness. Attributive gen., "unrighteous tools." **παραστήσατε** aor. imp. act. The previous pres. imp. calls for the discontinuation of an action. Aor. imp. here calls for an immediate decisive new action as a break from the past (Johnson; Bakker, 65). **ζῶντας** pres. act. part. ζάω (# 2409) to live; "alive, after being dead," a common classical expression (Lightfoot, *Notes*). ◆ **14 κυριεύσει** fut. ind. act. κυριεύω (# 3259) to be lord over (s.v. 9). ◆ **15 ἁμαρτήσωμεν** aor. subj. act. ἁμαρτάνω (# 279) to sin. Deliberative subj., "shall we sin?" Rhetorical question expecting the answer "no." **γένοιτο** aor. opt. mid. (dep.) γίνομαι (# 1181) to be, to become (s.v. 2). ◆ **16 παριστάνετε** pres. ind. act. παρίστημι (# 4225) to place beside (s.v. 13). It is used either as a term describing sacrifice or as a judicial term (BAGD). **ἤτοι** (# 2486) either. It has the notion of restriction (RG, 1154). ◆ **17 ἦτε** impf. ind. act. εἰμί (# 1639) to be. **ὑπηκούσατε** aor. ind. act. ὑπακούω (# 5634) to be obedient. **παρε-δόθητε** aor. ind. pass. παραδίδωμι (# 4140) to deliver over to, to pass on a teaching (TLNT). **τύπος** (# 5596) type, mark, copy, image, compendium, terse presentation (Fitzmyer, 449; Moo). Incorporation of the antecedent into the real cl., "to which form of doctrine you were delivered" (RWP). **διδαχῆς** gen. sing. (# 1439) teaching. Gen. of description or content. ◆ **18 ἐλευ-θερωθέντες** aor. pass. part. ἐλευθερόω (# 1802) to free, to make free. Aor. expresses logically antecedent action. Temp. part. ("after") or possibly causal. **ἐδουλώθητε** aor. ind. pass. δουλόω (# 1530) to serve. ◆ **19 ἀνθρώπινος** (# 474) human; here, "in human terms" (BAGD). **ἀσθέ-νεια** (# 819) weakness; here, "because of the difficulties of apprehension" (SH). **παρεστήσατε** aor. ind. act. παρίστημι (# 4225) to place beside. **μέλη** (# 3517) s.v. 13. **δοῦλος** (# 1528) servant. Acc. pl. pred. acc. in a double acc. construction: "as servants" (MT, 246; RG, 408f). **ἀκαθαρσίᾳ** dat. sing. (# *174*) uncleanness. Dat. as indir. obj. **ἀνομίᾳ** (# *490*) lawlessness. **παραστήσατε** aor. ind. act. παρίστημι (s.v. 16). **ἁγιασμός** (# *40*) sanctification, holiness, consecration. It refers to the process or state (Murray) of being set apart for God's service and the development and display of His characteristics (Cremer; TDNT; EDNT). ◆ **20 ἦτε** impf. ind. act. εἰμί (# *1639*) to be. **ἐλεύθερος** (# *1801*) free. ◆ **21 εἴχετε** impf. ind. act. ἔχω (# *2400*) to have. **ἐπαισχύνεσθε** pres. ind. mid. (dep.) ἐπαισχύνομαι (# *2049*) to be ashamed. ◆ **22 ἐλευθερωθέντες** aor. pass. part. ἐλευθερόω (# *1802*) to be free. Temp. or causal part. Aor. indicating logically antecedent action. **δουλωθέντες** aor. pass. part. δουλόω (# *1530*) to be a slave. Theol. pass. indicating God as the active subject. ◆ **23 ὀψώνιον** (# *4072*) provisions, wages of a soldier (C.C. Caragounis, "Ὀψώνιον: A Reconsideration of its Meaning," *NovT* 16 [1974]: 35-37; TDNT). For a description of soldier's pay s. Lightfoot, *Notes*; CC, 206-209; BC 5:428. **χάρισμα** (# *5922*) free gift, grace gift (s. 5:15). **ἐν** (# *1877*) in. Dat. is local, or better instr. ("through").

Romans 7

◆ **1 ἀγνοεῖτε** pres. ind. act. ἀγνοέω (# *51*) to be ignorant. **γινώσκουσιν** pres. act. part. γινώσκω (# *1182*) to know. He speaks to those who have a knowledge of a general principle of all law, or Roman law, or Jewish law (SH; Moo; Cranfield; Fitzmyer, 455-57; Dunn). Indir. obj. **κυριεύει** pres. ind. act. κυριεύω (# *3259*) to be lord over, to rule, w. gen. Gnomic pres. **ζῇ** pres. ind. act. ζάω (# *2409*) to live, to be alive. Gnomic. pres. ◆ **2 ὕπανδρος** (# *5635*) under (subjected to) a husband, married. The word may itself include the idea of subordination (Barrett). **ζῶντι** pres. act. part. (adj.) ζάω (# *2409*) "living husband" (Lightfoot, *Notes*). **δέδεται** perf. ind. pass. δέω (# *1313*) to bind. Perf. emphasizes the state or cond. (s. Rom. 3:21). **νόμῳ** dat. sing. νόμος (# *3795*) Instr. dat., "by law" (LIF, 84ff). **ἀποθάνῃ** aor. subj. act. ἀποθνῄσκω (# *633*) to die. Subj. used in a 3rd. class cond. cl. where the cond. is viewed as probable. **κατήργηται** perf. ind. pass. καταργέω (# *2934*) to render inoperative, to nullify, to annul. Perf. emphasizes she is completely absolved or discharged (SH). ◆ **3 ἄρα** (# *726*) then. **ζῶντος** pres. act. part. (temp.) ζάω (# *2409*) to live. Gen. abs., "while he is living." **μοιχαλίς** (# *3655*) adulteress. **χρηματίσει** fut. ind. act. χρηματίζω (# *5976*) to bear a name, to be called or named. The basic meaning is to do business, to negotiate. Then, to be called, to bear the name or title of. It also had a special sense of giving answer or communications as an oracle (SH). Gnomic fut. used to state what will customarily happen on the occasion (SMT, 36; GGBB, 571). **γένηται** aor. subj. mid. (dep.) γίνομαι (# *1181*) to become. Subj. in a 3rd. class cond. cl. which assumes the probability of the

cond. **ἀνδρί** dat. sing. ἀνήρ (# *467*) male, husband. Dat. of possession (Fitzmyer, 458). **ἀποθάνῃ** aor. ind. act. ἀποθνῄσκω (# *633*) to die. Subj. in a 3rd. class cond. cl. assuming the probability of the cond. **εἶναι** pres. inf. act. εἰμί (# *1639*) to be. Articular inf. used to express result. **γενομένην** aor. mid. (dep.) part. (adj.) γίνομαι (# *1181*) to become. ◆ **4 ὥστε** (# *6063*) therefore, consequently. It draws an inference or conclusion rather than a comparison from the preceding and introduces the actual relation w. respect to Christians who are in a position corresponding w. that of the wife (Meyer; Cranfield). **ἐθανατώθητε** aor. ind. pass. θανατόω (# *2506*) to put to death. **νόμῳ** (# *3795*) law s.v. 2. Dat. of respect or reference (BD, 105). **γενέσθαι** aor. mid. (dep.) inf. γίνομαι (# *1181*) to become. Inf. w. prep. **εἰς** (# *1650*) to express purp. **ἐγερθέντι** aor. pass. part. ἐγείρω (# *1586*) to rise; pass., to be raised. **καρποφορήσωμεν** aor. subj. act. καρποφορέω (# *2844*) to bear fruit. Subj. w. **ἵνα** (# *2671*) to express purp. **τῷ θεῷ** dat. sing. (# *2436*). Dat. of personal interest, "for God." ◆ **5 ἦμεν** impf. ind. act. εἰμί (# *1639*) to be. Impf. pictures the past life. **σαρκί** dat. sing. σάρξ (# *4922*) flesh, human nature as controlled and directed by sin as illustrated by the Jewish evil inclination (Murray; TDNT; NIDNTT; Kuss; DPL, 303-6; s. Rom. 6:6; Gal. 5:16). Some see the word as depicting a power sphere in which a person lives (Moo, 442f, 498-99). **πάθημα** (# *4077*) passion, strong physical desires (LN, 1:292; TDNT; EDNT). **ἁμαρτιῶν** gen. pl. ἁμαρτία (# *281*) sin. **ἐνηργεῖτο** impf. ind. mid. (dep.) ἐνεργέω (# *1919*) to work within, to be at work, to effect (BAGD). The pricks and stings of passion were active in our members (SH). Impf. pictures the continual action. **καρποφορῆσαι** aor. inf. act. καρποφορέω (# *2844*) to bear fruit. Articular inf. w. **εἰς** (# *1650*) to express purp. (Dunn) (s.v. 4). **θανάτῳ** dat. sing. θάνατος (# *2505*) death. Dat. of purp. or dat. of advantage (Moo). ◆ **6 κατηργήθημεν** aor. ind. pass. καταργέω (# *2934*) to render inoperative (s.v. 2). The meaning w. the prep. is "separated from," "discharged from" (Moo). **ἀποθανόντες** aor. act. part. ἀποθνῄσκω (# *633*) to die. Temp. or causal part. **κατειχόμεθα** impf. ind. pass. κατέχω (# *2988*) to hold down, to suppress, to hold fast, to confine, to restrain (Dunn). Impf. pictures the continual state or action in the past. **ὥστε** (# *6063*) so that, w. the pres. inf. act. **δουλεύειν** (# *1526*) indicating contemplated result (Moo). **καινότητι** (# *2786*) newness (s. 6:4). **παλαιότητι** dat. παλαιότας (# *4095*) obsoleteness, oldness. Gen. following these two words are gen. of apposition denoting that in which the newness or oldness consists (SH). **γράμματος** gen. sing. γράμμα (# *14*) letter of the alphabet, writing, legal code, written code; here referring to the OT as the legislation of the old covenant (Fitzmyer, 460). ◆ **7 ἐροῦμεν** fut. ind. act. λέγω (# *3306*) to say. **γένοιτο** aor. opt. mid. (dep.) γίνομαι (# *1181*) used in a construction rejecting a false conclusion (s. Rom. 3:4). **ἔγνων** aor. ind. act. γινώσκω (# 1182) to know. **εἰ μή** (# 502; 3590) except; used to introduce a contrary to fact cond. cl.: "if it were not through the Law." **τε γάρ** (# 5445; 1142) and in fact; denotes a second fact of the same kind as the preceding (**τε** also). The second fact serves as a proof or explanation to the first (**γάρ** for) (Godet). **ἐπιθυμία** (# 2123) desire, lust. Some see this as having strong sexual overtones (Robert H. Gundry, "The Moral Frustration of Paul Before His Conversion: Sexual Lust in Romans 7:1-25," PSEB, 228-45). **ᾔδειν** plperf. ind. act. οἶδα (# 3857) to know. Def. perf. w. pres. meaning and the plperf. expressing the impf., denoting the beginning of a continuing experience (Dunn). **ἐπιθυμήσεις** fut. ind. act. ἐπιθυμέω (# 2123) to desire, to long for, to covet. It includes every kind of illicit desire (SH). ◆ **8 ἀφορμή** (# 929) occasion, pretext, opportunity for something. Lit., the starting point or base of operations for an expedition, then generally the resources needed to carry through an undertaking (BAGD; GELTS, 74; TDNT). **λαβοῦσα** aor. act. part. λαμβάνω (# 3284) to take. Temp. part. or part. of means. **ἐντολή** (# 1953) commandment. **κατειργάσατο** aor. ind. mid. (dep.) κατεργάζομαι (# 2981) to achieve, to work out, to bring about (s. Rom. 5:3). ◆ **9 ἔζων** impf. ind. act. ζάω (# 2409) to live. He had no dread of punishment, no painful conscientiousness of sin (Hodge). **ἐλθούσης** aor. act. part. (temp.) ἔρχομαι (# 2262) to come. Gen. abs. Aor. denotes antecedent action. **ἀνέζησεν** aor. ind. act. ἀναζάω (# 2409) to revive, to live again, to regain life. ◆ **10 ἀπέθανον** aor. ind. act. ἀποθνήσκω (# 633) to die. **εὑρέθη** aor. ind. pass. εὑρίσκω (# 2351) to find; here in the sense of resulting in: "prove to be a cause for death to me" (BAGD). ◆ **11 λαβοῦσα** aor. act. part. λαμβάνω (# 3284) to take (s.v. 8). **ἐξηπάτησεν** aor. ind. act. ἐξαπατάω (# 1987) to deceive completely, to make someone lose the way (RWP). The prep. compound may be intensive ("completely") or perfective ("successfully") (MH, 309f). **ἀπέκτεινεν** aor. ind. act. ἀποκτείνω (# 650) to kill. ◆ **12 μέν** (# 3525) undoubtedly. This is intended to guard beforehand the unassailable character of the law (Godet). ◆ **13 ἐγένετο** aor. ind. mid. (dep.) γίνομαι (# 1181) to become. **γένοιτο** aor. opt. mid. (dep.) s.v. 7. **φανῇ** aor. subj. pass. φαίνω (# 5743) to appear. Subj. w. **ἵνα** (# 2671) to express purp. **κατεργαζομένη** pres. mid. (dep.) part. (# 2981) κατεργάζομαι s.v. 8. Circum. part. or part. of means. **γένηται** aor. subj. mid. (dep.) γίνομαι (# 1181). **ὑπερβολή** (# 5661) beyond measure, exceedingly. **ἁμαρτωλός** (# 283) sinful. ◆ **14 σάρκινος** (# 4921) fleshly. It denotes the material of which human nature is composed (SH). For adj. w. this suffix indicating the material of which something is made s. MH, 359, 378. **πεπραμένος** perf. pass. part. πράσσω (# 4556) to sell. Perf. emphasizes the state or cond. ("sold") and therefore his bondslave (Lightfoot, *Notes*). Part. as pred. adj. ◆ **15 κατεργάζομαι**

pres. ind. mid. (dep.) s.v. 8. **πράσσω** (# 4556) pres. ind. act. to do, to practice. The classification of the pres. tenses have to do with the question whether Paul is speaking as a believer or not. A mediating position is that they are gnomic, referring to either (GGBB, 391-92, 531-32). **μισῶ** pres. ind. act. μισέω (# 3631) to hate. **ποιῶ** pres. ind. act. ποιέω (# 4472) to do. ◆ **16 σύμφημι** (# 5238) pres. ind. act. to speak w., to agree, to consent. ◆ **17 οὐκέτι** (# 4033) no longer. **οἰκοῦσα** pres. act. part. οἰκέω (# 3861) to indwell. ◆ **18 οἶδα** (# 3857) perf. ind. act. Def. perf. w. pres. meaning, to know. **θέλειν** pres. inf. act. θέλω (# 2577) to desire. Inf. as subst. and subject of the vb. **παράκειται** pres. ind. mid. παράκειμαι (# 4154) to lie alongside, to lie at hand, to be within reach (SH). **κατεργάζεσθαι** pres. mid. (dep.) inf. κατεργάζομαι (# 2981) (s.v. 8). Articular inf. used as a noun. ◆ **20 οἰκοῦσα** pres. act. part. οἰκέω (# 3861) to live (s.v. 17). ◆ **21 θέλοντι** pres. act. part. θέλω (# 2527) to desire. Part. describes an ongoing characteristic. **ποιεῖν** pres. inf. act. ποιέω (# 4472) to do. Compl. inf. to the main vb. ◆ **22 συνήδομαι** pres. ind. mid. (dep.) (# 5310) to rejoice w. someone, to joyfully agree. **ἔσω** (# 2276) inner. ◆ **23 ἀντιστρατευόμενον** pres. mid. (dep.) part. (adj.) ἀντιστρατεύομαι (# 529) to make a military expedition or take the field against anyone, to oppose, to war against (T). For the struggle between the good and evil inclination in Judaism, s. 6:6. **νοός** gen. sing. νοῦς (# 3795) mind, the reflective intelligence (RWP). **αἰχμαλωτίζοντά** pres. act. part. αἰχμαλωτίζω (# 170) lit., to capture w. a spear, to take a prison of war, to subdue (LS). **ὄντι** pres. act. part. (adj.) εἰμί (# 1639) to be. ◆ **24 ταλαίπωρος** (# 5417) miserable, wretched, distressed, unhappy. It is an expression of despair or condemnation and can also describe the state of being pulled in two directions (TLNT; Dunn; CCFJ, 4:155). **ῥύσεται** fut. ind. mid. (dep.) ῥύομαι (# 4861) to rescue. The word is used to denote the act of the soldier who runs at his comrade's cry to rescue him from the hands of the enemy (Godet). ◆ **25 αὐτὸς ἐγώ** (# 899; 1609) I, myself. **τῷ ... νοΐ** dat. sing. νοῦς (# 3808) mind; dat. of reference (BD, 105).

Romans 8

◆ **1 ἄρα** (# 726) so, therefore, consequently, an inference drawn from that which preceded (Murray). **κατάκριμα** (# 2890) punishment following the sentence, a judgment against someone (BAGD; BS, 264-65; Preisigke, 1:752-53; Moo). For the textual problem s. TC, 515. ◆ **2 ζωή** (# 2437) life. The gen. expresses the effect wrought. The Spirit is the author and giver of life (Gifford). For various views on the meaning and connection of the words s. Cranfield. **ἠλευθέρωσεν** aor. ind. act. ἐλευθερόω (# 1802) to liberate, to make free (TDNT). ◆ **3 ἀδύνατος** (# 105) impossible. **ἐν ᾧ** (# 1877; 4005) in which, wherein; defining the point of the law's powerlessness. **πέμψας** aor. ind. act. πέμπω (# 4287) to send. Part. of manner. Aor. indicates logically antecedent action. **ὁμοίωμα** (# 3930) likeness (Moo). **περὶ ἁμαρτίας** (# 4309; 281) concerning sin. It could mean "as a sin offering" (Moo; Fitzmyer, 486; Dunn). **κατέκρινεν** pres. ind. act. κατακρίνω (# 3212) to judge, to condemn. ◆ **4 δικαίωμα** (# 1468) righteous demand, ordinance (s. 1:32). **πληρωθῇ** aor. subj. pass. πληρόω (# 4444) to fill, to fulfill. **περιπατοῦσιν** pres. act. part. περιπατέω (# 4344) to walk about, to conduct one's life (TDNT). Dat. of advantage. Pres. indicates a habit of life. ◆ **5 ὄντες** pres. act. part. εἰμί (# 1639) to be. Part. as subst. **φρονοῦσιν** pres. ind. act. φρονέω (# 5858) to think, to set one's mind or heart upon something, to employ one's faculty for thoughtful planning, w. the emphasis upon the underlying disposition or attitude (LN, 1:325). It denotes the whole action of the affections and will as well as of the reason (SH). ◆ **6 φρόνημα** (# 5859) way of thinking, mindset, aim, aspiration, striving (BAGD). **τῆς σαρκὸς** (# 4922) of the flesh; for this concept s. BBC; DPL, 303-6; gen. of description, the attitude characterized by and determined by (Moo). ◆ **7 διότι** (# 1484) because. **ἔχθρα** (# 2397) hatred, hostility, enmity, active hostility. **ὑποτάσσεται** pres. ind. pass. ὑποτάσσω (# 5718) pass., to be in subjection, to place oneself under. ◆ **8 ὄντες** pres. act. part. εἰμί (# 1639) to be. Part. as subst. expressing a characteristic. Pres. expresses a durative idea. **ἀρέσαι** aor. inf. act. ἀρέσκω (# 743) to please. Compl. inf. to the main vb. ◆ **9 ἐν πνεύματι** (# 4922) to be under the domination of the Spirit (SH). **εἴπερ** (# 1642) if indeed. This strengthens the ascensive force (GGBB, 694). **οἰκεῖ** pres. ind. act. οἰκέω (# 3811) to dwell. Pres. indicates a continual action. ◆ **10 εἰ** (# 1623) if, used is a 1st. class cond. cl. which assumes the reality of the cond. **σῶμα** (# 5293) body, the physical body (Meyer). ◆ **11 ἐγείραντος** aor. act. part. ἐγείρω (# 1586) to raise, to resurrect. **ἐγείρας** aor. act. part. **ζωοποιήσει** fut. ind. act. ζωοποιέω (# 4472) to make alive. **θνητός** (# 2570) mortal, subject to death. **ἐνοικοῦντος** pres. act. part. (adj.) ἐνοικέω (# 1940) to dwell in. Pres. indicates a continual indwelling. ◆ **12 ὀφειλέτης** (# 4050) one who owes a moral debt, debtor (s. 1:14). **κατά** (# 2848) in accordance with. **ζῆν** pres. inf. act. ζάω (# 2409) to live. Epex. inf. used to explain the debt. Pres. stresses the continual living. ◆ **13 ἀποθνήσκειν** pres. inf. act. ἀποθνήσκω (# 633) to die. Compl. inf. to the main vb. **πρᾶξις** (# 4552) deed, act. **θανατοῦτε** pres. ind. act. θανατόω (# 2506) to put to death. **ζήσεσθε** fut. ind. mid. ([dep.] s. BD, 42) ζάω (# 2409) to live. ◆ **14 ὅσος** (# 4012) as many as. **ἄγονται** pres. ind. pass. ἄγω (# 72) to lead. ◆ **15 ἐλάβετε** aor. ind. act. λαμβάνω (# 3284) to take, to receive. **δουλεία** (# 1525) servitude, slavery. **υἱοθεσία** (# 5625) adoption. The word indicates a total break w. the old family and a new family relation with all its

rights, privileges, and responsibilities. For the custom of adoption s. TDNT; OCD, 8f; Fransic Lyall, "Roman Law in the Writings of Paul - Adoption," *JBL* 88 (1969) 458-66; DNP, 1:122-24; RAC, 1:99-112; KP, 1:71-72; DGRA, 14-16; Buckland, 121-28; DPL, 15-18. **κράζομεν** pres. ind. act. κράζω (# 3189) to cry out. It was used in the LXX for urgent prayer and here denotes an urgent and sincere crying to God (Cranfield). Iterat. pres., "to cry again and again." **Ἀββά** (# 5) voc. sing. *'abba* (Aramaic) father. An Aramaic expression used in prayers and in the family circle (BAGD; NIDNTT, 1:614-15; Fitzmyer, 501; lit. on *"abba,"* 502-4; Dunn; AT, 503). ◆ **16 αὐτό** (# 899) himself. For this use of the pron. s. MT, 40f. **συμμαρτυρεῖ** pres. ind. act. συμμαρτυρέω (# 5210) to bear witness w. someone, to confirm, to testify in support of someone. Used in the papyri where the signature of each attesting witness is accompanied by the words, "I bear witness w. and I seal w." (MM). **τέκνον** (# 5451) child. It expresses the relation of nature and indicates community of life (Godet). ◆ **17 κληρονόμος** (# 3101) heir. Paul is still concerned to demonstrate the certainty of fut. salvation and argues that if we are heirs of God our inheritance is secure (Barrett). **συγκληρονόμος** (# 5169) fellow heir, co-heir. **εἴπερ** (# 1642) if indeed, seeing that (Cranfield; s. Rom. 3:30). **συμπάσχομεν** pres. ind. act. συμπάσχω (# 5224) to suffer together (BAGD). It indicates the daily anxieties, tensions and persecutions (Moo). **συνδοξασθῶμεν** aor. subj. pass. συνδοξάζω (# 5280) to glorify together. Subj. w. **ἵνα** (# 2671) to express purp. or the goal in view (Cranfield; Moo; Dunn). Theol. pass. indicating that God is the agent. ◆ **18 λογίζομαι** (# 3357) pres. ind. mid. (dep.) to consider, to reckon. **ἄξιος** (# 545) that which balances the scales, comparable, worthy (TDNT). **πάθημα** (# 4077) suffering. **πρός** (# 4639) the basic meaning w. acc., is "near," "toward," "against." Here, "in comparison w." (RG, 622f; BD, 124f). **μέλλουσαν** pres. act. part. (adj.) acc. fem. sing. μέλλω (# 3516) to be about to. "Coming," "about to be," w. inf. to express fut. **ἀποκαλυφθῆναι** aor. inf. pass. ἀποκαλύπτω (# 636) to reveal. ◆ **19 ἀποκαραδοκία** (# 638) watching eagerly w. outstretched head, eagerly waiting, eager expectation, confident hope and positive expectation (BAGD; D.R. Denton, "Ἀποκαραδοκία," *ZNW* 73 [1982]: 138-40). The sense is strengthened by the prep. in compound which denotes diversion from all other things and concentration on a single object and indicates a patience waiting (EH, 528; SH). **κτίσεως** gen. sing. κτίσις (# 3232) creation. **ἀποκάλυψις** (# 637) uncovering, unveiling, revelation. **ἀπεκδέχεται** pres. ind. mid. (dep.) ἀπεκδέχομαι (# 587) to await expectantly, but patiently. Prep. in compound is perfective w. the idea of readiness and preparedness. Pres. indicates the going on of the act until he comes (MH, 310). The word occurs in the apocryphal work *Acts of Paul* to describe Onesiphorus on the

outskirts of Lystra waiting for Paul's arrival from Iconium (MM). It is also used in *Test. of Abraham*, 16:3 where Death is called before God to be commissioned w. the task of going to Abraham, and Death trembles and waits (ἀπεκδεχόμενος) for the command of God.
◆ **20 ματαιότης** (# *3470*) vanity, aimlessness, the inability to reach a goal or achieve results (Trench, *Synonyms*, 180-84; TDNT; EH, 526; GELTS, 291). Dat. used here, possibly as dat. of association (GGBB, 160). **ὑπετάγη** aor. ind. pass. ὑποτάσσω (# *5718*) to submit (s.v. 7). **ἑκοῦσα** nom. fem. ἑκών (# *1776*) willing, unconstrained, gladly. It usually stands opposed to violence or compulsion (Cremer, 246). **ὑποτάξαντα** aor. act. part. ὑποτάσσω (# *5718*) to submit. Part. as subst. Aor. points to the specific act. The reference is to God rather than to Adam or Satan (Dunn; Moo). ◆ **21 ἐλευθερωθήσεται** fut. ind. pass. ἐλευθερόω (# *1802*) to liberate (s.v. 2). **φθορά** (# *5785*) corruption, deterioration. ◆ **22 συστενάζει** pres. ind. act. συστενάζω (# *5367*) to groan together, perhaps as an unintended prayer (BBC). **συνωδίνει** pres. ind. act. συνωδίνω (# *5349*) to suffer birth pains together, perhaps as an unintended prayer (BBC). The prep. in these two words indicates all the parts of which creation is made up (SH). Pres. indicates the continual action. ◆ **23 ἀπαρχή** (# *569*) firstfruit. The first portion of the harvest, regarded both as a first installment and as a pledge of the final delivery of the whole (Barrett). Gen. of apposition. The Holy Spirit is regarded as an anticipation of final salvation, and a pledge that we who have the Spirit shall in the end be saved (Barrett). **ἔχοντες** pres. act. part. ἔχω (# *2400*) to have. **στενάζομεν** pres. ind. act. στενάζω (# *5100*) to sigh, to groan. **υἱοθεσία** (# *5625*) adoption (s.v. 15). **ἀπεκδεχόμενοι** pres. mid. (dep.) part. (temp.) ἀπεκδέχομαι (# *587*) (s.v. 19). Pres. expressing contemporary action, "while eagerly awaiting." **ἀπολύτρωσις** (# *667*) redemption, release, a deliverance from the "ills that the flesh is heir to" (SH; s. Rom. 3:24). It refers to the final and complete deliverance of our earthly bodies. ◆ **24 ἐλπίδι** dat. sing. ἐλπίς (# *1828*) hope; "in hope." Dat. is not instr. but modal, referring to the fact that salvation bestowed in the past is characterized by hope (Murray; EH, 532-33). **ἐσώθημεν** aor. ind. pass. σῴζω (# *5392*) to save, to rescue. **βλεπομένη** pres. pass. part. (adj.) βλέπω (# *1063*) to see. ◆ **25 ὑπομονή** (# *5705*) patience, patient endurance (TDNT; TLNT). **ἀπεκδεχόμεθα** pres. ind. mid. (dep.) ἀπεκδέχομαι (# *587*) (s.v. 19). ◆ **26 συναντιλαμβάνεται** pres. ind. mid. (dep.) συναντιλαμβάνω (# *5269*) to lend a hand together w., at the same time w. one (RWP), to help, to come to the aid of someone, to take an interest in someone (BAGD; MM; NDIEC, 3:84-85; LAE, 87; TDNT; EDNT; Luke 10:40). **ἀσθενείᾳ** (# *819*) weakness. **προσευξώμεθα** aor. subj. mid. (dep.) προσεύχομαι (# *4667*) to pray. Deliberative subj. **δεῖ** pres. ind. act. (# *1256*); it is necessary, w. inf. giving a logical necessity.

αὐτὸ τὸ πνεῦμα the Spirit himself (s.v. 16). **ὑπερεντυγχάνει** pres. ind. act. ὑπερεντυγχάνω (# *5659*) to plead or intercede on behalf of someone. It is a picturesque word of rescue by one who happens on or happens upon another in trouble and in his behalf pleads w. "unuttered groanings" or w. "sighs that baffle words" (RWP). For intercession in the OT, Judaism, and in Jesus' teaching s. E.A. Obeng, "The Origins of the Spirit Intercession Motif in Romans 8:26," *NTS* 32 (1986): 621-32. Iterat. pres. **ἀλάλητος** (# *227*) unable to be spoken, sighs too deep for words; but not a reference to tongues (Dunn; Moo). Instr. dat. ◆ **27 ἐραυνῶν** pres. act. part. ἐραυνάω (# *2236*) to search, to examine. Part. as subst. emphasizing a particular trait. Pres. indicates an ongoing action. **οἶδεν** perf. ind. act. οἶδα (# *3857*) to know. Def. perf. w. pres. meaning. **κατὰ θεόν** (# *2848; 2536*) according to God. The prep. denotes the standard (Godet). **ἐντυγχάνει** pres. ind. act. ἐντυγχάνω (# *1961*) to intercede, to plead for. ◆ **28 οἴδαμεν** perf. ind. act. οἶδα (# *3857*) s.v. 27. The knowledge is the common assumption of faith (Dunn). **ἀγαπῶσιν** pres. act. part. dat. masc. pl. ἀγαπάω (# *26*) to love. Part. as subst. Dat. of advantage. **πάντα** nom. or acc. pl. πᾶς (# *4246*) all things, everything. The word could be the subject ("all things work together"), or the obj. ("God works all things"), or an acc. of respect ("God works in respect to all things" [Moo; Dunn]; for a discussion s. GGBB, 180-81). **συνεργεῖ** pres. ind. act. συνεργέω (# *5300*) to cooperate, to work together, to work w. one another, to assist (Gifford; CCFJ, 4:118). Josephus uses the noun in connection w. the Romans suffering a temporary setback at Gamala (TJ, 150-56), saying that the Jews viewed this as an "interposition of divine providence" (συνεργίαν θεοῦ) (Jos., *JW*, 4:26). Gnomic pres. describing a general truth. The variant reading ὁ θεός indicates that God is the one who works (s. TC, 518; Cranfield), which would be in accord to the teaching of the Pharisees (TJ, 73-74; Jos., *JW*, 2:162-63). **κατὰ πρόθεσιν** (# *2848; 4606*) acc. sing. πρόθεσις setting forth, plan, purpose, resolve, will (BAGD; TDNT; EDNT). W. the prep. ("according to His purpose"), it refers to God's purpose (Cranfield; Moo). **κλητοῖς** dat. pl. κλητός (# *3105*) called; dat. of advantage. Used to designate the person whose interest is affected (BD, 101). **οὖσιν** pres. act. part. (adj.) εἰμί (# *1639*) to be. Part. as subst. ◆ **29 ὅτι** (# *4022*) because. **οὕς** acc. pl. masc. ὅς (# *4005*) rel. pron. whom. Acc. as direct obj. It is not what He knew beforehand, but whom. God's choice was no surprise to Him. **προέγνω** aor. ind. act. 3rd. pers. sing. προγινώσκω (# *4589*) to know before, to take note of, to fix the regard upon (SH). **προώρισεν** aor. ind. act. προορίζω (# *4633*) to mark out w. a boundary beforehand, to predestine. Aor. views the completed act. **σύμμορφος** (# *5215*) conformed, having the same form w. It denotes an inward and not merely superficial conformity (RWP; TDNT). **εἰκόνος** gen. sing. εἰκών (# *1635*) image (TDNT; NIDNTT, 2:286-88). εἶναι pres. inf. act. εἰμί (# 1639) to be. Articular inf. used with εἰς (# 1650) to express purp. πρωτότοκος (# 4758) firstborn. In Judaism the firstborn was the most beloved, the most cherished, the most honored, the one w. the most ability (SB, 3:256-58). The term reflects on the priority and the supremacy of Christ (Murray; s. Col. 1:15). ◆ 30 προώρισεν aor. ind. act. προορίζω (# 4633) s.v. 29. ἐκάλεσεν aor. ind. act. καλέω (# 2813) to call. ἐδικαίωσεν aor. ind. act. δικαιόω (# 1467) to declare to be in the right, to justify (s. Rom. 2:13). ἐδόξασεν aor. ind. act. δοξάζω (# 1519) to glory. Aor. speaks of God who sees the end from the beginning and in whose decree and purpose all fut. events are comprehended and fixed (Hodge). ◆ 31 οὖν (# 4036) now, therefore, drawing an inference from the preceding. ἐροῦμεν fut. ind. act. λέγω (# 3306) to say. Used in a rhetorical question expecting a neg. answer. ὑπέρ (# 5642) for; here in the sense of "on our side." καθ' (# 2848) against; here in the sense of "be successful in standing against us." ◆ 32 γε (# 1145) an intensive, here magnifying the deed (RWP). ἐφείσατο aor. ind. mid. (dep.) φείδομαι (# 5767) to spare. παρέδωκεν aor. ind. act. παραδίδωμι (# 4140) to deliver over. χαρίσεται fut. ind. mid. (dep.) χαρίζομαι (# 5919) to give graciously, to give out of grace, to give help to those who do not deserve it (s. 5:15; EDNT). ◆ 33 ἐγκαλέσει fut. ind. act. ἐγκαλέω (# 1592) to call in, to bring a legal charge against someone (MM). In a rhetorical question expecting a neg. answer. δικαιῶν pres. act. part. δικαιόω (# 1467) to justify (s. Rom. 2:13). Part. used as a noun to emphasize a defining trait. Pres. emphasizes a contemporaneous action. ◆ 34 κατακρινῶν pres. act. part. κατακρίνω (# 3212) to condemn. Part. used as a noun to emphasize a defining trait. Pres. emphasizes a contemporaneous action. ἀποθανών aor. pass. part. ἀποθνήσκω (# 633) to die. Part. used as a noun to emphasize a defining trait. Aor. indicates logically antecedent action. ἐγερθείς aor. pass. part. ἐγείρω (# 1586) to raise up. δεξιᾷ dat. sing. δεξιός (# 1288) right hand; dat. of location, "at the right hand." This is a position of great honor. ἐντυγχάνει pres. ind. act. ἐντυγχάνω (# 1961) to intercede (s.v. 27). ◆ 35 χωρίσει fut. ind. act. χωρίζω (# 6004) to separate. This is a rhetorical question expecting a neg. answer. ἀπὸ τῆς ἀγάπης τοῦ Χριστοῦ from the love of Christ. Subjective gen. indicating the love Christ had in offering Himself (GGBB, 114). θλῖψις (# 2568) pressure, tribulation. στενοχωρία (# 5103) narrowness, distress. For these two words s. 2:9. διωγμός (# 1501) persecution. λιμός (# 3350) hunger. γυμνότης (# 1219) nakedness. κίνδυνος (# 3074) danger. μάχαιρα (# 3479) sword. ◆ 36 γέγραπται perf. ind. pass. γράφω (# 1211) to write. θανατούμεθα pres. ind. pass. θανατόω (# 2506) to kill, to die, to put to death. Pres. indicating continual action, "this happens all the time." It indicates being in constant danger of

being put to death. ὅλην τὴν ἡμέραν (# 3910; 3836; 2465) the whole day long. Dat. of time indicating the temp. extent. ἐλογίσθημεν aor. ind. pass. λογίζομαι (# 3357) to number, to count as. πρόβατα σφαγῆς (# 4585; 5375) sheep destined for slaughter, gen. of purp. (GGBB, 101). ◆ 37 ὑπερνικῶμεν pres. ind. act. ὑπερνικάω (# 5664) to conquer, to win a victory. The prep. compound intensifies the vb., "we are winning a most glorious victory," "supervictor" (BAGD; Fitzmyer, 534). It suggests a lopsided victory in which the enemy or opponent is completely routed. ἀγαπήσαντος aor. act. part. ἀγαπάω (# 26) to love. Subst. part. to emphasize a particular trait. Aor. emphasizes the logically necessary, antecedent action. ◆ 38 πέπεισμαι perf. ind. pass. πείθω (# 4275) to persuade; pass. to be persuaded. Perf. suggests a past action with continuing result. ἐνεστῶτα perf. pass. part. ἐνίστημι (# 1931) to place in, perf. to be at hand, to be present. Part. as subst. It signifies pres. events and circumstances (Cranfield). μέλλοντα pres. act. part. acc. n. pl. μέλλω (# 3516) about to be; here, "things in the future." δύναμις (# 1539) potentate. ◆ 39 ὕψωμα (# 5739) height, exaltation. βάθος (# 958) depth. Perhaps a merism or a ref. to the Greek concept of fate determining destiny (BBC). δυνήσεται fut. ind. mid. (dep.) δύναμαι (# 1538) to be able to. χωρίσαι aor. inf. act. χωρίζω (# 6004) to separate. Compl. inf. to the main vb. Aor. looks at the total action. ἐν (# 1877) in, describing the sphere of the love.

Romans 9

◆ 1 For the structure of Rom. 9-11, based on the quotations from the OT. s. James W. Aageson, "Scripture and Structure in the Development of the Argument of Romans 9-11," CBQ 48 (1986): 265-89. συμμαρτυρούσης pres. act. part. συμμαρτυρέω (# 5210) to witness together, to testify w., to testify to, to assure (Cranfield; s. Rom. 8:16). Gen. abs. Causal or temp. part., "while, or "because my conscience bears witness." μοι dat. sing. ἐγώ (# 1609) I, indicating the recipient of the testimony (Dunn). συνείδησις (# 5287) conscience (s. 2:15). ◆ 2 λύπη (# 3383) sorrow, grief as a state of mind (SH). μοί dat. sing. (# 1609) to me. Dat. of possession, "my sorrow." ἀδιάλειπτος (# 89) continually, increasing, unceasing (s. 1:9). ὀδύνη (# 3850) pain. It implies the anguish or smart of the heart which is the result of sorrow (SH). ◆ 3 ηὐχόμην impf. ind. mid. (dep.) εὔχομαι (# 2377) to pray, to wish; idiomatic impf., "I was on the point of wishing" (RWP; for the desiderative impf. s. IBG, 9). ἀνάθεμα (# 353) a thing or person devoted to destruction, accursed (Barrett; TDNT; SB, 3:260-61). συγγενής (# 2848) relative, kinsman.   ◆ 4 ὧν gen. pl. ὅς (# 4005) who, rel. pron. "to whom belong." υἱοθεσία (# 5625) adoption (s. 8:15). διαθήκη (# 1347) agreement, covenant, treaty (TDNT). Paul probably has in mind the covenant w. Abraham,

w. Israel through Moses, and w. David (Cranfield). **νομοθεσία** (# *3792*) giving of the law. **λατρεία** (# *3301*) religious service. The sum total of the levitical services instituted by the law (Godet) and the worship of the temple (Dunn; Cranfield). **ἐπαγγελία** (# *2039*) promise. The promises refer to the those made w. Abraham, including the land promise and the blessings on all families of the earth (Cranfield; Dunn). ◆ **5 πατήρ** (# *4252*) father. **τὸ κατὰ σάρκα** (# *2848; 4922*) the article as an adv. acc. strongly emphasizes the limitation: "insofar as the physical is concerned" (BD, 139). The Messiah's physical descent was through the family of David (s. 1:3). **ὢν** pres. act. part. εἰμί (# *1639*) to be. Subst. part. to emphasize a quality. For the various possible references to Christ or God the Father s. Cranfield; Fitzmyer, 548; SH; Dunn. **εὐλογητός** (# *2329*) blessed. ◆ **6 οὐχ οἶον** (# *4024; 3888*) rel. pron. qualitative sort or manner of, such as. Used here as an idiom: "but it is not as though" (AS). **ἐκπέπτωκεν** perf. ind. act. ἐκπίπτω (# *1738*) to fall out, to fall from its place; that is, perished and become of no effect (SH). ◆ **7 κληθήσεται** fut. ind. pass. καλέω (# *2813*) to call. ◆ **8 λογίζεται** pres. ind. pass. λογίζομαι (# *3357*) to be counted as. ◆ **9 ἐλεύσομαι** fut. ind. mid. (dep.) ἔρχομαι (# *2262*) to come. **ἔσται** fut. ind. mid. (dep.) εἰμί (# *1639*) to be. ◆ **10 Ῥεβέκκα** (# *4831*) Rebecca. Perhaps best to be taken as a nom. abs. providing the introduction to what is stated in verses 11 and 12 (Murray). **κοίτη** (# *3130*) bed, sexual intercourse (SB, 3:265-66). Used w. **ἔχουσα** pres. act. part. ἔχω (# *2400*) to have. As an idiom, "having" means "to conceive" (BAGD). ◆ **11 μήπω** (# *3609*) not yet. **γεννηθέντων** aor. pass. part. γεννάω (# *1164*) to bear; pass. to be born. Gen. abs. **πραξάντων** aor. act. part. πράσσω (# *4556*) to do. Gen. abs. **φαῦλος** (# *5765*) bad, foul. Worthlessness is the central notion (Trench, *Synonyms*, 317f). **ἐκλογή** (# *1724*) election, choice. **πρόθεσις** (# *4606*) purpose. This is in accord w. the teaching of the Pharisees concerning predestination (s. 8:28; Gerhard Maier, *Mensch und freier Wille nach den jüdischen Religionsparteien zwischen Ben Sira und Paulus* [Tübingen: J.C.B. Mohr, 1971], 1-23). **μένῃ** pres. subj. act. μένω (# *3531*) to remain. Pres. emphasizes the continual remaining. Subj. w. **ἵνα** (# *2671*) shows result. ◆ **12 καλοῦντος** pres. act. part. καλέω (# *2813*) to call. Part. as subst. **ἐρρέθη** aor. ind. pass. (dep.) λέγω (# *3306*) to say. **μείζων** comp. μέγας (# *3505*) large; comp., greater, here in the sense of greater in age or older. **δουλεύσει** fut. ind. act. δουλεύω (# *1526*) to serve as a slave, w. dat. **ἐλάσσονι** (# *1781*) comp. μικρός (# *3625*) small; comp., less, in the sense of age; that is, younger. ◆ **13 γέγραπται** perf. ind. pass. γράφω (# *1211*) to write. Perf. emphasizes the lasting and binding authority of that which was written (MM). **ἠγάπησα** aor. ind. act. ἀγαπάω (# *26*) to love. **ἐμίσησα** aor. ind. act. μισέω (# *3631*) to hate. The Heb. idiom means, "I prefer Jacob to Esau" (Mal. 1:2-3), but Paul

may again have taken the word literally (Barrett; Cranfield; Dunn; SB, 3:267). ◆ **14 ἐροῦμεν** fut. ind. act. λέγω (# *3306*) to say. **μή** (# *3590*) used in questions expecting the answer "no." **γένοιτο** aor. opt. mid. (dep.) γίνομαι (# *1181*) to become. The expression strongly denies a false conclusion (s. 3:4). ◆ **15 ἐλεήσω** fut. ind. act. ἐλεέω (# *1796*) to show mercy, to have compassion on someone in need and to seek to help (TLNT; TDNT; EDNT). **οἰκτιρήσω** fut. ind. act. οἰκτιρέω (# *3882*) to show compassion, to be inwardly moved to deep compassion (TDNT; EDNT). The first of these words expresses the compassion of the heart, the second the manifestation of that feeling (Godet). ◆ **16 ἄρα οὖν** (# *726; 4036*) therefore then, drawing an inference from the preceding. **θέλοντος** pres. act. part. gen. masc. sing. θέλω (# *2527*) to desire. Subst. part. Pres. describes an ongoing activity. Gen. could be obj. gen. of a word ("mercy") to be supplied (Cranfield), or it could be gen. of source, "God's mercy does not have as its source human effort." **τρέχοντος** pres. act. part. τρέχω (# *5556*) to run. The two words indicates human striving and may reflect the symbol of an athletic contest and sum up the totality of man's capacity (Michel; Dunn; PAM, 135-36). **ἐλεῶντος** pres. act. part. (adj.) ἐλεέω (# *1796*) to show mercy (s.v. 15). ◆ **17 ἐξήγειρα** aor. ind. act. ἐξεγείρω (# *1995*) to rise out, to rise up. It is used of God calling up the actors on the stage of history (SH). **ἐνδείξωμαι** aor. subj. mid. (dep.) ἐνδείκνυμι (# *1892*) to show, to demonstrate. **διαγγελῇ** aor. subj. pass. διαγγέλλω (# *1334*) to proclaim. ◆ **18 σκληρύνει** pres. ind. act. σκληρύνω (# *5020*) to harden. ◆ **19 μέμφεται** pres. ind. mid. (dep.) μέμφομαι (# *3522*) to blame, to find fault. **ἀνθέστηκεν** perf. ind. act. ἀνθίστημι (# *468*) to stand up against, to resist. ◆ **20 μενοῦνγε** (# *3529*) on the contrary (Thrall, 34f). **εἰ** pres. ind. act. εἰμί (# *1639*) to be. **ἀνταποκρινόμενος** pres. mid. (dep.) part. ἀνταποκρίνομαι (# *503*) to answer back, to talk back, to reply. Reciprocal action is expressed by the prep. compound (MH, 297). **πλάσμα** (# *4420*) that which is molded or formed (AS). **πλάσαντι** aor. act. part. πλάσσω (# *4421*) to form, to mold. Aor. used to show the action logically antecedent to the action of the main vb. The same root is used to heighten the contrast. **ἐποίησας** aor. ind. act. ποιέω (# *4472*) to make, to fashion. ◆ **21 κεραμεύς** (# *3038*) potter. **πηλός** (# *4384*) clay (GELTS, 375). Gen. is used w. the word **ἐξουσίαν** ("authority"); that is, "authority over the clay." **φύραμα** (# *5878*) lump of clay. For the use of clay and pottery in the OT and Judaism s. Moo. **ποιῆσαι** aor. inf. act. ποιέω (# *4472*) (s.v. 20). Epex. inf. to explain the authority. **σκεῦος** (# *5007*) vessel. **ἀτιμία** (# *871*) dishonor. That is, one vessel designed for noble, one for ignoble use (Barrett). Corinth, where Paul wrote the epistle of Romans, was a city known for its pottery (s. 2 Cor.4:7). ◆ **22 θέλων** pres. act. part. θέλω (# *2527*) to desire. Pres. to describe an ongoing activity.

Subst. part. **ἐνδείξασθαι** aor. inf. mid. (dep.) ἐνδείκνυμι (# *1892*) to show, to demonstrate, to show something in someone (BAGD). Compl. inf. to the main vb. **γνωρίσαι** aor. inf. act. γνωρίζω (# *1192*) to make known. **ἤνεγκεν** aor. ind. act. φέρω (# *5770*) to carry, to bear. **μακροθυμία** (# *3429*) longsuffering (s. Rom. 2:4). **κατηρτισμένα** perf. pass. part. (adj.) καταρτίζω (# *2936*) to make ready, to prepare. Perf. emphasizes the state or cond. (s. 3:21). Pass. (GGBB, 417-18) not mid. (Cranfield). **ἀπώλεια** (# *724*) ruin, destruction. ◆ **23 γνωρίσῃ** aor. subj. act. γνωρίζω (# *1192*) to make known. Subj. w. **ἵνα** (# *2671*) to express purp. **δόξα** (# *1518*) honor, glory. **ἔλεος** (# *1799*) mercy. **προητοίμασεν** aor. ind. act. προετοιμάζω (# *4602*) to prepare before. The prep. compound is temp. indicating antecedent action. ◆ **24 οὕς** acc. pl. ὅς (# *4005*) whom. "even us whom He has called." The rel. pron. is attracted to the gender of the personal pron. **ἐκάλεσεν** aor. ind. act. καλέω (# *2813*) to call (s.v. 7). ◆ **25 καλέσω** fut. ind. act. καλέω (# *2813*) to call. **ἠγαπημένην** perf. pass. part. ἀγαπάω (# *26*) to love. ◆ **26 ἔσται** fut. ind. mid. (dep.) εἰμί (# *1639*) to be. **ἐρρέθη** aor. ind. pass. λέγω (# *3306*) to say. **κληθήσονται** fut. ind. pass. s.v. 7. **ζῶντος** pres. act. part. (adj.) ζάω (# *2409*) to live. Pres. expresses a contemporary or continuous action. ◆ **27 ᾖ** pres. subj. act. εἰμί (# *1639*) to be. Subj. w. **ἐάν** (# *1569*) to express cond. **ἀριθμός** (# *750*) number. **ἄμμος** (# *302*) sand. **ὑπόλειμμα** (# *5698*) rest, remnant. **σωθήσεται** fut. ind. pass. σῴζω (# *5392*) to rescue, to save. ◆ **28 συντελῶν** pres. act. part. συντελέω (# *5334*) to bring to an end, to complete, to finish, to consummate. The prep. compound is perfective (MH, 325). **ποιήσει** fut. ind. act. ποιέω (# *4472*) to do, to make. ◆ **29 προείρηκεν** perf. ind. act. προλέγω (# *3306*) to say before. **ἐγκατέλιπεν** aor. ind. act. ἐγκαταλείπω (# *1593*) to leave behind. Used as a 2nd. class cond. cl. which is contrary to fact. **ἐγενήθημεν** aor. ind. pass. (dep.) γίνομαι (# *1181*) to become. **ὡμοιώθημεν** aor. ind. pass. ὁμοιόω (# *3929*) to be like. ◆ **30 ἐροῦμεν** (# *3306*) s.v. 14. **διώκοντα** pres. act. part. διώκω (# *1503*) to hunt, to pursue, to persecute. **κατέλαβεν** aor. ind. act. καταλαμβάνω (# *2898*) to lay hold, to obtain. ◆ **31 διώκων** pres. act. part. διώκω (# *1503*) to hunt. **ἔφθασεν** aor. ind. act. φθάνω (# *5777*) to arrive at. ◆ **32 προσέκοψαν** aor. ind. act. προσκόπτω (# *4684*) to cut against, to stumble on or at. **πρόσκομμα** (# *4682*) stumbling, offense. ◆ **33 γέγραπται** perf. ind. pass. γράφω (# *1211*) to write 13). **ἰδού** aor. imp. act. ὁράω (# *3972*) to see. **τίθημι** (# *5502*) pres. ind. act. to place. **σκάνδαλον** (# *4682*) a stumbling block, that which give offense (TDNT; DPL; 918-19; NTW, 111-14; TLNT). **πιστεύων** pres. act. part. πιστεύω (# *4409*) to believe. **καταισχυνθήσεται** fut. ind. pass. καταισχύνω (# *2875*) to be ashamed.

Romans 10

◆ **1 εὐδοκία** (# *2306*) good will, good pleasure, wish, or desire, inasmuch as a desire is usually directed toward something that causes satisfaction or favor (BAGD; TDNT; TLNT). **δέησις** (# *1255*) petition, request, prayer. ◆ **2 ζῆλος** (# *2419*) zeal, followed by the obj. gen. "zeal for God." **ἔχουσιν** pres. ind. act. ἔχω (# *2400*) to have, to possess. Durative pres. **ἐπίγνωσις** (# *2106*) knowledge, accurate knowledge. The prep. compound is directive (MH, 314). ◆ **3 ἀγνοοῦντες** pres. act. part. (causal) ἀγνοέω (# *51*) to be ignorant, not to know. For the prefix as a neg. s. Rom. 1:20. **ζητοῦντες** pres. act. part. ζητέω (# *2426*) to seek, to search for, to try to, w. inf. Pres. part. emphasizes the continuing search, and indicates a deliberate and sustained intention, reflecting their zeal (Dunn). **στῆσαι** aor. inf. act. ἵστημι (# *2705*) to cause to stand, to establish. It means to cause to stand erect as a monument raised, not to God's glory, but to their own (Godet). Compl. inf. to the main vb. **ἰδίαν** acc. sing. ἴδιος (# *2625*) own, individual, mine (Dunn). It indicates their own uprightness sought by deeds of the law (Fitzmyer, 583). **ὑπετάγησαν** aor. ind. pass. ὑποτάσσω (# *5718*) to put oneself under orders, to obey; pass., to be in subjection (RWP). ◆ **4 τέλος** (# *5465*) end, goal, completion. The word could mean Christ is the goal of the Law, not temporally but directively and teleologically (Robert Badenas, *Christ the End of the Law: Romans 10.4 in Pauline Perspective* [Sheffield: JSOT Press, 1985]; Cranfield; LIF, 134-36); or it could mean Christ is the end of the Law temporally (SH), or it could be a combination of both meanings (Dunn; Barrett). For these and other views s. Fitzmyer, 584; Badenas, 5-37. **πιστεύοντι** pres. act. part. πιστεύω (# *4409*)to believe. Subst. part. to emphasize a quality. Sing. emphasizes the individual nature of the belief. Dat. of advantage. ◆ **5 γράφει** pres. ind. act. γράφω (# *1211*) to write (DPL, 971-72). Hist. pres. to describe a past action more vividly. **ποιήσας** aor. act. part. ποιέω (# *4472*) to do. Part. as subst. Aor. part. emphasizes the logically antecedent action to the main vb. **ζήσεται** fut. ind. mid. (dep.) ζάω (# *2409*) to live. ◆ **6 εἴπῃς** aor. subj. act. λέγω (# *3306*). Aor. subj. w. neg. as a prohibition forbids the beginning of an action. **ἀναβήσεται** fut. ind. mid. (dep.) ἀναβαίνω (# *326*) to go up, to ascend. **καταγαγεῖν** aor. inf. act. κατάγω (# *2864*) to lead down. Inf. to express purp. The thought here is to precipitate the Incarnation. The Messiah has appeared, and it is therefore impossible to hasten His coming by perfect obedience to the law or penitence for transgressing it (Barrett). ◆ **7 καταβήσεται** fut. ind. mid. (dep.) καταβαίνω (# *2849*) to go down. **ἄβυσσος** (# *12*) abyss, depth, underworld (SH; TDNT). **ἀναγαγεῖν** aor. inf. act. ἀνάγω (# *343*) to lead up. Inf. used to express purp. This also is sheer impossibility, since the resurrection has already happened (Barrett). ◆ **8 ἐγγύς**

(# *1584*) near, used w. dat. **πίστεως** gen. sing. πίστις (# *4411*) faith. Obj. gen., gospel message concerning faith (RWP). **κηρύσσομεν** pres. ind. act. κηρύσσω (# *3062*) to preach. Pres. to indicate the ongoing activity of preaching. For a discussion of the OT passages s. Dunn. ◆ **9 ὁμολογήσῃς** aor. subj. act. ὁμολογέω (# *3933*) to agree, to confess, to proclaim. As a judicial term, the word indicates the binding and public declaration which settles a relationship w. legal force (Käsemann; TDNT; Dunn). Subj. w. **ἐάν** (# *1569*) in a 3rd. class cond. cl. assuming the probability of the cond. **κύριον Ἰησοῦν** (# *3261; 2652*) double acc., Jesus is Lord. The confession is the acknowledgment that Jesus shares the name and the nature, the holiness, the authority, power, majesty, and eternity of the One and only true God (Cranfield). For the background of the term κύριος and its reference to Yahweh s. J. Fitzmyer, "The Semitic Background of the New Testament *Kyrios*-Title," WA, 115-42; George Howard, "The Tetragram and the New Testament," *JBL* 96 (1977): 63-83; Cranfield; Dunn; GGBB, 187-88. **πιστεύσῃς** aor. subj. act. πιστεύω (# *4409*) to believe. Here the subj. is parallel to the preceding ὁμολογήσῃς. **ὅτι** (# *4022*) that, giving the content of the belief. **ἤγειρεν** aor. ind. act. ἐγείρω (# *1586*) to raise. **σωθήσῃ** fut. ind. pass. σώζω (# *5392*) to rescue, to save. Theol. pass. indicating that God saves. ◆ **10 πιστεύεται** pres. ind. pass. πιστεύω (# *4409*) to believe. **ὁμολογεῖται** pres. ind. pass. (# *3933*) to confess. Both pass. are impersonal: "it is believed"; that is, "one believes" (RG, 820). ◆ **11 πιστεύων** pres. act. part. πιστεύω (# *4409*) to believe. Part. as subst. **καταισχυνθήσεται** fut. ind. pass. καταισχύνομαι (# *2875*) to put to shame. ◆ **12 διαστολή** (# *1405*) division, difference. **πλουτῶν** pres. act. part. πλουτέω (# *4456*) to be rich. **ἐπικαλουμένους** pres. mid. (dep.) part. ἐπικαλέω (# *2126*) to call, to name. Mid., to call upon for aid; often used in calling on a divinity (BAGD). ◆ **13 ἐπικαλέσηται** aor. subj. mid. ἐπικαλέω (# *2126*) s.v. 12. Subj. w. indef. rel. cl., "whoever," "all who call." ◆ **14 ἐπικαλέσωνται** aor. subj. mid. ἐπικαλέω (# *2126*) s.v. 12. Subj. in a deliberative question. **ἐπίστευσαν** aor. ind. act. πιστεύω (# *4409*) to believe. **πιστεύσωσιν** aor. subj. act. Deliberative subj. used in a rhetorical question (SMT, 77). **ἤκουσαν** aor. ind. act. ἀκούω (# *201*) to hear. **ἀκούσωσιν** aor. subj. act.; deliberative subj. **κηρύσσοντος** pres. act. part. κηρύσσω (# *3062*) to preach. Subst. part. used to indicate a necessary trait. ◆ **15 κηρύξωσιν** aor. subj. act. κηρύσσω (# *3062*) to preach; deliberative subj. **ἀποσταλῶσιν** aor. subj. pass. ἀποστέλλω (# *690*) to send, to commission w. the authority of the one sending (TDNT; TLNT). Deliberative subj. **γέγραπται** perf. ind. pass. γράφω (# *1211*) to write. Perf. was used for documents w. abiding authority (MM). **ὡραῖος** (# *6053*) originally, seasonable, ripe, timely; then, beautiful, fair, lovely, pleasant (BAGD; Dunn). Perhaps the idea here is "timely," or "coming at

the right time" (Dunn). **εὐαγγελιζομένων** pres. mid. (dep.) part. εὐαγγελίζομαι (# *2294*) to proclaim good news (TDNT; NIDNTT, 2:107-114; TLNT; EDNT; GELTS, 184; CCFJ, 224). Subst. part. to describe a durative trait. ◆ **16 ὑπήκουσαν** aor. ind. act. ὑπακούω (# *5634*) to listen to, to obey, in the sense of give credence to. The word implies the idea of voluntary submission (SH). **ἐπίστευσεν** aor. ind. act. πιστεύω (# *4409*) to believe. Const. aor. to describe the state of Israel's belief. **ἀκοῇ** (# *198*) hearing, that which is heard, a message report (SH). ◆ **17 ἄρα** (# *726*) then, it follows. **ῥήματος** gen. sing. ῥῆμα (# *4839*) that which is spoken, word; w. obj. gen. or gen. of content. "The message which has Christ as its obj. or content." ◆ **18 μή** (# *3590*) Used in questions expecting the answer "no." **μενοῦνγε** (# *3529*) (s. 9:20). **ἐξῆλθεν** aor. ind. act. ἐξέρχομαι (# *2002*) to go out. **φθόγγος** (# *5782*) sound, vibration of a musical string (RWP). **πέρας** (# *4306*) boundary, limit. **οἰκουμένη** (# *3872*) earth, the inhabited earth. ◆ **19 ἔγνω** aor. ind. act. 3rd. pers. sing. γινώσκω (# *1182*) to know. **παραζηλώσω** fut. ind. act. παραζηλόω (# *4143*) to provoke to jealousy, to make jealous. **ἀσύνετος** senseless, not understanding. **παροργιῶ** fut. ind. act. παροργίζω (# *4239*) to provoke to anger. ◆ **20 ἀποτολμᾷ** pres. ind. act. ἀποτολμάω (# *703*) to be bold of oneself; that is, to assume boldness, to make bold (T). The prep. comp. is perfective; that is "carry daring to its limit" (MH, 298). **εὑρέθην** aor. ind. pass. εὑρίσκω (# *2351*) to find. **ζητοῦσιν** pres. ind. act. ζητέω (# *2426*) to find. **ἐμφανής** (# *1181*) visible, manifest. **ἐγενόμην** aor. ind. mid. (dep.) γίνομαι (# *1181*) to become. **ἐπερωτῶσιν** pres. act. part. dat. masc. pl. ἐπερωτάω (# *2089*) to ask for, to inquire. ◆ **21 ἐξεπέτασα** aor. ind. act. ἐκπετάννυμι (# *1736*) to spread out, to stretch out. **ἀπειθοῦντα** pres. act. part. (adj.) ἀπειθέω (# *578*) to contradict, to speak against. **ἀντιλέγοντα** pres. act. part. (adj.) ἀντιλέγω (# *515*) to speak against.

Romans 11

◆ **1 μή** (# *3590*) used in questions expecting the answer "no." **ἀπώσατο** aor. ind. mid. (dep.) ἀπωθέω (# *723*) to push away, to repel; mid. to push away from oneself, to reject, to repudiate. Used in the LXX where the thought of God's rejection of Israel was entertained, but with the assurance that He has *not* or will not reject His people (Dunn; Cranfield; GELTS, 59; DPL, 796-805). **γένοιτο** aor. opt. mid. (dep.) γίνομαι (# *1181*) to become; used in the expression strongly denying a false conclusion; "Certainly not!" (s. Rom. 3:4). Paul emphatically, almost indignantly, rejects the false implication (Fitzmyer, 603). **σπέρματος** (# *5065*) seed, here, nation. Gen. of family relationship. **φυλή** (# *5876*) tribe. ◆ **2 ἀπώσατο** aor. ind. mid. (dep.) ἀπωθέω (# *723*) to push away (s.v. 1). **προέγνω** aor. ind. act. 3rd. pers. sing. προγινώσκω (# *4589*) to foreknow, to know beforehand (s. Murray at 8:29; DPL, 310-11). οὐκ (# *4024*) neg. in a question expecting the answer "yes," "you know, don't you?" ἐν Ἠλίᾳ (# *1877*; *2460*) "in Elijah"; a rabbinic method of quotation denoting "in the passage of Scripture which contains the history of Elijah" (Godet; Cranfield; SB, 3:288). ἐντυγχάνει pres. ind. act. ἐντυγχάνω (# *1961*) to intercede, to plead w. (w. dat). The vb. means to meet w., then to meet w. for the purposes of conversation, to have an interview w., or to accuse (SH). Hist. pers. vividly describing the action as in progress. ◆ **3** ἀπέκτειναν aor. ind. act. ἀποκτείνω (# *650*) to kill. θυσιαστήριον (# *2603*) altar, place of sacrifice. κατέσκαψαν aor. ind. act. κατασκόπτω (# *2940*) to dig under or down, to tear down. ὑπελείφθην aor. ind. pass. ὑπολείπω (# *5699*) to leave behind. ζητοῦσιν pres. ind. act. ζητέω (# *2426*) to seek. ◆ **4** χρηματισμός (# *5977*) oracle, divine utterance or response (NDIEC, 1:77; 4:176). The word here emphasizes the localization; the awesomeness is probably the indirectness of the divine communication (Anthony Hanson, "The Oracle in Romans 11:4," *NTS* 19 [1973]: 301). Josephus uses the vb. (χρηματίζω) in the sense of "to receive a response from God" (CCFJ, 4:368-69; Jos., *Ant.* 3:212). κατέλιπον aor. ind. act. καταλείπω (# *2901*) to leave behind, to reserve. ἐμαυτῷ dat. ἐμαυτοῦ (# *1831*) refl. pron., for myself. It emphasizes the thought that the remnant is preserved by God Himself for His own gracious purpose (Gifford). Dat. of advantage or personal interest. ἑπτακισχίλιοι (# *2233*) seven thousand. ἔκαμψαν aor. ind. act. κάμπτω (# *2828*) to bend, to bow. γόνυ (# *1205*) knee. ◆ **5** οὕτως (# *4048*) so. It refers to the internal resemblance of the two facts, for the same principle is realized in both (Godet). οὖν καί (# *4036*; *2779*) then also. The words refer to the moral necessity in which one follows the other and indicates the addition of a new example to the former (Godet). λεῖμμα (# *3307*) rest, remnant (Dunn; Ronald E. Clements, "'A Remnant Chosen by Grace' [Romans 11:5]: The Old Testament Background and Origin of the Remnant Concept," PSEB, 106-21). ἐκλογή (# *1724*) selection, election. γέγονεν perf. ind. act. γίνομαι (# *1181*) to become. Perf. indicates an original action (God's choice of Israel) establishing a situation which still pertains. God's original choice of Israel still holds true into the present time, precisely because it was an election of grace (Dunn). ◆ **6** εἰ (# *1623*) if, introducing a 1st. class cond. cl. which assumes the reality of the cond. χάριτι dat. sing. χάρις (# *1562*) grace (TLNT; TDNT). Instr. dat. οὐκέτι (# *4033*) no longer. γίνεται pres. ind. mid. (dep.) γίνομαι (# *1181*). χάρις (# *1562*). Grace ceases to show itself as that which according to its nature it is; it becomes what according to its essence it is not. It gives up its specific character (Meyer). Pred. nom. without the article stresses the character. ◆ **7** ἐπιζητεῖ pres. ind. act. ἐπιζητέω (# *2118*) to seek for. ἐπέτυχεν aor. ind. act.

ἐπιτυγχάνω (# *2209*) to obtain, to reach, to hit upon. ἐπωρώθησαν aor. ind. pass. πωρόω (# *4800*) to harden, to cover w. a thick skin, to harden by covering w. a callous (T; SH; Dunn). Ingressive aor., "they became hardened." Theol. pass., "they were hardened by God" (Cranfield). ◆ **8** γέγραπται perf. ind. pass. γράφω (# *1211*) to write. Perf. indicates the abiding authority of the document (MM). ἔδωκεν aor. ind. act. δίδωμι (# *1443*) to give. κατανύξεως gen. sing. κατάνυξις (# *2919*) stupefaction. Derived from the vb. meaning to strike or pick violently, to stun (SH; GELTS, 240). The Hebrew expression behind this denotes a spirit of deep sleep and in Isa. 29:10 it denotes a state of spiritual insensibility (Cranfield). Gen. of description, or subj. gen., "a spirit which produces stupefaction." βλέπειν pres. inf. act. βλέπω (# *1063*) to see. Inf. of result. ἀκούειν pres. inf. act. ἀκούω (# *201*) to hear. Inf. of result. In both cases the vbs. speak not of physical, but of spiritual perception. ◆ **9** γενηθήτω aor. imp. pass. (dep.) γίνομαι (# *1181*) to become. τράπεζα (# *5544*) table. The original imagery is that a skin or cloth was spread out on the ground and the food was placed upon it, but the cloth could entangle the feet of those eating if they suddenly sprang up at the approach of danger (Cranfield; Fitzmyer, 606). παγίς (# *4075*) trap, snare. θήρα (# *2560*) a net used in hunting as a trap. σκάνδαλον (# *4998*) trap, offense used symbolically (BAGD; TDNT; TLNT). ἀνταπόδομα (# *501*) a recompense, a paying back, that which is paid back. ◆ **10** σκοτισθήτωσαν aor. imp. pass. σκοτίζω (# *5029*) to darken. Ingressive aor., "become dark." βλέπειν pres. inf. act. βλέπω (# *1063*) to see. Inf. of result. Their eyes are darkened so that they do not or cannot see. νῶτος (# *3822*) back. διὰ παντός (# *1328*; *4246*) continually, constantly (BAGD; Cranfield). σύγκαμψον aor. imp. act. συμκάμπτω (# *5159*) to bend together, to bow down, as of captives whose backs were bent under burdens (RWP). The idea is, "May their backs be always weak and feeble under the burden that they bear" (Fitzmyer, 607). ◆ **11** μή (# *3590*) neg. to introduce a question expecting the answer "no." ἔπταισαν aor. ind. act. πταίω (# *4760*) to stumble. πέσωσιν aor. subj. act. πίπτω (# *4406*) to fall. A man who stumbles may recover himself, or he may fall completely. The word is used here of a completely irrevocable fall—"to fall to rise no more"—as the sprawling on one's face puts a runner out of the race (SH; Dunn). Subj. w. ἵνα (# *2671*) to express result (Dunn). γένοιτο aor. opt. mid. (dep.) γίνομαι (# *1181*) to become; used in the construction emphatically denying a false conclusion (s. 3:4). παραπτώματι dat. sing. παράπτωμα (# *4183*) transgression, false step (TDNT; EDNT). Instr. dat. or dat. of cause. παραζηλῶσαι aor. inf. act. παραζηλόω (# *4143*) to make jealous, to provoke to jealously. Articular inf. w. εἰς (# *1650*) used to express purp., showing divine intention (Dunn). ◆ **12** ἥττημα (# *2488*) defeat, complete defeat, overthrow (GELTS, 200; CCFJ, 3:309). πόσῳ μᾶλλον (# *4531; 3437*) by how much more. For this type of argument s. Rom. 5:9. πλήρωμα (# *4445*) fullness. ◆ **13** ἐφ᾽ ὅσον (# *2093; 3525*) inasmuch as, insofar as (RWP). δοξάζω (# *1519*) pres. ind. act. to glorify. ◆ **14** εἴ πως (# *1623; 4803*) if by any means. The use of the particle w. purp. or aim is a kind of indir. discourse (RWP) and indicates hesitant expectation (Moo, ER.). παραζηλώσω aor. subj. act. or fut. ind. act. παραζηλόω (# *4143*) to make jealous (s.v. 11). σώσω aor. subj. act. or fut. ind. act. σῴζω (# *5392*) to rescue, to save. ◆ **15** ἀποβολή (# *613*) casting away. καταλλαγή (# *2903*) reconciling (APC, 186-223; TDNT; s. Rom. 5:10). πρόσλημψις (# *4691*) receiving. ◆ **16** ἀπαρχή (# *569*) firstfruit (s. Rom. 8:23). φύραμα (# *5878*) dough, lump. For the rabbinical practice based on Num. 15:18f; s. SB, 4:665f. ῥίζα (# *4844*) root. κλάδος (# *3080*) branch. ◆ **17** ἐξεκλάσθησαν aor. ind. pass. ἐκκλάω (# *1709*) to break off. Ind. w. εἰ (# *1623*) in a 1st. class cond. cl. which assumes the reality of the cond. Pass. could be theol. pass. ἀγριέλαιος (# *66*) wild olive tree (DPL, 642-44). ὤν pres. act. part. nom. masc. sing. εἰμί (# *1639*) to be. Part. could be concessive. ἐνεκεντρίσθης aor. ind. pass. ἐγκεντρίζω (# *1596*) to graft in. For the grafting of plants in the ancient world s. Cranfield; SB, 3:290-92; NW, 2, i:167–170; Columella, *De Re Rustica*, 5, 4-30; BBC). συγκοινωνός (# *1181*) participant, partner, one who shares something w. someone (BAGD; TDNT). πιότης (# *4404*) fatness. ἐλαία (# *1777*) olive tree (DPL, 642-44). ἐγένου aor. ind. mid. (dep.) 2nd. pers. sing. γίνομαι (# *1181*) to become. ◆ **18** κατακαυχῶ pres. imp. mid. (dep.) 2nd. pers. sing. κατακαυχάομαι (# *2878*) to boast against, to brag. The prep. compound indicates an action unfavorable to its object (MH, 316). Pres. imp. w. neg. indicates either stop an action in progress or do not make the action a habit (MKG, 272). βαστάζεις pres. ind. act. βαστάζω (# *1002*) to carry, to bear; fig. to support (BAGD). ◆ **19** ἐρεῖς fut. ind. act. λέγω (# *3306*) to say. οὖν (# *4036*) now, therefore, drawing an inference. ἐξεκλάσθησαν aor. ind. pass. ἐκκλάω (# *1709*) to break off. κλάδος (# *3080*) branch. Without the article, the character is emphasized, "beings who had the character of branches" (Godet). ἐγκεντρισθῶ aor. subj. pass. ἐγκεντρίζω (# *1596*) to graft in (s.v. 17). Subj. w. ἵνα (# *2671*) for purp. For the process of grafting and its relation to the figure of the olive tree s. Munck, 128-30. ◆ **20** καλῶς (# *2822*) adv. well; "true enough" (Barrett). τῇ ἀπιστίᾳ dat. sing. ἀπιστία (# *602*) unbelief, unfaithfulness. Dat. of cause, "on account of their disbelief" (Fitzmyer, 615). ἕστηκας perf. ind. act. ἵστημι (# *2705*) to stand. ὑψηλός (# *5734*) high. φρόνει pres. imp. act. φρονέω (# *5858*) to think, to set one's mind upon. φοβοῦ pres. imp. mid. (dep.) φοβέομαι (# *5828*) to be afraid, to fear. ◆ **21** φύσις (# *5882*) nature. ἐφείσατο aor. ind. mid.

(dep.) φείδομαι (# *5767*) w. gen., to spare. Ind. in a 1st. class cond. cl. which views the cond. as a reality. φείσεται fut. ind. mid. (dep.) φείδομαι (# *5767*) w. gen., to spare. ◆ **22** ἴδε aor. imp. act. ὁράω (# *3972*) to see, to look. χρηστότης (# *5983*) goodness, kindness (s. 2:4). ἀποτομία (# *704*) severity. The word comes from a vb. meaning "to cut right off," "to cut short" and emphasizes an unbending rigor (Godet). It was used in the papyri of the severe enacting of a law, as well as for the severity or difficulty involved in travelling up the Nile (MM; Preisigke, 1:198-99). Note Josephus' use of the adj. (ἀπότομος) to describe the character of Herod the Great as being "relentless in punishment" (ἐπὶ τιμωρία ἀπότομον), in contrast to Agrippa who had a gentle disposition (πραΰς) (Jos., *Ant.* 19:329-20). Plutarch used the term to describe how a father is to treat his children in mixing severity w. mildness (ἀποτομίαν τῇ πραότητι μιγνύναι) (Plutarch, *Moralia*, 13, d-e). πεσόντας aor. act. part. πίπτω (# *4406*) to fall; part. as subst. ἐπιμένης pres. subj. act. ἐπιμένω (# *2152*) to remain, to continue. Subj. used to express cond. ἐπεί (# *2075*) since, otherwise. ἐκκοπήσῃ fut. ind. pass. ἐκκόπτω (# *1716*) to cut out. ◆ **23** ἐπιμένωσιν pres. ind. act. ἐπιμένω (# *2152*) to remain. ἐγκεντρισθήσονται fut. ind. pass. ἐγκεντρίζω (# *1596*) to graft in (s.v. 17). ἐγκεντρίσαι aor. inf. act. Compl. inf. to the main vb., "God is able to...." ◆ **24** ἐξεκόπης aor. ind. pass. ἐκκόπτω (# *1716*) to cut out (s.v. 22). καλλιέλαιος (# *2814*) cultivated olive tree as opposed to wild olive tree (BAGD). πόσῳ μᾶλλον (# *4531; 3437*) by how much more? (s. 5:9). ἐγκεντρισθήσονται fut. ind. pass. ἐγκεντρίζω (# *1596*) to break off. ◆ **25** ἀγνοεῖν pres. inf. act. ἀγνοέω (# *51*) to be ignorant, not to know. Compl. inf. to the main vb. μυστήριον (# *3696*) mystery; the plan and purpose of God which was hidden in the past and impossible for human beings to discover but which is now made known by God (LN, 1:345; TDNT; EDNT; NIDNTT, 3:501-5; Cremer, 424f; Raymond E. Brown, *The Semitic Background of the Term, "Mystery" in New Testament Study,* [Philadelphia: Fortress Press, 1968]; C.C. Caragounis, *The Ephesian Mysterion: Meaning and Content* [Lund: Gleerup, 1977]). ἦτε pres. subj. act. εἰμί (# *1639*) to be. Subj. w. ἵνα (# *2671*) to express purp. φρόνιμος (# *5861*) wise. πώρωσις (# *4801*) the covering w. a callous, dulled perception, hardness (T; s. v. 7). μέρος (# *3538*) a part. γέγονεν perf. ind. act. (# *1181*) to become. ἄχρις οὗ (# *948; 4005*) w. aor. subj., until, until that (Godet; Cranfield). πλήρωμα (# *4445*) fullness. It denotes the full number of the elect from among the nations (Fitzmyer, 622). εἰσέλθῃ aor. subj. act. εἰσέρχομαι (# *1656*) to come into, to come in. ◆ **26** οὕτως (# *4048*) so, accordingly. It continues the thought of what precedes or draws out its implications (Murray). πᾶς Ἰσραήλ (# *4246; 2702*) all Israel. It refers to the forgiveness of the whole Jewish people or nation, the whole ethnic group in contrast to the saved rem-

nant of Jews in Paul's day and ours (Johnson). σωθήσεται fut. ind. pass. σώζω (# 5392) to save. The
restoration of Israel scattered throughout the Diaspora
was a common theme of Jewish expectation as seen by
such passages as Deut. 30:1-5; Jer. 23:3; 29:14; Ezek.
11:17; 36:24; Mic. 2:12; 4:6-7; Zech. 10:8-10; Bar. 4:37; 2
Macc. 2:18; Jub. 1:15; Pss. Sol. 17:26-28; 1QSa. 1:1-9
(Dunn). γέγραπται perf. ind. pass. γράφω (# 1211) to
write. Perf. indicates the abiding authority of the document (MM). ἥξει fut. ind. act. ἥκω (# 2457) to come, to
be present. ῥυόμενος pres. mid. (dep.) part. ῥύομαι
(# 4861) to rescue, to deliver. Pres. emphasizes a continuing trait. Subst. part. refers to Jesus as the Messiah
(SH). ἀποστρέψει fut. ind. act. ἀποστρέφω (# 608) to
turn. ἀσέβεια ungodliness (# 813) (s. 1:18). ◆ 27 διαθήκη (# 1347) treaty, covenant. This undoubtedly refers
to the new covenant (Fitzmyer, 625). ἀφέλωμαι aor.
subj. mid. ἀφαιρέω (# 904) to take away, to remove.
◆ 28 κατὰ τὸ εὐαγγέλιον (# 2295) according to the Gospel; the relation is thereby designated according to
which they are enemies (Meyer). ἐχθρός (# 2398) enemy. It points to the rejection of Israel w. which Paul is
dealing throughout this chapter (Murray). δι' ὑμᾶς
(# 1328; 5148) because of you; "for your advantage"
(Barrett). Prep. w. acc. is extended to the final cause
(BG, 37). ἀγαπητός (# 28) beloved. ◆ 29 ἀμεταμέλητος
(# 294) not to be sorry afterward, not to be regretted, irrevocable of something one does not take back
(BAGD). χάρισμα (# 5922) a gift of grace. God does not
go back on His acts of grace (Barrett; s. Rom. 5:15).
◆ 30 ἠπειθήσατε aor. ind. act. ἀπειθέω (# 578) to be disobedient. ἠλεήθητε aor. ind. pass. ἐλεέω (# 1796) to have
mercy or pity; pass., to obtain mercy or pity (TLNT;
TDNT). Theol. pass. indicating that God showed mercy. ἀπειθείᾳ dat. sing. (# 577) disobedience. Dat. of
cause. ◆ 31 ἠπείθησαν aor. ind. act. ἀπειθέω (# 578) to
be disobedient. τῷ ὑμετέρῳ ἐλέει (# 5629; 1799) by (because of) your mercy. For the various possible connec-
tions of this phrase and the interpretations of it s.
Cranfield. ἐλεηθῶσιν aor. subj. pass. ἐλεέω (# 1796) to
have mercy. Subj. w. ἵνα (# 2671) to express result or
purp. ◆ 32 συνέκλεισεν aor. ind. act. συγκλείω (# 5168)
to shut together, to shut together like a net (RWP). ἐλε-
ήσῃ aor. subj. act. ἐλεέω (# 1796) to have mercy (s.v. 30).
Subj. w. ἵνα (# 2671) expressing purp. ◆ 33 Ὦ (ὦ)
(# 6043) O! It is used in exclamations expressing very
strong emotion (BD, 81; RG, 461). βάθος (# 958) depth.
ἀνεξεραύνητος (# 451) unfathomable, unsearchable. For
the prefix used w. neg. s. Rom. 1:20; for the use of vb.
adjectives w. this ending s. M, 221f; MH, 188, 370f. The
word was used by the Church Fathers of God and His
attributes being unsearchable (PGL, 134). ἀνεξιχνίαστοι
(# 453) literally, not to be tracked out, incomprehensible, inscrutable (BAGD). Perhaps there is a reference to
the use of the word in Job (MM; GELTS, 35; Job 5:9; 9:10;

34:24; for its use in the Church Fathers s. PGL, 135).
◆ 34 ἔγνω aor. ind. act. γινώσκω (# 1182) to know. σύμ-
βουλος (# 5207) fellow counselor, advisor. ἐγένετο aor.
ind. mid. (dep.) γίνομαι (# 1181) to become.
◆ 35 προέδωκεν aor. ind. act. προδίδωμι (# 4594) to give
beforehand, to give in advance, to pay in advance
(MM; Dunn). If man could really be the first to do
something for God, he would make God his debtor
(Godet). ἀνταποδοθήσεται fut. ind. pass. ἀνταποδίδωμι
(# 500) to recompense, to give back, to repay. ◆ 36 ἐξ
(# 1666) from, out of. It refers to God as Creator (Godet). διά (# 1328) w. gen., through. It refers to the government of mankind. Everything is executed only
through Him (Godet). εἰς (# 1650) for. It refers to a final
goal (Godet). αὐτῷ dat. sing. αὐτός (# 899), to Him.
Dat. of personal interest. δόξα (# 1518) glory, honor, a
good reputation (TLNT; TDNT). It refers to the enhancing of God's glory and renown by praise, prayer, and
thanksgiving (Fitzmyer, 635).

Romans 12

◆ 1 παρακαλῶ pres. ind. act. παρακαλέω (# 4151)
to exhort, to encourage someone to do something. The
word was used of exhorting troops who were about to
go into battle. Here it is a request based on the apostolic
authority of Paul (MNTW, 134; Michel; Cranfield;
TDNT; CCFJ, 3:291-94). οὖν (# 4036) therefore. It refers
to the result of the whole previous argument (SH). οἰκτιρμός (# 3880) mercy, compassion, compassion and
pity arising from the miserable state of one in need
(TDNT; EDNT; Cremer; GELTS, 326). Pl. may reflect
the individual acts of compassion or it may be due to
the Heb. רַחֲמִים ("deep compassion") , which is an abstract pl. to be translated as sing. (Moo, ER.; NIDOTTE,
3:1093-95). διά (# 1328) prep. w. gen. informs the reader
that the divine mercies are the power by which this exhortation should take possession of one's will (Godet).
παραστῆσαι aor. inf. act. παρίστημι (# 4225) to present,
a t.t. for presenting a sacrifice; literally meaning "to
place beside" for any purpose (SH). Inf. in indir. discourse as obj. of the vb. Aor. indicates a specific act.
σῶμα (# 5393) body. It refers here to the physical body;
then v. 2 singles out the mind for renewal (SBT, 36). θυσία (# 2602) offering, sacrifice. For a description of how
the animals were tied to the altar and offered in the
Temple at Jerusalem during the daily burnt offering s.
M, Tamid 4:1-3; JPB, 104-5. Double acc., "present your
bodies as a sacrifice." ζῶσαν pres. act. part. (adj.) ζάω
(# 2409) to live. The living sacrifice stands in contrast to
those which were killed and refers to a constant dedication (Murray; Dunn). ἁγίαν acc. sing. ἅγιος (# 41)
holy, set apart from profane or daily use and dedicated
to the service of God (EDNT; TDNT). εὐάρεστος
(# 2298) well-pleasing, acceptable, w. dat. (BAGD).
λογικός (# 3358) pertaining to reason, rational, spiritu-

al. The use of our bodies is characterized by conscious, intelligent, consecrated devotion to the service of God (Murray). The word could mean "spiritual" in the sense of inner or real; "rational," in the sense of appropriate for human beings as rational and spiritual creatures of God; "rational," in the sense of acceptable to human reason; or "logical" in the sense of fitting the circumstances (Moo, ER.). For adjs. w. this suffix having the idea of "belonging to," "pertaining to," "w. the characteristics of" s. MH, 378. **λατρεία** (# 3301) service, worship; acc. in apposition to the object (SH).   ◆ **2** **συσχηματίζεσθε** pres. imp. pass. συσχηματίζω (# 5372) to form or mold after something. It refers to the external conformity (Dunn). The vb. indicates the adoption or imitation of a pose or received mode of conduct (Godet). Pres. imp. w. neg. **μή** (# 3590) indicates the discontinution of an action in progress or else that the action is not to be continually done (MKG, 272f). Permissive pass., "do not let yourselves be molded." **μεταμορφοῦσθε** pres. imp. pass. μεταμορφόω (# 3565) to transform, to change the inward reality; "but be transformed in your inmost nature" (SH). Prep. compound indicates change; that is, change in form (MH, 318). Permissive pass. and theol. pass. (Cranfield), "let yourselves be transformed by God." **ἀνακαινώσει** (# 364) dat. sing. ἀνακαίνωσις renewing. Instr. dat., "by the renewing." **νοός** gen. sing. νοῦς (# 3808) mind, the thinking power, reason in its moral quality and activity (Meyer). Obj. gen. **δοκιμάζειν** pres. inf. act. δοκιμάζω (# 1507) to prove by testing, to accept as approved after testing (TLNT). Inf. w. prep. **εἰς** (# 1650) expresses the purp. or result (MT, 143).   ◆ **3** **δοθείσης** aor. pass. part. δίδωμι (# 1443) to give. **ὄντι** pres. act. part. εἰμί (# 1639) to be. Part. as subst. Dat as indir. obj. **ὑπερφρονεῖν** pres. inf. act. ὑπερφρονέω (# 5672) to think over, above or beyond, to think highly of oneself, to be haughty. Inf. in indir. discourse; here, indir. neg. command (RWP). **δεῖ** pres. ind. act. (# 1256) it is necessary, giving a logical necessity. **φρονεῖν** pres. inf. act. φρονέω (# 5858) to think, to set the mind or attention on something (TDNT; EDNT; NIDNTT, 2:616-19). **σωφρονεῖν** pres. inf. act. σωφρονέω (# 5404) to be of sound mind, to be reasonable, sensible, to keep the proper measure, not going beyond the set boundaries; "to turn the energy of the mind to recognize its limits and respect them" (Godet; TDNT; TLNT). **ἐμέρισεν** aor. ind. act. μερίζω (# 3532) to measure. **μέτρον** (# 3586) measure.   ◆ **4** **καθάπερ** (# 2749) just as. **μέλη** (# 3517) member. **πρᾶξις** (# 4552) practice, function, activity (Dunn).   ◆ **5** **οἱ πολλοί** Semitic idiom meaning "all"; here, all of any worshiping community (Dunn). **καθ' εἷς** (# 3517; 1651) as to each one. A late idiom w. prep. is treated adverbially (RWP; BD, 160). **ἀλλήλων** (# 253) one another.   ◆ **6** **ἔχοντες** pres. act. part. ἔχω (# 2400) to have. The word here is determined by the imagery of the body (Dunn). Circum. or adj.

part. **διάφορος** (# 1427) differing. **ἀναλογία** (# 381) proportion, proportionate allowance, right relationship (BAGD; MM).   ◆ **7** **διακονία** (# 1355) ministry. The word indicates a personal ministry done in service to another (TDNT). Here it probably refers to the administration of alms and attendance to bodily wants (SH). It may also refer to the ministry of the Word (Murray). **διδάσκων** pres. act. part. διδάσκω (# 1438) to teach. Part. as subst.   ◆ **8** **παρακαλῶν** pres. act. part. παρακαλέω (# 4151) (s.v. 1). **μεταδιδούς** pres. act. part. μεταδίδωμι (# 3556) to give, to share w. someone. Part. as subst. **ἁπλότητι** dat. sing. ἁπλότης (# 605) sincerity, generously, liberally. It refers to openhanded and openhearted giving out of compassion and a singleness of purpose, not from ambition (SH; TLNT). Instr. dat. **προϊστάμενος** pres. act. part. προΐστημι (# 4613) to stand on the first place, to preside. **σπουδῇ** (# 1877) zeal. **ἐλεῶν** pres. act. part. ἐλεέω (# 1796) to show mercy. It probably means the person whose special function is to tend to the sick, relieve the poor, or care for the aged and disabled (Cranfield). **ἱλαρότητι** dat. sing. ἱλαρότης (# 2660) cheerfulness, gladness, graciousness. Instr. dat., "with an attitude of cheerfulness."   ◆ **9** **ἀνυπόκριτος** (# 537) without hypocrisy. For the prefix used as a neg. s. Rom. 1:20. **ἀποστυγοῦντες** pres. act. part. ἀποστυγέω (# 696) to despise, to hate bitterly. It expresses a strong feeling of horror and the prep. compound emphasizes the idea of separation (SH). The parts. in this section are to be viewed as imp. (VANT, 386-88; P. Kanjuparambil, "Imperatival Participles in Rom. 12:9-21," *JBL* 102 [1983]: 285-88). **κολλώμενοι** pres. mid. part. κολλάω (# 3140) to glue or cement together, to join firmly, to join oneself to (AS). Our attachment to the good is to be that of the devotion illustrated by the bond of marriage (Murray).   ◆ **10** **φιλόστοργος** (# 5789) authentically loving, tenderly devoted, full of tenderness (TLNT; TDNT). It denotes the delicate affections mutually rendered by those who cherish one another w. natural affection, as the innate love of a mother, or as the love between a man and wife, or as parents and children, brothers and sisters (Godet; TLNT; NDIEC, 2:100-103; 3:40-43; 4:136). **τῇ τιμῇ** (# 5507) in or w. honor. The result of true affection is that no one seeks his own honor or position, and everyone is willing to give honor to others (SH). **προηγούμενοι** pres. mid. (dep.) part. προηγέομαι (# 4605) to go before and show the way, to consider, to esteem. It either means to try to outdo one another in showing respect or to consider better, to esteem more highly (BAGD).   ◆ **11** **ὀκνηρός** (# 3891) idle, lazy, irksome, troublesome, not irked by the demands of (Murray). Josephus uses the word in reference to military attacks which slowed down because those fighting became soft and lost heart (Jos., *JW*, 4:584). The word was used in the LXX in Prov. 6:6, 9 of the lazy person who should learn from the ant (GELTS, 328). **ζέοντες** pres. act. part.

ζέω (# *2417*) to boil, to be fervent. **δουλεύοντες** pres. act. part. δουλεύω (# *1526*) to serve as a slave, w. dat. ◆ **12** τῇ ἐλπίδι (# *1828*) in hope. Dat. is loc., in the point of hope (EGT). **χαίροντες** pres. act. part. χαίρω (# *5897*) to be glad, to rejoice. **θλῖψις** (# *2568*) pressure, tribulation. **ὑπομένοντες** pres. act. part. ὑπομένω (# *5702*) to remain under, to endure w. patience. **προσκαρτεροῦντες** pres. act. part. προσκαρτερέω (# *4674*) to hold fast to, to persevere, to give attention to, to be faithful in (TDNT; TLNT). ◆ **13** χρεία (# *5970*) need. **κοινωνοῦντες** pres. act. part. κοινωνέω (# *3125*) to share in, to have fellowship w., to give or contribute a share in w. reference to financial or material contributions (Dunn; TDNT). **φιλοξενία** (# *5810*) hospitality, fond of strangers, to receive strangers and treat them as guests by providing lodging, food, and friendship (TLNT; TDNT; EDNT; RAC, 8:1061-123; DGRA, 619-21). This would be needful among the Christians who were travelling, especially in Rome (Cranfield; Dunn; NDIEC, 7:55). **διώκοντες** pres. act. part. διώκω (# *1503*) to pursue. ◆ **14** εὐλογεῖτε pres. imp. act. εὐλογέω (# *2328*) to bless, to invoke God's blessings upon them (Murray). Pres. imp. could be iterat. and calls for habitual action (s. 6:11). **καταρᾶσθε** pres. imp. mid. (dep.) καταράομαι (# *2933*) to curse, to invoke a curse. Pres. imp. w. neg. **μή** (# *3590*) forbids the habitual action. ◆ **15** κλαίειν pres. inf. act. κλαίω (# *3081*) to weep; inf. expresses the force of an imp. (RG, 1092f; IBG, 126). **κλαιόντων** pres. act. part. Part. as subst. ◆ **16** φρονοῦντες pres. act. part. φρονέω (# *5858*) to think. **ὑψηλός** (# *5734*) high, exalted. **ταπεινός** (# *5424*) low, humble (BBC). **συναπαγόμενοι** pres. mid. part. συναπάγω (# *5270*) to lead along w. one. pass. to be carried along w., as by a flood which sweeps everything along w. it and then to give oneself up to (SH). **γίνεσθε** pres. imp. mid. (dep.) γίνομαι (# *1181*) to become. **φρόνιμος** (# *1571*) wise (s. Matt. 10:16). ◆ **17** ἀποδιδόντες pres. act. part. ἀποδίδωμι (# *625*) to render, to give back, to pay back (BBC). **προνοούμενοι** pres. mid. part. προνοέω (# *4629*) to think before, to have regard for, to be preoccupied w. (Godet). ◆ **18** εἰρηνεύοντες pres. act. part. εἰρηνεύω (# *1644*) to practice peace, to live in peace. For vbs. ending w. this suffix, which expresses the notion of "being or behaving, or acting as," s. MH. 400. ◆ **19** ἐκδικοῦντες pres. act. part. ἐκδικέω (# *1688*) to secure someone's right, to avenge, to revenge. For the imp. sense of the part. in vv. 9-19 in a series of exhortations s.v. 9 (BG, 129f). **δότε** aor. imp. act. δίδωμι (# *1443*) to give. **γέγραπται** perf. ind. pass. γράφω (# *1211*) to write. **ἐμοί** dat. sing. ἐγώ (# *1609*) "I." Dat. of possession, emphatic by its position, "to me belongs...." **ἐκδίκησις** (# *1689*) revenge. **ἀνταποδώσω** fut. ind. act. ἀνταποδίδωμι (# *500*) to pay back, to recompense. Prep. compound expresses a reciprocal idea (MH, 297). ◆ **20** πεινᾷ pres. subj. act. πεινάω (# *4277*) to be hungry. **ψώμιζε** pres. imp. act.

ψωμίζω (# *6039*) to feed w. morsels; then to feed generally (AS). **διψᾷ** pres. subj. act. διψάω (# *1498*) to be thirsty. **πότιζε** pres. act. imp. ποτίζω (# *4540*) to give to drink. **ποιῶν** pres. act. part. ποιέω (# *4472*) to make. **ἄνθραξ** (# *472*) coal. **σωρεύσεις** fut. ind. act. σωρεύω (# *5397*) to pile up, to heap. For various views s. Cranfield; Dunn; Fitzmyer, 657-58; Moo, ER. ◆ **21** νικῶ pres. imp. pass. νικάω (# *3771*) to conquer, to overcome. **νίκα** pres. imp. act.

Romans 13

◆ **1** For the development of the argument in this section s. Robert H. Stein, "The Argument of Romans 15:1-7," *NovT* 31 (1989): 325-43; Moo, ER.). **πᾶσα ψυχή** (# *4246*; *6034*) every person, especially those at Rome (Cranfield). **ἐξουσία** (# *2026*) authority. Here a reference to governmental authorities rather than invisible angelic power (Murray, Appendix C). **ὑπερεχούσαις** pres. mid. (dep.) part. dat. fem. pl. ὑπέρχομαι (# *5660*) to have or hold over, to be above or supreme. Part. as subst. **ὑποτασσέσθω** pres. imp. pass. ὑποτάσσω (# *5718*) to place or rank under, to subject, to obey, w. dat. (TDNT; TLNT; DPL, 141-43). **οὖσαι** pres. act. part. εἰμί (# *1639*) to be. Part. as subst. **τεταγμέναι** perf. pass. part. τάσσω (# *5435*) to draw up an order, to arrange in place, to assign, to appoint (AS). Part. in a periphrastic construction. Perf. emphasizes the state or cond., "stand ordained by God" (RWP). ◆ **2** ὥστε (# *6063*) therefore. It presents the logical result (SH). **ἀντιτασσόμενος** pres. mid. (dep.) part. ἀντιτάσσω (# *530*) to arrange oneself opposite or against, to resist, w. dat. Part. as subst. **διαταγή** (# *1411*) ordinance. **ἀνθέστηκεν** perf. ind. act. ἀνθίστημι (# *468*) to take one's stand against, to withstand, w. dat. **ἀνθεστηκότες** perf. act. part. ἀνθίστημι (# *468*). **λήμψονται** fut. ind. mid. (dep.) λαμβάνω (# *3284*) to take. ◆ **3** ἄρχοντες pres. act. part. ἄρχω (# *807*) to rule. Subst. part. used as a noun. **φόβος** (# *5852*) fear, terror. **θέλεις** pres. ind. act. θέλω (# *2527*) to desire. **φοβεῖσθαι** pres. inf. mid. (dep.) φοβέομαι (# *5828*) to be afraid, to fear. **ποίει** pres. imp. act. ποιέω (# *4472*) to do. **ἕξεις** fut. ind. act. ἔχω (# *2400*) to have. ◆ **4** σοί dat. sing. σύ (# *5148*) you. "For you," "to you," ethical dat. (RWP). **ποιῇς** pres. subj. act. ποιέω (# *4472*) to do. Subj. w. ἐάν (# *1569*) in a 3rd. class cond. cl. which assumes the possibility of the cond. **φοβοῦ** pres. imp. mid. (dep.) φοβέομαι (# *5828*) to be afraid. **εἰκῇ** (# *1632*) without a cause, purposeless, in vain. **μάχαιρα** (# *3479*) sword. The sword is the symbol of the executive and criminal jurisdiction of a magistrate and is therefore used of the power of punishing inherent in the government (SH; Sherwin-White, 8-11). **φορεῖ** pres. ind. act. φορέω (# *5841*) to bear, to carry. Gnomic pres. **ἔκδικος** (# *1690*) avenging. Adj. as subst., "the avenger," "the one who punishes" (BAGD). **πράσσοντι** pres. act. part. πράσσω (# *4556*) to do, to practice. Pres. points to a lifestyle or habit of life. ◆ **5 ἀνάγκη** (# *340*) necessity, imposed either by the external cond. of things or by the law of duty, regard to one's advantage, custom, argument (T). **ὑποτάσσεσθαι** pres. inf. pass.(# *5718*) ὑποτάσσω s.v. 1. Epex. inf. explaining the necessity. **συνείδησις** (# *5287*) conscience (s. 2:15).   ◆ **6 φόρος** (# *5843*) tax. **τελεῖτε** pres. ind. act. τελέω (# *5464*) to fulfill, to pay. For taxation in the Roman Empire s. CC, 183f; A.H.M. Jones, *The Roman Economy,* 151-58. **λειτουργός** (# *3313*) minister, servant. **προσκαρτεροῦντες** pres. act. part. προσκαρτερέω (# *4674*) to attend constantly, to adhere to (TLNT; s. Rom. 12:12). Pres. part. describes a continuing trait of these servants of God. ◆ **7 ἀπόδοτε** aor. imp. act. ἀποδίδωμι (# *625*) to pay back. **ὀφειλή** (# *4051*) obligation, debt. Here it is the obligations we owe to those in authority in the state (Murray). **φόρος** (# *5843*) tax. **τέλος** (# *5465*) duty, toll, custom. This is the summary statement of the teaching. Governments fulfill a vital rule in God's plan. Thus there is an obligation to support them. ◆ **8 ὀφείλετε** pres. imp. act. ὀφειλέω (# *4053*) to owe, to be indebted to someone. **ἀγαπᾶν** pres. inf. act. ἀγαπάω (# *26*) to love. Articular inf. used as a noun. **ἀγαπῶν** pres. act. part. ἀγαπάω (# *36*) to love. **πεπλήρωκεν** perf. ind. act. πληρόω (# *4444*) to fill, to fulfill. ◆ **9 τό** (# *3836*) the article refers to the well-known commandments (Dunn). **μοιχεύσεις** fut. ind. act. μοιχεύω (# *3658*) to commit adultery. **φονεύσεις** fut. ind. act. φονεύω (# *5839*) to murder. **κλέψεις** fut. ind. act. κλέπτω (# *3096*) to steal. **ἐπιθυμήσεις** fut. ind. act. ἐπιθυμέω (# *2121*) to desire, to covet. For the use of the fut. under Semitic influence to express a categorical imp. s. BG, 94f; GGBB, 569-70. **ἀνακεφαλαιοῦται** pres. ind. pass. ἀνακεφαλαιόω (# *368*) to summarize, to sum up. A rhetorical term used of the summing up of a speech or argument and hence including a large number of separate details under one head (SH). **ἀγαπήσεις** fut. ind. act. ἀγαπάω (# *26*) to love. ◆ **10 ἐργάζεται** pres. ind. mid. (dep.) ἐργάζομαι (# *2237*) to work, to perform, to do. **πλήρωμα** (# *4445*) fulfillment, a complete fulfillment (Barrett). ◆ **11 εἰδότες** perf. act. part. οἶδα (# *3857*) to know. Def. perf. w. a pres. meaning. It is a reference to something well known and accepted by the readers (Dunn). **ὕπνου** gen. sing. ὕπνος (# *5678*) sleep. **ἐγερθῆναι** aor. inf. pass.ἐγείρω (# *1586*) to raise; pass. to rise. Inf. w. **ὥρα** (# *6052*) was a familiar construction to indicate the right time to do something (Dunn). **ἐγγύτερον** comp. ἐγγύς (# *1584*) near, close; comp., closer. **ἐπιστεύσαμεν** aor. ind. act. πιστεύω (# *4409*) to believe. Aor. views the time of belief at conversion. ◆ **12 προέκοψεν** aor. ind. act. προκόπτω (# *4621*) to put forward, to advance. **ἤγγικεν** perf. ind. act. ἐγγίζω (# *1581*) to draw near, to come close. **ἀποθώμεθα** aor. subj. mid. (dep.) ἀποτίθημι (# *700*) to put off. Hortatory subj. **ἐνδυσώμεθα** aor. subj. mid. (dep.) ἐνδύω (# *1907*) to put on, to clothe oneself

(BBC); hortatory subj. **ὅπλον** (# *3960*) weapon. ◆ **13 εὐσχημόνως** (# *2361*) adv., decently, becomingly. **περιπατήσωμεν** aor. subj. act. περιπατέω (# *4344*) to walk about, to conduct one's life. **κώμοις** dat. pl. κῶμος (# *3269*) carousing, reveling. It was used of a nocturnal, riotous procession of half-drunken and frolicking fellows who paraded through the streets w. torches and music honoring Bacchus or some other deity. Then it was used generally of feasts and drinking parties that went on late into the night and indulged in revelry (T; Dunn; for the "drinking bouts in Rome" s. LLAR, 49-51). **μέθαις** dat. pl. μέθη (# *3494*) drunkenness (TDNT; Philo, *De Ebriatate*). **κοίταις** dat. κοίτη (# *3130*) bed, sexual intercourse; here, unlawful sexual intercourse (SH). **ἀσελγείαις** dat. pl. ἀσέλγεια (# *816*) debauchery. The word contained the idea of shameless greed, animal lust, sheer self-indulgence which is such a slave to its so-called pleasures that it is lost to shame. It is one who acknowledges no restraints, who dares whatsoever his caprice and wanton petulance may suggest (NTW, 26f; Trench, *Synonyms,* 56). **ἔριδι** dat. sing. ἔρις (# *2251*) strife. **ζήλῳ** dat. sing. ζῆλος (# *2419*) envy. ◆ **14 ἐνδύσασθε** aor. imp. mid. (dep.)ἐνδύω (# *1907*) to put on (s.v. 12). **πρόνοια** (# *4630*) forethought, thought in advance, provision. **ποιεῖσθε** pres. inf. mid. ποιέω (# *4472*) to do. **ἐπιθυμίας** acc. pl. ἐπιθυμία (# *2123*) desire, lust (s. Rom. 7:7).

Romans 14

◆ **1 ἀσθενοῦντα** pres. act. part. ἀσθενέω (# *820*) to be weak. Part. denotes one whose faith falters (becomes weak) at a given moment and in a special case (Godet). The weak ones were probably Jewish Christians who refrained from certain kinds of food and observed certain days out of loyalty to the Mosaic Law (Moo, ER.). One of the subjects often discussed at a Roman dinner party was, "Why do Jews not eat pork?" (LLAR, 46). **προσλαμβάνεσθε** pres. imp. mid. (dep.) προσλαμβάνω (# *4689*) to take to oneself, to receive. The word is used of God receiving others into fellowship or companionship (SH). **διάκρισις** (# *1360*) distinguishing, quarrel; "welcome, but not for the purpose of getting into quarrels about opinions" (BAGD). **διαλογισμός** (# *1369*) thought, reasoning, questioning. ◆ **2 πιστεύει** pres. ind. act. πιστεύω (# *4409*) to believe, to have faith; that is, he is completely uninhibited by relics of a pagan or a Jewish past expressing itself in religious scruples (Barrett). **φαγεῖν** aor. inf. act. ἐσθίω (# *2266*) to eat. Inf. as obj. of the vb. **ἀσθενῶν** pres. act. part. ἀσθενέω (# *820*) to be weak (s.v. 1). Part. as subst. **λάχανον** (# *3303*) vegetable. The practice of vegetarianism for religious or philosophic reasons was well known in the ancient world (Dunn; NW, 2, i:212-14). ◆ **3 ἐσθίων** pres. act. part. ἐσθίω (# *2266*) to eat. Part. as subst. **ἐσθίοντα** pres. act. part. acc. masc. sing. Part. as subst. **ἐξουθενείτω** pres. imp. act. 3rd. pers. sing. ἐξουθενέω (# 2024) to consider as nothing, to treat w. contempt, to disregard, to despise, to disdain (BAGD). **ἐσθίοντα** pres. act. part. ἐσθίω (# 2266) to eat. **κρινέτω** pres. imp. act. 3rd. pers. sing. κρίνω (# 3212) to judge. **προσελάβετο** aor. ind. mid. (dep.) προσλαμβάνω (# 4689) to accept (s.v. 1). ◆ **4 εἰ** pres. ind. act. εἰμί (# 1639) to be. **κρίνων** pres. act. part. κρίνω (# 3212) to judge. **ἀλλότριος** (# 259) belonging to another, not one's own. **οἰκέτης** (# 3860) servant, household slave. **ἰδίῳ** dat. sing. ἴδιος (# 2625) one's own. "To his own master." Dat. of reference. It is to his own master that he is responsible (SH). **σταθήσεται** fut. ind. pass. ἵστημι (# 2705) pass. to stand. For the pass. deponent s. RG, 817. **δυνατεῖ** pres. ind. act. δυνατέω (# 1542) to be able, to be strong enough, w. inf. (BAGD). **στῆσαι** aor. inf. act. ἵστημι (# 2705) to cause to stand. Compl. inf. to the main vb. ◆ **5 παρ'** (# 4123) more than. The prep. shows preference (Dunn). The question probably had to do w. the Sabbath day observances (Dunn; Cranfield). **πληροφορείσθω** pres. imp. pass. πληροφορέω (# 4442) to fill completely, to convince fully; pass. to be fully convinced, assured, certain (BAGD). ◆ **6 φρονῶν** pres. act. part. φρονέω (# 5858) to think of, to esteem, to regard. Part. as subst. **ἐσθίων** pres. act. part. ἐσθίω (# 2266) to eat. Part. as subst. **εὐχαριστεῖ** pres. ind. act. εὐχαριστέω (# 2372) to thank, w. dat. ◆ **7 ἑαυτῷ** dat. sing. ἑαυτοῦ (# 1571) refl. pron. Dat. of advantage or personal interest. **ζῇ** pres. ind. act. ζάω (# 2409) to live. **ἀποθνήσκει** pres. ind. act. ἀποθνήσκω (# 633) to die. ◆ **8 τε** (# 5445) and. **ζῶμεν** subj. act. ζάω (# 2409) to live. Subj. w. ἐάν (# 1569) in a 3rd. class cond. cl. assuming the possibility of the cond. **κυρίῳ** dat. sing. κύριος (# 3261) Lord. Dat. of advantage or personal interest, "for the benefit or interest of the Lord." **ζῶμεν** pres. ind. act. ζάω (# 2409) to live. **ἀποθνήσκωμεν** pres. subj. act. ἀποθνήσκω (# 633) to die. Subj. in a 3rd. class cond. cl. **τοῦ κυρίου** (# 3261) gen. sing. Gen. of possession. **ἐσμέν** pres. ind. act. εἰμί (# 1639) to be. ◆ **9 ἀπέθανεν** aor. ind. act. ἀποθνήσκω (# 633) to die. **ἔζησεν** aor. ind. act. ζάω (# 2409) to live. **ζώντων** pres. act. part. **κυριεύσῃ** aor. subj. act. κυριεύω (# 3259) to be lord, to rule over, w. gen. Subj. w. ἵνα (# 2671) to express purp. ◆ **10 παραστησόμεθα** fut. ind. mid. (dep.) παρίστημι (# 4225) to stand, to stand beside, to stand before. **ἐξουθενεῖς** pres. ind. act. ἐξουθενέω (# 2024) to look down upon (s.v. 3). ◆ **11 γέγραπται** perf. act. pass. γράφω (# 1211) to write. **κάμψει** fut. ind. act. κάμπτω (# 2828) to bend. **ἐξομολογήσεται** fut. ind. mid. (dep.) ἐξομολογέω (# 2018) to confess, to acknowledge, to give praise. ◆ **12 δώσει** fut. ind. act. δίδωμι (# 1443) to give, to give an account. ◆ **13 κρίνωμεν** pres. subj. act. κρίνω (# 3212) to judge, hortatory subj. **κρίνατε** aor. imp. act. κρίνω (# 3212) to judge (BBC). **τιθέναι** pres. inf. act. τίθημι (# 5502) to place. **πρόσκομμα** (# 4682) stumbling, the opportunity to take offense or to make a misstep

(BAGD). **σκάνδαλον** (# 4998) snare, the stick which caused the trap to fall, cause of offense; it is that which trips us up or lures us into sin (NTW, 111-14; TDNT; TLNT). ◆ **14 πέπεισμαι** perf. ind. pass. πείθω (# 4275) to persuade; pass. to be persuaded, to have confidence. Perf. indicates the continuing state, "I have been persuaded and have confidence." The triple emphasis, "I know," "I am convinced," "in the Lord," is very forceful and makes it clear that the following statement is one on which Paul puts great stress (Dunn). **κοινόν** n. nom. sing. κοινός (# 3123) common, unclean, defiled. It is a t.t. to express those customs and habits which, although common in the world, were forbidden to the pious Jew (SH). **εἰ μή** (# 1623; 3590) except. **λογιζομένῳ** pres. mid. (dep.) part. λογίζομαι (# 3357) to consider, to suppose. **εἶναι** pres. inf. act. εἰμί (# 1639) to be. Compl. inf. to the preceding part. ◆ **15 βρῶμα** (# 1109) food. **λυπεῖται** pres. ind. pass. λυπέω (# 3382) to cause sorrow, to hurt. It expresses the painful and bitter feeling produced in the heart of the weak (Godet). **περιπατεῖς** pres. ind. act. περιπατέω (# 4344) to walk around, to conduct one's life. **ἀπόλλυε** pres. imp. act. ἀπόλλυμι (# 660) to ruin, to destroy. **ἀπέθανεν** aor. ind. act. ἀποθνήσκω (# 633) to die. ◆ **16 βλασφημείσθω** pres. imp. pass. βλασφημέω (# 1059) to slander, to speak evil of. Permissive pass. **ὑμῶν τὸ ἀγαθόν** (# 5148; 3836; 19) your good. It may refer to the inner freedom or to the Gospel and its benefits (Cranfield; Dunn). ◆ **17 βρῶσις** (# 1111) eating. **πόσις** (# 4530) drinking. ◆ **18 ἐν τούτῳ** (# 1877; 4047) in this; that is, by recognizing that food and drink are secondary matters (Barrett). **δουλεύων** pres. act. part. δουλεύω (# 1526) to serve as a slave. **εὐάρεστος** (# 2298) pleasing. **δόκιμος** (# 1511) approved, approved after examination (TDNT; TLNT). ◆ **19 διώκωμεν** pres. subj. act. διώκω (# 1503) to pursue, diligently follow. Hortatory subj., "let us pursue." **οἰκοδομή** (# 3869) building as a process; figurative of spiritual strengthening, edifying, building up (BAGD). ◆ **20 κατάλυε** pres. imp. act. καταλύω (# 2907) to tear down, to overthrow. It is the opposite of the building up involved in the word οἰκοδομή (Murray). Pres. imp. w. the neg. μή (# 3590) indicates the discontinuing of an action in progress or that the action should not be a habit (s. Rom. 6:12). **τῷ ἀνθρώπῳ** (# 476) Ethical dat., "in the judgement of the man who eats." **πρόσκομμα** (# 4682) stumbling, offense (s.v. 13). **ἐσθίοντι** pres. act. part. (adj.) ἐσθίω (# 2266) to eat. The words may refer to either the strong one or to the weak one (Dunn). ◆ **21 φαγεῖν** aor. inf. act. ἐσθίω (# 2266) to eat. Articular inf. used as subst., "the eating." **κρέας** (# 3200) meat. **πιεῖν** aor. inf. act. πίνω (# 4403) to drink. Articular inf. used as subst. **προσκόπτει** pres. ind. act. προσκόπτω (# 4684) to strike against a stone or other obstacle in the path. Here it indicates to be induced to sin (T). ◆ **22 ἔχε** pres. imp. act. ἔχω (# 2400) to have. **κρίνων** pres. act.

part. κρίνω (# 3212) to judge. Subst. part. Pres. used to describe a continuing trait. **δοκιμάζει** pres. ind. act. δοκιμάζω (# 1507) to approve of after testing and examining (SH). ◆ **23 διακρινόμενος** pres. mid. (dep.) part. διακρίνω (# 1359) to judge between, to hesitate, to waiver.

Romans 15

◆ **1 ὀφείλομεν** pres. ind. act. ὀφείλω (# 4053) to owe someone, to be a debtor, to be morally obligated (s. Rom. 1:14). **ἀσθένημα** (# 821) weak. **ἀδύνατος** (# 105) powerless, without strength. **βαστάζειν** pres. inf. act. βαστάζω (# 1002) to bear. Epex. inf. explaining the obligation. **ἀρέσκειν** pres. inf. act. ἀρέσκω (# 743) to please, w. dat. Epex. inf. ◆ **2 πλησίον** (# 4446) neighbor. Dat. w. vb. of pleasing. **ἀρεσκέτω** pres. imp. act. 3rd. pers. sing. ἀρέσκω (# 743) to please. **τὸ ἀγαθόν** (# 19) for the good, for his benefit (Meyer). The end or purpose of pleasing must be the promotion of what is absolutely to their good, further defined by their edification (SH; Fitzmyer, 702). ◆ **3 ἤρεσεν** aor. ind. act. ἀρέσκω (# 743) to please. **γέγραπται** perf. ind. pass. γράφω (# 1211) to write. Perf. indicates the continuing authority (MM). **ὀνειδισμός** (# 3869) reproach, reviling, insult. **ὀνειδιζόντων** pres. act. part. ὀνειδίζω (# 3944) to reproach, to heap insults upon (TLNT). Part. as subst. **ἐπέπεσαν** aor. ind. act. ἐπιπίπτω (# 2093) to fall upon. ◆ **4 ὅσα** nom. pl. ὅσος (# 4012) as great, how great, whatever. **προεγράφη** aor. ind. pass. προγράφω (# 1211) to write beforehand. The prep. "before" is in contrast to "today" (SH). **διδασκαλία** (# 1436) teaching; referring here to the act of teaching (BAGD). **ἐγράφη** aor. ind. pass. γράφω (# 1211) to write. **παράκλησις** (# 4155) consolation, encouragement (TDNT). **ἔχωμεν** pres. subj. act. ἔχω (# 2400) to have, to obtain. Subj. w. ἵνα (# 2671) to express purp. ◆ **5 δῴη** aor. opt. act. δίδωμι (# 1443) to give. The opt. is used to express a wish (s. MT, 120f; J. Gonda, *The Character of the Indo-European Moods* [Wiesbaden: Otto Harrassowitz, 1956]). **φρονεῖν** pres. inf. act. φρονέω (# 5858) to have in mind, to think of, to set one's mind upon. Subst. inf. as dir. obj. **κατὰ Χριστόν** (# 2848; 5986) according to Christ's example (Murray). ◆ **6 ὁμοθυμαδόν** (# 3924) of one accord, w. unity of mind (SH). **στόματι** dat. sing. στόμα (# 5125) mouth. Instr. dat. used figuratively (metonymy, cause for result) to refer to voice. **δοξάζητε** pres. subj. act. δοξάζω (# 1519) to glorify, to cause a good opinion about someone. Subj. w. ἵνα (# 2671) to express purp. ◆ **7 προσλαμβάνεσθε** pres. imp. mid. (dep.) προσλαμβάνω (# 4689) to receive, to welcome (s. Rom. 14:1). **προσελάβετο** aor. ind. mid. (dep.) προσλαμβάνω. ◆ **8 γεγενῆσθαι** perf. inf. pass. (dep.) γίνομαι (# 1181) to become. Inf. used in indir. disc. after vbs. of "saying" (BD, 203f) w. the acc. functioning as the subject to the inf. **βεβαιῶσαι** aor. inf. act. βεβαιόω (# 1011) to confirm, to make firm, to establish.

To establish a promise is to confirm by fulfilling it, to carry out or realize the promise (Godet; TLNT). **ἐπαγγελία** (# 2039) promise, referring here to the promises of the covenant. **πατέρων** gen. pl. πατήρ (# 4252) father. Gen. of poss., "promises belonging to the fathers" or obj. gen., "promises given to the fathers." The reference is probably to the aspect of the promise given to Abraham that all of the people of the earth would be blessed through his seed, that is, Christ (Gen. 12:3; 22:18). ◆ **9 δοξάσαι** aor. inf. act. δοξάζω (# 1519) to glorify (s.v. 6). Inf. to express purp. is to be related to the εἰς (# 1650) τό of v. 8 (Michel). **γέγραπται** perf. ind. pass. γράφω (# 1211) to write. **ἐξομολογήσομαι** fut. ind. mid. ἐξομολογέω (# 2018) to confess, to praise. **ψαλῶ** fut. ind. act. ψάλλω (# 6010) to play a stringed instrument w. the fingers, to sing to a harp, to sing a hymn, to sing praise (AS). ◆ **10 εὐφράνθητε** aor. imp. pass. (dep.) εὐφραίνομαι (# 2370) to rejoice. ◆ **11 αἰνεῖτε** pres. imp. act. αἰνέω (# 140) to praise. **ἐπαινεσάτωσαν** aor. imp. act. 2nd. pers. pl. ἐπαινέω (# 2046) to approve, to praise. Prep. in compound is directive (MH, 312). ◆ **12 ἔσται** fut. ind. mid. (dep.) εἰμί (# 1639) to be. **ῥίζα** (# 4844) root. **ἀνιστάμενος** pres. act. part. ἀνίστημι (# 482) to arise, to rise up, in the sense to appear or come (BAGD). **ἄρχειν** pres. inf. act. ἄρχω (# 806) to rule. Inf. to express purp. "He will come to rule...." **ἐλπιοῦσιν** fut. ind. act. ἐλπίζω (# 1827) to hope, to expect to receive. For the use of composite quotations by Paul s. Rom. 3:10. ◆ **13 πληρῶσαι** aor. opt. act. πληρόω (# 4444) to fill, to fulfill. For the opt. expressing a wish s.v. 5. **πιστεύειν** pres. inf. act. πιστεύω (# 4409) to believe. Articular inf. used as a noun. **περισσεύειν** pres. inf. act. περισσεύω (# 4355) to abound. Articular inf. used to express purp. ◆ **14 πέπεισμαι** perf. ind. pass. πείθω (# 4275) to persuade; pass., to be persuaded; perf., to have confidence. **μεστοί** (# 3550) full. **ἐστε** pres. ind. act. εἰμί (# 1639) to be. **ἀγαθωσύνη** (# 20) goodness. **πεπληρωμένοι** perf. pass. part. πληρόω (# 4444) to fill. **δυνάμενοι** pres. mid. (dep.) part. δύναμαι (# 1538) to be able. **νουθετεῖν** pres. inf. act. νουθετέω (# 3805) to admonish, to warn. It is the appeal to the mind where opposition is present. The person is led away from a false way through warning, instruction, reminder, teaching, and encouragement so his conduct is corrected (NIDNTT, 1:568-69; TDNT; EDNT; TLNT). Compl. inf. ◆ **15 τολμηρότερον** adv. comp. τόλμηρος (# 5529) bold, daring; comp., rather boldly. **ἔγραψα** aor. ind. act. γράφω (# 1211) to write. **μέρος** (# 3538) part, measure; "in some measure," "in part of the epistle" (SH). **ἐπαναμιμνήσκων** pres. act. part. ἐπαναμιμνήσκω (# 2057) to call back to mind again, to remind again (RWP). **δοθεῖσαν** aor. pass. part. δίδωμι (# 1443) to give. ◆ **16 εἶναι** pres. inf. act. εἰμί (# 1639) to be. Articular inf. used as a noun. **λειτουργός** (# 3313) minister, one who performs a public service, particularly a religious service (BAGD;

TDNT; NTW, 74-76; TLNT). ἱερουργοῦντα pres. act. part. ἱερουργέω (# 2646) to serve as a priest, to perform a sacred function, especially to sacrifice (SH). γένηται aor. subj. mid. (dep.) γίνομαι (# 1181) to become. προσφορά (# 4714) offering. εὐπρόσδεκτος pleasing, acceptable (# 2347). ἡγιασμένη perf. pass. part. ἁγιάζω (# 39) to sanctify, to set apart for divine purposes. ◆ **17** οὖν (# 4036) now, therefore, drawing a conclusion from the preceding. καύχησις (# 3018) boasting, glorying. ◆ **18** τολμήσω fut. ind. act. τολμάω (# 5528) to be bold, to dare. λαλεῖν pres. inf. act. λαλέω (# 3281) to speak. Compl. inf. to the main vb. κατειργάσατο aor. ind. mid. (dep.) κατεργάζομαι (# 2981) to accomplish, to produce. ὑπακοή (# 5633) obedience. ◆ **19** τεράτων gen. pl. τέρας (# 5469) wonder. κύκλῳ (# 3241) in a circle, roundabout. The idea in the word is that of a complete circle and Paul describes the territory already evangelized in Palestine, Syria, Asia Minor, and Greece as lying within a circle; that is, within the circle of the nations around the Mediterranean Sea (John Knox, "Romans 15:14-33 and Paul's Conception of His Apostolic Mission," *JBL* 83 [1964]: 11). πεπληρωκέναι perf. inf. act. πληρόω (# 4444) to fulfill, to fill up. To fill up the space lacking and preaching the gospel where others have not (Knox, 10). ◆ **20** φιλοτιμούμενον pres. mid. (dep.) part. φιλοτιμέομαι (# 5818) to be fond of honor, to have as one's ambition, to aspire (BAGD). εὐαγγελίζεσθαι pres. inf. mid. (dep.) εὐαγγελίζομαι (# 2294) to proclaim the good news, to preach the gospel. Compl. inf. to the preceding part. ὠνομάσθη aor. ind. pass. ὀνομάζω (# 3951) to name; here, "so named as to be worshipped" (SH). οἰκοδομῶ pres. subj. act. οἰκοδομέω (# 3868) to build, to erect a structure (BADG). ◆ **21** γέγραπται perf. ind. pass. γράφω (# 1211) to write. Perf. indicates the abiding authority of the document (MM). ἀνηγγέλη aor. ind. pass. ἀναγγέλλω (# 334) to proclaim. ὄψονται fut. ind. mid. (dep.) ὁράω (# 3972) to see. ἀκηκόασιν perf. ind. act. ἀκούω (# 201) to hear. συνήσουσιν fut. ind. act. συνίημι (# 5317) to comprehend, to understand. ◆ **22** ἐνεκοπτόμην impf. ind. pass. ἐγκόπτω (# 1601) to cut in, to hinder. Iterat. impf. pictures the repeated action. ἐλθεῖν aor. inf. act. ἔρχομαι (# 2262) to come. Articular inf. complements the main vb. ◆ **23** ἔχων pres. act. part. ἔχω (# 2400) to have. κλίμα (# 3107) territory, region, district. ἐπιποθία (# 2163) longing. ἐλθεῖν aor. inf. act. ἔρχομαι (# 2262) to come. Epex. inf. explaining his desire. ◆ **24** πορεύωμαι pres. subj. mid. (dep.) πορεύομαι (# 4513) to travel. διαπορευόμενος pres. mid. (dep.) part. διαπορεύομαι (# 1388) to travel through. θεάσασθαι aor. inf. mid. θεάομαι (# 2517) to see. προπεμφθῆναι aor. inf. pass. προπέμπω (# 4636) to send forth, to help on one's journey w. food or money by arranging for companions, means of travel, etc.; to send on one's way (BAGD; BBC). Inf. to express purp. ἐμπλησθῶ aor. subj. pass. ἐμπίμπλημι (# 1855) to fill.

◆ **25** πορεύομαι (# 4513) pres. ind. mid. (dep.) to travel. Pres. describes the action in progress. διακονῶν pres. act. part. διακονέω (# 1354) to serve. Part. used to express purp. ◆ **26** εὐδόκησαν aor. ind. act. εὐδοκέω (# 2305) to be well pleased, to think it good. κοινωνία (# 3126) fellowship, sharing, contribution (TDNT). ποιήσασθαι aor. inf. mid. ποιέω (# 4472) to do. ◆ **27** ὀφειλέτης (# 4050) debtor (s. Rom. 1:14). πνευματικός (# 4461) spiritual. ἐκοινώνησαν aor. ind. act. κοινόω (# 3125) to have a share in. ὀφείλουσιν pres. ind. act. ὀφείλω (# 4053) to be indebted to. σαρκικός (# 4920) fleshly, carnal. Here it has no evil associations. It is used with reference to tangible, material possessions (Murray). λειτουργῆσαι aor. inf. act. λειτουργέω (# 3310) to minister, to do a service (s.v. 16). ◆ **28** ἐπιτελέσας aor. act. part. ἐπιτελέω (# 2200) to complete, to bring to completion. σφραγισάμενος aor. mid. part. σφραγίζω (# 5381) to seal, to seal w. a sign of ownership and a guarantee of the correctness of the contents (BS, 238f; TDNT; EDNT; BBC; 2 Cor. 1:22; Eph. 1:13). ἀπελεύσομαι fut. ind. mid. (dep.) ἀπέρχομαι (# 599) to go away, to depart. ◆ **29** οἶδα (# 3857) pres. ind. act. to know. Def. perf. w. pres. meaning. ἐρχόμενος pres. mid. (dep.) part. ἔρχομαι (# 2262) to go. ἐλεύσομαι fut. ind. mid. (dep.) ἔρχομαι (# 2262) to come. ◆ **30** παρακαλῶ pres. ind. act. παρακαλέω (# 4151) to urge, to exhort, to encourage (s. 12:1). συναγωνίσασθαι aor. inf. mid. συναγωνίζω (# 5253) to fight or contend along w. someone, to strive together. It is the picture of wrestling in prayer (Michel). Compl. inf. to the main vb. ◆ **31** ῥυσθῶ aor. subj. pass. ῥύομαι (# 4861) to rescue, to deliver. Subj. w. ἵνα (# 2671) giving the content of the prayer. ἀπειθούντων pres. act. part. ἀπειθέω (# 578) to be unbelieving. εὐπρόσδεκτος (# 2144) well pleasing, acceptable, pleasant, welcome (BAGD). γένηται aor. subj. mid. (dep.) γίνομαι (# 1181) to become. ◆ **32** ἐλθών aor. act. part. ἔρχομαι (# 2262) to come. συναναπαύσωμαι aor. subj. mid. (dep.) συναναπαύομαι (# 5265) to rest together w., to refresh together. "I may rest and refresh my spirit w. you" (SH).

Romans 16

◆ **1** συνίστημι (# 5319) pres. ind. act. to commend, to introduce. Commendatory letters were well known in the ancient world (Barrett; NDIEC, 7:55, 90). οὖσαν pres. act. part. εἰμί (# 1639) to be. ◆ **2** προσδέξησθε aor. subj. mid. (dep.) προσδέχομαι (# 4657) to receive, to welcome. Subj. w. ἵνα (# 2671) to express purp. ἀξίως (# 547) worthily. παραστῆτε aor. subj. act. παρίστημι (# 4225) to stand beside, to help, to assist, to stand beside in order to hold up (Godet). χρῄζῃ pres. subj. act. χρῄζω (# 5974) to need, to have a need. Subj. w. ἵνα (# 2671) to express purp. πρᾶγμα (# 4547) helper. Masc. form of the word was used by the Romans for the legal representative of a foreigner. In Jewish communities it meant the legal representative or wealthy patron. Here it indicates the personal help given to Paul (SH; Michel). ἐγενήθη aor. ind. pass. (dep.) γίνομαι (# 1181) to become; here, she had become, she was. ◆ 3 ἀσπάσασθε aor. imp. mid. (dep.) ἀσπάζω (# 832) to greet. For a study of greetings sent in letters s. T.Y. Mullins, "Greetings as a New Testament Form," JBL 87 (1968): 418-26. συνεργός (# 5301) fellow worker. ◆ 4 οἵτινες nom. pl. ὅστις (# 4015) qualitative pron. signifying "as people who," "who, as such" (Godet; BG, 69). τράχηλος (# 5549) neck. ὑπέθηκαν aor. ind. act. ὑποτίθημι (# 5719) to place under (the axe of the executioner), to risk one's life for another (RWP). εὐχαριστῶ pres. ind. act. εὐχαριστέω (# 2373) to give thanks. ◆ 5 ἀπαρχή (# 569) firstfruit (s. 8:23). εἰς (# 1650) for. The prep. makes Christ the person to whom the firstfruits are offered (Godet). ◆ 6 ἐκοπίασεν aor. ind. act. κοπιάω (# 3159) to grow weary, to work w. effort (Godet). ◆ 7 συγγενής (# 5150) kinsman. Probably a reference to a fellow Jew (Barrett). συναιχμαλώτος (# 5257) fellow prisoner, fellow captive (s. Col. 4:10; Phlm. 23). ἐπίσημος (# 2168) splendid, outstanding. γέγοναν perf. ind. act. γίνομαι (# 1181) to become. ◆ 10 δόκιμος (# 1511) approved, approved after trial. ◆ 12 κοπιῶσας aor. act. part. κοπιάω (# 3159) to grow weary (s.v. 6). Aor. expresses antecedent action. Part. used as a noun. ἐκοπίασεν aor. ind. act. κοπιάω (# 3159) to grow weary. ◆ 13 ἐκλεκτός (# 1723) elect. ◆ 16 φίλημα (# 5799) kiss. For this custom s. TDNT; 1 Cor. 16:20. ◆ 17 σκοπεῖν pres. inf. act. σκοπέω (# 5023) to observe, to mark, to scrutinize (T); "to mark and avoid" (SH). Compl. inf. to complete the main vb., "I urge you to observe." διχοστασία (# 1496) division, offense, cause of stumbling (s. Rom. 14:13). ἐμάθετε aor. ind. act. μανθάνω (# 3443) to teach. ποιοῦντας pres. act. part. ποιέω (# 4472) to make, to create; here, "causing." Pres. indicates a contemporaneous action. Adj. part. to emphasize a trait. ἐκκλίνετε pres. imp. act. ἐκκλίνω (# 1712) to come away from someone, to shun, to avoid.

◆ 18 τοιοῦτος (# 5525) such a one. δουλεύουσιν pres. ind. act. δουλεύω (# 1526) to be a slave. Those who were slaves to their passions were ridiculed (BBC). χρηστολογία (# 5981) smooth, plausible speech, fair and insinuating speech (MM). εὐλογία (# 2330) praise, fine speaking, well-chosen (but untrue) words, false eloquence or flattery (BAGD). ἐξαπατῶσιν pres. ind. act. ἐξαπατάω (# 1987) to deceive (s. 7:11). ἄκακος (# 179) without evil, innocent. ◆ 19 ἀφίκετο aor. ind. mid. (dep.) ἀφικνέομαι (# 919) to reach, to come from, then to arrive at (RWP). εἶναι pres. ind. act. εἰμί (# 1639) to be. Compl. inf. to complete the main vb. ἀκέραιος (# 193) unmixed, simple, unsophisticated, innocent. ◆ 20 συντρίψει fut. ind. act. συντρίβω (# 5341) to rub together, to crush; "will throw him under your feet, that you may trample upon him" (SH). ἐν τάχει (# 5443) quickly. ◆ 21 ἀσπάζεται pres. ind. mid. (dep.) ἀσπάζομαι (# 832) to greet (s.v. 3). ◆ 22 γράψας aor. act. part. γράφω (# 1211) to write. Art. part. used as a noun. For the use of a secretary s. Dunn; Cranfield; Richard N. Longenecker, "Ancient Amanuenses and the Pauline Epistles," ND, 281-97; E. Randolph Richards, The Secretary in the Letters of Paul (Tübingen: J.C.B. Mohr [Paul Siebeck], 1991). ◆ 23 ξένος (# 3828) host, one, who extends hospitality. οἰκονόμος (# 3874) steward, manager, city treasurer (TDNT; BBC). ◆ 25 δυναμένῳ pres. mid. (dep.) part. δύναμαι (# 1538) to be able to. στηρίξαι aor. inf. act. στηρίσσω (# 5114) to make firm, to make stable, to establish. Compl. inf. to the main vb. ἀποκάλυψις (# 637) unveiling, revelation. σεσιγημένου perf. pass. part. σιγάω (# 4967) to be silent. Perf. part. emphasizes the state or cond.; here, a state of silence (RWP). ◆ 26 φανερωθέντος aor. pass. part. φανερόω (# 5746) to make clear, to manifest, to reveal. προφητικός (# 4738) prophetic. ἐπιταγή (# 2198) command, commandment. γνωρισθέντος aor. pass. part. γνωρίζω (# 1192) to make known.

1 Corinthians

1 Corinthians 1

◆ **1 κλητός** (# 3105) called. verbal adj. here w. a pass. meaning (BG, 47f). **ἀπόστολος** (# 693) apostle, one who is called by the Lord, commissioned by Him and carrying His authority (TDNT; TLNT; EDNT; Schrage; J. Andrew Kirk, "Apostleship Since Rengstorf: Towards a Synthesis," *NTS* 21 [1975]: 249-64; F.H. Agnew, "The Origin of the New Testament Apostle-Concept: A Review of Research," *JBL* 105 [1986]: 75-96). Nom. in apposition. **Χριστοῦ Ἰησοῦ** (# 5986; 2652) Gen. shows whom Paul represents as an apostle. **Σωσθένης** (# 5398) Sosthenes. Probably the Sosthenes of Acts 18:17. **ἀδελφός** (# 81) brother. The term "brother" here is probably more than the bond of brotherhood of all believers, referring to a colleague in the Christian mission; that is, one who makes the ministry his primary occupation (E. Earle Ellis, "Paul and His Co-Workers," *NTS* 17 [1971]: 445-52; MM; BS, 87-88). The article refers to one well-known. ◆ **2 ἐκκλησία** (# 1711) dat. sing. assembly, church, a group gathered together for a common cause. Here the Christian community in Corinth (Hering; TDNT; EDNT; Matt. 16:18). Indir. obj. Dat. shows to whom the letter was sent (Schrage). **τοῦ θεοῦ** (# 3836; 2536) of God. Gen. is poss. and at once a protest against party spirit; "the church of God," not of any one individual (RP). **οὔση** pres. act. part. adj. εἰμί (# 1639) to be. For the city of Corinth s. Acts 18:1; PIG, 200-51; SPC; ABD, 1:1134-39; J.B. Salmon, *Wealthy Corinth: A History of the City to 338 B.C.* (Oxford: Clarendon, 1984); DPL, 172-75; J. Murphy-O'Connor, *St. Paul's Corinth: Texts and Archaeology,* Good News Studies 6 (Wilmington, Del: Michael Glazier, 1983); "The Corinth That Paul Saw," *BA* 47 (1984): 147-59; J. Wiseman, *The Land of the Ancient Corinthians.* Studies in Mediterranean Archaeology 50 (Goeteborg, 1978); "Corinth and Rome 1: 228 B.C.–A.D. 267," ANRW 7/1 (1978): 438-548. **ἡγιασμένοις** perf. pass. part. ἁγιάζω (# 39) to sanctify, to consecrate, to separate from the secular for sacred use and purposes (TDNT; NIDNTT; EDNT; GELTS, 3). Perf. emphasizes the state or condition resulting from a previous action (VA, 245-59; NSV, 31-34). Theol. pass. In spite of the severe problems of the group at Corinth, they had been set apart by God for His use. Adj. part. used to emphasize quality. **κλητοῖς** (# 3105) called, s.v. 1; here dat. pl. **ἐπικαλουμένοις** pres. mid. (dep.) part. ἐπικαλέω (# 2126) to call upon, to invoke. Pres. emphasizes the habitual act which characterizes their life (Hodge). **αὐτῶν καὶ ἡμῶν** theirs and ours. The words could refer to "place," but it is better to take them w. "Lord." Christians share in a common holiness because they share a common Lord (Barrett). ◆ **3 χάρις** (# 5921) grace, the undeserved help to someone who is not worthy of the help and w. no thought of repayment (TLNT). Here it is the daily help (Rom. 5:15). **εἰρήνη** (# 1645) peace. The Heb. (שׁלום) word as used in greetings emphasizes wholeness and prosperity of life and personality (TDNT; NIDNTT; TLNT; EDNT; NIDOTTE; Schrage). ◆ **4 εὐχαριστῶ** pres. ind. act. εὐχαριστέω (# 2373) to give thanks. For Paul's thanksgiving in his letters s. P.T. O'Brien, "Thanksgiving and the Gospel in Paul," *NTS* 21 (1974): 144-55; "Thanksgiving Within the Structure of Pauline Theology," PSEB, 50-66; DPL, 728-30. Pres. indicates an habitual act. **πάντοτε** (# 4121) always. **περί** (# 4309) for, concerning, w. gen. The meaning often overlaps w. **ὑπέρ** (# 5642)(BD, 121). **ἐπί** (# 2093) because of, w. dat. It indicates the reason or basis of the thanksgiving (Hering; Fee). **χάριτι** (# 5921) s.v. 3; dat. sing. Here it may indicate the "grace gifts" (Fee). **δοθείσῃ** aor. pass. part. δίδωμι (# 1443) to give. Theol. pass. indicating that God is the giver. Aor. summarizes the giving (Schrage). The thanksgiving forms an introduction which in rhetoric was called the *exordium;* it compares to the prologue in poetry or the prelude in flute playing. Its purpose was to give the keynote and advance to the main subject. It often consisted of praise, blame, or exhortation (Aristotle, *Rhetoric,* III, iv:14 [1414b-1415a]; Quintilian, *Institutio Oratoria,* IV:I, 1-79; Schrage). ◆ **5 ὅτι** (# 4022) that. It gives an explanation of the giving of the grace (Fee; Schrage). **ἐν παντί** (# 1877; 4246) in everything, in every respect (Barrett). **ἐπλουτίσθητε** aor. ind. pass. πλουτίζω (# 4457) to make rich, to make exceedingly rich. Josephus used it of Herod the Great who greatly enriched (ἐπὶ μέγα ἐπλούτιζε) his sister Salome in his will because she had been loyal to him (Jos., *Ant.,* 17:147). **παντί** dat. sing. πᾶς (# 4246) all. It can include everything belonging, in kind, to the class designated by the noun; "every kind of," "all sorts of" (BAGD). **λόγῳ** dat. sing. λόγος (# 3364) speech, utterance. It refers to the gifts of utterance mentioned in 1 Cor. 12-14: knowledge, wisdom, tongues, prophecy, etc. (Fee; Schrage). **γνῶσις** (# 1194) knowledge. The first is the outward expression and the second the inward conviction (Lightfoot, *Notes*). ◆ **6 καθώς** (# *2777*) just as, inasmuch as. Produces not a mere parallel but rather an explanation of what precedes (RP). **τὸ μαρτύριον τοῦ Χριστοῦ** (# *3836; 3457; 3836; 5986*) the witness of Christ. The gen. could be either obj. ("the witness about Christ") or subjective ("the witness which Christ gives") (Schrage). **ἐβεβαιώθη** aor. ind. pass. βεβαιόω (# *1011*) to make firm, to make stable, to confirm, to authenticate, to guarantee, to verify, to prove to be true and certain (LN, 1:340; Schrage). It was used in the papyri in the sense of a legally guaranteed security (BS, 104-9; TLNT). The mystery of Christ was given legal force through the apostle (TDNT). ◆ **7 ὑστερεῖσθαι** pres. mid. (dep.) inf. ὑστερέω (# *5728*) to come short, to lack. Inf. w. **ὥστε** (# *6063*) to express contemplated result (BD, 197-98). It was what was to be looked for in the Corinthians (RP). **χάρισμα** (# *5922*) gift, that which was given out of grace. Empowerments given to the church from God or from the risen Lord (E.E. Ellis, "Spiritual Gifts in the Pauline Community," *NTS* 20 [1974]: 128-44; TDNT; EDNT; DPL, 340-41). **ἀπεκδεχομένους** pres. mid. (dep.) part. ἀπεκδέχομαι (# *587*) to wait eagerly but patiently for something. The double prep. in compound implies a degree of earnestness and intensity of expectation (Lightfoot; MH, 298, 310). Pres. emphasizes the continuous action and the part. expresses an attendant circumstance (Grosheide). **ἀποκάλυψις** (# *637*) unveiling, revelation (TLNT, 2:244-50). It is here followed by the obj. gen. ◆ **8 βεβαιώσει** fut. ind. act. βεβαιόω (# *1011*) to make firm (s.v. 6). **ἕως** (# *2401*) unto, until. **τέλος** (# *5465*) end, goal. The phrase moves easily from a temp. meaning to meaning "completely" (Barrett). **ἀνέγκλητος** (# *441*) without accusation, blameless (TDNT; MM; for the pref. expressing a neg. idea s. Moorhouse, 42-68). ◆ **9 δι' οὗ** through whom. The prep. is used of the principal cause and expresses the indir. calling of God through the gospel and not by a voice from heaven (Grosheide). **ἐκλήθητε** aor. ind. pass. καλέω (# *2813*) to call. Aor. points to the beginning; the call was effective, not just an invitation (Schrage). **κοινωνία** (# *3126*) fellowship, communion, participation. It expresses the blending of two wills into one common cause (TDNT; NIDNTT; EDNT; RAC, 9:1100-45; BBC). **Ἰησοῦ Χριστοῦ** (# *2652; 5986*) of Jesus Christ. The name reoccurs in every phrase of this preface (Godet). ◆ **10 παρακαλῶ** pres. ind. act. παρακαλέω (# *4151*) to entreat, to encourage. Used in the sense of a polite command (EDNT; Schrage; Conzelmann; s. Rom. 12:1). For the change a request formula makes to the body of the letter, s. John L. White, "Introductory Formulae in the Body of the Pauline Letter," *JBL* 90 (1971): 91-97, esp. 93-95; Wilhelm Wuellner, "Haggadic Homily Genre in I Corinthians 1-3," *JBL* 89 (1979): 199-204. **διά** w. gen., through; the instrument of the appeal

(RWP). **λέγητε** pres. subj. act. λέγω (# *3306*) to say, to speak. The phrase "to speak the same thing" had political overtones of warring factions coming to a reconciliation (s. Jos., *Ant.*, 18:375; Polybius, 5:140, 1; NW, 2:237), but was also used on a grave inscription of the harmonious life of a man and wife (Schrage). Subj. w. **ἵνα** (# *2671*) in indir. discourse after a vb. of command. Pres. calls for an habitual action. **ᾖ** pres. subj. act. εἰμί (# *1639*) to be. **σχίσμα** (# *5388*) split, division. The word pictures the destruction of unity through force and was used of a tear in a garment or political factions engaged in a struggle for power (Weiss; Schrage; L.L. Welborn, "On the Discord in Corinth: 1 Corinthians 1-4 and Ancient Politics," *JBL* 106 [1987]: 86-87; NDIEC, 1:28-29). Perhaps the divisions were also caused by differences in social stratifications (BBC). **ἦτε** pres. subj. act. εἰμί (# *1639*) to be. **κατηρτισμένοι** perf. pass. part. καταρτίζω (# *2936*) to put in order, to restore to its former condition, to put into proper condition. The word is used by Herodotus (5:28) for composing civil disorder (Barrett; BAGD; TDNT). Periphrastic perf. pass. part. (RWP). Perf. emphasizes the completed state or condition. **νοΐ** dat. sing. νοῦς (# *3808*) mind, the intellect in its judging faculty (Grosheide). **γνώμῃ** (# *1191*) dat. sing. opinion, judgment. It indicates the expressed opinion or condition (Grosheide). The former denotes the general principles, the latter the special application of those principles (Lightfoot, *Notes*). The terms call for harmony in the direction of the will and intentions (Schrage). ◆ **11 ἐδηλώθη** aor. ind. pass. δηλόω (# *1317*) to make clear, to make known. **περί** (# *4309*) w. gen., concerning. **ὑπό** (# *5679*) by, w. gen. giving the agent. **τῶν Χλόης** (# *3836; 5951*) The name Chloe means "a young green sprout" (LS, 1994) or "blond" (Schrage). This probably means "by slaves belonging to Chloe's household" (RP; Schrage). **ἔριδες** nom. pl. ἔρις (# *2251*) strife; here pl. "strifes," "contentions." The word points to quarrels and is the hot dispute, the emotional flame, that ignites whenever rivalry becomes intolerable (Morris; Welborn, *JBL* 106:87; TLNT). ◆ **12 δέ** (# *1254*) and, now. **ἕκαστος** (# *1667*) each. λέγει pres. ind. act. λέγω (# *3306*) to say, to speak. Iterative pres. indicating repeated and continual action. The political parties of the ancient world were named after individuals w. the gen. of the proper name (Welborn, *JBL* 106:90-91). For a discussion of the various parties which probably developed because of an overemphasis on wisdom, heightened by cultural, social, and material differences, and then fostered in house churches located in various parts of the city s. Schrage, 142-52; SPC, 153-72; Welborn, *JBL* 106:90-111. For Peter s. DPL, 702-3; for Apollos DPL, 37-39. ◆ **13 μεμέρισται** perf. ind. pass. μερίζω (# *3532*) to divide, to separate, to divide up and distribute, to split up into political parties (Barrett; Welborn, *JBL* 106:87). Perf. pictures the completed action or state.

It means, "he has already been divided up and distributed" (Lenski). This sentence could be a question expecting the answer "no," or it could be taken as a statement of fact (Schrage; Fee; Conzelmann). μή (# 3590) introduces a question expecting a neg. answer. ἐσταυρώθη aor. ind. pass. σταυρόω (# 5090) to crucify. εἰς τὸ ὄνομα (# 1659; 3950) "into the name." This was used as a t.t. w. the meaning, "to apply to the account of someone" (Schrage). ἐβαπτίσθητε aor. ind. pass. βαπτίζω (# 966) to baptize. ◆ **14** εὐχαριστῶ pres. ind. act. εὐχαριστέω (# 2373) to give thanks (s.v. 4). ἐβάπτισα aor. ind. act. βαπτίζω (# 966) to baptize. εἰ μή (# 1623; 3590) except, only (BD, 221). ◆ **15** εἴπῃ aor. subj. act. λέγω (# 3306) to say. Subj. w. ἵνα (# 2671) and μή to express neg. purp. ἐμόν (# 1847) my, placed before the noun for the sake of emphasis. ἐβαπτίσθητε aor. ind. pass. βαπτίζω (# 966) to baptize. ◆ **16** καί (# 2779) also. λοιπόν (# 3370) acc. sing. otherwise, besides that. Acc. of general reference, "as for anything else" (RWP). οἶδα perf. ind. act. (# 3857) to know. Def. perf. w. pres. meaning, here, to recall (Fee; s.v. 281-87). εἰ (# 1623) if. Used in an indir. question. ἐβάπτισα aor. ind. act. βαπτίζω (# 966) to baptize. ◆ **17** ἀπέστειλεν aor. ind. act. ἀποστέλλω (# 690) to send, to commission. to commission, someone to a special task and to empower him w. the authority of the one sending (TDNT; EDNT; s.v. 1). βαπτίζειν pres. act. inf. βαπτίζω (# 966) to baptize. Inf. either expresses purp. or explains the idea of sending. εὐαγγελίζεσθαι pres. mid. (dep.) inf. εὐαγγελίζομαι (# 2294) to bring good news, to preach the gospel (TDNT; TLNT; EDNT; RAC, 6:1107-60). σοφία (# 5053) dat. sing. wisdom, practical wisdom, a way of life (M.D. Goulder, "Σοφία in Corinthians," *NTS* 37 [1991]: 516-34; TDNT; EDNT); here, perhaps cleverness in speaking (BAGD; Welborn, *JBL*:106:87-101; DPL, 820-21). What is prohibited is the transformation of words into wisdom; the speech makes the wisdom attractive and effective (Schrage). Paul does not use worldly wisdom (Grosheide). He does not attempt to manipulate through his cleverly devised words and a gaudy, grandiloquent style (s. Michael A. Bullmore, *St. Paul's Theology of Rhetorical Style: An Examination of 1 Corinthians 2:1-5 in the Light of First Century Graeco-Roman Rhetorical Culture* [San Francisco: International Scholars Publications, 1995]). It may be, however, that Paul is rejecting the role of the human persuader and stressing his role as herald (Duane Liftin, *St. Paul's Theology of Proclamation* [SNTSMS 79] [Cambridge: Cambridge University, 1994]). κενωθῇ aor. subj. pass. κενόω (# 3033) to make empty, to make useless (TLNT). It indicates "to dwindle to nothing, vanish under the weight of rhetorical ornament and dialectic subtlety" (Lightfoot, *Notes*). σταυρός (# 5089) cross. The cross and crucifixion were a source of disdain, shame, and horror because death on a cross was for the worst of criminals (CNT, 180-269;

C; DPL, 192-99). ◆ **18** γάρ (# 1142) for. It gives a causal explanation. ὁ λόγος γὰρ ὁ τοῦ σταυροῦ (# 3664; 1142; 3836; 5089) "for the word of the" cross. The repeated article is almost demonstrative (RWP). The cross occupies a central place in proclaiming the gospel. It is both the crowning point of a life of self-renunciation and also the ordained instrument of salvation (Lightfoot, *Notes*). ἀπολλυμένοις pres. mid./pass. part. ἀπόλλυμι (# 660) to ruin, to be lost. The prep. in compound is perfective. Pres. indicates that the goal is ideally reached. A complete transformation of its subjects is required to bring them out of the ruin implicit in their state (M, 114f) Part. as subst. Dat. of ref. μωρία (# 3702) blunted, dull, stupid, stupidity, foolishness, nonsense (TLNT; TDNT; EDNT). A crucified Messiah, Son of God, or God must have seemed a contradiction in terms to anyone–Jew, Greek, Roman, or barbarian–and certainly was thought offensive and foolish (C, 10). Cicero said in his defense of C. Rabirius, whose trial was instituted by Julius Caesar, "The very word 'cross' should be far removed not only from the person of a Roman citizen but from his thoughts, his eyes and his ears" (*nomen ipsum crucis absit non modo a corpore civium Romanorum sed etiam a cogitatione, oculis, auribus*) (*Pro Rabirio*, 16; C, 42; also 41-45; BBC; NW 2, i:239). σωζομένοις pres. pass. part. σώζω (# 5392) to save, to rescue. Dat. of this part. includes an effective relation and the idea of an effect produced (Godet; Conzelmann). Theol. pass. indicating that God is the agent. Pres. indicated the ongoing process. ◆ **19** γέγραπται perf. ind. pass. γράφω (# 1211) to write. Perf. expresses the authoritative character of the document, "it stands written" (MM). ἀπολῶ fut. ind. act. ἀπόλλυμι (# 660) to ruin, to destroy (GELTS, 53). σύνεσις (# 5304) understanding, a bringing together, the faculty of putting two and two together (MNTW, 148f; TDNT). For the DSS s. 1 QS 3:15; 4:22; 1 QH 1:8. ἀθετήσω fut. ind. act. ἀθετέω (# 119) to do away w. that which has been laid down, to set aside, to disregard, to make void, to set at naught, to repudiate, to challenge an authority (AS; GELTS, 9; TLNT). ◆ **20** ποῦ (# 4544) where? The repetition of the word introduces three rhetorical questions which expect a neg. answer (Schrage). συζητητής (# 5186) one who questions, one who disputes and discusses, debator. The three expressions–"wise," "scribe," ("expert in law"), "debator"–describe human wisdom (Schrage). οὐχί (# 4049) not; a strengthened form of οὐ used in a question which expects the answer "yes." ἐμώρανεν aor. ind. act. μωραίνω (# 3701) to regard as foolish, to make foolish, to consider as nonsense, to make dumb (TLNT; Schrage). The timeless aor. (VA, 237) indicates the completed action. ◆ **21** ἐπειδή (# 2076) since, since then, because. ἐν τῇ σοφίᾳ τοῦ θεοῦ (# 1877; 3836; 5053; 3836; 2536) in the wisdom of God. The prep. ἐν indicates the sphere or could give the circumstances under which something takes place (A.J.M. Wedderburn, "ἐν τῇ σοφίᾳ τοῦ θεοῦ–1 Kor 1:21," ZNW 64 [1973]: 132-34; DPL, 967-73). Gen. of description: "divine wisdom," "godly wisdom." **ἔγνω** aor. ind. act. γινώσκω (# 1182) to know. **διὰ τῆς σοφίας** (# 1328; 3836; 5053) through wisdom. **εὐδόκησεν** aor. ind. act. εὐδοκέω (# 2305) to please, to have pleasure in; w. a following inf. The word in Paul implies strong volition, as well as taking pleasure in (Fee). **μωρίας** (# 3702) gen. sing. foolishness (s.v. 18). **κήρυγμα** (# 3060) proclamation, preaching. **σῶσαι** aor. act. inf. σῴζω (# 5392) to save, to rescue. Inf. explains what is pleasing to God. **πιστεύοντας** pres. act. part. πιστεύω (# 4409) to believe. Subst. part. ◆ **22 ἐπειδή** (# 2076) since, because. Causal conj., but only loosely subordinating (BD, 238; Schrage). **σημεῖον** (# 4956) sign (DPL, 875-76). **αἰτοῦσιν** pres. ind. act. αἰτέω (# 160) to ask. To ask for a sign implies a refusal to take God on trust (Barrett). For the Jews demanding a sign s. SB, 1:640, 726f; for signs in the DSS s. 1 QS 10:4; 1 QH 12:8; 15:20. **ζητοῦσιν** pres. ind. act. ζητέω (# 2426) to seek. Both pres. vbs. show the habitual action and describe what is always done. For the Greeks seeking after knowledge s. NW 2, i:238-39; DC XII, 39; XXXVII, 26. ◆ **23 ἡμεῖς** (# 1609) but we; for emphasis and contrast. **κηρύσσομεν** pres. ind. act. κηρύσσω (# 3062) to proclaim as a herald, to preach (TDNT; EDNT; NIDNTT, 3:48-68). Pres. indicates Paul's habitual practice. **ἐσταυρωμένον** perf. pass. part. σταυρόω (# 3062) to crucify (TDNT; C; EDNT). Perf. emphasizes the state or condition (s. 3:21). It refers primarily to the exalted Lord who, in His exaltation, remains the Crucified One (E.E. Ellis, "'Christ Crucified,'" RH, 70). **σκάνδαλον** acc. sing. (# 4998) the stick which an animal stumbled over, causing the trap to shut; stumbling block, cause of stumbling, something that trips men up (Barrett; TDNT; NTW, 111-14). It indicates the occasion for guilt and the cause of destruction (Schrage). **ἔθνεσιν** dat. pl. ἔθνος (# 1620) Gentile. Ethical dat., "in the opinion of." **μωρίαν** (# 3702) acc. sing. foolishness, nonsense, that which displays a senseless act or thinking or speaking (NIDNTT; TLNT). The two nouns are in apposition to the object. ◆ **24 αὐτοῖς** dat. pl. αὐτός (# 899) self. Ethical dat., "to them," or "to the called themselves" (Weiss). **τε ... καί** both ... and. ◆ **25 τὸ μωρὸν τοῦ θεοῦ** (# 3836; 3704; 3836; 2536) "the foolish thing of God" is that work of God which the world considers foolishness (Grosheide). **σοφώτερον** comp. of σοφός (# 5055) wise; comp., "wiser," followed by the gen. of comp.; wiser than men w. all their strength (Godet). **ἀσθενής** (# 476) weak, without strength. **ἰσχυρότερον** comp. ἰσχυρός (# 2708) strong; comp., "stronger." The definite article refers to the salvation work of the cross (Schrage). ◆ **26 βλέπετε** pres. ind. act. βλέπω (# 1063) to see, to look at. **γάρ** (# 1142) for. It is explanatory: "you can see what I mean" (Barrett).

κλῆσις (# 3104) calling. **οὐ πολλοί** (# 4024; 4498) not many. The term is not exclusive ("none at all!"), but is limiting. **κατά** (# 2848) according, according to the standard of. It speaks of wisdom gained according to the flesh; that is, according to natural and human abilities (Weiss). **δυνατός** (# 1543) powerful. **εὐγενεῖς** nom. pl. εὐγενής (# 2302) noble, well-born (TLNT, 1:95-96; NDIEC, 2:58-60). The social structure of the church at Corinth included those from all levels of society. There were those from the lower levels of society as well as some from the upper levels (Gerd Theissen, "Soziale Schichtung in der korinthischen Gemeinde. Ein Beitrag zur Soziologie des hellenistischen Urchristentums," ZNW 65 [1974]: 232-72; Dieter Sänger, "Die δυνατοί in 1 Kor 1:26," ZNW 76 [1985]: 285-91; David W.J. Gill, "Acts and the Urban Elites," BAFCS, 2:105-18, esp. 110-13; Fee). ◆ **27 ἐξ-ελέξατο** aor. ind. mid. (indir. mid., "for oneself") ἐκλέγομαι (# 1721) to pick out, to select, to choose for oneself (GGBB, 421). **καταισχύνη** pres. subj. act. καταισχύνω (# 2875) to put to shame, to humiliate, to disgrace (BAGD; LN, 1:310). The prep. in compound is perfective (RWP). Subj. w. ἵνα (# 2671) to express purp. ◆ **28 ἀγενῆ** (# 822) not of noble birth, low, insignificant. For the neg. force of the prefix s. Rom. 1:20. **ἐξουθενημένα** perf. pass. part. ἐξουθενέω (# 2024) to despise, to consider as nothing. For the force of the prep. in compound and the development of this word s. MH, 310. Perf. denotes not only quality, but also that the things which were once despised will continue to be despised (Grosheide). Part. as subst. **ἐξελέξατο** aor. ind. mid. ἐκλέγομαι (# 1721) to pick out (s.v. 27). **ὄντα** pres. act. part. εἰμί (# 1639) to be; **μὴ ὄντα** "the things which do not exist," "which are nonexistent." A more contemptible expression in Greek thinking was not possible. Being was everything (Weiss). Part. as subst. Acc. can be taken as another dir. obj. or as being in apposition to the two previous objects. **καταργήσῃ** aor. subj. act. καταργέω (# 2934) to put out of action, to make inactive, to reduce to nothing (TDNT; EDNT). Prep. in compound indicates an action unfavorable to its object (MH, 316). Subj. w. ἵνα (# 2671) to express purp. ◆ **29 ὅπως** (# 3968) w. subj. used to express intended results (BD, 196). Here it expresses neg. results. **καυχήσηται** aor. subj. mid. (dep.) καυχάομαι (# 3016) to boast, to glory. **πᾶσα σάρξ** all flesh, any flesh; w. the neg., no flesh; that is, "no one," an OT expression (Barrett). ◆ **30 ἐξ αὐτοῦ** from him; that is, "you are born of him in Christ Jesus" (Lightfoot, Notes). **ἐστε** pres. ind. act. εἰμί (# 1639) to be. **ἐγενήθη** aor. ind. pass. γίνομαι (# 1181) to become. Pass. can either denote "has been made" or "became" (Schrage; BD, 42). **σοφία** (# 5053) wisdom, s.v. 17. Christ is the true wisdom and union w. Him makes the believer truly wise (Hodge; for Christ as the wisdom of God s. PW; PRJ, 147-76). **ἡμῖν** dat. pl. ἐγώ (# 1609) I; "for us." Dat. of advantage. **δικαιοσύνη**

(# *1466*) righteousness, the status of being in the right before God (GW, 147; for the view that it means God's loving, gracious, loyal action which believers share in s. MRP, 155). ἁγιασμός (# *40*) holiness, sanctification (TDNT; EDNT). ἀπολύτρωσις (# *667*) redemption, release through the payment of a ransom price (TDNT; TLNT; EDNT; LDC). It was used for the release of prisoners by the payment of a price (Jos., *Ant.*, 12:27). Perhaps here pointing to the last great day, the consummation of redemption (Morris; Schrage) or it may refer to the present passion (LDC, 185-88). The last three terms are an explanation of the word "wisdom" (Lightfoot, *Notes*). ◆ **31 ἵνα** (# *2671*) w. subj. used here in an elliptical expression: "in order that it might come to pass, work out just as" (BD, 255). γέγραπται perf. ind. pass. s.v. 19. καυχώμενος pres. mid. (dep.) part. καυχάομαι (# *3016*) to boast. The cond. part. used as the subject of the cl. is due to Semitic influence (Barrett). καυχάσθω pres. mid. (dep.) imp. 3rd. pers. sing. καυχάομαι. The force here is a command, not permissive (GGBB, 486).

1 Corinthians 2

◆ **1 κἀγώ** (# *2743*) = καὶ ἐγώ "and I"; accordingly. It emphasizes the apostle's consistency w. the principles laid down in the preceding verses (RP). ἐλθών aor. act. part. (temp.) ἔρχομαι (# *2262*) to come. "When I came," giving simultaneous action (GGBB, 614; 624-25). ἦλθον aor. ind. act. 1st. pers. sing. ἔρχομαι to come (# *2262*). **καθ'** = κατά (# *2848*) w. acc., according to. It can indicate the nature or characteristic of a thing or manner (BAGD). ὑπεροχή (# *5667*) prominence, superiority, excellency. λόγος (# *3364*) word, speech. σοφία (# *5053*) wisdom. The two nouns are close together in meaning; eloquence is rational talk and wisdom is wordy cleverness (Barrett; for the role of the "persuader," s. Liftin and Bullmore as noted in 1:17). For the emphasis on oratory in education and the importance of a skilled speaker in the ancient world s. CC, 151ff; KP 4:1396-414; Aristotle, *Art of Rhetoric*; Quintilian (s. Liftin and Bullmore as noted in 1:17). καταγγέλλων pres. act. part. καταγγέλλω (# *2859*) to proclaim, to make a solemn proclamation (NIDNTT). Pres. emphasizes the continual action and the part. is a part. of manner. In his proclamation Paul placed no reliance upon eloquence or wisdom, but it does not mean he did not employ any kind of speech or wisdom. It is just that these were not prominent in his evangelism (Barrett). μυστήριον θεοῦ (# *3457; 2536*) the mystery of God, the counsel of God, unknown to man except by revelation, especially concerning His saving work and ultimate purposes in history (ZPEB, 4:327; TDNT; EDNT; DPL, 621-23; ABD, 4:941-42). Subjective gen. (Lightfoot, *Notes*). For the variant reading μαρτύριον ("testimony") s. TC, 545. ◆ **2 ἔκρινα** aor. ind. act. κρίνω (# *3212*) to judge, to

decide. It emphasizes a deliberate act of the will (Lietzmann). Aor. states a fact which had come to its conclusion when Paul arrived at Corinth. He had to go on preaching Christ (Grosheide). εἰδέναι perf. act. inf. οἶδα (# *3857*) to know. Def. perf w. pres. meaning; "to exhibit the knowledge of, recognize" (Lightfoot, *Notes*). Inf. used in indir. discourse. ἐν ὑμῖν in your midst. εἰ μή (# *1623; 3590*) except. καὶ τοῦτον and this one; specifies the point on which stress was laid, the effect being that of a climax (RP). ἐσταυρωμένον perf. pass. part. σταυρόω (# *5090*) to crucify (s. 1:23). Adj. part. without the article emphasizes the character. Perf. indicates the abiding results. ◆ **3 κἀγώ** (# *2743*) s.v. 1. Here it points again to Paul's arrival at Corinth (Weiss). ἀσθενείᾳ (# *819*) dat. sing. weakness. τρόμος (# *5571*) trembling. The words point to the anxiety or solicitude of mind arising out of a sense of his insufficiency, and of the infinite importance of his work (Hodge). Dat. of manner explaining his manner of life among them. ἐγενόμην aor. ind. mid. (dep.) γίνομαι (# *1181*) to become. Used w. πρός (# *4639*) to come to someone, to be w. someone. ◆ **4 πειθός** (# *4273*) persuasive. For the formation of this word s. RG, 157. Paul may be referring to the halakic and haggadic discussions current in Jewish Corinth rather than sophistic rhetoric in Hellenistic Corinth (Wilhem Wuellner, "Haggadic Homily Genre in I Corinthians 1-3," *JBL* 89 [1970]: 203). There may, however, be allusions to Greek rhetoric (Fee). ἀπόδειξις (# *618*) demonstration, argumentation, proof (GELTS, 49). In Greek rhetoric the word indicates a compelling decision demanded by the presupposition or premises (Fascher; Fee; Quintilan 5, 10:7; for the word as used in Josephus s. CCFJ, 1:179). The following genitives are both obj. (spirit and power are manifested) and subjective (the spirit and power bring proof and conviction) (Barrett). ◆ **5 ᾖ** pres. subj. act. εἰμί (# *1639*) to be. Subj. w. ἵνα (# *2671*) expresses purp. ἐν (# *1877*) in. The prep. marks the medium or sphere in which faith has its root (RP). ◆ **6 δέ** (# *1254*) but. Paul contrasted the wisdom which he speaks w. that of his opponents (Pearson). λαλοῦμεν pres. ind. act. λαλέω (# *4246*) to speak. Pres. indicates a present action as well as a common practice. τέλειος (# *5455*) having attained the end or purpose, full-grown, mature, adult (BAGD). αἰῶνος gen. sing. αἰών (# *172*) age, the course and current of this world's affairs (Trench, *Synonyms*, 217; TDNT; EDNT; RAC, 1:193-204; NIDNTT, 3:826-33). Gen. of source, indicating the origin, or the gen. may be descriptive, explaining the kind of wisdom. ἀρχόντων pres. act. part. ἄρχω (# *807*) to rule. Part. as subst. The part. refers to the human rulers of this world, the general men of authority (A.W. Carr, "The Rulers of this Age-I Cor. ii. 6-8," *NTS* 23 [October, 1976], 20-35; Gene Iller, "ΑΡΧΟΝΤΩΝ ΤΟΥ ΑΙΩΝΟΣ ΤΟΥΤΟΥ - A New Look at I Corinthians 2:6-8," *JBL* 91 [1972]: 522-28; BBC). καταργουμένων pres.

pass. part. adj. καταργέω (# 2934) to make idle, to put out of commission, to remove from power (s. 1:28). Pres. indicates a process in progress. Theol. pass. indicating that God is the one acting. ◆ **7** ἀλλά (# 247) but. It introduces the positive side again, and at the same time gives a strong neg. emphasis (Grosheide). θεοῦ gen. sing. θεός (# 2536) God. Placed before the noun for strong emphasis. Descriptive gen., "divine wisdom," or gen. of source, indicating the origin. The wisdom of God is the work of Christ in His crucifixion, as God's secret plan of redemption and the exalted Christ who presently mediates God's hidden wisdom to His people (E.E. Ellis, "'Wisdom' and 'Knowledge' in I Corinthians," *TB* 25 [1974]: 95). ἐν μυστηρίῳ (# 1877; 3696) in a mystery (s.v. 1). ἀποκεκρυμμένην perf. pass. part. ἀποκρύπτω (# 648) to veil, to hide. Adj. part. Perf. indicates the continuing state or condition. προώρισεν aor. ind. act. προορίζω (# 4633) to mark off w. boundaries beforehand, to predetermine, to predestinate (s. Rom 8:28-29). πρὸ τῶν αἰώνων (# 4574; 172) before the ages; that is, "before time." εἰς δόξαν ἡμῶν (# 1659; 1518; 1609) for our glory. The phrase indicates our complete salvation (RP). ◆ **8** ἔγνωκεν perf. ind. act. γινώσκω (# 1182) to know, to recognize, to discern. Perf. pictures the continuing results. ἔγνωσαν aor. ind. act. Ind. w. a contrary to fact cond. cl. (BD, 182; GGBB, 683; VA, 304-5). δόξης gen. sing. δόξα (# 1518) glory. Gen. is not only a gen. of quality, but indicates that only Christ rules over glory; this is a title for God Himself (Weiss). ἐσταύρωσαν aor. ind. act. σταυρόω (# 5090) to crucify (s. 1:23). ◆ **9** ἀλλά (# 247) but. The contrast may be between the ignorance expressed in v. 8, and knowing, as expressed in an elliptical construction introduced by ἀλλά and the vb. ἔγνωσαν (v. 8), which is to be understood (Bo Frid, "The Enigmatic ΑΛΛΑ in I Corinthians 2.9," *NTS* 31 [1985]: 603-11; Fee). καθώς (# 2777) just as, in accordance w. γέγραπται perf. ind. pass. γράφω (# 1211) to write. The source of Paul's quotation is not known. It may be from a Jewish liturgy, or be based on Isa. 64:4 (LXX 64:3) or Isa. 52:15, or be from an *Apocalypse of Elijah,* or an amalgamation of OT ideas (Pearson, 35; Fee; SB, 3:327-29; Klaus Berger, "Zur Diskussion über die Herkunft von I Kor. ii.9," *NTS* 24 [1978]: 270-83). It is reported that one rabbi said that the prophets prophesied only in respect of the Messianic era; but as for the world to come–"the eye hath not seen, O God, besides thee, what he hath prepared for him that waiteth for him" (b. Sanh. 99b). εἶδεν aor. ind. act. ὁράω (# 3972) to see. οὓς (# 4044) ear. ἤκουσεν aor. ind. act. ἀκούω (# 201) to hear. καρδία (# 2840) heart. The whole man is viewed from his intentionality; it is the source of the will, emotion, thoughts, and affections (PAT, 448; DPL, 768). ἀνέβη aor. ind. act. ἀναβαίνω (# 326) to go up, to arise, here "to enter into." ἡτοίμασεν aor. ind. act. ἑτοιμάζω (# 2286) to prepare. ἀγαπῶσιν

pres. act. part. ἀγαπάω (# 26) to love. Dat. of personal interest. ◆ **10** ἡμῖν dat. pl. (# 1609) ἐγώ I; "to us." Emphatic by its position in the sentence. ἀπεκάλυψεν aor. ind. act. ἀποκαλύπτω (# 636) to unveil, to reveal (TLNT, 2:244-50; TDNT; EDNT; NIDNTT, 3:309-12). διά (# 1328) w. gen., through. πνεῦμα (# 4460) spirit. Paul denies the views of Philo that the human spirit can know the divine spirit and can make known the things of God (PW, 122). ἐραυνᾷ pres. ind. act. ἐραυνάω (# 2236) to search, to penetrate, to examine, to investigate. Gnomic pres. indicating that which is always true (IBG, 8). βάθη acc. pl. βάθος (# 958) depth. The deep things of God designates God's essence, then His attributes, volitions, and plans (Godet). ◆ **11** οἶδεν perf. ind. act. οἶδα (# 3857) to know. Def. perf. w. pres. meaning. τὰ τοῦ ἀνθρώπου (# 3836; 476) the things belonging to man; the personal memories, reflections, motives of any human being; all the thoughts of which he is conscious (RP). τὰ τοῦ θεοῦ (# 3836; 2536) the things belonging to God. Used as parallel to the preceding. ἔγνωκεν perf. ind. act. γινώσκω (# 1182) to know. For a discussion of the two vbs. for "knowing" s. VA, 281-87. Perf. emphasizes the continuing knowledge. ◆ **12** τὸ πνεῦμα τοῦ κόσμου (# 4460; 3180) the spirit of the world. Qualitative gen., the spirit which animates the world (Lenski). ἐλάβομεν aor. ind. act. λαμβάνω (# 3284) to receive. εἰδῶμεν perf. subj. act. οἶδα (# 3857) to know. Perf w. pres. meaning. Subj. w. ἵνα (# 2671) for purp. χαρισθέντα aor. pass. part. χαρίζομαι (# 5919) to give as a gift of grace, to give graciously as a favor (BAGD; TDNT; EDNT). Aor. indicates that Paul is not speaking only of the future, but also of the present life of Christians (Barrett). ◆ **13** λαλοῦμεν pres. ind. act. λαλέω (# 3281) to speak (s.v. 6). διδακτός (# 1435) taught. A substantivized verbal adj. w. a pass. meaning, followed by the gen. designating the agent (MT, 234). "Not in words taught by human wisdom, but in words taught by the Spirit" (IBG, 40). ἀνθρώπινος (# 474) human. For an adj. w. this ending signifying material, origin, or kind s. MH, 359. πνευματικός (# 4461) spiritual, pertaining to the Spirit. For an adj. w. this ending s. MH, 378. The word can be n. ("spiritual things") or masc. ("spiritual persons") (RP; Barrett). For a discussion s. Birger A. Pearson, *The "Pneumatikos-Psychikos" Terminology in 1 Corinthians: A Study in the Theology of the Corinthian Opponents of Paul and Its Relation to Gnosticism,* SBLDS 12 (Missoula: Scholars Press, 1973). συγκρίνοντες pres. act. part. συγκρίνω (# 5173) to judge together. The vb. has various meanings which are possible in this passage: to bring together, to combine, compare, or explain, to interpret (BAGD; RP; Fee; GELTS, 446; TDNT; Schrage; for the meaning "to compare," "to measure oneself against," as used in Josephus s. CCFJ, 4:76). ◆ **14** ψυχικός (# 6035) soulish, pertaining to the soul or life, pertaining to behavior which is typical of human nature, in contrast w. that which is under the control of God's Spirit (LN, 1:509; TDNT). It describes the natural man who does not possess the Holy Spirit (TDNT; PAT, 334-46; for strong arguments rejecting the gnostic influence on Paul's use of this term s. Pearson, 7-14). **δέχεται** pres. ind. mid. (dep.) δέχομαι (# 1312) to receive. Pres. indicates the habitual action. **μωρία** (# 3702) foolishness, nonsense (s. 1:18). **δύναται** pres. ind. pass. δύναμαι (# 4024) to be able to, w. inf. Pres. indicating that which is always true. **γνῶναι** aor. act. inf. γινώσκω (# 1182) to know. **πνευματικῶς** (# 4462) adv. spiritually. Paul rejects Philo's view that man has within him, breathed into him by God, the capacity for knowing God and the higher truths of the universe. The wisdom of God comes only through the Holy Spirit (Pearson, 39). **ἀνακρίνεται** pres. ind. pass. ἀνακρίνω (# 373) to examine, used of judicial hearings, to conduct an examination, to examine and judge, to call to account, to discern (BAGD). Pres. indicates that which is always true. ◆ **15 πάντα** acc. pl. πᾶς (# 373) all, all things. The spiritual man is able to consider and appraise all things because he is not only inspired to understand what he sees; he is also furnished w. a moral standard by which all things may be measured (Barrett). ◆ **16 ἔγνω** aor. ind. act. 3rd. pers. sing. (# 1182) to know. **νοῦς** (# 3808) mind, thought, plan. A comprehensive name for the thoughts existing in the conscience (Schlatter). **ὅς** (# 4005) who, which; rel. pron. used to express purp. and followed by the fut. (BG, 118). **συμβιβάσει** fut. ind. act. συμβιβάζω (# 5204) to put together so as to draw an inference from, to conclude; here, to instruct (Lightfoot). **νοῦν Χριστοῦ** (# 3808; 5986) the mind of Christ, i.e., the thoughts, counsels, plans, and knowledge of Christ known through the agency of the Holy Spirit (RP). **ἔχομεν** pres. ind. act. ἔχω (# 2400) to have, to possess. Pres. indicates the continual possession.

1 Corinthians 3

◆ **1 κἀγώ** = καὶ ἐγώ (# 2743) and I; emphatic w. a slight contrast to the preceding (Grosheide). **ἠδυνήθην** aor. ind. pass. (dep.) δύναμαι (# 1538) to be able, w. inf. **λαλῆσαι** aor. act. inf. λαλέω (# 4246) to speak. **πνευματικός** (# 4461) spiritual, pertaining to the Spirit. Adj. as subst. **σάρκινος** (# 4921) fleshly, made of flesh, having the characteristics of flesh, associated w. flesh (s.v. 3). Paul avoids accusing them of not having the Spirit altogether, but at the same time he bitingly forces them to have to face up to their true condition (Fee). For nouns w. this ending denoting the material relation s. RP; Schrage. **νήπιος** (# 3758) infant, baby. Those unexperienced are often called "babes" (BBC). ◆ **2 γάλα** (# 1128) acc. sing. milk. Epictetus, who accuses those who do not put into practice what they have learned and who make moral decisions like children who are

satisfied with cookies (Epictetus 2, 16:25-27), then asks, "Are you not willing, at this late date, like children, to be weaned (ἀπογαλακτισθῆναι) and partake of more solid food (τροφῆς στερεωτέρας) and not cry for mammies and nurses?" (Epictetus 2, 16:39). **ἐπότισα** aor. ind. act. ποτίζω (# 4540) to give to drink. **βρῶμα** (# 1109) acc. sing. food, solid food. For similar terminology appearing in Philo s. Pearson, 29f; Fee. **οὔπω** (# 4037) not yet. **ἐδύνασθε** impf. ind. pass. (dep.) δύναμαι (# 1538) to be able to. **γάρ** (# 1142) and indeed. The word has an intensifying effect (Barrett). **ἔτι νῦν** (# 2284; 3814) even now. ◆ **3 σαρκικός** (# 4920) fleshly, pertaining to the flesh, controlled by the flesh. Words w. this ending denote an ethical or dynamic relation (RP). Flesh is the outlook orientated toward the self, that which pursues its own ends in self-sufficient independence of God (NIDNTT; TDNT; PRJ, 17-35; PAT, 49-95). In Judaism it refers to the evil inclination (SB, 3:330-32; TS, 471-82). Pred. nom. **ὅπου** (# 3963) where, insofar as. Causal use (BD, 238). **ζῆλος** (# 2419) envy, jealousy, resentment (LN, 1:760; DPL, 462-63). **ἔρις** (# 2251) strife (s. 1:11). It is the outward result of envious feeling (RP). **οὐχί** (# 4049) A strengthened form of οὐ used to introduce a question which expects the answer "yes." **κατά** (# 2848) according to; here, w. merely human motives or feelings. Your walk in life conforms to a merely human standard. The prep. denotes the measure or standard (Lightfoot, *Notes*). **περιπατεῖτε** pres. ind. act. περιπατέω (# 4344) to walk, to conduct one's life. Pres. points to an action which was taking place and indicates a continual action. ◆ **4 ὅταν** (# 4020) whenever. **λέγῃ** pres. subj. act. λέγω (# 3306) to say. Subj. in an indef. temp. cl. **οὐκ** (# 4024) used in questions expecting the answer "yes." **ἄνθρωπος** (# 476) human being. Pred. nom. without the article expressing the character or quality. ◆ **5 διάκονος** (# 1356) servant, minister, helper, messenger (LN, 1:460-61; TDNT; EDNT; NIDNTT, 3:544-49; CCFJ, 1:456; MM; Schrage). The word excludes personal authority and personal interest as well as emphasizing a relation to another (Schrage). **δι'** = διά (# 1328) w. gen., through, indicating an intermediate agent. **ἐπιστεύσατε** aor. ind. act. πιστεύω (# 4409) to believe. Ingressive aor., "to become a believer," "to come to belief." **ἑκάστῳ** dat. sing. ἕκαστος (# 1667) each (one), every (one) (# 1667) Dat. as indir. obj., "each as the Lord gave to him" (Grosheide). **ἔδωκεν** aor. ind. act. δίδωμι (# 1443) to give. ◆ **6 ἐφύτευσα** aor. ind. act. φυτεύω (# 5885) to plant. It indicates the founding of the church at Corinth (Schrage; S. Fujita, "The Metaphor of Plant in Jewish Literature of the Intertestamental Period," *JJS* 7 [1976]: 30-45). **ἐπότισεν** aor. ind. act. ποτίζω (# 4540) to give to drink, to water. **ηὔξανεν** impf. ind. act. αὐξάνω (# 889) to cause to grow. Impf. indicates the continuous blessing of God on the work of both Paul and Apollos

(RWP). ◆ **7 ὥστε** (# *6063*) therefore. Used w. ind. to draw an inference from the previous sentence (RG, 999; IBG, 144). **οὔτε ... οὔτε** (# *4046*) "neither ... nor." **φυτεύων** pres. act. part. φυτεύω (# *5885*) to plant (s.v. 6). Part. as subst. **ποτίζων** pres. act. part. ποτίζω (# *4540*) to give to drink (s.v. 6). Part. as subst. **αὐξάνων** pres. act. part. αὐξάνω (# *889*) to cause to grow. Part. as subst. and emphasized by its position in the sentence. ◆ **8 ἕν** (# *1651*) one; n., one thing. The aim, result, and motivating power of their work are identical (Barrett). **μισθός** (# *3635*) reward, wage, salary. For the idea of receiving rewards for work s. SB 4:484-500; TDNT; DPL, 819-20. **λήμψεται** fut. ind. mid. (dep.) λαμβάνω (# *3284*) to receive. ◆ **9 συνεργός** (# *5301*) fellow worker. The word w. gen. could mean "fellow workers w. God," or "fellow workers in God's service." The context indicates that Paul is speaking of the equal relation of God's workers w. one another (Victor Paul Furnish, "'Fellow Workers, in God's Service,'" *JBL* 80 [1961]: 364-70; TDNT; GGBB, 130; DPL, 183-88). **γεώργιον** (# *1176*) working field, cultivated land, field. For the agricultural picture s. *ZPEB*, 1:71-78; IDB, 1:56-59; OCD, 29-30; *ABD*, 1:95-98. **οἰκοδομή** (# *3869*) building (BDG; TDNT). Perhaps Paul could be referring to the many buildings and temples in Corinth. For architecture and buildings s. TDNT; *ZPEB*, 1:287-97; RAC, 1:1265-78; Acts 18:1. ◆ **10 δοθεῖσαν** aor. pass. part. (adj.) δίδωμι (# *1443*) to give. **ἀρχιτέκτων** (# *802*) architect, builder, master worker, skilled craftsman (Philo, *On Dreams* 2, 8). The master builder has the responsibility of the planning and construction of the building; therefore Paul is within his rights to require of preachers who come to labor on the builder's work site and add to his construction that they be strictly faithful to the canon that he has determined once for all (TLNT, 1:209-11). **θεμέλιος** (# *2529*) foundation. **ἔθηκα** aor. ind. act. τίθημι (# *5502*) to lay. **ἐποικοδομεῖ** pres. ind. act. ἐποικοδομέω (# *2224*) to build upon (BDG). Pres. pictures the continual action and is to be contrasted w. the previous aor. **βλεπέτω** pres. imp. act. βλέπω (# *1063*) to see, to beware. Pres. imp. calls for an habitual action. ◆ **11 ἄλλος** (# *2529*) another, another of the same kind. **δύναται** pres. ind. pass. (dep.) δύναμαι (# *1538*) to be able to, w. inf. **θεῖναι** aor. act. inf. τίθημι (# *5502*) to lay. **παρά** (# *4123*) w. acc., beside, along, beyond. In comparisons the sense is "than," "more than," "rather than" (DM, 108; IBG, 51; NIDNTT, 3:1201-02). **κείμενον** pres. mid. (dep.) part. κεῖμαι (# *3023*) to lie; of a foundation, to be laid (BAGD). Pres. implies "the one already in place" (Fee; Barrett). ◆ **12 χρυσός** (# *5996*) gold. **ἄργυρος** (# *738*) silver. **λίθος** (# *3345*) stone. **τίμος** (# *5508*) precious, expensive. Here it means valuable stones for building such as granite and marble (Hodge). For the use of precious metals and stone in building s. RAC 6:451-457; SB, 3:333-34. **ξύλος** (# *3833*)

wood. **χόρτος** (# *5965*) grass, hay. **καλάμη** (# *2811*) stalk, straw, used as a building material for thatching roofs (BAGD; SB, 3:334-45). ◆ **13 γενήσεται** fut. ind. mid. (dep.) γίνομαι (# *1181*) to become, to be. **ἡμέρα** (# *2465*) the day. The article refers to a day which is well-known (Schlatter). **δηλώσει** fut. ind. act. δηλόω (# *1317*) to make visible, to make plain, to make clear. **ὅτι** because. **πῦρ** (# *4786*) fire. **ἀποκαλύπτεται** pres. ind. mid./pass. (Fee) ἀποκαλύπτω (# *636*) to unveil, to reveal. The word "day" is the subject of the vb. Pres. used to express the fut. It is a confident assertion regarding the fut. (BD, 168; RP; VA, 230-33). **ὁποῖος** (# *3961*) what kind of, what sort of. **δοκιμάσει** fut. ind. act. δοκιμάζω (# *1507*) to approve after testing, to examine, to put to the proof, used particularly of metals which are tried by fire (Weiss; TDNT; TLNT; NDIEC, 1:131; 2:14; CCFJ, 1:517; GELTS, 119). ◆ **14 εἰ** (# *1623*) if. Used in a 1st. class cond. cl. where the cond. is assumed to be true. **μενεῖ** fut. ind. act. μένω (# *3531*) to remain. **ἐποικοδόμησεν** aor. ind. act. ἐποικοδομέω (# *2224*) to build upon. **λήμψεται** fut. ind. mid. (dep.) λαμβάνω (# *3284*) to receive. ◆ **15 κατακαήσεται** fut. ind. pass. κατακαίω (# *2876*) to burn up completely. Prep. in compound is perfective (MH, 316). **ζημιωθήσεται** fut. ind. pass. ζημιόω (# *2423*) pass., to suffer loss; here, he will lose his reward (Hodge). **αὐτός** (# *899*) he himself, emphatic. **σωθήσεται** fut. ind. pass. σῴζω (# *5392*) to rescue, to save. **ὡς** (# *6055*) **διὰ πυρός** (# *1328*; *4786*) as through fire. The prep. is to be taken in a local sense; that is, "as one who dashes through the flames safe, but w. the smell of fire upon him" (Barrett). ◆ **16 οἴδατε** perf. ind. act. οἶδα (# *3857*) to know. Def. perf. w. pres. meaning. The neg. introducing the question expects a positive answer, "yes." **ναός** (# *3724*) temple, dwelling place of a deity, the inward shrine or sanctuary. The reference is to the one temple of Jerusalem and there may be an allusion to the dissensions which are corrupting God's temple (Lightfoot, *Notes*). **οἰκεῖ** pres. ind. act. οἰκέω (# *3861*) to dwell. ◆ **17 φθείρει** pres. ind. act. φθείρω (# *5780*) to corrupt, to ruin, to spoil. Ind. in a 1st. class cond. cl. in which the reality of the cond. is assumed. **φθερεῖ** fut. ind. act. **οἵτινες** nom. pl. ὅστις (# *4015*) who, whoever, ones of such a nature (BG, 68). ◆ **18 ἐξαπατάτω** pres. imp. act. ἐξαπατάω (# *1987*) to deceive, to cheat. Prep. in compound is perfective, "to successfully deceive" (MH, 311). For the pres. imp. in the neg. s. Rom. 6:12. **εἰ** (# *1623*) if. It introduces a 1st. class cond. cl. in which the cond. is assumed to be true. **δοκεῖ** pres. ind. act. δοκέω (# *1506*) to think, to suppose, to assume. **εἶναι** pres. act. inf. εἰμί (# *1639*) to be. Inf. as obj. of the vb. **γενέσθω** aor. imp. mid. (dep.) γίνομαι (# *1181*) to become. **γένηται** aor. subj. mid. (dep.). Subj. w. **ἵνα** (# *2671*) in a purp. cl. ◆ **19 παρά** (# *4143*) w. dat., beside, with, in the presence of (DM, 108; NIDNTT, 3:1201-3). **γέγραπται** perf. ind. pass. γράφω (# *1211*) to write. Perf.

indicates the lasting authority of the written document (MM). **δρασσόμενος** pres. mid. (dep.) part. δράσσω (# 1533) to catch, to seize. **πανουργία** (# 4111) dat. sing. cunning, craftiness, trickery; literally, "readiness to do anything" (BAGD). ◆ **20 διαλογισμός** (# 1369) thought, reasoning. **μάταιος** (# 3469) empty, vain, useless. It expresses the aimlessness, the leading to no object or end (Trench, *Synonyms*, 180-84). For God destroying the wisdom of the wise, as seen in the DSS s. 1 QS 5:19f. ◆ **21 ὥστε** (# 6063) therefore. It draws a conclusion or inference from the preceding. **καυχάσθω** pres. imp. mid. (dep.) καυχάομαι (# 3016) to boast, to glory in something or someone. **πάντα** nom. n. pl. πᾶς (# 4246) all; here, all things. He puts no limit to their possessions in Christ (Morris). ◆ **22 ἐνεστῶτα** perf. act. part. ἐνίστημι (# 1931) to be present. Part. as subst. **μέλλοντα** pres. act. part. μέλλω (# 3516) to be about to. Part. as subst., "things that are coming." **πάντα ὑμῶν** (# 4246; 5148) all things are yours, all things belong to you. Pred. gen. (RWP).

1 Corinthians 4

◆ **1 λογιζέσθω** pres. imp. mid. (dep.) λογίζομαι (# 3357) to reckon, to count, to consider. **ἄνθρωπος** (# 476) man; used in the indef. sense, "one" or "a person" (Meyer; MM). **ὑπηρέτης** (# 5677) minister, helper, one who is in the service of another (TDNT; TLNT; Acts 13:5). **οἰκονόμος** (# 3874) steward, manager of a household; often a trusted slave was put in charge of the whole household. The word emphasizes that one is entrusted w. great responsibility and accountability (TDNT; NIDNTT, 2:253-55; TLNT). **μυστηρίων θεοῦ** (# 3696; 2536) of the mysteries of God (s. 2:1). Gen. expresses that which the steward was entrusted w. and what he is to administer. ◆ **2 ὧδε** (# 6045) in that case, on that showing; used here to draw an inference, "therefore." **λοιπός** (# 3370) rest, remaining, adv. acc. Used here either to strengthen the inference or to introduce a fresh point ("now"); the use would be progressive (Thrall, 26-28; Blomqvist, 100-103). **ζητεῖται** pres. ind. pass. ζητέω (# 2426) to seek, to look for. Gnomic pres. indicating that which is always true. **ἵνα** (# 2671) that. It introduces an epex. cl. which is the object of the vb. (Fee). **πιστός** (# 4412) faithful, dependable. **εὑρεθῇ** aor. subj. pass. εὑρίσκω (# 2351) to find. ◆ **3 ἐμοί** dat. sing. ἐγώ (# 1609) I. Ethical dat., "to me," "in my opinion." **ἐλάχιστον** superl. μικρός (# 1650) small. Elative, very small, very little; "it amounts to very little," "it counts for a very small matter" (RP; BAGD). (For the use of the prep. εἰς after the vb. εἰμί s. RG, 595f; KVS, 65.) **ἵνα** (# 2671) that. It introduces an epex. cl. which explains what is very small in his opinion. **ὑφ'** = ὑπό (# 5679) w. gen., by used w. a pass. vb. to show the agent. **ἀνακριθῶ** aor. subj. pass. ἀνακρίνω (# 373) to question, to examine, to interrogate; used of a judicial

examination before the final verdict is given (Weiss; s. 2:14). ◆ **4 σύνοιδα** perf. ind. act. συνοῖδα (# 5323). Def. perf. w. a pres. meaning, to share knowledge; here, to know about oneself, what is unknown to others (RP); "my conscience is clear" (Fee). **δεδικαίωμαι** perf. ind. pass. δικαιόω (# 1467) to justify, to declare to be in the right. The form could also be perf. mid.: "I have not justified myself." **ἀνακρίνων** pres. act. part. ἀνακρίνω (# 373) question (s.v. 3). Part. as subst. ◆ **5 ὥστε** (# 6063) therefore. It draws an inference from the preceding. **ἕως ἄν** (# 2401; 323) w. subj., until. **ἔλθη** aor. subj. act. ἔρχομαι (# 2262) to come. Subj. in an indef. temp. cl. **φωτίσει** fut. ind. act. φωτίζω (# 5881) to illumine, to bring to light. **φανερώσει** fut. ind. act. φανερόω (# 5894) to make visible, to reveal. **γενήσεται** fut. ind. mid. (dep.) γίνομαι (# 1181) to become, to be. **ἑκάστῳ** dat. sing. ἕκαστος (# 1667) each one. Dat. of advantage, "for each one." ◆ **6 ταῦτα** n. pl. οὗτος (# 4047) this; these things, referring to the figures of gardeners, builders, and stewards. For a discussion of this verse s. M.D. Hooker, "'Beyond the Things Which Are Written': An Examination of 1 Cor. 4:6," *NTS* 10 [1963]: 127-32. **μετεσχημάτισα** aor. ind. act. μετασχηματίζω (# 3571) to change the form of, to transform. Here the meaning seems to be, "I have applied these figures of speech to myself and Apollos" (Hooker, NTS 10:131). Paul may be using the rhetorical device of covert allusion to indicate the true character of the Christian workers (Benjamin Fiore, "'Covert Allusion' in 1 Corinthians 1-4," *CBQ* 47 [1985]: 85-102). **μάθητε** aor. subj. act. μανθάνω (# 3443) to teach, to instruct. Subj. w. **ἵνα** (# 2671) to express purp. **ὑπέρ** w. acc., beyond. **γέγραπται** perf. ind. pass. γράφω (# 1211) to write. It was used to refer to the authoritative character of that which stands written (MM). Paul may be referring to the Scripture passages which he has quoted or to his own teaching (Hooker, NTS 10:128ff). **εἰς ὑπὲρ τοῦ ἑνός ... κατὰ τοῦ ἑτέρου** (# 1651; 5642; 3836; 2848; 2283) each on behalf of one and against another (Barrett). **φυσιοῦσθε** pres. ind. pass. or pres. subj. pass., by irregular contraction (RWP) φυσιόω (# 5881) to puff up, to inflate, to blow up. ◆ **7 διακρίνει** pres. ind. act. διακρίνω (# 1359) to judge between two, to make a distinction, to make different (Weiss; MH, 302; Fee). This is probably best taken as a rhetorical question (Barrett). **ἔλαβες** aor. ind. act. λαμβάνω (# 3284) to receive. **καί** (# 2779) It throws emphasis on the vb. and w. the cond. particle represents the insistence on what is fact (RP). **καυχᾶσαι** pres. ind. mid. 2nd. sing. (dep.) καυχάομαι (# 3016) to boast. **λαβών** aor. act. part. (cond.) λαμβάνω (# 3284). ◆ **8 κεκορεσμένοι** perf. pass. part. κορέννυμι (# 3016) to satisfy w. food, to fill; pass., to be satisfied w. food, to have enough of. Used ironically: "you think you already have all the spiritual food you need" (BAGD). Part. in a periphrastic construction or as pred. adj. Perf.

emphasizes the completed state or condition. ἐπλουτή-σατε aor. ind. act. πλουτέω (# 4456) to be rich. Ingressive aor., "to become rich." χωρίς (# 6006) w. gen., without. ἐβασιλεύσατε aor. ind. act. βασιλεύω (# 996) to rule, to reign as a king. ὄφελον particle derived from ὀφείλω (# 4054) to owe; expressing an impossible wish (BD, 181; MKG, 252; RG, 1003f). συμβασιλεύσωμεν aor. subj. act. συμβασιλεύω (# 996) to rule together, to be a co-ruler. Subj. w. ἵνα (# 2671) to express purp. ◆ 9 δοκῶ pres. ind. act. δοκέω (# 1506) to think, to suppose, to assume. ἔσχατος (# 2274) last. ἀπέδειξεν aor. ind. act. ἀποδείκνυμι (# 617) to show, to expose to view, to exhibit. A technical word of bringing a person into the arena. The apostles were brought out to make the grand finale (Lightfoot, Notes). ἐπιθανάτιος (# 2119) condemned to die, used of criminals sentenced to death in the arena (PAM, 189). θέατρον (# 2519) theater, play, spectacle (Lightfoot, Notes). Gladiatorial games were held in Corinth as well as Rome (Schrage; RAC, 11:23-45; LLAR, 288-302). ἐγενήθημεν aor. ind. pass. γίνομαι (# 1181) to become, to be made. Paul uses the picture to illustrate the humility and indignity to which the apostles are subjected. God is the one who set up this spectacle and uses the weakness of His servants in order to demonstrate His power and strength (PAM, 189). ◆ 10 ἡμεῖς nom. pl. ἐγώ I (# 1609) we! Emphatic and contrasted w. ὑμεῖς. μωρός (# 3704) dull, stupid, foolish, ridiculous (s. 1:18; TLNT). Pred. nom. without the article stressing the character or quality. διά (# 1328) w. acc., because, on account of. φρόνιμος (# 5861) sensible, smart. pred. nom. ἔνδοξος (# 1902) honored, distinguished, eminent. Pred. nom. ἄτιμος (# 872) without honor. Paul assumes the position of one who has been humiliated and dishonored, but his opponents consider themselves as superior in all respects and intend that their conduct should dishonor or shame others (EC, 210-11). ◆ 11 καί ... καί (# 2779) "both ... and." Paul now describes himself as a socially and economically disadvantaged person (EC, 211-13). πεινῶμεν pres. ind. act. πεινάω (# 4277) to be hungry. διψῶμεν pres. ind. act. διψάω (# 1498) to be thirsty. γυμνιτεύομεν pres. ind. act. γυμνιτεύω (# 1217) to be naked, to be scantily clothed, to be poorly clothed (Schrage). κολαφιζόμεθα pres. ind. pass. κολαφίζω (# 3139) to hit w. the fist, to beat, not simply strike w. the fist, in an insulting manner (like slaves or a condemned man) (Barrett). ἀστατοῦμεν pres. ind. act. ἀστατέω (# 841) to be homeless, to be without a roof over one's head. ◆ 12 κοπιῶμεν pres. ind. act. κοπιάω (# 3159) to toil, to labor, to do hard work, to work till one is weary or exhausted (TLNT; TDNT). ἐργαζόμενοι pres. mid. (dep.) part. ἐργάζομαι (# 2237) to work. Greeks despised manual labor (NW, 2, i, 270; RAC, 1:585-90; TRE 3:622-24; EC, 212). Paul glories in it, and even the rabbis often worked to support themselves (RP; SB, 3:338). Part. of manner.

χερσίν dat. pl. χείρ (# 5931) hand. Instr. dat. λοιδορούμενοι pres. pass. part. λοιδορέω (# 3366) to abuse w. words. It was a common practice of speakers and politicians to insult and abuse their opponents (TDNT; TLNT). Temp. or concessive part. (Kistemaker). εὐλογοῦμεν pres. ind. act. εὐλογέω (# 2328) to bless. διωκόμενοι pres. pass. part. διώκω (# 1503) to pursue, to hunt, to persecute. Temp. or concessive part. ἀνεχόμεθα pres. ind. mid. (dep.) ἀνέχομαι (# 462) to endure, to forbear. ◆ 13 δυσφημούμενοι pres. mid./pass. part. δυσφημέω (# 1555) to defame, to slander. Temp. or concessive part. παρακαλοῦμεν pres. ind. act. παρακαλέω (# 4151) to encourage, to comfort. Humiliation suffered normally leads to anger, which is defined as a desire for revenge accompanied by pain and the recovering of one's own honor, but Paul instead blesses, endures, and conciliates (EC, 214). περικάθαρμα (# 4326) that which is cleansed all around, that which is removed–dirt and filth–as a result of a thorough cleansing; a base insult when applied to humans (TLNT; Jos., JW, 4:241; NW, 2, ii, 272). The word was also used of condemned criminals of the lowest class who were sacrificed as offerings for the cleansing of a city in the sense of a ransom (TDNT; Lightfoot, Notes; EGT; TLNT; GELTS, 374). ἐγενήθημεν aor. ind. pass. (dep.) γίνομαι (# 1181) s.v. 9. περίψημα (# 4370) that which is removed by the process of cleaning dirt off, scouring, scum. The previous word indicates a rinsing, this word a scraping of a dirty vessel (TLNT). It was used in the papyri in a letter conveying the greeting; "your humble and devoted servant" (MM). It was used in the baths as an ironical form of greeting, "your offscouring," meaning "your humble servant" (LLAR, 30). ◆ 14 ἐντρέπων pres. act. part. ἐντρέπω (# 1956) to shame, to make ashamed. Pres. part. expresses purp. (MT, 157). Pres. may also be viewed as conative, "I am not trying to shame you" (Barrett). νουθετῶν pres. act. part. νουθετέω (# 3805) to admonish, to correct through admonition (TDNT; EDNT). Parents are responsible to reprimand, admonish, and correct their children (TLNT, 2:550). Part. expresses purp. Pres. expresses a continuing action. ◆ 15 ἐάν (# 1569) if, w. subj. introduces a 3rd. class cond. cl. in which the assumption is left undetermined, but there is some expectation of realization (Funk, 2:683). μυρίους masc. acc. pl. μύριοι (# 3692) ten thousand; in masc. pl., innumerable (BAGD; Kistemaker). παιδαγωγός (# 4080) child trainer, guardian, a trusted slave who was in charge of getting the children to the teacher (Fee; Schrage; s. Gal. 3:24). ἔχητε pres. subj. act. ἔχω (# 2400) to have. Subj. w. ἐάν (# 1569) in cond. cl. πατέρας acc. pl. πατήρ (# 4252) father. In contrast to the guardians, the father has the authority and bears the responsibility for the children (Fee). ἐγέννησα aor. ind. act. γεννάω (# 1164) to bear, to produce. Paul describes himself as their father. The instructor acts as representative of the father, but can never take his place (Schlatter). ◆ **16 παρακαλῶ** pres. ind. act. παρακαλέω (# 4151) to urge, to exhort. **μιμητής** (# 3629) imitator, one who copies or mimics another, w. obj. gen. **μου**. Pred. nom. Children were to be like their father (DPL, 428-31). **γίνεσθε** pres. imp. mid. (dep.) γίνομαι (# 1181) to become, to be. Pres. imp. calls for an habitual action. ◆ **17 ἔπεμψα** aor. ind. act. πέμπω (# 4287) to send. Not the epistolary aor., because Timothy had not yet reached Corinth and was not the one who delivered this letter (s. 16:10) (Lietzmann). **ἀναμνήσει** fut. ind. act. ἀναμιμνήσκω (# 389) to bring to memory, to remind. Fut. is used in a rel. cl. expressing purp. (RG, 960). **ὁδός** (# 3847) way. Here it probably refers to Paul's teachings (Weiss), or to his general manner of life. **πανταχοῦ** (# 4116) everywhere. ◆ **18 ἐρχομένου** pres. mid. (dep.) part. ἔρχομαι (# 2262) to come. Gen. abs. expressing a neg. condition "as if I were not coming." It introduces a neg. thought of some Corinthians (Kistemaker). **ἐφυσιώθησάν** aor. ind. pass. φυσιόω (# 5881) to puff up (s.v. 6). Ingressive aor., "some have become arrogant" (Kistemaker). **τινες** nom. pl. (# 5516) τίς a certain one. "Certain ones." ◆ **19 ἐλεύσομαι** fut. ind. mid. (dep.) ἔρχομαι (# 2262) to come. **ταχέως** (# 5441) adv. quickly, soon. **θελήσῃ** aor. subj. act. θέλω (# 2527) to wish, to desire. Subj. in a 3rd. class cond. in which the cond. is viewed as a possibility. **γνώσομαι** fut. ind. mid. (dep.) γινώσκω (# 1182) to know, to recognize. **πεφυσιωμένων** perf. pass. part. φυσιόω (# 5881) to puff up (s.v. 6). Perf. emphasizes the completed state or condition (s. Rom. 3:21). ◆ **20 ἡ βασιλεία τοῦ θεοῦ** (# 993; 3836; 2536) the kingdom of God; that is, God's rule. The vb. to be supplied is either "is" or "does not operate" (Barrett; DPL, 524-26). ◆ **21 ἐν** (# 1877) with; instr. use of the prep. similar to the Hebraic use (BD, 117f; Lietzmann; Hering). **ῥάβδος** (# 4811) rod, staff, stick. The figure indicates severity and is intended as a warning (Lenski). **ἔλθω** aor. subj. act. ἔρχομαι (# 2262) s.v. 19. Deliberative subj., "should I come?" **πραΰτης** (# 4559) meekness, gentleness, restrained patience (s. Matt. 5:5).

1 Corinthians 5

◆ **1 ὅλως** (# 3914) actually (Barrett), universally, everywhere (Hering; Kistemaker). **ἀκούεται** pres. ind. pass. ἀκούω (# 201) to hear. Here, "is reported"; that is, commonly known to exist (Lightfoot, *Notes*). **πορνεία** (# 4518) fornication. It refers to general sexual acts outside of legal marriage (TDNT; DPL, 871-75; SB, 3:342-43). **καί** (# 2779) even. **τοιαύτη** (# 5525) nom. fem. sing. of such a kind, such as this. In this case it refers to incest. **ἥτις** (# 4015) nom. sing. which, in the consecutive sense "such as" (BG, 68f). **ἔθνος** (# 1620) Gentile; one who was not a Jew. **ὥστε** (# 6063) normally used w. acc. of the inf. to express results—"so that"—or here it may be epex., explaining the kind of fornication (IBG,

140). **γυναῖκά** fem. acc. sing. γυνή (# 1222) wife. **τινα τοῦ πατρός** his father's; the woman was perhaps the stepmother of the offender, whose father had perhaps died (Barrett). The separation of the gen. from its noun emphasizes both parts of speech (BD, 249). **ἔχειν** pres. act. inf. ἔχω (# 2400) to have. Pres. emphasizes the continual possession. Inf. w. **ὥστε** (# 6063) expressing result. They were living as man and wife without being married (Schrage). Both the OT (Lev. 18:7; 20:11) and the rabbis (M Sanhedrin 7:4; SB, 3:342-58; Schrage; Fee; NW, 2, i:274), as well as Roman law prohibited such unions (Lietzmann; RAC, 4:685f; Buckland, 115f; NW, 2, i:274-76; Fee). ◆ **2 πεφυσιωμένοι** perf. pass. part. φυσιόω (# 5881) to blow up, to puff up, to inflate; a term used to express pride, arrogance, and haughtiness (LN, 1:765). Part. in either pred. adj. or used in a periphrastic construction (VA, 484). Perf. emphasizes the state or condition. **οὐχί** (# 4049) strengthened form of οὐ in a question expecting the answer "yes." **μᾶλλον** (# 3437) rather. **ἐπενθήσατε** aor. ind. act. πενθέω (# 4291) to mourn, to express deep sorrow as one mourning for the dead. **ἵνα** (# 2671) that. Used to express desired result (RWP) or a consequence resulting from some quality—"such that" (BD, 192)—or it may be imperatival (Barrett; Kistemaker). **ἀρθῇ** aor. subj. pass. αἴρω (# 149) to lift up, to take away, to remove. **πράξας** aor. act. part. (adj.) πράσσω (# 4556) to do, to practice. For the variant reading ποιήσας (aor. act. part. ποιέω [# 4472] to do) s. TC, 550. ◆ **3 ἐγὼ μέν** (# 1609; 1142) emphatic, and I for my part (Fee). **ἀπών** pres. act. part. ἄπειμι (# 582) to be absent. Pres. shows simultaneous action. Concessive. part., "although I am absent." **τῷ σώματι** dat. sing. σῶμα (# 5393) body. Dat. of reference. The word "body" refers to Paul's physical presence or absence (PAT, 268; for a study showing the emphasis on the material aspect of the word s. SBT). **παρών** pres. act. part. (circum.) πάρειμι (# 4205) to be present. **τῷ πνεύματι** dat. sing. πνεῦμα (# 4460) spirit. Dat. of reference. **κέκρικα** perf. ind. act. κρίνω (# 3212) to judge, to pass judgment. Perf. emphasizes the continuing results of the decision reached. **παρών** pres. act. part. πάρειμι (# 4205). Concessive part. **τὸν οὕτως** (# 3836; 4048) the one who has so acted; under circumstances such as these (Lightfoot, *Notes*). **κατεργασάμενον** aor. mid. (dep.) part. κατεργάζομαι (# 2981) to do, to accomplish, to bring an action to fruition. Adj. part. as subst. ◆ **4 ἐν τῷ ὀνόματι** (# 1877; 3950) dat. sing. ὄνομα name. "In the name" could be taken w. the part. ("gathered together in the name"), w. the vb. ("I have passed judgment in the name" [v.3]), w. the part. ("the one who did this in the name" [v.3]), or w. the inf. ("to deliver in the name") (Fee; RWP). **συναχθέντων** aor. pass. part. συνάγω (# 5251) to gather together; pass., to be assembled. Gen. abs. temp. part. The aor. part. can express antecedent or contemporaneous time (GGBB, 614, 624-25).

◆ **5 παραδοῦναι** aor. act. inf. παραδίδωμι (# 4140) to deliver over, to turn over, used in a judicial sense. This appears to be a curse w. special reference to satanic affliction of the body (SBT, 143; LAE, 303f; TLNT, 3:19-21; James T. South, "A Critique of the 'Curse/Death' Interpretation of 1 Corinthians 5.1-8," NTS 39 [1993]: 540-44). Inf. as obj. of the vb., "I have judged, made a decision" (v. 3), or inf. in an indir. command (VANT, 382; Kistemaker). **τοιοῦτον** (# 5525) acc. sing., such a one. **ὄλεθρος** (# 3897) destruction; the prep. **εἰς** (# 1659) gives the goal of the delivering over, "for destruction." The word refers to destruction and death, often in connection w. God's judgment against sin (TDNT; SB, 3:358; J.T. South, "A Critique ...," NTS 39 [1993]: 543-44; CCFJ, 3:190-91). Some see this as a physical punishment, others see it as exclusion from the Christian community (Fee; Schrage; RWP; J.T. South, "A Critique ...," NTS 39 [1993]: 539-61). **σωθῇ** aor. subj. pass. σῴζω (# 5392) to rescue, to save. Subj. w. **ἵνα** (# 2671) to express purp. ◆ **6 καύχημα** (# 3017) boasting, uttered boasting (RP). **οἴδατε** perf. ind. act. οἶδα (# 3857) def. perf. w. a pres. meaning to know. Ind. used w. **οὐκ** (# 4024) in a question expecting the answer "yes." **ζύμη** (# 2434) leaven, yeast (s. Matt. 13:33; TDNT; NW, 2, i:277) Philo writes, "Leaven is forbidden because of the rising which it produces" and this is a symbol of being puffed up and arrogant (Philo, "On the Special Laws," 1:293). **φύραμα** (# 5878) acc. sing. that which is mixed or kneaded, a lump or batch of dough (BAGD). **ζυμοῖ** pres. ind. act. ζυμόω (# 2435) to leaven. Gnomic pres. indicating a proverbial truth. For the use of the proverbial saying s. Barrett; NW, 2, i:277. ◆ **7 ἐκκαθάρατε** aor. imp. act. ἐκκαθαίρω (# 1705) to clean out, to purge thoroughly. For the Jewish regulation regarding the removal of all leaven from the house before celebrating the Passover s. SB, 3:359-60. The prep. in compound is perfective (MH, 309f). Aor. imp. calls for a specific act w. a note of urgency (RWP). **παλαιός** (# 4094) old; that is, the leaven used in the period before Passover (Barrett). **ἦτε** pres. subj. act. εἰμί (# 1639) to be. Subj. w. **ἵνα** (# 2671) to express purp. **νέον** new, fresh. **ἐστε** pres. ind. act. εἰμί (# 1639) to be. **ἄζυμος** (# 109) unleavened. The purpose is that they might be a people without the leaven of such sin in their midst (Fee; Barrett). Pred. nom. without the art. emphasizes the quality or character. **καὶ γάρ** for also. The "also" introduces the obj. relation of things corresponding to the exhortation (Meyer). **πάσχα** (# 4247) Passover, Passover Lamb (ZPEB, 4:605-11; ABD, 6:755-64; M Pesahim). **ἐτύθη** aor. ind. pass. θύω (# 2604) to kill, to stay, to kill a sacrifice, to slaughter. **Χριστός** (# 5986) Christ, Messiah. Nom. sing. in apposition w. the subject. ◆ **8 ὥστε** (# 6063) therefore; it draws a conclusion from the preceding. **ἑορτάζωμεν** pres. subj. act. ἑορτάζω (# 2037) to celebrate a feast. Hortatory subj., "let us celebrate." **κακίας**

(# 2798) gen. sing. malice. This is the vicious disposition and the next word, **πονηρίας** (# 4504) (gen. sing. s.v. 1), is the active exercise of it (Lightfoot, Notes). Descriptive or qualitative gen. **ἄζυμος** (# 109) unleavened loaf. The pl. may be a reference to the unleavened cakes eaten at the Passover, or else indefinite: "unleavened elements" (RP). **εἰλικρινείας** (# 1636) gen. sing. sincerity, purity of motive, integrity, perfect purity describing the mind, the heart, one's conduct (TLNT; CCFJ, 2:26). Perhaps the literal meaning is "checked by sunlight," referring to vases of pottery which were checked against the sunlight to see if any cracks had been filled by wax (TDNT; NTW, 32f). "The good set of mind does not talk from both sides of its mouth ... but has one disposition, uncontaminated (εἰλικρινῆ) and pure" ("T. Benj.," Testaments of the Twelve Patriarchs, 6:5). Descriptive gen. or gen. of quality. ◆ **9 ἔγραψα** aor. ind. act. γράφω (# 1211) to write. Not an epistolary aor., but it refers to another letter (RP). **ἐν τῇ ἐπιστολῇ** (# 2186) in the letter. The article points to a well-known letter written by Paul (GGBB, 217). **συναναμίγνυσθαι** pres. mid. (dep.) inf. συναναμίγνυμι (# 5264) to mix together, to mix up w., to associate w. Inf. used to express purp. or used in indir. discourse. Pres. points to a regular association (Grosheide). **πόρνοις** dat. pl. πόρνος (# 4521) one who engages in illicit sexual activities, a sexually immoral pers. Corinth was well-known in the ancient world for this type of activity (ABD, 1:1138-39). Dat. of association. ◆ **10 πάντως** (# 4122) adv., at all, in general. The meaning here is "not in the abs. sense" (Barrett; s. BD, 224). **πλεονέκταις** dat. pl. πλεονέκτης (# 4431) a covetous pers., one who seeks to fulfill his unsatisfiable desires at all cost and at the expense of others (s. Rom. 1:29). Dat. of association. **ἅρπαξιν** dat. pl. ἅρπαξ (# 774) robber, extortioner, joined to the previous word w. one article indicating that both words form a single class of those who are absolutely selfish, covetous, and who sometimes get more than their just share of things (RP). Dat. of association. **εἰδωλολάτραις** dat. pl. εἰδωλολάτρης (# 1629) idol worshiper, idolater. Dat. of association. This catalogue of vices extends the apostle's prior prohibition of πόρνοι to include other vicious types (Peter S. Zaas, "Catalogues and Context: 1 Corinthians 5 and 6," NTS 34 [1988]: 622-26; esp. 626). **ἐπεί** (# 2075) since, used to introduce the conclusion of a suppressed cond. cl. which is contrary to fact (RG, 965; BD, 181). **ὠφείλετε** impf. ind. act. ὀφείλω (# 4083) to be under obligation (should, must, ought) to pay a debt, w. inf. **ἄρα** (# 726) in that case (RWP). **ἐξελθεῖν** aor. act. inf. ἐξέρχομαι (# 2002) to go out from, to depart. ◆ **11 ἔγραψα** aor. ind. act. γράφω (# 1211) to write. Epistolary aor. referring to the present letter. **ὀνομαζόμενος** pres. pass. part. ὀνομάζω (# 3951) to name, to bear the name of. His behavior shows that in truth he is not a Christian (Barrett). Concessive part., "although he is called" (Kistemaker). ἦ pres. subj. act. εἰμί (# 1639) to be. Subj. in a 3rd. class cond. cl. w. ἐάν (# 351) in which the cond. is assumed as a possibility. λοίδορος (# 3368) an abusive person, insulter, one who attacks another w. abusive language (TDNT; TLNT). μέθυσος (# 3500) drunkard. The nom. forms are pred. nom. without the art., emphasizing the character. τοιούτῳ dat. sing. τοιοῦτος (# 5525) such a one. Dat. of association. συνεσθίειν pres. act. inf. συνεσθίω (# 5303) to eat together. The prohibition evidently includes the church's common meal as well as private entertainment (Barrett). Inf. as obj. of the vb., giving an indir. command. ◆ 12 τί γάρ μοι (# 5515; 1142; 1609) "for what is it to me?" "for what business of mine is it?" τοὺς ἔξω (# 3836; 2032) those who are outside. An expression used by the rabbis to indicate those who belong to another religion (SB, 3:362). κρίνειν pres. act. inf. κρίνω (# 3212) to judge. Epex. inf. explaining what is not the apostle's business. οὐχί (# 4049) neg. introducing a question expecting a positive answer. τοὺς ἔσω (# 3836; 2276) those within, referring to believers. ◆ 13 κρινεῖ fut. ind. act. κρίνω (# 3212) to judge. ἐξάρατε aor. imp. act. ἐξαίρω (# 1976) to exclude, to remove, to drive away. Prep. in compound makes the vb. effective, "to put out completely." τὸν πονηρόν (# 3836; 4505) the evil one; or the article is used in a generic sense referring to the wicked in general (BD, 138). ἐξ ὑμῶν αὐτῶν "from yourselves." Perhaps here not reflex (MT, 194; BD, 150). For the quotation from Deut. in the various contexts and a possible word play between πόρνος and πονηρός, s. Peter S. Zaas, "'Cast Out the Evil Man From Your Midst,'" JBL 103 [1984]: 259-61.

1 Corinthians 6

◆ 1 τολμᾷ pres. ind. act. τολμάω (# 5528) to dare. Pres. indicates that the action was in process. πρᾶγμα (# 4547) acc. sing. matter, lawsuit. Some feel that the lawsuit of 1 Cor. 6 had to do w. the offender of 1 Cor. 5 (Will Deming, "The Unity of 1 Corinthians 5-6," JBL 115 [1996]: 289-312; DPL, 544-46). ἔχων pres. act. part. ἔχω (# 2400) to have. Pres. shows contemporary action. Temp. part., "when he has a lawsuit." κρίνεσθαι pres. mid./pass. inf. κρίνω (# 3212) to judge; the permissive mid. or pass., "allow yourselves to be judged" (BD, 165, 166). Pres. indicates that the trial was being held and no decision had yet been reached. Epex. inf. as obj. of the vb. ἐπί (# 2093) w. gen. before, in the presence of (RWP). ἄδικος (# 96) unrighteous. Adj. as subst., "the unrighteous ones." These were either pagan judges or Jewish judges who tried cases in the synagogue (Albert Stein, "Wo trugen die korinthischen Christen ihre Rechtshandel aus?" ZNW 59 [1968]: 86-90; SB, 3:364); or it refers to the character of judges or the juries who pronounce verdicts in civil cases (Bruce W. Winter, "Civil Litigation in Secular Corinth and the Church:

The Forensic Background to 1 Corinthians 6.1-8," NTS 37 [1991]: 559-72; esp. 562-64). The problem may have been that the upper-class believers were taking those of a lower class to court, where the ones w. a lower status were at a disadvantage (Alan C. Mitchell, "Rich and Poor in the Courts of Corinth: Litigiousness and Status in 1 Corinthians 6.1-11," NTS 39 [1993], 562-86). For the corruptness of the courts at that time s. Winter, "Civil Litigation," NTS 37 (1991): 562-66; Mitchell, "Rich and Poor," NTS 39 (1993): 580-81. ◆ 2 οὐκ (# 4042) neg. introducing a question expecting a positive answer: "you know, don't you?" οἴδατε perf. ind. act. οἶδα (# 3857) to know. Def. perf. w. pres. meaning. κρινοῦσιν fut. ind. act. κρίνω (# 3212) to judge (s. Dan. 7:22; SB, 3:363). κρίνεται pres. ind. pass. κρίνω (# 3212) to judge. Futuristic pres. used in a 1st. class cond. cl. which assumes the reality of the cond. ἀνάξιος (# 396) unworthy, not equal to the task, w. gen. (For the neg. prefix s. Rom. 1:20). Pred. adj. without the article emphasizing the quality or character. κριτήριον (# 3215) law court, tribunal, lawsuit, cause, law proceeding (Weiss), legal cause (Winter, "Civil Litigation," NTS 37 [1991]: 560). For the suf. and its meaning s. MH, 343. Gen. w. the adj. ἀνάξιος which express value (BD, 98). ἐλαχίστων gen. pl. superl. μικρός (# 1788) small, insignificant; superl., smallest. 1 Cor. 6 discusses the nature of civil litigation in Corinth with brother taking brother to court for the smallest causes (Winter, "Civil Litigation," NTS 37 [1991]: 560). ◆ 3 οὐκ (# 4024) neg. introducing a question expecting a positive answer. κρινοῦμεν fut. ind. act. κρίνω (# 3212) to judge. μήτιγε (# 3615) not to speak of (BD, 220). βιωτικός (# 1053) that which pertains to daily living. It means questions related to our life on earth or to the resources of life such as food, clothing, property, etc. (RP). ◆ 4 μὲν οὖν gives a contrast: "no, but" or "no, rather" (RP). ἔχητε pres. subj. act. ἔχω (# 2400) to have. Subj. in a 3rd. class cond. cl. assuming the possibility of the cond. ἐξουθενημένους perf. pass. part. ἐξουθενέω (# 2024) to consider as nothing, to despise, to reject w. contempt. It probably refers to those in the church who are little esteemed (Grosheide) rather than to those outside of the church. Paul seems to be using irony to indicate the actual high status of the Corinthian Christians (Winter, "Civil Litigation," NTS 37 [1991]: 570). καθίζετε pres. ind. or imp. act. καθίζω (# 2767) to cause to sit, to appoint. ◆ 5 ἐντροπή (# 1959) shame, a state of embarrassment resulting from what one has done or failed to do (LN, 1:310; GELTS, 155). οὕτως (# 4048) so. "Has it come to this that," "is it to such a degree true that?" (Lightfoot, Notes). ἔνι (# 1928) pres. ind. act. 3rd. sing. ἔνι shortened form of ἔνεστιν to be, to exist, to be found (BD, 49). οὐδείς (# 4029) no one, not even one. σοφός (# 5055) wise. Paul may be using irony to refer to the ones who claim wisdom but do not use it to bring peace among the parties (Schrage). They could have used their wisdom in a legal capacity as arbitrators (Winter, "Civil Litigation," *NTS* 37 [1991]: 568-69). **δυνήσεται** fut. ind. pass. δύναμαι (# *1538*) to be able to, w. inf. Fut. used to designate a sort of consequence resulting from some quality, "such that" (BD, 192). **διακρῖναι** aor. act. inf. διακρίνω (# *1359*) to judge between two, to decide. For the force of the prep. in compound s. MH, 302f. **ἀνὰ μέσον** (# *324; 3545*) between. **τοῦ ἀδελφοῦ αὐτοῦ** an abridged sentence conveying a reproach "must his brothers go before strangers?" (Lightfoot, *Notes*). ◆ **6 ἀλλά** (# *247*) but in reality. **κρίνεται** pres. ind. mid./pass. κρίνω (# *3212*) to judge (s.v. 1). **καὶ τοῦτο** and at that, and especially (BD, 151). Climactic force of the part. used w. acc. of general reference (RWP). **ἄπιστος** (# *603*) unbeliever. For the neg. force of the prefix s. Rom. 1:20. Perhaps there is a slight nuance of "unfaithful," along w. the connotation of "evil." ◆ **7 ὅλως** (# *3914*) adv., altogether, assuredly, actually. **ἥττημα** (# *2488*) defeat. The word was used of a judicial defeat in court (Schlatter); here used of moral and spiritual defeat (Weiss). **ὑμῖν** dat. pl. σύ (# *5148*). Dat. of disadvantage. **κρίμα** (# *3210*) judgment, lawsuit. **μεθ' ἑαυτῶν** (# *3552; 1571*) w. yourselves. The reflex. pron. emphasizes the idea of corporate unity (Lightfoot, *Notes*). **μᾶλλον** (# *3437*) adv., rather. **ἀδικεῖσθε** pres. ind. mid./pass. ἀδικέω (# *92*) to wrong someone, to treat someone unjustly. **ἀποστερεῖσθε** pres. ind. mid./pass. ἀποστρεφέω (# *691*) to defraud, to steal, to deprive, to take something from someone by means of deception or trickery (LN, 1:585; NDIEC, 2:47; 3:82). The two forms here are permissive mid. or pass. (MT, 56f; BD, 165). ◆ **8 ὑμεῖς** (# *5148*) you! Emphatic. **ἀδικεῖτε** pres. ind. act. ἀδικέω (# *92*) to wrong someone (s.v. 7). Both pres. indicate actions in progress. **καὶ τοῦτο** and that (# *2779; 4047*) (s.v. 6). ◆ **9 οὐκ** neg. introducing a question expecting a positive answer. **θεοῦ** (# *2536*) emphatic by its position. **κληρονομήσουσιν** fut. ind. act. κληρονομέω (# *3099*) to inherit, to enter into full possession of (Morris). **πλανᾶσθε** pres. imp. mid./pass. πλανάω (# *4414*) to lead astray, to mislead, to deceive. Permissive mid. or pass. (s.v. 1). Pres. imp. w. the neg. is used to stop an action in progress, "do not continue" (MKG, 272). **εἰδω-λολάτρης** (# *1629*) one who serves idols, idolater. **μοιχός** (# *3659*) adulterer. **μαλακός** (# *3434*) soft, effeminate; a t.t. for the passive partner in homosexual relations (Barrett; Conzelmann; RAC, 4:620-50; LAE, 164). **ἀρσενοκοίτης** (# *780*) a male who has sexual relations w. a male, homosexual (Rom. 1:26; NW 2, i:279-81; Schrage; Fee; MM; BAGD; also David E. Malick, "The Condemnation of Homosexuality in 1 Corinthians 6:9," *Bib Sac* 150 [1993]: 479-92; DPL, 413-14). The Jewish punishment for the sin of homosexuality was stoning (SB, 3:70-74). ◆ **10 κλέπτης** (# *3095*) one who steals, thief. **πλεονέκτης** (# *4431*) one desirous of

having more and seeking to fulfill his desires through all means (s. 5:10). **μέθυσος** (# *3500*) drunkard. **λοίδορος** (# *3368*) one who uses abusive language (s. 5:11). **ἅρπαξ** (# *774*) robber, one who uses force and violence in stealing (BAGD). For similar lists which were used in the ancient world in a popular game s. LAE, 316. ◆ **11 καί** (# *2779*) and, and it is true (Godet). **ταῦτα** (# *4047*) these things. The n. is contemptuous, "such abominations!" (EGT). **τινες** nom. pl. τις (# *5516*) a certain one; some. Paul narrows the picture from all to some (RWP). **ἦτε** impf. ind. act. εἰμί (# *1639*) to be. Impf. refers to their past condition. **ἀλλά** (# *247*) but; emphasizes strongly the contrast between their past and pres. and the demand their changed moral condition makes upon them (RP). **ἀπελούσασθε** aor. ind. mid. ἀπολούω (# *666*) to wash, to wash thoroughly. Prep. in compound points to the complete washing away and the aor. refers to a decisive action (Morris). Permissive mid., or mid. w. pass., meaning since the word in the NT only occurs in mid. (Fee). **ἡγιάσθητε** aor. ind. pass. ἁγιάζω (# *39*) to set apart for the use of God, to sanctify, to make holy. It does not refer to the process of ethical development, but means "you were claimed by God as His own and made a member of His holy people" (Barrett). **ἐδικαιώθητε** aor. ind. pass. δικαιόω (# *1467*) to justify, to declare righteous, to declare to be in the right (s. Rom. 2:13). **ἐν** (# *1877*) in, w. dat. Instr. dat. ◆ **12 ἔξεστιν** (# *2003*) pres. ind. act. impers., it is allowed, it is permitted, w. epex. inf. Paul is evidently quoting a common saying in Corinth (Weiss; Barrett; NW 2, i:281; SB, 3:365; Schrage; TDNT). **συμφέρει** pres. ind. act. συμφέρω (# *5237*) to bring together, to confer a benefit, to be advantageous or profitable or useful (BAGD). **ἐξουσιασθήσομαι** fut. ind. pass. ἐξουσιάζω (# *2027*) to bring under the power of someone, to put under the authority of someone. Volitive fut. involving a decision of the will (RG, 874). Permissive pass., "I will not allow myself to be." ◆ **13 βρῶμα** (# *1109*) food. **κοιλία** (# *3120*) dat. sing. stomach. Dat. of advantage. **καὶ ταύτην καὶ ταῦτα** both this (fem. referring to κοιλία) and these things (acc. pl. referring to βρώματα). **καταργήσει** fut. ind. act. καταργέω (# *2934*) to make ineffective, to do away w. The organs of digestion will be changed at the resurrection and the physical constitution of the resurrected body will be different from that of the mortal body (SBT, 54). **σῶμα** (# *5393*) body, the physical body, not a reference to the whole person w. his personality, but rather the physical body (SBT, 51-80). **πορνεία** (# *4518*) dat. sing. illicit sex, fornication, sexual immorality, prostitution (LN, 1:771; TDNT; EDNT; NIDNTT, 1:499-501; BBC). Dat. of personal interest. **κυρίῳ** dat. sing. κύριος (# *3261*) Lord. Dat. of personal interest or dat. of ownership. **σώματι** dat. sing. (# *5393*) Dat. of interest or advantage. The Lord is for the body in that He wants to rule it and use it as a tool for service

(Schrage). ◆ **14 καὶ ... καί** (# 2779) "both ... and." **ἤγειρεν** aor. ind. act. ἐγείρω (# 1586) to raise up. **ἐξεγερεῖ** fut. ind. act. ἐξεγείρω (# 1995) to raise up out of. ◆ **15 οὐκ** (# 4024) neg. introducing a question expecting a positive answer, "you know, don't you?" **μέλη** nom. pl. μέλος (# 3517) member; used in an ecclesiastical and figurative meaning, but the figure rests on a strictly physical definition (SBT, 61). Pred. nom. **ἄρας** aor. act. part. αἴρω (# 149) to take away, to take. Temp. or cond. part. **οὖν** (# 4036) therefore draws a conclusion from the premise of the previous statement. **ποιήσω** aor. subj. act. (deliberative subj.), or fut. ind. act. (RWP) ποιέω (# 4472) to make. **πόρνη** (# 4520) prostitute. Prostitutes were often well-educated, intellectual, artistic, and jovial; they entertained not only w. their sexual services, but w. stimulating and intellectual discussions, poetry, song and dance, and witty stories. They combined both fine intellectual and sensual pleasures. In Corinth and Megara there were even schools for prostitutes. They were often in the service of a deity, called the "foals of Aphrodite" (RAC, 3:1149-1213; Lukian, *Hetären Gespräche* [Köln: Bund Verlag, 1983]; TDNT; DGRA, 604-6; Schrage; Iwan Bloch, *Die Prostitution*, [Berlin: Luis Marcus Verlagsbuchhandlung, 1912], 209-538, esp. 283-310; Rosamund Seymour, *Stews and Strumpets: A Survey of Prostitution*, vol. 1 *Primitive, Classical and Oriental* [London: MacGibbon & Kee, 1961], 44-139, esp. 63-73). Athenaeus quoting (actually misquoting) from a speech of the orator Demosthenes (which he says was actually delivered by the advocate Apollodrus!) writes, "We have harlots (ἑταίρας) for pleasure, mistresses (παλλακάς) for concubinage, but wives to produce children legitimately and to have a faithful guardian of daily affairs" (Athenaeus, *Deipnosophistae*, 13:573b). He goes on to describe the prostitutes of Corinth, indicating that the city held a yearly festival for them at which time the prostitutes would carouse and get drunk (Athenaeus, *Deipnosophistae*, 13:573c-574c). Block, *Die Prostitution*, 476-538, discusses the use of prostitutes in pictures and literature of the Greek and Roman culture. **γένοιτο** aor. opt. mid. (dep.) γίνομαι (# 1181) to become, "let it not be," indicating a false conclusion (s. Rom 3:4). ◆ **16 οὐκ** (# 4024) neg. introducing a question expecting a positive answer. **κολλώμενος** pres. mid. part. κολλάω (# 3140) to join together, to unite. Dir. mid., "to join oneself. The word refers to sexual relations or to a close and intimate relationship (Schrage). Part. as subst. **πόρνη** (# 4520) dat. sing. s.v. 15. Dat. of association. **ἕν** (# 1651) nom. sing. n. εἰς (# 1651) one. **ἔσονται** fut. ind. mid. (dep.) εἰμί (# 1639) to be. **φησίν** pres. ind. act. φημί (# 5774) to say (SB, 3:365-66). **εἰς** (# 1659) **σάρκα μίαν** (# 4922; 1651) one flesh. The prep. in place of the pred. nom. is due to Semitic influence (MH, 462; KVS, 63). Becoming one flesh refers to physical union through sexual inter-

course (SBT, 62). ◆ **17 ἓν πνεῦμα** (# 1651; 4460) one spirit. Illicit union w. a harlot effects a oneness of physical relationship which contradicts the Lord's claim over the body and creates a disparity between the body and the spirit (still united to the Lord) (SBT, 69). ◆ **18 φεύγετε** pres. imp. act. φεύγω (# 5771) to flee. Pres. imp. indicates it is to be a continual and habitual fleeing. **ἁμάρτημα** (# 280) sin, sin as the act or result of the principle of sin. For the suf. indicating the result of an action s. MH, 355. **ἐάν** (# 351) used after a rel. pron. giving a generalization "whatever." **ποιήσῃ** aor. subj. act. ποιέω (# 4472) to make (s.v. 15). Subj. in an indef. rel. cl. **ἐκτός** (# 1760) w. gen., outside. **εἰς** (# 1659) against. Immorality arises within the body and has as its sole purpose its gratification (Grosheide). **ἁμαρτάνει** pres. ind. act. ἁματάνω (# 279) to sin. Gnomic pres. indicating a principle which is always true. ◆ **19 οὐκ** (# 4024) neg. introducing a question expecting a positive answer. **ναός** (# 3724) temple, the dwelling place of God, the inner sanctuary itself (Lenski). An allusion either to the temple in Jerusalem or to the temple of Aphrodite near Corinth (SBT, 78). Pred. nom. **οὗ** gen. sing. ὅς (# 4005) who, which, what; (# 4005) rel. pron. Gen. by attraction. **ἐστέ** pres. ind. act. εἰμι (# 1639) to be; w. gen; in the sense of "belonging to" (MT, 231). ◆ **20 ἠγοράσθητε** aor. ind. pass. ἀγοράζω (# 60) to buy, to buy at the market place. For the purchasing of slaves in the ancient world s. FCS, 37ff; for a discussion of the background of the term s. Schrage. **τιμῆς** gen. sing. τιμή (# 5507) price. Gen. of price; "bought w. a price." Theol. pass. **δοξάσατε** aor. imp. act. δοξάζω (# 1519) to cause one to have a good opinion of someone, to glorify (TLNT; TDNT). **δή** (# 1314) then, certainly. Used as an intensive particle in a command of exhortation indicating that the point at last is clear and may be assumed as true (RG, 1149; BD, 285). **ἐν** (# 1877) w. dat. Local, in. Instr., with. The physical body is man's means of concrete service for God (SBT, 244).

1 Corinthians 7

◆ **1 περί** (# 4309) w. gen., concerning. The expression **περὶ δέ** is used to introduce the subject matter about which the church at Corinth had written to Paul (s. 7:25; 8:1; 12:1; 16:1, 12 [Fee]). For the elliptical expression w. the gen. of the personal pron., gen. by attraction s. RP). **ἐγράψατε** aor. ind. act. γράφω (# 1211) to write. Paul now gives his opinion to questions the Corinthians had asked him (Grosheide). **καλόν** (# 2819) good, that which is useful or pleasing, that which is suitable or appropriate for a situation (T; NIDNTT; TDNT). For an analysis of the formula "better... than" s. G.F. Snyder, "The *Tobspruch* in the New Testament," *NTS* 23 [1976]: 117-20). **ἅπτεσθαι** pres. mid. (dep.) inf. ἅπτομαι (# 721) to touch, w. gen. Here it refers to sexual intercourse (Fee). Epex. inf. explaining what is καλον.

This may have been a slogan common among some at Corinth that Paul rejected (William E. Phipps, "Paul's Attitude toward Sexual Relations," *NTS* 28 [1982]: 125-31; Schrage; BBC). The sacral celibacy may have arisen among those who had been influenced by Egyptian religions which were prevalent in Corinth (Richard E. Oster, Jr., "Use, Misuse and Neglect of Archaeological Evidence in Some Modern Works on 1 Corinthians [1 Cor 7,1-5; 8,10; 11,2-16; 12,14-26]," *ZNW* 83 [1992]: 58-64). **γυναικός** gen. sing. γυνή (# *1222*) female, woman. ◆ **2 πορνείας** acc. sing. πορνεία (# *4518*) fornication, illicit sex. Acc. w. prep. **διά** (# *1328*) expressing cause. **ἐχέτω** pres. imp. act. 3. sing. ἔχω (# *2400*) to have. The imp. is hortatory, not merely permissive (RP). For a study showing that consecrated virginity was not a customary way of life in the most primitive communities, s. J. Massyngberde Ford, "St. Paul, The Philogamist (I Corinthians VII in Early Patristic Exegesis)," *NTS* 11 (1965): 326-48. ◆ **3 γυναικί** dat. sing. γυνή (# *1222*) wife. Dat. as indir. obj. **ὀφειλή** (# *4051*) obligation, debt, due. The specific obligation involved in the marital union and a euphemism for sexual intercourse (Lenski; Schrage). **ἀποδιδότω** pres. imp. act. ἀποδίδωμι (# *625*) to pay back, to pay one's dues, to render. Pres. imp. indicates habitual duty (Morris). The rabbis required that the marriage partners have regular sexual relations w. one another; generally on Friday night, which was the Sabbath (SB, 3:368-71; JPB, 211). **καί** (# *2779*) also. **ἀνδρί** dat. sing. ἀνήρ (# *467*) male, man, husband. Dat. as indir. obj. ◆ **4 ἐξουσιάζει** pres. ind. act. ἐξουσιάζω (# *2027*) to exercise authority over, w. gen. Pres. emphasizes a general statement which is always true. ◆ **5 ἀποστερεῖτε** pres. imp. act. ἀποστερέω (# *691*) to rob, to deprive. **εἰ μήτι** (# *1623; 3614*) except, unless in a given case, unless perhaps (M 169; BS, 204). **σύμφωνος** (# *5247*) agreement, consent. Gen. w. **ἐκ** (# *1666*) expressing cause. **πρὸς καιρόν** (# *4639; 2789*) for a time, for a period (no longer) (BD, 124). The rabbis taught that abstinence from sexual intercourse was allowable for generally one to two weeks, but disciples of the law may continue abstinence for thirty days, against the will of their wives, while they occupy themselves in the study of the law (M Ketuboth, 5:6). **σχολάσητε** aor. subj. act. σχολάζω (# *5390*) to have leisure time for, to devote oneself to something, w. dat. (Lightfoot, *Notes*). Subj. w. **ἵνα** (# *2671*) either used to express purp. (Fee) or used as an imp. (MT, 94f; IBG, 144-45). **προσευχῇ** (# *4666*) dat. sing. prayer. **πάλιν** (# *4099*) again. **ἐπὶ τὸ αὐτό** lit., for the same thing; here, be together. It refers to being sexually together as before (Lenski). **ἦτε** pres. subj. act. εἰμί (# *1639*) to be. Subj. w. **ἵνα** to express purp. **πειράζῃ** pres. subj. act. πειράζω (# *4279*) to tempt, to try to bring someone to a fall. Subj. w. **ἵνα** and the neg. to express neg. purpose. Pres. indicates that Satan may not keep on tempting you (RWP).

ἀκρασία (# *202*) lack of self-control, incontinence. Here in the sense of irrepressible desire for sexual relations (Barrett; TLNT; NW 2, i:288-90). Acc. w. **διά** (# *1328*), giving the cause or reason. ◆ **6 συγγνώμη** (# *5152*) concession, allowance, "I do not give this as a binding rule. I state it as what is allowable" (Lightfoot, *Notes*). **ἐπιταγή** (# *2198*) command. Temporary abstinence for prayer is not a command, but a concession (Fee). ◆ **7 θέλω** (# *2527*) pres. ind. act. to wish, to desire, w. inf. His desire is not only that they be unmarried, but that they also be able to control themselves (Weiss). At this time Paul may have been unmarried, a widower, or his wife may have left him and returned to her family because of his conversion to Christianity (Bruce). **εἶναι** pres. act. inf. εἰμί (# *1639*) to be. **χάρισμα** (# *5922*) acc. sing. gift, gracious gift, a gift given out of grace. **ἐκ** (# *1666*) w. gen., from. It gives the source of the gift. Paul's celibacy is a gift from God, not a requirement for all (Fee). ◆ **8 ἄγαμος** (# *23*) unmarried. Perhaps referring to widowers (Fee). For the neg. pref. s. Rom. 1:20. Indir. obj. **χήραις** dat. pl. χήρα (# *5939*) widow. The article may suggest that Paul has in mind the members of the Corinthian church who are widows, but it may also be a generalization (Barrett). According to the Roman law *Lex Papia Poppaea*, which was to encourage marriage and childbearing, a widow had two years to remarry (Roy Bowen Ward, "Musonius and Paul on Marriage," *NTS* 36 [1990]: 282-83; RCS, 2:52). **καλόν** (# *2819*) good. **μείνωσιν** aor. subj. act. μένω (# *3531*) to remain. Subj. w. **ἐάν** (# *351*) in a 3rd. class cond. cl. in which the cond. is viewed as possible. ◆ **9 εἰ** (# *1623*) if, w. ind. introduces a 1st. class cond. cl. in which the cond. is assumed to be true. **ἐγκρατεύονται** pres. ind. mid. (dep.) ἐγκρατεύω (# *1603*) to exercise self-control, to have power over oneself (TLNT, 1:60-62). **γαμησάτωσαν** aor. imp. act. γαμέω (# *1138*) to marry. Perhaps ingressive aor., "let them seek marriage" (Grosheide). **κρεῖττον** (# *3202*) comp. ἀγαθός (# *19*) good; comp., better. **γαμῆσαι** aor. act. inf. γαμέω (# *1138*) to marry (DPL, 594-600; BBC). Epex. inf. explaining what is better. **πυροῦσθαι** pres. pass. inf. πυρόω (# *4792*) to set on fire; pass. to be inflamed. It may mean "to burn w. sexual passion" (NW, 2, i:29193), but may possibly mean "to burn in Gehenna," because of falling into fornication (Bruce). In Roman society those w. erotic desires had recourse to *hetairai* and other prostitutes, but Paul rules this out (R. B. Ward, "Musonius and Paul on Marriage," *NTS* 36 [1990]: 285-86; s. also the discussion in 6:15). ◆ **10 γεγαμηκόσιν** perf. act. part. γαμέω (# *1138*) to marry. Perf. emphasizes a state or condition (s. Rom. 3:21). Part. as subst. Dat. as indir. obj. **παραγγέλλω** (# *4133*) pres. ind. act. to give orders, to command, to instruct. Both Paul and the church at Corinth knew the words of Jesus, and Paul gives an additional command, expecting obedience because he receives revelations from the Lord which he can communicate to the churches (Grosheide). χωρισθῆναι aor. pass. inf. χωρίζω (# 6004) to separate, to divide; pass. may have the meaning, to allow oneself to be, w. the sense of "to divorce" (Jerome Murphy-O'Connor, "The Divorced Woman in 1 Corinthians 7:10-11," *JBL* 100 [1981]: 602; Schrage; BAGD; BD, 165). The wife is separated, the husband puts away. Then in the converse point of view the believing wife is said to put away and the unbelieving husband is to be separated (Bengel). Inf. in indir. discourse. ◆ **11** καί (# 2779) even, actually; "if a separation *does* take place" (Barrett). χωρισθῇ aor. subj. pass. χωρίζω (# 6004) to separate (s.v. 10). Ingressive aor., "she gets separated" (RWP). Subj. w. ἐάν (# 1569) in a 3rd. class cond. cl. in which the cond. is viewed as possible. μενέτω pres. imp. act. 3rd. pers. sing. μένω (# 3531) to remain. τῷ ἀνδρί (# 3836; 467) to the husband. The definite article is used to denote previous reference; that is, "to her husband" (DM, 141; Funk, 556). καταλλαγήτω aor. imp. pass. καταλλάσσω (# 2904) to reconcile; pass. to be reconciled (V, 40-83; TLNT; EDNT). Prep. in compound is perfective, "to effect a thorough change back, to reconcile" (APC, 187ff). In Judaism it was possible for the wife to return to the husband before the bill of divorcement had been received (SB, 3:374). ἀφιέναι pres. act. inf. ἀφίημι (# 918) to send away, to divorce. Inf. as imp. or in indir. discourse. ◆ **12** τοῖς λοιποῖς (# 3836; 1254) dat. pl. "to the rest." Paul refers here to those who have unbelieving partners (Barrett). ἐγώ (# 1609) I. Paul means that he is not now repeating the teaching of Christ, who is not likely to have said anything on the subject. He is, however, w. inspiration speaking w. apostolic authority (RP). ἔχει pres. ind. act. ἔχω (# 2400) to have. Ind. w. εἰ (# 1623) in a 1st. class cond., which assumes the reality of the cond. ἄπιστος (# 603) unbelieving. συνευδοκεῖ pres. ind. act. συνευδοκέω (# 5306) to be pleased together w., to agree together, to approve, to consent to, w. inf. οἰκεῖν pres. act. inf. οἰκέω (# 3861) to live; here in the sense of being married. ἀφιέτω pres. imp. act. ἀφίημι (# 918) to send away (s.v. 11). ◆ **13** γυνή (# 1222) woman, wife. The context indicates that it is a Christian woman (Barrett). ◆ **14** ἡγίασται perf. ind. pass. ἁγιάζω (# 39) to separate, to sanctify, to set apart for God's service, to consecrate. He was set apart to the service of God as the guardian of one of His chosen ones (Hodge). As long as the marriage is maintained the potential for their realizing salvation remains (Fee). Perf. refers to the lasting condition (Grosheide). ἐν τῇ γυναικί (# 1877; 1222) in the wife; that is, through the close tie w. her (Grosheide). ἐπεὶ ἄρα (# 2075; 726) since otherwise, since on the contrary supposition it follows.... (Lightfoot, *Notes*). ἀκάθαρτος (# 176) not clean, unclean. ◆ **15** εἰ δέ but if. The particle introduces a cond. which is assumed to be true. χωρίζεται pres. ind.

pass. χωρίζω (# 6004) to separate (s.v. 10). In the papyri the word was used as a technical expression for divorce (BS, 247). χωριζέσθω pres. imp. pass. χωρίζω (# 6004) to separate. δεδούλωται perf. ind. pass. δουλόω (# 1530) to enslave, to be a slave, to be under bondage. Perf. stresses the continuing condition. ἐν τοῖς τοιούτοις (# 1877; 3836; 5525) in such cases. ἐν εἰρήνη in peace (# 1877; 1645) Prep. may be used in a double sense: "God has called you *into* a peace *in* which He wishes you to live" (IBG, 79). κέκληκεν perf. ind. act. καλέω (# 2813) to call. Perf. emphasizes the continuing results or condition (s. Rom. 3:21). ◆ **16** οἶδας perf. ind. act. οἶδα (# 3857) def. perf. w. pres. meaning, to know. εἰ (# 1623) if. Introduces a noun cl. as obj. of the vb. σώσεις fut. ind. act. σῴζω (# 5392) to save, to rescue. ◆ **17** εἰ μή (# 1623; 3590) except, only. This looks back to v. 15, which contemplates the possibility of separation in certain circumstances (Barrett; BD, 191). ἑκάστῳ dat. sing. ἕκαστος (# 1667) each one. The word is the subject of the main cl. but appears in the dat. through inverse attraction to the subordinate cl. (RG, 717; BD, 151). ἐμέρισεν aor. ind. act. μερίζω (# 3532) to divide, to distribute. Some manuscripts have μεμέρικεν (perf. ind. act. [Fee]), in which case the perf. looks at the completed action in the past and the continuing results in the present: "has assigned his lot in life once for all." Here the word refers entirely to the external conditions of life (Lightfoot, *Notes*). κέκληκεν perf. ind. act. καλέω (# 2813) to call (s.v. 15). περιπατείτω pres. imp. act. περιπατέω (# 4344) to walk about, to conduct one's life. Pres. emphasizes the continual or habitual action. διατάσσω (# 1411) pres. ind. mid. to command, to ordain, to order. The word was a military term (RWP), a t.t. used in connection w. wills, as well as a general word for commanding (MM). ◆ **18** περιτετμημένος perf. pass. part. (adj.) περιτέμνω (# 4362) to circumcise. Perf. stresses the state or condition. ἐκλήθη aor. ind. pass. καλέω (# 2813) to call. Theol. pass. indicating that God did the calling. ἐπισπάσθω pres. mid. (permissive mid.) imp. ἐπισπάω (# 2177) to draw to oneself; a medical t.t., "to pull over the foreskin." A method used to conceal circumcision (BAGD; BBC; SB, 4:33f; Leitzmann; 1 Macc. 1:15; Theodor Hoffner, *Das Sexualleben der Griechen und Römer von den Anfängen bis ins 8. Jahrhundert nach Christus* [Prag: J.G. Calve, 1938], 218-22). ἀκροβυστία (# 213) dat. sing. uncircumcision. κέκληται perf. ind. pass. καλέω (# 2813) to call. Perf. emphasizes the continuing result. περιτεμνέσθω pres. imp. pass. Permissive pass., "allow himself to be circumcised." ◆ **19** τήρησις (# 5499) keeping, watching, guarding. For nouns ending w. this suff. to express action s. MH, 373f. ἐντολῶν gen. pl. ἐντολή (# 1953) commandment. Obj. gen. ◆ **20** κλήσει dat. sing. κλῆσις (# 3104) calling. ᾗ dat. sing. fem. ὅς (# 4005) rel. pron. Loc. referring to the state in which he is when he is called by God to become a Christian (Barrett). ἐκλήθη aor. ind. pass. καλέω (# 2813) to call. μενέτω pres. imp. act. μένω (# 3531) to remain. ◆ 21 δοῦλος (# 1528) slave; nom. in apposition to the subject. ἐκλήθης aor. ind. pass. καλέω (# 2813) to call. σοι dat. sing. σύ (# 5148) you. Dat. of personal interest w. the vb. μελέτω pres. imp. act. 3rd. sing. μέλω (# 3508) impersonal vb. used w. dat., "to be a concern to someone." "Don't let it be a concern to you," "don't worry about it." Pres. imp. w. neg. calls for the stopping of an action in progress: "stop being concerned about it" (FCS, 175; Rom 6:12; MKG, 272). ἀλλ' (# 247) but. The word has here its full adversative force (FCS, 177). εἰ καί (# 1623; 2779) if, indeed (FCS, 178; Thrall, 81; IBG, 167). Introduces a 1st. class cond. cl. in which the cond. is assumed as true. δύνασαι pres. ind. pass. (dep.) 2nd.pers. sing. δύναμαι (# 1538) to be able to, w. inf. ἐλεύθερος (# 1801) free. γενέσθαι aor. mid. (dep.) inf. γίνομαι (# 1181) to become. For an extensive discussion of slavery in the ancient world w. the discussion of why and how a slave was set free, s. FCS, 29-125; SCS, 39-46; Buckland, 72-90; DPL, 881-83; Dale B. Martin, *Slavery as Salvation: The Metaphor in Pauline Christianity* (New Haven, Conn.: Yale Univ. Press, 1990). μᾶλλον (# 3437) rather, by all means. χρῆσαι aor. imp. mid. (dep.) χράομαι (# 5968) to use, to live according to. The object to be supplied could be God's calling: "by all means, live according to (your calling in Christ)." The believer's existence is no longer determined by his legal status, but if he is to be freed he is to make better use of his vocation (FCS, 175-79f; Grosheide). The obj. could also be "freedom," w. the idea being, "but if you are indeed able to become free, rather than staying a slave, take freedom" (Gregory W. Dawes, "'But If You Can Gain Your Freedom' (1 Corinthians 7:17-24)," *CBQ* 52 [1990]: 681-97, esp. 690; Fee; IBG, 167). ◆ 22 γάρ (# 1142) for. This introduces an explanation and further reason why they are not to worry about being in slavery (FCS, 177). κληθείς aor. pass. part. καλέω (# 2813) to call. Part. as subst. ἀπελεύθερος (# 592) freedman. The following gen. describes who had freed him and to whom he now belongs. There were certain rights and obligations that a freedman had to the one who had freed him. He bore the family name of the one providing the freedom; he lived in the house of his patron (*paramone*); he rendered service (*operae*); the patron gave him gifts (*munera*); and he was to render respect (*obsequium*) to the one freeing him. For these and the social standing of a freedman s. FCS, 72-82; Francis Lyall, "Roman Law in the Writings of Paul - The Slave and the Freedman," *NTS* 17 (1970): 73-79; SCS, 39-46; LLAR, 113-15. ◆ 23 τιμῆς gen. sing. (# 5507) (s. 6:20). Gen. of price. ἠγοράσθητε aor. ind. pass. ἀγοράζω (# 60) to buy at the market place, to purchase (s. 6:20; APC, 53-59; TDNT; NIDNTT, 1:267-68; TLNT). Theol. pass. indicates God did the purchasing

and the aor. looks at the completed transaction. ◆ 24 ἐν ᾧ (# 1877; 4005) in which. It refers to the state or condition. ἐκλήθη aor. ind. pass. καλέω (# 2813) to call. μενέτω pres. imp. act. μένω (# 3531) to remain. παρά (# 4123) w. dat., alongside of, in the presence of. All secular conditions, whether of family life, caste, or service are capable of being made the expression of a Christian character (RP). ◆ 25 παρθένος (# 4221) virgin. It has been suggested that the word here refers to young widows or widowers who have only been married once and the question had been raised whether a second marriage was wrong (J.M. Ford, "Levirate Marriage in St. Paul [I Cor. VII]," *NTS* 10 [1964]: 361-65). Another suggestion is that it refers to engaged couples w. the meaning "fiance" and the entire section (vvs. 25-38) concerns engagement and whether couples should marry or not (J.K. Elliott, "Paul's Teaching on Marriage in I Cor.: Some Problems Considered," *NTS* 19 [1973]: 219-25; Schrage; Fee). Others feel that it refers to married couples who refuse to have sexual intercourse for spiritual or ascetic reasons; while others feel Paul refers to marriageable virgins (Kistemaker). ἐπιταγή (# 2198) commandment, order; that is, an expressed command, whether a directly recorded saying of our Lord (as in v. 10) or a direct intimation to the apostle by revelation (Lightfoot, *Notes*). γνώμη (# 1191) opinion. The words γνώμην δίδωμι indicate the giving of advice (Schrage). Though Paul is giving his own opinion, it does not mean that this section is not inspired by the Holy Spirit. ἠλεημένος perf. pass. part. ἐλεέω (# 1796) to show mercy; pass., to receive mercy. The word means to see someone in need and to have pity and compassion on him and to kindly help him out of his need (TDNT; NIDNTT, 2:593-98; Trench, *Synonyms*, 166-71; TLNT; EDNT). Perf. views the completed state or condition and the part. could be causal (Barrett). Theol. pass. indicating that it was God who showed mercy. πιστός (# 4412) true, faithful, trustworthy. εἶναι pres. act. inf. εἰμί (# 1639) to be. Epex. inf. explaining the part., "pitied ... enough to be trustworthy" (Kistemaker). ◆ 26 νομίζω (# 3787) pres. ind. act. to suppose, to consider, to think, to be of the opinion, to regard something as presumably true, but without particular certainty (LN, 1:369). ὑπάρχειν pres. act. inf. ὑπάρχω (# 5639) to be, to exist. Inf. in indir. discourse. ἐνεστῶσαν perf. act. part. (adj.) ἐνίστημι (# 1931) to stand on, to be present. ἀνάγκη (# 340) necessity, compulsion of any kind, distress, calamity. It refers to the whole state of things between the first and second coming of Christ (Godet). Acc. w. διά (# 1328) giving the cause or reason. ὅτι (# 4022) used after the main vb. in a recitative sense equivalent to quotation marks (RWP). εἶναι pres. act. inf. εἰμί (# 1639) to be. Epex. inf. as noun explaining what is fitting, "the being so is good" (BD, 205-206). ◆ 27 δέδεσαι perf. ind. pass. 2nd. pers. sing.

δέω (# *1313*) to bind, w. dat. to indicate the pers. w. whom one is bound. Perf. indicates the continuing state resulting from a previous action. For the lively style of this section s. BD, 242. **ζήτει** pres. imp. act. ζητέω (# *2426*) to seek. Pres. imp. w. the neg. could mean, "do not immediately ...," or "do not always ...," or "do not continue ..." (MKG, 272). **λύσις** (# *3386*) loosing, releasing. **λέλυσαι** perf. ind. pass. 2nd. pers. sing. λύω (# *3395*) to loose, to release. ◆ **28 ἐὰν καί** (# *1569*; *2779*) and if. It introduces a 3rd. class cond. cl. w. subj. indicating the cond. is possible. For the meaning "although," s. BD, 190. **γαμήσῃς** aor. subj. act. γαμέω (# *1138*) to marry. Ingressive aor., "to get married." **γήμῃ** aor. subj. act. Subj. in a 3rd. class cond. cl. assuming the possibilities of the cond. **ἥμαρτεν** aor. ind. act. ἁμαρτάνω (# *279*) to sin. Gnomic aor. indicating that which is always true (Lietzmann; BD, 171; Funk, 621). **θλῖψις** (# *2568*) tribulation, pressure, affliction. **σαρκί** dat. sing. σάρξ (# *4922*) flesh. It refers to the total person as a created being (Schrage). Dat. of reference, instr. dat., dat. of disadvantage, or dat. of sphere. **ἕξουσιν** fut. ind. act. ἔχω (# *2400*) to have. **τοιοῦτος** (# *5525*) such as; nom. pl., such ones. **φείδομαι** (# *5767*) pres. ind. mid. (dep.) to spare. Conative pres., "I am trying to spare" (Barrett). ◆ **29 καιρός** (# *2789*) time, time period. **συνεσταλμένος** perf. pass. part. συστέλλω (# *5319*) to draw together, to limit, to shorten. The time has been drawn together so as to be small in amount (RP). Perf. part. in a periphrastic construction. The time stands shortened because the world is passing away (VA, 484). **τὸ λοιπόν** (# *3836*; *3370*) finally, henceforth. The word can be inferential or progressive (Blomqvist, 100-103; Thrall, 25-30). **ἵνα** (# *2671*) w. pres. subj. as imp.: "let them be" (Kistemaker; BD,195). **ἔχοντες** pres. act. part. ἔχω (# *2400*) to have. Part. w. **ὡς** (# *6055*) for an assumed condition (RWP) or concessive, "as though" (Kistemaker). **ὦσιν** pres. subj. act. εἰμί (# *1639*) to be. ◆ **30 κλαίοντες** pres. act. part. κλαίω (# *3081*) to weep, to cry. Part. as subst., "those crying." **χαίροντες** pres. act. part. χαίρω (# *5897*) to rejoice. Part. as subst. **ἀγοράζοντες** pres. act. part. ἀγοράζω (# *60*) to buy at the market. Part. as subst. **κατέχοντες** pres. act. part. κατέχω (# *2988*) to hold down, to hold firm, to possess; "as not entering upon full ownership." Earthly goods are a trust, not a possession (RP). ◆ **31 χρώμενοι** pres. mid. (dep.) part. χράομαι (# *5968*) to use, to make use of. For the use of the acc. w. this vb., which generally has the instr. as obj., s. RG, 476. **καταχρώμενοι** pres. mid. (dep.) part. καταχράομαι (# *2974*) to make full use of, to use to the utmost; "using it down to the ground," "using it completely up" (RP). The word occurs in the papyri of a woman accusing her husband of squandering her dowry (MM). It is used in Josephus in the sense of misusing something (CCFJ, 2:470). **παράγει** pres. ind. act. παράγω (# *4135*) to pass by, to pass alongside of, to pass

away. Pres. emphasizes the action in progress. **σχῆμα** (# *5386*) outward appearance, form, shape (BAGD; TDNT; NDIEC, 1:83; 4:169). The word occurs in Josephus w. the additional meanings: pomp, splendor, form of government, state, condition (CCFJ, 4:142-43). It indicates all that makes up the present world (Schrage). **κόσμος** (# *3180*) world. It refers to the world's resources and opportunities (Bruce). ◆ **32 ὑμᾶς** acc. pl. σύ (# *5148*) you. Acc. as subject of the inf. **ἀμέριμνος** (# *291*) without care, free from care, without worry or concern. For the neg. pref. s. Rom. 1:20. **εἶναι** pres. act. inf. εἰμί (# *1639*) to be. Compl. inf. w. vb. θέλω (# *2527*) to want to, to wish to. **μεριμνᾷ** pres. ind. act. μεριμνάω (# *3534*) to have care or concern, to worry about something. Gnomic pres. indicating a general truth (SMT, 8; Funk, 615). **ἀρέσῃ** aor. subj. act. ἀρέσκω (# *743*) to please, w. dat. Deliberative subj. w. **πῶς** (# *4802*) retained in an indir. question (RWP). ◆ **33 γαμήσας** aor. act. part. γαμέω (# *1138*) to marry. Part. as subst. **μεριμνᾷ** pres. ind. act. μεριμνάω (# *3534*) to have care. **τὰ τοῦ κόσμου** (# *3836*; *3180*) things belonging to the world; gen. of relationship (BD, 89). ◆ **34 μεμέρισται** perf. ind. pass. μερίζω (# *3532*) to divide. Perf. emphasizes the state or condition. **ᾖ** pres. subj. act. εἰμί (# *1639*) to be. **ἁγία** (# *41*) holy, dedicated, consecrated. **καὶ ... καί** (# *2779*) "both ... and." **σώματι** dat. sing. σῶμα (# *5393*) body. Dat. of reference. **πνεύματι** dat. sing. πνεῦμα (# *4460*) spirit. The passage indicates that the human spirit is distinct from the body (SBT, 140). **γαμήσασα** aor. act. part. nom. fem. sing. γαμέω (# *1138*) to marry. ◆ **35 αὐτῶν** gen. pl. αὐτός (# *899*) self; here, own. Refl. use of the pron. or possibly the intensive use (RG, 687). **σύμφορον** (# *5239*) that which is carried together, beneficial, advantageous, profitable. Here used as a noun, benefit, advantage (NDIEC, 1:59-61). **βρόχος** (# *1105*) noose, a noose or slipknot used for lassoing animals (RWP). **ἐπιβάλω** aor. subj. act. ἐπιβάλλω (# *2095*) to cast upon, to put upon w. the purpose of catching; "to cast a noose upon one" is a figurative expression originally borrowed from the chase, for the idea of depriving of freedom (bringing under, bending and limiting relations). "Not to direct you, like a domesticated animal" (Meyer; Barrett). Subj. w. **ἵνα** (# *2671*) in a neg. purp. cl. **εὔσχημον** (# *2363*) well-shaped, proper, good order, decorum, decency, dignity, respectability. The word denotes perfect fitness (Godet). The emphasis is sometimes on decent behavior, sometimes on order and beauty, sometimes on respectability and nobility (TLNT; TDNT; EDNT). **εὐπάρεδρος** (# *2339*) constant, devoted to; lit., well sitting beside. "For the good position beside the Lord" (RWP; BAGD). The vb. is used in 1 Cor. 9:13 for "waiting upon the altar" (Barrett). **κυρίῳ** dat. sing. κύριος (# *3261*) Lord. Dat. of personal interest. **ἀπερισπάστως** (# *597*) adv. unhindered; lit. without anything drawn around (RWP), without distraction. ◆ **36 ἀσχημονεῖν** pres. act. inf. ἀσχημονέω (# *858*) to act without decorum, to behave in a dishonorable way; it can sometimes have sexual overtones (NW, 2, i:304-05). For the adj. s.v. 35. Inf. as obj. of the vb. **ἐπί** (# *2093*) w. acc., toward. **τὴν παρθένον αὐτοῦ** (# *3836; 4221; 899*) his virgin. This refers either to a father and his daughter, to a man and woman who have entered upon a spiritual marriage and now live together without physical relations; or to a case of levirate marriage, and the word means "young widow"; or it refers to a man and woman who are an engaged couple (Barrett; Schrage; s. also v. 25). Ind. in a 1st. class cond. cl. in which the cond. is viewed as true. **ᾖ** pres. subj. act. εἰμί (# *1639*) to be. Subj. w. **ἐάν** (# *1569*) in a 3rd. class cond. in which the cond. is viewed as possible. **ὑπέρακμος** (# *5644*) past the bloom of youth, beyond marriageable age (NW 2, i:305-06). Prep. in compound may be understood to express intensification rather than the temp. sense; that is, w. strong passion, oversexed, sexually well-developed (BAGD; Barrett; LS, 1859; Schrage). **ὀφείλει** pres. ind. act. ὀφείλω (# *4053*) to be obligated, it is necessary. The word expresses a moral obligation w. inf. **γίνεσθαι** pres. mid. (dep.) inf. γίνομαι (# *1181*) to become. **ποιείτω** pres. imp. act. 3rd. pers. sing. ποιέω (# *4472*) to do. **γαμείτωσαν** pres. imp. act. 3rd. pers. pl. γαμέω (# *1138*) to marry. Pres. imp. points to a general truth. ◆ **37 ἕστηκεν** perf. ind. act. ἵστημι (# *2705*) to stand. **ἐν τῇ καρδίᾳ αὐτοῦ** (# *2840*) in his heart. Here the heart is the center of man from which decisions come (PAT, 328). **ἑδραῖος** (# *1612*) firm, steadfast. Adj. used adv. **ἔχων** pres. act. part. (adj.) ἔχω (# *2400*) to have. **ἀνάγκη** (# *340*) necessity (s.v. 26). **ἐξουσία** (# *2026*) authority. **κέκρικεν** perf. ind. act. κρίνω (# *3212*) to judge, to come to a decision, to decide. Perf. indicates the settled results of the decision. **τηρεῖν** pres. act. inf. τηρέω (# *5498*) to keep. The meaning is probably "to keep his virgin as she is" (Barrett). Inf. is used in indir. discourse giving the content of the decision. **καλῶς** (# *2822*) adv., well. For the adj., s.v. 1. **ποιήσει** fut. ind. act. ποιέω (# *4472*) to do. ◆ **38 ὥστε** (# *6063*) therefore, drawing a conclusion from the discussion. **γαμίζων** pres. act. part. γαμίζω (# *1139*) to give in marriage (s.v. 9). Vbs. w. this ending are generally causative ("to give in marriage"), but the word may also mean "to marry," "to enter into marriage" (MM; Weiss; Lietzmann). Part. as subst. **ἑαυτοῦ** gen. sing., his. The reflex. pronoun here appears to have lost reflexive force (IBG, 120). **ποιεῖ** pres. ind. act. ποιέω (# *4472*) to do. **κρεῖσσον** comp. ἀγαθός (s.v. 9). **ποιήσει** fut. ind. act. ποιέω (# *4472*) to do. ◆ **39 δέδεται** perf. ind. pass. δέω (# *1313*) to bind. Perf. emphasizes the state or condition resulting from the act of marriage. **ὅσον** (# *4012*) rel. pron. as much as, as long as. **ζῇ** pres. ind. act. ζάω (# *2409*) to live. **κοιμηθῇ** aor. subj. pass. κοιμάω (# *3121*) to go to sleep. The term for

Christian death (EGT). Ingressive aor., "to fall asleep." **ἐλευθέρα** (# *1801*) free. **ᾧ** masc. dat. sing. ὅς (# *4005*) who, which; rel. pron. "To whom." Dat. w. the following inf. **γαμηθῆναι** aor. pass. inf. γαμέω (# *1138*) to marry; pass., to be married to. Epex. inf. explaining the freedom of the widow (Funk, 663f). ◆ **40 μακαριωτέρα** comp. μακάριος (# *3421*) happy (TDNT; TLNT; Matt. 5:3); comp., happier. **μείνῃ** aor. subj. act. μένω (# *3531*) to stay. Subj. w. ἐάν in a 3rd. class cond. cl. in which the cond. is assumed to be possible or probable. **δοκῶ** pres. ind. act. δοκέω (# *1506*) to think. **ἔχειν** pres. act. inf. ἔχω (# *2400*) to have. Inf. as obj. of the vb. and used in indir. discourse.

1 Corinthians 8

◆ **1 περί** (# *4309*) w. gen., concerning, about. Paul begins to treat a second point about which the Corinthians had questioned him (Grosheide). **εἰδωλόθυτον** (# *1628*) that which was offered as a sacrifice to an idol. The word is of Jewish origin (TDNT). Various types of choice animals without blemish were offered to the gods. Part of the meat (the bones covered w. fat) was burned on the altar outside the temple, as the god's portion. Part of it was allotted the worshippers, and part of it was dedicated to the god and placed upon his special table. It could be used for a sacred banquet, w. the deity as the honored guest. What was left was sold at the marketplace (OCD, 944; Bruce; IMC, 7-66; Stirling Dow and David H. Gill, "The Greek Cult Table," *AJA* 69 [1965]: 103-14; David H. Gill, "*Trapezomata*: A Neglected Aspect of Greek Sacrifice," *HTR* 67 [1974]: 117-37; NDIEC, 2:36-37; 4:108; Schrage; BBC; DRU, 1:30-31; DPL, 424-26; Wendell L. Willis, *Idol Meat in Corinth: The Pauline Argument in 1 Corinthians 8 and 10*, SBLDS 68 [Chico, Ca.: Scholars Press, 1985]). The Jews called this meat from sacrifices for the dead "idols" (SB, 3:377). **οἴδαμεν** perf. ind. act. οἶδα (# *3857*) to know. Def. perf. w. pres. meaning. Paul uses the 1st. pers. pl. to include himself w. the readers (Lietzmann). **γνῶσις** (# *1194*) knowledge. Paul's use of knowledge is not something purely intellectual. It is knowledge which has results and leads to action, especially religious action (Grosheide). Here it is not a reference to gnosticism, which developed later (PCG, 39f; R.A. Horsley, "Gnosis in Corinth: 1 Corinthians 8. 1-6," *NTS* 27 [1980]: 32-51; DPL, 350-53). Paul is probably quoting a saying well known at Corinth, since the expression **οἴδαμεν ὅτι** ("we know that") is frequently used to introduce a well-known, generally accepted fact (BAGD, 556; IMC, 69-70; Schrage). **φυσιοῖ** pres. ind. act. φυσιόω (# *5881*) to puff up, to blow up like a billows, to cause someone to be proud, arrogant or haughty (LN, 1:765). Gnomic pres. emphasizing a general truth. **οἰκοδομεῖ** pres. ind. act. οἰκοδομέω (# *3868*) to build, to build up, to edify; gnomic pres. For a discussion of these terms s. IMC, 71-81. ◆ **2 δοκεῖ** pres. ind. act. δοκέω (# *1506*) to think, to suppose, w. inf. Paul uses the expression w. the meaning, "if anyone sets himself forth as one who ..." (IMC, 79). Ind. in a 1st. class cond. cl. in which the cond. is viewed as true. **ἐγνωκέναι** perf. act. inf. γινώσκω (# *1182*) to know. Perf. emphasizes an acquired knowledge that is one's possession. Inf. in indir. discourse. **ἔγνω** aor. ind. act. Ingressive aor., "come to know" (RWP). **δεῖ** (# *1256*) pres. ind. act. it is necessary; impers. w. inf., giving a logical necessity. **γνῶναι** aor. act. inf. γινώσκω (# *1182*) to know. ◆ **3 ἀγαπᾷ** pres. ind. act. ἀγαπάω (# *26*) to love. Ind. in a 1st. class cond. cl. in which the cond. is viewed as true. **ἔγνωσται** perf. ind. pass. γινώσκω (# *1182*) to know (s.v. 2). Perf. indicates, "he has come to be known and is still known by God" (Lenski). For the textual problem s. Fee. ◆ **4 βρῶσις** (# *1111*) eating. For nouns ending w. this suf. indicating action s. MH, 373. **εἰδωλοθύτων** gen. pl. (s.v. 1) that which was offered as a sacrifice to an idol. Obj. gen. **οἴδαμεν** perf. ind. act. (s.v. 1). **εἴδωλον** (# *1631*) idol. The statues of the gods lined the marketplace of Corinth and were made from marble, copper, gold, silver, ivory, or wood, w. eyes made out of precious stones (DRU, 1:37-40). Paul calls that which the statue represents an idol (Schlatter). Paul's use of the word conforms to the Jewish use of the term (Schrage; GELTS, 130; TDNT; SB, 3:48-60; 4, i:189-207; CCFJ, 2:22; CGP, 297). **οὐδείς** (# *4029*) no one, nobody, used as an adj. ("no"). **εἰ μή** (# *1623*; *3590*) except. **εἷς** (# *1651*) one. ◆ **5 εἴπερ** (# *1642*) if indeed, if after all. Here used in a concessive sense (BD, 237). **εἰσίν** pres. ind. act. εἰμί (# *1639*) to be. Used. w. the part. in a periphrastic construction. **λεγόμενοι** pres. pass. part. λέγω (# *3306*) to say; pass., to be called. "Those who continually are called gods" or "so-called gods" (Grosheide). **ὥσπερ** (# *6061*) just as indeed. **θεοὶ πολλοὶ καὶ κύριοι πολλοί** many gods and many lords (s. Acts 17:16). ◆ **6 εἷς θεός** (# *1651*; *2536*) one God, followed, in apposition, by **ὁ πατήρ** (# *3836*; *4252*) the Father. **ἐξ οὗ** from whom, indicates the origin. **εἰς** (# *1659*) **αὐτόν** (# *899*) unto Him, indicating the fut. goal (Schrage). **εἷς κύριος** (# *1659*; *3251*) one Lord, followed by the words in apposition Ἰησοῦς Χριστός (# *2652*; *5986*). Lord, a title used to indicate the deity of Jesus Christ. For a collection of the evidence proving that the Jews at the time of Christ used this term for God s. Joseph A. Fitzmyer, "Der semitische Hintergrund des neutesamentlichen Kyriostitels," *Jesus Christus in Historie und Theologie*, 267-98; s. also R.A. Horsley, "The Background of the Confessional Formula in 1 Kor 8:6," *ZNW* 69 (1978): 130-35. **δι' οὗ** (# *1328*; *4005*) through whom, indicating agency. **ἡμεῖς δι' αὐτοῦ** "we through Him." Like all men we are created by Christ, but we are also redeemed by Him (Grosheide). ◆ **7 ἡ γνῶσις** (# *1194*) the knowledge. The article points to the specific knowledge he is

discussing in this context. **συνηθείᾳ** (# *5311*) dat. sing. familiarity, custom (Schrage). Instr. dat. **ἐσθίουσιν** pres. ind. act. ἐσθίω (# *2266*) to eat. **συνείδησις** (# *5287*) conscience (s. Rom. 2:15; TDNT; TLNT; PAT, 402-446; NIDNTT 1:348-53; EDNT; J.M. Espy, "Paul's 'Robust Conscience' Re-examined," *NTS* 31 [1985]: 161-88; P.W. Gooch, "'Conscience' in 1 Corinthians 8 and 10," *NTS* 33 [1987]: 244-54; NDIEC, 3:85; Schrage). **οὖσα** pres. act. part. (causal) nom. fem. sing. εἰμί (# *1639*) to be. **μολύνεται** pres. ind. pass. μολύνω (# *3662*) to make dirty, to stain, to pollute, to contaminate, to defile. Here, in the sense of religious and moral contamination (Schrage). ◆ **8 παραστήσει** fut. ind. act. παρίστημι (# *4225*) to present, to present for approbation or condemnation (RP). It was a t.t. for bringing someone before a judge (Fee; Schrage). **φάγωμεν** aor. subj. act. ἐσθίω (# *2266*) to eat. Subj. w. **ἐάν** (# *1569*) in a 3rd. class cond. in which the cond. is viewed as possible. **ὑστερούμεθα** pres. ind. mid. (dep) ὑστερέω (# *5728*) to fall short, to lack (s. Rom. 3:23). **περισσεύομεν** pres. ind. act. περισσεύω (# *4355*) to have an abundance. ◆ **9 βλέπετε** pres. imp. act. βλέπω (# *1063*) to see, to see to it, to beware. **μή** (# *3590*) lest, w. aor. subj. to express a neg. imp. (BD, 184). **πρόσκομμα** (# *4682*) stumbling, hindrance. **γένηται** aor. subj. mid. (dep.) γίνομαι (# *1181*) to become. **ἀσθενέσιν** dat. pl. ἀσθενής (# *822*) weak. For a discussion of the weak s. IMC, 92-96; Schrage; Fee. Dat. of disadvantage. ◆ **10 ἴδῃ** aor. subj. act. ὁράω (# *3972*) to see. **ἔχοντα** pres. act. part. (adj.) ἔχω (# *2400*) to have. **εἰδώλειον** (# *1627*) idol temple, idol shrine. **κατακείμενον** pres. mid. (dep.) part. κατάκειμαι (# *2879*) to lie down, to recline at the table. In many of the temples dining rooms used for the sacred meal were also used for other cultural events, such as birthdays, etc. (Richard E. Oster, "Use, Misuse and Neglect of Archaeological Evidence," *ZNW* 83 [1992]: 64-67; SPC, 161-67; PIG, 210-25; James Wiseman, "Corinth and Rome I: 228 B.C.-A.D. 267," ANRW, 2.7.1:438-548, esp. 509-21; Acts 18:1). It would not be uncommon to be invited to a meal in the temple, as is evident from the invitation cards found among the papyri (Bruce; IMC, 39-45; NDIEC, 1:5-9; DPL, 306-10). **οὐχί** (# *4049*) neg. used to introduce a question which expects the answer "yes." **ἀσθενοῦς** gen. sing. (s.v. 9). W. part. in apposition to the personal pron. **ὄντος** pres. act. part. (causal) gen. sing. εἰμί (# *1639*) to be. **οἰκοδομηθήσεται** fut. ind. pass. οἰκοδομέω (# *3868*) to build up, to strengthen (s.v. 1). **ἐσθίειν** pres. act. inf. ἐσθίω (# *2266*) to eat. Articular inf. w. **εἰς** (# *1650*) to express result or purp. (RG, 1071-72; Kistemaker). ◆ **11 ἀπόλλυται** pres. ind. pass. ἀπόλλυμι (# *660*) to ruin; that is, "to come to sin." It means not to show oneself as a Christian (Grosheide). **ἀσθενῶν** pres. act. part. ἀσθενέω (# *820*) to be weak. Part. as subst. **ἀπέθανεν** aor. ind. act. ἀποθνήσκω (# *633*) to die. ◆ **12 ἁμαρτάνοντες** pres. act. part. ἁμαρτάνω (# *279*) to sin.

Cond. or temp. part., or part. of means. εἰς w. acc., against. τύπτοντες pres. act. part. τύπτω (# 5597) to wound, to strike w. the fist, staff, or whip (RWP). Cond. or temp. part., or part. of means. ἀσθενοῦσαν pres. act. part. (adj.) ἀσθενέω (# 820) to be weak. ◆ **13 διόπερ** (# 1478) therefore, for this very reason; w. ind. **σκανδαλίζει** pres. ind. act. σκανδαλίζω (# 4997) to cause one to stumble, to offend (TDNT; NTW, 111-14; TLNT). Ind. in a 1st. class cond. cl. in which the cond. is assumed to be true. **οὐ μή** (# 4024; 3590) not in anywise. For the use of this strong neg. s. M 188f; GGBB, 468-69. **φάγω** aor. subj. act. ἐσθίω (# 2266) to eat. **σκανδαλίσω** aor. subj. act. (# 4997) Subj. w. **ἵνα** (# 2671) to express purp.

1 Corinthians 9

◆ **1 οὐκ** (# 4024) used in questions expecting the answer "yes." "I am free, aren't I?" **ἐλεύθερος** (# 1801) free; the freedom of a Christian (Morris; TDNT). **ἑώρακα** perf. ind. act. ὁράω (# 3972) to see. Having seen the Lord was one of the prerequisites for apostleship (s. 1:1; TDNT; TLNT). Perf. indicates the continuing results of having seen. ◆ **2 εἰ** (# 1623) if; w. ind. used to introduce a 1st. class cond. cl. which is assumed to be true. **ἄλλοις** dat. pl. ἄλλος (# 257) other. "To others." Dat. of respect or relation, or ethical dat., "in the estimation of others" (Funk, 721f; MT, 238; Barrett). **ἀλλά γε** (# 247; 1145) but at least. A contrast used w. the emphatic article (BD, 226). **σφραγίς** (# 5382) seal, a confirming and guaranteeing sign as well as a sign of authority (TDNT; NIDNTT, 3:497-501; CCFJ, 4:142; EDNT; Schrage). ◆ **3 ἐμή** nom. sing. ἐμός (# 1847) my, emphatic by position. **ἀπολογία** (# 665) defense. Used elsewhere of defense in a law court (Barrett). **ἀνακρίνουσιν** pres. act. part. masc. dat. pl. ἀνακρίνω (# 373) to examine, perhaps in the sense of cross-examine. Conative pres., "to those who would like to examine me" (Barrett). Dat. of personal interest. ◆ **4 μὴ οὐκ** (# 3590; 4024) The first neg. is used in the question expecting the answer "no" and the second neg. negates the vb.: "you would not say that we do not have the authority, would you?" (BD, 220f; RG, 1173). **φαγεῖν** aor. act. inf. ἐσθίω (# 2266) to eat. **πεῖν** aor. act. inf. πίνω (# 4403) to drink. Epex. infs. used to explain the content of the authority. ◆ **5 ἀδελφή** (# 80) sister; that is, a sister in Christ, one who belongs to the same religious belief (NIDNTT 1:254; TDNT; EDNT). Double acc. as dir. obj. followed by a second acc; **γυναικός** (# 1222) wife. "A sister as wife." **περιάγειν** pres. act. inf. περιάγω (# 4310) to lead around. The word does not emphasize the traveling together on a journey but rather "to have constantly w. oneself"; that is, being married (Conzelmann). These were wives who would accompany their husbands on missionary trips (Schrage). Epex. inf. explaining the right or authority. ◆ **6 ἤ** (# 2445) or. The word continues the question. **ἐργάζεσθαι** pres. mid.

(dep.) inf. ἐργάζομαι (# 2237) to work; that is, to do manual labor. Epex. inf. ◆ **7 στρατεύεται** pres. ind. mid. (dep.) στρατεύω (# 5129) to be a soldier, to do military service, to serve in the army. Gnomic pres. emphasizing a timeless truth (SMT, 8). **ὀψωνίοις** dat. pl. ὀψώνιον (# 4072) provisions; soldiers' pay was probably a denarius a day, out of which they had to equip themselves, secure any simple luxuries, or bribe the centurions for remissions of duties (BC, 5:428; Rom. 6:23; Schrage). Instr. dat. **ποτέ** (# 4537) at any time, ever. **φυτεύει** pres. ind. act. φυτεύω (# 5885) to plant. **ἀμπελῶν** (# 308) vineyard. For the rules governing workers eating the harvest s. SB, 3:382. **ποιμαίνει** pres. ind. act. ποιμαίνω (# 4477) to shepherd a flock, to tend sheep. **ποίμνη** (# 4479) flock. **γάλακτος** gen. sing. γάλα (# 1128) milk. According to Jewish custom a herdsman was allowed to drink from the milk of the herd when he was far away from home w. the herd, or when he needed food (SB, 3:381-82). ◆ **8 μή** (# 3590) neg. introducing a question expecting a neg. answer (s.v. 4). **καί** (# 2779) also. **οὐ** (# 4024) neg. introducing a question expecting a positive answer. ◆ **9 γέγραπται** perf. ind. pass. γράφω (# 1211) to write. Perf. emphasizes the standing legal authority of that which was written (MM). **κημώσεις** fut. ind. act. κημόω (# 3055) to muzzle. Fut. is used under Semitic influence of the legal language of the OT and expresses a categorical imp. (BG, 94). The Jewish concern for animals distinguished them from other nations (SB, 3:382). **βοῦς** (# 1091) ox. The ox in Scripture implied all laboring species (D. Instone Brewer, "1 Corinthians 9:9-11: A Literal Interpretation of 'Do Not Muzzle the Ox,'" NTS 38 [1992]: 554-65). **ἀλοῶντα** pres. act. part. ἀλοάω (# 262) to thrash, to tread or trample out. Sledges were drawn by teams of oxen and encircled the pile of grain heaped in the center of the thrashing floor (ZPEB, 5:739; IDB, 4: 637). Adj. or temp. part., "while he is thrashing." **μή** (# 3590) neg. used to introduce questions expecting the answer no. **μέλει** pres. ind. act. μέλω (# 3508) to have concern. Used impersonally followed by the dat. of interest and the gen. for thing concerned. It may be that Paul is here talking about the application of the passage without disregarding the literal meaning of the passage (Fee; OTN, 39-51; s. Walter C. Kaiser, Jr., "The Current Crisis in Exegesis and the Apostolic Use of Deuteronomy 25:4 in 1 Corinthians 9:8-10," JETS 21 [1978]: 3-18). ◆ **10 δι' ἡμᾶς** (# 1328; 1609) because of us, for our sakes. Either a reference to men in general or specifically to teachers. **πάντως** (# 4122) adv., assuredly, entirely; that is, in every case (Grosheide). **γάρ** (# 1142) for. In replies it affirms what was asked, giving the reason for a tacit "yes," "to be sure," "just so" (BD, 236). **ἐγράφη** aor. ind. pass. γράφω (# 1211) to write. **ὀφείλει** pres. ind. act. ὀφείλω (# 4053) to be obligated to (ought, should). It generally shows a moral obligation. **ἀρο-**

τριῶν pres. act. part. ἀροτριάω (# 769) to plow. Part. as subst. ἀροτριᾶν pres. act. inf. Used to complete the main vb. showing what the obligation is. ἀλοῶν pres. act. part. ἀλοάω (# 262) to thrash (s.v. 9). Part. as subst. μετέχειν pres. act. inf. μετέχω (# 3576) to share in, to partake of. Inf. w. the vb. ὀφείλει. In the examples of sharing used by Paul there is an intrinsic connection between one's activity and one's recompense (Harry P. Nasuti, "The Woes of the Prophets and the Rights of the Apostle: The Internal Dynamics of 1 Corinthians 9," CBQ 50 [1988]: 250; DPL, 295-97). ◆ **11 ὑμῖν** dat. pl. σύ (# 5148) you. Dat. of personal interest ("for your benefit") or dat. of place ("among you"). **τὰ πνευματικά** (# 4461) spiritual things (s. 2:13). Here w. the analogy, "spiritual seed" (Fee). **ἐσπείραμεν** aor. ind. act. σπείρω (# 5062) to sow, to sow seeds. Ind. w. εἰ (# 1623) introducing a 1st. class cond. cl in which the cond. is assumed to be true. **μέγα** (# 3489) great; "no big thing," "is this something extraordinary that we should expect this?" (Fee). **τὰ σαρκικά** (# 4920) fleshly things; fleshly, pertaining to the flesh. For the meaning of this suf. s. MH, 378. The word here is not identical w. "sinful." The contrast is between heavenly and earthly, or between spiritual and the material and it refers to the earthly things necessary for living (Grosheide; Schrage). **θερίσομεν** fut. ind. act. θερίζω (# 2545) to harvest, to reap. Fut. w. εἰ (# 1623) meaning, "if subsequently, as actually happened, we ..." (BD, 189). ◆ **12 ὑμῶν** gen. pl. σύ (# 5148) you. Obj. gen., "over you" (RG, 500). **ἐξουσίας** gen. sing. ἐξουσία (# 2026) authority. Gen. after a vb. of sharing. **μετέχουσιν** pres. ind. act. μετέχω (# 3576) to share in (s.v. 10). Ind. in a 1st. class cond. cl. in which the cond. is viewed as true. **οὐ** neg. in a question expecting a positive answer. **ἐχρησάμεθα** aor. ind. mid. (dep.) χράομαι (# 5968) to use, to make use of, w. obj. in dat. **στέγομεν** pres. ind. act. στέγω (# 5095) to cover, to protect or keep by covering, to bear up against, to endure (T). **ἐγκοπή** (# 1600) a cutting, hindrance. Used in the papyri in the literal sense of cutting down (a tree) (MM; TLNT). **δῶμεν** aor. subj. act. δίδωμι (# 1443) to give. Subj. w. ἵνα (# 2671) to express purp. **εὐαγγελίῳ** dat. sing. εὐαγγέλιον (# 2295) good news, gospel. Indir. obj. ◆ **13 οὐκ** (# 4024) neg. introducing a question which expects a positive answer. **ἐργαζόμενοι** pres. mid. (dep.) part. ἐργάζομαι (# 2237) to work; here, to officiate in religious matters. Part. as subst. **τὰ ἐκ τοῦ ἱεροῦ** (# 2639) the things from the temple or holy place; that is, the altar or the sacrifice. Thus the last cl. defines the first (Grosheide). **ἐσθίουσιν** pres. ind. act. ἐσθίω (# 2266) to eat. Gnomic pres. giving a general truth. **θυσιαστηρίῳ** dat. sing. θυσιαστήριον (# 2603) altar, place of sacrifice. The suf. indicates the location where an action takes place, "at the altar" (MH, 342-43). Dat. is pure locative (RG, 521). **παρεδρεύοντες** pres. act. part. παραδρεύω (# 4204) to sit

constantly beside, to attend constantly (AS). In the papyri the word has a religious connotation (MM), but is also used of a young boy attending school (NDIEC, 4:33-5; Jos., JW, 1:78). Part. as subst. **συμμερίζονται** pres. ind. mid. (dep.) συμμερίζομαι (# 5211) to share a portion together. The customs Paul refers to were widespread in antiquity. The recompense was the eating of the temple food (H.P. Nasuti, "The Woes of the Prophets and the Rights of the Apostle," CBQ 50 [1988]: 251). Those who held sacred offices on behalf of others might reasonably expect to be provided for. This Jesus Himself recognized (Barrett). ◆ **14 οὕτως καί** (# 4048; 2779) so also. **διέταξεν** aor. ind. act. διατάσσω (# 1411) to give an order, to command. Aor. indicates that Paul was consciously alluding to a past origin in the teaching of Jesus (JNP, 96). The reference is probably to Luke 10:7 (Fee; s. 1 Tim. 5:18). **καταγγέλλουσιν** pres. act. part. masc. dat. pl. καταγγέλλω (# 2859) to proclaim, to make a solemn proclamation (NIDNTT, 3:44-48; CCFJ, 2:434-35). Dat. of favor or advantage (Godet). **ἐκ** (# 1666) w. gen., out of, from. The prep. gives the source of income. **ζῆν** pres. act. inf. ζάω (# 2409) to live. Inf. in indir. speech (BD, 200; IBG, 153). ◆ **15 ἐγὼ δέ** (# 1609; 1254) but I! (emphatic). The apostle now applies the principle to himself and gives a further reason for the renunciation of his undoubted rights (Hering). **κέχρημαι** perf. ind. mid. (dep.) χράομαι (# 5968) to use. Perf. indicates the continuing condition. The change from the aor. in v. 12 to the perf. brings it down to the pres. moment, "I have not availed myself" (RP). **ἔγραψα** aor. ind. act. γράφω (# 1211) to write. Epistolary aor., "I am writing" (Kistemaker). **γένηται** aor. subj. mid. (dep.) γίνομαι to become. Subj. w. ἵνα (# 2671) expressing purp. **ἐν ἐμοί** in my case (Barrett). **ἀποθανεῖν** aor. act. inf. ἀποθνήσκω (# 633) to die. Epex. inf. explaining what is better. **ἤ** (# 2445) than. Paul breaks the construction abruptly (MT, 343; Kistemaker). **καύχημα** (# 3017) boasting, reason or ground for boasting. **κενώσει** fut. ind. act. κενόω (# 3033) to make empty, to make void. ◆ **16 εὐαγγελίζωμαι** pres. subj. mid. (dep.) εὐαγγελίζομαι (# 2294) to proclaim good news, to evangelize (TDNT; NIDNTT, 1:107-15; EDNT; TLNT; MNTW, 41f). Subj. w. ἐάν (# 1569) in a 3rd. class cond. cl. in which the cond. is viewed as possible. **ἀνάγκη** (# 340) compulsion, necessity, distress. tribulation (GELTS, 27; BAGD; Siegfried Kreuzer, "Der Zwang des Boten–Beobachtungen zu Lk 14:23 und 1 Kor 9:16," ZNW 76 [1985]: 123-28). In the NT the word does not mean "fate" (TDNT; Gustav Stählin, "Das Schicksal im Neuen Testament und bei Josephus," JS, 321f). **ἐπίκειται** pres. ind. pass. ἐπίκειμαι (# 2130) to place upon, to lie upon. Pres. shows continuing relevance (Kistemaker), meaning "presses upon me" (RP). **οὐαί** (# 4026) woe, alas! An interjection denoting pain or displeasure (BAGD), w. dat. of disadvantage. **εὐαγγελίσωμαι** aor. subj. mid. (dep.)

εὐαγγελίζομαι. Subj. w. **ἐάν** (# 1569) in 3rd. class cond. cl. ◆ **17 ἑκών** (# 1776) willingly, gladly, of one's own freewill. **πράσσω** (# 4556) pres. ind. act. to do, to practice. Pres. emphasizes habitual action. Ind. is used in a 1st. class cond. cl. which assumes the reality of the cond. **μισθός** (# 3635) payment, reward. Paul's purpose is to intimate that he does not seek his reward in the receiving of financial compensation (Grosheide). **ἄκων** (# 220) unwilling, not of one's own freewill. The word indicates that Paul is a mere servant w. responsibilities to his master (Schrage). For the neg. prefix s. Rom. 1:20. **οἰκονομία** (# 3873) stewardship, responsibility. The word indicates the task given to responsible and faithful servants who were appointed over the economy or an area of responsibility in the household. The word stresses obligation, responsibility, and faithfulness of the servant to his master in carrying out the entrusted task (TDNT; TLNT; 4:1; for the use of the word in patristic writers s. PGL). **πεπίστευμαι** perf. ind. pass. πιστεύω (# 4409) to believe, to entrust. Perf. emphasizes the completed state or condition reaching to the pres. time. Theol. pass. indicating that God had entrusted him w. this responsibility. ◆ **18 μού** (# 1609) my, emphatic by position. **μισθός** (# 3635) payment for services, reward. Paul's pay is that he preaches the gospel as a servant for no pay (Schrage). **ἵνα** (# 2671) here it does not express purpose but gives the content of the reward (BD, 202). **εὐαγγελιζόμενος** pres. mid. (dep.) part. εὐαγγελίζομαι (# 2294) to proclaim good news (s.v. 16). **ἀδάπανος** (# 78) adv., without expense, free of charge. **θήσω** fut. ind. act. τίθημι (# 5502) to place, to present. **καταχρήσασθαι** aor. mid. (dep.) inf. καταχράομαι (# 2974) to make full use of, to use completely, to use to the uttermost, w. dat. Prep. in compound is perfective (RWP; s. 7:31). Articular inf. w. **εἰς** (# 1659) to express purp. ◆ **19 ὤν** pres. act. part. εἰμί (# 1639) to be. Concessive part. ("although I am free") or causal (Schrage). **ἐδούλωσα** aor. ind. act. δουλόω (# 1530) to enslave, to make a slave of someone. **πλείονας** comp. πολύς (# 4498) more; comp., the majority, or it had the meaning "others," "even more" (BD, 127). **κερδήσω** aor. subj. act. or fut. ind. act. (RWP) κερδαίνω (# 3045) to win. The rabbinic equivalent means "to make proselytes," "to win over" (Schrage; NTRJ, 352-54). Subj. w. **ἵνα** (# 2671) to express purp. ◆ **20 ἐγενόμην** aor. ind. mid. (dep.) γίνομαι (# 1181) to become. **τοῖς Ἰουδαίοις** (# 3836; 2681) the individual use of the article, "the Jews w. whom I had to deal on each occasion" (BD, 137). Dat. of respect, ethical dat., or dat. of advantage (Schrage). **ὑπό** (# 5679) w. acc., under. The law here is the Torah, as written in the Pentateuch and expounded by orthodox Jewish rabbis (MS, 135). ◆ **21 ἄνομος** (# 491) lawless, without the law; however, not in the sense of leading an unregulated and irresponsible life (MS, 135). The addition of the gen. **θεοῦ** indicates that the law of God is

something wider and more inclusive than law, in the sense of Torah (MS, 137). **ἔννομος** (# 1937) legal, subject to law, obedient to the law; "under legal obligation to Christ" (Barrett). For the relation of this to the spiritual life and walk according to the precepts of Christ s. MS, 137-48. **κερδάνω** aor. act. subj. κερδαίνω (# 3045) to win. ◆ **22 ἐγενόμην** aor. ind. mid. (dep.) γίνομαι (# 1181) to become. **γέγονα** perf. ind. act. The change from aor. to perf. is significant; this is the permanent result of this past action (RP). **πάντως** (# 4122) by all means; or "under any circumstance" (Schrage). **σώσω** fut. ind. act. σῴζω (# 5392) to rescue, to save. Fut. w. **ἵνα** (# 2671) in purp. cl. (MT, 100). ◆ **23 συγκοινωνός** (# 5171) one who shares together, fellow partaker, fellow participant. **γένωμαι** aor. subj. mid. (dep.) γίνομαι (# 1181) to become. Subj. w. **ἵνα** to express purp. For discussions of Paul's accommodating position s. PAL, 230-44; Peter Richardson, "Pauline Inconsistency: 1 Corinthians 9:19-23 and Galatians 2:11-14," NTS 26 (1980): 347-62. ◆ **24 οἴδατε** perf. ind. act. οἶδα (# 3857) to know. Def. perf. w. pres. meaning. **στάδιον** (# 5084) stadium, a running track which was a long parallelogram about 200 yards long and 30 yards wide. The Isthmian Games held near Corinth form the background for this passage (OCD, 1010f; Oscar Bronner, "The Apostle Paul and the Isthmian Games," BA 25 [1962]: 1-31; A.H. Harris, Sport in Greece and Rome, 27-33; DGRA, 1055f; Schrage; BBC). **τρέχοντες** pres. act. part. τρέχω (# 5556) to run. Part. as subst. **εἷς** (# 1651) one. The point is not that just one person is the winner, but rather "to run like one who is the winner" (Schrage). **λαμβάνει** pres. ind. act. λαμβάνω (# 3284) to receive. Gnomic pres., indicating a general truth. **βραβεῖον** (# 1092) prize. The prize given to the winner of an athletic contest. The prize was generally a wreath, but the winner was also rewarded w. fame and popularity. **τρέχετε** pres. act. imp. (# 5556) Pres. imp. calls for a constant attitude. **καταλάβητε** aor. subj. act. καταλαμβάνω (# 2898) to attain, to grasp and hold. Effective aor. w. the perfective use of the prep. in compound (RWP). The example of the runners in the arena sets the stage for the theme of self-control which follows (PAM, 87; Schrage). Subj. w. **ἵνα** (# 2671) to express purp. ◆ **25 ἀγωνιζόμενος** pres. mid. (dep.) part. ἀγωνίζομαι (# 76) to engage in an athletic contest, to strive. For the attitude of Greeks, Romans, and Jews toward the athletic contest s. PAM, 16-75; for the particular neg. attitude of the Jews s. SB, 4:401-405. Part. as subst. **πάντα** acc. πᾶς (# 4246) all; acc. of general reference, "in regards to all things." **ἐγκρατεύεται** pres. ind. mid. (dep.) ἐγκρατεύω (# 1603) to exercise self-control. Gnomic pres. emphasizing that which is always true. All the endeavors of the athlete are in vain if he has not trained his body and abstained from all that might in any way harm his physical condition. Paul seems to be referring to the training period during which time the athlete was under strict rules (PAM, 87; Schrage). **φθαρ-τός** (*# 5778*) perishable. **λάβωσιν** aor. act. subj. λαμβάνω (*# 3284*) to receive. Subj. w. **ἵνα** (*# 2671*) to express purp. **ἡμεῖς** (*# 1609*) we! Emphatic and contrastive. **ἄφθαρτος** (*# 915*) imperishable. Paul is not speaking of agonizing for the prize of eternal life, but rather for the goal of faithfully proclaiming the gospel (PAM, 87f). ◆ **26 τοίνυν** (*# 5523*) accordingly, therefore. It is used to draw an inference. **ἀδήλως** (*# 85*) uncertainly, aimlessly; "I do not run as one who has no fixed and certain goal" (PAM, 90; Weiss). **πυκτεύω** (*# 4782*) pres. ind. act. to fight w. the fist, to box (A.H. Harris, *Sport in Greece and Rome*, 22-25; DGRA, 974; Schrage). Paul turns to the picture of the boxer in order to reintroduce the principle of self-restriction and self-negation (PAM, 90). **ἀέρα** acc. ἀήρ (*# 113*) air. **δέρων** pres. act. part. δέρω (*# 1296*) to beat. The word could signify the failure of the pugilist to make his blows count or his carrying on mock contest as a shadow boxer (PAM, 90). Part. of manner, explaining how he does not box. ◆ **27 ὑπω-πιάζω** (*# 5724*) pres. ind. act. to strike under the eye, to beat black and blue (Schrage). **δουλαγωγῶ** pres. ind. act. δουλαγωγέω (*# 1524*) to lead into slavery, to make a slave or to treat one as a slave. The two vbs. give the picture of the athlete who does all to discipline himself and to keep his body under rigorous control in order that it might serve and not hinder his progress to the goal (PAM, 91). **μή πως** (*# 3590; 4803*) "lest by any means." **κηρύξας** aor. act. part. (temp.) κηρύσσω (*# 3062*) to preach, to proclaim as a herald (TDNT; EDNT). Aor. expressing antecedent time, "after I have preached." **ἀδόκιμος** (*# 99*) rejected as unusable. Used of metals and coins which were rejected for not standing the test (RWP; s. NDIEC, 1:61-62; TLNT). **γένωμαι** aor. subj. mid. (dep.) γίνομαι (*# 1181*) to become. Paul's fear is that he will be unfaithful in carrying out his commission of preaching the gospel as expected of him (PAM, 96).

1 Corinthians 10

◆ **1 γάρ** (*# 1142*) for. The explanatory γάρ and the voc. ἀδελφοί indicate that the present argument has close ties with the exhortation and warning that has just preceded (Fee). **ἀγνοεῖν** pres. act. inf. ἀγνοέω (*# 51*) not to know, to be ignorant. Used w. acc. as subject and supplementary to θέλω (*# 2527*). For the neg. force of the pref. s. Rom. 1:20. **πάντες** (*# 4246*) all. The main emphasis in vv. 1-4 rests on this word. Paul had received the same privileges (Bruce; Grosheide). **ἦσαν** impf. ind. act. εἰμί (*# 1639*) to be. **διῆλθον** aor. ind. act. διέρχομαι (*# 1451*) to go through, to pass completely through. Prep. in compound is perfective and local (MH, 301f). The OT clearly sees Israel's passing through the sea and the accompanying cloud as divine activity (Exod. 13:21; Ps. 105:39) (IMC, 129). ◆ **2 εἰς**

(*# 1659*) into. **ἐβαπτίσθησαν** aor. ind. pass. βαπτίζω (*# 966*) to baptize. It means to immerse in Moses; that is, to bring in close relationship w. Moses (Grosheide). Permissive pass., "to allow oneself to be ..." (MT, 57). A variant reading, which very well may be the best reading, is **ἐβαπτίσαντο** aor. ind. mid. (Fee; BD, 166). Permissive mid. ◆ **3 αὐτό** (*# 899*) the same. **πνευματικός** (*# 4461*) spiritual, that which pertains to the spirit. The word is either "spiritual" in contrast to material, or "spiritual" in its relation to the Holy Spirit. **βρῶμα** (*# 1109*) acc. sing. food. **ἔφαγον** aor. ind. act. ἐσθίω (*# 2266*) to eat. ◆ **4 ἔπιον** aor. ind. act. πίνω (*# 4403*) to drink. **πόμα** (*# 4503*) acc. sing. that which one drinks, drink. **ἔπινον** impf. ind. act. Impf. pictures the manner of action and shows the continual access to the supernatural source of supply (RWP; BD, 169). **ἀκολουθούσης** pres. act. part. (adj.) gen. fem. sing. ἀκολουθέω (*# 199*) to follow. For the Jewish tradition of the well which followed the Israelites in the wilderness and the Rock, s. SB, 4:406-08; Tg. Onk. and Rashi at Num. 21:16-19; Schrage; Fee; IMC, 133-38; for the DSS s. CD 6:3-9; 1QH 11:15. **πέτρα** (*# 4376*) rock (s. Matt. 16:18). In the OT God is often referred to as a Rock (Ps. 18:31, 46; 42:9; 78:35; 89:26; 95:1; 144:1; G. Henton Davies, "Psalm 95," *ZAW* 85 [1973]: 188-90), especially in the Song of Moses (Deut. 32:4, 15, 18, 30). **ἦν** impf. ind. act. εἰμί (*# 1639*) to be. It was not that Christ was the literal rock, but He was the spiritual rock that followed and from which Israel drank. The benefits enjoyed by the people are spiritual because they came from Christ, the source of all blessings (Grosheide; IMC, 138-42; TDNT). ◆ **5 πλείοσιν** dat. pl. πλείων (nom. masc. sing.) most; comp. of πολύς (*# 4498*) (BAGD). As subst., the majority. **εὐ-δόκησεν** aor. ind. act. εὐδοκέω (*# 2305*) to be pleased w. W. the prep. ἐν (*# 1877*) denotes a Semitic influence (BD, 111; KVS, 262-65). **κατεστρώθησαν** aor. ind. pass. καταστρώννυμι (*# 2954*) to stretch or spread down as of a couch, to lay low, as if by a hurricane (RWP), to strike down, to annihilate (CCFJ, 2:464). ◆ **6 τύπος** (*# 5596*) type, example. The word is used here in the sense of "an awful, warning example" (Barrett; NIDNTT, 3:903-7; TDNT; OTN, 53-57). Pred. nom. **ἡμῶν** gen. pl. ἐγώ (*# 1609*) I. Either obj. gen., "examples for us," or subjective gen., "examples of us" (Kistemaker; Fee). **ἐγενήθη-σαν** aor. ind. pass. (dep.) γίνομαι (*# 1181*) to become, to be. Instead of the usual sing. of the vb. after a n. pl. subject, the vb. here is pl. thought the attraction of the pred. (EGT). **εἶναι** pres. act. inf. εἰμί (*# 1639*) to be. Articular inf. w. εἰς (*# 1659*) and the neg. μή (*# 3590*) to express neg. purp., "that we should not be." **ἐπιθυμητής** (*# 2122*) one who lusts, one who has a strong desire. The noun is followed by the obj. gen., indicating the object of the strong desire. Words w. the ending -της indicate the agent performing an action (MH, 365-68). **ἐπεθύμησαν** aor. ind. act. ἐπιθυμέω (*# 2121*) to have strong desire, to lust after, to lust, to set one's heart upon, to long for (GELTS, 170; Exod. 20:17 LXX). Lust is strong desire of any sort, but in the NT it is more commonly used of evil passions than of good desires (Morris). Prep. in compound is directive. ◆ **7 εἰδωλολάτρης** (# 1629) one who worships and serves an idol, w. γίνομαι, to take part in idol worship (BAGD). **γίνεσθε** pres. imp. mid. (dep.) γίνομαι (# 1181) s.v. 6. Pres. imp. w. the neg. **μηδέ** (# 3593) is often used to stop an action in progress–"do not continue" (MKG, 272f)–or it forbids general conduct. **γέγραπται** perf. ind. pass. γράφω (# 1211) to write. The term in perf. was used of authoritative documents, "it standing written" (MM). **ἐκάθισεν** aor. ind. act. καθίζω (# 2767) to take one's seat, to sit. **φαγεῖν** aor. act. inf. ἐσθίω (# 2266) to eat. **πεῖν** aor. act. inf. πίνω (# 4403) to drink. The infs. express purp. **ἀνέστησαν** aor. ind. act. ἀνίστημι (# 482) to rise up, to get up. **παίζειν** pres. act. inf. παίζω (# 4089) to play, to amuse oneself, to dance. In this context it has strong overtones of sexual play (Fee; Kistemaker; Schrage). This activity, as well as the eating and drinking, were considered by the rabbis to be committing idolatry (SB, 3:410). ◆ **8 πορνεύωμεν** pres. subj. act. πορνεύω (# 4519) to engage in unlawful sexual acts, to commit fornication. Hortatory subj. ("let us not"). **ἐπόρνευσαν** aor. ind. act. πορνεύω (# 4519). **ἔπεσαν** aor. ind. act. πίπτω (# 4406) to fall. **μιᾷ ἡμέρᾳ** (# 1651; 2465) in one day. Dat. of time, indicating the period during which an action takes place. **εἴκοσι τρεῖς χιλιάδες** (# 1633; 5552; 5943) twenty-three thousand. ◆ **9 ἐκπειράζωμεν** pres. subj. act. ἐκπειράζω (# 1733) to try, to put to the test (s. Matt. 4:1). Prep. in compound is perfective and might suggest the daring of the act or an effort to put to a decisive test (MH, 309). Hortatory subj. **ἐπείρασαν** aor. ind. act. πειράζω (# 4279) to tempt. **ὄφεων** gen. pl. ὄφις (# 4058) snake. **ἀπώλλυντο** impf. ind. mid./pass. ἀπόλλυμι (# 660) to be destroyed, to perish. Impf. pictures the continual and repeated action, "they continue to perish day by day" (RWP). ◆ **10 γογγύζετε** pres. imp. act. γογγύζω (# 1197) to murmur, to mutter, to complain, to give audible expression to unwarranted dissatisfaction (Lenski; GELTS, 92). It contains the idea of God's judgment and condemnation of man who instead of giving God thanks and showing obedience sets himself up as a judge over God (TDNT; EDNT; Schrage). **καθάπερ** (# 2749) just as. **ἐγόγγυσαν** aor. ind. act. (# 1197). **καί** (# 2779) and, w. the result that (Barrett). **ἀπώλοντο** aor. ind. mid. (dep.) ἀπόλλυμι (# 660) to be destroyed. **ὀλοθρευτής** (# 3904) one who destroys, the destroyer. Perhaps a reference to the angel of destruction whom the rabbis called Mashhith (SB, 3:412-16; Jastrow, 2:851; DDD, 456-63; s. Exod. 12:23; TDNT). ◆ **11 τυπικῶς** (# 5595) adv., typically (s.v. 6; Schrage). **συνέβαινεν** impf. ind. act. συμβαίνω (# 5201) to happen, w. dat., which indicates to whom the events happened. Impf.

pictures the enumerated events in the process of happening; the sing. sums them up as one series (RP). **ἐγράφη** aor. ind. pass. γράφω (# 1211) s.v. 7. **νουθεσία** (# 3804) admonition, warning, instruction (TDNT; TLNT; EDNT; for the use in Jos. s. CCFJ, 3:157). **τὰ τέλη τῶν αἰώνων** (# 5465; 172) the ends of the ages. In Jewish writing the term means the beginning of redemption or the time of the Messiah's appearing or "the end," in general (SB, 3:416; Schrage). For the apparently general use of the term in the DSS s. 1 QS 4:16f. Paul believes he and his correspondents are living in the last days of world history before the breaking in of the Messianic Age (Barrett). **κατήντηκεν** perf. ind. act. καταντάω (# 2910) to come down to a meeting, to arrive at a goal, to come to. The word appears in the papyri as a t.t. for the inheritance that comes to an heir (TDNT; BAGD; MM). ◆ **12 ὥστε** (# 6063) therefore, thus then. It indicates that this exhortation to watchfulness is the inference to be drawn from the foregoing examples (Godet). **δοκῶν** pres. act. part. δοκέω (# 1506) to seem, to be of the opinion, to think, w. inf. Part. as subst., "the one who thinks." **ἑστάναι** perf. act. inf. ἵστημι (# 2705) to stand. **βλεπέτω** pres. imp. act. βλέπω (# 1063) to see, to beware. Pres. imp. indicates the necessity of continual watchfulness. **πέσῃ** aor. subj. act. πίπτω (# 4406) to fall; here, perhaps to fall into sin (Weiss). Subj. w. **μή** (# 3590) lest, in a neg. purp. or result cl. ◆ **13 πειρασμός** (# 4279) testing, trying, temptation. The vb. came to signify intentional trying w. the purpose of discovering what of good and evil, or power or weakness, was in a person or thing (Trench, *Synonyms*, 280; TLNT). **εἴληφεν** perf. ind. act. λαμβάνω (# 3284) to take, overtake, w. the emphasis here on its lying outside their willing or doing (Fee). The words imply that there was a certain temptation which had captured the Corinthians and which subdued them (Grosheide). **εἰ μή** (# 1623; 3590) except. **ἀνθρώπινος** (# 474) human, that which is according to human strength, bearable (Weiss; BAGD). The suf. signifies material or kind (MH, 359). **ἐάσει** fut. ind. act. ἐάω (# 1572) to allow, w. inf. and the subject of the inf. in the acc. **πειρασθῆναι** aor. pass. inf. πειράζω (# 4279) to test, to tempt, to try (TLNT). Pass. indicates that the temptation is from without. **ὑπέρ** (# 5642) w. acc., above, beyond. **ὅ** (# 4005) who, which. Rel. pron. which includes the unexpressed demonstrative pron. "Beyond that which" (BD, 154). **δύνασθε** pres. ind. pass. (dep.) δύναμαι (# 1538) to be able. **ποιήσει** fut. ind. act. ποιέω (# 4472) to do, to make. **σύν** (# 5250) w. dat., with, in connection w. It ties the two together, w. the temptation there is also the escape (Schrage). **ἔκβασις** (# 1676) a way out, escape (LS, 501; BAGD). In the papyri it has the meaning "end," "completion" (MM; Preisigke, 1:438; GELTS, 133). **δύνασθαι** pres. pass. (dep.) inf. δύναμαι (# 1538) to be able. **ὑπενεγκεῖν** aor. act. inf. ὑποφέρω (# 5722) to carry under, to bear, to endure. ◆ **14**

διόπερ (# *1478*) wherefore, for which very reason, "the conclusion of this" (Barrett; DM, 245; Blomqvist, 136f). **ἀγαπητοί** (# *28*) voc. pl. one who is loved, w. subject gen., "ones loved by me." The designation suggests that Paul's concern is motivated by genuine interest in them. **φεύγετε** pres. act. imp. φεύγω (# *5771*) to flee, to run from. Pres. imp. calls for a constant way of life. ◆ **15 φρόνιμος** (# *5861*) wise, understanding, sensible, the ability to make a decision, understanding resulting from insight and wisdom (TDNT; LN, 1:384). Indir. obj. **κρίνατε** aor. imp. act. κρίνω (# *3212*) to judge. **ὑμεῖς** (# *5148*) you yourself. ◆ **16 ποτήριον** (# *4539*) cup; the cup of blessing was a technical Jewish term used for the cup of wine drunk at the end of a meal. The most honored guest at the table took the cup, lifted it up, and said the benediction (Barrett; SB, 4:627ff; D. Cohn-Sherbok, "A Jewish Note on ΤΟ ΠΟΤΗΡΙΟΝ ΤΗΣ ΕΥΛΟΓΙΑΣ," *NTS* 27 [1981]: 704-709; Phillip Sigal, "Another Note to 1 Corinthians 10.16," *NTS* 29 [1983]: 134-39). **εὐλογοῦμεν** pres. ind. act. εὐλογέω (# *2328*) to bless. Pres. views the general Christian practice without going into details (RP). **οὐχί** (# *4049*) introduces a question expecting the answer "yes." **κοινωνία** (# *3126*) fellowship, to have in common w. someone, common participation (Barrett; NIDNTT, 1:639-44; RAC, 9:110-45; TDNT; esp. IMC, 167-212). **αἵματος τοῦ Χριστοῦ** gen. sing. (# *135; 3836; 5986*) obj. gen., "a participation in the blood of Christ," "participation in Christ's death"; that is, "committal to him who died for us" (RWP; IMC, 207). **τὸν ἄρτον** acc. sing. ἄρτος (# *788*) bread. Acc. by inverse attraction to the rel. pron. (BD, 154; RG, 717f). **κλῶμεν** pres. ind. act. κλάω (# *3089*) to break. Iterat. pres. referring to a repeated action. **σώματος τοῦ Χριστοῦ** (# *5393; 3638; 5986*) the body of Christ. A reference to the church as the body of Christ and the fellowship among believers (Lietzmann). The fellowship means the relationship established among members of a covenant and the obligations ensuing from it (IMC, 209). ◆ **17 ὅτι** (# *4022*) because. **οἱ πάντες** (# *4246*) the all; "we the whole, the whole number." These words are in apposition to the subject (RWP). **μετέχομεν** pres. ind. act. μετέχω (# *3576*) to share w., to be partners in. ◆ **18 κατὰ σάρκα** (# *2848; 4922*) according to the flesh; a reference to historical Israel (Conzelmann). **οὐχ** (# *4024*) introduces a question expecting a positive answer. **ἐσθίοντες** pres. act. part. ἐσθίω (# *2266*) to eat. Part. as subst. **θυσία** (# *2602*) sacrifice. **θυσιαστηρίου** gen. sing. θυσιαστήριον (# *2603*) altar, place of sacrifice. Obj. gen.; that is, joint participation in the sacrifice and the accompanying rites (IMC, 184-88, esp. 187). ◆ **19 οὖν** (# *4036*) then. It draws a consequence from v. 18 (Schrage). **εἰδωλόθυτον** (# *1628*) that which is sacrificed to an idol (s. 8:1). **τί** (# *5516*) anything, anything at all; that is, a real sacrifice (IMC, 189). ◆ **20 ἅ** pl. ὅς (# *4005*) who, which. Rel. pron. including the demonstrative pron. which is not expressed (s.v. 13). **δαιμονίοις** dat. pl. δαιμόνιον (# *1228*) demon. Dat. of advantage, "to demons." Heathen sacrifices were sacrifices to demons (TDNT; SB, 3:51-53; RAC, 9:546-797; NW 2, i:335-36). **γίνεσθαι** pres. mid. (dep.) inf. γίνομαι (# *1181*) to become (s.v. 6). Inf. completes the vb., "I do not want you to become partners with demons." This would involve becoming one with demons as well as giving tacit recognition of supernatural powers which are opposed to God (IMC, 191-92). ◆ **21 δύνασθε** pres. ind. pass. (dep.) δύναμαι (# *1538*) to be able to; "you are not able." Gnomic pres. emphasizes that which is always true. **ποτήριον** (# *4539*) cup, the common meal and the common drinking of the heathen created a close and meaningful relationship between the human partners and the god to whom they ate and drank. This was especially true when they drank from a common cup (RAC 2:41). **πίνειν** pres. act. inf. πίνω (# *4403*) to drink (s.v. 7). **τραπέζης** gen. sing. τράπεζα (# *5544*) table indicating a common meal (IMC, 15-17; s. 8:1). Gen. after a vb. of sharing. ◆ **22 ἤ** (# *2445*) or. **παραζηλοῦμεν** pres. ind. act. παραζηλόω (# *4143*) to provoke to jealousy, to cause one to be jealous (s. Deut 32:21). For the prep. compound s. MH 320. **μή** (# *3590*) introduces a question which expects the answer "no." **ἰσχυρότεροι** comp. ἰσχυρός (# *2708*) strong; comp., stronger, w. gen. **αὐτοῦ** (# *899*) as gen. of comparison, "stronger than he (is)." ◆ **23 ἔξεστιν** (# *2003*) pres. ind. act.; impersonal, it is lawful, it is allowed. **συμφέρει** pres. ind. act. (# *5237*) συμφέρω to bring together, to help, to confer a benefit, to be advantageous, profitable, or useful (BAGD). Gnomic pres. indicating that which is always true. **οἰκοδομεῖ** pres. ind. act. οἰκοδομέω (# *3868*) to build up, to edify. It means to cause to advance spiritually (Grosheide). ◆ **24 μηδείς** (# *3594*) no one. **τὸ ἑαυτοῦ** (# *1571*) the thing of himself, that which is his own, his own ends (Barrett). **ζητείτω** pres. imp. act. ζητέω (# *2426*) to seek. Pres. points to a habitual action. ◆ **25 μάκελλον** (# *3425*) stall or shop on the market-place where meat and other foods were sold. Because of the nearness to the temple, it was possible that some of the meat in the marketplace had been sacrificial offerings (Lietzmann; TDNT; H.J. Cadbury, "The *Macellum* of Corinth," *JBL* 53 [1934]: 134-41; C. K. Barrett, "Things Sacrificed to Idols," *NTS* 11 [1965]: 144; Schrage; SPC, 32, 37; BBC). **πωλούμενον** pres. pass. part. (adj.) πωλέω (# *4797*) to sell. A middle to lower class household in Corinth buying its supplies in the *macellum* would often make purchases that had no connection w. idolatry (Barrett, *NTS* 11 [1965]: 146). **ἐσθίετε** pres. imp. act. ἐσθίω (# *2266*) to eat. Imp. of permission, "you may eat" (RG, 948). For a discussion of Plutarch's arguments against eating meat s. PTW, 301-16. **ἀνακρίνοντες** pres. act. part. (circum.) ἀνακρίνω (# *373*) to examine, to make inquiry. The word was used in a judicial sense of conducting a hearing or investigation (BAGD). Jews were only allowed to buy meat from the Gentiles if it could be established that it was not meat offered to idols (SB, 3:420-21). **συνείδησις** (# 5287) conscience (s. Rom. 2:15; PAT, 416-20). ◆ **26 τοῦ κυρίου** (# 3261) belongs to the Lord. Emphatic by its position. **πλήρωμα** (# 4445) fullness, the total content. ◆ **27 εἰ** (# 1623) if. It views the possibility as a reality. **καλεῖ** pres. ind. act. καλέω (# 2813) to call, to invite. Christians were evidently frequently invited to dinners by the unbelievers and some of these dinners may have been connected w. heathen gods. (For a study of such invitations w. examples, s. Chan-Hie Kim, "The Papyrus Invitation," *JBL* 94 [1975]: 391-402; IMC, 39-45). **πορεύεσθαι** pres. mid. (dep.) inf. πορεύομαι (# 4513) to go. Inf. w. vb. **παρατιθέμενον** pres. pass. part. (adj.) παρατίθημι (# 4192) to place before, here in the sense to "serve." The unbeliever places the meat before the believer. ◆ **28 εἴπῃ** aor. subj. act. λέγω (# 3306) to say. Subj. w. **ἐάν** (# 351) in a 3rd. class cond. cl. in which the cond. is viewed as possible. **ἱερόθυτον** (# 2638) that which is sacrificed in a temple. It is different from the word in chapter 8:1; 10:19 and more appropriate on pagan lips or in pagan company (Bruce). **ἐσθίετε** pres. imp. act. ἐσθίω (# 2266) to eat. **μηνύσαντα** aor. act. part. μηνύω (# 3606) to make known, to give information, to reveal. The word implies private communication (Fee). Part. as subst. ◆ **29 τὴν ἑαυτοῦ** (# 1571) his own. **ἱνατί** (# 2672) why. **κρίνεται** pres. ind. pass. κρίνω (# 3212) to judge; pass., to be judged, to be exposed to judgment (Barrett). ◆ **30 χάριτι** dat. sing. χάρις (# 5921) grace, thanksgiving. Dat. of manner: "w. thanks," "w. thanksgiving" (BD, 106). The word "grace" not only meant the gift which was given, but the thanks which was expressed for the gift (TDNT). **μετέχω** (# 3576) pres. ind. act. to partake. Ind. in a 1st. class cond. cl. in which the cond. is assumed as actual. **βλασφημοῦμαι** pres. ind. pass. βλασφημέω (# 1059) to slander, to defame, to injure the reputation of someone (BAGD; TLNT). **οὗ** gen. ὅς (# 4005) "that which," rel. pron. used including the idea of the demonstrative pron. ◆ **31 ποιεῖτε** pres. ind./imp. act. ποιέω (# 4472) to do. The first form, **ποιεῖτε**, is pres. ind. act. The second **ποιεῖτε**, is pres. imp. and points to a habitual action. ◆ **32 ἀπρόσκοπος** (# 718) without offense, without causing others to stumble (RP). Used in the papyri in the sense of "free from hurt or harm" (MM) and "not causing injury" (Preisigke). **Ἰουδαίοις** dat. pl. Ἰουδαῖος (# 2681) Jew (s. Malcolm Love, "Who Were the IOUDAIOI?," *NovT* 18 [1976]: 101-30). Dat. of disadvantage. **γίνεσθε** pres. imp. mid. (dep.) γίνομαι (# 1181) to become. **ἐκκλησία** (# 1711) dat. sing. church. Dat. of disadvantage. ◆ **33 πάντα** acc. pl. πᾶς (# 4246) all. Acc. of general reference. **σωθῶσιν** aor. subj. pass. σῴζω (# 5392) to rescue, to save. Subj. w. **ἵνα** (# 2671) in a purp. cl.

1 Corinthians 11

◆ **1 μιμηταί** nom. pl. μιμητής (# 3629) imitator, one who mimics another; w. obj. gen. indicating who is to be imitated (DPL, 428-31). It is from the vb. μιμέομαι to imitate, to mimic. The ending of the noun indicates the agent who performs an action (MH, 365). Pred. nom. **γίνεσθε** pres. imp. mid. (dep.) γίνομαι (# 1181) to become, to be. Pres. imp. calls for an habitual conduct. **Χριστοῦ** gen. sing. Χριστος (# 5986) Christ. Obj. gen. Paul's appeal to the character of Jesus of Nazareth shows Paul's interest in the earthly life of Christ (JNP, 109). ◆ **2 ἐπαινῶ** pres. ind. act. ἐπαινάω (# 2046) to praise. **πάντα** acc. pl. πᾶς (# 4246) all. Acc. of reference, "in respect to all things. **μέμνησθε** perf. ind. mid. (dep.) μιμνήσκομαι (# 3630) to remember, w. obj. in gen. Perf. indicates that the Corinthians remembered continually (Grosheide). **παρέδωκα** aor. ind. act. παραδίδωμι (# 4140) to deliver over, to pass on. Often used in the sense of a teacher passing on material which he has (TDNT; TLNT; NIDNTT, 3:772-74; EDNT; DPL, 569-75, 989-90). **παράδοσις** (# 4142) tradition, that which is passed on. **κατέχετε** pres. ind. act. κατέχω (# 2988) to hold down, to hold fast, to possess (MM). ◆ **3 εἰδέναι** perf. act. inf. οἶδα (# 3857) to know. Def. perf. w. pres. meaning. Inf. completing the vb. θέλω (# 2527) pres. ind. act., I desire. **κεφαλή** (# 3051) head; in its metaphorical sense it may apply to the outstanding and determining part of a whole, but also to origin. Paul does not say that the man is the Lord of the woman; he says that he is the origin of her being (Barrett; TDNT; H. Wayne House, "Should a Woman Prophesy or Preach before Men?" *Bib Sac* 145 [1988]: 145-48; DPL, 375-77). Paul uses the word to set forth the hierarchical, social structure in God's economy (Bruce K. Waltke, "1 Corinthians 11:2-16: An Interpretation," *Bib Sac* 135 [1978]: 46-57, esp. 48). For a discussion of this passage s. Craig S. Keener, *Paul, Women and Wives* (Peabody, Mass.: Hendrikson, 1992), 19-100. ◆ **4 προσευχόμενος** pres. mid. (dep.) part. (adj.) προσεύχομαι (# 4662) to pray. **προφητεύων** pres. act. part. προφητεύω (# 4736) to speak for someone, to prophecy. **κατὰ κεφαλῆς** (# 2848; 3051) down from the head; that is, a head covering or veil hanging down from the head (Richard E. Oster, "When Men Wore Veils to Worship: The Historical Context of I Corinthians 11.4," *NTS* 34 [1988]: 486; RG, 606f; MT, 268). Some feel that Paul is not referring to a head covering as such, but rather to the wearing of long, loose flowing hair, which may have been the indication of a homosexual (Schrage). **ἔχων** pres. act. part. (adj.) ἔχω (# 2400) to have. **καταισχύνει** pres. ind. act. καταισχύνω (# 2875) to put to shame, to disgrace. Since the Christian man reflects the glory of Christ, were he to wear a veil concealing his head he would rob his own head of its chief function of reflecting the glory of Christ (Barrett). It was common for Roman men to wear their heads covered while performing religious duties. Numerous references by various writers attest to this, as well as statues, pictures, coins, etc. (Richard E. Oster, *NTS* 34 [1988]: 481-505; Richard E. Oster, "Use, Misuse and Neglect of Archaeological Evidence," *ZNW* 83 [1992]: 67-69; D.W.J. Gill, "The Importance of Roman Portraiture for Head-coverings in 1 Corinthians 11,2-16," *TB* 42 [1990]: 245-60; Cynthia L. Thompson, "Hairstyles, Head-coverings, and St. Paul: Portraits from Corinth," *BA* 51 [1988]: 99-115; NW, 2, i:340-43; Plutarch, "The Roman Questions," *Moralia*, 266 C-F). For the Jewish custom of men praying w. uncovered heads s. SB, 3:423-26. ◆ **5 προσευχομένη** pres. mid. (dep.) part. (adj.) προσεύχομαι (# 4662) to pray. **ἀκατακαλύπτῳ** dat. sing. ἀκατακάλυπτος (# 184) uncovered. For a Jewish woman to appear outside of the house w. an uncovered head was shameful and her husband could divorce her (SB, 3:427). The Jewish sense of a woman's head covering indicated the special hairstyle she was to wear–plaited hair held together w. bands and coverings (SB, 3:427-35). The women of Tarsus were to have their face covered when they appeared on the street. This was an old custom retained in Tarsus (DC, 33:48). It may be a reference to women wearing long, unkempt, flowing hair, as pagan women often did during the frenzied worship of some of the gods (Schrage; William J. Martin, "1 Corinthians 11:2-16: An Interpretation," AHG, 231-41). In the worship of the Greek deity Desponia, the women were not to have their hair braided, nor the men their head covered (NDIEC, 4:109-18). Dat. of manner. **ἓν γάρ ἐστιν καὶ τὸ αὐτό** "for it is one and the same thing" (RWP). **ἐξυρημένη** perf. pass. part. (adj.) ξυράω (# 3834) to shave. For the Jews a woman w. a shaved head was particularly ugly; a shaved head was a sign of adultery (SB, 3:434; Philo, *The Special Laws*, 3:36). In Cyprus a woman guilty of adultery was considered a harlot and her hair was cut off (DC, 64:3). A woman w. a shaved head was also the sign of mourning (DC, 64:16; *The Syrian Goddess*, 6; Barrett). Perf. indicates the state or condition. ◆ **6 κατακαλύπτεται** pres. ind. mid. κατακαλύπτω (# 2877) to cover oneself; mid., to cover oneself w. a veil. It may mean, "to have the head covered w. hair" (Schrage). Pres. expresses a general principle. Ind. in a 1st. class cond. cl. which assumes the reality of the cond. **κειράσθω** aor. imp. mid. κείρω (# 3025) to shear, to cut w. scissors (Lietzmann). Perhaps Paul in using sarcasm to indicate that when a woman will not wear a decent hairstyle, let her cut off all of her hair (Schrage). **αἰσχρός** (# 156) shame, disgrace, w. dat. of disadvantage, **γυναικί** dat. sing. γυνή (# 1222) woman. **κείρασθαι** aor. mid. (dep.) inf. κείρω (# 3025) Inf. w. the article is used as the subject of the cl. (Funk, 657). **ξυρᾶσθαι** pres. mid. inf. ξυράω (# 3834) to shave, to cut w. a razor (s.v. 5; Lietzmann; BAGD; MM). **κατακα-**

λυπτέσθω pres. imp. pass. κατακαλύπτω (# 2877) to cover. Pres. imp. indicates a general command. ◆ **7 ὀφείλει** pres. ind. act. ὀφείλω (# 4053) to be obligated to. "One ought to," "one is obligated to," w. inf. The word indicates moral obligation. **κατακαλύπτεσθαι** pres. mid. inf. κατακαλύπτω (# 2877) to cover. **εἰκών** (# 1635) image. **δόξα** (# 1518) glory. **ὑπάρχων** pres. act. part. (causal) ὑπάρχω (# 5639) to exist, to be. ◆ **8 γυναικός** gen. sing. γυνή (# 1222) s.v. 6 **ἀνδρός** gen. sing. ἀνήρ (# 467) male, man. ◆ **9 καὶ γάρ** for even, yes, even (BD, 236). **ἐκτίσθη** aor. ind. pass. κτίζω (# 3231) to create. **γυναῖκα** acc. sing. s.v. 8. **ἄνδρα** acc. sing. (s.v. 8). ◆ **10 ἐξουσίαν** (# 2026) authority, the right to perform an act. The covered head is the woman's authority to pray and worship since it shows her belonging and obedient to her husband (Schlatter; M.D. Hooker, "Authority on Her Head: An Examination of First Corinthians 11:10," *NTS* 10 [1964]: 410-16; DPL, 584-86). The statement may mean that the authority of the Corinthian woman was that she should wear a fitting hairstyle (Schrage). **ἔχειν** pres. act. inf. ἔχω (# 2400) to have. Inf. complementary to the vb. **ἐπὶ τῆς κεφαλῆς** (# 3051) upon her head. It is unclear whether this is to be understood in a literal or fig. sense. **διὰ τοὺς ἀγγέλους** (# 1328; 34) "because of the angels." Angels were considered to be the guardians of the order of creation (Hooker, *NTS* 10:412f; DPL, 20-21), and present at worship services (Schlatter). The misconduct of the women would be taken as a sign of rebellion (H. Wayne House, "Should a Woman Prophesy or Preach Before Men?" *Bib Sac* 145 [1988]: 158; Schrage). For Qumran parallels to angels being present at a worship service and the interpretation that the lack of covering for a woman signified a physical defect which excluded one from worship s. Fitzmyer, *Essays*, 187-204. ◆ **11 πλήν** (# 4440) however, nevertheless, in any case. It is used in an adversative and modifying sense to conclude a discussion and emphasize what is essential (BD, 234; Blomqvist, 82f). **χωρίς** (# 6006) w. gen., without, separated from. **ἐν κυρίῳ** (# 1877; 3261) in the Lord, or perhaps, in the Lord's intention; that is, that of the original creation and its restoration (Barrett). ◆ **12 διά** (# 1328) w. gen., through. **ἐκ τοῦ θεοῦ** (# 2536) from, out of God. The man is the woman's initial cause, she is his instrumental cause, but both owe their origin to God (RP). ◆ **13 κρίνατε** aor. imp. act. κρίνω (# 3212) to judge, to decide. **πρέπον** pres. act. part. nom. sing. πρέπω (# 4560) that which is fitting to the circumstances, that which is proper; followed by the acc. w. the inf. **ἀκατακάλυπτον** (# 184) uncovered (s.v. 5). **προσεύχεσθαι** pres. mid. (dep.) inf. προσεύχομαι (# 4667) to pray. ◆ **14 οὐδέ** (# 4028) used to introduce a question expecting a positive answer (RWP). **ἡ φύσις αὐτή** (# 3836; 5882; 899) nature herself. **κομᾷ** pres. subj. act. κομάω (# 3150) to have long hair, to let one's hair grow long. Subj. w. **ἐάν**

(# 1569) in a 3rd. class cond. cl. which assumes the possibility of the cond. ἀτιμία (# 871) dishonor. Jewish men wore middle length hair which was usually well-groomed (SB, 3:440-42). Sometimes long hair was associated w. homosexuality (Wiess; Philo, *The Special Laws*, 3:37), but long hair was not uncommon for philosophers, farmers, barbarians, etc. (DC, 35:11). ◆ **15 δόξα** (# 1518) glory, that which brings praise or honor (TLNT). **αὐτῇ** dat. sing. αὐτός (# 899) self, (her); dat. of advantage. **κόμη** (# 3151) long hair, the hairdo neatly held in place by means of ribbon or lace. What is required by these verses is an orderly hairdress which distinguishes a woman from a man (Grosheide; for pictures and a discussion of women's hairstyle s. Cynthia L. Thompson, "Hairstyles, Head-coverings, and St. Paul: Portraits from Corinth," *BA* 51 [1988]: 99-115). **ἀντί** (# 505) w. gen., instead of. **περιβολαίου** (# 4316) that which is thrown about, a wrap, a covering. Her hair is the covering (Schrage). **δέδοται** perf. ind. pass. δίδωμι (# 1443) to give. Perf. indicates the abiding state or condition. Perhaps the pass. is a theol. pass. ◆ **16 δοκεῖ** pres. ind. act. δοκέω (# 1506) to seem to be, to seem, to intend to be. Ind. in a 1st. class cond. cl. which views the cond. as true. **φιλόνεικος** (# 5809) strife-loving, contentious, quarrelsome. **εἶναι** pres. act. inf. εἰμί (# 1639) to be. Compl. inf. w. the vb. **συνήθεια** (# 5311) custom, habit, usage. He means we have no such custom such as women praying or prophesying w. head uncovered (Morris). ◆ **17 παραγγέλλων** pres. act. part. (temp.) παραγγέλλω (# 4133) to transmit a message along from one to another, to declare, to order, to charge. Used especially of the order of the military commander which is passed along the line by his subordinates (T, 343). Pres. indicating contemporaneous time, "in giving this charge." **ἐπαινῶ** pres. ind. act. ἐπαινέω (# 2046) to praise. **κρεῖσσον** (# 3202) comp. of ἀγαθός (# 19) good; comp., more prominent, preferable, more advantageous, better. **ἧσσον** (# 2482) functions as a comp. of κακός inferior, weaker, lesser, for the worse. For both of these words s. BAGD. **συνέρχεσθε** pres. ind. mid. (dep.) συνέρχομαι (# 5302) to come together. ◆ **18 πρῶτον μὲν** (# 4754; 3525) first of all, in the first place. It is not formally caught up by such a companion phrase as "in the next place," unless we so regard v. 34b (Bruce). **συνερχομένων** pres. mid. (dep.) part. συνέρχομαι (# 5302) to come together. Gen. abs. temp. part., "when you come together." The Corinthians came together in the various homes of the believers (SPC, 153-67; BBC; Bradley Blue, "Acts and the House Church," BAFS, 119-222). **σχίσμα** (# 5388) division (s. 1:10). **ὑπάρχειν** pres. act. inf. ὑπάρχω (# 5639) to exist, to be. Inf. in indir. discourse. **μέρος τι** (# 3538; 5516) partly. Acc. of extent, "to some part" (RWP). ◆ **19 δεῖ** pres. ind. act. δεῖ (# 1256) impersonal w. inf., it is necessary to, expressing logical necessity.

γὰρ καί for also, for precisely (Kistemaker). **αἵρεσις** (# 146) division, different opinion (MM). **εἶναι** pres. act. inf. εἰμί (# 1639) to be. **δόκιμος** (# 1511) that which is approved after examination, genuine, tested. approved (BS, 259-62; TDNT; TLNT). **φανερός** (# 5745) open to sight, visible, w. reference to outward appearance, manifest as opposed to concealed (AS, 104). Pred. nom. **γένωνται** aor. subj. mid. (dep.) γίνομαι (# 1181) to become. Subj. w. **ἵνα** (# 2671) expressing purp. Divisions are not good, but they are inevitable and show those who are truly Christ's (Fee). ◆ **20 συνερχομένων** pres. mid. (dep.) part. συνέρχομαι (# 5302) to come together. Gen. abs. **οὖν** (# 4036) therefore, then, now. The word indicates the continuation of the subject from one thought to another or the introduction of a new phase of thought (DM, 253). **τὸ αὐτό** (# 899) the same; here, "the same place." **κυριακός** (# 3258) belonging to the Lord. The word was used in the papyri in the sense of "belonging to Caesar" or "imperial" (Deissmann; BS, 217-19; LAE, 362f; TDNT; DPL, 578-79; Rev. 1:10). **δεῖπνον** (# 1270) dinner, the main meal. For the meal of the Greeks and the Romans s. Bengel; Lietzmann; LLAR, 35-53; PLR, 1:297-340. **φαγεῖν** aor. act. inf. ἐσθίω (# 2266) to eat. Inf. of purp. ◆ **21 ἕκαστος** (# 1667) each, each one for himself. It was not the Lord who was determining the celebration, but the individual (Conzelmann). **προλαμβάνει** pres. ind. act. προλαμβάνω (# 4624) to take before. Prep. here is temp., "each one takes it before others have theirs" (Barrett). For the examples in the papyri and the suggested weakening of the prep. in compound s. MM. **φαγεῖν** aor. act. inf. ἐσθίω (# 2266) to eat. Inf. w. prep. **ἐν** (# 1877) to indicate the area in which some were going ahead of others. They took what they had brought along and did not permit others, the poor, to eat from their portion (Grosheide). **ὃς μὲν … ὃς δέ** the one, the other. **πεινᾷ** pres. ind. act. πεινάω (# 4277) to be hungry. **μεθύει** pres. ind. act. μεθύω (# 3501) to be drunk. Pres. vividly points out the action that was in progress. It could also point to a habitual or repeated action. For a description of the common meal associated w. the Lord's Supper s. IDB, 2:53-54; DPL, 569-75, esp. 571-73; ABD, 1:90-91; 4:362-72. ◆ **22 μή** (# 3590) used in a question expecting the answer "no"; "it is certainly not that you do not have houses, is it?" **ἐσθίειν** pres. act. inf. ἐσθίω (# 2266) to eat. **πίνειν** pres. act. inf. πίνω (# 4403) to drink. Inf. w. prep. **εἰς** (# 1650) to express purp.; "for eating and drinking." At a Roman banquet, which was a three course meal, different qualities of food and drink were served to the different grades of guests, and the drinking sessions followed the meal (LLAR, 42-50). **καταφρονεῖτε** pres. ind. act. καταφρονέω (# 2969) to think down upon, to despise, w. obj. in gen. **καταισχύνετε** pres. ind. act. καταισχύνω (# 2875) to put to shame. Pres. could be conative, "Are you trying to put to shame?" (Barrett).

ἔχοντας pres. act. part. ἔχω (# 2400) to have. Adj. part. as a noun, "those who do not have." εἴπω aor. subj. act. λέγω (# 3306) to say. Deliberative subj., "what shall I say?" "what should I say?" ἐπαινέσω fut. ind. act. or aor. subj. act. ἐπαινέω (# 2046) to praise. For the struggle between the rich and poor and the social problems at the Lord's Supper in Corinth s. G. Theissen, "Soziale Integration und sakramentales Handeln," *NovT* 16 [1974]: 179-206. ◆ **23** ἐγώ (# 1609) I Strongly emphasized and stands in contrast to those at Corinth. παρέλαβον aor. ind. act. παραλαμβάνω (# 4161) to receive. The word corresponds to the t.t. in the rabbinical literature, *quibbel*, meaning to receive tradition which has been passed on (PRJ, 248; SB, 3:444). ἀπό (# 608) from. The prep. can indicate that Paul did not receive his information directly by revelation (Grosheide). It may be, however, that he received the interpretation of the information from the Lord (Barrett). παρέδωκα aor. ind. act. παραδίδωμι (# 4140) to pass on, to hand down to (TDNT; TLNT). The word corresponds to the rabbinical t.t. *masar* indicating the passing down of tradition. The words mean the chain of hist. tradition that Paul received goes back unbroken to the words of Jesus himself (Ladd, 389; for the use of *masar* in the DSS s. CD 3:3). ὅτι (# 4022) that. Introduces the content of that which was received. παρεδίδετο impf. ind. pass. παραδίδωμι (# 4140) to deliver over, to betray. Impf. implies that this betrayal was at that time still going on (Grosheide). ἔλαβεν aor. ind. act. λαμβάνω (# 3284) to take, to receive. ◆ **24** εὐχαριστήσας aor. act. part. εὐχαριστέω (# 2373) to give thanks. Temp. part., "after he had given thanks." ἔκλασεν aor. ind. act. κλάω (# 3089) to break. μού (# 1609) my. Strongly emphasized by its position. τὸ ὑπὲρ ὑμῶν which was (given) on behalf of you. The word to be supplied here is "given" (s. Luke 22:19). ποιεῖτε pres. imp. act. ποιέω (# 4472) to do. Pres. imp. emphasizes the repeated action. ἀνάμνησις (# 390) memorial, remembrance. The word indicates to call back again into memory a vivid experience (TDNT; CCFJ, 1:103-04; A.R. Millard, "Covenant and Communion in First Corinthians," AHG, 242-48, esp. 245-47). The object of recalling to memory is expressed by the obj. use of the poss. adj. (BD, 149). Paul's words mean that the Supper of the Lord was initiated to remind the disciples of the Lord of the work he had done (A.R. Millard, "Covenant and Communion in First Corinthians," 247). ◆ **25** ὡσαύτως (# 6058) likewise, in the same manner. ποτήριον (# 4539) cup. For the cup of blessing which the honored guest lifted up and the benediction, s. SB, 4: 630f; TDNT. δειπνῆσαι aor. act. inf. δειπνέω (# 1268) to dine, to eat the main meal. Inf. w. prep. μετά (# 3552) expressing time: "after they had eaten." διαθήκη (# 1347) covenant, treaty (s. Matt. 26:28; for the covenant setting of the Lord's Supper s. A.R. Millard, "Covenant and Communion in First

Corinthians," AHG, 242-48). ἐν τῷ ἐμῷ αἵματι "in my blood." Blood indicates a life given up in death, which was the penalty for breaking the covenant (Cleon Rogers, "The Covenant with Moses and its Historical Setting," *JETS* 14 [1971]: 152). ὁσάκις (# 4006) as often as, used w. ἐάν w. the meaning, "every time." The usual construction for a general temp. cl. of repetition (RWP). πίνητε pres. subj. act. πίνω (# 4403) to drink. Subj. in an indef. temp. cl. ◆ **26** γάρ (# 1142) for. Introduces the apostle's explanation of the Lord's command (RP). ἐσθίητε pres. subj. act. ἐσθίω (# 2266) to eat. Subj. w. ἐάν (# 1569) in an indef. temp. cl. καταγγέλλετε pres. ind. act. (# 2859) to proclaim. It is used in the sense of making a solemn announcement by word of mouth (Barrett; NIDNTT, 3:44-48). Pres. indicates a repeated action. ἄχρις (# 948) until. οὗ (# 4005) when. ἔλθη aor. subj. act. ἔρχομαι (# 2262) to come. Subj. may have an affinity w. a final cl. (BD, 193), w. the idea "until the goal is reached, that is till he comes" (Otfried Hofius, "'Bis dass er kommt:' I Kor. XI. 26," *NTS* 14 [1968]: 439-41). ◆ **27** ὥστε (# 6063) wherefore, it follows. The word is used to draw a conclusion. ὃς ἄν (# 4005; 323) whoever. ἐσθίῃ pres. subj. act. ἐσθίω (# 2266) to eat. ἀναξίως (# 397) adv., unworthily, not in accordance w. their value, in an unworthy manner (Grosheide; Fee). ἔνοχος (# 1944) guilty of, guilty of violating (Hering). When the dat. is used it indicates a crime of which one is guilty; when the gen. is used it indicates against which or against whom the crime is committed (Weiss). ἔσται fut. ind. mid. (dep.) εἰμί (# 1639) to be. ◆ **28** δοκιμαζέτω pres. imp. act. 3rd. pers. sing. δοκιμάζω (# 1507) to examine, to approve after examination (TDNT; TLNT). Pres. imp. calls for a repeated action. ἄνθρωπος (# 476) person, one. Used in an indefinite and at the same time general sense—"one" (BAGD). ἐσθιέτω pres. imp. act. 3rd. pers. sing. s.v. 26. πινέτω pres. imp. act. 3rd. pers. sing. πίνω (# 4403) to drink. ◆ **29** ἐσθίων pres. act. part. ἐσθίω (# 2266) to eat. Part. as subst. πίνων pres. act. part. πίνω (# 4403) to drink. Part. as subst. κρίμα (# 3210) judgment. The suf. indicates the result of an action; that is, the result of making a decision (MH, 355). ἑαυτῷ dat. ἑαυτοῦ (# 1571) himself; reflex. pron. Dat. of disadvantage. διακρίνων pres. act. part. διακρίνω (# 1359) to judge between, to determine, to distinguish. Cond. or causal part. (RWP). It could also be part. of manner, giving the manner in which they eat or drink. ◆ **30** ἀσθενής (# 822) weak, sickly. Pred. nom. ἄρρωστος (# 779) powerless, feeble, ill. Pred. nom. Without the article the pred. nom. stresses the cond. κοιμῶνται pres. ind. pass. κοιμάω (# 3121) to fall asleep, to die. Pres. indicates either an action in progress or a repeated action. ἱκανός (# 2653) a sufficient number, a large amount, many. ◆ **31** διεκρίνομεν impf. ind. act. διακρίνω (# 1359) to judge between (s.v. 29). Impf. ind. w. εἰ in a 2nd. class cond. cl. in which the cond. is viewed as contrary to fact. **ἐκρινόμεθα** impf. ind. pass. κρίνω (# 3212) to judge; pass., to be judged. Impf. ind. w. **ἄν** (# 323) in a 2nd. class cond. cl. ◆ **32 κρινόμενοι** pres. pass. part. κρίνω (# 3212) to judge (s.v. 31). Cond. part., "if we are being judged," "when we are being judged." **παιδευόμεθα** pres. ind. pass. παιδεύω (# 4084) to discipline, to train a child through discipline. It includes every aspect of causing a young person to become a mature responsible adult. For this figure of speech and the training of children in the ancient world s. TDNT; RAC, 6:502-59. **κατακριθῶμεν** aor. subj. pass. κατακρίνω (# 2891) to condemn, to reach a verdict or decision against someone. Subj. w. **ἵνα** (# 2671) in a neg. purp. cl. ◆ **33 ὥστε** (# 6063) wherefore, so. The word draws a conclusion from the previous discussion. **συνερχόμενοι** pres. mid. (dep.) part. συνέρχομαι (# 5302) to come together. Temp. or cond. part. **φαγεῖν** aor. act. inf. ἐσθίω (# 2266) to eat. Articular inf. w. **εἰς** (# 1650) expressing purp. **ἐκδέχεσθε** pres. imp. mid. (dep.) ἐκδέχομαι (# 1683) to wait upon, to wait in turn (RWP). It is implied that a proper distribution of food should first be made, and then that all should eat together (Barrett). Pres. imp. calls for an habitual action. ◆ **34 πεινᾷ** pres. ind. act. πεινάω (# 4277) to eat. Ind. in a 1st. class cond. cl. in which the cond. is viewed as a reality. **ἐν οἴκῳ** (# 3875) at home. **ἐσθιέτω** pres. imp. act. ἐσθίω (# 2266) to eat. **συνέρχησθε** pres. subj. mid. (dep.) συνέρχομαι (# 5302) to come together. Subj. **ἵνα** (# 2671) in a neg. purp. cl. **ὡς ἄν** whenever (# 6055; 323). **ἔλθω** aor. subj. act. ἔρχομαι (# 2262) to come. Subj. w. **ἄν** in an indef. temp. cl. **διατάξομαι** fut. ind. mid. (dep.) διατάσσω (# 1411) to put in order.

1 Corinthians 12

◆ **1 πνευματικός** (# 4421) spiritual. The suf. indicates that which pertains to the spirit (MH, 378f). The word can be either masc. (spiritual people) or n. spirit (spiritual things, gifts) (Pearson, 47f; Grosheide). **ἀγνοεῖν** pres. act. inf. ἀγνοέω (# 51) to be ignorant. Inf. complementary to the main vb. **θέλω** (# 2527) pres. ind. act., "I desire for you not to be ignorant." ◆ **2 ἦτε** impf. ind. act. εἰμί (# 1639) to be. **ἄφωνος** (# 936) without speech, dumb. **ὡς ἄν** (# 6055; 323) used w. impf. for the notion of repetition (RG, 974). **ἤγεσθε** impf. ind. pass. ἄγω (# 72) to lead. **ἀπαγόμενοι** pres. pass. part. ἀπάγω (# 552) to lead away, to carry away. It suggests moments of ecstasy experienced in heathen religion, when a human being is possessed by the supernatural (Barrett). The dangling construction is best understood by supplying ἦτε to form a periphrastic construction (Fee; Kistemaker). ◆ **3 ἐν** (# 1877) w. dat., in, through, in control of. **λαλῶν** pres. act. part. λαλέω (# 4246) to speak. Adj. part. as subst. **ἀνάθεμα** (# 353) that which is set apart for a deity, that which is abandoned by the gods, a curse, cursed (Grosheide; TDNT;

EDNT; GELTS, 28; RAC, 1:427-30). The reference is to demonic powers and the control of these powers over the lives of the Corinthians before they became Christians. It was possible that the demons used the gift of ecstatic speech to curse Jesus (Pearson, 49-50f; s. H. Wayne House, "Tongues and the Mystery Religions of Corinth," *Bib Sac* 140 [1983]: 134-50; Jouette M. Bassler, "1 Cor 12:3 - Curse and Confession in Context," *JBL* 101 [1982]: 415-18). **δύναται** pres. ind. pass. (dep.) δύναμαι (# 1538) to be able to, w. inf. Pres. indicates that which is always true. **εἰπεῖν** aor. act. inf. λέγω (# 3306) to say. Compl. inf. to the main vb. **Κύριος Ἰησοῦς** (# 3261; 2652) Jesus is Lord (s. 8:6). **εἰ μή** (# 1623; 3590) except. For the view that Paul is primarily referring to a ruler of the synagogue who is reported to have tutored a Jewish Christian to say these words in order to save membership in the community s. J.D.M. Derrett, "Cursing Jesus (1 Cor. 13:3): The Jews as Religious 'Persecutors,'" *NTS* 21 (1975): 544-54. ◆ **4 διαίρεσις** (# 1348) distribution, division, allotment (RP; BAGD; MM; GELTS, 103), difference, variety (Conzelmann). ◆ **5 διακονιῶν** gen. pl. διακονία (# 1355) service, ministry. Gen. of description. ◆ **6 ἐνέργημα** (# 1920) performance, that which was accomplished through energy. These are the results or effects of the working given by God (RP). **ἐνεργῶν** pres. act. part. (adj.) ἐνεργέω (# 1919) to perform, to be at work, to be effective, to produce. **τὰ πάντα ἐν πᾶσιν** "all things in all." The second "all" could be n. or masc. but the emphasis in the passage is on the working of God within men (Morris). ◆ **7 δίδοται** pres. ind. pass. δίδωμι (# 1443) to give. Pres. points to the habitual and repeated action. Theol. pass. indicating that God is the giver. **φανέρωσις** (# 5748) manifestation, a making clear. **συμφέρον** pres. act. part. n. sing. συμφέρω (# 5237) to bring together, to confer a benefit, to be advantageous, profitable or useful (BAGD). Used here w. prep. **πρός** meaning "w. a view to advantage," that is, "the profit of all" (RP). Part. as subst. ◆ **8 κατὰ τὸ αὐτὸ πνεῦμα** (# 2848; 3836; 899; 4460) according to the same Spirit. The prep. gives the norm or standard. ◆ **9 πίστις** (# 4411) faith. Faith here is to be connected w. the miracles referred to in the next few lines (Barrett). **ἴαμα** (# 2611) healing. Here, pl. relates to the different classes of sicknesses to be healed (Godet). ◆ **10 διάκρισις** (# 1360) a judging between things, distinguish, discerning. **γλῶσσα** (# 1185) tongue, language (Robert H. Gundry, "'Ecstatic Utterance' [N.E.B.]?" *JTS* 17 [1966], 299-307; DPL, 939-43; for lit. s. Fee). **ἑρμηνεία** (# 2255) interpretation. ◆ **11 ἐνεργεῖ** pres. ind. act. ἐνεργέω (# 1919) to work in, to energize. The word is often used of the working of the power of God in a miraculous way (MNTW, 46-54; s.v. 6). **διαιροῦν** pres. act. part. (adj.) διαιρέω (# 1349) to distribute (s.v. 4). **ἰδίᾳ** dat. ἴδιος (# 2625) individually, by oneself, privately. Dat. of advantage. **καθώς** (# 2777) just as, accordingly. **βούλεται** pres. ind. mid. (dep.) βούλομαι (# 1089) to will, to determine. Pres. emphasizes the habitual or repeated action. Christ gives not according to the merit or wishes of men, but according to his own will (Hodge). ◆ **12 καθάπερ** (# 2749) just as. **σῶμα** (# 5393) body. (For this comparison s. SBT, 235f; SPC, 165-67). **μέλη** nom. pl. μέλος (# 3517) member. **ὄντα** pres. part. act. εἰμί (# 1639) to be. Concessive part., "although they are many." **οὕτως καὶ ὁ Χριστός** (# 5986) so also is Christ. Paul draws a comparison and uses the corporate rather than the solely individual person of Christ (SBT, 235). ◆ **13 καὶ γάρ** (# 1609; 4246) for even, yes, even (BD, 236). **ἡμεῖς πάντες** we all. Paul includes himself as well as all believers (s. Samuel Byrskog, "Co-Senders, Co-Authors and Paul's Use of the First Person Plural," *ZNW* 87 [1996]: 230-50). **εἰς ἓν σῶμα** (# 1650; 1651; 5393) into one body. The prep. describes the result of the process (Barrett; Weiss). **ἐβαπτίσθημεν** aor. ind. pass. βαπτίζω (# 966) to baptize. Paul is not referring to water baptism but to the spiritual transformation which puts the believer in Christ, and which is the effect of receiving the gift of the Spirit at conversion (BHS, 130f). Aor. points to the event which has taken place. **ἐποτίσθημεν** aor. ind. pass. ποτίζω (# 4540) to cause to drink, to give to drink, to water, to irrigate (MH; BHS, 131). ◆ **14 τὸ σῶμα** (# 5393) Article w. the subject ("the body") is generic, "a body" (Barrett; GGBB, 253-54). **ἔστιν** pres. ind. act. εἰμί (# 1639) to be, to consist of. ◆ **15 εἴπῃ** aor. subj. act. λέγω (# 3306) to say. Subj. w. **ἐάν** (# 1569) in a 3rd. class cond. cl. which assumes the possibility of the cond. **ὅτι** because. **παρὰ τοῦτο** because of this, alongside of this, on that score, for that reason (IBG, 51). The prep. w. acc. is causal (RG, 616). The one neg., **οὐ** (# 4024), is to be taken w. the prep. ("not by asserting this"), and the other neg., **οὐκ** (# 4024), negates the rest of the sentence ("not to be of the body") (Fee; Kistemaker). ◆ **16 εἴπῃ** aor. subj. act. λέγω (# 3306) to say (s.v. 15). **οὖς** (# 4044) ear. ◆ **17 εἰ** (# 1623) if. Introduces a 1st. class cond. cl. which assumes the reality of the cond. for the sake of argument (VA, 294-304). **ἀκοή** (# 198) hearing. **ὄσφρησις** (# 4018) smelling. If the whole body were only one member the condition would be sad (Grosheide). ◆ **18 νυνὶ δέ** but now, but, as it is (RP). **ἔθετο** aor. ind. mid. (dep.) τίθημι (# 5502) to place, to put, to arrange (Kistemaker; BAGD). **ἓν ἕκαστον** (# 1651; 1667) each one. **ἠθέλησεν** aor. ind. act. θέλω (# 2527) to wish, to will. God made unity, but not uniformity. Aor. refers to the act of creation (RP). ◆ **19 εἰ** (# 1623) if. Introduces a 2nd. class cond. cl. which is contrary to fact. **ἦν** impf. ind. act. εἰμί (# 1639) to be. ◆ **20 νῦν δέ** (# 3815; 1254) but now (s.v. 18). The "now" is logical and the "but" is adversative (Fee). ◆ **21 εἰπεῖν** aor. act. inf. λέγω (# 3306) to say. Inf. complementary to the main vb. **σου** gen. sing. σύ (# 5198) you. Gen. w. the noun χρεία (# 5970), "to have need of you." ◆ **22 ἀλλά** (# 247) adversative

use, on the contrary (RWP). **πολλῷ μᾶλλον** by how much more. Dat. of comparison w. the positive of the adj. for the comparative (Kistemaker). **δοκοῦντα** pres. act. part. δοκέω (# 1506) to seem to be, to consider to be; generally w. inf. **ἀσθενέστερα** comp. ἀσθενής (# 822) weak; comp., weaker. The delicate organs, such as the eye, and invisible organs, such as the heart (Barrett). **ὑπάρχειν** pres. act. inf. ὑπάρχω (# 5639) to be, to exist. Inf. w. part., even though the two are separated (BD, 250). **ἀναγκαῖος** (# 338) necessary, indispensable (LN, 1:672; for the adj. s. TLNT). ◆ **23 δοκοῦμεν** pres. ind. act. δοκέω (# 1506) to seem to be (s.v. 22). Gnomic pres. indicating a common truth. **ἀτιμότερα** comp. ἄτιμος (# 872) without honor; comp., less honorable. **εἶναι** pres. act. inf. εἰμί (# 1639) to be. **τούτοις** dat. pl. οὗτος (# 5393) this person or thing. "To those." Indir. obj. **περισσοτέραν** comp. περισσός (# 4358) more; comp., greater. **περιτίθεμεν** pres. ind. act. περιτίθημι (# 4363) to place around, to clothe. Gnomic pres. pointing to that which is always true. **ἀσχήμων** (# 860) unpresentable, indecent, the unpresentable, that is, private, parts (BAGD). For the ancient world's ideas concerning the genitals s. RAC, 10:1-52. **εὐσχημοσύνη** (# 2362) decency, propriety, presentability. Here it is used in the sense of modesty (BAGD). ◆ **24 εὐσχήμων** (# 2362) presentable, decent. **συνεκέρασεν** aor. ind. act. συγκεράννυμι (# 5166) to mix together, to blend together. God mixed the members of the body in order that it might function harmoniously (Grosheide). **ὑστερουμένῳ** pres. mid./pass. part. ὑστερέω (# 5728) to come short, to fail, to be inferior, to lack. Part. as subst. **δούς** aor. act. part. δίδωμι (# 1443) to give. Part. of manner telling how the mixing was done. ◆ **25 ᾖ** pres. subj. act. εἰμί to be (# 1639). Subj. w. **ἵνα** (# 2671) to express purp., in this case a neg. purp. **σχίσμα** division, that which results from a splitting (s. 1:10). **μεριμνῶσιν** pres. subj. act. μεριμνάω (# 3534) to exercise care for, to exercise concern for. Subj. w. **ἵνα** (# 2671) to express purp. ◆ **26 πάσχει** pres. ind. act. πάσχω (# 4248) to suffer. **συμπάσχει** pres. ind. act. συμπάσχω (# 5224) to suffer together. **δοξάζεται** pres. ind. pass. δοξάζω (# 1519) to honor, to glorify; pass., to be honored, to be thought well of. **συγχαίρει** pres. ind. act. συγχαίρω (# 5176) to rejoice together. Vbs. in the pres. in this verse are gnomic, indicating that which is generally true. ◆ **27 ἐκ μέρους** (# 1666; 3538) from a part. The idiom here means "individually" (Barrett). ◆ **28 ἔθετο** aor. ind. mid. (dep.) τίθημι (# 5502) s.v. 18. **πρῶτον** (# 4754) acc. sing., first. **δεύτερον** (# 1309) acc. sing. secondly. **τρίτον** (# 5568) acc. sing. thirdly. The nouns in acc. are used adverbially. The notion of subordination is to be found in these words (Godet; Fee). **δύναμις** (# 1539) power; powerful act or deed (BAGD; DPL, 345-47, 876-77). **ἴαμα** (# 2611) healing. Gen. describing the gifts: "gifts which consist of ...." **ἀντιλήμψις** (# 516) helpful deeds,

assistance. The basic meaning of the word is "an undertaking on behalf of another" and is used both in the
papyri and the LXX in the sense of help, either from
God or from men (BS, 92; MM; GELTS, 41). **κυβέρνησις**
(# 3236) administration; lit. it refers to the steering of a
ship. The pl. here indicates proofs of ability to hold a
leading position in the church (BAGD; TDNT). In an
inscription the vb. is applied to the management of a
household (MM). ◆ **29 μή** (# 3590) neg. used to introduce a question in which the answer "no" is expected:
"all are not apostles, are they?" ◆ **30 διερμηνεύουσιν**
pres. ind. act. διερμηνεύω (# 1450) to translate, to interpret. ◆ **31 ζηλοῦτε** pres. imp. act. ζηλόω (# 2420) to
covet, to be zealous for, to earnestly desire. Believers
may desire a gift; the Spirit gives them as He wills (Bengel). **μείζονα** comp. μέγας (# 3505) large, great; comp.,
greater. **καθ' ὑπερβολήν** (# 2848; 5651) lit., according to
the excess. It is best taken to describe the "way" and
indicates "a way beyond all comparison" (RWP).

1 Corinthians 13

◆ **1 ἐάν** (# 1569) w. subj. The word introduces a
cond. which may be possible, "supposing that." **γλώσσαις** dat. pl. γλῶσσα (# 1185) tongue, language. Instr.
dat. **λαλῶ** pres. subj. act. λαλέω (# 4246) to speak. Subj.
in a 3rd. class cond. cl. **ἀγγέλων** gen. pl. ἄγγελος (# 34)
angel, heavenly being. Gen. of description. **ἀγάπη**
(# 27) love, love w. deep respect and admiration, which
is full of thoughtfulness and concern and always demonstrates itself, even to those who are inferior (TLNT,
1:8-22 w. extensive bibliography, 19-22; TDNT;
NIDNTT, 2:538-47; MNTW; Moffatt L, esp. 178-87;
Trench, *Synonyms*, 41-44; EDNT; DPL, 575-78; 1 John
2:5). This was evidently a missing ingredient among
many of the Corinthian believers and its lack caused
many of the difficulties in the church there. **γέγονα** perf.
ind. act. γίνομαι (# 1181) to become. Perf. would indicate what a person has become and continues to be.
χαλκός (# 5910) copper, brass, bronze. Used w. the following word to indicate a gong (BAGD; Conzelmann).
The Copper Bowl of Dodona, at the oracle of Dodona,
was said to sound (ἠχεῖν) all day long and therefore
was used to describe a person who talked incessantly
(NW, 2, i:369; OCD, 358). It has been suggested that the
background of Paul's statement is that of acoustic
vases used in the theaters to help improve the sound
(W.W. Klein, "Noisy Gong or Acoustic Vase? A Note on
1 Corinthians 13:1," *NTS* 32 [1986]: 286-89; SPC, 76-77).
Pred. adj. without the article stressing the character or
quality. **ἠχῶν** pres. act. part. ἠχέω (# 2490) to sound, to
ring, to echo, to roar. In connection w. the previous
word it indicated a gong which produced a hollow,
echoing, groaning noise (Weiss). **ἤ** or. It has been suggested that the translation should be, "If I speak ..., but
do not have love, I am a dinging piece of bronze rather

than a joyfully sounding cymbal" (Todd K. Sanders, "A
New Approach to 1 Corinthians 13:1," *NTS* 36 [1990]:
614-18). **κύμβαλον** (# 3247) cymbal. Cymbals played a
part in the Jewish worship service but an even greater
role in the heathen worship of the goddess Cybele and
Bacchus (TDNT; DGRA, 381f; MM; LAE, 164-66; Sanders, *NTS* 36 [1990]: 615). **ἀλαλάζον** pres. act. part. ἀλαλάζω (# 226) to sound loudly, to clash. Lit. used in the
sense of "raise a war cry, shouting w. triumphant or
joy" (AS; GELTS, 18; CCFJ, 1:59). ◆ **2 ἔχω** pres. subj.
act. ἔχω (# 2400) to have. Subj. w. ἐάν (# 1569) in a 3rd.
class cond. cl. which assumes the possibility of the
cond. For a discussion of the grammar s. GGBB, 471,
698. **εἰδῶ** perf. subj. act. οἶδα (# 3857) to know. Def. perf.
w. pres. meaning. **πᾶσαν τὴν γνῶσιν** (# 4246; 3836; 1194)
all knowledge, acc. sing. Used w. article it means, "all
that there is in its entirety" (BD, 144). **πᾶσαν τὴν πίστιν**
(# 4245; 3836; 4411) all the faith. **μεθιστάναι** pres. act.
inf. μεθίστημι (# 3496) to remove, to transfer from one
place to another. A proverbial expression meaning "to
make what seems impossible" (Barrett; s. Matt. 17:20).
Inf. w. ὥστε (# 6063) to express results. **οὐθέν** (# 4029)
nothing, an absolute zero (RWP). ◆ **3 ψωμίσω** aor. subj.
act. ψωμίζω (# 6039) to spend everything on food, or to
break into crumbs (Grosheide). The word lit. means, "I
feed w. small morsels," as a child, or invalid. The
meaning here is "if, for the purpose of alms giving, I
divide all my property in fragments" (Barrett). **ὑπάρχοντα** pres. act. part. acc. pl. ὑπάρχω (# 5639) to exist.
Part. in pl. as subst. means "goods," "possessions,"
"property." Although giving to charity was held in
high esteem by the rabbis and thought to gain great
merit, there were requirements prohibiting one from
giving all of his goods; for example, in a year he was
not to give more than 20% of his entire possessions (SB,
3:451; 4:536-58). **παραδῶ** aor. subj. act. παραδίδωμι
(# 4140) to give, to hand over. Subj. w. ἐάν (# 1569) in a
3rd. class cond. cl. which assumes the possibility of the
cond. **καυχήσωμαι** aor. subj. mid. (dep.) καυχάομαι
(# 3016) to boast, to glory. For a discussion of the variant reading (καυθήσομαι fut. ind. pass. καίω [# 2794] to
set fire, to burn) s. TC, 536f; Barrett; Weiss; Fee; J.K.
Elliott, "In Favour of καυθήσομαι at 1 Corinthians
13:3," *ZNW* 62 (1971): 297-98. **ὠφελοῦμαι** pres. ind. pass.
ὠφελέω (# 6067) to profit, to be of value. The gifts are
not valueless, but he is (RP). ◆ **4 μακροθυμεῖ** pres. ind.
act. μακροθυμέω (# 3428) to be longsuffering, to be
patient. It is a long holding out of the mind before it
gives room to action or passion - generally to passion
(Trench, *Synonyms*, 196). It is the steadfast spirit which
will never give in (NTW, 83; TDNT; EDNT). The idea of
the word is that it takes a long time before fuming and
breaking into flames. Pres. either emphasizes the continual state of action or is gnomic, indicating that which
is always true. **χρηστεύεται** pres. ind. mid. (dep.)

χρηστεύομαι (# *5980*) to be useful, to be kind and gracious, to show kindness, one who renders gracious, well-disposed service to others (EGT; TDNT; Trench, *Synonyms*, 323f; TLNT). In the second century, the spectacle of Christian love was so stunning for pagans that they called Christians not *christiani* but *chrestinai*, "made up of mildness or kindness" (TLNT, 3:515-16). For vbs. w. this ending, conveying the idea of being or behaving, or acting as s. MH, 400. ζηλοῖ pres. ind. act. ζηλόω (# *2420*) to be fervent, to boil w. envy, to be jealous (TDNT). περπερεύεται pres. ind. mid. (dep.) περπερεύομαι (# *4371*) to brag, to boast. One who talks a lot and acts presumptuously, to be a windbag. Ostentation is the chief idea and ostentatious boasting leads easily to the next point (RP; TDNT; NW 2, i:373; Fee). φυσιοῦται pres. ind. mid. φυσιόω (# *5881*) to puff up, to puff oneself out like a pair of bellows (RWP). ◆ **5** ἀσχημονεῖ pres. ind. act. ἀσχημονέω (# *858*) to behave indecently or in a shameful manner. Love is tactful and does nothing that would raise a blush (RP). ζητεῖ pres. ind. act. ζητέω (# *2426*) to seek. Pres. indicates a continual or habitual action. παροξύνεται pres. ind. pass. παροξύνω (# *4236*) to irritate, to promote to anger; pass., to be irritated, to be touchy, to become indignant (CCFJ, 3:327-28). Selfishness generates the irritability (EGT). λογίζεται pres. ind. mid. (dep.) λογίζομαι (# *3357*) to credit someone's account, to put to one's account for fut. payment. Here, "does not register (the evil)." Love stores up no resentment and bears no malice (RP; TDNT; MM). ◆ **6** χαίρει pres. ind. act. χαίρω (# *5897*) to rejoice. συγχαίρει pres. ind. act. συγχαίρω (# *5196*) to rejoice together, to join in rejoicing. Here the rejoicing is at the truth rather than w. the truth (Barrett). ◆ **7** στέγει pres. ind. act. στέγω (# *5095*) to cover (as a roof). The meaning is either to cover in the sense of to protect, as a roof, or to bear up as to support, as a roof (Barrett) or to endure, forbear, to put up w. (RP; Fee). πιστεύει pres. ind. act. πιστεύω (# *4409*) to believe. Love trusts that the motives of action are pure. ἐλπίζει pres. ind. act. ἐλπίζω (# *1827*) to hope. Love hopes that the motives of action are pure. ὑπομένει pres. ind. act. (# *5702*) to endure, to bear up patiently (TDNT; Trench, *Synonyms*, 195f). Love has this indefatigable capacity to endure despite the ingratitude, bad conduct, and problems that all communal living involves, and this without complaining or becoming discouraged (TLNT, 3:420). When the motives prove to be impure, love bears it with no resentment! ◆ **8** οὐδέποτε (# *4030*) never. πίπτει pres. ind. act. πίπτω (# *4406*) to fall, to fail. Pres. indicates a continual action, or is a gnomic pres. stating that which is always true. καταργηθήσονται fut. ind. pass. καταργέω (# *2934*) to render inoperative, to make ineffective or powerless. παύσονται fut. ind. mid. παύω (# *4264*) to cause to rest, to cause to cease. Possibly, "they shall make themselves cease or automatically cease of themselves" (RWP; HGS, 2, i:774-75). For the dying out and the little use of the gift of tongues in the post-apostolic church s. Cleon L. Rogers, Jr., "The Gift of Tongues in the Post-Apostolic Church," *Bib Sac* 122 (1965): 134-43; S.D. Currie, "'Speaking in Tongues': Early Evidence Outside the New Testament Bearing on GLOSSAIS LALEIN," *Interp* 19 (1965): 277-94. For a discussion of the grammar s. GGBB, 422-23. ◆ **9** ἐκ μέρους (# *1666*; *3528*) in part, partially. Both times the words are emphatic in this v. (RWP). ◆ **10** ἔλθῃ aor. subj. act. ἔρχομαι (# *2262*) to come. Subj. w. ὅταν (# *4020*) in an indef. temp. cl. καταργηθήσεται fut. ind. pass. καταργέω (# *2934*) to render inoperative (s.v. 8). ◆ **11** ἤμην impf. ind. act. εἰμί (# *1639*) to be. νήπιος (# *3758*) infant, child, minor. Pred. nom. ἐλάλουν impf. ind. act. λαλέω (# *4246*) to speak. Customary impf., "I used to speak." ἐφρόνουν impf. ind. act. φρονέω (# *5858*) to think. It points to the thoughts, interest, and the striving of a child (Lenski). Customary impf. ἐλογιζόμην impf. ind. mid. (dep.) λογίζομαι (# *3357*) to reckon (s.v. 5). γέγονα perf. ind. act. γίνομαι (# *1181*) to become. Not to be viewed as an aoristic perf. (BD, 177), but as a normal perf. emphasizing the resultant condition or state of the subject (M, 143f; RG, 900). κατήργηκα perf. ind. act. καταργέω (# *2934*) to render inoperative. Here it has the meaning "to put aside." ◆ **12** ἄρτι (# *785*) now. A contrast between this dispensation and the fut. (Grosheide). ἔσοπτρον (# *2269*) mirror. In Gr. literature a mirror symbolized clarity and self-recognition (Conzelmann). Mirrors of the ancient world were generally made from polished metal and the Corinthian mirrors were famous (RP; Conzelmann; DGRA, 1052f; BBC). For the report or legend of letting a mirror down in a spring before the temple of Demeter and looking in the mirror to see if the sick person was to get well or die, s. Pausanias, *Description of Greece*, 7:21, 22; 8:37, 7. αἴνιγμα (# *141*) riddle, an indistinct image (BAGD). πρός (# *4639*) w. acc., before, facing; here, "face to face." ἐπιγνώσομαι fut. ind. mid. (dep.) ἐπιγινώσκω (# *2105*) to know, to have specific knowledge. Prep. in compound is directive (MH, 312). ἐπεγνώσθην aor. ind. pass. ἐπιγινώσκω. The words bring out the inadequacy of man's present knowledge of God in contrast w. God's knowledge of man now and the knowledge of God that man will have in the future (Barrett). Theol. pass. ◆ **13** νυνί (# *3815*) now; logical not temp. μένει pres. ind. act. μένω (# *3531*) to remain. μείζων comp. μέγας (# *3505*) large; great. The comp. is used here to express the superl., "greatest" (GGBB, 299-300). For the contrast of Paul's treatment of love w. the ancient view of virtue, s. Gunther Bornkamm, "Der köstlichere Weg: 1 Kor. 13," *Gesammelte Aufsätze*, 1:93-112.

1 Corinthians 14

◆ **1 διώκετε** pres. imp. act. διώκω (# *1503*) to hunt, to pursue. Pres. imp. calls for a habitual action. **ζηλοῦτε** pres. imp. act. ζηλόω (# *2420*) to be zealous, to earnestly desire. **μᾶλλον** (# *3437*) adv., rather. Comp. may retain its comp. meaning or it may be used to express the superl. (Barrett). **προφητεύητε** pres. subj. act. προφητεύω (# *4736*) to speak for someone, to give a message for God, to prophesy (s. F. David Farnell, "Is the Gift of Prophecy for Today?"; "Does the New Testament Teach Two Prophetic Gifts?"; "When Will the Gift of Prophecy Cease?" *Bib Sac* 150 [1993]: 62-88, 171-202; DPL, 755-62). Subj. w. **ἵνα** (# *2671*) giving the content of **ζηλοῦτε**, expressing the aim of the pursuit and desire (Kistemaker; EGT). ◆ **2 λαλῶν** pres. act. part. λαλέω (# *3281*) to speak. Part. as subst. **γλώσσῃ** dat. sing. γλῶσσα (# *1185*) tongue, language (TDNT; s. 12:10). Instr. dat. **λαλεῖ** pres. ind. act. λαλέω (# *3281*) to speak. **ἀκούει** pres. ind. act. ἀκούω (# *201*) to hear. "No one hears;" that is, "no one can understand" (Barrett). However, it is possible that the vb. retains its normal meaning. **πνεύματι** dat. sing. πνεῦμα (# *4460*) spirit. If it refers to the Holy Spirit dat. is instr. (Bruce). If it is loc., it refers to the human spirit (Grosheide). ◆ **3 προφητεύων** pres. act. part. προφητεύω (# *4736*) to prophesy (s.v. 1). Part. as subst. **οἰκοδομή** (# *3869*) edification, building up. **παράκλησις** (# *4155*) exhortation, encouragement, consolation (MNTW, 128-35; TDNT; NIDNTT, 1:569-71). **παραμυθία** (# *4171*) encouragement, consolation, advice, stimulation and strength for overcoming difficulties (TLNT). A synonym w. the previous word. ◆ **4 λαλῶν** pres. act. part. λαλέω (# *4246*) to speak. Part. as subst. **ἑαυτόν** (# *1571*) himself. Chrysostom says, "What a difference between one person and the church" (RP). **ἐκκλησίαν** (# *1711*) church, assembly. Without the article it refers to the local assembly, the assembly of which he is one member (Barrett). **οἰκοδομεῖ** pres. ind. act. οἰκοδομέω (# *3868*) to edify, to build up. Pres. emphasizes the continual action, that which is habitual or always true. ◆ **5 θέλω** (# *2527*) pres. ind. act. to wish, to desire, to want, w. inf. expressing the object of the desire. In this v. it is also followed by **ἵνα** (# *2671*) w. the subj. (M 208). **προφητεύητε** pres. subj. act. προφητεύω (# *4736*) to speak for someone (s.v. 1). **ἐκτὸς εἰ μή** (# *1760; 1623; 3590*) except (Kistemaker; IBG, 83). **διερμηνεύῃ** pres. subj. act. διερμηνεύω (# *1450*) to translate. Prep. in compound may indicate either "being a go-between," or "thoroughness." One who interprets his own words intervenes between unintelligible utterance and the hearers (RP). For the subj. w. **εἰ** (# *1623*) s. VA, 309-11. **λάβῃ** aor. subj. act. λαμβάνω (# *3284*) to take, to receive. Ingressive aor., "may get edification" (RWP). Subj. w. **ἵνα** (# *2671*) to express either purp. or result. ◆ **6 νῦν δέ** and now. The particle is logical, not temp. (Weiss). **ἔλθω** aor. subj. act. ἔρχομαι

(# *2262*) to come. Subj. w. **ἐάν** (# *1569*) in a 3rd. class cond. cl. which assumes the possibility of the cond.: "in case," "suppose I were to come." **λαλῶν** pres. act. part. λαλέω (# *3281*) to speak. Part. of manner explaining how he would come to them. **ὠφελήσω** fut. ind. act. ὠφελέω (# *6067*) to profit, to benefit; here w. acc. **ἐὰν μή** (# *1569; 3590*) if not, except. **λαλήσω** aor. subj. act. λαλέω (# *3281*) to speak. **ἐν** (# *1877*) in, by, through. Instr. use of the prep. **ἀποκάλυψις** (# *637*) unveiling, revelation. **γνῶσις** (# *1194*) knowledge. **προφητεία** (# *4735*) dat. sing. prophecy. The proclamation of a prophet. The revelation and knowledge are the internal gifts of which prophecy and teaching are the external manifestation (RP). ◆ **7 ὅμως** (# *3940*) The word could be viewed as displaced and mean "nevertheless," "all the same"; or it could be viewed as an adv. and mean "likewise" (BD, 234; MT, 337; BAGD). **ἄψυχος** (# *953*) lifeless, inanimate. For the neg. force of the prefix s. Moorhouse, 47ff. **φωνή** (# *5889*) voice, sound. **αὐλός** (# *888*) flute. The word could refer to various types of wind instruments that were popular in social, religious, and military life (DGRA, 1131; RP). **κιθάρα** (# *3067*) lyre, a stringed musical instrument resembling our guitar. It was used in education, lyric poetry, religion, and entertainment (OCD, 709; Conzelmann; KP, 3:1580). There was a large music hall (*odeion*) located in Corinth which would seat around 18,000 (G.E. Wright, *Biblical Archaeology,* 262). This, however, was constructed south of the theater in the late 1st. century (SPC, 34; James Wiseman, "Corinth and Rome 228 B.C. - A.D. 267," ANRW, 2. 7. 1:527). **διαστολή** (# *1405*) difference, distinction. **φθόγγοις** dat. pl. φθόγγος (# *5782*) sound, musical sound, note. It could refer to the notes on a lyre or stops of a flute (OCD, 705-13). Dat. of sphere, "difference in sound." **δῷ** aor. subj. act. δίδωμι (# *1443*) to give. Subj. w. **ἐάν** (# *1569*) in a 3rd. class cond. cl. which assumes the possibility of the cond. **γνωσθήσεται** fut. ind. pass. γινώσκω (# *1182*) to know, to recognize. **αὐλούμενον** pres. pass. part. αὐλέω (# *884*) to play the flute. Part. as subst., "that which is being played on the flute." **κιθαριζόμενον** pres. pass. part. κιθαρίζω (# *3068*) to play on the harp or lyre used to create a harmonious melody. Pres. part. as subst. emphasizes the continuous contemporaneous action, "that which is being played on the lyre." ◆ **8 ἄδηλος** (# *83*) not clear, uncertain, indistinct. **σάλπιγξ** (# *4894*) trumpet used to signal movements of an army (BBC). **δῷ** aor. subj. act. δίδωμι (# *1443*) to give (s.v. 7). **παρασκευάσεται** fut. ind. mid. παρασκευάζω (# *4186*) to prepare; mid. to prepare oneself, to make oneself ready, to make preparations. Josephus describes the three trumpet calls which signal the various aspects of breaking camp and preparing for battle (Jos., *JW*, 2:279; 3:89-93; TJ, 105-6). **πόλεμος** (# *4483*) war, battle (Trench, *Synonyms,* 322). ◆ **9 οὕτως καί** (# *4048; 2779*) so also. He now applies the illustration. **εὔσημος** (# 2358) intelligible, that which is well-marked. The adv. was used in the papyri in the sense of "legible," "clearly" (MM; Preisigke, 1:621). **δῶτε** aor. subj. act. δίδωμι (# 1443) to give. Subj. w. **ἐάν** (# 1569) in a 3rd. class cond. cl. assuming the possibility of the cond. **γνωσθήσεται** fut. ind. pass. γινώσκω (# 1182) to know. **λαλούμενον** pres. pass. part. λαλέω (# 4246) to speak. Part. as subst. **ἔσεσθε** fut. ind. mid. (dep.) εἰμί (# 1639) to be. Used in a periphrastic construction which emphasizes the linear or continuous action (IBG, 18). **λαλοῦντες** pres. act. part. λαλέω (# 3281) to speak. ◆ **10 τοσαῦτα** (# 5537) so great. Here it indicates a number indefinite but very great (Meyer). **τύχοι** aor. opt. act. τυγχάνω (# 5593) to happen, to occur. Used in the idiom **εἰ τύχοι** as a 4th. class cond. cl.: "if it should happen" (RWP), "perhaps," "if it should turn out that way" (RWP; Kistemaker). **ἄφωνος** (# 936) without sound, voiceless; that is, "meaningless sound" (RP). ◆ **11 εἰδῶ** perf. subj. act. οἶδα (# 3857) to know. Def. perf. w. pres. meaning. Subj. in a 3rd. class cond. cl. which assumes the possibility or probability of the cond. **δύναμις** meaning (BAGD). **ἔσομαι** fut. ind. mid. (dep.) εἰμί (# 1639) to be. **λαλοῦντι** pres. act. part. dat. sing. λαλέω (# 3281) to speak. Part. as subst. Dat. of respect, "in the eyes of the speaker" (Kistemaker). **βάρβαρος** (# 975) barbarian. It denotes a man whose language sounds like "bar bar"; that is, whose language makes no sense (Morris). Herodotus wrote that Egyptians called those who did not speak their language "barbarians" (Herodotus, 2, 158:5; NW, 2, i:381). **λαλῶν** pres. act. part. λαλέω (# 4246) to speak. **ἐν ἐμοί** (# 1877; 1609) in my case, in my judgment (M, 103; BD, 118). ◆ **12 ἐπεί** (# 2075) because, since, in the NT it is regularly causal (BD, 238). **ζηλωτής** (# 2421) zealot, one who is zealous for something, enthusiast. Pred. nom. without the article stresses the character. **πνευμάτων** gen. pl. πνεῦμα (# 4460) spirit. Obj. gen., indicating the object of the strong desire. The pl. refers to the various manifestations of the Spirit (Lenski). **ζητεῖτε** pres. imp. act. ζητέω (# 2426) to seek, to seek after. Pres. imp. indicates the continuing of an action in progress or the continual action which is to be habitual (MKG, 272; VANT, 327-34). **περισσεύητε** pres. subj. act. περισσεύω (# 4355) to increase, to abound. The increase could be numerical or spiritual. Subj. w. **ἵνα** (# 2671) expressing purp. ◆ **13 διό** (# 1475) because of this, for this reason, therefore, drawing an inference from the previous discussion (BAGD; BD, 235). **λαλῶν** pres. act. part. λαλέω (# 4246) to speak. Part. as subst. **προσευχέσθω** pres. imp. mid. (dep.) 3rd. pers. sing. προσεύχομαι (# 4662) to pray. Pres. imp. could be iterative or habitual, giving instructions how the gift is to be used. **διερμηνεύῃ** pres. subj. act. διερμηνεύω (# 1450) to interpret (s.v. 5). The one who spoke in tongues evidently knew when he was going to use the gift, for he is to pray beforehand so he

may interpret so that the whole church may be edified. Subj. w. **ἵνα** (# 2671) giving the content of the prayer. ◆ **14 προσεύχωμαι** pres. subj. mid. (dep.) προσεύχομαι (# 4662) s.v. 13. Subj. w. **ἐάν** (# 1569) in a 3rd. class cond. cl. assuming the possibility or probability of the cond., "if I were to ...." **τὸ πνεῦμά μου** my spirit. It could refer to the human spirit of Paul (Barrett) the Holy Spirit, or the spiritual gift given by the Holy Spirit (Weiss; PAT, 190f). **νοῦς** (# 3808) mind, thinking, understanding; it is the constellation of thoughts and assumptions which make up the consciousness of the person and acts as the agent of rational discernment and communication (PAT, 450; TDNT; EDNT). **ἄκαρπός** (# 182) unfruitful, fruitless, sterile, profitless work. It does not mean that the mind did not function, but rather that the product of the mind did not bear fruit and did not edify. ◆ **15 τί οὖν ἐστιν** What then is the result of this discussion? (RP). **προσεύξομαι** fut. ind. mid. (dep.) προσεύχομαι (# 4662) to pray. Fut. is assertive or volitive, expressing the determined decision of Paul's will (SMT, 34; M, 150; RG, 874). **πνεύματι** dat. sing. πνευμα (# 4460) spirit; instr. dat. **νοΐ** dat. sing. νους (# 3808) mind (s.v. 14). **ψαλῶ** fut. ind. act. ψάλλω (# 6010) to sing a hymn, to sing praises. ◆ **16 εὐλογῇς** pres. subj. act. 2nd. pers. sing. εὐλογέω (# 2328) to speak well of, to praise, to bless, to give thanks. Subj. w. **ἐάν** (# 1659) in a 3rd. class cond. cl. assuming the possibility of the cond. **ἀναπληρῶν** pres. act. part. ἀναπληρόω (# 405) to fill. Here, to fill up the place; that is, "he who fills the role of" (Barrett). Part. as subst. **ἰδιώτης** (# 2626) unskilled, unlearned, a layman in contrast to an expert (BAGD; TDNT; TLNT; MM; Preisigke, 1:689f). **ἐρεῖ** fut. ind. act. λέγω (# 3306) to say. **ἀμήν** (# 297) amen, true. It was the Jewish and Christian custom to express agreement and concurrence w. the prayer by responding "amen" (SB, 3:456; Barrett; for the use of the term in the DSS s. 1 QS 1:20; 2:10, 18). **ἐπί** (# 2093) w. dat., to; that is, in response to. **ἐπειδή** (# 2076) since, because. **οἶδεν** perf. ind. act. οἶδα (# 3857) to know. Def. perf. w. pres. meaning. ◆ **17 μέν** (# 3525) followed by **ἀλλά** (# 247) to be sure, but (Fee). **καλῶς** (# 2822) adv., well. **εὐχαριστεῖς** pres. ind. act. εὐχαριστέω (# 2373) to give thanks. **οἰκοδομεῖται** pres. ind. pass. οἰκοδομέω (# 3868) to edify (s.v. 4). ◆ **18 μᾶλλον** (# 3437) adv. more, followed by the gen. of comparison w. the meaning, "more than." **λαλῶ** pres. ind. act. λαλέω (# 3281) to speak. ◆ **19 ἐν ἐκκλησίᾳ** (# 1711) in the gathering, in the church. The place where God's people gather to worship, a place of teaching and preaching of God's Word (Kistemaker). **θέλω** (# 2527) pres. ind. act. I wish, I prefer, w. inf. (RP; LAE, 187, 190). **πέντε** (# 4297) five, a round number, as used in Judaism (Barrett; SB, 3:461). **λαλῆσαι** aor. act. inf. λαλέω (# 3281) to speak. **κατηχήσω** aor. subj. act. κατηχέω (# 2994) to instruct, to teach, Paul only uses the word in the sense of theological instruction (Conzelmann). Subj. w. ἵνα (# 2671) to express purp. μυρίος (# 3692) ten thousand, innumerable, countless (BAGD). ◆ **20** παιδία nom. pl. παιδίον (# 4086) little child. Pred. nom. without the article stressing the character. γίνεσθε pres. imp. mid. (dep.) γίνομαι (# 1181) to become, to be. Pres. imp. w. the neg. is a command to stop an action in progress: "do not continue to be" (MKG, 72). φρεσίν dat. pl. φρήν (# 5856) only used here and in the pl. to mean "thinking," "understanding" (BAGD). Dat. of respect or reference, "in reference to understanding." κακία (# 2798) dat. sing. wickedness, maliciousness, and ill will (RP). Dat. of reference. νηπιάζετε pres. imp. act. νηπιάζω (# 3757) to be as a child (BAGD). It implies the need of innocence w. regard to evil (Fee). Pres. imp. calls for a constant attitude. τέλειος (# 5455) mature. Pred. nom. without the article stresses the character. ◆ **21** γέγραπται perf. ind. pass. γράφω (# 1211) to write. Perf. points to the continuing authority of that which stands written (MM). ἑτερόγλωσσος (# 2280) other tongue, strange language. Here, instr. dat. w. the prep. χείλεσιν dat. pl. χεῖλος (# 5927) lip. λαλήσω fut. ind. act. (# 4246) s.v. 4. εἰσακούσονταί fut. ind. mid. (dep.) εἰσακούω (# 1653) to hear into, to attend to w. obj. in gen. For the prep. in compound s. MH, 304. ◆ **22** ὥστε (# 6063) therefore. The word draws a conclusion from the previous. εἰς (# 1659) w. the vb. εἰμί it may have a Semitic meaning, "to serve as" (BD, 80; but also s. Barrett). σημεῖον (# 4956) acc. pl. sign. For a study of this v., s. J.P.M. Sweet, "A Sign for Unbelievers: Paul's Attitude to Glossolalia," *NTS* 13 (1967): 240-57. εἰσιν pres. ind. act. εἰμί (# 1639) to be. πιστεύουσιν pres. act. part. dat. pl. πιστεύω (# 4409) to believe. Part. as subst. Dat. of personal interest. ἄπιστος (# 603) unbelieving. Adj. as subst. Here, dat. of personal interest. ◆ **23** συνέλθη aor. subj. act. συνέρχομαι (# 5302) to come together, to assemble. Subj. w. ἐάν (# 1569) in a 3rd. class cond. cl. in which the cond. is viewed as possible. ἐπὶ τὸ αὐτό (# 2093; 3836; 899) to the same place, together. λαλῶσιν pres. subj. act. λαλέω (# 4246) to speak. Pres. indicates an action in progress. Subj. in a 3rd. class cond. cl. εἰσέλθωσιν aor. subj. act. εἰσέρχομαι (# 5302) to enter into. Subj. in a 3rd. class cond. cl. ἰδιῶται (# 2626) nom. pl. not understanding (s.v. 16). ἐροῦσιν fut. ind. act. λέγω (# 3306) to say. ὅτι (# 4022) It introduces either indir. discourse ("that"), or a direct quotation and then is used as quotation marks. μαίνεσθε pres. ind. mid. (dep.) μαίνομαι (# 3419) to be mad, to be crazy. The question introduced by the neg. οὐκ (# 4024) expects the answer "yes." ◆ **24** προφητεύωσιν pres. subj. act. προφητεύω (# 4736) to prophesy (s.v. 1). Subj. in a 3rd. class cond. cl. assuming the possibility of the cond. Pres. emphasizes the continual action, or is iterative. εἰσέλθη aor. subj. act. εἰσέρχομαι (# 1656) to enter (s.v. 23). ἐλέγχεται pres. ind. pass. ἐλέγχω (# 1794) to convict; to so present the evidence

that one is driven to the conclusion that the argument is correct (TDNT; T). ἀνακρίνεται pres. ind. pass. ἀνακρίνω (# 373) to examine, to cross-examine, to put through a course of questioning as when one is questioned and examined by a judge in a court (Lenski). ◆ **25** γίνεται pres. ind. mid. (dep.) (# 1181) to become. Pres. vividly pictures the action in progress. πεσών aor. act. part. πίπτω (# 4406) to fall down. Part. of manner explaining how the worship is carried on. προσκυνήσει fut. ind. act. προσκυνέω (# 4686) to worship, to fall down and worship. Used to designate the custom of prostrating oneself before a person and kissing his feet, the hem of his garment, the ground, etc.; w. obj. in dat. (BAGD; TDNT; EDNT). ἀπαγγέλλων pres. act. part. ἀπαγγέλλω (# 550) to solemnly declare. Part. of manner. ◆ **26** τί οὖν ἐστιν s.v. 15. συνέρχησθε pres. subj. mid. (dep.) συνέρχομαι (# 5302) to come together. Pres. is iterat. and points to a recurring action. Subj. w. ὅταν (# 4020) in an indef. temp. cl.: whenever, as often as. ψαλμός (# 6011) song, hymn. The word signifies the singing of praises to God (EGT). Those present may have composed a song or sung a Christian hymn (Grosheide). ἔχει pres. ind. act. ἔχω (# 2400) to have. Each one had these gifts because they were given by the Spirit (Grosheide). ἑρμηνεία (# 2255) translation, interpretation. πρός (# 4639) w. acc., for, leading to (IBG, 53). γινέσθω pres. imp. mid. (dep.) γίνομαι (# 1181) to happen. Pres. imp. is a command for habitual action. ◆ **27** εἴτε (# 1664) if, whether. The construction "whether... or" is begun but left unfinished (RP). κατά (# 2848) w. acc. used in a distributive sense, "by twos" (MT, 268). πλεῖστον adv. superl. πολύς (# 4498) great, much. Used as adverbial acc.: "at the most" (RWP). ἀνὰ μέρος (# 324; 3538) in turn (IBG, 67; MT, 265). In the Jewish synagogue service there were at least seven readers of Scripture who read at least three verses in turn (SB, 3:465f; 4:154-71; JPF, 2:927-33). εἷς (# 1651) one, someone. διερμηνευέτω pres. imp. act. διερμηνεύω (# 1450) to interpret (s.v. 5). ◆ **28** ᾖ pres. subj. act. εἰμί (# 1639) to be. Subj. in a 3rd. class cond. cl. assuming the possibility of the cond. διερμηνευτής (# 1449) translator, interpreter. σιγάτω pres. imp. act. σιγάω (# 4967) to be silent. Pres. indicates that he is not even to speak in a tongue once (RWP). The command indicates that the person could control the use of the gift. ἑαυτῷ dat. sing. ἑαυτοῦ (# 1571) himself. "To himself," or dat. of advantage (Kistemaker). λαλείτω pres. imp. act. λαλέω (# 3281) to speak. ◆ **29** λαλείτωσαν pres. imp. act. 3rd. pers. pl. λαλέω (# 3281) to speak. διακρινέτωσαν pres. imp. act. 3rd. pers. pl. διακρίνω (# 1359) to separate, to make a distinction, to pass judgment on, to test (BAGD; MM). ◆ **30** ἀποκαλυφθῇ aor. subj. pass. ἀποκαλύπτω (# 636) to reveal. Subj. in a 3rd. class cond. cl. assuming the possibility of the cond. Theol. pass. καθημένῳ pres. mid. (dep.) part. κάθημαι

(# 2764) to sit. Part. as subst. Dat. as indir. obj. It was the prophet who stood while the congregation sat (Lietzmann; s. Luke 4:16). ◆ **31** καθ' ἕνα (# 2848; 1651) one by one; distributive use of prep. (MT, 268). μανθά-νωσιν pres. subj. act. μανθάνω (# 3443) to learn. Subj. w. ἵνα (# 2671) to express purp. παρακαλῶνται pres. subj. pass. παρακαλέω (# 4151) to exhort, to encourage, to comfort (MNTW, 128-35). ◆ **32** πνεύματα προφητῶν (# 4460; 4737) pl., the spirits of the prophets (s.v. 12). It is the manifestation of the Spirit or the divine influence under which the prophets spoke (Hodge). ὑποτάσσεται pres. ind. mid. (dep.) ὑποτάσσω (# 5718) to be in subjection, to be obedient. The prophet exercised self-control and control over the gift. A preacher without self-control is no true prophet (RP). ◆ **33** ἀκαταστασία (# 189) disorder, disturbance, confusion. It could refer to disorder or confusion in the assembly (Barrett) or it could refer to the disorder if the Spirit was not in harmony w. Himself (Conzelmann). Here, descriptive gen. ὡς (# 6055) as. These words should not be taken w. the preceding but w. the words which follow (Grosheide). ◆ **34** γυναῖκες nom. pl. γυνή (# 1222) woman. ἐκκλησία (# 1711) church, assembly. Pl. here it refers to the local gathering. σιγάτωσαν pres. imp. act. σιγάω (# 4967) to be silent. ἐπιτρέπεται pres. ind. pass. ἐπιτρέπω (# 2205) to allow, w. inf. In the Jewish synagogue women were not allowed to speak in public and took no active part in the conduct of divine service (JPF, 2:920f; SB, 3:467f; BBC). ◆ **35** μαθεῖν aor. act. inf. μανθάνω (# 3443) to learn. θέλουσιν pres. ind. act. θέλω (# 2527) to desire (s.v. 19). Ind. in a 1st. class cond. cl. assuming the reality of the cond. ἐν οἴκῳ (# 1877; 3875) at home. ἰδίους acc. pl. ἴδιος (# 2625) own. ἐπερωτάτωσαν pres. imp. act. 3rd. pl. ἐπερωτάω (# 2089) to ask, to ask about something. Prep. in compound is directive (MH, 314). αἰσχρός (# 156) shameful, disgraceful. Plutarch wrote that not only the arm but the voice of a modest woman ought to be kept from the public, and she should feel shame at being heard, as at being stripped (Barrett; NW, 2, i:385-88; SB, 3:468-69). For a discussion on this passage in the light of other Scriptures dealing w. woman in church life s. PWC, 70-80; DPL, 590-92. λαλεῖν pres. act. inf. λαλέω (# 4246) s.v. 4. Epex. inf. explaining what is shameful. ◆ **36** ἐξῆλθεν aor. ind. act. ἐξέρχομαι (# 2002) to go out. κατήντησεν aor. ind. act. καταντάω (# 2918) to reach, to arrive. The question is, "were you the starting point of the gospel? Or were you its only destination?" Paul is attacking the abuses of the Corinthians by pointing out they were not the source of the gospel (RP). ◆ **37** δοκεῖ pres. ind. act. δοκέω (# 1506) to suppose, w. inf. Ind. in a 1st. class cond. cl. which assumes that the cond. is true. εἶναι pres. act. inf. εἰμί (# 1639) to be. ἐπιγινωσκέτω pres. imp. act. ἐπιγινώσκω (# 2105) to recognize, to acknowledge completely. κυρίου gen. sing. κύριος (# 3261).

Gen. could be poss. gen. or gen. of source. Emphatic by its word position. ἐντολή (# 1953) commandment. Paul is claiming inspiration and authority for his writing. ◆ **38** ἀγνοεῖ pres. ind. act. ἀγνοέω (# 51) to be ignorant, to disregard. Ind. in a 1st. class cond. cl. assuming the reality of the cond. ἀγνοεῖται pres. ind. pass. (# 51) to be ignored, to be disregarded (BAGD). ◆ **39** ὥστε (# 6063) therefore. The word sums up and draws a conclusion of the previous discussion. ζηλοῦτε pres. imp. act. ζηλόω s.v. 1. προφητεύειν pres. act. inf. προφητεύω (# 4736) to prophesy (s.v. 1). Inf. as obj. of the vb. λαλεῖν pres. act. inf. λαλέω (# 3281) to speak. Inf. as obj. of the vb. κωλύετε pres. imp. act. κωλύω (# 3266) to hinder, to restrain, to forbid. Pres. imp. w. neg. means either to stop an action in progress or it forbids a habitual action (MKG, 272f). ◆ **40** εὐσχημόνως (# 2361) adv., decently, properly (TLNT). τάξις (# 5423) orderly; w. the prep., "according to order" (TLNT, 2:10). Josephus uses the neg. of this word to say that the Roman army did not erect its camp in disorderly parties (Jos., JW, 3:77; CCFJ, 4:157-58). Josephus also uses the word to indicate that the Essenes only spoke "in turn" (Jos., *Wars*, 2:132). Paul uses the word to suggest that members of the church do things one at a time, not all at once (Barrett).

1 Corinthians 15

◆ **1** γνωρίζω (# 1192) pres. ind. act. to make known. "I draw your attention" (Barrett). The word was used to introduce a solemn statement (Conzelmann). εὐηγγελισάμην aor. ind. mid. (dep.) εὐαγγελίζομαι (# 2294) to proclaim good news (TDNT; EDNT; TLNT). Aor. views the total ministry of Paul, emphasizing the one gospel which he preached. παρελάβετε aor. ind. act. παραλαμβάνω (# 4161) to receive, to receive as authoritative teaching what was passed on (s. 11:23). ἑστήκατε perf. ind. act. ἵστημι (# 2705) to stand. Perf. pictures the abiding results. ◆ **2** σῴζεσθε pres. ind. pass. σῴζω (# 5392) to rescue, to save. Pres. indicates a continuous action which was being performed in the believers. Theol. pass. indicating that God is performing the action. τίνι λόγῳ (# 5515; 3364) by or in which word. The interrogative pron. is used here as a normal rel. pron. (RG, 737f). κατέχετε pres. ind. act. κατέχω (# 2988) to hold down, to hold fast. Ind. w. εἰ (# 1623) in a 1st. class cond. cl. assuming the reality of the cond. ἐκτὸς εἰ μή (# 1623; 1760; 3590) except (BD, 191). εἰκῇ (# 1632) adv., without cause, in vain, to no purpose, without due consideration (BAGD). ἐπιστεύσατε aor. ind. act. πιστεύω (# 4409) to believe. Not that Paul really entertains this as a serious possibility, but if the denial of the resurrection is carried to its logical conclusion, then it would be shown that their belief was fruitless, perhaps because it was exercised superficially or at random (Bruce). ◆ **3** παρέ-δωκα aor. ind. act. παραδίδωμι (# 4140) to deliver over, to pass on, to pass on authoritative teaching (for a detailed study of this passage s. RH, 76-89). **ἐν πρώτοις** (# *1877; 4755*) in the first place, first of all. The words may indicate priority either in time or importance (Barrett). **παρέλαβον** aor. ind. act. παραλαμβάνω (# *4161*) to receive (s. 11:23). **ἀπέθανεν** aor. ind. act. ἀποθνῄσκω (# *633*) to die. **ὑπέρ** (# *5642*) prep. w. gen., on behalf of, in lieu of; that is, "to deal w. our sins," "to expiate our sins" (NIDNTT, 3:1196-97). **κατὰ τὰς γραφάς** (# *1210*) according to the scriptures. The phrase can be taken to mean, "even as the whole tone of the O.T. so foretold concerning Him" (Kenneth O. Gangel, "According to the Scriptures," *Bib Sac* 125 [1968]: 123-28). ◆ **4 ἐτάφη** aor. ind. pass. θάπτω (# *2507*) to bury. **ἐγήγερται** perf. ind. pass. ἐγείρω (# *1586*) to raise. Perf. emphasizes that Christ is risen and indicates a continuing condition which has given rise to a new state of affairs. Christ continues in the risen state (McKay, 12; GI, 113). **τῇ ἡμέρᾳ τῇ τρίτῃ** (# *2465; 5569*) on the day the third. Dat. of time. ◆ **5 ὤφθη** aor. ind. pass. ὁράω (# *3972*) to see; pass., to be seen, to appear. The appearances were not just visions; he could be seen by human eyes (Grosheide; W.L. Craig, "The Historicity of the Empty Tomb of Jesus," *NTS* 31 [1985]: 39-67; Robert Stein, "Was the Tomb Really Empty?" *JETS* 20 [1977]: 27-29; DPL, 805-12). **εἶτα** (# *1663*) then, next; adv. denoting sequence (AS). ◆ **6 ἔπειτα** (# *2083*) thereupon, thereafter, then. **ἐπάνω** (# *2062*) above, over. For the use of the adv. w. numbers s. BD, 99. **πεντακόσιοι** (# *4296*) 500. **ἐφάπαξ** (# *2384*) at once, at one time. (from ἐπί and ἅπαξ). **πλείονες** nom. pl. comp. πολύς much, great (# *4498*) pl., the majority. **μένουσιν** pres. ind. act. μένω (# *3531*) to remain. **ἕως ἄρτι** (# *785; 2401*) until now. Paul was writing 20 years or so later (Barrett). **ἐκοιμήθησαν** aor. ind. pass. κοιμάω (# *3121*) pass., to fall asleep, to die. ◆ **7 πᾶσιν** dat. pl. πᾶς (# *4246*) all. Placed after the subst. to emphasize it (BD, 144). ◆ **8 ἔσχατον** (# *2274*) last. Used either in the sense that Paul is the last of those to be granted such an appearance, the last of the apostles, or that he refers to himself as the least of the apostles (PAA, 105). **ὡσπερεί** (# *6062*) like, as though, as it were. **ἔκτρωμα** (# *1765*) a fetus born before its time, stillborn child, child born abnormally before term, untimely birth, miscarriage (TLNT; NDIEC, 2:81-82; GELTS, 142; BAGD; Peter von der Osten-Sacken, "Die Apologie des pln Apostolats in 1 Kor 15, 1-11," *ZNW* 64 [1973]: 245-62; Markus Schaefer, "Paulus: 'Fehlgeburt' oder 'unvernünftiges Kind' - Ein Interpretationsvorschlag zu 1 Kor 15,8," *ZNW* 85 [1994]: 207-17; TDNT; EDNT; DPL, 49-51). The term points to the results of the birth and was used to indicate that which is incapable of sustaining life of its own volition but requires divine intervention if it is to continue. It emphasizes Paul's weakness and his dependence on God's grace (PAA, 104-105; Schlatter). It could refer to the abnormal

and sudden character of Paul's birth to the Christian faith and the apostolic ministry (TLNT, 1:466). **κἀμοί** = καὶ ἐμοί dat. κἀγώ (# *2743*) to me also. ◆ **9 ἐλάχιστος** superl. μικρός (# *1788*) small, little; superl., the smallest, the least. The true superl., followed by the gen. of comparison. Pred. nom. w. the article indicates that the subject and pred. are the same. **ἱκανός** (# *2653*) sufficient, capable, worthy, competent, fit (TLNT). **καλεῖσθαι** pres. pass. inf. καλέω (# *2813*) to call. Epex. inf. explaining the word **ἱκανός**. **διότι** (# *1484*) a strengthened form of ὅτι, because. **ἐδίωξα** aor. ind. act. διώκω (# *1503*) to hunt, to pursue, to persecute. ◆ **10 χάριτι** dat. sing. χάρις (# *5921*) grace, the help or favor granted to one who is undeserving and with no thought of any return (TDNT; TLNT; EDNT). Instr. dat. **θεοῦ** gen. sing. θεός (# *2536*) Gen. of source ("grace from God") or descriptive gen. ("godly or divine grace"). **ὅ** (# *4005*) rel. pron. n. The deliberate choice of the neuter stresses the thing, not the person: *"what* I am" (Kistemaker). **ἡ εἰς ἐμέ** The article is used as a rel. pron., "which was extended to me" (RP). **κενή** (# *3031*) empty, in vain, without success (TLNT). **ἐγενήθη** aor. ind. pass. (dep.) γίνομαι (# *1181*) to become, to be. **περισσότερον** comp. περισσός (# *4358*) more than sufficient, abundantly; comp., even more, so much more. Followed by comp. gen. **ἐκοπίασα** aor. ind. act. κοπιάω (# *3159*) to labor, to work to the point of exhaustion, to work hard (TDNT; TLNT). It points to the weariness which follows this straining of all his powers to the utmost (Trench, *Synonyms*, 378). ◆ **11 κηρύσσομεν** pres. ind. act. κηρύσσω (# *3062*) to preach, to proclaim as a herald (DPL, 755-57). Pres. denotes a constant fact (Godet). **ἐπιστεύσατε** aor. ind. act. πιστεύω (# *4409*) to believe. Aor. points to the fact of belief. ◆ **12 κηρύσσεται** pres. ind. pass. κηρύσσω (# *3062*). Ind. w. **εἰ** (# *1623*) in a 1st. class cond. cl. which assumes the reality of the cond. Pres. points to the continual proclamation. **ἐγήγερται** perf. ind. pass. ἐγείρω (# *1586*) to raise. Perf. means, "he lives at the present as the risen Savior" (Grosheide). **λέγουσιν** pres. ind. act. λέγω (# *3306*) to say. Pres. points to a continuous action in progress. **ἀνάστασις** (# *414*) resurrection, w. obj. gen. It is possible that the opponents of Paul who deny a resurrection of the dead were influenced by a Hellenistic, dualistic concept of afterlife current among the sacramentally oriented popular cults (J.H. Wilson, "The Corinthians Who Say There Is No Resurrection of the Dead," *ZNW* 59 [1968]: 103; for the views of resurrection in the ancient world s. RAC, 1:919-38; TDNT). ◆ **13 ἔστιν** pres. ind. act. εἰμί (# *1639*) to be. Ind. w. **εἰ** (# *1623*) in a 1st. class cond. cl. assuming for the sake of argument that the cond. is true. **ἐγήγερται** perf. ind. pass. ἐγείρω (# *1586*) to raise (s.v. 4). ◆ **14 ἐγήγερται** perf. ind. pass. ἐγείρω (# *1586*) to raise (s.v. 12). Ind. in a 1st. class cond. cl. assuming for the sake of argument the reality of the cond. **κενόν** (# *3031*) empty, without content, nothingness, absolute void (TLNT, 2:305; s.v. 10). Take out the resurrection, and there is nothing left (Barrett). **ἄρα** (# *726*) then. The word implies the inevitable nature of the conclusion (Grosheide). ◆ **15 εὑρισκόμεθα** pres. ind. pass. εὑρίσκω (# *2351*) to find; pass. to be found. The word is often used of moral judgments respecting character, and conveys the idea of discovering or detecting (RP). **ψευδόμαρτυς** (# *6020*) false witness. The following gen. is either obj. ("a false witness about God") or subjective gen. ("a false witness claiming to be from God"). Such a false witness would make his message a myth, a human composition which arises from human wishes; at the same time he would be claiming that his message was the word of God (Schlatter). **ἐμαρτυρήσαμεν** aor. ind. act. μαρτυρέω (# *3455*) to serve as a witness, to give witness. **κατά** (# *2848*) w. gen., against. **ἤγειρεν** aor. ind. act. ἐγείρω (# *1586*) to raise. **εἴπερ ἄρα** (# *725*; *1642*) if indeed; if, as they say, it is true (BD, 237). **ἐγείρονται** pres. ind. pass. ἐγείρω (# *1586*)to raise. Theol. pass. indicating that God raises the dead (Kistemaker). ◆ **16 εἰ γάρ** if indeed. Use. w. ind. in a 1st. class cond. cl. which assumes the reality of the cond. **ἐγήγερται** perf. ind. pass. ἐγείρω (# *1586*) to raise. ◆ **17 μάταιος** (# *3469*) vain, empty. The word emphasizes the aimlessness and the leading to no object or end (Trench, *Synonyms*, 180f; NIDNTT, 1:549-52). ◆ **18 κοιμηθέντες** aor. pass. part. κοιμάω (# *3121*) to sleep (s.v. 6). Part. as subst. **ἀπώλοντο** aor. ind. mid. (dep.) ἀπόλλυμι (# *660*) to ruin, to destroy, to perish. ◆ **19 ἠλπικότες** perf. act. part. ἐλπίζω (# *1827*) to hope (EH, 270-71). Part. could be used as a periphrastic perf. emphasizing the continual condition or state of hoping (RWP), or it could be considered as substitutive: "we are hopers" (Barrett). **ἐσμέν** pres. ind. act. εἰμί (# *1639*) to be. Ind. w. εἰ (# *1623*) in a 1st. class cond. assuming the reality of the cond. for the sake of argument. **ἐλεεινότεροι** comp. ἐλεεινός (# *1795*) pitiable, one who is to be pitied (TLNT). The comp. is used as a superl. ("most pitiable"), followed by the gen. of comparison (RP; BD, 33f). ◆ **20 νυνί** (# *3815*) now; not temp., but logical and returns to reality (Schlatter). **ἐγήγερται** perf. ind. pass. ἐγείρω (# *1586*) to raise (s.v. 4). **ἀπαρχή** (# *569*) firstfruit. The word means the first installment of the crop which foreshadows and pledges the ultimate offering of the whole (Barrett). The word was used in various ways: a birth certificate, a certificate of authorization, a yearly offering for a god, or inheritance tax (Preisigke, 1:157; MM; TLNT; TDNT; GELTS, 45; CCFJ, 1:164). Nom. in apposition to Christ. **κεκοιμημένων** perf. pass. part. κοιμάω (# *3121*) to sleep (s.v. 6). Part. as subst. Here, gen. of description or content. ◆ **21 ἐπειδή** (# *2076*) since, because. **δι'** (# *1328*) w. gen., through. ◆ **22 ὥσπερ** (# *6061*) as, just as. **ἀποθνῄσκουσιν** pres. ind. act. ἀποθνῄσκω (# *633*)

to die. Pres. describes action which reoccurs from time to time w. different individuals, as the iterative describes action repeated by the same agent (M, 114). **καί** (# *2779*) also. **πάντες** nom. pl. πᾶς (# *4246*) all. It is qualified by ἐν τῷ Χριστῷ. **ζῳοποιηθήσονται** fut. ind. pass. ζῳοποιέω (# *2443*) to make alive. Theol. pass., indicating it is God who makes alive. ◆ **23 ἕκαστος** (# *1667*) each. **τάγμα** (# *5413*) rank, order, often used in the military sense denoting a body of troops which can be disposed according to the decision of the commanding officer; or it could be applied to any sort of group and could also mean place or position (s. 14:40; Barrett). **ἔπειτα** (# *2083*) then, after, thereafter. **παρουσία** (# *4242*) dat. sing., presence, arrival, coming. The word was used as a technical expression for the arrival or visit of the king or emperor (LAE, 368; TLNT). It was also used for the appearance of a god (Conzelmann; TDNT). ◆ **24 εἶτα** (# *1663*) then, after this. The word may indicate that there is also to be an interval between his coming and the end (RP; Weiss). **τέλος** (# *5465*) completion, end. The word was used as a technical phrase denoting the final consummation (PRJ, 295). **παραδιδῷ** pres. subj. act. παραδίδωμι (# *4140*) to give over, to turn over to someone. Pres. pictures a fut. proceeding (RWP). Subj. w. ὅταν (# *4020*) ("whenever") in an indef. temp. cl. **τῷ θεῷ καὶ πατρί**. The definite article has here the force of demonstrative w. the meaning of a rel. pron.: "to the one who is God and Father" (Weiss). **καταργήσῃ** aor. subj. act. καταργέω (# *2934*) to make ineffective, to abolish, to bring to an end (TDNT). **ἀρχή** (# *794*) rule, ruler. The nouns here represent the evil powers under whose control the world has come (Barrett). ◆ **25 δεῖ** pres. ind. act. (# *1256*) impersonal, it is needful, w. inf. The necessity arises out of the sovereign plan of God (TDNT). **βασιλεύειν** pres. act. inf. βασιλεύω (# *996*) to rule, to carry out the duties of a king. **ἄχρι** (# *948*) w. gen., until. **θῇ** aor. subj. act. τίθημι (# *5502*) to place, to put. Subj. in an indef. temp. cl. ◆ **26 ἔσχατος ἐχθρός** (# *2398*) the last enemy. Either subject w. ὁ θάνατος (# *2505*) in apposition to "death"; death as the last enemy (s. Rev. 20:14; 21:4; J. Davis McCaughey, "The Death of Death [1 Corinthians 15:26]," RH, 246-61). **καταργεῖται** pres. ind. pass. καταργέω (# *2934*) to make ineffective (s.v. 24). Fut. pres. (VA, 230-32). ◆ **27 πάντα γάρ** (# *4246*; *1142*) the first word is emphatic (RP) and the particle gives a causal explanation. **ὑπέταξεν** aor. ind. act. ὑποτάσσω (# *5718*) to subject, to bring under control, to make subordinate (LN, 1:476; TLNT). **εἴπῃ** aor. subj. act. λέγω (# *3306*) to say. Used to introduce a scriptural quotation, "now when it says" (Barrett). **ὑποτέτακται** perf. ind. pass. ὑποτάσσω (# *5718*). **δῆλος** (# *1316*) clear, plain. **ἐκτός** (# *1760*) outside, expect. **ὑποτάξαντος** aor. act. part. ὑποτάσσω. Part. as subst. ◆ **28 ὑποταγῇ** aor. subj. pass. ὑποτάσσω (# *5718*) to subject (s.v. 27). Subj. in an indef. temp. cl.

αὐτός (# 899) himself. The word is used as an intensifying pronominal adj. (Funk, 562f). ὑποταγήσεται fut. ind. pass. ὑποτάσσω (# 5718). ὑποτάξαντι aor. act. part. ὑποτάσσω (# 5718). Part. as subst. ᾖ pres. subj. act. εἰμί (# 1639) to be. Subj. w. ὅταν (# 4020) in a purp. cl. Paul refers neither to pantheism nor universalism, but speaks of the new heaven and new earth in which all things are in harmony w. God (Barrett; Godet). ◆ 29 ἐπεί (# 2075) since, otherwise. τί (# 5515) what. ποιήσουσιν fut. ind. act. ποιέω (# 4472) to do. Here it means either "what will they have recourse to?" or "what will they gain?" (RP). βαπτιζόμενοι pres. pass. part. βαπτίζω (# 966) to baptize. Part. as subst. w. the article suggests a particular group, not all Christians (Barrett). ὑπέρ w. gen., for, on behalf of, because of. Perhaps the best explanation is that the prep. is to be taken as "because of," assuming he is referring to those who have been baptized because of the witness of those who have already died (John D. Reaume, "Another Look at 1 Corinthians 15:29, 'Baptised for the Dead,'" *Bib Sac* 152 [1995], 457-75; for literature regarding "baptism for the dead" s. NIDNTT, 3:1197; Conzelmann; ZPEB, 1:469f; TDNT; Joel R. White, "'Baptized on Account of the Dead:' The Meaning of 1 Corinthians 15:29 in its Context," *JBL* 116 [1997]: 487-99; Jerome Murphy-O'Connor, "Baptized for the Dead (I Cor., XV,29): Corinthian Slogan?" *RB* 88 [1981]: 532-43; B.M. Foschini, *Those Being Baptized for the Dead: 1 Cor 15:29, An Exegetical, Historical Dissertation* [Worchester, Mass.: Heffernan, 1951]; BBC). ὅλως (# 3914) at all, never. ἐγείρονται pres. ind. pass. ἐγείρω (# 1586) to raise (s.v. 4). Ind. in a 1st. class cond. cl. assuming for the sake of argument the reality of the cond. τί καί (# 5515; 2779) why then, why at all, still? (BD, 228). ◆ 30 ἡμεῖς (# 1609) we! Emphatic and contrastive. κινδυνεύομεν pres. ind. act. κινδυνεύω (# 3073) to be in danger. Pres. emphasizes the constant or continual state of danger. πᾶσαν ὥραν (# 4246; 6052) every hour. Acc. of time, "hourly," "all through every hour" (RWP). ◆ 31 καθ' ἡμέραν (# 2848; 2465) distributive use of the prep.: day after day, daily. ἀποθνῄσκω (# 633) pres. ind. act. to die. Here, "to be in danger of death," or it may mean that Paul abandons life daily, and knowing that he may die, continually prepares himself for death (Grosheide). νή (# 3755). Particle used in solemn oaths that means "truly," "yes" (RG, 1150). Followed by the acc. of the person or thing by which one swears or affirms: "yes, truly by my pride in you" (BAGD). ◆ 32 κατὰ ἄνθρωπον (# 2848; 476) in accordance w. human standards, on partly human terms (Barrett). ἐθηριομάχησα aor. ind. act. θηριομαχέω (# 2562) to fight w. wild animals. It is uncertain if Paul is speaking literally or figuratively. If figuratively, the beasts may have been the legalists or Judaizers (Robert E. Osborne, "Paul and the Wild Beasts," *JBL* 85 [1966]: 230; BBC). It may have been evil

men whose association corrupts. If there were no resurrection of the body, his struggles at Ephesus had been in vain (Abraham J. Malherbe, "The Beasts at Ephesus," *JBL* 87 [1968]: 80). Ind. w. εἰ (# 1623) in a 1st. class cond. cl. assuming the truth of the cond. μοι dat. ἐγώ (# 1609) I. Dat. of advantage. ὄφελος (# 4055) profit, benefit, good. φάγωμεν aor. subj. act. ἐσθίω (# 2266) to eat. πίωμεν aor. subj. act. πίνω (# 4403) to drink. The two subjs. are cohortative, "let us." αὔριον (# 892) tomorrow. ἀποθνῄσκομεν pres. ind. act. ἀποθνῄσκω (# 633) to die. Pres. expressing fut. time. For the quotation from Isa. 22:13 s. Barrett; for other parallels s. LAE, 296; Conzelmann; NW, 2, ii:396-400. ◆ 33 πλανᾶσθε pres. imp. pass. πλανάω (# 4414) to lead astray, to deceive. Pres. imp. w. the neg. μή (# 3590) is a command to stop an action in process. Pass. is permissive pass.: "Don't allow yourself to be deceived" (BD, 165). φθείρουσιν pres. ind. act. φθείρω (# 5780) to corrupt, to ruin. Gnomic pres. indicating that which is always true. ἦθος (# 2456) custom, way, moral, habit (BAGD). χρηστός (# 5982) useful, good (TLNT). ὁμιλία (# 3918) association, company (CCFJ, 3:200-01). κακός (# 2805) bad. A possible quotation from Menander's *Thais* (F.W. Danker, "Menander and the New Testament," *NTS* 10 [1964]: 365-68; NW, 2, ii:400-404). ◆ 34 ἐκνήψατε aor. act. imp. ἐκνήφω (# 1729) to become sober, to come to one's senses, to wake up. Prep. in compound points to sobriety attained out of drunkenness (MH, 309). Ingressive aor. imp. calls for immediate action (MKG, 272; VANT, 368). δικαίως (# 1469) adv., righteously, truly, really, indeed (Lietzmann, 194). ἁμαρτάνετε pres. imp. act. ἁμαρτάνω (# 279) to sin. Pres. imp. w. the neg. is a command not to continue an action in progress or a command not to always do an action (MKG, 272f). ἀγνωσία (# 57) ignorance, followed by the obj. gen., "ignorance of God." ἐντροπή (# 1959) shame, embarrassment, a state resulting from what one has or has not done (LN, 1:310). λαλῶ pres. ind. act. λαλέω (# 4246) to say, to speak. ◆ 35 ἐρεῖ fut. ind. act. λέγω (# 3306) to say. ἐγείρονται pres. ind. pass. (# 1586) to raise. Pres. to express fut. ποίῳ dat. sing. ποῖος (# 4481) what sort of, what kind of. σώματι dat. sing. σῶμα (# 5393) body. Instr. dat. ἔρχονται pres. ind. mid. (dep.) ἔρχομαι (# 2262) to come. Pres. to express fut. ◆ 36 ἄφρων (# 933) voc. sing. senseless, fool, one who is ignorant, one who does not have or use understanding (TDNT; GELTS, 74; CCFJ, 1:284). σπείρεις pres. ind. act. σπείρω (# 5062) to sow. ζῳοποιεῖται pres. ind. pass. ζῳοποιέω (# 2443) to make alive (s.v. 22). ἀποθάνῃ aor. sub. act. ἀποθνῄσκω (# 633) to die. Subj. w. ἐάν (# 1569) in a 3rd. class cond. cl. in which the cond. is assumed as possible. ◆ 37 γενησόμενον fut. mid. (dep.) part. γίνομαι (# 1181) to become. Adj. part., "the body that it will become." Perhaps Paul chose the analogy of the seed precisely because it implies continuity as well as discontinuity (Ronald J. Sider, "The Pauline Conception of the Resurrection Body in 1 Corinthians 15:35-54," *NTS* 21 [1975]: 432). γυμνός (# *1218*) naked, bare. κόκκος (# *3133*) grain. τύχοι aor. opt. act. τυγχάνω (# *5593*) to happen. Opt. in the idiom meaning "perhaps" (BAGD). σῖτος (# *4992*) wheat. λοιπός (# *3370*) rest, remaining. For rabbinic parallels using the analogy of bare grains arising w. many coverings to describe the resurrection s. PRJ, 305; SB, 3:475. ◆ **38** δίδωσιν pres. ind. act. δίδωμι (# *1443*) to give. ἠθέλησεν aor. ind. act. θέλω (# *2527*) to wish, to will, w. inf. God gives the seed a body in accordance w. His past decision at creation (Sider, *NTS* 21:432). καί (# *2779*) and. Perhaps epex., "that is...." σπέρμα (# *5065*) seed. ◆ **39** αὐτή (# *899*) fem. sing., same. κτῆνος (# *3229*) animal, a domesticated animal. Descriptive gen. of poss. gen. πτηνός (# *4764*) adj., feathered. Used as a subst. ("bird"). ἰχθύς (# *2716*) fish. The distinction made between different kinds of flesh was common to rabbinical thought, but not as familiar to Hellenistic thinking (SB, 3:475f; PRJ, 305f). ◆ **40** ἐπουράνος (# *2230*) heavenly, celestial; that is, upon heaven or existing in heaven (RWP), not the heavenly body of human beings or angels (Grosheide). ἐπίγειος (# *2103*) earthly, terrestrial; that is, the bodies of everything that lives on earth (Grosheide). ἕτερος (# *2283*) another, another of a different kind. δόξα (# *1518*) good opinion, reputation, brightness, splendor, glory (AS; TDNT; NIDNTT, 2:44-52; TLNT). ◆ **41** ἥλιος (# *2463*) sun. σελήνη (# *4943*) moon. ἀστήρ (# *843*) star. The lack of the article points to a characteristic of the class or of the single thing (BD, 132). γάρ (# *1142*) yes, and ... (Barrett). διαφέρει pres. ind. act. διαφέρω (# *1422*) to differ. The stars differed in brilliance or brightness (Conzelmann; Barrett). Gnomic pres. indicating a general truth. ◆ **42** οὕτως (# *4048*) so, thus. Paul now applies the preceding remarks (Grosheide). σπείρεται pres. ind. pass. σπείρω (# *5062*) to sow. φθορᾷ (# *5785*) dat. sing. corruption, that which is subject to decay. Corruption is also viewed as an evil power which affects all of creation as a result of Adam's sin (Sider, *NTS* 21:433). ἐγείρεται pres. ind. pass. ἐγείρω (# *1586*) to raise. ἀφθαρσίᾳ (# *914*) dat. sing. incorruption, that which is not subject to decay and control by sin. ◆ **43** ἀτιμίᾳ (# *871*) dat. sing. dishonor. The word was sometimes used of loss of the rights of citizenship. A corpse has no rights (Morris). ἀσθενείᾳ (# *819*) dat. sing. weakness. ◆ **44** ψυχικός (# *6035*) natural, that which pertains to the soul, a physical body which is suited to earthly life (SBT, 156) and is subject to sin (Sider, *NTS* 21:433ff). πνευματικός (# *4461*) spiritual, that which pertains to the spirit. It refers to a physical body renovated by the Spirit of God and therefore suited to heavenly immortality (SBT, 166; Sider, *NTS* 21:435). For the suf. which denotes an ethical or dynamic relation s. MH, 378. ◆ **45** γέγραπται perf. ind.

pass. γράφω (# *1211*) to write. Perf. denotes the abiding authoritative character of that which was written, "it stands written" (MM). ἐγένετο aor. ind. mid. (dep.) γίνομαι (# *1181*) to become, followed by the prep. w. acc. in the place of a pred. nom.: "the first Adam became a living soul" (MH, 462; BD, 86; KSV, 64). ζῶσαν aor. act. part. (adj.) ζάω (# *2409*) to live. ζωοποιοῦν pres. act. part. (adj.) ζωοποιέω (# *2443*) to make alive; part., life giving. It was in His saving work for men that Christ became a life-giving Spirit (Morris). ◆ **46** πρῶτον (# *4754*) first; nom. sing., pred. nom. πνευματικόν (# *4461*) spiritual. ἔπειτα (# *2083*) then. ◆ **47** ἐκ γῆς (# *1178*) out of the ground, earthly. The absence of the article stresses that the essential thing is the earth's specific quality (BD, 132). χοϊκός (# *5954*) dusty. The word stresses mortality due to earthly origin (SBT, 166). ◆ **48** οἷος (# *3888*) of what sort, such as; correlative pron. expressing quality (RG, 291, 731). ἐπουράνιος (# *2230*) heavenly, celestial. ◆ **49** ἐφορέσαμεν aor. ind. act. φορέω (# *5841*) to wear. Used in the papyri in the sense of wearing clothes, a breastplate, or a badge (MM; Preisigke, 2:700). εἰκόνα acc. sing. εἰκών (# *1635*) image (TDNT; NIDNTT, 2:286-88; TLNT; EDNT). φορέσομεν fut. ind. act. φορέω (# *5841*). The reading of the fut. is accepted instead of the aor. subj. since the context is didactic, instead of hortatory, giving a promise (Weiss; TC, 569). ◆ **50** φημί (# *5774*) pres. ind. act. to say. σάρξ καὶ αἷμα (# *4922*; *135*) flesh and blood. The phrase means our present mortal nature and refers to those who are still living (RP; Barrett; Fee). κληρονομῆσαι aor. act. inf. κληρονομέω (# *3099*) to inherit, to receive as an inheritance. Supplementary inf. w. δύναται (# *1538*). κληρονομεῖ pres. ind. act. κληρονομέω (# *3099*). Gnomic pres. stating a common truth. ◆ **51** πάντες οὐ here = οὐ πάντες not all of us. For the position of the neg. s. BD, 224; MT, 287. κοιμηθησόμεθα fut. ind. pass. κοιμάω (# *3121*) to sleep (s.v. 6). ἀλλαγησόμεθα fut. ind. pass. ἀλλαγάσσω (# *248*) to change, to alter. ◆ **52** ἄτομος (# *875*) indivisible because of smallness; here, "in a moment" (BAGD). ῥιπῇ (# *4846*) dat. sing. throwing, rapid movement. For example, casting a glance takes an extremely short time. Here, "in the twinkling of an eye" (BAGD). ἐν τῇ ἐσχάτῃ σάλπιγγι "at the last trumpet" (dat. sing. σάλπιγξ [# *4894*]). The last in a series of trumpets. According to the Jewish view the resurrection occurs w. the sound of the trumpet, w. seven trumpets sounded for the various stages of resurrection. At the seventh trumpet all were made alive and stood up on their feet (TDNT; SB, 3:481). σαλπίσει fut. ind. act. σαλπίζω (# *4895*) to sound a trumpet. Here used impersonally, "the trumpet will sound," "the trumpet shall trumpet" (RG, 392). ἐγερθήσονται fut. ind. pass. ἐγείρω (# *1586*) to raise. ἄφθαρτος (# *915*) incorruptible. ἀλλαγησόμεθα fut. ind. pass. ἀλλαγάσσω (# *248*) to change. ◆ **53** δεῖ (# *1256*) pres. ind. act. φθαρτός (# *5778*) corruptible, that which is subject to decay. ἐνδύσασθαι aor. mid. (dep.) inf. ἐνδύω (# *1907*) to put on, to put on as clothing. θνητός (# *2570*) mortal, that which is subject to death (M, 222). ἀθανασία (# *114*) immortality, that which is not subject to death. ◆ **54** ἐνδύσηται aor. subj. mid. (dep.) ἐνδύω (# *1907*) to put on (s.v. 53). Subj. w. ὅταν (# *4020*) in an indef. temp. cl. γενήσεται fut. ind. mid. (dep.) γίνομαι (# *1181*) to happen. γεγραμμένος perf. pass. part. γράφω (# *1211*) to write (s.v. 45). Part. as subst. κατεπόθη aor. ind. pass. καταπίνω (# *2927*) to drink down, to swallow down. Prep. in compound is perfective, "to swallow down completely." εἰς νῖκος (# *3777*) into victory. The translation of the Semitic phrase meaning forever, permanently, successfully (SL, 153-56; SB, 3:481f). ◆ **55** σου gen. sing. σύ (# *5148*) you; "your," emphatic by its position. θάνατε (# *2505*) voc. sing., O death! νῖκος (# *3777*) victory. κέντρον (# *3034*) sting. The word represents death as a venomous creature, a scorpion or a hornet, which is rendered harmless (RP). ◆ **56** ἁμαρτία (# *281*) sin. The article indicates the principle of sin. Death is not simply the result of decay; rather, it is the result of the deadly poison, sin itself, which became all the more energized in our lives through acquaintance with the law (Fee). ◆ **57** χάρις (# *5921*) grace, thanks. διδόντι pres. act. part. (adj.) δίδωμι (# *1443*) to give. Pres. emphasizes the certainty of the victory (Barrett). ◆ **58** ὥστε (# *6063*) therefore. It draws a conclusion from the previous. ἑδραῖος (# *1612*) firm, steadfast. Pred. nom. without the art. stresses the character. γίνεσθε pres. imp. mid. (dep.) γίνομαι (# *1181*) to become. Pres. imp. calls for constant action, attitude, or state. ἀμετακίνητος (# *293*) unmovable, not capable of being moved from its place. περισσεύοντες pres. act. part. περισσεύω (# *4355*) to abound, to be in abundance. Part. of manner. εἰδότες perf. act. part. (causal) οἶδα (# *3857*) to know. Def. perf. w. pres. meaning. κόπος (# *3160*) effort, labor (s.v. 10). κενός (# *3031*) empty, vain.

1 Corinthians 16

◆ **1** περὶ δέ "now concerning." The words introduce another topic that Paul is to deal with (s. 7:1). λογεία (# *3356*) collection, contribution. The word appears in the papyri in the sense of collection, particularly in the sense of religious collection for a god or temple (LAE, 105f; BS, 142f). The article refers to a specific collection. The Christians evidently had grave financial difficulties in the society of Jerusalem (Acts 6:1; Brian Capper, "The Palestinian Cultural Context of the Earliest Christian Community of Goods," BAFCS, 4:323-56; SB, 3:316-18; RP; Fee; DPL, 143-47). τῆς gen. sing. ὁ (# *3836*) the. Art. used as a relative pron. εἰς (# *1659*) w. acc., to, for. ὥσπερ (# *6061*) just as. διέταξα aor. ind. act. διατάσσω (# *1411*) to arrange, to order, to command, to give express commands (MH, 302). τῆς

Γαλατίας (# *3836*; *1130*) of Galatia. Perhaps referring to the Roman province and the churches that had been established there on Paul's first missionary journey. καί (# *2779*) also. ποιήσατε aor. imp. act. ποιέω (# *4472*) to do. Aor. imp. calls for a specific action. ◆ **2** κατά (# *2848*) w. acc.; the distributive use of the prep.: "on every first day of the week" (RP). μίαν σαββάτου (# *1651*; *4879*) a Hebraic expression for the first day of the week; that is, Sunday (Hering; Conzelmann; Fee; s. also the essays in FSLD, esp. D.R. de Lacey, "The Sabbath/Sunday Questions and the Law in the Pauline Corpus," FSLD, 159-95, esp. 184-86). τιθέτω pres. imp. act. 3rd. pers. sing. τίθημι (# *5502*) to set, to lay, used w. the prepositional phrase παρ' ἑαυτῷ; that is, "in his home" (RWP). Pres. imp. could be iterative pointing to the repeated acts, or it could call for a habit of life. θησαυρίζων pres. act. part. θησαυρίζω (# *2564*) to store up, to save up. Part. of means or manner explaining how each one is to lay aside. ὅ τι ἐάν whatever, the generalized rel. pron. εὐοδῶται pres. subj. pass. εὐοδόω (# *2338*) to send well on one's way, to be led along a good road. It then has the meaning "to get along well," "to prosper," "to succeed," and was used of having success in business (BAGD; Lietzmann; GELTS, 188). Subj. in an indef. rel. cl. ἔλθω aor. subj. act. ἔρχομαι (# *2262*) to come. Subj. w. ὅταν ("whenever") in an indef. temp. cl. γίνωνται pres. subj. mid. (dep.) γίνομαι (# *1181*) to become, to be. Subj. w. ἵνα (# *2671*) in a purp. cl. ◆ **3** παραγένωμαι aor. subj. mid. (dep.) παραγίνομαι (# *4134*) to arrive. Subj. w. ὅταν (# *4020*) in an indef. temp. cl., "whenever I arrive" (RWP). οὓς ἐάν (# *4005*; *1569*) whomever (pl.). δοκιμάσητε aor. subj. act. δοκιμάζω (# *1507*) to approve after examination, to accept as proven, to approve (BAGD; TDNT; GELTS, 119; TLNT; MM; NDIEC, 1:130-31; 2:14). In an inscription the vb. is almost a t.t. for passing as fit for a public office (MM). It was also used to indicate a government approved doctor (Preisigke, 1:395; NDIEC, 2:13-14). δι' ἐπιστολῶν (# *2186*) through letters, w. letters. Commendatory letters were well known in antiquity (Barrett; Conzelmann; NDIEC, 7:55, 90; s. 2 Cor. 3:1). πέμψω fut. ind. act. πέμπω (# *4287*) to send. ἀπενεγκεῖν aor. act. inf. ἀποφέρω (# *708*) to carry away, to take home, to bring to its destination. It was not the removal of the money from Corinth, but its being conveyed to Jerusalem that was the important point (RP). Inf. expressing purp. χάρις (# *5921*) grace, generosity, favor (TDNT; Trench, *Synonyms*, 167; TLNT). ◆ **4** ἄξιος (# *545*) that which is equal in weight, worthy, right. Paul would make the journey if circumstances were such that the work demanded him going (Grosheide). ᾖ pres. subj. act. εἰμί (# *1639*) to be. Subj. w. ἐάν (# *1569*) in a 3rd. class cond. cl. assuming the probability of the cond. κἀμέ = καὶ ἐμέ acc. sing. κἀγώ (# *2743*) as subject of the inf. πορεύεσθαι pres. mid. (dep.) inf. πορεύομαι (# *4513*) to travel, to make a journey. Epex. inf. w. the adj. **πορεύσονται** fut. ind. mid. (dep.). πορεύομαι (# 4513). ◆ **5 ἐλεύσομαι** fut. ind. mid. (dep.) ἔρχομαι (# 2262) to come. **διέλθω** aor. subj. act. διέρχομαι (# 1451) to pass through. **διέρχομαι** pres. ind. mid. (dep.). Pres. used to express the fut., "I am going to pass through" (BD, 168). ◆ **6 πρὸς ὑμᾶς** w. you. The prep. w. acc. denotes position (IBG, 52f). **τυχόν** aor. act. part. n. sing. τυγχάνω (# 5593) to happen, to occur. Aor. part. is used here as an adv., meaning "possibly," "perhaps" (RWP). **παραμενῶ** fut. ind. act. παραμένω (# 4169) to remain, to stay, to remain w. someone. The contrast is w. passing through Macedonia. **παραχειμάσω** fut. ind. act. παραχειμάζω (# 4199) to spend the winter. Once winter is past ships can sail again. The winter season would thus compel Paul to sojourn at Corinth (Grosheide). Land travel was generally closed from Nov. 11 to Mar. 10. Sea travel was considered very dangerous during this time (Brian Rapske, "Acts, Travel and Shipwreck," BAFCS, 2:3, 22). **προπέμψητε** aor. subj. act. προπέμπω (# 4636) to send forth, to help on one's journey w. food, money by arranging for companions, means of travel, etc. (BAGD). Subj. w. ἵνα (# 2671) to express purp. **οὗ ἐὰν** wherever, w. subj. **πορεύωμαι** pres. subj. mid. (dep.) πορεύομαι (# 4513) to go, to travel. Subj. in indef. spatial construction. ◆ **7 πάραδος** (# 4227) a passing visit; here, "in passing" (RP). **ἰδεῖν** aor. act. inf. ὁράω (# 3972) to see. Supplementary inf. **ἐπιμεῖναι** aor. act. inf. ἐπιμένω (# 2152) to remain, to stay for a time. Inf. as obj. of the vb. ἐλπίζω. **ἐπιτρέψῃ** aor. subj. act. ἐπιτρέπω (# 2205) to allow, to permit. Subj. w. ἐάν (# 1569) in a 3rd. class cond. cl. where the cond. is considered probable. ◆ **8 ἐπιμενῶ** fut. ind. act. ἐπιμένω (# 2152) to remain. **πεντηκοστῆ** (# 4300). Pentecost. Paul was using the Jewish calendar. For the Jewish celebration of Pentecost s. Acts 2:1. ◆ **9 θύρα** (# 2598) door. The term "door" is a metaphor for opportunity (Bruce; NW, 2, i:409-10). **μοι** dat. sing. ἐγώ (# 1609) I. Here, "to me," "for me." Dat. of advantage. **ἀνέῳγεν** perf. ind. act. ἀνοίγω (# 487) to open; perf., to stand open. The vb. is intransitive and means "stand wide open" (RWP). **ἐνεργής** (# 1921) effective, active, powerful. The opening of the door promises a rich field of labor (BAGD). The word was used of a mill in working order or things or persons which were active (MM; Preisigke, 1:488; CCFJ, 2:102). **ἀντικείμενοι** pres. mid. (dep.) part. (adj.) ἀντίκειμαι (# 512) to lie against someone, to oppose, to be in opposition, to resist. ◆ **10 ἔλθη** aor. subj. act. ἔρχομαι (# 2262) to come. Subj. w. ἐάν (# 1569) in a 3rd. class cond. cl. where the cond. is considered probable. **ἀφόβως** (# 925) without fear. Paul is not thinking about the outward dangers but about the opposition that he himself faced (Schlatter). **γένηται** aor. subj. mid. (dep.) γίνομαι (# 1181) to become. Subj. w. ἵνα (# 2671) as obj. of the vb. **ἐργάζεται** pres. ind. mid. (dep.) ἐργάζομαι

(# 2262) to carry out, to accomplish, to work at. Pres. indicates continual and habitual action. ◆ **11 ἐξουθενήσῃ** aor. subj. act. ἐξουθενέω (# 2024) to consider as nothing, to despise. Prep. in compound not only has a perfective force but it also makes the trans. idea clear (MH, 310). Subj. in a neg. command or prohibition. **προπέμψατε** aor. imp. act. προπέμπω (# 4636) to send on the way (s.v. 6). Aor. imp. calls for a specific action. **ἔλθῃ** aor. subj. act. ἔρχομαι (# 2262) to go. Subj. expressing purp. **ἐκδέχομαι** (# 1683) pres. ind. mid. (dep.) to expect, to wait for. The idea of the prep. in compound is "to be ready for" (MH, 310). ◆ **12 περὶ δὲ Ἀπολλῶ** (# 1254; 663) "now concerning Apollos." This may mean that the Corinthians in their letter had inquired about Apollos (Barrett). **πολλὰ** n. pl. (# 4498) great, much, used here as an adverb, earnestly, often. **παρεκάλεσα** aor. ind. act. παρακαλέω (# 4151) to exhort, to encourage, to ask. **ἔλθῃ** aor. subj. act. ἔρχομαι (# 2262). Subj. w. ἵνα (# 2671) as. obj. of the vb. **παρεκάλεσα**. **πάντως** (# 4122) adv., at all, simply; w. the neg., not at all, wholly not (Barrett; Kistemaker). **ἦν** impf. ind. act. εἰμί (# 1639). **θέλημα** (# 2525) wish, will. It refers to either God's will or the will or wish of Apollos (RP; Kistemaker). **ἔλθῃ** aor. subj. act. ἔρχομαι (# 2262). Subj. w. ἵνα (# 2671) in an epex. cl. explaining θέλημα. **ἐλεύσεται** fut. ind. mid. (dep.) ἔρχομαι (# 2262). **εὐκαιρήσῃ** aor. subj. act. εὐκαιρέω (# 2320) to find a good time, to have opportunity. Subj. w. ὅταν (# 4020) in an indef. temp. cl. ◆ **13 γρηγορεῖτε** pres. imp. act. γρηγορέω (# 1213) to watch, to stay awake, to be alert (GELTS, 93). Pres. imp. is a command for habitual action. **στήκετε** pres. imp. act. στήκω (# 5112) to stand, to stand fast. **ἀνδρίζεσθε** pres. imp. mid. (dep.) ἀνδρίζομαι (# 437) to conduct oneself in a manly or courageous way, to be brave, to display courage (BAGD; CCFJ, 1:117). The word is common in the LXX in exhortations (Josh. 1:6, 7, 9; GELTS, 34; RP). Aristotle uses the word to indicate the display of courage which he describes as the mean between fear and confidence (*Nichomachean Ethics* III, VI, 1, 12; NW 2, ii:411). The word was also used in the papyri in the exhortation, "therefore do not be fainthearted, but be courageous as a man" (MM; note also ἀνδραγαθέω "to act like a good man" as used in a letter to a philosopher telling him to finish his task and not be distracted by wealth or the charm of youth, NDIEC, 4:67-70). Josephus uses the term to describe the courageous fighting of the Jewish defenders of Jotapatha (Jos., *JW*, 3:268), and in his description of Titus telling his troops to be courageous, but using forethought and not running personal risks (Jos., *JW*, 5:316). It also appears in Titus' speech of encouragement to his soldiers as they are discouraged in their siege of Jerusalem (Jos., *JW*, 6:50). Pres. imp. calls for an habitual action. **κραταιοῦσθε** pres. imp. pass. κραταιόω (# 3194) to be strong, to become strong (BAGD). In the LXX it is used

w. ἀνδρίζομαι (2 Sam. 10:12 [LXX 2 Kings]; s. 1 Sam. 4:9 [LXX 1 Kings 4:9]). ◆ **14 ἐν ἀγάπη** (# 27) in or w. love. This was a basic, but lacking, ingredient among the believers at Corinth (s. ch. 13). **γινέσθω** pres. imp. mid. (dep.) γίνομαι (# 1181) to become. ◆ **15 παρακαλῶ** pres. ind. act. παρακαλέω (# 4151) to encourage, to urge (TDNT; TLNT; EDNT). **οἴδατε** perf. ind. act. οἶδα (# 3857) def. perf. w. a pres. meaning, to know. **ἀπαρχή** (# 569) firstfruit (s. 15:20). **ἔταξαν** aor. ind. act. τάσσω (# 5435) to appoint. They had appointed themselves to the service of their fellow Christians. It was a self-imposed duty (RP). ◆ **16 ὑποτάσσησθε** pres. subj. mid. (dir. mid., "subject yourselves") ὑποτάσσω (# 6718) to subject oneself, to be in subjection, w. dat. Subj. w. **ἵνα** (# 2671) as obj. of the vb. παρακαλῶ in v. 15. **συνεργοῦντι** pres. act. part. (adj.) συνεργέω (# 5300) to work w., to work together, to cooperate. **κοπιῶντι** pres. act. part. κοπιάω (# 3159) to labor, to work to the point of exhaustion (s. 15:10). ◆ **17 ἐπί** (# 2093) w. the dat., over, on the occasion of. **παρουσία** (# 4242) dat. sing. coming, arrival. **ὑστέρημα** (# 5729) lack, want, that which comes short. Paul could mean that he had missed his Christian friends, and this trio had renewed his acquaintance w. the city (Morris). **ἀνεπλήρωσαν** aor. ind. act. ἀναπληρόω (# 405) to fill up again, to supply. ◆ **18 ἀνέπαυσαν** aor. ind. act. ἀναπαύω (# 399) to give intermission from labor, to refresh (AS). **ἐπιγινώσκετε** pres. imp. act. ἐπιγινώσκω (# 2105) to recognize, to acknowledge. **τοιοῦτος** (# 5525) such a one, one belonging to this class or having this quality. ◆ **19 ἀσπάζονται** pres. ind. mid. (dep.) ἀσπάζομαι (# 832) to greet. **πολλά**

(# 4498) n. pl. used as an adv., heartily, s.v. 12. **τῇ κατ' οἶκον αὐτῶν ἐκκλησίᾳ** (# 3875; 1711) w. the church in their house. For the house church s. Bradley Blue, "Acts and the House Church," BAFCS, 2:119-222. ◆ **20 ἀσπάσασθε** aor. imp. mid. (dep.) ἀσπάζομαι (# 832) to greet. **φίλημα** (# 5799) kiss. In the ancient world it was customary to give a kiss as a greeting both at the meeting and at the departure. The kiss as symbol of love, fellowship, and thankfulness may have been at this time a liturgical act indicating the forgiveness which had been received and the willingness to partake of the Lord's Supper (William Klassen, "The Sacred Kiss in the New Testament: An Example of Social Boundary," *NTS* 39 [1993]: 122-35; KP, 3:381; TDNT; Conzelmann). ◆ **21 ἀσπασμός** (# 833) greeting. **τῇ ἐμῇ χειρὶ Παύλου** (# 5931; 4263) w. my hand, Paul. This means that the letter to this point has been inscribed by someone else, probably Sosthenes, and the rest by Paul (Fee). ◆ **22 φιλεῖ** pres. ind. act. φιλέω (# 5797) to love (TDNT; EDNT; TLNT). Ind. in a 1st. class cond. cl. which assumes the reality of the cond. **ἤτω** pres. imp. act. 3rd. pers. sing. εἰμί (# 1639) to be. **ἀνάθεμα** (# 353) anathema, dedicated for destruction, cursed. **Μαράναθα** (# 3448) or to be divided as μαρὰν ἀθά an Aramaic expression. The first possible division would be a pres. imp.–"Our Lord, come!"–understood as a prayer. The second possible division–"Our Lord comes!"–is fut. ind.; as perf. ind., "Our Lord is here!" is understood as a confession (ECC, 121-24; SB, 3:493-94; AT, 525, 629-30; TDNT; Fee).

2 Corinthians

2 Corinthians 1

◆ **1 οὖσῃ** pres. act. part. dat. fem. sing. εἰμί (# *1639*) to be. Rel. use of the part., "which is at Corinth." **οὖσιν** pres. act. part. dat. masc. pl. εἰμί. **ὅλῃ** dat. fem. sing. ὅλος (# *3910*) whole, entire, complete. **Ἀχαΐα** (# *938*) Achaia. It refers to the Roman province which included the whole of Greece (ZPEB, 1:35f; KP, 1:32-38; Strabo 17:3.25), and included Corinth as the capital, Cenchraea (s. Acts 18:1; DNP, 1:62-69) and Athens (Windisch). ◆ **2 χάρις** (# *5921*) grace. God's favor to those who do not deserve it (TDNT; EDNT; CPP, 132-33; Martin; Gordon D. Fee, "ΧΑΡΙΣ in II Corinthians 1:15," *NTS* 24 [1977-78]: 533-38). ◆ **3 εὐλογητός** (# *2329*) blessed, a Jewish ascription of praise to God acknowledging Him as the source of all blessing (TDNT; TDOT; NIDNTT, 1:206; EDNT; Furnish). **οἰκτιρμῶν** gen. pl. οἰκτιρμός (# *3880*) compassion, lament, or sorrow which arises from the pitiful state of the object; then the feeling of compassion and understanding. Used in Judaism to describe the character of God (TDNT; EDNT; SB, 3:494; Martin; Rom. 12:1). Gen. may be due to Semitic influence indicating character or attribute (BG, 14f). **παράκλησις** (# *4155*) encouragement, consolation, comfort. It is the standing beside a person to encourage him when he is undergoing severe testing (Hughes; MNTW; CCFJ, 3:296; Furnish; SB, 3:494). ◆ **4 παρακαλῶν** pres. act. part. παρακαλέω (# *4151*) to encourage, to comfort (s. Rom. 12:1). Part. as subst., "The one who encourages or stands beside to comfort." Pres. indicates a ongoing or characteristic activity. **ἐπί** (# *2093*) w. dat., on, on the occasion of. **θλίψει** dat. sing. θλῖψις (# *2568*) pressure, affliction, crushing (Plummer; Trench, *Synonyms*, 202f; Thrall; DPL, 919-21). **εἰς** (# *1650*) followed by the acc., w. the inf. to express purp. **δύνασθαι** pres. pass. (dep.) inf. δύναμαι (# *1538*) to be able to, w. inf. **θλίψει** dat. sing. θλῖψις (# *2568*). Used previously w. the article it means, "all tribulation actually encountered." Here, without the article, "in any which may be encountered," or "in any kind of affliction" (BD, 114; MT, 200). **ἧς** gen. fem. sing. ὅς (# *4005*) who, which, what; rel. pron. Gen. instead of the acc. is by attraction to the case of its antecedent (BD, 154). **παρακαλούμεθα** pres. ind. pass. παρακαλέω (# *4151*). Pres. points to the continual action; or it is iterat. and points to the comfort received every time trouble and afflictions arise. The 1st. pers. pl. in Paul's

letters may refer to himself and the recipients, or to a specific group within the community, or to Paul and his fellow-workers, or only to himself, i.e., a literary pl. For a discussion of this use, s. Thrall, 105-7; Samuel Byrskog, "Co-Senders, Co-Authors and Paul's Use of the First Person Plural," *ZNW* 87 (1996): 230-50. ◆ **5 περισσεύει** pres. ind. act. περισσεύω (# *4355*) to abound, to overflow. **πάθημα** (# *4077*) suffering. **τοῦ Χριστοῦ** (# *5986*) to follow Christ is to follow Him into suffering. In this too disciples must expect to be identified w. the master (Hughes; Martin). ◆ **6 θλιβόμεθα** pres. ind. pass. θλίβω (# *2567*) pass. to be afflicted, to suffer pressure (s.v. 4). **ὑπέρ** w. the gen., "w. a view to" (IBG, 65). It points to that which one wants to attain (BD, 121). **τῆς ὑμῶν παρακλήσεως** your comfort (# *4155*) obj. gen. **ἐνεργουμένης** pres. mid./pass. part. ἐνεργέω (# *1919*) to be effective; pass., is made to work by him who bestows it, to be effective (Furnish). Mid. may be better, "which makes itself felt," "takes effect" (Plummer; Barrett). **ὑπομονῇ** (# *5705*) remaining under, patience, endurance. It was used in the endurance of that which has come upon man against his will. In classical Gr. it is used also of the ability of a plant to live under hard and unfavorable circumstances. It was later used of that quality which enabled men to die for their god. (NTW, 59f; TDNT; RAC, 9:243-94; TLNT). **ὧν** gen. pl. ὅς (# *4005*) rel. pron. gen. pl. Gen. instead of the acc. because of attraction to the antecedent ("the same suffering"). **καί** (# *2779*) also. **πάσχομεν** pres. ind. act. πάσχω (# *4248*) to suffer. Pres. points to the continual or repeated suffering. ◆ **7 βέβαιος** (# *1010*) firm, certain, valid, guaranteed (TLNT; s. 1 Cor. 1:6). **εἰδότες** perf. act. part. (causal) οἶδα (# *3857*) to know. Def. perf. w. pres. meaning. **κοινωνός** (# *3128*) partner, one who has a common share w. another, common participant. Used in the papyri for a partner in business or a participant in a sacrifice (MM), w. gen. indicating the thing which is shared. Here it is the common sharing in the divine encouragement (Martin). **παράκλησις** (# *4155*) comfort, encouragement (s.v. 3). ◆ **8 θέλομεν** pres. ind. act. θέλω (# *2527*) to desire. **ἀγνοεῖν** pres. act. inf. ἀγνοέω (# *51*) to not know, to be ignorant. Paul uses this idiomatic expression to call attention to the second reason for his thanks (Martin). **ὑπέρ** (# *5642*) w. gen., concerning (IBG, 65). **γενομένης** aor. mid. (dep.) part. γίνομαι (# *1181*) to become, to happen. **Ἀσία** (# *823*) Asia; the

Roman province whose capital was Ephesus (Barrett). Paul may be referring to the riot in Ephesus or to the breakdown of law and order resulting in danger to him as suggested by his being exposed to wild beasts (s. 1 Cor. 15:32), or to a death sentence passed by the civil courts (Martin; Hughes). καθ' ὑπερβολήν (# 2848; 5651) lit., "a throwing beyond"; then "beyond measure," "exceedingly." ὑπέρ (# 5642) w. acc., above, beyond (IBG, 64); "beyond the normal power of endurance" (Hughes). ἐβαρήθημεν aor. ind. pass. βαρέω (# 976) to weigh down; pass., to be burdened down. Used in the papyri of misfortune or injustice (BAGD; MM). ἐξαπορηθῆναι aor. pass. inf. ἐξαπορέομαι (# 1989) to be without a way out, to be in utter despair. Prep. in compound is perfective (MH, 310). Inf. to express result, "so that we were utterly without way of escape" (Plummer). ζῆν pres. act. inf. ζάω (# 2409) to live, to remain alive, to continue to live. Gen. of the inf. w. the vb. explaining the despair, "even to live" (M, 217f). ◆ 9 ἀλλά (# 247) yes indeed, certainly. The word is confirmatory or emphatic (DM, 240). ἑαυτοῖς dat. pl. ἑαυτοῦ (# 1571) himself. Here, "within ourselves." For the strengthening of the reflex., which was frequent in Attic, s. BD, 148. ἀπόκριμα (# 645) response, verdict, death sentence. A t.t. used for an official decision in answer to the petition of an embassy (Martin; Colin J. Hemer, "A Note on II Cor. 1:9," TB 23 [1972]: 104f; MM; BS, 257; TDNT). τοῦ θανάτου (# 2505) gen. sing., of death. Appositional gen. describing the content of the decree (Furnish). ἐσχήκαμεν perf. ind. act. ἔχω (# 2400) to have. Perf. means "having gotten, I continue to have" and indicates that though the sentence was not immediately carried out, it remained in force (K.L. McKay, "Syntax in Exegesis," TB 23 [1972]: 48; Barrett; Furnish). The action completed in the past is conceived in terms of pres. time for the sake of vividness. This vivid perf. indicates the experience was a dreadful memory to Paul (RG, 896-97). Perf. may, however, have here the force of a pluperf. referring to the past (VA, 260-63; Furnish; Martin). ἵνα (# 2671) used here to express purp. not result; expresses God's purpose (Windisch). πεποιθότες perf. act. part. πείθω (# 4275) to persuade, perf. to have been persuaded, to trust in. ὦμεν pres. subj. act. εἰμί (# 1639) to be. Used in a periphrastic construction. The neg. suggests the discontinuance of an existing condition (Barrett). ἐγείροντι pres. act. part. ἐγείρω (# 1586) to rise. Perhaps an allusion or quotation from the second prayer of the Eighteen Petition Prayer which was quoted three times a day by every Israelite (HJP, 2, ii:85-89; JPF, 2:801; M, Berakoth 4:1-7, s. especially 5:2; SB, 4:208-49). ◆ 10 τηλικοῦτος (# 5496) so great. terrible. ἐρρύσατο aor. ind. mid. (dep.) ῥύομαι (# 4861) to rescue. The prep. seems to imply peril rather than death personified, but the use of this prep. w. the vb. is a common expression (s. Job

33:30; 2 Tim. 4:17, 18; Plummer). ῥύσεται fut. ind. mid. (dep.) ῥύομαι (# 4861) to rescue. ἠλπίκαμεν perf. ind. act. ἐλπίζω (# 1827) to hope. Perf. means, "towards whom we have set our hope, and continue to do so" (EGT). ◆ 11 συνυπουργούντων pres. act. part. συνυπουργέω (# 5348) to work together, to cooperate. The word could mean cooperation w. one another or cooperation w. God (Barrett). Part. in a gen. abs. which is either temp. ("while") or manner ("in that"). δέησις (# 1255) prayer, request. προσώπος (# 4725) face. Here it may have the meaning "person," "from many persons" (Plummer), or it may retain the lit. meaning "face" and be a picture of many upturned faces (RWP; Hughes). εἰς (# 1650) for, to; here in the sense of "the gracious gift for us." χάρισμα (# 5922) gracious gift; here it probably refers to his deliverance (Martin; Furnish). διὰ πολλῶν (# 1328; 4498) through many. The word may be viewed as masc., it may be taken w. following vb. ("may be thanked for by many") or w. the word χάρισμα, meaning "the gift which reached us by the agency of many" (IBG, 108). εὐχαριστηθῇ aor. subj. pass. εὐχαρίζω (# 2373) to give thanks. Subject of the pass. vb. is χάρισμα, i.e., Paul's deliverance (Bultmann) and the pass. is to be understood as "that you might give thanks for the gift" (Lietzmann, 197). ◆ 12 καύχησις (# 3018) boasting, glorying. The ending of the noun means "the act of glorying," but in v. 14 the word is "the thing boasted of" (RWP). μαρτύριον (# 3457) witness, testimony, evidence (Plummer). The word is an explanation of the previous pron. αὕτη. συνείδησις (# 5287) conscience (Rom. 2:15). ἁπλότητι (# 605) simplicity, frankness. For a defense of the variant reading ἁγιότητι (# 42) holiness s. Hughes; for the adopted reading s. TC, 575. εἰλικρινείᾳ (# 1636) without mixture, sincerity, purity, of good faith, candid (1 Cor. 5:8; TLNT; for a discussion of the etymology "judged by the sun," "determined by sunlight" s. GEW, 1:450; Hughes). τοῦ θεοῦ (# 2536) of God. Probably subjective gen., "God-given simplicity and sincerity" (Plummer). σαρκικός (# 4920) fleshly. Fleshly wisdom which is not the work of the Holy Spirit but of human nature, itself enlightened and unimproved, guided by the sinful lust of the flesh (Meyer; s. Rom. 7:14). ἀνεστράφημεν aor. ind. pass. ἀναστρέφω (# 418) pass., to turn back and forth, to conduct oneself, "to live in the sense of the practice of certain principles (BAGD). It is always used w. the kind of behavior more exactly described (MM; TLNT, 111-14). περισσοτέρως (# 4359) comp. of περισσός (# 4356) abundantly; comp., more abundantly, even more. Here in a elative sense, "especially" (BAGD). ◆ 13 ἄλλα (# 257) other things. γράφομεν pres. ind. act. γράφω (# 1211) to write. Pres. refers to all the letters that Paul writes (Hering). ἀλλ' ἤ (# 247; 2445) except (BD, 233). ἀναγινώσκετε pres. ind. act. ἀναγινώσκω (# 336) to read. ἐπιγινώσκετε pres. ind. act. ἐπιγινώσκω (# 2105) to acknowledge, to know w.

certainty. He is referring to the Corinthians' certain knowledge of his character through firsthand experience (Hughes). τέλος (# 5465) completion, end. ἕως τέλους (# 2401; 2445) to the end, perhaps w. the meaning "completely" (Barrett). ἐπιγνώσεσθε fut. ind. mid. (dep.) ἐπιγινώσκω (# 2105) to acknowledge. ◆ 14 ἐπέγνωτε aor. ind. act. ἐπιγινώσκω (# 2105) to acknowledge (s.v. 13). ἀπὸ μέρους (# 608; 3538) partially. The phrase determines the degree of recognition (Windisch). ὅτι (# 4022) that. Here it is not causal (Plummer), but it gives the content of knowledge. καύχημα (# 3017) boasting, ground of boasting (s.v. 12). The apostle shares the experience of the community because both share something which originates beyond them. For this reason Paul can write, "I hope ... that you can be proud of us, as we can be of you, on the day of the Lord Jesus" (PAA, 234). For this word and the boasting of the apostle s. PAA, 233-38; NIDNTT, 1:227-29; TDNT; TLNT. ◆ 15 πεποίθησις (# 4301) trust, confidence (s.v. 9). ἐβουλόμην impf. ind. mid. (dep.) βούλομαι (# 1089) to will, to decide to, w. inf. The word implies an act of will, a decision (Barrett). Impf. pictures his former state of mind (RWP). πρότερον (# 4728) adv., formerly, earlier, at first. ἐλθεῖν aor. act. inf. ἔρχομαι (# 2262) to come. δεύτερος (# 1311) second. χάρις (# 5921) grace, benefit, favor. They would have had two opportunities of receiving spiritual communication from him in person (Hughes; s.v. 2). σχῆτε aor. subj. act. ἔχω (# 2400) to have; aor. to get, to receive. (M, 110, 247). Subj. w. ἵνα (# 2671) in a purp. cl. ◆ 16 δι' ὑμῶν (# 1328; 5148) w. gen., through you (Plummer). διελθεῖν aor. act. inf. διέρχομαι (# 1451) to pass through. προπεμφθῆναι aor. pass. inf. προπέμπω (# 4636) to send forth, to outfit for a trip (s. 1 Cor. 16:6). Compl. infs. are to be taken w. the main vb. of v. 15 (ἐβουλόμην). ◆ 17 οὖν (# 4036) therefore. It introduces a false conclusion drawn by some of the readers (Thrall). βουλόμενος pres. mid. part. (causal) βούλομαι (# 1089) to desire (s.v. 15). μήτι ἄρα (# 3516; 726) Used to introduce a question in which an indignant neg. answer is called for (RWP): "You really don't think ... do you?" (Thrall; Barrett). τῇ ἐλαφρίᾳ (# 1786) lightness, fickleness, vacillation, irresponsibility (Furnish). ἐχρησάμην aor. ind. mid. (dep.) χράομαι (# 5968) to use. βουλεύομαι (# 1086) pres. ind. mid. (dep.) βουλεύω (# 1086) to make plans, to consider, to decide (Windisch). κατὰ σάρκα (# 2848; 4922) according to the flesh; that is, in a worldly manner, opportunistically (Furnish). ἵνα (# 2671) w. subj. Normally introduces a purp. cl., but in this case the idea of result is possible: "w. the result that" (Hughes; BD, 198). ᾖ pres. subj. act. εἰμί (# 1639) to be. ναί (# 4922) yes. The duplication of the words "yes" and "no" strengthens the picture of the untrustworthy man, who affirms just as fervently as he afterwards denies (Meyer). ◆ 18 πιστός (# 4412) faithful, trustworthy. There is an appeal to God's char-

acter as faithful, or covenant-keeping, and so He is the guarantor of His promises. This may be a word play on the Heb. word 'mn (אמן) (Martin). ◆ 19 γάρ (# 1142) for. The position of the word emphasizes the gen. τοῦ θεοῦ (# 2536) God's (BD, 251). "For it is this faithful God's Son" (Plummer). κηρυχθείς aor. pass. part. κηρύσσω (# 3062) to proclaim, to preach, to herald (TDNT; EDNT). ἐγένετο aor. ind. mid. (dep.) γίνομαι (# 1181) to become; here, to be. γέγονεν perf. ind. act. γίνομαι (# 1181) to become. Perf. emphasizes the continuing state or condition: "in Him—yes—was and continues to be reality" (Hughes). ◆ 20 ὅσος (# 4012) how many; rel. pron. indicating quantity. ἐπαγγελίαι (# 2039) promise. ἀμήν (# 297) A Heb. word meaning "true," "trustworthy"; suggesting solidity, firmness, and used as a strengthening and confirming statement (Martin; Barrett; NIDNTT, 1:97-100; TDNT; EDNT; DCH). The use of the article w. the word means "the customary amen" (Plummer). ◆ 21 βεβαιῶν pres. act. part. βεβαιόω (# 1011) to make a legal guarantee; appears often in the guarantee cl. of a bill of sale (Preisigke; MM; BS, 104-109; TLNT). χρίσας aor. act. part. χρίω (# 5987) to anoint. The anointing here refers to the anointing of the Holy Spirit at conversion which every believer receives (BHS, 131-34). ◆ 22 σφραγισάμενος aor. mid. part. (subst.) σφραγίζω (# 5381) to seal. Goods were sealed as a guarantee indicating not only ownership but also the correctness of the contents (BS, 239; MM; TDNT). δούς aor. act. part. δίδωμι (# 1443) to give. Subst. part. ἀρραβών (# 775) pledge, earnest, down payment. The term means a deposit which is in itself a guarantee that the full amount will be paid (Hughes; SB, 3:495). For the use of the Aramaic word ערב in the sense of "surety," or to act as a guarantor in commercial texts dealing w. the sale of property, a house, or note of indebtedness, s. AT, 315-16, 320-19, text # M 31, 32; V 45; MPAT, 142-43, text # 41; 148-49, text # 45; 150-51, text # 47; 156-57, text # 51; For the word taken over as a loan word in Gr. s. NW, 2, i:416-17; MM; NDIEC, 1:83. τοῦ πνεύματος (# 4460) of the Spirit. Here, gen. of apposition, "the guarantee consisting of the Spirit" (MT, 214). ◆ 23 ἐπικαλοῦμαι pres. ind. mid. (dep.) ἐπικαλέω (# 2126) to call upon someone, to invoke, to call upon someone as a witness. The article used w. the obj. θεόν may be the article of previous reference, meaning "I call this God the God whom I have just described" (Plummer). ἐπί (# 2093) w. acc., against. Used w. the vb. meaning, "he should punish me if I lie" (Lietzmann). φειδόμενος pres. mid. (dep.) part. φείδομαι (# 5767) to spare, to hold back. Followed by the gen., the part. can be casual or express purp. (RWP). ἦλθον aor. ind. act. ἔρχομαι (# 2262) to come, to go. ◆ 24 κυριεύομεν pres. ind. act. κυριεύω (# 3259) to be lord, to exercise authority. συνεργός (# 5301) fellow worker. χαρά (# 5915) joy. πίστις (# 4411) faith; here, instr. dat. (Barrett) or loc., indicating the sphere (Plummer). ἑστήκατε perf. ind. act. ἵστημι (# 2705) perf., to stand. It emphasizes the steadfastness.

2 Corinthians 2

◆ **1** ἔκρινα aor. ind. act. κρίνω (# 3212) to judge, to decide, to make up one's mind. ἐμαυτῷ dat. ἐμαυτοῦ (# 1831) myself. Vb. used w. the dat. of advantage, "I decided this for my own sake" (EGT; RG, 539; MT, 238). λύπη (# 1877) dat. sing. sorrow. The sorrow here is emotional and spiritual stress (Furnish). Dat. under Semitic influence w. the following vb. meaning, "to come w.," "to cause," "to bring" (Martin). ἐλθεῖν aor. act. inf. ἔρχομαι (# 2262) to come, to go. Epex. inf. explaining Paul's decision.   ◆ **2** λυπῶ pres. ind. act. λυπέω (# 3382) to cause sorrow, to make sorry. Ind. in a 1st. class cond. cl. assuming the reality of the cond. καί (# 2779) then. This word accepts the previous statement, and the question shows what a paradox it involves (Plummer). εὐφραίνων pres. act. part. εὐφραίνω (# 2370) to make happy, to make joyful, to cause one to have good thinking (RWP). Part. as subst. λυπούμενος pres. pass. part. λυπέω (# 3382). Part. as subst. ἐξ (# 1666) out of, from. The prep. may suggest "sorrow that arises from me, on my account" (Barrett). ◆ **3** ἔγραψα aor. ind. act. γράφω (# 1211) to write. "I wrote." The reference may be to a lost letter that Paul wrote between 1 and 2 Cor. or it may refer to 1 Cor., particularly to 1 Cor. 16:5ff (s. Hughes for a discussion of the identity of the epistle). αὐτό (# 899) pron. 3rd. pers. sing. n. The word here may be taken in three ways: 1. in adverbial acc. ("precisely this reason"); 2. the dir. obj. to the vb.; 3. a summary of the content of the letter ("I wrote to just this effect") (Barrett; Martin). ἐλθών aor. act. part. (temp.) ἔρχομαι (# 2262) to come. "When I come." Aor. indicates a logically antecedent action. σχῶ aor. subj. act. ἔχω (# 2400) to have, to receive (s. 1:15). Subj. w. ἵνα (# 2671) gives the neg. purp. of his writing. ἔδει impf. ind. act. δεῖ (# 1256) impersonal, it is necessary to, w. inf. Impf. used for an unrealized pres. obligation (RWP). χαίρειν pres. inf. act. χαίρω (# 5897) to rejoice. Compl. inf. to the main vb. πεποιθώς perf. act. part. πείθω (# 4275) to persuade; perf., to have confidence in, to be confident, to be persuaded. ὅτι (# 4022) that, gives the content of his confidence. ◆ **4** θλῖψις (# 2568) pressure, trouble, affliction (s. 1:4). συνοχῆς (# 5330) holding together, distress, anguish, a state of mental distress involving acute anxiety (LN, 1:315). The lit. meaning is compression and in the papyri it refers to "imprisonment" (MM; TDNT). ἔγραψα aor. ind. act. γράφω (# 1211) to write. διά (# 1328) w. the gen., through, with. It expresses attendant circumstances (IBG, 57). δάκρυον (# 1232) tear. These words are expressive of deep emotion and intense distress (Plum-

mer). λυπηθῆτε aor. subj. pass. λυπέω (# 3382) to cause sorrow (s.v. 2). Subj. w. ἵνα (# 2671) used in a neg. purp. cl. γνῶτε aor. subj. act.γινώσκω (# 1182) to know. Subj. w. ἵνα (# 2671) expressing purp. περισσοτέρως (# 4359) adv. comp. περισσός (# 4359) over and above; comp., much, more. Here, "especially" (s. 1:12). ◆ **5** εἰ (# 1623) if; introduces a 1st. class cond. cl. which assumes the cond. to be true. λελύπηκεν perf. ind. act. λυπέω (# 3382) to cause sorrow (s.v. 2). Perf. indicates that the pain continues to be felt (Windisch). ἀπὸ μέρους (# 608; 3538) in part, to some extent, partially (Furnish). The phrase may indicate either that not quite all the Corinthians had been distressed (Plummer), or it limits the extent of the effect (Barrett). ἐπιβαρῶ pres. subj. act. ἐπιβαρέω (# 2096) to weigh down, to burden. Perhaps here w. the meaning, "in order not to heap up too great a burden of words," "to exaggerate" (BAGD; Hughes). ◆ **6** ἱκανός (# 2653) sufficient, enough. The use of n. instead of the fem. may be explained as a Latinism w. the meaning satis ("sufficient") (Hughes). τοιούτῳ dat. τοιοῦτος (# 5525) such, such a person. ἐπιτιμία (# 2204) punishment, rebuke. The word does not have here the classical meaning of "possession of political rights," but the legal sense of "penalty" (Plummer; MM). ὑπὸ τῶν πλειόνων (# 5679; 4498) by the majority, by the main body of the church (Barrett; Thrall). ◆ **7** τοὐναντίον (# 5539) on the contrary. μᾶλλον (# 3437) rather. This word may indicate that there were still some who felt that punishment was insufficient (Plummer). χαρίσασθαι aor. mid. (dep.) inf. χαρίζομαι (# 5919) to be friendly to someone, to be gracious to someone, to graciously bestow a favor on someone (NDIEC, 1:64-66, 111; TDNT). It occurs in the LXX w. in the meaning "to give a gift." Here it has the meaning "to forgive" (TDNT; Windisch; CCFJ, 4:347-48). παρακαλέσαι aor. act. inf. παρακαλέω (# 4151) to encourage, to exhort, to urge on. It is the word used of the speeches of leaders urging soldiers and sailors courageously into battle (MNTW, 134; CCFJ, 3:291-94). Infs. used to express results. περισσότερος comp. περίσσος (# 4358) exceeding the usual number or size. Comp. used in the sense of superl., "greater," "even more"; here, "excessive sorrow" (BAGD), instr. dat. καταποθῇ aor. subj. pass. καταπίνω (# 2927) to swallow. The prep. is intensive, to swallow down, to swallow up completely or to engulf (Hughes). ◆ **8** παρακαλῶ pres. ind. act. παρακαλέω (# 4151) to encourage (s.v. 7). κυρῶσαι aor. act. inf. κυρόω (# 3263) to legally confirm, to ratify (BAGD). In the papyri the word was used before the confirmation of a sale or the ratification of an appointment (MM; NDIEC, 4:171). The call for the confirmation of love may have been a request for a formal act by the congregation to reinstate the offender in the community of the church and to assure him of their love (Hughes; Thrall). ◆ **9** ἔγραψα aor. ind. act. γράφω (# 1211) to write. γνῶ aor. subj. act. γινώσκω (# 1182) to know. Subj. w. ἵνα (# 2671) to express purp. Ingressive aor., "to come to know" (RWP). δοκιμή (# 1509) approval, proof. The word indicates the results of a test (TLNT). εἰς πάντα (# 1650; 4246) in every respect, in all things. ὑπήκοος (# 5675) obedience. Paul wanted to know the church's obedience to his apostolic authority (Bruce). ◆ 10 χαρίζεσθε pres. ind. mid. (dep.) χαρίζομαι (# 5919) to be friendly to someone (s.v. 7). κεχάρισμαι perf. ind. mid. (dep.) χαρίζομαι. Perf. denotes the continuing state or condition of forgiveness. εἴ τι κεχάρισμαι (# 5919) "if I have had anything to forgive." He is not suggesting doubt as to whether he has granted forgiveness, but stating a mere hypothesis (Plummer). δι' ὑμᾶς (# 1328; 5148) prep. w. the acc., because of you, on account of you. ἐν προσώπῳ Χριστοῦ (# 1877; 4725; 5986) lit., "before the face of Christ." It is a Semitic construction w. the meaning, "in the presence of" (Hughes). ◆ 11 πλεονεκτηθῶμεν aor. subj. pass. πλεονεκτέω (# 4430) to take advantage of, to outwit. The arrogant, greedy defrauding of someone, often through trickery and treacherous means (Martin; NTW; TDNT; TLNT, 3:117). Subj. w. ἵνα (# 2671) expresses neg. purp. or result. νόημα (# 3784) thought, purpose, design; in the sinister sense "devices," "wiles," "plots," i.e., "evil schemings." The word signifies the function of the intellective faculty (Hughes). ἀγνοοῦμεν pres. ind. act. ἀγνοέω (# 51) to be ignorant, to be unknowing. For the neg. pref., s. Moorhouse, 41-66. ◆ 12 ἐλθών aor. act. part. (temp.) ἔρχομαι (# 2262) to come, to go; here, to arrive. Aor. indicates logically antecedent action: "When I had come...." Τρῳάς (# 5590). The article indicates, "to the Troas where we had agreed to meet." (BD, 137). For an excellent article dealing w. the history and geography of Troas as well as the NT references to this important city s. C.J. Hemer, "Alexandria Troas," TB 26 (1975): 79-112; also Furnish. θύρα (# 2598) door. Used as a symbol of missionary opportunity. ἀνεῳγμένης perf. pass. part. ἀνοίγω (# 487) to open; perf. pass., to be standing open. Here was a Roman and cosmopolitan population, reinforced by temporary sojourners suffering in forced delays far from their homes in many parts of the Roman world (Hemer, TB, 26:103). ἐν κυρίῳ (# 3261) in the Lord. The Lord Christ is both the content of the apostle's message and also the sphere of his opportunity (Hughes). ◆ 13 ἔσχηκα perf. ind. act. ἔχω (# 2400) to have. Perf. may have the idea of an aor. (BD, 177), but Paul may have wished to accent the strain of his anxiety up to the time of the arrival of Titus (RG, 901). ἄνεσις (# 457) relief. τῷ πνεύματί μου (# 4460) in my spirit. Loc. dat. Paul writes of his inward distress through anxiousness to hear Titus's report concerning the Corinthians (SBT, 144). εὑρεῖν aor. act. inf. εὑρίσκω (# 2351) to find. Instr. use of the inf.: "by the not finding Titus as to me" (RWP; MT, 142; GGBB, 196-97). ἀποτα-

ξάμενος aor. mid. part. ἀποτάσσω (# 698) mid., to say good-by, to bid farewell to friends (Plummer). ἐξῆλθον aor. ind. act. ἐξέρχομαι (# 2002) to depart. ◆ 14 χάρις (# 5921) thanks, preceded by the dat. indicating to whom thanks is given. πάντοτε (# 4121) always. θριαμβεύοντι pres. act. part. θριαμβεύω (# 2581) to lead in a triumph. Subst. part. The picture is the triumphal entry of a military hero into the city of Rome. The victorious Roman general marched into the city in a long procession preceded by the city magistrates. They were followed by trumpeters, then the spoils taken from the enemy, followed by the king of the conquered country, then officials of the victorious army and musicians dancing and playing; and at last the general himself, in whose honor the whole wonderful pageant was taking place (ELR, 115-18; DGRA, 1163-67; KP, 5:973-75; H.S. Vesnel, Triumphus [Leiden, 1970]); Rory B. Egan, "Lexical Evidence on Two Pauline Passages," NovT 19 [1977]: 22-62; Lamar Wiliamson, Jr., "Led in Triumph: Paul's Use of Treambeuo," Interp. 22 [1968]: 322; TJ, 204-9; BBC; DPL, 946-54, esp. 952-54; Furnish; Martin; Thrall). Paul represents himself as one of the victorious general's soldiers sharing in the glory of his triumph (Barrett). ὀσμή (# 4011) fragrance, sweet smell. It was customary of the triumphal processions to be accompanied by the release of sweets odors from the burning of spices in the streets (Hughes). φανεροῦντι pres. act. part. φανερόω (# 5746) to manifest. The manifestation here is not in the eschatological sense, but in the missionary sense. Pres. parts. indicate contemporaneous action. ◆ 15 εὐωδία (# 2380) aroma, fragrance. ἐσμέν pres. ind. act. εἰμί (# 1639) to be. σῳζομένοις pres. pass. part. σῴζω (# 5392) to save, to rescue. ἀπολλυμένοις pres. pass. part. ἀπόλλυμι (# 660) to destroy; pass., to perish, to be perishing. Parts. used as nouns to emphasize a character trait. ◆ 16 ἐκ θανάτου εἰς θάνατον (# 2505) from death unto death. The rabbis used similar words concerning the law. For some it was a medicine unto healing and to others unto death (SB, 3:498; Barrett). ἱκανός (# 2653) sufficient, adequate. "Who is sufficient for these responsibilities?" What kind of minister ought he to be who preaches a gospel which may prove fatal to those who come in contact w. it? (Plummer). ◆ 17 οἱ πολλοί (# 4498) the majority. καπηλεύοντες pres. act. part. καπηλεύω (# 2836) to peddle, to pawn off a product for gain. The word is used in the LXX in Isa. 1:22 for those who mix wine w. water in order to cheat the buyers (Plummer). It is used in papyri for a wine dealer and for the running of a junk store (MM; Preisigke, 1:736; TLNT). The word refers to those who would peddle or merchandise the Word of God for profit (TLNT; NW, 2, i:420-21). ἀλλ' = ἀλλά (# 247) but. The repetition of this word gives emphasis in an ascending scale (Plummer). κατέναντι (# 2978) before, in the presence of. **ἐν Χριστῷ** (*# 1877; 5986*) in union or fellowship w. Christ (DPL, 433-38).

2 Corinthians 3

◆ **1 ἀρχόμεθα** pres. ind. mid. (dep.) 1st. per. pl. ἄρχομαι (*# 806*) to begin. This is sort of an echo of the supposed criticism (Plummer). **συνιστάνειν** pres. act. inf. συνίστημι (*# 5319*) to place together, to introduce, to commend. For the form s. BD, 46. **χρῄζομεν** pres. ind. act. χρῄζω (*# 5974*) to need. **συστατικός** (*# 5364*) recommendation. **ἐπιστολή** (*# 2186*) letter. Letters of recommendation were generally requests for help and hospitality for aid in seeking employment or instruction based on the virtues of the one introduced and the opportunity of the recipient to express his loyalty to the writer (William Baird, "Letters of Recommendation: A Study of II Corinthians 3:1-3," *JBL* 80 [1961]: 168f; LAE, 158; NDIEC, 7:55, 90; 1 Cor. 16:3). ◆ **2 ἐγγεγραμμένη** perf. pass. part. ἐγγράφω (*# 1582*) to write in, to inscribe. Adj. part. as pred. adj. **καρδίαις ἡμῶν** (*# 2840*) our hearts. A reference to Paul's own heart (Baird) or to both Paul and Timothy. **γινωσκομένη** pres. pass. part. γινώσκω (*# 1182*) to know. **ἀναγινωσκομένη** pres. pass. part. ἀναγινώσκω (*# 336*) to read. Pres. indicates continual reading, in an iterative sense. **ὑπὸ πάντων ἀνθρώπων** (*# 4246*) by all men. Paul is not referring to receiving the letter, but to carrying it. Like a papyrus roll, it is sealed within him to be revealed to all men when w. open heart he declares to them the Christian's faith (Baird, 170). ◆ **3 φανερούμενοι** pres. pass. part. φανερόω (*# 5746*) to make clear, to manifest. **διακονηθεῖσα** aor. pass. part. nom. fem. sing. διακονέω (*# 1354*) to serve, to minister to. The vb. is often used to mean, "to deliver a message" (BAGD). **ἐγγεγραμμένη** perf. pass. part. ἐγγράφω (*# 1211*) to write, to inscribe, to engrave. **μέλανι** n. dat. sing. μέλας (*# 3506*) black. The n. of the adj. has the meaning "ink." Ink could be blotted out or washed off (Plummer); instr. dat. For the making of ink and the use of ink by the rabbis s. SB, 3:499f; IDB, 4:918-19. **ζῶντος** pres. act. part. (adj.) ζάω (*# 2409*) to live. The Spirit of living God was the agent of the Corinthians' conversion (Barrett). **πλάξ** (*# 4419*) flat stone, tablet. Used in reference to the tablets of the law (BAGD). **καρδίαις σαρκίναις** fleshly hearts. Used in apposition to πλαξίν. The ending of the adj. **σαρκίναις** denotes the material out of which something is made (MH 378). ◆ **4 πεποίθησις** (*# 4301*) confidence. The subst. is derived from the perf. of πείθω. The word is emphatic by its position (Meyer). ◆ **5 ἱκανός** (*# 2653*) sufficient, qualified, capable (TLNT). **λογίσασθαι** aor. mid. (dep.) inf. λογίζομαι (*# 3357*) to consider, to reckon. Used here in its widest sense of carrying on any of the ordinary processes of reasoning (EGT). Inf. expresses either result or is a further explanation of **ἱκανοί**, "sufficient."

ἱκανότης (*# 2654*) sufficience, capability. The adj. was sometimes used in the LXX to translate *Shaddai* as the name of God (TDNT; TDOT; NIDOTTE), and the thought may be "our sufficiency comes from Sufficient One" (Plummer). ◆ **6 ἱκάνωσεν** aor. ind. act. ἱκανόω (*# 2655*) to make sufficient (TLNT; TDNT). Vbs. w. this ending are usually casual. The vb. is followed by the double acc. ("as ministers") (MT, 246f). Aor. points to the time when Paul was called to be an apostle (Plummer; NIDOTTE; 1:400-401). **διάκονος** (*# 1356*) servant, minister, messenger, envoy (OPSC, 27-32; DPL, 45-51; J.N. Collins, "Georgi's `Envoys' in 2 Cor. 11:23," *JBL* 93 [1974]: 88-96). **διαθήκη** (*# 1347*) covenant, agreement (s. Jer. 31:31-34; Matt. 26:28; DPL, 179-83). **γράμμα** (*# 1207*) that which was written, letter of the alphabet, letter. **ἀποκτέννει** pres. ind. act. ἀποκτέννω (*# 650*) to kill. For the form s. BAGD. The law demands perfect obedience and pronounces the sentence of death on the disobedient (Hodge; Windisch). **ζῳοποιεῖ** pres. ind. act. ζῳοποιέω (*# 2443*) to make alive. The indwelling Christ has replaced the old Torah written on tablets of stones and has become a Torah written within (PRJ, 226). ◆ **7 εἰ... πῶς οὐχὶ μᾶλλον** (v. 8). Here Paul uses an argument from the greater to the lesser (s. Rom 5:9). **διακονία τοῦ θανάτου** (*# 1355; 2505*) obj. gen., a ministry leading to death. **ἐντετυπωμένη** perf. pass. part. ἐντετυπόω (*# 1963*) to imprint, to engrave. For the rabbinical view of the tables engraved in stone s. SB 3:502-13. **ἐγενήθη** aor. ind. pass. γεννάω (*# 1181*) to become, to come into existence, to be. **δύνασθαι** pres. inf. pass. (dep.) δύναμαι (*# 1538*) to be able to, w. inf. Inf. expresses result. **ἀτενίσαι** aor. act. inf. ἀτενίζω (*# 867*) to gaze, to look intently. Compl. inf. to the preceding vb.; ("able to intently gaze"). The rabbis felt that the shining of Moses' face was either from the tablets of the law or from Moses' position as mediator, or even from Moses' humility (SB, 3:513-16). **καταργουμένην** pres. pass. part. καταργέω (*# 2934*) to render inoperative, to make of no effect, to do away w., to abolish. Pres. part. indicates the continual contemporary action that was taking place at that time. The glory was very transitory (Plummer). Theol. pass. ◆ **8 μᾶλλον** (*# 3437*) rather, even more. It introduces the conclusion of the argument started in v. 7. **ἔσται** fut. ind. mid. (dep.) εἰμί (*# 1639*) to be. This is a logical not a chronological fut. (Barrett). ◆ **9 κατάκρισις** (*# 2892*) condemnation, a judgment against someone. **περισσεύει** pres. ind. act. περισσεύω (*# 4355*) to abound, followed by the dat., indicating the area in which the abundance is found. ◆ **10 καὶ γάρ** for even. A more precise grounding of the previous statement (Meyer). **δεδόξασται** perf. ind. pass. δοξάζω (*# 1519*) to think well of, to glorify; pass., to be made glorious. **δεδοξασμένον** perf. pass. part. **μέρος** (*# 3538*) part. **ἐν τούτῳ τῷ μέρει** in this part, in respect to. **εἵνεκεν** = ἕνεκεν (*# 1915*) w. the gen., because of, on account of. **ὑπερ-**

βαλλούσης pres. act. part. gen. fem. sing. ὑπερβάλλω (# 5650) to go above and beyond, to surpass; pres. part., surpassing, extraordinary, outstanding (BAGD). ◆ **11** εἰ γάρ for if; a continuation of the explanation and support of this argument. καταργούμενον pres. pass. part. nom. n. sing. καταργέω (# 2934) to render inoperative (s.v. 7). The neuter refers to the entire ministry of the old covenant (Furnish). μένον pres. act. part. acc. n. sing. μένω (# 3531) to remain. Here, "that which remains." Pres. emphasizes the continual existence in contrast to that which is passing away. ◆ **12** ἔχοντες pres. act. part. ἔχω (# 2400) to have. παρρησία (# 4244) lit., speaking all, then speaking openly; then the further developed meanings, boldness, courage, great freedom (Barrett; TDNT; Windisch). χρώμεθα pres. mid. (dep.) subj. χράω (# 5968) to use. Hortative subj., "let us make use of." ◆ **13** καὶ οὐ Introduces an abbreviated main cl.: "we do not do as" (BD, 255). ἐτίθει impf. ind. act. τίθημι (# 5502) to place, customary impf. "used to place" (RWP). κάλυμμα (# 2749) that which covers, veil. πρός (# 4639) followed by the inf. indicates purp., "w. a view to" (MT, 144). ἀτενίσαι aor. act. inf. ἀτενίζω (# 867) to gaze (s.v. 7). εἰς τὸ τέλος "unto the end." They should not see the disappearing of the glory on Moses' face and recognize that this service was coming to an end (Schlatter; DPL, 620-21; L. Belleville, *Reflections of Glory: Paul's Polemic Use of the Moses Doxa Tradition in 2 Corinthians 3:12-18* [Sheffield: Academic Press, 1991]). καταργουμένου pres. pass. part. gen. n. sing. καταργέω (# 2934) to render inoperative. ◆ **14** ἐπωρώθη aor. ind. pass. πωρόω (# 4800) to harden, to make insensitive, to cover w. thick skin, to petrify (RWP). νόημα (# 3784) mind. Here the word means "the thinking faculty" (Plummer). ἀνάγνωσις (# 342) reading. A reference to the public reading of law. For the reading of the Scriptures in the synagogue s. JPF, 2:927-33; SB, 4:154-65. παλαιός (# 4094) old. ἀνακαλυπτόμενον pres. pass. part. ἀνακαλύπτω (# 365) to unveil, to reveal. Pres. part. indicates the continual or ongoing condition. Part. refers to the veil which is not lifted. The whole sentence illustrates the deep tragedy of Judaism. They hold the law high and read it in their worship service, yet they do not see that it is the document which only pronounces their condemnation (Windisch). They do not understand that in Christ the old covenant and its ministry are being annulled (Furnish; s. Heb. 8:7-13). ὅτι (# 4022) because. καταργεῖται pres. ind. pass. καταργέω (# 2934) to render inoperative, to do away w. ◆ **15** ἡνίκα (# 2471) when followed by ἄν (# 323) w. subj. introducing an indef. temp. cl., "whenever" (RWP; BD, 237). ἀναγινώσκηται pres. subj. pass. ἀναγινώσκω (# 336) to read, to read aloud. ἐπὶ τὴν καρδίαν upon the heart. The heart is viewed as a center of man's being, the spring of will and activity, the seat of affection and understanding (Hughes). κεῖται pres. ind. mid. (dep.) κεῖμαι

(# 3023) to lie. ◆ **16** ἐπιστρέψῃ aor. subj. pass. ἐπιστρέφω (# 2188) to turn; mid. and pass., to turn oneself. Prep. in compound is directive, "to turn to." The word gives a graphic parallel to the account in Exod. 34 where Moses turned from the people and went in before the Lord, thereupon removing the veil from his face. The word also involves the experience of evangelical conversion (Hughes). περιαιρεῖται pres. ind. pass. περιαιρέω (# 4311) to take away, to take away from around. The compound vb. expresses the removing of something which envelops (Plummer), but the prep. may be intensive; i.e., "to remove completely" (MH, 321; NIDNTT; TDNT). ◆ **17** οὗ (# 4023) rel. pron., where. ἐλευθερία (# 1800) freedom, liberty. The end of the dominance of the written law means liberty (Barrett; NIDNTT; TDNT). ◆ **18** πάντες nom. pl. πᾶς (# 4246) all. This stands in contrast to Moses and the old covenant. ἀνακεκαλυμμένῳ perf. pass. part. ἀνακαλύπτω (# 365) to unveil (s.v. 14). Perf. indicates the continual state resulting from a previous action. The veil, once lifted, remains lifted (Hughes). κατοπτριζόμενοι pres. part. mid. κατοπτρίζω (# 3002) to produce reflection (act.), to look at oneself in a mirror (mid.). Here, "to look at something as in a mirror, to contemplate something" (BAGD; s. esp. Thrall, excursus IV, "Mirror-Vision and Transformation," 1:290-95). The pres. part. shows that the beholding is continuous and free from interruption (Hughes). μεταμορφούμεθα pres. ind. pass. μεταμορφόω (# 3565) to transform, to change the inward reality to something else. (Trench, *Synonyms*, 264; TDNT; Plummer). ἀπὸ δόξης εἰς δόξαν from glory unto glory. Christians seeing in Jesus the image of God are not deified but transformed into the same image; the glory they share w. Him increasing from one stage of glory to a higher one (Barrett; DPL, 348-50). The character is continually being formed in the believer as he is conformed to the image of Christ, thus fulfilling one of the creation purposes of God (s. Gen. 1:26-28). ἀπὸ κυρίου πνεύματος from the Lord of the Spirit; i.e., from the Lord who sends the Spirit. Or it may be taken to mean, "of the Lord who is Spirit." For the varying interpretations of this phrase s. Hughes; Furnish; Thrall; Martin.

2 Corinthians 4

◆ **1** διὰ τοῦτο (# 1328; 4047) because of this. This is either a reference to the preceding (because the gospel is the good news of the glory of God), or it looks forward–because of what is said in the next cl. (Barrett). ἔχοντες pres. act. part. ἔχω (# 2400) to have, to possess. Epex. part. explaining the τοῦτο; (# 4047) or causal part. καθώς (# 2777) just as, in accordance w. ἠλεήθημεν aor. ind. pass. ἐλεέω (# 1796) to show mercy; pass., to be shown mercy, to obtain mercy (Trench, *Synonyms*,

169; TDNT; NIDNTT, 2:594; TLNT). ἐγκακοῦμεν pres. ind. act. 1st. pl. ἐγκακέω (# 1591) to give into evil, to conduct oneself badly, to become weary, to lose heart, to lose courage (TLNT). It is the fainthearted coward (RWP). The word is also used in the papyri in the sense of treating someone badly (Preisigke, 1:411). It became a Christian t.t. expressing the unflagging pursuit of the goal of service to neighbor, or of apostolic ministry, as well as the tautness of the determined heart that does not let up or lose courage (TLNT, 1:399). ◆ 2 ἀπειπάμεθα aor. ind. mid. (dep.) ἀπεῖπον (# 584) to speak forth, to speak off or away from, to renounce, to disown (RWP; BAGD). Aor. is timeless and does not mean that he had previously practiced what he says that he has renounced (Plummer). κρυπτός (# 3220) hidden. αἰσχύνη (# 158) shame. κρυπτὰ τῆς αἰσχύνης hidden things of shame; i.e., the things one hides because one is ashamed of them (Lietzmann). Gen. here could be gen. of quality ("the disgraceful secret ways," "shaming secret ways"), gen. of agent ("conduct concealed by shame"), gen. of apposition ("feelings of shame") or gen. of relationship ("hidden practices belonging to the category of disgraceful conduct") (Thrall; Bultmann). περιπατοῦντες pres. act. part. περιπατέω (# 4344) to walk, to conduct one's life. Part. of manner. πανουργία (πᾶν ἔργον) (# 4111) readiness to do anything. In an unfavorable sense, it has the meaning, cunning, craftiness, trickery. The man who practices this is ready to do anything, and is up to every trick (Hughes; TDNT). δολοῦντες pres. act. part. δολόω (# 1516) to use deceit, to use bait, to ensnare, to corrupt w. error, to falsify, to corrupt (RWP; T; Trench, *Synonyms*, 228-31). φανερώσει dat. sing. φανέρωσις (# 5748) openness, clearness, manifestation. The word is selected in opposition to "the hidden things of shame" (Plummer). Instr. dat. συνιστάνοντες pres. act. part. συνίστημι (# 5319) to place together, to introduce. συνείδησις (# 5287) conscience (s. Rom. 2:15). ◆ 3 εἰ (# 1623) if; w. the ind. assumes the reality of the cond. καί (# 2779) even, even if. With this construction there is sometimes a tone of contempt and the matter is belittled (RG, 1026). κεκαλυμμένον perf. pass. part. καλύπτω (# 2821) to veil, to hide. Perf. looks at the state or circumstance and is used w. an adj. (IBG, 18). ἀπολλυμένοις pres. pass. part. ἀπόλλυμι (# 660) to ruin; pass., to perish, to be lost. The durative vb. is perfective and indicates the inevitable doom and the fact that the goal is ideally reached. A complete transformation of its subjects is required to bring them out of the ruin implicit in their state (M, 114f). ◆ 4 ὁ θεός (# 2536) God. Here, "the god who is over this age" or "the god who controls this age," i.e., Satan (Martin; DPL, 862-67; DDD, 1369-80). αἰών (# 172) age. It refers to that floating mass of thoughts, opinions, maxims, speculations, hopes, impulses, aims, aspirations current in the world at any time (Trench, *Synonyms*, 217f; TDNT). ἐτύφλωσεν

aor. ind. act. τυφλόω (# 5604) to blind. νόημα (# 3784) thought, thinking, the ability to reason (s. 2:11; 3:14). ἄπιστος (# 603) unbelieving. The fault that leads to their destruction is their own (Barrett). εἰς (# 1650) w. the inf. can express either purp. or result (IBG, 143). αὐγάσαι aor. act. inf. αὐγάζω (# 878). The vb. has two meanings: to see distinctly or to gaze upon (Furnish); or, to illumine, to beam upon. Used in Lev. 13 and 14 w. the meaning, to appear bright (Hughes). φωτισμός (# 5895) illumination followed by the gen. of origin: "light from the gospel" (MT, 218). εἰκών (# 1635) image, the resemblance of something to a prototype from which it is derived and in whose essence it shares. Christ shares in God's being and is a perfect manifestation of that being (Hughes; TDNT; NIDNTT, 2:286-88; TLNT). ◆ 5 κηρύσσομεν pres. ind. act. κηρύσσω (# 3062) to preach, to proclaim, to proclaim as a herald (TDNT; EDNT). Iterative pres., "we preach Christ again and again"; or durative pres., "we are presently preaching Christ." κύριος (# 3261) Here, double acc., "Christ Jesus as Lord." ◆ 6 ὅτι (# 4022) because. This explains why they must preach Christ and not themselves (Plummer). ὁ θεός (# 3836; 2536) the God; the Creator of the old creation is also the Creator of the new creation. εἰπών aor. act. part. λέγω (# 3306) to speak. Adj. part. as subst. Aor. points to the specific act. λάμψει fut. ind. act. λάμπω (# 3290) to shine, to shine forth (TDNT). Fut. used to express the command is a translation of the Heb. jussive (BD, 183; BG, 94; DPL, 556-57). φωτισμός (# 3290) illumination, enlightenment; followed by the gen. of origin or subj. gen.: "the illumining which the knowledge of the glory produces" (Plummer). πρόσωπον (# 5895) face, countenance, pers. (BG, 184). ◆ 7 θησαυρός (# 2565) treasure, that which is valuable and expensive. ὀστράκινος (# 4017) made of clay, earthenware, pottery. Corinthian pottery was well known in the ancient world (Strabo, *Geography*, 8:6.23; Martin; ABD, 1:1136); Paul may have been referring to the small pottery lamps which were cheap and fragile, or he may have referred to earthenware vases or urns. The point seems to be that the valuable treasure is contained in weak, fragile, and valueless containers (Hughes; SB, 3:516; NW, 2, ii:436-38; Thrall; Furnish). The ending of the word signifies material out of which something was made (MH, 359). σκεύεσιν dat. pl. σκεῦος (# 5007) vessel. ὑπερβολή (# 5651) excess, abundance, extraordinary quality of character (BAGD). ᾖ pres. subj. act. εἰμί (# 1639) to be. Subj. w. ἵνα (# 2671) generally indicates purp., but here it may have a causal idea (BG, 140-41). ◆ 8 θλιβόμενοι pres. pass. part. θλίβω (# 2567) to subject to pressure, to afflict; that which presses upon or burdens the spirit (Trench, *Synonyms*, 202; TDNT). This part. and the following ones may be taken w. ἔχομεν (# 2400), explaining the circumstances of the possessing, or they may be taken as circum. and used as the ind. (Thrall). The first part. of the pair may be concessive ("although"), followed by the second part. used as the ind. οὐ (# 4024) not. The usual neg. w. the part. is μή and the use of οὐ (# 4024) may be the proper neg. for the statement of a downright fact (M, 231-32). στενοχωρούμενοι pres. pass. part. στενοχωρέω (# 1593) to pressure into a narrow place. It speaks of the narrowness of room, a confined space, and then painfulness of which this is the occasion (Trench, *Synonyms*, 203; TDNT). ἀπορούμενοι pres. mid. part. ἀπορέω (# 679) to be at a loss, to be in doubt, to be perplexed, to be despondent. In the papyri it was used of one who was ruined by creditors and thus at his wits' end (MM). ἐξαπορούμενοι pres. pass. (dep.) part. ἐξαπορέομαι (# 1989) to be completely baffled (Barrett). Prep. in compound is perfective and shows the despondency in its final result of despair (M, 237). ◆ 9 διωκόμενοι pres. pass. part. διώκω (# 1503) to hunt, to hunt down like an animal, to persecute. ἐγκαταλειπόμενοι pres. pass. part. ἐγκαταλείπω (# 1593) to desert, to abandon one in difficulty. The word occurs in the LXX in reference to God's promises not to forsake His own (Deut. 31:6-8; Josh. 1:5; 1 Chron. 28:20; Ps. 37:25, 28; GELTS, 126-27; Plummer; Bultmann). For a study on the background and significance of the antitheses, s. Thrall, 329-31. ◆ 10 πάντοτε (# 4121) always. νέκρωσις (# 3740) dying, the process of dying (Hughes; Martin), slaying, putting to death. It refers to Paul's constant exposure to death (Hodge). ἐν τῷ σώματι (# 5393) in the body; in the sense, in "my body." Loc. dat. describing the place of the dying. περιφέροντες pres. act. part. περιφέρω (# 4367) to carry about, to bear about. Pres. emphasizes the continual action. The missionaries were perpetually being delivered to death for Christ's sake. They were never free from peril (Plummer). φανερωθῇ aor. subj. pass. φανερόω (# 5746) to make clear, to manifest. Subj. w. ἵνα (# 2671) to express purp. ◆ 11 ἀεί (# 107) always. γάρ (# 1142) for. The particle gives an explanation of the preceding. ζῶντες pres. act. part. ζάω (# 2409) to live; "the living," "we are ever a living prey" (Plummer). Part. as subst. παραδιδόμεθα pres. ind. pass. παραδίδωμι (# 4140) to deliver over, to hand over. Pres. emphasizes the continual danger that is faced. διά (# 1328) w. acc., because. φανερωθῇ aor. subj. pass. φανερόω (# 5746) to make clear (s.v. 10). θνητός (# 2570) mortal, subject to death. It emphasizes the material weakness and transitoriness of the body (Meyer). ◆ 12 ὥστε (# 6063) therefore. It is used here as an inferential particle, meaning "and so, accordingly" (IBG, 144). ἐνεργεῖται pres. ind. mid./pass. ἐνεργέω (# 1919) to work, to be at work. If it is a dep. mid., the meaning is, "to be at work," to be working;" if pass., the meaning is, "to be made operative" (Furnish; Thrall). ◆ 13 ἔχοντες pres. act. part. ἔχω (# 2400) to have. Causal part. (Thrall). τὸ αὐτὸ πνεῦμα τῆς πίστεως the same

spirit, followed by the obj. gen., the spirit who engenders faith (Barrett). γεγραμμένον perf. pass. part. γράφω (# 1211) to write; perf., that which stands written. It refers to an authoritative document (MM; BS, 250). ἐπίστευσα aor. ind. act. πιστεύω (# 4409) to believe. Paul quotes Ps. 116:10 as rendered in the LXX (Hughes). ἐλάλησα aor. ind. act. λαλέω (# 4246) to speak. πιστεύομεν pres. ind. act. πιστεύω (# 4409) to believe. λαλοῦμεν pres. ind. act. λαλέω (# 3281) to speak. ◆ 14 εἰδότες perf. act. part. οἶδα (# 3857) to know. Def. perf. w. pres. meaning. The vb. expresses knowledge grasped directly or intuitively by the mind (Donald W. Burdick, "οἶδα and γινώσκω in the Pauline Epistles," ND, 344-56; VA, 281-87). ἐγείρας aor. act. part. ἐγείρω (# 1586) to raise up. Subst. use of the part. to describe a character trait. ἐγερεῖ fut. ind. act. ἐγείρω. παραστήσει fut. ind. act. παρίστημι (# 4225) to present; to present as a bride is presented to the bridegroom (Plummer). ◆ 15 πλεονάσασα aor. act. part. nom. fem. sing. πλεονάζω (# 4429) to make more through more, to expand, to become more, to increase. Perhaps the idea is increasing in number (IBG, 108). πλειόνων comp. πόλυς (# 4498) great, much; comp., more. Here, the majority, the many. εὐχαριστία (# 2374) thanksgiving. The acc. is the obj. of the vb. περισσεύσῃ aor. subj. act. περισσεύω (# 4355) to increase, to cause to abound, to make extremely rich (BAGD). ◆ 16 διό (# 1475) wherefore. ἐγκακοῦμεν pres. ind. act. ἐγκακέω (# 1591) to give into evil (s.v. 1). ἀλλ' εἰ (# 247; 1623) even though. W. ind. introduces a cond. assumed to be true. ἔξω (# 2032) outward; w. the article, "the external." ἡμῶν poss. gen. ἐγώ (# 1609). For the position of the pronoun s. BD, 148. διαφθείρεται pres. ind. pass. διαφθείρω (# 1425) to decay. Pres. pictures the process of continual decay. ἔσω (# 2032) inward; w. the article, "the inward." ἀνακαινοῦται pres. ind. pass. ἀνακαινόω (# 363) to renew again. Pres. emphasizes the continual renewal. ◆ 17 παραυτίκα (# 4194) momentary. It indicates a short amount of pres. time, including the temporary; i.e., till life ends or the Lord comes (Plummer; Windisch). ἐλαφρός (# 1787) light, not heavy (Matt. 11:30). Affliction for Jesus' sake, however crushing it may seem, is in fact light, a weightless trifle (Hughes). θλίψεως gen. θλῖψις (# 2568) pressure, tribulation, affliction. ὑπερβολή (# 5651) excess (s.v. 7). εἰς ὑπερβολήν for or to excess. The two phrases, καθ'ὑ. and εἰς ὑ., form a double expression which cannot lit. be translated. The meaning is "out of all proportion" (Barrett). βάρος (# 983) weight. Paul's choice of the expression ("the weight of glory") may be influenced by the fact that in Heb. "weight" and "glory" come from the same root (Bruce). κατεργάζεται pres. ind. mid. (dep.) κατεργάζομαι (# 2981) to produce, to accomplish. It implies a prolonged process, a working out (Plummer). ◆ 18 σκο-πούντων pres. act. part. σκοπέω (# 5023) to fix one's gaze upon, to concentrate one's attention upon.

Part. used as a gen. abs., circum. (Hughes). **βλεπόμενα** pres. pass. part. βλέπω (# 1063) to see. Adj. part., "the things being seen," i.e., "visible things." **πρόσκαιρος** (# 4672) for a time, temporary.

2 Corinthians 5

◆ **1 οἴδαμεν** perf. act. ind. οἶδα (# 3857) to know. Def. perf. w. pres. meaning (s. 4:14). **ἐπίγειος** (# 2103) upon the earth. Death involves the loss not only of physical corporeality, but also of earthly corporateness (M.J. Harris, ND, 319; DPL, 553-55). **σκήνους** gen. sing. σκῆνος (# 5011) tent. Gen. of apposition, "our earthly tent-dwelling," "the tent which forms our earthly house" (Harris, ND, 318). The figure of a tent picturing the human body suggests impermanence and insecurity. It is a common picture of earthly life and its setting in the body (Barrett). From a Jewish point of view the tent could be a reference to the Feast of Tabernacles, suggesting that the Christian would have to live in a booth before reaching the promised land (PRJ, 313). For other references to the figure of the tent, s. Windisch; Harris, ND, 318. **καταλυθῇ** aor. subj. pass. καταλύω (# 2907) to destroy. In reference to the tent metaphor it describes the act of dismantling a tent (Hughes). **οἰκοδομή** (# 3869) house, building. **ἐκ θεοῦ** from God. The phrase indicates the source of the building as contrasted w. the earthly tent. **ἔχομεν** pres. ind. act. ἔχω (# 2400) to have, to possess. For pres. w. the meaning, "to possess" s. M, 110. **ἀχειροποίητος** (# 942) vb. adj. (χείρ hand, ποιέω to make), not made w. hands, not handmade; i.e., not of this creation (Hughes), supernatural, spiritual (Plummer). **αἰώνιος** (# 173) eternal, everlasting; not in the sense of pre-existent but of indefinite durability (Plummer). ◆ **2 καὶ γάρ** (# 2779; 1142) for even, yes, even (BD, 326). **στενάζομεν** pres. ind. act. στενάζω (# 5100) to sigh, to groan because of an undesirable circumstance (BAGD). Pres. tense emphasizes the continual groaning in this life. **οἰκητήριον** a place of living. It denotes a permanent abode or home (s. the discussion in Jude 6; Plummer). **ἐπενδύσασθαι** aor. mid. (dep.) inf. ἐπενδύομαι (# 2086) to put on over, to put on upon oneself (RWP). Compl. inf. to the following part. **ἐπιποθοῦντες** pres. ind. act. ἐπιποθέω (# 2160) to desire, to long for something. For the intermediate state s. DPL, 438-41. ◆ **3 εἴ γε** (# 1145; 1623) of course if, if, indeed (Hughes; IBG, 165). **ἐνδυσάμενοι** aor. mid. (dep.) part. ἐνδύομαι (# 1907) to put on, to be clothed. For the variant reading, "to be unclothed" s. TC, 579f. **γυμνός** (# 1218) naked, unclothed. **εὑρεθησόμεθα** fut. ind. pass. εὑρίσκω (# 2351) to find; pass., to be found, to be discovered. Paul's desire not to be found naked reveals not only a characteristically Jewish horror of nakedness, but also that he does not use it in its normal Hellenistic sense (Barrett). ◆ **4 καὶ γάρ** s.v. 2. **ὄντες** pres.

act. part. εἰμί (# 1639) to be. Part. w. the article indicates the group to which the subject belongs–"we who are in the tent," i.e., the earthly body (Barrett). **στενάζομεν** pres. ind. act. στενάζω (# 5100) to groan (s.v. 2). The groaning expresses the desire to put on a new body (Martin). **βαρούμενοι** pres. pass. part. βαρέω (# 976) to make heavy, to burden, to weigh down. Part. used adverbially, we groan as weighed down since we are under a constant depressing burden (Lenski). **ἐφ' ᾧ** = ἐπὶ τούτῳ ὅτι (# 2093; 4005) in view of the fact that (M, 107), because (MT, 272). **θέλομεν** pres. ind. act. θέλω (# 2527) to want to, to desire to, w. inf. Pres. indicates a continual and constant wish. **ἐκδύσασθαι** aor. mid. (dep.) inf. ἐκδύομαι (# 1624) to take off, to be unclothed. **ἐπενδύσασθαι** aor. mid. (dep.) inf. ἐπενδύομαι to put on (in addition) (BAGD). **καταποθῇ** aor. pass. subj. καταπίνω (# 2927) to drink down, to swallow down; pass., to be swallowed up. Subj. w. ἵνα (# 2671) to express purp. **θνητός** (# 2570) that which is mortal. It refers to our entire mortal existence (Lenski). The ending of the vb. adj. indicates "libel to death" (RG, 1097; BD, 36). ◆ **5 κατεργασάμενος** aor. mid. (dep.) part. κατεργάζομαι (# 2981) to produce, to prepare, to produce a condition or atmosphere, to prepare one for a circumstance (Windisch). Part. as subst. **εἰς αὐτὸ τοῦτο** "for this very purpose." **θεός** (# 2536) God. The word here is in a position of emphasis (Hughes). **δούς** aor. act. part. δίδωμι (# 1443) to give. Substantival use of part. to emphasize a defining character trait. Aor. indicates antecedent action. **ἀρραβών** (# 775) earnest, down payment (s. 1:22; DPL, 262; MM). ◆ **6 θαρροῦντες** pres. act. part. θαρρέω (# 2509) to be of good cheer, to be of good courage, to be confident. Anacoluthon breaks the sentence structure, so the sentence begins again in v. 8 (Barrett). **πάντοτε** (# 4121) always; esp. in view of death. **εἰδότες** perf. act. part. οἶδα (# 3857) to know. Def. perf. w. pres. meaning (s. 4:14). **ἐνδημοῦντες** pres. act. part. (temp.) ἐνδημέω (# 1897) to be at home, to be among one's own people, to live in a place (RWP). Pres. expresses contemporaneous activity to the main vb. **ἐκδημοῦμεν** pres. ind. act. ἐκδημέω (# 1685) to be gone, to be away from home, to be abroad, to emigrate (Hughes). For the use of the words "be at home" and "to be abroad," "to be away from home," (MM; Preisigke, 1:441). **ἀπὸ τοῦ κυρίου** (# 698; 3261) "from the Lord." Paul is not saying that communion w. the Lord is nonexistent in this body, but the Christian is away from the Lord only in comparison with the prospect of seeing Him face to face (Martin). ◆ **7 διά** (# 1328) w. gen., through, by means of, in the manner of, according to (Furnish). **περιπατοῦμεν** pres. ind. act. περιπατέω (# 4344) to walk, to conduct one's life. **εἶδος** (# 1626) appearance. The word refers to the thing seen, the form or appearance of an object (Hughes). "We conduct our lives on the basis of faith, not the appearance of things" (Barrett). ◆ **8 θαρροῦμεν** pres.

ind. act. θαρρέω (# 2509) to be of good cheer. **εὐδοκοῦμεν** pres. ind. act. εὐδοκέω (# 2305) to be well-pleased, to consent. Here, "we wish rather," "we prefer" (BAGD). **ἐκδημῆσαι** aor. act. inf. ἐκδημέω (# 1685) to be gone (s.v. 6). Compl. inf. to the main vb. ◆ **9 φιλο-τιμούμεθα** pres. ind. mid. (dep.) φιλοτιμέομαι (# 5818) to love or honor; then to be ambitious, to devote oneself zealously to a cause, to be ambitious (Hughes). **εὐάρεστος** (# 2298) pleasing. The word is used in Titus 2:9 of slaves who give satisfaction to their masters (BAGD). **εἶναι** pres. inf. act. εἰμί (# 1639) to be. Inf. to express purp., "so that we are pleasing to him." ◆ **10 πάντας** acc. pl. πᾶς (# 4246) all. Used here w. the article it means "the sum total of us" (MT, 201; BG, 61). **φανερωθῆναι** aor. pass. inf. φανερόω (# 5746) to make clear, to manifest; pass., to be made manifest. They not only have to appear, but must have their whole character made manifest (Plummer). **δεῖ** (# 1256) pres. ind. act. it is necessary to, w. inf. giving a logical necessity. **ἔμπροσθεν** (# 1869) w. gen., before. **βῆμα** (# 1037) step, platform, tribunal. This was a tribunal where official decisions were given (RAC, 2:129-30); for a description of the judgment seat found at the city of Corinth s. IBD, 1:683-84; PIG, 225-27; Acts 18:12). The word was also used in the papyri in the official sense of tribunal or judgment seat (MM), suggesting here the place of judgment and reward (DPL, 516-17, 819-20). **κομίσηται** aor. subj. mid. κομίζω (# 3152) to bring; mid., to carry off, to get for oneself, to receive, to receive as recompense (BAGD). In the NT the mid. has the meaning, "to receive back" or "to receive what is one's own" (Hughes; MM). **τὰ διὰ τοῦ σώματος** the things (done) through the body. The phrase expresses personal agency in which the body acts as the subject of the doing (SBT, 187). This gives the body its positive meaning for eternity (Schlatter). **ἔπραξεν** aor. ind. act. πράσσω (# 4556) to do. Aor. pictures the whole life of the individual Christian seen as a unit. With the prep. the phrase means, "w. reference to what he did" (Hughes). **φαῦλος** (# 5765) worthless, bad, of no account, good-for-nothing. The word indicates the impossibility of any true gain ever coming forth; worthlessness is the central notion (Trench, *Synonyms*, 317; GELTS, 500). ◆ **11 εἰδότες** perf. act. part. (causal) οἶδα (# 3857) to know. Def. perf. w. pres. meaning (s. 4:14). **φόβον τοῦ κυρίου** (# 5832; 3261) "fear of the Lord." The fear excited by the thought of standing before the judgement seat of Christ and having one's whole life exposed and estimated (Plummer). It could, however, have reference to the OT concept of reverence or awe (Furnish; Thrall). Obj. gen. **πείθομεν** pres. ind. act. πείθω (# 4275) to persuade. Pres. may be conative, "we are trying to persuade" (Barrett; SMT, 8). **πεφανερώμεθα** perf. ind. pass. φανερόω (# 5746) to make manifest. **συνείδησις** (# 5287) conscience (s. Rom. 2:15). **πεφανερῶσθαι** perf. pass. inf. φανερόω (# 5746) to make clear

(s.v. 10). Perf. indicates Paul's true and integral self has been and continues to be manifested in the conscience of the Corinthians (Hughes). Compl. inf. to the main vb. ◆ **12 συνιστάνομεν** pres. ind. act. συνίστημι (# 5319) to commend **ἀφορμή** (# 929) occasion, basis of operation, a place to start from (Plummer). In the papyri the word was used w. the meanings, incitement, prompting, occasion, or opportunity (MM). **διδόντες** pres. act. part. δίδωμι (# 1443) to give. Circum. part. to be translated as a main vb. To be translated as a main vb. Paul is fond of continuing a construction begun w. a finite vb. by means of coordinated part. (BD, 245; IBG, 179; MT *Style*, 89). **καύχημα** (# 3017) a boast, the ground or matter of glorying (AS). **ἔχητε** pres. subj. act. ἔχω (# 2400) to have. The meaning is, "in order that you may have a refutation of those who glory in appearance and not in heart" (Hughes). Subj. w. ἵνα (# 2671) to express purp. ◆ **13 ἐξέστημεν** aor. ind. act. ἐξίστημι (# 2014) to stand out of oneself, to be beside oneself. The word indicates mental imbalance (Windisch). **θεῷ** dat. θεός (# 2536) God; dat. of advantage. **σωφρονοῦμεν** pres. ind. act. σωφρονέω (# 5404) to be sane, to be sensible, to be in control of one's faculties (TDNT; Trench, *Synonyms*, 69-72; TLNT). For an example of a heathen prophetess who did not utter her prophecies in wild ecstasy, but in self-control and moderation s. DC, 1:56. ◆ **14 ἀγάπη τοῦ Χριστοῦ** (# 27; 5986) either obj. gen. ("Paul's love for Christ" [Martin]), or subjective gen. ("Christ's love for Paul"). It is perhaps best taken as subjective gen., indicating the love which originates or ends w. God in Christ; i.e., Christ's love for him, which is prior to and the explanation of his love for Christ (Hughes; Barrett; RG, 499; also DPL, 575-77). Perhaps both ideas are intended (GGBB, 120). **συνέχει** pres. ind. act. συνέχω (# 5309) to hold together, to press together, to constrain. The vb. implies the pressure which confines, restricts, as well as controls (Plummer, Barrett). Pres. indicates the continual habit of life. **κρίναντας** aor. act. part. κρίνω (# 3212) to judge, to decide. Aor. may be perfective, indicating the judgment or decision which Paul had come to. The word points to a judgment formed in the past, perhaps at or soon after his conversion (Hughes). **ὑπὲρ πάντων** (# 5642; 4246) for all. The prep. could mean "for the benefit of" or "instead of," w. the idea of substitution, which fits the context better (Martin; Hughes; NIDNTT, 3:1196-97). **ἀπέθανεν, ἀπέθανον** aor. ind. act. ἀποθνήσκω (# 633) to die. **ἄρα** (# 726) therefore; "that means that" (Barrett; BD, 235). **οἱ πάντες** (# 4246) all; w. the article the word denotes the class named is taken as a whole; i.e., "the sum total of all" (BG, 61; MT, 201). ◆ **15 ἀπέθανεν** aor. ind. act. ἀποθνήσκω (# 633) to die. **ζῶντες** pres. act. part. ζάω (# 2409) to live. Part. as subst. **μηκέτι** = οὐκέτι (# 3600) no longer. **ἑαυτοῖς** dat. 3rd. pers. pl. ἑαυτοῦ (# 1571) reflex. pron. Dat. of advantage, "to live for the advantage of oneself." ζῶσιν pres. subj. act. ζάω (# 2409) to live. Subj. w. ἵνα (# 2671) to express purp. ἀποθανόντι aor. act. part. ἀποθνῄσκω (# 633) to die. Part. as subst. Aor. indicates an antecedent action to the main vb. Dat. of advantage or personal interest. ἐγερθέντι aor. pass. part. ἐγείρω (# 1586) to raise; pass., to be raised. Part. as subst. ◆ **16** ὥστε (# 6063) wherefore. The word is used to draw a conclusion. κατά (# 2848) w. acc., according to, according to the standard of. Both prep. phrases (κατὰ σάρκα) in this v. are to be taken w. the vbs. and not w. the nouns. It is fleshly knowledge that Paul repudiates (Barrett). εἰ καί (# 1623; 2779) even if. The words introduce a 1st. class cond. cl., which assumes the cond. to be true. It indicates that Paul and others really did have a knowledge of the historical Jesus Christ (John W. Fraser, "Paul's Knowledge of Jesus: II Cor. 5:16 Once More," NTS 17 [1971]: 300; Martin). ἐγνώκαμεν perf. ind. act. γινώσκω (# 1182) to know. Personal acquaintance of others is not what is meant here. Paul has a way of looking at, regarding, and understanding Christ; now he has a new way of understanding others, including Christ (Fraser, NTS 17:299). For arguments showing that Paul was not denying knowledge of the historical Jesus s. Barrett; JNP, 89ff; Hughes. νῦν οὐκέτι (# 3814; 4033) "now no longer." This does not mean that Paul had no interest in the historical Jesus, his example, teaching, and the traditions about Him. He knew about Jesus. The basic meaning is that Paul had a new, fuller understanding of the whole Christ, by the Spirit and by faith; and he sees others in a new way according to their standing w. him in the new creation (Fraser, NTS 17:312). ◆ **17** ὥστε (# 6063) wherefore. Paul draws a second conclusion. κτίσις (# 3232) creation. The one who is in Christ and has experienced the new birth is a part of the new creation. The rabbis used the term "new creature" to describe those whose sins had been forgiven (SB, 2:415; 3:519; for additional parallels w. rabbinic teaching regarding the new creation s. PRJ, 119ff; for DSS references s. Thrall). ἀρχαῖος (# 792) old, that which comes from an earlier time. παρῆλθεν aor. ind. act. παρέρχομαι (# 4216) to go by, to pass away. Perfective aor. points to the finality. γέγονεν perf. ind. act. γίνομαι (# 1181) to become. Perf. indicates the continuing state or condition (McKay). For a discussion of the new life in Christ s. Ladd, 479f. ◆ **18** καταλλάξαντος aor. act. part. καταλάσσω (# 2904) to effect a change, to exchange, to reconcile. Prep. in compound is perfective: "to effect a thorough change back" (MH, 298). Reconciliation indicates that Christ's death removed God's enmity against man (APC, 186-223; TDNT; NIDNTT, 3:166-69; DPL, 92-95; V; EDNT; Martin; Rom. 5:10). δόντος aor. act. part. δίδωμι (# 1443) to give. Aor. indicates antecedent or complete action. Adj. part. used to stress a defining trait. καταλλαγή (# 2903) reconciliation; here, gen. of description. It refers to the office and duty of an-

nouncing this reconciliation (Hodge). ◆ **19** ὡς ὅτι namely, that, how that. The force of the words is declarative of what has immediately preceded (Hughes; Alford; RG, 1033). κόσμος (# 3180) world, world of human beings. Acc. is the dir. obj. of the part. It is the world God reconciles. καταλλάσσων pres. act. part. καταλλάσσω (# 2904) to reconcile. Part. may be taken as part of a periphrastic impf. (Barrett; MT, 88). λογιζόμενος pres. mid. (dep.) part. λογίζομαι (# 3357) to place to one's account, to reckon. A formula used in rabbinic writing (SB, 3:121f) and a common formula in the papyri in the commercial sense of putting down to one's account (MM; Preisigke). αὐτοῖς dat. pl. αὐτός (# 899) self. "Against them"; dat. of disadvantage. The pl. pron. takes up the phrase "the world" (Barrett). παράπτωμα (# 4183) transgression, a false step, blunder (Trench, Synonyms, 245f; TDNT). θέμενος aor. mid. (dep.) part. τίθημι (# 5502) to place, to put. ◆ **20** ὑπέρ (# 5642) on behalf of, representing. Perhaps the prep. also has the idea of "in place of" (Hughes; s.v. 14). πρεσβεύομεν pres. ind. act. πρεσβεύω (# 4563) to be an ambassador, to carry out the office of an ambassador. For vbs. w. this ending, marking the exercise of a profession s. MH, 398. This was the regular word in the Greek east for envoys or the emperor's legate (MM; TDNT; LAE, 378; TLNT; Windisch; Martin; Margaret M. Mitchell, "New Testament Envoys in the Context of Greco-Roman Diplomatic and Epistolary Conventions: The Example of Timothy and Titus," JBL 111 [1992]: 644-51; NW, 2, i:451-55). ὡς (# 6055) as. Followed by the gen. abs. it gives a subjective view of that which is stated by the gen. abs., indicating that the statement is correct. It may be translated, "seeing that" (Plummer). παρακαλοῦντος pres. act. part. παρακαλέω (# 4151) to urge, to ask, to entreat. δεόμεθα pres. ind. mid. (dep.) δέομαι (# 1289) to ask, to request, to ask for a specific thing. Pres. indicates the continual or habitual action. It could be iterative, emphasizing the repeated action. καταλλάγητε aor. imp. pass. καταλάσσω (# 2904) to reconcile. Ingressive aor., "become reconciled to God" (Plummer); s.v. 18. Aor. imp. calls for a specific act w. a note of urgency. ◆ **21** γνόντα aor. act. part. γινώσκω (# 1182) to know. It expresses knowledge gained by experience (D.W. Burdick, ND, 344ff). Part. could be used in a concessive sense: "although he knew no sin." ἁμαρτίαν ἐποίησεν he made to be sin. The reference may be an allusion to the scapegoat on the Day of Atonement (Windisch), or it may refer to the suffering servant of Isa. 53 w. the idea of sacrifice prominent (Bruce; Martin). God placed our sins on the sinless Jesus and as our substitute God punished Him w. death (Lietzmann). γενώμεθα aor. subj. mid. (dep.) γίνομαι (# 1181) to become. Subj. w. ἵνα (# 2671) to express purp. δικαιοσύνη θεοῦ the righteousness of God. This is the righteousness both that God requires and that He provides in justification. Paul relates being in Christ to justification (GW, 141f).

2 Corinthians 6

◆ **1 συνεργοῦντες** pres. act. part. (causal) συνεργέω (# 5300) to work w. someone, to cooperate, to work together. The complement to be supplied to part. can only be "God" (Barrett; Martin). **παρακαλοῦμεν** pres. ind. act. παρακαλέω (# 4151) to encourage, to exhort; followed by the acc. w. the inf. (TDNT; EDNT). **κενός** (# 3031) empty, without results, in vain, without meaningful effect (Furnish; DPL, 320-22). **δέξασθαι** aor. mid. (dep.) inf. δέχομαι (# 1312) to receive. Aor. may point to the time of conversion. Paul exhorts them not to have accepted the grace of God in vain; i.e., not to show by their behavior now that they accepted it then to no profit (Plummer). The fear is not that they would lose their salvation, but that they would not effectively carry out the ministry of reconciliation which had been committed to them (s. 5:18). ◆ **2 λέγει** pres. ind. act. λέγω (# 3306) to say. It is used without a stated subject and it may mean either "He (God) says," or "it (Scripture) says" (Hughes). δέκτος (# 1283) acceptable, welcome, favorable (BAGD); verbal adj. **καιρῷ** dat. καιρός (# 2789) time, convenient time. Dat. of time, "at an acceptable time." **ἐπήκουσα** aor. ind. act. ἐπακούω (# 2052) to listen to, to hear. It is a t.t. for hearing prayer (Barrett) and thus answering it. **ἐβοήθησα** aor. ind. act. βοηθέω (# 1070) to help. **εὐπρόσδεκτος** (# 2347) easily acceptable, pleasant, welcome. Used of a time which is favorable for bringing God's grace to fruition (BAGD). **σωτηρία** (# 5401) salvation. Gen. in the phrase "day of salvation" could be gen. of direction or purp. (BD, 92): "a day for salvation," "a day for the proclamation of salvation." It would then refer again to the fulfilling of the ministry of reconciliation (s. 5:18). ◆ **3 μηδεμίαν** acc. fem. sing. μηδείς (# 3594) no. A strengthened form used w. another neg. w. the meaning, "no (offense) at all" (BAGD). **διδόντες** pres. act. part. δίδωμι (# 1443) to give. Pres. points to the habitual, continual action (MT, 343); or may be conative (Barrett; Martin). Part. picks up the construction of v. 1 (Martin). **προσκοπή** (# 4683) a striking against, an occasion of stumbling, to do something which causes others to stumble (T; DPL, 918-19). It indicates the causing of the foot to strike and the person to stumble (Lenski). **μωμηθῇ** aor. subj. pass. μωμάομαι (# 3699) to find a defect, to find fault w., to blame someone (Windisch; GELTS, 312). The word often implies ridicule as well as blame, w. disgrace as a result (Plummer). Subj. w. **ἵνα** (# 2671) to express purp. ◆ **4 ἐν παντί** (# 1877; 4246) in everything, in every way. **συνιστάνοντες** pres. act. part. συνίστημι (# 5319) to bring together, to recommend, to commend (s. 3:1). **θεοῦ διάκονοι** as ministers of God. The nom. means "as

God's servants we commend ourselves" (RG, 454). The word emphasizes the personal service rendered to another (TDNT; NIDNTT, 3:544-46; OPSC, 27-32). **θλῖψις** (# 2568) pressure, affliction (s. the discussion in 1:4; DPL, 18-20). **ἀνάγκη** (# 340) necessity, anguish. Here it is used in the sense of suffering; quite possibly it means "tortures" (Barrett). **στενοχωρία** (# 5103) narrow space, tight places (RWP), distress (s. 4:8). ◆ **5 πληγή** (# 4435) stripe, wound. **θυλακή** (# 5871) the place of guarding, prison (BAGD; BAFCS, 3:195-392; DPL, 752-54). **ἀκαταστασία** (# 189) instability, often from politics (RWP), disorders. These things consist of troubles inflicted by men (Plummer). **κόπος** (# 3160) work, labor. The word implies toil unto fatigue, the weariness which follows the straining of all powers to the utmost (Trench, *Synonyms*, 379). **ἀγρυπνία** (# 71) without sleep, sleeplessness. It refers to the times when Paul voluntarily went without sleep or shortened his hours of rest in order to devote more time to his evangelistic work, care of all the churches, and to prayer (Hughes). **νηστεία** (# 3763) fasting; the voluntary foregoing of food in order to get more work done (Plummer). This triplet consists of those troubles which Paul took upon himself in the prosecution of his mission (Plummer). ◆ **6 ἁγνότης** gen. fem. sing. ἁγνότης (# 55) purity. The word probably refers to purity of life and motive in the comprehensive sense (Hughes), perhaps in the sense of "innocence" (Barrett). **γνῶσις** (# 1184) knowledge. **μακροθυμία** (# 3429) longsuffering, patience. It describes the steadfast spirit which will never give in, which can endure delay and bear suffering. It is used of God's patience toward sinful men and of the attitude which Christians are to display (NTW, 83-85; TDNT). It refers to a long holding-out of the mind before it gives room to action or passion–generally to passion (Trench, *Synonyms*, 196). **χρηστότης** (# 5983) usefulness, kindness. **ἀνυπόκριτος** (# 537) without hypocrisy, love that is not entirely genuine, mingled w. insincerity or self-seeking (Hughes). For the prefix used to negate the word s. Moorhouse, 47ff. ◆ **7 διά** (# 1328) w. gen., through; followed by the gen. **ὅπλων** gen. pl. ὅπλον (# 3960) used only in the pl., weapons. **δικαιοσύνη** (# 1466) righteousness. The phrase refers either to the weapons provided by righteousness (subjective gen.), or to the weapons used in the defense of righteousness (Windisch; MRP, 161). **δεξιός** (# 1288) right; "for the right hand." **ἀριστερός** (# 754) left; "for the left hand." Together, then, "right hand and left hand weapons," offensive and defense armor, the shield being carried on the left arm (Plummer). ◆ **8 ἀτιμία** (# 871) dishonor, disgrace. **δυσφημία** (# 1556) slander, evil report. **εὐφημία** (# 2367) praise, good report. **πλάνος** (# 4418) deceiver. ◆ **9 ἀγνοούμενοι** pres. pass. part. ἀγνοέω (# 51) to be ignorant; pass., to be unknown. It refers to being nonentities, not worth knowing, without proper credentials

(Plummer). They did not receive recognition in the world of their day because the world, its literature, politics, and scholarship, took no notice of them. They were not the source of daily conversation and were not sought out as great orators (Windisch). ἐπιγινωσκόμενοι pres. pass. part. ἐπιγινώσκω (# 2105) to recognize, to acknowledge; pass., to be recognized. They received their recognition from God and hopefully from the Corinthians themselves (Barrett). ἀποθνῄσκοντες pres. act. part. ἀποθνῄσκω (# 633) to die. ἰδού aor. imp. act. ὁράω (# 3972) to see. "See!" "behold," suddenly and contrary to hope (Bengel). ζῶμεν pres. ind. act. ζάω (# 2409) to live, to be alive. As an apostle, Paul was like a man under sentence of death (Barrett). παιδευόμενοι pres. pass. part. παιδεύω (# 4084) to punish, to discipline. God disciplines His servants for their good (Barrett). θανατούμενοι pres. pass. part. θανατόω (# 2506) to kill, to put to death. S. Ps. 118:18, "the Lord hath chastened me sore; but he hath not delivered me over to death." Let believers regard their afflictions not as indications of God's disapprobation, but rejoice in them as opportunities graciously afforded them to glorify His name (Hodge). For a comparison of Paul's list of difficulties w. the list of his day s. Robert Hodgson, "Paul the Apostle and the First Century Tribulation Lists," *ZNW* 74 [1983]: 59-80. ◆ **10** λυπούμενοι pres. pass. part. λυπέω (# 3382) to cause pain or grief; pass., to be sorry, to be grieved. χαίροντες pres. act. part. (adj.) χαίρω (# 5897) to rejoice, to be glad. πτωχός (# 4777) poor, extremely poor, destitute poverty. It describes the abject poor who have lit. nothing and are in imminent danger of real starvation (NTW, 110; TDNT; DPL, 826-27). πλουτίζοντες pres. act. part. πλουτίζω (# 4457) to make rich, to make wealthy. ἔχοντες pres. act. part. ἔχω (# 2400) to hold down, to hold as a possession. For parallel statements in the ancient world s. Lietzmann; David L. Mealand, "'As Having Nothing, and Yet Possessing Everything' II Cor. 6:10c," *ZNW* 67 (1976): 277-79. κατέχοντες pres. act. part. κατέχω (# 2988) to possess, to hold, to keep in one's possession (BAGD). ◆ **11** στόμα (# 5125) mouth. ἀνέῳγεν perf. ind. act. ἀνοίγω (# 487) to open; perf., to be opened, to stand open. The phrase means, "I am speaking to you frankly, w. an open heart, hiding nothing of my life from you" (Hering). πεπλάτυνται perf. ind. pass. πλατύνω (# 4425) to make wide, to open wide; pass., to be wide open. To have the heart wide open means there are no secrets in it. Paul tells them, "there is room for you in it, and I long to have you there" (Barrett). ◆ **12** στενοχωρεῖσθε pres. ind. pass. στενοχωρέω (# 5102) to make narrow, to crowd, to restrict; pass., to be restricted. σπλάγχνον (# 5073) pl., inward parts. It properly refers to the contents of the breast–the heart, lungs, liver–and is used to describe the seat of the deepest emotions; the strongest word in Gr. for the feeling of compassion (Hughes;

MNTW, 156; TDNT; TLNT). ◆ **13** ἀντιμισθία (# 521) recompense, paying back. The use of the acc. here may be an adverbial acc. (IBG, 160) , or it may be acc. in apposition to the cl. (IBG, 35; MT, 245; Martin). ὡς τέκνοις λέγω I speak as to children. It is in the nature of things that paternal love should meet w. the response of filial love (Hughes). πλατύνθητε aor. imp. pass. πλατύνω (# 4425) to make wide (s.v. 11). ◆ **14** For the connection of 2 Cor. 6:14-7:1 s. Martin; J.A. Fitzmyer, "Qumran and the Interpolated Paragraph in 2 Cor 6:14-1:1," ESB, 205-17; γίνεσθε pres. imp. mid. (dep.) γίνομαι (# 1181) to become. Pres. imp. w. the neg. is used either to stop an action in progress or to prohibit a habitual action (MKG, 272f). ἑτεροζυγοῦντες pres. act. part. ἑτεροζυγέω (# 2282) to yoke w. a different yoke, to draft animals that need different kinds of yokes because they are of different species (BAGD), to use a double harness (Barrett). Paul is probably referring to the prohibitions found in Deut. 22:10. For the rabbinical development of this prohibition s. M, Kilaim 8:2f; SB, 3:521; Martin. The concept of the yoke was used in relation to marriage and in relation to teachers who agreed in their doctrine. A mixed marriage or cooperation w. one who had a different doctrine was considered to be unequally yoked (Schlatter). Part. w. this vb. is sometimes used to denote the beginning of a state or condition: "do not lend yourselves to ..." (BD, 180). For a discussion of a yoke s. ABD, 6:1026-27. ἄπιστος (# 603) unbelieving, unbeliever. Here, dat. of association or accompaniment (NTGS; GGBB, 160) used in connection w. the vb. ἑτεροζυγοῦντες (Windisch). μετοχή (# 3580) having a part in, partaking, partnership. κοινωνία (# 3126) fellowship, to have things in common or together (TDNT; RAC, 9:1100-45; NIDNTT, 1:639-44; EDNT). Paul's use of the prep. πρός (# 4639) w. the word may be Semitic (s. Sir. 13:2; Fitzmyer, ESB, 209). φωτί dat. sing. φῶς (# 5890) light. Dat. of advantage or associative dat. πρὸς σκότος w. darkness. For the term "darkness," particularly in the DSS s. John 1:5; Fitzmyer, ESB, 205-17; DPL, 598. This is a rhetorical question expecting the answer "no." ◆ **15** συμφώνησις (# 5245) harmony, agreement. The vb. related to this noun was used in the papyri w. the meaning "agree w.," "agree together" (MM). βελιάρ (# 1016) a Heb. word meaning "worthless" used in Jewish writings and the DSS to describe Satan, the prince of lawlessness, and darkness (Hughes; Bruce; Barrett; TDNT; SB, 3:521-22; Fitzmyer, ESB, 211-13; DDD, 322-27; Peter von der Osten-Sacken, *Gott und Belial: Traditionsgeschichtliche Untersuchungen zum Dualismus in den Texten von Qumran* [Göttingen: Vandenhoeck & Ruprecht, 1969]; DPL, 863-64). ◆ **16** συγκατάθεσις (# 5161) approval, accent, agreement, union. Used in the papyri of a decision arrived at by a group, an agreement (BAGD). ναός (# 3724) temple. The term was properly used of the innermost sanctuary of a temple where the divine presence was supposed to be located (Hughes; DPL, 924-25). As a community the believers constitute the temple of God; it's a concept found in the Qumran community (Fitzmyer, ESB, 213-14). ζῶντος pres. act. part. ζάω (# 2409) to live. εἶπεν aor. ind. act. λέγω (# 3306) to speak. ὅτι (# 4022) that. Used to introduce dir. speech and the equivalent of quotation marks (BD, 205; 246f). ἐνοικήσω fut. ind. act. ἐνοικέω (# 1940) to live in, to dwell in. ἐμπεριπατήσω fut. ind. act. ἐμπεριπατέω (# 1853) to walk about in, to walk about among. ἔσομαι fut. ind. mid. (dep.) εἰμί (# 1639) to be. For Paul's use of the OT in the Pharisaic practice of putting together various Scriptures to prove a point s. BE, 115ff. ἔσονται fut. ind. mid. (dep.) εἰμί (# 1639) to be. ◆ **17** ἐξέλθατε aor. imp. act. ἐξέρχομαι (# 2002) to go out. ἀφορίσθητε aor. imp. pass. ἀφορίζω (# 928) to separate; pass., to be separated. ἀκάθαρτος (# 176) unclean. ἅπτεσθε pres. imp. mid. (dep.) ἅπτομαι (# 721) to touch, w. gen. εἰσδέξομαι fut. ind. mid. (dep.) εἰσδέχομαι (# 1654) to receive, to receive w. favor (Plummer). ◆ **18** ἔσομαι, ἔσεσθε fut. ind. mid. (dep.) εἰμί (# 1639) to be. The prep. εἰς (# 1650) is used in a Hebraic way to introduce the pred. nom. (BG, 10f). παντοκράτωρ (# 4120) almighty, all powerful, omnipotent (s. Rev. 1:8).

2 Corinthians 7

◆ **1** ἔχοντες pres. act. part. ἔχω (# 2400) to have. Pres. points to the continuous possession. ἐπαγγελία (# 2039) promise. καθαρίσωμεν aor. subj. act. καθαρίζω (# 2751) to cleanse, to purify. For examples of this vb. used w. the prep. s. BS, 216f. Hortatory subj., "let us cleanse ourselves." Avoidance of ritual defilement was a major pre-occupation of the Essenes and affected many aspects of their life (ESB, 215; Martin; CD 6:17; 1QS 9:8-9; ABD, 2:621-625; TJ, 81-101). Aor. indicates that a complete break should be made (Hughes). μολυσμός (# 3663) that which stains, defilement, pollution. σαρκὸς καὶ πνεύματος flesh and spirit. The terms refer to the outward and inward man, both of whom would be contaminated by contact w. heathen forces (Schlatter). ἐπιτελοῦντες pres. act. part. ἐπιτελέω (# 2200) to complete, to perfect, to bring to the goal. The word can also refer to the discharging of religious duties (Barrett). The prep. in compound is directive, indicating the concentration of the vb.'s action upon some object (MH, 312). Pres. points to a continual advance in holiness (Hughes). ἁγιωσύνη (# 43) holiness (EDNT; TDNT). ἐν φόβῳ θεοῦ the fear of God. Obj. gen., God is the object of the fear or reverence. ◆ **2** χωρήσατε aor. imp. act. χωρέω (# 6003) to make room for, to provide a place for. "Make room for us in your hearts" (RWP). Aor. imp. calls for a specific act w. a note of urgency. ἠδικήσαμεν aor. ind. act. ἀδικέω (# 92) to wrong someone, to treat someone unjustly, to injure (BAGD).

ἐφθείραμεν aor. ind. act. φθείρω (# 5780) to corrupt, to ruin. It may refer to money, or morals, or doctrine (Plummer). ἐπλεονεκτήσαμεν aor. ind. act. πλεονέκτω (# 4430) to take advantage of someone in order to gain something, to defraud for the purpose of gain. It refers to the selfish attitude of one who is willing to go to any length to satisfy his selfishness (TDNT; NTW; TLNT). The three aors. point back to a definite occasion (Hughes). ◆ **3** κατάκρισις (# 2892) condemnation, the rendering of a decision against someone. προείρηκα perf. ind. act. προλέγω (# 4625) to say before. Prep. in compound is temp. εἰς (# 1650) w. articular inf. to express purp. (MT, 143). συναποθανεῖν aor. act. inf. συναποθνήσκω (# 5271) to die w. someone, to die together. συζῆν pres. act. inf. συζάω (# 5182) to live together. ◆ **4** παρρησία (# 4244) freedom in speaking, openness, boldness (s. 3:12). καύχησις (# 3018) boasting. πεπλήρωμαι perf. ind. pass. πληρόω (# 4444) to fill; pass., to be filled. Perf. indicates "I was filled then and am still" (Plummer). Dat. occurs here as instr. instead of the classical gen. (BD, 104). ὑπερπερισσεύομαι pres. ind. pass. ὑπερπερισσεύω (# 5668) to cause someone to overflow, pass. to overflow, to be overflowing (BAGD). ἐπί (# 2093) w. dat. "amid all my afflictions" (Plummer). ◆ **5** καὶ γάρ for even. ἐλθόντων aor. act. part. (temp.) ἔρχομαι (# 2262) to come, to go. Gen. abs. Aor. indicates antecedent action. "when we had come." ἔσχηκεν perf. ind. act. ἔχω (# 2400) to have. For the use of the perf. here, s. 2:13. ἄνεσις (# 457) relief. θλιβόμενοι pres. pass. part. θλίβω (# 2567) to exercise pressure on someone, to afflict. Part. used independently in the cl., and in this case w. the character of the ind. (M, 182; RG, 1135). μάχη (# 3480) battle, fight. The fights without were presumably against adversaries–Paul had many–whether Christian or non-Christian (Barrett). φόβος (# 5832) fear. The fears within were perhaps for the safety of Titus, who might have been carrying a large sum of money and was seriously overdue, and also for the success of the work in Corinth (Barrett; Windisch; Martin). ἔξωθεν... ἔσωθεν (# 2033; 2277) outward ... inward. ◆ **6** παρακαλῶν pres. act. part. παρακαλέω (# 4151) to encourage. Pres. refers to the habitual character of the comforting God. Part. as subst. to emphasize a defining trait. ταπεινός (# 5424) humble, used here in the psychological sense of downcast, depressed (Hughes). παρεκάλεσεν aor. ind. act. παρακαλέω (# 4151) to comfort, to encourage. παρουσία (# 4242) arrival. ◆ **7** παράκλησις (# 4155) comforting, consolation, comfort, encouragement. παρεκλήθη aor. ind. pass. παρακαλέω (# 4151) to comfort (s.v. 6). ἐφ᾽ ὑμῖν over you, upon you (RWP). ἀναγγέλλων pres. act. part. ἀναγγέλλω (# 334) to report, to announce. Part. is used as a nom. abs. (Lietzmann). ἐπιπόθησις (# 2161) longing, yearning. Prep. in compound is directive indicating a longing towards (RWP). ὀδυρμός (# 3851) lamentation, mourning. Evidently the expression of regret for having saddened Paul by the disorders tolerated in the church (Meyer). ζῆλος (# 2419) zeal, intense interest. ὥστε (# 6063) so that; w. inf. and the so-called subject of the inf. expresses result. μᾶλλον (# 3437) comp., rather. It is used either in the sense "I rejoiced rather than mourning," or "I rejoiced the more" (Barrett; Windisch). χαρῆναι aor. inf. pass. χαίρω (# 5897) to rejoice. ◆ 8 ὅτι (# 4022) because. εἰ καί if even, although. For this construction s. 4:3. ἐλύπησα aor. ind. act. λυπέω (# 3382) to cause pain, to make sorry. μεταμέλομαι (# 3564) pres. ind. pass. (dep.) to be sorry, to regret. The vb. indicates to change one's feelings about something (TDNT; Trench, *Synonyms*, 255-61; NIDNTT, 1:353-56). μετεμελόμην impf. ind. mid. (dep.) μεταμέλομαι Impf. is used in the concessive cl., w. the meaning "although I was in a regretful mood at first" (RWP). πρὸς ὥραν (# 4639; 6052) for a moment, for an hour. ◆ 9 ἐλυπήθητε aor. ind. pass. λυπέω (# 3382) to cause pain. μετάνοια (# 3567) repentance. It indicates the changing of one's thinking regarding a matter (TDNT; Windisch; NIDNTT). κατὰ θεόν (# 2848; 2536) according to God, in the way of God's will (Barrett). ζημιωθῆτε aor. subj. pass. ζημιόω (# 2423) to inflict injury or punishment; pass., to suffer damage or loss, to sustain injury. The pass. is the permissive pass. "to permit one's self to sustain loss" (BAGD). Subj. w. ἵνα (# 2671) for purp. ἐξ = ἐκ (# 1666) from. Used here in the causal sense: "because of us" (MT, 260). ◆ 10 λύπη (# 3383) pain, sorrow. ἀμεταμέλητος (# 294) vb. adj., not to be regretted. It refers either to repentance or to salvation or to both; i.e., "repentance-unto-salvation" (Hughes; Barrett). For the prefix as a neg. s. Moorhouse, 47ff. ἐργάζεται pres. ind. mid. (dep.) ἐργάζομαι (# 2237) to work, to produce. κατεργάζεται pres. ind. mid. (dep.) κατεργάζομαι (# 2981) to work out, to produce its fulfillment in. The compound is intensive and designed to emphasize the inevitability of the outworking of death in the sorrow of the world (Hughes). ◆ 11 λυπηθῆναι aor. pass. inf. λυπέω (# 3382) to sorrow. Articular inf. used as a noun (BD, 205f). πόσην acc. πόσος (# 4531) how large? κατειργάσατο aor. ind. mid. (dep.) κατεργάζομαι (# 2981) to work out (s.v. 10). σπουδή (# 5082) eagerness, earnestness, diligence. For the use of the word in the papyri and examples s. MM. ἀλλά but, yea. The word is used to introduce an additional point in an emphatic way (BD, 233). ἀπολογία (# 665) defense; i.e., a defense against an accusation (Barrett). ἀγανάκτησις (# 25) indignation. Here it indicates the indignation at the shame brought upon the church (Plummer). ἐπιπόθησις (# 2161) longing, yearning (s.v. 7). ζῆλον (# 2419) zeal. ἐκδίκησις (# 1689) vengeance, punishment. Perhaps it has the idea of requital, i.e., seeing that justice is done by bringing the guilty person to ecclesiastical discipline (Hughes). συνεστήσατε aor. ind. act. συνίστημι (# 5319) to

commend. ἁγνούς (# 54) pure, immaculate, without guilt. εἶναι pres. act. inf. εἰμί (# 1639) to be. Inf. used here w. the vb.: "you have demonstrated yourselves to be pure." For the construction s. BD. 209. πρᾶγμα (# 4547) matter, affair. ◆ 12 ἄρα (# 726) then, so, therefore, consequently (BD, 235). ἔγραψα aor. ind. act. γράφω (# 1211) to write. ἕνεκεν (# 1915) w. the gen., because of, on account of, for the sake of. ἀδικήσαντος aor. act. part. ἀδικέω (# 92) to wrong someone (s.v. 2). ἀδικηθέντος aor. pass. part. ἀδικέω pass., to be wronged. Subst. part., "the one who was wronged." The word has a strong legal flavor, w. the active voice accusing the person who was guilty and had wronged, and the pass. indicating the party against whom the crime was committed (Windisch). Followed by the gen. of the inf., for the sake of, on account of. Inf. to express purp. (IBG, 83; MT, 144). φανερωθῆναι aor. pass. inf. φανερόω (# 5746) to make clear, to manifest. ἐνώπιον (# 1967) in the presence of, before. ◆ 13 παρακεκλήμεθα perf. ind. pass. παρακαλέω (# 4151) to comfort (s.v. 6). Perf. means "we have been comforted and continue to be so" (Hughes). παράκλησις (# 4151) comforting, consolation. περισσοτέρως (# 4359) adv. strengthened by μᾶλλον (# 3437); meaning, "the more exceedingly." For examples of this construction s. Hughes; BD, 129; MT, 29. ἐχάρημεν aor. ind. pass. χαίρω (# 5897) to rejoice, to be glad. ἀναπέπαυται perf. ind. pass. ἀναπαύομαι (# 399) to refresh, to give rest. The compound vb. expresses a temporary relief–a truce as distinct from a peace (Plummer; MM). Perf. indicates that at the time of writing Titus was still in a state of refreshment (Hughes). ◆ 14 ὅτι (# 4022) because. W. the ind. introduces a cond. assumed to be true. κεκαύχημαι perf. ind. mid. (dep.) καυχάομαι (# 3016) to glory, to boast. Perf. brings out the fact that Paul kept up this boasting about the Corinthians when he was speaking to Titus (Lenski). κατησχύνθην aor. ind. pass. καταισχύνω (# 2875) to put to shame. ἐλαλήσαμεν aor. ind. act. λαλέω (# 4246) to speak. ἐγενήθη aor. ind. pass. (dep.) γίνομαι (# 1181) to become. Perfective aor., "our boasting before Titus proved to be the truth" (Barrett). ◆ 15 σπλάγχνα (# 5073) the inward parts, the affections (s. 6:12). περισσοτέρως (# 4359) abundantly. ἀναμιμνησκομένου pres. pass. part. (temp.) ἀναμιμνήσκω (# 389) to remind someone of something; pass., to remember to recall. Gen. abs. Pres. expressing contemporaneous action. τρόμος (# 5571) trembling. The phrase μετὰ φόβου καὶ τρόμου w. fear and trembling indicates a nervous anxiety to do one's duty (Plummer; however, s. Thrall). ἐδέξασθε aor. ind. mid. (dep.) δέχομαι (# 1312) to receive. ◆ 16 ἐν παντί (# 1877; 4246) in everything. θαρρῶ pres. ind. act. θαρρέω (# 2509) to be confident, to be courageous. The basic meaning of the word is "to dare," "to be bold or daring" (TDNT), but in the papyri was also used in the sense of "to have confidence in" (MM).

2 Corinthians 8

◆ **1 γνωρίζομεν** pres. ind. act. γνωρίζω (# 1192) to make known, to cause to know. Here, "we draw your attention to" (Barrett). **χάρις** (# 5921) grace. The word here means the generous giving on the part of Christians, which is considered as a gift of thanksgiving (GNT, 174f; TDNT; NIDNTT; EDNT; CPP, 138). **δεδομένην** perf. pass. part. δίδωμι (# 1443) to give. The grace of generosity was given to the churches by God (Lietzmann). Perf. emphasizes the state or condition w. ongoing results. The prep. ἐν has nearly the meaning of the dat.; i.e., "in the case of the churches" (BD, 118). Although the area of Macedonia, which included Philippi, Thessalonica, and Berea, had at one time been rich, the Romans had taken possession of the gold and silver mines and the country was like a lacerated and disjointed animal (Plummer). ◆ **2 δοκιμή** (# 1509) proof, test as of metal (RWP). **θλῖψις** (# 2568) pressure, affliction. **περισσεία** (# 4353) abundance, superfluity, surplus (LAE, 84). **κατὰ βάθους** (# 2848; 958) down to depth, rock bottom. Their poverty had already reached the lowest stage (Plummer; Barrett). **πτωχεία** (# 4775) poverty (s. 6:10). In many parts of the Roman Empire the bulk of the urban population seems to have been very poor, probably because of high taxes, high rent, and high food prices (Jones, 38; A.M.H. Jones, *The Greek City*, 269; RAC, 1:698-705; DPL, 826-27; BBC). **ἐπερίσσευσεν** aor. ind. act. περισσεύω (# 4355) to abound, to overflow. **ἁπλότητος** (# 605) generosity, liberality. The basic meaning of the word is "simplicity," "single-mindedness" and indicates the true open-heartedness and generosity toward others in which there is no duplicity of motive (Hughes; TLNT). ◆ **3 παρά** (# 4123) w. acc., beyond. **αὐθαίρετος** (# 882) (αὐτός + αἱρέω to choose) voluntarily, of one's own accord; i.e., spontaneously and voluntarily, out of one's own initiative, without request and without coercion (Windisch; Plummer). ◆ **4 παρακλήσεως** (# 4155) beseeching, urging. **δεόμενοι** pres. mid. (dep.) part. δέομαι (# 1289) to ask, to beg. **κοινωνία** (# 3126) fellowship, sharing (TDNT). **διακονία** (# 1355) ministry; here, **κοινωνίαν τῆς διακονίας** (relief work) was used in Greek-speaking Judaism as a t.t. for supplying the needs of the poor (Furnish; SB, 3:316; Klaus Berger, "Almosen für Israel: Zum historischen Kontext der paulinischen Kollekte," *NTS* 23 [1977]: 180-204; DPL, 143-47). **ἅγιος** (# 41) holy ones, saints. A term of honor used for the church in Jerusalem. ◆ **5 ἠλπίσαμεν** aor. ind. act. ἐλπίζω (# 1827) to hope, to expect. **ἔδωκαν** aor. ind. act. δίδωμι (# 1443) to give. Not only have they given grace and a proof of fellowship, but they have altogether

given their own selves (Bengel). **θελήματος θεοῦ** (# 2525; 2536) will of God. Everywhere in Paul's writings the impulse to faithful service is traced to God's grace (EGT). For a discussion of this collection s. DPL, 143-47. ◆ **6 εἰς** (# 1650) w. articular inf.; used here to introduce results: "in such a manner that we have urged" (BD, 207; RG, 1003; IBG, 141). **παρακαλέσαι** aor. act. inf. παρακαλέω (# 4151) to urge, to beseech, to ask. **ἵνα** (# 2671) that. It introduces the content of the request (Barrett). **προενήρξατο** aor. ind. mid. (dep.) προενάρχομαι (# 4599) to begin previously. **ἐπιτελέσῃ** aor. subj. act. ἐπιτελέω (# 2200) to complete, to bring to the goal. Prep. in compound is perfective (RWP). ◆ **7 περισσεύετε** pres. ind. act. περισσεύω (# 4355) to abound, to overflow; followed by dat. of reference, "to abound in reference to." **ἵνα** (# 2671) w. subj. to introduce an imp. (BD, 195f; MT, 94f; BG, 141f). ◆ **8 ἐπιταγήν** (# 2198) command. **διά** (# 1328) w. gen., through. This gives the motive which justifies the request. **γνήσιος** (# 1188) genuine, sincere. The primary sense ("born in wedlock") is overshadowed by derived application (MM). **δοκιμάζων** pres. act. part. δοκιμάζω (# 1507) to approve by testing, to accept as proven, to approve (BAGD; TLNT). Part. expressing purp. or manner. Conative pres., "attempting to," or "trying to test" (Martin). ◆ **9 γινώσκετε** pres. ind. act. γινώσκω (# 1182) to know. **δι'** = δία (# 1328) w. acc., because of. **ἐπτώχευσεν** aor. ind. act. πτωχεύω (# 4776) to be poor; ingressive aor., to become poor, to be reduced to abject poverty. Aor. makes it evident that the whole event of the Incarnation is referred to and viewed as one act (Fred. B. Craddock, "The Poverty of Christ; An Investigation of II Cor. 8:9," *Interp* 22 [1968]: 165ff). **ὤν** pres. act. part. εἰμί (# 1639) to be. Concessive part., "even though he was rich." **πτωχεία** (# 4775) poverty (s.v. 2). **πλουτήσητε** aor. subj. act. πλουτέω (# 4456) to be rich. Ingressive aor., "to become rich"; i.e., w. the heavenly riches of union w. God in Christ and the assurance of eternal life (Plummer). Subj. w. **ἵνα** (# 2671) to express purp. ◆ **10 γνώμη** (# 1191) opinion, advice. **δίδωμι** (# 1443) pres. ind. act. to give. **συμφέρει** pres. ind. act. συμφέρω (# 5237) to bring together, to be advantageous, profitable or useable (BAGD). **οἵτινες** pl. ὅστις (# 4015) who, those who. It is used to emphasize persons belonging to a certain class and emphasizes the characteristic quality (IBG, 124; BAGD). **ποιῆσαι** aor. act. inf. ποιέω (# 4472) to do, to make. Articular inf. used as a noun (BD, 205). **θέλειν** pres. inf. act. θέλω (# 2527) to desire. Inf. used as a subst. **προενήρξασθε** aor. ind. mid. (dep.) προενάρχομαι (# 4599) to begin previously (s.v. 6). **ἀπὸ πέρυσι** (# 608; 4373) last year, from last year (RWP). If Paul was writing these words in the autumn of A.D. 57, the Corinthian collection would have been initiated not less than some nine months, and up to as much as twenty-one months previously, depending on whether Paul is using the Roman or Jewish calendar (Hughes; Martin; Furnish). ◆ **11 ποιῆσαι** aor. act. inf. ποιέω (# *4472*) to do. Here, w. the meaning, "undertaking" (Furnish; Martin). Articular inf. used as dir. obj. of the vb. **ἐπιτελέσατε** aor. imp. act. ἐπιτελέω (# *2200*) to finish (s.v. 6). Aor. imp. calls for a specific act w. a note of urgency. **ὅπως** (# *3968*) in order that. **προθυμία** (# *4608*) readiness, forwardness, eagerness (RWP). **θέλειν** pres. act. inf. θέλω (# *2527*) to desire. Articular inf. used as a noun, explaining the readiness. **ἐπιτελέσαι** aor. act. inf. ἐπιτελέω (# *2200*) to complete (s.v. 6). **ἔχειν** pres. act. inf. ἔχω (# *2400*) to have; w. prep., "out of the having"; i.e., "according to one's resources," "according to your means" (MT, 144; Furnish; Martin). The construction is probably meant to accent the ability growing out of the possession of property (RG, 1074). ◆ **12 πρόκειται** pres. ind. mid. (dep.) πρόκειμαι (# *4618*) to lie before one. **καθὸ ἐάν** (# *2771; 1569*) according to whatever. The amount that a man may have is indef., therefore the subj. is used; but his not having is a definite fact, thus the ind. (Plummer; RG, 967). **ἔχῃ** pres. subj. act. ἔχω (# *2400*) to have. **εὐπρόσ-δεκτος** (# *2347*) acceptable, well-received. For the same principle in Judaism s. SB, 3:523. ◆ **13 ἄνεσις** (# *457*) relief. **ἰσότητος** (# *2699*) equality. Used here w. the prep. "according to equality" (Hughes; s.v. 11). ◆ **14 περίσ-σευμα** (# *4354*) abundance. **εἰς** (# *1650*) for. **γένηται** aor. subj. mid. (dep.) γίνομαι (# *1181*) to become. Subj. w. **ἵνα** (# *2671*) to express purp. The expression **γένηται εἰς** means "to be extended to" (Hughes). ◆ **15 γέγραπται** perf. ind. pass. γράφω (# *1211*) to write. **τὸ πολύ** (# *4498*) one must supply either ἔχω; i.e., "the one who has much" (RG, 1202), or the word "gathered"; i.e., "he who has gathered much." This arises from the context of the quotation from Exod. 16:18 (Hughes). **ἐπλεόνασεν** aor. ind. act. πλεονάζω (# *4429*) to have an abundance, to have more than enough. **ἠλαττόνησεν** aor. ind. act. ἐλαττονέω (# *1782*) to have little, to lack, to not have enough. ◆ **16 δόντι** aor. act. part. δίδωμι (# *1443*) to give (variant reading δίδοντι pres. act. part.). Aor. expresses antecedent action to the main vb. Adj. part. to express a defining trait. **αὐτήν** fem. acc. αὐτός (# *899*) same; here, the same zeal that I have myself, and have now described (Barrett). **σπουδή** (# *5082*) encouragement, exhortation. ◆ **17 ἐδέξατο** aor. ind. mid. (dep.) δέχομαι (# *1312*) to receive, to welcome. **σπουδαιότερος** comp. σπουδαῖος (# *5080*) zealous, eager, diligent (BAGD; TLNT). Elative comp., very zealous (BD, 127; MT, 30). **ὑπάρχων** pres. act. part. ὑπάρχω (# *5639*) to exist, to be. **αὐθαίρε-τος** (# *882*) of one's own accord (s.v. 3). **ἐξῆλθεν** aor. ind. act. ἐξέρχομαι (# *2002*) to go out, to depart; epistolary aor. which views the action as past at the time the letter is read and refers to Titus' present trip (MT, 72f). **πρός** to, unto. ◆ **18 συνεπέμψαμεν** aor. ind. act. συμπέμπω (# *5225*) to send together; epistolary aor., "we are now

sending" (Barret). **ἔπαινος** praise. **ἐν** (# *1877*) in, in the matter of. The prep. gives the sphere in which the praise occurs and the reason for the praise. ◆ **19 χειρο-τονηθείς** aor. pass. part. χειροτονέω (# *5936*) to stretch out the hand, to vote by holding up the hand, to elect, to appoint (MM; for the use in Josephus s. CCFJ, 4:355). The vb. may indicate that the churches elected by voting (Lenski) or it may simply point to the selection and appointment but not refer to ordination (Hughes; NDIEC, 1:123). For the use of the part. as continuing the construction begun w. the finite vb. s. BD, 245. **συνέκδη-μος** (# *5292*) traveling companion, one who goes out w. another. For a discussion of the identity of the person and his identification as Tychicus s. Hughes. **δια-κονουμένη** pres. pass. part. διακονέω (# *1354*) to minister (TDNT). The prep. can refer either to the brother appointed to promote the glory or to the fund being ministered to promote the glory (Plummer). **προθυμία** (# *4608*) readiness (s.v. 11). ◆ **20 στελλόμενοι** pres. mid. (dep.) part. στέλλω (# *5097*) to avoid, to take precautions. Perhaps the word is used here as a nautical metaphor w. the meaning to furl or shorten the sail when coming to shore or in order to avoid danger in navigation (Hughes). For the use of the part. as an example of anacoluthon s. RG, 431. **μωμήσηται** aor. subj. mid. (dep.) μωμέω (# *3699*) to blame. Subj. to express neg. purp., "lest anyone blame us" (RWP). **ἀδρότης** (# *103*) that which is thick or bulky, abundant wealth (Hughes). Here it refers to a large sum of money (Barrett). ◆ **21 προνοοῦμεν** pres. ind. act. προνοέω (# *4629*) to plan beforehand, to think of beforehand, to care for, to take into consideration. **καλά** pl. καλός (# *2819*) good, that which suits the occasion, that which is fitted to the purp. (TDNT). **ἐνώπιον** (# *1967*) in the presence of, before. ◆ **22 συνεπέμψαμεν** aor. ind. act. συμπέμπω (# *5225*) to send together (s.v. 18). **ἐδοκιμάσαμεν** aor. ind. act. δοκιμάζω (# *1507*) to approve after testing (TDNT; TLNT; EDNT). **σπουδαῖος** (# *5080*) zealous (s.v. 17). **ὄντα** pres. act. part. (adj.) acc. masc. sing. εἰμί (# *1639*) to be. **πολύ** n. of the adj. πολύς (# *4498*) used as an adv., more. **σπουδαιότερον** s.v. 17. **πεποίθησις** (# *4301*) confidence. **εἰς** (# *1650*) in, into, toward. ◆ **23 ὑπέρ** (# *5642*) for, concerning, about. For the prep. w. this meaning s. BD, 121; M, 105. **κοινωνός** (# *3128*) partner. **συνεργός** (# *5301*) fellow worker. **ἀπόστολος** (# *693*) official messenger, envoy. The word was used in Jewish writings to denote the official messenger who brought or delivered the collection (SB, 3:316f; TLNT; TDNT; DPL). **δόξα** (# *1518*) glory; here, glory of Christ; i.e., the glory belonging to Him or the glory designed for Him. ◆ **24 ἔνδειξις** (# *1893*) demonstration, evidence, proof. **καυχήσεως** (# *3018*) boasting. **ἐνδεικνύμενοι** pres. pass. part. ἐν-δείκνυμι (# *1892*) to demonstrate, to show proof, to give visible proof. **εἰς πρόσωπον** (# *1650; 4725*) to the face. A

Semitic expression meaning "in the presence of" (Hughes).

2 Corinthians 9

◆ **1 περισσός** (*# 4356*) superfluous. **γράφειν** pres. act. inf. γράφω (*# 1211*) to write. Articular inf. explains that which is superfluous. The article indicates that chapters 8 and 9 belong together. Pres. points to the act of writing: "it is superfluous for me to go on writing to you like this" (Barrett). ◆ **2 προθυμία** (*# 4608*) readiness (s. 8:11). **καυχῶμαι** pres. ind. mid. (dep.) καυχάομαι (*# 3016*) to boast, to glory. Pres. emphasizes Paul's continual boasting on their behalf (Plummer). **παρεσκεύασται** perf. ind. mid. παρασκευάζω (*# 4186*) to prepare, to make preparations, to make ready. Perf. emphasizes the past completed action w. the pres. continuing state: "stands prepared" (RWP). **ἀπὸ πέρυσι** (*# 608; 4373*) last year (s. 8:10). **ζῆλος** (*# 2419*) zeal. **ἠρέθισεν** aor. ind. act. ἐρεθίζω (*# 2241*) to stir up, to irritate, to stimulate, to excite. Here there is no bad sense, but the meaning is rather "to promote healthy rivalry," "to stimulate" (Martin; TLNT). **πλείονας** comp. πολύς (*# 4498*) many, great; comp., the majority. ◆ **3 ἔπεμψα** aor. ind. act. πέμπω (*# 4287*) to send. Epistolary aor., "I am sending." **ἀδελφός** (*# 81*) brother. Pl. here, the brothers. Article indicates those who were previously mentioned. **τὸ ὑπὲρ ὑμῶν** on your behalf. Article is repeated here in order to avoid misunderstanding (BD, 141). **κενωθῇ** aor. subj. pass. κενόω (*# 3033*) to empty, to make void; effective use of the aor., "to be proven empty" (Barrett; DM, 196f). Subj. w. **ἵνα** (*# 2671*) to express purp. **ἔλεγον** impf. ind. act. λέγω (*# 3306*) to say. Impf. emphasizes the repeated action. **καθὼς ἔλεγον** just as I repeatedly said (Plummer). **παρεσκευασμένοι** perf. pass. part. παρασκευάζω (*# 4186*) to prepare (s.v. 2). Part. w. the subj. of the vb. εἰμί to express the perf. subj. pass. in a final cl., "that you may really be prepared" (RWP). **ἦτε** pres. subj. act. εἰμί (*# 1639*) to be. ◆ **4 ἔλθωσιν** aor. subj. act. ἔρχομαι (*# 2262*) to come. Subj. w. **ἐάν** (*# 1569*) in a 3rd. class cond. cl. in which the cond. is viewed as probable. **εὕρωσιν** aor. subj. act. εὑρίσκω (*# 2351*) to find. **ἀπαρασκευάστος** (*# 564*) unprepared. **καταισχυνθῶμεν** aor. subj. pass. καταισχύνω (*# 2875*) to put to shame; pass., to be put to shame. Subj. w. **μή πως** (*# 3590; 4803*) in a purp. cl. ("lest somehow...") (BAGD). **ἵνα μὴ λέγω ὑμεῖς** "lest I say you," "not to mention you" (Martin; Furnish). A use of paralipsis, in which the writer pretends to pass over something which he in fact mentions (BD, 262; RG, 1199; Furnish). **ὑποστάσει** dat. fem. sing. ὑπόστασις (*# 5712*) basis, foundation, support, ground of hope or confidence, assurance, undertaking (Hughes; Furnish; Martin; s. Heb. 11:1). ◆ **5 ἀναγκαῖος** (*# 338*) necessary, compelling. **ἡγησάμην** aor. ind. mid. (dep.) ἡγέομαι

(*# 2451*) to consider. **παρακαλέσαι** aor. act. inf. παρακαλέω (*# 4151*) to ask, to urge, to encourage. **προέλθωσιν** aor. subj. act.προέρχομαι (*# 4601*) to go ahead, to go before. **προκαταρτίσωσιν** aor. subj. act. προκαταρτίζω (*# 4616*) to arrange beforehand, to organize beforehand. **προεπηγγελμένην** perf. pass. part. προεπαγγέλλω (*# 4600*) to promise before. Perf. part. emphasizes the continuing state: that which was promised before and the promise remains valid. **ἕτοιμος** (*# 2330*) ready. Used w. inf. to express purp. **εἶναι** pres. act. inf. εἰμί (*# 1639*) to be. **πλεονεξία** (*# 4432*) selfishness, greed. The word indicates the greedy grasping for more at the expense of others (NTW, 97-99; TLNT; TDNT). The idea here is, "ready as a gift and not as something wrung from you" (Barrett). ◆ **6 σπείρων** pres. act. part. σπείρω (*# 5062*) to sow, to sow seed. **φειδομένως** (*# 5768*) adv., sparingly. Developed from a part. from φείδομαι to spare, to be miserly, here, "in a miserly manner" (BAGD; Hughes). **θερίσει** fut. ind. act. θερίζω (*# 2545*) to reap, to gather a harvest. **ἐπ' εὐλογίαις**. The prep. has an adverbial force and the noun means a gift freely and spontaneously bestowed and thus constituting a blessing to the recipient. The total phrase is used as an adv. w. the meaning, generously, bountifully (Hughes). ◆ **7 προῄρηται** perf. subj. mid. προαιρέω (*# 4576*) mid. to determine beforehand, to decide. The word refers to the deliberate choosing (Plummer). **ἀνάγκη** (*# 340*) necessity, compulsion. **ἱλαρός** (*# 2659*) cheerful, joyful, glad (NDIEC, 4:169; GELTS, 213; Prov. 22:8 [LXX]; CCFJ, 2:382; TDNT). **δότης** (*# 1522*) one who gives, giver. Paul evidently alludes to Prov. 22:9. **ἀγαπᾷ** pres. ind. act. ἀγαπάω (*# 26*) to love. ◆ **8 δυνατεῖ** pres. ind. act. δυνατέω (*# 1542*) to make able, to enable, to be able. Pres. emphasizes the continual ability of God. **περισσεῦσαι** aor. act. inf. περισσεύω (*# 4355*) to abound, to have more than enough, to overflow. **αὐτάρκεια** (*# 894*) sufficiency, self-sufficiency. The word indicates being independent of external circumstances, especially of the services of other people (Plummer). For the use of the word in the ancient world, both among the Stoic philosophers and also the common people s. Windisch; Barrett; TDNT; MM; NW, 2, i:427-76; RAC, 1:1039-50. **ἔχοντες** pres. act. part. ἔχω (*# 2400*) to have. **περισσεύητε** pres. subj. act. περισσεύω (*# 4355*). Subj. w. **ἵνα** (*# 2671*) to express purp. **πᾶν ἔργον ἀγαθόν** every good work. The meaning here is that the less a man requires for himself, the greater means he will have for relieving the wants of others (Plummer). ◆ **9 γέγραπται** perf. ind. pass. γράφω (*# 1211*) to write. Perf. indicates the abiding authority of the document (MM). **ἐσκόρπισεν** aor. ind. act. σκορπίζω (*# 5025*) to scatter, to disperse, to distribute. **ἔδωκεν** aor. ind. act. δίδωμι (*# 1443*) to give. Gnomic aor. used in a proverb-like expression (Barrett). **πένης** (*# 4288*) poor. The word describes the man for whom life and living is a struggle; the man who is the reverse of the one who lives in affluence (NTW, 110). ◆ **10 ἐπιχορηγῶν** pres. act. part. ἐπιχορηγέω (# 2220) to supply, to furnish, to provide. **σπείροντι** pres. act. part. σπείρω (# 5062) to sow. **βρῶσις** (# 1111) eating. **χορηγήσει** fut. ind. act. χορηγέω (# 5961) to lead a chorus, to supply the chorus for a drama. A service which cost the persons who undertook it a large outlay; "to supply anything plentifully" (Plummer). **πληθυνεῖ** fut. ind. act. πληθύνω (# 4437) to increase, to multiply. **αὐξήσει** fut. ind. act. αὐξάνω (# 889) to increase, to cause to grow. **γένημα** (# 1163) produce; the yield of harvest, particularly the fruit or juice of the grapevine (Hughes). **δικαιοσύνη** (# 1466) righteousness; perhaps here in the sense of almsgiving, benevolence (SB, 3:52; MRP, 161), or it is used to connote righteousness of life of which charity is an expression (GW, 154). ◆ **11 πλουτιζόμενοι** pres. pass. part. πλουτίζω (# 4457) to make rich, to enrich. For the construction w. the part. s. BD 245f; Martin. **ἁπλότης** (# 605) liberality (s. 8:2). **κατεργάζεται** pres. ind. mid. (dep.) κατεργάζομαι (# 2981) to produce. **εὐχαριστία** (# 2374) thanksgiving. ◆ **12 διακονία** (# 1355) ministry, service. The meaning here is ministration, execution (Barrett). **λειτουργία** (# 3311) ministry, service. In classical Gr. the word was used of wealthy citizens who rendered the public service of financing choruses for dramas. In Jewish and in *koine* usage it indicated religious service or freewill service (Plummer; MM; TDNT; TLNT; Lietzmann). **προσαναπληροῦσα** pres. act. part. nom. fem. sing. προσαναπληρόω (# 4650) to fill, to fill up. Prep. in compound means to fill up by adding to (RWP). **ὑστέρημα** (# 5729) that which lacks, deficiency, shortcoming, need, want. **περισσεύουσα** pres. act. part. nom. fem. sing. περισσεύω (# 4355) to abound (s.v. 8). The collection has a twofold effect: it fills up what is lacking among their poorer brethren of the necessities of life as well as causing an overflow of praise and gratitude to God (Hughes). ◆ **13 δοκιμή** (# 1509) approval, that which has been tested and approved (s. 2:9). **δοξάζοντες** pres. act. part. δοξάζω (# 1519) to glorify, to cause one to think well of someone. **ὑποταγή** (# 5717) obedience, subordination of oneself. **ὁμολογία** (# 3934) confession. The word is used specifically to introduce or express a conviction; i.e., the obj. confession which especially has reference to confessing Christ or the teaching of His church (ECC, 17). **ἁπλότης** (# 605) liberality. The word indicates singleness of purp. leading to liberality in giving to others (Hughes; s. 2 Cor. 8:2). **κοινωνία** (# 3126) fellowship. Here it is used in the sense of participation in the collection (Barrett; s. 8:4). ◆ **14 δέησις** (# 1255) request, petition. The word implies special petition for the supply of wants (Plummer; Trench, *Synonyms*, 189). Dat. here indicates accompanying circumstances; i.e., the intercession accompanies their longing (Plummer). **ἐπιποθούντων** pres. act. part. ἐπιποθέω (# 2160) to long for someone, to earnestly desire

(Hering). Gen. abs. (RWP). **ὑπερβάλλουσαν** pres. act. part. ὑπερβάλλω (# 5650) to throw beyond, to surpass. Here it refers to the surpassing grace or generosity (Barrett). ◆ **15 ἀνεκ-διήγητος** (# 442) vb. adj., indescribable, not able to recount or to describe or to set forth in detail (Lenski; EDNT). God's exquisite working cannot be fully described w. human words (Windisch). For the neg. prefix s. Moorhouse, 47ff. **δωρεᾷ** (# 1561) gift, that which is freely given.

2 Corinthians 10

◆ **1 αὐτὸς δὲ ἐγώ** "now I myself." Paul is now calling attention to a specially personal matter (EGT). For a defense of the authenticity of chapters 10 through 13 s. Hughes. **παρακαλῶ** pres. ind. act. παρακαλέω (# 4151) to beseech. **πραΰτης** (# 4559) meekness. It denotes the humble and gentle attitude which expresses itself, in particular, in a patient submissiveness to offense, free from malice and desire for revenge (R. Leivestad, "The Meekness and Gentleness of Christ, II Cor. 10:1," *NTS* 12 [1966]: 159; NTW, 103f; TDNT; TLNT; Windisch). **ἐπιείκεια** (# 2117) fitting, suitable, reasonable, fair. When applied to authorities it denotes indulgence, equity, lenience. It also denotes a humble, patient steadfastness which is able to submit to injustice, disgrace, and maltreatment without hatred or malice, trusting God in spite of it all (Leivestad, 158; TDNT; Trench, *Synonyms*, 153-57; NTW, 38f; TLNT). These words indicate that Paul knew of the historical Jesus and is referring to His character (JNP, 108f; Martin). **πρόσωπον** (# 2848; 4725) face; here, "face to face," "present in person" (Hughes). **ταπεινός** (# 5424) low, humble. Used here in the bad sense meaning "downcast," expressing depression when it is the effect of the want of courage (Hodge). **ἀπών** pres. act. part. ἄπειμι (# 582) to be absent. Pres. expresses contemporaneous action. Concessive part., "even though I am absent"; or temp., "while I am absent." **θαρρῶ** pres. ind. act. θαρρέω (# 2509) to be confident, to be courageous. ◆ **2 δέομαι** (# 1289) pres. ind. mid. (dep.) to ask, to beg. **παρών** pres. act. part. πάρειμι (# 4205) to be present. Adverbial use of the part.: "when I am present." **θαρρῆσαι** aor. act. inf. θαρρέω (# 2509) to be confident. Articular inf. and the neg. expressing the dir. obj. of the vb. (RWP; BD, 105). Aor. inf. is the ingressive aor., "to become courageous." **πεποίθησις** (# 4301) having been persuaded, confidence. **ᾗ** dat. sing. ὅς (# 4005) who, which rel. pron. Instr. use, "with which," "by which." **λογίζομαι** (# 3357) pres. ind. mid. (dep.) to judge, to reckon, to think. **τολμῆσαι** aor. act. inf. τολμάω (# 5528) to be bold, to dare. Comp. inf. to the main vb. **λογιζομένους** pres. mid. (dep.) part. λογίζομαι (# 3357) to reckon. Subst. part. to emphasize a trait. Here ind. obj., "toward those who judge." **κατὰ σάρκα** (# 2848; 4922) according to flesh; i.e., according to fleshly principles. **περιπα-τοῦντας** pres. act. part. περιπατέω (# 4344) to walk, to walk about, to conduct one's life. ◆ **3 ἐν σαρκί** (# 1877; 4922) in the flesh; i.e., in the element of flesh. Living his life, like every other man, subject to the laws and limitations common to human flesh (Hughes; DPL, 304-6). For Paul's style of using the same word or word stem in close proximity s. BD, 258. **περιπατοῦντες** pres. act. part. s.v. 2. **στρατευόμεθα** pres. ind. mid. (dep.) στρατεύω (# 5129) to be a soldier, to serve as a soldier, often serving at their own expense. Here used fig. to describe the struggles and activities of the apostle (BAGD). ◆ **4 ὅπλα** pl. ὅπλον (# 3960) weapon, instrument of warfare. A general word used for both defensive and offensive weapons (TDNT; Windisch). For a brief description of the weapons of the Roman army s. ELR, 106; OCD, 121f; TJ, 106-10; DJG, 548-49. **στρατεία** (# 5127) expedition, campaign, warfare. Here, descriptive gen., "the weapons we use in our warfare" (BAGD). **σαρκικός** (# 4920) fleshly, pertaining to the flesh. The ending of the word indicates, "like the flesh" (MH, 378). **δυνατός** (# 1543) powerful. **θεῷ** dat. θεός (# 2536) Dat. indicates either personal interest, "to or for God"; i.e., employed on God's behalf (Barrett; BG, 20); or it may be viewed as an intensive dat. corresponding to the Hebraic construction that indicates a superl. force ("divinely powerful") (Hughes; IBG, 184; MH, 443). **καθαίρεσις** (# 2746) tearing down, pulling down, destroying. **ὀχύρωμα** (# 4065) stronghold, fortress. In the papyri the word also meant "prison" (MM). Paul may have had Prov. 21:22 in mind (Hughes). **λογισμός** (# 3361) calculation, reasoning, reflection, thought (BAGD). **καθαιροῦντες** pres. act. part. καθαιρέω (# 2747) to tear down, to destroy. ◆ **5 ὕψωμα** (# 5739) that which is lifted up, high, exalted. **ἐπαιρό-μενον** pres. mid. part. ἐπαίρω (# 2048) to lift up; mid., to exalt oneself. The metaphor here is from walls and towers standing defiantly and the vb. may be pass. ("erected") (Plummer). **αἰχμαλωτίζοντες** pres. act. part. αἰχμαλωτίζω (# 170) to take one captive w. a spear, to bring into captivity, to bring into subjection. Pres. points to the continual struggle and warfare. **νόημα** (# 3784) thought, purpose, design. **ὑπακοή** (# 5633) obedience. **τοῦ Χριστοῦ** (# 5986) obj. gen., obedience to Christ. ◆ **6 ἕτοιμος** (# 2289) ready. Used w. **ἔχοντες** pres. act. part. ἔχω (# 2400) to have; meaning here, to be ready, to be prepared. **ἐκδικῆσαι** aor. act. inf. ἐκδικέω (# 1688) to punish, to avenge (BAGD; TDNT). Epex. inf. explaining the readiness. **παρακοήν** (# 4157) disobedience. **ὅταν** (# 4020) used w. subj., when, whenever. **πληρωθῇ** aor. subj. pass. πληρόω (# 4444) to fill; pass., to be filled. The effective aor., "to reach completion" (Barrett). ◆ **7 κατὰ πρόσωπον** (# 2848; 4725) according to the face; i.e., "before your face." **βλέπετε** pres. ind. act., or better, pres. imp. act. βλέπω (# 1063) to look.

"Look at what is before your eyes," "face the obvious facts" (Hughes). **εἴ τις** (# 1623; 5516) if anyone. Used w. ind. to introduce a cond. which is assumed to be true. **πέποιθεν** perf. ind. act. πείθω (# 4275) w. a pres. meaning, to have confidence; i.e., to have been persuaded, to trust. **ἑαυτῷ** dat. sing. ἑαυτοῦ (# 1571) oneself; reflex. pron. "To have confidence or trust in oneself." **Χριστοῦ εἶναι** (# 5986; 1639) to be of Christ. pred. gen. used w. the inf. in indir. discourse "confidence that he belongs to Christ" (RWP). **εἶναι** pres. inf. act. εἰμί (# 1639) to be. **λογιζέσθω** pres. imp. mid. (dep.) λογίζομαι (# 3357) to think, to consider, to reckon. **ἑαυτοῦ** (# 1571) for himself. Let him then consider once more for himself (Meyer). For a study of Paul's opponents at Corinth s. Hughes; C.K. Barrett, "Paul's Opponents in Second Corinthians," *NTS* 17 (1971): 233-24; OPSC; DPL, 644-53. ◆ **8 ἐάν τε γάρ** (# 1569; 5445; 1142) for if. For the use of the particles here s. Thrall, 96; BD, 229f; Barrett. **περισσότερόν** comp. περισσός (# 4356) abundant; comp., somewhat more abundantly. **καυχήσωμαι** aor. subj. mid. (dep.) καυχάομαι (# 3016) to boast, to glory. **ἐξου-σία** (# 2026) authority. **ἧς** gen. sing. ὅς (# 4005) who, which, rel. pron. Gen. by attraction. **ἔδωκεν** aor. ind. act. δίδωμι (# 1443) to give. **οἰκοδομή** (# 3869) building up, edification. **καθαίρεσις** (# 2746) tearing down (s. Jer. 1:10). **αἰσχυνθήσομαι** fut. ind. pass. αἰσχύνω (# 159) to put to shame; pass., to be put to shame. ◆ **9 δόξω** aor. subj. act. δοκέω (# 1506) to appear, to seem to be. Subj. w. **ἵνα** (# 2671) to express purp. or result. **ὡσάν** = ὡς (# 6055) **ἄν** (# 323) as it were (M, 167). **ἐκφοβεῖν** pres. act. inf. ἐκφοβέω (# 1768) to terrify, to frighten to distraction. Prep. in compound is intensive (Hughes). Compl. inf. to complete the main vb. ◆ **10 ὅτι** (# 4022) equivalent to quotation marks introducing a dir. quotation. **φησίν** pres. ind. act. 3rd. pers. sing. φημί (# 5774) to say; i.e., "one says." It may be, however, that Paul is quoting a particular person (Barrett). **βαρεῖαι** nom. pl. βαρύς (# 987) heavy, weighty. **ἰσχυρός** (# 2708) strong. **παρουσία** (# 4242) presence. Followed by the gen. **τοῦ σώματος** (# 5393) it emphasizes the external presence; i.e., the visible and tangible presence in the physical body (SBT, 48). **ἀσθενής** (# 822) weak. **ἐξουθενημένος** perf. pass. part. ἐξουθενέω (# 2024) to despise, to consider of no account. Perf. emphasizes the state or condition; i.e., despised, counted as nothing. ◆ **11 λογιζέσθω** pres. imp. mid. (dep.) 3rd. pers. sing. λογίζομαι (# 3357) s.v. 7. **τοιοῦτος** (# 5525) such a one. **οἷος** (# 3888) what sort of. The pron. is qualitive (RWP). **παρόντες** pres. act. part. πάρειμι (# 4205) to be present (s.v. 2). ◆ **12 τολμῶμεν** pres. ind. act. τολμάω (# 5528) to be bold, to dare. (For a study of Paul's boasting in 2 Cor. 10-12 from a rhetoric prospective s. Christopher Forbes, "Comparison, Self-Praise and Irony: Paul's Boasting and the Conventions of Hellenistic Rhetoric," *NTS* 32 [1986]: 1-30.) **ἐγκρῖναι** aor. act. inf. ἐγκρίνω

(# *1605*) to judge among, to class or categorize. **συγ-κρῖναι** aor. act. inf. συγκρίνω (# *5173*) to judge together, to compare. Comparison was used as a rhetorical device (Forbes, *NTS* 32 [1986]: 2-8). **συνιστανόντων** pres. act. part. συνίστημι (# *5319*) to commend, to recommend (s. 3:1). **αὐτοί** pl. αὐτός (# *899*) "they themselves." **μετροῦντες** pres. act. part. μετρέω (# *3582*) to measure. Part. here in the role of a pred., "they do not realize that they are measuring themselves by their own standards" (MT, 160). **συνιᾶσιν** pres. ind. act. συνίημι (# *5317*) to understand, to comprehend, to realize. ◆ **13 ἄμετρος** (# *296*) unmeasured, immeasurable. The phrase here means, "we shall not boast excessively" (Barrett; IBG, 71). **καυχησόμεθα** fut. ind. mid. (dep.) καυχάομαι (# *3016*) (s.v. 8). An epistolary pl. (GGBB, 395). **μέτρον** (# *3586*) measure. **κανόνος** gen. masc. sing. κανών (# *2834*) rule, measuring rod, the fixed bounds of a territory (TDNT; Plummer). It may be that Paul has in mind the marked out lanes used by runners in athletic contests (Hughes). **οὗ** gen. sing. ὅς (# *4005*) who, which; rel. pron. Gen. by attraction (RG, 719). The repetition of **μέτρον** in the gen. may be due to attraction and the word may be considered as in apposition to the rel. pron. (Hughes). **ἐμέρισεν** aor. ind. act. μερίζω (# *3532*) to measure out, to distribute, to deal out, to assign. **ἐφικέσθαι** aor. mid. (dep.) inf. ἐφικνέομαι (# *2391*) to reach, to come to. Inf. is used to express result (Windisch). **ἄχρι** (# *948*) w. the gen., unto, as far as. ◆ **14 ἐφικνούμενοι** pres. mid. (dep.) part. ἐφικνέομαι (# *2391*) (s.v. 13). **ὑπερεκτείνομεν** pres. ind. act. ὑπερεκτείνω (# *5657*) to stretch out beyond, to overstretch. "We are not overextending ourselves beyond the limits set by God" (BAGD). **ἐφθάσαμεν** aor. ind. act. φθάνω (# *5777*) to arrive first, to come before others, to precede (Hughes). **ἐν τῷ εὐαγγελίῳ** (# *1877*; *2295*) in the gospel; i.e., in preaching the gospel as its ministers and envoys (Barrett). ◆ **15 ἄμετρα** (# *280*) without measure (s.v. 13). **καυχώμενοι** pres. mid. (dep.) part. καυχάομαι (# *3016*) to boast (s.v. 8). **ἀλλότρος** (# *259*) another, belonging to another (RWP). **κόπος** (# *3160*) work. **ἔχοντες** pres. act. part. ἔχω (# *2400*) to have. Circum. part. **αὐξανομένης** pres. pass. part. (temp.) αὐξάνω (# *889*) to cause to grow; pass., to grow, to increase. Gen. abs., "as your faith increases" (Barrett). Pres. expresses contemporaneous action. **μεγαλυνθῆναι** aor. pass. inf. μεγαλύνω (# *3486*) to make large, to magnify, to enlarge. Inf. used in indir. discourse, explaining what the **ἐλπίδα** is (RWP). **κανόνα** acc. sing. κάνων (s.v. 13). **εἰς περισσείαν** (# *4353*) unto abundance; i.e., in the highest degree possible (Lietzmann). Paul expected a brilliant and glorious triumph in Corinth (Windisch). ◆ **16 ὑπερέκεινα** (# *5654*) beyond; i.e., "the lands that lie beyond you" (BAGD; RG, 297). **εὐαγγελίσασθαι** aor. mid. (dep.) inf. εὐαγγελίζω (# *2294*) to proclaim the good news, to preach the gospel, to evangelize. **ἕτοιμος** (# *2289*) ready,

prepared. **καυχήσασθαι** aor. mid. (dep.) inf. καυχάομαι (# *3016*) to boast. The idea is, "without boasting of work already done in another's field" (Hughes). ◆ **17 καυχώμενος** pres. mid. (dep.) part. καυχάομαι (# *3016*) to boast. Subst. part. to emphasize a particular trait. **καυχάσθω** aor. imp. mid. (dep.) καυχάομαι. ◆ **18 συνιστάνων** pres. act. part. συνίστημι (# *5319*) to commend (s.v. 12). **δόκιμος** (# *1511*) approved, approved after a test (TLNT).

2 Corinthians 11

◆ **1 ὄφελον** (# *4054*) Oh that, would that (BAGD); for the form s. RG, 1003; BD, 37. The word has become a particle w. the impf. or aor. ind. used to express an unattainable wish (BD, 181). **ἀνείχεσθε** impf. ind. mid. (dep.) ἀνέχομαι (# *462*) to endure, to bear, to put up w. (BAG). **μου** gen. ἐγώ (# *1609*) I. "W. me," gen. following the vb. **μικρόν τι** (# *3625*; *5516*) adv., a little; acc. of general reference, "in reference to a little foolishness" (RG, 486). **ἀφροσύνη** (# *932*) lack of sense, foolishness, thoughtlessness (TDNT; EDNT). This was a t.t in Jewish wisdom lit., esp. Prov. and Eccl. (Martin; GELTS, 74), and was used in Josephus to mean "want of judgment," "stupidity," "folly" (CCFJ, 1:284). **ἀλλὰ καί** (# *247*; *2779*) but indeed. **ἀνέχεσθε** pres. ind./imp. mid. (dep.) ἀνέχομαι (# *462*) to endure, to bear (BAGD). The ind. appears to be better: "but indeed you do already bear w. me" (Hughes). ◆ **2 ζηλῶ** pres. ind. act. ζηλόω (# *2420*) to be jealous. **ζῆλος** (# *2420*) jealously. The word is taken up in a metaphor drawn from marriage (Barrett; Martin). Here, dat. of means or manner. **ἡρμοσάμην** aor. ind. mid. ἁρμόζω (# *764*) to fit together, to join, to harmonize, to give in marriage, to betroth (BAGD). Mid. is probably used purposely to bring out the apostle's personal interest (MM). **ἑνὶ ἀνδρί** (# *1651*; *467*) to one man. The emphasis is on the fact that there is one person, and only one, to whom the Corinthians owe their allegiance (Barrett). **παρθένος** (# *4221*) virgin. **ἁγνός** (# *54*) pure, chaste, undefiled. **παραστῆσαι** aor. act. inf. παρίστημι (# *4225*) to present. Inf. to express purp. ◆ **3 φοβοῦμαι** pres. ind. mid. (dep.) φοβέομαι (# *5828*) to fear, to be afraid. **μή** (# *3590*) followed by the subj., "lest by any means" (RWP). **ὄφις** (# *4058*) snake. **ἐξηπάτησεν** aor. ind. act. ἐξαπατάω (# *1987*) to deceive. Prep. in compound is perfective: "to completely deceive" (s. 1 Tim. 2:14). **πανουργία** (# *4111*) craftiness (s. 4:2). **φθαρῇ** aor. subj. pass. φθείρω (# *5780*) to corrupt. **νόημα** (# *3784*) thought, purpose, design. **ἁπλότης** (# *605*) simplicity, sincerity. **ἁγνότης** (# *55*) purity. ◆ **4 εἰ** (# *1623*) if; w. the ind. introduces a cond. which is assumed to be true. **ἐρχόμενος** pres. mid. (dep.) part. ἔρχομαι (# *2262*) to go, to come. Subst. part., w. the article pointing to a specific person who was well known to the readers. For a discussion s. Martin. **κηρύσσει** pres.

ind. act. κηρύσσω (# 3062) to proclaim, to proclaim as a herald (TDNT; NIDNTT, 3:48-68). ἐκηρύξαμεν aor. ind. act. κηρύσσω ἐλάβετε aor. ind. act. λαμβάνω (# 3284) to take. ἐδέξασθε aor. ind. mid. (dep.) δέχομαι (# 1312) to receive, to welcome. ἀνέχεσθε pres. ind. mid. (dep.) ἀνέχομαι (# 462) to put up with. ◆ 5 λογίζομαι (# 3357) pres. ind. mid. (dep.) to consider, to judge, to reckon. μηδέν = οὐδέν (# 3594) acc., no, no one; acc. of reference; "in reference to nothing," "in no way at all" (Barrett). ὑστερηκέναι perf. act. inf. ὑστερέω (# 5728) to come behind, to lack. Inf. in indir. discourse. ὑπερλίαν (# 5663) super, exceedingly, beyond measure. Paul's description is vibrant w. sarcasm–"extra-super-apostles"–and is an ironic restatement of the opponents claim to be apostles (Hughes; OPSC, 32). For the use of irony in rhetoric s. Forbes, "Comparison, Self-Praise and Irony," NTS 32 (1986): 10-13. ◆ 6 εἰ δὲ καί but even if. ἰδιώτης (# 2626) a private person, in contrast to one who holds an office or to one who has special ability or knowledge, a layman, one who is unskilled (TDNT; Barrett; RWP; TLNT). The word is followed by the dat. of reference. ἀλλ' οὐ τῇ γνώσει but not really in knowledge. ἐν παντί (# 1877; 4246) in every respect. φανερώσαντες aor. act. part. φανερόω (# 5746) to make clear, to manifest. ◆ 7 ἤ (# 2445) or. ἐποίησα aor. ind. act. ποιέω (# 4472) to do, to make. ταπεινῶν pres. act. part. ταπεινόω (# 5427) to make low, to bring low, to make humble. ὑψωθῆτε aor. subj. pass. ὑψόω (# 5738) to lift up, to exalt. Subj. w. ἵνα (# 2671) to express purp. ὅτι (# 4022) because. δωρεάν (# 1562) adv., freely, without charge. Emphatic juxtaposition "God's gospel," that most precious thing–for nothing!" (Plummer). εὐαγγελισάμην aor. ind. mid. (dep.) εὐαγγελίζομαι (# 2294) to proclaim good news, to preach the gospel, to evangelize (TDNT; TLNT; NIDNTT, 2:107-14). Active occurs infrequently, w. no difference in meaning (BAGD; BD, 163). ◆ 8 ἄλλος (# 257) other; i.e., in distinction to the churches in Corinth. ἐσύλησα aor. ind. act. συλάω (# 5195) to plunder. The word was used either for the robbing of temples or for the plundering of soldiers (Hughes; Barrett; Furnish). λαβών aor. act. part. λαμβάνω (# 3284) to take, to receive. Part. of means or manner explaining how he robbed the other churches. ὀψώνιον (# 4072) wages, pay. ὑμῶν διακονίαν for your service. ◆ 9 παρών pres. act. part. πάρειμι (# 4205) to be present. Temp. part. expressing contemporaneous time. ὑστερηθείς aor. pass. part. (# 5728) to lack. κατενάρκησα aor. ind. act. καταναρκάω (# 2915) to make or become numb, to be a burden. A noun based on the simplex of the vb. was used for an electric eel which numbed its victims by an electric shock (Lenski; LS). Prep. in compound is perfective (MH, 316). ὑστέρημα (# 5729) need, lack, want. προσανεπλήρωσαν aor. ind. act. προσαναπληρόω (# 4650) to fill up, to fill up in addition. Prep. in compound signifies the adding of some-

thing and may indicate that the gift from Macedonia supplemented the amount which Paul earned (Hughes). ἀβαρής (# 4) free from weight, not burdensome. ἐτήρησα aor. ind. act. τηρέω (# 5498) to guard, to keep. Aor. summarizes the past ministry of Paul. τηρήσω fut. ind. act. τηρέω. ◆ 10 ἔστιν pres. ind. act. εἰμί (# 1639) to be. The vb. is emphatic by its position in the sentence. ἀλήθεια Χριστοῦ the truth of Christ. The expression here reveals the intensity of Paul's feelings and is to be taken as a solemn assertion (Bruce; IBG, 112). καύχησις (# 3018) boasting. φραγήσεται fut. ind. pass. φράσσω (# 5852) to fence in, to stop, to block in. The figure may be that of blocking or barricading a road or damming a river; the central idea is blockage (Hughes; RWP). κλίμα (# 3107) province, district, region (BAGD). ◆ 11 διὰ τί (# 1328; 5515) why? οἶδεν perf. ind. act. οἶδα (# 3857) to know. Def. perf. w. pres. meaning. For this word s. ND, 344-56. ◆ 12 ποιήσω fut. ind. act. ποιέω (# 4472) to do. ἐκκόψω aor. subj. act. ἐκκόπτω (# 1716) to cut off, to remove, to destroy (BAGD; GELTS, 137; CCFJ, 2:56). Subj. w. ἵνα (# 2671) used to express purp. ἀφορμή (# 929) opportunity, base of operation (s. 5:12). θελόντων pres. act. part. (subst.) θέλω (# 2527) to wish, to desire, to want. καυχῶνται pres. ind. mid. (dep.) καυχάομαι (# 3016) to boast, to glory. εὑρεθῶσιν aor. subj. pass. εὑρίσκω (# 2351) to find; pass., to be found. Subj. w. ἵνα (# 2671) used to express purp. ◆ 13 τοιοῦτος (# 5525) such a one. ψευδαπόστολος (# 6013) false apostle, pseudo-apostle (DPL, 644-53). ἐργάτης (# 2239) one who works. δόλιος (# 1513) deceitful, tricky, cunning, treacherous. The basic meaning of the word is "bait for fish"; then, any cunning contrivance for deceiving or catching (LS). μετασχηματιζόμενοι pres. mid. part. μετασχηματίζω (# 3571) to transform one's outward appearance, to disguise, to transform. Mid., to change, disguise oneself (Barrett; TDNT; BAGD). Pres. points to that which Satan habitually does (Plummer). ◆ 14 θαῦμα (# 2512) wonder, marvel. μετασχηματίζεται pres. ind. mid. μετασχηματίζω (# 3571) to transform (s.v. 13). ἄγγελον φωτός (# 34; 5890) angel of light. Descriptive gen. indicating the character or perhaps the appearance. The term may have been used to indicate a messenger of God (Lietzmann; Schlatter). In the Jewish writing, The Life of Adam and Eve (Apocalypse), it is said that Satan transformed himself into the brightness of angels and came to Eve (Adam and Eve 9:1; OTP, 2:260; Martin). ◆ 15 διάκονοι αὐτοῦ (# 1356) "his ministers"; obj. gen., those who serve Satan. ἔσται fut. ind. mid. (dep.) εἰμί (# 1639) to be. ◆ 16 μή (# 3590) used w. aor. subj. in a neg. prohibition (RG, 933). δόξῃ aor. subj. act. δοκέω (# 1506) to suppose, to think. The prohibitive aor. subj. could be used to prevent an action from arising without involving the notion "immediately" (MKG, 273). Aor. implies that no one did (RG, 853). ἄφρων (# 933) fool, one who does not think. εἶναι pres.

act. inf. εἰμί (# 1639) to be. Inf. used in indir. discourse. εἰ δὲ μή γε and even if, otherwise (Barrett; BD, 191, 226). **δέξασθε** aor. imp. mid. (dep.) δέχομαι (# 1312) to accept, to receive, to welcome. **κἀγώ** = καί ἐγώ I also, I too. **μικρόν τι** s. the discussion in 11:1. **καυχήσωμαι** aor. ind. mid (dep.) subj. καυχάομαι (# 3016) to boast. Subj. w. **ἵνα** (# 2671) to express purp. ◆ **17 κατά** (# 2848) w. the acc., according to, according to the standard. Paul is not claiming to be uninspired, but the expression means, "in accordance w. the character or example of Christ" (Hughes). **ὑπόστασις** (# 5712) basis, confidence (s. Heb. 11:1), followed by the descriptive or adjectival gen. **τῆς καυχήσεως** (# 3018) boastful confidence (Barrett). ◆ **18 καυχῶνται** pres. ind. mid. (dep.) **καυχήσομαι** fut. ind. mid. (dep.) καυχάομαι (# 3016) to boast. For self-praise in rhetoric s. Forbes, "Comparison, Self-Praise and Irony," *NTS* 32 (1986): 8-10. ◆ **19 ἡδέως** (# 2452) adv., gladly, joyously. Paul is using irony of the sharpest kind (BD, 262). **ἀνέχεσθε** pres. ind. mid. (dep.) ἀνέχομαι (# 462) to endure, to bear w. someone, followed by the gen. **φρόνιμος** (# 5861) wise, understanding. **ὄντες** pres. act. part. εἰμί (# 1639) to be. Part. could be concessive ("although") or causal ("because you are sensible"). ◆ **20 ἀνέχεσθε** pres. ind. mid. (dep.) ἀνέχομαι (# 462) to bear w. **καταδουλοῖ** pres. ind. act. καταδουλόω (# 2871) to enslave. Used in a cond. cl. which assumes the reality of the cond. **κατεσθίει** pres. ind. act. κατεσθίω (# 2983) to eat up, to devour. Prep. in compound is perfective. The reference may be to one who takes advantage of the privilege of receiving help: "if anyone eats you out of house and home" (Barrett). **λαμβάνει** pres. ind. act. λαμβάνω (# 3284) to take, to receive; i.e., "catch you" as birds in a snare, or fish w. bait (Plummer). **ἐπαίρεται** pres. ind. mid. (dep.) ἐπαίρω (# 2048) to lift oneself up, to exalt oneself. The exaltation is essentially self-exaltation, carnal and worldly in character (Hughes). **δέρει** pres. ind. act. δέρω (# 1296) to skin, to strike. The reference may be to physical violence, or it may be used to express vb. affronts (Windisch; Hughes). Pres. of the vb. here may be explained as conative or tendential, and picture an attempted action, representing the idea of that which is intended or tends toward realization (DM, 186; BD, 167; RG, 880). The prep. used w. the vb. δέρει often directs to a part of the body to, or on, which an act is done (MT, 256). ◆ **21 κατὰ ἀτιμίαν** (# 2848; 871) according to dishonor. Here Paul used intense irony (RWP). **ὡς ὅτι** as that; i.e., "as people have been saying, that" (Hughes). **ἠσθενή-καμεν** perf. ind. act. ἀσθενέω (# 820) to be weak, to be powerless. The charge here may be of weakness caused by fear or caution (BAGD). **ἐν ᾧ** in whatever. In whatever matter any person exhibits real courage, the apostle does not fear comparison (Plummer). **τολμᾷ** pres. subj. act. 3rd. pers. sing. τολμάω (# 5528) to dare. **τολμῶ** pres. ind. act. 1st. pers. sing. **κἀγώ** = καί ἐγω I also, I too.

The personal pron. is strongly emphasized. ◆ **22** **ἑβραῖος** (# 1578) Hebrew. The term emphasizes the pure-blooded Jew; sometimes it can emphasize a Hebrew-speaking Jew or a Jew of Palestine (TDNT; Lietzmann; Windisch; Barrett; OPSC, 41-46). **Ἰσραηλίτης** (# 2703) Israelite. The term emphasizes the social and religious character as well as the national promises and blessings from God (Windisch; TDNT; OPSC, 46-49). **σπέρμα** (# 5065) seed descendant. The emphasis here may be from a theological point of view (Barrett), particularly emphasizing the promises made by God (Windisch). ◆ **23 διάκονοι Χριστοῦ** ministers of Christ. The gen. is obj. gen. those who minister or serve Christ. **παραφρονῶν** pres. act. part. παραφρονέω (# 4196) to be beside oneself, to be mentally deranged. "I am talking like a mad man" (MM). **ὑπέρ** (# 5642) over, beyond. Here used as an adv., more, to a higher degree, better (BD, 121; MT, 250). **κόπος** (# 3160) work, toil. The word emphasizes the weariness which follows on the straining of all of his powers to the utmost (Trench, *Synonyms*, 378). **περισσοτέρως** (# 4359) adv., comp. of περισσός (# 4356) abundant. Used here in the superl. sense as elative, very abundantly. It may mean, "more abundantly than most men" or "than you would believe" (Plummer). In the following vv. Paul describes in detail his affliction for Christ (DPL, 18-20). **φυλακή** (# 5871) prison, guarding. Places of confinement, both public and private, were used during the investigation as the accused awaited his trial. Most of the prisons were dark, w. very little room, no sanitary facilities, and inadequate food. For prisons in the ancient world s. BAFCS, 3:195-392; RAC, 9:318-45; DGRA, 240f; KP, 1:1053, 1496; OCD, 879, 1099; TDNT; PIP. **πληγή** (# 4435) strike, blow, wound, or bruise as the result of a blow (BAGD). **ὑπερβαλλόντως** (# 5649) adv., beyond measure, very exceedingly; built from the part. **θάνατος** (# 2505) death. pl., deaths; i.e., "situations in which I was in danger of death" (Barrett). **πολλάκις** (# 4490) often. ◆ **24 πεντάκις** (# 4294) five times. **τεσσαράκοντα** (# 5477) forty. **παρὰ μίαν** (# 4123; 1651) except one. This was the Jewish method of punishment based on Deut. 25:2f. The person had his two hands bound to a pillar on either side and his garments removed so that his chest was bare. With a whip made of a strap of calf hide and two other straps of donkey hide connected to a long handle, the person received one-third of the thirty-nine stripes in front and two-thirds behind while he was bending low. During this time the reader reads over and again Deut. 28:58 (M, Makkoth; SB, 3:527-30; Sven Gallas, "'Fünfmal vierzig weniger einen...': Die an Paulus vollzogenen Synagogalstrafen nach 2 Kor 11, 24," *ZNW* 81 [1990]: 178-91). **ἔλαβον** aor. ind. act. λαμβάνω (# 3284) to receive. ◆ **25 τρίς** (# 5565) three times. **ἐραβδίσθην** aor. ind. pass. ῥαβδίζω (# 4810) to beat w. rods. This refers to the Roman method of beating which was often used as police coercion (s. Acts 16:22; TDNT; RAC, 9:469-90; Furnish). In Paul's case it was probably a punishment prescribed by city magistrates (BAGD). ἅπαξ (# 562) once, one time. ἐλιθάσθην aor. ind. pass. λιθάζω (# 3342) to stone (s. the discussion in Acts 14:19). ἐναυάγησα aor. ind. act. ναυαγέω (# 3728) to suffer shipwreck. For the possible voyages during which Paul may have been involved in shipwrecks s. Hughes. νυχθήμερον (# 3819) night-day. This refers to the Heb. custom of reckoning the day of 24 hours from evening to evening. The word may be viewed as adverbial or as the dir. obj. of the vb. (Hughes). βυθός (# 1113) deep. πεποίηκα perf. ind. act. ποιέω (# 4472) to make. Aoristic or dramatic perf. to emphasize vividness (GGBB, 579). Perf. shows that the dreadful experience is vividly before the apostle's mind, and possibly indicates that the occurrence was recent (Plummer; M, 144). ◆ 26 ὁδοιπορία (# 3845) walking journey, journey. κίνδυνος (# 3074) danger. The following gen.s tell where the danger comes from. ποταμός (# 4532) river. The rivers were sometimes difficult to cross; some changed in a moment from half-dry riverbeds to rushing torrents (Barrett; Furnish). λῃστής (# 3334) robber, bandit, one who uses weapons and violence in robbing others. For a good description of bandits and robbers in the ancient world, s. Martin Hengel, *Die Zeloten* (Leiden: E.J. Brill, 1976), 25-47; TDNT; DJG, 688-98. Although the main highways were well-policed and relatively free of bandits, they still posed a threat, esp. to small groups of unarmed travelers (Furnish). γένος (# 1169) generation, contemporary, those descended from a common ancestor (BAGD). Here it refers to the Jews. ἐρημία (# 2244) desert, an isolated place. ψευδάδελφος (# 6012) false brother. ◆ 27 κόπος (# 3160) work (s.v. 23). μόχθῳ (# 3677) toil, labor. The word is active indicating struggle and toil (Plummer). ἀγρυπνία (# 71) wakefulness, the inability to sleep (Martin). It refers evidently to the sleepless nights Paul spent in work and ministry (Windisch). λιμός (# 3350) hunger. δίψος (# 1499) thirst. νηστεία (# 3763) fasting. The word refers to the foregoing of meals in order that Paul's work as a minister of Christ might not be interrupted (Hughes). It refers to going without food, either voluntarily or because of a hard life (Martin). ψῦχος (# 6036) cold. γυμνότης (# 1218) nakedness. Perhaps the last two descriptions recall Paul's being thrown into prison, or drenched by rain, or stripped by brigands (Plummer). ◆ 28 χωρίς (# 6006) apart, besides. παρεκτός (# 4211) external; i.e., the outward suffering, or it may imply an exception: "apart from the things that I have not mentioned" (Hughes). ἐπίστασις (# 2180) pressure, stress. The word here probably refers to the daily pressure of responsibility (Hughes). μέριμνα (# 3533) concern, care. ◆ 29 ἀσθενεῖ pres. ind. act. ἀσθενέω (# 820) to be weak. σκανδαλίζεται pres. ind. pass. σκανδαλίζω

(# 4997) to cause to stumble. The word means rather, to catch in a death trap; pass., to be caught. It refers to the moral offense that kills spiritually (Lenski). πυροῦμαι pres. ind. pass. πυρόω (# 4792) to set on fire, to enflame. When a brother stumbles, Paul is set on fire w. grief (RWP). ◆ 30 καυχᾶσθαι pres. mid. (dep.) inf. καυχάομαι (# 3016) to boast, to glory. Compl. inf. to the following impersonal vb. δεῖ pres. ind. act. (# 1256) it is necessary, w. inf. giving a logical necessity. τὰ τῆς ἀσθενείας (# 819) things belonging to my weakness. καυχήσομαι fut. ind. mid. (dep.) καυχάομαι. ◆ 31 οἶδεν perf. ind. act. οἶδα (# 3857) to know. Def. perf. w. a pres. meaning. ὤν pres. act. part. εἰμί (# 1639) to be. Subst. part. stressing the continual character. εὐλογητός (# 2329) blessed (s. 1:3). ψεύδομαι (# 6017) pres. ind. mid. (dep.) to lie. ◆ 32 ἐθνάρχης (# 1617) ethnarch. The term seems to refer to a representative of a subject people who has been given certain powers of control over his own people yet responsible to the foreign dominating power (TJ, 42-43; ISBE, 2:199; Furnish; Martin). For a discussion of Aretas in this passage s. Hughes; Martin; Furnish; and for the Nabateans in general s. HK, 62-68). ἐφρούρει impf. ind. act. φρουρέω (# 5864) to watch, to guard, to guard by posting sentries. Impf. pictures the continual action in the past. πιάσαι aor. act. inf. πιάζω (# 4389) to seize, to arrest. Inf. to express purp. (Barrett). Aor. points to the specific act of seizing. Perhaps Paul escaped from Damascus in A.D. 37 which would put his conversion around A.D. 34 (Hughes; Windisch). ◆ 33 θυρίδος gen. θυρίς (# 2600) window. A small opening in the wall is still shown as the little door through which St. Paul was let down (Plummer). σαργάνη (# 4914) basket, rope basket. ἐχαλάσθην aor. ind. pass. χαλάω (# 5899) to let down. διά (# 1328) w. gen., through. τεῖχος (# 1328) wall. ἐξέφυγον aor. ind. act. ἐκφεύγω (# 1767) to escape. Prep. in compound is perfective, indicating that the escape was successful.

2 Corinthians 12

◆ 1 καυχᾶσθαι pres. mid. (dep.) inf. καυχάομαι (# 3016) to boast. Complementary inf. to the following impersonal vb. Pres. indicates the continuing of the action, "I must go on boasting" (Martin). δεῖ pres. ind. act. (# 1256); it is necessary. συμφέρον pres. act. part. συμφέρω (# 5237) to be expedient. In Paul's usage the word points to the welfare not of the individual but of the Christian society (Barrett). Part. used as an acc. abs. (RG, 1130). ἐλεύσομαι fut. ind. mid. (dep.) ἔρχομαι (# 2262) to come. ὀπτασία (# 3965) vision. ἀποκάλυψις (# 637) unveiling, revelation. κυρίου gen. κύριος (# 3261). Here, of the Lord. Gen. could be subj. gen. (visions and revelations from the Lord [Barrett]) or it could be the obj. gen. (visions and revelations which have the Lord as their object [Hughes]). ◆ 2 ἄνθρωπος

(# 476) man. It was part of the rabbinic style to substitute an impersonal word–"man"–for the 1st. and 2nd. person when one talked of oneself (SB, 3:530f). ἔτος (# 2291) year. δεκατέσσαρες (# 1280) fourteen. This would make the year about A.D. 44, but the incident remains unknown in Paul's life (Martin). οἶδα (# 3857) perf. ind. act. Def. perf. w. a pres. meaning, to know. ἐκτός (# 1760) w. gen., out of. The possibility of separating the inner man from the body is presented in this v. (SBT, 146f). ἁρπαγέντα aor. pass. part. (adj.) ἁρπάζω (# 773) to seize, to snatch, to take by force, to catch up. For various parallels to Paul's experience s. Barrett; Windisch. τρίτου οὐρανοῦ (# 5569; 4041) the third heaven. Perhaps the expression means the highest heaven where the presence of God is. Paul was granted the sight of the glory that lies ahead and was thereby fortified to enter patiently all the suffering which awaited him (Hughes; SB, 5:531f; Martin; Furnish). ◆ 4 ἡρπάγη aor. ind. pass. ἁρπάζω (# 773) to seize (s.v. 2). παράδεισος (# 4137) paradise. The word refers to a blissful abode within the very courts of heaven itself (Hughes; Furnish; s. Luke 23:43). ἤκουσεν aor. ind. act. ἀκούω (# 201) to hear. ἄρρητος (# 777) verbal adj., unspeakable, unutterable. The word was often used of divine secrets not intended for human beings (Windisch; Barrett). ῥῆμα (# 4839) word. ἐξόν pres. act. part. nom. n. sing. ἔξεστι(ν) (# 2003) it is allowed. The word is to be taken in connection w. ἀνθρώπῳ (s.v. 2); "which it is not lawful for a man to speak" (Plummer). ◆ 5 ὑπέρ (# 5642) on behalf of, for the benefit of. καυχήσομαι fut. ind. mid. (dep.) καυχάομαι (# 3016) to glory. εἰ μή except. ἀσθενείαις (# 819) weakness. ◆ 6 ἐάν (# 1569) if. Used to introduce a cond. cl. in which the cond. is considered to be probable. θελήσω aor. subj. act. θέλω (# 2527) to wish, to will, to choose. The v. properly carries w. it an element of deliberate preference (Barrett). καυχήσασθαι aor. mid. (dep.) inf. καυχάομαι (# 3016) to glory. ἔσομαι fut. ind. mid. (dep.) εἰμί (# 1639) to be. ἄφρων (# 933) foolish, senseless, without reason. It expresses a want of mental sanity and sobriety, a reckless and inconsiderate habit of mind (AS). ἐρῶ fut. ind. act. λέγω (# 3306) to say. φείδομαι (# 5767) pres. ind. mid. (dep.) to spare, to refrain from doing something. Inf. as obj. is to be supplied, "refrain from boasting" (BAGD). Pres. could be taken as conative, "but I am trying to spare you" (Barrett). εἰς ἐμέ unto me. Used w. the following vb. in the sense, "to reckon to my account." The expression occurs often in commercial language (Lietzmann). λογίσηται aor. subj. mid. (dep.) λογίζομαι (# 3357) to reckon, to put to one's account. ὑπέρ beyond, more than. βλέπει pres. ind. act. βλέπω (# 1063) to see. ἐξ ἐμοῦ from me. ἀκούει pres. ind. act. ἀκούω (# 201) to hear. Pres. may be iterative or habitual. ◆ 7 ὑπερβολῇ (# 5651) excess, extraordinary quality or character; here, instr. dat. ἀποκάλυψις (# 637) revela-

tion. ὑπεραίρωμαι pres. subj. mid. ὑπεραίρω (# 5643) to lift up beyond, mid. to lift oneself up beyond, to exalt oneself. Prep. in compound has the sense of excess (MH, 326). Subj. w. ἵνα (# 2671) to express purp. w. the cl. placed first for emphasis (MT, Style, 94). ἐδόθη aor. ind. pass. δίδωμι (# 1443) to give. σκόλοψ (# 5022) stake used for impaling or torturing someone, a sharpened wooden staff, thorn, or splinter (Windisch; Barrett; Hughes). For a discussion as to what the thorn was s. Martin; Furnish; Hughes; Windisch; T.Y. Mullens, "The Thorn in the Flesh," JBL 76 (1957): 299f. σαρκί dat. fem. sing. σάρξ (# 4922) flesh. Dat. is either dat. of advantage ("for my flesh") or locative ("in my flesh") (RG, 538). κολαφίζῃ pres. subj. act. κολαφίζω (# 3139) to strike w. the fist, to beat (s. Mark 14:65). For a listing of the various interpretations given to this phrase s. Martin; BAGD. Pres. refers to either a constant buffeting or a reoccurrence (Hughes). ◆ 8 τρίς (# 5565) three times. παρεκάλεσα aor. ind. act. παρακαλέω (# 4151) to ask, to entreat. ἀποστῇ aor. subj. act. ἀφίστημι (# 923) to depart, to go away. The vb. is generally used of persons not things (Hughes). ◆ 9 εἴρηκεν perf. ind. act. λέγω (# 3306) to say. Perf. implies that the words remain w. Paul as an abiding source of assurance and comfort (Bruce; IBG, 15). ἀρκεῖ pres. ind. act. ἀρκέω (# 758) to be sufficient, to be enough, to be adequate for a particular purpose, w. the implication of leading to satisfaction (LN, 1:599). σοι dat. σύ (# 5148) you; here, for you. Dat. of advantage. ἡ χάρις μου (# 5921; 1609) my grace; the unmerited help for one undeserving w. no thought of recompense (TDNT; TLNT; EDNT; CCP). γάρ (# 1142) for, giving an explanation or reason. ἐν ἀσθενείᾳ (# 819) in weakness. This is to strengthen the contrast to δύναμις (# 1539) power. τελεῖται pres. ind. pass. τελέω (# 5464) to bring to completion, to bring to perfection. Pres. emphasizes the continuous action: "my power is being perfected in weakness" (M, 130). It may also be iterat.: "my power is repeatedly perfect in weakness." ἥδιστα superl. of the adv. ἡδέω (# 2452) gladly; elative use of the superl., very gladly. μᾶλλον (# 3437) rather. The comp. is not to be connected w. the previous adv. (BD, 129). καυχήσομαι fut. ind. mid. καυχάομαι (# 3016) to boast. ἐπισκηνώσῃ aor. subj. act. ἐπισκηνόω (# 2172) to take up one's residence, to abide, to dwell. Subj. w. ἵνα (# 2671) expresses result. There may be a reference to the Shekhina glory of God dwelling in a tent or tabernacle. Paul may mean that the power of God descends upon him and makes its abode in the frail tabernacle of his earthly body (Hughes). ἐπ' ἐμέ upon me, by me. ◆ 10 διό (# 1475) therefore. εὐδοκῶ pres. ind. act. εὐδοκέω (# 2305) to take pleasure in, to be content. Perhaps iterat. "I repeatedly take pleasure." ὕβρις (# 5615) insulting injury. It refers to treatment which is calculated publicly to insult and openly humiliate the person who suffers from it (MNTW, 83; TDNT; Plummer). **διωγμός** (# 1501) persecution. **στενοχωρία** (# 5103) distress (s. 6:4; 4:8). **ὑπὲρ Χριστοῦ** on behalf of Christ. **ὅταν** (# 4020) whenever. **ἀσθενῶ** pres. subj. act. ἀσθενέω (# 820) to be weak. Subj. in an indef. temp. cl. **δυνατός** (# 1543) strong, powerful. ◆ **11 γέγονα** perf. ind. act. γίνομαι (# 1181) to become. The vb. is emphatic and means that which was expected or predicted has come to pass (Plummer). **ἄφρων** (# 933) fool (s.v. 6). **ἠναγκάσατε** aor. ind. act. ἀναγκάζω (# 337) to compel. **ὤφειλον** impf. ind. act. ὀφείλω (# 4053) to be obligated, to be under moral obligation, to ought to. Impf. expresses an unfulfilled obligation (RWP; BD, 181). **συνίστασθαι** pres. pass. inf. συνίστημι (# 5319) to commend (s. 3:1). **ὑστέρησα** aor. ind. act. ὑστερέω (# 5728) to lack, to come behind. **ὑπερλίαν** (# 5663) exceedingly, beyond measure, super. **εἰ καί** if also, although. Cond. is treated as a matter of indifference (RG, 1026). ◆ **12 σημεῖα** (# 4956) sign (DPL, 875-77). **ἀποστόλου** gen. ἀπόστολος (# 693) apostle; gen., belonging to or characteristic of an apostle. **κατειργάσθη** aor. ind. pass. κατεργάζω (# 2981) to produce, to bring about. **σημείοις** dat. pl. σημεῖον (# 4956) sign. instr. dat. **τέρας** (# 5469) wonder. ◆ **13 ὅ** acc. ὅς (# 4005) who, what. Acc. of reference, in regard to what? wherein? **ἡσσώθητε** aor. ind. pass. ἐσσόομαι (# 2273) to make less, to make inferior; pass., to be defeated, to be weaker than or inferior to. Here, "in what respect, then, are you worse off than the other churches?" (BAGD). **ὑπέρ** (# 5642) w. acc., than. Prep. is used to express the comp. **κατενάρκησα** aor. ind. act. καταναρκάω (# 2915) to burden, to be a burden (s. 11:9). **χαρίσασθε** aor. imp. mid. χαρίζω (# 5919) to show grace, to forgive. **ἀδικία** (# 94) wrong, a wrong act. ◆ **14 ἰδού** aor. imp. act. ὁράω (# 3972) to see; here, behold! look! **τρίτον τοῦτο** (# 5569; 4047) "This is the third time." **ἑτοίμως** (# 2290) ready. Used w. the vb. ἔχω (# 2400) pres. ind. act. To have readiness; i.e., to be ready to do something. **ἐλθεῖν** aor. act. inf. ἔρχομαι (# 2262) to come, to go. For a discussion of Paul's third visit to Corinth s. Hughes, Martin. **καταναρκήσω** fut. ind. act. καταναρκάω (# 2915) to burden (s. 11:9). **ζητῶ** pres. ind. act. ζητέω (# 2426) to seek; followed by the pl. article w. the gen., "to seek after your possessions." Pres. indicates the continual and habitual action. **ὀφείλει** pres. ind. act. ὀφείλω (# 4053) to be obligated (s.v. 11). Gnomic pres. used to express customary actions and general truths (SMT, 8). **γονεῦσιν** (# 1204) dat. pl., parents. **θησαυρίζειν** pres. act. inf. θησαυρίζω (# 2564) to store up treasures, to accumulate money. Compl. inf. w. the vb. ὀφείλει. ◆ **15 ἥδιστα** (# 2452) (s.v. 9). **δαπανήσω** fut. ind. act. δαπανάω (# 1251) to spend money, to spend money freely, to consume, to use up (GELTS, 95). For the use of the word in the papyri s. MM; Preisigke, 1:319, and its use in Josephus (to use up, to consume, to eat up, to burn up, to waste, to squander, to spend lavishly) s. CCFJ, 1:407. **ἐκδαπανηθήσομαι** fut. ind. pass. ἐκδαπανάω

(# 1682) pass., to be spent out, to be utterly spent. Prep. in compound is perfective (RG, 596). Paul is ready to exhaust his energies in order to prove his love for the Corinthians (Martin). **περισσοτέρως** (# 4359) adv. comp. περισσός (# 4356) abundantly; comp., more abundantly. **ἧσσον** adv. comp. (# 2482) less. **ἀγαπῶμαι** pres. ind. pass. ἀγαπάω (# 26) to love (TLNT; TDNT; EDNT). ◆ **16 ἔστω** pres. imp. act. εἰμί (# 1639) to be. "Let it be." The previous sentence is to be considered the subject of the imp. (RG, 596). **κατεβάρησα** aor. ind. act. καταβαρέω (# 2851) to put weight on someone, to be burdensome, to put a burden on someone. **ὑπάρχων** pres. act. part. ὑπάρχω (# 5639) to be, to exist, to be by constitution (Hughes). **πανοῦργος** (# 4112) (πᾶν + ἔργον) every work; up to every trick, crafty and unscrupulous (Hughes). **δόλος** (# 1515) guile, craftiness, trickery (s. 4:2). **ἔλαβον** aor. ind. act. λαμβάνω (# 3284) to take, to catch. The metaphor is from hunting or fishing; he entrapped or caught them in his wiliness (Plummer). ◆ **17 μή** (# 3590) introduces a question expecting the answer "no." **τινα** acc. τις (# 5516) any, anyone. The anacoluthon is resumed by the personal pron. in the prep. phrase δι᾽ αὐτοῦ. "Anyone of whom I sent—I did not defraud you through him, did I?" For the construction s. RG, 436; IBG, 176; BG, 10; BD, 234. **ἀπέσταλκα** perf. ind. act. ἀποστέλλω (# 690) to send, to send as an authoritative representative. Perf. indicates that Paul had sent someone from time to time (M, 144) and is a perf. of repeated action or of broken continuity (RG, 893, 896). **ἐπλεονέκτησα** aor. ind. act. πλεονεκτέω (# 4430) to take advantage of someone, often out of selfish, greedy arrogance (NTW, 97-99; TLNT). ◆ **18 παρεκάλεσα** aor. ind. act. παρακαλέω (# 4151) to ask, to beseech, to exhort. **συναπέστειλα** aor. ind. act. συναποστέλλω (# 5273) to send someone w. another, to send together. **μήτι** (# 3614) interrogative particle used in questions expecting the answer "no" or "certainly not" (BD, 220). **οὐ** (# 4024) used in questions which expect the answer "yes." **περιεπατήσαμεν** aor. ind. act. περιπατέω (# 4344) to walk, to conduct one's life. **ἴχνεσιν** dat. pl. ἴχνος (# 2717) step, footstep. Used here in the pl., "in the same footsteps." ◆ **19 πάλαι** (# 4093) long ago, in the past time. Used w. pres. which gathers up past and pres. into one phrase: "you have been thinking all this?" (M, 119; RG, 89). **δοκεῖτε** pres. ind. act. δοκέω (# 1506) to suppose, to think. For the pres. s. the previous word. **ἀπολογούμεθα** pres. ind. mid. (dep.) ἀπολογέομαι (# 664) to defend oneself. This was a term used in law courts (Hughes). **κατέναντι** (# 2978) over against, before. **λαλοῦμεν** pres. ind. act. λαλέω (# 4246) to speak. **ἀγαπητός** (# 28) vb. adj., beloved. **οἰκοδομή** (# 3869) building up, edification. ◆ **20 φοβοῦμαι** (# 5828) pres. ind. mid. (dep.) to fear, to be afraid. **μή πως** (# 3590; 4803) lest, lest by any means. For the use of these words w. vbs. of fearing, s. RG, 99; SMT, 95. When followed by the subj. it indicates fear of an uncertain thing in the fut. (MT, 99). **ἐλθών** aor. act. part. ἔρχομαι (# 2262) to come, to go temp. or cond. part. **οὐχ οἴους** = οὐ τοιοῦτος + οἴους = (# 3888) not such ones as. **εὑρεθῶ** aor. subj. act. εὑρίσκω (# 2351) to find. **ἔρις** (# 2251) strife, quarreling. **ζῆλος** (# 2419) jealous, envying. **θύμος** (# 2596) anger, sudden flare-up of burning anger (Trench, *Synonyms*, 130). **ἐριθεία** (# 2249) selfishness, intrigue (s. Phil. 2:3). **καταλαλιά** (# 2896) speaking against someone, backbiting. **ψιθυρισμός** (# 6030) whispering (s. Rom. 1:29). **φυσίωσις** (# 5883) inflated opinion (Barrett). **ἀκαταστασία** (# 189) disorder. ◆ **21 πάλιν** (# 4099) again. The word could refer either to the part. or to the main vb. (Barrett; Hughes). **ἐλθόντος** aor. act. part. (temp.) ἔρχομαι (# 2262) to come. Gen. abs., "when I come" (BD, 218). **ταπεινώσῃ** aor. subj. act. ταπεινόω (# 5427) to make low, to humiliate. Aor. points to a specific act. Subj. used w. **μή** (# 3590) in a neg. purp. cl. which goes back to the vb. φοβοῦμαι in v. 20 (RWP). **πενθήσω** aor. subj. act. πενθέω (# 4291) to express sorrow for one who has died, to mourn. **προημαρτηκότων** perf. act. part. προαρματάνω (# 4579) to sin previously. Perf. part. indicates that the sinning began early and continued, and refers to persistence in sexual sin by the members of the Corinthian church during a previous period (Barrett; Hughes). **μετανοησάντων** aor. act. part. μετανοέω (# 3566) to change one's thinking, to repent. Aor. in contrast to the previous perf. indicates that the repentance which might have ended the sinning did not take place (Barrett). **ἀκαθαρσία** (# 174) uncleanness. The word refers to sexual sins of impurity. **πορνεία** (# 4518) fornication, illicit sexual activity (TDNT). **ἀσέλγεια** (# 816) not bridled, unrestrained, lawless insolence, sheer animal lust. It is the vice of a man who has no more shame than an animal in the gratification of his physical desires (NTW, 27; Trench, *Synonyms*, 53f). **ἔπραξαν** aor. ind. act. πράσσω (# 4556) to do, to practice. Aor looks at all the individual actions as a whole.

2 Corinthians 13

◆ **1 τρίτον τοῦτο** (# 5569; 4047) this third time (Hughes; Hodge). **ἐπί** (# 2093) w. gen., upon, on the basis of; "on the basis of the testimony." **δύο ... καὶ τριῶν** two or three. **σταθήσεται** fut. ind. pass. ἴστημι (# 2705) to stand; pass., to be established. **ῥῆμα** (# 4839) word, matter. The matter between Paul and the Corinthians is to be brought to conclusion by the third visit, which would be in line w. this statement from Deut. 19:15 (Windisch). ◆ **2 προείρηκα** perf. ind. act. προλέγω (# 4625) to say previously, to say beforehand, to tell in advance. It is possible that the idea of the word is "to warn" (Barrett). **παρών** pres. act. part. πάρειμι (# 4205) to be present. Temp. part. expressing contemporaneous action, "while I am present." **δεύτερον** (# 1309) sec-

ond, the second time. **ἀπών** pres. act. part. ἄπειμι (# 582) to be absent. **προημαρτηκόσιν** perf. act. part. προαμαρτάνω (# 4579) to sin beforehand (s. 12:21). **ἔλθω** aor. subj. act. ἔρχομαι (# 2262) to come, to go. **πάλιν** (# 4099) again; "for another visit" (IBG, 69). **φείσομαι** fut. ind. mid. (dep.) φείδομαι (# 5767) to spare. It primarily means to spare in battle–not to kill when the opportunity to do so exists. It then comes to mean "to have mercy upon" (Barrett). ◆ **3 ἐπεί** (# 2075) since. Used in a causal sense ("because"). **δοκιμή** (# 1509) proof, that which passes an examination. **ζητεῖτε** pres. ind. act. ζητέω (# 2426) to seek. Gen. indicates that which was to be proven: "proof that Christ is speaking in me." **λαλοῦντος** pres. act. part. λαλέω (# 4246) to speak. Adj. part., "proof of Christ speaking in me." **ἀσθενεῖ** pres. ind. act. ἀσθενέω (# 820) to be weak. **δυνατεῖ** pres. ind. act. δυνατέω (# 1542) be strong, to be mighty. ◆ **4 καὶ γάρ** (# 2779; 1142) for even (Hughes). **ἐσταυρώθη** aor. ind. pass. σταυρόω (# 5090) to crucify. **ζῇ** pres. ind. act. ζάω (# 2409) to live. **ἐκ** out of. The prep. here is used in the causal sense (MT, 259f). **καὶ γάρ** for also (Hughes), for indeed (Barrett). **εἰς ὑμᾶς** (# 1650; 5148) toward you. It is probably to be taken w. the v. ζήσομεν (Hughes). ◆ **5 ἑαυτούς** acc. pl. ἑαυτοῦ (# 1571) oneself; "yourselves." **πειράζετε** pres. imp. act. πειράζω (# 4279) to try, to examine, here, "to discover what kind of person someone is" (BAGD; Martin; TLNT; Trench, *Synonyms*, 280). **ἐστέ** pres. ind. act. εἰμί (# 1639) to be. **δοκιμάζετε** pres. imp. act. δοκιμάζω (# 1507) to test, to prove, to approve after examination. In the NT the word almost always implies proof as well as approval (Trench, *Synonyms*, 278; Hughes). **ἐπιγινώσκετε** pres. ind. act. ἐπιγινώσκω (# 2105) to recognize, to know. Prep. in compound is directive and directs the knowledge to the specific obj. (MH, 312). **εἰ μήτι** (# 1623; 3614) if perhaps, unless indeed. **ἀδόκιμος** (# 99) disapproved, rejected after examination, not usable. ◆ **6 ἐλπίζω** (# 1827) pres. ind. act. to hope. **γνώσεσθε** fut. ind. mid. (dep.) γινώσκω (# 1182) to recognize. ◆ **7 εὐχόμεθα** pres. ind. mid. (dep.) εὔχομαι (# 2377) to pray, followed by the inf. indicating the contents of the prayer. **ποιῆσαι** aor. act. inf. ποιέω (# 4472) to do, used w. the neg. The subject of the inf. is not clear; either "that you may do no evil thing," or "that God may do no harm" (Barret). **δόκιμος** (# 1511) approved, approved after testing. **φανῶμεν** aor. subj. act. φαίνω (# 5743) to appear. Subj. w. **ἵνα** (# 2671) to express purp. or result. **ποιῆτε** pres. subj. act. ποιέω (# 4472) to do. **ὦμεν** pres. subj. act. εἰμί (# 1639) to be. ◆ **8 ἀλήθεια** (# 237) truth. The word may be used here in a general sense (Barrett). ◆ **9 ὅταν** (# 4020) when, whenever. **ἀσθενῶμεν** pres. subj. act. ἀσθενέω (# 820) to be weak. **ἦτε** pres. subj. act. εἰμί (# 1639) to be. **εὐχόμεθα** pres. ind. mid. (dep.) εὔχομαι (# 2377) to pray. **κατάρτισις** (# 2937) perfecting, fitting together. It is used in the sense of setting bones or reconciling parties and refers here to the growth in holiness (Plummer). ◆ **10** ἀπών pres. act. part. ἀπείμι (# 582) to be absent. **παρών** pres. act. part. πάρειμι (# 4205) to be present. **ἀποτόμως** (# 705) adv. cut off, curt, sharply, severely (RWP; BAGD). **χρήσωμαι** aor. subj. mid. (dep.) χράομαι (# 5968) to use. **οἰκοδομή** (# 3869) building up, edification. **καθαίρεσις** (# 2746) tearing down, destroying. ◆ **11** λοιπόν (# 3370) finally, acc. of the adj. used as an adv. **χαίρετε** pres. imp. act. χαίρω (# 5897) to rejoice, used as a farewell greeting (GGBB, 493). **καταρτίζεσθε** pres. imp. pass. καταρτίζω (# 2936) to restore; pass., to be restored. **παρακαλεῖσθε** pres. imp. pass. παρακαλέω (# 4151) to exhort, to encourage (TDNT; MNTW, 134). **φρονεῖτε** pres. imp. act. φρονέω (# 5858) to think; here, "be of the same mind," "be harmonious in thought and aim" (Plummer). **εἰρηνεύετε** pres. imp. act. εἰρηνεύω (# 1644) to be peaceable, to live in peace. **ἔσται** fut. ind. mid. (dep.) εἰμί (# 1639) to be. ◆ **12** ἀσπάσασθε aor. imp. mid. (dep.) ἀσπάζομαι (# 832) to greet. **φίλημα** (# 5799) kiss. S. the discussion in 1 Cor. 16:20 concerning the holy kiss (ἁγίῳ φιλήματι). ◆ **13** ἡ κοινωνία τοῦ ἁγίου πνεύματος "the fellowship of the Holy Spirit." The gen. could be obj. gen. (the fellowship or participation which has the Holy Spirit as its obj.), or it could be subjective gen. (the fellowship or participation which comes from the Holy Spirit) (TDNT; Barrett).

Galatians

Galatians 1

◆ **1** For the possible rhetorical structure of the book s. Betz; Longenecker; Walter B. Russell, "Rhetorical Analysis of the Book of Galatians: Parts 1 & 2." *Bib Sac* 150 [1993]: 341-58, 416-39. ἀπόστολος (# 693) apostle, one sent w. a mission to be carried out w. the authority of the one sending (TDNT; TLNT; EDNT; DPL, 45-51; Longenecker; Betz, 74-75). ἀπ' = ἀπό (# 608) from. The prep. indicates source; Paul states that his apostleship did not have a group of men (pl.) as its source. διά (# 1328) through. The prep. denotes means or agency. It points to the medium through which one would have conveyed the office of his apostleship. ἐγείραντος aor. act. part. (adj.) ἐγείρω (# 1586) to raise. Aor. indicates logically antecedent action. The context indicates that the resurrection of Christ has a special bearing on Paul's apostleship: "I was commissioned by the risen and glorified Lord: I am in all respects an apostle, a qualified witness of His resurrection, and a signal instance of His power" (Lightfoot). ◆ **2** οἱ σὺν ἐμοὶ πάντες ἀδελφοί all the brothers with me. Though they are not mentioned by name they were evidently known to the churches, and the emphatic "all" indicates that they were solidly behind him and the letter (Betz). Γαλατία (# 1130) The term could refer to the geographical area (North Galatia), or better to the Roman province Galatia (South Galatia), which included the churches founded by Paul on his first mission journey (Acts 13-14). For the arguments concerning both views s. DPL, 323-26; Bruce; Longenecker; Fung; Betz; Guthrie, *New Testament Introduction*, 450-57; ABD, 2:870-72; Cilliers Breytenbach, *Paulus und Barnabas in der Provinz Galatia: Studien zu Apostelgeschichte 13f.; 16,6; 18,23 und den Adressaten des Galaterbriefes* (Leiden: E.J. Brill, 1996); James M. Scott, *Paul and the Nations: The Old Testament and Jewish Background of Paul's Mission to the Nations with Special Reference to the Destination of Galatians* (Tübingen: Mohr-Siebeck, 1995). ◆ **3** ὑμῖν dat. pl. σύ (# 5148) you. Dat. of advantage: "to you," "for you." ◆ **4** δόντος aor. act. part. δίδωμι (# 1443) to give, to bestow (s. 2:20). The idea involved is a delivering up of oneself for a specific purpose (Guthrie). Aor. part. describes logically antecedent action. ἐξέληται aor. subj. mid. (dep.) ἐξαιρέω (# 1975) to take out, to remove, to deliver (GELTS, 157). It denotes a rescue from the power of (Burton). Subj. w. ὅπως (# 3968) to express

purp. αἰών (# 172) age, the system of practices and standards associated w. secular society (LN, 1:508; EDNT; TDNT; NIDNTT, 3:826-33; Bruce). ἐνεστῶτος perf. act. part. ἵστημι (# 1931) to have come, to be present. The word points to the present transitory age (Lightfoot; Eadie). ◆ **5** ἀμήν (# 297) truly. Used to emphasize and substantiate a statement (TDNT; NIDNTT, 1:97-100; Matt. 5:18). ◆ **6** θαυμάζω pres. ind. act. (# 2513) to marvel, to wonder, to be astonished. The word indicates astonishment, irritation, and rebuke (Longenecker; T.Y. Mullins, "Formulas in New Testament Epistles," *JBL* 91 [1972]: 380), and was a rhetorical device used in law courts and politics to attack things done by the opposition party (Betz). Pres. points to the pres. continual attitude of Paul. οὕτως ταχέως (# 4048; 5441) so quickly. Paul was astonished at the speed (ταχέως [# 5441]) w. which the Galatians were responding to a counterfeit gospel (Guthrie; Mussner). μετατίθεσθε pres. ind. mid. (dep.) μετατίθημι (# 3572) to transfer, to remove, to desert, to change one's opinion. The word was used of desertion or revolt in a military or political defection and frequently had the idea of a change in religion, philosophy, or morals (Lightfoot; TDNT; Betz). καλέσαντος aor. act. part. (subst.) καλέω (# 2813) to call. Aor. points to the previous time when the Galatians received the gospel (Mussner). ἕτερον (# 2283) another. It expresses a difference in kind (Guthrie; TDNT; Lightfoot; Burton; J.K Elliot, "The Use of ἕτερος in the New Testament," *ZNW* 60 [1969]: 140-41). The rabbis used a similar term for those who had refused to receive traditions (Mussner). ◆ **7** εἰ μή (# 1623; 3590) except. The words limit that which went before (Ridderbos). ταράσσοντες pres. act. part. (subst.) ταράσσω (# 5429) to shake back and forth, to trouble, to disturb; used of political agitators who cause confusion and turmoil (TLNT; Longenecker). θέλοντες pres. act. part. (subst.) θέλω (# 2527) to wish, to desire, to want to, w. inf. Pres. of both parts. indicate actions still in progress; Paul hopes to be able to influence the decision of the Galatians (Betz; Burton). μεταστρέψαι aor. act. inf. μεταστρέφω (# 3570) to turn about, to change from one thing to another, to change to the opposite, to pervert (Burton; Lightfoot). It was also used as a political term, w. revolutionary action in view (Longenecker). Aor. indicates a complete and thorough change. Compl. inf. to the part. ◆ **8** εὐαγγελίζηται aor. subj. mid. (dep.) εὐαγγελίζομαι

(# 2294) to proclaim good news, to preach the gospel (TDNT; EDNT; TLNT; Bruce). Aor. may point to the act of a one-time preaching of the gospel. Subj. w. ἐάν (# 1569) expresses a 3rd. class cond. cl. which views the cond. as a possibility. εὐηγγελισάμεθα aor. ind. mid. (dep.) εὐαγγελίζομαι; an editorial "we" (GGBB, 394). ἀνάθεμα (# 353)accursed, dedicated for destruction (TDNT; GELTS, 28; Betz; RAC 8:1-29; MM). ἔστω pres. imp. act. 3rd sing. εἰμί (# 1639) to be. ◆ 9 προειρήκαμεν perf. ind. act. προλέγω (# 4625) to say beforehand, to said previously. Perf. points to the abiding authority of that say previously. The vb. expresses the communication of authorized Christian teaching (Guthrie). παρελάβετε aor. ind. act. παραλαμβάνω (# 4161) to receive. ◆ 10 πείθω pres. ind. act. (# 4275) to persuade, to win the favor of someone (Burton). Conative pres. indicating the trying or attempting (BD, 167; RG, 880). ζητῶ pres. ind. act. ζητέω (# 2426) to seek. ἀρέσκειν pres. act. inf. ἀρέσκω (# 743) to please, to cause pleasure. Compl. inf. Gives the content of the main vb. ζητῶ. ἤρεσκον impf. ind. act. ἀρέσκω. Ind. in a contrary to fact cond. cl. Impf. indicates an incomplete action. ἤμην impf. ind. act. εἰμί (# 1639) to be. ◆ 11 γνωρίζω pres. ind. act. (# 1192) to make known, to make clear, to certify. It has the effect of suggesting a somewhat formal statement to follow (Longenecker). εὐαγγελισθέν aor. pass. part. (adj.) εὐαγγελίζομαι s.v. 8. In this section Paul seems to be asserting that the historical roots of the Pauline churches did not extend back to the community of the Torah covenant, but had an independent foundation confirmed by the Jerusalem church, thereby proving the legitimacy of Gentile salvation outside the covenant Law (Donald J. Verseput, "Paul's Gentile Mission and the Jewish Community. A Study of the Narrative in Galatians 1 and 2," *NTS* 39 [1993]: 36-58, 38; B. Lategan, "Is Paul Defending His Apostleship in Galatians?" *NTS* 34 [1988]: 411-30; DPL, 681-88; George Lyons, *Pauline Autobiography: Toward a New Understanding* SBLDS 73 [Atlanta: Scholars Press, 1985]). ◆ 12 οὐδέ (# 4028) not, not even. The word indicates either "even I who so naturally might have been (taught of men) did not ..."; or it might mean, "I as little as the other apostles"; i.e., I (distinctly emphatic) as little as any others did not" (Ellicott; Burton). παρέλαβον aor. ind. act. παραλαμβάνω s.v. 9. ἐδιδάχθην aor. ind. pass. διδάσκω (# 1438) to teach. ἀποκαλύψεως (# 637) unveiling, revelation. The word indicates that it was an opening up of what was previously secret. The following gen. is best taken not as subjective–that Christ was revealing–but as obj. gen., indicating that Christ was the object of the revelation (Guthrie). ◆ 13 ἠκούσατε aor. ind. act. ἀκούω (# 201) to hear. ἀναστροφή (# 419) manner of life, way of life (Matera). It refers to Paul's ethical conduct (Ridderbos). ὑπερβολή (# 5651) throwing beyond, beyond measure, in excess. ἐδίωκον impf.

ind. act. διώκω (# 1503) to pursue, to hunt, to persecute. Impf. pictures the persistent and continual action in the past. ἐπόρθουν impf. ind. act. πορθέω (# 4514) to ravage, to destroy. It was used of soldiers ravaging a city (Burton). Conative impf., "I was trying to devastate it" (Matera). ◆ 14 προέκοπτον impf. ind. act. προκόπτω (# 4621) to cut forward (as in a forest), to blaze a way, to go ahead, to advance, to make progress (RWP; Longenecker; TDNT; TLNT). Customary impf. "I was continually advancing..." (GGBB, 548). Saul of Tarsus was so intent in his ambition to further the cause of Judaism that he did not hesitate to cut down all opposition and in this respect outstripped his contemporaries (Guthrie). ὑπέρ (# 5642) beyond, over, above. The prep. used w. the acc. designated that which excels or surpasses and is a type of comp. (BD, 121). συνηλικιώτης (# 5312) one of the same age, contemporary. γένει dat. γένος (# 1877) offspring, people. Here it has the connotation "of my people" (Ridderbos). περισσοτέρως (# 4359) adv., abundantly, extremely. ζηλωτής (# 2421) enthusiast, one who is zealous for a cause; followed by the gen. indicating that which one is zealous of. (For a study of the word s. TDNT; Hengel, *Zeloten*, 67-78; DJG, 696-97). ὑπάρχων pres. act. part. (causal) ὑπάρχω (# 5639) to be, to exist, to be by constitution (s. 2 Cor. 12:16). (Fung). πατρικός (# 4257) pertaining to a father, fatherly. For the meaning of the suf. s. MH, 378. παράδοσις (# 4142) passing on from one to another, tradition. In connection w. Judaism it refers to that body of oral teaching which was complementary to the written law and in fact possessed equal authority to the law (Guthrie; Longenecker; TLNT). ◆ 15 εὐδόκησεν aor. ind. act. εὐδοκέω (# 2305) to please, to be well-pleased, followed by the inf. ἀφορίσας aor. act. part. (subst.) ἀφορίζω (# 928) to divide w. a boundary, to mark off from others w. a boundary, to set apart. The idea here is "to set aside for special purpose" (Ridderbos). κοιλία (# 3120) body cavity, womb, i.e., "from before my birth," "before I had any impulses, any principles of my own" (Lightfoot). καλέσας aor. act. part. (subst.) καλέω (# 2813) to call. ◆ 16 ἀποκαλύψαι aor. act. inf. ἀποκαλύπτω (# 636) to unveil, to reveal. Inf. to express purp. Aor. points to a specific act. ἐν ἐμοί (# 1877; 1609) in me, to me, me. With vbs. of knowing and making known the prep. designates not only the person through whom the communication comes, but also the one who receives it (Ridderbos; BD, 118). εὐαγγελίζωμαι pres. subj. mid. εὐαγγελίζω s.v. 8. Subj. w. ἵνα (# 2671) used in a purp. cl. ἔθνεσιν pl. ἔθνος (# 1620) nation, pl. Gentiles. εὐθέως adv. immediately. προσανεθέμην aor. ind. mid. προσανατίθηνι (# 4651) lit., to lay on oneself in addition. When used w. the gen. it suggests the gaining of information by communicating w. others, to consult in order to give a skilled or authoritative interpretation (Guthrie; Lightfoot; Mussner;

J.D.G. Dunn, "The Relationship between Paul and Jerusalem according to Galatians 1 and 2," *NTS* 28 [1982]: 110). ◆ **17 ἀνῆλθον** aor. ind. act. ἀνέρχομαι (# 456) to go up. **ἀπῆλθον** aor. ind. act. ἀπέρχομαι (# 599) to go away. **εἰς Ἀραβίαν** (# 728) into Arabia. This probably refers to the Nabataean cities east of Damascus (Betz; Matera; 2 Cor. 11:32). **ὑπέστρεψα** aor. ind. act. ὑποστρέφω (# 5715) to return. Prep. in compound connotes "back" (MH, 327). ◆ **18 ἔπειτα** (# 2083) then. The word draws particular attention to the next event in order of sequence (Guthrie). **ἔτη** pl. ἔτος (# 2291) year. **ἀνῆλθον** aor. ind. act. ἀνέρχομαι (# 456) to go up. **ἱστορῆσαι** aor. act. inf. ἱστορέω (# 2707) to inquire, to visit places or persons, to get to know, perhaps w. the idea of finding out information (Burton; MM; Preisigke, 1:703; Otfried Hofius, "Gal 1,18: ἱστορῆσαι Κηφᾶν," *ZNW* 74 [1984]: 73-85; J.D.G. Dunn, "Once More - Gal 1,18: ἱστορῆσαι Κηφᾶν In Reply to Otfried Hofius," *ZNW* 76 [1985]: 138-39; Grave verbum, ut de re magna. Nochmals Gal 1,18: ἱστορῆσαι Κηφᾶν," *ZNW* 81 [1990]: 262-69; DPL, 701-3). Perhaps Paul wanted to find out about the earthly Jesus (Longenecker). Inf. to express purp. **ἐπέμεινα** aor. ind. act. ἐπιμένω (# 2152) to remain. For the prep. in compound s. MH, 312. ◆ **19 εἶδον** aor. ind. act. ὁράω (# 3972) to see. **εἰ μή** (# 1623; 3590) except. For the possible ways of understanding these words s. L. Paul Trudinger, "A Note on Galatians 1:19," *NovT* 17 (1975): 200-202. For a discussion of the various interpretations related to James, the brother of the Lord s. Eadie; Lightfoot, 252-91. ◆ **20 ψεύδομαι** pres. ind. mid. (dep.) (# 6017) to lie. For a comparison of Paul's statement to the oaths offered during Roman court procedures s. J. P. Sampley, "'Before God, I Do Not Lie' (Gal. 1:20)," *NTS* 23 (1977): 477-82. ◆ **21 ἦλθον** aor. ind. act. ἔρχομαι (# 2262) to come, to go. **κλίμα** (# 3107) region, area. ◆ **22 ἤμην** impf. ind. act. εἰμί (# 1639) to be. **ἀγνοούμενος** pres. pass. part. ἀγνοέω (# 51) to be ignorant, to not know; pass., to be unknown. Pres. stresses the continuity of the state of not knowing (Guthrie). ◆ **23 ἀκού-οντες** pres. act. part. ἀκούω (# 201) to hear. **ἦσαν** impf. ind. act. εἰμί (# 1639) to be. **διώκων** pres. act. part. s.v. 13. Subst. part. used to emphasize a trait. Pres. suggests a durative notion. **εὐαγγελίζεται** pres. ind. mid. (dep.) s.v. 8. Pres. indicates the continual action. **ἐπόρθει** impf. ind. act. s.v. 13. ◆ **24 ἐδόξαζον** impf. ind. part. δοξάζω (# 1519) to glorify, to cause one to think highly of another. Impf. indicates, "they began to glorify, and continued to do so." **ἐν ἐμοί** (# 1877; 1609) in me. The prep. constitutes the ground or basis of the action: "they found in me occasion and reason for praising God" (Burton).

Galatians 2

◆ **1 ἔπειτα** then s. 1:18. **ἐτῶν** gen. ἔτος (# 2291) year. **ἀνέβην** aor. ind. act. ἀναβαίνω (# 326) to go up (BBC).

μετά w. the gen., with, accompanied by. It suggests that Paul was the leader (Guthrie). **συμπαραλαβών** aor. act. part. συμπαραλαμβάνω (# 5221) to take along w., to take someone along as a travelling companion or helper. The word is applied to a private companion or minister who is not sent forth on the mission of an envoy, but is taken by the envoy on their authority (Ramsey; MM). ◆ **2 ἀνέβην** aor. ind. act. s.v. 1. **ἀποκάλυψις** (# 637) unveiling, revelation. Acc. w. the prep. **κατά** (# 2848), "in obedience to such a revelation" (Burton). **ἀνεθέμην** aor. ind. act. ἀνατίθημι (# 423) to declare, to communicate, to lay before someone for consideration, to relate w. a view to consulting (BAGD; Lightfoot). **κατ᾽ ἰδίαν** (# 2848) one's own; used in the idiomatic construction, "privately." **δοκοῦσιν** pres. act. part. δοκέω (# 1506) to seem to be, to appear. A shortened version of the construction **οἱ δοκοῦντες εἶναί τι** (v. 6) "those who seem to be something." It is used in the sense of "the authorities" and the word itself implies position of honor (Meyer; Guthrie), or it may be intended to be ironical (Longenecker; Betz). **μή** (# 3590) lest. Used w. the subj. to express a neg. purp. or to prohibit that which is feared (2 Cor. 12:20). **τρέχω** pres. subj. act. τρέχω (# 5556) to run. The preacher of the gospel is pictured as a runner of a race concerned about his eventual success or failure in the race. Pres. subj. expresses the fear of continuous fruitless effort into the fut. (PAM, 100f). **ἔδραμον** aor. ind. act. τρέχω. Ind. used of that which has already taken place or is entirely independent of the will. The fact of having run in the past is no longer dependent on the will of him who fears (BD, 188; PAM, 101; Schlier). ◆ **3 ὤν** pres. act. part. εἰμί (# 1639) to be. Concessive part. ("although"). **ἠναγκάσθη** aor. ind. pass. ἀναγκάζω (# 337) to exert pressure on someone, to compel, to coerce. Aor. is effective or resultative, affirming that an action attempted in the past was accomplished (SMT, 42). **περιτμηθῆναι** aor. pass. inf. περιτέμνω (# 4362) to circumcise (Neil. J. McEleney, "Conversion, Circumcision and the Law," *NTS* 20 [1974]: 319-41; TDNT; EDNT). ◆ **4 δέ** (# 1254) but. The structure and grammatical connection of this verse is not clear. For a discussion of the various possibilities s. Lightfoot; Burton; Mussner. **παρείσακτος** (# 4207) secretly brought in, smuggled in alongside of, sneaked in (BAGD). The word was used of spies or traitors who infiltrate an opposing camp (Longenecker) or it could simply mean "alien" or "foreign" (Eadie; MM). **ψευδάδελφος** (# 6012) false brother. **οἵτινες** pl. ὅστις (# 4015) who, one who. The word specifies the class to which one belongs (Ellicott; RG, 727). **παρεισῆλθον** aor. ind. act. παρέρχομαι (# 4209) to come in alongside of, to slip into. The word usually implies stealth (Burton). The metaphor is that of spies or traitors introducing themselves by stealth into the enemy's camp (Lightfoot). **κατασκοπῆσαι** aor. act. inf. κατακοπέω (# 2945) to spy out, to examine carefully. The word is used most frequently to imply treachery (Lightfoot; s. Josh. 2:2, 3). Aor. may refer to the act done before it was detected (Eadie). Inf. is used to express purp. ἐλευθερία (# 1800) freedom. καταδουλώσουσιν fut. ind. act. καταδουλόω (# 2871) to enslave, to bring down to bondage, to completely enslave. The prep. in compound is perfective (MH, 316). Fut. ind. expressing purpose (IBG, 139; VA, 413). ◆ 5 εἴξαμεν aor. ind. act. εἴκω (# 1634) to yield, to give into, to give way, to allow. ὑποταγῇ (# 5717) submission. Dat. of reference or respect, "we did not yield w. respect to the submission." The definite article refers to the matter under discussion, circumcision (Guthrie). διαμείνῃ aor. subj. act. διαμένω (# 1373) to remain permanently, to continue throughout. The idea of firm possession is enforced by the compound vb., the past tense, and the prep. (Lightfoot). ◆ 6 δοκούντων pres. act. part. δοκέω s.v. 2. εἶναι pres. act. inf. εἰμί (# 1639) to be. Compl. inf. completing the main vb. ὁποῖοί ποτε (# 3961; 4537) what kind of people they were. The general rel. pron. refers to quality (BD, 159; Schlier). διαφέρει pres. ind. act. διαφέρω (# 1422) it makes a difference, it matters. Used here w. the neg. οὐδέν (# 4029), "it makes no difference to me." δοκοῦντες pres. act. part. s.v. 2. προσανέθεντο aor. ind. mid. (dep.) προσανατίθημι (# 4707) to add something. In addition here it connotes, "to teach in addition to what I have already learned" (Burton). Paul means that no restrictions were set to, no further and extraneous requirements were laid upon the fundamental proclamation of the gospel (PAA, 146). For Paul's view of his apostleship and authoritative message in relation to the other apostles s. David M. Hay, "Paul's Indifference to Authority," *JBL* 88 (1969): 36-44; DPL, 45-51. ◆ 7 τοὐναντίον (# 5539) on the contrary. ἰδόντες aor. act. part. ὁράω (# 3972) to see. Temp. or causal part. πεπίστευμαι perf. ind. pass. πιστεύω (# 4409) to believe. pass. to be entrusted w. something. ἀκροβυστίας (# 213) foreskin, uncircumcision. περιτομή (# 4364) circumcised (DPL, 137-39). ◆ 8 ἐνεργήσας aor. act. part. ἐνεργέω (# 1919) to be at work, to be active, to effect, to produce results (Burton; Mussner). The vb. is followed by the dat. of advantage or instr. (GGBB, 163). εἰς (# 1650) into. The prep. points to the goal of the active working of God (Mussner). ἀποστολή (# 692) apostleship. The word is the act of fulfilling the commission, i.e., the establishment of Christian communities (PAA, 148; Robert Duncan Culver, "Apostles and the Apostolate in the New Testament," *Bib Sac* 134 [1977]: 131-43; s. 1:1). ἐνήργησεν aor. ind. act. ἐνεργέω (# 1919) to work effectively. ◆ 9 γνόντες aor. act. part. γινώσκω (# 1182) to know, to recognize. δοθεῖσαν aor. pass. part. δίδωμι (# 1443) to give. δοκοῦντες pres. act. part. δοκέω s.v. 2. στῦλος (# 5146) pillar. The metaphor was used by the Jews in speaking of the great teachers of the law (Bruce; Light-

foot; SB, 3:537). εἶναι pres. inf. act. εἰμί (# 1639) to be. δεξιός (# 1288) right, here in the sense of right hand. ἔδωκαν aor. ind. act. δίδωμι (# 1443) to give. κοινωνία (# 3126) fellowship (NIDNTT, 1:639-44; TDNT; RAC, 9:1100-45). In modern parlance this means that they all shook hands to signify agreement (Guthrie). ◆ 10 μνημονεύωμεν pres. subj. act. μνημονεύω (# 3648) to remember. ἐσπούδασα aor. ind. act. σπουδάζω (# 5079) to be diligent, to be eager. αὐτὸ τοῦτο (# 899; 4047) this very thing. ποιῆσαι aor. act. inf. ποιέω (# 4472) to do. Compl. inf. to the main vb. ἐσπούδασα. ◆ 11 ἦλθεν aor. ind. act. ἔρχομαι (# 2262) to come. ἀντέστην aor. ind. act. ἀνίστημι (# 468) to stand against, to oppose. κατεγνωσμένος perf. pass. part. καταγινώσκω (# 2861) to condemn; pass. to be condemned. Peter was condemned either by his own contradictory actions (Lightfoot) or by his own conscience. For this view as well as examples from the papyri s. MM; Schlier. ἦν impf. ind. act. εἰμί (# 1639) to be. ◆ 12 ἐλθεῖν aor. act. inf. ἔρχομαι (# 2262). Articular inf. w. the prep. πρό (# 4574) to express previous or antecedent time ("before") (MT, 144). συνήσθιεν impf. ind. act. συνεσθίω (# 5303) to eat w. someone, to eat together. Impf. expresses the habitual action of the past: "he used to eat regularly (w. Gentiles)." ἦλθον impf. ind. act. ἔρχομαι (# 2262) to come. ὑπέστελλεν impf. ind. act. ὑποστέλλω (# 5713) to withdraw. Inceptive impf., "he began to withdraw." ἀφώριζεν impf. ind. act. ἀφορίζω (# 928) to separate. φοβούμενος pres. mid. (dep.) part. φοβέομαι (# 5828) to fear, to be afraid. Causal part., "because he feared." ◆ 13 συνυπεκρίθησαν aor. ind. pass. (dep.) συνυποκρίνομαι (# 5347) to act as a hypocrite w. another. The basic meaning of the word is "to answer from under" and refers to actors who, in playing a part, spoke from under a mask. The actors hid their true selves behind the role they were playing. The word indicates the concealment of wrong feelings, character, etc., under the pretense of better ones (Burton; Guthrie; TDNT; TLNT, 3:406-13). συναπήχθη aor. ind. pass. συνάγω (# 5270) to lead away together. The pass. of the word suggests that Barnabas did not play an active part in the hypocrisy; but the meaning of the vb. implies that Barnabas was swept off his balance (Guthrie; DPL, 66-67). ◆ 14 εἶδον aor. ind. act. ὁράω (# 3972) to see. ὀρθοποδοῦσιν pres. ind. act. ὀρθοποδέω (# 3980) to walk correctly, to walk straight or upright. Followed by the prep., the verse means, "they were not walking on the straight path towards the truth of the gospel" (Mussner). εἶπον aor. ind. act. λέγω (# 3306) to speak, to say. ὑπάρχων pres. act. part. ὑπάρχω (# 5639) to exist, to be. ἐθνικῶς (# 1619) adv., in the manner of heathen. ζῆς pres. ind. act. ζάω (# 2409) to live. Ind. w. εἰ (# 1623) in a 1st. class cond. cl. assumes the reality of the cond. ἀναγκάζεις pres. ind. act. ἀναγκάζω (# 337) to be necessary. ἰουδαΐζειν pres. act. inf. ἰουδαΐζω (# 2678) to live as a Jew, to adopt Jewish customs (Lightfoot; DPL, 513-16). ◆ **15** φύσις (# *5882*) nature; here in the dat., "by nature," "by birth." The vb. to be supplied is to be taken as concessive: "though we are Jews by nature and not sinners of Gentile origin" (Burton; Mussner). ἁμαρτωλός (# *283*) sinner. ◆ **16** εἰδότες perf. act. part. οἶδα (# *3857*) def. perf. w. the pres. meaning to know. Pres. indicates that which is always true. Pass. points to the fact that one does not justify himself but is declared righteous by another. The neg. w. pres. indicates that justification can never at any time be achieved by works of the law. ἐὰν μή (# *1569; 3590*) if not, except. The expression is properly exceptive and introduces an exception related to the main vb. Here it can be translated "but only" (Burton; s. also William O. Walker, Jr., "Translation and Interpretation of ἐὰν μή in Galatians 2:16," *JBL* 116 [1997]:515-20). ἐπιστεύσαμεν aor. ind. act. πιστεύω (# *4409*) to believe. Possibly ingressive aor., "we have come to believe" (Ribberbos). δικαιωθῶμεν aor. subj. pass. δικαιόω (# *1467*) to justify (s. Rom. 2:13; DPL, 517-23)). Subj. w. ἵνα (# *2671*) to express purp. Theol. pass. indicating that God is the one who makes the declaration that someone is in the right. Aor. points to the specific act which takes place. δικαιωθήσεται fut. ind. pass. δικαιόω (# *1467*). Theol. pass., indicating that God is the subject. ◆ **17** ζητοῦντες pres. act. part. (temp.) ζητέω (# *2426*) to seek. Pres. indicates action contemporaneous to the main vb. δικαιωθῆναι aor. inf. pass. s.v. 16. Compl. inf. to the preceding part. εὑρέθημεν aor. ind. pass. εὑρίσκω (# *2351*) to find. ἆρα (# *727*) here to be taken as the interrogative particle rather than an inferential particle. It expresses bewilderment as to a possible conclusion: "is Christ then a minister of sin?" (Lightfoot; Mussner). γένοιτο aor. opt. mid. (dep.) γίνομαι (# *1181*) to be, to become. Let it not be, certainly not! This represents a characteristic Pauline refutation of an unthinkable suggestion (Guthrie). For a discussion of this phrase s. Rom. 3:4. ◆ **18** κατέλυσα aor. ind. act. καταλύω (# *2907*) to tear down, to destroy, to annul, to abrogate. Perhaps the 1st person is used for vividness (GGBB, 391). οἰκοδομῶ pres. ind. act. οἰκοδομέω (# *4099*) to build up. Pres. suggests a maxim which would always be true (Eadie). παραβάτης (# *4127*) one who goes beyond the boundary, transgressor. συνιστάνω pres. ind. act. συνίστημι (# *5319*) to constitute, to prove, Used w. the double acc. Used w. the reflex. pron. as one of the accs. It means "to prove to oneself something," "to recommend or present oneself as such" (Ridderbos). ◆ **19** ἐγώ (# *1609*) I. The idea here is, "I, Paul, the natural man, the slave of the old covenant" (Lightfoot). γάρ (# *1142*) for. This explicative shows how this rehabilitation of the law actually amounts to a transgression of its true principles (Ellicott). ἀπέθανον aor. ind. act. ἀποθνήσκω (# *633*) to die, followed by the dat. of

reference. ζήσω aor. subj. act. ζάω (# *2409*) to live. Followed by the dat. of advantage, "to live for God." συνεσταύρωμαι perf. ind. pass. συνσταυρόω (# *5365*) to crucify together. Perf. suggests that Paul is thinking of that specific completed event which marked his identification w. Christ and which has had an enduring effect upon his life (Guthrie). ◆ **20** ζῶ pres. ind. act. ζάω (# *2409*) to live. οὐκέτι (# *4033*) no longer. ζῇ pres. ind. act. ζάω. ἀγαπήσαντός aor. act. part. ἀγαπάω (# *26*) to love (TLNT; TDNT; EDNT). Causal part. ("because he loved") or adj. part. ("who loved"). Aor. indicates action logically antecedent to the main vb. παραδόντος aor. act. part. παραδίδωμι (# *4140*) to give over, to give. Christ's self-giving upon the cross was a definite act of love. ◆ **21** ἀθετῶ pres. ind. act. ἀθετέω (# *119*) to set aside, to reject. In the papyri it was used of loans which were repaid and cancelled and for the rejection of certain officials who were described as inefficient and incapable of doing their duty. It was also used of grain rejected by the inspector as unfit for food (MM). δωρεάν (# *1562*) adv., gratuitously; "without (giving or receiving) pay" (Burton). ἀπέθανεν aor. ind. act. ἀποθνήσκω s.v. 19.

Galatians 3

◆ **1** ἀνόητος (# *485*) foolish, without thinking. It describes acting in a spirit which manifests the absence of wisdom (Eadie). Paul does not accuse them of lacking intelligence but of an inability or a refusal to recognize the real situation (Matera; Betz). ἐβάσκανεν aor. ind. act. βασκαίνω (# *1001*) to bewitch, to cast a magic spell, to seek to bring damage to a person through an evil eye or a spoken word (Lightfoot; Betz; TDNT; MM; NW 2, ii:537-38). One ancient writer felt that one could ward off the evil spell by spitting three times (BAGD; for other magic texts s. GMP). Their new behavior was so strange that it appeared as if someone had put a spell on them (Bruce). προεγράφη aor. ind. pass. προγράφω (# *4592*) to write before, to write up in public. The word was used to describe all public notices or proclamations and indicates a public announcement in which the validity of a particular fact or cond. is proclaimed (Lightfoot; Ridderbos; TDNT). ἐσταυρωμένος perf. pass. part. σταυρόω (# *5090*) to crucify. The lack of the article stresses the character, "a crucified one." For a description of crucifixion in the ancient world s. C; TDNT. ◆ **2** μαθεῖν aor. act. inf. μανθάνω (# *3443*) to learn. ἐλάβετε aor. ind. act. λαμβάνω (# *3284*) to receive. ἀκοή (# *198*) hearing. ◆ **3** ἐναρξάμενοι aor. mid. (dep.) part. ἐνάρχω (# *1887*) to begin. Temp. part. refers to the moment of becoming a Christian (Longenecker). πνεύματι dat. sing. πνεῦμα (# *4460*) and σαρκί dat. sing. σάρξ (# *4922*) flesh, are dats. of instr. ἐπιτελεῖσθε pres. ind. mid./ pass. (# *2200*) ἐπιτελέω to accomplish, to complete, to finish, to come to the intended goal. ◆ **4** τοσαῦτα pl. τοσοῦτος (# 5537) so great, pl. so great things. ἐπάθετε aor. ind. act. πάσχω (# 4248) to experience. The word may mean "to experience evil" ("to suffer"), or it may be used in a neutral sense, "to experience" (Burton; Mussner). εἰκῇ (# 1632) in vain. εἴ γε καί if it be really. The phrase leaves a loophole for doubt, implying an unwillingness to believe on the part of the speaker w. some hope that the situation is not irretrievable (Lightfoot; Bruce). ◆ 5 ἐπιχορηγῶν pres. act. part. ἐπιχορηγέω (# 2220) to supply. The simple vb. means "to defray the expense of providing a chorus at the public feast" while the prep. expresses strongly the idea, "to supply abundantly" (Burton; s. 2 Cor. 9:10). Pres. implies the permanency of the action (Ellicott). ἐνεργῶν pres. act. part. ἐνεργέω (# 1919) to be energetic, to work. ◆ 6 καθώς (# 2777) just as. The word indicates that Paul is drawing a parallel between Abraham's justification and present-day justification (Mussner). ἐπίστευσεν aor. ind. act. πιστεύω (# 4409) to believe. ἐλογίσθη aor. ind. pass. λογίζομαι (# 3357) to place to one's account, to account, to reckon. Theol. pass. indicating that God is the subject (s. Achim Behrens, "Gen 15, 6 und das Vorverständnis des Paulus," *ZAW* 109 [1997]:327-41). For Abraham in Judaism s. Longenecker, 110-12; G. W. Hanson, *Abraham in Galatians: Epistolary and Rhetorical Contexts* (Sheffield: JSOT, 1989); DPL, 1-9; BCC; Betz, 139-40; Rom. 4:2. ◆ 7 γινώσκετε pres. ind. or imp. act. γινώσκω (# 1182) to know. ἄρα (# 726) so, therefore. It is used as a particle of inference. ◆ 8 προϊδοῦσα aor. act. part. προοράω (# 4632) to see beforehand, to foresee. The word indicates that the faith element in God's method of justification is timeless (Guthrie). δικαιοῖ pres. ind. act. δικαιόω (# 1467) to justify, to declare righteous (s. Rom. 2:13). Futuristic pres. (Longenecker). ἔθνος (# 1620) nation, Gentile. προευηγγελίσατο aor. ind. mid. (dep.) προευαγγελίζομαι (# 4603) to proclaim the good news beforehand. ὅτι (# 4022) recitative use introducing a direct quotation is equivalent to quotation marks. ἐνευλογηθήσονται fut. ind. pass. ἐνευλογέω (# 1922) to bless. For the term "blessing," "to bless" s. Cleon Rogers, "The Covenant with Abraham and Its Historical Setting," *Bib Sac* 127 (1970): 241-56.; TDOT; TDNT. ◆ 9 ὥστε (# 6063) therefore. The word draws a conclusion from the previous material. εὐλογοῦνται pres. ind. pass. εὐλογέω (# 2328) to bless. ◆ 10 ὅσος (# 4012) as many as. The word indicates those belonging to the same class. κατάρα (# 2932) curse (DPL, 199-200). This was the covenant curse for disobeying the Mosaic covenant (NIDNTT, 1:416; TDNT). γέγραπται pres. ind. pass. γράφω (# 1211) to write. Perf. indicates that the authority of the document is binding: "it stands written" (MM). ἐπικατάρατος (# 2129) curse, cursed. For a discussion of the Heb. word "curse" as used here in the quotation from Deut. 27:26 s. TDOT, 405-18; H. C.

Brichto, *The Problem of "Curse" in the Hebrew Bible* (Philadelphia: Society of Biblical Literature, 1968); DCH, 1:397-98). ἐμμένει pres. ind. act. ἐμμένω (# 1844) to remain in, to continue in. Pres. indicates the need for unbroken and continual observance of the whole law. γεγραμμένοις perf. pass. part. γράφω. ποιῆσαι aor. act. inf. ποιέω (# 4472). Articular inf. to express purp. Aor. indicates the complete action. ◆ 11 δικαιοῦται pres. ind. pass. s.v. 8. δῆλος (# 1316) clear, evident. ζήσεται fut. ind. mid. (dep.) ζάω (# 2409) to live. ◆ 12 ποιήσας aor. act. part. (subst.) ποιέω (# 2409) to do, to practice. Aor. indicates the complete action. ζήσεται fut. ind. mid. s.v. 11. ◆ 13 ἐξηγόρασεν aor. ind. act. ἐξαγοράζω (# 1973) to buy out of the marketplace, to redeem, to ransom from slavery (APC; TDNT; DPL, 784-86; ABD, 5:650-57). Prep. in compound is perfective: "to buy out," "to completely redeem." γενόμενος aor. mid. (dep.) part. γίνομαι (# 1181) to become, to be. Part. gives the means or way in which the action of the main vb. was accomplished. Aor. portrays a logically antecedent action. γέγραπται perf. ind. pass. s.v. 10 κρεμάμενος pres. mid. (dep.) part. κρεμάννυμι (# 3203) to hang. ξύλου wood, tree (s. Acts 10:39). For the view that Paul combines Deut. 21:22-23 w. a reference to Isaac in Gen. 22 s. Max Wilcox, "'Upon the Tree'–Deut. 21:22-23 in the New Testament," *JBL* 96 (1977): 85-99. ◆ 14 εὐλογία (# 2330) blessing. γένηται aor. subj. mid. (dep.) γίνομαι (# 1181) to become, to be. Subj. w. ἵνα (# 2671) to express purp. ἐπαγγελία (# 2039) promise. The following gen., τοῦ πνεύματος (# 4460), is obj. gen.; i.e., the promise which has the Spirit for its object (Eadie). λάβωμεν aor. subj. act. λαμβάνω (# 3284) to receive. ◆ 15 ὅμως (# 3940) even though, nevertheless; here, part of the following possible translation, "even though it is only a man's will, nevertheless." However, it may be used to introduce a comparison and have the translation "also," "likewise" (BD, 234). κεκυρωμένην perf. pass. part. κυρόω (# 3263) to validate, to ratify. The word was used in an inscription from Ephesus for a decree which was formally ratified (NDIEC, 4:171; s. other examples of officially ratified agreements: SIG, 2:81-86, inscription # 581:5, 85, 95; 3:341, inscription # 1185:10). διαθήκη (# 1347) agreement, treaty, covenant. However, it may mean "will," "testament" (Guthrie; APC; TDNT). For a discussion of the legal background and the problems involved s. Longenecker. ἀθετεῖ pres. ind. act. ἀθετέω (# 119) to annul (s. 2:21). ἐπιδιατάσσεται pres. ind. mid. (dep.) ἐπιδιατάσσομαι (# 2112) to add on to. The prep. in compound indicates "to make additional prescriptions," "to add a codicil to a testament" (Burton; Betz). Gnomic pres. here, indicating that which is always true. ◆ 16 ἐρρέθησαν aor. ind. pass. λέγω (# 3306) to say. Aor. points to a specific act. ◆ 17 τοῦτο δέ now this I say. Paul comes to his real purpose and proceeds to apply the figure of v. 15, arguing from the lesser to the greater; i.e., if this is true among human beings and their agreements it is even more true in respect to God and His promises (Ridderbos). **προκεκυρωμένην** perf. pass. part. προκυρόω (# 4623) to ratify beforehand, to confirm previously. Perf. points to the lasting authority of the legal ratification. **ἔτη** (# 2291) year. **γεγονώς** perf. act. part. γίνομαι (# 1181) to become. **ἀκυροῖ** pres. ind. act. ἀκυρόω (# 218) to make invalid, to annul either by rescinding or overriding (Burton; MM; BS, 228). **καταργῆσαι** aor. act. inf. καταργέω (# 2934) to render inoperative, to make of no effect. Inf. w. the prep. εἰς (# 1650) to express either purp. or result (MT, 143). ◆ **18 κληρονομία** (# 3100) inheritance. **οὐκέτι** no longer. **κεχάρισται** perf. ind. mid. (dep.) χαρίζομαι (# 5919) to give graciously (TDNT). Perf. indicates the lasting results. ◆ **19 παράβασις** (# 4126) stepping over the boundary, transgression. **χάριν** (# 5920) w. gen., on account of, because of. Cf. Ulrich Wilckens, "Zur Entwicklung des paulinischen Gesetzverständnis," *NTS* 28 (1982): 171. **προσετέθη** aor. subj. act. προστίθημι (# 4707) to add to. **ἔλθῃ** aor. subj. act. ἔρχομαι (# 2262) to come. Subj. in an indef. temp. cl. **τὸ σπέρμα** (# 5065) the seed, the offspring has already been identified as Christ in v. 16 (Guthrie). **ἐπήγγελται** perf. ind. pass. ἐπαγγέλλω (# 2040) to promise. **διαταγείς** aor. pass. part. διατάσσω (# 1411) to enact a law. The prep. δι' ("through") expresses an intermediate agent (GGBB, 434). It is a t.t. for the carrying out of laws and ordinances (Ridderbos). For the Jewish view concerning the activity of angels in the giving of the law s. SB, 3:554-56. ◆ **20 μεσίτης** (# 3542) mediator. On the meaning of this passage s. Longenecker; Betz; Burton; Guthrie; Mussner; U. Mussner, "Galater III, 20: Die Universalität des Heils," *NTS* 18 (1967): 258-70. ◆ **21 γένοιτο** aor. opt. mid. (dep.) γίνομαι (# 1181) to become, to be. Opt. used to deny a false conclusion (s. 2:17). **ἐδόθη** aor. ind. pass. δίδωμι (# 1443) to give. Ind. is used in a contrary to fact cond. cl. **δυνάμενος** pres. pass. (dep.) part. δύναμαι (# 1538) to be able to, w. inf. **ζωοποιῆσαι** aor. act. inf. ζωοποιέω (# 2443) to make alive. The purpose of the law was not to make alive, but to give Israel a rule of life in the promised land (LIF, 39-40). ◆ **22 συνέκλεισεν** aor. ind. act. συγκλείω (# 5168) to lock up together, to shut in on all sides. The vb. indicates no possibility of escape (Guthrie). **δοθῇ** aor. subj. pass. δίδωμι (# 1443) to give. Subj. w. ἵνα (# 2671) to express purp. **πιστεύουσιν** pres. act. part. (subst.) πιστεύω (# 4409) to believe. Dat. is the indir. object. ◆ **23 ἐλθεῖν** aor. act. inf. ἔρχομαι (# 2262) to go, to come. Aor. inf. w. the prep. to express antecedent time ("before") (MT, 144). **τὴν πίστιν** (# 5864) the faith; before the salvation given in Christ was revealed as the object of faith (Ridderbos). **ἐφρουρούμεθα** impf. ind. pass. φρουρέω (# 5864) to guard. The vb. carries the idea

of setting a protective guard (Guthrie). It has the idea of a garrison keeping watch over a town (MM; Preisigke, 2:707; GELTS, 505). **συγκλειόμενοι** pres. pass. part. συγκλείω s.v. 22. **μέλλουσαν** pres. act. part. μέλλω (# 3516) to be, about to be. It is used w. the inf. to express the fut. **ἀποκαλυφθῆναι** aor. pass. inf. ἀποκαλύπτω (# 636) to unveil, to reveal. Compl. inf. to the main vb. μέλλω, with an inf. expressing verbal action which is expected momentarily. ◆ **24 παιδαγωγός** (# 4080) custodian, male nursemaid. He was a slave employed in Gr. and Roman families to have general charge of a boy in the years from about 6 to 16, watching over his outward behavior and attending him both at home and whenever he left from home; as, for example, to school (Betz; Burton; Mussner; TDNT; TLNT; CC, 144f; DGRA, 847; Longenecker; R.N. Longenecker, "The Pedagogical Nature of the Law in Galatians 3:19-4:7," *JETS* 25 [1982]: 53-61; D.J. Lull, "'The Law Was Our Pedagogue': A Study in Galatians 3:19-25," *JBL* 105 [1986]: 481-98; N. H. Young, "*Paidagogos*: The Social Setting of a Pauline Metaphor," *NovT* 29 (1987): 150-76; LIF, 79-80; BBC; ABD, 2:312-17, particularly 313-14). **γέγονεν** perf. ind. act. γίνομαι (# 1181) to become. **δικαιωθῶμεν** aor. subj. pass. δικαιόω (# 1467) to justify (s. Rom. 2:13). Subj. w. ἵνα (# 2671) to express purp. Theol. pass., indicating that God is the One declaring to be in the right. ◆ **25 ἐλθούσης** aor. act. part. ἔρχομαι (# 2262) to come, to arrive. Gen. abs. Temp. part. aor. expressing a logically antecedent action to the main vb., "after faith has come." ◆ **26 ἐν Χριστῷ Ἰησοῦ** (# 1877) in Christ Jesus. For the use of the phrase in Paul s. Longenecker; DPL, 433-36. ◆ **27 ἐβαπτίσθητε** aor. ind. pass. βαπτίζω (# 966) to baptize. Baptism was the sign of an entry into a new kind of life (Guthrie). **ἐνεδύσασθε** aor. ind. mid. (dep.) ἐνδύομαι (# 1907) to put on, to put on a garment. Just as a garment which one puts on envelops the person wearing it and defines his appearance, so the person baptized in Christ is entirely taken up in Christ and in the salvation brought by Him (Ridderbos). ◆ **28 ἔνι** (# 1928). Used w. the neg. οὐκ (# 4024) it means "there is not" and is a statement of a fact rather than a possibility (RWP). **ἐλεύθερος** (# 1801) free. **ἄρσεν** (# 781) male. **θῆλυ** (# 2559) female. **ἐστε** pres. ind. act. εἰμί (# 1639) to be. Durative pres. to describe a present state in contrast to the past state. ◆ **29 κατ' ἐπαγγελίαν** (# 2848; 2039) according to promise. **κληρονόμος** (# 3101) heir. It does not mean that the believer receives the land promises of Abraham, but rather that he partakes of the blessing of justification which is through faith, the universal blessing promised to Abraham for the whole world.

Galatians 4

◆ **1 λέγω** pres. ind. act. λέγω (# 3306) to say, to tell; "I mean that." Paul begins w. an explanation of his reference to the heirs (Guthrie). **ἐφ' ὅσον χρόνον** (*# 2093; 4012; 5989*) for as long a time as, as long as. **κληρονόμος** (*# 3101*) heir. The term was used in the inscriptions of Asia Minor to refer to a son after he has succeeded to the inheritance as representative of his father, undertaking all the duties and obligations of his father (Ramsay). **νήπιος** (*# 3758*) infant; properly, "one without understanding" (Burton). Here it describes a minor at any stage and is used here in a legal sense (Lightfoot; Betz). **διαφέρει** pres. ind. act. διαφέρω (*# 1422*) to differ. **ὤν** pres. part. act. εἰμί (*# 1639*) to be. Concessive part., "although he is lord over all." ◆ **2 ἐπίτροπος** (*# 2208*) guardian, a general term referring to someone to whom the whole care of the underaged boy is entrusted; could also be a legal t.t. for a tutor (Betz; Ridderbos). **οἰκονόμος** (*# 3874*) steward, trustee. The word usually denotes a slave acting as a house steward for his principal, or a treasurer or administrator (Betz; Burton; NW, 2, ii:546-48). **προθεσμία** (*# 4607*) appointed day, fixed time. It was customary in the ancient world for the father to set a fixed time or day on which the son entered manhood (Lightfoot; Burton; Ramsay; DGRA, 462, 630f; Longenecker). **πατρός** (*# 4252*) father. Subjective gen. The father appoints the time. ◆ **3 οὕτως** (*# 4048*) so, thus. Paul now applies the illustration. **ἦμεν** impf. ind. act. εἰμί (*# 1639*) to be. **στοιχεῖον** (*# 5122*) rudimentary element. It may mean the elementary teaching, referring to the elementary truths of natural religion, or its elementary rules and regulations; or it may refer to elementary spirits; i.e., the spiritual forces behind the world (Guthrie; TDNT; Burton; Longenecker; Betz; s. Col. 2:8). **ἤμεθα** impf. ind. mid. εἰμί (*# 1639*). **δεδουλωμένοι** perf. pass. part. δουλόω (*# 1530*) to be a slave (DPL, 881-82). Perf. indicates the state of slavery. Part. in a past perf. periphrastic construction (RWP). ◆ **4 ἦλθεν** aor. ind. act. ἔρχομαι (*# 2262*) to come. **πλήρωμα** (*# 4445*) that which is filled up, fullness. It refers to the appointed time of the father (s.v. 2). God had prepared the whole world for the coming of His Son at this particular time in history (Guthrie). The coming of the Lord Jesus was not by chance at this time, but by divine plan and appointment. **ἐξαπέστειλεν** aor. ind. act. ἐξαποστέλλω (*# 1990*) to send out from, to send forth. The word indicates to send someone as an authoritative representative w. a specific task (TDNT; NIDNTT). **γενόμενον** aor. mid. (dep.) part. γίνομαι (*# 1181*) to become; here, to be born or to be. Part. defines the principle cl. (Ellicott). ◆ **5 ἐξαγοράσῃ** aor. subj. act. ἐξαγοράζω (*# 1973*) to buy out of the marketplace, to redeem (s. 3:13). Subj. w. **ἵνα** (*# 2671*) to express purp. **υἱοθεσία** (*# 5625*) adoption (DNP, 1:122-24; DPL, 15-18; ABD, 1:7-8). **ἀπολάβωμεν** aor. subj. act. ἀπολαμβάνω (*# 655*) to receive from someone, to receive. ◆ **6 ἐξαπέστειλεν** aor. ind. act. s.v. 4. **κρᾶζον** pres. act. part. κράζω (*# 3189*) to cry out. **ἀββά**

(*# 5*) (Aramaic) father. This was the language of the children, and a daily but polite form of address to the father (Mussner; TDNT; Longenecker; Rom. 8:15). ◆ **7 ὥστε** (*# 6063*) therefore. It is used to draw a conclusion from the previous, "it becomes apparent" (Ridderbos). **οὐκέτι** (*# 4033*) no longer. **εἶ** pres. ind. act. εἰμί (*# 1639*) to be. **κληρονόμος** (*# 3101*) heir. ◆ **8 εἰδότες** perf. act. part. οἶδα (*# 3857*) to know (s. 2:16). **ἐδουλεύσατε** aor. ind. act. δουλεύω (*# 1526*) to be enslaved. **οὖσιν** pres. act. part. εἰμί (*# 1639*) to be. Dat. indicates the one to whom they were enslaved. ◆ **9 γνόντες** aor. act. part. (temp.) γινώσκω (*# 1182*) to know. Aor. indicates antecedent action, "after you have come to know." **γνωσθέντες** aor. pass. part. **ἐπιστρέφετε** pres. ind. act. ἐπιστρέφω (*# 2188*) to turn to someone or something. The prep. in compound is directive. Progressive pres. points to an action which is in progress. **ἀσθενής** (*# 822*) weak, without strength. **πτωχός** (*# 4777*) poor, poor as a beggar, beggarly. The heathen religions were feeble and poor as beggars for they bring no rich endowment of spiritual treasures (Lightfoot). **πάλιν** (*# 4099*) anew, again. Used in the expression "once more," which strongly expresses the completeness of their reversion (Guthrie). **δουλεύειν** pres. act. inf. δουλεύω s.v. 8. A variant reading is **δουλεῦσαι** aor. act. inf. Compl. inf. to the main vb. ◆ **10 παρατηρεῖσθε** pres. ind. mid. παρατηρέω (*# 4190*) to observe closely, to watch carefully (Eadie); for the prep. in compound s. MH, 319. W. this vb. mid. and act. have the same meaning (BAGD). **μήν** (*# 3604*) month. The pl. here may be used for monthly reoccurring events (Burton). **ἐνιαυτός** (*# 1929*) year. For a detailed discussion of these religious elements s. Mussner; DPL, 402-4; FCRR. ◆ **11 φοβοῦμαι** pres. ind. mid. (dep.) φοβέομαι (*# 5828*) to be afraid, to fear. **μή πως** (*# 3590, 4803*) lest, used here w. the ind. following a vb. of fearing. Ind. indicates that the anxiety is directed toward something which has already taken place (BD, 188). **εἰκῆ** (*# 1632*) in vain. **κεκοπίακα** perf. ind. act. κοπιάω (*# 3159*) to labor, to toil, to work to exhaustion. Pres. draws attention to what Paul fears may be the permanent result of his past effort (Guthrie). ◆ **12 γίνεσθε** pres. imp. mid. (dep.) γίνομαι (*# 1181*) to become, to be. Paul appeals to the Galatians to become as he is in reference to freedom from the law and to the freedom which they have as sons of God (Schlier). **δέομαι** pres. ind. mid. (dep.) (*# 1289*) to beseech, to beg. **ἠδικήσατε** aor. ind. act. ἀδικέω (*# 92*) to wrong someone, to injure someone. ◆ **13 οἴδατε** perf. ind. act. οἶδα (*# 3857*) to know. Def. perf. w. pres. meaning. **ἀσθένεια** (*# 819*) weakness, disease, ailment. For the various views regarding Paul's sickness s. 2 Cor. 12:7; Lightfoot; Ramsay, 422f. **εὐηγγελισάμην** aor. ind. mid. (dep.) εὐαγγελίζομαι (*# 2294*) to preach the good news, to preach the gospel (TLNT; TDNT; EDNT). **πρότερον** (*# 4728*) the first time. The word can mean "at first" or "formerly" (Guthrie). ◆ **14 πειρασμός** (# *4280*) temptation, trial (TLNT; Trench, *Synonyms*, 208). **ἐξουθενήσατε** aor. ind. act. ἐξουθενέω (# *2024*) to consider as nothing, to despise. **ἐξεπτύσατε** aor. ind. act. ἐκπτύω (# *1746*) to spit out. The spitting out may refer to contempt and scorn, to an attempt to ward off evil spirits (BAGD), or to the fact that they did not spit out the message Paul preached (Mussner; MM). **ἐδέξασθε** aor. ind. mid. (dep.) δέχομαι (# *1312*) to receive, to welcome. ◆ **15 ποῦ** (# *4544*) where? Used to ask a question. **μακαρισμός** (# *3422*) happiness, blessedness (s. Matt. 5:3). **μαρτυρῶ** pres. ind. act. μαρτυρέω (# *3455*) to testify, to bear witness. **ἐξορύξαντες** aor. act. part. ἐξορύσσω (# *2021*) to dig out, to tear out. Aor. indicates an antecedent action. **ἐδώκατε** aor. ind. act. δίδωμι (# *1443*) to give. Used in a contrary to fact cond. cl. (RWP). ◆ **16 ὥστε** (# *6063*) therefore, so then. Used here w. a question, "can it be that I have become your enemy?" (Lightfoot). **γέγονα** perf. ind. act. γίνομαι (# *1181*) to become, to be. **ἀληθεύων** pres. act. part. ἀληθεύω (# *238*) to speak the truth. Part. indicates the means: "by speaking the truth." Pres. suggests contemporaneous action. ◆ **17 ζηλοῦσιν** pres. ind. act. ζηλόω (# *2420*) to be zealous, to busy oneself about someone, to take interest in; "they pay court to" (Lightfoot; s. 1:14). **καλῶς** (# *2822*) well; here, "in no honorable way" (Eadie). **ἐκκλεῖσαι** aor. act. inf. ἐκκλείω (# *1710*) to shut out, to exclude. **θέλουσιν** pres. subj. act. θέλω (# *2527*) to desire, to, to want to, w. inf. For the subj. form of this vb. s. BD, 46. **ζηλοῦτε** pres. subj. act. ζηλόω (# *2420*). Subj. w. ἵνα (# *2671*) to express purp. ◆ **18 ζηλοῦσθαι** pres. pass. inf. (# *2420*). **πάντοτε** (# *4121*) always; "but it is good to be courted fairly at all times" (Eadie). **παρεῖναι** pres. act. inf. πάρειμι (# *4205*) to be present. Inf. w. the prep. ἐν (# *1877*) to express contemporaneous time: "when I am present w. you" (MT, 144f). ◆ **19 πάλιν** (# *4099*) again. **ὠδίνω** pres. ind. act. (# *6048*) to have birth pains. For childbearing and the figure of childbearing in the ancient world s. RAC, 9:37-217. **μέχρις** (# *3588*) until. **μορφωθῇ** aor. subj. pass. μορφέω (# *3672*) to form; pass., to take on form, to be formed. The form means the essential form rather than outward shape. The idea is therefore formation of real Christlike character (Guthrie; TDNT). ◆ **20 ἤθελον** impf. ind. act. θέλω (# *2527*) to desire, to wish, to want to, w. inf. Impf. to express an unfulfilled desire, "I could wish" (RG, 886). **παρεῖναι** pres. inf. act. πάρειμι (# *4205*) to be present. **ἀλλάξαι** aor. act. inf. ἀλλάσσω (# *248*) to change. **ἀποροῦμαι** pres. ind. mid. ἀπορέω (# *679*) to be at a loss, to be at wits end, to be perplexed (s. Guthrie; Longenecker; Betz; Matera). **ἐν** (# *1877*) in; here, "in respect to you" (Burton). ◆ **21 λέγετε** pres. act. imp. λέγω (# *3306*) to say. **θέλοντες** pres. act. part. θέλω (# *2527*) s.v. 20. Pres. part. used to describe a present defining trait. **εἶναι** pres. act. inf. εἰμί (# *1639*) to be.

Compl. inf. to the main vb. ◆ **22 γέγραπται** perf. ind. pass. γράφω (# *1211*) to write. The form was used to express an authoritative document (MM). **ἔσχεν** aor. ind. act. ἔχω (# *2400*) to have. **παιδίσκη** (# *4087*) maidservant. **ἐλεύθερος** (# *1801*) free. ◆ **23 γεγέννηται** perf. ind. pass. γεννάω (# *1164*) to bear, to bear a child. **ἐπαγγελία** (# *2039*) promise. ◆ **24 ἀλληγορούμενα** pres. pass. part. ἀλληγορέω (# *251*) to allegorize, to use an allegory. Paul is using a historical event as an example. For the allegorical interpretation in Paul's time s. BE, 126ff; Eadie; TDNT; DPL, 635-37; Longenecker. **δουλεία** (# *1525*) bondage, slavery. **γεννῶσα** pres. act. part. s.v. 23. Adj. part. expressing timelessness (Burton). **ἥτις** (# *4015*) whoever, whatever. The indefinite rel. pron. denotes an attribute which essentially belongs to the nature of the antecedent (Ellicott). ◆ **25 τό** The article is n. and refers to Hagar as applied to the mountain (RWP). **συστοιχεῖ** pres. ind. act. συστοιχέω (# *5368*) to line up in the same rank (in a military sense); here, to correspond to (Guthrie). **δουλεύει** pres. ind. act. δουλεύω (# *1526*) to be in bondage, to be in slavery; i.e., in spiritual bondage w. her children just as Hagar was in social bondage w. her child Ishmael (Lightfoot). ◆ **26 ἥτις** which s.v. 24. ◆ **27 εὐφράνθητι** aor. pass. imp. εὐφραίνομαι (# *2370*) to rejoice. **στεῖρα** (# *5096*) sterile, barren. **τίκτουσα** pres. act. part. τίκτω (# *5503*) to bear a child. **ῥῆξον** aor. act. imp. ῥήγνυμι (# *4838*) to break. to burst, to break loose; here, to break forth. **βόησον** aor. act. imp. βοάω (# *1066*) to cry aloud. **ὠδίνουσα** pres. act. part. nom. fem. sing. ὠδίνω to have labor pains s.v. 19. **ἔρημος** (# *2245*) desolate. **μᾶλλον** (# *3437*) more, more than. **ἐχούσης** pres. act. part. ἔχω (# *2400*) to have. For Isa. 54:1 in the rabbinical literature s. SB, 3:574. ◆ **28 ἐπαγγελία** (# *2039*). Emphatic by its position and without the article the gen. here stresses the quality (Fung). ◆ **29 γεννηθείς** aor. pass. part. γεννάω (# *1164*) s.v. 23. **ἐδίωκεν** impf. ind. act. διώκω (# *1503*) to hunt, to persecute. Impf. pictures the continual action in the past. ◆ **30 ἔκβαλε** aor. imp. act. ἐκβάλλω (# *1675*) to throw out. **κληρονομήσει** fut. ind. act. κληρονομέω (# *3099*) to inherit. ◆ **31 διό** (# *1475*) therefore. It draws a conclusion from the previous discussion and summarizes the section. For a discussion of this allegory in relation to the argument of Galatians s. C. K. Barrett, "The Allegory of Abraham, Sarah, and Hagar in the Argument of Galatians," R, 1-16; Fung, 217-20.

Galatians 5

◆ **1 ἐλευθερία** (# *1800*) freedom. For the meaning of this word s. NIDNTT; TDNT; RAC, 8:269-306; DPL, 313-16. The dat. could be instr. (Bruce) or it may be a dat. of purp. or designation (Ridderbos). **ἠλευθέρωσεν** aor. ind. act. ἐλευθερόω (# *1802*) to free, to free from slavery. A slave was free under Gr. law, for he had freedom from seizure of property, freedom to act as his own legal person, freedom to earn his own living as he might choose, and freedom to dwell where he wished (FCS, 115). For a discussion of the ways in which a slave could be freed s. FSC, 88-120. **στήκετε** pres. imp. act. στήκω (# 5112) to stand fast. Pres. indicates a continual and habitual action. **ζυγός** (# 2433) yoke (SCS, 31-32; ABD, 6:1026-27). **δουλείας** (# 1525) slavery, bondage. **ἐνέχεσθε** pres. imp. mid. ἐνέχω (# 1923) to be had in, to be ensnared. Pres. calls for the stopping of as action in progress: "cease to be entangled" (Burton). Mid. voice could be permissive, "stop allowing yourselves to be entangled." ◆ **2 ἴδε** aor. act. imp. ὁράω (# 2623) to see; imp. used to draw attention: "look!" "see!" **ἐγὼ Παῦλος** I Paul; very emphatic, emphasizing Paul's authority (Schlier). **περιτέμνησθε** pres. subj. mid. περιτέμνω (# 4362) to circumcise (DPL, 137-38). Here the mid. is permissive: to allow oneself to be circumcised. **ὠφελήσει** fut. ind. act. ὀφελέω (# 6067) to be of value, to profit, to be an advantage, followed by the acc. of respect: "Christ will be an advantage to you in respect to nothing." ◆ **3 περιτεμνομένῳ** pres. mid. part. περιτέμνω (# 4362) s.v. 2. permissive mid. Pres. part. used to emphasize a present trait. **ὀφειλέτης** (# 4050) one who is morally obligated to fulfil a debt, debtor (s. Rom. 1:14). **ποιῆσαι** aor. act. inf. ποιέω (# 4472) to do. Epex. inf., "he is indebted to keep the whole law." ◆ **4 κατηργήθητε** aor. ind. pass. καταργέω (# 2934) to make idle or inactive, to render invalid; followed by the prep., "to be separated from," "to be loosed from" (AS). **δικαιοῦσθε** pres. ind. pass. δικαιόω (# 1467) to declare righteous, to justify. Conative pres. indicating an attempt, "you are trying to be justified" (DM, 186; GGBB, 535). **ἐξεπέσατε** aor. ind. act. ἐκπίπτω (# 1738) to fall out of. Originally used for the falling out of a flower; then, to be loosened from something, to loose one's grasp of (Ridderbos). To attempt to be justified by the law is to reject the way of grace - justification by faith. ◆ **5 ἀπεκδεχόμεθα** pres. ind. mid. (dep.) ἀπεκδέχομαι (# 587) to wait expectantly, earnestly but patiently, for someone or something. The first prep. in compound intensifies the vb. and the second one indicates, "to be receiving from a distance," "to be intently awaiting" (Burton; MM). ◆ **6 ἰσχύει** pres. ind. act. ἰσχύω (# 2710) to be strong, to have power. When used of things it means "to be serviceable" (Guthrie). **ἀκροβυστία** (# 213) foreskin, not circumcised. **ἐνεργουμένη** pres. mid. (dep.) part. ἐνεργέω (# 1919) to be active; mid., to demonstrate activity, to work, to work effectually. ◆ **7 ἐτρέχετε** impf. ind. act. τρέχω (# 5556) to run, to run a race (s. 2:2). **καλῶς** (# 2822) well. **ἐνέκοψεν** aor. ind. act. ἐγκόπτω (# 1601) to cut in, to hinder. The word suggests a breaking into or obstruction of the Galatian Christians in their course of following the truth. The picture is that of the runner who has allowed his progress to be blocked or who is still running, but on

the wrong course (PAM, 146f). **πείθεσθαι** pres. mid. (dep.) inf. πείθω (# 4275) to obey. The prep. is used to express results. ◆ **8 πεισμονή** (# 4282) persuasion. The word can have an active or pass. sense (Mussner). **καλοῦντος** pres. act. part. καλέω (# 2813) to call. The one who does the calling is obviously God (Bruce). Part. emphasizes the trait of God who calls. ◆ **9 ζύμη** (# 2434) yeast, leaven (s. Matt. 13:33). **φύραμα** (# 5878) that which is mixed, a lump or batch of dough (BAGD). **ζυμοῖ** pres. ind. act. ζυμόω (# 2435) to leaven, to ferment (s. 1 Cor. 5:6f). Gnomic pres. expresses the continuing truth of a proverb or saying. ◆ **10 πέποιθα** perf. ind. act. πείθω (# 4275) to be persuaded, to have confidence. For the instructions employed by Paul after this vb. s. Burton. **φρονήσετε** fut. ind. act. φρονέω (# 5858) to think, to hold an opinion, to set one's mind on something, to have an attitude or thought. **ταράσσων** pres. act. part. ταράσσω (# 5429) to shake back and forth, to disturb, to trouble. **βαστάσει** fut. ind. act. βαστάζω (# 1002) to carry, to bear. Paul thinks of the heavy weight which will press down upon those seeking to impose a load of Judaism on these Christians (Guthrie). **κρίμα** (# 3210) judgment. **ᾖ** pres. subj. act. εἰμί (# 1639) to be. ◆ **11 διώκομαι** pres. ind. pass. διώκω (# 1503) to hunt, to hunt down, to persecute. **ἄρα** (# 726) then; "so it appears!" The word introduces a false statement or inference which is here used ironically (Lightfoot). **κατήργηται** perf. ind. pass. κατεργέομαι s.v. 4. **σκάνδαλον** (# 4998) The arm or stick on which bait was fixed in a trap, that which trips one up, offense, cause of stumbling (NTW, 111-14; DPL, 918-19; TDNT). **σταυρός** (# 5089) cross. The gen. here can be either gen. of explanation ("cause of offense which the cross causes") or causal ("the offence which the cross causes") (Mussner). ◆ **12 ὄφελον** (# 4054) I would, oh, that, would that; a fixed form functioning as a particle to introduce unobtainable wishes (BAGD, 181f). Here it is used w. the fut. ind. for an obtainable wish, even though strictly speaking fulfillment is inconceivable and this impossibility is forgotten only for the moment (BD, 181, 194). **ἀποκόψονται** fut. ind. mid. (dep.) ἀποκόπτω (# 644) to cut off; here, to castrate. Paul expresses the wish that his opponents would not stop w. circumcision but would go on to emasculation (Burton; Betz; BCC). Perhaps there is also a reference to the practices of the ancient cult of Cybele (TDNT; BAGD; *De Dea Syria–The Syrian Goddess*, ed. Harold W. Attridge and Robert A. Oden [Missoula, Mont.: Scholars Press, 1976], 51; Strabo 13:4:14; NW, 2, ii:568-70). **ἀναστατοῦντες** pres. act. part. ἀναστατέω (# 415) to upset, to trouble, to disturb. It was used in the papyri in the sense of upsetting or disturbing one's mind (RWP; MM). ◆ **13 ἐκλήθητε** aor. ind. pass. καλέω (# 2813) to call. Theol. pass. indicating that God did the calling. **ἐλευθερία** (# 1800) freedom. Here, object of a vb. to be supplied (ἔχετε). **ἀφορμή** (# *929*) properly, it refers to the place from which an attack is made, a base of operation, opportunity, occasion (Burton; Guthrie; Longenecker). **δουλεύετε** pres. imp. act. δουλεύω (# *1526*) to perform the duties of a slave. **ἀλλήλοις** dat. ἀλλήλων (# *253*) one another; dat. of advantage. ◆ **14 πεπλήρωται** perf. ind. pass. πληρόω (# *4444*) to fulfil. **ἀγαπήσεις** fut. ind. act. ἀγαπάω (# *26*) to love (TLNT; TDNT; EDNT). **πλησίον** (# *4446*) neighbor. ◆ **15 δάκνετε** pres. ind. act. δάκνω (# *1231*) to bite. **κατεσθίετε** pres. ind. act. κατεσθίω (# *2983*) to eat up. The two vbs. in present are conative, indicating the attempt (Burton); and the indicatives are used in a cond. cl., which assumes the cond. as true. **βλέπετε** pres. imp. act. βλέπω (# *1063*) to see. **μή** (# *3590*) w. the subj. to express a neg. purp. **ἀναλωθῆτε** aor. subj. pass. ἀναλίσκω (# *384*) to consume, to devour. These vbs. suggest wild animals engaged in deadly struggles (Burton). ◆ **16 περιπατεῖτε** pres. imp. act. περιπατέω (# *4344*) to walk, to walk about, to conduct one's life. Pres. indicates a continual habitual action. **πνεύματι** dat. πνεῦμα (# *4460*) spirit. Dat. is either agency or means (GGBB, 165-66). **ἐπιθυμία** (# *2123*) desire, lust. Prep. in compound is directive. **οὐ μή** (# *4024; 3590*) used w. the subj. as a strong neg., "not at all" (M, 188ff). **τελέσητε** aor. subj. act. τελέω (# *5464*) to fulfill, to bring to the goal, to perform. ◆ **17 ἐπιθυμεῖ** pres. ind. act. ἐπιθυμέω (# *2121*) to desire, to yearn, to long for. The use of the vb. brings out the more active side of the lust of the flesh (Guthrie). **ἀντίκειται** pres. ind. mid. (dep.) ἀντίκειμαι (# *512*) to lie opposite, to oppose. Pres. indicates continual opposition. **θέλητε** pres. subj. act. θέλω (# *2527*) to desire to, to want to **ποιῆτε** pres. subj. act. ποιέω (# *4472*) to do, to make. Subj. w. **ἐάν** (# *1569*) to express purp. or result. For a discussion s. Mussner. ◆ **18 ἄγεσθε** pres. ind. pass. ἄγω (# *72*) to lead; pass., to be led. Here the Spirit is regarded as a guide to whom the believer is expected to submit himself (Guthrie). ◆ **19** For lists of virtues and vices s. DPL, 962-63; ABD, 6:857-59. **φανερός** (# *5745*) clear, manifest. **πορνεία** (# *4518*) illicit sexual activity (TDNT; FS, 24-28). **ἀκαθαρσία** (# *174*) uncleanness, impurity (FS, 29-30). **ἀσέλγεια** (# *816*) unrestrained living, unbridled acts of indecency which shock the public (Lightfoot; TDNT; FS, 31-33; s. 2 Cor. 12:21). ◆ **20 εἰδωλολατρία** (# *1630*) worship of idols, idolatry (FS, 33-36). **φαρμακεία** (# *5758*) the use of medicine or drugs, the use of drugs for magical purposes, magic, sorcery (FS, 36-39; Burton; Guthrie; GELTS, 499; Exod. 7:11, 22; 8:3, 14; Isa. 47:9; Rev. 9:21). **ἔχθρα** (# *2397*) hostility. **ἔρις** (# *2251*) strife. **ζῆλος** (# *2419*) jealousy. **θύμος** (# *2596*) anger, a terrible flare-up of temper (Trench, *Synonyms*, 130; TDNT; NIDNTT). **ἐριθεία** (# *2249*) selfishness, self-seeking ambition (FS, 39-42; s. 2 Cor. 12:20; Phil. 2:3). **διχοστασία** (# *1496*) dissension (FS, 56-58). **αἵρεσις**

(# *146*) faction. It is the result of the former divisions organized into factions and cliques (Eadie). ◆ **21 φθόνος** (# *5784*) envy, the desire to appropriate what another possesses. The word "jealousy" in v. 20 refers to the desire to be as well off as another, and the word "envy" refers to the desire to deprive another of what he has (Lightfoot; Eadie; NIDNTT). **μέθη** (# *3494*) drunkenness (FS, 60-62; s. Rom. 13:13; ABD, 4:650-55). **κῶμος** (# *3269*) carousing, drinking party (s. Rom. 13:13). **ὅμοιος** (# *3927*) that which is like another. **προλέγω** (# *4625*) pres. ind. act. to say beforehand, to tell forth, to tell publicly, to warn. The meaning here may be "to predict" (Burton). **προεῖπον** aor. ind. act. προλέγω (# *4625*) to say before. **τοιαῦτα** pl. acc. τοιοῦτος (# *5525*) of such a kind, such as this. **πράσσοντες** pres. act. part. πράσσω (# *4556*) to do, to practice. **κληρονομήσουσιν** fut. ind. act. κληρονομέω (# *3099*) to inherit. ◆ **22 καρπός** (# *2843*) fruit, that which is produced by growth (NIDNTT; TDNT). **πνεῦμα** (# *4460*) spirit. Here, gen. ("of the Spirit") indicates the source or cause of the fruit. For a study of the words used here s. FS, 63-127; DPL, 316-19. **ἀγάπη** (# *27*) love. The word includes both love for God and love for fellowman. It is a love which holds its object in high esteem and admiration and expresses itself in a concrete fashion. It is expressed to the lovely and unlovely and seeks the best for its object (TDNT; TLNT). **χαρά** (# *5915*) joy. In the Hellenistic world joy was related to happiness or pleasure, such as returning to one's homeland, but this joy is grounded in conscious relationship to God (TLNT; TDNT; EDNT; RAC, 8:348-418; TRE, 11:584-86; Longenecker; Burton). **εἰρήνη** (# *1645*) peace. Perhaps the word here combines the Greek and Heb. (שָׁלוֹם *shalom* [DCH; TDOT; NIDOTTE]) ideas giving the meaning of a wholeness of soul which issues in a tranquil disposition regardless of outward circumstances (TLNT; TDNT; EDNT; Longenecker; FS, 83-90). **μακροθυμία** (# *3429*) longsuffering, patient endurance under injuries inflicted by others. It describes the response of Christians towards circumstances and events, as well as God's patience endurance of the rebellion and sin of mankind (FS, 91-97; Lightfoot; NIDNTT; TDNT; s. Rom. 2:4). **χρηστότης** (# *5983*) kindness, gentleness. It refers to a kindly disposition toward one's neighbors, showing goodness and concern towards others, sympathetic kindness (FS, 97-102; TLNT; Lightfoot). **ἀγαθωσύνη** (# *20*) goodness. It refers to active goodness as an energetic principle; it is the generosity which springs from the heart that is kind and will always take care to obtain for others that which is useful or beneficial (Lightfoot; Trench, *Synonyms*, 231f; FS, 102-7; TLNT; TDNT; NIDNTT). **πίστις** (# *4411*) faith, faithfulness, reliability, loyalty (FS, 107-111). ◆ **23 πραΰτης** (# *4559*) meekness, gentle submissiveness, controlled strength, the ability to bear reproaches and slights without bitterness and resentment; the ability to provide a soothing influence on someone who is in a state of anger, bitterness and resentment against life (FS, 111-21; Burton; EDNT; TDNT; TLNT; 2 Cor. 10:1). ἐγκράτεια (# 1602) self-control, the holding in of passions and appetites, self-restraint (FS, 212-27; Eadie; Burton; RAC, 5:343-65; EDNT). ◆ **24 ἐσταύρωσαν** aor. ind. act. σταυρόω (# 5090) to crucify. Aor. points to a completed action in the past and most naturally refers to conversion (Guthrie). πάθημα (# 4077) passion, affections (Trench, *Synonyms*, 323). ἐπιθυμία (# 2123) desire, longing directed to a certain object (DNP, 2:542-44; TDNT). ◆ **25 ζῶμεν** pres. ind. act. ζάω (# 2409) to live. Ind. in a cond. cl. which views the cond. as real. **στοιχῶμεν** pres. subj. act. στοιχέω (# 5123) to stand in a row, to walk in a straight line, to behave properly. The word was used for movement in a definite line, as in military formation or dancing (Ridderbos). Here it means to walk in a straight line, to conduct oneself rightly (Burton). Pres. points to the continual and habitual action. Cohortatory subj., "let us walk." ◆ **26 γινώμεθα** pres. subj. mid. (dep.) γίνομαι (# 1181) to become; hortatory subj. used w. the neg. κενόδοξος (# 3030) empty glorying, vain glory, vain-minded. It refers to one who knows how or who attempts to achieve unfounded respect by big talk, boasting, and ambition (Mussner; Burton). **προκαλούμενοι** pres. mid. part. προκαλέω (# 4614) to invite or challenge to combat, to provoke (Eadie). **φθονοῦντες** pres. act. part. φθονέω (# 5783) to be envious (s.v. 21). The two parts. describe the means or manner of the action in the main vb.

Galatians 6

◆ **1 προλημφθῇ** aor. subj. pass. προλαμβάνω (# 4624) to overtake by surprise, to overpower before one can escape (Lightfoot; Eadie). παράπτωμα (# 4183) false step, transgression. The results of stepping aside may have been chosen because of its appropriateness to the Christian life as a walk by the Spirit (Guthrie). **καταρτίζετε** pres. imp. act. καταρτίζω (# 2936) to restore, to correct. It is used especially as a surgical term of setting a bone or joint; or in other contexts of the strengthening or sustaining of a worn down people, of the mixing of medicine, of a sailor outfitting his boat, of fishermen mending nets, or of politicians appeasing factions and restoring unity (Lightfoot; TLNT; Longenecker; Betz). πραΰτητος (# 4559) meekness, gentleness, submissiveness (s. 5:23; 2 Cor. 10:1). **σκοπῶν** pres. act. part. σκοπέω (# 5023) to look at, to observe, to consider, to give heed to. The vb. indicates being sharply attentive, very diligent; pres. indicates continually doing so (Ridderbos). **πειρασθῇς** aor. subj. pass. πειράζω (# 4279) to try, to attempt. Subj. may be used to express purp. or it may be used after a vb. of fearing. "Consider or give heed lest you be tempted"

(Burton). ◆ **2 ἀλλήλων** (# 253) gen. pl. one another. βάρη pl. acc. βάρος (# 983) burden, that which is heavy (BCC). **βαστάζετε** pres. imp. act. βαστάζω (# 1002) to carry, to bear, to carry away, to endure (MM). **ἀναπληρώσετε** fut. ind. act. ἀναπληρόω (# 405) to fill, to fill up, to fulfil. The prep. in compound gives the idea of a complete filling, of a filling up (Eadie). ◆ **3 δοκεῖ** pres. ind. act. δοκέω (# 1506) to think, to suppose. **εἶναι** pres. act. inf. εἰμί (# 1639) to be. Part. is temp. or temp. concessive, "when, although he is nothing" (Ellicott). **φρεναπατᾷ** pres. ind. act. φρεναπατάω (# 5854) to lead one's mind astray, to deceive. The word suggests the subjective fantasies which deceive (Lightfoot; RWP). ◆ **4 δοκιμαζέτω** pres. imp. act. δοκιμάζω (# 1507) to examine, to approve after testing or examination. The word was used for testing of metals to see whether they were pure (Guthrie). καύχημα (# 3017) the ground or reason for boasting. ◆ **5 φορτίον** (# 5845) burden, a load which one is expected to bear. It was used as a military term for a man's pack or a soldier's kit (Lightfoot). **βαστάσει** fut. ind. act. βαστάζω s.v. 2. ◆ **6 κοινωνείτω** pres. imp. act. κοινωνέω (# 3125) to share w. someone, to exercise fellowship. The apostle is thinking here especially of material things (Ridderbos). **κατηχούμενος** pres. pass. part. κατηχέω (# 2994) to instruct; pass. to be instructed, to be taught. **κατηχοῦντι** pres. act. part. κατηχέω (# 2994). Dat. of advantage used w. the main vb. **κοινωνείτω**. ◆ **7 πλανᾶσθε** pres. imp. pass. πλανάω (# 4414) to deceive, to lead astray. **μυκτηρίζεται** pres. ind. pass. μυκτηρίζω (# 3682) to turn up the nose at, to treat w. contempt, to ridicule. The idea is to make God ridiculous by outwitting Him and evading His laws (Betz; Burton; TLNT). ἐάν (# 1569) used to generalize the rel. pron. ("whatever"). **σπείρῃ** pres. subj. act. σπείρω (# 5062) to sow, to sow seeds. Gnomic pres. indicating that which is always true. **θερίσει** fut. ind. act. θερίζω (# 2545) to harvest, to gather. For the agricultural metaphor in the ancient world s. Longenecker. ◆ **8 σπείρων** pres. act. part. σπείρω s.v. 7. φθορά (# 5785) corruption, rottenness. No one would bother to harvest a field of decaying matter. The corruption stands for that which results in death (Guthrie). αἰώνιος (# 173) eternal. ◆ **9 ποιοῦντες** pres. act. part. ποιέω (# 4472) to do. **ἐγκακῶμεν** pres. subj. act. ἐγκακέω (# 1591) to grow weary, to give in to evil, to lose heart and become a coward, to conduct oneself badly (TLNT; Lightfoot; s. Luke 18:1). **καιρῷ** dat. καιρός (# 2789) season, time. Dat. of time, "in its own season," "at the time of harvest." It indicates there is an appointed time for the spiritual reaping (Guthrie). **θερίσομεν** fut. ind. act. s.v. 7. **ἐκλυόμενοι** pres. pass. part. ἐκλύω (# 1725) to loosen out, to relax, to faint, to be exhausted as a result of giving in to evil, to be physically or morally weak (TLNT; GELTS, 138; RWP). Cond. part. "we shall reap, if we do not lose heart"

(GGBB, 633). ◆ **10 ἄρα** (# *726*) so, then. It is used to draw a conclusion from the previous. **ἐργαζώμεθα** pres. subj. mid. (dep.) ἐργάζομαι (# *2237*) to be active, to work effectively. Hortatory subj., "let us work." **οἰκεῖος** (# *3858*) household, members of a household. ◆ **11** **ἴδετε** aor. imp. act. ὁράω (# *3972*) to see. **πηλίκος** (# *4383*) how large. **ἔγραψα** aor. ind. act. γράφω (# *1211*) to write. At this point Paul may have taken the pen from the amanuensis and added concluding remarks in his own handwriting, which consisted of larger letters than the smaller and neater script of the amanuensis (Guthrie; also Richard N. Longenecker, "Ancient Amanuenses," *ND*, 281-97; ABD, 1:172-73; s. Rom. 16:22). ◆ **12 ὅσος** (# *4012*) as many as. **θέλουσιν** pres. ind. act. θέλω (# *2527*) to desire to, w. inf. **εὐπροσωπῆσαι** aor. act. inf. εὐπροσωπέω (# *2349*) to play a good role, to please, to make a fair appearance (Burton). **ἐν σαρκί** (# *1877; 4922*) in the flesh. **ἀναγκάζουσιν** pres. ind. act. ἀναγκάζω (# *337*) to compel, to coerce (s. Gal. 2:3). Conative pres., "they are trying to coerce." **περιτέμνεσθαι** pres. pass. inf. περιτέμνω (# *4362*) to circumcise. **σταυρῷ** dat. σταυρός (# *5089*) cross. Causal dat., "because of the cross" (BD, 105). **διώκωνται** pres. subj. pass. διώκω (# *1503*) to hunt, to persecute; pass., to suffer persecution. Subj. w. **ἵνα** (# *2671*) to express purp. ◆ **13** **περιτεμνόμενοι** pres. pass. part. περιτέμνω (# *4362*) to circumcise. **φυλάσσουσιν** pres. ind. act. φυλάσσω (# *5875*) to guard, to observe. **καυχήσωνται** aor. subj. mid. (dep.) καυχάομαι (# *3016*) to glory, to boast. Subj. w. **ἵνα** (# *2671*) to express purp. ◆ **14 γένοιτο** aor. opt. mid. (dep.) γίνομαι (# *1181*) to be, to become. Followed by

the inf. **εἰ μή** (# 1623; 3590) except. **δι' οὗ** through which. **ἐσταύρωται** perf. ind. pass. σταυρόω (# *5090*) to crucify, to put to death by crucifixion. Perf. indicates the continuing and lasting state or cond. ◆ **15 περιτομή** (# *4364*) circumcision. **ἀκροβυστία** (# *213*) foreskin, uncircumcision. **κτίσις** (# *3232*) creation. ◆ **16 κανόνι** dat. κανών (# *2834*) rod, measuring rule, standard. For this word s. 2 Cor. 10:13. **στοιχήσουσιν** fut. ind. act. στοιχέω (# *5123*) to walk the line, to walk according to a standard (s. 5:25). **ἔλεος** (# *1799*) mercy (TDNT; TLNT). **καὶ ἐπὶ τὸν Ἰσραὴλ τοῦ θεοῦ** and upon the Israel of God. The phrase is not to be taken as an explanation of the preceding but as a separate entity or group. His thoughts turn to his own brethren after the flesh and he pauses to specify those who were once Israelites according to the flesh but now are the Israel of God (Ellicott). ◆ **17 λοιπός** (# *3836*) rest, remaining. Gen. here means, "in respect of remaining time" (RWP). **κόπος** (# *3160*) trouble. **παρεχέτω** pres. imp. act. παρέχω (# *4218*) to furnish, to provide, to cause. **στίγμα** (# *5116*) mark, brand. It was the custom to mark slaves by scars (Ramsay); religious tattooing also played a great role in antiquity (BAGD; *The Assyrian Goddess*, 59; Longenecker; Betz; Bruce). Paul is speaking of the permanent marks which he bore from persecution undergone in the service of Christ (Lightfoot; TDNT). **βαστάζω** pres. ind. act. (# *1002*) to carry, to bear. Pres. indicates the continual bearing. ◆ **18 ἀμήν** (# *297*) so let it be. A Hebraic word used to emphasize and confirm a statement. Paul means to add weight to his conclusion (Guthrie).

Ephesians

Ephesians 1

◆ **1 Παῦλος** Paul. Nom. in the address of a letter (s. Rom. 1:1). For a defense of the Pauline authorship s. A. van Roon, *The Authenticity of Ephesians* (Leiden: E.J. Brill, 1974; Barth; DPL, 240-42). **οὖσιν** pres. act. part. εἰμί (# 1639) to be. **ἅγιος** (# 41) saint; Dat. here indicates to whom this letter was written ("to the saints who are..."). The term "saints" means those who are cleansed by the blood of Christ and the renewal of the Holy Ghost, and thus separated from the world and consecrated to God (Hodge; TDNT; EDNT). **ἐν Ἐφέσῳ** (# 1877; 2387) in Ephesus. Although some manuscripts do not have this reading, because of the many personal references, such as the ref. to Paul himself, to the readers with "you" pl., to Paul's prayer request (6:19-20), and to Tychicus (6:21), there is little or no reason to consider the letter to be a circular letter sent to various cities (TC, 601; DPL, 243-45). **καί** (# 2779) and; epex., the "saints who are believers." ◆ **2 χάρις** (# 5921) grace, the undeserved and unmerited favor of God (TDNT; NIDNTT; EDNT; CPP). **εἰρήνη** (# 1645) peace. Probably to be understood in terms of the Heb. shalom (שלום) indicating spiritual prosperity (Barth; Lincoln; TDNT; NIDNTT; NIDOTTE, 4:130-35). ◆ **3 εὐλογητός** (# 2329) blessed. Verbal adjs. w. this ending indicate one who is worthy, i.e., "worthy of blessing" (Abbott; s. 2 Cor. 1:3). In the NT it is only used of God. **εὐλογήσας** aor. act. part. εὐλογέω (# 2328) to bless, to endow one w. the ability to succeed (TDOT, s.v. ברך, 280-308; DCH; TDNT; NIDOTTE, 1:757-67). Aor. expresses antecedent action to the main vb. **εὐλογία** (# 2330) dat. blessing; instr. dat., "with every blessing." **ἐπουράνιος** (# 2230) heavenly; here, "in the heavenlies." The term is to be understood in a local sense, indicating the sphere of the blessings which are related to the Spirit as well as the location of the exalted Christ. The term refers to heaven as seen in relation to the new age brought about in Christ. For this reason it is so closely linked w. the Spirit of that age (A.T. Lincoln, "A Reexamination of 'The Heavenlies' in Ephesians," *NTS* 19 [1973]: 468-83, 471; Barth; W. Hall Harris III, "`The Heavenlies' Reconsidered: Οὐρανός and Ἐπουράνιος in Ephesians," *Bib Sac* 148 [1991]: 72-89; DPL, 382). **ἐν Χριστῷ** (# 5986) in Christ (DPL, 433-36; Lincoln; Gnilka, 66-69). ◆ **4 καθώς** (# 2777) just as, because. Here the word combines the comp. and causal idea (Schlier; BD, 236). **ἐξελέξατο**

(# 1721) aor. ind. mid. (dep.) ἐκλέγω to choose out, to select. The word involves three ideas; the stem of the word indicates "the telling over"; prep. in compound indicates the rejection of some and acceptance of others; and the mid. voice indicates the talking to (for) himself (Lightfoot, *Notes*; GGBB, 421). **ἐν αὐτῷ** in him; dat. of sphere. **καταβολή** (# 2856) throwing down, foundation. For the various usages of the word s. Barth; TDNT. "Before the foundation of the world" means from all eternity (Abbott). **εἶναι** pres. act. inf. εἰμί (# 1639) to be. Inf. to express purp. **ἄμωμος** (# 320) without blame, unblemished; used of the absence of defects in sacrificial animals (BAGD; GELTS, 25). **κατενώπιον** (# 2979) in the presence of, prep. used w. a gen. (RG, 644). **ἐν ἀγάπη** (# 27) in love (TLNT; TDNT). The phrase is best understood as being joined w. the part. in v. 5 (Eadie); Alford understood it w. the preceding inf. ◆ **5 προορίσας** aor. act. part. προορίζω (# 4633) to mark out w. a boundary beforehand, to foreordain, to predestinate (TDNT; L.C. Allen, "The Old Testament Background of (προ) ὁρίζω in the New Testament," *NTS* 17 [1970]: 104-8). Causal part. giving the reason for the election (Abbott). **υἱοθεσία** (# 5625) adoption (Lincoln; Rom. 8:15; ABD, 1: 76-79; DPL, 15-18). The emphasis is on being an adult son in the family (John Crook, "*Patria Potestas*," *The Classical Quarterly* 17 [1967]: 113-22; Francis Lyall, "Roman Law in the Writings of Paul–Adoption," *JBL* 88 [1969]: 458-66; OCD, 8-9; DNP, 1:122-24). **εὐδοκία** (# 2306) good pleasure, satisfaction (Schnackenburg). The election and predestination is God's absolute act of free love grounded totally in Himself; nothing apart from Him gave His will its direction (Gaugler). ◆ **6 ἔπαινος** (# 2047) praise. **δόξης** gen. δόξα (# 1518) glory, honor, reputation (TLNT; TDNT; GELTS, 119). Obj. gen., the praise of God's excellence, nature, and activity (TLNT). **χάριτος** gen. sing. χάρις (# 5921) grace (s.v. 2; CPP, 134-35). Gen. could be gen. of source ("glory arising fr. His grace" [Gnilka]), or a type of obj. gen. ("glory or praise") which has His grace as the obj. (BD, 93). **ἧς** gen. ὅς (# 4005) who, which, rel. pron. Gen. by attraction to its antecedent (TC, 601). **ἐχαρίτωσεν** aor. ind. act. χαρίζω (# 5923) to bestow grace, to give grace. The word means "begracing w. grace" and indicates exclusive and abundant demonstration of grace (Barth; TDNT; EDNT; Robinson; s. Luke 1:28). **ἠγαπημένῳ** perf. pass. part. ἀγαπάω (# 26) to love (TDNT; TLNT). Pass. part. indicates the one who is in the state or condition of being loved, "the beloved." ◆ 7 ἀπολύτρωσις (# 667) purchasing w. a price, redemption (s. Rom. 3:24; Abbott; Lightfoot, *Notes*; Lincoln; DPL, 784-86). ἄφεσις (# 912) releasing, forgiveness. παράπτωμα (# 4183) falling aside, transgression. The word signifies the actual and numerous results and manifestations of our sinful nature (Eadie). κατὰ τὸ πλοῦτος τῆς χάριτος according to the wealth of His grace. The term πλοῦτος (# 4458) indicates an abundance of possessions exceeding the norm of a particular society (LN, 1:561). The gen. χάριτος (# 5921) indicates the content of the wealth. ◆ 8 ἧς (# 4005) s.v. 6. Gen. by attraction rather than acc; thus it is the obj. to the following vb. ἐπερίσσευσεν aor. ind. act. περισσεύω (# 4355) to cause to overflow, to cause to abound. φρόνησις (# 5860) understanding. It refers to the display of wisdom in operation (Simpson). It is the ability to discern modes of action w. a view to their results (Lightfoot, *Notes*). ◆ 9 γνωρίσας aor. act. part. (circum.) γνωρίζω (# 1192) to make known. Aor. describes contemporaneous action (GGBB, 625; VA, 382-85). προέθετο aor. mid. (dep.) ind. προτίθημι (# 4729) to place before. Prep. in compound can be local, i.e., "to set before oneself," "to purpose" (Abbott). ◆ 10 οἰκονομία (# 3873) household management, administration (TDNT; BAGD; TLNT). πλήρωμα (# 4445) fullness. Here, descriptive gen. ἀνακεφαλαιώσασθαι aor. pass. inf. ἀνακεφαλαιόω (# 368) to gather again under one head, to sum up, to gather up into one. For this word s. Barth; Robinson; Abbott; Lincoln. Prep. in compound refers to the prior dispersion of the elements and the noun of the vb. describes the ultimate aggregation into one; thus the whole compound involves the idea of unity brought out of diversity (Lightfoot; *Notes*). Epex. inf. to explain the preceding. Aor. points to a specific act. ◆ 11 ἐκληρώθημεν aor. ind. pass. κληρόω (# 3103) to appoint by lot; pass., to be appointed by lot, to be destined, to be chosen. The emphasis may either be on the concept of inheritance or more likely the concept of appointment (BAGD; MM; CCFJ, 2:506). προορισθέντες aor. pass. part. (adj.) s.v. 5. πρόθεσις (# 4606) purpose. ἐνεργοῦντος pres. act. part. ἐνεργέω (# 1919) to be effective, to be energetic, to work, to accomplish (Robinson). βουλήν (# 1087) counsel, will. It expresses counsel w. reference to action (Westcott). The word solemnly represents the almighty will as displayed in action (Ellicott). θέλημα (# 2525) will. It denotes the will in general (Westcott). ◆ 12 εἶναι pres. act. inf. εἰμί (# 1639) to be. Articular inf. w. εἰς (# 1650) to express purp. προηλπικότας perf. act. part. προελπίζω (# 4598) to hope before, to hope beforehand. The prep. in compound is temp. but its significance is not clear. It could indicate the hope before the event (EGT) or the hope of the Jewish Christians prior to the conversion of the heathen (Abbott; Barth); or it could refer to the hope or belief before Christ actually came (Westcott). Perf. indicates that the hope continues. Part. is in apposition to the subject of the inf., "we." ◆ 13 ἀκούσαντες aor. act. part. ἀκούω (# 201) to hear. πιστεύσαντες aor. act. part. πιστεύω (# 4409) to believe. Temp. parts. expressing contemporaneous action to the main vb.: "when you believed," "at the time you believed" (Simpson; RG, 860-61; MT, 61, 65; GGBB, 625; VA, 383-85). ἐσφραγίσθητε aor. ind. pass. σφραγίζω (# 5381) to seal. Seals indicated not only ownership, but also were used as a guarantee of the correctness of the contents. Jars, sacks of fruit, or grain were sealed (BS; 238-39; NDIEC, 2:191; BBC). ἐπαγγελία (# 2039) promise. Obj. gen. here, indicating what was sealed. ◆ 14 ἀρραβών (# 775) down payment, pledge. It indicates a deposit which in itself is a guarantee that the full amount will be paid. The down payment is of the same kind as the full payment (s. 2 Cor. 1:22; Abbott; DPL, 263; Lightfoot, *Notes*). κληρονομία (# 3100) inheritance. ἀπολύτρωσις (# 667) redemption (s.v. 7). περιποίησις (# 4348) possessing, possession, that which is one's own (NIDNTT). ◆ 15 ἀκούσας aor. act. part. (temp.) ἀκούω s.v. 13. Aor. indicates antecedent action which is logically necessary before the action of the main vb., "after I heard." ἀγάπη (# 27) love (TLNT; TDNT). ◆ 16 παύομαι pres. ind. mid. (παύω) (# 4264) to cease. εὐχαριστῶν pres. act. part. εὐχαριστέω (# 2373) to give thanks. Compl. part. to complete the main vb. μνεία (# 3644) remembrance. ποιούμενος pres. mid. part. ποιέω (# 4472) to make. Used (often in mid.) w. the previous noun as a periphrasis for a verb, w. the sense "to make mention of," esp. in the sense of mentioning someone in prayer (BAGD). ◆ 17 ἵνα (# 2671) that; introduces the content of the prayer. δώῃ aor. opt. act. δίδωμι (# 3972) to give. The volitive opt. is used to express a wish or desire in prayer (RG, 939f). Perhaps an attributed gen., "spiritual revelation" (GGBB, 90-91). For the view that the form is subj. rather that opt. s. BD, 187. ἀποκαλύψεως (# 637) unveiling, revelation. ἐπίγνωσις (# 2106) recognition, knowledge. The word means knowledge directed toward a particular object: perceiving, discerning, recognizing. Gen. following the word denotes the object of the knowledge (Robinson, 254). ◆ 18 πεφωτισμένους perf. pass. part. φωτίζω (# 5894) to enlighten, to illuminate, to give light. The word was used in pagan initiation rites and also in the LXX for God's instruction (APM, 19; GELTS, 511). It refers to the ministry of the Holy Spirit who continually illuminates spiritual truth (1QS 2; Gnilka). Perf. points to the continuous process (Barth). The grammatical structure of the part. could be an anacoluthon, a third predicate of the main vb., or an acc. abs. (RWP). εἰδέναι perf. act. inf. οἶδα (# 3857) to know (ND, 344ff). Def. perf. w. pres. meaning. Inf. w. εἰς (# 1650) to express purp. κλήσεως (# 3104) calling.

◆ **19 ὑπερβάλλον** pres. act. part. (adj.) ὑπερβάλλω (# *5650*) to throw beyond, to exceed, to surpass. **μέγεθος** (# *3490*) greatness. **δυνάμεως** (# *1539*) power, ability. Here, gen. of description. **πιστεύοντας** pres. act. part. πιστεύω (# *4409*) to believe. Subst. part. in apposition to the preceding word–"those who believe." **ἐνέργεια** (# *1918*) working of ability (Schlier; Robinson; TDNT). **κράτος** (# *3197*) might, power. The word refers to strength regarded as abundantly effective in relation to an end to be gained or dominion to be exercised; to power, to overcome what stands in the way (Westcott; Lincoln; TDNT). Here, descriptive gen. or attributed gen. "surpassing greatness of his power" (GGBB, 90). **ἰσχύς** (# *2709*) strength, strength which one has, in possession, ability; or latent power (Eadie; Schlier). ◆ **20 ἐνήργησεν** aor. ind. act. ἐνεργέω (# *1919*) to be at work, to work effectually. **ἐγείρας** aor. act. part. ἐγείρω (# *1586*) to raise. **καθίσας** aor. act. part. (temp.) καθίζω (# *2767*) to cause to sit, to seat. Aor. gives a logically antecedent action. **δεξιᾷ** (# *1288*) right, right hand. Christ seated at the right hand is His place of honor and authority (David M. Hay, *Glory at the Right Hand: Psalm 110 in Early Christianity* [Nashville; Abingdon, 1973]; APM, 9-22; for a critical approach to this theme s. W.R.G. Loader, "Christ at the Right Hand - Ps. CX.1 in the New Testament," *NTS* 24 [1978]: 199-217). **ἐπουράνιος** (# *2230*) heaven, heavenly place (s.v. 3). ◆ **21 ὑπεράνω** (# *5645*) high above, far above. **ἀρχή** (# *794*) rule, ruler. **κυριότης** (# *3262*) lordship, dominion. In Jewish writings these terms were used to designate angelic powers and their ranks (SB, 3:581; Abbott; Barth). Ephesus was well known for its occult practice of magic (s. Acts 19:19; C.E. Arnold, *Ephesians, Power and Magic: The Concept of Power in Ephesians in the Light of its Historical Setting* [Cambridge: University Press, 1989]; Peter Lampe, "Acta 19 im Spiegel der ephesischen Inschriften," *BZ* 36 [1992]: 69-70]. **ὀνομαζομένου** pres. pass. part. ὀνομάζω (# *3951*) to name. **μέλλοντι** pres. act. part. dat. sing. masc. μέλλω (# *3516*) to be about to, coming. ◆ **22 ὑπέταξεν** aor. ind. act. ὑποτάσσω (# *5718*) to subject. **πόδας** acc. πούς (# *4546*) feet. This is a sign of total subjection. **ἔδωκεν** aor. ind. act. δίδωμι (# *3972*) to give. The vb. is followed by the indirect object "he gave Him as head over all things to the church." Rather than speaking only of Christ as being the Head of the church, Paul refers to the cosmic rule of Christ and implies that Christ is the sovereign head of all things (George Howard, "The Head-Body Metaphors of Ephesians," *NTS* 20 [1974]: 353f; DPL, 77-82, 377-78). ◆ **23 πληρουμένου** pres. mid./pass. part. πληρόω (# *4444*) to fill. Part. could be pass. (Robinson), or it could also be mid.: "the one who fills for himself" (George Howard, "The Head-Body Metaphors of Ephesians," *NTS* 20 [1974]: 351; Abbott).

Ephesians 2

◆ **1 ὄντας** pres. act. part. εἰμί (# *1639*) to be. Circum. or concessive part., "although." **παράπτωμα** (# *4183*) transgression (s. 1:7). Here, dat. could be causal or sphere: "dead because of transgressions" or "dead in transgressions" (s. Eph. 1:7). ◆ **2 αἷς** dat. fem. pl. ὅς (# *4005*) who, which. Strictly speaking the antecedent of the rel. pron. is ἁμαρτίαις (# *281*), but logically αἷς refers to both sins and transgressions. **ποτε** (# *4537*) at that time, formerly. It refers to one's preconversion time. **περιεπατήσατε** aor. ind. act. περιπατέω (# *4344*) to walk about, to conduct one's life. Const. aor. views from a point the total past life in summary fashion. **αἰών** (# *172*) age. To be taken as a synonym w. **κόσμος** (# *3180*) to indicate both temp. and spatial aspects of fallen existence (Lincoln; s. Gal. 1:4). **ἀέρος** gen. ἀήρ (# *113*) air, atmosphere, the realm in which the evil powers operate (Abbott; Barth; Hodge). Obj. gen., "power over the air." **πνεύματος** gen. πνεῦμα (# *4460*) spirit. Gen. is best understood as being in apposition to the words τῆς ἐξουσίας τοῦ ἀέρος (Ellicott; for the worship of the occult in Ephesus s. Eph. 1:21), or it could be gen. of subordination: "the ruler over the spirit" (GGBB, 100, 103-4) **ἀπείθεια** (# *577*) disobedience. The phrase "sons of disobedience" is a Hebraic expression indicating the chief characteristic is that of disobedience (BG, 16). ◆ **3 ἀνεστράφημεν** aor. ind. pass. ἀναστρέφω (# *418*) to conduct one's life. The word refers to the social action whereas the vb. περιεπατήσατε in v. 2 is used more of personal action (Westcott). **ἐπιθυμία** (# *2123*) desires, strong lust (DNP, 2:542-44; EDNT). **σαρκός** gen. σάρξ (# *4922*) flesh. Subjective gen. indicates the source of the desires. **ποιοῦντες** pres. act. part. ποιέω (# *4472*) to do, to make. **διάνοια** (# *1379*) understanding, intelligence, mind, disposition, thought (BAGD). **ἤμεθα** impf. ind. mid. (dep.) εἰμί (# *1639*) to be. **φύσις** (# *5882*) nature. **ὀργή** (# *3973*) wrath, anger (s. Rom. 1:18). Here, gen. of destination, "children destined for wrath" (GGBB, 101). ◆ **4 πλούσιος** (# *4454*) rich (s. Eph. 1:7). **ὤν** pres. act. part. εἰμί (# *1639*). Causal part., "because he is rich in mercy." **ἐλέει** dat. ἔλεος (# *1799*) mercy, compassion, pity. The word indicates the emotion aroused by someone in need and the attempt to relieve the person and remove his trouble (NIDNTT; TDNT; Trench, *Synonyms*, 166f; TLNT). **ἠγάπησεν** aor. ind. act. ἀγαπάω (# *26*) to love (TDNT; TLNT). ◆ **5 ὄντας** pres. act. part. acc. masc. pl. εἰμί (# *1639*) to be. Temp. part. ("even when") (Lincoln). **συνεζωοποίησεν** aor. ind. act. συζωοποιέω (# *5188*) to make alive together w. The word is a synonym for the vb. ἐγείρω but it can also have the meaning "to keep alive" or "to preserve life" (Barth). The words in compound w. **σύν** indicate the relationship between Christ and the believer, and the participation with Christ (Lincoln). **σεσωσμένοι** perf. pass. part. σῴζω (# *5392*) to rescue, to save. Perf. points to the completed action w. a continuing result, thus emphasizing the continual state or condition. ◆ **6 συνήγειρεν** aor. ind. act. συνεγείρω (# *5283*) to raise together w. Believers not only receive life, they experience a resurrection (Eadie). Aor. points to a specific event that has taken place. **συνεκά-θισεν** aor. ind. act. συνκαθίζω (# *5154*) to cause to sit down together w. another. **ἐπουράνιος** (# *2230*) heavenly, heavenly places (s. 1:3). ◆ **7 ἐνδείξηται** aor. subj. pass. ἐνδείκνυμι (# *1892*) to demonstrate, to display, to put on display, to show, to prove (Schnackenburg). In the papyri it could have a quasi-legal sense of proving a petition or charge, or of proving that a charge was wrong (MM; Preisigke, 1:484). Josephus used the word to describe Herod Agrippa´s display of generosity to those of other nations (Jos., *Ant.*, 19:330; also CCFJ, 2:97-98). Subj. w. ἵνα (# *2671*) to express purp. (MacArthur). **ἐπερχομένοις** pres. mid. (dep.) part. ἐπέρχομαι (# *2088*) to come upon, approaching. The times after the coming of the Lord are viewed as being already approaching (Meyer). **ὑπερβάλλον** pres. act. part. ὑπερβάλλω (# *5650*) to throw beyond, to exceed, to surpass. Part. is used in the sense of surpassing, extraordinary, outstanding (BAGD). Adj. part., exceeding wealth. **χρηστότης** (# *5983*) usefulness, goodness, kindness. The word involves the idea of the exercise of kindness toward another (Abbott; Trench, *Synonyms*, 232f; TDNT). ◆ **8 χάριτι** dat. sing. χάρις (# *5921*) grace. Instr. dat., "by grace." The definite article appears w. the word because it is the grace already mentioned (Abbott). **σεσωσμένοι** perf. pass. part. s.v. 5. **διὰ πίστεως** (# *4411*) through faith. The prep. indicates the channel through which salvation comes (Ellicott). Faith is not viewed as a positive work or accomplishment of the individual (Gaugler). **θεοῦ** (# *2536*) of God. The gen. is emphasized by its position before the noun and stands in emphatic contrast w. the personal pron. ὑμῶν (Abbott). ◆ **9 ἔργων** gen. pl. ἔργον (# *2240*) work, deed. Gen. of source, "not out of their works." **καυχήσηται** aor. subj. mid. (dep.) καυχάομαι (# *3016*) to boast, to glory. Subj. w. ἵνα (# *2671*) in a neg. purp cl. ◆ **10 ποίημα** (# *4473*) that which is made, work. The word can also have the connotation of a "work of art," esp. a poetic product, including fiction. In the LXX it refers to God's creation work (Barth; Lincoln). **κτισθέντες** aor. pass. part. κτίζω (# *3231*) to create. The word points to God's new creation in Christ. For this aspect of Paul's teaching against its Jewish background s. PRJ, 119ff. **ἐπί** (# *2093*) w. the dat., for. The prep. indicates the goal or purp. It primarily designates movement ending in a definite spot (IBG, 50). **ἔργοις ἀγαθοῖς** (# *2240; 19*) good works. W. the prep. the phrase indicates the goal (Schnackenburg). **προητοίμασεν** aor. ind. act. προετοιμάζω (# *4602*) to prepare beforehand. Aor. points to a specific act that has taken place. The prep. refers to a period before the

action described in the part. κτισθέντες, and describes the means by which the end is secured according to divine arrangement (Eadie). **περιπατήσωμεν** aor. subj. act. περιπατέω (# *4344*) to walk. Subj. w. ἵνα (# *2671*) in a purp. cl. ◆ **11 διό** (# *1475*) therefore. **μνημονεύετε** pres. act. imp. μνημονεύω (# *3648*) to remember. The word calls for repentance, decision, and gratitude (Barth). **ὅτι** (# *4022*) that, gives the content of what is to be remembered. **ποτέ** (# *4537*) formerly. **ἔθνη** pl. ἔθνος (# *1620*) nation; pl. Gentile, the non-Jewish world. **ἐν σαρκί** (# *1877; 4922*) in the flesh. The words suggest the external and temporary nature of the distinction (Robinson). **λεγόμενοι** pres. pass. part. λέγω (# *3306*) to call. **ἀκροβυστία** (# *213*) foreskin, uncircumcision. **περιτομή** (# *4364*) circumcision (TDNT; Barth; NIDNTT). **χειρο-ποίητος** (# *5935*) verbal adj. handmade. ◆ **12 ἦτε** impf. ind. act. εἰμί (# *1639*) to be. **καιρός** (# *2789*) time, season. Here, dat. of time. **χωρίς** (# *6006*) without. **ἀπηλ-λοτριωμένοι** perf. pass. part. ἀπαλλοτριόω (# *558*) to estrange, to alienate, to separate from (Lincoln). Perf. indicates the state or condition. **πολιτεία** (# *4486*) citizenship, state, commonwealth. It indicates the government of Israel framed by God in which religion and polity were joined (Eadie). **ξένος** (# *3828*) stranger followed by the gen of separation "strange to something" (BD, 98). **διαθήκη** (# *1347*) covenant, treaty. **ἐπαγγελία** (# *2039*) promise. **ἔχοντες** pres. act. part. ἔχω (# *2400*) to have. **ἄθεος** (# *117*) without God, godless, atheist. The prefix negates the stem of the word (Moorhouse, 47ff). Thus they were separated from the Messianic covenants and redemption that was to come from God through the Jews. ◆ **13 νυνὶ δέ** (# *3815; 1254*) but now; introduces a contrast to their previous state. **ὄντες** pres. act. part. (subst.) εἰμί, s.v. 1. **μακράν ... ἐγγύς** (# *3426; 1584*) adv. Far and near were used in rabbinical writings to indicate, among other things, non-Jew (far) and Jews (near), or those who were righteous and near God or those who were godless and far away (SB, 3:585-87). **ἐγενήθητε** aor. ind. pass. γίνομαι (# *1181*) to become. **αἷμα** (# *135*) blood. Here, instr. dat., "through the blood." For a discussion of Eph. 2:13-17 in the light of Isa. 52:7 and 57:19 s. APM, 23-55. ◆ **14 αὐτός** (# *899*) He himself. The pronoun is used to strengthen the contrast. **ἡ εἰρήνη** (# *1645*) peace. S. also DPL, 698-99. The article used w. the pred. noun presents the pres. as something well-known or which alone merits such designation; i.e., the only thing to be considered (BD, 143). **ποιήσας** aor. act. part. ποιέω (# *4472*) to make. **ἀμ-φότεροι** (# *317*) both; i.e., both Jews and Gentiles (Abbott). The n. is used if it is not the individual but a general quality that is to be emphasized (BD, 76). **μεσό-τοιχον** (# *3546*) middle wall, dividing wall. For a discussion of the various views concerning the middle wall s. Barth; Lincoln; Schnackenburg; BBC. The context identifies the wall in four ways: it is the fact of separation between Israel and the nations; it has to do w. the law and its statutes and interpretations; it is experienced in the enmity between Jews and Gentiles; it also consists of the enmity of Jews and Gentiles alike against God (Barth). **φραγμός** (# 5850) fence, partition. It signified originally a fence or railing erected for protection rather than separation (Barth). **λύσας** aor. act. part. λύω (# 3395) to loose, to destroy, to break down. Temp. or causal part. or of means. Aor. points to the completed action. It also points to a logically antecedent action to the main vb. **ἔχθρα** (# 2397) enmity, hostility. **σαρκί** dat. sing. (# 4922) s.v. 3. It can refer either to His death on the cross or his life on earth. ◆ **15 νόμος** (# 3795) law. Here it would refer to the Law of Moses. **ἐντολῶν** gen. pl. ἐντολή (# 1953) commandment **δόγμα** (# 1504) decree. The law consisted of, was in decrees. **καταργήσας** aor. act. part. καταργέω (# 2934) to invalidate, to nullify, to annul, to make of no effect (Simpson). Temp. or causal part. **κτίσῃ** aor. subj. act. κτίζω (# 3231) to create. In rabbinic Judaism a heathen coming to know God is as though he had been newly created by whoever helped him to attain knowledge of God (APM, 42). Subj. w. **ἵνα** (# 2671) to express purp. **ποιῶν** pres. act. part. (temp.) ποιέω (# 4472) to do. Part. of result (GGBB, 639). ◆ **16 ἀποκαταλλάξῃ** aor. subj. act. ἀποκαταλάσσω (# 639) to change, to exchange, to turn from hostility to friendship, to reconcile. The double prep. in compound may be intensive (Abbott; Barth; V; Rom. 5:10), or there may be a hint at a restoration to a primal unity (Ellicott; s. Col. 1:20). **σταύρος** (# 5089) cross. The term reveals two things: Christ's death is shameful, not honorable, among men; it corresponds to death on the gallows. In addition, it is an execution which bore God's curse (Barth). **ἀποκτείνας** aor. act. part. ἀποκτείνω (# 650) to put to death, to kill. Part. of means. Aor. expresses logically antecedent action to the main vb. ◆ **17 ἐλθών** aor. act. part. ἔρχομαι (# 2262) to come. Part. of means. Aor. indicates antecedent action. **εὐηγγελίσατο** aor. ind. mid. (dep.) εὐαγγελίζομαι (# 2294) to proclaim good news. ◆ **18 δι' αὐτοῦ** through Him. **ἔχομεν** pres. ind. act. ἔχω (# 2400) to have, to possess. Pres. indicates continual possession. **προσαγωγή** (# 4643) entrance, access. The word was used of a solemn, unhindered approach to a deity and of access to a king's presence (Simpson; Lincoln). **ἀμφότεροι** (# 317) s.v. 14. "We both," referring to those near and far. ◆ **19 ἄρα** (# 726) therefore. The word marks the progress in the argument and has a connective sense implying a consequence. The double particles (ἄρα οὖν) in combination are intended to imply logical connection, the one simply reinforcing the other, w. both used to sum up the argument of the whole section (Thrall, 11; Eadie). **οὐκέτι** (# 4033) no longer. **πάροικος** (# 4230) one living alongside, alien. A resident alien was subject to only a part of the law of the land and enjoyed only corresponding legal protection according to the OT meaning (Barth; TDOT under גֵּר *ger*; Lincoln). **συμπολίτης** (# 5232) fellow citizen. **οἰκεῖος** (# 3858) one's own household, family. When used of persons it means "of one's family," strictly of kinsmen, sometimes loosely of familiar friends (Robinson). It refers to all members regardless of social or personal position. ◆ **20 ἐποικοδομηθέντες** aor. pass. part. (adj.) ἐποικοδομέω (# 2224) to build upon. Theol. pass. indicating God as the one who is active. **θεμέλιος** (# 2529) foundation. **τῶν ἀποστόλων καὶ προφητῶν** of apostles and prophets. Gen. of apposition. For a summary of the discussion of the grammar s. GGBB, 284-86. **ὄντος** pres. act. part. gen. masc. sing. εἰμί (# 1639) to be. **ἀκρογωνιαῖος** (# 214) foundation stone, cornerstone, keystone. The word could refer either to the cornerstone or to the keystone in an archway (TDNT; Lincoln; 1 Pet 2:6). ◆ **21 οἰκοδομή** (# 3869) building. **συναρμολογουμένη** pres. pass. part. συναρμολογέω (# 5274) to fit together. In construction terms it represents the whole of the elaborate process by which stones are fitted together: the preparation of the surfaces, including the cutting, rubbing, and testing; the preparation of the dowels and dowel holes, and finally the fitting of the dowels w. molten lead (Robinson, 262). **αὔξει** pres. ind. act. αὐξάνω (# 889) to increase, to grow. Pres. indicates the continual development, "is continuing to grow and develop." Though the building is structurally complete, it continues to grow w. the addition of individual stones. **ναός** (# 3724) temple, inner sanctuary. This is the result of the growth (Gaugler; DPL, 925). ◆ **22 συνοικοδομεῖσθε** pres. ind. pass. συνοικοδομέω (# 5325) to build together; pass., to be built together, i.e., together w. the others. Pres. is used because the building is still going on (Abbott). **κατοικητήριον** (# 2999) place of dwelling, a place of settling down. For the suf. indicating place or locality s. MH, 343. The prep. indicates the goal or intention.

Ephesians 3

◆ **1 τούτου χάριν** because of this, on account of this, for this reason. The reference is not only to building God's house on a firm foundation, but also to the unification of Jews and Gentiles (Barth). **δέσμιος** (# 1300) prisoner. Prisoners often had time to think, read, write, etc. (BAFCS, 3:323-67; CIC, 66-75; DPL, 752-54). **ἐθνῶν** pl. ἔθνος (# 1620) people, nation, pl. Gentile. ◆ **2 εἴ γε** (# 1145, 1623) if indeed, surely. The particles here are used to express assurance (Thrall, 87f). **ἠκούσατε** aor. ind. act. ἀκούω (# 201) to hear. Ind. in a 1st. class cond. cl. which assumes the reality of the cond. **οἰκονομία** (# 3873) administration, responsibility, management of a household. The term was used of the administrative responsibility given to a servant over a household (TLNT; TDNT). **χάριτος** gen. sing. χάρις

(# 5921) grace. Gen. gives the content of the responsibility. **δοθείσης** aor. pass. part. (adj.) δίδωμι (# 3972) to give. Theol. pass. indicating God is the giver. **εἰς ὑμᾶς** for you; i.e., for your benefit. ◆ **3 κατά** (# 2848) w. the acc., according to. Used here in an adverbial sense: "by way of revelation" to express the mode of the making known (Meyer). **ἀποκάλυψις** (# 637) unveiling, revealing, revelation. **ἐγνωρίσθη** aor. ind. pass. γνωρίζω (# 1192) to make known. **μυστήριον** (# 3696) mystery, that which a human being cannot know but which is revealed by God (TDNT; ZPEB, 4:327-30). **προέγραψα** aor. ind. act. προγράφω (# 4592) to write beforehand. It refers to the previous part of this letter (Schlier). **ἐν ὀλίγῳ** (# 1877; 3900) in a few words, in brief. ◆ **4 πρὸς ὅ** to that which, w. reference to; "w. reference to what I have said" (Abbott; Barth). **ἀναγινώσκοντες** pres. act. part. ἀναγινώσκω (# 336) to read. Temp. part., "when you read." Pres. shows contemporaneous action. **νοῆσαι** aor. act. inf. νοέω (# 3783) to perceive, to come to the knowledge of, to apprehend, to understand, to gain an insight into (BAGD). Supplementary inf w. the vb. **δύνασθε** pres. poss. ind. δύναμαι (# 1538) to be able. **σύνεσις** (# 5304) understanding, insight. ◆ **5 γενεά** (# 1155) generation. Dat. here could be dat. of time ("in other generations" [Robinson]) or it could be dat. of indirect object ("to other generation" [Barth]). **ἀπεκαλύφθη** aor. ind. pass. ἀποκαλύπτω (# 1192) to unveil, to reveal. ◆ **6 εἶναι** pres. act. inf. εἰμί (# 1639) to be. Epex. inf. explaining the content of the divine revelation. **συγκληρονόμος** (# 5169) fellow heir. **σύσσωμος** (# 5362) fellow members of a body, belonging to the same body. **συμμέτοχος** (# 5212) fellow partaker, co-sharer. The word was used in the papyri of those who were joint possessors of a house (MM; for the vb. s. NDIEC, 3:85-86). **ἐπαγγελία** (# 2039) promise. ◆ **7 ἐγενήθην** aor. ind. pass. (dep.) γίνομαι (# 1181) to become. **κατά** (# 2848) w. the acc., s.v. 3. **χάριτος** (# 1561) gift, followed by the gen. of apposition (Eadie) or the gen. of source. **δοθείσης** aor. pass. part. δίδωμι (# 3972) to give. Divine pass. indicting God as the agent. **ἐνέργεια** (# 1918) working, effectual working (Robinson). **δυνάμεως** gen. sing. δύναμις (# 1539) power. Gen. of description. ◆ **8 ἐλαχιστοτέρῳ** (# 1788) dat. comp. of the superl. ἐλάχιστος (BAGD) less than the least; "the smallester," "leaster" (Barth; GGBB, 302). The form was used to designate the deepest self-abasement (Eadie). Paul may be making an allusion to his own name (Simpson). For the form s. BD, 34. **ἐδόθη** aor. ind. pass. δίδωμι (# 3972) to give. Theol. pass. indicating that God is the giver. **εὐαγγελίσασθαι** aor. mid. (dep.) inf. εὐαγγελίζω (# 2294) to proclaim the good news, to preach the gospel. Inf. of purp. **ἀνεξιχνίαστος** (# 453) not able to track out, untraceable (s. Rom. 11:33). ◆ **9 φωτίσαι** aor. act. inf. φωτίζω (# 5894) to illuminate, to bring into light, to shed light upon. Inf. of purp. **ἀποκεκρυμμένου** perf.

pass. part. ἀποκρύπτω (# 648) to hide. Perf. part. indicates the state or condition, "that which was hidden." **κτίσαντι** aor. act. part. (adj.) κτίζω (# 3231) to create. ◆ **10 γνωρισθῇ** aor. subj. pass. γνωρίζω (# 1192) s.v. 3. Subj. w. ἵνα (# 2671) to express. purp. **ἐπουράνιος** (# 2230) heavenly (s. 1:3). **πολυποίκιλος** (# 4497) many-sided, variegated, very varied. The word was used to describe robes or hems (Robinson). ◆ **11 πρόθεσις** (# 4606) purpose, design. Gen. following the word could be descriptive gen. ("eternal purp."), poss. gen. ("the purpose that runs through the ages") [Abbott]); or it could be obj. gen., "purpose about the ages," "the design concerning the ages." For this view and a discussion of other views s. Barth. **ἐποίησεν** aor. ind. act. ποιέω (# 4472) to make, to do. Aor. points to the completion of the act, "to accomplish." ◆ **12 παρρησία** (# 4244) speaking freely, confidence, boldness. **προσαγωγή** (# 4643) entrance, access (s. 2:18). **πεποίθησις** (# 4301) having been persuaded, confidence. ◆ **13 διό** (# 1475) therefore. **αἰτοῦμαι** pres. ind. mid. (dep.) αἰτέω (# 160) to ask, to request. **ἐγκακεῖν** pres. act. inf. ἐγκακέω (# 1591) to give to evil, to be a coward, to be discouraged, to grow weary. **θλίψεσιν** dat. pl. θλῖψις (# 2568) pressure, tribulation, trouble. ◆ **14 κάμπτω** pres. ind. act. (# 2828) to bow. **γόνατα** acc. pl. γόνυ (# 1205) knee. For a discussion of the position of kneeling in prayer s. Barth. ◆ **15 πατριά** (# 4255) family, descendant from a common father. It always refers to a concrete group of people. For a discussion of the meaning of the term in this passage s. Barth; SB, 3:594. **ὀνομάζεται** pres. ind. pass. ὀνομάζω (# 3951) to name, to give a name to a thing. To have a family name indicated the possessing of all the rights and responsibilities belonging to that family. ◆ **16 δῷ** aor. subj. act. δίδωμι (# 3972) to give. Subj. w. ἵνα (# 2671) to give the content of Paul's prayer. **δυνάμει** dat. δύναμις power. Here, (# 1539) w. power, w. infused strength; instr. dat. (Ellicott; Abbott). **κραταιωθῆναι** aor. pass. inf. κραταιόω (# 3194) to strengthen, to fortify, to brace, to invigorate (Simpson; s. 1:19). **ἔσω** (# 2276) inner. ◆ **17 κατοικῆσαι** aor. act. inf. κατοικέω (# 2997) to dwell, to live in, to settle down. The vb. denotes permanent habitation as opposed to sojourning or an occasional visit (Barth). Inf. used as a type of apposition explaining the previous inf. (Schlier). **ἐρριζωμένοι** perf. pass. part. ῥιζόω (# 4845) to cause to take root; pass., to be or to become firmly rooted or fixed (BAGD). Perf. looks at the continuing state or condition. **τεθεμελιωμένοι** perf. pass. part. θεμελιόω (# 2530) to lay a foundation, to establish, to strengthen. The reference is the solid basement of the spiritual temple described in chapter 2 (Eadie). ◆ **18 ἐξισχύσητε** aor. subj. act. ἐξισχύω (# 2015) to be able, to be fully able, to be strong enough. Subj. w. ἵνα (# 2671) to express the content of the parallel prayer in v. 16. Prep. in compound is perfective and indicates a strength exerted till its object is attained (MH, 310). **καταλαβέσθαι** aor. mid. inf. καταλαμβάνω (# *2898*) to grasp mentally, to comprehend (Abbott). **πλάτος** breadth, width (# *4424*). **μῆκος** (# *3601*) length. **ὕψος** (# *5737*) height. **βάθος** (# *958*) depth. Each term refers fig. to God's love (GGBB, 286). ◆ **19 γνῶναί** aor. act. inf. γινώσκω (# *1182*) to know. **ὑπερβάλλουσαν** pres. act. part. ὑπερβάλλω (# *5650*) to throw beyond, to excel, to surpass. **πληρωθῆτε** aor. subj. pass. πληρόω (# *4444*) to fill. ◆ **20 δυ-ναμένῳ** pres. pass. (dep.) part. δύναμαι (# *1538*) to be able. Part. used as a noun. Dat. of advantage. Pres. describes a continuing trait. **ποιῆσαι** aor. act. inf. ποιέω (# *4472*) to do, to accomplish. Compl. inf. to the preceding part. **ὑπερεκπερισσοῦ** (# *5655*) superabundantly, quite beyond all measure, greatly exceeding all boundaries. The form is used as the highest form of comparison imaginable (BAGD). **αἰτούμεθα** pres. ind. mid. (dep.) αἰτέω (# *160*) to ask. **νοοῦμεν** pres. ind. act. νοέω (# *3783*) to understand (s.v. 4). **ἐνερ-γουμένην** pres. mid. (dep.) part. ἐνεργέομαι (# *1919*) to be active, to be effective (Robinson). ◆ **21 γενεά** generation (# *1155*). **ἀμήν** (# *297*) truly. Used after a statement to add confirmation (TDNT).

Ephesians 4

◆ **1 παρακαλῶ** pres. ind. act. παρακαλέω (# *4151*) to beseech, to exhort, to encourage. The word signifies a will of the writer that is at the same time warm, personal, and urgent (Barth; TDNT; NTW). **οὖν** (# *4036*) therefore. **δέσμιος** (# *1300*) prisoner. **ἀξίως** (# *547*) adv., worthily. The basic meaning of the word is, "that which balances the scales," "equivalent" (TDNT). **περι-πατῆσαι** aor. act. inf. περιπατέω (# *4344*) to walk about, to conduct one's life. Compl. inf. is used to express the content of Paul's urging. **ἧς** gen. sing. ὅς (# *4005*) who, which rel. pron. by attraction to its antecedent (RWP). **ἐκλήθητε** aor. ind. pass. καλέω (# *3104*) to call. ◆ **2 τα-πεινοφροσύνη** (# *5425*) lowly thinking, humility. The word refers to the quality of esteeming ourselves as small but at the same time recognizing the power and ability of God (TDNT; Trench, *Synonyms*, 148; NIDNTT; EDNT; RAC, 3:735ff). **πραΰτης** (# *4559*) meek, gentle. The humble and gentle attitude which expresses itself in a patient submissiveness to offense, free from malice and desire for revenge (s. Matt. 5:5; TDNT; NIDNTT; Gal. 5:22). **μακροθυμία** (# *3429*) long-suffering (s. Gal. 5:22). **ἀνεχόμενοι** pres. mid. (dep.) part. ἀνέχομαι (# *462*) to bear, to bear up, to hold oneself up. The word indicates giving patience to someone till the provocation is past (Eadie). Perhaps a part. of means (GGBB, 652). **ἀλλήλων** (# *253*) one another. ◆ **3 σπουδάζοντες** pres. act. part. σπουδάζω (# *5079*) to give diligence, to be eager, to make every effort. Part. of manner explaining how to conduct one's life. **τηρεῖν** pres. act. inf. τηρέω (# *5498*) to guard, to keep, to main-

tain (Schlier). Compl. inf. explaining the effort. **ἑνότης** (# *1942*) unity. **πνεύματος** gen. sing. πνεῦμα (# *4460*) Spirit. Subjective gen., indicating the source or agent producing the unity. **σύνδεσμος** (# *5278*) that which binds together, a bond. The word denotes that which keeps something together (Barth). ◆ **4 καθώς** (# *2777*) just as. **ἐκλήθητε** aor. ind. pass. καλέω (# *2813*) to call. **ἐλπίδι** dat. ἐλπίς (# *1828*) hope (EH, 598-601). **κλήσεως** gen. sing. κλῆσις (# *3104*) calling. Gen. of source, indicating that the hope arises fr. the calling. ◆ **5 βάπτισμα** (# *967*) baptism. It could refer to the baptism of the Spirit which places the believer in Christ, thus forming the body of Christ, the church. ◆ **6 εἷς** (# *1651*) one. ◆ **7 ἑκάστῳ** dat. sing. ἕκαστος (# *1667*) each. Dat. of the indir. obj. **ἐδόθη** aor. ind. pass. δίδωμι (# *3972*) to give. Theol.pass. **χάρις** (# *5921*) grace. Unity is not uniformity, but is quite consistent w. a variety of gifts and offices in the church (Eadie). **μέτρον** (# *3586*) measure. **δωρεά** (# *1561*) gift. ◆ **8 διό** (# *1475*) therefore [he says]. This formula introduces a citation from the OT and is characterized by the absence of a legalistic and polemic undertone. It is an urgent invitation to listen attentively (Barth; BE, 107ff). For a discussion of this section in relation to Ps. 68:18 s. APM, 56-86. **ἀναβάς** aor. act. part. (temp.) ἀναβαίνω (# *326*) to ascend, to go up. **ὕψος** (# *5737*) height. **ᾐχμαλώτευσεν** aor. ind. act. αἰχμαλω-τεύω (# *169*) to lead captive. The allusion is to a triumphal possession in which marched the captives taken in war (Eadie; Lincoln; 2 Cor. 2:14; W. Hall Harris III, *The Descent of Christ in Ephesians 4:7-11: An Exegetical Investigation with Special Reference to the Influence of Traditions About Moses Associated with Psalm 68:19* [Leiden: E.J. Brill, 1996]. For DSS and Jewish parallels s. APM, 60-63). **ἔδωκεν** aor. ind. act. δίδωμι (# *3972*) to give. ◆ **9 ἀνέβη** aor. ind. act. ἀναβαίνω (# *326*) to go up, to ascend. **κατέβη** aor. ind. act. καταβαίνω (# *2849*) to go down, to descend. **κατώτερος** (# *3005*) the lower parts, the lower regions. **γῆς** gen. γῆ earth. (# *1178*). "Of the earth," possibly a gen. of apposition (GGBB, 99-100, 112). The reference could be to the Incarnation and Christ's coming to earth (RWP; Barth; Hodge). ◆ **10 καταβάς** aor. act. part. καταβαίνω s.v. 9. **ὑπεράνω** (# *5645*) w. the gen., high above. **πληρώσῃ** aor. subj. act. πληρόω (# *4444*) to fill. Subj. w. ἵνα (# *2671*) to express purp. ◆ **11 ἔδωκεν** aor. ind. act. δίδωμι (# *3972*) to give. For a discussion of gifts s. DPL, 339-47. **ἀπόστολος** (# *693*) apostle. Those appointed by Jesus to be His official representatives (s. Rom. 1:1). **τοὺς μὲν ... τοὺς δέ** the one ... the other. **εὐαγγελιστής** (# *2296*) one who proclaims the good news, evangelist. An evangelist was one who proclaimed the gospel which he had received from the apostle. He was in particular a missionary who brought the gospel into new regions (Schlier; Barth; BBC; TDNT; NIDNTT; TLNT). **ποιμένας** acc. pl. ποιμήν (# *4478*) shepherd, pastor. The image of a shepherd w. his flock pictures the relation of a spiritual leader to those committed to his charge (Eadie). καί (# 2779) and. Often the word has the meaning "that is" or "in particular" and indicates that the shepherds and teachers are viewed as one common group; i.e., teaching shepherds (Barth; also GGBB, 284). διδάσκαλος (# 1437) teacher. ◆ 12 καταρτισμός (# 2938) equipping, qualification. The word was a medical t.t. for the setting of a bone (BAGD; for the vb. s. TLNT). The noun describes the dynamic act by which persons or things are properly conditioned (Barth; Lincoln). οἰκοδομή (# 3869) building, building up, edification. The word is an expression of development (Meyer). ◆ 13 μέχρι (# 3588) until, used to give the goal. καταντήσωμεν aor. subj. act. καταντάω (# 2918) to come to, to arrive at, to reach, to attain to, to come down to the goal. Subj. is used in an indef. temp. cl. w. a purp. idea (RWP). ἑνότης (# 1942) unity. ἐπίγνωσις (# 2106) knowledge, knowledge directed toward a particular object (Robinson). τέλειος (# 5455) that which has reached the set goal, perfect, mature. For a discussion of the various views regarding the perfect man s. Barth; Lincoln; DPL, 699-701. ἡλικία (# 3586) age, full age, ripeness of full age. The word can also mean development in stature but is best understood as mature age (Eadie; Abbott). πλήρωμα (# 4445) fullness. ◆ 14 μηκέτι (# 3600) no longer. ὦμεν pres. subj. act. εἰμί (# 1639) to be. Subj. w. ἵνα (# 2671) to express purp. νήπιος (# 3758) baby, immature. It refers to the immaturity of children compared to the perfection of the perfect man (Barth). κλυδωνιζόμενοι pres. pass. part. κλυδωνίζομαι (# 3115) to be driven by waves, to be agitated by waves (RWP). περιφερόμενοι pres. pass. part. περιφέρω (# 4367) to carry about, to carry around, to be borne to and fro. For this figure of speech s. Abbott; Lincoln. ἀνέμῳ dat. ἄνεμος (# 449) wind. Instr. dat. διδασκαλία (# 1436) teaching. Here, descriptive gen. or gen. of apposition (GGBB, 94f). κυβεία (# 3235) dice playing, cunning. It means wicked dice playing and refers to intentional fraud (BAGD; Barth; Ellicott; Lincoln). ἀνθρώπων gen. ἄνθρωπος (# 476) human being. Subjective gen. ("dice playing by men") or gen. of description ("human treachery"). πανουργία (# 4111) cleverness, trickery. μεθοδεία (# 3497) following after, deceit, scheming (RWP; Barth). πλάνη (# 4415) wandering, roaming. Used figuratively of wandering from the path of truth: error, delusion, deceit (BAGD). Descriptive gen. ◆ 15 ἀληθεύοντες pres. act. part. ἀληθεύω (# 238) to be truthful, to tell the truth, to deal truly. Vbs. ending in this suf. express the doing of an action signified by the corresponding noun (Abbott). With this vb. the relationship of quality passes to that of action (MH, 399). αὐξήσωμεν aor. subj. act. αὐξάνω (# 889) to grow, to increase. πάντα acc. πᾶς (# 4246) all. Acc. of general reference, "in respect to all things." It may, however, be

viewed adverbially: in every way, totally (Barth). κεφαλή (# 3051) head. ◆ 16 συναρμολογούμενον pres. pass. part. συναρμολογέω (# 5274) to join together, to fit together (s. 2:21). συμβιβαζόμενον pres. pass. part. συμβιβάζω (# 5204) to bring together by sinews, ligaments, joints (BAGD). It refers to a correlation as of a functioning organism (Simpson). ἁφή (# 913) joint, contact, touching; contact w. the supply (Abbott). ἐπιχορηγία (# 2221) supply. Here subjective gen. (Lincoln). The simple noun originally indicated a payment for the cost of bringing out a chorus at a public festival. Then it signified provisions for an army or expedition. The word. w. the prep. in compound was a t.t. describing the provision of food, clothing, etc., which a husband is obligated to make for his wife. Here it indicates that the body receives from the head what nourishment, life, and direction it needs (Barth; Robinson). ἐνέργεια (# 1918) function. It refers to the working process (Robinson). αὔξησις (# 890) growing, growth. ποιεῖται pres. ind. mid. ποιέω (# 4472) to do. Mid. is used of the body promoting its own growth (Abbott; BAGD). ◆ 17 μαρτύρομαι pres. ind. mid. (dep.) (# 3458) to testify, to bear witness. περιπατεῖν pres. act. inf. περιπατέω (# 4344) to walk about, to conduct one's life. Inf. is used either to express a command or as obj. of the vb. Pres. points to a habitual action. καθώς (# 2777) just as. ἔθνη pl. ἔθνος (# 1620) people, nation; pl., Gentiles, heathen, those who were not Jews. ματαιότης (# 3470) vanity, emptiness. The word contains the idea of aimlessness, the leading to no object or end (Trench, Synonyms, 180-84; TDNT). For the Jewish indictment of the Gentiles s. Barth; SB, 3:600; JPF, 2:106ff). νοῦς (# 3808) mind, thinking facility, reasoning capacity. ◆ 18 ἐσκοτωμένοι perf. pass. part. σκοτόω (# 5031) to darken. Perf. part. is used in a periphrastic construction indicating the continuing darkened condition. διανοίᾳ (# 1379) thinking through, understanding, intelligence, the mind as the organ of thinking (BAGD). ὄντες pres. act. part. εἰμί (# 1639) to be. ἀπηλλοτριωμένοι perf. pass. part. ἀπαλλοτριόω (# 558) to estrange, to alienate. Perf. emphasizes the continuing state or existence: being alienated from the life of God. It does not imply that they had at one time enjoyed that life; it means simply being aliens from it (Robinson). ἄγνοια (# 53) ignorance, lack of knowledge. It refers to the inability to comprehend and see the light (Barth). πώρωσις (# 4801) hardening (RWP; NIDNTT; Barth). οὖσαν pres. act. part. acc. fem. sing. εἰμί (# 1639). ◆ 19 ἀπηλγηκότες perf. act. part. ἀπαλγέω (# 556) to cease to feel pain or grief, to become callous, insensible to pain (T). The translation "past feeling" expresses the sense accurately (Abbott). The lack of moral feeling and discernment means the inability to exercise any restraint (Lincoln). παρέδωκαν aor. ind. act. παραδίδωμι (# 4140) to deliver over to, to hand over to. ἀσελγείᾳ (# 816) unrestrained living (s. Gal. 5:19). ἐργασία

(# 2238) working, producing, performance, practice (Robinson). ἀκαθαρσία (# 174) uncleanness, filthiness, impurity (Barth). πλεονεξία (# 4432) insatiable craving greed, consuming ambition, giving rein to appetites and desires which are against the laws of God and man (NTW, 99; Barth; TDNT; TLNT; s. Rom. 1:29). ◆ **20** ἐμάθετε aor. ind. act. μανθάνω (# 3443) to learn. Χριστός (# 5986) Christ. Just as a Jew learned the Torah, now the Christian learns Christ (Lincoln). ◆ **21** ἠκούσατε aor. ind. act. ἀκούω (# 201) to hear. ἐδιδάχθητε aor. ind. pass. διδάσκω (# 1438) to teach; pass., to be taught. ◆ **22** ἀποθέσθαι aor. mid. (dep.) inf. ἀποτίθημι (# 700) to put off, to remove as one puts off clothes. Epex. inf. explaining the teaching, or inf. as imp. The change of clothes imagery signifies an exchange of identities (Lincoln; GGBB, 605). Inf. is used to denote the substance of what they had been taught (Eadie). Aor. denotes a once and for all, definite, concluding action: the stripping off is to be done at once, and for good (Barth). ἀναστροφή (# 419) manner of life (s. 2:3). παλαιός (# 4094) old. φθειρόμενον pres. pass. part. φθείρω (# 5780) to corrupt. The whole character representing the former self was not only corrupt but growing ever more and more corrupt. This is indicated by the pres. (Westcott). Every trait of the old man's behavior is putrid, crumbling, or inflated like rotting waste or cadavers, stinking, ripe for being disposed of and forgotten (Barth). ἐπιθυμία (# 2123) strong desire, lust (DNP, 2:542-44). ἀπάτη (# 573) deceit. ◆ **23** ἀνανεοῦσθαι pres. pass. inf. ἀνανεόω (# 391) to make new again, to renew. Pres. emphasizes the continuing renewing. Epex. inf. or inf. as imp. ◆ **24** ἐνδύσασθαι aor. mid. (dep.) inf. ἐνδύομαι (# 1907) to put on. Often used in the sense of putting on a garment. This inf. gives the positive side of v. 22, the obj. of what they were taught. κτισθέντα aor. pass. part. κτίζω (# 3231) to create. ὁσιότης (# 4009) piety, holiness. It indicates fulfilling the divine demands which God places upon men (NIDNTT; TDNT; Ellicott). ἀλήθεια (# 237) truth. Here, gen. of description, "genuine holiness." ◆ **25** ἀποθέμενοι aor. mid. (dep.) part. ἀποτίθημι, s.v. 22. ψεῦδος (# 6022) lie. The sing. w. the article indicates a collective sense (Lincoln). λαλεῖτε pres. imp. act. λαλέω (# 3281) to speak. Pres. imp. points to a habitual action which is to characterize the life. πλησίον (# 4446) one who is close by, neighbor. ἀλλήλων (# 253) one another. μέλη pl. μέλος (# 3517) member. For the relation of this v. to Zech. 8:16 s. APM, 88-89. ◆ **26** ὀργίζεσθε pres. imp. pass. (dep.) ὀργίζομαι (# 3974) to be angry. For a refutation of the classification of the imp. as cond. s. GGBB, 491-92. A quotation from Ps. 4:5 (LXX; s. APM, 89-90). ἁμαρτάνετε pres. imp. act. ἁμαρτάνω (# 279) to sin. μή (# 3590) w. imp. forms a prohibition. ἐπιδυέτω pres. imp. act. ἐπιδύω (# 2115) to go down, to set. For the relation of this v. to Ps. 4:26b and Deut.

24:15 s. APM, 90-91. The day of anger should be the day of reconciliation (Barth). παροργισμός (# 4240) anger, angry mood; a violent irritation is meant, expressed by either hiding oneself from others or by flaming looks, harmful words, inconsiderate actions (Barth). ◆ **27** δίδοτε pres. imp. act. δίδωμι (# 3972) to give. τόπος (# 5536) place; here in the sense of place in your life or opportunity. διάβολος (# 1333) slanderer, devil (DDD, 463-73). Here, dat. indir. obj.–"an opportunity to" or "for the devil." ◆ **28** κλέπτων pres. act. part. κλέπτω (# 3096) to steal. Pres. part. indicates the continuous action, "the one stealing." Part. used as a noun, emphasizing this action as a character trait. μηκέτι (# 3600) no longer. κλεπτέτω pres. imp. act. (# 3096). Pres. imp. w. the neg. calls for the stopping of an action in progress. κοπιάτω pres. imp. act. κοπιάω (# 3159) to grow weary, to work w. effort, to labor (S). For the relation of this v. to Lev. 19:11 s. APM, 91-92. ἐργαζόμενος pres. mid. (dep.) part. ἐργάζομαι (# 2237) to work. Pres. indicates a contemporaneous action. Temp. part. "while working." ἔχῃ pres. subj. act. ἔχω (# 2400) to have. Subj. w. ἵνα (# 2671) used in a purp. cl. μεταδιδόναι pres. act. inf. μεταδίδωμι (# 3556) to give w., to share. Inf. to express purp. or result. χρεία (# 5970) need, necessity. ἔχοντι pres. act. part. dat. masc. sing. ἔχω (# 2400) to have. Subst. use of the pres. part. to indicate the contemporary trait as a characteristic. For the concept of sharing among the members of the Dead Sea community s. CD, 14:12f. ◆ **29** σαπρός (# 4911) rank, foul, putrid, rotten, worthless, disgusting (Simpson; Abbott). ἐκπορευέσθω pres. mid. (dep.) imp. ἐκπορεύομαι (# 1744) to go out, to come out. οἰκοδομή (# 3869) building, edification. δῷ aor. subj. act. δίδωμι (# 3972) to give. Subj. w. ἵνα (# 2671) to express purp. χάρις (# 5921) grace. Used w. this vb. it means to confer a favor, to give pleasure or profit. The meaning is, "that it may benefit the hearers" (Hodge). ἀκούουσιν pres. act. part. ἀκούω (# 201) to hear. ◆ **30** λυπεῖτε pres. imp. act. λυπέω (# 3382) to cause sorrow, to grieve. Pres. imp. w. the neg. μή (# 3590) is used to forbid a continual and habitual action. The Spirit who makes men attest to the truth is put to shame when the saints lie to one another and utter foul talk (Barth). For the relation of this v. to Isa. 63:10 s. APM, 92-93. ἐσφραγίσθητε aor. ind. pass. σφραγίζω (# 5381) to seal (s. 1:13). ἀπολύτρωσις (# 667) release through the payment of a price, redemption (s. Rom. 3:24). ◆ **31** πικρία (# 4394) bitterness. It is a figurative term denoting that fretted and irritable state of mind that keeps a man in perpetual animosity; that inclines him to harsh and uncharitable opinions of men and things; that makes him sour, crabby, and repulsive in his general demeanor; that brings a scowl over his face and infuses the words of his tongue w. venom (Eadie). θυμός (# 2596) anger. It expresses the temporary excitement or passion (Abbott;

Trench, *Synonyms*, 130f). ὀργή (# *3973*) wrath. It refers to the more subtle and deep-flowing anger (Abbott; Trench, *Synonyms*, 130f; TDNT). κραυγή (# *3199*) clamor, outcry, shouting. It is the cry of strife (Ellicott). βλασφημία (# *1060*) slander, speaking evil of someone. It is a more enduring manifestation of inward anger that shows itself in reviling (TLNT). These two words are the outward manifestation of the foregoing vices (Ellicott). ἀρθήτω aor. imp. pass. αἴρω (# *149*) to pick up and carry away, to take away, to make a clean sweep (RWP). κακία (# *2798*) malice, badness. It is a generic term that seems to signify "badhardiness," the root of all those vices (Eadie). ◆ **32** γίνεσθε pres. imp. mid. (dep.) γίνομαι (# *1181*) to become. χρηστός (# *5982*) useful, worthy, good, kind, benevolent (BAGD; TDNT; NIDNTT; Gal. 5:22). εὔσπλαγχνος (# *2359*) tenderhearted, compassionate. In the lit. and physical sense, "having healthy bowels." The inward organs were considered the seat of emotion and intention (Barth; TDNT; s. 1 Peter 3:8). χαριζόμενοι pres. mid. (dep.) part. χαρίζομαι (# *5919*) to forgive, to exercise grace in freely forgiving (TDNT; EDNT). καθώς (# *2777*) just as. ἐχαρίσατο aor. imp. mid. (dep.) χαρίζομαι to show grace by providing undeserved help to someone unworthy (TDNT; EDNT).

Ephesians 5

◆ **1** γίνεσθε pres. imp. mid. (dep.) γίνομαι (# *1181*) to become. Pres. imp. suggests way of life. μιμηταί pl. μιμητής (# *3629*) imitator. The following gen. describes whom to imitate. ἀγαπητά pl. ἀγαπητός (# *28*) beloved. ◆ **2** περιπατεῖτε pres. imp. act. περιπατέω (# *4344*) to walk about, to conduct one's life. Pres. imp. calls for habitual action. ἐν in. καθώς (# *2777*) just as. ἠγάπησεν aor. ind. act. ἀγαπάω (# *26*) to love (TLNT; TDNT; s. John 3:16). παρέδωκεν aor. ind. act. παραδίδωμι (# *4140*) to deliver over. Vb. expresses wherein his love was shown (Abbott; TLNT). ἑαυτοῦ (# *1571*) himself, a reflexive pronoun with the object and the subject being the same. προσφορά (# *4714*) offering. The word generally denotes offerings which consist of products from the field and trees (Barth). θυσία (# *2602*) sacrifice. The word describes the offering of animals from the flock or stable which were killed at the holy place and portions of which were burned upon the altar (Barth) ὀσμή (# *4011*) smell. εὐωδία (# *2380*) sweet odor, fragrance. The phrase "odor of fragrance" is a fig. designation for the acceptableness of the offering (Meyer). ◆ **3** πορνεία (# *4518*) illicit sexual activity (TLNT). ἀκαθαρσία (# *174*) uncleanness, impurity, filthiness (s. 4:19). πλεονεξία (# *4432*) greediness (s. 4:19). μηδέ (# *3593*) emphatic neg., not even. ὀνομαζέσθω pres. imp. pass. ὀνομάζω (# *3951*) to name; pass., to be named. Here, "let it not even be mentioned by name" (Ellicott). πρέπει pres. ind. act. πρέπω (# *4560*) to be fitting, to be proper. The

standard of that which is fitting to their position as saints. ◆ **4** αἰσχρότης (# *157*) shameful conduct (Abbott; Barth). μωρολογία (# *3703*) foolish talk, silly talk. It is that talk of fools which is foolishness and sin together (Trench, *Synonyms*, 121), a mere laugh aimed at even without wit (Bengel). εὐτραπελία (# *2365*) coarse jesting. It implies the dexterity of turning a discourse to wit or humor that ends in deceptive speech, so formed that the speaker easily contrives to wriggle out of its meaning or engagement (Eadie). After a banquet the guests would sit and talk making jokes; often there was a jester (*scurra, coprea*) who knew how to make plays on words (LLAR, 45-49; NW 2, i:627-30). Ephesus was especially known for producing facetious orators (Barth). ἀνῆκεν impf. ind. act. ἀνήκει (# *465*) impersonal, it is proper, it is fitting. Impf. is used of necessity, obligation, duty and is used here in the sense of what is (really) not proper but still happens (BD, 181). μᾶλλον (# *3437*) rather. εὐχαριστία (# *2374*) thanksgiving. Gratitude is here singled out as the basic structural feature of the Christian's ethic (Barth). ◆ **5** ἴστε perf. ind. act./imp. οἶδα (# *3857*) to know. Def. perf. w. pres. meaning. The form is probably best understood as imp. and perhaps a Hebraism used w. the following part., w. the meaning, "know of a surety" (M, 245; MH, 222; ND, 352; Barth; Gnilka). γινώσκοντες pres. act. part. γινώσκω (# *1182*) to know. πόρνος (# *4521*) one who practices sexual immorality, fornicator. ἀκάθαρτος (# *176*) one who is unclean. πλεονέκτης (# *4431*) one who is greedy (Rom. 1:29). ὅ ἐστιν that is to say. A formulaic phrase used without reference to the gender of the word explained or to that of the word which explains it (BD, 73). εἰδωλολάτρης (# *1629*) one who serves an idol, idolater. κληρονομία (# *3100*) inheritance. βασιλεία (# *993*) kingdom. The realm of Christ's and God's rule. ◆ **6** ἀπατάτω pres. imp. act. ἀπατάω (# *572*) to lead astray, to mislead, to deceive. Imp. in a neg. command indicating the stopping of an action in progress, or the forbidding of a continual action. κενός (# *3031*) empty, without content; empty words or words which have no inner substance or kernel of truth, hollow sophistries and apologies for sin (Trench, *Synonyms*, 180). Here, instr. dat. διὰ ταῦτα γάρ (# *1328; 4047; 1142*) refers not only to this v. but also to the previous vss. ὀργή (# *3973*) wrath. ἀπείθεια (# *577*) disobedience; υἱοὺς τῆς ἀπειθείας "sons of disobedience" is a Semitic expression indicating the chief characteristic of the person as disobedience (BG, 15f). ◆ **7** γίνεσθε pres. ind./imp. mid. (dep.) γίνομαι (# *1181*) to become. συμμέτοχος (# *5212*) fellow partaker, partner, one who shares together w. another. ◆ **8** ἦτε impf. ind. act. εἰμί (# *1639*) to be. ποτε (# *4537*) formerly. περιπατεῖτε pres. ind. act. περιπατέω (# *4344*) to walk, to conduct one's life. ◆ **9** καρπός (# *2843*) fruit; here, results. ἀγαθωσύνη (# *20*) goodness (Gal. 5:22). ◆ **10** δοκιμάζοντες pres. act.

part. δοκιμάζω (# 1507) to approve after examination, to arrange and execute a test, to accept and heed the results of a test, to carry out a careful examination, to find out by experience (Barth; TLNT; TDNT). εὐάρεστος (# 2298) well-pleasing, acceptable, followed by the dat. of advantage. ◆ 11 συγκοινωνεῖτε pres. imp. act. συγκοινωνέω (# 5170) to join in fellowship w. someone, to have part in a thing (Abbott). Pres. imp. w. the neg. μή (# 3590) forbids a continual or habitual act (MKG, 272f). ἄκαρπος (# 182) unfruitful. ἐλέγχετε pres. imp. act. ἐλέγχω (# 1794) to bring to light, to expose, to reveal hidden things, to convince, to reprove, to correct, to punish, to discipline. For the various meanings, s. Barth; TDNT; Robinson. ◆ 12 κρυφῇ (# 3225) hidden, secret. γινόμενα pres. mid. (dep.) part. γίνομαι (# 1181) to become. ◆ 13 ἐλεγχόμενα pres. pass. part. ἐλέγχω s.v. 11. φῶς (# 5890) light. φανεροῦται pres. ind. pass. φανερόω (# 5746) to make clear, to make known; pass., to become visible or known, to be revealed (BAGD). ◆ 14 φανερούμενον pres. pass. part. φανερόω s.v. 13. διὸ λέγει s. 4:8. Paul evidently uses a free adaptation of Isa. 26:19 and 61:1 (RWP; Eadie; s. esp. APM, 97-116). ἔγειρε pres. imp. act. ἐγείρω (# 1586) to rise, to wake up. καθεύδων pres. act. part. καθεύδω (# 2761) to sleep, to be asleep. Subst. use of the part. ἀνάστα aor. imp. act. ἀνίστημι (# 482) to stand up, to get up. ἐπιφαύσει fut. ind. act. ἐπιφαύσκω (# 2213) to shine upon. The means employed by the Messiah are compared to the rays of the rising sun. God's glory or light appearing over Israel exerted the life-giving power (Barth). ◆ 15 βλέπετε pres. ind. act. βλέπω (# 1063) to watch, to give heed. ἀκριβῶς (# 209) adv. answering the question how one should conduct one's life: accurately, carefully. περιπατεῖτε pres. ind. act. περιπατέω (# 4344) to walk about, to conduct one's life. Pres. points to the continual action. ἄσοφος (# 831) unwise, foolish. The applying of acquired knowledge (TDNT). ◆ 16 ἐξαγοραζόμενοι pres. mid. (dep.) part. ἐξαγοράζω (# 1973) to buy up at the market place. Either w. the meaning, "seizing the opportunity," "making your market to the full from the opportunity of this life" (Abbott); or w. the meaning, "buying back (at the expense of personal watchfulness and self-denial) the present time which is now being used for evil and godless purposes" (MM). καιρός (# 2789) time, referring to the brevity of life, or opportunity, referring to the diligent use of opportunities in life. πονηρός (# 4505) evil, active evil. ◆ 17 γίνεσθε pres. imp. mid. (dep.) γίνομαι (# 1181) to become. ἄφρων (# 933) without understanding, senseless. The word refers to imprudence or folly in action (Abbott). συνίετε pres. imp. act. συνίημι (# 5317) to understand; the ability to bring things together and see them in relation to one another. The saints are encouraged to make use of their reasoning power (Barth). ◆ 18 καί (# 2779) not continuative but a transition from a general fact to a

particular instance in daily life (Abbott; Alford). μεθύσκεσθε pres. imp. mid. (dep.) (# 3499) μεθύσκομαι to get drunk, to be drunk. In Philo's treatise, entitled *On Drunkenness*, he characterizes drunkenness generally as a mark of the blind and foolish man who is a slave to the material world (NIDNTT). Others describe drunkenness as producing inability to preserve one's self-control and forcing one to commit many distasteful acts (DC, 37:55). The religious aspects of drunkenness were seen in the Bacchus festivals in the worship of Dionysus (Barth; KP, 2:77-85; OCD 352f; DGRA, 410-14; DRU, 1:96-105; Cleon Rogers, "The Dionysian Background of Ephesians 5:18," *Bib Sac* 146 [1979]: 249-57). The neg. w. the pres. imp. calls for discontinuation of an action in progress or prohibition of a habitual action. οἴνῳ dat. οἶνος (# 3885) wine. Instr. dat. ἀσωτία (# 861) excess. The word indicated one who himself cannot save or spare, thus one who extravagantly squanders his means. Then it chiefly denoted a dissolute, debauched, profligate manner of living (Trench, *Synonyms*, 54f; also Jos., *JW*, 4:651f; MM; TDNT). The excesses and flagrant, senseless activities connected w. the religious celebrations to Dionysus were well-known to the ancient world. The worshipers felt that they were united, indwelt, and controlled by Dionysus who gave them special powers and abilities (s. the references above; s. also H.J. Rose, *Religion in Greece and Rome*, [New-York: Harper and Brothers, 1959], 60f; Rogers, *Bib Sac* 136 [1979]: 249-57). πληροῦσθε pres. imp. pass. πληρόω (# 4444) to fill; pass., to be filled. The idea of the word is "control." The indwelling Spirit of God is the one who should continually control and dominate the life of the believer. This stands in marked contrast to the worshipers of Dionysus. The pres. calls for a habitual and continuing action. Pass. could be permissive pass.: "allow yourselves to be ..." (BD, 165). This is further supported by imp. ◆ 19 λαλοῦντες pres. act. part. λαλέω (# 3281) to speak. The following four parts. indicate the outworking or practice of being filled w. the Spirit (Schlier; GGBB, 639, 650-51). ψαλμός (# 6011) song of praise, psalm. The vb. meant primarily the plucking of the strings, and the noun was used of sacred songs chanted to the accompaniment of instrumental music (Abbott; Eadie; Barth). ὕμνος (# 5631) hymn. It refers to sacred poetic compositions whose primary purpose is to praise (Eadie). ᾠδαῖς pl. ᾠδή (# 6046) song. This general word originally meant any kind of song but was specially used of lyric poetry (Abbott). ᾄδοντες pres. act. part. ᾄδω (# 106) to sing. ψάλλοντες pres. act. part. ψάλλω (# 6010) to sing (BAGD). ◆ 20 εὐχαριστοῦντες pres. act. part. εὐχαριστέω (# 2373) to be thankful, to give thanks. πάντοτε (# 4121) always. ◆ 21 ὑποτασσόμενοι pres. mid. (dep.) part. ὑποτάσσομαι (# 5718) to line oneself up under, to submit. Used in a military sense of soldiers submitting to their superior or slaves submitting to their masters. The word has primarily the idea of giving up one's own right or will; i.e., to subordinate oneself (RWP; TDNT; Barth). **ἀλλήλοις** dat. pl. ἀλλήλων (# 253) one another: "To one another." **φόβος** (# 5832) fear, reverence. ◆ **22 ἴδιος** (# 2625) one's own. ◆ **23 κεφαλή** (# 3051) head. The word speaks of authority and direction (Eadie). **σωτήρ** (# 5400) savior, protector. ◆ **24 ὑποτάσσεται** pres. ind. mid. (dep.) s.v. 21. Pres. points to the continual action or state. **οὕτως** (# 4048) so. ◆ **25 οἱ ἄνδρες** (# 467) voc. you men. The Attic Gr. used the nom. w. the article only in addressing inferiors in a rather harsh manner. However the NT does not follow this practice and uses the nom. w. the article as the voc. sometimes under Semitic influence (BD, 81f; MT, 31f). **ἀγαπᾶτε** pres. imp. act. ἀγαπάω (# 26) to love (TDNT; TLNT; EDNT). Pres. imp. calls for a continual habitual action. Love was not listed as a duty of the husband (BBC). **καθώς** (# 2777) just as. **ἠγάπησεν** aor. ind. act. (# 26). Aor. either points to the specific act of Christ giving Himself, or views His acts of love in summary fashion. **παρέδωκεν** aor. ind. act. s.v. 2. In a time when marriages were arranged and morals were loose, to fulfill the commands of subordination and love was not an easy task. For marriage and the home in the ancient world, including both Jewish and Gentile s. SB, 3:610-913; JPFC, 2:748-69; Barth, 655-62, 700-20; DPL, 393, 418-19, 587-89; BBC; W.K. Lacey, *The Family in Classical Greek* [London: Thames & Hudson, 1972]; Heinrich Greeven, "Ehe nach dem Neuen Testament," *NTS* 15 [1969]: 365-88. ◆ **26 ἀγιάσῃ** aor. subj. act. ἀγιάζω (# 39) to sanctify, to make holy, to set apart (EDNT; TDNT). Subj. w. **ἵνα** (# 2671) to express purp. For the relation of this word to the marriage ceremony s. Barth. **καθαρίσας** aor. act. part. καθαρίζω (# 2751) to cleanse. Aor. portrays logically antecedent actions, even though they may be temporally contemporary. Part. may suggests the means of the sanctification. It may also be temp. giving the time of the sanctification. **λουτρῷ** dat. λουτρόν (# 3373) bath. Since a bridal bath was the practice both among Jews and Gentiles, Paul may be making allusions to this custom (SB, 1:506; DGRA, 737; NW, 2, i:638). Barth's objection that such an allusion would mean that the bridegroom would be said to have given the bride a bath is to press the allusion too far (Barth, 694). Loc. or instr. dat. **ῥῆμα** (# 4839) word, spoken word. Perhaps the reference is to the gospel which is proclaimed. ◆ **27 παραστήσῃ** aor. subj. act. παρίστημι (# 4225) to present. Subj. w. **ἵνα** (# 2671) to express purp. **ἔνδοξος** (# 1902) glorious, splendor (LN, 1:696). **ἔχουσαν** pres. act. part. acc. fem. sing. ἔχω (# 2400) to have. **σπίλος** (# 5070) spot, speck, fleck, stain. **ῥυτίς** (# 4869) wrinkle, fold on the face. The terms used here are taken from physical beauty, health, and symmetry, to denote spiritual perfection (Eadie). **τοιοῦτος** (# 5525) such a thing. **ᾖ** pres. subj. act. εἰμί

(# 1639) to be. Subj. w. **ἵνα** (# 2671) to express purp. **ἄμωμος** (# 320) blameless. ◆ **28 ὀφείλουσιν** pres. ind. act. ὀφειλέω (# 4053) to owe someone a debt, to be obligated, to ought to. The word indicates moral obligation (TDNT). Pres. indicates the continual existence of the obligation. **ἀγαπᾶν** pres. act. inf. ἀγαπάω (# 26) to love. Compl. inf. used to complete the main vb. **ἀγαπῶν** pres. act. part. (# 26). Subst. part. used to describe a trait. It almost is used in a cond. sense ("if he loves"). Pres. may portray the contemporaneous action or the durative aspect: "the one who loves." ◆ **29 ἐμίσησεν** aor. aor. ind. act. μισέω (# 3631) to hate. Gnomic aor. expressing something which is always true. **ἐκτρέφει** pres. ind. act. ἐκτρέφω (# 1763) to nourish, to nourish children to maturity (T). Prep. in compound is perfective. Pres. of a linear vb. denotes the whole process leading up to an attained goal (M, 114). **θάλπει** pres. ind. act. θάλπω (# 2499) to cherish, to show affection and tender love. **καθώς** (# 2777) according to, just as. The manner and the extent of the care is to be identical to that of Christ for the church. ◆ **30 μέλη** nom pl. μέλος (# 3517) member. ◆ **31 ἀντὶ τούτου** (# 505; 4047) because of this, for this reason. **καταλείψει** fut. ind. act. καταλείπω (# 2901) to leave behind. **προσκολληθήσεται** fut. ind. pass. προσκολλάω (# 4681) to be glued to, to be joined to. The previous word suggests the complete separation from all former ties and this word gives the forming of a new relation. **ἔσονται** fut. ind. mid. (dep.) εἰμί (# 1639) to be. For the relation of this v. to Gen 2:24 s. APM, 117-52. ◆ **32 μυστήριον** (# 3696) mystery. The word refers to that which is incapable of being discovered by human nature but is revealed by God. Here it has to do w. the mystical union of Christ and His church (s. 3:3). ◆ **33 πλήν** (# 4440) in any case, however. The word is used for breaking off discussion and emphasizing what is important (BAGD). **ἀγαπάτω** pres. imp. act. ἀγαπάω (# 26) to love. **φοβῆται** pres. subj. mid. (dep.) φοβέομαι (# 5828) to reverence, to show respect. Subj. w. **ἵνα** (# 2671) to express an imperatival notion.

Ephesians 6

◆ **1 ὑπακούετε** pres. imp. act. ὑπακούω (# 5634) to listen to, to obey, w. dat. **γονεῦσιν** dat. pl. (# 1204) γονεύς parent. For the responsibilities of the family members and the conditions of family life in the society of the day s. Lincoln. **δίκαιος** (# 1465) right, acceptable, corresponds to the correct standard. ◆ **2 τίμα** pres. imp. act. τιμάω (# 5506) to count as valuable, to value, to honor, to revere (BAGD; TDNT). **ἐντολή** (# 1953) commandment. **ἐπαγγελία** (# 2039) promise. For the Jewish teaching regarding this commandment and the position of children in the family s. SB, 1:705-17; 3:614; JPFC, 2:769f; APM, 153-77, esp. 159-64. ◆ **3 εὖ** (# 2292) adv., well. **γένηται** aor. subj. mid. γίνομαι (# 1181) to become. Subj. w. **ἵνα** (# 2671) to express purp. or result. **ἔσῃ** fut.

ind. mid. (dep.) 2nd pers. sing. εἰμί (# 1639) to be. It is possible that the fut. is used here because there was no aor. subj. of the vb. (Abbott). μακροχρόνιος (# 3432) long-lived, long-timed (Eadie). ◆ **4 παροργίζετε** pres. imp. act. παροργίζομαι (# 4239) to anger, to provoke to anger. This involves avoiding attitudes, words, and actions which would drive a child to angry exasperation or resentment and thus rules out excessively severe discipline, unreasonably harsh demands, abuse of authority, arbitrariness, unfairness, constant nagging and condemnation, subjecting a child to humiliation, and all forms of gross insensitivity to a child's needs and sensibilities (Lincoln). Prep. in compound indicates an onward motion (MH, 320; Schlier; TDNT; s. 4:26). The neg. μή (# 3590) w. the pres. imp. is used to prevent a habitual action. **ἐκτρέφετε** pres. imp. act. ἐκτρέπω (# 1763) to nourish, to provide for w. tender care (s. 5:29). For the responsibility of the father for the children in a Jewish family s. JPFC, 2:769f. **παιδεία** (# 4082) education, child training, discipline. The word indicates the discipline used to correct the transgression of the laws and ordinances of the Christian household (Trench, *Synonyms*, 112; TDNT; TLNT; for the development of the concept in Greek culture s. Werner Jaeger, *Paideia: The Ideals of Greek Culture* [Oxford: Basil Blackwell, 1939-45]). **νουθεσία** (# 3804) admonition. It refers to the training by word - by the word of encouragement, when this is sufficient, but also that of remonstrance, reproof, and blame, where these may be required (Trench, *Synonyms*, 112; TDNT). ◆ **5 ὑπακούετε** pres. imp. act. ὑπακούω (# 5634) s.v. 1. **φόβος** (# 5832) fear, reverence. **τρόμος** (# 5571) tremble. The words only express anxious solicitude about the performance of duty, so that there is no allusion to the hardness of the service (Abbott). **ἁπλότης** (# 605) simplicity, sincerity, uprightness (BAGD). It indicates purity of intention and whole-hearted devotion in service (TLNT). ◆ **6 ὀφθαλμοδουλία** (# 4056) eye service. It is labor when the master is present, but relaxation and laziness as soon as he is gone (Eadie). **ἀνθρωπάρεσκος** (# 473) men pleaser, one who tries to please men at the sacrifice of principle (BAGD). **ποιοῦντες** pres. act. part. ποιέω (# 4472) to do. Pres. portrays a contemporaneous action. Part. of means or manner. ◆ **7 εὔνοια** (# 2334) good will, benevolent feelings w. good intentions (TLNT). It suggests the ready good will which does not wait to be compelled (Robinson). **δουλεύοντες** pres. act. part. δουλεύω (# 1526) to serve, to be a slave. Part. of means or manner, explaining how one is not to serve as a man pleaser. ◆ **8 εἰδότες** perf. act. part. (causal) οἶδα (# 3857) to know. **ἕκαστος** (# 1667) each. **ποιήσῃ** aor. subj. act. ποιέω (# 4472) to do. Subj. in an indef. rel. cl. **κομίσεται** fut. ind. mid. (dep.) κομίζω (# 3152) to receive, to receive back; i.e., to receive as deposit. Hence here it implies an adequate return (Abbott). **εἴτε … εἴτε**

(# 1664) whether … or. **ἐλεύθερος** (# 1801) free, one who has been freed from slavery, but has certain responsibilities to the one freeing him (LLAR, 114-15). ◆ **9 ποιεῖτε** pres. ind. act. ποιέω s.v. 8. **ἀνιέντες** pres. act. part. ἀνίημι (# 479) to loosen up, to relax; to let up on (RWP). **ἀπειλή** (# 581) threatening. **προσωπολημψία** (# 4721) the accepting of one's person, partiality. ◆ **10 τοῦ λοιποῦ** (# 3836) finally, for the remaining. For a discussion of the section 6:10-17 in the light of the OT s. APM, 178-212. **ἐνδυναμοῦσθε** pres. imp. pass. ἐνδυναμόω (# 1904) to empower; pass., to be strengthened. **κράτος** (# 3197) strength. **ἰσχύς** (# 2709) might. For these two words s. 1:19. ◆ **11 ἐνδύσασθε** aor. imp. mid. (dep.) ἐνδύομαι (# 1907) to put on, to clothe oneself. **πανοπλία** (# 4110) full armor, complete armor. This included such things as shield, sword, lance, helmet, greaves, and breastplate (T); for a description of a Roman soldier and his armor s. CC, 207f; Jos., *JW*, 3:93ff; TJ, 106-10; BBC. Since a soldier's armor was often a display of splendor Barth prefers the translation, "the splendid armor" (Barth, 793-95). **τοῦ θεοῦ** (# 2536) of God; gen. of source or origin indicating that God provides the armor (Eadie). **δύνασθαι** aor. mid. (dep.) inf. δύναμαι (# 1538) to be able to, w. inf. Inf. of purp. or result. **στῆναι** aor. act. inf. ἵστημι (# 2705) to stand. Compl. inf. completing the idea of the preceding vb. The word could be used in a military sense indicating either "to take over," "to hold a watch post"; or it could also mean to stand and hold out in a critical position on a battlefield (Barth). **μεθοδεία** (# 3497) scheming, craftiness. **διάβολος** (# 1333) slanderer, devil. ◆ **12 πάλη** (# 4097) struggle, wrestling. The word refers particularly to a hand-to-hand fight (Barth). Wrestling was a fight characterized by trickery, cunning, and strategy (DGRA, 817; KP, 4:1436; CC, 143f). **κοσμοκράτωρ** (# 3179) world ruler. For a discussion of the spiritual warfare in the DSS s. 1QM. ◆ **13 ἀναλάβετε** aor. imp. act. ἀναλαμβάνω (# 377) to take up. The word was used as a military t.t. describing the last preparation and final step necessary before the actual battle begins (Barth). Aor. imp. demands an immediate action. **δυνηθῆτε** aor. subj. pass. (dep.) δύναμαι (# 1538) to be able. Subj. w. ἵνα (# 2671) used in a purp. cl. **ἀντιστῆναι** aor. act. inf. ἀντίστημι (# 468) to spend against, to resist. **κατεργασάμενοι** aor. mid. (dep.) part. κατεργάζομαι (# 2981) to accomplish, to carry out. Although the word may mean "to carry to victory," it here means not only having made all necessary preparations, but indicates having done everything which the crisis demands, in order to quell the foe and maintain position (Eadie; Barth). **στῆναι** aor. inf. act. ἵστημι (# 2705) to stand. Inf. used to express purp. ◆ **14 στῆτε** aor. imp. act. ἵστημι (# 2705) to stand. Ingressive aor., "take your stand" (RWP). **περιζωσάμενοι** aor. mid. (dep.) part. περιζώννυμι (# 4322) to bind around oneself. The Roman soldiers wore one of at least three wide belts or girdles–the breech-like leather apron worn to protect the lower abdomen; or the sword belt, which was buckled on together w. the sword as the decisive step in the process of preparing oneself for battle; and the special belt or sash designating an officer or high official (Barth; TDNT). ὀσφῦς (# 4019) hips. ἐνδυσάμενοι aor. mid. part. (dep.) s.v. 11. θώρακα acc. θώραξ (# 2606) breastplate. The word denotes a piece of armor that can mean everything worn at different periods to protect the body between the shoulders and the loins. The average Roman soldier wore a piece of metal, but those who could afford it used the very best available–a scale or chain mail that covered chest and hips (Barth; DGRA, 711f; TJ, 106-107). ◆ **15** ὑποδησάμενοι aor. mid. (dep.) part. ὑποδέομαι (# 5686) to bind under, to strap on. It may refer to the Roman soldiers' shoe, which was thickly studded w. hobnails. Or it may refer to the more elegant shoe, the *calceus*, worn by men of higher rank (DGRA, 233f). πόδας acc. πούς (# 4546) foot; acc. of general reference. ἑτοιμασία (# 2288) preparation, readiness. However, the word may in this context have the meaning "firmly" and express solidity, firmness, solid foundation (Barth). ◆ **16** ἀναλαβόντες aor. act. part. ἀναλαμβάνω (# 377) to take up s.v. 13. θυρεός (# 2599) shield. It refers to the large door-shaped shield, in contrast to the small round convex shield. The reference is to the Roman soldier's *scutum* which had an iron frame and sometimes a metal boss in the center at the front. Often the several layers of leather were soaked in water before the battle in order to put out the incendiary missiles of the enemy (Barth; TJ, 110). δυνήσεσθε fut. ind. mid. (dep.) δύναμαι (# 1538) to be able to, w. a following inf. βέλη acc. pl. βέλος (# 1018) dart, arrow. The term could be used of any type of missile (Barth). πεπυρωμένα perf. pass. part. πυρόω (# 4792) to set on fire. Perf. pass. part. indicates that the arrows were set on fire and are burning. These were arrows or spears tipped w. fabric and dipped in pitch (Barth; s. also Jos., JW, 3:173). σβέσαι aor. act. inf. σβέννυμι (# 4931) to put out, to quench. Compl. inf. ◆ **17** περικεφαλαία (# 4330) a protection around the head, helmet. The Roman soldier wore a bronze helmet equipped w. cheek pieces. The helmet was a heavy, decorative, and expensive item w. an inside lining of felt or sponge which made the weight bearable. Nothing short of an axe or hammer could pierce the heavy helmet (Barth; TDNT; TJ, 107). σωτηρίον (# 5402) salvation; here, gen. of apposition. δέξασθε aor. imp. mid. (dep.) δέχομαι (# 1312) to take, to

receive. μάχαιρα (# 3479) sword. It signifies the short, straight sword used by the Roman soldier (Barth; DGRA, 557; TDNT; TJ, 107-108). ◆ **18** προσευχή (# 4666) request, prayer, petition. It is generally a petition for particular benefits or a petition arising from a particular need (Trench, *Synonyms*, 189; NIDNTT; TDNT). προσευχόμενοι pres. mid. (dep.) part. προσεύχομαι (# 4667) to pray. This is the general word which is used for making a petition to a divine being. (NIDNTT; TDNT; Trench, *Synonyms*, 188f). καιρός (# 2789) time, occasion, opportunity. εἰς αὐτό (# 1650; 899) for this. ἀγρυπνοῦντες pres. act. part. ἀγρυνέω (# 70) to stay awake, to lie sleepless, to pass a sleepless night, to suffer from insomnia, to be watchful, to be vigilant (Barth). προσκαρτέρησις (# 4675) perseverance, constancy, diligence, persistence (LAE, 102; TLNT). The vb. was used in the papyri in the sense of holding out or waiting; e.g., waiting until one's trial came before the court or diligently remaining at one's work (Preisigke, 2:403-4). ◆ **19** δοθῇ aor. subj. pass. δίδωμι (# 1443) to give. ἄνοιξις (# 489) opening. στόμα (# 5125) mouth. παρρησία (# 4244) speaking everything, speaking openly, boldness (TDNT). γνωρίσαι aor. act. inf. γνωρίζω (# 1192) to make known. Inf. as subj. of the pass. vb. μυστήριον (# 3696) mystery (s. 3:3). ◆ **20** πρεσβεύω pres. ind. act. (# 4563) to be an ambassador or envoy. To travel or work as an ambassador is to reveal the riches, power, and dignity of the government one represents, but Paul's chain is one of prisoner iron. The word could also refer to imprisonment, and because an ambassador normally would not be arrested, Paul indicates the wrong he is suffering. Finally, a delegate who is in prison knows that the end of his mission is near (Barth). παρρησιάσωμαι aor. mid. (dep.) subj. παρρησιάζω (# 4245) to speak everything, to speak openly and frankly, to speak boldly, to be bold. δεῖ (# 1256) it is necessary, w. inf. λαλῆσαι aor. act. inf. λαλέω (# 3281) to speak. Compl. inf. to the main vb. ◆ **21** εἰδῆτε perf. subj. act. οἶδα (# 3857) to know. Def. perf. w. pres. meaning. γνωρίσει fut. ind. act. s.v. 19. ἀγαπητός (# 28) beloved. ◆ **22** ἔπεμψα aor. ind. act. πέμπω (# 4287) to send. εἰς αὐτὸ τοῦτο for this very reason. γνῶτε aor. subj. act. γινώσκω (# 1182) to know. Subj. w. ἵνα (# 2671) to express purp. παρακαλέσῃ aor. subj. act. παρακαλέω (# 4151) to comfort, to encourage (TDNT; MNTW, 134). ◆ **24** ἀγαπώντων pres. act. part. ἀγαπάω (# 26) to love. ἀφθαρσία (# 914) not corruptible, incorruption. The word does not point merely to time, but to character (Abbott).

Philippians

Philippians 1

◆ **1** For the letter form s. Rom. 1:1. δοῦλοι Χριστοῦ Ἰησοῦ (# 1528; 5986; 2652) slaves of Christ Jesus. The term may be used in the Hellenistic context of a slave who serves his master, or in the OT sense of being the servant of the Lord (Hawthorne; Silva). οὖσιν pres. act. part. (adj.) εἰμί (# 1639) to be. Φίλιπποι (# 5804) Philippi. The city, founded by Philip of Macedonia and the scene of the battle between Crasus and Brutus against Octavian and Anthony, was located on the *Via Egnatia*, the famous road between Rome and the East. It had become a Roman colony w. *libertas* (self-governing), *immunitas* (freedom from tribute and taxes), *Ius Italicum* (under the laws of Italy) and was the home of many retired Roman soldiers (s. Acts 16:12; NW, 2, i:653-54; PIG, 32-47; P, 1-113; PSCZP; Hawthorne; s.v. Phil. 1:27). σύν (# 5250) with, w. dat. The prep. implies close fellowship or cooperation (DM, 111). ἐπίσκοπος (# 2176) overseer, superintendent, bishop. The word was used for one who had the responsibility of oversight. It is important to note that Paul here uses the pl. and that elsewhere the term is used interchangeably w. "elder" (NIDNTT; TDNT; Lightfoot, 95-99; Gnilka; ZPEB, 1:617-20; Vincent; 1 Tim. 3:1, 8). For the view that these were local terms used in Philippi for the leaders of the "religious guilds" s. P, 140-47. ◆ **3** εὐχαριστῶ pres. ind. act. εὐχαριστέω (# 2373) to give thanks. Iterative pres. μνείᾳ (# 3644) remembrance, mention. Used w. the prep. to express the thought, "as often as I make mention of you (in prayer)" (BAGD; Silva). The prep. ἐπί may have a causal meaning, "I thank my God because of your every remembrance of me" (Hawthorne). ◆ **4** πάντοτε (# 4121) every time, always. δέησις (# 1255) request, petition; generally a specific petition arising from a need. ποιούμενος pres. mid. part. ποιέω (# 4472) to make. Mid. voice of this vb. forms a periphrasis equivalent to a simple verb, i.e., "to pray" (BG, 72f). Pres. indicates a contemporaneous action to the main vb. Temp. part., "while making mention." ◆ **5** κοινωνία (# 3126) fellowship, sharing. The word signifies "your cooperation toward, in aid of the gospel." The word refers not only to financial contribution, but also denotes cooperation w. the apostle in the widest sense, whether in sympathy or in suffering or in active labor (Hawthorne; Lightfoot; TDNT; NIDNTT; RAC, 9:1100-45). ◆ **6** πεποιθώς perf. act. part. πείθω (# 4275)

to persuade. Perf. to be convinced, to be sure, to be certain. For the construction of the vb. followed by a noun cl. s. BD, 204. Part. may have a faint causal force (Ellicott). αὐτὸ τοῦτο (# 899; 4047) this thing, just this (and nothing else) (BD, 151). ἐναρξάμενος aor. mid. (dep.) part. (subst.) ἐνάρχομαι (# 1887) to begin. Prep. in compound represents the action of the vb. as more directly concentrated on the object (Ellicott). ἔργον ἀγαθόν (# 2240; 19) good work. It may refer to God's work of salvation (Silva), or to their sharing in the advancement of the gospel (Hawthorne). ἐπιτελέσει fut. ind. act. ἐπιτελέω (# 2200) to complete, to bring to the goal. Prep. in compound is directive and the vb. indicates, "will carry it on towards completion, and finally complete" (Vincent). ἄχρι (# 948) until. ◆ **7** καθώς (# 2777) just as. The word has a slight causal sense and is often used to introduce new ideas (Gnilka). ἐστιν δίκαιον (# 1639; 1465) it is right. Although the expression may have been a daily figure of speech (Lohmeyer) the word does contain an ethical and general moral sense which has its foundation in the moral relation of man to God (Vincent; MRP, 148). φρονεῖν pres. act. inf. φρονέω (# 5858) to be minded, to think, to be concerned for, to feel. The word denotes a general disposition of mind including both feeling and thought, emotions and mind (Vincent; Hawthorne). Epex. inf. explaining what is right. ἔχειν pres. act. inf. ἔχω (# 2400) to have. Articular inf. w. the prep. διά (# 1328) in a causal sense. For a discussion of the subject of the inf. s. GGBB, 196. The words form an expression of heartfelt love on the part of the apostle toward his readers (Meyer). δεσμός (# 1301) bond. ἀπολογία (# 665) defense, defense against a judicial accusation. The word may be more general, including all of Paul's efforts—whatever put forth—to defend the gospel (Vincent). βεβαίωσις (# 1012) that on which one can walk solid, firm, and durable, guarantee, confirmation, a legal t.t. for guaranteeing or furnishing security (TLNT; BAGD; BS, 104-109; MM). συγκοινωνός (# 5171) sharers together w. someone, fellow partakers. ὄντας pres. act. part. (causal) εἰμί (# 1639) to be. ◆ **8** ἐπιποθῶ pres. ind. act. ἐπιποθέω (# 2160) to long for, to yearn after. Prep. in compound signifies direction; w. the idea of straining after the object being thereby suggested, the idea implied is eagerness (Lightfoot). σπλάγχνον (# 5073) the inward parts; i.e., the heart, liver, lungs which were collectively regarded as the seat of feeling. The strongest word in Gr. for the feeling of compassion (Vincent; MNTW, 156f; TDNT; NIDNTT; TLNT; EDNT). ◆ 9 προσεύχομαι pres. ind. mid. (dep.) (# 4667) to pray. For the prayer words and syntactical constructions s. PIP, 173f. DPL. ἔτι (# 2285) yet. μᾶλλον (# 3437) more. The phrase "more and more" accentuates their need for unremitting progress (PIP, 209). περισσεύῃ pres. subj. act. περισσεύω (# 4355) to overflow, to abound. Pres. is progressive and expresses the desire, "may continue to abound" (Vincent). Subj. w. ἵνα (# 2671) to express the content of the prayer. ἐπίγνωσις (# 2106) knowledge, recognition. Prep. in compound indicates a knowledge directed toward an object. Here the word indicates a firm conception of those spiritual principles which would guide them in their relations w. one another and the world (EGT). αἴσθησις (# 151) insight, perception, discernment. The word was originally used of sense perception, but is applicable to the inner world of sensibility, referring to moral and spiritual perception related to practical applications (EGT; Lightfoot). It refers to the ability to make proper moral decisions in the midst of a vast array of differing and difficult choices (Hawthorne). ◆ 10 δοκιμάζειν pres. act. inf. δοκιμάζω (# 1507) to approve after careful testing (TDNT; TLNT). Articular inf. w. the prep. εἰς (# 1650) could express either purp. or result (MT, 143). διαφέροντα pres. act. part. διαφέρω (# 1422) to differ. Here it refers to what is worthwhile, excellent, vital (PIP, 209). εἰλικρινής (# 1637) unmixed, pure, genuine, sincere, moral integrity, perfect purity describing the mind, heart, and conduct (TLNT; Hawthorne). The etymology "tested by sunlight" is possible but uncertain (GEW, 1:459; Vincent; Lohmeyer; TDNT; TLNT). ἀπρόσκοπος (# 718) without stumbling, without offense. The word means either "not stumbling" or "not causing others to stumble" (Vincent). ◆ 11 πεπληρωμένοι perf. act. part. πληρόω (# 4444) to fill. Perf. views the completed state or condition. ἔπαινος (# 2047) praise. ◆ 12 γινώσκειν pres. act. inf. γινώσκω (# 1182) to know, to realize. Compl. inf. to the main vb. βούλομαι (# 1089) pres. ind. mid. (dep.) to desire, to want. τὰ κατ' ἐμέ the things regarding me, my affairs (Hawthorne). μᾶλλον (# 3437) rather; here, rather than the reverse, as might have been anticipated (Lightfoot). προκοπή (# 4620) cutting forward, advance, progress, furtherance (TLNT). For the vb. s. Gal. 1:14. ἐλήλυθεν perf. act. ind. ἔρχομαι (# 2262) to come, to go. ◆ 13 φανερός (# 5745) clear, manifest. γενέσθαι aor. mid. (dep.) inf. γίνομαι (# 1181) to become. Inf. used w. ὥστε (# 6063) to express actual result (BD, 197f). πραιτώριον (# 4550) praetorian guard, praetorium. The word refers either to the elite troops or to the headquarters used by such troops. They were select troops designed to guard the person of the emperor (Vincent; Lightfoot; Gnilka; ZPEB, 4:832-34; CC, 198f;

KP, 4:1116-17; DGRA, 957-58). ◆ 14 πλείονας comp. πολύς (# 4498) great, many; comp. the majority (BD, 127). πεποιθότας perf. act. part. πείθω (# 4275) to encourage (s.v. 6). περισσοτέρως (# 4359) adv. comp. περισσός abundantly (s. 2 Cor. 2:4). Here it denotes the increased zeal of the brethren when stimulated by St. Paul's endurance (Lightfoot). τολμᾶν pres. act. inf. τολμάω (# 5528) to dare. Inf. expresses actual results (s.v. 13). ἀφόβως (# 925) adv., fearless. λαλεῖν pres. act. inf. λαλέω (# 3281) to speak. Inf. used to complement the previous inf. ◆ 15 καί (# 2779) and. Used here in a contrasting force and to introduce another and a different class (Vincent). φθόνος (# 5784) envy. ἔρις (# 2251) strife, discord, contention. This was the intended result of their proclamation. εὐδοκία (# 2306) goodwill. The word refers to the good motives and well wishes from which an action comes (TDNT; Gnilka). κηρύσσουσιν pres. ind. act. κηρύσσω (# 3062) to proclaim. ◆ 16 οἱ μὲν … οἱ δέ the ones … the others. ἐξ ἀγάπης out of love, giving the motivation. εἰδότες perf. act. part. (causal). οἶδα (# 3857) to know. Def. perf. w. a pres. meaning. ἀπολογίαν (# 665) defense (s.v. 7). κεῖμαι (# 3023) pres. ind. mid. (dep.) to lie, to recline. Figuratively, to be appointed, to be destined (BAGD). ◆ 17 ἐριθεία (# 2249) selfishness. Originally, the character of one who worked for pay. A hired worker was looked down upon because his laboring was wholly for his own interest (EGT; s. 2:3). καταγγέλλουσιν pres. ind. act. καταγγέλλω (# 2859) to proclaim, to proclaim w. authority. Prep. in compound is perhaps intensive: "making fully known" (Ellicott; Vincent; NIDNTT). ἁγνῶς (# 56) adv., purely. W. neg. οὐχ (# 4024), w. mixed or impure motives (Lightfoot). οἰόμενοι pres. mid. (dep.) part. (causal) οἴομαι (# 3887) to suppose, to imagine. It denotes a belief or judgment based principally upon one's own feelings, or the peculiar relations of outward circumstances to oneself (Vincent). θλῖψις (# 2568) pressure, tribulation. ἐγείρειν pres. act. inf. ἐγείρω (# 1586) to raise up. Used in the context "to make my chains gall me" (Lightfoot; Silva). ◆ 18 γάρ (# 1142) then, assuredly (Thrall, 44). πλήν (# 4440) except, but, nevertheless. The particle is used in an adversative sense (Blomqvist, 75-100; Thrall, 20f). τρόπος (# 5573) manner, fashion. εἴτε (# 1664) whether. πρόφασις (# 4733) pretense, pretext, excuse. The word indicates the ostensible reason for which a thing is done, and generally points to a false reason as opposed to the truth (MM; BAGD; TLNT; GELTS, 408). Here it is using the name of Christ as a cover or mask for personal and selfish ends (Vincent). Dat. here expresses the manner (Ellicott). καταγγέλλεται pres. ind. pass. καταγγέλλω (# 2859) to proclaim (s.v. 17). ἀλλὰ καί The two particles are combined in a progressive sense: further, what is more, moreover (Thrall, 14ff). χαρήσομαι fut. ind. mid. (BD, 42) χαίρω (# 5897) to be glad, to rejoice. Volitive fut. indicating a decision of the will (RG, 889). It is a progressive fut. which affirms that an action will be in progress in fut. time (SMT, 32). ◆ **19 οἶδα** (# 3857) perf. ind. act. Def. perf. w. a pres. meaning, to know. The word speaks of the possession of knowledge which is grasped directly or intuitively by the mind (ND, 344f). **τοῦτο** (# 4047) this; this state of things, these perplexities and annoyances (Lightfoot). **ἀποβήσεται** fut. ind. mid. (dep.) ἀποβαίνω (# 609) to come from, to come back, to turn out (RWP). **ἐπιχορηγία** (# 2221) supply (Eph. 4:16; Gal. 3:5). ◆ **20 ἀποκαραδοκία** (# 638) intense expectation, earnest watching. The word is composed of the prep. "away," the noun "head," and the vb. "to watch," and indicates watching something w. the head turned away from other objects (Vincent). It indicates the concentrated intense hope which ignores other interests and strains forward as w. outstretched head (EGT; s. Rom. 8:19; Gnilka). **αἰσχυνθήσομαι** fut. ind. pass. αἰσχύνομαι (# 159) to be ashamed, to be put to shame. **παρρησία** (# 4244) speaking all things, forthrightness of speech; then more broadly, boldness, esp. the courage appropriate to the free man, which acts openly even in a hostile atmosphere (Beare). **μεγαλυνθήσεται** fut. ind. pass. μεγαλύνω (# 3486) to make large, to magnify. ◆ **21 ζῆν** pres. act. inf. ζάω (# 2409) to live. Articular inf. is the subject of the sentence: "the act of living" (GGBB, 601). Continuous pres. (Vincent). **ἀποθανεῖν** aor. act. inf. ἀποθνήσκω (# 633) to die. Articular inf. used as the subject. **κέρδος** (# 3046) gain, profit. The word was used of something advantageous and in the pl. sometimes refers to money (BAGD; MM; for the other examples s. Lohmeyer). For a discussion of this v. s. D. W. Palmer, "'To Die Is Gain,' Philippians 1:21," *NovT* 18 (1975): 203-18. ◆ **22 ζῆν** pres. act. inf. ζάω (# 2409) to live. **αἱρήσομαι** fut. ind. mid. (dep.) αἱρέομαι (# 145) to take; to pick; mid., to choose. For the view that Paul may have contemplated "voluntary death" s. CIC, 96-125. **γνωρίζω** (# 1192) pres. ind. act. to understand, to know, to declare, to make known. The latter meaning is better in this context (Lightfoot; Vincent). ◆ **23 συνέχομαι** pres. ind. pass. συνέχω (# 5309) to hold together, to hem in on both sides. The idea is that of a strong pressure bearing upon him from two sides, keeping him motionless (EGT; Lightfoot). **δέ** (# 1254) and, now. It introduces an explanation and at the same time separates it from that which is to be explained (Vincent). **ἐπιθυμία** (# 2123) desire. **ἔχων** pres. act. part. ἔχω (# 2400) to have, to possess. **ἀναλῦσαι** aor. act. inf. ἀναλύω (# 386) to break up, to unloose, to undo. It is used of loosening a ship from its moorings, of breaking camp, and of death (Vincent). Epex. inf. w. the prep. **εἰς** (#1650) is used to supply the limits of the noun ἐπιθυμίαν (MT, 143). **εἶναι** pres. act. inf. εἰμί (# 1639) to be. Epex. inf. **μᾶλλον** (# 3437) more, to a greater degree. **κρεῖσσον** (# 3202) comp. ἀγαθός (s. 1 Cor. 7:9); stronger,

better. ◆ **24 ἐπιμένειν** pres. act. inf. ἐπιμένω (# 2152) to remain, to stay. Prep. in compound implies rest in a place and hence a more protracted stay (Ellicott). Epex. inf., "It is more necessary to remain...." **ἀναγκαιότερον** comp. ἀναγκαῖος (# 338) necessary; comp., more necessary. **δι᾽ ὑμας** for you, for your sake. ◆ **25 πεποιθώς** perf. act. part. (causal) πείθω (# 4275) to be convinced, to persuade (s.v. 6). **μενῶ** fut. ind. act. μένω (# 3531) to remain. **παραμενῶ** fut. ind. act. παραμένω (# 4169) to remain w. someone, to stand by. In Koine the word often had the idea "to remain in service," "to remain at someone's disposal" (NDIEC, 4:98-99; MM; Preisigke, 2:252; Lohmeyer). ◆ **26 καύχημα** (# 3017) ground or reason for boasting. Here it is their knowledge and possession of the gospel (EGT). **περισσεύη** pres. subj. act. περισσεύω (# 4355) to overflow, to abound. Subj. w. ἵνα (# 2671) is used to express purp. **παρουσία** (# 4242) arrival, presence. ◆ **27 ἀξίως** (# 547) adv. worthily (Eph. 4:1; for examples of "acting or living worthy" of a city council, god, gods, etc. s. P, 136-37). **πολιτεύεσθε** pres. imp. mid. (dep.) πολιτεύω (# 4488) to be a citizen, to conduct oneself as a citizen. Paul may be alluding to the fact that the city of Philippi had the Roman status of *colonia*, which meant that the city was a mini-Rome w. many Latin inscriptions (s.v. 1; DGRA, 315-20; IDB 1:657; s. also A.N. Sherwin-White, *The Roman Citizenship* [Oxford; Clarendon Press, 1973]; esp. P, 114-39). For vbs. w. this suf., meaning "to play the part of," "to act as," s. MH, 398-400. Pres. imp. calls for a continual and habitual action. **ἐλθών** aor. act. part. ἔρχομαι (# 2262) to come; to go. **ἰδών** aor. act. part. ὁράω (# 3972) to see. Parts. could be cond., temp., or translated as a main vb. (Vincent). **ἀπών** pres. act. part. ἄπειμι (# 582) to be away from, to be absent. **στήκετε** pres. ind. act. στήκω (# 5112) to stand, to stand firm, to hold one's ground. The word indicates the determination of a soldier who does not budge one inch from his post (Lohmeyer). **ψυχῇ** (# 6034) soul. It indicates the mind as the seat of sensation and desire (Vincent; TDNT; PAT). **συναθλοῦντες** pres. act. part. συναθλέω (# 5254) to contend or struggle along w. someone (BAGD). ◆ **28 πτυρόμενοι** pres. pass. part. πτύρω (# 4769) to frighten, to startle, to terrify. The metaphor is of a timid horse (Lightfoot). Perhaps there is an allusion to Cassius who at the battle of Philippi committed suicide at the fear of defeat (CAH, 10:24). **ἀντικειμένων** pres. mid. (dep.) part. ἀντίκειμαι (# 512) to line up against, to oppose, to be an adversary. **ἥτις** (# 4015) which, "seeing it is." The rel. pronoun has an explanatory force and takes its gender from the predicate, but agrees logically w. the part. in the nom. (Vincent). **ἔνδειξις** (# 1893) evidence, proof, w. dat. of disadvantage **αὐτοῖς** (GGBB, 143-44). The word was used as an Attic law term (EGT). **ἀπώλεια** (# 724) destruction. Here it is the destruction which consists in the loss of eternal life (Vincent; TDNT). ◆ **29 ἐχαρίσθη** aor. ind. pass. χαρίζομαι (# *5919*) to give graciously. "God has granted you the high privilege of suffering for Christ; this is the surest sign that He looks upon you w. favor" (Lightfoot). **πιστεύειν** pres. act. inf. πιστεύω (# *4409*) to believe. **πάσχειν** pres. act. inf. πάσχω (# *4248*) to suffer. Articular inf. is used as the subject of the vb. ◆ **30 ἀγών** (# *74*) conflict, struggle. The word pictures Paul's apostolic life of service (RAM, 183). **ἔχοντες** pres. act. part. ἔχω (# *2400*) to have. **οἷος** (# *3888*) which kind of. **εἴδετε** aor. ind. act. ὁράω (# *3972*) to see. **ἀκούετε** pres. ind. act. ἀκούω (# *201*) to hear.

Philippians 2

◆ **1 παράκλησις** (# *4155*) comfort, consolation, exhortation, encouragement (TDNT; MNTW, 128ff). **παραμύθιον** (# *4172*) encouragement, esp. as consolation or alleviation (BAGD). Prep. in compound may have the force of "aside"; i.e., "the converse which draws the mind aside from care" (MM). **κοινωνία** (# *3126*) fellowship. **σπλάγχνα** (# *5073*) tender affection, mercy (s. Phil. 1:8). **οἰκτιρμός** (# *3880*) compassion. It signifies the manifestation of tender feelings in compassionate yearnings and action (Lightfoot). ◆ **2 πληρώσατε** aor. imp. act. πληρόω (# *4444*) to fill. The particle **ἵνα** (# *2671*) (that) is used to introduce the object of the request and blends in the purpose of making it (Ellicott; s. also BD, 199f). **φρονῆτε** pres. subj. act. φρονέω (# *5858*) to think, to hold an opinion, to have thoughts or an attitude, to be minded or disposed (BAGD). Pres. implies a continual, habitual attitude. **ἔχοντες** pres. act. part. ἔχω (# *2400*) to have. **σύμψυχος** (# *5249*) harmonious, united in spirit (BAGD). The following words appear on the gravestone of a man and his wife: "we spoke the same things, we thought the same things, and we go the inseparable way to Hades" (Lohmeyer; BS, 256). **φρονοῦντες** pres. act. part. φρονέω (# *5858*) to think. ◆ **3 ἐριθεία** (# *2249*) selfishness, selfish ambition. The word is related to a noun which originally meant "a day laborer" and was used esp. of those cutting and binding wheat or of those who were spinners or weavers. The word later denotes the attitude of those who worked for wages; particularly it denoted a self-seeking pursuit of political office by unfair means. It then came to be used of party squabbles, of the jockeying for position and the intrigue behind place and power. Finally, it meant selfish ambition, the ambition which has no conception of service but only aimed at profit and power (BAGD; TDNT; GEW, 1:558; NTW, 39ff). **κενοδοξία** (# *3029*) empty praise, vainglory. It refers to personal vanity; it is the person who is conceited without reason, deluded, ambitious for his own reputation, challenging others to rivalry, jealous himself and willing to fight to prove his idea is right (Lightfoot; Hawthorne; s. Gal. 5:26). **ταπεινοφροσύνη** (# *5425*) lowly thinking, humility. The word indicates the recog-

nition of one's insufficiency but the powerful sufficiency of God (TDNT; NIDNTT; Gnilka). **ἀλλήλους** acc. pl. ἀλλήλων (# *253*) one another. **ἡγούμενοι** pres. mid. (dep.) part. ἡγέομαι (# *2451*) to consider, to count as. The word implies a conscious, sure judgment resting on a careful weighing of the facts (Vincent). **ὑπερέχοντας** pres. act. part. ὑπερέχω (# *5660*) w. the gen., to have over and beyond, to excel or surpass, to be superior (RWP; Ellicott). ◆ **4 τὰ ἑαυτῶν** (# *1571*) the things of others; i.e., others, different from those named. For the contrast s. BD, 161. **ἕκαστος** (# *1667*) each, each one. **σκοποῦντες** pres. act. part. σκοπέω (# *5023*) to look at, to consider, to regard as one's aim. Used w. the article and reflex. pron. it means to consult one's own interest (Lightfoot). ◆ **5 φρονεῖτε** pres. imp. act. φρονέω (# *5858*) to think (s.v. 2). **ἐν ὑμῖν** in you; i.e., in your community (of faith and love), in your common life (Beare). ◆ **6 μορφῇ** (# *3671*) form. The outward display of the inner reality or substance. Here it refers to the outward display of the divinity of the preexistent Christ, in the display of His glory as the image of the Father. For a study of this word s. Martin, 99-133; Lightfoot, esp. 127-33; TDNT; NIDNTT; T. F. Glasson, "The Notes on the Philippians' Hymn: 2:6-11," *NTS* 21 (1974): 133-39; Vincent, 78ff. **ὑπάρχων** pres. act. part. ὑπάρχω (# *5639*) to be, to exist. The word expresses continuance of an antecedent state or condition (AS); concessive part. (GGBB, 634-35). **ἁρπαγμός** (# *772*) a prize, something to hold onto. The word has either an active sense ("robbing") or a pass. sense ("prize gained through robbery"). Perhaps the meaning is that Christ did not use His equality w. God in order to snatch or gain power and dominion, riches, pleasure, or worldly glory. He did not reach out of His favored place and grasp at authority (Meyer; Martin, 152). For detailed studies on this difficult word s. Martin, 134-64; Lightfoot, 133-38; Glasson, 133-37; DPL, 106-7; TDNT. **ἡγήσατο** aor. ind. mid. (dep.) ἡγέομαι (# *2451*) to consider. For the view that the vb. in connection w. the previous noun means "to treat as a piece of good fortune," "to regard as a lucky find," "to prize highly," "to welcome eagerly," s. Martin, 143f; Lightfoot, 138. **εἶναι** pres. act. inf. εἰμί (# *1639*) to be. For a discussion of the article s. GGBB, 220. **ἴσα** (# *2698*) equal, exactly equal, equal in number, size, quality. The acc. pl. can be used as an adv. which in turn is used here as an adj. w. the vb. εἰμί (BAGD; BD, 224; TDNT). The acc. is used w. the articular inf. ("to be equal w. God") to form the acc. of object in a double acc. construction: "He did not regard the being equal w. God (acc. of object) as a robbing (pred. acc.)." For this construction s. BD, 86; RG, 479ff. ◆ **7 ἑαυτοῦ** (# *1571*) himself, reflexive pronoun. The word is emphasized by its position in the sentence. **ἐκένωσεν** aor. ind. act. κενόω (# *3033*) to empty, to make empty, to make of no effect. The word does not mean He emptied Himself of His deity, but rather He emptied Himself of the display of His deity for personal gain (Vincent; Martin, 195; for a study of the word s. TDNT; Martin, 165-96; NIDNTT). **δοῦλος** (*# 1528*) slave. **λαβών** aor. act. part. λαμβάνω (*# 3284*) to take. Part. of means (GGBB, 630). **ὁμοίωμα** (*# 3930*) likeness. The phrase expresses the fact that His mode of manifestation resembled what men are. The apostle views Him solely as He could appear to men (Vincent). This, however, does not deny His true humanity. **γενόμενος** aor. mid. (dep.) part. γίνομαι (*# 1181*) to become. **σχῆμα** (*# 5386*) outward appearance. The word was used of a king who exchanges his kingly robe for sackcloth (BAGD; Lightfoot, 127-33; NIDNTT; TDNT; Martin, 207f). **εὑρεθείς** aor. pass. part. εὑρίσκω (*# 2351*) to find. The parts. are of manner and indicate how Christ emptied Himself. ◆ **8 ἐταπείνωσεν** aor. ind. act. ταπεινόω (*# 5427*) to make low, to humble. **ὑπήκοος** (*# 5675*) obedient. **μέχρι** (*# 3588*) until, unto. "Even unto death," i.e., to the extent of death (Vincent). **δέ** (*# 1254*) and even, yea. It introduces another and more striking detail of the humiliation and leads on to a climax–not only death but a death of suffering, shameful and accursed, the most ignominious of deaths (Vincent; Ellicott). For the horrors and the attitude of the ancient world toward the despicable death by crucifixion, a form of punishment reserved for slaves, rebels and the lowest criminals s. Blinzler; C; ABD, 1:1207-10; 1 Cor. 1:18. ◆ **9 διό** (*# 1475*) wherefore; in consequence of this voluntary humiliation, in fulfillment of divine law which He Himself enunciated (Lightfoot; Martin, 231ff). **ὑπερύψωσεν** aor. ind. act. ὑπερυψόω (*# 5671*) to exalt, to exalt above and beyond, to highly exalt. The force of the prep. in compound is not to describe a different stage in Christ's existence in a comp. sense, but to contrast His exaltation w. the claim of other high powers, and thereby to proclaim His uniqueness and absoluteness (Martin, 241; Beare). **ἐχαρίσατο** aor. ind. mid. (dep.) χαρίζομαι (*# 5919*) to give out of grace, to grant graciously. Now, after a career of self-humbling and obedience, there comes to Him in the Father's good pleasure the very thing He might have grasped (Martin, 236). ◆ **10 γόνυ** (*# 1205*) knee. **κάμψῃ** aor. subj. act. κάμπτω (*# 2828*) to bend, to bow. Subj. w. **ἵνα** (*# 2671*) to express purp. or result (GGBB, 474). **ἐπουράνιος** (*# 2230*) heavenly, heaven (s. Eph. 1:3). **ἐπίγειος** (*# 2103*) earthly, on the earth. **καταχθόνιος** (*# 2973*) under the earth. Christ is acknowledged as Lord of all angelic forces, esp. malevolent demons. They are compelled to admit that He is victor, and they show their submission by prostrating before Him (Martin, 261; for a discussion of this threefold division of the universe s. Martin 257-65). ◆ **11 γλῶσσα** (*# 1185*) tongue. **ἐξομολογήσηται** aor. subj. mid. (dep.) ἐξομολογέω (*# 2018*) to admit openly, to acknowledge, to recognize, to acclaim (Martin, 263; TDNT; Beare). Subj. w.

ἵνα (from v. 10) is used to express purp. **εἰς δόξαν θεοῦ πατρός** for the glory of God the Father. The Lord Jesus was neither selfish nor did He seek vainglory, but even in His exaltation all praise, honor, and power finally belonged to God the Father (Martin, 273). For lit. on this passage s. Martin, 320-39; Hawthorne, 71-75. ◆ **12 ὥστε** (*# 6063*) wherefore, so then, consequently. This particle draws a conclusion from the preceding. As Christ was perfectly obedient, therefore w. like subjection to Him the readers are to carry out their own salvation (Vincent). **ἀγαπητός** (*# 28*) beloved. **καθώς** (*# 2777*) just as. **πάντοτε** (*# 4121*) always. **ὑπηκούσατε** aor. ind. act. ὑπακούω (*# 5634*) to answer the door, to obey as a result of listening, to obey, to be obedient. Prep. in compound contains the idea of submission (MH, 327; Vincent). **παρουσία** (*# 4242*) presence. **πολλῷ μᾶλλον** much more. **ἀπουσία** (*# 707*) absence. **τρόμος** (*# 5571*) trembling. The expression "w. fear and trembling" indicates a nervous and trembling anxiety to do right (Lightfoot). **σωτηρία** (*# 5401*) salvation; perhaps a figure for the changed life that is produced by the inward change caused by salvation. **κατεργάζεσθε** pres. imp. mid. (dep.) κατεργάζομαι (*# 2981*) to work out, to work on to the finish. Prep. in compound is perfective and views the linear progress down to the goal: "work on to the finish" (RWP; M, 114ff). ◆ **13 θεός** (*# 2536*) God. The word is placed first as the subject, not as the pred.; God is the agent (Meyer). **γάρ** (*# 1142*) for. It gives the reason for the entire previous v. and supplies at once the stimulus to and the corrective of the precept in the preceding (Vincent; Lightfoot). **ἐνεργῶν** pres. act. part. ἐνεργέω (*# 1919*) to work effectually and productively, to put forth power. The word describes the energy and the effective power of God Himself in action (Vincent; MNTW, 46-54). **θέλειν** pres. act. inf. θέλω (*# 2527*) to desire. **ἐνεργεῖν** pres. act. inf. (*# 1919*). The articular infs. are used as the direct obj. to the preceding part. For the syntactical difficulties here s. GGBB, 602-3. **εὐδοκία** (*# 2306*) good pleasure, satisfaction; "in fulfillment of His benevolent purpose" (Lightfoot; s. Phil. 1:15). ◆ **14 ποιεῖτε** pres. imp. act. ποιέω (*# 4472*) to do. **γογγυσμός** (*# 1198*) murmuring, an expression of dissatisfaction, grumbling, muttering in a low voice. The word was used in the LXX for the murmuring of Israel against God (T; TDNT; GELTS, 92; NDIEC, 143-44; s. also 3 Bar. 8:5; 13:4). It is the kind of grumbling action that promotes ill will instead of harmony and good will (Hawthorne). **διαλογισμός** (*# 1369*) inward questioning, dispute, discussion, skeptical questioning or criticism (Vincent). It refers to the intellectual rebellion against God (Lightfoot). ◆ **15 γένησθε** aor. subj. mid. (dep.) γίνομαι (*# 1181*) to be, to become. **ἄμεμπτος** (*# 289*) unblamed, without blame (s. Eph. 1:4; Trench, *Synonyms*, 379). **ἀκέραιος** (*# 193*) unmixed, unadulterated, pure, sincere. The word was used of pure wine and of unalloyed metal (Lightfoot). ἄμωμος (# 320) without spot, without blemish (Trench, *Synonyms*, 380). μέσον (# 3545) in the midst of, in the middle of. The n. as an adv. was used as a prep. w. the gen. (RG, 644). γενέα (# 1155) generation. σκολιός (# 5021) curved, crooked. διεστραμμένης perf. pass. part. διαστρέφω (# 1406) twisted, distorted, to twist in two. It denotes an abnormal moral cond. Perf. expresses a state or cond. consequent to an action (Vincent; Matt. 17:17). φαίνεσθε pres. ind. mid. (dep.) φαίνομαι (# 5743) to shine, to give light, to be bright; mid., to appear, to be visible, to make one's appearance, to show oneself (BAGD). Pres. points to the continual action. φωστήρ (# 5891) luminary, the light given off by heavenly bodies, mainly the sun and moon–the light or great lights (Trench, *Synonyms*, 164; TDNT; s. also Gen. 1:14, 16; for Qumran parallels s. also 1QS 10:3; 1QM 10:11; 1QH 1:11; 7:25; 9:26). For the Jewish teaching regarding those who shine as luminaries s. SB, 1:236; 3:621. ◆ 16 λόγον ζωῆς word of life. Gen. of source or gen. of apposition, i.e., the word which brings life and which is life. ἐπέχοντες pres. act. part. ἐπέχω (# 2091) to hold fast, to hold forth. The latter sense would be "to hold out," and the metaphor may be that of offering food or wine (Lightfoot; MM). Part. expresses means. Pres. expresses contemporaneous action. καύχημα (# 3017) reason for boasting, ground of glorying. It is not a boasting in meritorious effort, but the sign of the completion of a divinely assigned commission (PAM, 104; Lohmeyer). κενός (# 3031) empty, in vain. The word fits well into the picture of the runner and his eventual success or failure in the race (PAM, 100). ἔδραμον aor. ind. act. τρέχω (# 5556) to run. The word pictures Paul's work as an apostle spreading the gospel w. the figure of a runner. The word indicates the strenuous effort and exertion involved. Paul's fear is that his own interest might impede the gospel; or that either the threatened introduction of the law as a condition for salvation or the possibility of unfaithfulness on the part of the Philippians might make his efforts fruitless (PAM, 107). ἐκοπίασα aor. ind. act. κοπιάζω (# 3159) to work hard, to labor. This vb. is qualified by the preceding and both vbs. designate the intense labor and efforts of Paul toward the one goal (PAM, 109f). ◆ 17 καί (# 2779) even. The word refers to the whole cl. (Vincent). σπένδομαι pres. ind. σπένδω (# 5064) pass. to pour out as a drink offering. A drink offering, usually a cup of wine, was poured out on the ground to honor deity. Paul is again referring to the prospect of martyrdom which he faces, and thinks of himself–his life's blood–as a libation poured forth to God (Beare). θυσία (# 2602) sacrifice. The prep. can mean "upon the sacrifice," or "in addition to the sacrifice" (Vincent). λειτουργία (# 3311) service, religious or sacred service. For the development of this word s. Lightfoot; BS, 140f; TDNT. χαίρω

(# 5897) pres. ind. act. to rejoice. συγχαίρω (# 5176) pres. ind. act. to rejoice together, to rejoice w. someone. ◆ 18 χαίρετε pres. ind. act. χαίρω (# 5867) to rejoice. συγχαίρετε pres. imp. act. συγχαίρω (# 5176) to rejoice together. ◆ 19 ἐλπίζω (# 1827) pres. ind. act. to hope. ταχέως (# 5441) quickly, soon. πέμψαι aor. act. inf. πέμπω (# 4287) to send. Compl. inf. explains the content of Paul's hope. εὐψυχῶ pres. subj. act. εὐψυχέω (# 2379) to be glad, to have courage. In the papyri the word is found in the salutation of a letter of condolence (MM). Subj. w. ἵνα (# 2671) expresses purp. γνούς aor. act. part. γινώσκω (# 1182) to know. Temp. part., "when I know," "after I know." ◆ 20 ἰσόψυχος (# 2701) likeminded, having the same mind, having equal power confident (Gnilka). The word may have the meaning, "precious as life" (LS, 75). γνησίως (# 1189) adv., genuinely; legitimate, not spurious, birth (RWP). μεριμνήσει fut. ind. act. μεριμνάω (# 3534) to give one's thoughts to a matter, to be concerned (EGT). Fut. points to the time when Timothy would come to them (Ellicott). ◆ 21 πάντες nom. pl. πᾶς (# 4246) all. The article w. the adj. excludes any exception (Lohmeyer; RG, 773f). τὰ ἑαυτῶν (# 1571) their own things. This stands in stark contrast to the things of Jesus Christ. ζητοῦσιν pres. ind. act. ζητέω (# 2426) to seek. Pres. could be customary ("this is your long standing practice") or progressive ("this is your present practice"). ◆ 22 δοκιμή (# 1509) approval, acceptance after being tested (TDNT). γινώσκετε pres. ind. act. γινώσκω (# 1182) to know. ἐδούλευσεν aor. ind. act. δουλεύω (# 1526) to serve as a slave, to serve. ◆ 23 ὡς (# 6055) w. ἄν (# 323) = ὅταν whenever, as soon as. The construction is temp. and indicates the uncertainty which surrounds the whole prospect (EGT; BD, 237f). πέμψαι aor. act. inf. πέμπω (# 4287) to send. Compl. inf. gives the content of the hope. ἀφίδω aor. subj. act. ἀφοράω (# 927) to look away, to see. Prep. in compound implies looking away from the pres. circumstances to what is going to happen, which will decide the question of his sending Timothy (Vincent). ἐξαυτῆς (# 1994) at once, immediately, soon thereafter. ◆ 24 πέποιθα perf. ind. act. πείθω (# 4275) to persuade; perf. w. the pres. meaning, to be convinced, to be sure, to be certain (BAGD). Perf. expresses a state or cond.: "I am convinced" (BD, 176). ἐλεύσομαι fut. ind. mid. (dep.) ἔρχομαι (# 2262) to come. ◆ 25 ἀναγκαῖος (# 338) compelling, necessary. ἡγησάμην aor. ind. mid. (dep.) ἡγέομαι (# 2451) to lead, to consider. συνεργός (# 5301) fellow worker. συστρατιώτης (# 5369) fellow soldier. ἀπόστολος (# 693) missionary; not apostle in the official or technical sense, but a messenger sent on a special commission (Vincent). λειτουργός (# 3313) minister. The word was used of a public official in civil service; then it was also used for one ministering in religious ceremonies (s.v. 17; TDNT; NIDNTT). χρεία (# 5970) need. πέμψαι aor. act. inf. πέμπω (# 4287) to send. Inf. in indir. speech after the vb. ἡγησάμην. ◆ **26** ἐπειδή (# *2076*) since, since then, because. It presents the reason for Paul feeling compelled to send Epaphroditus (Ellicott). ἐπιποθῶν pres. act. part. ἐπιποθέω (# *2160*) to yearn after, to long for (s. 1:8). Part. used in a periphrastic impf. construction: "he was yearning after" (RWP). ἀδημονῶν pres. act. part. ἀδημονέω (# *86*) to be distressed. Although the root meaning of the word is not clear (GEW, 1:20), the word describes the confused, restless, half-distracted state which is produced by physical derangement, or by mental distress like grief, shame, disappointment, etc. (Lightfoot). ἡκούσατε aor. ind. act. ἀκούω (# *201*) to hear. ἠσθένησεν aor. ind. act. ἀσθενέω (# *820*) to be without strength, to be weak, to be sick. ◆ **27** καὶ γάρ (# *2779; 1142*) for even, yes, even (BD, 236). παραπλήσιον (# *4180*) w. the dat., near to. ἠλέησεν aor. ind. act. ἐλεέω (# *1796*) to have mercy, to show mercy. λύπη (# *3383*) sorrow. σχῶ aor. subj. act. ἔχω (# *2400*) to have; aor., to get, to receive (M, 110). Subj. w. ἵνα (# *2671*) in a neg. purp. cl. ◆ **28** σπουδαιοτέρως adv., comp. of σπουδαίως (# *5081*) w. haste; comp., w. special urgency (BAGD). W. increased eagerness, on account of this circumstance (Lightfoot). ἔπεμψα aor. ind. act. πέμπω (# *4287*) to send. Epistolary aor. (EGT). ἰδόντες aor. act. part. (temp.) ὁράω (# *3972*) to see. Aor. gives the logically antecedent action to the main verb. πάλιν (# *4099*) again. The word is to be taken w. the main vb. χαρῆτε rather than w. the part. (Vincent). χαρῆτε aor. subj. pass. (dep.) χαίρω (# *5897*) to rejoice. ἀλυπότερος comp. ἄλυπος (# *267*) without grief, free from sorrow; comp., less sorrowful. The joy felt by the Philippians will mitigate the sorrow (in his confinement) of the sympathizing apostle (Ellicott). For the neg. character of the alpha privative s. Moorhouse, 47ff. ὦ pres. subj. act. εἰμί (# *1639*) to be. Subj. w. ἵνα (# *2671*) used in a purp. cl. ◆ **29** προσδέχεσθε pres imp. mid. (dep.) προσδέχομαι (# *4657*) to receive, to receive favorably, to welcome. τοιοῦτος (# *5525*) such a one, one w. such characteristics. ἔντιμος (# *1952*) in honor, prized, precious; pred. acc. in a double acc. construction: "hold such ones in honor" (RWP). ◆ **30** ἤγγισεν aor. ind. act. ἐγγίζω (# *1581*) to come near, to draw near, to be near. παραβολευσάμενος aor. mid. (dep.) part. παραβολεύομαι (# *4129*) to gamble, to play the gambler, to expose oneself to danger. The word has connotations of humbling or playing dice by which high sums were often at stake (OCD, 338f). The word was used in the papyri of one who, in the interest of friendship, had exposed himself to dangers as an advocate in legal strife by taking his client's causes, even up to emperors (MM; LAE, 88). The word was later used of merchants who, for the sake of gain, exposed themselves to death (PGL, 1008). The word was used of a fighter in the arena who exposed himself to the dangers of the arena (PGL, 1009). In the post-apostolic church a

group called the *paraboloni* risked their lives by nursing the sick and burying the dead (Lightfoot; Vincent). For the use of the dat. w. this vb. s. M, 64. ἀναπληρώσῃ aor. subj. act. ἀναπληρόω (# *405*) to fill up, to make complete, to fill a gap, to replace. Used of a person w. the gen. it means, "to make up for someone's absence or lack," "to represent one who is absent" (BAGD). ὑστέρημα (# *5729*) that which is lacking, deficiency. There is no rebuke in the word, since the only deficiency is that they could not be w. him themselves, to do him service (Beare). λειτουργία (# *3311*) service, ministry (s.v. 17).

Philippians 3

◆ **1** τὸ λοιπόν (# *3370*) finally. With this Paul probably intends to draw to a close the general admonitions and then takes up specific matters in the latter part of the letter (Victor Paul Furnish, "The Place and Purpose of Philippians 3," *NTS* 10 [1963]: 80-88). τὰ αὐτά (# *899*) the same things. Paul perhaps means the same warning and directives Epaphroditus and Timothy would orally communicate when they visit the Philippians in person. (Furnish, NTS 10:86). The opponents here were those who stressed the need of circumcision and were probably from the small Jewish group in Philippi who formed a sort of Jewish commonwealth (P, 132-36, 231-34). They offered the Christians a legal religion in Judaism (P, 134-39). γράφειν pres. act. inf. γράφω (# *1211*) to write. Epex. inf. is used as a noun explaining the word. ὀκνηρός (# *3891*) causing fear or reluctance, troublesome (BAGD). ἀσφαλής (# *855*). The word is taken from a vb. meaning "to trip up," "to overthrow," "to cause to fall or stumble." With the neg. prefix the adj. is used to describe anything which has stability and firmness enough not to be overthrown. It carries then the idea of certain, dependable knowledge (Furnish, *NTS* 10: 83; s. Luke 1:4). ◆ **2** βλέπετε pres. imp. act. βλέπω (# *1063*) to look, to beware of, to consider, to take proper notice of, to pay attention to, to learn your lesson from (Hawthorne). Pres. imp. calls for habitual action: "continually be on the lookout for" (Vincent). κύνας acc. pl. κύων (# *3264*) dog. The Jews considered dogs to be the most despised and miserable of all creatures and used this word to describe Gentiles. Perhaps the Jews used this designation because of the herds of dogs which prowled about eastern cities, without a home and without an owner, feeding on the refuge and filth of the streets, quarreling among themselves and attacking the passerby (Lightfoot; SB, 3:621; 1:722-26; TDNT; OCD, 358; KP, 2:1245-49). Paul uses the term here of those who prowl around the Christian congregations, seeking to win converts (Beare). ἐργάτης (# *2239*) worker. Instead of doing good works, they do evil works. κατατομή (# *2961*) incision, mutilation. Used in contrast to circumcision (RWP). ◆ **3** περιτομή

(# 4394) circumcision (s. Gal. 2:3). **λατρεύοντες** pres. act. part. λατρεύω (# 3302) to minister, to serve (TDNT). Subst. part., giving the character. **καυχώμενοι** pres. mid. part. καυχάομαι (# 3016) to boast, to glory. **πεποιθότες** perf. act. part. πείθω (# 4275) to persuade; perf., to be persuaded, to be confident, to have confidence (s. 2:24). ◆ **4 καίπερ** (# 2788) even though, although. It is used to clarify the concessive sense of the part. (BD, 219; Blomqvist, 47). **ἔχων** pres. act. part. ἔχω (# 2400) to have. Concessive use of the part. **πεποίθησις** (# 4301) trusting, confidence. **δοκεῖ** pres. ind. act. δοκέω (# 1506) to suppose, to seem, to think. Here, "if anyone is disposed to think" (Vincent). **πεποιθέναι** perf. act. inf. πείθω (# 4275) to persuade (s.v. 3). **μᾶλλον** (# 3437) more, to a higher degree.   ◆ **5 περιτομῇ** (# 4364) circumcision. Here, dat. of respect: "w. respect to circumcision an eighth-day one" (BD, 105; often called dat. of reference s. DM, 85; MT, 238). **ὀκταήμερος** (# 3862) eighth day, on the eighth day. The normal procedure was circumcision on the eighth day after birth, but under certain circumstances the circumcision could be on the ninth, tenth, eleventh or twelfth day (SB, 4:23ff; M, Shabbath 19:5). **φύλη** (# 5876) tribe. A Roman citizen in Philippi was a "member" of the Roman "tribe of Voltinia," but Paul contrasts his citizenship by saying he was from the tribe of Benjamin (P, 122-27; RI, 24; 128, nr. 55; 226, nr. 157; 247-49, nr. 180; 181; Sherwin-White, *Roman Citizenship* [s. Phil. 1:27], 155-57). **Ἑβραῖος** (# 1578) Hebrew. The term emphasized not only the rights and privileges belonging to the Jewish nation, but also that those who lived in the Diaspora (outside of Palestine) had remained true to the religious practices and their language. Paul was trained in the use of the Heb. tongue by Heb.-speaking parents (Vincent; Lightfoot; JPFC, 1:184-225; MM). **νόμος** (# 3795) law. Used here without the article. It emphasizes law in the abstract, as a principle of action (Lightfoot). **φαρισαῖος** (# 5757) Pharisee. For a discussion of their beliefs s. TJ, 70-76. ◆ **6 ζῆλος** (# 2419) zeal. **διώκων** pres. act. part. διώκω (# 1503) to pursue, to persecute. **γενόμενος** aor. mid. (dep.) part. γίνομαι (# 1181) to become. **ἄμεμπτος** (# 289) without blame (s. 2:15).   ◆ **7 ἦν** impf. ind. act. εἰμί (# 1639) to be. **κέρδη** nom. pl. κέρδος (# 3046) profit, gain (s. 1:21). **ἥγημαι** perf. ind. mid. (dep.) ἡγέομαι (# 2451) to consider, to reckon, to count as (s. 2:6). Perf. indicates a completed action w. continuing results: "I have counted (and they are now to me)" (Ellicott). **ζημία** (# 2422) loss. Used for a loss at sea (Acts 27:10) and used in the papyri of a commercial or business loss (MM).   ◆ **8 μενοῦνγε** (# 3529) the presence of so many particles is clearly for the purp. of emphasis (DM, 255) and could be translated, "yes the previous is true, but more than that I also ...." **εἶναι** pres. inf. act. εἰμί (# 1639) to be. Compl. inf. to the main vb. **ὑπερέχον** pres. act. part. acc. n. sing. ὑπερέχω (# 5660) to surpass,

excel. The n. sing. is used as an abstract noun followed by the gen., "the surpassing greatness" (BAGD; BD, 138; s. 2:3). **γνώσεως** (# 1194) knowledge. It is the personal knowledge and acquaintance w. Christ. It is the knowledge of one who loves and knows himself beloved (Bear). **ἐζημιώθην** aor. ind. pass. ζημιόω (# 2423) pass., to suffer loss. Aor. points to the definite period of Paul's conversion. In that great crisis he lost all his legal possessions (Vincent). **σκύβαλον** (# 5032) refuse. It refers to such things as a half-eaten corpse; filth, like lumps of manure or human excrement; the portion of food rejected by the body as unnourishing; or to the scraps or leavings of a feast, the food thrown away from the table (Lightfoot; Hawthorne; TDNT; TLNT; MM; NW, 2, i:701). **ἡγοῦμαι** pres. ind. mid. (dep.) ἡγέομαι (# 2451) to count, to reckon. **κερδήσω** aor. subj. act. κερδέω (# 3045) to gain, to win. Subj. w. ἵνα (# 2671) to express purp.   ◆ **9 εὑρεθῶ** aor. subj. pass. εὑρίσκω (# 2351) to find; pass. to be found. The idea involved is a revelation of true character (EGT). Subj. w. ἵνα to express purp. **ἔχων** pres. act. part. ἔχω (# 2400) to have. **διὰ πίστεως Χριστοῦ** "through faith of Christ"; obj. gen. ("my faith in Christ") or subjective gen. ("faithfulness of Christ") (GGBB, 114). **ἐπὶ τῇ πίστει** on the basis of faith, resting upon faith (Vincent). ◆ **10 γνῶναι** aor. act. inf. γινώσκω (# 1182) to know, to recognize; to know personally through experience, to appropriate. The word often implies a personal relation between the knower and the known, involving the influence of the object of knowledge upon the knower (Vincent; TDNT; ND, 344ff; NIDNTT). Inf. to express purp. or perhaps intended result (Funk, 706). **δύναμιν τῆς ἀναστάσεως** the power of the resurrection. Gen. of means; i.e., the power which caused the resurrection. **κοινωνία** (# 3126) fellowship. **πάθημα** (# 4077) suffering. **συμμορφιζόμενος** pres. pass. part. συμμορφίζομαι (# 5214) to grant or invest w. the same form; pass., to be conformed to, to take on the same form as. This seems to be a reference to the kind of death Paul was to die (BAGD; Meyer).   ◆ **11 εἴ πως** if perhaps. The word of hope or desire (SMT, 111; BD, 191). **καταντήσω** aor. subj. act. καταντάω (# 2918) to reach, to arrive at a destination. **ἐξανάστασις** (# 1983) resurrection, rising up.   ◆ **12 οὐχ ὅτι** not that. The words serve to correct a false impression that might have arisen from his preceding words. **ἔλαβον** aor. ind. act. λαμβάνω (# 3284) (RWP), to receive, to obtain. Aor. points to the time of Paul's conversion; "not as though by my conversion I did once attain" (Lightfoot). **τετελείωμαι** perf. ind. pass. τελέω (# 5457) to reach the goal, to perfect; pass, to be perfect. The perfection referred to is moral and spiritual perfection (Vincent). Perf. describes his pres. state: "not as though I were now already perfected" (Lightfoot). **διώκω** pres. ind. act. (# 1503) to pursue. **καταλάβω** aor. subj. act. καταλαμβάνω (# 2898) to seize, to grasp, to lay hold of. Subj. w. the particle εἰ (# 1623) in a 3rd. class cond. cl., which is a sort of purp. cl. or aim (RWP; RG, 1917). ἐφ' ᾧ for which, for the reason that, because (BD, 123). The phrase can also express purp. ("whereunto") (Lightfoot). κατελήμφθην aor. ind. pass. καταλαμβάνω (# 2898) to reckon, to consider. ◆ 13 κατειληφέναι perf. act. inf. καταλαμβάνω (# 2898) to take hold of. Prep. in compound is perfective, "to grant completely" (RWP). ἓν δέ but one thing. The vb. λέγω could be supplied (Lohmeyer) or the vb. ποιέω is to be understood (Vincent). ὀπίσω (# 3958) behind. ἐπιλανθανόμενος pres. mid. (dep.) part. ἐπιλανθάνομαι (# 2140) to forget. Prep. in compound is directive (MH, 312). ἐπεκτεινόμενος pres. mid. (dep.) part. ἐπικτείνομαι (# 2085) to stretch oneself out for or toward. The metaphor is from the foot race. The word pictures the body of the racer bent forward, his hand outstretched toward the goal and his eye fastened upon it. (Vincent). The vb. is followed by the dat. ◆ 14 σκοπός (# 5024) a mark on which to fix the eye, goal. Paul is evidently referring to the goal of a foot race. For a description of the stadium and the foot race s. DGRA, 105f; Oscar Bronner, "The Apostle Paul and the Isthmian Games," BA 25 (1962): 1-31. The prep. has the sense of the goal (Lohmeyer; PAM, 141). βραβεῖον (# 1092) prize, a prize awarded the winner at the games. ἄνω (# 529) above, upward. The word could be an adv. telling where the calling comes from, or it could point to the direction in which the calling leads: upward, heavenward (PAM, 149). κλήσεως (# 3104) calling. ◆ 15 ὅσος (# 4012) as many as, those who. τέλειος (# 5455) perfect, mature. The word refers to grown men, as opposed to children (Lightfoot). φρονῶμεν pres. subj. act. φρονέω (# 5858) to think, to have an attitude (s. 2:2). Cohortative subj., "Let us have this attitude ..." ἑτέρως (# 2284) adv., otherwise. ἀποκαλύψει fut. ind. act. ἀποκαλύπτω (# 636) to unveil, to reveal. ◆ 16 πλήν (# 4440) nevertheless. The word is used at the conclusion of a section in order to bring out the main point of discussion: "just one thing more" (RG, 1187; Blomqvist, 75ff). ἐφθάσαμεν aor. ind. act. φθάνω (# 5777) to come to, to arrive at, to attain. Dramatic aor. used to express what has just taken place (RG, 842). στοιχεῖν pres. act. inf. στοιχέω (# 5123) to walk in line, to march in battle order. The word refers to walking according to principles of a system (Vincent; TDNT). Inf. used in the sense of an imp. This construction generally follows an imp. and the command is carried on by the inf. (RG, 943; BD, 196f; IBG, 126). ◆ 17 συμμιμητής (# 5213) fellow imitator. γίνεσθε pres. imp. mid. (dep.) γίνομαι (# 1181) to become. σκοπεῖτε pres. imp. act. σκοπέω (# 5023) to look at, to fix one's attention upon, to mark. Here, to mark and follow (Lightfoot). περιπατοῦντας pres. act. part. περιπατέω (# 4344) to walk, to conduct one's life. καθώς (# 2777) just as. τύπος (# 5596) that which is formed by a blow or impression, pattern,

type, example (T; TDNT). ◆ 18 περιπατοῦσιν pres. ind. act. περιπατέω (# 4344) to walk, to conduct one's life. κλαίων pres. act. part. κλαίω (# 3081) to cry, to weep, to weep audibly. The heart of St. Paul's grief would lie in the fact that they degraded the true doctrine of liberty (Lightfoot). σταυρός (# 5069) cross. Here obj. gen., they oppose the cross. ◆ 19 ἀπώλεια (# 724) ruin, destruction. κοιλία (# 3120) stomach. For a description of the luxury of Roman eating s. DGRA, 303-309; LAE, 164f. The word may be used as a general term to include all that belongs most essentially to the bodily, fleshly life of man and therefore inevitably perishes (EGT). αἰσχύνη (# 158) shame. ἐπίγειος (# 2103) earthly, upon the earth. φρονοῦντες pres. act. part. φρονέω (# 5858) to think, to consider (s. 2:2). ◆ 20 πολίτευμα (# 4487) citizenship. The word means either the state, the constitution, to which as citizens we belong, or the functions which as citizens we perform (Lightfoot; Vincent; TDNT; P, 127-34; s. 1:27). ὑπάρχει pres. ind. act. ὑπάρχω (# 5639) to exist, to be (s. 2 Cor. 12:16). ἀπεκδεχόμεθα pres. ind. mid. (dep.) ἀπεκδέχομαι (# 587) to expect anxiously, to await eagerly. Preps. in compound indicate the eager but patient waiting (s. Gal. 5:5). The Christian "citizenship" is not connected to a fictitious "tribe," like the Roman Voltinia, but has real roots in heaven, and the Lord will soon come for His "citizens" (P, 130-31). ◆ 21 μετασχηματίσει fut. ind. act. μετασχηματίζω (# 3571) to refashion, to change, to change the outward form or appearance. The meaning of the word could be illustrated by changing a Dutch garden, not merely into an Italian garden, but by transforming it into something wholly different, like a city (Trench, Synonyms, 263; Lightfoot, 130f). ταπεινώσεως (# 5428) lowliness, humble, insignificant. σύμμορφος (# 5215) conformed; the changing of the inward and outward substance, conforming to or w. something (s. 2:6). ἐνέργεια (# 1918) working. The act. and productive power of God at work (s. 2:13; MNTW, 46-54). δύνασθαι pres. mid. (dep.) inf. δύναμαι (# 1410) to be able to. Epex. inf. explaining the productive power (Hawthorne). ὑποτάξαι aor. act. inf. ὑποτάσσω (# 5718) to place under, to subdue, to subject, to place under one's authority. Epex. inf. αὐτός (# 899) himself. The pron. is used here in a reflex. sense (BD, 148).

Philippians 4

◆ 1 ὥστε (# 5718) wherefore, therefore. It draws a conclusion from Phil. 3:17-21 (EGT). ἀγαπητός (# 28) beloved. ἐπιπόθητος (# 2182) longed for, desired (s. Phil. 1:8). The word is a verbal adj. (RWP; M, 221; MH, 370). στήκετε pres. imp. act. στήκω (# 5112) to stand, to stand firm (s. 1:27). ◆ 2 παρακαλῶ pres. ind. act. παρακαλέω (# 4151) to beseech, to urge, to encourage (TDNT; MNTW, 128ff). φρονεῖν pres. act. inf. φρονέω (# 5858) to be minded, to have an attitude or disposition, to think

(s. 2:2). For the speculations regarding the two women s. Hawthorne. ◆ **3 ναί** (# 3721) yes, yea. The particle is a confirmation of an assertion (Ellicott; RG, 1150). **ἐρωτῶ** pres. ind. act. ἐρωτάω (# 2263) to ask, to request, to ask something of someone. For examples in the papyri s. BS, 276ff; MM. **γνήσιε** voc. γνήσιος (# 1188) legitimately born, genuine, true, sincere (s. 2:20). **σύζυγε** voc. σύζυγος (# 5187) yoked together, yokefellow. Some view this as a proper name, "Synzygus" (Vincent). **συλλαμβάνου** pres. imp. mid. (dep.) συλλαμβάνομαι (# 5197) to take and bring together, to lay hold of, to help, to assist (MM). **συνήθλησαν** aor. ind. act. συναθλέω (# 5254) to fight alongside, to contend w. someone against a common enemy, to labor together. **καί** (# 2779) also. The word may be retrospective, referring to the true yokefellows (Lightfoot), or it may be pleonastic, i.e., superfluous (BD, 228). **λοιπός** (# 3370) rest. **συνεργός** (# 5301) fellow worker. ◆ **4 χαίρετε** pres. imp. act. χαίρω (# 5897) rejoice. Pres. imp. calls for a continual and habitual action. **πάντοτε** (# 4121) always. **ἐρῶ** fut. ind. act. λέγω (# 3306) to speak. ◆ **5 τὸ ἐπιεικές** (# 2117) reasonableness in judging. The word signifies a humble, patient steadfastness which is able to submit to injustice, disgrace, and maltreatment without hatred and malice, trusting in God in spite of it all (Leivestad, 158; s. 2 Cor. 10:1; Trench, *Synonyms*, 154). **γνωσθήτω** aor. imp. pass. γινώσκω (# 1182) to know. A pass. imp.: "let your attitude be known," "allow your attitude to be known." **ἐγγύς** (# 1584) near. The word could imply near in space or near in time. Here the phrase probably expresses general expectation of the speedy second coming of Christ (Vincent). ◆ **6 μεριμνᾶτε** pres. imp. act. μεριμνάω (# 3534) to be anxious, to be troubled, to care for something, to be fretful (Beare). **προσευχῇ** (# 4666) prayer. **δέησις** (# 1255) request; generally a request arising from a specific need. **εὐχαριστία** (# 2374) thanksgiving. It expresses that which ought never to be absent from any of our devotions–namely, the grateful acknowledgement of past mercies, as distinguished from the earnest seeking of fut. (Trench, *Synonyms*, 191). **αἴτημα** (# 161) request, a thing asked for. The word in the pl. indicates the several objects of the request (Lightfoot; Trench, *Synonyms*, 191). **γνωριζέσθω** pres. imp. pass. γνωρίζω (# 1192) to make known. ◆ **7 ὑπερέχουσα** pres. act. part. ὑπερέχω (# 5660) to rise above, to be superior, to surpass (Vincent; s. 2:3). **φρουρήσει** fut. ind. act. φρουρέω (# 5864) to guard. The word, a military term picturing soldiers standing on guard duty, refers to the guarding of the city gate from within as a control on all who went out (BAGD; EGT). Fut. preceded by an imp. and joined by **καί** has the character of a result cl. in a Semitic type of cond. cl.: "make your request known, then the peace of God will guard your hearts" (Beyer, 238-55; BD, 227). **καρδία** (# 2840) heart. The heart is the center of each person, from which thoughts and affection flow (PAT, 326).

νόημα (# 3784) thought, act of the will which issues from the heart (Vincent; PAT, 327). ◆ **8 τὸ λοιπόν** (# 3370) finally. **ὅσα** pl. ὅσος (# 4012) whatever. **ἀληθής** (# 239) truth. **σεμνός** (# 4948) worthy of respect or honor, noble, dignified, reverent. The word implies that which is majestic and awe-inspiring (BAGD; Trench, *Synonyms*, 347; Lohmeyer). **ἁγνός** (# 54) morally pure, undefiled. In the LXX it signifies ceremonial purification (Vincent; Lohmeyer; Trench, *Synonyms*, 333). **προσφιλής** (# 4713) acceptable, pleasing, lovely. It refers to those things whose grace attracts (EGT). **εὔφημος** (# 2368) well-sounding, praiseworthy, attractive, appealing (BAGD). **ἀρετή** (# 746) virtue; the most comprehensive Gr. term for moral excellence and the central theme of Gr. ethics (Beare; TDNT; NIDNTT; Cremer; PS, 152ff; PIGC, 1:1-12). For a comparison of Paul and Stoicism, esp. Seneca, s. Lightfoot, 270-333; PS; Beare, 42f). **ἔπαινος** (# 2047) praise. **λογίζεσθε** pres. imp. mid. (dep.) λογίζω (# 3357) to consider, to reckon, to take into account, to think on; "use your facilities upon them" (Ellicott; Vincent). Pres. calls for a continual or habitual action. ◆ **9 καί** (# 2779) also. The word here is ascensive, but its other occurrences in this v. are copulative ("and") (Ellicott). **ἐμάθετε** aor. ind. act. μανθάνω (# 3443) to learn. **παρελάβετε** aor. ind. act. παραλαμβάνω (# 4161) to receive, to receive tradition or that which is passed on (TDNT). **ἠκούσατε** aor. ind. act. ἀκούω (# 201) to hear. **εἴδετε** aor. ind. act. ὁράω (# 3972) to see. The last two vbs.–"heard and saw"–refer to Paul's personal contact w. the Philippians (Vincent). **πράσσετε** pres. imp. act. πράσσω (# 4556) to do, to practice. The vb. contains the idea of continuity and repeated action (Trench, *Synonyms*, 361). Pres. calls for a continual practicing. **ἔσται** fut. ind. mid. (dep.) εἰμί (# 1639) to be. For the construction of the imp. plus **καί** plus the fut., forming a type of cond. cl. w. the fut. used in a result cl., s.v. 7. ◆ **10 ἐχάρην** aor. ind. pass. χαίρω (# 5897) to rejoice, to be glad; epistolary aor. (Vincent). Paul intentionally places the "thank you" at the end of the letter after he had developed "their partnership in his imprisonment" (CIC, 127-47). **μεγάλως** (# 3487) adv., greatly. **ἤδη ποτέ** (# 2453; 4537) now at last. The word indicates an indef. delay, but has more the notion of culmination rather than time (RG, 1147). **ἀνεθάλετε** aor. ind. act. ἀναθάλλω (# 352) to sprout again, to shoot up, to blossom again, to put forth new shoots (RWP; Lightfoot). Prep. in compound probably contains a causative idea (MH, 295). **φρονεῖν** pres. act. inf. φρονέω (# 5858) to think (s. 2:2). Inf. as obj. of the vb. "You caused your thought for me to sprout and bloom afresh, like a tree putting out fresh shoots after the winter" (Vincent). **ἐφ' ᾧ** upon which, upon whom. The phrase could indicate the obj. of their thinking (Ellicott) or it could be taken as causal (BD, 123). **ἐφρονεῖτε** impf. ind. act. φρονέω (# 5858) to think. Impf. emphasizes the continual action in the past: "you were all along taking thought"

(Vincent). **ἠκαιρεῖσθε** impf. ind. mid. (dep.) ἀκαιρέομαι (# *177*) to have no opportunity, to lack opportunity, to lack a convenient time. The church at Philippi had sent a monetary gift to Paul via Epaphroditus, which was perhaps to help take care of his expenses during his time in prison in Rome. This included food and rent for his accommodations, which was probably rather expensive (BAFCS, 3:227-42). For an enlightening discussion on the financial relationship between the Philippian church and Paul in the light of Roman social customs s. PSCZP, 126-224. ◆ **11 οὐχ ὅτι** not that. It is used to avoid a misunderstanding, "my meaning is not..." (Meyer). **ὑστέρησις** (# *5730*) coming short, lack. **ἐγώ** (# *1609*) "I"; strongly emphatic. **ἔμαθον** aor. ind. act. μανθάνω (# *3443*) to learn. Effective aor. pointing to the completion of the process. **αὐτάρκης** (# *895*) content, self-sufficiency, having enough. The word indicates independence of external circumstances and often means the state of one who supports himself without aid from others (Lightfoot; BAGD). The word indicates an inward things (Vincent). **εἶναι** pres. inf. act. εἰμί (# *1639*) to be. Inf. as obj. of the vb. ἔμαθον. ◆ **12 ταπεινοῦσθαι** pres. pass. inf. ταπεινόω (# *5427*) to make low; pass., to be brought low. Here it has to do w. the physical rather than the moral or spiritual and is used in respect to the needs of daily life (EGT). Inf. is used as obj. of the vb. **περισσεύειν** pres. act. inf. περισσεύω (# *4355*) to overflow, to abound. **μεμύημαι** perf. ind. pass. μυέω (# *3679*) to initiate; pass. to be initiated, to be instructed. A t.t. of the mystery religions (BAGD). Perf. emphasizes the completed action w. a continuing state or result. **χορτάζεσθαι** pres. pass. inf. χοράζω (# *5963*) to fill, pass. to be full. The word was used primarily of feeding and fattening animals in a stall (Vincent). **πεινᾶν** pres. act. inf. πεινάω (# *4277*) to be hungry. Perhaps he spent days in hunger during his time in prison, even though he was entitled to the grain distribution in Rome (BAFCS, 3:242). **ὑστερεῖσθαι** pres. mid. (dep.) inf. ὑστερέομαι (# *5728*) to come short, to fall behind, to lack, to suffer need. ◆ **13 ἰσχύω** (# *2710*) pres. ind. act. to be strong, to have strength, to be able. **ἐνδυναμοῦντι** pres. act. part. ἐνδυναμόω (# *1904*) to empower, to give strength, to infuse strength into someone (Vincent). ◆ **14 πλήν** (# *4440*) nevertheless, however (s. 3:16). **καλῶς** (# *2822*) well. **ἐποιήσατε** aor. ind. act. ποιέω (# *4472*) to do. **συγκοινωνήσαντες** pres. act. part. συγκοινωνέω (# *5170*) to participate in something w. someone, to share together w. someone (s. Phil. 1:7). **θλῖψις** (# *2568*) pressure, trouble, tribulation. ◆ **15 καί** (# *2779*) and. It marks the transition to his first experience of their generosity (EGT). **Φιλιππήσιοι** (# *5803*) voc. pl. Paul evidently coined this spelling to

the Latin character of the city. The normal term was Φίλιππεύς (P, 116-18). **ἀρχῇ** (# *794*) beginning. **ἐξῆλθον** aor. ind. act. ἐξέρχομαι (# *2002*) to go out. **ἐκοινώνησεν** aor. ind. act. κοινωνέω (# *3125*) to have fellowship, to share, to be a partner. **εἰς λόγον** as to an account. He used a metaphor from the business world. The Philippians by their contributions had "opened an account" w. him (Vincent; for the commercial t.t. s. BAGD; LAE, 117; MM). **δόσεως** gen. sing. δόσις (# *1521*) giving. The word is very common in financial transactions to refer to a payment or an installment (MM; Preisigke.) **λήμψεως** (# *3331*) receiving. This was also a t.t. in the business world and meant the receiving of a payment; it was used in connection w. the word **δόσεως** in the sense of credit and debit (Vincent; MM; Lohmeyer; P, 147-52). ◆ **16 ἅπαξ** (# *562*) once. **δίς** (# *1489*) twice. Used together in the sense of, "not merely once, but twice" (Vincent). **χρεία** (# *5970*) need. **ἐπέμψατε** aor. ind. act. πέμπω (# *4287*) to send. ◆ **17 ἐπιζητῶ** pres. ind. act. ἐπιζητέω (# *2118*) to seek after. Prep. in compound is directive, indicating the concentration of the action upon some object (MH, 312). **δόμα** (# *1517*) that which is given, gift. **πλεονάζοντα** pres. act. part. πλεονάζω (# *4429*) to increase, to become more, to multiply. The commercial or business metaphor continues; their earthly investment accrues heavenly dividends. Business investments were common in Rome. ◆ **18 ἀπέχω** (# *600*) pres. ind. act. to have in full, to receive in full. The word was also a commercial t.t., meaning "to receive a sum in full and give a receipt for it." For examples s. BAGD; MM; BS, 229; LAE, 111. **πεπλήρωμαι** perf. ind. pass. πληρόω (# *4444*) to fill; pass., to be filled. Perf. emphasizes the continuing state. **δεξάμενος** aor. mid. (dep.) part. δέχομαι (# *1312*) to receive. Aor. part. expresses contemporaneous action: "when I received." **ὀσμή** (# *4011*) smell. **εὐωδία** (# *2380*) aroma, fragrance; ὀσμὴν εὐωδίας was a t.t. indicating the acceptance and pleasantness of a sacrifice (Gnilka). **δεκτήν** acc. sq. δεκτός (# *1283*) acceptable. **εὐάρεστος** (# *2298*) pleasing. ◆ **19 πληρώσει** fut. ind. act. πληρόω (# *4444*) to fulfill, to supply. **ἐν δόξῃ** in glory. Used here as adv., indicating the mode or manner of the fulfillment–gloriously–in such a way that His glory will be manifested (Vincent). ◆ **20 θεῷ** dat. sing. θεός (# *2536*). Dat. of advantage or personal interest. ◆ **21 ἀσπάσασθε** aor. imp. mid. (dep.) ἀσπάζομαι (# *832*) to greet, to give greetings. ◆ **22 μάλιστα** (# *3436*) especially. **οἱ ἐκ τῆς Καίσαρος οἰκίας** the members of Caesar's household. Probably slave and freedmen attached to the palace (Lightfoot, esp. 171-78; DPL, 83-84). ◆ **23 χάρις** (# *5921*) grace. The daily unmerited help from the Lord Jesus.

Colossians

Colossians 1

◆ **1** For the structure of ancient letters s. Rom. 1:1. Τιμόθεος (# *5512*) Timothy (s. Bruce; 1 Tim. 1:1). He is mentioned not as a joint author, but to indicate that he too preaches the same true gospel (O'Brien). For a defence of the Pauline authorship of the book s. O'Brien; UTMC, 175-229. ◆ **2** ἐν Κολοσσαῖς (# *1877; 3145*) in Colossae. A city of Asia Minor located on the south bank of the Lycus River in the Lycus Valley, near the neighboring towns of Laodicea and Hierapolis (ABD, 1:1089; DPL, 147-52; Dunn, 20-23). As Herodotus describes Xerxes' march westward in 480 B.C., he says, "He came to Colossae, a great city of Phrygia (πόλιν μεγάλην Φρυγίης), situated at a spot where the river Lycus plunges into a chasm and disappears. The river, after flowing underground for about five Stadia, reappears once more and empties itself into the Maeander" (Herodotus, *History*, 7.30; O'Brien; Bruce; NW, 2, i:714-15; ANTC, 155-61). Antiochus III (223-187 B.C.) transported about two thousand Jews from Mesopotamia to Phrygia and Lydia (Jos., *Ant.*, 12:147-53) and some may have been Essenes who settled in the area of Colossae (TJ, 82-83). ἅγιος (# *41*) holy. The adjs. can be taken w. the noun ("the holy brothers") or it can be taken as a noun indicating a definite class of people, "the holy ones" (Moule; Martin, NCB). πιστός (# *4412*) The adj. can mean "believing" or "faithful." The latter sense is perhaps preferable and has the idea of trustworthy, steadfast, unswerving (Lightfoot; Dunn). ◆ **3** εὐχαριστοῦμεν pres. ind. act. εὐχαριστέω (# *2373*) to give thanks. The pl. could be an epistolary pl. ("I thank") or a real pl., "Timothy and I thank" (Moule). The expression of congratulatory thanksgiving was a characteristic feature of ancient letter writing (Dunn). πάντοτε (# *4121*) always. It could be taken either w. the part. or w. the main vb. The latter is probably more accurate (Lohse). προσευχό-μενοι pres. mid. (dep.) part. προσεύχομαι (# *4667*) to pray. Iterative pres. points to a repeated action. ◆ **4** ἀκούσαντες aor. act. part. ἀκούω (# *201*) to hear. Aor. indicates antecedent action. Part. could be temp. ("after we heard") or causal, "because we heard" (Martin, NCB). He heard from Epaphras, since the apostle had no direct personal knowledge of the Colossian church (Lightfoot). ἔχετε pres. ind. act. ἔχω (# *2400*) to have. ◆ **5** διά (# *1328*) w. acc. because. ἐλπίδα acc. ἐλπίς (# *1828*) hope (TDNT; EH). The prep. phrase can be taken either w. the main vb. as the ground of thanksgiving, or w. the words πίστιν and ἀγάπην, indicating the reason for these (Abbott; Eadie; Moule). For the psychological necessity of hope in one's life s. Basil Jackson, "Psychology, Psychiatry and the Pastor: Relationships Between Psychiatry, Psychology, and Religion," *Bib Sac* 132 [1975]: 3-15. ἀποκειμένην pres. mid. (dep.) part. ἀπόκειμαι (# *641*) to put up, to store up, to put away for one's use. As an extension of a royal Persian custom, Hellenistic rulers would store up goods for faithful servants (Lohse; TDNT). προηκούσατε aor. ind. act. προακούω (# *4578*) to hear beforehand, to hear previously; i.e., they had heard the gospel before they had heard the false teaching (Moule). ἀληθείας (# *237*) truth. Here, gen. of quality belonging to λόγος, "the word of truth" (Abbott). ◆ **6** παρόντος pres. act. part. (adj.) πάρειμι (# *4205*) to arrive and be present (Lohmeyer). The prep. combines the idea of the gospel being present w. the idea of the gospel coming to them (Abbott; Lightfoot). κάθως (# *2777*) just as. καρποφορού-μενον pres. mid. part. καρποφορέω (# *2844*) to bear fruit. Mid. emphasizes that the gospel bears fruit of itself. Part. is used in a periphrastic construction emphasizing the continuity of the process (RWP). αὐξανόμενον pres. mid. (dep.) part. αὐξάνω (# *889*) to grow, to increase, to develop. The word refers to the outward expansion, while the previous part. refers to the personal inner working (Abbott). ἀφ' ἧς ἡμέρας (# *608; 4005; 2465*) from which day. The fruitfulness and growing started on the day they received the grace of God (Lohse). ἠκούσατε aor. ind. act. ἀκούω (# *201*) to hear. Aor. points to the specific time when they heard the gospel. ἐπέγνωτε aor. ind. act. ἐπιγινώσκω (# *2105*) to know, to recognize. It implies not so much developed knowledge as active conscience recognition, of taking knowledge of (Abbott; Dunn). Ingressive aor., "you came to know." χάρις (# *5921*) grace. It refers to God's unmerited and undeserved help to someone in need, here indicating the message of salvation in the gospel (TDNT; NIDNTT; EDNT). ἐν ἀληθείᾳ (# *1877; 237*) in truth; i.e., the grace of God as it truly is (Moule). ◆ **7** ἐμάθετε aor. ind. act. μανθάνω (# *3443*) to learn. ἀγαπη-τός (# *28*) one who is loved, beloved. σύνδουλος (# *5281*) fellow slave. πιστός (# *4412*) faithful. διάκονος (# *1356*) minister, one who ministers to the needs of another (TDNT). As a native of Colossae (Col. 4:12), Epaphras had been the evangelist of the Lycus valley where there were now flourishing churches (O'Brien). ◆ **8 δηλώσας** aor. act. part. δηλόω (# 1317) to make plain, to make clear. **ἐν πνεύματι** (# 1877; 4460) in the Spirit. It is to be connected w. ἀγάπη and expresses the ground of their love, which was not individual sympathy, personal acquaintance or the like, but belonged to the sphere of the Holy Spirit's influence (Abbott). ◆ **9 διὰ τοῦτο** (# 1328; 4047) for this reason. **καί** (# 2779) also. The word is to be taken w. the main vb. (Lohse). **ἠκούσαμεν** aor. ind. act. s.v. 6. **παυόμεθα** pres. ind. mid. (dep.) παύομαι (# 4264) to cease. For the 1st. pers. pl. s.v. 3. **προσευχόμενοι** pres. mid. (dep.) part. προσεύχομαι s.v. 3. **αἰτούμενοι** pres. mid. part. αἰτέω (# 160) to ask, to request. Mid. indicates that one is asking something for himself. Mid. was often used in a commercial sense and also of requests addressed to God (BD, 165f; M, 160f). **ἵνα** (# 2671) that. W. subj. used to introduce the content of the prayer (Lohse). **πληρωθῆτε** aor. subj. pass. πληρόω (# 4444) to fill. Pass. is used as a substitute for God's name: "may God fill you" (Lohse). Pass. is followed here by the acc. (BD, 87). **ἐπίγνωσις** (# 2106) knowledge. **τὴν ἐπίγνωσιν τοῦ θελήματος** knowledge of the will of God. The knowledge here is not of other worlds but of the will of God (Lohse). The concept of knowledge in Colossians is related more to the concept of knowledge found in the OT and the DSS than that in the gnostic philosophy (Edwin Yamauchi, "Qumran and Colosse," *Bib Sac* 121 [1964]: 141-52; DPL, 352-53; for specific references in the DSS and other literature s. also NIDNTT; Dunn; Eph. 1:17). **σοφία** (# 5053) wisdom (DPL, 966-73). The word indicated for the Gr. the mental excellency in its highest and fullest sense (Lightfoot; Abbott). The OT concept of wisdom (חכמה) was that of applying the knowledge of God's will to life's situations (TDNT; Lohse; NIDOTTE, 2:130-34; 4:1276-85). **σύνεσις** (# 5304) understanding, insight. The word refers to putting together the facts and information and drawing conclusions and seeing relationships. **πνευματικῇ** (# 4461) spiritual. The prevailing meaning of the word in the NT is "of, or belonging to the Holy Spirit" (Eadie; for the suf. of the adj. s. MH, 378). The phrase is best taken w. the vb. **πληρωθῆτε**, meaning to be filled w. the knowledge of God by having spiritual knowledge and discernment (Harris). ◆ **10 περιπατῆσαι** aor. act. inf. περιπατέω (# 4344) to walk about, to conduct one's life (Dunn). Inf. to express intended or potential results (IBG, 141; BD, 197f; S. Lewis Johnson, Jr., "Spiritual Knowledge and Walking Worthily of the Lord," *Bib Sac* 118 [1961]: 342). According to the teaching of the Dead Sea community, those who walked according to the spirit of truth will walk pleasing before God. For this teaching and the references in the DSS s. Lohse. **ἀρεσκεία** (# 742) pleasing. The word, often used in a neg. sense of trying to gain

favor from someone, describes that cringing, subservient attitude of one who would do anything to please a benefactor (Abbott; Johnson, 342; MM; TDNT; Dunn). **καρποφοροῦντες** pres. act. part. καρποφορέω s.v. 6. Pres. indicates that fruit-bearing for believers is to be a continuous thing; the act. voice may point to external diffusion or it may simply direct attention away from the inherent energy of the fruit-bearing instrument, the Christian (Johnson, 342). **αὐξανόμενοι** pres. mid. part. αὐξάνω s.v. 6. **ἐπίγνωσις** (# 2106) knowledge. Dat. here could be either loc. ("growing in knowledge"), or it could be instr., "growing by knowledge." The simple instr. dat. represents the knowledge of God as the dew or the rain which nurtures the growth of the plant (Lightfoot). ◆ **11 δύναμις** (# 1539) power, might. **δυναμούμενοι** pres. pass. (dep.) part. δυναμόω (# 1540) to make powerful, to strengthen. **κράτος** (# 3197) strength, might. It refers to the inherent strength which displays itself in the rule over others (TDNT; GEW, 2:8; s. Eph. 1:19). Here it refers to the might which is characteristic of His glory (Eadie; Moule) and is a Semitic construction meaning "His glorious might," w. the word "glory" indicating the awesome radiance of deity (Dunn). **μακροθυμία** (# 5705) patience, longsuffering. It refers to the self-restraint which does not hastily revenge a wrong (Lightfoot; TDNT; NTW, 83-85; s. Gal. 5:22; Rom.2:4). ◆ **12 εὐχαριστοῦντες** pres. act. part. s.v. 3. **ἱκανώσαντι** aor. act. part. ἱκανόω (# 2655) to make sufficient, to qualify, to authorize. Adj. use of part. to emphasize a quality. Aor. indicates antecedent action. This is a qualification for inheritance due solely to the grace of God (Johnson, 344). For the textual problem s. TC, 620. **μερίδα** acc. μερίς (# 3535) part, portion. **κλῆρος** (# 3102) lot. The phrase is not exactly equivalent to the word κληρονομία since it designates only the allotted part. Gen. here is either apposition ("the portion which consists in the lot") or it is partitive, "to have a share in the lot" (Abbott). For the teaching of inheritance in the DSS s. Lohse. **φωτί** dat. φῶς (# 5890) light. The inheritance is in the light because He who is the Light dwells there and fills heaven w. His marvelous light (Johnson, 344). ◆ **13 ἐρρύσατο** aor. ind. mid. (dep.) ῥύομαι (# 4861) to rescue, to deliver. For the relation of rescuing or deliverance w. the OT and the Dead Sea community s. Lohse. **ἐξουσία** (# 2026) authority. The word properly means liberty of action, i.e., freedom to do something without any hindrance. In relation to others it means authority and here refers to the characteristic and ruling principle under which they dwelt before conversion to Christ (Abbott; TDNT). **μετέστησεν** aor. ind. act. μεθίστημι (# 3496) to remove from one place to another, to transfer. The word was often used to signify deportation of a body of men or the removal of them to form a colony (Eadie). **βασιλεία** (# 993) kingdom (DPL, 524-26). **τοῦ υἱοῦ** (# 5626) son.

Here possessive gen., "belonging to the Son." τῆς ἀγάπης (# 27) obj. gen., "the Son who is the object of His love (Abbott). ◆ 14 ἐν ᾧ (# 1877; 4047) in whom. The reference is to Christ and the rel. sentence speaks of the new life which we have received in Christ (Lohse). ἀπολύτρωσις (# 667) redemption, complete release based on the payment of a price (s. Rom. 3:24; LAE, 327; also the references to the DSS listed by Lohse). τὴν ἄφεσιν τῶν ἁμαρτιῶν forgiveness of sin, obj. gen. Epex. acc. explaining redemption (Harris). ◆ 15 εἰκών (# 1635) image, copy. In Gr. thought an image shares in reality what it represents. Christ is the perfect likeness of God. The word contains the idea of representation and manifestation (TLNT; NIDNTT; Moule; Lightfoot; TDNT; Lohse; Bruce; PGL, 410-16). The word points to His revealing the Father and His pre-existence (O'Brien). For pre-existence in Judaism s. Bruce; DPL, 743-46. ἀόρατος (# 548) not capable of being seen, invisible. It was a central point of Jewish theology that God cannot be seen (Dunn). πρωτότοκος (# 4758) firstborn. The word emphasizes the pre-existence and uniqueness of Christ as well as His superiority over creation. The term does not indicate that Christ was a creation or a created being. (For this important word s. Lohse; Lightfoot; Abbott; Moule; Martin; PRJ, 150-53; SB, 3:626; TLNT; EDNT; TDNT; NIDNTT; GELTS, 410; PGL, 1201-3; GI, 122-26; CEJC, 53f; Bruce; O'Brien.) κτίσεως (# 3232) creation. ◆ 16 ἐν αὐτῷ in Him. The prep. denotes Christ as the sphere within which the work of creation takes place (Bruce). All the laws and purposes which guide the creation and government of the universe reside in Him (Lightfoot). The prep. is possibly both instr. and local (Moule). He is not in all things, but all things are in Him, a difference that is not insignificant (Fred B. Craddock, "'All Things in Him': A Critical Note on Col. 1.15-20," NTS 12 [1965]: 78-80). ἐκτίσθη aor. ind. pass. κτίζω (# 3231) to create. ὁρατός (# 3971) visible. ἀόρατος (# 548) invisible. εἴτε … εἴτε whether. κυριότης (# 3262) lordship. ἀρχαί fem. pl. ἀρχή (# 794) beginning, ruler. δι' αὐτοῦ through Him. The prep. w. the gen. describes Christ as the immediate instrument of creation (Abbott; Lightfoot). εἰς αὐτὸν for Him, unto Him. The prep. indicates that Christ is the goal of creation (Lohse). The rabbis taught that the world was created for the Messiah (SB, 3:626). ἔκτισται perf. ind. pass. κτίζω (# 3231) to create. Perf. emphasizes the duration and persistence of the act of creation (Ellicott). ◆ 17 αὐτός (# 899) The pron. is used emphatically–He Himself, in contrast to the created things (Abbott). Here it means "He and no other" (MT,40). πρό (# 4574) before. The prep. could refer to priority in time or in rank but here the idea of time is here more suitable. Used w. the pres. of the vb., the idea expresses immutability of existence; i.e., "His existence is before all things" (Abbott; Moule; Lightfoot). συνέστηκεν perf.

ind. act. συνίστημι (# 5319) to place together, to stand together, to hold together, to cohere. God Himself is the principal of cohesion in the universe (Lightfoot), the unifying band which encompasses everything and holds it together. This applies not only to the largest things of the universe, but also to its smallest things (Lohse). ◆ 18 κεφαλή head (DPL, 377-78; BBC). ἀρχή (# 794) beginning, origin. The word refers to priority in time and to originating power (Lightfoot; Moule). γένηται aor. subj. mid. (dep.) γίνομαι (# 1181) to become, to be. The purp. cl. means, "that He Himself in all things (material and spiritual) may come to hold the first place" (RWP). πρωτεύων pres. act. part. πρωτεύω (# 4750) to be first, to have first place, to hold the chief place. For the quotation from Meander–"Never does a house fail to come to grief, where woman takes the lead in everything"–s. MM. ◆ 19 εὐδόκησεν aor. ind. act. εὐδοκέω (# 2305) to be pleased. The subject here is God. πλήρωμα (# 4445) fullness. The word denotes completeness and was used for a ship's crew (Dunn; GELTS; DPL, 320). It could refer either to the totality of the divine powers and attributes (Lightfoot) or perhaps better to the fullness of saving grace and power which belongs to one constituted as savior (Eadie; S. Lewis Johnson, "From Enmity to Amity," Bib Sac 119 [1962]: 141-42). κατοικῆσαι aor. act. inf. κατοικέω (# 2997) to live, to dwell, to settle down. The word indicates permanent abode (Lightfoot). The aor. could be ingressive aor., "to take up one's permanent abode" (Lightfoot, 142). ◆ 20 ἀποκαταλλάξαι aor. act. inf. ἀποκαταλλάσσω (# 639) to exchange hostility for friendship, to reconcile. (Johnson, 143; TDNT; NIDNTT; V; APC, 186-233; MNTW, 10ff). Prep. in compound has the meaning "back" and implies a restitution to a state from which one has fallen. The meaning is "to effect a thorough change back" (MH, 298; Lightfoot). Inf. can be epex., explaining what was pleasing to Him, or inf. of purpose. εἰρηνοποιήσας aor. act. part. εἰρηνοποιέω (# 1647) to make peace. The part. describes the means of the reconciliation. The insertion of the part. indicates that reconciliation is not to be thought of as a cosmic miracle which merely changed the state of the universe outside of man, but shows that reconciliation is primarily concerned w. the restoration of relationships (R.P. Martin, "Reconciliation and Forgiveness in Colossians," RH, 113; O'Brien). Peace is more than an end to hostilities. It has a positive content, pointing to the presence of positive blessings and concerned w. the spiritual blessing and prosperity of the whole man (VANT, 251; DPL, 697-98). αἷμα (# 135) blood, referring to a life given up in a violent death, and in this context denoting life offered up sacrificially and voluntarily in death (Harris). σταυρός (# 5089) cross. Here gen. of reference or relationship (Harris). ◆ 21 καί (# 2779) and, also. The word indicates that this message of reconciliation is also applicable to those at the church of Colossae (Lohse). **ποτέ** (# *4537*) once, formerly. **ὄντας** pres. act. part. εἰμί (# *1639*) to be. **ἀπηλλοτριωμένους** perf. pass. part. ἀπαλλοτριόω (# *558*) to estrange, to alienate. Part. used in a periphrastic construction w. the perf. It expresses more forcibly the settledness of the alienation (Abbott; s. Eph. 2:12). **ἐχθρός** (# *2398*) hostility. The adj. is act. rather than pass. (Lightfoot). **διανοίᾳ** (# *1379*) mind. Here dat. of reference. The hostile minds of the Colossian Christians have turned into a willing and glad subservience; and the ultimate result of this interchange of attitude toward God will be perfection in sanctification (Ladd, 455). ◆ **22 νυνί** (# *3815*) now. **ἀποκατηλλάγητε** aor. ind. pass. ἀποκαταλάσσω s.v. 20. The vb. has a soteriological meaning which embraces both the overcoming of the cosmic hostility through the lordship of Christ and the restoration of sinful men to God's favor and family (Martin, RH, 114). For a discussion of the pass. as a variant reading s. TC, 621f; Lohse. **παραστῆσαι** aor. act. inf. παρίστημι (# *4225*) to present. Inf. can express either purp. or result. The picture here may be a sacrificial metaphor (Moule). It may be a legal word indicating that one is placed before a court of justice (Lohse; Dunn). **ἄμωμος** (# *320*) without spot, without blemish. In the LXX the word was used as a t.t. to designate the absence of anything amiss in a sacrifice, anything which would render it unworthy to be offered (Trench, *Synonyms*, 379; GELTS, 25). **ἀνέγκλητος** (# *441*) without accusation, unaccused, free from any charge at all. It is a legal word indicating that there is no legal or judicial accusation which can be brought against a person (Trench, *Synonyms*, 381; TDNT; Abbott; Lohse; O'Brien). **κατενώπιον** (# *2979*) before; "right down in the eye of" (RWP). ◆ **23 εἴ γε** (# *1145; 1623*) if, assuming that (Abbott). The particle introduces a cond. cl. which the author assumes to be true, thus expressing confidence rather than doubt (Dunn; Harris). **ἐπιμένετε** pres. ind. act. ἐπιμένω (# *2152*) to remain, to continue. Prep. in compound adds to the force of the linear action of the pres.: "to continue and then some" (RWP). **τεθεμελιωμένοι** perf. pass. part. θεμελιόω (# *2530*) to lay the foundation of something; pass., to be founded. Perf. emphasizes the completed state or condition. **ἑδραῖος** (# *1612*) firm. This word refers to the firmness of the structure (Abbott). For DSS parallels to the figure of a building used to describe the people of God s. Lohse. **μετακινούμενοι** pres. mid./pass. part. μετακινέω (# *3560*) to move from one place to another, to shift from one place to another, to move away (transitive) (BAGD; MM). Pres. stresses the "not constantly shifting" (Abbott). **ἠκούσατε** aor. ind. act. ἀκούω (# *201*) to hear. **κηρυχθέντος** aor. pass. part. κηρύσσω (# *3062*) to preach, to proclaim, to herald, to proclaim as a herald (TDNT; NIDNTT; TLNT). **ἐγενόμην** aor. ind. mid. (dep.) γίνομαι (# *1181*) to become. ◆ **24 χαίρω** pres. ind. act.

(# *5897*) to rejoice. W. the temp. **νῦν** (# *3814*) it refers to the present condition of Paul as he was in prison (Harris). **πάθημα** (# *4077*) that which is suffered, suffering. The suf. in the word indicates a pass. idea or the result of an action (MH, 355). **ὑπὲρ ὑμῶν** (# *5642; 5148*) on behalf of you, for you. The prepositional phrase is to be connected w. the word παθήμασιν (Eadie). **ἀνταναπληρῶ** pres. ind. act. ἀνταναπληρόω (# *499*) to fill up. The idea of the prep. in compound may be reciprocal or may signify that the supply comes from an opposite quarter; or it may contain the idea of substituting for that which is lacking (MH, 297; Lightfoot; Lohse; S. Lewis Johnson, "The Minister of the Mystery," *Bib Sac* 119 [1962]: 228ff). **ὑστέρημα** (# *5729*) lacking, that which is lacking. **θλίψεων** gen. pl. θλίψις (# *2568*) pressure, tribulation, affliction. The sufferings of Paul were the afflictions of Christ, who suffered in and w. Paul because of his identification w. Christ in mystical union (Johnson, 231; for a discussion of the various interpretations s. Moule; O'Brien). **σαρκί** dat. σάρξ (# *4922*) flesh. **σώματος** (# *5393*) body. **ἐκκλησία** (# *1711*) assembly, a group called together for a specific reason–church. Here it refers to the universal church composed of all believers. ◆ **25 ἐγενόμην** aor. ind. mid. (dep.) γίνομαι (# *1181*) to become. **οἰκονομία** (# *3873*) stewardship. The word indicated the responsibility, authority, and obligation given to a household slave (s. Lohse; J. Reumann, "OIKONOMIA - Terms in Paul in Comparison with Lukian Heilsgeschichte," *NTS* 13 [1967]: 147-67; Bruce; O'Brien; Dunn; TDNT; TLNT; EDNT). **δοθεῖσαν** aor. pass. part. (adj.) δίδωμι (# *1443*) to give. Theol. pass. indicating God as the giver. **πληρῶσαι** aor. act. inf. πληρόω (# *4444*) to fill, to fulfill. The word has the sense of doing fully, carrying to completion (Moule). Inf. of purp. Aor. points to the specific act. ◆ **26 μυστήριον** (# *3696*) mystery, that which is hidden and undiscoverable by human means, but that which has been revealed by God (Eph. 3:3; Johnson, 231f; Lohse; Moule; O'Brien; Dunn). **ἀποκεκρυμμένον** perf. pass. part. (adj.) ἀποκρύπτω (# *648*) to hide, to veil, to conceal. Perf. part. emphasizes the state or condition. **ἀπό** from. The prep. is doubtless temp. (Lightfoot). **αἰώνων** gen. pl. αἰών (# *172*) age. The pl. here indicates successive periods of time (TDNT). **γενεῶν** gen. pl. γενεά (# *1155*) generation; an age includes many generations (Abbott). **ἐφανερώθη** aor. ind. pass. φανερόω (# *5746*) to make clear, to manifest. ◆ **27 ἠθέλησεν** aor. ind. act. θέλω (# *2527*) to desire, to want to, w. inf. **γνωρίσαι** aor. act. inf. γνωρίζω (# *1192*) to make known. Compl. inf. to the main vb. **δόξης** gen. sing. δόξα (# *1518*) glory. The word became a comprehensive word for God's glorious presence (Moule; NIDNTT; TDNT). **ἔθνεσιν** dat. pl. ἔθνος (# *1620*) folk, nation, Gentile. **ἐν ὑμῖν** (# *1877; 5148*) in you, among you. For Christ to be among the Gentiles involved being in those who believed (Johnson, 232). ◆ **28 καταγγέλλομεν** pres. ind. act. καταγγέλλω (# *2859*) to proclaim. The word indicates an official proclamation (Lohmeyer; NIDNTT). Pres. emphasizes the continual and habitual action. **νουθετοῦντες** pres. act. part. νουθετέω (# *3805*) to admonish, to correct through instruction and warning (TDNT; TLNT; EDNT). Part. of manner defining more nearly the manner or accompaniments of the proclamation (Ellicott). **πάντα ἄνθρωπον** each or every man. The threefold repetition of the phrase is for emphasis. **διδάσκοντες** pres. act. part. διδάσκω (# *1438*) to teach. **παραστήσωμεν** aor. subj. act. s.v. 22. Subj. w. **ἵνα** (# *2671*) to express purp. **τέλειος** (# *5455*) perfect, mature (Lohse). ◆ **29 κοπιῶ** pres. ind. act. κοπιάω (# *3159*) to work, to labor, to labor w. wearisome effort, to work to exhaustion (T; TDNT). **ἀγωνιζόμενος** pres. mid. (dep.) part. ἀγωνίζομαι (# *76*) to strive, to exert effort. The athletic picture behind this word emphasizes Paul's missionary work, w. all its attendant toil, tireless exertion, and struggles against all manner of setbacks and opposition (PAM, 175). **ἐνέργεια** (# *1918*) working, effectual working. The word is used of the effective working of God's power (MNTW, 46-54). **ἐνεργουμένην** pres. mid. (dep.) part. ἐνεργέω (# *1919*) to work effectively, to be effectual (TDNT).

Colossians 2

◆ **1 θέλω** pres. ind. act. (# *2527*) to wish, to desire to, to want to, w. inf. **εἰδέναι** perf. act. inf. οἶδα (# *3857*) to know. Def. perf. w. pres. meaning. **ἡλίκον** (# *2462*) how great. **ἀγών** (# *74*) struggle. The picture is that of an athletic contest which is strenuous and demanding. The struggle here is not the struggle against God, but the intense effort of the one praying as he struggles within himself and against those who oppose the gospel (PAM, 113f, 123f; BBC). **ἑόρακαν** perf. ind. act. ὁράω (# *3972*) to see. For the form of this vb. s. BD, 44. **ἐν σαρκί** (# *1877; 4922*) in the flesh. This is to be taken w. the noun πρόσωπόνμου and implies that they had a knowledge of Him, though not a personal one (Abbott). ◆ **2 ἵνα** (# *2671*) that. The word introduces the purp. of the struggle. **παρακληθῶσιν** aor. subj. pass. παρακαλέω (# *4151*) to comfort, to encourage (Phil. 2:1). **συμβιβασθέντες** aor. pass. part. συμβιβάζω (# *5204*) to bring together, to unite, to knit together. The meaning here could be to instruct, to teach (Dibelius; Lohse; TDNT). Part. of manner. **πληροφορία** (# *4443*) full assurance, firm conviction, confidence. The gen. is descriptive, the wealth consists of conviction (Moule). **συνέσεως** (# *5304*) understanding, insight. **ἐπίγνωσις** (# *2106*) knowledge. **μυστήριον** (# *3696*) mystery. The gen. **τοῦ θεοῦ** (# *2536*) is possessive and the next gen. **Χριστοῦ** (# *5986*) Christ, is in apposition to the word μυστηρίον (Moule; Lightfoot). ◆ **3 θησαυρός** (# *2565*) storehouse, treasure. The imagery may be from Jewish apocalyptic

ideas of heavenly treasures, hidden from the human eye (Dunn; 1 Enoch 18:1). **γνώσεως** (# *1194*) knowledge. **ἀπόκρυφος** (# *649*) hidden. It is in Christ that all the treasures of divine wisdom and knowledge have been stored up–formerly in hiding, but now are displayed to those who have come to know Christ (Bruce). ◆ **4 ἵνα** (# *2671*) that, in order that. The conjunction may express purp. ("I say this in order that ..."), or equally possible w. an imperatival sense: "Let no one ..." (MT, 102). **παραλογίζηται** pres. subj. mid. (dep.) παραλογίζομαι (# *4165*) to reckon wrong, to cheat by false reasoning (T). The word was used in the papyri of a keeper of a state library who had shown a willingness to make a wrong use of certain documents. Paul uses the word here to point to drawing an erroneous conclusion from the reasoning submitted (MM; for the use in Josephus of the meaning "to deceive" s. CCFJ, 3:300). Prep. in compound has the idea of counting beside or counting aside, w. the idea of miscalculating (MH; 319; RWP). Subj. w. **ἵνα** (# *2671*) to express purp. **πιθανολογία** (# *4391*) dat. sing. persuasive speech. The word was used by classical writers for probable reasoning opposed to demonstration (Abbott). The word is used in the papyri in a court case of those who sought persuasive words to keep things obtained by robbery (Lohse; MM). The terminology used here is practically equivalent to our English expression, "to talk someone into something," "to use plausible sounding, but actually specious arguments," as one would hear at the marketplaces (Dunn; S. Lewis Johnson, "Beware of Philosophy," *Bib Sac* 119 [1962]: 304). Instr. dat. ◆ **5 γάρ** (# *1142*) for. The particle gives the reason why Paul, who was unknown to the Colossians and not present w. them, can give such a warning. Through the Holy Spirit he is so bound to them as though he were w. them (Dibelius). **ἄπειμι** pres. ind. act. (# *582*) to be away from someone, to be absent. **χαίρων** pres. ind. act. χαίρω (# *5897*) to rejoice. **βλέπων** pres. act. part. (temp.) βλέπω (# *1063*) to see. Pres. expresses contemporaneous action. "I am with you rejoicing and seeing you." **τάξιν** (# *5423*) an orderly arrangement; used in the military sense of a rank or orderly array (Lightfoot; Lohse). **στερέωμα** (# *5106*) that which is firm, hard, solid. For the development in meaning s. GEW 2:790f. Here it is probably a continuation of the military metaphor and means a solid front, a close phalanx (Lightfoot). ◆ **6 παρελάβετε** aor. ind. act. παραλαμβάνω (# *4161*) to receive, to receive through transmission, to receive through teaching; equivalent to the rabbinical terms for receiving and passing on tradition (Johnson, 305f; Lohse; TDNT). **περιπατεῖτε** pres. imp. act. περιπατέω (# *4344*) to walk about, to walk, to conduct life in accord w. the truth of Paul's preaching and not in accord w. enticing words of heretics (Johnson, 306). Pres. calls for a continual and habitual action. For a brief discussion of the so called

"Colossian heresy" s. BTNT, 304-5; 400-12; DPL, 350-53, also 148-50. ◆ **7** ἐρριζωμένοι perf. pass. part. ῥιζόω (# 4845) to cause to take root; pass., to be or to become firmly rooted or fixed. The word was also used in the metaphor of the building and pictured the firm and solid foundation (BAGD; Lohse; TDNT). Perf. points to the past completed action w. continuing results or condition and pictures the settled state brought about by conversion. The following parts. in the pres. emphasize the continuing development which is always advancing (Abbott). ἐποικοδομούμενοι pres. pass. part. ἐποικοδομέω (# 2224) to build up, to build up upon (BDG). βεβαιούμενοι pres. pass. part. βεβαιόω (# 1011) to make firm, to establish, to strengthen (BAGD; TDNT; TLNT). Pres. gives the idea of being more and more established (Abbott). πίστις (# 4411) faith. The word could be used in the subjective sense so the dat. would be instr. ("by your faith"). Faith would be, as it were, the cement of the building (Lightfoot). It is, however, more probable that faith is to be taken in its obj. sense, referring to the doctrines of the Christian faith (Eadie; Johnson, 303). ἐδιδάχθητε aor. ind. pass. διδάσκω (# 1438) to teach. περισσεύοντες pres. act. part. περισσεύω (# 4355) to overflow, to abound. εὐχαριστία (# 2374) dat. sing. thanksgiving. ◆ **8** βλέπετε pres. imp. act. βλέπω (# 1063) to watch, to see; here, "Look out!" "Beware!" The word is normally followed by μή plus the subj., but the ind. ἔσται in this case shows that the danger is real (Lightfoot). ἔσται fut. ind. mid. (dep.) εἰμί (# 1639) to be. συλαγωγῶν pres. act. part. συλαγωγέω (# 5194) to carry off as booty or captive. The word meant "to kidnap" (Dibelius; Johnson, 306), and here depicts carrying someone away from the truth into the slavery of error (BAGD). φιλοσοφία (# 5814) philosophy. It was used among Jewish writers in the sense of "teaching," "an intellectual movement" (Dunn; CCFJ; BBC). κενός (# 3031) empty. ἀπάτη (# 573) deceit. παράδοσις (# 4142) tradition, that which is given over from one to another (TDNT; TLNT). ἄνθρωπος (# 476) man; man-made tradition to be contrasted w. the true, living, divine tradition just alluded to (Moule). στοιχεῖα (# 5122) component parts of a series, elementary things. The word could refer to elemental powers–cosmic spirits–or more probably to elementary teaching (Johnson, 308; Moule; Dibelius; Lohse; TDNT). For studies regarding the heresy at Colossae s. Martin, 12ff; Martin, NCB, 9-19; Andrew J. Bandstra, "Did the Colossian Errorists Need a Mediator?" ND, 329-43; NW, 21, i:722-26; also the various articles in CC; Dunn, 23-35. ◆ **9** κατοικεῖ pres. ind. act. κατοικέω (# 2997) to settle down, to be at home (s. Col. 1:19). Pres. indicates the continual state and points to the pres. reality (Lohse). πλήρωμα (# 4445) fullness (s. Col. 1:19). θεότη (# 2540) divine nature, deity. The word differs from the expression "Godhead" in Rom. 1:20 in that it emphasizes not so much

divine attributes but divine nature or essence. Divine glory did not merely gild Him, lighting up His person for a season w. a splendor not His own; He was and is absolute and perfect God (Trench, *Synonyms*, 8; TDNT; Lightfoot; EDNT; O'Brien). σωματικῶς (# 5395) adv., bodily. The word refers to the human body of Christ (Johnson, 310), indicating also the full humanity of Jesus a humanity which was not simply a covering for His deity (Lohse; TDNT; Moule; Lohmeyer; O'Brien). ◆ **10** πεπληρωμένοι perf. pass. part. πληρόω (# 4444) to fill, to make full. Perf. is used in a periphrastic construction accentuating the abiding results of believers' completeness through union w. the exalted Lord. In Him they find their needs fully met (Johnson, 310). κεφαλή (# 3051) head. The word here probably denotes primarily supremacy, but it also emphasizes that the head is the center of vital force, the source of all energy and life (Lightfoot; DPL, 377-78). ἀρχή (# 794) beginning, principality, power. ◆ **11** περι-ετμήθητε aor. ind. pass. περιτέμνω (# 4362) to circumcise (s. Gal. 2:3). περι-τομή (# 4364) circumcision. ἀχειροποίητος (# 942) not made w. hands. ἀπέκδυσις (# 589) putting off. Prep. in compound expresses a complete putting off and laying aside (Abbott). σάρκος gen. sing. σάρξ (# 4922) flesh. The reference here could be to putting off the fleshly nature of man, the crucifixion of the old man (S. Lewis Johnson, "The Sufficiency of Union with Christ," *Bib Sac* 120 [1963]: 15), or it could be a reference to the physical death or crucifixion of Christ (Moule; SBT, 41f). ◆ **12** συνταφέντες aor. pass. part. συνθάπτω (# 5313) to bury together. συνηγέρθητε aor. ind. pass. συνεγείρω (# 5283) to raise up together w. someone, to be co-resurrected. ἐνέργεια (# 1918) effective working, divine working (s. Col. 1:29). ἐγείραντος aor. act. part. ἐγείρω (# 1586) to raise up, to resurrect. The rite of baptism typified the reality of death and resurrection. Death is the neg. side, resurrection is the positive (Johnson, 16). ◆ **13** ὄντας pres. act. part. εἰμί (# 1639) to be. Pres. part. to emphasize a continuing trait. παράπτωμα (# 4183) transgression (s. Eph. 2:1). Dat. here could be loc. or instr., describing either the circumstances (Moule) or the reason for their being dead (Lightfoot). ἀκροβυστία (# 213) foreskin, uncircumcision. συνεζωοποίησεν aor. ind. act. συζωοποιέω (# 5188) to make alive together (s. Eph. 2:5; for the usage in Jewish writings s. Dunn). χαρισάμενος aor. mid. (dep.) part. χαρίζομαι (# 5919) to grant as a favor, to give graciously, to forgive out of grace (Abbott; TDNT; NIDNTT; TLNT; CPP). ◆ **14** ἐξαλείψας aor. act. part. ἐξαλείφω (# 1981) to wash over, to wipe out. The word was used for wiping out the memory of an experience, or for canceling a vote, annulling a law, or canceling a charge or debt. It was also used for washing out the writing on a papyrus (NTW, 46-48; MM; Preisigke, 1:507; Moule; BBC). καθ' (# 2848) w. the gen., against. χειρόγραφον (# 5934) handwriting.

It was used as a t.t. for a written acknowledgment of debt. It is an I.O.U., a statement of indebtedness personally signed by the debtor (Abbott; Moule; LAE, 334). For a description of the Jewish certificate of indebtedness and for its use in Jewish apocalyptical writings refering to a book where the good and bad deeds of a person were recorded s. Dunn; SB, 3:628; Lohse. δόγμα (# *1504*) decree. The word referred to a legal obligation, a binding law or edict placed in a public place for all to see (TDNT; Lohmeyer; Lohse; Martin, NCB; NDIEC, 4:146; Dunn). Here dat. of description, a document containing or consisting of decrees (IBG, 45; MT, 219). ὑπεναντίος (# *5641*) opposed, against, hostile, directly opposed. It described the active hostility (Lightfoot). ἦρκεν perf. ind. act. αἴρω (# *149*) to take away. Perf. stands in contrast to the aor. in this section and fixes attention on the pres. state of freedom resulting from the action which was esp. before the apostle's mind (Abbott). μέσον (# *3545*) middle, combined w. the vb., a strong expression meaning "and put out of sight" (Lightfoot). προσηλώσας aor. act. part. προσηλόω (# *4669*) to nail to. Modal part. describing the manner in which Christ removed the handwriting. He nailed the Mosaic Law with all its decrees to His cross and it died w. Him (Ellicott). σταυρός (# *5089*) cross. ◆ **15** ἀπεκδυσάμενος aor. mid. (dep.) part. ἀπεκδύομαι (# *588*) to strip off, to put off as one puts off a garment. Christ divested Himself at the cross of the evil power which had struggled w. Him so strongly during His ministry in attempts to force Him to abandon the pathway of the cross (Johnson, 20; Dunn). ἐδειγμάτισεν aor. ind. act. δειγματίζω (# *1258*) to display, to expose, to display as a victor displays his captives or trophies in a triumphal procession (Lightfoot). παρρησία (# *4244*) openness, boldness, confidence (Abbott; Lightfoot). θριαμβεύσας aor. act. part. θριαμβεύω (# *2581*) to lead in a triumph. It pictures a victorious general leading his prisoners in a triumphal procession (Moule; TJ, 204-9: s. 2 Cor. 2:14; also Rory B. Egan, "Lexical Evidence of Two Pauline Passages," *NovT* 19 [1977]: 34-62; R. Yates, "Colossians 2.15: Christ Triumphant," *NTS* 37 (1991): 573-91. For a study of these vs. s. Ralph P. Martin, "Reconciliation and Forgiveness in Colossians," RH, 116-24). ◆ **16** κρινέτω pres. imp. act. κρίνω (# *3212*) to judge, to take one to task (Abbott). Pres. imp. w. the neg. μή (# *3590*) calls for the stopping of an action in progress or indicates that an action should not be a habitual one (MKG, 272f). βρῶσις (# *1111*) eating. πόσις (# *4530*) drinking. Here it refers to indulgence in wine (Dibelius). The idea that man could serve deity or draw near to deity or prepare oneself for the reception of a revelation through ascetic living and fasting was widespread in the ancient world (Lohse). μέρος (# *3538*) part. Used in the construction ἐν μέρει to mean "in respect to", "in the matter of" (Abbott). ἑορτή (# *2038*) festival. Here it

refers chiefly to the annual festival like the Passover, Pentecost, etc. (Lightfoot). νεομηνία (# *3741*) new moon (DPL, 402-4). This describes the monthly festival and the following word σαββάτων refers to the weekly holy day (Lightfoot). ◆ **17** σκιά (# *5014*) shadow. The word refers either to a shadow which in itself has no substance but indicates the existence of a body which casts the shadow (Abbott), or it indicates a dim outline, a sketch of an object in contrast w. the object itself. This would mean that the OT ritual observances were dim outlines of the NT redemptive truths (S. Lewis Johnson, "The Paralysis of Legalism," *Bib Sac* 120 [1963]: 112). For the use of the figure of a shadow in Josephus and rabbinical writings s. SB, 3:628. μελλόντων pres. act. part. μέλλω (# *3516*) to be about to. Subst. part. Here it means "things coming." ◆ **18** καταβραβευέτω pres. imp. act. καταβραβεύω (# *2857*) to decide against someone as an umpire would, to deprive of the prize, to give judgment against someone (BAGD; Abbott; Lohse; Preisigke, 1:744; Lohmeyer). θέλων pres. act. part. θέλω (# *2527*) to want to, to desire to, w. inf. Vb. here followed by the prep. could be taken as a septuagintism and be translated "being bent upon" (Fred O. Francis, "Humility and Angelic Worship in Colossians 2:18," CAC, 167). ταπεινοφροσύνη (# *5425*) lowliness, humility. The word was often used in connection w. fasting, and several Jewish Christian writings specify that the consequence of this ascetic practice is entrance into the heavenly realm (Francis, CAC, 168ff). θρησκεία (# *2579*) worship. The word can be used in a variety of ways but stands for the act of worship (Francis, CAC, 180). ἄγγελος (# *34*) angel. Here the word is normally taken as obj. gen. ("the worship given to angels"), but it is also possible (Dunn) that the gen. is subj. gen. and refers to the worship the angels performed (Francis, CAC, 177-80). ἑόρακεν perf. ind. act. s.v. 1. ἐμβατεύων pres. act. part. ἐμβατεύω (# *1836*) to enter into, to penetrate. Perhaps the meaning here is the entering into heavenly spheres as a sort of superspiritual experience. For various contexts in which this word appears and a discussion of this interpretation s. CAC, 171-76; cf. PLG, 453; for other views s. also Abbott; Lohse; Johnson, 111; Dunn. φυσιούμενος pres. pass. part. φυσιόω (# *5881*) to puff up, to blow up; pass, to be puffed up. Their profession of humility was a cloak for excessive pride (Lightfoot). νοῦς (# *3808*) mind, thinking facility. ◆ **19** κρατῶν pres. act. part. κρατέω (# *3195*) to hold fast to someone, to remain closely united w. someone (BAGD; Lohse). κεφαλή (# *3051*) head; here the Head regarded as a title, so that a person is at once suggested, and the rel. pronoun that follows is masc. (Lightfoot). σῶμα (# *5393*) body. Here it refers to the church as the body of Christ, consisting of the saints and deriving its unity and growth from Christ (SBT, 224; DPL, 76-82). ἁφῶν gen. pl. ἁφή (# *913*) ligament.

The word could refer to the nerves (Meyer) or to the joints of the body as contacts between the members (Lightfoot). For a study of the word s. Eph. 4:16; Robinson; Lightfoot; O'Brien. **σύνδεσμος** (# *5278*) band, that which binds together. Given the figure of the church being the body of Christ, these words refer to believers in the body of Christ, who are to exercise their spiritual gift in the church for the edification of the whole body (Johnson, 115). **ἐπιχορηγούμενον** pres. pass. part. ἐπιχορηγέω (# *2220*) to furnish or provide, to support; pass., to be supported, to receive help (BAGD). **συμβιβαζόμενον** pres. pass. part. s.v. 2. **αὔξει** pres. ind. act. αὔξω (# *889*) to grow. Pres. emphasizes the continual growth. **αὔξησις** (# *890*) growth. Cognate acc. here being the acc. of the inner content used for emphasis (BD, 84f; RG, 478; DM,94). Growth does not come through a denial of certain foods, but rather growth comes from God. ◆ **20 ἀπεθάνετε** aor. ind. act. ἀποθνήσκω (# *633*) to die. Ind. in a 1st class cond. cl. which views the cond. as true. **στοιχεῖον** (# *5122*) elementary teaching s.v. 8. **ζῶντες** pres. act. part. ζάω (# *2409*) to live. Part. used w. **ὡς** (# *6055*) is concessive ("as though"). The particle here gives the subjective motivation of the subject or action: w. the assertion that, on the pretext that, w. the thought that you are still living (BD, 219). **δογματίζεσθε** pres. ind. mid. δογματίζω (# *1505*) to issue a decree. Permissive mid., "why are you allowing yourselves to be subjected to authoritative decrees?" (RG, 808; MT, 57). ◆ **21 ἄψῃ** aor. subj. mid. (dep.) ἅπτομαι (# *721*) to touch, to take hold of, to grasp. **γεύσῃ** aor. subj. mid. (dep.) γεύομαι (# *1174*) to taste, to partake of, to enjoy. **θίγῃς** aor. subj. act. θιγγάνω (# *2566*) to touch. For a comparison of the words for "touch" and the first word's use in a sexual sense s. Lightfoot; Abbott; Schweizer. The prohibition concerning purity has a strong Jewish flavor (Dunn). ◆ **22 ἀπόχρησις** (# *712*) consuming, consumption, using up. The prep. in compound is perfective–completely using up (MH, 299; Ellicott). **ἔνταλμα** (# *1945*) commandment. **διδασκαλία** (# *1436*) teaching, doctrine. ◆ **23 ἔχοντα** pres. act. part. ἔχω (# *2400*) to have. Part. is used w. ἐστιν to form a periphrastic pres. ind. (RWP), pointing out that the character of the precepts is such that a word of wisdom belongs to them (Abbott). **ἐθελοθρησκία** (# *1615*) The word could mean "self-chosen worship" (Francis; CAC, 181f; MH, 290; BD, 64; BBC). **ταπεινοφροσύνη** (# *5425*) lowliness; s.v. 18. **ἀφειδία** (# *910*) unsparing, severity, hard treatment (S. Lewis Johnson, "Human Taboos and Divine Redemption," *Bib Sac* 120 [1963]: 210). **πλησμονή** (# *4447*) filling up, satisfaction, gratification, but it may be used in the bad sense, indulgence of the flesh (BAGD; Lightfoot; Abbott).

Colossians 3

◆ **1 συνηγέρθητε** aor. ind. pass. συνεγείρω (# *5283*) to raise up together; pass. to be co-resurrected. Ind. used in a cond. cl. which assumes the reality: "if then (as is the case) you were raised together w. Christ" (EGT). Aor. looks at the completed action. **ἄνω** (# *539*) above; "the things above." The words are used to mean the heavenly world (Lohse; TDNT; DPL, 382). For a contrast between things above and things below in Jewish writings s. SB, 1:395, 977; 2:116, 133, 430; 3:630. **ζητεῖτε** pres. imp. act. ζητέω (# *2426*) to seek. Pres. imp. suggests a continual and habitual action. **δεξιᾷ** (# *1288*) right, right hand (Eph. 1:20). **καθήμενος** pres. mid. (dep.) part. κάθημαι (# *2764*) to sit. The sitting at the right hand was considered a place of honor (Schweizer). ◆ **2 φρονεῖτε** pres. imp. act. φρονέω (# *5858*) to think, to be minded. The vb. in this v. differs from that employed in the preceding in referring more to an inner disposition, while the former is practical pursuit (Eadie). ◆ **3 ἀπεθάνετε** aor. ind. act. ἀποθνήσκω (# *633*) to die. **κέκρυπται** perf. ind. pass. κρύπτω (# *3221*) to hide. The idea of life being hidden in God suggests three thoughts: secrecy where the believer's life is nurtured by secret springs; safety, "w. Christ in God" marking a double protection; and identity, the believer being identified w. the risen Lord (Johnson, 212). Perf. views the completed state arising from a past action. ◆ **4 ὅταν** (# *4020*) w. subj., whenever. **φανερωθῇ** aor. subj. pass. φανερόω (# *5746*) to make plain or clear, to manifest. Here it refers to the coming of the Lord, at which time the veil will be removed so that the things now hidden from our eyes will be illuminated in a bright light (Lohse). **φανερωθήσεσθε** fut. ind. pass. φανερόω (# *5746*). ◆ **5 νεκρώσατε** aor. imp. act. νεκρόω (# *3739*) to put to death. The meaning here, comparable to Rom. 6:11, contains the idea "reckon as dead" (Bruce). **μέλη** pl. μέλος (# *3517*) member. The members of the body were used to carry out the desires. According to the rabbis there are as many commandments and restraints in the law as the body has members and the evil impulse is said to be king over 248 members (Schweizer); the two great passions which the evil inclination plays the most upon are idolatry and adultery (S. Schechter, *Some Aspects of Rabbinic Theology,* 250). **πορνεία** (# *4518*) illicit sex, sexual activity apart from marriage. Sexual activity was often connected w. the idolatrous worship of false gods (TDNT; DPL, 871-75; Gal. 5:19). **ἀκαθαρσία** (# *174*) uncleanness, filthiness (DPL, 776; Gal. 5:19). **πάθος** (# *4079*) passion. The word indicates a drive or force which does not rest until it is satisfied (Trench, *Synonyms,* 324). **ἐπιθυμίαν** (# *2123*) desire, lust. The word, wider in meaning than the previous word, reaches to all evil longing (Lightfoot; DNP, 2:542-44). **πλεονεξία** (# *4432*) insatiable selfishness, greed (NTW, 97; TDNT; TLNT). **εἰδωλολατρία** (# *1630*) idolatry. The accs. in this v. are accs. of general reference: "put to death the members in reference to ..." (DM, 93; RG, 486). ◆ **6 ἔρχεται** pres. ind. mid. (dep.) ἔρχομαι (# 2262) to come. Fut. pres. used to emphasize the certainty of the fut. event. **ὀργή** (# 3973) wrath, anger. It refers to the deep-seated anger of God which displays itself in eternal punishment to come upon those who practice sexual sins, uncontrolled greed, and service to idols (TDNT; NIDNTT; DPL, 991-92; Lohse). ◆ **7 περιεπατήσατε** aor. ind. act. περιπατέω (# 4344) to walk about, to conduct one's life. The vb. used w. the prep. indicates "to take part in" (BAGD). Constative aor. summing up their whole life of the past (RWP; DM, 196; Funk, 620f). **ἐζῆτε** impf. ind. act. ζάω (# 2409) to live. Customary impf. indicating the continual action of the past: "you used to live." ◆ **8 ἀπόθεσθε** aor. imp. mid. (dep.) ἀποτίθημι (# 700) to take off from oneself, to change one's clothes, to remove one's clothes from oneself, to put off. **θυμός** (# 2596) anger. It refers to a burning anger which flares up and burns w. the intensity of a fire (Trench, *Synonyms*, 130f; TDNT). **κακία** (# 2798) malice. It refers to the vicious nature which is bent on doing harm to others (Lightfoot; Trench, *Synonyms*, 37ff; TDNT). **βλασφημία** (# 1060) slander. It indicates the attempt to belittle and cause someone to fall into disrepute or to receive a bad reputation (TLNT; TDNT; for examples from the DSS s. Lohse). **αἰσχρολογία** (# 155) filthy talk, dirty speech, abusive language (Lightfoot; MM). ◆ **9 ψεύδεσθε** pres. imp. mid. (dep.) ψεύδομαι (# 6017) to lie. Pres. imp. w. the neg. **μή** (# 3590) forbids a manner of life. **ἀπεκδυσάμενοι** aor. mid. (dep.) part. ἀπεκδύομαι (# 588) to take off completely, to strip off of oneself. Causal part. contains the motive for the preceding exhortation (Abbott). Paul means that if the old man really has been put off, one must not at a critical moment revert to the way one acted before his conversion. For this and a discussion of the origin of Paul's metaphor, along w. various parallel usages, s. P. W. van der Horst, "Observations on a Pauline Expression," *NTS* 19 (1973): 185, 181-87. **παλαιός** (# 4094) old. **πρᾶξις** (# 4552) deed. The pl. describes the individual deeds which characterized the former life. ◆ **10 ἐνδυσάμενοι** aor. mid. (dep.) part. ἐνδύομαι (# 1907) to put on oneself, to cloth oneself. Causal part. (Hendriksen). **νέος** (# 3742) new. The word only expresses newness in point of time (Abbott; Lightfoot; Trench, *Synonyms*, 219f). **ἀνακαινούμενον** pres. pass. part. ἀνακαινόω (# 363) to make new again, to renew. The idea of "new" is that of newness in quality (s. Rom. 12:2; TDNT). The prep. in compound does not suggest the restoration of the original state, but its contrast of late (Abbott). Pres. points to the continual action: "which is ever being renewed" (Lightfoot). Pass. indicates that the action is performed by another. **ἐπίγνωσις** (# 2106) knowledge; thorough knowledge

(Abbott; s. 1:9). **εἰκόνα** acc. sing. εἰκών (# 1635) image (TDNT; NIDNTT; TLNT; EDNT). **κτίσαντος** aor. act. part. κτίζω (# 3231) to create. **αὐτόν** (# 899) him. The reference is to the new man rather than man in general (Ellicott). ◆ **11 ὅπου** (# 3963) where. **περιτομή** (# 4364) circumcision. **ἀκροβυστία** (# 213) foreskin, uncircumcision. **βάρβαρος** (# 975) barbarian. The word properly denoted one who spoke an inarticulate, stammering, unintelligible language and was adopted by Gr. exclusiveness and pride to stigmatize the rest of mankind, denoting one who was not a Gr. (Lightfoot; Lohse, TDNT; BBC; Rom. 1:14). **ἐλεύθερος** (# 1801) free, one who had been freed from slavery. ◆ **12 ἐνδύσασθε** aor. imp. mid. (dep.) s.v. 10. **ἐκλεκτός** (# 1723) chosen, elect. If God chose them as members of His new creation, they must fulfill the command to conduct themselves accordingly. **ἠγαπημένοι** perf. pass. part. ἀγαπάω (# 26) to love (TLNT; TDNT; EDNT). Perf. points to a past completed action w. a continuing state or result. **σπλάγχνον** (# 5073) heart. It denotes esp. the nobler inward parts—heart, liver, and lungs—and figuratively refers to the seat of the emotion (Abbott; MNTW, 156; TDNT; s. Phil. 1:8). **οἰκτιρμός** (# 3880) compassion (s. Phil. 2:1). **χρηστότης** (# 5983) kindness. It is kindness expressed in attitude and deed, the friendly and helpful spirit which seeks to meet the needs of others through kind deeds (TDNT; s. Gal. 5:22). **ταπεινοφροσύνη** (# 5425) lowliness in thinking, humility. It is the recognizing of one's own weakness, but also the recognition of the power of God (TDNT; NIDNTT). **πραΰτης** (# 4559) meekness. The word indicates an obedient submissiveness to God and His will, w. unwavering faith and enduring patience displaying itself in a gentle attitude and kind acts toward others, and this often in the face of opposition. It is the restrained and obedient powers of the personality brought into subjection and submission to God's will by the Holy Spirit (s. Gal. 5:23). **μακροθυμία** (# 3429) longsuffering. It is a long holding out of the mind before it gives room to action or passion. It indicates the patient longsuffering in bearing injustices or unpleasant circumstances without revenge or retaliation but w. a view or hope to a final goal or betterment (Trench, *Synonyms*, 196; TDNT; Gal. 5:23). ◆ **13 ἀνεχόμενοι** pres. mid. (dep.) part. ἀνέχομαι (# 462) to endure, to bear w., to put up w. someone (BAGD; Dunn). Part. describes the manner or means. Pres. emphasizes the continual action. **χαριζόμενοι** pres. mid. (dep.) part. χαρίζομαι (# 5919) to be gracious, to forgive (Eph. 4:32; TLNT; EDNT; CPP). **ἑαυτοῖς** = ἀλλήλοις. For the reflex. pron. used instead of the reciprocal pron. s. BD, 150; MT, 37f. The reflex. pron. here may suggest the performance of an act faintly resembling that of Christ, namely, of each one toward all—themselves included, Christians being members one of another (Ellicott). **ἔχῃ** pres. subj. act. ἔχω (# 2400) to have.

Pres. has the idea of "having" rather than the idea of "getting" as expressed by the aor. (M, 110). Subj. w. ἐάν (# 1569) in a 3rd. class cond. cl. where the cond. is viewed as possible. **μομφή** (# 3664) blame, cause for complaint. The vb. from which this noun is taken means "to find fault w. someone," "to be dissatisfied w. someone," and refers most commonly to errors of omission; so the noun here is regarded as a debt which needs to be remitted (Lightfoot; TDNT). **ἐχαρίσατο** aor. ind. mid. (dep.) χαρίζομαι (# 5019). Aor. points to the completed action. **καθὼς ... οὕτως** (# 2777; 4048) just as ... so. There should be the same attitude on both sides. ◆ **14 ἐπί** (# 2093) w. the dat. The prep. could mean "in addition to," "on top of all the others," or it may have an elative force and mean "above all;" i.e., love is the most important moral quality in the believer's life (Moule; S. Lewis Johnson, "Christian Apparel," *Bib Sac* 121 [1964]: 30). **σύνδεσμος** (# 5278) that which binds or holds something together, bond. **τελειότης** (# 5456) perfection, complete maturity. Gen. here could be an obj. gen. ("the bond producing perfection" [MT, 212; Lohse]), or it could be a type of descriptive gen.: "the bond which signifies or indicates perfection." The word here refers to the full expression of the divine life in the community, devoid of bitter words and angry feelings, and freed from the ugly defects of immorality and dishonesty (Bruce). ◆ **15 βραβευέτω** pres. imp. act. 3rd. pers. sing. βραβεύω (# 1093) to referee, to be an umpire, to call a decision, to decide between; then in a fig. sense to direct, to administer, to control. Either an athletic stadium or a judicial setting is the background (EDNT; TDNT; MM; Lohse; Lightfoot; O'Brien). **ἐκλήθητε** aor. ind. pass. καλέω (# 2813) to call. **εὐχάριστος** (# 2375) thankful. The word indicates the obligation of being thankful to someone for a favor done. The thankfulness arises out of the grace of God and that which He has done (TDNT). **γίνεσθε** pres. imp. mid. (dep.) γίνομαι (# 1181) to become. Pres. indicates a continual action pointing to a habit of life. ◆ **16 ἐνοικείτω** pres. imp. act. 3rd. pers. sing. ἐνοικέω (# 1940) to live in, to dwell in, to take up one's residence in, to make one's home among (Moule; Preisigke, 1:493). **πλουσίως** adv. (# 4455) extravagantly rich, richly. **διδάσκοντες** pres. act. part. διδάσκω (# 1438) to teach. This and the following parts. could be taken as impvs., or as part. of means or manner (Harris). **νουθετοῦντες** pres. act. part. νουθετέω (# 3805) to admonish, to correct one who is at fault through admonition (s. 1:28). **ψαλμός** (# 6011) psalm. It was often used of the psalms in the OT and has the idea of a song w. musical accompaniment (Trench, *Synonyms*, 296; Lightfoot; Lohse). **ὕμνος** (# 5631) hymn. The word is used of a song which is a praise to God (Trench, *Synonyms*, 297f; Lightfoot). **ᾠδαῖς** dat. pl. ᾠδή (# 6046) song. This is the general word for any kind of a song (Trench, *Synonyms*,

300f; Lightfoot). The three dats. are to be taken w. the part. **ᾄδοντες** rather that w. **διδάσκοντες** or **νουθετοῦντες**. **ᾄδοντες** pres. act. part. ᾄδω (# 106) to sing. ◆ **17 ἐάν** (# 1569) w. the subj. generalizes the object: whatever, everything whatever (RWP). **ποιῆτε** pres. subj. act. ποιέω (# 4472) to do. **εὐχαριστοῦντες** pres. act. part. εὐχαριστέω (# 2373) to give thanks. ◆ **18 ὑποτάσσεσθε** pres. imp. mid. ὑποτάσσω (# 5718) mid. to be in subjection, to subject oneself. Submission for Paul is a voluntary submission based on one's own recognition of God's order (Crouch, 110; DPL, 418-19; s. Eph. 5:21). For references to the position of women in the ancient world s. Crouch, 107; Tal Ian, *Jewish Women in Greco-Roman Palestine* (Tübingen: J. C. B. Mohr, 1994). **ἀνῆκεν** impf. ind. act. ἀνήκω (# 465) it is fitting, it is proper. Impf. w. a pres. meaning in an expression of necessity, obligation, or duty (BD, 181; RG, 919f; MT, 90f). ◆ **19 ἀγαπᾶτε** pres. imp. act. ἀγαπάω (# 26) to love (TDNT; TLNT; EDNT). Pres. imp. calls for a continual attitude and positive expression. **πικραίνεσθε** pres. imp. pass. πικραίνω (# 4393) to make bitter, to embitter, to become bitter. The vb. has the idea of being sharp, harsh, and bitter. It speaks of friction caused by impatience and thoughtless nagging. If love is absent, such obedience will not be secured by perpetual irritation and faultfinding (TDNT; Moule; Eadie). Pres. imp. w. the neg. **μή** (# 3590) forbids a habitual action. ◆ **20 ὑπακούετε** pres. imp. act. ὑπακούω (# 5634) to listen to, to obey. **γονεῖς** (# 1204) (pl.) parents. **εὐάρεστός** (# 2298) well-pleasing, commendable. The word is generally used in the Bible to mean "pleasing to God" (Moule). ◆ **21 ἐρεθίζετε** pres. imp. act. ἐρεθίζω (# 2241) to excite, to provoke, to irritate (Abbott). **ἀθυμῶσιν** pres. subj. act. ἀθυμέω (# 126) to be without courage or spirit, to lose heart, to become spiritless; "to go about their task in a listless, moody, sullen frame of mind" (Lightfoot). A child frequently irritated by over-severity or injustice to which, nevertheless, it must submit, acquires a spirit of sullen resignation leading to despair (Abbott). ◆ **22 ὑπακούετε** pres. imp. act. ὑπακούω (# 5634) to be obedient. **ὀφθαλμοδουλία** (# 4056) eye service. It might mean merely such service as can be seen; i.e., superficial work–not dusting behind the ornaments, not sweeping under the wardrobe; but the context suggests instead going through the outward movements of the work without a corresponding keenness of will behind them (Moule). The word could also have the idea of "when the master's eye is upon you" (S. Lewis Johnson, "The New Man in the Old," *Bib Sac* 121 [1964]: 113). **ἀνθρωπάρεσκος** (# 473) men-pleaser, one who tries to please men at the sacrifice of principle (BAGD). **ἁπλότης** (# 605) singleness. The phrase used here means "w. undivided service" (Lightfoot; TLNT). **καρδία** (# 2840) heart. Here descriptive gen. **φοβούμενοι** pres. mid. (dep.) part. φοβέομαι (# 5828) to be afraid, to fear, to fear the Lord (Christ) is the leading principle of Christian conduct (Lohse). ◆ **23 ἐάν** (# 1569) w. the subj. and the rel. pron., whatever (s.v. 17). **ποιῆτε** pres. subj. act. s.v. 17. Subj. w. indef. rel. cl. **ἐργάζεσθε** pres. imp. mid. (dep.) ἐργάζομαι (# 2237) to work, to work energetically, to work diligently (Lightfoot). ◆ **24 εἰδότες** perf. act. part. οἶδα (# 3857) to know. Def. perf. w. a pres. meaning. **ἀπολήμψεσθε** fut. ind. mid. (dep.) ἀπολαμβάνω (# 655) to receive from someone. The prep. denotes that the recompense comes immediately from Christ, its possessor (Eadie). **ἀνταπόδοσις** (# 502) receiving from another in return, recompensing, requital. Prep. in compound expresses the idea of full, complete return (Hendriksen). **κληρονομία** (# 3100) inheritance. Here gen. of apposition, the reward which consists in the inheritance. There is a special point in the word, inasmuch as slaves could not be inheritors of an earthly possession (Abbott). **δουλεύετε** pres. imp. or ind. act. δουλεύω (# 1526) to serve as a slave. The form could be either imp. (Lohse; Moule) or ind. (Lightfoot). Pres. in either case suggests a continuous or ongoing activity. ◆ **25 ἀδικῶν** pres. act. part. ἀδικέω (# 92) to commit an unrighteous act, to wrong (TDNT). The sentence is an explanation and gives a general law applicable to all. **κομίσεται** fut. ind. mid. κομίζω (# 3152) to carry off; mid. to bear for oneself, to receive, to receive a recompense (AS; BAGD). **ἠδίκησεν** aor. ind. act. ἀδικέω (# 92). **προσωπολημψία** (# 4721) the accepting of one's face or person, partiality (Moule; TDNT).

Colossians 4

◆ **1 ἰσότης** (# 2699) equality, fairness. **παρέχεσθε** pres. imp. mid. (dep.) παρέχομαι (# 4218) to give, to grant; mid. to show oneself to be something. Here, "exhibit on your part fairness to the slaves." The idea is reciprocation, the master's duty as corresponding to the slaves (Lightfoot; BAGD; BD, 166). ◆ **2 προσκαρτερεῖτε** pres. imp. act. προσκαρτερέω (# 4674) to adhere to, to persist in, to busy oneself w., to busily engage in, to be devoted to (BAGD; TDNT; MM; TLNT). **γρηγοροῦντες** pres. act. part. γρηγορέω (# 1213) to be awake, to stay awake, to be watchful, to be vigilant. Perhaps Paul was reminded of the literal sleep which he had heard about in the story of the Passion or Transfiguration (Moule). **ἐν αὐτῇ** (# 1877; 899) in it; i.e., in prayer. **εὐχαριστία** (# 2374) thanksgiving. ◆ **3 προσευχόμενοι** pres. mid. (dep.) part. προσεύχομαι (# 4667) to pray. **ἅμα** (# 275) to gather at the same time; "praying at the same time also for us" (BD, 220). **ἵνα** (# 2671) that; gives the content of the prayer. **ἀνοίξῃ** aor. subj. act. ἀνοίγω (# 487) to open. Subj. w. **ἵνα** (# 2671). The picture of an open door stood for opportunity. For rabbinical examples s. SB, 3:631; TDNT. **θύρα** (# 2598) door. Here in the sense of opportunity. **λόγου** (# 3364) the word; here obj. gen., "a door

for preaching" (RWP). **λαλῆσαι** aor. act. inf. λαλέω (# 3281) to speak. Compl. inf. **μυστήριον** (# 3696) mystery (s. Col. 1:26; Eph. 3:3). **δέδεμαι** perf. ind. pass. δέομαι (# 1313) to bind. Perf. emphasizes the continuing state or cond. ◆ **4 φανερώσω** aor. subj. act. φανερόω (# 5746) to make clear, to manifest. (# 1256) **δεῖ** pres. ind. act. impersonal, it is necessary; w. acc. and inf. giving a logical necessity (AS; for the meaning "need," "to have a need," and earlier usages of the word s. GEW, 1:375). **λαλῆσαι** aor. act. inf. s.v. 3. Compl. inf. ◆ **5 περιπατεῖτε** pres. imp. act. περιπατέω (# 4344) to walk about, to walk, to conduct one's life. **ἔξω** (# 2032) outside. The expression "those outside" is equivalent to the rabbinical term denoting those who belong to another religious group and is used here to denote those who are non-Christians (SB, 3:362; TDNT; Lohse). **καιρός** (# 2789) time, opportunity. The word does not emphasize a point of time but rather a space of time filled w. all kinds of possibilities (TDNT; Lohse). **ἐξαγοραζόμενοι** pres. mid. (dep.) part. ἐξαγοράζω (# 1973) to buy at the marketplace. Prep. in compound is probably intensive and the obj. of the vb. is viewed as commodity to be eagerly bought (s. Eph. 5:16; Moule; Lightfoot). ◆ **6 πάντοτε** (# 4121) always. **ἅλατι** dat. ἅλος (# 229) salt. **ἠρτυμένος** perf. pass. part. ἀρτύω (# 789) to season. The figure of speech as salt was used in the ancient world of sparkling conversation, speech dotted w. witty or clever remarks (Hendriksen; Moule; Lohse; BBC; SB, 3:631). Here it indicates speech which gives a flavor to the discourse and recommends it to the pallet as well as speech which preserves from corruption and renders wholesome (Lightfoot). **εἰδέναι** perf. act. inf. οἶδα (# 3857) to know. Def. perf. w. a pres. meaning. Inf. to express results. **πῶς** (# 4802) how? The conversation must not only be opportune in regards to time; it must also be appropriate as regards the person (Lightfoot). **δεῖ** (# 1256) pres. ind. act. it is necessary s.v. 4. **ἀποκρίνεσθαι** pres. mid. (dep.) inf. ἀποκρίνομαι (# 646) to answer. ◆ **7 τὰ κατ' ἐμὲ πάντα** the things related to me, my affairs. **γνωρίσει** fut. ind. act. γνωρίζω (# 1192) to make known. **ἀγαπητός** (# 28) beloved. **πιστός** (# 4412) true, faithful. **διάκονος** (# 1356) minister (s. 1:23). **σύνδουλος** (# 5281) fellow servant. ◆ **8 ἔπεμψα** aor. ind. act. πέμπω (# 4287) to send. **γνῶτε** aor. subj. act. γινώσκω (# 1182) to know. Subj. w. **ἵνα** (# 2671) to express purp. **παρακαλέσῃ** aor. subj. act. παρακαλέω (# 4151) to exhort, to encourage, to comfort (TDNT; MNTW, 128ff). ◆ **9 γνωρίσουσιν** fut. ind. act. γνωρίζω s.v. 7. **ὧδε** (# 6045) here. ◆ **10 ἀσπάζεται** pres. ind. mid. (dep.) ἀσπάζομαι (# 832) to greet. **συναιχμάλωτός** (# 5257) fellow prisoner. The term denotes properly a prisoner of war but also occurs in the general sense (TDNT; Moule). **ἀνεψιός** (# 463) cousin (Lightfoot). **ἐλάβετε** aor. ind. act. λαμβάνω (# 3284) to receive. **ἐντολάς** acc. pl. ἐντολή

(# *1953*) command. **ἔλθῃ** aor. subj. act. ἔρχομαι (# *2262*) to come. **δέξασθε** aor. imp. mid. (dep.) δέχομαι (# *1312*) to receive, to welcome. ◆ **11 λεγόμενος** pres. pass. part. λέγω (# *3306*) to say; pass., to be called. "W. the name." **ὄντες** pres. pass. part. εἰμί (# *1639*) to be. **περιτομή** (# *4364*) circumcision. **συνεργός** (# *5301*) fellow worker. **ἐγενήθησάν** aor. ind. pass. (dep.) γίνομαι (# *1181*) to become. **παρηγορία** (# *4219*) encouragement, comfort. The word appears on gravestones and in one letter of condolence where it means "comfort" (MM; Lohse; Lightfoot). ◆ **12 ἐξ ὑμῶν** (# *1666*; *5148*) one who belongs to you, who is one of you; i.e., a native or at least an inhabitant of Colossae (Lightfoot). **ἀγωνιζόμενος** pres. mid. (dep.) part. ἀγωνίζομαι (# *76*) to struggle, to agonize. It is the zeal and intensity of prayer which is emphasized (PAM, 123). **σταθῆτε** aor. subj. pass. ἵστημι (# *2705*) to place, pass, to stand. The word conveys the idea of standing firm (Abbott). **τέλειος** (# *5455*) perfect, mature. **πεπληροφορημένοι** perf. pass. part. πληροφορέω (# *4442*) to fill completely, pass. to be fully convinced, to be assured through. Rich, gratifying insight into all spiritual matters is meant, understanding which not only penetrates the mind, but also fills the heart w. satisfying conviction (Hendriksen; BAGD). **θέλημα** (# *2525*) will. ◆ **13 μαρτυρῶ** pres. ind. act. μαρτυρέω (# *3455*) to witness, to testify. **ἔχει** pres. ind. act. ἔχω (# *2400*) to have. Pres. indicates his present and continual possession. **πόνος** (# *4506*) labor, strenuous work. It is labor that does not stop short of demanding the soul strength of a man–and this exerted to the uttermost, if he is to accomplish the task which is set before him. It is the standing word by which the labors of Hercules are expressed (Trench, *Synonyms*, 378). ◆ **14 ἀσπάζεται** pres. ind. mid. (dep.) ἀσπάζομαι (# *832*) to greet. **ἰατρός** (# *2620*) doctor, physician. For information concerning

physicians and medicine in the ancient world s. RAC, 1:720-24; OCD, 660-64; DGRA, 747-48; Preisigke, 3:123; ZPEB, 4:788f; AIA; NDIEC, 2:10-25; BBC. **ἀγαπητός** (# *28*) beloved. ◆ **15 ἀσπάσασθε** aor. imp. mid. ἀσπάζομαι (# *832*) to greet. **Νύμφαν** (# *3809*) Numpha, personal name. The manuscript evidence is divided as to whether the name refers to a woman or a man (TC, 627; Lightfoot). **τὴν κατ' οἶκον** at home, at one's house. The use of the home for Christian assembly is well attested in the NT period (Martin; Lightfoot; BAFCS, 2:119-222). ◆ **16 ὅταν** (# *4020*) w. subj., when, whenever. **ἀναγνωσθῇ** aor. subj. pass. ἀναγινώσκω (# *336*) to read. **ποιήσατε** aor. imp. act. ποιέω (# *4472*) to do, to make. **ἀναγνωσθῇ** aor. subj. pass. Subj. w. ἵνα (# *2671*) to express purp. or result. **τὴν ἐκ Λαοδικείας** (# *3294*) the letter that is at Laodicea (BD, 225). For the suggestion that the Laodicean letter was written by Epaphras s. C.P. Anderson, "Who Wrote the 'Epistle From Laodicea'?" *JBL* 85 (1966): 436-40. **ἀναγνῶτε** aor. subj. act. ἀναγινώσκω (# *336*) to read. Subj. w. ἵνα (# *2671*) to express purp. or result. ◆ **17 εἴπατε** aor. imp. act. λέγω (# *3306*) to say. **βλέπε** pres. imp. act. βλέπω (# *1063*) to see, to take heed, to keep an eye on (RWP). **διακονία** (# *1355*) ministry, service (TDNT). **παρέλαβες** aor. ind. act. παραλαμβάνω (# *4161*) to receive, to receive from someone. The word suggests a mediate rather than a direct reception; Archippus received the charge immediately from St. Paul, though ultimately from Christ (Lightfoot). **πληροῖς** pres. subj. act. πληρόω (# *4444*) to fulfill. Pres. points to a continual action. It refers to a lifetime job. (RWP). ◆ **18 ἀσπασμός** (# *833*) greeting. **μνημονεύετε** pres. imp. act. μνημονεύω (# *3648*) to remember. The vb. is followed by the gen. **δέσμος** (# *1301*) bond. The chain clanked afresh as Paul took the pen to sign the salutation (RWP; also DPL, 752-54).

1 Thessalonians

1 Thessalonians 1

◆ **1** τῇ ἐκκλησίᾳ Θεσσαλονικέων to the church of the Thessalonians. Dat. as indir. obj.in a letter. For the letter style, s. Rom. 1:1. For the city of Thessalonica s. Acts 17:1; PIG, 78-116; Wanamaker; Bruce; NW, 2, i:767-68; FAP, 297-317; DPL, 933-34. For a summary of the bibliography s. Jeffrey A. D. Weima and Stanley E. Porter, *1 and 2 Thessalonians: An Annotated Bibliography* (Leiden: E.J. Brill, 1998). ἐν (# 1877) in. The prep. could be local, emphasizing that the church is in the atmosphere of the divine (Frame). They live in Him day by day. All their deeds are done in Him (Morris). The prep. could also be taken in an instr. sense, to mean that for the believer salvation lies in what God accomplished by Christ's life, death, and resurrection (Best; Wanamaker; Richard). For the rhetorical structure of 1 Thess., s. Wanamaker; John S. Kloppenborg, "Φιλαδελφία, θεοδίδακτος and the Dioscuri: Rhetorical Engagement in 1 Thessalonians 4.9-16," *NTS* 39 (1993): 265-89, w. lit. ◆ **2** εὐχαριστοῦμεν pres. ind. act. εὐχαριστέω (# 2373) to give thanks, to thank. Pres. stresses the continual action (DPL, 728-29). πάντοτε (# 4121) always. μνεία (# 3644) remembrance, mention. The word indicates remembrance in a special case, "the direction of the memory to some particular object" (Lightfoot, *Notes*). ποιούμενοι pres. mid. part. ποιέω (# 4472) to make. Used in connection w. the previous noun to mean "making mention," "remembering." For examples in the papyri and inscriptions s. Milligan. This is the first of three modal parts. describing the nature of the perpetual thanksgiving (Milligan). ἀδιαλείπτως (# 90) constantly, without interruption, unceasingly. The word was used of that which was continually and repeatedly done; e.g., the uninterrupted necessary payment of hard taxes, the continual service or ministry of an official, a continual uninterrupted cough (Presigke; MM), repeated military attacks (Jos., *JW*, 1:252), the continual failing of a military effort (Jos., *JW*, 3:241), the regular and consistent production of fruit (Jos., *JW*, 3:519), or the constant pounding of a battering ram against a city wall (TJ, 181; Jos., *JW*, 5:298-302) (s. Rom. 1:9). ◆ **3** μνημονεύοντες pres. act. part. μνημονεύω (# 3648) to remember, w. obj. in gen. The vb. regularly means to call something to mind, or to make mention of it (Moore). ὑμῶν gen. pl. σύ (# 5148) your. The word is placed emphatically at the head of three phrases and should be taken w. each (Best). ἔργον (# 2240) work. The word refers to active work (Lightfoot). The word could also involve the results of the activity, an achievement (Best). The word comprehends the whole Christian life work as it is ruled and energized by faith (Milligan). πίστεως gen. sing. πίστις (# 4411) faith, faithfulness. Subj. gen., "the work produced by faith." κόπος (# 3160) labor. The word denotes arduous, wearying toil involving sweat and fatigue (Moore); it emphasizes the weariness which follows on this straining of all of one's powers to the utmost (Trench, *Synonyms*, 378). ὑπομονή (# 5705) endurance. It is the spirit which bears things not simply w. resignation, but w. blazing hope. It is the spirit which bears things because it knows that these things are leading to a goal of glory (NTW, 60; TDNT; NIDNTT; TLNT). The gens. here–faith, love, and hope–are subj. gen., "that which is produced by faith, hope and love" (MT, 211). ἔμπροσθεν (# 1869) in the presence of. ◆ **4** εἰδότες perf. act. part. οἶδα (# 3857) to know. Def. perf. w. pres. meaning. For the meaning of this word s. ND, 344-56; VA, 281-87. ἠγαπημένοι perf. pass. part. ἀγαπάω (# 26) to love. Perf. pass. part. stresses continuing love which God shows to men (Morris). ἐκλογή (# 1724) choosing, election. ◆ **5** ὅτι (# 4022) because, since. It introduces the first reason for Paul's certitude that the community has been called by God (Richard). ἐγενήθη aor. ind. pass. (dep.) γίνομαι (# 1181) to become, to come. The word is significant as pointing to a result reached through the working of an outside force (Milligan). εἰς ὑμᾶς unto you, to you. Prep. w. the acc. is used here as an equivalent to the dat. (RG, 594). οὐκ ... ἐν λόγῳ μόνον not in word alone; i.e., "our preaching was not merely declamation, a hollow and heartless rhetoric" (Lightfoot, *Notes*). δύναμις (# 1539) power. The word is generally used by Paul of divine energy (Moore). πληροφορία (# 4443) dat. sing. full assurance, conviction, confidence (Lightfoot, *Notes*; Wanamaker; s. Col. 4:12). οἴδατε perf. ind. act. οἶδα (# 3867) to know (s.v. 4). οἷος (# 3888) what sort of, what kind of, what manner of. The qualitative pron. brings out the interest and advantage of those for whom that power was exercised (Milligan). ἐγενήθημεν aor. ind. pass. (dep.) γίνομαι (# 1181) to become. The sense here is "came to be," "proven to be" (Ellicott). ἐν ὑμῖν in your midst. δι' ὑμᾶς because of you, for your sake. ◆ **6 μιμηταί** nom. pl. μιμητής (# 3629) imitator, one who imitates another particularly by following one's example or one's teaching (TDNT; von Dobschütz). **ἐγενήθητε** aor. ind. pass. (dep.) γίνομαι (# 1181) to become (s.v. 5). **δεξάμενοι** aor. mid. part. δέχομαι (# 1312) to receive, to welcome. Part. expresses contemporaneous or identical action: "in that you welcomed" (Frame). **θλίψις** (# 2568) pressure, tribulation (TDNT). **χαρά** (# 5915) joy. Gen. following this word is a gen. of originating cause: "joy inspired by, preceding from the Holy Spirit" (Milligan). ◆ **7 ὥστε** (# 6063) w. inf. used here to introduce a result cl. which expresses actual and far-reaching rather than merely contemplated results (Milligan; Funk, 707; Richard). **γενέσθαι** pres. mid. inf. (dep.) γίνομαι (# 1181) to become. **τύπος** (# 5596) example, type. Originally the word denoted the mark left by a blow. Then it was used in the ethical sense of a pattern of conduct; but more usually, as here, of an example to be followed (TDNT; EDNT; TLNT). **πιστεύουσιν** pres. act. part. dat. pl. πιστεύω (# 4409) to believe. Indir. obj. Articular part. to stress a characterizing trait. ◆ **8 ἐξήχηται** perf. ind. pass. ἐξηχέω (# 2010) to thunder, to sound forth, to sound out. The word suggests an echoing like thunder or sounding out as a trumpet (Moore; Lightfoot; Milligan; GELTS, 160). Although the metaphor is not clear, the word indicates that a sound is made and it is heard spreading out from a center (Best). Perf. denotes the continuing activity (Morris) or lasting effect. **τόπῳ** dat. sing. τόπος (# 5536) place. The definite article w. **θεός** (# 2536) God, indicates their faith in the true God and contrasts their present attitude to God w. their past pagan attitude to idols (Frame). **ἐξελήλυθεν** perf. ind. act. ἐξέρχομαι (# 2002) to go out. Perf. indicates the continuing result. **χρεία** (# 5970) need, necessity. **ἔχειν** pres. act. inf. ἔχω (# 2400) to have. W. the preceding noun, "to have a need." Inf. w. ὥστε (# 6063) to express result. **λαλεῖν** pres. act. inf. λαλέω (# 3281) to speak. Compl. inf. is used to explain the need. ◆ **9 αὐτοί** (# 899) they themselves; people generally (Moore). **ἀπαγγέλλουσιν** pres. ind. act. ἀπαγγέλλω (# 550) to report. Pres. indicates a continuous and repeated action. **ὁποῖος** (# 3961) what sort of. **εἴσοδος** (# 1658) entrance. The word indicates here the act of entering rather than the means of entering and points to the nature of the entrance–how happy and successful it was (Milligan). **ἔσχομεν** aor. ind. act. ἔχω (# 2400) to have. **ἐπεστρέψατε** aor. ind. act. ἐπιστρέφω (# 2188) to turn oneself to or toward (BBC). Prep. in compound is directive. **εἴδωλον** (# 1631) idol. The worship of the Caesar was prominent in the city as well as the cults of Dionysus, Serapis, Isis, Zeus, Aphrodite, Demeter, and especially the cult of Cabirus, which had become the chief cult of Thessalonica (Charles Edson, "Cults of Thessalonica," *HTR* 41 [1948]: 153-204; K.P. Donfried, "The Cults of Thessal-

onica and the Thessalonian Correspondence," *NTS* 31 [1985]: 336-56; PIG, 96-99; FAP, 331-33, 336-39; NDIEC, 1:29-32; for the Cabirus worship, s. OCD, 186; GGR, 2:101-03; KP, 3:34-38; FAP, 336; Edson, *HTR* 41 [1948]: 188-204). **δουλεύειν** pres. act. inf. δουλεύω (# 1526) to serve. Inf. to express result or purp. **ζῶντι** pres. act. part. ζάω (# 2409) to live. Part. used as an adj. The living God is not merely one who is alive but one who gives life, both the life of creation and the new life of redemption (Best). **ἀληθινός** (# 240) genuine, true, real. Adj. w. this ending express the material out of which anything is made, therefore the word signifies "genuine," made up of that which is true and is used to distinguish the true God from idols and all other false gods (Trench, *Synonyms*, 27). ◆ **10 ἀναμένειν** pres. act. inf. ἀναμένω (# 388) to wait, to wait for. The leading thought here seems to be to wait for one whose coming is expected, perhaps w. the added idea of patience and confidence (Milligan). The emphasis on the eschatological hope may have arisen from their former concern for life after death in the mystery religions. For example, Cabirus was thought to have been killed by his two brothers, but was expected to return again to the city and help the poor (FAP, 336, 339-40). Pres. points to the continual waiting. Inf. to express purp. or result; parallel to the inf. in v. 9. **ἤγειρεν** aor. ind. act. ἐγείρω (# 1586) to raise. **ῥυόμενον** pres. mid. (dep.) part. ῥύομαι (# 4861) to rescue, to deliver. The word indicates a deliverance and the avoidance of great danger (Moore). **ὀργῆς** gen. sing. ὀργή (# 3973) wrath, deepseated anger (TDNT; Morris; DPL, 991-92; BBC). **ἐρχομένης** pres. mid. (dep.) part. ἔρχομαι (# 2262) to come, to go. Part. is emphatic by position and emphasizes the approaching anger (Best). Pres. part. emphasize the contemporaneous action.

1 Thessalonians 2

◆ **1 οἴδατε** perf. ind. act. οἶδα (# 3857) to know. Def. perf. w. a pres. meaning. "You yourselves know." **εἴσοδος** (# 1658) entrance (s. 1:9). **κενή** nom. sing. κενός (# 3031) empty, vain. The reference is to the essential content of the apostle's preaching rather than to its results (Milligan; Marshall). The word suggests hollow, empty, wanting in purp. and earnestness (Lightfoot, *Notes*; Trench, *Synonyms*, 180). **γέγονεν** perf. ind. act. γίνομαι (# 1181) to become. Perf. indicates the lasting effects of Paul's preaching (Lightfoot, *Notes*; Best). ◆ **2 προπαθόντες** aor. act. part. προπάσχω (# 4634) to suffer beforehand, to suffer previously. Aor. indicates antecedent action. Paul refers to the shameful treatment that he received in Philippi at the hands of the Roman officials (s. Acts 16:19-40). **ὑβρισθέντες** aor. pass. part. ὑβρίζω (# 5614) to abuse, to treat shamefully. The word expresses insulting and outrageous treatment, and esp. treatment which is calculated publicly to insult and openly to humiliate the person who suffers from it (MNTW, 83; TDNT). Both parts. are to be taken w. the main vb. and are either temp. ("after having suffered previously and having been shamefully treated") or concessive, "although" (Frame). **οἴδατε** perf. ind. act. οἶδα (# 3857) to know. Def. perf. w. pres. meaning. **ἐπαρρησιασάμεθα** aor. ind. mid. (dep.) παρρησιάζομαι (# 4245) to speak freely, to speak all things, to be bold and courageous. The word was used in classical Gr. to signify freedom of speech or expression, often w. a political connotation (Moore; TDNT; EDNT; TLNT). **λαλῆσαι** aor. act. inf. λαλέω (# 3281) to speak. Compl. inf. to the main vb., or could be considered to be an inf. of purp. (Richard). **ἀγών** (# 74) conflict, effort. The word implies the intense effort and strenuous exertion in Paul's preaching of the gospel, esp. in the face of hostility and conflict w. the Jews at Thessalonia (PAM, 112-14). ◆ **3 παράκλησις** (# 4155) exhortation, encouragement, appeal. The word implies an appeal, having for its object the direct benefit of those addressed, which may be either hortatory or conciliatory depending on circumstances. The word was used to encourage soldiers before going into battle and it was said that encouragement was necessary for hired soldiers; but for those who fight for life and country no exhortation is required (Milligan; MNTW, 128f; TDNT). **ἐκ πλάνης** (# 1666; 4415) out of error. The word is used either in the active sense of deceit, the leading astray, or in the pass. sense of error (Lightfoot, *Notes*; Best). **ἐξ ἀκαθαρσίας** (# 1666; 174) out of impurity. The word could refer to sexual or moral impurity but here it is more general and means that Paul does not preach from any impure motives: ambition, pride, greed, popularity (Best). **ἐν δόλῳ** (# 1877; 1515) in guile. The word meant a bait or trap, then any form of strategy (Moore; Milligan). So many wandering charlatans (γόητες) made their way about the Greek world, peddling their religious or philosophical nostrums and living at the expense of their devotees, that it was necessary for Paul and his friends to emphasize, by contrast, the purity of their motives and actions (Bruce). ◆ **4 καθώς** (# 2777) The word is to be taken in connection w. **οὕτως** (# 4048) meaning "just as ..., so ...." **δεδοκιμάσμεθα** perf. ind. pass. δοκιμάζω (# 1507) to prove, to approve after examination or testing. The word was used in classical Gr. w. the technical sense to describe the passing of fit for election to a public office (Milligan; TDNT; TLNT). Perf. indicates a lasting approval and not something over and done w. (Moore). **πιστευθῆναι** aor. pass. inf. πιστεύω (# 4409) to entrust. Inf. is explanatory serving to define more nearly that to which the approval was directed (Ellicott). **λαλοῦμεν** pres. ind. act. λαλέω (# 3281) to speak. **ἀρέσκοντες** pres. act. part. ἀρέσκω (# 743) to please someone. The word is found in inscriptions to people who have served their fellow

citizens; it conveys the sense of service and obedience (Moore). Pres. indicates contemporaneous action. Part. of manner. **δοκιμάζοντι** pres. act. part. (adj.). δοκιμάζω (# 1507) to prove. Here is Paul's inner life in its totality of thought and intention which God scrutinizes (Best). ◆ **5 ποτε** (# 4537) ever; here used w. the neg., never. **κολακεία** (# 3135) flattery. The word contains the idea of deception for selfish ends. It is flattery not merely for the sake of giving pleasure to others but for the sake of self-interest. It is deception by slick eloquence, the idea being to win over the hearts in order to exploit them (Lightfoot, *Notes*; Moore; Frame; Milligan; TLNT; BBC). Dio Chrysostom explains in a speech before the Emperor Trajan (of whom he says, "you delight in truth and frankness [ἀλήθεια καὶ παρρησία] rather than flattery and guile," *The Third Discourse*, 2), "... even those flatterers who openly follow the business acknowledge that to play the flatterer is of all things most distasteful" (*The Third Discourse*, 16); then he adds, "Furthermore, flattery seems neither reputable nor honorable even when practiced to gain distinction, or from some other worthy motive. Nay, of all vices, I may say, flattery will be found to be the meanest" (αἰχίστην) (*The Third Discourse*, 17). For other occurrences of the word in Dio Chrysostom s. DCNT, 200f. For other ancient condemnations of flattery s. NW, 2, i:773-74, and for the word in Josephus s. CCFJ, 2, 514. **ἐγενήθημεν** aor. ind. pass. (dep.) γίνομαι (# 1181) to become; here, to demonstrate oneself as (s. 1:5). **οἴδατε** perf. ind. act. οἶδα (# 3857) to know. Def. perf. w. a pres. meaning. **πρόφασις** (# 4733) cloak, pretense. The word denotes that which one puts on for appearance, w. the definite design to color or to cloak something else. It therefore denotes pretext, the outward show (Lünemann). The import of the word may be actual motive, meaning "we did not act w. a motive of greed" (Wanamaker). **πλεονεξία** (# 4432) greed, selfishness. It is the disregard for the rights of others in order to meet one's own selfish desires for more and more (TDNT; NTW, 97f). Gen. shows what the material of the cloth consists of. ◆ **6 ζητοῦντες** pres. act. part. ζητέω (# 2426) to seek. Pres. points to a continual and habitual action. ◆ **7 δυνάμενοι** pres. pass. (dep.) part. δύναμαι (# 1538) to be able to, w. inf. Concessive part. which qualifies the fact–"we never came requiring honor"–by asserting the principle that the demand for honor inheres in their place as Christ's apostles (Frame). **βάρος** (# 983) weight, burden. Here the word is used in the sense of honor, authority, dignity, importance. The aspect of the word is closely related to the Heb. root *kbd* כבד (Milligan; Best; DCH). **εἶναι** pres. inf. act. εἰμί (# 1639) to be. Compl. inf. to the preceding part. **ἐγενήθημεν** aor. ind. pass. (dep.) γίνομαι (# 1181) to become. **ἤπιος** (# 2413) gentle. For the variant reading **νήπιος** (# 3758) infants, and the textual problem s. TC, 639f. **ὡς** (# 6055) used w.

the comparative particle and the subj., implying a standing contingency; i.e., "as it may be at any time" (Milligan). **τροφός** (# *5577*) one who nourishes or feeds. nurse, wet nurse, nursing mother (Best; for a parallel in the DSS s. 1QH 7, 20f; 9, 29-32). A wet nurse in the ancient world not only had strict contractual stipulation, but often came to be a very trusted person whose influence lasted a lifetime (RAC, 1:381-85; "Engagement of a Wet Nurse"; No. 146, CPJ, 2:15-19; NDIEC, 2:7-10; A.J. Malherbe, "'Gentle as a Nurse': The Cynic Background of 1 Thes. 2," *NovT* 12 [1970]: 203-17; DC, *Thirty-Second Discourse*; NW, 2, i:771-72; BBC). **θάλπη** pres. subj. act. θάλπω (# *2499*) to warm, to foster, to nourish, to cherish. In Deut. 22:6 it is used of a bird warming her eggs (Moore; Milligan; GEW, 1:651). ◆ **8 ὁμειρόμενοι** pres. mid. (dep.) part. ὁμείρομαι (# *3916*) to have a kindly feeling, to long for someone. The derivation of the word is uncertain (Lightfoot, *Notes*; Morris; MH, 251; Richard). It is used on a grave inscription describing the parents' sad yearning for their dead child and seems to indicate deep affection and great attraction (Moore; MM). **εὐδοκοῦμεν** pres. ind. act. εὐδοκέω (# *2305*) to be well-pleased, to be gladly determined. The word draws attention to the hearty goodwill attending the writer's attitude (Milligan). Although the form is pres. ind. it is probably a case where the impf. is used without the augment (Best; BD, 37). **μεταδοῦναι** aor. act. inf. μεταδίδωμι (# *3556*) to share. It is the giving of something by which the giver retains one part and the receiver another so that they both share in the matter (von Dobschütz). **ψυχάς** acc. pl. ψυχή (# *6034*) soul, life. The word signifies here the life of the individual person which is shared w. another. It is the life of the individual as it is manifested in behavior and refers to the observable totality of Paul's earthly existence (PAT, 346f). **διότι** (# *1484*) therefore, because. The word apparently always has a causal force in the NT (Milligan). **ἀγαπητός** (# *28*) beloved, dear. **ἐγενήθητε** aor. ind. pass. (dep.) γίνομαι (# *1181*) to become. ◆ **9 μνημονεύετε** pres. imp. act. μνημονεύω (# *3648*) to remember. **κόπος** (# *3160*) exhausting labor (s. 1:3). **μόχθος** (# *3677*) toil. The word refers to the trouble and pain of arduous work; the leading notion is that of struggling to overcome difficulties (Moore; Lightfoot, *Notes*). **ἐργαζόμενοι** pres. mid. (dep.) part. ἐργάζομαι (# *2237*) to work. There were no paid teachers in Palestine. It was necessary therefore for a rabbi to have some other means of income than the gifts that might now and then be made to him (Morris; s. also the rabbinical examples quoted by Morris; Best). There was probably a high rate of unemployment in Thessalonica at that time, but Paul had found work in his trade and through his work contacts had won many to the new faith (FAP, 334; BBC; DPL, 925-27). **πρός** (# *4639*) prep. used w. the inf. to indicate

purp. (MT, 144; BG, 135). **ἐπιβαρῆσαι** aor. act. inf. ἐπιβαρέω (# *2096*) to place a weight on someone, to be burdensome, to make demands (Moore; Milligan). **ἐκηρύξαμεν** aor. ind. act. κηρύσσω (# *3062*) to proclaim, to preach. Although Paul does not mention it, the church at Philippi had sent him financial support several times (Bruce; Phil 4:15-16). ◆ **10 ὁσίως** (# *4010*) adv., piously, holy. The word describes one's duty toward God (Lightfoot, *Notes*; Trench, *Synonyms*; 328f; TDNT; NIDNTT). **δικαίως** (# *1469*) adv., righteously. The word describes one's duties toward men but it also stresses a righteous life before God (Lightfoot, *Notes*; Best). **ἀμέμπτως** (# *290*) adv., blamelessly. **πιστεύουσιν** pres. act. part. πιστεύω (# *4409*) to believe. Part. used to emphasize a characterizing trait. Dat. here could be dat. of reference ("in reference to you believers"), or dat. of advantage ("to the benefit of you believers") or loc. ("among you believers"). For the various views s. Best. ◆ **11 καθάπερ** (# *2749*) just as, in accordance w. The first part of the word marks comparison and the last part the latitude of the application. It introduces a confirmatory appeal to the individual experience of the hearers (Ellicott; Milligan). **οἴδατε** pres. ind. act. οἶδα (# *3857*) to know. Defective perf. w. a pres. meaning ◆ **12 παρακαλοῦντες** pres. act. part. παρακαλέω (# *4151*) to exhort, to encourage, to console. The word means to exhort to a particular line of conduct (Lightfoot, *Notes*; TDNT; s.v. 3). Part. of manner. **παραμυθούμενοι** pres. mid. (dep.) part. παραμυθέομαι (# *4170*) to encourage. The word means to encourage to continue in a course (Milligan). Part. of manner. **μαρτυρόμενοι** pres. mid. (dep.) part. μαρτυρέω (# *3458*) to witness. Part. describe the content of the knowledge. Pres. describes the durative action, "continually exhorting." **περιπατεῖν** pres. act. inf. περιπατέω (# *4344*) to walk, to conduct one's life. Articular inf. w. the prep. εἰς (# *1650*) to express either purp. (Morris) or the content of the command or entreaty (M, 219). **ἀξίως** (# *547*) adv., worthily (s. Eph. 4:1). **καλοῦντος** pres. act. part. καλέω (# *2813*) to call. Part. used as an adj. to emphasize this as a trait of God. For the variant reading of the aor. part. s. TC, 630; Best. ◆ **13 The second καί** (# *2779*) in the expression κ. ὑμεῖς indicates a reciprocal relation between writers and readers (Frame), and does not necessarily indicate that Paul was answering a letter from the Thessalonians (Morris; Moore). **εὐχαριστοῦμεν** pres. ind. act. εὐχαριστέω (# *2373*) to give thanks. **ἀδιαλείπτως** (# *90*) without interruption, continually, regularly (s. 1:2; Rom. 1:9). **παραλαβόντες** pres. act. part. παραλαμβάνω (# *4161*) to receive, to receive from another; a t.t. used for the reception of tradition which was conveyed (TDNT; TLNT; s. Col. 2:6). **ἀκοή** (# *198*) hearing, report, message (Best). **παρ' ἡμῶν** (# *4123; 1609*) from us. The phrase is to be connected w. the part. and indicates the immediate source of the message delivered and received, while the emphatic **τοῦ θεοῦ** (# 2536) from God, is added to point to its real source (Milligan). The gen. "from God" is therefore a subj. gen.–"preceding from God, having God as its author"–as its emphatic position requires (Lightfoot, *Notes*). **ἐδέξασθε** aor. ind. mid. (dep.) δέχομαι (# 1312) to receive. to welcome. **καθώς** (# 2777) just as. **ἀληθῶς** (# 242) adv., truly. **ἐνεργεῖται** pres. ind. mid. (dep.) ἐνεργέομαι (# 1919) to work effectually, to work efficiently and productively. The word is used to describe the energy and effective power of God Himself (MNTW, 46-54; TDNT). **πιστεύουσιν** pres. act. part. dat. masc. pl. πιστεύω (# 4409) to believe. Subst. part. used to emphasize a trait. ◆ **14 μιμηταί** (# 3629) imitator (s. 1:6). **ἐγενήθητε** aor. pass. (dep.) ind. γίνομαι (# 1181) to become (s.v. 5). **οὐσῶν** pres. act. part. εἰμί (# 1639) to be. **ἐπάθετε** aor. ind. act. πάσχω (# 4248) to suffer. For a discussion of the suffering of the church at Thessalonica s. Wanamaker. **ἴδιος** (# 2625) one's own. **συμφυλέτης** (# 5241) countryman. This expression may be in part geographical and include Thessalonian Jews, but it points to a large Gentile element in the opposition (Morris). ◆ **15 ἀποκτεινάντων** aor. act. part. ἀποκτείνω (# 650) to kill. **ἐκδιωξάντων** aor. act. part. (adj.) ἐκδιώκω (# 1691) to hunt down, to hunt out, to persecute. Prep. in compound may connote to drive out w. the intention of persecuting (Moore). Aor. indicates action antecedent to the main vb. **ἀρεσκόντων** pres. act. part. ἀρέσκω (# 743) to please (s.v. 4). Pres. indicates contemporaneous action. **ἐναντίος** (# 1885) opposing, contrary to, hostile toward. ◆ **16 κωλυόντων** pres. act. part. κωλύω (# 3266) to hinder, to prevent, to forbid. Pres. would be conative as well as indicating a continual action: "they are continually trying to hinder." **ἔθνεσιν** dat. pl. ἔθνος (# 1620) nation, Gentile. **λαλῆσαι** aor. act. inf. λαλέω (# 3281) to speak. Compl. inf. to the main vb. **σωθῶσιν** aor. subj. pass. σώζω (# 5392) to rescue, to save. Subj. w. **ἵνα** (# 2671) to express purp. **εἰς** (# 1650) to, into. The prep. is used w. the articular inf. to express purp. (Ellicott; Morris; NT, 143). **ἀναπληρῶσαι** aor. act. inf. ἀναπληρόω (# 405) to fill up, to fill up to the full. The word means "to fill up the measure" of their sins, implying that the process of filling had already begun, drop after drop being poured into the cup of their guilt (Lightfoot, *Notes*). **πάντοτε** (# 4121) always. **ἔφθασεν** aor. ind. act. φθάνω (# 5777) to arrive, to reach. The word could have two meanings here. It could mean anger hangs over them and is just about to fall on them: or it could mean anger has fallen on them and they now experience it. For a discussion of these two meanings as well as the meaning of the aor. s. Best. **ὀργή** (# 3973) wrath, anger (TDNT; NIDNTT). **εἰς** (# 1650) to, toward. The phrase means either "at last" or "to the end" (Morris). ◆ **17 ἀπορφανισθέντες** aor. pass. part. ἀπορφανίζομαι (# 682) to make one an orphan by separation. The word

could be used of a parentless child, or of childless parents, and even in a general sense of any severe deprivation or desolation (Moore): "we are like children who have lost their parents" (Lightfoot, *Notes*; Bruce; Richard; TDNT). Pass. points out that the situation was forced (von Dobschütz). Aor. implies a single action and not a continued state (Best). **καιρός** (# 2789) time, period of time, space of time. **προσώπῳ οὐ καρδίᾳ** dat. of reference marking the true limiting power of the case, the metaphorical place to which the action is restricted (Ellicott). **προσώπῳ** dat. sing. πρόσωπον (# 4725) face, person, indicating what the outward connection or relationship is. **καρδία** (# 2840) heart, the place of the affections and of the inner connection in life (von Dobschütz). **περισσοτέρως** (# 4359) comp. adv. περισσός more abundantly. The adv. could have the true comp. force, "the more fervently," or it could be elative, "excessively" (Frame). **ἐσπουδάσαμεν** aor. ind. act. σπουδάζω (# 5079) to make haste, to endeavor. **ἰδεῖν** aor. act. inf. ὁράω (# 3972) to see. Compl. inf. to the main vb.: "we make haste to see you." **ἐπιθυμία** (# 2123) desire, longing. ◆ **18 διότι** (# 1484) because (s.v. 8). **ἠθελήσαμεν** aor. ind. act. θέλω (# 2527) to wish, to desire. The word probably points to the will which proceeds from inclination (T; Morris). **ἐλθεῖν** aor. act. inf. ἔρχομαι (# 2262) to come, to go. Compl. inf. to the main vb.: "I desire to come." **ἐγώ** (# 1609) I. This is the first of a number of instances where Paul speaks for himself alone in these letters (Moore). Paul's name is used to guarantee the correctness of the **ἠθελήσαμεν** (von Dobschütz; for a discussion of the "we" sections in the Thessalonian letters s. von Dobschütz, 67f; Milligan, 131f). **ἅπαξ** (# 562) once. **δίς** (# 1489) twice. The two words used together form an idiomatic expression meaning "and that more than once," "several times" (Morris; Best). **ἐνέκοψεν** aor. ind. act. ἐγκόπτω (# 1601) to cut in. The word was originally used of breaking up a road to render it impassable; later it was used in a military sense of making a break through the enemy's line. It was also used in the athletic sense of cutting in on someone during a race. The general meaning of the word is "to hinder" (Milligan; Moore; TDNT; s. Gal. 5:7). **Σατανᾶς** (# 4928) Satan (DDD, 1369-80; TDNT; DPL, 852-67). ◆ **19 καυχήσεως** (# 3018) boasting. **οὐχί** (# 4049) strengthened form of οὐ used in questions expecting the answer "yes" (BD, 220f). The words "it is certainly you, isn't it?" form a rhetorical parenthesis interjected into the main sentence to draw special attention to the position of the Thessalonians (Milligan). **ἔμπροσθεν** (# 1869) before, in the presence of. **παρουσία** (# 4242) coming, presence. ◆ **20 γάρ** (# 1142) yes, indeed. The particle is used to introduce the answer to a rhetorical question and in such cases it affirms what was asked, giving the reason for a tacit "yes" (BD, 236).

1 Thessalonians 3

◆ **1 διό** (# *1475*) therefore, on which account: "on account of this very fervent desire, which I was unable to gratify" (Lightfoot, *Notes*). **μηκέτι** (# *3600*) no longer. **στέγοντες** pres. act. part. στέγω (# *5095*) to cover, to ward off by covering (e.g., a roof covering a house both conceals and wards off), to endure, to bear up under (Milligan; Morris; Best). Part. is either temp. or causal. **εὐδοκήσαμεν** aor. ind. act. εὐδοκέω (# *2305*) to be well pleased, to willingly determine, to consider it good (s. 2:8). **καταλειφθῆναι** aor. pass. inf. καταλείπω (# *2901*) to leave behind, to forsake. The idea here is "willing to be forsaken" (Moore). ◆ **2 ἐπέμψαμεν** aor. ind. act. ἐμπέμπω (# *4287*) to send. The vb. is used w. the prep. εἰς and the articular inf. to express purp. (Frame). **τοῦ Χριστοῦ** (# *5986*) of Christ. Gen. is either subjective or obj. gen. or could indicate both; i.e., Christ is the author and the content of the gospel (Best). **στηρίξαι** aor. act. inf. στηρίσσω (# *5114*) to support, to strengthen, to establish. The word has the idea of putting in a buttress as a support (Morris). Inf. to express purp. **παρακαλέσαι** aor. act. inf. παρακαλέω (# *4151*) to exhort, to encourage (s. 2:12). **ὑπέρ** (# *5642*) on behalf of, for the advantage of (Morris). ◆ **3 σαίνεσθαι** pres. pass. inf. σαίνω (# *4883*) to shake or wag; used esp. of a dog wagging the tail to allure, to fascinate, to flatter, to beguile, to draw aside from the right path (Lightfoot, *Notes*; Best; Milligan; Wanamaker; Bruce). The word occurs in Josephus in the sense of "to caress," "to stroke" (CCFJ, 3:8; Jos., *JW*, 6.336). Inf. to express purp. (Richard). **θλῖψις** (# *2568*) pressure, tribulation (TDNT). **κείμεθα** pres. ind. mid. (dep.) κεῖμαι (# *3023*) to lie, to place; used as a perf. pass. of τίθημι w. the meaning "to be appointed, "to be destined" (Best; Milligan; Moore). ◆ **4 ἦμεν** impf. ind. act. εἰμί (# *1639*) to be. **προελέγομεν** impf. ind. act. προλέγω (# *4625*) to say beforehand, to foretell. Prep. in compound is predictive while the impf. denotes repeated action (Frame). **μέλλομεν** pres. ind. act. μέλλω (# *3516*) to be about to. The word is used w. the pres. inf. to denote a durative fut. ind. or an impending event: "we are going to ..." (MKG, 307f). **θλίβεσθαι** pres. pass. inf. θλίβω (# *2567*) to put under pressure; pass., to suffer tribulation. **καθώς** (# *2777*) just as. **ἐγένετο** aor. ind. mid. (dep.) γίνομαι (# *1181*) to happen, to come to pass. **οἴδατε** perf. ind. act. οἶδα (# *3857*) to know. Def. perf. w. a pres. meaning. ◆ **5 διὰ τοῦτο** (# *1328; 4047*) for this reason. **κἀγώ** (# *2743*) I also (Morris). It could also mean "I actually sent ...," or "that is in fact why I sent ..." (IBG, 167). **στέγων** pres. act. part. (causal) στέγω (# *5095*) to cover, to pass over in silence; fig., to endure, to stand. "Since I could bear it no longer" (BAGD; MM). Aor. indicates antecedent action to the main vb. **ἔπεμψα** aor. ind. act. πέμπω (# *4287*) to send. **εἰς** (# *1650*) used w. the articular inf. to express purp. **γνῶναι** aor. act. inf. γινώσκω (# *1182*) to

know. Ingressive aor., "to come to know" (RWP; ND, 344f). **μή πως** (# *3590; 4803*) lest. Used to express neg. purp., particularly in an expression of apprehension. It is used w. the subj. if the anxiety is directed toward warding off something still dependent on the will, and w. the ind. if directed toward something which is entirely independent of the will. With the subj. it expresses feared results (BD, 188; RG, 988). **ἐπείρασεν** aor. ind. act. πειράζω (# *4279*) to test, to try, to tempt. (Trench, *Synonyms*, 278-81; TLNT). Ind. is used to express fear regarding a pres. inevitable reality (MT, 99). **πειράζων** pres. act. part. (subst.) πειράζω (# *4279*) **κενός** (# *3031*) empty. **γένηται** aor. subj. mid. (dep.) γίνομαι (# *1181*) to be, to become. Subj. expresses a fear of an uncertain thing in the fut. (MT, 99). **κόπος** (# *3160*) labor, wearying work (s. 1:3). ◆ **6 ἄρτι** (# *785*) now, just now. **ἐλθόντος** aor. act. part. ἔρχομαι (# *2262*) to come, to go. Aor. indicating antecedent action to the main vb. Temp. part. gen. abs., "Now that Timothy has come." **εὐαγγελισαμένου** aor. mid. (dep.) part. εὐαγγελίζομαι (# *2294*) to bring good news. This is the only place in the NT where the vb. is used without a full and direct reference to the gospel, which is Jesus Christ (Best; Milligan, 141-44; TDNT). **μνεία** (# *3644*) mention, remembrance. Used w. the main vb. in the sense of "to hold," "to maintain a recollection." Here it indicates a kindly remembrance toward their former teachers (Milligan). **ἐπιποθοῦντες** pres. act. part. ἐπιποθέω (# *2160*) to long for, to yearn after. Prep. in compound is directive (Lightfoot, *Notes*; s. Phil. 1:8). Part. further expands the preceding words and gives an example of their kindly remembrance (Ellicott; von Dobschutz). **ἰδεῖν** aor. act. inf. ὁράω (# *3972*) to see. Compl. inf. **καθάπερ** (# *2749*) just as (s. 2:11). ◆ **7 διὰ τοῦτο** because of this, for that reason. This is a transitional phrase taking up the preceding whole of v. 6 (Best). **παρεκλήθημεν** aor. ind. pass. παρακαλέω (# *4151*) to comfort. **ἐφ' = ἐπί** (# *2093*) w. the dat., because, because of. The prep. frequently denotes the basis for a state of being, action, or result, esp. w. verbs of emotion (BD, 123). **ἀνάγκη** (# *340*) necessity, distress, affliction. The word is used of outward calamities or distresses (Milligan). **θλῖψις** (# *2568*) pressure. ◆ **8 ζῶμεν** pres. ind. act. ζάω (# *2409*) to live; "we live once more," i.e., in spite of this distress and affliction (Lightfoot, *Notes*). **στήκετε** pres. ind. act. στήκω (# *5112*) to stand, to stand firm, to stand fast, to be steadfast (BAGD). ◆ **9 εὐχαριστία** (# *2374*) thanksgiving, thanks. **δυνάμεθα** pres. ind. pass. (dep.) δύναμαι (# *1538*) to be able. **ἀνταποδοῦναι** aor. act. inf. ἀνταποδίδωμι (# *500*) to render, to give back as an equivalent. Prep. in compound implies the adequacy of the return (Lightfoot, *Notes*; Moore). **χαίρομεν** pres. ind. act. χαίρω (# *5897*) to rejoice. Pres. denotes continual action. **ἔμπροσθεν** (# *1869*) before, in the presence of. ◆ **10 νυκτὸς καὶ ἡμέρας** (# *3816; 2779; 2465*) night time and daytime, night and day, gen. of time. The emphasis is not on the duration but on the kind of time (GGBB, 123-24). ὑπερεκπερισσοῦ (# 5655) adv., more than out of bounds, overflowing all bounds, exceedingly, super-abundantly (RWP; Best; s. Eph. 3:20). δεόμενοι pres. mid. (dep.) part. δέομαι (# 1289) to make a request, to pray. The word embodies a sense of personal need and is very common in petitions addressed to ruling sovereigns as distinguished from those addressed to magistrates (Milligan; PIP, 191f). ἰδεῖν aor. ind. act. ὁράω (# 3972) to see. Compl. inf. to the main vb. Aor. points to a specific act. καταρτίσαι aor. act. inf. καταρτίζω (# 2936) to fit together, to join together, to restore, to repair, to equip. The word had a variety of usages depending upon the context. It was used to reconcile political factions; it was a surgical term for setting bones. It was used for repairing nets (s. Mark 1:19), and making military and naval preparations (Best; Lightfoot, *Notes*; TDNT). ὑστέρημα (# 5729) that which is lacking, deficiency. ◆ **11** For a discussion of the background and form of intercessory wish prayers, s. PIP, 22-44. αὐτὸς δέ now [God] Himself. Although this was a conventional liturgical form of address, Paul adds a new depth of meaning and invokes the august majesty and unique power of almighty God, the original creator and direct controller of events (PIP, 54; BBC). κατευθύναι aor. opt. act. κατευθύνω (# 2985) to make straight. The word refers to the leveling or removal of those obstacles which Satan has used to obscure the path (Lightfoot, *Notes*; Milligan). Opt. was often used to express a wish in prayers (PIP, 32f; M, 165; RG, 939f; BD, 194; GGBB, 482). ◆ **12** πλεονάσαι aor. opt. act. πλεονάζω (# 4429) to make more, to increase. περισσεύσαι aor. opt. act. περισσεύω (# 4355) to cause to overflow. τῇ ἀγάπῃ (# 27) The dat. could be dat. of reference or loc. or perhaps instr. (Ellicott). ◆ **13** στηρίξαι aor. act. inf. στηρίσσω (# 5114) to establish εἰς τὸ στηρίξαι. The prep. and the aor. inf. w. the article expresses purp. For the meaning of the word "establish," s.v. 2. ἄμεμπτος (# 289) blameless. The prayer gains sublimity in that they must be prepared to stand blameless in holiness before God as judge, the searcher of the inward motives of men, who tests and tries their hearts (PIP, 62; Frame). ἁγιωσύνη (# 43) holiness. The word indicates the state or cond. of holiness (Lightfoot, *Notes*). παρουσία (# 4242) coming, arrival. The word was used as a near t.t. for the visit of a king or emperor or for the appearance of a god (MM; LAE, 370ff; TDNT).

1 Thessalonians 4

◆ **1** λοιπὸν οὖν (# 3370) finally; "as our last matter" (Best; s. Phil. 3:1). ἀδελφοί voc. pl. ἀδελφός (# 81) brother. The term is an organizing metaphor that portrays the community as a family, thus linking together people who often had no previous contact (Wanama-

ker). ἐρωτῶμεν pres. ind. act. ἐρωτάω (# 2263) to ask, to request. The word lays stress on the person asked rather than on the thing asked for and it conceives the request in a question form (Milligan; Morris). παρακαλοῦμεν pres. ind. act. παρακαλέω (# 4151) to beseech, to exhort. ἵνα (# 2671) that. The word introduces the content of the request. καθώς (# 2777) just as. παρελάβετε aor. ind. act. παραλαμβάνω (# 4161) to receive, to receive from another, to receive tradition or teaching (s. Col. 2:6). τὸ πῶς (# 4802) how. The article is used to introduce an indir. question (RWP; BD, 140). δεῖ (# 1256) pres. ind. act. it is necessary to, an impersonal expression w. inf. giving a logical necessity. περιπατεῖν pres. act. inf. περιπατέω (# 4344) to walk, to walk about, to conduct one's life. Compl. inf. ἀρέσκειν pres. act. inf. ἀρέσκω (# 743) to please. Pres. emphasizes the continual or habitual action. καθώς (# 2777) just as, introducing a parenthetical cl. περιπατεῖτε pres. ind. act. περιπατέω (# 4344) to conduct one's life. περισσεύητε pres. subj. act. περισσεύω (# 4355) to overflow, to abound. ◆ **2** παραγγελία (# 4132) order, command, instruction. The word often denotes a word of command received from a superior officer that may be passed on to others. Here the pl. points to special precepts or rules of living which the writers had laid down when in Thessalonica, and in which they had referred to the Lord Jesus as the one alone through whom they could be put into effect (Milligan). ἐδώκαμεν aor. ind. act. δίδωμι (# 1443) to give. ◆ **3** τοῦτο γάρ ἐστιν θέλημα τοῦ θεοῦ for this is the will of God. The τοῦτο is to be taken as the subj. and the θέλημα τοῦ θεοῦ is the pred. nom. (Richard; Wanamaker). The omission of the article followed by the gen. may be due to the Semitic influence of the *status constructus* (BD, 135). To please God is to do His will (Bruce). ἁγιασμός (# 40) sanctification. The process of becoming holy (Moore). ἀπέχεσθαι pres. mid. inf. ἀπέχω (# 600) to hold oneself from, to abstain. Inf. is explanatory, defining the neg. side of sanctification (Ellicott). πορνεία (# 4518) sexual sin, illicit sexual activity. Sex was often linked to pagan religious practice (Best; TDNT; Lightfoot, *Notes*) Loose morals were a continuous problem in the Greco-Roman world (J. Carcopino, *Daily Life in Ancient Rome*, 76-100; BBC; DPL, 871-72). ◆ **4** εἰδέναι perf. act. inf. οἶδα (# 3857) to know. Def. perf. w. a pres. meaning. The vb. was often used to describe know-how, the possession of knowledge or skill necessary to accomplish a desired goal (ND, 347). The word might mean, in this context, "to respect" (Frame). σκεῦος (# 5007) vessel. In this context the word could mean either "body," "wife," or perhaps "life" (Best; Morris; TDNT; T; Holz), or perhaps it has the sense of controlling one's sexual urge, or mastering oneself (J. Whitton, "A Neglected Meaning for *Skeuos* in 1 Thessalonians 4.4," *NTS* 28 [1982]:142-43). κτᾶσθαι pres. mid. (dep.) inf. κτάομαι

(# 3227) to acquire. Although the perf. generally means "to possess" some examples from the papyri indicates the same meaning in the pres. (MM; Milligan; TDNT; Morris). It is possible that the word reflects a Heb. idiom and has the sense, "to possess a woman sexually" (Best; TDNT). ◆ **5 πάθει** dat. πάθος (# 4079) passion. **ἐπιθυμία** (# 2123) lust, desire. Paul does not forbid the natural impulse of desire, but rather "passion of lust," "lustful passion," a cond. where sense has been converted into the ruling principle or into passion (Lunemann). **καθάπερ** (# 2749) just as (s. the discussion in 2:11). **ἔθνη** nom. pl. ἔθνος (# 1620) Gentile. **εἰδότα** perf. act. part. οἶδα (# 3857) to know (s.v. 4). Adj. part. to emphasize a trait. ◆ **6 ὑπερβαίνειν** pres. act. inf. ὑπερβαίνω (# 5648) to go beyond, to exceed the proper limits, to transgress. With acc. of a person the verb means "to get the better of, to override" (Lightfoot, *Notes*). Inf. may be used to express results or purp., or it may be used parallel to the other inf. in the section (Frame; Best). **πλεονεκτεῖν** pres. act. inf. πλεονεκτέω (# 4430) to claim more, to have more than one's due, to defraud, to selfishly attempt to gain more at all costs and by all means, disregarding others and their rights (Moore; TDNT; NTW, 97ff; NIDNTT; BBC). **πρᾶγμα** (# 4547) matter. In this case it could mean in matters of sex (TDNT; Best). **ἔκδικος** (# 1690) one who carries out that which is right, avenger. The word was used in the papyri for the office of an official legal representative (MM; Preisigke 1:443; 3:110; Milligan). The word may be a compound developed from a prep. phrase w. the meaning, "just as after a legal decision," and the word would thus refer to one who carries out a sentence (MH, 311). **προείπαμεν** aor. ind. act. προλέγω (# 4625) to say previously, to say beforehand. The word is not used here in the sense of "prophesy," "predict" (Best). **διεμαρτυράμεθα** aor. ind. mid. (dep.) διαμαρτύρομαι (# 1371) to solemnly declare, to warn, to insist (Wanamaker; Bruce). Prep. in compound has the idea of "thoroughly" (MH, 302). ◆ **7 ἐκάλεσεν** aor. ind. act. καλέω (# 2813) to call. Consummative aor. views the completion of the action. **ἀκαθαρσία** (# 174) uncleanness, filthiness, impurity. The prep. used w. the noun means for the purp. of (Moore). **ἐν** (# 1877) in. The prep. indicates the state of holiness resulting from the calling (Frame). ◆ **8 τοιγαροῦν** (# 5521) for that very reason then, therefore (BAGD; for its position in usage s. Blomqvist, 130). **ἀθετῶν** pres. act. part. ἀθετέω (# 119) lit., to do away w. what has been laid down; to reject, to set aside, to spurn, to despise (Milligan; Frame). Nom. part. to emphasize a trait, "the one who despises this." Pres. indicates a continuing action. **ἀθετεῖ** pres. ind. act. ἀθετέω (# 119). **διδόντα** pres. act. part. δίδωμι (# 1443) to give. Adj. or nominal use of part. Pres. describes the continual or the continually repeated action. ◆ **9 φιλαδελφία** (# 5789) love for the brothers.

χρεία (# 5970) need. **ἔχετε** pres. ind. act. ἔχω (# 2400) to have. **γράφειν** pres. act. inf. γράφω (# 1211) to write. Compl. inf. **θεοδίδακτος** (# 2531) taught of God. The word points not so much to one divine communication as to divine relationship established between believers and God; hence, it is as those who have been born of God and whose hearts are in consequence filled by God's spirit that the Thessalonians for their part can no longer help loving (Milligan). For the verbal adj. w. this ending s. M, 221; MH, 370; and for the compound having an instr. sense ("God-taught") s. MH, 271. **ἀγαπᾶν** pres. act. inf. ἀγαπάω (# 26) to love. Articular inf. w. εἰς (# 1650) to express purp. or result. **ἀλλήλων** (# 253) reciprocal pron., one another. ◆ **10 καὶ γάρ** for also, for indeed. The phrase marks this statement as an advance upon the preceding one: "You are not only taught the lesson, but you also practice it" (Lightfoot, *Notes*). **ποιεῖτε** pres. ind. act. ποιέω (# 4472) to do. **παρακαλοῦμεν** pres. ind. act. παρακαλέω (# 4151) to exhort. **περισσεύειν** pres. act. inf. περισσεύω (# 4355) to excel. Compl. inf. to the main vb. **μᾶλλον** (# 3437) more. ◆ **11 φιλοτιμεῖσθαι** pres. mid. (dep.) inf. φιλοτιμέομαι (# 5818) to make it one's ambition, to be zealous, to strive eagerly, to consider it an honor (MM; Milligan; BAGD; NDIEC, 1:87-88). The infs. in v. 11 connected by καί (# 2779) are epex., giving concrete examples of how love of others applies to daily life (Richard). **ἡσυχάζειν** pres. act. inf. ἡσυχάζω (# 2483) to be at rest, to be quiet, to remain silent; i.e., to live quietly. Compl. inf. to the main vb. The context suggests that Paul is speaking to those who were busybodies w. their brotherly love and he directs such people to learn to behave and quietly get on w. their own work (Moore; BBC). **πράσσειν** pres. act. inf. πράσσω (# 4556) to do, to practice. **ἴδιος** (# 2625) private, one's own. **ἐργάζεσθαι** pres. mid. (dep.) inf. ἐργάζομαι (# 2237) to work. Compl. inf. to the main vb. Although the Gr. generally looked down on manual labor as the work of slaves, the Jews had no such attitude. The emphasis here, however, is not on manual labor opposed to some other form but upon working as opposed to idling (Moore; RAC, 1:585-90; KP, 1:490-94). Paul seems to be warning against the prevalent and popular idea of living from public or private support (FAP, 334-35, 338-39; Wanamaker). **παρηγγείλαμεν** aor. ind. act. παραγγέλλω (# 4133) to charge, to order, to instruct. In classical writers the word was used of the orders of military commanders, which here brings out the authority w. which the apostle spoke (Milligan). ◆ **12 περιπατῆτε** pres. subj. act. περιπατέω (# 4344) to walk, to conduct one's life. Subj. w. ἵνα (# 2671) to express purp. **εὐσχημόνως** (# 2361) decently, becomingly. **πρός** (# 4639) toward; w. an eye to (Frame). **ἔξω** (# 2032) outside. "Those outside" reflects a rabbinic expression and means anyone and everyone not within the Christian community (Moore). **ἔχητε** pres.

subj. act. ἔχω (# 2400) to have. Parallel to the previous vb., w. subj. expressing purp. ◆ **13 θέλομεν** pres. ind. act. θέλω (# 2527) to desire. **ἀγνοεῖν** pres. act. inf. ἀγνοέω (# 51) not to know, to be ignorant. Compl. inf. to the main vb.: "We desire for you not to be ignorant." **κοιμωμένων** pres. mid. (dep.) part. κοιμάω (# 3121) to sleep, to fall asleep. Pres. is probably timeless and denotes a class, "the sleepers" (Frame; Morris). **λυπῆσθε** pres. subj. pass. (dep.) λυπέω (# 3382) to grieve, to pain; pass., to become sad, to be sorrowful, to be distressed. Pres. signifies a continuing sorrow (Morris). **λοιπός** (# 3370) remaining; here, "the others." **ἔχοντες** pres. act. part. ἔχω (# 2400) to have. The general hopelessness of the pagan world in the presence of death is almost too well-known to require illustration (Milligan; Lightfoot, *Notes*; Morris; LAE, 176-78; Gerhard Pfohl, *Römische Grabinschriften* [Munich: Ernst Heimeran, 1969]; G. Pfohl, *Griechische Inschriften*, 11-42; FAP, 339-40). One common motif was the sorrowing parents waving good-bye to their daughter sitting in a boat, about to depart for the underworld. **ἐλπίς** (# 1828) hope (EH, 447-51). Here hope for a reunion in the afterlife. ◆ **14 εἰ** (# 1623) if. The word introduces a cond. of the first class, assuming the death and resurrection of Jesus to be true (RWP; GGBB, 694). **γάρ** (# 1142) for, drawing a conclusion or inference from the cond. **πιστεύομεν** pres. ind. act. πιστεύω (# 4409) to believe. **ἀπέθανεν** aor. ind. act. ἀποθνήσκω (# 633) to die. **ἀνέστη** aor. ind. act. ἀνίστημι (# 482) to rise. **κοιμηθέντας** aor. pass. part. κοιμάω (# 3121) to sleep. **ἄξει** fut. ind. act. ἄγω (# 72) to lead, to bring. The prep. phrase is to be taken w. this vb., "God will bring through Jesus those who have fallen asleep" (Moore). ◆ **15 ζῶντες** pres. act. part. (adj.) ζάω (# 2409) to live. Pres. used to stress a trait. **περιλειπόμενοι** pres. pass. part. περιλείπω (# 4335) to leave, to leave behind. Pres. indicates that the action is viewed as going on to the limit of time designated by the prep. **εἰς** (# 1650) (Frame). **παρουσία** (# 4242) arrival, coming (s. 3:13). **οὐ μή** not in anywise. **φθάσωμεν** aor. subj. act. φθάνω (# 5777) to precede, to go before. Aor. subj. used w. the emphatic neg. **οὐ μή** (# 4024; 3590) has the sense of an emphatic fut. ind. (SMT, 78; RG, 939f). **κοιμηθέντας** aor. pass. part. (# 3121) (s.v. 13). ◆ **16 κέλευσμα** (# 3026) command, shout. The word was used in a variety of ways. It is the cry made by the ship's master to its rowers, or by a charioteer to his horses. When used w. military or naval personnel, it was a battle cry. In most places it denotes a loud, authoritative cry, often one uttered in the thick of great excitement (Morris; Lightfoot, *Notes*; BBC). In the Roman army, at the sound of the third trumpet a herald, standing at the right of the commander, called out three times to ask if the soldiers were ready for war; the troops shouted loud and lustily, "We are ready!" (TJ, 106; Jos., *JW.*, 3.91-93). **ἀρχάγγελος** (# 791) archangel. It

was a term for those of the uppermost rank (Best). **σάλπιγγι** dat. σάλπιγξ (# 4894) trumpet. The trumpet was used by the Jews in their festival and was associated w. theophanies, the End, and w. the resurrection of the dead (Best; TDNT; for the three trumpets in the Roman army as they broke camp s. TJ, 105-6). **καταβήσεται** fut. ind. mid. (dep.) καταβαίνω (# 2849) to come down. **ἀναστήσονται** fut. ind. mid. (dep.) ἀνίστημι (# 482) to rise. **πρῶτον** (# 4754) first. ◆ **17 ἔπειτα** (# 2083) then, following. The word denotes the speedy following of the event specified upon what has gone before (Milligan; Ellicott). **ζῶντες** pres. act. part. ζάω (# 2409) to live. **περιλειπόμενοι** pres. pass. part. περιλείπω (# 4335) to leave behind. **ἁρπαγησόμεθα** fut. ind. pass. ἁρπάζω (# 773) to snatch up, to seize, to carry off by force, to rapture. The word often denotes the emotion of a sudden swoop, and usually that of a force which cannot be resisted (Morris). **ἀπάντησις** (# 561) meeting. The word had a technical meaning in the Hellenistic world related to the visits of dignitaries to cities where the visitor would be formally met by the citizens, or a deputation of them, who went out from the city and would then ceremonially escort him back into the city (Best). **ἀέρα** acc. sing. ἀήρ (# 113) air. **πάντοτε** (# 4121) always. **ἐσόμεθα** fut. ind. mid. (dep.) εἰμί (# 1639) to be. ◆ **18 ὥστε** (# 6063) therefore. **παρακαλεῖτε** pres. imp. act. παρακαλέω (# 4151) to encourage.

1 Thessalonians 5

◆ **1 χρόνος** (# 5989) time. The word expresses simply duration, time viewed in its extension (Milligan; Best; Morris; TDNT). **καιρός** (# 2789) originally the opportunity for doing, or avoiding to do, anything. It is time w. reference to both its extent and character and refers to the kind of events that are taking place (Lightfoot, *Notes*; Milligan; Morris; TDNT). **ἔχετε** pres. ind. act. ἔχω (# 2400) to have; here, to have need. **γράφεσθαι** pres. pass. inf. γράφω (# 1211) to write. ◆ **2 ἀκριβῶς** (# 209) accurately, precisely, well (Moore; s. Luke 1:3). **ἡμέρα κυρίου** (# 2465; 3261) day of the Lord. This could refer to the day of the Lord in the OT sense (Bruce), or it could refer to the day of the Lord Jesus and be a reference to the rapture as described in 4:15-18. Note the repeated use of Lord, meaning the Lord Jesus Christ, in these verses. ◆ **3 ὅταν** (# 4020) used. w. the subj., when, whenever. **λέγωσιν** pres. subj. act. λέγω (# 3306) to say, to speak. **ἀσφάλεια** (# 854) safety. The word occurs in the papyri as a law term: bond, security (Milligan; MM). **αἰφνίδιος** (# 167) sudden, suddenly. The word could be an adj. ("sudden destruction comes upon them"), or it could be used as an adv., "all of a sudden" (Frame). **ἐφίσταται** pres. ind. mid. (dep.) ἐφίστημι (# 2392) to approach, to appear, to come upon. It is used of misfortunes which suddenly come upon someone (BAGD). **ὄλεθρος** (# 3897) destruction, disaster, ruin. The word is used in the LXX, particularly in the prophets to mean an eschatological destruction (TDNT; NIDNTT). ὠδίν (# 6047) birth pain. The term was used in the pl. in the OT and Jewish writings to describe the pain, anxiety, or distress associated particularly w. divine judgment (BBC; Richard). γαστρί dat. γαστήρ (# 1143) stomach. ἐχούσῃ pres. act. part. ἔχω (# 2400) to have. Used in the expression "to have something in the stomach," w. the meaning "to be pregnant." οὐ μή (# 4024; 3590) certainly not. ἐκφύγωσιν aor. subj. act. ἐκφύγω (# 1767) to escape, to escape completely. For the subj. w. the emphatic neg. s. 4:15. ◆ **4** ἵνα (# 2671) used w. the subj. to express result (IBG, 142; BD, 198; RG, 998; MT, 103f; BG, 122). κλέπτης (# 3095) thief; fig. to show surprise. καταλάβῃ aor. subj. act. καταλαμβάνω (# 2898) to seize, to seize w. danger for them (BAGD). ◆ **5** υἱοὶ φωτός (# 5626; 5890) sons of light. The word "son" followed by the gen. is a Semitic construction meaning "to be characterized by that thing" (Morris; BG, 15ff; BS, 161-66). For the use of the term "sons of light" in the DSS, s. 1QM; 1QS 1:9; 2:16; 3:13, 24, 25; s. also the discussion in John 1:5. νυκτός (# 3816) and σκότους (# 5030) of night, of darkness. Gen. points to the sphere to which the subjects belong (Milligan). For the term "sons of darkness" in the DSS s. 1QM; 1QS 1:10; John 1:5. ◆ **6** ἄρα (# 726) therefore, then. Paul uses this to introduce a new stage in the argument (Best). καθεύδωμεν pres. subj. act. καθεύδω (# 2761) to sleep, cohortative subj. used w. the neg. μή (3590) indicating a prohibition. γρηγορῶμεν pres. subj. act. γρηγορέω (# 1213) to stay awake, to watch, to be vigilant. The word signifies the proper attitude of the Christian (Moore). Cohortative subj. Pres. indicates a continuing attitude: "Let us continue to remain vigilant, in contrast to the others who continue to sleep." νήφωμεν pres. subj. act. νήφω (# 3768) to be sober, not to be under the influence of drink. The word points to a cond. of moral alertness, the sense of being so exercised and disciplined that all fear of sleeping again is removed (Milligan; TDNT; Best). ◆ **7** καθεύδοντες pres. act. part. καθεύδω (# 2761) to sleep. νυκτός gen. sing. νύξ (# 3816) night; gen. of time, "during the night." Gen. specifies the time within which something occurs, "nighttime action" (MT, 235; DM, 77; BD, 99f; RG, 494f). μεθυσκόμενοι pres. pass. (dep.) part. μεθύσκομαι (# 3499) to get drunk, to make drunk (s. Eph. 5:18). μεθύουσιν pres. ind. act. μεθύω (# 3501) to be drunk. Pres. points to that which generally happens. ◆ **8** ὄντες pres. act. part. εἰμί (# 1639) to be. ἐνδυσάμενοι aor. mid. (dep.) part. ἐνδύω (# 1907) to clothe oneself, to put on. Aor. part. expresses identical or contemporaneous action in relation to the main vb. (Ellicott; Frame; GGBB, 624-25). θώρακα acc. sing. θώραξ (# 2606) breastplate (s. Eph. 6:14). πίστεως (# 4411) and ἀγάπης (# 27) faith and love, are epexegetical gens. explaining the

breastplate (von Dobschütz; Best). περικεφαλαίαν (# 4330) that which goes around the head, helmet (s. Eph. 6:17). ἐλπίδα acc. ἐλπίς (# 1828) hope, oppositional to περικεθαλαίαν (von Dobschütz). ◆ **9** ἔθετο aor. ind. mid. τίθημι (# 5502) to place, to destine (Best; MT, 55; BD, 165). ὀργή (# 3973) wrath, anger. περιποίησις (# 4348) obtaining, acquiring (Morris; Moore). διά (# 1328) w. the gen., through. The phrase is to be taken w. π. σωτηρίας (von Dobschütz). ◆ **10** ἀποθανόντος aor. act. part. ἀποθνήσκω (# 633) to die. ὑπέρ for. For the prep. in relation to the death of Christ as compared to other prep. s. IBG, 63; M, 105; BG, 96). εἴτε (# 1664) whether. It is used as an alternative cond. of a 3rd. class cond. cl. w. the pres. subj. (RWP; RG, 1017; BD, 187). γρηγορῶμεν pres. subj. act. γρηγορέω (# 1213) to watch. καθεύδωμεν pres. subj. act. καθεύδω (# 2761) to sleep. ζήσωμεν aor. subj. act. ζάω (# 2409) to live. Aor. points to this life as a definite fact secured for us by the equally definite death of our Lord (Milligan). ◆ **11** διό (# 1475) therefore. παρακαλεῖτε pres. imp. act. παρακαλέω (# 4151) to encourage, to comfort (s. 2:12). ἀλλήλων (# 253) one another. οἰκοδομεῖτε pres. imp. act. οἰκοδομέω (# 3868) to build up, to edify. καθώς (# 2777) just as. ποιεῖτε pres. ind. act. ποιέω (# 4472) to do. ◆ **12** ἐρωτῶμεν pres. act. ind. ἐρωτάω (# 2263) to ask, to request (s. 4:1). εἰδέναι perf. act. inf. οἶδα (# 3857) to know. Def. perf. w. pres. meaning (ND, 344ff). κοπιῶντας pres. act. part. κοπιάω (# 3159) to grow weary, to work w. effort. The word refers to both bodily and mental labor (Milligan; s. 1:3). προϊσταμένους pres. mid. (dep.) part. προΐστημι (# 4613) to stand before someone. The word has two possible meanings, either "to preside, lead, direct" or "to protect, to care for" (Best; TDNT; MM). νουθετοῦντας pres. act. part. νουθετέω (# 3805) to put one in mind, to advise, to warn, to admonish. The word is used for the admonition and correction of those who are in error (Moore; TDNT). ◆ **13** ἡγεῖσθαι pres. mid. (dep.) inf. ἡγέομαι (# 2451) to consider, to esteem (Morris; for examples in the papyri, s. MM). ὑπερεκπερισσοῦ (# 5655) adv., exceedingly, very highly (Moore; s. also 3:10). εἰρηνεύετε pres. imp. act. εἰρηνεύω (# 1644) to exercise peace, to be at peace. Vbs. w. this suf. are often causative or connote the possession of a quality that sometimes leads to action (MH, 399f). ◆ **14** παρακαλοῦμεν pres. ind. act. παρακαλέω (# 4151) to encourage. (s. 2:12). νουθετεῖτε pres. imp. act. νουθετέω (# 3805) to warn, to exhort (s.v. 12; BBC). ἄτακτος (# 864) without rank, out of rank, disorderly. The word was primarily a military term used of the soldier who is out of step or rank, or of the army moving in disarray. Then it was used more generally of whatever is out of order. In this passage the special reference would seem to be the idleness and neglect of duty which characterized certain members of the Thessalonian church in view of the shortly expected parousia

(Milligan, esp. 152-54; Morris; Best; s. also 4:11). **παρα-μυθεῖσθε** pres. imp. mid. (dep.) παραμυθέομαι (# *4170*) to encourage (s. 2:12). **ὀλιγόψυχος** (# *3901*) fainthearted, worried, discouraged, fearful (Best). **ἀντέχεσθε** pres. mid. imp. ἀντέχω (# *504*) to lay hold of, to hold firmly to. For this as well as examples from the papyri s. Milligan; MM. **ἀσθενής** (# *822*) without strength, weak (Best). **μακροθυμεῖτε** pres. imp. act. μακροθυμέω (# *3428*) to be longsuffering. It indicates not giving way to a short or quick temper toward those who fail, but being patient and considerate of them (Milligan; TDNT; NTW, 83ff; Trench, *Synonyms*, 195). ◆ **15 ὁρᾶτε** pres. imp. act. ὁράω (# *3972*) to see, to see to it. The combination of 2nd. and 3rd. pers. in this construction conveys the idea that the whole group is being held responsible for the conduct of each individual. They are not only to abstain from retaliation, but to see that none of their number retaliates (Morris; Frame). **μή** (# *3590*) that, lest. The neg. is used in an expression of apprehension and the subj. indicates that anxiety is directed toward warding off something still dependent on the will (BD, 188; MT, 98). **ἀντί** (# *505*) w. the gen., instead of, in return for. **ἀποδῷ** aor. subj. act. ἀποδίδωμι (# *625*) to give back, to pay back. **πάντοτε** (# *4121*) always. **διώκετε** pres. imp. act. διώκω (# *1503*) to hunt, to pursue, to seek eagerly (Best). ◆ **16 χαίρετε** pres. imp. act. χαίρω (# *5897*) to rejoice. Pres. imp. calls for a continual attitude of rejoicing. ◆ **17 ἀδιαλείπτως** (# *90*) adv., without interruption, unceasingly, constantly (s. 1:2; BBC). **προσεύχεσθε** pres. imp. mid. (dep.) προσεύχομαι (# *4667*) to pray. This is the more comprehensive term for prayer and can include the other words for prayer (Morris; TDNT). ◆ **18 ἐν παντί** (# *1877*; *4246*) in every circumstance. This includes even persecutions and trials (Milligan). **εὐχαριστεῖτε** pres. imp. act. εὐχαριστέω (# *2373*) to give thanks. **τοῦτο** (# *4047*) this. Grammatically it could refer only to the last injunction, but it is more likely that Paul means all three commands to be regarded as a unity (Moore). ◆ **19 σβέννυτε** pres. imp. act. σβέννυμι (# *4931*) to put out (a fire), to quench. ◆ **20 προφητεία** (# *4735*) prophecy. The gift of speaking for God. **ἐξουθενεῖτε** pres. imp. act. ἐξουθενέω (# *2024*) to consider as noth-

ing, to make absolutely nothing of, to downgrade, to despise (Morris). ◆ **21 πάντα** nom. pl. πᾶς (# *4246*) all; all things. Here it is unlimited and refers to "all things whatsoever" (Lightfoot, *Notes*). **δοκιμάζετε** pres. imp. act. δοκιμάζω (# *1507*) to approve after testing (s. the discussion in 2:4). **κατέχετε** pres. imp. act. κατέχω (# *2988*) to hold fast, to lay hold of, to take possession of (MM; Milligan, 155-57). ◆ **22 εἶδος** (# *1626*) visible form, outward show. The word could also be used in the sense of kind, species, class (Milligan). **πονηρός** (# *4505*) evil. The word could be taken either as an adj. or a noun (Ellicott; Morris). **ἀπέχεσθε** pres. imp. mid. ἀπέχω (# *600*) to hold oneself from, to abstain. ◆ **23 ἁγιάσαι** aor. opt. act. ἁγιάζω (# *39*) to sanctify. For the use of the opt. in prayers to express a wish s. PIP, 32f. **ὁλοτελής** (# *3911*) wholly, entirely, quite completely. The word not only implies entirety but involves the further idea of completion (Lightfoot, *Notes*; Moore). **ὁλόκληρος** (# *3908*) whole, complete, undamaged, intact (BAGD). The point is that no part of the Christian personality should be lacking in consecration (Frame). For the possible construction of the entire s. PIP, 39; Best. **ἀμέμπτως** (# *290*) adv., blamelessly. **παρουσία** (# *4242*) arrival, coming (s. 3:13). **τηρηθείη** aor. opt. pass. τηρέω (# *5498*) to keep. The word has a sense of protecting, watching over, and guarding (Moore). ◆ **24 καλῶν** pres. act. part. καλέω (# *2813*) to call. **ποιήσει** fut. ind. act. ποιέω (# *4472*) to do. ◆ **25 προσεύχεσθε** pres. imp. mid. (dep.) προσεύχομαι (# *4667*) to pray (s.v. 17). ◆ **26 ἀσπάσασθε** pres. imp. mid. (dep.) ἀσπάζομαι (# *832*) to greet. **φίλημα** (# *5799*) kiss. Here, instr. dat., "with a kiss." The kiss was used in the ancient world as a form of greeting (Best; Moore; TDNT; s. 1 Cor. 16:20). ◆ **27 ἐνορκίζω** (# *1941*) pres. ind. act. to adjure, to cause someone to swear by something, to put someone on their oath (BAGD; Morris). The vb. is followed by the inf. (BD, 199f.) and the one by whom the oath is sworn is in the acc. (BD, 83; RG, 483f.). **ἀναγνωσθῆναι** aor. pass. inf. ἀναγινώσκω (# *336*) to read. From the context it is clear that it is a public reading or a reading aloud (Milligan). **ἐπιστολή** (# *2186*) letter.

2 Thessalonians

2 Thessalonians 1

◆ **1-2** For the introduction s. 1 Thess. 1:1, and for the slight differences s. Bruce. ◆ **3** εὐχαριστεῖν pres. act. inf. εὐχαριστέω (# 2373) to give thanks (P.T. O'Brien, "Thanksgiving and the Gospel in Paul," *NTS* 21 [1974]: 144-55). ὀφείλομεν pres. ind. act. ὀφείλω (# 4053) to be obligated, w. inf. The word implies a special, personal obligation rather than one arising out of the nature of things (Best); "we owe it to God" (Moore). For parallels to the necessity and propriety of giving thanks, esp. in the midst of persecution s. Roger D. Aus, "The Liturgical Background of the Necessity and Propriety of Giving Thanks According to II Thess. 1:3," *JBL* 92 (1973): 432-38. πάντοτε (# 4121) always. καθώς (# 2777) just as. The word is slightly causal and resumes and explains the obligation to give thanks (Frame). ἄξιον (# 545) fitting. The word indicates that this thanksgiving is also appropriate in the circumstances (Moore). ὑπεραυξάνει pres. ind. act. ὑπεραυξάνω (# 5647) to grow abundantly, to grow over and beyond. It is a figure of the tree of faith growing above measure (RWP). Prep. in compound intensifies and magnifies the normal meaning of the word (Best; Bruce; MH, 326). πλεονάζει pres. ind. act. πλεονάζω (# 4429) to increase. ἕκαστος (# 1667) each one. ἀλλήλων (# 253) one another, reflexive pron. ◆ **4** ὥστε (# 6063) used w. the inf. to express results. αὐτοὺς ἡμᾶς (# 899; 1609) we ourselves. The words are emphatic and may form a contrast. For the various interpretations s. Best; Richard. Acc. as subj. of the inf. ἐγκαυχᾶσθαι pres. mid. (dep.) inf. ἐγκαυχάομαι (# 1595) to boast. Inf. w. ὥστε to express actual results. The boasting done by Paul was the result of his readers' ever increasing faith and love (Wanamaker). ἐν ταῖς ἐκκλησίαις (# 1877; 1711) in the churches. The prep. ἐν may be used for the normal dat. ("to the churches"), but it may also have its normal local meaning: "within the churches," "among the churches" (MT, 264). ὑπέρ (# 5642) concerning. ὑπομονή (# 5705) patience, endurance. The word indicates a remaining under, i.e., a bearing up under difficult circumstances. It is the Spirit which can bear things, not simply w. resignation but w. blazing hope. It is not the patience which grimly waits for the end, but the patience which radiantly hopes for the dawn (NTW, 60; TDNT; NIDNTT; TLNT). διωγμός (# 1501) persecution. θλίψεσιν dat. pl. θλῖψις (# 2568)

persecution inflicted by the enemies of the gospel; the latter is more general and denotes tribulation of any kind (Lightfoot, *Notes*). ἀνέχεσθε pres. ind. mid. (dep) ἀνέχομαι (# 462) to hold oneself up, to endure (MH, 295). Pres. indicates that trouble did not end for the converts w. the expulsion of the missionaries (Moore). ◆ **5** ἔνδειγμα (# 1891) evidence, proof, the means by which one knows that something is a fact (LN, 1:341). In Josephus the word is used in the sense of a denunciation, indication, or proof (CCFJ, 2:98; s. Jos., *Ant.*, 13:306, 19:133) and the noun ἐνδείκτης is used in 2 Macc. 4:1 of an informer (GELS, 150). The ending of the word denotes a result which has been reached–a thing proved–but frequently in similar cases where the abstract gives place to the concrete the word can hardly be distinguished from evidence, the actual proof by and appeal to facts (Milligan; but for a different opinion s. Lightfoot, *Notes*). κρίσεως (# 3213) judging, judgment. καταξιωθῆναι aor. pass. inf. καταξιόω (# 2921) to consider or declare worthy. The strengthened form of the vb. means "to declare to be worthy," "to deem worthy" (Morris). Articular inf. w. εἰς (# 1650) to express purp. or result. ὑπέρ (# 5642) for, for the sake of which, in the name of which, in the interest of which (Moore; Morris). πάσχετε pres. ind. act. πάσχω (# 4248) to suffer. Pres. denotes the sufferings are still going on (Frame). ◆ **6** εἴπερ (# 1642) if on the whole, provided that. The word introduces a cond. cl. which assumes the reality of the cond. (RWP; von Dobschütz). παρά (# 4123) w. dat. The reference is to the righteous judgment of God. ἀνταποδοῦναι aor. act. inf. ἀνταποδίδωμι (# 500) to pay back again, to recompense. The prep. in compound conveys the thought of a full and due requital (Morris). θλίβουσιν pres. act. part. (subst.) dat. pl. θλίβω (# 2567) to put one under pressure, to cause tribulation, to persecute. Pres. indicates that the affliction was in process. Dat. of disadvantage. ◆ **7** θλιβομένοις pres. pass. part. θλίβω (# 2567) to put under pressure (s.v. 6). ἄνεσις (# 457) loosening, relaxing. In classical Gr. it could refer to the release of a bowstring and so comes to mean relaxation and recreation in general. It is the relaxing of the cords of endurance now tightly drawn (Moore; Milligan). Here it is the lifting of the pressure caused by their persecution (Bruce). ἀποκάλυψις (# 637) unveiling, revelation (Milligan, 149f; TDNT). ◆ **8** πῦρ (# 4786) fire. φλογός gen. φλόξ (# 5825) flame. The flaming fire emphasizes the glory of the Lord's appearance and may be a reference to judgment (Best; Lightfoot, *Notes*; von Dobschütz; BBC). **διδόντος** pres. act. part. (adj.) δίδωμι (# *1443*) to give. Pres. to indicate contemporaneous action to the appearing of Christ. **ἐκδίκησις** (# *1689*) vengeance. The word indicates full, complete punishment (Milligan). **εἰδόσιν** perf. act. part. οἶδα (# *3857*) to know. Def. perf. w. a pres. meaning (ND, 344f). **ὑπακούουσιν** pres. act. part. ὑπακούω (# *5634*) to listen to, to obey. The prep. in compound has the idea of submission (MH, 327). ◆ **9 οἵτινες** nom. pl. ὅστις (# *4015*) who. The rel. pron. is generic indicating ones who belong to such a class: "such people" (Best; MT, 47f; IBG, 123f; MKG, 174f). **δίκη** (# *1472*) the standard to which a thing is to conform, right, law, judicial hearing. It then came to express the results of the lawsuit, execution of a sentence, punishment (Milligan; TDNT; GW, 99; NIDNTT; Preisigke, 1:383-85; TLNT). **τίσουσιν** fut. ind. act. τίνω (# *5514*) to suffer, to pay a penalty. The word means to pay a price by way of recompense (Moore). **ὄλεθρος** (# *3897*) destruction, ruination. The word does not mean annihilation, but implies the loss of all things that give worth to existence (MM; Best; TDNT; s. 1 Thess. 5:3). Acc. is in apposition to the word **δίκην** (RWP). **αἰώνιος** (# *173*) eternal. The adj. lit. means agelong and everything depends on the length of the age. In the NT there is never a hint that the coming age has an end (Morris; GW, 186-89; NIDNTT; TDNT). **ἰσχύς** (# *2709*) strength, might, power (s. Eph. 1:19). ◆ **10 ὅταν** (# *4020*) w. subj., when, whenever. **ἔλθῃ** aor. subj. act. ἔρχομαι (# *2262*) to come, to go. **ἐνδοξασθῆναι** aor. pass. inf. ἐνδοξάζω (# *1901*) to glorify. The prep. in compound is repeated after the vb. and could have either a local meaning ("in"), an instr. meaning ("by means of"), or a causal meaning ("because of") (Best). The prep. is used to express purp. **θαυμασθῆναι** aor. pass. inf. θαυμάζω (# *2513*) to marvel, to wonder; pass., to be marveled at. Inf. is to express purp. **πιστεύσασιν** aor. act. part. masc. pl. dat. πιστεύω (# *4409*) to believe. Aor. part. focuses attention on the past act of belief (Best). **ἐπιστεύθη** aor. ind. pass. πιστεύω (# *4409*) to believe. **μαρτύριον** (# *3457*) witness. ◆ **11 εἰς ὅ** to this end, w. this in mind. The expression conveys the idea of purp. (Morris; Moore). **προσευχόμεθα** pres. ind. mid. (dep.) προσεύχομαι (# *4667*) to pray (s. 1 Thess. 5:17). **πάντοτε** (# *4121*) always, constantly. **ἵνα** (# *2671*) that. The particle introduces the content of the prayer. **ἀξιώσῃ** aor. subj. act. ἀξιόω (# *546*) to consider worthy, to reckon as worthy. Subj. w. ἵνα. **κλήσεως** gen. sing. κλῆσις (# *3104*) calling. Gen. is used after the vb. **ἀξιώσῃ**. **πληρώσῃ** aor. subj. act. πληρόω (# *4444*) to fill. Here it has the sense of accomplishing (Moore). **εὐδοκία** (# *2306*) good pleasure, resolve, consent, desire (BAGD; TDNT). **ἀγαθωσύνη** (# *20*) goodness. Here, obj. gen., "delight in well doing" (Lightfoot, *Notes*; s. Gal.

5:22). ◆ **12 ἐνδοξασθῇ** aor. pass. subj. ἐνδοξάζω (# *1901*) to glorify (s.v. 10). Subj. w. **ὅπως** (# *3968*) to express purp.

2 Thessalonians 2

◆ **1 ἐρωτῶμεν** pres. ind. act. ἐρωτάω (# *2263*) to ask, to request (s. the discussion in 1 Thess. 4:1). **παρουσία** (# *4242*) arrival, coming (s. 1 Thess. 3:13). **ἐπισυναγωγή** (# *2093*) meeting, assembling, gathering together, collection, collecting together (LAE, 103f). The prep. in compound is directive (MH, 312). The word is used in 2 Macc 2:7 indicating a fut. time when God shall gather His people together. ◆ **2 εἰς** (# *1650*) w. the articular inf.; is used either to express purp. (RWP) or to introduce the object of the vb. (Best; MT, 143). **ταχέως** (# *5441*) quickly, hastily (Lightfoot, *Notes*). **σαλευθῆναι** aor. pass. inf. σαλεύω (# *4888*) to shake, to cause to move to and fro, to cause to waiver; pass., to be shaken, to be make to waver or totter, like the shaking of a foundation (BAGD; Wanamaker). By aor. the suddenness of the shock is emphasized (Moore). **νοῦς** (# *3808*) mind, understanding, the reasoning faculty, man's power of judgment (Best; TDNT). **θροεῖσθαι** pres. pass. inf. θροέω (# *2583*) pass., to be inwardly aroused, to be disturbed, to be frightened (BAGD). Pres. points to a continued state of agitation following upon a definite shock received and describes a state of jumpiness (Milligan; Morris). **πνεῦμα** (# *4460*) spirit. It could refer here to some type of spiritual revelation (Lightfoot, *Notes*). **λόγος** (# *3364*) word. A general expression which could refer to prophecy or sermon or any verbal communication (Moore). **ὡς** (# *6055*) before **ὅτι** (# *4022*) to the effect that (MT, 137). **ἐνέστηκεν** perf. ind. act. ἐνίστημι (# *1931*) to place in, to stand in; perf., to be at hand, to be pres. The word could be translated, "is now pres.," and the vb. is sometimes contrasted w. vb.s expressing the fut. idea (Morris; RWP). ◆ **3 ἐξαπατήσῃ** aor. subj. act. ἐξαπατάω (# *1987*) to deceive, to deceive completely, to deceive successfully (MH, 311). Subj. w. the neg. **μή** (# *3590*) to express a prohibition. Subj. of prohibition occurs in the 3rd. pers., esp. in cls. of fear or warning (DM, 171; SMT, 76). **τρόπος** (# *5573*) manner. Used in the expression, "in no way" (Milligan). **ἔλθῃ** aor. subj. act. ἔρχομαι (# *2262*) to come. **ἀποστασία** (# *686*) falling away, rebellion, revolt, apostasy (Best; Moore; TDNT; TDNT; BBC). **ἀποκαλυφθῇ** aor. subj. pass. ἀποκαλύπτω (# *636*) to unveil, to reveal. The word is very significant, not only as marking the superhuman character of the one spoken of, but as placing it in mocking counterpart to the revelation of the Lord Jesus Himself (Milligan). **ἀνομία** (# *490*) lawlessness. The word describes the condition not of one living without law, but of one who acts contrary to law (Milligan; Best; for a discussion of the Antichrist s. ZPEB, 1:179-81; DPL, 592-94; for the Jewish teaching regarding the

Antichrist named Armilis who was identified w. the Christ of Christianity s. SB, 3:637-40). Gen. here is of Semitic influence and is used as an adj. describing the main quality or character (BG, 14f; MT, 208; Best). υἱός (# 5626) son. Used in a Semitic construction followed by the gen. describing the character or quality (BG, 15f; MH, 441). ἀπωλεία (# 724) ruin, doom, destruction. The Semitic construction means, "he who is destined to be destroyed" (Moore; Best). ◆ 4 ἀντικείμενος pres. mid. (dep.) part. ἀντίκειμαι (# 512) to lie against, to oppose. Pres. part. indicates a constant habitual opposing or a lifestyle. ὑπεραιρόμενος pres. mid. (dep.) part. ὑπεραίρω (# 5643) to lift up; mid., to lift oneself up, to exalt oneself, to exalt oneself exceedingly, to exalt oneself above measure (Lightfoot, *Notes*). λεγόμενον pres. pass. part. λέγω (# 3306) to say, to call. σέβασμα (# 4934) an object of worship. The ending of the noun indicates a pass. idea: something which is reverenced, something which is worshiped; and the word includes anything at all that could be worshiped (MH, 355; Morris; TDNT). ὥστε (# 6063) so that. Used w. the inf. to express results. αὐτόν (# 899) himself. ναός (# 3724) temple, sanctuary, the innermost part of the temple (Best). καθίσαι aor. act. inf. καθίζω (# 2767) to sit, to take one's seat. Inf. to express result. ἀποδεικνύντα pres. act. part. ἀποδείκνυμι (# 617) to show off, to exhibit, to display, to prove, to nominate or proclaim to an office. Part. of manner or attendant circum. Here, "proclaiming himself that he is God" (Milligan; Best). ἑαυτόν (# 1571) himself. ὅτι that, introducing the content of his proclamation. ◆ 5 μνημονεύετε pres. ind. act. μνημονεύω (# 3648) to remember, to call to remembrance (s. 1 Thess. 1:3). The vb. is used in a question introduced by the neg. particle which expects the answer "yes": "you remember don't you?" ὢν pres. act. part. εἰμί (# 1639) to be. ἔλεγον impf. ind. act. λέγω (# 3306) to say. ◆ 6 νῦν (# 3814) now. The word can be logical, introducing a new point, but it is almost certainly temp. in the pres. context (Best). κατέχον pres. act. part. κατέχω (# 2988) to hold down, to restrain. Though many explanations for the restrainer have been offered (Morris; Best; BBC; Milligan, 155-57) in light of the supernatural character of "the one holding back," the use of the masc. article in v. 7 (the n. article here is because the Gr. word for "spirit" is n.) may suggest that "the restrainer" is the Holy Spirit (TDNT; and for ancient interpretations in this regard s. PGL, 731; Milligan). ἀποκαλυφθῆναι aor. pass. inf. ἀποκαλύπτω (# 636) to reveal (s.v. 3). Articular inf. w. εἰς (# 1650) to express purp. καιρός (# 2789) time, opportunity, the moment appointed by God (Moore). ◆ 7 μυστήριον (# 3696) mystery, that which was unknown and incapable of being known by man except through a revelation of God (TDNT; ZPEB, 4:327-30; Best). ἐνεργεῖται pres. ind. mid. ἐνεργέω (# 1919) to work, to work effec-

tively. The word is often used of supernatural working (Best). μόνον (# 3667) only. ὁ κατέχων pres. act. part. κατέχω (# 2988) The masc. article may refer to the pers. of the Holy Spirit (s.v. 6). ἄρτι (# 785) until. μέσος (# 3545) midst. γένηται aor. subj. mid. (dep.) γίνομαι (# 1181) to become, to be. The phrase means "to be removed," "to be taken away." For this meaning, as well as a discussion of the passage relating the restrainer to God, s. Roger D. Aus, "God's Plan and God's Power: Isaiah 66 and the Restraining Factor of 2 Thess. 2:6-7," *JBL* 96 (1977): 537-53. ◆ 8 καὶ τότε and then. ἀποκαλυφθήσεται fut. pass. ind. ἀποκαλύπτω (# 636) to unveil, to reveal (s.v. 3). ἄνομος (# 491) lawless (s.v. 3). ἀνελεῖ fut. ind. act. ἀναιρέω (# 359) to take away, to do away w., to destroy (BAGD). στόματος gen. sing. στόμα (# 5125) mouth. καταργήσει fut. ind. act. καταργέω (# 2934) to render inactive, to abolish, to bring to naught, to put out of commission. ἐπιφανείᾳ (# 2211) manifestation, glorious appearance. The word usually has some idea of striking splendor and was often used by the Greeks of a glorious manifestation of the gods (Morris; T; LAE, 373; Milligan, 148f). ◆ 9 κατ' = κατά (# 2848) according to. The prep. not only refers to the norm, but indicates the source or cause of the miracle (von Dobschütz). ἐνέργεια (# 1918) word, effective work. The word was often used of supernatural work (TDNT). τέρασιν dat. pl. τέρας (# 5469) wonder (BBC). ◆ 10 ἀπάτη (# 573) deception, deceitfulness. ἀδικία (# 94) unrighteousness, wrongdoing. The combination of deceit and unrighteousness is evidence here of an active, aggressive power (Milligan). ἀπολλυμένοις pres. mid. (dep.) part. ἀπόλλυμι (# 660) to destroy, to ruin. Pres. of the vb. perfectized by the prep. has the sense of inevitable doom, indicating that the goal is ideally reached w. a complete transformation of its subjects required to bring them out of the ruin implicit in their state (M, 114f). ἀνθ' ὧν (# 505; 4005) because (Lightfoot, *Notes*). ἐδέξαντο aor. ind. mid. (dep.) δέχομαι (# 1312) to receive, to receive gladly, to welcome. σωθῆναι aor. pass. inf. σῴζω (# 5392) to rescue, to save. ◆ 11 διὰ τοῦτο (# 1328; 4047) for this reason. πέμπει pres. ind. act. πέμπω (# 4287) to send. Fut. pres. to emphasize the certainty of the fut. event. πλάνη (# 4415) delusion, error. εἰς used w. the articular inf. to express purp. (von Dobschütz; Milligan). πιστεῦσαι aor. act. inf. πιστεύω (# 4409) to believe. τῷ ψεύδει the lie. dat. following. Article may refer back to the claim of deity by the Antichrist. ◆ 12 κριθῶσιν aor. pass. subj. κρίνω (# 3212) to judge. Here, "to be judged," "to be condemned" (Best). Subj. ἵνα to express purp. or result. πιστεύσαντες aor. act. part. πιστεύω (# 4409) to believe. εὐδοκήσαντες aor. act. part. εὐδοκέω (# 2305) to have pleasure in, to delight in. Aor. suggests antecedent action to the main vb., thus providing a cause for the judgment. Substantival use of the part. to emphasize a characterizing trait. ◆ **13** ὀφείλομεν pres. ind. act. ὀφείλω (# 4053) to be obligated, to owe a debt, ought to (s. 1:3). εὐχαριστεῖν pres. act. inf. εὐχαριστέω (# 2373) to give thanks (s. 1:3). Compl. inf to the main vb. ἠγαπημένοι perf. pass. part. ἀγαπάω (# 26) to love. Perf. emphasizes the continual state. εἵλατο aor. ind. mid. (dep.) αἱρέομαι (# 145) to choose, to elect; mid., to choose for oneself. ἀπαρχή (# 794) firstfruit. σωτηρία (# 5401) sanctification. ◆ **14** εἰς ὅ unto which, whereunto. The phrase is to be taken w. the whole of the previous expression–"salvation … truth" (Morris). ἐκάλεσεν aor. ind. act. καλέω (# 2813) to call. περιποίησις (# 4348) possessing, obtaining. τοῦ κυρίου of the Lord; possessive gen. ◆ **15** ἄρα (# 726) therefore. The practical conclusion is drawn from what has just been said (Milligan). στήκετε pres. imp. act. στήκω (# 5112) to stand, to stand fast. κρατεῖτε pres. ind. act. κρατέω (# 3195) to hold, to hold fast. παράδοσις (# 4142) tradition, that which is passed on. Here it refers to the teaching of the apostle (TDNT; Moore; Best). ἐδιδάχθητε aor. ind. pass. διδάσκω (# 1438) to teach. Const. aor. focusing on the act of teaching, or consummative aor. focusing on the completion of the continuing results of the action. ◆ **16** ἀγαπήσας aor. act. part. subst. ἀγαπάω (# 26) to love. Aor. indicates antecedent action. δούς aor. act. part. δίδωμι (# 1443) to give. παράκλησις (# 4155) encouragement, comfort. Here it refers to consolation and encouragement in the present (Lightfoot, *Notes*). ◆ **17** παρακαλέσαι aor. opt. act. παρακαλέω (# 4151) to encourage, to comfort (TDNT; BAGD; MNTW, 128). στηρίξαι aor. opt. act. στηρίσσω (# 5114) to strengthen, to support (s. 1 Thess. 3:2).

2 Thessalonians 3

◆ **1** τὸ λοιπόν (# 3370; 3836) finally, as our last matter (Best; s. also Phil. 3:1). προσεύχεσθε pres. imp. mid. (dep.) προσεύχομαι (# 4667) to pray. Pres. means "pray continually" (Morris). λόγος (# 3364) the word. Here, the word of the Lord. Gen. κυρίου could be subjective ("the word from the Lord"), or obj. ("word concerning the Lord"). τρέχῃ pres. subj. act. τρέχω (# 5556) to run. Subj. w. ἵνα to express the content of the prayer. The word was used in the LXX of the running of a warrior in battle; the picture of the word as the authorized messenger of the Lord is then further applied to the prophets as His "runners" (PAM, 49; GELTS, 480). Paul uses the word here to express his dominating concern for the free course of the gospel. The important thing here is the swift progress of the Word - if any image is intended it is that of the urgent herald (PAM, 108). δοξάζηται pres. subj. pass. δοξάζω (# 1519) to think well of, to have a good opinion of, to glorify; pass., to be glorified. The triumphant onrush of the gospel brings glory to God, and in its success His glory is seen because it is God who spreads the gospel and brings it

to success or glory (Best). καθώς (# 2777) just as. πρὸς ὑμᾶς w. you, as in your case (Frame). ◆ **2** ῥυσθῶμεν aor. subj. pass. ῥύομαι (# 4861) to rescue, to deliver. To express his second request Paul uses a term which often has the idea of deliverance w. power; however, the use of the prep. here lays stress perhaps on the deliverance rather than on the power from which it is granted (Milligan; Morris). Subj. w. ἵνα (# 2671) to express purp. ἄτοπος (# 876) out of place, odd, unbecoming, outrageous. The word was used in the papyri in one instance to describe those who had pulled to pieces a farmer's sheaves of wheat and thrown them to the pigs; and in another incident it was used of parents who publicly announced their prodigal son's misdeeds, "lest he should insult us, or do anything else amiss" (i.e., outrageous) (MM; Preisigke, 1:234). ἡ πίστις (# 4411) the faith. The word w. the article may signify the body of Christian teaching, or it may be used in the sense of trust (Morris). ◆ **3** στηρίξει fut. ind. act. στηρίσσω (# 5114) to establish, to support, to make firm (s. 1 Thess. 3:2). φυλάξει fut. ind. act. φυλάσσω (# 5875) to guard, to protect. The Lord will also protect them from external assaults (Milligan). ◆ **4** πεποίθαμεν perf. ind. act. πείθω (# 4275) to persuade, to have been persuaded, to trust. Perf. emphasizes a state of trust (RWP; s. also Phil. 1:6). παραγγέλλομεν pres. ind. act. παραγγέλλω (# 4133) to command, to charge, to instruct. For the noun s. 1 Thess. 4:2. ποιήσετε fut. ind. act. ποιέω (# 4472) to do. ◆ **5** κατευθύναι pres. opt. act. κατευθύνω (# 2985) to make straight, to guide (s. 1 Thess. 3:11). ◆ **6** στέλλεσθαι pres. mid. inf. στέλλω (# 5097). The word originally meant "to get ready," "to equip," esp. in reference to equipping an army for an expedition or for sailing. Then it came to mean "to bring together" or "to gather up," as for instance one gathers or tucks up clothes. From this comes the sense of an inner gathering-up or withdrawal, and so of flinching and avoiding. Here it is withdrawal from brethren who are out of step (BAGD; Moore; Milligan). περιπατοῦντος pres. act. part. περιπατέω (# 4344) to walk about, to conduct one's life. παράδοσις (# 4142) tradition, teachings that were passed down. It refers to the authoritative teaching of the apostle (TLNT). παρελάβοσαν aor. ind. act. παραλαμβάνω (# 4123) to receive, to receive that which is passed on (TLNT; s. Col. 2:6; 1 Cor. 11:23). ◆ **7** οἴδατε pres. ind. act. οἶδα (# 3857) to know. Defective perf. w. a pres. meaning. δεῖ pres. ind. act. (# 1256) it is necessary to, Impersonal vb. w. inf. The word indicates a logical necessity arising from the circumstances (AS). μιμεῖσθαι pres. mid. (dep.) inf. μιμέομαι (# 3628) to imitate, to mimic (s. 1 Thess. 1:6; BBC). ἠτακτήσαμεν aor. ind. act. ἀτακέω (# 863) to be out of rank, to be out of order, to be disorderly, to be idle, to be a loafer (s. the discussion in 1 Thess. 5:14; Best). ◆ **8** δωρεάν (# 1562) freely, without paying, gratis. One example in the papyri speaks of labor or work as gratis or at reduced wages (Milligan; MM; Moore). For the situation at Thessalonica s. 1 Thess. 4:11. ἐφάγομεν aor. ind. act. ἐσθίω (# 2266) to eat. The phrase "to eat bread" is evidently a semitism and means "to get a living" (Morris). κόπος (# 3160) toil, working until one is weary. μόχθος (# 3677) labor, toil, hardship in working. For these two words s. 1 Thess. 2:9; AS. ἐργαζόμενοι pres. mid. (dep.) part. ἐργάζομαι (# 2237) to work. ἐπιβαρῆσαι aor. act. inf. ἐπιβαρέω (# 2096) to be heavy, to be burdensome (s. 1 Thess. 2:9). ◆ 9 ἔχομεν pres. ind. act. ἔχω (# 2400) to have. τύπος (# 5596) type, example (s. 1 Thess. 1:7; TDNT). δῶμεν aor. subj. act. δίδωμι (# 1443) to give. Subj. w. ἵνα (# 2671) to express purp. μιμεῖσθαι pres. mid. (dep.) inf. μιμέομαι (# 3628) to imitate. Articular inf. w. εἰς (# 1650) to express purp. or result. ◆ 10 καί (# 2779) also. "Not only did we set before you our own example, but we gave you a positive precept to this effect, when at Thessalonica" (Lightfoot, Notes). ἦμεν impf. ind. act. εἰμί (# 1639) to be. Impf. indicates continuing action in the past time, for Paul had repeatedly used this injunction in his preaching (Morris). παρηγγέλλομαι pres. ind. mid. (dep.) παραγγέλλω (# 4133) to command, to give orders. ὅτι recitative use equivalent to quotation marks in a direct quote (RWP). θέλει pres. ind. act. θέλω (# 2527) to desire. Iterative pres., "repeatedly desires not to work." ἐργάζεσθαι pres. mid. (dep.) inf. ἐργάζομαι (# 2237) to work. Compl. inf. to the main vb. ἐσθιέτω pres. imp. act. 3rd. sing. ἐσθίω (# 2266) to eat (Best; Moore). ◆ 11 ἀκούομεν pres. ind. act. ἀκούω (# 201) to hear. περιπατοῦντας pres. act. part. περιπατέω (# 4344) to work around, to waste one's energy, to be a busybody. Here Paul uses a play on words, "busybodies instead of busy." These people were not simply idle, they were meddling in the affairs of others (Morris; Best; Moore), either wasting time or, being troublemakers (BBC). περιεργαζομένους pres. mid. (dep.) part. περιεργάζομαι (# 4318) to do something unnecessary or useless, to be useless. ◆ 12 τοιούτοις (# 5525) such a one. παραγγέλλομεν pres. ind. act. παραγγέλλω (# 4133) to instruct, direct or command (BAGD). παρακαλοῦμεν pres. ind. act. παρακαλέω (# 4133) to encourage, to urge, to exhort. ἡσυχία (# 2484) quietness, calmness. The expression suggests a manner of life which is to characterize an activity and signifies the calm and contentment which are the opposite of being a busybody (Moore). ἐργαζόμενοι pres. mid. (dep.) part. ἐργάζομαι (# 2237) to work. ἐσθίωσιν pres. subj. act. ἐσθίω (# 2266) to eat. ◆ 13 ἐγκακήσητε aor. subj. act. ἐγκακέω (# 1591) to behave badly in, to be cowardly, to lose courage, to faint (RWP). Aor. subj. is used w. the neg. μή (# 3590) in a prohibition to forbid a thing not yet done; the aor. is ingressive (RG, 852). καλοποιοῦντες pres. act. part. καλοποιέω (# 2818) to do good, to do the noble thing, to do the fair (honorable) thing. The word "good" carries w. it the thought not only of what is right in itself, but of what is perceived to be right and so exercises an attractive power (Milligan; MM; BAGD). ◆ 14 ὑπακούει pres. ind. act. ὑπακούω (# 5634) to listen to, to obey. σημειοῦσθε pres. imp. mid. σημειόω (# 4957) to mark, to signify, to mark out, to take note of; "put a tag on that man." Used exclusively in the mid. (RWP; Lightfoot, Notes; Moore; MM; BAGD). συναναμίγνυσθαι pres. mid. inf. συναναμίγνυμι (# 5264) to mix up together, to associate w. someone. The first prep. in compound denotes combination, and the second prep. denotes interchange (Lightfoot, Notes). Inf. used as an indirect command (RWP). ἐντραπῇ aor. subj. pass. ἐντρέπω (# 1956) to turn about, to make one turn about, pass. to put someone to shame (Moore). Subj. w. ἵνα (# 2671) to express purp. ◆ 15 ἡγεῖσθε pres. imp. mid. (dep.) ἡγέομαι (# 2451) to consider, to reckon. νουθετεῖτε pres. imp. act. νουθετέω (# 3805) to admonish, to correct (s. 1 Thess. 5:12). ◆ 16 δώη aor. opt. act. δίδωμι (# 1443) to give. Opt. is used to express a wish or desire. τρόπος (# 5573) manner, way. ◆ 17 ἀσπασμός (# 833) greeting. Paul's greeting in his own hand suggests that the autographs of these letters exhibited two hands, one in the body and the other in the subscription. Paul may have used an amanuensis (Richard N. Longenecker, "Ancient Amanuensis," ND, 290f. s. Rom. 16:22). σημεῖον (# 4956) sign, mark, token, signification; the means of authentication. This is the way he indicates that his letters are genuine (Morris; BBC).

1 Timothy

1 Timothy 1

◆ **1** ἐπιταγή (# 2198) command, commission. The word connotes an order, and is used of royal commands which must be obeyed; in the papyri it occurs in commands given by a god (NDIEC, 2:86; 3:23, 68; MM; Kelly; Spicq; NIDNTT). ◆ **2** γνήσιος (# 1188) genuine, true, legitimate, born in lawful wedlock. Since Timothy's father was a Gentile and his mother a Jewess, his birth according to Jewish teaching would be illegitimate, but his relation to Paul, as son to father, was genuine (Schlatter; Kelly; s. JTJ, 275-76; Spicq; ABD, 558-60; Lea and Griffin). ἐν πίστει (# 1877; 4411) in faith, in the sphere of Christian faith. The stress is on spiritual character, faith in and loyalty to Christ (Lock; Ellicott). ἔλεος (# 1799) mercy, compassion, pity. It is the emotion aroused by affliction which comes undeservedly on someone else. It has special and immediate regard to the misery which is the consequence of sin and is the effort, which only the continued perverseness of man can hinder or defeat, to assuage and entirely remove such misery (TLNT; TDNT; NIDNTT; Trench, *Synonyms*, 169). ◆ **3** καθώς (# 2777) just as. Used in an elliptical construction in which the act of writing is understood as the last part of the construction; "as I urged, so now I write" (Lock; MM). παρεκάλεσα aor. ind. act. παρακαλέω (# 4151) to urge, to exhort. προσμεῖναι aor. act. inf. προσμένω (# 4693) to remain, to stay on. Prep. in compound could have a locative sense: "to remain with someone" (MH, 324). Compl. inf., here as obj. of the vb. παρεκάλεσα. πορευόμενος pres. mid. (dep.) part. (temp.) πορεύομαι (# 4513) to journey, to travel. Pres. expresses contemporary action to the main vb. ("when or while I was going"), and may indicate that he left Timothy enroute to Ephesus and charged him to abide there (Guthrie). If Paul were not the author it would seem very strange to mention such specific geographical information and instructions. παραγγείλῃς aor. subj. act. παραγγέλλω (# 4133) to command, to charge, to instruct, to pass on commands from one to another. It is a military term meaning to give strict orders and emphasizes that the commanding was to be done authoritatively (Guthrie; Kelly; Ellicott). Subj. w. ἵνα (# 2671) to express purp. ἑτεροδιδασκαλεῖν pres. act. inf. ἑτεροδιδασκαλέω (# 2281) to teach another doctrine, to teach something totally different (Ellicott). Compl. inf. to the main vb. The oppo-

nents in the pastoral epistles were not gnostic, but rather Jews or Jewish Christians who were teachers of the law who taught Jewish myths and genealogies and that the Resurrection had already occurred, and who forbade marriage and enjoined abstinence from food. They may have been quite successful. ◆ **4** προσέχειν pres. act. inf. προσέχω (# 4668) to turn one's mind to, to pay attention to, to give heed to, to be concerned about, to occupy oneself w.; obj. in dat. (BAGD). Inf. parallel to the preceding inf. (s.v. 3). μῦθος (# 3680) myth, fable, legendary stories, fiction (NIDNTT, 2:643-47; TDNT; Dibelius). γενεαλογία (# 1157) genealogy, the tracing of one's ancestors or family tree. In postexilic Judaism there was a keen interest in family trees, and this played a part in controversies between Jews and Jewish Christians (Kelly; Jastrow, 1:575; M, Kidd. 4:1-14; Lea and Griffin; for a lengthy discussion of genealogies in the ancient world s. RAC, 9:1145-268). The dats. are direct objs. to the vb. ἀπέραντος (# 596) endless, unrestrained (Guthrie). ἐκζήτησις (# 1700) seeking out, speculation; out-of-the-way researches, useless speculation (Lock; BAGD). παρέχουσιν pres. ind. act. παρέχω (# 4218) to cause, to bring about, to give rise to (BAGD). Gnomic pres., "they always give rise to." μᾶλλον (# 3437) rather. οἰκονομία (# 3873) administration, the entrusting of responsibility to a trusted person, office of stewardship; they do not help to carry out the stewardship entrusted to them by God (Lock; Kelly; TLNT; TDNT). ◆ **5** δέ (# 1254) however, in contrast τέλος (# 5465) goal, purpose. παραγγελία (# 4132) instruction, command (s.v. 3). συνειδήσεως (# 5287) conscience. The word indicates self-judgment (Guthrie; s. Rom. 2:15; PAT, 458f). ἀνυπόκριτος (# 537) without hypocrisy (s. 2 Cor. 6:6). ◆ **6** ἀστοχήσαντες aor. act. part. (circum.) ἀστοχέω (# 846) to miss the mark, to swerve, to fail to aim at. The word suggests taking no pains to aim at the right path (Lock; Kelly). Josephus wrote that the Essenes seldom err (ἀστοχοῦσιν) in their predictions (Jos., JW, 2:159; CCFJ, 1:256; for other uses of the word s. NW, 2, i:819; MM; Spicq). Aor. indicates antecedent action to the main vb. Nominal use of part. to emphasize a particular trait. ἐξετράπησαν aor. ind. pass. ἐκτρέπω (# 1762) to turn or twist aside, to turn away. The word was used as a medical t.t., "to be dislocated" (BAGD: MM). ματαιολογία (# 3467) vain or useless talk, idle chatter, empty argument (Kelly; MM). ◆ **7** θέλοντες pres. act. part. θέλω (# 2527) to desire, to want. Part. could be concessive ("although they desire"), or causal ("because they desire"). Pres. expresses a contemporaneous action. εἶναι pres. act. inf. εἰμί (# 1639) to be. Compl. inf. to the preceding part. νομοδιδάσκαλος (# 3791) law teachers, a term from Judaism (s. Luke 5:17; Acts 5:34). They sought popularity not only in their subtle and detailed exegesis, but also in a strict legalism and ascetic demands (Jeremias), using the Law as a means to produce righteousness (LIF, 174). νοοῦντες pres. act. part. νοέω (# 3783) to understand, to comprehend. Pres. w. the neg. μή (# 3590) stresses their continuing inability to understand. Part. has a slight antithetical or perhaps even concessive force (Ellicott). λέγουσιν pres. ind. act. λέγω (# 3306) to say. Cust. pres. describing an iterative or ongoing action. διαβεβαιοῦνται pres. ind. mid. (dep.) διαβεβαιόομαι (# 1331) to confidently affirm, to strongly affirm, to speak confidently, to insist. Cust. pres. The vb. means to make assertion, or to give one's opinion in a firm, dogmatic tone (BAGD; Fairbairn). Prep. in compound means "thoroughly" (MH, 302). ◆ **8** οἴδαμεν pres. ind. act. οἶδα (# 3857) to know. Def. perf. w. pres. meaning. καλός (# 2819) good, suitable, useful (NIDNTT; TDNT). νομίμως (# 3789) lawfully; i.e., agreeably to the design of the law (Ellicott) χρῆται pres. subj. mid. (dep.) χράομαι (# 5968) to use, to make use of, followed by the dat. as the obj. ◆ **9** εἰδώς perf. act. part. οἶδα (# 3857) to know. Def. perf. w. pres. meaning. Used to express knowledge grasped directly by the mind (ND, 344; VA, 281-87). κεῖται pres. ind. pass. (dep.) κεῖμαι used as pass. of τίθημι (# 3023) to place (BAGD). Here used for the introduction or enactment of a law "to establish" (Fairbairn). ἀνυπότακτος (# 538) not made subject, independent, undisciplined, disobedient, rebellious (BAGD). ἀσεβής (# 815) ungodly, irreverent, irreligious. ἁμαρτωλός (# 283) sinful. ἀνόσιος (# 495) unholy. It speaks of one's lack of inner purity (Ellicott; NIDNTT; TDNT). βέβηλος (# 1013) that which is accessible to everybody, the opposite of inaccessible or sacred, profane (TLNT; Spicq). It speaks of irreverent and contemptuous behavior toward the things more particularly associated w. the name of God (Fairbairn). πατρολῴας (# 4260) one who kills one's father, one who smites one's father. μητρολῴας (# 3618) one who smites or strikes one's mother. The words speak of a most unnatural and shameful violation of the honor due to parents; whether or not it might issue in fatal consequences, it is considered a transgression of the fifth commandment (Fairbairn). ἀνδροφόνος (# 439) murderer. ◆ **10** πόρνος (# 4521) one who practices sexual immorality, an immoral person (BAGD; TDNT; NIDNTT). ἀρσενοκοίτης (# 780) homosexual (s. Rom. 1:26-27; 1 Cor. 6:9; DPL, 413-14). ἀνδραποδιστής (# 435) to catch a man by the foot, manstealer, kidnapper. It in-

cludes all who exploit other men and women for their own selfish ends (RWP; EGT; BBC). ψεύστης (# 6026) liar. ἐπίορκος (# 2156) one who commits perjury, perjurer. The force of the prep. in compound may be "against"; i.e., against one's oath (MH, 314f). ὑγιαινούσῃ pres. act. part. ὑγιαίνω (# 5617) to be healthy, to be sound. The word denotes the wholesomeness or healthiness of true Christian teaching (Guthrie; Kelly). διδασκαλία (# 1436) teaching. ἀντίκειται pres. ind. mid. (dep.) ἀντίκειμαι (# 512) to sit against, to be contrary, to be opposite. ◆ **11** μακάριος (# 3421) blessed. It describes God as containing all happiness in Himself and bestowing it to men (Lock). δόξης gen. sing. δόξα (# 1518) glory. Attributive gen. describes an attribute or quality: "glorious gospel." Frequently viewed as a Semitic influence (BDF, # 165). θεοῦ (# 2536) of God. This gen. describes the source. ἐπιστεύθην aor. ind. pass. πιστεύω (# 4409) to believe; pass., to be entrusted w. theol. pass. indicating God is the agent. ◆ **12** ἔχω (# 2400) pres. ind. act. to have. χάριν ἔχω "I thank." ἐνδυναμώσαντι aor. act. part. ἐνδυναμόω (# 1904) to empower, to give strength, to enable. Aor. suggests that the writer's thoughts pass back to the particular time when he received increasing inward strength (EGT). It expresses antecedent action to the main vb. There may be a causal nuance ("to him, because"). πιστός (# 4412) faithful, trustworthy. ἡγήσατο aor. ind. mid. (dep.) ἡγέομαι (# 2451) to consider, to reckon, to count. Used w. a double acc., "to consider someone something." θέμενος aor. mid. (dep.) part. τίθημι (# 5502) to place, to appoint. Aor. expresses antecedent action. διακονία (# 1355) ministry, service (TDNT; NIDNTT). ◆ **13** πρότερον (# 4728) formerly, previously; acc. of general reference of the articular comp.: "as to the former time" (RWP). ὄντα pres. act. part. εἰμί (# 1639) to be. Part. could be temp. ("while," "when I was") or concessive, "though I was" (Ellicott). βλάσφημος (# 1061) blasphemer, one who slanders God. In Jewish teaching they were condemned to hell (BBC). διώκτης (# 1502) one who pursues as a hunter, persecutor. ὑβριστής sadist, a violent person. The word indicates one who in pride and insolence deliberately and contemptuously mistreats, wrongs, and hurts another person just to hurt and deliberately humiliate the person. It speaks of treatment which is calculated publicly to insult and openly to humiliate the person who suffers it. The word is used in Rom. 1:30 to describe a man of arrogant insolence, and pictures one of the characteristic sins of the pagan world (MNTW, 77-85; TDNT; NIDNTT; EDNT). The LXX uses the word to translate the Heb. לִיץ, which is arrogance manifested as contempt for other people and their ideas (Michael V. Fox, "Words for Folly," *ZAH* 10 [1997]: 4-12, esp. 7-8). ἠλεήθην aor. ind. pass. ἐλεέω (# 1796) to show mercy, to show compassion and pity, pass. to obtain mercy, to be shown pity (TDNT; EDNT; TLNT). Theol. pass. indicating that God showed mercy. **ἀγνοῶν** pres. act. part. ἀγνοέω (# 51) to be ignorant. Paul is availing himself of the distinction, conventional in Judaism (Lev. 22:14; Num. 15:22-31) and also in the Qumran sect, between unwitting and presumptuous sins, linking unbelief w. his ignorance. He does not claim that as a result he was without guilt, but mentions the fact as explaining how his career prior to his conversion became the object of God's compassion rather than His wrath (Kelly). **ἐποίησα** aor. ind. act. ποιέω (# 4472) to do, to make. ◆ **14 ὑπερεπλεόνασεν** aor. ind. act. ὑπερπλεονάζω (# 5670) to abound over and beyond, to be present in great abundance, to abound exceedingly. Prep. in compound means "above its usual measure" and is an attempt to express the superabundance of divine grace (Lock; Guthrie). ◆ **15 πιστὸς ὁ λόγος** faithful saying. This is the first of the five faithful sayings in the Pastoral Epistles. For a discussion s. George Knight III, *The Faithful Sayings in the Pastoral Epistles* (Grand Rapids: Baker, 1979). The art. could refer back or better to the following (GGBB, 220). **ἀποδοχή** (# 628) reception, acceptance, approval. In Koine Greek the word indicates the acceptance and recognition which someone or something has found (Dibelius; MM). **σῶσαι** aor. act. inf. σῴζω (# 5392) to rescue, to save. Inf. here to express purp. Aor. looks at the whole process of salvation. **πρῶτος** (# 4755) first, foremost, chief. Here the word is used in the sense of greatest (Fairbairn). Pres. "I am," not "I was." The sinner remains a sinner even if forgiven; the past is always there as a stimulus to deeper penitence and service (Lock; Kelly). ◆ **16 ἠλεήθην** aor. ind. pass. ἐλεέω (# 1796) to have mercy; pass., to receive mercy. **ἐνδείξηται** aor. subj. mid. (dep.) ἐνδείκνυμι (# 1892) to point out, to demonstrate. Prep. in compound suggest a more complete demonstration than the simple vb. It is the laying of the index finger, as it were, on the object (MH, 305). Subj. w. ἵνα (# 2671) to express purp. **μακροθυμία** (# 1892) longsuffering, patience (s. Gal. 5:22). **μελλόντων** pres. act. part. μέλλω (# 3516) to be about to. Used w. inf. to express the durative fut. (MKG, 307). **πιστεύειν** pres. act. inf. πιστεύω (# 4409) to trust. Compl. inf. to the part. Used w. the prep. w. the dat. to mean, "to repose one's trust upon," suggesting more of the state, whereas the acc. emphasizes more the initial act of faith (M, 68; Lock). **αἰώνιος** (# 173) eternal, everlasting. Everlasting life emphasizes life of the age to come, containing a temp. reference, but stressing the qualitative character. Although Paul regards eternal life as predominately eschatological, he also sees it as a pres. possession of the believer, the result of the indwelling Spirit (GW, 118ff). ◆ **17 ἄφθαρτος** (# 915) incorruptible; i.e., immune from decay, immortal (Kelly). **ἀόρατος** (# 548) not able to be seen, invisible. ◆ **18 παρατίθεμαι** pres. ind. mid. (dep.)

παρατίθημι (# 4192) to place beside; mid., to entrust, to pledge, to deposit w. another. The term here is a banking figure suggesting that one is depositing something valuable (RWP; MM). **προαγούσας** pres. act. part. προάγω (# 4575) to go before, to lead before. The phrase may be translated "relying on the prophecies once made about you," or "the prophecies which pointed me to you" (Kelly; Lock). **στρατεύῃ** pres. subj. act. στρατεύω (# 5129) to fight as a soldier, to war as a soldier. Subj. w. ἵνα (# 2671) to express purp. **στρατεία** (# 5127) military expedition, or campaign, warfare. Here, cognate acc. or acc. of content: "to fight a fight" (MT, 245; BD, 84f; RG, 477f). ◆ **19 ἔχων** pres. act. part. ἔχω (# 2400) to have, to possess (M, 110). **ἀπωσάμενοι** aor. mid. part. ἀπωθέω (# 723) to push away from oneself, to push aside, to reject, to repudiate. In the NT it occurs only as mid. The word implies a violent rejection (Guthrie; BAGD). **ἐναυάγησαν** aor. ind. act. ναυαγέω (# 3728) to make shipwreck, to suffer shipwreck. Paul himself had suffered shipwreck at least four times by the time he wrote this epistle. He had on each occasion lost everything except his life (EGT; Acts 27). ◆ **20 παρέδωκα** aor. ind. act. παραδίδωμι (# 4140) to deliver over to (TLNT). **παιδευθῶσιν** aor. subj. pass. παιδεύω (# 4084) to train through discipline. The word conveys the idea of stern punishment rather than instruction (Kelly). Subj. w. ἵνα (# 2671) to express purp. and/or result. **βλασφημεῖν** pres. act. inf. βλασφημέω (# 1059) to ridicule, to slander, to slander God, to blaspheme (TLNT). Inf. as obj. of the vb. **παιδευθῶσιν**.

1 Timothy 2

◆ **1 Παρακαλῶ** pres. ind. act. παρακαλέω (# 4151) to urge, to exhort (s. Rom. 12:1). **πρῶτον πάντων** first of all. The words relate not to primacy of time but to primacy of importance (Guthrie). **ποιεῖσθαι** pres. mid. (dep.) inf. ποιέω (# 4472) to make, to do. The word is used in a causative sense (BAGD; s. 1 Thess. 1:2). Compl. inf. to the main vb.: "I beseech you to do." **δέησις** (# 1255) intercession, petition. The vb. from which the noun is derived had the meaning "to chance upon"; then, "to have an audience w. a king"; to have the good fortune to be admitted to an audience, so "to present a petition." The word was a regular term for a petition to a superior and in the papyri it was constantly used of any writing addressed to the king (Lock; Guthrie; MM; BS, 121f; Preisigke; TDNT). **ἔντευξις** (# 1950) prayer, intercessory prayer (BAGD). **εὐχαριστίας** (# 2374) thanksgiving. ◆ **2 ὑπεροχή** (# 5667) prominence, a place of prominence or authority, used of prominent officials. The word was used in Hellenistic Gr. to indicate the prominent position of a person (BAGD; MM; Dibelius; Spicq; NW, 2. i:841-42). Since Jews did not worship the Roman gods they were to pray for the emperor (BBC). **ὄντων** pres. act. part. εἰμί (# 1639) to be.

Subst. part. to emphasize a quality. ἵνα (# 2671) introduces the result or purp. of the prayer (Lock). For references to Jewish prayers for those in authority s. Dibelius. ἤρεμος (# 2475) quiet, tranquil. ἡσύχιος (# 2485) quiet. For the desire in the ancient world to live a peaceable life, s. NW, 2. i:842-47. διάγωμεν pres. subj. act. διάγω (# 1341) to lead, to conduct. εὐσεβείᾳ (# 2354) godliness, religious devotion. It refers to the true reverence toward God which comes from knowledge. It is a right attitude to God and to God's holiness, majesty, and love (Lock; MNTW, 66-77; Trench, *Synonyms*, 172ff; TDNT; NIDNTT; RAC, 6:985-1052). σεμνότης (# 4949) gravity. The word denotes moral earnestness, affecting outward demeanor as well as interior intention (Kelly; Trench, *Synonyms*, 347f). ◆ 3 τοῦτο (# 4047) this. The word refers to the idea of universal prayer for all men (Guthrie; EGT). καλόν (# 2819) good (s. 1 Tim. 1:8; Lock, 22f). ἀπόδεκτος (# 621) acceptable. ἐνώπιον (# 1967) before, in the presence of. ◆ 4 θέλει pres. ind. act. θέλω (# 2527) to wish, to desire, w. inf. σωθῆναι aor. pass. inf. σῴζω (# 5392) to save. Compl. inf. w. the vb. θέλει (Guthrie). ἐπίγνωσις (# 2106) recognition, knowledge, knowledge directed to a particular object. ἐλθεῖν aor. inf. act. ἔρχομαι (# 2262) to come, to go. Compl. inf. parallel to the preceding inf. ◆ 5 μεσίτης (# 3542) mediator, go-between (s. Gal. 3:20). ἄνθρωπος (# 476) man. The lack of the article emphasizes the character: one possessing the nature and in his work manifesting the attributes of humanity (Fairbairn). ◆ 6 δούς aor. act. part. δίδωμι (# 1443) to give. Aor. expresses antecedent action. Articular part. used as a noun. ἀντίλυτρον (# 519) ransom, the price paid for the release of a slave. Prep. in compound implies an exchange (EGT; s. Matt 20:28 or Mark 10:45; TDNT; I. Howard Marshall, "The Development of the Concept of Redemption in the New Testament," *RH*, 153-69; Dibelius). μαρτύριον (# 3457) witness. καιρός (# 2789) time, opportunity, season. The dat. here is locative: "in its due seasons" (RWP). ◆ 7 ἐτέθην aor. ind. pass. τίθημι (# 5502) to place, to appoint, to commission. κῆρυξ (# 3061) herald, preacher. The herald was someone who had important news to bring. He often announced an athletic event or religious festival, or functioned as a messenger, the bringer of some news or command from the king's court. He was to have a strong voice and proclaim his message w. vigor, without lingering to discuss it. The herald's most important qualification was that he faithfully represent or report the word of the one by whom he had been sent. He was not to be original; his message was to be that of another (Victor Paul Furnish, "Prophets, Apostles, and Preachers: A Study of the Biblical Concept of Preaching," *Inter.* 17 [1963]: 55; TDNT; NIDNTT; TLNT). For the use of the nom. in this construction, εἰς ὅ ἐτέθην, s. RG, 40. ψεύδομαι (# 6017) pres. ind. mid.

(dep.) to lie. For the import of Paul's statement s. Gal. 1:20. ἐθνῶν gen. pl. ἔθνος (# 1620) nation; pl., Gentiles, non-Jews. Obj. gen. ἐν (# 1877) in. The prep. indicates the sphere in which the apostle performs his mission (Ellicott). ◆ 8 βούλομαι (# 1089) pres. ind. mid. (dep.) to purpose, to determine, to will, w. inf. The apostolic authority is represented in this expression (Bengel). προσεύχεσθαι pres. mid. (dep.) inf. προσεύχομαι (# 4667) to pray. τοὺς ἄνδρας acc. pl. ἀνήρ (# 467) man, male. The word is used here to emphasize the responsibilities of the male members of the congregation. τόπος (# 5536) place. The expression is used for public worship (RW). ἐπαίροντας pres. act. part. ἐπαίρω (# 2048) to lift toward, to raise up. Pres. expresses contemporaneous action. Part. of means, "I desire all to pray by lifting up hands." The most general attitude for prayer in antiquity for pagans, Jews, and Christians alike was to stand w. hands outstretched and lifted up, the palms turned upward (Kelly; SB, 2:261; 4:645; DGRA, 16; MM). While there were specific prayer times there were also daily prayers in the home and frequent spontaneous prayers. The expectation was that God does hear and answer prayers (ABD, 5:449). ὅσιος (# 4008) holy. The word stood for what was in accord w. divine direction and providence. The word describes the pious, pure, and clean action which is in accordance w. God's command. The hands are holy which have not been given over to deeds of wicked lust (Huther; NIDNTT; Trench, *Synonyms*, 328; TDNT). ὀργή (# 3973) anger, wrath. διαλογισμός (# 1369) a thinking back and forth, deliberation. The word then came to mean doubting or disputing. In relation to prayer in this section the meaning "doubting" is possible (Guthrie); or in relation to the idea of holy hands it could have the meaning "disputing," "quarrelsomeness" (Kelly). ◆ 9 ὡσαύτως (# 6058) just as, likewise. καταστολή (# 2950) clothing, apparel. The word could be understood in a wider sense: demeanor, deportment (MM; Ellicott; ABD, 2:235-38). For a discussion of this passage s. Craig S. Keener, *Paul, Women and Wives* (Peabody, Mass: Hendrickson, 1992), 101-32. For the status of women in Judaism and the ancient world s. Tal Ilan, *Jewish Women in Greco-Roman Palestine* (Tübingen: J. B. C. Mohr, 1994); Eva Cantarella, *The Role of Women in Greek and Roman Antiquity* (Baltimore: The John Hopkins University Press, 1987); J. P. V. D. Balsdon, *Roman Women: Their History and Habits* (London: The Bodley Head, 1977). κόσμιος (# 3177) well-arranged, well-ordered, moderate, modest. αἰδοῦς (# 133) modesty. The word connotes fem. reserve in matters of sex. In the word is involved an innate moral repugnance to the doing of the dishonorable. It is "shamefastness" which shrinks from transgressing the limits of womanly reserve and modesty, as well as from dishonor would justly attach thereto (Kelly;

Trench, *Synonyms*, 68; 71f). σωφροσύνη (# *5408*) sobriety, self-control. It stands basically for perfect self-mastery in the physical qualities; as applied to women it too had a definitely sexual nuance. It is that habitual inner self-government, w. its constant reign on all the passions and desires (Kelly; Trench, *Synonyms*, 72; TDNT; TLNT; GELTS, 467). κοσμεῖν pres. act. inf. κοσμέω (# *3175*) to put in order, to arrange, to adorn. Compl. inf. to the main vb. βούλομαι (s.v. 8). πλέγμα (# *4427*) that which is woven or plaited. Here it refers to hairstyles; i.e., plaited hair. Instr. dat. Both Jewish and Gentile women were noted for their elaborate hairstyles (SB, 3:428ff; DGRA, 328-30; BBC). In Philo's description of pleasure coming in the guise of a prostitute, he describes such a woman as having her hair in curious and elaborate plaits, her eyes w. pencil lines, her eyebrows smothered w. paint, her costly raiment embroidered lavishly w. flowers, and w. bracelets and necklaces of gold and jewels hanging around her (Philo, *The Sacrifices of Abel and Cain*, 21). μαργαρίτης (# *3449*) pearl. Pearls were considered to have had the top rank among valuables, worth three times the value of gold. Pearls were esp. prized by women, who used them to adorn their hair, as rings and earrings, or to decorate their garments and even their sandals (Pliny, *Natural History*, 9:106-23; KP, 3:1020-21; TDNT). ἱματισμός (# *2669*) garment, clothing. πολυτελής (# *4500*) very costly, very expensive. The best garments could cost as much as seven thousand denarii. For those of inferior quality for commoners and slaves the cost would be between eight hundred and five hundred denarii (the average wage of the working man was one denarius a day). Tarsus was an important weaving center and its garments were classified as some of the best in the ancient world. For information regarding clothes and the cloth industry in the Roman Empire s. Jones, 350-64. ◆ **10** πρέπει pres. ind. act. πρέπω (# *4560*) to be clearly seen, to resemble, to be fitting or becoming, to suit (AS). ἐπαγγελλομέναις pres. mid. (dep.) part. ἐπαγγέλλω (# *2040*) to announce, to proclaim, to profess, to lay claim to, to give oneself out as an expert in something (BAGD). Pres. emphasizes continual action. Adj. part. emphasizes a trait. θεοσέβεια (# *2537*) reverence toward God. The emphasis in this section is on the fact that true beauty and beautification is not in the outward appearance (Dibelius). ◆ **11** ἡσυχία (# *2484*) quietness, silence. The word expresses quietness in general (T). For the relation of this command to the commands of Paul in 1 Cor. s. PWC, 74ff. μανθανέτω pres. imp. act. 3rd pers. sing. μανθάνω (# *3443*) to learn. In that culture most women were not well educated (BBC). ὑποταγῇ (# *5717*) submission (PWC, 72f). ◆ **12** διδάσκειν pres. act. inf. διδάσκω (# *1438*) to teach. Compl. inf. to the main vb. ἐπιτρέπω (# *2205*) pres. ind. act. to allow, to permit. Pres. emphasizes the continual action and

points to an abiding attitude. It could also be a gnomic pres. (GGBB, 525). For a discussion of the passage s. Ann Bowman, "Women in Ministry: An Exegetical Study of 1 Timothy 2:11-15," *Bib Sac* 149 (1992): 193-213; DPL, 590-92; HSB, 665-71. αὐθεντεῖν pres. act. inf. αὐθεντέω (# *883*) to act on one's own authority, to exercise authority, to have mastery, to be an autocrat, to be dominating (AS; MM; Preisigke; Dibelius; LAE, 88f; G.W. Knight, "ΑΥΘΕΝΤΕΩ in Reference to Women in 1 Tim 2:12," *NTS* 30 [1984]: 143-57). Compl. inf. to the main vb. εἶναι pres. act. inf. εἰμί (# *1639*) to be. Compl. inf. to the main vb. ◆ **13** ἐπλάσθη aor. ind. pass. πλάσσω (# *4421*) to form, to fashion, to mold, to create. This an argument from the chronological order of creation (BBC). ◆ **14** ἠπατήθη aor. ind. pass. ἀπατάω (# *572*) to deceive, to trick, to mislead. ἐξαπατηθεῖσα aor. pass. part. ἐξαπατάω (# *1987*) to deceive completely, to deceive successfully (MH, 311; A.C. Perriman, "What Eve Did, What Women Shouldn't Do," *TB* 44 [1993]: 143-57; BBC). παράβασις (# *4126*) stepping over the boundary, transgression. γέγονεν perf. ind. act. γίνομαι (# *1181*) to become. Perf. expresses an abiding state (Guthrie). ◆ **15** σωθήσεται fut. ind. pass. σῴζω (# *5392*) to save, to rescue. Rescue from the penalty of sin. τεκνογονία (# *5450*) childbearing. The use of the definite article here may be a reference to the birth of the Savior (Ellicott; but also s. Guthrie). For a survey article s. Andreas J. Köstenberger, "Ascertaining Women's God-Ordained Roles: An Interpretation of 1 Timothy 2:15," *Bulletin for Biblical Research* 7 (1997): 107-44; R. C. and C. C. Kroeger, *I Suffer Not a Woman: Rethinking 1 Timothy 2:11-15 in Light of Ancient Evidence* (Grand Rapids: Baker, 1992); BBC; Lea and Griffin. ἁγιασμός (# *40*) sanctification. The word is used here in the act. sense and would refer to the living of a godly life.

1 Timothy 3

◆ **1** ἐπισκοπή (# *2175*) office of bishop (NIDNTT; TDNT; ABD, 2:768-69; ZPEB, 1:617-20; DPL, 131-37; BBC). ὀρέγεται pres. ind. mid. ὀρέγω (# *3977*) to stretch oneself out, to aspire to, to desire. In the NT it only occurs in the mid. w. dat. (TLNT; Guthrie; BAGD). ἐπιθυμεῖ pres. ind. act. ἐπιθυμέω (# *2121*) to set one's heart on, to desire (Guthrie). ◆ **2** δεῖ (# *1256*) pres. ind. act. Impersonal vb., it is necessary. The word speaks of logical necessity according to the needs or circumstances (TDNT; AS). ἐπίσκοπος (# *2176*) overseer, bishop, pastor. The art. here is generic (GGBB, 229). In the LXX it was used of one who watches over something or someone, guardian, supervisor, inspector (GELTS, 174; Num. 4:16, 31:14; Judg. 9:28; 2 Kings [2 Sam.] 11:15; s. also CCFJ, 2:174; *JosAsen*, 15:7; 21:11; for the use in the papyri s. BS, 230-31; MM). In the early Church Fathers it was used to denote function rather than the status of anyone who exercised supervision or control, as well as to denote a member of a body exercising oversight and government in a church, equivalent to πρεσβύτερος (PGL, 532-33). ἀνεπίλημπτος (# 455) not able to be taken hold of, irreproachable, beyond reproach, beyond criticism, unimpeachable (LN, 1:436; CCFJ, 1:120). The word implies not only that the man is of good report, but that he is deservedly so (AS; MM; Priesigke; Spicq). Plutarch used the word to describe the character of one who teaches children (*Moralia, The Education of Children*, 4b-c; 7; also NW 2, i:866-68). ἄνδρα acc. sing. ἀνήρ (# 467) man. "A husband of one wife," "one-woman man." The difficult phrase probably means that he is to have one wife at a time (Robert L. Saucy, "The Husband of One Wife," *Bib Sac* 131 [1974]: 229-40: SB, 3:647-50; Eldon Glasscock, "'The Husband of One Wife' Requirement in 1 Timothy 3:2," *Bib Sac* 140 [1983]: 255; C.E. B. Cranfield, "The Church and the Divorce and Remarriage of Divorced Persons in Light of Mark 10:1-12," *The Bible and the Christian Life* [Edinburgh: T. &. T. Clark, 1985], 229-34; Craig S. Keener, *...And Marries Another: Divorce and Remarriage in the Teaching of the New Testament* [Peabody, Mass: Hendrickson, 1991], 83-103). The phrase could mean "faithful to his one wife" (Lea and Griffin). νηφάλιος (# 3767) sober, sober-minded, clearheaded. The word originally connotes abstinence from alcohol, but here it has a wider, metaphorical sense (Kelly). σώφρων (# 5409) self-controlled (MM; TDNT). κόσμιος (# 3177) orderly (s. 1 Tim. 2:5). It implies well-ordered demeanor, the orderly fulfillment of all duties, and the ordering of the inner life from which these spring. φιλόξενος (# 5811) hospitable. In his official capacity he has the duty of keeping open house both for delegates traveling from church and for ordinary needy members of the congregation (Kelly; BBC). διδακτικός (# 1434) able to teach, skillful in teaching. The suffix stresses the verbal force and can be either intransitive or causal; here, "apt at teaching" (MH, 379). ◆ **3** πάροινος (# 4232) one who sits long at his wine, one who is a slave of drink (RW; Kelly). πλήκτης (# 4438) not a giver of blows, not given to violence (Kelly). ἐπιεικής (# 2117) equity, lenient, kindly, forebearing (s. 2 Cor. 10:1; Phil. 4:5). ἄμαχος (# 285) without fighting, not a fighter, not contentious (RW; Guthrie). ἀφιλάργυρος (# 921) not a lover of money. ◆ **4** ἴδιος (# 2526) one's own. καλῶς (# 2822) adv., well. προϊστάμενον pres. mid. (dep.) part. προΐστημι (# 4613) to stand before, to rule over, to manage. In that culture the authority of the father was exceedingly great (BBC). ἔχοντα pres. act. part. ἔχω (# 2400) to have. ὑποταγή (# 5717) submission. σεμνότης (# 4949) dignity, stateliness. It describes the characteristic of the one who carries himself w. the perfect blend of dignity and courtesy, independence and humility toward his fellowmen (MNTW, 143; Trench, *Synonyms*, 344f). The word avoids the suggestion of sternness yet retains the

idea of natural respect (Guthrie). ◆ **5** προστῆναι aor. act. inf. προΐστημι (# 4613) to rule, to manage, to govern. Inf. as obj. of the vb. οἶδεν. ἐπιμελήσεται fut. ind. mid. (dep.) ἐπιμελέω (# 2150) to care for, to exercise concern for. Prep. in compound is directive (RW). ◆ **6** νεόφυτος (# 3745) newly planted, recent convert. The word was used in a literal sense of newly planted trees (BS, 220f). τυφωθείς aor. pass. part. τυφόω (# 5605) to wrap in smoke, to puff up; pass., to be clouded w. pride (AS). The part. could be causal or temp. κρίμα (# 3210) judgment. ἐμπέσῃ aor. subj. act. ἐμπίπτω (# 1860) to fall into. διάβολος (# 1333) slanderer, devil (DDD, 463-73; DPL, 865). Gen. here could be obj. gen.–condemnation reserved for the devil (the judgment meted out for the sin of pride)–or subjective gen.–condemnation wrought by the devil (the condemnation brought about by the further intrigues of the devil when a man is lured into his grasp by pride). ◆ **7** ἔξωθεν (# 2033) outside; "those outside" is a term used for unbelievers (s. Col. 4:5). ὀνειδισμός (# 3944) reproach, disgrace, insult. παγίδα acc. sing. παγίς (# 4075) trap, snare. Here the gen. τοῦ διαβόλου is subjective gen. "the snare made by the devil" (Ellicott). ◆ **8** ὡσαύτως (# 6058) likewise. σεμνός (# 4948) serious, dignified, stately (s.v. 4). δίλογος (# 1474) double-tongued. The word could mean "tale-bearer," suggesting the idea of gossiper (Guthrie: Lock); or it could be "consistent in what one says"; i.e., not saying one thing while thinking another, or not saying one thing to one man and a different thing to the next (Kelly). προσέχοντας pres. act. part. προέχω (# 4668). Used w. the dat., to turn one's mind to, to occupy oneself w. Here, to be addicted to much wine (BAGD). Pres. points to an habitual action. αἰσχροκερδής (# 153) greedy of gain. The gain may become shameful when a man makes the acquisition of it, rather than the glory of God, his prime object (EGT; Plutarch, *Moralia, On Love of Wealth*). ◆ **9** τῆς πίστεως gen. πίστις (# 4411) the faith, referring to a known body of belief. Gen. gives the content or substance of the mystery; i.e., the mystery, the substance of which is Christian faith (Guthrie; Schlatter). συνείδησις (# 5287) conscience (s. Rom. 2:15; TDNT; AT, 402ff; 458f). ◆ **10** δοκιμαζέσθωσαν pres. imp. pass. 3rd. pers. pl. δοκιμάζω (# 1507) to approve after testing or examining (TDNT; MM). εἶτα (# 1663) then. διακονείτωσαν pres. imp. act. 3rd. pers. pl. διακονέω (# 1354) to serve as a deacon, to minister. ἀνέγκλητος (# 441) without charge, blameless, without accusation, irreproachable. For examples of this word in the papyri s. MM; Preisigke. ὄντες pres. act. part. εἰμί (# 1639) to be. Part. could be cond. ("if they are beyond reproach"), subst. ("those who are blameless") (GGBB, 633), or causal ("because they are beyond reproach"). In either case the qualifications are met. ◆ **11** διάβολος (# 1333) slanderous. ◆ **12** ἔστωσαν pres. imp. act. 3rd. pers. pl.

εἰμί (# 1639) to be. ◆ 13 διακονήσαντες aor. act. part. διακονέω (# 1354) to serve, to minister. βαθμός (# 957) step, base, foundation (e.g., pedestal). The word is used here in a fig. sense and may refer to standing in the sight of God; or it may refer to the reputation and influence of the deacons in the congregation (Guthrie; Kelly). περιποιοῦνται pres. ind. mid. περιποιέω (# 4347) to make besides; mid. to achieve, to gain for oneself, to acquire for oneself (RW). παρρησία (# 4244) speaking all, confidence, assurance, boldness (TDNT). ◆ 14 ἐλπίζων pres. act. part. ἐλπίζω (# 1827) to hope. Part. may be concessive, "although I hoped" (Ellicott). Pres. gives a contemporaneous action. ἐλθεῖν aor. act. inf. ἔρχομαι (# 2262) to come. Compl. inf. to the preceding part. Aor. points to a specific act. τάχει dat. sing. τάχος (# 5443). ἐν τάχει means "quickly, at once without delay" (BAGD); "sooner than I at one time thought" (Fairbairn). ◆ 15 βραδύνω (# 1094) pres. subj. act. to hesitate, to delay. Subj. in a third-class cond. cl. expressing that which may be possible (RW). εἰδῇς perf. subj. act. οἶδα (# 3857) to know. Def. perf. w. pres. meaning. The word was used to describe know-how; i.e., the possession of knowledge or skill necessary to accomplish a desired goal (ND, 347f). It is followed by an indirect question. ἀναστρέφεσθαι pres. mid. (dep.) inf. ἀναστρέφω (# 418) to conduct oneself, to behave. Compl. inf. to the impersonal δεῖ (# 1256) pres. ind. act. it is necessary, w. inf. It refers fig. to human conduct; acting or behaving in the sense of practicing certain principles. The principle is often more exactly described with a following phrase–at times w. a prep. phrase as here or in 1 Pet. 1:17 (BAGD). The word could well apply to the discharge of official duties and aptly covers conduct expected from, and the mutual relations of, all the groups discussed (Guthrie; Kelly; Lock; MM). ἥτις (# 4015) which indeed; the explanatory use of the indef. rel. (Ellicott; RG, 960). ζῶντος pres. act. part. ζάω (# 2409) to live. Adj. use of the part., "living God." στῦλος (# 5146) pillar. ἑδραίωμα (# 1613) foundation, buttress, bulwark. For various views related to this v. s. Guthrie; Kelly; Lock. ◆ 16 ὁμολογουμένως (# 3935) adv. confessedly, by common consent. The word is a pres. part, expressing the unanimous convictions of Christians (Kelly; ECC, 129f). εὐσέβεια (# 2354) godliness, piety, religion. The word may include the thought of doctrine as well as of life (Lock; Kelly). For a discussion of the rhythm of this hymn s. GGBB, 341-42. ἐφανερώθη aor. ind. pass. φανερόω (# 5746) to make visible, to manifest. σαρκί dat. sing. σάρξ (# 4922) flesh; He appeared on earth as a real man (Kelly). The word does not indicate the nature of natural man opposed to God, but in connection w. the OT use of the word it indicates the earthly existence of Jesus (Jeremias). ἐδικαιώθη aor. ind. pass. δικαιόω (# 1467) to justify, to declare righteous, to vindicate. If the word πνεύματι (# 4460) is taken to be parallel to σαρ-

κί, the meaning is "declared righteous and shown to be in fact Son of God, in respect to his spiritual nature," and a reference to the Resurrection is implied. If the word πνεύματι denotes the Holy Spirit, it means "he was declared righteous through, or by means of, the Holy Spirit" (Kelly; MRP, 371f). ὤφθη aor. ind. pass. ὁράω (# 3972) to see; pass. to be seen, to appear. ἐκηρύχθη aor. ind. pass. κηρύσσω (# 3062) to reach, to proclaim as a herald. ἐπιστεύθη aor. ind. pass. πιστεύ-ω (# 4409) to believe. ἀνελήμφθη aor. ind. pass. ἀναλαμβάνω (# 377) to receive up. The vb. is used of the ascension (Acts 1:2, 11, 22). Aor. points to a specific action that is completed.

1 Timothy 4

◆ 1 ῥητῶς (# 4843) adv., expressly, clearly, unmistakably; "in express terms." The word indicates that the elements of fut. events have been distinctly made known (Guthrie; Lock). ὕστερος (# 5731) later, latter, last. καιρός (# 2789) period of time, season (TDNT; Trench, Synonyms, 209; NIDNTT). ἀποστήσονται fut. ind. mid. (dep.) ἀφίστημι (# 923) to go away, to withdraw, to fall away, to become apostate. Gen. τῆς πίστεως indicates that which they leave and is used in the obj. sense–Christian doctrine, sound teaching (Kelly). προσέχοντες part. act. part. προσέχω (# 4668). Used w. the dat. to give one's attention to, to devote oneself to, to give heed to (s. 1 Tim. 1:4). πνεῦμα (# 4460) spirit. Here, dat. pl. These are evidently supernatural evil spirits who work through individuals and they stand in contrast to the Spirit mentioned immediately before (Guthrie; EGT; Fairbairn). πλάνος (# 4418) leading astray, deceptive, deceiving, seducing. διδασκαλία (# 1436) teaching. δαιμόνιον (# 1228) demon. ◆ 2 ὑποκρίσει dat. ὑπόκρισις (# 5694) hypocrisy, play-acting, deception (TLNT). Instr. dat. ψευδολόγος (# 6016) false speaker, a speaker of that which is not true. This word expresses perhaps more than "liar" by the notion of definite false statements. κεκαυστηριασμένων perf. pass. part. καυστηράζω (# 3013) to brand w. a red hot iron, to sear. The idea of the word may be that these are people in the service of Satan and consequently have their conscience stamped w. the brand marking his ownership (BBC; Lea and Griffin). Another possible interpretation is that their conscience has been cauterized, i.e., made insensible to the distinction between right and wrong (Kelly). Perf. looks at the completed action and its lasting effects. συνείδησις (# 5287) conscience (TLNT; TDNT; EDNT). ◆ 3 κωλυόντων pres. act. part. κωλύω (# 3266) to hinder, to forbid. γαμεῖν pres. act. inf. γαμέω (# 1138) to marry. Inf. in indir. discourse as obj. of the part.: "forbidding to marry." ἀπέχεσθαι pres. mid. (dep.) inf. ἀπέχω (# 600) to hold oneself apart from, to abstain from, w. gen. These people may have insisted that the new age had already been introduced by Christ, and so failed to distinguish the present times which the resurrection of Jesus had initiated from the consummation to be inaugurated by the yet fut. resurrection (William L. Lane, "First Timothy IV.1-3: An Early Instance of Over-Realized Eschatology," *NTS* 11 [1965]: 164-69). βρῶμα (# 1109) that which is eaten, food. ἔκτισεν aor. ind. act. κτίζω (# 3231) to create. μετάλημψις (# 3563) receiving, reception, sharing. (MH, 318). εὐχαριστία (# 2374) thanksgiving. ἐπεγνωκόσι perf. act. part. ἐπιγινώσκω (# 2105) to recognize, to know, to know thoroughly. Prep. in compound is directive. ◆ **4** κτίσμα (# 3233) creation, creature. ἀπόβλητος (# 612) to be thrown away, rejected, refused. Verbal adj. here has a pass. sense (RW). ◆ **5** πᾶν (# 4246) everything, used w. the sing. κτίσμα (# 3233) creation, created thing. This suffix refers to the product of the verbal action. λαμβανόμενον pres. pass. part. λαμβάνω (# 3284) to take, receive. ἁγιάζεται pres. ind. pass. ἁγιάζω (# 39) to cause to be set apart, to remove from profane or common use; to sanctify (TDNT; NIDNTT). ἔντευξις (# 1950) prayer, request (s. 2:1). ◆ **6** ὑποτιθέμενος pres. mid. (dep.) part. ὑποτίθημι (# 5719) to lay down something; mid., to suggest or point out something (BAGD). Part. could have a cond. force ("if you suggest" [Ellicott]) or it could be modal ("by suggesting"). ἔσῃ fut. ind. act. εἰμί (# 1639) to be. ἐντρεφόμενος pres. pass. part. ἐντρέφω (# 1957) to nourish in. The metaphor is that of feeding, w. the idea of reading and inwardly digesting. Pres. part. suggests a continuing process (Lock; Guthrie). διδασκαλία (# 1436) teaching. παρηκολούθηκας perf. ind. act. παρακολουθέω (# 4158) to follow, to follow beside. The word combines the idea of understanding w. that of practicing perseveringly (Lock). ◆ **7** βέβηλος (# 1013) permitted to be trodden, accessible to everyone, profane, unhallowed (BAGD; AS; s. 1 Tim. 1:9). γραώδης (# 1212) characteristic of old women. It is the sarcastic epithet frequent in philosophical polemic that conveys the idea of limitless credulity (Kelly). μῦθος (# 3680) myth, tale; here such as old women tell children but quite unfit for strong young men who have been trained to discipline themselves (Lock; Spicq). παραιτοῦ pres. imp. mid. (dep.) παραιτέομαι (# 4148) to refuse, to turn away from, to decline, to have nothing to do w. The word suggest a strong refusal. γύμναζε pres. imp. act. γυμνάζω (# 1214) to exercise. It is not the self-centered ascetic struggle of the individual for his moral and religious perfection, but the training necessary for the unhindered pursuit of God's purposes. Enemies may have accused Paul of moral laxity since he refused to follow their demands of abstention, but his exercise was a rigorous development and application of all his strength and ability to serve the glory of God w. every thought and action (AM, 174f). εὐσέβεια (# 2354) godliness, piety (TDNT; NIDNTT; MNTW, 66-77; EDNT; Spicq, 1.482-92; s. 1 Tim. 2:2). ◆ **8** σωματικός (# 5394) bodily, that which

pertains to the body. γυμνασία (# 1215) exercise. Bodily exercise refers back to the errors of the heretics against which the author has been warning. It is best to see in this phrase not the Hellenistic culture of the body, but an external dualistic asceticism as propounded by the heretics and reflected in the warnings contained in v. 3 (AM, 173; TDNT; Jeremias). ὀλίγος (# 3900) little, that which is numerically small and lasts only a short time (Schlatter). ὠφέλιμος (# 6068) useful, profitable. ἐπαγγελία (# 2039) promise. The struggle of Paul and Timothy is not to gain eternal life, but to honor and glorify God, to proclaim and demonstrate His faithfulness to the promise of life. The promise of life to all men is the basis and motive for their life's task (AM, 175ff). ἔχουσα pres. act. part. ἔχω (# 2400) to have. μελλούσης pres. act. part. μέλλω (# 3516) to be about to; "the coming age" (Lane, *NTS* 11 [1965]: 166). ◆ **9** ἄξιος (# 545) worthy, w. a following gen. ἀποδοχή (# 628) reception, acceptance; i.e., acceptance as true. ◆ **10** κοπιῶμεν pres. ind. act. κοπιάω (# 3159) to work hard, to work until one is weary. ἀγωνιζόμεθα pres. ind. mid. (dep.) ἀγωνίζομαι (# 76) to struggle, to exert oneself. The two words speak of Paul's tremendous effort and exertions in the proclamation of the gospel (AM, 171-77). Pres. describes the continuous action. ἠλπίκαμεν perf. ind. act. ἐλπίζω (# 1827) to hope. Perf. implies a state of hope: "because we have fixed our hope" (Guthrie). ζῶντι pres. act. part. ζάω (# 2409) to live. Pres. indicates that God is living and therefore able to give life now and hereafter (Lock). μάλιστα (# 3436) especially. ◆ **11** παράγγελλε pres. imp. act. παραγγέλλω (# 4133) to transmit a message, to order, to command (s. 1 Tim. 1:3). δίδασκε pres. imp. act. διδάσκω (# 1438) to teach. Pres. indicates the continuation of an action and the continual, habitual carrying out of the command (Bakker; MKG, 271ff): "continue to command and to teach." ◆ **12** νεότης (# 3744) youth. καταφρονείτω pres. imp. act. 3rd sing. καταφρονέω (# 2969) to think down, to despise, to underrate. In the ancient world a person between 30 and 40 years old could be considered young (Kelly). One rabbi said that a person at 30 was fit for authority and at 40 he was fit for discernment (M, Aboth 5:21). τύπος (# 5596) type, example, thus taking the role of a father (BBC). γίνου pres. imp. mid. (dep.) γίνομαι (# 1181) to become. ἀναστροφή (# 419) behavior. Here dat. of sphere w. prep. ἐν ἁγνείᾳ (# 48) purity. The word covers not only chastity in matters of sex, but also the innocence and integrity of heart denoted by the related noun in 2 Cor. 6:6 (Kelly). The word refers to purity of act and thought (Lock). ◆ **13** πρόσεχε pres. imp. act. προσέχω (# 4668) (s.v. 1), to give attendance to, w. dat.; implies preparation in private (Guthrie). Pres. calls for a continual action. ἀνάγνωσις (# 342) reading, audible reading. Used w. the vb. it implies a wise choice of the passages to be read; a power of correct exposition (Lock). **παράκλησις** (# *4155*) exhortation, encouragement (TDNT; NIDNTT). **διδασκαλία** (# *1436*) teaching, doctrine. Dat. w. the vb. ◆ **14 ἀμέλει** pres. imp. act. ἀμελέω (# *288*) to be unconcerned about something, to neglect. For the pref. as a neg. s. Moorhouse, 47ff. Pres imp. could mean, "do not immediately," "do not always," "do not continue" (MKG, 272). **χάρισμα** (# *5922*) a result of grace, free gift, grace gift. It denotes special endowment of the Spirit enabling the recipient to carry out some function in the community (Kelly; TDNT; NIDNTT; DPL, 341). **ἐδόθη** aor. ind. pass. δίδωμι (# *1443*) to give. Theol. pass. indicating that God was the giver. **προφητεία** (# *4735*) speaking for someone, prophecy (DPL, 755-62). **μετά** (# *3552*) with. The prep. does not express instr. or means but merely accompaniment (RWP; EGT). **ἐπίθεσις** (# *2120*) placing upon, laying on. **πρεσβυτέριον** (# *4564*) assembly of elders, presbytery. This may be the rendering of a Heb. t.t. which meant the leaning or the pressing on of elders, which in effect meant the leaning of elders upon someone w. the object of making him an elder or rabbi. In a Christian context it would mean elder ordination or formal ordination to an office (Kelly). ◆ **15 μελέτα** pres. imp. act. μελετάω (# *3509*) to take care, to practice, to cultivate, to take pains w. something, to think about, to meditate upon (BAGD). **ἴσθι** pres. imp. act. εἰμί (# *1639*) to be; "be in them." It is a construction expressing absorption in anything. The mind is to be as immersed in these pursuits as the body in the air it breathes (Guthrie). **προκοπή** (# *4620*) advance, progress (s. Phil 1:12). The expression is a favorite word in Stoic writers of a pupil's progress in philosophy (Lock). **φανερός** (# *5745*) clear, obvious, manifest. **ᾖ** pres. subj. act. εἰμί (# *1639*) to be. Subj. w. **ἵνα** (# *2671*) is used to express purp. ◆ **16 ἔπεχε** pres. imp. act. ἐπέχω (# *2091*) to hold upon, to give heed to, to give attention to, to fix attention upon. For examples from the papyri s. MM; Preisigke. **διδασκαλία** (# *1436*) teaching. The article may refer to Timothy's ability to teach, if the word is understood in an active sense. In the pass. sense it refers to that which is taught or a body of teaching (BAGD). **ἐπίμενε** pres. imp. act. ἐπιμένω (# *2152*) to remain upon, to continue. Prep. in compound is directive indicating the concentration of the vb.'s action upon some object (MH, 312). **ποιῶν** pres. act. part. ποιέω (# *4472*) to make. Pres. expressing continuing action. Part. is modal ("by doing this"). **σώσεις** fut. ind. act. σῴζω (# *5392*) to rescue, to save. **ἀκούοντας** pres. act. part. (subst.) ἀκούω (# *201*) to hear, here w. gen. as obj.

1 Timothy 5

◆ **1 ἐπιπλήξῃς** aor. subj. act. ἐπιπλήσσω (# *2159*) to strike upon, to strike at, to rebuke sharply. The word contains a note of severity; to censure severely (MM; Guthrie). Aor. subj. is used w. the neg. in a prohibition

and implies that an action is not yet existent and should not arise (MKG, 273). **παρακάλει** pres. imp. act. παρακαλέω (# *4151*) to encourage, to exhort. **νεωτέρους** comp. νέος (# *3742*) young, comp., younger. "The younger men." ◆ **2 ἀδελφάς** acc. fem. pl. ἀδελφή (# *80*) sister. **ἁγνείᾳ** (# *48*) purity, chastity (s. 4:12). ◆ **3 χήρα** (# *5939*) widow. Care and protection of widows and orphans had long been recognized as an ethical obligation in Judaism and the same view had been adopted by the church from the beginning (HOG, 162; JPF, 787-91; BBC; Bruce W. Winter, "Providentia for the Widows of 1 Timothy 5:3-16," *TB* 39 [1988]: 83-99; J. M. Bassler, "The Widow's Tale: A Fresh Look at 1 Tim. 5:3-16," *JBL* 103 [1984]: 23-41). **τίμα** pres. imp. act. τιμάω (# *5506*) to honor, to show respect; The word would also carry the idea of support in this context (EGT; Schlatter). **ὄντως** (# *3953*) actually, really; adv. from the pres. part. of εἰμί. Paul means widows who have no other means of support, no opportunity for marriage, and who have given themselves to the service of the Lord (Jeremias; Guthrie; HOG, 162). ◆ **4 ἔκγονος** (# *1681*) descendant, grandchild (Guthrie). **μανθανέτωσαν** pres. imp. act. 3rd. pers. pl. μανθάνω (# *3443*) to learn. The subject of the pl. vb. is "such children and grandchildren" (Lock). **ἴδιος** (# *2625*) one's own. **εὐσεβεῖν** pres. act. inf. εὐσεβέω (# *2355*) to show piety, to show reverence, to fulfill one's religious obligations (s. 1 Tim. 2:2; MM). **ἀμοιβάς** acc. pl. ἀμοιβή (# *304*) return, recompense (MM). **ἀποδιδόναι** pres. act. inf. ἀποδίδωμι (# *625*) to give back, to return, to render. Used w. the noun it means to make a worthy requital (Guthrie). **πρόγονος** (# *4591*) parent, forefather, ancestor (BAGD). **ἀπόδεκτος** (# *621*) acceptable. ◆ **5 μεμονωμένη** perf. pass. part. μονόω (# *3670*) to leave alone; pass., to be left alone. Perf. looks at the continual cond. or state. **ἤλπικεν** perf. ind. act. ἐλπίζω (# *1827*) to hope. Perf. conveys the meaning "has fixed her hope and keeps it in the direction of God" (RW; Guthrie). **προσμένει** pres. ind. act. προσμένω (# *4693*) to remain w. something, to remain, to continue, to abide in. Pres. emphasizes the continual action. **δέησις** (# *1255*) request. ◆ **6 σπαταλῶσα** pres. act. part. σπαταλάω (# *5059*) to live a luxurious life, to give oneself to pleasure. The word connotes abandonment to pleasure and comfort (Kelly; BBC; s. James 5:5). **ζῶσα** pres. act. part. ζάω (# *2409*) to live. Part. expresses contemporaneous action. **τέθνηκεν** perf. ind. act. θνήσκω (# *2569*) to die, perf. to be dead. ◆ **7 παράγγελλε** pres. imp. act. παραγγέλλω (# *4133*) to command, to instruct (s. 1 Tim. 1:3). **ἀνεπίλημπτος** (# *455*) without reproach, irreproachable; (s. 1 Tim. 3:2). **ὦσιν** pres. subj. act. εἰμί (# *1639*) to be. ◆ **8 ἴδιος** (# *2625*) one's own; the near relatives (EGT). **μάλιστα** (# *3436*) especially. **οἰκεῖος** (# *3858*) household. It refers to the members of one's household and immediate family circle (Guthrie; EGT). **προνοεῖ** pres. ind. act. προνοέω (# *4629*) to think of beforehand, to provide for. The obj. of the vb. is in the gen. For examples in the papyri s. MM; Priesigke; esp. NDIEC, 8:106-16. **ἤρνηται** perf. ind. mid. (dep.) ἀρνέομαι (# 766) to deny. **ἄπιστος** (# 603) unbeliever; here, gen. of comparison. **χείρων** (# 5937) comp. κακός bad; comp., worse. He is worse than an unbeliever because unbelievers perform their duty (both Jew and Gentile), and because he not only has the law of nature but the law of Christ to guide him (Lock; JFC, 2:761; M, Ketuboth 5:8-9; Epictetus, 3, 18f). Provision for widows is part of everyday kinship and has become for Paul the crowning expression of genuine faith in action within the Christian household (NDIEC, 8:115). ◆ **9 καταλεγέσθω** pres. imp. pass. καταλέγω (# 2899) to write down in a list, to enroll. It is a t.t. for being placed on a recognized list or catalogue (Kelly). **ἔλαττον** (# 1781) comp. μίκρος little; comp., less than. **ἔτος** (# 2291) year. Here gen. of comparison or gen. of quality (RG, 516; BD, 99). **γεγονυῖα** perf. act. part. nom. fem. sing. γίνομαι (# 1181) to become. To the Jews old age began w. the 60th year; Orientals regarded it as the time for retiring for quiet contemplation (SB, 3:653; BBC; Lock). ◆ **10 μαρτυρουμένη** pres. pass. part. μαρτυρέω (# 3455) to witness, to testify. **ἐτεκνοτρόφησεν** aor. ind. act. τεκνοτροφέω (# 5442) to rear children. **ἐξενοδόχησεν** aor. ind. act. ξενοδοχέω (# 3827) to welcome strangers, to show hospitality (ABD, 3:299-301). **ἔνιψεν** aor. ind. act. νίπτω (# 3782) to wash. The washing of the feet was a service to visitors which occupied a great place in Eastern hospitality. The mistress of the house would act as a servant to the servants of God (Kelly; EGT). **θλιβομένοις** pres. pass. part. θλίβω (# 2567) to put under pressure, to bring about distress; pass., to be in distress. **ἐπήρκεσεν** aor. ind. act. ἐπαρκέω (# 2064) to help, to aid, to assist, to relieve. **ἐπηκολούθησαν** aor. ind. act. ἐπακολουθέω (# 2051) to follow after. Prep. in compound is directive (MH, 312). The vbs. in this v. are used in first class cond. cls. which assume the reality of the cond. ◆ **11 παραιτοῦ** pres. imp. mid. (dep.) παραιτέομαι (# 4148) to decline, to refuse; here, to refuse to put on the list entitled to special guardianship and sustenance on the part of the church (Fairbairn). **ὅταν** (# 4020) w. the subj., when, whenever. **καταστρηνιάσωσιν** aor. subj. act. καταστρηνιάω (# 2952) to feel the impulse of sexual desire; here, to feel sensuous impulses that alienate from Christ (RW; BAGD). **θέλουσιν** pres. ind. act. θέλω (# 2527) to desire. **γαμεῖν** pres. act. inf. γαμέω (# 1138) to marry. Compl. inf. to the preceding vb. ◆ **12 ἔχουσαι** pres. act. part. ἔχω (# 2400) to have. **κρίμα** (# 3210) judgment. The meaning is that the widows who forsook their sacred obligation in order to marry would be deserving of censure. For such action would amount to casting aside their first faith, i.e., their pledge of service (Guthrie). **ἠθέτησαν** aor. ind. act. ἀθετέω (# 119) to set aside, to regard as void, to annul (s. Gal. 2:21).

◆ **13 ἅμα** (# 275) at the same time. Used here in the phrase ἅμα δὲ καί (BAGD). **ἀργός** (# 734) not working, idle. **μανθάνουσιν** pres. ind. act. μανθάνω (# 3443) to learn. The vb. w. a substitutive denoting a profession or occupation was an idiomatic construction signifying qualification as such and such (e.g., a doctor, wrestler, etc.). (Kelly). **περιερχόμεναι** pres. mid. (dep.) part. περιέρχομαι (# 4320) to go about, to go around. The word may mean that the younger widows were going around misusing their opportunities in visitation (Guthrie; EGT). **φλύαρος** (# 5827) gossipy, loose talkers; i.e., babbling out whatever might come into their mind (Fairbairn). **περίεργος** (# 4319) overcareful, taking needless trouble, busybodies (Kelly). The word marks a meddling habit, a perverted activity that will not content itself w. minding its own concerns, but must busy itself about those of others (Ellicott; s. 2 Thess. 3:11). **λαλοῦσαι** pres. act. part. (adj.) λαλέω (# 3281) to speak. **δέοντα** pres. act. part. δεῖ (# 1256) it is necessary. τὰ δέοντα things which are necessary; w. the neg. μή (# 3590) things which are not proper (EGT). ◆ **14 βούλομαι** (# 1089) pres. ind. mid. (dep.) to will, to desire w. inf. Jewish formal law and accepted Jewish custom undoubtedly agreed that a widow's remarriage was both permissible and desirable and she was only required to wait long enough for it to be ascertained that she was not already pregnant at the time of the second marriage. There were in Judaism, however, some groups which considered a widow's abstinence from remarriage to be a pious and proper act (JFC, 2:787-88f). **τεκνογονεῖν** pres. act. inf. τεκνογονέω (# 5449) to bear children. **οἰκοδεσποτεῖν** pres. inf. act. οἰκοδεσποτέω (# 3866) to rule over the house, to manage the household, to be master of a house. **ἀφορμή** (# 929) a starting point, a base of operation, opportunity (AS; s. 2 Cor. 5:12). **ἀντικειμένῳ** pres. mid. (dep.) part. (subst.) ἀντίκειμαι (# 512) to lie against, to oppose, to be an adversary. **λοιδορία** (# 3367) abuse, reproach, railing, insult (TLNT). **χάριν** (# 5920) prep. w. gen., on account of, because of. ◆ **15 ἐξετράπησαν** aor. ind. pass. ἐκτρέπομαι (# 1762) to turn from, to go astray, to turn out of the true path (Lock). **ὀπίσω** (# 3958) w. gen., after, behind; i.e., they follow behind or after Satan (EGT). ◆ **16 ἐπαρκείτω** pres. imp. act. 3rd. pers. sing. ἐπαρκέω (# 2064) to help, to assist. **βαρείσθω** pres. imp. pass. βαρέω (# 976) to burden; pass., to be burdened. The word is used of financial burdens and refers here to financial support (Kelly). **ἐπαρκέσῃ** aor. subj. act. ἐπαρκέω (# 2064). ◆ **17 καλῶς** (# 2822) adv. well. **προεστῶτες** perf. act. part. προΐστημι (# 4613) to stand first, to rule. The word means general superintendence and describes the duties allotted to all presbyters (Guthrie). **διπλῆς** gen. sing. διπλοῦς (# 1486) double. **τιμή** (# 5507) honor (Schlatter), remuneration (Kelly; EGT). **ἀξιούσθωσαν** pres. imp. pass. ἀξιόω (# 546) to consider worthy, to hold as worthy. **κοπιῶντες** pres. imp. pass. κοπιάω (# 3159) to work, to labor, to work until one is exhausted. **λόγος** (# 3364) word; here, those who preach and teach (Guthrie). **διδασκαλία** (# 1436) teaching, doctrine. ◆ **18 γραφή** (# 1210) writing, Scripture (TDNT). **βοῦς** (# 1091) ox, cow. **ἀλοῶντα** pres. act. part. (adj.) ἀλοάω (# 262) to thrash. **φιμώσεις** fut. ind. act. φιμόω (# 5821) to muzzle (1 Cor. 9:9, ἀλοάω). The fut. is used to express a prohibition and is used in the legal language of the OT almost always as a categorical imp. (BS, 118; RW). **μισθός** (# 3635) wage, salary. ◆ **19 κατηγορία** (# 2990) that which is brought against someone, charge, legal accusation (MM; Priesigke). **παραδέχου** pres. imp. mid. (dep.) παραδέχομαι (# 4138) to entertain. **ἐκτὸς εἰ μή** except when (BS, 118). ◆ **20 ἁμαρτάνοντας** pres. imp. act. ἁμαρτάνω (# 279) to miss the mark, to sin. **ἔλεγχε** pres. imp. act. ἐλέγχω (# 1794) to bring to light, to expose, to demonstrate or prove to convince or convict someone, to reprove or correct. Here it may have the connotation of refuting (BAGD). **λοιπός** (# 3370) remaining, rest. **ἔχωσιν** pres. subj. act. ἔχω (# 2400) to have. Subj. w. ἵνα (# 2671) to express purp. ◆ **21 διαμαρτύρομαι** (# 1371) pres. ind. mid. (dep.) to charge solemnly; to declare solemnly. Prep. in compound has the idea of "thoroughly" (MH, 302). **ἐκλεκτός** (# 1723) chosen, elect. **ἵνα** (# 2671) w. subj., that. It introduces the content of Paul's charge to Timothy. **φυλάξῃς** aor. subj. act. φυλάσσω (# 5875) to guard, to observe, to keep. **προκρίμα** (# 4622) a judgment before hand, prejudice. **ποιῶν** pres. act. part. ποιέω (# 4472) to do, to make. Part. of manner or epex. part. explaining the command. **πρόσκλισις** (# 4680) inclining toward, partiality (RW). ◆ **22 ταχέως** (# 5441) quickly, adv. τάχυς. **ἐπιτίθει** pres. imp. act. ἐπιτίθημι (# 2202) to place upon, to lay hands upon. **κοινώνει** pres. imp. act. κοινωνέω (# 3125) to have fellowship w., to participate. **ἀλλότριος** (# 259) belonging to another, not one's own. **ἁγνός** (# 54) pure (s. 1 Tim. 4:12). **τήρει** pres. imp. act. τηρέω (# 5498) to keep. ◆ **23 μηκέτι** (# 3600) no longer. **ὑδροπότει** pres. imp. act. ὑδροποτέω (# 5621) to drink water. The command to abstain from drinking water exclusively may have been due to the fact that contaminated water contributed to Timothy's indigestion (Guthrie). Epictetus used the word in a positive command–drink only water to show one's ability in restraint (Epictetus, 3:13, 21). **χρῶ** pres. imp. mid. (dep.) χράομαι (# 5968) to use. **στόμαχος** (# 5126) stomach. **πυκνός** (# 4781) often, frequently. **ἀσθένεια** (# 819) sickness, weakness. For the text of a memorandum requesting the purchase of a jar of wine according to the doctor's orders s. SP, 1:396-97. ◆ **24 πρόδηλος** (# 4593) clear, evident, openly plain before all. (RW). **προάγουσαι** pres. act. part. nom. fem. pl. προάγω (# 4575) to go ahead. **κρίσις** (# 3213) judgment. ◆ **25 ὡσαύτως** (# 6058) likewise. **πρόδηλα** n. nom. pl.

(# 4593) s.v. 24. **ἄλλως** (# 261) otherwise. **ἔχοντα** pres. act. part. ἔχω (# 2400) to have; "those having it otherwise" (RWᵧ). **δύνανται** pres. ind. pass. (dep.) δύναμαι (# 1538) to be able to, w. inf. **κρυβῆναι** aor. pass. inf. κρύπτω (# 3221) to hide. Compl. inf. to the main vb.

1 Timothy 6

◆ **1 ὅσος** (# 4012) as many as. The pron. indicates those who belong to a particular class or group. **ζυγός** (# 2433) yoke. The metaphor "under the yoke" indicated slavery by capture, since the captives were made to pass underneath three spears lashed together to form a doorway outline, thus requiring them to bow their heads and "pass under the yoke" (SCS, 31; ABD, 6:1026-27). For ancient discourses on slavery s. DC 10. 14, 15; Seneca, *Epistle* 47; 1 Cor. 7:21; Philemon 21; DPL, 881-83). **δεσπότης** (# 1305) master. **ἡγείσθωσαν** pres. imp. mid. (dep.) ἡγέομαι (# 2451) to consider, to reckon, to deem. **διδασκαλία** (# 1436) teaching, doctrine. **βλασφημῆται** pres. subj. pass. βλασφημέω (# 1059) to slander, to blaspheme. Subj. w. ἵνα (# 2671) to express purp. or result. ◆ **2 ἔχοντες** pres. act. part. ἔχω (# 2400) to have. **καταφρονείτωσαν** pres. imp. act. καταφρονέω (# 2969) to think down upon, to despise. The word means to treat without the full consideration due to the other man's station (Kelly). Pres. imp. w. the neg. is to prohibit a continual or habitual action (MKG, 272f). **μᾶλλον** (# 3437) comp., rather, more. The word is intensive and indicates that the Christian master should be served more, i.e., better (Ellicott; RW). **δουλευέτωσαν** pres. ind. act. δουλεύω (# 1526) to serve. **εὐεργεσία** (# 2307) working well, good service, good deed, benefit. The word refers to the human kindness not of masters but of slaves as shown by their better service (Lock). This benefit is a gift to the master (BBC). **ἀντιλαμβανόμενοι** pres. mid. (dep.) part. ἀντιλαμβάνω (# 514) to take part in, to devote oneself to, to practice; here, "those who devote themselves to kindness" (BAGD). **δίδασκε** pres. imp. act. διδάσκω (# 1438) to teach. **παρακάλει** pres. imp. act. παρακαλέω (# 4151) to encourage, to exhort. Pres. imp. calls for a continual or habitual action. ◆ **3 ἑτεροδιδασκαλεῖ** pres. ind. act. ἑτεροδιδασκαλέω (# 2281) to teach another doctrine, to teach a completely different doctrine, to teach a false or heretical doctrine (Fairbairn). **προσέρχεται** pres. ind. mid. (dep.) προσέρχομαι (# 4665) to come to, to approach, to attach oneself to, to consent (Guthrie). The vbs. in the ind. are used in a first-class cond. cl. which assumes the reality of the cond. **ὑγιαίνουσιν** pres. act. part. ὑγιαίνω (# 5617) to be in good health, to be healthy, to be sound (s. 3 John 2). **εὐσέβεια** (# 2354) godliness (s. 1 Tim. 4:7). ◆ **4 τετύφωται** perf. ind. pass. τυφόω (# 5605) to be puffed up, to be proud (s. 1 Tim. 3:6). **ἐπιστάμενος** pres. pass. (dep.) part. ἐπίσταμαι (# 2179) to know, to understand. **νοσῶν** pres. act. part. νοσέω

(# 3796) to be sick, to be ailing w., to have a morbid craving for something (BAGD). The disease is intellectual curiosity about trifles (EGT). ζήτησις (# 2428) seeking, speculation. It denotes the preoccupation w. pseudo-intellectual theorizing (Kelly; s. 1 Tim. 1:4). λογομαχία (# 3363) word war, strife of words. φθόνος (# 5784) envy. ἔρις (# 2251) strife. βλασφημία (# 1060) slander, blasphemy (TLNT). ὑπόνοια (# 5707) suspicion, conjecture. Prep. in compound suggests the idea of thoughts making their way into the mind (MH, 327). ◆ 5 διαπαρατριβή (# 1384) a mutual rubbing or irritation alongside, protracted quarreling, persistent wrangling (RW; EGT; Kelly; MH, 303). διεφθαρμένων perf. pass. part. διαφθείρω (# 1425) to corrupt. Perf. emphasizes the completed state or cond. νοῦς (# 3808) mind, understanding. ἀπεστερημένων perf. pass. part. ἀποστρέφω (# 691) to steal, to rob, to derive. νομιζόντων pres. act. part. νομίζω (# 3787) to suppose. πορισμός (# 4516) means of gain. εἶναι pres. act. inf. εἰμί (# 1639) to be. ◆ 6 αὐτάρκεια (# 894) contentment, self-sufficiency. The word was a t.t. in Gr. philosophy used to denote the wise man's independence of circumstances (Kelly; Dibelius; Spicq; Phil. 4:11). ◆ 7 εἰσηνέγκαμεν aor. ind. act. εἰσφέρω (# 1650) to bring into. ἐξενεγκεῖν aor. act. inf. ἐκφέρω (# 1766) to carry out of. For Jewish and Gentile parallels s. Kelly; SB, 3:655; NW, 2, i:944-48. ◆ 8 ἔχοντες pres. act. part. ἔχω (# 2400) to have. Adj. part. to emphasize a quality or characterizing trait. διατροφή (# 1418) food, nourishment. σκέπασμα (# 5004) that which covers, clothing. ἀρκεσθησόμεθα fut. ind. pass. ἀρκέω (# 758) pass., to be content, to be satisfied. The fut. probably has an imp. sense as used in the legal language of the OT (BG, 94; EGT). ◆ 9 βουλόμενοι pres. mid. (dep.) part. βούλομαι (# 1089) to will, to purpose, w. inf. πλουτεῖν pres. act. inf. πλουτέω (# 4456) to be rich, to be wealthy. Compl. inf. to the preceding part. (DPL, 826-27; BBC). ἐμπίπτουσιν pres. ind. act. ἐμπίπτω (# 1860) to fall into. Pres. indicates that which always or normally happens. πειρασμός (# 4280) temptation. παγίδα sing. acc. παγίς (# 4075) snare, trap. ἐπιθυμία (# 2123) strong desire. ἀνόητος (# 485) irrational (s. Gal. 3:1). βλαβερός (# 1054) harmful, injuring. βυθίζουσιν pres. ind. act. βυθίζω (# 1112) to drag to the bottom, to submerge, to drown. The image is of drowning someone in the sea (Kelly; RW). ὄλεθρος (# 3897) destruction. ἀπώλεια (# 724) ruin. The two words are used in the sense of ruin that suggests irretrievable loss (Guthrie). ◆ 10 ῥίζα (# 4844) root. Pred. nom. without the article emphasizes the character or quality (s. John 1:1; also GGBB, 265). κακός (# 2805) evil. The pl. here emphasizes evils of all kinds (Kelly). φιλαργυρία (# 5794) love of money. The writer of The Sentences of Pseudo-Phocylides says, "Love of money is the mother of all evil (ἡ φιλοχρημοσύνη μήτηρ κακότητος ἁπάσης). Gold and silver are always a lure for men. Gold, originator of evil

(κακῶν ἀρχηγέ) destroyer of life, crushing all things, would that you were not a desirable calamity to mortals! For your sake there are battles and plunderings and murders, and children become enemies of their parents and brothers (the enemies) of their kinsmen" (The Sentences of Pseudo-Phocylides, 42-45; SPP, 91; for other parallels to this proverbial saying s. Lock; Kelly; Dibelius; NW, 2, i:953-59; DCNT, 211; s. 1 Tim. 3:8). ὀρεγόμενοι pres. mid. part. ὀρέγω (# 3977) to reach out after something, to desire something. Obj. is in the gen. (s. 1 Tim. 3:1). ἀπεπλανήθησαν aor. ind. pass. ἀποπλανάω (# 675) to lead astray. περιέπειραν aor. ind. act. περιπείρω (# 4345) to pierce completely (RW). ◆ 11 φεῦγε pres. imp. act. φεύγω (# 5771) to flee. Pres. imp. suggests a continual or habitual action. δίωκε pres. imp. act. διώκω (# 1503) to hunt, to pursue. ὑπομονή (# 5705) patience, endurance (s. 2 Thess. 1:4). πραϋπαθία (# 4557) gentleness, meekness (s. 2 Cor. 10:1; Gal. 5:23). ◆ 12 ἀγωνίζου pres. imp. mid. (dep.) ἀγωνίζομαι (# 76) to carry on a contest, to strive, to struggle, to fight. The word includes the effort put forth in the proclamation of the gospel (AM, 178f). ἀγών (# 74) struggle, contest. In opposition to those who crave material riches, Timothy is to strive after righteousness, godliness, faith, love, patience, and meekness (AM, 178). ἐπιλαβοῦ aor. imp. mid. (dep.) ἐπιλαμβάνω (# 2138) to lay hold on, to get a good grip on (RW). This does not appear as a fut. prize lying at the end of the ἀγών, but as that to be grasped and retained in the pres. struggle of faith (AM, 179f). ἐκλήθης aor. ind. pass. καλέω (# 2813) to call. ὡμολόγησας aor. ind. act. ὁμολογέω (# 3933) to agree to, to confess. ὁμολογία (# 3934) agreement, confession. It is the acknowledging of Jesus as the Messiah (ECC, 133). ◆ 13 παραγγέλλω (# 4133) pres. ind. act. to instruct, to command, to charge (s. 1:3). ζωογονοῦντος pres. act. part. ζωογονέω (# 2441) to give life to, to make alive. μαρτυρήσαντος aor. act. part. μαρτυρέω (# 3455) to give witness to, to testify. ◆ 14 τηρῆσαι aor. act. inf. τηρέω (# 5498) to keep. Inf. is used to express the obj. of the vb. παραγγέλλω and is used in a indir. command (RW). ἄσπιλος (# 834) without spot. ἀνεπίλημπτος (# 455) irreproachable (s. 3:2). ἐπιφάνεια (# 2211) manifestation, appearance. The word was a t.t. in the language of contemporary Hellenistic religion for the self-disclosure of a god or king (Kelly; also 2 Thess. 2:8). ◆ 15 καιρός (# 2789) time, season, opportune time. δείξει fut. ind. act. δείκνυμι (# 1259) to show. μακάριος (# 3421) happy, blessed. δυνάστης (# 1541) potentate. The word was used of one who exercised sovereignty in his own power (Guthrie). βασιλευόντων pres. act. part. (subst.) βασιλεύω (# 995) to be a king, to rule as king. κυριευόντων pres. act. part. (subst.) κυριεύω (# 3259) to be a lord, to rule as a lord. ◆ 16 ἀθανασία (# 114) not able to die, immortality (BS, 293). οἰκῶν pres. act. part. οἰκέω (# 3861) to dwell.

ἀπρόσιτος (# 717) unapproachable (SB, 3:656). εἶδεν aor. ind. act. ὁράω (# 3972) to see. ἰδεῖν aor. act. inf. ὁράω (# 3972) to see. Compl. inf. to the following vb. δύναται pres. ind. pass. (dep.) δύναμαι (# 1538) to be able to, w. inf. κράτος (# 3197) power (s. Eph. 1:19). ◆ **17** πλούσιος (# 4454) rich, wealthy. **παράγγελλε** pres. imp. act. παραγγέλλω (# 4133) to give orders, to instruct, to command (BAGD; s. 1:3). ὑψηλοφρονεῖν pres. act. inf. ὑψηλοφρονέω (# 5735) to think exalted, to think highly, to be proud and haughty. ἠλπικέναι perf. act. inf. ἐλπίζω (# 1827) to hope. Perf., to place one's hope upon something or someone and rest there–to have hope and continue to hope (Ellicott). ἀδηλότης (# 84) uncertainty. From the adj. meaning, unseen, unobserved, not manifest, indistinct (AS). παρέχοντι pres. act. part. παρέχω (# 4218) to give, to grant, to cause, to bring about something for someone (BAGD). πλουσίως (# 4455) richly, adv. πλουσίος. ἀπόλαυσις (# 656) enjoying, enjoyment, pleasure. ◆ **18** ἀγαθοεργεῖν pres. act. inf. ἀγαθοεργέω (# 14) to do that which is good, to do good works, to do deeds inherently noble and praiseworthy (Fairbairn). εὐμετάδοτος (# 2331) sharing well, generous, ready to impart (MM). κοινωνικός (# 3127) ready to share, giving or sharing generously (BAGD; MH, 378). ◆ **19** ἀποθησαυρίζοντας pres. act. part. ἀποθησαυρίζω (# 631) to store up, to amass a treasure. Prep. in compound implies that the rich are to take from their own plenty, and by devoting it to the service of God and the relief of the poor, actually to treasure it up as a good foundation for the future (Ellicott; Kelly). θεμέλιος (# 2529) foundation. μέλλον pres. act. part. μέλλω (# 3516) to be about to. Here, for that which is coming, for the future. ἐπιλάβωνται aor. subj. mid. ἐπιλαμβάνω (# 2138) to grasp, to take hold of. ὄντως (# 3953) adv., truly (from the part. of εἰμί). ◆ **20** παραθήκη (# 4146) that which is placed beside, deposit, trust. It is a legal term connoting something which is placed on trust in another man's keeping (Kelly; BBC; MM). φύλαξον aor. act ind. φυλάσσω (# 5875) to guard. ἐκτρεπόμενος pres. mid. (dep.) part. ἐκτρέπω (# 1762) to go out of the way, to run away from. Part. describes manner or means. βέβηλος (# 1013) that which is accessible to all, profane (s. 1:9). κενοφωνία (# 3032) empty talking, uttering emptiness (RWP). ἀντίθεσις (# 509) opposition, objection, contradiction. ψευδώνυμος (# 6024) falsely named. γνῶσις (# 1194) knowing, knowledge. ◆ **21** ἐπαγγελλόμενοι pres. mid. (dep.) part. ἐπαγγέλλω (# 2040) to announce, to proclaim, to profess. ἠστόχησαν aor. ind. act. ἀστοχέω (# 846) to miss the mark, to fail, to deviate (s. 1:6).

2 Timothy

2 Timothy 1

◆ **1** κατ' (*# 2848*) according to. It gives the standard by which God chose him and to which his apostleship must be true (Lock). Prep. also denotes the obj. and intention of the appointment: to further, to make known, the promise of eternal life (Ellicott). ἐπαγγελία (*# 2039*) promise. ζωή (*# 2437*) life. Gen. here gives the content of the promise. For a study of the concept of eternal life s. GW, 163-201; TDNT; NIDNTT. ἐν (*# 1877*) in. Prep. indicates that the source and sphere of life is in Christ Jesus. ◆ **2** ἀγαπητός (*# 28*) beloved. τέκνον (*# 5451*) child. A term of endearment. ἔλεος (*# 1799*) mercy (s. 1 Tim. 1:2). ◆ **3** ἔχω pres. ind. act. (*# 2400*) to have. χάριν ἔχω τῷ θεῷ "I have thanks to God," "I give thanks to God." The word, indicating the gratitude of the one who receives a favor from a benefactor, was a common expression of that day (TLNT; Spicq). λατρεύω (*# 3302*) pres. ind. act. to serve. The word, used esp. of carrying out religious duties–particularly of a cultic nature–was used in the sense of worship (BAGD; TDNT; TLNT). Pres. emphasizes the continual unbroken habit of life: "I have been serving" (RWP). πρόγονος (*# 4591*) forbearer. The statement must be understood to mean that Paul thought of Judaism in such close connection w. Christianity that his present worship of God is in a sense a continuation of his own Jewish worship (Guthrie). ἐν (*# 1877*) in. Local prep. giving the spiritual sphere in which the worship was offered (Ellicott). συνείδησις (*# 5287*) conscience (s. Rom. 2:15). ἀδιάλειπτος (*# 89*) without interruption, unceasing (s. 1 Thess. 1:2; Josephus, *Wars*, 5:71; 279; 298; MM). μνεία (*# 3644*) remembrance, mention (s. 1 Thess. 1:2). δέησις (*# 1255*) request, prayer. νυκτὸς καὶ ἡμέρας (*# 3816; 2779; 2465*) night and day. Here gen. of time indicating within which or during which an action takes place (GGBB, 122-24). ◆ **4** ἐπιποθῶν pres. act. part. ἐπιποθέω (*# 2160*) to have a strong desire for, to yearn after (Spicq). Prep. in compound is directive (s. Phil. 1:8). ἰδεῖν aor. act. inf. ὁράω (*# 3972*) to see. Compl. inf. to the preceding part. μεμνημένος perf. pass. (dep.) part. μιμνῄσκομαι (*# 3630*) to remind oneself, to recall to mind, to remember, w. gen. Perf. emphasizes the continuing state. Temp. or causal part. δάκρυον (*# 1232*) tear. ἵνα (*# 2671*) w. subj., that. Introduces the purp. of Paul wanting to see Timothy (Kelly). πληρωθῶ aor. subj. pass. πληρόω (*# 4444*) to fill; pass., to be filled. ◆ **5** ὑπόμνησις (*# 5704*) remem-bering, reminder. The word is used properly of an external reminder (Lock). λαβών aor. act. part. λαμβάνω (*# 3284*) to receive. Aor. suggests a logically antecedent action to the main vb. The phrase, "having received a reminder," may suggest that Paul had just had news of Timothy (Guthrie). ἀνυπόκριτος (*# 537*) without hypocrisy, genuine. It was a genuine principle, the opposite of a hypocritical or wavering profession (Fairbairn). ἐνῴκησεν aor. ind. act. ἐνοικέω (*# 1940*) to live in, to dwell in (s. Col. 3:16). μάμμη (*# 3439*) grandmother. The mother and grandmother played a vital part in the early training of the young children (JTJ, 102; BBC). For the use of the names Lois and Eunice s. Spicq. πέπεισμαι perf. ind. pass. πείθω (*# 4275*) to persuade, to be persuaded; perf., I stand persuaded (RWP). Perf. emphasizes the continuing result. ◆ **6** αἰτία (*# 162*) cause, reason. ἀναμιμνῄσκω (*# 389*) pres. ind. act. to remind, to cause to remember. Prep. in compound is causative (MH, 295). ἀναζωπυρεῖν pres. act. inf. ἀναζωπυρέω (*# 351*) to stir up smoldering embers into a living flame, to keep at white heat (Lock). The word means either "to kindle afresh" or "to keep a full flame" (AS; MH, 296; RWP). Paul's statement does not necessarily contain a censure since fire in the ancient world was never kept at a continual blaze, but rather kept alive through glowing coals which were then rekindled through a flame by a bellows whenever the situation demanded flame (TDNT; OCD, 439; Lev. 6:9). Compl. inf. to the preceding vb. χάρισμα (*# 5922*) gift, grace gift. ἐπίθεσις (*# 2120*) laying on. ◆ **7** ἔδωκεν aor. ind. act. δίδωμι (*# 1443*) to give. δειλία (*# 1261*) cowardice, timidity, lack of courage, faintheartedness, fear (TLNT; Spicq). σωφρονισμός (*# 5406*) self-discipline, the power to keep oneself in hand, free from all excitement or hesitation (Lock; TDNT; EDNT; GPT, 179-80; TLNT). It has to do with character and conduct and is the general virtue or knowledge of what to do and what to avoid (TLNT). ◆ **8** οὖν (*# 4036*) therefore, drawing a logical conclusion from the preceding. ἐπαισχυνθῇς aor. subj. pass. ἐπαισχύνομαι (*# 2049*) to be ashamed of, to experience or feel shame or disgrace, w. attention focused upon that which causes shame (LN: 310). Aor. subj. w. a neg. μή (*# 3590*) to form a prohibition designed to prevent an action from arising (MKG, 273). μαρτύριον (*# 3457*) witness, here in the sense of witness through the proclamation of the gospel leading to his imprisonment. **δέσμιος** (# 1300) prisoner. To show sympathy to a prisoner and to offer him help could be very dangerous since it involved one in the charges against the prisoner (BAFCS, 3:388-92). **συγκακοπάθησον** aor. imp. act. συγκακοπαθέω (# 5155) to suffer evil together, to take one's share of evil treatment (AS). Disciples were to share in the sufferings of the teacher (BBC). Aor. imp. calls for a specific act w. a note of urgency (MKG, 272). ◆ **9 σώσαντος** aor. act. part. σώζω (# 5392) to save, to rescue. Both parts. are logically antecedent to the governing imp. (v. 8). Both describe saving and calling as characterizing traits of God. **καλέσαντος** aor. act. part. καλέω (# 2813) to call. **κλῆσις** (# 3104) calling. **ἴδιος** (# 2625) one's own. **πρόθεσις** (# 4606) facing before, purpose. **δοθεῖσαν** aor. pass. part. δίδωμι (# 1443) to give. **αἰώνιος** (# 173) eternal. This may be a reference to the earliest promise of triumph for the woman's seed (Gen. 3:15), or to the grace of the preexistent Christ (Guthrie). ◆ **10 φανερωθεῖσαν** aor. pass. part. φανερόω (# 5746) to make visible, to make clear, to manifest. **ἐπιφάνεια** (# 2211) manifestation, appearing (s. 1 Tim. 6:14; 2 Thess. 2:8; TDNT; Dibelius). Here are two thoughts, the divine intervention of a Savior in an hour of need and the dawning of a new light (Lock). **καταργήσαντος** aor. act. part. καταργέω (# 2934) to render inoperative, to make inactive, to annul. **μέν ... δέ** (# 3525; 1254) on the one hand ... on the other hand. The particles indicate connection and contrast (Fairbairn). **φωτίσαντος** aor. act. part. φωτίζω (# 5894) to illuminate, to flood w. light, to bring to light (Kelly). The two parts. indicate the meaning or manner in which the manifestation was accomplished. **ἀφθαρσία** (# 914) incorruptibility, immortality. ◆ **11 ἐτέθην** aor. ind. pass. τίθημι (# 5502) to place, to appoint, to commission. **κῆρυξ** (# 3061) proclaimer, herald, preacher (s. 1 Tim. 2:7). ◆ **12 καί** (# 2779) also. **πάσχω** (# 4248) pres. ind. act. to suffer. Pres. indicates a continual action going on at the pres. time. **ἐπαισχύνομαι** pres. ind. mid. (dep) (# 2049) s.v. 8. **οἶδα** (# 3857) perf. ind. act. to know. Def. perf. w. present meaning (s. VA, 281-87). **ᾧ** dat. ὅς (# 4005) who; "whom," rel. pron. used as obj. of the vb., but the antecedent is not expressed. Paul knows Jesus Christ whom he has trusted (RWP). **πεπίστευκα** perf. ind. act. πιστεύω (# 4409) to believe, to trust in. Perf. indicates "in whom I have put my trust, and still do put it" (Ellicott). **παραθήκη** (# 4146) that which is committed to another, deposit. It is a legal term connoting something one person places in trust to another's keeping; e.g., money, a person, a harvest of grain, a secret. The deposit belonged to the one making it and the one receiving it was obligated to be faithful and guard it like something sacred and divine (TLNT; Kelly; BBC; Lock, 90f; Lea and Griffin; s. 1 Tim. 6:20). The word is best understood as that which God entrusted to Paul and the present vb. focuses attention on God's ability to guard

(Guthrie; Kelly). **φυλάξαι** aor. act. inf. φυλάσσω (# 5875) to guard, to protect, to keep watch over, to keep guard. For references s. LS; TDNT. Compl. inf. to the adj. **δυνατός** (# 1543) able; "he is able to keep." ◆ **13 ὑποτύπωσις** (# 5721) model, example. The word denotes an outline sketch or ground plan used by an artist, or in literature the rough draft forming the basis of a fuller exposition (Kelly; Spicq). **ἔχε** pres. imp. act. ἔχω (# 2400) to have, to hold. **ὑγιαινόντων** pres. act. part. ὑγιαίνω (# 5617) to be healthy, to be sound. **ἤκουσας** aor. ind. act. ἀκούω (# 201) to hear. **ἐν** (# 1877) in. Prep. specifies the principles in which the example is to be held (Ellicott). ◆ **14 φύλαξον** aor. imp. act. φυλάσσω (# 5875) to guard (s.v. 12). **ἐνοικοῦντος** pres. act. part. ἐνοικέω (# 1940) to dwell in. ◆ **15 οἶδας** perf. ind. act. 2nd. pers. sing. οἶδα (# 3857) to know. Def. perf. w. pres. meaning (VA, 281-87). **ἀπεστράφησαν** aor. ind. pass. (dep.) ἀποστρέφω (# 695) to turn away from, to desert. Vb. is a pass. deponent and has its obj. in the acc. (RG, 484f). ◆ **16 δώη** aor. opt. act. δίδωμι (# 1443) to give, to grant. Opt. expresses a wish or prayer. **ἔλεος** (# 1799) mercy (s.v. 2). **ἀνέψυξεν** aor. ind. act. ἀναψύχω (# 434) to cool again, to refresh. The idea is that the presence of his friend provided a special tonic (Guthrie; RWP). **ἅλυσις** (# 434) chain. For prisons and prison conditions in the ancient world s. RAC, 9:318-45; BAFCS, 3; CIC, 27-95. **ἐπαισχύνθη** aor. ind. pass. ἐπαισχύνομαι (# 2049) s.v. 12. ◆ **17 γενόμενος** aor. mid. (dep.) part. γίνομαι (# 1181) to become, to be, to arrive. Temp. part., "when he arrived and was there" (Ellicott). Aor. points to a specific action. **σπουδαίως** (# 5081) adv., diligently, eagerly. **ἐζήτησεν** aor. ind. act. ζητέω (# 2426) to seek; effective aor. (RWP). **εὗρεν** aor. ind. act. εὑρίσκω (# 2351) to find. ◆ **18 δώη** aor. opt. act. δίδωμι (# 1443) to give (s.v. 16). **εὑρεῖν** aor. act. inf. εὑρίσκω (# 2351) to find. Compl. inf. to the main vb.: "May God give to find." **ὅσος** (# 4012) as many as, which one, those belonging to this class or group. **διηκόνησεν** aor. ind. act. διακονέω (# 1354) to minister, to serve. **βέλτιον** (# 1019) adv. comp. ἀγαθός good. The word can be taken as a true comp., "better than I" (RG, 165), or it can mean "well" (BAGD; BD, 127).

2 Timothy 2

◆ **1 ἐνδυναμοῦ** pres. imp. pass. ἐνδυναμόω (# 1904) to empower; pass. to be strong. **ἐν** (# 1877) in. Prep. is probably instr., "by means of" or "in the power of" (Kelly). ◆ **2 ἤκουσας** aor. ind. act. ἀκούω (# 201) to hear. **παράθου** aor. imp. mid. (dep.) παρατίθημι (# 4192) to place to another's trust, to entrust, to deposit, to commit for safe keeping (MM). **ἱκανός** (# 2653) that which reaches or arrives at a certain standard, sufficient, capable (GEW 1:719f; TDNT; LS). **ἔσονται** fut. ind. mid. (dep.) εἰμί (# 1639) to be. **διδάξαι** aor. act. inf. διδάσκω (# 1438) to teach. Compl. inf. to the adj. **ἱκανοί**.

Here w. the inf., "capable to teach." ◆ **3 συγκακοπάθη-σον** aor. imp. act. συγκακοπαθέω (# *5155*) to suffer evil together, to endure affliction together, to take one's share of rough treatment (Kelly). **στρατιώτης** (# *5132*) soldier. The Roman soldier–always ready to faithfully obey his commander without grumbling and complaining; constantly in training whatever hardships must be endured; fighting bravely, never leaving his post even if it meant death; working with his company as a unit, carrying out his specific task-was the one who received the praise from his commander and was rewarded for his service. He was a good soldier! (TJ, 114; also DPL, 952-53). ◆ **4 στρατευόμενος** pres. mid. (dep.) part. στρατεύομαι (# *5129*) to be a soldier. For a description of the life, training, and discipline of Roman soldiers s. Jos. *JW*, 3:70-109; TJ, 101-14. This emphasizes the total commitment required of a follower (BBC). **ἐμπλέκεται** pres. ind. mid. ἐμπλέκω (# *1861*) to entangle; mid., to entangle oneself. Lit. of sheep; fig. of worldly pursuits (BAGD). The word pictures a soldier's weapon entrammelled in his cloak (Guthrie). **πραγματεία** (# *4548*) affair, pursuit. The soldier does not let himself get involved in the preoccupations of civil life (Kelly). As applied to ministers this command requires wholehearted devotion to their work (Lock). **στρατολογήσαντι** aor. act. part. (subst.) στρατολογέω (# *5133*) to enlist soldiers. Aor. expresses logically antecedent action. It was the general's duty to see that his soldiers were well equipped and provided w. food and shelter (DC, 3:67f). **ἀρέσῃ** aor. subj. act. ἀρέσκω (# *743*) to please. The Christian soldier has only one goal and purpose–wholehearted devotion to the given task, the effort to please his Lord (PAM, 169). Subj. w. ἵνα (# *2671*) used in a purp. cl. ◆ **5 ἀθλῇ** pres. subj. act. ἀθλέω (# *123*) to compete in a contest. Subj. in a 3rd. class cond. cl. which assumes the possibility or probability of the cond. **στεφανοῦται** pres. ind. pass. στεφανόω (# *5110*) to crown one w. a victor's crown. **νομίμως** (# *3789*) adv., lawfully. The athlete's adherence to the laws of the contest was mandatory; he was not allowed to lighten his struggle by bypassing the rules. When applied to Timothy this meant that he as an athlete of Christ must also be prepared to suffer. The word also suggests the rejection of the heretics who do not contend lawfully (PAM, 170f). The training period could last 10 months out of a year (BBC). **ἀθλήσῃ** aor. subj. act. ἀθλέω (# *123*) to compete in a contest. Subj. in a 3rd. clas cond. cl. ◆ **6 κοπιῶντα** pres. act. part. κοπιάω (# *3159*) to work, to work until one is exhausted. Adj. use of the part.: hard-working farmer, farmer who is exhausted from his work. **γεωργός** (# *1177*) farmer. **δεῖ** (# *1256*) pres. ind. act. it is necessary to, impers. vb. w. the acc. and inf. giving a logical necessity. **μεταλαμβά-νειν** pres. act. inf. μεταλαμβάνω (# *3561*) to partake, to share. Compl. inf. to the preceding impers. vb. ◆ **7 νόει**

pres. imp. act. νοέω (# *3783*) to understand, to think over, to consider; i.e., "work out what I am getting at" (Kelly). **δώσει** fut. ind. act. δίδωμι (# *1443*) to give. **σύνε-σις** (# *5304*) insight, understanding. ◆ **8 μνημόνευε** pres. imp. act. μνημονεύω (# *3648*) to remember, to call to memory. **ἐγηγερμένον** perf. pass. part. ἐγείρω (# *1586*) to rise; pass., to be raised. Perf. points to the continual state; i.e., he was raised and continues to live. Timothy was to remember not just the mere fact of the Resurrection, but was to keep Christ in mind as a living, risen Lord who is able to give His life to the believer (Lock). ◆ **9 κακοπαθῶ** pres. ind. act. κακοπαθέω (# *2802*) to suffer trouble. Pres. emphasizes that which is continually taking place. **δεσμός** (# *1301*) bond. **κακοῦργος** (# *2806*) evil worker, criminal. The word is used for the criminals who were crucified alongside Jesus (Luke 23:32f), and in technical legal parlance it was reserved for burglars, murderers, traitors, and the like (Kelly; TLNT; Spicq). **δέδεται** perf. ind. pass. δέω (# *1313*) to bind. Perf. emphasizes that the Word of God is not bound, i.e., has not been and is not now bound (Ellicott). ◆ **10 ὑπομένω** (# *5702*) pres. ind. act. to remain under, to endure, to endure patiently (s. 1 Thess. 1:3). Pres. indicates a habit of life. **ἐκλεκτός** (# *1723*) elect, chosen. **τύχωσιν** aor. subj. act. τυγχάνω (# *5593*) to reach, to obtain, followed by the gen. Subj. w. ἵνα (# *2671*) to express purp. ◆ **11 πιστός** (# *4412*) faithful, trustworthy. **συναπεθάνομεν** aor. ind. act. συναποθνήσκω (# *5271*) to die together. Ind. is used in a 1st. class cond. cl. which assumes the cond. as a reality. **συζήσομεν** fut. ind. act. συζάω (# *5182*) to live together, to live w. someone. ◆ **12 συμβασιλεύσομεν** fut. ind. act. συμβασιλεύω (# *5203*) to be king together, to rule w. someone. **ἀρνη-σόμεθα** fut. ind. mid. (dep.) ἀρνέομαι (# *766*) to deny. Redundant mid. (GGBB, 419). ◆ **13 ἀπιστοῦμεν** pres. ind. act. ἀπιστέω (# *601*) to be unfaithful, to be untrustworthy. For the alpha prefix s. Moorhouse, 47ff. **μένει** pres. ind. act. μένω (# *3531*) to remain. **ἀρνήσασθαι** aor. mid. (dep.) inf. (# *766*) (s.v. 12). ◆ **14 ὑπομίμνησκε** pres. imp. act. ὑπομιμνῄσκω (# *5703*) to call to remembrance, to remind someone of something. **διαμαρτυρόμενος** pres. mid. (dep.) part. διαμαρτύρομαι (# *1371*) to solemnly charge someone (s. 1 Tim. 5:21). **λογομαχεῖν** pres. act. inf. λογομαχέω (# *3362*) to wage a word war. To argue or quarrel about the meaning or use of words (LN, 1:440). Inf. is used to give the content of the charge. Pres. w. the neg. could indicate the stopping of an action in progress or it could prohibit the carrying on of such an action. **χρήσιμος** (# *5978*) useful. **κατα-στροφή** (# *2953*) dat. sing. turning against, overturning, subverting, demoralizing (Kelly). **ἀκουόντων** pres. act. part. ἀκούω (# *201*) to hear. Subst. part. is an obj. gen. ◆ **15 σπούδασον** aor. imp. act. σπουδάζω (# *5079*) to give diligence. The word contains the notion of persistent zeal (Guthrie). **δόκιμος** (# *1511*) approved after examination or testing (TDNT; BS, 259-62; TLNT; MM; Preisigke). παραστῆσαι aor. act. inf. παρίστημι (# 4225) to stand alongside of, to present. Compl. inf. to the main vb.: "be diligent to present." ἐργάτης (# 2239) worker. ἀνεπαίσχυντος (# 454) not being ashamed, having no occasion to be ashamed of (Fairbairn). ὀρθοτομοῦντα pres. act. part. ὀρθοτομέω (# 3982) to cut along a straight line, to cut a straight road, to handle correctly (TLNT). The metaphor could be that of plowing a straight furrow, or of a road foreman making his road straight, or of a mason squaring and cutting a stone to fit in its proper place, or the cutting of a sacrifice or household food (Lock; EGT; Kelly; Spicq; MM). Part. of manner. ◆ **16** βέβηλος (# 1013) available for everyone, profane (s. 1 Tim. 4:7). κενοφωνία (# 3032) empty or vain talking. In the ancient world useless talking was believed to be caused by a sickness of the soul that demonstrated itself either in the quantity or quality of speech (RAC, 10:829-37). περιΐστασο pres. imp. act. περιΐστημι (# 4325) to shift around, to avoid, to shun (MH, 231). ἐπὶ πλεῖον (# 2093; 4498) far the more; i.e., they will arrive at an ever greater measure of, become more and more deeply involved in, godlessness (BAGD). προκόψουσιν fut. ind. act. προκόπτω (# 4621) to set before, to advance, to make progress (s. Gal. 1:14). ἀσέβεια (# 813) godlessness (TDNT). ◆ **17** γάγγραινα (# 1121) gangrene, cancer, spreading ulcer. It is a disease by which any part of the body suffering from inflammation becomes so corrupted that unless a remedy be seasonably applied the evil continually spreads, attacks other parts, and at last eats away at the bones (T). The metaphor illustrates insidiousness. Nothing could more suitably describe the manner of advancement of most false teachings, whether ancient or modern (Guthrie). νομή (# 3786) pasture, grazing, feeding. It is used of a spreading sore (AS). ἕξει fut. ind. act. ἔχω (# 2400) to have. It will spread further into the church and corrupt others (Lock). Ὑμέναιος καὶ Φίλητος Hymenaeus and Philetus. They may have been ringleaders of the trouble in Ephesus (Lea and Griffin; ABD, 3:348-49). ◆ **18** ἠστόχησαν aor. ind. act. ἀστοχέω (# 846) to miss the mark, to go astray (s. 1 Tim. 1:6). λέγοντες pres. act. part. (modal) λέγω (# 3306) to say, to claim. γεγονέναι perf. act. inf. γίνομαι (# 1181) to become. Inf. used in indir. discourse. ἀνάστασις (# 414) resurrection. ἀνατρέπουσιν pres. ind. act. ἀνατρέπω (# 426) to over turn, to upset, to break down, to ruin (MM). ◆ **19** μέντοι (# 3530) however. The particle gives a strong adversative sense (RWP; Blomqvist, 27). στερεός (# 5104) solid, hard, firm, steadfast, strong (BAGD). θεμέλιος (# 2529) foundation. ἕστηκεν perf. ind. act. ἵστημι (# 2705) to stand; perf., to remain standing. ἔχων pres. act. part. ἔχω (# 2400) to have. Causal part., "because it has." σφραγίς (# 5382) seal. The allusion is to the practice of placing on a building, or its foundation stone, an

inscription or other sign to indicate its owner's purpose (Kelly). ἔγνω aor. ind. act. γινώσκω (# 1182) to know (ND, 344ff). ὄντας pres. act. part. εἰμί (# 1639) to be. ἀποστήτω aor. imp. act. 3rd. pers. sing. ἀφίστημι (# 923) to depart, to leave; "let everyone stand off from" (RWP). Aor. calls for a definite break. ἀδικία (# 94) unrighteousness. ὀνομάζων pres. act. part. ὀνομάζω (# 3951) to name. ◆ **20** σκεύη pl. σκεῦος (# 5007) vessel. In a household there were various kinds of vessels, some for cooking, some for water or wine, some for lamps, but all had a specific use (s. Erika Brödner, *Wohnen in der Antike* [Darmstadt: Wissenschaftliche Buchgesellschaft, 1989], 87-92; DPL, 966-67). χρυσοῦς (# 5997) golden. ἀργυροῦς (# 739) silver. ξύλινος (# 3832) wooden. The suf. of the adj. signifies material (MH, 359, 378). ὀστράκινος (# 4017) made out of clay, earthenware, pottery. ἀτιμία (# 871) dishonor. ◆ **21** ἐκκαθάρῃ aor. subj. act. ἐκκαθαίρω (# 1705) to clean out, to cleanse completely. Subj. in a cond. cl. w. ἐάν (# 1569). The purging out relates either to the false teachers or to inward purification (Guthrie). ἔσται fut. ind. mid. (dep.) εἰμί (# 1639) to be. ἡγιασμένον perf. pass. part. ἁγιάζω (# 39) to separate, to sanctify, to set apart for holy use (TDNT; NIDNTT). Perf. looks at the completed state or condition. εὔχρηστος (# 2378) for good use, useful. δεσπότης (# 1305) master, ruler, lord. The term denotes absolute ownership and uncontrolled power. ἡτοιμασμένον perf. pass. part. ἑτοιμάζω (# 2286) to prepare. ◆ **22** νεωτερικός (# 3754) youthful, that which pertains to youth. For the suffix s. MH, 378. ἐπιθυμία (# 2123) strong desire, passion. φεῦγε pres. imp. act. φεύγω (# 5771) to flee. Pres. imp. could have an iterative force; it calls for a continuous action which indicates a habit of life. δίωκε pres. imp. act. διώκω (# 1503) to pursue. εἰρήνη (# 1645) peace. ἐπικαλουμένων pres. mid. part. ἐπικαλέω (# 2126) to call upon. ◆ **23** μωρός (# 3704) foolish, stupid. ἀπαίδευτος (# 553) without discipline, without training, uninstructed, uneducated (BAGD). ζήτησις (# 2428) questioning, speculation. παραιτοῦ pres. imp. mid. (dep.) παραιτέομαι (# 4148) to refuse, to reject. εἰδώς perf. act. part. (causal) οἶδα (# 3857) to know. Def. perf. w. pres. meaning; "because you know that...." γεννῶσιν pres. ind. act. γεννάω (# 1164) to give birth to, to produce. Pres. points to that which happens continually. μάχας acc. pl. (# 3480) fight, strife. ◆ **24** δεῖ (# 1256) pres. ind. act. it is necessary, w. a following inf. μάχεσθαι pres. mid. (dep.) inf. μάχομαι (# 3481) to fight. Compl. inf. to the preceding impers. vb. The word was generally used of armed combatants, or those who engage in hand-to-hand struggle. It was then used of those who engage in a war of words; i.e., to quarrel, to wrangle, to dispute (T). ἤπιος (# 2473) gentle. εἶναι pres. act. inf. εἰμί (# 1639) to be. This inf. is parallel to the first one. διδακτικός (# 1434) skillful in teaching (s. 1 Tim. 3:2). ἀνεξίκακος

(# 452) bearing up evil, ready to put up w. evil, patient of wrong. The word denotes an attitude of patient forbearance toward those who are in opposition (Guthrie; Kelly; Ellicott; RWP). ◆ **25 πραΰτης** (# 1877) meekness, gentle, submissiveness. It denotes the humble and gentle attitude which expresses itself, in particular, in a patient submissiveness to offense, a freedom from malice and desire for revenge (s. 2 Cor. 10:1). **παιδεύοντα** pres. act. part. παιδεύω (# 4084) to train, to train by discipline, to instruct. **ἀντιδιατιθεμένους** pres. mid. (dep.) part. (subst.) ἀντιδιατίθημι (# 507) to place oneself in opposition, to oppose (MH, 297). **μήποτε** (# 3607) if perhaps, in the hope that (Ellicott; BD, 188). **δῴη** aor. opt. act. δίδωμι (# 1443) to give. The problematic construction may mean "it may be that he will give" (IBG, 15; MT, 129; BD, 118; RWP). **μετάνοια** (# 3567) a change of mind or attitude, repentance (Kelly; TDNT; NIDNTT). **ἐπίγνωσις** (# 2106) recognition, acknowledgment, knowledge. ◆ **26 ἀνανήψωσιν** aor. subj. act. ἀνανήψω (# 392) to sober up, to return to sobriety, to return to one's senses. The metaphor implies some previous duping by evil influences, as in the case of intoxication; the devil's method is to numb the conscience, confuse the senses and paralyze the will (Guthrie; Kelly). **παγίς** (# 4075) snare, trap. **ἐζωγρημένοι** perf. pass. part. ζωγρέω (# 2436) to capture alive, to make captive (Lea and Griffin).

2 Timothy 3

◆ **1 γίνωσκε** pres. imp. act. γινώσκω (# 1182) to know; to recognize (Lock). The pres. imp. is used in an idiomatic way (s. VANT, 352-53). **ἔσχατος** (# 2274) last. **ἐνστήσονται** fut. ind. mid. (dep.) ἐνίστημι (# 1931) to stand on, to be at hand, to set in (RWP; Ellicott). **καιρός** (# 2789) period of time, season, a particular time. **χαλεπός** (# 5901) difficult, dangerous. The demon-possessed of Gadara were dangerous (Matt. 8:28); Herod the Great resisted the seduction attempts of Cleopatra, knowing how vicious (χαλεπήν) she was to everyone (Jos., Ant., 15:98; CCFJ, 4:343-45; TLNT; Spicq). The reference is not merely to the outward dangers, but the evils that mark them (Ellicott). For the Jewish teachings and description of the difficulties of the last times s. SB, 4:977-1015; b. Sanh. 97a. ◆ **2 ἔσονται** fut. ind. mid. (dep.) εἰμί (# 1639) to be. **φίλαυτος** (# 5796) lover of oneself, self-loving. This was a trait rejected by Stoics and others (BBC). **φιλάργυρος** (# 5795) money-loving. **ἀλαζών** (# 225) bragger, boaster. It is one who brags and boasts about his accomplishments and in his boasting overpasses the limits of truth, stressing the fact to magnify himself in his attempt to impress others (MNTW, 38-42; Trench, Synonyms, 98-102; TDNT; TLNT; Spicq). **ὑπερήφανος** (# 5662) haughty, arrogant, one who shows himself above his fellow (Trench, Synonyms, 101f; TDNT). **βλάσφημος** (# 1061) abusive

speech, slanderer. **γονεῦσιν** (# 1204) parents. **ἀπειθής** (# 579) disobedient. **ἀχάριστος** (# 940) not thankful, ungrateful. **ἀνόσιος** (# 495) unholy, wicked (s. 1 Tim. 1:9). ◆ **3 ἄστοργος** (# 845) unloving, without family affection, without love of kindred, destitute of love toward those whom nature itself loves. The vb. without the neg. pref. denotes primarily and properly the love between parents and children (Ellicott; AS). **ἄσπονδος** (# 836) without a truce. It denotes a hostility that allows no truce (Guthrie). The word denotes a man who cannot bring himself to come to terms w. other people (Kelly; Trench, Synonyms, 193f). **διάβολος** (# 1333) slanderous (s. 1 Tim. 3:11). Those who promote quarrels in hope that they may gain from them (Lock). **ἀκρατής** (# 203) without power, without self-control, w. respect to tongue, appetite, and everything else. **ἀνήμερος** (# 466) not tamed, uncivilized fear, savage. **ἀφιλάγαθος** (# 920) without laws for good, haters of good. ◆ **4 προδότης** (# 4595) traitor, betrayer. The word was used of one who is a traitor to his oath or one who abandons another in danger (LS; MH, 323). **προπετής** (# 4637) one who falls before or ahead, hasty, reckless, one who is ready to precipitate matters by hasty speech or action (Fairbairn; Lock). It indicates lack of control or quickness, whether good or bad; and with respect to action it refers to those who are impulsive, who get carried away (hotheads!) like a bolting horse; people who make themselves known by their violence, who wreck everything, who take wild chances (TLNT). **τετυφωμένοι** perf. pass. part. τυφόω (# 5605) to fill with smoke, to be conceited (s. 1 Tim. 6:4; BAGD; MM). **φιλήδονος** (# 5798) pleasure-lover. **μᾶλλον** (# 3437) rather. **φιλόθεος** (# 5806) God-lover. ◆ **5 ἔχοντες** pres. act. part. ἔχω (# 2400) to have. **μόρφωσις** (# 3673) shaping, bringing into shape, embodiment, outline, outward form, resemblance (Phil. 2:6; LS; BAGD; TDNT; EDNT). **εὐσέβεια** (# 2354) reverence of God, godliness (s. 1 Tim. 2:2). **ἠρνημένοι** perf. mid. (dep.) part. ἀρνέομαι (# 766) to deny. The word involves always more than an act of the mind; it means putting into practice (EGT). **καί** (# 2779) and; the word here seems to retain its proper force by specifying those in particular who were to be avoided (Ellicott). **ἀποτρέπου** pres. imp. mid. ἀποτρέπω (# 706) to turn from, to turn oneself away from. The vb. is a strong one, implying that Timothy is to avoid them w. horror (Kelly). Pres. imp. indicates that this should be a continual habit of life. ◆ **6 ἐνδύνοντες** pres. act. part. ἐνδύνω (# 1905) to enter in, to creep in, to run one's way in. The word implies insidious methods (Guthrie). **αἰχμαλωτίζοντες** pres. act. part. αἰχμαλωτίζω (# 170) to take captive at spear point, to make a prisoner of war, to capture. The word here denotes getting complete possession of (Huther). **γυναικάριον** (# 1220) little woman, silly or idle woman. Perhaps since women in that culture were often uneducated, they were easy prey for false teachers (BBC). The word is a diminutive and expresses contempt (Fairbairn). σεσωρευμένα perf. pass. part. σωρεύω (# 5397) to heap or pile up, to overwhelm. Perf. emphasizes the continual state or condition. ἀγόμενα pres. pass. part. ἄγω (# 72) to lead, to drive. ἐπιθυμία (# 2123) strong desire, lust. Here, instr. dat. used w. the pass. ποικίλος (# 4476) many-colored, variegated, various, diversified. ◆ 7 πάντοτε (# 4121) always. μανθάνοντα pres. act. part. (adj.) acc. n. pl. μανθάνω (# 3443) to learn through instruction (BAGD). Part. in n. pl. refers to the women of v. 6, who apparently desired to listen to other people's advice, but their minds had become so fickle and warped that they had become incapable of obtaining the knowledge of the truth (Guthrie). Pres. points to their continual habit. μηδέποτε (# 3595) never. ἐπίγνωσις (# 2262) recognition, knowledge (s. Col. 1:9). ἐλθεῖν aor. act. inf. ἔρχομαι (# 2106) to go. Compl. inf. to the following part. δυνάμενα pres. mid. (dep.) part. (adj.) δύναμαι (# 1538) to be able to. The adj. part. without art. stresses the character. ◆ 8 τρόπος (# 5573) manner; adverbial acc.: in which manner (RWP). Ἰάννης καὶ Ἰαμβρῆς For Jewish references concerning Jannes and Jambres s. SB, 3:660-64; CD 5:18; ABD, 3:638-40; ZPEB, 3:403-5. ἀντέστησαν aor. ind. act. ἀνθίστημι (# 468) to stand against, to withstand, to oppose. οὕτως (# 4048) so. It refers rather to the degree of their hostility than to the manner in which it was expressed (EGT). κατεφθαρμένοι perf. pass. part. καταφθείρω (# 2967) to corrupt, to corrupt completely, to ruin; pass., to be perverted, to be depraved (BAGD; for examples in the papyri, s. MM). νοῦς (# 3808) mind, understanding. ἀδόκιμος (# 99) rejected after trial, disqualified (s. 1 Cor. 9:27). πίστις (# 4411) faith. W. the art. the word may refer to the body of Christian teaching and indicate that these had examined the faith and rejected its teaching. ◆ 9 προκόψουσιν fut ind. act. προκόπτω (# 4621) to cut before, to make progress, to advance (s. 2:16). ἐπὶ πλεῖον (# 2093; 4498) "farther, very far" (Lock). ἄνοια (# 486) without understanding, foolishness, faithlessness. ἔκδηλος (# 1684) clear, evident, very clear. Prep. in compound is perfective (MH, 311). ἔσται fut. ind. mid. (dep.) εἰμί (# 1639) to be. ἐγένετο aor. ind. mid. (dep.) γίνομαι (# 1181) to become. ◆ 10 παρηκολούθησας aor. ind. act. παρακολουθέω (# 4158) to follow along, to follow closely, to accompany, w. dat. The word is also a t.t. defining the relation of a disciple to his master–study at close quarter, follow in spirit, carefully note w. a view to reproducing, and so "take as an example" (Kelly; TDNT; EDNT). διδασκαλία (# 1436) teaching, doctrine. Here dat. w. the vb. παρηκολούθησας. ἀγωγῇ (# 73) manner of life, the way one leads his life. The word denotes general behavior, which a man's closest associate can never fail to know in all its aspects (Guthrie). πρόθεσις (# 4606) purpose; i.e., the guiding motive

of his life and work (Kelly). μακροθυμία (# 3429) longsuffering, patient endurance (s. Gal. 5:22; Rom. 2:4). ὑπομονή (# 5705) bearing under, patience, patient and hopeful endurance (2 Thess. 1:4; RAC, 9:243-94; TLNT). ◆ 11 διωγμός (# 1501) persecution. πάθημα (# 4077) that which is suffered, suffering. οἷα pl. n. οἷος (# 3888) which kind, which sort of. ἐγένετο aor. ind. mid. (dep.) γίνομαι (# 1181) to become, to be. ὑπήνεγκα aor. ind. act. ὑποστρέφω (# 5722) to bear by being under, to carry or be under a heavy load, to hold out, to endure. (For examples s. LS.) ἐρρύσατο aor. ind. mid. (dep.) ῥύομαι (# 4861) to rescue. ◆ 12 καί...δέ (# 2779; 1254) but even, yea (Ellicott). θέλοντες pres. act. part. θέλω (# 2527) to desire, to want to, to wish, w. inf. ζῆν pres. act. inf. ζάω (# 2409) to live. Compl. inf. to the preceding part. εὐσεβῶς (# 2357) adv. godly, godfearingly. It denotes living in the right attitude to God and things divine. It can sometimes have the meaning of loyalty or true religion (MNTW, 66-76; s. 1 Tim. 2:2). διωχθήσονται fut. ind. pass. διώκω (# 1503) to hunt, to follow after, to persecute. ◆ 13 γόητες nom. pl. γόης (# 1200) sorcerer, juggler; here more in the sense of swindler; to give incantations by howling, one who practices magic art, sorcerer, cheat (Ellicott; MM; BAGD; TDNT; Spicq; DPL, 580-83). Josephus uses the word to describe Theudas, who during the time of Fadus persuaded a large number of Jews to sell their possessions and follow him in rebellion against Rome (Jos., Ant. 20:97; for other examples of the word in Jos. s. CCFJ, 1:390). προκόψουσιν fut. ind. act. προκόπτω to advance. χεῖρον acc. χείρων (# 5937) worse. πλανῶντες pres. act. part. πλανάω (# 4414) to lead astray, to deceive. πλανώμενοι pres. pass. part. πλανάω (# 4414) to lead astray, to deceive. Adj. part. or part. of means explaining how they make their advancement. ◆ 14 μένε pres. imp. act. μένω (# 3531) to remain. Pres. imp. calls a constant and continual habit of life. ἔμαθες aor. ind. act. μανθάνω (# 3443) to learn. ἐπιστώθης aor. ind. pass. πιστεύω (# 4413) to make reliable; pass., to be assured of, to be convinced of (RWP). εἰδώς perf. act. part. οἶδα (# 3857) to know (ND, 344ff; VA, 281-87). Def. perf. w. pres. meaning. ◆ 15 ὅτι (# 4022) that; it introduces the obj. of the vb. οἶδας and presents a second fact which Timothy was to take into consideration (Ellicott). βρέφος (# 1100) child. The Jewish parents' duty was to teach children in their fifth year the Law (Lock; M, Aboth 5:21; SB, 3:664-66). ἱερά acc. pl. ἱερός (# 2641) sacred. The term τὰ ἱερὰ γράμματα is the name for the Holy Scriptures of OT used among Greek-speaking Jews (Dibelius; but s. also Guthrie; Lock). δυνάμενα pres. pass. part. δύναμαι (# 1538) to be able, w. inf. ("which are able to"). Adj. part. used as a subst. σοφίσαι aor. act. inf. σοφίζω (# 5054) to impart wisdom, to make wise. Compl. inf. to the preceding part. ◆ 16 γραφή (# 1210) writing, Scripture (TDNT; Schlatter; Guthrie;

Lea and Griffin). **θεόπνευστος** (# 2535) God-breathed, breathed into by God, inspired. The rabbinical teaching was that the Spirit of God rested on and in the prophets and spoke through them, so that their words did not come from themselves but from the mouth of God; they spoke and wrote in the Holy Spirit (Lea and Griffin). The early church was in entire agreement with this view (Kelly; SB, 4:435-51; ZPEB, 2:286-93; TDNT; Schlatter; Gerhard Delling, "Die biblische Prophetie bei Josephus," JS, 109-21; TLNT). Pred. adj. without the art. indicating the character: "every Scripture is inspired and profitable" (GGBB, 313-14; Daniel B. Wallace, "The Relation of Adjective to Noun in Anarthrous Constructions in the New Testament," *NovT* 26 [1984]: 128-67). **ὠφέλιμος** (# 6068) profitable. **ἐλεγμός** (# 1791) proving, convicting, reproof; i.e., for refuting error and rebuking sin (Kelly; Lock). **ἐπανόρθωσις** (# 2061) setting up straight in addition, setting right, correction. It is the setting upright on their feet (Lock; for examples in the papyri s. MM; Preisigke). **παιδεία** (# 4082) training, instruction, discipline. ◆ **17 ἄρτιος** (# 787) fit, complete, capable, sufficient; i.e., able to meet all demands (BAGD). **ἦ** pres. subj. act. εἰμί (# 1639) to be. Subj. w. **ἵνα** (# 2671) to express purp. **ἐξηρτισμένος** perf. pass. part. ἐξαρτίζω (# 1192) to completely outfit, fully furnish, fully equip or supply. The word was used of documents–or of a wagon or rescue boat–which were completely outfitted, or of a machine sold in good condition; i.e., capable of performing the service expected of it (MM; Preisigke; LS; TLNT). Prep. in compound is effective (MH, 308ff).

2 Timothy 4

◆ **1 διαμαρτύρομαι** pres. ind. mid. (dep.) (# 1371) to solemnly charge (s. 1 Tim 5:21). **μέλλοντος** pres. act. part. μέλλω (# 3516) to be about to. The word was used w. the inf. to express a durative fut. (MKG, 307). **κρίνειν** pres. act. inf. κρίνω (# 3212) to judge. Compl. inf. to the preceding part. **ζῶντας** pres. act. part. (subst.) ζάω (# 2409) to live. **ἐπιφάνεια** (# 2211) appearance, manifestation. The word was used in reference to the appearance of a god (s. 1 Tim. 6:14). ◆ **2 κήρυξον** aor. imp. act. κηρύσσω (# 3062) to proclaim as a herald, to preach (s. 1 Tim. 2:7). Not "begin to preach," but "preach as your first priority" (GGBB, 721). **ἐπίστηθι** aor. imp. pass. ἐφίστημι (# 2392) to take one's stand, to stand by, to be at hand. The word was also used in a military sense–to stay at one's post–but here it means to be at one's task and indicates that the Christian minister must always be on duty (Kelly; Guthrie). **εὐκαίρως** (# 2323) adv., well-timed, suitably, conveniently; i.e., when it is convenient (BAGD). **ἀκαίρως** (# 178) not well-timed, inconveniently; i.e., when it is inconvenient (BAGD). **ἔλεγξον** aor. imp. act. ἐλέγχω (# 1794) to prove w. demonstrative evidence, to convict, to reprove. It is so to rebuke another, w. such effectual feel-

ing of the victorious arms of the truth, as to bring one if not always to a confession, yet at least to a conviction of sin (Trench, *Synonyms*, 13; TDNT; EDNT). **ἐπιτίμησον** aor. imp. act. ἐπιτιμάω (# 2203) to rebuke. The word denotes in the NT usage the idea of censure and sharp rebuke (Guthrie; Trench, *Synonyms*, 13; TDNT). **παρακάλεσον** aor. imp. act. παρακαλέω (# 4151) to urge, to encourage, to exhort, to admonish (s. Rom. 12:1). **μακροθυμία** (# 3429) longsuffering, patient endurance (s. 2 Tim. 3:10). ◆ **3 ἔσται** fut. ind. mid. (dep.) εἰμί (# 1639) to be. **καιρός** (# 2789) season, period of time. **ὑγιαινούσης** pres. act. part. ὑγιαίνω (# 5617) to be well, to be in good health, to be sound. **διδασκαλία** (# 1436) teaching, doctrine. **ἀνέξονται** fut. ind. mid. (dep.) ἀνέχω (# 462) to bear up, to endure, to put up w. **ἐπιθυμία** (# 2123) strong desire, lust. **ἐπισωρεύσουσιν** fut. ind. act. ἐπισωρεύω (# 2197) to pile upon, to heap upon. **κνηθόμενοι** pres. mid. part. κνήθομαι (# 3117) to tickle, to scratch, to itch; pass., to feel an itching. It is used fig. of curiosity that looks for interesting and spicy bits of information. This itching is relieved by the message of the new teachers (BAGD; MM). **ἀκοή** (# 198) hearing, ear. Here, acc. of general reference: being tickled in reference to the hearing (Kelly). ◆ **4 ἀποστρέψουσιν** fut. ind. act. ἀποστρέφω (# 695) to turn away from. **μῦθος** (# 3680) myth (s. 1 Tim. 1:4). **ἐκτραπήσονται** fut. ind. mid. ἐκτρέπω (# 1762) to turn away from, to turn aside from (s. 1 Tim. 1:6). ◆ **5 νῆφε** pres. imp. act. νήφω (# 3768) to be sober; i.e., to be in a vigilant, wakeful, considerate frame of mind, taking heed of what is happening and pursuing a course w. calm and steady aim (Fairbairn). **κακοπάθησον** aor. imp. act. κακοπαθέω (# 2802) to suffer evil, to suffer hardship (s. 2 Tim. 1:8). **ἔργον** (# 2240) work, activity. **ποίησον** aor. imp. act. ποιέω (# 4472) to do. Aor. imp. calls for a specific act w. a note of urgency. **εὐαγγελιστής** (# 2296) one who proclaims the good news, evangelist. The word was found on a non-Christian inscription w. the meaning, "a proclaimer of oracle" (TDNT). The word, however, occurs primarily of those who preach the gospel (TDNT; PGL; TLNT). **διακονία** (# 1355) ministry, service. **πληροφόρησον** aor. imp. act. πληροφορέω (# 4442) to carry full, to make full, to fulfill, to accomplish (LAE, 86f). Aor. imp. calls for a specific act w. a note of urgency. ◆ **6 σπένδομαι** pres. ind. pass. (# 5064) to offer, to pour out as a drink offering (Phil. 2:17; Kelly). Pres. points to an action in progress. **ἀναλύσεως** gen. ἀνάλυσις (# 385) lifting up, departure. The word is used as a euphemism for death and evokes the picture of a ship weighing anchor, or of a soldier or traveler striking camp (Kelly). Departure after a meaningful and fruitful life (BAGD). Gen. of description. **ἐφέστηκεν** perf. ind. act. ἐφίστημι (# 2392) to be present, to be at hand (s.v. 2). ◆ **7 ἀγών** (# 74) struggle, fight. **ἠγώνισμαι** perf. ind. mid. (dep.) ἀγωνίζομαι (# 76) to struggle, to exert effort (PAM, 182ff). Perf. conveys a sense of finality (Guthrie) w. the results extending to the present. **δρόμος** (# 1536) foot race, race (PAM, 183f). **τετέλεκα** perf. ind. act. τελέω (# 5464) to finish, to complete, to arrive at the goal. **τετήρηκα** perf. ind. act. τηρέω (# 5498) to keep. The expression means to remain faithful or true (PAM, 183). ◆ **8 λοιπόν** (# 3370) finally. Adv. acc. **ἀπόκειται** pres. ind. pass. ἀπόκειμαι (# 641) to be laid away (RWP). The word appeared not only in an athletic context, but was also used of the award made to loyal subjects by oriental sovereigns for services rendered (Guthrie; Dibelius; Kelly). This, however, is not the certainty of the man who now looks forward to a merited reward. It is rather the certainty of faith and hope (PAM, 184). **στέφανος** (# 5109) crown. **ἀποδώσει** fut. ind. act. ἀποδίδωμι (# 625) to give, to give back, to recompense. Prep. in compound does not necessarily convey any sense of due. Here the prep. only seems to allude to the reward having been laid up and being taken out of some reserve treasure (Ellicott). **κριτής** (# 3216) judge. **ἠγαπηκόσι** perf. act. part. ἀγαπάω (# 26) to love. ◆ **9 σπούδασον** aor. imp. act. σπουδάζω (# 5079) to make haste, to be zealous or eager, to give diligence, to do one's best (AS; Kelly; s. 2 Tim. 2:15). Aor. imp. calls for a specific act w. a note of urgency. **ἐλθεῖν** aor. act. inf. ἔρχομαι (# 2262) to go. Compl. inf. to the preceding vb.: "hurry to come." **ταχέως** (# 5441) adv., quickly. For help to those in prison s. B. M. Rapske, "The Importance of Helpers to the Imprisoned Paul in the Book of Acts," TB 42 (1991): 3-30; esp. 23-29. ◆ **10 ἐγκατέλιπεν** aor. ind. act. ἐγκαταλείπω (# 1593) to abandon, to desert, to leave one in the lurch, to forsake. **ἀγαπήσας** aor. act. part. ἀγαπάω (# 26) to love. **ἐπορεύθη** aor. ind. pass. (dep.) πορεύομαι (# 4513) to travel. ◆ **11 ἀναλαβών** aor. act. part. ἀναλαμβάνω (# 377) to take up, to pick up (RWP). Aor. describes a logically antecedent action to the following vb. Temp. part., "After picking up ...." **ἄγε** pres. imp. act. ἄγω (# 72) to lead, to take, to bring. **εὔχρηστος** (# 2378) useful, serviceable (Guthrie). ◆ **12 ἀπέστειλα** aor. ind. act. ἀποστέλλω (# 690) to send. ◆ **13 φαιλόνης** cloak. It was a large, sleeveless outer garment made of a single piece of heavy material w. a hole in the middle for the head. It was used for protection against cold and rain, particularly by travelers. It may have been that Paul needed it because winter was at hand and his dungeon was cold (Kelly; DGRA, 848; BAFCS, 3:199). **ἀπέλιπον** aor. ind. act. ἀπολείπω (# 657) to leave behind. **φέρε** pres. imp. act. φέρω (# 5770) to carry, to bring. **βιβλία** acc. pl. βιβλίον (# 1046) book. **μάλιστα** (# 3436) especially. **μεμβράνα** (# 3521) parchment, pergament. The word denotes a piece of skin or vellum prepared for writing purposes and was a t.t. for a codex or leaf book made of parchment (Kelly). Paul may have been referring to

OT Scriptures (Charles C. Ryrie, "Especially the Parchments," Bib Sac 117 [1960]: 246f). In a late Christian papyrus letter the writer sends parchments worth 14 talents of silver to a Christian brother as well as a tunic and cloak (Oxyrhynchus Papyri # 2156). ◆ **14 χαλκεύς** (# 5906) one who works w. copper; coppersmith, smith. The word does not mean that he only worked in copper. The term also came to be used of workers in any kind of metal (EGT). **ἐνεδείξατο** aor. ind. mid. (dep.) ἐνδείκνυμι (# 1892) to show, to demonstrate, to do something to someone. **ἀποδώσει** fut. ind. act. ἀποδίδωμι (# 625) to give back, to repay in kind. ◆ **15 φυλάσσου** pres. imp. mid. φυλάσσω (# 5875) to guard; mid., to guard oneself, to be on one's guard. **λίαν** (# 3336) greatly, violently. **ἀντέστη** aor. ind. act. ἀνθίστημι (# 468) to stand against, to oppose. ◆ **16 ἀπολογία** (# 665) legal defense. **παρεγένετο** aor. ind. mid. (dep.) παραγίνομαι (# 4134) to be alongside of, to stand by, to support. Aor. points to a specific act. The vb. is a t.t. for a witness or advocate standing forward in court on a prisoner's behalf (Kelly). **λογισθείη** aor. opt. pass. λογίζομαι (# 3357) to reckon, to place to one's account. Opt. used to express a wish. ◆ **17 παρέστη** aor. ind. act. παρίστημι (# 4225) to stand by one's side. **ἐνεδυνάμωσεν** aor. ind. act. ἐνδυναμόω (# 1904) to empower, to strengthen. **κήρυγμα** (# 3060) proclamation, that which is proclaimed or preached. **πληροφορηθῇ** aor. subj. pass. (# 4442) s.v. 5. Subj. w. ἵνα (# 2671) to express purp. or result. **ἀκούσωσιν** aor. subj. act. ἀκούω (# 201) to hear. **ἐρρύσθην** aor. ind. pass. ῥύομαι (# 4861) to rescue. **στόμα** (# 5125) mouth. **λέοντος** gen. sing. λέων (# 3329) lion. For a discussion of the problems involved in the words of Paul s. Guthrie. ◆ **18 ῥύσεται** fut. ind. mid. (dep.) ῥύομαι (# 4861) to save. **πονηρός** (# 4505) evil, active evil. **σώσει** fut. ind. act. σώζω (# 5392) to save, to rescue. **ἐπουράνιος** (# 2230) heavenly (s. Eph. 1:3). ◆ **19 ἄσπασαι** aor. imp. mid. (dep.) ἀσπάζομαι (# 832) to greet. ◆ **20 ἔμεινεν** aor. ind. act. μένω (# 3531) to remain. **ἀπέλιπον** aor. ind. act. (# 657) s.v. 13. **ἀσθενοῦντα** pres. act. part. ἀσθενέω (# 820) to be weak, to be sick. Pres. expresses contemporaneous activity to the main vb. Causal part., "because he was sick." ◆ **21 σπούδασον** aor. imp. act. (# 4704) s.v. 9. Aor. imp. calls for a specific act w. a note of urgency. **χειμών** (# 5930) winter. Shipping was completely closed down from November 10 to March 10. It was extremely hazardous from September 15 to November 10 and March 11 to May 26. The danger was due to the winter storms sweeping the Mediterranean. A delay by Timothy would cause him to have to wait until spring (BBC; ABD; SSAW, 270-96). **ἐλθεῖν** aor. act. inf. ἔρχομαι (# 2262) to come, to go. Compl. inf. to the governing vb.

Titus

Titus 1

◆ **1 κατά** (# *2848*) according to; i.e., "for (the furtherance of the faith of God's elect" (Ellicott). Faith could indicate reasonable faith in Christ, faithfulness, trustworthiness, or faith as a creed or body of truth held as the revelation of God. For **πίστις** (# *4411*) in the Pastoral Epistles s. Quinn, 271-76. **ἐκλεκτός** (# *1723*) chosen, elect. The concept occurs often in the DSS (1 Qp Hab 10:13; 4Q 171:1; 4Q 164; 1QH 14:15; Quinn). **ἐπίγνωσις** (# *2106*) recognition, knowledge (Quinn, 276-82; Col. 1:9). **εὐσέβεια** (# *2354*) godliness, reverence for God (Quinn, 282-90; 1 Tim. 2:2). ◆ **2 ἐπ'** = ἐπί (# *2093*) upon. The prep. suggests that such hope is the basis on which the superstructure of Christian service is built (Guthrie). **ἐπηγγείλατο** aor. ind. mid. (dep.) ἐπαγγέλλομαι (# *2040*) to promise. **ἀψευδής** (# *950*) not a liar, one who does not lie, without deceit, truthful (GELTS, 75; Quinn). It was used in the discussion of the Greek oracles as to whether the gods could lie (Quinn; NW, 2, ii:1012). For the negating pref. s. Moorhouse, 47ff. ◆ **3 ἐφανέρωσεν** aor. ind. act. φανερόω (# *5746*) to make clear, to manifest. **καιρός** (# *2789*) time, season of time, opportune time. **ἴδιος** (# *2625*) one's own. **κήρυγμα** (# *3060*) that which is proclaimed, proclamation. **ἐπιστεύθην** aor. ind. pass. πιστεύω (# *4409*) to believe, to trust; pass. to entrust (1 Tim. 1:11). **ἐπιταγή** (# *2198*) command (1 Tim. 1:1). ◆ **4 γνήσις** (# *1188*) legitimate, true. **κοινή** (# *3123*) common, that which all share in. ◆ **5 χάριν** (# *5921*) prep. w. gen.: because of, on account. **ἀπέλιπον** aor. ind. act. ἀπολείπω (# *657*) to leave behind. **λείποντα** pres. act. part. λείπω (# *3309*) to leave; Subst. part.; i.e., "the things remaining," "the things that are lacking." **ἐπιδιορθώσῃ** aor. subj. mid. ἐπιδιορθόω (# *2114*) to set straight thoroughly in addition to; to set in order. For the prep. in compound s. RWP; MH, 313. Subj. w. **ἵνα** (# *2671*) to express purp. **καταστήσῃς** aor. subj. act. καθίστημι (# *2770*) to appoint. **πρεσβυτέρους** (# *4565*) elder. For elders in the Pastorals and today s. Lea and Griffin, 159-62; TDNT; EDNT. **διεταξάμην** aor. ind. mid. (dep.) διατάσσω (# *1411*) to give orders to, to appoint, to arrange, to ordain. ◆ **6 ἀνέγκλητος** (# *441*) without indictment, unchangeable, above reproach. **ἔχων** pres. act. part. ἔχω (# *2400*) to have. **κατηγορία** (# *2990*) accusation. **ἀσωτία** (# *861*) inability to save, one who wastes his money often, w. the implication of wasting it on pleasures and so ruining himself;

luxurious living, extravagant squandering of means (Lock; Trench, *Synonyms*, 53f; TDNT; Eph. 5:18). **ἀνυπότακος** (# *538*) independent, unruly, insubordinate. ◆ **7 δεῖ** (# *1256*) pres. ind. act. it is necessary to, w. inf. giving a logical necessity. **ἐπίσκοπος** (# *2176*) overseer, bishop (1 Tim. 3:1, 2). **ἀνέγκλητος** (# *441*) blameless, irreproachable (BAGD; MM; 1 Tim. 3:10). **εἶναι** pres. act. inf. εἰμί (# *1639*) to be. Compl. inf. to the impersonal vb. δεῖ. **οἰκονόμος** (# *3874*) manager of household or family, steward. The word emphasizes the commitment of a task and its responsibility to someone. It is a metaphor drawn from contemporary life and pictures the manager of a household or estate (Guthrie; TDNT; HOG; 1 Cor. 4:1; Gal. 4:2). **αὐθάδης** (# *881*) self-willed, obstinate in one's own opinion, arrogant, refusing to listen to others. It is the man who obstinately maintains his own opinion or asserts his own rights and is reckless of the rights, feelings, and interests of others (Lock; Trench, *Synonyms*, 349f; MM; TDNT; TLNT). Theophrastus describes such a person as one who, when asked a question, answers, "Leave me alone!"; or when he is greeted, he expresses no thank you; or when he sells something, he does not give the price but says, "What do I get?"; or when he stumbles on the street, he curses the stones; he is not willing to wait for anyone and is even capable of not once praying to the gods (Theophrastus, *Characters*, 15:1-11; NW, 2, ii:1013-14). **ὀργίλος** (# *3975*) inclined to anger, quick-tempered (BAGD). Words w. this ending often denote habit or custom (Ellicott). **πάροινος** (# *4232*) given to drink, heavy drinker (Kelly; 1 Tim. 3:3). Dionysus' drunken worship was well known on Crete. A leader in the church should not be confused w. a worshiper of this pagan god (BBC). **πλήκτης** (# *4438*) one who strikes, fighter. The word could be quite literal: "not hasty to strike an opponent" (Lock; 1 Tim. 3:3). **αἰσχροκερδής** (# *153*) greedy of shameful gain; i.e., making money discreditable, adopting one's teaching to the hearers in hope of getting more from them; or perhaps it refers to engaging in discreditable trade (Lock; 1 Tim. 3:8). ◆ **8 φιλόξενος** (# *5811*) lover of strangers, hospitable (BBC: ABD, 3:299-301). **φιλάγαθος** (# *5787*) lover of that which is good. It denotes devotion to all that is best (Kelly). **ὅσιος** (# *4008*) devout, holy (1 Tim. 2:8). **σώφρονα** (# *5409*) holy, devout (1 Tim. 2:8). **ἐγκρατής** (# *1604*) control over oneself. It means complete self-mastery, controlling all passionate impulses and keeping the will loyal to the will of God (Lock, esp. 148; Gal. 5:23). ◆ **9** ἀντεχόμενον pres. mid. (dep.) part. ἀντέχω (# *504*) to hold on to, to hold fast. Prep. in compound appears to involve a faint idea of holding out against something hostile or opposing. This, however, passes into steadfast application (Ellicott). It could also mean to take an interest in, to pay attention to (BAGD; MM). πίστος (# *4412*) reliable, trustworthy (Guthrie). δυνατός (# *1543*) able. ἦ pres. subj. act. εἰμί (# *1639*) to be. Subj. w. ἵνα (# *2671*) in a purp. cl. παρακαλεῖν pres. act. inf. παρακαλέω (# *4151*) to exhort, to urge. Compl. inf. to preceding verbal adj. δυνατός, "to be able to exhort." (Rom. 12:1). διδασκαλία (# *1436*) teaching, doctrine. Here, instr. dat. ὑγιαινούσῃ pres. act. part. ὑγιαίνω (# *5617*) to be well, to be healthy, to be sound. ἀντιλέγοντας pres. act. part. ἀντιλέγω (# *515*) to speak against, to oppose, to object. Subst. part., "those who speak against." ἐλέγχειν pres. act. inf. ἐλέγχω (# *1794*) to convict, to reprove (2 Tim. 4:2). Compl. inf. parallel to the preceding inf. ◆ **10** εἰσίν pres. ind. act. εἰμί (# *1639*) to be. γάρ (# *1142*) "for" giving the reason for the necessary traits. ματαιολόγοι (# *3468*) worthless words, evil talkers; i.e., using impressive language w. little or no solid content of truth (Kelly; 2 Tim. 2:16). φρεναπάτης (# *5855*) deceiver of the mind, deceiver of thinking, deceiver, seducer. μάλιστα (# *3436*) especially. περιτομή (# *4364*) circumcision. ◆ **11** ἐπιστομίζειν pres. act. inf. ἐπιστομίζω (# *2187*) to put something on the mouth, to muzzle, to silence. Compl. inf. to the impersonal vb. δεῖ (# *1256*) pres. ind. act. "It is necessary to muzzle them." ἀνατρέπουσιν pres. ind. act. ἀνατρέπω (# *426*) to turn upside down, to upset (2 Tim. 2:18). διδάσκοντες pres. act. part. διδάσκω (# *1438*) to teach. Part. gives the means or manner. αἰσχρός (# *156*) shameful, ugly, dishonest (BAGD). κέρδος (# *3046*) gain, profit. ◆ **12** ἐξ αὐτῶν from them. Paul quotes from Epimenides of Cnossus, in Crete, a religious teacher and worker of wonders of the sixth century B.C. (ABD, 1:1206; Kelly; Lock; Dibelius; OCD, 399; KP, 2:319). ἴδιος αὐτῶν προφήτης one of their own prophets. Epimenides, a famous figure of Crete, was considered a prophet. Because a well-known Cretian condemns his own people, the apostle cannot be charged w. censoriousness for his exposures (Guthrie). For the character of the Cretan as seen by ancient writers s. NW, 2, ii:1017-27; Callimachus, *Jov.* 8; BBC; ABD, 1:1206. ψεύστης (# *6026*) liar. θηρίον (# *2563*) wild animal, beast. γαστέρες pl. γαστήρ (# *1143*) stomach. ἀργαί pl. ἀργός (# *734*) inactive, lazy. The expression "lazy belly" describes their uncontrolled greed (Guthrie; for gluttony in the ancient world s. RAC, 9:345-90). ◆ **13** αἰτία (# *162*) reason, cause. ἔλεγχε pres. imp. act. ἐλέγχω (# *1794*) to reprove (2 Tim. 4:2). ἀποτόμως (# *705*) adv., severely, sharply. ὑγιαίνωσιν pres. subj. act. ὑγιαίνω (# *5617*) to be well, to

be healthy, to be sound. Subj. w. ἵνα (# *2671*) to express purp. ◆ **14** προσέχοντες pres. act. part. προσέχω (# *4668*) to give heed to, to devote oneself to (1 Tim. 1:4). μῦθος (# *3680*) myth (1 Tim. 1:4). ἐντολαῖς dat. pl. ἐντολή (# *1953*) command, rule. ἀποστρεφομένων pres. mid. part. ἀποστρέφω (# *695*) to turn away; mid., to turn oneself from something, to reject; to repudiate (BAGD). ◆ **15** μεμιαμμένοις perf. pass. part. μιαίνω (# *3620*) to stain, to defile, to pollute. Perf. points to a past completed action w. a continuing result, state or condition. νοῦς (# *3808*) mind, understanding. συνείδησις (# *5287*) conscience. ◆ **16** ὁμολογοῦσιν pres. ind. act. ὁμολογέω (# *3933*) to confess, to profess. εἰδέναι perf. act. inf. οἶδα (# *3857*) to know. Def. perf. w. pres. meaning. Compl. inf. to the preceding vb. ἀρνοῦνται pres. mid. (dep.) ind. ἀρνέομαι (# *766*) to deny. βδελυκτός (# *1008*) detestable, abominable. It is an expression of disgust at their hypocrisy (Guthrie). ὄντες pres. act. part. εἰμί (# *1639*) to be. ἀπειθής (# *579*) disobedient. ἀδόκιμος (# *99*) rejected after trial, disqualified (2 Tim. 3:8).

Titus 2

◆ **1** λάλει pres. imp. act. λαλέω (# *3281*) to speak. Pres. imp. calls for a habitual action. ἅ acc. pl. ὅς (# *4005*) who, which. Here, "the things," "the things which." πρέπει pres. ind. act. πρέπω (# *4560*) it is fitting. The word indicates that which is fitting or suitable to a particular context. ὑγιαινούσῃ pres. act. part. ὑγιαίνω (# *5617*) to be well, to be healthy, to be sound. διδασκαλίᾳ (# *1436*) teaching, doctrine; here dat. of respect. Correct doctrine should produce correct relationships. This counteracts any suspicion against the believers (BBC). ◆ **2** πρεσβύτης (# *4566*) one who is older, an older man. This does not refer to the office of elder, but to an age group (HOG, 171). νηφαλίος (# *3767*) sober. It refers here to general restraint in indulging desires (Kelly; 1 Tim. 3:2). εἶναι pres. act. inf. εἰμί (# *1639*) to be. Inf. used as an imp. (Quinn), or epex. (GGBB, 607). σεμνός (# *4948*) dignified (1 Tim. 3:8). ◆ **3** πρεσβῦτις (# *4567*) older woman. ὡσαύτως (# *6058*) likewise. κατάστημα (# *2949*) demeanor, deportment, behavior. The word describes a state of mind (Guthrie). ἱεροπρεπής (# *2640*) that which is suitable to holiness, reverence, temple-like; like people engaged in sacred duties, like those employed in sacred service. They are to carry into daily life the demeanor of priestesses in a temple (Lock; MM; Dibelius). διάβολος (# *1333*) slanderer (2 Tim. 3:3). δεδουλωμένας perf. pass. part. δουλόω (# *1530*) to be enslaved. Perf. emphasizes the completed state or condition. The warning against slanderous talk and addiction to wine reflect a popular stereotype of an old woman. Drunkenness among women was especially abhorred in Roman tradition (Spicq; HOG, 172; Quinn). καλοδιδάσκαλος (# *2815*) teacher in good. The word does not refer to formal instruction, but rather the advice and encouragement they can give privately, by word and example (Kelly). ◆ **4 σωφρονίζωσιν** pres. subj. act. σωφρονίζω (# 5405) to teach someone self-control, to train someone in self-control (Lock, 148f; TDNT; TLNT; Quinn, 304-15; esp. 314-15). Subj. w. ἵνα (# 2671) to express purp. **νέας** acc. pl. νέος (# 3742) young; young women. **φίλανδρος** (# 5791) husband-loving **φιλότεκνος** (# 5817) children-loving. ◆ **5 ἁγνός** (# 54) chaste (1 Tim. 5:22). **οἰκουργός** (# 3877) working at home, housekeeping. In a Jewish household the married woman had to grind flour, bake, launder, cook, nurse children, make the beds, spin wool, keep the house and be responsible for hospitality and the care of guests (M, Ketuboth 5:5; JPF, 2:761ff; SB, 3:667). **ὑποτασσομένας** pres. mid. (dep.) part. ὑποτάσσομαι (# 5718) to be in subjection (Eph. 5:21). **βλασφημῆται** pres. subj. pass. βλασφημέω (# 1059) to slander, to speak lightly of sacred things, to blaspheme (AS; TDNT; EDNT; TLNT). ◆ **6 νεωτέρους** comp. νέος (# 3742) young; comp., younger. **ὡσαύτως** likewise. **παρακάλει** pres. imp. act. παρακαλέω (# 4151) to urge, to exhort (Rom. 12:1). Pres. imp. calls for a repeated action. **σωφρονεῖν** pres. act. inf. σωφρονέω (# 5404) to be of sound mind, to exercise self-control, to have one's total life under control of the mind (s.v. 4; Lock. 148ff; TDNT). Compl. inf. to the preceding vb. ◆ **7 παρεχόμενος** pres. mid. part. παρέχω (# 4218) to show oneself to be something (BAGD); mid. w. a double acc. **τύπος** (# 5596) example, type, model. **διδασκαλία** (# 1436) teaching, doctrine. **ἀφθορία** (# 917) not corrupt, sincerity, not tainted. It is purity of motive, without desire of gain or respect of persons and purity of doctrine (Lock; Guthrie; MM). **σεμνότης** (# 4949) dignity (1 Tim. 2:2). ◆ **8 λόγος** (# 3364) word, speech. The word denotes the content of what is said (Guthrie). **ὑγιής** (# 5618) healthy, sound. **ἀκατάγνωστος** (# 183) without accusation, unable to be accused, that which cannot be condemned; beyond reproach, preaching beyond reproach (BAGD; MM). **ὁ** (# 3836) the; "he that is on the contrary part" (Lock). **ἐντραπῇ** aor. subj. pass. ἐντρέφω (# 1956) mid., to turn one on himself and so be ashamed (to blush) (RWP; 2 Thess. 3:14). **ἔχων** pres. act. (causal) part. ἔχω (# 2400) to have. **λέγειν** pres. act. inf. λέγω (# 3306) to say. Compl. inf. **φαῦλος** (# 5765) bad, worthless. ◆ **9 δεσπότης** (# 1305) master. **εὐάρεστος** (# 2298) well-pleasing. **ἀντιλέγοντας** pres. act. part. ἀντιλέγω (# 515) to speak against, to answer back, to talk back. ◆ **10 νοσφιζομένους** pres. mid. (dep.) part. νοσφίζομαι (# 3802) to set apart for oneself, to separate or lay on one's side, to embezzle (RWP; Kelly). **ἐνδεικνυμένους** pres. mid. (dep.) part. ἐνδείκνυμι (# 1892) to show oneself, to demonstrate, to show forth. **ἀγαθήν** acc. fem. sing. ἀγαθός (# 19) good. The adj. could be attributive ("good faith") or it could be the predicate ("showing faith to be good") (GGBB, 188-89). **κοσμῶσιν** pres. subj.

act. κοσμέω (# 3175) to put in order, to adorn. The word is used of the arrangement of jewels in a manner that sets off their full beauty (Guthrie). ◆ **11 ἐπεφάνη** aor. ind. pass. ἐπιφαίνω (# 2210) to appear; pass., to be made clear, to be made manifest. The essential meaning of the word is "to appear suddenly." It is used particularly of divine interposition, especially aid, and of the dawning of light upon darkness (Lock; MM). **σωτήριος** (# 5403) saving, delivering, bringing salvation. Followed by the dat., the word means "bringing deliverance to"; the phrase **πᾶσιν ἀνθρώποις** ("to all men") belongs to the noun showing the universal scope of Christian salvation (Guthrie; BAGD; DPL, 858-62). ◆ **12 παιδεύουσα** pres. act. part. παιδεύω (# 4084) to train by discipline, to train a child, to instruct. **ἵνα** (# 2671) so that. The particle w. subj. introduces the purpose of the training. **ἀρνησάμενοι** aor. mid. (dep.) part. ἀρνέομαι (# 766) to deny, to say no to. **ἀσέβεια** (# 813) godlessness, the rejection of all that is reverent and has to do with God (TDNT). **ἐπιθυμία** (# 2123) strong desire, lust. **σωφρόνως** (# 5407) adv., w. self-control (s.v. 6). **δικαίως** (# 1469) adv., righteously. **εὐσεβῶς** (# 2357) adv., godly, reverently. **ζήσωμεν** aor. subj. act. ζάω (# 2409) to live. Subj. in the ἵνα (# 2671) cl. Aor. calls for a specific act w. a note of urgency. ◆ **13 προσδεχόμενοι** pres. mid. (dep.) part. προσδέχομαι (# 4657) to expect, to wait for, to eagerly wait for. **μακαρίαν** acc. μακάριος (# 3421) blessed, happy. **ἐπιφάνεια** (# 2211) appearance (2 Thess. 2:8). ◆ **14 ἔδωκεν** aor. ind. act. δίδωμι (# 1443) to give. The act of giving himself indicates Christ's willing, gracious gift of himself. Aor. points to the act of giving Himself. **λυτρώσηται** aor. subj. mid. λυτρόω (# 3390) to obtain release by the payment of a price, to redeem, to ransom (Matt. 20:28; RAC, 6:54-219). Aor. points to the specific act. **ἀνομία** (# 490) lawlessness. **καθαρίσῃ** aor. subj. act. καθαρίζω (# 2751) to cleanse. Subj. w. ἵνα (# 2671) used in purp. cl. **περιούσιος** (# 4342) chosen, special; i.e., something that belongs in a special sense to oneself (Guthrie). **ζηλωτής** (# 2421) zealous. ◆ **15 παρακάλει** pres. imp. act. παρακαλέω (# 4151) to encourage, to exhort. **ἔλεγχε** pres. imp. act. ἐλέγχω (# 1794) to convince, to convict, to reprove (2 Tim. 4:2). **ἐπιταγή** (# 2198) command, order; here, "w. all impressiveness" (BAGD). **περιφρονείτω** pres. imp. act. 3rd. pers. sing. περιφρονέω (# 4368) to think around someone, to despise someone, to overlook, to disregard (MH, 321).

Titus 3

◆ **1 ὑπομίμνησκε** pres. imp. act. ὑπομιμνήσκω (# 5703) to call to remembrance, to remind someone of something. Pres. imp. could be iterative (Quinn). **ἀρχαῖς** dat. pl. ἀρχή (# 794) ruler. **ἐξουσία** (# 2026) authority. **ὑποτάσσεσθαι** pres. mid. (dep.) inf. ὑποτάσσομαι (# 5718) to be in subjection. **πειθαρχεῖν** pres. act. inf. πειθαρχέω (# 4272) to be obedient. Infs. in indir. discourse after the vb. ὑπομίμνησκε. ἕτοιμος (# 2289) prepared, ready. ◆ **2** βλασφημεῖν pres. act. inf. βλασφημέω (# 1059) to slander, to treat w. contempt, to blaspheme. Infs. parallel to the infs. in the preceding v. ἄμαχος (# 285) without fighting. εἶναι pres. act. inf. εἰμί (# 1639) to be. ἐπιεικής (# 2117) forbearing, reasonable, fair (2 Cor. 10:1; Phil. 4:5). ἐνδεικνυμένους pres. mid. (dep.) part. ἐνδείκνυμι (# 1892) to demonstrate, to display. πραΰτης (# 4559) meekness, mildness, patient trust in the midst of difficult circumstances (2 Cor. 10:1). ◆ **3** ἦμεν impf. ind. act. εἰμί (# 1639) to be. ποτέ (# 4537) formerly. ἀνόητος (# 485) without understanding, foolish. ἀπειθής (# 579) disobedient. πλανώμενοι pres. pass. part. πλανάω (# 4414) to deceive, to lead astray. The word suggests a false guide leading astray (Guthrie). δουλεύοντες pres. act. part. δουλεύω (# 1526) to be in slavery to. Adj. part. as pred. adj. ἐπιθυμία (# 2123) strong desire, lust. ἡδοναῖς dat. pl. ἡδονή (# 2454) pleasure. ποικίλος (# 4476) many-colored, variegated, various. κακία (# 2798) evil (TDNT; NIDNTT). φθόνος (# 5784) envy. διάγοντες pres. act. part. διάγω (# 1341) to live, to spend time. στυγητός (# 5144) hated, hateful, detestable. μισοῦντες pres. act. part. μισέω (# 3631) to hate. ἀλλήλους acc. pl. ἀλλήλων (# 253) one another. ◆ **4** χρηστότης (# 5983) kindness, goodness (Gal. 5:22). φιλανθρωπία (# 5792) love of mankind, love toward men, generosity. While generosity was sometimes attributed to God inscriptions show that in the Hellenistic age it was the most prized of the stock virtues acclaimed in rulers (Kelly; TLNT). ἐπεφάνη aor. ind. act. ἐπιφαίνω (# 2210) to appear. Often used of the sun or stars appearing (BAGD). ◆ **5** τῶν gen. pl. ὁ (# 3836) The definite article is used here as a rel.; i.e., "not as a result of works, those in righteousness which we did" (RWP; GGBB, 213-15). ἐποιήσαμεν aor. ind. act. ποιέω (# 4472) to do. ἔλεος (# 1799) mercy (1 Tim. 1:2). ἔσωσεν aor. ind. act. σώζω (# 5392) to rescue, to save. λουτρόν (# 3373) bath, washing (Eph. 5:26; Fairbairn). παλιγγενεσία (# 4098) a birth again, regeneration, new birth. The term was current in Stoicism for periodic restorations of the natural world. It was also used in an eschatological sense–especially by the Jews–of the renewing of the world in the time of the Messiah; but here the word takes on a new meaning in view of the Christian new birth, which is applied not cosmically but personally (Guthrie; BAGD; Lock; Dibelius; TDNT; NIDNTT; RAC, 9:43-171; Matt. 19:28). ἀνακαίνωσις (# 364) renewing, making new (Col. 3:10). ◆ **6** ἐξέχεεν aor. ind. act. ἐξέχω (# 1772) to pour out. πλουσίως (# 4455) adv., richly. ◆ **7** δικαιωθέντες aor. pass. part. δικαιόω (# 1467) to declare righteous, to justify (Rom. 2:13; 5:1). Either temp. part. ("after having been justified"), or causal ("because we have been justified"). κληρονόμος (# 3101) heir. γενηθῶμεν aor. subj. pass. γεννάω (# 1181) to be born. Subj. w. ἵνα (# 2671) to express

result or purp. For an attempt to explain the teaching in light of Philo s. Stephen Charles Mott, "Greek Ethics and Christian Conversion: The Philonic Background of Titus II 10-14 and III 37," *NovT* 20 (1978): 22-48. ◆ **8** τούτων gen. pl. οὗτος (# 4047) this. Here, these things; refers to all that has been included in the previous part of the letter (Guthrie). βούλομαι (# 1089) pres. ind. mid. (dep.) to determine, to will. διαβεβαιοῦσθαι pres. mid. (dep.) inf. διαβεβαιόομαι (# 1331) to speak confidently, to insist, to confirm, to make a point of (Lock; 1 Tim. 1:7). Compl. inf. to the main vb.: "I desire to insist." Pres. calls for a continual action. φροντίζωσιν pres. subj. act. φροντίζω (# 5863) to take thought of, to give heed to. Subj. w. ἵνα (# 2671) to express result or purp. προΐστασθαι pres. mid. (dep.) inf. προΐστημι (# 4613) to stand before, to take the lead in, to be careful to busy oneself w. The word has a technical meaning: "to practice a profession" (RWP; Kelly). Compl. inf. to the preceding vb. πεπιστευκότες perf. act. part. πιστεύω (# 4409) to believe. ὠφέλιμος (# 6068) useful, profitable, serviceable. ◆ **9** μωρός (# 3704) dull, stupid, foolish (AS). ζήτησις (# 2428) questioning, speculation (1 Tim. 1:4). γενεαλογία (# 1157) genealogy (1 Tim. 1:4). ἔρις (# 2251) strife. μάχας acc. pl. μάχη (# 3480) fight, controversy. νομικός (# 3788) pertaining to law, legal. The word here refers to the Mosaic Law (Guthrie). περιΐστασο pres. imp. mid. 2nd. pers. sing. περιΐστημι (# 4325) act., to place around; mid., to go around so as to avoid; to step around, to stand aside, to turn oneself about; to avoid, to shun (RWP; MM; 2 Tim. 2:16). ἀνωφελής (# 543) useless, unprofitable. μάταιος (# 3469) futile. ◆ **10** αἱρετικός (# 148) heresy, heretical; having the power of choice, a self-chosen party, sect, or faction. δεύτερος (# 1311) second. νουθεσία (# 3804) admonition, warning. It is the attempt to cause a person to correct his wrong by warning or counsel (TDNT; 1 Cor. 10:11; Eph. 6:4). παραιτοῦ pres. imp. mid. (dep.) παραιτέομαι (# 4148) to ask from, to beg off, to avoid (RWP; 1 Tim. 4:7; 5:11). ◆ **11** εἰδώς perf. act. part. οἶδα (# 3857) to know. Def. perf. w. pres. meaning. ἐξέστραπται perf. ind. mid. ἐκστρέφω (# 1750) to turn from, to turn inside out, to twist, to divert (RWP). τοιοῦτος (# 5525) such a one. ἁμαρτάνει pres. ind. act. ἁμαρτάνω (# 279) to sin. ὤν pres. act. part. nom. masc. sing. εἰμί (# 1639) to be. αὐτοκατάκριτος (# 896) condemnation of oneself, selfcondemned; he is condemned by his own action (Lock). ◆ **12** ὅταν (# 4020) used w. the subj., when, whenever. πέμψω aor. subj. act. πέμπω (# 4287) to send. σπούδασον aor. imp. act. σπουδάζω (# 5079) to hurry, to endeavor, to do one's best (Kelly). Nicopolis was on the Greek side of the Adriatic coast, 200 miles east of Italy (BBC; ABD, 4:1108). ἐλθεῖν aor. act. inf. ἔρχομαι (# 2262) to go. Compl. inf. to the main vb., "Hurry to come!" κέκρικα perf. ind. act. κρίνω (# 3212) to judge, to determine, to decide. Perf. looks at the settled decisions already reached. **παραχειμάσαι** aor. mid. (dep.) inf. παραχειμάζω (# 4199) to spend the winter (BAGD; MM). Inf. in indir. speech as obj. of the vb. Const. aor. views the action in its totality. ◆ **13 νομικός** (# 3788) pertaining to the law, lawyer. The word may be used of an expert in either Heb. or Roman law. Here it probably refers to a Roman lawyer (ABD, 6:1074-75; LAW, 3:2532-59). If one did not know the laws of a city, he consulted a lawyer (Guthrie; TDNT; MM; Preisigke). **σπουδαίως** (# 5081) speedily, hurriedly, earnestly, diligently. **πρόπεμψον** aor. imp. act. προπέμπω (# 4636) to send forth, to send on. The word often had the idea of supplying one w. money for material needs for a trip

(Rom. 15:24; 1 Cor. 16:6). **λείπῃ** pres. subj. act. λείπω (# 3309) to leave behind, to lack. Subj. w. ἵνα (# 2671) expresses result. The word suggests that Titus was in a position to provide material assistance (Guthrie). ◆ **14 μανθανέτωσαν** pres. imp. act. μανθάνω (# 3443) to learn. **προΐστασθαι** pres. mid. (dep.) inf. προΐστημι (# 4613) s.v. 8. **ἀναγκαῖος** (# 338) necessary. **ὦσιν** pres. subj. act. εἰμί (# 1639) to be. Subj. w. ἵνα (# 2671) to express purp. or result. **ἄκαρπος** (# 182) fruitless. ◆ **15** **ἀσπάζονται** pres. ind. mid. (dep.) ἀσπάζομαι (# 832) to greet. **ἄσπασαι** aor. imp. mid. (dep.) ἀσπάζομαι (# 832). **φιλοῦντας** pres. act. part. φιλέω (# 5797) to love.

Philemon

Philemon 1

◆ **1 δέσμιος** (*# 1300*) prisoner (CIC). **Χριστοῦ Ἰησοῦ** "of Jesus Christ." Gen. could be gen. of cause, gen. of purpose, or gen. of possesion (CIC, 151-57). Poss. gen. expresses to whom Paul belonged and indicates that the writing is not simply to be looked at as a private letter, but w. a message which those who receive it are obligated to obey (Lohse). It also indicates that Paul was a "willing prisoner," who gave up his freedom voluntarily (CIC, 155-57). **ἀγαπητός** (*# 28*) beloved. **συνεργός** (*# 5301*) fellow worker. The term is a frequent name given to Paul's colleagues in the work of the gospel. Just how Philemon had labored w. Paul in missionary service is unclear (Martin, NCB). ◆ **2 ἀδελφῇ** (*# 80*) sister. Since at that time the women had to do w. the business of the house, it was important to her what Paul had to say about the slave Onesimus (Stuhlmacher; Lohse; s. Titus 2:5; DPL, 881-83). **συστρατιώτης** (*# 5369*) fellow soldier; one who engaged in the same conflicts, faced the same dangers, fought for the same goals, and was loyal, refusing to desert his post, regardless of the consequences he might face (CIC, 164-70, 172-74; TDNT). **τῇ κατ' οἶκόν σου ἐκκλησίᾳ** to the church in your house. For the house church s. Col. 4:15; Harris; Stuhlmacher, 70-75. ◆ **3 χάρις** (*# 5921*) grace (EDNT; CPP); the undeserved help from God. **ὑμῖν** dat. pl. σύ (*# 5148*) you; here, "to you." Dat of advantage. ◆ **4 εὐχαριστῶ** pres. ind. act. εὐχαριστέω (*# 2373*) to give thanks. It was a common feature of Hellenistic letters that the sender praised the gods for the health and well-being of his addressees, and assured them of his prayers on their behalf. Paul gives a distinctly Christian content to the formula by the way in which he goes on to describe the reason for his thankfulness (Martin, NCB; Lohse; LAE, 184f; P.T. O'Brien, *Introductory Thanksgivings in the Letters of Paul* [Leiden: E.J. Brill, 1977]). **πάντοτε** (*# 4121*) always. **μνεία** (*# 3644*) mention, remembrance. **ποιούμενος** pres. mid. (dep.) part. ποιέω (*# 4472*) to make. The construction means "to make mention in prayer" (Moule; s. 1 Thess. 1:2). ◆ **5 ἀκούων** pres. act. part. ἀκούω (*# 201*) to hear. Part. could be causal ("because I hear"), and indicates the cause of Paul's giving thanks (Vincent; O'Brien). **πίστις** (*# 4411*) faith, faithfulness, loyalty (Bruce). **ἔχεις** pres. ind. act. ἔχω (*# 2400*) to have. Pres. indicates the present continuing possession. **πρός** (*# 4639*) toward. The prep. sig-

nifies direction: forward to, toward. Here it is used of faith which aspires toward Christ (Lightfoot; Vincent; Ellicott). **εἰς πάντας τοὺς ἁγίους** unto all the saints. The prep. denotes arrival and so contact (Lightfoot, but s. also MT, 256). ◆ **6 ὅπως** (*# 3968*) that, in order that. The particle introduces either the aim and purpose of Paul's prayer (Lightfoot) or else simply gives the content of Paul's prayer (Lohse; Bruce; O'Brien). **κοινωνία** (*# 3126*) fellowship, sharing. The word could mean generosity or participation; the main idea is that Philemon's faith is to show itself in loving service (Martin, NCB; TDNT; NIDNTT; RAC, 9:1100-45). **πίστεώς** (*# 4411*) faith. Gen. here can be an obj. gen. For a discussion of the various problems and interpretations s. Moule; Stuhlmacher. **ἐνεργής** (*# 1921*) active, effective, productive. (TDNT; MNTW, 46-54). **γένηται** aor. subj. mid. (dep.) γίνομαι (*# 1181*) to become. **ἐπίγνωσις** (*# 2106*) recognition, acknowledgment, knowledge. **παντὸς ἀγαθοῦ** (*# 4246; 19*) of every good. The words may refer to that which is God's will and generally refers to something which is done or performed (Moule; Stuhlmacher). ◆ **7 ἔσχον** aor. ind. act. ἔχω (*# 2400*) to have, aor. to get, to receive (M, 110). Aor. expresses forcibly the moment of joy which Paul experienced when he heard this good news about Philemon (EGT). **παράκλησις** (*# 4155*) encouragement, comfort. **σπλάγχνον** (*# 5073*) the inner organs, heart. The term is used here to denote the total person and his personality at the deepest level (Martin, NCB; Lohse; TLNT; TDNT). **ἀναπέπαυται** perf. mid. (dep.) inf. ἀναπαύομαι (*# 399*) to cause to rest, to refresh. The word implies relaxation, and refreshment as a preparation for the renewal of labor or suffering (Lightfoot). Hospitality was a necessary virtue (BBC). **ἀδελφέ** voc. ἀδελφός (*# 81*) brother. The place of the word here makes it emphatic (EGT). ◆ **8 διό** (*# 1475*) therefore. **παρρησία** (*# 4244*) speaking all things, openness, boldness, frankness, candor (TLNT; TDNT; O'Brien). **ἔχων** pres. act. part. ἔχω (*# 2400*) to have. Concessive part., "although" (IBG, 102). **ἐπιτάσσειν** pres. act. inf. ἐπιτάσσω (*# 2195*) to command. Compl. inf. to the preceding part. When a slave ran away, he could be sought through a wanted list, and if anyone recognized him and caught him he was to bring him back to his owner, who could punish the slave as he wished. In such a case it was also possible for one to intercede w. the master for the slave. For examples and references s. Lohse; s. also John M.G. Barclay, "Paul, Philemon and the Dilemma of Christian Slave-Ownership," *NTS* 37 (1991): 161-86. For a text describing two runaway slaves s. Moule, 34ff; and for two similar letters written in behalf of a slave s. NW, 2, ii:1059-60; Pliny, *Letters*, 9:21; 24. For texts concerning the crucifixion of a slave, a curse against a fugitive slave, and the government's pursuit of runaway slaves s. NDIEC, 8:1-46. For a text much similar to Paul's letter to Philemon, except the slave is to be caught, bound hand and foot and returned to the owner s. NDIEC, 8:24-26. It could be, however, that Onesimus was not a runaway slave (*fugitivus*), but someone who appealed to Paul as a friend of his master (*amicus domini*), asking for intersession on his behalf (Peter Lampe, "Keine 'Sklavenflucht' des Onesimus," *ZNW* 76 [1985]: 135-37; Brian M. Rapske, "The Prisoner Paul in the Eyes of Onesimus," *NTS* 37 [1991]: 187-203; s. also Dunn; Sara C. Winter, "Paul's Letter to Philemon," *NTS* 33 [1987]: 1-15). ἀνῆκον pres. act. part. ἀνήκω (# 465) to come up to, to pertain to; that which is required, that which is fitting, i.e. one's duty (Martin, NCB). ◆ **9 μᾶλλον** (# 3437) rather. παρακαλῶ pres. ind. act. παρακαλέω (# 4151) to urge, to beseech. The vb. contains the idea of a request (TDNT; Lohse). τοιοῦτος (# 5525) such a one. For the construction of this section s. Lightfoot; O'Brien; Harris. ὤν pres. act. part. εἰμί (# 1639) to be. Causal part., "because I am." πρεσβύτης (# 4566) old man, ambassador. The sense requires Paul's invoking his authority as an ambassador (Martin, NCB; O'Brien; Bruce; Harris), or he may appeal to his position as an "old man," who would be dependent on others, as well as have a right to demand respect and honor (CIC, 157-64). νυνί (# 3815) now. δέσμιος (# 1300) prisoner. ◆ **10 παρακαλῶ** pres. ind. act. παρακαλέω (# 4151) to beseech. Used w. the prep. here in the sense of making a request on behalf of someone (Lohse; Stuhlmacher). ἐγέννησα aor. ind. act. γεννάω (# 1164) to bear, to give birth. Here it is the metaphor of fatherhood: "of whose conversion I was the instrument" (Vincent; Moule). For references to the DSS and rabbinical literature concerning the metaphor of spiritual parenthood s. Stuhlmacher; SB, 3:340f; TDNT; BBC. ◆ **11 ποτέ** (# 4537) formerly. ἄχρηστος (# 947) useless, unserviceable. εὔχρηστος (# 2378) useful, serviceable, profitable. Perhaps a word play on the Latin name Onesimus. ◆ **12 ἀνέπεμψα** aor. ind. act. ἀναπέμπω (# 402) to send again, to send back (BAGD; Moule). Epistolary aor., which is translated by the pres. in English. It indicates that Onesimus carried the letter (Lightfoot; Stuhlmacher; BD, 172). σπλάγχνον (# 5073) inward organs, heart, "my very heart" (Lightfoot; s.v. 7; s. Phil 2:1). ◆ **13 ἐβουλόμην** impf. ind. mid. (dep.) βούλομαι (# 1086) to desire, to wish. The word involves the idea of purpose, deliberation, desire, mind (Lightfoot; TDNT).

κατέχειν pres. act. inf. κατέχω (# 2988) to retain, to keep. Although the word is capable of several meanings, the idea in this construction is "to keep w. me" (Lohse; LAE, 331; TDNT; Stuhlmacher). διακονῇ pres. subj. act. διακονέω (# 1354) to wait on, to minister to, to minister (TDNT). εὐαγγέλιον (# 2295) good news, gospel. Gen. here may be subjective, indicating that his bonds arise from the gospel (Lohmeyer), or it may mean "my imprisonment for the gospel" (Moule). ◆ **14 χωρίς** (# 6006) w. the gen., without. γνώμη (# 1191) opinion, consent. The word was used often in the papyri in this sense (Stuhlmacher; Dibelius; Priesigke; MM). ἠθέλησα aor. ind. act. θέλω (# 2527) to wish, to desire. Aor. describes a definite completed action (Lightfoot; EGT). ποιῆσαι aor. act. inf. ποιέω (# 4472) to do. ἀνάγκη (# 340) pressure, necessity, compulsion. ἀγαθόν σου (# 19; 5148) (the benefit arising from you; i.e., the good I should get from the continued presence of Onesimus, which would be owing to you (Lightfoot). ᾖ pres. subj. act. εἰμί (# 1639) to be. ἑκούσιος (# 1730) voluntary. Used here w. the prep.: "of one's own free will" (BAGD; GELTS, 139). ◆ **15 τάχα** (# 5440) perhaps. ἐχωρίσθη aor. ind. pass. χωρίζω (# 6004) to separate, to depart (by escaping). Pass. may be a divine pass, in Heb. a mode of expression to denote the hidden action of God (Martin, NCB). αἰώνιος (# 173) eternal. In this context it appears to mean permanently, for good (Moule). ἀπέχῃς pres. subj. act. ἀπέχω (# 600) to have. The word was a commercial t.t. meaning to receive a sum in full and give a receipt for it. Here the idea is "to keep," "to keep for oneself" (BAGD; Ellicott). ◆ **16 οὐκέτι** (# 4033) no longer. ὑπὲρ δοῦλον (# 1528) beyond a slave, more than a slave (RWP). ἀγαπητός (# 28) beloved (s.v. 1). μάλιστα (# 3436) especially. πόσῳ δὲ μᾶλλον (# 4531; 1254; 3437) how much rather. Having first said "most of all to me," he goes a step further: "more than most of all to thee" (Lightfoot). ἐν σαρκί (# 1877; 4922) in the flesh; i.e., "as a man" (Martin, NCB). ◆ **17 ἔχεις** pres. ind. act. ἔχω (# 2400) to have. Ind. is used in a first class cond. cl. which assumes the cond. as a reality. κοινωνός (# 3128) sharer, partner. The word denotes those who have common interest, common feelings, and common work (Lightfoot; s.v. 6). προσλαβοῦ aor. mid. imp. προσλαμβάνω (# 4689) mid., to take to oneself, to receive or accept into one's society, home, or circle of acquaintances (BAGD). ◆ **18 ἠδίκησέν** aor. ind. act. ἀδικέω (# 92) to act unjustly, to wrong someone, to injure. ὀφείλει pres. ind. act. ὀφειλέω (# 4053) to owe someone a debt. ἐλλόγα pres. imp. act. ἐλλογάω (# 1823) to place on someone's account. Imp. is a polite request. The word was a commercial t.t. meaning, "to charge to someone's account" (MM; Preisigke; BAGD; Dibelius; Lohse; O'Brien; BBC). ◆ **19 ἔγραψα** aor. ind. act. γράφω (# 4211) to write. Epistolary aor. ("I am writing"). ἀποτίσω fut. ind. act. ἀποτίθημι (# 702) to repay, to pay back. The word is a legal t.t. and appears in promissory notes (Lohse; LAE, 331f). λέγω (# 3306) pres. subj. act. to say. Subj. w. ἵνα (# 2671) to express purp. προσοφείλεις pres. ind. act. προσοφειλέω (# 4695) to owe a debt beside, to owe in addition to (Ellicott). ◆ 20 ναί (# 3721) yes. ὀναίμην aor. opt. mid. (dep.) ὀνίνημι (# 3949) to benefit, to profit. Opt. here to express a wish; it was used in the formula "may I have joy, profit or benefit" and w. the gen. of the person or thing that is the source of the joy or profit (BAGD; MM). ἀνάπαυσον pres. imp. act. (# 399) (s.v. 7). ◆ 21 πεποιθώς perf. act. part. (causal) πείθω (# 4275) to persuade, perf. to be persuaded, to have confidence (Dunn; s. Phil. 1:6). ὑπακοῇ (# 5633) listening to, obedient. ἔγραψα aor. ind. act. γράφω (# 1211) to write. εἰδώς perf. act. part. (causal) οἶδα (# 3856) to know. Def. perf. w. a pres. meaning. (Harris). ποιήσεις fut. ind. act. ποιέω (# 4472) to do. For general discussions of slavery in the ancient world, and esp. of slaves obtaining their freedom s. FCS; Lohse; Stuhlmacher, 42-48; DC, 1-15; Seneca, *Letters to Lucilus*, 47; DGRA, 1034-42; KP, 5:230-34; CC, 109-112; SCA, 27-46; also 1 Cor. 7:21). ◆ 22 ἅμα (# 275) at the same time, besides. ἑτοίμαζε pres. imp. act. ἑτοιμάζω (# 2286) to prepare, to prepare a guest room (Stuhlmacher). Imp. as a polite request. ξενία (# 3825) lodging, a place of entertainment. It may denote quarters in an inn or a room in a private house (Lightfoot). ἐλπίζω (# 1827) pres. ind. act. to hope. χαρισθήσομαι fut. ind. pass. χαρίζομαι (# 5919) to give graciously, to grant somebody to someone (Lightfoot; Moule). Pass. suggests that it is God alone who can secure Paul's release, though Paul relies on the prayers of the community to entreat God for this favor (Martin, NCB). ◆ 23 ἀσπάζεται pres. ind. mid. (dep.) ἀσπάζομαι (# 832) to greet. συναιχμάλωτός (# 5257) fellow captive. ◆ 24 συνεργός (# 5301) fellow worker (s.v. 1). For a discussion of churches in homes in the ancient Christian world s.v. 2.

Hebrews

Hebrews 1

◆ **1** πολυμερῶς (# 4495) adv., in many ways, in many parts. The word points to the fragmentary character of former revelation; it came in multiple segments or portions (Attridge; Weiss). The revelation of God was essentially progressive (EGT). πολυτρόπως (# 4502) adv. in many ways, in various manners. It could refer both to the various geographical locations of the revelation as well as to the various methods of disclosure–direct revelation, dreams, visions, etc.–thus stressing the diversity of God´s Word (Buchanan; Westcott; Michel; Attridge). πάλαι (# 4093) formerly, of time. The word describes something completed in the past. Here the thought is of the ancient teachings long since sealed (Westcott). The alliteration of the words w. π is difficult to reproduce in translation, but alliteration was a common practice of that time (Attridge; Lane; Braun). λαλήσας aor. act. part. (temp.) λαλέω (# 3281) to speak; w. dat., to speak to. Aor. indicating antecedent time, "after he had spoken." Aor. points to a completed act. πατράσιν dat. pl. πατήρ (# 4252) father; here, "to the fathers." ἐν τοῖς προφήταις (#1877; 4737) by means of the prophets. The prep. is instr. and could refer to the teaching of inspiration which viewed the prophets as being indwelt by the Holy Spirit (Michel; Westcott). The prep. could also be taken as local, indicating that God spoke in the prophets as His authorized speakers (Weiss). ◆ **2** ἐπ᾽ ἐσχάτου (#2093; 2274)at the end. ἐπ᾽ ἐσχάτου τῶν ἡμερῶν τούτων the last of these days. The rabbinic term indicated the time of the Messiah (SB, 3:617; Buchanan; Hughes; Lane; Attridge). ἐλάλησεν aor. ind. act. λαλέω (# 3281) to speak. Aor. used both of God speaking by the prophets and also His speaking by Christ, indicates that God has finished speaking in both cases (Hughes). Christ is the ultimate Word of God (BBC; s. also DLNT, 111-15). ἐν υἱῷ (#1877; 5626) in one who is a son. The absence of the article fixes attention upon the nature and not upon the personality of the mediator of a new revelation. God spoke to us in one who has this character–that He is Son (Westcott; GGBB, 245). For other examples of this in Heb. s. 3:6; 5:8. ἔθηκεν aor. ind. act. τίθημι (# 5502) to place, to appoint. κληρονόμος (# 3101) heir. The word is derived from the term "lot" and referred to a situation in which lots were drawn to divide property or select a winner; the one who drew the lot was the heir. The word came

to be used for dividing the property that a father left to his children when he died. Only one son meant only one heir. Christ is the heir of all things precisely because God has only one Son, so only one heir (Buchanan; Hughes; TDNT). ἐποίησεν aor. ind. act. ποιέω (# 4472) to make, to create. αἰών (# 172) age. According to rabbinical use, the word refers not only to the periods of time, but also to the content of the world (Michel; SB, 3:671f; Bruce). ◆ **3** ὤν pres. act. part. (circum.) εἰμί (# 1639) to be. The word refers to the absolute and timeless existence (RWP). ἀπαύγασμα (# 575) radiance. The active meaning has the idea of emitting brightness, so it means that the *shekinah* glory of God radiated from Him. Pass. idea is not so much that of reflection, but rather the radiation through the source of the light. It is as the sun radiates its rays of light (RWP; Hughes; Michel; Westcott; Attridge; Weiss; TDNT). δόξα (# 1518) glory. Here, obj. gen. or gen. of content. It refers to the brilliant radiancy from the person of God (TDNT; NIDNTT; TLNT; DLNT, 396-98). χαρακτήρ (# 5917) impression, stamp. It refers to an engraved character or impress made by a die or a seal. It also indicates the characteristic trait or distinctive mark. It was used w. special reference to any distinguishing peculiarity and hence indicated an exact reproduction (Hughes; BAGD; MM; TDNT; GELTS, 513). ὑπόστασις (# 5712) essence, substance, nature, reality (Grässer; s. 11:1; GELTS, 495). Here, gen. of description: "the exact representation of his substance." φέρων pres. act. part. (circum.) φέρω (# 5770) to carry. "He carries all things continually." The concept is dynamic and not static. The Son's work of upholding involves not only support, but also movement. He is the One who carries all things forward on their appointed course (Hughes; Bruce; Michel). Pres. indicates continual action (Attridge). τὰ πάντα (# 4246)all things. ῥήματι dat. sing. ῥῆμα (# 4839) word, spoken word. Dat. of instr., "by means of His word." καθαρισμός (# 2752) cleansing, purification. ποιησάμενος aor. mid. part. (temp.) ποιέω (# 4472) to make. The use of the mid. suggests that Christ Himself in His own person made the purification (Westcott). Aor. points to the completed action. Aor. expresses action which occurred before the main vb. ἐκάθισεν aor. ind. act. καθίζω (# 2767) to sit down, to take one's seat. This indicates that his work is finished. δεξιά (# 1288) right, w. prep. ἐν in a local sense:

"on the right hand." For the concept of Christ sitting at the right hand, s. Eph. 1:20. For a discussion of Christ's exaltation s. DLNT 360-61; BBC; Kistemaker; Hughes; ABD, 5:724. μεγαλωσύνη (# 3488) majesty. ἐν ὑψηλοῖς pl. (# 1877; 5734) high; equivalent to the term "in heaven" (Michel). ◆ 4 τοσοῦτος (# 5537) so great, so much. Dat. of instr. used w. the comp., "by how much more" (RWP). κρείττων (# 3202) comp. ἀγαθός good; comp., better, superior. The word is characteristic of this epistle (13 times) and the idea is superiority in dignity, worth, or advantage, the fundamental idea being power and not goodness (Westcott; Grässer). The following gen. is the object to which the comparison is made–"greater than angels." γενόμενος aor. mid. (dep.) part. γίνομαι (# 1181) to become, to be. Part. could be causal. ὅσῳ dat. ὅσος (# 4012) as great, how great, as much, how much. Used as a correlative w. the comp. in the sense, "by as much … as" (BAGD; RWP). ἄγγελος (# 34) angel. Angels and demons played a significant part in Judaism (AVB, 62-73; DDD, 81-96; Moore, *Judaism*, 1:401-13; TS, 135-83; TDNT; EDNT; NIDNTT; RAC, 5:53-258; TRE, 9:580-615; Attridge; Grässer; 1 Enoch 40; 64-69; Jub. 2:2; 10:1-14; 1QS 3:20, 21, 24; 4:12; 1QSb 4:25-26; GCDSS, 397). διαφορώτερον comp. διάφορος (# 1427) different; comp. excellent, more excellent. παρ' = παρά (# 4123) than. Prep. w. acc. after a comp. (MT, 251; IBG, 51). κεκληρονόμηκεν perf. ind. act. κληρονομέω (# 3099) to inherit, perf. to have inherited, to be an heir (Buchanan; Michel; TDNT). For a discussion of a ring structure beginning and ending with the Son's exaltation s. John P. Meier, "Structure and Theology in Heb. 1:1-14," *Biblica* 66 (1985): 168-89. ◆ 5 εἶπεν aor. ind. act. λέγω (# 3306) to speak. ποτε (# 4537) ever. εἶ pres. ind. act. 2nd. pers. sing. εἰμί (# 1639) to be. σύ (# 5148) you, emphatic. σήμερον (# 4958) today. A quotation from Ps. 2:7. The day spoken of here is the day of His glorious victory and vindication. The resurrection, ascension, and glorification should be viewed as forming a unity, each one contributing to the exaltation of the Son to transcendental heights of power and dignity (Hughes) For a discussion of the OT quotes, probably from the LXX s. EJH, 121-47; DLNT, 841-50; Leonhard Goppelt, *Typos: The Typological Interpretation of the Old Testament in the New* (Grand Rapids: Eerdmans, 1982), 161-97. γεγέννηκα perf. ind. act. γεννάω (# 1164) to give birth to, to bear. This begetting is the begetting of the incarnate Son that marks the completion and acceptance of His redeeming mission to our world (Hughes). ἔσομαι fut. ind. mid. (dep.) εἰμί (# 1639) to be. ἔσται fut. ind. mid. (dep.) (# 1639) The vb. εἰμί w. the prep. εἰς (# 1650) can have the idea of "to serve as …." (KVS, 65). ◆ 6 ὅταν (# 4020) when, whenever. εἰσαγάγῃ aor. subj. act. εἰσάγω (# 1652) to lead into. The word is probably a Hebraism w. the meaning, "to bring something into the world," referring either to a birth or to the entrance into

the fut. world. Here it refers either to the Incarnation or to the enthronement (Michel; Riggenbach). πρωτότοκος (# 4758) firstborn. In this context the word is a title of honor expressing priority in rank (Lane; Michel; TDNT; Hughes; Weiss; TLNT; BBC). οἰκουμένη (# 3876) world, inhabited world. The context requires the word to be understood as the heavenly world of eschatological salvation into which the Son entered at His ascension (Lane). προσκυνησάτωσαν aor. imp. act. προσκυνέω (# 4686) to fall on the knees before someone, to worship, w. the dat. (TDNT; NIDNTT). ◆ 7 πρός (# 4637) w. acc., to. ποιῶν pres. act. part. ποιέω (# 4472) to do. Part. as subst. πνεῦμα (# 4460) wind. λειτουργός (# 3313) minister. The description here may be understood in two ways, either as personification, as when the wind storm and fire do His word, or as referring to real persons; i.e., the angels can take the form of wind or fire (Delitzsch; Hughes; SB, 3:678-79). πῦρ (# 4786) fire. φλόγα acc. sing. φλόξ (# 5825) flame. There are two points the writer makes: (1) angels are changeable and temporal, but the Son is eternal and unchangeable; (2) angels are servants, but the Son is Master (Grässer). In Jewish lit. "angels" serve the Creator, here they serve the Son (EJH, 225; BBC). ◆ 8 ὁ θεός (# 2436) voc., O God. The art. w. the voc. is due to Semitic influence (BG, 11; MT, 34). The Son is called "God" by God (EJH, 228; BTNT, 376) αἰών (# 172) age. Used here in the expression to mean eternal (TDNT). ῥάβδος (# 4811) scepter. εὐθύτης (# 2319) strictness, uprightness. ◆ 9 ἠγάπησας aor. ind. act. 2nd. pers. sing. ἀγαπάω (# 26) to love. δικαιοσύνη righteousness. (# 1466) ἐμίσησας aor. ind. act. 2nd. per. sing. μισέω (# 3631) to hate. Aor. could apply to the life and ministry of the incarnate Son on earth (Westcott; Hughes; Riggenbach). ἀνομία (# 490) lawlessness. διὰ τοῦτο because of this. ἔχρισεν aor. ind. act. χρίω (# 5987) to anoint. The idea is the crowning of the sovereign w. joy as at the royal banquet (Westcott; TDNT). ἔλαιον (# 1778) oil. ἀγαλλίασις (# 21) joy, gladness. Here, gen. of description indicating the oil which was used on occasions of gladness. παρά (# 4123) more than, above, used in a comp. μέτοχος (# 3581) partner, comrade, colleague. The reference here is not to angels but to believers who will share His reign in the age to come (Kent). ◆ 10 κατ' ἀρχάς (# 2848) at the beginning, in the beginning. ἐθεμελίωσας aor. ind. act. 2nd. pers. sing. θεμελιόω (# 2530) to lay a foundation. εἰσιν pres. ind. act. εἰμί (# 1639) to be. For the OT quotation s. Heb. 1:10-12. Indirectly predictive "Messianic Prophecy," OTN, 81-94, 106-8. ◆ 11 ἀπολοῦνται fut. ind. mid. (dep.) ἀπόλλυμι (# 660) to perish. διαμένεις pres. ind. act. διαμένω (# 1373) to remain, to continue throughout. Pres. w. prep. in compound emphasizes the permanent continual existence (MH, 301f). ἱμάτιον (# 2668) garment. παλαιωθήσονται fut. ind. pass. παλαιόω (# 4096) pass., to grow old, to become old, frequently in the sense of becoming use-less (BAGD). ◆ **12 ὡσεί** (# *6059*) just as. **περιβόλαιον** (# *4316*) that which one wraps around oneself, cloak. The word suggests a costly robe (Westcott). **ἑλίξεις** fut. ind. act. ἑλίσσω (# *1813*) to roll up, to fold together. **ἀλλαγήσονται** fut. ind. pass. ἀλλάσσω (# *248*) to change, to change clothes. **εἶ** pres. ind. act. 2nd. pers. sing. εἰμί (# *1639*) to be. Used in the sense of "remain"; i.e., "but you remain (are) the same." **ἔτη** nom. pl. ἔτος (# *2291*) year. **ἐκλείψουσιν** fut. ind. act. ἐκλείπω (# *1722*) to leave off, to fail. For the prep. in compound s. MH, 309. ◆ **13 εἴρηκεν** perf. ind. act. λέγω (# *3306*) to speak. **κάθου** pres. imp. mid. (dep.) καθίζω s.v. 3. Imp. as an invita-tion. **δεξιός** (# *1288*) right, right hand; here, "on the right (hand)." The right hand was a place of privileged honor (s. Eph. 1:20; Heb. 1:3). **θῶ** aor. subj. act. τίθημι (# *5502*) to set, to place. **ἐχθρός** (# *2398*) one who active-ly hates, enemy. **ὑποπόδιον** (# *5711*) footstool, double acc. used w. the vb. (Michel). **ποδῶν** gen. pl. πούς (# *4546*) foot. The figure arose from the oriental custom of the victor putting his foot on the neck of the defeated enemy (N. Lightfoot). ◆ **14 λειτουργικός** (# *3312*) min-istering. The suf. of the word suggests belonging to, pertaining to, w. the characteristic of (MH, 378). **διακο-νία** (# *1355*) service (TDNT). The rabbinical term, "an-gel of service or ministry," was used of angels who protected or accompanied a person (SB, 3:608f). **ἀπο-στελλόμενα** pres. pass. part. ἀποστέλλω (# *690*) to send out, to commission, to send as an authoritative repre-sentative (TDNT; TLNT; EDNT). **διά** (# *1328*) w. the acc., because of. **μέλλοντας** pres. act. part. μέλλω (# *3516*) to be about to. The word is used w. the inf. to express the fut. (MKG, 307f). **κληρονομεῖν** pres. act. inf. κληρονομέω (# *3099*) to inherit. Angels ministered on behalf of the one who inherited a greater name ("for those who inherit salvation"). There was a common concept of guardians assigned to the righteous by God (BBC). **σωτηρία** (# *5401*) salvation. Here it is salvation in its ultimate and broadest sense (Michel; TDNT; NIDNTT; NTW, 114f). For the use of the OT by the au-thor of Hebrews s. Lightfoot, 63; BE; Weiss, 171-81; Lane, cxii-cxxiv; esp. EJH; DLNT, 1072-75.

Hebrews 2

◆ **1 δεῖ** (# *1256*) pres. ind. act. impersonal, it is nec-essary, used w. the acc. and the inf. The word marks the logical necessity ("we must" [Westcott]). **περισσοτέρως** (# *4359*) adv., more abundantly, more earnestly (BD, 33). The word here could have almost an elative sense, "w. extreme care" (Moffatt). **προσέχειν** pres. act. inf. προσέχω (# *4668*) to give heed to, to give attention to, w. dat. Compl. inf. to the impersonal vb. The word is com-monly used of bringing a ship to land (EGT), or to mean "to remain on course" (Weiss). **ἀκουσθεῖσιν** aor. pass. part. ἀκούω (# *201*) to hear. **παραρυῶμεν** aor. pass.

subj. παραρρέω (# *4184*) to flow by. The word was used to describe a river that flows by a place or flows aside from its normal channel, flooding or escaping it. It was used of something slipping from one's memory, of a ring slipping from one's finger, or of a crumb going down the wrong way. It also indicated a ship drifting away (Hughes; Buchanan; Moffatt; Michel; Westcott; Weiss; BAGD; MM). In Prov. 3:21 (LXX) it means to lose sight of advice and wisdom (Lane). Pass. means to get or to find oneself in a state of flowing or passing by; i.e., referring to an object that requires close attention (Del-itzsch). Subj. w. **μήποτε** (# *3607*) in a neg. purp. cl. to ex-press anxiety or apprehension and to ward off something still dependent on the will (BD, 188; GGBB, 676). ◆ **2 λαληθείς** aor. pass. part. λαλέω (# *3281*) to speak. Subst. part., "that which was spoken." It refers to the Law of Moses which was given through angels (Weiss; s. Gal. 3:19; Acts 7:38, 53). **ἐγένετο** aor. ind. mid. (dep.) γίνομαι (# *1181*) to become. Ind. in a 1st. class cond. cl. assuming the reality of the cond. **βέβαιος** (# *1010*) firm, dependable, reliable, guaranteed. The word was used in the papyri in a technical sense for a legal guarantee (BS, 107; BAGD; TDNT; TLNT; s. 1 Cor. 1:6). **παράβασις** (# *4126*) stepping beside, transgres-sion, infringement (Lane). **παρακοή** (# *4157*) hearing beside, disobedience. It implies an unwillingness to lis-ten to the voice of God and relates to the hearing men-tioned in v. 1 (Lane). Both expressions here involve an expressed rejection of the divine will (Riggenbach). **ἔλαβεν** aor. ind. act. λαμβάνω (# *3284*) to receive. Ind. in a 1st. class cond. cl. assuming the reality of the cond. **ἔνδικος** (# *1899*) just, that which conforms to the right. Prep. in compound indicates that the word stands in antithesis to the term ἄδικος (MH, 307). **μισθαποδοσία** (# *3632*) giving back w. payment, a paying back, rec-ompense, retribution. The word indicates a full recom-pense as punishment (Riggenbach). ◆ **3 ἐκφευξό-μεθα** fut. ind. mid. (dep.) ἐκφεύγομαι (# *1767*) to flee from, to escape. The rhetorical question used in the apodosis involves an *a fortiori* argument: "If the earlier message of God is such a serious matter, then how can the readers avoid their just desserts for neglecting what was delivered by the Son?" (Attridge). **τηλικαύ-της** gen. πηλικοῦτος (# *5496*) so great, so large, so im-portant. **ἀμελήσαντες** aor. act. part. ἀμελέω (# *288*) to be unconcerned about, to neglect, not to put oneself out, to be indifferent to, to lose interest in, w. gen. (TLNT). Cond. part., "if we neglect." Aor. indicates a logically antecedent action. **σωτηρία** (# *5401*) salvation s. Heb. 1:14. **λαβοῦσα** aor. act. part. nom. fem. sing. λαμβάνω (# *3281*) to take. **λαλεῖσθαι** pres. pass. inf. λαλέω (# *3284*) to speak. Epex. inf. describing the beginning. Pass. here is the divine pass, implying that it is God who spoke (Hughes). **ἀρχὴν λαβοῦσα λαλεῖσθαι** lit., having received a beginning to be spoken, "having begun to be spoken" (RWP). ἀκουσάντων aor. act. part. ἀκούω (# 201) to hear. This came to the author and his contemporaries from those who heard, and probably means that they received it from the ear and eyewitnesses, those who saw and heard the very words of Jesus (Buchanan). This information plainly rules out the possibility of any firsthand apostle or disciple as the writer of our epistle (Hughes). ἐβεβαιώθη aor. pass. ind. βεβαιόω (# 1011) to make firm, to confirm, to guarantee. A t.t. indicating legal security and validity (s.v. 2; TLNT; MM). ◆ 4 συνεπιμαρτυροῦντος pres. act. part. (temp.) συνεπιμαρτυρέω (# 5296) to witness together w. someone, to join in giving additional testimony. Gen. abs. Pres. indicating contemporaneous action, "while God endorsed their witness" (RWP; Lane). σημεῖον (# 4956) sign. The word indicates that the event is not an empty ostentation of power; it is significant in pointing beyond itself to the reality of the mighty hand of God in operation (Hughes; DPL, 875-77; DLNT, 1093-95). τέρας (# 5469) wonder. ποικίλος (# 4476) various, variegated, manifold. δύναμις (# 1539) power, miracle. The word emphasizes the dynamic character of the event, w. particular regard to its outcome or effect (Hughes). μερισμός (# 3536) dividing, distribution. The following gen. could be a subjective gen. ("distribution which the Holy Spirit gives"), or perhaps better obj. gen. ("distribution of the Holy Spirit"); the reference is God's distribution of spiritual gifts to His people (Bruce). κατά (# 2848) w. acc., according to, in accordance w. θέλησις (# 2526) will, willing. The word describes the active exercise of will (Westcott). ◆ 5 ὑπέταξεν aor. ind. act. ὑποτάσσω (# 5718) to subordinate, to subject to one's authority. οἰκουμένη (# 3876) inhabited earth. μέλλουσαν pres. act. part. μέλλω (# 3516) to be about to. The world to come was considered by the rabbis to be the age of Messiah, the time when the Messiah would rule as king from His throne at Jerusalem (Buchanan; SB, 5:799-976; Michel). The term refers to the coming age, when Christ at His return shall establish His rule as the promised Davidic king (Kent). λαλοῦμεν pres. ind. act. λαλέω (# 3281) to speak. Pres. indicates the action in progress, i.e., the subject matter about which he is writing. ◆ 6 διεμαρτύρατο aor. ind. mid. (dep.) διαμαρτύρομαι (# 1371) to testify, to solemnly testify, to solemnly declare (MH, 302). For a discussion of the quotations showing the inadequacy of the old order s. George B. Caird, "The Exegetical Method of the Epistle to the Hebrews,"*Canadian Journal of Theology* 5 (1959): 47ff. πού (# 4543) where, somewhere. It is characteristic of the author that he is not concerned to provide a precise identification of the sources from which he quotes. It is sufficient for him that he is quoting from Holy Scripture, whose inspiration and authority he accepts without question (Hughes). τις (# 5516) someone. μιμνήσκῃ pres. ind. mid. (dep.) 2nd.

pers. sing. μιμνήσκομαι (# 3630) to remember, w. gen. ἐπισκέπτῃ pres. ind. mid. (dep.) 2nd. pers. sing. ἐπισκέπτομαι (# 2170) to look upon, to visit, to consider, to watch over. The word is used almost exclusively in the LXX, as in the NT, of a visitation for good (Westcott; GELTS, 174; Attridge). ◆ 7 ἠλάττωσας aor. ind. act. ἐλαττόω (# 1783) to make less, to make lower, to reduce in rank (Buchanan). It could mean to make lower than God, or as the LXX takes it, "lower than the angels, or heavenly beings" (Lane; Donald R. Glenn, "Psalm 8 and Hebrews 2: A Case Study in Biblical Hermeneutics and Biblical Theology," in *Walvoord: A Tribute*, ed. Donald K. Campbell [Chicago: Moody Press, 1982], 46-47). βραχύς (# 1099) a little. The word could have a temp. force, "for a little while" (Bruce; Grässer). παρ' = παρά (# 4123) w. the acc., than. For the prep. used in a comp. construction, s. 1:4, 9. δόξα (# 1518) glory (TDNT; TLNT). Here instr. dat. ἐστεφάνωσας aor. ind. act. στεφανόω (# 5110) to crown. ◆ 8 ὑπέταξας aor. ind. act. ὑποτάσσω s.v. 5. ὑποκάτω (# 5691) under. ὑποτάξαι aor. act. inf. ὑποτάσσω s.v. 5. Articular inf. is used w. a prep. to express time ("when"). Although the aor. inf. w. the prep. ἐν (# 1877) generally expresses antecedent time, while the pres. inf. expresses contemporaneous time, the context must decide; here it could be translated, "putting everything in subjection" (MT, 145; GGBB, 595). ἀφῆκεν aor. ind. act. ἀφίημι (# 918) to leave out, to omit. ἀνυπότακτος (# 538) not subjected. The verbal adj. here has a pass. sense and can indicate a possibility as well as a reality (Attridge; RWP). οὔπω (# 4037) not yet. The phrase indicates that there will come a time when this is a reality. ὁρῶμεν pres. ind. act. ὁράω (# 3972) to see. ὑποτεταγμένα perf. pass. part. ὑποτάσσω s.v. 5. Compl. part. w. vb. ὁρῶμεν. Perf. emphasizes the completed state or cond. ◆ 9 βραχύ (# 1099) temp., a little while (s.v. 7). παρ' = παρά s.v. 7. ἠλαττωμένον perf. pass. part. ἐλαττόω (# 1783) to make less (s.v. 7). Perf. emphasizes the completed state or condition and that the human nature Christ assumed He still retains (Westcott). βλέπομεν pres. ind. act. βλέπω (# 1063) to see. πάθημα (# 4077) suffering. δόξα (# 1518) glory (s. 1:3). ἐστεφανωμένον perf. pass. part. στεφανόω s.v. 7. ὅπως (# 3968) in order that. Particle introduces a purp. cl. which is to be taken w. πάθημα (Moffatt; Bruce). χάριτι θεοῦ by the grace of God, instr. dat. For a discussion of the textual variant, χωρὶς θ., s. Michel; TC, 664. ὑπέρ (# 5642) w. the gen., for, for the benefit of. γεύσηται aor. subj. mid. (dep.) γεύομαι (# 1174) to taste, to taste of, w. gen. The vb. is used in this common idiomatic sense to mean, "to experience something to the full" (Hughes). ◆ 10 ἔπρεπεν impf. ind. act. πρέπω (# 4560) used impersonally, it is fitting, it is appropriate, w. inf. It was appropriate that action taken to help man should include suffering, since suffering is mankind's common lot (Montefiore; Westcott). δι' = διά

(# *1328*) w. the acc., because of. **δι'** = διά (# *1328*) w. the gen., through. The phrases indicate that the sufferings and death of Jesus are not accidental; they form part of the eternal world purpose of God (Moffatt). **ἀγαγόντα** (# *72*) aor. act. part. ἄγω to lead. Part. could refer to Christ who leads sons into glory, or it could refer to the subject of the inf.: God the Father who leads sons into glory (Hughes, 101f; Michel). Aor. part. could express coincident action ("by bringing in" [MT, 80]), or it could be explained as a proleptic aor. which envisages the work of Christ and its consequences for mankind as a unit (Hughes, 102). **ἀρχηγός** (# *795*) leader, pioneer. In Gr. writings it was used of a hero who founded a city, gave it its name, and became its guardian. It also denoted one who was head of a family or founder of a philosophic school. The term also had a distinct military connotation referring to a commander of an army who went ahead of his men and blazed the trail for them. The idea here is of a leader who opens up a new way (N. Lightfoot; TDNT; EDNT; GELTS, 64; MM; Preisigke; Michel; Weiss; Lane; Attridge; Grässer; J. Julius Scott, "*Archegos* in the Salvation History of the Epistle to the Hebrews," *JETS* 29 [1986]: 47-54; George Johnston, "Christ as Archegos," *NTS* 27 [1980/81]: 381-85; BBC). Acc. is to be taken as the obj. of the inf. **τελειῶσαι** aor. act. inf. τελειόω (# *5457*) to complete, to initiate, to perfect, to qualify. To make Jesus fully qualified as the pioneer of their salvation required passing through suffering (Buchanan; Michel; Weiss; Attridge; Lane; TDNT; EDNT). Christ's perfection may be understood as a vocational process by which He is made complete or fit for His office (Attridge; Moisés Silva, "Perfection and Eschatology in Hebrews," *WTJ* 39 [1976]: 60-62). ◆ **11 ἁγιάζων** pres. act. part. ἁγιάζω (# *39*) to sanctify, to consecrate (TDNT; EDNT; NIDNTT). **ἁγιαζόμενοι** pres. pass. part. ἁγιάζω. With the double use of the vb. there is an emphasis on the action of both the sanctifier and the sanctified. **ἑνός** gen. εἷς (# *1651*) one. **ἐξ ἑνός** from one, from one source. The one could refer to God, indicating that He is the source (Bruce); or it could refer to Abraham or Adam, indicating the humanity of Christ (Hughes). **αἰτία** (# *162*) cause, reason. **δι' ἣν αἰτίαν** for this reason, because, since. **ἐπαισχύνεται** pres. ind. mid. (dep.) ἐπαισχύνομαι (# *2049*) to be ashamed. ◆ **12 ἀπαγγελῶ** fut. ind. act. ἀπαγγέλλω (# *550*) to proclaim, to announce (NIDNTT). **μέσος** (# *3545*) middle. **ἐκκλησία** (# *1711*) assembly, congregation. In the OT context of Ps. 22:22, it was not the church but the community of friends invited to share in the thanksgiving meal. **ὑμνήσω** fut. ind. act. ὑμνέω (# *5630*) to praise, to sing the praise of someone (AS). The fut. is a Semitic impf. expressing confidence. The psalmist is confident that God will deliver him and promises to recount this deliverance before his friends at a banquet. ◆ **13 ἔσομαι** fut. ind. mid.

(dep.) εἰμί (# *1639*) to be. **πεποιθώς** perf. act. part. πείθω (# *4275*) to persuade; perf., to be persuaded, to be convinced (s. Phil. 1:6). Perf. part. is used in a periphrastic fut perf. construction (RWP). **παιδίον** (# *4086*) child, little child. **ἔδωκεν** aor. ind. act. δίδωμι (# *1443*) to give. ◆ **14 ἐπεί** (# *2075*) since. **παιδία** pl. (# *4086*) children (s.v. 13). It refers to men and women, creatures of flesh and blood (Bruce). **κεκοινώνηκεν** perf. ind. act. κοινωνέω (# *3125*) to share in, w. gen. Perf. describes the constant human situation (Hughes; Westcott). **αἷμα** (# *135*) blood. **σαρκός** gen. σάρξ (# *4922*) flesh. The expression "flesh and blood" was the post-biblical Heb. designation for men or human beings (Delitzsch). **παραπλησίως** (# *4181*) adv., coming near. nearly, resembling, in like manner, likewise (Attridge). **μετέσχεν** aor. ind. act. μετέχω (# *3576*) to have a part in, to share (TLNT; TDNT). Aor. points to the historical event of the Incarnation, when the Son of God assumed this human nature and thus Himself became truly man and so truly one w. mankind (Hughes; VANT, 136-40). **αὐτῶν** gen. αὐτός (# *899*) self; here gen. used as obj. of the vb., referring to flesh and blood. **καταργήσῃ** aor. subj. act. καταργέω (# *2934*) to render inoperative, to nullify, to make idle or ineffective, to render impotent as though no longer existing (Hewitt). The depiction of Jesus as champion (ὁ ἀρχηγός) who crushed the tyrant, who possessed the power of death in order to rescue those whom he had enslaved, may call to mind the exploits of Hercules (Lane). **κράτος** (# *3197*) power, control (TDNT; s. Eph. 1:19). **ἔχοντα** pres. act. part. ἔχω (# *2400*) to have. For rabbinical teaching regarding Satan and his angels and their power over death s. Michel; SB 1:144f; Buchanan. Here is a paradox–Jesus suffered and overcame death; the devil, wielding death in his hand, succumbed (Bengel). **διάβολος** (# *1333*) adversary, devil (DDD, 463-73; Grässer). ◆ **15 ἀπαλλάξῃ** aor. subj. act. ἀπαλλάσσω (# *557*) to change from, to set free from (Grässer). The word was used in the papyri for the release from a position of responsibility; e.g., a marriage contract, the superintendence of land under lease, the release from a municipal office, or the release of a slave (MM; Preisigke; CCFJ, 1:159-61; Weiss. **ὅσος** (# *4012*) as many as (BAGD). **φόβῳ** dat. sing. φόβος (# *5832*) fear. Instr. dat. (RWP). **θάνατος** (# *2505*) death. Here, obj. gen., "fear of death." Dio Chrysostom speaks of the fear of death as being so intense that many have anticipated it, and that tyrants constantly live in this fear (DC, 6:42-45). Epictetus asks, "Where can I go to escape death?" and answers by saying, "I cannot avoid death" (Epictetus, *Discourses*, 24, 28:9). Seneca says, "When death is feared, the fear is always there" (*Ita si timenda mors est, semper timenda est*) (Seneca, *Epistles*, 30:17). For other views of the fear of death in the ancient world s. NW, 2, ii:1084-88; DRU, 1:68-76; Attridge. **ζῆν** pres. act. inf. ζάω (# *2409*) to live.

Inf. as subst. διὰ παντὸς τοῦ ζῆν through the whole of life, all through the living. For the prep. and the inf. here s. IBG, 56; RWP; MT, 144; Attridge. ἔνοχος (# 1944) held in, subject to. ἦσαν impf. ind. act. εἰμί (# 1639) to be. δουλεία (# 1525) slavery, bondage. ◆ **16 δήπου** (# 1327) certainly, surely. ἐπιλαμβάνεται pres. ind. mid. (dep.) ἐπιλαμβάνομαι (# 2138) to take hold of, to seize, to take to oneself. The word may have in this context the sense of, to help, to assist, to draw someone to oneself to help, to take hold of to help (Bruce; Moffatt; Lane; TDNT; for a discussion of the various meanings and implications of the word s. Hughes). ◆ **17 ὅθεν** (# 3854) from there, therefore, wherefore. This seems to be a favorite word of the writer of this epistle (Riggenbach). ὤφειλεν impf. ind. act. ὀφείλω (# 4063) to be obligated ("one must"). The word often implies moral necessity (AS; TDNT). κατὰ πάντα (# 2848; 4246) in every respect. ὁμοιωθῆναι aor. pass. inf. ὁμοιόω (# 3929) to make like; pass., to become like. This likeness is nothing less than complete identification–assimilation, not simulation (Hughes). ἐλεήμων (# 1798) merciful, sympathetic (TDNT; NIDNTT; TLNT). γένηται aor. subj. mid. (dep.) γίνομαι (# 1181) to become. The vb. suggests the notion of a result reached through the action of what we regard as a law (Westcott). Subj. w. ἵνα (# 2671) to express purp. ἀρχιερεύς (# 797) high priest. For the term in Judaism s. Michel, 165f; Westcott, 137-41; Attridge, 97-103; SB, 3:696-700; TDNT; NIDNTT; Mikeal C. Parsons, "Son and High Priest: A Study in the Christology of Hebrews," *Evangelical Quarterly* 60 (1988): 200-208; William R. Loader, *Sohn und Hoherpriester: Eine traditionsgeschichtliche Untersuchung zur Christologie des Hebräerbriefes* (Neukirchen-Vluyn: Neukirchner Verlag, 1981). τὰ πρὸς τὸν θεόν w. reference to the things that pertain to God; acc. of reference. The expression points to all man's relations towards God (Westcott; Riggenbach). εἰς (# 1650) used w. the articular inf. to express purp. ἱλάσκεσθαι pres. mid. (dep.) inf. ἱλάσκομαι (# 2661) to satisfy, to render well disposed, to conciliate, to propitiate (Hughes; APC, 125-85; TDNT; NIDNTT; Riggenbach). ◆ **18 πέπονθεν** perf. ind. act. πάσχω (# 4248) to suffer. Perf. serves to emphasize that though the temptation Christ suffered in the flesh is a thing of the past, yet its effect–compassion and understanding as He aids us in the hour of our temptation–is permanent (Hughes). πειρασθείς aor. pass. part. πειράζω (# 4279) to test, to tempt (TLNT). Part. describes the manner in which the suffering took place (Moffatt). Aor. points to the completion of the action. δύναται pres. ind. pass. (dep.) δύναμαι (# 1538) to be able to, w. inf. πειραζομένοις pres. pass. part. πειράζω (# 4279) to tempt. Pres. part. points to the continuous action taking place at the time. Part. as subst. Ind. obj. of the following vb. βοηθῆσαι aor. act. inf. βοάω (# 1070)

to help, to help someone in need (Michel). Compl. to the main vb., "He is able to help."

Hebrews 3

◆ **1 ὅθεν** (# 3854) wherefore, therefore; lit., from which, meaning that the following argument could be deduced from the conclusion reached above (Buchanan). κλῆσις (# 3104) calling. Here gen. w. the word μέτοχοι. Emphatic by its position. ἐπουράνιος (# 2230) heavenly (s. Eph. 1:3). μέτοχος (# 3581) one who shares, partner, associate (TLNT; TDNT; Grässer; RAC, 10:142-52). κατανοήσατε aor. imp. act. κατανοέω (# 2917) to put the mind down on a thing, to fix the mind on something, to consider. The word expresses attention and continuous observation and regard (RWP; Westcott). Aor. imp. calls for a specific act w. a note of urgency. ἀπόστολος (# 693) one who is commissioned as an authoritative representative, apostle (s. 1 Cor. 1:1; TLNT; EDNT; TDNT; Hughes; Michel; Lane). ἀρχιερέα acc. ἀρχιερεύς (# 797) high priest (s. 2:17). ὁμολογία (# 3934) confession, contract, agreement. It denotes a binding expression of obligation and commitment, the response of faith to the action of God (Lane; Attridge; ECC; Weiss; TDNT; EDNT). ◆ **2 ὄντα** pres. act. part. (adj.) masc. acc. sing. εἰμί (# 1639) to be. ποιήσαντι aor. act. part. ποιέω (# 4472) to do, to make. Here the word has the idea, "to appoint." The word could be used of action that one undertakes or states of being that one brings about (BAGD: Hughes; Moffatt). Part. as subst. Dat. of personal interest after the adj. πιστόν. ◆ **3 πλείονος** comp., πολύς (# 4498) great; comp., greater, followed by the gen. of comparison. δόξα (# 1518) glory. παρά (# 4123) than. For the prep. used in a comp. construction s. Heb. 1:4. ἠξίωται perf. ind. pass. ἀξιόω (# 546) to consider worthy. Perf. looks at the state or condition. Pass. could be a theol. pass. indicating that God is the agent. ὅσος (# 4012) how much, as much as. Used in a comp. expression denoting measure and degree (AS). καθ' = κατά (# 2848) according to. Used in the comp. construction w. the meaning, "as much more … as" (BAGD). πλείονα comp. (# 4498). τιμή (# 5507) honor. οἶκος (# 3875) house, dwelling; here gen. of comp., "than the house." κατασκευάσας aor. act. part. (subst.) κατασκευάζω (# 2941) to equip, to make ready, to construct, to furnish. The word expresses more than the mere construction of the house. It includes the supply of all necessary furniture and equipment and was used of God's creative activity (Westcott; Michel; Attridge; Mary Rose D'Angelo, *Moses in the Letter to the Hebrews*, SBL Dissertation Series #2 [Missoula, Mont.: Scholars, 1976], 164-77; MM). ◆ **4 κατασκευάζεται** pres. ind. pass. κατασκευάζω (# 2941) (s.v. 3). Gnomic pres. indicating that which, as a general rule, always occurs (SMT, 8). θεός (# 2536) God. pred. nom. ("… is God"). The lack of the article w. the pred. nom. emphasizes character or quality (s. John 1:1). ◆ **5 θεράπων** (# 2544) server, minister. The word suggests a personal service freely rendered. It denotes both the willing service rendered as well as the relationship between the one serving and the one served. It also emphasizes an honorable and dignified office. In this case it may have been taken over from the LXX as a translation of the Heb. word "servant" (עֶבֶד *'ebed*) (TDNT; EGT; Hughes; Riggenbach; NIDOTTE, 3:304-9; BBC; DLNT, 777-82). **λαληθησομένων** fut. pass. part. λαλέω (# 3281) to speak. The word indicates that the position of Moses pointed beyond itself to a future and higher revelation (Moffatt; Michel). ◆ **6 Χριστός** (# 5986) Anointed One, Messiah, Christ. Subject of the unexpressed pres. vb. "is faithful" (Westcott). **ἐσμεν** pres. ind. act. εἰμί (# 1639) to be. **ἡμεῖς** nom. pl. ἐγώ (# 1609) we. Emphatic and contrastive. **παρρησία** (# 4244) saying all, freedom of speech, boldness, confident (Michel; Grässer; Lane; TDNT; TLNT; S.B. Morrow, "Παρρησία and the New Testament," *CBQ* 44 [1982]: 431-46; GELTS, 361). Because Jesus is a faithful high priest in the service of God, Christians have the right to approach God and can openly acknowledge their faith as the basis of an unshakable hope (Lane). **καύχημα** (# 3017) boasting. The following gen. **ἐλπίδος** may be described as a gen. of content or definition. The Christian's hope described is the theme of our boasting or glorying (Hughes). **μέχρι** (# 3588) w. gen., until. **βέβαιος** (# 1010) firm; here adverbial acc., firmly. For the variant readings and textual problem here s. TC, 665. **κατάσχωμεν** aor. subj. act. κατέχω (# 2988) to hold down, to hold fast to. ◆ **7 διό** (# 1475) wherefore, therefore. The particle introducing the quotation looks backward as well as forward (Michel). **λέγει** pres. ind. act. λέγω (# 3306) to say. **ἀκούσητε** aor. subj. act. ἀκούω (# 201) to hear. Subj. w. **ἐάν** (# 1569) in a 3rd. class cond. cl. where the cond. is considered as possible. ◆ **8 σκληρύνητε** pres./aor. subj. act. σκληρύνω (# 5020) to dry out, to dry up, to make hard, to harden (Michel). Both pres. and aor. forms are the same. **παραπικρασμός** (# 4177) embittering, exasperation, rebellion. The word is a translation of the Heb. name *Meribah* which in Heb. means "conflict" or "rebellion." **κατά** (# 2848) w. the acc. used in a temp. sense, at (IBG, 58). **πειρασμός** (# 4280) test, trial. It is a translation of the Heb. name *Massah* meaning "tempting" or "testing" (Buchanan; Montefiore; Hughes). ◆ **9 οὗ** (# 4023) where, adv. of place. **ἐπείρασαν** aor. ind. act. πειράζω (# 4279) to try to test, to tempt (TLNT). **πατέρες** nom. pl. πατήρ (# 4252) father. Used here to establish a close identity w. the readers. **ἐν δοκιμασίᾳ** (# 1877; 1508) by temptation, proof, testing; instr. use of the prep. The word implies a testing which is intended to bring out the good (TDNT). **εἶδον** aor. ind. act. ὁράω (# 3972) to see. ◆ **10 τεσσαράκοντα** (# 5477) forty. **ἔτη** acc. pl. ἔτος (# 2291) year, acc. of time. The words "forty

years" could be taken either w. what precedes ("your fathers put me to the test and saw my works for forty years"), or it could be taken w. what follows ("for forty years I was provoked") (Hughes). **προσώχθισα** aor. ind. act. προσωχθίζω (# 4696) to loath, to be burdened down, to be laden w. grief, to be exhausted, to be indignant (Buchanan). The vb. is followed by the dat. **πλανῶνται** pres. ind. pass. πλανάω (# 4414) to lead astray; pass., to go astray, to wander astray. Iterative pres., "They repeatedly err." **ἔγνωσαν** aor. ind. act. γινώσκω (# 1182) to know. The word here is not so much the understanding of the revelatory acts of God and His leading as it is obedience to God's command (Riggenbach). **ὁδός** (# 3847) way; here in the sense of God's demands. ◆ **11 ὡς** (# 6055) as, according as. **ὤμοσα** aor. ind. act. ὀμνύω (# 3923) to swear. **ὀργῇ** (# 3973) wrath, anger. **εἰ** (# 1623) if. The word is the translation of the Heb. particle and the equivalent of a strong neg. (MT, 333; MH, 468). This construction is in accord w. the Semitic idiom used in the taking of an oath (Buchanan; Michel; Attridge). **εἰσελεύσονται** fut. ind. mid. (dep.) εἰσέρχομαι (# 1656) to go into. **κατάπαυσις** (# 2923) rest (TDNT; Michel, 183f; Weiss, 268-73; O. Hofius, *Katapausis. Die Vorstellung vom endzeitlichen Ruheort im Hebräerbrief* [Tübingen, 1970]; GELTS, 241; Kaiser, 153-75). **μου** gen. ἐγώ (# 1609) I. Subjective gen., "the rest which I provide." ◆ **12 βλέπετε** pres. imp. act. βλέπω (# 1063) to see, to see to it, to beware. When the word is followed by the neg. **μήποτε** (# 3607) and ind., it expresses a warning and fear regarding a pres. inevitable reality, indicating the warning should be taken very seriously (MT, 99; Riggenbach). **ἔσται** fut. ind. mid. (dep.) εἰμί (# 1639) to be. **πονηρός** (# 4505) evil, wicked. **ἀπιστία** (# 602) unbelief; here gen. of quality, indicating that unbelief characterizes the evil heart (Westcott). **ἀποστῆναι** aor. act. inf. ἀφίστημι (# 923) to fall away, to depart, to leave, to step aside from. Articular inf. w. the prep. **ἐν** (# 1877) is used here epexegetically to indicate the content of an evil heart (MT, 146; RG, 1073). **ζῶντος** pres. act. part. ζάω (# 2409) to live. The construction without the article fixes attention upon the character (Westcott). Pres. part. indicates the unending existence of God. ◆ **13 παρακαλεῖτε** pres. imp. act. παρακαλέω (# 4151) to encourage, to beseech (Attridge; s. Rom. 12:1). Pres. imp. calls for a repeated or continual action. **ἑαυτούς** acc. pl. ἑαυτοῦ (# 1571) oneself. The reflex. pron. is deliberately used here instead of the reciprocal pron. ἀλλήλων w. the purp. of emphasizing the close unity of the Christian body (Westcott), but it may be that the two pron. are used interchangeably (Hughes). **καθ** = κατά (# 2848) w. the acc. used distributively. **καθ' ἑκάστην ἡμέραν** at each day; i.e., every day, daily (IBG, 59; Westcott; Hughes). **ἄχρις οὗ** (# 948; 4005) as long as, while (RWP). **καλεῖται** pres. ind. pass. καλέω (# 2813) to call. **σκληρυνθῇ** aor. subj. pass. σκληρύνω (# 5020) to harden (s.v. 8). Subj. w. ἵνα (# 2671) in a neg. purp. cl. Pass. could perhaps be understood as a pass. of permission ("allow or permit oneself to be hardened"). ἀπάτη (# 573) deceitfulness. Here dat. of means used w. a pass. vb. ◆ **14 μέτοχος** (# 3581) partner, sharer, partaker. For a discussion of this phrase s. Hughes; Michel. **γεγόναμεν** perf. ind. act. γίνομαι (# 1181) to become. Perf. signifies that the readers have become and consequently now are partakers of Christ (Hughes). **ἐάνπερ** (# 1570) if at least (Westcott). **ὑπόστασις** (# 5712) that which underlies, ground, basis. The word then means confidence, assurance, conviction and refers to the reality, essence, or nature of something; or to the groundwork or basis of hope (Bruce; Buchanan; Grässer; Attridge). Here it is the foundation of the Christian's assurance of faith (Weiss). **κατάσχωμεν** aor. subj. act. κατέχω (# 2988) to hold down, to hold fast. ◆ **15 λέγεσθαι** pres. pass. inf. λέγω (# 3306) to speak. Articular inf. w. the prep. ἐν (# 1877) could be temp. or causal (MT, 146). **ἀκούσητε** pres. subj. act. ἀκούω (# 291) to hear. **σκληρύνητε** pres./aor. subj. act. σκληρύνω (# 5020) to harden. ◆ **16 τίνες** nom. pl. τίς (# 5515) who? Interrogative pron. introducing a rhetorical question. **ἀκούσαντες** aor. act. part. ἀκούω (# 201) to hear. Part. could be concessive: "although they had heard." Aor. describes antecedent action. **παρεπίκραναν** aor. ind. act. παραπικραίνω (# 4176) to provoke, to exasperate, to be disobedient, to rebel (BAGD). **ἐξελθόντες** aor. act. part. ἐξέρχομαι (# 2002) to go out. ◆ **17 προσώχθισεν** aor. ind. act. προσωχθίζω (# 4696) to loathe (s.v. 10). **ἁμαρτήσασιν** aor. act. part. masc. pl. dat. ἁμαρτάνω (# 279) to sin. **κῶλον** (# 3265) body, corpse. **ἔπεσεν** aor. ind. act. πίπτω (# 4406) to fall. Const. aor. looking at the process over forty years. **ἐρήμῳ** dat. sing. ἔρημος (# 2245) desert. Loc. dat. ◆ **18 ὤμοσεν** aor. act. ind. ὄμνυμι (# 3923) to swear. **εἰσελεύσεσθαι** fut. mid. (dep.) inf. εἰσέρχομαι (# 1656) to enter. Inf. in indir. discourse; used in an abbreviated Semitic cond. cl. expressing an oath: "If they shall enter …" i.e., "they shall surely not enter into…." **ἀπειθήσασιν** aor. act. part. ἀπειθώ (# 578) to be disobedient; unbelief passed into action (Westcott). ◆ **19 βλέπομεν** pres. ind. act. βλέπω (# 1063) to watch. **ἠδυνήθησαν** aor. ind. pass. δύναμαι (# 1538) to be able to, w. inf. Their exclusion from Canaan was not only a fact but a moral necessity (Westcott). **εἰσελθεῖν** aor. act. inf. εἰσέρχομαι (# 1656) to enter. **ἀπιστία** (# 602) unbelief. Used w. the prep. δι' = διά (# 1328) and the acc.: "because of disbelief."

Hebrews 4

◆ **1 φοβηθῶμεν** aor. subj. pass. (dep.) φοβέομαι (# 5828) to be afraid, to fear. Cohortative subj. is used to express a command or excitation in the 1st. pers.: "let us fear." **οὖν** (# 4036) therefore, drawing the logical implication from the preceding. **μήποτε** (# 3607) lest. Used

after a vb. of fear expressing anxiety, and w. subj. indicating fear of an uncertain thing (MT, 99). **καταλειπομένης** pres. pass. part. καταλείπω (# 2901) to leave behind; pass., to be left behind. Here the sense is of being left open (Bruce). Gen. abs. Part. could express cause or could be concessive (Riggenbach). **ἐπαγγελία** (# 2039) promise (TDNT; NIDNTT; Michel). **εἰσελθεῖν** aor. act. inf. εἰσέρχομαι (# 1656) to enter, to go into. Epex. inf. explaining what the promise is. **κατάπαυσιν** (# 2923) rest (s. 3:11). **δοκῇ** pres. subj. act. δοκέω (# 1506) to appear, to seem, to suppose. The word could also have a forensic idea, "to be found" (Michel; Riggenbach). Subj. in a cl. of fear (GGBB, 477). **ὑστερηκέναι** perf. act. inf. ὑστερέω (# 5728) to fall short, to be late, to come behind, to fall behind. The vb. pictures someone in a company marching together w. others who march faster than he can. He cannot keep up, so he falls behind. Falling behind in religious matters means not being able to fulfill all the demands or commandments, being negligent, failing to qualify or measure up (Buchanan). Perf. marks not only a present or past defeat, but an abiding failure (Westcott). ◆ **2 ἐσμεν** pres. ind. act. εἰμί (# 1639) to be. **εὐηγγελισμένοι** perf. pass. part. εὐαγγελίζομαι (# 2294) to proclaim good news; pass, to have good news proclaimed to someone. Part. is used to form the periphrastic perf. ind. pass. Perf. emphasizes the completeness of the evangelization that has taken place, and thus leaves no room for any excuse that evangelization had been inadequate or deficient (Hughes). **καθάπερ** (# 2749) just as. **κἀκεῖνοι** = καὶ ἐκεῖνοι (# 2797) those also. **ὠφέλησεν** aor. ind. act. ὠφελέω (# 6067) to profit, to be profitable. **ἀκοή** (# 198) hearing. Here descriptive gen. emphasizes that the word or message is associated w. hearing; the implication is that the message is intended for people to hear and so must be proclaimed (Hughes). **συγκεκερασμένους** perf. pass. part. συγκεράννυμι (# 5166) to mix together, to blend, to unite. For the textual problem here s. PC; TC, 665; Hughes. **ἀκούσασιν** aor. act. part. ἀκούω (# 201) to hear. Aor. part. describes antecedent action. Subst. part. used as ind. obj.: "to those who have heard." ◆ **3 εἰσερχόμεθα** pres. ind. mid. (dep.) εἰσέρχομαι (# 1656) to enter. Although pres. could be used as a futuristic pres., it is better to take it as an expression of a pres. fact (Westcott). Pres. could express the idea, "we are already in process of entering" (Montefiore). **πιστεύσαντες** aor. act. part. πιστεύω (# 4409) to believe. **εἴρηκεν** perf. ind. act. λέγω (# 3306) to speak. **ὤμοσα** aor. ind. act. ὄμνυμι (# 3923) to swear, to take an oath. **ὀργή** (# 3973) anger, wrath. **εἰσελεύσονται** fut. ind. mid. (dep.) εἰσέρχομαι (# 1656). For the Semitic expression of the oath implying a strong negative s. 3:11. **κατάπαυσις** (# 2923) rest. s.v. 3:11. **καίτοι** (# 2792) used w. the part. expressing a concessive idea: although. **καταβολή** (# 2856) laying down, foundation. **γενηθέντων** aor. pass.

(dep.) part. γίνομαι (# 1181) to become. Here contains the sense, "to be completed," "to be finished." ◆ **4 εἴρηκεν** perf. ind. act. λέγω to say. **που** (# 4543) where, somewhere. **ἕβδομος** (# 1575) seventh. Day is implied; "the seventh day," i.e., the Sabbath. In the synagogue liturgy for the beginning of the Sabbath, the recital of Ps. 95:1-11 was followed by Gen. 2:1-3 (Lane). **κατέπαυσεν** aor. ind. act. καταπαύω (# 2924) to rest. ◆ **5 ἐν τούτῳ** (# 1877; 4047) in this, here. **εἰσελεύσονται** fut. ind. mid. (dep.) εἰσέρχομαι (# 1656) to enter. ◆ **6 ἐπεί** (# 2075) since, because. **ἀπολείπεται** pres. ind. pass. ἀπολείπω (# 657) to remain over, to leave behind; pass., to be left over. **εἰσελθεῖν** aor. act. inf. εἰσέρχομαι (# 1656) to enter. Compl. inf. explains what remains to be done. **πρότερον** (# 4728) formerly. **εὐαγγελισθέντες** aor. pass. part. s.v. 2. **εἰσῆλθον** aor. ind. act. εἰσέρχομαι (# 1656) to enter. **δι'** = διά (# 1328) w. acc., because, because of. **ἀπείθεια** (# 577) unpersuaded, disobedient. Active expression of unbelief is manifested in disobedience (Westcott; BBC). ◆ **7 ὁρίζει** pres. ind. act. ὁρίζω (# 3988) to mark out w. a boundary, to appoint, to designate. **σήμερον** (# 4958) today. **λέγων** pres. act. part. λέγω (# 3306) to say. **τοσοῦτος** (# 5537) so long. Used in the temp. expression, "after so long a time." **προείρηται** perf. ind. pass. προλέγω (# 4625) to say before, to say previously. **ἀκούσητε** aor. subj. act. ἀκούω (# 210) to hear. **σκληρύνητε** aor. subj. act. σκληρύνω (# 5020) to harden (TLNT, GELTS, 429). Aor. subj. w. the neg. **μή** (# 3590) to express a prohibition. ◆ **8 Ἰησοῦς** (# 2652) Joshua. **κατέπαυσεν** aor. ind. act. καταπαύω (# 2924) to give rest. Ind. is used here in a 2nd. class cond. cl. expressing that which is contrary to fact. **ἐλάλει** impf. ind. act. λαλέω (# 4246) to speak. "He would not speak," "he would not be speaking" (RWP). ◆ **9 ἄρα** (# 726) so then. The word draws a conclusion from the preceding argument. **ἀπολείπεται** pres. ind. pass. ἀπολείπω s.v. 6. **σαββατισμός** (# 4878) sabbath rest. The term stresses the special aspect of festivity and joy, expressed in the adoration and praise of God (Lane; s. also the various essays on the Sabbath in FSLD). **λαῷ** dat. λαός (# 3295) people. Dat. ind. obj., "for the people of God." ◆ **10 εἰσελθών** aor. act. part. εἰσέρχομαι (# 1656) to enter. **κατέπαυσεν** aor. ind. act. καταπαύω (# 2924) to rest, to cease. **ἴδιος** (# 2625) one's own. ◆ **11 σπουδάσωμεν** aor. subj. act. σπουδάζω (# 5079) to be in a hurry, to make haste, to be in earnest, to concentrate one's energies on the achievement of a goal, to endeavor (Hughes). Subj. is hortatory expressing a command ("let us"). **οὖν** (# 4036) therefore, drawing a logical conclusion from the preceding. **εἰσελθεῖν** aor. act. inf. εἰσέρχομαι (# 1656) to enter. Compl. inf. to the preceding main vb., "let us endeavor to enter." **ὑπόδειγμα** (# 5682) example. The word is used here in the sense of a warning sign (Michel). The word refers not to an example of disobedience, but to an example of

falling into destruction as a result of disobedience (BAGD). **πέσῃ** aor. subj. act. πίπτω (# 4406) to fall. Subj. w. **ἵνα** (# 2671) to express purp. **ἀπείθεια** disobedience s.v. 6. ◆ **12 ζῶν** pres. act. part. (adj.) ζάω (# 2409) to be alive, living; without the art. expressing the quality. The word is emphatic by its position. **ἐνεργής** (# 1921) energetic, active, productive. The word is used of activity that produces results and often for divine activity that produces results (MNTW, 46ff; TDNT). **τομώτερος** comp. τομός (# 5533) sharp; comp., sharper. **ὑπέρ** (# 5642) than. The word is used in a comp. construction: sharper beyond, sharper than. **μάχαιρα** (# 3479) sword (s. Eph. 6:17). **πᾶσαν** acc. sing. πᾶς (# 4246) any; pl., all. **δίστομος** (# 1492) double-edged, two-edged. **διϊκνούμενος** pres. mid. part. διϊκνέομαι (# 1459) to pass through, to pierce, to penetrate (cf. Exod. 26:28; LXX). **μερισμός** (# 3536) dividing. **ἁρμός** (# 765) joint. **μυελός** (# 3678) marrow. The expressions serve to convey effectively the notion of the extreme penetrative power of the word of God, to the very core of one's being (Hughes; Lane). **κριτικός** (# 3217) capable of making a decision, discerning, able to judge, followed by the obj. gen. **ἐνθύμησις** (# 1927) thought, reflection, feelings, idea (BAGD). The word refers to the action of the affections and is related to the will (Westcott; Michel). **ἔννοια** (# 1936) thought, intent. The word refers to the action of reason (Westcott). ◆ **13 κτίσις** (# 3232) creature. **ἀφανής** (# 905) hidden, not manifest. **γυμνός** (# 1218) naked, open. **τετραχηλισμένα** perf. pass. part. τραχηλίζω (# 5548) to lay bear, to expose. The figure of speech behind the word is not clear. It has been suggested that it refers to bending back the neck of a sacrificial victim to make ready for the final stroke; or it may refer to the wrestler's art of seizing one by the throat, rendering him limp and powerless. For these suggestions w. references to usage s. Riggenbach; Michel; Hughes; Bruce; Delitzsch; Grässer; Weiss; Attridge. **πρὸς ὃν ἡμῖν ὁ λόγος** w. whom our matter is, w. whom our final reckoning has to be made (Bruce). For the meaning, "w. reference to which our message applies," "which word applies to us," as well as a discussion of other interpretations s. Buchanan. ◆ **14 ἔχοντες** pres. act. part. (causal) ἔχω (# 2400) to have, to possess. Pres. indicates contemporary action to the main vb. **ἀρχιερεύς** (# 797) high priest. This could be a contrast w. the high priest of the OT, or w. the high priest of Judaism at the time of writing (BBC; DLNT, 962-67). **μέγας** (# 3489) great, indicating might (Grässer). **διεληλυθότα** perf. act. part. διέρχομαι (# 1451) to pass through, to go through. Perf. indicates that he has passed through the heavens and is still there. **κρατῶμεν** pres. subj. act. κρατέω (# 3195) to be in control of, to exercise power over, to hold to, to hold fast, followed by the gen. **ὁμολογία** (# 3934) confession, profession. ◆ **15 ἔχομεν** pres. ind. act. ἔχω (# 2400) to have, to possess. **δυνάμενον** pres.

mid. (dep.) part. δύναμαι (# 1538) to be able to, w. inf. **συμπαθῆσαι** aor. act. inf. συμπαθέω (# 5217) to share the experience of someone, to sympathize w. someone. Compl. inf. to the preceding part. The word is not to be understood in a psychological, but in an existential sense. The exalted one suffers together w. the weakness of the one tempted (Michel). **ἀσθένεια** (# 819) weakness. **πεπειρασμένον** perf. pass. part. πειράζω (# 4279) to tempt, to test, to try. Perf. emphasizes the completed state and continuing results. **ὁμοιότης** (# 3928) likeness. The word emphasizes exact correspondence (Michel; GELTS, 332; TDNT). ◆ **16 προσερχώμεθα** pres. subj. mid. (dep.) προσέρχομαι (# 4665) to come to, to draw near. The word was used in the LXX for the priestly approach to God in service (Westcott; GELTS, 400). Cohortative subj., "let us always come near." Pres. emphasizes that the privilege is always available. **παρρησία** (# 4244) speaking all things, boldness, confidence, assurance (s. 3:6; TLNT). **τῷ θρόνῳ τῆς χάριτος** throne of grace; i.e., a throne characterized by grace. **λάβωμεν** aor. subj. act. λαμβάνω (# 3284) to receive. Subj. used to express purp. **ἔλεος** (# 1799) mercy, compassion, compassionate help (TDNT; TLNT; s. 1 Tim. 1:2). **εὕρωμεν** aor. subj. act. εὑρίσκω (# 2351) to find. Subj. w. ἵνα (# 2671) to express purp. **εὔκαιρος** (# 2322) convenient, good time, well timed; at the right time, at the right moment (Delitzsch; Michel; Preisigke; MM; TLNT; GELTS, 186; Luke 22:6). Josephus uses the word of Herod the Great waiting for the right time to talk to his sons about who would succeed him (Jos., *Ant.* 16:80; for other examples s. CCFJ, 2:232). **βοήθεια** (# 1069) help, help given to one in need (s. 2:18).

Hebrews 5

◆ **1 γάρ** (# 1142) for. It introduces the grounds for the preceding and gives an explanation of how Christ was tried (Attridge). **λαμβανόμενος** pres. pass. part. λαμβάνω (# 3284) to take. **καθίσταται** pres. ind. pass. καθίστημι (# 2770) to constitute, to appoint. Pass. implies that he does not appoint himself (Hughes). Adj. part. without the art. stresses the character. Gnomic pres. referring to that which is always true. **τὰ πρὸς τὸν θεόν** in reference to things pertaining to God, in reference to things in relation to God. **προσφέρῃ** pres. subj. act. προσφέρω (# 4712) to carry to, to offer. The word was used in a religious sense of bringing an offering or sacrifice to God. Subj. w. ἵνα (# 1142) to express purp. **δῶρον** (# 1565) gift. **θυσία** (# 2602) sacrifice. The expressions are best understood here as a general description of the offerings over which the high priest officiated (Hughes; DLNT, 1069-72). ◆ **2 μετριοπαθεῖν** pres. act. inf. μετριοπαθέω (# 3584) to moderate one's feelings, to have feelings in the right measure. The word was used in Aristotelian philosophical tradition in the sense of moderating one's feelings or passions so as to avoid ex-

cess, either of enthusiasm or impassivity. The word indicates that an earthly high priest is not to pass over the sin of his passion and pity for the sinner but rather to have a controlled feeling of sympathy (Michel; Buchanan; Hughes). It indicates that compassion or sympathy is innate to the priest's nature (TLNT). Compl. inf. to the following part. **δυνάμενος** pres. mid. (dep) part. δύναμαι (# 1538) to be able to, w. inf. Adj. part. used to describe the character of one who is taken or appointed to be a high priest. **ἀγνοοῦσιν** pres. act. part. dat. masc. pl. ἀγνοέω (# 51) to be without understanding, to be ignorant. **πλανωμένοις** pres. pass. part. πλανάω (# 4414) to go astray, to wander (BAGD). The two parts. used w. a single article refer to a single class or category of those sinning; i.e., those who erred through ignorance (N. Lightfoot; Monteriore; Westcott). **περίκειται** pres. ind. pass. περίκειμαι (# 4329) to be surrounded by, to be encompassed by. It is like a millstone around his neck (Mark 9:42; Luke 17:2), or like a chain around him (Acts 28:20) (RWP). **ἀσθένεια** (# 819) weakness. ◆ **3 ὀφείλει** pres. ind. act. ὀφείλω (# 4053) to be obligated. The word speaks of moral obligation; i.e., "he must," "he is bound" in the very nature of things, in virtue of his constitution and of his office (Westcott). Gnomic pres., indicating that which is always true (SMT, 8). **καθώς** (# 2777) just as, as. **προσφέρειν** pres. act. inf. προσφέρω (# 4712) to offer (s.v. 1). ◆ **4 τιμή** (# 5507) honor. The word was used in Josephus to describe the honor of the office of high priest (Josephus, *Ant.*, 3:188; Michel). **καλούμενος** pres. pass. part. καλέω (# 2813) to call. **καθώσπερ** (# 2778) just as. The author may have had in mind the leading sacerdotal families of Jerusalem in his day, who were not descendants of Aaron but had sought for themselves the high priestly office and been elevated to it by Herod the Great. Such men, though approved by the state, were not approved by God (Hughes). ◆ **5 ἐδόξασεν** aor. ind. act. δοξάζω (# 1519) to glorify. **γενηθῆναι** aor. pass. (dep.) inf. γίνομαι (# 1181) to become. Inf. may be epex. explaining the main vb.; i.e., "Christ did not take for Himself the honor of becoming high priest." Or it may be used to express result, "that He might become a high priest" (IBG, 127). **λαλήσας** aor. act. part. λαλέω (# 3281) to speak. Part. as subst. Aor. indicates the completed action of the event. **εἶ** pres. act. ind. 2nd. pers. sing. εἰμί (# 1639) to be. **γεγέννηκα** perf. ind. act. γεννάω (# 1164) to beget, to become the father of. Perf. indicates the state or condition. ◆ **6 ἐν ἑτέρῳ** (# 1877; 2283) in another place. **λέγει** pres. ind. act. λέγω (# 3306) to say. **τάξις** (# 5423) rank, order. ◆ **7 δέησις** (# 1255) prayer. **ἱκετηρία** (# 2656) supplication, petition. The word properly denotes an olive branch entwined w. wool borne by suppliants. The olive branch was the sign of the suppliant (Westcott; BAGD; MM; Attridge; TDNT). **δυνάμενον** pres. mid. (dep.) part. δύναμαι (# 1538) to be able. **σῴζειν** pres. act.

inf. σῴζω (# 5392) to save. δάκρυον (# 1232) tear. Later rabbinic piety identified three kinds of prayers; i.e., entreaty, crying, and tears. It is said that entreaty is offered in a quiet voice, crying w. a raised voice, but tears are higher than all (Moffatt). προσενέγκας aor. act. part. (adj.) προσφέρω to offer s.v. 1. εἰσακουσθείς aor. pass. part. (adj.) εἰσακούω (# 1653) to hear, to answer; pass., to be heard. ἀπό (# 608) from; to be understood here in the sense of "arising from," "as the result of" (Hughes). εὐλάβεια (# 2325) godly fear. The word marks that careful and watchful reverence that pays regard to every circumstance (Westcott; Michel; for various interpretations of the passage s. Hughes; Bruce). ◆ 8 καίπερ (# 2788) w. the part., although. ὤν pres. act. part. εἰμί (# 1639) to be. Concessive part. υἱός (# 5626) son; the honored position as the heir and future owner (s. Heb 1:2). ἔμαθεν aor. ind. act. μανθάνω (# 3443) to learn. Discipline–even physical–was an essential part of Greek education (BBC). ἀφ᾽ ὧν = ἀπὸ τούτων ἅ from these things which. ἔπαθεν aor. ind. act. πάσχω (# 4248) to suffer. ὑπακοή (# 5633) obedience. The article indicates the particular obedience required of him in the days of his flesh (EGT). ◆ 9 τελειωθείς aor. pass. part. τελειόω (# 5457) to complete, to perfect. Part. could be temp. or causal. His perfection consisted in the retention of his integrity in the face of every kind of assault, thereby establishing his integrity (Hughes; for a study of this word and its contextual backgrounds s. Michel; TDNT; A. Wikgren, "Patterns of Perfection in the Epistle to the Hebrews," NTS 6 [1960]: 159-67). ἐγένετο aor. ind. mid. (dep.) γίνομαι (# 1181) to become. ὑπακούουσιν pres. act. part. ὑπακούω (# 5634) to obey, to be obedient. αἴτιος (# 165) cause, reason, author. For various examples of the word esp. from Philo s. Bruce; N. Lightfoot; Westcott; Attridge; NW, 2, ii:1105-6. ◆ 10 προσαγορευθείς aor. pass. part. προσαγορεύω (# 4641) to designate, to greet, to salute, to hail. The word contains the idea of a formal and solemn ascription of a title (BAGD; MM; EGT; Westcott; for a milder sense of the word–"mention" or "greet"–s. NDIEC, 1:61-62; 64-66; 4:245-50). κατὰ τὴν τάξιν after the order of. ◆ 11 περὶ οὗ (# 4309; 4005) concerning whom, concerning which. The author refers to the priesthood of Christ in the order of Melchizedek (Hughes). For a discussion s. BTNT, 380-93; ABD 4:684-88; DDD, 1047-53; DLNT, 729-31. ἡμῖν dat. pl. ἐγώ (# 1609) I. Here, "to us," "for us." Dat. indicates the obligation, what it is incumbent on us to undertake (EGT). δυσερμήνευτος (# 1549) difficult to explain, difficult to interpret, hard to explain (Moffatt; Michel; EGT). λέγειν pres. ind. act. λέγω (# 3306) to say. Epex. inf. explaining the adj. νωθρός (# 3821) dull, slow, sluggish. The word was used of the numbed limbs of a sick lion (EGT). In the LXX it is used of one who is lazy (GELTS, 320; Prov. 22:29; TLNT). In the papyri the corresponding vb. is used of sickness

(MM). γεγόνατε perf. ind. act. γίνομαι (# 1181) to become. It is not a question of what they are by nature, but of what they have become by default, the implication being that this was not the case w. them originally (Hughes). Perf. signifies the state or condition. ἀκοαῖς dat. pl. ἀκοή (# 198) hearing; dat. of reference, "in reference to hearing." ◆ 12 ὀφείλοντες pres. act. part. ὀφείλω (# 4053) to be obligated, one must. Concessive part., "although you are obligated." εἶναι pres. act. inf. εἰμί (# 1639) to be. Compl. inf. to the preceding part. διὰ τὸν χρόνον (# 1328; 5989) because of the time. Because of the length of time that they had been believers, they should have made progress in their religious condition (Grässer). χρείαν ἔχετε you have need. διδάσκειν pres. act. inf. διδάσκω (# 1438) to teach. Articular inf. w. gen., indicating the area of need: "you have need that someone teach you." στοιχεῖον (# 5122) basic element (Michel; TDNT). ἀρχή (# 794) beginning. Here, gen. of definition (Bruce) or descriptive gen. ("original elements"). Here it denotes the foundational teaching (Spicq; EGT). τῶν λογίων τοῦ θεοῦ the oracles of God. The phrase might refer to the new revelation given by Christ to His apostles; but it more naturally seems to refer to the collected writings of the OT (Westcott). γεγόνατε perf. ind. act. γίνομαι (# 1181) to become. ἔχοντες pres. act. part. ἔχω (# 2400) to have. χρείαν ἔχοντες having need. The following gen. indicates the area of need. γάλα (# 1128) milk. The word can be compared to the rabbinical term "suckling," referring to young students (EGT; Spicq; TDNT; DLNT, 736-38). στερεός (# 5104) solid. τροφή (# 5575) food. ◆ 13 μετέχων pres. act. part. μετέχω (# 3576) to partake, to partake, followed by the gen. Used here of eating and drinking (BAGD). Subst. use of the part. w. πᾶς (# 4246) to emphasize a defining trait: "any one who partakes." ἄπειρος (# 586) unskilled. It describes a person who lacks experience, is untried, or ignorant (Buchanan). λόγου δικαιοσύνης word of righteousness. The phrase has been taken to refer to an infant's inability to speak correctly (Riggenbach), or in the sense of the righteousness of Christ imputed to the believer (Hughes). ◆ 14 τέλειος (# 5455) perfect, mature. It refers to those who should assume adult responsibilities. The author is using terms of human development to describe the readers' development in faith (Buchanan; BBC; for a parallel in the DSS s. 1QS 1:10-11). ἕξις (# 2011) habit. It refers to a habit of body or mind indicating not the process but the result; the condition, produced by past exercise, is now habitual, the disposition of character (EGT; Westcott; Spicq; Attridge). It could be taken as referring to the ability gained through exercise (Weiss). αἰσθητήριον (# 152) faculty, sense organ like seeing, tasting, smelling, hearing (Attridge; NW, 2, ii:1110-11). Used here of spiritual sensitivity (Hughes). γεγυμνασμένα perf. pass. part. γυμνάζω (# 1214) to exercise, to train by exercise. The word gives an athletic image of exercising naked (Attridge). ἐχόντων pres. act. part. (adj.) ἔχω (# 2400) to have. διάκρισις (# 1360) distinguishing, deciding, making a judgment between two things. The goal of the training is distinguishing good and evil (Attridge). For the force of the prep. in compound s. MH, 303. Because the readers had been believers for a time, they should have known that to return to Judaism was a bad choice–they would not be able to go on to maturity! S. Barnabas Lindars, "The Rhetorical Structure of Hebrews," *NTS* 35 (1989): 382-406; esp. 384-90.

Hebrews 6

◆ **1** διό (# 1475) therefore. ἀφέντες aor. act. part. ἀφίημι (# 918) to leave. The part. could be means, "in that we leave." The leaving does not mean to despise or abandon the elementary doctrines. The point is that the beginning is not a stopping place; it is the door to progress and the springboard to achievement (Hughes). τὸν ... τοῦ Χριστοῦ λόγον the word of the beginning of Christ. The gen. τοῦ Χριστοῦ could be subjective gen.; i.e., Christ's initial teachings (Buchanan; Hughes; J.C. Adam, "Exegesis of Hebrews 6:1f," *NTS* 13 [1967]: 378-85). τῆς ἀρχῆς (# 794) of the beginning, elementary. τελειότης (# 5456) perfection, maturity (s. 5:14). The word goes back to the motif of babes and adults (5:12-14), and denotes that maturity of thought and commitment the writer attempts to inculcate in the addressees (Attridge). φερώμεθα pres. subj. pass. φέρω (# 5770) to carry; pass., to be carried. Cohortative subj., "let us be carried." The pass. gives the thought of personal surrender to an active influence (Westcott). It is not a matter of the learners being carried by their instructors, but of both being carried forward together by God. It is a divine pass. implying the agency of God (Hughes; BG, 76). θεμέλιον (# 2529) foundation, basis. καταβαλλόμενοι pres. mid. (dep.) part. καταβάλλω (# 2850) to cast down; mid., to lay a foundation. μετάνοια (# 3567) change of mind, repentance. Here, gen. of description or gen. of apposition. νεκρός (# 3738) dead. ἔργον (# 2240) work, deed. ◆ **2** βαπτισμῶν (# 968) washing. The pl. here evidently refers to the various washing to be found in Judaism (BBC). For this as well as evidence that the matters here refer primarily to Judaism s. J.C. Adam cited in v. 1; Lane; for various interpretations of the pl. s. Hughes. διδαχή (# 1439) teaching. ἐπίθεσις (# 2120) placing upon, laying on. For the Jewish teaching regarding the laying on the hands s. SB, 2:647f; TDNT. ἀνάστασις (# 414) resurrection. κρίμα (# 3210) judgment. ◆ **3** ποιήσομεν fut. ind. act. ποιέω (# 4472) to do. ἐάνπερ (# 351) if. The 2nd particle used w. the cond. particle emphasizes that the action is in spite of opposition: "if, in spite of opposition, God permits," if indeed, if after all (RG, 1154; BD, 237). ἐπιτρέπῃ pres. subj.

act. ἐπιτρέπω (# 2205) to allow, to permit. ◆ **4** ἀδύνατος (# 105) impossible. The word is forceful, emphatic, and the affirmation is unequivocal (Attridge; TLNT; Spicq). The adj. is used w. the inf. that occurs in v. 6. ἅπαξ (# 562) once, once for all. φωτισθέντας aor. pass. part. φωτίζω (# 5894) to enlighten, to illuminate. Aor. looks at the completed event. Illumination indicates that God gives understanding and spiritual light (Michel; Hughes; BBC; HSB s. for the different options BTNT). Temp. part. ("after"). γευσαμένους aor. mid. (dep.) part. γεύομαι (# 1174) to taste of, to taste, w. gen. The vb. expresses a real and conscious enjoyment of the blessings apprehended in their true character (Westcott; Hughes). Temp. part. ("after"). δωρεά (# 1561) gift. ἐπουράνιος (# 2230) heavenly (s. Eph. 1:3). μέτοχος (# 3581) sharer, participant. γενηθέντας aor. pass. (dep.) part. γίνομαι (# 1181) to become. Temp. part. ("after"). ◆ **5** γευσαμένους aor. mid. (dep.) part. γεύομαι to taste of (s.v. 4). ῥῆμα (# 4839) that which is spoken, word. μέλλοντος pres. act. part. adj. μέλλω (# 3516) to about to, coming. ◆ **6** παραπεσόντας aor. act. part. (cond.) παραπίπτω (# 4178) to fall beside, to go astray, to miss; later in a theological use, to fall away, to commit apostasy (BAGD; GELTS, 355). It implies nothing of their previous spiritual condition. It only suggests that they are going astray or missing what Christ has provided (Hughes; BBC; DLNT, 73-76). This is parallel to all the preceding parts. It could refer to those who might turn back to Judaism and try to make a "new start" in order to avoid persecution. ἀνακαινίζειν pres. act. inf. ἀνακαινίζω (# 362) to renew again, to make new again. Epex. inf. explaining what is impossible. εἰς (# 1650) unto. Prep. gives the direction or the goal. ἀνασταυροῦντας pres. act. part. acc. masc. pl. ἀνασταυρόω (# 416) to crucify again, to lift up on a cross. Causal part. indicates why it is impossible for such people to repent and make a new beginning (Hughes; Bruce). For the force of the prep. in compound, meaning "again" s. MH, 295; (or perhaps better "up," in the sense of "to put *up* on a stake" [Lindars, "The Rhetorical Structure of Hebrews," *NTS* 35 (1989): 37; Braun; Weiss; CCFJ, 1:109]). ἑαυτοῖς dat. pl. ἑαυτός (# 1571) oneself; dat. of advantage, "for themselves." παραδειγματίζοντας pres. act. part. παραδειγματίζω (# 4136) to expose publicly, to make a public example of, to expose to disgrace (RWP; BAGD; Weiss). If the readers were to return again to Judaism, no possibility existed for them to begin their spiritual life anew. This would require a recrucifixion of Christ, putting Him to open shame. For this reason they must continue toward maturity despite the difficulties, problems, and persecutions that attend their walk. ◆ **7** πιοῦσα aor. act. part. (adj.) πίνω (# 4403) to drink. Gnomic aor. ἐρχόμενον pres. mid. (dep.) part. (adj.) ἔρχομαι (# 2262) to come, to go. Iterat. pers. ὑετός (# 5624) rain. τίκτουσα pres. act. part. τίκτω (# 5503) to bear, to bring forth, to produce. **βοτάνη** (# 1083) vegetation, green plants. **εὔθετος** (# 2310) well-suited, conveniently placed, suitable (BAGD). **δι'** = διά (# 1328) w. acc., because of, on whose account. The owners are intended or it refers to those whom the owners meant to supply (EGT). **γεωργεῖται** pres. ind. pass. γεωργέω (# 1175) to cultivate. **μεταλαμβάνει** pres. ind. act. μεταλαμβάνω (# 3561) to receive w. someone, to partake, to share in. Gnomic. pres. ◆ **8 ἐκφέρουσα** pres. act. part. ἐκφέρω (# 1766) to carry out, to bring forth, to produce. Part. could be cond., "if it produces." **ἄκανθα** (# 180) thorn. **τρίβολος** (# 5560) thistle; lit., "three-pointed." For the use of these terms in the LXX s. EGT; GELTS, 480; GELRS, 295. **ἀδόκιμος** (# 99) disapproved, rejected after examination (s. 1 Cor. 9:27). **κατάρα** (# 2932) curse. **ἐγγύς** (# 1584) near; "nigh unto a curse," in Gen. 3:17ff. Thorns and thistles follow the cursing of the land for man's sake (Bruce). **καῦσις** (# 3011) burning. ◆ **9 πεπείσμεθα** perf. ind. pass. πείθω (# 4275) to persuade; pass., to be persuaded; perf., to have confidence (s. Phil. 1:6). **κρείσσονα** (# 3202) pl. comp. ἀγαθός good; comp., better. "Better things." **ἐχόμενα** pres. mid. part. ἔχω (# 2400) to have. Mid. to hold oneself fast, to belong to, to accompany. The mid. is used of inner belonging and close association; the "to" of belonging and the "w." of association are expressed by the gen. (BAGD). **εἰ καί** (# 1623; 2779) if also, although. The words introduce a concessive condition of the 1st. class (RWP). **λαλοῦμεν** pres. ind. act. λαλέω (# 4246) to speak. ◆ **10 ἐπιλαθέσθαι** aor. mid. (dep.) inf. ἐπιλανθάνομαι (# 2140) to forget, w. the gen. Epex. inf. explaining the word **ἄδικος**. **ἐνεδείξασθε** aor. ind. mid. ἐνδείκνυμι (# 1892) to demonstrate. The prep. in compound suggests more than the simplest demonstration–laying the index finger, as it were, on the object (MH, 305). **εἰς** (# 1650) for. This implies that their coming to the assistance of their brethren is evidence of their willingness to identify themselves w. the stigma attached to the name of Jesus, and thus of the genuineness of their love for Him (Hughes). **διακονήσαντες** aor. act. part. διακονέω (# 1354) to minister, to serve, perhaps to offer financial help (BBC). **διακονοῦντες** pres. act. part. διακονέω. Pres. part. emphasizes the continuous action going on at the pres. time. ◆ **11 ἐπιθυμοῦμεν** pres. ind. act. ἐπιθυμέω (# 2121) to long for, to yearn for, to give a strong desire (Attridge). **ἕκαστος** (# 1667) each one. **αὐτός** (# 899) the same. **σπουδή** (# 5082) earnestness, endeavor, diligence, great zeal (Attridge). **ἐνδείκνυσθαι** pres. mid. inf. ἐνδείκνυμι s.v. 10. Inf. expresses the object of what is desired. **πληροφορία** (# 4443) fullness, full assurance (TLNT; MM; Michel). ◆ **12 νωθρός** (# 3821) dull (s. 5:11). **γένησθε** aor. subj. mid. (dep.) γίνομαι (# 1181) to become, to be. Subj. in a neg. purp. cl. **μιμητής** (# 3629) imitator. **διά** (# 1328) w. gen., through. **μακροθυμία** (# 3429) longsuffering, pa-

tience, patient endurance (s. Gal. 5:22; Rom. 2:4). **κληρονομούντων** pres. act. part. κληρονομέω (# 3099) to inherit. Part. as subst. **ἐπαγγελία** (# 2039) promise. ◆ **13 ἐπαγγειλάμενος** aor. mid. (dep.) part. ἐπαγγέλομαι (# 2040) to promise, to make a promise. Temp. part., contemporaneous action, "when God promised." For this concept s. DLNT, 967-70; C. Rose, "Verheissung und Erfüllung: Zum Verständnis von ἐπαγγελία im Hebräerbrief,"*Biblische Zeitschrift* 33 (1989): 178-91; R. Worley, "God's Faithfulness to Promise: The Hortatory Use of Commisive Language in Hebrews," (Ph. D. dissertation, Yale University, 1981). **ἐπεί** (# 2075) since, because. **εἶχεν** aor. ind. act. ἔχω (# 2400) to have. **μείζων** (# 3505) greater. **ὀμόσαι** aor. act. inf. ὀμνύω (# 3923) to swear by followed by the prep. **καθ'** = κατά (# 2848) w. the gen. **ὤμοσεν** aor. ind. act. (# 3505) The fact that God swore by Himself indicates that He binds Himself to His word by His eternal person (Cleon Rogers, "The Covenant with Abraham and Its Historical Setting," *Bib Sac* 127 [1970]: 214-56; Michel; Buchanan; Attridge; Philo, *The Sacrifices of Abel and Cain*, 91-94; BBC). Concerning God's oath Philo says, "And it is so that while with us the oath gives warrant for our sincerity, it is itself guaranteed by God. For the oath does not make God trustworthy; it is God that assures the oath. Why then did it seem well … to represent God as binding Himself by an oath? It was to convince created man of his weakness and to accompany conviction with help and comfort" (Philo, *The Sacrifices of Abel and Cain*, 93-94). ◆ **14 λέγων** pres. act. part. λέγω (# 3306) to say. Used as quotation marks for dir. discourse. **μήν** (# 3605) surely. **εὐλογῶν** pres. act. part. εὐλογέω (# 2328) to bless. **εὐλογήσω** fut. ind. act. εὐλογέω. Part. and the finite vb. are used as a translation of the Heb. inf. abs., giving emphasis and certainty to the expression; "I shall certainly bless you" (BG, 128; BD, 218). **πληθύνων** pres. act. part. πληθύνω (# 4437) to increase, to multiply. **πληθύνω** fut. ind. act. πληθύνω. ◆ **15 μακροθυμήσας** aor. act. part. μακροθυμέω (# 3428) to endure patiently, to be longsuffering (s. Gal. 5:22). **ἐπέτυχεν** aor. ind. act. ἐπιτυγχάνω (# 2209) w. gen., to arrive at, to obtain. **ἐπαγγελία** (# 2039) promise. ◆ **16 ὀμνύουσιν** pres. ind. act. ὀμνύω (# 3923) to swear. Gnomic pres. **ἀντιλογία** (# 517) controversy, dispute, contradiction (EGT). **πέρας** (# 4306) end, boundary; "(as) an end of all disputing" (BAGD). **βεβαίωσις** (# 1012) confirming, confirmation, legal guarantee. The word was a technical expression for a legal guarantee (BS, 104-9; TDNT; MM; Hughes). **ὁ ὅρκος** (# 3992) oath. W. the article the oath just mentioned, the oath God swore to Abraham. ◆ **17 ἐν ᾧ** (# 1877; 4005) in which, wherefore, wherein, i.e., in this method of appeal to remove all doubt and gainsaying (Westcott; EGT). **περισσότερον** (# 4358) adv., more abundantly, more convincingly. It is probably best to take the adv. in its emphatic and elative sense, "especially" (Hughes). **βουλόμενος** pres. mid. (dep.) part. βούλομαι (# *1086*) to purpose, to will, w. inf. **ἐπιδεῖξαι** aor. act. inf. ἐπιδείκνυμι (# *2109*) to point out, to demonstrate. Compl. inf. to the preceding part.: "desiring to demonstrate." Prep. in compound may be directive (MH, 312), or it may suggest, "to show in addition" (RWP). **κληρονόμοις** dat. pl. κληρονόμος (# *3101*) heir. Here, dat. ind. obj. **ἀμετάθετος** (# *292*) not able to be removed, unchangeable, immutable. The word belongs to the legal terminology of the time and signifies a ruling or contract incapable of being set aside or annulled. Here it refers to God's irrevocable purpose as expressed in the promise and confirmed by the oath (Hughes). **ἐμεσίτευσεν** aor. ind. act. μεσιτεύω (# *3541*) to intervene, to act as a mediator, sponsor, or surety. Intransitively it is used to pledge oneself as surety (RWP; Riggenbach; Michel). **ὅρκος** (# *3992*) oath (BBC). ◆ **18** **πρᾶγμα** (# *4547*) thing, matter. **ἀμετάθετος** unchangeable. **ἀδύνατος** (# *105*) impossible. **ψεύσασθαι** aor. mid. (dep.) inf. ψεύδομαι (# *6017*) to lie. **ἔχωμεν** pres. subj. act. ἔχω (# *2400*) to have. Subj. w. ἵνα (# *2671*) in a purp. cl. **καταφυγόντες** aor. act. part. καταφύγω (# *2966*) to flee, to flee for refuge. In the LXX (Deut. 4:42; 19:5; Josh. 20:9) used for fleeing from the avenger to the asylum of the cities of refuge (EGT). **κρατῆσαι** aor. act. inf. κρατέω (# *3195*) to hold fast, to seize. The idea is to lay hold on and cling to that which has been taken (Westcott). Inf. expresses either purp. or result. The obj. of the vb. is in the gen. **ἐλπίδος** (# *1828*) hope (TDNT; EH). **προκειμένης** pres. mid. (dep.) part. πρόκειμαι (# *4618*) to set before, to lie before. ◆ **19** **ἄγκυρα** (# *46*) anchor (SSAW, 250-58). In the Gr. Hellenistic world the anchor represented hope (Moffatt; EGT; Michel; RAC, 1:440-43; BBC). **ἀσφαλής** (# *855*) safe. The word indicates what is outwardly safe (Michel). **βεβαίαν** fem. acc. βέβαιος (# *1010*) firm, established, steadfast. The word indicates what is firm within itself (Michel; TLNT). **εἰσερχομένην** pres. mid. (dep.) part. εἰσέρχομαι (# *1656*) to go into. **ἐσώτερον** (# *2278*) within, inside of. **καταπέτασμα** (# *2925*) curtain, veil. The reference is to the Holy of Holies (Hughes; Michel; Weiss). Clearly the veil is understood primarily as enclosing the presence of God (Attridge). ◆ **20** **ὅπου** (# *3963*) where. **πρόδρομος** (# *4596*) one who runs before, forerunner. The word was used esp. of the men or troops which were sent to explore in advance of an army or firstfruits (Westcott; Bruce; Spicq; BBC). **εἰσῆλθεν** aor. ind. act. εἰσέρχομαι (# *1656*) to go into. **τάξις** (# *5423*) order. For literature and a discussion of the priesthood of Melchizedek, s. Hughes; Lane; Weiss; Attridge; ABD, 4:684-86; Bruce Demarest, *A History of Interpretation of Hebrews 7:1-10 from the Reformation to the Present* (Tübingen: Mohr, 1976); NIDOTTE, 4:934-36; DLNT, 129-31.

Hebrews 7

◆ **1** **οὗτος** (# *4047*) this one. **ὕψιστος** (# *5736*) superl., highest, most high. In this case, the most high God was not the title of some heathen deity, but the same sovereign God whom Abraham worshipped; used in the LXX of God (Hughes; Attridge; Lane). **συναντήσας** aor. act. part. (subst.) συναντάω (# *5267*) to meet. **ὑποστρέφοντι** pres. act. part. (temp.) ὑποστρέφω (# *5715*) to return. Dat. here is used because the vb. **συναντήσας** takes its object in the dat. **κοπή** (# *3158*) slaughter; here defeat or defeating (BAGD; Bruce; EGT). **εὐλογήσας** aor. act. part. (subst.) εὐλογέω (# *2328*) to bless. ◆ **2** **ᾧ καί** to whom also. **δεκάτη** (# *1281*) tenth. The offering of a tithe of the spoils to the gods was a custom of antiquity (EGT; Grässer; NW, 2, ii:1126-30). In the *Testament of Levi* it is reported that as Jacob had a vision and made Levi a priest, he paid a tenth of all he had (*T. Levi* 9:1-4; 1Q21:14-22; AT, 196-97). **ἐμέρισεν** aor. ind. act. μερίζω (# *3532*) to divide. **ἑρμηνευόμενος** pres. pass. part. (adj.) ἑρμηνεύω (# *2257*) to interpret. **δικαιοσύνη** (# *1466*) righteousness. Josephus also interprets the name of Melchizedek, the founder of Jerusalem, as Righteous King, and adds, "in virtue thereof he was the first to officiate as priest of God" (Jos., *JW.*, 6:438; *Ant.*, 1:180). **ἔπειτα** (# *2083*) then. **Σαλήμ** (# *4889*) Salem. The word refer to the city of Jerusalem (Riggenbach; Bruce; Jos., *Ant.*, 1:180). **βασιλεὺς εἰρήνης** (# *995; 1645*) King of Peace. Philo has the same view: "Melchizedek, too, has God made both king of peace, for that is the meaning of `Salem,' and His own priest (Philo, *Allegorical Interpretation*, 79; SB, 3:692-93). ◆ **3** **ἀπάτωρ** (# *574*) without a father. **ἀμήτωρ** (# *298*) without a mother. The words indicate that father and mother were unknown (Riggenbach; NDIEC, 1:90-91). In rabbinical writings such expressions could mean that the father and mother had died and the child was an orphan (SB, 3:693). **ἀγενεαλόγητος** (# *37*) without genealogy. The fact that his genealogy was not known would have disqualified him for a Levitical priesthood (SB, 3:693). The argument from silence plays an important part in rabbinical interpretation of Scripture where, for exegetical purposes, nothing must be regarded as having existed before the time of its first biblical mention (Bruce; SB, 3:694; BBC). **μήτε … μήτε** (# *3612*) neither … nor. **ἀρχή** (# *794*) beginning. **ἔχων** pres. act. part. ἔχω (# *2400*) to have. **ἀφωμοιωμένος** perf. pass. part. ἀφομοιόω (# *926*) to make like, to produce a facsimile or copy. The likeness is in the picture from Genesis, not in the man himself (RWP). **μένει** pres. ind. act. μένω (# *3531*) to remain, to continue. **διηνεκής** (# *1457*) without interruption, continually. In referring to a dynasty this word means that the family would never fail to have a male heir to rule (Buchanan). ◆ **4** **θεωρεῖτε** pres. imp. act. θεωρέω (# *2555*) to see, to observe, to consider. The word expresses the regard of attentive contemplation (Westcott). Although the form of the vb. can be ind. or imp., the imp. would be stronger in this context (Hughes). **πηλίκος** (# 4383) how great. **δεκάτη** (# 1281) tenth. **ἔδωκεν** aor. ind. act. δίδωμι (# 1443) to give. **ἀκροθίνιον** (# 215) the top of the heap, spoils, the best part of the spoils. After a victory the Greeks gathered the spoils in a heap and the top or the best part of the heap was presented to the gods (EGT; Riggenbach; NW, 2, ii:1138-39). **πατριάρχης** (# 4256) the one who ruled a tribe, patriarch. The definite article used w. the word contains the sense of the great patriarch or our great patriarch (Hughes). ◆ **5 ἱερατεία** (# 2632) priesthood. The word emphasize the worth or honor of the office (Michel; TDNT; Lane; DLNT, 963-67). **λαμβάνοντες** pres. act. part. λαμβάνω (# 3284) to receive. **ἐντολή** (# 1953) command, commandment. **ἔχουσιν** pres. ind. act. ἔχω (# 2400) to have. **ἀποδεκατοῦν** pres. act. inf. ἀποδεκατόω (# 620) to take a tenth from someone, to receive a tithe. Used in Gen. 28:22; Matt. 23:23; Lk. 11:42. Epex. inf. to explain the content of the command. **κατά** (# 2848) w. acc., according to, in accord w. the standard of. **νόμος** (# 3795) law. It refers to the Law as the sum of the commandments (Lane; DLNT, 646-47). **καίπερ** (# 2788) although. **ἐξεληλυθότας** perf. act. part. ἐξέρχομαι (# 2002) to go out, to descend from. **ὀσφύς** (# 4019) waist, hip, loins. The Hebrews considered this the place of the reproductive organs and the expression, "to go forth from someone's loins," means to be someone's son or descendant (BAGD; GELTS, 341; T). ◆ **6 γενεαλογούμενος** pres. mid. (dep.) part. γενεαλογέομαι (# 1156) to trace one's genealogical descent, to have one's genealogical descent from someone, to count or reckon someone's genealogy from another (EGT). **δεδεκάτωκεν** perf. ind. act. δεκατόω (# 1282) to take or receive the tithe. **ἔχοντα** pres. act. part. ἔχω (# 2400) to have. **ἐπαγγελία** (# 2039) promise. **εὐλόγηκεν** perf. ind. act. εὐλογέω (# 2328) to bless (s.v. 1). That this higher status is permanent may be indicated by the two perfs. here in v. 6. (Bruce). For the so-called perf. of allegory, used of a past but still relevant event s. IBG, 15ff; GGBB, 582. ◆ **7 χωρίς** (# 6006) w. gen., without. **ἀντιλογίας** (# 517) contradiction, opposition, quarrel (MM). **ἔλαττον** (# 1781) comp. μικρός little; comp., lesser, inferior. **κρείττονος** (# 3202) comp., (s. 6:9); better, superior. **εὐλογεῖται** pres. ind. pass. εὐλογέω to bless (s.v. 1). ◆ **8 ἀποθνήσκοντες** pres. act. part. ἀποθνήσκω (# 633) to die. Anarthrous part. is used as an attributive and emphasizes the character; "mortal men" (RG, 1105f; Hughes). Pres. indicates an action that occurs repeatedly. **λαμβάνουσιν** pres. ind. act. λαμβάνω (# 3284) to receive. **μαρτυρούμενος** pres. pass. part. (adj.) μαρτυρέω (# 3455) to witness; pass., to be witnessed, to be reported (BS, 265; BD, 164). **ζῇ** pres. ind. act. ζάω (# 2409) to live. ◆ **9 εἰπεῖν** aor. act. inf. λέγω (# 3306) to speak. **ὡς ἔπος εἰπεῖν** so to speak; an idiomatic expression often

found in Philo. Here it could mean, "one might almost say" or "to use just the right word" (BAGD). The phrase is used to limit a startling statement and the inf. could express conceived result (RWP); or it could be an example of the so-called inf. abs. (MT, 136). **λαμβάνων** pres. act. part. (subst.) λαμβάνω (# 3284) to receive. **δεδεκάτωνται** perf. ind. pass. δεκατόω (# 1282) to collect, to receive tithes; pass., to pay a tenth. ◆ **10 ὀσφῦς** (# 4019) loins. **ἦν** impf. ind. act. εἰμί (# 1639) to be. **συνήντησεν** aor. ind. act. συναντάω (# 5267) to meet (s.v. 1). ◆ **11 τελείωσις** (# 5459) perfection, reaching the goal. The OT law and the Levitical system could not produce forgiveness or an eschatological completion or the holiness of heart demanded by God (Michel; TDNT). **ἱερωσύνη** (# 2648) priesthood. **αὐτῆς** (# 899) "on the basis of it," i.e., "the Levitical priesthood" "in association w. it" (Hughes). **ἦν** impf. ind. act. εἰμί (# 1639) to be. Ind. in a 2nd. class cond. cl. which is contrary to fact (Attridge). **νενομοθέτηται** perf. ind. pass. νομοθετέομαι (# 3793) to enact a law, to furnish w. law (RWP; BAGD). **ἀνίστασθαι** pres. mid. (dep.) inf. ἀνίστημι (# 482) to rise up. Mid. is used intransitively (RWP). If the form is taken as pass., the meaning of the vb. is trans.: "to be raised up" (BAGD). **λέγεσθαι** pres. pass. inf. λέγω (# 3306) to say. ◆ **12 μετατιθεμένης** pres. pass. part. μετατίθημι (# 3572) to change, to transfer. For the idea of change involved in the compound prep. s. MH, 318. Gen. abs., either cond. or temp. **ἀνάγκη** (# 340) necessity. **καί** (# 2779) also. **μετάθεσις** (# 3557) changing, transfer, change. **γίνεται** pres. ind. mid. (dep.) γίνομαι (# 1181) to become. ◆ **13 ἐφ'** = ἐπί (# 2093) upon, concerning, w. reference to (EGT). **λέγεται** pres. ind. pass. λέγω (# 3306) to say. **φυλή** (# 5876) tribe. **μετέσχηκεν** perf. ind. act. μετέχω (# 3576) to share w., to be a partaker of, to belong to, w. gen. The choice of this word points to the voluntary assumption of humanity by the Lord. It is not said simply that He was born of another tribe: He was born that way of His own will (Westcott; s. 2:14). The perf. expresses a condition of fact, both historic and official; undoubtedly it is intended to accentuate the abs. incompatibility, resulting from His birth, between Christ and the priesthood as far as the O.T. requirements were concerned (Spicq; Hughes). **προσέσχηκεν** perf. ind. act. προσέχω (# 4668) w. dat., to give attention to, to attend to, to serve at. **θυσιαστήριον** (# 2603) the place of sacrifice, altar. ◆ **14 πρόδηλος** (# 4593) before all, obvious. It is an intensified adj. which means "it is perfectly obvious" (Hughes). **ἀνατέταλκεν** perf. ind. act. ἀνατέλλω (# 422) to spring up, to arise. The word refers to rising as the sun, moon, and stars arise, and is also used to describe the sprouting or growing of plants, hair, and disease; it was used metaphorically where the imagery reflects the rising or growth of stellar bodies or planets, the idea being that the subjects would arise or had arisen to prominence or prosperity, and would increase in prominence. For this reason the word easily applied to a king or to the expected Messiah (Buchanan; Michel). The Messiah arose from the tribe of Judah, not from Levi (s. references to the Jewish lit. in Weiss; Braun; Gen 49:10). εἰς (# 1650) to, unto, concerning. The prep. is applied to the direction of the thought (EGT). ἐλάλησεν aor. ind. act. λαλέω (# 3282) to speak. ◆ 15 περισσότερον (# 4358) comp. περισσός (# 4356) more; comp., especially. κατάδηλος (# 2867) quite clear, evident. Prep. in compound is perfective. ὁμοιότης (# 3928) likeness. ἀνίσταται pres. ind. mid./pass. ἀνίστημι (# 482) to rise up (s.v. 11). ◆ 16 σάρκινος (# 4921) fleshly. Adjs. w. this ending signify material, origin, or kind (MH, 359). The enactment was fleshly inasmuch as it had to do only w. the flesh. It caused the priesthood to be implicated w. and dependent on fleshly descent (EGT; Michel). γέγονεν perf. ind. act. γίνομαι (# 1181) to be, to become. ἀκατάλυτος (# 186) not able to be destroyed, indestructible. ◆ 17 μαρτυρεῖται pres. ind. pass. μαρτυρέω (# 3455) to bear witness, to testify. Pass. may be the divine or theol. pass. used to imply God as the subject (BG, 76). ὅτι (# 4022) used as quotation marks to introduce dir. discourse. ◆ 18 ἀθέτησις (# 120) setting aside, annulling, cancellation. The word was a legal term used in the papyri for the cancellation or annulment of a legal enactment. Here it suggests cancellation has taken place (BS, 228f; Preisigke; MM; Hughes; Bruce). γίνεται pres. ind. mid. (dep.) γίνομαι (# 1181) to become. προαγούσης pres. act. part. προάγω (# 4575) to go before, to precede. Part. used in an adjectival sense to mean "former." ἐντολή (# 1953) commandment. ἀνωφελής (# 543) uselessness, without profit. The commandment was useless in that it was unable to help men draw near to God or to effect the justification of sinners before God (EGT; Hughes). ◆ 19 ἐτελείωσεν aor. ind. act. τελειόω (# 5457) to perfect, to bring to perfection, to bring to the goal. ἐπεισαγωγή (# 2081) bringing in, introduction. The word was used in Josephus w. the idea of "replacement." It is said that King Artaxerxes would quell his love for his former wife by replacing (ἐπεισαγωγή) her with another (Jos., *Ant.*, 11:196; Moffatt). Prep. in compound connotes "in addition to," "over and beyond"; i.e., a bringing in, in addition to (Bruce). κρείττονος gen. sing. κρείττων (# 3202) comp., better. κρείττονος ἐλπίδος better hope, obj. gen. ἐγγίζομεν pres. ind. act. ἐγγίζω (# 1581) to come near, to draw near. Pres. indicates that which is continually possible. ◆ 20 καθ᾽ ὅσον (# 2848; 4012) according to, how much, inasmuch as. ὁρκωμοσία (# 3993) taking of an oath. εἰσίν ... γεγονότες. Perf. act. part. of γίνομαι (# 1181) is used in a periphrastic perf. act. construction. The periphrasis marks the possession as well as the impartment of the office: they have been made priests and they act as priests (Westcott). ◆ 21 διὰ τοῦ λέγοντος (# 1328) through the one who

said. ὤμοσεν aor. ind. act. ὀμνύω (# 3923) to swear, to take an oath. μεταμεληθήσεται fut. ind. pass. (dep.) μεταμέλομαι (# 3564) to be sorry, to repent out of sorrow (EGT; Trench, *Synonyms*, 241; TDNT). ◆ 22 κατὰ τοσοῦτο (# 2848; 5537) "according to so much," "by so much." κρείττονος (# 3202) better (s.v. 19). διαθήκης (# 1347) contract, covenant, agreement, testament (Michel; TDNT; NIDNTT). γέγονεν perf. ind. act. γίνομαι (# 1181) to become. ἔγγυος (# 1583) surety, guarantee. The word means a bond, bail, collateral, or some kind of guarantee that a promise will be fulfilled. The word was used in the papyri in legal and promissory documents to designate a guarantor or one who stands security. Jesus Himself is our security that there will be no annulment of this new and better covenant (Buchanan; Bruce; TDNT; TLNT; Spicq; Michel, MM; BBC). ◆ 23 πλείονες comp. pl. πολύς (# 4498) many, many in number–not many at one and the same time but many in succession (EGT). εἰσίν γεγονότες (s.v. 20). διά (# 1328) used w. the acc. of the inf. to express cause. θανάτῳ dat. sing. θάνατος (# 2505) death; instr. dat., "by death." παραμένειν pres. act. inf. παραμένω (# 4169) to remain alongside of, to continue, to remain in office or serve (Moffatt; for its use in the papyri s. MM; NDIEC, 4:98-99). Epex. inf. explaining what was prevented. κωλύεσθαι pres. pass. inf. κωλύω (# 3266) to hinder, to prevent. ◆ 24 μένειν pres. act. inf. μένω (# 3531) to remain, to continue. Pres. indicates the unending and continuing action or state. Articular inf. is used w. prep. διά (# 1328) to express cause or reason. ἀπαράβατος (# 563) not able to be passed on to another, intransmittable, nontransferable. The priesthood of Christ does not pass to another precisely because it is a perpetual priesthood (Hughes; Bruce; Moffatt). ἱερωσύνη (# 2648) priesthood. ◆ 25 ὅθεν (# 3854) therefore. καί (# 2779) also. σῴζειν pres. act. inf. σῴζω (# 5392) to rescue (TDNT; EDNT; TLNT). Compl. inf. to the main vb. παντελής (# 4117) complete. The phrase εἰς τὸ παντελές ("unto completeness") can have a temp. sense ("for all time"), a qualitative sense that emphasizes full completeness ("fully and completely"); or both ideas may be contained and expressed in the phrase (Hughes; Michel; Attridge). δύναται pres. ind. pass. (dep.) δύναμαι (# 1538) to be able to, w. inf. προσερχομένους pres. mid. (dep.) part. προσέρχομαι (# 4665) to approach, to come to, w. dat. Part. as subst. Pres. emphasizes the continual activity. πάντοτε (# 4121) always. ζῶν pres. act. part. ζάω (# 2409) to live. Causal part. w. pres. indicating a continued action, "because He continually lives." εἰς (# 1650) w. articular inf. to express purp. ἐντυγχάνειν pres. act. inf. ἐντυγχάνω (# 1961) to make intercession, to intercede for another. It was sometimes used of bringing a petition before a king on behalf of another (EGT; Hughes; TDNT; MNTW, 54-56). Pres. indicates a continual action; or it is iterative indicating a repeated action. Since rabbinical scholars assigned an intercessory function to the angels, it may be that the readers were tempted to worship angels as intercessors. Therefore the writer makes it perfectly plain that Christ is the sole mediator and intercessor. To rely upon angels or saints or any other finite being for intercession is not only futile, but also betrays a failure of confidence in the adequacy of Christ as our intercessor (Hughes). ◆ **26 τοιοῦτος** (# *5525*) such a one; "such a high priest." The word refers to what preceded, indicating the one who is absolute in power and eternal in being (Westcott). **καί** (# *2779*) indeed. The word emphasizes the thought: "Such a high priest exactly befitted us" (Hughes; Westcott). **ἔπρεπεν** impf. ind. act. πρέπω (# *4560*) w. the dat., to be suited for, to be fit for. **ἀρχιερεύς** (# *797*) high priest. **ὅσιος** (# *4008*) holy, pious (TDNT; NIDNTT). **ἄκακος** (# *179*) without evil. The word describes the absence of all that is bad and wrong (Hughes). **ἀμίαντος** (# *299*) without defilement, stainless, untainted. The word implies not merely ritual purity, but real ethical cleanliness (RWP; BBC). **κεχωρισμένος** perf. pass. part. χωρίζω (# *6004*) to separate. The separation is due to His perfect qualities; he is separated in a class separate from sinners. Perf. suggests that He is permanently separated from them (Hewitt). **ὑψηλότερος** comp. of ὑψηλός (# *5734*) high, lofty; comp., higher, followed by the gen. of comparison. **γενόμενος** aor. mid. (dep.) part. (adj.) γίνομαι (# *1181*) to become. ◆ **27 ἔχει** pres. ind. act. ἔχω (# *2400*) to have. **καθ' ἡμέραν** (# *2465; 2848*) daily. **ἀνάγκη** (# *340*) necessity. **πρότερον** (# *4728*) first, first of all. The adv. is used for comparison between two things (RWP). **ἴδιος** (# *2625*) one's own. **ἀναφέρειν** pres. act. inf. ἀναφέρω (# *429*) to bring up, to offer. Epex. inf. explaining the necessity. The high priest does not offer the daily sacrifices personally, but he is responsible (BBC). **ἔπειτα** (# *2083*) then; "after that." **ἐποίησεν** aor. ind. act. ποιέω (# *4472*) to do. Aor. points to the one-time completed action. **ἐφάπαξ** (# *2384*) once for all. **ἀνενέγκας** aor. act. part. ἀναφέρω (# *429*) to offer up, to sacrifice. Temp. part., aor. indicating logically antecedent action ("after"). Aor. points to a specific and complete act. ◆ **28 καθίστησιν** pres. ind. act. καθίστημι (# *2770*) to constitute, to appoint. Pres. indicates that at the same time this epistle was being written the Levitical priesthood was still functioning, w. the implication that the Jerusalem temple was still standing (Hughes). **ἀρχιερεύς** (# *797*) high priest. Here acc. pl. in a double acc. construction: "appoint men as high priests." **ἔχοντας** pres. act. part. ἔχω (# *2400*) to have. **ἀσθένεια** (# *819*) weakness. **ὁρκωμοσία** (# *3993*) oath, taking of an oath, oath taking (Westcott). **μετά** (# *3552*) w. the acc., after. **υἱός** (# *5626*) son. The lack of the article emphasizes the character or quality: one who is a son; s. Heb

1:2. **τετελειωμένον** perf. pass. part. τελειόω (# *5457*) to perfect, to make perfect, to bring to the goal (s. 5:9).

Hebrews 8

◆ **1 κεφάλαιον** (# *3049*) pertaining to the head. The word can refer to the sum, as of numbers added up from below to the head of the column, where the result is set down as the summary or synopsis. However, the word could also mean the chief point, as of a capstone or capital of a pillar, and thus mean main thing, main point (Buchanan; EGT; Michel; BAGD; Westcott; Lane; NTNT, 227-28). **ἐπί** (# *2093*) w. dat., in the matter of (RWP). **λεγομένος** pres. pass. part. λέγω (# *3306*) to say; here, "that which is being discussed," "the things being talked about." **τοιοῦτον** (# *5525*) such a one. Adj. looks forward, but is also retrospective (Attridge). **ἔχομεν** pres. ind. act. ἔχω (# *2400*) to have. Pres. points to the continual possession. **ἐκάθισεν** aor. ind. act. καθίζω (# *2767*) to take one's seat, to sit down. For the concept of sitting at the right hand s. Eph. 1:20. **δεξιᾷ** (# *1288*) right; "on the right hand," the place of honor (also s. Heb. 1:13). **μεγαλωσύνη** (# *3488*) majesty. ◆ **2 τῶν ἁγίων** (# *41*) n. gen. pl., the holy things; i.e., the sanctuary (Hughes; Michel). **λειτουργός** (# *3313*) minister, one who ministers in religious matters; a word used in the LXX and Jewish lit. for the priest (TDNT; TLNT; Grässer; Attridge). **σκηνή** (# *5008*) tent, tabernacle. The word is used in the fourth gospel in contrast not to what is false, but to what is symbolic (EGT; for an extended discussion of this v. in relation to Heb. 9:11 s. Hughes, 283-90). **ἔπηξεν** aor. ind. act. πήγνυμι (# *4381*) to fix, to fasten as the pegs of a tent, to pitch a tent (RWP). **κύριος** (# *3261*) Lord. ◆ **3 εἰς** (# *1650*) w. the articular inf. to express purp. **προσφέρειν** pres. act. inf. προσφέρω (# *4712*) to bring to, to offer. Pres. emphasizes an action repeatedly done. **καθίσταται** pres. ind. pass. καθίστημι (# *2770*) to appoint. Gnomic pres. **ὅθεν** (# *3854*) whereafter, and so. **ἀναγκαῖος** (# *338*) necessity, necessary. **ἔχειν** pres. act. inf. ἔχω (# *2400*) to have. The so-called subject of the inf. in the acc. case is **τοῦτον** (# *4047*) this one (this priest), and refers to Christ. **καί** (# *2779*) also. **προσενέγκη** aor. subj. act. προσφέρω (# *4712*) to offer, to bring to. Aor. emphasizes that Christ's offering was once for all, consistent w. the author's repeated emphasis on the singularity of Christ's sacrifice offered (Bruce; Spicq; Hughes). Subj. in an indef. rel. cl. ◆ **4 ἦν** impf. ind. act. εἰμί (# *1639*) to be. Ind. in a 2nd. class cond. cl. expresses here a contrary-to-fact statement. **ὄντων** pres. act. part. (causal) εἰμί (# *1639*) to be. Gen. abs. ("Since there are") **προσφερόντων** pres. act. part. προσφέρω to offer (s.v. 3). Substantival use of part. to emphasize their actions as priests offering sacrifices. Iterat. pres. **κατά** (# *2848*) w. the acc., according to, according to the standard of. It was the law which regulated all that concerns the earthly priesthood, and by this law Christ is excluded from priestly office, not being of the tribe of Levi (EGT). ◆ **5 οἵτινες** (# *4015*) which one; i.e., those belonging to this class. The qualitative rel. pronoun emphasizes the character of the Levitical priesthood (Westcott). **ὑπόδειγμα** (# *5682*) pattern, copy (Grässer; Attridge; Lane). **σκιᾷ** (# *5014*) shadow. It could be taken w. the preceding dat. as a hendiadys: a shadowy outline, a shadowy reflection, or a shadowy suggestion (Lane). **λατρεύουσιν** pres. ind. act. λατρεύω (# *3302*) to minister, to perform religious service. **ἐπουράνιος** (# *2230*) heavenly; here, "the heavenly things" (s. Eph. 1:3). **καθώς** (# *2777*) just as. **κεχρημάτισται** perf. ind. pass. χρηματίζω (# *5976*) to warn, to instruct. The word used in the papyri of official pronouncements by magistrates and of a royal reply to a petition as well as an answer of an oracle. In the NT it is used of divine communications (AS; BS, 122; MM). **μέλλων** pres. act. part. μέλλω (# *3516*) to be about to, w. inf. Part. used to express an imp. It is a future under Semitic influence and a translation of the Heb. imp. (BG, 94). **ἐπιτελεῖν** pres. act. inf. ἐπιτελέω (# *2200*) to end, to complete, to bring to completion; here, to erect the tent. Esp. of the performance of rituals and ceremonies (BAGD). **σκηνή** (# *5008*) tent, booth, lodging or dwelling for nomads. Here tabernacle (BAGD). **ὅρα** pres. imp. act. ὁράω (# *3972*) to see. **φησίν** pres. ind. act. φημί (# *5774*) to say, introducing direct discourse. **ποιήσεις** fut. ind. act. ποιέω (# *4472*) to do. **τύπος** (# *5596*) type, pattern. This was the stamp or impression struck from a die or seal; hence, a figure, draft, sketch, or pattern (EGT; TLNT; TDNT; Leonhard Goppelt, *TYPOS: The Typological Interpretation of the Old Testament in the New,* 161-70). **δειχθέντα** aor. pass. part. (adj.) δείκνυμι (# *1259*) to show. Pass. here is the divine or theol. pass. indicating God as the One who did the action (Hughes; BG, 76). Aor. indicates the completed action. ◆ **6 νυνί** (# *3815*) now. The particle is logical rather than temp., but the temp. factor is inevitably involved in the argument (Hughes). **διαφορωτέρας** comp. διάφορος (# *1427*) differing, excellent, comp. more excellent. **τέτυχεν** perf. ind. act. τυγχάνω (# *5593*) to attain, to obtain. Perf. emphasizes the continual possession. The vb. is followed by the gen. of **λειτουργία** (# *3311*) service, ministry, religious or sacred service (TDNT; TLNT). **ὅσος** (# *4012*) as much; here, "by how much"; instr. case of the rel. (RWP). **καί** (# *2779*) also. **κρείττονος** (# *3202*) better (s. 7:19). **μεσίτης** (# *3542*) mediator, arbitrator, go-between (Michel, Bruce). **ἥτις** (# *4015*) which. The antecedent of the rel. pron. is **διαθήκη** (# *1347*) covenant. The new priest brings a better ministry based on a new covenant. This rel. properly indicates the class or kind to which an object belongs (RG, 727). **ἐπαγγελία** (# *2039*) promise. **νενομοθέτηται** perf. ind. pass. νομοθετέω (# *3793*) to legislate, to enact by law, to ordain by law. Perf. emphasiz-

es the continuing result. For this word s. Hughes. ◆ **7 πρώτη** fem. nom πρῶτος (# *4755*) first, i.e., the first covenant. **ἄμεμπτος** (# *289*) blameless, faultless. **δεύτερος** (# *1311*) second. For a summary discussion of the new covenant s. Kaiser, *Toward an Old Testament Theology* (Grand Rapids: Zondervan, 1978), 231-35; ABD, 4:1088-94; BTNT, 400-3; DLNT, 248-50; ABD; Susanne Lehne, *The New Covenant in Hebrews,* JSNTSS 44 (Sheffield: JSOT, 1990). **ἐζητεῖτο** impf. ind. pass. ζητέω (# *2426*) to seek. The vb. is used in the second part of a contrary to fact cond. cl. **τόπος** (# *5536*) place, room, occasion, followed by the gen ("room for," "occasion for"). ◆ **8 μεμφόμενος** pres. mid. (dep.) part. μέμφομαι (# *3522*) to blame, to find fault w. **αὐτός** (# *899*) self; here, acc. pl. them; i.e., the Israelites. **ἰδού** pres. imp. act. ὁράω (# *3922*) to see. Used to draw attention. **ἔρχονται** pres. ind. mid. (dep.) ἔρχομαι (# *2262*) to come. Pres. used to emphasize the certainty of the future event. **συντελέσω** fut. act. ind. συντελέω (# *5334*) to bring to completion, to accomplish, to establish. **ἐπί** (# *2093*) w. acc., upon. ◆ **9 κατά** (# *2848*) w. acc., according to. The second covenant was not only to be second, but of a different type (Westcott). The people were not able to fulfill the condition for the Mosaic covenant; therefore God changes the conditions for receiving blessing. **ἐποίησα** aor. ind. act. ποιέω (# *4472*) to do, to make; here in the sense of establish. **ἐπιλαβομένου** aor. mid. (dep.) part. ἐπιλαμβάνω (# *2138*) to grasp, to take hold of, w. gen. indicating the part affected (RWP). Temp. part., gen. abs. indicating the time (BD, 218): "when I took them ...." **ἐξαγαγεῖν** aor. act. inf. ἐξάγω (# *1974*) to lead out. Inf. to express purp. **ἐνέμειναν** aor. act. ind. ἐμμένω (# *1844*) to remain in, to continue in. Israel was continually disobedient. **ἠμέλησα** aor. act. ind. ἀμελέω (# *288*) to have no concern for, to neglect (s. Heb. 2:3). ◆ **10 αὕτη** (# *4047*) this. The pron. is used as the subject of the vb. to be supplied (ἐστιν); "this is ...." **διαθήσομαι** fut. ind. mid. (dep.) διατίθημι (# *1416*) to make a covenant. Used w. dat. **διδούς** pres. act. part. δίδωμι (# *1443*) to give. Part. may be temp. or manner or means of making the covenant: "I will make a covenant even by putting..." (Westcott). **διάνοια** (# *1379*) mind, understanding, intellect (EGT; RWP). **ἐπί** (# *2093*) w. acc., upon. **ἐπιγράψω** fut. act. ind. ἐπιγράφω (# *2108*) to write upon. **ἔσομαι** fut. ind. mid. (dep.) εἰμί (# *1639*) to be. **εἰς** (# *1650*) to. Prep. is used with the vb. εἰμί for the thought, "to serve as." Although this is a Hebraic use of the prep., there are also examples in Koine apart from Semitic influence (LAE, 120f; M, 71f). **ἔσονται** fut. ind. mid. (dep.) εἰμί (# *1639*) to be. **μοι** dat. ἐγώ (# *1609*) I. "To me," dat. of advantage. ◆ **11 διδάξωσιν** aor. subj. act. διδάσκω (# *1438*) to teach. **πολίτης** (# *4489*) citizen, fellow citizen. **γνῶθι** aor. imp. act. γινώσκω (# *1182*) to know. **ὅτι** (# *4022*) because. **εἰδήσουσιν** fut. perf. act. ind. οἶδα (# *3857*) to know; def. perf. w. pres. meaning.

For the fut. perf. form s. RG, 361. **μικρός** (# *3625*) small. **μεγάλου** gen. sing. μέγας (# *3489*) great. Two adjs. used in a superlat. sense: "from the least to the greatest." ◆ **12 ἵλεως** (# *2664*) gracious, merciful. **ἔσομαι** fut. ind. mid. (dep.) εἰμί (# *1639*) to be. **ἀδικία** (# *94*) unrighteousness. **μνησθῶ** aor. subj. pass. μιμνήσκομαι (# *3630*) to remember. Divine pass. indicating God as the agent. ◆ **13 πεπαλαίωκεν** perf. ind. act. παλαιόω (# *4096*) to declare or treat as old or obsolete; pass., to become old or obsolete. The word was used in the papyri for a temple and a wall that had become old and obsolete and needed repair (Priesigke, 2:224; MM; BBC). **καινήν** fem. acc. καινός (# *2785*) new. **παλαιούμενον** pres. pass. part. παλαιόω (# *4096*). **γηράσκον** pres. act. part. γηράσκω (# *1180*) to grow old. The word refers to the decay of old age (RWP). **ἐγγύς** (# *1584*) near. **ἀφανισμός** (# *907*) disappearing, vanishing away. The word is suggestive of utter destruction and abolition and was used in the LXX of God destroying the enemies in the Promised Land (Deut. 7:2) (EGT; GELTS, 72; HR, 1:182). Josephus used the word of cities that disappeared by destruction (Jos., *Ant.*, 17:306) or of attempts to destroy ("cause to disappear") the ancestry or heritage of the Jews (Jos., *Ant.*, 19:174; CCFJ, 1:275).

Hebrews 9

◆ **1 εἶχε** impf. ind. act. ἔχω (# *2400*) to have. **πρώτη** (# *4755*) first. The word is to be understood as modifying the unexpressed word διαθήκη (Hughes). **δικαίωμα** (# *1468*) that which is demanded by righteousness, regulation, ordinance (Westcott; Michel; Lane). **λατρεία** (# *3301*) worship, ministry, religious service. Rather than the acc. pl. ("regulations for cultic worship"), the word is to be understood as a gen. sing. modifying the word δικαιώματα (Hughes; Riggenbach; Lane). **ἅγιος** (# *41*) holy place, sanctuary. For a study contrasting the old order w. the work of Christ s. Norman H. Young, "The Gospel according to Hebrews 9," *NTS* 27 (1980/81): 198-210. **κοσμικός** (# *3176*) pertaining to the world, earthly. Here the word could mean mundane or material (Bruce). ◆ **2 σκηνή** (# *5008*) tent, tabernacle. **κατεσκευάσθη** aor. ind. pass. κατασκευάζω (# *2941*) to outfit w. vessels, to equip, to prepare, to furnish (s. 3:3). **ἧ** fem. dat. sing. ὅς (# *4005*) rel. pron., which; "in which." **λυχνία** (# *3393*) lampstand. It refers to the menorah placed at the south side of the Holy Place; it was made of gold, w. three branches springing from either side of the main stem; the main stem and all six branches each supported a flower-shaped lamp holder (Exod. 25:31ff; 37:17ff; Bruce; ND, 708; SB, 3:705-18; ABD, 4:141-43). **τράπεζα** (# *5544*) table (SB, 3:718-19). **πρόθεσις** (# *4606*) placing before, setting out. **ἄρτος** (# *788*) bread. The expression lit. means "the setting out of the bread (loaves)"; "the bread set forth in two rows" (Lightfoot; for a discussion of the regulations concern-

ing the showbread s. SB, 3:719-28). **ἅγια** n. pl. ἅγιος (# *41*) holy. The Holy Place (Hughes). ◆ **3 μετά** (# *3552*) w. the acc. "after," "behind." **δεύτερον** (# *1311*) second. **καταπέτασμα** (# *2925*) curtain, veil. **λεγομένη** pres. pass. part. λέγω (# *3306*) to say; pass., to be called. **Ἅγια Ἁγίων** The Holy of Holies. The translation of the Heb. idiom equivalent to a superl.: the most Holy Place (EGT; Attridge). ◆ **4 χρυσοῦς** (# *5997*) golden. **ἔχουσα** pres. act. part. ἔχω (# *2400*) to have. **θυμιατήριον** (# *2593*) altar of incense. The word has also been understood to mean the censer, or incense shovel, and some have thought to connect the altar of incense to the Holy Place in a theol. sense and point out a special doctrinal association between the altar of incense and the Holy of Holies. For a discussion of this problem s. Hughes; SB, 3:728ff; Lane. **κιβωτός** (# *3066*) box, chest, ark (EGT). **διαθήκη** (# *1347*) covenant. Here gen. of content: "box which contained the covenant" (SB, 3:737-41). **περικεκαλυμμένην** perf. part. pass. περικαλύπτω (# *4328*) to cover, to cover on all sides. **πάντοθεν** (# *4119*) all around. **χρυσίον** (# *5991*) gold. Here, instr. dat.: "covered on all sides w. gold." **στάμνος** (# *5085*) pitcher, jar. The rabbis believed that in the fut. Elijah would restore to Israel the container of manna, the flask of sprinkling water, and the jar of anointing oil (Buchanan). **ῥάβδος** (# *4811*) stick, staff. **βλαστήσασα** aor. act. part. βλαστάνω (# *1056*) to sprout, to bud. Aor. part. indicating antecedent action. **πλάκες** nom. pl. πλάξ (# *4419*) flat stone, tablet. ◆ **5 ὑπεράνω** (# *5645*) w. gen., above. **Χερούβ** (# *5938*) cherub. The cherubim are the carriers of the divine glory and shekinah. (Michel; SB, 3:168f; TDNT; NIDOTTE, 2:717; DDD, 362-67; ABD, 1: 899-900). The cherubim were two figures made of beaten gold standing at either end of the mercy seat, with which they were integrally connected, and facing inward toward each other, their wings stretched out and overarching the mercy seat (Exod. 25:17ff; Hughes). **κατασκιάζοντα** pres. act. part. κατασκιάζω (# *2944*) to overshadow. **ἱλαστήριον** (# *2663*) place of propitiation (s. Rom. 3:25); mercy seat. The mercy seat was a slab of pure gold, two and one-half cubits long by one and a half cubits wide, which fit exactly over the top of the ark of the covenant (Hughes; Bruce; SB, 3:165-85). **περὶ ὧν** (# *4309*; *4005*) concerning which things. **κατὰ μέρος** (# *2848*; *3538*) in detail; the distributive use of the prep. (RWP). ◆ **6 κατεσκευασμένων** perf. pass. part. κατασκευάζω (# *2941*) to prepare, to make ready; here in the (temp.) sense of furnish, equip (BAGD). Gen. abs. Perf. indicates the resulting condition or state. **διὰ παντός** (# *1328*; *4246*) through all, i.e., continually. The phrase seems to express the continuous, unbroken permanence of a characteristic habit (Westcott). **εἰσίασιν** pres. ind. act. 3rd. pers. pl. εἴσειμι (# *1655*) to go into. **λατρεία** (# *3301*) religious service (s.v. 1; TDNT; TLNT). **ἐπιτελοῦντες** pres. part. act. ἐπιτελέω (# *2200*) to bring to conclusion, to complete, to fulfill, to perform. The vb. is used by various writers for the accomplishing of religious services (EGT). ◆ **7 δεύτερος** (# 1311) second; i.e., the second tent or the Holy of Holies. **ἅπαξ** (# 562) once. **ἐνιαυτός** (# 1929) year. Here gen. of time: "once for each year" (RWP). **χωρίς** (# 6006) w. gen., without. **ὅ** nom. sin. **ὅς** (# 4005) which, referring to the word αἵματος. **προσφέρει** pres. ind. act. προσφέρω (# 4712) to bring to, to offer, to offer a sacrifice, to sacrifice. Pres. customary or iterat., indicating what continually happened year after year. **ὑπέρ** (# 5642) w. gen., on behalf of. **ἀγνόημα** (# 52) ignorance, sin of ignorance, error. The word refers to those sins committed inadvertently or in ignorance, unintentionally or through human frailty (Lev. 4:1f; 5:17f), as distinct from those who sin in deliberate and rebellious defiance of God and His law (Hughes; Michel; Moffatt; SB, 3:176-78; Attridge). ◆ **8 δηλοῦντος** pres. act. part. δηλόω (# 1317) to make clear. Gen. abs. Used here to express attendant circumstance ("and thus"). **μήπω** (# 3609) not yet. **πεφανερῶσθαι** perf. pass. inf. φανερόω (# 5746) to make plain, to manifest. Inf. is used in indir. discourse explaining the part. of the gen. abs. **τῶν ἁγίων** (# 41) sanctuary. Here the word is used to comprise the Holy Place and the Holy of Holies together (Bruce). **ἐχούσης** pres. act. part. (temp.) ἔχω (# 2400) to have. Gen. abs. expressing contemporaneous action, "while the outer tabernacle is standing." **στάσις** (# 5087) standing. Used w. the previous part., the phrase means "retaining its status" (Bruce; Westcott). ◆ **9 παραβολή** (# 4130) parable, symbol, figure (TDNT). **εἰς** (# 1650) unto (Riggenbach). **καιρός** (# 2789) time, time period. **ἐνεστηκότα** perf. part. act. ἐνίστημι (# 1931) to be present. **καθ'ἣν** (# 2848; 4005) according to which. The rel. pron. refers to the word **παραβολή** (# 4130). It is in accordance w. the parabolic significance of the tabernacle and its arrangements that gifts and sacrifices were offered which could purge only the flesh, not the conscience (EGT). **προσφέρονται** pres. ind. pass. προσφέρω to offer. Pres. implies that the temple ritual has not yet been discontinued (Hughes). **δυνάμεναι** pres. pass. (dep.) part. δύναμαι (# 1538) to be able to, w. inf. Adj. part. used to emphasize a particular trait. Pres. stresses the continual inability. **συνείδησις** (# 5287) conscience (s. Rom. 2:15; 1 Cor. 8:7). A defiled conscience is an obstacle to worhsip that the Aaronic priesthood could not overcome (DLNT, 242). **τελειῶσαι** aor. act. inf. τελειόω (# 5457) to perfect (s. 5:9). Compl. inf. to the preceding part. Aor. indicates the total inability to reach the intended goal. **λατρεύοντα** pres. act. part. λατρεύω (# 3302) to worship, to perform religious services (TDNT). ◆ **10 μόνον** (# 3667) only. **ἐπί** (# 2093) w. dat., in the matter of (RWP). **βρῶμα** (# 1109) food. **πόμα** (# 4503) drink. **διάφορος** (# 1427) different. The expression "meats and drink" denotes food laws in general (Bruce; Moffatt; JBP, 214-17). **βαπτισμός** (# 968)

washing. **δικαίωμα** regulation s.v. 1. **μέχρι** (# 3588) w. gen., until. **διόρθωσις** (# 1451) setting straight, restoring that which is out of line, improvement, reformation, new order (Hughes; BAGD). **ἐπικείμενα** pres. part. mid. (dep.) or pass. ἐπίκειμαι (# 2130) to lay upon, to impose (RWP). ◆ **11 παραγενόμενος** aor. part. mid. (dep.) παραγίνομαι (# 4134) to come, to appear (Hughes; Westcott). Temp. part., "when Christ appeared." Aor. suggests logically necessary activity preceding the main vb. **ἀρχιερεύς** (# 797) high priest. Pred. nom. ("in his role as"). **γενομένων** aor. mid. (dep.) part. γίνομαι (# 1181) to become, to be. **ἀγαθός** (# 19) good. **διά** (# 1328) w. gen., through. The prep. is best understood not in the local sense, but in the instr. sense ("by means of" [EGT]). **μείζονος** comp. μέγας (# 3489) great; comp., greater. **τελειοτέρας** comp. τέλειος (# 5455) perfect; comp., more perfect. **χειροποίητος** (# 5935) made w. hands, thus pure, perfect, changeless (BBC). **κτίσις** (# 3232) creation. Here gen. of source or origin. ◆ **12 τράγος** (# 5543) goat, male goat, he-goat. **μόσχος** (# 3675) calf. The goat was used for the people's sacrifice. The calf was used for the sacrifice for the high priest and his house (Michel; Grässer; Attridge; SB, 3:175-78; Lev. 16; M, Yoma, 3-7; b Yoma, 61a; BBC). **δέ** (# 1254) but, adversative. **ἴδιος** (# 2625) one's own, own. **εἰσῆλθεν** aor. ind. act. εἰσέρχομαι (# 1656) to go in. **ἐφάπαξ** (# 2384) once for all. The prep. in compound gives a directive strengthening (MH, 315). **ἅγια** sanctuary (s.v. 8). **αἰώνιος** (# 173) eternal. **λύτρωσις** (# 3391) redeeming, releasing by the payment of a price (s. Rom 3:24; Bruce; Hughes). **εὑράμενος** aor. mid. (dep.) part. εὑρίσκω (# 2351) to find, to obtain, to secure. Aor. part. means that Christ entered into the heavenly sanctuary after He had secured an eternal redemption; the securing of our eternal redemption took place at the cross and was followed by His entry into heaven (Hughes). ◆ **13 ταῦρος** (# 5436) steer, young bull. Here gen. of source ("blood coming from"). **σποδός** (# 5075) ashes. **δάμαλις** (# 1239) young female calf, heifer. **ῥαντίζουσα** pres. act. part. (adj.) ῥαντίζω (# 4822) to sprinkle. The ashes of a heifer were obtained by burning a red heifer outside of the camp according to a specially prescribed process. The ashes were mixed w. water, as necessity arose, to be sprinkled on persons who had become defiled by touching a corpse or being in a tent where there was a corpse (Num. 19). This ceremonial impurity disqualified one for intercourse w. men or God (Buchanan; Moffat; Lane; Grässer; ABD, 3:115-16; J. Bowman, "Did the Qumran Sect Burn the Red Heifer?" *RQ* 1 [1958]: 73-74; D.P. Wright, "Purification from Corpse Contamination in Numbers 31:19-24 ," *VT* 35 [1985]: 213-33; M Para). **κεκοινωμένους** perf. part. pass. κοινόω (# 3124) to make common, to defile. Perf. part. looks at the state or condition. **ἁγιάζει** pres. ind. act. ἁγιάζω (# 39) to sanctify, to set apart, to remove from the common or profane, thus qualifying the person again for worshipping God (EGT; EDNT; TDNT). Gnomic ("always cleanses") or iterative ("cleanses repeatedly"). **πρός** (# 4639) w. acc., w. a view to, for. **καθαρότης** (# 2755) purity, cleanliness. ◆ **14 μᾶλλον** (# 3437) more. For this type of rabbinical argument (from the lesser to the greater) s. Rom. 5:9; Attridge; Lane. **προσήνεγκεν** aor. ind. act. προσφέρω (# 4712) to bring a sacrifice. **ἄμωμος** (# 320) unblemished, without blemish (Hughes; s. Col. 1:22). The word was used of the Levitical sacrifices, but now has an ethical significance explaining how the blood of Christ should not merely furnish ceremonial cleansing (EGT). **καθαριεῖ** fut. ind. act. καθαρίζω (# 2751) to cleanse. The word marks what the object is itself–clean, ceremonially or morally (Westcott). Logical fut. used in this type argument (Riggenbach; Buchanan). The word was used in the papyri for religious cleansing (BS 216f). **συνείδησις** (# 5287) conscience. **ἀπὸ νεκρῶν ἔργων** (# 608; 3738; 2240) from dead works; i.e., "from works that lead to death" (Lane). **λατρεύειν** pres. act. inf. λατρεύω (# 3302) to serve, to do religious service, to minister (TLNT; TDNT; EDNT; AS, 226). Articular inf. w. the prep. **εἰς** (# 1650) to express purp. **ζῶντι** pres. act. part. (adj.) ζάω (# 2409) to live. Dat. follows the vb. **λατρεύειν**. For the use of the ashes of a heifer in relation to the death of Christ s. v. 13; Hughes, 326ff. ◆ **15 διὰ τοῦτο** (# 1328; 4047) because of this. It refers to Christ's effectiveness in offering sacrifice and cleansing from sin so that the believer might worship the living God (Buchanan). **μεσίτης** (# 3542) mediator. **ὅπως** (# 3968) w. subj. to express purp. (MT, 105). **γενομένου** aor. mid. (dep.) part. (causal) γίνομαι (# 1181) to be, to become. Gen. abs., "because death has occurred." **ἀπολύτρωσις** (# 667) a releasing by the payment of a price, redemption (s. Rom. 3:24). **ἐπί** (# 2093) w. dat, upon; here, by, under. **παράβασις** (# 4126) transgression. Here, gen. (ablative) expresses the idea of separation (Riggenbach). **λάβωσιν** aor. subj. act. λαμβάνω (# 3284) to receive. Subj. w. **ὅπως** (# 3968) to express purp. or result. **κεκλημένοι** perf. part. pass. καλέω (# 2813) to call. Perf. indicates the completed state or condition. **κληρονομία** (# 3100) inheritance. Gen. here is to be taken w. the word **ἐπαγγελία** (# 2039) promise, giving a further definition or content of the promise (Westcott). ◆ **16 ἀνάγκη** (# 340) necessity. **φέρεσθαι** pres. pass. inf. φέρω (# 5770) to bring; pass., to be brought. Compl. inf., "it is necessary to be brought." The word is probably used here in the legal technical sense: to be registered or to be publicly known (Bruce; Michel; MM; TDNT). **διαθεμένου** aor. mid. (dep.) part. διατίθημι (# 1416) to make a covenant, to make a testament. For a detailed discussion of the meaning of the word **διαθήκη** here s. Hughes; Bruce; Lane; Buchanan; Attridge. ◆ **17 βέβαιος** (# 1010) firm, guaranteed. Used here in the legal sense of valid (BAGD; TLNT; Riggenbach).

ἐπεί (# 2075) since, because. **μήποτε** (# 3607) never. **ἰσχύει** pres. ind. act. ἰσχύω (# 2710) to have strength, to be in force. For the legal term s. Michel; Riggenbach; Hughes. **ζῆ** pres. ind. act. ζάω (# 2409) to live. The presents here are gnomic, indicating what is always true. ◆ **18 ὅθεν** (# 3854) wherefore. **χωρίς** (# 6006) w. gen., without. **ἐγκεκαίνισται** perf. ind. pass. ἐγκαινίζω (# 1590) to renew, to inaugurate. The idea of the word is to introduce something new, to initiate, w. the concepts of inauguration and dedication closely related (Hughes). Perf. not in an aoristic sense, but rather to describe what stands written in Scripture–a marked feature of the author's style (M, 142; Michel; Riggenbach). ◆ **19 λαληθείσης** aor. pass. part. (temp.) λαλέω (# 3281) to say, to speak. Gen. abs. Aor. indicating antecedent time ("after"). **ἐντολή** (# 1953) commandment. **κατά** (# 2848) w. acc., according to. **λαβών** aor. act. part. λαμβάνω (# 3284) to take. **μόσχος** (# 3675) calf (GELTS, 310). The Heb. term "oxen" (פר) used in Exod. 24:5 is applicable to bovine animals of any age (Hughes; NIDOTTE, 3:670-72). The related word is used in the Ugaritic language w. the meaning "young cow" (Joseph Aisleitner, *Wörterbuch der Ugaritischen Sprache*, 259f; Cyrus H. Gordon, *Ugaritic Textbook*, #2122, prr III; 3:471). **τράγος** (# 5543) goat. The text is unclear. Despite an impressive combination of witnesses, many manuscripts omit this word. To omit is probably the best reading (Hughes; Bruce; TC, 668-69). If the omission is original, there is an imitation of v. 12. If the omission is not original there is either an accidental omission through a homeoteleuton or a deliberate omission in order to conform to Exod. 24:5. **μετά** (# 3552) w. gen. with. **ἔριον** (# 2250) wool. **κόκκινος** (# 3132) scarlet. **ὕσσωπος** (# 5727) hyssop, marjoram. The hyssop was apparently tied w. the scarlet wool to a cedar stick, thus forming a sprinkling implement which was dipped in the blood diluted with water. Although water and scarlet wool and hyssop are not mentioned in the Exodus account, there is no reason why this common method of sprinkling should not have been used by Moses in the procedure described in Exod. 24 (Hughes; Delitzsch; POB, 160-62; PB, 96-97; NIDOTTE, 1:334-35). **ἐράντισεν** aor. ind. act. ῥαντίζω (# 4822) to sprinkle (SB, 3:742). ◆ **20 ἐνετείλατο** aor. ind. mid. (dep.) ἐντέλλομαι (# 1948) to command. ◆ **21 σκεῦος** (# 5007) vessel. **λειτουργία** (# 3311) ministry, worship service (TLNT). **τῷ αἵματι** (# 135) w. the blood, dat. of instr. **ὁμοίως** (# 3931) adv., likewise. **ἐράντισεν** aor. ind. act. ῥαντίζω (# 4822) to sprinkle. ◆ **22 σχεδόν** (# 5385) almost. **καθαρίζεται** pres. ind. pass. καθαρίζω (# 2751) to purify (s.v. 14). Gnomic pres., indicating what is always true. **αἱματεκχυσία** (# 136) blood shedding, shedding of blood. The word may have been coined by the author, but is related to the expressions ἐκχεῖν αἷμα (to pour out blood) and ἔκχυσις αἵματος (the pouring out of blood), which appear in the LXX (Bruce; Michel; Grässer; DLNT, 274-78). **γίνεται** pres. ind. mid. (dep.) γίνομαι (# 1181) to become. Gnomic pres. indicating what is always true. **ἄφεσις** (# 912) releasing, forgiving, forgiveness. The expression here may have been a proverbial expression since it occurs in the rabbinical writings; i.e., "does not atonement come through the blood?" or "surely atonement can be made only w. the blood" (Bruce; Buchanan). ◆ **23 ἀνάγκη** (# 340) necessity, necessary. **ὑπόδειγμα** (# 5682) pattern, copy. **τούτοις** dat. pl. οὗτος (# 4047) instr. dat., "by these things." By these rites or by the different materials of cleansing depicted from Heb. 9:19ff. (Hughes; Michel). **καθαρίζεσθαι** pres. pass. inf. καθαρίζω (# 2751) to cleanse. Epex. inf. describing **ἀνάγκη**. **ἐπουράνιος** (# 2230) heavenly; here pl., "the heavenly things." **κρείττοσιν** dat. pl. (# 3202) comp. ἀγαθός good; comp., better. **παρά** (# 4123) used in the comp. sense, than. ◆ **24 χειροποίητος** (# 5935) made w. hands. **εἰσῆλθεν** aor. ind. act. εἰσέρχομαι (# 1656) to enter. **ἅγια** sanctuary s.v. 2. **ἀντίτυπος** (# 531) copy, antitype. The word lit. means "answering to the type" and here means a counterpart of reality (Moffatt). **ἀληθινός** (# 240) true, genuine. **ἐμφανισθῆναι** aor. pass. inf. ἐμφανίζω (# 1872) to make visible; pass., to become visible, to appear to someone. Prep. in compound is local: "to appear in the presence of." Inf. to express purp. **πρόσωπον** (# 4725) face, presence. **ὑπὲρ ἡμῶν** (# 5642; 1609) for us, on our behalf. For Christ's appearing in the presence of God s. Hughes, 329-54, esp. 349f. ◆ **25 προσφέρῃ** pres. subj. act. προσφέρω (# 4712) to bring to, to offer a sacrifice. (s.v. 7). Subj. w. **ἵνα** (# 2671) in a neg. purp. cl. Pres. emphasizes the continuous action and may be viewed here as iterat: "to offer Himself over and over again." **ὥσπερ** (# 6061) as, just as. **εἰσέρχεται** pres. ind. mid. (dep.) εἰσέρχομαι (# 1656) to enter. **ἐνιαυτός** (# 1929) yearly; the distributive use of the prep–"year after year," "every year the same thing." **ἀλλότριος** (# 259) belonging to another, not one's own. The blood provided by our high priest for the atonement of mankind was human blood–moreover, His own blood (Hughes). ◆ **26 ἐπεί** (# 2075) since, since in that case (Westcott). The word introduces causal cls. (MT, 318). **ἔδει** impf. ind. act. δεῖ (# 1256) it is necessary; impf., it would have been necessary. The construction is a 2nd-class cond. cl. (contrary to fact) w. the cond. omitted in an elliptical construction: "since, if that were true, it would be necessary for Him to suffer often" (RWP; RG, 963). **παθεῖν** aor. act. inf. πάσχω (# 4248) to suffer. Inf. is used to explain the necessity. **καταβολή** (# 2856) foundation. **κόσμος** (# 3180) world, here in the sense of creation. **ἅπαξ** (# 562) once for all. **συντελεία** (# 5333) completion, consummation (Grässer; s. 5:9). **ἀθέτησις** (# 120) putting away (s. 7:18). **ἁμαρτία** (# 281) sin. Here obj. gen. Prep. **εἰς** (# 1650) indicates the aim, goal, or purpose. **πεφανέρωται** perf. ind. pass. φανερόω

(# 5746) to appear. The vb. indicates a public manifestation and appearance of Christ before the world similar to the emergence of the high priest out of the sanctuary (Michel; BBC). Perf. emphasizes the completed action w. continuing results. ◆ **27 καθ'** = κατά (# 2846) according to so much; i.e., inasmuch as, just as. **ἀπόκειται** pres. ind. mid. (dep.) ἀπόκειμαι (# 641) to be put away, to appoint, to reserve for someone, to destine (BAGD). It was used on a tombstone which reads, "After a good life I departed home, where a place of piety has been reserved for me" (NDIEC, 4:23). Pres. indicates a truth which is continually true. **ἅπαξ** (# 562) once, one time. **ἀποθανεῖν** aor. act. inf. ἀποθνήσκω (# 633) to die. Epex. inf. explaining what is appointed. Aor. points to the fact of death as a conclusive act. **μετά** (# 3552) w. the acc., after. **κρίσις** (# 3213) judging, judgment. The rabbis taught that those born are appointed to die and those who die to live again and those who live again to be judged (Michel; Buchanan; M, Aboth 4:11, 22). ◆ **28 οὕτως** (# 4048) so. The comparison extends to both terms, the dying once and the judgment. The results of Christ's life are settled. In Christ's case the result is that He appears a second time without sin unto salvation, the sin having been destroyed by His death (EGT). **προσενεχθείς** aor. pass. part. προσφέρω s.v. 7. Temp. part. ("after"). **ἀνενεγκεῖν** aor. act. inf. ἀναφέρω (# 429) to take up and carry away, to take away. Articular inf. w. **εἰς** (# 1651) to express purp. **ἐκ δευτέρου** (# 1666; 1311) a second time. Prep. is used temporarily (IBG, 72f.) **χωρίς** (# 6006) without; i.e., "without any further sin laid upon Him," or "unburdened further by any sin" (Delitzsch). **ὀφθήσεται** fut. ind. pass. ὁράω (# 3972) to see; pass., to appear. **ἀπεκδεχομένοις** pres. mid. (dep.) part. ἀπεκδέχομαι (# 587) to eagerly but patiently expect or await (s. Phil. 3:20). The word is used in the NT to refer to a fut. manifestation of the glory of Christ (Westcott).

Hebrews 10

◆ **1 σκιά** (# 5014) shadow. It refers to the outline or shadow cast by the object which is the reality (Grässer; Riggenbach; Michel; BBC). **ἔχων** pres. act. part. ἔχω (# 2400) to have. Part. could be taken as causal. **μελλόντων** pres. act. part. μέλλω (# 3516) to be about to. Part. is used as a substitutive: "the future things," "the things about to come." **εἰκόνα** acc. sing. εἰκών (# 1635) image. The image is the real object that casts the law's shadow (Buchanan; Hughes; Michel). **πρᾶγμα** (# 4547) that which is done, matter, thing; i.e., the real object. It expresses the good things which are coming so far as they were embodied (Westcott). **κατ᾽ ἐνιαυτόν** (# 2846; 1929) yearly (s. 9:25). **προσφέρουσιν** pres. ind. act. προσφέρω (# 4712) to bring a sacrifice, to offer. Pres. points to the continually repeated sacrifices. **εἰς τὸ διηνεκές** (# 1457) continually, without interruption (s. Heb. 7:3). **δύναται** pres. ind. pass. (dep.) δύναμαι (# 1538) to be able to. **προσερχομένους** pres. mid. (dep.) part. προσέρχομαι (# 4665) to come to, to approach. Part. is used as a substitutive: "those approaching," "those who continually draw near" (s. 4:16). **τελειῶσαι** aor. act. inf. τελέω (# 5457) to perfect, to complete, to bring to the goal (s. Heb. 5:9). Compl. inf. w. vb. **δύναται**. ◆ **2 ἐπεί** (# 2075) since, for otherwise. Used in an elliptical construction of a contrary to fact cond. cl. (s. 9:26; BD, 238f). **ἐπαύσαντο** aor. ind. mid. (dep.) παύομαι (# 4264) to cease. **προσφερόμεναι** pres. pass. part. προσφέρω s.v. 1. Part. is used supplementarily to complete the action of the vb. **ἐπαύσαντο**. This sentence should be taken as a question: "For if it were otherwise, would they have not cease to be offered?" (Bruce). **διά** (# 1328) used w. acc. of the articular inf. to express cause. **ἔχειν** pres. act. inf. ἔχω (# 2400) to have. **μηδεμία** (# 3594) not one, no. The word is to be taken as negating the noun **συνείδησιν**. **ἔτι** (# 2285) yet, any longer. Used in the neg. expression meaning "more"; i.e., "no more." **συνείδησις** (# 5287) conscience, consciousness. The expression connotes the Hebrews sense of a burdened, smitten heart, which became most pronounced on the Day of Atonement (Lane). **λατρεύοντας** pres. act. part. λατρεύω (# 3302) to worship (TLNT; TDNT). Part. is used as a substitutive and is the so-called subject of the inf. **ἅπαξ** (# 562) once for all. **κεκαθαρισμένους** perf. pass. part. καθαρίζω (# 2751) to cleanse. Part. could be cond. or causal. Perf. suggests a cleansing that is permanent (Hughes). ◆ **3 ἐν αὐταῖς** (# 1877; 899) in these; i.e., "in the sacrifices." **ἀνάμνησις** (# 390) remembering, reminder. The word means a calling to mind of sins whereby men are put in remembrance of them by a divine institution (Westcott). ◆ **4 ἀδύνατος** (# 105) impossible. **αἷμα** (# 135) blood. **ταῦρος** (# 5436) steer, bull. **τράγος** (# 5543) goat, male goat. **ἀφαιρεῖν** pres. act. inf. ἀφαιρέω (# 904) to take away from, to take away, to remove. Pres. points to a continual action and emphasizes what is always true. ◆ **5 διό** (# 1475) wherefore. **εἰσερχόμενος** pres. mid. (dep.) part. εἰσέρχομαι (# 1656) to enter, to go into. The expression in Jewish lit. could refer to one's birth (Michel; Attridge; Braun). Temp. part., w. pres. indicating contemporaneous time: "when He came." The words are considered prophetic, depicting beforehand the mind of Christ regarding OT sacrifice and His own mission (EGT). **λέγει** pres. ind. act. λέγω (# 3306) to say. Christ Himself speaks from Ps. 40:6-8 (Hewitt). **θυσία** (# 2602) offering. It refers to the Heb. non-bloody offering–the meal offering (EGT). **προσφορά** (# 4714) offering. **ἠθέλησας** aor. ind. act. θέλω (# 2527) to desire. **κατηρτίσω** aor. act. ind. mid. 2nd. pers. sing. καταρτίζω (# 2936) to prepare. The words, "a body you have prepared for me," were evidently taken from the LXX and are an interpretative paraphrase of the Heb. text. The Gr. translators could have regarded the Heb. word as an instance of a part for the whole;

the digging or hollowing-out of the ears is part of the total work of fashioning a human body (Bruce). Or the ears may have been taken as a symbol of obedience as the organ that receives the divine will w. the body the organ that fulfills the divine will (Riggenbach). Perhaps there is an illusion to the custom of piercing a slave's ears, the sign he had voluntarily refused his liberty and was willing and ready to hear and execute God's command (s. Exod. 21:1-6; Deut. 15:17; Hughes; Attridge; TLNT: GELTS, 243; Walter C. Kaiser, Jr. "The Abolition of the Old Order and Establishment of the New: Ps. 40:6-8 and Hebrews 10:5-10," in *Tradition and Testament: Essays in Honor of Charles Lee Feinberg*, ed. John S. and Paul D. Feinberg [Chicago: Moody, 1981], 19-37). For a very good study of this passage from a typological view, w. a discussion of the textual problems s. OTN, 53-67. ◆ **6 ὁλοκαύτωμα** (# 3906) total or whole offering, burnt offering. **περὶ ἁμαρτίας** (# 4309; 281) concerning sin; i.e., sin offering. The phrase occurs frequently in Lev. to denote sin offering (EGT). **εὐδόκησας** aor. ind. act. 2nd. pers. sing. εὐδοκέω (# 2305) w. the acc. to be pleased w. ◆ **7 εἶπον** aor. ind. act. λέγω (# 3306) to say. **ἰδού** aor. imp. act. ὁράω (# 2627) to see. Here in the sense of "behold!," "look!" **ἥκω** pres. ind. act. (# 2457) The vb. has the meaning of a perfect: "I have come," "I am present" (BAGD; Westcott). **κεφαλίδι** dat. sing. κεφαλίς (# 3053) roll, diminutive of the word κεφαλη. It points to the head or knob of the rod around which the scroll was wound (Bruce; Attridge; Grässer). For various interpretations regarding the literal meaning of the word s. Hughes; Michel. The words **κεφαλίδι βιβλίου** signify the books of Moses in which the will of God and the way of obedience were written (Hughes). **γέγραπται** perf. ind. pass. γράφω (# 1211) to write; perf., it stands written. Perf. signifies the legal binding authority of a document (MM). **περὶ ἐμοῦ** (# 4309; 1609) concerning me. **ποιῆσαι** aor. act. inf. ποιέω (# 4472) to do. Articular inf. is used to express purp. It indicates that which is closely connected w. the action as its motive (Westcott, 342). **θέλημά** (# 2525) will. ◆ **8 ἀνώτερον** (# 542) adv., higher up. Here it means, "in the former part of the quotation" (EGT). **λέγων** pres. act. part. λέγω (# 3306) to say. **ὅτι** (# 4022) used to introduce a direct quotation and the equivalent of quotation marks. **κατά** (# 2848) w. acc., according to, according to the standard of. **προσφέρονται** pres. ind. pass. προσφέρω s.v. 1. ◆ **9 εἴρηκεν** perf. ind. act. λέγω (# 3306) to speak. Perf. expresses completed action, indicating that what the speaker said stands henceforth on permanent record (Bruce). **ἰδού** aor. ind. act. (s.v. 7). **ἥκω** pres. ind. act. to come s.v. 7. **ποιῆσαι** aor. act. inf. ποιέω (# 4472) to do, to accomplish. Articular inf. to express purp.: "I have come to do your will." **ἀναιρεῖ** pres. ind. act. ἀναιρέω (# 359) to lift up, to take away, to remove, to abolish. The word was used in classical Gr.

of the destruction, abolition, or repeal of laws, governments, customs, etc. (EGT; Westcott; Michel; Weiss; Grässer). **πρῶτος** (# 4755) first. **δεύτερος** (# 1311) second. **στήσῃ** aor. subj. act. ἵστημι (# 2705)to place, to establish. Subj. w. **ἵνα** (# 2671) to express purp. ◆ **10 ἐν** (# 1877) in, by. Instr. use of the prep. can also have a causal tinge (BD, 118). **ᾧ** dat. sing. ὅς (# 4005) rel. pron., who, which. "By which will" means by the will of God thus fulfilled by Christ (Bruce). **ἡγιασμένοι** perf. pass. part. ἁγιάζω (# 1639) to set apart, to sanctify (TDNT; EDNT). Part. is used in a perf. pass. periphrastic construction emphasizing the completed state or condition (RWP). **ἐσμέν** pres. ind. act. εἰμί (# 1639) to be. **προσφορά** (# 4714) offering. **ἐφάπαξ** (# 2384) once for all. Prep. in compound gives a directive strengthening force (MH, 315). The word is found in the papyri where the context may suggest a meaning, "at one time" (MM; Preisigke). ◆ **11 πᾶς** (# 4246) every. **ἕστηκεν** perf. ind. act. ἵστημι (# 2705) perf. to stand. The idea of standing is of a work still to be done, of service still to be rendered (Westcott). **καθ' ἡμέραν** (# 2846; 2465) daily. **λειτουργῶν** pres. act. part. λειτουργέω (# 3310) to perform religious service. The word was used in classical Gr. to mean, "to supply public offices at one's own cost"; then generally, "to serve the state," "to do a service." It was then used of service done by a priest and indicated the fulfillment of an office. The word has a definite representative character and corresponds to the function to be discharged (AS; NTW, 72f; BS, 140; TDNT; TLNT; Westcott, 230-33). Part. of manner. **τὰς αὐτάς** the same. **πολλάκις** (# 4490) frequently, time after time. **προσφέρων** pres. act. part. προσφέρω (# 4712) to offer. Pres. suggests contemporary action to the main vb. The action of presenting the sacrifice is continually repeated. **αἵτινες** fem. pl. ὅστις (# 4015) which, which one. Rel. pron. properly indicates the class or kind to which an object belongs (RG, 727). **οὐδέποτε** (# 4030) never. **δύνανται** pres. ind. pass. (dep.) δύναμαι (# 1538) to be able to, w. inf. **περιελεῖν** aor. act. inf. περιαιρέω (# 4311) to take from around, to remove utterly (RWP). Aor. expresses finality. ◆ **12 προσενέγκας** aor. act. part. προσφέρω (# 4712) to sacrifice. Temp. part. ("after"). **εἰς τὸ διηνεκές** (# 1457) continually, unbroken, perpetually, forever (s. 7:3; AS). **ἐκάθισεν** aor. ind. act. καθίζω (# 2767) to take one's seat. **δεξιᾷ** dat. sing. δεξιός (# 1288) right; here, "on the right." This is the position of honor (s. Eph. 1:20; SB, 4, i:452-65). His place in heaven, enabling Him to exercise the ministry of the new covenant, is the basis of the assurance that the community now possesses full access to God (Lane). ◆ **13 τὸ λοιπόν** (# 3370) henceforth; i.e., "for the rest," "for the future"–all the remaining time till the end of the pres. world. Here, acc. of the extent of time (Delitzsch; RWP). **ἐκδεχόμενος** pres. mid. (dep.) part. ἐκδέχομαι (# 1683) to await, to wait for. Prep. in compound has a

perfective idea, indicating that one is ready and prepared to deal with the situation when it arrives (MH, 310). Temp. part. ("while He waits"). **τεθῶσιν** aor. subj. pass. (dep.) τίθημι (# 5502) to place, to put. Subj. in a purp. and indef. temp. cl. (RWP). **ὑποπόδιον** (# 5711) footstool (Jam. 2:3; Isa. 66:1). Here fig., to subject him to the other, so that the other can put his foot on the subject's neck (BAGD; MM). Here it is the death and atoning sacrifice of the high priest that enables victory, not the death or defeat of the enemy. ◆ **14 μιᾷ προσφορᾷ** (# 1651; 4714) by one offering; dat. of instr. **τετελείωκεν** perf. ind. act. τελειόω (# 5457) to complete, to perfect (s. Heb. 5:9). Perf. indicates a one-time event w. a continuing result completed in the process depicted by the part. (Michel). **ἁγιαζομένους** pres. pass. part. ἁγιάζω to sanctify (s.v. 10). ◆ **15 μαρτυρεῖ** pres. ind. act. μαρτυρέω (# 3455) to witness, to bear witness. For the writer of Hebrews the truth of one kind of testimony required confirmation by another; in this case, by the testimony of the Scriptures. The testimony of the Scripture is the testimony of God (NTCW, 218, 221). **εἰρηκέναι** perf. act. inf. λέγω (# 3306) to say. Inf. w. **μετά** (# 3552) expressing time ("after"). For the significance of the perf. s.v. 9. ◆ **16 αὕτη** nom. fem. οὗτος (# 4047) this. The vb. εἰμί must be supplied; i.e., "this is the covenant." **διαθήκη** (# 1347) covenant. **διαθήσομαι** fut. ind. mid. (dep.) διατίθημι (# 1416) to make an agreement, to make a treaty, to make a covenant. **πρός** (# 4639) w. acc., with. **μετά** (# 3552) w. acc., after. **λέγει** pres. ind. act. λέγω (# 3306) to say. **διδούς** pres. act. part. δίδωμι (# 1443) to give. Part. could be temp. or it could express means or manner. **ἐπί** w. the acc., upon. **νόμος** (# 3795) law. **διάνοια** (# 1379) mind (s. 8:10). **ἐπιγράψω** fut. act. ind. ἐπιγράφω (# 2108) to write upon. **αὐτός** (# 899) oneself; them (the laws). It is not just the writing but the inner ability to know and obey the laws. ◆ **17 ἁμαρτία** (# 281) sin. **ἀνομία** (# 490) lawlessness, iniquity. **μνησθήσομαι** fut. ind. pass. μιμνήσκω (# 3630) w. the gen., to remember. Fut. is used here instead of the subj. of the LXX and 8:12 because the writer emphasizes the extension of the forgetting to all futurity (EGT). It is not just forgetting in the sense of not remembering, but in the sense of not holding the sins against the believer. Thus there is no need to atone for sin. **οὐ μή ... ἔτι** no longer, no more. ◆ **18 ὅπου** (# 3963) where. **ἄφεσις** (# 912) forgiveness. **οὐκέτι** (# 4033) no longer. **προσφορά** (# 4714) offering. **περί** (# 4309) w. gen., concerning, for. ◆ **19 ἔχοντες** pres. act. part. (causal) ἔχω (# 2400) to have. Pres. indicates a continual possession. **παρρησία** (# 4244) boldness, confidence, assurance (s. 3:6). **εἴσοδος** (# 1658) entrance. **τῶν ἁγίων** (# 41) sanctuary (s. 9:1). The expression designates the innermost sanctuary of the Holy of Holies into which, under the old dispensation, the people were forbidden to enter (Hughes). **ἐν** (# 1877) by. ◆ **20 ἥν** fem. acc. ὅς (# 4005) rel. pron., which, referring to the entrance. **ἐνεκαίνισεν** aor. ind. act. ἐγκαινίζω (# 1590) to inaugurate, to dedicate. The word is used in the LXX of the inauguration or dedication of the altar, of the temple, of the kingdom (1 Sam. 11:14), or of a house (Deut. 20:5) (GELTS, 126; TLNT; Grässer; Westcott; Heb. 9:18). **πρόσφατος** (# 4710) freshly slaughtered, fresh, new, recent. The word means not only newly fresh, but also retaining a freshness that cannot grow old (Grässer; Westcott; Buchanan; GELTS, 406). **ζῶσαν** pres. act. part. ζάω (# 2409) to live. It is living as a way of being in fellowship w. a person (Westcott; Michel). **καταπέτασμα** (# 2925) that which falls down, curtain, veil. ◆ **21 ἱερέα** acc. sing. ἱερεύς (# 2636) priest. **μέγας** (# 3489) great. Great in position as the Son of God and in his effective sacrifice that atones completely. **ἐπί** (# 2093) w. acc., over. **οἶκος** (# 3875) house, household; referring here to the worshipping community. ◆ **22 προσερχώμεθα** pres. subj. mid. (dep.) προσέρχομαι (# 4665) to come to, to draw near (s. 4:16). Cohortative subj., "let us draw near." **ἀληθινός** (# 240) truthful, in the sense of sincere. **πληροφορία** (# 4443) full assurance. **ῥεραντισμένοι** perf. pass. part. ῥαντίζω (# 4822) to sprinkle, to cleanse. Some would see this going back to the cleansing through the red heifer (Num. 19; BAGD; Attridge). The word occurs in Lev. 6:27; Ps. 51:7; 2 Kings 9:33 (4 Kings 9:33 LXX), each time associated w. blood (HR, 2:1248). In the first two references it refers to blood in the sacrificial system for the cleaning of sin; in the latter it refers to Jezebel's blood splattered on the wall. Perf. indicates a completed state or condition. **λελουσμένοι** perf. pass. part. λούω (# 3374) to wash. The parts. do not express conditions of approach to God yet to be achieved, but conditions already possessed (EGT). **ὕδατι** (# 5623) dat. sing. ὕδωρ water. Instr. dat., "w. water." ◆ **23 κατέχωμεν** pres. subj. act. κατέχω (# 2988) to hold down, to hold fast. Cohortatory subj. **ὁμολογία** (# 3934) confession, agreement (ECC; TDNT). **ἀκλινής** (# 195) unwavering, not leaning (RWP). **ἐπαγγειλάμενος** aor. mid. (dep.) part. ἐπαγγέλλομαι (# 2040) to promise. Subst. use of the part., "the one who promised." Aor. indicates antecedent action. ◆ **24 κατανοῶμεν** pres. subj. act. κατανοέω (# 2917) to place the mind down upon, to consider, to consider thoughtfully (s. Heb. 3:1). Hortatory subj. ("let us"). **ἀλλήλους** acc. pl. ἀλλήλων (# 253) one another, refl. pron. **παροξυσμός** (# 4237) irritating, inciting, stimulation (EGT; RWP; Michel). **ἀγάπη** (# 27) love. Here, obj. gen. **καλῶν ἔργων** (# 2819; 2240) good works. Here, obj. gen. This is to be the result of the stimulation. ◆ **25 ἐγκαταλείποντες** pres. act. part. ἐγκαταλείπω (# 1593) to leave in the lurch, to forsake. Part. of manner describing the main vb. **κατανοῶμεν**. **ἐπισυναγωγή** (# 2191) a gathering together, assembly. Prep. in compound indicates the common responsibility (Michel). The term here should be understood as

simply the regular gathering together of Christian believers for worship and exhortation in a particular place (Hughes; BBC). Part. of manner or part. as imp. Customary pres. indicates an habit of life (GGBB, 521-22). **ἔθος** (# 1621) custom, habit. **τισίν** dat. pl. τις (# 5516) someone, some (pl.). The dat. may be possession ("the custom of some") or dat. of reference ("the custom in reference to some"). **παρακαλοῦντες** pres. act. part. παρακαλέω (# 4151) to encourage, to entreat (s. Rom. 12:1). **τοσούτῳ** dat. τοσοῦτος (# 5537) so much. Used in the expression **μᾶλλον ὅσῳ** (# 3437; 4012) meaning, "by so much more." It is a instr. dat. or dat. of measure or degree: "by so much the more as" (RWP). **βλέπετε** pres. ind. act. βλέπω (# 1063) to see. **ἐγγίζουσαν** pres. act. part. ἐγγίζω (# 1581) to draw near, to come near. ◆ **26 ἑκουσίως** (# 1731) adv. willingly, voluntarily, deliberately, intentionally. **ἁμαρτανόντων** pres. act. part. ἁμαρτάνω (# 279) to sin. Gen. abs. used to express a cond. **λαβεῖν** aor. inf. act. λαμβάνω (# 3284) to take, receive, to obtain. Inf. w. prep. μετά (# 3552) w. a temp. meaning ("after"). **ἐπίγνωσις** (# 2106) knowledge, recognition. **ἀλήθεια** (# 237) truth. Here obj. gen., "knowledge of the truth"; the truth that is known. **ἀπολείπεται** pres. ind. pass. ἀπολείπω (# 657) to leave off, to leave behind; pass., to be left behind, to remain. The concept of a willful sin without a sacrifice is an OT teaching also reflected in Judaism (s. Num 15:31; Michel; Moffat; Hughes). ◆ **27 φοβερός** (# 5829) fearful. **ἐκδοχή** (# 1693) expectation. **ζῆλος** (# 2419) zeal. The phrase may be translated, "zeal of fire" or "fiery zeal" (Hughes). **ἐσθίειν** pres. act. inf. ἐσθίω (# 2266) to eat. Compl. inf. w. the following part. to express the fut. **μέλλοντος** pres. act. part. μέλλω (# 3516) to be about. **ὑπεναντίος** (# 5641) one who opposes, adversary. ◆ **28 ἀθετήσας** aor. act. part. ἀθετέω (# 119) to place aside, to reject, to annul. **τις** (# 5516) anyone. **χωρίς** (# 6006) w. gen., without. **οἰκτιρμός** (# 3880) compassionate mercy, heartfelt mercy (s. Phil 2:1; TDNT). **δυσίν** dat. δύο (# 1545) two. **τρισίν** dat. τρές (# 5552) three. **ἀποθνήσκει** pres. ind. act. ἀποθνήσκω (# 633) to die. Gnomic pres. indicating that which is generally true. ◆ **29 πόσος** (# 4531) how much? The argument from the less to the greater was common in rabbinical arguments (Moffatt; s. Rom. 5:9). **δοκεῖτε** pres. ind. act. δοκέω (# 1506) to suppose. **χείρονος** gen. of comp. χείρων (# 5937) worse. **ἀξιωθήσεται** fut. ind. pass. ἀξιόω (# 546) to consider worthy of, followed by the gen. **τιμωρία** (# 5513) punishment. **καταπατήσας** aor. act. part. καταπατέω (# 2922) to trample, to stomp upon. The word indicates treatment w. the utmost contempt (Hughes). **κοινός** (# 3123) common, profane. It denotes the opposite of ἅγιος (Michel). **ἡγησάμενος** aor. mid. (dep.) part. ἡγέομαι (# 2451) to consider, to count as. **ἡγιάσθη** aor. ind. pass. ἁγιάζω (# 39) to separate, to set apart for divine use, to sanctify. **ἐνυβρίσας** aor. act. part.

ἐνυβρίζω (# 1964) to treat w. utter contempt, to arrogantly insult (TDNT; MNTW, 77-85). ◆ **30 οἴδαμεν**
pres. ind. act. οἶδα (# 3857) to know. Def. perf. w. pres.
meaning. **εἰπόντα** aor. act. part. λέγω (# 3306) to say. **ἐκδίκησις** (# 1689) avenging, revenge. **ἀνταποδώσω** fut.
ind. act. ἀνταποδίδωμι (# 500) to pay back. Prep. in
compound indicates payment back w. the same thing
or in the like manner. **κρινεῖ** fut. ind. act. κρίνω (# 3212)
to judge. ◆ **31 φοβερός** (# 5829) fearful. **ἐμπεσεῖν** aor.
act. inf. ἐμπίπτω (# 1860) to fall in, to fall into. Inf. is
used as the subject of the vb. εἰμι, which is understood.
ζῶντος pres. act. part. ζάω (# 2409) to live. Adj. part.
without the art., indicating the quality of character.
◆ **32 ἀναμιμνῄσκεσθε** pres. imp. mid. (dep.) ἀναμιμνῄσκω (# 389) to remind oneself, to remember. **πρότερον** (# 4728) former, first. Since the distinction between
comp. and superl. had been weakened in Koine, the
phrase may be translated "the first days"; i.e., the time
when they first responded to the message of the gospel
(Hughes). **φωτισθέντες** aor. pass. part. φωτίζω (# 5894)
to make light, to enlighten. **ἄθλησις** (# 124) fighting,
conflict, struggle. **ὑπεμείνατε** aor. ind. act. ὑπομένω
(# 5702) to remain under, to patiently bear, to patiently
and hopefully endure (s.v. 36). **πάθημα** (# 4077) suffering. ◆ **33 τοῦτο μέν … τοῦτο δέ** partly so … and partly
so. By being made a public spectacle through reproach
and tribulations, and partly by becoming sharers with
those who were so treated. The acc. of general reference
is used w. the particles for contrast (RWP). **ὀνειδισμός**
(# 3944) reproach, revile, insult. **θλῖψις** (# 2568) pressure, trouble, affliction. **θεατριζόμενοι** pres. pass. part.
θεατρίζω (# 2518) to bring upon the stage, to hold up to
derision, to put to shame, to dispose publicly. It means
that they had been held up to public derision, scoffed
and sneered at, accused of crime and vice, unjustly suspected and denounced (RWP; BAGD; Moffat; Michel).
κοινωνός (# 3128) partner, sharer. **ἀναστρεφομένων** pres.
pass. (dep.) part. ἀναστρέφομαι (# 418) to conduct one's
life, to be treated. **γενηθέντες** aor. pass. (dep.) part. γίνομαι (# 1181) to become. ◆ **34 δέσμιος** (# 1300) prisoner.
συνεπαθήσατε aor. act. ind. συμπαθέω (# 5217) to suffer
together, to suffer w. someone. **ἁρπαγή** (# 771) seizing,
plundering. The word implies that their own property
either had been confiscated by the authorities or plun-
dered in some mob riot (Moffatt). **ὑπαρχόντων** pres. act.
part. ὑπάρχω (# 5639) n. pl. part., possessions. **χαρά**
(# 5915) joy. **προσεδέξασθε** aor. ind. mid. (dep.) προσδέχομαι (# 4657) to accept. **γινώσκοντες** pres. act. part. γινώσκω (# 1182) to know. **ἔχειν** pres. act. inf. ἔχω (# 2400)
to have. Inf. in indir. disc., as the object of the part.
γινώσκοντες. κρείττονα (# 3202) better; comp. ἀγαθός (s.
9:23). **ὕπαρξις** (# 5638) possession. **μένουσαν** pres. act.
part. μένω (# 3531) to remain, to abide. ◆ **35 ἀποβάλητε**
aor. subj. act. ἀποβάλλω (# 610) to throw away. Aor.
subj. is used w. the neg. μή (# 3590) in a prohibitive

sense, implying that the action does not yet exist and
should not arise (MKG, 273). **παρρησία** (# 4244) boldness, confidence (s. 3:6). **ἔχει** pres. ind. act. ἔχω (# 2400)
to have. Fut. pres. indicating the certainty of the coming reward. **μισθαποδοσία** (# 3632) payment, reward,
recompense. ◆ **36 ὑπομονή** (# 5705) patient endurance.
It is the spirit that can bear things not simply w. resignation but w. blazing hope; it is not the spirit that sits
statically enduring in one place, but the spirit that
bears all things because it knows that these things are
leading to a goal of glory (NTW, 60; TDNT; NIDNTT;
TLNT; DLNT, 326-30; GELTS, 494). This sets the stage
for Heb. 11, recounting those who had received God's
promises but who had to patiently wait in faith for the
fulfillment. **ἔχετε** pres. ind. act. ἔχω (# 2400) to have.
χρεία (# 5970) need; followed by the gen., "to have
need of something." **ποιήσαντες** aor. act. part. (temp.)
ποιέω (# 4472) to do. Aor. expressing logically antecedent action ("after"). **κομίσησθε** aor. subj. mid. (dep.) κο-
μίζομαι (# 3152) to receive. Here the word indicates
receiving the fulfillment of a promise (Hughes).
◆ **37 ἔτι μικρὸν ὅσον ὅσον** a very little; "only for a very
little while" (BD, 160). **ἐρχόμενος** pres. mid. (dep.) part.
(subst.) ἔρχομαι (# 2262) to go. **ἥξει** fut. ind. act. ἥκω
(# 2457) to come. **χρονίσει** fut. ind. act. χρονίζω (# 5988)
to delay. ◆ **38 ζήσεται** fut. ind. act. ζάω (# 2409) to live.
ὑποστείληται aor. subj. mid. ὑποστέλλω (# 5713) to
draw oneself back, to withdraw oneself, to shrink back.
Subj. w. ἐάν (# 1569) in a third class cond. cl. that assumes the possibility of the cond. **εὐδοκεῖ** pres. ind. act.
εὐδοκέω (# 2305) to delight in, to have pleasure in.
◆ **39 ἐσμέν** pres. ind. act. εἰμί (# 1639) to be. **ὑποστολή**
(# 5714) shrinking, timidity. Used here in the expression, "we do not belong to those who are timid"
(BAGD). **ἀπώλεια** (# 724) ruin, destruction. **περιποίησις**
(# 4348) possession. The term indicates what one
makes one's own, either by keeping or by gaining
(Hughes).

Hebrews 11

◆ **1 ἔστιν** pres. ind. act. εἰμί (# 1639) to be. The emphatic position of the word may suggest a definition
style (Michel). **πίστις** (# 4411) faith. It is the holding
fast, in patient waiting, to what Christ has done as high
priest, and it refers retrospectively to Heb. 10:39 where
the context gave the nuance of steadfast faithfulness to
God and His word of promise (Weiss; Lane; Attridge;
Dieter Lührmann, "Pistis im Judentum," ZNW 64
(1973): 19-38; DLNT, 364-65; BBC). **ἐλπιζομένων** pres.
pass. part. ἐλπίζω (# 1827) to hope (EH, 628-32). Subst.
part., "things hoped for." **ὑπόστασις** (# 5712) assurance. The word has a number of connotations and usages: essence, reality, substance, foundation, or
confidant assurance, hope or guarantee, attestation, as
in documents that attest or provide evidence of owner-

ship. For these meanings as well as other references s. Hughes; Michel; Attridge; Grässer; TDNT; TLNT; MM; GELTS, 495; GELRS, 303. **πρᾶγμα** (# 4547) matter, thing. **ἔλεγχος** (# 1793) evidence, proof. The word was used in the papyri of legal proofs of an accusation (MM; Preisigke; TDNT). Faith offers the full certainty of proof for what is not seen (Grässer). **βλεπομένων** pres. pass. part. (subst.) βλέπω (# 4063) to see. ◆ **2 ἐν** (# 1877) by. Instr. prep. **ταύτῃ** (# 4047) this, i.e., faith. **ἐμαρτυρή-θησαν** aor. ind. pass. μαρτυρέω (# 3455) to bear witness. Pass. may be the so-called theol. pass., indicating that it is God who bears witness concerning the elders (BG, 76). **πρεσβύτερος** (# 4565) elder. These were the men and women of old who received the divine commendation for faith of this kind (Bruce; DLNT, 38-40). Josephus tells of Judas Maccabaeus, who saw his troops shrinking from the battle because of their small number, and encouraged them w. the example of their forefathers, "who because of their righteousness and their struggles on behalf of their own laws and children had many times defeated many tens of thousands" (Jos., Ant., 12:290-91). ◆ **3 πίστει** dat. sing. πίστις (# 4411) faith (s.v. 1). Dat. of instr., "by faith." The use of this word in the chapter will serve as an introductory or a transition marker. **νοοῦμεν** pres. ind. act. νοέω (# 3783) to understand. The word expresses a mental perception in distinction from a sensuous perception (Westcott). **κατηρτίσθαι** pres. pass. inf. καταρτίζω (# 2936) to outfit, to perfect. The word expresses the manifoldness and the unity of all creation. The tense suggests that the original lesson of creation remains for abiding use and application (Westcott). The word was used in Hellenistic literature to describe the act of creation and in this sense has a solemn tone (Michel). Inf. is used in indir. disc. **αἰών** (# 172) age, world (TDNT). **ῥῆμα** (# 4839) that which is spoken, word. Here instr. dat. **φαινομένων** pres. mid. (dep.) part. φαίνομαι (# 5743) to appear, to be visible. **βλεπόμενον** pres. pass. part. βλέπω (# 4063) to see. **γεγονέναι** perf. inf. mid. (dep.) γίνομαι (# 1181) to become. Inf. to express results (RG, 1003; BD, 207f). The neg. should be taken w. inf. so the translation would be, "so that what is seen has not come into being from things which appear" (Hughes). ◆ **4 πλείονα** comp. πολύς (# 4498) much, great; comp., better. **παρά** (# 4123) than. For the prep. used in a comp. construction s. 1:4. **προσήνεγκεν** aor. ind. act. προσφέρω (# 4712) to bring to, to offer, to sacrifice. **τῷ θεῷ** (# 2536) to God, dat. ind. obj. For the textual problem s. TC, 671. **ἐμαρ-τυρήθη** aor. ind. pass. μαρτυρέω (# 3455) to witness. Aor. points to the event in the narrative. **εἶναι** pres. act. inf. εἰμί (# 1639) to be. Inf. in indir. disc. **μαρτυροῦντος** pres. act. part. (temp.) μαρτυρέω to testify, to bear witness. Gen. abs. Pres. indicating contemporary action. **ἐπί** (# 2093) concerning, w. respect to. For the textual variations in this v. s. Bruce; TC, 671-72. **ἀποθανών** aor.

act. part. ἀποθνῄσκω (# 633) to die. Part. could be concessive, "although He died." **λαλεῖ** pres. ind. act. λαλέω (# 4246) to speak. Pres. indicates a continual action, "Although he died, he continues to speak." ◆ **5 με-τετέθη** aor. ind. pass. μετατίθημι (# 3572) to change, to transpose, to transfer, to remove from one place to another, to translate (EGT). **ἰδεῖν** aor. ind. act. ὁράω (# 3872) to see. Here used in a fig. sense, "to see death"; i.e., to die. Articular inf. to express result. **ηὑρίσκετο** perf. ind. pass. εὑρίσκω (# 2351) to find; pass., to be found, to be. The Jewish view was that Enoch was taken to heaven and did not die (SB, 3:744-45; Jos., Ant., 1:85; ABD, 2:508; BBC). **μεμαρτύρηται** perf. ind. pass. μαρτυρέω to witness. (s.v. 2). **εὐαρεστηκέναι** perf. act. inf. εὐαρεστέω (# 2297) to be well pleasing to. Inf. in indir. discourse. ◆ **6 χωρίς** (# 6006) w. gen., without. **ἀδύ-νατος** (# 105) impossible. **εὐαρεστῆσαι** aor. act. inf. s.v. 5. Epex. inf. explaining what is impossible. **πιστεῦσαι** aor. act. inf. πιστεύω (# 4409) to believe. Inf. explains what is necessary. **δεῖ** (# 1256) pres. ind. act. it is necessary to, w. inf. Impersonal vb. The word speaks of the binding and logical necessity. **προσερχόμενον** pres. mid. (dep.) part. προσέρχομαι (# 4665) to come to, to approach. Subst. part., "the ones approaching God," used of the worshipers of God (Attridge; s. 4:16). **ἐκζητοῦσιν** pres. act. part. ἐκζητέω (# 1699) to search out, to seek after. Prep. in compound always seems to denote that the seeker finds, or at least exhausts his powers of seeking (MH, 310). **μισθαποδότης** (# 3633) one who gives a reward, one who pays back a reward. **γίνεται** pres. ind. mid. (dep.) γίνομαι (# 1181) to become. ◆ **7 χρημα-τισθείς** aor. pass. part. χρηματίζω (# 5976) to give divine instruction, to warn (s. 8:5). **μηδέπω** (# 3596) not yet. **βλεπομένων** pres. act. part. βλέπω (# 1063) to see. **εὐλα-βηθείς** aor. pass. (dep.) part. εὐλαβέω (# 2326) to be afraid; to reverence, to respect out of reverence, respect, or regard (BAGD); to take hold well or carefully, to act circumspectly or w. reverence, to beware, to reverence (RWP; AS; Michel). **κατεσκεύασεν** aor. ind. act. κατασκευάζω (# 2941) to make ready, to build, to construct, to erect, to create. It is a favorite word for the construction of a ship (BAGD). **κιβωτός** (# 3066) ark. **κατέκρινεν** aor. ind. act. κατακρίνω (# 2891) to pass judgment against, to condemn. **κατὰ πίστιν** (# 2848; 4411) according to the standard of faith. The prep. can also connote "by virtue of," "on the ground of," "in consequence of" (IBG, 59; EGT). **ἐγένετο** impf. ind. mid. (dep.) γίνομαι (# 1181) to become. **κληρονόμος** (# 3101) heir. ◆ **8 καλούμενος** pres. pass. part. καλέω (# 2813) to call. Part. could be temp., "when he was called." For the call of Abraham according to Jewish tradition s. The Apocalypse of Abraham, 1-8, Jub. 12:1-31. For Abraham in Hebrews s. DLNT, 1-6. **ὑπήκουσεν** aor. ind. act. ὑπα-κούω (# 5634) to listen to, to obey. **ἐξελθεῖν** aor. act. inf. ἐξέρχομαι (# 2002) to go out, to go forth from. Inf. is used to explain the obedience. ἤμελλεν impf. ind. act. μέλλω (# 3516) to be about to, w. inf. The word is used w. inf. to express the future, and the impf. w. the inf. expresses futurity or intention reckoned from a moment in the past (MKG, 307). λαμβάνειν pres. act. inf. λαμβάνω (# 3284) to receive. Compl. inf. to the main vb. εἰς (# 1650) for. κληρονομία (# 3100) inheritance. ἐξῆλθεν aor. ind. act. ἐξέρχομαι (# 2002) to go out. ἐπιστάμενος pres. mid. (dep.) part. ἐπίσταμαι (# 2179) to know, to understand. Concessive part., "even though he did not know." Aor. describes antecedent time. ποῦ (# 4544) where? ἔρχεται pres. ind. mid. (dep.) ἔρχομαι (# 2262) to go. Pres. used to describe vivid action. ◆ 9 παρῴκησεν aor. ind. act. παροικέω (# 4228) to dwell alongside of, to be a foreigner residing in a foreign country. Such foreigners had certain legal rights, even though they were considered only temporary or foreign residents (TDNT; NIDOTTE, 1:836-39; Michel; s. Eph. 2:19). ἀλλότριος (# 259) foreigner, stranger. σκηναῖς dat. pl. σκηνή (# 5008) tent. κατοικήσας aor. act. part. κατοικέω (# 2997) to reside, to dwell, to be at home. συγκληρονόμος (# 5169) fellow heir. Gen. here due to the preceding prep. μετά (# 3552) with. ◆ 10 ἐξεδέχετο impf. ind. mid. (dep.) ἐκδέχομαι (# 1683) to await expectantly. Prep. in compound means to be ready, to be prepared to deal w. the situation (EGT). θεμέλιος (# 2529) foundation. ἔχουσαν pres. act. part. ἔχω (# 2400) to have. τεχνίτης (# 5493) craftsman, artificer, designer, maker (Bruce; Michel; Hughes; Attridge). δημιουργός (# 1321) public workman, constructor, maker. The first word refers to the plan and this word to its execution (Westcott; Bruce; Michel; Attridge). The vb. was used in a Christian papyrus of Jesus Christ as the Creator of all things (ὁ δημιουργήσας τὰ πάντα) (NDIEC, 2:149-51; PGL, 343) ◆ 11 αὐτή (# 899) herself. καταβολή (# 2856) casting down. Used as a t.t. for the sowing of seed and here in the idiom, "to receive the sowing of the seed," meaning "to conceive." στεῖρα (# 5096) barren, incapable of bearing children. σπέρμα (# 5065) seed, sperm. ἔλαβεν aor. ind. act. λαμβάνω (# 3284) to receive. παρά (# 4123) beyond, past. ἡλικία (# 2461) age; "beyond the season of age" (RWP). ἡγήσατο aor. ind. mid. (dep.) ἡγέομαι (# 2451) to consider, to reckon as, to count as. ἐπαγγειλάμενον aor. mid. part. ἐπαγγέλλω (# 2040) to promise. Subst. part., "the one who promised." ◆ 12 διό (# 1475) therefore. ἑνός gen. εἷς (# 1651) one; one who stands at the beginning of a long series. Abraham was known as "the One" (Michel; Delitzsch). It serves to contrast the small beginning w. the abundant result (Attridge). ἐγεννήθησαν aor. ind. pass. γεννάω (# 1164) to bear; pass., to be born. (For the variant reading ἐγενήθησαν aor. ind. pass. [dep.] γίνομαι [# 1181] to be, to become s. Delitzsch; Bruce.) νενεκρωμένου perf. pass. part. νεκρόω (# 3739) to make dead, to treat as dead, to consider dead; "as good as

dead" (RWP; Bruce). καθώς (# 2777) just as. ἄστρα nom. pl. ἄστρον (# 849) constellation; star. πλήθει dat. sing. πλῆθος (# 4436) quantity, number. Dat. is either loc. ("in number") or dat. of reference ("in reference to quantity"). ἄμμος (# 302) sand. παρά (# 4123) w. the acc., along, alongside of. χεῖλος (# 5927) lip, shore. ἀναρίθμητος (# 410) unable to be counted, innumerable. ◆ 13 κατά (# 2848) w. the acc., according to; i.e., in accordance w. the principle of faith (Hughes). ἀπέθανον aor. ind. act. ἀποθνῄσκω (# 633) to die. λαβόντες aor. act. part. λαμβάνω (# 3284) to receive, to obtain; i.e., to obtain the fulfillment of the promise (Michel). πόρρωθεν (# 4523) from afar, from a long distance away. ἰδόντες aor. act. part. ὁράω (# 3972) to see. ἀσπασάμενοι aor. mid. (dep.) part. ἀσπάζομαι (# 832) to greet. They hailed them from afar, as those on board ship descry friends on shore and wave in recognition (EGT); or they greet the fulfillment still far off, as a wanderer who sees his native city on the horizon (Riggenbach). ὁμολογήσαντες aor. act. part. ὁμολογέω (# 3933) to agree, to confess. Aor. indicates logically antecedent action. ξένος (# 3828) foreigner. παρεπίδημος (# 4215) one who makes his home alongside of, one from another country, pilgrim, one who stays for a while in a strange place. The word was used in the LXX and in the papyri for those who settled in a particular district only for a time (MM; BS, 149; Preisigke; BAGD; TLNT). ◆ 14 τοιαῦτα acc. pl. τοιοῦτος (# 5525) such a one. λέγοντες pres. act. part. λέγω (# 3306) to say. ἐμφανίζουσιν pres. ind. act. ἐμφανίζω (# 1872) to manifest, to show, to make clear. πατρίδα acc. sing. πατρίς (# 4258) fatherland. ἐπιζητοῦσιν pres. ind. act. ἐπιζητέω (# 2118) to seek after. Prep. in compound indicates direction (EGT). ◆ 15 ἐκεῖνος (# 1697) that one; i.e., the earthly country. Gen. here is used after the vb. ἐμνημόνευον impf. ind. act. μνημονεύω (# 3648) to remember, to be mindful of something. Ind. used in a contrary to fact cond. cl. ἐξέβησαν aor. ind. act. ἐκβαίνω (# 1674) to go out. εἶχον aor. ind. act. ἔχω (# 2400) to have. ἀνακάμψαι aor. act. inf. ἀνακάμπτω (# 366) to bind back, to turn back again. Inf. used to explain the word καιρός. ◆ 16 νῦν (# 3814) now; i.e., "the truth is," "as it is" (Bruce). ὀρέγονται pres. ind. mid. (dep.) ὀρέγομαι (# 3977) to stretch oneself out for; fig., to desire, to aspire, to strive for, to yearn for (RWP; BAGD; s. 1 Tim. 3:1). Present vbs. in this context indicate the continual habitual attitude of life. ἐπουράνιος (# 2230) heavenly (s. Eph. 1:3). ἐπαισχύνεται pres. ind. mid. (dep.) ἐπαισχύνομαι (# 2049) to be ashamed. ἐπικαλεῖσθαι pres. mid./pass. inf. ἐπικαλέω (# 2126) to call upon, to name. If the vb. is taken as mid., the meaning is, "God is not ashamed of them to call Himself their God." If pass., "God is not ashamed of them to be called their God." Epex. inf. explaining the main vb. ἡτοίμασεν aor. ind. act. ἑτοιμάζω (# 2286) to prepare, to make ready.

◆ 17 **προσενήνοχεν** perf. ind. act. προσφέρω (# 4712) to offer, to offer as a sacrifice. Perf. indicates this as an abiding example (BD, 177). **πειραζόμενος** pres. pass. part. πειράζω (# 4279) to try, to examine, to test (TLNT; TDNT). Pass. is divine pass. indicating that Abraham was tested by God (Hughes; BG, 76). **μονογενής** (# 3666) unique, only one of the kind, only (TDNT; NIDNTT). **προσέφερεν** aor. ind. act. προσφέρω (# 4712) to offer. **ἐπαγγελία** (# 2039) promise. Here, w. the def. art., "the well-known promises." **ἀναδεξάμενος** aor. mid. (dep.) part. ἀναδέχομαι (# 346) to receive, to gladly receive. Temp. or causal part. Aor. indicates logically antecedent action. The idea suggested here seems to be of welcoming and cherishing a divine charge that involves a noble responsibility (Westcott). "After having received the promises," or "because he had received the promises"; or adj. part., "who received...." ◆ 18 **ἐλαλήθη** aor. ind. pass. λαλέω (# 3281) to speak. **κληθήσεται** fut. ind. pass. καλέω (# 2813) to call. **σπέρμα** (# 5065) seed. ◆ 19 **λογισάμενος** aor. mid. (dep.) part. λογίζομαι (# 3357) to consider, to reckon. Vb. is used by Paul in the sense of calculating or reckoning on the basis of firm evidence. The word denotes inward conviction, persuasion, not simply a more or less reliable opinion (Hughes). Part. could be used to express the cause or reason and explains why Abraham had the courage to sacrifice Isaac, even though the action seemed certain to ruin the fulfillment of God's promise (Moffatt). **ἐγείρειν** pres. act. inf. ἐγείρω (# 1586) to raise. Compl. inf. to the following adj. **δυνατός** (# 1543) capable, able; "that God was able to raise." **ὅθεν** (# 3854) wherefore. **παραβολῇ** (# 4130) dat. parable, analogy; used here adverbially–"figuratively speaking" (Hughes; Michel; Westcott). **ἐκομίσατο** aor. ind. mid. κομίζω (# 3152) to obtain or get, to receive. ◆ 20 **περί** (# 4309) concerning. **μελλόντων** pres. act. part. μέλλω (# 3516) to be about to. Subst. part: "future, coming things." **εὐλόγησεν** aor. ind. act. εὐλογέω (# 2328) to bless. ◆ 21 **ἀποθνῄσκων** pres. act. part. (temp.) ἀποθνῄσκω (# 633) to die. Pres. indicates that he was in the process of dying when he spoke; "while he was dying," "on his death bed." **ἕκαστος** (# 1667) each one. **εὐλόγησεν** aor. ind. act. εὐλογέω (# 2328) to bless. **προσεκύνησεν** aor. ind. act. προσκυνέω (# 4686) to worship. **ἐπί** (# 2093) w. the acc., on, upon. **ἄκρον** (# 216) top. **ῥάβδος** (# 4811) stick, staff. ◆ 22 **τελευτῶν** pres. act. part. (temp.) τελευτάω (# 5462) to come to the end, to expire, to die. Pres. indicates that he was in the process of dying. **ἔξοδος** (# 2016) way out, departure. **ἐμνημόνευσεν** aor. ind. act. μνημονεύω s.v. 15. **ὀστέον** (# 4014) bone. **ἐνετείλατο** aor. ind. mid. (dep.) ἐντέλλομαι (# 1948) to instruct, to command. ◆ 23 **γεννηθείς** aor. pass. part. γεννάω (# 1164) to bear; pass., to be born. Temp. part., "when (after) he was born." **ἐκρύβη** aor. ind. pass. κρύπτω (# 3221) to hide. For a discussion of Moses s.

DLNT,778-82; ABD, 4:918-20.**τρίμηνος** (# 5564) three months; acc. of time, "for three months." **πατέρων** gen. pl. πατήρ (# 4252) father, parent. **διότι** (# 1484) because. **εἶδον** aor. ind. act. ὁράω (# 3972) to see. **ἀστεῖος** (# 842) beautiful, handsome, pretty, charming (GELTS, 67). It describes an attractive comeliness that is uncommonly striking (Hughes; Bruce). **ἐφοβήθησαν** aor. ind. pass.(dep.) φοβέομαι (# 5828) to be afraid, to fear. **διάταγμα** (# 1409) command, order. ◆ 24 **μέγας** (# 3489) large; here in the sense of adult, mature. **γενόμενος** aor. mid. (dep.) part. γίνομαι (# 1181) to be, to become. Aor. part. describes antecedent action. **ἠρνήσατο** aor. ind. mid. (dep.) ἀρνέομαι (# 766) to say no to, to deny, to refuse. **λέγεσθαι** pres. inf. pass. λέγω (# 3306) to say; pass., to be called. ◆ 25 **μᾶλλον** (# 3437) rather. **ἑλόμενος** aor. mid. (dep.) part. αἱρέω (# 145) to lift up; mid., to choose. **συγκακουχεῖσθαι** pres. pass. inf. συγκακέω (# 5156) to suffer evil together, to suffer w. someone. Inf. is used to explain the choosing. **πρόσκαιρος** (# 4672) for a time, temporary, fleeting. **ἔχειν** pres. act. inf. ἔχω (# 2400) to have. **ἁμαρτία** (# 281) sin. Here subjective gen., emphatic by its position. **ἀπόλαυσις** (# 656) enjoyment, pleasure; w. ἔχω ("to have pleasure"). For the meaning of the word as "enjoyment" in the papyri and inscriptions s. MM; Preisigke; BAGD; NDIEC, 2:195, 205. ◆ 26 **μείζονα** (# 3505) greater. **ἡγησάμενος** aor. mid. (dep.) part. ἡγέομαι (# 2451) to consider, to reckon. **θησαυρός** (# 2565) treasure; here gen. of comp. **ὀνειδισμός** (# 3944) reproach, reviling, disgrace, insult. **ἀπέβλεπεν** impf. ind. act. ἀποβλέπω (# 611) to look away from. Used w. the prep. εἰς (# 1650): to look to. Impf. emphasizes the continuous action in the past time. The word was used of keeping one's attention fixed upon something, as an artist fixes his attention on the object or model he is reproducing in painting or sculpture (Bruce). **μισθαποδοσία** (# 3632) recompense, reward. ◆ 27 **κατέλιπεν** aor. ind. act. καταλείπω (# 2901) to leave behind, to leave. **φοβηθείς** aor. pass. (dep.) part. φοβέομαι (# 5828) to able afraid, to fear (BBC). Aor. indicates logically antecedent action. **θυμός** (# 2596) anger, wrath (TDNT). **βασιλέως** gen. sing. βασιλεύς (# 995) king. Gen. of source, "of the king" "the wrath from the king." **ἀόρατος** (# 548) invisible, not able to be seen; here, "the invisible one"; i.e., God. **ὁρῶν** pres. act. part. (causal) ὁράω (# 3972) to see. Pres. expressing contemporaneous action to the main vb., "because he could see." **ἐκαρτέρησεν** aor. act. ind. καρτερεω (# 2846) to be strong, to hold out, to endure. ◆ 28 **πεποίηκεν** perf. ind. act. ποιέω (# 4472) to do. Here in the sense of celebrating the Passover. Perf. indicates that the celebration was the inauguration of a divine institute (Spicq; Westcott; Bruce). **πρόσχυσις** (# 4717) pouring, sprinkling, followed by the obj. gen. **ὀλοθρεύων** pres. act. part. ὀλοθρεύω (# 3905) to destroy. Subst. part., "destroyer," "the one who destroys." **πρω-**

τότοκος (# 4758) firstborn. **θίγῃ** aor. subj. act. θιγγάνω (# 2566) to touch, w. gen. Subj. w. ἵνα (# 2671) in a neg. purp. cl. ◆ **29 διέβησαν** aor. ind. act. διαβαίνω (# 1329) to go through, to pass through. **ἐρυθρός** (# 2261) red. **ξηρός** (# 3831) dry. **πεῖρα** (# 4278) attempt, try. **λαβόντες** aor. act. part. λαμβάνω (# 3284) to take. Temp. part., "when the Egyptians made an attempt." **κατεπόθησαν** aor. ind. pass. καταπίνω (# 2927) to swallow down, to engulf. The prep. in compound is intensive: "they were totally engulfed," "overwhelmed" (Hughes). ◆ **30 τεῖ-χη** nom. pl. τεῖχος (# 5446) wall; pl., of circular walls (BAGD). **ἔπεσαν** aor. ind. act. πίπτω (# 4406) to fall. Aor. viewing the event in a narrative. **κυκλωθέντα** aor. pass. part. κυκλόω (# 3240) to encircle. Temp. part., "after they were encircled." ◆ **31 πόρνη** (# 4520) prostitute, whore. **συναπώλετο** aor. ind. mid. συναπόλλυμι (# 5272) to destroy together, to be destroyed together. **ἀπειθήσα-σιν** aor. act. part. ἀπειθέω (# 578) to be disobedient. **δε-ξαμένη** aor. mid. (dep.) part. δέχομαι (# 1312) to welcome, to receive. **κατάσκοπος** (# 2946) spy. ◆ **32 λέγω** (# 3306) pres. ind. act. to say. Pres. suggests continuous activity: "Why do I still speak?" The form could be taken as pres. subj. and be deliberative (Attridge). **ἐπιλείψει** fut. ind. act. ἐπιλείπω (# 2142) to fall upon, to fail. **διηγούμενον** pres. mid. (dep.) part. διηγέομαι (# 1455) to narrate, to tell about, to carry a discussion through. The words are lit., "will leave me telling about" (RWP). This is a common rhetorical device, allowing the author to summarize (BBC). Part. could be cond., "If I were to tell about"(GGBB, 633). Pres. indicates incomplete action. ◆ **33 κατηγωνίσαντο** aor. ind. mid. (dep.) κατηγωνίζω (# 2865) to struggle against, to overcome, to subdue. Prep. in compound not only carries the idea of "against," but also that the action is unfavorable to an object (MH, 316). Aor. in a narrative pointing to the completed action. **εἰργάσαντο** aor. ind. mid. (dep.) ἐργάζομαι (# 2237) to work effectively. The vb. is used w. the noun δικαιοσύνην in the LXX to mean "to practice justice" (Ps. 15:2), and is used of doing what is right in reference to personal integrity (Hughes). **ἐπέτυχον** aor. ind. act. ἐπιτυγχάνω (# 2209) to obtain, to receive, w. gen. **ἔφραξαν** aor. ind. act. φράσσω (# 5852) to fence in, to block up, to stop (RWP). **στόμα** (# 5125) mouth. ◆ **34 ἔσβεσαν** aor. ind. act. σβέννυμι (# 4931) to quench, to put out a fire. **ἔφυγον** aor. ind. act. φεύγω (# 5771) to flee. Perfective aor. indicates the success in fleeing; i.e., "to escape." **στόματα** mouth, edge (s.v. 33). **μάχαιρα** (# 3479) sword. **ἐδυναμώθησαν** aor. ind. pass. δυναμόω (# 1540) to make strong, to be strong. Ingressive aor., "to become strong," "they became mighty." **ἀσθένεια** (# 819) weakness. **ἐγενήθησαν** aor. ind. pass. (dep.) γίνομαι (# 1181) to become. **πολέμῳ** dat. sing. πόλεμος (# 4483) war, battle. **παρεμβολάς** acc. pl. παρεμβολή (# 4213) encampment, barracks, armies in a battle line, army (RWP). **ἔκλιναν** aor. ind. act. κλίνω (# 3111) to

make to bend, to bow, to turn to flight (AS). **ἀλλότριος** (# 259) foreign. ◆ **35 ἔλαβον** aor. ind. act. λαμβάνω (# 3284) to take, to receive. **ἀνάστασις** (# 414) resurrection. **ἐτυμπανίσθησαν** aor. ind. pass. τυμπανίζω (# 5594) to torture. The root meaning of the word is "to beat," "to strike," or "to pound." A related noun means a kettle drum w. a skin stretched taut for striking. Those who were tortured might either be beaten directly or stretched over a wheel and whirled while being afflicted w. rods to break their limbs until they died (Buchanan; Westcott; Attridge; Michel; BBC; BAGD). **προσ-δεξάμενοι** aor. mid. (dep.) part. προσδέχομαι (# 4657) to accept, to receive. **ἀπολύτρωσις** (# 667) release by the payment of a price, release (s. Rom. 3:24). **κρείττονος** (# 3202) comp., better (s. 9:23). **τύχωσιν** aor. subj. act. τυγχάνω (# 5593) to receive, to obtain. ◆ **36 ἕτερος** (# 2283) other. **ἐμπαιγμός** (# 1849) mocking, heaping derision upon a person by sarcastically imitating him. **μαστίγων** gen. pl. μάστιξ (# 3465) scourging, whipping w. a scourge. **πεῖραν ἔλαβον** (# 4278; 3284) s.v. 29. The expression "received the trial" is the same idiom used in the LXX Deut. 28:56 to describe a woman so delicate that she would not risk setting her foot on the ground. These "others" were not that delicate (Buchanan). **ἔτι δέ** yea, moreover. The expression is commonly used to indicate a climax (EGT). **δεσμός** (# 1301) bonds. **φυλακή** (# 5871) prison (BAFCS, 3:9-112, 195-392; CIC). ◆ **37 ἐλιθάσθησαν** aor. ind. pass. λιθάζω (# 3342) to stone. **ἐπειράσθησαν** aor. ind. pass. πειράζω to try, to tempt. For the suspected textual variation s. Hughes; Riggenbach. This could be an inadvertent scribal dittography of the following. The more general word "tempted" seems somewhat out of place in the midst of the enumeration of the violent deaths suffered (TC). **ἐπρίσθησαν** aor. ind. pass. πρίζω (# 4569) to saw into. The tradition that the prophet Isaiah suffered death by being sawed in two w. a wooden saw is found in other writings, as well as the Talmudic books and the pseudepigraphic Jewish work, *The Martyrdom of Isaiah*, in which it is recounted that during this terrible ordeal "Isaiah neither cried aloud nor wept, but his lips spoke w. the Holy Spirit until he was sawn in two" (*The Martyrdom of Isaiah*, 5:14; Hughes; SB, 3:747). **φόνος** (# 5840) murder. Instr. prep. ἐν (# 1877); "by murder of the sword." **ἀπέθανον** aor. ind. act. ἀποθνῄσκω (# 1877) to die. **περιῆλθον** aor. ind. act. περιέρχομαι (# 4320) to go about. **μηλωτή** (# 3603) sheepskin, used of the cloak worn by prophets (BAGD). **αἴγειος** (# 128) of a goat. Adjs. w. this suf. "of, or belonging to" (MH, 336). **δέρμα** (# 1293) skin; i.e., animal hide that was processed. **ὑστε-ρούμενοι** pres. mid. (dep.) part. ὑστερέω (# 5728) to lack, to suffer need. **θλιβόμενοι** pres. pass. part. θλίβω (# 2567) to put under pressure, to cause distress, to afflict. **κακουχούμενοι** pres. pass. part. κακουχέω (# 2807) to mishandle, to treat evilly, to ill treat. ◆ **38 ὧν** gen.

masc. pl. ὅς (# 4005) who, which, rel. pron.; "of whom." ἦν impf. ind. act. εἰμί (# 1639) to be. κόσμος (# 3180) world. ἐρημία (# 2244) desert. πλανώμενοι pres. mid. (dep.) part. πλανάω (# 4414) to wander, to wander aimlessly; they wandered like lost sheep hunted by wolves (RWP). ὄρεσιν dat. pl. (# 4001) ὄρος hill, mountain. Used here as a remote or isolated place (BAGD). σπήλαιον (# 5068) cave. ὀπαῖς dat. pl. ὀπή (# 3956) opening, hole, den. They were unfit for civilized society; the truth was that civilized society was unfit for them (Bruce). For an account of the persecuted who lived in caves and dens and wandered about the mountains s. 1 Macc. 2:29-38; Jos., *Ant.*, 12:271-78. ◆ 39 μαρτυρηθέντες aor. pass. part. μαρτυρέω (# 3455) to witness; pass., to be witnessed, to be attested by witness (Hughes; Westcott). Concessive part. ("although"). ἐκομίσαντο aor. ind. mid. κομίζω (# 3152) to get back, to recover (s.v. 19). ◆ 40 προβλεψαμένου aor. mid. part. (causal) προβλέπω (# 4587) to see before, to exercise forethought, to foresee, to provide. gen. abs. χωρίς (# 6006) w. gen., without. τελειωθῶσιν aor. subj. pass. τελειόω (# 5457) to bring to the goal, to complete, to perfect (s. 5:9).

Hebrews 12

◆ 1 τοιγαροῦν (# 5521) therefore, then, consequently. A triple compound inferential particle to draw a conclusion of emphasis, making Heb. 12:1-3 the climax of the whole argument about the better promises (RWP; Lane). τοσοῦτος (# 5537) such a one, so great. ἔχοντες pres. act. part. ἔχω (# 2400) to have. Causal part., "because we have...." περικείμενον pres. mid. (dep.) part. περίκειμαι (# 4329) to lie around, to spread around, to surround. The competitors feel the crowd towering above them (Westcott). νέφος (# 3751) cloud. Aristophanes in his play, *The Frogs*, uses concept of clouds as witnesses. The picture of a cloud describing a crowded group of people is a common classical figure and expresses not only the great number of people, but also the unity of the crowd in their witness (Michel; Grässer; NW, 2, ii:1209-10). μαρτύρων gen. pl. μάρτυς (# 3459) witness, spectator (BAGD; Attridge). The witness was to confirm and attest to the truth of a matter (NTCW; DLNT, 1204-5; TDNT; Grässer; Attridge). ὄγκος (# 3839) bulk, mass, weight. An athlete would strip for action both by the removal of superfluous flesh through rigorous training and by the removal of all clothes (Hughes). ἀποθέμενοι pres. mid. (dep.) part. ἀποτίθημι (# 700) to lay aside from oneself, to lay aside one's clothing. Part. w. force of an imp. (Lane; VANT, 385-88). εὐπερίστατος (# 2342) The word could have a variety of meanings: (1) easily avoided; (2) admired, lit., well-surrounded; (3) easily surrounding, besetting; (4) dangerous, lit., having easy distress. The picture here may be that of putting off a long heavy robe that

would be a hindrance in running. For this word s. MH, 282; Michel; Westcott; MM; Hughes; Grässer; Attridge; TLNT. ὑπομονή (# 5705) patient endurance (s. 10:36). τρέχωμεν pres. subj. act. τρέχω (# 5556) to run. Cohortative subj., "let us run." Pres. calls for the continuing of the action in progress, "let us continue to run," "let us keep on running." προκείμενον pres. mid. (dep.) part. πρόκειμαι (# 4618) to lie before. ἀγών (# 74) struggle, contest, race (PAM; Grässer; Attridge; Weiss). ◆ 2 ἀφορῶντες pres. act. part. ἀφοράω (# 927) to look away from one thing and concentrate on another, to look away to. Part. of manner describing how we are to run. ἀρχηγός (# 795) pioneer, author, leader (s. 2:10; Michel; Westcott; Grässer; NDIEC, 4:217). He is the leader of those who run faith's race (Attridge). τελειωτής (# 5460) perfecter, one who brings to the goal (s. Heb. 5:9; Grässer). Christ is the Perfecter of the faith in which the readers share (Attridge). ἀντί (# 505) for the sake of, because of. Prep. can also have the idea of exchange or substitution. For a discussion of the meaning of the prep. here s. Hughes; NIDNTT, 3:1179-80. προκειμένης pres. mid. (dep.) part. πρόκειμαι (# 4618) to lie about, to be set before. ὑπέμεινεν aor. ind. act. ὑπομένω (# 5702) to patiently endure. σταυρός (# 5089) cross. The addressees are called to follow in Christ's footsteps; with this in view, Christ endured a far more severe trial–a cross–than Moses or the addressees had to face (Attridge). αἰσχύνη (# 158) shame, disgrace. καταφρονήσας aor. act. part. καταφρονέω (# 2969) to think down on something, to despise, to treat as contemptible; or in a positive sense, to brave, to be unafraid (Lane). Part. may be concessive ("although") or express manner, indicating how He endured. ἐν δεξιᾷ (# 1288) on the right. The noun "hand" is to be supplied. κεκάθικεν perf. ind. act. καθίζω (# 2767) to take one's seat, to sit down. Perf. indicates that He is still there (s. 1:3). ◆ 3 ἀναλογίσασθε aor. imp. mid. (dep.) ἀναλογίζομαι (# 382) to reckon up, to count up, to consider. The vb. can also include the idea of meditation (Michel). Aor. imp. calls for a specific act w. a note of urgency. τοιαύτη (# 5525) such a one. ὑπομεμενηκότα perf. act. part. ὑπομένω s.v. 2. Perf. part. suggests the abiding effect of Christ's redemptive suffering (Hughes). ἁμαρτωλός (# 283) sinful, sinner. εἰς (# 1650) against. ἀντιλογία (# 517) speaking against, hostility (Hughes). κάμητε aor. subj. act. κάμνω (# 2827) to grow weary. Ingressive aor. to become weary. Subj. w. ἵνα (# 2671) in a neg. purp. cl. ἐκλύω pres. pass. part. ἐκλύομαι (# 1725) to untie, to dissolve, to release; pass., to become weary or slack, to give out (BAGD). The word was used in a number of contexts: to spill water; to be physically weak–described as having limp, soft, or lifeless hands–to have a weak heart; or to be morally lax. Here, "do not slacken" when you undergo trials at God's hands. Providential training through correction is designed for your good (TLNT). Part. further describes the weariness of the main vb. ◆ **4 οὔπω** (# *4037*) not yet. **μέχρις** (# *3588*) w. gen., unto, unto the point of. **ἀντικατέστητε** aor. ind. act. ἀντικαθίστημι (# *510*) to stand in opposition against (in line of battle) (RWP). **πρός** (# *4639*) against. **ἀνταγωνιζόμενοι** pres. mid. (dep.) part. ἀνταγωνίζομαι (# *497*) to struggle against. The metaphor is still that of the athletic contest, but now shifts from the race track to the boxing ring (Hughes). ◆ **5 ἐκλέλησθε** perf. ind. mid. (dep.) ἐκλανθάνομαι (# *1720*) to cause to forget; mid., to forget, to forget completely. Prep. in compound is perfective w. the perf. indicating a complete forgetting (MH, 311; Grässer). **παράκλησις** (# *4155*) encouragement, exhortation (s. Phil. 2:1). **διαλέγεται** pres. ind. mid. (dep.) διαλέγομαι (# *1363*) to reason w., to converse w. followed by the dat. The utterance of Scripture is treated as the voice of God conversing w. men (Westcott). **ὀλιγώρει** pres. imp. act. ὀλιγωρέω (# *3902*) to think little of, to think lightly, to make light of something, to neglect (BAGD; MM; Preisigke). **παιδεία** (# *4082*) discipline, instructive discipline. In Judaism a father was required to provide for the instruction of his sons and daughters and to teach them good behavior. Whipping was accepted, along w. other disciplinary measures (JPF, 2:770f; TDNT; BBC; Grässer; SB, 3:747; DNP, 2:663-74). **ἐκλύου** pres. imp. pass. ἐκλύω (# *1725*) to release (s.v. 3). Pres. imp. w. the neg. **μηδέ** (# *3593*) could call for the stopping of an action in progress, or it could call for a general attitude of life. **ἐλεγχόμενος** pres. pass. part. ἐλέγχω (# *1794*) to reprove, to rebuke, to reproach, to state that someone has done wrong, w. the implication that there is adequate proof of such wrongdoing (NL, 1:436). Temp. part., "when you are reproved." ◆ **6 παιδεύει** pres. ind. act. παιδεύω (# *4084*) to discipline, to chasten. The word can refer to instruction, even to the actual dealing out of blows (MM). For the concept of suffering being the chastisement or discipline from God s. Michel; TDNT. **μαστιγοῖ** pres. ind. act. μαστιγέω (# *3463*) to beat w. a whip, to scourge. **παραδέχεται** pres. ind. mid. (dep.) παραδέχομαι (# *4138*) to accept, to receive. ◆ **7 ὑπομένετε** pres. ind. act. ὑπομένω (# *5702*) to patiently endure (s. 10:36) **προσφέρεται** pres. ind. mid. (dep.) προσφέρω (# *4712*) to carry oneself toward, to deal w. someone. **παιδεύει** pres. ind. act. παιδεύω (# *4084*) to discipline. Gnomic pres. showing the general expectation; or iterative, that the discipline is repeatedly given. ◆ **8 ἐστε** pres. ind. act. εἰμί (# *1639*) to be. Ind. in a 2nd. class cond. cl. giving a contrary to fact statement. **μέτοχος** (# *3581*) participant, partner. **γεγόνασιν** perf. ind. act. γίνομαι (# *1181*) to become. Perf. shows that the chastisement was personally accepted and permanent in its effect (Westcott). **ἄρα** (# *726*) therefore. **νόθος** (# *3785*) illegitimate. The word not only indicates a father insufficiently interested to inflict

on children the discipline that fits his legitimate children (Moffatt); it also is to be taken in the legal sense, that an illegitimate child does not enjoy the inheritance rights and the rights to participate in family worship (Spicq; Hughes; Lane). ◆ **9 εἴτα** (# *1663*) then, besides this (Hughes). **εἴχομεν** impf. ind. act. ἔχω (# *2400*) to have. Customary impf., "we are used to having" (RWP). **παιδευτής** (# *4083*) one who exercises discipline; one who instructs through discipline. The acc. is a double acc.: "fathers as ones who discipline." **ἐνετρεπόμεθα** impf. ind. mid. (dep.) ἐντρέπω (# *1956*) to fear, to reverence. Customary impf. **ὑποταγησόμεθα** fut. ind. pass. ὑποτάσσω (# *5718*) to subject, to be in subjection, to be in submission, to submit oneself. **ζήσομεν** fut. ind. act. ζάω (# *2409*) to live. ◆ **10 κατά** (# *2848*) w. acc., for. The prep. indicates the purp. of a few days and is a description for the whole earthly life (Michel). **δοκοῦν** pres. act. part. acc. n. sing. δοκέω (# *1506*) to seem, to seem to be good; "according to the thing seeming good to them" (RWP). **ἐπαίδευον** impf. ind. act. παιδεύω (# *4084*) to discipline. **συμφέρον** pres. act. part. συμφέρω (# *5237*) to differ, to be better. Part. is used as a substitutive, "that which is best," "for our advantage" (EGT). **μεταλαβεῖν** aor. act. inf. μεταλαμβάνω (# *3561*) to partake of, to have a share in, w. gen. Articular inf. w. the prep. **εἰς** (# *1650*) to express purp. **ἀγιότη** (# *42*) holiness. ◆ **11 πρός...τὸ παρόν** (# *4639*; *4205*) for the present. **δοκεῖ** pres. ind. act. δοκέω s.v. 10. **εἶναι** pres. act. inf. εἰμί (# *1639*) to be. Compl. inf., "it seems to be." **λύπη** (# *3383*) pain, sorrow. **ὕστερον** (# *5731*) afterwards. **καρπός** (# *2843*) fruit. **εἰρηνικός** (# *1646*) pertaining to peace, peaceful. **γεγυμνασμένοις** perf. pass. part. γυμνάζω (# *1214*) to exercise, to train (s. 5:14). Perf. part. indicates the completed state or cond. **ἀποδίδωσιν** pres. ind. act. ἀποδίδωμι (# *625*) to give back, to repay, to yield. For rabbinical parallels regarding the results of suffering s. Bruce; Braun; Weiss. **δικαιοσύνη** (# *1466*) righteousness. Here attributive gen. describing the kind of fruit. ◆ **12 παρειμένας** perf. pass. part. (adj.) παρίημι (# *4223*) to let fall at the side, to slacken, to weaken; pass. to be listless, drooping (BAGD). **παραλελυμένα** perf. pass. part. (adj.) παραλύω (# *4168*) to loosen on the side, to dissolve, to paralyze, to undo; pass., to be weak, to be lame (RWP; BAGD). **γόνατα** acc. pl. γόνυ (# *1205*) knee. The figure of the boxer, wearied and beaten, who drops his hands in weakness was commonplace in antiquity (Lane; Attridge; NW, 2, ii:1220-21). **ἀνορθώσατε** aor. imp. act. ἀνορθόω (# *492*) to set up straight, to set upright or straighten again, to revive (EGT). Aor. imp. calls for a specific action w. a note of urgency. ◆ **13 τροχία** (# *5579*) track of a wheel, track made by the feet of runners. Here it could have the meaning "running lane," developing the athletic imagery (Hughes; Attridge; Lane). **ὀρθός** (# *3981*) straight. **ποιεῖτε** pres. imp. act. ποιέω (# *4472*) to do, to make.

ποσίν (# 4546) dat. pl. πούς foot; dat. of advantage, "for your feet." χωλός (# 6000) lame. ἐκτραπῇ aor. subj. pass. ἐκτρέπω (# 1762) to turn from, to turn aside. The word could have the idea of turning aside in a race or it could be a medical image of putting a limb out of joint (Hughes; Westcott; Michel). ἰαθῇ aor. subj. pass. ἰάομαι (# 2615) to heal; pass., to be healed. Subjs. w. ἵνα (# 2671) are used here to express purp. ◆ **14 διώκετε** pres. imp. act. διώκω (# 1503) to hunt, to follow after, to pursue. ἁγιασμός (# 40) holiness, in this epistle explained as a drawing near to God w. a cleansed conscience (10:10, 22), a true acceptance of Christ's sacrifice as bringing the worshiper into fellowship w. God (EGT; EDNT). ὄψεται fut. ind. mid. (dep.) ὁράω (# 3972) to see. ◆ **15 ἐπισκοποῦντες** pres. act. part. ἐπισκοπέω (# 2174) to watch over, to watch out for. The word expresses the careful regard of those who occupy a position of responsibility as a physician or a superintendent (Westcott). ὑστερῶν pres. act. part. ὑστερέω (# 5728) to lack, to come short, to fail. ῥίζα (# 4844) root. πικρία (# 4392) bitterness. The root of bitterness in Deut. 29:18 probably referred to anything that led to idolatry and apostasy (Buchanan; BBC). Here gen. of description. ἄνω (# 539) up. φύουσα pres. act. part. φύω (# 5886) to sprout, to spring up. ἐνοχλῇ pres. subj. act. ἐνοχλέω (# 1943) to trouble, to trouble w. a crowd, to annoy, to harass (s. Acts 15:19; RWP; Hughes). Subj. in a neg. purp. cl. μιανθῶσιν aor. subj. pass. μιαίνω (# 3620) to stain, to defile. ◆ **16 πόρνος** (# 4521) immoral. βέβηλος (# 1013) profane, irreligious, impious (TLNT). Ἠσαῦ (# 2481) Esau. βρῶσις (# 1111) food. ἀπέδετο aor. ind. mid. (dep.) ἀποδίδωμι (# 625) to sell. πρωτοτόκια (# 4757) birthright, the privilege of the firstborn son (TDNT; EDNT; Attridge; Lane). ◆ **17 ἴστε** perf. ind. act. 2nd. pers. pl. οἶδα (# 3857) to know. Def. perf. w. a pres. meaning. μετέπειτα (# 3575) afterwards. θέλων pres. act. part. θέλω (# 2527) to desire to, to want to, w. inf. Concessive part. κληρονομῆσαι aor. act. inf. κληρονομέω (# 3099) to inherit. εὐλογία (# 2330) blessing. ἀπεδοκιμάσθη aor. ind. pass. ἀποδοκιμάζω (# 627) to reject after examination, to reject completely. μετάνοια (# 3567) change of mind, repentance. τόπος (# 5536) room, place, opportunity. εὗρεν aor. ind. act. εὑρίσκω (# 2351) to find. καίπερ (# 2788) although. Particle is used in a concessive cl. δάκρυον (# 1232) tear. ἐκζητήσας aor. act. part. ἐκζητέω (# 1699) to seek out, to look for. ◆ **18 προσεληλύθατε** perf. ind. act. προσέρχομαι (# 4665) to come to, to draw near (s. 4:16). ψηλαφωμένῳ pres. pass. part. ψηλαφάω (# 6027) to handle, to touch; here, to the mountain which may be touched (Hughes). κεκαυμένῳ perf. pass. part. καίω (# 2794) to burn. πῦρ (# 4786) fire. γνόφος (# 1190) darkness, blackness, thick darkness (Westcott). ζόφος (# 2432) darkness, deep gloom (AS). θύελλα (# 2590) storm, hurricane (RWP). ◆ **19 σάλπιγγος** gen. sing. σάλπιζ

(# 4894) trumpet. ἦχος (# 2491) sound. φωνή (# 5889) voice. ῥῆμα (# 4839) word. ἀκούσαντες aor. act. part. ἀκούω (# 201) to hear. παρῃτήσαντο aor. ind. mid. (dep.) παραιτέομαι (# 4148) to beg, to ask for, to request. προστεθῆναι aor. pass. inf. προστίθημι (# 4707) to place to, to add to. Inf. in indir. discourse (DUR). ◆ **20 ἔφερον** impf. ind. act. φέρω (# 5770) to carry, to bear, to endure. διαστελλόμενον pres. act. part. διαστέλλω (# 1403) to command, to order. Pres. presents the command as ringing constantly in their ears (Westcott). κἄν (# 2829) = καὶ ἄν if even. θηρίον (# 2563) animal. θίγῃ aor. subj. act. θιγγάνω (# 2566) to touch, w. gen. λιθοβοληθήσεται fut. pass. inf. λιθοβολέω (# 3344) to throw stones at, to stone. ◆ **21 φοβερός** (# 5829) terrible, fearful. ἦν impf. ind. act. εἰμί (# 1639) to be. φανταζόμενον pres. mid. (dep.) part. φαντάζομαι (# 5751) to appear. εἶπεν aor. ind. act. λέγω (# 3306) to say. ἔκφοβός (# 1769) terrified. Prep. in compound is perfective. ἔντρομος (# 1958) trembling. ◆ **22 προσεληλύθατε** perf. ind. act. προσέρχομαι (# 4665) to come to (s. Heb. 4:16). ὄρει dat. sing. ὄρος (# 4001) mountain. ζῶντος pres. act. part. ζάω (# 2409) to live. Adj. part., "living God." μυριάς (# 3689) myriad, ten thousand. It indicates a number that cannot be counted, "tens of thousands" (Hughes). πανήγυρις (# 4108) festive gathering. The word indicated the great gathering for a festival occasion. In the OT it was for the religious festivals. In the Gr. world it was a gathering for large athletic contests (Michel; Attridge). ◆ **23 πρωτότοκος** (# 4758) firstborn (TDNT). They are firstborn ones, enjoying the rights of firstborn sons because of their union w. Christ, the firstborn (Kent). ἀπογεγραμμένων perf. pass. part. ἀπογράφω (# 616) to write off, to enroll. κριτής (# 3216) judge. τετελειωμένων perf. pass. part. τελειόω (# 5457) to bring to the goal, to perfect (s. 5:9). ◆ **24 μεσίτης** (# 3542) mediator. ῥαντισμός (# 4823) sprinkling. κρεῖττον (# 3202) better (s. 9:23). λαλοῦντι pres. act. part. λαλέω (# 3281) to speak. παρά (# 4123) used in a comp. to mean "than." ◆ **25 βλέπετε** pres. imp. act. βλέπω (# 1063) to see, to beware, to take heed. παραιτήσησθε aor. subj. mid. (dep.) παραιτέομαι (# 4148) to ask, to request, to refuse (s.v. 19). Subj. in a neg. purp. cl. λαλοῦντα pres. act. part. λαλέω (# 3281) to speak. ἐξέφυγον aor. ind. act. ἐκφεύγω (# 1767) to flee from, to flee from successfully, to escape. Prep. in compound is perfective. Aor. is complexive, emphasizing the completion of the action. παραιτησάμενοι aor. mid. (dep.) part. παραιτέομαι to beg, to ask for. χρηματίζοντα pres. act. part. χρηματίζω (# 5976) to give divine instruction, to warn (s. 8:5). ἀποστρεφόμενοι pres. mid. (dep.) part. ἀποστρέφω (# 695) to turn away from, to turn from; mid., to turn away from someone, to repudiate, reject (BAGD). ◆ **26 ἐσάλευσεν** aor. ind. act. σαλεύω (# 4888) to shake. τότε (# 5538) formerly, at that time. ἐπήγγελται perf. ind. mid. (dep.) ἐπαγγέλομαι (# 2040) to promise. Perf. indi-

cates that the promise is still valid. **λέγων** pres. act. part.
λέγω (# 3306) to say. Used here to introduce direct discourse. **ἅπαξ** (# 562) once; "yet once more." **σείσω** fut.
ind. act. σείω (# 4940) to shaken, to cause to tremble (s.
Matt. 21:10). **μόνον** (# 3667) alone. ◆ **27 δηλοῖ** pres. ind.
act. δηλόω (# 1317) to make clear. **σαλευομένων** pres.
pass. part. s.v. 26. **μετάθεσις** (# 3557) removing. **πεποιη-
μένων** perf. pass. part. ποιέω (# 4472) to do, to make.
μείνῃ aor. subj. act. μένω (# 3531) to remain. Subj. w. **ἵνα**
(#2671) to express purp. or result. **σαλευόμενα** pres.
pass. part. s.v. 26. ◆ **28 ἀσάλευτος** (# 810) not able to be
shaken, unshakable. **παραλαμβάνοντες** pres. act. part.
παραλαμβάνω (# 4161) to receive. **ἔχωμεν** pres. subj. act.
ἔχω (# 2400) to have. Used in the expression χάριν ἔχω
(to be grateful). Horatory subj., "let us be grateful."
λατρεύωμεν pres. subj. act. λατρεύω (# 3302) to worship,
to serve. Hortatory subj. **εὐαρέστως** (# 2299) well-
pleasing. **εὐλάβεια** (# 2325) reverence (s. 5:7). **δέος**
(# 1290) awe. It is the apprehension of danger, as in a
forest (RWP). ◆ **29 πῦρ** (# 4786) fire. **καταναλίσκον**
pres. act. part. καταναλίσκω (# 2914) to consume completely. Prep. in compound is perfective.

Hebrews 13

◆ **1 φιλαδελφία** (# 5789) brotherly love, referring
to the affection of natural siblings; used also of the love
among believers (Attridge; Grässer; BAGD; TDNT; s.
Rom. 12:10). **μενέτω** pres. imp. act. μένω (# 3531) to remain. The use of the vb. suggests that the bond had
been in danger of being severed (Westcott). Pres. calls
for a continual and consistent action. ◆ **2 φιλοξενία**
(# 5810) entertaining of strangers, hospitality. Since
there were very few inns, the entertainment and showing of hospitality to travellers was an important part of
Jewish home life (JPFC, 2:762; RAC, 8:1061-123; TDNT;
TLNT; DLNT, 501-7; BBC; NW, 2, ii:1231-36; Grässer;
Weiss; s. Rom. 12:13). An inscription from a Christian
grave in Cappadocia tells of the Deaconess Maria, who
"in accordance w. the statement of the apostle reared
children, practiced hospitality (ἐξενοδόχησεν), washed
the feet of the saints, distributed her bread to the afflicted" (NDIEC, 2:193-95). **ἐπιλανθάνεσθε** pres. imp. mid.
(dep.) ἐπιλανθάνω (# 2140) to forget, w. gen. Pres. imp.
w. the neg. **μή** (# 3590) means, "do not go on being un-
mindful" of hospitality (Hughes). **ἔλαθον** aor. ind. act.
λανθάνω (# 3291) to escape notice, to do something
without knowing it (BAGD). **ξενίσαντες** aor. act. part.
ξενίζω (# 3826) to entertain strangers, to show hospitality. Part. is used compl. to the main vb. to give the
meaning, "some escaped notice when entertaining angels" (RWP). Those who entertained heavenly beings
include Abraham and Sarah, Lot, Gideon, Manoah,
and others (Attridge; Grässer; Weiss). ◆ **3 μιμνῄσκεσθε**
pres. imp. mid. (dep.) μιμνῄσκομαι (# 3630) to remember; here in the sense, "remember to care for them."

Pres. imp. suggests that the action should continue.
συνδεδεμένοι perf. pass. part. συνδέω (# 5279) to bind
together; pass., to be bound w. another, to be a fellow
prisoner. Perf. views the completed state or condition.
κακουχουμένων pres. pass. part. κακουχέω (# 2807) to
mishandle, to treat evilly. **ὄντες** pres. act. part. εἰμί
(# 1639) to be. Causal part., "because, since you are."
◆ **4 τίμιος** (# 5508) honorable. **γάμος** (# 1141) marriage.
κοίτη (# 3130) bed, figuratively, marriage bed, sexual
intercourse. **ἀμίαντος** (# 299) undefiled. **πόρνος** (# 4521)
immoral. The word designates those persons who indulge in sexual relationships outside the marriage
bond, both heterosexual and homosexual (Hughes).
μοῖχος (# 3659) adulterous. This word indicates those
who are unfaithful to their marriage vows; thus the
two adjs. cover all who licentiously engage in forbidden practices (Hughes). **κρινεῖ** fut. ind. act. κρίνω
(# 3212) to judge. ◆ **5 ἀφιλάργυρος** (# 921) without a
love for money (s. 1 Tim. 6:10). **τρόπος** (# 5573) manner,
manner of life, disposition. "Let your turn of mind be
free from love of money, content w. what you have"
(EGT). **ἀρκούμενοι** pres. pass. part. (circum.) ἀρκέω
(# 758) to have enough; pass., to be content. **παροῦσιν**
pres. act. part. πάρειμι (# 4205) to be present, to be at
hand. **εἴρηκεν** perf. ind. act. λέγω (# 3306) to speak. Perf.
indicates that the statement has been made and its authority continues. **ἀνῶ** aor. subj. act. ἀνίημι (# 479) to
send up, to send back, to let go, to leave without support (AS). **ἐγκαταλίπω** aor. subj. act. ἐγκαταλείπω
(# 1593) to leave someone in distress, to leave in the
lurch, to desert. Subj. in emphatic neg. cls. ◆ **6 ὥστε**
(# 6063) w. inf. to introduce a result cl. **θαρροῦντας** pres.
act. part. θαρρέω (# 2509) to be courageous, to be bold,
to be confident. Modal part. describing the manner in
which one can speak. **λέγειν** pres. act. inf. λέγω (# 3306)
to say; "so that we can confidently say." **βοηθός** (# 1071)
helper, one who brings help in the time of need. **φοβηθή-
σομαι** fut. ind. mid. (dep.) φοβέομαι (# 5828) to be
afraid. **ποιήσει** fut. ind. act. ποιέω (# 4472) to do. ◆ **7**
μνημονεύετε pres. imp. act. μνημονεύω (# 3648) to remember, to be mindful of, w. gen. Here in the sense,
"remember to honor them." **ἡγουμένων** pres. mid.
(dep.) part. ἡγέομαι (# 2451) to lead. Subst. use of part.,
"leaders." **οἵτινες** nom. pl. ὅστις (# 4015) rel. pron. generalizing or generic rel. pron. Here indicating belonging to a certain class: whoever, such a one (BAGD).
ἐλάλησαν aor. ind. act. λαλέω (# 3281) to speak; here,
perhaps, to proclaim. **ἀναθεωροῦντες** pres. act. part.
ἀναθεωρέω (# 355) to look back upon, to scan closely
(Moffatt), to look back carefully on, to contemplate
(Hughes; Attridge). Part. as imp. or manner explaining
how they are to be remembered. **ἔκβασις** (# 1676) going
out, away out, end. The phrase can mean either the end
of one's life or, more probably, the successful outcome
or result of one's way of life (BAGD). **ἀναστροφή** (# 419)

manner of life. **μιμεῖσθε** pres. imp. mid. (dep.) μιμέομαι (# 3628) to imitate. **πίστις** (# 4411) faith; here not just in the sense of their body of beliefs, but their practice in daily life. ◆ **8 ἐχθές** (# 2396) yesterday. **σήμερον** (# 4958) today. The formula "yesterday and today" is a common expression in the OT for continuity (Attridge; Exod. 5:14; 2 Sam. 15:20). **αἰών** (# 172) age. **εἰς τοὺς αἰῶνας** (# 1650; 172) into the ages; i.e., forever. Both the person of Jesus remains the same (Grässer), and the gospel message proclaimed by the deceased leaders (Lane). ◆ **9 ποικίλος** (# 4476) varying, diverse. **ξέναις** dat. pl. ξένος (# 3828) foreign, strange. **παραφέρεσθε** pres. imp. pass. παραφέρω (# 4195) to carry along, to lead away. Pass. would be permissive pass. **καλός** (# 2819) good. The words "it is" are to be supplied. **βεβαιοῦσθαι** pres. pass. inf. βεβαιόω (# 1011) to make firm, to confirm, to make stable (TLNT; TDNT; EDNT). **βρῶμα** (# 1109) food. **ὠφελήθησαν** aor. ind. pass. ὀφείλω (# 6067) to be profitable, to be useful. **περιπατοῦντες** pres. act. part. περιπατέω (# 4344) to walk about, to conduct one's life. ◆ **10 ἔχομεν** pres. ind. act. ἔχω (# 2400) to have. **θυσιαστήριον** altar, place of sacrifice. **φαγεῖν** aor. act. inf. ἐσθίω (# 2266) to eat. Epex. inf. explaining what is lawful. **ἔχουσιν** pres. ind. act. ἔχω (# 2400) to have. **ἐξουσία** (# 2026) that which is legal, lawful, authority, prerogative. **σκηνή** (# 5008) tent, tabernacle. **λατρεύοντες** pres. act. part. λατρεύω (# 3302) to serve religiously, to perform religious service (TDNT; EDNT). ◆ **11 εἰσφέρεται** pres. ind. pass. εἰσφέρω (# 1662) to bring in. **ζῷον** (# 2442) living creature, animal. **κατακαίεται** pres. ind. pass. κατακαίω (# 2876) to burn, to burn completely, to burn down, to burn up. **ἔξω** (# 2932) outside. **παρεμβολή** (# 4213) camp. ◆ **12 διό** (# 1475) therefore, wherefore. **ἁγιάσῃ** aor. subj. act. ἁγιάζω (# 39) to set apart, to sanctify (EDNT; TDNT). **ἴδιος** (# 2525) one's own. **πύλη** (# 4783) gate. He refers to the gate of the city of Jerusalem which, bounded by its walls, corresponds to the holy ground of the wilderness camp (Hughes). **ἔπαθεν** aor. ind. act. πάσχω (# 4248) to suffer. Christ's suffering outside the city gates is for the sanctification of His people. ◆ **13 τοίνυν** (# 5523) therefore. The inferential particle draws a conclusion from the preceding. **ἐξερχώμεθα** pres. subj. mid. (dep.) ἐξέρχομαι (# 2002) to go out. Hortatory subj., "let us go out." Pres. expresses vividly the immediate effort (Westcott). This could be a call for the readers to refuse to go back into Judaism (Hughes; Westcott). **ὀνειδισμός** (# 3944) reproach, insult. **φέροντες** pres. act. part. φέρω (# 5770) to bear. ◆ **14 ἔχομεν** pres. ind. act. ἔχω (# 2400) to have. **μένουσαν** pres. act. part. (adj.) μένω (# 3531) to remain. **μέλλουσαν** pres. act. part. μέλλω (# 3516) to be about to. Adj. part., "coming." **ἐπιζητοῦμεν** pres. ind. act. ἐπιζητέω (# 2118) to search for. Pres. indicates a continual action. ◆ **15 ἀναφέρωμεν** pres. subj. act. ἀναφέρω (# 429) to bring up, to offer up.

Cohortative subj., "let us offer up." **θυσία** (# 2602) sacrifice. **αἴνεσις** (# 139) praise. **διὰ παντός** (# 1328; 4246) through all, continually. A rabbinical tradition teaches that all the Mosaic sacrifices would end except the thank offering, and all prayers would cease except the prayer of thanksgiving (Hughes; Michel; SB, 1:246). **καρπός** (# 2843) fruit. **χειλέων** gen. pl. χεῖλος (# 5927) lip. **ὁμολογούντων** pres. act. part. ὁμολογέω (# 3933) to confess, to profess. The word carries the idea of proclamation (Michel) as well as praise (MM). ◆ **16 εὐποιΐα** (# 2343) good deed, doing good. **κοινωνία** (# 3126) fellowship, sharing (s. Phil. 1:5). **ἐπιλανθάνεσθε** pres. imp. mid. (dep.) ἐπιλανθάνομαι (# 2140) to forget something, w. gen. Pres. imp. w. the neg. **μή** (# 3590) is used to forbid a habitual action. **τοιαύταις** dat. pl. τοιοῦτος (# 5525) such, of this kind; "w. such sacrifices." **εὐαρεστεῖται** pres. ind. mid. (dep.) εὐαρεστέω (# 2297) to be well-pleased w. Pres. indicates what is always true. ◆ **17 πείθεσθε** pres. imp. mid. (dep.) πείθω (# 4275) to obey. **ἡγουμένοις** pres. mid. (dep.) part. ἡγέομαι (# 2451) to lead. Subst. part., "leaders." **ὑπείκετε** pres. imp. act. ὑπείκω (# 5640) to give in, to yield, to submit. **ἀγρυπνοῦσιν** pres. ind. act. ἀγρυπνέω (# 70) to be without sleep, to seek after sleep, to be watchful (RWP). **ἀποδώσοντες** fut. act. part. ἀποδίδωμι (# 625) to give an account, to render account. **ποιῶσιν** pres. subj. act. ποιέω (# 4472) to do. **στενάζοντες** pres. act. part. στενάζω (# 5100) to groan. **ἀλυσιτελής** (# 269) unprofitable, harmful. ◆ **18 προσεύχεσθε** pres. imp. mid. (dep.) προσεύχομαι (# 4667) to pray. **πειθόμεθα** pres. ind. mid. (dep.) πείθω (# 4275) to be persuaded, to have confidence, to be confident. **συνείδησις** (# 5287) conscience (s. Rom. 2:15). **ἔχομεν** pres. ind. act. ἔχω (# 2400) to have. **καλῶς** (# 2822) adv., good, clear. **θέλοντες** pres. act. part. θέλω (# 2527) to desire. **ἀναστρέφεσθαι** pres. mid. (dep.) inf. ἀναστρέφω (# 418) to conduct one's life. ◆ **19 περισσοτέρως** (# 4359) adv., more earnestly. **παρακαλῶ** pres. ind. act. παρακαλέω (# 4151) to beseech. **ποιῆσαι** aor. act. inf. ποιέω (# 4472) to do. Compl. inf., "I beseech you to do ...." **τάχιον** comp. τάχεως (# 5441) soon. Adj. is used as an adv., "sooner." **ἀποκατασταθῶ** aor. subj. pass. ἀποκαθίστημι (# 635) to restore back again. Subj. w. **ἵνα** (# 2671) to express purp. ◆ **20 ἀναγαγών** aor. act. part. ἀναγάγω (# 343) to lead up, to bring again. **ποιμένα** acc. sing. ποιμήν (# 4478) shepherd. **πρόβατον** (# 4585) sheep. **μέγας** (# 3489) great, in terms of his position and effectiveness. **αἰώνιος** (# 173) eternal. ◆ **21 καταρτίσαι** aor. opt. act. καταρτίζω (# 2936) to equip. The word includes the thoughts of the harmonious combination of different powers, the supply of that which is defective, and the amendment of that which is faulty (Westcott). Opt. used to express a wish for the future (RWP). **ποιῆσαι** aor. act. inf. ποιέω (# 4472) to do. Articular inf. is used w. the prep. **εἰς** (# 1650) to express purp. **ποιῶν** pres. act. part. ποιέω

(# *4472*) to do. **εὐάρεστος** (# *2298*) well-pleasing. **ἐνώ-πιον** (# *1967*) before, in the presence of. ◆ **22 παρακαλῶ** pres. ind. act. παρακαλέω (# *4151*) to beseech. **ἀνέχεσθε** pres. imp. mid. (dep.) ἀνέχομαι (# *462*) to hold oneself back from (RWP), to endure, to bear w. **βραχέων** gen. pl. βραχύς (# *1099*) short. Used w. the prep. **διά** (# *1328*) to mean "in few words" (Westcott). **ἐπέστειλα** aor. ind. act. ἐπιστέλλω (# *2182*) to send a letter to, to write. ◆ **23 γινώσκετε** pres. imp. act. γινώσκω (# *1182*) to know. **ἀπολελυμένον** perf. pass. part. ἀπολύω (# *668*) to release. Although the word has a variety of meanings, its most frequent sense in the NT is that of releasing from custody persons who were under arrest or in prison (Hughes). **τάχιον** (# *5441*) soon. **ἔρχηται** pres. subj. mid. (dep.) ἔρχομαι (# *2262*) to come. Subj. w. **ἐάν** (# *1569*) to express cond. **ὄψομαι** fut. ind. mid. (dep.) ὁράω (# *3972*) to see. ◆ **24 ἀσπάσασθε** aor. imp. mid. (dep.) ἀσπάζομαι (# *832*) to greet. **ἡγουμένους** pres. mid. (dep.) part. ἡγέομαι (# *2451*) to lead (s.v. 7). Subst. part., "leaders."

James

James 1

◆ **1** Ἰάκωβος (# *2610*) James. This James was the half-brother of Jesus (s. Mark 6:3-5; Mayor; Martin, xxxi-lxix; JMM; DLNT, 545-47). He grew up in a poor family w. at least 7 children, but before the resurrection of the Lord Jesus, he was not a believer (John 7:5; 1 Cor. 15:7). He was evidently small in stature (Mark 15:40) and led a very austere life (Eusebius, *Church History*, 2:23). After his conversion he became a leader in the church at Jerusalem (Gal. 2:9; Acts 15). He was called "the righteous (Just) one" and it was said of him that "his knees grew hard like a camel's because of his constant worship of God, kneeling and asking forgiveness for his people" (Eusebius, *Church History*, 2:23). While Ananus (Annas) was the high priest, just after the death of Porcius Festus, James was killed for his faith by being thrown down from the pinnacle of the temple in Jerusalem, then stoned and hit in the head with a club. As he was being stoned, he cried out, "I beseech thee, O Lord, God and Father, forgive them, for they know not what they do!" One of the priest called out, "Stop! What are you doing? The Just (ὁ δίκαιος) is praying for you" (Eusebius, *Church History*, 2:23; Jos., *Ant.*, 20:197-207). He was a man of righteousness, faith, patience, obedience, and prayer, as reflected in his life and letter. For a summary of the theology of the book s. Davids, 35-57; Martin, lxxvii-xcviii). θεοῦ καὶ κυρίου Ἰησοῦ Χριστοῦ of God and the Lord Jesus Christ. Emphatic by the position. Gen. indicating ownership of the slave. He calls his half-brother "Lord." δοῦλος (# *1528*) slave, one owned by another who stands in service to his master (DLNT, 1098-1102). Here he does not call himself "righteous" ("just") (δίκαιος), as others had, but rather "slave" (δοῦλος). Without the art. the character is stressed. δώδεκα (# *1557*) twelve. φυλαῖς dat. pl. φυλή (# *5876*) tribe. διασπορᾷ (# *1420*) scattering, dispersion, diaspora. The term indicates one living in a foreign country (Mussner; Dibelius; s. 1 Pet. 1:1). The term could refer to Jewish Christians living outside of Palestine (Mayor; Martin; Ropes; DLNT, 287-300). The article is used here since the dispersion, though not mentioned earlier, is well known (GGBB, 225). χαίρειν pres. act. inf. χαίρω (# *5897*) to greet. Independent use of inf. noun according to the letter style of the day: "greetings!" Perhaps there is a play on the words χαρεῖν and χαράν forming a transition to the body of the letter w. a new subject (Davids; Martin). ◆ **2** χάρα (# *5915*) joy. This is not the detachment of the Greek philosopher, but the eschatological joy of those expecting the intervention of God at the end of the age (Davids; TLNT; GELTS, 513; Adamson, 88-89). ἡγήσασθε aor. imp. mid. ἡγέομαι (# *2451*) to consider, to deem as, to reckon as. Obj. of vb. is placed first for emphasis (Mussner). Aor. is perhaps used because the writer is thinking of each special case of temptation (Ropes; Mayor). It could be ingressive aor., "begin to consider ..." (GGBB, 720). ἀδελφοί μου (# *81; 1609*) "my brothers"; a term of affection and inclusion. ὅταν (# *4020*) w. subj., whenever, indicating an indef. temp. cl. πειρασμός (# *4280*) trial, temptation. Sometimes the word is used regarding outward trials and inward temptations (Tasker; Mayor; TDNT; NIDNTT; TLNT). περιπέσητε aor. subj. act. περιπίπτω (# *4346*) to fall into, to encounter; usually of misfortunes, robbers, tortures, sickness; here, "become involved in various kinds of trials" (BAGD; Martin). Subj. w. ὅταν (# *4020*) in an indef. temp. cl. indicating that the trails may occur at any time. ποικίλος (# *4476*) many-colored, variegated, various, varied. ◆ **3** γινώσκοντες pres. act. part. (causal) γινώσκω (# *1182*) to know. Pres. describes contemporaneous action. The content of the knowledge is given in the following ὅτι (# *4022*) cl. δοκίμιον (# *1510*) trying, testing, proving, means of testing (Davids; Mayor). Pass. has the idea of "approved after testing," "tested and approved," "the genuine part" (BS, 259ff; IBG, 96; Ropes; Dibelius; BTNT, 418; TLNT). κατεργάζεται pres. ind. mid. (dep.) κατεργάζομαι (# *2981*) to accomplish, to bring about, to produce, to create (BAGD). Epictetus wrote, "It is difficulties (περιστάσεις) that show what men are" (Epictetus, 1:24). Gnomic pres. indicating a general truth, or iterative pres. indicating that this happens repeatedly. ὑπομονή (# *5705*) patience, faithful endurance (Martin; s. Heb. 10:36; TLNT). ◆ **4** τέλειον (# *5455*) perfection. Here James continues the OT idea of perfection as a right relationship w. God expressed in undivided obedience and unblemished life (Adamson; Martin). ἐχέτω pres. imp. act. 3rd. pers. sing. ἔχω (# *2400*) to have. Pres. imp. calls for the continuation of an action in progress. ἦτε pres. subj. act. εἰμί (# *1639*) to be. Subj. w. ἵνα (# *2671*) to express purp. ὁλόκληρος (# *3908*) complete in all its parts, entire; used of sacrificial animals without any defect, or of good health

(TLNT; CCFJ, 3:196; NDIEC, 1:132-35; 4:161-62; MM). The word indicates the entirety of all the Christian virtues (Mussner). **λειπόμενοι** pres. mid. part. λείπω (# 3309) to be left behind, to lack. Circum. part., perhaps indicating the result. ◆ **5 λείπεται** pres. ind. pass. λείπω (# 3309) s.v. 4. It picks up the part. of v. 4 to form a transition (Davids). Ind. w. εἰ (# 1623) in a 1st. class cond. cl. which presupposes a standing fact (Martin). **αἰτείτω** pres. imp. act. 3rd. pers. sing. αἰτέω (# 160) to ask, to petition. Imp. as a command, "He must ask God" (GGBB, 486). **διδόντος** pres. act. part. δίδωμι (# 1443) to give. Adj. part. "God who gives freely." Iterat. pres. suggests that He gives over and over again. **ἁπλῶς** (# 607) adv., simply, unconditionally, without bargaining. Here the word could possibly mean "generously," derived from the noun meaning "liberality," from the idea of frankness and open-heartedness (Mayor). Perhaps the best translation here is "freely" (Adamson), or perhaps "purely and simply," emphasizing that it is a pure gift (TLNT, 1:172-73); for the meaning "simplicity" used in a text concerning worshippers of men who approach him "in simplicity" s. NDIEC, 3:20-21. **πᾶσιν** dat. pl. πᾶς (# 4246) all. Dat. indir. obj., "to all"; anyone can ask, wisdom will be given to all who ask. **ὀνειδίζοντος** pres. act. part. ὀνειδίζω (# 3943) to rebuke, to reprove, to reproach, to insult. **δοθήσεται** fut. ind. pass. δίδωμι (# 1443) to give. Pass. would be the divine pass., indicating that God is the giver (BG, 236). ◆ **6 αἰτείτω** pres. imp. act. 3rd. pers. sing. αἰτέω (# 160) to ask (s.v. 5). **πίστις** (# 4411) faith. Here it does not denote constancy in the Christian religion as in v. 3. Here it means confidence in prayer–the petitioner's faith, his belief and trust that God will heed his prayer and grant it, or only in His superior wisdom deny it (Adamson; Ropes). For the grammatical structure of the cond. cl. followed by the imp. s. Mussner; Beyer, 238. **διακρινόμενος** pres. mid. (dep.) part. διακρίνω (# 1359) to divide, to be at variance w. oneself, to waver, to doubt (Ropes). **ἔοικεν** perf. ind. act. w. pres. meaning ἔοικα (# 2036) to be like, to resemble, w. dat. (BAGD; MM). **κλύδων** (# 3114) wave; i.e., "the surge of the sea," "the billowing sea" (Ropes). **θαλάσσης** gen. sing. θάλλασσα (# 2498) sea. Gen. of description. **ἀνεμιζομένῳ** pres. pass. part. (adj.) ἀνεμίζω (# 448) to drive w. the wind (Dibelius). **ῥιπιζομένῳ** pres. pass. part. (adj.) ῥιπίζω (# 4847) to fan, most often of fanning a flame (Mayor); here, to toss (Dibelius). ◆ **7 οἰέσθω** pres. imp. mid. (dep.) 3rd. pers. sing. οἴομαι (# 3887) to suppose. The word is often used in a neg. sense, indicating wrong judgment or conceit (Ropes). **λήμψεται** fut. ind. mid. (dep.) λαμβάνω (# 3284) to receive. ◆ **8 ἀνήρ** (# 467) male, man. The word is used here in the sense of a person (Dibelius). **δίψυχος** (# 1500) double-souled, double-minded; i.e., "w. soul divided between faith and the world" (Ropes; Adam-

son; Oscar S. J. Seitz, "Antecedents and Significance of the Term *Dipsychos*," *JBL* 66 [1947]: 215). **ἀκατάστατος** (# 190) not having stability, unsettled, unstable. Polybius uses it both of political disturbance and of individual character (Mayor). The word indicates vacillation in all activity and conduct (Dibelius). **ὁδός** (# 3847) ways, here manner of life, conduct. ◆ **9 καυχάσθω** pres. imp. mid. (dep.) καυχάομαι (# 3016) to boast, to boast over a privilege or possession. The word is used in the OT of any proud and exulting joy (Ropes). **ταπεινός** (# 5424) low, low degree, humble position. The word is used in the LXX to translate the Heb. word עָנִי for "poor," "without possessions" (Dibelius; GELTS, 468; TLNT). There were many poor people in Jerusalem at that time and a large section of the population lived chiefly or entirely on charity or relief. Many begged in order to survive (JTJ, 11-12, 109-19). **ὕψει** dat. sing. ὕψος (# 5737) height, exaltation. It refers to the pres. spiritual status which, by virtue of his relation to Christ, the Christian now enjoys (Adamson). ◆ **10 πλούσιος** (# 4454) rich, very rich, wealthy. There were some very rich people in Jerusalem at that time as evidenced by their elaborate homes, clothing, slaves, banquets, etc. This was especially true among some of the religious leaders, such as the Sadducees in line to high priest (JTJ, 87-99; JMM, 230-58). The family of Ananus, the high priest at the time of James' death, was very rich, but ruthless (Jos., *Ant.*, 20:207). **ταπείνωσις** (# 5428) lowliness, humiliation. **ἄνθος** (# 470) flower. **χόρτος** (# 5965) grass. **παρελεύσεται** fut. ind. mid. (dep.) παρέρχομαι (# 4216) to pass along the side of, to pass away, to disappear (Ropes). ◆ **11 ἀνέτειλεν** aor. ind. act. ἀνατέλλω (# 422) to rise up, to rise. Gnomic aor., indicating that which generally happens (Ropes). **καύσων** (# 3014) burning heat. The word may refer to the blistering east wind called **Sirocco** (Mayor; Ropes; Adamson). This wind came out of the eastern desert, scorching all plant life in its way. Frequently the Hebrew equivalent קדים occurs as a sign of divine judgment (Ezek 27:26; NIDOTTE, 3:872; GELTS, 251). **ἐξήρανεν** aor. ind. act. ξηραίνω (# 3830) to dry, to dry out, to wither. **ἐξέπεσεν** aor. ind. act. ἐκπίπτω (# 1738) to fall off. The word was used in the LXX of flowers falling from the stem (Mayor). **εὐπρέπεια** (# 2346) outward beauty. The word is used to suggest fitness between the object and its relations, sometimes gaining a stateliness or majesty (Ropes). **ἀπώλετο** aor. ind. mid. (dep.) ἀπόλλυμι (# 660) to ruin, to come to ruin, to be destroyed. **πορεία** (# 4512) way. The word could be used in the sense of business journey, but here it refers to the rich man's whole way of life (Dibelius). **μαρανθήσεται** fut. ind. pass. μαρανθέω (# 3447) to wither, to waste away. The picture of the rich withering continues the simile of the fading flower; the picturesque vb. may depict the dying of a flower or the decaying of plants like roses or ears of corn (Adamson; Ropes). The reference is to the loss of riches and earthly prosperity, not to eternal destiny (Ropes). ◆ **12 μακάριος** (# *3421*) blessed, happy (TDNT; TLNT; GELTS, 286). The idea expressed here is familiar in Judaism: "Happy is the man who can withstand the test, for there is none whom God does not prove" (Adamson; s. for example Prov. 8:32, 34; TDOT 1:445-48; also Matt. 5:3). **ὑπομένει** pres. ind. act. ὑπομένω (# *5702*) to endure, to patiently and triumphantly endure, to show constancy under (Ropes). It is not the patience that can sit down and bow its head, letting things descend upon it in passive endurance until the storm is passed. It is the spirit that can bear things, not simply w. resignation, but w. blazing hope (NTW, 60). **πειρασμός** (# *4280*) trial. **δόκιμος** (# *1511*) approved after testing (s.v. 3). **γενόμενος** aor. mid. (dep.) part. γίνομαι (# *1181*) to become. Temp. part. ("after being approved"), not cond. (Dibelius; Ropes). **λήμψεται** fut. ind. mid. (dep.) λαμβάνω (# *3284*) to receive. **στέφανον τῆς ζωῆς** (# *5109; 2437*) crown of life. The crown spoken of here, a head wreath or circlet, was the victor's prize in the Gr. games; it might also be given to someone the public wished to honor and worn in religious and secular feasts (Adamson; Ropes; TDNT). Gen. here could be descriptive (a living crown), in contrast to a perishable crown, or it could be an appositional gen. (the crown is life). For a discussion of the various possibilities s. Dibelius; Mayor. **ἐπηγγείλατο** aor. ind. mid. (dep.) ἐπαγγέλλω (# *2040*) to promise. **ἀγαπῶσιν** pres. act. part. ἀγαπάω (# *26*) to love (TDNT; TLNT; EDNT). Part. used as a noun to emphasize the verbal notion as a trait. Little did James know as he wrote these words that he too would soon be a martyr. ◆ **13 πειραζόμενος** pres. pass. part. (temp.) πειράζω (# *4279*) to try, to tempt (TDNT; TLNT). Here the word is used to mean, "temptation to sin" (Ropes). Pres. indicates a contemporaneous action, "while in the temptation." **λεγέτω** pres. imp. act. λέγω (# *3306*) to say. **ὅτι** (# *4022*) that, used as quotation marks to introduce a dir. quotation. **ἀπὸ θεοῦ** (# *608; 2536*) from God. The prep. expresses the remoter rather than the nearer cause (Mayor). **πειράζομαι** pres. ind. mid. (dep.) πειράζω (# *4279*) to tempt. Gnomic or iterative pres., indicating that which generally happens or happens over and over. **ἀπείραστος** (# *585*) not able to be tempted; invincible to assault of evils (Ropes; Peter H. Davids, "The Meaning of *Apeirastos* in James 1:13," *NTS* 24 [1978]: 386-92). **κακῶν** gen. pl. κακός (# *2805*) evil thing. Subjective gen., "not tempted by evil things"; or gen. of means, indicating the means by which God is tempted (GGBB, 125). **πειράζει** pres. ind. act. πειράζω (# *4279*) to tempt. Gnomic pres. **αὐτός** (# *899*) he, himself; used to strengthen the contrast. ◆ **14 ἕκαστος** (# *1667*) each. **πειράζεται** pres. ind. pass. πειράζω (# *4279*) to tempt. **ἴδιος** (# *2625*) one's own. **ἐπιθυμία** (# *2123*) desire,

strong desire directed toward an object, lust (TDNT; DNP, 2:542-44). **ἐξελκόμενος** pres. pass. part. ἐξέλκω (# *1999*) to draw out, to draw away, to lure. **δελεαζόμενος** pres. pass. part. δελεάζω (# *1284*) to entice or catch by the use of bait. These words were applied to the hunter or, esp., the fisherman who lures his prey from its retreat and entices it by bait into his trap, hook, or net (Ropes; Adamson). In like manner the first effect of lust is to draw the man out of his original repose, the second to allure him to a definite bait (Mayor). For the comparison of James' teaching regarding lust and desire w. the Jewish teaching regarding the "evil inclination" s. Mussner; SB, 4:466-83; PRJ, 17-35. ◆ **15 εἶτα** (# *1663*) then. The word introduces the practical result of the temptation arising from lust (Ropes). **συλλαβοῦσα** aor. act. part. (temp.) συλλαμβάνω (# *5197*) to become pregnant, to conceive. If the previous words refer to the enticement of a prostitute, then this word pictures the result of yielding to her seductive temptations (Mussner). Aor. indicates logically antecedent action. **τίκτει** pres. ind. act. τίκτω (# *5503*) to give birth, to bear. Gnomic pres. **ἀποτελεσθεῖσα** aor. pass. part. ἀποτελέω (# *699*) to come to completion, to come to maturity, to be fully grown. The word connotes completeness in parts and function accompanying full growth as opposed to a rudimentary or otherwise incomplete state (Adamson; Ropes). **ἀποκύει** pres. ind. act. ἀποκύω (# *652*) to cease being pregnant, to give birth to. The word is frequently used of animals; otherwise it is a medical rather than a literary word (Ropes). Prep. in compound denotes cessation (Mayor; MH, 298). ◆ **16 πλανᾶσθε** pres. imp. mid./pass. πλανάω (# *4414*) to lead astray, to deceive. Mid. or pass. could be permissive: "Don't allow yourselves to be deceived." **ἀγαπητός** (# *28*) beloved, a term of endearment. ◆ **17 δόσις** (# *1521*) giving. **δώρημα** (# *1564*) that which is given, gift. **τέλειος** (# *5455*) perfect, in the sense of complete. **ἄνωθεν** (# *540*) from above. **καταβαῖνον** pres. act. part. καταβαίνω (# *2849*) to come down. The part. can be adj. or periphrastic (GGBB, 648). Pres. is gnomic or pictures an action that is repeated. **πατρός** gen. sing. πατήρ (# *4252*) father. **φώτων** gen. pl. φῶς (# *5890*) light. The word generally refers to the light given heavenly bodies; and it describes God as the cosmic Father and Creator of the heavenly bodies (Mayor; Ropes; Dibelius; Martin; BBC). **ἔνι** = ἔνειμι (# *1928*) pres. ind. act. to be in, to be present (on this contracted form, which also may be considered a strengthened form of the prep. s. BAGD; BD, 49; MH, 306; RG, 313). It is not just the fact that is negated but also the possibility (Mayor). **παραλλαγή** (# *4164*) variation. It is used in Gr. for the setting of the teeth in a saw, for stones set alternately, or for a sequence of beacons or seasons; generally it denotes some regularity or system in change (Adamson). **τροπή** (# *5572*) turning. Here gen. of definition, "a variation consisting in turning." ἀποσκίασμα (# 684) shadow. The word can mean the shadow cast by an object, as in an eclipse, or the act of overshadowing; or it can mean a reflected image (Adamson; Dibelius; Mayor; Ropes). God's benevolence is like a light that cannot be extinguished, eclipsed, or "shadowed out" in any way at all. Nothing can block God's light, interrupt the flow of His goodness, or put us "in shadow" so that we are out of the reach of His radiance (Adamson). ◆ **18 βουληθείς** aor. pass. part. βούλομαι (# 1089) to counsel, to decide after counsel, to will. Here it refers to the free sovereign, creative will or decision, decree of God (Mussner; TDNT). Temp. part. ("after deciding"), or causal ("because he decided"). Aor. indicates a logically antecedent action. **ἀπεκύησεν** aor. ind. act. ἀποκυέω = ἀποκύω (# 652) to give birth, to bear (s.v. 15). Although the contract vb. generally refers to birth through a woman, it is used here in reference to God giving birth (Mussner; Adamson). **εἶναι** pres. act. inf. εἰμί (# 1639) to be. Articular inf. w. εἰς (# 1650) used to express purp. or result. **ἀπαρχή** (# 569) firstfruit. Collective noun referring to the group (Martin). Pred. acc. in with the inf., "that we should be firstfruits." **τινα** acc. sing. τις (# 5516) as it were, so to say, a kind of (BD, 158). **κτίσμα** (# 3233) creation. Here partitive gen., "which is a part of His creatures" (GGBB, 85-86). ◆ **19 ἴστε** pres. imp. act. 2nd. pers. pl. οἶδα (# 3857) to know. Def. perf. w. pres. meaning. **ἔστω** pres. imp. act. εἰμί (# 1639) to be. **ταχύς** (# 5444) quick, swift, fast. **ἀκοῦσαι** aor. act. inf. ἀκούω (# 201) to hear. Articular inf. w. the prep. εἰς (# 1650) can express purp. or result, or it can mean, "w. reference to hearing" (Ropes). **βραδύς** (# 1096) slow. **λαλῆσαι** aor. act. inf. λαλέω (# 3281) to speak. Articular inf. w. the prep. εἰς (# 1650) in the sense of "w. reference to" (Ropes). **ὀργή** (# 3973) anger, wrath. It refers to deep-seated anger (TDNT). ◆ **20 θεοῦ** gen. sing. θεός (# 2536) God. Here the gen., "God's righteousness," refers not to the righteousness that is part of His character, but to the way of life, in deed and thought, that He requires in us (Adamson; Lenski). **ἐργάζεται** pres. ind. mid. (dep.) ἐργάζομαι (# 2237) to work, to do, to practice (Ropes). Pres. indicates what is continually true. ◆ **21 διό** (# 1475) therefore. **ἀποθέμενοι** aor. mid. (dep.) part. ἀποτίθημι (# 700) to put off, to strip off. It is a metaphor for the putting off of clothes (Mayor). **ῥυπαρία** (# 4864) dirtiness, filthiness. The word was used of dirty clothes and moral defilement (Mayor; Ropes). **περισσεία** (# 4353) overabundance, excess. **κακία** (# 2798) evil, wickedness. Here gen. of apposition. The phrase calls attention to the fact that wickedness is in reality an excrescence on character, not a normal part of it (Ropes). **πραΰτης** (# 4559) meekness, mildness, gentleness. It is the humble and gentle attitude expressing itself in a patient submissiveness to offense, free from malice and desire for revenge. The word stands in con-

trast to the term ὀργή (Mussner; Gal. 5:23; 2 Cor. 10:1; Matt. 5:5). **δέξασθε** aor. imp. mid. (dep.) δέχομαι (# 1312) to receive, to accept. **ἔμφυτος** (# 1875) implanted. It is the word for an implanting not at birth, but later in life. It is used metaphorically for what is sent into a man to be, or for what he grows to be, a part of his nature (Adamson, 98-100). **δυνάμενον** pres. pass. (dep.) part. δύναμαι (# 1538) to be able to, w. inf. **σῶσαι** aor. act. inf. σώζω (# 5392) to rescue, to save. ◆ **22 γίνεσθε** pres. imp. mid. (dep.) γίνομαι (# 1181) to become. Pres. indicating continual action calls for a habit of life; thus, "become and continue to be ...." **ποιηταί** nom. pl. ποιητής (# 4475) one who performs an action, one who does something, doer. The expression would be the same as the Semitic phrase "to do the law," meaning to observe the law or to fulfill the law. For examples s. Dibelius. **ἀκροατής** (# 212) one who hears. In the Jewish home, the education process, and in the synagogue worship, the hearing of the Law read aloud played an important part in Jewish life (JPFC, 2:800f; 945-77; Dibelius). The rabbis also stressed very strongly the necessity of keeping the Law (M, Aboth 1,17; 5:14; for other examples s. Mussner; SB, 3:84-88, 753). **παραλογιζόμενοι** pres. mid. (dep.) part. παραλογίζομαι (# 4165) to reason beside the point, to misjudge, to miscalculate, to deceive oneself, to cheat in reckoning, to deceive through fallacious reasoning (MM; MH, 319; GELTS, 354). ◆ **23 ἔοικεν** perf. act. ind. ἔοικα (# 2036) to be like (s.v. 6). **κατανοοῦντι** pres. act. part. κατανοέω (# 2917) to put the mind down upon, to consider attentively, to take note of, to look at (RWP; Ropes). **πρόσωπον** (# 4725) face. **γένεσις** (# 1161) birth, origin, natural, mortal. The word indicates the face one received at birth and the gen. here is either gen. of attribute or perhaps of source (Mussner; Adamson; Ropes). **ἔσοπτρον** (# 2269) mirror. Mirrors were generally highly polished metal, frequently w. an ivory or bone handle as well as with a decorated covering (s. 1 Cor. 13:12; Mayor; BBC; LAW, 2859). For the "mirror of remembrance" s. DLNT, 815-16. ◆ **24 κατενόησεν** aor. ind. act. κατανοέω (# 2917) to consider attentively (s.v. 23). **ἀπελήλυθεν** perf. ind. act. ἀπέρχομαι (# 599) to go away. The force of the perf. here is to express an immediate, a swift result (Adamson; Ropes). **εὐθέως** (# 2311) adv., immediately. **ἐπελάθετο** aor. ind. mid. (dep.) ἐπιλανθάνομαι (# 2140) to forget. **ὁποῖος** (# 3961) what sort of, what kind of. **ἦν** impf. ind. act. εἰμί (# 1639) to be. ◆ **25 παρακύψας** aor. act. part. παρακύπτω (# 4160) to stoop down and look into in order to see something exactly and recognize (Mussner). Here it means "bending over the mirror in order to examine it more minutely," "hearing into it" (Mayor). **τέλειον** (# 5455) perfect. **ἐλευθερία** (# 1800) freedom (Adams, 33f). Here gen. of attribute (Mussner). **παραμείνας** pres. act. part. παραμένω (# 4169) to stay beside, to remain, to continue (s. Phil.

1:25). ἐπιλησμονή (# 2144) forgetfulness. γενόμενος aor. mid. (dep.) part. γίνομαι (# 1181) to become, to be. ποιητής (# 4475) doer. ἔργον (# 2240) work. Gen. here is a certain emphasis, "a doer who does" (Ropes). ποίησις (# 4472) doing. ἔσται fut. ind. mid. (dep.) εἰμί (# 1639) to be. ◆ 26 δοκεῖ pres. ind. act. δοκέω (# 1506) to seem. θρησκός (# 2580) religious, pious. The word denotes the scrupulous observance of religious exercise–in action or words–sincerely or hypocritically performed in the guise of devout religion. The word describes one who stands in awe of the gods and is tremendously scrupulous in regard to them (Adamson; Mayor; Ropes; TDNT). εἶναι pres. act. inf. εἰμί (# 1639) to be. χαλιναγωγῶν pres. act. part. χαλιναγωγέω (# 5902) to lead w. a bridle, to bridle. The picture is that of a man putting the bridle in his own mouth, not in that of another (RWP). ἀπατῶν pres. act. part. ἀπατάω (# 572) to deceive. μάταιος (# 3469) vain, empty, nonproductive, useless, dead (Mussner; TDNT). θρησκεία (# 2579) piety, religious worship. The word expresses the worship of God, religion, especially expressed in religious service or cult (BAGD; MM; s. also the adj. in this v.). ◆ 27 ἀμίαντος (# 299) without defilement, undefiled, free from contamination (AS). ἐπισκέπτεσθαι pres. mid. (dep.) inf. ἐπισκέπτομαι (# 2170) to look upon, to visit, to provide help for. The word often was used for the visiting of the sick (Mayor; Ropes). ὀρφανός (# 4003) orphan. χήρα (# 5939) widow. For the needs of the orphans and widows particularly in Judaism s. Mussner; Mayor; JPFC, 2:78ff; DLNT, 1220-21. θλῖψις (# 2568) stress, pressure, affliction. ἄσπιλος (# 834) without a spot, unstained. τηρεῖν pres. act. inf. τηρέω (# 5498) to observe, to keep, to guard. Epex. inf. explaining the nature of true piety or worship. κόσμος (# 3180) world system (TDNT; NIDNTT).

James 2

◆ 1 προσωπολημψία (# 4721) the receiving of one's face, partiality (s. Rom. 2:11; Davids; Mayor). ἔχετε pres. imp. act. ἔχω (# 2400) to have, to possess. Pres. imp. w. the neg. μή (# 3590) could call for the stopping of a habit or an action in progress. δόξης gen. sing. δόξα (# 1518) glory. Gen. has been variously interpreted as having an obj., a subjective, or a qualitative force and has been connected to the various substitutives in the sentence. For various interpretations s. Mayor; Adamson; Dibelius; Ropes; Davids; Martin. ◆ 2 εἰσέλθῃ aor. subj. act. εἰσέρχομαι (# 1656) to come into. Subj. w. ἐάν (# 1569) in a 3rd. class cond. cl. indicating the possibility or probability of the cond. συναγωγή (# 5252) gathering, assembly meeting (Davids; Martin). χρυσοδακτύλιος (# 5993) w. a golden ring on the finger. It was common to wear rings in the ancient world either as a signet ring or as a piece of jewelry for adornment. Sometimes more than one ring was worn, and the so-

cial status of a person could be noted by the quality of his ring (DGRA, 95-97; M, Kelim 11:8, 12:1; Pliny, NH, 33:24-25; NW 2, ii:1276-81). ἐσθής (# 2264) garment, clothes. λαμπρός (# 3287) shining. Some robes were said to have been made from silver that would glisten in the sunlight (s. Acts 12:21). The word here could refer to elegant and luxurious clothes or of fresh and clean clothes without any reference to costliness (Ropes). εἰσέλθῃ aor. subj. act. εἰσέρχομαι (# 1656) to come. Subj. w. ἐάν (# 1569) in a 3rd. class cond. cl. expressing probability. πτωχός (# 4777) poor, abject poverty, poor as a beggar (NTW, 109-11; BAGD; TDNT; s. 1:9). ῥυπαρός (# 4865) filthy, dirty. The normal toga of the Romans was white, as was the robe of the Jews, and political candidates wore even brighter white produced by rubbing the garment with chalk. The white toga had to be cleaned and when this was neglected the Romans called it sordida, and those who wore such garments sordidati s. DGRA, 1137; Mayor; Mussner. ◆ 3 ἐπιβλέψητε aor. subj. act. ἐπιβλέπω (# 2098) to look upon, to direct one's attention to, to look w. attention or interest or respect or favor (Adamson). φοροῦντα pres. act. part. (adj.) φορέω (# 5841) to carry, to wear, to wear clothes. ἐσθῆτα pl. (# 2264) garment, clothes (s.v. 2). εἴπητε aor. subj. act. λέγω (# 3306) to say, to speak to. Subjs. in this section are used in a third-class cond. cl. assuming the possibility of the cond. κάθου pres. imp. mid. (dep.) κάθημαι (# 2764) to sit. Imp. as an invitation or polite request to take an honored seat. It has been supposed that in the type of synagogue referred to here the cultic center was located close to the entrance, so the distinguished person is immediately provided a seat "here," while the poor man must either take his seat near the sanctuary or else be satisfied w. a place to stand over "there" in that part of the building further from the entrance and the cultic center (Dibelius). καλῶς (# 2822) adv., well, rightly. Here, "please," or "in a good place" (Adamson). πτωχῷ dat. sing. (# 4777) beggar (s.v. 2). Dat. indir. obj. Art. indicates it is the poor man previously mentioned. εἴπητε aor. subj. act. λέγω (# 3306) to say, to speak to. Subjs. w. ἐάν (# 1569) in this section are used in a 3rd. class cond. cl. assuming the possibility of the cond. στῆθι aor. imp. act. ἵστημι (# 2705) to stand; ingressive aor., "to take one's stand" (RWP). ὑπό (# 5679) w. the acc., under, down against, down beside (RWP). ὑποπόδιον (# 5711) footstool. This could have been something like what was found in a synagogue of the 2nd. or 3rd. century–a stone bench running along the walls, w. a lower tier for the feet of those sitting on the bench (Adamson). ◆ 4 διεκρίθητε aor. ind. pass. διακρίνω (# 1359) to judge between two, to face both ways, to be divided against oneself, to waiver, to distinguish. The vb. has numerous meanings; here the best seems to be "to make a distinction," "to make differences." The neg. οὐ (# 4024), "not," used in the question expects the answer "yes" and the words could be translated, "You have made differences, haven't you?" ἐν ἑαυτοῖς (# 1877; 1571) "in (among) yourselves"; can mean either distinctions between church members or the subjective opinion one makes within himself (Mussner; Adamson; Dibelius; MM). ἐγένεσθε aor. ind. mid. (dep.) γίνομαι (# 1181) to become. κριταί nom. pl. κριτής (# 3216) judge. διαλογισμός (# 1369) reasoning. The word includes purpose as well as deliberation, and the gen. here is gen. of quality, "judges w. evil thoughts" (Ropes). ◆ 5 ἀκούσατε aor. imp. act. ἀκούω (# 201) to hear. ἐξελέξατο aor. ind. mid. (dep.) ἐκλέγομαι (# 1721) to pick out, to choose out; mid. to choose for oneself. πτωχός (# 4777) poor, poor as a beggar. τῷ κόσμῳ (# 3180) world. Dat. could be locative indicating the place ("in the world"), dat. of respect ("those poor in respect to worldly goods") [Dibelius; GGBB, 145-46]), or it could be an ethical dat. ("poor in the opinion of the world," i.e., in the world's judgment [Mayor; BD, 103; MT, 239; Martin]). πλούσιος (# 4454) rich, wealthy. ἐν πίστει (# 1877; 4411) in faith. The phrase could mean "abounding in faith" (Mayor) or "in virtue of faith" or better "in the realm of faith" (Ropes; Adamson). κληρονόμος (# 3101) heir. βασιλείας (# 993) kingdom. Gen. here gives content of the inheritance. ἐπηγγείλατο aor. ind. mid. (dep.) ἐπαγγέλομαι (# 2040) to promise. ἀγαπῶσιν pres. act. part. ἀγαπάω (# 26) to love. Adj. part. as subst. Dat. of personal interest. ◆ 6 ἠτιμάσατε aor. ind. act. ἀτιμάζω (# 869) to treat without honor, to dishonor. τὸν πτωχόν (# 4777) the poor. The art. could point to a specific person or used w. the adj. to stress the quality, not simply generic (GGBB, 233; RG, 408; Ropes; Martin). καταδυναστεύουσιν pres. ind. act. καταδυναστεύω (# 2872) to exercise power against someone, to oppress. For a description of the wealthy class as well as the middle class and poor class in Jerusalem (to which the teachers of the law or the scribes often belonged) at this time s. JTJ, 87-119. ἕλκουσιν pres. ind. act. ἕλκω (# 1816) to drag. κριτήριον (# 3215) place where cases are judged, tribunal, law court, court of justice. ◆ 7 αὐτοί nom. pl. αὐτός (# 899) self; "they themselves"; perhaps for emphasis. βλασφημοῦσιν pres. ind. act. βλασφημέω (# 1059) to slander, to blaspheme. ἐπικληθέν aor. pass. part. ἐπικαλέω (# 2126) to call upon; pass., to be called upon, to be named. ◆ 8 μέντοι (# 3530) indeed. The particle has both an adversative meaning (but, nevertheless, however) and an affirmative meaning (verily, really) (Ropes; Adamson). τελεῖτε pres. ind. act. τελέω (# 5464) to fulfill, to keep. βασιλικός (# 997) pertaining to a king, royal, sovereign, excellent, supreme, an imperial edict. For various interpretations of this word s. Adamson; Mayor; Ropes; Dibelius; Davids. ἀγαπήσεις fut. ind. act. ἀγαπάω (# 26) to love (TDNT; TLNT; EDNT). Fut. under Semitic influence is used as a categorical imp.

(BG, 94). πλησίον (# 4446) neighbor. καλῶς (# 2822) adv. well, acceptable, morally good, pleasing to God, unobjectionable (BAGD). ποιεῖτε pres. ind. act. ποιέω (# 4472) to do. Pres. indicates a practice in progress. ◆ 9 προσωπολημπτεῖτε pres. ind. act. προσωπολημπτέω (# 4719) to show partiality (s.v. 1 for the noun). Ind. is used in a 1st. class cond. assuming the reality of the cond. It is possible to sin in other ways than by showing partiality (GGBB, 686). ἐργάζεσθε pres. ind. mid. (dep.) ἐργάζομαι (# 2237) to work, to do. ἐλεγχόμενοι pres. pass. part. ἐλέγχω (# 1794) to convict, to convince w. overwhelming evidence. παραβάτης (# 4127) transgressor, one who steps across a boundary (TDNT). ◆ 10 ὅστις (# 4015) w. subj., whoever. For this use w. subj. s. RG, 956f; BD, 192. τηρήσῃ aor. subj. act. τηρέω (# 5498) to guard, to keep. πταίσῃ aor. subj. act. πταίω (# 4760) to stumble, to trip. Stumbling means to make a mistake, to go astray, to sin (BAGD). ἐν ἑνί (# 1877; 1651) in one point. The word is n. since νόμον is not used of single precepts (Ropes). γέγονεν perf. ind. act. γίνομαι (# 1181) to become. Perf. indicates the continuing results of the action ("he has become guilty of all points"), ever remaining so (Lenski). ἔνοχος (# 1944) in the power of, guilty, liable to the penalty (BAGD; Martin). Here the following gen. indicates the authority or law against which one has transgressed (Dibelius; Mayor). Stricter rabbis taught that the Torah, even in its separate statutes, is immutable and indivisible (Adamson; SB, 3:755). ◆ 11 εἰπών aor. act. part. λέγω (# 3306) to speak. Part. as a subst. μοιχεύσῃς aor. subj. act. μοιχεύω (# 3658) to commit adultery. φονεύσῃς aor. subj. act. φονεύω (# 5839) to murder. For εἰ ... οὐ (# 1623; 4024) s. M, 171. The sense of the expression may be concessive ("although") (SNT, 179f). γέγονας perf. ind. act. γίνομαι (# 1181) to become. ◆ 12 λαλεῖτε pres. imp. act. λαλέω (# 3281) to speak. ποιεῖτε pres. imp. act. ποιέω (# 4472) to do. ἐλευθερίας (# 1800) freedom, liberty. Here gen. of description. The prep. διά (# 1328) here indicates the state or condition in which one does or suffers something; i.e., "under the law of liberty" (Ropes). μέλλοντες pres. act. part. μέλλω (# 3516) to be about to, w. inf. describing a certain fut. action (Martin). κρίνεσθαι pres. pass. inf. κρίνω (# 3212) to judge. Part. w. the inf. means "those who are going to be judged by the law of liberty," signifying not just a fut. event but a deliberate choice of the law of liberty (and mercy) in preference to the old ruthless rigor of the Law (Adamson). ◆ 13 κρίσις (# 3213) judgment. ἀνέλεος (# 447) without mercy, merciless (on the form s. Mayor; MM). ποιήσαντι aor. act. part. ποιέω (# 4472) to do; here, to show mercy. ἔλεος (# 1799) mercy, pity (TLNT; TDNT; EDNT). κατακαυχᾶται pres. ind. mid. (dep.) κατακαυχάομαι (# 2878) to boast against someone, to triumph over (Mayor; Dibelius; Mussner). For rabbinical parallels and Jewish emphasis on mercy and pity s. Adamson; SB, 1:203. ◆ **14** ὄφελος (# *4055*) profit, use, advantage. The expression was commonly used to introduce a rhetorical dialogue (Davids; Martin). **λέγῃ** pres. subj. act. λέγω (# *3306*) to say. It is used in presenting this one's claim to be approved of men and of God (Ropes). Subj. w. **ἐάν** (# *1569*) in a 3rd. class cond. cl. indicating the possibility of the cond. Pres. stresses the continual claim, "if a person keeps on saying he or she has faith but keeps on having no works" (Martin). **ἔχειν** pres. act. inf. ἔχω (# *2400*) to have. Inf. in indir. discourse. **ἔργα** acc. pl. ἔργον (# *2240*) work. The word seems here to be a recognized term for good works (Ropes; Mayor; Adamson, 34-38). For discussions on faith and works in this section s. Martin, 82-84; Davids; HSB, 696-99; DPL, 457-61; JMM, 195-227. **ἔχῃ** pres. subj. act. ἔχω (# *2400*) to have, to possess. **δύναται** pres. ind. mid. (dep.) δύναμαι (# *1538*) to be able to. **ἡ πίστις** (# *4411*) the faith. The art. could be the art. of previous reference meaning, "the previously mentioned faith" (IBG, 111). **σῶσαι** aor. act. inf. σῴζω (# *5392*) to rescue, to save. Compl. inf. to the main vb., "is not able to save." Aor. signifies ... "achieve salvation for him" (Adamson). ◆ **15** ἀδελφή (# *80*) sister. **γυμνός** (# *1218*) naked. The term does not necessarily imply absolute nakedness; it was used of a person wearing only an undertunic and meant someone poorly clad (Mayor). **ὑπάρχωσιν** pres. subj. act. ὑπάρχω (# *5639*) to exist, to be. **λειπόμενοι** pres. pass. part. λείπω (# *3309*) to lack; pass., to be lacking (followed by the gen.). **ἐφήμερος** (# *2390*) for the day. The phrase implies food for the day or the day's supply of food (MM; for examples s. Dibelius). ◆ **16** εἴπῃ aor. subj. act. λέγω (# *3306*) to say. **ὑπάγετε** pres. imp. act. ὑπάγω (# *5632*) to go away, to depart. **ἐν εἰρήνῃ** (# *1877; 1645*) "in peace." The expression "go in peace" is a Jewish expression for good-by and as an address to beggars; the Hebrew expression may still be heard today in the streets of Jerusalem w. the same effect. It signals the end of the encounter (Ropes; Adamson). **θερμαίνεσθε** pres. imp. mid./pass. θερμαίνω (# *2548*) to warm oneself, to be warm. The word was commonly used of the effect of warm clothes (Ropes). **χορτάζεσθε** pres. imp. pass. χορτάζω (# *5963*) to feed until one is full; pass., to be filled. The word has the general meaning of satisfying hunger (Mayor; MM). **δῶτε** aor. subj. act. δίδωμι (# *1443*) to give. Subj. in a 3rd. class cond. cl. dependent on the **ἐάν** (# *1569*) in v. 15 (Martin). **ἐπιτήδεια** acc. pl. ἐπιτήδειος (# *2201*) necessity; pl., the necessities of the body, the necessaries of life (RWP). **σῶμα** (# *5393*) body. Here, obj. gen. ("for the body") or gen. of description ("bodily needs"). **ὄφελος** (# *4055*) benefit, good; here, "what good does it do?" (BAGD; s.v. 14). The expected answer to this rhetorical question is negative–there is no benefit in simple words. ◆ **17** οὕτως (# *4048*) likewise. This is used in making the application (Ropes). **καθ᾽ ἑαυτήν** (# *2848*;

1571) in itself, in reference to itself, inwardly (Dibelius; Mayor; Adamson). ◆ **18** ἐρεῖ fut. ind. act. λέγω (# *3306*) to say. A common way to introduce the opinion of an imaginary opponent (BBC). **ἔχεις** pres. ind. act. ἔχω (# *2400*) to have. Pres. indicates the present possession. **δεῖξον** aor. imp. act. δείκνυμι (# *1259*) to show. For a discussion concerning the ones referred to here by the personal prons. **Σὺ, κἀγώ** "you and I"; s. Ropes; Adamson; Martin. **δείξω** fut. ind. act. δείκνυμι. (# *1259*). Aor. imp w.fut. used as a type of Semitic cond. cl. (Beyer, 238-55). ◆ **19** πιστεύεις pres. ind. act. πιστεύω (# *4409*) to believe. Pres. indicates the condition or state of belief. **ὅτι** (# *4022*) that, giving the content of the belief and used w. the vb. here to suggest this is not a call to personal trust in God, but simply a belief that God exists (Martin). **ποιεῖς** pres. ind. act. ποιέω (# *4472*) to do. **καλῶς ποιεῖς** idiomatic expression meaning, "you do well"; "that is good." **δαιμόνιον** (# *1228*) demon, evil spirit. **πιστεύουσιν** pres. ind. act. πιστεύω (# *4409*) to believe. **φρίσσουσιν** pres. ind. act. φρίσσω (# *5857*) to bristle. It was used of the physical signs of terror, esp. of the hair standing on end. The word often expresses only a high degree of awe or terror (Mayor; GELTS, 507-8). The demons go even further than the one who makes the claim concerning his faith. Gnomic pres. indicates what is always true. ◆ **20** θέλεις pres. ind. act. θέλω (# *2527*) to desire. **γνῶναι** aor. act. inf. γινώσκω (# *1162*) to know. Compl. inf. to the main vb. **ἄνθρωπε** voc. sing. ἄνθρωπος (# *476*) man. The term is used here in a derogatory sense. **κενέ** voc. sing. κενός (# *3031*) empty, deficient. The word is used of a man who cannot be depended upon, whose deeds do not correspond to his words; hence, of boasters and impostors (Mayor). **ἀργή** fem. nom. ἀργός (# *734*) inactive, barren, unprofitable, unproductive of salvation (Ropes). ◆ **21** ἐδικαιώθη aor. ind. pass. δικαιόω (# *1467*) to declare righteous, to pronounce to be in the right, to justify (TDNT; Rom. 2:13; Bengel; Lenski). **ἀνενέγκας** aor. act. part. ἀναφέρω (# *429*) to offer up, to sacrifice. **θυσιαστήριον** (# *2603*) place of sacrifice, altar. ◆ **22** συνήργει impf. ind. act. συνεργέω (# *5300*) to cooperate, to work together. **ἐτελειώθη** aor. ind. pass. τελειόω (# *5457*) to bring to completion, to bring to maturity, to perfect, to consummate. As the tree is perfected by its fruits, so faith is by its works (Mayor). Works do not animate faith; but faith produces works, and works perfect faith. Faith itself is perfected; i.e., shown to be true, by works (Bengel). ◆ **23** ἐπληρώθη aor. ind. pass. πληρόω (# *4444*) to make full, to fulfill. **λέγουσα** pres. act. part. λέγω (# *3306*) to say. **ἐπίστευσεν** aor. ind. act. πιστεύω (# *4409*) to believe. **ἐλογίσθη** aor. ind. pass. λογίζομαι (# *3357*) to place to one's account, to reckon. Aor. points to a specific act. **ἐκλήθη** aor. ind. pass. καλέω (# *2813*) to call. ◆ **24** ἐξ ἔργων (# *1666; 2240*) from works. Though neither ignored nor belittled, faith is regarded as complementing works, w. which it must be combined. The contrast is between faith minus works, and works minus faith–not between faith and works (Adamson). δικαιοῦται pres. ind. pass. δικαιόω (# 1467) to justify. ◆ **25 ὁμοίως** (# 3931) adv., in like manner. **πόρνη** (# 4520) whore, prostitute. For the view that Rahab (Josh. 2:1-21) provided lodging for strangers or travelers s. D.J. Wiseman, "Rahab of Jericho," *TB* 14 (1964): 8-11; for the Jewish views on Rahab s. Adamson; Davids; SB, 1:20-23. ἐδικαιώθη aor. ind. pass. δικαιόω (# 1467) to justify. ὑποδεξαμένη pres. mid. (dep.) part. ὑποδέχομαι (# 5685) to receive, to welcome, to entertain as a guest. ἐκβαλοῦσα pres. act. part. ἐκβάλλω (# 1675) to send out, to lead out without the connotation of force (BAGD). The part. could be causal or circum. ◆ **26 γάρ** (# 1142) for. The particle is used to introduce the supporting argument. The relationship between vs. 25 and 26 is this: Rahab was justified by works; she could not have been justified in any other way, for without works faith is dead. Therefore, the faith of Rahab is presupposed (Dibelius). πνεῦμα (# 4460) spirit, breath. The word refers to the vital principle by which the body is animated (Ropes). A dead faith is like a corpse and therefore cannot save (Mussner).

James 3

◆ **1 διδάσκαλος** (# 1437) teacher. The word is used perhaps in the sense of rabbi, indicating one who had studied the law and its application to life and was engaged in teaching others (TDNT; Adamson; Herschel Shanks, "Is the Title 'Rabbi' Anachronistic in the Gospels?" *JQR* 53 [1963]: 337-45). γίνεσθε pres. imp. mid. (dep.) γίνομαι (# 1181) to become. εἰδότες perf. act. part. οἶδα (# 3857) def. perf. w. pres. meaning, to know. Causal part., "because you know ...." μεῖζον comp. μέγας (# 3489) great; comp., greater. κρίμα (# 3210) judgment, results of a judicial decision, condemnation, sentence of punishment (Dibelius). The teacher's condemnation is greater than that of others because having, or professing to have, clear and full knowledge of duty, he is the more bound to obey it (Ropes). λημψόμεθα fut. ind. mid. (dep.) λαμβάνω (# 3284) to take. James uses the 1st. pers. pl. because he himself is a teacher in the church and knows that he must some day give account to the divine Judge for his teaching (Mussner). ◆ **2 πολλά** acc. pl. πολύς (# 4498) great, much; "many." This may be acc. of general reference, "in reference to many things" (RWP). πταίομεν pres. ind. act. πταίω (# 4760) to stumble, to offend (s. 2:10). Pres. could be iterat., indicating an action that occurs over and again. οὗτος (# 4047) this one. τέλειος (# 5455) perfect, mature. δυνατός (# 1543) able to. χαλιναγωγῆσαι aor. act. inf. χαλιναγωγέω (# 5902) to bridle (s. 1:26). Compl. inf. to the preceding verbal adj. ◆ **3** ἵππος (# 2691) horse. The gen. here is dependent on the

word **χαλινούς** but is put first because it contains the new emphatic idea (Ropes). χαλινός (# 5903) bridle, bit. The word is used of the bridle proper (or reins), the bit, and, as perhaps here, of the whole bridle, including both (Ropes). For a description of bridles and bits in the ancient world s. DGRA, 548. The word used here was also used of a particular type of rope connected to sails of a ship (DGRA, 790). πείθεσθαι pres. mid. (dep.) inf. πείθω (# 4275) to obey. Articular inf. w. prep. εἰς (# 1650) to express purp. μετάγομεν pres. ind. act. μετάγω (# 3555) to change the direction, to guide (RWP). Pres. used to express what is always true. ◆ **4 ἰδού** pres. imp. act. ὁράω (# 3972) to see. It calls attention to the following. πλοῖον (# 4450) ship. τηλικαῦτα nom. pl. τηλικοῦτος (# 5496) so great. ὄντα pres. act. part. εἰμί (# 1637) to be. ὑπό (# 5679) w. gen., by. The frequent use of the prep. in connection w. the word ἀνέμων and similar words suggest that here it retains something of its local force, not simply "by," but "under" (Mayor). ἄνεμος (# 449) wind. σκληρός (# 5017) harsh, stiff, strong (Ropes). ἐλαυνόμενα pres. pass. part. ἐλαύνω (# 1785) to drive. The word is used of wind or of sailors rowing or sailing a boat (AS). μετάγεται pres. ind. pass. μετάγω (# 3555) to steer. ἐλάχιστος (# 1788) The superl. of μικρός (small) is used in an elative sense, "very small" (BAGD; BD, 33). πηδάλιον (# 4382) rudder. The rudder of an ancient ship was like an oar w. a very broad blade; ships generally had two rudders placed on each side of the stern, not at the ship's extremity. Both rudders were managed by the same steersman to prevent confusion (DGRA, 788-89; Pliny, NH, 7:57; SSAW, 224-28). ὁρμή (# 3995) impetus, impulse. The word was used of the origin of motion either moral or physical. The word could mean here either the pressure or touch of the steersman or it could refer to his impulse (Mayor; TDNT; MM). εὐθύνοντος pres. act. part. εὐθύνω (# 2316) to direct, to guide, to steer. βούλεται pres. ind. mid. (dep.) βούλομαι (# 1089) to decide, to will. For examples of the use of the two figures of the control of a horse and a ship s. Dibelius; Ropes; Martin; NW, 2, ii:1302-3. ◆ **5 οὕτως** (# 4048) so, thus. The word introduces the application of the examples. γλῶσσα (# 1185) tongue. μικρός (# 3625) small. μέλος (# 3517) member. μεγάλα nom. pl. μέγας (# 3489) great, great thing. Sometimes the adj. is written in connection w. the following vb. αὐχεῖ pres. ind. act. αὐχέω (# 902) to boast. The phrase is used here in the sense not of an empty boast, but of a justified, though haughty, sense of importance (Ropes; Dibelius; Mussner). ἰδού pres. imp. act. ὁράω (# 2627) to see. ἡλίκος (# 2462) what size. In this context the n. means "how small" and the fem. "how much," "how large" (Ropes; Mayor). πῦρ (# 4786) fire. ὕλη (# 5627) woods, forest. It has been suggested that the word means thicket or brush (L.E. Elliott-Binns, "The Meaning of ὕλη in James III.5," *NTS*

2 [1956]: 48-50; Dibelius). For examples paralleling James' illustration of fire s. Dibelius; Ropes. ἀνάπτει pres. act. ind. ἀνάπτω (# 409) to set on fire, to ignite. ◆ **6 γλῶσσα** (# 1185) tongue. **κόσμος** (# 3180) world, here followed by the gen. τῆς ἀδικίας (# 94) (world) of injustice. For the various interpretations of this phrase s. Mayor; Ropes; Dibelius; Davids. **καθίσταται** pres. ind. mid. or pass. καθίστημι (# 2770) to place, to set. Pass. means "is constituted" and the mid. means "presents itself" (RWP; Mayor). **σπιλοῦσα** pres. act. part. σπιλόω (# 5071) to stain, to defile. **φλογίζουσα** pres. act. part. φλογίζω (# 5824) to set in flames, to inflame, to set on fire. **τροχός** (# 5580) wheel, cycle, circle (GELTS, 482). **γένεσις** (# 1161) origin, birth. The phrase has been variously interpreted; e.g., "the cycle of the coming," signifying little more than life (Dibelius), the whole circle of life (Mussner). Others see the phrase as eschatological, signifying the course (of time) ordained by God for the present era, now in its last days, so the phrase means "sets afire all that revolving time brings to birth" (Adamson). For examples s. Ropes; Mayor; Martin; Dibelius; SB, 1:820. **φλογιζομένη** pres. pass. part. φλογίζω (# 5824). **γεέννης** gen. sing. γέεννα (# 1147) (Heb.) the valley of Henna, Gehenna, hell. The valley of Henna just outside Jerusalem was the city garbage dump used as a picture of hell, the place of punishment for the wicked (TDNT; s. Mk. 9:43; Luke 12:5). ◆ **7 φύσις** (# 5882) nature. **θηρίον** (# 2563) wild animal. **πετεινόν** (# 4374) bird. **ἑρπετόν** (# 2260) crawling animal, reptile. **ἐνάλιος** (# 1879) sea creature (Adamson). **δαμάζεται** pres. ind. pass. δαμάζω (# 1238) to tame, gnomic pres. Pres. points to the continual possibility of taming wild animals. **δεδάμασται** perf. pass. ind. δαμάζω (# 1238). Perf. points to the completed action and the two tenses could be translated, "is from time to time, and has actually been, tamed" (Ropes). **φύσις** (# 5882) nature. Dat. here is used in the sense of "in subjection to," and the term itself here denotes "humankind" (Ropes). Both pagan and Heb. was proud of man's lordship over the animal world (Adamson). **ἀνθρώπινος** (# 474) human. ◆ **8 δαμάσαι** aor. act. inf. δαμάζω (# 1238) to tame. Compl. inf. to the main vb. **δύναται** pres. ind. pass. (dep.) δύναμαι (# 1538) to be able to, w. inf. **ἀκατάστατος** (# 190) restless, not quiet, like the least tameable beasts (Mayor). **μεστή** fem. nom. μεστός (# 3550) w. gen., full. **ἰοῦ** gen. sing. ἰός (# 2675) poison. **θανατηφόρος** (# 2504) death bearing. ◆ **9 εὐλογοῦμεν** pres. act. inf. εὐλογέω (# 2328) to bless. Pres. is customary, indicating what one usually does (s. Eph. 1:3). **καταρώμεθα** pres. ind. mid. (dep.) καταράω (# 2933) to curse. **ὁμοίωσις** (# 3932) likeness. **θεοῦ** gen. θεός (# 2536) God. Attributed gen., "(likeness) of God." **γεγονότας** perf. act. part. γίνομαι (# 1181) to become, to be. Perf. looks at the completed action or state of man being in the image of God. ◆ **10 ἐξέρχεται** pres. ind.

mid. (dep.) ἐξέρχομαι (# 2002) to go out. **κατάρα** (# 2932) curse. **χρή** (# 5973) pres. ind. act. impersonal vb., it is necessary, it ought to be, there is a need. Followed by inf.; occurs only here in the NT (BAGD; BD, 181; MM). The necessity expressed by this word signifies a need resulting from time or circumstances or from the fitness of things (AS; T; Mayor). Here it denotes the incongruity of blessing and cursing coming out of the same mouth (RWP). **γίνεσθαι** pres. mid. (dep.) inf. γίνομαι (# 1181) to become. ◆ **11 μήτι** (# 3614) Particle used in a question which expects the answer "no" (Mussner). **πηγή** (# 4380) spring, fountain, well. The word is used w. the definite article; it is suggested that among country folk the spring or well has a prominent individuality (Adamson). **ὀπή** (# 3956) opening. The word is used elsewhere of a cleft in a rock (Mayor; s. Heb. 11:38). **βρύει** pres. ind. act. βρύω (# 1108) to gush forth. The word, meaning "to teem," "full of bursting," is ordinarily used of the swelling buds of plants and so figuratively of various kinds of fullness. Here the thought is of the gushing forth of water (Ropes; Mayor). **γλυκύς** (# 1184) sweet. **πικρός** (# 4395) bitter. Here the word may suggest a case where a salty source above the outlet has contaminated the good water (Adamson). ◆ **12 δύναται** pres. ind. pass. (dep.) δύναμαι (# 1538) to be able to. **συκῆ** (# 5190) fig, fig tree. **ἐλαία** (# 1777) olive. **ποιῆσαι** aor. act. inf. ποιέω (# 4472) to produce. **ἄμπελος** (# 306) vine, grapevine. These three fruits–fig, olive, and grape–found all over the Near East, are particularly associated w. Palestine (Adamson; Martin). **ἁλυκός** (# 266) salty. ◆ **13 σοφός** (# 5055) wise. A t.t. for the teacher; in Jewish usage one who has a knowledge of practical moral wisdom resting on a knowledge of God (Ropes). By contrast, the Gr. philosophical term meant theoretical wisdom (GPT, 179). **ἐπιστήμων** (# 2184) understanding. The word implies expert or professional knowledge (Tasker). The use of the interrogative is a Semitic construction taking the place of a condition (Mayor; Mussner; Beyer, 167). **δειξάτω** aor. imp. act. δείκνυμι (# 1259) to show, to demonstrate. **ἀναστροφή** (# 419) manner of life, conduct. **πραΰτης** (# 4559) meekness, gentleness. The opposite of arrogance, it indicates the submissiveness to offense that is free from malice and desire for revenge (Matt. 5:5; 2 Cor. 10:1; Gal. 5:23). ◆ **14 ζῆλος** (# 2419) zeal, envy, jealousy, resentment, a particularly strong feeling of resentment and jealousy against someone (LN, 1:760). The idea is of a fierce desire to promote one's own opinion to the exclusion of others (Ropes). **πικρός** (# 4395) bitter, embittered, harsh. **ἔχετε** pres. ind. act. ἔχω (# 2400) to have; to have bitter jealousy in one's heart (BAGD). **ἐριθεία** (# 2249) selfish ambition. The word suggests the vice of a leader who creates a party for his own pride: it is partly ambition, partly rivalry (Dibelius; NTW, 39f; TDNT; Phil.

2:3). **κατακαυχᾶσθε** pres. imp. mid. (dep.) κατακαυχάομαι (# *2878*) to boast against, to boast arrogantly. The word is used sometimes w. the gen. to denote the triumph of one principle over another. Prep. in compound is either intensive or indicates an unfavorable action (Mayor; MH, 316). Pres. imp. w. the neg. **μή** (# *3590*) indicates either the stopping of an action in progress or prohibits the habitual action. **ψεύδεσθε** pres. imp. mid. (dep.) ψεύδομαι (# *6017*) to lie. ◆ **15 σοφία** (# *5053*) wisdom. **ἄνωθεν** (# *540*) from above. **κατερχομένη** pres. mid. (dep.) part. (adj.) κατέρχομαι (# *2982*) to come down. **ἐπίγειος** (# *2103*) earthly, on the earth (Adamson). **ψυχικός** (# *6035*) natural; i.e., pertaining to the natural life of men and animals alike; unspiritual (Ropes; Adamson). **δαιμονιώδης** (# *1229*) demonic (Adamson). ◆ **16 ἀκαταστασία** (# *189*) disorder, disturbance, trouble, instability. The word sometime had political associations in the meaning "anarchy." Here it would refer to the disorder caused by those who w. their false wisdom trouble the group of believers by demanding their own rights and exercising a party spirit (Ropes; Adamson; Mussner). **φαῦλος** (# *5765*) bad, foul, vile. **πρᾶγμα** (# *4547*) matter, thing. ◆ **17 ἁγνή** fem. nom. ἁγνός (# *54*) pure. The word implies sincere, moral and spiritual integrity (Adamson). **εἰρηνικός** (# *1646*) peaceable, loving, and promoting peace. **ἐπιεικής** (# *2117*) gentle, reasonable in judging. The word signifies a humble patience, a steadfastness able to submit to injustice, disgrace, and maltreatment without hatred and malice, trusting in God in spite of all of it (s. 2 Cor. 10:1; NTW, 38f). **εὐπειθής** (# *2340*) easily persuaded, willing to yield, compliant. The opposite of the word is "disobedient." The word is used of submission to military discipline and for observance of legal and moral standards in ordinary life; i.e., one who willingly submits to a fatherly will (MM; Adamson; Mayor). **μεστή** nom. fem. μεστός (# *3550*) full. Full in the sense that it is characterized by what follows. **ἐλέους** (# *1799*) merciful. **ἀδιάκριτος** (# *88*) undivided, unwavering, wholehearted w. reference to the evil situation described in vs. 9 and 10 (Ropes). **ἀνυπόκριτος** (# *537*) without hypocrisy, not hypocritical. ◆ **18 δικαιοσύνη** (# *1466*) righteousness. The gen. here could be gen. of definition or apposition, indicating that the fruit is righteousness (Mayor). Some view it as a subjective gen. or gen. of source, indicating that fruit is the product of righteousness and the source of the fruit (Ropes). **σπείρεται** pres. ind. pass. σπείρω (# *5062*) to sow (Dibelius). **ποιοῦσιν** pres. act. part. ποιέω (# *4472*) to do. The dat. is either dat. of agency ("sown by those who do peace" [Mussner]) or it is dat. of advantage ("for peaceable people" [Dibelius; Mayor; Martin]).

James 4

◆ **1 πόθεν** (# *4470*) where, from where. **πόλεμος** (# *4483*) war. **μάχαι** nom. pl. μάχη (# *3480*) battle, fight. The first word pictures the chronic state or campaign of war while the second presents the separate conflicts or battles of the war (RWP). **ἐντεῦθεν** (# *1949*) from here. It is used to indicates the reason or source (BAGD). **ἡδονῶν** gen. pl. ἡδονή (# *2454*) lust, pleasure. Although the word has a strong philosophical flavor (GPT, 75-78; TDNT), it is to be taken here in a practical and bad sense (Adamson; Mussner). **στρατευομένων** pres. mid. (dep.) part. στρατεύομαι (# *5129*) to carry on a campaign, to fight a military battle. **μέλεσιν** dat. pl. μέλος (# *3517*) member. Here the pl. is used collectively as the abode of the passions (Adamson). ◆ **2 ἐπιθυμεῖτε** pres. ind. act. ἐπιθυμέω (# *2121*) to desire, to long for. **ἔχετε** pres. ind. act. ἔχω (# *2400*) to have; here, to possess. **φονεύετε** pres. ind. act. φονεύω (# *5839*) to murder. **ζηλοῦτε** pres. ind. act. ζηλόω (# *2420*) to be zealous, to hotly desire, to possess, to covet (Ropes; s. James 3:14). **δύνασθε** pres. ind. pass. (dep.) δύναμαι (# *1538*) to be able to, w. inf. **ἐπιτυχεῖν** aor. act. inf. ἐπιτυγχάνω (# *2209*) to obtain (Mayor). Compl. inf. to the main vb. **μάχεσθε** pres. ind. mid. (dep.) μάχομαι (# *3481*) to fight a battle. **πολεμεῖτε** pres. ind. act. πολεμέω (# *4482*) to wage war. **ἔχετε** pres. ind. act. ἔχω (# *2400*) to have; here, to possess. **αἰτεῖσθαι** pres. mid. inf. αἰτέω (# *160*) to ask, to ask for one's self. For a discussion of the significance of the mid. voice s. Mayor; M, 160. Articular inf. is used w. the prep. **διά** (# *1328*) w. acc. to express cause. ◆ **3 αἰτεῖτε** pres. ind. act. αἰτέω (# *160*) to ask; mid. = "to ask for one's self." **λαμβάνετε** pres. ind. act. λαμβάνω (# *3284*) to receive. **κακῶς** (# *2809*) adv., evilly, wrongly. **αἰτεῖσθε** pres. ind. mid. αἰτέω (# *160*) to ask. **δαπανήσητε** aor. subj. act. δαπανέω (# *1251*) to spend, to spend freely. The obj. of this vb. is the means of securing enjoyment for which they pray; throughout the passage money is esp. in mind (Ropes). Subj. w. **ἵνα** (# *2671*) to express the purp. of the asking and at the same time indicating the reason or cause for asking (Mussner). ◆ **4 μοιχαλίδες** voc. pl. μοιχαλίς (# *3655*) adulteress, one who is unfaithful to the marriage vows. The term was a figure of speech, particularly in the OT (esp. in Hosea; THAT, 1:518-20; TDOT, 4:99-104) to indicate unfaithfulness to God and the practice of idolatry, here the false god is the world (Adamson). **οἴδατε** perf. ind. act. οἶδα (# *3857*) to know. Def. perf. w. a pres. meaning. **ὅτι** (# *4022*) introducing the content of the knowledge. **φιλία** (# *5802*) friendship. The word involves the idea of loving as well as of being loved (Mayor). **κόσμος** (# *3180*) world. Here obj. gen., friendship to or with the world. **ἔχθρα** (# *2397*) enmity, active hostility. **τοῦ θεοῦ** (# *2536*) obj. gen., "(hostility) against God." **βουληθῇ** aor. subj. pass. (dep.) βούλομαι (# *1089*) to will, to want, to desire to, w. inf. The word has the connotation of preference or choosing one thing before another (Mussner; TDNT). **εἶναι** pres. act. inf. εἰμί (# *1639*) to be. **καθίσταται** pres. ind. pass. καθίστημι (# *2770*) to be constituted, to be rendered (RWP; s. 3:6). ◆ **5 δοκεῖτε** pres. ind. act. δοκέω (# *1506*) to suppose, to think. **κενῶς** (# *3036*) adv., emptily; i.e., "without meaning all that it says" (Ropes). **γραφή** (# *1210*) writing, Scripture. For a discussion of the source of the quotation s. Mayor; Ropes; Adamson; Davids; Martin. **φθόνος** (# *5784*) envy, malice, or envy arising out of ill will, jealousy (Mayor; Adamson; Trench, *Synonyms*, 34). **ἐπιποθεῖ** pres. ind. act. ἐπιποθέω (# *2160*) to strongly desire. **κατῴκισεν** aor. ind. act. κατοικίζω (# *3001*) to cause to dwell, to take up one's dwelling. For a discussion of the difficulties of this v. s. Adamson; S.S. Laws, "The Scripture Speaks in Vain; A Reconsideration of James IV.5," *NTS* 20 (1973-74): 220ff; Martin; Davids. ◆ **6 μείζονα** acc. comp. μέγας (# *3505*) great; comp., greater. **δίδωσιν** pres. ind. act. δίδωμι (# *1443*) to give. Iterat. pres., "to give over and again," or gnomic indicating what is always true. **ὑπερήφανος** (# *5662*) haughty, one who thinks above and beyond that which is proper, arrogant. The word sometimes signifies the arrogant rich (Adamson; 1QH, 6:36; CD, 1:15). **ἀντιτάσσεται** pres. ind. mid. (dep.) ἀντιτάσσω (# *530*) to stand against, to oppose. Pres. indicates what is always true. **ταπεινός** (# *5424*) low, humble. ◆ **7 ὑποτάγητε** aor. imp. pass. ὑποτάσσω (# *5718*) to submit, to align oneself under the authority of another. **ἀντίστητε** aor. imp. act. ἀνθίστημι (# *468*) to oppose. Ingressive aor., "take one's stand against." Aor. imp. calls for urgent action (RWP). **διάβολος** (# *1333*) slanderer, devil. **φεύξεται** fut. ind. mid. (dep.) φεύγομαι (# *5771*) to flee. The use of the imp. followed by the fut. forms a Semitic cond. cl.: "When you take your stand against the devil, then he will flee from you" (Beyer, 253; Mussner). ◆ **8 ἐγγίσατε** aor. imp. act. ἐγγίζω (# *1581*) to come near, to draw near. **ἐγγιεῖ** fut. ind. act. ἐγγίζω. For the construction of an imp. followed by the fut., building a type of cond. cl. s.v. 7. **καθαρίσατε** aor. imp. act. καθαρίζω (# *2751*) to cleanse, to purify. **ἁμαρτωλός** (# *283*) sinful, sinner. **ἁγνίσατε** aor. imp. act. ἁγνίζω (# *49*) to purify, to make pure. **δίψυχος** (# *1500*) doubleminded (s. 1:8). ◆ **9 ταλαιπωρήσατε** aor. imp. act. ταλαιπωρέω (# *5415*) to undergo hardship, to endure misery. Here it is used intransitively–be miserable, feel miserable–and refers to the inner attitude of repentance (Mayor; Dibelius; Mussner; Adamson). **πενθήσατε** aor. imp. act. πενθέω (# *4291*) to mourn. The word expresses a self-contained grief, never violent in its manifestation (Ropes). The word is often connected w. κλαίω and describes the mourning that cannot be hidden. It describes not only a grief bringing ache to the heart, but also a grief bringing tears to the eyes (MNTW, 137; Mussner). **κλαύσατε** aor. imp. act. κλαίω (# *3081*) to cry, to weep. **γέλως** (# *1152*)

laughter. The word indicates the leisurely laughter of gods and men in their pleasures. It is the laughter of a fool who believes in his own autonomy and who rejects God as the one determining reality (Mussner; TDNT). **πένθος** (# *4292*) sorrow, mourning. **μετατραπήτω** aor. pass. imp. 3rd. pers. sing. μετατρέπω (# *3573*) to turn about, to turn into. Prep. in compound has the idea of change (MH, 318). **κατήφεια** (# *2993*) dejection, downcast, dismay. It describes the condition of one w. eyes cast down like the publican in Luke 18:13 (Mayor; Adamson). ◆ **10 ταπεινώθητε** aor. imp. pass. ταπεινόω (# *5427*) to make low, to humble. The form is pass. but the meaning is reflex., "to humble oneself" (Adamson). **ὑψώσει** fut. ind. act. ὑψόω (# *5738*) to make high, to exalt, to make high, to lift up. Imp. followed by the fut. is a Semitic cond. construction (Beyer, 252f). ◆ **11 καταλαλεῖτε** pres. imp. act. καταλαλέω (# *2895*) to talk against, to defame, to speak evil of. It usually is applied to harsh words about the person who is absent (Ropes). **καταλαλῶν** pres. act. part. καταλαλέω. Part. as subst. **κρίνων** pres. act. part. κρίνω (# *3212*) to judge. **καταλαλεῖ** pres. ind. act. καταλαλέω (# *2895*). **κρίνει** pres. ind. act. κρίνω (# *3212*) to judge. **εἰ** pres. ind. act. εἰμί (# *1639*) to be. **ποιητής** (# *4475*) one who performs an act, doer. The construction ποιητής νόμου means "lawgiver" (Ropes). ◆ **12 εἷς** (# *1651*) one, used emphatically. **νομοθέτης** (# *3794*) lawgiver, one who makes a law. **δυνάμενος** pres. pass. (dep.) part. δύναμαι (# *1538*) to be able to, w. inf. **σῶσαι** aor. act. inf. σῴζω (# *5392*) to rescue, to save. **ἀπολέσαι** aor. act. inf. ἀπόλλυμι (# *660*) to destroy, to ruin. **εἰ** pres. ind. act. εἰμί (# *1639*) to be. **κρίνων** pres. act. part. κρίνω (# *3212*) judge. **πλησίον** (# *4446*) the next one, neighbor. ◆ **13 ἄγε** pres. imp. act. ἄγω (# *72*) to lead. Imp. here is an interjection w. the meaning "come now!" "see here!" and a somewhat brusque address (Mayor; Ropes). **λέγοντες** pres. act. part. λέγω (# *3306*) to say. **σήμερον** (# *4958*) today. **ἤ** (# *2445*) or. The word indicates the choice in planning. **αὔριον** (# *892*) tomorrow. **πορευσόμεθα** fut. ind. mid. (dep.) πορεύομαι (# *4513*) to travel, to go on a journey. There were three kinds of merchants: the old Hellenistic mariners, sea and caravan traders, and those who combined domestic w. foreign trade (Adamson). **εἰς τήνδε τὴν πόλιν** into this city. The old demonstrative form **τήνδε** (# *3840*) this has the force of the particular as opposed to the general–"we will go to this city"–pointing it out on the map (Mayor). **ποιήσομεν** fut. ind. act. ποιέω (# *4472*) to do, to spend time. **ἐνιαυτός** (# *1929*) year. **ἐμπορευσόμεθα** fut. ind. mid. (dep.) ἐμπορεύομαι (# *1864*) to conduct business, to carry on business as a merchant. **κερδήσομεν** fut. ind. act. κερδέω (# *3045*) to make a profit, to profit, to gain. ◆ **14 ἐπίστασθε** pres. ind. mid. (dep.) ἐπίστημι (# *2179*) to know, to understand. **ποῖος** (# *4481*) of what character; is it secure or precarious? (Ropes). **ἀτμίς**

(# 874) vapor, steam, smoke. The word was used of steam from a kettle or of smoke the wind carried away; it graphically depicts the transience of life (Adamson; Mussner; Mayor). **ἐστε** pres. ind. act. εἰμί (# 1639) to be. **φαινομένη** pres. mid./pass. part. φαίνω (# 5743) to show. Mid. to show oneself; pass. to be shown, to reveal. Here it is used in the sense, to appear. **ἀφανιζομένη** pres. pass. part. ἀφανίζω (# 906) to render invisible or unrecognizable. ◆ **15 λέγειν** pres. act. inf. λέγω (# 3306) to say. **ἀντὶ τοῦ λέγειν ὑμᾶς** instead of your saying. The thought of v. 13 is resumed (Adamson; Dibelius). **θελήσῃ** aor. subj. act. θέλω (# 2527) to will. **ζήσομεν** fut. ind. act. ζάω (# 2409) to live. **ποιήσομεν** fut. ind. act. ποιέω (# 4472) to do. ◆ **16 νῦν δέ** (# 3814; 1254) but now, but actually, in point of fact; in contrast to what they ought to do (Ropes). **καυχᾶσθε** pres. ind. mid. (dep.) καυχάομαι (# 3016) to boast, to glory. **ἀλαζονεία** (# 224) bragging, pretentious, arrogant, arrogant words. The word refers to empty boasting that seeks to impress. It is extravagant claims which one cannot fulfill (BAGD; MNTW, 38-42; TDNT). **καύχησις** (# 3018) boasting. ◆ **17 εἰδότι** perf. act. part. οἶδα (# 3857) to know. Def. perf. w. pres. meaning. **ποιεῖν** pres. act. inf. ποιέω (# 4472) to do. Inf. explains the knowledge, "He knows to do." **ποιοῦντι** pres. act. part. ποιέω (# 4472) to do; here in the sense of practice. The dat. is dat. of disadvantage and indicates that such a one is guilty of sin (Mayor). Pres. indicates a habit of life.

James 5

◆ **1 ἄγε** pres. imp. act. ἄγω (# 72) to lead; here, come now! (s. 4:13). **πλούσιοι** voc. pl. πλούσιος (# 4454) rich (s. 1:10). Adj. as subst. **κλαύσατε** aor. imp. act. κλαίω (# 3081) to cry, to weep. Aor. imp. calls for a specific act w. a note of urgency. **ὀλολύζοντες** pres. act. part. ὀλολύζω (# 3909) to howl, to cry aloud. The word is used in the LXX as the expression of violent grief (Mayor; Joel 1:5, 13; Isa. 13:6; 14:31; 15:3; 16:7; Jer. 4:8; Mussner; TDNT; NIDOTTE, 1:976-77; 4:866-84; BTNT, 434-35). Part. of manner describing the crying. **ταλαιπωρία** (# 5416) misery. **ἐπερχομέναις** pres. mid. (dep.) part. (adj.) ἐπέρχομαι (# 2088) to come upon. Fut. pres. showing the certainty of a fut. event, or progressive pres. picturing the action in progress. ◆ **2 σέσηπεν** perf. ind. act. σήπω (# 4960) to be rotten. Perf. indicates the state or condition: "is rotten" (Ropes). **ἱμάτιον** (# 2668) garment. The wealth of the rich was often evident in their type of clothes (s. James 1:10). **σητόβρωτος** (# 4963) moth-eaten. The word occurs in a papyrus that refers to moth-eaten files (NDIEC, 1:77). **γέγονεν** perf. ind. act. γίνομαι (# 1181) to become. The perfs. are of prophetic anticipation rather than historical record (Adamson; Martin). ◆ **3 χρυσός** (# 5996) gold. **ἄργυρος** (# 738) silver. **κατίωται** perf. ind. pass. κατιόω (# 2995) to rust, to rust out, to rust through, of gold and silver tarnished,

corroded (BAGD; s. Strabo 16, 2, 42; Epictetus 4, 6, 14; NW, 2, ii:1336-39). Prep. in compound is perfective, "to rust through down to the bottom" (RWP). **ἰός** (# 2675) poison, rust (Mayor). **ἔσται** fut. ind. mid. (dep.) εἰμί (# 1639) to be. **φάγεται** fut. ind. mid. (dep.) ἐσθίω (# 2266) to eat. **πῦρ** (# 4786) fire. **ἐθησαυρίσατε** aor. act. ind. θησαυρίζω (# 2564) to treasure up, to store up. For rabbinical and DSS parallels of fire being God's judgment s. Mussner; SB, 4:866f. **ἐσχάταις ἡμέραις** (# 2274; 2465) last days. There may be irony here, for the treasure in mind is not their riches, but the misery that awaits them (Martin; Davids) ◆ **4 ἰδού** pres. imp. act. ὁράω (# 2627) to see. **μισθός** (# 3635) wage, pay. **ἐργατῶν** gen. pl. ἐργάτης (# 2239) one who works, worker. **ἀμησάντων** aor. act. part. (adj.) ἀμάω (# 286) to reap, to mow. Aor. points to the specific act which they do. **χώρα** (# 6001) field. **ἀπεστερημένος** perf. pass. part. ἀποστερέω (# 691) steal, to hold back. The vb. indicates not just delay, but complete default (Adamson; RWP). Perf. looks at the completed state or condition. **ἀφ' ὑμῶν** (# 608; 5148) from you, by you. **κράζει** pres. ind. act. κράζω (# 3189) to cry out. Pres. indicates the continual crying out. Both the OT (Lev. 19:13; Deut. 24:14) and rabbinic teaching required that the workers be paid at the end of the day (SB, 1:832; Matt. 20:87). The withholding of wages is one of the four sins that are said to cry to heaven (Mayor; Adamson). **βοαί** nom. pl. βοή (# 1068) cry. **θερισάντων** aor. act. part. θερίζω (# 2545) to reap, to harvest. **ὦτα** acc. pl. οὖς (# 4044) ear. **σαβαώθ** (# 4877)(Heb.) armies, hosts (TWOT; TDOT; NIDOTTE, 4:1297-98). **εἰσεληλύθασιν** perf. ind. act. εἰσέρχομαι (# 1656) to come into. Perf. emphasizes that the cries that come to the ears of the Lord remain, so that He does not forget and they are not in vain. ◆ **5 ἐτρυφήσατε** aor. ind. act. τρυφάω (# 5587) to live in luxury. The word literally means "to break down" and denotes soft luxury, not necessarily wanton vice (Ropes). Const. aor. summarizes their total life (M, 109). **ἐσπαταλήσατε** aor. ind. act. σπαταλάω (# 5059) to give oneself to pleasure. The prominent idea is that of self-indulgence without distinct reference to squandering (Mayor; s. 1 Tim. 5:6). **ἐθρέψατε** aor. ind. act. τρέφω (# 5555) to feed, to fatten, to nourish. **καρδία** (# 2840) heart. Here heart refers to stomach; cf. Ernst Lerle, "Καρδία als Bezeichnung für den Mageneingang," ZNW 76 (1985): 292-94. **σφαγή** (# 5375) slaughter. The imagery of the slaughter of the rich is found in 1 Enoch 94:7-9: 1QH 15:17-18; 1QS 10:19; 1QM 1:9-12; CD 19:15, 19; Martin; Davids. ◆ **6 κατεδικάσατε** aor. ind. act. καταδικάω (# 2868) to give a sentence against someone, to condemn. **ἐφονεύσατε** aor. ind. act. φονεύω (# 5839) to kill, to murder. **ἀντιτάσσεται** pres. ind. mid. (dep.) ἀντιτάσσω (# 530) to stand against, to oppose. Pres. brings the action before our eyes and makes us dwell upon this, as the central point, in contrast w. the accompanying circumstances (Mayor). ◆ **7** μακροθυμήσατε aor. imp. act. μακροθυμέω (# *3428*) to patiently endure. The word describes the attitude that can endure delay, bear suffering, and never give in (NTW, 84; TDNT; Gal. 5:22). Aor. imp. calls for a specific act w. a note of urgency. παρουσία (# *4242*) arrival, coming. The word was used of the appearance of a god, or the arrival of someone of high rank (BAGD; TLNT; LAE, 372). γεωργός (# *1177*) farmer. ἐκδέχεται pres. ind. mid. (dep.) ἐκδέχομαι (# *1683*) to wait for something or someone. Gnomic pres. indicating what is common to farmers. τίμιος (# *5508*) precious, valuable. καρπός (# *2843*) fruit. γῆ (# *1178*) earth. μακροθυμῶν pres. act. part. μακροθυμέω (# *3428*) to be patient. λάβῃ aor. subj. act. λαμβάνω (# *3284*) to receive. Subj. in an indef. temp. cl. πρόϊμος (# *4611*) early. ὄψιμος (# *4069*) late. The early rain normally begins in Palestine late October or early November, and is anxiously awaited because, as a necessity for the germination of seed, it is the signal for sowing. In the spring the maturing of the grain depends on the late rain, light showers that fall in April and May. Without these even heavy winter rains will not prevent failure of crops (Ropes; Mayor; Martin; GB, 41-66; SB, 3:758-59; BBC; ABD, 5:119, 122-25). ◆ **8** μακροθυμήσατε aor. imp. act. μακροθυμέω (# *3428*) to patiently endure. στηρίξατε aor. imp. act. στηρίζω (# *5114*) to strengthen, to make stable. ἤγγικεν perf. ind. act. ἐγγίζω (# *1581*) to come near, to draw near. ◆ **9** στενάζετε pres. imp. act. στενάζω (# *5100*) to groan. Pres. imp. w. the neg. μή (# *3590*) calls for the discontinuing of a action in progress or prohibits habitual action. κριθῆτε aor. subj. act. κρίνω (# *3212*) to judge. Subj. w. ἵνα (# *2671*) in a neg. purp. cl. ἰδού aor. imp. act. ὁράω (# *3972*)to see. ἕστηκεν perf. ind. act. ἵστημι (# *2705*) to stand. ◆ **10** ὑπόδειγμα (# *5682*) example. λάβετε aor. imp. act. λαμβάνω (# *3284*) to take. κακοπάθεια (# *2801*) suffering, hardship, suffering evil. μακροθυμία (# *3429*) patient endurance. ἐλάλησαν aor. ind. act. λαλέω (# *3281*) to speak. ὀνόματι κυρίου (# *3590*; *3261*) "in the name of the Lord." The prophets were messengers of the Lord and consequently had to face suffering; yet they waited patiently and expectantly (Martin). ◆ **11** ἰδού aor. imp. act. ὁράω (# *3972*) to see. μακαρίζομεν pres. ind. act. μακαρίζω (# *3420*) to consider happy, to consider blessed. The word refers to the prevalent habit of considering constancy worthwhile (Ropes). ὑπομείναντας aor. act. part. ὑπομένω (# *5702*) to remain under, to be patient in adverse circumstances (NTW, 60; TDNT; NIDNTT; Heb. 10:36). ἠκούσατε aor. ind. act. ἀκούω (# *201*) to hear. τέλος (# *5465*) goal, purpose, outcome, result. τέλος κυρίου the conclusion wrought by the Lord to his trouble (Rope; Adamson; s. Job 42:12-17). εἴδετε aor. ind. act. ὁράω (# *3972*) to see. πολύσπλαγχνος (# *4499*) very kind, very pitiful, very sympathetic, extremely compassionate (Mayor;

MNTW, 156f; TDNT; Davids). οἰκτίρμων (# *3881*) compassion. Both words stand in sharp contrast to the normal reaction of someone undergoing trials similar to Job's. ◆ **12** ὀμνύετε pres. imp. act. ὀμνύω (# *3923*) to swear. ὅρκος oath (s. Matt. 5:33). Pres. imp. w. the neg. μή (# *3590*) prohibits an habitual action. ἤτω pres. imp. act. εἰμί (# *1639*) to be. πέσητε aor. subj. act. πίπτω (# *5679*) to fall; here used in a fig. sense, to come under condemnation (BAGD) and thus face ruin. Subj. w. ἵνα (# *2671*) in a neg. purp. cl. ◆ **13** κακοπαθεῖ pres. ind. act. κακοπαθέω (# *2802*) to suffer misfortune, to suffer trouble. προσευχέσθω pres. imp. mid. (dep.) προσεύχομαι (# *4667*) to pray. Pres. imp. calls for an habitual action. εὐθυμεῖ pres. ind. act. εὐθυμέω (# *2313*) to be happy, to feel good. ψαλλέτω pres. imp. act. ψάλλω (# *6010*) to sing, to sing praises, to play on a harp (Adamson). ◆ **14** ἀσθενεῖ pres. ind. act. ἀσθενέω (# *820*) to be weak, to be sick. προσκαλεσάσθω aor. imp. mid. προσκαλέω (# *4673*) to call one alongside, to summon. mid., to call to one's side. For a discussion s. BTNT, 433-34. προσευξάσθωσαν aor. imp. mid. (dep.) προσεύχομαι (# *4667*) to pray. Aor. imp. calls for a specific act w. a note of urgency. ἀλείψαντες aor. act. part. ἀλείφω (# *230*) to anoint. The word is used basically for an outward anointing of the body (TDNT; Martin). Aor. part. can express antecedent time ("after anointing pray"), or it can express contemporaneous time as a circum. part in the sense of an imp. ("anoint and pray") (Mussner; BG, 129f; Martin; DLNT, 48-50). ἔλαιον (# *1778*) oil, olive oil. Generally, oil was used as a curative by the ancients, including the rabbis (Adamson; TDNT; Mayor, Ropes; SB, 4:553; Martin). ◆ **15** εὐχή (# *2376*) prayer. πίστεως gen. sing. πίστις (# *4411*) faith. Gen. of description. σώσει fut. ind. act. σῴζω (# *5392*) to rescue, to save, to heal. Here the word has the idea, "to restore to health" (Ropes). κάμνοντα pres. act. part. (subst.) acc. masc. sing. κάμνω (# *2827*) to be ill. ἐγερεῖ fut. ind. act. ἐγείρω (# *1586*) to raise. The word means, "raise from the bed of sickness to health" (Ropes). κἄν (# *2829*) = καὶ ἄν and if, and. ᾖ pres. subj. act. εἰμί (# *1639*) to be. πεποιηκώς perf. act. part. ποιέω (# *4472*) to do. Perf. part. is used in a periphrastic perf. subj. act. in a condition of 3rd. class, which indicates the possibility of sin being related to the sickness (RWP). ἀφεθήσεται fut. ind. pass. ἀφίημι (# *918*) to forgive. The pass. is the so-called theol. or divine pass., indicating that God is the one who forgives (BG, 76). ◆ **16** ἐξομολογεῖσθε pres. imp. mid. (dep.) ἐξομολογέω (# *2018*) to openly agree to, to confess. The confession is to be not only to the elders but to one another, i.e., probably to those they have wronged (Adamson). εὔχεσθε pres. imp. mid. (dep.) εὔχομαι (# *2377*) to pray. ἰαθῆτε aor. subj. pass. ἰάομαι (# *2615*) to heal. Theol. pass. indicating that God is the one who heals (s.v. 15). Subj. w.ὅπως (# *3968*) may give the content of the prayer, or express purp. **ἰσχύει** pres. ind. act. ἰσχύω (# *2710*) to be strong, to be powerful, to have power, to be competent, to be able (BAGD). **δέησις** (# *1255*) request, prayer. **ἐνεργουμένη** pres. mid./pass. part. ἐνεργέω (# *1919*) to be effective, to produce (MNTW, 46; TDNT). For a discussion of whether the form is mid. or pass., and the suggested translation–"the prayer of a righteous man is very powerful in its operation" s. Adamson 205-10; Mayor; Ropes; Martin; Davids).   ◆ **17 ὁμοιοπαθής** (# *3926*) like feelings, of similar feelings, circumstances, experiences w. the same nature as someone (BAGD). The word indicates that the power of Elijah's prayer lay not in his supernatural greatness, but rather in his humanity–the prophet was only a human being like we are (Mussner; s. 1 Kings 17:1; 18:41-45); for references to Elijah in Judaism, s. Davids; ABD, 2:465-66. **προσευχή** (# *4666*) prayer. Here instr. dat. **προσηύξατο** aor. ind. mid. (dep.) προσεύχομαι (# *4667*) to pray. **βρέξαι** aor. act. inf. βρέχω (# *1101*) to rain. Inf. in indir. disc. indicating

the content of the prayer. **ἔβρεξεν** aor. ind. act. βρέχω (# *1101*). **ἐνιαυτός** year (# *1929*). **μήν** (# *3604*) month. ◆ **18 προσηύξατο** aor. ind. mid. (dep.) προσεύχομαι (# *4667*) to pray. **ὑετός** (# *5624*) rain. **ἔδωκεν** aor. ind. act. δίδωμι (# *1443*) to give. **ἐβλάστησεν** aor. ind. act. βλαστέω (# *1056*) to sprout, to bring forth.   ◆ **19 πλανηθῇ** aor. subj. pass. πλανάω (# *4414*) to go astray. **ἐπιστρέψῃ** aor. subj. act. ἐπιστρέφω (# *2188*) to turn around, to turn to convert. Aor. points to a specific act. The two subjs. are in a 3rd. class cond. cl. assuming the possibility of the cond.   ◆ **20 γινωσκέτω** pres. imp. act. γινώσκω (# *1182*) to know, to recognize. **ἐπιστρέψας** aor. act. part. ἐπιστρέφω (# *2188*) to turn away. Aor. points to a specific act. **πλάνη** error (# *4415*). **σώσει** fut. ind. act. σῴζω (# *5392*) to save. **καλύψει** fut. ind. act. καλύπτω (# *2821*) to cover, to hide, to veil. **πλῆθος** (# *4436*) a great number, multitude; many. **ἁμαρτιῶν** gen. pl. ἁμαρτία (# *281*) sin. Gen. of content, "a multitude of sins." This suggests the extent of the forgiveness (Davids; Martin).

1 Peter

1 Peter 1

◆ **1** ἀπόστολος (# 693) apostle, an official representative who was appointed and authorized by the one sending (TDNT; Best; TLNT; EDNT; 1 Cor. 1:1). For the omission of the article, w. all of the substantives in this v. indicating a stereotype epistolary introduction s. BD, 137. ἐκλεκτός (# 1723) elect. Verbal adj. from the vb. ἐκλέκτω meaning "to pick out, to select" (RWP). The word was used in the papyri in our sense of the word: select, choice (Beare). παρεπίδημος (# 4215) one who lives alongside of, sojourner, foreigner temporarily living in a place; staying for a while in a strange place (BAGD; TLNT; GELTS, 358). The word is used of temporary residents, not permanent settlers who have a deep attachment and a higher allegiance in another sphere (Beare). The word emphasizes both alien nationality and temporary residents (Stibbs; Hort, 154-56; BS, 149; NIDNTT; TDNT; TLNT; TDOT, 2:443-48, DCH, 2:372-73; NIDOTTE, 1:836-39; ZPEB, 2:119-22). διασπορά (# 1402) dispersion, scattering, diaspora. The Jewish diaspora came about through deportation and voluntary movement to a foreign land. The people generally lived in their own settlement or quarters in a foreign land but were still vitally joined to the land of Palestine and the city of Jerusalem w. her temple. There was always the hope for the eschatological regathering of those who had been scattered. Peter uses the term for believers who are scattered throughout the world, yet have a heavenly fatherland and a hope of one day being gathered in to this land (Goppelt; SB, 2:490; TDNT; RAC, 3:972-82; DLNT, 287-300; JPF, 1:177-215; HJP, 3, i:1-176; BAFCS, 5). Πόντου, Γαλατίας, Καππαδοκίας, Ἀσίας, καὶ Βιθυνίας Pontus, Galatia, Cappadocia, Asia, and Bithynia. These were all Roman provinces in Asia Minor and the order of the listing here may have been the route of the one who delivered the letter (Hort; Davids; Michaels; GAM, 89-426; DNP, 2:698-702; ABD, 1:750-53; 1:870-71; 2:870-72; 5:401-2). Years after Peter had written this letter, Pliny the Younger was put in charge of Bithynia and wrote to the Emperor Trajan concerning the Christians (*Christiani*). He tried to make them recant by force and have them acknowledge the pagan gods, bow down before the image of the emperor, and curse (*maledixerunt*) Christ. Some did, others did not, so Pliny asked for advice. He writes, "It seems to me to be necessary to get advice, because many in every age group, every status of life, and both male and female are now in danger and will be in the future. This plague of superstition has spread over cities and over the fields and villages, but I believe that its advance can be stopped" (Pliny the Younger, *Letters*, Book 10, Letter 16) ◆ **2** πρόγνωσις (# 4590) knowing beforehand, foreknowledge. God's foreknowledge is much more than knowing what will happen in the future; it includes, as reflected in the language of LXX (s. the LXX w. the aor. ind. act. "He knows (knew)..." in Num. 16:5; Judg. 9:6; Amos 3:2), His effective choice (Kelly; Michaels; Rom. 8:28-29). ἁγιασμός (# 40) holiness, sanctification. W. the prep. ἐν (# 1877) as instr. πνεῦμα (# 4460) spirit. The word could refer to the human spirit, but by the analogy of the other cls., it refers to the Holy Spirit (Hort). Subjective gen. here indicates that the Spirit produces the sanctification (Michaels). ὑπακοή (# 5633) obedience. ῥαντισμόν (# 4823) sprinkling. It is probably a reference to Exod. 24:3-8 (Best). πληθυνθείη aor. opt. pass. πληθύνω (# 4437) to multiply. Opt. to express a wish or desire (MT, 120f). Peter prays for the multiplication of grace and peace that the trials through which the Asiatic Christians are about to pass may result in a manifold increase of grace and peace (Hort). ◆ **3** εὐλογητός (# 2329) blessed (s. Eph. 1:3). ἀναγεννήσας aor. act. part. ἀναγεννάω (# 335) to regenerate, to cause to be born again. The idea of a new beginning through a new birth w. the infusion of divine life was a widespread idea in the ancient world. It was present in the mystery religions and in Judaism. A proselyte to Judaism was regarded as a newborn baby (Best; RAC, 9:153-55; Schelkle; Goppelt; SB, 3:763; for a parallel in the DSS s. 1QH3, 19-23). Part. gives the reason why God is blessed (Schelkle). ζῶσαν pres. act. part. (adj.) ζάω (# 2409) to live. Life is a quality or characteristic of the hope here spoken of, not its obj. (Hort). Pres. indicates an abiding quality. A living hope is never extinguished by untold circumstances, just as living waters flow fresh from a perennial spring (Selwyn). ◆ **4** κληρονομία (# 3100) inheritance. The word can mean a property already received as well as one that is expected. But here the inheritance is kept for the believer, not on earth but in heaven, and is another name for that salvation which is ready to be revealed (Bigg; Hort; Kelly). ἄφθαρτος (# 915) imperishable, not corruptible, not liable to pass away (Beare). It has been suggested that the main idea of the word is "to injure, to spoil," and the chief idea in mind is the ravaging of a land by a hostile army (Hort). ἀμίαντος (# 299) unstained, undefiled; here, being unstained by evil (Beare). ἀμάραντος (# 278) unfading. The word was used of flowers and suggests a supernatural beauty that time does not impair. The three verbal adjs. indicate that the inheritance is untouched by death, unstained by evil, unimpaired by time. It is composed of immortality, purity, and beauty (Beare). τετηρημένην perf. pass. part. (adj.) τηρέω (# 5498) to guard, to keep, to take care of, to reserve. Perf. indicates the state or condition and underlines the fact that the inheritance already exists and is being preserved for those who are now being guarded (v. 5) (Best). ◆ 5 φρουρουμένους pres. pass. part. φρουρέω (# 5864) to guard, to watch over. The term is a military term indicating the guarding done by soldiers. Pres. emphasizes our need for continual protection in the unending struggle of the soul. They are being guarded by God's power, the guarantee of the final victory (Beare; Stibbs; Grudem). σωτηρία (# 5401) salvation. The word indicates deliverance or preservation bestowed by God, more specifically deliverance from His wrath at the final judgment (Kelly). The term here suggests salvation in its broadest sense (TDNT; NIDNTT). ἕτοιμος (# 2289) ready, prepared. ἀποκαλυφθῆναι aor. pass. inf. ἀποκαλύπτω (# 636) to unveil, to reveal. (BAGD). Pass. would be the theol. or divine pass., indicating that God is the one who does the action. Inf. to express purp. Aor. points to a specific event. καιρῷ ἐσχάτῳ (# 2798; 2274) in the last time. The word καιρῷ indicates the fit or appointed time or moment (Bigg). The word ἐσχάτῳ ("last") means simply "last in order of time" (Bigg). ◆ 6 ἐν ᾧ (# 1877; 4005) in which, in which circumstance, wherefore. For a discussion of the antecedent of the rel. pron. s. Selwyn; Brox; Michaels. ἀγαλλιᾶσθε pres. ind. mid. (dep.) ἀγαλλιάομαι (# 22) to rejoice, to be glad. This vb. appears to be used always w. the connotation of a religious joy, a joy that springs from the contemplation of God or God's salvation (Beare; TDNT; Hort; Kelly). ὀλίγος (# 3900) a little, a little while, a short while (Kelly). δέον pres. act. part. δεῖ (# 1256) it is necessary. Part. is used w. the cond. particle εἰ (# 1623), which can be taken as a concessive cl. ("although" [Beare]), or it can be taken as a 1st-class cond. cl. bordering on a causal cl. ("since" [BD, 189; Kelly]). λυπηθέντες aor. pass. part. λυπέω (# 3382) to cause pain, to cause sorrow, to put to grief. The word expresses not suffering but the mental effect of suffering (Hort). Part. could be concessive, "although." ποικίλος (# 4476) various, diversified, manifold, different kinds. πειρασμός (# 4280) trial. The word here could mean the undeserved suffering from without (Bigg). For a discussion of persecution s. DLNT, 907-15. ◆ 7 δοκίμιον (# 1507) tried,

approved after trial, genuineness. The genuine element in their faith was proven by a process similar to that of metal refining and is found to be something more precious than these precious metals (Selwyn; s. also Jam. 1:3; BS, 259f; TLNT). πίστις (# 4411) faith. Obj. gen. here, denoting the obj. of the process of testing (Michaels), or it could be an attributed gen., "genuine faith" (GGBB, 90). πολυτιμότερον comp. πολύτιμος (# 4501) costly, precious; comp., more precious, of greater price. χρυσίον (# 5992) gold. In the ancient world gold was considered the most expensive and rarest of all metals. It was used in the worship of the gods, and was very prominent in the temple of Jerusalem, where the true God was worshipped. Emperors and heros were known for their lavish use of gold. Under Augustus and Nero the price of the Roman gold coin, the *aureus*, was worth 45 denarii (a Roman soldier got 225 denarii a year and one denarius was considered to be a day's wage (RAC, 11:895-930; KP, 2:841-42; RE, 190-227; Pliny, NH, 33:4-94; NW, 2, ii:1343-49). All of this indicates that a tried, genuine faith is extremely valuable! The known quantity in this statement is the preciousness of gold–a genuine faith is much more precious than that (GGBB, 112). Gen. of comparison. ἀπολλυμένου pres. mid. (dep.) part. ἀπόλλυμι (# 660) to destroy, to ruin, to perish. πῦρ (# 4796) fire. Pliny describes how metals are mined, cleaned, fired, and ground to a powder, then put in a smelting furnace. The slag (*scoria*) from gold was pounded again and fired a second time; "the crucibles for this are made of tasconium, which is a white earth resembling clay. No other earth can stand the blast of air, the fire, or the intensely hot material" (Pliny, NH, 33:69). δοκιμαζομένου pres. pass. part. δοκιμάζω (# 1507) to approve after examination (TLNT). εὑρεθῇ aor. subj. pass. εὑρίσκω (# 2351) to find. Subj. w. ἵνα (# 2671) used to express purp. ἀποκάλυψις (# 637) unveiling, revelation. W. the prep. ἐν (# 1877) used in a temp. sense, "at the revelation of Jesus Christ." Ἰησοῦ Χριστοῦ (# 2652; 5986) of Jesus Christ, gen. sing. Obj. gen. indicating that He will be revealed. ◆ 8 ἰδόντες aor. act. part. ὁράω (# 3972) to see. For the variant reading s. TC, 687. Aor. indicates a completed action, but logically antecedent to the main vb. Part. is concessive ("although"). The word here refers to physical or eyesight (Selwyn). ἀγαπᾶτε pres. ind. act. ἀγαπάω (# 26) to love (TDNT; TLNT; EDNT). Pres. indicates the continual and contemporary action. ὁρῶντες pres. act. part. ὁράω (# 3972) to see. Pres. indicates the continual action. Concessive part. ("although"). The first statement (ἰδόντες) indicates that Christ and the salvation he brings are hidden until his revelation; the second statement (ὁρῶντες) focuses more on the various ordeals now confronting Peter and his readers (Michaels). πιστεύοντες pres. act. part. (circum.) πιστεύω (# 4409) to believe. The neg. μή (# 3590) used w. the part. here is introduced as it were hypothetical, merely to bring out the full force of believing (Hort; Selwyn). ἀγαλλιᾶσθε pres. imp. mid. (dep.) ἀγαλλιάομαι (# 22) to rejoice (s.v. 6). χαρά (# 5915) joy. Here instr. dat. ἀνεκλάλητος (# 443) unspeakable, inexpressible, ineffable, vb. adj. The word contains the sense of a divine mystery exceeding the powers of speech and thought (Beare; Davids). This joy defies all human efforts at understanding or explanation (Michaels). The joy is based on the expectation of future deliverance. δεδοξασμένη perf. pass. part. δοξάζω (# 1519) to glorify; pass., to be glorified. Here the idea is to be endowed w. glory from above (Selwyn, 253-58; TDNT; NIDNTT; EDNT; TLNT). ◆ 9 κομιζόμενοι pres. mid. part. κομίζω (# 3152). mid., to receive, to obtain. τέλος (# 5465) goal. ψυχῶν gen. pl. ψυχή (# 6034) soul. Obj. gen., "salvation of your souls." This is not a special part of man's structure, but is man as a whole; it is a Jewish rather than a Gr. or modern usage of the word (Best). ◆ 10 ἐξεζήτησαν aor. ind. act. ἐκζητέω (# 1699) to seek out. Prep. in compound is intensive. ἐξηραύνησαν aor. ind. act. ἐξεραυνάω (# 2001) to search out. Prep. in compound is intensive. "Seeking out" is the more general term, "searching out" the minute and sedulous process of thought and investigation which subserve the seeking (Hort). The two vbs. taken together give emphatic expressing to the earnestness w. which enlightenment was sought (Beare; MH, 310). προφητεύσαντες aor. act. part. (adj.) προφητεύω (# 4736) to speak for, to speak forth, to prophesy (TDNT; EDNT; DLNT, 670-76). ◆ 11 ἐραυνῶντες pres. act. part. ἐραυνάω (# 2236) to search. Part. of manner. τίνα acc. sing. τίς (# 5515) what? ποῖος (# 4481) what sort of. Indef. pron. suggests a definite period, almost a date to be fixed, while this word suggests the general outward circumstances to be expected (Beare; BS, 155). For the view that the words should be translated "what person or time" s. Grudem. ἐδήλου impf. ind. act. δηλόω (# 1317) to make clear, to make plain. Though the word is often used of declarations through articulate language, it is still more often used of any indirect kind of communication (Hort). Impf. indicates continual action in the past time. προμαρτυρόμενον pres. mid. (dep.) part. προμαρτύρομαι (# 4626) to testify beforehand (Selwyn). τὰ εἰς Χριστὸν παθήματα (# 1650; 5986; 4077) the sufferings to Christ; i.e., the sufferings in store for Christ (Kelly). It is quite possible that we have a reference to the words recorded in Luke 24:26-27 (Bigg). For a discussion of the passages in 1 Peter that point to the words of Christ and support Petrine authorship of the epistle and the authenticity of the gospel passages s. R.H. Gundry, "'Verba Christi' in 1 Peter: Their Implications Concerning the Authorship of 1 Peter and the Authenticity of the Gospel Tradition," *NTS* 13 (1967): 336-50; R.H. Gundry, "Further Verba on 'Verba Christi' in 1 Peter,"

Bib 55 [1974]: 211-32. πάθημα (# 4077) suffering. For suffering as a theme in 1 Peter s. DLNT, 1135-38. δόξα (# 1518) glory; pl., glorious deeds, triumphs (Selwyn). ◆ 12 ἀπεκαλύφθη aor. ind. pass. ἀποκαλύπτω (# 636) to reveal, to unveil (Selwyn, 250ff). Theol. pass. indicating that God did the revealing. διηκόνουν impf. ind. act. διακονέω (# 1354) to serve, to minister to, to render service to, to help by performing certain duties (LN, 1:460). It was used of delivering a message (Michaelis). Impf. points to the continual or customary action in the past. ἀνηγγέλη aor. ind. pass. ἀναγέλλω (# 334) to report, to set forth, to tell, to declare, to proclaim (Selwyn; NIDNTT). εὐαγγελισαμένων aor. mid. part. εὐαγγελίζω (# 2294) to proclaim good news, to evangelize, to preach the gospel (TDNT; TLNT; EDNT). ἀποσταλέντι aor. pass. part. (subst.) dat. sing. ἀποστέλλω (# 690) to send, to send as an official authoritative representative of the one sending (TDNT; NIDNTT; EDNT; TLNT). ἐπιθυμοῦσιν pres. ind. act. ἐπιθυμέω (# 2121) to desire, to long for, to eagerly desire. The vb. is fairly strong and consistent w. a longing not yet fulfilled (Kelly). Pres. indicates the continual action that has not reached fulfillment. ἄγγελος (# 34) angel, heavenly messenger, heavenly being. παρακύψαι aor. act. inf. παρακύπτω (# 4160) to stretch forward the head, esp. through a window or door, sometimes inward, more often outward. When used figuratively, it commonly implies a rapid and cursory glance. The word means to bend down to look and often suggests a fleeting glance; i.e., "to peep," "to catch a glimpse of" (Hort; Kelly). The main idea here rests on their intense interest in what has taken place and on the limitations of their power and knowledge (Michaels). ◆ 13 διό (# 1475) therefore. This is the usual particle when an author passes from statement to inference (Selwyn). ἀναζωσάμενοι aor. mid. (dep.) part. ἀναζώννυμι (# 350) to bind up, to gather up, to gird up. The word refers to the habit of the Orientals, who quickly gather up their loose robes w. a girdle or belt when in a hurry or at the start of a journey because the easterners' long flowing robes would impede physical activity unless tucked under the belt (RWP; Best; BBC; Michaels). One worker describes tavern keepers who worked in front of their taverns w. their tunics belted high (DC, 72:2). ὀσφύας acc. pl. ὀσφῦς (# 4019) hip. διάνοια (# 1379) mind. More than mere intellectual faculties, the word indicates that which guides and directs conduct (Best). This is a call for the readers to be alert and ready in their whole spiritual and mental attitude (Kelly). νήφοντες pres. act. part. νήφω (# 3768) to be sober. In the NT the word generally denotes self-control and the clarity of mind which goes w. it (Kelly; s. 2 Tim. 4:5; 1 Thess. 5:6). τελείως (# 5458) adv., perfectly, unreservedly. The adv. is best taken w. the main vb. ἐλπίσατε (Selwyn). ἐλπίσατε aor. imp. act. ἐλπίζω (# 1827) to hope, to set one's hope upon something. **φερομένην** pres. pass. part. φέρω (# 5770) to carry, to bear, to bring. Pres. part. pictures the process, "that is being brought" (RWP). Although a pres. part. can have a fut. force, it is used here in keeping w. the writer's conviction that the object of their hope is already virtually within his readers' grasp (Kelly). **χάρις** (# 5921) grace (TDNT; EDNT). The word is used here concretely of the eschatological consummation (Beare). **ἀποκαλύψει Ἰησοῦ Χριστοῦ** (# 637; 2652; 5986) at the revelation of Jesus Christ (s.v. 7). ◆ **14** **ὑπακοή** (# 5633) obedient hearing, obedience (Brox). Gen. of description, "obedient children," a trait highly valued (BBC). **συσχηματιζόμενοι** pres. mid. (dep.) part. συσχηματίζομαι (# 5372) to form together, to conform (s. Rom. 12:2). The mid. could be is a direct mid., "do not fashion yourselves" (RWP). Mid. could also be a permissive mid., "do not allow yourselves to be fashioned." Part. is used to convey a command and conforms to the rabbinic Heb. practice of using part. to express rules of conduct and even religious precepts (Kelly; for this use of the part. w. imp. sense s. David Daube in Selwyn, 467-88; GI, 165-68; MT *Style*, 128f; VANT, 386). **πρότερον** (# 4728) former, previous. **ἄγνοια** (# 53) ignorance; it is a moral and religious defect, nothing less than rebellion against God (Hort; Michaels). **ἐπιθυμία** (# 2123) strong desire, lust (TDNT; DNP, 2:542-44). ◆ **15 κατά** (# 2848) according to, prep. w. acc. **καλέσαντα** aor. act. part. καλέω (# 2813) to call. **ἅγιος** (# 41) separate, marked off, holy. The word indicates the display of the character of God whose perfect attributes separate Him from His creation (Kelly; NIDNTT; TDNT). Pred. adj. used in the cl., "just as the one who called you is holy." **πᾶς** (# 4246) every, each. All inclusive here, referring to all aspects of life. **ἀναστροφή** (# 419) conduct, active life. The word is used of public activity, life in relation to others. Being holy as members of a holy people, they were to show themselves holy in every kind of dealing w. other men (Beare; Hort; BS, 194). **γενήθητε** aor. imp. pass. (dep.) γίνομαι (# 1181) to become. Aor. may be taken as ingressive: began to be, become (Beare; RWP). ◆ **16 διότι** (# 1484) therefore. **γέγραπται** perf. ind. pass. γράφω (# 1211) to write. Perf. emphasizes the continuing results, "it stands written." The word was used of legal documents whose validity continued (MM). **ἔσεσθε** fut. ind. mid. (dep.) εἰμί (# 1639) to be. The fut. here is volitive and is used like an imp. (RWP; BG, 94). **ὅτι** (# 4022) causal, because. **ἅγιος** (# 41) holy. This trait of God should also characterize the believer's life. ◆ **17 ἐπικαλεῖσθε** pres. ind. mid. ἐπικαλέω (# 2126) to call, to call upon, to invoke, to appeal to (Selwyn). **ἀπροσωπολήμπτως** (# 719) adv., impartially, without showing respect or favoritism, (Bigg). **κρίνοντα** pres. act. part. (adj.) κρίνω (# 3212) to judge. Without the article the character is stressed. **ἔργον** (# 2240) work, here deed.

παροικία (# 4229) temporary residency, temporary stay. The word denotes residence in a place without taking out or being granted citizen rights (Kelly; Hort; s. 1:1; TDNT; EDNT; GELTS, 360). **ἀναστράφητε** aor. imp. pass. ἀναστρέφω (# 418) to conduct one's life (s.v. 15). ◆ **18 εἰδότες** perf. act. part. οἶδα (# 3857) to know. Def. perf. w. a pres. meaning. Part. may be causal. Christian reverence rests upon the knowledge of redemption, four aspects of which are now enumerated; (1) its cost in the death of Christ, (2) its transcendent origin, (3) its certification in Christ's resurrection, (4) its fruit in the church's faith and hope in God (Selwyn). **φθαρτός** (# 5778) subject to decay, corruptible. **ἀργύριον** (# 736) silver; here instr. dat. or dat. of means (Beare). **χρυσίον** (# 5992) gold; instr. dat. or dat. of means. Silver and gold were used as money to set slaves free (BAGD; RWP). The price of a slave in the Roman Empire ran from 700,000 to 200 sesertii (a worker in Rome could earn 3 sesertrii a day) (ERE, 348-50, 354). **ἐλυτρώθητε** aor. ind. pass. λυτρόω (# 3390) to release, to procure a release by a ransom, to deliver by the payment of a price, to redeem. For the Jews the picture of redemption would be God's deliverance from Egypt. For the Gentiles it would be the picture of a slave whose freedom was purchased w. a price (Hort; Beare; TDNT; NIDNTT; GW, 70f; APC; NTW, 76-83; LAE, 319-27; NTRJ, 268-84; LDC; ABD, 6:71-72; TLNT; NDIEC, 3:72-75; GELTS, 286). **μάταιος** (# 3469) vain, vanity. The idea is that which lacks reality (Beare). **ἀναστροφή** (# 419) manner of life (s.v. 15). **πατροπαράδοτος** (# 4261) that which is passed on from fathers, inherited. ◆ **19 τίμιος** (# 5508) valuable, precious, costly. **ἀμνός** (# 303) lamb. **ἄμωμος** (# 320) blameless. **ἄσπιλος** (# 834) spotless, without stain. Perhaps Peter has the Passover lamb in mind (Hort). It was required to be without blemish. ◆ **20 προεγνωσμένου** perf. pass. part. adj. προγινώσκω (# 4589) to know beforehand, to foreknow (s. 1:2). **καταβολή** (# 2856) foundation. **κόσμος** (# 3180) world. **φανερωθέντος** aor. pass. part. (adj.) φανερόω (# 5746) to make clear, to make plain, to manifest. **ἐπ' ἐσχάτου τῶν χρόνων** (# 2093; 2274; 5989) in the last times. **δι' ὑμᾶς** (# 1328; 5148) because of you, for your sake. ◆ **21 ἐγείραντα** aor. act. part. (adj.) ἐγείρω (# 1586) to raise up. Aor. points to a specific act that is complete. **δόντα** aor. act. part. δίδωμι (# 1443) to give, to grant. **ὥστε** (# 6063) w. inf. can express intended or contemplated results (Selwyn; BD, 197). Since the book deals w. the believer's pilgrim life and persecution on earth, w. emphasis on faith and eschatological hope, it is felt that this cl. is a sort of climax to the whole passage (William J. Dalton, "'So That Your Faith May also Be Your Hope,'" RH, 262-74; s. esp. 272f). **τὴν πίστιν ὑμῶν καὶ ἐλπίδα** your faith and hope; could be taken as the subject to the inf. ("so that your faith and hope may be in God"), or the word **ἐλπίδα** may be considered as the pred. ("so that your faith may also be your hope in God") (Dalton, RH, 272). **εἶναι** pres. act. inf. εἰμί (# 1639) to be. Inf. is used to express intended results. ◆ **22 ἡγνικότες** perf. act. part. ἁγνίζω (# 49) to make pure, to purify, to cleanse. In the LXX the word generally has a ceremonial reference, but it can also have the sense of moral purification (GELTS, 4; TDNT; EDNT). Perf. emphasizes the completed state or condition (Selwyn; Beare). **ὑπακοή** (# 5633) obedient. Dat. w. **ἐν** (# 1877) expresses sphere of the purification, or better, it is instr., giving the means. **ἀλήθεια** (# 237) truth. Here obj. gen., "obedient to the truth." **φιλαδελφία** (# 5789) brotherly love. **ἀνυπόκριτος** (# 537) unhypocritical, without hypocrisy. **ἀγαπήσατε** aor. imp. act. ἀγαπάω (# 26) to love (TLNT; TDNT). Aor. imp. calls for a specific action w. a note of urgency. **ἐκτενῶς** (# 1757) adv., earnestly. The fundamental idea is earnestness, zealousness (doing a thing not lightly and perfunctorily, but, straining, as it were) (Hort; TLNT). ◆ **23 ἀναγεγεννημένοι** perf. pass. part. ἀναγεννάω (# 335) to regenerate (s.v. 3). **σπορά** (# 5076) seed. The contrast is between human seed that produces mortal human life and divine seed that produces eternal life (Best). **φθαρτός** (# 5778) perishable, subject to decay and destruction (BAGD). **ἄφθαρτος** (# 915) incorruptible (s.v. 4). **ζῶντος** pres. act. part. ζάω (# 2409) to live (s.v. 3). **μένοντος** pres. act. part. μένω (# 3531) to remain. ◆ **24 χόρτος** (# 5965) grass. **ἄνθος** (# 470) flower. **ἐξηράνθη** aor. ind. pass. ξηραίνω (# 3830) to dry up; pass., to be withered. **ἐξέπεσεν** aor. ind. act. ἐκπίπτω (# 1738) to fall off. Aor. vividly expresses the rapid blooming and fading of herbage (Kelly). ◆ **25 εὐαγγελισθέν** aor. pass. part. εὐαγγελίζω (# 2294) to proclaim the good news.

1 Peter 2

◆ **1 ἀποθέμενοι** aor. mid. (dep.) part. ἀποτίθημι (# 700) to put off, to put away. The part. shares the imp. force of the governing vb. (Beare; s. 1:14). The word is applied to any kind of rejection, esp. of what is in any way connected w. the person, body, or mind, whether clothing or hair (Hort). **κακία** (# 2798) wickedness. The word is an all-inclusive term (Kelly). **δόλος** (# 1515) cunning, deceit by using trickery and treachery (LN, 1:759). It comes from a vb. meaning, "to catch w. bait" (RWP). **ὑπόκρισις** (# 5694) hypocrisy, pretense. **φθόνος** (# 5784) envy. The vb. was used often in secular Gr. to express the envy that makes one man begrudge another something he himself desires but does not possess. It is sadness occasioned by the thought of another's good and aggression in seeking to do harm, at least through slander (NIDNTT; TLNT). **καταλαλιά** (# 2896) speaking against someone. The vb. means "to run down," "to disparage," and was used by Aristophanes of a slave who blabs his master's secrets (Selwyn; Bigg). ◆ **2 ἀρτιγέννητος** (# 786) recently born, new-

born. **βρέφος** (# 1100) baby, infant. The word is used of a nursing baby (Goppelt). **λογικός** (# 3358) that which pertains to a word. There are three possible renderings of this word: (1) of the word; (2) reasonable, rational; (3) spiritual (Best; TDNT; Michaels). However, it seems hardly creditable that he is not also consciously referring back to God's Word, about which he was so concerned in 1:22-25 (Kelly). **ἄδολος** (# 100) without deceit, pure, unadulterated, uncontaminated. The word is commonly used in this sense of corn, wheat, barley, oil, wine, and farm products (Beare; Kelly; MM; BBC; DLNT, 737-38). **γάλα** (# 1128) milk. The many-breasted goddesses of the heathen religions who were to sustain and nourish life were widespread in the ancient world. The rabbis also compared the Law to milk (Goppelt; Beare; TDNT; Montefiore, 163f; Selwyn, esp. 308; RAC, 2:657-64). **ἐπιποθήσατε** aor. imp. act. ἐπιποθέω (# 2160) to long for, to desire, to crave. Prep. in compound indicates intensive desire directed toward an object (s. Ps. 42:1). **αὐξηθῆτε** aor. subj. pass. αὐξάνω (# 889) to cause to grow; pass., to grow. Subj. w. **ἵνα** (# 2671) to express purp. ◆ **3 ἐγεύσασθε** aor. ind. mid. (dep.) γεύομαι (# 1174) to taste. The ind. is used in a cond. cl. of the 1st class which accepts the reality of the cond. **χρηστός** (# 5982) useful, good, gracious. ◆ **4 προσερχόμενοι** pres. mid. (dep.) part. προσέρχομαι (# 4665) to come to. Pres. part. is used because stones keep coming, one after another (Bigg). **ζῶντα** pres. act. part. ζάω (# 2409) to live. For the figure of a living stone s. Beare; Selwyn. **ἀποδεδοκιμασμένον** perf. pass. part. ἀποδοκιμάζω (# 627) to reject after examination, to examine and deem useless. **παρὰ θεῷ** (# 4123; 2536) by the side of God, who looks at it, in contrast w. the rejection by men (RWP). **ἐκλεκτός** (# 1723) chose, choice, select, elect (s. 1:1; Hort). **ἔντιμος** (# 1952) precious, costly, expensive, valuable, highly valued (Hort; GELTS, 155). ◆ **5 αὐτοὶ ὡς λίθοι** (# 899; 6055) you also are yourselves like living stones (Kelly; Hort). **ζῶντες** pres. act. part. (adj.) ζάω (# 2409) to live. **οἰκοδομεῖσθε** pres. ind. pass. οἰκοδομέω (# 3868) to build, to erect a building. **πνευματικός** (# 4461) spiritual, pertaining to the Spirit; "suited for the Spirit." **ἱεράτευμα** (# 2633) priesthood. **ἀνενέγκαι** aor. act. inf. ἀναφέρω (# 429) to bring up, to offer, to offer sacrifice. **πνευματικὰς θυσίας** spiritual sacrifices. These are sacrifices which consist of praise and thanksgiving, charity and mutual sharing, and which are inspired by the Spirit (Kelly). **εὐπρόσδεκτος** (# 2347) acceptable. ◆ **6 διότι** (# 1484) therefore. **περιέχει** pres. ind. act. περιέχω (# 4321) impersonal, it is included. The word was used in the papyri concerning a will, as "in the will as it stands written" (MM; Beare). **γραφῇ** (# 1210) writing, Scripture. **ἰδού** pres. imp. mid. ὁράω (# 3972) to see. Imp. used to draw attention. **τίθημι** (# 5502) pres. ind. act. to lay. **ἀκρογωνιαῖος** (# 214) lying at the extreme corner. **λίθον ἀκρογωνιαῖον** foundation stone, cornerstone, chief cornerstone, capstone. The word refers either to a massive cornerstone placed at the upper corner of the building in order to bind the walls firmly together, or to the keystone in the middle of an archway (Beare; TDNT). πιστεύων pres. act. part. subst. πιστεύω (# 4409) to believe. οὐ μή (# 3590; 4024) not at all. The two negatives form a strong denial (M, 187ff). καταισχυνθῇ aor. subj. pass. καταισχύνω (# 2875) to put to shame. Subj. w. the double neg. ◆ 7 ἡ τιμή (# 5507) the honor. The honor includes their privileged status here and now as well as triumph over their mocking assailants and their salvation on the last day (Kelly). For a discussion of the grammatical difficulties and various interpretations s. Hort; Michaels. πιστεύουσιν pres. act. part. πιστεύω (# 4409) to believe; "to you who are believing." Part. is in apposition to the personal pron. ὑμῖν dat. pl. οὐ (# 5148) you. Dat. is personal advantage or possession. ἀπιστοῦσιν pres. act. part. ἀπιστεύω (# 601) to be unbelieving. ἀπεδοκίμασαν aor. ind. act. ἀποδοκιμάζω (# 627) to reject after examination (s.v. 4). οἰκοδομοῦντες pres. act. part. οἰκοδομέω (# 3868) to build. Subst. part., "the builders." ἐγενήθη aor. ind. pass. (dep.) γίνομαι (# 1181) to become. γωνία (# 1224) corner. ◆ 8 πρόσκομμα (# 4682) stumbling. The stone of stumbling is the loose stone lying in the way against which the traveler strikes his foot (Hort). προσκόπτουσιν pres. ind. act. προσκόπτω (# 4684) to cut against, to stumble. ἀπειθοῦντες pres. act. part. ἀπειθέω (# 578) to disobey. The word carries a strong sense of refusal to believe (Kelly). εἰς ὅ (# 1650; 4005) unto which. ἐτέθησαν aor. ind. pass. τίθημι (# 5502) to place, to put, to appoint. ◆ 9 γένος (# 1169) generation, race. βασίλειος (# 994) kingly, royal. The word could be taken as an adj. modifying ἱεράτευμα, or it can be taken as a substantive, either w. the meaning royal house, palace, or a group of kings (Best; Kelly; Goppelt; J.H. Elliott, The Elect and Holy. An Exegetical Examination of I Peter 2:4-10 [Leiden: E.J. Brill, 1966]). ἱεράτευμα (# 2633) priesthood (E. Best, "Spiritual Sacrifice: General Priesthood in the New Testament," Interp. 14 [1960]: 273-99). περιποίησις (# 4348) possession, private possession (TLNT; GELTS, 371) . ἀρετάς acc. pl. ἀρετή (# 746) virtue, the ability to do heroic deeds. When the word is applied to deity it does not denote virtues or intrinsic qualities, but the manifestations of divine power; i.e., His mighty and glorious deeds, the virtue needed when virtue was called for (TDNT; Goppelt; Kelly; Hort; Beare; BS, 95f; MM; NDIEC, 4:67-69; PIGC, 1:1-2). ἐξαγγείλητε aor. subj. act. ἐξαγγέλλω (# 1972) to tell out, to tell forth. The word often has the additional force of declaring things unknown (Hort). In the LXX the word is used w. the sense of cultic proclamation, or the rehearsal in adoring language of God's righteousness and praises (Kelly). Subj. w. ὅπως (# 3968) to express purp. καλέσαντος aor. act. part. (subst.) καλέω (# 2813)

to call. The word refers to the effective call of God. θαυμαστός (# 2515) wonderful, marvelous. The marvelous light could refer to the future revelation of the glory at the coming of Jesus Christ (Michaels). ◆ 10 ποτε (# 4537) then, at that time, formerly. ἠλεημένοι perf. pass. part. ἐλεέω (# 1796) to be merciful; pass., to obtain mercy, to have mercy and pity showed upon one. Perf. emphasizes the completed state or cond. The contrast of the perf. w. the following aor. stresses the contrast between the long antecedent state and the single event of conversion that ended it (Hort). ἐλενθέντες aor. pass. part. ἐλεέω (# 1796). ◆ 11 ἀγαπητός (# 28) verbal adj. loved one, beloved. παρακαλῶ pres. ind. act. παρακαλέω (# 4151) to urge, to encourage, to beseech (s. Rom. 12:1). πάροικος (# 4230) alien. It denotes a man who lives in a foreign country (Kelly). παρεπίδημος (# 4215) foreigner, stranger, temporary sojourner. This word suggests a visitor making a brief stay (Kelly; s. 1:1). As long as we are in this world, our lives as Christians should display a certain detachment (Stibbs). ἀπέχεσθαι pres. mid. (dep.) inf. ἀπέχομαι (# 600) to hold oneself away from, to abstain. Inf. in indir. disc. after the main vb. The obj. of the vb. is in gen., indicating what one is not to indulge in (Beare). σαρκικός (# 4920) fleshly, that which pertains to the flesh; i.e., the impulses belonging to the selfish and lower side of human nature (Selwyn). For the significance of the suf. s. MH, 378f. ἐπιθυμία (# 2123) strong desire, lust. στρατεύονται pres. ind. mid. (dep.) στρατεύομαι (# 5129) to fight, to carry on a military campaign, to wage war. Pres. emphasizes the continual warfare. ◆ 12 ἀναστροφή (# 419) manner of life, conduct, behavior (s. 1:15). ἔθνεσιν pl. ἔθνος (# 1620) nation; pl. heathen–those who have no knowledge of the true God, Gentiles. ἔχοντες pres. act. part. ἔχω (# 2400) to have. Pres. indicates the continual possession and could have an imp. force (Beare). καταλαλοῦσιν pres. ind. act. καταλαλέω (# 2895) to speak evil of (Hort). κακοποιός (# 2804) evildoer. It denotes the doing of mischief or injury, either to a specific person or object, or else absolutely. It is a wicked man who does evil in such a way that he is liable for punishment from the magistrate (Hort; Bigg). ἐποπτεύοντες pres. act. part. ἐποπτεύω (# 2227) to look upon, to observe, to be a spectator, to view carefully, to watch over a period of time. Pres. indicates a longer period of time and includes the observer's memory and reflection upon the deeds. The thought is of spiritual insight to be gained in the future, through the influence of the good works (RWP; Selwyn; Beare). Part. could be temp. ("when") or causal ("because they observe"). δοξάσωσιν aor. subj. act. δοξάζω (# 1519) to hold a high opinion of, to glorify. Subj. w. ἵνα (# 2671) is used to express purp. ἐπισκοπή (# 2175) visitation. The word is used in the OT either in the sense of visit, or a visitation for blessing (GELTS, 175); here, however, the visitation must be one of judgment (Hort; Best). ◆ **13** ὑποτάγητε aor. imp. pass. ὑποτάσσω (# 5718) to be in subjection, to submit oneself, to be subject to. The believer is to submit to civil authority (DLNT, 230-33). ἀνθρώπινος (# 474) human, that which is made by human beings, that which proceeds from men. For the suf. of the word s. MH, 378f. κτίσις (# 3232) creation, institution. The word may refer to institutions men have created (Best), or to creation by God, w. the previous adj. having the force "among man," so that the phrase means, "to every (divine) institution among men" (Hort). διὰ τὸν κύριον because of the Lord, for the Lord's sake (Kelly). βασιλεῖ dat. sing. βασιλεύς (# 995) king, emperor (Beare). ὑπερέχοντι pres. act. part. ὑπερέχω (# 5660) to send out above, to have it over, to be supreme. The word refers to the head of public administration, not deity (Beare). ◆ **14** ἡγεμόσιν dat. pl. ἡγεμών (# 2450) governor. The word has various applications but was specially applied about this time to governors of provinces, or proconsuls, whether appointed by the emperor or the senate (Hort; Best; BBC). πεμπομένοις pres. pass. part. πέμπω (# 4287) to send. Gnomic pres. stating a general truth. ἐκδίκησις (# 1689) punishment, legal punishment, avenging (Bigg). κακοποιῶν (# 2804) evildoer (s.v. 12). obj. gen., "punishment for evildoers." ἔπαινος (# 2047) praise. Governors demanded order in the home because many thought that the house is like a small city, and insubordination in one led to insubordination in the other (Balch, 94). ἀγαθοποιός (# 18) doing good, upright, one who does right as opposed to an evildoer (BAGD). Here, obj. gen., "praise for those who do good." ◆ **15** ἀγαθοποιοῦντας pres. act. part. ἀγαθοποιέω (# 18) to do good, to do right. Part. further defines the will of God and gives the manner or means "by showing yourselves to be good subjects," "by active beneficence" (Beare). φιμοῦν pres. act. inf. φιμόω (# 5821) to muzzle, to put to silence, to gag, to restrain (Hort). Epex. inf. explaining the will of God. ἄφρων (# 933) foolish, without reason, those who are senseless in what they are prone to say about Christianity (Stibbs). Here, gen. of description. ἀγνωσία (# 57) ignorant. The word suggests culpable ignorance rather than mere lack of knowledge (Best). ◆ **16** ἐλεύθερος (# 1801) free, freedman. To describe the ideal life in terms of freedom meant much for the ancient world because of its clear distinction between the slave and free man. The freedman could live with the family of the one freeing him, take the family name, and even receive his part of the inheritance, but he was always indebted to the one freeing him and was to always show respect (Best; LLAR, 114-15; ABD, 2:855-59; DPL, 881; A.M. Duff, *Freedmen in the Early Roman Empire*, Oxford, 1928). ἐπικάλυμμα (# 2127) that which covers over, veil, cloak. Here it signifies "pretext" (Hort). ἔχοντες pres. act. part. ἔχω (# 2400) to have. Circum. part., perhaps

w. imp. force. κακία (# 2798) evil. Obj. gen. here, indicating that which is covered up. ἐλευθερία (# 1800) freedom, liberty. θεοῦ δοῦλοι slaves to God. A freedman could become the slave of the one freeing him (DLNT, 1086-87). ◆ **17** τιμήσατε aor. imp. act. τιμάω (# 5506) to honor. Const. aor. denotes the total action w. special emphasis on carrying it to its final point (RWP; VANT, 375-77), but it may be better to view the aor. imp. as expressing a more urgent and authoritative force than the pres. (VANT, 374-75; Hort). ἀδελφότης (# 82) brotherhood. The word has the concrete sense of a band of brothers (Hort; RAC, 2:631-40; TDNT; NIDNTT; DC, 38:15; NW, 2, ii:1357). ἀγαπᾶτε pres. imp. act. ἀγαπάω (# 26) to love. φοβεῖσθε pres. imp. mid. (dep.) φοβέομαι (# 5828) to fear, to be afraid. τιμᾶτε pres. imp. act. τιμάω (# 5506) to honor. Pres. imp. calls for a continual attitude. ◆ **18** οἰκέται voc. pl. οἰκέτης (# 3860) household servant. The word denotes household slaves, many of whom might be well-educated and hold responsible positions in their households (Best; Goppelt; s. Philemon). The nom. w. the article is used as a voc. (Beare; M, 70). ὑποτασσόμενοι pres. mid. (dep.) part. ὑποτάσσω (# 5718) to submit. Part. is used as an imp. (Selwyn; Daube in Selwyn, 467-88). παντί (# 4246) used w. φόβῳ (# 5832) in all fear. Not fear of the masters to whom they are subject, but fear of God. It is the spirit of reverence toward Him that induces respect and faithfulness to duty in the sphere of human relationships (Beare). δεσπότης (# 1305) master, ruler, one who has complete authority. ἐπιεικέσιν dat. pl. ἐπιεικής (# 2117) mild, gentle (s. Phil. 4:5). καί (# 2779) even. σκολιός (# 5021) bent, crooked, severe, hard to deal w., harsh (Kelly; Selwyn; Phil. 2:15). ◆ **19** χάρις (# 5921) grace, thanks, excellence. The word is used here in the sense of that which is admirable, enhancing the esteem in which those who display it are held (Beare; TDNT). συνείδησις (# 5287) conscience (s. Rom. 2:15; RAC, 10:1025-107). ὑποφέρει pres. ind. act. ὑποφέρω (# 5722) to bear up under, to endure, to put up w. (Kelly; Goppelt). λύπας acc. pl. λύπη (# 3383) pain, sorrow. πάσχων pres. act. part. πάσχω (# 4248) to suffer. Part. could be temp. Mere endurance is no cause for pride. Slaves, like school boys, sometimes vied w. one another in the ability to endure corporal punishment without flinching. If the beating is deserved, there is no glory in bearing it; but to show patience in the face of injustice is true evidence of Christian character (Beare). ἀδίκως (# 97) adv., unjustly. ◆ **20** ποῖος (# 4481) what kind of, what sort of. κλέος (# 3094) reputation, prestige, glory, credit (Kelly; Selwyn). ἁμαρτάνοντες pres. act. part. (temp.) ἁμαρτάνω (# 279) to sin, to do wrong (Bigg). κολαφιζόμενοι pres. pass. part. κολαφίζω (# 3139) to strike w. the fist, to beat, to treat roughly. Since the word was used of Christ and His suffering (s. Matt. 26:67; Mark 14:65), Peter may be comparing the beating of a slave to the suffering Christ endured (Selwyn; Schelkle; TDNT). Temp. or circum. part. ὑπομενεῖτε fut. ind. act. ὑπομένω (# 5702) to endure, to patiently endure. ἀγαθοποιοῦντες pres. act. part. ἀγαθοποιέω (# 16) to do good, to do that which is right. πάσχοντες pres. act. part. πάσχω (# 4248) to suffer. Both temp. parts. Pres. indicates an action in progress. ◆ 21 τοῦτο (# 4047) this; i.e., the patient and cheerful endurance of maltreatment when you least deserve it (Kelly). ἐκλήθητε aor. ind. pass. καλέω (# 2813) to call. The divine pass. indicates that it is God who calls. In calling us "to his eternal glory" (5:10), "out of darkness into his marvelous light" (2:9), God also calls us to the exercise of this patient endurance of suffering that we have done nothing to deserve. In this very respect, Christ has given us a model of Christian conduct (Beare). ἔπαθεν aor. ind. act. πάσχω (# 4248) to suffer. ὑπολιμπάνων pres. act. part. ὑπολιμπάνω (# 5701) to leave behind. ὑπογραμμός (# 5681) copy, example. The word is used in 2 Macc. 2:28 of the outlines of a sketch the artist fills in w. detail. It is also used as the model of handwriting to be copied by the school boy, then fig. of a model of conduct for imitation (Bigg; Beare). ἐπακολουθήσητε aor. subj. act. ἐπακολουθέω (# 2051) to follow after, to follow upon, to follow closely (RWP). Subj. w. ἵνα (# 2671) is used to express purp. (RWP). or the cl. is epex. explaining the pattern or example (Beare). ἴχνεσιν dat. pl. ἴχνος (# 2717) footprint. In the pl. it means the line of footprints. To follow a man's footprints is to move in the direction he is going (Kelly). ◆ 22 ἁμαρτία (# 281) sin. ἐποίησεν aor. ind. act. ποιέω (# 4472) to do. The phrase ἁμαρτίαν ἐποίησεν ("to do sin") means to sin. εὑρέθη aor. ind. pass. εὑρίσκω (# 2351) to find. δόλος deceit (s.v. 1). στόμα (# 5125) mouth. ◆ 23 λοιδορούμενος pres. pass. part. λοιδορέω (# 3366) to abuse, to revile, to use vile and abusive language against someone, to heap abuse upon someone, to insult (TLNT; TDNT; T; GELTS, 284). Pres. part. indicates something done over and over. Part. could be concessive ("although he was repeatedly being ridiculed"), or it could be temp. ("while he was continually being ridiculed"). ἀντελοιδόρει impf. ind. act. ἀντιλοιδορέω (# 518) to return abuse, to give back abusive language in return. For the prep. in compound indicating reciprocal action s. MH, 297. Impf. is used for repeated incidence (RWP). πάσχων pres. act. part. πάσχω (# 4248) to suffer. ἠπείλει impf. ind. act. ἀπειλέω (# 580) to threaten. Impf. is either inchoative ("he did not begin to threaten") or iterative, emphasizing the repeated action (RWP). παρεδίδου impf. ind. act. παραδίδωμι (# 4140) to deliver over, to give over to, to entrust, to commit. κρίνοντι pres. act. part. κρίνω (# 3212) to judge. δικαίως (# 1469) adv., righteously, according to justice. Christ accepted without rebellion the unjust treatment meted out to Him, confident of vindication before God (Beare).

◆ 24 αὐτός (# 899) himself. ἀνήνεγκεν aor. ind. act. ἀναφέρω (# 429) to bear up, to bear away. Peter stresses the redemptive significance of Jesus' death by his use of OT sacrificial language (Best; Selwyn). ξύλον (# 3833) wood, tree. This is referring to His death on the cross (TDNT; Gal. 3:13). ἀπογενόμενοι aor. mid. (dep.) part. ἀπογίνομαι (# 614) to get away from, to die, to depart. The word is followed by the dat. of reference; i.e., to die in reference to sin (Selwyn; RWP). ζήσωμεν aor. subj. act. ζάω (# 2409) to live. μώλωπι dat. sing. μώλωψ (# 3698) whelp, bruise, wound caused by blows. The word denotes the welt or discolored swelling left by a blow from a fist or whip. The word strictly means a cut that bleeds; he thinks here of the lashing that draws blood (BAGD; Kelly; Beare). Instr. dat. ἰάθητε aor. ind. pass. ἰάομαι (# 2615) to heal. Peter, like Isaiah, uses physical healing as a metaphor for religious conversion; s. v. 25 (Michaels). ◆ 25 ἦτε impf. ind. act. εἰμί (# 1639) to be. πρόβατον (# 4585) sheep, echoing perhaps Isa. 53:6. πλανώμενοι pres. pass. (dep.) part. πλανάω (# 4414) to wander, to wander away, to go astray. Part. is used in periphrastic construction emphasizing the continual action in the past: "you were going astray" (Beare). ἐπεστράφητε aor. ind. pass. ἐπιστρέφω (# 2188) to turn, to return. ποιμένα acc. sing. ποιμήν (# 4478) shepherd (TDNT). ἐπίσκοπος (# 2176) overseer, guardian, bishop (Best; Kelly; TDNT; NIDNTT; DLNT, 224-25; 1 Tim. 3:1). The word interprets the metaphor of shepherd, combining the ideas of God's close and tireless scrutiny of the human heart w. the protecting care of His people (Michaels).

1 Peter 3

◆ 1 ὁμοίως (# 3931) adv., likewise, in like manner, referring to the passage on slaves. ὑποτασσόμεναι pres. mid. (dep.) part. ὑποτάσσομαι (# 5718) to be in subjection, to subject oneself. Circum. part. as imp. (s. 1:14; Balch, 97-98). Submission of wives to their husbands should be viewed in the light of the society of that day, esp. in the light of the wild activities of women in the worship of Dionysus (Lat. Bacchus) and Isis (Balch, 63-80; DDD, 855-60; NP, 3:651-64). ἴδιος (# 2625) one's own. ἀνδράσιν dat. pl. ἀνήρ (# 467) husband. Alexander the Great told his mother that it is proper for the wife to be submissive to her own husband; and Plutarch says that wives are to subordinate themselves, and the man is to exercise control "as the soul controls the body, by entering into her feelings and being knit to her through goodwill" (Balch, 98-99; s. Col. 3:18). ἵνα (# 2671) w. fut. (BD, 186-87). ἀπειθοῦσιν pres. ind. act. ἀπειθέω (# 578) to be disobedient, to disobey (s. 2:8). The ind. is used in a 1st. class cond. cl. assuming the reality of the cond. This reference to pagan husbands should be understood against the social background in which a wife was expected to accept the customs and religious rites of her husband (Balch, 99). **ἀναστροφή** (# 419) conduct, behavior; proper relations w. associates (Balch, 100; BBC; s. 1:15; Tal Ilan, *Jewish Women in Greco-Roman Palestine*, [Tübingen: J. C. B. Mohr: 1994], 59-61, 128-29; Tal Ilan, "How Women Differed," *BAR* 24 [1998]: 38-39, 68). **ἄνευ** (# 459) w. gen., without. There is a play on the word **λόγος**. The wives are to remain silent–"without a word"–so that the husbands disobedient to "the word" may be converted (Balch, 99). **κερδηθήσονται** fut. ind. pass. κερδέω (# 3045) to win, to gain. Here the vb. means to win over to a point of view (Selwyn; TDNT; Goppelt; David Daube, "Κερδαίνω as a Missionary Term," *HTR* 40 [1947]: 109-20; Balch, 99-100). ◆ **2 ἐποπτεύσαντες** aor. act. part. ἐποπτεύω (# 2227) to look at, to observe (s. 2:12). Temp. or causal part. **ἁγνήν** acc. sing. ἁγνός (# 54) pure, clean, chaste. Here it indicates the irreproachable conduct of the wife (Kelly). ◆ **3 ἔστω** pres. imp. act. εἰμί (# 1639) to be. **ἔξωθεν** (# 2033) outward. **ἐμπλοκή** (# 1862) plaited, braiding. **τριχῶν** gen. pl. θρίξ, τριχός (# 2582) hair. The braiding of the hair, along with bright clothes, was important in the cult of Artemis of Ephesus and the cult of Isis (Balch, 101-2). **περίθεσις** (# 4324) placing around, wearing. **χρυσίον** (# 5992) gold, gold jewelry. For references of writers in the ancient world who also spoke against the superficial preoccupation of women w. dress, jewelry, etc., s. Kelly; Goppelt; Selwyn, 432-39; Balch, 101f. **ἔνδυσις** (# 1906) putting on. **ἱμάτιον** (# 2668) garment, clothes. ◆ **4 κρυπτός** (# 3220) hidden. **ἄφθαρτος** (# 915) incorruptible (s. 1:4). **πραέως** gen. sing. πραΰς (# 4558) meek, gentle, controlled strength. The word refers to the humble and gentle attitude that expresses itself in a patient submissiveness; it could be used in the context of a meek and quiet spirit as a response to slander (Balch, 102-3; s. Matt. 5:5; Gal. 5:23). **ἡσύχιος** (# 2485) quiet. **πνεῦμα** (# 4460) spirit, disposition (Selwyn). Here gen. of definition (Beare). **ἐνώπιον τοῦ θεοῦ** (# 1967; 2536) in the presence of God. This stands in sharp contrast to the normal human experience. **πολυτελής** (# 4500) very valuable, costly. ◆ **5 οὕτως** (# 4048) so, thus, in this way. **ποτε** (# 4537) at that time, formerly. **ἅγιαι** nom. pl. ἅγιος (# 41) holy. **ἐλπίζουσαι** pres. act. part. (adj.) nom. fem. pl. ἐλπίζω (# 1827) to hope. **ἐκόσμουν** impf. ind. act. κοσμέω (# 3175) to put in order, to adorn. Here it refers to the correctness of a well-fitted garment, in no way outlandish or provocative. Christian women should dress themselves in good taste, appropriately (TLNT, 2:322; Col 3:18). For clothing in the ancient world s. ABD, 2: 235-38. Impf. indicates customary action, "they used to adorn themselves" (RWP). **ὑποτασσόμεναι** pres. mid. (dep.) part. ὑποτάσσομαι (# 5718) to submit. Part. of manner indicating how they adorned themselves. ◆ **6 Σάρρα** (# 4925) Sarah. Sarah is used as an example of this adorning w. a quiet spirit and of submission to her hus-

band (Balch, 103). **ὑπήκουσεν** aor. ind. act. ὑπακούω (# 5634) to listen to, to obey. **καλοῦσα** pres. act. part. καλέω (# 2813) to call. Temp. part. ("when she called him"), but it also gives an explanation of her obedience. For the example of Sarah calling Abraham lord in Jewish lit. s. Balch, 103-5; Michaels. **ἐγενήθητε** aor. ind. pass. (dep.) γίνομαι (# 1181) to become. The vb. γίνομαι insinuates that they were formerly pagans (Kelly). Aor. points to a one-time act (Goppelt). **ἀγαθοποιοῦσαι** pres. act. part. ἀγαθοποιέω (# 16) to do good. **φοβούμεναι** pres. mid. (dep.) part. φοβέομαι (# 5828) to be afraid, to have fear. Parts. provide proof that they have become Sarah's children, "in that you do good and are not a prey to terror" (Beare; Goppelt). **πτόησις** (# 4766) frightening, terrifying. The word means fluttering, excitement, perturbation of spirit caused by any passion, but more esp. by fear (Bigg). The acc. seems to be used as a cognate acc. (Beare). Wives must fear God and not be terrified of those in house or city who oppose their faith (Balch, 105). ◆ **7 συνοικοῦντες** pres. act. part. συνοικέω (# 5324) to live together. Part. used as an imp. (Selwyn). **γνῶσις** (# 1194) understanding. Here it means Christian insight and tact, a conscious sensitivity to God's will (Kelly; Beare). **ἀσθενεστέρῳ** comp. ἀσθενής (# 822) weak; comp., weaker. Here it may be weaker in the physical sense (Selwyn; Best; Beare; BBC). **σκεῦος** (# 5007) vessel, jar, instrument. The word may refer to the physical body (Selwyn; Schelkle). Dat. here could be the obj. of the part. συνοικοῦντες or be taken w. the part. ἀπονέμοντες (Michaels). **γυναικεῖος** (# 1221) female, woman. The n. adj. is used w. the article to denote an abstract noun (Selwyn). **ἀπονέμοντες** pres. act. part. ἀπονέμω (# 671) to assign, to show, to pay respect. Used here in the sense of showing honor to someone (BAGD). Used in the papyri in the sense of rendering one his dues, or showing gratitude (MM; NDIEC, 1:61-62; Preisigke, 1:190). Josephus uses the word to describe the honors Titus paid his troops after the destruction of Jerusalem (Jos., *JW*, 7:15; for other uses in Josephus s. CCFJ, 1:201). **συγκληρονόμος** (# 5169) fellow heir, joint heir; followed by the obj. gen., "fellow heirs of the grace of life," i.e., God's gracious gift of eternal life (Bigg). **ἐγκόπτεσθαι** pres. pass. inf. ἐγκόπτω (# 1601) to cut in on, to hinder (s. Gal. 5:7; 1 Thess. 2:18; TDNT; NIDNTT). Articular inf. w. the prep. εἰς (# 1650) to express purp. (RWP). **προσευχάς** acc. pl. προσευχή (# 4666) prayer. ◆ **8 τὸ τέλος** (# 5465) used adverbially, finally. In this adverbial sense the word always seems to introduce a fresh point, not simply summarize what has gone before. Here it affects the transition from specific ethical duties to a general statement of Christian character (Selwyn). **ὁμόφρων** (# 3939) like-minded; i.e., of that inward unity of attitude in spiritual things which make schism unthinkable (Beare); peace in all relations at home (BBC).

συμπαθής (# *5218*) full of sympathy, sharing in feeling. The word denoted a readiness to enter into and share the feelings of others and to unite alike in sorrow and in joy (Kelly; Beare). φιλάδελφος (# *5790*) love of brother, brotherly love. εὔσπλαγχνος (# *2359*) compassionate, compassionate tenderness (s. Eph. 4:32; TDNT; MNTW, 156f). ταπεινόφρων (# *5426*) humble minded (s. Phil. 2:3; TDNT; TLNT). ◆ **9** ἀποδιδόντες pres. act. part. ἀποδίδωμι (# *625*) to give back, to pay back. Part. is used as an imp. λοιδορία (# *3367*) railing, abuse, insult. τοὐναντίον (# *5539*) = τὸ ἐναντίον on the contrary (RWP). εὐλογοῦντες pres. act. part. εὐλογέω (# *2328*) to bless. Part. of manner. ἐκλήθητε aor. ind. pass. καλέω (# *2813*) to call (s. 2:21). Const. aor. w. the emphasis on the event and no reference to time. εἰς τοῦτο (# *1650; 4047*) for, unto this. It could refer to the previous context, or look forward to the inheritance of a blessing (Davids). κληρονομήσητε aor. subj. act. κληρονομέω (# *3099*) to inherit. Subj. w. ἵνα (# *2671*) to express purp. The idea here is of an inheritance as a free gift that comes, unmerited, to the recipient (Kelly). ◆ **10** θέλων pres. act. part. (subst.) θέλω (# *2527*) to desire to, w. inf. ἀγαπᾶν aor. act. inf. ἀγαπάω (# *26*) to love. ἰδεῖν aor. act. inf. ὁράω (# *3972*) to see. Compl. inf. to the preceding part. παυσάτω aor. imp. act. παύω (# *4264*) to cease, to stop. Here, to keep the tongue from evil (BAGD). For the change from the 2nd. pers. imp. of the LXX to the 3rd. pers. s. Selwyn. λαλῆσαι aor. act. inf. λαλέω (# *3281*) to speak. Compl. inf. to the preceding vb. δόλος (# *1515*) deceit (s. 2:1). ◆ **11** ἐκκλινάτω aor. imp. act. 3rd. pers. sing. ἐκκλίνω (# *1712*) to turn from, to turn away from. ποιησάτω aor. imp. act. ποιέω (# *4472*) to do. ζητησάτω aor. imp. act. ζητέω (# *2426*) to seek. διωξάτω aor. imp. act. διώκω (# *1503*) to hunt, to pursue. The words enjoin the same active and persistent effort on behalf of peace as enjoined in the beatitude in Matt. 5:9 (Selwyn). ◆ **12** ὀφθαλμός (# *4057*) eye. ὦτα nom. pl. οὖς (# *4044*) ear. δέησις (# *1255*) request, prayer. ποιοῦντας pres. act. part. ποιέω (# *4472*) to do. Pres. emphasizes the continual doing of something. Subst. part. without the art. stresses the character. ◆ **13** καί (# *2779*) besides. After the quotation from Psalm 34, the resumption is rapid and effects a swift and easy entrance into the new theme (Selwyn). κακώσων fut. act. part. (subst.) κακόω (# *2805*) to do evil to someone, to harm someone. The fut. part. has the idea, "who is going to harm you?" (Kelly). ζηλωτής (# *2421*) zealot, enthusiast, one who exercises zeal for an object (Selwyn; Best; DJG, 696-97). γένησθε aor. subj. mid. (dep.) γίνομαι (# *1181*) to become. Subj. w. ἐάν (# *1569*) in a 3rd. class cond. cl. which views the cond. as possible. ◆ **14** πάσχοιτε pres. opt. act. πάσχω (# *4248*) to suffer. The opt. is used in a cond. of the 4th class to imply that there is no certainty of fulfillment of the condition, "if perchance" (RWP; Best; BD, 195; BG, 111). There is no contradiction between this statement and 1 Peter 4:12ff, and no evidence that the letter should be divided into different writings. For arguments against viewing 1 Peter 4:12ff as a separate writing s. Kelly. μακάριος (# *3421*) happy, blessed, fortunate (TDNT; BAGD; NIDNTT). φοβηθῆτε aor. subj. pass. (dep.) φοβέομαι (# *5828*) to be afraid, to fear. Subj. w. the neg. μή (# *3590*) used to form a prohibition. ταραχθῆτε aor. subj. pass. ταράσσω (# *5429*) to shake, to disturb, to trouble. ◆ **15** ἁγιάσατε aor. imp. act. ἁγιάζω (# *39*) to sanctify; to venerate and adore Him, thus dispelling all fear of man (Beare). ἕτοιμος (# *2289*) ready, prepared. ἀεί (# *107*) always. ἀπολογία (# *665*) defense. The word was often used of the argument for the defense in a court of a law, and though the word may have the idea of a judicial interrogation in which one is called to answer for the manner in which he has exercised his responsibility (Beare), the word can also mean an informal explanation or defense of one's position. The word would aptly describe giving an answer to the skeptical, abusive, or derisive inquiries of ill-disposed neighbors (Kelly). αἰτοῦντι pres. act. part. αἰτέω (# *160*) to ask. Pres. would be iterative, "every time someone asks." Part. as subst., "the one asking." λόγος (# *3364*) account, a rational account of (Selwyn). ἐλπίδος gen. sing. ἐλπίς (# *1828*) hope (EH). In this letter hope is used almost as an equivalent for faith (s. 1:21; Best). ◆ **16** ἀλλά (# *247*) but, however. πραΰτης (# *4559*) meekness, gentleness. συνείδησις (# *5287*) conscience. ἔχοντες pres. act. part. ἔχω (# *2400*) to have. Pres. can mean to possess, to maintain. Part. is used as an imp. (Beare). καταλαλεῖσθε pres. ind. pass. καταλαλέω (# *2895*) to speak evil against. Pres. could be iterat., indicating an action that occurred repeatedly: "every time you are slandered." καταισχυνθῶσιν aor. subj. pass. καταισχύνω (# *2875*) to put to shame. Perhaps Peter was thinking of his personal experience at Pentecost, when the Jews first scoffed but then were pierced to the heart (Acts 2:13, 37) (Hort). Subj. w. ἵνα (# *2671*) in a purp. cl. ἐπηρεάζοντες pres. act. part. ἐπηρεάζω (# *2092*) to threaten, to mistreat, to abuse, to insult, to treat wrongfully, to deal despitefully w. someone. For examples from the papyri s. MM. ἀναστροφή (# *419*) behavior, conduct (s. 1:15). ◆ **17** κρεῖττον (# *3202*) n. comp. ἀγαθός good; comp., better. ἀγαθοποιοῦντας pres. act. part. ἀγαθοποιέω (# *16*) to do good. Part. is acc. pl., agreeing w. the subj. of the inf.; and causal, giving the reason for suffering. θέλοι pres. opt. act. θέλω (# *2527*) to desire. Opt. is used in a 4th class cond. cl. (s.v. 14). πάσχειν pres. act. inf. πάσχω (# *4248*) to suffer. Compl. inf. to main vb. κακοποιοῦντας pres. act. part. (causal) κακοποιέω (# *2803*) to do evil, to do wrong. For interpretation of this v. as referring to eschatological judgment s. J.R. Michaels, "Eschatology in 1 Peter 3:17," *NTS* 13 [1967]: 394-401. ◆ **18** ὅτι καὶ Χριστός because Christ also. This introduces a new application of the imitation of Christ–we pass from the patient Christ to the victorious Christ (Selwyn). ἀπέθανεν aor. ind. act. ἀποθνήσκω (# 633) to die. For the variant reading ἔπαθεν aor. ind. act. πάσχω (# 4248) to suffer s. TC, 692f; Selwyn; Kelly; Goppelt. προσαγάγῃ aor. subj. act. προσφέρω (# 4642) to lead or bring to, to introduce, to provide access for, to bring about a right relationship. Subj. w. ἵνα (# 2671) to express purp. or result. The word had various usages. It could denote the bringing of a person before a tribunal or presenting him at a royal court; it also denoted the ritual act of bringing a sacrifice to God or the consecration of persons to God's service (Kelly; TDNT; Eph. 2:18). θανατωθείς aor. pass. part. (circum.) θανατόω (# 2506) to put to death. σαρκί dat. sing. σάρξ (# 4922) flesh. The expression refers to the reality of Christ's physical death; the dat. is dat of reference (Selwyn). ζῳοποιηθείς aor. pass. part. ζῳοποιέω (# 2443) to make alive. The expression "in reference to spirit" could refer either to the Holy Spirit or to the spirit of Christ (Best). ◆ **19** ἐν ᾧ (# 1877; 4005) in which. The rel. pron. could refer to the word πνεύματι or it can refer to the state or circumstances (Selwyn, 315f; Reicke, 138; Best). φυλακῇ (# 5871) prison. πνεῦμα (# 4460) spirit. For a discussion of the identity s. DLNT, 1118-19. πορευθείς aor. pass. (dep.) part. πορεύομαι (# 4513) to go. ἐκήρυξεν aor. ind. act. κηρύσσω (# 3062) to proclaim, to preach. For various discussions and literature on this difficult passage s. Goppelt; Best; Selwyn, 314-62; Sherman E. Johnson, "The Preaching to the Dead," *JBL* 79 [1960]: 48-51; Bo Reicke, *The Disobedient Spirit and Christian Baptism* (Copenhagen, 1946); W.J. Dalton, *Christ's Proclamation to the Spirits* (Rome, 1965); Michaels; Davids; Brox; Grudem. ◆ **20** ἀπειθήσασιν aor. act. part. ἀπειθέω (# 578) to be disobedient (s. 2:8). ἀπεξεδέχετο impf. ind. mid. (dep.) ἀπεκδέχομαι (# 587) to earnestly and eagerly await w. expectancy, to wait out the time (Beare; Gal. 5:5). μακροθυμία (# 3429) longsuffering, patience (s. Rom. 2:4; Gal. 5:22). κατασκευαζομένης pres. pass. part. (temp.) κατασκευάζω (# 2941) to make ready, to build, to construct. Gen. abs. Pres. expressing contemporaneous time. κιβωτός (# 3066) box, ark. διεσώθησαν aor. ind. pass. διασῴζω (# 1407) to save through, to bring safe through (RWP; Acts 27:43). δι' ὕδατος (# 1328; 5623) through water. Prep. could be taken in a local sense–"they were brought to safety by passing through water"–or it could be taken in an instr. sense (Kelly). ◆ **21** ἀντίτυπος (# 531) antitype, n. adj. used as a noun (Goppelt). The word connotes the exactness of correspondence between the stamp and the die (Sewlyn; MM; Heb. 9:24). σῴζει pres. ind. act. σῴζω (# 5392) to save, to rescue. The saving by baptism Peter mentions here is symbolic not actual, as Peter hastens to explain (RWP). Baptism is the occasion and sign of transition from an old way of life to another that is marked by a new ethic. In accepting baptism the per-

son is affirming willingness to share in the known experience of baptized persons–suffering and treatment w. suspicion and hostility. This indicates that the main theme of 1 Peter is not baptism, but rather suffering (David Hill, "On Suffering and Baptism in 1 Peter," *Nov T* 17 [1976]: 181-89; for those who attempt to make this v. the key to 1 Peter and view the book as a baptismal instructional sermon s. Oscar S. Brooks, "I Peter 3:21-The Clue to the Literary Structure of the Epistle," *Nov T* 16 [1974]: 290-305; for Jewish parallels related to baptismal catechism for Jewish proselytes s. NTRJ, 106-40). ἀπόθεσις (# 629) putting off, putting away. ῥύπος (# 4866) filth, dirt. ἐπερώτημα (# 2090) question, inquiry, pledge, declaration of commitment. In the papyri there is evidence that this word was a t.t. in making a contract, denoting the pledge or undertaking given by one of the parties in answer to formal questions. The word then implies the registering of agreement to conditions or demands. Baptism is a response or commitment to God (DLNT, 117-19). Here the pledge is an assent to certain conditions; it may imply a confession of faith as well as the willingness to accept the new duties (David Hill, *NovT* 17, 187f; Reicke; Kelly; Michaels; TLNT; MM; Preisigke, 1:538). δι' ἀναστάσεως (# 1328; 414) through the resurrection. Baptism is a symbolic picture of the resurrection of Christ as well as our own spiritual renewal (RWP). ◆ **22** δεξιός (# 1288) right hand. For the meaning of being on the right hand s. Eph. 1:20. πορευθείς aor. pass. (dep.) part. πορεύομαι (# 4513) to go. Temp. part., "after he went." ὑποταγέντων aor. pass. part. (circum.) ὑποτάσσω (# 5718) to subject, to be in subjection, w. dat. Gen abs. ἀγγέλων καὶ ἐξουσιῶν καὶ δυνάμεων angels and authorities and powers. The designations embrace all ranks of spiritual beings (Beare; TDNT).

1 Peter 4

◆ **1** οὖν (# 4036) therefore. This word introduces the main lesson to be drawn from 3:18-22 (Bigg). παθόντος aor. act. part. πάσχω (# 4248) to suffer. Gen. abs., circum. or temp. ἔννοια (# 1936) thought, principle, counsel, mind, resolve. The principle of thought and feeling here referred to is the dying life voluntarily accepted and put on as armor, and finding expression in the meek and courageous pursuit of the spiritual life (Selwyn; Bigg). For the philosophical meaning of the word s. GPT 57. ὁπλίσασθε aor. imp. mid. (dep.) ὁπλίζομαι (# 3959) to arm oneself w. weapons. The idea of the word is, "put on as your armor" (Selwyn), "arm yourselves w. the same insight" (Goppelt). παθών aor. act. part. πάσχω (# 4248) to suffer. Part. used here as a noun, "the one who has suffered." For a discussion of this as a reference to Christ s. Michaels. πέπαυται perf. ind. mid. (dep.) παύομαι (# 4264) to cease. The word seem to have been a proverbial expression related to

Romans 6:7 w. the suffering taken to mean dying in the sense of dying to sin (Best; Beare; Stibbs). Perf. stresses the cond. or state. ◆ **2** εἰς τό in order that. The words introduce a purp. cl. (RWP). μηκέτι (# 3600) no longer. ἐπιθυμία (# 2123) strong desire, lust, passion. θέλημα (# 2525) will. Here dat. of advantage, indicating personal interest. These two dat. could also express the rules by which man shapes his life (Bigg). ἐπίλοιπος (# 2145) remaining. βιῶσαι aor. act. inf. βιόω (# 1051) to live. ◆ **3** ἀρκετός (# 757) sufficient. The sense of the word is "more than sufficient," "far too much" (Beare). The word may be used ironically to mean "more than enough" (Kelly; Goppelt). παρεληλυθώς perf. act. part. παρέρχομαι (# 4216) to go by, to pass by. One after another, the three perfs. in this v. emphasize the thought that this past of theirs is a closed chapter; that part of the story is over and done w. (Beare). βούλημα (# 1088) will, wish. κατειργάσθαι perf. mid. (dep.) inf. κατεργάζομαι (# 2981) to produce, to work, to accomplish. πεπορευμένους perf. mid. (dep.) part. πορεύομαι (# 4513) to go. The word is used here in sense of the Hebrew word הָלַךְ ("to walk," "to conduct one's life") (Bigg; Selwyn; TDNT; TDOT, 3:391-92). ἀσέλγεια (# 816) unbridled and unrestrained living. The word describes the spirit that knows no restraints and dares whatever caprice and wanton insolence suggest (NTW 26; TDNT; Gal. 5:19). ἐπιθυμία (# 2123) lust, passion. οἰνοφλυγία (# 3886) wine bubbling up, drunkenness. The context shows that the word means habitual drunkards (RWP; Selwyn). κῶμος (# 3269) drunken party, reveling. The word originally referred to a band of friends who accompanied home a victor in the games. They rejoiced and sang his praises. But the word degenerated until it came to mean a carousal, a band of drunken revellers swaying and singing their way through the streets (NTW, 27; BBC; LLAR, 49-51). The public parties and revelings were associated w. the cult of certain gods, esp. Dionysus (Selwyn; DDD, 480-90; s. Eph. 5:18). πότος (# 4542) drinking, drinking parties. ἀθέμιτος (# 116) abominable, unrighteous, lawless. εἰδωλολατρία (# 1630) worship of idols, idolatry. The prominence here is on sexual and alcoholic excess, w. the stress on idolatry (Kelly). ◆ **4** ἐν ᾧ in which thing, wherein, in which manner of life (Bigg). ξενίζονται pres. ind. pass. ξενίζω (# 3826) to entertain, to entertain strangers, to astonish, to surprise; pass., to be entertained as a guest (BAGD). The word has the idea of being surprised or entertained by the novelty of a thing or being surprised or upset at a new turn of events (Selwyn). The word also includes the thought of taking offense, as ignorant people often feel an unreasonable resentment at anything that does not fit into the pattern of life familiar to them. The matter of this resentful astonishment is expressed by the gen. abs. that follows (Beare). συντρεχόντων pres. act. part. συντρέχω (# 5340) to run

together. The metaphor suggests joining in a mad race (Beare). Gen. abs. describes that which is considered to be thought strange. ἀσωτία (# 861) wasteful, riotous living, dissipation (TDNT; s. Eph. 5:18). ἀνάχυσις (# 431) pouring forth. The word was used of the rock pools filled up by the sea at high tide (Selwyn), or of a swamp formed by the pouring of waters. Here it has the active verbal sense followed by the obj. gen. ("outpouring of profligacy"), w. the thought of the life of paganism as a feverish pursuit of evil wherein men vie to pour forth profligate living (Beare). βλασφημοῦντες pres. act. part. βλασφημέω (# 1059) to defame someone, to injure the reputation of someone, to blaspheme (BAGD). Circum. part. to be translated as a main vb., "they consider it strange and defame you." ◆ **5** ἀποδώσουσιν fut. ind. act. ἀποδίδωμι (# 625) to pay back, to give account. ἑτοίμως (# 2290) adv., ready. ἔχοντι pres. act. part. ἔχω (# 2400) to have. Dat. here indicates to whom account is rendered, "to the one who stands ready." For this construction s. Kelly; RWP; Acts 21:13. κρῖναι aor. act. inf. κρίνω (# 3212) to judge. Inf. is epex. explaining the readiness. ζῶντας pres. act. part. (subst.) ζάω (# 2409) to live. νεκρός (# 3738) dead. The phrase, "the living and the dead" means "all men" (Best). ◆ **6** νεκροῖς dat. pl. (# 3738) s.v. 5 "to the dead." The reference may be to those who are spiritually dead, but it seems better to understand the term as referring to those to whom the gospel was preached and have since died (Stibbs). εὐηγγελίσθη aor. ind. pass. εὐαγγελίζω (# 2294) to proclaim the good news, to evangelize, to preach the gospel. κριθῶσι aor. subj. pass. κρίνω (# 3212) to judge. Subj. w. ἵνα (# 2671) is used in a purp. cl. ζῶσι pres. subj. act. ζάω (# 2409) to live. For the omission of the moveable nu (ν) s. GGP, 1:114. κατὰ θεόν (# 2848; 2536) according to God. The phrase either could mean "in the eyes of God" (Kelly) or "in God's likeness," "as God lives," i.e., eternally (Selwyn). ◆ **7** ἤγγικεν perf. ind. act. ἐγγίζω (# 1581) to come near; perf., to be at hand. σωφρονήσατε aor. imp. act. σωφρονέω (# 5404) to be sound in mind. The word connotes the cool head and balanced mind to exercise self-control or moderation (Beare; Selwyn; GPT, 179f; TDNT; TLNT). νήψατε aor. imp. act. νήφω (# 3768) to be sober, to keep a clear head (Kelly). ◆ **8** πρὸ πάντων (# 4574; 4246) before all things, above all. ἐκτενής (# 1756) strenuous, intense (s. 1:22). ἔχοντες pres. act. part. ἔχω (# 2400) to find. καλύπτει pres. ind. act. καλύπτω (# 2821) to cover, to hide. The proverbial expression may be a quotation or adaptation of Prov. 10:12 (Best; Beare). Gnomic pres., indicating that which is constantly true. πλῆθος (# 4436) multitude. ◆ **9** φιλόξενος (# 5811) hospitality, entertaining of strangers. The lack of a network of decent hotels for ordinary people resulted in a readiness to provide board and lodging for friends and other suitable sponsored travelers that was more highly esteemed than it is today (Kelly; for Jewish parallels s. SB, 3:297; and in general RAC, 8:1061-123; TDNT). γογγυσμός (# *1198*) murmuring, complaining, grumbling. These words add a sharp twang of realism. Then as now guests could overstay or otherwise abuse their host's welcome; it is a good reminder that hospitality can be an exasperating chore, to be shouldered cheerfully if it is to be worthwhile (Kelly).   ◆ **10** ἕκαστος (# *1667*) each one. καθώς (# *2777*) just as. ἔλαβεν aor. ind. act. λαμβάνω (# *3284*) to receive. χάρισμα (# *5922*) gift, gracious gift, grace gift (s. 1 Cor. 1:7; DPL, 339-47; TDNT; NIDNTT). διακονοῦντες pres. act. part. διακονέω (# *1354*) to minister, to serve. οἰκονόμος (# *3874*) steward. The word denotes a slave who was responsible for managing his master's property or household and for distributing wages, food, etc. to its members (Kelly; s. 1 Cor. 4:1; TDNT; TLNT). ποικίλος (# *4476*) many-colored, manifold, variegated.   ◆ **11** λαλεῖ pres. ind. act. λαλέω (# *3281*) to speak. Ind. in a 1st. class cond. assuming the truth of the cond. λόγον (# *3359*) utterance, oracle. The word sometimes means "Scripture," and in classical Gr. it means any divine utterance (Selwyn). διακονεῖ pres. ind. act. διακονέω (# *1354*) to serve. ἰσχύς (# *2709*) strength, might. χορηγεῖ pres. ind. act. χορηγέω (# *5961*) to supply. The word originally meant to be in a chorus. Then it meant "to supply a chorus" and so produce a play at one's own risk. Finally it simply meant to furnish or supply anything (Selwyn). δοξάζηται pres. subj. pass. δοξάζω (# *1519*) to glorify. Subj. w. ἵνα (# *2671*) used to express purp.   ◆ **12** ἀγαπητός (# *28*) one loved, beloved. ξενίζεσθε pres. imp. pass. ξενίζω (# *3826*) to entertain, to entertain strangers (s.v. 4). πύρωσις (# *4796*) burning, fiery. The word was often used in the sense of a purifying or refining fire (Goppelt). πειρασμός (# *4280*) trial, ordeal. γινομένη pres. mid. (dep.) part. (subst.) γίνομαι (# *1181*) to become. ξένος (# *3828*) strange, foreign. συμβαίνοντος pres. act. part. (temp.) συμβαίνω (# *5201*) to happen, to occur. Gen. abs.   ◆ **13** καθό (# *2771*) insofar; far as, according to which thing (RWP). κοινωνεῖτε pres. ind. act. κοινωνέω (# *3125*) to share in, to have fellowship. πάθημα (# *4077*) suffering. χαίρετε pres. imp. act. χαίρω (# *5897*) to be happy, to rejoice. Pres. imp. calls for continual rejoicing. ἀποκάλυψις (# *637*) revelation. χαρῆτε aor. subj. act. χαίρω (# *5897*) to rejoice. Subj. w. ἵνα (# *2671*) in a purp. cl. ἀγαλλιώμενοι pres. mid. (dep.) part. ἀγαλλιάομαι (# *22*) to be exuberantly happy (s. 1:6). Part. w. the imp. is emphatic, "rejoice w. rapture" (Selwyn).   ◆ **14** ὀνειδίζεσθε pres. ind. pass. ὀνειδίζω (# *3943*) to revile, to insult. The word, used in the LXX for reproaches heaped on God and His saints by the wicked, in the NT becomes associated w. the indignities and maltreatment Christ had to endure (Kelly). ἀναπαύεται pres. ind. mid. ἀναπαύω (# *399*) to give rest, to refresh.   ◆ **15** πασχέτω pres. imp.

act. 3rd. sing. πάσχω (# *4248*) to suffer. φονεύς (# *5838*) murder. κλέπτης (# *3095*) thief. κακοποιός (# *2804*) evildoer. ἀλλοτριεπίσκοπος (# *258*) one who looks after the affairs of another, agitator, mischief maker, meddling in domestic affairs (Kelly; Best; Michaels; Balch, 93-94).   ◆ **16** αἰσχυνέσθω pres. imp. pass. αἰσχύνω (# *159*) to put to shame; pass., to be put to shame. δοξαζέτω pres. imp. act. δοξάζω (# *1519*) to glorify.   ◆ **17** ἄρξασθαι pres. mid. (dep.) inf. ἄρχομαι (# *806*) to begin. The construction of the inf. is unusual and may be in apposition or epex. (RWP). ἀπειθούντων pres. act. part. ἀπειθέω (# *578*) to be disobedient (s. 2:8).   ◆ **18** μόλις (# *3660*) w. difficulty, scarcely. The words do not imply doubt about the salvation of Christians, but emphasize the greatness of God's effort in saving them (Best). σώζεται pres. ind. pass. σώζω (# *5392*) to save. ἀσεβής (# *815*) ungodly. ἁμαρτωλός (# *283*) sinner. φανεῖται fut. ind. mid. (dep.) φαίνομαι (# *5743*) to appear.   ◆ **19** ὥστε (# *6063*) therefore, wherefore. The word sums up the thought of the entire paragraph (Beare). καί (# *2779*) also. The word introduces a new thought; the certainty of divine justice is a call to a complete serenity of faith in God (Selwyn). πάσχοντες pres. act. part. (subst.) πάσχω (# *4248*) to suffer. κτίστης (# *3234*) creator. παρατιθέσθωσαν pres. imp. pass. παρατίθημι (# *4192*) to deliver over to, to entrust, to entrust for safe keeping. ἀγαθοποιΐα (# *17*) active well-doing (Kelly).

1 Peter 5

◆ **1** παρακαλῶ pres. ind. act. παρακαλέω (# *4151*) to beseech, to encourage (Rom. 12:1). συμπρεσβύτερος (# *5236*) fellow elder. Here the word πρεσβύτερος (# *4565*) elder, denotes the officials who acted as pastoral leader of the congregations (Kelly; TDNT; Michaels; BBC; DLNT, 1090-93). μάρτυς (# *3459*) witness. παθημάτων gen. pl. πάθημα (# *4077*) suffering. μελλούσης pres. act. part. (subst.) μέλλω (# *3516*) to be about to. ἀποκαλύπτεσθαι pres. pass. inf. ἀποκαλύπτω (# *636*) to reveal. Compl. inf. to the preceding part. κοινωνός (# *3128*) partner, sharer.   ◆ **2** ποιμάνατε aor. imp. act. ποιμαίνω (# *4477*) to shepherd. Aor. may be ingressive ("take up the task of shepherding" [Beare]), or it may call for a specific act w. a note of urgency (VANT, 371-79). ἐπισκοποῦντες pres. act. part. ἐπισκοπέω (# *2174*) to oversee (s. 1 Tim. 3:1). ἀναγκαστῶς (# *339*) forced, constrained. ἑκουσίως (# *1731*) willingly. αἰσχροκερδῶς (# *154*) adv., shameful gain, shamefully greedy (LN, 1:292; TLNT). προθύμως (# *4610*) zealously, eagerly. The word is extremely strong and expresses enthusiasm and devoted zeal (Kelly).   ◆ **3** κατακυριεύοντες pres. act. part. κατακυριεύω (# *2894*) to lord it over someone, to domineer, to exercise complete control. Prep. in compound indicates that the action is unfavorable to an object (MH, 316). κλῆρος (# *3102*) lot, charge. The word probably refers to the flock or those who were put in charge of the flock (Best; Beare). **τύπος** (# 5596) pattern, example. **γινόμενοι** pres. mid. (dep.) part. γίνομαι (# 1181) to become. ◆ **4 φανερωθέντος** aor. pass. part. φανερόω (# 5746) to appear. **ἀρχιποίμην** (# 799) chief shepherd, master shepherd. The designation on a wooden mummy label, as well as in other writings, indicates it was not an uncommon designation (LAE, 99-101; Michaels). **κομιεῖσθε** fut. ind. mid. (indir. mid) κομίζω (# 3152) to bring; mid., to get for oneself, to receive, to obtain (BAGD). **ἀμαράντινος** (# 277) unfading (s. 1 Pet. 1:4). ◆ **5 ὁμοίως** (# 3931) adv., likewise. **νεώτεροι** voc. pl. comp. νέος (# 3742) new, young; comp., younger. Adj. as subst., "young men." **ὑποτάγητε** aor. imp. pass. (dep.) ὑποτάσσομαι (# 5718) to submit, to be in subjection. **ταπεινοφροσύνη** (# 5425) lowly thinking, humility (TDNT; TLNT). **ἐγκομβώσασθε** aor. imp. mid. (dep. or dir. mid.) ἐγκομβόομαι (# 1599) to tie or fasten something on oneself firmly w. a clasp, knot, or bow. The word was also used of a slave who tied on an apron; then the idea may be that of wearing humility as a slave's apron (TLNT; Selwyn; Beare). **ὑπερήφανος** (# 5662) showing oneself above others, proud, arrogant (AS). The proud person has a heart that is puffed up, who compares himself to others and, reckoning he is above them, scorns them (TLNT). **ἀντιτάσσεται** pres. ind. mid. (dep.) ἀντιτάσσω (# 530) to line up against, to oppose, to resist. **ταπεινός** (# 5424) lowly, humble. ◆ **6 ταπεινώθητε** aor. imp. pass. ταπεινόω (# 5427) to make low, to humble; pass., to humble oneself, to humble (TLNT; TDNT; EDNT; DLNT, 961-63). Aor. calls for a specific act w. a note of urgency. **κραταιός** (# 3193) strong, mighty (Eph. 1:19). **ὑψώσῃ** aor. subj. act. ὑψόω (# 5738) to exalt, to lift up, to make high. Subj. w. **ἵνα** (# 2671) to express purp. or result. Aor. points to the event. ◆ **7 πᾶσαν τὴν μέριμναν ὑμῶν** (# 4246; 3533; 5148) your total care. The adj. πᾶς w. noun and its art. stresses the total aspect of the noun (BAGD). The word **μέριμναν** indicates worry, anxiety. It is the translation for the Heb. יהב (yehab) in Ps. 54:23 (LXX) (55:23 Heb.), where the meaning of the Heb. is uncertain. The meaning would be, "a burden, load of trouble that comes from our lot in life." The meaning of the word "care" is uncertain and may mean, "casting all your troubles that come from your lot in life on the Lord" (BDB; Marvin Tate, *Psalms 51-100,* Word Biblical Commentary [Dallas: Word, 1990]. Note the Vulgate translation of the Heb. in Ps. 54:23, *curam tuam* ["your trouble"].) The words are emphatic by their position in the cl. **ἐπιρίψαντες** aor. act. part. ἐπιρίπτω (# 2166) to throw at, to throw something upon something else; e.g., to throw clothes on an animal for riding (Luke 19:35); to throw a mantle on someone (Jos., *Ant.,* 8:353 [Elijah throws his mantle on Elisha]; BAGD; for the LXX s. GELTS, 173). Part. is to be closely connected w. the imp. **ταπεινώθητε** (either as imp., or as part. of man-

ner), showing that the true Christian attitude is not neg. self-abandonment or resignation, but involves as the expression of one's self-humbling the trusting of oneself and one's troubles to God (Kelly). This is probably a quotation from Ps. 55:22 (54:23 LXX; 55:23 Heb.). The aor. imp. of the LXX ἐπίρριψον (Heb. הַשְׁלֵךְ), is the part. ἐπιρίψαντες in Peter and the word "all" (πᾶσαν) has been added. **μέλει** (# 3508) pres. ind. act. to have concern, to have a care, impersonally w. the dat. (BAGD). **αὐτῷ** dat. sing. αὐτός (# 899) self; "(there is constant care and concern) to him." ◆ **8 νήψατε** aor. imp. act. νήπω (# 3768) to be sober. **γρηγορήσατε** aor. imp. act. γρηγορέω (# 1213) to stay awake, to be watchful, to be on the alert. Aor. imp. rings sharply: "be alert!" Confidence in God must not lead to slackness; the spiritual warfare that they wage demands vigilance (Beare). **ἀντίδικος** (# 508) legal adversary, opponent in a law suit. The word then denotes an enemy in general (Kelly). **διάβολος** (# 1333) slanderer, devil (TDNT; DDD). **λέων** (# 3329) lion, the most ferocious animal (BBC). **ὠρυόμενος** pres. mid. (dep.) part. (adj.) ὠρύομαι (# 6054) to roar. Pres. pictures the continual roaring of Satan as a lion. **περιπατεῖ** pres. ind. act. περιπατέω (# 4344) to walk about. **ζητῶν** pres. act. part. ζητέω (# 2426) to seek, to look for. **καταπιεῖν** aor. act. inf. καταπίνω (# 2927) to swallow down, to eat up, to devour. The word lit. means "to drink down," but it can be used of an animal swallowing its prey (Jonah 2:1; Kelly). Epex. inf. explaining his seeking, or it could express purp. ◆ **9 ἀντίστητε** aor. imp. act. ἀντίστημι (# 468) to stand up against, to withstand, to resist. Aor. could be ingressive, "take your stand against." **στερεός** (# 5104) compact, solid, firm, steadfast (Selwyn; Kelly). **εἰδότες** perf. act. part. (causal) οἶδα (# 3857) to know. Def. perf. w. pres. meaning. **ἀδελφότης** (# 82) brotherhood (s. 2:17; MM). **ἐπιτελεῖσθαι** pres. mid./pass. inf. ἐπιτελέω (# 2200) to complete, to perform, to lay something upon someone (BAGD); mid. the meaning can be, "is required," "to pay in full" (MT, 55), w. the idea of knowing how to pay "the same tax of suffering" (Bigg). The mid. could also mean "to fulfill a religious duty," "to perform the obligations of piety." The gen. **παθημάτων** would be a gen. of definition and the meaning would be "to make the same fulfillment (of duty toward God) of sufferings" (Beare). If the pass. is adopted, the phrase might be translated, "knowing that the same tax of suffering will be paid by our brotherhood" (Best). The inf. is used as the obj. of the vb. εἰδότες. ◆ **10 καλέσας** aor. act. part. (subst.) καλέω (# 2813) to call. Aor. points to a completed action. **παθόντας** aor. act. part. πάσχω (# 4248) to suffer. Temp. part., "after you have suffered." **καταρτίσει** fut. ind. act. καταρτίζω (# 2936) to put in order, to mend, to reestablish, to make whole. The word could be used in a medical sense of setting a broken bone, or of repairing and refitting a damaged vessel (Sewlyn; Beare; TDNT; Gal. 6:1). **στηρίξει** fut. ind. act. στηρίζω (# 5114) to set up, to fix firmly, to establish, to strengthen (BAGD; MM). **σθενώσει** fut. ind. act. σθενόω (# 4964) to strengthen, to make strong (Kelly; BAGD). **θεμελιώσει** fut. ind. act. θεμελιόω (# 2530) to make a foundation, to provide a solid foundation, to ground firmly (Goppelt). ◆ **12 λο-γίζομαι** (# 3357) pres. ind. act. to reckon, to count as, to regard. This does not imply that others have doubted the ability of Silvanus, but it emphasizes Peter's confidence in his fidelity (Best; Michaels). **ἔγραψα** aor. ind. act. γράφω (# 1211) to write; epistolary aor., "I am writing" (Beare). **παρακαλῶν** pres. act. part. παρακαλέω (# 4151) to encourage (s.v. 1). **ἐπιμαρτυρῶν** pres. act. part. ἐπιμαρτυρέω (# 2148) to testify, to affirm, to supply evidence that, to confirm that fact by evidence (Selwyn; Goppelt). **εἶναι** pres. act. inf. εἰμί (# 1639) to be.

Inf. in indir. discourse. **στῆτε** aor. imp. act. ἵστημι (# 2705) to stand; ingressive aor., "take your stand" (RWP). For the structure of the v. s. Michaels. ◆ **13 ἀσπάζεται** pres. ind. mid. (dep.) ἀσπάζομαι (# 832) to greet. **Βαβυλών** (# 956) Babylon. This could be the literal city of Babylon, a designation for the city of Rome, or a metaphor for both the actual city (Rome) and for an experience of alienation not necessarily linked to any place (Michaels; Davids; Brox; DLNT, 111-12). **συνεκλεκτή** (# 5293) fem. adj., fellow elect. The fem. could refer to the local church from which the letter was written (Kelly). **Μᾶρκος** (# 3453) Mark. John Mark is intended, but was not the physical son but rather the spiritual son of Peter (Best). ◆ **14 ἀσπάσασθε** aor. imp. mid. (dep.) ἀσπάζομαι (# 832) to greet. **φίλημα** (# 5799) kiss (s. 1 Cor. 16:20). **ἀγάπη** (# 27) love. Here gen. of description.

2 Peter

2 Peter 1

◆ **1** ἀπόστολος (# 693) apostle, one appointed by another to carry out a task on behalf of, in the name of, and with the authority of the one who appoints (TDNT; EDNT; TLNT; s. Rom. 1:1). Nom. in apposition to Simon Peter and without the art. stresses the character. ἰσότιμος (# 2700) w. the same honor, equal in value, equal in privilege, status or rank in civil life. Here the word could have the meaning "equal privilege" or "equally privileged"; i.e., a faith that carries equal privileges (Mayor), or equal in status or rank (Bauckham; Grundmann). ἡμῖν dat. pl. ἐγώ (# 1609) I; "w. us." The contrast could be between Jews and Gentiles who have equal privileges; but it is almost certainly between the apostles, who had been eyewitnesses of the original revelation (cf. 2 Pet. 1:16), and the Christians of the second or even third generation (Kelly; Bigg). λαχοῦσιν aor. act. part. λαγχάνω (# 3275) to obtain by lot, to obtain. The word implies a gift of favor, and God gives to all Christians equal privileges in His city (Bigg). πίστις (# 4411) faith. Here it is not the faith as a body of doctrine, but the faith or God-given capacity to trust Him that brings a man salvation (Green). δικαιοσύνη (# 1466) righteousness. τοῦ θεοῦ (# 2536) of God. Subjective gen., God is the one who dispenses righteousness. The one definite art. governing the two nouns θεοῦ, Ἰησοῦ indicates that they are the same person, thus stressing the deity of Jesus (GGBB, 270-77).
◆ **2** πληθυνθείη aor. opt. pass. πληθύνω (# 4437) to multiply, to increase; pass., to be multiplied, to grow, to increase as here–"may grace and peace be yours in ever greater measure" (BAGD). Opt. is used to express a wish or desire (RWP; GGBB, 483; s. 1 Peter 1:2). ἐπίγνωσις (# 2106) knowledge directed toward a particular object which can imply a more detailed or fuller knowledge (Mayor, 171-74; Bauckham). ◆ **3** θείας gen. sing. θεῖος (# 2521) godly, divine. The term "divine power" was a phrase used for God. A parallel expression is found in the decree of Stratonicea, an inscription in honor of Zeus and Hekate (BS, 460-68; MM). δυνάμεως gen. sing δύναμις (# 1539) power. Gen. as subject of the part. δεδωρημένης. εὐσέβεια (# 2354) godliness, true religion that displays itself in reverence before what is majestic and divine in worship, and in a life of active obedience which befits that reverence (MNTW, 67ff; TDNT; NIDNTT; s. 1 Tim. 2:2). δεδωρημένης perf. mid.

(dep.) part. δωρέομαι (# 1563) to give as a gift, to grant, to bestow (BAGD; GELTS, 124; MM). Gen. abs., circum. part. translated as a main vb. Perf. emphasizes the continuing nature of what was given. καλέσαντος aor. act. part. καλέω (# 2813) to call. ἀρετή (# 746) virtue, excellence, the display of divine power and divine acts (s. 1 Peter 2:9). Dat. here could be either instr. ("by") or dat. of advantage ("to," "for") (RWP). ◆ **4** δι' ὧν (# 1328; 4005) through which things. The antecedent of the rel. pron. would be the words δόξῃ and ἀρετῇ (Bigg). τίμιος (# 5508) honorable, precious, valuable. μέγιστος (# 3492) greatest, magnificent; elative superl., very great. ἐπάγγελμα (# 2041) that which was promised, promise. δεδώρηται perf. ind. mid. (dep.) δωρέομαι (# 1563) to give as a gift (s.v. 3). γένησθε aor. subj. mid. (dep.) γίνομαι (# 1181) to become, to be. Subj. w. ἵνα (# 2671) is used to express purp. κοινωνός (# 3128) partner, sharer, partaker (TDNT; EDNT). φύσις (# 5882) nature. Peter does not mean that man is absorbed into deity but rather that they who partake of Christ will partake of the glory to be revealed (Green; Kelly). ἀποφυγόντες aor. act. part. ἀποφεύγω (# 709) to escape, to escape completely. ἐπιθυμία (# 2123) strong desire, lust, passion (DNP, 2:542-44). φθορά (# 5785) corruption. The basic meaning of the word denotes not a sudden destruction owing to external violence, but a dissolution brought on by means of internal decay–"rottenness" (Mayor, 175-79). ◆ **5** σπουδή (# 5082) haste, effort (TLNT; Bauckham). παρεισενέγκαντες aor. act. part. παρεισφέρω (# 4210) to bring in alongside of. Used idiomatically w. the word σπουδήν to express the idea of bringing in every effort. We are to bring into this relationship, alongside what God has done, every ounce of determination we can muster (Green; Bigg; Kelly; Mayor; BS, 361). ἐπιχορηγήσατε aor. imp. act. ἐπιχορηγέω (# 2220) to supply in addition to, to outfit the chorus w. additional (complete) supplies (RWP). Aor. imp. calls for a specific action w. a note of urgency. Prep. in compound seems to have an accumulative force: "to add further supplies," "to provide more than was expected or could be demanded" (Mayor), "to give lavishly, w. generosity" (Kelly; Green; Bigg; s. Gal. 3:5; 1 Peter 4:11). ἐν (# 1877) w. dat., in. The sense is: since you have faith, let it not be wanting in virtue, etc. (Huther). πίστις (# 4411) faith. Here it is to be understood subjectively of loyal adhesion to Christian teaching rather than that teaching itself (Kelly). **ἀρετή** (# 746) virtue, moral energy. In classical times the word meant the god-given power or ability to perform heroic deeds–whether military, athletic, or artistic accomplishments or the conducting of one's life. This ability needed to be demonstrated again in each situation that presents a challenge. The basic meaning of the word indicates the quality by which one stands out as being excellent. In ethics Aristotle held that it was the right behavior, or mean, between two extremes. The Stoics connected it w. nature, teaching that the excellency of virtue was living harmoniously w. nature (Mayor; TDNT; BBC; GPR, 25; KP, 1:530-31). **γνῶσις** (# 1194) knowing, knowledge. ◆ **6 ἐγκράτεια** (# 1602) self-control; lit., "holding himself in" (RWP; Gal. 5:23). ◆ **7 φιλαδελφία** (# 5789) brotherly love, affection for one's fellow believer in Christ. In the NT the term has acquired a highly specialized meaning which restricts the range of reference to fellow believers (LN, 1:292; for references to the word φιλάδελφος from Bithynia in a non-Christian context s. NDIEC, 2:103; 3:87). ◆ **8 ταῦτα** nom. pl. οὗτος (# 4047) this; "these things;" i.e., "the possession of these qualities and their continued increase" (Mayor). **ὑπάρχοντα** pres. act. part. ὑπάρχω (# 5639) to be, to exist. **πλεονάζοντα** pres. act. part. πλεονάζω (# 4429) to abound, to increase. In the classical writers the word is a term of disparagement implying excess–to be or to have more than enough, to exaggerate. But to fervent Christianity there can be no excess of good (Mayor). Pres. emphasizes the continual action. **ἀργός** (# 734) not active, inactive, idle. **ἄκαρπος** (# 182) not fruitful, unfruitful. **καθίστησιν** pres. ind. act. καθίστημι (# 2770) to bring a person to a place, to make (Bigg). ◆ **9 πάρεστιν** pres. ind. act. πάρειμι (# 4205) to be by, to be present. **τυφλός** (# 5603) blind. **μυωπάζων** pres. act. part. μυωπάζω (# 3697) to be short-sighted. The word refers to the involuntary contraction of the half-closed eyes of a short-sighted man; the word may be a correction or limitation of the idea of being blind (Mayor; for eye diseases s. DNP, 2:277-79). On the other hand, the meaning may be "shutting the eyes to the truth," the intention being to emphasize the responsibility of the believer (Kelly; NW, 2, ii:1387; Bauckham). **λήθη** (# 3330) forgetfulness. **λαβών** aor. act. part. λαμβάνω (# 3284) to take, to receive. Used in the expression, "having received forgetfulness," i.e., "to forget." Part. could be causal, "because he has forgotten" (Bigg). **καθαρισμός** (# 2752) cleansing, purifying. **πάλαι** (# 4093) old. ◆ **10 διὸ μᾶλλον** (# 1475; 3437) wherefore the more (Bigg). **σπουδάσατε** aor. imp. act. σπουδάζω (# 5079) to be in a hurry, to give diligence, to exert effort, to apply oneself to, to actively involve oneself w. (TLNT). The word stresses the urgency of his plea that they should determine to live for God (Green). Aor. imp. calls for a specific action w. a note of urgency.

βέβαιος (# 1010) firm, secure. Used w. inf. in the sense of, to make firm, to certify, to confirm, to attest. In the papyri the word was a t.t. for a legal guarantee (Mayor; BS, 107; TDNT; TLNT; s. 1 Cor. 1:6). **κλῆσις** (# 3104) calling. **ἐκλογή** (# 1724) selection, election, choosing. **ποιεῖσθαι** pres. mid. inf. ποιέω (# 4472) to do, to make. Mid. could indicate "to make," or "to do something for or of oneself" (BAGD). Used w. the adj. in the sense of "to make certain," "to give a guarantee." The holy life is the guarantee demonstrating one's calling and election to others. The inf. is epex. or compl. explaining the vb. σπουδάσατε. **ποιοῦντες** pres. act. part. ποιέω (# 4472) to make. Part. could be means ("by doing this") or cond. ("if you continually do this"). **οὐ μή** (# 4024; 3590) never in any wise. **πταίσητε** aor. subj. act. πταίω (# 4760) to stumble. Subj. w. double neg. for a strong negation. **ποτε** (# 4537) ever; after οὐ μή, not ever, never. ◆ **11 πλουσίως** (# 4455) adv., richly. **ἐπιχορηγηθήσεται** fut. ind. pass. ἐπιχορέω (# 2220) to supply in addition to (s.v. 5). **εἴσοδος** (# 1658) the way in, entrance. **βασιλεία** (# 993) kingdom. ◆ **12 μελλήσω** fut. act. ind. μέλλω (# 3516) to be about to, to be on the point of doing something. The vb. is used w. the inf. to express the idea, "I shall take care to remind you." This thought of the duty of reminding his readers appears again in verses 13 and 15, and in 3:1 (Mayor; RWP). **ἀεί** (# 107) always, ever. The word implies a prospect of frequent communication between them (Mayor). **ὑπομιμνήσκειν** pres. act. inf. ὑπομιμνήσκω (# 5703) to remember. **καίπερ** (# 2788) although. Used w. the part. to express concession. **εἰδότας** perf. act. part. οἶδα (# 3857) to know (ND, 344f). Def. perf. w. a pres. meaning. **ἐστηριγμένους** perf. pass. part. στηρίζω (# 5114) to set up, to formally establish, to strengthen. Perf. indicates the settled state or condition. Part. is used to express concession. **παρούσῃ** pres. act. part. πάρειμι (# 4205) to be present. ◆ **13 ἡγοῦμαι** pres. ind. mid. (dep.) ἡγέομαι (# 2451) to consider, to think. **ἐφ' ὅσον** (# 2093; 4012) for as long as. **σκήνωμα** (# 5013) tent. For the concept of the tent picturing the body s. 2 Cor. 5:1; Mayor. **διεγείρειν** pres. act. inf. διεγείρω (# 1444) to wake out of sleep, to stir up. Prep. in compound is perfective: to stir up or wake up thoroughly (RWP; Mayor). Epex. inf. to explain that which Peter considers to be right. **ὑπόμνησις** (# 5704) remembering, reminder. ◆ **14 εἰδώς** perf. act. part. οἶδα (# 3857) to know. Def. perf. w. a pres. meaning. Causal part., "because I know." **ταχινός** (# 5442) speedy, soon, swiftly. The word here could mean either suddenly or soon (Bigg). **ἀπόθεσις** (# 629) putting off. The word could be used for the idea of putting off clothing (Bigg; Kelly; TDNT). **ἐδήλωσέν** aor. ind. act. δηλόω (# 1317) to reveal, to make clear (BAGD). For a discussion of the prophecy to which he refers s. Bauckham. ◆ **15 σπουδάσω** fut. ind. act. σπουδάζω (# 5079) to give diligence (s.v. 10). **καί** (# 2779) even. Here he speaks of making provision for them after his death (Mayor). ἑκάστοτε (# 1668) every time, on each occasion; i.e., whenever there is need (Mayor). ἔξοδος (# 2016) departure, exodus. The word is used to indicates death (Bigg; Green). ποιεῖσθαι pres. mid. inf. ποιέω (# 4472) to do, to make. Used w. the noun μνήμη (# 3647) remembering, w. the meaning, to recall, to remember. Inf. is used to complete the idea of the main vb., "to make an effort to recall." ◆ 16 σεσοφισμένοις perf. pass. part. (adj.) σοφίζω (# 5054) to make wise, to be wise, to behave wisely, to cleverly contrive, to concoct subtly, to reason out subtly (Mayor; Kelly; BAGD). Here in the sense of cleverly devised, calculated to manipulate. Perf. indicates a state or condition. μῦθος (# 3680) myth, fable. The word stood for mythical stories about gods, the creation of the world, miraculous happenings, etc. (Kelly; NIDNTT; TDNT; Bigg; Mayor; GPT, 120f). Apparently the mockers of 2 Pet. 3:3 said the Christian hope of the glories to come rested on factitious prophecies (Mayor). ἐξακολουθήσαντες aor. act. part. ἐξακολουθέω (# 1979) to follow after, to follow out, to rest upon, w. dat. Josephus uses the word to indicate that Moses did not give the Law like others did who followed myths (τοῖς μύθοις ἐξακολουθήσαντες) (Jos., Ant., 1:21-23; NW, 2. ii:1389-91; for the papyri usages s. MM). Aor. indicates that the action was not done at all. ἐγνωρίσαμεν aor. ind. act. γνωρίζω (# 1192) to make known. Aor. points to a completed action. παρουσία (# 4242) coming. The word was often used as a term for the appearance of a god or arrival of a king or ruler (Schelkle; TDNT; TLNT; 1 Thess. 3:13). ἐπόπτης (# 2228) one who sees w. his eyes, eyewitness (s. Luke 1:2). γενηθέντες aor. act. part. γίνομαι (# 1181) to become, to be. Aor. points to the specific event. μεγαλειότης (# 3484) majesty. The word means divine majesty and is used here to express it as revealed in the transfiguration of Jesus (Green). ◆ 17 λαβών aor. act. part. (temp.) λαμβάνω (# 3284) to take, to receive. Aor. points to the completed event. τιμή (# 5507) honor. Here the word denotes the exalted status which the proclamation of sonship implies, while δόξαν points to the ethereal radiance of the transfigured Jesus, a participation in that splendor of light which according to OT conceptions belongs to God's very being (Kelly; Mayor). ἐνεχθείσης aor. pass. part. φέρω (# 5770) to bring, to bear. The sense of the word is to make a word, speech, announcement, charge, and it is used of a divine proclamation, whether dir. or indir. (BAGD). τοιόσδε (# 5524) such, such as this, of this kind. The word refers to what follows as so unique (BAGD). μεγαλοπρεπής (# 3485) magnificent, sublime, majestic. The word was used in the papyri as a term of honor and respect for political personalities. As preparations were made for the reception of a Roman senator in Egypt the instructions were, "let him be received w. special magnificence" (MM; Mayor;

TLNT; NDIEC, 2:108-9). It was common for the Jews to use such statements when referring to God Himself (Schelkle; Bauckham). δόξης gen. sing. δόξα (# 1518) glory. Gen. of description. ἀγαπητός (# 28) one who is loved, beloved. εὐδόκησα aor. ind. act. εὐδοκέω (# 2305) to be well-pleased, to be satisfied w. The word suggests the good pleasure of the Father alighting and remaining on Jesus (Green). ◆ 18 ἠκούσαμεν aor. ind. act. ἀκούω (# 201) to hear, to listen to. ἐνεχθεῖσαν aor. pass. part. φέρω (# 5770) to carry, to take. Temp. part., "when we were taken." ὄντες pres. act. part. εἰμί (# 1639) to be. Temp. part., "when (while) we were on the holy mountain." Pres. points to the event as taking place at the same time as the main vb. ◆ 19 ἔχομεν pres. ind. act. ἔχω (# 2400) to have. βεβαιότερον comp. βέβαιος (# 1010) firm, certain; comp., more certain, more sure. For this word, s.v. 10. Peter is saying that the Holy Scriptures are more certain than experience. He is saying, "If you don't believe me, go to the Scriptures" (Green). προφητικός (# 4738) prophetic, that which pertains to the message of a prophet. The prophetic word was a current expression embracing the OT as a whole and not simply the prophets proper (Kelly). καλῶς (# 2822) adv., well. ποιεῖτε pres. ind. act. ποιέω (# 4472) to do. προσέχοντες pres. act. part. προσέχω (# 4668) to hold the mind on something, to give heed to (RWP). The part. could be understood either as cond. ("if you give heed"), or it could express the manner or means of doing well ("by giving heed to"). λύχνῳ dat. sing. λύχνος (# 3394) lamp. φαίνοντι pres. act. part. φαίνω (# 5743) to shine. Pres. emphasizes the continual shining. αὐχμηρός (# 903) dry and parched, dirty, dark, murky. The word does not imply absolute darkness, but dingy and dusky obscurity, in contrast to the brightness of Messiah's rising (Isa. 60:3; Rom. 13:12; Mayor; BBC; RWP; MM). The word may also connote "dirty" since that which is dirty is destitute of brightness; thus light shows up the dirt and makes possible its removal (T; Green). τόπος (# 5536) place. The phrase αὐχμηρῷ τόπῳ describes the world as it at exists at present, which in the NT is regularly characterized as darkness (Kelly). ἕως οὗ (# 2401; 4005) until, until which time. Temp. conjunction w. subj. is a normal construction for fut. (RWP; Mayor). διαυγάσῃ aor. subj. act. διαυγάζω (# 1419) to shine through, to break, to dawn (BAGD). The word is used of the first streaks of dawn breaking through the darkness (Mayor). Subj. in an indef. temp. cl. φωσφόρος (# 5892) light bringing, light bringer, the morning star; i.e., the planet Venus. The imagery lay ready at hand, for the famous prophecy in Num. 24:17-"there shall come a star out of Jacob"-was understood in Judaism to point to the Messiah (Kelly); the coming of the Messiah is also compared to the dawn in Malachi 4:2 (Mayor). For the eschatological and messianic interpretation of Num. 24:17 in the DSS

s. 1 QM11, 6-7f. In Greek and Roman times the term was applied not only to the morning star (Venus), but also to royal and divine persons (Green; KP, 5:1179-80; MM). **ἀνατείλῃ** aor. subj. act. ἀνατέλλω (# 422) to rise, to arise. **ἐν ταῖς καρδίαις** in your hearts. This phrase could possibly be connected w. the part. of v. 20 to mean, "knowing this first and foremost in your hearts." Or the rising of the morning star in Christian hearts at the dawning of the day may mean the glow of anticipation in Christian hearts when "the finds of the approaching Day are manifest to Christians" (Green; Mayor). ◆ **20 γινώσκοντες** pres. act. part. γινώσκω (# 1182) to know. Part. could be causal, or else continues the construction of v. 19 ("you do well giving heed"), defining the spirit and feeling w. which the Scriptures should be read: "recognizing this truth first of all..." (Mayor). Pres. indicates a continuing knowledge. **πᾶσα** nom. sing. πᾶς (# 4246) all. Used w. the neg. **οὐ** (# 4024) in the sense of "not even one" (BG, 151; RG, 753). In the sing. the word πᾶς without the article means "every," in a distributive sense: "every single one" (BG, 61). **προφητεία** (# 4735) the message of a prophet, prophecy. **γραφή** (# 1210) writing, Scripture. Normally in the NT the word denotes the OT (Kelly). **ἴδιος** (# 2625) one's own. It was the mark of a false prophet to speak "his own thing" of from himself (Mayor). **ἐπίλυσις** (# 2146) releasing, solving, explaining, interpreting. The word almost comes to mean inspiration (Green; Mayor; MM). The gen. (ablative) here indicates source. Peter is talking about the divine origin of Scripture, not about its proper interpretation (Green). **γίνεται** pres. ind. mid. (dep.) γίνομαι (# 1181) to become. ◆ **21 θέλημα** (# 2525) will. Here instr. dat. **ἠνέχθη** aor. ind. pass. φέρω (# 5770) to bear. The word was used of bearing, conveying, or uttering a divine proclamation and it could also have the sense of "to produce," "to bring forth" (BAGD; T). Aor. indicates the completed action. **φερόμενοι** pres. pass. part. φέρω (# 5770) to carry; pass., to be carried, to be borne along. Pres. describes the action as it was in progress. The word was used of a ship carried along by the wind (s. Acts 27:15, 17). The metaphor here is of prophets raising their sails, the Holy Spirit filling them and carrying their craft along in the direction He wished. Men spoke; God spoke (Green). The part. expresses contemporaneous time. **ἐλάλησαν** aor. ind. act. λαλέω (# 3281) to speak. For references to the inspiration of the Scripture s. 2 Tim. 3:16.

2 Peter 2

◆ **1 ἐγένοντο** aor. ind. mid. (dep.) γίνομαι (# 1181) to become, to appear, to arise. **καί** (# 2779) also, too. In addition to the holy men who spoke the inspired Word of God there were also some in Israel—now history was repeating itself (Green). **ψευδοπροφήτης** (# 6021) false

prophet. The compound in the word may either mean falsely named—a sham or counterfeit—or it may mean falsely doing the work implied—to speak falsely, and either meaning would suit the word, for to prophesy falsely in the narrow sense was one of the marks of a pretender prophet (Mayor). **ἔσονται** fut. ind. mid. (dep.) εἰμί (# 1639) to be. **ψευδοδιδάσκαλος** (# 6015) false teacher (Mayor, CLXII-CLXXX). They are the antithesis of the apostles, teaching a false message of human invention rather than the apostolic message based on the divine words (Bauckham). **οἵτινες** nom. pl. ὅστις (# 4015) whoever; who belongs to a particular class or group. **παρεισάξουσιν** fut. ind. act. παρεισάγω (# 4206) to bring into alongside of, to smuggle in. The word may signify to bring in secretly, w. the 1st prep. in compound giving the idea of creeping along under some sort of cover (Bigg; s. Gal. 2:4). **αἵρεσις** (# 146) heresy, false teaching. The term was used for a school of thought and could designate the particular teaching of such a school (Bauckham). **ἀπώλεια** (# 724) destruction. Here gen. of product, indicating what the teachings produce (GGBB, 106-7). **ἀγοράσαντα** aor. act. part. (adj.) ἀγοράζω (# 60) to buy at the marketplace, to buy, to purchase, to redeem, to pay a price for buying (TDNT; TLNT; DLNT, 1001-4). The price of their redemption had been paid, but they had not taken it by faith (Blum). **δεσπότης** (# 1305) lord, master, one who holds authority over another. **ἀρνούμενοι** pres. pass. part. (adj.) ἀρνέω (# 766) to deny. **ἐπάγοντες** pres. act. part. ἐπάγω (# 2042) to bring upon. **ταχινός** (# 5442) quick, sudden, soon. ◆ **2 ἐξακολουθήσουσιν** fut. ind. act. ἐξακολουθέω (# 1979) to follow, to follow after. **αὐτῶν** gen. pl. αὐτός (# 899) self; "their." The pron. refers to the false teachers, whose bad example will be largely followed (Mayor). **ἀσέλγεια** (# 816) unbridled living. The pl. may denote either different forms or repeated habitual acts of lasciviousness (Bigg; s. 1 Peter 4:3; Gal. 5:19). **δι᾽ οὕς** (# 1328; 4005) because of whom. The reference is clearly to the many backsliders (Kelly). **ἡ ὁδὸς τῆς ἀληθείας** (# 3847; 237) the way of truth. The phrase refers to the teaching of the truth, the correct teaching, the correct religion (Schelkle). Here the expression denotes the Christian message and way of life that are inevitably brought into discredit when their adherents identify themselves w. patently immoral courses (Kelly). Gen. of description. **βλασφημηθήσεται** fut. ind. pass. βλασφημέω (# 1059) to injure the reputation of someone, to defame, to blaspheme (TDNT; TLNT). ◆ **3 πλεονεξία** (# 4432) uncontrolled greed, insatiable greed (TDNT; NTW, 97; Rom. 1:29; 2 Cor. 9:5; 1 Thess. 2:5). **πλαστός** (# 4422) made up, factitious. The word was used in the papyri of a forged contract (MM; Mayor), and Josephus uses the word for falsified documents or writings (Jos., *Life*, 177, 337; CCFJ, 3:419). **ἐμπορεύσονται** fut. ind. mid. (dep.) ἐμπορεύομαι (# 1864) to travel as a merchant, to travel on business, to carry on business, to trade in, to cheat, to make a gain of, to exploit (Kelly; Mayor). **κρίμα** (# 3210) the decision of a judgment, verdict, condemnation, judgment. **ἔκπαλαι** (# 1732) for a long time, from of old. **ἀργεῖ** pres. ind. act. ἀργέω (# 733) to be not working, to be idle. The judgment is not idle, but already active in the punishment of others, and gathering up for these false teachers (Mayor). **νυστάζει** pres. ind. act. νυστάζω (# 3818) to nod, to sleep, to nap. The word was used of God's judgement which would come on the unrighteous (Isa. 5:27 LXX; Bauckham). Pres. points to an action in progress, "their destruction is not napping." In the OT, implicit in the phrase "God slumbers" is a disbelief in his existence (Jerome H. Neyrey, "The Form and Background of the Polemic in 2 Peter," *JBL* 99 [1980]: 415). ◆ **4 ἁμαρτησάντων** aor. act. part. (adj.) ἁμαρτάνω (# 279) to sin. **ἐφείσατο** aor. ind. mid. (dep.) φείδομαι (# 5767) w. gen. to spare. Ind. is used in a 1st. class cond. cl. which assumes the reality of the cond. **σειρά** (# 4937) chain, rope. The variant σιρός (# 4987) is properly a pit for the storage of grain, but was used for a large bin that held edible roots or for a pit made for trapping a wolf (Mayor). **ζόφος** (# 2432) dark, darkness. **ταρταρώσας** aor. act. part. ταρταρόω (# 5434) to confine in Tartarus. Tartarus was the name in classical mythology for the subterranean abyss in which rebellious gods and other such beings, like the Titans, were punished. The word, however, was taken over into Hellenistic Judaism and used in the book of Enoch (1 Enoch 20:2) in connection w. fallen angels; it is the angel Uriel who rules Tartarus (Kelly; Mayor; Bigg; KP, 5:530-31; NW, 2, ii:1399-1403; DLNT, 459-62; GELTS, 469). **παρέδωκεν** aor. ind. act. παραδίδωμι (# 4140) to deliver over, to hand over, to confine. **κρίσις** (# 3213) judging. **τηρουμένους** pres. pass. part. (adj.) τηρέω (# 5498) to keep. ◆ **5 ἀρχαῖος** (# 792) ancient. Here, gen. as obj. of the vb. φείδομαι. **ἐφείσατο** aor. ind. mid. (dep.) φείδομαι (# 5767) to spare. **ὄγδοος** (# 3838) eighth; Noah w. seven others, he being the eighth (BD, 130). **δικαιοσύνη** (# 1466) righteousness. The word denotes here the just or upright moral behavior (Kelly). **κήρυκα** acc. sing. κήρυξ (# 3061) preacher, herald (s. 1 Tim. 2:7). **ἐφύλαξεν** aor. ind. act. φυλάσσω (# 5875) to guard, to watch over, to protect. **κατακλυσμός** (# 2886) flood, deluge. Often as a judgment (BBC). **ἀσεβής** (# 815) ungodly, impious (s. Rom. 4:5). **ἐπάξας** aor. act. part. ἐπάγω (# 2042) to bring upon. Temp. part., expressing contemporaneous action. ◆ **6 Σοδόμων καὶ Γομόρρας** (# 5047; 2779; 1202) of Sodom and Gomorrah; gen. of apposition (BD, 92; Mayor; GGBB, 97; ABD, 6: 99-103). **τεφρώσας** aor. act. part. τεφρόω (# 5491) to reduce to ashes; or perhaps here, better, to cover w. ashes (Mayor). The Roman historian Dio Cassius used the word to describe the inner part of Mount Vesuvius that was constantly growing brittle

and being reduced to ashes so that the center section over time settled and became concave (Dio Cassius, *Roman History,* 66:21, 2). **καταστροφή** (# 2953) overturning, destruction. Here, instr. dat. **κατέκρινεν** aor. ind. act. κατακρίνω (# 2891) to pronounce a verdict against someone, to sentence to punishment, to condemn. The vb. continues the cond. of the 1st. cond. cl., beginning w. v. 4, which assumes the reality of the cond. (RWP). **ὑπόδειγμα** (# 5682) pattern, example. **μελλόντων** pres. act. part. (adj.) μέλλω (# 3516) to be about to. used w. the inf. to form the fut. **ἀσεβεῖν** pres. act. inf. ἀσεβέω (# 814) to live ungodly, to be impious; to commit impious deeds (s.v. 5; BAGD). For the variant reading ἀσεβής (# 815) ungodly; here, "ungodly men," which would give the sense, "unto ungodly men of things about to be," i.e., of things in store for them s. RWP; TC, 702. **τεθεικώς** perf. act. part. τίθημι (# 5502) to place, to make, to constitute. Perf. emphasizes that the example still has lasting validity. ◆ **7 δίκαιος** (# 1465) righteous. Jewish tradition interpreted Abraham's plea on behalf of the righteous in Sodom to refer to Lot and so could speak of him as a righteous man (Bauckham; SB, 3:769-71). **καταπονούμενον** pres. pass. part. καταπονέω (# 2930) to wear down through exhausting work, to trouble greatly. **ἄθεσμος** (# 118) lawless. It pictures them as being rebels against the law of nature and conscience, not Moses' Law (Bigg). **ἀσέλγεια** (# 816) licentiousness, unbridled living; here, "in unbridled living" (s.v. 2). Prep. phrase (**ἐν ἀσελγείᾳ**) indicates the sphere in which their conduct displayed itself. **ἀναστροφή** (# 419) behavior, conduct (s. 1 Peter 1:15). **ἐρρύσατο** aor. ind. mid. (dep.) ῥύομαι (# 4861) to rescue. ◆ **8 βλέμμα** (# 1062) sight. The word is generally subjective, in that the eye reveals to outsiders the inner feeling of man. The idea would be, "the righteousness of man showed itself in his shrinking from the sights and sounds which met him on every side"; lit., "righteous in look and in hearing he tortured himself at their lawless deeds while he lived among them" (Mayor). Here instr. dat. **ἀκοή** (# 198) hearing. Here instr. dat. **ἐγκατοικῶν** pres. act. part. (temp.) ἐγκατοικέω (# 1594) to live or dwell among. Pres. describes contemporary action. **ἄνομος** (# 491) lawless. **ἔργοις** dat. pl. ἔργον (# 2240) work, deed. **ἐβασάνιζεν** impf. ind. act. βασανίζω (# 989) to torture, to torment. Impf. pictures the continual action of the past time. The rabbis generally viewed Lot as one who despised God and was given over to immorality (SB, 3:769-71). Compare, however, the statements recorded in the Genesis Apocryphon (1 Qap Gen, XXI 5-7): "pasturing his herds he (Lot) reached Sodom and he bought himself a house in Sodom and settled in it. But I remained in the hill country of Bethel, and it grieved me that my nephew Lot had parted from me" (*Aramaic Text from Qumran with Translations and Annotations by B. Jongeling, C.J. Labuschagne, A.S. Van Der*

Voude [Leiden: E.J.Brill, 1976], 105; AT, 165-87; MPAT, 100-127). ◆ **9 οἶδεν** perf. ind. act. οἶδα (# 3857) to know. Def. perf. w. a pres. meaning. **εὐσεβής** (# 2356) God-fearing, godly, devout (s. 1:3). **ῥύεσθαι** pres. mid. (dep.) part. ῥύομαι (# 4861) to punish. Epex. inf. to the main vb., "He knows how to save." The original sense of the word was "to cut short" and was used of pruning a tree; later it took on the meaning "to correct" and then "to punish" and was used of the punishment of slaves as well as divine punishment (BAGD; MM; Kelly). **κολαζομένους** pres. pass. part. κολάζω (# 3134) to punish. Pres. part could be contemporaneous, describing the punishment before the last judgement, or it could be a futuristic pres. and refer to the final judgement (Bauckham). **τηρεῖν** pres. act. inf. τηρέω (# 5498) to keep. Vs. 4-9 present a list of biblical figures who could not hide from God and did not escape divine judgement, thus indicating that God's past judgement are grounds for His future action (Jerome H. Neyrey, "The Form and Background of the Polemic in 2 Peter," *JBL* 99 [1980]: 427-28). ◆ **10 μάλιστα** (# 3436) especially. **ὀπίσω** (# 3958) w. gen., after. The phrase **τοὺς ὀπίσω σαρκός** "them (that walk) after the flesh" suggests sodomy (Green). **ἐπιθυμία** (# 2123) strong desire, lust, passion. **μιασμός** (# 3622) pollution. The gen. here could be obj. gen. ("in their hankering after pollution"), but if it is subjective it would mean "in lust which pollutes" (Kelly). **πορευομένους** pres. mid. (dep.) part. πορεύομαι (# 4513) to walk, to go. **κυριότη** (# 3262) lordship. **καταφρονοῦντας** pres. act. part. καταφρονέω (# 2969) to think down upon, to despise. The false teachers despised the power and majesty of the Lord (Bigg). **τολμητής** (# 5532) one who dares, one who is brazen; headstrong daredevils, shameless and headstrong. The word smacks of the reckless daring that defies God and man (Mayor; Green). **αὐθάδης** (# 881) self-pleasing, arrogant. The word is used for an obstinate fellow determined to please himself at all costs (Green; RWP; s. Titus 1:7). **δόξα** (# 1518) glory; here, "glorious ones." The word could refer to angelic beings, either those heavenly beings in God's service or celestial beings, probably the fallen angels (Kelly; HSB, 727-29). **τρέμουσιν** pres. ind. act. τρέμω (# 5554) to tremble, to be afraid to (GELTS, 479). The vb. is completed by the compl. part. rather than by an inf. (RWP). Pres. indicates a continual action. **οὐ** (# 4024) **βλασφημοῦντες** pres. act. part. βλασφημέω (# 1059) to defame, blaspheme (TLNT; TDNT). ◆ **11 ὅπου** (# 3963) where, in a case in which, whereas, seeing that (Mayor). **ἰσχύς** (# 2709) strength, indwelling strength (RWP; s. Eph. 1:19). **μείζονες** (# 3505) comp. μέγας great; comp., greater, superior. **ὄντες** pres. act. part. εἰμί (# 1639) to be. Concessive part. ("although"). **φέρουσιν** pres. ind. act. φέρω (# 5770) to bear, to bring. Pres. emphasizes a continual attitude which is negated by the neg. particle **οὐ**

(# 4024). **βλάσφημος** (# 1061) defamation, railing, blaspheming (TLNT). ◆ **12 ἄλογος** (# 263) without reason, irrational. They have physical but not intellectual life; they are not better than the brutes that perish (Bigg). **ζῷα** nom. pl. ζῷον (# 2442) living creature, animal, beast. **γεγεννημένα** perf. pass. part. (adj.) γεννάω (# 1164) to bear; pass. to be born. Perf. emphasizing the continuing state of life after birth. **φυσικός** (# 5879) natural, pertaining to nature, in accordance w. nature; here used in the sense of "mere creatures of instinct, born to be caught and killed" (BAGD). **ἅλωσις** (# 274) capture. **φθορά** (# 5785) corruption, destruction. The combination of the vb. w. the noun makes it almost certain that destruction is meant (Bigg). **ἀγνοοῦσιν** pres. ind. act. ἀγνοέω (# 51) to be without knowledge, to be ignorant. These have no more knowledge than brute beasts would have (Kelly). **βλασφημοῦντες** pres. act. part. βλασφημέω (# 1059) to blaspheme. **φθαρήσονται** fut. ind. pass. φθείρω (# 5780) to corrupt, to decay, to destroy, to devastate (Mayor, 175ff; s. 1:4). ◆ **13 ἀδικούμενοι** pres. mid./pass. part. ἀδικέω (# 92) to commit injustice, to do wrong; mid. or pass., to suffer injustice, to be damaged, to be harmed (Kelly). The phrase "being defrauded of the wages of fraud" has been vindicated by a parallel example from the papyri, which reads, "when this has been done [in the context, 'when a receipt has been given'], we shall not be defrauded" (Green). It could also mean that they suffer recompense for their wrongdoing (Bauckham). **μισθός** (# 3635) wage, recompense. **ἀδικία** (# 94) unrighteousness, fraud. **ἡδονή** (# 2454) pleasure. In the NT the word always means sensual gratification (Bigg). **ἡγούμενοι** pres. mid. (dep.) part. ἡγέομαι (# 2451) to consider, to reckon, to count. **τρυφή** (# 5588) indulgence, reveling. Daytime debauchery was frowned on even in degenerate Roman society (Green; Kelly). Dio Chrysostom quotes Alexander the Great as saying that other men "had all been well-nigh ruined in soul by luxury and idleness and were slaves of money and pleasure" (DC 4:6). **σπίλος** (# 5070) spot, blot, a disfiguring spot (Bigg). **μῶμος** (# 3700) blemish. The accusation is one of riotous misbehavior at banquets, and since the correspondents participated in these it would seem to be some kind of community celebration (Kelly) **ἐντρυφῶντες** pres. act. part. ἐντρυφάω (# 1960) to live in luxury, to revel (for the wild parties, and banqueting s. LLAR, 33-53; Petronius, *Satyrica*; Athenaeus, *The Deipnosophists*). **ἀπάτη** (# 573) deception. Perhaps the meaning here is dissipations, so the transition from guile or deception to sinful pleasure was natural and easy (Kelly). **συνευωχούμενοι** pres. mid. (dep.) part. συνευωχέομαι (# 5307) to feed well, to feed abundantly, to eat together, to feast w. (RWP). Part. denotes the circumstances of the preceding action (Mayor). ◆ **14 ἔχοντες** pres. act. part. (adj.) ἔχω (# 2400) to have. **μεστός** (# 3550) full. This is a vivid expression which means that their eyes are always looking for a woman with whom to commit adultery (Bauckham). Plutarch, in discussing compliance says, "And so, as the orator said that the shameless man (ἀναίσχυντον) had harlots (πόρνας), not maidens (κόρας the word can also mean "pupils of the eyes), in his eyes, so the compliant man ...." (Plutarch, "On Compliancy," *Moralia*, 528, E; NW, 2, ii:1406-07; Bauckham). **μοιχαλίδος** (# 3655) adulteress. The connotation is probable more general, w. the meaning "loose woman" (Kelly; DJG, 643; DPL, 871-75). **ἀκατάπαυστος** (# 188) without succession, not pausing; unable to stop (RWP). **δελεάζοντες** pres. act. part. δελεάζω (# 1284) to trap by using bait, to ensnare. **ἀστήρικτος** (# 844) without firmness, unstable. They lack a firm foundation in faith and discipline and so are liable to be unsettled by scandalous conduct or erroneous teaching (Kelly; Green). **γεγυμνασμένην** perf. pass. part. γυμνάζω (# 1214) to exercise, to do bodily exercise, to be familiar w. Lit., to exercise naked. Here, "a heart trained in greed" (BAGD). Gen. used after the part. denotes familiarity w. anything (Bigg). **πλεονεξία** (# 4432) greediness, avarice, unsuitableness (TLNT). **ἔχοντες** pres. act. part. (adj.) ἔχω (# 2400) to have. **κατάρα** (# 2932) curse. The Hebraic expression "children of curse" meant "accursed creatures" (Kelly; Bigg); i.e., "God's curse on them." These men rest under the curse of God, as do all who fail to trust in Christ, who bore man's curse (Green). ◆ **15 καταλείποντες** pres. act. part. καταλείπω (# 2901) to leave off, to abandon. **εὐθεῖαν** acc. sing. εὐθύς (# 2318) straight. Upright conduct is pictured in the Bible as a straight path (Kelly). **ἐπλανήθησαν** aor. ind. pass. πλανάω (# 4414) to go astray, to follow the wrong path. **ἐξακολουθήσαντες** aor. act. part. ἐξακουθέω (# 1979) to follow after (s. 1:16). Part. of means ("by following after") or causal ("because they followed after"). **Βαλαὰμ τοῦ Βοσόρ** (# 962; 1082) Balaam son of Bosor. Perhaps there is a play on the name Bosor and the Heb. word for flesh (בָּשָׂר bsr), indicating Balaam's immoral character (Bauckham; BBC; ABD, 1: 569-72). **ἀδικία** (# 94) unrighteousness, fraud. Gen. here could be subjective or obj. gen., either reward prompted by fraud or reward which has fraud or unrighteousness as its object. **ἠγάπησεν** aor. act. ind. ἀγαπάω (# 26) to love. ◆ **16 ἔλεγξις** (# 1792) rebuke. **ἔσχεν** aor. ind. act. ἔχω (# 2400) to have; aor., to get. **παρανομία** (# 4175) beyond the law, transgression. The word indicates not a general defiance of law, but rather a breech of a particular law (Mayor). **ὑποζύγιον** (# 5689) being under a yoke. The term was used for a beast of burden, specifically for a donkey (BS, 160f; ABD, 6: 1026-27). **ἄφωνος** (# 936) not having a sound, speechless, dumb. **φθεγξάμενον** aor. mid. (dep.) part. (adj.) φθέγγομαι (# 5779) to make a sound, to speak. The vb. is esp. used of a portentous prophetic utterance (Bigg). **ἐκώλυσεν** aor. ind. act. κωλύω (# 3266) to hinder. **παρα-**

φρονία (# 4197) beyond understanding, madness. It is being beside one's wits (RWP). The v. suggests that he who was bribed by Balak to curse Israel was rebuked for his own disobedience by the disobedience of the ass and thus hindered from receiving the promised reward (Mayor). ◆ **17 εἰσιν** pres. ind. act. εἰμί (# 1639) to be. **πηγαί** nom. pl. πηγή (# 4380) spring. **ἄνυδρος** (# 536) waterless. **ὁμίχλη** (# 3920) fog, mist. **λαίλαπος** gen. λαίλαψ (# 3278) storm, squall (s. Mark 4:37; Luke 8:23). **ἐλαυνόμεναι** pres. pass. part. (adj.) ἐλαύνομαι (# 1785) to drive, to blow. **ζόφος** (# 2432) darkness, gloom. **τετήρηται** perf. ind. pass. τηρέω (# 5498) to keep. ◆ **18 ὑπέρογκος** (# 5665) swelling, inflated. The word means unnaturally swollen. They used big, ponderous words in their discourses. Ostentatious verbosity was their weapon to ensnare the unwary and licentiousness was the bait on their hook (Green). **ματαιότη** (# 3470) vanity, futility. Their words amount to nothing of significance, w. the gen. a descriptive gen. (Green). **φθεγγόμενοι** pres. mid. (dep.) part. φθέγγομαι (# 5779) to make a sound, to speak. (s.v. 16). **δελεάζουσιν** pres. ind. act. δελεάζω (# 1284) to bait, to entice. **ὀλίγως** (# 3903) adv., very recently, in a small degree; slightly, a little (Kelly; Mayor). **ἀσελγείαις** dat. pl. ἀσέλγεια (# 816) unrestraint greed. unbridled desire. Here instr. dat. **ἀποφεύγοντας** pres. act. part. ἀποφεύγω (# 709) to escape from. **πλάνη** (# 4415) error. The word stands specifically for idolatry or paganism (Kelly; TDNT). **ἀναστρεφομένους** pres. mid. (dep.) part. ἀναστρέφομαι (# 418) to conduct one's life, to live. ◆ **19 ἐλευθερία** (# 1800) freedom, liberty. **ἐπαγγελλόμενοι** pres. mid. (dep.) part. ἐπαγγέλλομαι (# 2040) to promise. **ὑπάρχοντες** pres. act. part. ὑπάρχω (# 5639) to be, to exist. The word denotes continuance of an antecedent state or condition (AS; s. 2 Cor. 12:16). **φθορά** (# 5785) corruption, destruction. **ἥττηται** perf. ind. pass. ἡττάομαι (# 2487) to be inferior, to be defeated, to be overcome. **δεδούλωται** perf. ind. pass. δουλόω (# 1530) to enslave. The imagery derives directly from the ancient practice of enslaving an enemy defeated in battle as a prisoner (Kelly). Perf. indicates the continuing condition of being a slave. ◆ **20 ἀποφυγόντες** aor. act. part. ἀποφεύγω (# 709) to escape from. **μίασμα** (# 3621) pollution. **ἐπίγνωσις** (# 2106) recognition, knowledge. **ἐμπλακέντες** aor. act. part. ἐμπλέκω (# 1861) to unweave, to entangle. **ἥττῶνται** pres. ind. pass. ἡττάομαι (# 2487) to be inferior (s.v. 19). **γέγονεν** perf. ind. act. γίνομαι (# 1181) to become, to be. **χείρονα** (# 5937) worse. They are worse off at the end than they were at the beginning; the reference is to a lost apostate (Blum). ◆ **21 κρεῖττον** (# 3202) comp. ἀγαθός good; comp., better. **ἐπεγνωκέναι** perf. act. inf. ἐπιγινώσκω (# 2105) to know. Inf. is used epexegetically to explain that which is better. **ἐπιγνοῦσιν** aor. act. part. ἐπιγινώσκω (# 2105) to know. Dat. pl. agrees w. the pron. **αὐτοῖς** (RWP). **ὑποστρέψαι** aor. act. inf. ὑποστρέφω (# 5715) to turn back. **παραδοθείσης** aor. pass. part. παραδίδωμι (# *4140*) to deliver over, to commit. The word was almost a t.t. for the passing on of tradition (TDNT). ◆ **22 συμβέβηκεν** perf. ind. act. συμβαίνω (# *5201*) to happen. The dramatic perf. treats what is certain to befall as already accomplished (Kelly). **παροιμία** (# *4231*) proverb. **κύων** (# *3264*) dog. **ἐπιστρέψας** aor. act. part. ἐπιστρέφω (# *2188*) to turn to. The part. needs to be translated as a finite vb. (GGBB, 55). **ἐξέραμα** (# *2000*) that which is thrown out, vomit (s. Prov. 26:11). **ὗς** (# *5725*) pig, hog. Both are unclean animals. **λουσαμένη** aor. mid. part. λούω (# *3374*) to wash oneself. Temp. part., "after having been washed." The word means "having bathed itself in mud" (Bigg). **κυλισμός** (# *3243*) wallowing. **βόρβορος** (# *1079*) mud, mire, filth, slime (BAGD). Epictetus says of those who refuse to keep themselves clean, "go and talk to a pig, that he may wallow no more in mud!" (Epictetus, 4: 11, 29; Bauckham).

2 Peter 3

◆ **1 δεύτερος** (# *1311*) second. **γράφω** (# *1211*) pres. ind. act. to write. **διεγείρω** (# *1444*) pres. ind. act. to awaken, to stir up (s. 1:13). **ὑπόμνησις** (# *5704*) remembering, reminder. **εἰλικρινής** (# *1637*) pure, unmixed, sincere. The word was used of things unmixed, air as well as ethical purity (Mayor; s. Phil. 1:10). **διάνοια** (# *1379*) thinking, understanding. The phrase was used by Plato to mean pure reason, uncontaminated by the seductive influence of the senses (Green; GPT, 37). ◆ **2 μνησθῆναι** aor. pass. inf. μιμνήσκομαι (# *3630*) to remind. Inf. to express purp., here the purp. of his writing. Inf. could also be taken as epex. defining the vb. διεγείρω (Mayor). **προειρημένων** perf. pass. part. προλέγω (# *4625*) to say before. **ῥῆμα** (# *4839*) word. **ἐντολῆς** (# *1953*) commandment. The construction of the gen. τῆς τῶν ἀποστόλων ὑμῶν ἐντολῆς τοῦ κυρίου is not entirely clear, but probably could be translated, "of the commandment of the Lord transmitted by the apostles" (BD, 93). ◆ **3 γινώσκοντες** pres. act. part. γινώσκω (# *1182*) to know. Part. could be understood here as having the force of an imp. (Mayor). **ἐλεύσονται** fut. ind. mid. (dep.) ἔρχομαι (# *2262*) to come. **ἐσχάτων τῶν ἡμερῶν** (# *2274*; *2465*) last days. **ἐμπαιγμονῇ** (# *1848*) scoffing, making fun of through mockery. **ἐμπαίκτης** (# *1851*) one who makes fun through mockery, mocker, scoffer. The phrase "mockers w. (in) mockery," i.e., "scoffers shall come w. scoffing" reflects a strong Hebraic influence on the analogy of the Heb. inf. abs. (Bigg; MT, *Style*, 142f). **ἐπιθυμία** (# *2123*) strong desire, lust, passion. **πορευόμενοι** pres. mid. (dep.) part. (adj.) πορεύομαι (# *4513*) to walk, to come. ◆ **4 λέγοντες** pres. act. part. λέγω (# *3306*) to say. **ποῦ** (# *4544*) where? "what has become of?" This is a traditional formula for expressing skepticism (Kelly). **ἐπαγγελία** (# *2039*)

promise. **παρουσία** (# *4242*) coming (s. 1:16). Obj. gen. gives the content of the promise. **ἐκοιμήθησαν** aor. ind. pass. (dep.) κοιμάομαι (# *3121*) to sleep, to fall asleep. The term is used as a metaphor for dying (Kelly). **διαμένει** pres. ind. act. διαμένω (# *1373*) to remain, to remain through, to continue. Pres. emphasizes the continual unbroken action: "All things continue as they have." **ἀρχή** (# *794*) beginning. **κτίσεως** gen. sing. κτίσις (# *3232*) creation. They maintain that God's promise is unreliable and God's universe a stable, unchanging system where events like the parousia just do not happen (Green). Gen. of description. ◆ **5 λανθάνει** pres. ind. act. λανθάνω (# *3291*) to escape notice of, to be hidden from; "for they shut their eyes to this fact that..." (Mayor; RWP; Kelly). **θέλοντας** pres. act. part. θέλω (# *2527*) to desire, to wish. The part. has here almost an adverbial sense (RWP). **ἦσαν** impf. ind. act. εἰμί (# *1639*) to be. **ἔκπαλαι** (# *1732*) for a long time, long ago. **συνεστῶσα** perf. act. part. συνίστημι (# *5319*) to consist (s. Col. 1:17). **λόγος** (# *3364*) word. Here dat. of means or instr. ◆ **6 κατακλυσθείς** aor. pass. part. κατακλύζω (# *2885*) to surge over completely, to inundate, to flood. Part. of means or manner explaining how the world was destroyed. **ἀπώλετο** aor. ind. mid. (dep.) ἀπόλλυμι (# *660*) to ruin, to destroy. ◆ **7 νῦν** (# *3814*) now, present. **τεθησαυρισμένοι** perf. pass. part. θησαυρίζω (# *2564*) to treasure up, to store up, to reserve. The sense of the metaphor here is "to set apart for," "destined for" (Mayor). Perf. emphasizes the completed state or condition. **εἰσίν** pres. ind. act. εἰμί (# *1639*) to be. **πῦρ** (# *4786*) fire. **τηρούμενοι** pres. pass. part. τηρέω (# *5498*) to guard, to watch. **κρίσις** (# *3213*) judging. **ἀπώλεια** (# *724*) ruin, destruction. **ἀσεβής** (# *815*) ungodly, impious. ◆ **8 λανθανέτω** pres. imp. act. 3rd pers. sing. λανθάνω (# *3291*) to escape notice (s.v. 5). **ἔτη** nom. pl. ἔτος (# *2291*) year. This is a quotation from Ps. 90:4. The idea is that in God's eyes a long period may appear short. God does not reckon time as man does (BBC; Bauckham; also his discussion of the Jewish background and the various interpretations). ◆ **9 βραδύνει** pres. ind. act. βραδύνω (# *1094*) to be slow, to delay. For examples in the papyri s. MM. **βραδύτης** (# *1097*) slowness, delay. **ἡγοῦνται** pres. ind. mid. (dep.) ἡγέομαι (# *2451*) to consider, to think, to count (as if delay sprang from impotence or unwillingness to perform [Bigg]). **μακροθυμεῖ** pres. ind. act. μακροθυμέω (# *3428*) to be longsuffering and patient. It is the Spirit who could take revenge, but who utterly refuses to do so (NTW, 84; TDNT; Rom. 2:4). The delay of punishment rests on God's long-suffering, which had an extensive history in Jewish tradition and was not unknown in Greek thinking (Jerome H. Neyrey, "The Form and Background of the Polemic in 2 Peter," *JBL* 99 [1980] : 424-27). **βουλόμενος** pres. mid. (dep.) part. βούλομαι (# *1089*) to wish, to desire, to want to, w. inf.

ἀπολέσθαι aor. mid. (dep.) inf. ἀπόλλυμι (# 660) to perish. μετάνοια (# 3567) change of thinking, repentance (s. Matt. 3:2). χωρῆσαι aor. act. inf. χωρέω (# 6003) to make room, to have room for. The apparent delay of God is rooted in God's desire that all have room, i.e., opportunity for repentance. ◆ 10 ἥξει fut. ind. act. ἥκω (# 2457) to come. The vb. is placed for strong emphasis at the beginning of the sentence (Kelly). ῥοιζηδόν (# 4853) adv., w. a hissing or crackling sound. The word is onomatopoeic, expressing the whizzing sound produced by rapid motion through the air of shrill rushing sounds–the hissing of a snake, the whirl of a bird's wings, the hurtling of an arrow–and then is used for the rushing movement itself or the accompanying crash or roar. Here probably the roaring of flame is meant (Bigg; Mayor; Jos. JW, 3:248). παρελεύσονται fut. ind. mid. (dep.) παρέρχομαι (# 4216) to pass by, to go away, to pass away. στοιχεῖον (# 5122) an element. Things arranged in a row: the letters of the alphabet, or the elements of nature. Here it clearly means physical elements (Bigg). It could refer to the elements of earth, air, fire, and water or the heavenly bodies such as sun, moon, and stars (Green); or it may refer to the atomic particles that are the basic structure of nature. καυσούμενα pres. mid. (dep.) part. καυσόομαι (# 3012) to burn, to melt. The word was employed by medical writers to express feverish heat. It may be intended to denote a conflagration arising from internal heat, such as a volcano (Mayor). λυθήσεται fut. ind. pass. λύω (# 3395) to loosen, to disintegrate. The word is used of breaking up a structure, as well as of dissolving a compound into its elements (Mayor). εὑρεθήσεται fut. ind. pass. εὑρίσκω (# 2351) to find; here, will be found. The meaning here may be that the earth and man's achievements will be discovered and exposed to divine judgment (Kelly; Mayor). ◆ 11 λυομένων pres. pass. part. (causal) λύω (# 3395) to loosen. Gen. abs. Pres. is either the futuristic pres., or else the process of dissolution is pictured (RWP). ποταπός (# 4534) what sort of, what kind of. In the context the word hints that great things are expected of the readers; "how outstandingly excellent" (Kelly). δεῖ (# 1256) pres. ind. act. it is necessary, used w. the acc. and the inf. ὑπάρχειν pres. act. inf. ὑπάρχω (# 5639) to be, to exist as (s. 2:19). ἀναστροφή (# 419) walk, life's practice, manner of living, way of life. εὐσέβεια (# 2354) godliness, a life of piety, respect, and reverence. ◆ 12 προσδοκῶντας pres. act. part. προσδοκέω (# 4659) to await expectantly, to look forward to. σπεύδοντας pres. act. part. σπεύδω (# 5067) to hasten, to accelerate, to desire, to be eager for (Mayor; Kelly; Bigg; HSB, 731-32). δι' ἥν (# 1328; 4005) because of which. The destruction takes place because God's day has arrived (Green). πυρούμενοι pres. pass. part. πυρέω (# 4792) to set on fire; pass., to be on fire, to burn. λυθήσονται fut. ind. pass. λύω (# 3395) to loose. καυσούμενα

pres. pass. part. καυσόω (# 3012) pass., to be consumed by heat, to burn up. Circum. or temp. part., describing what is taking place at the time of the action of the main vb. τήκεται pres. ind. pass. τήκω (# 5494) to melt, to make liquid; pass., to be melted. Pres. is futuristic (Bigg). ◆ 13 ἐπάγγελμα (# 2041) that which is promised, promise. προσδοκῶμεν pres. ind. act. προσδοκέω (# 4659) to await; to look forward to. Inclusive "we" (GGBB, 398). κατοικεῖ pres. ind. act. κατοικέω (# 2997) to settle down, to dwell, to be at home at (s. Rev. 21:1). ◆ 14 ταῦτα (# 4047) (s. 1:8); "these things," i.e., a freshly created heaven and earth where God's will is paramount (Kelly). προσδοκῶντες pres. act. part. προσδοκέω (# 4659) to earnestly await, to expect (s.v. 12). σπουδάσατε aor. imp. act. σπουδάζω (# 5079) to give diligence, to make an effort (s. 1:10). ἄσπιλος (# 834) spotless. ἀμώμητος (# 318) blameless. αὐτῷ dat. sing. αὐτός (# 899) self; "him." The dat. may be taken w. the adj. ("spotless and blameless in His sight"), or w. the inf. ("to be found by Him") (Bigg). εὑρεθῆναι aor. pass. inf. εὑρίσκω (# 2351) to find. The inf. is used to complete the vb. σπουδάσατε. ἐν εἰρήνῃ (# 1877; 1645) in peace. This describes the state of reconciliation w. God the restored sinner enjoys (Kelly). ◆ 15 μακροθυμία (# 3429) long-suffering, patient endurance (s. Gal. 5:22; RAC, 9:254f). ἡγεῖσθε pres. mid. (dep.) imp. ἡγέομαι (# 2451) to consider, to count, followed by the double acc. ὁ ἀγαπητὸς ἡμῶν ἀδελφός (# 28; 1609; 81) "our beloved brother." The phrase refers not simply to a fellow Christian, but in this case to a fellow apostle (Kelly). δοθεῖσαν aor. pass. part. δίδωμι (# 1443) to give. The pass. is a theol. or divine pass. indicating that God is the subject (BG, 76). ἔγραψεν aor. ind. act. γράφω (# 1211) to write. Peter may be referring to Paul's letter to the Romans, or he may be alluding simply to Paul's constant teaching in all his letters (Green). ◆ 16 λαλῶν pres. act. part. λαλέω (# 3281) to speak. δυσνόητος (# 1554) difficult to understand, hard to understand. ἀμαθής (# 276) untaught. The word brings out the moral value of teaching, trained habits of reflection, and disciplined good sense (Bigg). ἀστήρικτος (# 844) unstable. στρεβλοῦσιν pres. ind. act. στρεβλόω (# 5137) to twist, to torture. The fig. sense seems to flow from the notion of twisting or warping rather than that of torturing on the rack. The result is then false and distorted (Mayor; Bauckham; BAGD). λοιπός (# 3370) rest. γραφάς acc. pl. γραφή (# 1210) Scripture, referring to the inspired, authoritative writings (Bauckham). Peter gives a very high place to Paul's writings. They are included in "the other scriptures" (Green; Bauckham; Blum). ἀπώλεια (# 724) destruction. ◆ 17 προγινώσκοντες pres. act. part. προγινώσκω (# 4589) to know beforehand, to know in advance. Part. could be causal. φυλάσσεσθε pres. imp. mid. (dep.) φυλάσσω (# 5875) to guard, to keep watch; mid. to guard oneself. Pres. imp. calls for a continual action. **ἄθεσμος** (# *118*) lawless (s. 2:7). **πλάνη** (# *4415*) error. **συναπαχθέντες** aor. pass. part. συναπάγω (# *5270*) to lead away together, to carry away together. **ἐκπέσητε** aor. subj. act. ἐκπίπτω (# *1738*) to fall out of, to dislodge. Subj. w. ἵνα (# *2671*) is used in a neg. purp. cl. **στηριγμός** (# *5113*) fixedness, firmness, steadfastness, firm stance. It connotes fixity as opposed to movement, and is used in conscious contrast to ἀστήρικτοι above, the characteristic of heretics and their dupes. Stability, or being firmly established in the faith, is clearly a quality he greatly esteems (Kelly). ◆ **18 αὐξάνετε** pres. imp. act. αὐξάνω (# *889*) to grow, to advance. **ἐν** in. Prep. could express either the sphere of growth or the means by which one grows. **γνώσει** dat. sing. γνῶσις (# *1194*) knowledge. **τοῦ κυρίου** (# *3261*) of the Lord. Gen. could be obj. ("knowledge about...") or subjective ("knowledge from...").

1 John

1 John 1

◆ 1 ἦν impf. ind. act. εἰμί (# 1639) to be. ἀρχή (# 794) beginning. The beginning here could refer to the beginning of creation, or beginning in the abs. sense; word emphasizes the preexistence and divine character, or beginning of the Christian preaching, or the beginning of Jesus' ministry (Schnackenburg; Marshall; Brown; Klauck; Smalley; Strecker). ἀκηκόαμεν perf. ind. act. ἀκούω (# 201) to hear. ἑωράκαμεν perf. act. ind. ὁράω (# 3972) to see. The perfs. express an act in the past w. lasting results. It indicates that a revelation has been made in terms men can understand and the results are abiding (Marshall; Brooke; JG, 344). The 1st pers. pl. "we" could mean the writer of the epistle and his companions, but it more probably means "we all," "we disciples of Christ" (JG, 311; Schnackenburg, 52-58; Brown; Klauck, 73-78). ὀφθαλμός (# 4057) eye. Instr. dat. here, "w. our eyes." ἐθεασάμεθα aor. ind. mid. (dep.) θεάομαι (# 2517) to look at, to behold. The vb. expresses the calm, intentional continuous contemplation of an object (Westcott; s. John 1:14). ἐψηλάφησαν aor. act. ind. ψηλαφέω (# 6027) to grope or feel after in order to find, like one blind or in the dark; hence, "to handle, to touch." The idea of searching sometimes disappears altogether; here it naturally suggest all the evidence available for sense perception other than hearing and sight. The author is claiming a physical contact w. Jesus (Brooke; Brown; Klauck). Perhaps this is to combat a type of Docetism (DLNT, 306-9). ζωῆς gen. sing. ζωή (# 2437) life (Strecker; Klauck). Gen. could indicate the content of the word or, as gen. of quality could indicate "the living word"; it could indicate the object ("the life-giving word"), or it could be an epex. gen. ("the word which is life") (Stott; Marshall; Brown). **◆ 2** ἐφανερώθη aor. ind. pass. φανερόω (# 5746) to make clear, to manifest; pass., to be revealed. The vb. is used of the revelation of the Lord at His first coming, the Incarnation (Westcott; Schnackenburg; Klauck). ἑωράκαμεν perf. ind. act. ὁράω (# 3972) to see. μαρτυροῦμεν pres. ind. act. μαρτυρέω (# 3455) to be a witness, to testify. Pres. indicates the continuing action. ἀπαγγέλλομεν pres. ind. act. ἀπαγγέλλω (# 550) to report, to declare, to report w. reference to the eyewitness source of a message (Bultmann). V. 2 forms a parenthesis the writer inserted to make clear beyond all possible mistake that the life to which John bears witness was revealed by

God in the historical person of Jesus (Marshall). ἐφανερώθη aor. ind. pass. φανερόω (# 5746) to be revealed. **◆ 3** ἑωράκαμεν perf. ind. act. ὁράω (# 3972) to see. ἀκηκόαμεν perf. ind. act. ἀκούω (# 201) to hear. ἀπαγγέλλομεν pres. ind. act. ἀπαγγέλλω (# 550) to report (s.v. 2). This is the main vb. of the sentence began in v. 1. κοινωνία (# 3126) fellowship. The word indicates the setting aside of private interest and desire and the joining in w. another or others for common purposes (TDNT; NIDNTT; RAC, 9:1100-45; Smalley; Klauck; DLNT, 373-74; NDIEC, 3:19; GELTS, 261). ἔχητε pres. subj. act. ἔχω (# 2400) to have. Subj. w. ἵνα (# 2671) to express purp. **◆ 4** ταῦτα nom. pl. οὗτος (# 4047) this; "these things." The reference is to the entire contents of the letter (Brooke; Marshall), or to the apostolic message in vv. 1-3 (Westcott). γράφομεν pres. ind. act. γράφω (# 1211) to write. Pres. used w. the emphatic personal pron. ἡμεῖς (# 1609) (for the text variant s. TC, 709) means the writer is writing the letter in solidarity w. all the representatives of orthodoxy in the church (Smalley). In v. 5 the "we" refers to the author and other ministers, while in v. 6 it is inclusive (the author and audience) (GGBB, 396). ᾖ pres. subj. act. εἰμί (# 1639) to be, used w. part. πεπληρωμένη perf. pass. part. πληρόω (# 4444) to fill, to make full. Part. in a periphrastic perf. pass. subj. construction stressing the state of completion in the purp. cl. (RWP). The assurance of knowing that they possess eternal life would make their joy full, so he writes to the group and presents certain criteria for them to know that they have this life. The ones who keep themselves from habitual sin and idols can know that they have eternal life. **◆ 5** ἀγγελία (# 32) report, message. The word may suggest that the message contains a conception of God men could not have formed without His help. It is a revelation and not a discovery (Brooke). ἀκηκόαμεν perf. ind. act. ἀκούω (# 201) to hear. Perf. indicates the abiding results of the hearing. ἀναγγέλλομεν pres. ind. act. ἀναγγέλλω (# 334) to announce. Prep. in compound has the additional idea of bringing the tidings up to or back to the person receiving them. It is the recipient who is prominent in this vb. (Westcott). Pres. indicates the action in progress. ὅτι (# 4022) that. This conj. introduces the content of the announcement. φῶς (# 5890) light and σκοτία (# 5028) darkness. That God is light is a penetrating description of the being and nature of God, indicating that He is absolute in His glory, truth, and holiness (Smalley; Klauck; Strecker, 76-83; DLNT, 657-59). ◆ **6 ἐάν** (# *1569*) if. The five cond. cls. introduced by this word are followed by the aor. subj. or pres. subj. In each case the cond. is a supposition that is possible: "if this should happen" (JG, 371-74; Marshall). **εἴπωμεν** aor. subj. act. λέγω (# *3306*) to say. "If we should say." In vv. 6, 8, and 10, the phrase introduces three statements of false doctrine (JG, 372). **ἔχομεν** pres ind. act. ἔχω (# *2400*) to have, to possess. **περιπατῶμεν** pres. subj. act. περιπατέω (# *4344*) to walk about, to conduct one's life. The word is comparable to the Heb. word הָלַךְ, "to walk" (TDOT; NIDOTTE), and is used in the sense of practical, ethical dealing (Schnackenburg). Pres. indicates an habitual manner of life–"to live habitually in darkness"–an attitude of mind issuing in specific acts of wrongdoing, as well as a determination to choose sin (darkness) rather that God (light) as one's constant sphere of existence (Smalley). **ψευδόμεθα** pres. ind. mid. (dep.) ψεύδομαι (# *6017*) to lie. **ποιοῦμεν** pres. ind. act. ποιέω (# *4472*) to do, to practice. In Jewish writings "to do the truth" indicated doing right, or being faithful, esp. concerning truth as revealed in the Law; but for Christians Christ has replaced the Law (Brown; Klauck). ◆ **7 περιπατῶμεν** pres. subj. act. περιπατέω (# *4344*) to conduct one's life (s.v. 6). The cond. cls. in vv. 7 and 9 introduce the hypothesis of pres. and continuous Christian life–"on the supposition that we are walking or confessing" (JG, 372)–involving a present general reality (GGBB, 663). "Walking in the light" is the conscious and sustained endeavor to live a life in conformity w. the revelation of God who is light, esp. as that revelation has been made finally and completely in Jesus Christ. And this is the necessary condition of fellowship (Brooke). **κοινωνία** (# *3126*) fellowship (s.v. 3). **ἔχομεν** pres. ind. act. ἔχω (# *2400*) to have. **μετ'** = μετά (# *3552*) with. **ἀλλήλων** (# *253*) one another; "w. one another." Although the phrase could mean fellowship between God and man, John's general use indicates that he takes the fellowship of Christians as the visible sign of fellowship w. God (Westcott; Schnackenburg). **αἷμα** (# *135*) blood. For a study of the term "blood" in the Scripture s. APC, 108-124; BBC; A.M. Stibbs, *The Meaning of the Word "Blood" in Scripture* [London: The Tyndale Press, 1962]. **καθαρίζει** pres. ind. act. καθαρίζω (# *2751*) to cleanse. The vbs. suggest that God does more than forgive; He erases the stain of sin. Pres. suggests it is a continuous process (Stott). ◆ **8 εἴπωμεν** aor. subj. act. λέγω (# *3306*) to say (s.v. 6). **ἔχομεν** pres. ind. act. ἔχω (# *2400*) to have. Pres., "to possess." To have no sin is the equivalent of a sinless character or disposition (Smalley). **πλανῶμεν** pres. ind. act. πλανάω (# *4414*) to lead astray, to cause to wander, to mislead, to deceive (BAGD). To deceive or lead ourselves astray is either to deceive oneself, or to deceive those in the

Christian community (Brown). ◆ **9 ὁμολογῶμεν** pres. subj. act. ὁμολογέω (# *3933*) to say the same thing, to agree, to concede, to admit, to confess, to acknowledge (ECC, 13-20; TDNT; EDNT; GELTS, 332). Iterative pres., indicating a repeated acknowledgment of sin. Subj. may suggest implicit uncertainty or a generalization of the "we" (GGBB, 698). **πιστός** (# *4412*) faithful. It refers here to God's fidelity or reliability in the keeping of His word (Brown). **δίκαιος** (# *1465*) righteous, just. God acts according to the standard of His holiness and can forgive sin because its penalty has been paid by the death of Christ. **ἀφῇ** aor. subj. act. ἀφίημι (# *918*) to release, to forgive (TDNT; NIDNTT). The subject cl. indicates the way in which God expresses His faithfulness and justice and is equivalent to an inf. of result (Marshall; BD, 198). **καθαρίσῃ** aor. subj. act. καθαρίζω (# *2751*) to purify, to cleanse. Perhaps John thought of the words of Jesus as He responded to Peter's request to be completely washed: "A person who has had a bath needs only to wash his feet; his whole body is clean" (John 13:10 NIV). **ἀδικία** (# *94*) unrighteousness. ◆ **10 εἴπωμεν** aor. subj. act. λέγω (# *3306*) to say; here in the sense "to claim." **ἡμαρτήκαμεν** perf. ind. act. ἁμαρτάνω (# *279*) to sin. Perf. points to the abiding results of a past action (GGBB, 577). For a discussion of sin in 1 John 5:16 s. DLNT, 1095-97. **ψεύστης** (# *6026*) one who lies, liar. **ποιοῦμεν** pres. ind. act. ποιέω (# *4472*) to make; here, "to make someone a liar" (Smalley; Brown).

1 John 2

◆ **1 τεκνία** voc. pl. τεκνίον (# *5448*) little child, small child. The dim. form is used for affection: "dear children" (Marshall). **γράφω** (# *1211*) pres. ind. act. to write. Pres. indicates the writing of this letter. **ἁμάρτητε** aor. subj. act. ἁμαρτάνω (# *279*) to sin. Aor. indicates a single act, not a state, of sin (Westcott). Subj. w. ἵνα (# *2671*) is used in a neg. purp. cl. (GGBB, 472). **ἁμάρτῃ** aor. subj. act. ἁμαρτάνω (# *279*) to sin. Subj. in an 3rd. class cond. cl. which assumes the possibility of the cond. **παράκλητος** (# *4156*) helper. In rabbinical literature the word could indicate one who offers legal aid or who intercedes on behalf of someone else; in the pres. context the word undoubtedly signifies a legal advocate or counsel for the defense (Marshall; Schnackenburg; Brooke; Klauck; BBC; TDNT; John 14:16). **ἔχομεν** pres. ind. act. ἔχω (# *2400*) to have. Pres. indicates continual possession. **πρός** (# *4639*) to, with, by. Prep. denotes both presence with and a relationship towards: "in the presence of the Father" (Brown; NIDNTT, 3:1204-6). ◆ **2 ἱλασμός** (# *2662*) satisfaction, propitiation. Since the idea is to placate the wrath of God, the pres. passage means that Jesus propitiates w. respect to our sins (Marshall; Stott; Brown; Smalley; Rom. 3:25). **περί** concerning, for. The phrase **περὶ τῶν ἁμαρτιῶν** (# *4309; 281*) could refer to sin offering as in the OT, or mean "in reference to sin" (NIDNTT, 3:1203). ◆ **3 γινώσκομεν** pres. ind. act. γινώσκω (# 1182) to know. **ἐγνώκαμεν** perf. act. ind. γινώσκω (# 1182) to know. The tenses here are significant; we learn to perceive more and more clearly that our knowledge is genuine through its abiding results in a growing willingness to obey (Brooke). **ἐντολάς** acc. pl. ἐντολή (# 1953) commandment. **τηρῶμεν** pres. subj. act. τηρέω (# 5498) to guard, to keep. The word has the idea of observing or holding something fast in memory (Schnackenburg). Subj. w. **ἐάν** (# 1569) is used in a 3rd. class cond. cl. which views the cond. as a possibility. ◆ **4 λέγων** pres. act. part. λέγω (# 3306) to say. Subst. part., to emphasize a defining character trait. The change from the pl. to the sing. suggests that the principle is being applied and tested in the life of the individual believer (Smalley). **ἔγνωκα** perf. ind. act. γινώσκω (# 1182) to know. Perf. stresses the abiding state or cond. **τηρῶν** pres. act. part. τηρέω (# 5498) to keep. Concessive use of part. Pres. indicates a continual action. **ψεύστης** (# 6026) one who lies, liar. ◆ **5 τηρῇ** pres. subj. act. τηρέω (# 5498) to keep. Subj. w. the generalized or indef. rel. pron. **ὅς ἄν**, meaning "whoever keeps." **ἀληθῶς** (# 242) adv., truly. **ἡ ἀγάπη τοῦ θεοῦ** the love of God. The gen. could be subjective gen. ("God's love for man"), obj. gen. ("man's love for God"), or gen. of quality ("God's kind of love") (Marshall). For the meaning of the term "love," s. 1 Cor. 13:1; Oda Wischmeyer, "Agape in der ausserchristlichen Antike," *ZNW* 69 [1978]: 212-38; TLNT; TDNT; EDNT. **τετελείωται** perf. ind. pass. τελειόω (# 5457) to bring to the goal, to perfect. Proleptic perf. used to refer to a state resulting from an antecedent action yet to come (GGBB, 581). True love for God is expressed not in sentimental language or mystical experience, but in moral obedience. The proof of love is loyalty. Such love is perfected (Stott). **γινώσκομεν** pres. ind. act. γινώσκω (# 1182) to know. **ἐσμεν** pres. ind. act. εἰμί (# 1639) to be. ◆ **6 λέγων** pres. act. part. (subst.) λέγω (# 3306) to say. **μένειν** pres. act. inf. μένω (# 3531) to remain. The pres. of this vb. indicates a continual abiding in Him (s. John 15:4; Schnackenburg, 105-10). Inf. is used as indir. disc. after the part. **ὀφείλει** pres. ind. act. ὀφείλω (# 4053) to be morally obligated; "he ought to," w. inf. **καθώς** (# 2777) just as. **ἐκεῖνος** (# 1697) that one, i.e. Christ. **περιεπάτησεν** aor. ind. act. περιπατέω (# 4344) to walk, to conduct one's life (s. 1:6). Aor. sums up the total life of Jesus. **οὕτως** (# 4048) so, in like manner. **περιπατεῖν** pres. act. inf. περιπατέω (# 4344). Inf. as obj. or complementary to the vb. ὀφείλει. Pres. indicates a continual action. ◆ **7 ἀγαπητοί** voc. pl. ἀγαπητός (# 28) one who is loved, beloved. **καινήν** acc. sing. καινός (# 2785) new, novel, new in kind (RWP; Trench, *Synonyms*, 219-25; Schnackenburg; John 13:34). **παλαιός** (# 4094) old, ancient; i.e., old in time. For example Deut. 6:5; Lev. 19:18. **εἴχετε** aor. ind. act. ἔχω (# 2400) to have. **ἠκούσατε**

aor. ind. act. ἀκούω (# 201) to hear. ◆ **8 ἀληθής** (# 239) true, genuine. The word expresses not only the truth of the logical content; it says the newness of the commandment to love was actually manifested in Christ and in those who received the letter (Schnackenburg). **ὅτι** (# 4022) that. It could be epex., explaining the new commandment ("namely, that the darkness is passing away"), causal ("because the darkness is passing away"); or perhaps both ideas are intended (Brown). **παράγεται** pres. ind. mid. (dep.) παράγομαι (# 4135) to pass away. Pres. indicates that the process has already begun and the darkness is passing away (Brooke). **φῶς** (# 5890) light. **ἀληθινός** (# 240) true, genuine. **φαίνει** pres. ind. act. φαίνω (# 5743) to shine. Customary pres., indicating that this is an ongoing state (GGBB, 522). ◆ **9 λέγων** pres. act. part. λέγω (# 3306) to say. Subst. part. to emphasize a defining trait. **εἶναι** pres. act. inf. εἰμί (# 1639) to be. Inf. in indir. discourse. **μισῶν** pres. act. part. μισέω (# 3631) to hate. Subst. part. to emphasize a defining trait. **ἄρτι** (# 785) now, at the pres. time. ◆ **10 ἀγαπῶν** pres. act. part. ἀγαπάω (# 26) to love (s.v. 5). Subst. part. to emphasize a defining trait, "the one who continually expresses loves." **μένει** pres. ind. act. μένω (# 3531) to remain (s.v. 6). **σκάνδαλον** (# 4998) stumbling. ◆ **11 μισῶν** pres. act. part. μισέω (# 3631) to hate. **περιπατεῖ** pres. ind. act. περιπατέω (# 4344) to walk about, to conduct one's life. Pres. pictures the pres. continual action, "he is walking about." **οἶδεν** perf. ind. act. οἶδα (# 3857) to know. Def. perf. w. a pres. meaning. **ὑπάγει** pres. ind. act. ὑπάγω (# 5632) to go. The idea is not that of preceding to a definite point, but of leaving the pres. scene (Westcott). **ἐτύφλωσεν** aor. ind. act. τυφλόω (# 5604) to make blind, to cause to be blind, to blind. ◆ **12 γράφω** (# 1211) pres. ind. act. to write. Pres. could indicate the letter that John is now writing, stressing the progressive writing, "I am writing." **ἔγραψα** aor. ind. act. γράφω to write. The aor. could be an epistolary aor., referring to the present writing but stressing the completed action as they read the letter; or it could refer to another letter written in the past. For a discussion of the views regarding the tenses of the vb. γράφω s. Marshall; Schnackenburg; Plummer; Brown; Smalley. **ὅτι** (# 4022) that. This particle is used six times in vv. 12-14. They could be causal ("because") or they could indicate the content of that which John is writing. **ἀφέωνται** perf. ind. pass. ἀφίημι (# 918) to release, to forgive. Perf. indicates that the sins have been and remain forgiven (Scott). Pass. could be the theol. pass., indicating that God is the one who forgives the sins. **διά** (# 1328) w. acc., because; "because God is the one who forgives the sins." ◆ **13 ἐγνώκατε** perf. ind. act. γινώσκω (# 1182) to know. Perf. indicates the continuing results of the knowledge. **τὸν ἀπ' ἀρχῆς** (# 608; 794) the one who was from the beginning. Art. used with a prep. phrase. **νεανίσκος** (# 3734) young man. The word could indicates either someone young in the faith or physically young. **νενικήκατε** perf. act. ind. νικάω (# 3771) to bring about a victory, to achieve the victory, to conquer. Perf. indicates the pres. consequence of a past event (Stott). **τὸν πονηρόν** (# 4505) the evil one. It is a clear reference to the devil (Brown). ◆ **14 ἔγραψα** aor. ind. act. γράφω (# 1211) to write. Aor. could be epistolary aor., referring to the pres. letter; or it could indicates a previous writing (s.v. 12). **ἐγνώκατε** perf. ind. act. γινώσκω (# 1182) to know. **μένει** pres. ind. act. μένω (# 3531) to remain (s.v. 6). **νενικήκατε** perf. ind. act. νικάω (# 3771) to conquer (s.v. 13). ◆ **15** **ἀγαπᾶτε** pres. imp. act. ἀγαπάω (# 26) to love. Pres. imp. commonly used to forbid an action or attitude of life (GGBB, 487). **κόσμος** (# 3180) world, world system. The word can signify mankind organized in rebellion against God (Marshall; Schnackenburg, 133-37; TDNT; HSB, 733-34). **ἡ ἀγάπη τοῦ πατρός** the love of the Father. The gen. could be subjective gen. ("the love from the Father"), obj. gen. ("the love for the Father"), or descriptive ("fatherly love"). ◆ **16 ἐπιθυμία** (# 2123) strong desire, lust, passion (TDNT; DNP, 2:542-44). **σαρκός** gen. sing. σάρξ (# 4922) flesh. The word here could refer to the fallen human nature in general, to a disposition of hostility toward God (Smalley; Brown). Gen. could be gen. of source ("desires arising fr. the fallen human nature") or gen. of description ("fleshly desire"). **ὀφθαλμῶν** gen. pl. ὀφθαλμός (# 4057) eye. Gen. of source or subjective gen, indicating that the eyes are the agent of the desires (Smalley). **ἀλαζονεία** (# 224) pride, boasting arrogance. It means the braggadocio who exaggerates what he possesses in order to impress other people. Such a person stood on the pier and told his friends how much he had invested in shipping; then sent his boy to the bank although he has only one drachma in his account! (Marshall; MNTW, 38-42; Trench, *Synonyms*, 98-102f; TLNT; Klauck). **βίος** (# 1050) life, life substances or goods, possessions. Obj. gen. here, indicating the boasting about one's goods or livelihood. ◆ **17 παράγεται** pres. ind. mid. (dep.) παράγομαι (# 4135) to pass away (s.v. 8). **ποιῶν** pres. act. part. ποιέω (# 4472) to do. Subst. part. to emphasize a defining trait. **θέλημα** (# 2525) will. **μένει** pres. ind. act. μένω (# 3531) to remain (s.v. 6). ◆ **18 παιδίον** (# 4086) little child, dear child (s.v. 1). **ἐσχάτη ὥρα** (# 2274; 6052) last hour. **ἠκούσατε** aor. ind. act. ἀκούω (# 201) to hear. **ἀντίχριστος** (# 532) Antichrist. Prep. could refer either to one who comes instead of Christ or one who opposes Christ. The lack of the art. stresses the category or quality (Schnackenburg; MT, 132; DLNT, 50-53). **ἔρχεται** pres. ind. mid. (dep.) ἔρχομαι (# 2262) to come; "he is coming." **γεγόνασιν** perf. ind. act. γίνομαι (# 1181) to become. Here, "to have come to be," "to have arisen" (Brooke). **ὅθεν** (# 3854) therefore, for this reason. **γινώσκομεν** perf. ind. act. γινώσκω (# 1182) to

know, to recognize. ◆ **19 ἐξῆλθαν** aor. ind. act. ἐξέρχομαι (# 2002) to go out. They either left the doctrine or left the fellowship. For a discussion of the problem in the community and the purpose of the letter to address these s. DLNT, 587-99. **ἦσαν** impf. ind. act. εἰμί (# 1639) to be. Ind. in a contrary to fact cond. cl. **μεμενήκεισαν** plperf. ind. act. μένω (# 3531) to remain (s.v. 6). Plperf. expresses the continuance of the contingent results up to the time of speaking (M, 148). The plperf. often lacks the augment in Koine (BD, 36). **φανερωθῶσιν** aor. pass. subj. φανερόω (# 5746) to manifest, to bring to light, to reveal. Subj. w. **ἵνα** (# 2671) in a purp. cl. Possibly an imperatival **ἵνα** (GGBB, 476-77). John not only relates the fact of their departure from the fellowship, but discerns a purpose in it. The heretics left of their own volition, but behind the secession was the divine purp. that they should be made manifest. Their departing was their unmasking. What is counterfeit cannot remain forever hidden (Stott). **ἐξ ἡμῶν** (# 1666; 1609) of us. ◆ **20 καί** (# 2779) and yet. The word has here an adversative force ("but") (Marshall; BD, 227; JG, 135f). **χρίσμα** (# 5984) anointing. The word, which expresses not the act of anointing, but that w. which it is performed, marks the connection of Christians w. their Head and refers to the Holy Spirit (Westcott; TDNT; Marshall; Smalley; DLNT, 48-50). **οἴδατε** perf. ind. act. οἶδα (# 3857) to know. Def. perf. w. a pres. meaning. ◆ **21** **ἔγραψα** aor. act. ind. γράφω (# 1211) to write. Epistolary aor., "I am writing." **ὅτι** (# 4022) that. **οἴδατε** perf. ind. act. οἶδα (# 3857) to know. Def. perf. w. pres. meaning. **ψεῦδος** (# 6022) liar. ◆ **22 ψεῦδος** (# 6022) liar. **εἰ μή** (# 1623; 3590) if not, except. **ἀρνούμενος** pres. mid. (dep.) part. (subst.) ἀρνέομαι (# 667) to say no to, to deny. **τὸν πατέρα καὶ τὸν υἱόν** the Father and the Son. Art. is par excellence (GGBB, 233). The one who rejects the Son also rejects the Father (Smalley). ◆ **23 ἀρνούμενος** pres. mid. (dep.) part. ἀρνέομαι (# 667) to say no to, to deny. **ὁμολογῶν** pres. act. part. ὁμολογέω (# 3933) to agree, to confess (s. 1:9). Subst. part. w. art. to indicate a defining trait. **ἔχει** pres. ind. act. ἔχω (# 2400) to have. Gnomic pres. (GGBB, 522). ◆ **24 ἠκούσατε** aor. ind. act. ἀκούω (# 201) to hear and accept what has been heard. **μενέτω** pres. imp. act. 3rd. pers. sing. μένω (# 3531) to remain (s.v. 6). **μείνῃ** aor. subj. act. μένω (# 3531) to remain. Subj. w. **ἐάν** (# 1569) in a 3rd. class cond. cl. which views the cond. as possible (s. 1:6). **ἠκούσατε** aor. ind. act. ἀκούω (# 201) to express. **μενεῖτε** fut. ind. act. μένω (# 3531) to remain. It is significant that μένω expresses a continuing relationship (Marshall). ◆ **25 ἐπαγγελία** (# 2039) announcement, promise, pledge (BAGD; Schnackenburg). **ἐπηγγείλατο** aor. ind. mid. (dep.) ἐπαγγέλομαι (# 2040) to promise, to pledge, to pledge oneself to do something. ◆ **26 ἔγραψα** aor. ind. act. γράφω (# 1211) to write. **πλανώντων** pres. act. part. πλανάω (# 4414) to lead astray, to deceive. Part. has a conative force, "trying to deceive" (Marshall). Pres. indicates an unfulfilled attempt. ◆ **27 ἐλάβετε** aor. ind. act. λαμβάνω (# 3284) to receive, to accept. **μένει** pres. ind. act. μένω (# 3531) to remain. **ἔχετε** pres. ind. act. ἔχω (# 2400) to have. **διδάσκῃ** pres. subj. act. διδάσκω (# 1438) to teach. Subj. w. ἵνα (# 2671) used epexegetically to explain what the need is. **ἐδίδαξεν** aor. ind. act. διδάσκω (# 1438) to teach. **μένετε** pres. imp. act. μένω (# 3531) to remain. ◆ **28 μένετε** pres. imp. act. μένω (# 3531) to remain. **φανερωθῇ** aor. subj. pass. φανερόω (# 5746) to appear (s.v. 19). Subj. w. ἐάν (# 1569) in a 3rd. class cond. cl. and a clear reference to the second coming of Christ at any time (RWP). **σχῶμεν** aor. subj. act. ἔχω (# 2400) to have. Subj. w. ἵνα (# 2671) in a purp. cl. **παρρησία** (# 4244) speaking everything, openness, boldness, confidence. The word originated from the political scene and meant openness in speaking. It was soon taken into the ethical area and closely connected w. the concept of friendship. Philo used the word regarding a slave whose good conscience gave him openness and confidence w. his master. The person who has been cleansed from sin and continues in love also has freedom of speech w. his Master who rules the whole world (Schnackenburg; TLNT; TDNT; GELTS, 361; Heb. 3:6). **αἰσχυνθῶμεν** aor. subj. pass. αἰσχύνω (# 159) to shame; pass., to be put to shame, to be made ashamed. Subj. w. ἵνα (# 2671) in a neg. purp. cl. **παρουσία** (# 5746) presence, coming (s. 1 Thess. 3:13). ◆ **29 εἰδῆτε** perf. subj. act. οἶδα (# 3857) to know. Def. perf. w. pres. meaning. Subj. in a 3rd. class cond. cl., normally meaning that the cond. is viewed as possible. Here the intention may not be to question the certainty that He is just, but to turn the audience toward self-interrogation: Have they realized that He is just? (Brown). **γινώσκετε** pres. ind. act. γινώσκω (# 1182) to know. **ποιῶν** pres. act. part. (subst.) ποιέω (# 4472) to do. Pres. indicates a continual action. **γεγέννηται** perf. ind. pass. γεννάω (# 1164) to bear; pass., to be born. The child exhibits the parents' character because he shares the parents' nature (Stott). Perf. indicates the abiding result.

1 John 3

◆ **1 ἴδετε** aor. imp. act. ὁράω (# 3972) to see. The vb. is followed by an indir. statement as a means of arousing the readers' attention (Marshall). He invites his readers to contemplate the same truth as presented before them in an intelligent shape (Westcott). **ποταπήν** acc. sing. ποταπός (# 4534) what kind of. The word is used often of something admirable in character (Brooke). The word meant originally "of what country," and seems always to imply astonishment (Scott; Plummer). **δέδωκεν** perf. ind. act. δίδωμι (# 1443) to give. The word signifies an unearned gift. Perf. indicates that what they had received is permanent

and abiding (Brooke; Schnackenburg). **τέκνα** nom. pl. τέκνον (# 5451) child. Nom. w. vb. of calling. It was a great privilege to be the child of a kind, loving father. Because the child had the nature of his father, he should behave like his father (BBC; DLNT, 1115-17). **κληθῶμεν** aor. subj. pass. καλέω (# 2813) to call; pass., to be named. Subj. w. ἵνα (# 2671) could be used here to express either purp. (Westcott) or results (RWP). **ἐσμέν** pres. ind. act. εἰμί (# 1639) to be. **γινώσκει** pres. ind. act. γινώσκω (# 1182) to know. Pres. indicates a continual action. **ἔγνω** aor. ind. act. γινώσκω (# 1182) to know. ◆ **2 οὔπω** (# 4037) not yet. **ἐφανερώθη** aor. ind. pass. φανερόω (# 5746) to make clear, to manifest, to reveal. **ἐσόμεθα** fut. ind. mid. (dep.) εἰμί (# 1639) to be. **οἴδαμεν** perf. ind. act. οἶδα (# 3857) to know. Def. perf. w. pres. meaning. **φανερωθῇ** aor. subj. pass. φανερόω (# 5746) to appear. The subject of the vb. could be either Jesus Himself or it could refer to τί ἐσόμεθα (Marshall; Schnackenburg; Westcott). **ὅμοιος** (# 3927) like. This likeness of man redeemed and perfected to God is the likeness of the creature reflecting the glory of the Creator (Westcott). **ἐσόμεθα** fut. ind. mid. (dep.) εἰμί (# 1639) to be. **ὀψόμεθα** fut. ind. mid. (dep.) ὁράω (# 3972) to see. For the ambiguous construction s. Marshall; Brown; Smalley. ◆ **3 ἔχων** pres. act. part. ἔχω (# 2400) to have, to possess. Subst. part., "the one having hope." **ἐλπίδα** acc. sing. ἐλπίς (# 1828) hope; here in the sense of confidence, is the confident expectation that the believer will share fully in God's eternal life (Smalley; EH). **ἁγνίζει** pres. ind. act. ἁγνίζω (# 49) to purify. The word originally had a cultic meaning, indicating withdrawal from the profane and dedication to God–to make ceremonially ready. The term, however, also took on an ethical character (Schnackenburg; TDNT; EDNT; Smalley). The hope of appearing before God's presence, and of seeing Christ as He is, necessarily inspires its recipients w. the desire of putting away every defilement that clouds the vision of God (Brooke). **ἑαυτοῦ** (# 1571) refl. pron., himself. **καθώς** (# 2777) just as. ◆ **4 ποιῶν** pres. act. part. ποιέω (# 4472) to do, to continue to do, to practice. Subst. part., "the one practicing." **ἀνομία** (# 281) that which is without the law, lawlessness. **ποιεῖ** pres. ind. act. ποιέω (# 4472) to do. ◆ **5 οἴδατε** perf. ind. act. οἶδα (# 3857) to know. Def. perf. w. a pres. meaning. **ὅτι** (# 4022) that, giving the content of the knowledge. **ἐφανερώθη** aor. ind. pass. φανερόω (# 5746) to appear. **ἄρῃ** aor. subj. act. αἴρω (# 149) to lift up, to take away, to remove completely. Subj. w. ἵνα (# 2671) used in a purp. cl. ◆ **6 μένων** pres. act. part. (subst.) μένω (# 3531) to remain. Pres. indicates continual action. **ἁμαρτάνει** pres. ind. act. ἁμαρτάνω (# 279) to sin. Pres. indicates habitual action. It has been suggested that here John intends a potential view, that the one remaining in Him should not live in sin (Smalley). **ἁμαρτάνων** pres. act. part. ἁμαρτάνω

(# 279) to sin. **ἑώρακεν** perf. ind. act. ὁράω (# 3972) to see. Perf. means to see and to experience the continual results of having seen. **ἔγνωκεν** perf. ind. act. γινώσκω (# 1182) to know. The vb. ὁράω lays stress on the obj., which appears and is grasped by the mental vision; the vb. γινώσκω stresses the subsequent subjective apprehension of what is grasped in the vision, or unfolded gradually in experience (Brooke). ◆ **7 πλανάτω** pres. imp. act. πλανάω (# 4414) to lead astray, to deceive. **ποιῶν** pres. act. part. ποιέω (# 4472) to do, to practice. Subst. part. indicates habitual action. ◆ **8 ποιῶν** pres. act. part. ποιέω (# 4472) to do. **διάβολος** (# 1333) devil, adversary (DDD, 464-73). **ἁμαρτάνει** pres. ind. act. ἁμαρτάνω (# 279) to sin. Pres. indicates continual, habitual action. It began in the past but continues in the pres. (GGBB, 519-20). **ἐφανερώθη** aor. ind. pass. φανερόω (# 5746) to appear. **λύσῃ** aor. subj. act. λύω (# 3395) to loose, to destroy. The word suggests destruction by undoing or dissolving that which forms the bond of cohesion (Brooke). Subj. w. **ἵνα** (# 2671) in a purp. cl. ◆ **9 γεγεννημένος** perf. pass. part. γεννάω (# 1164) to bear; pass., to be born (s. 2:29). **ποιεῖ** pres. ind. act. ποιέω (# 4472) to do. **μένει** pres. ind. act. μένω (# 3531) to remain. **δύναται** pres. ind. mid. (dep.) δύναμαι (# 1538) to be able. **ἁμαρτάνειν** pres. act. inf. ἁμαρτάνω (# 279) to sin. For a discussion of the use of the pres. here s. GGBB, 522, 524; S. Kubo, "I John 3:9: Absolute or Habitual?," *AUSS* 7 (1969): 47-56. **γεγέννηται** perf. ind. pass. γεννάω (# 1164) to be born. Perf. marks not only the single act of birth, but the continuous presence of its efficacy (Westcott). The v. indicates the abiding influence of His seed within everyone who is born of God, as that which enables John to affirm without fear of contradiction that one cannot go on living in sin. Indeed, "if he should thus continue in sin, it would indicate that he has never been born again" (Stott); for a discussion of this v. w. various viewpoints s. Marshall; Smalley; Brown; HSB, 736-39. ◆ **10 φανερός** (# 5745) clear, evident, conspicuous (MM). **ποιῶν** pres. act. part. ποιέω (# 4472) to do. **ἀγαπῶν** pres. act. part. ἀγαπάω (# 26) to love. ◆ **11 ἀγγελία** (# 32) report, message (s. 1:5). **ἠκούσατε** aor. ind. act. ἀκούω (# 201) to hear. **ἀγαπῶμεν** pres. subj. act. ἀγαπάω (# 26) to love. Subj. w. **ἵνα** (# 2671) in a cl. explaining ἀγγελία (RWP; GGBB, 476). Pres. would indicate a continual, habitual attitude of love. **ἀλλήλους** acc. pl. ἀλλήλων (# 253) one another, reciprocal pron. ◆ **12 ἦν** impf. ind. act. εἰμί (# 1639) to be. **χάριν τίνος** (# 5515; 5920) for the sake of what? wherefore? (RWP). **ἔσφαξεν** aor. ind. act. σφάζω (# 5377) to slaughter, to kill, to butcher, to murder. Although the word was used often of the slaying of animals, particularly for sacrifice, this is not the sense here. It is used here of violent killing (Schnackenburg; Marshall; RWP). Cain is used here as a typical OT example of wickedness. The heretical group may have

been vegetarian, so John may be deliberately pointing to the fact that Cain worked the soil (Smalley). ◆ **13 θαυμάζετε** pres. imp. act. θαυμάζω (# 2513) to be amazed, to wonder, to marvel. Aor. would emphasize the immediate feeling aroused by a particular thought, or action (s. 3:7). Here the pres. is used of the continuous feeling stirred up by the whole temper of men (Westcott; Brooke). The vb. is followed by the particle **εἰ** (# 1623) ("if," "that") (BD, 237). **μισεῖ** pres. ind. act. μισέω (# 3631) to hate. ◆ **14 οἴδαμεν** pref. ind. act. οἶδα (# 3857) to know. Def. perf. w. pres. meaning. **μεταβεβήκαμεν** perf. ind. act. μεταβαίνω (# 3553) to pass over from one place to another, to transfer, to migrate (RWP). Perf. indicates the permanency of the step of salvation (Schnackenburg). **ἀγαπῶμεν** pres. ind. act. ἀγαπάω (# 26) to love. Pres. indicates habitual action. **ἀγαπῶν** pres. act. part. ἀγαπάω (# 26) to love. Subst. part., "the one (not) loving." Pres. indicates a habit of life. **μένει** pres. ind. act. μένω (# 3531) to remain. ◆ **15 μισῶν** pres. act. part. μισέω (# 3631) to hate. **ἀνθρωποκτόνος** (# 475) one who kills a human being, murderer. **οἴδατε** perf. ind. act. οἶδα (# 3857) to know. Def. perf. w. pres. meaning. **ἔχει** pres. ind. act. ἔχω (# 2400) to have, to possess. Pres. points to possession. **μένουσαν** pres. act. part. (adj.) acc. fem. sing. μένω (# 3531) to remain. Pres. stresses continuing action. ◆ **16 ἐγνώκαμεν** perf. ind. act. γινώσκω (# 1182) to know (s.v. 6). **ἔθηκεν** aor. ind. act. τίθημι (# 5502) to place. Used here in the Semitic sense of, "to lay down one's life," "to give one's life" (Marshall; Brooke; Bultmann; Gaugler). **ὀφείλομεν** pres. ind. act. ὀφείλω (# 4053) to be morally obligated. **θεῖναι** aor. act. inf. τίθημι (# 5502) to lay down. Compl. inf. to the main vb. Aor. involves a single action of giving up one's life. The variant reading of the pres. τιθέναι would indicate a continuing willingness to do so out of love (Brown). ◆ **17 ἔχῃ** pres. subj. act. ἔχω (# 2400) to have, to possess. **βίος** (# 1050) life; i.e., things pertaining to life, like possessions or wealth (Houlden; Schnackenburg). **θεωρῇ** pres. subj. act. θεωρέω (# 2555) to see. **ἔχοντα** pres. act. part. ἔχω (# 2400) to have. **κλείσῃ** aor. subj. act. κλείω (# 3091) to shut up, to lock. The word perhaps suggests that a barrier raised against the natural human feelings is exposed by the contemplation of such cases (Brooke). **σπλάγχνον** (# 5073) the inward organs, tender mercy, strong compassion (s. Phil. 1:8; TDNT; MNTW, 156; TLNT). **ἡ ἀγάπη τοῦ θεοῦ** the love of God; God's own love, which comes and dwells in the genuine believer and is the source of the love in the believing community (Holden). **μένει** pres. ind. act. μένω (# 3531) to remain. ◆ **18 ἀγαπῶμεν** pres. subj. act. ἀγαπάω (# 26) to love. Hortatory subj., "let us love." **γλῶσσα** (# 1185) tongue, language, speech; w. mere outward expression as opposed to the genuine movement of our whole being (Westcott). ◆ **19 γνωσόμεθα** fut. ind. mid. (dep.)

γινώσκω (# 1182) to know. ἐκ τῆς ἀληθείας ἐσμέν we are from the truth; i.e., "we draw the power of our being from the Truth as its source" (Westcott). This is the origin of our belief. ἔμπροσθεν (# 1869) before. πείσομεν fut. ind. act. πείθω (# 4275) to persuade, to reassure, to set at rest, to appease (Marshall; Stott). καρδία (# 2840) heart. The word is used here in the sense of conscience (Marshall). ◆ **20** καταγινώσκῃ pres. subj. act. καταγινώσκω (# 2861) to know something against someone, to condemn. Subj. w. ὅτι ἐάν (# 4022; 1569) viewed as a generalizing rel., in a 3rd. class cond. cl. w. the cond. viewed as possible (Smalley). μείζων (# 3505) comp. μέγας great; comp., greater. W. the gen., "greater than." Our conscience is by no means infallible; its condemnation may often be unjust. We can, therefore, appeal from our conscience to God who is greater and more knowledgeable. Indeed He knows all things, including our secret motives and deepest resolves, and, it is implied, He will be more merciful toward us than our own heart (Stott). γινώσκει pres. ind. act. γινώσκω (# 1182) to know. Pres. indicates God's knowledge is continual. ◆ **21** καταγινώσκῃ pres. subj. act. καταγινώσκω (# 2861) to condemn. παρρησία (# 4244) openness, confidence, assurance (s. 2:28). ἔχομεν pres. ind. act. ἔχω (# 2400) to have. ◆ **22** αἰτῶμεν pres. subj. act. αἰτέω (# 160) to ask, to request. Subj. in an indef. rel. cl. λαμβάνομεν pres. ind. act. λαμβάνω (# 3284) to take. τηροῦμεν pres. ind. act. τηρέω (# 5498) to guard, to keep, to obey. ἀρεστός (# 744) pleasing, vb. adj. Here, "the things pleasing." ποιοῦμεν pres. ind. act. ποιέω (# 4472) to do. ◆ **23** πιστεύσωμεν aor. subj. act. πιστεύω (# 4409) to believe. Subj. w. ἵνα (# 2671) used in an epex. cl. explaining what His commandment is. ἀγαπῶμεν pres. subj. act. ἀγαπάω (# 26) to love. Parallel to the previous vb. ἔδωκεν aor. ind. act. δίδωμι (# 1443) to give. ◆ **24** τηρῶν pres. act. part. τηρέω (# 5498) to observe, to hold, to obey. μένει pres. ind. act. μένω (# 3531) to remain. γινώσκομεν pres. ind. act. γινώσκω (# 1182) to know. οὗ gen. sing. ὅς (# 4005) who, which; rel. pron. gen. because it is attracted to the case of πνεύματος (# 4460). ἔδωκεν aor. ind. act. δίδωμι (# 1443) to give.

1 John 4

◆ **1** πιστεύετε pres. imp. act. πιστεύω (# 4409) to believe. Pres. imp. w. μή (# 3590) could call for the stopping of an action in progress. ἀλλά (# 247) but, rather. δοκιμάζετε pres. imp. act. δοκομάζω (# 1507) to prove by trial, to test (TDNT; TLNT; EDNT). τὰ πνεύματα (# 4460) the spirits. Pl. may indicate the spirit of error and spirit of truth, or the Holy Spirit and the evil spirit (Smalley, Brown; s. 1 Cor. 12:10). For a treatment of the word πνεῦμα in 1 John s. Schnackenburg, 209-15. ψευδοπροφήτης (# 6021) false prophet. ἐξεληλύθασιν perf. ind. act. ἐξέρχομαι (# 2002) to go out from. Perf. expresses the continued agency, not the single fact, of

their departure (Westcott). ◆ **2** γινώσκετε pres. ind. act. γινώσκω (# 1182) to know. The vb. is to be taken as ind. rather than imp. (Marshall). ὁμολογεῖ pres. ind. act. ὁμολογέω (# 3933) to agree, to confess. ἐληλυθότα perf. act. part. ἔρχομαι (# 2262) to come. Predicated acc. of the part. used after the vb. ὁμολογεῖ (RWP; for this construction s. Stott; Marshall). Perf. indicates that the coming of Christ in the flesh was well-known; the effects of the Incarnation were lasting (Schnackenburg; Brooke; McKay). ◆ **3** ὁμολογεῖ pres. ind. act. ὁμολογέω (# 3933) to confess. ἀκηκόατε perf. ind. act. ἀκούω (# 201) to hear. ἔρχεται pres. ind. mid. (dep.) ἔρχομαι (# 2262) to come, to go. Pres. here also has a fut. implication. ◆ **4** νενικήκατε perf. ind. act. νικάω (# 3771) to conquer, to be victorious. μείζων (# 3505) s.v. 20. κόσμος (# 3180) world. In v. 3 the word means more the area inhabited by man, in v. 4 it refers to sinful mankind, and in v. 5 the stress is more on the sinful principle found in such people (Marshall; TDNT). ◆ **5** διὰ τοῦτο (# 1328; 4047) because of this. λαλοῦσιν pres. ind. act. λαλέω (# 3281) to speak. ἀκούει pres. ind. act. ἀκούω (# 201) to hear. Followed by the gen., "to listen to," "to hear." The world recognizes its own people and listens to a message originating in its own circle. This explains their popularity (Stott). ◆ **6** ἐσμεν pres. ind. act. εἰμί (# 1639) to be. γινώσκων pres. act. part. γινώσκω (# 1182) to know. πλάνη (# 4415) error. Descriptive gen. or obj. gen. The word here can have the meaning, "cause of error." For this and other parallels to the spirits of truth and perversity s. Marshall; Schnackenburg, 211f; TDNT; NIDNTT. ◆ **7** ἀγαπῶμεν pres. subj. act. ἀγαπάω (# 26) to love. Hortatory subj., "let us love." ἀγαπῶν pres. act. part. ἀγαπάω. γεγέννηται perf. ind. pass. γεννάω (# 1164) to bear; pass., to be born. Perf. emphasizes the continuing results of the new birth. γινώσκει pres. ind. act. γινώσκω (# 1182) to know. Pres. indicates continual knowledge. ◆ **8** ἀγαπῶν pres. act. part. ἀγαπάω (# 26) to love. God has the quality of love (GGBB, 45, 245, 264). For the term "love" and its relation to the person and nature of God s. 2:5; Schnackenburg, 231-39; Marshall. ◆ **9** ἐφανερώθη aor. ind. pass. φανερόω (# 5746) to make clear, to make evident, to reveal. The word conveys the thought of the manifestation of what was previously hidden (Marshall). μονογενής (# 3666) only one of its kind, single one, only, unique (Marshall; Smalley; Brown; s. John 3:16). ἀπέσταλκεν perf. ind. act. ἀποστέλλω (# 690) to send, to send an official authoritative representative to do a specific task (TNDT). Perf. indicates that God the Father sent Him and we now enjoy the blessings of the mission (Westcott). ζήσωμεν aor. subj. act. ζάω (# 2409) to live. Subj. w. ἵνα (# 2671) used in a purp. cl. ◆ **10** ἀγάπη (# 27) love; here, the quality of true love. True love is selfless (Brooke). For a discussion of the meaning of love s. DLNT, 694-700. ἠγαπήκαμεν perf.

ind. act. ἀγαπάω (# 26) to love. The use of the perf. perhaps stresses that it is not our continuing love for God which should be central, but the love revealed historically to us in Jesus (Marshall). ἠγάπησεν aor. ind. act. ἀγαπάω (# 26) to love. The change from the perf. to the aor. stresses the historic manifestation of the love rather than the continuing effect of God's act (Marshall). ἀπέστειλεν aor. ind. act. ἀποστέλλω (# 690) to send. ἱλασμός (# 2662) satisfaction, propitiation (s. 2:2). ◆ 11 ἠγάπησεν aor. ind. act. ἀγαπάω (# 26) to love. ὀφείλομεν pres. ind. act. ὀφείλω (# 4053) to be morally obligated, to owe a debt that must be paid, to have to do something; "we must, ought." ἀγαπᾶν pres. act. inf. ἀγαπάω (# 26) to love. Compl. inf. to the main vb. ◆ 12 πώποτε (# 4799) at any time, ever. τεθέαται perf. ind. mid. (dep.) θεάομαι (# 2517) to see, to behold (s. 1:1). Here the thought is of the continuous beholding that answers to abiding fellowship (Westcott). ἀγαπῶμεν pres. subj. act. ἀγαπάω (# 26) to love. Subj. w. ἐάν (# 1569) is used in a 3rd.-class cond. cl. which views the cond. as possible. μένει pres. ind. act. μένω (# 3531) to remain. τετελειωμένη perf. pass. part. τελειόω (# 5457) to bring to completion, to bring to the goal, to perfect (s. 2:5). ◆ 13 γινώσκομεν pres. ind. act. γινώσκω (# 1182) to know. ἐκ τοῦ πνεύματος αὐτοῦ from His Spirit. The possession of the Spirit indicates that the believer is in Him. δέδωκεν perf. ind. act. δίδωμι (# 1443) to give. Perf. emphasizes the completed action w. the continuing results. ◆ 14 τεθεάμεθα perf. ind. mid. (dep.) θεάομαι (# 2517) to see (s.v. 12). μαρτυροῦμεν pres. ind. act. μαρτυρέω (# 3455) to witness. ἀπέσταλκεν perf. ind. act. ἀποστέλλω (# 690) to send (s.v. 9). σωτήρ (# 5400) savior; here, double acc., "He sent the Son as Savior of the world." κόσμος (# 3180) world. Obj. gen. here. ◆ 15 ὁμολογήσῃ aor. subj. act. ὁμολογέω (# 3933) to confess. Subj. w. ἐάν (# 1569) to express cond. Aor. points to a specific action. ◆ 16 ἐγνώκαμεν perf. ind. act. γινώσκω (# 1182) to know. Perf. indicates we have come to know and still know (Marshall). πεπιστεύκαμεν perf. ind. act. πιστεύω (# 4409) to believe. Perf. indicates that the recognition of the love of God is considered to be a lasting and settled conviction (Schnackenburg). ἔχει pres. ind. act. ἔχω (# 2400) to have. μένων pres. act. part. μένω (# 3531) to remain. μένει pres. ind. act. ◆ 17 τετελείωται perf. ind. pass. τελειόω (# 5457) to bring to completion (s.v. 12). παρρησία (# 4244) openness, confidence, assurance (s. 2:28). ἔχωμεν pres. subj. act. ἔχω (# 2400) to have. Subj. used either as in a purp. cl. or in apposition to ἐν τούτω or w. the ὅτι cl., the latter of which would make this cl. a parenthesis (RWP; Westcott). κρίσεως (# 3213) judging, judgment. ἐσμεν pres. ind. act. εἰμί (# 1639) to be. ◆ 18 φόβος (# 5832) fear. τελεία fem. nom. τέλειος (# 5455) perfect. ἔξω (# 2032) outside, out. βάλλει pres. ind. act. βάλλω (# 965) to cast out, to drive out, to turn

out of doors (RWP). κόλασις (# 3136) punishment. The word indicates the disciplinary chastisement of the wrongdoer (Westcott). φοβούμενος pres. mid. part. φοβέομαι (# 5828) to be afraid, to have fear. τετελείωται perf. ind. pass. τελέω (# 5457) to perfect. ◆ 19 ἀγαπῶμεν pres. subj. act. ἀγαπάω (# 26) to love. Cohortatory subj., "let us love." πρῶτος (# 4755) first. ἠγάπησεν aor. ind. act. ἀγαπάω (# 26) to love. Aor. may point to a specific act of love. ◆ 20 εἴπῃ aor. subj. act. λέγω (# 3306) to say. Subj. w. ἐάν (# 1569) is used in a 3rd. class cond. cl. viewing the cond. as a possibility. ἀγαπῶ pres. ind. act. ἀγαπάω (# 26) to love. μισῇ pres. subj. act. μισέω (# 3631) to hate. ψεύστης (# 6026) liar. ἀγαπῶν pres. act. part. ἀγαπάω. ἑώρακεν perf. ind. act. ὁράω (# 3972) to see. δύναται pres. ind. mid. (dep.) δύναμαι (# 1538) to be able to. ἀγαπᾶν pres. act. inf. ἀγαπάω. Compl. inf. to the main vb. ◆ 21 ἐντολή (# 1953) command. ἔχομεν pres. ind. act. ἔχω (# 2400) to have. ἀγαπῶν pres. act. part. ἀγαπάω (# 26) to love. ἀγαπᾷ pres. subj. act. ἀγαπάω. Subj. w. ἵνα (# 2671) gives the content of the command. This concept was common in the Greek world (BBC).

1 John 5

◆ 1 πιστεύων pres. act. part. πιστεύω (# 4409) to believe. ὅτι (# 4022) that. The particle introduces the content of what is believed. γεγέννηται perf. ind. pass. γεννάω (# 1164) to bear; pass., to be born (s.1 John 2:29; RAC, 9:43-171). ἀγαπῶν pres. act. part. ἀγαπάω (# 26) to love. γεννήσαντα aor. act. part. γεννάω. ἀγαπᾷ pres. subj. act. ἀγαπάω. γεγεννημένον perf. pass. part. γεννάω. This new birth, which brings us into believing recognition of the eternal Son, also involves us in a loving relationship w. the Father and His other children. The part. here refers to every child of God (Stott). Perf. indicates the continuing state. ◆ 2 γινώσκομεν pres. ind. act. γινώσκω (# 1182) to know. ὅταν (# 4020) w. subj., whenever. ἀγαπῶμεν pres. ind. act. ἀγαπάω (# 26) to love (following ὅτι). ἀγαπῶμεν pres. subj. act. ἀγαπάω. ποιῶμεν pres. subj. act. ποιέω (# 4472) to do. Subjs. are used in an indef. temp. cl. (RWP; Schnackenburg). ◆ 3 ἡ ἀγάπη τοῦ θεοῦ love of God. Obj. gen., love which has God as the object. The main idea here may be that our love for God must find expression in keeping the commandment to love one another (Brown). τηρῶμεν pres. subj. act. τηρέω (# 5498) to keep, to observe, to obey. For a discussion of the commandments s. DLNT, 238-41. Subj. w. ἵνα (# 2671) used in an explanatory cl. defining our love for God. βαρεῖαι nom. pl. βαρύς (# 987) heavy, burdensome. The word suggests the idea of a heavy and oppressive burden (Brooke). ◆ 4 γεγεννημένον perf. pass. part. n. nom. sing. γεννάω (# 1164) to be born. πᾶν τὸ γεγεννημένον ἐκ τοῦ θεοῦ everyone who has been born of God. The n. phrase is possibly meant in a generalizing sense or the use may be influenced by the fact that the Gr. words for "child" are n. (Marshall). **νικᾷ** pres. ind. act. νικάω (# 3771) to conquer, to gain a victory, to overcome. **νικήσασα** aor. act. part. νικάω. Aor. could point to a definite act or fact (Brooke). **πίστις** (# 4411) faith. ἡ πίστις ἡμῶν our faith. Our faith enables us to overcome the world. It acts as a weapon of war, and its force consists in the fact that its content is the true nature of Jesus (Houlden). ◆ **5 νικῶν** pres. act. part. νικάω (# 3771) to conquer. εἰ μή (# 1623; 3590) except, if not. **πιστεύων** pres. act. part. πιστεύω (# 4409) to believe. ◆ **6 ἐλθών** aor. act. part. (subst.) ἔρχομαι (# 2262) to come, to go. **αἷμα** (# 135) blood. Perhaps the best explanation of the meaning of the term here is that it refers to the bloody death upon the cross (Plummer; Westcott; Marshall; Brooke; for various explanations of vv. 6-8 s. Brown; Smalley; Ben Witherington III, "The Waters of Birth: John 3:5 and 1 John 5:6-6," *NTS* 35 [1989]: 155-60; HSB, 739-40). **μαρτυροῦν** pres. act. part. μαρτυρέω (# 3455) to be a witness, to testify. ◆ **7 τρεῖς** (# 552) three. **μαρτυροῦντες** pres. act. part. (# 3455) μαρτυρέω to witness. On sale documents often several witnesses signed (BBC). For a discussion of the textual problem in vs. 7 and 8 s. TC, 716-18. ◆ **9 λαμβάνομεν** pres. ind. act. λαμβάνω (# 3284) to receive. **μείζων** (# 3505) comp. μέγας greater (s. 3:20). In John 5:36 the word indicates the greater credence; in this v. it indicates the stronger, obligating power of the divine witness (Schnackenburg). **μεμαρτύρηκεν** perf. ind. act. μαρτυρέω (# 3456) to be a witness, to bear witness, to testify. ◆ **10 πιστεύων** pres. act. part. πιστεύω (# 4409) to believe. The vb. constructed w. dat. usually expresses acceptance of the statement rather than surrender to the person (Brooke). **πεποίηκεν** perf. ind. act. ποιέω (# 4472) to do. **πεπίστευκεν** perf. ind. act. πιστεύω (# 4409) to believe. Perf. indicates the abiding affects. **μεμαρτύρηκεν** perf. ind. act. μαρτυρέω (# 3456) to witness. Perf. stresses the continuing results. ◆ **11 ἔδωκεν** aor. ind. act. δίδωμι (# 1443) to give. ◆ **12 ἔχων** pres. act. part. ἔχω (# 2400) to have, to possess. Pres. of the vb. indicates continual possession (M, 110). The word is used to describe our personal possession of the Father through confessing the Son (Stott). **ἔχει** pres. ind. act. ἔχω (# 2400) to have. ◆ **13 ἔγραψα** aor. ind. act. γράφω (# 1211) to write. The word could be epistolary aor., referring to the whole epistle, or it could refer to the immediately preceding section, either vv. 1-12 or vv. 5-12 (Marshall). **εἰδῆτε** perf. subj. act. οἶδα (# 3857) to know. Def. perf. w. pres. meaning. Subj. w. ἵνα (# 2671) in a purp. cl. ὅτι (# 4022) that, giving the content of the knowledge. **πιστεύουσιν** pres. ind. act. πιστεύω (# 4409) to believe. ◆ **14 παρρησία** (# 4244) openness, confidence (s. 1 John 2:28). **ἔχομεν** pres. ind. act. ἔχω (# 2400) to have. ἐάν τι (# 1569; 5516) whatever, if anything. The particle introduces a 3rd. class cond. cl.

(RWP). **αἰτώμεθα** pres. ind. mid. (dep.) αἰτέομαι (# 160) mid., to ask for oneself, to request. **ἀκούει** pres. ind. act. ἀκούω (# 201) to hear. ◆ **15 ἐάν** (# 1569) if. Particle used w. the ind. in a 1st. class cond. cl. has almost a causal sense (BD, 189; MT 115f; RWP). **αἰτώμεθα** pres. ind. mid. (dep.) αἰτέομαι (# 160) to ask. Mid. suggests asking for oneself. Subj. in an indef. rel. cl. **αἴτημα** (# 161) that which is asked, request. **ᾐτήκαμεν** perf. ind. act. αἰτέομαι (# 160) to ask, to request. Perf. indicates the results of asking. ◆ **16 ἴδῃ** aor. subj. act. ὁράω (# 3972) to see. Subj. w. ἐάν (# 1569) is used in a 3rd. class cond. cl. which views the condition as a possibility. **ἁμαρτάνοντα** pres. act. part. ἁμαρτάνω (# 279) to sin. For a discussion of the sin unto death s. Stott; Westcott; Marshall; Smalley; Brown; HSB, 742-44; DNLT, 1095-97. **αἰτήσει** fut. ind. act. αἰτέω (# 160) to ask. **δώσει** fut. ind. act. δίδωμι (# 1443) to give. **ἁμαρτάνουσιν** pres. act. part. ἁμαρτάνω (# 279) to sin. **ἐρωτήσῃ** aor. subj. act. ἐρωτάω (# 2263) to ask about, to request information about (Westcott). Subj. w. ἵνα (# 2671) as obj. of the vb. λέγω. ◆ **17 ἀδικία** (# 94) unrighteousness. ◆ **18 οἴδαμεν** perf. ind. act. οἶδα (# 3857) to know. Def. perf. w. pres. meaning. **γεγεννημένος** perf. pass. part. γεννάω (# 1164) to give birth. **ἁμαρτάνει** pres. ind. act. ἁμαρτάνω (# 279) to sin. **γεννηθείς** aor. pass. part. γεννάω (# 1164) to be born. **τηρεῖ** pres. ind. act. τηρέω (# 5498) to keep. **πονηρός** (# 4505) evil, mean. The word refers to active evil (TDNT; Trench, *Synonyms*, 315f). **ἅπτεται** pres. ind. mid. (dep.) ἅπτομαι (# 721) to touch, w. gen. The vb. means to lay hold of someone in order to harm him (Marshall). ◆ **19 οἴδαμεν** perf. ind. act. οἶδα (# 3857) to know. Def. perf. w. pres. meaning. **ὅλος** (# 3910) whole, total. **κεῖται** pres. ind. mid. (dep.) κεῖμαι (# 3023) to lie (RWP). ◆ **20 οἴδαμεν** perf. ind. act. οἶδα (# 3857) to know. Def. perf. w. pres. meaning. **ἥκει** pres. ind. act. ἥκω (# 2457) to have come. Perf. pres., "the Son of God has come." **δέδωκεν** perf. ind. act. δίδωμι (# 1443) to give. **διάνοια** (# 1379) knowing, understanding. The faculty of knowing or discerning the ability to reason correctly used in Gr. philosophy of syllogistic reasoning (Brooke; Westcott; GPT, 37). **γινώσκωμεν** pres. subj. act. γινώσκω (# 1182) to know. Subj. w. ἵνα (# 2671) in a purp. cl. **ἀληθινός** (# 240) true, genuine. **οὗτος** (# 4047) this one. The pron. clearly refers to Jesus (Marshall; s. also GGBB, 326-27). ◆ **21 φυλάξατε** aor. imp. act. φυλάσσω (# 5875) to guard, to keep. The use of the act. w. the reflex. pron. may be regarded as emphasizing the duty of personal effort (Westcott). **εἰδώλων** (# 1631) image, idol, false god. The presence of idols in the ancient world is witnessed to not only by the geographical description of Strabo and Pausanias, but also in literature, art, theater, music, and the various archaeological discoveries (s. Acts 17:16; DPL, 424-26).

2 John

2 John

◆ **1 πρεσβύτερος** (# *4565*) old, elder. John may indicate by the term that he was a vernerated old man in the community, or better that he was an elder, or leader in the church (Smalley; Brown; TDNT; EDNT; NIDNTT; DLNT, 219-26). The art. indicates that he was well known. **ἐκλεκτός** (# *1723*) chosen, selected (s. 1 Peter 1:1). The phrase "to the elect lady" could refer to a specific person or it could be a personification indicating some local church (Stott; Westcott; Marshall; Brown; Smalley; HSB, 745-46). **τέκνοις** dat. pl. τέκνον (# *5451*) child. **τοῖς τέκνοις αὐτῆς** to her children. This would refer to the members of the church (Marshall). **ἀγαπῶ** pres. ind. act. ἀγαπάω (# *26*) to love. Pres. expresses a continuing love. **ἐγνωκότες** perf. act. part. γινώσκω (# *1182*) to know. Perf. emphasizes the continuing results of having known. For a rhetorical analysis s. Duane F. Watson, "A Rhetorical Analysis of 2 John according to Greco-Roman Convention," *NTS* 35 (1989): 104-30. ◆ **2 ἀλήθεια** (# *237*) truth. Here the word refers to the divine reality and signifies what is ultimately real; namely, God himself. Hence, it can refer to the expression of God in His incarnate Son and in the Christian message (Schnackenburg; Marshall). **μένουσαν** pres. act. part. (adj.) μένω (# *3531*) to remain. Pres. indicates the permanant character of the truth. **ἔσται** fut. ind. mid. (dep.) εἰμί (# *1639*) to be. **εἰς τὸν αἰῶνα** (# *1650; 172*) forever. ◆ **3 χάρις** (# *5921*) grace (EDNT; TLNT; TDNT). **ἔλεος** (# *1799*) mercy (s. 1 Tim. 1:2). ◆ **4 ἐχάρην** aor. ind. pass. χαίρω (# *5897*) to rejoice, to be glad. Aor. is not epistolary, but refers back to the time when the elder met the members of the church (Marshall). **λίαν** (# *3336*) greatly, very much, very. **ὅτι** (# *4022*) that. The word gives not only the content of the rejoicing but also the reason for rejoicing (Bultmann). **εὕρηκα** perf. ind. act. εὑρίσκω (# *2351*) to find. Perf. strongly suggests personal experience (Marshall). **τέκνον** (# *5451*) child. **περιπατοῦντας** pres. act. part. περιπατέω (# *4344*) to walk about, to conduct one's life. **καθώς** (# *2777*) just as. The sentence introduced by this word explains how the walk of these church members can be called a walk in the truth (Schnackenburg). **ἐντολή** (# *1953*) commandment (DLNT, 238-41). **ἐλάβομεν** aor. ind. act. λαμβάνω (# *3284*) to receive. ◆ **5 ἐρωτῶ** pres. ind. act. ἐρωτάω (# *2263*) to ask, to request. **γράφων** pres. act. part. (circum.) γράφω (# *1211*) to write. For let-

ters and their form s. DLNT, 649-54. **εἴχομεν** impf. ind. act. ἔχω (# *2400*) to have. **ἀγαπῶμεν** pres. subj. act. ἀγαπάω (# *26*) to love. Subj. w. ἵνα (# *2671*) in a cl. describing the content of the request. **ἀλλήλων** (# *253*) reciprocal pron., one another. ◆ **6 ἀγάπη** (# *27*) love (TDNT; TLNT; EDNT). Love means living according to the Father's commands (Marshall). **περιπατῶμεν** pres. subj. act. περιπατέω (# *4344*) to conduct one's life. Subj. w. ἵνα (# *2671*) in a cl. explaining what the commandment is. **ἠκούσατε** aor. act. ind. ἀκούω (# *201*) to hear. **περιπατῆτε** pres. subj. act. περιπατέω (# *4344*) to walk. Subj. w. ἵνα (# *2671*) to express the content of the command. ◆ **7 πλάνος** (# *4418*) deceiver, one who leads not only to wrong opinion but also to wrong action (Westcott). **ἐξῆλθον** aor. ind. act. ἐξέρχομαι (# *2002*) to go out. **ὁμολογοῦντες** pres. act. part. (subst.) ὁμολογέω (# *3033*) to agree to, to profess. The vb. is used w. the double acc. and has to do w. the messianic character of Jesus; John uses the word in order to correct faulty or inadequate messianic ideas current in his time (ECC, 105). **ἐρχόμενον** pres. mid. (dep.) part. ἔρχομαι (# *2262*) to come, to go. Here indir. discourse is suggested by the part. (GGBB, 646). **ὁ πλάνος καὶ ὁ ἀντίχριστος** "the deceiver and the Antichrist." Pred. nom. w. art. indicates that the nouns are the same as the subject, **οὗτος** (# *4047*) this one; a generic force here, "such a person is..." (GGBB, 332). John identifies the heretical members w. the deceiver and the antichrist (Smalley; Brown). ◆ **8 βλέπετε** pres. imp. act. βλέπω (# *1063*) to see, to beware, to watch out. **ἀπολέσητε** aor. subj. act. ἀπόλλυμι (# *660*) to lose, to suffer loss. Subj. w. μή (# *3590*) in a neg. purp. cl. For a discussion of the textual problem s. TC. **εἰργασάμεθα** aor. ind. mid. (dep.) ἐργάζομαι (# *2237*) to work. **μισθός** (# *3635*) pay. The metaphor seems to be taken from the payment of labor, since this word refers to a workman's wage (Stott). **πλήρης** (# *4441*) full, complete. **ἀπολάβητε** aor. subj. act. ἀπολαμβάνω (# *655*) to take away, to receive. The word was used in the papyri of receiving what is due (MM). ◆ **9 προάγων** pres. act. part. προάγω (# *4575*) to go before, to run ahead. Perhaps this is a sarcastic reference to the way in which the false teachers themselves proudly claim to be offering advanced teaching; the elder claims that they have advanced beyond the boundaries of true Christian belief (Marshall). **μένων** pres. act. part. μένω (# *3531*) to remain. **ἐν τῇ διδαχῇ τοῦ**

Χριστοῦ in the teaching of Christ. Gen. subj. ("the teaching from Christ") or better, obj. gen. ("the teaching about Christ"). ἔχει pres. ind. act. ἔχω (# 2400) to have. Pres. indicates a present possession. ◆ 10 ἔρχεται pres. ind. mid. (dep.) ἔρχομαι (# 2262) to come. φέρει pres. ind. act. φέρω to carry. λαμβάνετε pres. imp. act. λαμβάνω (# 3284) to receive, to show hospitality to. Pres. imp. w. the neg. μή (# 3590) could call for the stopping of an action in progress, or call for a continual or habitual action (GGBB, 725). It was common in the ancient world to receive traveling teachers in the home and offer them shelter and lodging (BBC; DLNT, 501-7). χαίρειν pres. act. inf. χαίρω (# 5897) to give greeting. The giving of greetings indicates entering into fellowship w. the one greeted, and to welcome a false teacher was to express solidarity w. them (Schackenburg; Marshall). Inf. is used in indir. discourse as the obj. of the vb. λέγετε pres. imp. act. λέγω (# 3306) to speak, to say. Pres. imp. w. the neg. μή (# 3590) could call for the stopping of an action in progress, or call for a continual or habitual action. Used here in connection w. the inf., meaning "to give greeting." John's instruction may relate not only to an official visit of false teachers, but to extending them an official welcome rather than merely private hospitality (Stott). ◆ 11 λέγων pres. act. part. λέγω (# 3306) to say; here, "the one saying," "the one who says." χαίρειν pres. act. inf. χαίρω (# 5897) to rejoice. κοινωνεῖ pres. ind. act. κοινωνέω (# 3125) to have fellowship, to share in. Housing an apostate was seen as collaborating with him (BBC). ◆ 12 ἔχων pres. act. part. ἔχω (# 2400) to have. Concessive part., "although I have." γράφειν pres. act. inf. γράφω (# 1211) to write. ἐβουλήθην aor. ind. pass. (dep.) βούλομαι (# 1086) to will, to want to. χάρτου gen. sing. χάρτης (# 5925) paper. A leaf of papyrus was prepared for writing by cutting the pith into stripes and pasting together (RWP). μέλας (# 3506) black, black ink (s. 3 John 13). ἐλπίζω (# 1827) pres. ind. act. to hope. γενέσθαι aor. mid. (dep.) inf. γίνομαι (# 1182) to become. Inf. to present the content of the hope. λαλῆσαι aor. act. inf. λαλέω (# 3281) to speak. Compl. inf. to the main vb. πεπληρωμένη perf. pass. part. πληρόω (# 4444) to make full, to fulfill, to complete. ᾖ pres. subj. act. εἰμί (# 1639) to be. Subj. w. perf. part. to form the perf. subj. pass. ◆ 13 ἀσπάζεται pres. ind. mid. (dep.) ἀσπάζομαι (# 832) to greet.

3 John

3 John

◆ **1** πρεσβύτερος (# *4565*) old, older one, elder comp. of πρέσβυς (s. 2 John 1). The use of the article indicates he is well known or familiar (GGBB, 225). ἀγαπητός (# *28*) one who is loved, beloved. The name "Gaius" was very prominent in the Roman Empire and occurs several times in the NT (Acts 19:29; 1 Cor. 1:14) (Plummer; Brooke; Brown). It is not known who this Gaius was, but it is clear from the terms in which John writes that he occupied a position of responsibility and leadership in the local church (Stott; Smalley; Klauck; ABD, 2:869). ἐν ἀληθείᾳ (# *1877; 237*) in truth. Dat. w. prep. ἐν could be used as an adv. ("truly"), or here it may be theological, since belief in Christ as the truth makes one a child of God and constitutes the basis of love (Brown). ◆ **2** ἀγαπητέ voc. sing. ἀγαπητός (# *28*) beloved. περὶ πάντων (# *4309; 4246*) in all respects (Marshall). The phrase is to be taken w. the inf. εὐοδοῦσθαι. The writer prays for the prosperity of Gaius in all respects. The thought may be of the public and social work of Gaius as well as his personal health (Brooke; Westcott). εὔχομαι (# *2377*) pres. ind. mid. (dep.) to pray, to wish (Marshall; Strecker; DLNT, 941-48). σε acc. sing. σύ (# *5148*) you, used as the subject of the inf. εὐοδοῦσθαι pres. pass. inf. εὐοδόω (# *2338*) pass., to be led along a good road, to get along well, to prosper, to succeed (BAGD; MM). Inf. in indir. discourse as obj. of the vb. εὔχομαι. ὑγιαίνειν pres. act. inf. ὑγιαίνω (# *5617*) to be well, to be in good health. It was a common greeting and desire expressed in letters for the recipient to be in good health (LAE, 187f; Schnackenburg; Strecker; MM; NIDNTT; TDNT; for the general concept of health and well-being in the ancient world s. RAC, 10:902-45). καθώς (# *2777*) just as. The wish is that Gaius' outward prosperity may correspond to the condition of his soul (Schnackenburg). ◆ **3** ἐχάρην aor. ind. pass. (dep.) χαίρω (# *5897*) to be happy, to rejoice, to be glad. The vb. occurs in letters of that day (Klauck). ἐρχομένων pres. mid. (dep.) part. ἔρχομαι (# *2262*) to come. Gen. abs. temp. part., "when the brothers came." Pres. indicates repetition and shows that several visits had been paid to the elder, possibly by different groups of Christians (Marshall; Brown). μαρτυρούντων pres. act. part. μαρτυρέω (# *3455*) to bear witness to, to testify about, w. dat. (DLNT, 1204-5) ἀληθεία (# *237*) truth (s. 2 John 2). They confirmed the fact that Gaius was faith-ful to the truth of the Christain gospel (Smalley). The identity of the brothers is not clear. They may have returned to the elder w. a report, or they may have been a group from another area (Brown). καθώς (# *2777*) as, just as, how, that. The word may introduce the content of the report ("how," "as"), or it may be a statement of the elder's assurance ("indeed") (Smalley; Marshall; Brown). περιπατεῖς pres. ind. act. περιπατέω (# *4344*) to walk about, to conduct one's life. Pres. indicates continual or habitual action. ◆ **4** μειζοτέραν (# *3504*) greater comp. ending on the comp. μείζων fr. μέγας large, great. Used w. gen. to mean "greater than." The Koine Greek has a number of the popular new formations of double comp. and double superl. (BD, 33f; M, 236; Brown). τούτων gen. pl. οὗτος (# *4047*) this; Pl., "these things," is a gen. of comparison. The τούτων refers to the content of the ἵνα (# *2671*) cl. and would normally be sing. (GGBB, 331-33). περιπατοῦντα pres. act. part. περιπατέω (# *4344*) to walk about. Pres. indicates the continual habitual conducting of one's life. Compl. part. completing the vb. ἀκούω (# *201*) to hear. ◆ **5** ἀγαπητέ (# *28*) beloved (s.v. 2). ποιεῖς pres. ind. act. ποιέω (# *4472*) to do, to practice; w. πιστόν (# *4412*) faithful; "to act faithfully." Pres. may be a futuristic pres., "you will demonstrate fidelity," implying that Gaius is being encouraged to offer hospitality to a group that includes missionaries employed by the Elder (Brown). ἐργάσῃ aor. subj. mid. (dep.) 2nd. pers. sing. ἐργάζομαι (# *2237*) to work. The use of the indef. rel. pron. ὅ (# *4005*) w. the subj. implies an unspecified number of ways or occasions of helping the brothers (Marshall). ξένος (# *3828*) stranger, guest (TLNT). The fact that brethren who were strangers were helped is emphasized by the use of the acc. of general reference: "and that too," "especially" (RWP; Westcott; Plummer; Smalley; DLNT, 501-507; J. Koenig, *New Testament Hospitality: Partnership with Strangers as Promise and Mission* [Philadelphia: Fortress, 1985]). ◆ **6** ἐμαρτύρησαν aor. ind. act. μαρτυρέω (# *3455*) to witness. The dat. that follows is used to express the obj. of the witness, the thing to which one testifies. Aor. may indicate a single instance of testimony or it may be complexive, covering a series of testimonies (Brown). ἐνώπιον (# *1967*) w. gen., in the presence of. The absence of the art. w. the word ἐκκλησίας denotes a meeting of the church at which the witness was borne (Brooke), or it may simply indicate the church in general (Smalley). **καλῶς** (# 2822) adv., well. **ποιήσεις** fut. ind. act. ποιέω (# 4472) to do. The expression καλῶς ποιήσεις is an idiom that means "please," "kindly," and was used often in the papyri to express a polite request (MM; Marshall; Brown; Strecker). **προπέμψας** aor. act. part. προπέμπω (# 4636) to send forth, to send someone on their way. The sending of missionaries on their way involved providing for their journey–supplying them w. food and money to pay for their expenses, washing their clothes and generally helping them to travel as comfortably as possible (Marshall; Brown; Strecker; BAGD). For a study regarding the support of wandering ministers and missionaries in the early church s. Gerd Theissen, "Legitimation und Lebensunterhalt: Ein Beitrag zur Soziologie Urchristlicher Missionare," *NTS* 21 (1975): 192-221; DLNT, 392-93, 769-70. Part. used epex. explaining the "doing well." **ἀξίως** (# 547) adv. w. gen., worthily; here, "worthily of God"; i.e., worthily of their dedication to the service of God (Westcott).   ◆ 7 **ὑπέρ** (# 5642) for, on behalf of, concerning. These went out in the service or name (ὄναμα) of Christ (SB, 3:779; Klauck; Brown) to make Him known (Smalley). **ἐξῆλθον** aor. ind. act. ἐξέρχομαι (# 2002) to go out; to go out from the church (or from God) into the world, regarded as a field for evangelism (Marshall). **λαμβάνοντες** pres. act. part. λαμβάνω (# 3284) to take, to receive. Pres. indicates habitual and customary action. It was their custom to carry out the spirit of the commission of the Twelve (Matt. 10:5ff) and of the tradition established by Paul. They had, therefore, a special claim on hospitality and help of the churches in places through which they had to pass (Brooke; Westcott). **ἐθνικός** (# 1618) pagan, heathen, unbeliever (Smalley). That these missionaries were supported by fellow Christians stands in marked contrast both to the wandering philosophers of the day and to the beggar priests of the Syrian goddess, who went out on behalf of the goddess and returned triumphantly boasting that "each journey brought in seventy bags" (LAE, 109; Bultmann; Schnackenburg; Klauck; BBC).   ◆ 8 **ἡμεῖς** nom. pl. ἐγώ (# 1609) I; "we." Emphatic pers. pron. Pl. includes the writer, readers and believers in general. **οὖν** (# 4036) therefore, drawing a conclusion from the previous. **ὀφείλομεν** pres. ind. act. ὀφείλω (# 4053) to be morally obligated, to owe a debt; w. inf., giving the moral obligation. Pres. indicates a continual obligation. **ὑπολαμβάνειν** pres. act. inf. ὑπολαμβάνω (# 5696) to take up under in order to raise up, to bear on high, to take up and carry away, to receive hospitality, to welcome, to support. The word is often used in the sense of receiving w. hospitality, and esp. of supporting (T; Brooke). The related noun ὑπόλημψις was used in the papyri for that which was given to a worker for taking over a job (Preisigke, 2:665). Christians should finance

Christian enterprises which the world will not, or should not be asked to, support. Indeed, Christians have a moral obligation to do so. They must support their brethren to whom the world should not be asked to contribute. **τοιοῦτος** (# 5525) such a one; here, "of such a kind" (Brown). **συνεργός** (# 5301) fellow worker. As sharers in the truth themselves, they must prove to be fellow workers in practice, working together w. the missionaries for the benefit of the truth (Marshall). **γινώμεθα** pres. subj. mid. (dep) γίνομαι (# 1181) to become, to be. An inclusive "we" to include both the author and the readers. Subj. w. **ἵνα** (# 2671) to express purp. **ἀλήθεια** (# 237) truth. Dat. here w. the noun **συνεργοί** could mean either "fellow-workers w. the truth" or "on behalf of, for the truth," or "in cooperation w." (Schnackenburg; Brown).   ◆ 9 **ἔγραψα** aor. ind. act. γράφω (# 1211) to write. Aor. is not the epistolary aor., but refers to a previous letter (Smalley; Brown). John had probably written to the church where Diotrephes was and requested support for the itinerant missionaries; Diotrephes rejects him and his request (Smalley; Brown; BBC). For a discussion of the disagreement over polity and over doctrine between John and Diotrephes s. Smalley. **φιλοπρωτεύων** pres. act. part. φιλοπρωτεύω (# 5812) to be fond of the first position, to wish to be first, to like to be the leader, w. gen. The word expresses ambition, the desire to have the first place in everything (BAGD; Brooke). Adj. part., "the-liking-to-be-first Diotrephes" (Brown). Pres. indicates the continual and habitual attitude. **αὐτῶν** gen. pl. αὐτός (# 899) self. Gen. w. the part., "to be first over them." Pl. is according to sense and refers to the church (Smalley; Brown). **Διοτρέφης** (# 1485) Diotrephes. The name was not overly common, but was a name for kings and those of noble birth and means "Zeus-nurtured," "Come from Zeus" (Brown; Klauck; for views as to who he was s. Klauck, 106-10; Strecker, 365-68). **ἐπιδέχεται** pres. ind. mid. (dep.) ἐπιδέχομαι (# 2110) to accept, to receive gladly (Klauck; GELTS, 169; 1 Macc. 12:8). The word can mean either "to accept the authority of" or "to welcome." The pl. **ἡμᾶς** will refer to the elder and his associates (Marshall). Pres. indicates a continuing attitude.   ◆ 10 **ἔλθω** aor. subj. act. ἔρχομαι (# 2262) to come. Subj. w. **ἐάν** (# 1569) in a 3rd. class cond. cl. assuming the possibility of the cond. **ὑπομνήσω** fut. ind. act. ὑπομιμνήσκω (# 5703) to call to memory, to remind, to bring up (Brown). John will remind either the congregation or Diotrephes of the deeds, since the deeds reveal the character. **ποιεῖ** pres. ind. act. ποιέω (# 4472) to do. Pres. points to an action in progress. **λόγοις πονηροῖς** (# 3364; 4505) with evil words, instr. dat. **φλυαρῶν** pres. act. part. φλυαρέω (# 5826) to talk nonsense (about), to babble, to bring unjustified charges against. It was used in polemic debate to denounce the inaneness of an argument: "O

Cleon, stop spouting silliness" (Ω Κλέων, παῦσαι φλυαρῶν) (TLNT, 3:466). The word emphasizes the emptiness of the charges (BAGD; MM; Brooke; 1 Tim. 5:13). Temp. part., "when he spreads nonsense about us w. evil words." ἀρκούμενος pres. mid. (dep.) part. ἀρκέω (# 758) to be enough, to be satisfied, to be content. Part. could be causal, "because he is not satisfied w. that." αὐτός (# 899) he, himself. ἐπιδέχεται pres. ind. mid. (dep.) ἐπιδέχομαι (# 2110) to accept (s.v. 9). Pres. points to a continual or repeated action. βουλομένους pres. mid. (dep.) part. (subst.) βούλομαι (# 1086) to want to, to desire to. Pres. points to the continual desire. κωλύει pres. ind. act. κωλύω (# 3266) to forbid. Pres. may be iterative and point to a repeated action. ἐκβάλλει pres. ind. act. ἐκβάλλω (# 1675) to throw out, to put out. The vbs. in the pres. here may be conative, "he is trying to" (Westcott; but s. Marshall; Schnackenburg). ◆ 11 μιμοῦ pres. imp. mid. (dep.) μιμέομαι (# 3628) to mimic, to imitate. Pres. imp. calls for a continual action, "keep on or continue imitating." ἀγαθοποιῶν pres. act. part. ἀγαθοποιέω (# 16) to do good, to practice what is right (Smalley). Part. as subst. κακοποιῶν pres. act. part. κακοποιέω (# 2803) to do evil. Part. as subst. ἑώρακεν perf. act. ind. ὁράω (# 3972) to see. Perf. stresses the state, condition, or continual outworking of having seen. ◆ 12 Δημήτριος (# 1320) Demetrius. The name means "belonging to Demeter," the Greek goddess of fruits and crops, and indicates this Demetrius was of pagan background (Smalley; Strecker). He may have been in the church with Diotrephes or a travelling missionary (Smalley; Brown: Klauck). Here, dat. of advantage w. the vb. μεμαρτύρηται perf. ind. pass. μαρτυρέω (# 3455). Perf. implies that the testimony to Demetrius had been given over a period of time and was still effective (Smalley). ◆ 13 εἶχον impf. ind. act. ἔχω (# 2400) to have. γράψαι aor. act. inf. γράφω (# 1211) to write. Aor. expresses the writing of a single letter containing what the writer felt obliged to say. Pres. inf. indicates the continuation of the pres. letter (Marshall). Inf. as obj. of the main vb. εἶχον. μέλανος gen. sing. μέλας (# 3506) black, ink. The ink used was a writing fluid whose chief ingredient was soot or black carbon. It was mixed w. gum or oil for use on parchment, or w. a metallic substance for use on papyrus (ZPEB, 2:279). κάλαμος (# 2812) reed, reed pen used for writing (Marshall; Brooke). ◆ 14 εὐθέως (# 2311) immediately, soon. ἰδεῖν aor. act. inf. ὁράω (# 3972) to see. Inf. as obj. of the vb. ἐλπίζω. στόμα (# 5125) mouth. Here used in the expession "face to face." Perhaps John feared that Diotrephes would intercept the letter and learn the strategy based on Demetrius, and this may be the reason why he did not want to write any more (Brown). λαλήσομεν fut. ind. act. λαλέω (# 3281) to say, to speak. ◆ 15 ἀσπάζονται pres. ind. mid. (dep.) ἀσπάζομαι (# 832) to greet. ἀσπάζου pres. imp. mid. (dep.) Pres. imp. may be iterative: "greet each one." For the form of 2 and 3 John in relation to ancient letter writing s. Robert W. Funk, "The Form and Structure of Second and Third John," JBL 86 (1967): 424-30; Joseph A. Fitzmyer, "Some Notes on Aramaic Epistolography," JBL 93 (1974): 201-25.

Jude

Jude

◆ **1 δοῦλος** (# *1528*) slave, servant. **ἀδελφὸς Ἰακώβου** brother of James. This makes him the half brother of Jesus (DLNT, 611-21, 1004-6). **ἠγαπημένοις** perf. pass. part. ἀγαπάω (# *26*) to love (TDNT; TLNT; EDNT). Perf. suggests that they were not only once but continued to be the objects of God's love and care (Kelly). **τετηρημένοις** perf. pass. part. τηρέω (# *5498*) to keep safe, to guard, to watch over. The vb. used in a friendly sense means, "to keep safe from harm," "to preserve." It expresses the watchful care given to someone (Mayor). Perf. emphasizes the continuing watchful care. **κλητός** (# *3105*) vb. adj., called. ◆ **2 ἔλεος** (# *1799*) mercy, pity (s. 1 Tim. 1:2). **εἰρήνη** (# *1645*) peace. **πληθυνθείη** aor. opt. pass. πληθύνω (# *4437*) to multiply, to increase. Opt. is used to express a wish (s. 1 Pet. 1:2), "May ... be multiplied." ◆ **3 σπουδή** (# *5082*) haste, diligence, effort, earnestness. **ποιούμενος** pres. mid. part. ποιέω (# *4472*) to make, to do. The vb. was used in connection w. a noun to build the verbal idea found in the noun (M, 159). **γράφειν** pres. act. inf. γράφω (# *1211*) to write. Compl. inf. to the main vb. **κοινός** (# *3123*) common, that which all believers share commonly. **σωτηρία** (# *5401*) salvation. **ἀνάγκη** (# *340*) compulsion, necessity. **ἔσχον** aor. act. ind. ἔχω (# *2400*) to have; aor., to receive. For the distinction between the pres. and the aor. s. M, 110; Kelly. **γράψαι** aor. act. inf. γράφω (# *1211*) to write. Aor. contrasted w. the preceding pres. inf. implies that the new epistle had to be written at once and could not be prepared for at leisure, like the one he had previously contemplated (Mayor). Epex. inf. to explain the necessity. **παρακαλῶν** pres. act. part. παρακαλέω (# *4151*) to urge, to encourage, to beseech. It is the word used of speeches of leaders and soldiers who urge each other on. It is used of words that sent fearful and hesitant soldiers and sailors courageously into battle (MNTW, 134). **ἐπαγωνίζεσθαι** pres. mid. (dep.) inf. ἐπαγωνίζω (# *2043*) to struggle for, to contend for, to exercise great effort and exertion for something. The word was used of athletic contests and the struggle and effort for the athletes in their games (Kelly; 1 Cor. 9:24-27). Prep. in compound denotes direction (MH, 312), and the word following in the dat. denotes the cause on behalf of which one fights (Kelly). Inf. is used as the obj. of the vb. **παρακαλῶν**. **ἅπαξ** (# *562*) once for all (Mayor). **παραδοθείσῃ** aor. pass. part. (adj.) παραδίδωμι (# *4140*) to deliver over, to hand down, to commit and entrust (TDNT; TLNT). The word is used for handing down authorized tradition in Israel (s. 1 Cor. 15:1-3). Jude is therefore saying that the Christian apostolic tradition is normative for the people of God (Green). **πίστις** (# *4411*) faith. The word here indicates the body or truth. The dat. here is to be related to the vb. **ἐπαγωνίζεσθαι** (Kelly). ◆ **4 παρεισέδυσαν** aor. ind. act. παρεισδύω (# *4208*) to slip in alongside of secretly. (For this sinister and secretive word s. Green; Gal. 2:4; 2 Pet. 2:1.) **πάλαι** (# *4093*) long ago. **προγεγραμμένοι** perf. pass. part. προγράφω (# *4592*) to write down beforehand, to write down previously, i.e., "written before (in God's book of judgment)." The word is intended to show that they are already doomed to punishment as enemies of God (Mayor; Kelly; SB, 2:173). Perf. indicates the continuing authority of that which was written (MM). **κρίμα** (# *3210*) that which was decided upon, judgment. **ἀσεβής** (# *815*) ungodly, impious (s. 2 Pet. 2:5). **μετατιθέντες** pres. act. part. μετατίθημι (# *3572*) to transpose, to change from one place to another, to transfer. Pres. could be conative, "they are trying to change." **ἀσέλγεια** (# *816*) unbridled living. **δεσπότης** (# *1305*) lord, master. **ἀρνούμενοι** pres. mid. (dep.) part. ἀρνέομαι (# *766*) to say no to, to deny. ◆ **5 ὑπομνῆσαι** aor. act. inf. ὑπομιμνήσκω (# *5703*) to cause someone to remember, to remind. Compl. inf. to the main vb. **βούλομαι** (# *1089*) pres. ind. mid. (dep.) to desire. **εἰδότας** perf. act. part. οἶδα (# *3857*) to know. Def. perf. w. a pres. meaning. Part. could be concessive, "although you know," and justifying the reminder. They only need to be reminded of truths already known, so that it is unnecessary to write at length. **λαός** (# *3295*) a people, nation. The word is used without the article–"a people"–indicating that not all the ones who left Egypt were believers (Green). **σώσας** aor. act. part. σώζω (# *5392*) to rescue, to deliver, to save. Temp. part., "after he saved." **δεύτερος** (# *1309*) the second time. The phrase could mean "the next time" or be an adverbial acc., "afterwards." Here the word marks a strong contrast and sharpens the point of the warning (Bigg; Green; RWP; Kelly). **πιστεύσαντας** aor. act. part. (subst.) πιστεύω (# *4409*) to believe. Aor. points to the completed action. **ἀπώλεσεν** aor. act. ind. ἀπόλλυμι (# *660*) to ruin, to destroy. ◆ **6 τηρήσαντας** aor. act. part. τηρέω (# *5498*) to keep, to guard (s.v. 1). **ἀρχή** (# *794*) dominion, office, authority. The word could indicate either the office of the angels or their domain, sphere of rule; or it could indicate the spiritual state in which they were created–they were made different from humanity but forfeited this original state when they left their own habitation (Kelly; Mayor; Green). ἀπολιπόντας aor. act. part. ἀπολείπω (# 657) to leave, to desert, to leave behind, to forsake. οἰκητήριον (# 3863) place of living, dwelling place. The ending of the word indicates the place of action (MH, 343; RG, 154). κρίσις (# 3213) judging. μεγάλης acc. pl. μέγας (# 3489) great. δεσμός (# 1301) band, bond, chain. Chains signified shame and humiliation (CIC, 48; BAFCS, 3:206-9). ἀϊδίοις dat. pl. ἀΐδιος (# 132) eternal, everlasting. ζόφος (# 2432) darkness, gloom (BAFCS, 3:199-202; CIC, 33-35; DLNT, 459-62, 657-59; Cicero, *Against Verres*, 2, 5:160). τετήρηκεν perf. ind. act. τηρέω (# 5498) to guard, to keep. Extensive perf. emphasizing the completed action or process from which a present state is the result (GGBB, 577). The word is used here in a neg. sense w. a punitive meaning, "to keep in custody" (s.v. 1; Mayor). Prisoners were generally kept in a prison until the final sentence was carried out (BAFCS, 3; CIC). ◆ **7** ὅμοιος (# 3927) like, similar. τρόπος (# 5573) manner. The phrase is a vb. acc. meaning "likewise," "in like manner." τούτοις masc. dat. pl. οὗτος (# 4047) this; "to these," "w. these." Since the word is masc. it cannot refer to the cities Sodom and Gomorrah (Kelly) and evidently refers to the angels of v. 6. It was a common understanding among many of the Jewish rabbis that the beings referred to in Gen. 6 were angelic beings (1 Enoch 6:24; Jubilees 5:1; DSS 1Qap Gen. 2:1; CD 2:17-19; BBC; SB, 3:780). For more discussion of this passage and its relatioinship to Gen. 6:1-4 s. DDD, 1499-510; particularly Claus Westermann, *Genesis 1-11: A Continental Commentary* (Minneapolis: Fortress, 1994), 363-83. ἐκπορνεύσασαι aor. act. part. ἐκπορνεύω (# 1745) to indulge in excessive immorality. Prep. in compound may be intensive (T) or it may suggest that this immorality was against the course of nature (Green; DLNT, 1088-90). ἀπελθοῦσαι aor. act. part. ἀπέρχομαι (# 599) to go after. ὀπίσω (# 3958) behind, after. The participial phrase would emphasize their bent and determination for unnatural sexual acts. Prep. in compound indicates the turning aside from the right way (Huther). πρόκεινται pres. ind. mid. (dep.) πρόκειμαι (# 4618) to lie before, to be exposed to public view. The word was used of a corpse lying in state (BAGD). δεῖγμα (# 1257) example, sample. The word was used in the papyri of samples of corn or wheat (MM). These are laid out before all as a sample or warning of judgment (Bigg). πῦρ (# 4786) fire. αἰώνιος (# 173) eternal, everlasting. Pres. of the vb. plus this adj. are intended to impress on readers that the appalling effects of the catastrophe are still visible for all to see and note w. dread (Kelly). δίκη

(# 1472) punishment. Here it would indicate a judicial sentence passed by a judge (MM). ὑπέχουσαι pres. act. part. (adj.) ὑπέχω (# 5674) to undergo punishment (BAGD; MM). ◆ **8** ὁμοίως (# 3931) adv., likewise. This introduces the comparison between examples that they knew about and the spiritual spies about whom he is writing. μέντοι (# 3530) notwithstanding; in spite of the dreadful fate of the three groups just mentioned (Kelly). ἐνυπνιαζόμενοι pres. mid. (dep.) part. ἐνυπνιάζω (# 1965) to dream. The word may indicates that in the false teachers' delusion and blindness, they take the real for the unreal and the unreal for the real (Mayor; BBC), which would emphasize their false source of revelation. But the word may also stress the fact that they are asleep to God's judgment and entertained by the temp. allusive and imaginary character of the pleasures of their lusts. μιαίνουσιν pres. ind. act. μιαίνω (# 3620) to stain, to defile. The word often is used of moral defilement or pollution (Kelly). Pres. part. indicates a continual habitual action. κυριότης (# 3262) lordship, authority. The word indicates the majestic power that a lord uses in ruling (BAGD). ἀθετοῦσιν pres. ind. act. ἀθετέω (# 119) to set aside, to do away w., to nullify, to not recognize as valid, to despise (Mayor; s. Gal. 2:21). δόξα (# 1518) glory; here, "glorious ones." The word refers here to angelic beings. They are the angels, whom these persons blaspheme by supposing that they had created the world in opposition to the will of the true God (Mayor; Kelly). βλασφημοῦσιν pres. act. ind. βλασφημέω (# 1059) to revile, to defame, to blaspheme (TLNT; TDNT). ◆ **9** ἀρχάγγελος (# 791) archangel. The Jews considered Michael to be the highest among the angels and to be the representative of God (SB, 3:831; ABD, 1:253-55; DDD, 150-53). διάβολος (# 1333) devil (DDD, 463-73). διακρινόμενος pres. mid. (dep.) part. διακρίνομαι (# 1359) to take issue w., to dispute. διελέγετο impf. ind. mid. (dep.) διαλέγομαι (# 1363) to argue, to dispute. Impf. pictures the continuous action in the past time. ἐτόλμησεν aor. ind. act. τολμάω (# 5528) to dare. ἐπενεγκεῖν aor. act. inf. ἐπιφέρω (# 2214) to bring upon, to pronounce. βλασφημία (# 1060) railing, blasphemy. Michael did not dare pronounce a judgment of reproach upon Satan. εἶπεν aor. ind. act. λέγω (# 3306) to say. ἐπιτιμῆσαι aor. opt. act. ἐπιτιμάω (# 2203) to rebuke. This was a word of command used by Jesus that brought the hostile powers under control (s. Matt. 17:18). Opt. is used in a wish. ◆ **10** ὅσος (# 4012) how much, how great, which things. οἴδασιν perf. ind. act. οἶδα (# 3857) to know. Def. perf. w. a pres. meaning. βλασφημοῦσιν pres. ind. act. βλασφημέω (# 1059) to blaspheme. Pres. indicates a continual or repeated action that has become a habit of life. For an example s. BBC. φυσικῶς (# 5880) naturally, by instinct. ἄλογα (# 263) without reason, without rationality. ζῷα (# 2442) living creature, animal (for all three words s. 2 Pet. 2:12). ἐπίστανται pres. ind. mid. (dep.) ἐπίστημι (# 2179) to understand. φθείρονται pres. ind. pass. φθείρω (# 5780) to corrupt, to ruin, to destroy. The natural antithesis here would have been "these things they admire and delight in." For this Jude substitutes, by a stern irony, "these things are their ruin" (Mayor; s. 2 Peter 1:4). ◆ **11** οὐαί (# 4026) woe. The word is an imprecation of doom also found in 1 Cor. 9:16, frequently in the gospels, and repeatedly in 1 Enoch 94-100 (Kelly; DJG, 80-81). ἐπορεύθησαν aor. ind. pass. (dep.) πορεύομαι (# 4513) to go, to travel along. The word is used to indicates a manner of life. πλάνη (# 4415) error, wandering (s. 1 John 1:8). μισθός (# 3635) wage, reward, pay. Here gen. of price, "for pay or gain." Like Balaam they were greedy for money (Green). ἐξεχύθησαν aor. ind. pass. ἐκχέω (# 1772) to pour out. Pass. used to express either the outward sweeping movement of a great crowd, or the surrender to an overwhelming motive on the part of an individual (Mayor). ἀντιλογία (# 517) speaking against, hostility, rebellion. ἀπώλοντο aor. ind. mid. ἀπόλλυμι (# 660) to perish. Aor. is a dramatic way of saying that their fate is already settled (Kelly). So in these three pictures from the OT we see three leading characteristics of the errorists. Like Cain they were devoid of love. Like Balaam they were prepared in return for money to teach others that sin did not matter, leaders in sin. Like Korah they were careless of the ordinances of God and insubordinate to church leaders (Green; BBC). ◆ **12** οὗτος (# 4047) this, this one. The same phrase ("these are") reoccurs in vs. 16 and 19 to signal the beginning of an independent description of the false teachers. In v. 16 the statement is balanced by something said on the other side, introduced w. a conj. "but" (Green; Alford). σπιλάδες nom. pl. σπιλάς (# 5069) spot (s. 2 Peter 2:13). The better meaning here is "hidden rocks." The word was used to denote rocks in the sea close to shore and covered w. water and so were dangerous to vessels (Kelly; Mayor). συνευωχούμενοι pres. mid. part. συνευώχομαι (# 5310) to come together to have a feast, to eat a feast together (s. 2 Peter 2:13). The meaning here is that at these meals the false teachers are liable to undermine the faith and decent comportment of their fellow Christians, much as submerged reefs can wreck ships (Kelly). ἀφόβως (# 925) adv., without fear, fearless, without respect. ποιμαίνοντες pres. act. part. ποιμαίνω (# 4477) to shepherd, to care for as a shepherd. Here the sense is "to fatten, to indulge" (Mayor). νεφέλαι nom. pl. νεφέλη (# 3749) cloud. ἄνυδρος (# 536) waterless, without water. ἄνεμος (# 449) wind. παραφερόμεναι pres. pass. part. παραφέρω (# 4195) to carry by. The picture here is that of clouds being blown by and passing on without bringing the long hoped-for and refreshing rains. The suggestion is that the errorists are all show and no substance; they have nothing to give to those

foolish enough to listen to them (Kelly). δένδρον (# 1285) tree; used here fig. of people. φθινοπωρινός (# 5781) belonging to late autumn. The word describes trees as they are at the close of autumn–dry, leafless, without fruit, w. bare branches and all growth sapped at the approach of winter (T; Kelly). ἄκαρπος (# 182) without fruit, fruitless; late autumn would be toward the end of the harvest, and the image here is of the harvest come and almost gone, yet these trees have no fruit on them. They are worthless and disappointing. δίς (# 1489) twice. ἀποθανόντα aor. act. part. ἀποθνήσκω (# 633) to die, to be dead. The trees were twice dead, in the sense of being sterile and then of being actually lifeless (Kelly). ἐκριζωθέντα aor. pass. part. ἐκριζόω (# 1748) to uproot. Such trees were commonly torn up by the roots and disposed of by burning; the uprooting of trees is a favorite OT metaphor of judgment (Ps. 52:5; Prov. 2:22; Kelly; Green). ◆ **13** κῦμα (# 3246) wave. ἄγριος (# 67) untamed, wild. θαλάσσης gen. sing. θάλασσα (# 2498) sea. Descriptive gen. ἐπαφρίζοντα pres. act. part. ἐπαφρίζω (# 2072) to foam up, to cause to splash like foam. The word refer to the seaweed and other refuse borne on the crest of the waves and thrown up on the beach, to which is compared the overflowing of ungodliness (Mayor; s. Isa. 57:20). αἰσχύνη (# 158) shame. ἀστέρες nom. pl. ἀστήρ (# 843) star. πλανήτης (# 4417) wandering. The figure of the wandering star is used in the Book of Enoch (1 Enoch 43, 44, 48, etc.), and describes shooting stars that fall out of the sky to be engulfed in darkness (Mayor; Green). ζόφος τοῦ σκότους (# 2432; 5030) black darkness. The darkness of ancient prisons was well-known (BAFCS, 3; CIC; s.v. 6). τετήρηται perf. ind. pass. τηρέω (# 5498) to keep. ◆ **14** προεφήτευσεν aor. act. ind. προφητεύω (# 4736) to deliver the message of a prophet, to speak forth, to prophesy. ἕβδομος (# 1575) the seventh. In Gen. 5:21 Enoch is listed as the seventh after Adam and is designated as the seventh from Adam in Enoch 60:8; 93:3; Jub 7:39 (Mayor; Green; HSB, 754-56). λέγων pres. act. part. λέγω (# 3306) to say. Used here to introduce dir. discourse ἰδού aor. imp. mid. ὁράω (# 3972) to see. Imp. used here to call attention. ἦλθεν aor. act. ind. ἔρχομαι (# 2262) to go. For a discussion s. DLNT, 867. μυριάς (# 3689) myriad, ten thousand. This refers to the angels who accompany God, esp. in judgment (Kelly). ◆ **15** ποιῆσαι aor. act. inf. ποιέω (# 4472) to do. This vb. is used w. the noun κρίσις (# 3213) to form a vb. idea contained in the noun; lit. "to make judgment," "to do judgment." Inf. is used to express purp. ἐλέγξαι aor. act. inf. ἐλέγχω (# 1794) to convict w. proof. ἀσέβεια (# 815) godless, irreverence (s.v. 4). ἠσέβησαν aor. ind. act. ἀσεβέω (# 814) to conduct an irreligious life, to be ungodly. σκληρός (# 5017) hard, harsh. The word always conveys a grave reproach; it indicates a character harshly inhumane and uncivil (Trench, *Synonyms*, 48). ἐλάλησαν aor. ind. act. λαλέω (# *3281*) to speak. ἁμαρτωλός (# *283*) sinful, sinner. Jude's quotation from Enoch (Enoch 1:9) does not mean that the Book of Enoch was regarded as inspired or equal w. Scripture. An inspired man might well use contemporary ideas that were not contrary to revelation (Green, 49); for a study of the comparison between Enoch 1:9 and the quotation in Jude s. Carroll D. Osborne, "The Christological Use of I Enoch I.9 in Jude 14,15," *NTS* 23 (1977): 334-41. ◆ **16** γογγυστής (# *1199*) one who grumbles, one who murmurs and complains (s. 1 Cor. 10:10; Phil. 2:14). μεμψίμοιρος (# *3523*) complaining of one's lot, grumbling about one's condition in life. The word was used to describe a standard Gr. character: "You're satisfied by nothing that befalls you; you complain at everything. You don't want what you have got; you long for what you haven't got. In winter you wish it were summer, and in summer that it were winter. You are like the sick folk, hard to please, and one who complains about his lot in life" (s. Green's quotation from Lucian, Cynic, XVII). The word indicates one who complained against the God who has appointed each man his fate (TDNT; MM). ἐπιθυμία (# *2123*) strong desire, lust, passion (DNP, 2:542-44; TDNT; EDNT). πορευόμενοι pres. mid. (dep.) part. πορεύομαι (# *4513*) to go (s.v. 11). ὑπέρογκος (# *5665*) excessive size, puffed up, swollen. The word is generally used of great or even excessive size, and in later writers it is also used of big words and arrogant speech and demeanor (Mayor; GELTS, 490). θαυμάζοντες pres. act. part. θαυμάζω (# *2513*) to marvel, to wonder, to admire. The expression is used to translate the Heb. idiom, "to take, or raise, a man's countenance," i.e., to do honor or show favor to him. The formula had its origin in the oriental custom of making one to rise from the ground as a token of welcome. This imagery soon disappeared and the expression meant "to show favoritism toward" or "to curry favor w." (Kelly). ὠφέλεια (# *6066*) profit, gain, advantage. χάριν (# *5920*) w. gen., on account of, for the sake of. ◆ **17** μνήσθητε aor. imp. pass. μιμνήσκομαι (# *3630*) to remember, to recall to memory. προειρημένων perf. pass. part. προλέγω (# *4625*) to say beforehand, to speak prior to the events predicted, to foretell (Kelly). Perf. indicates the lasting result of the prediction. ◆ **18** ἔλεγον impf. ind. act. λέγω (# *3306*) to say. Impf. is customary ("they used to say"), or it pictures the interaction ("they continued to say from time to time"). ἔσονται fut. ind. mid. (dep.) εἰμί (# *1639*) to be. ἐμπαίκτης (# *1851*) one who makes fun by mocking, mocker, scoffer. πορευόμενοι pres. mid. (dep.) part. πορεύομαι (# *4513*) to go (s.v. 11). ἀσέβεια (# *813*) godlessness. ◆ **19** ἀποδιορίζοντες pres. act. part. ἀποδιορίζω (# *626*) to make a boundary between someone and to separate from this one, to make a distinction, to make a division, to cause division. The word would indicate divisive distinctions made

between themselves and other people (Green). It could also mean that by their ungodly living they divide those in the assembly, w. some being or about to be taken by their error. ψυχικός (# *6035*) worldly-minded. The word implies that these men follow their natural lusts and appetites without restraint or control. ἔχοντες pres. act. part. ἔχω (# *2400*) to have, to possess. These do not have the Spirit of God and therefore live unrestrained lives. ◆ **20** ἐποικοδομοῦντες pres. act. part. ἐποικοδομέω (# *2224*) to build up, to edify. The part. could express the means or the manner of guarding oneself and expresses contemporaneous time. ἁγιωτάτῃ superl. ἅγιος (# *41*) holy; superl.; most holy, holiest. The superl. is used w. an elative force, "very holy" (MT, 31). The most holy faith would be the body of truth or faith that has been once delivered to the saints (s.v. 3), upon which one is to build his life. προσευχόμενοι pres. mid. part. (dep.) προσεύχομαι (# *4667*) to pray. The Christian must not only study the Scripture if he is to grow in the faith and be of use to others, but he must also pray in the Spirit; for the battle against false teaching is not won by argument (Green). ◆ **21** τηρήσατε aor. imp. act. τηρέω (# *5498*) to keep (s.v.1). προσδεχόμενοι pres. mid. (dep.) part. προσδέχομαι (# *4657*) to earnestly expect, to look forward to, to wait for. Pres. part. expresses contemporary action and could be temp.: "while you are awaiting." ἔλεος (# *1799*) mercy. ◆ **22** ἐλεᾶτε pres. imp. act. ἐλεάω (# *1796*) to show pity, to be merciful, to see someone in dire need and to have compassion and try to help them (TDNT; TLNT; EDNT). For the textual problems in vv. 22 and 23 s. TC, 727ff. διακρινομένους pres. mid. part. διακρίνω (# *1359*) to dispute. The word may also have the meaning "to doubt," "to waiver," and the meaning might be "to show pity on the waiverers" (Green). ◆ **23** σώζετε pres. imp. act. σώζω (# *5392*) to rescue, to save. ἁρπάζοντες pres. act. part. ἁρπάζω (# *773*) to seize, to snatch. The figure of snatching them from fire may have been suggested by the allusion to the punishment of Sodom and Gomorrah (Mayor). ἐλεᾶτε pres. imp. act. ἐλεάω (# *1796*) to show mercy. μισοῦντες pres. act. part. μισέω (# *3631*) to hate. ἐσπιλωμένον perf. pass. part. ἐσπιλόω (# *5971*) to stain, to defile, to contaminate. Perf. emphasizes the state or result. χιτών (# *5945*) the garment worn next to the body, i.e., undergarment. Then it referred to any garment. The idea seems to be that they are so corrupt that their very clothes are defiled (Green). ◆ **24** δυναμένῳ pres. mid. (dep.) part. δύναμαι (# *1538*) to be able to, w. inf. Subst. part., "the one who is able." φυλάξαι aor. act. inf. φυλάσσω (# *5875*) to guard, to protect w. guards. The idea of protection and safety seems to be prominent here (T). ἄπταιστος (# *720*) without stumbling, not falling. The word is used of a sure-footed horse that does not stumble or of a good man who does not make moral lapses

(Green). This would be the stumbling into the grievous sins of the spiritual spies. στῆσαι aor. act. inf. ἵστημι (# 2705) to place, to present. κατενώπιον (# 2979) before the face of, in the presence of. ἄμωμος (# 320) without blame. ἀγαλλίασις (# 21) rejoicing, exaltation. The word has special eschatological overtones denoting the jubilation of God's chosen people at His final manifestation (Kelly; s. 1 Peter 1:6). ◆ **25 μεγαλωσύνη** (# 3488) greatness, majesty. ἀμήν (# 297) truly, amen. The word regularly closes doxologies and sets a seal on this confident attribution of glory to the One to whom it belongs–the God who is able! (Green). For general remarks regarding the book of Jude s. D.J. Rowstone, "The Most Neglected Book in the New Testament," *NTS* 21 [1975]: 554-63).

Revelation

Revelation 1

◆ **1** Robert L. Muse, *The Book of Revelation : An Annotated Bibliography* (Books of the Bible, vol. 2), 1996; ABD, 5:694-708; DLNT, 1025-38; Stanley J. Grenz, *The Millenial Maze* (Downers Grove, Ill.: InterVarsity, 1972). ἀποκάλυψις (# 637) the act of uncovering, unveiling, revealing, revelation (TLNT; DLNT, 1024; Hort; Swete). The word is often used to describe a type of Jewish lit. of the first century B.C., which arose under persecution. It used many symbols and was published under the name of an important OT person (TRE, 3:189-289; OTP, 1:3-4; W.G. Rollins, "The New Testament and Apocalyptic," *NTS* 17 [1971]: 454-76; James Kallas, "The Apocalypse - An Apocalyptic Book?" *JBL* 86 [1967]: 69-80; Bruce W. James, "More about the Apocalypse as Apocalyptic," *JBL* 87 [1968]: 325-27; Allen Dwight Callahan, "The Language of Apocalypse," *HTR* 88 [1995]: 453-70; Stephen H. Travis, "The Value of Apocalyptic," *TB* 30 [1979]: 53-76; David E. Aune, *The New Testament in Its Literary Environment* [Philadelphia: Westminster Press, 1987], 226-52; J.J. Collins, "Apocalyptic in Literature" in *Early Judaism and Its Modern Interpreters* edited by Robert Kraft and George W.E. Nickelsburg (Atlanta: Scholars Press, 1986), 345-70; ABD, 1:279-92; 5:703-4; Thomas; Charles; Mounce). The book of Revelation does not fit all of the characteristics of the apocalyptic lit. of the time, but its subject matter and symbols must be viewed in the light of the OT, especially the book of Daniel (G.K. Beale, "The Influence of Daniel upon the Structure and Theology of John's Apocalypse," *JETS* 27 [1984]: 413-23). The nom. could be viewed as a title of the book. Ἰησοῦ Χριστοῦ (# 2652; 5986) Jesus Christ. Gen. here could be either obj. ("a revelation of Jesus Christ"), w. Him as the object; or it could be subjective gen., which fits better here–Jesus Christ is the One who received the revelation and is passing it on to John (Charles; Bousset; Aune; GGBB, 120-21). The subjective gen. is supported by the context as well as other uses in titles like *The Apocalypse of Ezra* (Gr. text); *The Apocalypse of Baruch* (Gr. text); *The Apocalypse of Abraham,*. ἔδωκεν aor. ind. act. δίδωμι (# 1443) to give. αὐτῷ dat. sing. αὐτός (# 899) dat. sing. self; "to Him." It refers to Jesus Christ, who received the revelation. Dat. as in;gdir. obj. δεῖξαι aor. act. inf. δείκνυμι (# 1259) to show. This word is characteristic of our author when it means to communicate a divine revelation

by means of visions (Charles). Aor. points to a specific act and summarizes the total action. Inf. of purp. δεῖ (# 1256) pres. ind. act. it is necessary, w. inf. giving a logical necessity. The word denotes the sure fulfillment of the purpose of God revealed by the prophets (Swete). γενέσθαι aor. mid. (dep.) inf. γίνομαι (# 1181) to happen, to come to pass. Inf. w. vb. δεῖ. Culmative aor. summing up the various events and looking at them as a total. τάχει dat. sing. τάχος (# 5443) speed, swiftness. W. prep. used as adv. quickly, suddenly, soon. The word indicates rapidity of execution (Walvoord). The cl., "the things which are about to happen suddenly" indicates a detailed account of events that must transpire in God's program to replace other earthly, temporary kingdoms w. the everlasting kingdom. This is the goal toward which this book moves (Thomas). καί (# 2779) and. Under Semitic influence it can be translated as a rel. "which He made known through signs" (AASS, 91; for general studies on the language of the Apocalypse s. Aune, clx-ccvii; MKG; AASS; Daryl D. Schmidt, "Semitisms and Septuagintalisms in the Book of Revelation," *NTS* 37 [1991]: 592-603; Stanley E. Porter, "The Language of the Apocalypse in Recent Discussion," *NTS* 35 [1989]: 582-603; Allen Dwight Callahan, "The Language of Apocalypse," *HTR* 88 [1995]: 453-70; VA, 111-61; MT, *Style*, 145-59; Charles; S. Thompson, *The Apocalypse and Semitic Syntax* (Cambridge, 1985). ἐσήμανεν aor. ind. act. σημαίνω (# 4955) to signify. The word strictly means to show by some sort of sign, and it is esp. used of any intimation given by the gods to men, esp. concerning the fut. (Hort; Aune). ἀποστείλας aor. act. part. ἀποστέλλω (# 690) to send, to send a commissioned authoritative representative on a specific mission (TDNT; EDNT; TLNT). Circum. part. or part. of means. ◆ **2** ἐμαρτύρησεν aor. ind. act. μαρτυρέω (# 3455) to testify to, to bear witness, to provide information about a person or event concerning which the speaker has direct knowledge (LN, 1:418; DLNT, 1204-5). Aor. could be const., referring either to John's past testimony or summarizing the events of the book of Revelation; or it could be an epistolary aor. (Thomas; AASS, 40). εἶδεν aor. ind. act. ὁράω (# 3972) to see. Const. aor. summing up the things which he saw. ◆ **3** μακάριος (# 3421) happy, blessed (s. Matt. 5:3). ἀναγινώσκων pres. act. part. (subst.) ἀναγινώσκω (# 336) to read, to read aloud. This is not the private student, but the public reader (Charles; Swete; Aune; Paul J. Achtemeier, "*Omne verbum sonat*: The New Testament and the Oral Environment of Late Western Antiquity," *JBL* 109 [1990]: 3-27; M. Slusser, "Reading Silently in Antiquity," *JBL* 111 [1992]: 499). Iterat. pres., "at the various times of reading." ἀκούοντες pres. act. part. ἀκούω (# *201*) to hear, to listen to. Subst. part., "the ones who hear." The public reading of Scripture, taken over from Jewish practice, was a necessity since manuscripts were not readily available (Mounce; Thomas; Aune; s. Acts 13:15; M, Megilla 4:1-4; Justin Martyr, *Apog.* 1:67; for reading silently s. Frank D. Gilliard, "More Silent Reading in Antiquity: *Non Omne Verbum Sonabat*," *JBL* 112 [1993]: 689-94). προφητεία (# *4735*) the message of a prophet, prophecy. Descriptive gen., indicating the nature of John's writing (Thomas), or gen. of apposition, "the words of the prophecy" (GGBB, 99). The use of the art. is deitic (GGBB, 221). τηροῦντες pres. act. part. (subst.) τηρέω (# *5498*) to keep, to observe. The two parts. governed by the one article indicate one group, those who hear are to keep the things written (GGBB, 270-90). It could be that καί (# *2779*) and, is to be understood as epex. to the part. ἀκούντες, meaning, "those who hear, that is those who obey." This would be a common explanation of the Heb. word שָׁמַע ("to hear"), for it means not only to hear with the ears but to hear in the sense of "to obey." γεγραμμένα perf. pass. part. γράφω (# *1211*) to write. Perf. stresses the state or condition and often the authority of a legal document (MM). ἐγγύς (# *1584*) near. ◆ **4** ταῖς ἑπτὰ ἐκκλησίαις ταῖς ἐν τῇ Ἀσίᾳ (# *2231*; *1711*; *1877*; *823*) "to the seven churches in Asia." These churches were chosen as typical assemblies with regard to their histories and spiritual states (Thomas; for the view that the seven churches depict periods of church history s. Thomas, 505-15; SCA, 231-50; for each city s. the vs. in Rev. 2-3; NDIEC, 3:51-58). ἀπό (# *608*) from. The prep. is normally followed by the gen. Here the names of God are to be treated as an undeclinable noun and as such are probably intended to be treated as a paraphrase of the tetragrammaton, Y-H-W-H, "He who is" (Aune; Ford; Mounce; Swete; GGBB, 62-64). ὤν pres. act. part. εἰμί (# *1639*) to be. Subst. part. w. the art., "The One who is." Pres. part. indicates the Eternal One, who exists forever. ἦν impf. ind. act. εἰμί (# *1639*) to be. Impf. ind. is used to indicate continual existence in the past (Thomas). ἐρχόμενος pres. mid. (dep.) part. (subst.) ἔρχομαι (# *2262*) to come. Pres. used to express fut., "He who is already on His way may arrive at any moment" (Thomas). In the Gr. world similar titles for the gods are found. In the oracle of the Peleiae (doves) at Dodona it is said, "Zeus who was, Zeus who is, Zeus who will be" (Ζεὺς ἦν, Ζευγς ἐστίν, Ζεὺς ἔσται) (Pausanias, *Description of Greece*, 10, 12:10; Charles; for other examples s. NW, 2, ii:1455-57). πνεῦμα (# *4460*) spirit. The ex-

pression "the seven Spirits before His throne" goes back to Zech. 4:1-10 and refers to the Holy Spirit and His activity in the world (Thomas; Mounce; Aune). ◆ **5** ὁ μάρτυς ὁ πιστός (# *3459*; *4412*) the faithful witness. Nom. in apposition to Jesus Christ, though in Greek it is in the gen. (GGBB, 62). This evidently is a reference to Ps. 89:37 (BBC) and indicates that Jesus Christ is the seed of David and will sit on the throne of David that will endure forever as the sun (Ps. 89:36; Thomas). The use of the art. is par excellence. He is the preeminent one deserving praise (GGBB, 223). πρωτότοκος (# *4758*) firstborn, indicating a place of prominence and privilege (TLNT; GELTS, 410; Aune; s. Col. 1:15). Nom. is in apposition to Jesus Christ. ἄρχων pres. act. part. (subst.) ἄρχω (# *807*) to be at the beginning; part., ruler, prince. The resurrection carried w. it the potential lordship over all humanity and the words, "the ruler of the kings of the earth," stand appropriately at the head of a book representing the glorified Christ as presiding over the destinies of nations (Swete). Pres. indicates continual action. ἀγαπῶντι pres. act. part. (subst.) dat. masc. sing. ἀγαπάω (# *26*) to love. Pres. indicates the continual love. Dat. of personal interest. λύσαντι aor. act. part. (subst.) λύω (# *3395*) to loose, to release. Aor. points to the completed act. The one art. w. two subst. parts. indicates that the same person is intended. For the variant reading λούσαντι (aor. act. part. λούω (# *3374*) to wash) s. TC, 731. αἵματι dat. sing. αἷμα (# *135*) blood. Instr. dat. w. prep. ἐν (# *1877*) "by His blood" (Ford). The blood speaks of the sacrificed life as the ransom or payment for release (Swete; s. 1 Pet. 1:18-19). ◆ **6** ἐποίησεν aor. ind. act. ποιέω (# *4472*) to make, to constitute. Aor. looks at the completed work of Christ and sums up the application of this to each believer as they believe. βασιλεία (# *993*) kingdom. This is a collective designation for all believers in Christ (Thomas). Double acc., "to make us a kingdom" (GGBB, 181-89). ἱερεύς (# *2636*) priest. This is the individual appointment of the believer as priest to serve God. It is a kingdom of subjects with direct priestly access to God (Thomas; Aune). τῷ θεῷ (# *2536*) dat. sing. θεός (# *2536*) God. "to, for God." Dat. of personal interest (cf. Exod. 19:5-6). ἀμήν (# *297*) amen. Hebrew אָמֵן (*amen*) meaning truly. The word was used in affirmation of other words and is an acknowledgment of that which is valid (DCH, 1:317-18; GELTS, 24; RAC-Supplement, 310-23). In the synagogue it is the response of the community to the prayers uttered by the leader (Ford; DJGE, 493; also 21, 28, 37, 59, 94-96). In the DSS it is said that those entering into the covenant shall repeat after the priest, saying "amen, amen" (אמן אמן) (1QS, 1:20; 2:10, 18). The Aramaic expression was used as a formal conclusion of an inscription as well as occurring on "magic bowels" (AT, 513). ◆ **7** ἔρχεται pres. ind. mid. (dep.) ἔρχομαι (# *2262*) to go. Futuristic pres. in a prophetic pronouncement indicating vividness and confident assertion (VANT, 225; GGBB, 535-37; for a discussion of the parousia s. DLNT, 856-75, particularly 869-72). **νεφελῶν** gen. pl. νεφέλη (# 3749) cloud. Not simply that He has a surrounding of clouds, but that He compels all the clouds into His retinue (Hort). It may be that the clouds are not the ordinary clouds of nature, but clouds in heaven seen in the vision around the throne of God. In any case the cloud in Heb. thought is commonly associated w. the divine presence (Exod. 13:21; 16:10; Matt. 17:5; Acts 1:9) (Aune; Mounce; Dan. 7:13; Jastrow, 2:1095; SB, 1:956; 1QM 12:9). **ὄψεται** fut. ind. mid. (dep.) ὁράω (# 3972) to see. **πᾶς ὀφθαλμός** (# 4246; 4057) every eye. This is all-inclusive and indicates those at the time of His coming. **καί** (# 2779) and. It could be ascensive, "even," "also." **οἵτινες** nom. pl. ὅστις (# 4015) who, indicating those belonging to a class or group (BAGD; GGBB, 343-45; JG, 303). This would refer the Jewish nation as indicated in Zech. 12:10, a part of those who will see Him. The statement of remorse by the nation of Israel as they see Him is Isa. 53. **ἐξεκέντησαν** aor. ind. act. ἐκκεντέω (# 1708) to pierce. The word is used in John 19:37, where there they looked to Him in amazement. They will look to Him for forgiveness and salvation (JG, 247). In the gospel the main reference is to the crucifixion, whereas here it is eschatological (Charles). **κόψονται** fut. ind. mid. (dep.) κόπτομαι (# 3164) to smite the chest in sorrow as a sign of mourning or remorse. **φυλαί** nom. pl. φυλή (# 5876) tribe. The whole world joins in the remorseful mourning as stated in Zech. 12:12. **ναί** (# 3721) yes. This is the Greek statement of confirmation and approval followed by the Heb. "amen" (s.v. 6), thus forming an expression of vigorous approval (Mounce). ◆ **8 ἐγώ** (# 1609) I; emphatic, "I and no other!" **Ἄλφα** (# 270) alpha; the first letter of the Gr. alphabet. The art. τό w. the pred. nom. indicates that the subject and pred. are the same and interchangeable (GGBB, 41-42). **Ω** (# 6042) omega; the last letter of the Gr. alphabet. The phrase "A...Ω" is seen to express not only eternity, but infinitude, the boundless life embracing all while transcending all (Swete). The phrase A...Ω was often used in magic texts to indicate eternity or the name of a deity (GMP, 106-07, 194, 299; David E. Aune, "The Apocalypse Of John and Greco-Roman Revelatory Magic," NTS 33 [1987]: 481-501; esp. 489-91; RAC, 1:1-4; Aune). A parallel construction was used in Hebrew: the aleph and the tau, meaning "from the beginning to the end" (SB, 3:789). **ὤν** pres. act. part. εἰμί (# 1639) to be (s.v. 4). **ἦν** impf. ind. act. εἰμί (# 1639) to be. **ἐρχόμενος** pres. mid. (dep.) part. ἔρχομαι (# 2262) to go. **παντοκράτωρ** (# 4120) the almighty, the omnipotent. It is a title expressing the rule and dominion God has over all. The word stresses God's supremacy over all things more than the related idea of divine omnipotence, without denying His omnipotence (SCA). It em-

phasizes that He is creator and sustainer of the universe (s. esp. Hildebrecht Hommel, "Pantokrator: Schöfer und Erhalter," Sebasmata: Studien zur antiken Religionsgeschichte und zum frühen Christentum, [Tübingen: J.C.B Mohr (Paul Siebeck), 1983] 1:131-77). The word was used in secular literature to describe the attributes of the gods and is probably used here in contrast to the Roman emperor's self-designation as αὐτοκράτωρ (autokrator), a designation that appears on numerous Roman milestones along the Roman roads of Asia Minor (D.H. French, "The Roman Road-System of Asia Minor," ANRW, 2, 7.2:714-20; Mounce; Ford; TDNT; MM; DDD, 35-41). The word is used in the LXX to translate צְבָאוֹת (Seba'oth, army, heavenly army KB³, 934-35; TDOT; GELTS, 349) and שַׁדַּי (Shaddai, almighty, TDOT). Kenneth L. Barker, "YHWH SABAOTH: The Lord Almighty," The NIV: The Making of a Contemporary Translation ed. Kenneth L. Barker (Grand Rapids: Zondervan, 1986), 109-10; ABD, 4:1005, 1008. It was used in apocalyptic lit. as a designation of the God of Israel (T. Abraham 8:3; 15:12; 3 Bar. 1:3; Letter of Aristeas, 185). ◆ **9 συγκοινωνός** (# 5171) fellow partaker, one who shares together. **θλίψει** dat. sing. θλῖψις (# 2568) pressure, trouble, distress, tribulation (TDNT; Trench, Synonyms, 202; MM; NDIEC, 84). The use of the article suggests that both suffering and glory unite those who suffer w. the kingdom (GGBB, 287). **ὑπομονή** (# 5705) patience, patient endurance, bearing up under pressure (TLNT; TDNT). **ἐγενόμην** aor. ind. mid. (dep.) γίνομαι (# 1181) to become, to be. **νήσῳ** dat. sing. νῆσος (# 3762) island. **καλουμένη** pres. pass. part. καλέω (# 2813) to call, to name. The island of Patmos was a small, rocky island about 8 miles long and 5 miles wide, located in the Aegean Sea some 40 miles southwest of Miletus. It may have been a penal settlement to which the Roman authorities sent offenders (LSC, 82-92; LSCA, 27-30; KP, 4:549; IBD, 3:677; ABD, 5:178-79; Charles; Swete; Mounce; Caird; Thomas; BBC). **διά** (# 1328) w. acc., because of. John was sent to Patmos as a prisoner because of his preaching of the gospel in Ephesus and the rest of Asia (Thomas; LSCA, 28-29; ABD, 5:179). ◆ **10 ἐγενόμην** aor. ind. mid. (dep.) γίνομαι (# 1181) to become. **ἐν πνεύματι** (# 1877; 4460) in the Spirit. The phrase denotes the prophet under inspiration, but not in the sense of ecstatic frenzy (Swete; Richard L. Jeske, "Spirit and Community in the Johannine Apocalypse," NTS 31 [1985]: 452-66). **κυριακός** (# 3258) pertaining to the Lord, the Lord's Day. This could be a reference to Sunday, or it could be an eschatological reference to the Day of the Lord so that the prophet was stationed as a spectator amid the very scenes of the great judgment itself (Seiss; W. Stott, "A Note on the Word KURIAKE in Revelation I. 10," NTS 12 [1965]: 70-75; K.A. Strand, "Another Look at `Lord's Day' in the Early Church and in Revelation I.10," NTS

13 [1967]: 174-81; R.J. Bauckham, "The Lord's Day," FSLD, 221-50; Aune; BBC; DLNT, 679-86). **ἤκουσα** aor. ind. act. ἀκούω (# 201) to hear. **ὀπίσω** (# 3958) behind, w. gen. **σάλπιγγος** gen. sing. σάλπιγξ (# 4894) trumpet. Gen. of description, indicating a sound as loud and clear as a trumpet's blast, signaling the necessity to submit to whatever is commanded (Thomas). ◆ **11** **λεγούσης** pres. act. part. (adj.) gen. fem. sing. λέγω (# 3306) to speak. The part. agrees w. the dependent gen. **σάλπιγγος** rather than the noun **φωνὴν** (Mounce). **βλέπεις** pres. ind. act. βλέπω (# 1063) to see. Pres. vividly describes the vision he is seeing at that time. **γράψον** aor. imp. act. γράφω (# 1211) to write. Aor. imp. calls for a specific act w. a note of urgency. **βιβλίον** (# 1046) book, a papyrus scroll (Harrington). **πέμψον** aor. imp. act. πέμπω (# 4287) to send. (For the writing and sending of letters in the ancient world s. NDIEC, 7:1-57; LSC 1-49; RAC, 2:564-85; KP, 2:324-27; for Roman roads in the province of Asia s. GAM, 164-79; D.H. French, "The Roman Road-system of Asia Minor," ANRW, 2, 7.2:698-729; ABD, 4:290-93.) The messenger would arrive in Ephesus first (BBC). ◆ **12 ἐπέστρεψα** aor. ind. act. ἐπιστρέφω (# 2188) to turn around, to turn toward. **βλέπειν** pres. act. inf. βλέπω (# 1063) to see. Inf. of purp., "in order to see." **ἐλάλει** impf. ind. act. λαλέω (# 3281) to speak. Impf. emphasizes the continual action in the past time. **ἐπιστρέψας** aor. act. part. ἐπιστρέφω (# 2188). Temp. part. expressing contemporaneous action. Since it is related to an aor. main vb. the action is contemporaneous, though the turning around is logically antecedent. **εἶδον** aor. ind. act. ὁράω (# 3972) to see. **λυχνία** (# 3393) lampstand. The Mosaic lampstand for the Tabernacle, that which stood (one or more) in the later temples and in the vision of Zech. 6:2, had seven branches, but here we have seven distinct lampstands, each w. its one light. It has nothing to do w. candlesticks but is a kind of lamp w. a wick and oil (Hort; Mounce; Swete). **χρυσοῦς** (# 5991) golden, made of gold (BAGD). The very precious metal was often used in connection w. the heavenly or divine (SCA). Note Enoch's vision described in 1 Enoch 14. ◆ **13 μέσῳ** dat. sing. μέσον (# 3545) middle. **ὅμοιος** (# 3927) like. **ἐνδεδυμένον** perf. pass. part. (adj.) ἐνδύω (# 1907) to put on; pass., to be clothed. **ποδήρη** (# 4468) reaching to the foot. The word is used in Exod. 28:4 for the blue-purple outward robe of the high priest that reached down to his feet (Bousset; Mounce; GELTS, 383). The word is also used in Ezek. 9:2 where it is applied to the man charged w. setting a mark upon some of the Jerusalemites before the destruction of the city. Of the two possible emphases–a priestly ministry or one of dignity and mercy in the face of impending judgment–the latter is more likely the choice, since nowhere else in the book does Christ appear in a priestly capacity (Robert L. Thomas, "The Glorified Christ on Patmos," *Bib Sac* 122 [1965]: 243;

Thomas). **περιεζωσμένον** perf. pass. part. περιζώννυμι (# 4322) to be girded round about, to wear a wide belt around oneself. **μαστός** (# 3466) breast. The ordinary girding for one actively engaged was at the loins, but the Levitical priests were girded higher up–about the breast–favoring a calmer, more majestic movement. Josephus writes, "This robe is a tunic descending to the ankles, enveloping the body and with long sleeves tightly laced round the arms; they gird it at the breast, winding to a little above the armpits the sash, which is of a breadth of about four fingers and has an open texture giving the appearance of a serpent's skin. Therein are interwoven flowers of diverse hues, of crimson and purple, blue and fine linen, but the warp is purely of fine linen" (Jos., *Ant.*, 3:153-54; JPB, 92-102; for descriptions of the priestly garments s. Philo, *The Life of Moses*, 2:117-18; *On the Special Laws I*, 84-85; NW 2, ii:1460-62). In like manner the angels who carry out the judgment of God have their breasts girded w. golden girdles (s. 15:6). **ζώνη** (# 2438) girdle, belt. The girdle or wide belt is often considered the symbol of strength and activity (SCA; Swete). ◆ **14 τρίχες** nom. pl. θρίξ (# 2582) hair. **λευκαί** nom. pl. λευκός (# 3328) white. **ἔριον** (# 2250) wool. **χιών** (# 5946) snow. In Dan. 7:9 the Ancient of Days is described as having hair like pure wool and raiment white as snow. The ascriptions of the titles and attributes of God to Christ is an indication of the exalted Christology of the Apocalypse. The hoary head was worthy of honor and conveyed the idea of wisdom, dignity (Lev. 19:32; Prov. 16:31), and longevity (SCA; Mounce; Thomas). **φλόξ** (# 5825) flame. **πυρός** gen. sing. πῦρ (# 4786) fire. Descriptive gen. The eyes as a flame of fire indicated the penetrating glance that flashed w. quick intelligence and, when need arose, w. righteous wrath (Swete; SCA; for examples from the ancient world s. NW, 2, ii:1463-67). ◆ **15 χαλκολίβανον** (# 5909) gold ore, fine brass or bronze. The meaning of the word is somewhat uncertain, but it is best understood as an alloy of gold or fine brass. In any case the shining bronze-like feet portray strength and stability (Mounce; Swete; BAGD; Ford). **κάμινος** (# 2825) oven. **πεπυρωμένης** perf. pass. part. (adj.) πυρόω (# 4792) to set on fire, to burn. Perf. emphasizes the completed state or results, "having been burned," "having been refined." The idea may be "glowing," indicating that the metal is not only the finest and brightest, but also aglow as if still in the crucible (Swete). **φωνή** (# 5889) sound, voice. Within John's hearing, waves of the Aegean Sea pounded endlessly on the shores of Patmos; the expression "as the sound of many waters" suggests a powerful force, as in Ps. 93:4; Isa. 17:13 (Thomas). ◆ **16 ἔχων** pres. act. part. ἔχω (# 2400) to have. Adj. part., "holding seven stars." Independent use of the part. (GGBB, 653). **δεξιᾷ** dat.sing. δεξιός (# 1288) right. **χείρ** (# 5931) hand. **ἀστέρας** acc. pl. ἀστήρ (# 843) star.

The idea of Him holding the seven stars in His right hand may symbolize Christ's absolute authority over the churches, or that he keeps them safe (Charles; Thomas). στόμα (# 5125) mouth. ῥομφαία (# 4855) sword. This is properly the long and heavy broad sword w. which the Thracians and other barbarous nations were armed; it symbolizes the irresistible power of divine judgment (SCA; Mounce). δίστομος (# 1492) two-edged, double-edged, w. a cutting edge on both sides. ὀξεῖα fem. noun ὀξύς (# 3955) sharp. ἐκπορευομένη pres. mid. (dep.) part. (adj.) ἐκπορεύομαι (# 1744) to go out. ὄψις (# 4071) appearance, outward appearance, face. In the context its primary reference is to the face but should not be limited to that alone (Mounce). φαίνει pres. ind. act. φαίνω (# 5743) to shine; "as the sun shines in His might" (Swete). Gnomic pres. This may be a reference to the Shekinah glory of the OT and Judaism (TS, 37-65; s. Enoch's vision of one whose robe was "shining more brightly than the sun, it was whiter than any snow" 1 Enoch 14:20). ◆ **17** εἶδον aor. ind. act. ὁράω (# 3972) to see. ἔπεσα aor. ind. act. πίπτω (# 4406) to fall. Enoch too fell down in fear (1 Enoch 14:24) ἔθηκεν aor. ind. act. τίθημι to place. λέγων pres. act. part. λέγω (# 3306) to say. Pleonastic or redundant part. used as the Heb. לֵאמֹר (l'mr), for an introductory formula that could be translated, "with these words," "thus" (AASS, 69-70; but s. VA, 138-39). φοβοῦ pres. imp. mid. (dep.) φοβέομαι (# 5828) to be afraid. Pres. imp. w. the neg. μή (# 3590) indicates the stopping of an act in progress: "stop being afraid," given that the appearance of an angelic being is often a source of apprehension. ὁ πρῶτος καὶ ὁ ἔσχατος (# 4755; 2779; 2274) the first and the last. The expression "I am the first and the last" is the expression of absolute Godhead (s. Isa. 41:4; 44:6; 48:12; SCA; Ford). Pred. nom. w. art. indicates the subject and the pred. are the same. ◆ **18** ζῶν pres. act. part. (subst.) ζάω (# 2409) to live. Pres. indicates continual unending life. ἐγενόμην aor. ind. mid. (dep.) γίνομαι (# 1181) to become. κλείς (# 3090) key. ᾅδου gen. sing. ᾅδης (# 87) Hades, death, the place of the dead (TDNT; NIDNTT; SB, 4:1016-65; DLNT, 459-62; DDD, 726-27). Descriptive gen. To have the keys of death and of Hades is to possess authority over their domain. The claim to possess potentially the key of death is made by Christ Himself in John 5:28; the Apocalypse connects the actual possession of the keys w. His victory over death. They are from that moment in His keeping (Swete). Pluto, Greek god of the underworld, was thought to have the key to Hades, which he would lock up so no one could get out (Pausanias, *Description of Greece*, 5, 20:3; NW, 2, ii:1468-70). In Greek and Roman mythology Charon, the old, ugly, stubble-bearded ferryman, waited with his blue boat to let the dead who had been buried get in for their trip to the underworld, from which they never returned (DNP, 2:1107-8; RAC,

2:1040-61). What a contrast w. the One who was dead but now is alive and holds the key to Hades! ◆ **19** γράψον aor imp. act. γράφω (# 1211) to write. Aor. imp. calls for a specific act w. a note of urgency. οὖν (# 4036) therefore. It draws a conclusion from the preceding. εἶδες aor. ind. act. ὁράω (# 3972) to see. εἰσίν pres. ind. act. εἰμί (# 1639) to be. μέλλει pres. ind. act. μέλλω (# 3516) to be about to, w. the inf. to express the fut. γενέσθαι aor. mid. (dep.) inf. γίνομαι (# 1181) to become, to happen. The wording may be based on Isa. 48:6 or Dan. 2:29 (Daryl D. Schmidt, "Semitisms and Septuagintalisms in the Book of Revelation," *NTS* 37 [1991]: 599; Swete). This v. gives the threefold division of the book of Revelation: (1) "the things which you saw" refer to the vision of the glorified Christ, esp. vv. 11-18; (2) "the things which are" refer to the letters to the churches in chapters 2 and 3; (3) and "the things which will happen, come to pass after these things" refer to the events described in 4-22 (Charles; Lohse; Walvoord; Govett; Scott; Bousset; Robert L. Thomas, "John's Apocalyptic Outline," *Bib Sac* 123 [1966]: 334-41; Thomas; for the view that this v. gives the narrative structure of the book s. J. Ramsey Michaels, "Revelation 1:19 and the Narrative Voices of the Apocalypse," *NTS* 37 [1991]: 604-20). ◆ **20** μυστήριον (# 3696) mystery (TDNT; EDNT; DLNT, 782-84). Here acc. of respect or general ref. (GGBB, 204). εἶδες aor. ind. act. ὁράω (# 3972) to see. ἄγγελος (# 34) messenger, angel. The word could refer to heavenly beings who are guardians of the churches, or to the churches personified as messengers, or to human beings as messengers of God (Thomas; Mounce; Swete; Charles; LSCA, 32-34; Aune; BBC).

Revelation 2

◆ **1** ἄγγελος (# 34) angel, messenger (s. 1:20). Ἔφεσος (# 2387) Ephesus. For a survey of the seven churches s. ABD, 5:1143-44. For the city of Ephesus s. Acts 18:19; G.H.R. Horsley, "The Inscriptions of Ephesus and the New Testament," *Nov T* 34 (1992): 105-68; Steven Friesen, "The Cult of the Roman Emperors in Ephesus: Temple Wardens, City Titles, and the Interpretation of the Revelation of John," *Ephesus–Metropolis of Asia: An Interdisciplinary Approach to its Archaeology, Religion, and Culture*, Helmut Koester, ed.; HTS 41 (Valley Forge, Pa.: Trinity Press, 1996), 229-50; Steven J. Friesen, "Revelation, Realia, and Religion: Archaeology in the Interpretation of the Apocalypse," *Harvard Theological Review* 88 (1995): 291-314; DNP, 3:1078-85; Aune; ABD, 2:542-49; RI, 153; DLNT, 146-47. γράψον aor. imp. act. γράφω (# 1211) to write. Aor. imp. calls for a specific act w. a note of urgency. The writings to the seven churches may have been a type of royal or imperial edict in the mode of a prophetic message or wake-up call (*Weckruf*) included in the whole book rather than individual letters sent separately to the individual churches (Robert L. Muse, "Revelation 2-3: A Critical Analysis of Seven Prophetic Messages," *JETS* 29 [1986]: 147-61; Wiard Popkes, "Die Funktion der Sendschreiben in der Johannes-Apokalypse. Zugleich ein Beitrag zur Spätgeschichte der neutestamentlichen Gleichnisse," *ZNW* 74 [1983]: 90-107; David E. Aune, "The Form and Function of the Proclamations to the Seven Churches [Revelation 2-3]," *NTS* 36 [1990]: 182-204; Aune). **τάδε** n. pl. acc. of the demonstrative pronoun ὅδε (# 3840) was obsolete in Koine Greek and similar to the obsolete English phrase "thus saith." It was used to introduce with great solemnness a prophetic message or a royal letter or edict (Aune; Aune, "The Form and Function of the Proclamations to the Seven Churches [Revelation 2-3]," *NTS* 36 [1990]: 187-89; GGBB, 328). They seem to be similar to covenant lawsuits (BBC). **λέγει** pres. ind. act. λέγω (# 3306) to say. **κρατῶν** pres. act. part. (subst.) κρατέω (# 3195) to have power over, to hold, to grasp, to hold fast; the opposite of "to let go" (Ford; Thomas). **ἀστέρας** (# 843) star (s. 1:16). **δεξιᾷ** (# 1288) right (s. 1:16); here "right hand." **περιπατῶν** pres. act. part. (subst.) περιπατέω (# 4344) to walk about. The Lord patrols the ground and is ever there when needed; His presence is not localized but coextensive w. the church (Swete). Pres. indicates the continual action. **μέσῳ** (# 3545) middle (s. 1:13). **λυχνία** (# 3393) lampstand. **χρυσῶν** gen. pl. χρυσοῦς (# 5991) golden. ◆ **2 οἶδα** (# 3857) perf. ind. act. to know. Def. perf. w. a pres. meaning (VA, 281-87). The **οἶδα** cl. introduces the *narratio*, i.e., a description of the situation of each community that serves as the basis for the *dispositio*, or response, that immediately following (Aune, "The Form and Function of the Proclamations to the Seven Churches (Revelation 2-3)," *NTS* 36 [1990]: 190). **κόπος** (# 3160) laborious work, toil. The word signifies not merely labor, but labor unto weariness, or to the point of exhaustion (Hort; SCA; TLNT; Trench, *Synonyms*, 378; s. 1 Thess. 2:9). **ὑπομονή** (# 5705) patience, endurance under difficult circumstances (TLNT; TDNT). **δύνη** pres. ind. pass. (dep.) δύναμαι (# 1538) to be able to, w. inf. **βαστάσαι** aor. act. inf. βαστάζω (# 1002) to take up, to carry, to bear; fig., to bear, to endure (BAGD). **ἐπείρασας** aor. ind. act. πειράζω (# 4279) to try, to examine. **λέγοντας** pres. act. part. (subst.) λέγω (# 3306) to say; here in the sense "to claim." **ἀπόστολος** (# 693) one sent or commissioned to carry out a duty w. the authority of the one sending (TDNT; EDNT; TLNT). For a discussion as to who these might be s. Thomas; LSCA, 39-41. **οὐκ εἰσίν** (# 4024; 1639) "and they are not." The words are a Hebraism, for "not being" (Charles). **εὗρες** aor. ind. act. εὑρίσκω (# 2351) to find, to discover. **ψευδεῖς** (# 6014) lying, liars. ◆ **3 ἔχεις** pres. ind. act. ἔχω (# 2400) to have. **ἐβάστασας** aor. ind. act. βαστάζω (# 1002) to take up (s.v. 2). **κεκοπίακες** perf.

ind. act. κοπιάω (# 3159) to be weary, to work and labor to the point of weariness. The word implies strenuous and exhausting labor. Here it could mean weary morally; i.e., to allow oneself to become weary (Hort; SCA; TLNT). Perf. looks at the continuing results of the labor. ◆ **4 ἔχω** (# 2400) pres. ind. act. to have. **ὅτι** (# 4022) that, used to introduce a dir. obj. cl. (GGBB, 454). **κατά** (# 2848) against. **ἀφῆκες** aor. ind. act. ἀφίημι (# 918) to leave, to forsake. ◆ **5 μνημόνευε** pres. imp. act. μνημονεύω (# 3648) to remember, to call to remembrance. **οὖν** (# 4036) now, therefore. **πόθεν** (# 4470) from where. **πέπτωκας** perf. ind. act. πίπτω (# 4406) to fall. **μετανόησον** aor. imp. act. μετανοέω (# 3566) to change one's thinking, to think differently, to repent (TDNT; TLNT). Pres. imp. ("repent!") stands in contrast to the aor. imp. ("repent!"), and suggests a continuing attitude over against a decisive break. "Bear in mind the loving relationships you once enjoyed and make a clean break w. your present manner of life!" (Mounce). **ποίησον** aor. imp. act. ποιέω (# 4472) to do. Aor. imp. calls for a specific act w. a note of urgency. **ἔρχομαι** (# 2262) pres. ind. mid. (dep.) to come. Pres. describes a fut. event that will happen w. certainty. **σοι** dat. sing. σύ (# 5148) you; "to you." The dat. could be taken as dat. of disadvantage (Swete) or dat. of destination (GGBB, 148). **κινήσω** fut. ind. act. κινέω (# 3075) to move. **τόπος** (# 5536) place. **μετανοήσῃς** aor. subj. act. μετανοέω (# 3566) to repent. Subj. w. **ἐάν** (# 1569) is used in a 3rd. class cond. cl. which assumes that the cond. is possible, but is not sure whether it will be fulfilled. ◆ **6 ἔχεις** pres. ind. act. 2nd sing. ἔχω (# 2400) to have. **μισεῖς** pres. ind. act. 2nd. sing. μισέω (# 3631) to hate. **μισῶ** pres. ind. act. **Νικολαΐτης** (# 3774) Nicolaitan. For a discussion of the identity of the Nicolaitans s. Mounce; Ford; Swete; Thomas; LSCA, 87-94; Roman Heiligenthal, "Wer waren die `Nikolaiten'? Ein Beitrag zur Theologiegeschichte des frühen Christentums," *ZNW* 82 (1991): 133-37; HSB, 759-61. ◆ **7 ἔχων** pres. act. part. ἔχω (# 2400) to have. **οὖς** (# 4044) ear. **ἀκουσάτω** aor. imp. act. ἀκούω (# 201) to hear. The "hearing formula" is intended as an encouragement and a call to those who have remained faithful and stood firm in spite of the problems (Anne-Marit Enroth, "The Hearing Formula in the Book of Revelation," *NTS* 36 [1990]: 598-608, esp. 604). Aor. imp. calls for a specific act w. a note of urgency. **λέγει** pres. ind. act. λέγω (# 3306) to say. **νικῶντι** pres. act. part. (subst.) dat. masc. sing. νικάω (# 3771) to be victor, to gain a victory, to be victorious. This seems to be a term applicable to all believers rather than to a limited or special group (Thomas). Dat. of respect ("in respect to the one who is victorious") or dat. as indir. obj., followed by the resumptive pron. **αὐτῷ** dat. sing. αὐτός (# 899) " to him." **δώσω** fut. ind. act. δίδωμι (# 1443) to give; here in the sense "to allow." **φαγεῖν** aor. act. inf. ἐσθίω (# 2266) to eat. Inf. of purp. **ξύλου τῆς ζωῆς** (# 3833;

2437) tree of life. There may be a reference to a tree of life in the OT and Jewish writings (Gen. 3; The Life of Adam and Eve, 19:2; 22:4; 28:4; 1 Enoch 24-25; T. Levi, 18:10-11; Pss. Sol. 14:3); or there may be an allusion to the wood of life, that is, the cross of Christ which brings life (LSCA, 42-44; RAC, 2:25-26). It may refer to Artemis; a date palm and a tree were often associated w. her and her worship (LSCA, 41-47; LSC, 248-49; DNP, 2:53-58; 2:506; DDD, 167-80; Aune). παραδείσῳ dat. sing. παράδεισος (# 4137) paradise, a Persian word meaning a park or enclosed garden. According to rabbinical teaching there was a threefold paradise: the paradise of Adam where the tree of life stood; the paradise of the souls in heaven which was the abode of the redeemed between death and the resurrection; and the eschatological paradise where the souls of the righteous would be. The eschatological paradise was considered the paradise of Adam restored w. the tree of life (SB, 3:792f; 4:1144-65; Ford; Aune; ABD, 5:154-55; GELTS, 351; s. Luke 23:43). The reference may also be to the asylum that was available in the Temple of Artemis in Ephesus (LSCA, 48-52). ◆ 8 γράψον aor. ind. act. γράφω (# 1211) to write. Σμύρνα (# 5044) Smyrna. The word means "myrrh." The myths and local traditions suggest a city of suffering (LSCA, 58-59; Thomas; ABD, 6:73-75). The city was also noted for its faithfulness to its political rulers. Cicero called Smyrna "where our most faithful and oldest allies are" (Cicero, *The Eleventh Philippian Oration*, 5; LSC, 254-55; LSCA, 70). The city was also known for its beauty, w. its stone-paved streets, lovely trees and the hill Pagos, which w. its buildings was like a crown in the city (LSC, 256-60; LSCA, 59-60, 73; Thomas; NW, 2, ii:1472-74; Bean, 20-30; ANTC, 55-62; Aune). The builders, however, had made a grave error in not placing canals under the paved streets and the sewage often filled the streets, especially after a heavy rain (Strabo, *Description of Greece*, 14 i:36-37). The city was also a place of learning and considered the birthplace of Homer (Thomas; LSCA, 57). Cybele was its patron goddess (LSC, 264-65; Thomas). It was also the city where the aged bishop Polycarp was martyred as he uttered the immortal words, "Eighty-six years I have been His servant, and He has done me no wrong. How can I blaspheme my King who saved me?" (ὀγδοήκοντα καὶ ἓξ ἔτη ἔχω δουλεύων αὐτῷ, καὶ οὐδέν με ἠδίκησεν; καὶ πῶς δύναμαι βλασφημῆσαι τὸν βασιλέα μου, τὸν σώσαντά με; (The Mart. Pol., 8:3; Beasley-Murray; Johannes Bapt. Bauer, *Die Polykarpbriefe. Kommentar zu den Apostolischen Vätern*, ed. N. Brox, G. Kretschmar und K. Niederwimmer [Göttingen: Vandenhoeck & Ruprecht, 1995]; Gerd Buschmann, *Das Martyrium des Polykarp: Kommentar zu den Apostolischen Vätern* [Göttingen: Vandenhoeck & Ruprecht, 1998]). The city's destruction was prophesied in the Sibylline Oracles (Sib. Or., 3:340, 365; 5:122-23). λέγει pres. ind. act. λέγω (# 3306) to say,

to speak. ἔσχατος (# 2274) last (s. 1:17). ἐγένετο aor. ind. mid. (dep.) γίνομαι (# 1181) to become, to be. ἔζησεν aor. ind. act. ζάω (# 2409) to live. Ingressive aor. "He was dead, but He became alive." The purpose of this statement is to fix attention upon the fact of the resurrection. As the Lord rose, so will His martyrs triumph over death (Swete). ◆ 9 οἶδα (# 3857) perf. ind. act. to know. Def. perf. w. pres. meaning. θλῖψις (# 2568) pressure, trouble, tribulation (s. 1:9). πτωχεία (# 4775) poverty, extreme and abject poverty (s. 2 Cor. 8:2; NTW, 109-111). πλούσιος (# 4454) rich, very rich, wealthy. Here there is a parenthesis in thought: "I know your trial and your poverty (yet you are [in reality] rich)" (GGBB, 53-54). εἶ pres. ind. act. εἰμί (# 1639) to be. βλασφημία (# 1060) slander, railing, blasphemy (TLNT). λεγόντων pres. act. part. λέγω (# 3306) to say, to make a claim. Subst. part. w. the prep. ἐκ (# 1666), indicating the source of the accusations. εἶναι pres. act. inf. εἰμί (# 1639) to be. Inf. in indir. discourse. These were evidently Jews in the physical sense, but w. no spiritual relation to God (LSCA, 6; Thomas). συναγωγή (# 5252) synagogue, gathering. Σατανᾶ gen. sing. Σατανᾶς (# 4928). Satan. Gen. of description indicating the character of the assembly. The reference is not to a building, but to the people who gather there and plan their assault on the church, putting themselves at the disposal of the devil to carry out his will (Thomas; also Aune, Excursus 2B: "Anatolian Jewish Communities and Synagogues," 1:168-72; BBC). ◆ 10 φοβοῦ pres. imp. mid. (dep.) φοβέομαι (# 5828) to be afraid. Pres. imp. w. neg. μηδέν (# 3594) can indicate the stopping of an action in progress, or call for a constant attitude. μέλλεις pres. ind. act. μέλλω (# 3516) to be about to, w. the inf. to express the immediate fut. πάσχειν pres. act. inf. πάσχω (# 4248) to suffer. ἰδού aor. imp. act. ὁράω (# 3972) to see. The word directs special attention to the announcement and signals a declaration that is oracular in nature (Thomas). βάλλειν pres. act. inf. βάλλω (# 965) to throw, to cast. Inf. w. μέλλει to express immediate fut. διάβολος (# 1333) devil. (DDD, 463-73) φυλακή (# 5871) prison. In the ancient world prisons were the place where the accused awaited sentencing, either of execution or banishment (BBC; Mounce; BAFCS, 3). πειρασθῆτε aor. pass. subj. πειράζω (# 4879) to tempt, to try. The word can indicate a trial of virtue by means of affliction or adversity by Satan's intervention (TLNT, 2:82). Subj. w. ἵνα (# 2671) to express purp. ἕξετε fut. ind. act. ἔχω (# 2400) to have. ἡμερῶν gen. pl. ἡμέρα (# 2465) day. Gen. of description, "a ten-day tribulation." The ten days should probably be seen as a limited, intermediate period of suffering, expected to terminate in judgement and death (LSCA, 70; also Thomas). γίνου pres. imp. mid. (dep.) γίνομαι (# 1181) to become; to "prove thyself loyal and true, to the extent of being ready to die for my sake" (Swete). Pres.

imp. calls for a continual attitude. ἄχρι (# 948) w. gen., unto; "up to and including" (LSCA, 71). δώσω fut. ind. act. δίδωμι (# 1443) to give. στέφανος (# 5109) crown. This evidently refers to a wreath given to a victorious athlete or worn by a pagan priest or priestly magistrate of a city, or given to officials at the arrival of a dignitary; or it could be an illusion to the physical appearance of the city of Smyrna (Swete, Hort, LSC, 256-60; LSCA, 72-77; Thomas). ζωῆς gen. sing. ζωή (# 2437) life. Epex. gen. or gen. of apposition, indicating what the wreath is. In this regards it seems that the crown of life refers to the wreath given in victory (Thomas; LSCA, 76-77; Aune, Excursus 2C: "Ancient Wreath and Crown Imagery," 1:172-75). ◆ **11** ἔχων pres. act. part. (subst.) ἔχω (# 2400) to have. ἀκουσάτω aor. imp. act. ἀκούω (# 201) to hear (s.v. 7). νικῶν (# 3771) pres. act. part. to overcome (s.v. 7). Subst. part. w. a generic art. describing a distinguishing trait (GGBB, 230). ἀδικηθῇ aor. subj. pass. ἀδικέω (# 92) to harm, to injure. Subj. w. the double neg. οὐ μή (# 4024; 3590) in an emphatic denial. This is the strongest way to negate something in Greek (GGBB, 468). θανάτου τοῦ δευτέρου (# 2505; 1311) second death. It refers to an unending punishment (Thomas; SB, 3:830-31). ◆ **12** Πέργαμος (# 4307) Pergamum. The name of the city probably means "mountain," given its location some 1,300 feet between two tributaries of the Caicus River. In 133 BC Attalus III left the city to the Romans, who made it the original capital of the province of Asia. It was a wealthy and important city known for its impressive library rivalling the famous library in Alexandria. Because the king of Pergamum was not able to get papyrus, he developed the use of animal skins. That led to the making of books in a codex form. The library was finally given to Cleopatra by Anthony and moves to Alexandria. Pergamum was the home of the famous physician Galen. The city of Pergamum was a stronghold of idolatry. It was famous for the great altar to Zeus which had a frieze around the base of the altar depicting the gods of Greece in victorious combat against the giants of the earth (symbolizing the triumph of civilization over barbarianism) (Werner Müller, *Der Pergamon-Altar* [Leipzig: Veb E.A. Seemann Buch-und Kunstverlag, 1978]). The shrine of Asklepios, the god of healing, attracted people from all over the world (DNP, 2:94-100; RAC, 1:795-99; BBC; GLH, 83-101). Of greatest import for the Christians living in Pergamum was the fact that it was the official center in Asia for the imperial cult (Lily Ross Taylor, *The Divinity of the Roman Emperor* [Middletown, Conn.: American Philological Association, 1931]; DDD, 1342-52; P. Herz, "Bibliographie zum römischen Kaiserkult [1955-1975]," ANRW 2, 16, 2:833-910; GGR, 2:177-85; 384-95; RAC, 14:1047-93; S.F.R. Price, *Rituals and Power: The Roman Imperial Cult in Asia Minor* [Cambridge: University Press, 1984]; S.F.R. Price, "Gods and Emperors: The

Greek Language of the Imperial Cult," *JHS* 104 [1984]: 79-95); Aune; Thomas; LSC, 281-315; LSCA, 78-105; Bean, 45-69; KP, 4:626-32; ANTC, 30-49; DRU, 2:17-74; Strabo, *Geography of Greece*, 13, 4:1-4; NW, 2, ii:1481-86; ABD, 5:228-30. In A. D. 74 Vespasian provided special privileges for physicians and teachers, but in A.D. 93/94 Domitian passed a law prohibiting the misuse of these privileges through greed (RI, 102-4; DLNT, 320-26). γράψον aor. imp. act. γράφω (# 1211) to write (s.v. 1). λέγει pres. ind. act. λέγω (# 3306) to say. ἔχων pres. act. part. ἔχω (# 2400) to have. ῥομθαία (# 4855) sword (s. 1:16). δίστομος (# 1492) two-edged. ὀξεῖαν acc. sing. ὀξύς (# 3955) sharp. The sword was the symbol of absolute authority, invested w. the power of life and death (LSC, 291). ◆ **13** οἶδα (# 3857) perf. ind. act. to know. Def. perf. w. pres. meaning. κατοικεῖς pres. ind. act. κατοικέω (# 2997) to settle down, to live. Pres. indicates continual action. Prep. in compound (κατά "down") is perfective, indicating "to dwell permanently." ὁ θρόνος τοῦ Σατανᾶ (# 2585; 4928) the throne of Satan. This may refer to the large hill or acropolis seen as one approaches the city (Charles), or it could refer to the tremendous and influential idol worship in the city (s.v. 12), w. special stress on emperor worship (Thomas; LSCA, 84-87; LAE, 346-47, w. two inscriptions from Pergamum; NW, 2, ii:1486; Aune; HSB, 757-58; DDD, 1379). Society was permeated w. pagan religion that determined the holidays and dominated everything from sports to everyday life. κρατεῖς pres. ind. act. κρατέω (# 3195) to hold, to grasp, to hold fast (s.v. 1). Pres. indicates the continual action. ὄνομα (# 3950) name. The term indicates one's person, and in this context "to hold My name" indicates to be faithful (Thomas). ἠρνήσω aor. ind. act. ἀρνέω (# 766) to say no, to deny. Aor. points to a specific example of how they were holding His name and the idea of a completed action stresses that they had not at all been unfaithful. For the resistance of Jews and the early Christians to the worship of the emperor s. LAE, 338-46; LSCA, 86-87; RAC, 14:1077-90. ἀπεκτάνθη aor. pass. ind. ἀποκτείνω (# 650) to kill. The person of Antipas is unknown, but as the aor. suggests this was a specific incident (LSCA, 86). κατοικεῖ pres. ind. act. κατοικέω (# 2997) to dwell. ◆ **14** ἔχω (# 2400) pres. ind. act. to have. ἔχεις pres. ind. act. (s.v. 6). κρατοῦντας pres. act. part. (subst.) κρατέω (# 3195) to hold to. Βαλαάμ (# 962) Balaam. The meaning of the name has been explained as, "without a people," "because he destroyed the people," or "because he swallowed up the people" (SB, 3:793; Thomas). In later Jewish writings the name may have been a reference to Jesus, but in general Balaam was used as a type of a magician or deceiver who misuses the gift of prophecy for material gain and attempts through syncretistic religion to cause the people of God to sin (b Sahn 106a; JNTU, 68-103; BBC; ABD, 1:571-72; also Jos., *Ant.*, 4:129-30;

Aune). ἐδίδασκεν impf. ind. act. διδάσκω (# *1438*) to teach. βαλεῖν aor. act. inf. βάλλω (# *965*) to throw. Inf. as obj. of the vb. ἐδίδασκεν. σκάνδαλον (# *4998*) lit., trap; enticement to sin (LN, 1:775). Here, "to entice the sons of Israel to sin" (BAGD). φαγεῖν aor. act. inf. ἐσθίω (# *2266*) to eat. εἰδωλόθυτον (# *1628*) sacrifices offered to idols, that which is slain for a sacrifice (SCA). There may be a reference here to the sacrifices and festivals of the pagan religion at Pergamum (LSCA, 90; DLNT, 528-30; Aune, Excursus 2D: "Eating Food Sacrificed to Idols," 1:191-94). πορνεῦσαι aor. act. inf. πορνεύω (# *4519*) to engage in sexual activities. The infs. are used after the vb. ἐδίδασκεν, or could be viewed as epex., explaining how he enticed the people to sin. ◆ **15** οὕτως (# *4048*) so, thus. The application and parallel is now drawn. ἔχεις pres. ind. act. ἔχω (# *2400*) to have. καί (# *2779*) also. κρατοῦντας pres. act. part. (subst.) κρατέω (# *3195*) to hold. Some have viewed those holding the teaching of Balaam and those holding the teaching of the Nicolaitans as being the same (LSCA, 87-94), but it seems better to view them as two groups (Thomas). This teaching could have been an antinomian movement and may have been connected w. the special pressures of emperor worship and pagan society (LSCA, 94; s. Aune, Excursus 2A: "The Nicolaitans," 1:148-49; HSB, 759-61). ◆ **16** μετανόησον aor. imp. act. μετανοέω (# *3566*) to repent (s.v. 5). ἔρχομαι (# *2262*) pres. ind. mid. (dep.) to come. Pres. used to describe a certain fut. event. ταχύς (# *5444*) adv., quickly, soon. πολεμήσω fut. ind. act. πολεμέω (# *4482*) to wage war, to fight against. ῥομφαία τοῦ στόματός (# *4855*; *5125*) sword of (my) mouth. Instr. dat. w. prep. ἐν (# *1877*). ◆ **17** ἔχων pres. act. part. ἔχω (# *2400*) to have. ἀκουσάτω aor. imp. act. ἀκούω (# *201*) to hear. λέγει pres. ind. act. λέγω (# *3306*) to say. νικῶντι pres. act. part. νικάω (# *3771*) to overcome. δώσω fut. ind. act. δίδωμι (# *1443*) to give. μάννα (# *3445*) manna (ABD, 4:511; TDNT; GELTS, 290). κεκρυμμένου perf. pass. part. κρύπτω (# *3221*) to hide. It was a Jewish teaching that in the messianic time the Messiah would send manna from heaven, and in the future age manna would be the food of the righteous (SB, 3:793-94; Mounce; LSCA, 94-95; Aune). In the context here the hidden manna alludes to the proper and heavenly food in contrast to the unclean food supplied by the Balaamites. While the promise is primarily eschatological, it is not without immediate application for a persecuted people (Mounce). δώσω fut. ind. act. δίδωμι (# *1443*) to give. ψῆφος (# *6029*) stone. λευκός (# *3328*) white. There were various usages of a white stone in the ancient world; e.g., a jewel, the judicial *calculus Minervae*, the casting vote of acquittal, a token of admission, membership or recognition, an amulet, a token of gladiatorial discharge (LSCA, 96-102). Perhaps in the context it is best to take the white stone as a token of admission

to a banquet. Many such tokens were little tablets of wood, metal, or stone distributed to the poor in Rome by the emperors to insure a regular supply of corn. Or they were given to the victor at games and to gladiators who won the admiration of the public and had been allowed to retire from further combat. Here the white stone as a symbol of the triumph of faith would be considered a token for admission to the messianic feast (Mounce; LSC, 39ff; Thomas; Aune; BBC). γεγραμμένον perf. pass. part. γράφω (# *1211*) to write. οἶδεν perf. ind. act. οἶδα (# *3857*) to know (s.v. 2). Def. perf. w. pres. meaning. λαμβάνων pres. act. part. (subst.) λαμβάνω (# *3284*) to receive. The new name symbolizes the individual's entry into a new life, status, or personality (LSCA, 103); for the use of amulets w. names in the magic texts s. Aune. ◆ **18** Θυάτειρα (# *2587*) Thyatira. The not so important city founded by Seleucus I as a defense against Lysimachus was located about 35 miles inland southeast of Pergamum. The city had various trade guilds or unions, such as unions for clothiers, bakers, tanners, potters, linen workers, wool merchants, slave traders, coppersmiths and dyers (s. Acts 16:14; LAC, 316-53; LSCA, 106-11; ANTC, 51-62; Thomas; Charles; Swete; BBC; Aune; ABD, 6:546). γράψον aor. ind. act. γράφω (# *1211*) to write. λέγει pres. ind. act. λέγω (# *3306*) to say, to speak. ἔχων pres. act. part. ἔχω (# *2400*) to have. ὀφθαλμός (# *4057*) eye. φλόγα acc. sing. φλόξ (# *5825*) flame. πυρός gen. πῦρ (# *4786*) fire. χαλκολίβανον (# *5909*) something like gold ore, fine brass or bronze (BAGD; s. 1:15). Dat. here due to the preceding adj. ὅμοιος (# *3927*) like; "like unto fine brass." It has been suggested that the metal here is an alloy of copper w. metallic zinc and was made in Thyatira (LSCA, 111-17). ◆ **19** διακονία (# *1355*) ministry. ὑπομονή (# *5705*) patience endurance, perseverance (TLNT; TDNT). πλείονα comp. πολύς (# *4498*) great, much; comp., more than. πρώτων gen. pl. πρῶτος (# *4755*) first. Gen. of comparison, "than the first one." ◆ **20** ἀφεῖς pres. ind. act. ἀφίημι (# *918*) to allow, to tolerate. λέγουσα pres. act. part. λέγω (# *3306*) to call; here, "to claim to be." προφῆτις (# *4739*) prophetess. The "prophetess" Jezebel is considered a prominent woman claiming the gift of divine prophecy and leading many in pagan worship and pagan feasts that often led to sexual promiscuity. She may have been connected w. the cult of Sibyl or Jewish magic and been influential in the trade guilds of the city. She apparently taught that a Christian could join a guild and participate in its feasts (LSCA, 117-23; Thomas; Mounce; DLNT, 1210-11; BBC). διδάσκει pres. ind. act. διδάσκω (# *1438*) to teach. πλανᾷ pres. ind. act. πλανάω (#*4414*) to lead astray, to deceive. πορνεῦσαι aor. act. inf. πορνεύω (# *4519*) to commit adultery. Inf. to show result, "she taught so that they commit adultery and eat." φαγεῖν aor. act. inf. ἐσθίω (# *2266*) to eat. εἰδωλόθυτα (# *1628*) sacrifice offered to an idol (s.v. 14). ◆ **21 ἔδωκα** aor. ind. act. δίδωμι (# 1443) to give. **μετανοήσῃ** aor. subj. act. μετανοέω (# 3566) to repent. Subj. w. **ἵνα** (# 2671) to express purp. **θέλει** pres. ind. act. θέλω (# 2527) to desire. Potential ind., "yet she does not want to repent" (GGBB, 452). **μετανοῆσαι** aor. act. inf. μετανοέω (# 3566) to repent. **πορνεία** (# 4518) immorality. The word here means wanton behavior, including fornication (Joseph Jenses, "Does Porneia Mean Fornication? A Critique of Bruce Malina," *Nov T* 20 [1978]: 168-84; DLNT, 1088-90). ◆ **22 ἰδού** aor. imp. act. ὁράω (# 3972) to see. **βάλλω** (# 965) pres. ind. act. to throw, to cast. Pres. used to describe a fut. event that is certain. **κλίνη** (# 3109) bed. The bed is not a funeral bier or a dining couch of the guild feast, but a bed of sickness or pain. Disease as a punishment for sin was an accepted view (Mounce; Thomas). **μοιχεύοντας** pres. act. part. μοιχεύω (# 3658) to commit adultery (DLNT, 714-17). **μετανοήσωσιν** aor. subj. act. μετανοέω (# 3566) to repent. Subj. w. **ἐάν** (# 1569) in a 3rd. class cond. cl. which assumes the probability of the cond. ◆ **23 ἀποκτενῶ** fut. ind. act. ἀποκτείνω (# 650) to kill. **γνώσονται** fut. ind. mid. (dep.) γινώσκω (# 1182) to know. **ἐραυνῶν** pres. act. part. ἐραύνω (# 2236) to search. Pres. indicates habitual and continual action. **νεφρός** (# 3752) kidney. Kidneys were regarded as the seat of the emotions, just as the heart was the seat of the intelligence or will. Hence, the speaker w. divine omniscience will prove that no deceit or sophistry of any kind can escape him (Ford). **δώσω** fut. ind. act. δίδωμι (# 1443) to give. ◆ **24 λοιπός** (# 3370) rest, remaining. **ἔχουσιν** pres. ind. act. ἔχω (# 2400) to have. **ἔγνωσαν** aor. ind. act. γινώσκω (# 1182) to know. **βαθέα** acc. pl. βαθύς (# 960) deep, depth. **λέγουσιν** pres. ind. act. λέγω (# 3306) to say. **βάλλω** (# 965) pres. ind. act. to throw. **βάρος** (# 983) burden (s. Acts 15:28, 29). ◆ **25 πλήν** (# 4440) except, only. **ἔχετε** pres. ind. act. ἔχω (# 2400) to have. **κρατήσατε** aor. imp. act. κρατέω (# 3195) to hold (s.v. 1). **ἄχρι[ς]** (# 948) until, until which time. **ἥξω** fut. ind. act. ἥκω (# 2457) to come. Used in an indef. temp. cl. The form can be either fut. ind. act. or aor. subj. act. (RWP). ◆ **26 νικῶν** pres. act. part. νικάω (# 3771) to overcome (s.v. 7). **τηρῶν** pres. act. part. τηρέω (# 5498) to keep, to guard, to observe. **δώσω** fut. ind. act. δίδωμι (# 1443) to give. ◆ **27 ποιμανεῖ** fut. ind. act. ποιμαίνω (# 4477) to shepherd. The word should be taken here in the sense of wheeling the shepherd's staff or club to ward off attacks of marauding beasts (Mounce). **ῥάβδος** (# 4811) stick, staff. **σιδηροῦς** (# 4971) iron. **σκεύη** (# 5007) vessel. **κεραμικός** (# 3039) pottery, earthenware. **συντρίβεται** pres. ind. pass. συντρίβω (# 5341) to crush together, to smash (s. Ps. 2:9). ◆ **28 εἴληφα** perf. ind. act. λαμβάνω (# 3284) to take. **δώσω** fut. ind. act. δίδωμι (# 1443) to give. **ἀστέρα** acc. sing. ἀστήρ (# 843) star. **πρωϊνός** (# 4748) morning (GELTS, 409); ἀστέρα πρωϊνόν, morning star.

For extra biblical references to morning star s. Aune. In addition to authority over the nations the overcomer is promised the morning star, perhaps a symbol of sovereignty among the Romans (BBC). No completely satisfactory answer for this symbol has been offered (Mounce; s. also his listing of various possibilities). ◆ **29 ἔχων** pres. act. part. ἔχω (# 2400) to have. **ἀκουσάτω** aor. imp. act. ἀκούω (# 201) to hear (s.v. 7).

Revelation 3

◆ **1 Σάρδεις** (# 4915) Sardis. Viewed as one of the great cites of primitive history, and in the Greek view long considered the greatest of all cities, Sardis was located 45 miles east of Smyrna in the Hermus River valley. It was founded about 700 B.C. and was the ancient capital of Lydia and because of its location was considered to be invincible. Under the rule of King Croesus (560-46 B.C.), famous for his riches–especially his gold (s. C.J. Hemer, "The Sardis Letter and the Croesus Tradition," *NTS* 19 [1972]: 94-97)–the city was defeated by Cyrus of Persia due to the city guards' failed caution. Herodotus relates how the city was fortified except for one area w. a sheer cliff. As one of the Persian soldiers observed a guard of the city retrieving his dropped helmet, the Persian figured he too could climb up the cliff; along with others he did, and took the city by surprise attack (Herodotus, 1:84). Polybius describes the fall of the city to Antiochus III in 214 B.C. occurring similarly from careless negligence. At an unguarded point in the wall, considered impossible to take, some brave and cunning soldiers put ladders against that spot one night and at dawn entered the city as the main force struck at the city's main gate (Polybius, 7:15-18). When the city was rebuilt in the time of Alexander the Great, it was dedicated to a local Asiatic goddess Cybele, who was worshipped along with Artemis and Attis, among others (NDIEC, 1:21-23). There was also an active Jewish population in the city (LSCA, 134-38; Helga Bottermann, "Die Synagoge von Sardis: Eine Synagoge aus dem 4. Jahrhundert?" *ZNW* [1990]: 103-21). The city and eleven others were destroyed by a tremendous surprise earthquake in A.D. 17 in the middle of the night (LSCA, 134; Pliny, NH, 2, 86:200; Tacitus, *Annals*, 2, 47:1-3). But Sardis was rebuilt (ANTC, 63-78; LSCA, 127-52; LSC, 354-90; Bean, 217-29; NW, 2, ii:1492-93; Thomas; Mounce; Aune; ABD, 6:73-75; BBC). **γράψον** aor. imp. act. γράφω (# 1211) to write. **λέγει** pres. ind. act. λέγω (# 3306) to say. **ἔχων** pres. act. part. ἔχω (# 2400) to have. **ἀστέρας** (# 843) star (s. 2:28). **οἶδά** (# 3857) perf. ind. act. to know. Def. perf. w. pres. meaning. **ὄνομα** (# 3950) name, used here in the sense of reputation (LSCA, 143). **ἔχεις** pres. ind. act. ἔχω (# 2400) to have. **ζῇς** pres. ind. act. ζάω (# 2400) to live. Cybele and Attis were worshipped through the *taurobolium*, a rite by which the worshipper was rejuvenated w. the life force of a bull slain over him and by bathing in its blood. Cybele and Attis were also the guardians of the grave, and the afterlife was originally seen as a reunion w. the Earth Mother. The serpents associated w. the goddess Cybele were seen emerging from the earth to shed their skin, a sign they possessed the power of rejuvenation (LSCA, 138-40; Mounce; LSC, 363-65f; DDD, 405-6; DNP, 2:247-48; GGR, 2:640-57; RAC, 1:889-99; DRU, 1:110-11). **εἶ** pres. ind. act. εἰμί (# 1639) to be. ◆ **2 γίνου** pres. imp. mid. (dep.) γίνομαι (# 1181) to become. Pres. imp. calls for a continual attitude as a habit of life. **γρηγορῶν** pres. act. part. γρηγορέω (# 1213) to be awake, to be watchful, be alert. Adj. part. used as pred. nom. (AASS, 52; VA, 491). Although the city of Sardis was considered to be a natural citadel and incapable of capture, there were several times in the city's history that the city fell because of self-confidence and failure to watch (s.v. 1; LSC, 354-62; Mounce; C.J. Hemer, "The Sardis Letter and the Croesus Tradition," *NTS* 19 [1972]: 94-97). The earthquake of A.D. 17 surprised the city in the middle of the night (s.v. 1). **στήρισον** aor. imp. act. στηρίζω (# 5114) to make firm, to strengthen, to establish. Aor. imp. calls for a specific act w. a note of urgency. **τὰ λοιπά** n. acc. pl. λοιπός (# 3370) rest, remaining. Though the words are n., they should be translated as "those who remain," "the rest," referring to those who are not yet dead, but who may be at the point of death (LSC, 166; Thomas). **ἔμελλον** impf. ind. act. μέλλω (# 3516) to be about to. Used w. inf. to express the fut. Impf. w. inf. expresses futurity or intention reckoned from a moment in the past (MKG, 307). **ἀποθανεῖν** aor. act. inf. ἀποθνήσκω (# 633) to die. Aor. points to the act of dying. **εὕρηκα** perf. ind. act. εὑρίσκω (# 2351) to find. Perf. indicates the continuing results. **πεπληρωμένα** perf. pass. part. (adj.) πληρόω (# 4444) to fill, to be filled. Their works have not measured up to God's standard (RWP). Perf. stresses the abiding condition. **ἐνώπιον** (# 1967) before. ◆ **3 μνημόνευε** pres. imp. act. μνημονεύω (# 3648) to remember. **εἴληφας** perf. ind. act. λαμβάνω (# 3284) to receive. The word represents the faith as a trust. Perf. calls attention to the abiding responsibility of the trust received (Swete). **ἤκουσας** aor. ind. act. ἀκούω (# 201) to hear. Aor. looks back to the moment when faith came by hearing (Swete). **τήρει** pres. imp. act. τηρέω (# 5498) to keep, to watch, to guard. Pres. calls for a continual watchful attitude. **μετανόησον** aor. imp. act. μετανοέω (# 3566) to change one's thinking, to repent (s. 2:5). **γρηγορήσῃς** aor. subj. act. γρηγορέω (# 1213) to be watchful. Subj. w. **ἐάν** (# 1569) is used in a 3rd. class cond. cl. which views the cond. as a possibility. **ἥξω** fut. ind. act. ἥκω (# 2457) to come (note the history of the city alluded to, s. vs. 1-2). **οὐ μή** (# 4024; 3590) not in any wise. **γνῷς** aor. subj. act. γινώσκω (# 1182) to know. Subj. w. double neg. for strong denial. **ποίαν** acc. sing. ποῖος (# 4481) what kind

of. The acc. here is acc. of time but looks more at a point of time rather than a long duration (RG, 470f; RWP; Mounce). ◆ **4 ἔχεις** pres. ind. act. ἔχω (# 2400) to have. **ἐμόλυναν** aor. ind. act. μολύνω (# 3662) to soil. The language recalls the inscription found in Asia Minor announcing that soiled garments disqualified the worshiper and dishonored the god (Ford). It is also often noted that since the manufacture and dying of woolen goods was a principle trade in Sardis, an allusion to defiled garments would be immediately recognized. It is unlikely, however, that any more than a general reference to the danger of contaminating the Christian witness by accommodation to the prevailing standards of a pagan city is in mind (Mounce). **περιπατήσουσιν** fut. ind. act. περιπατέω (# 4344) to walk about. **λευκός** (# 3328) white. The raiment here spoken of is the heavenly raiment or else the symbol of inner purity (Charles; Ford). The priest who served in the temple at Jerusalem wore black clothes and veiled himself in black if he had a blemish; but if he had no blemish, he wore white and was allowed to serve (M, Middoth, 5:4). For the views regarding the white garments and the possibility they refer here to the white-clad attendants of the conqueror walking in his triumphal procession s. LSC, 386-88; LSCA, 147. ◆ **5 νικῶν** pres. act. part. (subst.) νικάω (# 3771) to win a victory, to be victorious, to overcome. **περιβαλεῖται** fut. ind. mid. (dep.) περιβάλλω (# 4314) to throw clothes around oneself, to clothe oneself. **οὐ μή** in no way (s.v. 3). **ἐξαλείψω** fut. ind. act. ἐξαλείφω (# 1981) to wipe out, to blot out. The OT book of life was a register of all who held citizenship in the theocratic community of Israel. The idea was also common in the secular world, where all Gr. and Roman cities of that time kept a list of citizens according to their class or tribe in which new citizens were entered and from which degraded citizens were expunged (Mounce; Ford; LSC, 385-86; LSCA, 148-50; BBC). Fut. w. the double neg. οὐ μή (# 4024; 3590) forms a strong denial as to what will not happen. The promise here is positive, that these will not in any way have their names blotted out (Thomas). **ὁμολογήσω** fut. ind. act. ὁμολογέω (# 3933) to confess, to acknowledge, to profess. ◆ **6 ἔχων** pres. act. part. ἔχω (# 2400) to have. **ἀκουσάτω** aor. imp. act. ἀκούω (# 201) to hear. For this formula s. Rev. 2:7. **λέγει** pres. ind. act. λέγω (# 3306) to speak. ◆ **7 Φιλαδελφεῖ** (# 5788) Philadelphia. The city was located on an important trade route, but its founding is somewhat uncertain. The city was destroyed by the great earthquake of A.D. 17 (s.v. 1), and even though it was rebuilt w. generous aid from Tiberius people often lived outside the city in the open for protection (LSC, 401-12; LSCA, 153-77; Aune; Thomas; Strabo, *Geography*, 12, 8:18; 13, 4:8). **γράψον** aor. imp. act. γράφω (# 1211) to write. **ἀληθινός** (# 240) true, genuine. **ἔχων** pres. act. part. ἔχω (# 2400) to have. **κλεῖν** acc. sing. κλεῖς (# 3090) key. **κλεῖν Δαυίδ**. The key of David is a metaphorical expression indicating complete control over the royal household (Thomas; Mounce; Swete). **ἀνοίγων** pres. act. part. ἀνοίγω (# 487) to open. **κλείσει** fut. ind. act. κλείω (# 3091) to shut, to lock. **κλείων** pres. act. part. κλείω (# 3091) to shut. For a description of keys and locks in the ancient world and how they worked and were used as a symbol of power s. OCD, 573; KP, 5:18f; TDNT.   ◆ **8 οἶδα** (# 3857) perf. ind. act. to know. Def. perf. w. pres. meaning. **ἰδού** aor. ind. act. ὁράω (# 3972) to see. **δέδωκα** perf. ind. act. δίδωμι (# 1443) to give. **ἠνεωγμένην** perf. pass. part. ἀνοίγω (# 487) to open. Perf. indicates the continuing condition, "a door standing open." The metaphor of the open door indicated the opportunity for preaching the gospel (Swete; SCA; LSCA, 162; s. 1 Cor. 16:9). **δύναται** pres. ind. pass. (dep.) δύναμαι (# 1538) to be able to, w. inf. **κλεῖσαι** aor. act. inf. κλείω (# 3091) to shut. **ἔχεις** pres. ind. act. ἔχω (# 2400) to have, to possess. **ἐτήρησας** aor. ind. act. τηρέω (# 5498) to keep (s.v. 3). **ἠρνήσω** aor. ind. mid. (dep.) ἀρνέομαι (# 766) to say no, to deny. The aor. forms refer to some distinct occasions in the past when, being put to the test, they had proved themselves faithful to Him (SCA).   ◆ **9 ἰδού** aor. ind. act. ὁράω (# 3972) to see. **διδῶ** pres. ind. act. A late omega form for δίδωμι (# 1443) to give (RWP). The word could be understood as having a Heb. meaning w. a causative idea, "I will make," and pres. indicating fut. (AASS, 13; 34; Thomas; Charles; LSCA, 163). **λεγόντων** pres. act. part. (subst.) λέγω (# 3306) to say, to claim. **εἶναι** pres. act. inf. εἰμί (# 1639) to be. Inf. in indir. discourse. **ψεύδονται** pres. ind. mid. (dep.) ψεύδομαι (# 6017) to lie. Pres. indicates an habitual action. **ποιήσω** fut. ind. act. ποιέω (# 4472) to do. **ἥξουσιν** fut. ind. act. ἥκω (# 2457) to come. **προσκυνήσουσιν** fut. ind. act. προσκυνέω (# 4686) to worship. **γνῶσιν** aor. subj. act. γινώσκω (# 1182) to know; here, "to acknowledge." **ὅτι** (# 4022) that; gives the content of the knowledge. **ἠγάπησα** aor. ind. act. ἀγαπάω (# 26) to love. The use of the personal pronoun **ἐγώ** (# 1609) focuses the attention on the subject. Perhaps some doubted Christ's love for the church (GGBB, 323).   ◆ **10 ἐτήρησας** aor. ind. act. τηρέω (# 5498) to keep. **ὑπομονή** (# 5705) remaining under, patient endurance. It is the spirit which can bear things not simply w. resignation, but w. blazing hope (NTW, 60; TDNT; NIDNTT; RAC, 9:255ff). **τηρήσω** fut. ind. act. τηρέω (# 5498) to keep. **πειρασμός** (# 4280) testing, temptation. Descriptive gen. here, indicating the nature of the hour. It could be a reference to a local persecution, but it is more in keeping w. the context and nature of Revelation to view this as the period of tribulation preceding the coming of Christ to the earth. The prep. **ἐκ** (# 1666) means that these would be kept from entering this period (Thomas). **μελλούσης** pres. act. part. μέλλω (# 3516) to be about to. The word is used w.

inf. to express fut. **ἔρχεσθαι** pres. pass. inf. ἔρχομαι (# 2262) to come. **οἰκουμένης** pres. pass. (subst.) part. οἰκέω (# 3876) to live. The word is used for the inhabited earth. **πειράσαι** aor. act. inf. πειράζω (# 4279) to try. **κατοικοῦντας** pres. act. (subst.) part. κατοικέω (# 2997) to dwell, to live on the earth.   ◆ **11 ἔρχομαι** (# 2262) pres. ind. mid. (dep.) to come. Pres. used to describe a fut. event w. great certainty. **ταχύς** (# 5444) quickly, soon. **κράτει** pres. imp. act. κρατέω (# 3195) to hold fast, to grasp. **ἔχεις** pres. ind. act. ἔχω (# 2400) to have, to possess. **λάβῃ** aor. subj. act. λαμβάνω (# 3284) to take. Subj. w. **ἵνα** (# 2671) is used in a neg. purp. cl. **στέφανος** (# 5109) crown; here as a symbol of reward (DLNT, 1040).   ◆ **12 νικῶν** pres. act. part. νικάω (# 3771) to be victorious. **ποιήσω** fut. ind. act. ποιέω (# 4472) to do. **στῦλος** (# 5146) pillar. The metaphor of being a pillar in a temple is current in most languages and conveys the idea of stability and permanence (Mounce). The background may be that of the coronation of a king, which connects the believer w. the symbol of royal stability (Richard H. Wilkinson, "The ΣΤΥΛΟΣ of Revelation 3:12 and Ancient Coronation Rites," *JBL* 107 [1988]: 498-501). **ἐξέλθῃ** aor. subj. act. ἐξέρχομαι (# 2002) to go out. To a city that had experienced devastating earthquakes so that people fled into the countryside to establish temporary dwellings there, the promise of permanence within the New Jerusalem would have a special meaning (Mounce; LSC, 396f). Aor. subj. w. the double neg. **οὐ μή** (# 4024; 3590) stressing a strong denial (GGBB, 468). **γράψω** fut. ind. act. γράφω (# 1211) to write. **καταβαίνουσα** pres. act. part. (adj.) καταβαίνω (# 2849) to come down. For the New Jerusalem s. Rev. 21:2.   ◆ **13 ἔχων** pres. act. part. ἔχω (# 2400) to have, to possess. **ἀκουσάτω** aor. imp. act. ἀκούω (# 201) to hear. The hopelessness of those who have no promise of an heavenly city is well illustrated by an inscription from a Philadelphia cemetery dated towards the end of the first century A.D. It reads, "Lysimachos made this grave for the lovely Antiochis, who died too early. Be of good cheer, for this is the same end (τὸ τέλος) for everyone" (GIZ, 25-26).   ◆ **14 Λαοδίκει** (# 3293) Laodicea. It was the most important city in the Lycus Valley and was located on an main trade route not far from Hierapolis and Colossae. It was named by Antioch II (261-46 B.C.) for his wife Laodice. An affluent Jewish population is attested by Cicero in his defense of the governor Flaccus, who seized 20 pounds of gold the Jews were going to send to Jerusalem (Cicero, *Pro Flacco*, 68; LSCA, 182-84; ANTC, 137; LSC, 420-22; Aune). The city was also a rich banking center and a manufacturing center, especially noted for its fine soft black wool which brought in much revenue (Strabo, *Geography*, 12, 8:16). It was also famous for its medical school where Demosthenes (surnamed Philalethes), a well-known ophthalmologist had studied (LSCA, 198; KP, 1:1487;

KGH, 2:431-33). There must have been a sizable and influential Jewish community in the city (LSCA, 182-86). Strabo relates how the whole area was constantly in danger of earthquakes; in the nearby village of Carura, where there were fountains of "boiling-hot waters" (ζεστῶν ὑδάτων), a brothel keeper and a large number of women were staying in the inns of the village when an earthquake struck at night and he and all of the women disappeared from sight (Strabo, *Geography*, 12, 8:16-17). **γράψον** aor. imp. act. γράφω (# 1211) to write. **ὁ Ἀμήν** (# 297) the amen. The word conveys the idea of firmness, stability, and credibility (s. 1:6, 7). It has been suggested that the word goes back to Prov. 8:30 and is a transliteration of אָמוֹן (*'amon*), master workman, architect (Lou H. Silberman, "Farewell to O AMHN," *JBL* 82 [1963]: 213-15; LSCA, 185; for a study of the word and its use in Prov. 8:30 s. Cleon L. Rogers III, "The Meaning and Significance of the Hebrew Word אָמוֹן in Proverbs 8,30," *ZAW* 109 [1997]: 208-21). **ὁ μάρτυς ὁ πιστὸς καὶ ἀληθινός** (# 4412; 2779; 240) The faithful (trustworthy, reliable) and true (genuine) witness. This element in the character of Christ contrasts strongly w. the faithlessness and inconsistency of the Laodiceans in relation to the faith they professed (Beasley-Murray). **ἀρχή** (# 794) beginning, first, originator, initiator. The word here does not refer to time, but to the source of creation (Thomas; s. Col. 1:18). **κτίσεως** gen. sing. κτίσις (# 3232) creation. Obj. gen.: "He is the one who began creation!" ◆ **15 οἶδα** (# 3857) perf. ind. act. to know. Def. perf. w. pres. meaning. **ψυχρός** (# 6037) cold. **εἶ** pres. ind. act. εἰμί (# 1639) to be. **ζεστός** (# 2412) boiling, hot. **ὄφελον** (# 4054) Particle used to express an unattainable wish about the pres.: "I would that you were..." (RWP; BD, 37; 181-82). **ἧς** impf. ind. act. εἰμί (# 1639) to be. Cold water was useful as well as water that was boiling hot. The hot springs here may be those of Hierapolis (Strabo, *Geography*, 13, 4:14), some six miles from Laodicea, and the cold water may be that of Colossae (LSCA, 186-88). ◆ **16 χλιαρός** (# 5950) warm, lukewarm. The contrast here is between the hot medicinal waters of Hierapolis and the cold, pure waters of Colossae. As the hot water flowed to Laodicea through pipes, it cooled and was probably only lukewarm when it arrived (LSCA, 188-91; Stanley E. Porter, "Why the Laodiceans Received Lukewarm Water [Revelation 3:15-18]," *TB* 38 [1987]: 143-49). Thus, the church in Laodicea was providing neither refreshment for its spiritual weary nor healing for the spiritual sick. It was totally ineffective and thus distasteful to the Lord (Mounce; BBC; Ford). **μέλλω** (# 3516) pres. ind. act. to be about to. **ἐμέσαι** aor. act. inf. ἐμέω (# 1840) to vomit, to reject w. disgust (RWP; SCA). ◆ **17 λέγεις** pres. ind. act. λέγω (# 3306) to say, to claim. **ὅτι** (# 4022) Used after the vb. λέγεις to introduce dir. speech and equivalent to quotation marks. **πλούσιος** (# 4454) rich,

wealthy. For a discussion of poverty and wealth s. DLNT, 1051-53; DJG, 701-10; M. Hengel, *Property and Riches in the Early Church* (Philadelphia: Fortress, 1974). **πεπλούτηκα** perf. ind. act. πλουτέω (# 4456) to become rich, to be rich; my wealth is due to my own exertion (Swete). The city of Laodicea was known for its wealth (Ford; LSC, 416ff; Mounce). Perf. indicates the continuing state. **ἔχω** (# 2400) pres. ind. act. to have. **χρείαν ἔχω** "I have no need." **οἶδας** (# 3857) perf. ind. act. οἶδα to know. Def. perf. w. pres. meaning. **εἶ** pres. ind. act. εἰμί (# 1639) to be. **ταλαίπωρος** (# 5417) miserable, wretched, unfortunate. The vb. and noun are used in the LXX to refer to ravaged lands, devastated countries, and pillaging and ravaging (Mic. 2:4; Joel 1:10; Jer.4:20; Zech. 11:2-3; GELTS, 468); here the adj. refers to the misery associated w. suffering and deprivation (TLNT; s. Rom. 7:24; for the word in Josephus s. CCFJ, 4:155). **ἐλεεινός** (# 1795) pitiable, miserable. The word indicates one set forth as an object of extreme pity; it is the feeling of one who is moved by the sight of another's suffering and in a way shares in it—compassion (TLNT; TDNT; SCA). **πτωχός** (# 4777) poor, extremely poor, poor as a beggar. **τυφλός** (# 5603) blind. Laodicea was widely known for its medical school and particularly famous for an eye salve made from Phrygian powder mixed w. oil (Mounce; LSC, 419f; Ford; KP, 1:733-34; DNP, 2:277-79; R.P. Jackson, "Eye Medicine in the Roman Empire," ANRW, 2, 37, 3:2226-51; LSCA, 196-99; OCD, 752; s.v 14, 18). **γυμνός** (# 1218) naked. The city was famous for its garments of glossy black wool (Ford; LSC, 416; LSCA, 199-201). To be poor, destitute, and blind in the ancient world—or in any society—is to be at one's wits end, without hope, destitute and in dire need! ◆ **18 συμβουλεύω** (# 5205) pres. ind. act. to give counsel, to advise. **ἀγοράσαι** aor. act. inf. ἀγοράζω (# 60) to buy, to buy at the market. Compl. inf. explaining the content of the counsel. **πεπυρωμένον** perf. pass. part. πύρόω (# 4792) to burn; pass., to be refined. **πλουτήσῃς** aor. subj. act. πλουτέω (# 4456) to be rich. Subj. w. ἵνα (# 2671) to express purp. **περιβάλῃ** aor. subj. mid. (dir. mid., "to clothe oneself") περιβάλλω (# 4314) to clothe. Subj. w. ἵνα (# 2671) to express purp. **φανερωθῇ** aor. subj. pass. φανερόω (# 5746) to make known, to make clear; pass., to be manifest, to be revealed. Subj. w. ἵνα (# 2671) and μή (# 3590) to express neg. purp. **αἰσχύνη** (# 158) shame. **γυμνότη** (# 1219) nakedness. In the biblical world nakedness was a symbol of judgment and humiliation (Mounce). **κολλούριον** (# 3141) salve, eye salve. The word was used of a yellow salve to treat discharges, wounds, bruises, and weals (*Oxyrhynchus Papyri*, 8:110-15, # 1088); but it was also used for eye salve (DMTG, 207; KP, 3:272; RAC, 1:972-75; KGH, 2:432-33; NDIEC, 3:56-57; LSCA, 196-99; LSC, 419, 429; Pliny, *NH*, 34:105-6). An inscription mentions four types of eye salve, such as myrrh and nardensalve (RI, 298). The

Phrygian powder was apparently applied to the eyes in the form of a doughy paste (Mounce; s.v. 17). ἐγχρῖσαι aor. act. inf. ἐγχρίζω (# 1608) to anoint w. salve. In an inscription from Melitus the account is given of a blind man who is told to mix blood from a white rooster w. honey and apply it as eye salve for 3 days, after which he was able to see again (κολλύριον συντρῖψαι ... ἐπιχρεῖσαι ... ἀνέβλεψεν) (SIG, 3:322-33 # 1173). Compl. inf. w. vb. συμβουλεύω. βλέπῃς pres. subj. act. βλέπω (# 1063) to see. Subj. w. ἵνα (# 2671) to express purp. or intended result. The local facts of the city are used to present Christ as the source of the remedy for the church's hidden needs of spiritual wealth, vision, and holiness (LSCA, 2001). ◆ **19 ὅσος** (# 4012) how many; those belonging to the same class or group (BAGD). **φιλῶ** pres. subj. act. φιλέω (# 5797) to be fond of, to love. The word refers to affection, pure and simple–attachment, sympathy, and good will–always marked by a kindly attitude; and here it is a tenderer word than ἀγαπᾶν (TLNT, 1:10; SC). In the case of the Philadelphian church, He *esteemed* (ἠγάπησε) it; in the case of the Laodicean, He *loves* it (φιλεῖ). The former is w. His judgment; the latter w. gratuitous affection (Bengel). **ἐλέγχω** (# 1794) pres. ind. act. to rebuke, to state that someone has done wrong, w. the implication that there is adequate proof of such wrongdoing and the person is convinced and brought to the acknowledgement of his fault (LN, 1:436; SC). **παιδεύω** (# 4084) pres. ind. act. to discipline, to train as a child (TDNT; PIGC). Customary pres. indicating that which He habitually does. **ζήλευε** pres. imp. act. ζηλεύω (# 2418) to be zealous. **μετανόησον** aor. imp. act. μετανοέω (# 3566) to repent (s. 2:5). ◆ **20 ἰδού** aor. imp. act. ὁράω (# 3972) to see. **ἕστηκα** perf. ind. act. ἵστημι (# 2705) to place; perf., to stand. **κρούω** (# 3218) pres. ind. act. to knock. No one dared to enter a house without first knocking and being invited to enter. Perhaps the people were accustomed to having travellers knock at their door, or they may have recalled the Romans forcing their way into houses demanding food and lodging (SB, 3:798; LSCA, 201-5). Pres. indicates the continual knocking. **ἀκούσῃ** aor. subj. act. ἀκούω (# 201) to hear. Subj. w. ἐάν (# 1569) is used in a 3rd. class cond. cl. which assumes the cond. to be possible. **ἀνοίξῃ** aor. subj. act. ἀνοίγω (# 487) to open. **εἰσελεύσομαι** fut. ind. mid. (dep.) εἰσέρχομαι (# 1656) to come in; to come in toward a person (GGBB, 380-82). **δειπνήσω** fut. ind. act. δειπνέω (# 1268) to eat, to eat a meal, to partake of a banquet. The word refers to the meal at the end of the day, the principal meal and the usual occasion for hospitality (Swete). For a description of a Jewish banquet s. SB, 4, ii:611-39; for a Hellenistic or Greek eating and drinking and dinner (δεῖπνον) s. KGH, 2:42-69; DGRA, 303-6; for a Roman dinner (*coena*) s. DGRA, 306-9; LLAR, 32-53;DJG, 796-800. The reference may be to the eschatological ban-

quet of the Messiah or may simply indicate close friendship and fellowship. ◆ **21 νικῶν** pres. act. part. (subst.) νικάω (# 3771) to overcome. **δώσω** fut. ind. act. δίδωμι (# 1443) to give. **καθίσαι** aor. act. inf. καθίζω (# 2767) to sit, to cause to sit. Inf. of purp. or result. For a discussion of sitting at the right hand in light of Ps. 110:1 s. David M. Hay, *Glory at the Right Hand: Psalm 110 in Early Christianity* (Nashville: Abingdon Press, 1973) in general, particularly, 80-81. **ἐνίκησα** aor. ind. act. νικάω (# 3771) to overcome. **ἐκάθισα** aor. ind. act. καθίζω (# 2767) to sit. ◆ **22 ἔχων** pres. act. part. (subst.) ἔχω (# 2400) to have. **ἀκουσάτω** aor. imp. act. ἀκούω (# 201) to hear (s.v. 6).

Revelation 4

◆ **1 μετὰ ταῦτα** (# 3552; 4047) after these things. This transition marker marks the beginning of a new vision and the change is from the church on earth to a vision of heaven's court (Thomas). **εἶδον** aor. ind. act. ὁράω (# 3972) to see. **ἰδού** aor. imp. act. ὁράω (# 3972) to see. The phrase **εἶδον, καὶ ἰδού** ("I saw and behold") serves to introduce a new vision of special importance (Swete; Charles). **ἠνεῳγμένη** perf. pass. part. ἀνοίγω (# 487) to open. Perf. could suggest that the door had been opened and left that way for John's arrival (Mounce). **ἤκουσα** aor. ind. act. ἀκούω (# 201) to hear. **σάλπιγγος** gen. sing. σάλπιγξ (# 4894) trumpet. For a discussion of the trumpet voice and visions s. DLNT, 1182-84. **λαλούσης** pres. act. part. (adj.) λαλέω (# 3281) to speak. **λέγων** pres. act. part. λέγω (# 3306) to say. Pleonastic part. under Semitic influence (s. 1:17). **ἀνάβα** aor. imp. act. ἀναβαίνω (# 326) to go up. Aor. imp. calls for a specific act w. a note of urgency. **δείξω** fut. ind. act. δείκνυμι (# 1259) to show, to exhibit. **δεῖ** (# 1256) pres. ind. act. it is necessary, w. inf. The vision that follows in an anticipation of a fut. yet to be accomplished a prophecy of the things to take place after the present time, as described in Revelation 2-3. V. 1 signals a decisive turn to the fut. (Swete; Bousset; Harrington; 1:19). **γενέσθαι** aor. mid. (dep.) inf. γίνομαι (# 1181) to happen. ◆ **2 εὐθέως** (# 2311) adv., immediately. **ἐγενόμην** aor. ind. mid. (dep.) γίνομαι (# 1181) to happen. **ἰδού** aor. imp. act. ὁράω (# 3972) to see. **ἔκειτο** impf. ind. mid. (dep.) κεῖμαι (# 3023) to lie, to stand. The vb. is used as the pass. of the vb. τίθημι (RWP; Swete). **καθήμενος** pres. mid. (dep.) part. κάθημαι (# 2764) to sit. John is allowed to see the throne room of the heavenly palace where his eyes fall first on the ruler's throne, the kind used by kings and presiding judges. The one enthroned in heaven can only be the King of all kings who ruled and Judge of the whole world (Lohse). ◆ **3 καθήμενος** pres. mid. (dep.) part. κάθημαι (# 2764) to sit. **ὁράσει** dat. sing. ὅρασις (# 3970) sight, appearance. Dat. of reference or respect, "in reference to appearance." **ἰάσπιδι** dat. sing. ἴασπις (# 2618) jasper stone. Perhaps this ancient stone was a translucent rock crystal found in a variety of colors (Pliny, NH, 37:115-17); or perhaps a diamond, suggesting such qualities as majesty, holiness, or purity (BAGD; Mounce). Dat. after the adj. ὅμοιος (# *3927*) similar, like. σάρδιον (# *4917*) carnelian, sardius stone. This was a blood-red stone said to be named after Sardis, near where it was found, and one of the most commonly used gems in the ancient world (Pliny, NH, 37:105-7). The stone may be interpreted as wrath or judgment (Mounce). ἶρις (# *2692*) rainbow, rainbow-colored. The word may indicate the halo of emerald encircling the throne (Swete). κυκλόθεν (# *3239*) w. gen., encircling. σμαράγδινος (# *5039*) made of emerald. Pliny writes that there are twelve kinds of smaragdus, or emeralds, and he gives a description of each (Pliny, NH, 37:62-75). If the rainbow that surrounded the throne was a halo, then the emerald is usually pictured as green; otherwise it is a colorless crystal that would refract a rainbow of prismatic colors and speak of God's mercy (Mounce; Ford). ◆ **4** καθημένους pres. mid. (dep.) part. (adj.) κάθημαι (# *2764*) to sit. περιβεβλημένους perf. pass. part. (adj.) περιβάλλω (# *4314*) to throw around; pass., to be clothed. λευκός (# *3328*) white. κεφαλάς acc. pl. κεφαλή (# *3051*) head. χρυσοῦς (# *5991*) golden. The 24 elders clothed in white robes w. golden crowns could represent the church (Seiss; Walvoord; Scott), or the faithful of all ages (Charles). Others would interpret them as being an exalted angelic order who serve and adore God as an angelic priesthood (Mounce; Govett; Thomas; Aune, Excursus 4A: "The Twenty-Four Elders," 287-92). ◆ **5** ἐκπορεύονται pres. ind. mid. (dep.) ἐκπορεύομαι (# *1744*) to go out from, to proceed from. Pres. vividly describes the action of the vision in progress. ἀστραπή (# *847*) lightning. βροντή (# *1103*) thunder. The thunderstorm is in Heb. poetry a familiar symbol of the divine power and glory (Swete). λαμπάδες nom. pl. λαμπάς (# *3286*) torch (s. Exod. 20:18 LXX: καὶ πᾶς λαὸς ἑώρα τὴν φωνὴν καὶ τὰς λαμπάδας; s. also Charles). πυρός gen. sing. πῦρ (# *4786*) fire. Descriptive gen. καιόμεναι pres. pass. part. (adj.) καίομαι (# *2794*) to burn; pass. to be burning. ◆ **6** ὑάλινος (# *5612*) made of glass. κρύσταλλος (# *3223*) crystal. It was a pavement of glass resembling an expanse of water clear as rock crystal (Swete; ABD, 5:1059). μέσος (# *3545*) middle. κύκλος (# *3241*) circle, encircling, around. It is an adv. in the loc. used here as a prep. This seems to mean that one of the four living creatures was on each of the four sides of the throne, either stationary or moving rapidly around (RWP). The exact location is a bit uncertain but "in the midst" apparently means in the immediate vicinity. Thus, they surround the throne as an inner circle (Mounce). The vision may be that of the mercy seat so the living creatures form a part of the throne; they are in the midst of the throne as constituents of it and the Lamb is in the midst of the throne as

its occupant (Robert G. Hall, "Living Creatures in the Midst of the Throne: Another Look at Revelation 4.6," *NTS* 36 [1990]: 614-18). ζῷα nom. pl. ζῷον (# *2442*) living, that which is alive, living creature. It refers to beings that are not human and yet not really animals of the usual kind (BAGD). Josephus uses the word for earthly animals (CCFJ, 2:280), but also for the cherubim on the mercy seat whom he says were winged creatures (ζῷα δέ ἐστι πετεινά) in a form unlike any man's eyes have seen (Jos., *Ant.*, 1:137; R. Hall, *NTS* 36 [1990]: 610-11). For a comparison to Ezekiel's vision s. SB, 3:799-800; for a discussion of their identity s. Thomas; Mounce. γέμοντα pres. act. part. γέμω (# *1154*) to be full of. ἔμπροσθεν (# *1869*) in front. ὄπισθεν (# *3957*) behind, in back of. ◆ **7** λέοντι dat. sing. λέων (# *3329*) lion. μόσχος (# *3675*) a young steer, calf. ἔχων pres. act. part. ἔχω (# *2400*) to have. πρόσωπον (# *4725*) face. ἀετός (# *108*) eagle. The four forms suggest the noblest, strongest, wisest, and swiftest in the animal world (Swete). The beings here are heavenly creatures who serve and worship God. πετομένῳ pres. mid. (dep.) part. (adj.) πέτομαι (# *4375*) to fly. ◆ **8** ἓν καθ' ἓν αὐτῶν one by one of them, one after the other (BAGD). ἔχων pres. act. part. ἔχω (# *2400*) to have. ἀνά (# *324*) each one, one by one, the distributive use of the prep. (BAGD). πτέρυγας acc. pl. πτέρυξ (# *4763*) wing. ἕξ (# *1971*) six. κυκλόθεν (# *3239*) all around, from all sides. ἔσωθεν (# *2277*) within. γέμουσιν pres. ind. act. γέμω (# *1154*) to be full of. ἀνάπαυσις (# *398*) ceasing, pause, rest. ἔχουσιν pres. ind. act. ἔχω (# *2400*) to have. ἡμέρας καὶ νυκτός (# *2465*; *2779*; *3816*) day and night. Gen. of time, describing the time in which the action took place (GGBB, 122-23); in this case, "continually, in the nighttime and in the daytime." λέγοντες pres. act. part. λέγω (# *3306*) to say. παντοκράτωρ (# *4120*) almighty (s. Rev. 1:8). ἦν impf. ind. act. εἰμί (# *1639*) to be (s. 1:4). ὤν pres. mid. part. εἰμί. ἐρχόμενος pres. mid. (dep.) part. ἔρχομαι (# *2262*) to come. ◆ **9** ὅταν (# *4020*) when, whenever. δώσουσιν fut. ind. act. δίδωμι (# *1443*) to give. εὐχαριστία (# *2374*) thanksgiving. καθημένῳ pres. mid. (dep.) part. κάθημαι (# *2764*) to sit. ζῶντι pres. act. part. ζάω (# *2409*) to live. ◆ **10** πεσοῦνται fut. ind. mid. (dep.) πίπτω (# *4406*) to fall, to fall down. καθημένου pres. mid. (dep.) part. κάθημαι (# *2764*) to sit. προσκυνήσουσιν fut. ind. act. προσκυνέω (# *4686*) to worship. ζῶντι pres. act. part. ζάω (# *2409*) to live. βαλοῦσιν fut. ind. act. βάλλω (# *965*) to throw. λέγοντες pres. act. part. λέγω (# *3306*) to say. ◆ **11** εἶ pres. ind. act. εἰμί (# *1639*) to be. λαβεῖν aor. act. inf. λαμβάνω (# *3284*) to take, to receive. Inf. is used in explaining the adj. ἄξιος (# *545*) worthy. ἔκτισας aor. ind. act. κτίζω (# *3231*) to create. ἦσαν impf. ind. act. εἰμί (# *1639*) to be. Impf. views the state of creation, i.e., creation's existence, and the following aor. pass. looks at the fact of the beginning of its existence (Thomas;

Ladd). **ἐκτίσθησαν** aor. ind. pass. κτίζω (# 3231) to create. Theol. pass. indicates God was the agent.

Revelation 5

◆ **1 εἶδον** aor. ind. act. ὁράω (# 3972) to see. **δεξιός** (# 1288) right. **καθημένου** pres. mid. (dep.) part. (subst.) κάθημαι (# 2764) to sit. **βιβλίον** (# 1046) book, scroll, document. This is a term used for writing material of papyrus, leather, skin, or parchment (Ford). **γεγραμμένον** perf. pass. part. γράφω (# 1211) to write. Perf. indicates the completed action and was often used of legal authoritative documents whose authority continued (MM; TDNT). **ἔσωθεν** (# 2277) within. **ὄπισθεν** (# 3957) on the back. That the scroll is also written on the back indicates how extensive and comprehensive are the decrees of God (Mounce). **κατεσφραγισμένον** perf. pass. part. κατασφραγίζομαι (# 2958) to seal, to seal up, to seal completely and securely (Swete). **σφραγίς** (# 5382) seal. Seals were used as a stamping device in place of signatures to validate a document. The impression was normally made on clay, wax, or some other soft material (Ford; TDNT; Max Kaser, *Roman Private Law* [Durban, South Africa: Butterworths, 1968], 42-43; LAW, 1094-98, 2795; DLNT, 1084-86; BBC; DGRA, 95-96). According to Roman law a testament or will was sealed w. seven seals by seven witnesses (Bousset; Emmet Russell, "A Roman Law Parallel to Rev. V," *Bib Sac* 115 [1958]: 258-64; Buckland, 238f). The testimony of witnesses not present at a trial was also sealed, then opened by the court and read aloud (s. Max Kaser, *Das römische Zivilpozessrecht* [München: Verlag C.H. Beck, 1966], 283). The book spoken of here seems to be the book of God's decrees containing the full account of what God in His sovereign will has determined as the destiny of the world (Mounce; Bousset; Thomas; Roland Bergmeier, "Die Buchrolle und das Lamm [Apk 5 und 10]," *ZNW* 76 [1985]: 225-42). Note also the Greek style "double document," where a summary is attached to the top of the longer form of the document (Anthony J. Saldarini, "Babatha's," *BAR* 24 [1998]: 36). ◆ **2 εἶδον** aor. ind. act. ὁράω (# 3972) to see. **ἰσχυρός** (# 2708) strong. **κηρύσσοντα** pres. act. part. (adj.) κηρύσσω (# 3062) to proclaim, to cry out as a herald (TDNT; EDNT). **ἀνοῖξαι** aor. act. inf. ἀνοίγω (# 487) to open. **λῦσαι** aor. act. inf. λύω (# 3395) to loose, to remove. Epex. infs. explaining the adj. ἄξιος (# 545) worthy. Aor. points to a specific act. ◆ **3 ἐδύνατο** impf. ind. pass. (dep.) δύναμαι (# 1538) to be able to, w. inf. **ὑποκάτω** (# 5691) down under, underneath. **ἀνοῖξαι** aor. act. inf. ἀνοίγω (# 487) to open. Compl. inf. to the main vb. **βλέπειν** pres. act. inf. βλέπω (# 1063) to see. Compl. inf. to the main vb. ◆ **4 ἔκλαιον** impf. ind. act. κλαίω (# 3081) to cry, to weep aloud, to wail. The word is frequently used to mean professional mourning (Ford). Impf. pictures the continual action. **εὑρέθη** aor.

ind. pass. εὑρίσκω (# 2351) to find. **ἀνοῖξαι** aor. act. inf. ἀνοίγω (# 487) to open. Epex. inf. explaining the adj. **ἄξιος** (# 545) worthy. **βλέπειν** pres. act. inf. βλέπω (# 1063) to see. ◆ **5 εἷς** (# 1651) one. **κλαῖε** pres. imp. act. κλαίω (# 3081) to cry. Pres. imp. w. neg. μή (# 3590) calls for the stopping of an action in progress. **ἰδού** aor. ind. act. ὁράω (# 3972) to see. **ἐνίκησεν** aor. ind. act. νικάω (# 3771) to win a victory, to be victor, to overcome. Consummative aor. stressing the cessation or completion of the act (GGBB, 559-60). **λέων** (# 3329) lion. The lion, an emblem of strength, majesty, courage, authority, and menace, as well as symbolic of intellectual excellence, was often applied to the Messiah as the national ruler from the tribe of David (Ford; Cleon L. Rogers, Jr., "The Davidic Covenant in Acts-Revelation," *Bib Sac* 151 [1994]: 83; TDOT; SB, 3:801; Charles; BBC. **φυλή** (# 5876) tribe. **ῥίζα** (# 4844) root. The word suggests a stump of a tree that has been cut down, out of which develops a "root" that eventually becomes a tree again (s. Isa 11:1; s. the DSS text 6Q8, 2 where the sons of Noah are referred to as "roots" which will produce again; s. AT, 265; MPAT, 78-79). The connotation here is that the nation of Israel has been cut down, but now One from the dynasty of David has the right to rule so that the tree will flourish again (Cleon L. Rogers, Jr., "The Davidic Covenant in Acts-Revelation," *Bib Sac* 151 [1994]: 83; Kenneth E. Pomykala, *The Davidic Dynasty Tradition in Early Judaism: Its History and Significance for Messianism* [Atlanta, Ga.: Scholars Press, 1995]). **ἀνοῖξαι** aor. act. inf. ἀνοίγω (# 487) to open. The word is used of unrolling a book (Charles). Inf. to express purp. or result. ◆ **6 εἶδον** aor. ind. act. ὁράω (# 3972) to see. **μέσος** (# 3545) in the middle. **ζῶον** (# 2442) living creature. **ἀρνίον** (# 768) lamb, little lamb (s. John 1:29; Donald Guthrie, "The Lamb in the Structure of the Book of Revelation," *Vox Evangelica* 12 [1981]: 64-71; Aune, Excursus 5A: "Christ as Lamb," 1:367-73; BTNT, 193-94; DLNT, 641-44; DJG, 432-34). This word for lamb is used exclusively in Rev. of the resurrected and victorious Christ, the crucified Messiah (Mounce; Bergmeier, "Die Buchrolle und das Lamm [Apk 5 und 10]," *ZNW* 76 [1985]: 230-35). **ἑστηκός** perf. act. part. ἵστημι (# 2705) to stand. **ἐσφαγμένον** perf. past. part. σφάζω (# 5377) to slaughter, to slaughter a sacrifice. Perf. indicates the lasting effects. The Lamb has been offered, yet it stands erect and alive in the sight of heaven (Swete). **ἔχων** pres. act. part. (adj.) ἔχω (# 2400) to have. Some have felt that the use of the part. shows Semitic or LXX influence and is like the prep. ל (lᵉ) denoting possession (AASS, 109-10; Daryl D. Schmidt, "Semitisms and Septuagintalisms in the Book of Revelation," *NTS* 37 [1991]: 603; but s. Beyer, 208-9). **κέρας** (# 3043) horn. The horn is proverbially a symbol of courage, strength, and might (Ford; TDNT; SB, 2:110-11; Rogers, "Davidic Covenant in the Gospels," *Bib Sac*

150 [1993]: 467). ὀφθαλμός (# 4057) eye. The seven horns stress that He is omnipotent and the seven eyes stress that He is omniscient (Thomas). John sees a lamb w. seven horns and seven eyes bearing the wounds of sacrificial slaughter, yet standing in readiness for action. In one brilliant stroke John portrays his central theme of NT; revelation–victory through sacrifice (Mounce; s. also DLNT, 283-84). ἀπεσταλμένοι perf. pass. part. ἀποστέλλω (# 690) to send, to send as an official representative (EDNT; TDNT). The vb. has reference to the mission of the Spirit (Swete). ◆ 7 ἦλθεν aor. ind. act. ἔρχομαι (# 2262) to come. εἴληφεν perf. ind. act. λαμβάνω (# 3284) to receive, to take. Rather than being an aoristic, perf., here the perf. is like a highly dramatic historical pres. (K.L. McKay, "Syntax in Exegesis," TB 23 [1972]: 54; NSV, 50). καθημένου pres. mid. (dep.) part. (subst.) κάθημαι (# 2764) to sit. ◆ 8 ἔλαβεν aor. ind. act. λαμβάνω (# 3284) to receive, to take. ἔπεσαν aor. ind. act. πίπτω (# 4406) to fall; here, to fall down in worship. ἔχοντες pres. act. part. ἔχω (# 2400) to have. κιθάρα (# 3067) harp. This is the general term for a kind of harp or lyre (Ford; Thomas; s. 1 Cor. 14:7). φιάλας acc. pl. φιάλη (# 5786) bowl. This was a flat, shallow cup or bowl for drinking or libations (Mounce). χρυσᾶς acc. pl. χρυσοῦς (# 5991) golden. γεμούσας aor. act. part. γέμω (# 1154) to be full of. θυμίαμα (# 2592) incense. In Judaism the angels were considered to be the carriers of the prayers of men (SB, 3:807-8). Incense was used to produce fragrant perfumes both in secular and liturgical life (Ford; s. Matt. 2:11). ◆ 9 ᾄδουσιν pres. ind. act. ᾄδω (# 106) to sing. During the Hellenistic period a new kind of music was introduced to the Greek world. Concerts in great amphitheaters w. huge choirs and professional singers accompanied by instrumental music played on stringed instruments, flutes, percussion instruments and even a water organ, were staged. Large choirs made up of virgins sang at weddings and the singers in the temples of worship were often under special protection of the king (KGH, 2:622-43). ᾠδή (# 6046) song. The idea of a new song grows out of the use of the expression in the Psalms. Every new act of mercy calls forth a new song of gratitude and praise (Mounce). Judaism taught that Israel will first sing a new song in the days of the Messiah as a song of praise for the miracle of deliverance (SB, 3:801-2). The hymns were to encourage those undergoing persecution (DLNT, 524-25). ἄξιος (# 545) worthy. εἶ pres. ind. act. εἰμί (# 1639) to be. λαβεῖν aor. act. inf. λαμβάνω (# 3284) to receive. The inf. is used to explain the adj. ἄξιος. ἀνοῖξαι aor. act. inf. ἀνοίγω (# 487) to open. ἐσφάγης aor. ind. pass. σφάζω (# 5377) to slaughter. ἠγόρασας aor. ind. act. ἀγοράζω (# 60) to buy at the marketplace, to redeem. γλώσσης gen. sing. γλῶσσα (# 1185) tongue, language. ◆ 10 ἐποίησας aor. ind. act. ποιέω (# 4472) to do, to make, to constitute. βασιλεύσουσιν fut. ind. act.

βασιλεύω (# 996) to be a king, to rule as king, to reign. ◆ 11 εἶδον aor. ind. act. ὁράω (# 3972) to see. ἤκουσα aor. ind. act. ἀκούω (# 201) to hear. κύκλῳ (# 3241) encircling, round about. ἦν impf. ind. act. εἰμί (# 1639) to be. ἀριθμός (# 750) number. Now it is the innumerable host of angels who lift their voices in a great doxology of praise. Their number is an apocalyptic symbol for countless thousands (Mounce). μυριάδες nom. pl. μυριάς (# 3689) sing., myriad, 10,000; pl., a very large undefined number (BAGD). This is the largest single number used in Greek. The double use refers to an innumerable number (BBC). ◆ 12 λέγοντες pres. act. part. λέγω (# 3306) to say. ἐσφαγμένον perf. pass. part. σφάζω (# 5377) to slaughter. Perf. indicates the abiding effects. λαβεῖν aor. act. inf. λαμβάνω (# 3284) to receive. Inf. explaining the adj. ἄξιον (# 545) worthy. δύναμις (# 1539) power. ἰσχύς (# 2709) strength, might (s. Eph. 1:19). εὐλογία (# 2330) praise (Bousset). ◆ 13 κτίσμα (# 3233) that which is created, creation. ἤκουσα aor. ind. act. ἀκούω (# 201) to hear. λέγοντας pres. act. part. λέγω (# 3306) to say. ◆ 14 ἔλεγον impf. ind. act. λέγω (# 3306) to say. Inceptive impf., "they began to say," or iterat. impf., "they said over and over again." ἔπεσαν aor. ind. act. πίπτω (# 4406) to fall. προσεκύνησαν aor. ind. act. προσκυνέω (# 4686) to worship. For worship in Rev. s. DLNT, 1235-38.

Revelation 6

◆ 1 εἶδον aor. ind. act. ὁράω (# 3972) to see. ἤνοιξεν aor. ind. act. ἀνοίγω (# 487) to open, to break the seal. With the opening of the first seal the beginning of the seven-year tribulation period is described. The Jews considered this a time of unprecedented trouble and judgment that preceded the messianic salvation. This time of judgment for Israel and for the whole world was called the "birth pains of the Messiah," indicating ever increasing severity of judgement until the Messiah appears (s. Matt. 24:8; esp. SB, 4:858-80, 976-1015; Moore, Judaism, 2:360-63; b. Sanh., 98a-97a; b. Shab., 118a; M, Sota 9:15). ἀρνίον (# 768) lamb (s. 5:6). It is the lamb who controls the world's destiny and pours out his wrath upon the world. σφραγίδων gen. pl. σφραγίς (# 5382) seal (s. 5:1). ἤκουσα aor. ind. act. ἀκούω (# 201) to hear. ζῷον (# 2442) living creature. λέγοντος pres. act. part. λέγω (# 3306) to say. βροντή (# 1103) thunder. Here gen. of description. ἔρχου pres. imp. mid. (dep.) ἔρχομαι (# 2262) to come. Imp. as invitation. Pres. imp. is often used w. a vb. of motion (VANT, 341-45). ◆ 2 εἶδον aor. ind. act. ὁράω (# 3972) to see. ἰδού aor. imp. act. ὁράω (# 3972) to see. ἵππος (# 2691) horse. The rabbis believed the appearance of a white horse was a favorable sign. In the later rabbinic writings the coming of the Messiah was associated w. the sight of a horse. Perhaps war horses were associated w. the messianic woes, i.e., the suffering that would precede the advent of the Messiah (Ford). **λευκός** (# *3328*) white. **καθήμενος** pres. mid. part. κάθημαι (# *2764*) to sit. **ἔχων** pres. act. part. (adj.) ἔχω (# *2400*) to have (s. 5:6). **τόξον** (# *5534*) bow. The bow is not only the weapon of the Parthians, the most feared enemies of the Romans, but in general a weapon of attack all nations feared. It is part of the typical cavalry equipment of all Oriental armies and the particular weapon of the king (Mathias Rissi, "The Rider on the White Horse," *Interp.* 18 [1964]: 414; BBC). In the OT this was a sign of divine judgment. **ἐδόθη** aor. ind. pass. δίδωμι (# *1443*) to give. **στέφανος** (# *5109*) crown. **ἐξῆλθεν** aor. ind. act. ἐξέρχομαι (# *2002*) to go out. **νικῶν** pres. act. part. νικάω (# *3771*) to conquer. Part. of manner describing his going out. Pres. may be conative, "trying to conquer." **νικήση** aor. subj. act. νικάω (# *3771*) to be the victor, to overcome, to conquer. Subj. w. **ἵνα** (# *2671*) used in a purp. cl. Some have felt that the rider on the white horse is Christ himself (Zane Hodges, "The First Horseman of the Apocalypse," *Bib Sac* 119 [1962]: 324-34), or the Antichrist–the "man of sin" (Rissi, Inter. 18:407-18; Mounce; Walvoord; Ford); or else not specific individual but a peace movement that can only offer a temporary peace (Thomas). ◆ **3 ἤνοιξεν** aor. ind. act. ἀνοίγω (# *487*) to open. **ἤκουσα** aor. ind. act. ἀκούω (# *201*) to hear. **λέγοντος** pres. act. part. λέγω (# *3306*) to say. **ἔρχου** pres. imp. act. ἔρχομαι (# *2262*) to come. ◆ **4 ἐξῆλθεν** aor. ind. act. ἐξέρχομαι (# *2002*) to come out. **πυρρός** (# *4794*) fiery, red. The color represents bloodshed and sin (Ford). **καθημένῳ** pres. mid. (dep.) part. κάθημαι (# *2764*) to sit. **ἐδόθη** aor. ind. pass. δίδωμι (# *1443*) to give. **λαβεῖν** aor. act. inf. λαμβάνω (# *3284*) to take. Epex. inf. explaining that which was given. **σφάξουσιν** fut. ind. act. σφάζω (# *5377*) to slaughter. The term indicates death by violence. Fut. ind. is used here in an epex. explanatory purp. cl. (RWP). For the use here of the ind. rather than the subj. s. MT, 100. **ἐδόθη** aor. ind. pass. δίδωμι (# *1443*) to give. **μάχαιρα** (# *3479*) sword. This was the short Roman sword symbolic of violent death, war, and the power of the authorities to punish evildoers (Mounce; Ford). ◆ **5 ἤνοιξεν** aor. ind. act. ἀνοίγω (# *487*) to open. **ἤκουσα** aor. ind. act. ἀκούω (# *201*) to hear. **λέγοντος** pres. act. part. λέγω (# *3306*) to say. **ἔρχου** pres. imp. act. ἔρχομαι (# *2262*) to come (s.v. 1). **ἰδού** aor. imp. act. ὁράω (# *3972*) to see. **μέλας** (# *3506*) black. This color is symbolic of mourning, affliction, or famine (Ford; Mounce). **καθήμενος** pres. mid. (dep.) part. κάθημαι (# *2764*) to sit. **ἔχων** pres. act. part. ἔχω (# *2400*) to have. **ζυγός** (# *2433*) scales. The beam of a pair of scales (Swete). This suggests rationing or famine (BBC). ◆ **6 ἤκουσα** aor. ind. act. ἀκούω (# *201*) to hear. **λέγουσαν** aor. ind. act. λέγω (# *3306*) to say. **Χοῖνιξ** (# *5955*) quart. This was a dry measure of about a quart, approximately 1.92 pints. One of these was a man's daily ration (Ford). **σῖτος** (# *4992*) grain. Grain was the mainstay of daily food. Here gen. of con-

tent. **δηνάριον** (# *1324*) denarius (DGRA, 393-94). This Roman silver coin equivalent to one day's wages indicates here that enough wheat to feed one man for one day cost a full day's wages. The cost of wheat here is five to twelve times its normal price, indicating famine (Ford; Mounce). Gen. of price here in a distributive sense, "per denarius" (MKG, 189; GGBB, 122). **κριθῶν** gen. pl. κριθή (# *3208*) barley. Barley, primarily the food of the poor, was relatively cheaper than wheat (Swete). For a discussion of prices for wheat and barley, especially in Rome–and grain shortages s. ERE, 120-237, 345-47; BAFCS, 2:59-78; JTJ, 120-23. **ἔλαιον** (# *1778*) oil, olive oil. **ἀδικήσῃς** aor. subj. act. ἀδικέω (# *92*) to injure, to do harm to. Subj. w. the neg. **μή** (# *3590*) is used to express a prohibition or neg. command. Ingressive aor., "do not begin to hurt" (Thomas). ◆ **7 ἤνοιξεν** aor. ind. act. ἀνοίγω (# *487*) to open. **ἤκουσα** aor. ind. act. ἀκούω (# *201*) to hear. **λέγοντος** pres. act. part. λέγω (# *3306*) to say. **ἔρχου** pres. imp. act. ἔρχομαι (# *2262*) to come (s.v. 1). **ἰδού** aor. imp. act. ὁράω (# *3972*) to see. ◆ **8 εἶδον** aor. ind. act. ὁράω (# *3972*) to see. **ἰδού** aor. imp. act. ὁράω (# *3972*) to see. **χλωρός** (# *5952*) green, pale. The word means a yellowish green, but refers here to the color of a corpse or the blanched appearance of a person struck w. terror (Ford; Mounce). **καθήμενος** pres. mid. (dep.) κάθημαι (# *2764*) to sit. **ἐπάνω** (# *2062*) upon, on. **ᾅδης** (# *87*) Hades, the place of the dead, the underworld (s. Rev. 1:18). **ἠκολούθει** impf. ind. act. ἀκολουθέω (# *199*) to follow after, to follow. **ἐδόθη** aor. ind. pass. δίδωμι (# *1443*) to give. **ἀποκτεῖναι** aor. act. inf. ἀποκτείνω (# *650*) to kill. Epex. inf. to explain **ἐξουσία** (# *2026*) the authority that was given. **ῥομφαία** (# *4855*) sword. This was the sword w. the large blade (s. Rev. 1:16). The word is used w. prep. **ἐν** (# *1877*) in an instr. sense, "w. the sword." **λιμός** (# *3350*) hunger. **θάνατος** (# *2505*) death; here, plague. **θηρίον** (# *2563*) wild animal, wild beast. Death by wild beasts would be expected in a land decimated by war and famine (Mounce). ◆ **9 ἤνοιξεν** aor. ind. act. ἀνοίγω (# *487*) to open. **εἶδον** aor. ind. act. ὁράω (# *3972*) to see. **ὑποκάτω** (# *5691*) under, underneath. **θυσιαστήριον** (# *2603*) place of offering, altar. **ἐσφαγμένων** perf. pass. part. σφάζω (# *5377*) to slaughter, to slay. The souls of the slaughtered ones are seen under the altar because in the Levitical rite the blood was poured out at the foot of the altar (Swete). For a discussion of persecution s. DLNT, 908-14. **εἶχον** impf. ind. act. ἔχω (# *2400*) to have. ◆ **10 ἔκραξαν** aor. ind. act. κράζω (# *3189*) to scream out, to cry. **λέγοντες** pres. act. part. λέγω (# *3306*) to say. **ἕως πότε** (# *2401*; *4536*) until when?, how long? These words echo through the OT: Ps. 6:3; 13:1-2; 35:17; 74:9-10; Isa. 6:11; Jer. 47:6; Zech. 1:12 (Harrington). 1 Enoch gives a description of those who cry out to the Almighty God for vengeance (1 Enoch 9:3-11). **δεσπότης** (# *1305*) lord, master, ruler, one who exercises absolute authority.

ἀληθινός (# *240*) true, genuine. **κρίνεις** pres. ind. act. κρίνω (# *3212*) to judge. **ἐκδικεῖς** pres. ind. act. ἐκδικέω (# *1688*) to avenge, to revenge, to execute vengeance. For a study of the imprecatory prayers in Rev. s. Thomas, 1:517-24. **κατοικούντων** pres. act. part. (subst.) κατοικέω (# *2997*) to reside, to dwell. ◆ **11 ἐδόθη** aor. ind. act. δίδωμι (# *1443*) to give. **στολή** (# *5124*) robe. The word refers to any stately robe and as long, sweeping garments they eminently would have this stateliness about them. Always or almost always it refers to a garment reaching to the feet, or else train-like, sweeping the ground (Trench, *Synonyms*, 186). **ἐρρέθη** aor. ind. pass. λέγω (# *3306*) to say. Pass. is the divine or theol. pass. indicating that God is the one who does the action (BG, 76). **ἀναπαύσονται** fut. ind. mid. (dep.) ἀναπαύομαι (# *399*) to cease, to pause, to rest. Fut. mid. used in the subfinal cl. is to be preferred rather than the aor. mid. subj. (RWP). **πληρωθῶσιν** aor. subj. pass. πληρόω (# *4444*) to fill, to fulfill. **σύνδουλος** (# *5281*) fellow slave. **μέλλοντες** pres. act. part. μέλλω (# *3516*) to be about to. The vb. is used w. the inf. to express the immediate fut. **ἀποκτέννεσθαι** pres. pass. inf. ἀποκτείνω (# *650*) to kill. ◆ **12 εἶδον** aor. ind. act. ὁράω (# *3972*) to see. **ἤνοιξεν** aor. ind. act. ἀνοίγω (# *487*) to open. **σεισμός** (# *4939*) earthquake. Earthquakes were often used to introduce God's judgment (s. Richard Bauckham, "The Eschatological Earthquake in the Apocalypse of John," *Nov T* 19 [1977]: 224-33; Amos Nur and Hagai Ron, "Earthquake! Inspiration for Armageddon," *BAR* 23 [1997]: 48-55; Isa. 24:17-23; also Rev. 3:7, 14 for earthquakes in Asia Minor). **ἐγένετο** aor. ind. mid. (dep.) γίνομαι (# *1181*) to happen, to occur, to be. **σάκκος** (# *4884*) sackcloth. It was the rough cloth made from the hair of a black goat and worn in times of mourning (Mounce). **τρίχινος** (# *5570*) made of hair. **σελήνη** (# *4943*) moon. ◆ **13 ἀστέρες** nom. pl. ἀστήρ (# *843*) star. **ἔπεσαν** aor. ind. act. πίπτω (# *4406*) to fall. **γῆ** (# *1178*) earth. **συκῆ** (# *5190*) fig tree. **βάλλει** pres. ind. act. βάλλω (# *965*) to throw, to cast. Gnomic pres. picturing that which is always true. **ὄλυνθος** (# *3913*) fig, unripe fig. The word means the green figs that appear in winter and of which, though some ripen, many drop off in spring (Swete). **ἄνεμος** (# *449*) wind. **σειομένη** pres. pass. part. σείω (# *4940*) to shake. The world and its well-being depend on the faithfulness w. which the heavenly luminaries fulfill their roles. When the sun, moon, and stars forsake this order, the end of the world is at hand (Charles). ◆ **14 ἀπεχωρίσθη** aor. ind. pass. ἀποχωρίζω (# *714*) to tear apart, to rip apart. **βιβλίον** (# *1046*) book, scroll, roll. **ἑλισσόμενον** pres. pass. part. ἑλίσσω (# *1813*) to roll up. The image is of a rent papyrus, whereupon the divided portions curl and form a roll on either side (Charles). **ὄρος** (# *4001*) mountain. **νῆσος** (# *3762*) island. **ἐκινήθησαν** aor. ind. pass. κινέω (# *3075*) to move. ◆ **15 μεγιστάν** (# *3491*) great one,

mighty one, magistrate, the civil official in authority (Swete). **χιλίαρχος** (# *5941*) leaders of a thousand soldiers, tribune. The term was commonly used of the military tribune no matter how many he commanded. The word refers to the military authorities (Ford; Swete). **πλούσιοι** (# *4454*) rich, wealthy. **ἰσχυρός** (# *2708*) powerful. **δοῦλος** (# *1528*) slave. **ἐλεύθερος** (# *1801*) freeman, free, those who were no longer slaves. The seven conditions of life are named, covering the whole fabric of society from the emperor down to the meanest slave (Swete). **ἔκρυψαν** aor. ind. act. κρύπτω (# *3221*) to hide. **σπήλαιον** (# *5068*) cave. ◆ **16 λέγουσιν** pres. ind. act. λέγω (# *3306*) to say. **πέσετε** aor. imp. act. πίπτω (# *4406*) to fall. **κρύψατε** aor. imp. act. κρύπτω (# *3221*) to hide. **πρόσωπον** (# *4725*) face. **καθημένου** pres. mid. (dep.) κάθημαι (# *2764*) to sit. **ὀργή** (# *3973*) wrath, anger. **ὀργῆς τοῦ ἀρνίου** wrath of the lamb. The "wrath of the lamb" is a deliberate paradox by which John intends to goad his readers into theological alertness (Caird; DLNT, 1238-41). ◆ **17 ἦλθεν** aor. ind. act. ἔρχομαι (# *2262*) to come. **δύναται** pres. ind. mid. (dep.) δύναμαι (# *1538*) to able to. **σταθῆναι** aor. pass. inf. ἵστημι (# *2705*) to stand, to hold one's ground (Swete). Compl. inf. to the main vb.

Revelation 7

◆ **1 εἶδον** aor. ind. act. ὁράω (# *3972*) to see. **μετὰ τοῦτο εἶδον** "after this I saw." The phrase introduces another part of the vision (s. Rev. 4:1). The vision he now describes, between the opening of the sixth and seventh seal, contrasts the preparedness of God's people w. the unbeliever's unreadiness (Swete; Thomas). **ἑστῶτας** perf. act. part. (adj.) ἵστημι (# *2705*) perf., to stand. **γωνία** (# *1224*) corner. **κρατοῦντας** pres. act. part. (adj.) κρατέω (# *3195*) to hold, to grasp, to have power over. **ἄνεμος** (# *449*) wind. **πνέη** pres. subj. act. πνέω (# *4463*) to blow. The subj. w. **ἵνα** (# *2671*) is used in a neg. purp. cl. (RWP). **μήτε** (# *3612*) neither. The four winds as destructive agents of God are a regular feature in apocalyptic literature (Mounce; Charles). Enoch sees three gates: through one the winds blow good things on the earth, but through the other two the winds blow violence and sorrow upon the earth (1 Enoch 34:2-3; note 1 Enoch 76 where he describes the easterly winds, the southerly winds, the northly winds, and the westerly winds; for Pliny's description of the four winds s. Pliny, *NH*, 2:119-21). ◆ **2 εἶδον** aor. ind. act. ὁράω (# *3972*) to see. **ἀναβαίνοντα** pres. act. part. ἀναβαίνω (# *326*) to come down. **ἀνατολή** (# *242*) rising; the rising of the sun indicates the east. **ἔχοντα** pres. act. part. ἔχω (# *2400*) to have. **σφραγίς** (# *5382*) seal. To the prophet's contemporaries, a seal would have suggested the branding of cattle or the tattooing of slaves and soldiers, esp. those in the service of the emperor who could be recognized by this mark if they deserted; the marking of a soldier or the member of a guild on the hand, brow, or neck to seal him as a religious devotee, i.e., a member of a sacred militia. The mark in this case was a sign of consecration to the deity; it could refer to the mark prophets might have worn on their forehead, either painted or tattooed; or it could refer to the phylactery worn on the forehead and hand (Ford). In describing the worship at Heiropolis, it is said that all of the worshippers are marked (στίζονται "tattooed"), some on their wrist and some on their necks (s. *De Dea Syria*, 59). The idea of a seal would be to mark one's property and show ownership as well as protection (Swete; Thomas). **ζῶντος** pres. act. part. ζάω (# 2409) to live. **ἔκραξεν** aor. ind. act. κράζω (# 3189) to scream, to cry out. **οἷς ἐδόθη αὐτοῖς** to whom it was given to them. This may reflect the Hebraic construction of the resumptive pron. (MH, 434f; PAPC, 41; AASS, 111-12). **ἐδόθη** aor. ind. pass. δίδωμι (# 1443) to give. The theol. or divine pass. indicates God is the subject of the action. **ἀδικῆσαι** aor. act. inf. ἀδικέω (# 92) to harm, to injure. Inf. to explain that which was given. ◆ **3 λέγων** pres. act. part. λέγω (# 3306) to say (for the use of the pleonastic part. s. Rev. 1:17). **ἀδικήσητε** aor. subj. act. ἀδικέω (# 92) to harm. Subj. w. the neg. μή (# 3590) to form a prohibition or neg. command. **σφραγίσωμεν** aor. subj. act. σφραγίζω (# 5381) to seal. Aor. subj. in a temp. cl. of indefinite action for the fut. (RWP). **μέτωπον** (# 3587) between the eyes, forehead. ◆ **4 ἤκουσα** aor. ind. act. ἀκούω (# 201) to hear. **ἀριθμός** (# 750) number. **τεσσεράκοντα τέσσαρες χιλιάδες** (# 5475; 5477; 5942) 144,000. It seems best to view the number as literal, since it is difficult to find any objective meaning for a symbolical interpretation. This select group from Israel were to spread the Word of God during the tribulation (Thomas). It was a hope of the Jews that the tribes of Israel would be gathered again (HSB, 761-63; Albert Geyser, "The Twelve Tribes in Revelation: Judean and Judeo Christian Apocalypticism," *NTS* 28 [1982]: 388-99; Ezek. 37; Hos. 3:4-5; Sirach 33:1; Tob. 13:10, 13; 2 Macc. 1:27; Jubil. 1:15; 1 Enoch 90:23). **ἐσφραγισμένων** perf. pass. part. σφραγίζω (# 5381) to seal. **φυλή** (# 5876) tribe. The tribes are to be taken as members of the literal nation of Israel (Thomas). The names of Dan and Ephraim are not found in the following list, perhaps because of their connection w. idolatry (SB, 3:804-5; Thomas). ◆ **9 μετὰ ταῦτα** (# 3552; 4047) after these things. It marks a new vision. **εἶδον** aor. ind. act. ὁράω (# 3972) to see. **ἰδού** aor. imp. act. ὁράω (# 3972) to see. **ἀριθμῆσαι** aor. act. inf. ἀριθμέω (# 749) to count; pass. to be counted. Compl. inf. to the main vb. **ἐδύνατο** impf. ind. pass. (dep.) δύναμαι (# 1538) to be able to, w. inf. **γλῶσσαν** (# 5876) tongue, speech. **ἑστῶτες** perf. act. part. ἵστημι (# 2705) perf., to stand. **ἀρνίον** (# 768) lamb (cf. Rev. 5:6). **περιβεβλημένους** perf. pass. part. περιβάλλω (# 4314) to cast around; pass., to be

clothed. **στολάς** acc. pl. (# 5124) robe (s. 6:11). **λευκός** (# 3328) white. **φοίνικες** nom. pl. φοῖνιξ (# 5836) palm branch. The palm is a sign of festive joy. One inscription describes how, out of gratitude to the gods, the inhabitants of a city decreed that thirty boys should daily sing prescribed hymns as they were "clothed in white and crowned w. a twig, likewise holding a twig in their hands" (BS, 370). ◆ **10 κρά-ζουσιν** pres. ind. act. κράζω (# 3189) to call. Pres. indicates a continual or repeated action. **λέγοντες** pres. act. part. λέγω (# 3306) to say (s. 1:17). **σωτηρία** (# 5401) salvation. **θεῷ** dat. sing. θεός (# 2536) God. Dat. of possession: salvation belongs to Him as the victor. **ἡμῶν** gen. pl. ἐγώ (# 1609) I; our. **καθημένῳ** pres. mid. (dep.) part. (adj.) κάθημαι (# 2764) to sit. ◆ **11 εἰστήκεισαν** plperf. ind. act. ἵστημι (# 2705) to stand. The plperf. is used like an impf. (RWP). **κύκλῳ** dat. sing. κύλος (# 3241) encircling, in a circle, round about. Dat. of place used as adv. explaining where they were standing. **ζῴων** gen. pl. ζῷον (# 2442) living creature. **ἔπεσαν** aor. ind. act. πίπτω (# 4406) to fall, to fall down. **προσεκύνησαν** aor. ind. act. προσκυνέω (# 4686) to worship. ◆ **12 λέγοντες** pres. act. part. λέγω (# 3306) to say. **εὐλογία** (# 2330) blessing. **εὐχαριστία** (# 2374) thanksgiving. **ἰσχύς** (# 2709) strength, might (s. Eph. 1:19). ◆ **13 ἀπεκρίθη** aor. ind. pass. (dep.) ἀποκρίνομαι (# 646) to answer. **περιβεβλημένοι** perf. pass. part. περιβάλλω (# 4314) to cast around; pass., to be clothed. **πόθεν** (# 4470) from where? **ἦλθον** aor. ind. act. ἔρχομαι (# 2262) to come. **πόθεν ἦλθον** "where have they come from?" ◆ **14 εἴρηκα** perf. ind. act. λέγω (# 3306) to say. Aoristic perf. used as a simple past tense without concern for present consequences (GGBB, 578). **οἶδας** perf. ind. act. οἶδα (# 3857) to know. Def. perf. w. pres. meaning. **εἶπεν** aor. ind. act. λέγω (# 3306) to say. **ἐρχόμενοι** pres. mid. (dep.) part. ἔρχομαι (# 2262) to come, to go. **θλῖψις** (# 2568) tribulation. For a discusiion s. DLNT, 1179-82; BBC. **ἔπλυναν** aor. ind. act. πλύνω (# 4459) to wash. **ἐλεύκαναν** aor. ind. act. λευκαίνω (# 3326) to whiten, to make white (GELTS, 280). The idea of making robes white by washing them in blood is a striking paradox. It is the sacrifice of the lamb upon the cross that supplies white garments for the saints (Mounce; s. M, Middoth 5:4). ◆ **15 εἰσιν** pres. ind. act. εἰμί (# 1639) to be. **λατρεύουσιν** pres. ind. act. λατρεύω (# 3302) to perform worshipful service (TDNT). **ἡμέρας καὶ νυκτός** (#2465; 2779; 3816) gen. of time, day and night (s. 4:8). **ναῷ** dat. sing. ναός (# 3724) temple, sanctuary. **καθήμενος** pres. mid. (dep.) part. κάθημαι (# 2764) to sit. **σκηνώσει** fut. ind. act. σκηνεύω (# 5012) to live in a tent, to tabernacle (John 1:14). The setting may be the Feast of Tabernacles (Thomas). ◆ **16 πεινάσουσιν** fut. ind. act. πεινάω (# 4277) to be hungry. **διψήσουσιν** fut. ind. act. διψάω (# 1498) to be thirsty. **πέσῃ** aor. subj. act. πίπτω (# 4406) to fall. **καῦμα** (# 3008) burning, scorching. ◆ **17 μέσος** (# 3545) middle. Used in the phrase **ἀνὰ** μέσον between, amongst (Swete). **ποιμανεῖ** fut. ind. act. ποιμαίνω (# 4477) to shepherd (DLNT, 1090-93) . **ὁδηγήσει** fut. ind. act. ὁδηγέω (# 3842) to lead along the way, to guide, to lead. **πηγάς** gen. sing. πηγή (# 4380) spring. The word order in the phrase emphasizes life–"to life's water springs" (Swete). **ἐξαλείψει** fut. ind. act. ἐξαλείφω (# 1981) to wipe away. **δάκρυον** (# 1232) tear; here, "every single tear."

Revelation 8

◆ **1 ὅταν** (# 4020) when. Temp. particle is not used here in the indef. sense ("whenever"); rather, as was common in the Koine, writers used this particle w. the aor. ind. for a definite occurrence (RG, 973). **ἤνοιξεν** aor. ind. act. ἀνοίγω (# 487) to open, to break a seal. **σφραγίς** (# 5382) seal. **ἐγένετο** aor. ind. mid. (dep.) γίνομαι (# 1181) to be. **σιγή** (# 4968) silence. **οὐρανός** (# 4041) heaven. **ἡμιώριον** (# 2469) half an hour. The silence is a dramatic pause that makes even more impressive the judgment about to fall upon the earth. Although a thirty-minute period is a relatively short period, it would form an impressive break in such a rapidly moving drama (Mounce; Seiss). It could be silence so that the prayers of the saints on earth may be heard (Charles), or silence out of reverence just before the judgement of God falls (Lohse; Thomas; s. Zech. 2:13; Zeph. 1:7-8; 1QpHab 13:2-4). ◆ **2 εἶδον** aor. ind. act. ὁράω (# 3972) to see. **ἑστήκασιν** aor. ind. act. ἵστημι (# 2705) to stand. Enoch lists the names of the archangels as Sur'el (Uriel), Raphael, Raguel, Michael, Saraqa'el and Gabriel (1 Enoch 20; SB, 3:805-807). **ἐδόθησαν** aor. ind. pass. δίδωμι (# 1443) to give. Theol. pass. indicates that God is the one who gives. ◆ **3 ἦλθεν** aor. ind. act. ἔρχομαι (# 2262) to come. **ἐστάθη** aor. ind. pass. ἵστημι (# 2705) to stand. Ingressive aor., "he took his place" (RWP). **θυσιαστήριον** (# 2603) a place for sacrifices, altar. **ἔχων** pres. act. part. ἔχω (# 2400) to have. **λιβανωτός** (# 3338) golden censer or fire pan. The word usually means incense but here it appears to signify a censer (Ford). **χρυσοῦς** (# 5991) golden. **ἐδόθη** aor. ind. pass. δίδωμι (# 1443) to give (s.v. 2). **θυμίαμα** (# 2592) incense (s. 5:8). **δώσει** fut. ind. act. δίδωμι (# 1443) to give, to add. The fut. is used in a purp. cl. (MT, 100). ◆ **4 ἀνέβη** aor. ind. act. ἀναβαίνω (# 326) to go up. **καπνός** (# 2837) smoke. The meeting of the incense and the hot coals produces the fragrant smoke cloud, the symbol of divine acceptance (Swete). ◆ **5 εἴληφεν** perf. ind. act. λαμβάνω (# 3284) to take. For the use of the perf. s. 5:7. **ἐγέμισεν** aor. ind. act. γεμίζω (# 1153) to fill, to make full of, to fill up. **πῦρ** (# 4786) fire. **ἔβαλεν** aor. ind. act. βάλλω (# 965) to throw. **ἐγένοντο** aor. ind. mid. (dep.) γίνομαι (# 1181) to be. **βροντή** (# 1103) thunder. **ἀστραπή** (# 847) lightning. **σεισμός** (# 4939) earthquake (s. 6:12). ◆ **6 ἔχοντες** pres. act. part. (adj.) ἔχω (# 2400) to have. (s. 5:6). **ἡτοίμασαν** aor. ind. act. ἑτοιμάζω (# 2286) to prepare. **σαλπίσωσιν**

aor. subj. act. σαλπίζω (# 4895) to blow the trumpet. For various used of trumpets in the OT and in an eschatological sense s. Ford. Subj. w. ἵνα (# 2671) to express purp. ◆ **7 ἐσάλπισεν** aor. ind. act. σαλπίζω (# 4895) to blow the trumpet. **ἐγένετο** aor. ind. mid. (dep.) γίνομαι (# 1181) to be. **χάλαζα** (# 5898) hail. **μεμιγμένα** perf. pass. part. μείγνυμι (# 3502) to mix. **ἐβλήθη** aor. ind. pass. βάλλω (# 965) to throw. The syntax of the v. suggests that the blood-red storm appeared in heaven before it was cast upon the earth (Mounce). **κατεκάη** aor. ind. pass. κατακαίω (# 2876) to burn down, to burn up. Prep. in compound is perfective, "to burn down," "to burn up completely." **χόρτος** (# 5965) grass. **χλωρός** (# 5952) green. Only one-third of the land and its vegetation is devastated by fire. The fraction would indicate that although God is bringing punishment upon the earth, it is not yet complete and final (Mounce). ◆ **8 ἐσάλπισεν** aor. ind. act. σαλπίζω (# 4895) to blow the trumpet. This plague could suggest war or contamination of the water supply (BBC). **καιόμενον** pres. pass. part. καίω (# 2794) to set on fire; pass., to be burning, to burn. **ἐβλήθη** aor. ind. pass. βάλλω (# 965) to throw. **ἐγένετο** aor. ind. mid. (dep.) γίνομαι (# 1181) to become. ◆ **9 ἀπέθανεν** aor. ind. act. ἀποθνήσκω (# 633) to die. **ἔχοντα** pres. act. part. ἔχω (# 2400) to have. **διεφθάρησαν** aor. ind. pass. διαφθείρω (# 1425) to corrupt, to destroy. Prep. in compound is perfective. ◆ **10 ἐσάλπισεν** aor. ind. act. σαλπίζω (# 4895) to blow the trumpet. **ἔπεσεν** aor. ind. act. πίπτω (# 4406) to fall. **ἀστήρ** (# 843) star. **καιόμενος** pres. pass. part. καίω (# 2794) to burn. **λαμπάς** (# 3286) torch. **ποταμός** (# 4532) river. **πηγή** (# 4380) spring. Now the fresh water supply is smitten (Swete). ◆ **11 λέγεται** pres. ind. pass. λέγω (# 3306) to say; pass., to be called. **ἄψινθος** (# 952) wormwood. The word is used among medical writers (DMTG, 88). It is called wormwood after the strong bitter taste of the plant of that name. Wormwood symbolizes God's punishment; or bitterness, suffering, and sorrow (EDNT; Mounce; FFB, 198; ZPEB, 5:969; WTM, 2:517; ABD, 6:973). **ἐγένετο** aor. ind. mid. (dep.) γίνομαι (# 1181) to become. **ἐπικράνθησαν** aor. ind. pass. πικραίνω (# 4393) to make bitter, to cause to be bitter. ◆ **12 ἐσάλπισεν** aor. ind. act. σαλπίζω (# 4895) to blow the trumpet. **ἐπλήγη** aor. ind. pass. πλήσσω (# 4448) to strike, to smite. **σελήνη** (# 4943) moon. **σκοτισθῇ** aor. subj. pass. σκοτίζω (# 5029) to blacken, to darken. **φάνῃ** aor. subj. act. φαίνω (# 5743) to shine. Subj. w. ἵνα (# 2671) used in purp. cls. ◆ **13 εἶδον** aor. ind. act. ὁράω (# 3972) to see. **ἤκουσα** aor. ind. act. ἀκούω (# 201) to hear. **ἀετός** (# 108) eagle. The word may also be used for a vulture, which in this context would symbolize impending doom. The vulture hovers in mid-heaven, visible to all, and cries out in a great voice so that none will fail to hear (Mounce). **πετομένου** pres. mid. (dep.) part. πέτομαι (# 4375) to fly. **μεσουράνημα** (# 3547) at the zenith, in the meridian, i.e., in mid-heaven (Ford; Swete). **λέγοντος** pres. act. part. (subst.) λέγω (# 3306) to say. **κατοικοῦντας** pres. act. part. κατοικέω (# 2997) to dwell, to inhabit, to live. **μελλόντων** pres. act. part. μέλλω (# 3516) to be about to. It is used w. the inf. to express the immediate fut. **σαλπίζειν** pres. act. inf. σαλπίζω (# 4895) to blow a trumpet.

Revelation 9

◆ **1 ἐσάλπισεν** aor. ind. act. σαλπίζω (# 4895) to blow the trumpet. **εἶδον** aor. ind. act. ὁράω (# 3972) to see. **ἀστήρ** (# 843) star (s. 1 Enoch 21). **πεπτωκότα** perf. act. part. πίπτω (# 4406) to fall. Dramatic perf. (s. Rev. 5:7; DM, 204; Mounce). **ἐδόθη** aor. ind. pass. δίδωμι (# 1443) to give. The theol. or divine pass. indicates that God is the one who gives. **κλείς** (# 3090) key (s. Rev. 1:18; 3:7). **φρέατος** (# 5853) pit, well, shaft (Ford; esp. the references to the DSS: 1 QS 9:16, 22; 10:19). **ἄβυσσος** (# 12) bottomless, abyss; lit., unfathomable deep. It is a place of imprisonment for disobedient spirits and according to rabbinic thought it was the entrance to Gehenna, narrow at the top but wide as one went down (Ford; Swete; Charles; SB, 3:809; 4, ii:1083-93; HSB, 763-65; DLNT, 459-61). ◆ **2 ἤνοιξεν** aor. ind. act. ἀνοίγω (# 487) to open. **ἀνέβη** aor. ind. act. ἀναβαίνω (# 326) to go up, to ascend. **καπνός** (# 2837) smoke. **φρέατος** (# 5853) furnace. **κάμινος** (# 2825) furnace, kiln, fiery oven (BAGD; ABD, 4:38-39). **ἐσκοτώθη** aor. ind. pass. σκοτόω (# 5031) to darken. As the smoke rises it blots out the sun and darkens the atmosphere of the earth (Mounce). ◆ **3 ἐξῆλθον** aor. ind. act. ἐξέρχομαι (# 2002) to come out. **ἀκρίδες** (# 210) locust, grasshopper. Throughout the OT the locust is a symbol of destruction, and among the ancients the locust plague was viewed as a sign of the wrath of the gods (*deorun irae pestis ea intellegitur*); for locusts "are seen of exceptional size, and also they fly w. such a noise of wings that they are believed to be birds, and they obscure the sun, making the nations gaze upward in anxiety lest they should settle over all their lands" (Pliny, *NH*, 11:104). Bred in the desert, they invade cultivated areas in search of food. They may travel in a column a hundred feet deep and up to four miles long, leaving the land stripped bare of all vegetation (Mounce; FFB, 53; ZPEB, 3:948-50; Pliny, *NH*, 11:101-8). These are probably demons or fallen angels who assume a locust-like form (Thomas; BTNT, 173-74). **ἐδόθη** aor. ind. pass. δίδωμι (# 1443) to give. **ἔχουσιν** pres ind. act. ἔχω (# 2400) to have. **σκορπίος** (# 5026) scorpion; a lobster-like vermin some four or five inches long, it had a claw on the end of the tail that secreted a poison on contact. It should be noted that the demonic locusts of the first woe have the power rather than the appearance of scorpions (Mounce; FFB, 70; ZPEB, 5:297; NW, 2, ii:1521-23; Pliny, NH, 11:86-91). ◆ **4 ἐρρέθη** aor. ind. pass. λέγω (# 3306) to say. **ἀδικήσουσιν** fut. ind. act.

ἀδικέω (# 92) to injure, to harm. **χόρτος** (# 5965) grass. **χλωρός** (# 5952) green. **εἰ μή** (# 1673; 3590) except. **ἔχουσι** pres. ind. act. ἔχω (# 2400) to have. **σφραγίς** (# 5382) seal. **μέτωπον** (# 3587) forehead. ◆ **5 ἐδόθη** aor. ind. pass. δίδωμι (# 1443) to give. **ἀποκτείνωσιν** pres./aor. subj. act. ἀποκτείνω (# 650) to kill. Subj. w. ἵνα (# 2671) to express purp. **βασανισθήσονται** fut. ind. pass. βασανίζω (# 989) to torment, to torture. Fut. w. ἵνα (# 2671) expressing purp. (GGBB, 571; VA, 415). **μῆνας** acc. pl. μήν (# 3604) month. Acc. of time describing the extent of time. It is best to see this as a literal space of five months (Thomas). **βασανισμός** (# 990) torturing, torture. The word has the idea of punishment (Mounce). **σκορπίος** (# 5026) scorpion (s.v. 3). Here gen. of description. Pliny says that the poisonous wound of a scorpion is a slow, torturous death and almost always fatal to women and children–but to men only in the morning before the poison has been warmed by the sun (Pliny, *NH*, 11:86-89). **παίσῃ** aor. subj. act. παίω (# 4091) to strike. Subj. w. ὅταν (# 4020) in an indef. temp. cl., whenever. ◆ **6 ζητήσουσιν** fut. ind. act. ζητέω (# 2426) to seek, to look for. **εὑρήσουσιν** fut. ind. act. εὑρίσκω (# 2351) to find. **ἐπιθυμήσουσιν** fut. ind. act. ἐπιθυμέω (# 2121) to long for, to yearn after. **ἀποθανεῖν** aor. act. inf. ἀποθνήσκω (# 633) to die. Inf. is used as the obj. of the vb. ἐπιθυμήσουσιν. **φεύγει** pres. ind. act. φεύγω (# 5771) to flee, to escape. Pres. could perhaps be designated an historical pres. in the fut. ("death keeps fleeing from them"), or it could be an iterat. pres. indicating a repeated action. ◆ **7 ὁμοίωμα** (# 3930) likeness, shape (Swete). **ἵπποις** dat. pl. ἵππος (# 2691) horse. Dat. w. adj. ὅμοια. **ἡτοιμασμένοις** perf. pass. part. (adj.) ἑτοιμάζω (# 2286) to prepare. Perf. stresses the state or condition, "in a state of readiness." **πόλεμος** (# 4483) war. ◆ **8 εἶχον** impf. ind. act. ἔχω (# 2400) to have. **τρίχας** acc. pl. θρίξ (# 2582) hair. **ὀδόντες** nom. pl. ὀδούς (# 3848) teeth. **λεόντων** gen. pl. λέων (# 3329) lion. **ἦσαν** impf. ind. act. εἰμί (# 1639) to be. ◆ **9 θώρακας** acc. pl. θώραξ (# 2606) chest, breastplate. **σιδηρός** (# 4969) iron, of iron, made of iron. The scaly backs and flanks of the insects resembled iron coats of mail. The word points to the material of which such armor was ordinarily made, and at the same time indicates the hopelessness of any effort to destroy assailants so well-protected (Swete). **πτερύγων** gen. pl. πτέρυξ (# 4763) wing. **ἁρμάτων** gen. pl. ἅρμα (# 761) wagon, chariot. **τρεχόντων** pres. act. part. τρέχω (# 5556) to run. For Pliny's view of this type of plague s.v. 3. ◆ **10 ἔχουσιν** pres. ind. act. ἔχω (# 2400) to have. **οὐρά** (# 4038) tail. Perhaps a reference to the rearward archery of the Parthians (BBC). **κέντρον** (# 3034) goad for an ox, sting. **ἀδικῆσαι** aor. act. inf. ἀδικέω (# 92) to injure, to harm. In Italy the swarms of locusts were so bad that a law declared that war should be made upon them three times a year by crushing the eggs, then the grubs, and at last the fully grown insects. The law had the penalty of a deserter for the man who held back (Pliny, NH, 11:105). Epex. inf. explaining the authority or power that they have. **μῆνας** acc. pl. (# 3604) Acc. of time (s.v. 5). ◆ **11 ἔχουσιν** pres. ind. act. ἔχω (# 2400) to have. **Ἑβραϊστί** (# 1580) in Hebrew. **Ἀβαδδών** (# 3) Abaddon. The Heb. word אֲבַדּוֹן (abaddon), from אבד, means "destruction" and is used to refer to death or to the abode of the dead and can be parallel to Sheol (SB, 3:810; DCH, 1:101; s. also 1QH 3:19, 32; 1QM 18:17). In 4Q 286 (Berakot² frag. 3, col. 2. line 7), the text gives the curses issued by the Community Counsel of Belial and says "And [cursed be ... an]gel of the pit (חשׁה) and the sp[irit of des]truction (ורוח האבדון) in all the designs of your [guilty] inclination" (DSST, 435; DSSE, 160; Robert Eisenmann and Michael Wise, *The Dead Sea Scrolls Uncovered* [Dorset, England: Element Books Ltd, 1992], 222-30; ABD, 1:6; DDD, 1; TDOT, 1:23). **Ἀπολλύων** (# 661) Destroyer. The title or name does not necessarily refer to Satan, but to the demonic leader of the locust (Thomas). ◆ **12 οὐαί** (# 4026) woe, alas. Interjection denoting pain or displeasure, here used as a subst. (BAGD). The last three of the seven trumpets are looked upon as three woes because of their terrible destructive power (Ladd). **ἀπῆλθεν** aor. ind. act. ἀπέρχομαι (# 599) to go out, to go forth, to go away. **ἰδού** aor. imp. act. ὁράω (# 3972) to see. **ἔρχεται** pres. ind. mid. (dep.) ἔρχομαι (# 2262) to come. ◆ **13 ἐσάλπισεν** aor. ind. act. σαλπίζω (# 4895) to sound a trumpet. **ἤκουσα** aor. ind. act. ἀκούω (# 201) to hear. **μίαν** acc. sing. εἷς (# 1651) one. Here it means a single or solitary voice (Mounce). **κεράτων** gen. pl. κέρας (# 3043) horn. The horns on the altar were the symbol of God's power (Ford). **θυσιαστήριον** (# 2603) place where sacrifices are made, altar. **χρυσοῦς** (# 5991) golden. ◆ **14 λέγοντα** pres. act. part. λέγω (# 3306) to say. **ἔχων** pres. act. part. ἔχω (# 2400) to have. **λῦσον** aor. imp. act. λύω (# 3395) to loose, to release. Aor. imp. calls for a specific act w. a note of urgency. **δεδεμένους** perf. pass. part. (adj.) δέω (# 1313) to bind. Perf. emphasizes the state or condition. **ποταμός** (# 4532) river. ◆ **15 ἐλύθησαν** aor. ind. pass. λύω (# 3395) to release. **ἡτοιμασμένοι** perf. pass. part. ἑτοιμάζω (# 2286) to prepare (s.v. 7). **μήν** (# 3604) month. **ἐνιαυτός** (# 1929) year. **ἀποκτείνωσιν** pres. subj. act. ἀποκτείνω (# 650) to kill. Subj. w. ἵνα (# 2671) to express purp. ◆ **16 ἀριθμός** (# 750) number. **στράτευμα** (# 5128) army. **ἱππικός** (# 2690) pertaining to a horse, horseman. The army consisted of cavalry (Swete). **ἤκουσα** aor. ind. act. ἀκούω (# 201) to hear. ◆ **17 εἶδον** aor. ind. act. ὁράω (# 3972) to see. **ἵππος** (# 2690) horse. **ὅρασις** (# 3970) appearance, vision. **καθημένους** pres. mid. (dep.) part. κάθημαι (# 2764) to sit. **θώρακας** (# 2606) breastplate (s.v. 9). **πύρινος** (# 4791) fiery, made of fire (Swete). **ὑακίνθινος** (# 5610) hyacinth-colored, i.e., dark blue, a dusky blue color as of sulphurous

smoke (BAGD; MM). **θειώδης** (# 2523) sulphur, sulphur-colored, hence, yellow. Today brimstone is known as sulphur. It is difficult to determine whether the breastplates were of three colors each or whether each breastplate was of a single color; i.e., some red, some blue, some yellow (Mounce). **λέων** (# 3329) lion. **στόμα** (# 5125) mouth. **ἐκπορεύεται** pres. ind. mid. ἐκπορεύομαι (# 1744) to go out, to come out. **πῦρ** (# 4786) fire. **καπνός** (# 2837) smoke. **θεῖον** (# 2520) brimstone, sulphur. ◆ **18 πληγῶν** gen. pl. πληγή (# 4435) stripe, wound, calamity, plague (AS). **ἀπεκτάνθησαν** aor. ind. pass. ἀποκτείνω (# 650) to kill. **ἐκπορευομένου** pres. mid. (dep.) part. ἐκπορεύομαι (# 1744) to go out. ◆ **19 οὐρά** (# 4038) tail. **ὄφεσιν** dat. pl. ὄφις (# 4058) snake. Dat. w. adj. **ἔχουσαι** pres. act. part. ἔχω (# 2400) to have. Adj. part., "having heads (which) ...." **ἀδικοῦσιν** pres. ind. act. ἀδικέω (# 92) to injure, to harm. ◆ **20 λοιπός** (# 3370) rest. **ἀπεκτάνθησαν** aor. ind. pass. ἀποκτείνω (# 650) to kill. **μετενόησαν** aor. ind. act. μετανοέω (# 3566) to change one's mind, to change one's thinking, to repent. **προσκυνήσουσιν** fut. ind. act. προσκυνέω (# 4686) to worship. Fut. ind. could be used here to express result rather than purp. (RG, 992). **δαιμόνιον** (# 1228) demon (DDD, 445-55). **εἴδωλον** (# 1631) idol, false god (DLNT, 528-30). **χρυσᾶ** nom. pl. χρυσοῦς (# 5991) made of gold. **ἀργυροῦς** (# 735) silver. **χαλκοῦς** (# 5905) brass. **λίθινος** (# 3343) made of stone. **ξύλινος** (# 3832) wooden, made of wood. **δύνανται** pres. ind. pass. (dep.) δύναμαι (# 1538) to be able to, w. inf. **βλέπειν** pres. act. inf. βλέπω (# 1063) to see. **ἀκούειν** pres. act. inf. ἀκούω (# 201) to hear. **περιπατεῖν** pres. act. inf. περιπατέω (# 4344) to walk about. ◆ **21 μετενόησαν** aor. ind. act. μετανοέω (# 3566) to change one's mind. **φόνος** (# 5840) murder. **φάρμακον** (# 5760) magic art, sorcery. The use of drugs either for divination or for healing (BAGD; MM; DLNT, 701-5; Ford; DMTG, 324-30; s. Gal. 5:20). It is suggested that here the word has the special sense of magic spells inciting to illicit lust (EGT). Pliny describes the use of many superstitious and magical practices to bring about healing (Pliny, NH, 28), one being "that snake bites and scorpion stings are relieved by intercourse, but the act does harm to the woman" (Pliny, NH, 28:44); for further remedies against snake bites and scorpion stings s. Pliny, NH, 28: 149-55. **πορνεία** (# 4518) unlawful sexual intercourse, immorality (s. 2:21). **κλέμμα** (# 3092) stealing, theft.

Revelation 10

◆ **1 εἶδον** aor. ind. act. ὁράω (# 3972) to see. **ἰσχυρός** (# 2708) strong, powerful. **καταβαίνοντα** pres. act. part. (adj.) καταβαίνω (# 2849) to come down, to descend. **περιβεβλημένον** perf. pass. part. (adj.) περιβάλλω (# 4314) to cast about, to be clothed, to be enveloped. This word is used of encircling or throwing an embankment around a city, or clothing someone; in this context it indicates that the angel is encircled by a cloud (Ford). **νεφέλη** (# 3749) cloud (s. Rev. 1:7). **ἶρις** (# 2692) rainbow (s. 4:3). Here the word refers to the ordinary rainbow of many colors connected w. the cloud, due in this instance to the shining of the angel's face (Swete). **στῦλος** (# 5146) pillar. **πῦρ** (# 4786) fire. Some have taken this other angel as being Christ himself (Seiss; Scott), but others regard him as a true angelic being (Mounce; Thomas). ◆ **2 ἔχων** pres. act. part. (adj.) ἔχω (# 2400) to have. **βιβλαρίδιον** (# 1044) little book, a very small book. **ἠνεῳγμένον** perf. pass. part. ἀνοίγω (# 487) to open. Perf. pass. part. means having been opened and remaining so, i.e., "standing open." **ἔθηκεν** aor. ind. act. τίθημι (# 5502) to place, to put. **δεξιός** (# 1288) right. **εὐώνυμος** (# 2381) left. ◆ **3 ἔκραξεν** aor. ind. act. κράζω (# 3189) to cry out in a loud voice. **λέων** (# 3329) lion. **μυκᾶται** pres. ind. mid. (dep.) μυκάομαι (# 3681) to roar. The word is used of a low, deep sound like the lowing of an ox or the growl of thunder. The word may have been preferred here to indicate that the voice of the angel had not only volume but depth, at once compelling attention and inspiring awe (Swete). **ἐλάλησαν** aor. ind. act. λαλέω (# 3281) to speak. **βροντή** (# 1103) thunder. ◆ **4 ἐλάλησαν** aor. ind. act. λαλέω (# 3281) to speak. **ἤμελλον** impf. ind. act. μέλλω (# 3516) to be about to. The word is used w. inf. to express the immediate fut. Impf. here is inchoative, meaning "I was on the point of beginning to write" (RWP). **γράφειν** pres. inf. act. γράφω (# 1211) to write. **ἤκουσα** aor. ind. act. ἀκούω (# 201) to hear. **λέγουσαν** pres. act. part. λέγω (# 3306) to say. **σφράγισον** aor. imp. act. σφραγίζω (# 5381) to seal, to seal up (s. Rev. 5:1). **ἐλάλησαν** aor. ind. act. λαλέω (# 3281) to say. **γράψῃς** aor. subj. act. γράφω (# 1211) to write. Subj. w. the neg. **μή** (# 3590) is a prohibition or neg. command: "do not start to write." ◆ **5 εἶδον** aor. ind. act. ὁράω (# 3972) to see. **ἑστῶτα** perf. act. part. ἵστημι (# 2705) perf., to stand. **ἦρεν** aor. ind. act. αἴρω (# 149) to lift up. This is the typical Hebrew expression for swearing an oath. ◆ **6 ὤμοσεν** aor. ind. act. ὄμνυμι (# 3923) to take an oath, to swear. **ζῶντι** pres. act. part. ζάω (# 2409) to live. **ἔκτισεν** aor. ind. act. κτίζω (# 3231) to create. **χρόνος** (# 5989) time. The word here means "delay"–"there shall be delay no longer." Now nothing stands in the way of the final dramatic period of human history (Mounce). **οὐκέτι** (# 4033) no longer. **ἔσται** fut. ind. mid. (dep.) εἰμί (# 1639) to be. ◆ **7 ὅταν** (# 4020) w. subj., whenever. **μέλλῃ** pres. subj. act. μέλλω (# 3516) to be about to, w. inf. to express the immediate fut. Subj. w. **ὅταν** (# 4020) used in an indef. temp. cl. **σαλπίζειν** pres. act. inf. σαλπίζω (# 4895) to blow the trumpet. **ἐτελέσθη** aor. ind. pass. τελέω (# 5464) to bring to the goal, to complete, to bring to completion. The proleptic use of the aor., as here, occurs in vivacious speech of that which is annunciated as a consequence of a cond.

and expressed as already came to pass., the cond. regarded as fulfilled, "whenever he sounds the trumpet" (BG, 84f). **εὐηγγέλισεν** aor. ind. act. εὐαγγελίζω (# 2294) to proclaim the good news, to deliver good news (TDNT; TLNT; EDNT). ◆ **8 ἤκουσα** aor. ind. act. ἀκούω (# 201) to hear. **λαλοῦσαν** pres. act. part. λαλέω (# 3281) to speak. **λέγουσαν** pres. act. part. λέγω (# 3306) to say. **ὕπαγε** pres. imp. act. ὑπάγω (# 5632) to go; "go now." This is a Hebraic construction (Charles). **λάβε** aor. imp. act. λαμβάνω (# 3284) to take. **βιβλίον** (# 1046) book, small book. **ἠνεῳγμένον** perf. pass. part. ἀνοίγω (# 487) to open (s.v. 2). ◆ **9 ἀπῆλθα** aor. ind. act. ἀπέρχομαι (# 599) to go out, to go away from. John left his position by the door and went to the angel (RWP). **λέγων** pres. act. part. λέγω (# 3306) to say. **δοῦναι** aor. act. inf. δίδωμι (# 1443) to give. Inf. used in indir. discourse after the vb. **λέγων** to express a command (RWP). **λάβε** aor. imp. act. λαμβάνω (# 3284) to take. **κατάφαγε** aor. imp. act. κατεσθίω (# 2983) to eat down, to eat up completely. **πικραίνω** fut. ind. act. πικρανέω (# 4393) to make bitter. Imp. followed by the fut. is a Hebraic form of a cond. cl. in which the fut. expresses the result of having filled the command. For the construction s. Phil. 4:7; Beyer, 238-55. **κοιλία** (# 3120) stomach. **ἔσται** fut. ind. mid. (dep.) εἰμί (# 1639) to be. **γλυκύς** (# 1184) sweet. **μέλι** (# 3510) honey. ◆ **10 ἔλαβον** aor. ind. act. λαμβάνω (# 3284) to take. **κατέφαγον** aor. ind. act. κατεσθίω (# 2983) to eat down. **ἦν** impf. ind. act. εἰμί (# 1639) to be. **ἔφαγον** aor. ind. act. ἐσθίω (# 2266) to eat. The effective use of the aor., "after I had finished eating." **ἐπικράνθη** aor. ind. pass. πικραίνω (# 4393) to make bitter. Ingressive aor., "my stomach became bitter." If he would be admitted into part of God's secrets, the seer must be prepared for very mixed sensations; the first joy of fuller knowledge would be followed by sorrow deeper and more bitter than those of ordinary men (Swete). ◆ **11 λέγουσιν** pres. ind. act. λέγω (# 3306) to say. "They say to me." It is best to take the expression as an indefinite pl. or the equivalent of the pass., "it was said" (Mounce). **δεῖ** (# 1256) pres. ind act. it is necessary, w. acc. and the inf., expressing a logical necessity. **προφητεῦσαι** aor. act. inf. προφητεύω (# 4736) to speak forth, to prophesy. Inf. used to explain what is necessary. **ἐπί** (# 2093) about, concerning (Mounce). **ἔθνεσιν** dat. pl. ἔθνος (# 1620) nation. **γλῶσσα** (# 1185) tongue, speech, language.

Revelation 11

◆ **1 ἐδόθη** aor. ind. pass. δίδωμι (# 1443) to give. **κάλαμος** (# 2812) reed. This served as a surveyor's rule or measuring rod and it might have been the cane growing along the Jordan valley which was known as the "giant reed" of Mediterranean lands. It grows in swampy areas and sometimes may reach twelve, fifteen, or even twenty feet in height (Ford; FFB, 171).

ῥάβδος (# *4811*) staff. λέγων pres. act. part. λέγω (# *3306*) to say. Pleonastic use of the part. ἔγειρε pres. imp. act. ἐγείρω (# *1586*) to rise, to get up. For the idiomatic use of the pres. imp. of this vb. s. VANT, 348-49. μέτρησον aor. imp. act. μετρέω (# *3582*) to measure. Aor. imp. calls for a specific act w. a note of urgency. Measuring the courts was a way of praising the building's magnificence (BBC). ναός (# *3724*) temple, sanctuary. θυσιαστήριον (# *2603*) place where offerings or sacrifices are made, altar. προσκυνοῦντας pres. act. part. προσκυνέω (# *4686*) to worship. ◆ **2** αὐλή (# *885*) court. ἔξωθεν (# *2033*) outside. The outer court of the temple in Jerusalem is called the Court of the Gentiles (Ford; JTJ, 23-24). ἔκβαλε aor. imp. act. ἐκβάλλω (# *1675*) to throw out, to cast out. The word is used here in the sense of exclusion—exclude it from the sanctuary though the other courts are included (Swete). μετρήσῃς aor. subj. act. μετρέω (# *3582*) to measure. Neg. μή (# *3590*) w. the subj. indicates a prohibition or a neg. command. ἐδόθη aor. ind. pass. δίδωμι (# *1443*) to give. πατήσουσιν fut. ind. act. πατέω (# *4251*) to walk upon, to tread down, to trample. μήν (# *3604*) month. τεσσεράκοντα [καὶ] δύο (# *5477*; *1545*) forty-two. The designation "forty two months" is equal to three-and-one-half years, half of the seven-year period of tribulation. ◆ **3** δώσω fut. ind. act. δίδωμι (# *1443*) to give. προφητεύσουσιν fut. ind. act. προφητεύω (# *4736*) to prophesy. The construction, "I shall give and they shall prophesy" is a Hebraic construction meaning "I will commission (or give permission to) my two witnesses to prophesy" (Charles). περιβεβλημένοι perf. pass. part. περιβάλλω (# *4314*) to throw about, to clothe. σάκκος (# *4884*) sack, sackcloth. The fabric from which a sack is made is usually dark in color; hence, it is especially suited to be worn as a mourning garment (BAGD). Perhaps they were wailing over the sins of Israel (BBC). As latter-day prophets the two witnesses wear the rough garb of their ancient predecessors (Zech. 13:4). Their message is to call to repentance (Mounce). There are various views as to the identity of the two witnesses: merely symbolic, Enoch and Elijah, Moses and Elijah, or two others like them (Thomas). ◆ **4** εἰσιν pres. ind. act. εἰμί (# *1639*) to be. ἐλαία (# *1777*) olive tree. λυχνία (# *3393*) lampstand. ἑστῶτες perf. act. part. ἵστημι (# *2705*) to stand. ◆ **5** θέλει pres. ind. act. θέλω (# *2527*) to desire, to want to, w. inf in a 1st class cond. cl. ἀδικῆσαι aor. act. inf. ἀδικέω (# *92*) to injure, to harm. ἐκπορεύεται pres. ind. mid. (dep.) ἐκπορεύομαι (# *1744*) to go out, to come out of. Pres. could be iterat., indicating that fire would come out of their mouth every time someone would seek to harm them. κατεσθίει pres. ind. act. κατεσθίω (# *2983*) to eat up, to consume completely, to devour. θελήσῃ aor. subj. act. θέλω (# *2527*) to desire, to want to, w. inf. οὕτως (# *4048*) so, thus. δεῖ (# *1256*) pres. ind. act. w. the acc. and the inf., it is necessary. ἀποκτανθῆναι

aor. pass. inf. ἀποκτείνω (# *650*) to kill. ◆ **6** ἔχουσιν pres. ind. act. ἔχω (# *2400*) to have. κλεῖσαι aor. act. inf. κλείω (# *3091*) to close, to shut up. Epex. inf. explaining the word ἐξουσία (# *2026*) authority. ὑετός (# *5624*) rain. βρέχῃ pres. subj. act. βρέχω (# *1101*) to rain. Subj. w. ἵνα (# *2671*) is used in a neg. purp. cl. which may be considered a result cl. ἔχουσιν pres. ind. act. ἔχω (# *2400*) to have. στρέφειν pres. act. inf. στρέφω (# *5138*) to turn, to change. Epex. inf. explaining the authority. πατάξαι aor. act. inf. πατάσσω (# *4250*) to strike, to hit. πληγῇ (# *4435*) blow, plague. ὁσάκις (# *4006*) as often as. Used w. the particle ἐάν (# *1569*) and the subj. to express an indef. temp. cl. θελήσωσιν pres. subj. act. θέλω (# *2527*) to desire; "as often as they will" (RWP). ◆ **7** ὅταν (# *4020*) w. subj., whenever. τελέσωσιν aor. subj. act. τελέω (# *5464*) to complete, to finish. Subj. in an indef. temp. cl., "whenever." θηρίον (# *2563*) animal, wild animal. ἀναβαῖνον pres. mid. part. ἀναβαίνω (# *326*) to go up, to ascend. ἄβυσσος (# *12*) bottomless pit, abyss (s. Rev. 9:1). ποιήσει fut. ind. act. ποιέω (# *4472*) to make. πόλεμος (# *4483*) war. νικήσει fut. ind. act. νικέω (# *3771*) to gain the victory, to be victor, to overcome. ἀποκτενεῖ fut. ind. act. ἀποκτείνω (# *650*) to kill. ◆ **8** πτῶμα (# *4773*) that which is fallen, corpse, dead body. πλατεῖα (# *4423*) wide street, open street. καλεῖται pres. ind. pass. καλέω (# *2813*) to call; pass., to be called, to have the name. πνευματικῶς (# *4462*) spiritually, pertaining to the Spirit. Perhaps the idea here is not allegorically, but rather how the Spirit of God interprets. ὅπου (# *3963*) where. Here the word is used as a pron., "the place where." ἐσταυρώθη aor. ind. pass. σταυρόω (# *5090*) to crucify. ◆ **9** βλέπουσιν pres. ind. act. βλέπω (# *1063*) to see. ἐκ τῶν λαῶν (# *1666*; *3295*) some of the peoples. The expression is to be taken as a partitive gen. (Mounce). ἥμισυ (# *2468*) half. ἀφίουσιν pres. ind. act. ἀφίημι (# *4024*) to leave, to allow. τεθῆναι aor. pass. inf. τίθημι (# *5520*) to place, to put. μνῆμα (# *3645*) grave. ◆ **10** κατοικοῦντες pres. act. part. κατοικέω (# *2997*) to reside, to dwell. χαίρουσιν pres. ind. act. χαίρω (# *5897*) to rejoice. εὐφραίνονται pres. ind. mid. (dep.) εὐφραίνομαι (# *2370*) to be happy. πέμψουσιν fut. ind. act. πέμπω (# *4287*) to send. ἀλλήλοις dat. pl. ἀλλήλων (# *253*) one another; "to one another." ἐβασάνισαν aor. ind. act. βασανίζω (# *989*) to torment, to torture. κατοικοῦντας pres. act. part. κατοικέω (# *2997*) to inhabit, to dwell. ◆ **11** εἰσῆλθεν aor. ind. act. εἰσέρχομαι (# *1656*) to come into, to enter. ἔστησαν aor. ind. act. ἵστημι (# *2705*) to stand. ἐπέπεσεν aor. ind. act. ἐπιπίπτω (# *2158*) to fall upon. θεωροῦντας pres. act. part. (subst.) θεωρέω (# *2555*) to see, to behold, to watch. ◆ **12** ἤκουσαν aor. ind. act. ἀκούω (# *201*) to hear. λεγούσης pres. act. part. (adj.) λέγω (# *3306*) to speak. ἀνάβατε aor. imp. act. ἀναβαίνω (# *326*) to come up, to ascend. ἀνέβησαν aor. ind. act. ἀναβαίνω νεφέλη (# *3749*) cloud. ἐθεώρησαν aor. ind. act. θεωρέω (# *2555*) to see.

◆ **13** ἐγένετο aor. ind. mid. (dep.) γίνομαι (# 1181) to be, to become, to happen, to come about. σεισμός (# 4939) earthquake (s. 6:12). ἔπεσεν aor. ind. act. πίπτω (# 4406) to fall. ἀπεκτάνθησαν aor. ind. pass. ἀποκτείνω (# 650) to kill. ὄνομα (# 3950) name; here, people, person. For the use of the word in this sense s. BS, 196f. ἔμφοβος (# 1873) afraid, scared. ἐγένοντο aor. ind. mid. (dep.) γίνομαι (# 1181) to become. ἔδωκαν aor. ind. act. δίδωμι (# 1443) to give. ◆ **14** ἀπῆλθεν aor. ind. act. ἀπέρχομαι (# 599) to go away, to pass. ἰδού aor. imp. act. ὁράω (# 3972) to see. ἔρχεται pres. ind. mid. (dep.) ἔρχομαι (# 2262) to come, to go. ταχύς (# 5444) quickly, soon. ◆ **15** ἐσάλπισεν aor. ind. act. σαλπίζω (# 4895) to blow the trumpet. ἐγένοντο aor. ind. mid. (dep.) γίνομαι (# 1181) to become. λέγοντες pres. act. part. λέγω (# 3306) to say. Χριστός (# 5986) anointed, Messiah, Christ. βασιλεύσει fut. ind. act. βασιλεύω (# 996) to be king, to rule as a king, to reign. ◆ **16** καθήμενοι pres. mid. (dep.) part. κάθημαι (# 2764) to sit. ἔπεσαν aor. ind. act. πίπτω (# 4406) to fall down. προσεκύνησαν aor. ind. act. προσκυνέω (# 4686) to worship. ◆ **17** λέγοντες pres. act. part. λέγω (# 3306) to say. εὐχαριστοῦμέν pres. ind. act. εὐχαριστέω (# 2373) to give thanks, to praise w. thanks (BAGD). παντοκράτωρ (# 4120) almighty (s. 1:8). ὤν pres. act. part. εἰμί (# 1639) to be. ἦν impf. ind. act. εἰμί (# 1639) to be. εἴληφας perf. ind. act. λαμβάνω (# 3284) to take. Perf. may indicate that God has taken the power permanently (Mounce). ἐβασίλευσας aor. ind. act. βασιλεύω (# 996) to rule (s.v. 15). Const. aor. ◆ **18** ὠργίσθησαν aor. ind. pass. ὀργίζω (# 3974) to make angry; pass., to be angry. ἦλθεν aor. ind. act. ἔρχομαι (# 2262) to come. ὀργή (# 3973) wrath, anger. κριθῆναι aor. pass. inf. κρίνω (# 3212) to judge. δοῦναι aor. act. inf. δίδωμι (# 1443) to give. Infs. here used to explain the word καιρός (# 2789) time, season. μισθός (# 3635) reward, wage, pay. φοβουμένοις pres. mid. (dep.) part. (subst.) φοβέομαι (# 5828) to fear, to have reverence for someone, to show reverence to someone. διαφθεῖραι aor. act. inf. διαφθείρω (# 1425) to destroy, to corrupt. Prep. in compound is perfective, "to utterly destroy." Epex. inf. explaining the word καιρός. διαφθείροντας pres. act. part. διαφθείρω (# 1425) to destroy. ◆ **19** ἠνοίγη aor. ind. act. ἀνοίγω (# 487) to open. ὤφθη aor. ind. pass. ὁράω (# 3972) to see; pass., to be seen, to appear. κιβωτός (# 3066) box, ark. διαθήκη (# 1347) agreement, treaty, covenant. In the OT the ark of the covenant was a symbol of the abiding presence of God (Mounce). ἀστραπή (# 847) lightning. ἐγένοντο aor. ind. mid. (dep.) γίνομαι (# 1181) to happen. βροντή (# 1103) thunder. σεισμός (# 4939) earthquake (s. 6:12). χάλαζα (# 5898) hail.

Revelation 12

◆ **1** ὤφθη aor. ind. pass. ὁράω (# 3972) to see; pass., to be seen, to appear. περιβεβλημένη perf. pass. part. περιβάλλω (# 4314) to cast about, to clothe; pass., to be

clothed. σελήνη (# 4943) moon. ὑποκάτω (# 5691) w. gen., under. στέφανος (# 5109) crown. ἀστέρων gen. pl. ἀστήρ (# 843) star. δώδεκα (# 1557) twelve. Of all the various interpretations of the woman the most fitting is to view her as representing the nation Israel. In the OT the image of a woman is a classic symbol for Zion, Jerusalem, and Israel (Ford; Scott; Bousset; SB, 3:574-75, 812; Thomas; DLNT, 1209-10; HSB, 767-68). The twelve stars may be an allusion to the twelve tribes of Israel (Mounce). ◆ **2** ἔχουσα pres. act. part. ἔχω (# 2400) to have. ἐν γαστρὶ ἔχουσα to have something in the stomach, i.e., to be pregnant. κράζει pres. ind. act. κράζω (# 3189) to scream, to cry out w. a loud voice. This evidently refers to the first coming of the Messiah and his birth, and the hist. pres. here gives a vivid description of the event. ὠδίνουσα pres. act. part. ὠδίνω (# 6048) to have birth pains, to be in labor. Adj. or causal part., indicating why she was screaming. βασανιζομένη pres. pass. part. βασανίζω (# 989) to torment, to be in pain. Adj. or causal part. τεκεῖν aor. act. inf. τίκτω (# 5503) to bear a child, to give birth. Epex. inf. explaining the pain of the woman. For the relation of this to Israel and the OT, as well as to Jewish lit. s. Roger D. Aus, "The Relevance of Isaiah 66,7 to Revelation 12 and 2 Thessalonians 1," *ZNW* 67 (1976): 252-68; Thomas. ◆ **3** ὤφθη aor. ind. pass. ὁράω (# 3972) to see. ἰδού aor. imp. act. ὁράω (# 3972) to see. δράκων (# 1532) dragon, monster, serpent. The word was used often in the magic papyri (MM). Both Josephus and the LXX use the term to describe the snake that Moses' staff turned into and the snake that the Egyptian magicians produced (Jos. *Ant.*, 2:272, 285, 287; Exod. 7:9, 10, 12; GELTS, 121; DDD, 504-509; 1404-12; DLNT, 127-29). It also occurs in Isa. 27:1 for the Leviathan who will be killed by God when He delivers His people. John does not leave us in doubt as to the identity of this monster–he is "the old serpent, he that is called the Devil and Satan" (v. 9; Mounce; cf. 20:2). πυρρός (# 4794) fiery, red. ἔχων pres. act. part. (adj.) ἔχω (# 2400) to have; here in the sense of to possess. κέρατα acc. pl. κέρας (# 3043) horn. The horn was a symbol of strength. διάδημα (# 1343) diadem, a royal crown. The royal crown was a symbol of political power and authority denoting sovereignty (Swete). ◆ **4** οὐρά (# 4038) tail. σύρει pres. ind. act. σύρω (# 5359) to drag, to sweep. ἔβαλεν aor. ind. act. βάλλω (# 965) to throw. ἔστηκεν perf. ind. act. ἵστημι (# 5112) to stand. μελλούσης pres. act. part. μέλλω (# 3516) to be about to. Used w. inf. to express immediate fut. τεκεῖν aor. act. inf. τίκτω (# 5503) to give birth. ὅταν (# 4020) w. subj., whenever. τέκῃ aor. subj. act. τίκτω (# 5503) to give birth. Subj. in an indef. temp. cl. καταφάγη aor. subj. act. κατεσθίω (# 2983) to eat up, to consume, to devour. Subj. w. ἵνα (# 2671) to express purp. ◆ **5** ἔτεκεν aor. ind. act. τίκτω (# 5503) to give birth. ἄρσην (# 781) male, male child. μέλλει pres. ind.

act. μέλλω (# 3516) to be about to, w. inf. to express the immediate fut. **ποιμαίνειν** pres. act. inf. ποιμαίνω (# 4477) to shepherd, to lead, to rule. **ῥάβδος** (# 4811) staff. **σιδηροῦς** (# 4969) made of iron. **ἡρπάσθη** aor. ind. pass. ἁρπάζω (# 773) to seize, to snatch, to take away. Theol. pass., indicating that God did the action. ◆ **6 ἔφυγεν** aor. ind. act. φεύγω (# 5771) to flee. **ἔχει** pres. ind. act. ἔχω (# 2400) to have. **ἡτοιμασμένον** perf. pass. part. ἑτοιμάζω (# 2286) to prepare. Perf. pass. means "to stand prepared"; i.e., "that which has been prepared and now stands ready." **ἀπό** describes the ultimate agent (GGBB, 433). **τρέφωσιν** pres. subj. act. τρέφω (# 5555) to nourish. Subj. w. **ἵνα** (# 2671) used in a purp. cl. Pl. may be impersonal and equivalent to a pass. **ἡμέρας χιλίας διακοσίας ἑξήκοντα** thousand two hundred and sixty days. Acc. of time. ◆ **7 ἐγένετο** aor. ind. mid. (dep.) γίνομαι (# 1181) to become. **πόλεμος** (# 4483) war. **πολεμῆσαι** aor. act. inf. πολεμέω (# 4482) to conduct war, to fight. The nom. used w. the inf. may be the result of a Hebraic construction (Charles; AASS, 60-63). Inf. may indicate result: "there was war ... so that ...," or the inf. may be epex. explaining what the war was. **ἐπολέμησεν** aor. ind. act. πολεμέω (# 4482) to fight. ◆ **8 ἴσχυσεν** aor. ind. act. ἰσχύω (# 2710) to be strong, to be strong enough, to be able. The dragon's supreme effort was not just a failure, but resulted in his final expulsion from heaven (Swete). **εὑρέθη** aor. ind. pass. εὑρίσκω (# 2351) to find. ◆ **9 ἐβλήθη** aor. ind. pass. βάλλω (# 965) to throw. **ὄφις** (# 4058) snake, serpent (DDD, 1404-12). **ἀρχαῖος** (# 792) old, ancient. **καλούμενος** pres. pass. part. καλέω (# 2813) to call. **πλανῶν** pres. act. part. (subst.) πλανάω (# 4414) to lead astray, to deceive. Pres. part. indicates a continuous action that has become a habitual character. For the two names plus a further description s. NDIEC, 1:92. **οἰκουμένη** (# 3876) inhabited earth, the world in the sense of its inhabitants, mankind (BAGD). **ἐβλήθη** aor. ind. pass. βάλλω (# 965) to throw. **ἐβλήθησαν** aor. ind. pass. βάλλω (# 965) to throw. ◆ **10 ἤκουσα** aor. ind. act. ἀκούω (# 201) to hear. **λέγουσαν** pres. act. part. λέγω (# 3306) to say. **ἐγένετο** aor. ind. mid. (dep.) γίνομαι (# 1181) to become. **ἐβλήθη** aor. ind. pass. βάλλω (# 965) to throw. **κατήγωρ** (# 2992) one who brings a legal charge against another, accuser. **κατηγορῶν** pres. act. part. (subst.) κατηγορέω (# 2989) to bring a legal accusation, to accuse. Pres. indicates an habitual action, "the constant accuser." ◆ **11 ἐνίκησαν** aor. ind. act. νικάω (# 3771) to be a victor, to overcome. **διά** (# 1328) w. acc., because of. Prep. here gives the ground, not the means, of their victory (Mounce). **αἷμα** (# 135) blood. Here blood refers to the life of Christ poured out in death. **ἀρνίον** (# 768) lamb. **ἠγάπησαν** aor. ind. act. ἀγαπάω (# 26) to love. Their nonattachment to life was carried to the extent of being ready to die for their faith (Swete). ◆ **12 εὐφραίνεσθε** pres. imp. mid. (dep.)

εὐφραίνομαι (# 2370) to rejoice, to be happy. **σκηνοῦντες** pres. act. part. σκηνόω (# 5012) to tabernacle, to pitch one's tent; to live in a residence; emphasizing the presence of God (GELTS, 428; Mounce). **οὐαί** (# 4026) woe. Instead of the normal dat., the acc. which follows may be acc. of general ref. "woe to the earth." **κατέβη** aor. ind. act. καταβαίνω (# 2849) to go down; effective aor. "he did go down" (RWP). **ἔχων** pres. act. part. ἔχω (# 2400) to have. **θυμός** (# 2596) anger, burning anger (Trench, *Synonyms*, 131f). **εἰδώς** perf. act. part. οἶδα (# 3857) to know. Def. perf. w. pres. meaning. Causal part., "because." **ἔχει** pres. ind. act. ἔχω (# 2400) to have. ◆ **13 εἶδεν** aor. ind. act. ὁράω (# 3972) to see. **ἐδίωξεν** aor. ind. act. διώκω (# 1503) to hunt, to pursue, to persecute. This indicates the tremendous persecution to be suffered by Israel in the tribulation period. **ἔτεκεν** aor. ind. act. τίκτω (# 5503) to give birth. ◆ **14 ἐδόθησαν** aor. ind. pass. δίδωμι (# 1443) to give. The pass. is the theol. or divine pass., indicating that God is the one who gives. **πτέρυγες** nom. pl. πτέρυξ (# 4763) wing. **ἀετοῦ** gen. sing. ἀετος (# 108) eagle. Gen. of description. **πέτηται** pres. subj. mid. (dep.) πέτομαι (# 4375) to fly. Subj. w. **ἵνα** (# 2671) used in a purp. cl. **τρέφεται** pres. ind. pass. τρέφω (# 5555) to care for, to nourish. **ἥμισυ** (# 2463) half. The words indicate that the nation Israel will be protected from total destruction for the last three-and-one-half years of the Tribulation. ◆ **15 ἔβαλεν** aor. ind. act. βάλλω (# 965) to throw. **στόμα** (# 5125) mouth. **ὀπίσω** (# 3958) behind, after. **ποταμός** (# 4532) river. **ποταμοφόρητος** (# 4533) to be carried by the river, to be swept away by the river. **ποιήσῃ** aor. subj. act. ποιέω (# 4472) to do. Vb. is used in connection w. the noun to express the vb. action contained in the noun. Subj. w. **ἵνα** (# 2671) to express purp. ◆ **16 ἐβοήθησεν** aor. ind. act. βοηθέω (# 1070) to help. **ἤνοιξεν** aor. ind. act. ἀνοίγω (# 487) to open. **κατέπιεν** aor. ind. act. καταπίνω (# 2927) to swallow down, to swallow up completely. ◆ **17 ὠργίσθη** aor. ind. pass. ὀργίζω (# 3974) to make angry; ingressive aor., "to become angry." **ἀπῆλθεν** aor. ind. act. ἀπέρχομαι (# 599) to go out, to go away from, to depart. **ποιῆσαι** aor. act. inf. ποιέω (# 4472) to do. Inf. is used to express intent or purp. **λοιπός** (# 3370) rest. **σπέρμα** (# 5065) seed. **τηρούντων** pres. act. part. τηρέω (# 5498) to watch, to keep, to observe. **ἐχόντων** pres. act. part. ἔχω (# 2400) to have. ◆ **18 ἐστάθη** aor. ind. pass. ἵστημι (# 2705) to stand. **ἄμμος** (# 302) sand, beach. **θάλασσα** (# 2498) sea.

Revelation 13

◆ **1 εἶδον** aor. ind. act. ὁράω (# 3972) to see. **θάλασσα** (# 2498) sea. The sea is an apt symbol of the agitated surface of unregenerate humanity and esp. of the seething cauldron of national and social life, out of which the great historical movements of the world arise (Swete). The term, however, may be understood as the abyss–the source–of the satanic forces (Johnson; Thomas; Mounce). θηρίον (# 2563) beast, monster, wild animal, esp. of the ones hunted, hostile, and odious to man (LS, 800). Herodotus uses the word for birds, pigs, cats, as well as for wild animals such as sharks (LTH, 167-68; Herodotus, 6:44). The word describes the qualities of the dangerous person who is vicious, cruel, cunning, to be feared and unpredictable in his actions. This is the monstrous person in whom the political power of the world is finally concentrated as represented in Daniel 7 and as "the man of sin" in 2 Thess. 2:3 (Walvoord; Seiss; ZPEB, 1:180f; Johnson; Thomas). ἀναβαῖνον pres. act. part. (adj.) ἀναβαίνω (# 326) to go up, to arise, to ascend. ἔχον pres. act. part. (adj.). ἔχω (# 2400) to have. For the use of this vb. in Rev. s. Rev. 5:6. κέρας (# 3043) horn. διάδημα (# 1343) diadem, royal crown. These two figures represent the mighty political power and also stand for kings and their kingdom, as in Daniel 7 (Walvoord; Thomas). βλασφημία (# 1060) speaking evil of some one, blasphemy (TLNT; TDNT). ◆ 2 εἶδον aor. ind. act. ὁράω (# 3972) to see. ἦν impf. ind. act. εἰμί (# 1639) to be. παρδάλει dat. sing. πάρδαλις (# 4230) leopard. Dat. w. adj. ἄρκος (# 759) bear. λέων (# 3329) lion. This beast combines the characteristics of Daniel's beasts, in which the leopard (or panther) indicates agility, cat-like vigilance, craft, and fierce cruelty, while the feet of the bear indicate the slow strength and power to crush. The lion blends massive strength w. feline dexterity, as a power follows up a stealthy and perhaps unobserved policy of repression w. the sudden terrors of a hostile edict (Swete). ἔδωκεν aor. ind. act. δίδωμι (# 1443) to give. δράκων (# 1532) dragon. The great political leader receives his power, rule and leadership directly from Satan. ◆ 3 μίαν ἐκ τῶν κεφαλῶν (# 1651; 1666; 3051) one of the heads. This takes up the narrative of v. 1 and the vb., to be supplied, is εἶδον (Swete). ἐσφαγμένην perf. pass. part. σφαγίζω (# 5377) to slay, to slaughter, to kill. The use of this word indicates that the deadly wound was like that of the slain Lamb (Bousset; Swete). Perf. indicates the condition. πληγή (# 4435) blow, wound. W. the following gen. τοῦ θανάτου (# 2505) it is descriptive; death wound, lethal wound (Ford). ἐθεραπεύθη aor. ind. pass. θεραπεύω (# 2543) to heal. Here there is the political death and resurrection of the beast (Scott). ἐθαυμάσθη aor. ind. pass. θαυμάζω (# 2513) to cause someone to wonder, to cause to marvel. ὀπίσω (# 3958) behind, after. W. the pregnant use of the prep. it means, "all the earth wondered at and followed the beast" (RWP). ◆ 4 προσεκύνησαν aor. ind. act. προσκυνέω (# 4686) to worship. ἔδωκεν aor. ind. act. δίδωμι (# 1443) to give. προσεκύνησαν aor. ind. act. προσκυνέω. λέγοντες pres. act. part. λέγω (# 3306) to say. δύναται pres. ind. pass. (dep.) δύναμαι (# 1538) to be able to, w. inf. πολεμῆσαι aor. act. inf. πολεμέω (# 4482) to wage war, to

fight against. ◆ 5 ἐδόθη aor. ind. pass. δίδωμι (# 1443) to give. λαλοῦν pres. act. part. (adj.) λαλέω (# 3281) to speak. ποιῆσαι aor. act. inf. ποιέω (# 4472) to do; here, to carry out his work. During the forty-two months the beast actively carries out the will of the dragon (Mounce; Swete). Epex. inf. explaining the authority or power. μῆνας acc. pl. μήν (# 3604) month. Acc. of time, "for forty two months." It indicates the last three and one-half years of the Tribulation. ◆ 6 ἤνοιξεν aor. ind. act. ἀνοίγω (# 487) to open. Const. aor. includes the whole career of the wild animal (RWP; Thomas). στόμα (# 5125) mouth. βλασφημῆσαι aor. act. inf. βλασφημέω (# 1059) to ridicule, to slander, to blaspheme (TLNT; TDNT; EDNT). Inf. of purp. Aor. points to a specific act. σκηνή (# 5008) tent, habitation, dwelling place, tabernacle. To blaspheme the name of God is to speak evil of all that He is and stands for. The name sums up the person. His tabernacle is His dwelling place (Mounce). σκηνοῦντας pres. act. part. (subst.) σκηνόω (# 5012) to live in a tent, to tabernacle, to dwell. ◆ 7 ἐδόθη aor. ind. pass. δίδωμι (# 1443) to give. ποιῆσαι aor. act. inf. ποιέω (# 4472) to make. πόλεμος (# 4483) war. νικῆσαι aor. act. inf. νικάω (# 3771) to win a victory, to conquer, to overcome. ◆ 8 προσκυνήσουσιν fut. ind. act. προσκυνέω (# 4686) to worship. αὐτός (# 899) him. The masc. pronoun indicates that the beast is a person. κατοικοῦντες pres. act. part. κατοικέω (# 2997) to live, to dwell, to reside. γέγραπται perf. ind. pass. γράφω (# 1211) to write. Perf. indicates the continuing results and binding authority of what is written (MM). βιβλίῳ dat. sing. βιβλίον (# 1046) book, little book. ἀρνίον (# 768) lamb. ἐσφαγμένου perf. pass. part. σφαγίζω (# 5377) to slay, to slaughter. Perf. indicate the abiding condition. καταβολή (# 2856) foundation, laying of a foundation. The foundation of the world refers to the creation of the visible order (Mounce; s. Eph. 1:4). ◆ 9 ἀκουσάτω aor. imp. act. ἀκούω (# 201) to hear. ◆ 10 αἰχμαλωσία (# 168) one taken captive at spear point, captivity. ὑπάγει pres. ind. act. ὑπάγω (# 5632) to go forth. Gnomic pres. indicating the statement of a general truth. The proverbial style of the v. could be translated, "if any man leads into captivity, into captivity he goes." Thus, the v. would stress that the enemies of God's people would be requited for their persecution of believers in the same form they employed (captivity for captivity, sword for sword) (Mounce). μάχαιρα (# 3479) sword. ἀποκτανθῆναι aor. pass. inf. ἀποκτείνω (# 650) to kill. δεῖ (# 1256) pres. ind. act. "it is necessary," w. acc. and inf., indicating a logical necessity. ἀποκτανθῆναι aor. pass. inf. ἀποκτείνω (# 650) to kill. ◆ 11 θηρίον (# 2563) wild beast, beast, monster (s.v. 1). The second beast introduced is the religious leader or false prophet. ἀναβαῖνον pres. act. part. ἀναβαίνω (# 326) to come up, to ascend. εἶχεν impf. ind. act. ἔχω (# 2400) to have. κέρας (# 3043) horn. ὅμοιος (# 3927) like. ἀρνίον (# 768) lamb. The second beast is a pseudochrist, a religious antichrist promoting the worship of the first beast (Swete; Thomas; Ladd). **ἐλάλει** impf. ind. act. λαλέω (# 3281) to speak. Impf. pictures the customary action. **δράκων** (# 1532) dragon. ◆ **12 ποιεῖ** pres. ind. act. ποιέω (# 4472) to do. **κατοικοῦντας** pres. act. part. κατοικέω (# 2997) to dwell, to live. Subst. part., "those who live on the earth." **προσκυνήσουσιν** fut. ind. act. προσκυνέω (# 4686) to worship. The false prophet, who is a religious leader also inspired of Satan, causes the world to worship the man of sin who has set himself up as God (s. 2 Thess. 2:4f). **ἐθεραπεύθη** aor. ind. pass. θεραπεύω (# 2543) to heal. ◆ **13 ποιεῖ** pres. ind. act. ποιέω (# 4472) to do, to make. **ποιῇ** pres. subj. act. ποιέω (# 4472) to make, to cause. Subj. w. **ἵνα** (# 2671) could either be a purp. or result cl. (RWP). **καταβαίνειν** pres. act. inf. καταβαίνω (# 2849) to come down. Inf. used to complete the vb. **ποιῇ.** ◆ **14 πλανᾷ** pres. ind. act. πλανάω (# 4414) to lead astray, to deceive. **κατοικοῦντας** pres. act. part. (subst.) κατοικέω (# 4686) to dwell. **ἐδόθη** aor. ind. pass. δίδωμι (# 1443) to give. **ποιῆσαι** aor. act. inf. ποιέω (# 4472) to do. Epex. inf. explaining what was given, or it could be taken as the subject of the vb. **λέγων** pres. act. part. λέγω (# 3306) to say. Pleonastic part. s. 1:17. **ποιῆσαι** aor. act. inf. ποιέω (# 4472) to do, to make. Inf. in indir. discourse after the part. **λέγων. εἰκών** (# 1635) image. **ἔζησεν** aor ind. act. ζάω (# 2409) to live. ◆ **15 ἐδόθη** aor. ind. pass. δίδωμι (# 1443) to give. **δοῦναι** aor. act. inf. δίδωμι. Epex. inf. explaining what was given, or it could be taken as the subject of the vb. **λαλήσῃ** aor. subj. act. λαλέω (# 3281) to speak. Subj. w. **ἵνα** (# 2671) expressing purp. or result. **ποιήσῃ** aor. subj. act. ποιέω (# 4472) to do. The second beast is given the power to animate the image of the first beast. He gives to it the breath of life and the image speaks (Mounce). **προσκυνήσωσιν** aor. subj. act. προσκυνέω (# 4686) to worship. Subj. w. **ἐάν** (# 1569) is used in a 3rd. class cond. cl. which views the cond. as a possibility. **ἀποκτανθῶσιν** aor. subj. pass. ἀποκτείνω (# 650) to kill. ◆ **16 ποιεῖ** pres. ind. act. ποιέω (# 4472) to do. **πλούσιος** (# 4454) rich, wealthy. **πτωχός** (# 4777) poor, poor as a beggar. **ἐλεύθερος** (# 1801) free; those who had been set free from slavery. **δῶσιν** aor. subj. act. δίδωμι (# 1443) to give. **χάραγμα** (# 5916) brand, mark. For various usages of the brand in the ancient world, such as the branding of a slave, a soldier, a worshiper s. Rev. 7:2; Mounce; BS 242; LAE, 341f; Ford, TDNT; BBC. ◆ **17 δύνηται** pres. subj. pass. (dep.) δύναμαι (# 1538) to be able to, w. inf. Subj. w. **ἵνα** (# 2671) is in a purp. cl. or the cl. is the obj. of the vb. **ἀγοράσαι** aor. act. inf. ἀγοράζω (# 60) to buy. **πωλῆσαι** aor. act. inf. πωλέω (# 4797) to sell. **ἔχων** pres. act. part. ἔχω (# 2400) to have. ◆ **18 ἔχων** pres. act. part. ἔχω (# 2400) to have. **νοῦς** (# 3808) understanding, comprehension. **ψηφισάτω** aor. imp. act. ψηφίζω (# 6028) to count up, to calculate; lit.,

to count w. pebbles, to reckon (MM). **ἑξακόσιοι ἑξήκοντα ἕξ** (# 1971, 1980, 2008) six hundred sixty-six. For the use of numbers and their meaning s. NW 2, ii:1570-71. The actual meaning of the number remains a mystery. For suggestions s. Thomas; Mounce; Johnson; HSB, 773-74.

Revelation 14

◆ **1 εἶδον** aor. ind. act. ὁράω (# 3972) to see. **ἰδού** aor. imp. act. ὁράω. The words **εἶδον καὶ ἰδού,** "and I saw and behold," introduce a new and dramatic part of the vision (s. Rev. 4:1; 6:2; Mounce). **ἀρνίον** (# 768) lamb (s. 5:6). **ἑστός** perf. act. part. ἵστημι (# 2705) to stand. That the lamb is standing forms a contrast w. the beast who are rising. It indicates being established, standing firm, holding one's ground (Ford). **ἔχουσαι** pres. act. part. ἔχω (# 2400) to have. **γεγραμμένον** perf. pass. part. (adj.) γράφω (# 1211) to write, to inscribe. Perf. indicates the continuing result of the authoritative writing. The seal consists in the name of God inscribed on the brow. This inscription declares that the person so inscribed is God's own possession (Charles). The scene is an obvious contrast to the beast of chapter 13 whose followers are stamped w. his mark on the right hand or forehead (Mounce). Adj. part. **μετώπων** (# 3587) forehead, brow. ◆ **2 ἤκουσα** aor. ind. act. ἀκούω (# 201) to hear. **βροντή** (# 1103) thunder. **κιθαρῳδός** (# 3069) one who plays on a harp, harpist. **κιθαριζόντων** pres. act. part. κιθαρίζω (# 3068) to play the harp. **κιθάρα** (# 3067) harp (Rev. 5:8). ◆ **3 ᾄδουσιν** pres. ind. act. ᾄδω (# 106) to sing (s. Rev. 5:9). **ᾠδή** (# 6046) song (s. Rev. 5:9). **ζῷον** (# 2442) living creature. **ἐδύνατο** impf. ind. pass. (dep.) δύναμαι (# 1538) to be able to, w. inf. Impf. used of unfulfilled action. **μαθεῖν** aor. act. inf. μανθάνω (# 3443) to learn. **εἰ μή** (# 1623; 3590) except. **ἠγορασμένοι** perf. pass. part. ἀγοράζω (# 60) to buy, to redeem, to purchase (APC, 50f; TDNT). ◆ **4 ἐμολύνθησαν** aor. ind. pass. μολύνω (# 3662) to defile, to soil, to stain. **παρθένος** (# 4221) virgin. It seems best to take this description of chastity in a fig. sense, indicating that they have kept themselves pure from all defiling relationships w. the pagan world. They have resisted the seduction of the great harlot, Rome, w. whom the kings of the earth have committed fornication (Mounce). **ἀκολουθοῦντες** pres. act. part. (subst.) ἀκολουθέω (# 199) to follow, to follow after, to be a disciple of someone, w. dat. **ὅπου ἄν** (# 3963; 323) w. subj., wherever. **ὑπάγῃ** pres. subj. act. ὑπάγω (# 5632) to go forth, to go. Subj. w. **ἄν** (# 323) in an indef. spatial cl. **ἠγοράσθησαν** aor. ind. pass. ἀγοράζω (# 60) to buy at the marketplace, to purchase, to redeem. **ἀπὸ τῶν ἀνθρώπων** (# 608; 476) from men, from among men. Prep. here denotes not separation but extraction (Swete). **ἀπαρχή** (# 569) firstfruits. In the OT until the firstfruits of harvest or flock were offered to God the rest of the crop could not be put to profane or secular use (Ford; s. 1 Cor. 15:20). ◆ **5 στόμα** (# *5125*) mouth. **εὑρέθη** aor. ind. pass. εὑρίσκω (# *2351*) to find. **ἄμωμος** (# *320*) unblemished. This Levitical sacrificial term means unspoiled by any flaw. If unblemished continues the metaphor of the firstfruits, it would refer to flock rather than crop and Lamb (Ford). ◆ **6 εἶδον** aor. ind. act. ὁράω (# *3972*) to see. **πετόμενον** pres. mid. (dep.) part. (adj.) πέτομαι (# *4375*) to fly. **μεσουράνημα** (# *3547*) mid-heaven (s. 8:13). **ἔχοντα** pres. act. part. ἔχω (# *2400*) to have. **εὐαγγέλιον** (# *2295*) good news, good tidings. It is not the gospel of God's redeeming grace in Christ Jesus but, as the following vv. show, a summons to fear, honor, and worship the creator (Mounce). **εὐαγγελίσαι** aor. act. inf. εὐαγγελίζω (# *2294*) to proclaim good news. Inf. expresses purp.; or it could also be epex., explaining what the angel has (RWP; Swete). **καθημένους** pres. mid. (dep.) part. κάθημαι (# *2764*) to sit. For the variant reading κατοικοῦντες ("the ones dwelling on the earth") rather than "the ones sitting on the earth" s. Charles. **ἔθνος** (# *1620*) nation. **φυλή** (# *5876*) tribe. **γλῶσσα** (# *1185*) tongue, language. ◆ **7 λέγων** pres. act. part. λέγω (# *3306*) to say. **φοβήθητε** aor. imp. pass. (dep.) φοβέομαι (# *5828*) to fear, to show respect, to show reverence. Aor. imp. calls for a specific act w. a note of urgency. **δότε** aor. imp. act. δίδωμι (# *1443*) to give. **ἦλθεν** aor. ind. act. ἔρχομαι (# *2262*) to come. **κρίσεως** gen. sing. κρίσις (# *3213*) judging, judgment. **προσκυνήσατε** aor. imp. act. προσκυνέω (# *4686*) to worship, w. dat. The eternal gospel calls upon men to fear and honor the creator, for the hour of judgment is at hand. God has revealed himself in nature so that men are without excuse (Mounce). **ποιήσαντι** aor. act. part. ποιέω (# *4472*) to create, to make. Adj. part. as subst. **πηγή** (# *4380*) spring. ◆ **8 ἠκολούθησεν** aor. ind. act. ἀκολουθέω (# *199*) to follow. **ἔπεσεν** aor. ind. act. πίπτω (# *4406*) to fall. The ancient Mesopotamian city of Babylon had become the political and religious capital of a world empire renowned for its luxury and moral corruption. Above all it was the great enemy of the people of God. For the early church, Rome was a contemporary Babylon (Mounce), but it is probably better to view this as the literal city of Babylon (Thomas; DLNT, 111-12, 1067). **θυμοῦ** gen. sing. θυμός (# *2596*) anger, burning anger. Gen. explaining what the **οἴνου** is. **πορνεία** (# *4518*) immorality, illicit sexual activity. **πεπότικεν** perf. ind. act. ποτίζω (# *4540*) to give to drink, to cause to drink. The drinking of the wine indicates the intoxicating influence of Babylon's vices (Ford). Perf. indicates the lasting result. ◆ **9 ἠκολούθησεν** aor. ind. act. ἀκολουθέω (# *199*) to follow, w. dat. **λέγων** pres. act. part. λέγω (# *3306*) to say. Pleonastic part. (s. Rev. 1:17). **θηρίον** (# *2563*) wild beast, monster (s. Rev. 13:1). **εἰκών** (# *1635*) image. **λαμβάνει** pres. ind. act. λαμβάνω (# *3284*) to receive. **χάραγμα** (# *5916*) brand, mark. ◆ **10 πίεται** fut. ind. mid. (dep.) πίνω (# *4403*) to drink.

The pron. **αὐτός** (# *899*) emphasizes the person who worships the beast, and not anyone else. The author probably means that one cannot drink one cup and not the other; the two are linked. The consequence of drinking Babylon's cup is the inescapable necessity of drinking the Lord's (Ford). **κεκερασμένου** perf. pass. part. κεράννυμι (# *3042*) to mix. The word was used of the preparation of wine by the addition of various spices; the word later came to mean "properly prepared" (Mounce; Charles). **ἄκρατος** (# *204*) full strength, unmixed, undiluted, not diluted w. water. The words mean that those who worship the image will drink the wine of God's wrath poured out in full strength, untempered by God's mercy and grace (Mounce). **ποτήριον** (# *4539*) cup. **ὀργή** (# *3973*) wrath, anger. This word refers more to the settled feeling of righteous indignation, whereas the word θυμός (s. vv. 8, 10) refers to the white heat of God's anger (Mounce; Swete; Trench, *Synonyms*, 131ff). **βασανισθήσεται** fut. ind. pass. βασανίζω (# *989*) to torment, to torture. **θείῳ** dat. θεῖον (# *2520*) sulphur. ◆ **11 καπνός** (# *2837*) smoke. **βασανισμός** (# *990*) torturing pain, suffering. **ἀναβαίνει** pres. ind. act. ἀναβαίνω (# *326*) to go up, to ascend. Pres. connected w. the temp. designation "forever" indicates a continual unbroken action. **ἔχουσιν** pres. ind. act. ἔχω (# *2400*) to have. **ἀνάπαυσις** (# *398*) stopping, resting, ceasing, relief. The word was used in the papyri w. the idea of relief from public duties; the word contains the idea of temporary rest as a preparation for fut. toil (MM). **ἡμέρας καὶ νυκτός** (# *2465; 2779; 3816*) day and night. The time indicator is gen. of time indicating the kind of time within which something takes place (RG, 495; MT, 235; DM, 77; BD, 99f; GGBB, 155-57). **προσκυνοῦντες** pres. act. part. (subst.) προσκυνέω (# *4686*) to worship. **λαμβάνει** pres. ind. act. λαμβάνω (# *3284*) to receive. ◆ **12 τηροῦντες** pres. act. part. (subst.) τηρέω (# *5498*) to keep, to observe. **πίστιν Ἰησοῦ** (# *4411; 2652*) faith of Jesus. Obj. gen., "faith in Jesus." ◆ **13 ἤκουσα** aor. ind. act. ἀκούω (# *201*) to hear. **λεγούσης** pres. act. part. λέγω (# *3306*) to say. **γράψον** aor. imp. act. γράφω (# *1211*) to write. **μακάριος** (# *3421*) happy, blessed (s. Matt. 5:3). **ἀποθνήσκοντες** pres. act. part. ἀποθνῄσκω (# *633*) to die. **ἵνα** (# *2671*) w. subj., possibly an imperatival use of ἵνα (GGBB, 477). The word here passes into the meaning "in that" rather than "in order that" (Swete). **ἀναπαήσονται** fut. ind. mid. (dep.) ἀναπαύομαι (# *399*) to have relief, to cease, to rest. **κόπος** (# *3160*) toil, labor, hard work that produces weariness (s. Rev. 2:2). **ἀκολουθεῖ** pres. ind. act. ἀκολουθέω (# *199*) to follow. ◆ **14 εἶδον** aor. ind. act. ὁράω (# *3972*) to see. **ἰδού** aor. imp. act. ὁράω (# *3972*) to see. **εἶδον καὶ ἰδού** "and I saw and behold" (s.v. 1). **νεφέλη** (# *3749*) cloud (s. Rev. 1:7). **λευκή** (# *3328*) white. **καθήμενον** pres. mid. (dep.) part. κάθημαι (# *2764*) to sit. This is none other than the risen Christ (Mounce). **ἔχων** pres. act. part. ἔχω (# *2400*) to have. **χρυσοῦς** (# 5991) golden. The crown or wreath given to a victor was golden; this designates the Messiah as the one who has conquered and thereby won the right to act in judgment (Mounce; Trench, *Synonym*, 78-81; esp. NIDNTT). **δρέπανον** (# 1535) sickle. **ὀξύς** (# 3955) sharp. ◆ **15 ἐξῆλθεν** aor. ind. act. ἐξέρχομαι (# 2002) to come out. **ναός** (# 3724) temple, sanctuary. The angel that delivers the divine command to commence the harvest comes out from the temple, that most holy place of the presence of God. Judgment upon sin is a necessary function of righteousness (Mounce). **κράζων** pres. act. part. κράζω (# 3189) to scream. **καθημένῳ** pres. mid. (dep.) part. κάθημαι (# 2764) to sit. **πέμψον** aor. imp. act. πέμπω (# 4287) to send. Ingressive aor., "start at once." **θέρισον** aor. imp. act. θερίζω (# 2545) to harvest. Ingressive aor., "begin at once." **ἦλθεν** aor. ind. act. ἔρχομαι (# 2262) to come. **θερίσαι** aor. act. inf. θερίζω. Epex. inf. explaining the word ὥρα. The classical image of reaping to symbolize death and destruction is very common (EGT). **ἐξηράνθη** aor. ind. pass. ξηραίνω (# 3830) to dry, to be dry. Here the word indicates perfect ripeness (Swete). **θερισμός** (# 2546) harvest. ◆ **16 ἔβαλεν** aor. ind. act. βάλλω (# 965) to cast, to throw. **ἐθερίσθη** aor. ind. pass. θερίζω (# 2545) to harvest. ◆ **17 ἐξῆλθεν** aor. ind. act. ἐξέρχομαι (# 2002) to go out. **ἔχων** pres. act. part. ἔχω (# 2400) to have. ◆ **18 θυσιαστήριον** (# 2603) altar. **ἐφώνησεν** aor. ind. act. φωνέω (# 5888) to make a sound, to call out. **ἔχοντι** pres. act. part. ἔχω (# 2400) to have. **λέγων** pres. act. part. λέγω (# 3306) to say. **πέμψον** aor. imp. act. πέμπω (# 4287) to send. **τρύγησον** aor. imp. act. τρυγάω (# 5582) to gather ripe fruit, esp. to pick grapes (BAGD). **βότρυς** (# 1084) grapes, bunch of grapes. **ἄμπελος** (# 306) grape vine. **ἤκμασαν** aor. ind. act. ἀκμάζω (# 196) to be ripe, to be in the prime, to be at the peak. (GEW, 1:53; Mounce). **σταφυλή** (# 5091) the ripe, grape cluster (Swete). ◆ **19 ἔβαλεν** aor. ind. act. βάλλω (# 965) to throw. **ἐτρύγησεν** aor. ind. act. τρυγάω (# 5582) to gather ripe fruit (s.v. 18). **ληνός** (# 3332) trough, vat, wine press (AS; s. Matt. 21:33). ◆ **20 ἐπατήθη** aor. ind. pass. πατέω (# 4251) to walk, to walk on, to trample. In biblical days grapes were trampled in a trough, which had a duct leading to a lower basin where the juice collected. The treading of grapes was a familiar figure for the execution of divine wrath upon the enemies of God (Mounce; Isa. 63:3) since crushed grapes and their juice look like spilled blood (BBC). **ληνός** (# 3332) winepress. **ἔξωθεν** w. gen., outside. **ἐξῆλθεν** aor. ind. act. ἐξέρχομαι (# 2002) to go out. **χαλινός** (# 5903) bridle. **ἵππος** (# 2691) horse. **στάδιον** (# 5084) stadion. A stadion measures 670 feet so that the distance here would be approximately 184 miles (Mounce). When Jerusalem was taken by Titus, Josephus says that the Roman soldiers slew all they met and made the whole city run w. blood so much so that

the fire of many houses was quenched w. these men's blood (Govett; BBC; Jos., *JW.*, 6:406).

Revelation 15

◆ **1 εἶδον** aor. ind. act. ὁράω (# 3972) to see. **ἄλλο** (# 257) another. The words ἄλλο σημεῖον (# 4956) look back to Rev. 12:1 and 12:3 (Swete). **θαυμαστός** (# 2515) amazing, that which causes wonder. **ἔχοντας** pres. act. part. ἔχω (# 2400) to have. **πληγάς** acc. pl. πληγή (# 4435) blow, wound, plague. **ἐτελέσθη** aor. ind. pass. τελέω (# 5464) to bring to conclusion, to complete. ◆ **2 εἶδον** aor. ind. act. ὁράω (# 3972) to see. **ὑάλινος** (# 5612) glassy, crystal (s. Rev. 4:6). **μεμιγμένην** perf. pass. part. (adj.) μείγνυμι (# 3502) to mix. Perf. indicates the condition. **νικῶντας** pres. act. part. (subst.) νικάω (# 3771) to gain victory, to be victor, to overcome. **θηρίον** (# 2563) wild beast, monster. **εἰκόνος** gen. sing. (# 1635) image (s. Rev. 14:9). **ἀριθμός** (# 750) number. **ἑστῶτας** perf. act. part. ἵστημι (# 2705) to stand. The phrase could mean "standing on" or "standing by." This scene of the victors standing on the heavenly sea w. harps in their hands and praising God recalls Israel's song of triumph over Egypt on the shore of the Red Sea in Exod. 15 (Charles). **ἔχοντας** pres. act. part. ἔχω (# 2400) to have. **κιθάρα** (# 3067) harp, lyre. ◆ **3 ᾄδουσιν** pres. ind. act. ᾄδω (# 106) to sing. **ᾠδή** (# 6046) song. **ἀρνίου** gen. sing. (# 768) lamb (s. Rev. 14:1). Gen. could give the content of the song, indicating whom the song is about. **θαυμαστός** (# 2515) marvelous, awe-inspiring. **παντοκράτωρ** (# 4120) almighty (s. Rev. 1:8). ◆ **4 φοβηθῇ** aor. subj. pass. (dep.) φοβέομαι (# 5828) to fear, to show respect, to reverence. Subj. w. double neg. οὐ μή (# 4024; 3590). **δοξάσει** fut. ind. act. δοξάζω (# 1519) to glorify. **ὅσιος** (# 4008) undefiled by sin, free from wickedness, pure, holy (T; NIDNTT; Trench, *Synonym*, 328f; TDNT). **ἥξουσιν** fut. ind. act. ἥκω (# 2457) to come. **προσκυνήσουσιν** fut. ind. act. προσκυνέω (# 4686) to worship. **δικαίωμα** (# 1468) righteous deed. A reference to the acts of God which meet His standards of faithfulness and loyalty to His person and word. It could refer also to God's judgments in a judicial sense (TDNT; Ford; Charles). **ἐφανερώθησαν** aor. ind. pass. φανερόω (# 5746) to make clear, to manifest, to reveal. ◆ **5 εἶδον** aor. ind. act. ὁράω (# 3972) to see. **ἠνοίγη** aor. ind. pass. ἀνοίγω (# 487) to open. **ναός** (# 3724) temple, sanctuary. **σκηνή** (# 5008) tent, tabernacle. The word refers to the dwelling place of God. **μαρτύριον** (# 3457) testimony. ◆ **6 ἐξῆλθον** aor. ind. act. ἐξέρχομαι (# 2002) to go out, to come out. **ἐνδεδυμένοι** perf. pass. part. ἐνδύομαι (# 1907) to dress, to put on clothes, to be clothed. **λίνον** (# 3351) linen. **καθαρός** (# 2754) pure, clean. **λαμπρός** (# 3287) shining. The robes of linen, pure and shiny, denote the noble and sacred nature of their office (Mounce). **περιεζωσμένοι** perf. pass. part. (adj.) περιζώννυμι (# 4322) to be girded around, to wear a wide belt which held up the long flowing garments. **στῆθος** (# *5111*) breast, chest. **ζώνας** acc. pl. ζώνη (# *2438*) wide belt, girdle. **χρυσοῦ** (# *5991*) golden. The golden girdles are symbolic of royal and priestly functions (Mounce; s. Rev. 1:13). ◆ **7 ζῷον** (# *2442*) living creature. **ἔδωκεν** aor. ind. act. δίδωμι (# *1443*) to give. **φιάλη** (# *5786*) bowl. This was a wide shallow bowl like a deep saucer (Mounce; T; NBD, 1310). **γεμούσας** pres. act. part. (adj.) γέμω (# *1154*) to be full, to be full of. **ζῶντος** pres. act. part. (adj.) ζάω (# *2409*) to live. ◆ **8 ἐγεμίσθη** aor. ind. pass. γεμίζω (# *1153*) to fill up, to make full. **καπνός** (# *2837*) smoke. **ἐδύνατο** impf. ind. mid. (dep.) δύναμαι (# *1539*) to be able to. **εἰσελθεῖν** aor. act. inf. εἰσέρχομαι (# *1656*) to go into. **τελεσθῶσιν** aor. subj. pass. τελέω (# *5464*) to complete. Subj. used in an indef. temp. cl.

Revelation 16

◆ **1 ἤκουσα** aor. ind. act. ἀκούω (# *201*) to hear. **λεγούσης** pres. act. part. λέγω (# *3306*) to say. **ναός** (# *3724*) temple, sanctuary. **ὑπάγετε** pres. imp. act. ὑπάγω (# *5632*) to go forth. Pres. imp. w. a vb. of motion. **ἐκχέετε** pres. imp. act. ἐκχέω (# *1772*) to pour out, to empty out. **φιάλας** acc. pl. (# *5786*) bowl (s. Rev. 15:7). For a discussion of this series of judgment s. DLNT, 132-33. **θυμός** (# *2596*) anger, burning, blistering anger (s. Rev. 14:8, 10). ◆ **2 ἀπῆλθεν** aor. ind. act. ἀπέρχομαι (# *599*) to go forth, to go out. **ἐξέχεεν** aor. ind. act. ἐκχέω (# *1772*) to pour out. **ἐγένετο** aor. ind. mid. (dep.) γίνομαι (# *1181*) to become, to happen, to come to pass. **ἕλκος** (# *1814*) sore, abscess, boil. This is the word used in the LXX of the boils w. which God smote the Egyptians (Ford; Mounce; GELTS, 144). For Pliny's description of the treatment of boils and carbuncles s. Pliny, NH, 30:107-108; DMTG, 147-48. **ἔχοντας** pres. act. part. ἔχω (# *2400*) to have. **χάραγμα** (# *5916*) brand, mark. **θηρίον** (# *2563*) beast, monster. **προσκυνοῦντας** pres. act. part. προσκυνέω (# *4686*) to worship. **εἰκών** (# *1635*) image. ◆ **3 ἐξέχεεν** aor. ind. act. ἐκχέω (# *1772*) to pour out. **ἐγένετο** aor. ind. mid. (dep.) γίνομαι (# *1181*) to become, to happen. **ἀπέθανεν** aor. ind. act. ἀποθνήσκω (# *633*) to die. ◆ **4 ἐξέχεεν** aor. ind. act. ἐκχέω (# *1772*) to pour out. **ποταμός** (# *4532*) river. **πηγή** (# *4380*) spring. **ἐγένετο** aor. ind. mid. (dep.) γίνομαι (# *1181*) to become, to happen. ◆ **5 ἤκουσα** aor. ind. act. ἀκούω (# *201*) to hear. **λέγοντος** pres. act. part. λέγω (# *3306*) to say. **εἶ** pres. ind. act. εἰμί (# *1639*) to be. **ὤν** pres. act. part. εἰμί. **ἦν** impf. ind. act. εἰμί. **ὅσιος** (# *4008*) pure, holy (s. Rev. 15:4). **ἔκρινας** aor. ind. act. κρίνω (# *3212*) to judge. ◆ **6 ἐξέχεεν** aor. ind. act. ἐκχέω (# *1772*) to pour out. **[δ]έδωκας** perf. ind. act. δίδωμι (# *1443*) to give. **πιεῖν** aor. act. inf. πίνω (# *4403*) to drink. Epex. inf. after the vb. δέδωκας (RWP). **ἄξιοί εἰσιν** (# *514*; *1639*) they are worthy; i.e., it is what they deserve (Mounce). ◆ **7 ἤκουσα** aor. ind. act. ἀκούω (# *201*) to hear. **θυσιαστήριον** (# *2603*) place of sacrifice, altar. **ναί** (# *3721*) yes, yea. **παντοκράτωρ** (# *4120*) al-

mighty (s. Rev. 1:8). **ἀληθινός** (# *240*) true, genuine. **δίκαιος** (# *1465*) just, righteous. **κρίσις** (# *3213*) judging, judgment. ◆ **8 ἐξέχεεν** aor. ind. act. ἐκχέω (# *1772*) to pour out. **ἐδόθη** aor. ind. pass. δίδωμι (# *1443*) to give. The vb. is used in the sense of, "he was given authority," "he was allowed." **καυματίσαι** aor. act. inf. καυματίζω (# *3009*) to burn, to scorch (Ford; Swete). Epex. inf. ◆ **9 ἐκαυματίσθησαν** aor. ind. pass. καυματίζω (# *3009*) to burn. **καῦμα** (# *3008*) heat, scorching. The cognate acc. retained w. a pass. vb. (RWP). **ἐβλασφήμησαν** aor. ind. act. βλασφημέω (# *1059*) to speak evil of, to blaspheme (TLNT; TDNT). **ἔχοντος** pres. act. part. ἔχω (# *2400*) to have. **πληγάς** (# *4435*) blow, wound, plague (s. Rev. 15:1). **μετενόησαν** aor. ind. act. μετανοέω (# *3566*) to change one's mind, to change one's thinking, to repent. **δοῦναι** aor. act. inf. δίδωμι (# *1443*) to give. Inf. to express actual or realized results. ◆ **10 πέμπτος** (# *4286*) fifth. **ἐξέχεεν** aor. ind. act. ἐκχέω (# *1772*) to pour out. **ἐγένετο** aor. ind. mid. (dep.) γίνομαι (# *1181*) to become. **ἐσκοτωμένη** perf. pass. part. (adj.) σκοτόω (# *5031*) to make dark, to darken. Perf. indicates the condition. **ἐμασῶντο** perf. ind. mid. (dep.) μασάομαι (# *3460*) to chew, to gnaw. The word indicates that the pain caused by the scorching heat of the fourth plague and the malignant sores of the first was such that men chewed their tongues in agony. The phrase was used as an indication of intolerable pain (Swete; s. Matt. 8:12). **γλῶσσα** (# *1185*) tongue. **πόνος** (# *4506*) pain, agony. ◆ **11 ἐβλασφήμησαν** aor. ind. act. βλασφημέω (# *1059*) to speak evil of, to blaspheme (TLNT; TDNT). **πόνος** (# *4506*) pain. **ἑλκῶν** gen. pl. (# *1814*) boils, sores (s.v. 2). **μετενόησαν** aor. ind. act. μετανοέω (# *3566*) to change one's mind, to change one's thinking, to repent. ◆ **12 ἐξέχεεν** aor. ind. act. ἐκχέω (# *1772*) to pour out. **ἐξηράνθη** aor. ind. pass. ξηραίνω (# *3830*) to dry, to dry up. **ἑτοιμασθῇ** aor. subj. pass. ἑτοιμάζω (# *2286*) to prepare, to make ready. Subj. w. ἵνα (# *2671*) in purp. cl. **ἀνατολή** (# *424*) rising, **ἀνατολῆς ἡλίου** (# *2463*) rising of the sun, i.e., the east (s. Matt. 2:1). ◆ **13 εἶδον** aor. ind. act. ὁράω (# *3972*) to see. **στόμα** (# *5125*) mouth. **δράκων** (# *1532*) dragon. **θηρίον** (# *2436*) beast. **ψευδοπροφήτης** (# *6021*) false prophet. **ἀκάθαρτος** impure, unclean. **βάτραχος** (# *1005*) frog. The frog was classified as an unclean animal, an abomination (Lev. 11:10, 41; Ford; FFB, 33). The unclean spirits proceed from the mouths of the unholy triumvirate, suggesting the persuasive and deceptive propaganda that in the last days will lead men to commit unconditionally to the cause of evil (Mounce). ◆ **14 εἰσίν** pres. ind. act. εἰμί (# *1639*) to be. **ποιοῦντα** pres. act. part. ποιέω (# *4472*) to do, to perform. **ἐκπορεύεται** pres. ind. mid. (dep.) ἐκπορεύομαι (# *1744*) to go out, to proceed from. **συναγαγεῖν** aor. act. inf. συνάγω (# *5251*) to lead together, to gather together, to assemble. Inf. to express purp. **πόλεμος** (# *4438*) war. ◆ **15 ἰδού** aor. imp. act. ὁράω (# *3972*) to see. **ἔρχομαι**

(# 2262) pres. ind. mid. (dep.) to come. **κλέπτης** (# 3095) thief. The emphasis is on the unexpected coming. **μακάριος** (# 3421) blessed, happy. **γρηγορῶν** pres. act. part. (subst.) γρηγορέω (# 1213) to be awake, to watch. **τηρῶν** pres. act. part. τηρέω (# 5498) to keep, to protect. **γυμνός** (# 1218) naked. For Jewish abhorrence s. BBC. **περιπατῇ** pres. subj. act. περιπατέω (# 4344) to walk about. As the priest kept watch in the temple, so an officer of the temple went around every watch w. a lighted torch before him. If any watch did not stand up and say to him, "O officer of the Temple Mount, peace be to thee!" and it was manifest that he was asleep, he would beat him w. his staff and he had the right to burn his raiment (M, Middoth, 1:2). **βλέπωσιν** pres. subj. act. βλέπω (# 1063) to see. The pl. used impersonally gives the vb. the force of a pass., "his shame is seen." **ἀσχημοσύνη** (# 859) shamefulness, indecency. The word is probably an euphemism for private parts (Mounce; BAGD).
◆ **16 συνήγαγεν** aor. ind. act. συνάγω (# 5251) to gather together, to lead together, to assemble. **καλούμενον** pres. pass. part. καλέω (# 2813) to call. ◆ **17 ἐξέχεεν** aor. ind. act. ἐκχέω (# 1772) to pour out. **ἀέρα** acc. sing. ἀήρ (# 113) air. **ἐξῆλθεν** aor. ind. act. ἐξέρχομαι (# 2002) to go out, to come out of. **λέγουσα** pres. act. part. λέγω (# 3306) to say. **γέγονεν** perf. ind. act. γίνομαι (# 1181) to be, to become. Perf. could be translated, "it is done," "it has come to pass." The voice is esp. appropriate in this connection, since these plagues are the last; there remain no further manifestations of this kind (Swete). ◆ **18 ἐγένοντο** aor. ind. mid. (dep.) γίνομαι (# 1181) to be, to become. **ἀστραπή** (# 847) lightning. **βροντή** (# 1103) thunder. **σεισμός** (# 4939) earthquake. **οἷος** (# 3888) of such a kind. **ἀφ᾿ οὗ** (# 608; 4005) from when, ever since. **τηλικοῦτος** (# 5496) so large, so great. ◆ **19 μέρη** acc. pl. μέρος (# 3538) part, section. Here used with γίνομαι the idea is that the city split into three parts. **ἔπεσαν** aor. ind. act. πίπτω (# 4406) to fall, to fall down. **ἐμνήσθη** aor. ind. pass. μιμνήσκομαι (# 3630) to remember; pass., to be remembered. **δοῦναι** aor. act. inf. δίδωμι (# 3937) to give. Inf. expressing result. **ποτήριον** (# 4539) cup. **ὀργή** (# 2596) wrath, anger (s. Rev. 14:10). **θυμοῦ τῆς ὀργῆς** (# 2596; 3937) fierce wrath. Descriptive gen. ◆ **20 νῆσος** (# 3762) island. **ἔφυγεν** aor. ind. act. φεύγω (# 5771) to flee. **εὑρέθησαν** aor. ind. pass. εὑρίσκω (# 2351) to find. ◆ **21 χάλαζα** (# 5898) hail. **ταλαντιαῖος** (# 5418) talent. The talent varied in weight among different peoples at different times. The range seems to be from about sixty pounds to over a hundred (Mounce). **καταβαίνει** pres. ind. act. καταβαίνω (# 2849) to go down, to descend. **ἐβλασφήμησαν** aor. ind. act. βλασφημέω (# 1059) to speak evil of, to blaspheme (TLNT; TDNT). **σφόδρα** (# 5379) very much, extremely, greatly, very.

Revelation 17

◆ **1 ἦλθεν** pres. ind. act. ἔρχομαι (# 2262) to go. **ἐχόντων** pres. act. part. ἔχω (# 2400) to have. **φιάλη** (# 5786) bowl (s. Rev. 15:7). **ἐλάλησεν** aor. ind. act. λαλέω (# 3281) to speak. **λέγων** pres. act. part. λέγω (# 3306) to say. **δεῦρο** (# 1306) come here! **δείξω** fut. ind. act. δείκνυμι (# 1259) to show. **κρίμα** (# 3210) sentence, judgment. **πόρνη** (# 4520) prostitute, whore. In the Old Testament and prophetic literature prostitution and adultery were equal to idolatry and denoted religious apostasy (Hos. 1:2; Ford; Mounce). The harlot here is Rome, denoting the corrupt apostate religious system headed by the false prophet who is the second beast of Rev. 13. Some, however, consider a literal Babylon as the center of idol worship (Thomas). **καθημένης** pres. mid. part. κάθημαι (# 2764) to sit. **ἐπὶ ὑδάτων πολλῶν** (# 2093; 5623; 4498) upon many waters (s. Rev. 13:1).
◆ **2 ἐπόρνευσαν** aor. ind. act. πορνεύω (# 4519) to engage in immoral acts, to engage in unlawful sex. Again the picture is one of religious apostasy. **ἐμεθύσθησαν** aor. ind. pass. μεθύσκω (# 3499) to be drunk; pass. to be made drunk. Aor. could be ingressive: to enter in the state of drunkenness, to get drunk. The figure indicates the intoxicating and controlling aspects of the false religion. **κατοικοῦντες** pres. act. part. κατοικέω (# 2997) to live, to reside, to dwell. **πορνεία** (# 4518) immorality, unlawful sexual activity (s. 2:21). Here gen. of definition, explaining the word **οἴνου**. ◆ **3 ἀπήνεγκεν** aor. ind. act. ἀναφέρω (# 708) to carry off. **ἔρημος** (# 2245) desert. **εἶδον** aor. ind. act. ὁράω (# 3972) to see. **καθημένην** pres. mid. (dep.) part. κάθημαι (# 2764) to sit. **θηρίον** (# 2563) wild animal, beast. **κόκκινος** (# 3132) scarlet, crimson. The color, popular in the Roman Empire, indicated luxurious and haughty splendor (EGT; TDNT). **γέμον[τα]** pres. act. part. γέμω (# 1154) to be full. **βλασφημία** (# 1060) blasphemy. **ἔχων** pres. act. part. ἔχω (# 2400) to have. **κέρας** (# 3043) horn. The image suggests the close union of the political and religious powers in the last days. ◆ **4 ἦν** impf. ind. act. εἰμί (# 1639) to be. **περιβεβλημένη** perf. pass. part. περιβάλλω (# 4314) to cast about, to be clothed. **πορφυροῦς** (# 4526) purple. **κόκκινος** (# 3132) scarlet. Purple was often used of royal garments and scarlet was a color of magnificence (Mounce; ABD, 5:556-60; L. B. Jensen, "Royal Purple of Tyre," *Journal of Ancient Near Eastern Society* 22 [1963]: 104-18). **κεχρυσωμένη** perf. pass. part. χρυσόω (# 5998) to inlay w. gold, to cover w. gold. **μαργαρίτης** (# 3449) pearl (s. 1 Tim. 2:9). **ἔχουσα** pres. act. part. ἔχω (# 2400) to have. **ποτήριον** (# 4539) cup. **χρυσοῦς** (# 5992) golden. **βδέλυγμα** (# 1007) that which stinks, abomination, that which is detestable. The word is used in the LXX of the moral and ceremonial impurity connected w. idolatrous practices (Mounce). **ἀκάθαρτος** (# 176) impure, unclean. **πορνεία** (# 4518) immoral sexual acts. Either gen. of source explaining the source of the impu-

rity, or descriptive gen. indicating the kind of impurity–sexual impurity. ◆ **5 μέτωπον** (# 3587) forehead, brow. **γεγραμμένον** perf. pass. part. γράφω (# 1211) to write, to inscribe. ◆ **6 εἶδον** aor. ind. act. ὁράω (# 3972) to see. **μεθύουσαν** pres. act. part. μεθύω (# 3501) to get drunk. The metaphor of getting drunk on the blood of the saints and the blood of the witnesses of Jesus portrays the wanton slaughter of a great number of believers, along w. the intoxicating effect it produced upon the murderous harlot (Mounce). This depicts the tremendous persecution of true believers by the apostate religion of the last days (DLNT, 907-14). **ἐθαύμασα** aor. ind. act. θαυμάζω (# 2513) to be amazed, to wonder. **ἰδών** aor. act. part. ὁράω (# 3972) to see. **θαῦμα** (# 2512) wonderment. ◆ **7 ἐθαύμασας** aor. ind. act. θαυμάζω (# 2513) to be amazed. **ἐρῶ** fut. ind. act. λέγω (# 3306) to tell. **βαστάζοντος** pres. act. part. βαστάζω (# 1002) to carry, to bear. **ἔχοντος** pres. act. part. ἔχω (# 2400) to have. ◆ **8 εἶδες** aor. ind. act. ὁράω (# 3972) to see. **ἦν** impf. ind. act. εἰμί (# 1639) to be. **ἦν καὶ οὐκ ἔστιν καὶ μέλλει ἀναβαίνειν** "who was and is not and is about to arise." This phrase is perhaps an intentional antithesis to Rev. 1:4, "the one who was and is" (Swete). **μέλλει** pres. ind. act. μέλλω (# 3516) to be about to. Used w. inf. to express the fut. **ἀναβαίνειν** pres. act. inf. ἀναβαίνω (# 326) to go up, to ascend. **ἀβ-ύσσος** (# 12) bottomless pit, abyss (s. 9:1). **ἀπώλεια** (# 724) destruction, ruin. **ὑπάγει** pres. ind. act. ὑπάγω (# 5632) to go forth. **θαυμασθήσονται** fut. ind. pass. θαυμάζω (# 2513) to be amazed, to wonder w. the amazement of a horrible surprise; the world will still wonder and admire (Swete). **κατοικοῦντες** pres. act. part. κατοικέω (# 2997) to live, to dwell. **γέγραπται** perf. ind. pass. γράφω (# 1211) to write. **καταβολή** (# 2856) foundation (s. Rev. 13:8). **βλεπόντων** pres. act. part. βλέπω (# 1063) to see. Temp. part., "when they see." The gen. pl. agrees w. the gen. pl. of the rel. pron **ὧν**. (RWP). **ἦν** impf. ind. act. εἰμί (# 1639) to be. **παρέσται** fut. ind. act. παρειμί (# 4205) to be present, to come. ◆ **9 νοῦς** (# 3808) mind, understanding. The formula is a call to vigilance and close attention (Swete). **ἔχων** pres. act. part. ἔχω (# 2400) to have. **ὅπου** (# 3963) where. **κάθηται** pres. ind. mid. (dep.) κάθημαι (# 2764) to sit. **βασιλεύς** (# 995) king. The reference is either to seven world empires (Seiss) or to seven emperors of the Roman Empire (Govett; Mounce; Ford). Others have viewed this as various forms of government of the Roman Empire (Scott). ◆ **10 ἔπεσαν** aor. ind. act. πίπτω (# 4406) to fall, to fall down. **οὔπω** (# 4037) not yet. **ὅταν** (# 4020) w. subj., whenever. **ἔλθη** aor. subj. act. ἔρχομαι (# 2262) to go, to come. Subj. used in an indef. temp. cl. **δεῖ** (# 1256) pres. ind. act. it is necessary, w. acc. and inf. **μεῖναι** aor. inf. act. μένω (# 3531) to remain. ◆ **11 ὄγδοός** (# 3838) eight. The beast himself is an eighth king and at the same time one of the seven. He is Antichrist, not simply another Roman emperor. His period of hegemony is

the Great Tribulation preceding the return of the Messiah (Mounce). **ὑπάγει** pres. ind. act. ὑπάγω (# 5632) to go on. ◆ **12 εἶδες** aor. ind. act. ὁράω (# 3972) to see. **ἔλαβον** aor. ind. act. λαμβάνω (# 3284) to take. The ten kings who are yet to receive their power refer to the European kingdoms of a revived Roman Empire. The political beast of Revelation 13 will be one of these leaders (Scott). ◆ **13 γνώμη** (# 1191) opinion, purpose. The unity of the ten appears in their support of the beast (Swete). **ἔχουσιν** pres. ind. act. ἔχω (# 2400) to have. Pres. to describe the certainty of a fut. event. **διδόασιν** pres. ind. act. 3rd pl. δίδωμι (# 1443) to give. ◆ **14 ἀρνίον** (# 768) lamb. **πολεμήσουσιν** fut. ind. act. πολεμέω (# 4482) to wage war. **νικήσει** fut. ind. act. νικάω (# 3771) to gain the victory, to be victor, to overcome, to conquer. **κύριος κυρίων** (# 3261) Lord of lords. Gen. may be gen. of ruling, "He is the Lord who rules over lords." Perhaps this is a circumlocution for the superlative (GGBB, 298). The word or root κύριος is used 22 times in Rev. to show Christ as the true ruler. For the parallel passage in Daniel s. G.K. Beale, "The Origin of the Title 'King of Kings and Lord of Lords' in Revelation 17:14," *NTS* 31 (1985): 618-20. **κλητός** (# 3105) called. **ἐκλεκτός** (# 1723) chosen, elect. ◆ **15 εἶδες** aor. ind. act. ὁράω (# 3972) to see. **οὗ** (# 4023) where. **κάθηται** pres. ind. mid. (dep.) κάθημαι (# 2764) to sit. **ὄχλος** (# 4063) crowd, multitudes. **ἔθνη** nom. pl. ἔθνος (# 1620) nation. **γλῶσσα** (# 1185) tongue, language. The fourfold groupings stresses universality (Mounce). For the fig. of the sea representing people and nations s. Rev. 13:1. ◆ **16 εἶδες** aor. ind. act. ὁράω (# 3972) to see. **μισήσουσιν** fut. ind. act. μισέω (# 3631) to hate. **ἠρημωμένην** perf. pass. part. ἐρημόω (# 2246) to desolate, to make into a desert or desolate place. **ποιήσουσιν** fut ind. act. ποιέω (# 4472) to make. **φάγονται** fut. ind. mid. (dep.) ἐσθίω (# 2266) to eat. **κατακαύσουσιν** fut. ind. act. κατακαύομαι (# 2876) to burn down, to burn up, to completely destroy by fire. The political forces will turn against the false religious system and completely destroy it. ◆ **17 ἔδωκεν** aor. ind. act. δίδωμι (# 1443) to give. **ποιῆσαι** aor. act. inf. ποιέω (# 4472) to make. **δοῦναι** aor. act. inf. δίδωμι (# 1443) to give. **τελεσθήσονται** fut. ind. pass. τελέω (# 5464) to bring, to the goal, to complete. ◆ **18 εἶδες** aor. ind. act. ὁράω (# 3972) to see. **ἔχουσα** pres. act. part. ἔχω (# 2400) to have.

Revelation 18

◆ **1 μετὰ ταῦτα** (# 3552; 4047) after these things. **εἶδον** aor. ind. act. ὁράω (# 3972) to see. **καταβαίνοντα** pres. act. part. καταβαίνω (# 2849) to come down, to descend. **ἔχοντα** pres. act. part. ἔχω (# 2400) to have. **ἐφωτίσθη** aor. ind. pass. φωτίζω (# 5894) to light up, to illuminate. So recently has he come from the Presence that in passing he flings a broad belt of light across the dark earth (Swete). ◆ **2 ἔκραξεν** aor. ind. act. κράζω

(# 3189) to cry, to scream, to cry out w. a loud voice. **ἔπε-σεν** aor. ind. act. πίπτω (# 4406) to fall (s. Rev. 14:8; Isa. 21:9). The proleptic aors. are repeated like a solemn dirge or lament of the damned (RWP). **ἐγένετο** aor. ind. mid. (dep.) γίνομαι (# 1181) to become. **κατοικητήριον** (# 2999) place of living, habitation. **φυλακή** (# 5871) prison, place of banishment. **ὄρνεον** (# 3997) bird. **ἀκάθαρτος** (# 176) unclean. **μεμισημένου** perf. pass. part. μισέω (# 3631) to hate. ◆ **3 θυμός** (# 2596) anger, wrath, burning anger (s. 14:8, 10). **πορνεία** (# 4518) immortality, unlawful sexual acts. The figure is also used for apostasy and idolatry (s. Rev. 17:1). **πέπωκαν** perf. ind. act. πίνω (# 4540) to drink. Perf. would indicate the continuing results. **ἐπόρνευσαν** aor. ind. act. πορνεύω (# 4519) to commit immorality. **ἔμπορος** (# 1867) merchant. **στρῆνος** (# 5140) strong, mighty, arrogant; complacent luxury and self-indulgence w. accompanying arrogance and wanton exercise of strength (Mounce; GEW, 2:890ff; Swete). **ἐπλούτησαν** aor. ind. act. πλουτέω (# 4456) to be wealthy. Ingressive aor., "they became wealthy." ◆ **4 ἤκουσα** aor. ind. act. ἀκούω (# 201) to hear. **λέγουσαν** pres. act. part. λέγω (# 3306) to say. **ἐξέλθατε** aor. imp. act. ἐξέρχομαι (# 2002) to come out, to depart from. **συγκοινωνήσητε** aor. subj. act. συγκοινέω (# 5170) to be a partner, to be a co-partner w. (s. 1 John 1:3). Subj. w. ἵνα (# 2671) in a neg. purp. cl. **πληγῶν** gen. pl. πληγή (# 4435) blow, wound, plague. **λάβητε** aor. subj. act. λαμβάνω (# 3284) to take. Subj. w. ἵνα (# 2671) here used in a neg. purp. cl. The neg. μή (# 3590) in an expression of apprehension is combined in classical Gr. w. the subj. if the anxiety is directed toward warding off something still dependent on the will (BD, 188). ◆ **5 ἐκολλήθησαν** aor. ind. pass. κολλάω (# 3140) to stick to, to join to. The idea here is "joined to one another till they reach heaven, till the ever-growing mass rose sky high" (Swete). **ἐμνημόνευσεν** aor. ind. act. μνημονεύω (# 3648) to remember. **ἀδίκημα** (# 93) unrighteous act, injustice. ◆ **6 ἀπόδοτε** aor. imp. act. ἀποδίδωμι (# 625) to pay back. **διπλώσατε** aor. imp. act. διπλόω (# 1488) to double, to make double. **διπλᾶ** acc. pl. διπλοῦς (# 1487) double (BAGD). **κατὰ τὰ ἔργα αὐτῆς** (# 2848; 2240; 899) according to her deeds. In this v. there is precise compensation: double punishment for double crimes (Ford). **ποτήριον** (# 4539) cup. **ἐκέρασεν** aor. ind. act. κεράννυμι (# 3042) to mix. **κεράσατε** aor. imp. act. κεράννυμι, to mix, to mix a drink in preparation for drinking (s. Rev. 14:10). **διπλοῦν** acc. sing. neut. διπλοῦς (# 1487) double. ◆ **7 ὅσα** (# 4012) how much, as much as (AS). **ἐδόξασεν** aor. ind. act. δοξάζω (# 1519) to glorify. **ἐστρηνίασεν** aor. ind. act. στρηνιάω (# 5139) to live a proud and luxurious and sensuous life (s.v. 3). The term occurs in the papyri of bulls running wild (BAGD). **τοσοῦτος** (# 5537) so much, so great. **δότε** aor. imp. act. δίδωμι (# 1443) to give. **βασανισμός** (# 990) torture, torment, pain. **πένθος** (# 4292) mourning. **κάθημαι**

(# 2764) pres. ind. mid. (dep.) to sit, to sit established. **βασίλισσα** (# 999) queen. Nom. in apposition, "I sit as queen." **χήρα** (# 5939) widow. **οὐ μή** (# 4024; 3590) w. subj., not ever, never in any wise. **ἴδω** aor. subj. act. ὁράω (# 3972) to see. Subj. w. double neg. for a strong denial. ◆ **8 ἥξουσιν** fut. ind. act. ἥκω (# 2457) to come. **πληγή** (# 4435) plague, blow. **θάνατος** (# 2505) death. **πένθος** (# 4292) mourning. **λιμός** (# 3350) hunger, famine. **πῦρ** (# 4786) fire. **κατακαυθήσεται** fut. ind. pass. κατακαύομαι (# 2876) to burn down, to consume completely w. fire, to burn up. **ἰσχυρός** (# 2708) strong. **κρίνας** aor. act. part. κρίνω (# 3212) to judge. ◆ **9 κλαύσουσιν** fut. ind. act. κλαίω (# 3081) to weep, to cry aloud. **κόψονται** fut. ind. mid. κόπτω (# 3164) to beat, to cut, mid., to beat upon oneself, to beat one's breast as an act of mourning, to mourn for someone (BAGD). **πορνεύσαντες** aor. act. part. πορνεύω (# 4519) to commit immorality (s.v. 3). **στρηνιάσαντες** aor. act. part. στηνιάζω (# 5137) to live a proud and luxurious life (s.v. 3, 7). Adj. part. as subst. **ὅταν** (# 4020) w. subj., when, whenever. **βλέπωσιν** pres. subj. act. βλέπω (# 1063) to see. **καπνός** (# 2837) smoke. **πύρωσις** (# 4796) burning. ◆ **10 μακρόθεν** (# 3427) from afar off. **ἑστηκότες** perf. act. part. ἵστημι (# 2705) to stand. **λέγοντες** pres. act. part. λέγω (# 3306) to say. **ἦλθεν** aor. ind. act. ἔρχομαι (# 2262) to come. **κρίσις** (# 3213) judging, judgment. ◆ **11 κλαίουσιν** pres. ind. act. κλαίω (# 3081) to cry. **πενθοῦσιν** pres. ind. act. πενθέω (# 4291) to lament, to mourn. **γόμος** (# 1203) ship's cargo, merchandise (MM). **ἀγοράζει** pres. ind. act. ἀγοράζω (# 60) to buy, to purchase. For the position of Rome as a city of trade s. BBC; ABD, 6:629-33. **οὐκέτι** (# 4033) no longer. ◆ **12 ἄργυρος** (# 738) silver. Gen. of material describing the material out of which the cargo is made. **τίμιος** (# 5508) costly, expensive. **μαργαρίτης** (# 3449) pearl (s. 1 Tim. 2:9). **βύσσινος** (# 1115) linen. **πορφύρα** (# 4525) purple garment. **σιρικόν** (# 4986) silk. **κόκκινον** (# 3132) scarlet. **ξύλον** (# 3833) wood. **θύϊνος** (# 2591) wood of a citrus tree. This wood, imported from North Africa where it grew freely near the Atlas mountains, was much prized for its veining, which in the best specimens simulated the eyes of the peacock's tail or the stripes of the tiger and spots of the panther or the seeds of parsley. At Rome citrus wood was much sought after for dining tables, but it was also used for veneer and for small works of art made out of the hard roots of the tree (Swete; Pliny, *NH*, 13:96-102; for a description of the citron tree s. FFB, 190f). **σκεῦος** (# 5007) vessel. **ἐλεφάντι-νος** (# 1840) ivory. **τιμιωτάτου** superl. τίμιος (# 5508) costly, precious; used in the elative sense, "extremely expensive." **χαλκός** (# 5910) brass. **σίδηρος** (# 4970) iron. **μάρμαρος** (# 3454) marble. ◆ **13 κιννάμωμον** (# 3077) cinnamon. **ἄμωμον** (# 319) spice. This was a plant from India used as perfume (Pliny, *NH*, 12:48). **θυμίαμα** (# 2592) incense. **μύρον** (# 3693) myrrh. **λίβανος**

(# 3337) frankincense (s. Matt. 2:11). **οἶνος** (# 3885) olive oil. **ἔλαιον** (# 4947) fine flour. The fine flour imported for the use of the wealthy (Swete). **κτῆνος** (# 3229) cattle. **πρόβατον** (# 4585) sheep. **ἵππος** (# 2691) horse. **ῥέδη** (# 4832) chariot. A chariot from Gaul w. four wheels (Swete; RWP). **σῶμα** (# 5393) body, human being; here, slave. ◆ **14 ὀπώρα** (# 3967) fruit, the autumn fruit ripe for ingathering (Swete). **ἐπιθυμία** (# 2123) strong desire, lust, passion. **ἀπῆλθεν** aor. ind. act. **ἀπέρχομαι** (# 599) to go away, to pass. **λιπαρός** (# 3353) oily, fat, costly, rich, luxury, sleek (BAGD; Ford). The word may refer to the rich and dainty food (Swete). **λαμπρός** (# 3287) bright, shining. This may refer to the gay attire and costly furniture which were the fruits of Roman conquest and policy (Swete). **ἀπώλετο** aor. ind. mid. (dep.) **ἀπόλλυμι** (# 660) to destroy. **οὐκέτι** (# 4033) no longer. **οὐ μή** (# 4024; 3590) not at all. **εὐρήσουσιν** fut. ind. act. εὑρίσκω (# 2351) to find. The impersonal 3rd. pers. is equal to a pass. ◆ **15 πλουτή-σαντες** aor. act. part. (adj.) πλουτέω (# 4456) to be rich, to become rich. **στήσονται** fut. ind. mid. ἵστημι (# 2705) to stand. **κλαίοντες** pres. act. part. (circum.) κλαίω (# 3081) to weep, to weep aloud. **πενθοῦντες** pres. act. part. πενθέω (# 4291) to lament. ◆ **16 λέγοντες** pres. act. part. λέγω (# 3306) to say. **περιβεβλημένη** perf. pass. part. (adj.) περιβάλλω (# 4314) to cast about, to clothe. **βύσσινος** (# 1115) linen. **πορφυροῦς** (# 4528) purple, purple garment. **κεχρυσωμένη** perf. pass. part. (adj.) χρυσόω (# 5998) to cover w. gold, to overlay w. gold, to decorate w. gold. ◆ **17 ἠρημώθη** aor. ind. pass. ἐρημόω (# 2246) to turn into a desert, to make desolate, to devastate. **κυβερνήτης** (# 3237) one who guides a ship, steersman, pilot. The steersman held both rudders to keep them parallel (DRAG, 788-89; SSAW, 224-28). For a discussion of sea travel s. DPL, 945; SSAW). **τόπος** (# 5536) place. **πλέων** pres. act. part. πλέω (# 4434) to travel w. a ship, to sail. Subst. part. "He who sails" is the merchant w. his goods or the chance passenger (Swete). **ναύτης** (# 3731) sailor. **ἐργάζονται** pres. inf. mid. (dep.) ἐργάζομαι (# 2237) to work; here, those who gain their living by the sea, and it may refer to all those who earn their living in connection w. the maritime industry (Mounce). **ἔστησαν** aor. ind. act. ἵστημι (# 2705) to stand. ◆ **18 ἔκραζον** impf. ind. act. κράζω (# 3189) to cry out. Inceptive impf., "they began to cry out." **βλέποντες** pres. act. part. βλέπω (# 1063) to see. Part. could be temp. ("when they see") or it could be causal ("because they see"). **λέγοντες** pres. act. part. λέγω (# 3306) to say. ◆ **19 ἔβαλον** aor. ind. act. βάλλω (# 965) to throw. **χοῦς** (# 5967) dirt. **ἔκραζον** impf. ind. act. κράζω (# 3189) to cry out. **κλαίοντες** pres. act. part. κλαίω (# 3081) to cry. Part. of manner explaining how they cry. **πενθοῦντες** pres. act. part. πενθέω (# 4291) to lament. Part. of manner. **λέγοντες** pres. act. part. λέγω (# 3306) to say. **ἐπλούτησαν** aor. ind. act. πλουτέω (# 4456) to gain wealth. **ἔχοντες** pres. act. part. ἔχω

(# 2400) to have. **τιμιότητος** (# 5509) costliness. **ἠρημώθη** aor. ind. pass. ἐρημόω (# 2246) to turn into a desert. ◆ **20 εὐφραίνου** pres. imp. mid. εὐφραίνω (# 2370) to rejoice. **ἔκρινεν** aor. ind. act. κρίνω (# 3212) to judge. **κρίμα** (# 3210) judgment. ◆ **21 ἦρεν** aor. ind. act. αἴρω (# 149) to lift up. **μύλινος** (# 3684) millstone (ABD, 4:831-32). **ἔβαλεν** aor. ind. act. βάλλω (# 965) to throw. **λέγων** pres. act. part. λέγω (# 3306) to say. **ὅρμημα** (# 3996) rushing; instr. dat. "w. a rushing," like a stone whizzing through the air (Swete). The great millstone does not fall, but is violently hurled into the sea. This stresses how suddenly and spectacularly the judgment of God will be executed, not only upon an ancient city but ultimately upon the entire anti-Christian world in its opposition to God (Mounce). **βληθήσεται** fut. ind. pass. βάλλω (# 965) to throw. **εὐρεθῇ** aor. subj. pass. εὑρίσκω (# 2351) to find. Subj. w. οὐ μή (# 4024; 3590) in an emphatic neg. cl. ◆ **22 κιθαρῳδός** (# 3069) harp player. **μουσικός** (# 3676) pertaining to music, musician. The word means skilled in music and here it may refer either to instrumentalists or vocalists (Swete). **αὐλήτης** (# 886) flute player. **σαλπιστής** (# 4896) trumpet player. **ἀκουσθῇ** aor. subj. pass. ἀκούω (# 201) to hear. Music was used both for entertainment and religion (Mounce; Swete; s. 5:9). Subj. w. οὐ μή (# 4024; 3590) in an emphatic neg. cl. **τεχνίτης** (# 5493) skilled worker. It may refer to an artist in metal, in stone, or even in textile fabrics (Swete). **τέχνη** (# 5492) craft, skill. **εὐρεθῇ** aor. subj. pass. εὑρίσκω (# 2351) to find. Subj. w. οὐ μή (# 4024; 3590) in an emphatic neg. cl. **μύλος** (# 3685) mill. The word here apparently means the whole apparatus as distinguished from the millstone. The sound of the mill is best explained as the sound made by the mill (Swete). **ἀκουσθῇ** aor. ind. pass. ἀκούω (# 201) to hear. ◆ **23 λύχνος** (# 3394) lamp. **φάνῃ** aor. subj. mid. φαίνω (# 5743) to shine; mid., to appear. Subj. w. οὐ μή (# 4024; 3590) in an emphatic neg. cl. **ἀκουσθῇ** aor. subj. pass. ἀκούω (# 201) to hear. Subj. w. οὐ μή (# 4024; 3590) in an emphatic neg. cl. **ἔμπορος** (# 1867) merchant. The word may refer to merchants who deal in foreign exports and imports (Mounce). **ἦσαν** impf. ind. act. εἰμί (# 1639) to be. **μεγιστάν** (# 3491) the great ones. **φαρμακεία** (# 5758) use of drugs either as medicine, poison, or magic (s. Rev. 9:21). **ἐπλανήθησαν** aor. ind. pass. πλανάω (# 4414) to lead astray, to deceive. ◆ **24 εὐρέθη** aor. ind. pass. εὑρίσκω (# 2351) to find. **ἐσφαγμένων** perf. pass. part. σφάζω (# 5377) to slaughter, to kill.

Revelation 19

◆ **1 ἤκουσα** aor. ind. act. ἀκούω (# 201) to hear. **λεγόντων** pres. act. part. λέγω (# 3306) to say. **ἀλληλουϊά** (# 252) Hallelujah! praise the Lord! praise God. Transliteration of the Heb. הלל, a piel imp. of הלל (hll) w. the suff. יָהּ (yh), a shortened form of Yahweh. The basic meaning of the vb. is "to be bright," and the causative meaning of the piel imp. means, lit., "make Yahweh bright," that is, "illuminate the Lord by casting a bright light on Him and His works!" "Praise Yahweh!" "Praise the Lord!" (Oda Hagemeyer, "Preiset Gott!" *BibLeb* 11 (1970):145-49; THAT; TDOT; DCH). **θεοῦ** gen. sing. θεός (# 2536) God. Gen. could be possession ("salvation, deliverance belongs to our God") or gen. of source ("Salvation, deliverance is from our God"). ◆ **2 ἀληθινός** (# 240) true. **κρίσις** (# 3213) judgment. **ἔκρινεν** aor. ind. act. κρίνω (# 3212) to judge. **πόρνη** (# 4520) prostitute, whore. **ἔφθειρεν** aor. ind. act. φθείρω (# 5780) to corrupt. Complexive aor. summing up her deeds. **πορνεία** (# 4518) immorality, illicit sexual acts (s. Rev. 2:21). **ἐξεδίκησεν** aor. ind. act. ἐκδικέω (# 1688) to avenge, to procure justice for someone, to punish (BAGD). **τὸ αἷμα** (# 135) blood. The blood of someone often indicates a violent death; here, "the violent death of His slaves." ◆ **3 δεύτερον** (# 1309) a second time. **εἴρηκαν** perf. ind. act. λέγω (# 3306) to say. **καπνός** (# 2837) smoke. **ἀναβαίνει** pres. ind. act. ἀναβαίνω (# 326) to go up, to ascend. ◆ **4 ἔπεσαν** aor. ind. act. πίπτω (# 4406) to fall, to fall down. **ζῷα** nom. pl. ζῷον (# 2442) living creature. **προσεκύνησαν** aor. ind. act. προσκυνέω (# 4686) to worship. **καθημένῳ** pres. mid. (dep.) part. κάθημαι (# 2764) to sit. **λέγοντες** pres. act. part. λέγω (# 3306) to say. ◆ **5 ἐξῆλθεν** aor. ind. act. ἐξέρχομαι (# 2002) to go out. **λέγουσα** pres. act. part. λέγω (# 3306) to say. **αἰνεῖτε** pres. imp. act. αἰνέω (# 140) to praise. Pres. imp. indicates a continual praise. **φοβούμενοι** pres. mid. (dep.) part. (subst.) φοβέομαι (# 5828) to be afraid, to fear, to reverence (TDNT). ◆ **6 ἤκουσα** aor. ind. act. ἀκούω (# 201) to hear. **βροντή** thunder. **λεγόντων** pres. act. part. λέγω (# 3306) to say. **ἐβασίλευσεν** aor. ind. act. βασιλεύω (# 996) to be king, to reign as a king, to rule. **παντοκράτωρ** (# 4120) almighty (s. Rev. 1:8). ◆ **7 χαίρωμεν** pres. subj. act. χαίρω (# 5897) to rejoice. Hortatory subj., "let us rejoice." **ἀγαλλιῶμεν** pres. subj. act. ἀγαλλιάω (# 22) to be glad, to rejoice exuberantly. Hortatory subj. **δώσωμεν** fut. ind. act. δίδωμι (# 1443) to give. The variant reading would be aor. subj. and would be grammatically parallel to the preceding subj. (TC, 762). **ἦλθεν** aor. ind. act. ἔρχομαι (# 2262) to go. **γάμος** (# 1141) marriage, wedding. **ἀρνίον** (# 768) lamb. For references to wedding customs s. Rev. 21:2. **ἡτοίμασεν** aor. ind. act. ἑτοιμάζω (# 2286) to prepare. W. a reflexive pron. **ἑαυτήν** (# 1571), "she has prepared herself." ◆ **8 ἐδόθη** aor. ind. pass. δίδωμι (# 1443) to give, to allow. **περιβάληται** aor. subj. mid. περιβάλλω (# 4314) to throw around, to be clothed. **βύσσινος** (# 1115) linen. **λαμπρός** (# 3287) bright, shining. **καθαρός** (# 2754) pure. **δικαίωμα** (# 1468) righteous deeds, acts of righteousness. The expression here is the sum of the saintly acts of Christ's members wrought in them by His Holy Spirit and regarded as making up the clothing of His mythical body (Swete; Charles;

Thomas). ◆ **9 λέγει** pres. ind. act. λέγω (# 3306) to say. **γράψον** aor. imp. act. γράφω (# 1211) to write. **μακάριος** (# 3421) happy, blessed. **δεῖπνον** (# 1270) banquet. For an excellent description of both the preparation and the different parts of a Jewish banquet s. SB 4:611-39. **κεκλημένοι** perf. pass. part. καλέω (# 2813) to call, to invite. It was not only an honor to be invited to a wedding feast, but it was also very impolite and discourteous to reject an invitation. **ἀληθινός** (# 240) true, genuine. ◆ **10 ἔπεσα** aor. ind. act. πίπτω (# 4406) to fall down. **προσκυνῆσαι** aor. act. inf. προσκυνέω (# 4686) to worship. Inf. is used to express intended purp. **ὅρα** pres. imp. act. ὁράω (# 3972) to see. An elliptical expression w. the words "do not do it" understood; i.e., "see that you do not do it" (RWP). **ἐχόντων** pres. act. part. ἔχω (# 2400) to have. **Ἰησοῦς** (# 2652) Jesus. Here, subjective gen.: the witness borne by Jesus. By His life and death Jesus has demonstrated to His followers what it means to bear faithful witness to the message revealed by God (Mounce). **προσκύνησον** aor. ind. act. προσκυνέω (# 4686) to worship. **προφητεία** (# 4635) prophecy. Obj. gen., "prophecy given by the Spirit." The testimony of Jesus is the substance of what the Spirit inspires Christian prophets to speak (Thomas; Beasley-Murray; Mounce; Swete; HSB, 776-77). ◆ **11 εἶδον** aor. ind. act. ὁράω (# 3972) to see. **ἠνεῳγμένον** perf. pass. part. ἀνοίγω (# 487) to open. Perf. part. indicates "to have been opened and now stands open." **ἰδού** aor. imp. act. ὁράω (# 3972) to see. **ἵππος** (# 2691) horse. **λευκός** (# 3328) white. **καθήμενος** pres. mid. (dep.) part. κάθημαι (# 2764) to sit. **καλούμενος** pres. pass. part. καλέω (# 2813) to call; pass., to be called, to have the name. **κρίνει** pres. ind. act. κρίνω (# 3212) to judge. **πολεμεῖ** pres. ind. act. πολεμέω (# 4482) to wage war. The Messiah now returns to the earth as the divine warrior and conquering king (BBC). ◆ **12 ὀφθαλμός** (# 4057) eye. **φλόξ** (# 5825) flame. **πῦρ** (# 4786) fire (s. 1:14). **διάδημα** (# 1343) diadem, the crown of royalty, a kingly crown. **ἔχων** pres. act. part. ἔχω (# 2400) to have; to possess. Independent use of the part., "he had a name" (GGBB, 653). **ὄνομα** (# 3950) name. The name signified the character of the person as well as the character of His kingly rule (TDNT). Here the name no one knows indicates the name that can be known only when the apocalypse is fulfilled when it will be revealed: "Jesus Christ is Lord" (Ford). **γεγραμμένον** perf. pass. part. γράφω (# 1211) to write. **οἶδεν** perf. ind. act. οἶδα (# 3857) to know. Def. perf. w. pres. meaning. **εἰ μή** (# 1623; 3590) except. ◆ **13 περιβεβλημένος** perf. pass. part. περιβάλλω (# 4314) to be clothed. **βεβαμμένον** perf. pass. part. βάπτω (# 970) to dip. Perf. indicates a past completed action w. a continuing state or results. The blood staining the garment of the conquering Messiah is not His own, but the blood of the enemy shed in conflict (Mounce; Isa. 63:1-6). **κέκληται** perf. ind. pass.

καλέω (# 2813) to call. ◆ **14 στράτευμα** (# 5128) army.
ἠκολούθει impf. ind. act. ἀκολουθέω (# 199) to follow, to
follow after, w. dat. **ἐνδεδυμένοι** perf. pass. part. ἐνδύω
(# 1907) to put on clothes; pass., to be clothed. **βύσσινος**
(# 1115) linen. **λευκός** (# 3328) white. **καθαρός** (# 2754)
pure. ◆ **15 ἐκπορεύεται** pres. ind. mid. (dep.) ἐκπορεύομαι (# 1744) to go out, to come out. **ῥομφαία** (# 4855)
sword, a large broad sword (s. 1:16). **ὀξεῖα** nom. sing.
ὀξύς (# 3955) sharp. **πατάξῃ** aor. subj. act. πατάσσω
(# 4250) to smite. Subj. w. **ἵνα** (# 2671) used in a purp.
cl. (Charles). **ποιμανεῖ** fut. ind. act. ποιμαίνω (# 4477) to
shepherd, to rule, to govern. **ῥάβδος** (# 4811) stick, staff,
scepter. **σιδηροῦς** (# 4971) iron. The Messiah's rod is a
rod of iron; it is strong and unyielding in its mission of
judgment (Mounce). **πατεῖ** pres. ind. act. πατέω (# 4251)
to tread. **ληνός** (# 3332) trough, winepress. **οἶνος**
(# 3885) wine. **θυμός** (# 2596) anger, burning anger.
ὀργή (# 3973) wrath, deep-seated, righteous wrath. It
shows the futility of resistance. **παντοκράτωρ** (# 4120)
almighty (s. 1:8). ◆ **16 ἔχει** pres. ind. act. ἔχω (# 2400)
to have. **μηρός** (# 3611) thigh. **γεγραμμένον** perf. pass.
part. γράφω (# 1211) to write. The inscription **βασιλεὺς
βασιλέων καὶ κύριος κυρίων** (# 995; 2779; 3261) "King of
kings, and Lord of lords" was probably the name written on that part of the garment that fell open across the
thigh (Mounce). ◆ **17 εἶδον** aor. ind. act. ὁράω (# 3972)
to see. **ἑστῶτα** perf. act. part. ἵστημι (# 2705) to stand.
ἔκραξεν aor. ind. act. κράζω (# 3189) to scream, to cry
out w. a loud voice. **λέγων** pres. ind. act. λέγω (# 3306)
to say. **ὄρνεον** (# 3997) bird. **πετομένοις** pres. mid. (dep.)
part. πέτομαι (# 4375) to fly. **μεσουράνημα** (# 3547) mid-
heaven (s. 8:13). **δεῦτε** (# 1307) come here. **συνάχθητε**
aor. imp. pass. συνάγω (# 5251) to gather together, to
lead together, to assemble. **δεῖπνον** (# 1270) feast, banquet. **θεοῦ** (# 2536) of God; it is the supper of God in the
sense that God will provide it (Mounce). ◆ **18 φάγητε**
aor. subj. act. ἐσθίω (# 2266) to eat. Subj. w. **ἵνα** (# 2671)
used in a purp. cl. **σάρκας** acc. pl. σάρξ (# 4922) flesh; pl.
pieces of flesh (RWP). **χιλίαρχος** (# 5941) commander
of a thousand (s. Rev. 6:15; Mark 6:21). **καθημένων** pres.
mid. (dep.) part. κάθημαι (# 2764) to sit. ◆ **19 εἶδον** aor.
ind. act. ὁράω (# 3972) to see. **θηρίον** (# 2563) wild animal, beast. **στράτευμα** (# 5128) army. **συνηγμένα** perf.
pass. part. συνάγω (# 5251) to gather together, to assemble. Perf. pass. part. indicates to be assembled, to
stand assembled. **ποιῆσαι** aor. act. inf. ποιέω (# 4472) to
do. Inf. to express purp. **πόλεμος** (# 4483) war. The political leader described in Rev. 13 as the first beast as-
sembles his forces for war and the battle takes place at
Armageddon, the hill (mountain) of Meggido over-
looking the fertile valley of Jezreel. Meggido was the
important stronghold guarding not only the valley, but
also the famous trade route, *Via Maris*, from Egypt to
Damascus. ◆ **20 ἐπιάσθη** aor. ind. pass. πιάζω (# 4389)
to seize, to take hold of. The word was used of arresting

someone and taking him into custody and of catching
animals (BAGD). **ψευδοπροφήτης** (# 6021) false prophet. The religious leader who is the second beast of Rev.
13. **ποιήσας** aor. act. part. ποιέω (# 4472) to do. **ἐπλάνη-
σεν** aor. ind. act. πλανάω (# 4414) to lead in the wrong
way, to lead astray, to deceive. **λαβόντας** aor. act. part.
λαμβάνω (# 3284) to receive, to take. **χάραγμα** (# 5916)
brand, mark. **προσκυνοῦντας** pres. act. part. προσκυνέω
(# 4686) to worship. **εἰκών** (# 1635) image. **ζῶντες** pres.
act. part. ζάω (# 2409) to live. Pres. describes contemporary action, "while still alive." **ἐβλήθησαν** aor. ind. pass.
βάλλω (# 965) to throw, to cast. **λίμνη** (# 3349) lake. **πῦρ**
(# 4786) fire. **καιομένης** pres. pass. part. καίω (# 2794) to
burn; pass., to be burning. **θεῖον** (# 2520) brimstone,
sulphur. ◆ **21 ἀπεκτάνθησαν** aor. ind. pass. ἀποκτείνω
(# 650) to kill. **ῥομφαία** (# 4855) sword (s. 1:16). **καθημένου** pres. mid. (dep.) part. κάθημαι (# 2764) to sit. **ἐξ-
ελθούσῃ** aor. act. part. ἐξέρχομαι (# 2002) to go out.
ἐχορτάσθησαν aor. ind. pass. χορτάζω (# 5963) to feed, to
fatten; pass., to be filled, to be satisfied. The supper of
God is ready, and the vultures gorge themselves on the
flesh of the wicked (Mounce).

Revelation 20

◆ **1 εἶδον** aor. ind. act. ὁράω (# 3972) to see. **καταβαίνοντα** pres. act. part. καταβαίνω (# 2849) to come
down, to descend. **ἔχοντα** pres. act. part. ἔχω (# 2400) to
have. **κλείς** (# 3090) key. The key symbolized the authority over a place (s. Rev. 1:18; 3:7). **ἄβυσσος** (# 12)
bottomless pit, abyss (s. 9:1). The abyss stands here in
sharp contrast w. the lake (19:20); the locked dungeon
w. its black and bottomless depths forms an antithesis
to the open shallow pool of fire (Swete). **ἅλυσις** (# 268)
chain. ◆ **2 ἐκράτησεν** aor. ind. act. κρατέω (# 3195) to
exercise power, to take into custody, to arrest (BAGD;
Mounce). **δράκων** (# 1532) dragon. **ὄφις** (# 4058) snake.
ἀρχαῖος (# 792) old, ancient. **ἔδησεν** aor. ind. act. δέω
(# 1313) to bind. Aor. points to the completed action.
χίλιοι (# 5943) thousand. **ἔτη** acc. pl. ἔτος (# 2291) year.
Acc. of time indicating the extent of time, "for a thousand years." For a brief discussion of the views on this
v. s. HSB, 778-80; Ray Summers, "Revelation 20: An Interpretation," *RevExp* 57 (1960): 176-83; Hans Bietenhard, "The Millenial Hope in the Early Church," *SJT* 6
(1953): 12-30; Charles E. Hill, "Regnum Caelorum:
Chiliasm, Non-Chialism and the Doctrine of the 'Intermediate State in the Early Church,'" unpub. dissertation Cambridge, 1988; R. Fowler White, "Reexamining
the Evidence for Recapulation in Rev. 20:1-10," *WTJ* 51
(1989): 319-44; Harold W. Hoehner, "Evidence from
Revelation 20," in *A Case for Premillennialism: A New
Consensus*, ed. by Donald K. Campbell and Jeffrey L.
Townsend (Chicago: Moody Press, 1992), 235-62;
DLNT, 738-47. ◆ **3 ἔβαλεν** aor. ind. act. βάλλω (# 965)
to cast. **ἔκλεισεν** aor. ind. act. κλείω (# 3091) to shut up,

to lock. Aor. points to the completed action. **ἐσφράγισεν** aor. ind. act. σφραγίζω (# 5381) to seal. The sealing would indicate the authoritative placing of a seal so that no one is allowed in or out (Matt. 27:66). The purp. of sealing the entrance to a prison was to prevent any attempt at escape or rescue passing unobserved (Swete). The activity of Satan is completely removed from the earth a thousand years (Walvoord). **πλανήσῃ** aor. subj. act. πλανάω (# 4414) to lead astray, to deceive. Subj. w. ἵνα (# 2671) could be used either in a purp. or result cl. **τελεσθῇ** aor. subj. pass. τελέω (# 5464) to complete. Subj. in a temp. cl. **δεῖ** (# 1256) pres. ind. act. it is necessary, impersonal w. acc. and inf., expressing a logical necessity. **λυθῆναι** aor. pass. inf. λύω (# 3395) to loose, to release. The release will be brief in comparison w. the captivity (Swete). This indicates the completion of the 1000 years. ◆ **4 εἶδον** aor. ind. act. ὁράω (# 3972) to see. **ἐκάθισαν** aor. ind. act. καθίζω (# 2767) to take one's seat, to sit. **κρίμα** (# 3210) judgment. **ἐδόθη** aor. ind. pass. δίδωμι (# 1443) to give, to grant. Theol. pass. indicating that God is the one who gave. **πεπελεκισμένων** perf. pass. part. (subst.) πελεκίζω (# 4282) to cut one's head off w. a double-edge ax, to behead. The ax was the instrument of execution in the Roman republic (Mounce). **προσεκύνησαν** aor. ind. act. προσκυνέω (# 4686) to worship. **θηρίον** (# 2536) wild beast, monster (s. 13:1). **εἰκών** (# 1635) image. **ἔλαβον** aor. ind. act. λαμβάνω (# 3284) to take, to receive. **χάραγμα** (# 5916) brand, mark. **μέτωπον** (# 3587) forehead, brow. **ἔζησαν** aor. ind. act. ζάω (# 2509) to come to live. **ἐβασίλευσαν** aor. ind. act. βασιλεύω (# 996) to be king, to rule, to reign. Aor. could be ingressive aor., "they began to reign." The rabbis made a distinction between the days of the Messiah and the eternal kingdom, and debated the length of the days of the Messiah. Some said 600 years, others said 1000 years, others 2000 or 7000 years; but a very old tradition going back to Rabbi Eliezer Hyrkanus (ca. A.D. 90) or earlier, taught that the rule of the Messiah was 1000 years (SB, 3:824-27; Lohse; TS, 681; b. Sanh. 99a). ◆ **5 λοιπός** (# 3370) rest. These were the wicked who did not have a part in the first resurrection (Thomas). **ἔζησαν** aor. ind. act. ζάω (# 2409) to come to live. **τελεσθῇ** aor. subj. pass. τελέω (# 5464) to complete. **ἡ ἀνάστασις ἡ πρώτη** (# 414; 4755) the first resurrection. Jewish teaching claimed there would be a resurrection of those in the land of Israel, and after that a general resurrection for the Last Judgement (SB, 3:827-30). The idea here seems to correspond, to some extent, to the Jewish view, where the first resurrection refers to the resurrection of the righteous (Thomas; Johnson; DLNT, 1015-20). ◆ **6 μακάριος** (# 3421) happy, blessed. **ἔχων** pres. act. part. (subst.) ἔχω (# 2400) to have. **ὁ δεύτερος θάνατος** (# 1311; 2505) the second death. The second death may be spiritual death beyond physical death (Thomas). Rabbinical teaching said

some would be excluded from the resurrection and be delivered over to eternal destruction, which amounted to the second death (SB, 3:830-31). **ἔχει** pres. ind. act. ἔχω (# 2400) to have. **ἔσονται** fut. ind. mid. (dep.) εἰμί (# 1639) to be. **βασιλεύσουσιν** fut. ind. act. βασιλεύω (# 996) to rule (s.v. 4). ◆ **7 ὅταν** (# 4020) w. subj., when. **τελεσθῇ** aor. subj. pass. τελέω (# 5464) to complete. Subj. in an indef. temp. cl. **λυθήσεται** fut. ind. pass. λύω (# 3395) to loosen (s.v. 3). ◆ **8 ἐξελεύσεται** fut. ind. mid. (dep.) ἐξέρχομαι (# 2002) to go out. **πλανῆσαι** aor. act. inf. πλανάω (# 4414) to lead astray, to deceive. Inf. used to express purp. **γωνία** (# 1224) corner. **τὸν Γὼγ καὶ Μαγώγ** (# 1223; 2779; 3408) Gog and Magog. It seems that the designations refer to the enemies of God (Thomas). For a discussion of Jewish views of the names Gog and Magog and the activity before, during, and after the days of the Messiah s. SB, 3:813-40; ABD, 2:1056; DDD, 708-11, 999-1001. **συναγαγεῖν** aor. act. inf. συνάγω (# 5251) to lead together, to gather, to assemble. Inf. to express purp. **πόλεμος** (# 4483) war. **ἀριθμός** (# 750) number. **ἄμμος** (# 302) sand. ◆ **9 ἀνέβησαν** aor. ind. act. ἀναβαίνω (# 326) to go up, to ascend. **πλάτος** (# 4424) breadth. **ἐκύκλευσαν** aor. ind. act. κυκλεύω (# 3238) to encircle. **παρεμβολή** (# 4213) camp. The word signifies either a camp or an army marching or engaged in battle (Swete). **ἠγαπημένην** perf. pass. part. ἀγαπάω (# 26) to love. **κατέβη** aor. ind. act. καταβαίνω (# 2849) to come down. **πῦρ** (# 4786) fire. **κατέφαγεν** aor. ind. act. κατεσθίω (# 2983) to eat up, to consume completely. Prep. in compound is perfective. ◆ **10 διάβολος** (# 1333) devil (DDD, 463-73). **πλανῶν** pres. act. part. πλανάω (# 4414) to deceive. Part. is used here as a noun: "the deceiver," "the one who deceives them." **ἐβλήθη** aor. ind. pass. βάλλω (# 965) to throw, to cast. **λίμνη** (# 3349) lake. **πυρός** gen. sing. πῦρ (# 4786) fire. Gen. of description. **θεῖον** (# 2520) brimstone, sulphur. **ὅπου** (# 3963) where? Here it is used as a rel. pron. **ψευδοπροφήτης** (# 6021) false prophet. **βασανισθήσονται** fut. ind. pass. βασανίζω (# 989) to torment, to torture, to cause pain. ◆ **11 εἶδον** aor. ind. act. ὁράω (# 3972) to see. **λευκός** (# 3328) white. The great white throne marks the final judgment of the unbeliever and takes the place after the millennial reign of Christ and the judgement of Satan. The absolute purity of this supreme court is symbolized by the color of the throne (Swete). **καθήμενον** pres. mid. (dep.) part. κάθημαι (# 2764) to sit. **ἔφυγεν** aor. ind. act. φεύγω (# 5771) to flee. Earth and heaven flee away before the awesome grandeur of God seated upon the throne of judgment (Mounce). **εὑρέθη** aor. ind. pass. εὑρίσκω (# 2351) to find. ◆ **12 εἶδον** aor. ind. act. ὁράω (# 3972) to see. **ἑστῶτας** perf. act. part. ἵστημι (# 2705) to stand. **βιβλία** (# 1046) nom. pl. βιβλίον book. **ἠνοίχθησαν** aor. ind. pass. ἀνοίγω (# 487) to open. **ἐκρίθησαν** aor. ind. pass. κρίνω (# 3212) to judge. **γεγραμμένων** perf. pass. part. γράφω (# 1211) to write.

Perf. indicates "that which stands written." The sentence of the judge is not arbitrary; it rests upon written evidence; the books that were opened contain, so it seems, a record of the deeds of every human being who came up for judgment (Swete). ◆ **13 ἔδωκεν** aor. ind. act. δίδωμι (# 1443) to give. **ᾅδης** (# 87) Hades, the grave, the underworld as the place of the dead (s. Rev. 1:18). **ἐκρίθησαν** aor. ind. pass. κρίνω (# 3212) to judge. **ἕκαστος** (# 1667) each one. ◆ **14 ἐβλήθησαν** aor. ind. pass. βάλλω (# 965) to throw. **λίμνη** (# 3349) lake. **πυρός** gen. sing. πῦρ (# 4786) fire. Enoch sees a place that was burning and flaming and was a pain to look at. He was told that this was the prison house of the angels (1 Enoch 21:7-10).

Revelation 21

◆ **1 εἶδον** aor. ind. act. ὁράω (# 3972) to see. **ἀπῆλθαν** aor. ind. act. ἀπέρχομαι (# 599) to go away, to depart, to pass away. In rabbinical literature some taught that the world would be renovated and made new so that it would return to its original state after creation, cleansed from sin and evil. Others taught that the earth would return to the original chaos and would then be recreated w. a new existence. Others taught that the earth would be completely destroyed and the new heaven and new earth would be a totally new creation (SB, 3:842-47; Moore, *Judaism*, 2:338ff). At this time the purpose and plan of God's creating mankind will be fulfilled through redemption. Created in the image of God, mankind is to have unbroken fellowship w. God, to rule the earth, and to be God's representative on earth. Sin, however, did not allow these purposes to be completely realized; but the Messiah came as the Redeemer (גֹּאֵל, go'el, s. TDOT; NIDOTTE), and paid the price for the release from the slavery of sin to restore the broken fellowship. Now He has defeated the enemies of God and restored the earth to God's complete possession and provided for mankind to be the true representative of God on the new earth. ◆ **2 εἶδον** aor. ind. act. ὁράω (# 3972) to see. **Ἰερουσαλὴμ καινήν** (# 2647; 2785) New Jerusalem. For the Jewish writing found in the DSS describing the New Jerusalem or heavenly Jerusalem s. DSST, 129-35; AT, 214-22; MPAT, 46-65. **καταβαίνουσαν** pres. act. part. (adj.) καταβαίνω (# 2849) to come down, to descend. **ἡτοιμασμένην** perf. pass. part. ἑτοιμάζω (# 2286) to prepare. Perf. pass. part. indicates "to have been prepared and to stand ready." **νύμφη** (# 3811) bride. **κεκοσμημένην** perf. pass. part. κοσμέω (# 3175) to make orderly, to put in order, to adorn, to decorate, to make beautiful or attractive (BAGD). In preparation for the marriage and the arrival of the groom the bride was bathed and oiled, perfumed, her hair was fixed, and she was adorned w. her wedding garment. For marriage preparations s. JPF, 2:752-60; SB, 1:500-517; 2:373-99. ◆ **3**

ἤκουσα aor. ind. act. ἀκούω (# 201) to hear. **λεγούσης** pres. act. part. λέγω (# 3306) to say. **ἰδού** aor. ind. act. ὁράω (# 3972) to see. **σκηνή** (# 5008) tent, tabernacle. **σκηνώσει** fut. ind. act. σκηνόω (# 5012) to live in a tent, to tabernacle. The word indicates the abiding presence of God (Mounce). **ἔσονται** fut. ind. mid. (dep.) εἰμί (# 1639) to be. ◆ **4 ἐξαλείψει** fut. ind. act. ἐξαλείφω (# 1981) to wipe away, to wipe out. Predictive fut. giving a promise. **δάκρυον** (# 1232) tear. **πᾶν δάκρυον** every individual single tear. This would be tears of sorrow, not tears of joy. **ἔσται** fut. ind. mid. (dep.) εἰμί (# 1639) to be. **πένθος** (# 4292) sorrow, mourning. **κραυγή** (# 3199) shouting, outcry, crying in grief or anxiety (MM). **πόνος** (# 4506) pain. **ἀπῆλθαν** aor. ind. act. ἀπέρχομαι (# 599) to go away, to pass away. Aor. w. prep. in compound is perfective, "completely gone." ◆ **5 εἶπεν** aor. ind. act. λέγω (# 3306) to say. **καθήμενος** pres. mid. (dep.) part. κάθημαι (# 2764) to sit. **ἰδού** aor. imp. act. ὁράω (# 3972) to see. **ποιῶ** pres. ind. act. ποιέω (# 4472) to do. **γράψον** aor. imp. act. γράφω (# 1211) to write. ◆ **6 εἶπεν** aor. ind. act. λέγω (# 3306) to say. **γέγοναν** perf. ind. act. γίνομαι (# 1181) to become. "They have come to pass." Not only are the sayings mentioned in v. 5 faithful and true, but they have come to pass and their results continue on in the fut. **ἀρχή** (# 794) beginning. **τέλος** (# 5465) end. **διψῶντι** pres. act. part. (subst.) διψάω (# 1498) to thirst, to be thirsty. **δώσω** fut. ind. act. δίδωμι (# 1443) to give. **πηγή** (# 4380) spring, fountain. **δωρεάν** (# 1562) freely, without cost. In the arid climate of Palestine a spring of cool water would be a vivid symbol of refreshment and satisfaction (Mounce). ◆ **7 νικῶν** pres. act. part. (subst.) νικάω (# 3771) to be a victor, to conquer, to overcome. **κληρονομήσει** fut. ind. act. κληρονομέω (# 3099) to inherit. **ἔσται** fut. ind. mid. (dep.) εἰμί (# 1639) to be. ◆ **8 δειλός** (# 1264) cowardly. **ἄπιστος** (# 603) unfaithful, unbelieving. **ἐβδελυγμένοις** perf. pass. part. (subst.) βδελύσσομαι (# 1009) to pollute, to defile, to make detestable, to commit abomination; perf. pass. part., "to be detestable." The word indicates persons whose very natures have been saturated w. the abominations they practiced in their lifetime. The context suggests that in this case the abominations are not merely idolatrous acts, but the monstrous and unnatural vices of heathendom (Swete). **φονεύς** (# 5838) murderer. **πόρνος** (# 4521) immoral person, one who practices sexual immorality. **φαρμακός** (# 5761) one who mixes and uses drugs either for sorcery or magic practices (s. 9:21). **εἰδωλολάτρης** (# 1629) one who worships idols, idolater. **ψευδέσιν** dat. pl. ψευδής (# 6014) liar. The dat. pls. are indir. objs., dependant on the vb. δώσω in v. 6; or they are dat. of disadvantage. **μέρος** (# 3538) part. **λίμνη** (# 3349) lake. **καιομένη** pres. pass. part. καίομαι (# 2794) to burn; pass., to be burning. **πυρί** dat. sing. πῦρ (# 4786) fire. **θεῖον** (# 2520) brimstone, sulphur. Enoch saw a similar fearful place, a great burning fire and Ura'el, one of the holy angels asked him why he was so afraid. Enoch responds, "I am frightened because of this terrible place and the spectacle of this painful place"; and the angel replies, "This place is a prison house of the angels; they are detained here forever" (1 Enoch 21:7-10). ◆ **9 ἦλθεν** aor. ind. act. ἔρχομαι (# 2262) to come, to go. **ἐχόντων** pres. act. part. ἔχω (# 2400) to have. **φιάλη** (# 5786) bowl. **γεμόντων** pres. act. part. γέμω (# 1154) to be full of. **πληγή** (# 4435) blow, wound, plague. **ἔσχατος** (# 2274) last. **ἐλάλησεν** aor. ind. act. λαλέω (# 3281) to speak. **λέγων** pres. act. part. λέγω (# 3306) to say. **δεῦρο** (# 1306) come here. **δείξω** fut. ind. act. δείκνυμι (# 1259) to show. **νύμφη** (# 3811) bride. **ἀρνίον** (# 768) lamb. ◆ **10 ἀπήνεγκέν** aor. ind. act. ἀποφέρω (# 708) to carry away. **ἔδειξέν** aor. ind. act. δείκνυμι (# 1259) to show. **καταβαίνουσαν** aor. act. part. καταβαίνω (# 2849) to descend, to come down. ◆ **11 ἔχουσαν** pres. act. part. ἔχω (# 2400) to have. **δόξα** (# 1518) glory, brilliance. The word refers to the shining radiance coming from the presence and glory of God–the Shekinah (Mounce; TDNT; NIDNTT; TLNT; TS, 37-65). **φωστήρ** (# 5891) radiance, luminary. The word means something in which light is concentrated and from there radiates (Swete). **τιμιωτάτῳ** superl. τίμιος (# 5508) precious, costly; superl., extremely expensive, very expensive. **ἰάσπιδι** dat. sing. ἴασπις (# 2618) jasper. In antiquity the designation "jasper" was used for any opaque precious stone. The point of the comparison is the brilliance and sparkle of a gem, and the reference could be to a diamond (Mounce). **κρυσταλλίζοντι** pres. act. part. (adj.) κρυσταλλίζω (# 3222) to sparkle and shimmer like a crystal. ◆ **12 ἔχουσα** pres. act. part. ἔχω (# 2400) to have. **τεῖχος** (# 5446) wall. **μέγας** (# 3489) great, mighty. **πυλών** (# 4784) gate. **ἐπιγεγραμμένα** perf. pass. part. (adj.) ἐπιγράφω (# 2108) to write upon, to inscribe upon. **φυλή** (# 5876) tribe. ◆ **13 ἀνατολή** (# 424) rising, east (s. Matt. 2:1). **βορρᾶς** (# 1080) north wind, north. **νότος** (# 3803) south, south wind. **δυσμός** (# 1553) going down, west. ◆ **14 ἔχων** pres. act. part. ἔχω (# 2400) to have. **θεμέλιος** (# 2529) foundation. Each foundation was probably a stout oblong block like the stones that may still be seen in the lower rows of the Herodian masonry in Jerusalem (Ford). ◆ **15 λαλῶν** pres. act. part. λαλέω (# 3281) to speak. **εἶχεν** impf. ind. act. ἔχω (# 2400) to have. **μέτρον** (# 3586) measure. **κάλαμος** (# 2812) reed, rod (s. 11:1). **χρυσοῦς** (# 5991) golden. **μετρήσῃ** aor. subj. act. μετρέω (# 3582) to measure. Subj. w. ἵνα (# 2671) in a purp. cl. ◆ **16 τετράγωνος** (# 5481) square, four corners. **κεῖται** pres. ind. mid. (dep.) κεῖμαι (# 3023) to lie. **μῆκος** (# 3501) length. **πλάτος** (# 4424) width. **ἐμέτρησεν** aor. ind. act. μετρέω (# 3582) to measure. **στάδιον** (# 5084) stadion, furlong. A stadion is about 607 English feet; thus the city would be about 1,400 miles in each direction (Mounce). **ὕψος** (# 5737)

height. **ἴσος** (# 2698) equal. ◆ **17 ἐμέτρησεν** aor. ind. act. μετρέω (# 3582) to measure. **πηχῶν** gen. pl. πῆχυς (# 4388) cubit. A cubit is roughly the length of a man's forearm and 144 cubits would be 14 miles in height (Mounce). ◆ **18 ἐνδώμησις** (# 1908) structure, building (Ford; Mounce). **καθαρός** (# 2754) pure, clean. **ὕαλος** (# 5613) glass. ◆ **19 κεκοσμημένοι** perf. pass. part. (adj.) κοσμέω (# 3175) to adorn. Perf. indicates the abiding quality. **ἴασπις** (# 2618) jasper. **σάπφιρος** (# 4913) sapphire. This is a blue transparent precious stone (Ford). **χαλκηδών** (# 5907) agate, chalcedony. This gem is taken to be of a green color (Charles; Ford; BAGD). **σμάραγδος** (# 5040) emerald. This is a bright green transparent precious stone, the most valued variety of beryl (Ford). ◆ **20 πέμπτος** (# 4286) fifth. **σαρδόνυξ** (# 4918) onyx, sardonyx. This was a layered stone of red and white, prized for its use in making cameos (Mounce). **σάρδιον** (# 4917) sardus, carnelian. This was a blood-red stone commonly used for engraving (Mounce; Ford). **χρυσόλιθος** (# 5994) gold stone, topaz, chrysolite. The ancients seemed to have used this term for the yellow topaz (Ford; Charles). **ὄγδοος** (# 3838) eight. **βήρυλλος** (# 1039) beryl. This was a green stone ranging from transparent sea-green to opaque blue (Ford; Mounce). **ἔνατος** (# 1888) ninth. **τοπάζιον** (# 5535) topaz, a greenish yellow or gold. In ancient times it was often used in the making of seals and gems (Ford; Mounce). **χρυσόπρασος** (# 5995) chrysoprase. This is an apple green, finely grained hornstone, a variety of quartz, highly translucent (Ford). **ἑνδέκατος** (# 1895) eleventh. **ὑάκινθος** (# 5611) jacinth. It was a bluish-purple stone similar to the modern sapphire (Mounce; BAGD). **δωδέκατος** (# 1558) twelfth. **ἀμέθυστος** (# 287) amethyst, a variety of quartz, in color clear, transparent purple or bluish-violet. It got its name as an antidote for drunkenness (Mounce; Ford). For a description of these stones s. NBD, 631-34; IBD, 2:898-905; Pliny, NH, 27: N. Hillyer, "Precious Stones in the Apocalypse," NIDNTT, 3:395-98; William W. Reader, "The Twelve Jewels of Revelation 21:19-20: Tradition History and Modern Interpretations," *JBL* 100 (1981): 433-57; NW 2, ii:1656-65. ◆ **21 μαργαρίτης** (# 3449) pearl. **ἀνά** (# 324) each one, distributive use of the prep. **ἦν** impf. ind. act. εἰμί (# 1639) to be. **πλατεῖα** (# 4423) street, broad street. **διαυγής** (# 1420) transparent, clear. ◆ **22 εἶδον** aor. ind. act. ὁράω (# 3972) to see. **ναός** (# 3724) temple, sanctuary. **παντοκράτωρ** (# 4120) almighty (s. 1:8). **ἀρνίον** (# 768) lamb. ◆ **23 σελήνη** (# 4943) moon. **φαίνωσιν** aor. subj. act. φαίνω (# 5743) to shine. Subj. w. ἵνα (# 2671) in a purp. cl. **ἐφώτισεν** aor. ind. act. φωτίζω (# 5894) to illuminate, to cause to shine, to give light. **λύχνος** (# 3394) lamp. ◆ **24 περιπατήσουσιν** fut. ind. act. περιπατέω (# 4344) to walk about. **ἔθνος** (# 1620) nation. **φέρουσιν** pres. ind. act. φέρω (# 5770) to carry, to bring. ◆ **25 οὐ μή** (# 4024; 3590) never in any wise.

κλεισθῶσιν aor. subj. pass. κλείω (# 3091) to close, to lock, to shut. The gates would be closed for security at night (Ford). One is reminded of the Isaianic declaration concerning the restored Jerusalem, "your gates shall be open continually" (Isa. 60:11) (Mounce). The Roman god Janus was to guard the door of a house or building (KP, 2:1311-14; OCD, 561; LAW, 2:1357). **νύξ** (# 3816) night. **ἔσται** fut. ind. mid. (dep.) εἰμί (# 1639) to be. ◆ **26 οἴσουσιν** fut. ind. act. φέρω (# 5770) to carry. ◆ **27 εἰσέλθῃ** aor. subj. act. εἰσέρχομαι (# 1656) to go in, to come in. **κοινός** (# 3123) common, profane. **ποιῶν** pres. act. part. ποιέω (# 4472) to do. **βδέλυγμα** (# 1007) that which is detestable, abomination. **ψεῦδος** (# 6022) liar. **εἰ μή** (# 1623; 3590) except. **γεγραμμένοι** perf. pass. part. γράφω (# 1211) to write. Perf. indicates the abiding results or condition. **βιβλίον** (# 1047) book. **ζωή** (# 2437) life. Gen. here could be gen. of content or obj. gen., the book which leads to life. **ἀρνίον** (# 768) lamb. Poss. gen.

Revelation 22

◆ **1 ἔδειξεν** aor. ind. act. δείκνυμι (# 1259) to show. **ποταμός** (# 4532) river. **λαμπρός** (# 3287) brilliant, bright. **κρύσταλλον** (# 3223) crystal. **ἐκπορευόμενον** pres. mid. (dep.) part. ἐκπορεύομαι (# 1744) to go out. **ἀρνίον** (# 768) lamb. ◆ **2 πλατεῖα** (# 4423) wide street. Probably one is meant to think of one main broad street in contrast to the narrow streets in Eastern cities (Ford). **ἐντεῦθεν** (# 1949) from here. **ἐκεῖθεν** (# 1696) from there. **ξύλον** (# 3833) tree. For Enoch's vision of various trees, one being the tree of wisdom, which was the tree that Adam and Eve ate from in the Garden of Eden s. 1 Enoch 29-32. **ποιοῦν** pres. act. part. (adj.) ποιέω (# 4472) to make, to bear. Pres. indicates a repeated action. **δώδεκα** (# 1557) twelve. **μήν** (# 3604) month. **ἕκαστος** (# 1667) each. **ἀποδιδοῦν** pres. act. part. ἀποδίδωμι (# 625) to give back, to give, to render. **φύλλον** (# 5877) leaf. **θεραπεία** (# 2542) healing. Since sickness has been banned, this must refer to a promoting of the nations as an ongoing service in the new creation (Thomas). ◆ **3 κατάθεμα** (# 2873) curse. The word may refer to that which is cursed (Swete). **ἔσται** fut. ind. mid. (dep.) εἰμί (# 1639) to be. **λατρεύσουσιν** fut. ind. act. λατρεύω (# 3302) to worship, to worship by serving. ◆ **4 ὄψονται** fut. ind. mid. (dep.) ὁράω (# 3972) to see. **μετώπων** (# 3587) forehead, brow. ◆ **5 ἔσται** fut. ind. mid. (dep.) εἰμί (# 1639) to be. **ἔχουσιν** pres. ind. act. ἔχω (# 2400) to have. **λύχνος** (# 3394) lamp. **φωτίσει** fut. ind. act. φωτίζω (# 5894) to illuminate, to shine, to give light. **βασιλεύσουσιν** fut. ind. act. βασιλεύω (# 996) to be king, to rule as king, to reign. For a discussion of the new Jerusalem s. DLNT, 564-65. ◆ **6 εἶδον** aor. ind. act. ὁράω (# 3972) to see. **ἀληθινός** (# 240) true, genuine. **ἀπέστειλεν** aor. ind. act. ἀποστέλλω (# 690) to send, to send as an official authoritative representative. **δεῖξαι** aor. act. inf. δείκνυμι (# 1259) to show. Inf. used to express

purp. **δεῖ** (# 1256) pres. ind. act. it is necessary. **γενέσθαι** aor. mid. (dep.) inf. γίνομαι (# 1181) to happen, to become, to come to pass. **ἐν τάχει** (# 1877; 5443) quickly. The prep. phrase is used adverbially. ◆ **7 ἰδού** aor. imp. act. ὁράω (# 3972) to see. **ἔρχομαι** (# 2262) pres. ind. mid. (dep.) to come. **ταχύς** (# 5444) quickly. **μακάριος** (# 3421) happy, blessed. **τηρῶν** pres. act. part. τηρέω (# 5498) to keep. Pres. looks at a continual keeping. **βιβλίον** (# 1046) book. ◆ **8 κἀγὼ Ἰωάννης** (# 2743; 2722) "and I John." John now attests that he has actually heard and seen all the things recorded in the book (Mounce). **ἀκούων** pres. act. part. ἀκούω (# 201) to hear. **βλέπων** pres. act. part. βλέπω (# 1063) to see. **ἤκουσα** aor. ind. act. ἀκούω (# 201) to hear. **ἔβλεψα** aor. ind. act. βλέπω (# 1063) to see. **ἔπεσα** aor. ind. act. πίπτω (# 4406) to fall down. **προσκυνῆσαι** aor. act. inf. προσκυνέω (# 4686) to worship. Inf. to express purp. **δεικνύοντός** pres. act. part. δείκνυμι (# 1259) to show. ◆ **9 λέγει** pres. ind. act. λέγω (# 3306) to say. **ὅρα** pres. imp. act. ὁράω (# 3972) to see. For this construction and the meaning s. 19:10. **σύνδουλος** (# 5281) fellow slave. **τηρούντων** pres. act. part. τηρέω (# 5498) to keep (s.v. 7). **προσκύνησον** aor. imp. act. προσκυνέω (# 4686) to worship (s. Rev. 5:14). ◆ **10 σφραγίσῃς** aor. subj. act. σφραγίζω (# 5381) to seal. For the meaning of sealing s. Rev. 5:1. The neg. **μή** (# 3590) w. aor. subj. is used in a neg. command or prohibition (GGBB, 469). **προφητεία** (# 4735) prophecy. **καιρός** (# 2789) time, appointed time. **ἐγγύς** (# 1584) near. ◆ **11 ἀδικῶν** pres. act. part. ἀδικέω (# 92) to do injustice, to do unrighteousness. Part. used as a noun indicating he whose habit it is to do wrong-"the wrongdoer"–w. special reference perhaps to the persecutor (Swete). **ἀδικησάτω** aor. imp. act. ἀδικέω (# 92) to do unrighteousness. **ῥυπαρός** (# 4865) dirty, filthy. **ῥυπανθήτω** aor. imp. pass. ῥυπαίνω (# 4862) to soil, to make dirty, to defile (BAGD). The filthy disregard purity of life or even common decency. Aors. here indicate the permanent state into which these have entered; there is henceforth no break in the downward course, which is viewed as a single act (Swete). **ποιησάτω** aor. imp. act. ποιέω (# 4472) to do; here in the sense of act or practice. The actions demonstrate the character of the person. **ἁγιασθήτω** aor. imp. act. ἁγιάζω (# 39) to make holy, to sanctify, to set apart. (NIDNTT; TDNT; EWNT). ◆ **12 ἰδού** aor. imp. act. ὁράω (# 3972) to see. **ἔρχομαι** (# 2262) pres. ind. mid. (dep.) to come. **ταχύς** (# 5444) quickly. **μισθός** (# 3635) reward, wage, pay. **ἀποδοῦναι** aor. act. inf. ἀποδίδωμι (# 625) to give, to pay, to render. Inf. used to express purp. ◆ **13 ἔσχατος** (# 2274) last. **ἀρχή** (# 794) beginning. **τέλος** (# 5465) end, completion, goal (s. Rev. 1:8). ◆ **14 πλύνοντες** pres. act. part. πλύνω (# 4459) to wash. **στολάς** acc. pl. στολή (# 5124) robe. The word refers to a long flowing stately robe (Trench, *Synonyms*, 186; TDNT). **ἵνα** (# 2671) that, in order that. The word is used to introduce a purp. cl. expressed first by the fut. ind. rather than by the aor. subj. (RWP). **ἔσται** fut. ind. mid. (dep.) εἰμί (# *1639*) to be. **ξύλον** (# *3833*) tree. **πυλών** (# *4784*) gate. **εἰσέλθωσιν** aor. subj. act. εἰσέρχομαι (# *1656*) to go into, to enter. ◆ **15 ἔξω** (# *2032*) outside, without. **κύνες** nom. pl. κυνών (# *3264*) dog (s. Phil. 3:2). **φαρμακός** (# *5761*) one who mixes drugs either for magic or for sorcery (s. 9:21). **πόρνος** (# *4521*) immoral person, one who commits sexual acts of immorality. **φονεύς** (# *5838*) murderer. **εἰδωλολάτρης** (# *1629*) idol worshiper. **φιλῶν** pres. act. part. φιλέω (# *5797*) to be fond of, to love. **ποιῶν** pres. act. part. ποιέω (# *4472*) to do. ◆ **16 ἔπεμψα** aor. ind. act. πέμπω (# *4287*) to send. **μαρτυρῆσαι** aor. act. inf. μαρτυρέω (# *3455*) to witness, to testify (NTCW). Inf. to express purp. **ῥίζα** (# *4844*) root (s. 5:5). **ἀστήρ** (# *843*) star. **λαμπρός** (# *3287*) bright, shining, brilliant. **πρωϊνός** (# *4748*) morning, star, Venus. (s. 2 Pet. 1:19). ◆ **17 πνεῦμα** (# *4460*) spirit. **νύμφη** (# *3811*) bride. The Spirit is the Holy Spirit and the bride is the church. It is the testimony of the church empowered by the Holy Spirit that constitutes the great evangelizing force of this age (Mounce). **λέγουσιν** pres. ind. act. λέγω (# *3306*) to say. **ἔρχου** pres. imp. mid. (dep.) ἔρχομαι (# *2262*) to go, to come. **ἀκούων** pres. act. part. ἀκούω (# *201*) to hear. **εἰπάτω** aor. imp. act. λέγω (# *3306*) to say. **διψῶν** pres. act. part. διψάω (# *1498*) to thirst, to be thirsty. **ἐρχέσθω** pres. imp. pass. (dep.) ἔρχομαι (# *2262*) to come. Imp. as invitation and permission, "let him come." **θέλων** pres. act. part. θέλω (# *2527*) to desire, to want to. **λαβέτω** aor. imp. act. λαμβάνω (# *3284*) to take, to receive. **δωρεάν** (# *1562*) without cause, freely, without charge. ◆ **18 μαρτυρῶ** pres. ind. act. μαρτυρέω (# *3455*) to bear witness, to testify. The speaker is still surely Jesus. He has borne testimony through the book by His angel,

and now He bears it in person (Swete). **ἀκούοντι** pres. act. part. ἀκούω (# *201*) to hear. **προφητεία** (# *4735*) prophecy (Thomas; Robert L. Thomas, "The Spiritual Gift of Prophecy in Rev. 22:18," *JETS* 32 [1989]: 201-16; DLNT, 970-77). **βιβλίον** (# *1046*) book. **ἐπιθῇ** aor. subj. act. ἐπιτίθημι (# *2202*) to place upon, to place in addition, to add to. For the meaning of the prep. in compound, s. MH, 312f. Subj. w. **ἐάν** (# *1569*) in a 3rd. class cond. cl. which views the cond. as a possibility. **ἐπιθήσει** fut. ind. act. ἐπιτίθημι (# *2202*). **πληγή** (# *4435*) blow, wound, plague. **γεγραμμένας** perf. pass. part. γράφω (# *1211*) to write. Perf. indicates the continuing authority of that which was written (MM; TDNT). ◆ **19 ἀφέλῃ** aor. subj. act. ἀφαιρέω (# *904*) to take away, to take away from, to deduct from. For examples in the papyri s. MM; Preisigke. **μέρος** (# *3538*) part. **ξύλον** (# *3833*) tree. ◆ **20 λέγει** pres. ind. act. λέγω (# *3306*) to say. **μαρτυρῶν** pres. act. part. μαρτυρέω (# *3455*) to witness (s.v. 18). **ναί** (# *3721*) yes, yes (s. Rev. 1:7). **ἔρχομαι** (# *2262*) pres. ind. mid. (dep.) to come. Pres. used to describe a fut. event to emphasize the certainty or immediacy (GGBB, 536). **ταχύς** (# *5444*) adv., quickly, soon. **ἀμήν** (# *297*) amen (s. Rev. 1:7; EWNT). **ἔρχου** pres. imp. mid. (dep.) ἔρχομαι (# *2262*) to come. Imp. as a petition or prayer, or both. ◆ **21 χάρις** (# *5921*) grace. The benediction is pronounced upon all who have listened to the book as it was read aloud in the churches of Asia (Mounce). Grace is the only ground on which any can stand for eternity (Govett). **πάντων** gen. pl. πᾶς (# *4246*) all; "with all." Through clouds and sunshine, by night and by day, in all times and circumstances, His unfailing grace is their support and strength. It is grace from beginning to end, from otherwise hopeless ruin till complete redemption (Scott).

For additional textbooks on New Testament Greek look for these outstanding titles:

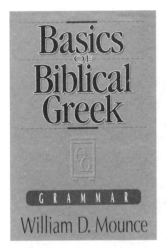

Basics of Biblical Greek

Grammar and Workbook

William D. Mounce

Basics of Biblical Greek takes an integrated approach to teaching and learning New Testament Greek. Students immediately start working with verses from the New Testament, tying the lessons directly to the biblical text. It makes learning Greek a natural process and shows from the very beginning how an understanding of Greek helps in understanding the New Testament. Written from the student's perspective, this approach combines the best of the deductive and inductive methods. The workbook features a parsing section and is usefully perforated with hole-punched pages for loose-leaf binders.

Grammar (Hardcover): 0-310-59800-1
Workbook (Softcover): 0-310-40091-0

Greek Grammar Beyond the Basics

An Exegetical Syntax of the New Testament

Daniel B. Wallace

Depth, accuracy, relevancy, and up-to-date presentation make this intermediate Greek grammar the finest available—equipping students of the New Testament with the skills they need to do biblical exegesis. Written by a world-class authority on Greek grammar, it links grammar and exegesis to provide today's student, expositor, or professor with solid exegetical and linguistic foundations.

Greek Grammar Beyond the Basics integrates the technical requirements for proper Greek interpretation with the actual interests and needs of Bible students. It is the first truly exegetical syntax in which the author constantly has an eye on the role of syntax in exegesis.

Hardcover: 0-310-37340-9

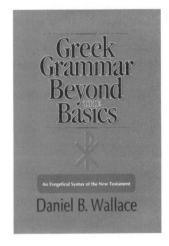

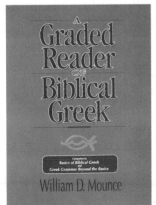

A Graded Reader of Biblical Greek

Companion to Basics of Biblical Greek and Greek Grammar Beyond the Basics

William D. Mounce

This multipurpose volume serves as a companion to *Basics of Biblical Greek, Greek Grammar Beyond the Basics,* and *Biblical Greek Exegesis.* It contains annotated readings from the New Testament designed for second-year Greek students. Sections from the Greek New Testament are presented in order of increasing difficulty, and unfamiliar forms and constructions are annotated.

Softcover: 0-310-20582-4

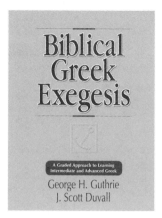

Biblical Greek Exegesis

A Graded Approach to Learning Intermediate and Advanced Greek

George H. Guthrie and J. Scott Duvall

Biblical Greek Exegesis teaches syntax and exegesis using examples from the New Testament text rather than from textbook sentence constructions. This real-world approach retains student interest by relating their Greek training directly to their future ministry.

Using the first nine New Testament sections of William D. Mounce's *Graded Reader of Biblical Greek*, the first section of *Biblical Greek Exegesis* asks the student to translate, identify syntactical elements in the text, and diagram the text. The second part of the book takes the student through a twelve-step process of exegesis, based largely on a grammatical and semantic analysis of the text, and concludes by helping students prepare preaching/teaching outlines on the various New Testament passages.

Softcover: 0-310-21246-4

The Morphology of Biblical Greek

A Companion to Basics of Biblical Greek and
An Analytical Lexicon to the Greek New Testament

William D. Mounce

The Morphology of Biblical Greek shows how Greek word forms (even the most "irregular" ones) are derived by means of a limited set of rules. It explains why Greek words "do what they do" in a way that second-year Greek students can understand. It also includes paradigms, principal parts, and an index of all words in the New Testament with their morphological category.

Hardcover: 0-310-41040-1

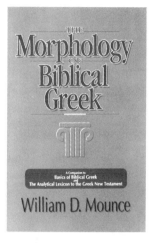

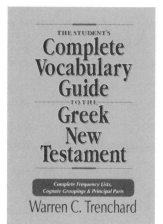

The Student's Complete Vocabulary Guide to the Greek New Testament

Complete Frequency Lists, Cognate Groupings, and Principal Parts

Warren C. Trenchard

The Student's Complete Vocabulary Guide to the Greek New Testament is the most complete book of its kind. Designed for both reference and study, it covers the entire vocabulary of the Greek New Testament—not just the words that occur most frequently. Words are arranged by frequency and in a separate section by cognates. Principal parts for all verbs found in the New Testament are also listed. A new revised edition being published October 1998 adds the Goodrick-Kohlenberger numbers to the index.

Softcover: 0-310-22695-3

ZondervanPublishingHouse
Grand Rapids, Michigan
http://www.zondervan.com

A Division of HarperCollinsPublishers

Available at your local Christian or college bookstore

We want to hear from you. Please send your comments about this book to us in care of the address below. Thank you.

ZondervanPublishingHouse
Grand Rapids, Michigan 49530
http://www.zondervan.com